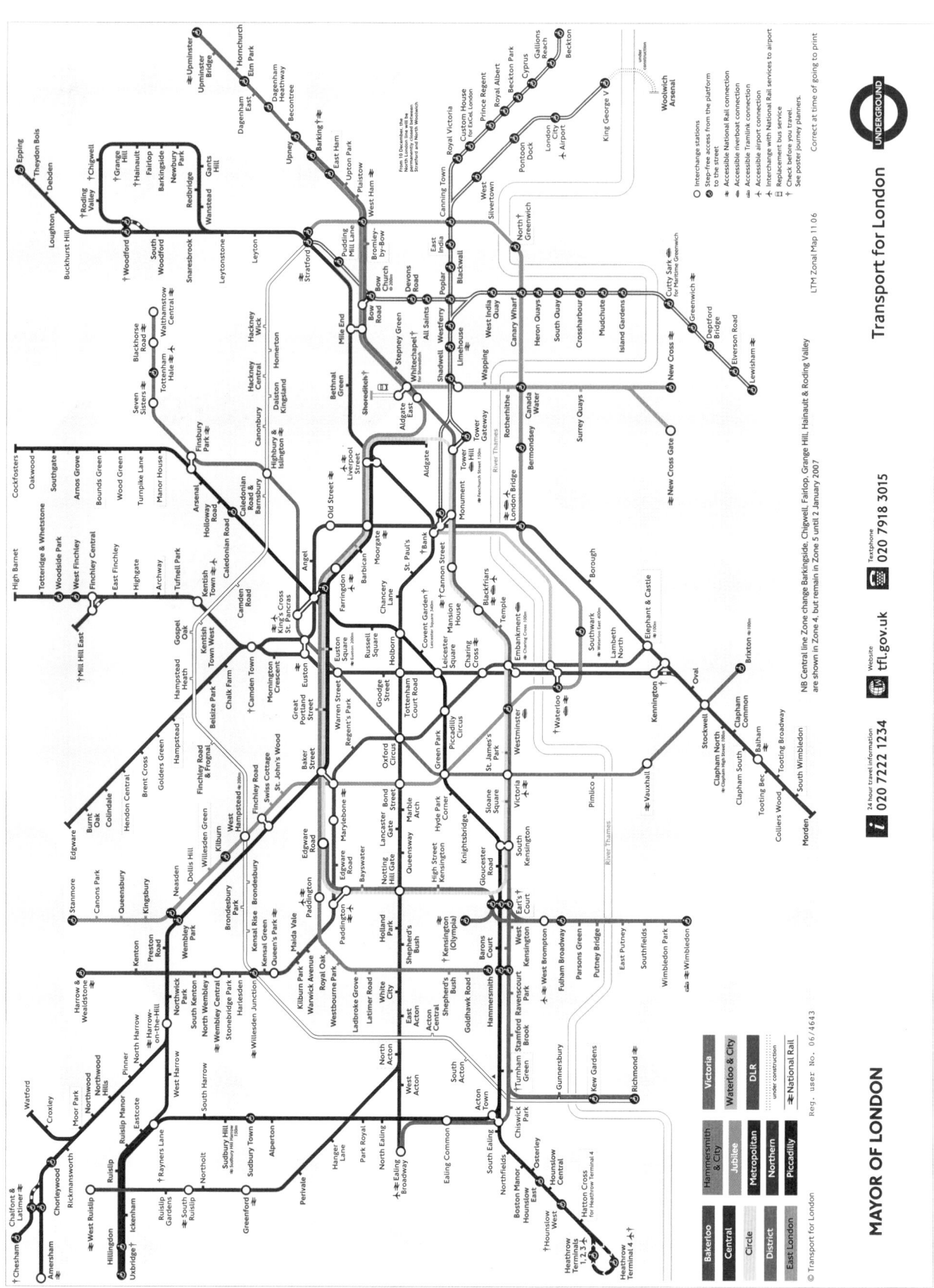

MAYOR OF LONDON

Transport for London

i 24 hour travel information **020 7222 1234**

Website **tfl.gov.uk**

Textphone **020 7918 3015**

Reg. user No. 06/4643

LTM Zonal Map 11.06

Correct at time of going to print

NB Central line Zone change Barkingside, Chigwell, Fairlop, Grange Hill, Hainault & Roding Valley are shown in Zone 4, but remain in Zone 5 until 2 January 2007

○ Interchange stations
Ⓓ Step-free access from the platform to the street
⟶ Accessible National Rail connection
⟶ Accessible riverboat connection
⟵ Accessible Tramlink connection
✈ Accessible airport connection
⟶ Interchange with National Rail services to airport
R Replacement bus service
† Check before you travel. See poster journey planners.

From 18 December, the North London line will be permanently closed between Stratford and North Woolwich

© Transport for London

Bakerloo	Hammersmith & City	Victoria
Central	Jubilee	Waterloo & City
Circle	Metropolitan	DLR
District	Northern	under construction
East London	Piccadilly	National Rail

PHILIP'S

STREET ATLAS

London

First published 2000 by

Philip's, a division of
Octopus Publishing Group Ltd
2–4 Heron Quays
London E14 4JP

Third edition 2007
First impression 2007
LONCA

© Philip's 2007

OS Ordnance Survey®

This product contains driver restriction information derived from Teleatlas
© TeleatlasDRI

The information for the speed camera locations is used with permission of the London Safety Camera Partnership and is correct at the time of publishing. New sites will be installed by the LSCP, for the latest list visit www.lscp.org.uk

Printed and bound in Spain
by Cayfosa-Quebecor.

Contents

II	Our Top 10 Tips to avoid parking penalties
V	Mobile speed camera sites
VI	**Key to map pages**
VIII	Administrative and Postcode boundaries
X	**Route planning**
XXVIII	**Key to map symbols**
1	**Street maps**
228	**Keys to enlarged map pages and symbols**
229	**Enlarged street maps**
271	**Index**
398	**List of numbered locations**
412	Hospitals
413	Places of interest
414	Shopping, theatres, cinemas
416	Central London buses
418	Local rail and London Underground

Digital Data

The exceptionally high-quality mapping found in this atlas is available as digital data in TIFF format, which is easily convertible to other bitmapped (raster) image formats.

The index is also available in digital form as a standard database table. It contains all the details found in the printed index together with the National Grid reference for the map square in which each entry is named.

For further information and to discuss your requirements, please contact james.mann@philips-maps.co.uk

Our Top 10 Tips
to avoid parking penalties

Parking fines 2005/6	
Borough	fines
1 Westminster	715085
2 Camden	448085
3 Kensington and Chelsea	294932
4 Lambeth	255066
5 Wandsworth	245475
6 Ealing	212656
7 Islington	210685
8 Newham	188465
9 Barnet	168681
10 Hammersmith and Fulham	165196
11 Hackney	140966
12 Waltham Forest	140216
13 Southwark	135045
14 Haringey	134551
15 Brent	133561
16 Enfield	100087
17 Redbridge	95966
18 Hounslow	92764
19 Croydon	86534
20 Harrow	83303
21 Tower Hamlets	72858
22 Richmond upon Thames	72526
23 Bromley	69538
24 Bexley	65739
25 Kingston upon Thames	63980
26 Lewisham	63250
27 Hillingdon	61211
28 Merton	56860
29 Sutton	48965
30 Greenwich	48892
31 Barking and Dagenham	42416
32 Havering	40141
33 City of London	37478
34 Transport for London	304305
	5,095,478

When it comes to parking, London's streets are mean and its traffic regulators keen. Lucky motorists might find a marked bay, or at night a patch of single line, but that could just be the start of the problem. It's all too easy to pick the wrong space or the wrong time of day.

Getting a ticket for over-staying, or using a suspended bay or a resident's only space, is invariably expensive and sometimes the pain doesn't end there. What's the worst that can happen? Well, the car could be clamped or towed away. But in either case it's excruciatingly costly and time-consuming to retrieve the vehicle, especially after 10pm, when London black cab prices go through the roof.

Why has parking become so hazardous? The whole process used to be much less complex, and far easier to understand. The hours of parking control were fairly standard right across the capital, and enforcement was also uniform, with traffic wardens attached to the police service. Then came the Road Traffic Act 1991, which took responsibility away from the police and into the hands of local authorities.

The post-code lottery

Since 1994 parking in London has been run by the borough councils. Most choose to employ private contractors to operate the parking penalty service. In common with all other companies,

these outfits are in pursuit of profit – and they haven't been disappointed. Parking fines are big business in London these days.

Latest figures show that more than five million parking penalties were levied on motorists in 2005/6 (see table). In bald terms, that's nearly one for every person living in Greater London. These penalties produced an income for the boroughs of some £279 million in a year. Once the operators have taken their slice, the money goes into the coffers of London's 33 boroughs as well as Transport for London, which has recently stepped up its enforcement activities, especially on red routes.

There is huge variation among the 32 boroughs, with central London by far the riskiest place to park. Westminster held the 2005 record for issuing the greatest number of fines, even though its total of 715,085 was about 100,000 less than the previous year. The fewest parking fines were given in the City of London.

There is one piece of good news. A third fewer cars were clamped than in 2004/5 – nearly 50,000 fewer. But there was a sharp 18% increase in cars removed to pounds. To acknowledge this grim statistic, Philip's London street atlases are now the first to locate Car Pounds on the maps using this symbol: 🏢

The figures also reveal the trend-setters among the boroughs:

Camden for the most cars clamped.

Westminster for the most cars removed to pounds.

The boroughs where the number of tickets issued grew the fastest were: Ealing (+55%), Enfield (+47%) and Hackney (+46%)

The boroughs who saw the biggest falls were: Greenwich (-21%), Richmond (-25%) and Islington (-26%)

The sheer number of different authorities shelling out penalties can make the London street parking issue seem baffling. Arrangements in Richmond

Top 10 Tips

1 **Check borough boundaries.** One common pitfall for London's drivers is to pump cash into a meter belonging to one borough while being parked in another. This is especially problematic around the London museums. Numerous visitors perfectly willing to pay the charge have fed money into a meter belonging to the Royal Borough of Kensington and Chelsea when they have inadvertently parked in a bay operated by Westminster council. The signage, campaigners claim, is inadequate – so beware.

2 **Keep plenty of loose change if you intend to use parking meters.** If a parking attendant happens along while you have toddled off to find the correct coinage you have no defence against a ticket.

3 **If you've been caught fair and square,** pay the ticket within 14 days to take advantage of the cash discount scheme. Prompt settlement usually means coughing up just half the full amount.

4 **Assume nothing.** Just because you are often permitted to park on single yellow lines after 6.30 doesn't mean it is always so. There are an increasing number of parking places reserved for 'residents only' and these are frequently governed by a 10pm rule. Moreover some zones are 24 hour no parking areas. Look for signs to indicate what rules apply to the parking space before moving into it. Don't forget that some parking areas are watched by cameras that can capture your licence plate, so don't imagine you are safe to contravene regulations on the basis that parking attendants will have ended their shift. If you have received a penalty charge notice in an area where the signs outlining the regulations on parking are obscured by trees or even missing then you may have grounds for appeal. Take photographs as evidence before embarking on the appeals process.

5 **If you return to your vehicle while a parking attendant is in the process of writing the ticket** don't hesitate to drive off if you can do so without endangering anyone. Parking offences are not criminal offences, so you are not leaving the scene of a crime. The relevant legislation makes it clear that the completed ticket must be either given to the driver or attached to the vehicle. If not, the ticket is invalid.

6 **There are loopholes** in parking regulations to capitalise upon. A ticket is invalid if the parking attendant is not wearing full uniform, including a hat, or if his identification number is not clearly visible. There might be discrepancies in the ticket regarding the timings or your vehicle. Sometimes the markings on the road are awry or the position of the meter is misleading. If the parking attendant is present request that he makes a note of your objections as this may assist in any pending appeals process.

7 **Don't be afraid to appeal** against a penalty that in your view has been wrongly issued. The number of appeals is surprisingly small (fewer than 1%) and yet more than 60% are successful. It generally costs nothing to appeal so what have you got to lose? At first glance the process is daunting but stick with it if you feel you have been unfairly targeted with a ticket. Whatever you do, don't ignore it! See 'How to appeal' on the following page.

8 **When cars are clamped or towed retrieve the vehicle fast** – within 24 hours if possible. This is an expensive business because drivers must pay the penalty charge notice as well as a fee to release the vehicle. If it's not recovered promptly expect a daily charge for 'storage' on top. Afterwards, study the timings on the ticket. Most councils permit a 15 or 20 minute grace period after a parking ticket has run out before clamping or towing. Anything less than that is grounds for appeal. Remember, if you return to your vehicle before the clamp is locked or before the wheels are raised from the ground if it is being towed then the penalty charge notice is invalid.

9 **Look out for cashless parking zones.** Some are already on trial in central London. Drivers can ring a database to establish an arrival time. Then the clock starts running until the driver calls again to signal departure. The amount due is automatically debited from the driver's account. There's no doubt that new technology will play its part on the parking scene in the over-crowded capital. And it's sensible recognition at last that drivers may have many talents but are not as yet blessed with the foresight to know the precise moment that they will return to their vehicles.

10 **Don't forget the other offences.** London drivers not only have to be careful about parking. There's the congestion charge to consider as well as fines for using bus lanes illegally and other moving traffic fines orchestrated by local authorities. Congestion charge boundaries, bus lanes, red lights and yellow box junctions are generally monitored by enforcement cameras and evidence is extremely difficult to dispute.

Parking on a suspended bay will almost certainly result in your car being towed to the borough pound.

may be substantially different to those in Redbridge. Charges and hours of operation for meters and ticket machines vary hugely, sometimes even on opposite sides of the same street. So there's 'stranger danger' not only for those from outside London, or suburbanites driving into central London, but even for Inner Londoners crossing borough borders.

But that isn't what most alarms the average motorist. There's a widely held belief that wardens have quotas to fill, and can get bonuses for over-achieving. Examples of predatory behaviour are

legendary. Favourite times for ticketing are the first and last 10 minutes of the controlled period, when wardens are often seen out in large numbers. There have been reports of tickets being issued to removal vans during house moves, to security company vans when rogue burglar alarms are clanging, and to numerous traders unloading goods for their shops – sometimes in the middle of the night.

In short, it is not only motorists who have broken parking regulations that are being fined, but also the unwary and the downright unlucky - in the right place, at the right time but with a wrong-minded attendant in the vicinity.

Some of the villains have been weeded out. Certain boroughs are ensuring those patrolling the streets have undergone a re-education process that will cast them as a friend to the motorist rather than a foe. It's not in your best interest to assume the whole system is unfair and take out your frustrations upon the parking attendant who just might have ticketed you legitimately.

However, the activities of a few parking regulators deserve close scrutiny. Clampers in particular have earned themselves a cowboy image that is finally arousing the interest of the legislators. A House of Commons Transport Committee Report has urged that operators should 'consider restricting clamping to persistent offenders and unregistered vehicles'. There's even talk in the document that towing a car may be incompatible with our human rights. That's perhaps why the number of cars being clamped in the capital has gone down by some 50,000.

Of course, there are always reasons to justify a harsh parking regime. It keeps London traffic on the move, making

Clamping rates are falling but you are still at risk – especially in Camden and Westminster.

How to appeal

■ **Begin with a letter sent by recorded delivery within 14 days.** That generally means the clock will stop on the prompt payment discount scheme and it will still be available if the initial appeal is unsuccessful – although some councils claim the reduced amount isn't open to those who embark on this route. Keep copies of the correspondence and any supporting evidence you send with it. Always quote the Penalty Charge Notice number. If you hear nothing for more than 56 days then the council is deemed out of time and the ticket should be cancelled.

■ **Do not pay any part of the fine if you are intending to appeal.** Once payment is received by the authority the case is closed.

■ If your appeal is turned down don't accept a letter couched in general terms. Write back to ask about the specifics of your case. The council will either stand by the notice and issue a Notice of Rejection or allow the appeal.

■ If the authority endorses the ticket its next step is to issue a Notice to Owner and that should happen within six months. According to the Road Traffic Act of 1991 the owner is liable for violations linked to his vehicle. Disturbingly, it is only at this stage that many motorists discover they are being pursued for a parking offence. If you are the sole driver of a vehicle that hasn't been stolen the ticket has clearly not been either attached to the vehicle or handed to you, the driver, as the

law demands. Respond within 28 days filing the relevant information. This is known as Formal Representation. (If you do not answer in the specified time the council may well up the fine and send in the bailiffs to recover the amount.)

■ If this petition is rejected by the local authority then it's time to take the case to the Parking and Traffic Appeals Service. You can select a postal or personal adjudication. Internet advice favours face time with the adjudicator as local councils are known to frequently cave in at the prospect of putting evidence before an official tribunal on the grounds of cost, although there's no guarantee of this happening. The adjudicator's decision is final as there is no recourse to law.

journey times more predictable and curtailing traffic mayhem. That's the official line – which never mentions just how valuable the income generated by parking penalties is to the enforcers. Further, authorities don't talk about targets in relation to parking fines, rather 'baseline performance indicators'.

So if you are going to park in London, especially in the centre, beware, be aware – and know your rights. If you do get fined and you think you have a case, be prepared to appeal. Fewer than 1% of motorists did appeal in 2004/5 (do we detect money-raising by inertia?),

but over 60% of those appeals were allowed. Remember, if you do not get a response to your appeal within 56 days, your appeal is automatically allowed.

Helpful information

The Knowledge A telephone advisory service run by off-duty London taxi drivers. They will help with problems including parking and directions. The number is 0906 265 6565 (premium rate) or try *www.theknowledge.com*

Transport for London (TfL) Responsible for 360 miles of roads, 4,600 traffic lights and London's red routes. It is also a fine-issuing authority. Contact Tfl on 0207 2221234 or *www.tfl.gov.uk.*

www.ticketbusters.co.uk is a website devoted to assisting London motorists, offering tailored advice on parking ticket appeals.

www.parkingticket.co.uk also offers support for London drivers.

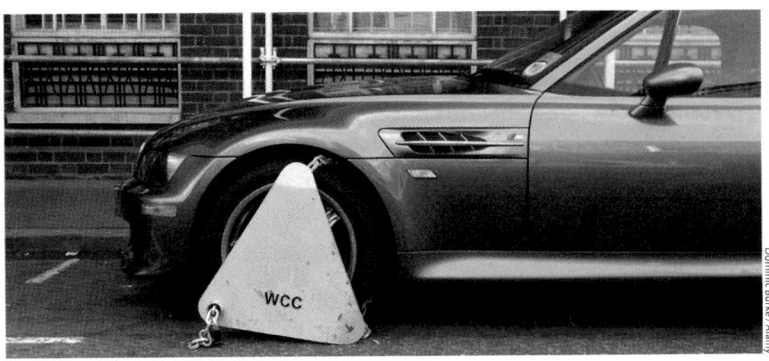

Mobile speed camera sites

This table lists the sites where the local safety camera partnership may enforce speed limits through the use of mobile cameras or detectors. These are usually set up on the roadside or a bridge spanning the road and operated by a police or civilian enforcement officer.

Barking & Dagenham

A13
Alfreds Way IG11
Alfreds Way IG12
Ripple Rd IG11
Ripple Rd RM9

A406
Barking Relief Rd IG11

A1153
Porters Avenue RM8

B178
Ballards Rd RM10

Barnet

A5
Hendon Broadway NW9

A406
North Circular Rd N3

Unclassified
Oakleigh Rd South N11

Bexley

A20
Sidcup Rd SE9

Unclassified
Abbey Rd DA17
Bellegrove Rd DA16
Erith Rd DA17
Farady Avenue DA14
King Harolds Way DA17
Lower Rd DA17
Penhill Rd DA5
Pickford Lane DA7
Well Hall Rd SE9
Woolwich Rd DA17

Brent

A5
Edgware Rd NW2

A406
North Circular Rd NW2
North Circular Rd NW10

A4006
Kenton Rd HA3

Unclassified
Crest Rd NW2
Fryent Way, Kingsbury NW9
Hillside NW10
Kingsbury Rd NW9
Watford Rd, Wembley HA0
Watford Rd, Sudbury HA0
Woodcock Hill HA3

Bromley

A20
Sidcup By-Pass DA14

A213
Croydon Rd SE20

A222
Bromley Rd BR2
Bromley Rd BR3

Unclassified
Beckenham Rd BR3
Burnt Ash Lane BR1
Crystal Palace Park Rd SE26
Elmers End Rd BR3
Main Rd TN16
Sevenoaks Way BR5
Wickham Way BR3

Camden

A501
Euston Rd NW1

Chadwell

M11
Chadwell IG8

City of Westminster

A40
Westway W2

Unclassified
Great Western Rd W11
Millbank SW1
Vauxhall Bridge Rd SW1

Croydon

A22
Godstone Rd CR8

A215
Beulah Hill SE19

A217
Garratt Lane SW18

Unclassified
Brigstock Rd CR7
Coulsdon Rd, Coulsdon CR5
Long Lane, Addiscombe CR0
Portnalls Rd, Coulsdon CR5
Thornton Rd CR0

Ealing

A40
Perivale UB6
Western Avenue UB5
Western Avenue UB6

Unclassified
Greenford Rd, Greenford UB6
Greenford Rd, Southall UB1
Horn Lane W3
Lady Margaret Rd UB1
Ruislip Rd UB5
Uxbridge Rd UB2

Egham

M25
Egham TW20

Elmbridge

M25
Byfleet KT14

Enfield

A10
Great Cambridge Rd N18

A110
Enfield Rd EN2

Unclassified
Fore Street N9

Forest Hill

Unclassified
Stanstead Rd SE23

Greenwich

A20
Sidcup Rd SE9

Unclassified
Beresford Street SE18
Court Rd SE9
Creek Rd SE10
Glenesk Rd SE9
Rochester Way SE3
Rochester Way SE9
Woolwich Church Street SE18

Hackney

A10
Stamford Hill N16

Unclassified
Clapton Common E5
Seven Sisters Rd N4
Upper Clapton Rd E5

Hammersmith & Fulham

A40
Westway W2
Westway W12

A219
Scrubs Lane W12

Unclassified
Fulham Palace Rd SW6
Uxbridge Rd W12

Haringey

A503
Seven Sisters Rd N15

Unclassified
Belmont Rd N15
Bounds Green Rd N11
Seven Sisters Rd N4
White Hart Lane N22

Harrow

Unclassified
Alexandra Avenue HA2
Harrow View HA3
Honeypot Lane NW9
Porlock Avenue HA2
Uxbridge Rd, Harrow Weald HA3
Watford Rd HA1

Havering

Unclassified
Brentwood Rd, Romford RM1
Chase Cross Rd RM5
Eastern Avenue RM14
Eastern Avenue East RM14
Hall Lane RM14
Ingrebourne Gardens, Upminster RM14
Ockenden Rd RM14
Parkstone Avenue, Hornchurch RM11
Wingletye Lane RM11

Hillingdon

M25
Colnbrook SL3
West Drayton UB7

A40
Western Avenue, Ruislip UB10

A312
Hayes UB3

Unclassified
Church Hill, Harefield UB9
Cowley Rd, Uxbridge UB8
Cowley High Rd UB8
Joel Street, Northwood Hills HA6
Kingshill Avenue, Hayes UB4
Park Rd UB8
Stockley Rd UB7
Uxbridge Rd, Hayes UB4

Hounslow

A4
Great West Rd, Brentford TW8
Great West Rd, Hounslow TW7
Great West Rd, Hounslow W4

A315
High Street TW8

Unclassified
Castle Way, Hanworth TW13
Great West Rd TW5
Harlington Rd West TW14
Hatton Rd, Bedfont TW14

Islington

Unclassified
Holloway Rd N19
Seven Sisters Rd N4
Upper Street N1

Kensington & Chelsea

Unclassified
Barlby Rd W10
Chelsea Embankment SW3
Chesterton Rd W10
Holland Park Avenue W11
Holland Villas Rd W14
Kensington Park Rd W11
Kensington Rd SW7
Ladbroke Grove W11
Latimer Rd W10
Royal Hospital Rd SW3
Sloane Street SW1
St Helens Gardens W10

Kingston upon Thames

A3
Kingston By-Pass SW20

A240
Kingston Rd KT4

Unclassified
Manor Drive North KT3
Richmond Rd KT2

Lambeth

Unclassified
Atkins Rd SW12
Brixton Hill SW2
Brixton Rd SW9
Clapham Rd SW9
Herne Hill Rd SE24
Kennington Park Rd SE11
Kings Avenue SW4
Streatham High Rd SW16

Lewisham

A21
Bromley Rd BR1

Unclassified
Brockley Rd SE4
Brockley Rd SE23
Bromley Rd SE6
Brownhill Rd SE6
Burnt Ash Hill SE12
Lee High Rd SE12
Lewisham Way SE4
Westwood Hill SE26

Merton

A298
Bushey Rd SW20

Unclassified
Central Rd SM4
High Street, Colliers Wood SW19
Hillcross Avenue SM4
London Rd CR4
Martin Way SM4
Martin Way SW20
Ridgway Place SW19
West Barnes Lane SW20

Newham

A13
Alfreds Way IG11

A124
Barking Rd E6

A1020
Royal Albert Dock Way E6
Royal Docks Rd E6

Unclassified
Barking Rd E13
Romford Rd E7

Redbridge

A406
Southend Rd IG8

Unclassified
Manford Way, Hainault IG7
Woodford Avenue IG8
Woodford Rd E18

Richmond upon Thames

A205
Upper Richmond Rd West SW14

Unclassified
Kew Rd TW9
Sixth Cross Rd TW2
Uxbridge Rd TW12

Ruislip

Unclassified
Field End Rd HA4

Runnymeade

M25
Runnymede TW20

Southwark

Unclassified
Albany Rd SE5
Alleyn Park SE21
Brenchley Gardens SE15
Camberwell New Rd SE5
Denmark Hill SE5
Kennington Park Rd SE11
Linden Grove SE15
Old Kent Rd SE1
Old Kent Rd SE14
Old Kent Rd SE17
Peckham Rye SE15
Salter Rd SE16
Southwark Pk Rd SE16
Sunray Avenue SE24

Spelthorne

M25
Staines TW18

Sutton

A232
Cheam Rd SM1

B272
Foresters Drive SM6

B278
Green Lane SM4

B279
Tudor Drive SM4

Unclassified
Malden Rd SM3
Middleton Rd SM5
Beddington Lane CR0
Cheam Common Rd KT4

Tower Hamlets

A102
Homerton High Street E9

Unclassified
Bow Rd E3
Cambridge Heath Rd E2
Manchester Rd E14
Mile End Rd E1
Upper Clapton Rd E5
Westferry Rd E14

Waltham Forest

Unclassified
Chingford Rd E4
Chingford Rd E17
Hoe Street E17
Larkshall Rd E4

Wandsworth

A3
Kingston Rd SW15

A214
Trinity Rd SW18

A3220
Latchmere Rd SW11

Unclassified
Battersea Park Rd SW11
Garratt Lane SW18
Upper Richmond Rd SW15

Windsor & Maidenhead

M25
Wraysbury TW19

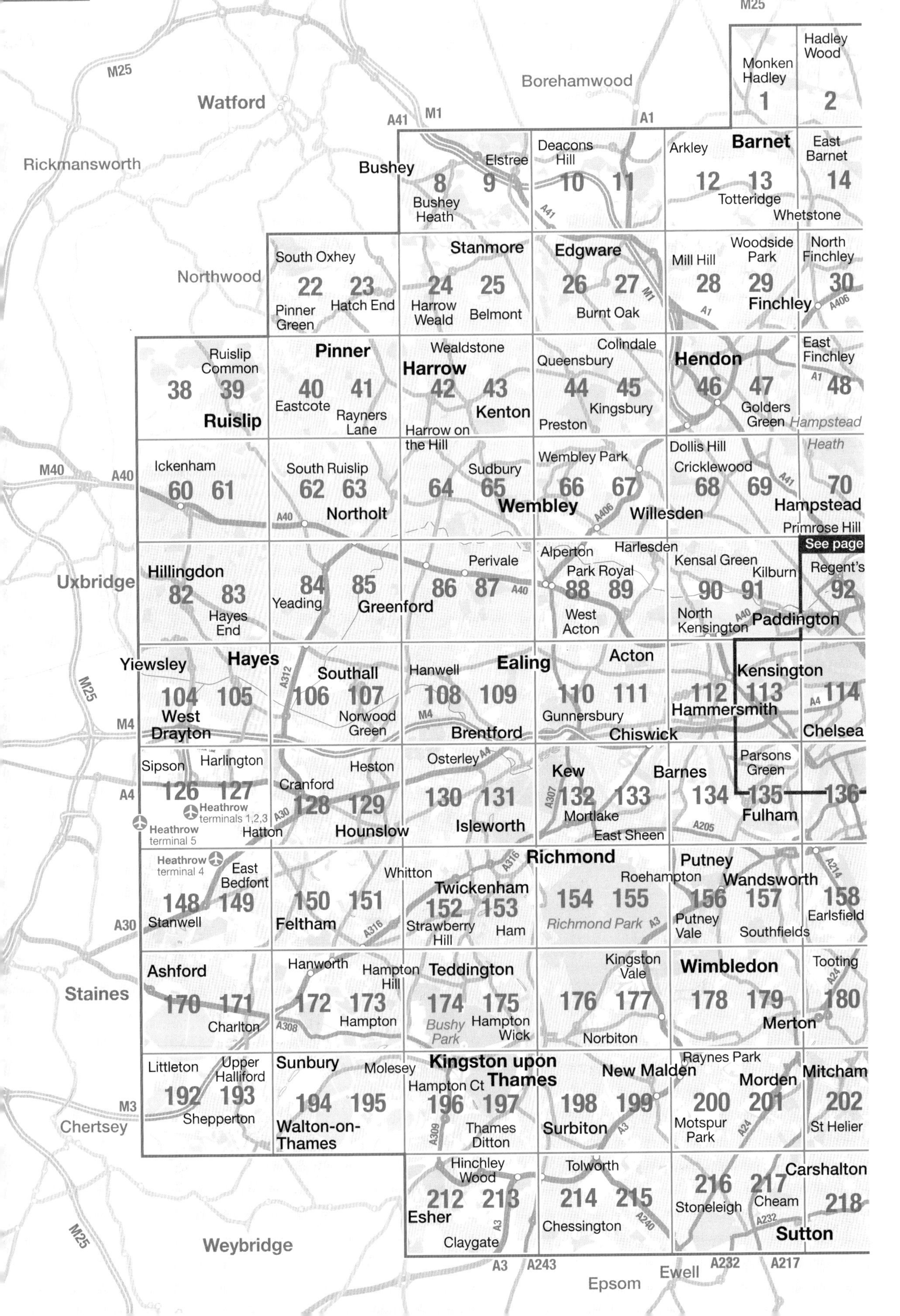

Potters Bar

M25

M25

Watford

Borehamwood

Rickmansworth

Monken Hadley **1** | Hadley Wood **2**

A41 | M1 | A1

Bushey **8** | Elstree **9** | Deacons Hill **10** | **11** | Arkley | **Barnet** | East Barnet **14**

Bushey Heath | | | | **12** | **13** | Totteridge

Whetstone

Northwood | South Oxhey **22** | **23** Hatch End | Stanmore **24** | **25** | Edgware **26** | **27** | Mill Hill **28** | Woodside Park **29** | North Finchley **30**

Pinner Green | Harrow Weald | Belmont | Burnt Oak | | **Finchley** | A406

Ruislip Common **38** | **39** | **Pinner** **40** | **41** | Wealdstone **42** | **43** | Colindale Queensbury **44** | **45** | **Hendon** **46** | **47** | East Finchley **48**

Ruislip | Eastcote | Rayners Lane | **Harrow** | **Kenton** | Kingsbury | Golders Green | Hampstead

| | Harrow on the Hill | Preston

Ickenham **60** | **61** | South Ruislip **62** | **63** | **64** | Sudbury **65** | Wembley Park **66** | **67** | Dollis Hill Cricklewood **68** | **69** | Heath

A40 | | **Northolt** | | **Wembley** | **Willesden** | A41 | Hampstead **70**

Primrose Hill

Uxbridge | Hillingdon **82** | **83** | **84** | **85** | Perivale **86** | **87** A40 | Alperton Park Royal **88** | **89** | Harlesden | Kensal Green **90** | Kilburn **91** | See page **92**

| Hayes End | Yeading | **Greenford** | | West Acton | North Kensington | **Paddington** | Regent's

Yiewsley | **Hayes** **104** | **105** | Southall **106** | **107** | Hanwell **108** | **109** | **Ealing** **110** | **111** | Acton **112** | **113** | **114**

West Drayton | | Norwood Green | M4 | **Brentford** | Gunnersbury | **Hammersmith** | A4 | Chelsea

Kensington

Chiswick

Sipson | Harlington **126** | **127** | Cranford **128** | **129** | Osterley **130** | **131** | Kew **132** | **133** | **134** | Parsons Green **135** | **136**

Heathrow terminals 1,2,3 | Heston | | Mortlake | Barnes | | **Fulham**

Heathrow terminal 5 | Hatton | **Hounslow** | **Isleworth** | East Sheen | A205

A4

Heathrow terminal 4 | East Bedfont **148** | **149** | **150** | **151** | Whitton | **Richmond** | **154** | **155** | Roehampton **Putney** **156** | **157** | **Wandsworth** **158**

A30 | Stanwell | **Feltham** | A316 | Twickenham **152** | **153** | Richmond Park A3 | Putney Vale | Southfields | Earlsfield

Strawberry Hill | Ham

Ashford **170** | **171** | Hanworth **172** | **173** | Teddington **174** | **175** | Kingston Vale **176** | **177** | **Wimbledon** **178** | **179** | Tooting **180**

| Charlton | A308 | Hampton | Bushy Park | Hampton Wick | Norbiton | | **Merton**

Littleton | Upper Halliford **192** | **193** | Sunbury **194** | **195** Molesey | **Kingston upon Thames** **196** | **197** | New Malden **198** | **199** | Raynes Park **200** | **201** Morden | Mitcham **202**

M3 | Shepperton | **Walton-on-Thames** | Hampton Ct | Thames Ditton | **Surbiton** | Motspur Park | St Helier

Chertsey

Hinchley Wood **212** | **213** | Tolworth **214** | **215** | **216** | **217** | Carshalton Cheam **218**

Weybridge | **Esher** | Chessington | Stoneleigh | A232 | **Sutton**

Claygate

A3 | A243 | Ewell | A232 | A217

Epsom

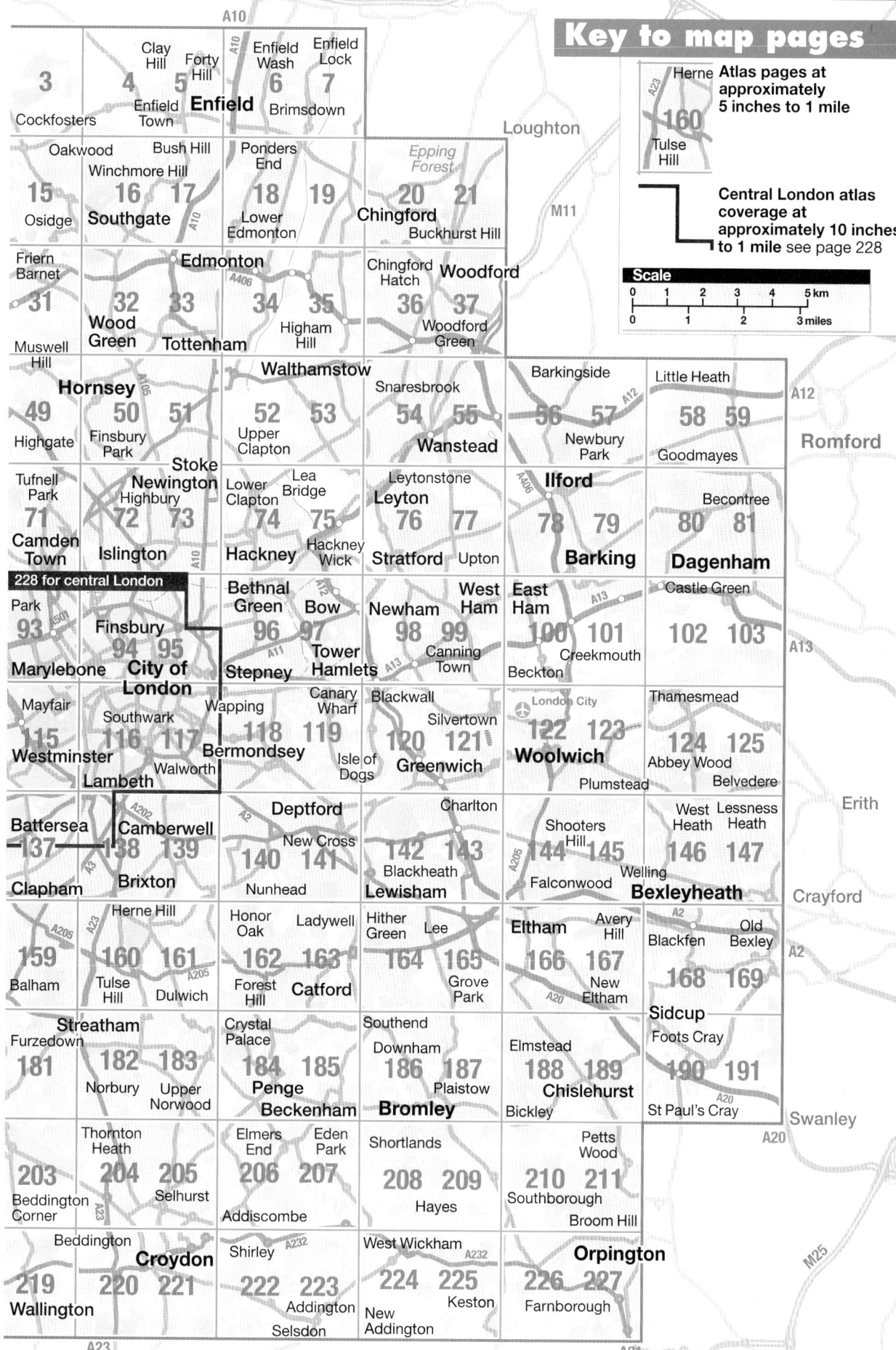

Key to map pages

Herne
160
Tulse
Hill

Atlas pages at
approximately
5 inches to 1 mile

Central London atlas
coverage at
approximately 10 inches
to 1 mile see page 228

Scale

0	1	2	3	4	5 km

| 0 | 1 | 2 | 3 miles |

M25
A10
M11
Loughton

3
Cockfosters

Clay
Hill
4
Enfield
Town

Forty
Hill
5
Enfield

Enfield
Wash
6
Brimsdown

Enfield
Lock
7

Epping
Forest

Oakwood
15
Osidge

Bush Hill
Winchmore Hill
16 **17**
Southgate

Ponders
End
18 **19**
Lower
Edmonton

20 **21**
Chingford
Buckhurst Hill

A12
Romford

Friern
Barnet
31
Muswell
Hill

Edmonton
32 **33**
Wood
Green
Tottenham

34 **35**
Higham
Hill

Chingford
Hatch
36 **37**
Woodford
Woodford
Green

Hornsey
49
Highgate

50 **51**
Finsbury
Park

Walthamstow
52 **53**
Upper
Clapton

Snaresbrook
54 **55**
Wanstead

Barkingside
56 **57**
Newbury
Park

Little Heath
58 **59**
Goodmayes

A12

Tufnell
Park
71
Camden
Town

Stoke
Newington
Highbury
72 **73**
Islington

Lower
Clapton
Lea
Bridge
74 **75**
Hackney
Hackney
Wick

Leytonstone
Leyton
76 **77**
Stratford
Upton

Ilford
78 **79**
Barking

Becontree
80 **81**
Dagenham

Park
93
Marylebone

228 for central London
Finsbury
94 **95**
City of
London

Bethnal
Green Bow
96 **97**
Stepney
Tower
Hamlets

West
Newham **Ham**
98 **99**
Canning
Town

East
Ham
100 **101**
Beckton
Creekmouth

Castle Green
102 **103**

A13

Mayfair
115
Westminster
Lambeth

Southwark
116 **117**
Walworth

Wapping
118 **119**
Bermondsey
Isle of
Dogs

Canary
Wharf
Blackwall
Silvertown
120 **121**
Greenwich

London City
122 **123**
Woolwich
Plumstead

Thamesmead
124 **125**
Abbey Wood
Belvedere

Erith

Battersea
137
Clapham

Camberwell
138 **139**
Brixton

Deptford
140 **141**
New Cross
Nunhead

Charlton
142 **143**
Blackheath
Lewisham

Shooters
Hill
144 **145**
Falconwood
Welling

West Lessness
Heath Heath
146 **147**
Bexleyheath

Crayford

159
Balham

Herne Hill
160 **161**
Tulse
Hill Dulwich

Honor
Oak Ladywell
162 **163**
Forest
Hill **Catford**

Hither
Green Lee
164 **165**
Grove
Park

Eltham
166 **167**
New
Eltham

Avery
Hill
Blackfen
168 **169**
Sidcup

A2
Old
Bexley

A2

181
Furzedown

Streatham
182 **183**
Norbury Upper
Norwood

Crystal
Palace
184 **185**
Penge
Beckenham

Southend
Downham
186 **187**
Bromley
Plaistow

Elmstead
188 **189**
Chislehurst
Bickley

Foots Cray
190 **191**
St Paul's Cray

Swanley

A20

203
Beddington
Corner

Thornton
Heath
204 **205**
Selhurst

Elmers Eden
End Park
206 **207**
Addiscombe

Shortlands
208 **209**
Hayes

Petts
Wood
210 **211**
Southborough
Broom Hill

219
Wallington

Croydon
220 **221**

Shirley
222 **223**
Addington
Selsdon

West Wickham
224 **225**
New Keston
Addington

Orpington
226 **227**
Farnborough

M25

A23
A21
A20
A10
A23
A3
A13
A205

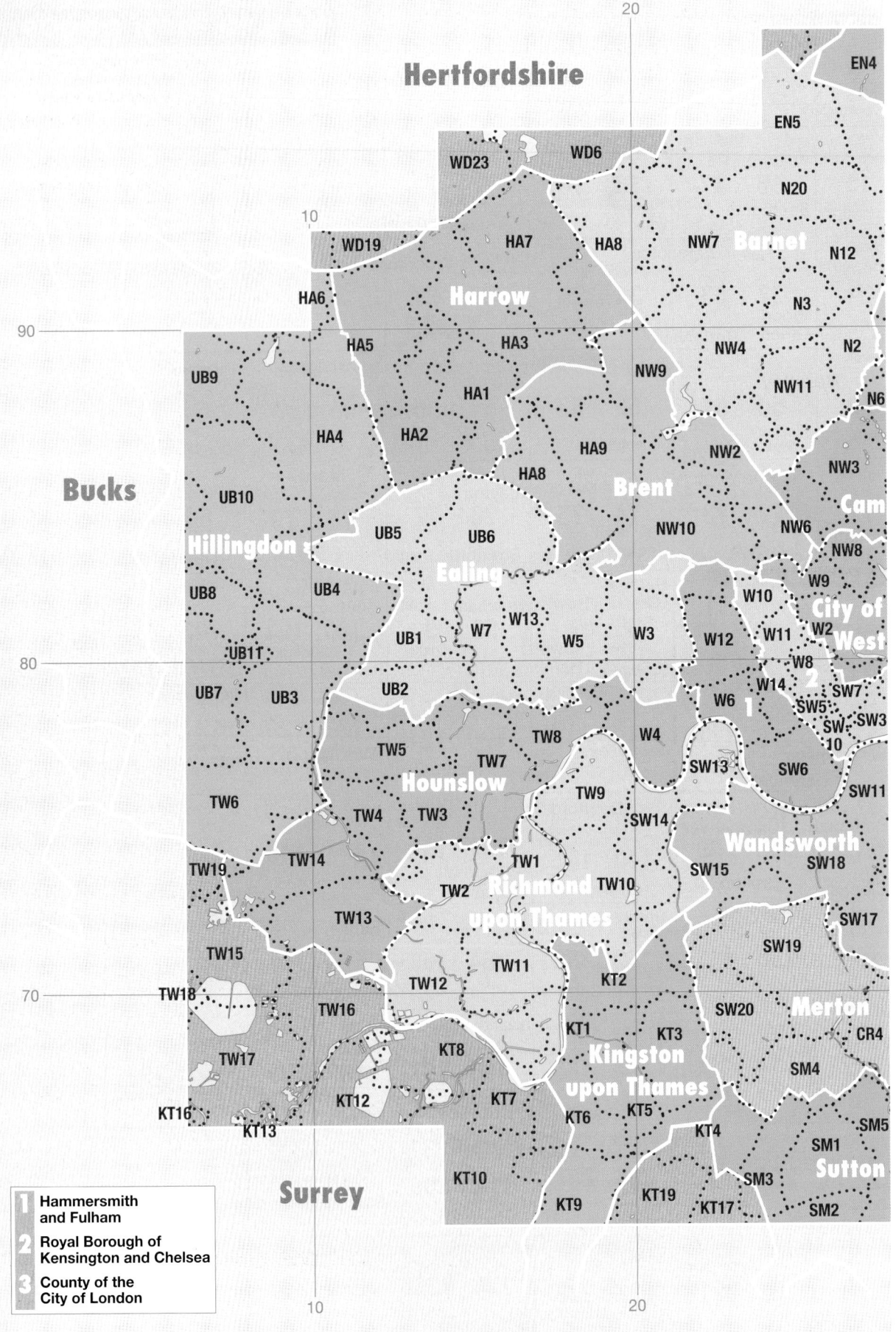

Hertfordshire

WD23 WD6

EN4

EN5

N20

WD19 HA7 HA8 NW7 Barnet N12

HA6 N3

Harrow HA3 NW9 N2

HA5 NW4 N6

UB9 HA1 NW11

Bucks HA4 HA2 NW2 NW3

UB10 HA9 Cam

Hillingdon HA8 Brent NW10 NW6 NW8

UB5 UB6 Ealing NW10 W9

UB8 UB4 W10 City of

W7 W13 W5 W3 W12 W11 West

UB1 W2

UB11 W8

UB7 UB3 UB2 W6 W14 SW7

W4 SW5 SW3

TW5 TW8 SW10

TW7 SW13 SW6 SW11

TW6 Hounslow TW9

TW4 TW3 SW14

TW19 TW14 SW15 SW18 Wandsworth

TW1 SW17

TW2 Richmond TW10

TW13 upon Thames SW19

TW15 TW11 KT2

TW18 SW20 Merton

TW16 KT1 KT3 CR4

TW17 KT8 Kingston SM4

KT12 KT7 upon Thames

KT16 KT6 KT5 SM5

KT13 KT4 SM1 Sutton

SM3 SM2

KT10 KT9 KT19 KT17

Surrey

1 Hammersmith
and Fulham

2 Royal Borough of
Kensington and Chelsea

3 County of the
City of London

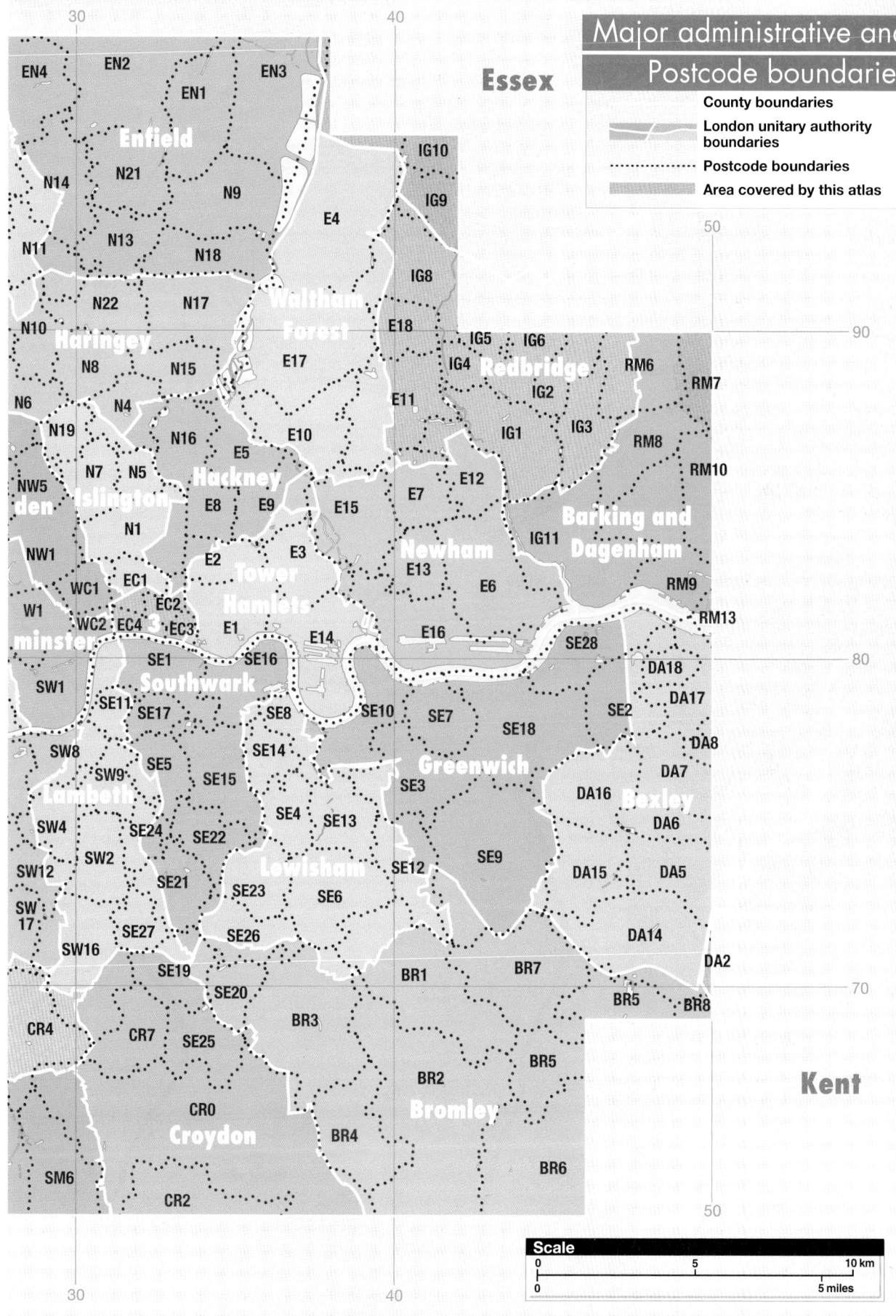

Major administrative and Postcode boundaries

County boundaries
London unitary authority boundaries
Postcode boundaries
Area covered by this atlas

Essex

Kent

EN4 EN2 EN1 EN3
Enfield
N14 N21 N9
N11 N13 N18
N22 N17 **Waltham Forest**
N10 E4
Haringey N15 E17
N8 E18
N6 N4 E11
N19 N16 E5 E10
N7 N5 **Hackney** E12
NW5 E8 E9 E15 E7
den Islington N1 E13 **Newham**
NW1 E2 E3 E6
WC1 EC1 **Tower Hamlets** E16
W1 EC2
WC2 EC4 EC3 E1 E14
minster SE16
SE1 **Southwark**
SW1 SE11 SE17 SE8 SE10 SE7 SE18
SW8 SE14
SW9 SE5 SE15 SE3 **Greenwich**
Lambeth SE4 SE13 SE9
SW4 SE24 SE22
SW2 SE12
SW12 SE21
SW17 SE23 SE6 **Lewisham**
SW16 SE27
SE19 SE26 BR1 BR7
SE20
CR4 CR7 SE25 BR3
CR0 BR2 **Bromley**
Croydon BR4
SM6 BR6
CR2

IG10
IG9
IG8
IG5 IG6
Redbridge RM6 RM7
IG4
IG2
IG1 IG3 RM8 RM10
Barking and Dagenham
IG11 RM9 RM13
SE28
DA18
DA17
SE2 DA8
DA7
DA16 **Bexley** DA6
DA15 DA5
DA14
DA2
BR5 BR8
BR5

Scale
0   5   10 km
0   5 miles

30   40   50   90   80   70   50

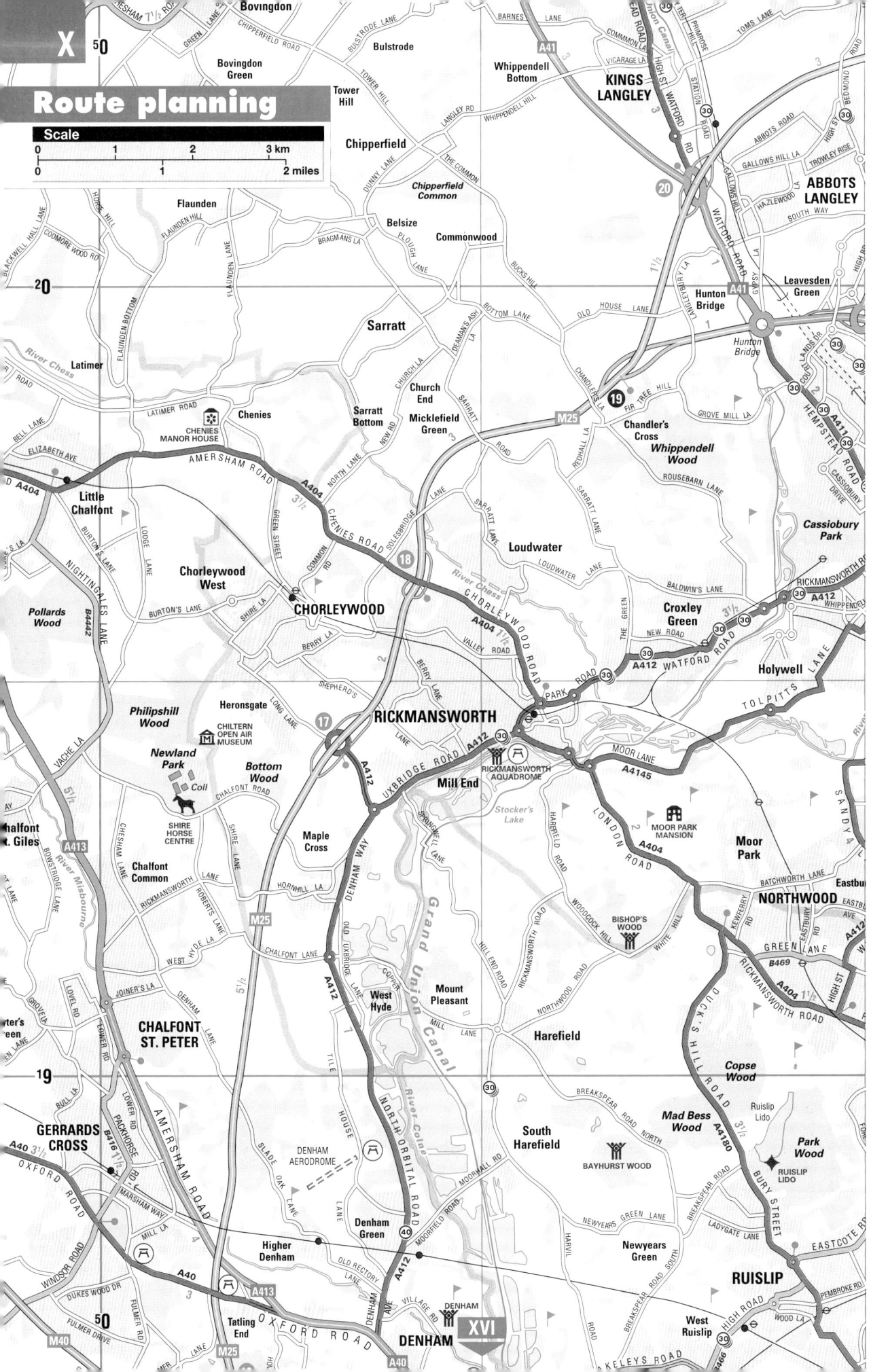
X
Route planning
Scale
0
1
2
3 km
0
1
2 miles
Bovingdon
Bovingdon Green
Bulstrode
Tower Hill
Chipperfield
Chipperfield Common
Whippendell Bottom
KINGS LANGLEY
ABBOTS LANGLEY
Flaunden
Belsize
Commonwood
Sarratt
Leavesden Green
Hunton Bridge
Latimer
Chenies
CHENIES MANOR HOUSE
Church End
Micklefield Green
Sarratt Bottom
Chandler's Cross
Whippendell Wood
Little Chalfont
Chorleywood West
CHORLEYWOOD
Loudwater
Cassiobury Park
Croxley Green
Pollards Wood
Holywell
Philipshill Wood
Heronsgate
CHILTERN OPEN AIR MUSEUM
RICKMANSWORTH
RICKMANSWORTH AQUADROME
Newland Park
Bottom Wood
Mill End
Stocker's Lake
SHIRE HORSE CENTRE
Maple Cross
MOOR PARK MANSION
Moor Park
Chalfont Common
NORTHWOOD
BISHOP'S WOOD
Grand Union Canal
West Hyde
Mount Pleasant
CHALFONT ST. PETER
Harefield
Copse Wood
GERRARDS CROSS
South Harefield
Mad Bess Wood
Ruislip Lido
Park Wood
RUISLIP LIDO
DENHAM AERODROME
BAYHURST WOOD
Denham Green
Higher Denham
Newyears Green
RUISLIP
Tatling End
DENHAM
West Ruislip
XVI
River Chess
River Colne
River Misbourne
M25
M40
A40
A41
A404
A412
A413
A4145
A4180
B4442
B469
B416
AMERSHAM ROAD
CHENIES ROAD
CHORLEYWOOD ROAD
UXBRIDGE ROAD
DENHAM WAY
NORTH ORBITAL ROAD
LONDON ROAD
MOOR LANE
WATFORD ROAD
RICKMANSWORTH ROAD
DUCK'S HILL ROAD
OXFORD ROAD
HIGH ROAD
BURY STREET
NIGHTINGALES LANE
17
18
19
20

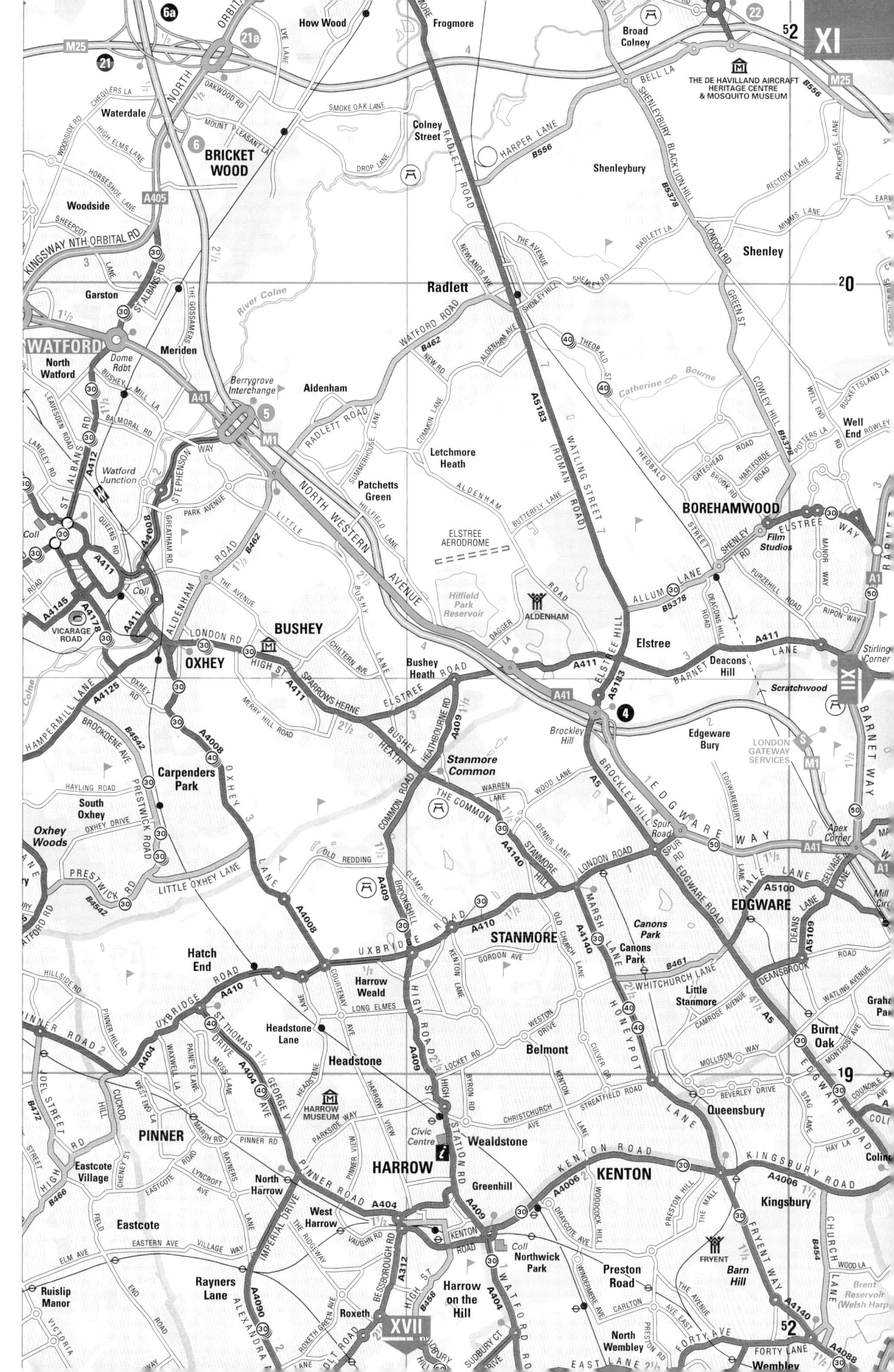
XI
52
M25
6a
21
21a
22
How Wood
Frogmore
Broad Colney
THE DE HAVILLAND AIRCRAFT HERITAGE CENTRE & MOSQUITO MUSEUM
BELL LA
B556
NORTH ORBITAL
CHEQUERS LA
OAKWOOD RD
LYE LANE
SMOKE OAK LANE
MOUNT PLEASANT LA
Waterdale
Colney Street
HARPER LANE
SHENLEYBURY
BLACK LION HILL
Shenleybury
WOODSIDE RD
HIGH ELMS LANE
6
BRICKET WOOD
DROP LANE
RADLETT ROAD
B5378
HORSESHOE LANE
A405
Woodside
SHEEPCOT
RECTORY LANE
PACKHORSE LANE
MIMMS LANE
KINGSWAY NTH ORBITAL RD
RADLETT LA
LONDON RD
Shenley
NEWLANDS AVE
THE AVENUE
Garston
ST ALBANS RD
THE GOSSAMERS
River Colne
Radlett
SHENLEY HILL
SHENLEY RD
20
GREEN ST
WATFORD
Dome Rdbt
Meriden
WATFORD ROAD
B462
NEW RD
ALDENHAM AVE
THEOBALD ST
North Watford
BUSHEY MILL LA
Berrygrove Interchange
Aldenham
Catherine Bourne
A41
5
LEAVESDEN ROAD
BALMORAL RD
M1
RADLETT ROAD
COMMON LANE
SUMMERHOUSE LANE
A5183
(ROMAN ROAD)
WATLING STREET
COWLEY HILL
WELL END
BUCKETTSLAND LA
Well End
ROWLEY
LANGLEY RD
ST ALBANS RD
A412
Watford Junction
STEPHENSON WAY
Letchmore Heath
Patchetts Green
THEOBALD
GATESHEAD ROAD
BROOK RD
HARTFORDE ROAD
POTTERS LA
QUEENS RD
PARK AVENUE
NORTH WESTERN AVENUE
LITTLE
HILLFIELD LANE
ALDENHAM
BUTTERFLY LANE
ELSTREE AERODROME
BOREHAMWOOD
STREET
SHENLEY RD
Film Studios
ELSTREE WAY
Coll
A4008
GREATHAM RD
ROAD
A411
BUSHY
Hilfield Park Reservoir
ALDENHAM
ROAD
ALLUM LANE
B5378
DEACONS HILL ROAD
FURZEHILL ROAD
MANOR WAY
BARNET
A1
A4145
A4178
VICARAGE ROAD
Coll
THE AVENUE
ALDENHAM
BUSHEY
LONDON RD
OXHEY
HIGH ST
CHILTERN AVE
LANE
Bushey Heath
DAGGER LA
Elstree
ELSTREE HILL
RIPON WAY
A411
LANE
BARNET
Deacons Hill
Stirling Corner
XII
Scratchwood
HAMPERMILL LANE
A4125
OXHEY RD
SPARROWS HERNE
MERRY HILL ROAD
ELSTREE ROAD
HEATHBOURNE RD
A409
4
Brockley Hill
Edgeware Bury
LONDON GATEWAY SERVICES
BARNET WAY
BROOKDENE AVE
B4542
BUSHEY HEATH
Stanmore Common
Carpenders Park
OXHEY
HAYLING ROAD
PRESTWICK ROAD
South Oxhey
OXHEY DRIVE
Oxhey Woods
WARREN LANE
WOOD LANE
A5
THE COMMON
COMMON ROAD
BROCKLEY HILL
EDGWARE WAY
EDGWAREBURY LANE
Apex Corner
DENNIS LANE
Spur Road
SPUR RD
A41
PRESTWICK RD
LITTLE OXHEY LANE
OLD REDDING
CLAMP HILL
A409
BROOKSHILL
A4140
STANMORE HILL
LONDON ROAD
EDGWARE ROAD
HALE LANE
SELVAGE LANE
A5100
Mill Hill Circus
LANE
A4008
UXBRIDGE ROAD
A410
STANMORE
OLD CHURCH LANE
MARSH LANE
A4140
Canons Park
EDGWARE
DEANS LANE
A5109
Hatch End
HILLSIDE RD
COURTENAY AVE
Harrow Weald
GORDON AVE
KENTON LANE
WHITCHURCH LANE
B461
Little Stanmore
DEANSBROOK
ROAD
WATLING AVENUE
Graham Park
UXBRIDGE ROAD
A410
PINNER HILL RD
LONG ELMES
WESTON DRIVE
HONEYPOT
CAMROSE AVENUE
A5
Burnt Oak
MONTROSE AVE
PINNER ROAD
A404
WAXWELL LA
PAINE'S LANE
ST THOMAS DRIVE
MOSS LANE
Headstone Lane
HIGH ROAD
LOCKET RD
Belmont
CULVER GR
MOLLISON WAY
JOEL STREET
CUCKOO HILL
WEST END LA
GEORGE V AVE
HEADSTONE
Headstone
HARROW VIEW
BYRON RD
KENTON LANE
STREATFIELD ROAD
BEVERLEY DRIVE
Queensbury
STAG LANE
EDGWARE ROAD
COUNDALE AVE
19
B472
HARROW MUSEUM
PARKSIDE WAY
HIGH ST
CHRISTCHURCH AVE
COLIN
PINNER
MARSH RD
PINNER RD
Civic Centre
Wealdstone
STATION RD
KENTON ROAD
HAY LA
Colindale
HIGH ST
B466
Eastcote Village
CHENEY ST
EASTCOTE RD
LYNCROFT AVE
RAYNERS LANE
North Harrow
PINNER VIEW
PINNER ROAD
HARROW
KENTON
A4006
WOODCOCK HILL
PRESTON HILL
THE MALL
KINGSBURY ROAD
A4006
Kingsbury
Greenhill
FIELD END
Eastcote
LANE
West Harrow
IMPERIAL DRIVE
THE RIDGEWAY
A404
VAUGHN RD
KENTON
A409
DRAYCOTE AVE
FRYENT
FRYENT WAY
EASTERN AVE
VILLAGE WAY
BESSBOROUGH RD
ROAD
Coll
Northwick Park
Preston Road
Barn Hill
B454
CHURCH LANE
ELM AVE
WOOD LA
Ruislip Manor
Rayners Lane
A4090
ALEXANDRA
A312
HIGH ST
B458
Harrow on the Hill
A404
WATFORD ROAD
WINDERMERE AVE
CARLTON AVE EAST
THE AVENUE
A4140
Brent Reservoir (Welsh Harp)
VICTORIA
Roxeth
ROXETH GREEN AVE
XVII
SUDBURY CT
North Wembley
PRESTON RD
FORTY AVE
FORTY LANE
A4088
Wembley
EAST LANE
52

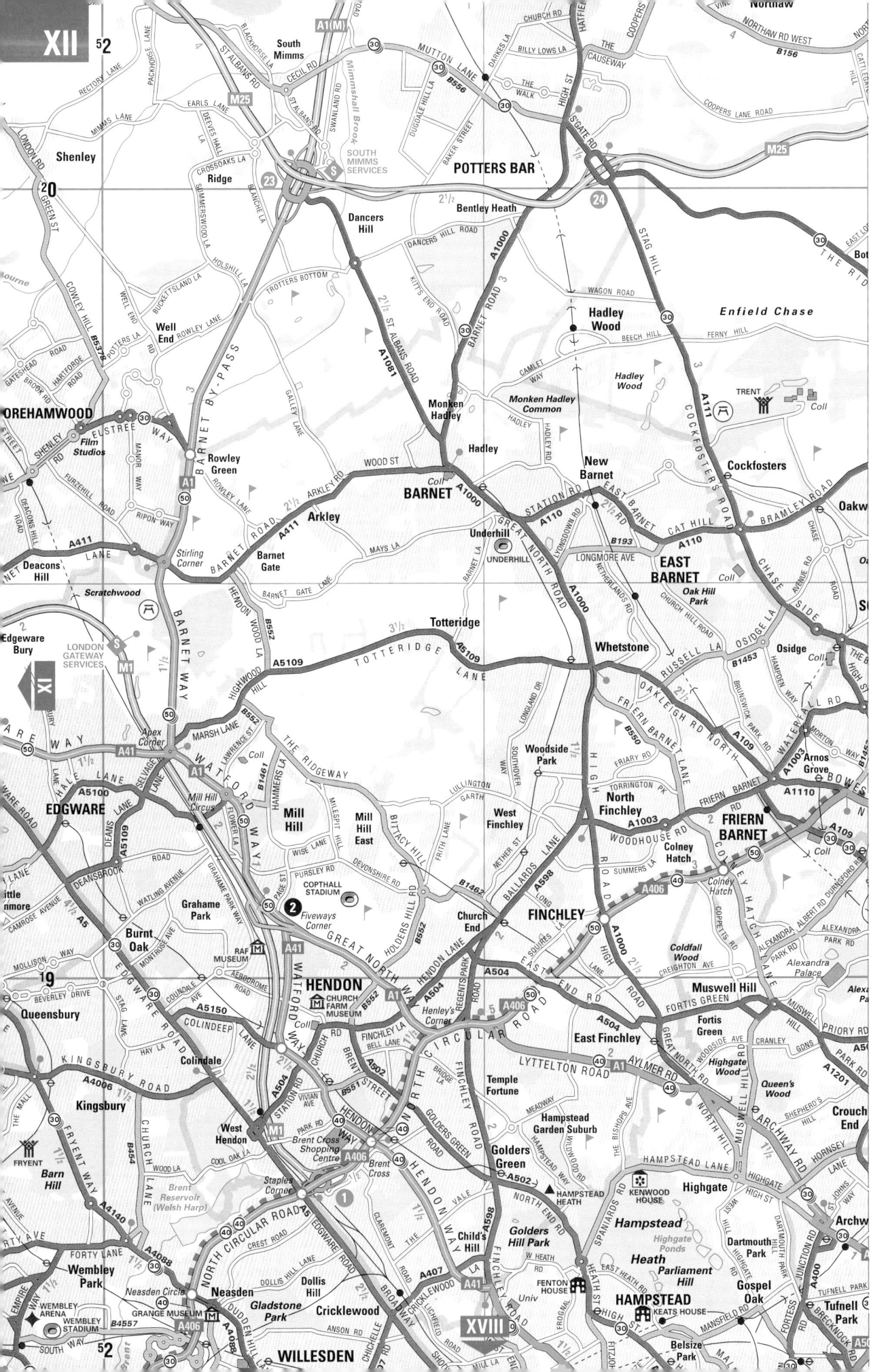

XII
South Mimms
MUTTON LANE
DARKES LA
CHURCH RD
BILLY LOWS LA
THE CAUSEWAY
NORTHAW RD WEST
B156
COOPERS LANE ROAD
RECTORY LANE
PACKHORSE LANE
BLACKHORSE LA
ST ALBANS RD
CECIL RD
A1(M)
M25
EARLS LANE
MIMMS LANE
DEEVES HALL LA
SWANLAND RD
Mimmshall Brook
DUGDALE HILL LA
BAKER STREET
B556
THE WALK
HIGH ST
S'GATE RD
LONDON RD
Shenley
CROSSOAKS LA
Ridge
SOUTH MIMMS SERVICES
POTTERS BAR
Bentley Heath
GREEN ST
SUMMERSWOOD LA
BLANCHE LA
Dancers Hill
DANCERS HILL ROAD
A1000
STAG HILL
HOLSHILL LA
TROTTERS BOTTOM
KITTS END ROAD
WAGON ROAD
Hadley Wood
Enfield Chase
COWLEY HILL
B5378
WELL END RD
BUCKETTSLAND LA
Well End
ROWLEY LANE
POTTERS LA
ST. ALBANS ROAD
A1081
BARNET ROAD
BEECH HILL
FERNY HILL
GATESHEAD ROAD
HARTFORDE ROAD
BROOK RD
BARNET BY-PASS
GALLEY LANE
CAMLET WAY
Hadley Wood
A111
COCKFOSTERS ROAD
TRENT
Monken Hadley
Monken Hadley Common
HADLEY RD
OREHAMWOOD
ELSTREE WAY
SHENLEY RD
Film Studios
MANOR WAY
Rowley Green
Hadley
New Barnet
Cockfosters
WOOD ST
ARKLEY RD
BARNET
A1000
STATION RD
EAST BARNET RD
CAT HILL
BRAMLEY ROAD
A1
FURZEHILL ROAD
RIPON WAY
ROWLEY LANE
Arkley
Underhill
UNDERHILL
A110
LYONSDOWN RD
B193
LONGMORE AVE
EAST BARNET
CHASE SIDE
DEACONS HILL ROAD
A411
LANE
Deacons Hill
Stirling Corner
BARNET ROAD
A411
Barnet Gate
MAYS LA
BARNET LA
GREAT NORTH ROAD
NETHERLANDS RD
Oak Hill Park
CHURCH HILL ROAD
BARNET GATE LANE
Scratchwood
HENDON WOOD LA
B552
Totteridge
A1000
Edgeware Bury
LONDON GATEWAY SERVICES
M1
BARNET WAY
A5109
TOTTERIDGE LANE
Whetstone
RUSSELL LA
OSIDGE LA
Osidge
B1453
HIGHWOOD HILL
OAKLEIGH RD NORTH
BRUNSWICK PARK RD
HAMPDEN WAY
IX
Apex Corner
MARSH LANE
B552
LAWRENCE ST
THE RIDGEWAY
LONGLAND DR
FRIERN BARNET LANE
B550
A109
WATERFALL RD
Arnos Grove
A41
WATFORD WAY
Woodside Park
FRIARY RD
A1003
BOWES
HALE LANE
A5100
SELVAGE LANE
B1461
HAMMERS LA
LULLINGTON GARTH
SOUTHOVER
TORRINGTON PK
FRIERN BARNET RD
A1110
EDGWARE
DEANS LANE
Mill Hill Circus
FLOWER LA
Mill Hill
MILESPIT HILL
Mill Hill East
BITTACY HILL
FRITH LANE
West Finchley
North Finchley
A1003
FRIERN BARNET
A5109
WISE LANE
WOODHOUSE RD
Colney Hatch
A109
DEANSBROOK ROAD
WATLING AVENUE
GRAHAME PARK WAY
PURSLEY RD
DEVONSHIRE RD
NETHER ST
BALLARDS LANE
SUMMERS LA
COLNEY HATCH LANE
CAMROSE AVENUE
A5
Grahame Park
COPTHALL STADIUM
B1462
A598
A406
Colney Hatch
Fiveways Corner
Church End
FINCHLEY
Burnt Oak
MONTROSE AVE
PAGE ST
GREAT NORTH WAY
HOLDERS HILL RD
B552
SQUIRES LA
HIGH ROAD
A1000
COPPETTS RD
ALEXANDRA PARK RD
MOLLISON WAY
RAF MUSEUM
AERODROME ROAD
HENDON LANE
REGENTS PARK ROAD
Coldfall Wood
CREIGHTON AVE
Alexandra Palace
BEVERLEY DRIVE
EDGWARE ROAD
STAG LANE
COUNDALE AVE
HENDON
CHURCH FARM MUSEUM
A504
EAST END RD
Muswell Hill
FORTIS GREEN
Queensbury
A5150
COLINDEEP LANE
Henley's Corner
A406
Fortis Green
MUSWELL HILL
PRIORY RD
HAY LA
Colindale
CHURCH RD
FINCHLEY LA
BELL LANE
NORTH CIRCULAR ROAD
A504
East Finchley
CRANLEY
KINGSBURY ROAD
A4006
A502
BRENT STREET
LYTTELTON ROAD
AYLMER RD
WOODSIDE AVE
Highgate Wood
Temple Fortune
GREAT NORTH RD
Kingsbury
STATION RD
VIVIAN AVE
B551
BRIDGE LA
FINCHLEY ROAD
Queen's Wood
MUSWELL HILL RD
SHEPHERD'S HILL
Crouch End
THE MALL
FRYENT WAY
CHURCH LANE
West Hendon
PARK RD
HENDON WAY
GOLDERS GREEN ROAD
MEADWAY
Hampstead Garden Suburb
NORTH HILL
ARCHWAY RD
HORNSEY LANE
FRYENT
Brent Cross Shopping Centre
COOL OAK LA
WOOD LA
A406
Brent Cross
HAMPSTEAD WAY
WILDWOOD RD
THE BISHOPS AVE
Golders Green
HAMPSTEAD LANE
Barn Hill
B454
Brent Reservoir (Welsh Harp)
Staples Corner
HENDON WAY
A502
HAMPSTEAD HEATH
KENWOOD HOUSE
Highgate
HIGHGATE
HIGH ST
A4140
NORTH CIRCULAR ROAD
EDGWARE ROAD
CLAREMONT
VALE
NORTH END RD
SPANIARDS RD
Hampstead
Highgate Ponds
Dartmouth Park
JUNCTION RD
Archway
CREST ROAD
Child's Hill
Golders Hill Park
W HEATH RD
Heath
Parliament Hill
FORTY LANE
A4088
A598
Wembley Park
A407
A41
DOLLIS HILL LANE
Dollis Hill
FENTON HOUSE
Univ
EAST HEATH RD
HIGHGATE RD
DARTMOUTH PARK HILL
A400
Gospel Oak
TUFNELL PARK
Neasden Circle
Neasden
CRICKLEWOOD LA
Gladstone Park
Cricklewood
HEATH ST
HAMPSTEAD
KEATS HOUSE
MANSFIELD RD
Tufnell Park
WEMBLEY ARENA
GRANGE MUSEUM
WEMBLEY STADIUM
B4557
A406
DUDDEN HILL LA
ANSON RD
CHICHELE RD
BROADWAY
XVIII
FROGNAL
HIGH ST
Belsize Park
BRECKNOCK RD
SOUTH WAY
WILLESDEN

Bury Green
CHESHUNT
LEE VALLEY
WALTHAM ABBEY
Cattlegate
Waltham Cross
Holdbrook
Wood Green
Crews Hill
Whitewebbs Park
CAPEL MANOR
Freezy Water
FORTY HALL
Clay Hill
Forty Hill
Enfield Wash
Enfield Lock
High Beach
Sewardstone
Gordon Hill
QUEEN ELIZABETH STADIUM
Enfield Highway
Brimsdown
ENFIELD
World's End
Grange Park
Bush Hill Park
Ponders End
King George's Reservoir
Sewardstonebury
Chingford Green
SOUTHGATE
Grovelands Park
Winchmore Hill
CHINGFORD
William Girling Reservoir
PICKETT'S LOCK
Friday Hill
Palmers Green
Lower Edmonton
Great Cambridge Junction
Pymmes Park
Cooks Ferry
Woodford Wells
Chingford Hatch
Bowes Park
EDMONTON
Angel Edmonton
Clockhouse Junction
NEW RIVER STADIUM
Hall Lane
Higham's Park
Hale End
WOODFORD
Banbury Reservoir
WHITE HART LANE
WALTHAMSTOW STADIUM
WOOD GREEN
BRUCE CASTLE MUSEUM
Woodford Green
Crooked Billet
Higham Hill
Waterworks Corner
Noel Park
TOTTENHAM
Bruce Grove
Reservoirs
West Green
Tottenham Hale
WALTHAMSTOW
Snaresbrook
Seven Sisters
VESTRY HOUSE MUSEUM
HORNSEY
Harringay
South Tottenham
Stroud Green
WANSTEAD
Finsbury Park
Stamford Hill
Upper Clapton
Green Man Interchange
Leytonstone
STOKE NEWINGTON
Clapton
BRISBANE ROAD
EMIRATES STADIUM
Lea Bridge
Hackney Marsh
LEYTON
Wanstead Flats
Shacklewell
Nags Head
Highbury
Clapton Park
Lea Interchange
Mkt
Canonbury
Temple Mills
Forest Gate
M25
A10
A406
A12
A503
XIV
XIX
54

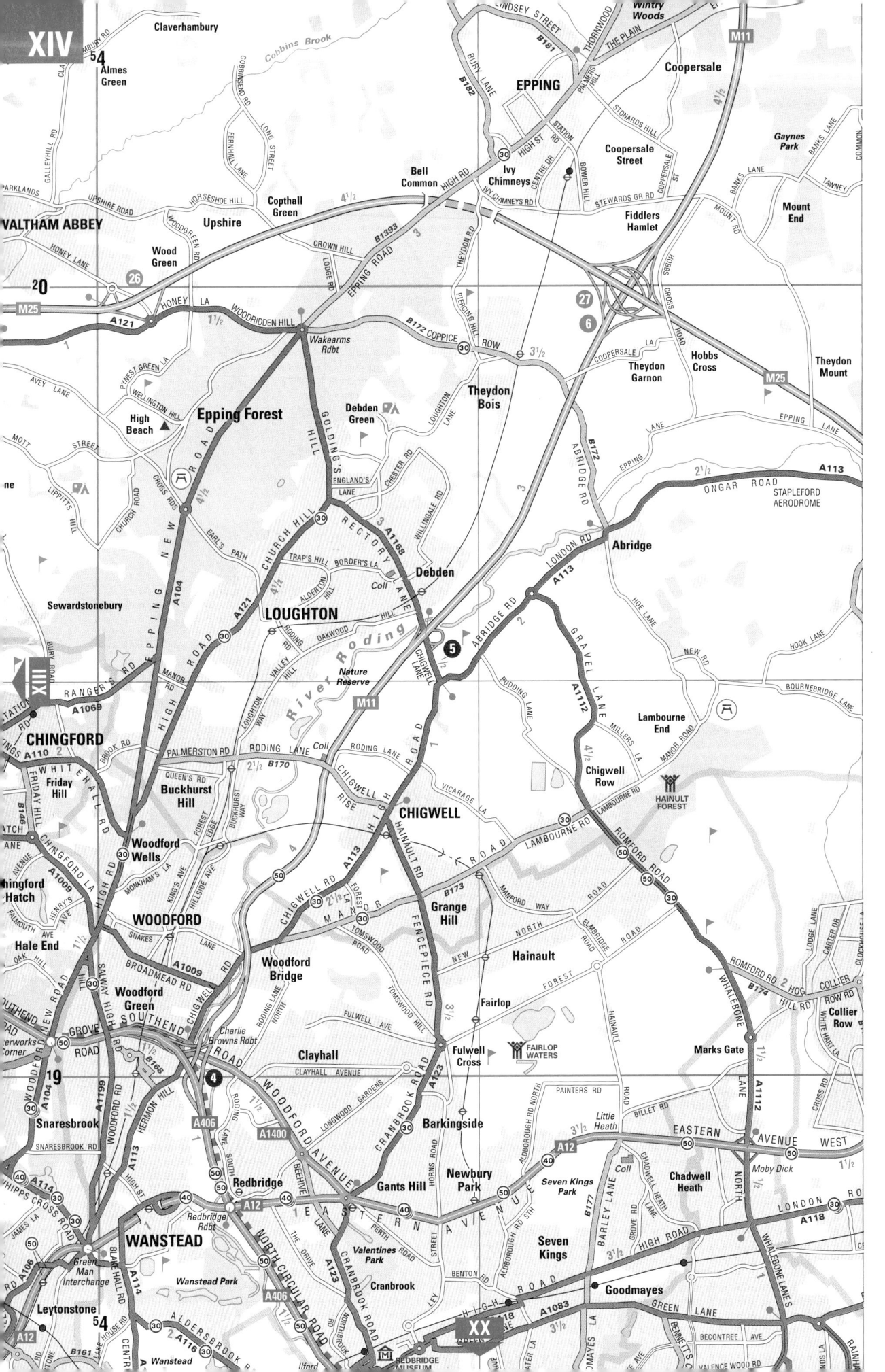
Claverhambury
Almes Green
Cobbins Brook
EPPING
Coopersale
Wintry Woods
THE PLAIN
M11
Coopersale Street
Gaynes Park
Bell Common
Ivy Chimneys
Copthall Green
Upshire
WALTHAM ABBEY
Fiddlers Hamlet
Mount End
Wood Green
M25
A121
B1393
B172
Wakearms Rdbt
Theydon Garnon
Hobbs Cross
Theydon Mount
Theydon Bois
Debden Green
High Beach
Epping Forest
A113
ONGAR ROAD
STAPLEFORD AERODROME
Abridge
Debden
LOUGHTON
Sewardstonebury
River Roding
Nature Reserve
Lambourne End
CHINGFORD
Friday Hill
Buckhurst Hill
Chigwell Row
HAINAULT FOREST
CHIGWELL
Woodford Wells
Chingford Hatch
WOODFORD
Grange Hill
Hale End
Woodford Bridge
Hainault
Woodford Green
Fairlop
Charlie Browns Rdbt
Clayhall
Fulwell Cross
FAIRLOP WATERS
Marks Gate
Collier Row
Snaresbrook
Barkingside
Little Heath
EASTERN AVENUE WEST
Redbridge
Gants Hill
Newbury Park
Seven Kings Park
Chadwell Heath
Moby Dick
Redbridge Rdbt
WANSTEAD
Valentines Park
Seven Kings
Green Man Interchange
Wanstead Park
Cranbrook
Goodmayes
Leytonstone
REDBRIDGE MUSEUM
Ilford
Wanstead
XX
XIII
A104
A1009
A406
A12
A1400
A123
A1112
A118
A1083
A114
A116
A1199
A106
A1069
A110
A1168
B173
B170
B174
B177
B168
B182
B181
B146
B161
19
20
54

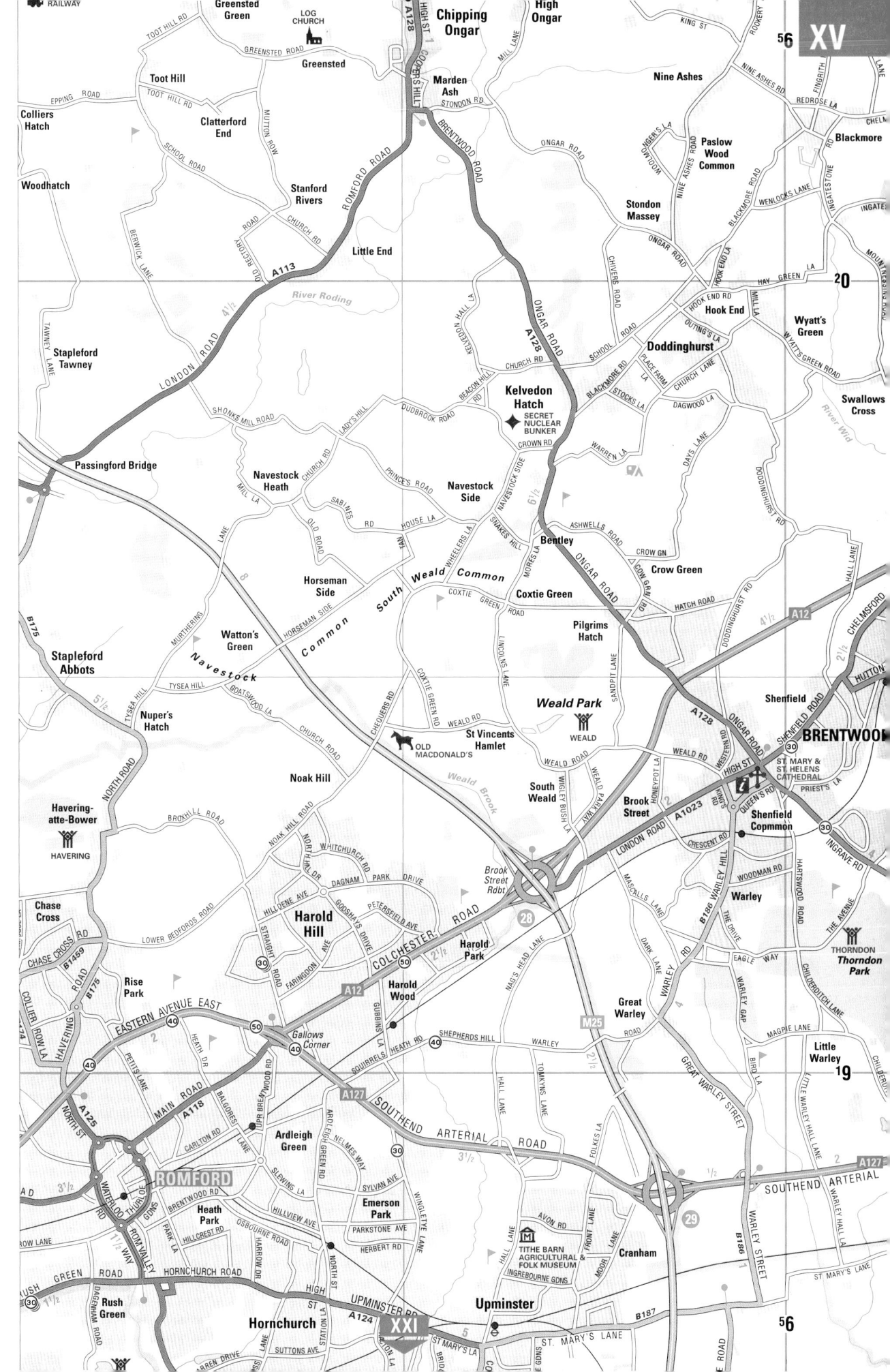

RAILWAY
XV
56
20
19
56
Greensted Green
LOG CHURCH
Greensted
TOOT HILL RD
GREENSTED ROAD
Chipping Ongar
High Ongar
A128
HIGH ST
COOPERS HILL
MILL LANE
Marden Ash
STONDON RD
BRENTWOOD ROAD
KING ST
ROOKERY
Nine Ashes
NINE ASHES RD
FINGRITH
REDROSE LA
Blackmore
Toot Hill
TOOT HILL RD
EPPING ROAD
Colliers Hatch
Clatterford End
MUTTON ROW
SCHOOL ROAD
Woodhatch
ROMFORD ROAD
Stanford Rivers
CHURCH RD
ROAD
OLD RECTORY
BERWICK LANE
Little End
A113
River Roding
ONGAR ROAD
WOOLMONGER'S LA
NINE ASHES ROAD
Paslow Wood Common
BLACKMORE ROAD
WENLOCKS LANE
INGATESTONE RD
Stondon Massey
ONGAR ROAD
CHIVERS ROAD
HOOK END LA
HAY GREEN LA
HOOK END RD
Hook End
MILL LA
OUTING'S LA
Wyatt's Green
WYATT'S GREEN ROAD
Doddinghurst
SCHOOL ROAD
KELVEDON HALL LA
ONGAR ROAD
A128
CHURCH RD
TAWNEY LANE
Stapleford Tawney
LONDON ROAD
PLACE FARM LA
CHURCH LANE
BLACKMORE RD
STOCKS LA
DAGWOOD LA
Kelvedon Hatch
SECRET NUCLEAR BUNKER
BEACON HILL RD
DUDBROOK ROAD
SHONKS MILL ROAD
LADY'S HILL
Swallows Cross
River Wid
CROWN RD
WARREN LA
DAYS LANE
Passingford Bridge
Navestock Heath
CHURCH RD
MILL LA
PRINCE'S ROAD
Navestock Side
NAVESTOCK SIDE
DODDINGHURST RD
SABINES RD
HOUSE LA
OLD ROAD
LANE
SNAKES HILL
Bentley
ASHWELLS ROAD
CROW GN
COW GRN RD
Crow Green
MORES LA
ONGAR ROAD
WHEELERS LA
South Weald Common
HALL LANE
Horseman Side
COXTIE GREEN ROAD
Coxtie Green
HATCH ROAD
A12
CHELMSFORD
HORSEMAN SIDE
Pilgrims Hatch
DODDINGHURST RD
B175
MURTHERING
Watton's Green
Navestock Common
LINCOLNS LANE
SANDPIT LANE
Stapleford Abbots
TYSEA HILL
GOATSWOOD LA
COXTIE GREEN RD
CHEQUERS RD
HUTTON
Shenfield
Weald Park
WEALD
Nuper's Hatch
CHURCH ROAD
WEALD RD
St Vincents Hamlet
OLD MACDONALD'S
A128
ONGAR ROAD
SHENFIELD ROAD
BRENTWOOD
WEALD ROAD
WEALD RD
WESTERN RD
HIGH ST
ST MARY & ST HELENS CATHEDRAL
PRIEST'S LA
NORTH ROAD
Noak Hill
Weald Brook
South Weald
WIGLEY BUSH LA
WEALD PARK WAY
HONEYPOT LA
Brook Street
A1023
KINGS RD
QUEEN'S RD
Shenfield Copmmon
INGRAVE RD
Havering-atte-Bower
HAVERING
BROXHILL ROAD
NOAK HILL ROAD
NORTH HILL DR
WHITCHURCH RD
LONDON ROAD
CRESCENT RD
Brook Street Rdbt
MASCALLS LANE
WOODMAN RD
HARTSWOOD ROAD
DAGNAM PARK DRIVE
HILLDENE AVE
GODSHALLS DRIVE
PETERSFIELD AVE
Warley
B186
WARLEY HILL
THE AVENUE
Chase Cross
LOWER BEDFORDS ROAD
Harold Hill
COLCHESTER ROAD
28
THE DRIVE
THORNDON
Thorndon Park
CHASE CROSS RD
B1459
STRAIGHT ROAD
FARINGDON AVE
Harold Park
NAG'S HEAD LANE
DARK LANE
EAGLE WAY
WARLEY RD
WARLEY GAP
CHILDERDITCH LANE
Rise Park
B175
A12
Harold Wood
GUBBINS LA
Great Warley
M25
COLLIER ROW LA
HAVERING ROAD
EASTERN AVENUE EAST
Gallows Corner
SHEPHERDS HILL
WARLEY
MAGPIE LANE
Little Warley
HEATH DR
PETITS LANE
HEATH RD
SQUIRRELS
UPR BRENTWOOD RD
TOMKYNS LANE
HALL LANE
GREAT WARLEY STREET
BIRD LA
LITTLE WARLEY HALL LANE
A125
NORTH ST
MAIN ROAD
A118
BALGORES LANE
A127
SOUTHEND ARTERIAL ROAD
ARDLEIGH GREEN RD
Ardleigh Green
NELMES WAY
FOLKES LA
CARLTON RD
A127
SOUTHEND ARTERIAL
WARLEY HALL LA
ROMFORD
SLEWINS LA
SYLVAN AVE
Emerson Park
WINGLETYE LANE
29
WATERLOO RD
THURLOE GDNS
BRENTWOOD RD
Heath Park
HILLVIEW AVE
PARKSTONE AVE
AVON RD
FRONT LANE
MOOR LANE
WARLEY STREET
B186
HILLCREST RD
OSBOURNE ROAD
HARROW DR
HERBERT RD
NORTH ST
HALL LANE
TITHE BARN AGRICULTURAL & FOLK MUSEUM
Cranham
ROM VALLEY WAY
PARK LA
INGREBOURNE GDNS
ST MARY'S LANE
RUSH GREEN ROAD
HORNCHURCH ROAD
HIGH ST
UPMINSTER RD
Upminster
B187
Rush Green
DAGENHAM ROAD
Hornchurch
A124
STATION LA
XXI
ST MARY'S LA
ST. MARY'S LANE
SUTTONS AVE

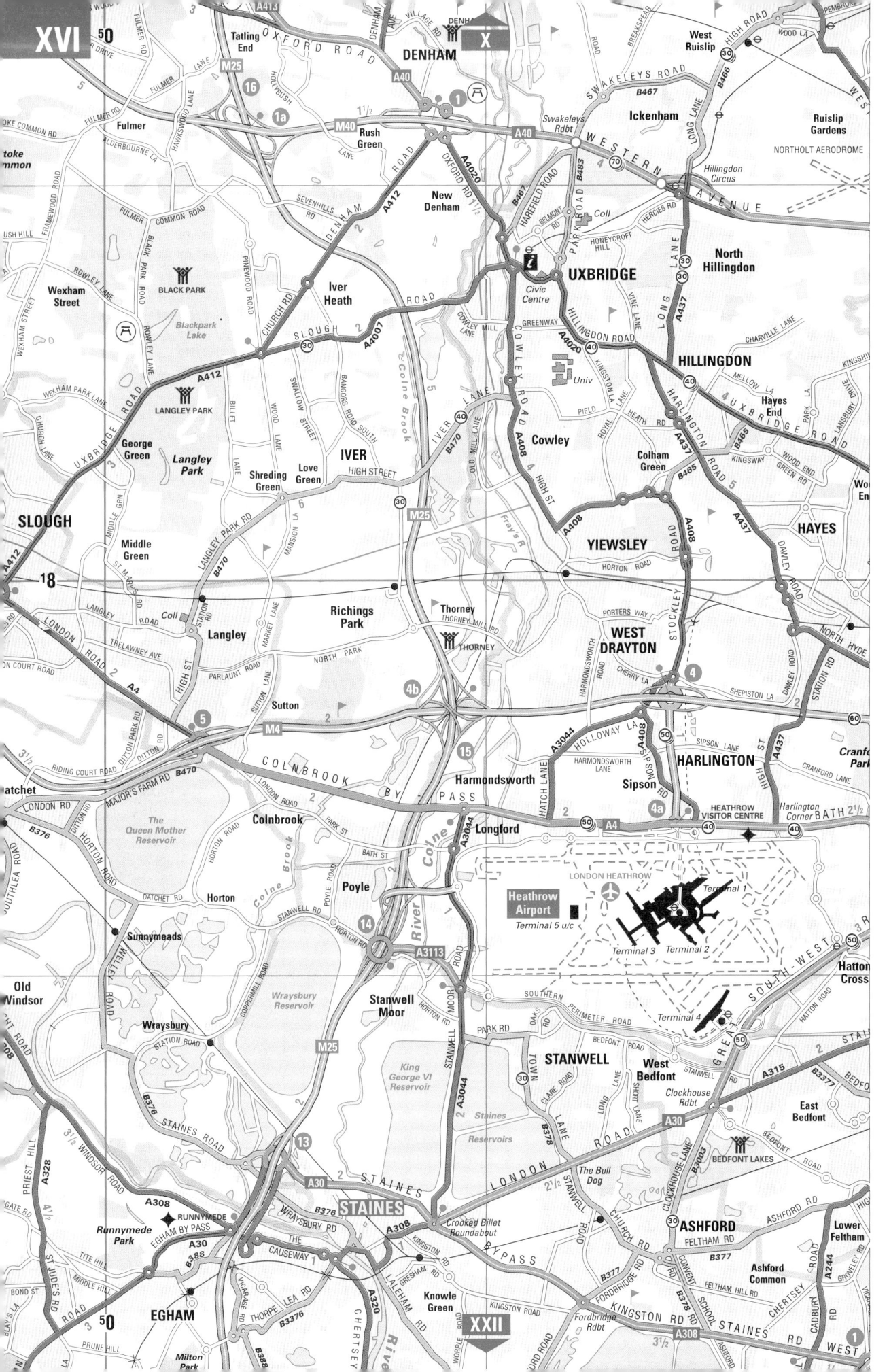
Tatling End
OXFORD ROAD
DENHAM
X
West Ruislip
HIGH ROAD
SWAKELEYS ROAD
Ickenham
Fulmer
Rush Green
M40
A40
Swakeleys Rdbt
WESTERN AVENUE
Ruislip Gardens
NORTHOLT AERODROME
Hillingdon Circus
New Denham
SEVENHILLS RD
DENHAM ROAD
FULMER COMMON ROAD
HARFIELD ROAD
PARK ROAD
Coll
HONEYCROFT HILL
North Hillingdon
UXBRIDGE
Civic Centre
Wexham Street
BLACK PARK
Blackpark Lake
Iver Heath
SLOUGH ROAD
PINEWOOD ROAD
CHURCH RD
ROWLEY LANE
BLACK PARK ROAD
LONG LANE
HILLINGDON ROAD
GREENWAY
COWLEY ROAD
Univ
HILLINGDON
CHARVILLE LANE
UXBRIDGE ROAD
Hayes End
WEXHAM PARK LANE
LANGLEY PARK
George Green
Langley Park
Colne Brook
IVER
IVER LANE
Cowley
Colham Green
HARLINGTON ROAD
Shreding Green
Love Green
HIGH STREET
SLOUGH
Middle Green
LANGLEY PARK RD
YIEWSLEY
HORTON ROAD
STOCKLEY ROAD
HAYES
DAWLEY ROAD
Richings Park
Thorney
THORNEY
Langley
WEST DRAYTON
NORTH HYDE
LONDON ROAD
A4
NORTH PARK
PARLAUNT ROAD
Sutton
M4
HARLINGTON
SIPSON LANE
HOLLOWAY LA
Sipson
SHEPISTON LA
Cranford Park
CRANFORD LANE
COLNBROOK BY PASS
Harmondsworth
HARMONDSWORTH LANE
HATCH LANE
Datchet
MAJOR'S FARM RD
RIDING COURT ROAD
The Queen Mother Reservoir
Colnbrook
Longford
HEATHROW VISITOR CENTRE
Harlington Corner
BATH ROAD
LONDON HEATHROW
Heathrow Airport
Terminal 5 u/c
Terminal 1
Terminal 2
Terminal 3
Terminal 4
Poyle
Horton
River Colne
Sunnymeads
Hatton Cross
GREAT SOUTH-WEST ROAD
Old Windsor
Wraysbury Reservoir
Stanwell Moor
SOUTHERN PERIMETER ROAD
Wraysbury
STATION ROAD
King George VI Reservoir
STANWELL
West Bedfont
PARK RD
Clockhouse Rdbt
East Bedfont
Staines Reservoirs
STAINES ROAD
WINDSOR ROAD
LONDON ROAD
BEDFONT LAKES
The Bull Dog
RUNNYMEDE
Runnymede Park
EGHAM BY PASS
STAINES
Crooked Billet Roundabout
ASHFORD
FELTHAM RD
Lower Feltham
THE CAUSEWAY
Ashford Common
Knowle Green
KINGSTON ROAD
Fordbridge Rdbt
EGHAM
THORPE LEA RD
XXII
STAINES RD WEST
Milton Park

Ruislip Manor
Roxeth
XI
Harrow on the Hill
North Wembley
Wembley Park
South Ruislip
South Harrow
Sudbury
WEMBLEY
WEMBLEY ARENA
WEMBLEY STADIUM
GRANGE MUSEUM
Neasden Circle
Polish War Memorial
NORTHOLT
Target Rdbt
Stonebridge Park
Alperton
Stonebridge
Perivale
Greenford Rdbt
White Hart Rdbt
GREENFORD
LONDON MOTORCYCLE MUSEUM
Hangar Lane
Park Royal
Yeading
Grand Union Canal
EALING
West Acton
Gipsy Corner
Ossie Garvin Rdbt
Hayes Town
Dormer's Wells
Drayton Green
ACTON
SOUTHALL
West Ealing
HANWELL
South Acton
Norwood Green
Osterley Park
Gunnersbury Park
Northfields
Chiswick Rdbt
HESTON SERVICES
GRIFFIN PARK
STEAM MUS.
Kew Bridge
BRENTFORD
OSTERLEY PARK (N.T.)
HESTON
Gillette Corner
MUSIC MUS.
Kew
CHISWICK
North Hyde
Osterley
Public Record Office
Syon Park
SYON HOUSE
ROYAL BOTANIC GARDENS (KEW)
Grove Park
Waggoners Rdbt
Cranford
Henlys Rdbt
Civic Centre
North Sheen
Chiswick Br
Hounslow West
HOUNSLOW
Woodlands
Richmond Circus
Chalkers Corner
Mortlake
Old Deer Park
Manor Circus
ISLEWORTH
East Sheen
RICHMOND
Twickenham Br
Hounslow Heath
RUGBY MUS.
TWICKENHAM
Richmond Br
St Margarets
Richmond Hill
Whitton
THE STOOP
MARBLE HILL HOUSE
Roads in Richmond Park open in daylight hours only
Richmond Park
FELTHAM
TWICKENHAM
Petersham
HAM HOUSE (N.T.)
River Thames
Hanworth Park
Ham
Robin Hood
Apex Corner
Kingston Vale
HANWORTH
TEDDINGTON
XXIII
KINGSTON UPON THAMES
KEMPTON

XVIII
XII
XVII
XXIV
52
18
HAMPSTEAD
KEATS HOUSE
Tufnell Park
Gladstone Park
Cricklewood
GRANGE MUSEUM
WILLESDEN
Belsize Park
Kentish Town
Swiss Cottage
West Hampstead
FREUD
Stonebridge Park
Brondesbury
Kilburn
Primrose Hill
JEWISH MUSEUM
CAMDEN TOWN
Stonebridge
Harlesden
LONDON ZOO
Kensal Rise
St. John's Wood
LORDS
Regents Park
Park Royal
Maida Vale
CRICKET
St Pancras
Euston
Old Oak Common
Grand Union Canal
Marylebone
MADAME TUSSAUD'S
Wormwood Scrubs Park
WEST LONDON STADIUM
Marylebone Flyover
MARYLEBONE
Gipsy Corner
West Acton
East Acton
Westbourne Park
Paddington
PADDINGTON
MUSEUM OF BRANDS
White City
LOFTUS ROAD
Savoy Circus
Bayswater
ACTON
Notting Hill
Hyde Park
Mayfair
ROYAL ACADEMY
NATIONAL GALLERY
Kensington Gardens
KENSINGTON PALACE
Green Park
St James's Palace
South Acton
Bedford Park
Shepard's Bush
Holland Park
APSLEY HOUSE
BUCKINGHAM PALACE
St James's Park
Hyde Park Corner
Knightsbridge
ROYAL ALBERT HALL
NATURAL HISTORY
WESTMINSTER ABBEY
Olympia
HAMMERSMITH
Victoria
TATE BRITAIN
CHELSEA
Chiswick Rdbt
NATIONAL ARMY MUSEUM
RANELAGH GDNS
Pimlico
Hammersmith Br
Hammersmith Broadway
Earls Court
Kew Bridge
CHISWICK
Hogarth Rdbt
THE QUEEN'S CLUB
Chelsea Br
CHISWICK HOUSE
Public Record Office
STAMFORD BRIDGE
Albert Br
CHILDREN'S ZOO
Battersea Br
Battersea Park
Grove Park
FULHAM
Parsons Green
WETLANDS CENTRE
River Thames
Barnes Br
BARNES
CRAVEN COTTAGE
WESTLAND HELIPORT
BATTERSEA
Chiswick Br
North Sheen
Mortlake
Putney Br
Hurlingham Park
Clapham Junction
CLAPHAM
Chalkers Corner
Manor Circus
Red Rover
Wandsworth Br
RICHMOND
East Sheen
PUTNEY
Wandsworth Gyratory
Clapham Common
WANDSWORTH
Richmond Hill
Roehampton
Putney Heath
West Hill
Wandsworth Common
Balham
Grange Mills
Roads in Richmond Park open in daylight hours only
Richmond Park
Tibbet's Corner
Southfields
Earlsfield
Putney Vale
Upper Tooting
Tooting Bec Common
Robin Hood
Wimbledon Park
WIMBLEDON L.T.A.
TENNIS MUSEUM
WIMBLEDON STADIUM
Tooting Bec
Kingston Vale
Wimbledon Common
WIMBLEDON
Tooting
Furzedown
Crooked Billet
Collier's Wood
Coombe
KINGSTON UPON THAMES
Coombe Lane
Norbiton
NEW MALDEN
MITCHAM
Morden Hall Park
Raynes
Bushey Mead

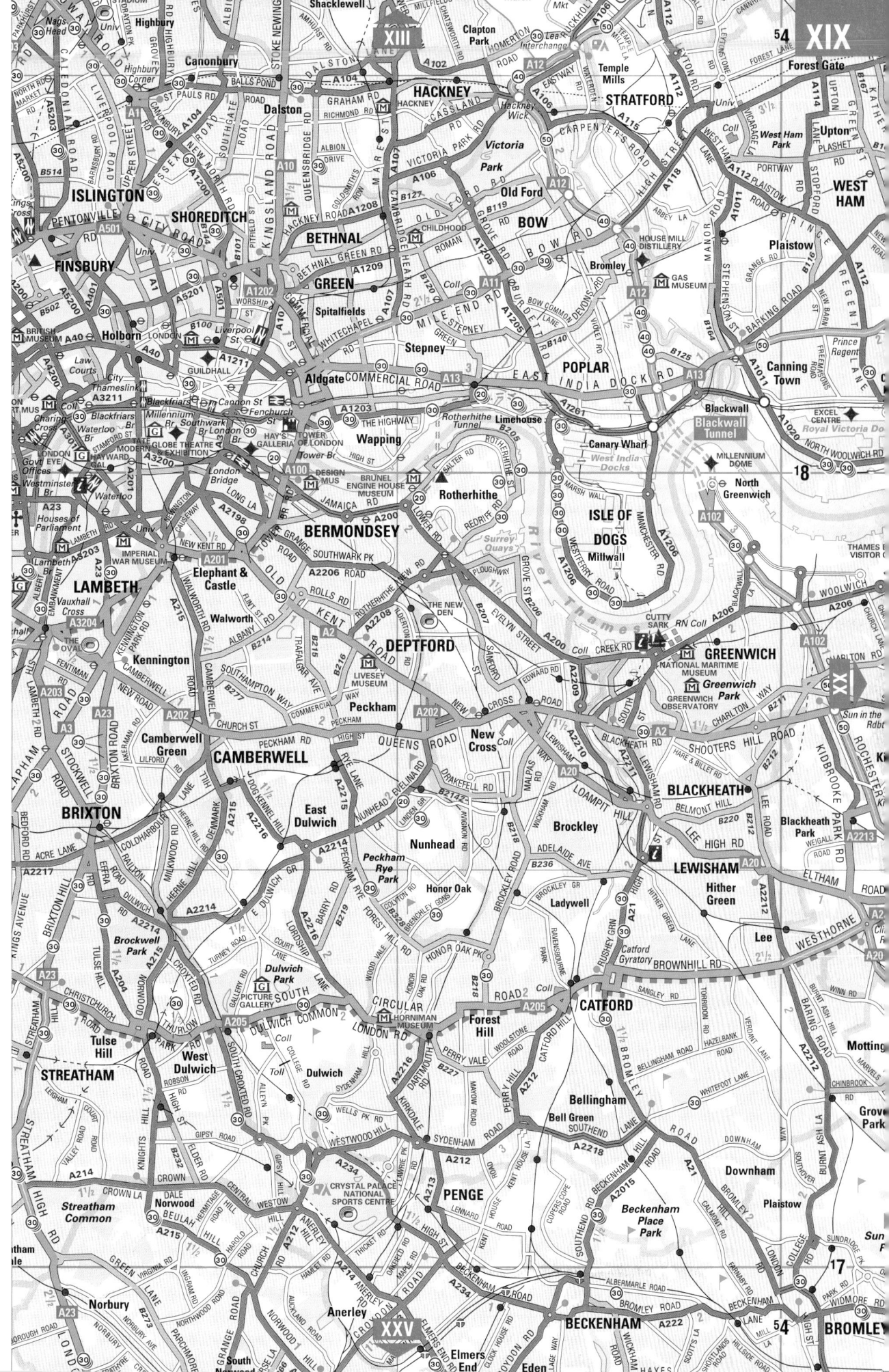
XIX
54
XIII
XX
XXV
18
17
Highbury
Canonbury
Shacklewell
Clapton Park
Lea Interchange
Temple Mills
Forest Gate
HACKNEY
Hackney Wick
Dalston
STRATFORD
Upton
West Ham Park
Victoria Park
Old Ford
ISLINGTON
SHOREDITCH
BETHNAL GREEN
BOW
WEST HAM
Plaistow
FINSBURY
Bromley
House Mill Distillery
Gas Museum
Spitalfields
Holborn
Stepney
Liverpool St
British Museum
POPLAR
Canning Town
Prince Regent
Law Courts
Guildhall
City Thameslink
Aldgate
Blackfriars
Cannon St
Fenchurch St
Limehouse
Blackwall
Blackwall Tunnel
ExCeL Centre
Royal Victoria Dock
Charing Cross
Millennium Br
Southwark Br
London Br
Tower of London
Wapping
Rotherhithe Tunnel
Canary Wharf
West India Docks
Millennium Dome
North Greenwich
London Eye
Westminster Br
Waterloo
Globe Theatre & Exhibition
Tate Modern
Hay's Galleria
Tower Br
Design Mus
Brunel Engine House Museum
Rotherhithe
Houses of Parliament
London Bridge
BERMONDSEY
ISLE OF DOGS
Millwall
Surrey Quays
Imperial War Museum
Lambeth Br
Elephant & Castle
LAMBETH
Vauxhall Cross
River Thames
Walworth
The New Den
Cutty Sark
The Oval
Kennington
DEPTFORD
GREENWICH
National Maritime Museum
Greenwich Park
Greenwich Observatory
Livesey Museum
Peckham
New Cross
Camberwell Green
CAMBERWELL
BLACKHEATH
Sun in the Sands
BRIXTON
East Dulwich
Nunhead
Brockley
Blackheath Park
Peckham Rye Park
LEWISHAM
Honor Oak
Ladywell
Hither Green
Brockwell Park
Lee
Catford Gyratory
Dulwich Park
Picture Gallery
Horniman Museum
CATFORD
Tulse Hill
West Dulwich
Forest Hill
Dulwich
Mottingham
STREATHAM
Bellingham
Bell Green
Grove Park
Crystal Palace National Sports Centre
PENGE
Downham
Streatham Common
Norwood
Beckenham Place Park
Plaistow
Norbury
Anerley
BECKENHAM
BROMLEY
South Norwood
Elmers End
Eden Park

XX
XIV
XIX
XXVI
Goodmayes
GREEN LANE
A1083
BECONTREE AVE
VALENCE WOOD RD
RAINHAM RD N
FRIZLANDS LA
Cranbrook
A406
Wanstead Flats
ALDERSBROOK RD
A116
Ilford Interchange
REDBRIDGE MUSEUM
ILFORD
Loxford
LOXFORD LANE
A123
ILFORD LANE
CAPEL ROAD
Manor Park
ROMFORD ROAD
A118
CHURCH RD
Little Ilford
LITTLE ILFORD LA
Forest Gate
FOREST LANE
CANNHALL RD
LEYTONSTONE RD
WOODFORD RD
CENTRE RD
A114
Univ
Fair Cross
LONGBRIDGE ROAD
A124
GOODMAYES LA
LODGE AVE
BECONTREE AVE
BENNETTS CASTLE LA
WOOD LANE
B191
Becontree
OXLOW LA
PARSLOES AVE
A1240
HEATHWAY
REEDE RD
Mayesbrook Park
PORTERS AVE
A1153
UPNEY LA
HEDGEMANS RD
WOODWARD RD
DAGENHAM AVE
BROAD ST
BALLARDS ROAD
Plashet
PLASHET GR
B109
A117
HIGH ST NORTH
B167
KATHERINE RD
GREEN ST
UPTON LANE
BROWNING ROAD
A406
NORTHERN RELIEF RD
BARKING
Castle Green
RIPPLE RD
RIPPLE ROAD
A123
EASTBURY MANOR HOUSE
Ripple Road
Heathway
Coll
West Ham Park
Upton
PLASHET RD
B165
Upton Park
BURGES RD
Barking Flyover
BARKING ROAD
VICARAGE LA
WEST HAM LANE
PORTWAY
A112
PLAISTOW ROAD
WEST HAM
BOLEYN GD (UPTON PARK)
STOPFORD RD
A124
Wallend
EAST HAM
HIGH ST SOUTH
ST PAULS RD
GASCOIGNE RD
EDWARDS RD
KING RD
MOVERS LA
A13
Movers Lane
BASTABLE AVENUE
ALFRED'S WAY
THAMES ROAD
RENWICK ROAD
RIVER RD
Barking Creek
Creekmouth
A1011
MANOR ROAD
Plaistow
PRINCE REGENT LANE
CENTRAL PARK RD
NEW CITY ROAD
B167
GRANGE RD
B116
LONSDALE AVENUE
NEWHAM WAY
A112
BARKING ROAD
NEW BARN ST
STEPHENSON ST
B164
Beckton Alps
TOLLGATE ROAD
Beckton
WOOLWICH MANOR WAY
Prince Regent
FREEMASONS ROAD
STANSFELD RD
Canning Town
Custom House
A1011
A13
River Thames
Blackwall
EXCEL CENTRE
Blackwall Tunnel
Royal Victoria Dock
A112
Royal Albert Dock
CITY AIRPORT
King George V Dock
A1020
NORTH WOOLWICH RD
A112
ALBERT RD
MILLENNIUM DOME
North Greenwich
Silvertown
Thames Barrier
North Woolwich
OLD STATION RAILWAY MUSEUM
Woolwich Ferry
A102
THAMES BARRIER VISITOR CENTRE
WOOLWICH
WOOLWICH ROAD
Univ
PLUMSTEAD RD
Plumstead
THE VALLEY
HILLREACH
CHARLTON CHURCH LANE
B210
Charlton
A206
GREENWICH
NATIONAL MARITIME MUSEUM
Greenwich Park
GREENWICH OBSERVATORY
A102
CHARLTON RD
CHARLTON PARK LA
Woolwich Common
ACADEMY ROAD
NIGHTINGALE PL
HERBERT RD
BURRAGE ROAD
PLUMSTEAD COMMON ROAD
GRIFFIN RD
A206
PLUMSTEAD HIGH ST
LAKEDALE ROAD
CROSSNESS PUMPING STATION
A2041
CARLYLE RD
Thamesmead
EASTERN WAY
A2016
WESTERN WAY
NATHAN WAY
YARNTON WAY
PICARDY MANORWAY
Abbey Wood
EYNSHAM DR
A2041
HARROW MANOR WAY
GILBERT RD
ABBEY ROAD
Belvedere
B213
McLEOD RD
BASILDON RD
KNEE HILL
BOSTALL HILL
NEW RD
PICARDY RD
ERITH
WOOLWICH RD
A206
Lessness Heath
Bostall Woods
West Heath
BEDONWELL RD
KING HAROLDS WAY
KING'S HIGHWAY
East Wickham
A209
WICKHAM LANE
LODGE HILL
LONGLEIGH LA
OKEHAMPTON CRES
BROOK ST
BELMONT RD
HEATH RD
GLENMORE ROAD
Shooters Hill
CHAUCER RD
WICKHAM ST
SHOOTERS HILL ROAD
A205
A207
Sun in the Sands Rdbt
B211
CHARLTON WAY
SHOOTERS HILL ROAD
HARE & BILLET RD
B212
KIDBROOKE PARK RD
ROCHESTER WAY
Kidbrooke
BROAD WALK
Eltham Common
WELL HALL ROAD
SHOOTERS HILL
DOVER RD
BELLEGROVE RD
Welling
NEW ROAD
PARK VIEW RD
BRAMPTON ROAD
PICKFORD LANE
BELVEDERE RD
WOOLWICH RD
ERITH ROAD
LONG LANE
BLACKHEATH
BELMONT HILL
B220
B212
LEE ROAD
LEE HIGH RD
Blackheath Park
Kidbrooke Intc
ROCHESTER WAY
A2213
WEIGALL ROAD
A2
Oxleas Wood
WELLINGWAY
HOOK LANE
A207
Falconwood
EAST ROCHESTER WAY
WESTWOOD LA
CROOK LOG
B'WAY
Bexleyheath
LEWISHAM
A20
ELTHAM ROAD
AVENUE
RELIEF ROAD
MOUNT RD
RIEFIELD RD
A2
Danson Park
THE RED HOUSE
DANSON RD
UPTON RD
ALBION RD
GRAVEL HILL
LATHAM RD
Hither Green
A2212
ELTHAM HILL
ELTHAM
BEXLEY RD
Danson Interchange
BEXLEY
A205
Yorkshire Grey
A210
Coll
Avery Hill
A210
BLACKFEN ROAD
Blackfen
A221
PENHILL RD
BRIDGEN RD
B2210
PARKHILL RD
Old Bexley
BOURNE RD
Lee
WESTHORNE
Cliftons Rdbt
A20
ELTHAM PALACE
COURT RD
A208
DAYS LANE
WILLERSLEY AVE
SHERWOOD PK AVE
PARK AVE
MARLBOROUGH
HALFWAY STREET
B2214
A222
HURST ROAD
HURST ROAD
FOOTSCRAY ROAD
AVERY HILL RD
New Eltham
SIDCUP ROAD
A211
B263
GREEN LANE
TORRIDON RD
HAZELBANK ROAD
VERDANT LANE
BURNT ASH HILL
BARING ROAD
WINN RD
A2212
Mottingham
Coll
MARVELS LANE
B226
GROVE PK RD
MOTTINGHAM RD
SOUTHWOOD RD
LONGLANDS ROAD
FARADAY AVE
LANSDOWN RD
BEXLEY LANE
WHITEFOOT LANE
CHINBROOK RD
Grove Park
DUNKERY ROAD
WILLIAM BAREFOOT DR
Longlands
MAIN RD
STATION RD
SIDCUP
RECTORY LA
NORTH CRAY ROAD
A223
North Cray
Joydens Wood
DOWNHAM WAY
SOUTHOVER
BURNT ASH LA
WHITE HORSE HILL
A208
ELMSTEAD LANE
RED HILL
B263
SIDCUP BY-PASS ROAD
A20
SIDCUP HILL
A211
Downham
Elmstead Wood
Coll
Elmstead
Foots Cray
GRAY RD
A21
BROMLEY HILL
CALMONT RD
Plaistow
Sundridge Park
SUNDRIDGE AVE
YESTER ROAD
WILLOW GR
ASHFIELD LA
FERRY ST
Frognal Corner
Scadbury Park Nature Reserve
EDGINGTON WAY
Critnall's Corner
Chislehurst Common
CHISLEHURST
MAIDSTONE ROAD
Ruxley
Upper Ruxley

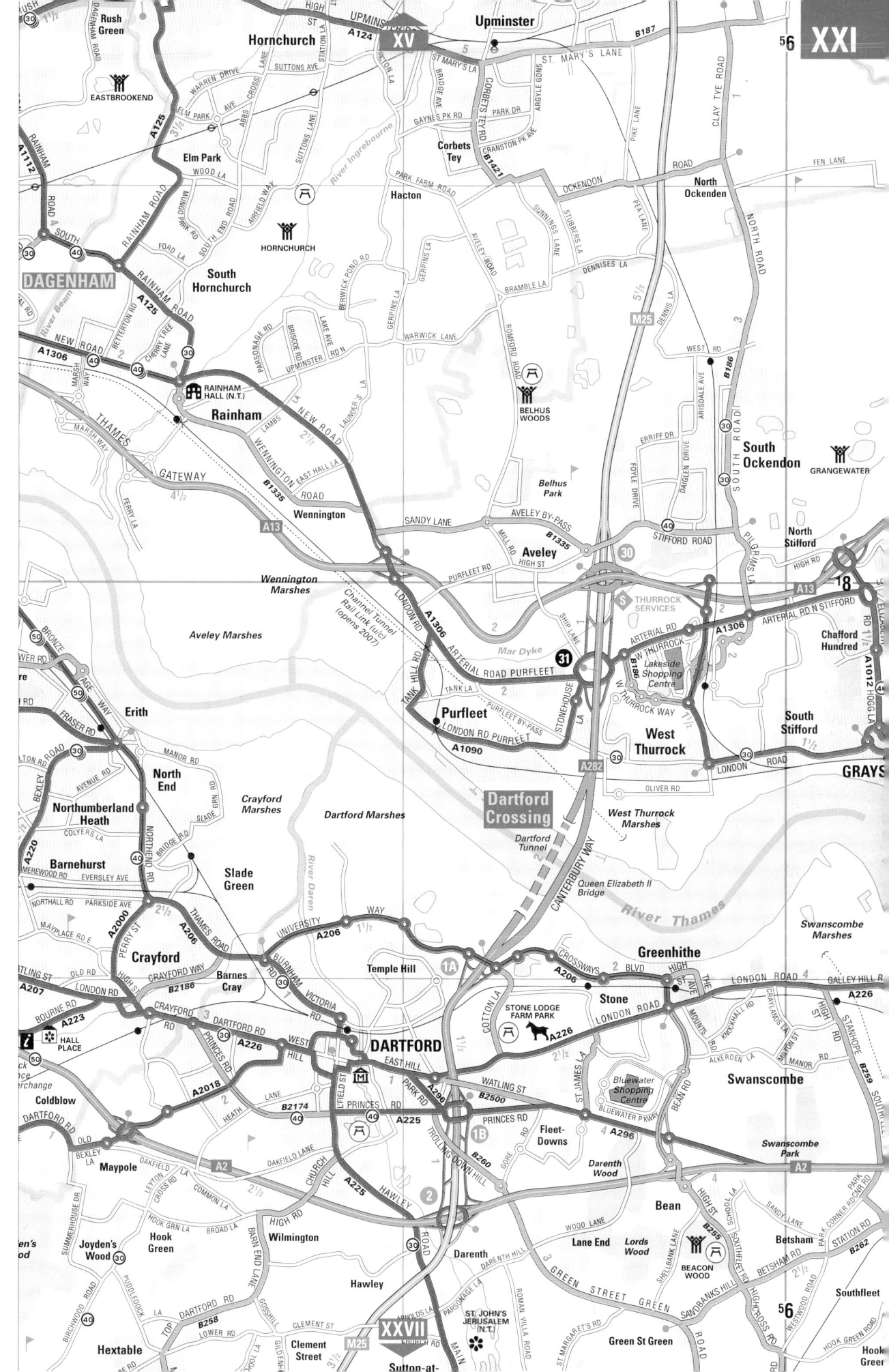

XV

Rush Green

Upminster

B187

Hornchurch

A124

EASTBROOKEND

St. Mary's La

CORBETS TEY RD

Clay Tye Road

FEN LANE

Corbets Tey

B1421

North Ockenden

OCKENDON ROAD

NORTH ROAD

Elm Park

Hacton

Warren Drive

River Ingrebourne

M25

DAGENHAM

South Hornchurch

HORNCHURCH

WEST RD

B186

South Ockendon

GRANGEWATER

A1306

NEW ROAD

RAINHAM HALL (N.T.)

BELHUS WOODS

South Ockendon

Rainham

Belhus Park

Stifford Road

North Stifford

A13

THAMES

GATEWAY

Wennington

Aveley By-Pass

B1335

Aveley High St

30

THURROCK SERVICES

A13

18

Wennington Marshes

Channel Tunnel Rail Link (u/c) (opens 2007)

LONDON RD

A1306

ARTERIAL ROAD PURFLEET

Mar Dyke

31

W Thurrock

Chafford Hundred

A1012

Aveley Marshes

TANK LA

Purfleet

West Thurrock

South Stifford

GRAYS

Erith

A1090 LONDON RD PURFLEET

A282

West Thurrock

London Road

Northumberland Heath

Barnehurst

North End

Crayford Marshes

Dartford Marshes

Dartford Crossing

Dartford Tunnel

West Thurrock Marshes

River Thames

Swanscombe Marshes

Slade Green

River Daren

Queen Elizabeth II Bridge

CANTERBURY WAY

A220

Crayford

A206

A206

Temple Hill

1A

CROSSWAYS

A206

Greenhithe

Stone

A226

Swanscombe

A226

Barnes Cray

Stone Lodge Farm Park

London Road

HALL PLACE

DARTFORD

A226

Bluewater Shopping Centre

Swanscombe Park

Coldblow

A2018

A225

A296

Fleet-Downs

A296

A2

Bean

A2

Maypole

Joyden's Wood

Hook Green

Wilmington

Darenth

Darenth Wood

Lane End

Lords Wood

BEACON WOOD

Betsham

Hextable

XXVII

M25

Clement Street

ST. JOHN'S JERUSALEM (N.T.)

Green St Green

Southfleet

Sutton-at-

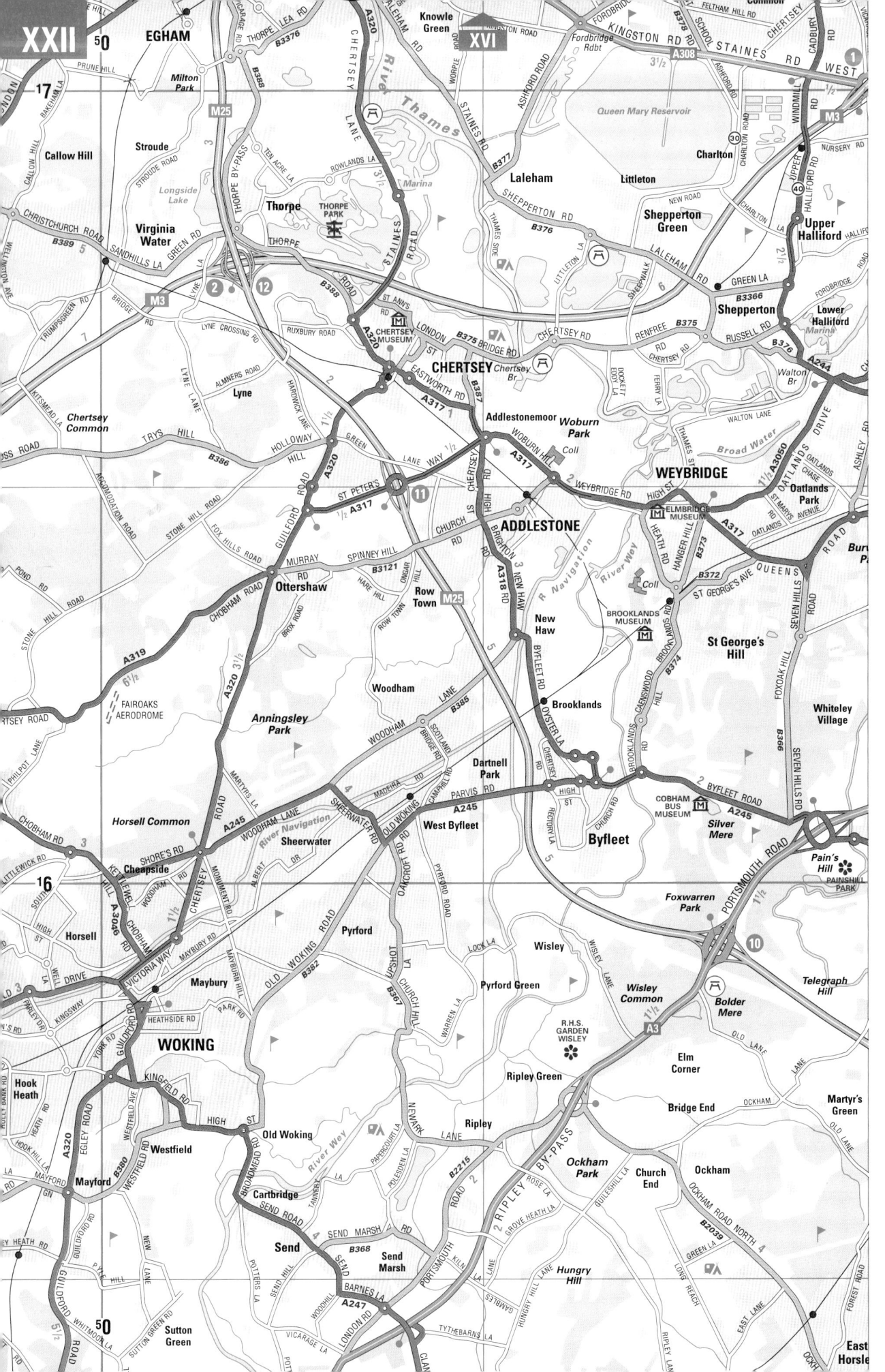

XVI
EGHAM
Milton Park
Knowle Green
Stroude
Callow Hill
Longside Lake
Thorpe
THORPE PARK
Virginia Water
Marina
River Thames
Laleham
Littleton
Queen Mary Reservoir
Charlton
Shepperton Green
Upper Halliford
Shepperton
Lower Halliford
Marina
CHERTSEY MUSEUM
CHERTSEY
Chertsey Br
Walton Br
Lyne
Chertsey Common
Addlestonemoor
Woburn Park
Coll
Broad Water
WEYBRIDGE
ELMBRIDGE MUSEUM
Oatlands Park
ADDLESTONE
Ottershaw
Row Town
R Navigation
River Wey
Coll
BROOKLANDS MUSEUM
New Haw
St George's Hill
Woodham
Brooklands
FAIROAKS AERODROME
Anningsley Park
Whiteley Village
Dartnell Park
Horsell Common
Sheerwater
River Navigation
West Byfleet
COBHAM BUS MUSEUM
Silver Mere
Byfleet
Cheapside
Pain's Hill
PAINSHILL PARK
Foxwarren Park
Horsell
Pyrford
Wisley
Telegraph Hill
Maybury
Pyrford Green
Wisley Common
Bolder Mere
R.H.S. GARDEN WISLEY
WOKING
Elm Corner
Hook Heath
Ripley Green
Bridge End
Martyr's Green
Westfield
Old Woking
Ripley
River Wey
Ockham Park
Church End
Ockham
Mayford
Cartbridge
Send
Send Marsh
Hungry Hill
Sutton Green
East Horsley
M25
M3
A3
A320
A308
A317
A318
A319
A245
A247
A244
A3050
A3046
B3376
B388
B377
B376
B389
B386
B375
B387
B3366
B3121
B373
B372
B374
B385
B365
B382
B367
B380
B2215
B2039
B368
KINGSTON RD
STAINES RD WEST
CHERTSEY LANE
STAINES ROAD
SHEPPERTON RD
CHRISTCHURCH ROAD
GUILDFORD ROAD
CHOBHAM ROAD
PORTSMOUTH ROAD
RIPLEY BY-PASS
OCKHAM ROAD NORTH
SEVEN HILLS RD
WEYBRIDGE RD
BYFLEET ROAD

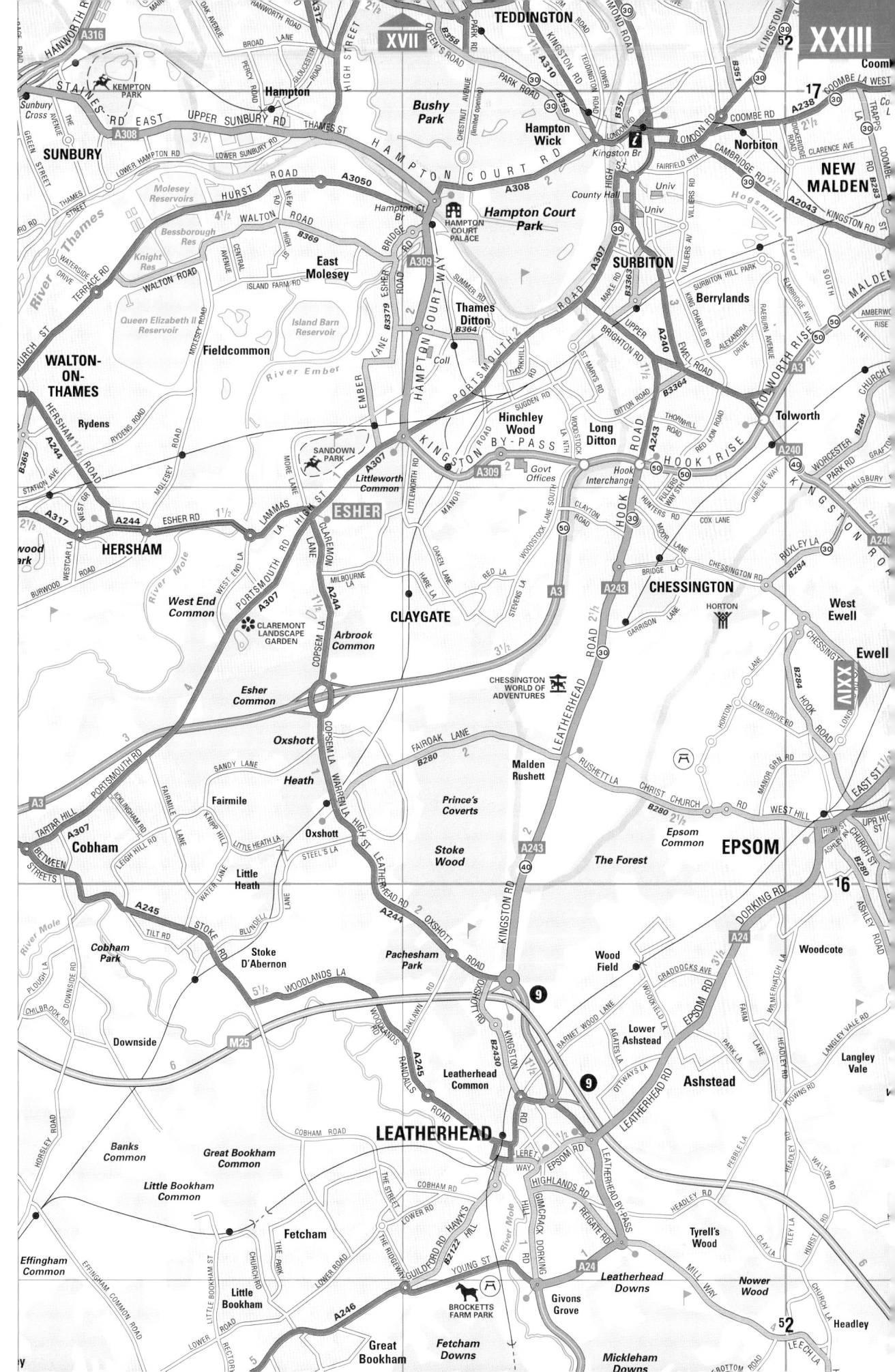
XVII
XXIV
TEDDINGTON
Hampton
Sunbury Cross
SUNBURY
Bushy Park
Hampton Wick
Kingston Br
Norbiton
NEW MALDEN
County Hall
Univ
Hampton Ct Br
HAMPTON COURT PALACE
Hampton Court Park
Molesey Reservoirs
Bessborough Res
Knight Res
River Thames
East Molesey
SURBITON
Berrylands
Queen Elizabeth II Reservoir
Island Barn Reservoir
Thames Ditton
Coll
Fieldcommon
River Ember
WALTON-ON-THAMES
Rydens
SANDOWN PARK
Hinchley Wood
Long Ditton
Tolworth
Littleworth Common
Govt Offices
Hook Interchange
ESHER
HERSHAM
River Mole
West End Common
CLAREMONT LANDSCAPE GARDEN
Arbrook Common
CLAYGATE
CHESSINGTON
HORTON
West Ewell
Ewell
CHESSINGTON WORLD OF ADVENTURES
Esher Common
Oxshott
Heath
Malden Rushett
Fairmile
Prince's Coverts
Cobham
Oxshott
Little Heath
Stoke Wood
Epsom Common
EPSOM
The Forest
Cobham Park
Stoke D'Abernon
Pachesham Park
Wood Field
Woodcote
Downside
Lower Ashstead
Leatherhead Common
Ashstead
Langley Vale
LEATHERHEAD
Banks Common
Great Bookham Common
Little Bookham Common
Fetcham
Tyrell's Wood
Effingham Common
Leatherhead Downs
Nower Wood
Little Bookham
BROCKETTS FARM PARK
Givons Grove
Headley
Great Bookham
Fetcham Downs
Mickleham Downs
M25
A3
A24
A243
A244
A245
A246
A307
A308
A309
A240
A3050
A316
A317
A2043
A238
B280
B284
B2430
B2122
B3379
B369
B364
B3364
B3363
B358
B357
B351
B365
B283
HAMPTON COURT RD
KINGSTON BY-PASS
PORTSMOUTH RD
HOOK RISE
LEATHERHEAD RD
KINGSTON RD
DORKING RD
EPSOM RD
WOODLANDS LA
HIGH ST
LONDON RD
EWELL RD
UPPER BRIGHTON RD
CHESSINGTON RD
HOOK ROAD
WALTON ROAD
HURST ROAD
UPPER SUNBURY RD
STAINES RD EAST
COOMBE LA WEST
KINGSTON RD
TOLWORTH RISE
RUSHETT LA
CHRIST CHURCH RD
WEST HILL
FAIROAK LANE
STOKE RD
GUILDFORD RD
YOUNG ST
MILL WAY
HIGHLANDS RD
REIGATE RD
LEATHERHEAD BY-PASS
CRADDOCKS AVE
COBHAM ROAD
17
16
52

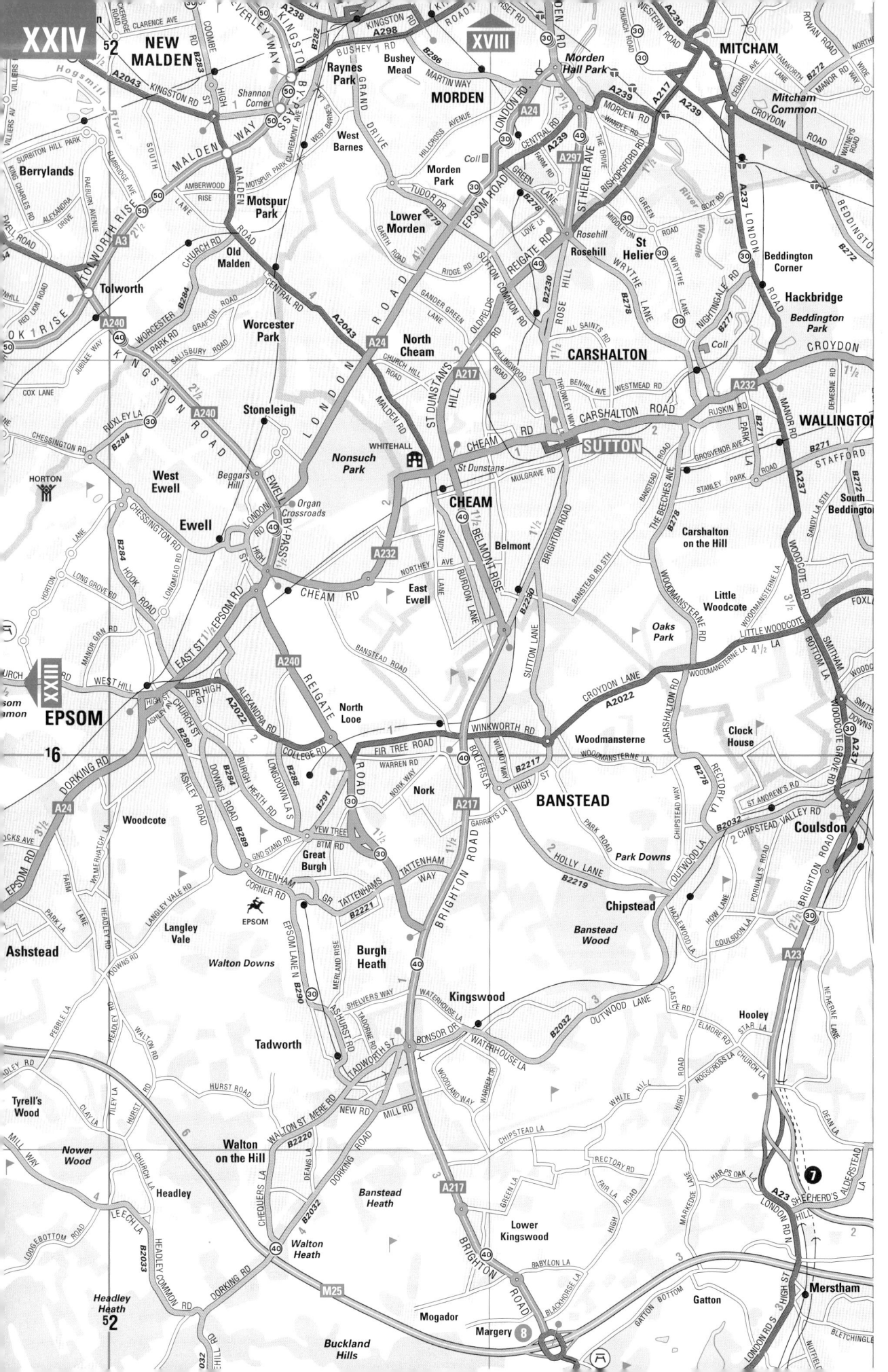
XVIII
XXIII
NEW MALDEN
Raynes Park
Bushey Mead
MORDEN
Morden Hall Park
MITCHAM
Mitcham Common
Shannon Corner
West Barnes
Morden Park
Berrylands
Motspur Park
Lower Morden
Old Malden
Rosehill
St Helier
Beddington Corner
Tolworth
Hackbridge
Beddington Park
Worcester Park
North Cheam
CARSHALTON
Stoneleigh
WALLINGTON
WHITEHALL
Nonsuch Park
SUTTON
St Dunstans
HORTON
West Ewell
Beggars Hill
Organ Crossroads
CHEAM
South Beddington
Ewell
Belmont
Carshalton on the Hill
East Ewell
Little Woodcote
Oaks Park
EPSOM
North Looe
Woodmansterne
Clock House
Nork
BANSTEAD
Woodcote
Coulsdon
Great Burgh
Park Downs
Chipstead
Langley Vale
Ashstead
Banstead Wood
Burgh Heath
Walton Downs
Kingswood
Hooley
Tadworth
Tyrell's Wood
Walton on the Hill
Nower Wood
Headley
Banstead Heath
Lower Kingswood
Walton Heath
Merstham
Headley Heath
Gatton
Mogador
Margery
Buckland Hills
M25
A23
A24
A217
A240
A232
A2043
A3
A22
A297
A239
A236
A237
A2022

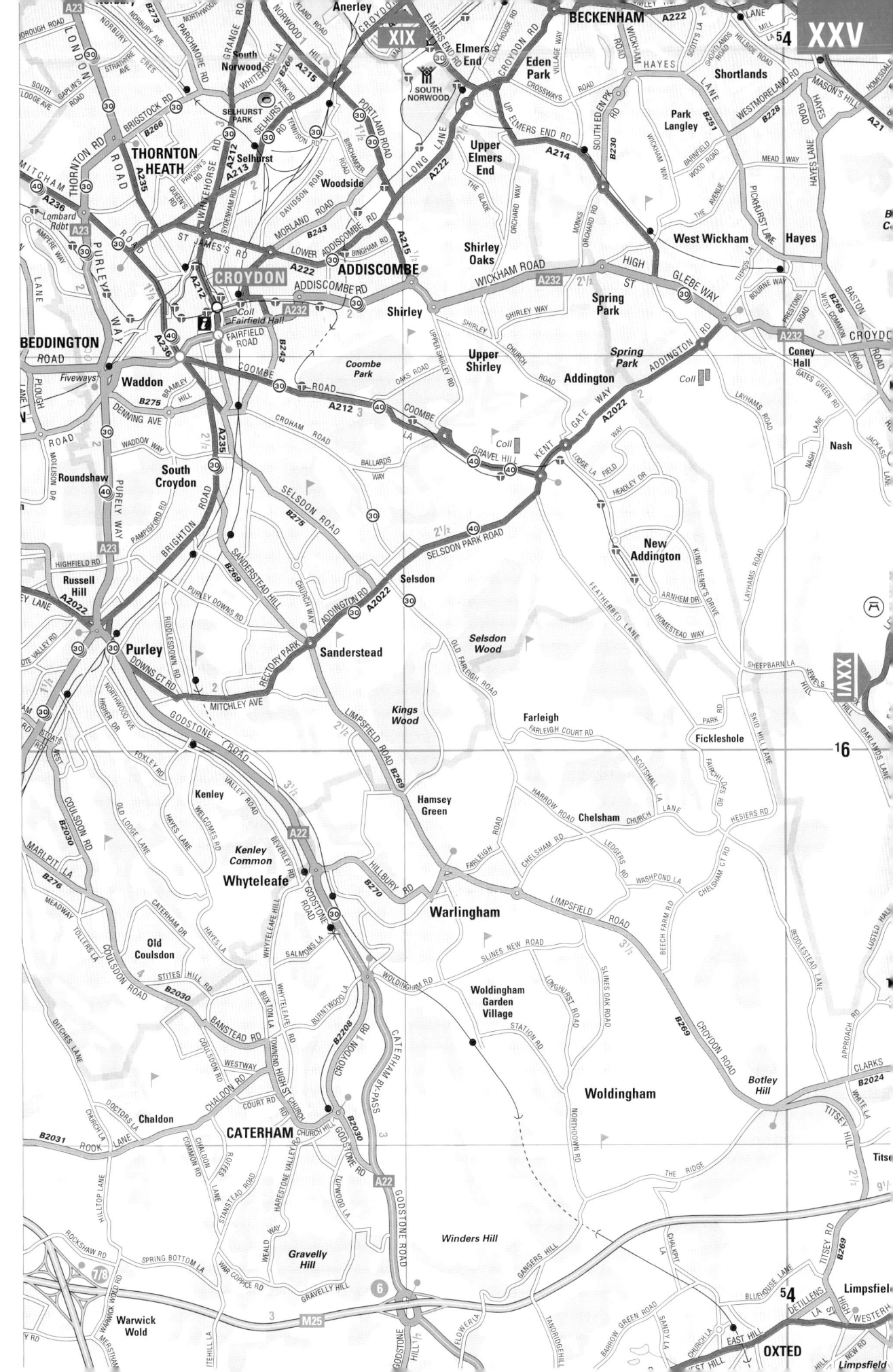
Anerley
BECKENHAM
XIX
Elmers End
Eden Park
Shortlands
South Norwood
SOUTH NORWOOD
Selhurst Park
SELHURST PARK
Park Langley
THORNTON HEATH
Selhurst
Upper Elmers End
Woodside
Lombard Rdbt
West Wickham
Hayes
Shirley Oaks
CROYDON
ADDISCOMBE
Shirley
Spring Park
Coll
Fairfield Hall
BEDDINGTON
Upper Shirley
Coney Hall
Coombe Park
Fiveways
Waddon
Addington
Nash
Roundshaw
South Croydon
New Addington
Russell Hill
Selsdon
Purley
Sanderstead
Selsdon Wood
Kings Wood
Farleigh
Fickleshole
Kenley
Hamsey Green
Chelsham
Kenley Common
Whyteleafe
Warlingham
Old Coulsdon
Woldingham Garden Village
Woldingham
Botley Hill
Chaldon
CATERHAM
Winders Hill
Gravelly Hill
Warwick Wold
Limpsfield
OXTED
XXVI
A23
A22
A212
A213
A215
A222
A232
A235
A236
A214
A2022
A21
B273
B266
B243
B275
B269
B276
B2030
B2031
B2208
B2024
B270
B230
B251
B228
B265
M25
LONDON ROAD
BRIGSTOCK RD
THORNTON RD
PURLEY WAY
WHITEHORSE RD
ST JAMES'S RD
LOWER ADDISCOMBE RD
ADDISCOMBE RD
WICKHAM ROAD
GLEBE WAY
ADDINGTON RD
SELSDON PARK ROAD
SELSDON ROAD
BRIGHTON ROAD
GODSTONE ROAD
LIMPSFIELD ROAD
CROYDON ROAD
COULSDON ROAD
CATERHAM BY-PASS
COOMBE ROAD
CROHAM ROAD
GRAVEL HILL
KENT GATE WAY
FEATHERBED LANE
KING HENRY'S DRIVE
SKID HILL LANE
LAYHAMS ROAD
CHURCH LANE
SLINES NEW ROAD
WOLDINGHAM RD
NORTHDOWN RD
THE RIDGE
TITSEY HILL
CHALDON RD
ROOK LANE
MITCHLEY AVE
SANDERSTEAD HILL
HIGHFIELD RD
UP ELMERS END RD
LONG LANE
PORTLAND ROAD
16
54

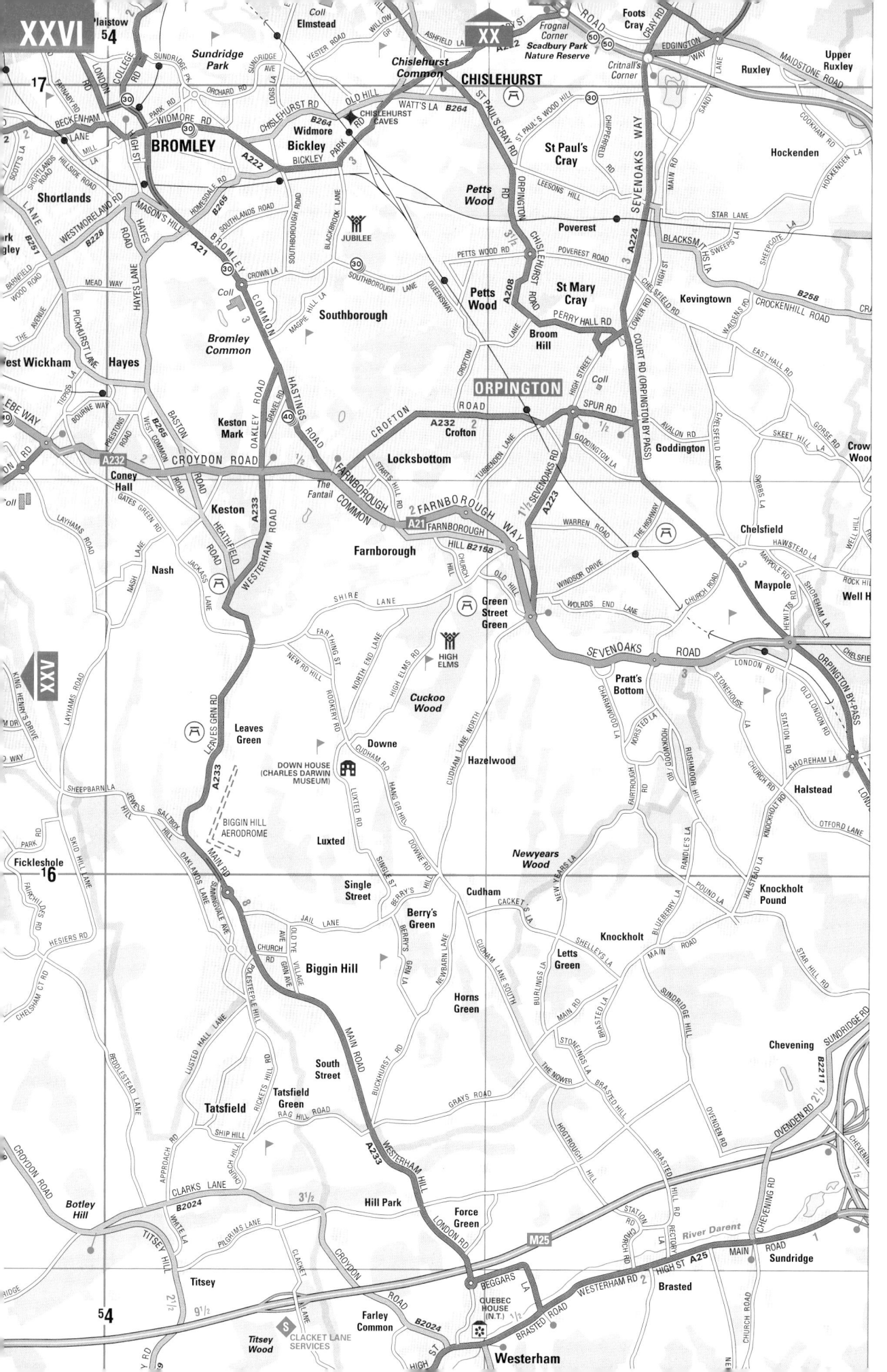

BROMLEY
CHISLEHURST
ORPINGTON
Bickley
Widmore
Shortlands
Hayes
Keston
Farnborough
Locksbottom
Petts Wood
St Paul's Cray
St Mary Cray
Southborough
Bromley Common
Chislehurst Common
Sundridge Park
Plaistow
Elmstead
Frognal Corner
Scadbury Park Nature Reserve
Foots Cray
Ruxley
Upper Ruxley
Hockenden
Poverest
Kevingtown
Broom Hill
Goddington
Crofton
Keston Mark
Coney Hall
Nash
Chelsfield
Maypole
Green Street Green
Pratt's Bottom
Halstead
Leaves Green
Downe
DOWN HOUSE (CHARLES DARWIN MUSEUM)
Hazelwood
Cuckoo Wood
BIGGIN HILL AERODROME
Luxted
Cudham
Newyears Wood
Knockholt Pound
Knockholt
Single Street
Berry's Green
Letts Green
Biggin Hill
Horns Green
Chevening
South Street
Tatsfield Green
Tatsfield
Hill Park
Force Green
Botley Hill
Titsey
Titsey Wood
CLACKET LANE SERVICES
Farley Common
QUEBEC HOUSE (N.T.)
Westerham
Brasted
Sundridge
Fickleshole
River Darent
A21
A232
A233
A208
A223
A224
A222
A25
M25
B2024
B2158
B2211
B258
B264
B265
B228
B251
JUBILEE
HIGH ELMS
CHISLEHURST CAVES
XX
XXV

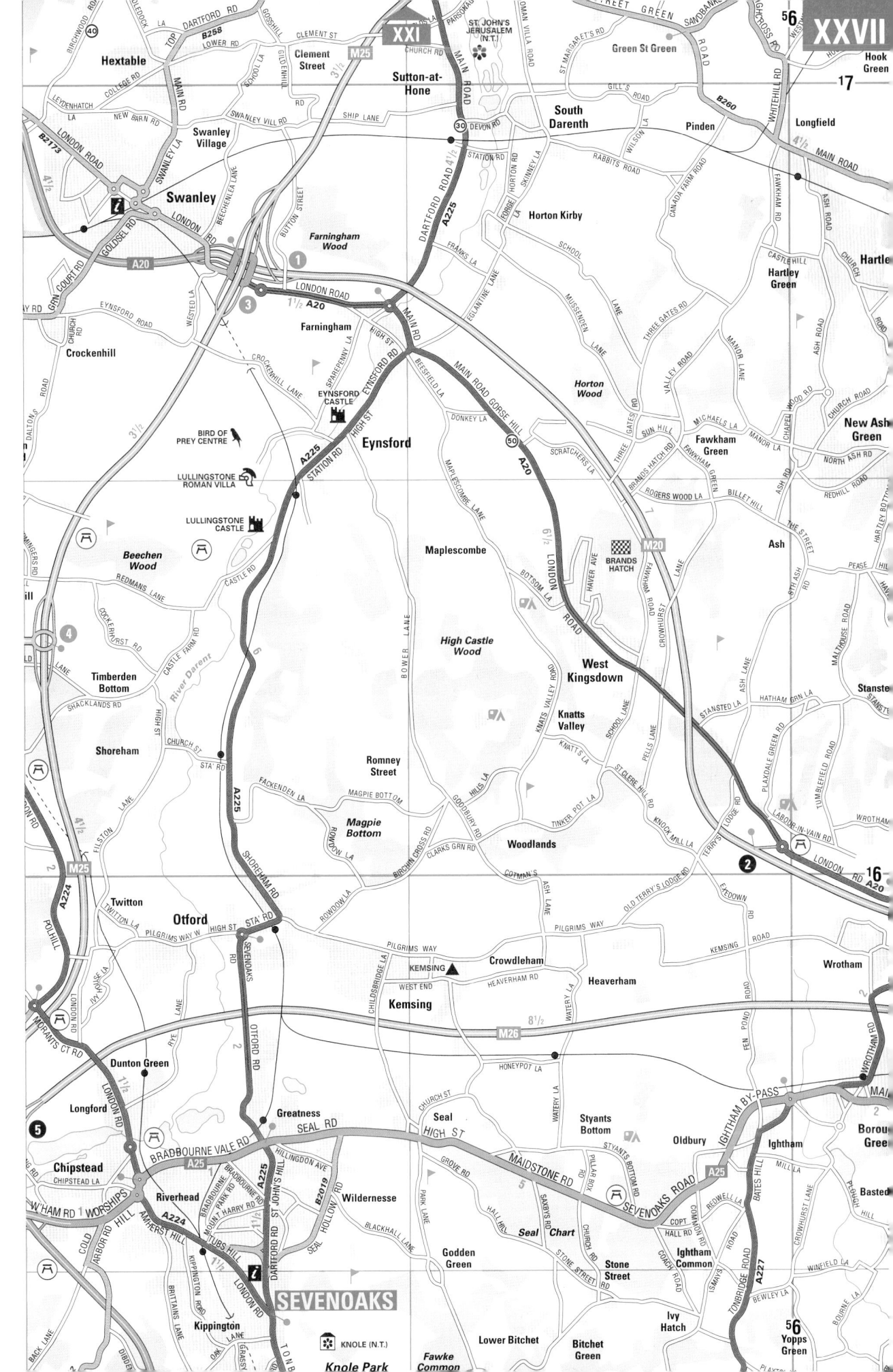

XXVII
XXI
56
17
16
Hextable
Clement Street
Sutton-at-Hone
ST JOHN'S JERUSALEM (N.T.)
Green St Green
Hook Green
South Darenth
Pinden
Longfield
Swanley Village
Swanley
Farningham Wood
Horton Kirby
Hartley Green
Farningham
Crockenhill
EYNSFORD CASTLE
Eynsford
BIRD OF PREY CENTRE
LULLINGSTONE ROMAN VILLA
LULLINGSTONE CASTLE
Horton Wood
Fawkham Green
New Ash Green
Ash
Beechen Wood
Maplescombe
BRANDS HATCH
High Castle Wood
West Kingsdown
Timberden Bottom
Knatts Valley
Shoreham
Romney Street
Magpie Bottom
Woodlands
Twitton
Otford
KEMSING
Crowdleham
Heaverham
Kemsing
Wrotham
Dunton Green
Longford
Greatness
Seal
Styants Bottom
Oldbury
Ightham
Chipstead
Riverhead
Wildernesse
Seal Chart
Godden Green
Stone Street
Ightham Common
SEVENOAKS
Kippington
KNOLE (N.T.)
Knole Park
Fawke Common
Lower Bitchet
Bitchet Green
Ivy Hatch
Yopps Green
M25
M20
M26
A20
A225
A224
A25
A227
B258
B260
B2173
B2019
LONDON ROAD
DARTFORD ROAD
MAIN ROAD
SEVENOAKS ROAD
MAIDSTONE RD
IGHTHAM BY-PASS
SEAL RD
BRADBOURNE VALE RD
TONBRIDGE ROAD
PILGRIMS WAY
River Darent

Key to map symbols

Roads

 Motorway with junction number

Primary route – single, dual carriageway

A road – single, dual carriageway

B road – single, dual carriageway

Through-route – single, dual carriageway

Minor road – single, dual carriageway

Road under construction

Rural track, private road or narrow road in urban area

Path, bridleway, byway open to all traffic, road used as public path

Tunnel, covered road

 Speed camera – single, multiple

 Congestion Charge Zone boundary
Roads within the zone are outlined in green

 Gate or obstruction, car pound

  Parking, park and ride

 Road junction name

 Pedestrianised, restricted access area

Public transport

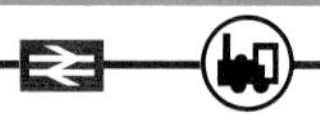

Railway station, private rail station

London Underground station, Docklands Light Railway station

Tramway or miniature railway

Bus or coach station, tram stop

Scale

4.83 inches to 1 mile   1:13 118

0   220yds   440yds   660yds   ½ mile

0   250m   500m   750m   **1km**

Emergency services

  Ambulance, police, fire station

 Hospital, accident and emergency entrance

General features

Market, public amenity site

Sports stadium

Information centre, post office

VILLA   House   Roman, non-Roman antiquity

100   .304   House number, spot height – metres

Christian place of worship

Mosque, synagogue

Other place of worship

Houses, important buildings

Woods, parkland/common

 123   Adjoining page number

Leisure facilities

Camp site, caravan site

Golf course, picnic site, view point

Boundaries

NW6 ......   Postcode boundaries

Westminster   County and unitary authority boundaries

Water features

Barking Creek   Water name

Tidal water

River or canal – minor, major

Stream

Water

Abbreviations

Acad	Academy	Coll	College	Glf Crs	Golf Course	Obsy	Observatory	Sh Ctr	Shopping Centre
Allot Gdns	Allotments	Ct	Court	Drv Rng	Golf Driving Range	Pav	Pavilion	Sp	Sports
Bndstd	Bandstand	Crem	Crematorium			Pk	Park	Stad	Stadium
Btcl	Botanical	Crkt	Cricket	Gn	Green	Pl Fld	Playing Field	Sw Pool	Swimming Pool
Bwg Gn	Bowling	Ent	Enterprise	Gd	Ground	Pal	Royal Palace		
Cemy	Cemetery	Ex H	Exhibition Hall	Hort	Horticultural	PH	Public House	Tenn Cts	Tennis
Ctr	Centre			Ind Est	Industrial Estate	Recn Gd	Recreation Ground	TH	Town Hall
C Ctr	Civic Centre	Fball	Football	Inst	Institute	Resr	Reservoir	Trad Est	Trading Estate
CH	Club House	Gdns	Gardens	Int	Interchange	Ret Pk	Retail Park	Univ	University
Ctry Pk	Country Park	Glf C	Golf Course			Sch	School	YH	Youth Hostel

Ct	Law Court
L Ctr	Leisure Centre
LC	Level Crossing
Liby	Library
Mkt	Market
Meml	Memorial
Mon	Monument
Mus	Museum
Nat Res	Nature Reserve

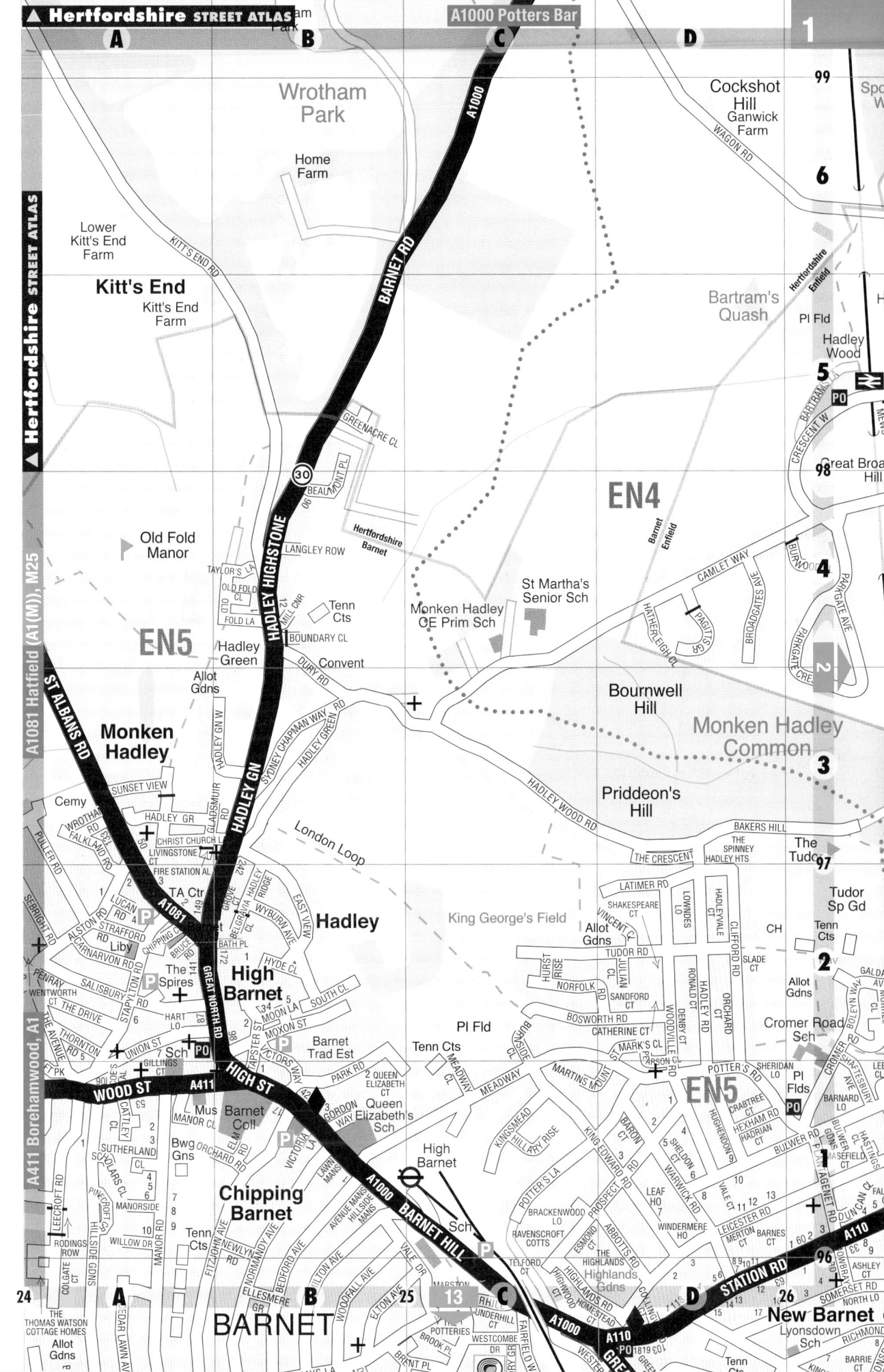

A1000 Potters Bar
Wrotham Park
Home Farm
Lower Kitt's End Farm
Kitt's End
Kitt's End Farm
Cockshot Hill
Ganwick Farm
WAGON RD
KITT'S END RD
BARNET RD
A1000
Bartram's Quash
Hertfordshire Enfield
Pl Fld
Hadley Wood
GREENACRE CL
BEAUMONT PL
Old Fold Manor
EN4
EN5
Hertfordshire Barnet
Barnet Enfield
HADLEY HIGHSTONE
LANGLEY ROW
TAYLOR'S LA
OLD FOLD CL
FOLD LA
MILL CNR
BOUNDARY CL
Tenn Cts
Monken Hadley CE Prim Sch
St Martha's Senior Sch
CAMLET WAY
HATHERLEIGH CL
PAGITT'S GR
BROADGATES AVE
PARKGATE AVE
PARKGATE CRES
Great Broad Hill
Hadley Green
Convent
DURY RD
Allot Gdns
Bournwell Hill
Monken Hadley Common
Monken Hadley
ST ALBANS RD
HADLEY GN
SYDNEY CHAPMAN WAY
HADLEY GREEN RD
HADLEY WOOD RD
Priddeon's Hill
BAKERS HILL
London Loop
SUNSET VIEW
Cemy
HADLEY GR
CHRIST CHURCH LA
LIVINGSTONE CT
FIRE STATION AL
TA Ctr
A1081
THE CRESCENT
THE SPINNEY
HADLEY HTS
The Tudor
Tudor Sp Gd
LATIMER RD
SHAKESPEARE CT
LOWNDES CT
HADLEYVALE CT
King George's Field
Hadley
WYBURN AVE
EAST VIEW
High Barnet
Liby
The Spires
GREAT NORTH RD
TUDOR RD
CLIFFORD RD
CH
SLADE CT
Allot Gdns
NORFOLK RD
SANDFORD CT
BOSWORTH RD
CATHERINE CT
Cromer Road Sch
Barnet Trad Est
Pl Fld
Tenn Cts
MEADWAY
WOOD ST
A411
HIGH ST
Mus
Barnet Coll
Queen Elizabeth's Sch
Bwg Gns
Chipping Barnet
High Barnet
A1000
BARNET HILL
Sch
STATION RD
A110
New Barnet
Lyonsdown Sch
BARNET
Allot Gdns
A1081 Hatfield (A1(M)), M25
A411 Borehamwood, A1
Highlands Gdns
EN5
PO

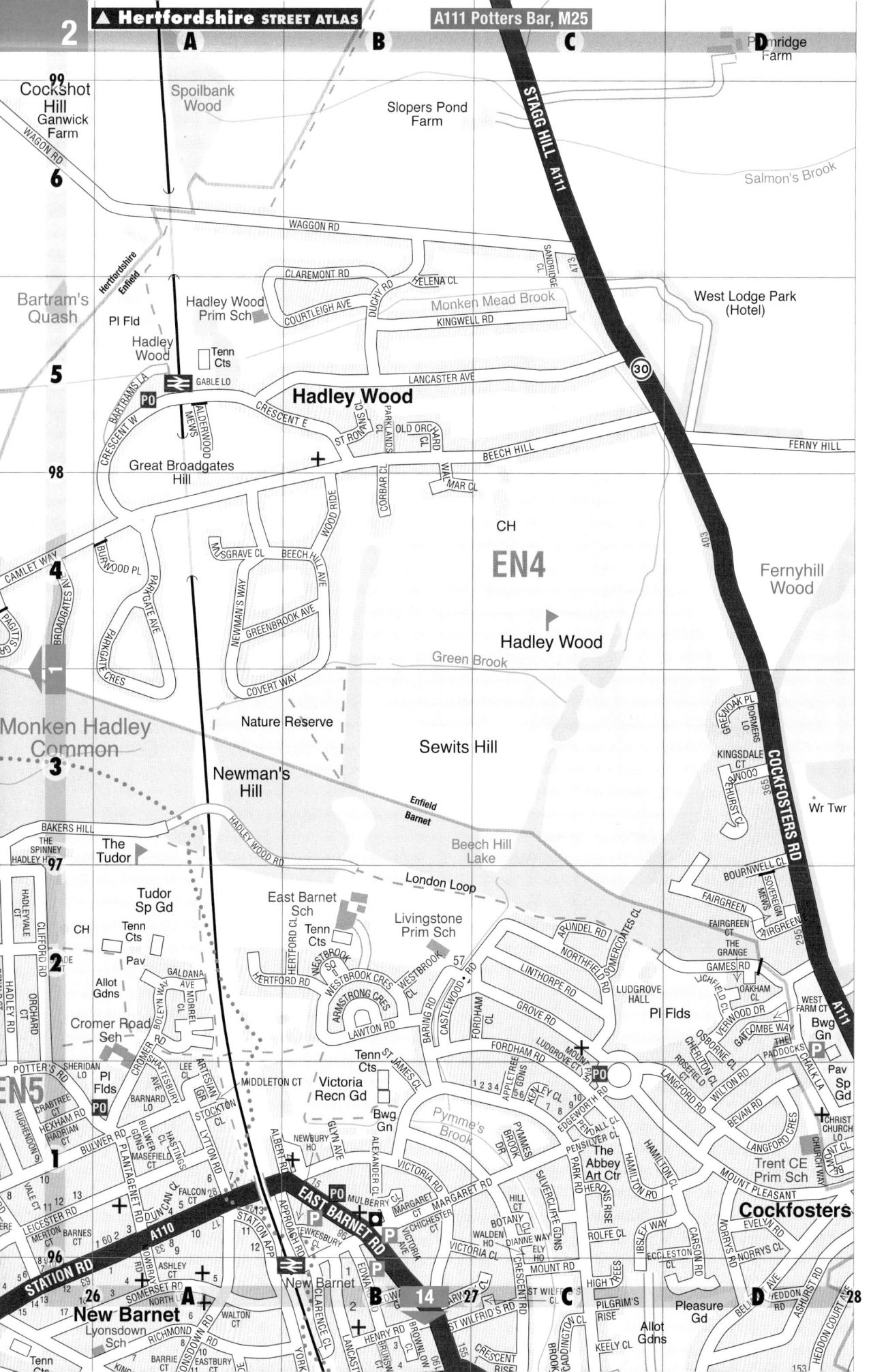
Cockshot Hill
Ganwick Farm
Spoilbank Wood
Slopers Pond Farm
Plumridge Farm
STAGG HILL
A111
Salmon's Brook
WAGON RD
WAGGON RD
SANDRIDGE CL
CLAREMONT RD
HELENA CL
DUCHY RD
COURTLEIGH AVE
Monken Mead Brook
KINGWELL RD
West Lodge Park (Hotel)
Bartram's Quash
Pl Fld
Hadley Wood Prim Sch
Hadley Wood
Tenn Cts
GABLE LO
LANCASTER AVE
Hadley Wood
BARTRAMS LA
PO
CRESCENT W
ALDERWOOD MEWS
CRESCENT E
ST RONANS CL
PARKLANDS CL
OLD ORCHARD CL
BEECH HILL
FERNY HILL
Great Broadgates Hill
CORBAR CL
WALMAR CL
WOOD RIDE
CH
EN4
CAMLET WAY
BURWOOD PL
MUSGRAVE CL
BEECH HILL AVE
PARKGATE AVE
BROADGATES AVE
PAGITTS GR
NEWMAN'S WAY
GREENBROOK AVE
PARKGATE CRES
COVERT WAY
Fernyhill Wood
Hadley Wood
Green Brook
Monken Hadley Common
Nature Reserve
Sewits Hill
GREENOAK PL
DORMERS LO
KINGSDALE CT
COOMBEHURST CL
COCKFOSTERS RD
Newman's Hill
Enfield
Barnet
Wr Twr
BAKERS HILL
THE SPINNEY
HADLEY HTS
The Tudor
HADLEY WOOD RD
Beech Hill Lake
London Loop
BOURNWELL CL
SOVEREIGN MEWS
Tudor Sp Gd
East Barnet Sch
FAIRGREEN
FAIRGREEN CT
Livingstone Prim Sch
Tenn Cts
CH
HADLEYVALE CT
CLIFFORD RD
Tenn Cts
Pav
Allot Gdns
HERTFORD CL
WESTBROOK SQ
HERTFORD RD
WESTBROOK CRES
WESTBROOK CL
ARMSTRONG CRES
ARUNDEL RD
NORTHFIELD RD
SOMERCOATES CL
LINTHORPE RD
THE GRANGE
GAMES RD
LICHFIELD CL
OAKHAM CL
WEST FARM CT
GALDANA AVE
BOLEYN WAY
MORREL CL
HADLEY RD
ORCHARD RD
Cromer Road Sch
CROMER RD
SHAFTESBURY AVE
LAWTON RD
BARING RD
CASTLEWOOD RD
FORDHAM CL
GROVE RD
LUDGROVE HALL
Pl Flds
VERWOOD DR
GATCOMBE WAY
THE PADDOCKS
Bwg Gn
OSBORNE CL
CHERITON CL
ROSEFIELD CT
LANGFORD RD
WILTON RD
CHALK LA
Pav
Sp Gd
POTTER'S RD
SHERIDAN LO
Pl Flds
LEE CL
ARTESIAN GR
MIDDLETON CT
Tenn Cts
ST JAMES CL
Victoria Recn Gd
FORDHAM RD
LUDGROVE CT
MOUNT PDE
APPLETREE GDNS
KENLEY CL
EDGEWORTH RD
PENDALL CL
PENSILVER CL
EN5
CRABTREE CT
HEXHAM RD
HADRIAN CT
HUGHENDON
BARNARD LO
BULWER RD
BULWER GDNS
PLANTAGENET RD
HASTINGS CL
MASEFIELD CT
STOCKTON CL
LYTTON RD
Bwg Gn
NEWBURY HO
GLYN AVE
ALEXANDER CL
ALBERT RD
Pymme's Brook
PYMMES BROOK DR
The Abbey Art Ctr
HAMILTON RD
HAMILTON CL
BEVAN RD
LANGFORD CRES
CHRIST CHURCH LO
CHURCH WAY
Trent CE Prim Sch
MOUNT PLEASANT
Cockfosters
VALE CT
LEICESTER RD
MERTON CT
BARNES CT
DUNCAN CL
FALCON CT
STATION APP
APPROACH RD
EAST BARNET RD
MULBERRY CL
MARGARET CT
VICTORIA RD
MARGARET RD
CHICHESTER CT
HILL CT
BOTANY CL
SILVERCLIFFE GDNS
PARK RD
HERONS RISE
IBSLEY WAY
CARSON RD
EVELYN RD
NORRYS RD
NORRYS CL
STATION RD
A110
TEWKESBURY
VICTORIA AVE
WALDEN HO
DIANNE WAY
ELY HO
VICTORIA CL
CRESCENT RD
MOUNT RD
ROLFE CL
ECCLESTON CL
ASHLEY CT
SOMERSET RD
NORTH
New Barnet
EDWARD
HIGH TREES
ST WILFRID'S CL
ST WILFRID'S RD
PILGRIM'S RISE
Pleasure Gd
Allot Gdns
BELMONT AVE
HEDDON RD
ASHURST RD
HEDDON COURT AVE
New Barnet
Lyonsdown Sch
RICHMOND RD
WALTON CT
LYONSDOWN RD
BARRIE CT
EASTBURY CT
CLARENCE CL
YORK
LANCASTER
HENRY RD
BRUNSWICK
BROMLOW
CRESCENT RISE
CADDINGTON CL
BROOK
KEELY CL
Tenn Cts

1
14

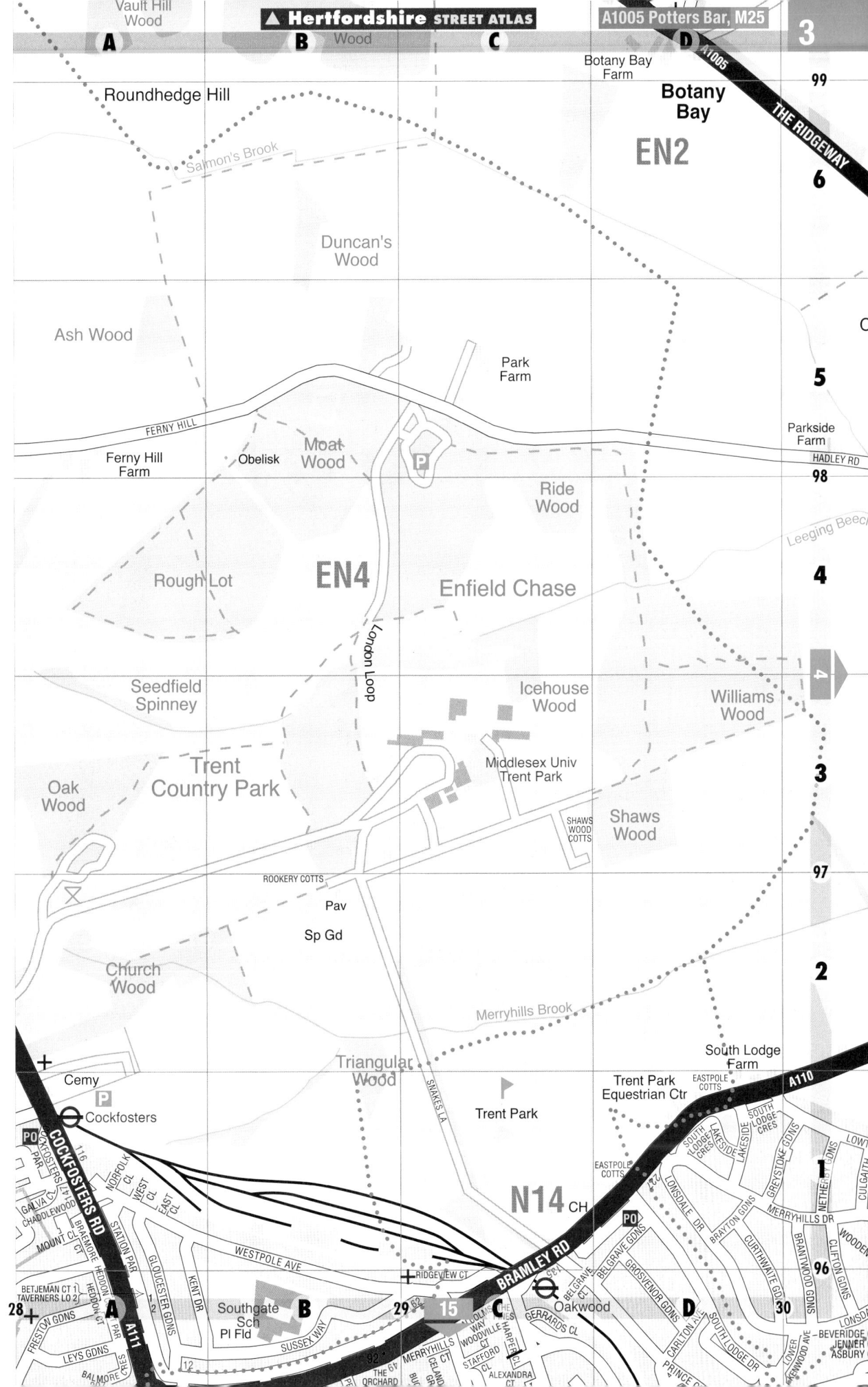

Vault Hill Wood

Wood

A B C D

Roundhedge Hill

Botany Bay Farm

99

Salmon's Brook

Botany Bay

EN2

6

Duncan's Wood

Park Farm

5

Ash Wood

FERNY HILL

Ferny Hill Farm

Obelisk

Moat Wood

Parkside Farm

HADLEY RD

98

THE RIDGEWAY

A1005

C

P

Ride Wood

Leeging Beech

EN4

Enfield Chase

4

Rough Lot

Seedfield Spinney

Icehouse Wood

Williams Wood

4

London Loop

Oak Wood

Trent Country Park

Middlesex Univ Trent Park

Shaws Wood

3

SHAWS WOOD COTTS

ROOKERY COTTS

97

Pav

Sp Gd

Church Wood

2

Merryhills Brook

South Lodge Farm

A110

Triangular Wood

Trent Park Equestrian Ctr

EASTPOLE COTTS

Cemy

P

SNAKES LA

Trent Park

EASTPOLE COTTS

SOUTH LODGE CRES

LAKESIDE

SOUTH LODGE CRES

1

Cockfosters

COCKFOSTERS RD

116

NORFOLK CL

WEST CL

EAST CL

N14 CH

PO

LONSDALE DR

GREYSTOKE GDNS

BRAYTON GDNS

CURITHWAITE GD

MERRYHILLS DR

BRANTWOOD GDNS

CLIFTON GDNS

WOODEND

96

GALVIA CL

CHADDLEWOOD

BRACMORE CT

MOUNT CL

HEDDON CT

STATION PAR

GLOUCESTER GDNS

KENT DR

WESTPOLE AVE

RIDGEVIEW CT

BRAMLEY RD

BELGRAVE GDNS

GROSVENOR GDNS

CARLTON AVE

SOUTHLODGE DR

LOWER

KENWOOD AVE

LONSDA

30

BEVERIDGE C

JENNER C

ASBURY C

A111

BETJEMAN CT 1

TAVERNERS LO 2

FRESTON GDNS

HEDDON CT

Southgate Sch Pl Fld

SUSSEX WAY

29

15

Oakwood

GERRARDS CL

WOODVILLE

STAFFORD

HARPER CL

ALEXANDRA

BELGRAVE WAY

BELGRAVE CT

D

28

LEYS GDNS

BALMORE

A

THE ORCHARD

MERRYHILLS

ICELAND

92

49

B

C

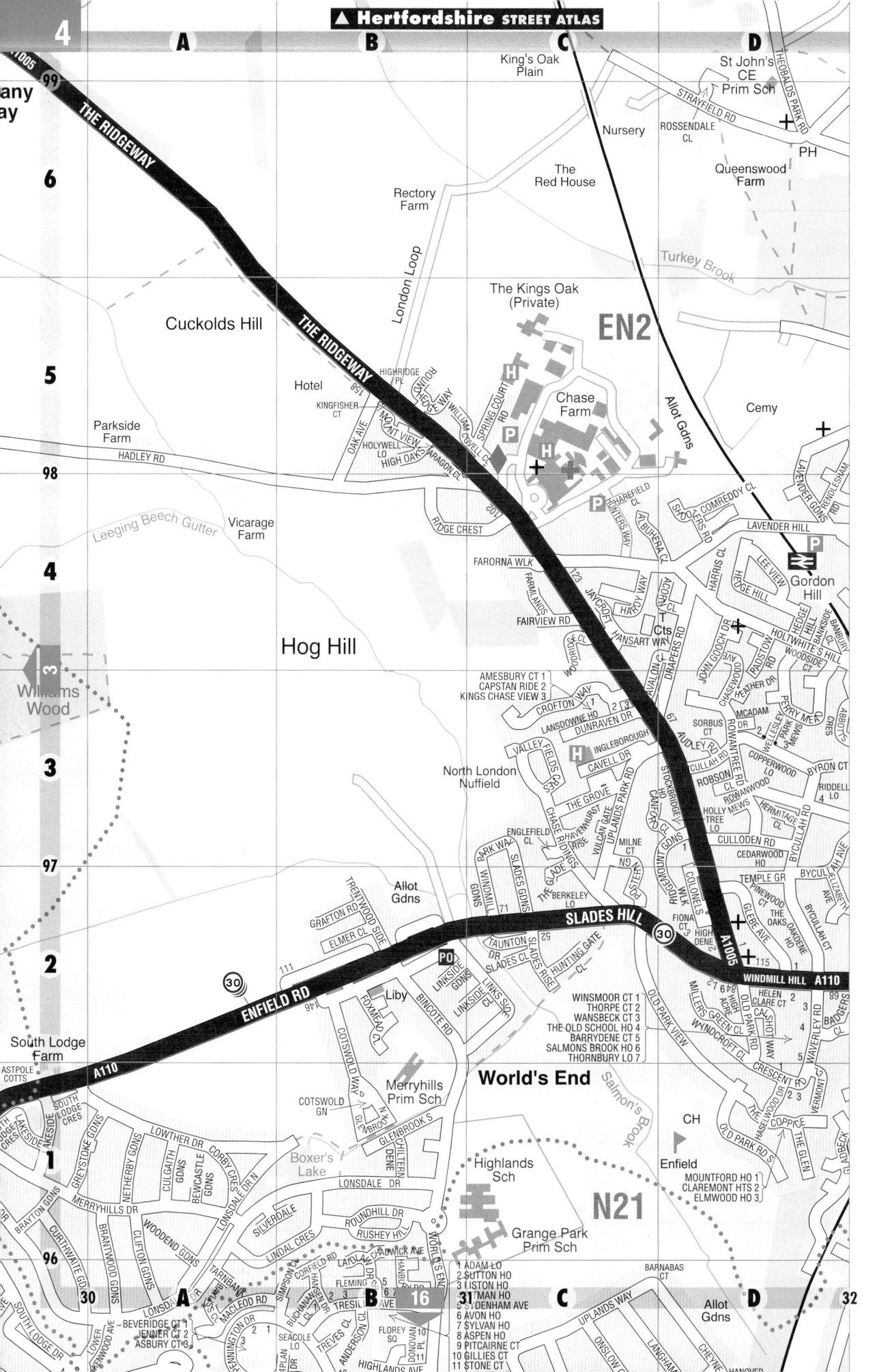

A   B   C   D

99

THE RIDGEWAY

Cuckolds Hill

King's Oak Plain

St John's CE Prim Sch

THEOBALDS PARK RD

STRAYFIELD RD

ROSSENDALE CL

PH

Nursery

The Red House

Queenswood Farm

Turkey Brook

EN2

London Loop

Rectory Farm

The Kings Oak (Private)

6

5

THE RIDGEWAY

HIGHRIDGE PL

Hotel

KINGFISHER CT

OAK AVE

MONT VIEW

HIGH OAKS

HOLYWELL LO

ARAGON CL

SPRING COURT RD

ROUND WAY

WILLIAM COVELL CL

Chase Farm

H

P

H

P

Allot Gdns

Cemy

Parkside Farm

HADLEY RD

98

RIDGE CREST

HAREFIELD CL

ALBUHERA CL

HUNTERS WAY

HARRIS CL

BROOKERS RD

COMREDDY CL

LAVENDER HILL

LAVENDER GDNS

RENDLESHAM

P

Leeging Beech Gutter

Vicarage Farm

FARORNA WLK

FAIRVIEW RD

FARMLANDS

JAYCROFT

WOODRIDINGS

HANSART WAY

ACORN CL

DRAPERS RD

LEE VIEW

HOGE HILL

HOLTWHITE'S HILL

WOODSIDE CT

BANKSIDE

BANBURY

HEDGE

ABBOTT'S

CRES

4

Hog Hill

Cts

JOHN GOOCH DR

CHASEWOOD

FEATHER DR

MCADAM DR

PERRY MEAD

PARK MEWS

BYRON CT

Williams Wood

3

AMESBURY CT 1
CAPSTAN RIDE 2
KINGS CHASE VIEW 3

CROFTON WAY

LANSDOWNE HO

DUNRAVEN DR

INGLEBOROUGH

VALLEY FIELDS CRES

CAVELL DR

SORBUS CT

ROWANTREE RD

CULLAH RD

ROBSON

ROWANWOOD

WELLESLEY LO

COPPERWOOD

HOLLY MEWS

HERMITAGE RD

CULLAH RD

RIDDELL LO

North London Nuffield

H

AUDLEY RD

97

THE GROVE

ENGLEFIELD CL

CHASE RIDINGS

RAVENHURST RISE

VULCAN GATE

UPLANDS PARK RD

STOCKBRIDGEУ

CANFORD

MILNE CT

TREE LO

CULLODEN RD

CEDARWOOD RD

TEMPLE GR

TRINEWOOD RD

THE OAKS

BYCULLAH AVE

BYCULLAH RD

OAKDENE

2

PARK WAY

GRAFTON RD

TRENTWOOD SIDE

ELMER CL

Allot Gdns

WINDMILL GDNS

SLADES GDNS

THE BERKELEY LO

SLADES HILL

COLONELS WLK

FIONA CT

HIGH DENE

GLEBE AVE

A1005

WINDMILL HILL A110

30

ENFIELD RD

30

A110

Liby

FOXMEAD

BINCOTE RD

LINKSIDE GDNS

LINKSIDE CL

LINKS SIDE

PO

TAUNTON

SLADES CL

SLADES RISE

HUNTING GATE CL

WINSMOOR CT 1
THORPE CT 2
WANSBECK CT 3
THE OLD SCHOOL HO 4
BARRYDENE CT 5
SALMONS BROOK HO 6
THORNBURY LO 7

OLD PARK VIEW

MILLERS GREEN CL

WINDCROFT CL

OLD PARK RD

HELEN CLARE CT

WAVERLEY RD

BADGERS

1

South Lodge Farm

ASTPOLE COTTS

SOUTH LODGE CRES

LAKESIDE

GREYSTOKE GDNS

LOWTHER DR

CORBY CRES

NETHERBY GDNS

CULGAITH GDNS

BEWCASTLE GDNS

LONSDALE DR N

COTSWOLD WAY

COTSWOLD GN

Merryhills Prim Sch

GLENBROOK S

CHILTERN DENE

World's End

CH

Enfield

MOUNTFORD HO 1
CLAREMONT HTS 2
ELMWOOD HO 3

THE HASLEWOOD RD

OLD PARK RD S

COPPICE

THE GLEN

96

30

BRAYTON GDNS

CURTHWAITE GDNS

SOUTH LODGE DR

MERRYHILLS DR

BRANTWOOD GDNS

CLIFTON GDNS

WOODEND GDNS

LONSDALE DR

SILVERDALE

LINDAL CRES

Boxer's Lake

LONSDALE DR

ROUNDHILL DR

RUSHEY HILL

WORLD'S END

Highlands Sch

N21

Grange Park Prim Sch

BARNABAS CT

Allot Gdns

A   B   16   31   C   D

30   32

BEVERIDGE CT 1
JENNER CT 2
ASBURY CT 3

LONSDAY

MACLEOD RD

BUCHANAN CT

CORFIELD RD

FLEMING

TRESILIAN AVE

HANBURY

1 ADAM LO
2 SUTTON HO
3 LISTON HO
4 DENHAM AVE
6 AVON HO
7 SYLVAN HO
8 ASPEN HO
9 PITCAIRNE CT
10 GILLIES CT
11 STONE CT

PENNINGTON DR

SEACOLE CL

ANDERSON RD

TREVES CL

DONOVAN PL

FLOREY SQ

HIGHLANDS AVE

UPLANDS WAY

ONSLOW

CHEYNE

LANGHAM

HANOVER

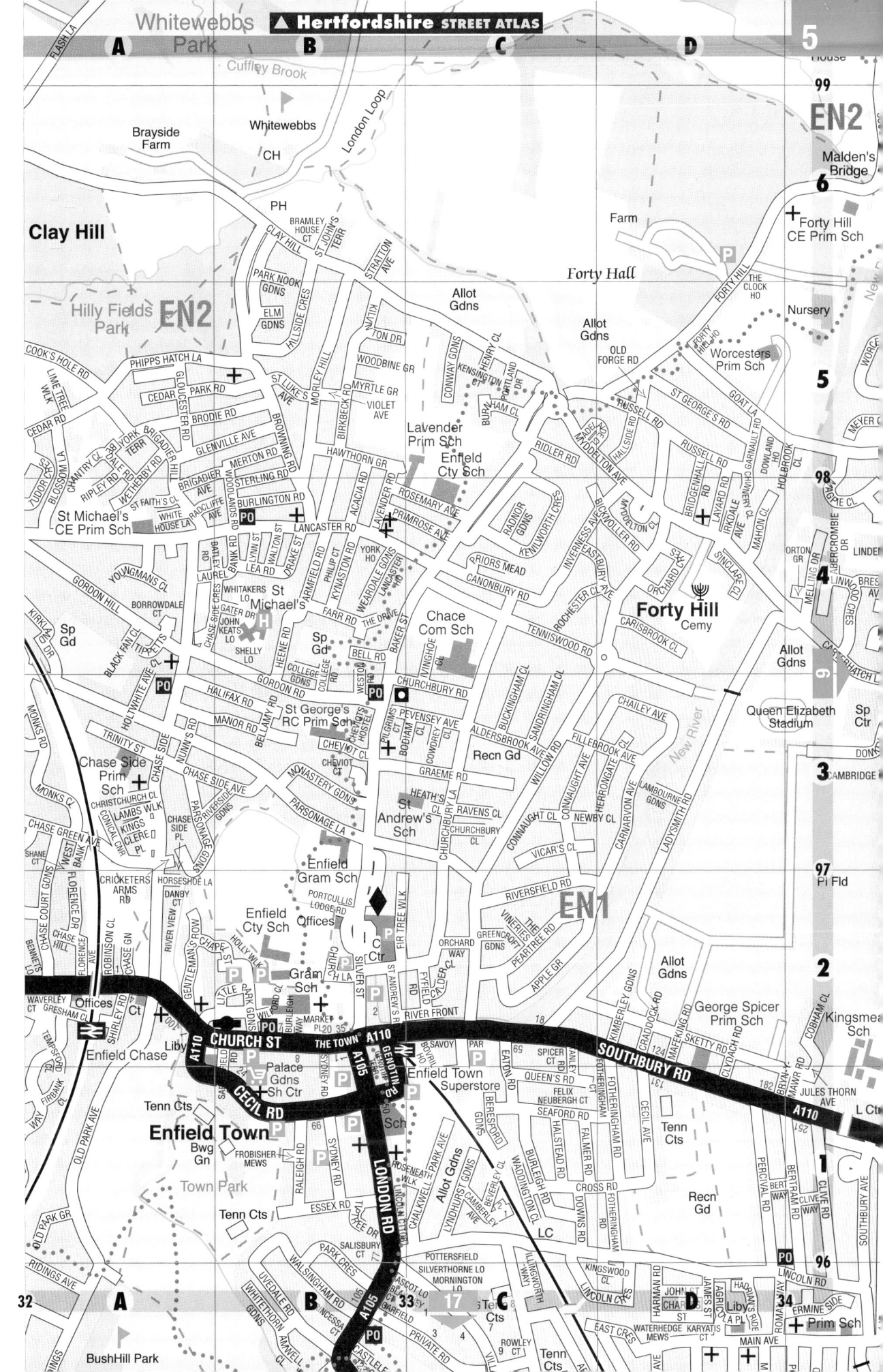
Whitewebbs Park
A
B
C
D
Cuffley Brook
FLASH LA
Whitewebbs
Brayside Farm
CH
London Loop
PH
Clay Hill
BRAMLEY HOUSE CT
ST JOHN'S TERR
CLAY HILL
STRATTON AVE
PARK NOOK GDNS
ELM GDNS
HILLSIDE CRES
Hilly Fields Park
EN2
Allot Gdns
Forty Hall
Farm
Malden's Bridge
Forty Hill CE Prim Sch
FORTY HILL
THE CLOCK HO
Nursery
Worcesters Prim Sch
OLD FORGE RD
COOK'S HOLE RD
PHIPPS HATCH LA
LIME TREE WLK
CEDAR RD
GLOUCESTER RD
PARK RD
CEDAR
BRODIE RD
GLENVILLE AVE
ST LUKE'S AVE
MORLEY HILL
BIRKBECK RD
WOODBINE GR
MYRTLE GR
VIOLET AVE
CONWAY GDNS
KENSINGTON CT
HENRY CL
PORTLAND DR
BURNHAM CL
Lavender Prim Sch
Enfield Cty Sch
RUSSELL RD
ST GEORGE'S RD
GOAT LA
HALLSIDE RD
MYDDELTON AVE
RIDLER RD
DOWLAND HO
HOLBROOK CL
GARNAULT RD
BLOSSOM LA
TUDOR CL
CHANTRY CL
YORK TERR
BRIGADIER HILL
RIPLEY RD
WETHERBY RD
MERTON RD
STERLING RD
BRIGADIER AVE
BROWNING RD
HAWTHORN GR
ACACIA RD
LAVENDER RD
ROSEMARY AVE
PRIMROSE AVE
RADNOR GDNS
KENILWORTH CRES
BICKWOLLER RD
MYDDELTON CL
BRIDGENHALL RD
LAYARD RD
IRKDALE AVE
MAHON CL
St Michael's CE Prim Sch
ST FAITH'S CL
WHITE HOUSE LA
RADCLIFFE AVE
BURLINGTON RD
PO
LANCASTER RD
YORK HO
INVERNESS AVE
EASTBURY AVE
ORCHARD CL
SINCLARE CL
ABERCROMBIE DR
ORTON GR
MELLING DR
YOUNGMANS CL
BATLEY RD
BANK RD
LYNN ST
WALTON ST
DRAKE ST
ARMFIELD RD
PHILIP CT
KYNASTON RD
WEARDALE GDNS
LANCASTER HO
PRIORS MEAD
CANONBURY RD
GORDON HILL
LAUREL
LEA RD
BORROWDALE CT
WHITAKERS LO
St Michael's
GATER DR
JOHN KEATS LO
SHELLY LO
FARR RD
THE DRIVE
Chace Com Sch
ROCHESTER CL
Forty Hill
Cemy
CARISBROOK CL
TENNISWOOD RD
Allot Gdns
Sp Gd
BLACK FAN CL
TIPPETTS
HOLTWHITE AVE
HEENE RD
COLLEGE GDNS
COLLEGE RD
BELL RD
BAKER ST
WESTON RD
VINGHOE CL
CHURCHBURY RD
BUCKINGHAM CL
SANDRINGHAM CL
CHAILEY AVE
Queen Elizabeth Stadium
Sp Ctr
GORDON RD
HALIFAX RD
MANOR RD
BELLAMY RD
St George's RC Prim Sch
CHEVIOTS HOSTEL
PILGRIMS CT
BODIAM CL
PEVENSEY AVE
COWDREY CL
ALDERSBROOK AVE
WILLOW RD
FILLEBROOK AVE
New River
MONKS RD
TRINITY ST
NUNN'S RD
CHEVIOT CL
CHEVIOT CT
Recn Gd
CAMBRIDGE
Chase Side Prim Sch
CHASE SIDE
CHASE SIDE AVE
MONASTERY GDNS
GRAEME RD
CONNAUGHT AVE
HERRONGATE CL
LAMBOURNE GDNS
LADYSMITH RD
MONKS CL
CHRISTCHURCH CL
LAMBS WLK
KINGS CLERE PL
CONICAL CNR
PARSONAGE GDNS
RIVERSIDE GDNS
PARSONAGE LA
HEATH'S CL
St Andrew's Sch
RAVENS CL
CHURCHBURY LA
CHURCHBURY CL
CONNAUGHT CL
NEWBY CL
CARNARVON AVE
CHASE GREEN AVE
WEST BANK
SHANE CT
VICAR'S CL
Enfield Gram Sch
RIVERSFIELD RD
EN1
Pl Fld
CHASE COURT GDNS
FLORENCE DR
CRICKETERS ARMS RD
HORSESHOE LA
DANBY CT
RIVER VIEW
PORTCULLIS LODGE RD
Enfield Cty Sch
Offices
FIR TREE WLK
C Ctr
THE VINERIES
PEARTREE RD
GREENCROFT GDNS
ORCHARD WAY
CALDER CL
APPLE GR
Allot Gdns
KIMBERLEY GDNS
CRADDOCK RD
George Spicer Prim Sch
COBHAM CL
Kingsmead Sch
BENNETS LO
CHASE HILL
FLORENCE AVE
ROBINSON CL
CHASE GN
GENTLEMAN'S ROW
CHAPEL ST
HOLLY WLK
LITTLE PARK GDNS
Gram Sch
CHURCH LA
SILVER ST
ST ANDREW'S RD
FYFIELD RD
RIVER FRONT
WAVERLEY CT
GRESHAM CL
Offices
SHIRLEY RD
Ct
MARKET PL
CHURCH ST
THE TOWN
A110
A105
GENOTIN RD
SAVOY
PAR
EATON RD
SPICER CT
QUEEN'S RD
FOTHERINGHAM CT
SOUTHBURY RD
MAFEKING RD
SKETTY RD
CLYDACH RD
BRYN-Y-MAWR RD
JULES THORN AVE
L Ctr
TEMPSFORD
FIRBANK CL
Enfield Chase
Liby
Palace Gdns Sh Ctr
CECIL RD
SYDNEY RD
Enfield Town
Superstore
FELIX NEUBERGH CT
SEAFORD RD
HALSTEAD RD
FALMER RD
FOTHERINGHAM RD
CECIL AVE
Tenn Cts
Sch
Enfield Town
Bwg Gn
FROBISHER MEWS
RALEIGH RD
SYDNEY RD
LONDON RD
ROSENEATH WLK
CHALKWELL PARK AVE
Allot Gdns
LYNDHURST GDNS
CAMBERLEY AVE
BEVERLEY CL
BERESFORD GDNS
WADDINGTON CL
BURLEIGH RD
CROSS RD
DOWNS RD
Recn Gd
PERCIVAL RD
BERTRAM RD
BERT WAY
CLIVE WAY
CLIVE RD
SOUTHBURY AVE
OLD PARK AVE
Town Park
ESSEX RD
TAPTREE DR
LINCOLN CT
LC
OLD PARK GR
RIDINGS AVE
SALISBURY CT
PARK CRES
POTTERSFIELD
SILVERTHORNE LO
MORNINGTON LO
ILLINGWORTH WAY
KINGSWOOD CL
LINCOLN CRES
HARMAN RD
JOHN ST
CHARLES ST
JAMES ST
AGRICOLA PL
HADRIAN'S RIDE
ROMAN WAY
LINCOLN RD
ERMINE SIDE
Prim Sch
WALSINGHAM RD
UVEDALE RD
WHITETHORN GDNS
PRINCESSA CT
ASCOT LO
GARFIELD
PRIVATE RD
ROWLEY CT
EAST CRES
WATERHEDGE MEWS
KARYATIS CT
MAIN AVE
AMWELL CL
CASTLELEE
BushHill Park
99
6
5
98
4
3
97
2
1
96
32
33
17
34

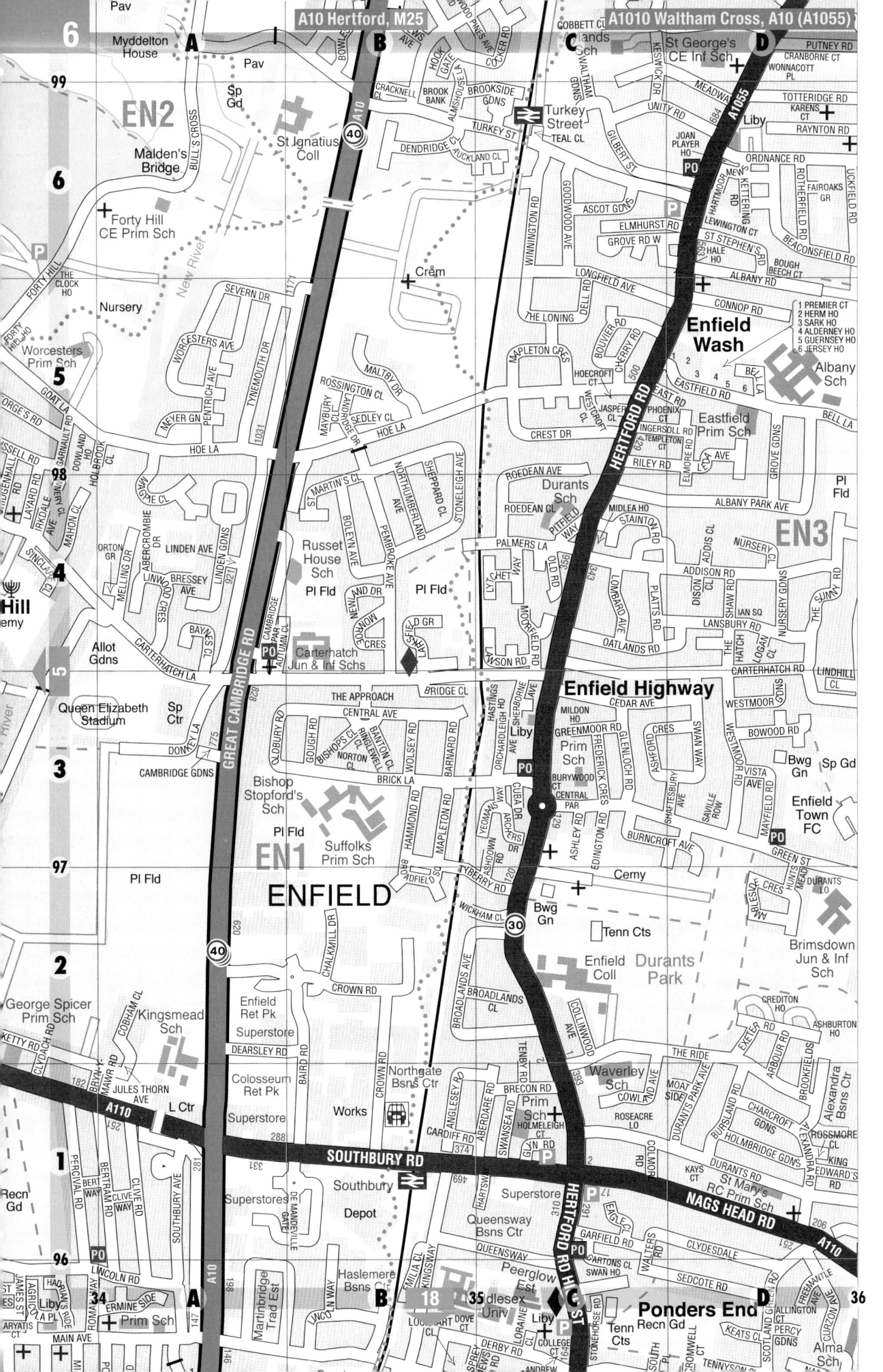

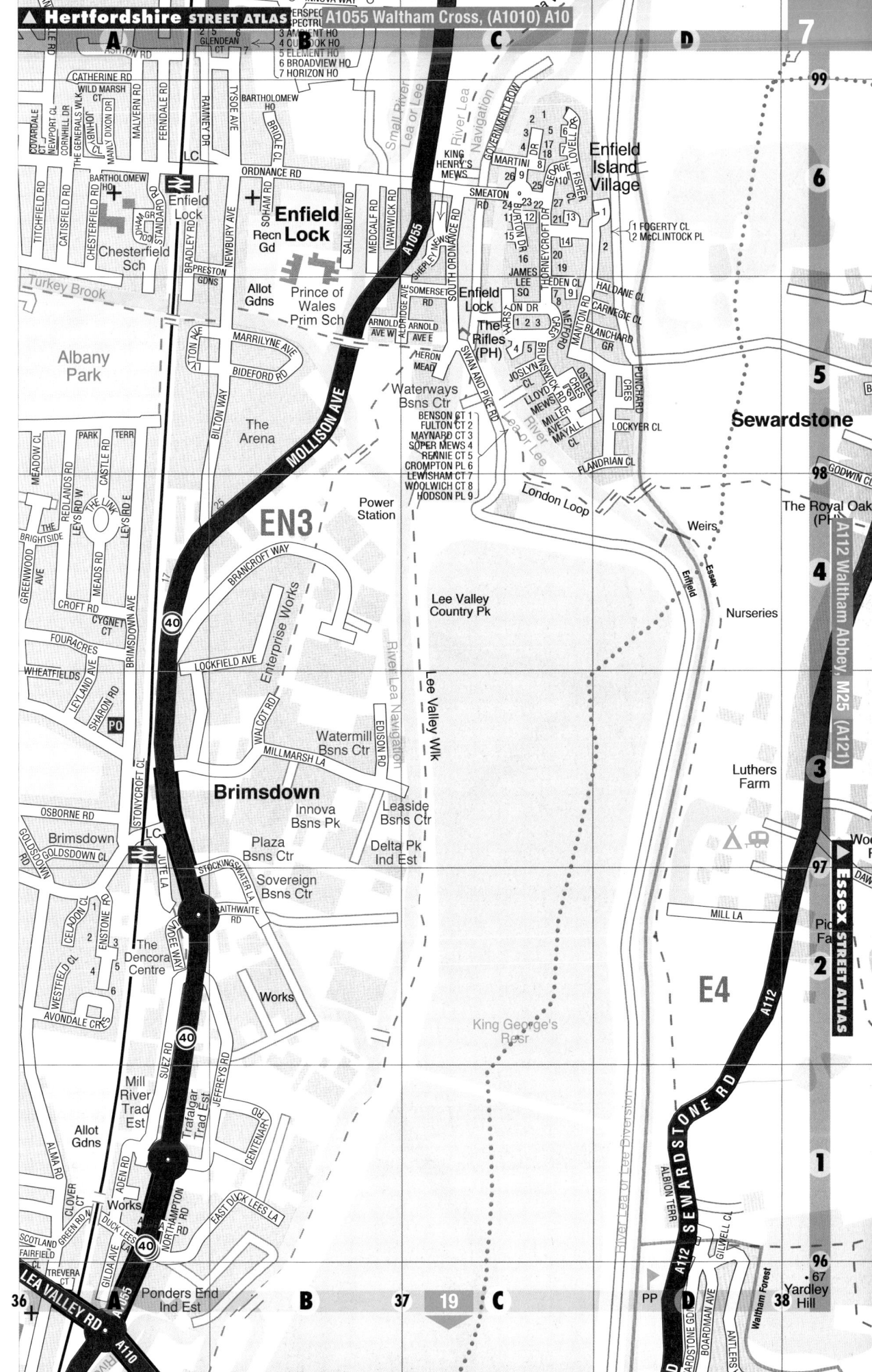
Enfield Lock
Enfield Island Village
Albany Park
The Arena
EN3
Power Station
Lee Valley Country Pk
Sewardstone
The Royal Oak (PH)
Nurseries
Luthers Farm
Brimsdown
Innova Bsns Pk
Plaza Bsns Ctr
Sovereign Bsns Ctr
Leaside Bsns Ctr
Delta Pk Ind Est
Watermill Bsns Ctr
Enterprise Works
The Dencora Centre
Mill River Trad Est
Trafalgar Trad Est
Ponders End Ind Est
King George's Resr
E4
Weirs
London Loop
Waterways Bsns Ctr
Prince of Wales Prim Sch
Chesterfield Sch
Recn Gd
Allot Gdns
Turkey Brook
MOLLISON AVE
A1055
A112
SEWARDSTONE RD
LEA VALLEY RD
A110
Lee Valley Wlk
River Lea Navigation
River Lea or Lee Diversion
ORDNANCE RD
1 FOGERTY CL
2 McCLINTOCK PL
BENSON CT 1
FULTON CT 2
MAYNARD CT 3
SOPER MEWS 4
RENNIE CT 5
CROMPTON PL 6
LEWISHAM CT 7
WOOLWICH CT 8
HODSON PL 9
3 AMBIENT HO
4 OUTLOOK HO
5 ELEMENT HO
6 BROADVIEW HO
7 HORIZON HO
A112 Waltham Abbey, M25 (A121)
▲ Essex STREET ATLAS
Yardley Hill
Waltham Forest
Enfield
Essex

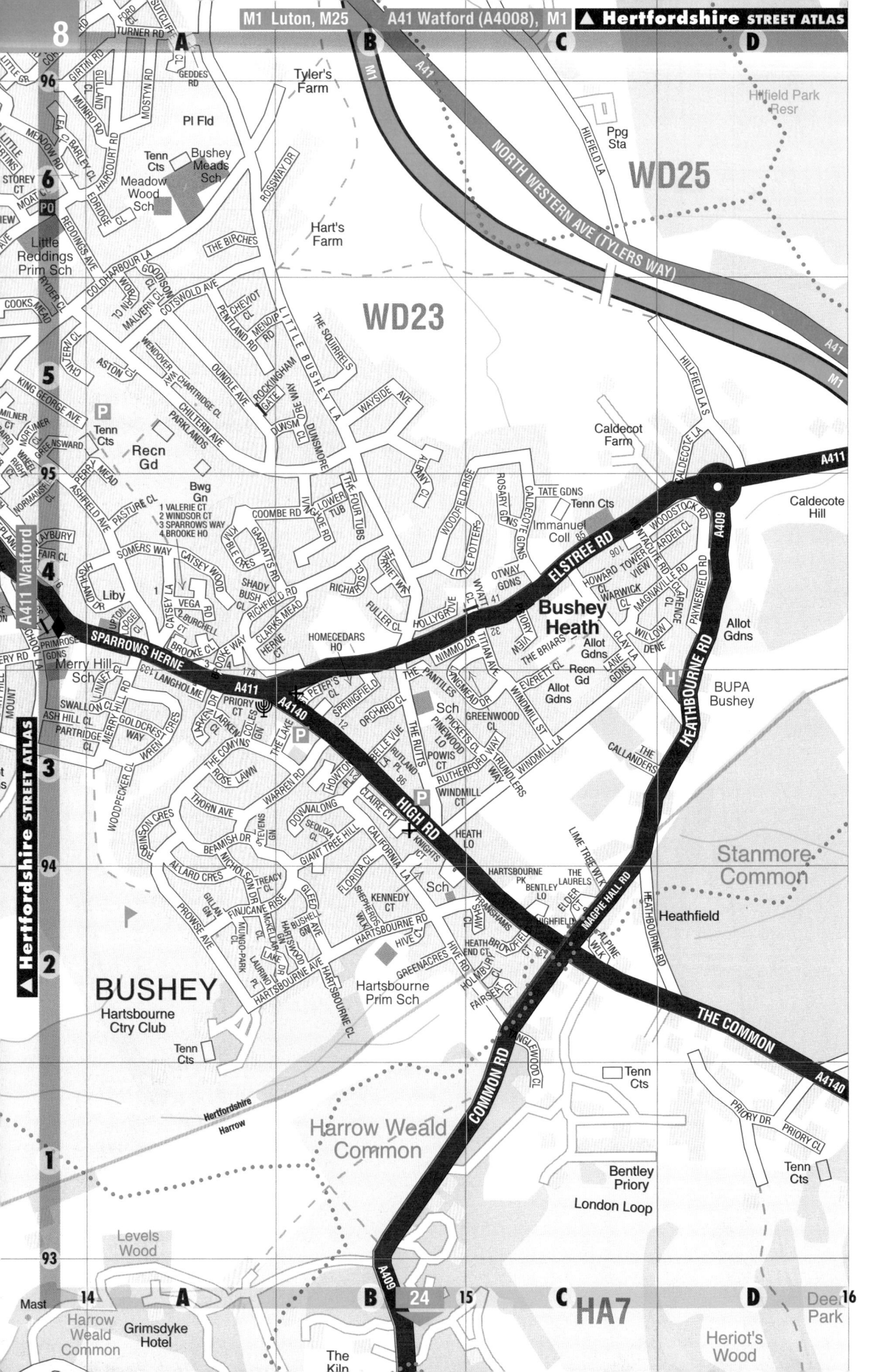
WD25
WD23
HA7
Bushey Heath
BUSHEY
Hartsbourne Ctry Club
Harrow Weald Common
Stanmore Common
Heathfield
Bentley Priory
London Loop
Tyler's Farm
Hart's Farm
Caldecot Farm
Caldecote Hill
Hilfield Park Resr
Ppg Sta
Bushey Meads Sch
Meadow Wood Sch
Little Reddings Prim Sch
Merry Hill Sch
Immanuel Coll
BUPA Bushey
Hartsbourne Prim Sch
Levels Wood
Grimsdyke Hotel
Heriot's Wood
Deer Park
The Kiln
Mast
NORTH WESTERN AVE (TYLERS WAY)
SPARROWS HERNE
ELSTREE RD
HIGH RD
HEATHBOURNE RD
THE COMMON
COMMON RD
A411 Watford
Hertfordshire
Harrow
1 VALERIE CT
2 WINDSOR CT
3 SPARROWS WAY
4 BROOKE HO

A   B   C   D

Home Farm

96

A5183

B5378   ALLUM L

Aldenham Ctry Pk

Laboratory

P

LISTER COTTS

DAGGER LA

6

Cem

ELSTREE HILL N

Aldenham Resr

Sailing Club   Pav

Sp Gd   Tenn Cts

ROMELAND CT

THE BARTONS

St Nicholas CE Prim Sch

ROMELAND   ST NICHOLAS CL

NEW RD

TREE CT TREE CT

Elstree

WD6

LANDS' END

HIGH ST

GEORGES MEAD

5

WATFORD RD

PH

SCHUBERT RD   BRITTEN CD   RODGERS CL

PO   A411

SUMMER GR

VALENTINE CT

FORTUNE LA

MAY GDNS

DELIUS CL   WEBBER CL   BEEHIVE

Tenn Cts

95   The L

ELSTREE RD

Lismirrane Ind Pk

BEETHOVEN RD   DYLAN   COATES RD   ELGAR CL   ELSTREE HILLS S   WEST VIEW GDNS   SULLIVAN WAY

Edgwarebury House Farm

WD23

Hertfordshire   Harrow

NORTH WESTERN AVE (WATFORD BY-PASS)

CENTENNIAL AVE

Centennial Pk

A5183

4

Centennial Ct

10

London Loop

Brockleyhill Farm

A5

4

Hertfordshire   Barnet

M1

3

Sp Gd

Brockley Grange

Tenn Cts

BROCKLEY HILL HO

94

HA8

Annandale

A41 EDGWARE WAY (WATFORD BY-PASS)

Works   **HA7**

SIR HENRY FLOYD CT

Royal National Orthopaedic

H

NUTT GR

2

Grove Farm

Pear Wood Cottages

BROCKLEY HILL

THE LIMES   Limes House

WOOD LA

Wood Farm

Pear Wood

Crkt Gd

CH

Brockley Hill

1

LANCASTER HO   Pav

RINGFIELD CL   HILLTOP WAY   PARK LA

Tenn Cts

Cloisters Wood

Springbok House

Tenn Cts

NEWLANDS CL   GRANTHAM CL   HAMLYN CL   GREEN LA

BROOMFIELD HO 1   FALLOWFIELD CT 2   HILL HO 3   WELLINGTON HO 4   FALLOWFIELD   LITTLE COMMON

DENNIS LA

JULIUS CAESAR WAY

AUGUSTUS CL   CLAUDIUS CL

Barnet   Harrow

BROCKLEY

A5

STANMORE HILL

Stanmore Hall

30

A4140

PINE CL

Stanmore Hall

93

16   A   B   17   **25**   C   D   18

HERIOTS CL   OLD FORGE CL   SPRING LAKE   St Johns   DENNIS LA   HALL   GLANLEAM RD   KERRY   REENGLASS RD   BERRY HILL   CHEVALIER CL   FAUNA CL   REES DR   PARTRIDGE   FANNA CL

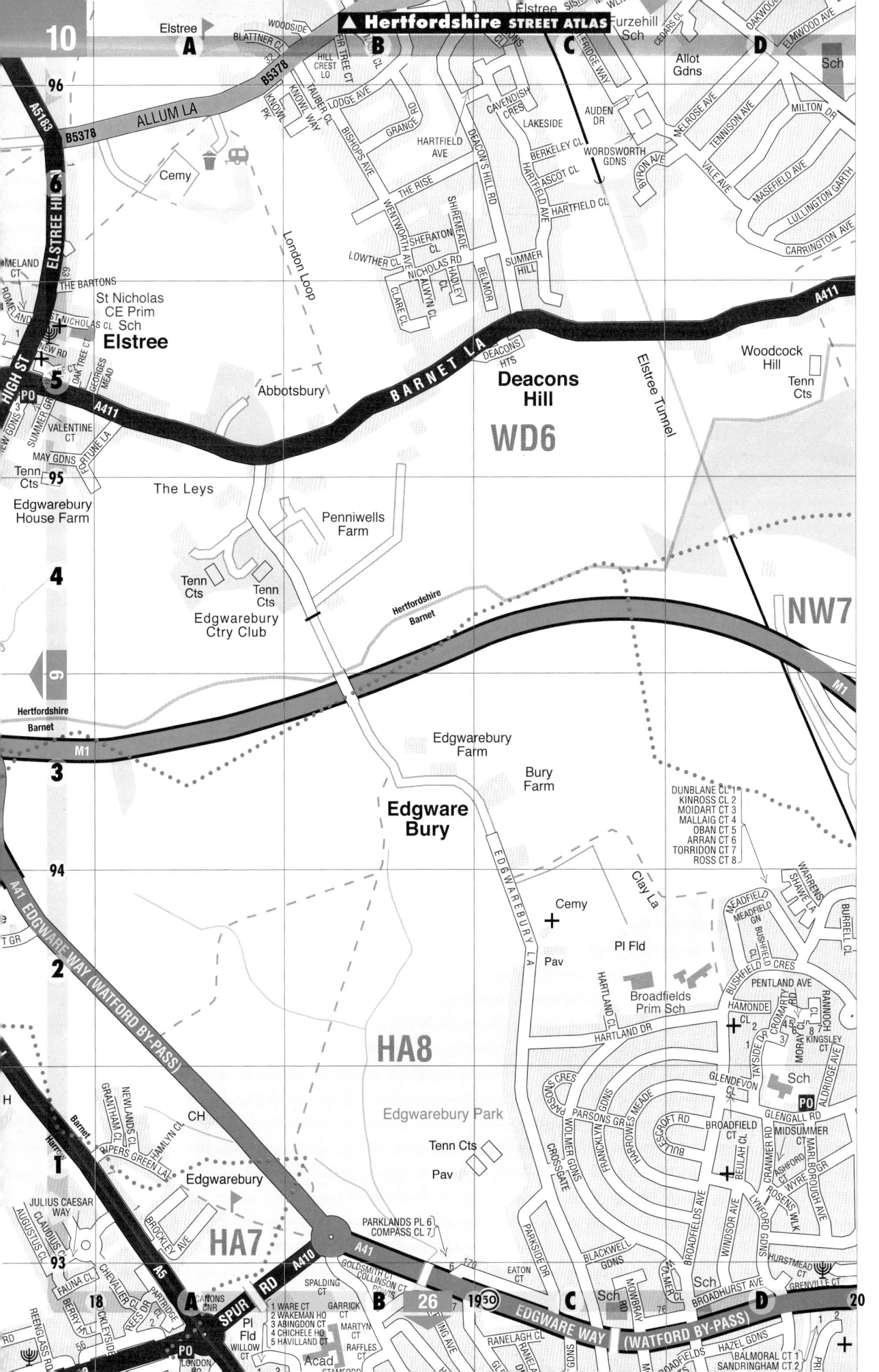

A   B   C   D

96

95

94

93

Elstree

WOODSIDE
BLATTNER CL
B5378
KNOWL WAY
KNOWL PK
FIR TREE CT
HILL CREST LO
TAUBER CL
LODGE AVE

ALLUM LA
B5378

A5183

ELSTREE HILL

Cemy

London Loop

BISHOPS AVE
THE RISE
GRANGE
HARTFIELD AVE
WENTWORTH AVE
LOWTHER CL
SHIREMEADE
SHERATON CL
NICHOLAS RD
ALWYN CL
CLARE CL
HADLEY

DEACON'S HILL RD
ASCOT CL
HARTFIELD CL
HARTFIELD AVE
SUMMER HILL
BELMOR
BERKELEY CL

CAVENDISH CRES
LAKESIDE
WORDSWORTH GDNS
AUDEN DR
BYRON AVE

Elstree
Furzehill Sch
CEDARS CL
FRIDGE WAY
Allot Gdns
NELROSE AVE
TENNISON AVE
VALE AVE
MASEFIELD AVE
CARRINGTON AVE
MILTON DR
LULLINGTON GARTH
OAKWOOD
ELMWOOD AVE
Sch

MELAND CT
ROMELAND
THE BARTONS
St Nicholas
CE Prim Sch
Elstree
ST NICHOLAS CL
NEW RD
OAK TREE C
GEORGES MEAD
HIGH ST
PO
SUMMER GR
VALENTINE CT
MAY GDNS
FORTUNE LA
Tenn Cts

A411
A411

BARNET LA

Deacons Hill

WD6

Abbotsbury

DEACONS HTS
Elstree Tunnel
Woodcock Hill
Tenn Cts

A411

The Leys
Penniwells Farm

Hertfordshire
Barnet

Tenn Cts   Tenn Cts
Edgwarebury
Ctry Club

Edgwarebury
House Farm

6
Hertfordshire
Barnet

M1

M1

NW7

Edgwarebury
Farm

Bury
Farm

**Edgware
Bury**

DUNBLANE CL 1
KINROSS CL 2
MOIDART CT 3
MALLAIG CT 4
OBAN CT 5
ARRAN CT 6
TORRIDON CT 7
ROSS CT 8

A41
EDGWARE WAY (WATFORD BY-PASS)

EDGWAREBURY LA

Clay La

MEADFIELD
MEADFIELD GN
BUSHFIELD DR
WARRENS LA
SHAWE LA
BURRELL CL

Cemy
Pav
Pl Fld

Broadfields
Prim Sch

HARTLAND CL
HARTLAND DR

HA8

Edgwarebury Park

Tenn Cts
Pav

PENTLAND AVE
HAMONDE CL
RANNOCH CL
CROMARTY RD
TAYSIDE DR
MORAY CL
KINGSLEY CT
BUSHFIELD CRES

GLENDEVON CL
Sch
PO
ALDRIDGE CL
GLENGALL RD
BROADFIELD CT
MIDSUMMER
ASHFORD
WYRE CT
ROSENS WLK
BEULAH CL
CRAMER RD
MARLBOROUGH AVE

NEWLANDS CL
GRANTHAM CL
HAMLYN CL
PIPERS GREEN LA
CH
Barnet
Harrow

HA7
JULIUS CAESAR WAY
CLAUDIUS CL
AUGUSTUS CL
FAUNA CL
BERRY HILL
CHEVALIER CL
REES DR
PARTRIDGE
BROCKLEY AVE
GARRICK
Edgwarebury

A5

A410
SPUR RD
A41

1 WARE CT
2 WAKEMAN HO
3 ABINGDON CT
4 CHICHELE HO
5 HAVILLAND CT

PARKLANDS PL 6
COMPASS CL 7

GOLDSMITH CL
COLLINSON CT

PARSONS CRES
WOLMER GDNS
CROSSGATE
PARSONS GR
FRANCKLYN GDNS
HARROWES MEADE
BULLESCROFT RD
BROADFIELDS AVE
WINDSOR AVE
LYNEG GDNS
PARKSIDE DR
BLACKWELL GDNS
HAZEL GDNS
MOWBRAY RD
BROADHURST AVE
HURSTMEAD CT
GRENVILLE CT
BALMORAL CT 1
SANDRINGHAM CT 2

**EDGWARE WAY
(WATFORD BY-PASS)**

26   19   50   C   D   20

Acad

PO
LONDON

18   A   B   C   D

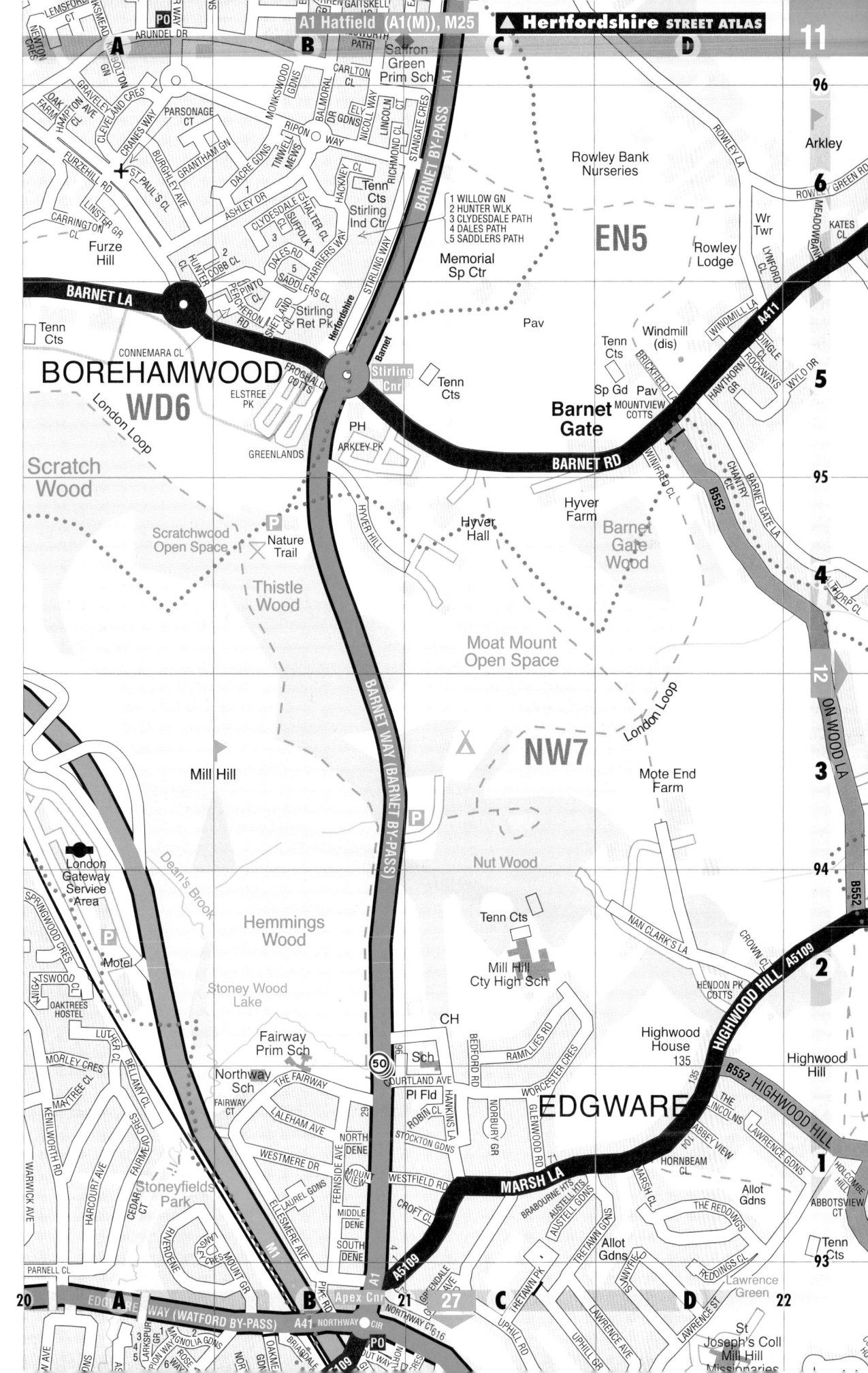
BOREHAMWOOD
WD6
EN5
NW7
EDGWARE
Barnet Gate
Arkley
Furze Hill
Scratch Wood
Scratchwood Open Space
Nature Trail
Thistle Wood
Moat Mount Open Space
Mill Hill
London Gateway Service Area
Hemmings Wood
Stoney Wood Lake
Nut Wood
Mill Hill Cty High Sch
Highwood House
Highwood Hill
Mote End Farm
Hyver Hall
Hyver Farm
Barnet Gate Wood
Rowley Bank Nurseries
Rowley Lodge
Memorial Sp Ctr
Windmill (dis)
Saffron Green Prim Sch
Fairway Prim Sch
Northway Sch
Stoneyfields Park
St Joseph's Coll Mill Hill
BARNET LA
BARNET RD
BARNET BY-PASS
BARNET WAY (BARNET BY-PASS)
MARSH LA
HIGHWOOD HILL
EDGWARE WAY (WATFORD BY-PASS)
London Loop
1 WILLOW GN
2 HUNTER WLK
3 CLYDESDALE PATH
4 DALES PATH
5 SADDLERS PATH
Stirling Cnr
Apex Cnr
A1
A411
A5109
B552
M1
A41
96
95
94
93
6
5
4
3
2
1
20
21
22
12
27

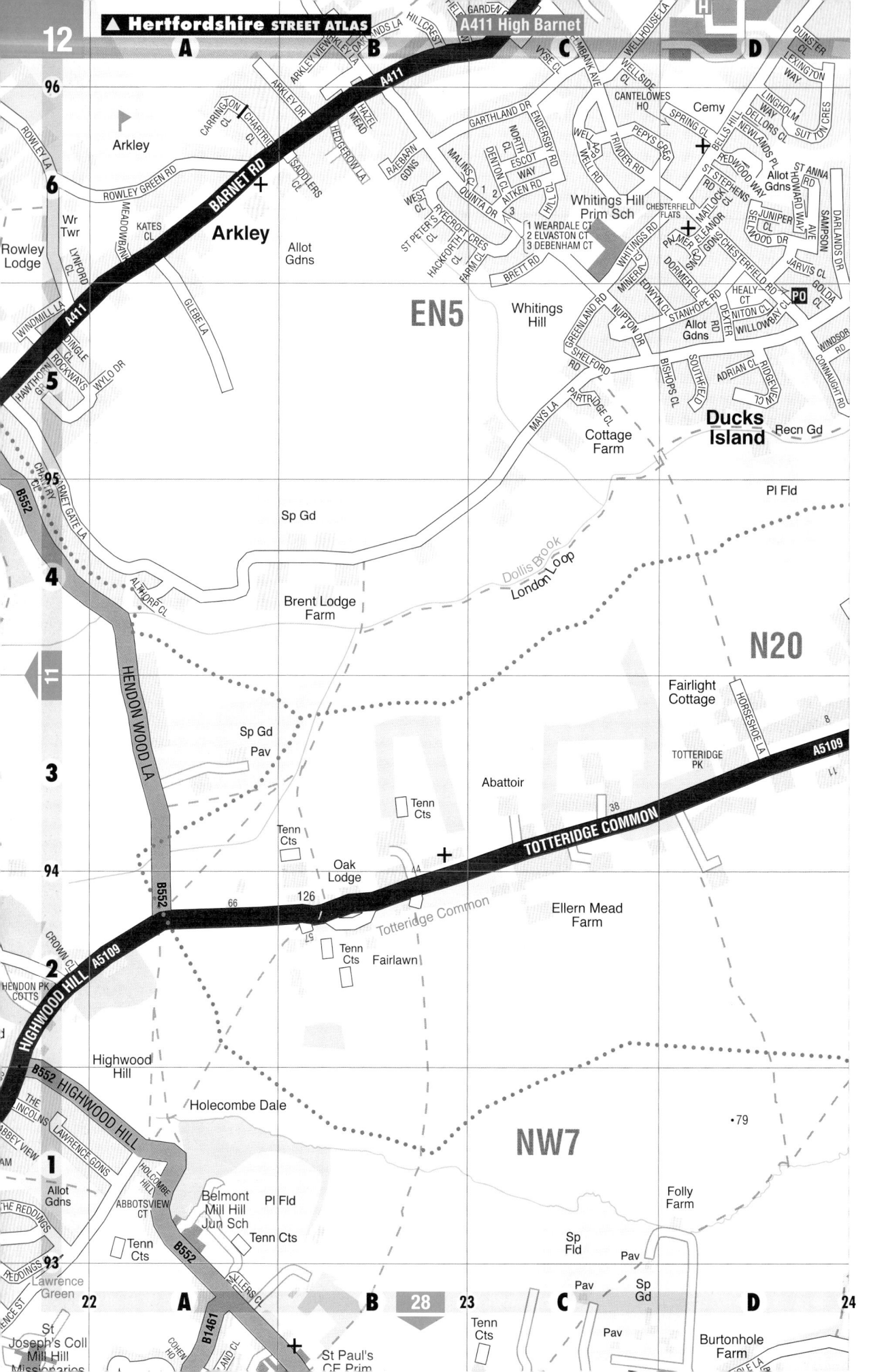
A411 High Barnet
A
B
C
D
96
6
5
95
4
3
94
2
1
93
22
23
24
28
11
Arkley
Barnet Rd
A411
Rowley Green Rd
Rowley La
Rowley Lodge
Wr Twr
Kates Cl
Meadowbank
Lynford Cl
Windmill La
Dingle Cl
Rockways
Wylo Dr
Hawthorn Gr
Allot Gdns
Glebe La
Arkley Dr
Carrington Cl
Chartridge Cl
Saddlers Cl
Hedgerow La
Hazel Mead
Hillcrest
Arkley View
Oaklands La
Raebarn Gdns
Garthland Dr
Malins Cl
North Cl
Denton Cl
Escot Way
Aitken Rd
Endersby Rd
Quinta Dr
Hill Cl
West Cl
St Peter's Cl
Ryecroft Cres
Hackforth Cl
Farm Cl
Brett Rd
1 Weardale Ct
2 Elvaston Ct
3 Debenham Ct
Whitings Hill Prim Sch
Whitings Hill
EN5
Vyse Cl
Elmbank Ave
Wellhouse La
Wellside Cl
Cantelowes Ho
Well Rd
Trimder Rd
Pepys Cres
Spring Cl
Cemy
Bells Hill
Newlands Pl
Dellors Cl
Lingholm Way
Lexington Way
Dunster Cl
Sutton Cres
Redwood Way
St Stephens Rd
Matlock Ct
Chesterfield Flats
Chesterfield Rd
Eleanor Gdns
Palmer Ct
Allot Gdns
St Anna Rd
Howard Way
Juniper Cl
Selwood Dr
Sampson Ave
Darlands Dr
Jarvis Cl
Golda Cl
PO
Whitings Rd
Minerva Cl
Edwyn Cl
Dormer Cl
Stanhope Rd
Healy Ct
Niton Cl
Willowbay Cl
Dexter Rd
Greenland Rd
Nupton Dr
Shelford Rd
Bishops Cl
Southfield
Adrian Cl
Ridgeview Cl
Windsor Rd
Connaught Rd
Partridge Cl
Mays La
Cottage Farm
Ducks Island
Recn Gd
Pl Fld
Chantry Cl
Barnet Gate La
B552
Sp Gd
Dollis Brook
London Loop
Althorp Cl
Brent Lodge Farm
N20
Hendon Wood La
Fairlight Cottage
Horseshoe La
Totteridge Pk
A5109
Sp Gd
Pav
Abattoir
Tenn Cts
Totteridge Common
Oak Lodge
Ellern Mead Farm
Fairlawn
Crown Cl
Hendon Pk Cotts
Highwood Hill
Highwood Hill
Holecombe Dale
NW7
Folly Farm
The Lincolns
Lawrence Gdns
Abbey View
Holcombe Hill
Abbotsview Ct
Belmont Mill Hill Jun Sch
Pl Fld
Tenn Cts
The Reddings
Reddings
Lawrence Green
Millers Cl
B1461
Sp Fld
Pav
Sp Gd
Burtonhole Farm
St Joseph's Coll Mill Hill Missionaries
St Paul's CE Prim

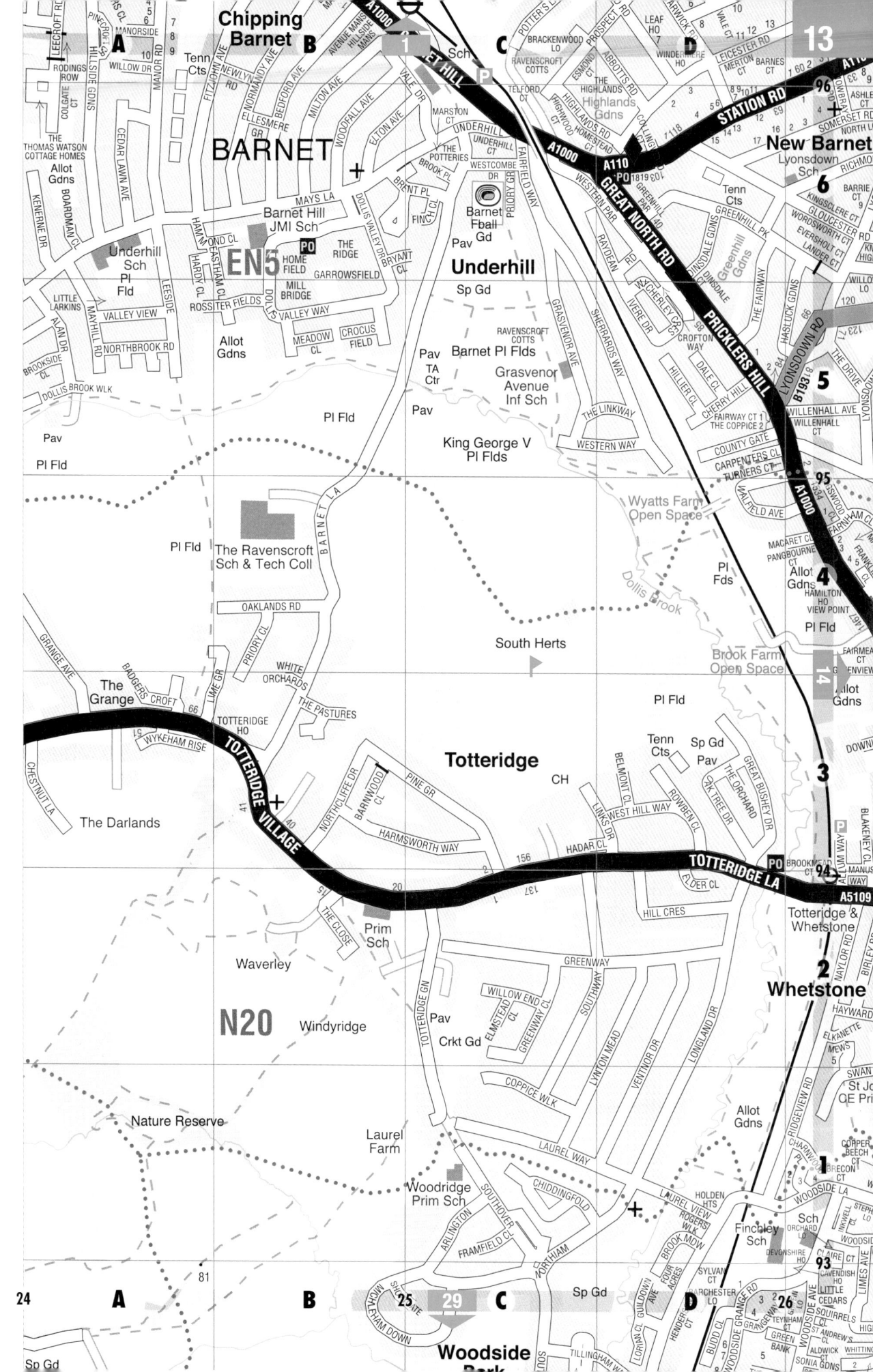
Chipping Barnet
BARNET
EN5
N20
New Barnet
Underhill
Totteridge
Whetstone
Woodside Park
Barnet Hill JMI Sch
Underhill Sch
Barnet Fball Gd
Barnet Pl Flds
Grasvenor Avenue Inf Sch
King George V Pl Flds
The Ravenscroft Sch & Tech Coll
South Herts
Wyatts Farm Open Space
Brook Farm Open Space
Dollis Brook
Highlands Gdns
Greenhill Gdns
The Grange
The Darlands
Waverley
Windyridge
Nature Reserve
Laurel Farm
Woodridge Prim Sch
Finchley Sch
Totteridge & Whetstone
Lyonsdown Sch
Allot Gdns
Pl Fld
Sp Gd
Tenn Cts
Pav
TA Ctr
Prim Sch
Crkt Gd
A1000
A110
A5109
B193
STATION RD
GREAT NORTH RD
PRICKLERS HILL
TOTTERIDGE LA
TOTTERIDGE VILLAGE
BARNET LA
MAYS LA
LYONSDOWN RD
DOLLIS VALLEY DR
VALLEY VIEW
NORTHBROOK RD
DOLLIS BROOK WLK
GRASVENOR AVE
SHERRARDS WAY
WESTERN WAY
THE LINKWAY
FAIRFIELD WAY
OAKLANDS RD
PRIORY CL
WHITE ORCHARDS
THE PASTURES
BADGERS CROFT
WYKEHAM RISE
GRANGE AVE
CHESTNUT LA
NORTHCLIFFE DR
BARNWOOD CL
PINE GR
HARMSWORTH WAY
WEST HILL WAY
LINKS DR
HADAR CL
ROWBEN CL
OAK TREE DR
THE ORCHARD
GREAT BUSHEY DR
ELDER CL
HILL CRES
GREENWAY
SOUTHWAY
WILLOW END
ELMSTEAD CL
GREENWAY CL
LYNTON MEAD
VENTNOR DR
LONGLAND DR
COPPICE WLK
LAUREL WAY
LAUREL VIEW
TOTTERIDGE GN
THE CLOSE
CHIDDINGFOLD
SOUTHOVER
ARLINGTON
FRAMFIELD CL
NORTHIAM
MICHLEHAM DOWN
BROOK MDW
FOUR ACRES
GUILDOWN AVE
RIDGEVIEW RD
WOODSIDE LA
NAYLOR RD
ALLUM WAY
BLAKENEY CL
WOODSIDE AVE
LIMES AVE
A B C D
1 2 3 4 5 6
24 25 26 29 81 93 94 95 96 14

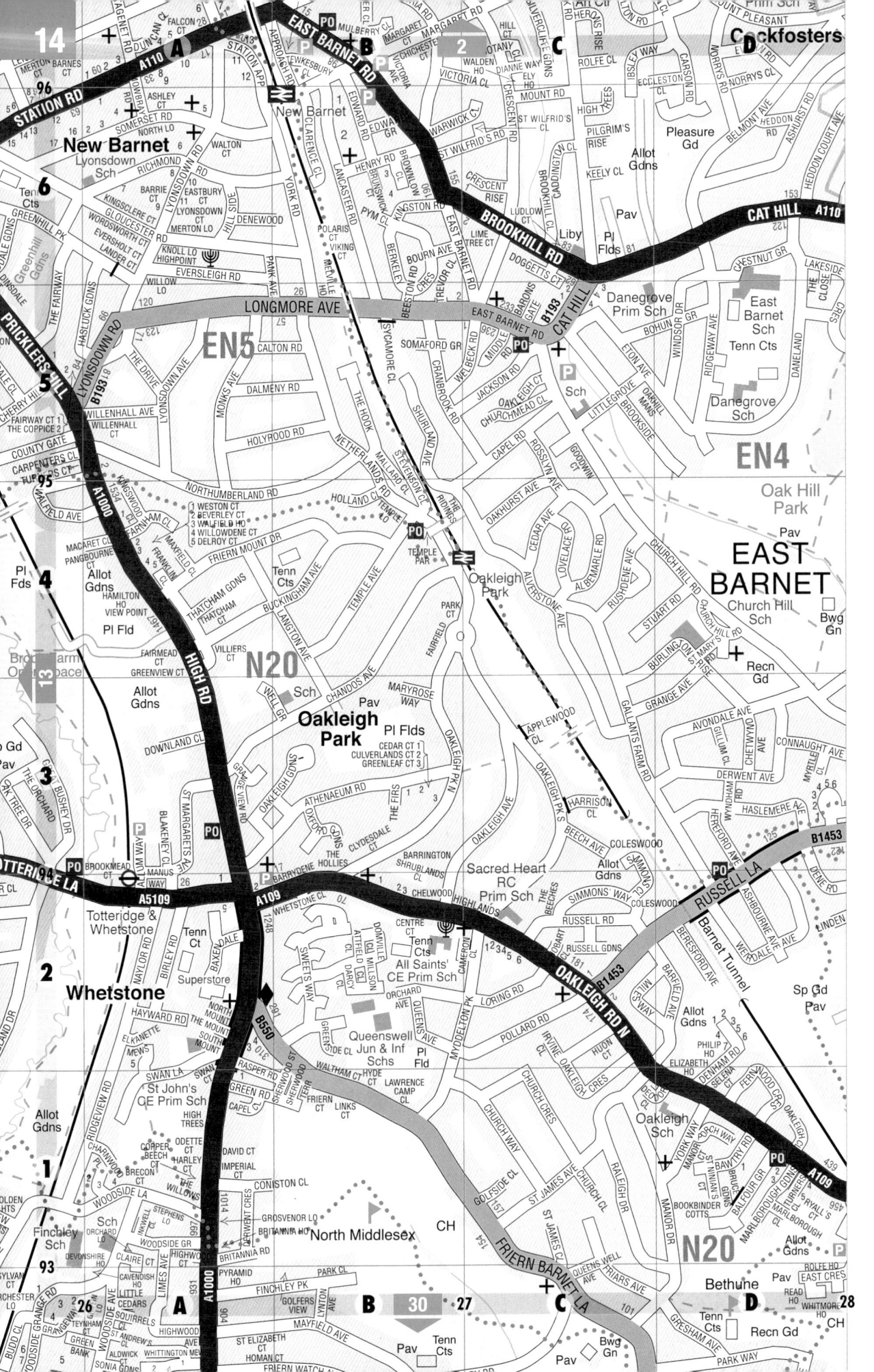

New Barnet
Cockfosters
EAST BARNET
Oakleigh Park
Whetstone
EN5
EN4
N20
STATION RD
A110
EAST BARNET RD
BROOKHILL RD
CAT HILL
LONGMORE AVE
PRICKLERS HILL
LYONSDOWN RD
B193
A1000
HIGH RD
TOTTERIDGE LA
A5109
A109
OAKLEIGH RD N
B1453
RUSSELL LA
Barnet Tunnel
FRIERN BARNET LA
B550
Lyonsdown Sch
Danegrove Prim Sch
East Barnet Sch
Danegrove Sch
Oak Hill Park
Church Hill Sch
Sacred Heart RC Prim Sch
All Saints' CE Prim Sch
Queenswell Jun & Inf Schs
St John's CE Prim Sch
Oakleigh Sch
Finchley Sch
Totteridge & Whetstone
North Middlesex
Pleasure Gd
Allot Gdns
Pl Flds
Tenn Cts
Recn Gd
Bethune
Superstore
NORTHUMBERLAND RD
FRIERN MOUNT DR
CHANDOS AVE
CHURCH HILL RD
OAKLEIGH PK N
OAKLEIGH PK S
GALLANTS FARM RD
WOODSIDE LA
FINCHLEY PK
MAYFIELD AVE
GRESHAM AVE
PARK WAY
MANOR DR
RALEIGH DR
CHURCH WAY
MYDDELTON PK
2
13
30

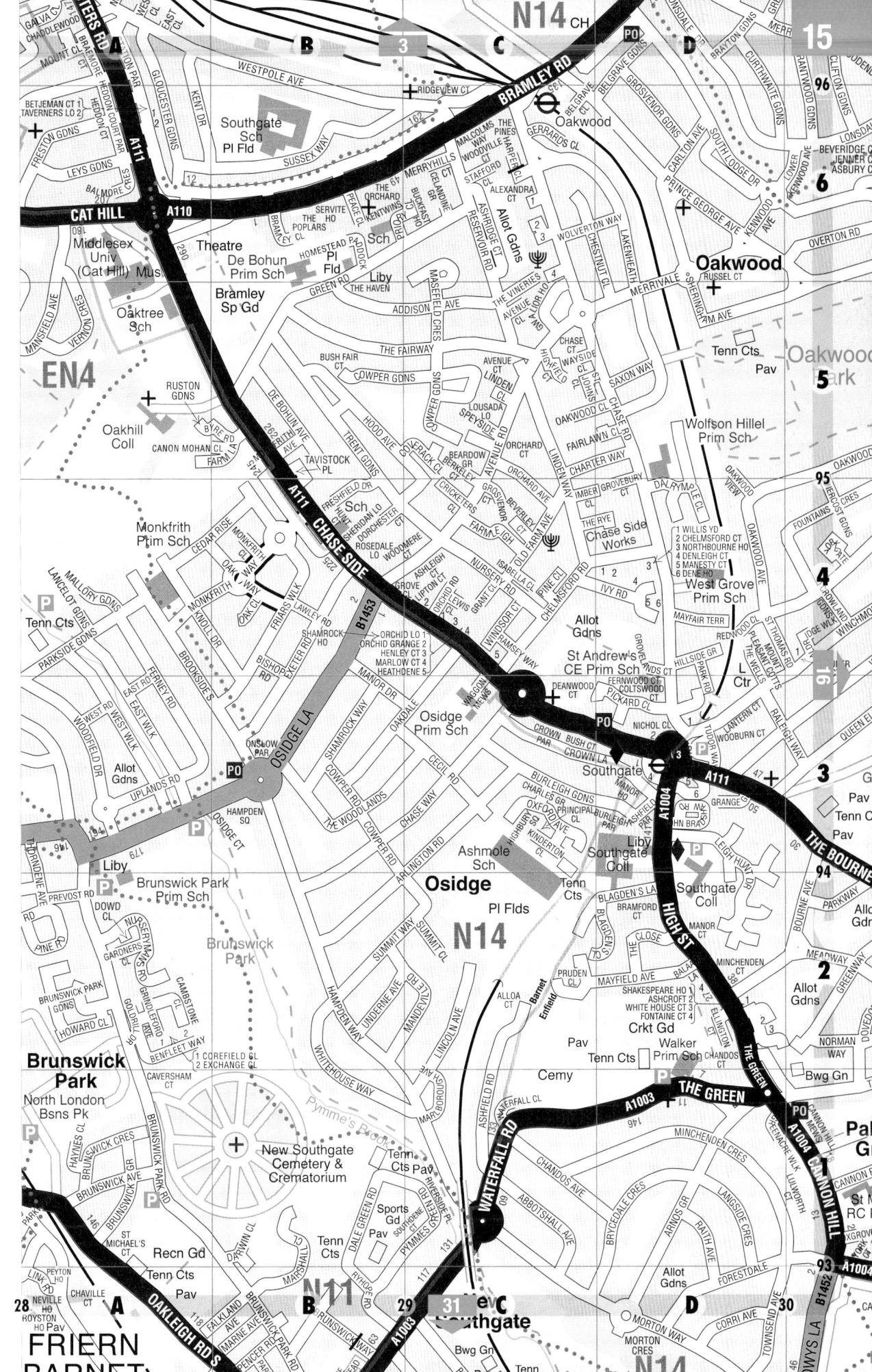

15
N14
A
B
C
D
3
Westpole Ave
Bramley Rd
Oakwood
Southgate Sch
Pl Fld
Sussex Way
Cat Hill
A110
A111
Middlesex Univ (Cat Hill)
Mus
Theatre
De Bohun Prim Sch
Bramley Sp Gd
Oaktree Sch
EN4
Oakhill Coll
Monkfrith Prim Sch
Chase Side
Osidge La
B1453
Osidge Prim Sch
Osidge
N14
Ashmole Sch
Pl Flds
Southgate
Southgate Coll
Liby
High St
A1004
The Bourne
The Green
A1003
Walker Prim Sch
Crkt Gd
Cemy
Brunswick Park
Brunswick Park Prim Sch
North London Bsns Pk
New Southgate Cemetery & Crematorium
Pymme's Brook
Waterfall Rd
Oakleigh Rd S
Friern Barnet
New Southgate
N11
Recn Gd
Sports Gd
Tenn Cts
Pav
Allot Gdns
Chase Side Works
West Grove Prim Sch
St Andrew's CE Prim Sch
Wolfson Hillel Prim Sch
Oakwood Park
L Ctr
Cannon Hill
Bwg Gn
28
29
30
31
93
94
95
96
4
5
6
2
16

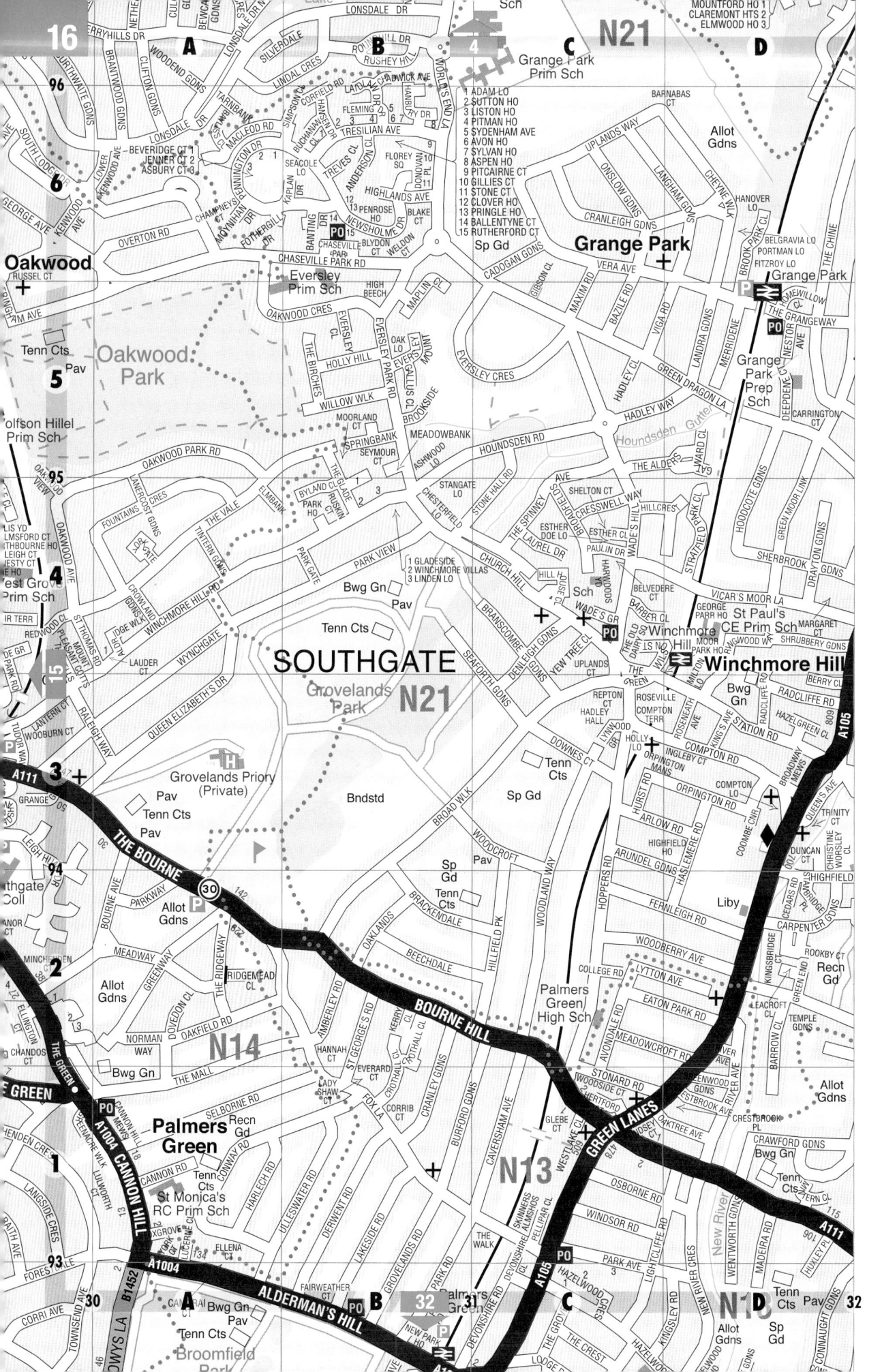
N21
Oakwood
Oakwood Park
Grange Park
SOUTHGATE
Grovelands Park
Winchmore Hill
Palmers Green
N14
N13
THE BOURNE
BOURNE HILL
GREEN LANES
CANNON HILL
ALDERMAN'S HILL
Grovelands Priory (Private)
Eversley Prim Sch
Grange Park Prim Sch
Palmers Green High Sch
St Monica's RC Prim Sch
St Paul's CE Prim Sch
Grange Park Prep Sch
Broomfield Park

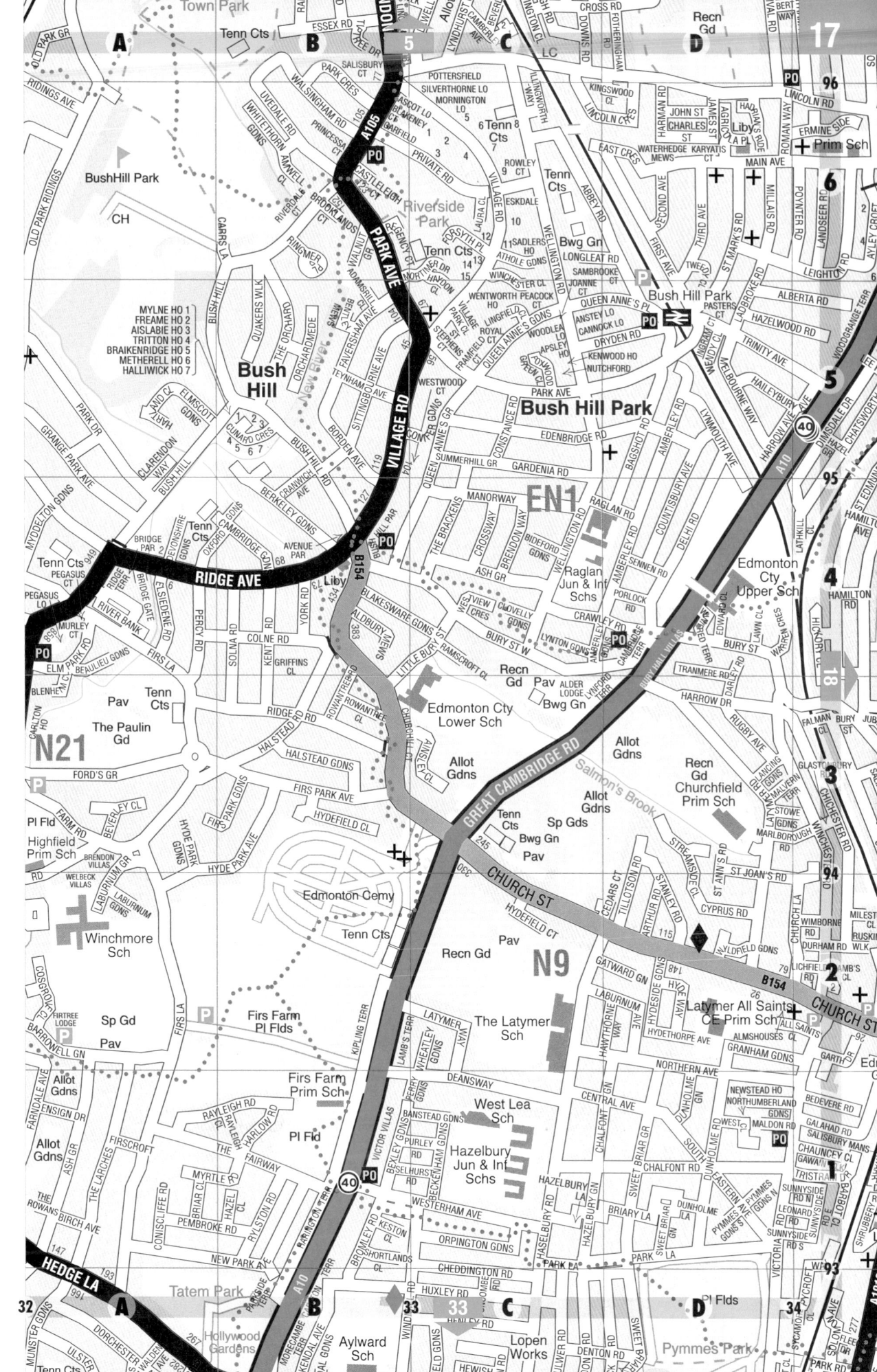
A
B
C
D
5
Town Park
Tenn Cts
ESSEX RD
OLD PARK GR
RIDINGS AVE
OLD PARK RIDINGS
BushHill Park
CH
Recn Gd
CROSS RD
DOWNS RD
FOTHERINGHAM RD
LC
SALISBURY CT
PARK CRES
WALSINGHAM RD
UVEDALE RD
WHITETHORN GDNS
PRINCESSA CT
ANNVELL CL
POTTERSFIELD
SILVERTHORNE LO
MORNINGTON LO
ASCOT LO
BLAKENEY CT
GARFIELD
PRIVATE RD
A105
CASTLELEIGH CT
RIVERDALE CT
BROOKLANDS CT
Riverside Park
RINGMER PL
CARRS LA
PARK AVE
REGENCY CT
FORSYTH PL
Tenn Cts
LAURA CL
VILLAGE RD
ESKDALE
ROWLEY CT
Tenn Cts
ILLINGWORTH WAY
KINGSWOOD CL
LINCOLN CRES
ABBEY RD
WELLINGTON RD
SADLERS HO
Bwg Gn
LONGLEAT RD
ATHOLE GDNS
SAMBROOKE CT
WINCHESTER CL
JOANNE CT
WENTWORTH PEACOCK HO
QUEEN ANNE'S PL
HARMAN RD
JOHN ST
CHARLES ST
JAMES ST
AGRICOLA PL
HADRIANS RIDE
Liby
ROMAN WAY
LINCOLN RD
ERMINE SIDE
Prim Sch
EAST CRES
WATERHEDGE MEWS
KARYATIS CT
MAIN AVE
SECOND AVE
FIRST AVE
THIRD AVE
ST MARK'S RD
MILLAIS RD
POYNTER RD
LANDSEER RD
AYLEY CROFT
LEIGHTON RD
ALBERTA RD
HAZELWOOD RD
Bush Hill Park
PASTERS CT
LADBROKE RD
TWEED WAY
MYLNE HO 1
FREAME HO 2
AISLABIE HO 3
TRITTON HO 4
BRAIKENRIDGE HO 5
METHERELL HO 6
HALLIWICK HO 7
BUSH HILL
QUAKERS WLK
THE ORCHARD
ORCHARDMEDE
Bush Hill
New River
FAVERSHAM AVE
TEYNHAM AVE
SITTINGBOURNE AVE
ADAMSRILL CL
BENTLEY MEWS
MORTIMER DR
HAYDON CL
VILLAGE PARK CL
ST STEPHENS CT
FRAMFIELD CT
LINGFIELD CL
ROYAL CT
QUEEN ANNE'S GDNS
WOODLEA LO
APSLEY HO
FOXWOOD GREEN CL
ANSTEY LO
CANNOCK LO
DRYDEN RD
KENWOOD HO
NUTCHFORD
INGRAM CT
WENDY CL
MELBOURNE WAY
TRINITY AVE
HAILEYBURY AVE
HARROW AVE
WOODGRANGE TERR
DIMSDALE DR
CHATSWORTH
WESTWOOD CT
PARK AVE
Bush Hill Park
CONSTANCE RD
EDENBRIDGE RD
BAGSHOT RD
AMBERLEY RD
LYNMOUTH AVE
VILLAGE RD
COWPER GDNS
QUEEN ANNE'S GR
SUMMERHILL GR
GARDENIA RD
A10
40
95
HAZEL GR
ST EDMUND
HAMILTON AVE
PARK DR
GRANGE PARK AVE
HARTWOOD CL
ELMSCOTT GDNS
CLARENDON WAY
BUSH HILL
CUNARD CRES
BUSH HILL RD
CRANWICH AVE
BERKELEY GDNS
BORDEN AVE
MANORWAY
THE BRACKENS
CROSSWAY
BRENDON WAY
EN1
RAGLAN RD
COUNTISBURY AVE
DELHI RD
MYDDELTON GDNS
Tenn Cts
PEGASUS CT
PEGASUS LO
BRIDGE PAR
DEVONSHIRE GDNS
Tenn Cts
OXFORD GDNS
CAMBRIDGE GDNS
AVENUE PAR
BUSH HILL PAR
B154
BIDEFORD GDNS
ASH GR
Raglan Jun & Inf Schs
AMBERLEY RD
SENNEN RD
Edmonton Cty Upper Sch
HAMILTON RD
LATHKILL CL
RIDGE AVE
RIDGE TERR
BRIDGE GATE
ELSIEDENE RD
PERCY RD
SOLNA RD
KENT RD
YORK RD
Liby
BLAKESWARE GDNS
WESTVIEW CRES
CLOVELLY GDNS
PORLOCK RD
CRAWLEY RD
EDWARD CL
LAWN CL
WARREN CRES
HICKORY CL
MURLEY CT
RIVER BANK
FIRS LA
ALDBURY MEWS
BURY ST W
LYNTON GDNS
CAMBRIDGE TERR
BURY ST
18
ELM PARK RD
BEAULIEU GDNS
BLENHEIM CL
COLNE RD
GRIFFINS CL
LITTLE BURY ST
RAMSCROFT CL
Recn Gd
Pav
ALDER LODGE
Bwg Gn
LYNFORD TERR
BURY HALL VILLAS
TRANMERE RD
DARLEY RD
HARROW DR
RUGBY AVE
FALMAN CL
BURY ST
CARLTON HO
Pav
Tenn Cts
The Paulin Gd
N21
RIDGE RD
ROWANTREE RD
ROWANTREE CL
CHURCHILL CT
Edmonton Cty Lower Sch
ANSLEY CL
HALSTEAD RD
HALSTEAD GDNS
Allot Gdns
GREAT CAMBRIDGE RD
Salmon's Brook
Allot Gdns
Recn Gd
Churchfield Prim Sch
LANCING GDNS
GLASTONBURY
MALVERN TERR
3
FORD'S GR
FIRS PARK AVE
FIRS PARK GDNS
BEVERLEY CL
Pl Fld
FARM RD
HYDEFIELD CL
Allot Gdns
Tenn Cts
Sp Gds
Bwg Gn
Pav
STOWE GDNS
MARLBOROUGH RD
CHICHESTER RD
WINCHESTER RD
Highfield Prim Sch
BRENDON VILLAS
LABURNUM GR
HYDE PARK GDNS
HYDE PARK AVE
WELBECK VILLAS
LABURNUM GDNS
Edmonton Cemy
CHURCH ST
HYDEFIELD CT
CEDARS CT
TILLOTSON RD
ARTHUR RD
STANLEY RD
STREAMSIDE CL
ST ANN'S RD
ST JOAN'S RD
CYPRUS RD
94
CHURCH LA
WIMBORNE RD
DURHAM RD
MILESTONE CL
RUSKIN WLK
Winchmore Sch
Tenn Cts
Recn Gd
Pav
N9
WYLDFIELD GDNS
LICHFIELD RD
LAMB'S CL
2
COSGROVE CL
FIRTREE LODGE
Sp Gd
Pav
BARROWELL GN
FIRS LA
Firs Farm Pl Flds
KIPLING TERR
LAMB'S TERR
WHEATLEY GDNS
LATYMER WAY
The Latymer Sch
GATWARD GN
LABURNUM AVE
HAWTHORNE WAY
HYDESIDE GDNS
HYDE WAY
Latymer All Saints CE Prim Sch
ALL SAINTS' CL
HYDETHORPE AVE
ALMSHOUSES
GRANHAM GDNS
GARTH RD
CHURCH ST
FARNDALE AVE
Allot Gdns
ENSIGN DR
Firs Farm Prim Sch
DEANSWAY
PERRY GDNS
West Lea Sch
NORTHERN AVE
CENTRAL AVE
DUNHOLME GN
NEWSTEAD HO
NORTHUMBERLAND GDNS
BEDEVERE RD
Allot Gdns
ASH GR
THE LARCHES
FIRSCROFT
RAYLEIGH RD
RAYLEIGH CL
HARLOW RD
THE FAIRWAY
Pl Fld
VICTOR VILLAS
BANSTEAD GDNS
BEXLEY GDNS
PURLEY RD
BECKENHAM GDNS
SELHURST RD
Hazelbury Jun & Inf Schs
CHALFONT WAY
SWEET BRIAR GR
CHALFONT RD
SOUTH EASTERN AVE
DUNHOLME RD
WEST CL
MALDON RD
GALAHAD RD
SALISBURY MANS
CHAUNCEY CL
GAWAIN CL
TRISTRAM DR
1
THE ROWANS
BIRCH AVE
CONISCLIFFE RD
BRIAR CL
MYRTLE RD
HAZEL CL
RYLSTON RD
PEMBROKE RD
HARRINGTON TERR
WESTERHAM AVE
KESTON CL
HAZELBURY LA
HAZELBURY GN
HASELBURY RD
BRIARY LA
SWEET BRIAR GN
DUNHOLME LA
PYMMES GDNS S
PYMMES GDNS N
SUNNYSIDE RD N
LEONARD RD
SUNNYSIDE RD E
SUNNYSIDE RD S
BARBOT CL
SHRUBBERY
HEDGE LA
NEW PARK AVE
BROMLEY RD
SHORTLANDS CL
ORPINGTON GDNS
CHEDDINGTON RD
PARK LA
PARK LA
VICTORIA RD
PYCROFT WAY
93
Tatem Park
PARKSIDE TERR
HUXLEY RD
Pl Flds
32
33
34
MUNSTER GDNS
DORCHESTER
ULSTER
Tenn Cts
WALDEN
Hollywood Gardens
A10
MORECAMBE TERR
KENDAL AVE
Aylward Sch
HENLEY RD
Lopen Works
HEWISH
DENTON RD
Pymmes Park
SYCAMORE
SOLONA
PARK RD

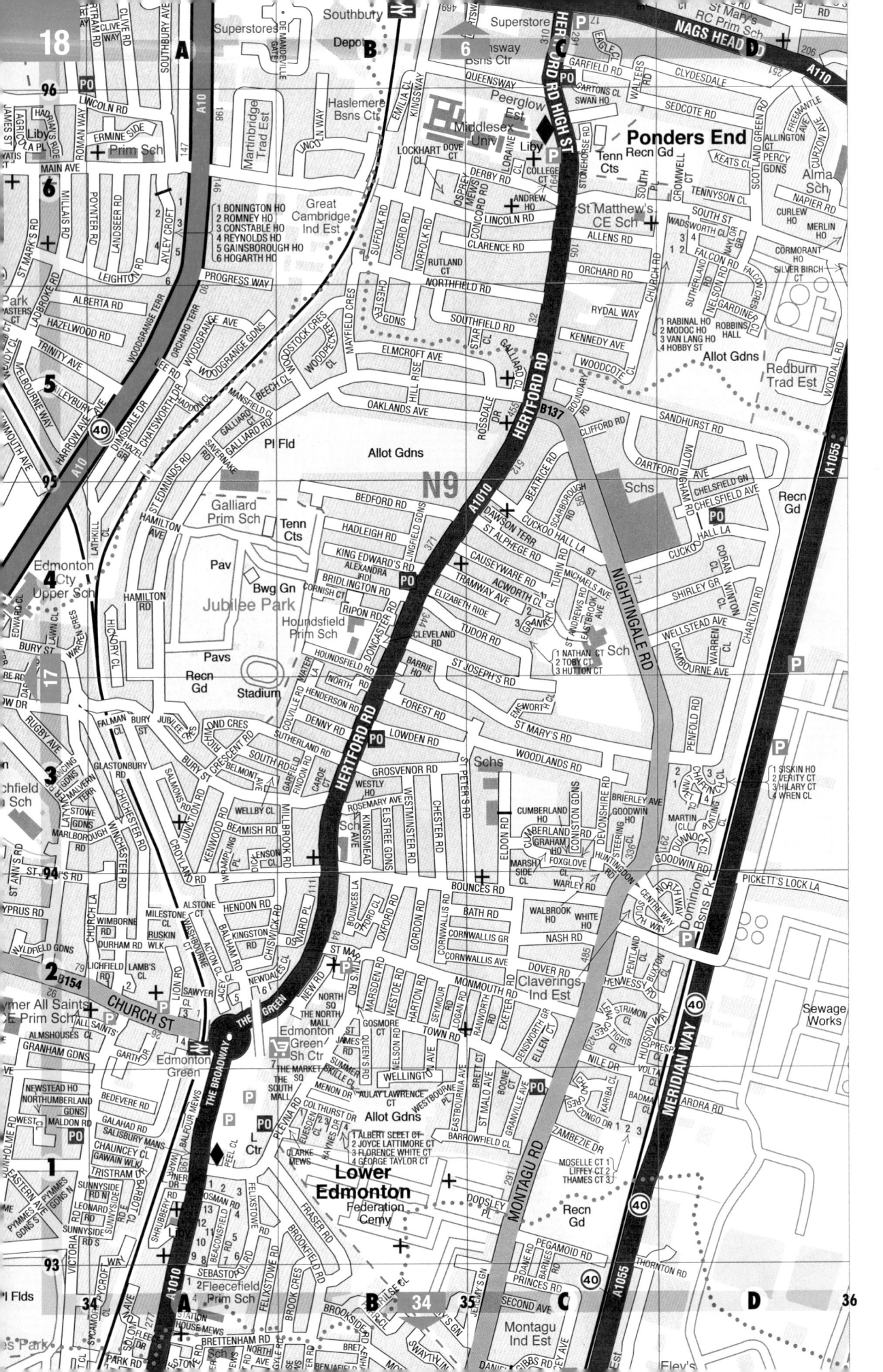
Southbury
Superstores
Depot
Superstore
Queensway Bsns Ctr
NAGS HEAD
St Mary's RC Prim Sch
A110
A10
LINCOLN RD
ERMINE SIDE
Prim Sch
MAIN AVE
Liby
Martinbridge Trad Est
Haslemere Bsns Ctr
Peerglow Est
Middlesex Univ
Ponders End
Recn Gd
Tenn Cts
QUEENSWAY
GARFIELD RD
CLYDESDALE
SEDCOTE RD
SWAN HO
KEATS CL
PERCY GDNS
Alma Sch
NAPIER RD
TENNYSON CL
SOUTH ST
St Matthew's CE Sch
ALLENS RD
ORCHARD RD
RYDAL WAY
KENNEDY AVE
WOODCOTE CL
LINCOLN RD
CLARENCE RD
NORTHFIELD RD
SOUTHFIELD RD
DERBY RD
Great Cambridge Ind Est
1 BONINGTON HO
2 ROMNEY HO
3 CONSTABLE HO
4 REYNOLDS HO
5 GAINSBOROUGH HO
6 HOGARTH HO
PROGRESS WAY
LEIGHTON RD
ALBERTA RD
HAZELWOOD RD
TRINITY AVE
WOODGRANGE TERR
WOODGRANGE AVE
WOODGRANGE GDNS
ELMCROFT AVE
OAKLANDS AVE
HERTFORD RD
HERTFORD RD HIGH ST
B137
A1010
Allot Gdns
Redburn Trad Est
SANDHURST RD
CLIFFORD RD
DARTFORD AVE
CHELSFIELD AVE
Recn Gd
A1055
N9
Pl Fld
Allot Gdns
BEDFORD RD
HADLEIGH RD
KING EDWARD'S RD
Galliard Prim Sch
Tenn Cts
Edmonton Cty Upper Sch
Pav
Bwg Gn
Jubilee Park
Houndsfield Prim Sch
Pavs
Recn Gd
Stadium
NIGHTINGALE RD
Schs
CUCKOO HALL LA
SHIRLEY GR
WELLSTEAD AVE
CAMBOURNE AVE
CAUSEYWARE RD
TRAMWAY AVE
TUDOR RD
ST JOSEPH'S RD
FOREST RD
LOWDEN RD
ST MARY'S RD
WOODLANDS RD
GROSVENOR RD
1 NATHAN CT
2 TOBY CT
3 HUTTON CT
Sch
1 SISKIN HO
2 VERITY CT
3 HILARY CT
4 WREN CL
Schs
BOUNCES RD
PICKETT'S LOCK LA
Dominion Bsns Pk
MERIDIAN WAY
Sewage Works
Claverings Ind Est
MONMOUTH RD
TOWN RD
NASH RD
DOVER RD
CHURCH ST
B154
THE BROADWAY
THE GREEN
Edmonton Green
Edmonton Green Sh Ctr
L Ctr
Allot Gdns
1 ALBERT SLEET CT
2 JOYCE LATTIMORE CT
3 FLORENCE WHITE CT
4 GEORGE TAYLOR CT
Lower Edmonton
Federation Cemy
Recn Gd
MONTAGU RD
MOSELLE CT 1
LIFFEY CT 2
THAMES CT 3
Fleecefield Prim Sch
Montagu Ind Est
PEGAMOID RD
PRINCES RD
THORNTON RD
BRETTENHAM RD
34
35
36
A
B
C
D
1
2
3
4
5
6
93
94
95
96
17
34
6
40

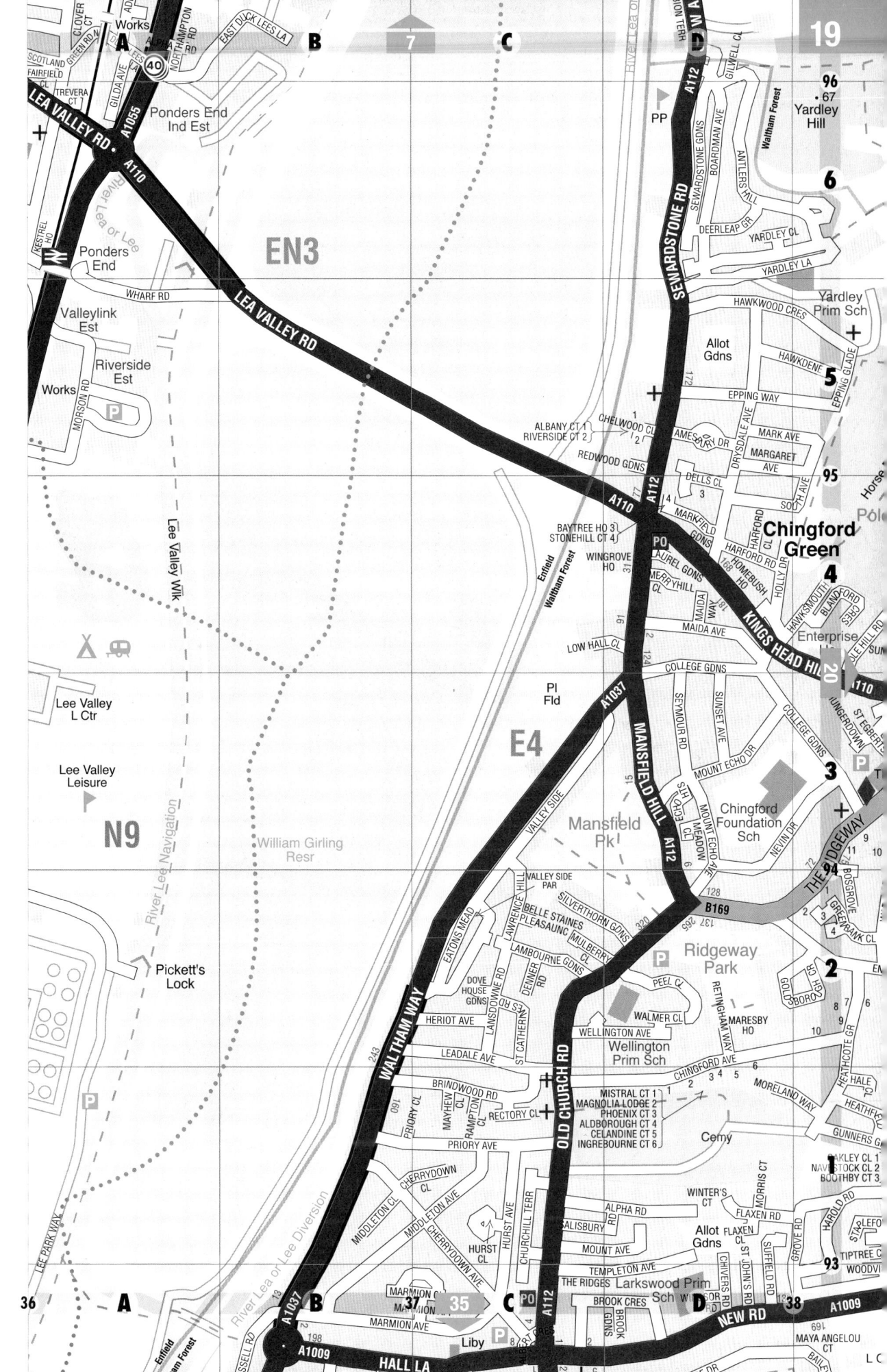
A
B
7
C
D
96
67
Yardley Hill
6
Works
CLOVER CT
SCOTLAND GREEN RD N
FAIRFIELD CL
TREVERA CT
GILDA AVE
ALPHA RD
NORTHAMPTON RD
EAST DUCK LEES LA
40
A1055
Ponders End Ind Est
LEA VALLEY RD
A110
River Lea or Lee
KESTREL HO
Ponders End
WHARF RD
EN3
Valleylink Est
Riverside Est
Works
MORSON RD
PP
A112
BION TERR
GILWELL CL
SEWARDSTONE GDNS
BOARDMAN AVE
ANTLERS HILL
Waltham Forest
SEWARDSTONE RD
DEERLEAP GR
YARDLEY CL
YARDLEY LA
Yardley Prim Sch
HAWKWOOD CRES
Allot Gdns
HAWKDENE
EPPING GLADE
5
EPPING WAY
ALBANY CT 1
RIVERSIDE CT 2
CHELWOOD CL
AMESBURY DR
DRYSDALE AVE
MARK AVE
MARGARET AVE
REDWOOD GDNS
DELLS CL
SOUTH AVE
95
Horse
A110
BAYTREE HO 3
STONEHILL CT 4
MARKFIELD GDNS
HARFORD CL
Chingford Green
PO
WINGROVE HO
LAUREL GDNS
HARFORD RD
HOMEBUSH HO
HOLLY DR
4
MERRYHILL CL
MAIDA WAY
KINGS HEAD HILL
HAWKSMOUTH
BLANDFORD CRES
Enfield
Waltham Forest
MAIDA AVE
LOW HALL CL
Enterprise
COLLEGE GDNS
20
Lee Valley Wlk
Pl Fld
A1037
SEYMOUR RD
SUNSET AVE
COLLEGE GDNS
Lee Valley L Ctr
E4
MOUNT ECHO DR
3
MANSFIELD HILL
Lee Valley Leisure
VALLEY SIDE
Mansfield Pk
Chingford Foundation Sch
N9
River Lee Navigation
William Girling Resr
MEADOW CL
MOUNT ECHO AVE
NEVIN DR
THE RIDGEWAY
94
VALLEY SIDE PAR
BELLE STAINES PLEASAUNCE
SILVERTHORN GDNS
B169
BOSGROVE
GREENBANK CL
EATONS MEAD
LAWRENCE HILL
MULBERRY CL
LAMBOURNE GDNS
Ridgeway Park
2
Pickett's Lock
DOVE HOUSE GDNS
LANSDOWNE RD
DENNER RD
PEEL CL
WALMER CL
RETINGHAM WAY
MARESBY HO
WALTHAM WAY
HERIOT AVE
ST CATHERINES RD
WELLINGTON AVE
Wellington Prim Sch
LEADALE AVE
OLD CHURCH RD
CHINGFORD AVE
HEATHCOTE GR
HALE CL
BRINDWOOD RD
MORELAND WAY
MISTRAL CT 1
MAGNOLIA LODGE 2
PHOENIX CT 3
ALDBOROUGH CT 4
CELANDINE CT 5
INGREBOURNE CT 6
PRIORY CL
MAYHEW CL
RAMPTON CL
RECTORY CL
HEATHFIELD
GUNNERS GR
Cemy
PRIORY AVE
OAKLEY CL 1
NAVESTOCK CL 2
BOOTHBY CT 3
1
CHERRYDOWN CL
WINTER'S CT
MORRIS CT
FLAXEN RD
HAROLD RD
MIDDLETON CL
MIDDLETON AVE
CHERRYDOWN AVE
HURST AVE
CHURCHILL TERR
ALPHA RD
SALISBURY RD
Allot Gdns
FLAXEN CL
ST JOHN'S RD
SUFFIELD RD
GROVE RD
STAPLEFORD
HURST CL
MOUNT AVE
93
TIPTREE C
WOODVILLE
River Lea or Lee Diversion
LEE PARK WAY
TEMPLETON AVE
THE RIDGES
Larkswood Prim Sch
CHIVERS RD
36
A
B
MARMION CL
37
35
C
PO
A112
BROOK CRES
BROOK GDNS
D
38
A1009
NEW RD
MARMION AVE
Liby
MAYA ANGELOU CT
A1037
A1009
HALL LA
Enfield
Waltham Forest
RUSSELL RD
ALBERT CRES

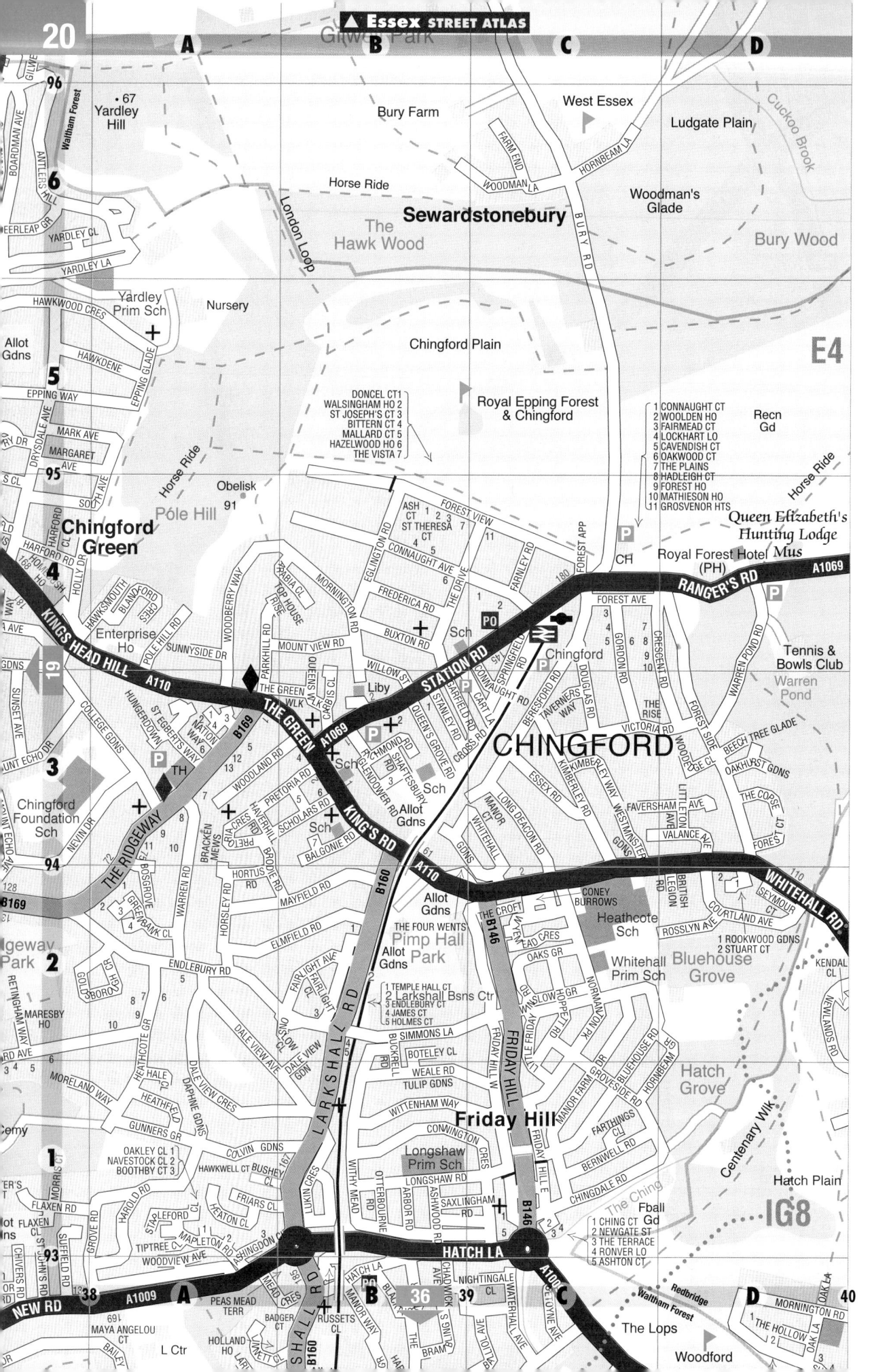

20
Essex STREET ATLAS
A
B
C
D
Gilwell Park
Yardley Hill
Bury Farm
West Essex
Ludgate Plain
Cuckoo Brook
Waltham Forest
BOARDMAN AVE
ANTLERS HILL
FARM END
HORNBEAM LA
WOODMAN LA
Horse Ride
Woodman's Glade
Sewardstonebury
London Loop
The Hawk Wood
BURY RD
Bury Wood
YARDLEY CL
YARDLEY LA
HAWKWOOD CRES
Yardley Prim Sch
Nursery
Allot Gdns
HAWKDENE
EPPING GLADE
Chingford Plain
E4
EPPING WAY
DOCEL CT 1
WALSINGHAM HO 2
ST JOSEPH'S CT 3
BITTERN CT 4
MALLARD CT 5
HAZELWOOD HO 6
THE VISTA 7
Royal Epping Forest & Chingford
1 CONNAUGHT CT
2 WOOLDEN HO
3 FAIRMEAD CT
4 LOCKHART LO
5 CAVENDISH CT
6 OAKWOOD CT
7 THE PLAINS
8 HADLEIGH CT
9 FOREST HO
10 MATHIESON HO
11 GROSVENOR HTS
Recn Gd
DRYSDALE AVE
MARK AVE
MARGARET AVE
SOUTH AVE
Horse Ride
Obelisk
Pole Hill
Chingford Green
HARFORD CL
HARFORD RD
HOLLY DR
ASH CT
ST THERESA CT
FOREST VIEW
EGLINGTON RD
CONNAUGHT AVE
FARNLEY RD
FOREST APP
Queen Elizabeth's Hunting Lodge Mus
Royal Forest Hotel (PH)
CH
RANGER'S RD
A1069
KINGS HEAD HILL
HAWKSMOUTH
BLANDFORD CRES
WOODBERRY WAY
ARABIA CL
TOP HOUSE RISE
MORNINGTON RD
FREDERICA RD
THE DRIVE
FOREST AVE
Enterprise Ho
POLE HILL RD
SUNNYSIDE DR
PARKHILL RD
MOUNT VIEW RD
BUXTON RD
Sch
PO
Chingford
GORDON RD
CRESCENT RD
WARREN POND RD
Tennis & Bowls Club
Warren Pond
19
A110
THE GREEN
THE GREEN WLK
QUEENS WLK
CARBIS CL
WILLOW ST
Liby
STATION RD
SPRINGFIELD RD
CONNAUGHT RD
DOUGLAS RD
TAVERNERS WAY
BERESFORD RD
THE RISE
VICTORIA RD
FOREST SIDE
BEECH TREE GLADE
SUNSET AVE
COLLEGE GDNS
HUNGERDOWN
ST EGBERTS WAY
NATION WAY
B169
WOODLAND RD
A1069
RICHMOND RD
SHAFTESBURY
QUEEN'S GROVE RD
STANLEY RD
GARFIELD RD
CART LA
CROSS RD
CHINGFORD
WOODBEGE CL
OAKHURST GDNS
THE COPSE
MOUNT ECHO DR
TH
PRETORIA RD
GLENDOWER RD
Allot Gdns
ESSEX RD
KIMBERLEY RD
KIMBERLEY WAY
WESTMINSTER GDNS
FAVERSHAM AVE
LITTLETON AVE
VALANCE AVE
FOREST CT
Chingford Foundation Sch
NEVIN DR
THE RIDGEWAY
BRACKEN MEWS
HAVERHILL RD
SCHOLARS RD
BALGONIE RD
KING'S RD
MANOR CT
WHITEHALL GDNS
LONG DEACON RD
BRITISH LEGION RD
WHITEHALL RD
SEYMOUR CT
BOSGROVE
WARREN RD
HORSLEY RD
HORTUS RD
BRODIE RD
MAYFIELD RD
B160
A110
Allot Gdns
THE CROFT
CONEY BURROWS
Heathcote Sch
COURTLAND AVE
ROSSLYN AVE
1 ROOKWOOD GDNS
2 STUART CT
GREENBANK CL
ELMFIELD RD
THE FOUR WENTS
Pimp Hall Park
B146
OAKS GR
Whitehall Prim Sch
Bluehouse Grove
KENDAL CL
Ridgeway Park
ENDLEBURY RD
GOLDSBOROUGH CR
RETINGHAM WAY
MARESBY HO
FAIRLIGHT AVE
FAIRLIGHT CL
Allot Gdns
1 TEMPLE HALL CT
2 Larkshall Bsns Ctr
3 ENDLEBURY CT
4 JAMES CT
5 HOLMES CT
LARKSHALL RD
WINSLOW GR
HOPPETT RD
NORMANTON PK
NEWLANDS RD
SIMMONS LA
BUCKRELL RD
BOTELEY CL
FRIDAY HILL W
LITTLE FRIDAY RD
FRIDAY HILL
DALE VIEW AVE
DALE VIEW GDN
ONSLOW CL
HEATHCOTE GR
HALE CL
MORELAND WAY
HEATHFIELD
DAPHNE GDNS
DALE VIEW CRES
WEALE RD
TULIP GDNS
WITTENHAM WAY
MANOR FARM DR
GROVESIDE RD
BLUEHOUSE RD
HORNBEAM GR
Hatch Grove
GUNNERS GR
Cemy
Friday Hill
CONNINGTON CRES
FARTHINGS CL
Centenary Wlk
OAKLEY CL 1
NAVESTOCK CL 2
BOOTHBY CT 3
COLVIN GDNS
HAWKWELL CT
BUSHEY CL
Longshaw Prim Sch
BERNWELL RD
FRIDAY HILL E
MORRIS CT
LUKIN CRES
WITHY MEAD
OTTERBOURNE RD
LONGSHAW RD
ARBOR RD
ASHWOOD RD
CHINGDALE RD
Hatch Plain
FLAXEN RD
FLAXEN CL
HAROLD RD
GROVE RD
STAPLEFORD CL
HEATON CL
FRIARS CL
SAXLINGHAM RD
The Ching
Fball Gd
IG8
1 CHING CT
2 NEWGATE ST
3 THE TERRACE
4 RONVER LO
5 ASHTON CT
CHIVERS RD
ST JOHN'S RD
SUFFIELD RD
TIPTREE CL
MAPLETON RD
ASHINGDON CL
WOODVIEW AVE
HATCH LA
NEW RD
A1009
PEAS MEAD TERR
MEAD CRES
LARKSHALL RD
HATCH LA
MANOR WAY
36
CHADWICK AVE
NIGHTINGALE CL
WATERHALL AVE
A1009
CLAYTON AVE
Redbridge
Waltham Forest
The Lops
Woodford
MORNINGTON RD
OAK LA
THE HOLLOW
MAYA ANGELOU CT
BADGER CT
RUSSETS CL
HOLLAND HO
L Ctr
BAILEY
B160
38
39
40
93
94
95
96

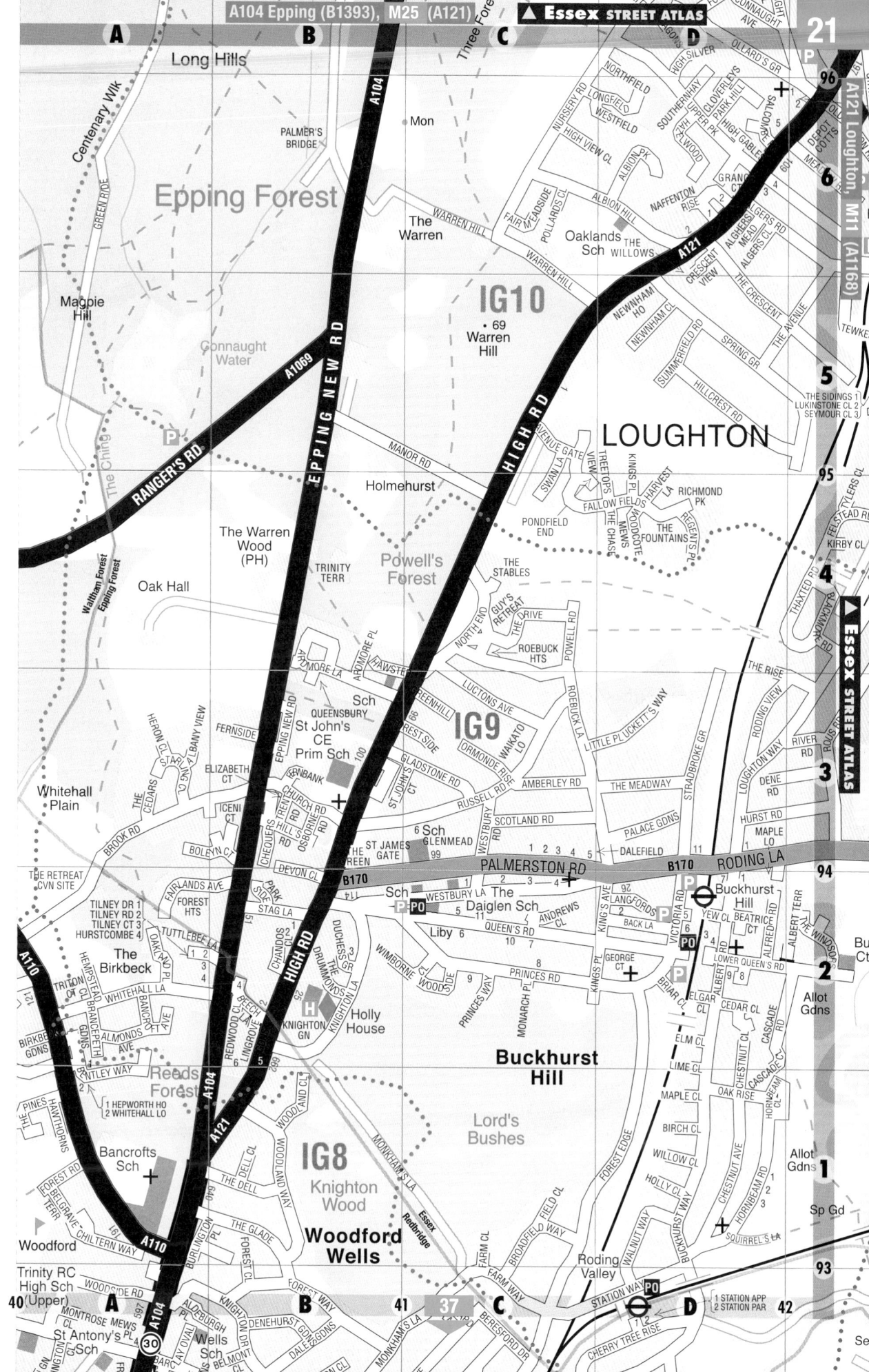
A104 Epping (B1393), M25 (A121)
Essex STREET ATLAS
Long Hills
Epping Forest
The Warren
Magpie Hill
Connaught Water
IG10
69 Warren Hill
LOUGHTON
Holmehurst
The Warren Wood (PH)
Powell's Forest
Oak Hall
Sch
St John's CE Prim Sch
IG9
Whitehall Plain
Oaklands Sch
PALMERSTON RD
RODING LA
Buckhurst Hill
The Daiglen Sch
Liby
The Birkbeck
Holly House
Buckhurst Hill
Reeds Forest
Lord's Bushes
Bancrofts Sch
IG8
Knighton Wood
Woodford Wells
Woodford
Trinity RC High Sch (Upper)
St Antony's Sch
Wells Sch
Roding Valley
Allot Gdns
Sp Gd
A121 Loughton, M11 (A1168)
Essex STREET ATLAS
1 STATION APP
2 STATION PAR
THE SIDINGS 1
LUKINSTONE CL 2
SEYMOUR CL 3
TILNEY DR 1
TILNEY RD 2
TILNEY CT 3
HURSTCOMBE 4
1 HEPWORTH HO
2 WHITEHALL LO
40
41
42
37
93
94
95
96
A
B
C
D
1
2
3
4
5
6

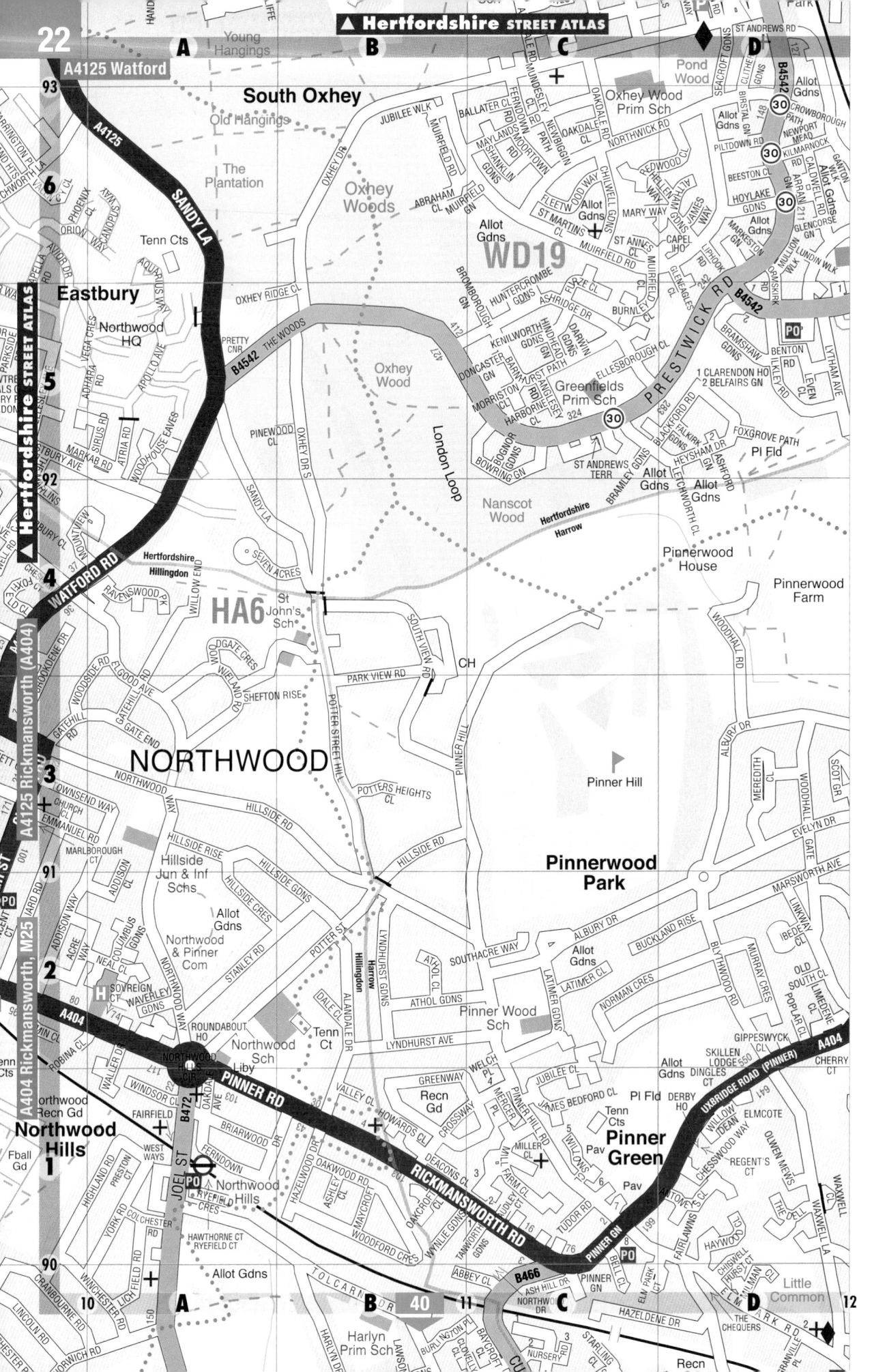
A4125 Watford
South Oxhey
Young Hangings
Old Hangings
The Plantation
Oxhey Woods
Pond Wood
Oxhey Wood Prim Sch
WD19
Eastbury
Northwood HQ
Tenn Cts
SANDY LA
A4125
B4542 THE WOODS
PRETTY CNR
OXHEY RIDGE CL
OXHEY DR
JUBILEE WLK
MUIRFIELD RD
NORTHWICK RD
PRESTWICK RD
B4542
Oxhey Wood
Greenfields Prim Sch
London Loop
Nanscot Wood
Hertfordshire
Harrow
Hillingdon
Allot Gdns
Pinnerwood House
Pinnerwood Farm
ST ANDREWS TERR
FOXGROVE PATH
Pl Fld
HA6
St John's Sch
SEVEN ACRES
WATFORD RD
SOUTH VIEW RD
PARK VIEW RD
CH
SHEFTON RISE
NORTHWOOD
POTTER STREET HILL
PINNER HILL
Pinner Hill
POTTERS HEIGHTS CL
WOODHALL RD
ALBURY DR
EVELYN DR
MARSWORTH AVE
Pinnerwood Park
HILLSIDE RD
Hillside Jun & Inf Schs
Northwood & Pinner Com
SOUTHACRE WAY
BUCKLAND RISE
A4125 Rickmansworth (A404)
A404 Rickmansworth, M25
A404
NORTHWOOD HILLS CIR
PINNER RD
Northwood Sch
Tenn Ct
Pinner Wood Sch
LYNDHURST AVE
Recn Gd
RICKMANSWORTH RD
UXBRIDGE ROAD (PINNER)
Pinner Green
PINNER GN
Northwood Recn Gd
Northwood Hills
Fball Gd
JOEL ST
B472
Allot Gdns
B466
Harlyn Prim Sch
Little Common
Recn
A
B
C
D
93
6
5
92
4
3
91
2
1
90
10
11
12
40

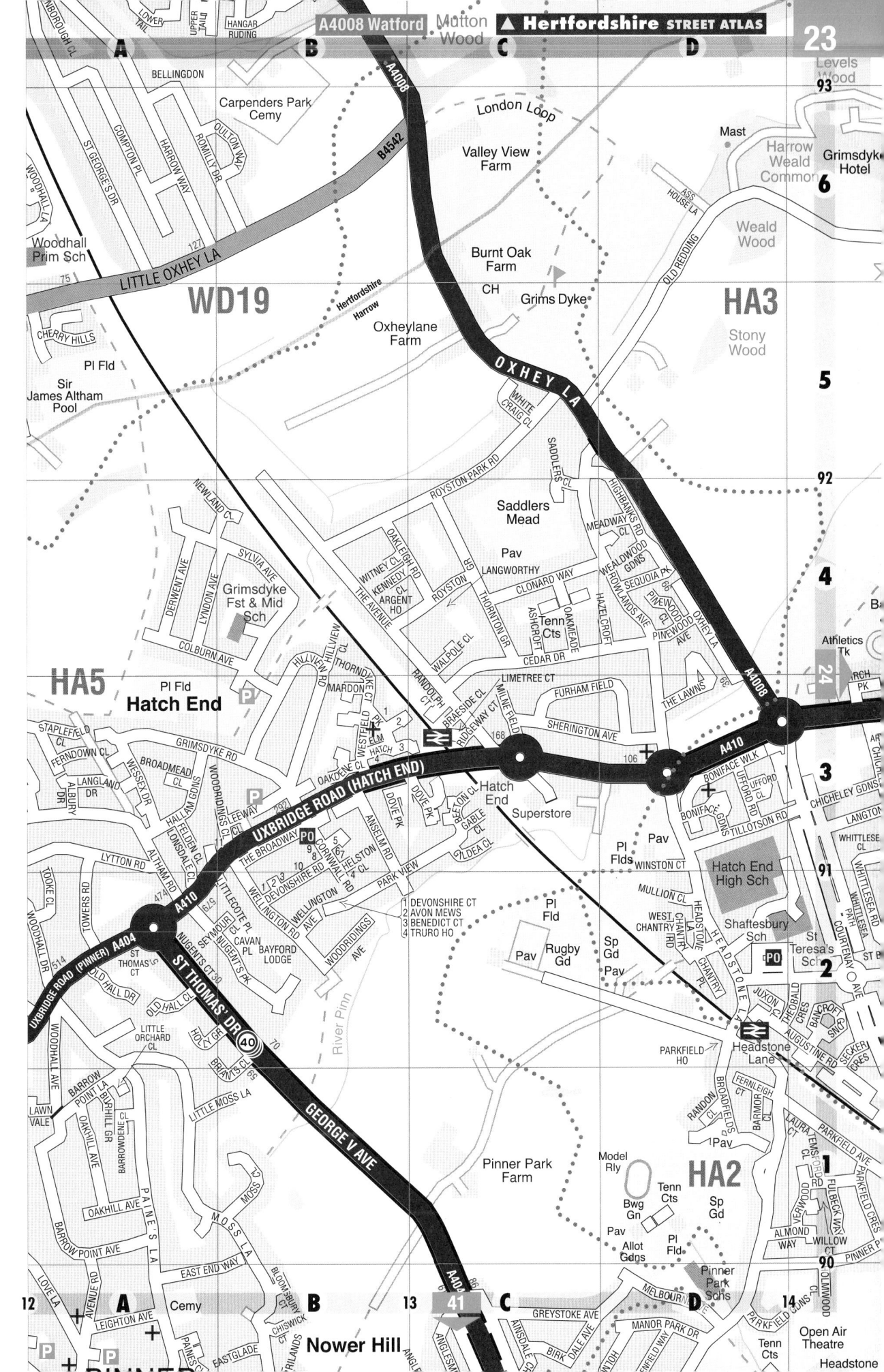
Mutton Wood
Levels Wood
Bellingdon
Carpenders Park Cemy
London Loop
Valley View Farm
Mast
Harrow Weald Common
Grimsdyke Hotel
Weald Wood
Woodhall Prim Sch
LITTLE OXHEY LA
Burnt Oak Farm
Grims Dyke
WD19
HA3
Hertfordshire
Harrow
Oxheylane Farm
Stony Wood
Pl Fld
Sir James Altham Pool
OXHEY LA
Saddlers Mead
Grimsdyke Fst & Mid Sch
Tenn Cts
Athletics Tk
HA5
Hatch End
UXBRIDGE ROAD (HATCH END)
Superstore
Hatch End High Sch
Shaftesbury Sch
St Teresa's Sch
1 DEVONSHIRE CT
2 AVON MEWS
3 BENEDICT CT
4 TRURO HO
Rugby Gd
River Pinn
Headstone Lane
GEORGE V AVE
ST THOMAS' DR
UXBRIDGE ROAD (PINNER) A404
Pinner Park Farm
Model Rly
HA2
Bwg Gn
Allot Gdns
Pinner Park Schs
Open Air Theatre
Nower Hill
Cemy
PINNER

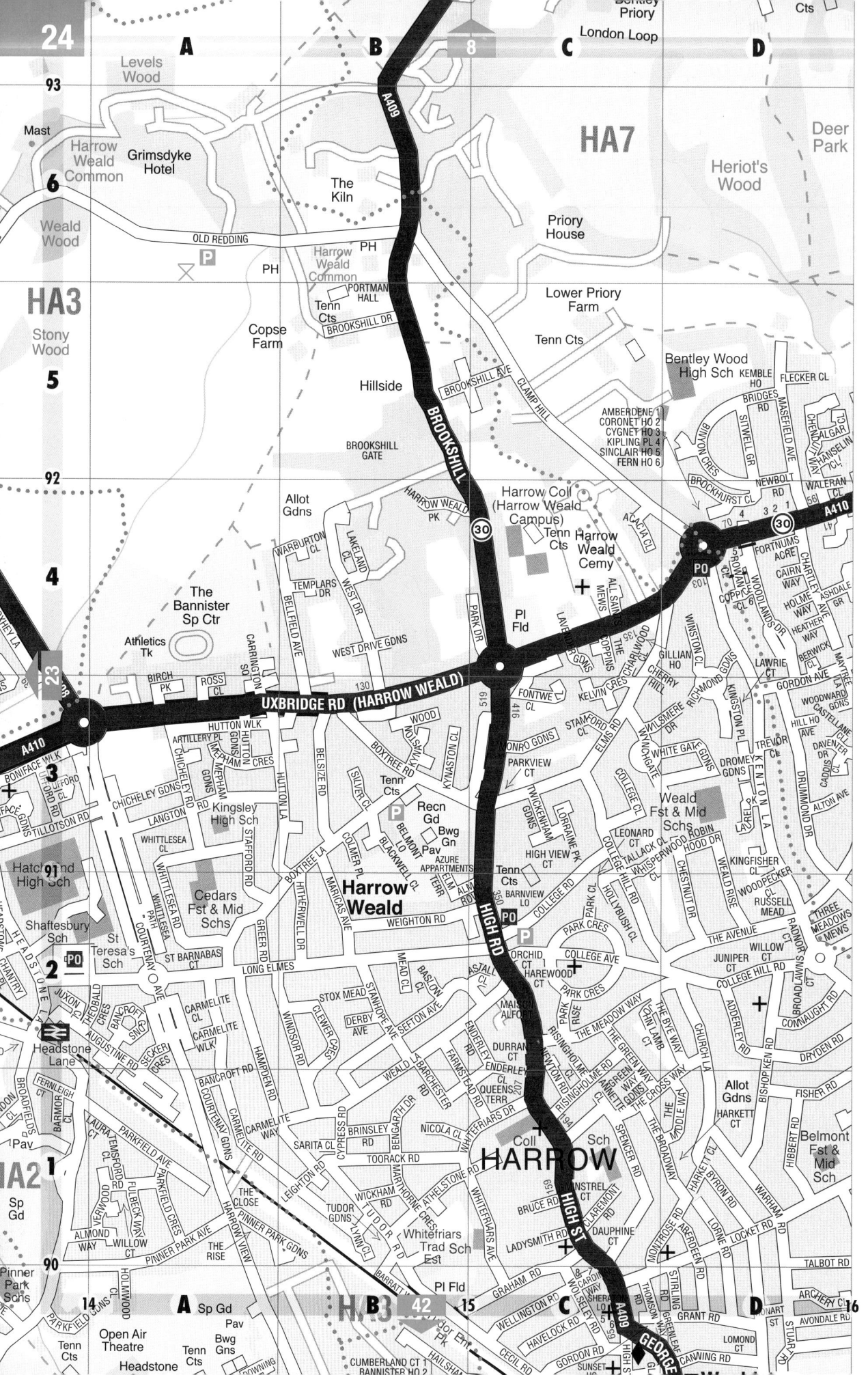
A
B
C
D
8
London Loop
Bentley Priory
Levels Wood
93
Mast
Harrow Weald Common
Grimsdyke Hotel
6
Weald Wood
OLD REDDING
A409
The Kiln
HA7
Deer Park
Heriot's Wood
Priory House
Lower Priory Farm
Harrow Weald Common
PH
PORTMAN HALL
Tenn Cts
BROOKSHILL DR
HA3
Stony Wood
5
Copse Farm
Hillside
BROOKSHILL
BROOKSHILL AVE
CLAMP HILL
Tenn Cts
Bentley Wood High Sch
KEMBLE HO
FLECKER CL
BRIDGES RD
MASEFIELD AVE
AMBERDENE 1
CORONET HO 2
CYGNET HO 3
KIPLING PL 4
SINCLAIR HO 5
FERN HO 6
BROOKSHILL GATE
BINYON CRES
SITWELL GR
NEWBOLT RD
WALERAN CL
BROCKHURST CL
92
Allot Gdns
HARROW WEALD PK
Harrow Coll (Harrow Weald Campus)
Tenn Cts
Harrow Weald Cemy
ACACIA CL
A410
30
WARBURTON CL
LAKELAND CL
FORTNUMS ACRE
CAIRN WAY
CHARTLEY AVE
ASHDALE GR
4
TEMPLARS DR
WEST DR
PARK DR
Pl Fld
ALL SAINTS MEWS
PO
ROWAN CL
COPPICE CL
WOODLANDS DR
HOLME WAY
HEATHER WAY
The Bannister Sp Ctr
Athletics Tk
BELLFIELD AVE
WEST DRIVE GDNS
CARRINGTON SQ
LAVENDER GDNS
THE COPPINS
CHARLWOOD CL
GILLIAN HO
WINSTON CL
LAWRIE CT
BERWICK CL
MAYTREE LA
GORDON AVE
23
BIRCH PK
ROSS CL
130
UXBRIDGE RD (HARROW WEALD)
519
416
FONTWELL CL
KELVIN CRES
CHERRY HILL
RICHMOND GDNS
KINGSTON PL
WOODWARD GDNS
CASTELLANE CL
HUTTON WLK
WOOD
ARTILLERY PL
HUTTON GDNS
MEPHAM CRES
BOXTREE RD
KYNASTON CL
STAMFORD CL
ELMS RD
WILSMERE DR
WYNCHGATE
HILL HO AVE
DAVENTER DR
TREVOR CL
CADDIS CL
3
BONIFACE WLK
CHICHELEY RD
MEPHAM GDNS
BELSIZE RD
HUTTON LA
SILVER CL
MONRO GDNS
PARKVIEW CT
WHITE GATE GDNS
DROMEY GDNS
KENTON LA
ALTON AVE
CHICHELEY GDNS
LANGTON
Kingsley High Sch
Tenn Cts
Recn Gd
Bwg Gn
Pav
TWICKENHAM GDNS
LORRAINE PK
COLLEGE CL
Weald Fst & Mid Schs
DRUMMOND DR
TILLOTSON RD
WHITTLESEA CL
BELMONT LO
BLACKWELL CL
AZURE APPARTMENTS
ELM TERR
HIGH VIEW CT
LEONARD CT
TALLACK CL
WHISPERWOOD CL
ROBIN HOOD DR
KINGFISHER CL
WOODPECKER CL
RUSSELL MEAD
91
Hatch End High Sch
WHITTLESEA RD
STAFFORD RD
BOXTREE LA
HITHERWELL DR
MARICAS AVE
COLMER PL
Harrow Weald
ALMA ROW
Tenn Cts
BARNVIEW LO
COLLEGE RD
COLLEGE HILL RD
HOLLYBUSH CL
CHESTNUT DR
WEALD RISE
THE AVENUE
THREE MEADOWS MEWS
Cedars Fst & Mid Schs
Shaftesbury Sch
WEIGHTON RD
HIGH RD
350
PO
PARK CL
PARK CRES
HEADSTONE LA
St Teresa's Sch
COURTENAY AVE
ST BARNABAS CT
GREER RD
LONG ELMES
MEAD CL
ORCHID CT
HAREWOOD CT
COLLEGE AVE
WILLOW CT
JUNIPER CT
COLLEGE HILL RD
RADNOR CT
BROADLAWNS CT
2
CHANTRY PL
JUXON CL
THEOBALD CRES
BANCROFT GDNS
CARMELITE CL
STOX MEAD
STANHOPE AVE
BASLOW CL
ASTALL CL
MAISON ALFORT
PARK RISE
PARK CRES
THE MEADOW WAY
JOHN LAMB CT
THE BYE WAY
CHURCH LA
ADDERLEY RD
CONNAUGHT RD
Headstone Lane
AUGUSTINE RD
SECKER CRES
CARMELITE WLK
WINDSOR RD
CLEWER CRES
DERBY AVE
SEFTON AVE
ENDERLEY RD
DURRANT CT
RISINGHOLME CL
KENTON RD
THE GREEN WAY
BISHOP KEN RD
DRYDEN RD
FERNLEIGH CT
BROADFIELDS
BARMOR CL
BANCROFT RD
HAMPDEN RD
WEALD LA
BARCHESTER RD
FARMSTEAD RD
ENDERLEY CL
QUEENS TERR
207
RISINGHOLME RD
ANNETTE CL
GREEN WAY GDNS
THE CROSS WAY
Allot Gdns
FISHER RD
Pav
LAURA CT
PARKFIELD AVE
COURTENAY GDNS
CARMELITE RD
CARMELITE WAY
CYPRESS RD
BRINSLEY RD
BENGARTH DR
NICOLA CL
WHITEFRIARS DR
194
SPENCER RD
THE MIDDLE WAY
THE BROADWAY
HARKETT CT
HIBBERT RD
Belmont Fst & Mid Sch
1
HA2
TEMSFORD CL
FULBECK WAY
PARKFIELD CRES
SARITA CL
TOORACK RD
Coll
HARROW
Sch
HARKETT CL
BYRON RD
WARHAM RD
Sp Gd
VERWOOD RD
LEIGHTON RD
THE CLOSE
WICKHAM RD
MARTHORNE CRES
ATHELSTONE RD
WHITEFRIARS AVE
159
MINSTREL CT
BRUCE RD
HIGH ST
CLAREMONT RD
ALMOND WAY
WILLOW CT
PINNER PARK AVE
THE RISE
HARROW VIEW
PINNER PARK GDNS
TUDOR GDNS
LYNN CL
TUDOR RD
Whitefriars Trad Est
Sch
LADYSMITH RD
DAUPHINE CT
MONTROSE RD
ABERDEEN RD
LORNE RD
LOCKET RD
90
Pinner Park Schs
HOLMWOOD CL
BARRATT WAY
Pl Fld
GRAHAM RD
CARDINAL WAY
SHERATON LO
THOMSON WAY
STIRLING RD
GREENLEAF
TALBOT RD
ARCHERY CL
14
A
Sp Gd
B
42
15
C
WELLINGTON RD
WOLSELEY RD
D
AVONDALE RD
16
GRANT RD
BONNART ST
STUART RD
PARKFIELD GDNS
Pav
Open Air Theatre
Bwg Gns
Tenn Cts
Tenn Cts
Headstone
DOWNING
CUMBERLAND CT 1
BANNISTER HO 2
HAILSHAM
CECIL RD
HAVELOCK RD
GORDON RD
SUNSET
HIGH ST
GEORGE
LOMOND CT
CANNING RD

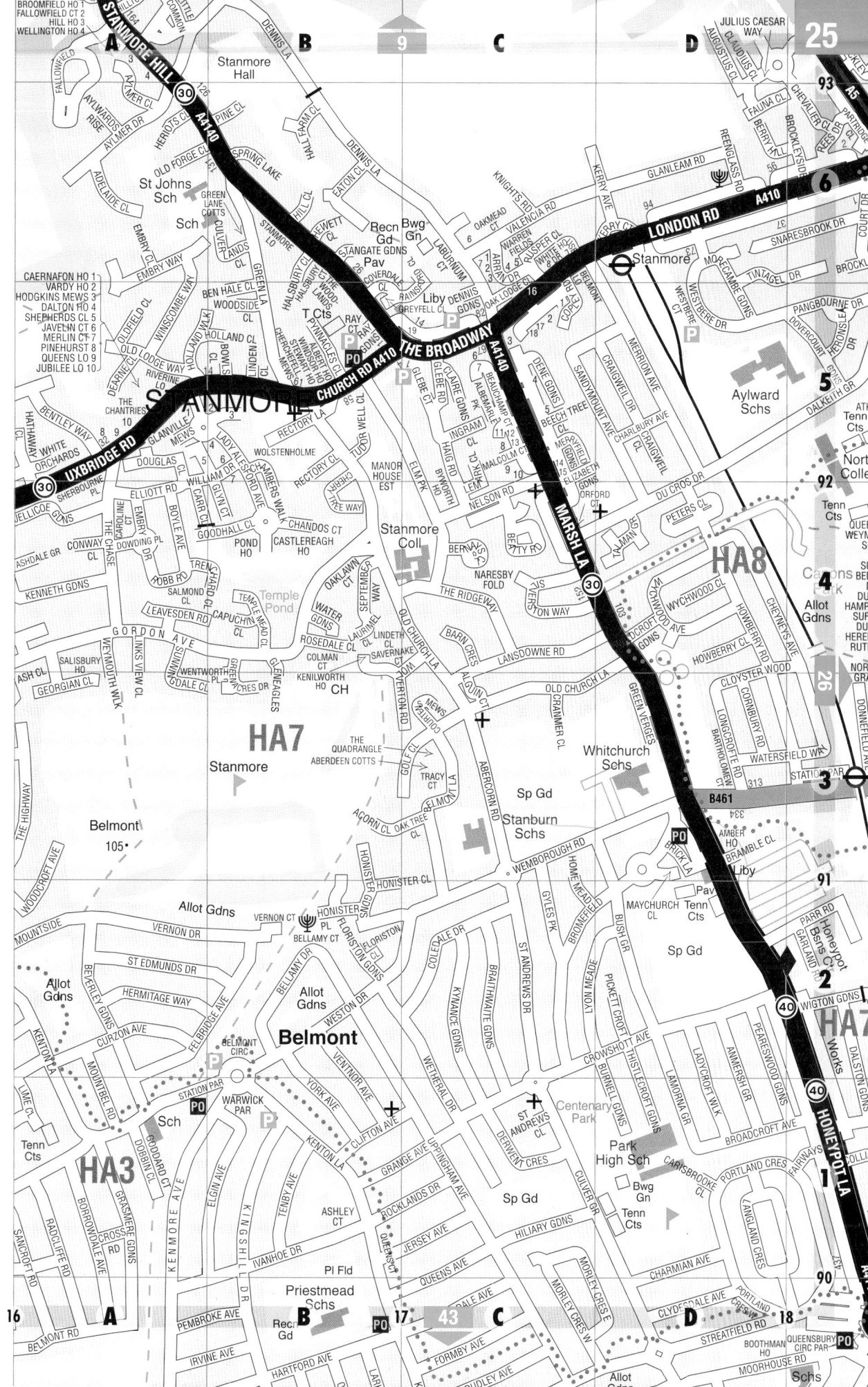

STANMORE
HA7
HA8
HA3
Belmont
Stanmore Hall
St Johns Sch
Stanmore Coll
Aylward Schs
Whitchurch Schs
Stanburn Schs
Park High Sch
Priestmead Schs
Centenary Park
Temple Pond
STANMORE HILL
UXBRIDGE RD
CHURCH RD A410
THE BROADWAY
LONDON RD
MARSH LA
HONEYPOT LA
A4140
A410
A5
B461
BROOMFIELD HO 1
FALLOWFIELD CT 2
HILL HO 3
WELLINGTON HO 4
CAERNAFON HO 1
VARDY HO 2
HODGKINS MEWS 3
DALTON HO 4
SHEPHERDS CL 5
JAVELIN CT 6
MERLIN CT 7
PINEHURST 8
QUEENS LO 9
JUBILEE LO 10

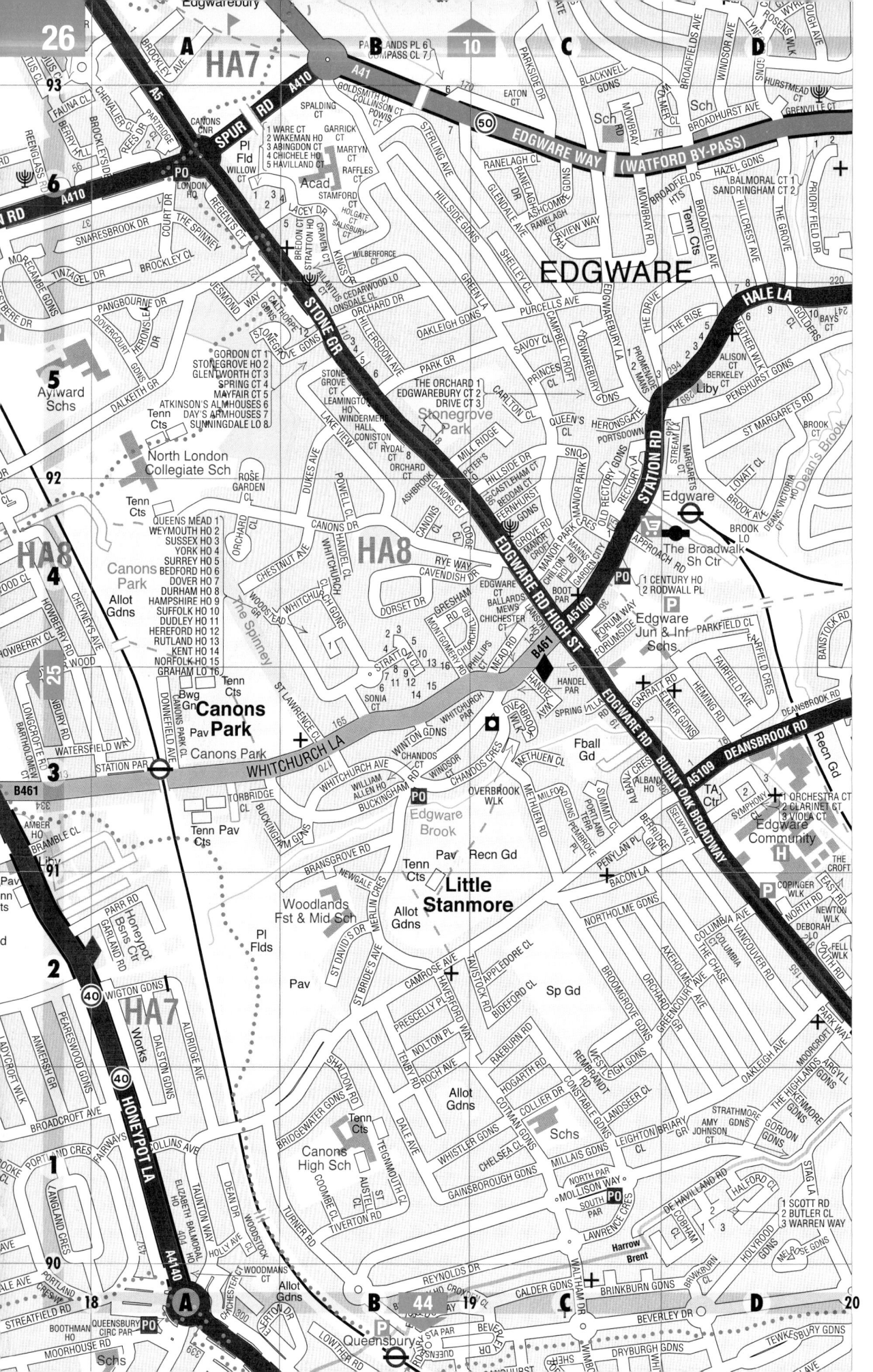
Edgwarebury
A
B
C
D
HA7
10
PARKLANDS PL 6
COMPASS CL 7
A41
A5
A410
SPUR RD
CANONS CNR
EATON CT
BLACKWELL GDNS
PARKSIDE DR
MOWBRAY
BROADFIELDS AVE
WINDSOR AVE
HURSTMEAD CT
GRENVILLE CT
BROADHURST AVE
GOLDSMITH CT
COLLINSON CT
POWIS CT
SPALDING CT
1 WARE CT
2 WAKEMAN HO
3 ABINGDON CT
4 CHICHELE HO
5 HAVILLAND CT
GARRICK CT
MARTYN CT
RAFFLES CT
Acad
STAMFORD CT
HOLGATE CT
SALISBURY CT
STERLING AVE
HILLSIDE GDNS
EDGWARE WAY
(WATFORD BY-PASS)
RANELAGH CL
RANELAGH DR
GLENDALE AVE
ASHCOMBE GDNS
FAIRVIEW WAY
MOWBRAY RD
BROADFIELDS HTS
HAZEL GDNS
BALMORAL CT 1
SANDRINGHAM CT 2
HILLCREST AVE
THE GROVE
PRIORY FIELD DR
Tenn Cts
BROADFIELD AVE
EDGWARE
Pl Fld
WILLOW CT
PO
LONDON HO
REGENTS CT
THE SPINNEY
COURT DR
SNARESBROOK DR
BROCKLEY CL
BROCKLEY AVE
CHEVALIER CL
FAUNA CL
BERRY HILL
BROCKLEYSIDE
REES DR
PARTRIDGE CL
REENGLASS RD
LACEY DR
BREDON CT
STATION HO
CRAVEN CT
KINGS DR
WILBERFORCE CT
CEDARWOOD LO
LONSDALE CL
ORCHARD DR
ATLANTUS CL
SHELLEY CL
GREEN LA
PURCELLS AVE
CAMPBELL CROFT
EDGWAREBURY LA
THE DRIVE
THE RISE
HALE LA
BAYS CT
GOLDERS CL
MORECAMBE GDNS
TINTAGEL DR
JESMOND WAY
CALTHORPE GDNS
PANGBOURNE DR
DOVERCOURT GDNS
HERONSLEA DR
DALKEITH GR
STONEGROVE GDNS
STONE GR
HILLERSDON AVE
OAKLEIGH GDNS
SAVOY CL
PRINCES CL
EDGWAREBURY GDNS
PROMENADE MANS
ALISON CT
BERKELEY CT
HEATHER WLK
PENSHURST GDNS
Liby
GORDON CT 1
STONEGROVE HO 2
GLENTWORTH CT 3
SPRING CT 4
MAYFAIR CT 5
ATKINSON'S ALMHOUSES 6
DAY'S ARMHOUSES 7
SUNNINGDALE LO 8
PARK GR
THE ORCHARD 1
EDGWAREBURY CT 2
DRIVE CT 3
CARLTON CL
STONE GROVE CT
LEAMINGTON HO
WINDERMERE HALL
CONISTON CT
RYDAL CT
ORCHARD CT
Stonegrove Park
MILL RIDGE
QUEEN'S CL
HERONSGATE
PORTSDOWN
STATION RD
STREAM LA
ST MARGARETS RD
BROOK CT
Aylward Schs
North London Collegiate Sch
Tenn Cts
ROSE GARDEN CL
DUKES AVE
LAKE VIEW
POWELL CL
ASHBROOK
CANONS CT
ST PETER'S CL
HILLSIDE DR
CASTLEHAM CT
BEDDAN CT
FERNHURST GDNS
MANOR PARK GDNS
OLD RECTORY GDNS
RECTORY LA
MARGARETS CT
LOVATT CL
Dean's Brook
DEANS VICTORIA HO
BROOK AVE
BROOK LO
Edgware
The Broadwalk Sh Ctr
APPROACH RD
QUEENS MEAD 1
WEYMOUTH HO 2
SUSSEX HO 3
YORK HO 4
SURREY HO 5
BEDFORD HO 6
DOVER HO 7
DURHAM HO 8
HAMPSHIRE HO 9
SUFFOLK HO 10
DUDLEY HO 11
HEREFORD HO 12
RUTLAND HO 13
KENT HO 14
NORFOLK HO 15
GRAHAM LO 16
ORCHARD CL
CHESTNUT AVE
CANONS DR
HANDEL CL
WHITCHURCH CL
HA8
CANONS CL
LODGE CL
GROVE RD
MANOR CROFT
MANOR PARK CRES
CHILTON RD
MANNS RD
GARDEN CITY
1 CENTURY HO
2 RODWALL PL
Canons Park
Allot Gdns
The Spinney
WOODSTEAD GR
WHITCHURCH GDNS
RYE WAY
CAVENDISH DR
DORSET DR
GRESHAM RD
MONTGOMERY RD
CHURCHILL PL
EDGWARE CT
BALLARDS MEWS
CHICHESTER CT
LANSON
BOOT PAR
A5100
EDGWARE RD HIGH ST
FORUM WAY
FORUMSIDE
Edgware Jun & Inf Schs
PARKFIELD CL
FAIRFIELD CRES
BANSTOCK RD
CHEYNEYS AVE
HOWBERRY RD
HOWBERRY CL
LONGCROFT RD
BARTHOLOMEW CL
25
STRATTON CL
SONIA CT
PHILLIPS CT
MEAD RD
B461
HANDEL WAY
HANDEL PAR
SPRING VILLA RD
GARRATT RD
ELMER GDNS
HEMING RD
FAIRFIELD AVE
DEANSBROOK RD
Recn Gd
Bwg Gn
Tenn Cts
Canons Park
Pav
DONNEFIELD AVE
CANONS PARK CL
ST LAWRENCE CL
WHITCHURCH LA
WHITCHURCH PAR
WINTON GDNS
OVERBROOK WLK
METHUEN CL
Fball Gd
ALBANY CRES
ALBANY HO
EDGWARE RD
BURNT OAK BROADWAY
A5109
TA Ctr
SYMPHONY CL
1 ORCHESTRA CT
2 CLARINET CT
3 VIOLA CT
Edgware Community
H
THE CROFT
WATERSFIELD WAY
STATION PAR
B461
CHANDOS CT
WHITCHURCH AVE
WILLIAM ALLEN HO
WINDSOR CT
CHANDOS CRES
BUCKINGHAM RD
OVERBROOK WLK
METHUEN RD
MILFORD GDNS
PORTLAND TERR
SUMMIT CL
BERRIDGE GN
SELWYN CT
AMBER HO
BRAMBLE CL
TORBRIDGE CL
Tenn Pav Cts
BUCKINGHAM GDNS
Edgware Brook
Pav
Recn Gd
PEMBROKE PL
PENYLAN PL
BACON LA
Liby
BRANSGROVE RD
NEWGALE GDNS
Tenn Cts
Little Stanmore
COPINGER WLK
NORTH RD
EAST RD
NEWTON WLK
DEBORAH LO
FELL WLK
SOUTH RD
PARR RD
Honeypot Bsns Ctr
GARLAND RD
Woodlands Fst & Mid Sch
MERLIN CRES
Allot Gdns
NORTHOLME GDNS
COLUMBIA AVE
COLUMBIA CT
VANCOUVER RD
THE CHASE
AXEHOLME AVE
Pl Flds
ST DAVID'S DR
ST BRIDE'S AVE
CAMROSE AVE
HAVERFORD WAY
APPLEDORE CL
TAVISTOCK RD
BIDEFORD CL
Sp Gd
BROOMGROVE GDNS
ORCHARD GR
GREENCOURT AVE
PARK WAY
WIGTON GDNS
HA7
Pav
PRESCELLY PL
NOLTON PL
TENBY RD
ROCH AVE
RAEBURN RD
HOGARTH RD
REMBRANDT RD
WESTLEIGH GDNS
OAKLEIGH AVE
MOORCROFT GDNS
THE HIGHLANDS
ARGYLL GDNS
KENMORE GDNS
Works
PEARESWOOD GDNS
ANMERSH GR
DALSTON GDNS
ALDRIDGE AVE
HONEYPOT LA
SHALDON RD
BRIDGEWATER GDNS
Tenn Cts
Canons High Sch
DALE AVE
Allot Gdns
COTMAN GDNS
COLLIER DR
CONSTABLE GDNS
Schs
LANDSEER CL
STRATHMORE GDNS
AMY JOHNSON CT
GORDON GDNS
BROADCROFT AVE
FAIRWAYS
COLLINS AVE
PORTLAND CRES
LANGLAND CRES
WHISTLER GDNS
CHELSEA CL
MILLAIS GDNS
LEIGHTON CL
BRIARY GR
TEIGNMOUTH CL
COOMBE CL
AUSTELL CL
ST
GAINSBOROUGH GDNS
NORTH PAR
MOLLISON WAY
SOUTH PAR
DE HAVILLAND RD
HALFORD CL
STAG LA
1 SCOTT RD
2 BUTLER CL
3 WARREN WAY
ELIZABETH HO
BALMORAL HO
TAUNTON WAY
DEAN DR
HOLLY AVE
WOODSTOCK CL
TURNER RD
TIVERTON RD
LAWRENCE CRES
COBHAM CL
Harrow Brent
HOLYROOD GDNS
MELROSE GDNS
A4140
WOODMANS CT
CHICHESTER CT
Allot Gdns
REYNOLDS DR
CROYDON CL
CALDER GDNS
BRINKBURN GDNS
BRINKBURN CL
WALTHAM DR
STREATFIELD RD
PORTLAND CRES W
BOOTHMAN HO
QUEENSBURY CIRC PAR
MOORHOUSE RD
Schs
FLETON DR
44
STA PAR
BEVERLEY DR
Queensbury
LOWTHER RD
DRYBURGH GDNS
TEWKESBURY GDNS
20
18
19
93
92
91
90
6
5
4
3
2
1

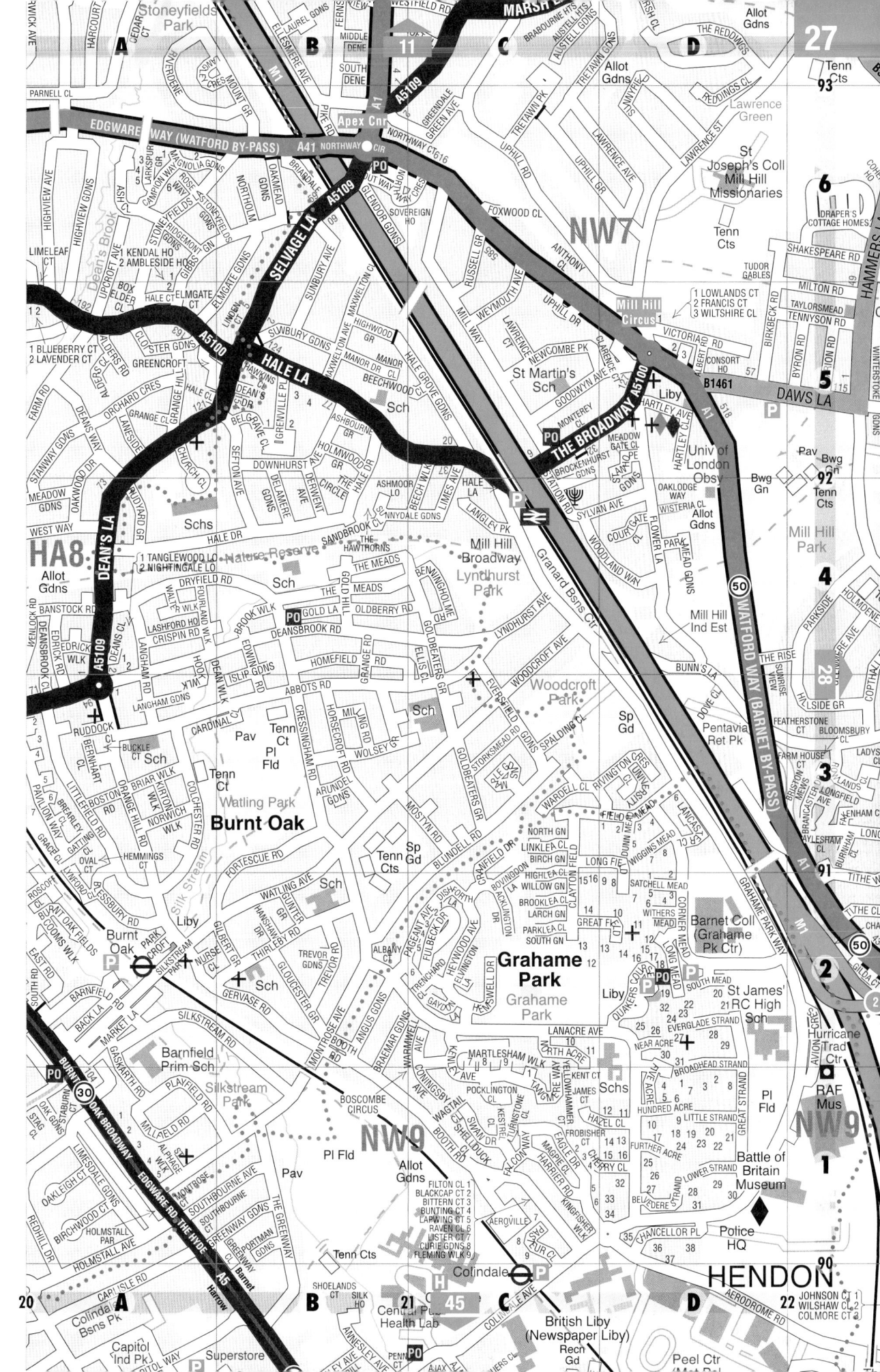

Stoneyfields Park
EDGWARE WAY (WATFORD BY-PASS)
Apex Cnr
NW7
St Joseph's Coll Mill Hill Missionaries
Lawrence Green
Mill Hill Circus
DAWS LA
SELVAGE LA
HALE LA
DEAN'S LA
THE BROADWAY
St Martin's Sch
Univ of London Obsy
Mill Hill Park
HA8
Mill Hill Broadway
Lyndhurst Park
Nature Reserve
WATFORD WAY (BARNET BY-PASS)
Mill Hill Ind Est
Woodcroft Park
Pentavia Ret Pk
Watling Park
Burnt Oak
Grahame Park
Barnet Coll (Grahame Pk Ctr)
St James' RC High Sch
Hurricane Trad Ctr
RAF Mus
NW9
Battle of Britain Museum
Barnfield Prim Sch
Silkstream Park
BURNT OAK BROADWAY
EDGWARE RD THE HYDE
Colindale
Police HQ
HENDON
Colindale Bsns Pk
Capitol Ind Pk
Superstore
Central Public Health Lab
British Liby (Newspaper Liby)
Peel Ctr
AERODROME RD

11
28
45

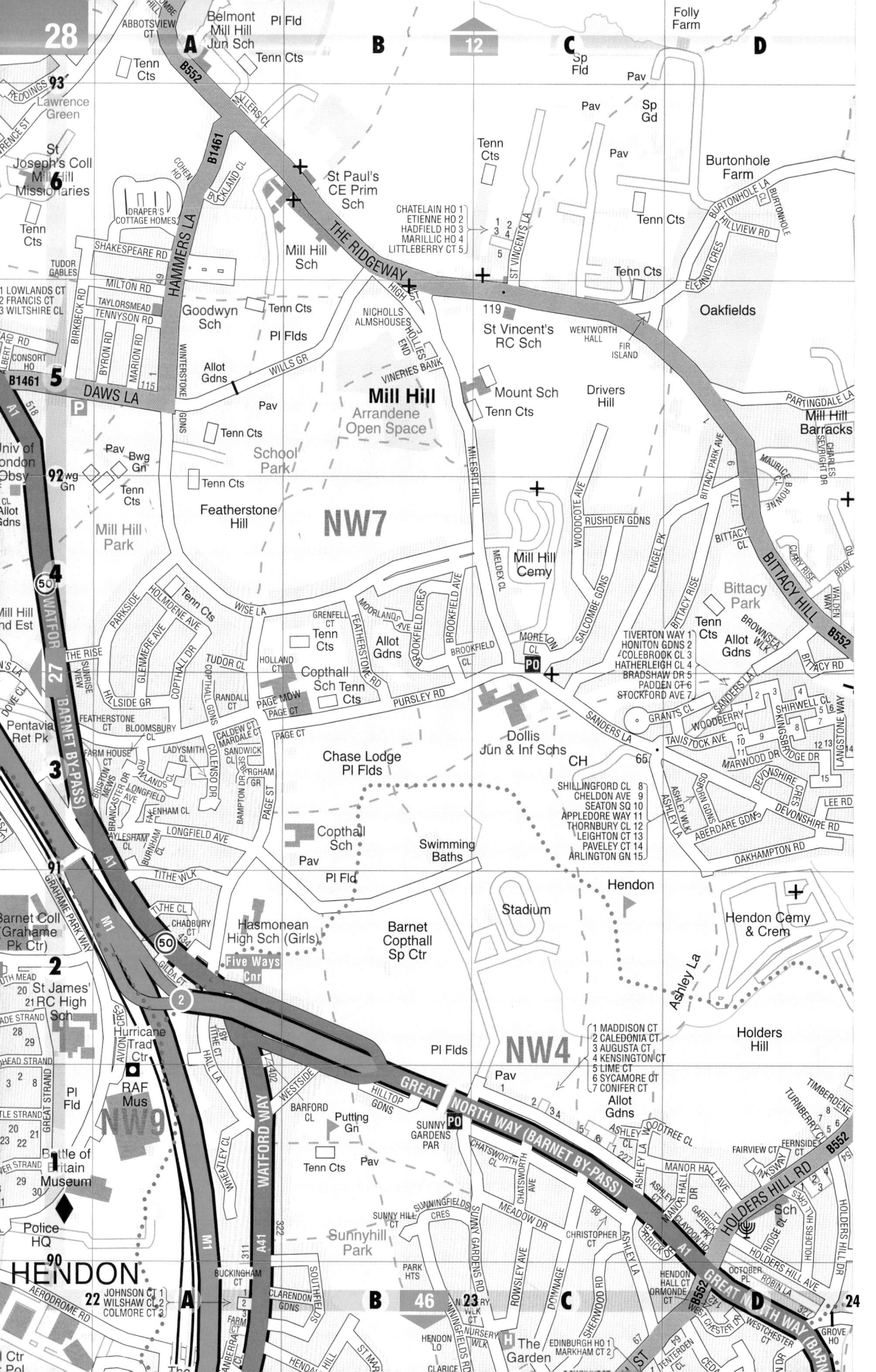
12
A
B
C
D
Belmont Mill Hill Jun Sch
Pl Fld
Folly Farm
Abbotsview Ct
Tenn Cts
Sp Fld
Pav
Sp Gd
Lawrence Green
St Joseph's Coll Mill Hill Missionaries
St Paul's CE Prim Sch
Burtonhole Farm
The Ridgeway
Hammers La
Mill Hill Sch
Draper's Cottage Homes
Shakespeare Rd
Milton Rd
Tennyson Rd
Taylorsmead
Tudor Gables
1 Lowlands Ct
2 Francis Ct
3 Wiltshire Cl
Chatelain Ho 1
Etienne Ho 2
Hadfield Ho 3
Marillic Ho 4
Littleberry Ct 5
St Vincents La
Goodwyn Sch
Pl Flds
Nicholls Almshouses
St Vincent's RC Sch
Wentworth Hall
Fir Island
Oakfields
Burtonhole La
Hillview Rd
Eleanor Cres
Daws La
Wills Gr
Allot Gdns
Vineries Bank
Mill Hill
Arrandene Open Space
Mount Sch
Drivers Hill
Partingdale La
Mill Hill Barracks
School Park
Featherstone Hill
NW7
Mill Hill Park
Univ of London Obsy
Mill Hill Cemy
Rushden Gdns
Woodcote Ave
Salcombe Gdns
Engel Pk
Bittacy Park Ave
Bittacy Hill
Bittacy Park
Bittacy Rise
Wise La
Holmdene Ave
Parkside
The Rise
Glenmere Ave
Copthall Dr
Tudor Cl
Copthall Sch
Moorland Ave
Featherstone Rd
Brookfield Cres
Brookfield Ave
Pursley Rd
Page St
Page Mdw
Tiverton Way 1
Honiton Gdns 2
Colebrook Cl 3
Hatherleigh Cl 4
Bradshaw Dr 5
Padden Ct 6
Stockford Ave 7
Sanders La
Dollis Jun & Inf Schs
Chase Lodge Pl Flds
Shillingford Cl 8
Cheldon Ave 9
Seaton Sq 10
Appledore Way 11
Thornbury Cl 12
Leighton Ct 13
Paveley Ct 14
Arlington Gn 15
Devonshire Rd
Oakhampton Rd
Pentavia Ret Pk
Watford Way (Barnet By-Pass)
Longfield Ave
Swimming Baths
Hendon
Stadium
Hendon Cemy & Crem
Barnet Coll (Grahame Pk Ctr)
Hasmonean High Sch (Girls)
Barnet Copthall Sp Ctr
Ashley La
Holders Hill
Five Ways Cnr
St James' RC High Sch
Hurricane Trad Ctr
RAF Mus
NW9
NW4
1 Maddison Ct
2 Caledonia Ct
3 Augusta Ct
4 Kensington Ct
5 Lime Ct
6 Sycamore Ct
7 Conifer Ct
Great North Way (Barnet By-Pass)
Watford Way
Putting Gn
Sunny Gardens Par
Battle of Britain Museum
Police HQ
Sunnyhill Park
HENDON
Johnson Ct 1
Wilshaw Cl 2
Colmore Ct 3
Aerodrome Rd
Holders Hill Rd
46
24

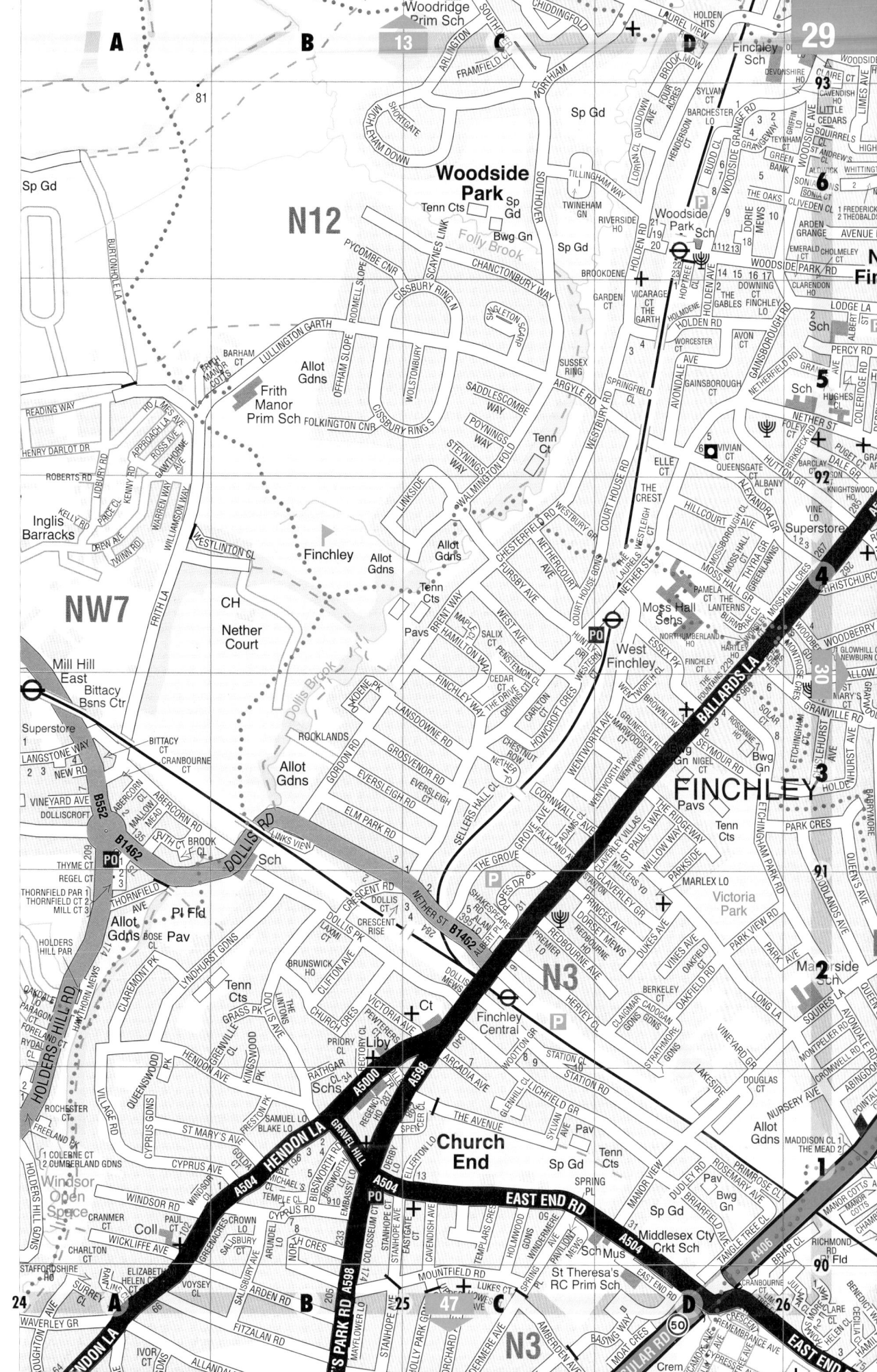
29
13
47
30
24
25
26
A
B
C
D
Woodside Park
N12
NW7
N3
FINCHLEY
Church End
West Finchley
Finchley Central
Mill Hill East
Inglis Barracks
Frith Manor Prim Sch
Nether Court
Finchley
Woodridge Prim Sch
Finchley Sch
Woodside Park Sch
Moss Hall Schs
Victoria Park
Marlborough Sch
Middlesex Cty Crkt Sch
St Theresa's RC Prim Sch
Windsor Open Space
Folly Brook
Dollis Brook
Bittacy Bsns Ctr
Superstore
Allot Gdns
Sp Gd
Tenn Cts
BALLARDS LA
HENDON LA
EAST END RD
DOLLIS RD
NETHER ST
HOLDERS HILL RD
GRAVEL HILL
REGENTS PARK RD
FRITH LA
WOODSIDE PARK RD
HOLDEN RD
ARGYLE RD
CHANCTONBURY WAY
LULLINGTON GARTH
CISSBURY RING N
CISSBURY RING S
CHURCH CRES
VICTORIA AVE
STATION RD
LICHFIELD GR
THE AVENUE
PRIMROSE CL
NURSERY AVE
A504
A5000
A598
A406
B1462
B552

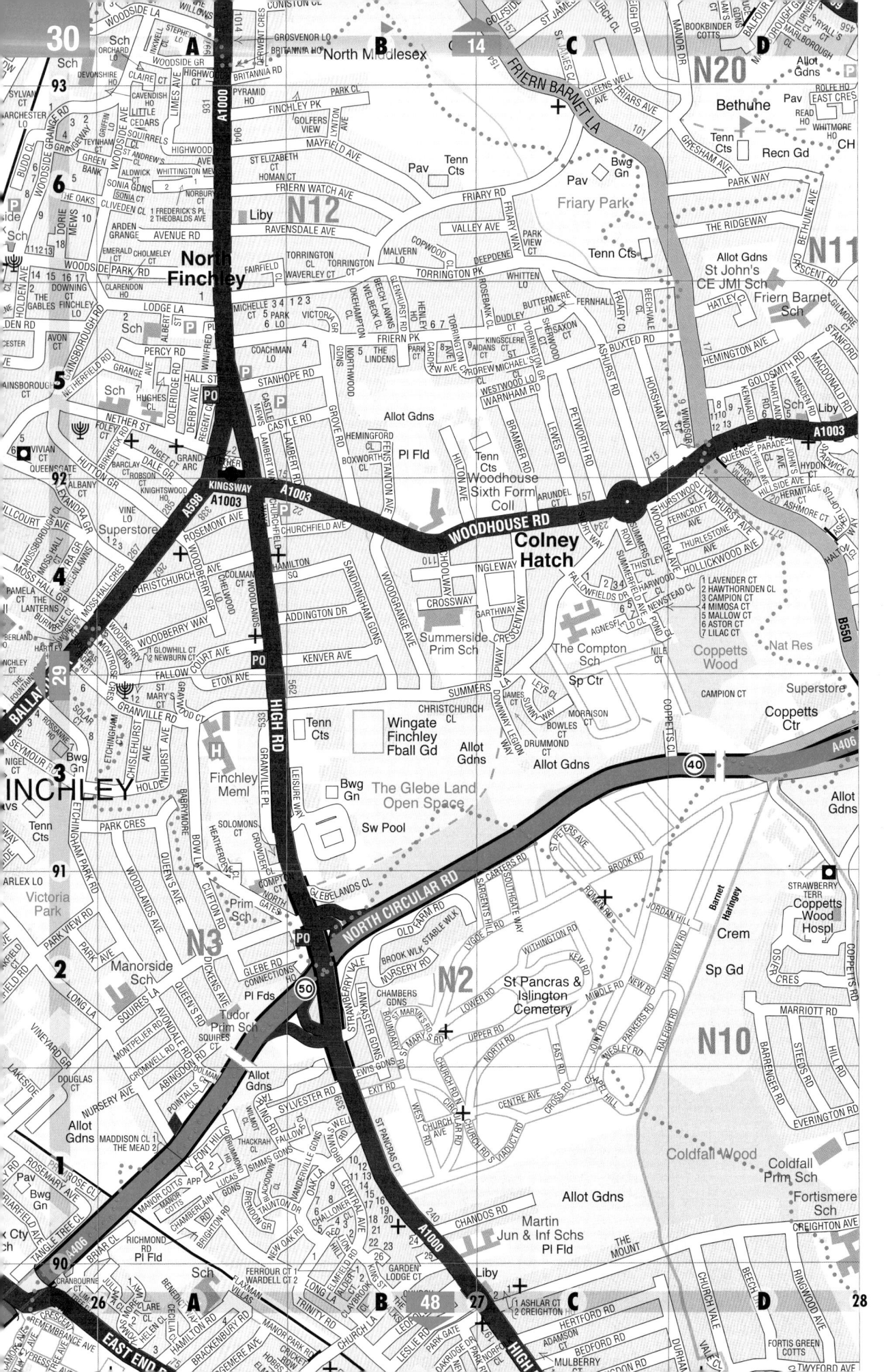
A
B
C
D
14
N20
N12
N11
N3
N2
N10
North Middlesex
North Finchley
Colney Hatch
FINCHLEY
Bethune
Friary Park
Friern Barnet Sch
St John's CE JMI Sch
Woodhouse Sixth Form Coll
Summerside Prim Sch
The Compton Sch
Coppetts Wood
Coppetts Ctr
Wingate Finchley Fball Gd
The Glebe Land Open Space
Sw Pool
Finchley Meml
Manorside Sch
Tudor Prim Sch
Victoria Park
St Pancras & Islington Cemetery
Crem
Coppetts Wood Hospl
Coldfall Wood
Coldfall Prim Sch
Fortismere Sch
Martin Jun & Inf Schs
Nat Res
Superstore
Barnet
Haringey
FRIERN BARNET LA
WOODHOUSE RD
NORTH CIRCULAR RD
HIGH RD
KINGSWAY
A1000
A1003
A598
A406
B550
40
50
93
92
91
90
6
5
4
3
2
1
29
48
26
27
28

15
FRIERN
BARNET
N11
New
Southgate
N14
Arnos Park
N13
OAKLEIGH RD S
A1003
A5109
A1110
Betstyle
Circus
BOWES RD
Arnos
Grove
WILMER WAY
B1452
POWYS LA
A1004
Broomfield
Sch
Bowes
Prim Sch
BOWES RD (NORTH C
A406
TELFORD RD (NORTH CIRCULAR RD)
FRIERN BARNET RD
STATION RD
A109
Superstore
Friern Bridge
Ret
Pk
Bounds
Green
Ind Est
PINKHAM WAY NORTH CIRCULAR RD
Colney
Hatch
COLNEY HATCH LA
Hollickwood
Park
1 CROMWELL HO
2 SYDNEY HO
3 CLEEVE CT
4 QUEENSLAND CT
5 NEALE CT
6 BRISBANE CT
7 MELBOURNE CT
8 SLADE CT
9 CONSTANCE CT
Hollickwood
Prim Sch
Muswell Hill
St Martin of Porres
RC Prim
Sch
Wood Green Tunnel
Allot
Gdns
Alexandra Park
Sch
Rhodes Avenue
Prim Sch
Recn Gd
DURNSFORD RD
ALBERT RD
BOUNDS GREEN RD
BROWNLOW RD
B106
Bounds
Green
Enfield
Haringey
Barnet
N22
N10
Coppetts
Wood
Prim Sch
ALEXANDRA PARK RD
ALEXANDRA PARK RD
The
Lake
Alexandra
Palace
Mast
N8
90
Norfolk
House
Sch
Our Lady
of Muswell
RC Prim Sch
Blanche
Nevile Sch
Muswell Hill
Fortismere
Sch
(South Wing)
MUSWELL HILL BDWY
B550
QUEENS AVE
ALEXANDRA PALACE WAY
Alexandra Park
The
Grove
49
32
28
29
30
A
B
C
D
1
2
3
4
5
6

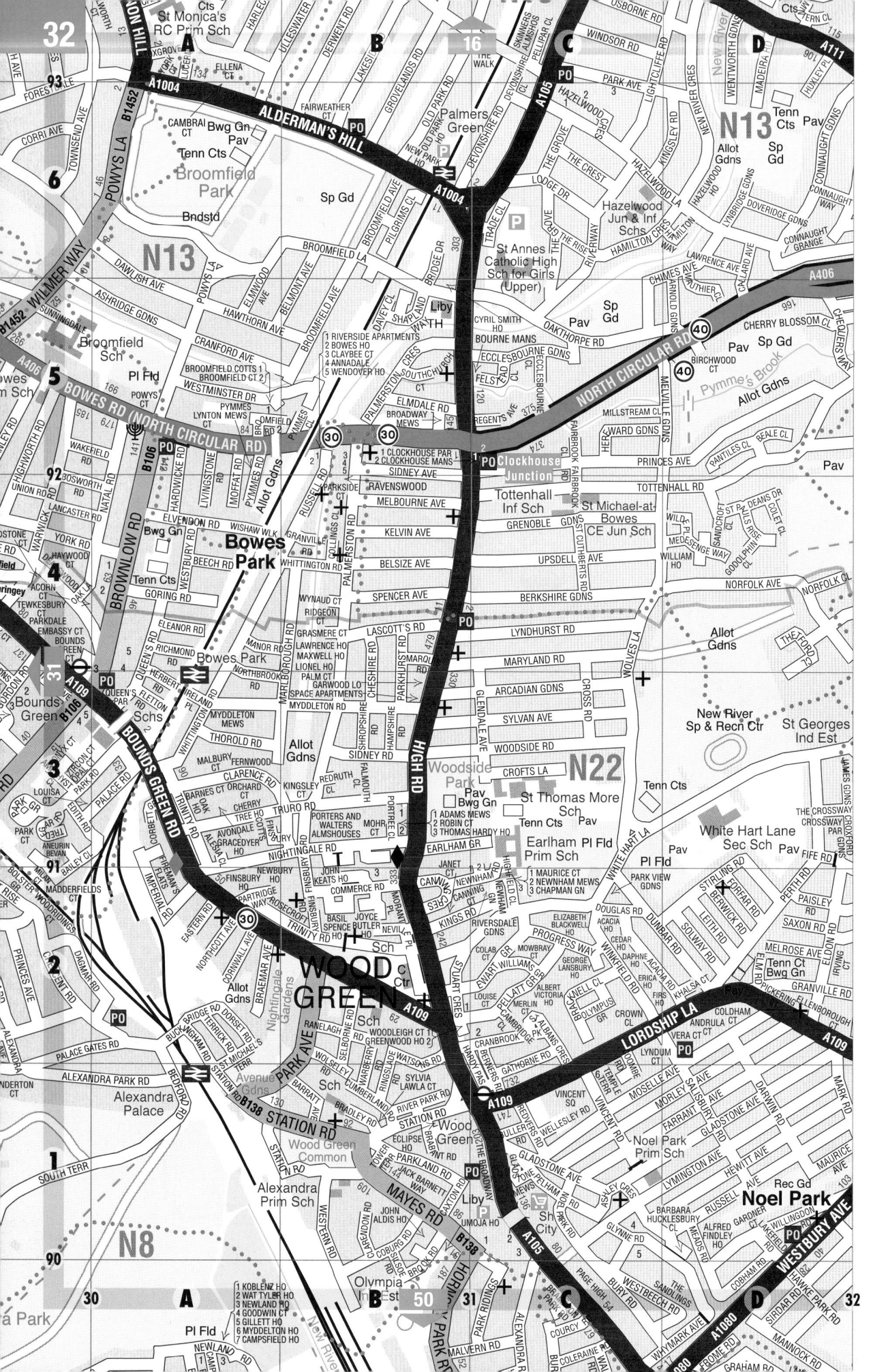

Broomfield Park
Bowes Park
Palmers Green
Wood Green
Alexandra Palace
Noel Park
Clockhouse Junction
N13
N22
N8
Alderman's Hill
North Circular Rd
Bowes Rd (North Circular Rd)
High Rd
Lordship La
Bounds Green Rd
Station Rd
Mayes Rd
Westbury Ave
Wilmer Way
Powys La
Brownlow Rd
White Hart Lane Sec Sch
St Thomas More Sch
New River Sp & Recn Ctr
St Georges Ind Est
Tottenhall Inf Sch
St Michael-at-Bowes CE Jun Sch
St Annes Catholic High Sch for Girls (Upper)
Hazelwood Jun & Inf Schs
Earlham Prim Sch
Alexandra Prim Sch
Noel Park Prim Sch
Broomfield Sch
Wood Green Common
Woodside Park
Olympia Ind Est
16
31
50

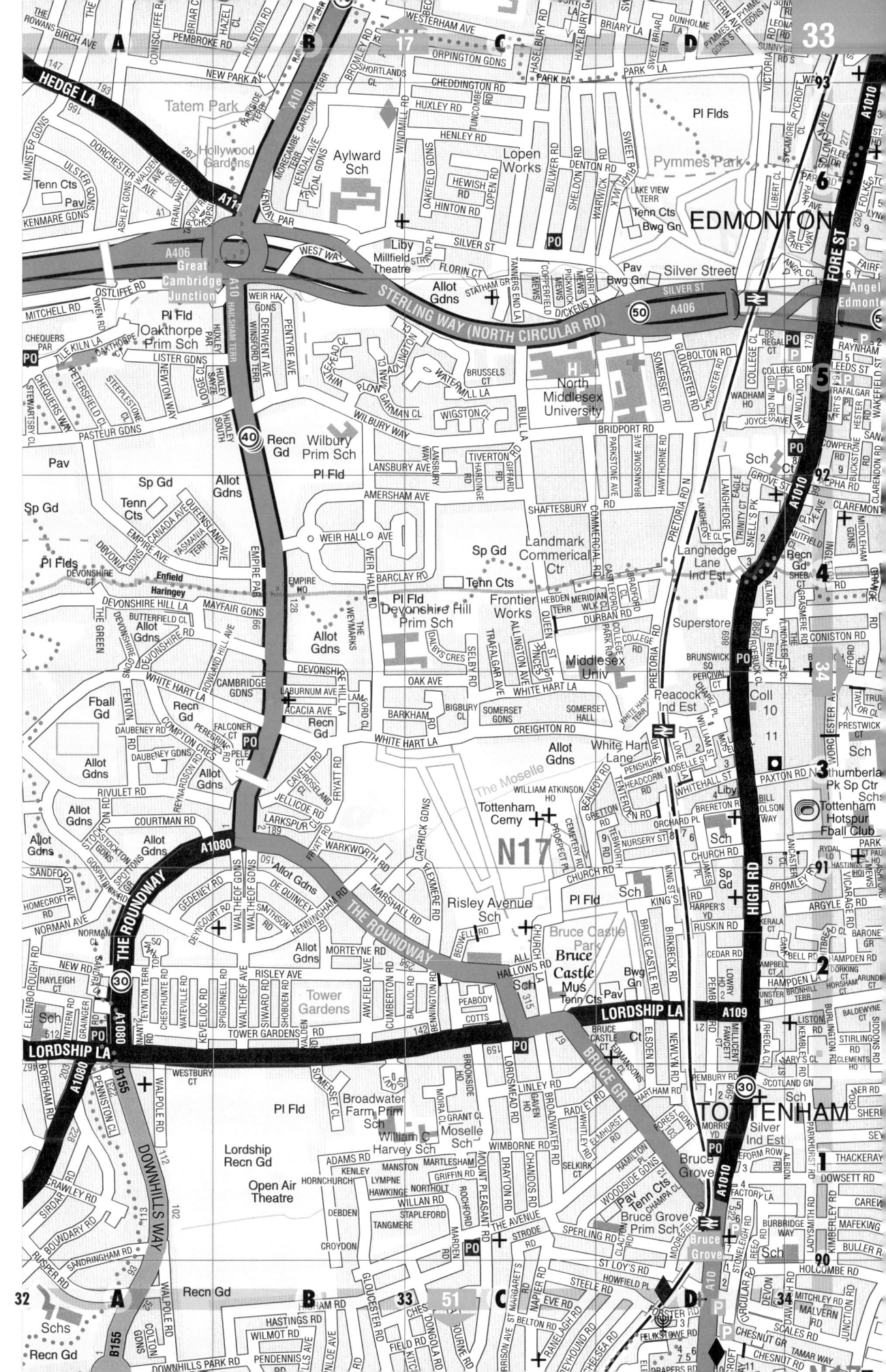

Edmonton
Federation Cemy
18
A
B
C
D
93
Pl Flds
6
EDMONTON
Fleecefield Prim Sch
Station House Mews
Brettenham Rd
Park Rd
Fore St
A1010
Lyndhurst Rd
St Peter's Ave
Morley Ave
Fairfield Rd
Hythe Cl
Tenn Cts
Recn Gd
Bwg Gn
Aberdeen Rd
Cavendish Rd
Montagu Gdns
Montagu Cres
Cameron Cl
Craig Park Rd
Jeremy's Gn
Swaythling Cl
Montagu Ind Est
Pegamoid Rd
Princes Rd
Second Ave
Gibbs Rd
Stacey Ave
First Ave
Rays Ave
Rays Rd
B137
A1055
Thornton Rd
Rainstar Est
Nobel Rd
Kynoch Rd
Eley's Est
N18
Eley Rd
Conduit La
Derby Rd
Kenninghall Rd
New Park Est
Kenninghall
Cooks Ferry
Angel Edmonton
A406
50
Angel Road (North Circular Road)
Angel Rd Works
Angel Road
Advent Way
Argon Rd
Banksia Rd
Raynham Rd
Leeds St
Raynham Terr
Raynham Prim Sch
Pl Fld
Upton Rd
Hampshire Cl
Berkshire Gdns
Shillibeer Ct
Culpepper Cl
Leopold Rd
Albany Rd
Yorkshire Gdns
Ladysmith Rd
5
College Cl
Wadham Ho
Joyce Ave
Sandal Rd
Sayesbury La
Thornaby Gdns
Upper Edmonton
Alston Rd
Broadberry Ct
Stockton Rd
Leyburn Rd
Middleham Rd
Kimberley Rd
Dyson's Rd
Hawley Rd
Ravenside Ret Pk
Stonehill Bsns Pk
Blackwood Ave
Greenway Ave
Superstore
Glover Dr
Whitehurst Dr 1
Greyswood Ave 2
Silvermere Dr
Lea Valley Trad Est
Towpath Rd
Anthony Way
Rivermead Rd
Kingsway Est
92
Alpha Rd
Claremont St
Langhedge La
Langhedge Lane Ind Est
Recn Gd
Sheba Ct
4
Willoughby La
Elm Lea Trad Est
Leeside Rd
Brantwood Rd
Meridian Way
Edmonton Wharf
Coniston Rd
Burleigh Ct
Triumph Trad Est
Royal London Est
Hotspur Ind Est
Lake Bsns Ctr
Sp Gd
Sp Ctr
Tenn Cts
Bwg Gns
Nrthmbrlnd Park Ind Est
Leeside Trad Est
Mowlem Trad Est
Leeside Works
Canal Bridge
33
Coll
10
11
Northumberland Pk
Trulock Ct
Prestwick Ct
Sch
Scotswood Wlk
Farningham Ct
Morpeth Wlk
Willoughby Park Rd
Heybourne Rd
Leeside Ind Est
Garman Rd
N17
3
Paxton Rd
Northumberland Pk Sp Ctr
Schs
Tottenham Hotspur Fball Club
Almond Rd
Rothbury Wlk
Haynes Cl
Willoughby Mews
Park Avenue Rd
Unicorn Works
Recn Gd
40
Liby
Sch
Church Rd
91
Sp Gd
Park La
High Rd
Bromley Rd
Vicarage Rd
Argyle Rd
Northumberland Park
Manor Rd
Asplins Rd
Marigold Rd
LC
Allot Gdns
Marsh La
Tottenham Marshes
Lee Flood Relief Channel
River Lee Navigation
River Lea or Lee Diversion
Ruskin Rd
Baronet Rd
Foyle Rd
Romney Cl
Crowhurst Ct
Sinnott Rd
Travers Cl
Gurney Cl
Cedar Rd
2
Hampden Rd
Hampden La
Fiske Ct
Lansdowne Rd
Allot Gdns
Depot
B179
A109
Liston Rd
Glendish Rd
Halefield Rd
Coleraine Park Prim Sch
Sutton Rd
The Mile End
Lee Cl
Recn Gd
Poynton Rd
Scotland Gn
Rosebery Ave
Sherringham Ave
Seymour Ave
Thackeray Ave
Dowsett Rd
Norfolk Rd
Riverhead Cl
Kestrel Ct
Worcester Rd
Woolston Cl
Lockwood Way
Gloucester Rd
Clarence Rd
Blackhorse La
30
TOTTENHAM
Silver Ind Est
Rosebery Ind Pk
Pymme's Brook
Haringey
Waltham Forest
1
Carew Rd
Mafeking Rd
Buller Rd
Park View Rd
Watermead Way
Lockwood Reservoir
Lancaster Rd
Goldsmith Rd
Shakespeare Rd
Uplands Ave
Bruce Grove
90
Holcombe Rd
Lea Valley Technopark
Allot Gdns
Millmead Ind Ctr
Uplands Bsns Pk
A10
34
A
Down Lane Park
B
52
35
C
D
36
Malvern Rd
Scales Rd
Chesnut Rd
Tamar Way
Ashley Rd
Burdock Rd
Tenn Cts
Lockwood Ind Pk
Priestley Way
Forest Trad Est
Highams Lodge Bsns Ctr
Blackhorse Mews

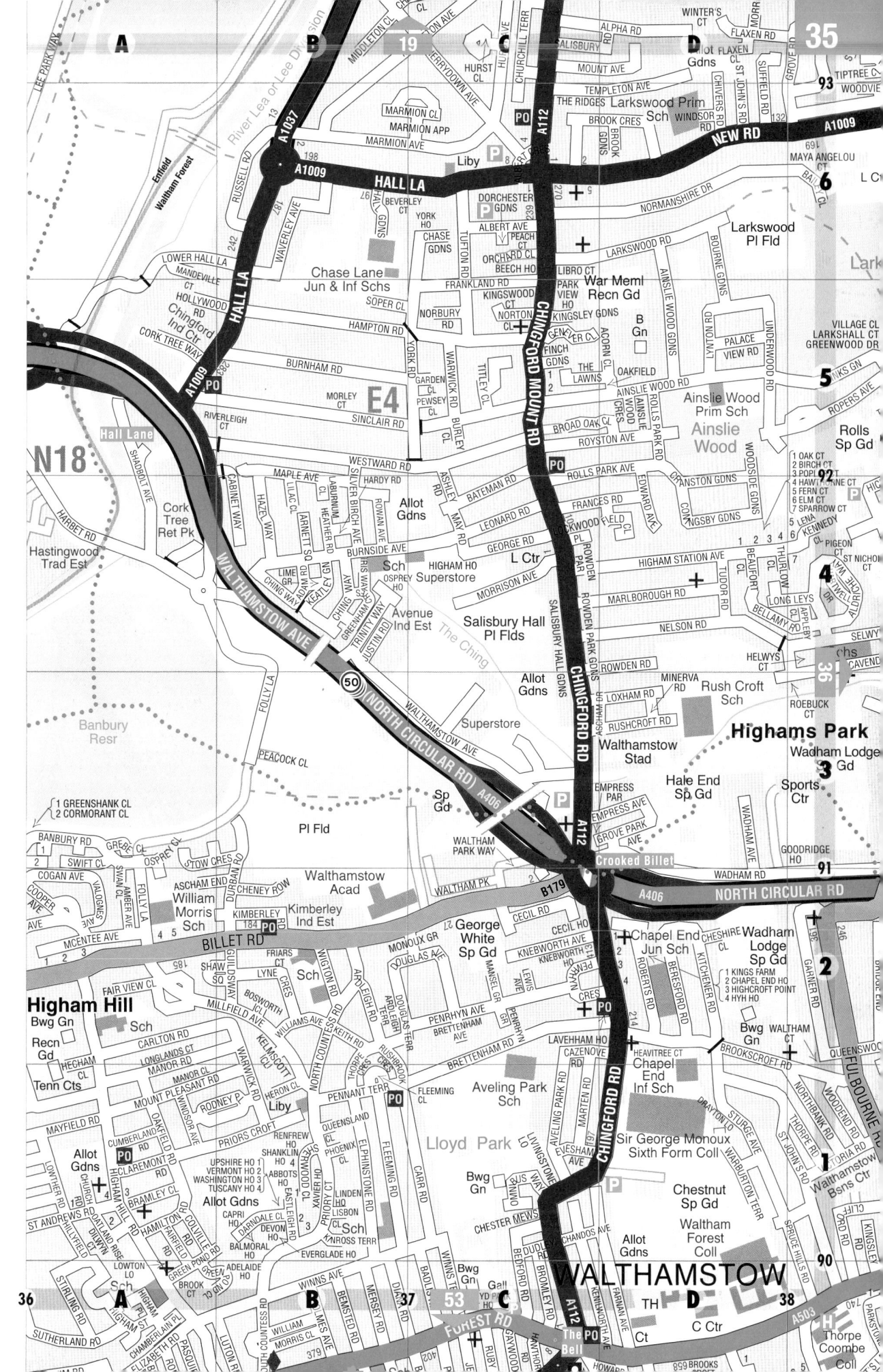

35
A
B
19
C
D
LEE PARK WAY
River Lea or Lee Diversion
MIDDLETON CL
CHERRYDOWN AVE
HURST CL
CHURCHILL TERR
SALISBURY
ALPHA RD
WINTER'S CT
FLAXEN RD
Allot Gdns
FLAXEN CL
MOUNT AVE
TEMPLETON AVE
ST JOHN'S RD
SUFFIELD RD
GROVE RD
TIPTREE CT
WOODVIEW
93
CHIVERS RD
THE RIDGES
Larkswood Prim Sch
WINDSOR RD
BROOK CRES
BROOK GDNS
MARMION CL
MARMION APP
MARMION AVE
A1037
A112
A1009
NEW RD
PO
Liby
ALBERT CRES
Enfield
Waltham Forest
RUSSELL RD
HALL LA
MAYA ANGELOU CT
BAILEY CL
6
NORMANSHIRE DR
DORCHESTER GDNS
BEVERLEY CT
YORK HO
CHASE GDNS
TUFTON RD
ALBERT AVE
PEACH CT
ORCHARD CL
BEECH HO
Larkswood Pl Fld
LARKSWOOD RD
LOWER HALL LA
MANDEVILLE CT
WAVERLEY AVE
HALL GDNS
Chase Lane Jun & Inf Schs
LIBRO CT
FRANKLAND RD
War Meml Recn Gd
PARK VIEW HO
KINGSWOOD CT
NORTON CL
KINGSLEY GDNS
AINSLIE WOOD GDNS
BOURNE GDNS
HOLLYWOOD RD
Chingford Ind Ctr
SOPER CL
HAMPTON RD
NORBURY RD
B Gn
LAWTON RD
PALACE VIEW RD
UNDERWOOD RD
VILLAGE CL
LARKSHALL CT
GREENWOOD DR
CORK TREE WAY
BURNHAM RD
YORK RD
WARWICK RD
TITLEY CL
GENEVER CL
FINCH GDNS
THE LAWNS
ACORN CL
OAKFIELD
CHINGFORD MOUNT RD
LINKS GN
5
ROPERS AVE
MORLEY CT
E4
GARDEN CL
PEWSEY CL
BURLEY CL
AINSLIE WOOD RD
AINSLIE WOOD CRES
Ainslie Wood Prim Sch
RIVERLEIGH CT
SINCLAIR RD
BROAD OAK CL
ROYSTON AVE
ROLLS PARK RD
Ainslie Wood
Rolls Sp Gd
Hall Lane
N18
SHADBOLT AVE
WESTWARD RD
ROLLS PARK AVE
1 OAK CT
2 BIRCH CT
3 POPLAR CT
4 HAWTHORNE CT
5 FERN CT
6 ELM CT
7 SPARROW CT
92
MAPLE AVE
HARDY RD
ASHLEY RD
BATEMAN RD
CRANSTON GDNS
WOODSIDE GDNS
CABINET WAY
HAZEL WAY
LILAC CL
LABURNUM CL
SILVER BIRCH AVE
HEATHER RD
ROWAN AVE
Allot Gdns
MAY RD
LEONARD RD
FRANCES RD
EDWARD AVE
CONINGSBY GDNS
Cork Tree Ret Pk
HARBET RD
ARNETT SQ
LOCKWOOD PL
FIELD CL
LENA KENNEDY CL
PIGEON CT
ST NICHOLAS CT
Hastingwood Trad Est
BURNSIDE AVE
Sch
GEORGE RD
L Ctr
HIGHAM STATION AVE
BEAUFORT CL
THURLOW CL
HIGHAM HO
Superstore
ROWDEN PAR
4
LIME GR
ADAM RD
KEATLEY GN
CHING WAY
OSPREY HO
MORRISON AVE
TUDOR RD
MARLBOROUGH RD
LONG LEYS
APPLEBY CL
BELLAMY RD
CARDWELL DR
ALDRIDGE WAY
WALTHAMSTOW AVE
GREENHAM CL
IRIS WAY
TRINITY WAY
JUSTIN RD
Avenue Ind Est
Salisbury Hall Pl Flds
The Ching
NELSON RD
SELWYN
SALISBURY HALL GDNS
ROWDEN PARK GDNS
HELWYS CT
36
CAVENDISH
ROWDEN RD
CHINGFORD RD
50
(NORTH CIRCULAR RD)
Allot Gdns
MINERVA RD
Rush Croft Sch
FOLLY LA
LOXHAM RD
ROEBUCK CT
Banbury Resr
Superstore
ASCHAM DR
RUSHCROFT RD
Walthamstow Stad
Highams Park
Wadham Lodge Sp Gd
3
PEACOCK CL
Hale End Sp Gd
Sports Ctr
EMPRESS PAR
EMPRESS AVE
Sp Gd
A406
1 GREENSHANK CL
2 CORMORANT CL
Pl Fld
GROVE PARK AVE
WALTHAM PARK WAY
WADHAM AVE
GOODRIDGE HO
BANBURY RD
GREBE CL
OSPREY CL
SWIFT CL
STOW CRES
Crooked Billet
91
COGAN AVE
VALOGNES AVE
SWAN CL
AMBER AVE
ASCHAM END
DURBAN RD
CHENEY ROW
Walthamstow Acad
WALTHAM PK
WADHAM RD
NORTH CIRCULAR RD
B179
COOPER AVE
William Morris Sch
KIMBERLEY RD
Kimberley Ind Est
CECIL RD
CECIL HO
George White Sp Gd
Chapel End Jun Sch
CHESHIRE CL
Wadham Lodge Sp Gd
McENTEE AVE
BILLET RD
FRIARS CT
MONOUX GR
KNEBWORTH AVE
KNEBWORTH HO
ROBERTS RD
BERESFORD RD
KITCHENER RD
1 KINGS FARM
2 CHAPEL END HO
3 HIGHCROFT POINT
4 HYH HO
2
GARNER RD
SHAW SQ
GUILDSWAY
LYNE CRES
DOUGLAS AVE
MANSEL GR
LEWIS AVE
PENRHYN AVE
Higham Hill
FAIR VIEW CL
BOSWORTH CL
ARDLEIGH RD
ARDLEIGH TERR
DOUGLAS TERR
PENRHYN GR
Bwg Gn
Recn Gd
MILLFIELD AVE
WILLIAMS AVE
KEITH RD
BRETTENHAM AVE
LAVENHAM HO
CAZENOVE RD
HEAVITREE CT
BROOKSCROFT RD
WALTHAM CT
QUEENSWOOD
CARLTON RD
LONGLANDS CT
MANOR RD
HECHAM CL
MANOR CL
MOUNT PLEASANT RD
WARWICK RD
KELMSCOTT CL
NORTH COUNTESS RD
THORPE CRES
RUSHBROOK CRES
BRETTENHAM RD
Chapel End Inf Sch
FULBOURNE RD
Tenn Cts
RODNEY PL
HERON CL
Liby
PENNANT TERR
FLEEMING CL
Aveling Park Sch
NORTHBANK RD
WOODEND RD
MAYFIELD RD
CUMBERLAND RD
OAKFIELD RD
WINDSOR AVE
PRIORS CROFT
QUEENSLAND CL
RENFREW HO
SHANKLIN HO
PHOENIX CL
ELPHINSTONE RD
FLEEMING RD
CARR RD
Lloyd Park
AVELING PARK RD
MARTEN RD
LIVINGSTONE LO
DRAYTON LO
STURGE AVE
Sir George Monoux Sixth Form Coll
WARBURTON TERR
THORPE RD
ST JOHN'S RD
VICTORIA RD
Walthamstow Bsns Ctr
Allot Gdns
CLAREMONT RD
HIGHAM HILL RD
UPSHIRE HO 1
VERMONT HO 2
WASHINGTON HO 3
TUSCANY HO 4
ABBOTS HO
EASTLEIGH RD
SHERWOOD CL
XAVIER HO
EVESHAM AVE
1
LOWTHER RD
CHURCH RD
BRAMLEY CL
Allot Gdns
LINDEN HO
LISBON HO
Bwg Gn
BUS WAY
Chestnut Sp Gd
CLIFFORD RD
KINGSLEY RD
ST ANDREWS RD
OATLAND RISE
HAMILTON RD
COLVILLE RD
CAPRI HO
DARNDALE CL
DEVON HO
PRIORY CT
Sch
CHESTER MEWS
CHANDOS AVE
Waltham Forest Coll
HILLYFIELD
DILWYN CT
FAIRFIELD RD
GREEN POND RD
BALMORAL HO
KINROSS TERR
EVERGLADE HO
DUDLEY RD
Allot Gdns
LOWTON LO
ADELAIDE HO
WINNS AVE
WINNS TERR
BADLIS RD
BROMLEY RD
FARNAN AVE
SPRUCE HILLS RD
90
Sch
BROOK CT
GREEN POND CL
Bwg Gn
Gall
BEDFORD RD
KENILWORTH AVE
WALTHAMSTOW
STIRLING RD
HIGHAM PL
HIGHAM ST
36
A
B
37
53
C
D
38
TH
A503
PARKSTONE
FOREST RD
YD PI HO
C Ctr
SUTHERLAND RD
CHAMBERLAIN PL
ELIZABETH RD
NORTH COUNTESS RD
WILLIAM MORRIS CL
ELMES AVE
BEMSTED RD
MERSEY RD
DIANA RD
RUBY RD
GAYWOOD RD
A112
The Bell
Ct
Thorpe Coombe
Coll
LUTON RD
HOWARD
BROOKS

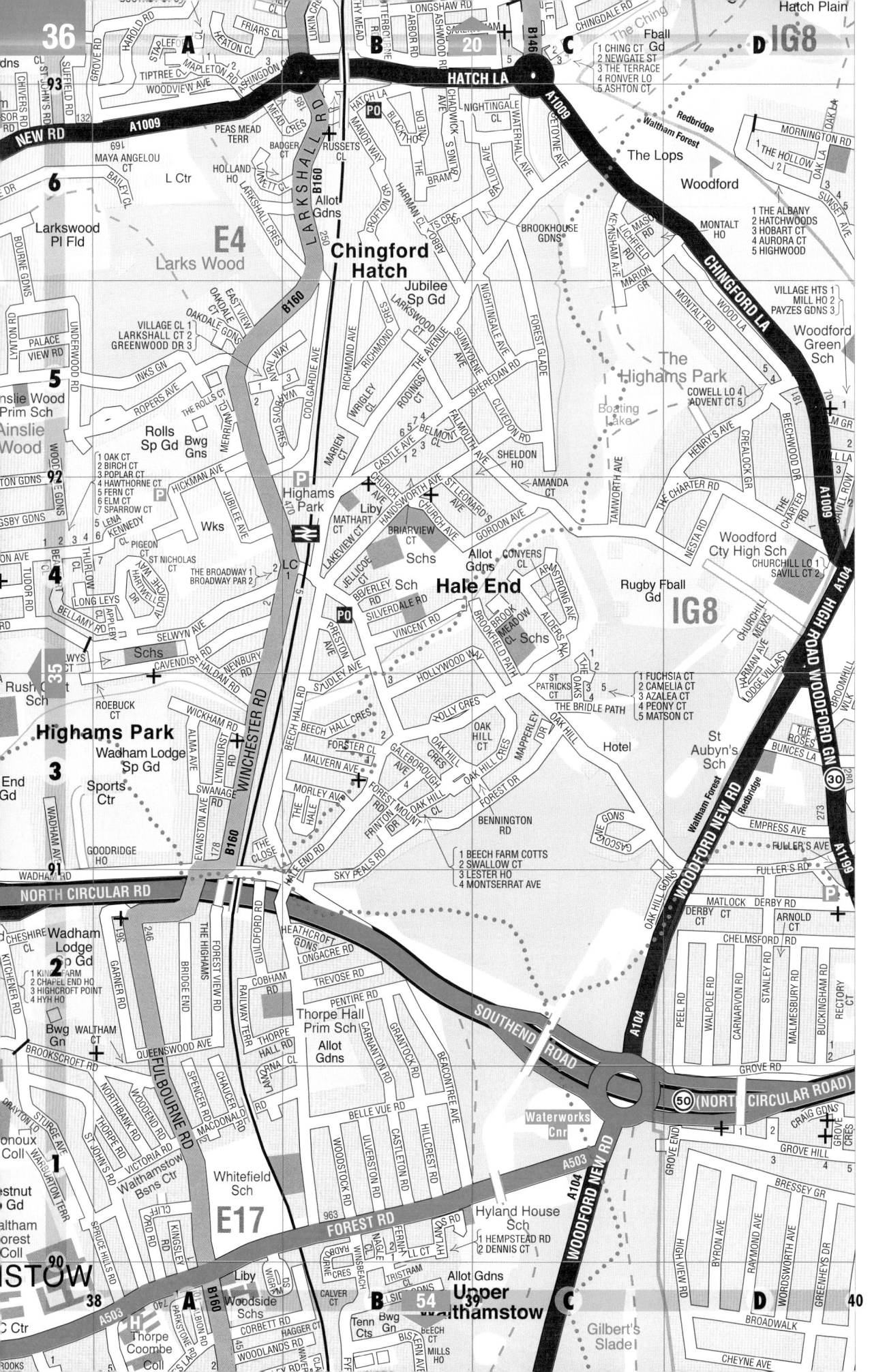
Hatch Plain
IG8
A
B
C
D
20
Fball Gd
The Ching
HATCH LA
A1009
B146
LONGSHAW RD
CHINGDALE RD
1 CHING CT
2 NEWGATE ST
3 THE TERRACE
4 RONVER LO
5 ASHTON CT
FRIARS CL
HEATON CL
HAROLD RD
GROVE RD
MAPLETON RD
ASHINGDON CL
TIPTREE C
WOODVIEW AVE
SUFFIELD RD
ST JOHN'S RD
CHIVERS RD
93
NEW RD
PEAS MEAD TERR
MAYA ANGELOU CT
BADGER CT
HOLLAND HO
LINNETT CL
L Ctr
BAILEY CL
6
Larkswood Pl Fld
E4
Larks Wood
LARKSHALL RD
LARKSHALL CRES
B160
RUSSETS CL
HATCH LA
PO
MANOR WAY
Allot Gdns
CROFTON GR
HARMAN CL
CHADWICK AVE
NIGHTINGALE CL
WATERHALL AVE
SETOYNE AVE
BALLIOL AVE
BROOKHOUSE GDNS
Redbridge
Waltham Forest
The Lops
Woodford
MORNINGTON RD
THE HOLLOW
OAK LA
SUNSET AVE
1 THE ALBANY
2 HATCHWOODS
3 HOBART CT
4 AURORA CT
5 HIGHWOOD
MONTALT HO
KEYNSHAM AVE
LICHFIELD RD
MASON RD
MARION GR
CHINGFORD LA
MONTALT RD
WOOD LA
Chingford Hatch
Jubilee Sp Gd
LARKSWOOD CT
RICHMOND AVE
RICHMOND CRES
THE AVENUE
SUNNYDENE AVE
NIGHTINGALE AVE
FOREST GLADE
VILLAGE HTS 1
MILL HO 2
PAYZES GDNS 3
Woodford Green Sch
BOURNE GDNS
UNDERWOOD RD
PALACE VIEW RD
VILLAGE CL 1
LARKSHALL CT 2
GREENWOOD DR 3
OAKDALE CT
OAKDALE GDNS
EAST VIEW
INKS GN
5
Ainslie Wood Prim Sch
Ainslie Wood
ROPERS AVE
THE ROLLS CT
MERRIAM CL
AVRIL WAY
WARBOYS CRES
COOLGARDIE AVE
WRIGLEY CL
RODINGS CT
SHEREDAN RD
CLIVEDON RD
The Highams Park
Boating Lake
COWELL LO 4
ADVENT CT 5
Rolls Sp Gd
Bwg Gns
1 OAK CT
2 BIRCH CT
3 POPLAR CT
4 HAWTHORNE CT
5 FERN CT
6 ELM CT
7 SPARROW CT
92
WOODSIDE GDNS
HICKMAN AVE
JUBILEE AVE
Wks
MARIEN CT
CASTLE AVE
BELMONT CL
FALMOUTH AVE
SHELDON HO
AMANDA CT
TAMWORTH AVE
HENRY'S AVE
CREALOCK GR
BEECHWOOD DR
THE CHARTER RD
A1009
MILL LA
SAVILL ROW
ELM GR
Highams Park
Liby
CHURCH AVE
HANDSWORTH AVE
ST LEONARD'S AVE
GORDON AVE
CHURCH AVE
MATHART CT
BRIARVIEW CT
LAKEVIEW CT
Schs
Allot Gdns
CONYERS CL
ARMSTRONG AVE
NESTA RD
Woodford Cty High Sch
CHURCHILL LO 1
SAVILL CT 2
A104
KENNEDY CL
PIGEON CT
ST NICHOLAS CT
THE BROADWAY 1
BROADWAY PAR 2
LC
THURLOW CL
TUDOR RD
4
HARTWELL DR
ALDRIDGE WAY
LONG LEYS
APPLEBY
BELLAMY RD
JELLICOE
BEVERLEY RD
Sch
Hale End
SILVERDALE RD
VINCENT RD
BROOKFIELD PATH
BROOK MEADOW CL
Schs
ALDERS AV
Rugby Fball Gd
IG8
CHURCHILL MEWS
HARMAN AVE
LODGE VILLAS
HIGH ROAD WOODFORD GN
BROOMHILL WLK
SELWYN AVE
35
Schs
CAVENDISH RD
NEWBURY RD
HALDAN RD
PRESTON AVE
STUDLEY AVE
HOLLYWOOD WAY
THE OAKS
ST PATRICKS CT
1 FUCHSIA CT
2 CAMELIA CT
3 AZALEA CT
4 PEONY CT
5 MATSON CT
THE BRIDLE PATH
Rush Croft Sch
ROEBUCK CT
Highams Park
WICKHAM RD
ALMA AVE
LYNDHURST RD
WINCHESTER RD
BEECH HALL RD
BEECH HALL CRES
HOLLY CRES
OAK HILL CT
OAK HILL CRES
MAPPERLEY DR
OAK HILL
Hotel
St Aubyn's Sch
THE ROSES
BUNCES LA
Wadham Lodge Sp Gd
3
Sports Ctr
SWANAGE RD
FORSTER CL
MALVERN AVE
GALEBOROUGH AVE
FOREST MOUNT RD
OAK HILL CL
FOREST DR
BENNINGTON RD
WOODFORD NEW RD
30
MORLEY AVE
THE HALE
FRINTON DR
GASCOYNE GDNS
EMPRESS AVE
FULLER'S AVE
WADHAM AVE
GOODRIDGE HO
EVANSTON AVE
THE CLOSE
HALE END RD
SKY PEALS RD
1 BEECH FARM COTTS
2 SWALLOW CT
3 LESTER HO
4 MONTSERRAT AVE
FULLER'S RD
A1199
91
WADHAM RD
NORTH CIRCULAR RD
OAK HILL GDNS
MATLOCK CT
DERBY CT
DERBY RD
ARNOLD CT
CHESHIRE CL
Wadham Lodge Sp Gd
KITCHENER RD
GARNER RD
THE HIGHAMS
FOREST VIEW RD
BRIDGE END
GUILDFORD RD
HEATHCROFT GDNS
LONGACRE RD
TREVOSE RD
CHELMSFORD RD
2
1 KING'S FARM
2 CHAPEL END HO
3 HIGHCROFT POINT
4 HYH HO
COBHAM RD
PENTIRE RD
Thorpe Hall Prim Sch
CARNANTON RD
GRANTOCK RD
SOUTHEND ROAD
PEEL RD
WALPOLE RD
CARNARVON RD
STANLEY RD
MALMESBURY RD
BUCKINGHAM RD
RECTORY CT
Bwg Gn
WALTHAM CT
QUEENSWOOD AVE
RAILWAY TERR
THORPE HALL RD
Allot Gdns
BEACONTREE AVE
A104
GROVE RD
BROOKSCROFT RD
NORTHBANK RD
WOODEND RD
FULBOURNE RD
SPENCER RD
CHAUCER RD
LAMORNA CL
MACDONALD RD
50
(NORTH CIRCULAR ROAD)
CRAIG GDNS
GROVE CRES
DRAYTON LO
STURGE AVE
THORPE RD
ST JOHN'S RD
VICTORIA RD
BELLE VUE RD
Waterworks Cnr
GROVE END
GROVE HILL
1
WARBURTON TERR
Walthamstow Bsns Ctr
Whitefield Sch
WOODSTOCK RD
ULVERSTON RD
CASTLETON RD
HILLCREST RD
A503
WOODFORD NEW RD
A104
BRESSEY GR
CLIFFORD RD
KINGSLEY RD
E17
FOREST RD
Hyland House Sch
1 HEMPSTEAD RD
2 DENNIS CT
HIGH VIEW RD
BYRON AVE
RAYMOND AVE
WORDSWORTH AVE
GREENHEYS DR
90
SPRUCE HILLS RD
Liby
TRISTRAM
Allot Gdns
Upper Walthamstow
38
A
B
54
39
C
D
40
Woodside Schs
CALVER CT
A503
Thorpe Coombe
CORBETT RD
HAGGER CT
Tenn Cts
Bwg Gn
BEECH CT
MILLS HO
BROADWALK
Gilbert's Slade
PARKSTONE RD
ALBION RD
WOODLANDS RD
CHEYNE AVE

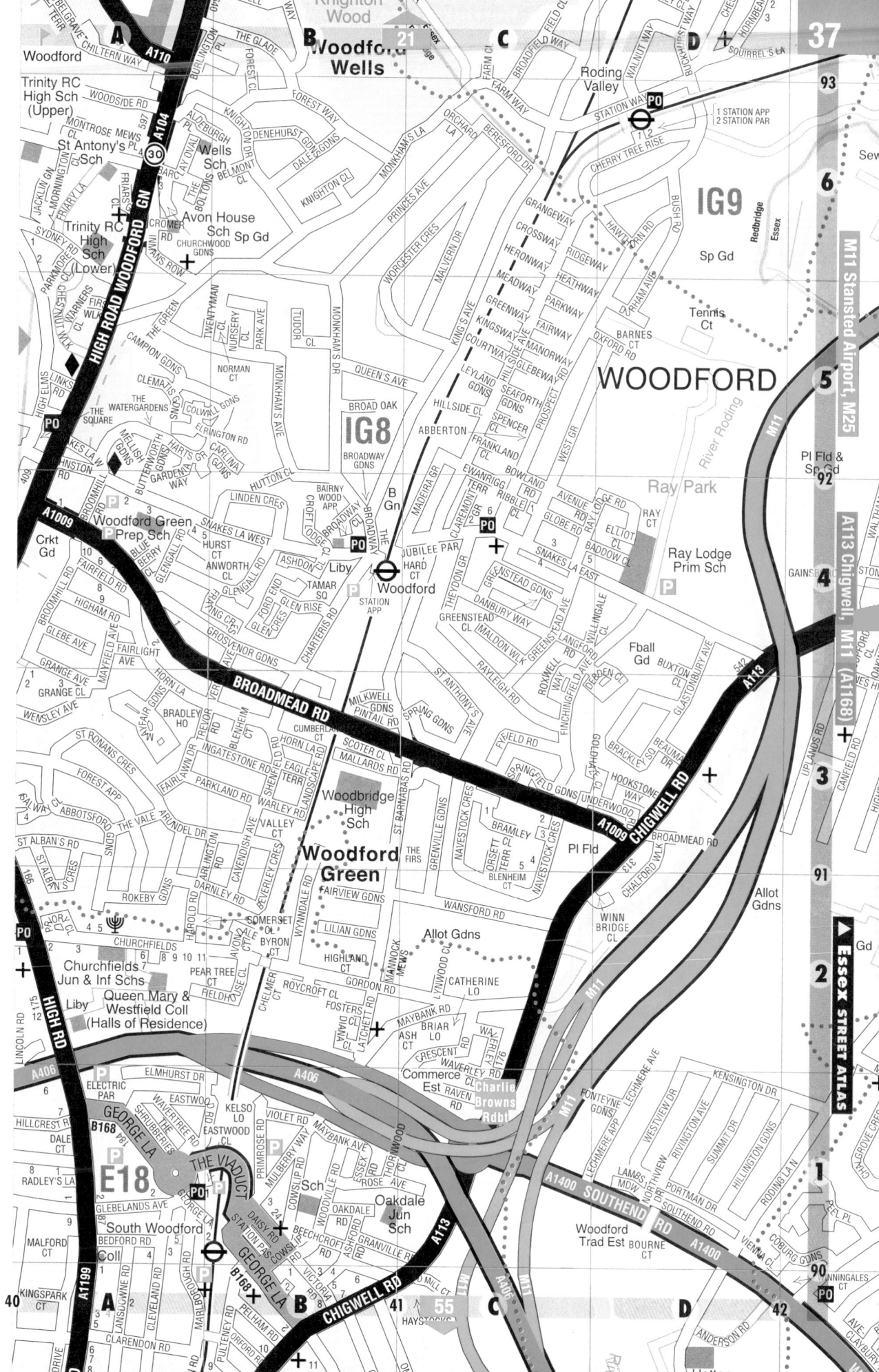

Woodford Wells
Roding Valley
IG9
WOODFORD
IG8
Woodford Green
Woodford
Ray Park
E18
South Woodford
Charlie Browns Rdbt
M11 Stansted Airport, M25
A113 Chigwell, M11 (A1168)
Essex STREET ATLAS
HIGH ROAD WOODFORD GN
BROADMEAD RD
CHIGWELL RD
SOUTHEND RD
HIGH RD
Redbridge
Essex

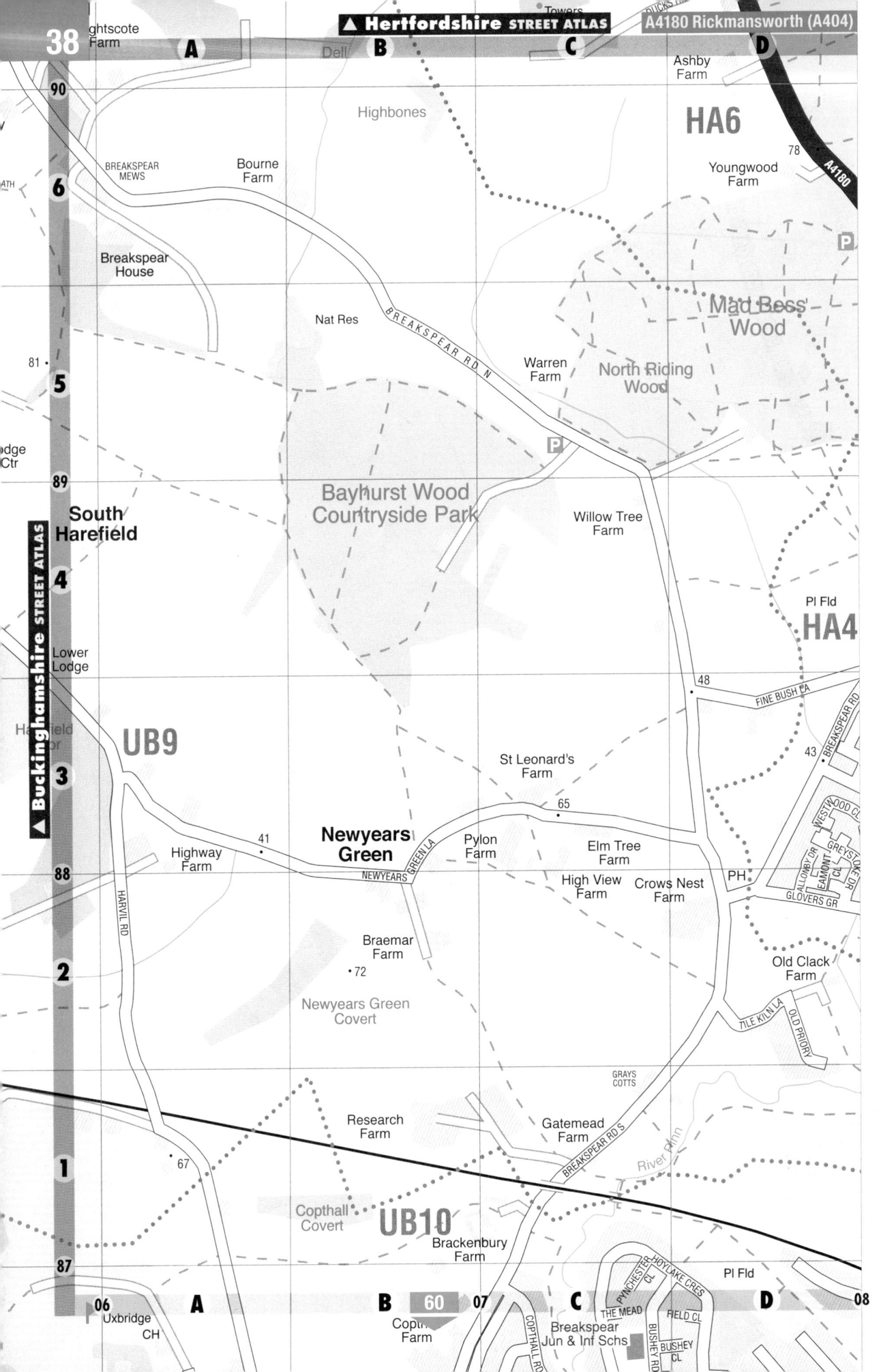

ghtscote Farm

A

Dell

B

Towers

C

Ashby Farm

D

90

Highbones

HA6

6

BREAKSPEAR MEWS

Bourne Farm

78

Youngwood Farm

A4180

Breakspear House

Nat Res

Mad Bess Wood

81

5

Warren Farm

North Riding Wood

BREAKSPEAR RD N

89

South Harefield

P

Bayhurst Wood Countryside Park

Willow Tree Farm

odge Ctr

4

Lower Lodge

Pl Fld

HA4

48

FINE BUSH LA

UB9

43

BREAKSPEAR RD

3

Highway Farm

41

Newyears Green

St Leonard's Farm

65

Pylon Farm

Elm Tree Farm

WESTWOOD CL

GREYSTONE DR

Harefield or

GREEN LA

NEWYEARS

High View Farm

Crows Nest Farm

PH

ALLONBY DR

EAMONT CL

GLOVERS GR

88

HARVIL RD

2

Braemar Farm

72

Old Clack Farm

TILE KILN LA

OLD PRIORY

Newyears Green Covert

GRAYS COTTS

Research Farm

Gatemead Farm

BREAKSPEAR RD S

River Pinn

1

67

Copthall Covert

UB10

Brackenbury Farm

Pl Fld

87

06

A

Uxbridge CH

B

60

07

C

Copth Farm

Breakspear Jun & Inf Schs

PYNCHESTER CL

HOYLAKE CRES

THE MEAD

FIELD CL

BUSHEY RD

BUSHEY CL

COPTHALL RD

D

08

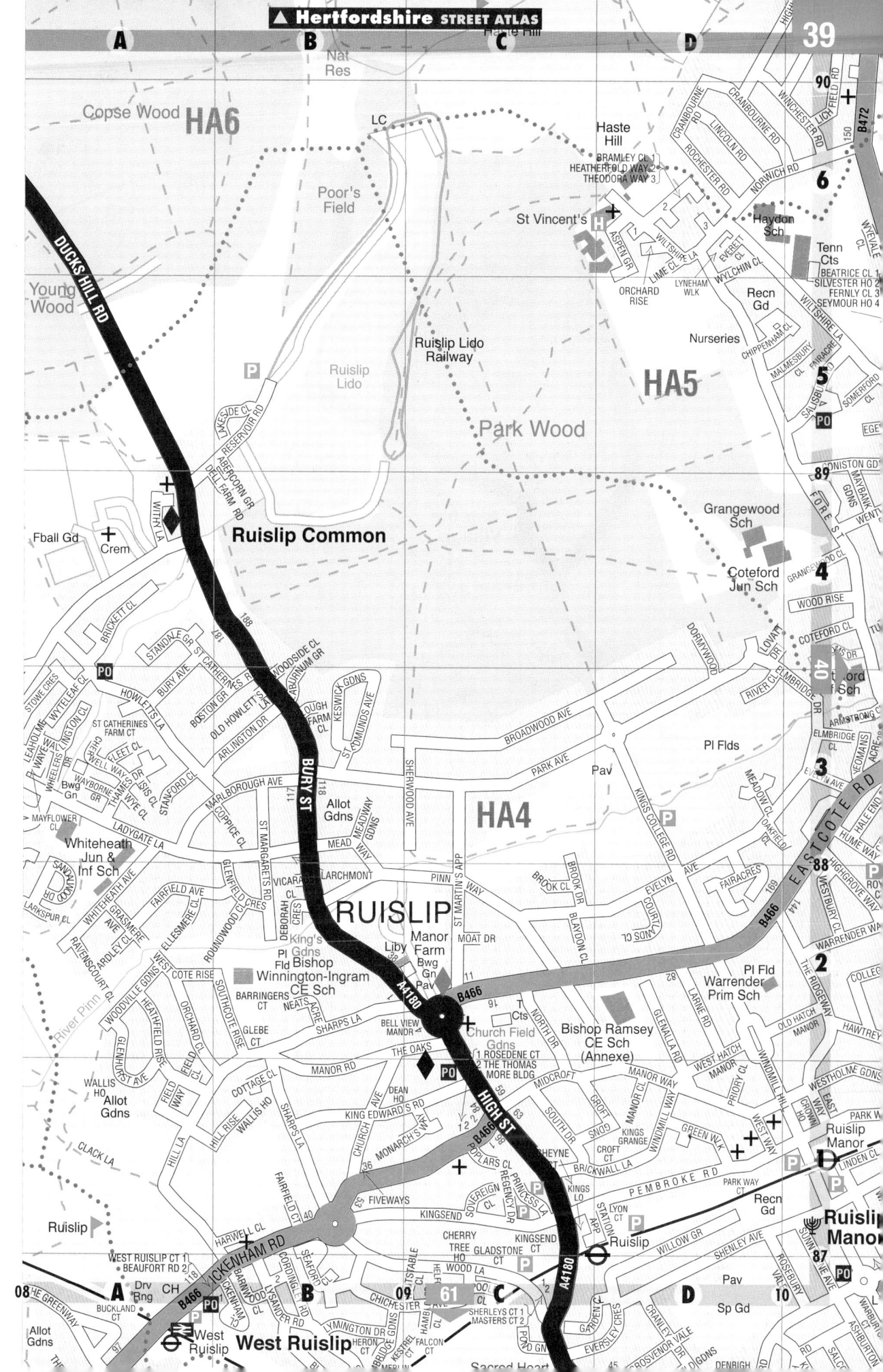

A   B   C   D

90

6

Copse Wood   **HA6**

Nat
Res

LC

Haste
Hill

BRAMLEY CL 1
HEATHERFOLD WAY 2
THEODORA WAY 3

Poor's
Field

St Vincent's

Haydon
Sch

Tenn
Cts

BEATRICE CL 1
SILVESTER HO 2
FERNLY CL 3
SEYMOUR HO 4

ASPEN GR
WILTSHIRE LA
EVERETT CL
WYLCHIN CL
LIME CL
LYNEHAM WLK
ORCHARD RISE

Recn
Gd

CHIPPENHAM CL

Nurseries

CONISTON GDNS

Young
Wood

Ruislip Lido
Railway

Ruislip
Lido

Park Wood

HA5

Grangewood
Sch

Coteford
Jun Sch

WOOD RISE

MALMESBURY CL
SALISBURY
SOMERFORD
EGE
FAIRACRE
FORE
GRANGEWOOD

5

89

4

P

LAKESIDE CL
RESERVOIR RD
ABERCORN GR
DELL FARM RD

Ruislip Common

Fball Gd

Crem

WITHY LA

BRICKETT CL
STANDALE GR
ST CATHERINES RD
WOODSIDE CL
LABURNUM GR
KESWICK GDNS
OUGH FARM CL
ST EDMUNDS CL

40

P

P0

DORMYWOOD

LOWATT
RIVER CL
ELMBRIDGE DR
ford Sch
ELMBRIDGE
CL
Sch

Whiteheath
Jun &
Inf Sch

STOWE CRES
WYTELEAF CL
HOWLETTS LA
BURY AVE
BOSTON GR
OLD HOWLETT'S LA
ARLINGTON DR
MARLBOROUGH AVE
ST MARGARETS RD
COPPICE CL
GLENFIELD CRES

Broadwood Ave

Park Ave

Pav

Pl Flds

HA4

ELMBRIDGE DR
ARMSTRONG
EVELYN AVE
YEOMANS
ACRE
HALF ACRE
HUME WAY
HIGHGROVE WAY
WESTBURY CL

3

88

EASTCOTE RD

B466

P

LEAHOLME
WAYE WAY
WHEELERS DR
CHELL WAY
FLEET CL
THAMES
WYE CL
SIS CL
WAYBORNE GR
STANFORD CL
LADYGATE LA
MEAD
MEADWAY GDNS
KESWICK GDNS
SHERWOOD AVE

Allot
Gdns

Mayflower
CL

Bwg
Gn

LARCHMONT

PINN WAY
MOAT DR

BROOK DR
BROOK CL
BLAYDON CL
EVELYN CT
FAIRACRES
LARNE RD
GLENALLA RD
KINGS COLLEGE RD
MEADOW CL
OAKFIELD

Pl Fld
Warrender
Prim Sch

THE RIDGEWAY
COLLEG
WARRENDER RD

2

FAIRFIELD AVE
ELLESMERE CL
WEST COTE RISE
ROUNDWOOD RD
SOUTHCOTE RISE
VICARAGE RD
DEBORAH CL

RUISLIP

King's
Pl Gdns

Fld Bishop
Winnington-Ingram
CE Sch

Manor
Farm

Liby

Bwg
Gn
Pav

ST MARTIN'S APP
NORTH DR
WEST HATCH MANOR

Bishop Ramsey
CE Sch
(Annexe)

OLD HATCH MANOR
HAWTREY
WINDMILL HILL
PRIORY CL
MANOR WAY

WESTHOLME GDNS
GROWN
EAST

River Pinn

RAVENSCOURT CL
ARDLEY CL
WOODVILLE GDNS
HEATHFIELD RISE
ORCHARD CL
GLENHURST AVE
GRASMERE AVE
BARRINGERS CT
NEATSACRE
SHARPS LA
GLEBE CT
FIELD

BELL VIEW
MANOR

Church Field
Gdns

1 ROSEDENE CT
2 THE THOMAS MORE BLDG

MIDCROFT
SOUTH DR
CHEYNE
CROFT CT
KINGS GRANGE
GREEN WLK
WEST WAY

PARK WAY
Ruislip
Manor

LINDEN CL

WALLIS
HO

Allot
Gdns

A4180

THE OAKS

DEAN
HO

P0

COTTAGE CL
CHURCH AVE
KING EDWARD'S RD
MANOR RD
HILL RISE
WALLIS HO
SHARPS LA
MONARCH'S WAY

BRICKWALL LA

WEST WAY

P

D

P

Ruisli
Manor

CLACK LA

Ruislip

FAIRFIELD CT
HARWELL CL
FIVEWAYS
KINGSEND
CHERRY TREE CT
GLADSTONE CT
SOVEREIGN CT
REGENCY DR
PRINCESS DR
POPLARS CL
KINGSEND
LYON CT
KINGS LO
STATION APP

HIGH ST

PEMBROKE RD
Park Way
Recn
Gd

WILLOW GR
SHENLEY AVE
ROSEBURY
SIMM

87

P0

08   A   B   09   61   C   D   10

Drv Rng
CH
B466
P0
WEST RUISLIP CT 1
BEAUFORT RD 2
ICKENHAM RD
CORDING
OKENHAM
SEAFORD
LYSANDER RD
BARNW
CHICHESTER
SHERLEYS CT 1
MASTERS CT 2
POOL
WOOD LA
CONSTABLE
KESTREL
HELFORD
FALCON
HERON
LYMINGTON DR
HAMBI
MERLIN
A4180
POND GN
EVERSLEY VALE
GROSVENOR VALE
DIGONS
DENBIGH
CRANLEY
GARDEN
Pav
Sp Gd

THE GREENWAY
BUCKLAND CT
Allot
Gdns
West
Ruislip

West Ruislip

Sacred Heart

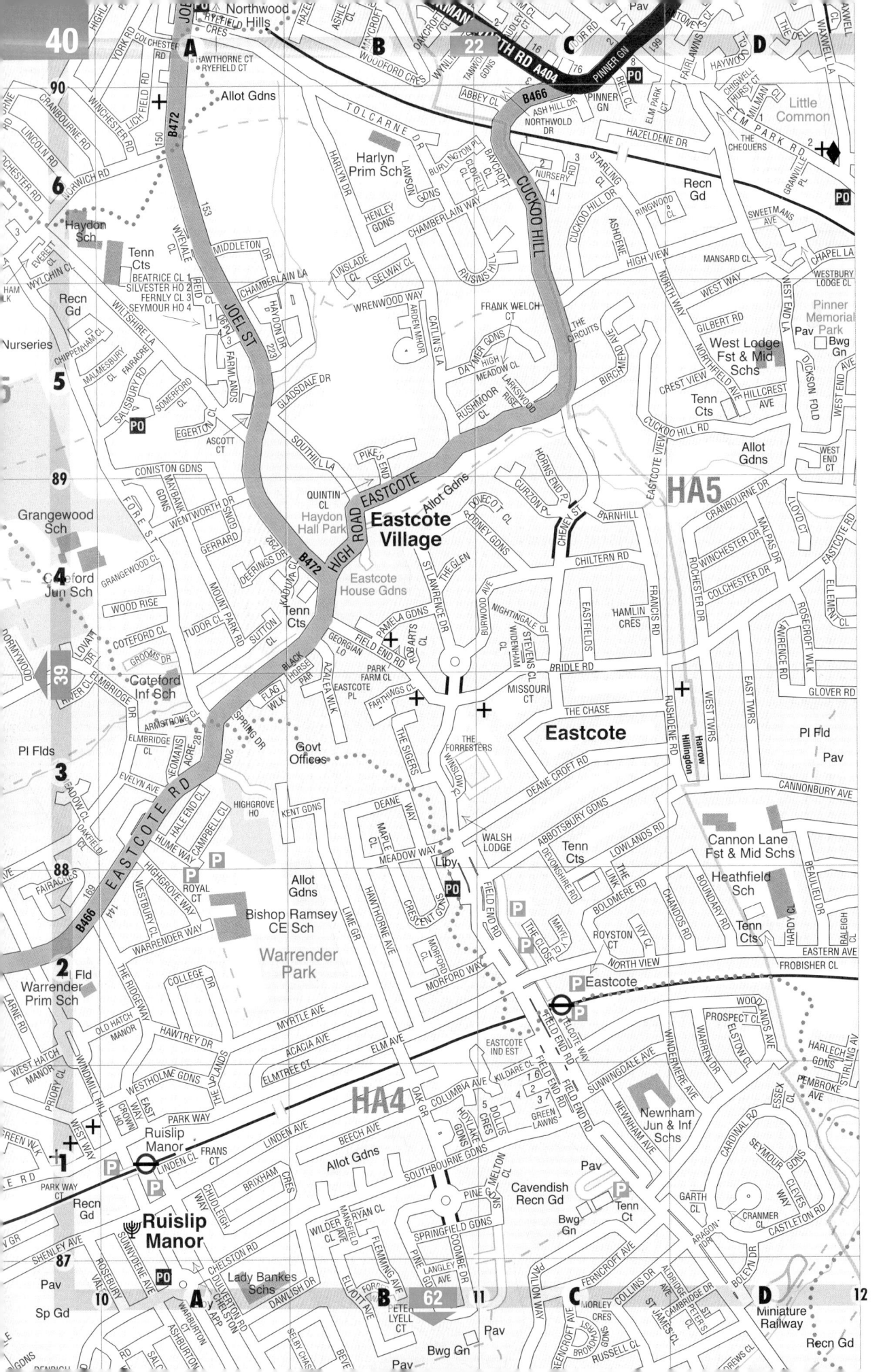

A
B
C
D
22
Northwood Hills
Allot Gdns
Harlyn Prim Sch
Little Common
Recn Gd
Haydon Sch
Tenn Cts
Recn Gd
Nurseries
Pinner Memorial Park
West Lodge Fst & Mid Schs
Grangewood Sch
Coteford Jun Sch
Haydon Hall Park
Eastcote Village
Eastcote House Gdns
Coteford Inf Sch
Pl Flds
Govt Offices
Eastcote
HA5
Pl Fld
Pav
Cannon Lane Fst & Mid Schs
Heathfield Sch
Bishop Ramsey CE Sch
Warrender Park
Warrender Prim Sch
Allot Gdns
Liby
HA4
Newnham Jun & Inf Schs
Ruislip Manor
Cavendish Recn Gd
Lady Bankes Schs
Miniature Railway
Recn Gd
Sp Gd
Bwg Gn
JOEL ST
HIGH ROAD EASTCOTE
EASTCOTE RD
CUCKOO HILL
FIELD END RD
B472
B466
A404
39
62
90
89
88
87
6
5
4
3
2
1
10
11
12

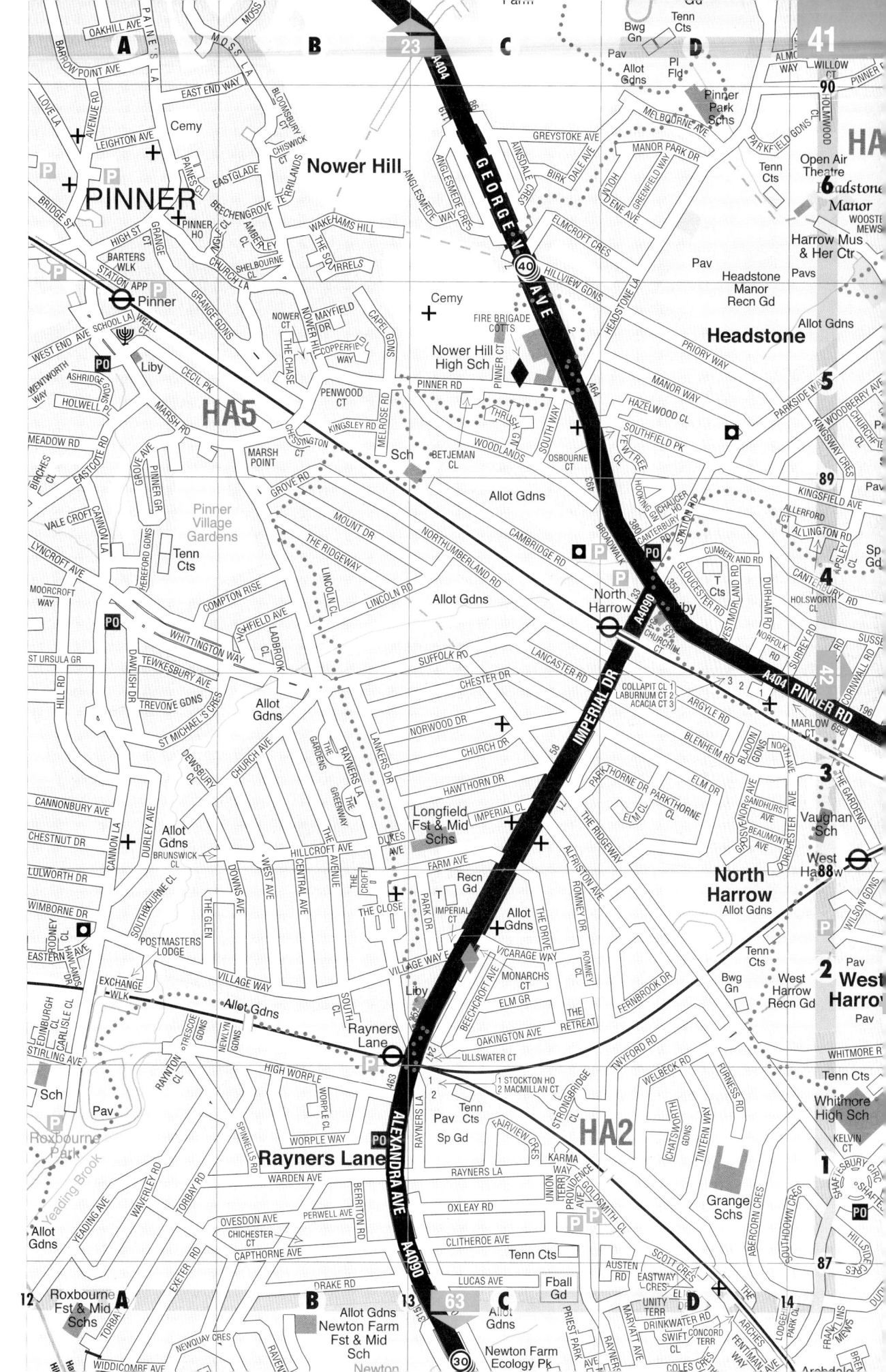
A
B
C
D
23
63
90
89
88
87
6
5
4
3
2
1
12
13
14
A404
A4090
PINNER
Nower Hill
Headstone
North Harrow
Rayners Lane
HA5
HA2
West Harrow
OAKHILL AVE
PAINE'S LA
MOSS LA
MOSS CL
BARROW POINT AVE
EAST END WAY
LOVE LA
AVENUE RD
LEIGHTON AVE
Cemy
BLOOMSBURY CT
CHISWICK CT
EASTGLADE
TERRILANDS
BRIDGE ST
HIGH ST
BARTERS WLK
STATION APP
Pinner
GRANGE CT
PINNER HO
CHURCH LA
BEECHENGROVE
AMBERLEY CL
SHELBOURNE CL
GRANGE GDNS
WAKEHAMS HILL
THE SQUIRRELS
NOWER CT
NOWER HILL
MAYFIELD DR
CAPEL GDNS
COPPERFIELD WAY
THE CHASE
WEST END AVE
SCHOOL LA
WEALL CT
Liby
CECIL PK
WENTWORTH WAY
ASHRIDGE GDNS
HOLWELL PL
MARSH RD
MEADOW RD
BIRCHES CL
EASTCOTE RD
GROVE AVE
PINNER GR
VALE CROFT
CANNON LA
Pinner Village Gardens
Tenn Cts
LYNCROFT AVE
HEREFORD GDNS
MOORCROFT WAY
ST URSULA GR
HILL RD
DAWLISH DR
TEWKESBURY AVE
TREVONE GDNS
ST MICHAEL'S CRES
WHITTINGTON WAY
COMPTON RISE
HIGHFIELD AVE
LADBROOK CL
MARSH POINT
CHESSINGTON CT
GROVE RD
MOUNT DR
THE RIDGEWAY
LINCOLN CL
LINCOLN RD
NORTHUMBERLAND RD
PENWOOD CT
KINGSLEY RD
MELROSE RD
Sch
PINNER RD
BETJEMAN CL
WOODLANDS
THRUSH GN
SOUTH WAY
OSBOURNE CT
Allot Gdns
CAMBRIDGE RD
Nower Hill High Sch
FIRE BRIGADE COTTS
PINNER CT
GEORGE V AVE
ANGLESMEDE CRES
ANGLESMEDE WAY
AINSDALE CRES
GREYSTOKE AVE
BIRKDALE AVE
MELBOURNE AVE
MANOR PARK DR
HOLLYDENE AVE
GREENFIELD WAY
ELMCROFT CRES
HILLVIEW GDNS
HEADSTONE LA
PRIORY WAY
MANOR WAY
HAZELWOOD CL
SOUTHFIELD PK
YEW TREE CL
HOOKING GN
CHAUCER HO
CANTERBURY RD
STATION RD
BROADWALK
Pinner Park Schs
Bwg Gn
Pav
Pl Fld
Tenn Cts
PARKFIELD GDNS
HOLMWOOD CL
Open Air Theatre
Headstone Manor
WOOSTER MEWS
Harrow Mus & Her Ctr
Headstone Manor Recn Gd
Pavs
PARKSIDE WAY
WOODBERRY AVE
KINGSWAY CRES
KINGSFIELD AVE
ALLERFORD CT
ALLINGTON RD
CANTERBURY RD
HOLSWORTH CL
CUMBERLAND RD
GLOUCESTER RD
WESTMORLAND RD
DURHAM RD
NORFOLK RD
SURREY RD
CORNWALL RD
CHURCHILL CT
North Harrow
SUFFOLK RD
LANCASTER RD
CHESTER DR
NORWOOD DR
CHURCH DR
HAWTHORN DR
IMPERIAL DR
COLLAPIT CL
LABURNUM CT
ACACIA CT
ARGYLE RD
BLENHEIM RD
BLADON GDNS
NORTH AVE
PINNER RD
MARLOW CT
PARKTHORNE DR
PARKTHORNE CL
ELM DR
ELM CL
THE RIDGEWAY
SANDHURST AVE
BEAUMONT AVE
GROSVENOR AVE
DORCHESTER AVE
THE GARDENS
Vaughan Sch
West Harrow
ALFRISTON AVE
ROMNEY DR
DEWSBURY CL
CHURCH AVE
RAYNERS LA
THE GREENWAY
LANKERS DR
CANNONBURY AVE
CHESTNUT DR
DURLEY AVE
BRUNSWICK CL
LULWORTH DR
WIMBORNE DR
RODNEY CL
EASTERN AVE
HAWLANDS DR
SOUTHBOURNE CL
POSTMASTERS LODGE
DOWNS AVE
WEST AVE
CENTRAL AVE
THE AVENUE
HILLCROFT AVE
DUKES AVE
FARM AVE
Longfield Fst & Mid Schs
IMPERIAL CL
Recn Gd
THE CROFT
THE CLOSE
PARK DR
IMPERIAL CT
THE DRIVE
VICARAGE WAY
MONARCHS CT
ELM GR
BEECHCROFT AVE
OAKINGTON AVE
THE RETREAT
FERNBROOK DR
EXCHANGE WLK
VILLAGE WAY
VILLAGE WAY E
SOUTH CL
EDINBURGH CL
CARLISLE CL
STIRLING AVE
TRESCOE GDNS
NEWLYN GDNS
RAYNTON CL
Rayners Lane
ULLSWATER CT
HIGH WORPLE
WORPLE CL
WORPLE WAY
1 STOCKTON HO
2 MACMILLAN CT
STRONGBRIDGE CL
TWYFORD RD
WELBECK RD
FURNESS RD
CHATSWORTH GDNS
TINTERN WAY
Whitmore High Sch
WHITMORE RD
Pav
Sp Gd
FAIRVIEW CRES
KARMA WAY
UNION TERR
PROVIDENCE AVE
GOLDSMITH CL
Grange Schs
ABERCORN CRES
SOUTHDOWN CRES
KELVIN CT
SHAFTESBURY CIRC
HILLSIDE CRES
Roxbourne Park
Yeading Brook
Sch
YEADING AVE
WAVERLEY RD
TORBAY RD
SPINNELLS RD
WARDEN AVE
BERRITON RD
ALEXANDRA AVE
RAYNERS LA
OXLEAY RD
OVESDON AVE
PERWELL AVE
CHICHESTER CT
CAPTHORNE AVE
CLITHEROE AVE
EXETER RD
DRAKE RD
LUCAS AVE
Fball Gd
AUSTEN RD
EASTWAY CRES
SCOTT CRES
ELLIOT DR
UNITY TERR
DRINKWATER RD
SWIFT CL
CONCORD TERR
COLES CRES
FENTIMAN WAY
THE ARCHES
LODGE PARK CL
FRANKLINS MEWS
Roxbourne Fst & Mid Schs
TORBAY
NEWQUAY CRES
WIDDICOMBE AVE
Newton Farm Fst & Mid Sch
Newton Farm Ecology Pk
PRIEST PARK AVE
MARYATT AVE
RAYNERS

24
HA2
HA3
HA1
Pinner Park Schs
Headstone Manor
Harrow Mus & Her Ctr
Headstone Manor Recn Gd
Headstone
Open Air Theatre
Whitefriars Trad Est
Tudor Ent Pk
Waverley Ind Pk
Wealdstone
Harrow & Wealdstone
Greenhill
Phoenix Ind Est
Ind Est
HARROW
St Georges Sh & L Ctr
St Ann's Ctr
Harrow-on-the-Hill
Harrow Coll
Quainton Hall Sch
Norbury Sch
Vaughan Sch
West Harrow
North Harrow
West Harrow Recn Gd
Whitmore High Sch
Grange Schs
St Anselm's RC Prim Sch
The John Lyon Sch
Harrow Sch
The Grove Open Space
Capital Ring
Harrow on the Hill
Roxeth
Bowden House
HIGH ST
GEORGE GANGE WAY
RAILWAY APP
STATION RD
SHEEPCOTE RD
A409
A404
PINNER RD
A4005
GREENHILL WAY
COLLEGE RD
B458
LOWLANDS RD
TYBURN LA
KENTON RD
PETERBOROUGH RD
A312
BESSBOROUGH RD
LOWER RD
ROXETH HILL
PINNER PARK AVE
PINNER PARK GDNS
HEADSTONE GDNS
HEADSTONE DR
MARLBOROUGH HILL
CUNNINGHAM PK
KINGSFIELD AVE
CANTERBURY RD
WHITMORE RD
SHAFTESBURY CIRC
SHAFTESBURY AVE
1 JARDINE HO
2 HILLBOROUGH CT
3 DRUMMOND CT
4 LITTLE CT
5 CHESTNUT CT
1 CROWN CT
2 CHILTERN HO
WORDSWORTH CT 1
CHARLES CRES 2
KINGSFIELD RD 3
BURRELL CT 4
HANOVER CT 5
KINGSFIELD CT 6
LEYS CL 1
CHILTERN CT 2
MILES LO 3
HOLLY LO 4
CUNNINGHAM CT 5
CUMBERLAND CT 1
BANNISTER HO 2
POPPY CT 3
KARMAN CT 4
AMBASSADOR HO 5
CHURCH PAR 6
CENTURY HO 7
REGENCY LO 8
1 CLARENDON HO
2 BEVERLEY CT
90
89
88
87
14
15
16
A
B
C
D
1
2
3
4
5
6
41
64

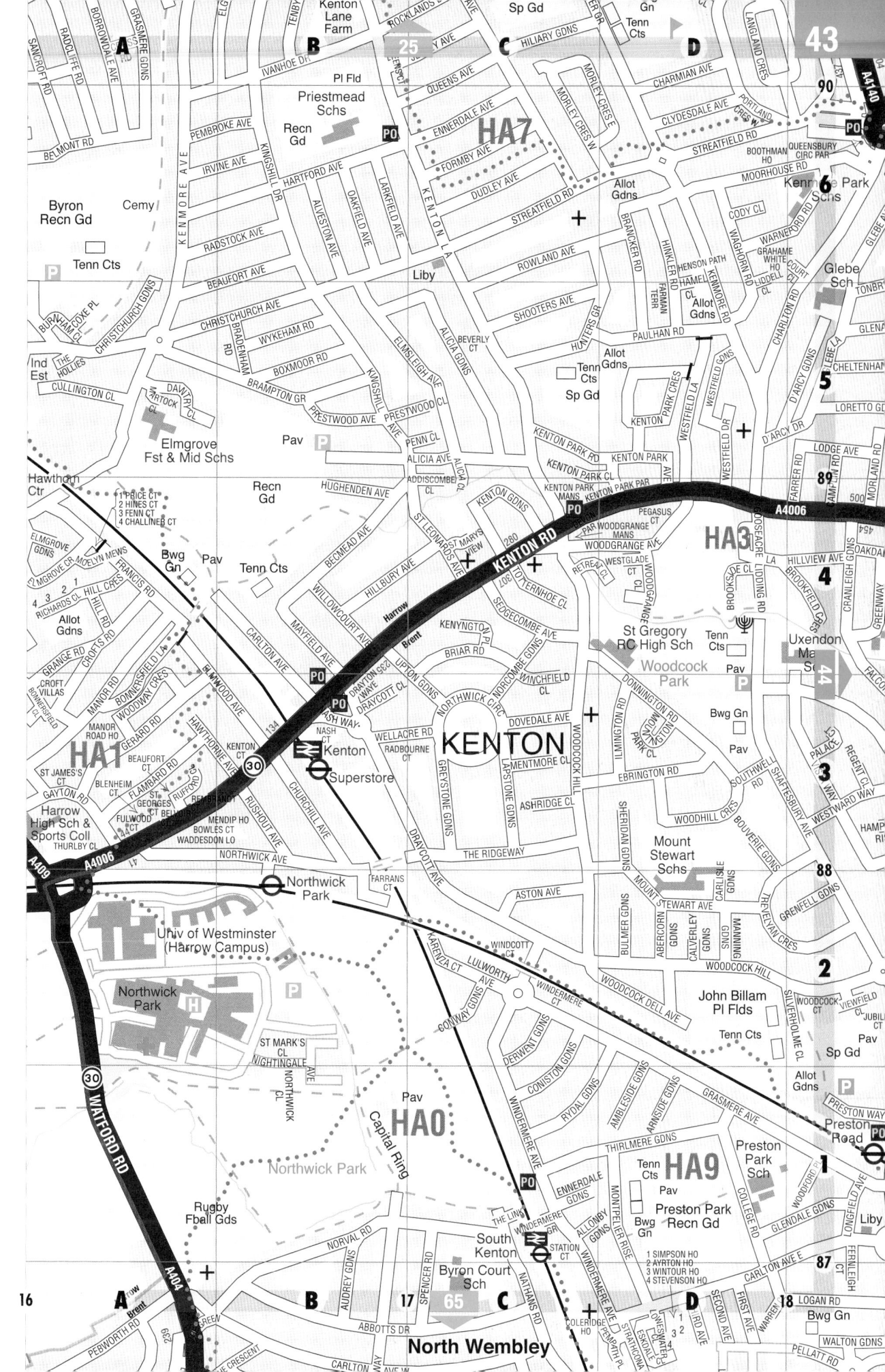
A
B
C
D
25
Kenton Lane Farm
Sp Gd
Tenn Cts
Gn
SANCROFT RD
RADCLIFFE RD
BORROWDALE AVE
GRASMERE GDNS
TENBY
ROCKLANDS
IVANHOE DR
HILIARY GDNS
LANGLAND CRES
Pl Fld
QUEENS AVE
CHARMIAN AVE
MORLEY CRES E
MORLEY CRES W
Priestmead Schs
Recn Gd
PO
ENNERDALE AVE
HA7
CLYDESDALE AVE
PORTLAND CRES W
STREATFIELD RD
90
A4140
PEMBROKE AVE
BELMONT RD
FORMBY AVE
BOOTHMAN HO
QUEENSBURY CIRC PAR
MOORHOUSE RD
IRVINE AVE
HARTFORD AVE
DUDLEY AVE
Kenmore Park Schs
6
Byron Recn Gd
Cemy
KENMORE AVE
KINGSHILL DR
ALVESTON AVE
OAKFIELD AVE
LARKFIELD AVE
KENTON LA
STREATFIELD RD
Allot Gdns
BRANCKER RD
HINKLER RD
HENSON PATH
HAMEL CL
KENMORE RD
WAGHORN RD
CODY CL
WARNEFORD RD
GRAHAME WHITE HO
LIDDELL CL
COURT CL
GLEBE AVE
RADSTOCK AVE
ROWLAND AVE
Tenn Cts
Liby
FARMAN TERR
Allot Gdns
Glebe Sch
P
BEAUFORT AVE
CHRISTCHURCH GDNS
CHRISTCHURCH AVE
BRADENHAM RD
WYKEHAM RD
SHOOTERS AVE
CHARLTON RD
TONBRIDGE
GLENALMOND
BURNHAM CL
COXE PL
BEVERLY CT
ALICIA GDNS
ELMSLEIGH AVE
HUNTERS GR
PAULHAN RD
Allot Gdns
WESTFIELD GDNS
GLEBE LA
D'ARCY GDNS
CHELTENHAM
Ind Est
THE HOLLIES
BOXMOOR RD
Tenn Cts
Sp Gd
PARK CRES
5
CULLINGTON CL
DAWTRY CL
MARTOCK CL
BRAMPTON GR
PRESTWOOD AVE
KINGSHILL AVE
PRESTWOOD CL
KENTON
WESTFIELD LA
WESTFIELD DR
LORETTO GDNS
D'ARCY DR
Elmgrove Fst & Mid Schs
Pav
PENN CL
KENTON PARK RD
KENTON PARK AVE
LODGE AVE
Hawthorn Ctr
ALICIA AVE
ALICIA CL
ADDISCOMBE CL
KENTON PARK CL
FARRER RD
CAMPLIN RD
MORLAND RD
89
Recn Gd
HUGHENDEN AVE
KENTON GDNS
KENTON PARK MANS
KENTON PARK PAR
A4006
500
1 PRICE CT
2 HINES CT
3 FENN CT
4 CHALLINER CT
ST LEONARDS AVE
BECMEAD AVE
ST MARYS VIEW
280
KENTON RD
DEVON
PEGASUS CT
WOODGRANGE MANS
WOODGRANGE AVE
HA3
454
ELMGROVE GDNS
MOELYN MEWS
Bwg Gn
Pav
Tenn Cts
HILLBURY AVE
TOTTERNHOE CL
RETREAT CL
WESTGLADE CT
WOODGRANGE CL
BROOKSIDE CL
GOOSEACRE LA
LIDDING RD
HILLVIEW AVE
OAKDALE
ELMGROVE CR
FRANCIS RD
HILL CRES
RICHARDS CL
HILL RD
WILLOWCOURT AVE
Harrow
Brent
307
SEDGECOMBE AVE
BROOKFIELD CRES
CRANLEIGH GDNS
GREENWAY
4
Allot Gdns
CROFTS RD
GRANGE RD
BONNERSFIELD LA
CARLTON AVE
MAYFIELD AVE
KENYNGTON PL
BRIAR RD
NORCOMBE GDNS
St Gregory RC High Sch
Tenn Cts
Uxendon Manor Sch
44
FALCON
Woodcock Park
Pav
CROFT VILLAS
BONNERSFIELD CL
MANOR RD
WOODWAY CRES
ELMWOOD AVE
DRAYTON WAYE
DRAYCOTT CL
UPTON GDNS
WINCHFIELD CL
ILMINGTON RD
DONNINGTON RD
Bwg Gn
Pav
MANOR ROAD HO
GERARD RD
HAWTHORNE AVE
134
ASH WAY
NASH CT
WELLACRE RD
NORTHWICK CIRC
DOVEDALE AVE
NEWINGTON PARK CL
PALACE GDNS
REGENT CL
HA1
BEAUFORT CT
KENTON CT
30
Kenton
RADBOURNE CT
KENTON
MENTMORE CL
WOODCOCK HILL
EBRINGTON RD
SOUTHWELL RD
SHAFTESBURY AVE
VISTA WAY
3
ST JAMES'S CT
GAYTON RD
BLENHEIM CT
FLAMBARD RD
RUFFORD CL
Superstore
CHURCHILL AVE
GREYSTONE GDNS
LAPSTONE GDNS
ASHRIDGE CL
WOODHILL CRES
WESTWARD WAY
HAMPDEN RISE
Harrow High Sch & Sports Coll
ST GEORGES CT
BELVOIR CT
REMBRANDT CT
MENDIP HO
BOWLES CT
WADDESDON LO
RUSHOUT AVE
FULWOOD CT
THURLBY CL
44
DRAYCOTT AVE
THE RIDGEWAY
SHERIDAN GDNS
Mount Stewart Schs
BOUVERIE GDNS
A409
A4006
41
NORTHWICK AVE
88
Northwick Park
FARRANS CT
ASTON AVE
MOUNT STEWART AVE
CARLISLE GDNS
TREVELYAN CRES
GRENFELL GDNS
Univ of Westminster (Harrow Campus)
KARENZA CT
WINDCOTT CT
BULMER GDNS
ABERCORN GDNS
CALVERLEY GDNS
MANNING GDNS
2
Northwick Park
H
P
LULWORTH AVE
WINDERMERE CT
WOODCOCK DELL AVE
WOODCOCK HILL
John Billam Pl Flds
SILVERHOLME CL
WOODCOCK CT
VIEWFIELD CL
JUBILEE CT
CONWAY GDNS
Tenn Cts
Pav
ST MARK'S CL
NIGHTINGALE AVE
NORTHWICK CL
DERWENT GDNS
CONISTON GDNS
Sp Gd
Allot Gdns
30
WATFORD RD
Pav
RYDAL GDNS
AMBLESIDE GDNS
ARNSIDE GDNS
GRASMERE AVE
PRESTON WAY
Capital Ring
HA0
WINDERMERE AVE
THIRLMERE GDNS
Preston Road
Preston Park Sch
Tenn Cts
HA9
WOODFORD PL
1
Northwick Park
PO
ENNERDALE GDNS
MONTPELIER RISE
Pav
COLLEGE RD
LONGFIELD AVE
Rugby Fball Gds
THE LINK
WINDERMERE GR
ALLONBY GDNS
Preston Park Recn Gd
Bwg Gn
GLENDALE GDNS
Liby
NORVAL RD
South Kenton
STATION CT
1 SIMPSON HO
2 AYRTON HO
3 WINTOUR HO
4 STEVENSON HO
CARLTON AVE E
FERNLEIGH CT
87
AUDREY GDNS
SPENCER RD
Byron Court Sch
NATHANS RD
WINDERMERE AVE
SECOND AVE
FIRST AVE
THIRD AVE
WARREN RISE
Harrow
Brent
A404
A
B
17
65
C
D
18
LOGAN RD
Bwg Gn
PEBWORTH RD
239
GREEN
ABBOTTS DR
COLERIDGE HO
PEMPATH PL
STRATHCONA RD
ESKDALE CL
LOWESWATER CL
North Wembley
CRESCENT
CARLTON AVE W
WAY
WALTON GDNS
PELLATT RD

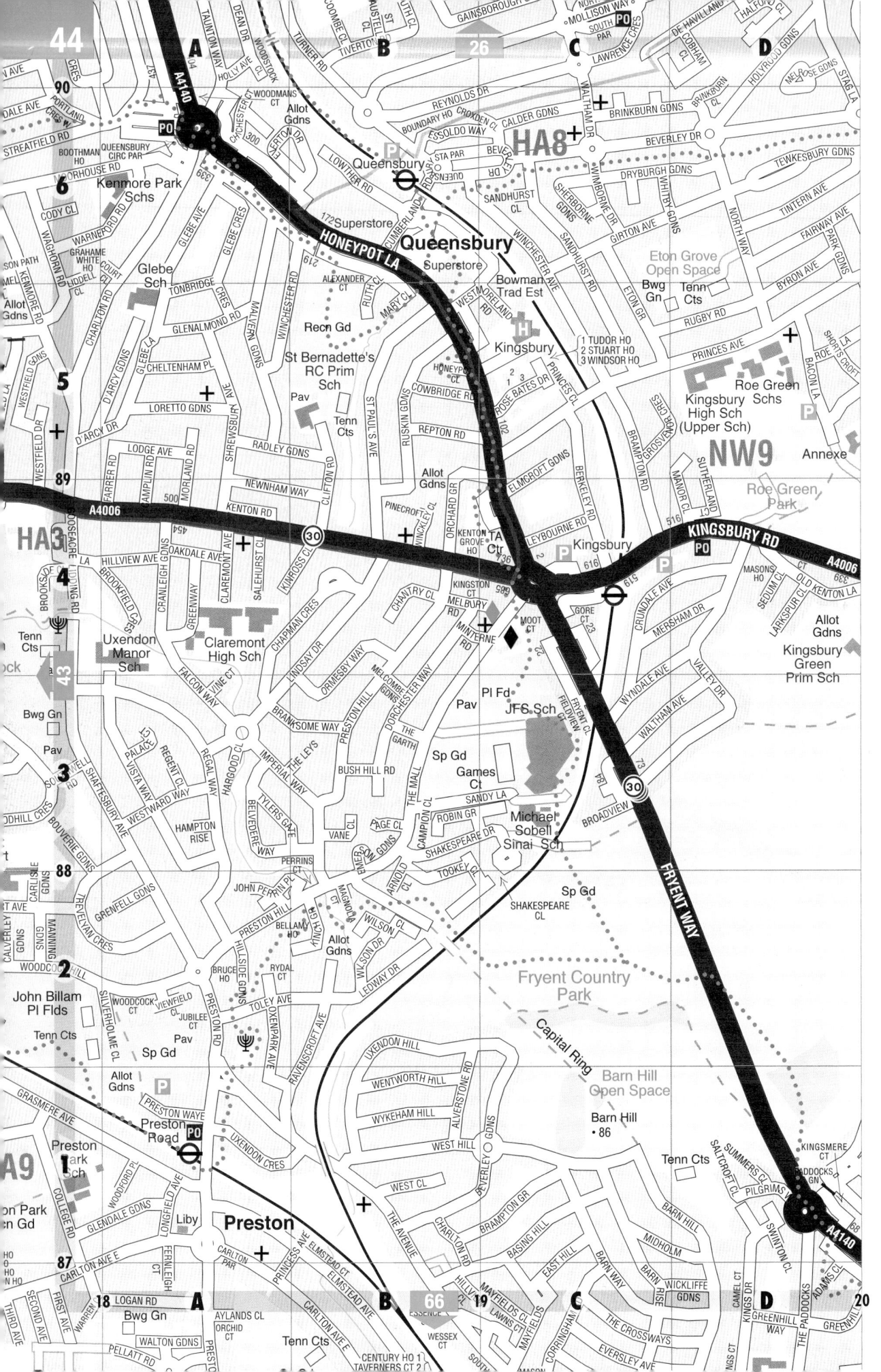

A
B
C
D
26
HA8
HA3
NW9
A4140
A4006
HONEYPOT LA
KINGSBURY RD
FRYENT WAY
Queensbury
Kenmore Park Schs
Glebe Sch
St Bernadette's RC Prim Sch
Recn Gd
Superstore
Bowman Trad Est
Kingsbury
Eton Grove Open Space
Roe Green Schs
Kingsbury High Sch (Upper Sch)
Annexe
Roe Green Park
Allot Gdns
Kingsbury Green Prim Sch
Claremont High Sch
Uxendon Manor Sch
JFS Sch
Michael Sobell Sinai Sch
Fryent Country Park
Capital Ring
Barn Hill Open Space
Barn Hill
• 86
John Billam Pl Flds
Preston Road
Preston Park Sch
Preston
Liby
Tenn Cts
Bwg Gn
Pav
Sp Gd
Games Ct
Pl Fd
43
1 TUDOR HO
2 STUART HO
3 WINDSOR HO
90
89
88
87
6
5
4
3
2
1
18
19
20
66

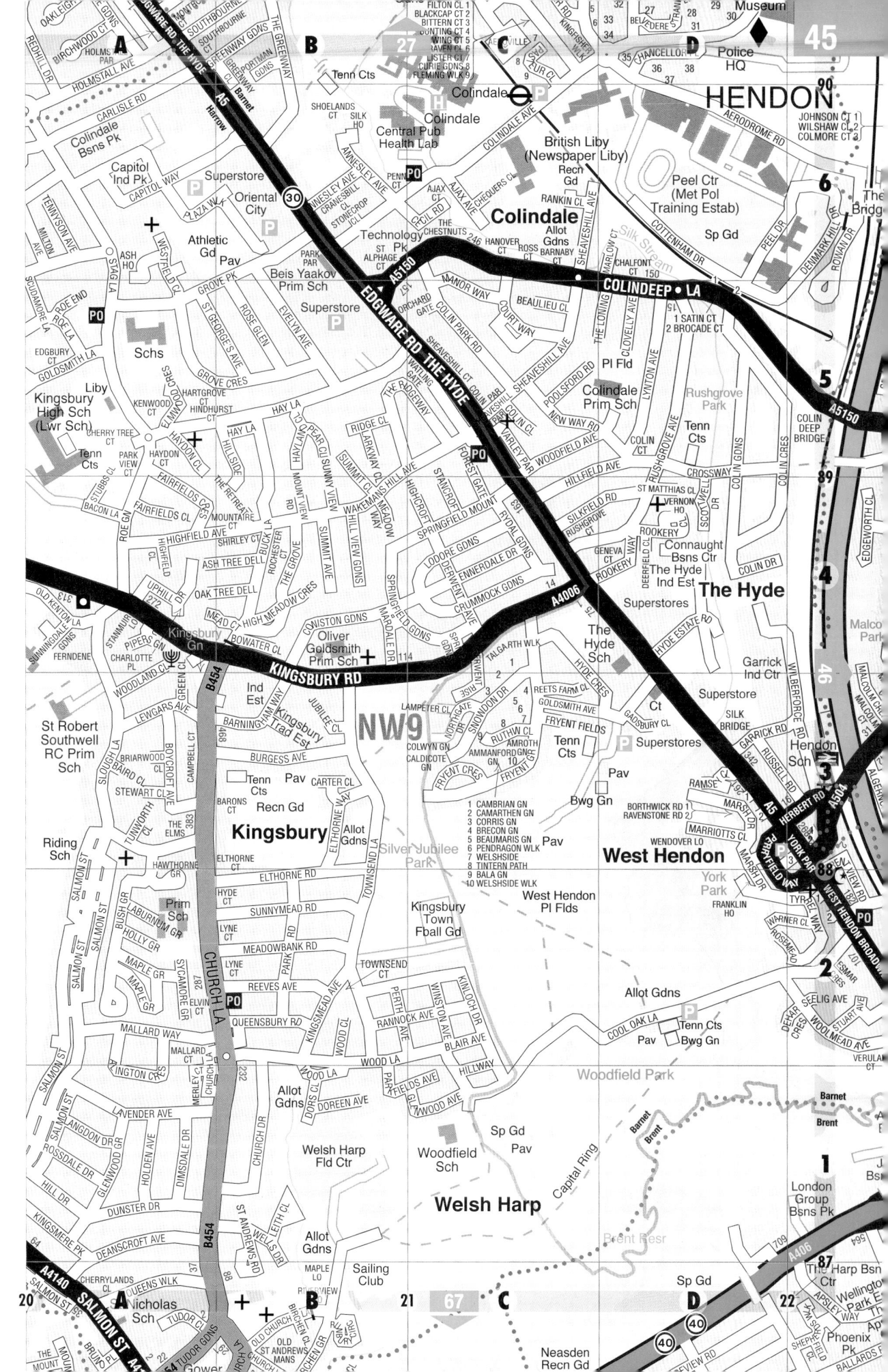
HENDON
Colindale
The Hyde
West Hendon
Kingsbury
NW9
Welsh Harp
Colindale Bsns Pk
Capitol Ind Pk
Oriental City
Athletic Gd
Beis Yaakov Prim Sch
Central Pub Health Lab
British Liby (Newspaper Liby)
Peel Ctr (Met Pol Training Estab)
Police HQ
Museum
Colindale Prim Sch
Rushgrove Park
Kingsbury High Sch (Lwr Sch)
Oliver Goldsmith Prim Sch
Connaught Bsns Ctr
The Hyde Ind Est
The Hyde Sch
Garrick Ind Ctr
Hendon Sch
Kingsbury Trad Est
St Robert Southwell RC Prim Sch
Riding Sch
Silver Jubilee Park
Kingsbury Town Fball Gd
West Hendon Pl Flds
York Park
Woodfield Park
Woodfield Sch
Welsh Harp Fld Ctr
Sailing Club
Brent Resr
London Group Bsns Pk
Neasden Recn Gd
St Nicholas Sch
EDGWARE RD THE HYDE
COLINDEEP LA
KINGSBURY RD
CHURCH LA
A5
A5150
A4006
B454
A4140
A406
A504
1 CAMBRIAN GN
2 CAMARTHEN GN
3 CORRIS GN
4 BRECON GN
5 BEAUMARIS GN
6 PENDRAGON WLK
7 WELSHSIDE
8 TINTERN PATH
9 BALA GN
10 WELSHSIDE WLK
1 FILTON CL
2 BLACKCAP CT
3 BITTERN CT
4 BUNTING CT
5 WING CT
6 RAVEN CL
7 LISTER CT
8 CURIE GDNS
9 FLEMING WLK
1 JOHNSON CT
2 WILSHAW CL
3 COLMORE CT
1 SATIN CT
2 BROCADE CT
1 BORTHWICK RD
2 RAVENSTONE RD
27
46
67
A
B
C
D
1
2
3
4
5
6
20
21
22
87
88
89
90

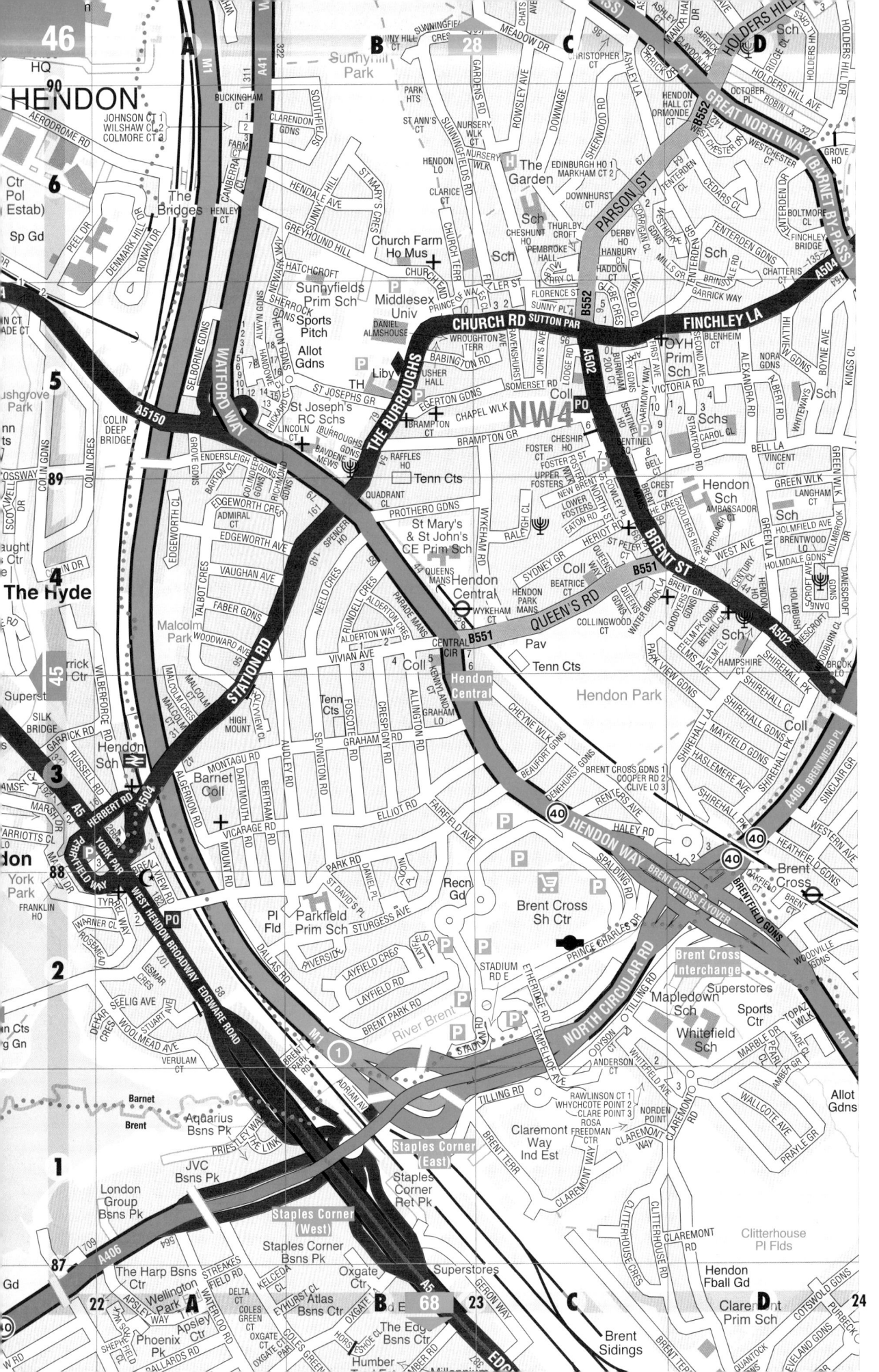
HENDON
NW4
The Hyde
28
45
68
A
B
C
D
6
5
4
3
2
1
90
89
88
87
22
23
24
Sunnyhill Park
Church Farm Ho Mus
Middlesex Univ
Sunnyfields Prim Sch
Sports Pitch
Allot Gdns
St Joseph's RC Schs
St Mary's & St John's CE Prim Sch
Hendon Central
Hendon Park
Malcolm Park
Barnet Coll
Hendon Sch
York Park
Parkfield Prim Sch
Brent Cross Sh Ctr
Brent Cross
Brent Cross Interchange
Brent Cross Flyover
Mapledown Sch
Whitefield Sch
Claremont Way Ind Est
Clitterhouse Pl Flds
Hendon Fball Gd
Claremont Prim Sch
Staples Corner (East)
Staples Corner (West)
Staples Corner Ret Pk
Staples Corner Bsns Pk
Aquarius Bsns Pk
JVC Bsns Pk
London Group Bsns Pk
The Harp Bsns Ctr
Wellington Park
Apsley Ctr
Phoenix Pk
Atlas Bsns Ctr
Oxgate Ctr
The Edge Bsns Ctr
Brent Sidings
River Brent
Barnet
Brent
The Bridges
Colin Deep Bridge
Silk Bridge
Hendon Central
Tenn Cts
Pav
Recn Gd
Pl Fld
Superstores
Sports Ctr
Allot Gdns
WATFORD WAY
GREAT NORTH WAY (BARNET BY-PASS)
CHURCH RD
FINCHLEY LA
THE BURROUGHS
STATION RD
BRENT ST
QUEEN'S RD
HENDON WAY
NORTH CIRCULAR RD
WEST HENDON BROADWAY
EDGWARE ROAD
PARSON ST
SUTTON PAR
HOLDERS HILL
A1
A41
A5
A406
A502
A504
A5150
B551
B552
M1

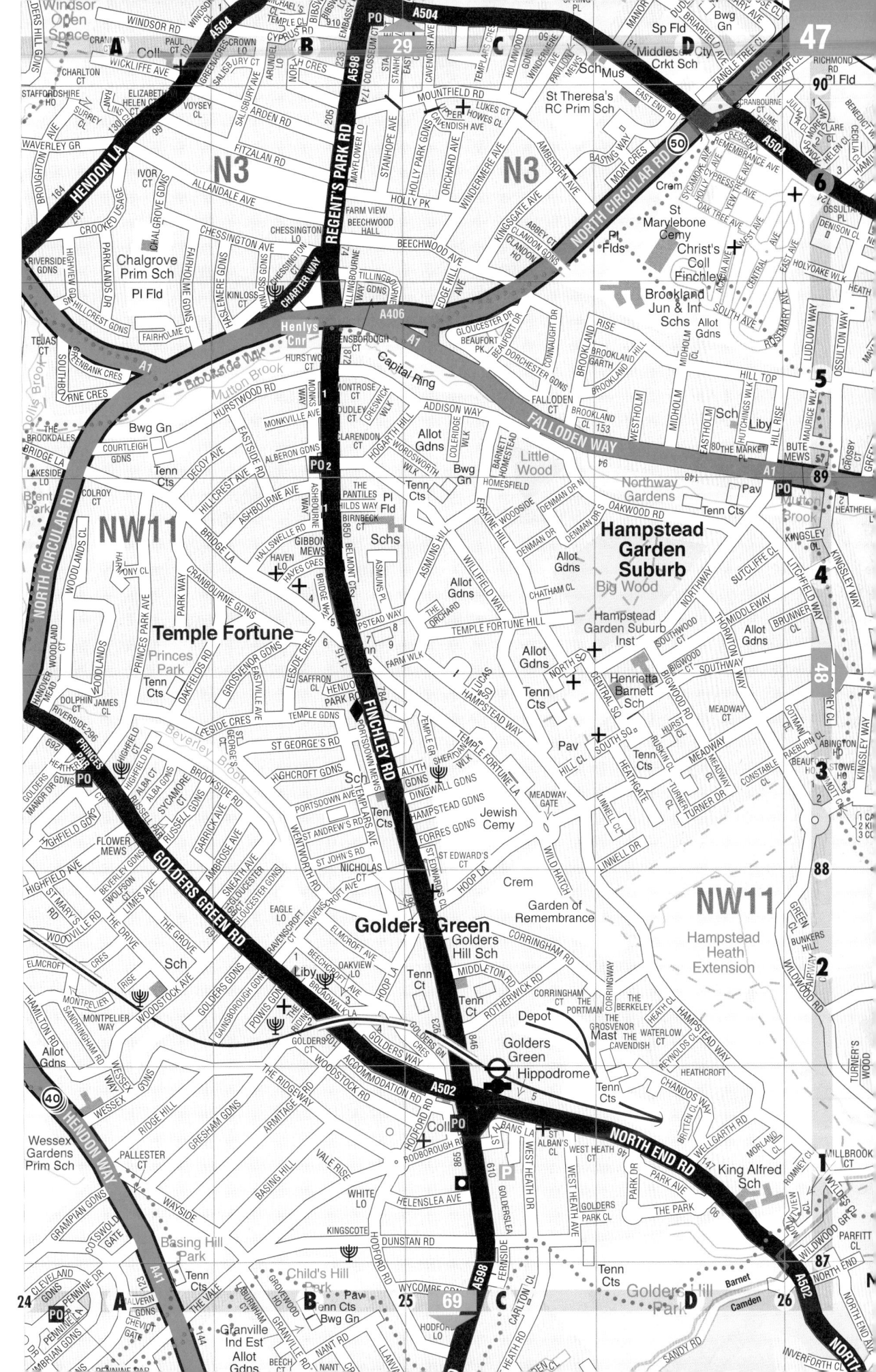
A
B
C
D
29
48
69
1
2
3
4
5
6
24
25
26
87
88
89
90
N3
N3
NW11
NW11
Hampstead
Garden
Suburb
Temple Fortune
Golders Green
REGENT'S PARK RD
FINCHLEY RD
HENDON LA
NORTH CIRCULAR RD
GOLDERS GREEN RD
NORTH END RD
HENDON WAY
FALLODEN WAY
A504
A598
A406
A1
A502
A41
A406
Henlys
Cnr
Capital Ring
Mutton Brook
Brookside Wlk
Beverley Brook
Windsor Open Space
Chalgrove Prim Sch
St Theresa's RC Prim Sch
Middlesex Cty Crkt Sch
St Marylebone Cemy
Christ's Coll Finchley
Brookland Jun & Inf Schs
Little Wood
Northway Gardens
Big Wood
Hampstead Garden Suburb Inst
Henrietta Barnett Sch
Princes Park
Jewish Cemy
Crem
Garden of Remembrance
Golders Hill Sch
Golders Green Hippodrome
Hampstead Heath Extension
King Alfred Sch
Wessex Gardens Prim Sch
Basing Hill Park
Child's Hill Park
Golders Hill Park
Granville Ind Est
Barnet
Camden
Allot Gdns
Tenn Cts
Bwg Gn
Pl Fld
Depot
Mast
Sch
Liby
Coll
Pav
PO

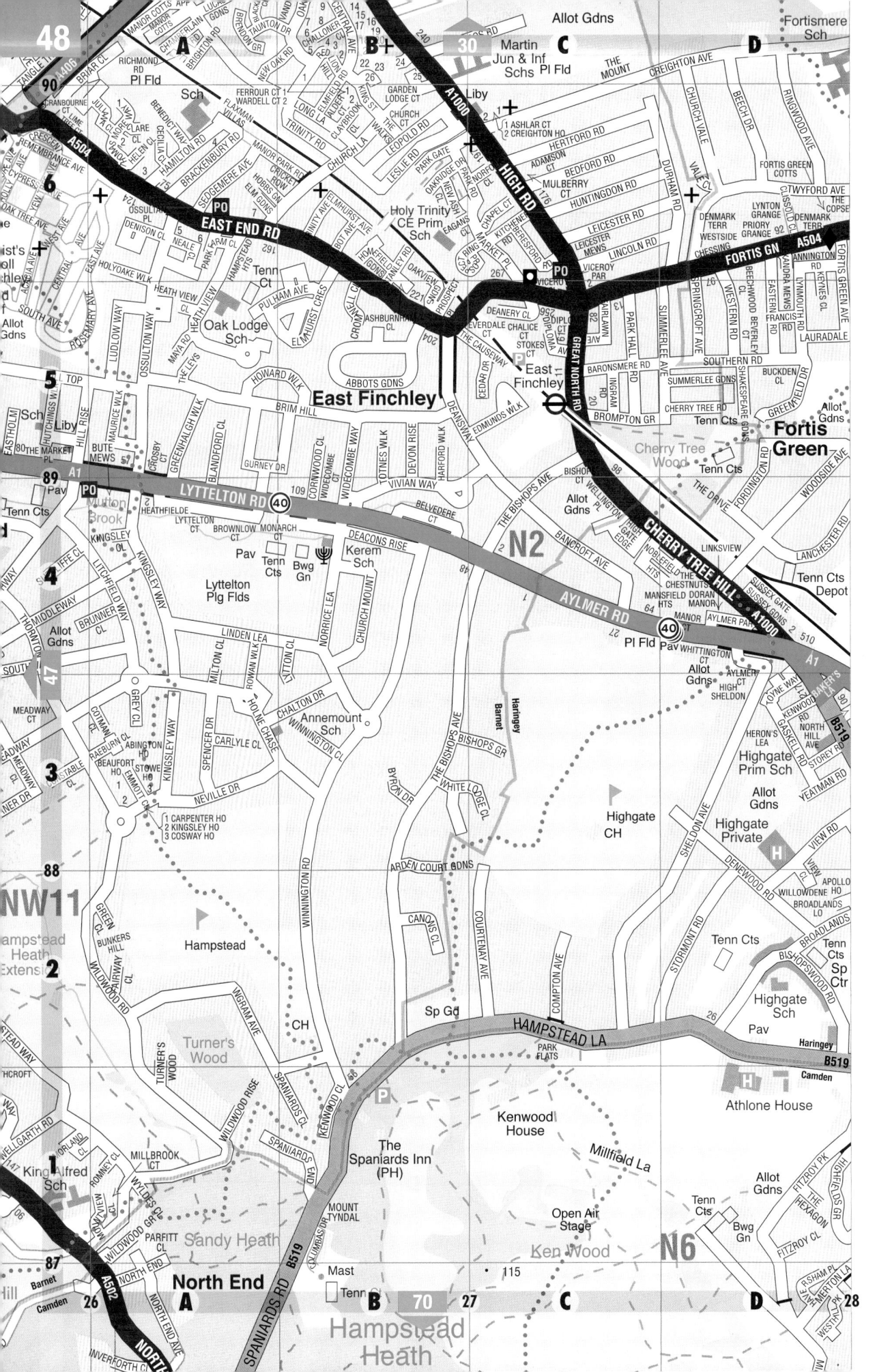

A
B
C
D
30
Allot Gdns
Fortismere Sch
Martin Jun & Inf Schs
Pl Fld
THE MOUNT
CREIGHTON AVE
A406
90
RICHMOND RD
Pl Fld
BRIAR CL
Sch
FLAXMAN VILLAS
FERROUR CT
WARDELL CT
GARDEN LODGE CT
CHURCH CT
Liby
A1000
1 ASHLAR CT
2 CREIGHTON HO
HERTFORD RD
CHURCH VALE
BEECH DR
RINGWOOD AVE
FORTIS GREEN COTTS
A504
REMEMBRANCE AVE
CYPRESS AVE
BRACKENBURY RD
HAMILTON RD
SEDGEMERE AVE
MANOR PARK RD
TRINITY RD
CHURCH LA
LEOPOLD RD
LESLIE RD
PARK GATE
OAKRIDGE DR
NEW ASH CL
PARK RD
HIGH RD
ADAMSON CT
BEDFORD RD
MULBERRY CT
HUNTINGDON RD
DURHAM RD
VALE CL
TWYFORD AVE
6
EAST END RD
PO
Holy Trinity CE Prim Sch
ELMHURST AVE
EAGANS CL
CHAPEL CT
KITCHENER RD
LEICESTER RD
LEICESTER MEWS
LINCOLN RD
DENMARK TERR
WESTSIDE
LYNTON GRANGE
PRIORY GRANGE
CHESSING
FORTIS GN
ANNINGTON RD
FORTIS GREEN AVE
OSSULTON PL
DENISON CL
NEALE CL
HAMPSTEAD HTS
Tenn Ct
HOLYOAKE WLK
HEATH VIEW CL
HEATH VIEW
PULHAM AVE
ELMHURST CRES
OAKVIEW GDNS
PROSPECT
MARKET PL
VICEROY PAR
SPRINGCROFT AVE
WESTERN RD
BEECHWOOD AVE
BEVERLEY CT
EASTERN RD
SANDRA MEWS
LYNMOUTH RD
KEYNES CL
Allot Gdns
SOUTH AVE
ROSEMARY AVE
LUDLOW WAY
OSSULTON WAY
Oak Lodge Sch
MAYA RD
ASHBURNHAM CL
DEANERY CL
EVERDALE CT
CHALICE CT
STOKES CT
DIPLOMA AVE
GREAT NORTH RD
FAIRLAWN AVE
PARK HALL RD
SUMMERLEE AVE
FRANCIS RD
LAURADALE
THE CAUSEWAY
East Finchley
5
TOP
THE LEYS
HOWARD WLK
ABBOTS GDNS
CEDAR DR
SOUTHERN RD
BARONSMERE RD
INGRAM RD
SUMMERLEE GDNS
SHAKESPEARE GDNS
BUCKDEN CL
GREENFIELD DR
Sch
Liby
HUTCHINGS WLK
HILL RISE
MAURICE WLK
BRIM HILL
East Finchley
DEANSWAY
EDMUNDS WLK
BROMPTON GR
CHERRY TREE RD
Tenn Cts
Allot Gdns
Fortis Green
EASTHOLM
THE MARKET PL
80
BUTE MEWS
CROSBY CT
GREENHALGH WLK
BLANDFORD CL
GURNEY DR
CORNWOOD CL
WIDECOMBE CT
WIDECOMBE WAY
TOTNES WLK
DEVON RISE
HARFORD WLK
Cherry Tree Wood
Tenn Cts
FORDINGTON RD
WOODSIDE AVE
89
A1
Pav
PO
LYTTELTON RD
40
109
VIVIAN WAY
BISHOPS CT
WELLINGTON PL
98
THE DRIVE
Tenn Cts
Mutton Brook
HEATHFIELDE
LYTTELTON CT
BROWNLOW CT
MONARCH CT
BELVEDERE CT
DEACONS RISE
THE BISHOPS AVE
Allot Gdns
HIGH GATE EDGE
CHERRY TREE HILL
LINKSVIEW
LANCHESTER RD
KINGSLEY CL
Pav
Tenn Cts
Bwg Gn
Kerem Sch
N2
BANCROFT AVE
NOBLEFIELD HTS
THE CHESTNUTS
Tenn Cts Depot
4
LITCHFIELD WAY
KINGSLEY WAY
Lyttelton Plg Flds
NORRICE LEA
CHURCH MOUNT
48
AYLMER RD
MANSFIELD HTS
DORAN MANOR
SUSSEX GATE
SUSSEX GDNS
MIDDLEWAY
BRUNNER CL
Allot Gdns
LINDEN LEA
64
MANOR CT
AYLMER PAR
A1000
510
THORNTON WAY
47
MILTON CL
ROWAN WLK
27
Pl Fld
Pav
WHITTINGTON CT
Allot Gdns
AYLMER CT
HIGH SHELDON
TOYNE WAY
KENWOOD RD
BAKER'S LA
MEADWAY CT
GREY CL
COTMAN CL
KINGSLEY WAY
SPENCER DR
HOLNE CHASE
CHALTON DR
Annemount Sch
WINNINGTON CL
Barnet
Haringey
HERON'S LEA
GASKELL RD
NORTH HILL AVE
B519
3
CONSTABLE CL
RAEBURN CL
ABINGTON HO
BEAUFORT HO
STOWE HO
EMMOTT CL
CARLYLE CL
NEVILLE DR
BISHOPS GR
BYRON DR
WHITE LODGE CL
Highgate Prim Sch
STOREY RD
YEATMAN RD
Allot Gdns
Highgate CH
1 CARPENTER HO
2 KINGSLEY HO
3 COSWAY HO
SHELDON AVE
Highgate Private
VIEW RD
88
ARDEN COURT GDNS
DENEWOOD RD
VIEW CL
APOLLO HO
WILLOWDENE
BROADLANDS LO
NW11
Hampstead Heath Extension
GREEN CL
BUNKERS HILL
Hampstead
WINNINGTON RD
CANONS CL
COURTENAY AVE
STORMONT RD
Tenn Cts
BROADLANDS
BISHOPSWOOD RD
Tenn Cts
Sp Ctr
2
FAIRWAY CL
WILDWOOD RD
WIGRAM AVE
COMPTON AVE
Highgate Sch
CH
Sp Gd
HAMPSTEAD LA
26
Pav
Haringey
Turner's Wood
PARK FLATS
B519
Camden
TURNER'S WOOD
SPANIARDS CL
KENWOOD CL
WILDWOOD RISE
Kenwood House
Athlone House
SPANIARDS END
The Spaniards Inn (PH)
Millfield La
1
MILLBROOK CT
King Alfred Sch
ROMNEY CL
WYLDES CL
MOUNT TYNDAL
Open Air Stage
Tenn Cts
Bwg Gn
Allot Gdns
FITZROY PK
HIGHFIELDS GR
THE HEXAGON
FITZROY CL
WILDWOOD GR
PARFITT CL
Sandy Heath
SPANIARDS RD
COLUMBAS DR
Ken Wood
N6
87
Barnet
Camden
A502
NORTH END
North End
NORTH END AVE
Mast
115
Tenn Cts
26
70
27
28
Hampstead Heath
INVERFORTH CL
MERTON LA
WESTHILL PK

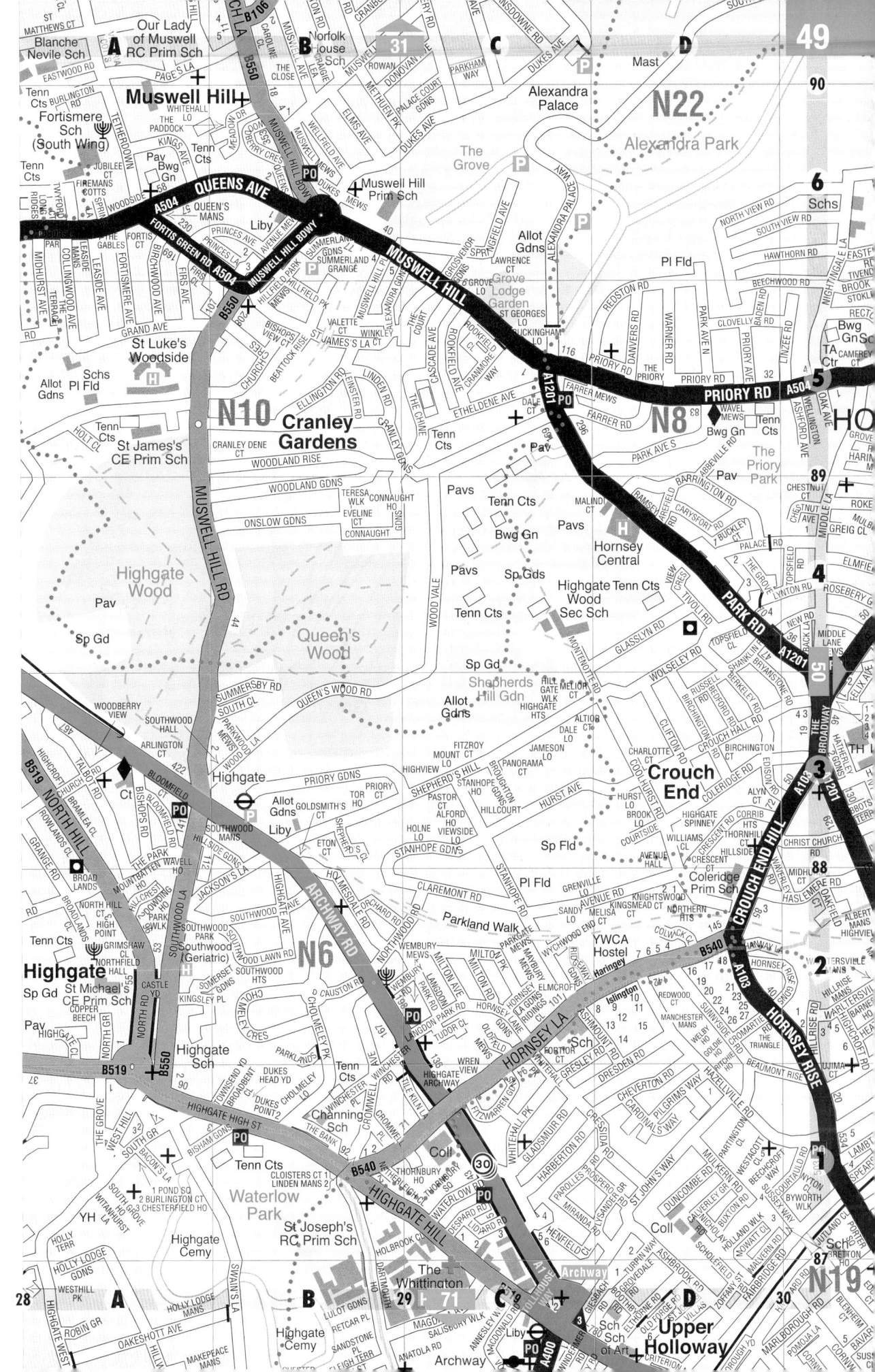

A
B
C
D
31
90
Muswell Hill
Our Lady of Muswell RC Prim Sch
Blanche Nevile Sch
Norfolk House Sch
Fortismere Sch (South Wing)
Alexandra Palace
Mast
N22
Alexandra Park
The Grove
Muswell Hill Prim Sch
QUEENS AVE
MUSWELL HILL
MUSWELL HILL RD
PRIORY RD
PARK RD
Allot Gdns
Grove Lodge Garden
6
Schs
Pl Fld
5
N10
Cranley Gardens
N8
St Luke's Woodside
St James's CE Prim Sch
Highgate Wood
Queen's Wood
The Priory Park
89
Hornsey Central
Highgate Wood Sec Sch
4
50
Shepherds Hill Gdn
Crouch End
Highgate
3
88
Coleridge Prim Sch
Parkland Walk
YWCA Hostel
N6
ARCHWAY RD
HORNSEY LA
HORNSEY RISE
CROUCH END HILL
Highgate
St Michael's CE Prim Sch
Highgate Sch
2
Channing Sch
Waterlow Park
St Joseph's RC Prim Sch
Highgate Cemy
The Whittington
Archway
Upper Holloway
N19
87
1
28
A
B
29
71
C
D
30

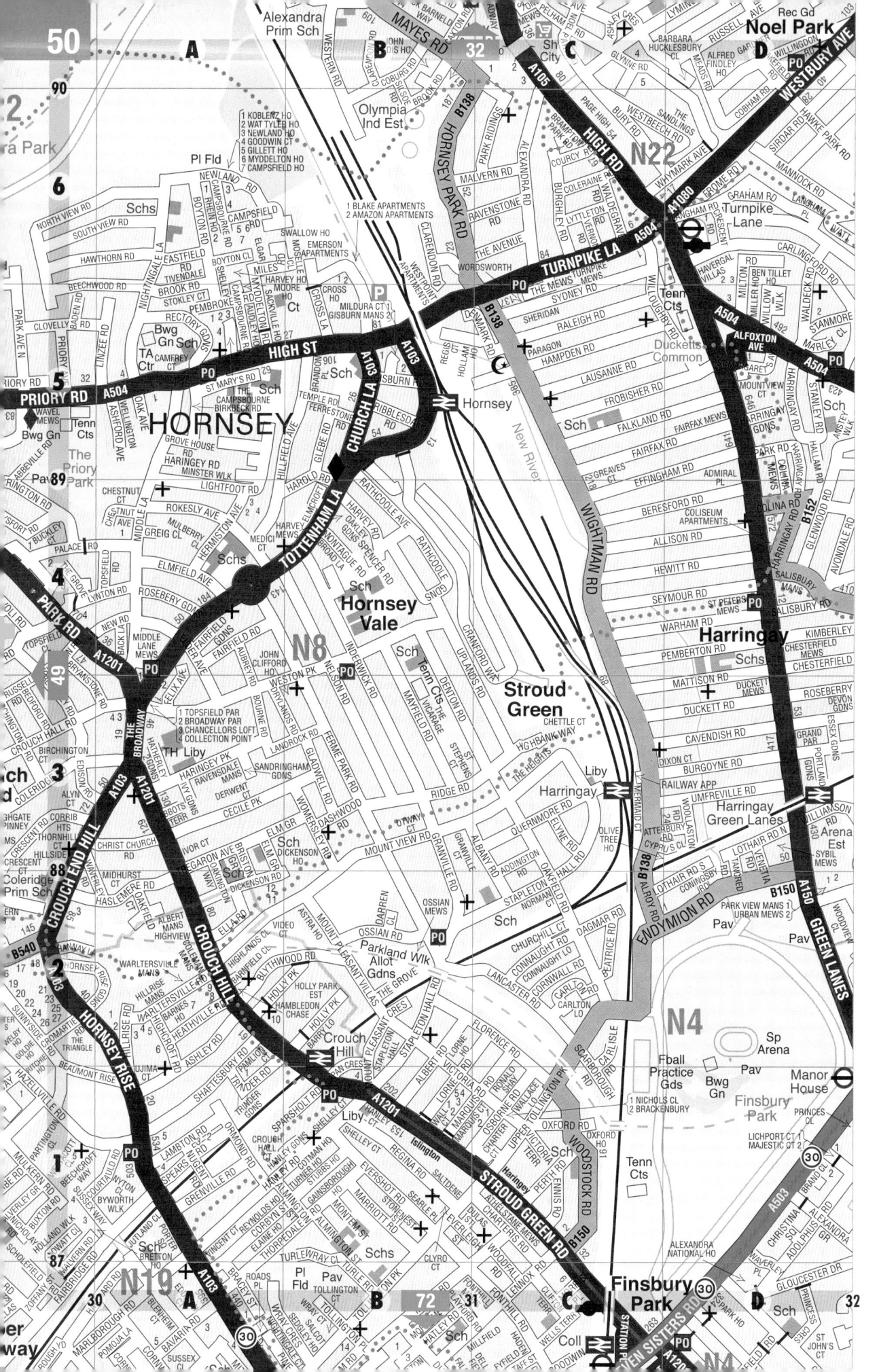

A
B
C
D
32
90
6
5
89
4
49
3
88
2
1
87
30
72
31
Noel Park
N22
Turnpike Lane
HORNSEY
Hornsey
Hornsey Vale
N8
Stroud Green
Harringay
Harringay Green Lanes
Crouch Hill
N4
N19
Finsbury Park
Manor House
New River
Olympia Ind Est
Alexandra Prim Sch
Sh City
Ducketts Common
The Priory Park
Parkland Wlk
Fball Practice Gds
Sp Arena
Coleridge Prim Sch
HIGH ST
HIGH RD
PRIORY RD
TURNPIKE LA
TOTTENHAM LA
CHURCH LA
PARK RD
CROUCH END HILL
HORNSEY RISE
CROUCH HILL
STROUD GREEN RD
WIGHTMAN RD
HORNSEY PARK RD
GREEN LANES
WESTBURY AVE
ENDYMION RD
THE BROADWAY
MAYES RD
SEVEN SISTERS RD
A504
A105
A1080
A103
A1201
B138
B150
A503
A150
B152
B540

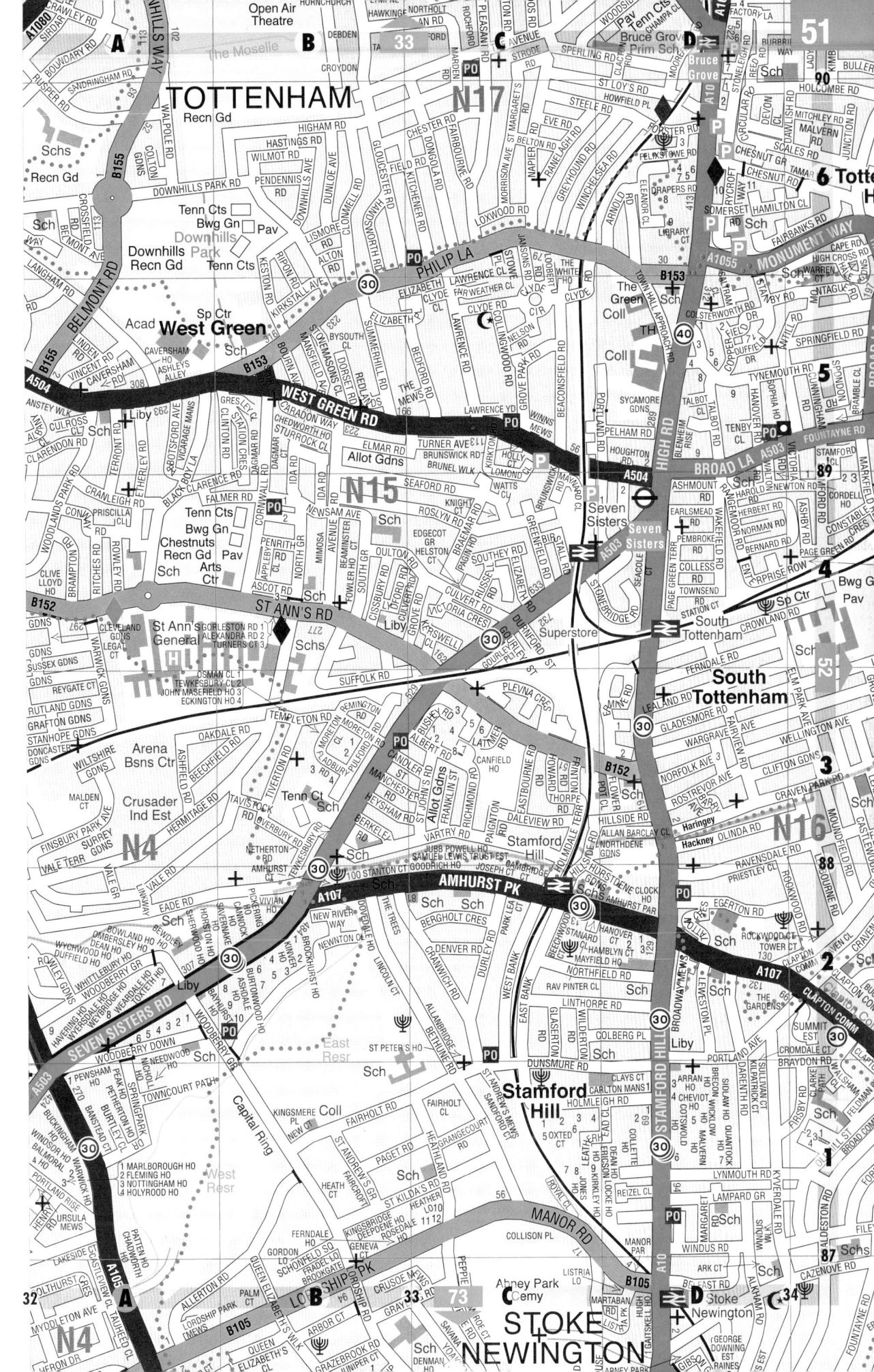

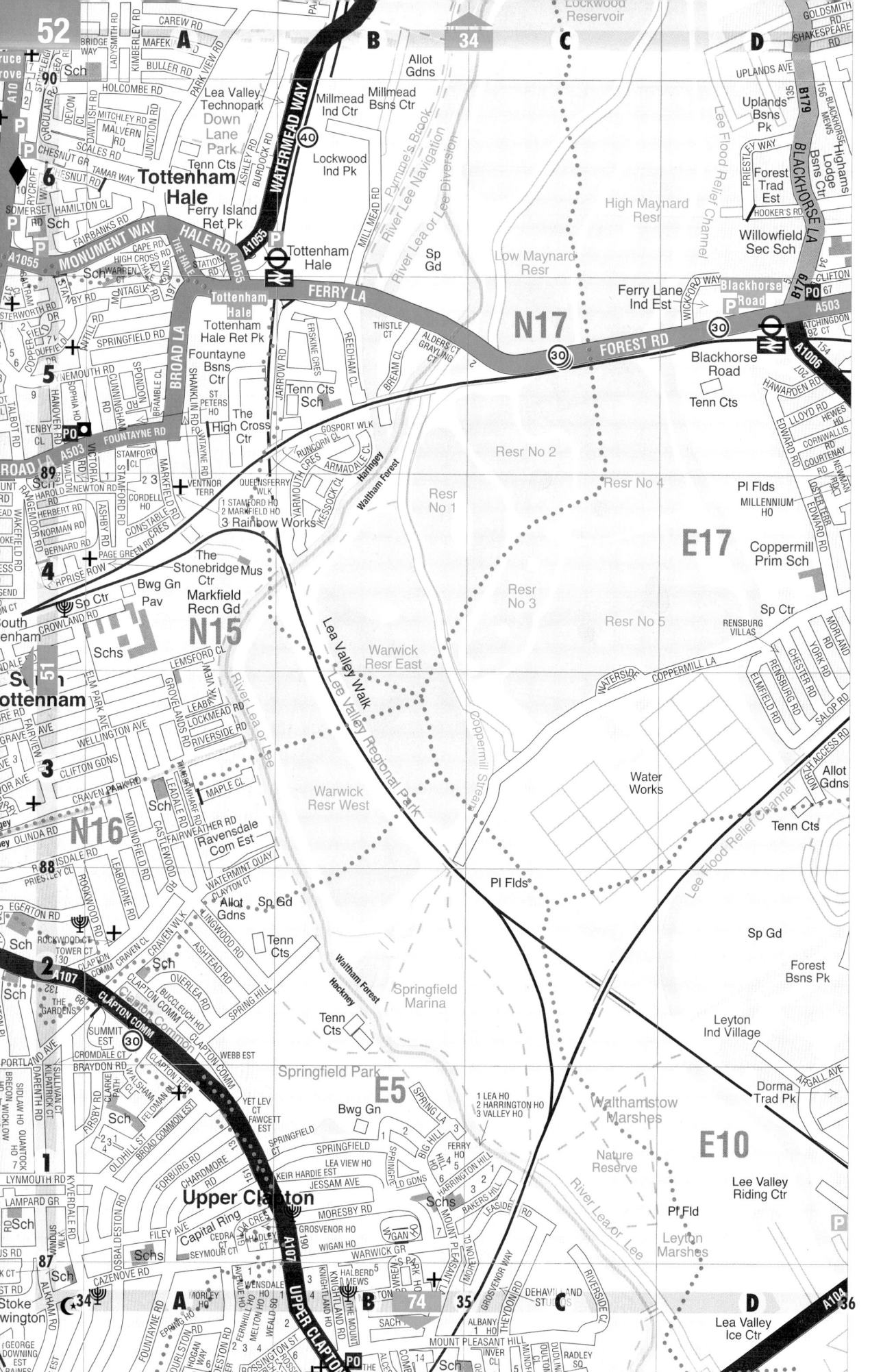

A
B
C
D
34
35
36
51
74
90
89
88
87
6
5
4
3
2
1
Lockwood Reservoir
GOLDSMITH RD
SHAKESPEARE RD
CAREW RD
BRIDGE WAY
LADYSMITH RD
KIMBERLEY RD
MAFEKING RD
BULLER RD
PARK VIEW RD
Sch
HOLCOMBE RD
CIRCULAR RD
DEVON CL
DAWLISH RD
MITCHLEY RD
MALVERN RD
SCALES RD
JUNCTION RD
Lea Valley Technopark
Down Lane Park
Tenn Cts
ASHLEY RD
BURDOCK RD
WATERMEAD WAY
40
Millmead Ind Ctr
Millmead Bsns Ctr
Allot Gdns
Lockwood Ind Pk
Pymme's Brook
River Lee Navigation
River Lea or Lee Diversion
MILL MEAD RD
UPLANDS AVE
Uplands Bsns Pk
PRIESTLEY WAY
Forest Trad Est
HOOKER'S RD
B179
BLACKHORSE LA
Highams Lodge Bsns Ctr
Lee Flood Relief Channel
High Maynard Resr
Low Maynard Resr
Willowfield Sec Sch
CHESNUT GR
CHESNUT RD
TAMAR WAY
Tottenham Hale
RYCROFT WAY
SOMERSET RD
HAMILTON CL
FAIRBANKS RD
Ferry Island Ret Pk
MONUMENT WAY
HALE RD
A1055
HIGH CROSS RD
WARREN CT
THE HALE
STATION RD
Tottenham Hale
Sp Gd
River Lea or Lee
FERRY LA
Ferry Lane Ind Est
WICKFORD WAY
Blackhorse Road
A503
A1006
MONTAGUE RD
STANBY RD
COPPERFIELD DR
DUFFIELD DR
ANTILL RD
SPRINGFIELD RD
BROAD LA
Tottenham Hale Ret Pk
Fountayne Bsns Ctr
JARROW RD
ERSKINE CRES
REEDHAM CL
THISTLE CT
ALDERS CT
GRAYLING CT
BREAM CL
N17
30
FOREST RD
Blackhorse Road
Tenn Cts
HAWARDEN RD
LLOYD RD
HEWES HO
CORNWALLIS RD
COURTENAY RD
EDWARD RD
TENBY CL
HANOVER RD
SOPHIA HO
CUNNINGHAM RD
SPONDON RD
BRAMBLE CL
SHANKLIN RD
ST PETERS HO
The High Cross Ctr
Tenn Cts Sch
GOSPORT WLK
RUNCORN CL
ARMADALE CL
YARMOUTH CRES
KESSOCK CL
Haringey
Waltham Forest
PO
FOUNTAYNE RD
BROAD LA
VICTORIA RD
STAMFORD CL
STAMFORD RD
MARKFIELD RD
VENTNOR TERR
QUEENSFERRY WLK
1 STAMFORD HO
2 MARKFIELD HO
3 Rainbow Works
Resr No 2
Resr No 4
Resr No 1
Pl Flds
MILLENNIUM HO
E17
Coppermill Prim Sch
HAROLD RD
NEWTON RD
CORDELL HO
CONSTABLE CRES
WAKEFIELD RD
HERBERT RD
NORMAN RD
BERNARD RD
ASHBY RD
PAGE GREEN RD
The Stonebridge Ctr
Mus
PRISE ROW
Bwg Gn
Pav
Sp Ctr
Markfield Recn Gd
CROWLAND RD
Schs
N15
Resr No 3
Resr No 5
Sp Ctr
RENSBURG VILLAS
MORLAND RD
South Tottenham
LEMSFORD CL
ELM PARK AVE
GROVELANDS RD
LEABANK VIEW
LOCKMEAD RD
RIVERSIDE RD
Lea Valley Walk
Lee Valley Regional Park
Warwick Resr East
WATERSIDE
COPPERMILL LA
CHESTER RD
YORK RD
RENSBURG RD
ELMFIELD RD
SALOP RD
FAIRVIEW RD
WELLINGTON AVE
CLIFTON GDNS
CRAVEN PARK RD
MAPLE CL
Coppermill Stream
Water Works
NORTH ACCESS RD
Allot Gdns
Tenn Cts
OLINDA RD
N16
Sch
MOUNDFIELD RD
LEADALE RD
CASTLEWOOD RD
FAIRWEATHER RD
Ravensdale Com Est
Warwick Resr West
RISDALE RD
PRIESTLEY CL
ROOKWOOD RD
LEABOURNE RD
WATERMINT QUAY
CLAYTON CT
Allot Gdns
Sp Gd
Pl Flds
EGERTON RD
ROCKWOOD CT
TOWER CT
CLAPTON COMM
CRAVEN CL
CRAVEN WLK
LINGWOOD RD
ASHTEAD RD
Tenn Cts
Sp Gd
Forest Bsns Pk
A107
THE GARDENS
CLAPTON COMM
Clapton Common
OVERLEA RD
BUCCLEUCH HO
SPRING HILL
Waltham Forest
Hackney
Springfield Marina
Tenn Cts
Leyton Ind Village
SUMMIT EST
CROMDALE CT
PORTLAND AVE
BRAYDON RD
CLARKE PATH
WALSHAM CL
CLAPTON TERR
WEBB EST
Springfield Park
E5
Dorma Trad Pk
ARGALL AVE
SIDLAW HO
BRECON HO
WICKLOW HO
QUANTOCK HO
KILPATRICK CT
DARENTH RD
FIRSBY RD
OLDHILL ST
BROAD COMMON EST
FELDMAN CL
YET LEV CT
FAWCETT EST
SPRINGFIELD CT
Bwg Gn
SPRING LA
BIG HILL
1 LEA HO
2 HARRINGTON HO
3 VALLEY HO
Walthamstow Marshes
Nature Reserve
E10
Lee Valley Riding Ctr
LYNMOUTH RD
FORBURG RD
CHARDMORE RD
SPRINGFIELD
LEA VIEW HO
KEIR HARDIE EST
JESSAM AVE
FERRY HO
HILL HO
HARRINGTON HILL
BAKERS HILL
LEASIDE RD
Upper Clapton
LAMPARD GR
KYVERDALE RD
OSBALDESTON RD
FILEY AVE
Capital Ring
CEDRA CT
GILDA CRES
HADLEY CT
MORESBY RD
GROSVENOR HO
WIGAN HO
WARWICK GR
Schs
MOUNT PLEASANT LA
MORETON CL
GROSVENOR WAY
Pf Fld
Leyton Marshes
River Lea or Lee
SEYMOUR CT
CAZENOVE RD
HALBERD MEWS
PARK HO
WENSDALE HO
Schs
Sch
Stoke Newington
ALKHAM RD
MORLEY HO
FOUNTAYNE RD
EPPING HO
DURLSTON RD
HOGAN WAY
FERNHILL HO
MELTON HO
WEALD SQ
ROSSINGTON ST
UPPER CLAPTON RD
KNIGHTLAND RD
THE MOUNT
SACH RD
DEHAVILLAND STUDIOS
THEYDON RD
RIVERSIDE CL
ALBANY HO
MOUNT PLEASANT HILL
INVER CL
RADLEY SQ
Lea Valley Ice Ctr
A104
GEORGE DOWNING EST
PO

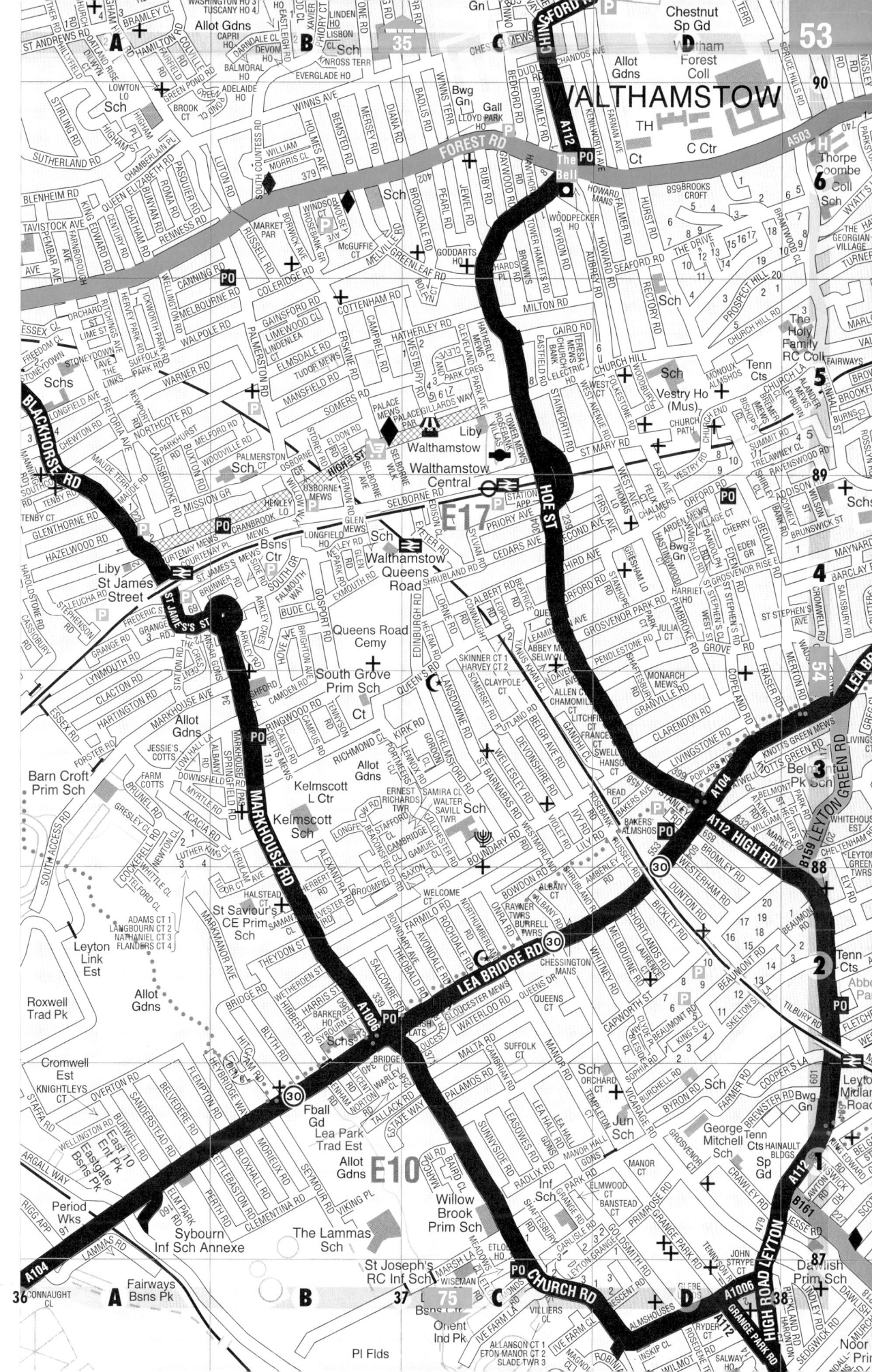

53
WALTHAMSTOW
Chestnut Sp Gd
Waltham Forest Coll
Allot Gdns
TH
C Ctr
Ct
Thorpe Coombe
Coll
Sch
The Bell
FOREST RD
A503
A112
CHINGFORD RD
HOE ST
BLACKHORSE RD
MARKHOUSE RD
LEA BRIDGE RD
HIGH RD
HIGH ROAD LEYTON
LEYTON GREEN RD
B159
B161
A104
A1006
CHURCH RD
GRANGE PARK RD
E17
E10
Walthamstow Central
Walthamstow Queens Road
St James Street
Leyton Midland Road
Liby
Queens Road Cemy
South Grove Prim Sch
Kelmscott L Ctr
Kelmscott Sch
St Saviour's CE Prim Sch
Barn Croft Prim Sch
Leyton Link Est
Roxwell Trad Pk
Cromwell Est
East 10 Ent Pk
Eastgate Bsns Pk
Period Wks
Sybourn Inf Sch Annexe
Fball Gd
Lea Park Trad Est
Willow Brook Prim Sch
The Lammas Sch
St Joseph's RC Inf Sch
Fairways Bsns Pk
Orient Ind Pk
Pl Flds
George Mitchell Sch
Jun Sch
Inf Sch
Dawlish Prim Sch
The Holy Family RC Coll
Vestry Ho (Mus)
Tenn Cts
Belmont Pk Sch
Bwg Gn
Gall
LLOYD PARK
WINNS AVE
HIGHAM ST
SUTHERLAND RD
BLENHEIM RD
TAVISTOCK AVE
PEMBAR AVE
QUEEN ELIZABETH RD
CHURCH HILL
ST MARY RD
SELBORNE RD
HIGH ST
PRIORY AVE
CEDARS AVE
GROSVENOR PARK RD
LINDEN HO
PALMERSTON RD
COPPERMILL
ESSEX CL
MAYNARD
BARCLAY RD
CHURCH LA
SOMERS RD
WARNER RD
HAZELWOOD RD
GLENTHORNE RD
CLACTON RD
MARKHOUSE AVE
SHRUBLAND RD
LEA HALL RD
CAPWORTH ST
COOPER'S LA
CRAWLEY RD
PRIMROSE RD
MANOR RD
BRIDGE RD
THEYDON ST
VICARAGE RD
BAKERS AVE
LIVINGSTONE RD
CLARENDON RD
ALMSHOUSES
A
B
C
D
35
54
75
36
37
38
87
88
89
90
1
2
3
4
5
6

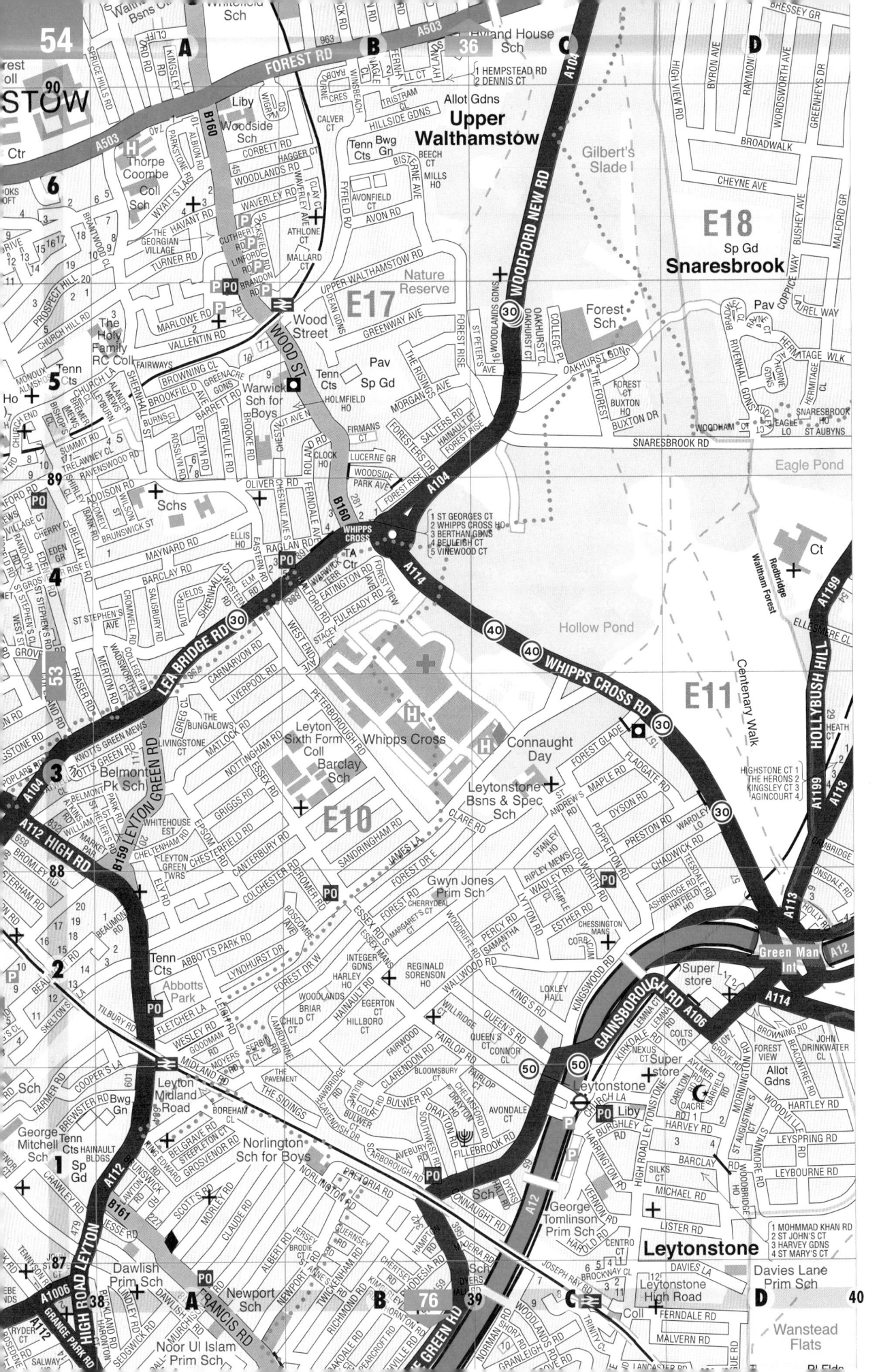
FOREST RD
A503
B160
Woodside Sch
Thorpe Coombe
Coll Sch
Upper Walthamstow
Allot Gdns
WOODFORD NEW RD
A104
Gilbert's Slade
E18
Sp Gd
Snaresbrook
E17
Nature Reserve
Wood Street
WOOD ST
Warwick Sch for Boys
The Holy Family RC Coll
Forest Sch
SNARESBROOK RD
Eagle Pond
WHIPPS CROSS
1 ST GEORGES CT
2 WHIPPS CROSS HO
3 BERTHAN GDNS
4 BEULEIGH CT
5 VINEWOOD CT
A114
Hollow Pond
WHIPPS CROSS RD
Redbridge
Waltham Forest
E11
Centenary Walk
HOLLYBUSH HILL
A1199
LEA BRIDGE RD
Leyton Sixth Form Coll
Barclay Sch
Whipps Cross
Connaught Day
Leytonstone Bsns & Spec Sch
E10
Belmont Pk Sch
LEYTON GREEN RD
B159
A112 HIGH RD
Gwyn Jones Prim Sch
HIGHSTONE CT 1
THE HERONS 2
KINGSLEY CT 3
AGINCOURT 4
Green Man Int
A12
A113
GAINSBOROUGH RD A106
Super store
Abbotts Park
Tenn Cts
Leyton Midland Road
George Mitchell Sch
Norlington Sch for Boys
Leytonstone
Allot Gdns
1 MOHMMAD KHAN RD
2 ST JOHN'S CT
3 HARVEY GDNS
4 ST MARY'S CT
George Tomlinson Prim Sch
Leytonstone
Davies Lane Prim Sch
Leytonstone High Road
Wanstead Flats
Dawlish Prim Sch
Newport Sch
FRANCIS RD
HIGH ROAD LEYTON
Noor Ul Islam Prim Sch
36
53
76
40
90
89
88
87
39
38

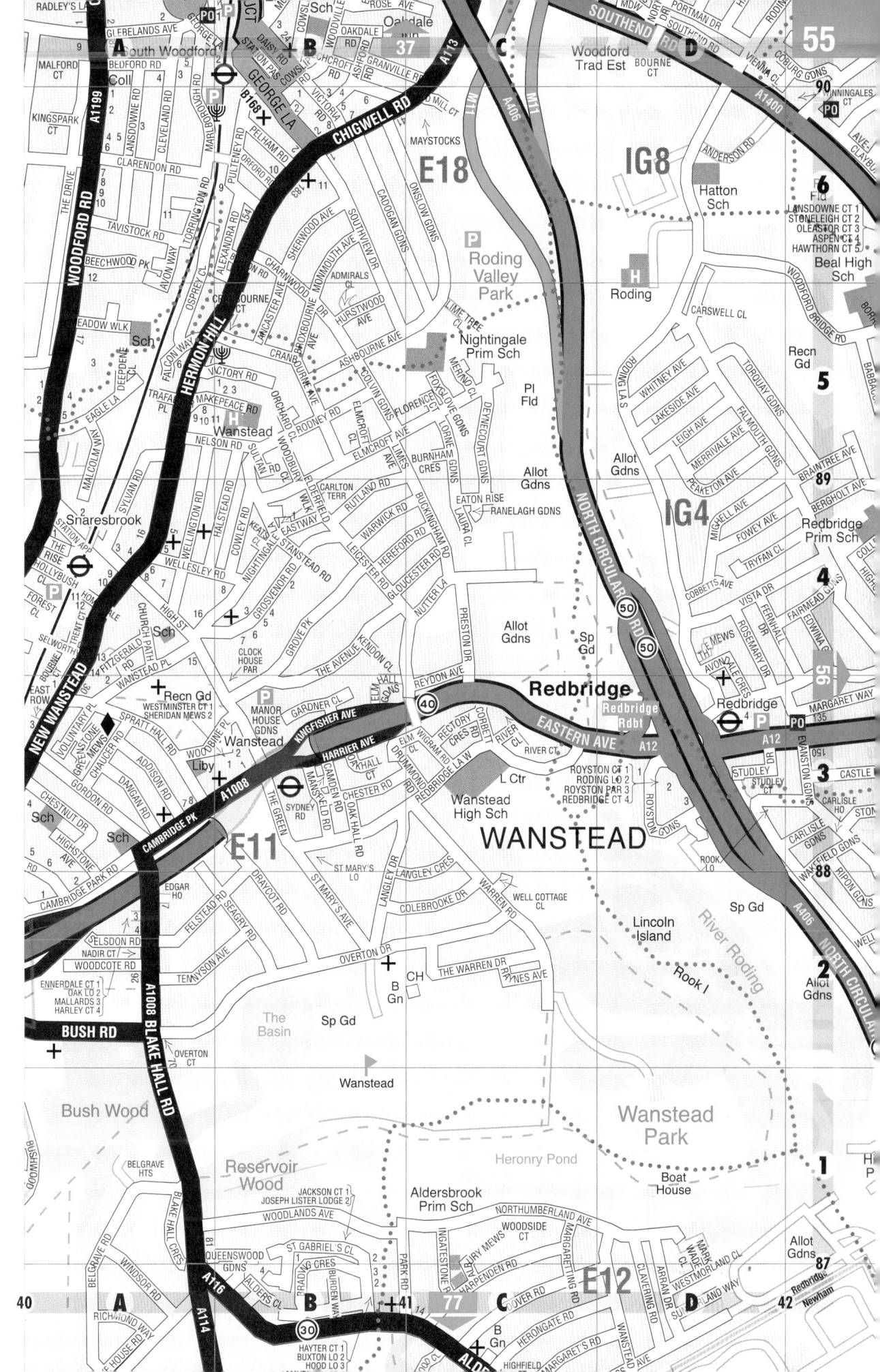
South Woodford
Woodford Trad Est
E18
IG8
Hatton Sch
Roding Valley Park
Roding
Nightingale Prim Sch
Wanstead
Snaresbrook
Recn Gd
Redbridge
Redbridge Rdbt
Eastern Ave
Kingfisher Ave
Harrier Ave
Cambridge Pk
Wanstead High Sch
WANSTEAD
E11
IG4
Redbridge Prim Sch
Beal High Sch
Lincoln Island
River Roding
Rook I
Wanstead Park
Heronry Pond
Boat House
Bush Wood
Reservoir Wood
The Basin
Sp Gd
Aldersbrook Prim Sch
E12
Woodford Rd
New Wanstead
Hermon Hill
Chigwell Rd
George La
North Circular Rd
Southend Rd
Blake Hall Rd
Bush Rd
Northumberland Ave
Woodlands Ave
Overton Dr
Allot Gdns
Pl Fld
L Ctr
Liby
37
56
77
40
41
42
A
B
C
D
1
2
3
4
5
6
Redbridge
Newham

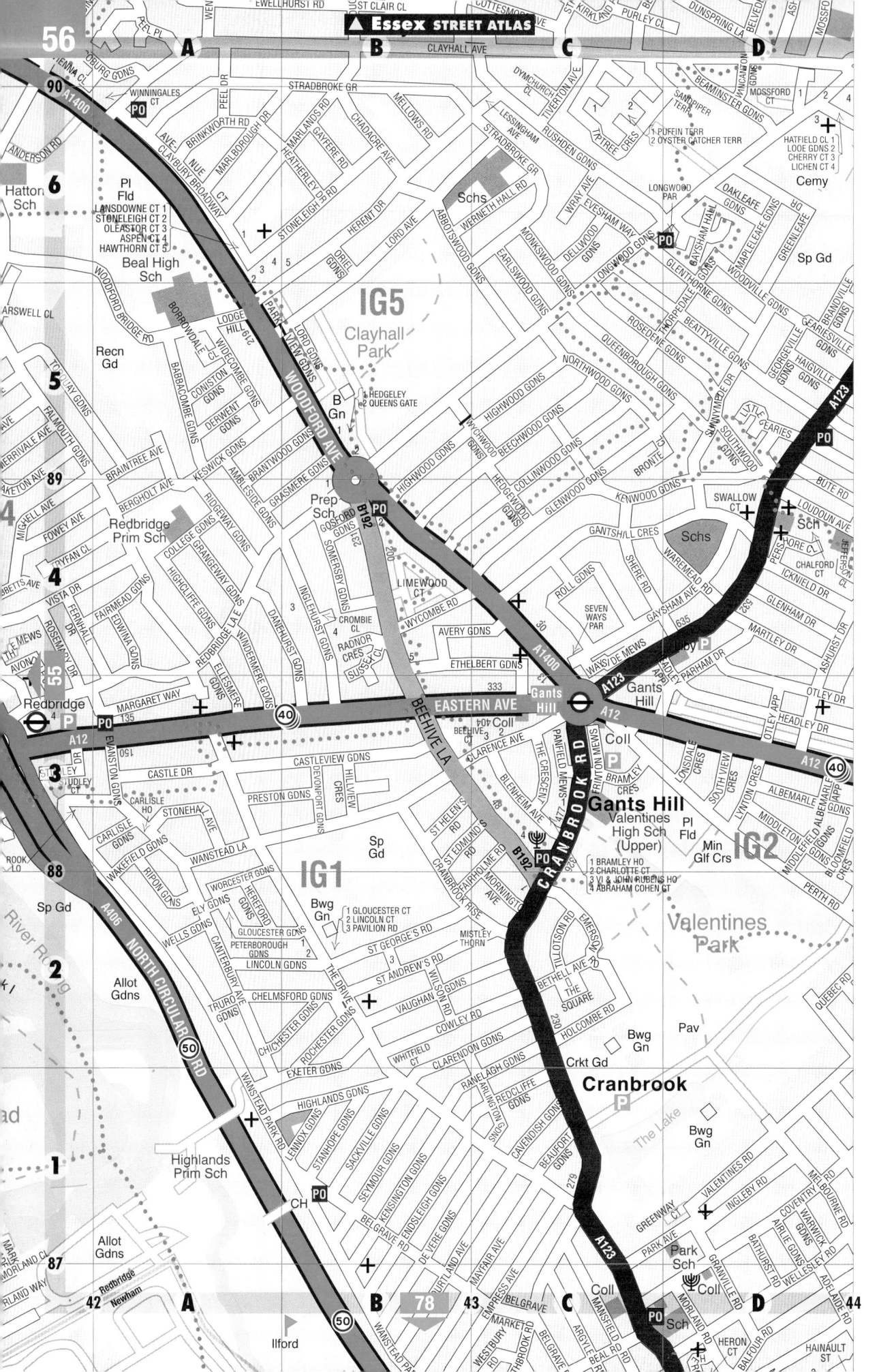
A
B
C
D
90
89
88
87
6
5
4
3
2
1
42
43
44
55
78
CLAYHALL AVE
STRADBROKE GR
WOODFORD AVE
WOODFORD BRIDGE RD
Beal High Sch
Hatton Sch
Pl Fld
Recn Gd
IG5
Clayhall Park
Prep Sch
Redbridge Prim Sch
Schs
Sp Gd
Cemy
LANSDOWNE CT 1
STONELEIGH CT 2
OLEASTOR CT 3
ASPEN CT 4
HAWTHORN CT 5
1 PUFFIN TERR
2 OYSTER CATCHER TERR
HATFIELD CL 1
LOOE GDNS 2
CHERRY CT 3
LICHEN CT 4
1 HEDGELEY
2 QUEENS GATE
LONGWOOD PAR
SEVEN WAYS PAR
GANTSHILL CRES
EASTERN AVE
Gants Hill
BEEHIVE LA
CRANBROOK RD
Redbridge
IG1
IG2
Gants Hill
Valentines High Sch (Upper)
Min Glf Crs
Valentines Park
1 BRAMLEY HO
2 CHARLOTTE CT
3 VI & JOHN RUBENS HO
4 ABRAHAM COHEN CT
1 GLOUCESTER CT
2 LINCOLN CT
3 PAVILION RD
NORTH CIRCULAR RD
Allot Gdns
River Roding
Highlands Prim Sch
Cranbrook
Crkt Gd
Bwg Gn
Pav
The Lake
Park Sch
Coll
Ilford
Redbridge
Newham
A12
A123
A1400
A406
B192

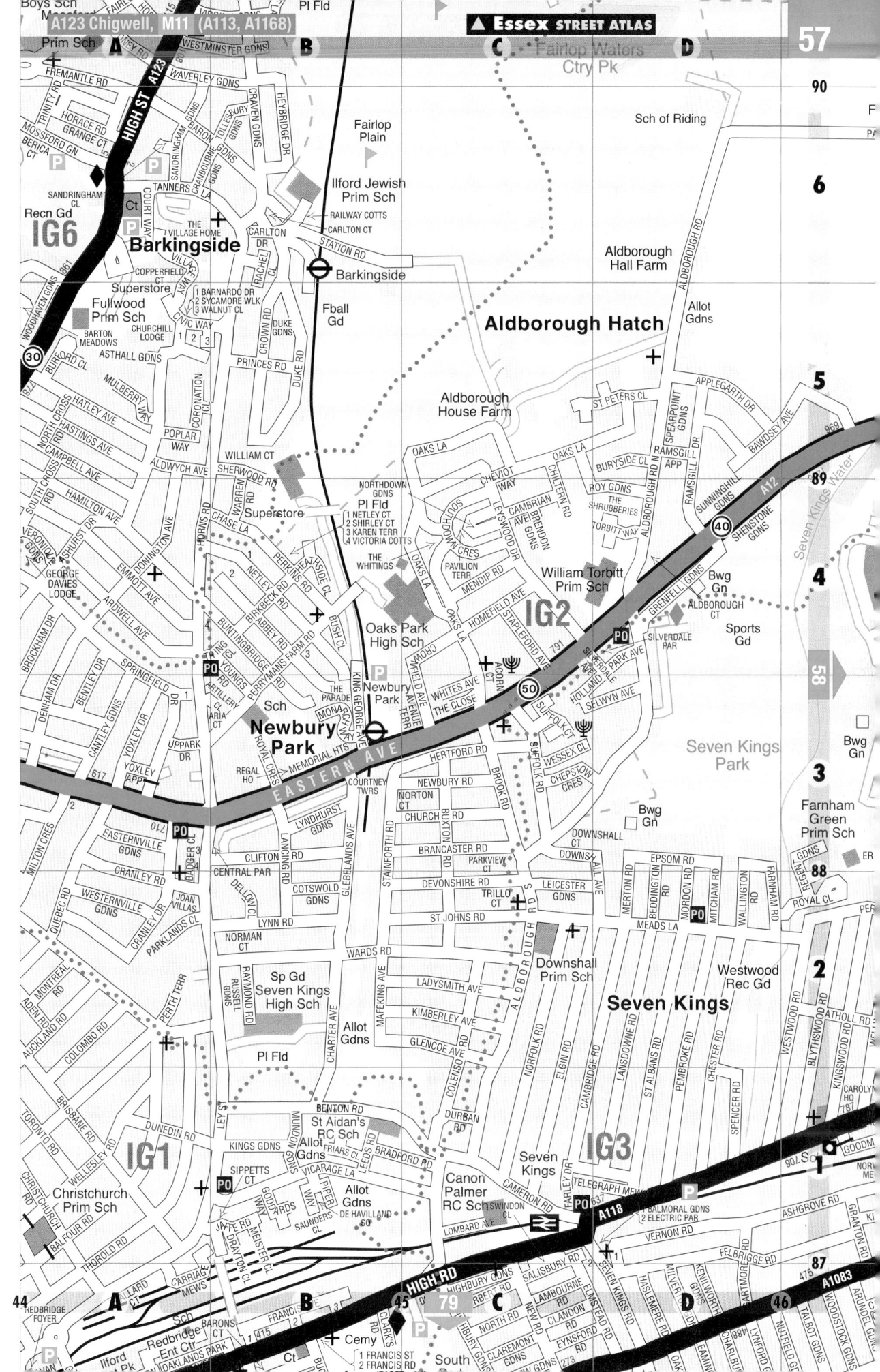
Fairlop Waters
Ctry Pk
Sch of Riding
Fairlop
Plain
Ilford Jewish
Prim Sch
RAILWAY COTTS
CARLTON CT
STATION RD
Barkingside
IG6
Recn Gd
Barkingside
HIGH ST
A123
WESTMINSTER GDNS
WAVERLEY GDNS
FREMANTLE RD
TRINITY RD
HORACE RD
GRANGE CT
MOSSFORD GN
BERICA CT
SANDRINGHAM CL
TANNERS
COURT WAY
THE VILLAGE HOME
CARLTON DR
RACHEL CL
CRAVEN GDNS
HEYBRIDGE DR
TOLLESBURY GDNS
CRANBOURNE GDNS
SANDRINGHAM GDNS
COPPERFIELD CT
Superstore
1 BARNARDO DR
2 SYCAMORE WLK
3 WALNUT CL
Fullwood
Prim Sch
BARTON MEADOWS
CHURCHILL LODGE
CIVIC WAY
ASTHALL GDNS
WOODHAVEN GDNS
BURFORD CL
MULBERRY WAY
CORONATION CL
PRINCES RD
CROWN RD
DUKE GDNS
DUKE RD
Fball
Gd
Aldborough Hatch
Aldborough
Hall Farm
ALDBOROUGH RD
Allot
Gdns
Aldborough
House Farm
ST PETERS CL
APPLEGARTH DR
SPEARPOINT GDNS
BAWDSEY AVE
RAMSGILL APP
RAMSGILL DR
BURYSIDE CL
OAKS LA
CHEVIOT WAY
CHILTERN RD
ROY GDNS
THE SHRUBBERIES
TORBITT WAY
ALDBOROUGH RD N
SUNNINGHILL GDNS
SHENSTONE GDNS
A12
Seven Kings Water
HATLEY AVE
HASTINGS AVE
NORTH CROSS RD
CAMPBELL AVE
HAMILTON AVE
SOUTH CROSS RD
POPLAR WAY
ALDWYCH AVE
WILLIAM CT
SHERWOOD RD
NORTHDOWN GDNS
Pl Fld
1 NETLEY CT
2 SHIRLEY CT
3 KAREN TERR
4 VICTORIA COTTS
Superstore
WARREN RD
CHASE LA
HORNS RD
DONINGTON AVE
EMMOTT AVE
ASHURST DR
VERONICA GDNS
GEORGE DAVIES LODGE
SOUTHDOWN CRES
LEYSWOOD DR
CAMBRIAN AVE
BRENDON GDNS
PAVILION TERR
MENDIP RD
THE WHITINGS
OAKS LA
William Torbitt
Prim Sch
Bwg Gn
ALDBOROUGH CT
Sports Gd
SILVERDALE PAR
IG2
HOMEFIELD AVE
STAPLEFORD AVE
PERKINS RD
HEATHSIDE CL
NETLEY RD
BIRKBECK RD
ABBEY RD
BUNTINGBRIDGE RD
PERRYMANS FARM RD
BUSH CL
ARDWELL AVE
SPRINGFIELD DR
BROCKHAM DR
BENTLEY DR
DENHAM DR
CANTLEY GDNS
YOXLEY DR
UPPARK DR
YOXLEY APP
Oaks Park
High Sch
CROWHILL AVE
WHITES AVE
THE CLOSE
AVENUE TERR
ACORN CT
PARK AVE
SILVERDALE AVE
HOLLAND AVE
SELWYN AVE
SUFFOLK CT
WESSEX CL
SUFFOLK RD
CHEPSTOW CRES
Newbury
Park
THE PARADE
KING GEORGE AVE
MONKCHESTER
ARTILLERY CL
ARIA CT
YOUNGS RD
Sch
Newbury
Park
MEMORIAL HTS
ROYAL CRES
REGAL HO
EASTERN AVE
COURTNEY TWRS
HERTFORD RD
NEWBURY RD
NORTON CT
CHURCH RD
BUXTON RD
BROOK RD
Seven Kings
Park
Bwg Gn
58
Farnham
Green
Prim Sch
REGENT GDNS
ROYAL CL
ER
MILTON CRES
EASTERNVILLE GDNS
BADGER CL
CRANLEY RD
WESTERNVILLE GDNS
JOAN VILLAS
CENTRAL PAR
DELLOW CL
PARKLANDS CL
CRANLEY DR
LYNDHURST GDNS
LANCING RD
CLIFTON RD
COTSWOLD GDNS
GLEBELANDS AVE
STAINFORTH RD
BRANCASTER RD
PARKVIEW CT
DEVONSHIRE RD
TRILLO CT
ST JOHNS RD
LYNN RD
NORMAN CT
WARDS RD
DOWNSHALL CT
DOWNSHALL AVE
LEICESTER GDNS
EPSOM RD
MERTON RD
BEDDINGTON RD
MORDON RD
MITCHAM RD
WALLINGTON RD
FARNHAM RD
MEADS LA
QUEBEC RD
MONTREAL RD
ADEN RD
AUCKLAND RD
COLOMBO RD
PERTH TERR
RUSSELL GDNS
RAYMOND RD
Sp Gd
Seven Kings
High Sch
CHARTER AVE
Allot
Gdns
MAFEKING AVE
LADYSMITH AVE
KIMBERLEY AVE
GLENCOE AVE
ALDBOROUGH RD S
Downshall
Prim Sch
Seven Kings
Westwood
Rec Gd
NORFOLK RD
ELGIN RD
CAMBRIDGE RD
LANSDOWNE RD
ST ALBANS RD
PEMBROKE RD
CHESTER RD
SPENCER RD
WESTWOOD RD
BLYTHSWOOD RD
ATHOLL RD
KINGSWOOD RD
Pl Fld
TORONTO RD
BRISBANE RD
DUNEDIN RD
WELLESLEY RD
IG1
LEYS CL
BENTON RD
MUNDON GDNS
St Aidan's
RC Sch
COLENSO RD
DURBAN RD
IG3
KINGS GDNS
Allot
Gdns
FRIARS CL
LEEDS RD
BRADFORD RD
SIPPETTS CT
VICARAGE LA
Seven
Kings
TELEGRAPH MEWS
Canon
Palmer
RC Sch
CAMERON RD
FARLEY DR
Christchurch
Prim Sch
CHRISTCHURCH RD
BALFOUR RD
THOROLD RD
GODDARDS WAY
PIPERS WAY
Allot
Gdns
DE HAVILLAND SQ
SAUNDERS CL
JAYE RD
DRAYTON CL
MEISTER CL
SWINDON CL
LOMBARD AVE
A118
1 BALMORAL GDNS
2 ELECTRIC PAR
ASHGROVE RD
VERNON RD
FELBRIGGE RD
GRANTON RD
CARRIAGE MEWS
ALLARD CT
REDBRIDGE FOYER
HIGH RD
79
HIGHBURY GDNS
SALISBURY RD
LAMBOURNE RD
CLANDON RD
ELMSTEAD RD
SEVEN KINGS RD
HASLEMERE RD
MILVERTON GDNS
KENILWORTH GDNS
GARTMORE RD
NORTH RD
NEW RD
CLAREMONT GDNS
EYNSFORD RD
A1083
TALBOT GDNS
WOODSTOCK GDNS
ARUNDEL GDNS
NUTFIELD GDNS
LYNFORD GDNS
Sch
BARONS CT
FRANCIS
Redbridge
Ent Ctr
OAKLANDS PARK
Ilford
Cemy
1 FRANCIS ST
2 FRANCIS RD
South
44
45
46
90
89
88
87
6
5
4
3
2
1
A
B
C
D

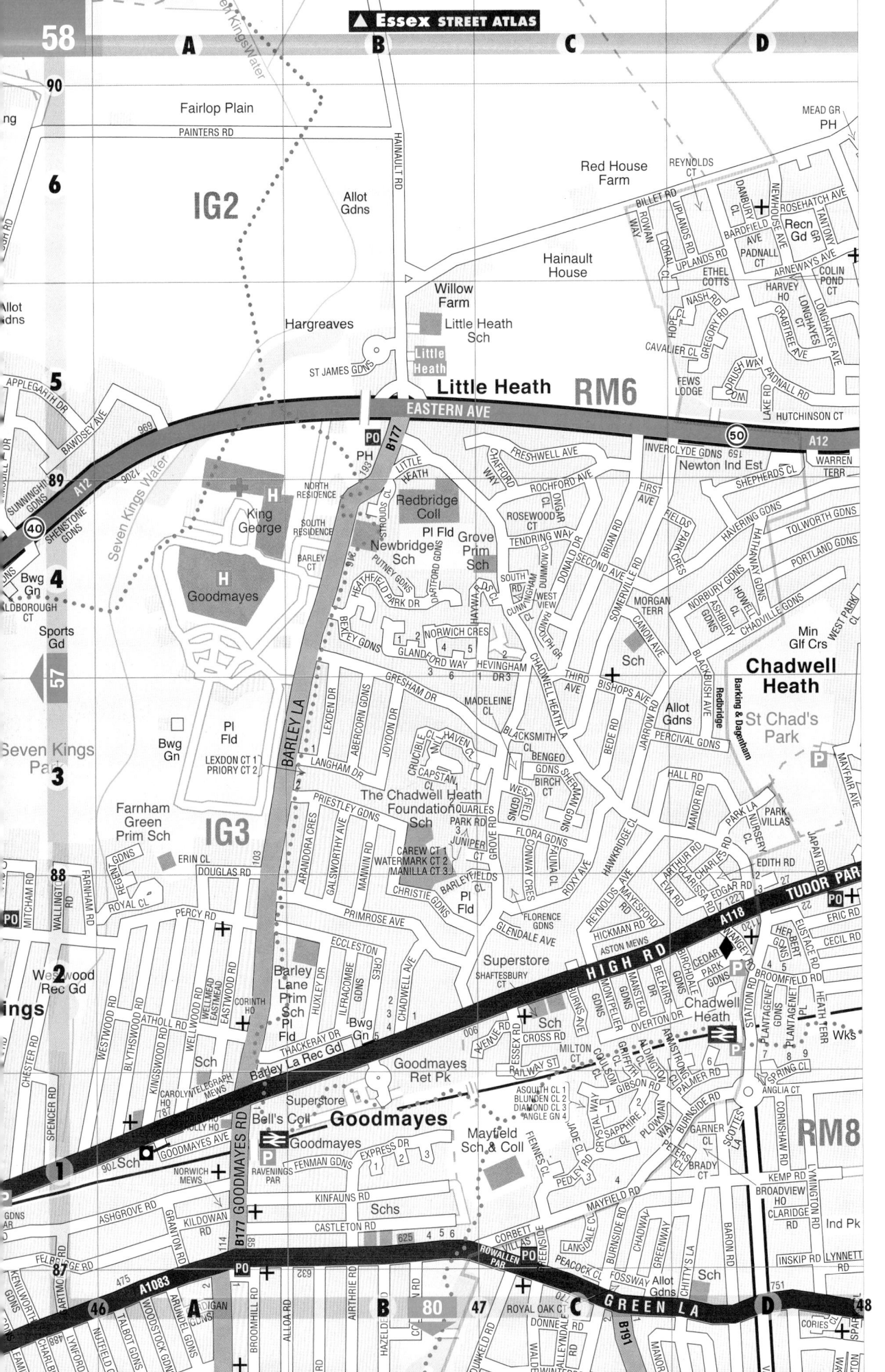

A   B   C   D

90

ng

6

Fairlop Plain

PAINTERS RD

IG2

Allot
Gdns

Hargreaves

ST JAMES GDNS

Little
Heath

5

Allot
dns

APPLEGARTH DR

BAWDSEY AVE

SUNNINGH
GDNS

89

SHENSTONE GDNS

A12

40

Bwg
Gn

LDBOROUGH
CT

4

Sports
Gd

57

Seven Kings
Par

3

Farnham
Green
Prim Sch

IG3

88

MITCHAM RD

FARNHAM RD

WALLINGT
GDNS

P.O

Westwood
Rec Gd

2

ings

HAINAULT RD

Willow
Farm

Little Heath
Sch

Little Heath

EASTERN AVE

B177

PO

PH

North
Residence

King
George

H

South
Residence

BARLEY CT

H

Goodmayes

Pl
Fld

Bwg
Gn

LEXDON CT 1
PRIORY CT 2

BARLEY LA

LEXDON DR

ABERCORN GDNS

GALSWORTHY AVE

PRIESTLEY GDNS

MANNIN
LANGHAM DR

ARANDORA CRES

ERIN CL

REGENT
GDNS

DOUGLAS RD

ROYAL CL

PERCY RD

WESTWOOD RD

WELLMEAD
RD

ATHOLL RD

EASTMEAD

WELLWOOD RD

Sch

CORINTH
HO

HUXLEY DR

ILFRACOMBE
GDNS

Barley
Lane
Prim Sch
Pl
Fld

Bwg
Gn 5

THACKERAY DR

Barley La Rec Gd

KINGSWOOD RD

BLYTHSWOOD RD

SPENCER RD

CHESTER RD

CAROLYN
HO

TELEGRAPH
MEWS

HOLLY HO

NORWICH
MEWS

GOODMAYES AVE

P

Bell's Coll

Goodmayes

Sch

B177 GOODMAYES RD

1

GDNS

87

ASHGROVE RD

KENILWORTH

46

A1083

GRANTON RD

KILDOWAN
RD

BROOMHILL RD

475

632

A

LOGAN

ARUNDEL GDNS

WOODSTOCK GDNS

NUTFIELD GDNS

TALBOT RD

LYNFORD

CHARLB

FELBRIDGE RD

Hainault
House

Red House
Farm

BILLET RD

REYNOLDS
CT

UPLANDS RD

ETHEL
COTTS

CORAL CL

HOPE
CL

NASH RD

CAVALIER CL

GREGORY RD

MEAD GR
PH

DANBURY
CL

BARDFIELD
AVE

NEWHOUSE AVE
AVE

ROSEHATCH AVE

TANTONY

Recn
Gd

PADNALL
CT

ARNEWAYS AVE

COLIN
POND
CT

HARVEY
HO

LONGHAYES
CT

CRABTREE
AVE

LONGHAYES
AVE

BRUSH WAY

COM

LAKE RD

PADNALL RD

FEWS
LODGE

HUTCHINSON CT

RM6

50

A12

WARREN
TERR

Newton Ind Est

INVERCLYDE GDNS

SHEPHERDS CL

FIRST
AVE

FIELDS
PARK CRS

HAVERING GDNS

HATHWAY GDNS

TOLWORTH GDNS

PORTLAND GDNS

WEST PARK

FRESHWELL AVE

CHAFFORD
WAY

ROCHFORD AVE

ONGAR
RD

ROSEWOOD
CT

TENDRING WAY

BRIAN RD

SECOND AVE

DONALD DR

NORBURY
GDNS

ASHBURY

HOWELL
CL

CHADVILLE GDNS

Min
Glf Crs

Chadwell
Heath

Redbridge
Coll

Pl Fld

Newbridge
Sch

Grove
Prim
Sch

STROUDS CL

LITTLE
HEATH

HEATHFIELD
PARK DR

PUTNEY GDNS

DARTFORD RD

BEXLEY GDNS

1 2
NORWICH CRES
4 5
GLANDFORD WAY
6
HEVINGHAM
1 DR 3

GRESHAM DR

JOYDON DR

CRUCIBLE
CL HAVEN CL

MADELEINE
CL

CAPSTAN
CL

QUARLES
PARK RD

JUNIPER
GT

CAREW CT 1
WATERMARK CT 2
MANILLA CT 3

3

BARLEYFIELDS

Pl
Fld

GROVE RD

FLORA GDNS

CONWAY CRES

GLENDALE AVE

FLORENCE
GDNS

ROXY AVE

CHADWELL AVE

ECCLESTON
CRES

PRIMROSE AVE

CHRISTIE GDNS

The Chadwell Heath
Foundation
Sch

WESTFIELD
GDNS

BLACKSMITH
CL

BENGEO
GDNS

BIRCH
CT

CHADWELL HEATH LA

THIRD
AVE

BISHOPS AVE

BEDE RD

SHERMAN GDNS

HALL RD

MANOR RD

HAWKRIDGE AVE

RANDOLPH GR

HAYWA
RD

CUNN

SOUTH
RD

WEST
VIEW

WEST

SOMERVILLE RD

MORGAN
TERR

CANON
AVE

Sch

JARROW RD

PERCIVAL GDNS

Allot
Gdns

Redbridge

Barking & Dagenham

St Chad's
Park

P

MAYFAIR AVE

PARK LA

NURSERY

PARK
VILLAS

ARTHUR RD

EVA RD

CLARISSA
RD

CHARLES RD

EDGAR RD

JAPAN GDNS

EDITH RD

3 27

TUDOR PAR

A118

HER
BERT
GDNS

EUSTACE RD

CECIL RD

ERIC RD

Superstore

SHAFTESBURY
CT

Aston Mews

HIGH RD

BELFAIRS
GDNS

MANSTEAD
GDNS

MONTPELIER
GDNS

Sch

AVENUE RD

ESSEX RD

CROSS RD

RAILWAY ST

MILTON
CT

REYNOLDS
RD

HICKMAN
RD

WAVESFORD
RD

ARTHUR RD

GRIFFIN
RD

COULSON CL

GIBSON RD

BURNS AVE

OVERTON DR

ARMSTRONG RD

BIRCHDALE
GDNS

CEDAR
PARK
GDNS

Chadwell
Heath

STATION RD

PLANTAGENET
GDNS

HEATH TERR

Wks

P

Goodmayes
Ret Pk

Superstore

DIAMOND CL 3
ANGLE GN 4

ASQUITH CL 1
BLUNDEN CL 2

Mayfield
Sch & Coll

CRYSTAL WAY

SAPPHIRE
CL

JADE CL

PEDLEY RD

PLOWMAN
WAY

BROADWAY

PETERS
CL

BRADY
CT

GARNER
CL

BURNSIDE RD

SCOTTES
LA

CORNSHAW RD

ANGLIA CT

SPRING CL

RM8

RAVENINGS
PAR

FENMAN GDNS

EXPRESS
DR

1 2

KINFAUNS RD

Schs

CASTLETON RD

625 4 5 6

CORBETT
VILLAS

GREENSIDE

BURNSIDE RD

CHADWAY

GREENWAY

LANGLANDS

PEACOCK CL

P.O

ROWALLEN PAR

ROYAL OAK LA

DONNE

DUNKELD RD

WALDEN

WINTERB

FOSSWAY

Allot
Gdns

CHITTY'S LA

B

80

47

C

GREEN LA

B191

MANOR

KEMP RD

CLARIDGE
RD

LYMINGTON
RD

Ind Pk

BROADVIEW
HO

BARON RD

INSKIP RD

LYNNETT
RD

751

D

48

CORIES

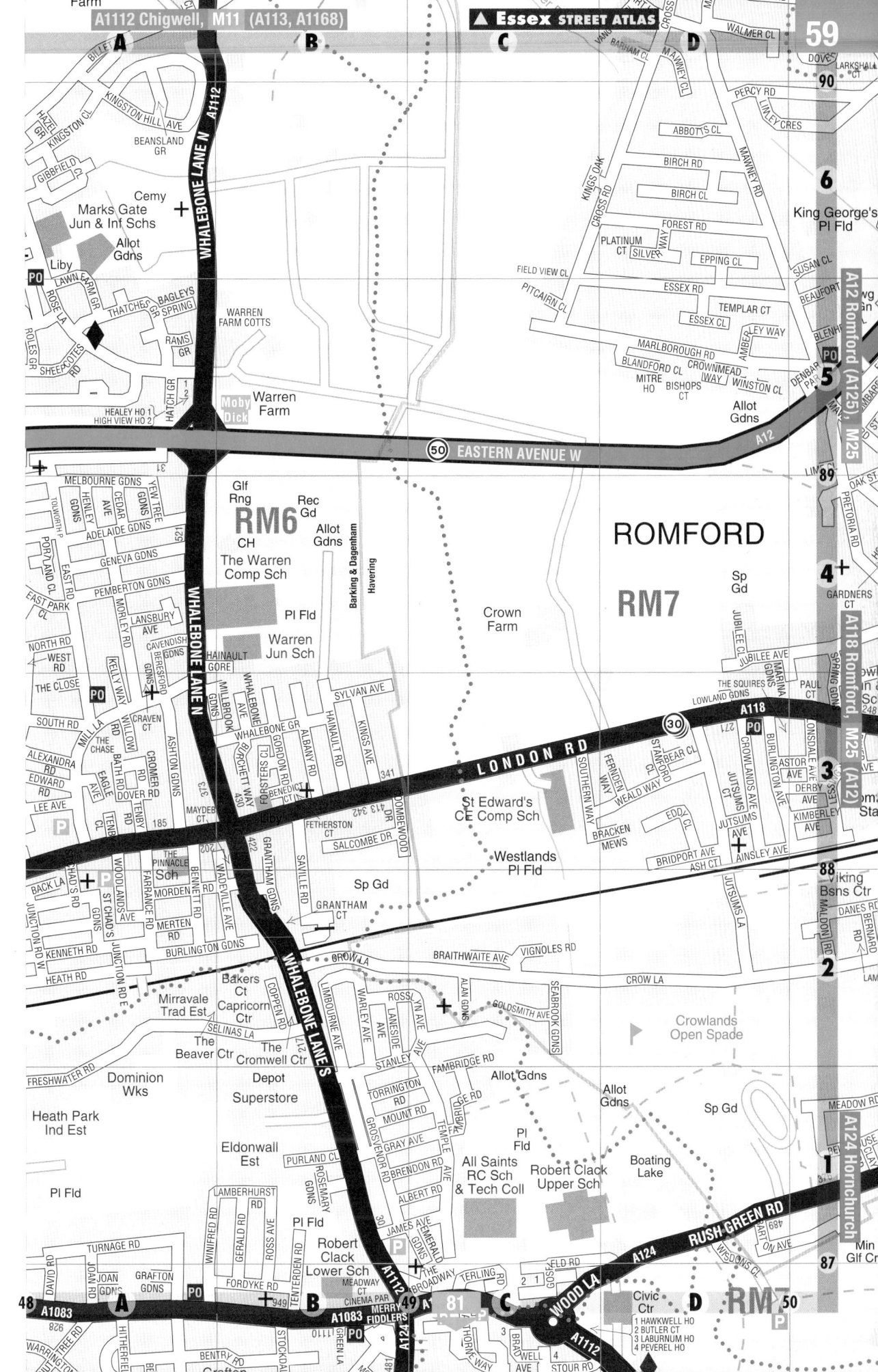
A
B
C
D
Farm
BILLET
KINGSTON HILL AVE
KINGSTON CL
HAZEL GR
BEANSLAND GR
GIBBFIELD CL
A1112
WHALEBONE LANE N
Cemy
Marks Gate Jun & Inf Schs
Allot Gdns
Liby
PO
LAWN FARM GR
ROSE LA
THATCHES GR
BAGLEYS SPRING
RAMS GR
ROLES GR
SHEEPCOTES RD
WARREN FARM COTTS
HATCH GR
HEALEY HO 1
HIGH VIEW HO 2
Moby Dick
Warren Farm
WALMER CL
BARHAM CL
MAWNEY CL
CROSS RD
DOVES
LARKSHALL CT
90
PERCY RD
LINLEY CRES
ABBOTTS CL
BIRCH RD
BIRCH CL
MAWNEY RD
KINGS OAK
6
King George's Pl Fld
FOREST RD
PLATINUM CT
SILVER WAY
EPPING CL
FIELD VIEW CL
PITCAIRN CL
SUSAN CL
ESSEX RD
BEAUFORT
TEMPLAR CT
ESSEX CL
AMBERLEY WAY
MARLBOROUGH RD
BLANDFORD CL
CROWNMEAD WAY
MITRE HO
BISHOPS CT
WINSTON CL
DENBAR PAR
BLENHEIM
PO
5
Allot Gdns
A12 Romford (A125), M25
50
EASTERN AVENUE W
A12
89
LIME CL
OAK ST
PRETORIA RD
MELBOURNE GDNS
YEW TREE GDNS
HENLEY GDNS
CEDAR AVE
TOLWORTH P
ADELAIDE GDNS
Glf Rng
RM6
Rec Gd
Allot Gdns
CH
The Warren Comp Sch
ROMFORD
PORTLAND CL
EAST RD
GENEVA GDNS
PEMBERTON GDNS
EAST PARK CL
MORLEY RD
LANSBURY AVE
Pl Fld
Barking & Dagenham
Havering
Crown Farm
RM7
Sp Gd
4
GARDNERS CT
NORTH RD
WEST RD
CAVENDISH GDNS
BERESFORD GDNS
Warren Jun Sch
HAINAULT GORE
JUBILEE CL
JUBILEE AVE
A118 Romford, M25 (A12)
THE CLOSE
KELLY WAY
PO
WHALEBONE AVE
MILLBROOK GDNS
SYLVAN AVE
THE SQUIRES
MARINA GDNS
SPRING GDNS
PAUL CT
LOWLAND GDNS
A118
SOUTH RD
CRAVEN CT
WILLOW RD
MILL LA
THE CHASE
ASHTON GDNS
WHALEBONE GR
HAINAULT RD
KINGS AVE
30
PO
ALEXANDRA RD
EDWARD RD
CROMER RD
BATH RD
EAGLE AVE
DOVER RD
BURCHETT WAY
FORSTERS CL
GORDON RD
ALBANY RD
BENEDICT CT
LONDON RD
SOUTHERN WAY
FERNDEN WAY
STANFORD CL
BEAR CL
CROWLANDS AVE
BURLINGTON AVE
ASTOR AVE
LONSDALE AVE
3
LEE AVE
TENBY RD
MAYDEB CT
Liby
DOOMBEWOOD DR
FETHERSTON CT
St Edward's CE Comp Sch
WEALD WAY
JUTSUMS CT
DERBY AVE
KIMBERLEY AVE
P
THE PINNACLE Sch
SALCOMBE DR
BRACKEN MEWS
EDDY CL
JUTSUMS AVE
BRIDPORT AVE
ASH CT
AINSLEY AVE
Westlands Pl Fld
88
Viking Bsns Ctr
BACK LA
ST CHAD'S RD
WOODLANDS AVE
ST CHAD'S GDNS
FARRANCE RD
MORDEN RD
BENNETT RD
WADEVILLE AVE
GRANTHAM GDNS
SAVILLE RD
Sp Gd
GRANTHAM CT
JUTSUMS LA
DANES RD
BERNARD RD
MALDON RD
JUNCTION RD W
KENNETH RD
MERTEN RD
BURLINGTON GDNS
HEATH RD
JUNCTION RD E
CROW LA
BRAITHWAITE AVE
VIGNOLES RD
CROW LA
2
Bakers Ct
Mirravale Trad Est
Capricorn Ctr
COPPEN RD
WHALEBONE LANE S
LIMBOURNE AVE
WARLEY AVE
ROSSLYN AVE
ALAN GDNS
GOLDSMITH AVE
SEABROOK GDNS
Crowlands Open Space
SELINAS LA
The Beaver Ctr
The Cromwell Ctr
LANESIDE AVE
STANLEY AVE
FAMBRIDGE RD
FRESHWATER RD
Dominion Wks
Depot
Superstore
TORRINGTON RD
MOUNT RD
Allot Gdns
Allot Gdns
Sp Gd
MEADOW RD
Heath Park Ind Est
GROSVENOR RD
TEMPLE AVE
Pl Fld
Eldonwall Est
GRAY AVE
PURLAND CL
ROSEMARY GDNS
BRENDON RD
All Saints RC Sch & Tech Coll
Robert Clack Upper Sch
Boating Lake
1
A124 Hornchurch
Pl Fld
LAMBERHURST RD
ALBERT RD
WINIFRED RD
GERALD RD
ROSS AVE
TENTERDEN RD
Pl Fld
JAMES AVE
EMERALD GDNS
RUSH GREEN RD
A124
WISDONS CL
Min Glf Cr
TURNAGE RD
DAVID RD
JOAN RD
JOAN GDNS
GRAFTON GDNS
Robert Clack Lower Sch
PO
FORDYKE RD
THE BROADWAY
TERLING RD
87
48
A1083
MEADWAY CT
CINEMA PAR
MERRY FIDDLERS
49
81
WOOD LA
Civic Ctr
RM7
50
1 HAWKWELL HO
2 BUTLER CT
3 LABURNUM HO
4 PEVEREL HO
A1083
PO
A124
A1112
BENTRY RD
STOCKDALE
GREEN LA
HITHERFIELD
WARRINGTON
BRADWELL AVE
STOUR RD
P

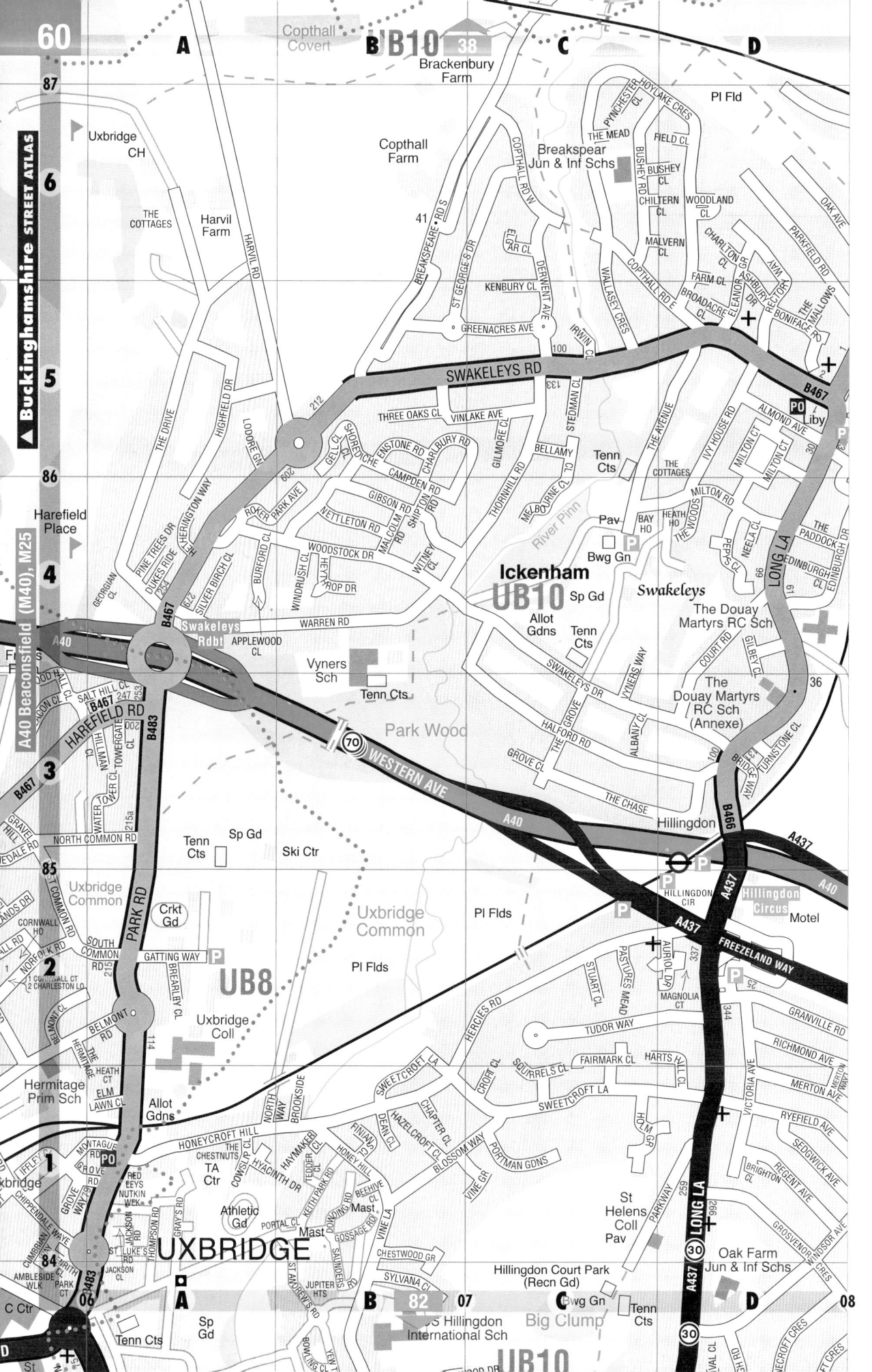
Buckinghamshire STREET ATLAS
A40 Beaconsfield (M40), M25
UB10
38
Copthall Covert
Brackenbury Farm
A
B
C
D
87
86
85
84
6
5
4
3
2
1
Uxbridge CH
Copthall Farm
Breakspear Jun & Inf Schs
Pl Fld
THE COTTAGES
Harvil Farm
HARVIL RD
PYNCHESTER CL
HOYLAKE CRES
THE MEAD
FIELD CL
BUSHEY RD
BUSHEY CL
CHILTERN CL
WOODLAND CL
MALVERN CL
COPTHALL RD W
COPTHALL RD E
BREAKSPEARE RD S
ST GEORGE'S DR
ELGAR CL
DERWENT AVE
KENBURY CL
GREENACRES AVE
IRWIN CL
WALLASEY CRES
CHARLTON CL
FARM CL
BROADACRE CL
ELEANOR GR
ASHBURY DR
RECTORY WAY
BONIFACE RD
THE MALLOWS
PARKFIELD RD
OAK AVE
SWAKELEYS RD
B467
PO
Liby
THE DRIVE
HIGHFIELD DR
LODORE GN
THREE OAKS CL
VINLAKE AVE
GILMORE CL
STEDMAN CL
BELLAMY CL
THE AVENUE
IVY HOUSE RD
ALMOND AVE
MILTON CT
MILTON RD
GELL CL
SHOREDITCH CL
ENSTONE RD
CHARLBURY RD
CAMPDEN RD
GIBSON RD
NETTLETON RD
SHIPTON RD
MALCOLM RD
THORNHILL RD
MELBOURNE CL
Tenn Cts
THE COTTAGES
HERRINGTON WAY
ROKER PARK AVE
WOODSTOCK DR
WITNEY CL
River Pinn
Pav
BAY HO
HEATH HO
THE WOODS
PEPYS CL
NEELA CL
THE PADDOCK
EDINBURGH CL
EDINBURGH DR
LONG LA
Harefield Place
PINE TREES DR
DUKES RIDE
GEORGIAN CL
SILVER BIRCH CL
BURFORD CL
WINDRUSH CL
HEYTHROP DR
WARREN RD
Bwg Gn
Ickenham
UB10
Sp Gd
Swakeleys
The Douay Martyrs RC Sch
Allot Gdns
Swakeleys Rdbt
APPLEWOOD CL
A40
Vyners Sch
COURT RD
GILBEY CL
VYNERS WAY
SWAKELEYS DR
The Douay Martyrs RC Sch (Annexe)
HARFIELD RD
SALT HILL CL
HILLMAN CL
TOWERGATE CL
B483
Park Wood
WESTERN AVE
70
THE GROVE
HALFORD RD
ALBANY CL
GROVE CL
THE CHASE
TURNSTONE CL
BRIDGE WAY
B466
Hillingdon
A437
WATER TOWER CL
GRAVEL HILL
NORTH COMMON RD
Tenn Cts
Sp Gd
Ski Ctr
Uxbridge Common
ST COMMON RD
CORNWALL HO
Crkt Gd
PARK RD
Pl Flds
HILLINGDON CIR
Hillingdon Circus
Motel
FREEZELAND WAY
NORFOLK RD
SOUTH COMMON RD
GATTING WAY
BREARLEY CL
UB8
Pl Flds
STUART CL
PASTURES MEAD
AURIOL DR
MAGNOLIA CT
1 CORNWALL CT
2 CHARLESTON LO
BELMONT CL
BELMONT RD
Uxbridge Coll
HERCIES RD
TUDOR WAY
GRANVILLE RD
RICHMOND AVE
THE HERMITAGE
HEATH CT
ELM LAWN CL
Hermitage Prim Sch
Allot Gdns
CROFT CL
SQUIRRELS CL
FAIRMARK CL
HARTS HALL CL
MERTON AVE
MERTON WAY
SWEETCROFT LA
NORTH WAY
BROOKSIDE
HOLM GR
VICTORIA AVE
RYEFIELD AVE
HONEYCROFT HILL
THE CHESTNUTS
TA Ctr
COWSLIP CL
HYACINTH DR
HAYMAKER CL
TEDDER CL
HAZELCROFT CL
CHAPTER CL
DEAN CL
FINIAN CL
BLOSSOM WAY
PORTMAN GDNS
SEDGWICK AVE
MONTAGUE RD
GROVE WAY
IFFLEY CL
CHIPPENDALE WAYE
NUTKIN WLK
REDLEYS
KEITH PARK RD
HONEY HILL
BEEHIVE CL
VINE GR
PARKWAY
St Helens Coll Pav
LONG LA
BRIGHTON CL
REGENT AVE
GROSVENOR CRES
WINDSOR AVE
Uxbridge
Athletic Gd
Mast
DOWDING RD
GOSSAGE RD
VINE LA
PORTAL CL
ST LUKE'S RD
JACKSON RD
THOMPSON RD
GRAY'S RD
UXBRIDGE
CHESTWOOD GR
SYLVANA CL
SAUNDERS RD
JUPITER HTS
ST ANDREW'S RD
Hillingdon Court Park (Recn Gd)
Bwg Gn
Tenn Cts
Oak Farm Jun & Inf Schs
CUMBRIAN WAY
AMBLESIDE WLK
PARK CT
JACKSON CL
Sp Gd
Tenn Cts
C Ctr
82
07
06
08
Big Clump
Hillingdon International Sch
BOWLING CL
UB10

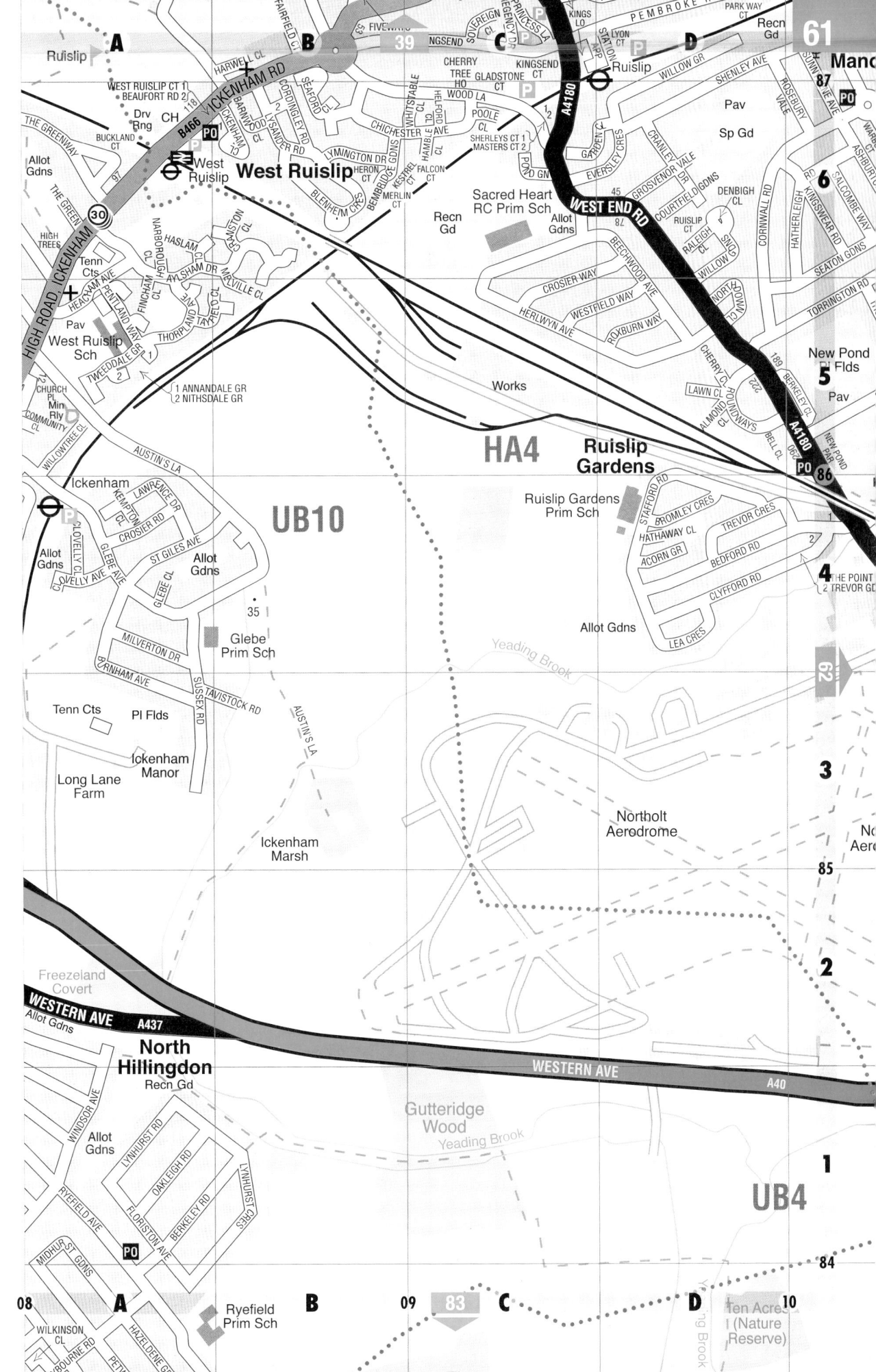
West Ruislip
Ruislip Gardens
HA4
UB10
UB4
Ickenham
North Hillingdon
Northolt Aerodrome
Ickenham Marsh
Ickenham Manor
Long Lane Farm
Gutteridge Wood
Freezeland Covert
Yeading Brook
Ruislip
West Ruislip Sch
Sacred Heart RC Prim Sch
Ruislip Gardens Prim Sch
Glebe Prim Sch
Ryefield Prim Sch
Ten Acres (Nature Reserve)
New Pond Pl Flds
Works
WESTERN AVE
A40
A437
A4180
B466
WEST END RD
HIGH ROAD, ICKENHAM
ICKENHAM RD
AUSTIN'S LA
SUSSEX RD
BURNHAM AVE
MILVERTON DR
TAVISTOCK RD
GLEBE AVE
ST GILES AVE
CLOVELLY AVE
CROSIER RD
LAWRENCE DR
KEMPTON CL
BEECHWOOD AVE
CROSIER WAY
WESTFIELD WAY
HERLWYN AVE
ROXBURN WAY
STAFFORD RD
BROMLEY CRES
HATHAWAY CL
ACORN GR
TREVOR CRES
BEDFORD RD
CLYFFORD RD
LEA CRES
SHENLEY AVE
WILLOW GR
CORNWALL RD
HATHERLEIGH RD
KINGSWEAR RD
SALCOMBE WAY
SEATON GDNS
TORRINGTON RD
LYNHURST RD
OAKLEIGH RD
BERKELEY RD
FLORISTON AVE
RYEFIELD AVE
WINDSOR AVE
LYNHURST CRES
MIDHURST GDNS
WILKINSON CL
HAZELDENE GDNS
1 ANNANDALE GR
2 NITHSDALE GR
1 THE POINT
2 TREVOR GDNS
08
09
10
84
85
86
87
A
B
C
D
1
2
3
4
5
6

39
62
83

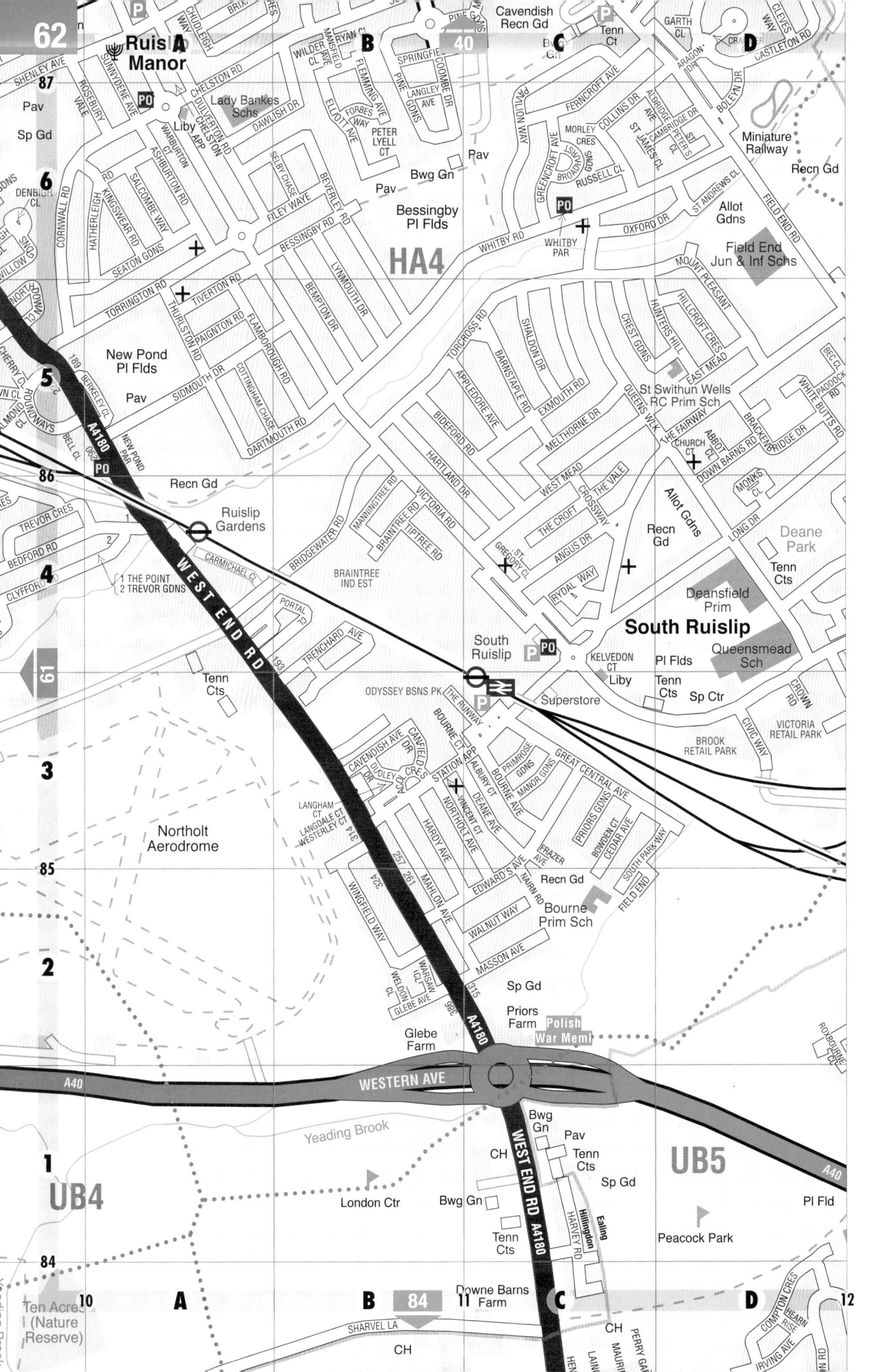
Ruislip Manor
Cavendish Recn Gd
Tenn Ct
40
A
B
C
D
87
Pav
Sp Gd
6
5
86
4
3
85
2
1
84
10
11
12
61
84
SHENLEY AVE
ROSEBURY VALE
SUNNYDENE AVE
CHUDLEIGH WAY
CHELSTON RD
DULVERTON RD
CHELSTON APP
Lady Bankes Schs
DAWLISH DR
WILDER CL
RYAN CL
MANSFIELD AVE
FLEMMING AVE
ELLIOTT AVE
FORBES WAY
PETER LYELL CT
SPRINGFIELD
PINE GDNS
LANGLEY AVE
COOMBE DR
PINE GDNS
Pav
Bwg Gn
Pav
Bessingby Pl Flds
HA4
PAVILION WAY
FERNCROFT AVE
GREENCROFT AVE
MORLEY CRES
BROADHURST GDNS
RUSSELL CL
COLLINS DR
ST JAMES CL
ALDRIDGE AVE
CAMBRIDGE DR
PETERS CL
ST CL
GARTH CL
ARAGON DR
CRANLEY
CASTLETON RD
CLEVES WAY
BOLEYN DR
Miniature Railway
Recn Gd
Allot Gdns
ST ANDREWS CL
OXFORD DR
WHITBY PAR
WHITBY RD
FIELD END RD
Field End Jun & Inf Schs
MOUNT PLEASANT
HILLCROFT CRES
HUNTERS HILL
CREST GDNS
EAST MEAD
St Swithun Wells RC Prim Sch
DENBIGH CL
CORNWALL RD
HATHERLEIGH RD
KINGSWEAR RD
ASHBURTON RD
WARBURTON CT
SALCOMBE WAY
SEATON GDNS
TORRINGTON RD
THURLSTON RD
TIVERTON RD
PAIGNTON RD
FLAMBOROUGH RD
SELBY CHASE
FILEY WAYE
BEVERLEY RD
BESSINGBY RD
BEMPTON DR
LYNMOUTH DR
TORCROSS RD
SHALDON DR
BARNSTAPLE RD
APPLEDORE AVE
EXMOUTH RD
BIDEFORD RD
HARTLAND DR
MELTHORNE DR
QUEENS WLK
THE FAIRWAY
ABBOT CL
CHURCH CT
DOWN BARNS RD
BRACKENBRIDGE DR
WHITE BUTTS RD
PADDOCK RD
BEC CL
MONKS CL
LONG DR
Deane Park
Tenn Cts
New Pond Pl Flds
Pav
SIDMOUTH DR
COTTINGHAM CHASE
DARTMOUTH RD
BERKELEY CL
ROUNDWAYS
BELL CL
NEW POND PAR
A4180
Recn Gd
Ruislip Gardens
TREVOR CRES
BEDFORD RD
CLYFFORD RD
1 THE POINT
2 TREVOR GDNS
CARMICHAEL CL
WEST END RD
MANNINGTREE RD
BRAINTREE RD
VICTORIA RD
TIPTREE RD
BRIDGEWATER RD
BRAINTREE IND EST
WEST MEAD
THE VALE
CROSSWAY
THE CROFT
ANGUS DR
ST GREGORY CL
RYDAL WAY
Allot Gdns
Recn Gd
Deansfield Prim
South Ruislip
Queensmead Sch
PORTAL CL
TRENCHARD AVE
Tenn Cts
South Ruislip
KELVEDON CT
Liby
Pl Flds
Tenn Cts
Sp Ctr
Superstore
ODYSSEY BSNS PK
THE RUNWAY
BOURNE CT
CROWN RD
VICTORIA RETAIL PARK
BROOK RETAIL PARK
CIVIC WAY
CAVENDISH AVE
CANFIELD DR
DUDLEY DR
ACOL CRES
STATION APP
ALBURY CT
PRIMROSE GDNS
MANOR GDNS
BOURNE AVE
GREAT CENTRAL AVE
LANGHAM CT
LANGDALE CT
WESTERLEY CT
VINCENT CT
DEANE AVE
NORTHOLT AVE
HARDY AVE
PRIORS GDNS
BOWDEN CT
CEDAR AVE
SOUTH PARK WAY
Northolt Aerodrome
MAHLON AVE
WINGFIELD WAY
EDWARD'S AVE
FRAZER AVE
NAIRN RD
Recn Gd
FIELD END
Bourne Prim Sch
WALNUT WAY
MASSON AVE
Sp Gd
Priors Farm
Polish War Meml
WELDON CL
WARSAW CL
GLEBE AVE
Glebe Farm
ROXBOURNE CL
A40
WESTERN AVE
Bwg Gn
Pav
Yeading Brook
CH
Tenn Cts
UB5
Sp Gd
UB4
London Ctr
Bwg Gn
HARVEY RD
Hillingdon
Ealing
Tenn Cts
Pl Fld
Peacock Park
Downe Barns Farm
Ten Acres (Nature Reserve)
SHARVEL LA
CH
CH
COMPTON CRES
HEARN RISE
IRVING AVE

A
B
C
D
41
85
64
12
13
14
87
6
5
86
4
3
85
2
84
1
Allot Gdns
Roxbourne Fst & Mid Schs
Hillingdon
Harrow
YEADING AVE
WAVERLEY
TORBAY RD
OVESDON AVE
CHICHESTER CT
CAPTHORNE AVE
BERRITON RD
OXLEAY RD
CLITHEROE AVE
GOLDSMITH CL
Grange Schs
ABERCORN CRES
SOUTHDOWN CRES
HILLSIDE CRES
A4090
Tenn Cts
Fball Gd
LUCAS AVE
DRAKE RD
EXETER RD
Allot Gdns
Newton Farm Fst & Mid Sch
Newton Park
Allot Gdns
Newton Farm Ecology Pk
AUSTEN RD
EASTWAY CRES
ELIOT DR
UNITY TERR
DRINKWATER RD
SWIFT CL
CONCORD TERR
SCOTT CRES
THE ARCHES
FENTIMAN WAY
LODGEHILL PARK CL
FRANKLINS MEWS
BREMBER RD
Archdale Bsns Ctr
STANLEY RD
PRIEST PARK AVE
RAYNERS LA
MARYATT AVE
COLES CRES
THORNLEY DR
ROXETH GREEN AVE
EASTCOTE AVE
EASTLEIGH AVE
MAPLE AVE
BARNABY CL
ST MARGARET'S AVE
THE VIADUCT
SHERWOOD
GREENWOOD
NEWQUAY CRES
WIDDICOMBE AVE
LYNTON RD
LULWORTH GDNS
KINGS RD
RAVENSWOOD CRES
CLOVELLY WAY
LULWORTH CL
Tenn Cts
Pav
The Roxbourne
Alexandra Sch
NEWTON CL
LEAFIER DR
JASMINE GDNS
ABBOTS DR
MONKS CL
SANDRINGHAM CRES
CROSS RD
MINEHEAD CT
MINEHEAD RD
TITHE FARM CL
TITHE FARM AVE
HA2
Recn Gd
PARKFIELD CRES
DUNSTER WAY
WOOD CL
MALVERN AVE
MERLINS AVE
HODSON CL
HAMILTON CRES
JORDAN CL
ROWE WLK
ALEXANDRA AVE
Schs
EASTCOTE LA
WINKLEY CT
ALEXANDRA CL
Cemy
REVEREND CL
MEADOW GATE
GROVELANDS CL
FINDON CL
PARK MEAD
BEECHWOOD CIRC
BEECHWOOD AVE
BEECHWOOD GDNS
CORBIN'S LA
BARNETTS
VALENTINE RD
CRANE CL
PO
Liby
WHITBY RD
WARGRAVE RD
CARSDALE RD
DUNCAN RD
WYVENHOE RD
KINGSLEY
A312 NORTHOLT RD
RUFUS CL
WELL CL
LEAMINGTON CRES
THISTLEDENE AVE
STUART AVE
VELDENE WAY
STIVEN CRES
BODMIN CL
KINGS ROAD BGLWS
1 CORNELL HO
2 MEAD FIELD
3 STRADBROOK CL
WINDSOR AVE
WINDSOR CRES
TORRINGTON CT
TORRINGTON DR
LEATH
SALE RD
South Harrow
1 TREGENNA CT
2 PARK GATES
3 ARUNDEL CT
PARK LA
BRENDON GDNS
ROXETH GR
Welldon Park Schs
WOOD END AVE
ROYAL CRES
PALACE RD
PRIMROSE CL
MIRREN CL
SALTER CL
ROSEBERY AVE
BROOKSIDE CL
TREGENNA AVE
CORFE AVE
BALMORAL RD
Alexandra Park
PADDOCKS CL
STATION PAR
WESTWOOD AVE
RAGLAN TERR
STROUD GATE
CADOGAN CL
JUBILEE DR
PRINCES WAY
Ind Est
BRACKENHILL
DIAMOND RD
THE COURT
VICTORIA RD
FIELD END RD
HOLYROOD AVE
WARWICK AVE
KENILWORTH AVE
IVY CL
LUDLOW CL
WALTON AVE
EARLSMEAD
CARLYON AVE
Fball Gd
Earlsmead Fst & Mid Sch
ARUNDEL DR
Superstores
HA4
Chancerygate Bsns Ctr
STONEFIELD CL
Ind Est
STONEFIELD WAY
BRADFIELD RD
SOMERVELL RD
A312
Northolt Park
HOLLYDALE CL
NEW CT
DORCHESTER RD
HALSBURY RD W
STATION PAR
CLAUSON AVE
ADCOCK GR
Tenn Cts
1 SALISBURY CT
2 FOLKESTONE CT
3 PONTEFRACT CT
4 SEDGEFIELD CT
THE HEIGHTS
WINCANTON CRES
DANEMEAD GR
PETT'S HILL
READING RD
FLORISTON CT
MORTON CT
SHERIDAN TERR
A4090
DONCASTER DR
MALLET DR
MARTIN DR
GREENACRE CL
DONCASTER GDNS
GAYLOR RD
Allot Gdns
DABBS HILL LA
Ealing
SILVERDALE CL
HORNBEAM CL
PERCEVAL CT 1
HILL CT 2
CHURCHILL CT 3
WARWICK CT 4
LANARK CT 5
NEWMARKET AVE
BANGOR CL
MILDRED AVE
RABOURNMEAD DR
GRAHAM CT
THE LINK
WHEATSHEAF CL
WILSMERE DR
SANDOWN WAY
EPSOM CL
HURST CL
KEMPTON AVE
Sch
THE MOUNT
WOOD END LA
GRAINGER CL
NEWNHAM AVE
PERTH CL
ASCOT CL
REDCAR CL
Pl Fld
HUNTINGDON CL
PLUMPTON CL
FONTWELL CL
RIPON CL
WETHERBY CL
BAYSHILL RISE
NEWBURY WAY
NEWBURY CL
CARTMEL CT
EASTCOTE LA
Northolt High Sch
SOUTHWELL AVE
CHELTENHAM
THIRSK CL
HOLMWOOD CL
EGGARDON CT
LANCASTER RD
HAYDOCK AVE
HAYDOCK GN
ANSON TERR
BLENHEIM RD
Masts
GIRTON RD
CONEYGROVE PATH 1
VINCENTS PATH 2
PRIORS FIELD 3
RIDGEWAY WLK 4
SHEPHERDS PATH 5
FORLONG PATH 6
Willow Tree Prim Sch
GOODWOOD DR
SUSSEX CRES
Allot Gdns
LEWES CL
UB5
SIVERST CL
Pl Fld
ARNOLD RD
OWEN CL
BUTTERCUP CL
ABBOTT CL
MILLWAY GDNS
Sch
TENBY GDNS
EASTCOTE LANE N
BRIAR CRES
RIBBLESDALE AVE
GONVILLE CRES
NEW PARK
STROUD FIELD
ATTEWOOD RD
BRUFFS MDW
WINNINGS WLK
PALMER CL
POPPY CL
BLUEBELL CL
HOLLOWFIELD WLK
ACRE PATH
LAYMEAD CL
FORTUNES MEAD
COWINGS MEAD
WILLOW TREE CL
Northolt
THE FARMLANDS
WELLINGTON HO
MANDEVILLE RD
BADMINTON CL
GIRTON CL
GLAMIS WAY
ORIEL WAY
CASTLE RD
FREEMAN CL
GAUNTLET CL
YEOMAN RD
ISLIP MANOR RD
EASTCOTE LA
MOAT FARM RD
BELVUE CL
CARR RD
LORDSHIP RD
MANOR GATE
Islip Manor Park
PO
BELVUE RD
STATION PAR
SANDRINGHAM RD
CHERRY GDNS
Allot Gdns
ISLIP GDNS
PETWORTH CL
Belvue Bsns Ctr
Northolt Trad Est
Grand Union
DUKES AVE
MANOR AVE
DALE CT
ALDERNEY GDNS
LYTTON CL
KINGSMEAD DR
COURT FARM RD
SUMMIT RD
Grand Union Canal Wlk
FAIRWAY DR
HAREWOOD CL
HAREWOOD AVE
CHURCH LO
CHURCH RD
VICARAGE CL
CHURCH RD
EALING RD
NORTHOLT
FORT RD
John Chilton Sch
West London Acad
WESTERN AVE
KINGSTON CL
CARISBROOKE CT
Belvue Park
ROWDELL RD
MOHAMMEDI PK COMPLEX
TAUNTON RD
FAIRWAY DR
Aladdin Workspace
West London Acad
DIAS HO
Target Rdbt
ESKDALE AVE
RECTORY
WESTWAY CT
A40
MOORLANDS
BISHOPS DR
GARDEN CL
SARAH CT
GULLIVER CL
Belvue Sch
Golf Range
BRIDPORT RD
DERBY RD
The Metropolitan Ctr
HALIFAX RD
NORWICH
LONG DR
CHARTWELL
STANLEY AVE
LINCOLN

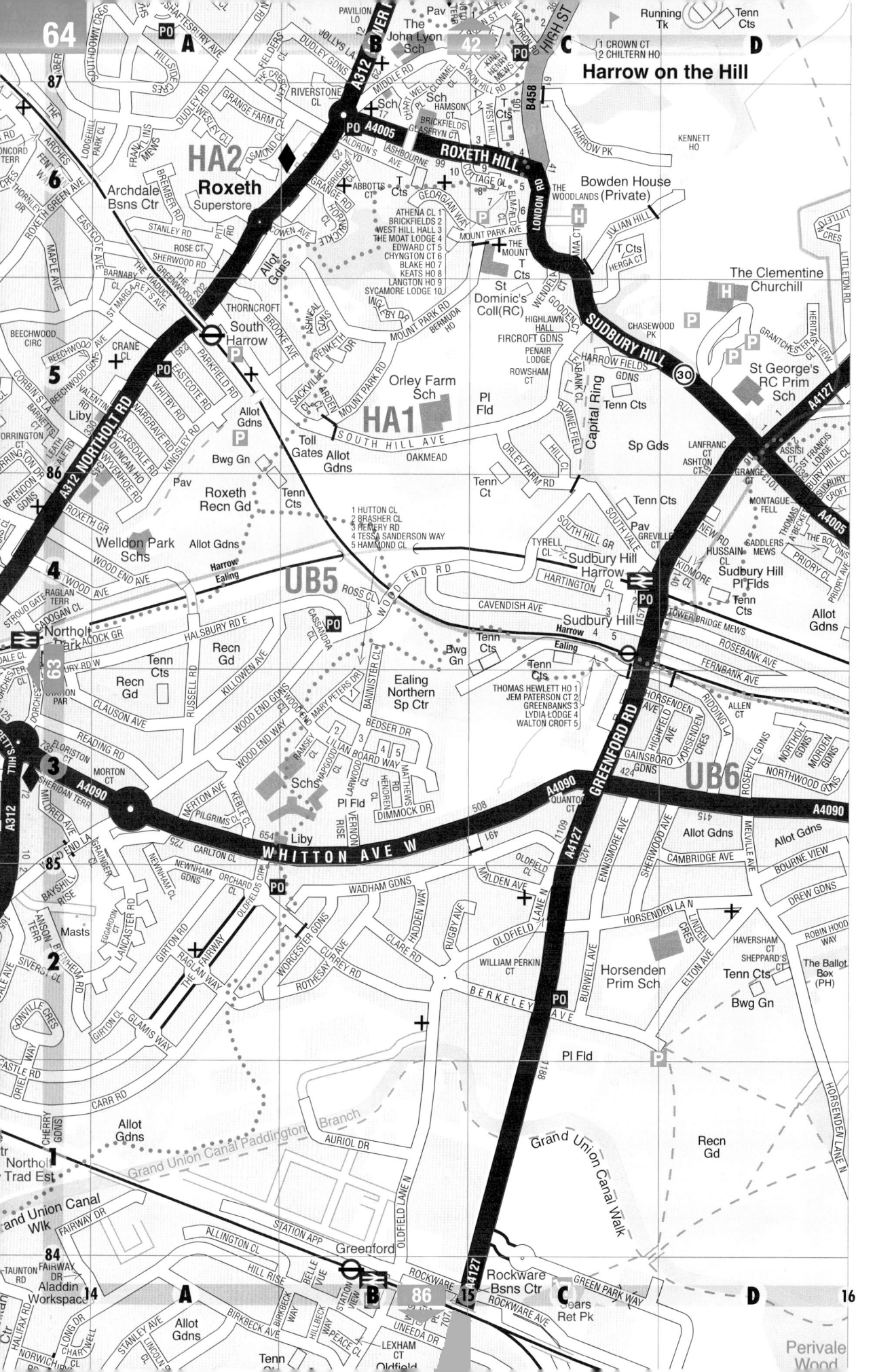

42
A
B
C
D
1 CROWN CT
2 CHILTERN HO
Harrow on the Hill
Running Tk
Tenn Cts
The John Lyon Sch
Pav
PAVILION LO
HIGH ST
SHAFTESBURY AVE
SOUTHDOWN CRES
HILLSIDE GDNS
DUDLEY GDNS
JOLLYS LA
FIELDERS CL
THE CRESCENT
RIVERSTONE CL
MIDDLE RD
CHARTWELL PL
CLONMEL CL
BYRON HILL RD
KING HENRY MEWS
WALDRON RD
Sch
HAMSON CT
BRICKFIELDS
GLASFRYN CT
WEST HILL
B458
HARROW PK
KENNETT HO
A312
A4005
ROXETH HILL
ASHBOURNE AVE
LONDON RD
COTTAGE CL
ELMFIELD CL
DUDLEY RD
WESLEY CL
GRANGE FARM CL
FRANKLINS MEWS
LODGEHILL PARK CL
OSMOND CL
HA2
Roxeth
Superstore
Archdale Bsns Ctr
BREMBER RD
STANLEY RD
ROSE CT
SHERWOOD RD
PITT RD
COWEN AVE
Allot Gdns
BRIGADE CL
GRANGE RD
HORNBUCKLE CL
ABBOTTS CT
T Cts
GEORGIAN WAY
ATHENA CL 1
BRICKFIELDS 2
WEST HILL HALL 3
THE MOAT LODGE 4
EDWARD CT 5
CHYNGTON CT 6
BLAKE HO 7
KEATS HO 8
LANGTON HO 9
SYCAMORE LODGE 10
MOUNT PARK AVE
THE MOUNT
THE WOODLANDS
Bowden House (Private)
JULIAN HILL
HERGA CT
St Dominic's Coll(RC)
WENDELA CT
GOODEN CT
HIGHLAWN HALL
FIRCROFT GDNS
PENAIR LODGE
ROWSHAM CT
SUDBURY HILL
CHASEWOOD PK
The Clementine Churchill
GRANTCHESTER CL
HERITAGE VIEW
LITTLETON CRES
St George's RC Prim Sch
A4127
30
HARROW FIELDS GDNS
Capital Ring
Tenn Cts
Sp Gds
LANFRANC CT
ASHTON CT
GRANGE CT
ASSISI CT
ST FRANCIS LODGE
SUDBURY CROFT
MONTAGUE FELL
THOMAS A'BECKET RD
THE BOLTONS
SADDLERS MEWS
PRIORY CL
6
EASTCOTE AVE
MAPLE AVE
ROXETH GREEN AVE
THORNLEY DR
CONCORD TERR
ARCHES
BARNABY CL
THE VIADUCT
THE GREENWOODS
ST MARGARET'S AVE
THORNCROFT
BROOKE AVE
South Harrow
ASHNEAL GDNS
PENKETH DR
INGLEBY DR
MOUNT PARK RD
BERMUDA HO
Orley Farm Sch
Pl Fld
HA1
SOUTH HILL AVE
OAKMEAD
ORLEY FARM RD
HILL CL
RUNNELFIELD
5
BEECHWOOD CIRC
BEECHWOOD GDNS
CRANE CL
CORBIN'S LA
BARNETTS CT
PARKFIELD RD
EASTCOTE RD
WHITBY RD
WARGRAVE RD
CARSDALE RD
DUNCAN HO
WYVENHOE RD
KINGSLEY RD
NORTHOLT RD
Liby
Toll Gates
Allot Gdns
Bwg Gn
Pav
Roxeth Recn Gd
Tenn Cts
Tenn Ct
86
BRENDON DR
ROXETH GR
Welldon Park Schs
Allot Gdns
1 HUTTON CL
2 BRASHER CL
3 REMERY RD
4 TESSA SANDERSON WAY
5 HAMMOND CL
SOUTH HILL GR
SOUTH VALE
TYRELL CL
Sudbury Hill Harrow
HARTINGTON CL
GREVILLE CT
NEW RD
HUSSAIN CL
KIDMORE
Sudbury Hill Pl Flds
Tenn Cts
Allot Gdns
4
WOOD END AVE
RAGLAN TERR
STROUD GATE
CADOGAN CL
Harrow
Ealing
UB5
ROSS CL
WOOD END RD
CAVENDISH AVE
Sudbury Hill
TOWER BRIDGE MEWS
ROSEBANK AVE
FERNBANK AVE
Northolt Park
63
ACOCK GR
HALSBURY RD E
HALSBURY RD W
CASSANDRA CL
Recn Gd
Tenn Cts
Recn Gd
KILLOWEN AVE
RUSSELL RD
STATION PAR
CLAUSON AVE
BANNISTER CL
Bwg Gn
Tenn Cts
Tenn Cts
Ealing Northern Sp Ctr
THOMAS HEWLETT HO 1
JEM PATERSON CT 2
GREENBANKS 3
LYDIA LODGE 4
WALTON CROFT 5
HORSENDEN AVE
HIGHFIELD AVE
HORSENDEN CRES
RIDDING LA
ALLEN CT
GAINSBORO GDNS
UB6
ROSEHILL GDNS
NORTHOLT GDNS
MORDEN GDNS
NORTHWOOD GDNS
READING RD
FLORISTON CL
MORTON CT
WOOD END GDNS
WOOD END WAY
MARY PETERS DR
BEDSER DR
LILLIAN BOARD WAY
HAPGOOD CL
LARWOOD CL
HENDREN CL
MATTHEWS RD
DIMMOCK DR
Schs
Pl Fld
3
SHERIDAN TERR
A4090
MERTON AVE
PILGRIMS CL
KEBLE CL
RAMSEY CL
GREENFORD RD
QUANTOCK CT
424
415
A4090
2
MILDRED AVE
WOOD END LA
GRAINGER CL
CARLTON CL
Liby
RISE
VERNON RISE
WHITTON AVE W
508
491
OLDFIELD CL
1109
1420
ENNISMORE AVE
SHERWOOD AVE
Allot Gdns
MELVILLE AVE
CAMBRIDGE AVE
Allot Gdns
BOURNE VIEW
85
BAYSHILL RISE
NEWNHAM CL
NEWNHAM GDNS
ORCHARD CL
OLDFIELDS CIR
WADHAM GDNS
MALDEN AVE
DREW GDNS
ROBIN HOOD WAY
Masts
EGGARDON CT
LANCASTER RD
ANSON TERR
2
BRETHEM RD
SIVERS CL
GIRTON RD
THE FAIRWAY
RAGLAN WAY
WORCESTER GDNS
CURREY RD
ROTHESAY AVE
HADDEN WAY
CLARE RD
RUGBY AVE
OLDFIELD LANE N
WILLIAM PERKIN CT
HORSENDEN LA N
LINDEN CRES
ELTON AVE
HAVERSHAM CT
SHEPPARD'S CT
The Ballot Box (PH)
Tenn Cts
Bwg Gn
Horsenden Prim Sch
BURWELL AVE
BERKELEY AVE
GONVILLE CRES
GIRTON CL
GLAMIS WAY
ORIEL WAY
CASTLE RD
Pl Fld
1188
CARR RD
CHERRY GDNS
Allot Gdns
Grand Union Canal Paddington Branch
AURIOL DR
Grand Union Canal Walk
Recn Gd
HORSENDEN LANE N
1
Northolt Trad Est
Grand Union Canal Wlk
FAIRWAY DR
STATION APP
ALLINGTON CL
OLDFIELD LANE N
Greenford
84
TAUNTON RD
FAIRWAY DR
Aladdin Workspace
14
HILL RISE
BELLE VUE
STATION VIEW
ROCKWARE AVE
86
A4127
15
Rockware Bsns Ctr
GREEN PARK WAY
Sears Ret Pk
16
HALIFAX RD
LONG DR
CHARTWELL
STANLEY AVE
LINCOLN
Allot Gdns
BIRKBECK AVE
BIRKBECK WAY
HILLBECK WAY
PEACE CL
UNEEDA DR
LEXHAM CT
Tenn
Oldfield
Perivale Wood
NORWICH

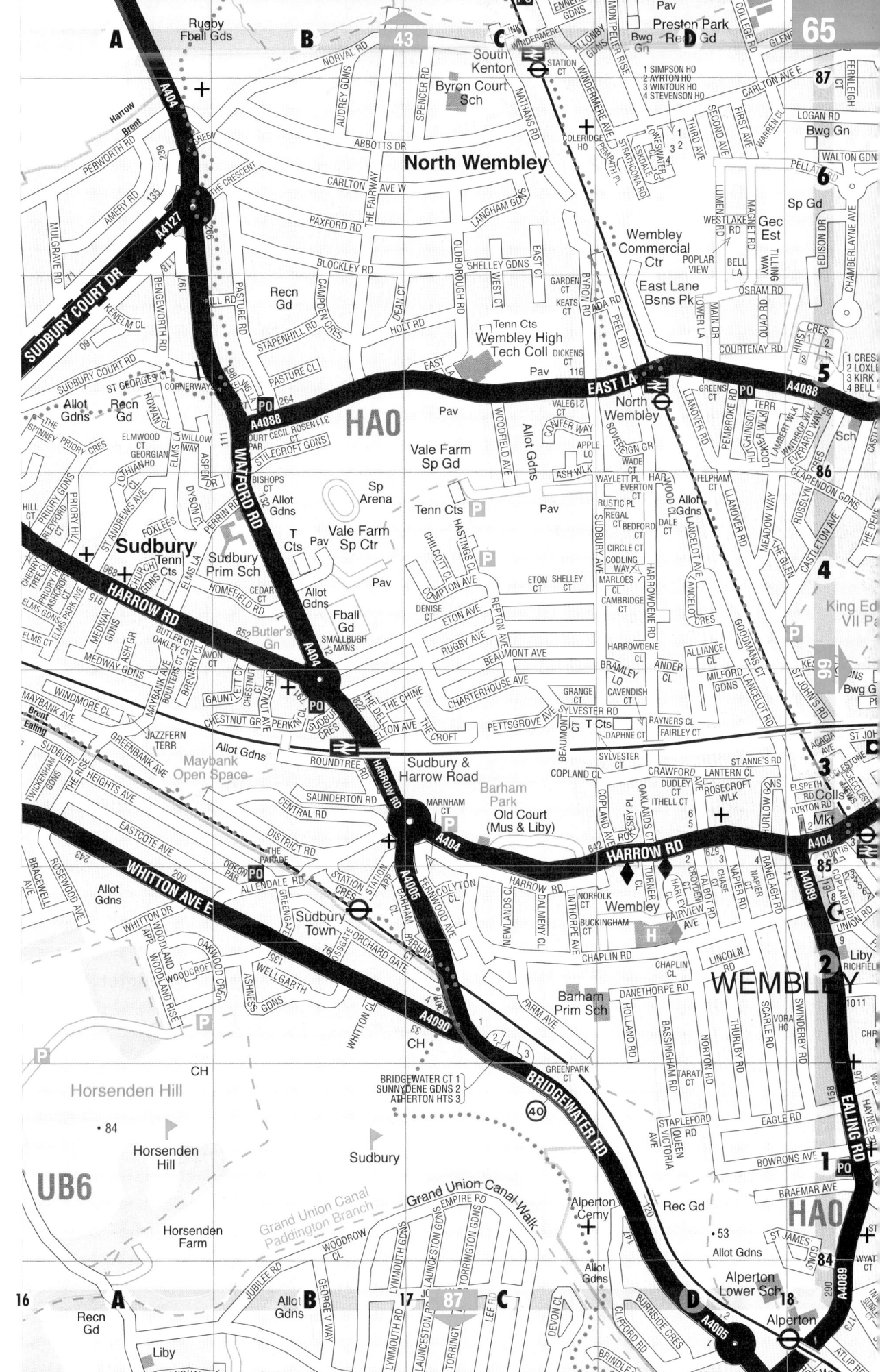
A
B
C
D
43
87
Rugby Fball Gds
South Kenton
Preston Park
Byron Court Sch
North Wembley
Wembley Commercial Ctr
East Lane Bsns Pk
Gec Est
Sp Gd
Bwg Gn
Recn Gd
Tenn Cts
Wembley High Tech Coll
HA0
Vale Farm Sp Gd
Sp Arena
Vale Farm Sp Ctr
Fball Gd
Allot Gdns
Sudbury
Sudbury Prim Sch
Butler's Gn
Maybank Open Space
Sudbury & Harrow Road
Barham Park
Old Court (Mus & Liby)
Sudbury Town
Wembley
WEMBLEY
Barham Prim Sch
King Edward VII Park
Horsenden Hill
Horsenden Farm
Sudbury
UB6
Grand Union Canal Paddington Branch
Grand Union Canal Walk
Alperton Cemy
Alperton Lower Sch
Alperton
Rec Gd
Liby
Recn Gd
A404
A4127
A4088
A4005
A4090
A4089
SUDBURY COURT DR
WATFORD RD
HARROW RD
WHITTON AVE E
BRIDGEWATER RD
EALING RD
EAST LA
NORVAL RD
ABBOTTS DR
CARLTON AVE W
PAXFORD RD
BLOCKLEY RD
HOLT RD
STAPENHILL RD
PASTURE CL
ETON AVE
RUGBY AVE
BEAUMONT AVE
CHARTERHOUSE AVE
ROUNDTREE RD
SAUNDERTON RD
CENTRAL RD
DISTRICT RD
EASTCOTE AVE
HEIGHTS AVE
WINDMORE CL
MAYBANK AVE
CHAPLIN RD
DANETHORPE RD
EAGLE RD
BOWRONS AVE
BRAEMAR AVE
FARM AVE
WOODROW CL
EMPIRE RD
LOGAN RD
CARLTON AVE E
BRIDGEWATER CT 1
SUNNYDENE GDNS 2
ATHERTON HTS 3
1 SIMPSON HO
2 AYRTON HO
3 WINTOUR HO
4 STEVENSON HO
16
17
18
84
85
86
87
88

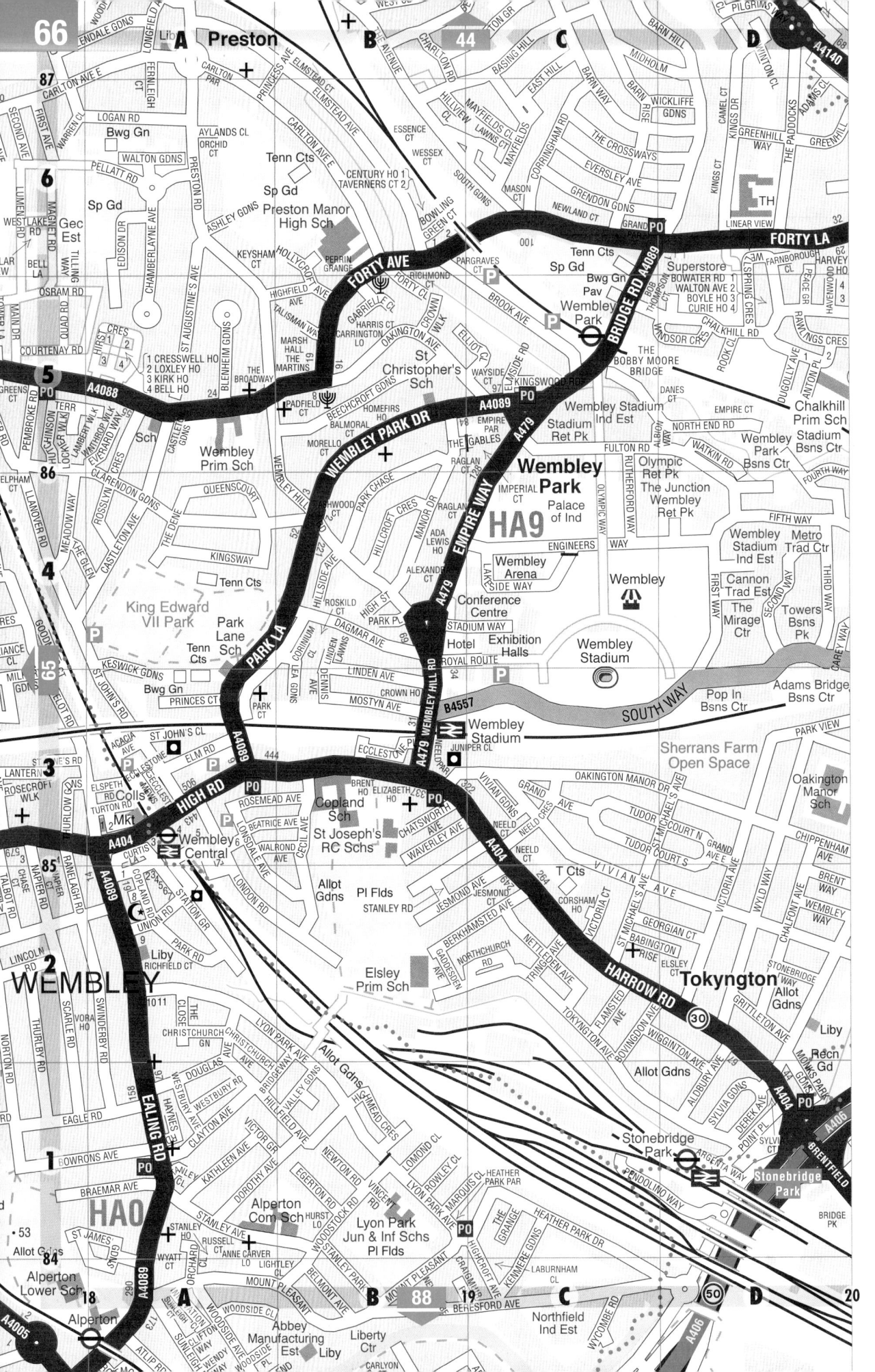

66
Preston
44
A
B
C
D
Wembley Park
HA9
Wembley
Wembley Stadium
Wembley Arena
Conference Centre
Exhibition Halls
Wembley Central
Wembley Stadium
Tokyngton
Stonebridge Park
Alperton
WEMBLEY
HA0
88
65
FORTY AVE
FORTY LA
BRIDGE RD A4089
A4088
A4089
WEMBLEY PARK DR
EMPIRE WAY
A479
PARK LA
HIGH RD
A404
HARROW RD
EALING RD
SOUTH WAY
B4557
WEMBLEY HILL RD
A4140
A406
A4005
Preston Manor High Sch
St Christopher's Sch
Wembley Prim Sch
King Edward VII Park
Park Lane Sch
Copland Sch
St Joseph's RC Schs
Elsley Prim Sch
Alperton Com Sch
Lyon Park Jun & Inf Schs
Oakington Manor Sch
Chalkhill Prim Sch
Alperton Lower Sch
Sherrans Farm Open Space
Wembley Stadium Ind Est
Stadium Ret Pk
Olympic Ret Pk
The Junction Wembley Ret Pk
Palace of Ind
Wembley Park Bsns Ctr
Stadium Bsns Ctr
Wembley Stadium Ind Est
Metro Trad Ctr
Cannon Trad Est
The Mirage Ctr
Towers Bsns Pk
Adams Bridge Bsns Ctr
Pop In Bsns Ctr
Northfield Ind Est
Abbey Manufacturing Est
Liberty Ctr
Superstore
THE BOBBY MOORE BRIDGE
Gec Est
Allot Gdns
Pl Flds
Tenn Cts
Sp Gd
Bwg Gn
Liby
Mkt
Colls
Hotel

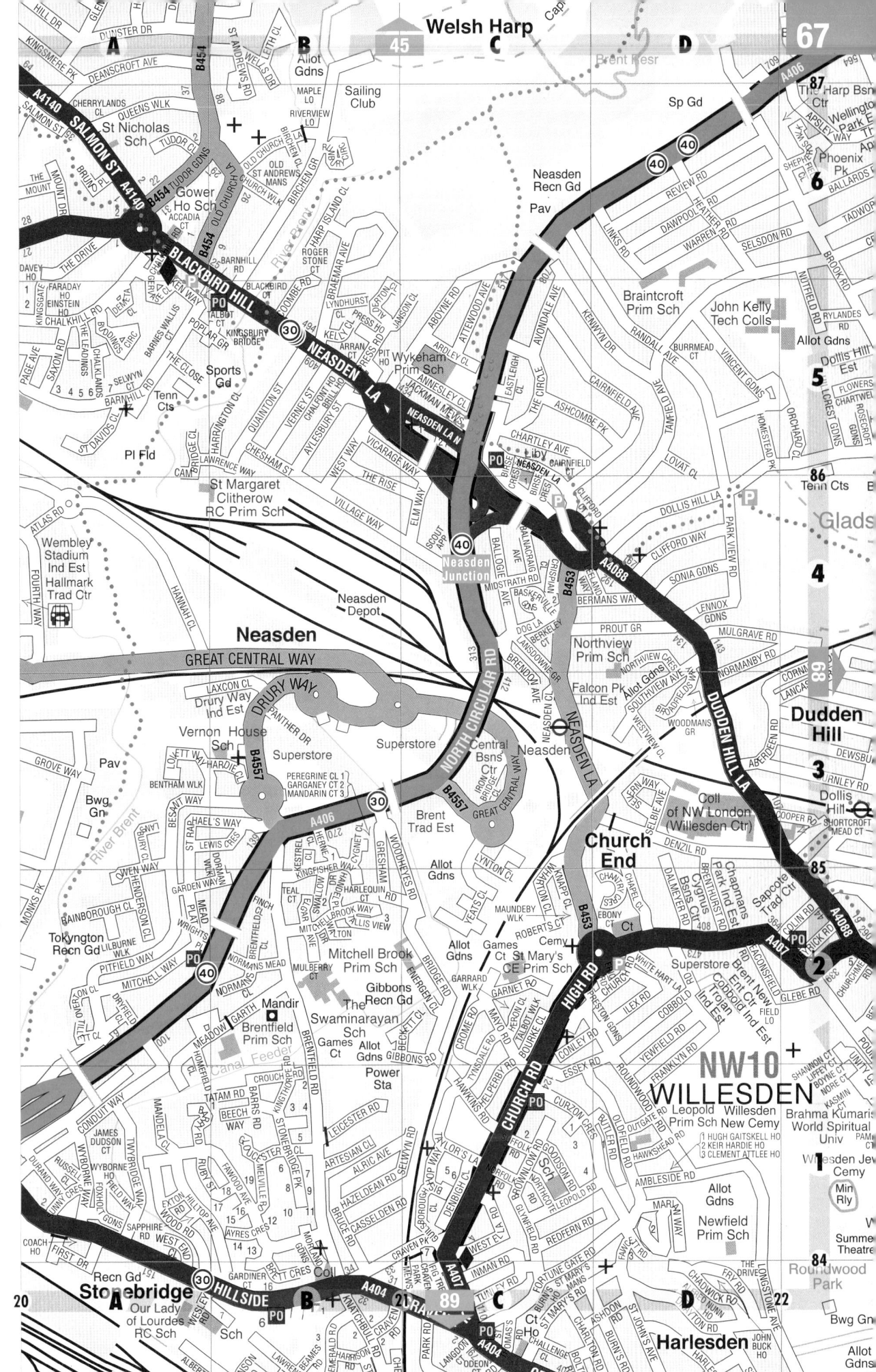
Welsh Harp
45
A
B
C
D
Brent Resr
Allot Gdns
Sailing Club
Sp Gd
The Harp Bsns Ctr
Phoenix Pk
St Nicholas Sch
SALMON ST
A4140
B454
Gower Ho Sch
BLACKBIRD HILL
NEASDEN LA
Neasden Recn Gd
Pav
Braintcroft Prim Sch
John Kelly Tech Colls
Allot Gdns
Dollis Hill Est
Wykeham Prim Sch
Sports Gd
Tenn Cts
Pl Fld
St Margaret Clitherow RC Prim Sch
Liby
Neasden Junction
Wembley Stadium Ind Est
Hallmark Trad Ctr
Neasden Depot
Neasden
GREAT CENTRAL WAY
NORTH CIRCULAR RD
Northview Prim Sch
Falcon Pk Ind Est
Allot Gdns
DUDDEN HILL LA
Dudden Hill
Dollis Hill
Drury Way Ind Est
DRURY WAY
Vernon House Sch
Superstore
Central Bsns Ctr
Neasden
Pav
Bwg Gn
A406
Brent Trad Est
Church End
Coll of NW London (Willesden Ctr)
River Brent
Tokyngton Recn Gd
Allot Gdns
Games Ct
St Mary's CE Prim Sch
Cemy
Sapcote Trad Ctr
A4088
A407
Superstore
Mitchell Brook Prim Sch
Gibbons Recn Gd
Mandir
The Swaminarayan Sch
Brentfield Prim Sch
Games Ct
Allot Gdns
Power Sta
HIGH RD
CHURCH RD
NW10
WILLESDEN
Leopold Prim Sch
Willesden New Cemy
Brahma Kumaris World Spiritual Univ
Willesden Jewish Cemy
Allot Gdns
Newfield Prim Sch
Summer Theatre
Roundwood Park
Stonebridge
HILLSIDE
A404
Our Lady of Lourdes RC Sch
Sch
Recn Gd
Coll
89
Harlesden
Bwg Gn
Allot Gdns
20
21
22
87
86
85
84
6
5
4
3
2
1
68

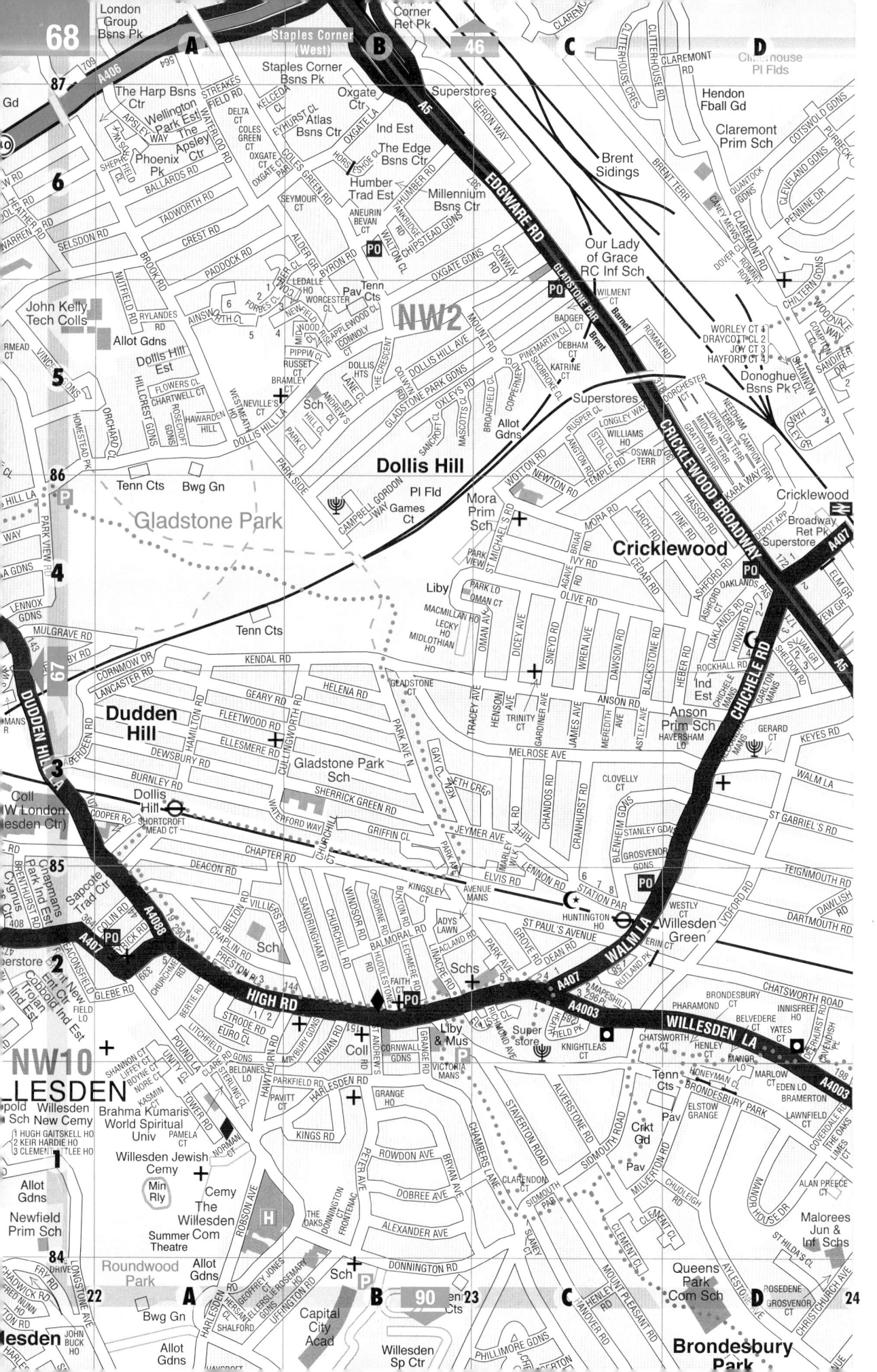

London Group Bsns Pk
Staples Corner (West)
Staples Corner Bsns Pk
Corner Ret Pk
46
Clitterhouse Pl Flds
A
B
C
D
A406
A5
87
The Harp Bsns Ctr
Wellington Park Est
The Apsley Ctr
Phoenix Pk
Atlas Bsns Ctr
Oxgate Ctr
Ind Est
Superstores
The Edge Bsns Ctr
Humber Trad Est
Millennium Bsns Ctr
Hendon Fball Gd
Claremont Prim Sch
Brent Sidings
EDGWARE RD
6
STREAKES FIELD RD
WATERLOO RD
DELTA CT
COLES GREEN CT
OXGATE CT
OXGATE CT PAR
KELCEDA CL
EYHURST CL
COLES GREEN RD
OXGATE LA
HORSESHOE CL
HUMBER RD
GERON WAY
CLITTERHOUSE CRES
CLITTERHOUSE RD
CLAREMONT RD
BRENT TERR
COTSWOLD GDNS
CLEVELAND GDNS
PENNINE DR
QUANTOCK GDNS
CANEY MEWS
CLAREMONT RD
DOVER CL
ROMNEY ROW
APSLEY WAY
SHEPHERD CL
BALLARDS RD
TADWORTH RD
CREST RD
SELSDON RD
HEATHER RD
WARREN RD
PADDOCK RD
BROOK RD
NUTFIELD RD
SEYMOUR CT
ANEURIN BEVAN CT
TANKRIDGE RD
CHIPSTEAD GDNS
WALTON CL
ALDER GR
BYRON RD
PO
Our Lady of Grace RC Inf Sch
OXGATE GDNS
CONWAY RD
GLADSTONE PAR
WILMENT CT
Barnet
Brent
John Kelly Tech Colls
Allot Gdns
RYLANDES RD
AINSWORTH CL
FORBES CL
LEDALLE HO
WORCESTER CL
Pav
Tenn Cts
NEWFIELD RISE
APPLEWOOD CL
CONNOLY CT
NW2
MOUNT RD
BADGER CT
DEBHAM CT
ROMAN RD
WORLEY CT 1
DRAYCOTT CL 2
JOY CT 3
HAYFORD CT 4
CHILTERN GDNS
WOODVALE WAY
Donoghue Bsns Pk
SANDIFER DR
SHANNON CL
Dollis Hill Est
FLOWERS CL
CHARTWELL CT
ROSECROFT GDNS
HAWARDEN HILL
HILLCREST GDNS
ORCHARD CL
HOMESTEAD PK
5
NEVILLE'S CT
BRAMLEY CT
RUSSET CT
PIPPIN CL
DOLLIS HTS
THE CRESCENT
COLWYN RD
DOLLIS HILL AVE
GLADSTONE PARK GDNS
OXLEYS RD
PINEMARTIN CL
SHOBROKE CL
KATRINE CT
Superstores
DORCHESTER CT
NEEDHAM TERR
JOHNSTON TERR
MIDLAND TERR
GRATTON TERR
CAMPION TERR
KARA WAY
DOLLIS HILL LA
Sch
ST ANDREW'S CL
HILL CL
PARK CL
SANCROFT CL
MASCOTTS CL
BROADFIELD CL
COPPERMEAD CL
Allot Gdns
RUSPER CL
LONGLEY WAY
WILLIAMS HO
STOLL CL
OSWALD TERR
LANGTON RD
TEMPLE RD
CRICKLEWOOD BROADWAY
86
Tenn Cts
Bwg Gn
Gladstone Park
PARK SIDE
Dollis Hill
Pl Fld
CAMPBELL GORDON WAY
Games Ct
Mora Prim Sch
WOTTON RD
NEWTON RD
ST MICHAEL'S RD
PARK VIEW
MORA RD
BRIAR RD
LARCH RD
PINE RD
HASSOP RD
Cricklewood
Broadway Ret Pk
Superstore
DEPOT APP
A407
ELM GR
PARK VIEW RD
4
LENNOX GDNS
MULGRAVE RD
Liby
PARK LO
OMAN CT
MACMILLAN HO
LECKY HO
MIDLOTHIAN HO
OMAN AVE
DICEY AVE
SNEYD RD
AGAVE RD
IVY RD
OLIVE RD
CEDAR RD
ASHFORD RD
OAKLANDS PAS
OAKLANDS RD
HOWARD RD
SHELDON RD
VAN GR
Tenn Cts
WREN AVE
DAWSON RD
BLACKSTONE RD
HEBER RD
ROCKHALL RD
CHICHELE RD
CARLTON MANS
Ind Est
CHICHELE MANS
67
DUDDEN HILL LA
CORNMOW DR
LANCASTER RD
KENDAL RD
GEARY RD
HELENA RD
GLADSTONE CT
Dudden Hill
HAMILTON RD
FLEETWOOD RD
ELLESMERE RD
DEWSBURY RD
CULLINGWORTH RD
PARK AVE N
TRACEY AVE
HENSON AVE
TRINITY CT
GARDINER AVE
JAMES AVE
MEREDITH AVE
ASTLEY AVE
ANSON RD
Anson Prim Sch
HAVERSHAM LO
ALEXANDRA MANS
GERARD CT
KEYES RD
ABERDEEN RD
3
BURNLEY RD
Gladstone Park Sch
GAY CL
KENNETH CRES
MELROSE AVE
CHANDOS RD
CRANHURST RD
CLOVELLY CT
WALM LA
Coll (NW London Willesden Ctr)
Dollis Hill
SHORTCROFT MEAD CT
COOPER RD
SHERRICK GREEN RD
WATERFORD WAY
CHURCHILL CT
GRIFFIN CL
JEYMER AVE
PARK AVE
MARLEY WLK
LENNON RD
RIFFEL RD
BLENHEIM GDNS
STANLEY GDNS
GROSVENOR GDNS
ST GABRIEL'S RD
85
Sapcote Trad Ctr
Chapmans Park Ind Est
BRENTHURST RD
CHAPTER RD
DEACON RD
VILLIERS RD
BELTON RD
SANDRINGHAM RD
CHURCHILL RD
WINDSOR RD
OSBORNE RD
BUXTON RD
KINGSLEY CT
AVENUE MANS
ELVIS RD
STATION PAR
PO
TEIGNMOUTH RD
DAWLISH RD
DARTMOUTH RD
COLIN RD
A4088
A407
CHAPLIN RD
PRESTON RD
Sch
ADYS LAWN
ACLAND RD
BALMORAL RD
LECHMERE RD
LINACRE RD
PARK AVE
GROVE RD
DEAN RD
ST PAUL'S AVENUE
HUNTINGTON HO
WALM LA
Willesden Green
WESTLY CT
LYDFORD RD
ERIN CT
RUTLAND PK
2
GLEBE RD
CHURCHMEAD RD
BERTIE RD
HIGH RD
HUDDLESTONE RD
FAITH CT
Schs
A4003
MAPESHILL PL
HEATHFIELD PK
CHATSWORTH ROAD
BRONDESBURY CT
PHARAMOND CT
BELVEDERE CT
INNISFREE HO
YATES CT
HENLEY CT
CHATSWORTH CT
WILLESDEN LA
DEERHURST RD
CAVENDISH RD
NW10
WILLESDEN
STRODE RD
EURO CL
LITCHFIELD GDNS
MAYBURY GDNS
GOWAN RD
Coll
CORNWALL GDNS
GRANGE RD
Liby & Mus
Super store
RICHMOND AVE
KNIGHTLEAS CT
MANOR LO
MARLOW CT
EDEN LO
BRAMERTON
SHANNON CT
LIFFEY CT
BOYNE CT
NORE CT
KASMIN CT
UNITY CL
POUND LA
CLARE RD
BELDANES LO
PARKFIELD RD
HARLESDEN RD
PAVITT CT
VICTORIA MANS
GRANGE HO
Tenn Cts
HONEYMAN CL
BRONDESBURY PARK
ELSTOW GRANGE
LAWNFIELD CT
COVERDALE RD
THE OAKS
LIMES CT
Willesden New Cemy
Brahma Kumaris World Spiritual Univ
1 HUGH GAITSKELL HO
2 KEIR HARDIE HO
3 CLEMENT ATTLEE HO
PAMELA CT
TOWER RD
STERLING CL
KINGS RD
STAVERTON ROAD
ALVERSTONE RD
SIDMOUTH ROAD
Crkt Gd
Pav
1
Allot Gdns
Willesden Jewish Cemy
NORMAN CT
Min Rly
ROWDON AVE
BRYAN AVE
CHAMBERS LANE
CLARENDON CT
MILVERTON RD
CHUDLEIGH RD
MANOR HOUSE DR
ALAN PREECE CT
Newfield Prim Sch
Cemy
The Willesden Com
Summer Theatre
ROBSON AVE
H
DONNINGTON CT
FRONTENAC
PETER AVE
DOBREE AVE
ALEXANDER AVE
SIDMOUTH PAR
SLANEY CT
CLEMENT CL
Malorees Jun & Inf Schs
84
Roundwood Park
Allot Gdns
THE OAKS
GEOFFREY JONES CT
ROSEMARY HO
ELLERSLIE GDNS
UFFINGTON RD
Sch
DONNINGTON RD
MOUNT PLEASANT RD
HENLEY RD
Queens Park Com Sch
AYLESTONE AVE
ST HILDA'S CL
ROSEDENE
GROSVENOR CT
CHRISTCHURCH AVE
22
A
B
90
23
C
D
24
Bwg Gn
HARLESDEN RD
HERSANT CL
SHALFORD
Capital City Acad
Willesden Sp Ctr
HANOVER RD
PHILLIMORE GDNS
Brondesbury Park
Allot Gdns
JOHN BUCK HO
LONGSTONE AVE
CHADWICK RD
FRY RD
Willesden

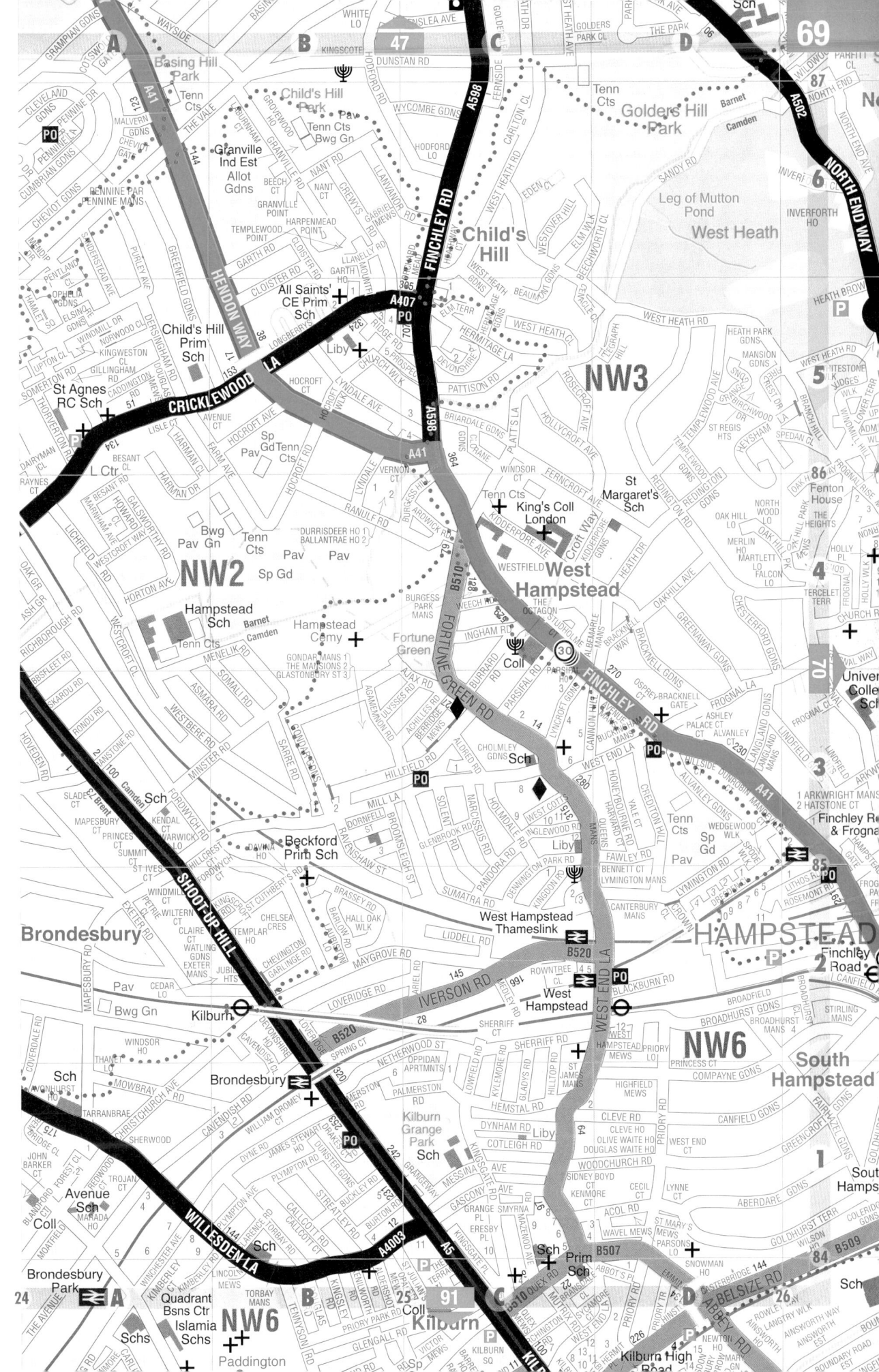
47
A
B
C
D
Basing Hill Park
Child's Hill Park
Golders Hill Park
Leg of Mutton Pond
West Heath
Child's Hill
Granville Ind Est
Allot Gdns
All Saints' CE Prim Sch
Child's Hill Prim Sch
St Agnes RC Sch
HENDON WAY
FINCHLEY RD
CRICKLEWOOD LA
NORTH END WAY
A41
A598
A407
A502
NW3
NW2
NW6
King's Coll London
St Margaret's Sch
West Hampstead
Hampstead Sch
Hampstead Cemy
Fortune Green
FORTUNE GREEN RD
Fenton House
Univer Colle
Beckford Prim Sch
SHOOT-UP HILL
Brondesbury
Kilburn
West Hampstead Thameslink
IVERSON RD
WEST END LA
HAMPSTEAD
Finchley Road
South Hampstead
Kilburn Grange Park
WILLESDEN LA
Brondesbury Park
Quadrant Bsns Ctr
Islamia Schs
BELSIZE RD
ABBEY RD
Barnet
Camden
Brent
70
24
26
84
91
Kilburn

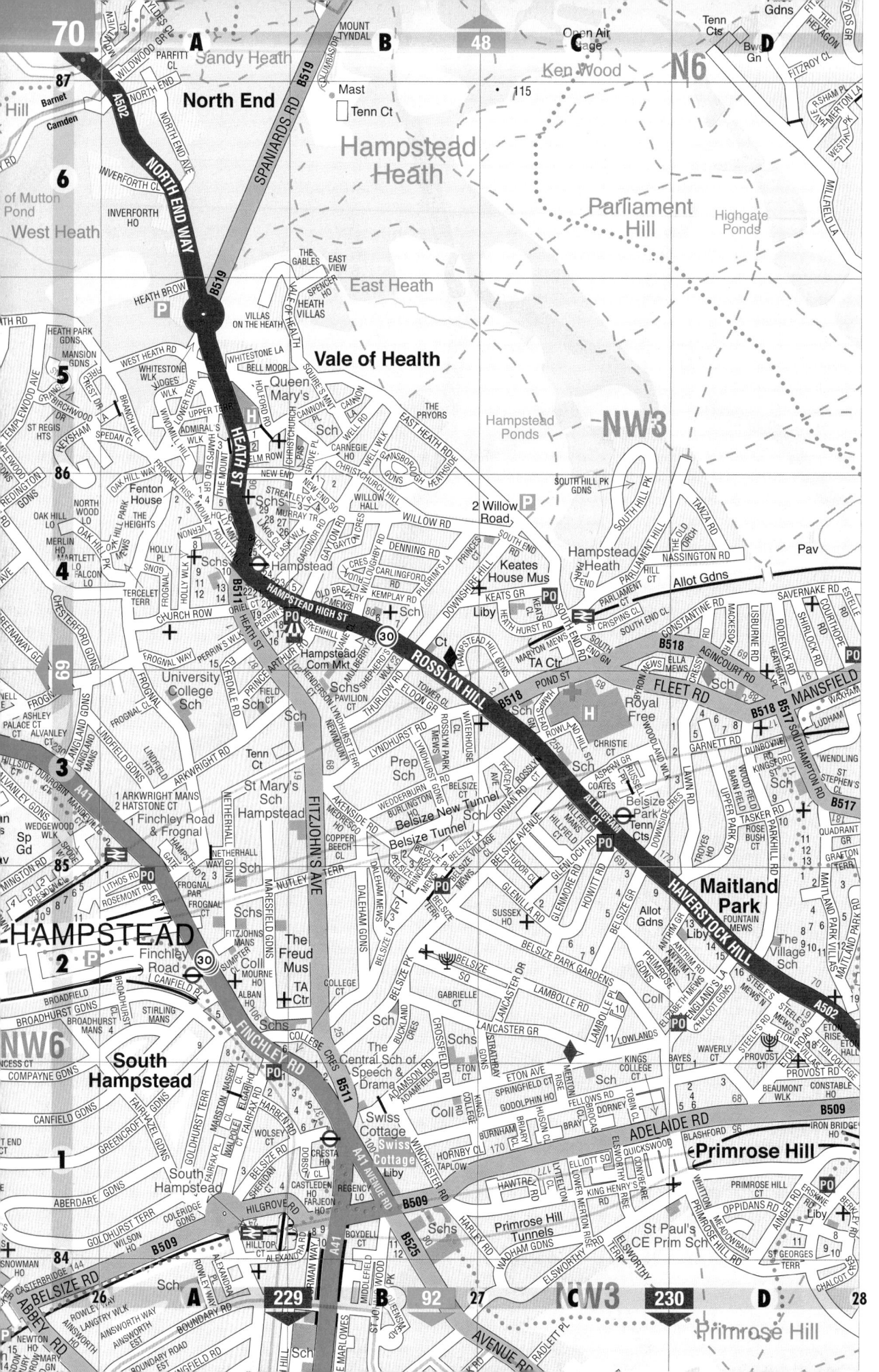
A
B
C
D
48
N6
Sandy Heath
Mount Tyndal
Open Air Stage
Ken Wood
Tenn Cts
Bwg Gn
Gdns
The Hexagon
Fitzroy Cl
North End
Mast
Tenn Ct
115
Hampstead Heath
Parliament Hill
Highgate Ponds
Millfield La
87
Barnet
Camden
Hill
6
of Mutton Pond
West Heath
Inverforth Cl
Inverforth Ho
Parfitt Cl
Wildwood Gr
North End
North End Ave
North End Way
A502
Spaniards Rd
B519
Columbas Dr
Heath Brow
P
East Heath
The Gables
East View
Spencer Ho
Heath Villas
Vale of Health
Villas on the Heath
Whitestone La
Bell Moor
Heath Park Gdns
Mansion Gdns
5
West Heath Rd
Whitestone Wlk
Judges' Wlk
Templewood Ave
Grange Gdns
Birchwood Dr
St Regis Hts
Heysham La
Spedan Cl
Branch Hill
Queen Mary's
Holford Rd
Christchurch Hill
Squire's Mnt
Cannon Pl
Cannon La
Well Rd
Carnegie Ho
Well Wlk
Sch
The Pryors
East Heath Rd
Hampstead Ponds
NW3
Gainsborough Gdns
Heathside
Upper Terr
Lower Terr
Admiral's Wlk
Windmill Hill
Hampstead Gr
Heath St
Elm Row
Grove Pl
New End
New End Sq
Streatley Pl
Murray Ter
Willow Hall
Willow Rd
2 Willow Road
South Hill Pk Gdns
South Hill Pk
Tanza Rd
The Old Orch
Parliament Hill
86
Redington Gdns
Oak Hill Way
Fenton House
The Heights
North Wood Lo
Oak Hill Lo
Oak Hill Park
Oak Hill Pk
Merlin Ho
Martlett Lo
Falcon Lo
4
Frognal Rise
Holly Bush Vale
Holly Pl
Holly Wlk
Schs
Hampstead
Gayton Rd
Gayton Cres
Denning Rd
Willoughby Rd
Carlingford Rd
Kemplay Rd
Pilgrim's La
Princes Ct
South End Rd
Keates House Mus
Downshire Hill
Keats Gr
Keats Cl
Liby
PO
Hampstead Heath
Parliament Hill
Nassington Rd
Allot Gdns
Pav
Tercelet Terr
Church Row
Frognal
Oriel Ct
Hampstead High St
Perrin's Ct
Perrin's Wlk
Old Brewery Mews
Greenhill
Hampstead Com Mkt
Heath Hurst Rd
South End Gn
St Crispins Cl
South End Cl
Constantine Rd
Mackeson Rd
Lisburne Rd
Roderick Rd
Shirlock Rd
Courthope Rd
Savernake Rd
Estelle Rd
30
Rosslyn Hill
Ct
Hampstead Hill Gdns
Maryon Mews
TA Ctr
B518
Ella Mews
Cressy Rd
Agincourt Rd
Heathgate
Fleet Rd
Mansfield
Waxham
Chesterford Gdns
Frognal Way
69
Frognal Gdns
Frognal Cl
University College Sch
Lindfield Gdns
Ellerdale Rd
Prince Arthur Rd
Field Ct
Henderson Ct
Lyndhurst Terr
Shepherd's Wlk
Mulberry Cl
Schs
Pavilion Ct
Thurlow Rd
Eldon Gr
Tower Cl
Pond St
Royal Free
H
Christie Ct
Woodland Wlk
Southampton Rd
B517
Ludham
Dunboyne Rd
Kingsford St
Wendling
St Stephen's Cl
Ashley Palace Ct
Alvanley Ct
Langland Gdns
Langland Mans
Lindfield Hts
Arkwright Rd
Tenn Ct
Newmount
Lyndhurst Rd
Rosslyn Park Mews
Lyndhurst Gdns
Waterhouse Cl
Prep Sch
Belsize Ct
Perceval Ave
Ornan Rd
Rowland Hill St
Aspern Gr
Russell Ct
Coates Ct
Allingham Ct
Belsize Park
Tenn Cts
Downside Cres
Lawn Rd
Upper Park Rd
Garnett Rd
Wood Field
Barn Field
Tasker Rd
Rose Bush Ct
Troyes Ho
Parkhill Rd
Quadrant Gr
Grafton Terr
3
Hillside Ct
Dunrobin Ct
Mandeville Ct
Alvanley Gdns
Wedgewood Wlk
Sp Gd
A41
1 Arkwright Mans
2 Hatstone Ct
Finchley Road & Frognal
St Mary's Sch Hampstead
Wedderburn Ho
Burlington Ho
Belsize New Tunnel
Belsize Tunnel
Akenside Rd
Medresco Ho
Copper Beech Cl
Belsize La
Belsize Village
Belsize Mews
Belsize Avenue
Tudor Cl
Hillfield Mans
Hillfield Ct
Glenloch Rd
Glenmore Rd
Howitt Rd
Haverstock Hill
Maitland Park
85
Lithos Rd
Rosemont Rd
Dresden Cl
Hampstead Gate
Netherhall Way
Netherhall Gdns
Frognal Par
Frognal Ct
Nutley Terr
Fitzjohn's Ave
Daleham Mews
Daleham Gdns
Glenilla Rd
Sussex Ho
Belsize Gr
Allot Gdns
Antrim Gr
Antrim Mans
Antrim Rd
Fountain Mews
Liby
The Village Sch
Maitland Park Villas
Maitland Park Rd
Hampstead
Fitzjohns Mans
Maresfield Gdns
The Freud Mus
Belsize Park Gardens
2
Finchley Road
Sumpter Cl
Coll
Mourne Ho
Alban Ho
TA Ctr
College Ct
Belsize Pk
Belsize Sq
Gabrielle Ct
Lancaster Dr
Lamboll Rd
Lambolle Pl
Primrose Gdns
Elizabeth Mews
England's La
Chalcot Gdns
Steele's Mews N
Steele's Mews S
Steele's Rd
Eton Rd
Eton Rise
Eton Villas
Eton College Rd
Eton Hall
A502
Canfield Pl
Broadfield
Broadhurst Gdns
Broadhurst Mans
Broadhurst Cl
Stirling Mans
Sch
Buckland Cres
Crossfield Rd
Lancaster Gr
Lowlands
Waverly Ct
Provost Ct
Provost Rd
Constable Ho
NW6
South Hampstead
Compayne Gdns
Finchley Rd
Naseby Cl
Marston Cl
Elgar Ho
Harben Rd
College Cres
B511
The Central Sch of Speech & Drama
Adamson Rd
Adamfields
Eton Ct
Strathray Gdns
Eton Ave
Springfield Ct
Godolphin Ho
Merton Rise
Kings College Ct
Bayes Ct
Beaumont Wlk
Canfield Gdns
Fairhazel Gdns
Greencroft Gdns
Goldhurst Terr
Walpole Ct
Fairfax Rd
Fairfax Pl
Wolsey Ct
Swiss Cottage
Coll
Kings College Rd
Burnham
Briary Cl
Huson Cl
Fellows Rd
Brocas Cl
Dorney
Tobin Cl
Bray
Adelaide Rd
B509
Iron Bridge Ho
Blashford
Primrose Hill
1
Belsize Rd
Dobson Cl
Cresta Ho
Regency Lo
A41 Avenue Rd
Hornby Cl
Taplow
Elliott Sq
Quickswood
Conybeare
Lower Merton Rise
King Henry's Rd
Elsworthy Rise
Whitton
Primrose Hill Ct
Oppidans Rd
Ainger Rd
Erskine Rd
Berkley Rd
Aberdare Gdns
Coleridge Gdns
Hilgrove Rd
Sheridan Ct
Castleden Ho
Farjeon Ho
Boydell Ct
Winchester Rd
Hawtrey Rd
Primrose Hill Tunnels
Wadham Gdns
St Paul's CE Prim Sch
Meadowbank
Primrose Hill Rd
St Georges Terr
Chalcot Cres
84
Goldhurst Terr
Wilson Ho
Snowman Ho
Casterbridge
Hilltop Ct
Alexandra Rd
B525
Harley Rd
Elsworthy Rd
Elsworthy Terr
26
Abbey Rd
Rowley Way
Langtry Wlk
Ainsworth Way
Ainsworth Est
Boundary Rd
Boundary Road Est
229
92
27
230
28
Middlefield
St John's Wood Pk
Marlowes
Avenue Rd
Radlett Pl
Newton Ho
Sch

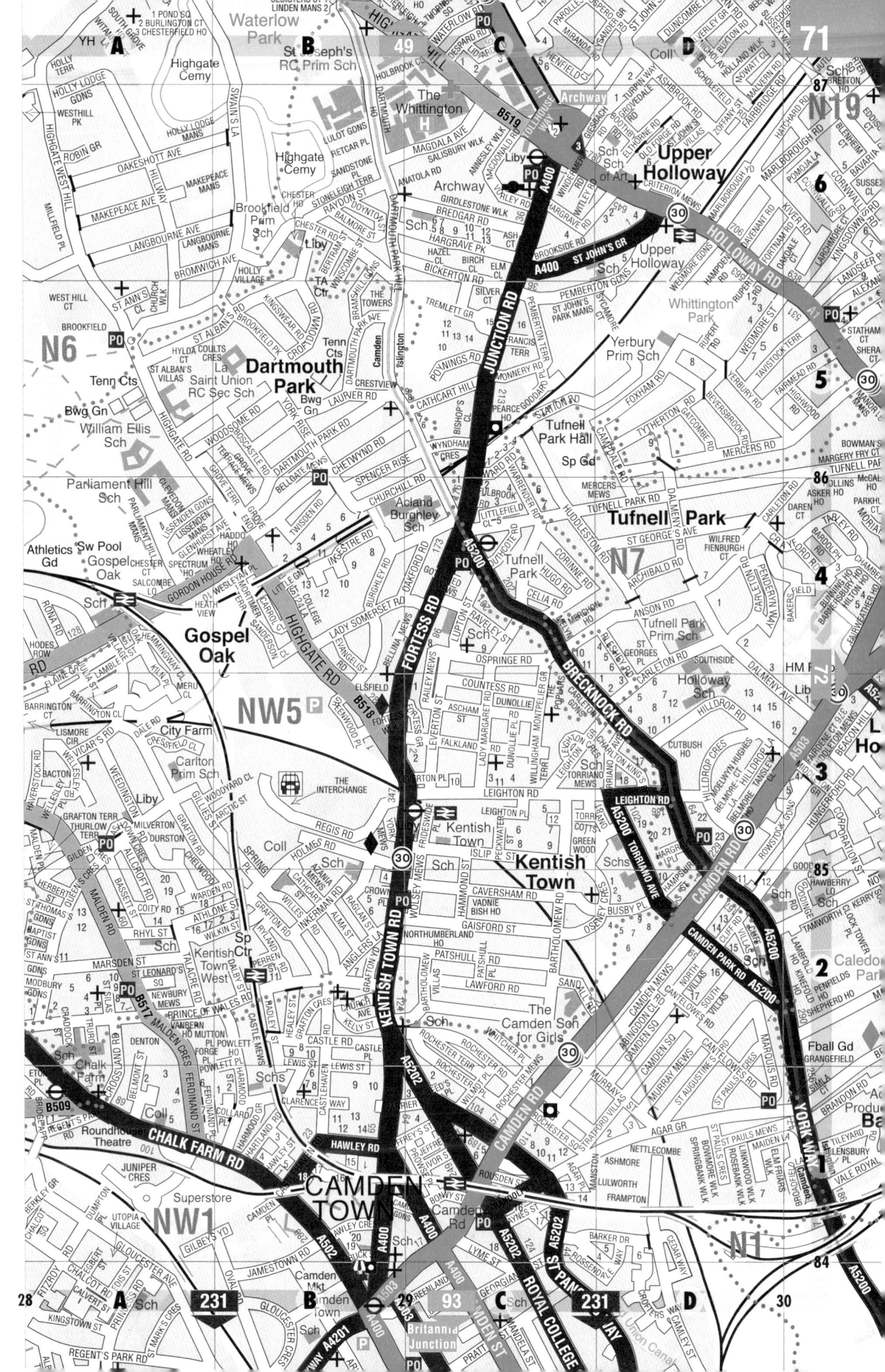

A
B
C
D
49
Waterlow Park
Highgate Cemy
St Joseph's RC Prim Sch
The Whittington
Archway
Upper Holloway
N19
Whittington Park
Yerbury Prim Sch
N6
Dartmouth Park
Saint Union RC Sec Sch
William Ellis Sch
Parliament Hill Sch
Tufnell Park Hall
Tufnell Park
Acland Burghley Sch
Gospel Oak
N7
Tufnell Park Prim Sch
Holloway Sch
NW5
City Farm
Carlton Prim Sch
The Interchange
Kentish Town
Kentish Town West
The Camden Sch for Girls
Roundhouse Theatre
Chalk Farm
CHALK FARM RD
CAMDEN TOWN
Superstore
NW1
Camden Mkt
Camden Town
Camden Rd
N1
Britannia Junction
Union Canal
JUNCTION RD
HOLLOWAY RD
FORTESS RD
KENTISH TOWN RD
BRECKNOCK RD
CAMDEN RD
HIGHGATE RD
YORK WAY
ROYAL COLLEGE ST
TUFNELL PARK RD
DARTMOUTH PARK HILL
LEIGHTON RD
TORRIANO AVE
CAMDEN PARK RD
HAWLEY RD
MALDEN RD
GORDON HOUSE RD
72
28
29
30
231
93

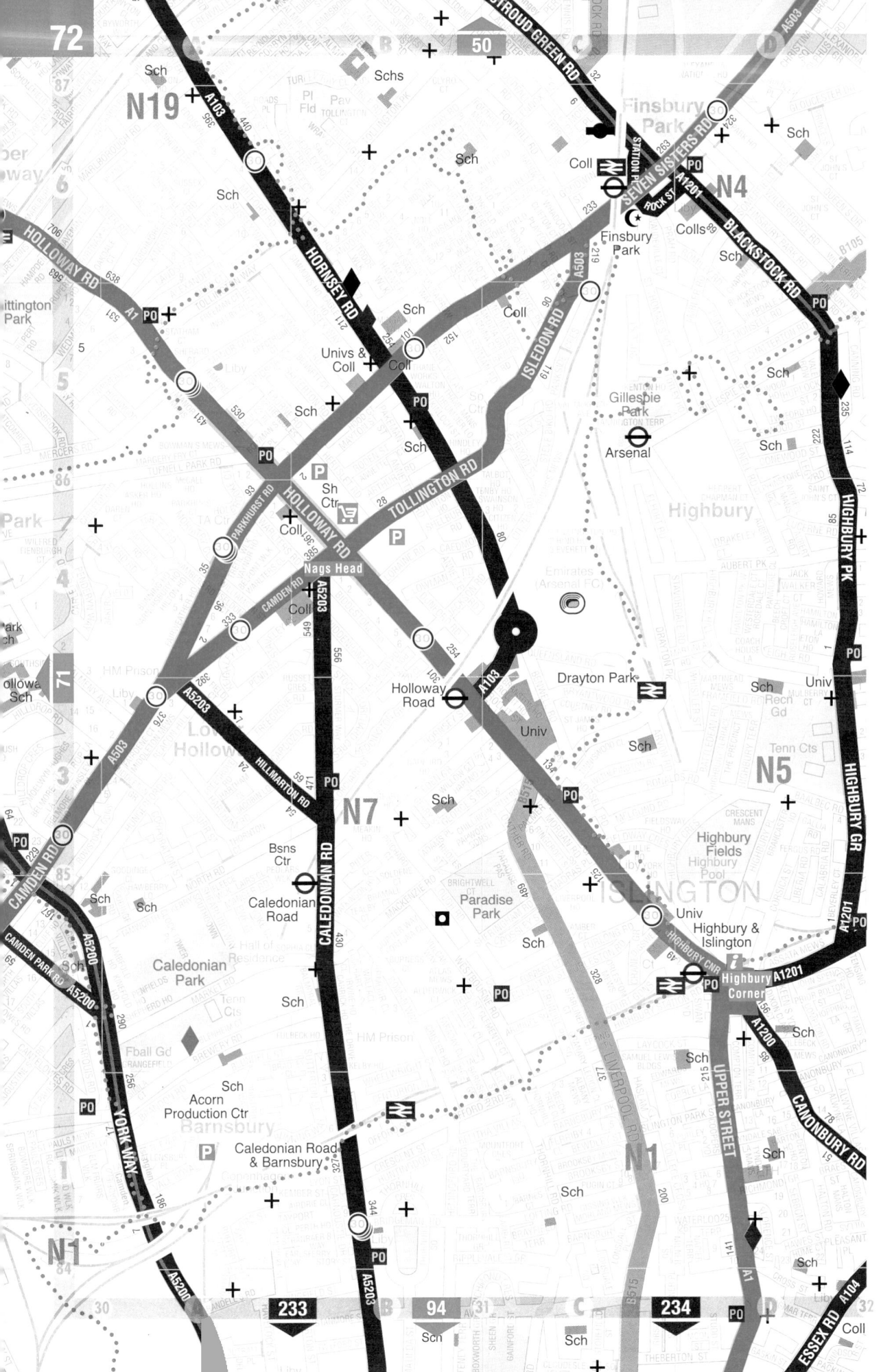

50
N19
Finsbury Park
Stroud Green Rd
Seven Sisters Rd
Station Pl
Rock St
N4
Blackstock Rd
Hornsey Rd
Holloway Rd
Tollington Rd
Isledon Rd
Camden Rd
Parkhurst Rd
Nags Head
Caledonian Rd
Hillmarton Rd
Gillespie Park
Arsenal
Highbury
Emirates (Arsenal FC)
Drayton Park
Holloway Road
N7
N5
Highbury Pk
Highbury Gr
Highbury Fields
Highbury Pool
Islington
Highbury & Islington
Highbury Corner
Caledonian Road
Caledonian Park
Paradise Park
HM Prison
Camden Park Rd
York Way
Liverpool Rd
Upper Street
Canonbury Rd
Barnsbury
Caledonian Road & Barnsbury
Acorn Production Ctr
N1
Essex Rd
233
94
234
71

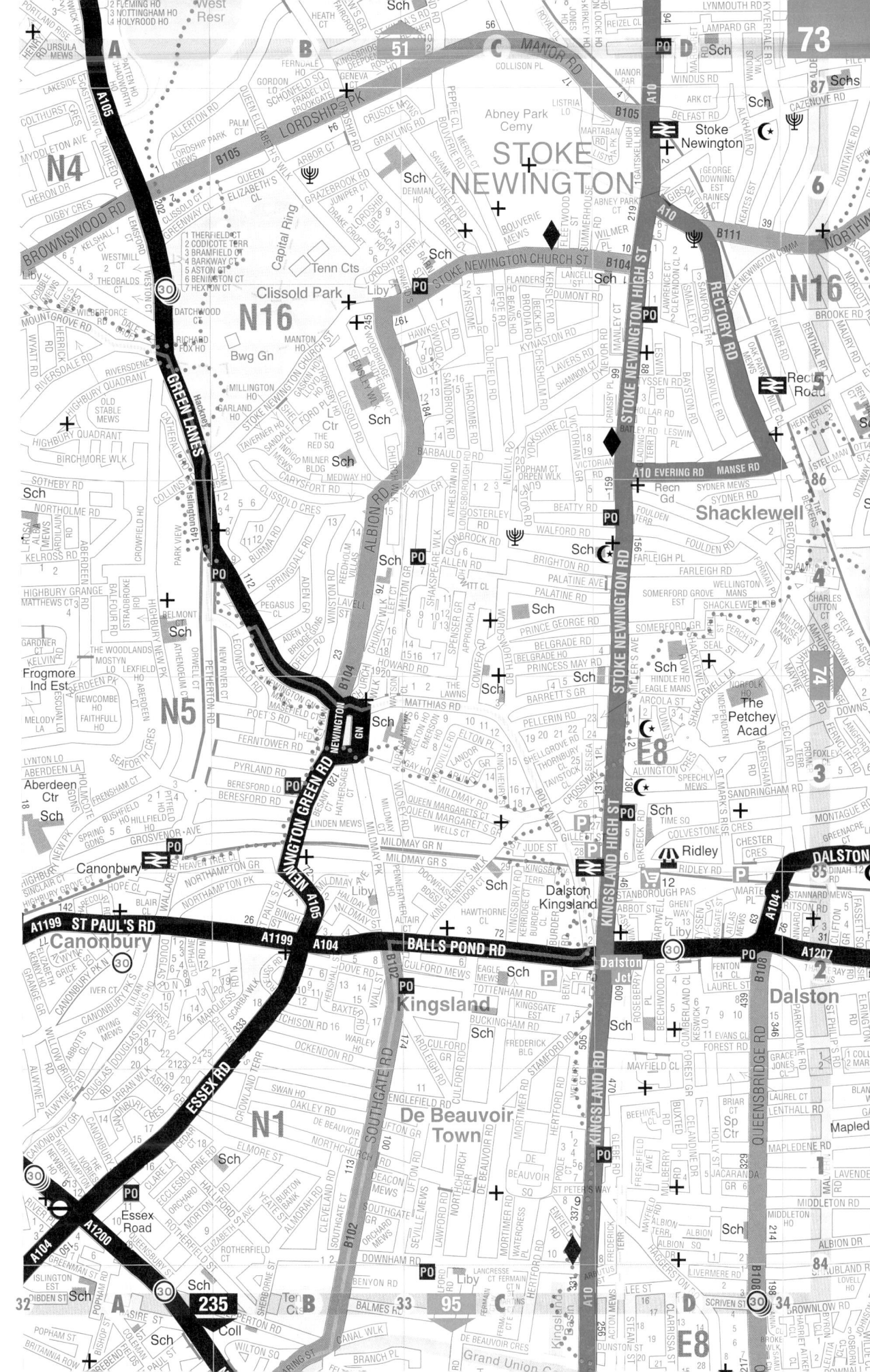
51
STOKE NEWINGTON
Abney Park Cemy
MANOR RD
LORDSHIP PK
BROWNSWOOD RD
GREEN LANES
Clissold Park
Capital Ring
Tenn Cts
STOKE NEWINGTON CHURCH ST
STOKE NEWINGTON HIGH ST
Stoke Newington
RECTORY RD
Rectory Road
N16
N4
N5
N1
E8
ALBION RD
EVERING RD
MANSE RD
Shacklewell
NEWINGTON GREEN RD
NEWINGTON GN
KINGSLAND HIGH ST
KINGSLAND RD
Dalston Kingsland
Dalston Jct
DALSTON
Dalston
BALLS POND RD
ST PAUL'S RD
Canonbury
Frogmore Ind Est
Aberdeen Ctr
ESSEX RD
Essex Road
SOUTHGATE RD
Kingsland
De Beauvoir Town
QUEENSBRIDGE RD
The Petchey Acad
Ridley
74
235
95
Grand Union C
Kingsland Basin
A
B
C
D
1
2
3
4
5
6
32
33
34

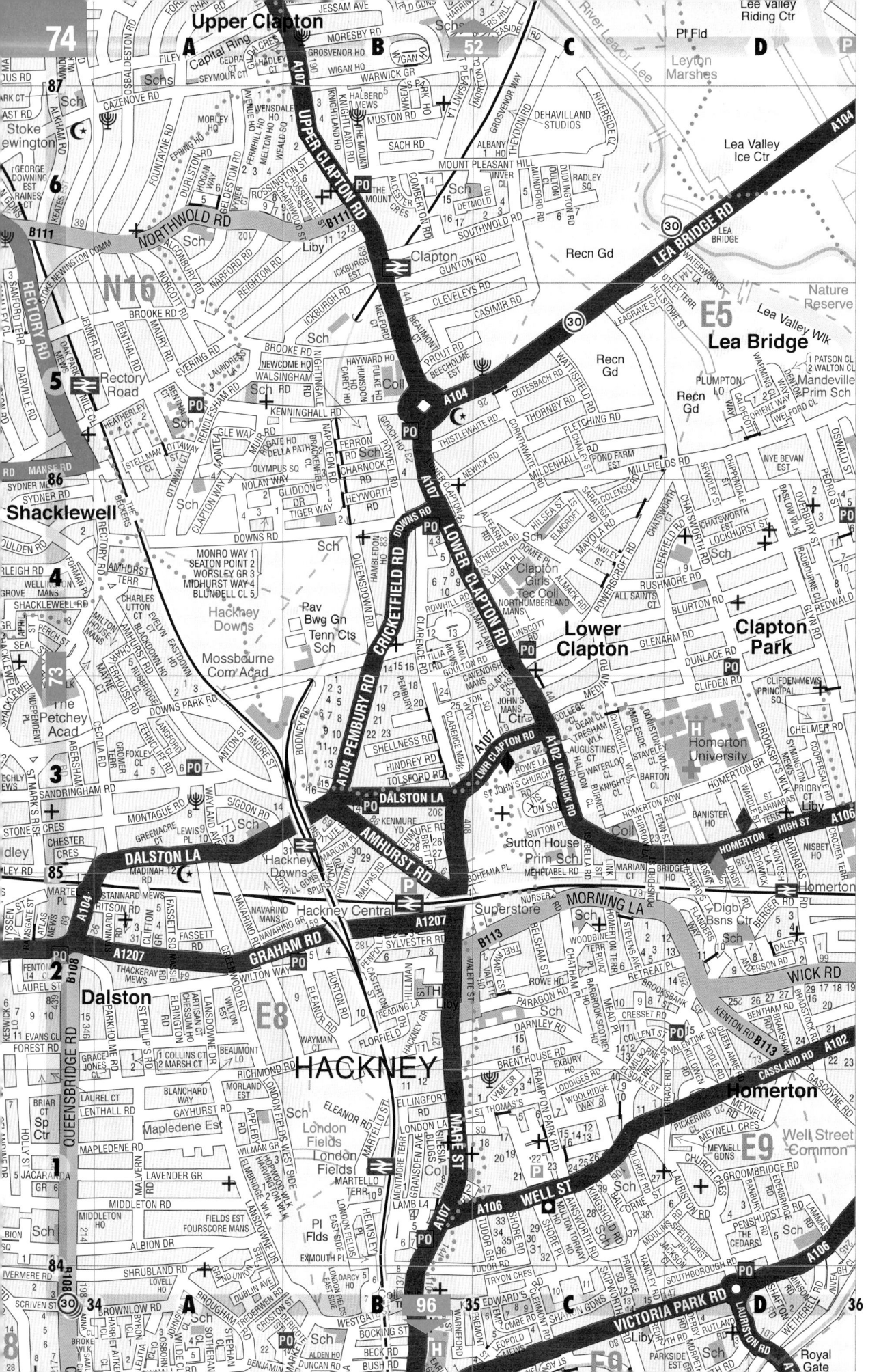
Upper Clapton
A
B
C
D
52
Lee Valley
Riding Ctr
Leyton
Marshes
River Lea or Lee
UPPER CLAPTON RD
A107
NORTHWOLD RD
B111
Stoke
Newington
N16
RECTORY RD
Rectory
Road
Clapton
LEA BRIDGE RD
A104
E5
Lea Bridge
Lea Valley
Ice Ctr
Nature
Reserve
Lea Valley Wlk
Mandeville
Prim Sch
Recn Gd
DEHAVILLAND
STUDIOS
MOUNT PLEASANT HILL
SOUTHWOLD RD
CLEVELEYS RD
Shacklewell
LOWER CLAPTON RD
CRICKETFIELD RD
DOWNS RD
Hackney
Downs
Mossbourne
Com Acad
The
Petchey
Acad
Lower
Clapton
Clapton
Park
Clapton
Girls
Tec Coll
Homerton
University
PEMBURY RD
DALSTON LA
AMHURST RD
URSWICK RD
A102
Sutton House
HOMERTON HIGH ST
A106
Homerton
Hackney Central
MORNING LA
B113
GRAHAM RD
A1207
Dalston
QUEENSBRIDGE RD
B108
E8
HACKNEY
WICK RD
CASSLAND RD
Homerton
E9
Well Street
Common
MARE ST
WELL ST
London
Fields
Mapledene Est
VICTORIA PARK RD
LAURISTON RD
Royal
Gate
96
34
35
36
1
2
3
4
5
6
73
84
85
86
87

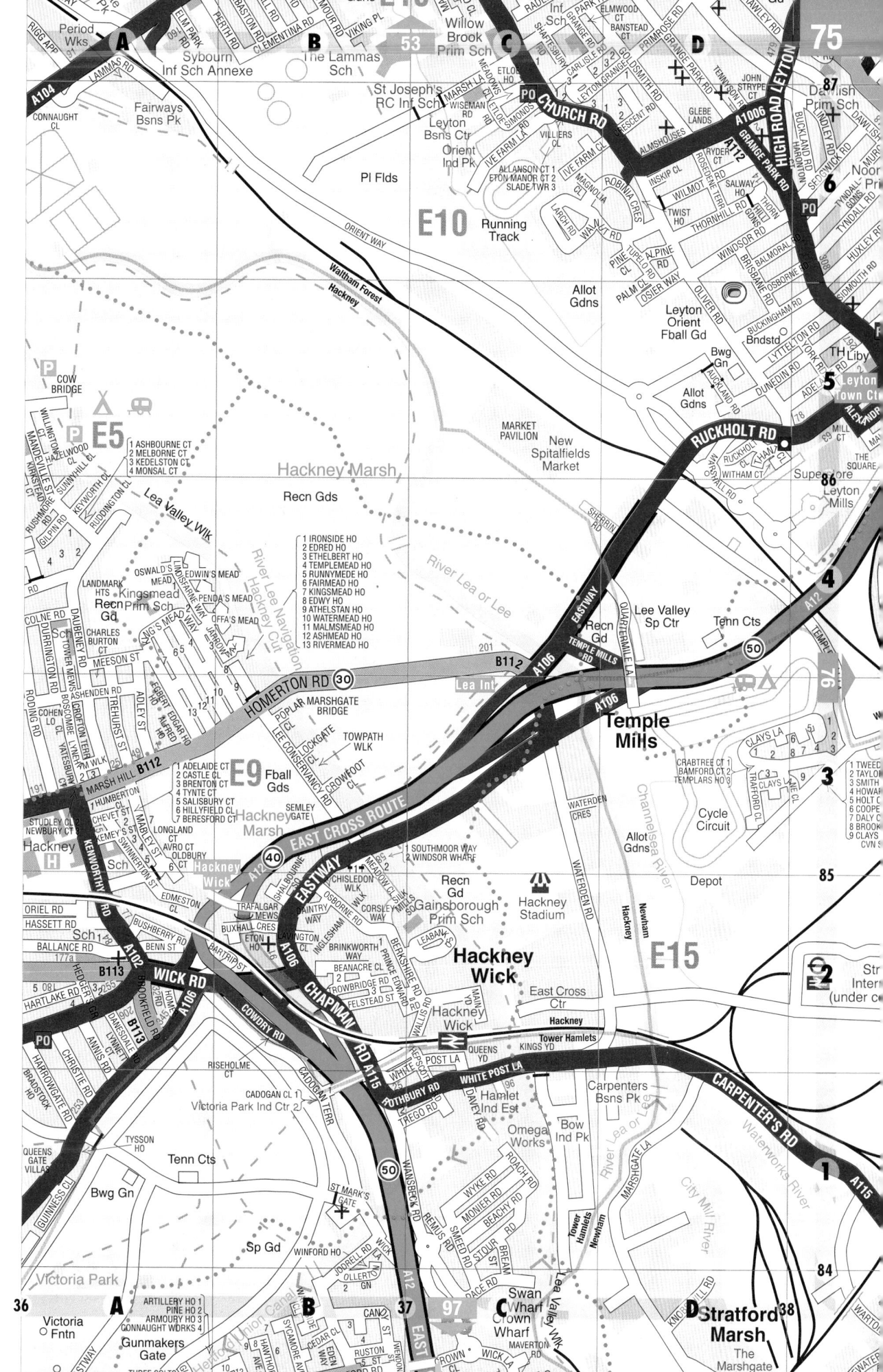

53
Period Wks
Sybourn Inf Sch Annexe
The Lammas Sch
Willow Brook Prim Sch
Inf Sch
Fairways Bsns Pk
St Joseph's RC Inf Sch
Leyton Bsns Ctr
Orient Ind Pk
CHURCH RD
HIGH ROAD LEYTON
A1006
A112
A104
Dawlish Prim Sch
Pl Flds
E10
Running Track
ORIENT WAY
Waltham Forest
Hackney
Allot Gdns
Leyton Orient Fball Gd
Bwg Gn
Bndstd
Liby
Leyton Town Ctr
RUCKHOLT RD
MARKET PAVILION
New Spitalfields Market
Hackney Marsh
Recn Gds
Superstore
Leyton Mills
COW BRIDGE
E5
Lea Valley Wlk
River Lee Navigation Hackney Cut
River Lea or Lee
Kingsmead Prim Sch
Recn Gd
Lee Valley Sp Ctr
Tenn Cts
EASTWAY
TEMPLE MILLS RD
A106
A12
B112
HOMERTON RD
Lea Int
76
Temple Mills
MARSHGATE BRIDGE
TOWPATH WLK
E9
Fball Gds
Hackney Marsh
EAST CROSS ROUTE
Channelsea River
Cycle Circuit
Allot Gdns
Depot
Hackney
Hackney Wick
Recn Gd
Gainsborough Prim Sch
Hackney Stadium
Hackney Wick
E15
East Cross Ctr
Hackney
Tower Hamlets
WICK RD
A102
B113
CHAPMAN RD
A115
WHITE POST LA
CARPENTER'S RD
Carpenters Bsns Pk
Hamlet Ind Est
Omega Works
Bow Ind Pk
Victoria Park Ind Ctr
Tenn Cts
Bwg Gn
Sp Gd
Victoria Park
Waterworks River
City Mill River
Lea Valley Wlk
Hertford Union Canal
Swan Wharf
Crown Wharf
Stratford Marsh
The Marshgate
Victoria Fntn
Gunmakers Gate
97
36
37
38
84
85
86
87

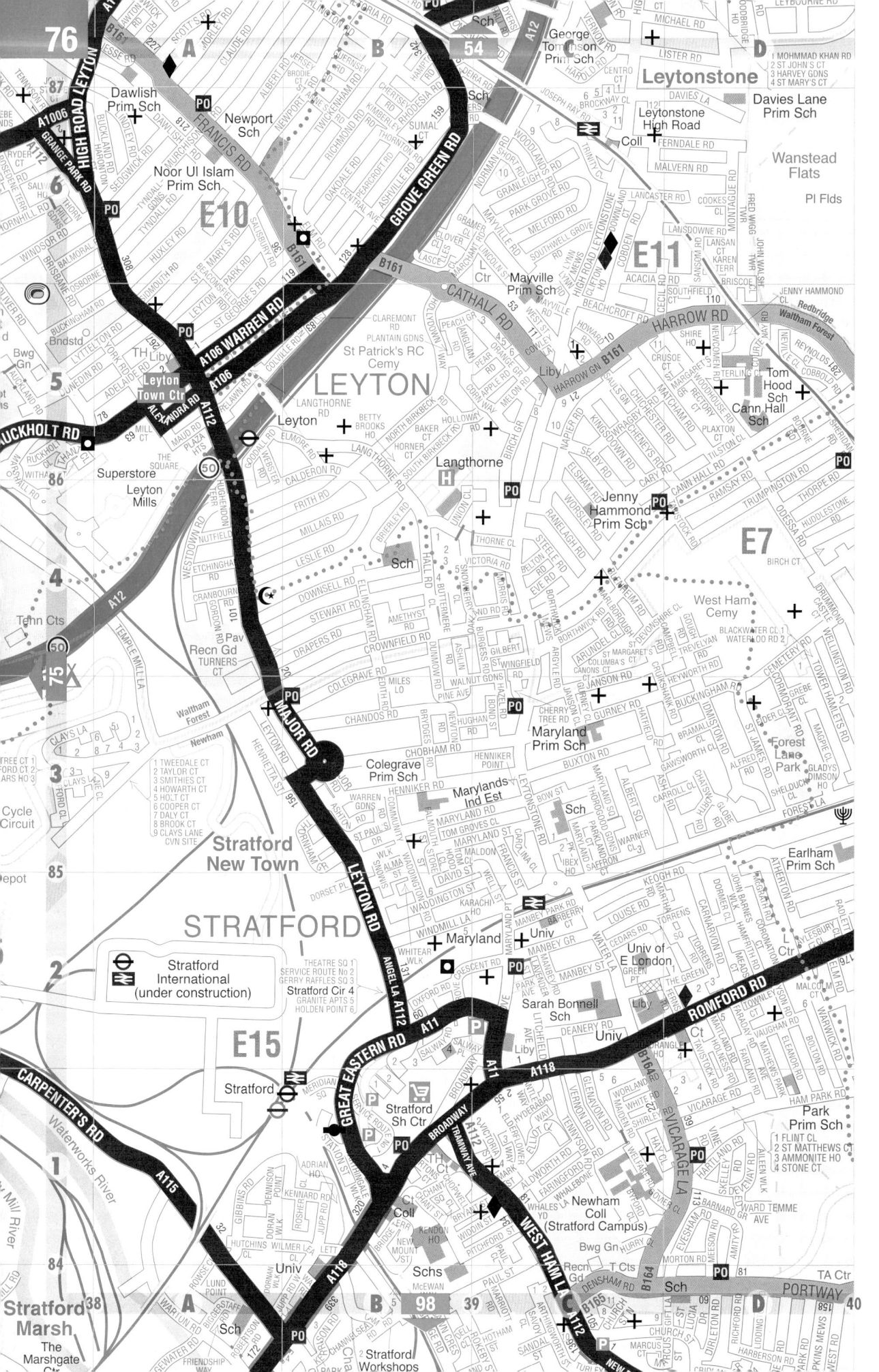
54
A
B
C
D
Leytonstone
Wanstead Flats
Pl Flds
E10
E11
E7
E15
LEYTON
STRATFORD
Stratford New Town
Stratford Marsh
HIGH ROAD LEYTON
GROVE GREEN RD
FRANCIS RD
A106 WARREN RD
HARROW RD
CATHALL RD
MAJOR RD
LEYTON RD
ANGEL LA A112
GREAT EASTERN RD
ROMFORD RD
BROADWAY
WEST HAM LA
CARPENTER'S RD
VICARAGE LA
PORTWAY
A12
A11
A118
A115
B161
B164
Dawlish Prim Sch
Newport Sch
Noor Ul Islam Prim Sch
George Tomlinson Prim Sch
Leytonstone High Road
Davies Lane Prim Sch
Mayville Prim Sch
St Patrick's RC Cemy
Leyton
Langthorne
Jenny Hammond Prim Sch
Tom Hood Sch
Cann Hall Sch
West Ham Cemy
Leyton Town Ctr
Superstore
Leyton Mills
Tennis Cts
Recn Gd
Colegrave Prim Sch
Marylands Ind Est
Maryland Prim Sch
Forest Lane Park
Earlham Prim Sch
Cycle Circuit
Stratford International (under construction)
Maryland
Univ
Univ of E London
Sarah Bonnell Sch
Stratford
Stratford Sh Ctr
Park Prim Sch
Newham Coll (Stratford Campus)
Stratford Workshops
The Marshgate
Waterworks River
1 MOHMMAD KHAN RD
2 ST JOHN'S CT
3 HARVEY GDNS
4 ST MARY'S CT
1 TWEEDALE CT
2 TAYLOR CT
3 SMITHIES CT
4 HOWARTH CT
5 HOLT CT
6 COOPER CT
7 DALY CT
8 BROOK CT
9 CLAYS LANE CVN SITE
THEATRE SQ 1
SERVICE ROUTE No 2
GERRY RAFFLES SQ 3
Stratford Cir 4
GRANITE APTS 5
HOLDEN POINT 6
1 FLINT CL
2 ST MATTHEWS CT
3 AMMONITE HO
4 STONE CT
75
98
38
39
40
84
85
86
87

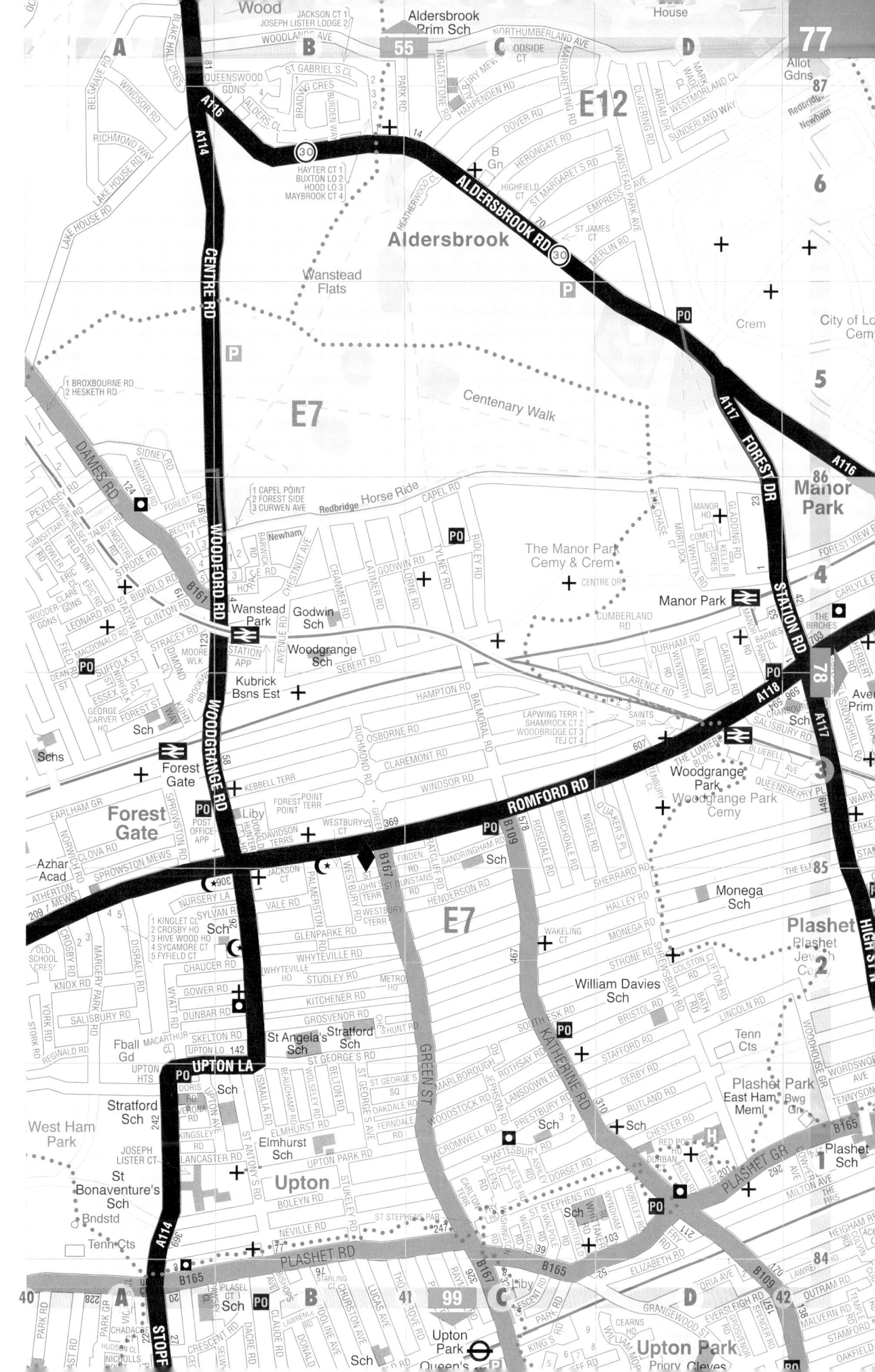
Wood
Aldersbrook Prim Sch
House
Allot Gdns
E12
Aldersbrook
Wanstead Flats
Centenary Walk
E7
Crem
City of London Cem
Manor Park
Redbridge
Newham
The Manor Park Cemy & Crem
Wanstead Park
Godwin Sch
Woodgrange Sch
Kubrick Bsns Est
Forest Gate
Woodgrange Park
Woodgrange Park Cemy
Monega Sch
Plashet
Plashet Jewish Cemy
William Davies Sch
Tenn Cts
Plashet Park
East Ham Meml
Plashet Sch
Azhar Acad
West Ham Park
Stratford Sch
St Bonaventure's Sch
St Angela's Sch
Elmhurst Sch
Upton
Upton Park
Fball Gd
A116
A114
A117
A118
B161
B165
B167
B109
ALDERSBROOK RD
CENTRE RD
WOODFORD RD
WOODGRANGE RD
ROMFORD RD
FOREST DR
STATION RD
UPTON LA
GREEN ST
KATHERINE RD
PLASHET RD
PLASHET GR
DAMES RD
CAPEL RD
Redbridge Horse Ride
WOODLANDS AVE
NORTHUMBERLAND AVE
PARK RD
LAKE HOUSE RD
RICHMOND WAY
WINDSOR RD
BELGRAVE RD
BLAKE HALL CRES
DOVER RD
HERONGATE RD
ST MARGARET'S RD
WANSTEAD PARK AVE
EMPRESS AVE
MERLIN RD
WESTMORLAND CL
SUNDERLAND WAY
CLAVERING RD
ARRAN DR
HAMPTON RD
OSBORNE RD
CLAREMONT RD
WINDSOR RD
RICHMOND RD
BALMORAL RD
SEBERT RD
GODWIN RD
LATIMER RD
CRANMER RD
LORNE RD
TYLNEY RD
RIDLEY RD
DURHAM RD
ALBANY RD
CARLTON RD
CLARENCE RD
SALISBURY RD
QUEENSBERRY PL
BLUEBELL AVE
HENDERSON RD
SHERRARD RD
HALLEY RD
MONEGA RD
STRONE RD
BRISTOL RD
STAFFORD RD
DERBY RD
RUTLAND RD
CHESTER RD
LINCOLN RD
SHREWSBURY RD
WOODHOUSE GR
CROMWELL RD
WOODSTOCK RD
MARLBOROUGH RD
LANSDOWN RD
SHAFTESBURY RD
ST STEPHENS RD
GLENPARKE RD
WHYTEVILLE RD
STUDLEY RD
KITCHENER RD
GROSVENOR RD
ST GEORGE'S RD
ELMHURST RD
UPTON PARK RD
BOLEYN RD
NEVILLE RD
CHAUCER RD
GOWER RD
DUNBAR RD
SKELTON RD
SALISBURY RD
KNOX RD
EARLHAM GR
CLOVA RD
SPROWSTON MEWS
GRANGEWOOD ST
OUTRAM RD
HIGH ST N
Upton Park
Queen's

55
78
99

A
B
C
D
56
100
77
Allot Gdns
Redbridge
Newham
Ilford
City of London Cemy
Crem
Alders Brook
Manor Park
FOREST DR
STATION RD
FOREST VIEW RD
ROMFORD RD
RABBITS RD
Liby & Mus
Prim Sch
LITTLE ILFORD LA
E12
Little Ilford
Little Ilford Park
Wks
Avenue Prim Sch
Essex Prim Sch
Monega Sch
Plashet
Plashet Jewish Cemy
HIGH ST N
BROWNING RD
Kensington Prim Sch
EAST AVE
Plashet Park
East Ham Meml
Plashet Sch
PLASHET GR
East Ham
E6
Tenn Cts
IG1
ILFORD
Ilford Interchange
ILFORD HILL
NORTH CIRCULAR RD
ILFORD LA
Maytime Sch
Park Sch
Coll
The Exchange
STATION RD
Rec Gd
Uphall Prim Sch
Pl Fld
Allot Gdns
IG11
Riverside Works
River Roding
Pacific Wharf
Superstore
Sports Gd
Bwg Gn
THE WILLOWS
Barking Flyover
LONDON RD
ABBEY RD
HIGHBRIDGE RD
Recn Gd
Barking & Dagenham
Redbridge
A116
A117
A118
A123
A124
A406
B165
B109
RON LEIGHTON WAY

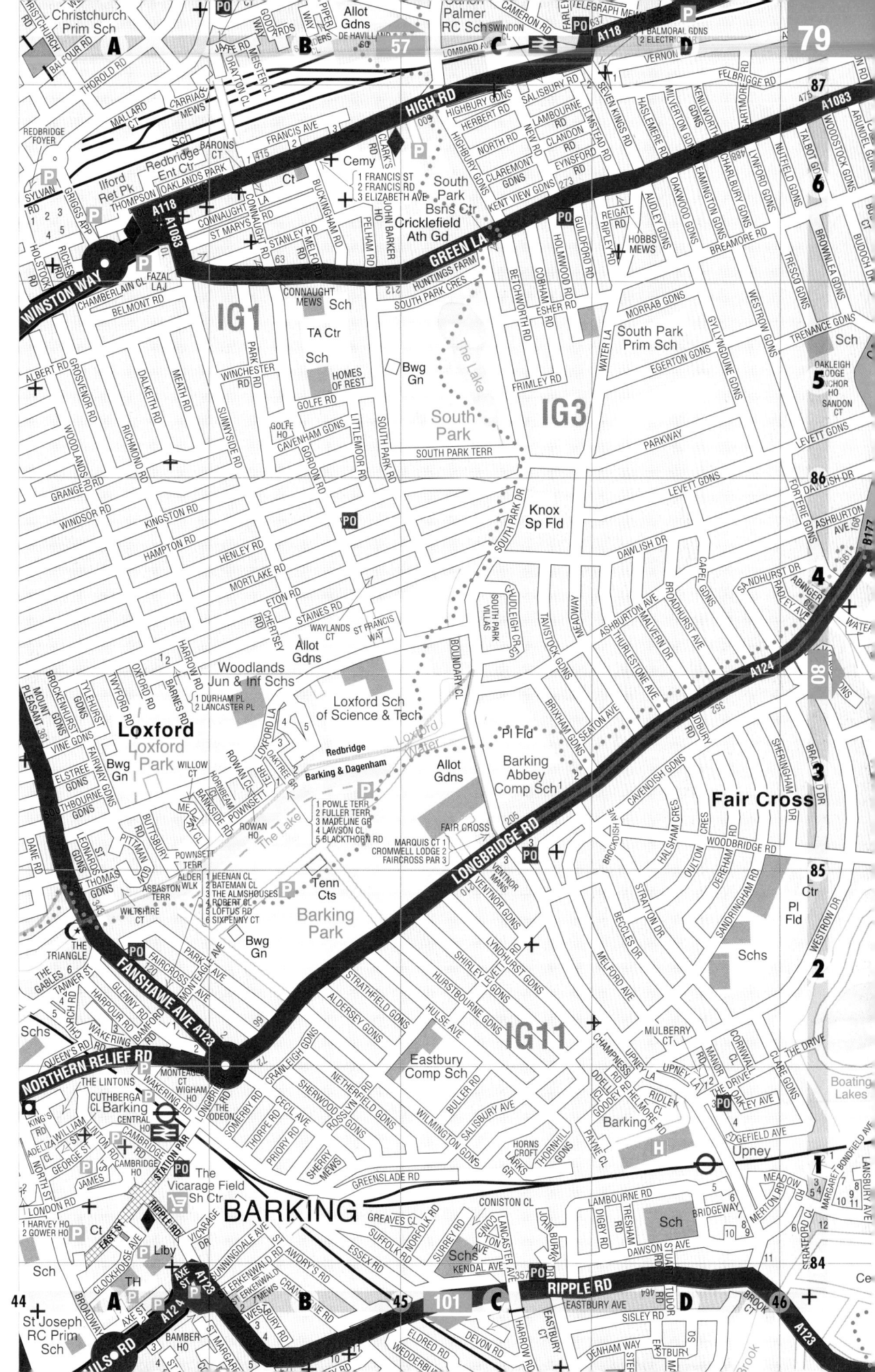

Christchurch Prim Sch
Allot Gdns
Palmer RC Sch
HIGH RD
GREEN LA
WINSTON WAY
IG1
IG3
IG11
South Park
South Park Bsns Ctr
Cricklefield Ath Gd
South Park Prim Sch
Knox Sp Fld
Loxford
Loxford Park
Woodlands Jun & Inf Schs
Loxford Sch of Science & Tech
Redbridge
Barking & Dagenham
Barking Abbey Comp Sch
Fair Cross
LONGBRIDGE RD
FANSHAWE AVE A123
NORTHERN RELIEF RD
Barking Park
Eastbury Comp Sch
BARKING
The Vicarage Field Sh Ctr
Upney
RIPPLE RD
St Joseph RC Prim Sch
Boating Lakes

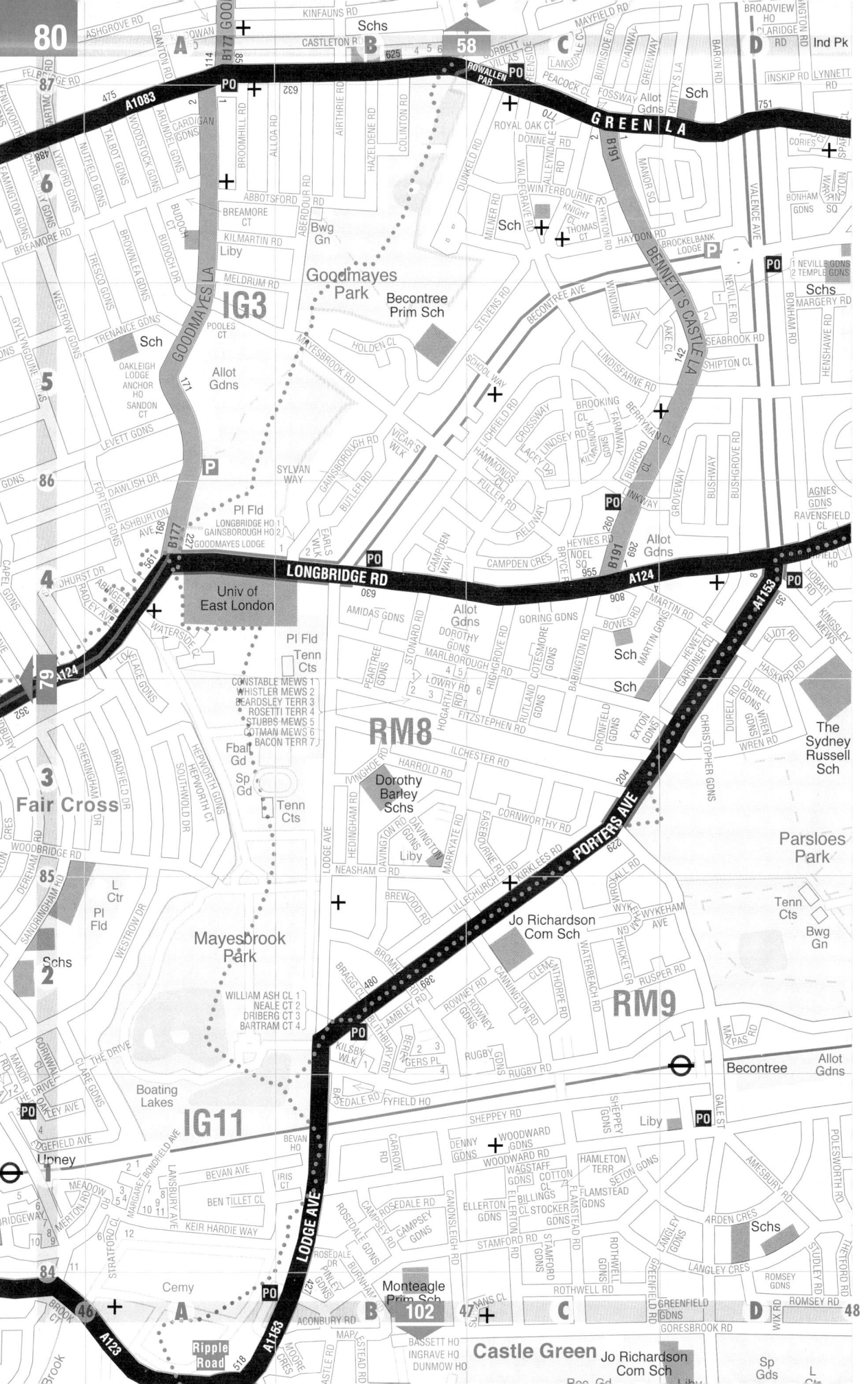
58
GREEN LA
A1083
Goodmayes Park
Becontree Prim Sch
IG3
GOODMAYES LA
BENNETT'S CASTLE LA
BECONTREE AVE
LONGBRIDGE RD
A124
Univ of East London
RM8
Dorothy Barley Schs
PORTERS AVE
A1153
Parsloes Park
The Sydney Russell Sch
Jo Richardson Com Sch
RM9
Mayesbrook Park
Fair Cross
Boating Lakes
IG11
Becontree
Upney
LODGE AVE
Monteagle Prim Sch
Castle Green
Ripple Road
A123
79
102

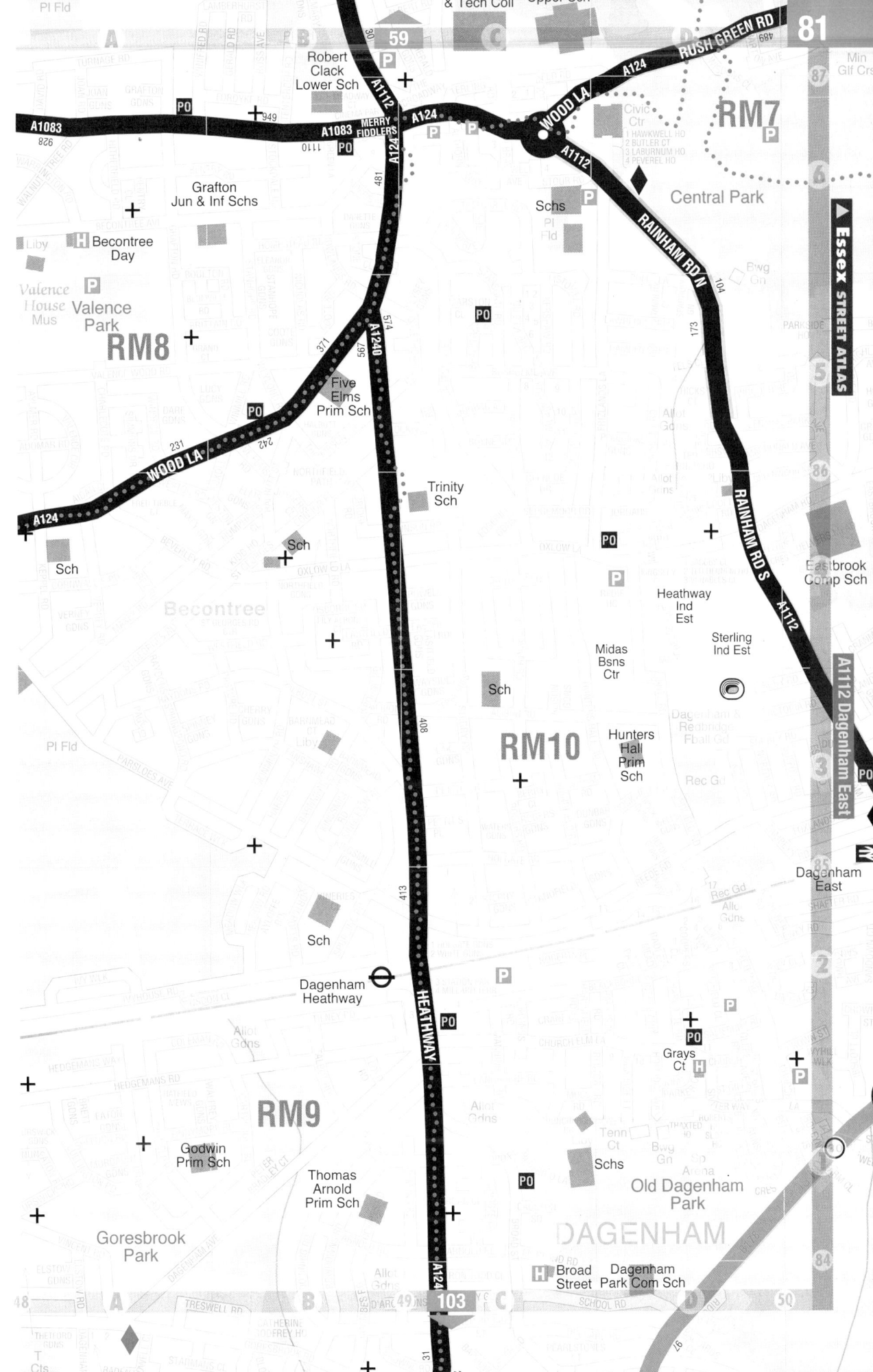

59
Robert Clack Lower Sch
& Tech Coll
Upper Sch
RUSH GREEN RD
A124
WOOD LA
Civic Ctr
RM7
Min Glf Crs
A1083
MERRY FIDDLERS
A1112
Grafton Jun & Inf Schs
Schs
Central Park
Liby
Becontree Day
RAINHAM RD N
Valence House Mus
Valence Park
RM8
A1240
Five Elms Prim Sch
Essex STREET ATLAS
WOOD LA
Trinity Sch
RAINHAM RD S
Sch
Eastbrook Comp Sch
Heathway Ind Est
Becontree
Sterling Ind Est
Midas Bsns Ctr
Sch
RM10
Hunters Hall Prim Sch
Dagenham & Redbridge Fball Gd
Rec Gd
A1112 Dagenham East
Pl Fld
Dagenham East
Sch
Dagenham Heathway
HEATHWAY
Allot Gdns
Grays Ct
RM9
Godwin Prim Sch
Schs
Old Dagenham Park
Thomas Arnold Prim Sch
Goresbrook Park
DAGENHAM
Broad Street
Dagenham Park Com Sch
103

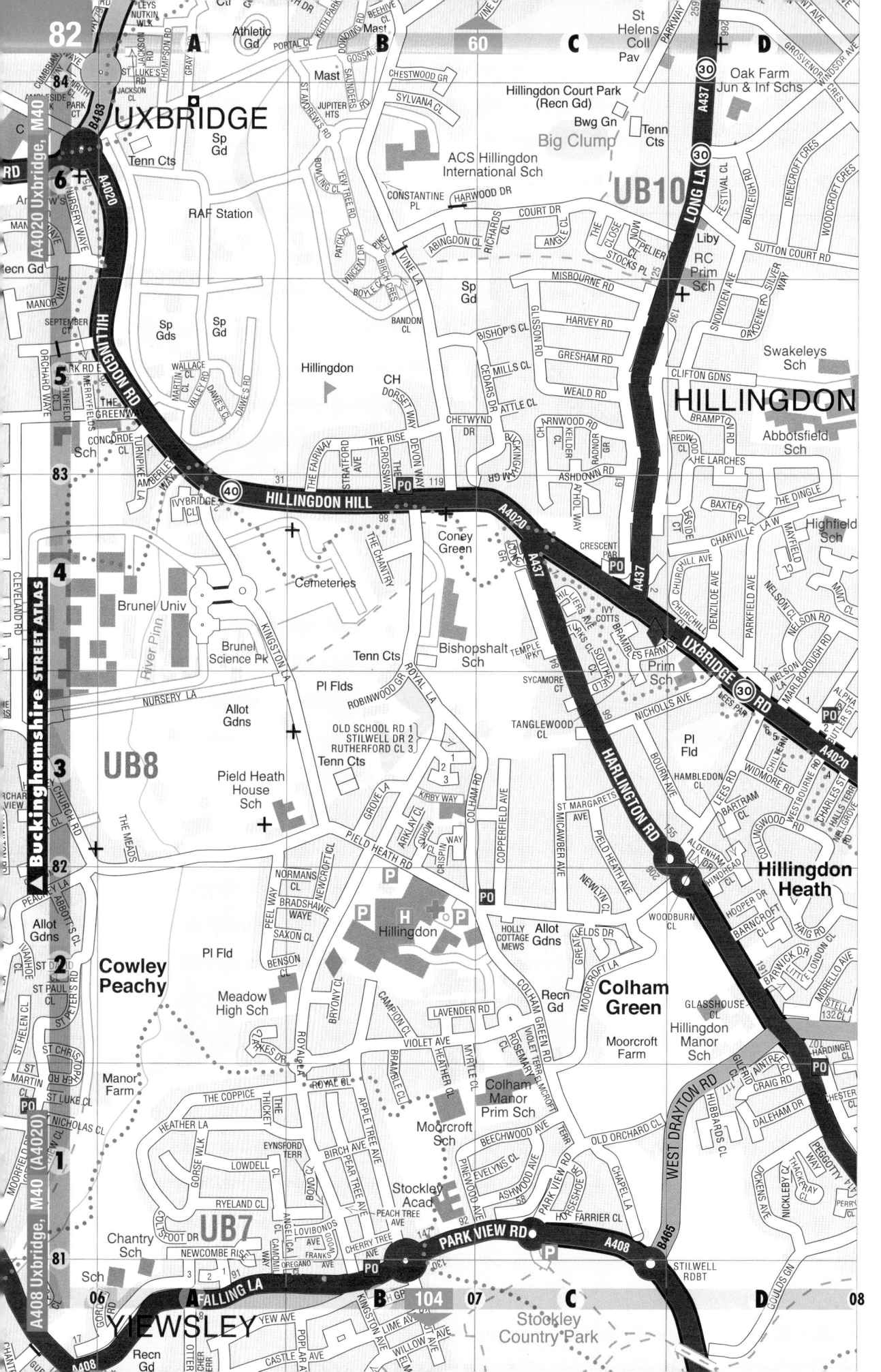
82
60
104
A
B
C
D
UXBRIDGE
HILLINGDON
Hillingdon Heath
Colham Green
Cowley Peachy
YIEWSLEY
UB10
UB8
UB7
St Helens Coll Pav
Oak Farm Jun & Inf Schs
Hillingdon Court Park (Recn Gd)
Bwg Gn
Tenn Cts
Big Clump
ACS Hillingdon International Sch
Athletic Gd
Mast
RAF Station
Sp Gd
Sp Gds
Tenn Cts
Hillingdon
CH
Swakeleys Sch
Abbotsfield Sch
Highfield Sch
Liby
RC Prim Sch
Coney Green
Cemeteries
Brunel Univ
Brunel Science Pk
River Pinn
Bishopshalt Sch
Pl Flds
Allot Gdns
Pield Heath House Sch
Prim Sch
Pl Fld
Meadow High Sch
Hillingdon
Recn Gd
Moorcroft Farm
Hillingdon Manor Sch
Manor Farm
Colham Manor Prim Sch
Moorcroft Sch
Stockley Acad
Chantry Sch
Sch
Recn Gd
Stockley Country Park
STILWELL RDBT
HILLINGDON RD
HILLINGDON HILL
UXBRIDGE RD
HARLINGTON RD
LONG LA
PARK VIEW RD
FALLING LA
WEST DRAYTON RD
KINGSTON LA
ROYAL LA
PIELD HEATH RD
COLHAM GREEN RD
VINE LA
NURSERY LA
COURT DR
A4020
A437
A408
B483
B465
A4020 Uxbridge, M40
Buckinghamshire STREET ATLAS
A408 Uxbridge, M40 (A4020)
06
07
08
81
82
83
84
1
2
3
4
5
6

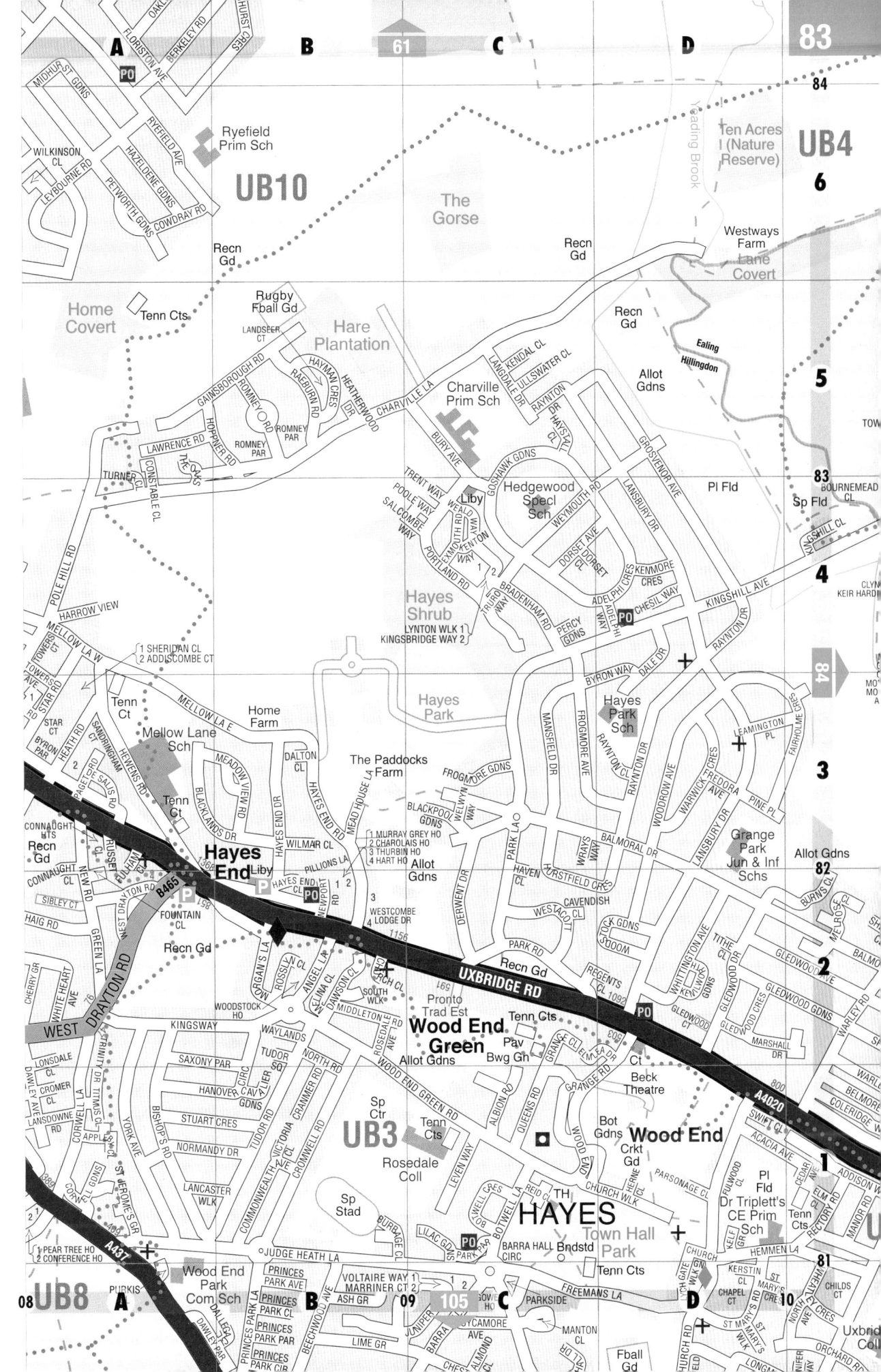
A
B
61
C
D
84
UB10
UB4
Ryefield Prim Sch
The Gorse
Ten Acres (Nature Reserve)
Yeading Brook
Westways Farm
Lane Covert
Recn Gd
Home Covert
Tenn Cts
Rugby Fball Gd
Hare Plantation
Allot Gdns
Ealing
Hillingdon
Charville Prim Sch
Hedgewood Specl Sch
Liby
Pl Fld
Sp Fld
Hayes Shrub
Hayes Park
Hayes Park Sch
Home Farm
Mellow Lane Sch
The Paddocks Farm
Grange Park Jun & Inf Schs
Hayes End
UXBRIDGE RD
WEST DRAYTON RD
Pronto Trad Est
Wood End Green
Beck Theatre
Sp Ctr
UB3
Rosedale Coll
Sp Stad
Bot Gdns
Wood End
Crkt Gd
HAYES
Town Hall Park
Dr Triplett's CE Prim Sch
Wood End Park Com Sch
UB8
105
Fball Gd
A4020
A437
B465
6
5
4
3
2
1
84
83
82
81
08
09
10

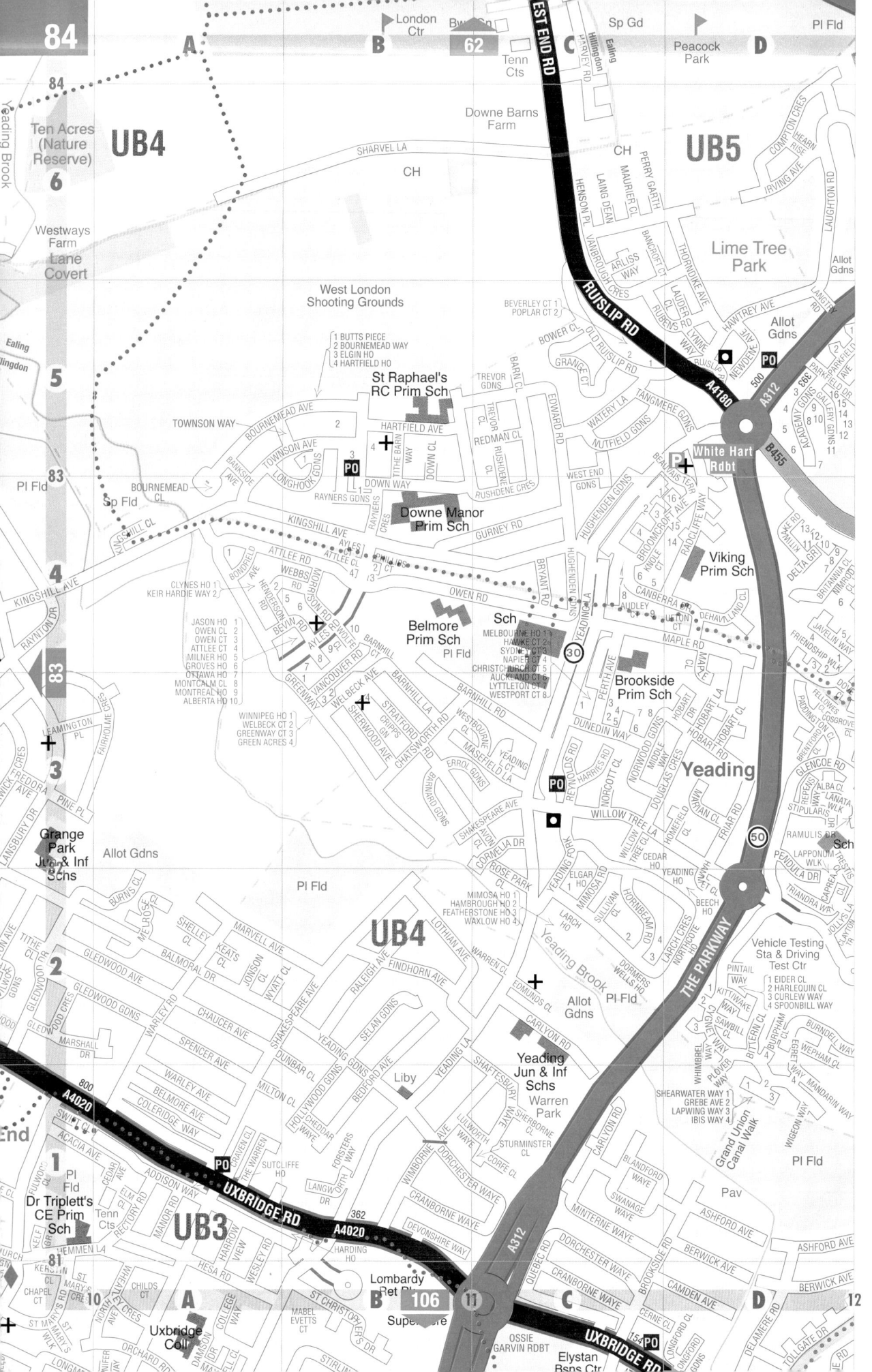

UB4
UB5
UB3
Ten Acres (Nature Reserve)
Yeading Brook
Westways Farm
Lane Covert
West London Shooting Grounds
Downe Barns Farm
SHARVEL LA
CH
WEST END RD
RUISLIP RD
A4180
Lime Tree Park
Peacock Park
St Raphael's RC Prim Sch
Downe Manor Prim Sch
Belmore Prim Sch
Brookside Prim Sch
Viking Prim Sch
White Hart Rdbt
Yeading
Grange Park Jun & Inf Schs
Allot Gdns
Pl Fld
Yeading Jun & Inf Schs
Warren Park
Liby
THE PARKWAY
A312
B455
UXBRIDGE RD
A4020
Lombardy Ret Pk
OSSIE GARVIN RDBT
Elystan Bsns Ctr
Dr Triplett's CE Prim Sch
Uxbridge Coll
Vehicle Testing Sta & Driving Test Ctr
Grand Union Canal Walk
KINGSHILL AVE
OWEN RD
BOURNEMEAD AVE
HARTFIELD AVE
TOWNSON AVE
GURNEY RD
MAPLE RD
WILLOW TREE LA
YEADING LA
BARNHILL RD
SHAKESPEARE AVE
GLEDWOOD AVE
BALMORAL DR
CHAUCER AVE
SPENCER AVE
WARLEY AVE
BELMORE AVE
COLERIDGE WAY
ASHFORD AVE
BERWICK AVE
CAMDEN AVE
CRANBORNE WAYE
DORCHESTER WAYE
MINTERNE WAYE
1 BUTTS PIECE
2 BOURNEMEAD WAY
3 ELGIN HO
4 HARTFIELD HO
JASON HO 1
OWEN CL 2
OWEN CT 3
ATTLEE CT 4
MILNER HO 5
GROVES HO 6
OTTAWA HO 7
MONTCALM CL 8
MONTREAL HO 9
ALBERTA HO 10
WINNIPEG HO 1
WELBECK CT 2
GREENWAY CT 3
GREEN ACRES 4
MELBOURNE HO 1
HAWKE CT 2
SYDNEY CT 3
NAPIER CT 4
CHRISTCHURCH CT 5
AUCKLAND CT 6
LYTTLETON CT 7
WESTPORT CT 8
MIMOSA HO 1
HAMBROUGH HO 2
FEATHERSTONE HO 3
WAXLOW HO 4
1 EIDER CL
2 HARLEQUIN CL
3 CURLEW WAY
4 SPOONBILL WAY
SHEARWATER WAY 1
GREBE AVE 2
LAPWING WAY 3
IBIS WAY 4
BEVERLEY CT 1
POPLAR CT 2
CLYNES HO 1
KEIR HARDIE WAY 2

62
83
106

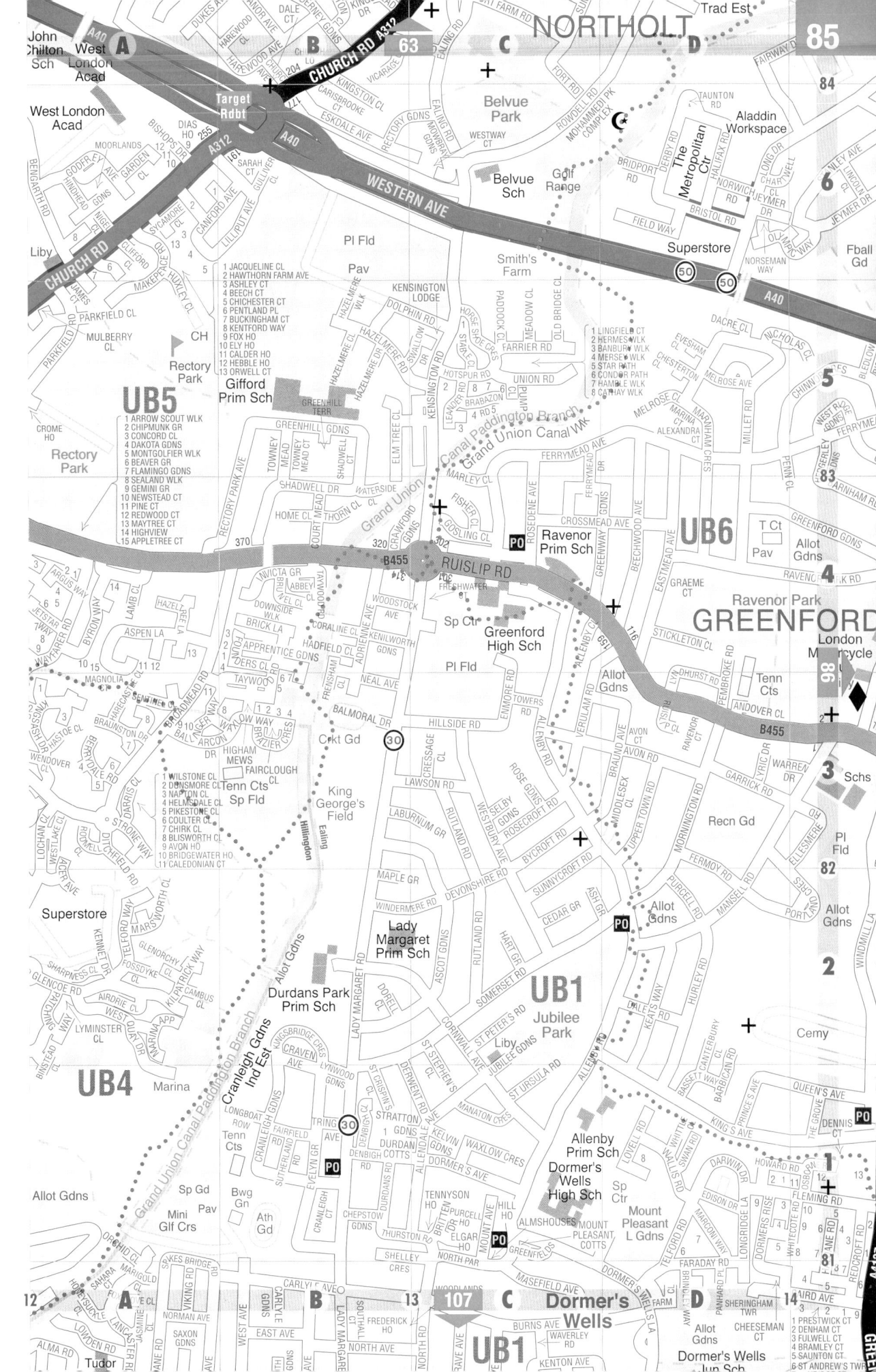

NORTHOLT
Trad Est
A
B
C
D
63
John Chilton Sch
West London Acad
West London Acad
Target Rdbt
CHURCH RD A312
A40
A312
WESTERN AVE
Belvue Park
Belvue Sch
Golf Range
MOHAMMEDI PK COMPLEX
Aladdin Workspace
The Metropolitan Ctr
Superstore
Smith's Farm
Fball Gd
Pl Fld
Pav
KENSINGTON LODGE
Rectory Park
Gifford Prim Sch
CH
Liby
UB5
1 JACQUELINE CL
2 HAWTHORN FARM AVE
3 ASHLEY CT
4 BEECH CT
5 CHICHESTER CT
6 PENTLAND PL
7 BUCKINGHAM CT
8 KENTFORD WAY
9 FOX HO
10 ELY HO
11 CALDER HO
12 HEBBLE HO
13 ORWELL CT
1 ARROW SCOUT WLK
2 CHIPMUNK GR
3 CONCORD CL
4 DAKOTA GDNS
5 MONTGOLFIER WLK
6 BEAVER GR
7 FLAMINGO GDNS
8 SEALAND WLK
9 GEMINI GR
10 NEWSTEAD CT
11 PINE CT
12 REDWOOD CT
13 MAYTREE CT
14 HIGHVIEW
15 APPLETREE CT
1 LINGFIELD CT
2 HERMES WLK
3 BANBURY WLK
4 MERSEY WLK
5 STAR PATH
6 CONDOR PATH
7 HAMBLE WLK
8 CATHAY WLK
Grand Union Canal Paddington Branch
Grand Union Canal Wk
Ravenor Prim Sch
UB6
RUISLIP RD
B455
Sp Ctr
Greenford High Sch
Pl Fld
Ravenor Park
GREENFORD
London Motorcycle Museum
Tenn Cts
Allot Gdns
T Ct
Pav
Crkt Gd
Tenn Cts Sp Fld
King George's Field
Hillingdon
Ealing
1 WILSTONE CL
2 DUNSMORE CL
3 NAPTON CL
4 HELMSDALE CL
5 PIKESTONE CL
6 COULTER CL
7 CHIRK CL
8 BLISWORTH CL
9 AVON HO
10 BRIDGEWATER HO
11 CALEDONIAN CT
Superstore
Lady Margaret Prim Sch
Durdans Park Prim Sch
Recn Gd
Schs
UB1
Jubilee Park
Cemy
Liby
Cranleigh Gdns Ind Est
UB4
Marina
Allot Gdns
Sp Gd
Mini Glf Crs
Pav
Bwg Gn
Ath Gd
Tenn Cts
Allenby Prim Sch
Dormer's Wells High Sch
Sp Ctr
Mount Pleasant L Gdns
ALMSHOUSES
1 PRESTWICK CT
2 DENHAM CT
3 FULWELL CT
4 BRAMLEY CT
5 SAUNTON CT
6 ST ANDREW'S TWR
Dormer's Wells
107
UB1
Allot Gdns
Dormer's Wells Jun Sch
Tudor
84
6
5
83
4
98
3
82
2
1
81
12
13
14

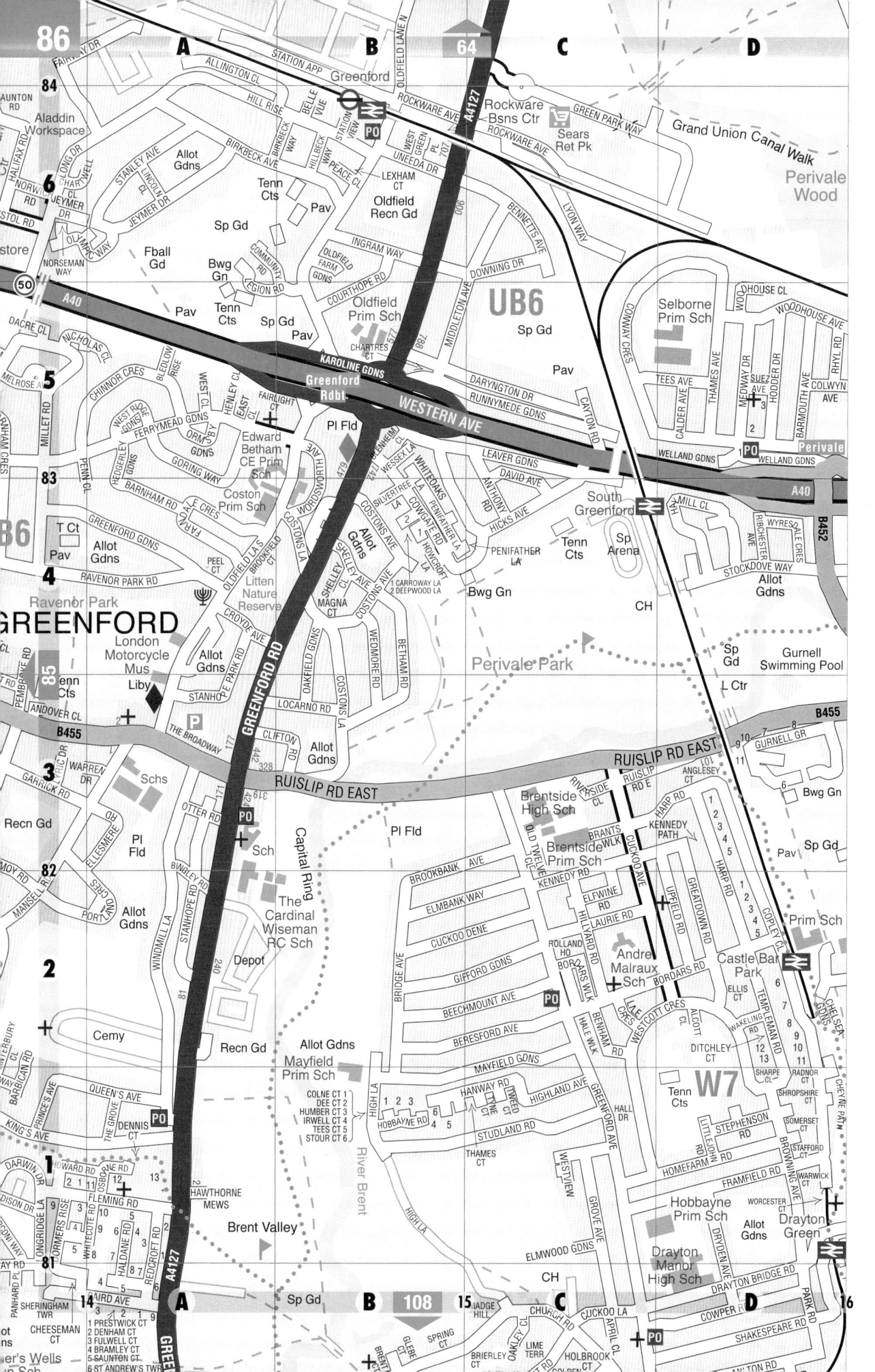

Greenford
Rockware Bsns Ctr
Sears Ret Pk
Grand Union Canal Walk
Perivale Wood
Aladdin Workspace
Oldfield Recn Gd
UB6
Selborne Prim Sch
Oldfield Prim Sch
Greenford Rdbt
WESTERN AVE
Edward Betham CE Prim Sch
Coston Prim Sch
South Greenford
Sp Arena
Litten Nature Reserve
GREENFORD
Ravenor Park
London Motorcycle Mus
Perivale Park
Gurnell Swimming Pool
RUISLIP RD EAST
GREENFORD RD
Brentside High Sch
Brentside Prim Sch
Capital Ring
The Cardinal Wiseman RC Sch
Andre Malraux Sch
Castle Bar Park
Mayfield Prim Sch
W7
Hobbayne Prim Sch
Drayton Green
Drayton Manor High Sch
Brent Valley
River Brent
A40
A4127
B455
B452
64
85
108

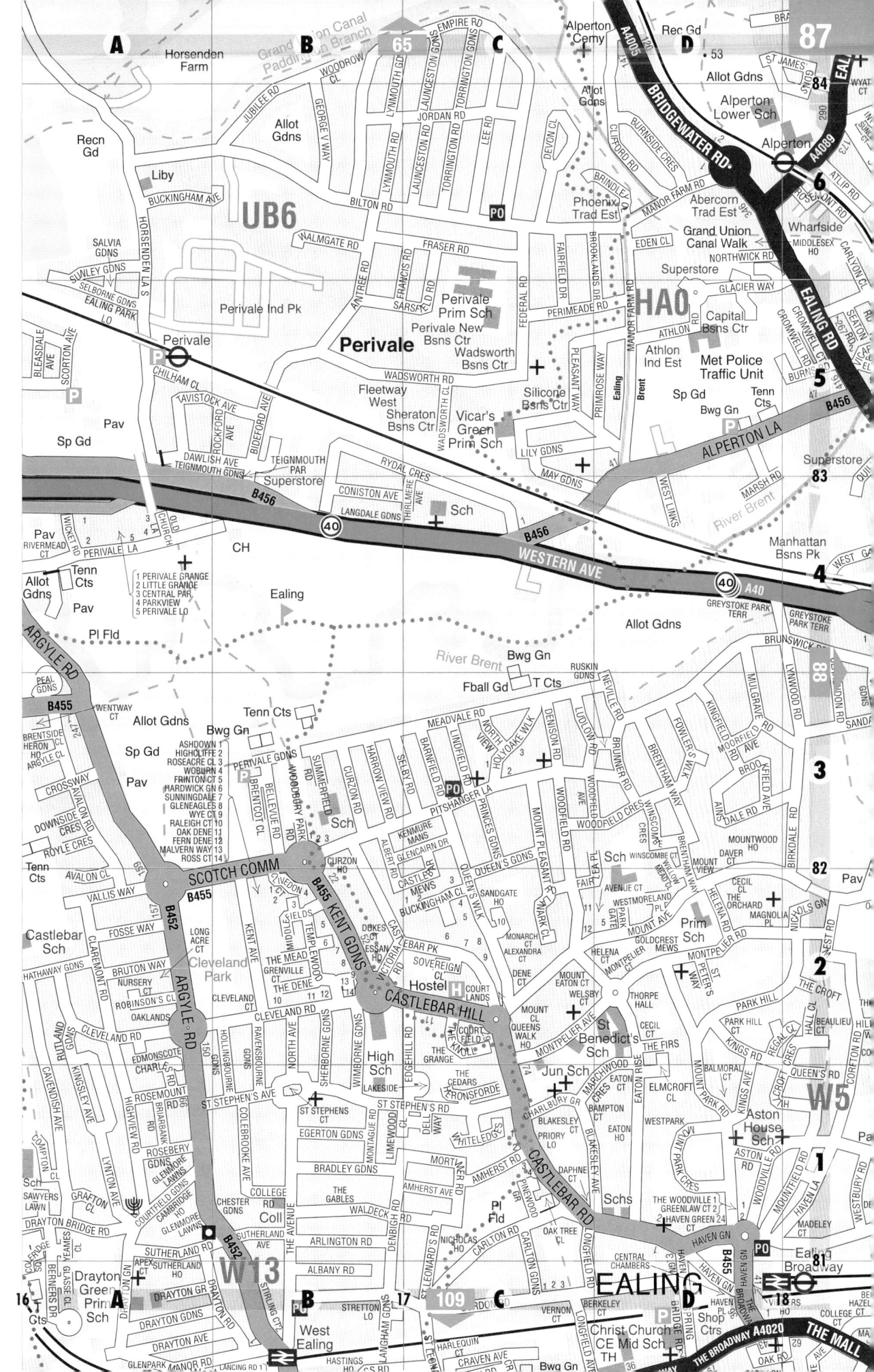

87
A
B
C
D
65
Horsenden Farm
Grand Union Canal Paddington Branch
WOODROW CL
EMPIRE RD
LYNMOUTH GDNS
LAUNCESTON GDNS
TORRINGTON GDNS
Alperton Cemy
A4005
Rec Gd
ST JAMES' GDNS
Allot Gdns
JUBILEE RD
GEORGE V WAY
Allot Gdns
JORDAN RD
LEE RD
LYNMOUTH RD
LAUNCESTON RD
TORRINGTON RD
DEVON CL
CLIFFORD RD
BURNSIDE CRES
BRIDGEWATER RD
Alperton Lower Sch
Alperton
A4089
ATLIP RD
Recn Gd
Liby
BUCKINGHAM AVE
BILTON RD
UB6
PO
BRINDLEY CL
Phoenix Trad Est
MANOR FARM RD
Abercorn Trad Est
6
Wharfside
SALVIA GDNS
HORSENDEN LA S
WALMGATE RD
FRASER RD
EDEN CL
Grand Union Canal Walk
NORTHWICK RD
MIDDLESEX HO
SUNLEY GDNS
SELBORNE GDNS
EALING PARK LO
ANTREE RD
FRANCIS RD
SARSFIELD RD
Perivale Prim Sch
FEDERAL RD
FAIRFIELD DR
BROOKLANDS DR
HA0
Superstore
GLACIER WAY
EALING RD
Perivale Ind Pk
PERIMEADE RD
ATHLON RD
Capital Bsns Ctr
CROMWELL RD
Perivale
Perivale New Bsns Ctr
Wadsworth Bsns Ctr
Athlon Ind Est
Met Police Traffic Unit
BLEASDALE AVE
SCORTON AVE
CHILHAM CL
WADSWORTH RD
PLEASANT WAY
PRIMROSE WAY
Ealing
Brent
BURNS RD
5
Fleetway West
Silicone Bsns Ctr
Sp Gd
Tenn Cts
TAVISTOCK AVE
ROCKFORD AVE
BIDEFORD AVE
Sheraton Bsns Ctr
Vicar's Green Prim Sch
WADSWORTH CL
Bwg Gn
B456
Pav
Sp Gd
LILY GDNS
ALPERTON LA
DAWLISH AVE
TEIGNMOUTH GDNS
TEIGNMOUTH PAR
RYDAL CRES
Superstore
MAY GDNS
Superstore
83
CONISTON AVE
THIRLMERE AVE
MARSH RD
LANGDALE GDNS
Sch
WEST LINKS
River Brent
B456
40
Pav
RIVERMEAD CT
WICKET RD
PERIVALE LA
OLD CHURCH LA
CH
WESTERN AVE
Manhattan Bsns Pk
Allot Gdns
Tenn Cts
1 PERIVALE GRANGE
2 LITTLE GRANGE
3 CENTRAL PAR
4 PARKVIEW
5 PERIVALE LO
Ealing
A40
4
GREYSTOKE PARK TERR
Pav
Allot Gdns
ARGYLE RD
Pl Fld
BRUNSWICK RD
River Brent
Bwg Gn
RUSKIN GDNS
PEAL GDNS
Fball Gd
T Cts
88
B455
WENTWAY CT
Allot Gdns
Tenn Cts
MEADVALE RD
NORTH VIEW
HOLYOAKE WLK
DENISON RD
LUDLOW RD
NEVILLE RD
KINGFIELD RD
MULGRAVE RD
LYNWOOD RD
BRENTSIDE
HERON HO
ARGYLE CL
Sp Gd
Bwg Gn
ASHDOWN 1
HIGHCLIFFE 2
ROSEACRE CL 3
WOBURN 4
FRINTON CT 5
HARDWICK GN 6
SUNNINGDALE 7
GLENEAGLES 8
WYE CT 9
RALEIGH CT 10
OAK DENE 11
FERN DENE 12
MALVERN WAY 13
ROSS CT 14
PERIVALE GDNS
SUMMERFIELD RD
CURZON RD
HARROW VIEW RD
SELBY RD
BARNFIELD RD
LINDFIELD RD
BRUNNER RD
BRENTHAM WAY
FOWLER'S WLK
MOORFIELD AVE
3
CROSSWAY
AVALON RD
Pav
BRENTCOT CL
BELLEVUE RD
WOODBURY PARK RD
PITSHANGER LA
PRINCES GDNS
WOODFIELD RD
WOODFIELD AVE
WOODFIELD CRES
WINSCOMBE CRES
BROOKFIELD AVE
AINSDALE RD
DOWNSIDE CRES
ROYLE CRES
Sch
KENMURE MANS
GLENCAIRN DR
ALBERT RD
MOUNT PLEASANT RD
MOUNTWOOD HO
BIRKDALE RD
Tenn Cts
AVALON CL
SCOTCH COMM
CURZON HO
CASTLEBAR MEWS
QUEEN'S GDNS
LEA PL
Sch
WINSCOMBE CT
MOUNT VIEW
DAVER CT
82
Pav
VALLIS WAY
B455
KENT GDNS
BUCKINGHAM CL
QUEEN'S WLK
SANDGATE HO
PARK CL
AVENUE CT
CECIL CT
THE ORCHARD
MAGNOLIA PL
Castlebar Sch
FOSSE WAY
B452
LONG ACRE CT
CLAREMONT RD
KENT AVE
MIDDLEFIELDS
TEMPLEWOOD
DUKES CT
LESSAR HO
CASTLEBAR PK
WESTMORELAND PL
PARK GATE
MOUNT AVE
Prim Sch
HELENA RD
NICHOLS GN
HATHAWAY GDNS
Cleveland Park
THE MEAD
GRENVILLE CT
THE DENE
VICTORIA RD
SOVEREIGN CL
MONARCH CT
ALEXANDRA CT
GOLDCREST MEWS
HELENA CT
MONTPELIER CT
MONTPELIER RD
2
THE CROFT
BRUTON WAY
NURSERY CT
ROBINSON'S CL
OAKLANDS
CLEVELAND CT
Hostel
COURTLANDS
CASTLEBAR HILL
DENE CT
MOUNT EATON CT
WELSBY CT
THORPE HALL
ST PETER'S WAY
PARK HILL
CLEVELAND RD
RUTLAND GDNS
ARGYLE RD
CLEVELAND RD
NORTH AVE
SHERBORNE GDNS
WIMBORNE GDNS
MOUNT CL
QUEENS WALK HO
MONTPELIER AVE
St Benedict's Sch
CECIL CT
THE FIRS
PARK HILL CT
KINGS RD
BEAULIEU CT
EDMONSCOTE
CHARLES
HOLLINGBOURNE GDNS
RAVENSBOURNE GDNS
High Sch
EDGEHILL RD
COURTFIELD
THE KNOLL
THE GRANGE
BALMORAL CT
QUEEN'S RD
CAVENDISH AVE
KINGSLEY AVE
ROSEMOUNT RD
ST STEPHEN'S AVE
LAKESIDE
THE CEDARS
HERONSFORDE
Jun Sch
MARCHWOOD CRES
EATON CT
EATON RISE
ELMCROFT CL
MOUNT PARK RD
W5
HIGHVIEW RD
BRIARBANK RD
COLEBROOKE AVE
ST STEPHENS CT
ST STEPHEN'S RD
CHARLBURY GR
BLAKESLEY CT
BAMPTON CT
EATON HO
WESTPARK
Aston House Sch
ROSEBERY GDNS
GLENMORE LAWNS
EGERTON GDNS
MONTAGUE RD
LIMEWOOD
DELL WAY
WHITELEDGES
PRIORY LO
MOUNT PARK CRES
ASTON RD
WOODVILLE RD
MOUNTFIELD RD
HAVEN LA
1
COMPTON CL
COURTFIELD GDNS
CAMBRIDGE HO
LYNTON AVE
BRADLEY GDNS
MORTIMER RD
AMHERST RD
CASTLEBAR RD
DAPHNE CT
Sch
SAWYERS LAWN
GRAFTON CL
CHESTER GDNS
COLLEGE RD
THE GABLES
AMHERST AVE
Pl Fld
PINEWOOD GR
Schs
THE WOODVILLE 1
GREENLAW CT 2
HAVEN GREEN 24
MADELEY CT
DRAYTON BRIDGE RD
Coll
WALDECK RD
DENBIGH RD
OAK TREE CL
HAVEN GN
PO
SUTHERLAND RD
SUTHERLAND AVE
THE AVENUE
ARLINGTON RD
NICHOLAS HO
CARLTON RD
LONGFIELD RD
CENTRAL CHAMBERS
B455
Ealing Broadway
81
W13
B452
Drayton Green Prim Sch
APEX CT
SUTHERLAND HO
DRAYTON GR
ALBANY RD
ST LEONARD'S RD
CARLTON GDNS
EALING
16
A
B
109
C
D
18
DRAYTON GDNS
DRAYTON RD
STIRLING CT
STRETTON LO
17
GORDON RD
VERNON CT
BERKELEY CT
HAVEN PL
VILLIERS HO
COLLEGE CT
DRAYTON AVE
West Ealing
LANGHAM GDNS
HARLEQUIN CT
Christ Church CE Mid Sch
Shop Ctrs
A4020
THE BROADWAY
THE MALL
OAK RD
GLENPARK
MANOR RD
LANCING RD
HASTINGS HO
CRAVEN AVE
Bwg Gn

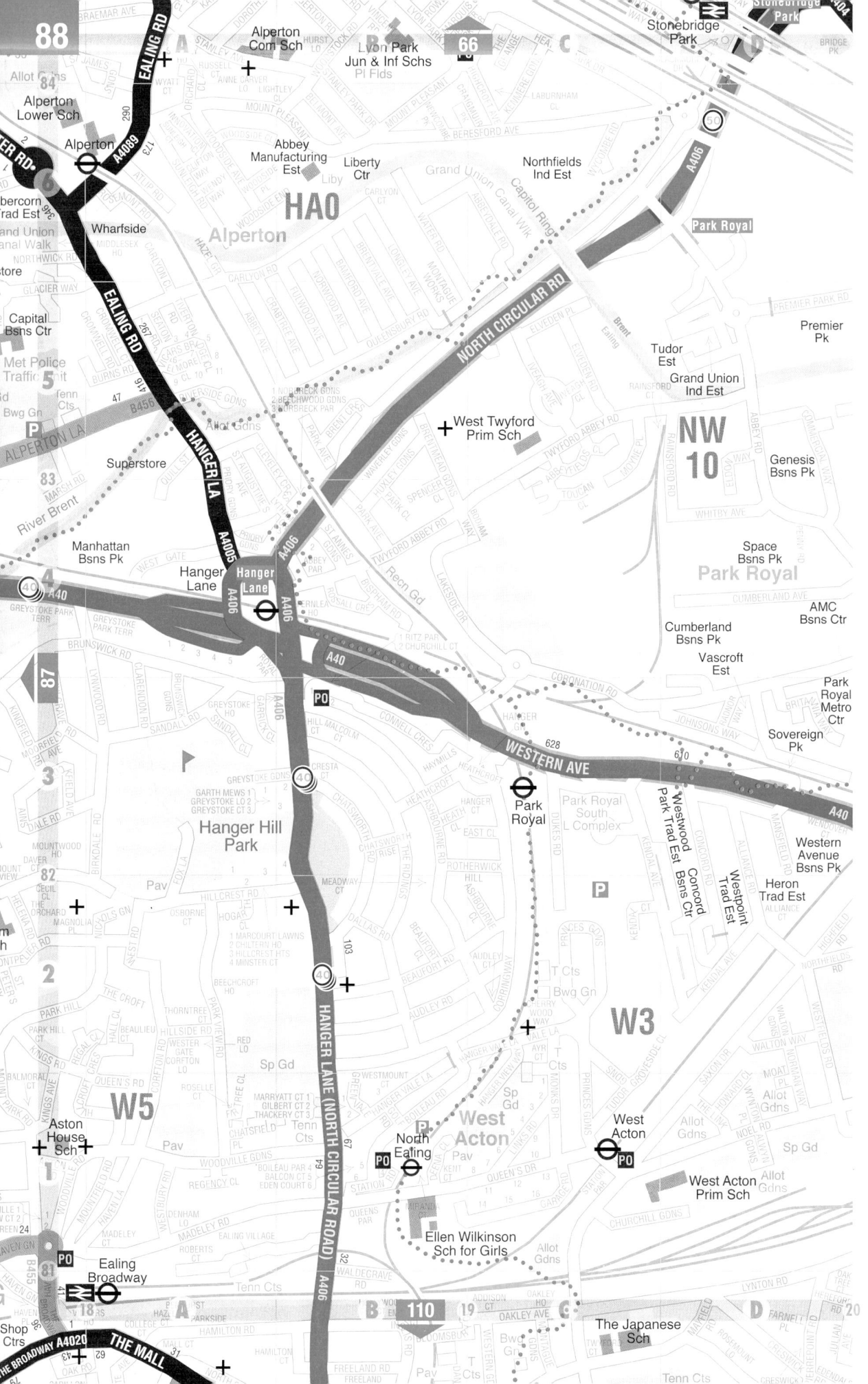

Alperton Com Sch
Lyon Park Jun & Inf Schs
Pl Flds
66
Stonebridge Park
Alperton Lower Sch
Alperton
EALING RD
A4089
Abbey Manufacturing Est
Liberty Ctr
Northfields Ind Est
Grand Union Canal Wlk
Capital Ring
A406
HA0
Alperton
Park Royal
Abercorn Trad Est
Wharfside
Grand Union Canal Walk
Capital Bsns Ctr
Met Police Traffic Unit
NORTH CIRCULAR RD
Tudor Est
Grand Union Ind Est
Premier Pk
West Twyford Prim Sch
NW10
Genesis Bsns Pk
ALPERTON LA
B456
Allot Gdns
Superstore
HANGER LA
River Brent
Manhattan Bsns Pk
A4005
Hanger Lane
Space Bsns Pk
Park Royal
A40
AMC Bsns Ctr
Cumberland Bsns Pk
Vascroft Est
Recn Gd
87
Park Royal Metro Ctr
Sovereign Pk
WESTERN AVE
Hanger Hill Park
Park Royal
Park Royal South L Complex
Westwood Park Trad Est
Concord Bsns Ctr
Westpoint Trad Est
Western Avenue Bsns Pk
Heron Trad Est
W3
W5
HANGER LANE (NORTH CIRCULAR ROAD)
Aston House Sch
North Ealing
West Acton
West Acton
West Acton Prim Sch
Ellen Wilkinson Sch for Girls
Ealing Broadway
110
The Japanese Sch
THE BROADWAY A4020
THE MALL

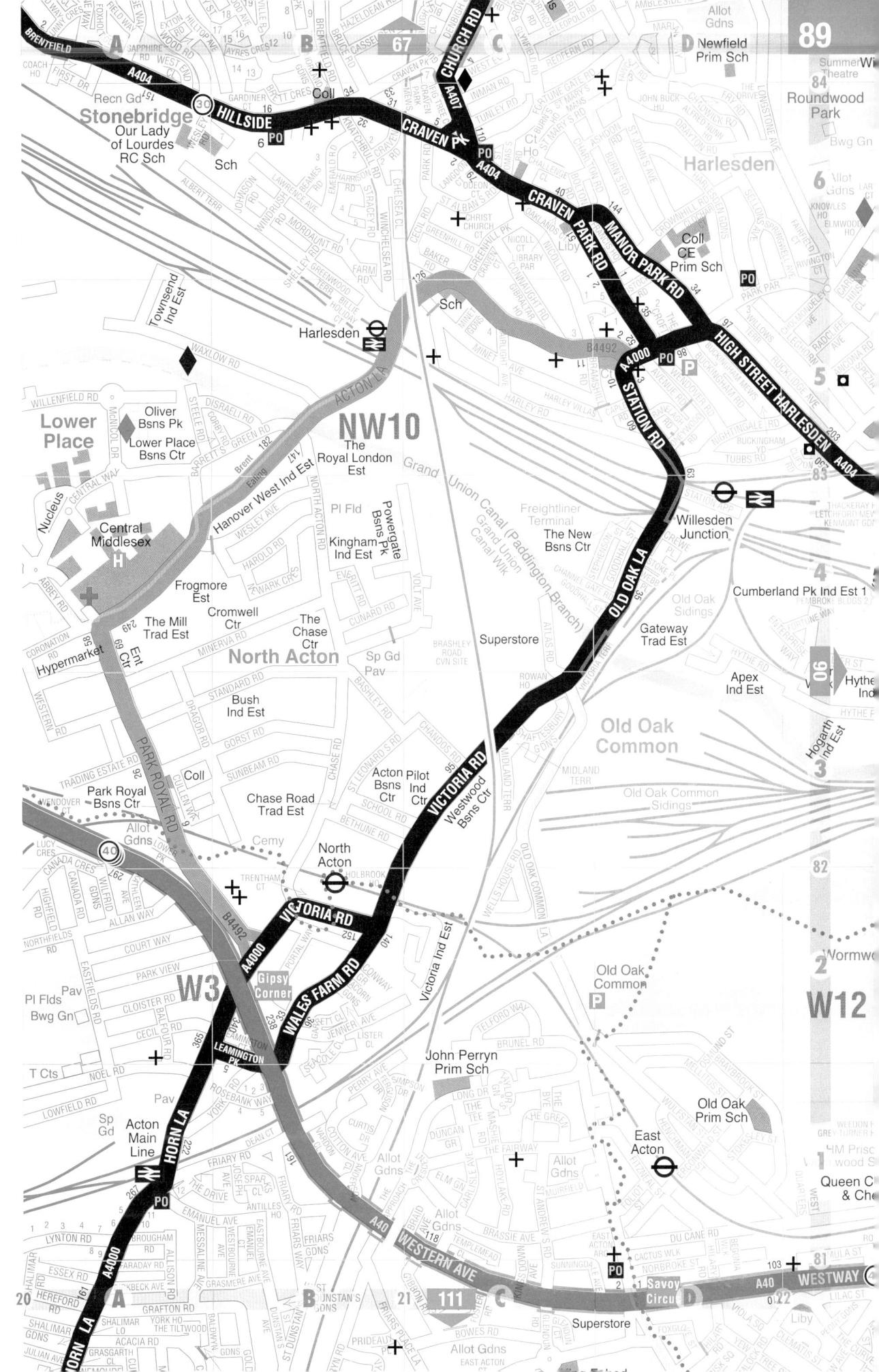
Stonebridge
Our Lady of Lourdes RC Sch
Recn Gd
HILLSIDE
CRAVEN PK
CHURCH RD
A404
A407
Newfield Prim Sch
Roundwood Park
Harlesden
Coll CE Prim Sch
CRAVEN PARK RD
MANOR PARK RD
HIGH STREET HARLESDEN
STATION RD
A4000
B4492
Harlesden
Townsend Ind Est
WAXLOW RD
Lower Place
Oliver Bsns Pk
Lower Place Bsns Ctr
NW10
The Royal London Est
Grand Union Canal (Paddington Branch)
Grand Union Canal Wlk
Freightliner Terminal
The New Bsns Ctr
Willesden Junction
Hanover West Ind Est
Central Middlesex
Nucleus
Frogmore Est
Cromwell Ctr
The Mill Trad Est
Kingham Ind Est
Powergate Bsns Pk
Pl Fld
OLD OAK LA
Old Oak Sidings
Cumberland Pk Ind Est
Gateway Trad Est
Superstore
North Acton
The Chase Ctr
Sp Gd Pav
Hypermarket
Ent Ctr
Bush Ind Est
Apex Ind Est
Old Oak Common
Hogarth Ind Est
PARK ROYAL RD
Park Royal Bsns Ctr
Coll
Chase Road Trad Est
Acton Bsns Ctr
Pilot Ind Ctr
VICTORIA RD
Westwood Bsns Ctr
Old Oak Common Sidings
Allot Gdns
Cemy
North Acton
VICTORIA RD
WALES FARM RD
Victoria Ind Est
W3
Gipsy Corner
Old Oak Common
W12
John Perryn Prim Sch
Old Oak Prim Sch
East Acton
Acton Main Line
HORN LA
LEAMINGTON PK
WESTERN AVE
A40
WESTWAY
Savoy Circus
Superstore
Allot Gdns
Liby
67
111
90
A B C D
1 2 3 4 5 6
20 21 22
81 82 83 84

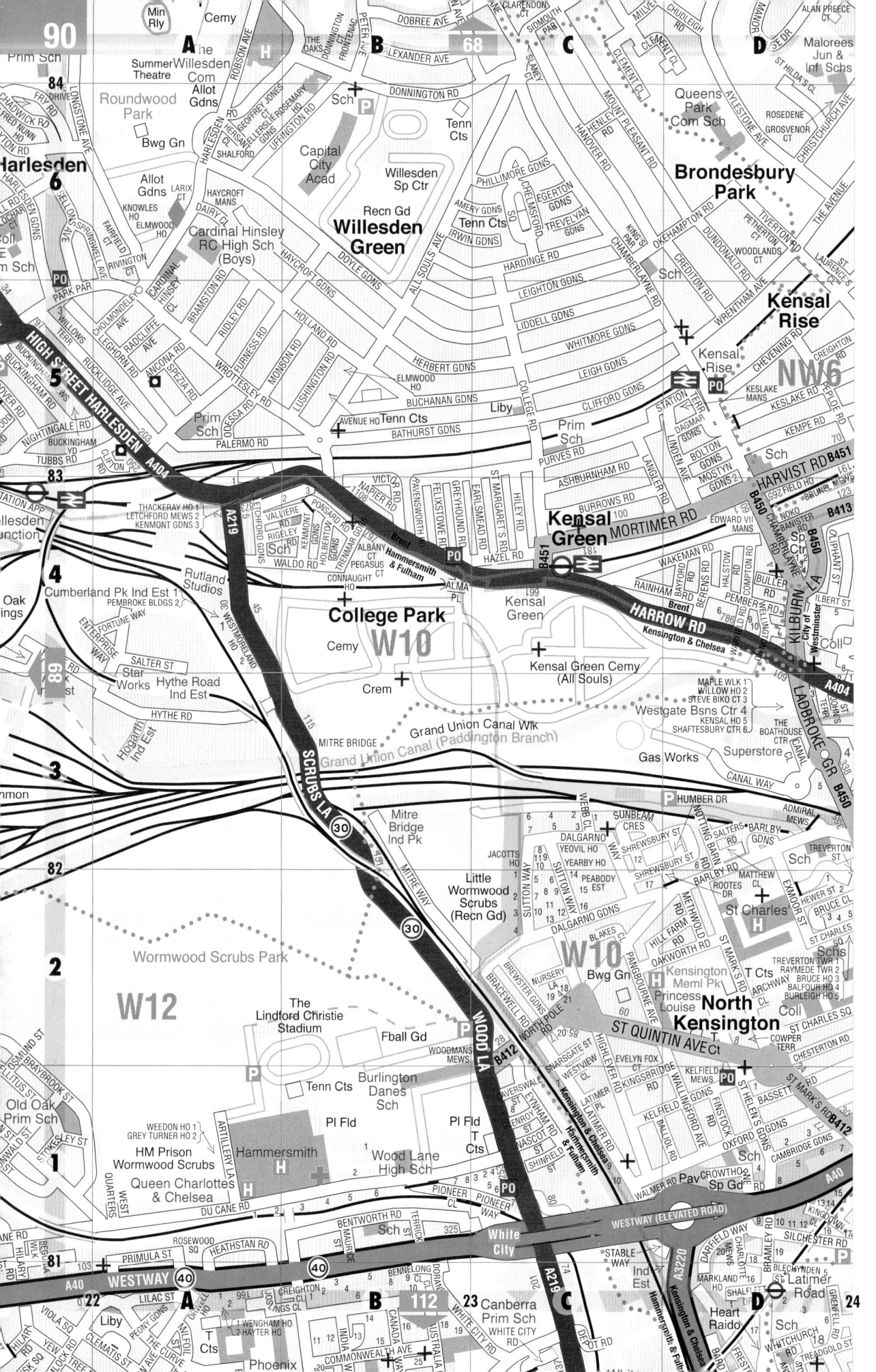
Harlesden
Willesden Green
Brondesbury Park
Kensal Rise
Kensal Green
College Park
North Kensington
White City
Wormwood Scrubs Park
W12
W10
NW6
HIGH STREET HARLESDEN
HARROW RD
SCRUBS LA
WOOD LA
WESTWAY
WESTWAY (ELEVATED ROAD)
ST QUINTIN AVE
MORTIMER RD
LADBROKE GR
KILBURN LA
CHAMBERLAYNE RD
HARVIST RD
Grand Union Canal (Paddington Branch)
Grand Union Canal Wlk
Kensal Green Cemy (All Souls)
Willesden Sp Ctr
Capital City Acad
Cardinal Hinsley RC High Sch (Boys)
Roundwood Park
Queens Park Com Sch
Malorees Jun & Inf Schs
Little Wormwood Scrubs (Recn Gd)
The Lindford Christie Stadium
HM Prison Wormwood Scrubs
Hammersmith
Queen Charlottes & Chelsea
Burlington Danes Sch
Wood Lane High Sch
Mitre Bridge Ind Pk
Hythe Road Ind Est
Rutland Studios
Cumberland Pk Ind Est
Star Works
Hogarth Ind Est
Gas Works
Superstore
St Charles'
Kensington Meml Pk
Princess Louise
Canberra Prim Sch
Latimer Road
Old Oak Prim Sch
Willesden Junction
A404
A219
A40
A3220
B450
B451
B412
B413
68
89
112
24
A
B
C
D
1
2
3
4
5
6
81
82
83
84
22
23

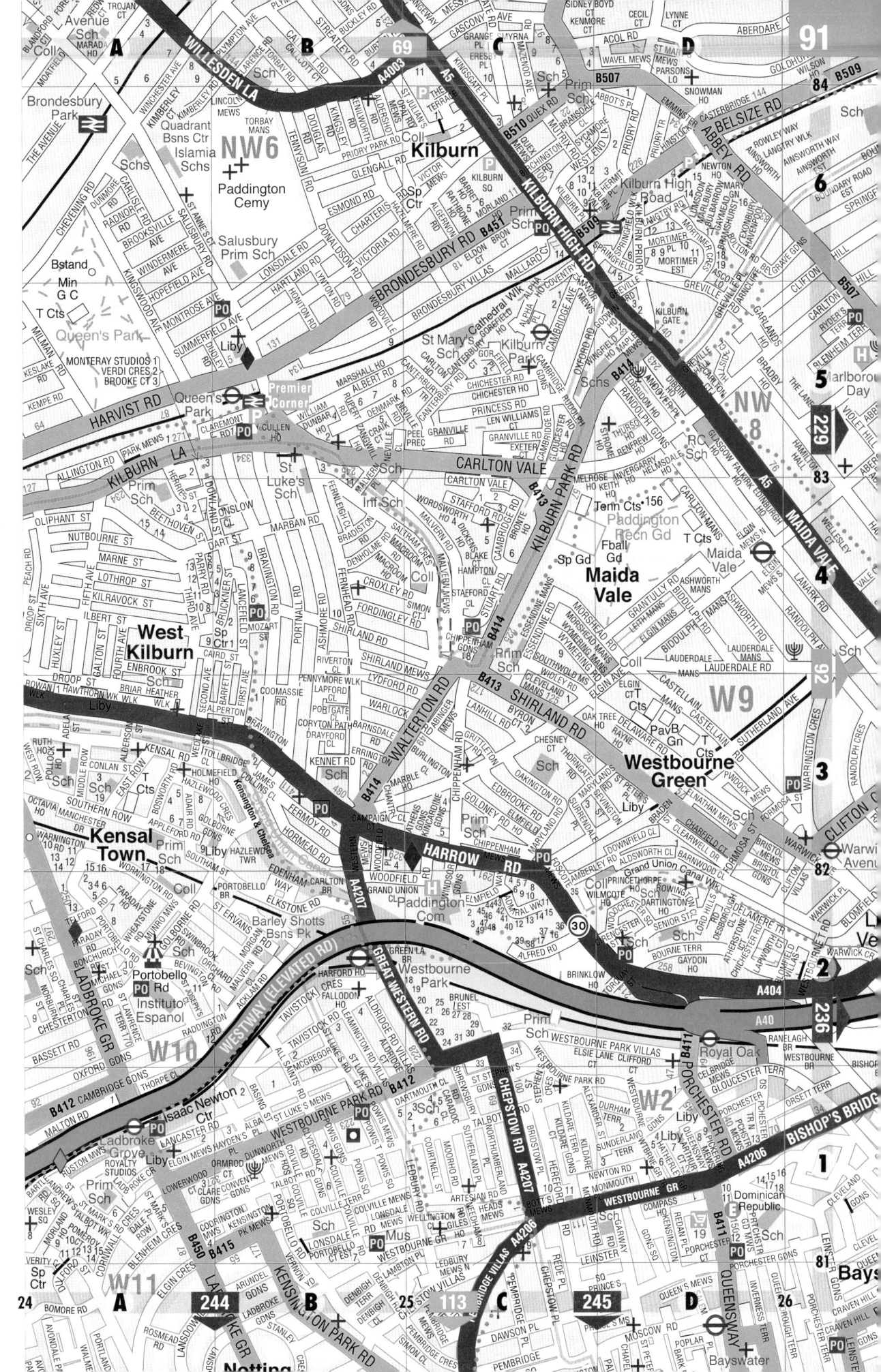

Kilburn
NW6
Paddington Cemy
Salusbury Prim Sch
Brondesbury Park
Queen's Park
Kilburn High Road
Kilburn Park
Maida Vale
West Kilburn
Westbourne Green
Kensal Town
Paddington Recn Gd
NW8
W9
W10
W2
W11
Royal Oak
Westbourne Park
Ladbroke Grove
Portobello Rd Instituto Espanol
Barley Shotts Bsns Pk
Paddington Com
Dominican Republic
Bayswater
Warwick Avenue
Isaac Newton Ctr
Premier Corner
WILLESDEN LA
KILBURN HIGH RD
MAIDA VALE
HARROW RD
WESTWAY (ELEVATED RD)
GREAT WESTERN RD
CHEPSTOW RD
WESTBOURNE GR
BISHOP'S BRIDGE
PORCHESTER RD
QUEENSWAY
KENSINGTON PARK RD
LADBROKE GR
KILBURN PARK RD
SHIRLAND RD
CARLTON VALE
BRONDESBURY RD
HARVIST RD
KILBURN LA
ABBEY RD
BELSIZE RD
WALTERTON RD
WESTBOURNE PARK RD
A5
A404
A40
A4207
A4206
B413
B414
B450
B412
69
229
92
236
244
113
245
A
B
C
D
1
2
3
4
5
6
24
25
26

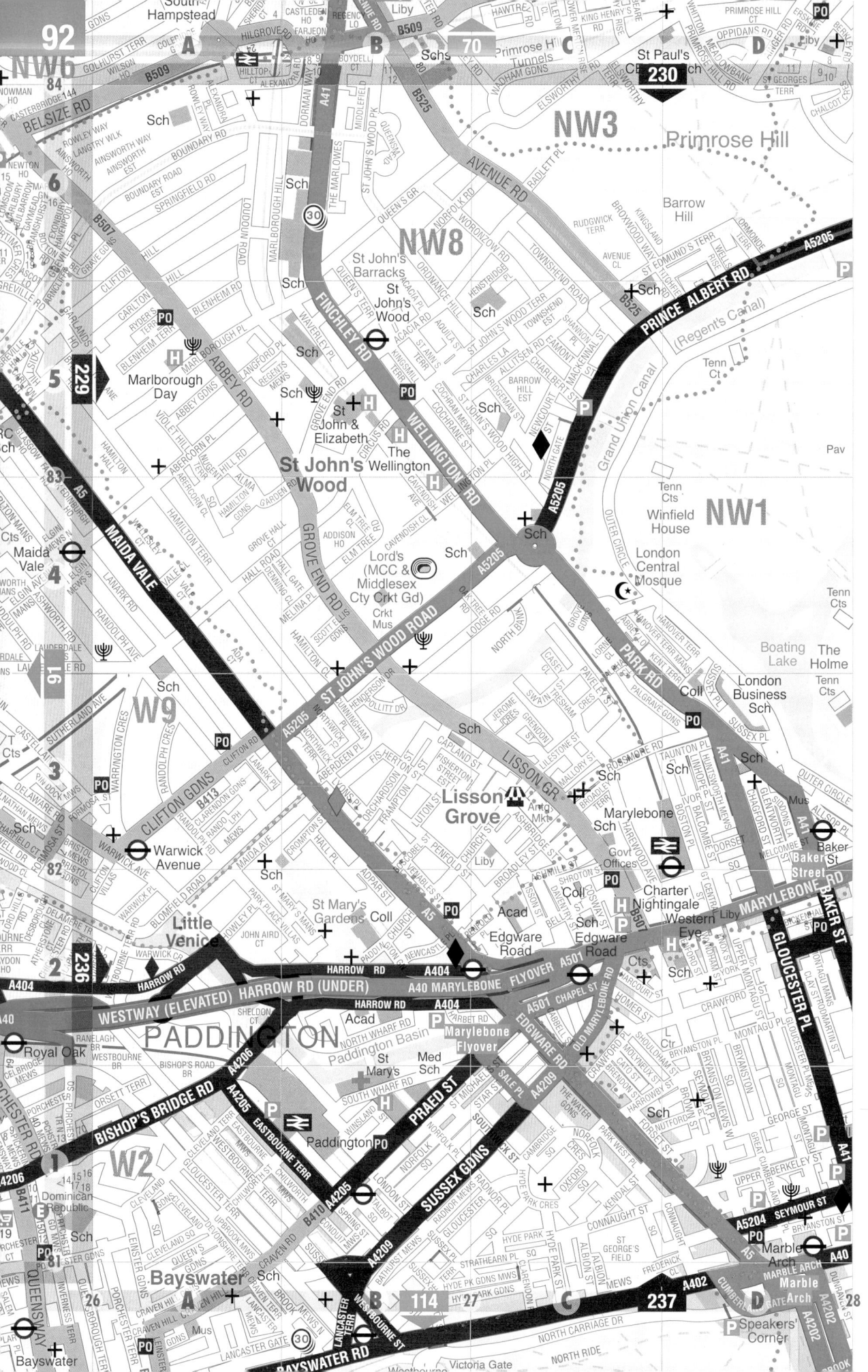

NW6
NW3
NW8
NW1
W9
W2
PADDINGTON
Primrose Hill
St John's Wood
Lisson Grove
Little Venice
South Hampstead
Hilgrove Rd
Golhurst Terr
Belsize Rd
Boundary Rd
Springfield Rd
Loudoun Road
Marlborough Hill
Abbey Rd
Finchley Rd
Wellington Rd
Avenue Rd
Prince Albert Rd
Regent's Canal
Grand Union Canal
Outer Circle
Park Rd
Maida Vale
Grove End Rd
St John's Wood Road
Lord's (MCC & Middlesex Cty Crkt Gd)
Crkt Mus
London Central Mosque
Winfield House
Barrow Hill
Boating Lake
The Holme
London Business Sch
Marylebone
Marylebone Rd
Baker St
Baker Street
Gloucester Pl
Edgware Rd
Edgware Road
Harrow Rd
Westway (Elevated) Harrow Rd (Under)
A40 Marylebone Flyover
Marylebone Flyover
Paddington Basin
St Mary's
Paddington
Praed St
Sussex Gdns
Bishop's Bridge Rd
Eastbourne Terr
Westbourne Terr
Royal Oak
Warwick Avenue
Clifton Gdns
Maida Vale
Marlborough Day
St John & Elizabeth
The Wellington
St John's Barracks
St Mary's Gardens
Charter Nightingale
Western Eye
Antq Mkt
Govt Offices
Bayswater
Queensway
Bayswater Rd
Marble Arch
Speakers' Corner
North Carriage Dr
North Ride
Victoria Gate
Dominican Republic
St Paul's Church
Primrose Hill Tunnels
70
230
229
91
236
237
114
84
83
82
81
26
27
28
A
B
C
D
1
2
3
4
5
6

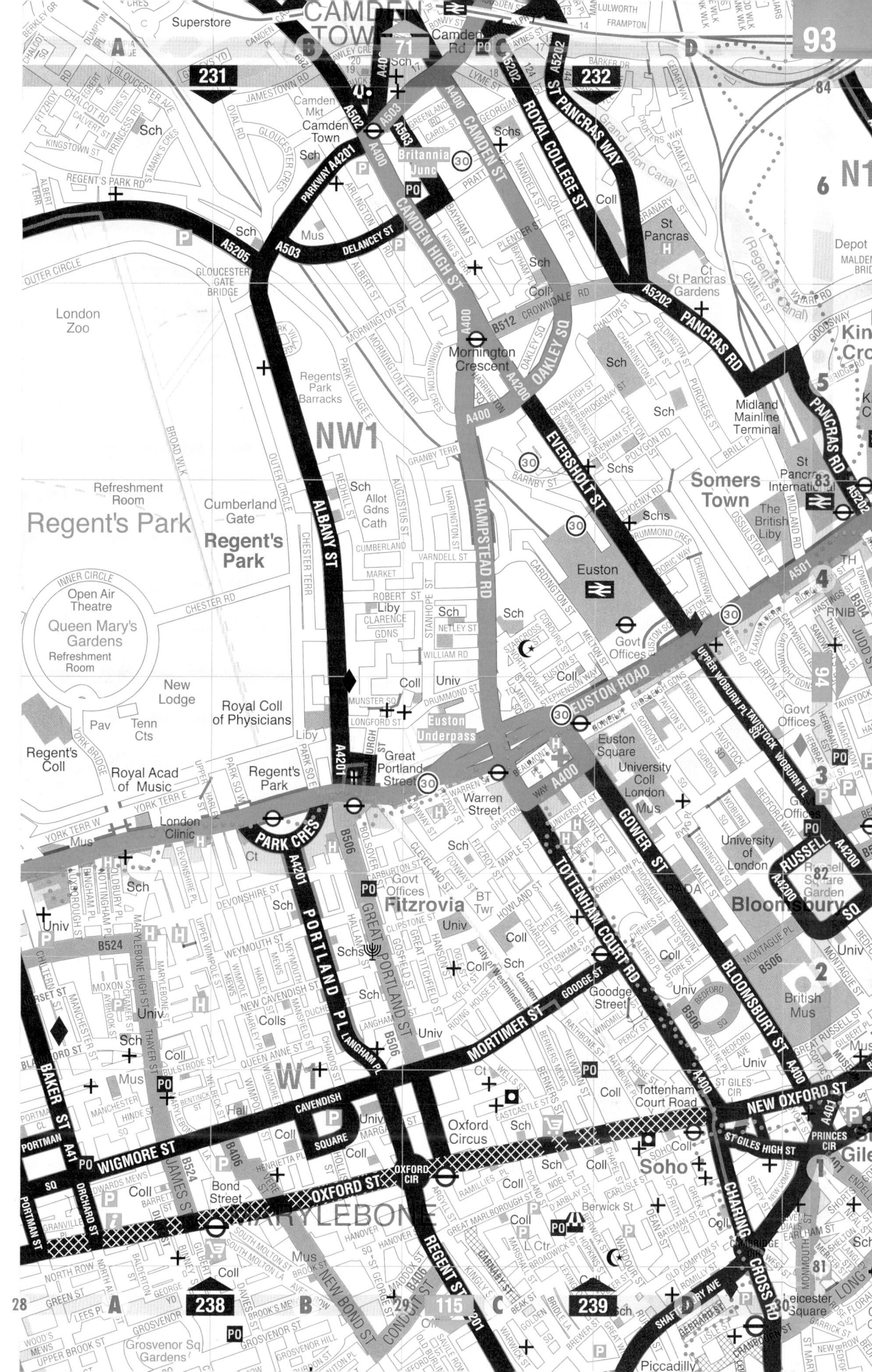
Camden Town
Regent's Park
NW1
London Zoo
Regent's Park
Queen Mary's Gardens
Open Air Theatre
Somers Town
Euston
Fitzrovia
Bloomsbury
Soho
W1
MARYLEBONE
Oxford Circus
Tottenham Court Road
Warren Street
Great Portland Street
Mornington Crescent
Euston Square
Goodge Street
Bond Street
St Pancras International
Midland Mainline Terminal
The British Liby
British Mus
University of London
University Coll London
Royal Coll of Physicians
Royal Acad of Music
Regent's Coll
London Clinic
EUSTON ROAD
OXFORD ST
TOTTENHAM COURT RD
GOWER ST
HAMPSTEAD RD
ALBANY ST
PORTLAND PL
CAMDEN HIGH ST
CAMDEN ST
ROYAL COLLEGE ST
ST PANCRAS WAY
PANCRAS RD
EVERSHOLT ST
BAKER ST
WIGMORE ST
MORTIMER ST
REGENT ST
NEW OXFORD ST
CHARING CROSS RD
BLOOMSBURY ST
231
232
238
239
71
115
94
84
83
82
81
28
29
30

A
B
C
D
233
72
234
84
N1
6
5
4
3
2
1
93
82
81
YORK WAY
CALEDONIAN RD
B514 COPENHAGEN ST
RICHMOND AVE
Barnard Park
LIVERPOOL RD
UPPER ST
ESSEX RD
ISLINGTON GN
Camden Pas
Depot
MALDEN LANE BRIDGE
King's Cross
King's Cross (Thameslink)
ISLINGTON
Pentonville
PENTONVILLE RD
Angel
Midland Mainline Terminal
St Pancras International
PANCRAS RD
Somers Town
The British Liby
ST JOHN ST
GOSWELL RD
FINSBURY
City Univ
KING'S CROSS RD
ROSEBERY AVE
Family Records Ctr
St Pancras
WC1
HUNTER ST
Coram's Fields
GUILFORD ST
GRAY'S INN RD
FARRINGDON RD
CLERKENWELL RD
Clerkenwell
EC1
Russell Square
University of London
Bloomsbury
THEOBALD'S RD
Gray's Inn
SOUTHAMPTON ROW
British Mus
Holborn
HIGH HOLBORN
HOLBORN VIADUCT
Smithfield Mkt
Farringdon
NEW OXFORD ST
St Giles
KINGSWAY
WC2
Lincoln's Inn Fields
CHANCERY LA
Royal Courts of Justice
Covent Garden
ALDWYCH
STRAND
Somerset House
Temple
VICTORIA EMBANKMENT
BLACKFRIARS UNDERPASS
Blackfriars
City Thameslink
LUDGATE HILL
NEWGATE
St Barts
240
116
241
30
31
32

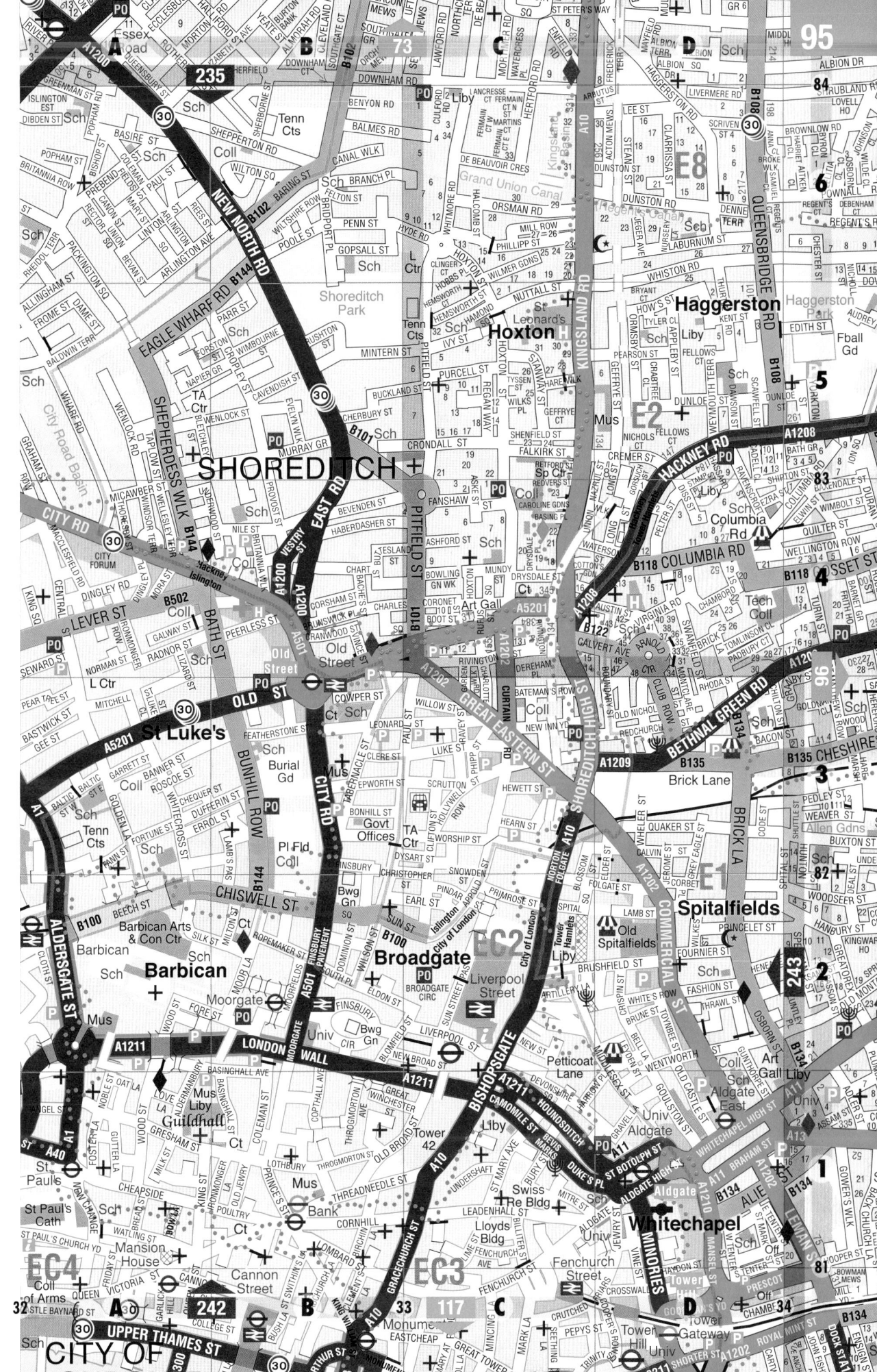

A
B
C
D
73
235
117
242
243
96
Essex Road
NEW NORTH RD
EAST RD
CITY RD
CITY RD
OLD ST
GREAT EASTERN ST
SHOREDITCH HIGH ST
KINGSLAND RD
QUEENSBRIDGE RD
HACKNEY RD
BETHNAL GREEN RD
COLUMBIA RD
COMMERCIAL ST
BRICK LA
BISHOPSGATE
LONDON WALL
ALDERSGATE ST
CHISWELL ST
LEVER ST
PITFIELD ST
BUNHILL ROW
BATH ST
SHEPHERDESS WLK
EAGLE WHARF RD
WENLOCK RD
MOORGATE
MINORIES
GRACECHURCH ST
UPPER THAMES ST
HOUNDSDITCH
CHEAPSIDE
CORNHILL
LEADENHALL ST
FENCHURCH ST
THREADNEEDLE ST
Grand Union Canal
Regent's Canal
City Road Basin
Kingsland Basin
SHOREDITCH
Hoxton
Haggerston
Haggerston Park
Shoreditch Park
St Luke's
Barbican
Broadgate
Spitalfields
Old Spitalfields
Brick Lane
Whitechapel
Aldgate
Aldgate East
Petticoat Lane
Liverpool Street
Moorgate
Old Street
Bank
Cannon Street
Fenchurch Street
Tower Hill
Tower Gateway
Monument
Mansion House
Guildhall
St Paul's
St Paul's Cath
Tower 42
Lloyds Bldg
Swiss Re Bldg
Barbican Arts & Con Ctr
Bunhill Fields
Burial Gd
Govt Offices
Columbia Rd
Tech Coll
CITY OF
E8
E2
E1
EC2
EC3
EC4
1
2
3
4
5
6

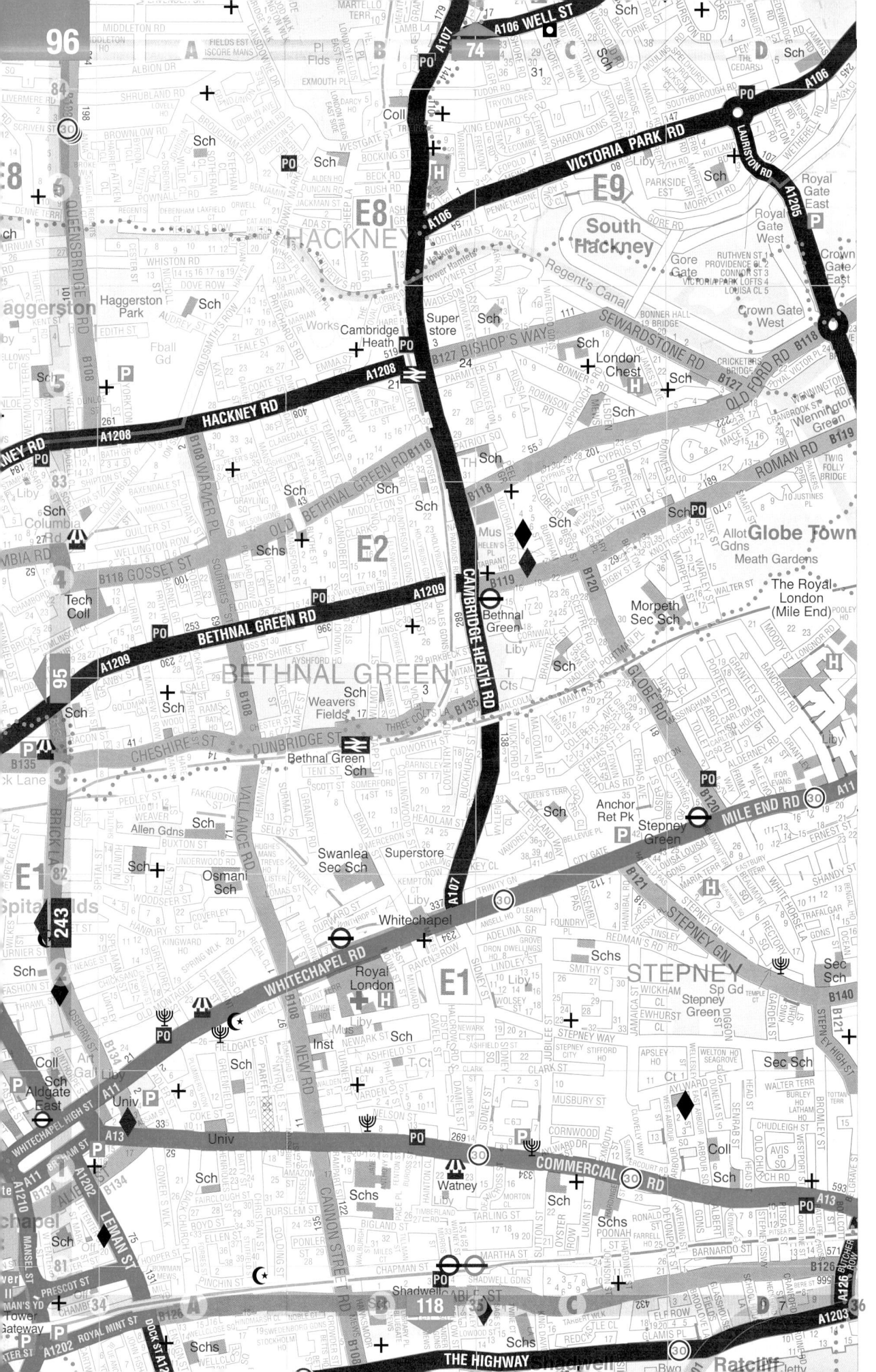
74
A106 WELL ST
VICTORIA PARK RD
LAURISTON RD
A1205
E9
South Hackney
Regent's Canal
E8
HACKNEY
Haggerston
Haggerston Park
QUEENSBRIDGE RD
HACKNEY RD
A1208
Cambridge Heath
BISHOP'S WAY
SEWARDSTONE RD
OLD FORD RD
London Chest
ROMAN RD
Globe Town
Meath Gardens
The Royal London (Mile End)
Morpeth Sec Sch
E2
OLD BETHNAL GREEN RD
GOSSET ST
BETHNAL GREEN RD
A1209
CAMBRIDGE HEATH RD
Bethnal Green
BETHNAL GREEN
Weavers Fields
CHESHIRE ST
DUNBRIDGE ST
95
GLOBE RD
MILE END RD
Stepney Green
Anchor Ret Pk
VALLANCE RD
Allen Gdns
Osmani Sch
Swanlea Sec Sch
Superstore
Whitechapel
WHITECHAPEL RD
Royal London
E1
Spitalfields
243
STEPNEY
Stepney Green
NEW RD
CANNON STREET RD
COMMERCIAL RD
A13
Watney
Aldgate East
WHITECHAPEL HIGH ST
LEMAN ST
PRESCOT ST
ROYAL MINT ST
Tower Gateway
Shadwell
118
THE HIGHWAY
Ratcliff
A1203
136

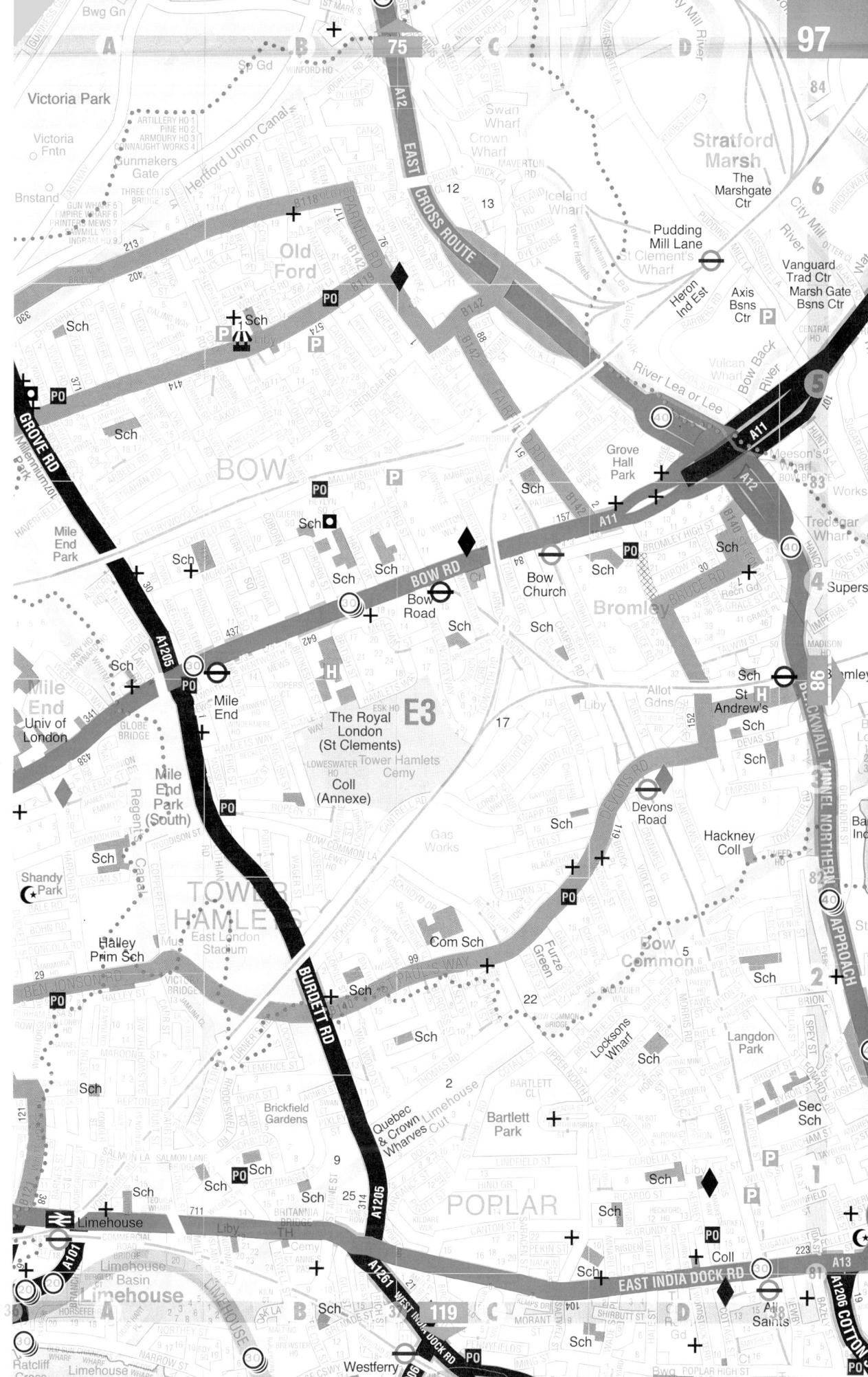
Victoria Park
Victoria Fntn
Bnstand
Gunmakers Gate
Hertford Union Canal
Old Ford
BOW
Mile End Park
Mile End
Univ of London
Mile End Park (South)
Regent's Canal
Shandy Park
Halley Prim Sch
TOWER HAMLETS
East London Stadium
Brickfield Gardens
The Royal London (St Clements)
Tower Hamlets Cemy
Coll (Annexe)
E3
Gas Works
Com Sch
Furze Green
Bow Common
Locksons Wharf
Langdon Park
Bartlett Park
Quebec & Crown Wharves
Limehouse Cut
POPLAR
Limehouse
Limehouse Basin
Westferry
Ratcliff Cross
EAST INDIA DOCK RD
BURDETT RD
GROVE RD
BOW RD
FAIRFIELD RD
EAST CROSS ROUTE
BLACKWALL TUNNEL NORTHERN APPROACH
Swan Wharf
Crown Wharf
Iceland Wharf
St Clement's Wharf
Stratford Marsh
The Marshgate Ctr
Pudding Mill Lane
Heron Ind Est
Axis Bsns Ctr
Vanguard Trad Ctr
Marsh Gate Bsns Ctr
City Mill River
Vulcan Wharf
Bow Back River
River Lea or Lee
Grove Hall Park
Meeson's Wharf
Tredegar Wharf
Bow Church
Bow Road
Bromley
Devons Road
St Andrew's
Hackney Coll
Sec Sch
All Saints
Mile End Park
Millennium Park
Lea Valley Wlk
75
119
A12
A11
A1205
A1261
A13
B140
B142
B119
B118

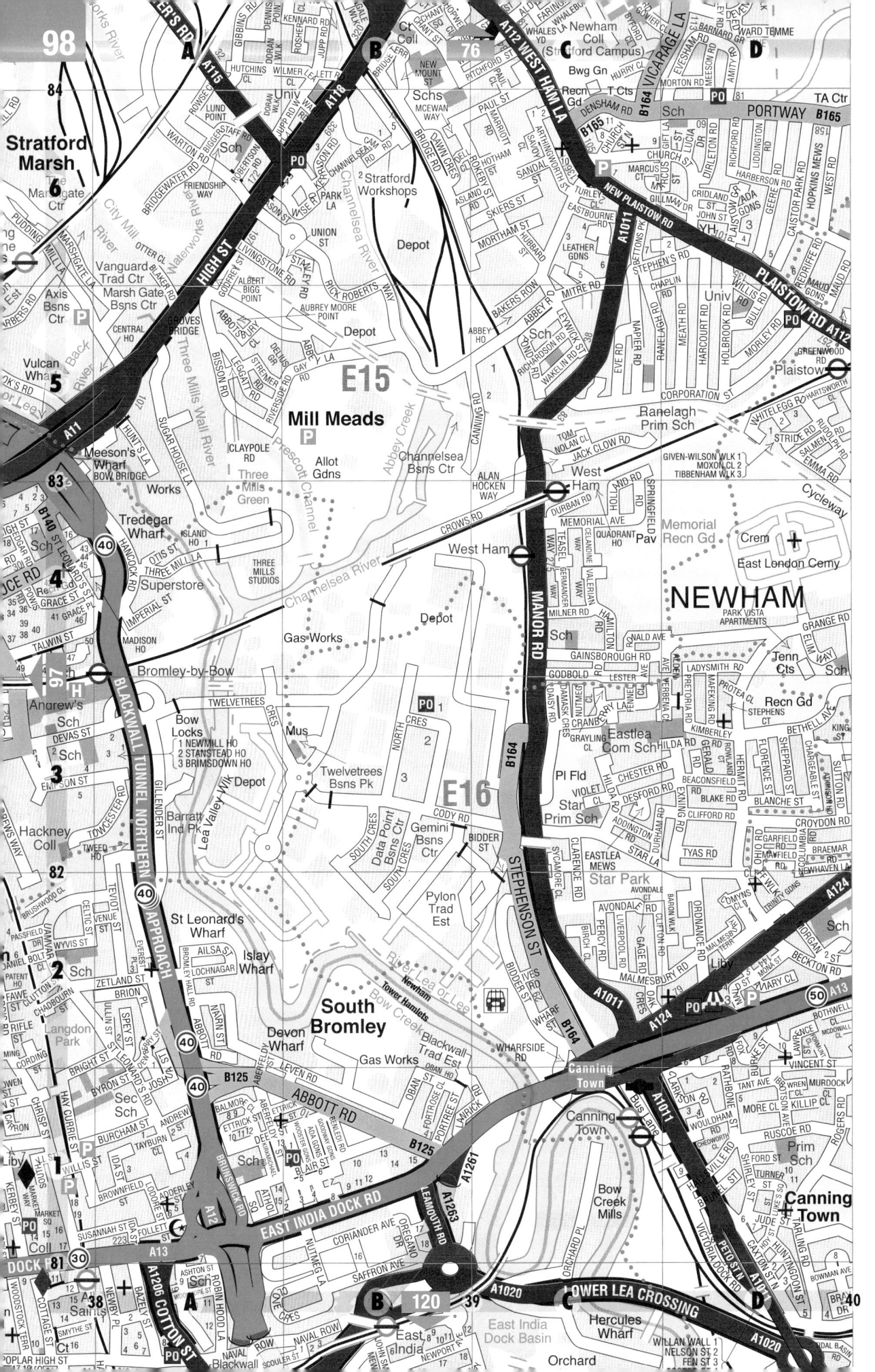

A
B
C
D
76
120
Stratford Marsh
Marshgate Ctr
Vanguard Trad Ctr
Marsh Gate Bsns Ctr
Axis Bsns Ctr
Vulcan Wharf
Meeson's Wharf
BOW BRIDGE
Tredegar Wharf
Works
Superstore
Bromley-by-Bow
Bow Locks
1 NEWMILL HO
2 STANSTEAD HO
3 BRIMSDOWN HO
Depot
Barratt Ind Pk
Hackney Coll
Langdon Park
St Leonard's Wharf
Islay Wharf
Devon Wharf
South Bromley
Gas Works
Blackwall Trad Est
Mill Meads
Allot Gdns
Three Mills Green
THREE MILLS STUDIOS
Gas Works
Mus
Twelvetrees Bsns Pk
Data Point Bsns Ctr
Gemini Bsns Ctr
Pylon Trad Est
E15
E16
Stratford Workshops
Channelsea Bsns Ctr
Newham Coll (Stratford Campus)
Ranelagh Prim Sch
West Ham
Memorial Recn Gd
Crem
East London Cemy
NEWHAM
PARK VISTA APARTMENTS
Tenn Cts
Recn Gd
Eastlea Com Sch
Star Prim Sch
EASTLEA MEWS
Star Park
Pl Fld
Plaistow
Cycleway
Canning Town
Bow Creek Mills
Hercules Wharf
East India Dock Basin
East India
Blackwall
Orchard
All Saints
HIGH ST
A11
A12
A13
A112 WEST HAM LA
PORTWAY B165
NEW PLAISTOW RD
PLAISTOW RD A112
A1011
MANOR RD
B164
STEPHENSON ST
BLACKWALL TUNNEL NORTHERN APPROACH
ABBOTT RD
B125
EAST INDIA DOCK RD
LOWER LEA CROSSING
A1020
A124
A1206 COTTON ST
Channelsea River
Three Mills Wall River
Prescott Channel
Abbey Creek
River Lea or Lee
Bow Creek
City Mill River
Waterworks River
Lea Valley Wlk
Newham
Tower Hamlets

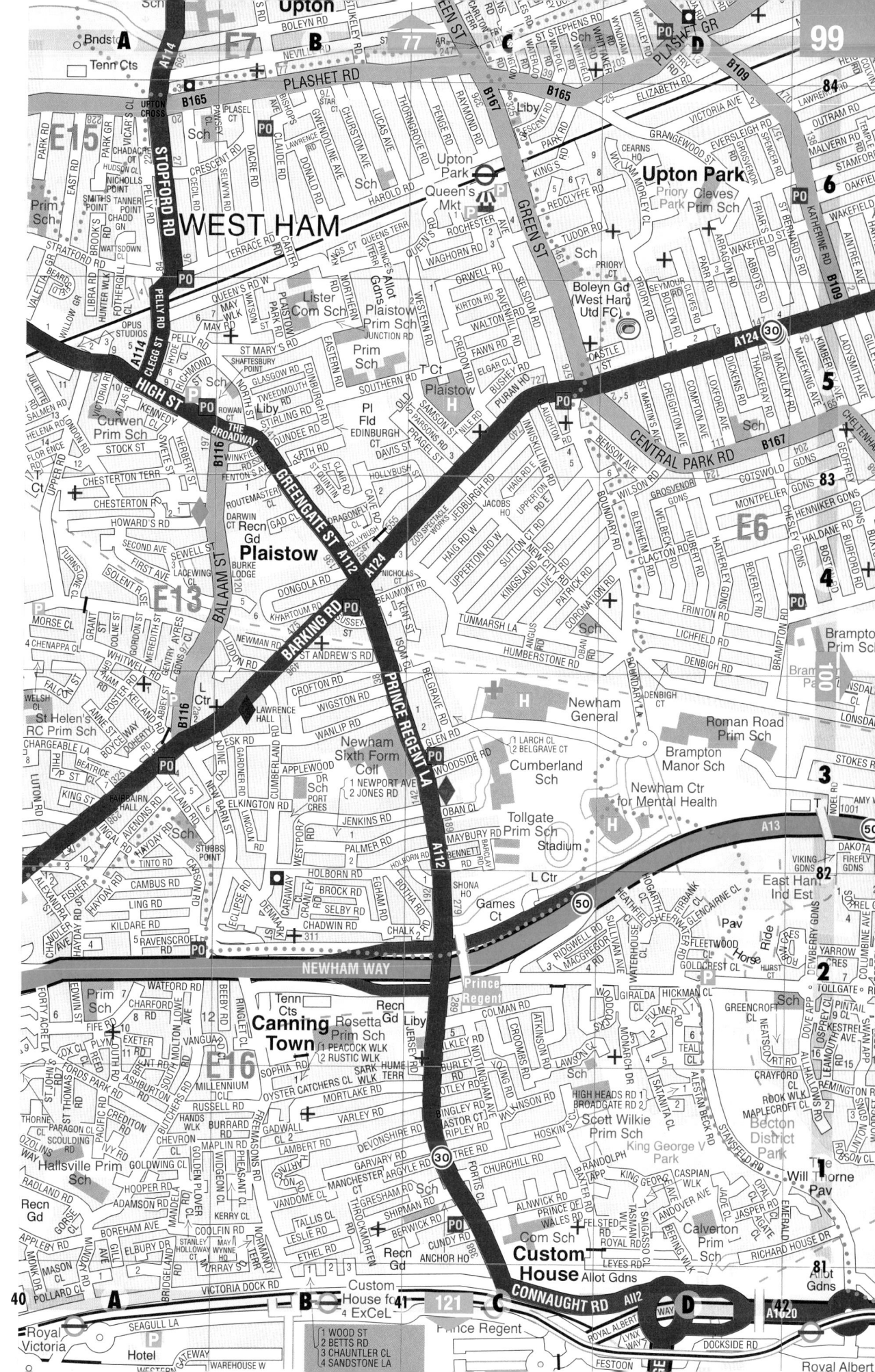

Upton
WEST HAM
Upton Park
Plaistow
E13
E15
E6
E16
E7
Canning Town
Custom House
Newham General
Newham Sixth Form Coll
Cumberland Sch
Brampton Manor Sch
Newham Ctr for Mental Health
Tollgate Prim Sch
Roman Road Prim Sch
East Ham Ind Est
Becton District Park
King George V Park
Scott Wilkie Prim Sch
Calverton Prim Sch
Hallsville Prim Sch
Rosetta Prim Sch
Boleyn Gd (West Ham Utd FC)
Lister Com Sch
Plaistow Prim Sch
Curwen Prim Sch
St Helen's RC Prim Sch
Priory Park
Cleves Prim Sch
Queen's Mkt
Upton Park
Prince Regent
Custom House for ExCeL
Royal Victoria
Royal Albert
Will Thorne Pav
GREEN ST
PLASHET RD
STOPFORD RD
HIGH ST
BARKING RD
GREENGATE ST
PRINCE REGENT LA
CENTRAL PARK RD
NEWHAM WAY
CONNAUGHT RD
BALAAM ST
VICTORIA DOCK RD
A13
A112
A124
A114
B165
B167
B116
A1020
77
100
121
84
83
82
81
40
41
42

E6
78
EAST HAM
Central Park
Wallend
Barking Flyover
IG11
NORTH CIRCULAR RD
BARKING RD
HIGH ST S
NEWHAM WAY
WOOLWICH MANOR WAY
ROYAL DOCKS RD
ROYAL ALBERT WAY
Beckton
Beckton Alps
Beckton Ret Pk
Beckton Triangle Ret Pk
Gateway Ret Pk
Gooseley's Pl Flds
East Ham Jewish Cemy
Brampton Prim Sch
Langdon Sch
Town Quay Wharf
North Beckton Prim Sch
East Beckton Dist Ctr
Kingsford Com Sch
New Becton Park
Becton District Park
Winsor Prim Sch
Gallions Prim Sch
Gallions Reach
Beckton Park
Cyprus
Univ of East London
Royal Albert
Calverton Prim Sch
East Ham Ind Est
Roman Road Prim Sch

99
122
44

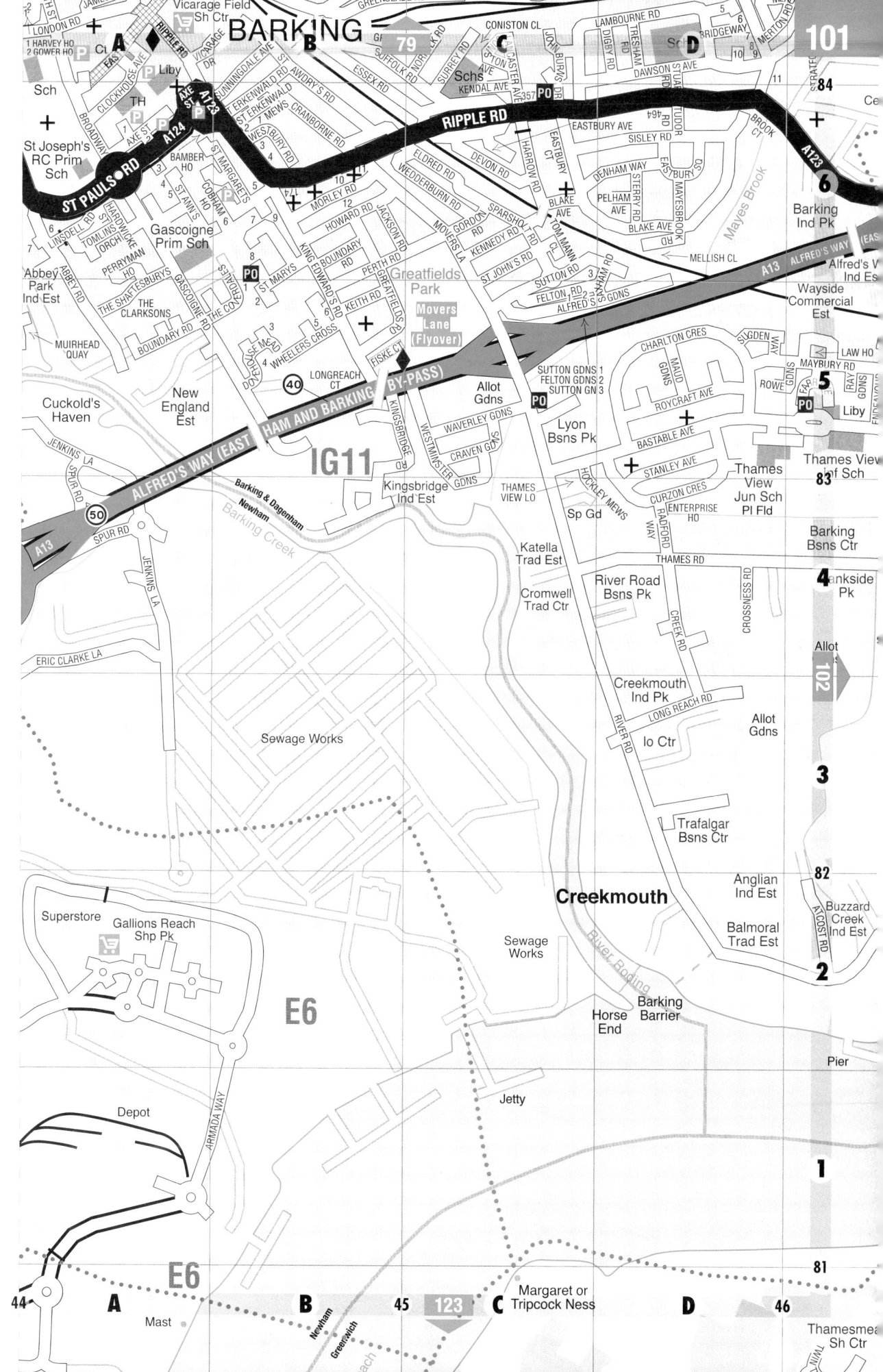

BARKING
Vicarage Field Sh Ctr
RIPPLE RD
St Joseph's RC Prim Sch
Gascoigne Prim Sch
Abbey Park Ind Est
Greatfields Park
Movers Lane (Flyover)
ALFRED'S WAY (EAST HAM AND BARKING BY-PASS)
New England Est
Cuckold's Haven
IG11
Kingsbridge Ind Est
Lyon Bsns Pk
Barking Ind Pk
Wayside Commercial Est
Thames View Jun Sch
Thames View Inf Sch
Barking Bsns Ctr
River Road Bsns Pk
Katella Trad Est
Cromwell Trad Ctr
Creekmouth Ind Pk
Sewage Works
Trafalgar Bsns Ctr
Creekmouth
Anglian Ind Est
Balmoral Trad Est
Buzzard Creek Ind Est
Barking Barrier
Horse End
Superstore
Gallions Reach Shp Pk
E6
Depot
Jetty
Margaret or Tripcock Ness
Mast
Thamesmead Sh Ctr
Barking Creek
River Roding
Mayes Brook

79
102
123

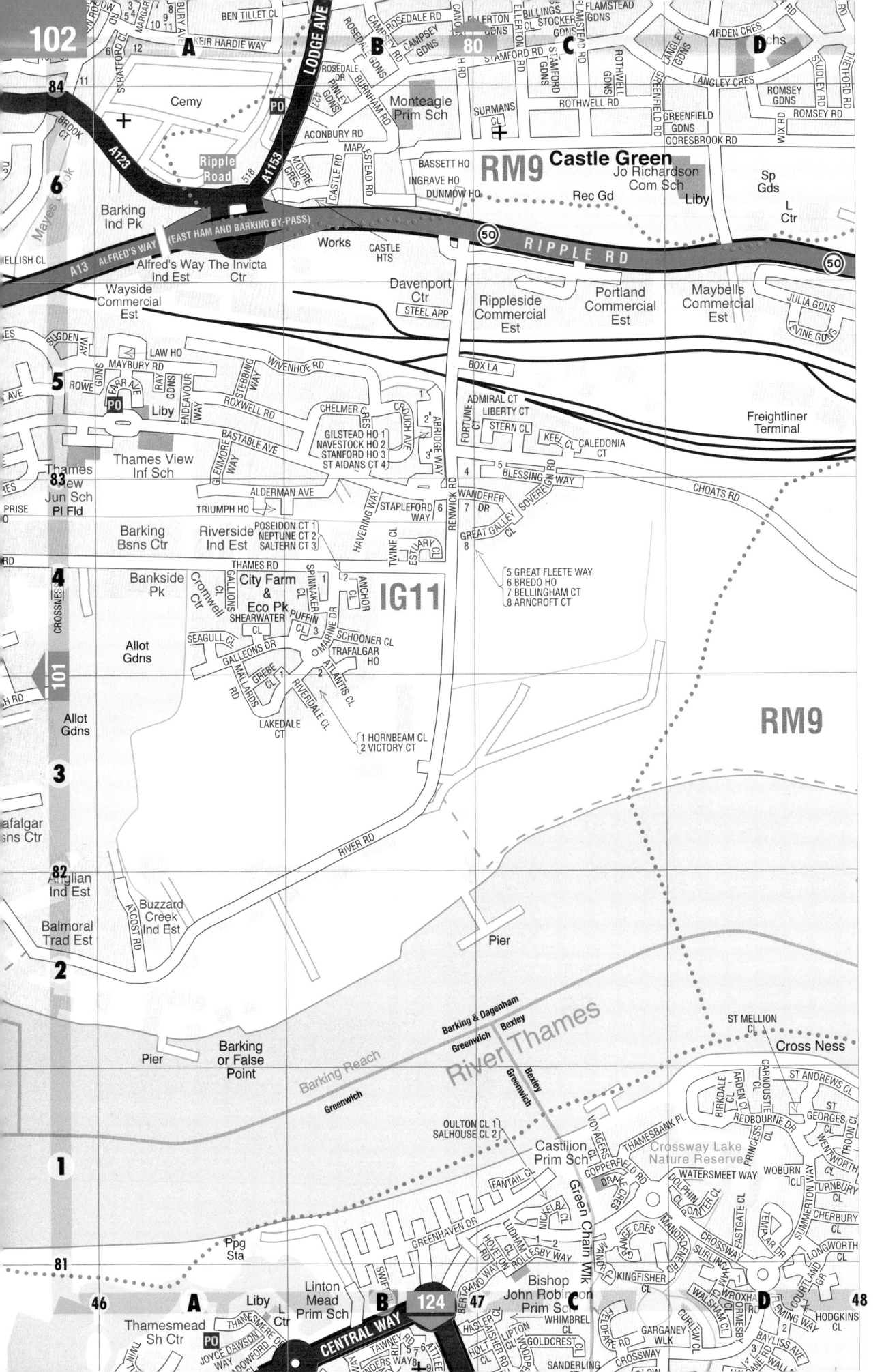
A
B
C
D
80
84
6
5
83
4
101
3
82
2
1
81
46
47
48
124
BEN TILLET CL
KEIR HARDIE WAY
BURY AVE
STRATFORD CL
LODGE AVE
ROSEDALE GDNS
CAMPSEY RD
ROSEDALE RD
CAMPSEY GDNS
ROSEDALE DR
PINLEY GDNS
BURNHAM RD
ELLERTON GDNS
ELLERTON RD
BILLINGS CL
STOCKER GDNS
FLAMSTEAD GDNS
FLAMSTEAD RD
STAMFORD RD
STAMFORD GDNS
ROTHWELL GDNS
ROTHWELL RD
GREENFIELD RD
GREENFIELD GDNS
LANGLEY GDNS
ARDEN CRES
LANGLEY CRES
Schs
ROMSEY GDNS
ROMSEY RD
STUDLEY RD
THETFORD RD
WIX RD
GORESBROOK RD
Cemy
A123
A1153
A13
Ripple Road
Monteagle Prim Sch
SURMANS CL
ACONBURY RD
MAPLESTEAD RD
MOORE CRES
CASTLE RD
BASSETT HO
INGRAVE HO
DUNMOW HO
RM9
Castle Green
Jo Richardson Com Sch
Liby
Rec Gd
Sp Gds
L Ctr
BROOK CT
Mayes Brook
Barking Ind Pk
ALFRED'S WAY
(EAST HAM AND BARKING BY-PASS)
Works
CASTLE HTS
50
RIPPLE RD
ELLISH CL
Alfred's Way Ind Est
The Invicta Ctr
Wayside Commercial Est
Davenport Ctr
STEEL APP
Rippleside Commercial Est
Portland Commercial Est
Maybells Commercial Est
JULIA GDNS
LEVINE GDNS
SILGDEN WAY
LAW HO
MAYBURY RD
ROWE GDNS
FARR AVE
RAY GDNS
ENDEAVOUR WAY
STEBBING WAY
WIVENHOE RD
ROXWELL RD
BOX LA
PO
Liby
CHELMER CRES
CROUCH AVE
ABRIDGE WAY
FORTUNE CT
ADMIRAL CT
LIBERTY CT
STERN CL
KEEL CL
CALEDONIA CT
Freightliner Terminal
GILSTEAD HO 1
NAVESTOCK HO 2
STANFORD HO 3
ST AIDANS CT 4
BASTABLE AVE
GLENMORE WAY
Thames View Inf Sch
Thames View Jun Sch
Pl Fld
BLESSING WAY
SOVEREIGN RD
CHOATS RD
ALDERMAN AVE
RENWICK RD
WANDERER DR
TRIUMPH HO
STAPLEFORD WAY
HAVERING WAY
GREAT GALLEY CL
PRISE
Barking Bsns Ctr
Riverside Ind Est
POSEIDON CT 1
NEPTUNE CT 2
SALTERN CT 3
TWINE CL
ESTUARY CL
THAMES RD
5 GREAT FLEETE WAY
6 BREDO HO
7 BELLINGHAM CT
8 ARNCROFT CT
Bankside Pk
Cromwell Ctr
GALLIONS CL
City Farm & Eco Pk
SPINNAKER CL
ANCHOR CL
IG11
CROSSNESS
SHEARWATER CL
PUFFIN CL
MARINE DR
SCHOONER CL
SEAGULL CL
GALLEONS DR
TRAFALGAR HO
Allot Gdns
MALLARDS RD
GREBE CL
ATLANTIS CL
RIVERDALE CL
LAKEDALE CT
1 HORNBEAM CL
2 VICTORY CT
RM9
afalgar
sns Ctr
RIVER RD
Anglian Ind Est
Buzzard Creek Ind Est
ATCOST RD
Balmoral Trad Est
Pier
Barking & Dagenham
Bexley
Greenwich
River Thames
Barking Reach
Barking or False Point
Pier
ST MELLION CL
Cross Ness
ST ANDREWS CL
BIRKDALE CL
ARDEN CL
CARNOUSTIE CL
ST GEORGES CL
REDBOURNE DR
PRINCESS CL
WENTWORTH CL
TROON CL
THAMESBANK PL
VOYAGERS CL
OULTON CL 1
SALHOUSE CL 2
Castilion Prim Sch
Crossway Lake Nature Reserve
COPPERFIELD RD
DRAKE CRES
WATERSMEET WAY
WOBURN CL
TURNBURY CL
DOLPHIN CL
POYNTER CL
FANTAIL CL
Green Chain Wlk
EASTGATE CL
TEMPLAR DR
SUMMERTON WAY
CHERBURY CL
NICKELBY CL
GRANGE CRES
MANORDENE RD
CROSSWAY
SURLINGHAM CL
LONGWORTH CL
GREENHAVEN DR
LUDHAM CL
HOVETON RD
ROLLESBY WAY
COURTLAND GR
Ppg Sta
KINGFISHER CL
WROXHAM RD
ORMESBY
WALSHAM CL
FLEMING WAY
HODGKINS CL
BERTRAND WAY
Bishop John Robinson Prim Sch
Linton Mead Prim Sch
Liby
L Ctr
Thamesmead Sh Ctr
THAMESMERE DR
JOYCE DAWSON WAY
DOWFORD
CENTRAL WAY
TAWNEY RD
ATTLEE
HASLER CL
LIPTON CL
WHIMBREL CL
GOLDCREST CL
FELDFARE RD
GARGANEY WLK
CURLEW CL
BAYLISS AVE
SANDERLING
CROSSWAY
Ripple Road
518
427

DAGENHAM
Old Dagenham Park
Goresbrook Park
Thomas Arnold Prim Sch
Allot Gdns
Broad Street
Dagenham Park Com Sch
RM10
RM9
IG11
SE28
SE2
RM13
Merrielands Ret Pk
Gore's Bridge Superstore
Marsh Green Prim Sch
Motor Works
Dagenham Dock
Channel Tunnel Rail Link
Thames Gateway Pk
Dagenham Breach
Horse Shoe Corner
Power Sta
Ind Est
Works
Jetties
Jetty
River Thames
Beam River
Halfway Reach
Crossness Pumping Station
Drv Rng
Riverside
RIPPLE RD
NEW RD
A1306
A1240
A13
B178
A1306 Rainham
A13 Stanford-le-Hope, M25 Tilbury (A1089)
Essex STREET ATLAS
Barking & Dagenham
Havering
Bexley
CHOATS MANOR WAY
CHEQUERS LA
KENT AVE
HINDMANS WAY
THUNDERER RD
BREACH LA
BALLARDS RD
OVAL RD N
OVAL RD S
BEAM AVE
THIRD AVE
SECOND AVE
FIRST AVE
CENTRE RD
CROSBY RD
REVIEW RD
WHITEBARN LA
SCHOOL RD
ORCHARD RD
MORLAND RD
DAGENHAM AVE
VINCENT RD
ELSTOW GDNS
ELSTOW RD
THETFORD GDNS
TRESWELL RD
GORESBROOK RD
STARMANS CL
BADEN
1 CASTLE CT
2 PAVILION CT
HORSEBRIDGE CL
SCRATTONS TERR
SHAW AVE
MORRISON RD
MERRIELANDS CRES
CHEQUERS PAR
PRINCESS PAR
SIERRA DR
EAST ENTRANCE
THAMES AVE
FIESTA DR
LYTHAM CL
FAIRWAY DR
CHART HILLS CL
SUNNINGDALE CL
A B C D
84 83 82 81
48 49 50
81 125

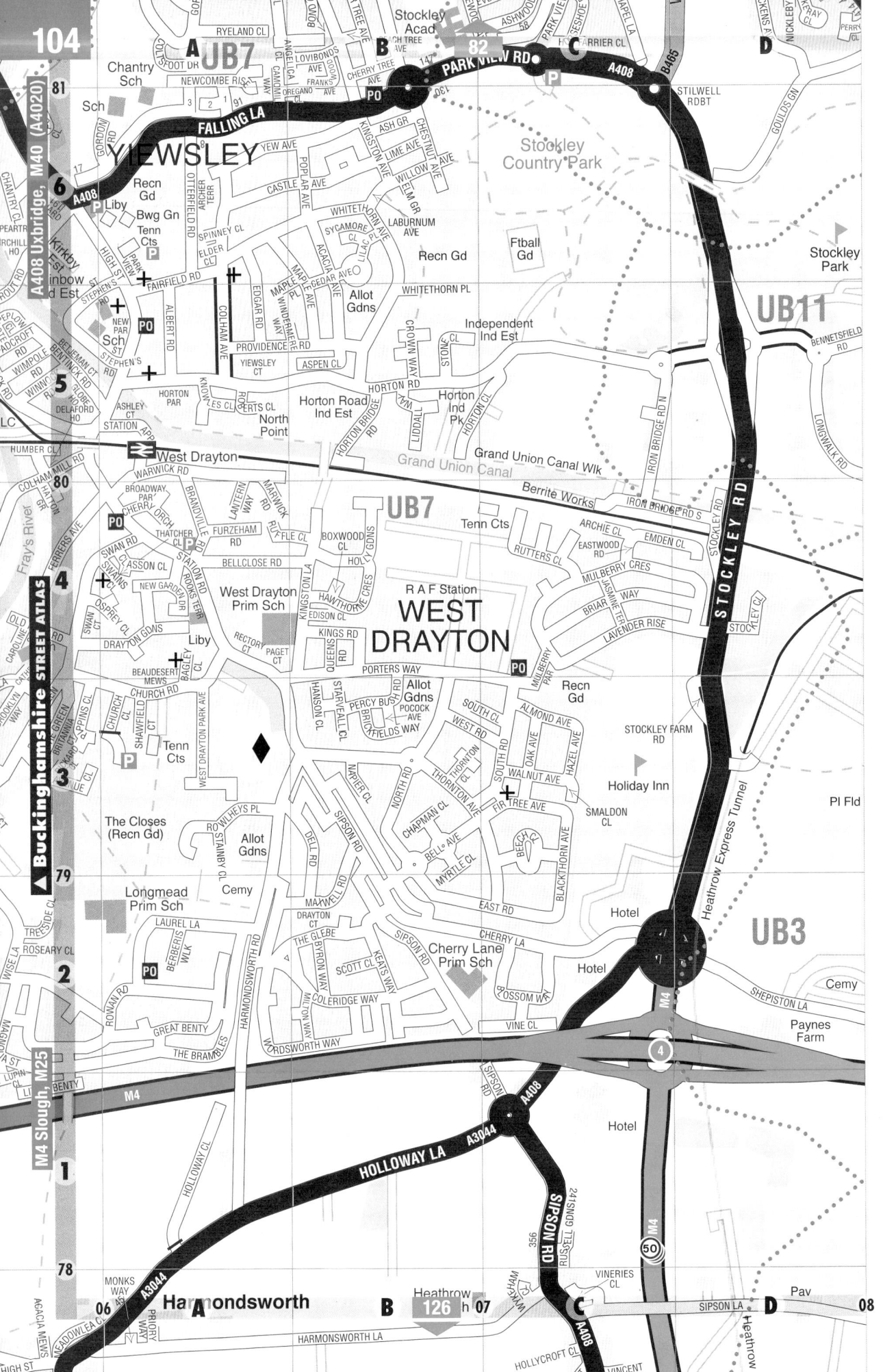

A
B
C
D
UB7
82
Stockley Acad
RYELAND CL
COLTSFOOT DR
NEWCOMBE RISE
LOVIBONDS AVE
FRANKS AVE
CHERRY TREE AVE
ANGELICA CL
CAMOMILE WAY
OREGANO CL
PARK VIEW RD
A408
B465
FARRIER CL
STILWELL RDBT
GOULDS GN
NICKLEBY
Chantry Sch
Sch
FALLING LA
YIEWSLEY
YEW AVE
ASH GR
LIME AVE
KINGSTON AVE
CHESTNUT AVE
WILLOW AVE
ELM GR
CASTLE AVE
POPLAR AVE
GORDON RD
Recn Gd
Liby
Bwg Gn
Tenn Cts
OTTERFIELD RD
ARCHER TERR
SPINNEY CL
ELDER CL
WHITETHORN AVE
SYCAMORE CL
LILAC PL
LABURNUM AVE
ACACIA AVE
MAPLE AVE
CEDAR AVE
Recn Gd
Stockley Country Park
Ftball Gd
Stockley Park
HIGH ST
PARK VIEW
FAIRFIELD RD
ST STEPHEN'S RD
NEW PAR
Sch
ALBERT RD
COLHAM AVE
EDGAR RD
MAPLE PL
WINDERMERE WAY
Allot Gdns
WHITETHORN PL
UB11
BENNETSFIELD RD
Independent Ind Est
CROWN WAY
STONE CL
PROVIDENCE RD
YIEWSLEY CT
ASPEN CL
HORTON RD
HORTON PAR
KNOWLES CL
ROBERTS CL
Horton Road Ind Est
North Point
HORTON BRIDGE RD
LIDDALL WAY
Horton Ind Pk
HORTON CL
IRON BRIDGE RD N
LONGWALK RD
ASHLEY CT
STATION APP
HUMBER CL
West Drayton
Grand Union Canal
Grand Union Canal Wlk
Berrite Works
IRON BRIDGE RD S
STOCKLEY RD
COLHAM MILL RD
WARWICK RD
HATTON GR
BROADWAY PAR
CHERRY ORCH
BRANDVILLE RD
LANTERN WAY
MARWICK RD
RUFFLE CL
BOXWOOD CL
HOLLY GDNS
UB7
Tenn Cts
ARCHIE CL
EASTWOOD RD
EMDEN CL
RUTTERS CL
Fray's River
FERRERS AVE
THATCHER CL
FURZEHAM RD
SWAN RD
ASSON CL
STATION RD
BELLCLOSE RD
MULBERRY CRES
JASMINE TER
BRIAR WAY
LAVENDER RISE
STOCKLEY CL
NEW GARDEN DR
ROOKS TERR
West Drayton Prim Sch
KINGSTON LA
HAWTHORNE CRES
R A F Station
WEST DRAYTON
OSPREY CL
SWAN CT
DRAYTON GDNS
Liby
EDISON CL
KINGS RD
QUEENS RD
RECTORY CT
PAGET CT
BAGLEY CL
BEAUDESERT MEWS
PORTERS WAY
MULBERRY PAR
Recn Gd
CHURCH RD
HANSON CL
STARVEALL CL
PERCY BUSH RD
Allot Gdns
POCOCK AVE
BRICKFIELDS WAY
SOUTH CL
WEST RD
ALMOND AVE
STOCKLEY FARM RD
CHURCH CL
SHAWFIELD CT
Tenn Cts
WEST DRAYTON PARK AVE
OAK AVE
HAZEL AVE
SOUTH RD
Holiday Inn
Pl Fld
NAPIER CL
NORTH RD
THORNTON CL
THORNTON AVE
WALNUT AVE
FIR TREE AVE
SMALDON CL
Heathrow Express Tunnel
The Closes (Recn Gd)
ROWLHEYS PL
STAINBY CL
Allot Gdns
SIPSON RD
DELL RD
CHAPMAN CL
BELL AVE
MYRTLE CL
BEECH CL
BLACKTHORN AVE
Longmead Prim Sch
Cemy
MAXWELL RD
DRAYTON CT
EAST RD
Hotel
UB3
TREESIDE CL
LAUREL LA
BERBERIS WLK
THE GLEBE
BYRON WAY
ROSEARY CL
CHERRY LA
Cherry Lane Prim Sch
SCOTT CL
KEATS WAY
Hotel
Cemy
HARMONDSWORTH RD
ROWAN RD
COLERIDGE WAY
MILTON WAY
BOSSOM WAY
SHEPISTON LA
M4
Paynes Farm
GREAT BENTY
THE BRAMBLES
WORDSWORTH WAY
VINE CL
4
SIPSON RD
M4
A408
Hotel
HOLLOWAY CL
HOLLOWAY LA
A3044
SIPSON RD
RUSSELL GDNS
50
VINERIES CL
MONKS WAY
Harmondsworth
Heathrow
126
WYKEHAM CL
SIPSON LA
Pav
06
07
08
MEADOWLEA CL
PRIORY WAY
HARMONSWORTH LA
HOLLYCROFT CL
VINCENT
HIGH ST
ACACIA MEWS
Heathrow
81
80
79
78
6
5
4
3
2
1
A408 Uxbridge, M40 (A4020)
Buckinghamshire STREET ATLAS
M4 Slough, M25

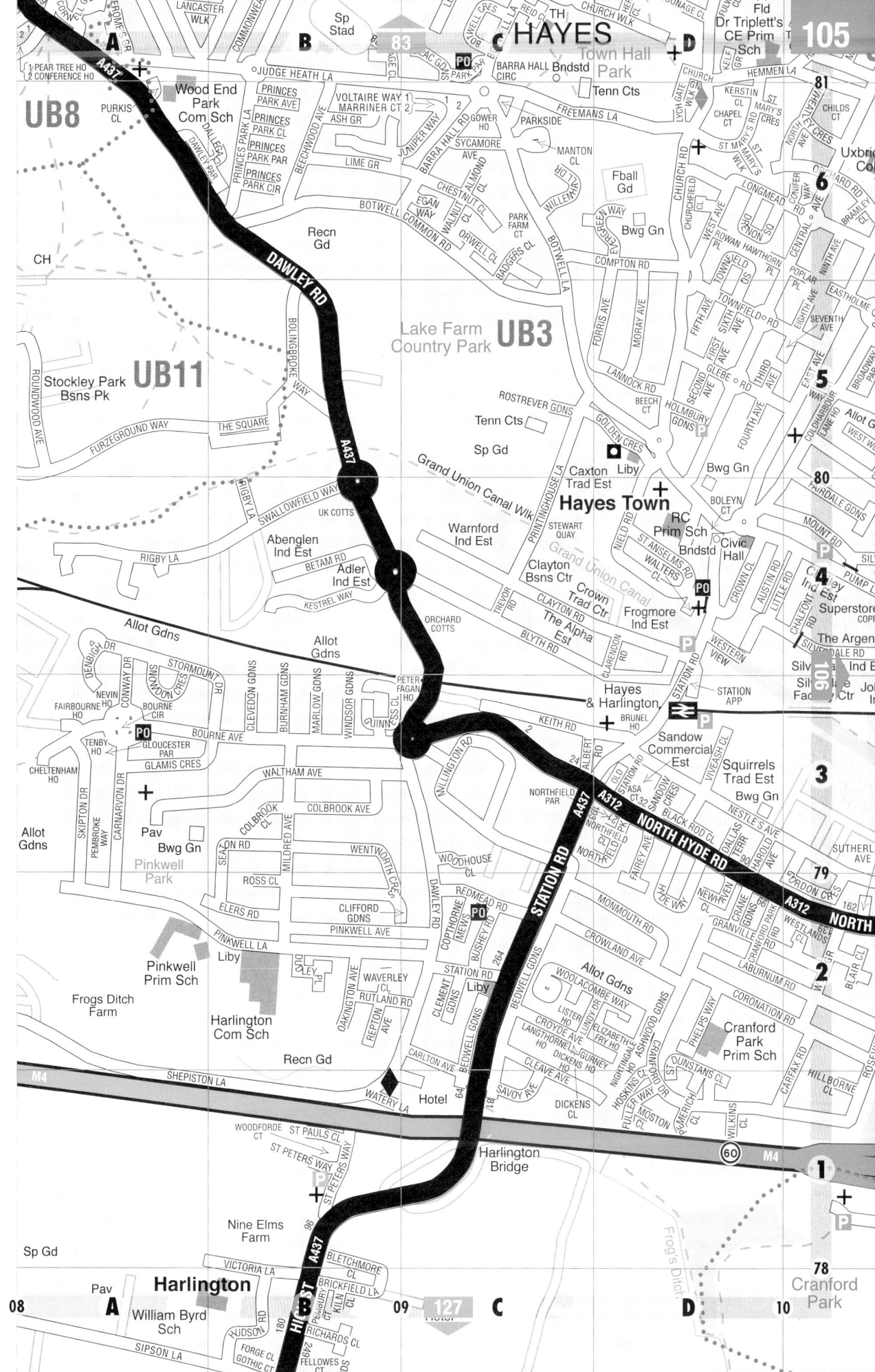

HAYES
Town Hall Park
UB8
UB11
UB3
Wood End Park Com Sch
Dr Triplett's CE Prim Sch
Lake Farm Country Park
Stockley Park Bsns Pk
DAWLEY RD
A437
Grand Union Canal Wlk
Grand Union Canal
Hayes Town
Caxton Trad Est
Warnford Ind Est
Abenglen Ind Est
Adler Ind Est
Clayton Bsns Ctr
Crown Trad Ctr
The Alpha Est
Frogmore Ind Est
RC Prim Sch
Civic Hall
Hayes & Harlington
Sandow Commercial Est
Squirrels Trad Est
NORTH HYDE RD
A312
STATION RD
Pinkwell Park
Pinkwell Prim Sch
Harlington Com Sch
Frogs Ditch Farm
Cranford Park Prim Sch
M4
Harlington Bridge
Nine Elms Farm
Harlington
William Byrd Sch
HIGH ST
Cranford Park
Frog's Ditch
Recn Gd
Allot Gdns
Sp Gd
Bwg Gn
Fball Gd
Tenn Cts
Liby
Hotel
Pav
CH
BARRA HALL CIRC
JUDGE HEATH LA
BOTWELL LA
BOTWELL COMMON RD
FREEMANS LA
CHURCH RD
COMPTON RD
PRINTINGHOUSE LA
FURZEGROUND WAY
ROUNDWOOD AVE
SWALLOWFIELD WAY
RIGBY LA
BOURNE AVE
WALTHAM AVE
COLBROOK AVE
PINKWELL LA
PINKWELL AVE
SHEPISTON LA
WATERY LA
ST PETERS WAY
VICTORIA LA
SIPSON LA
CORONATION RD
LABURNUM RD
WESTERN VIEW
KEITH RD
DAWLEY RD
BEDWELL GDNS
ASHWOOD GDNS
WOOLACOMBE WAY
CROWLAND AVE
MONMOUTH RD
BLACK ROD CL
NESTLE'S AVE
TOWNFIELD RD
GLEBE RD
LONGMEAD RD
HEMMEN LA

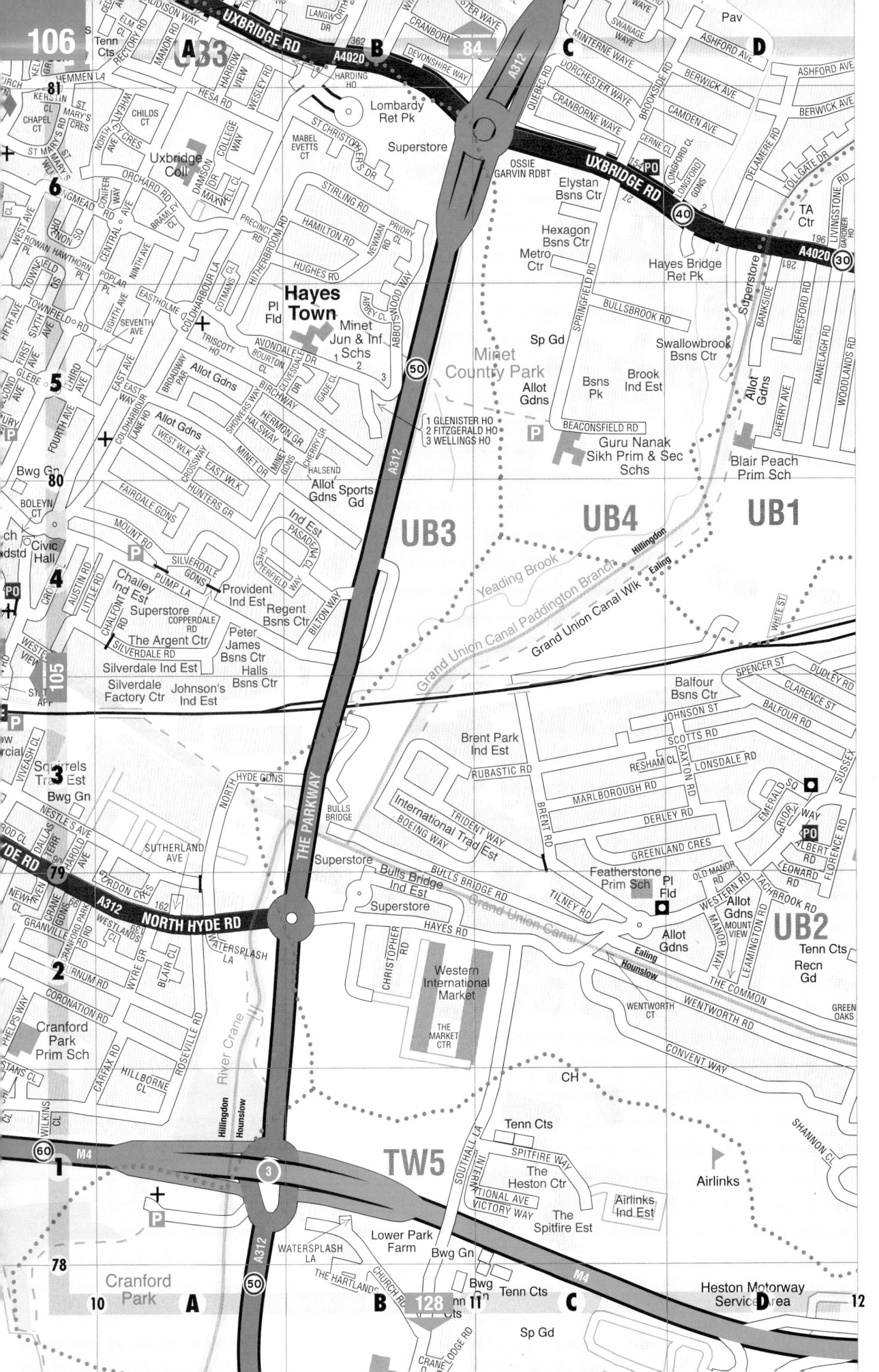

UXBRIDGE RD
A4020
UB3
Hayes Town
Minet Country Park
UB4
UB1
UB3
Lombardy Ret Pk
Superstore
Uxbridge Coll
OSSIE GARVIN RDBT
Elystan Bsns Ctr
Hexagon Bsns Ctr
Metro Ctr
Hayes Bridge Ret Pk
Minet Jun & Inf Schs
Allot Gdns
Bsns Pk
Brook Ind Est
Swallowbrook Bsns Ctr
Guru Nanak Sikh Prim & Sec Schs
Blair Peach Prim Sch
1 GLENISTER HO
2 FITZGERALD HO
3 WELLINGS HO
Yeading Brook
Grand Union Canal Paddington Branch
Grand Union Canal Wlk
Civic Hall
Provident Ind Est
Regent Bsns Ctr
Chailey Ind Est
Peter James Bsns Ctr
Halls Bsns Ctr
The Argent Ctr
Silverdale Ind Est
Silverdale Factory Ctr
Johnson's Ind Est
THE PARKWAY
A312
Squirrels Trad Est
Brent Park Ind Est
International Trad Est
Balfour Bsns Ctr
NORTH HYDE RD
Bulls Bridge Ind Est
Superstore
Featherstone Prim Sch
Grand Union Canal
UB2
Western International Market
THE MARKET CTR
Cranford Park Prim Sch
River Crane
TW5
M4
The Heston Ctr
Airlinks Ind Est
The Spitfire Est
Airlinks
Lower Park Farm
Heston Motorway Service Area
Cranford Park

84
105
128

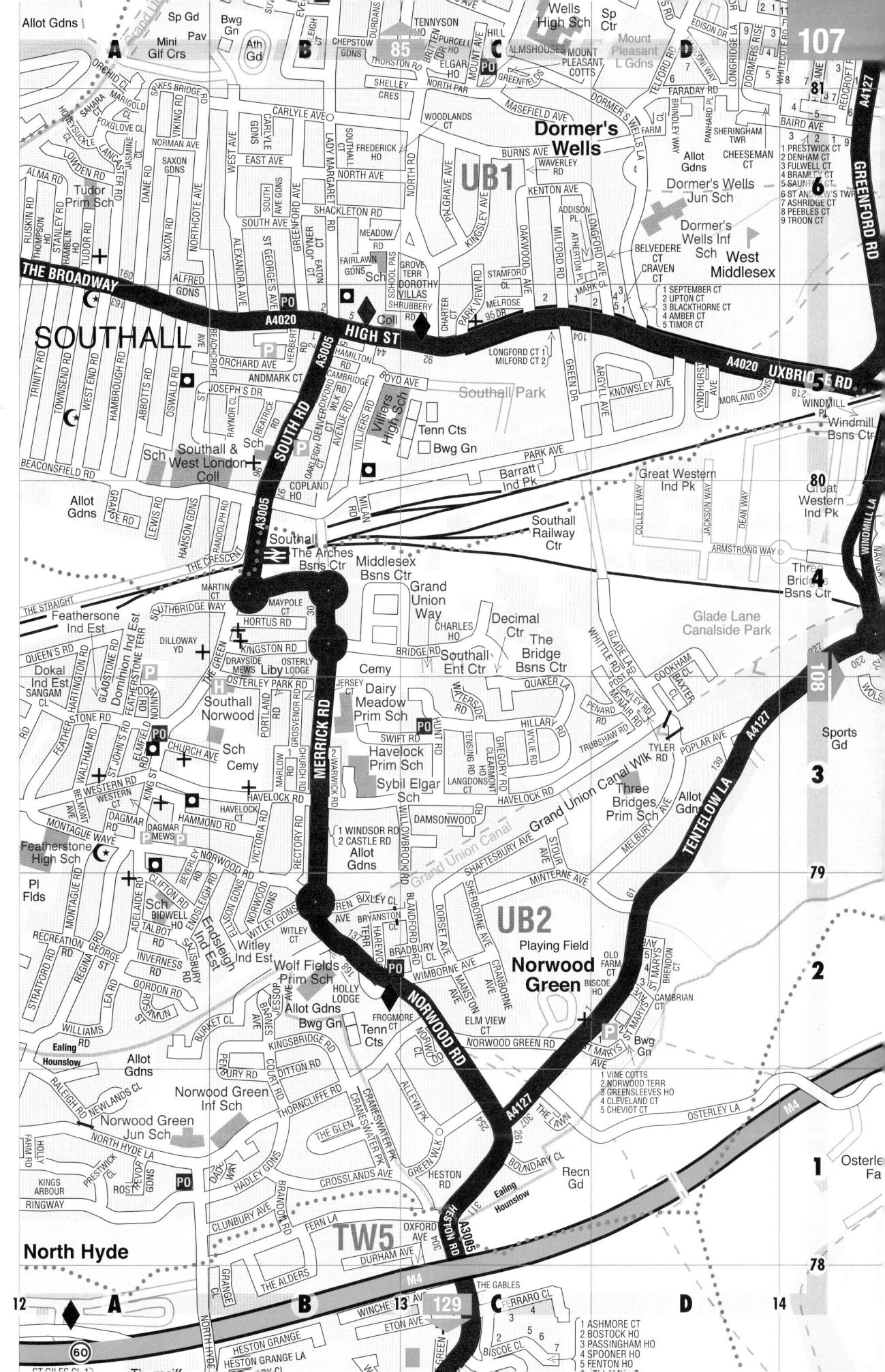

A
B
C
D
85
SOUTHALL
Dormer's Wells
UB1
UB2
TW5
Norwood Green
North Hyde
THE BROADWAY
HIGH ST
A4020
UXBRIDGE RD
GREENFORD RD
A4127
SOUTH RD
A3005
MERRICK RD
NORWOOD RD
TENTELOW LA
HESTON RD
M4
Grand Union Canal
Southall Park
Glade Lane Canalside Park
Southall & West London Coll
Villiers High Sch
Dormer's Wells Jun Sch
Dormer's Wells Inf Sch
West Middlesex
Tudor Prim Sch
Featherstone High Sch
Dairy Meadow Prim Sch
Havelock Prim Sch
Sybil Elgar Sch
Three Bridges Prim Sch
Wolf Fields Prim Sch
Norwood Green Inf Sch
Norwood Green Jun Sch
Southall Norwood
Great Western Ind Pk
Southall Railway Ctr
Middlesex Bsns Ctr
The Arches Bsns Ctr
Grand Union Way
Decimal Ctr
The Bridge Bsns Ctr
Southall Ent Ctr
Three Bridges Bsns Ctr
Windmill Bsns Ctr
Dominion Ind Est
Featherstone Ind Est
Dokal Ind Est
Endsleigh Ind Est
Witley Ind Est
Barratt Ind Pk
Playing Field
Recn Gd
Sports Gd
1 PRESTWICK CT
2 DENHAM CT
3 FULWELL CT
4 BRAMLEY CT
5 SAUNTON CT
6 ST ANDREW'S TWR
7 ASHRIDGE CT
8 PEEBLES CT
9 TROON CT
1 SEPTEMBER CT
2 UPTON CT
3 BLACKTHORNE CT
4 AMBER CT
5 TIMOR CT
1 WINDSOR RD
2 CASTLE RD
1 VINE COTTS
2 NORWOOD TERR
3 GREENSLEEVES HO
4 CLEVELAND CT
5 CHEVIOT CT
1 ASHMORE CT
2 BOSTOCK HO
3 PASSINGHAM HO
4 SPOONER HO
5 FENTON HO
Ealing
Hounslow
108
129
60
12
13
14
81
80
79
78
6
5
4
3
2
1

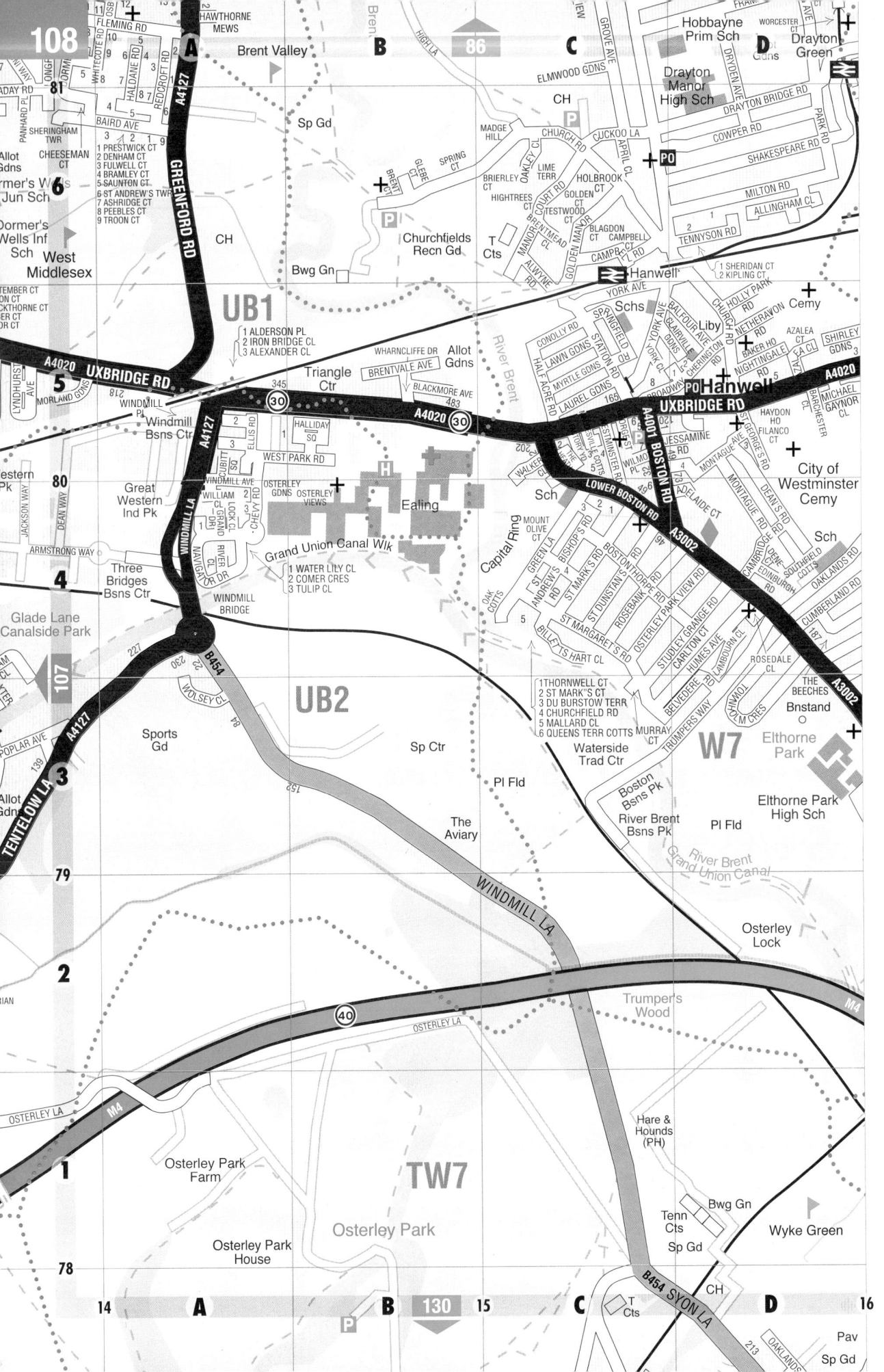

Brent Valley
Sp Gd
Hobbayne Prim Sch
Drayton Green
Drayton Manor High Sch
DRAYTON BRIDGE RD
COWPER RD
SHAKESPEARE RD
MILTON RD
ALLINGHAM CL
TENNYSON RD
ELMWOOD GDNS
CH
CHURCH RD
CUCKOO LA
APRIL CL
HOLBROOK CT
GOLDEN CT
TESTWOOD CT
BLAGDON CT
CAMPBELL CT
GOLDEN MANOR
BRENTMEAD CL
ALWYNE RD
MANOR COURT RD
OAKLEY CL
LIME TERR
BRIERLEY CT
HIGHTREES CT
MADGE HILL
SPRING CT
GLEBE CT
BRENT CT
Churchfields Recn Gd
T Cts
Bwg Gn
Hanwell
1 SHERIDAN CT
2 KIPLING CT
GREENFORD RD
A4127
CH
West Middlesex
Dormer's Wells Inf Sch
Dormer's Wells Jun Sch
Allot Gdns
CHEESEMAN CT
SHERINGHAM TWR
BAIRD AVE
FLEMING RD
HAWTHORNE MEWS
WHITECOTE RD
HALDANE RD
REDCROFT RD
1 PRESTWICK CT
2 DENHAM CT
3 FULWELL CT
4 BRAMLEY CT
5 SAUNTON CT
6 ST ANDREW'S TWR
7 ASHRIDGE CT
8 PEEBLES CT
9 TROON CT
UB1
1 ALDERSON PL
2 IRON BRIDGE CL
3 ALEXANDER CL
A4020 UXBRIDGE RD
LYNDHURST AVE
MORLAND GDNS
WINDMILL PL
Windmill Bsns Ctr
Triangle Ctr
WHARNCLIFFE DR
BRENTVALE AVE
BLACKMORE AVE
Allot Gdns
River Brent
HALLIDAY SQ
WEST PARK RD
ELLIS RD
CUBITT SQ
WINDMILL AVE
OSTERLEY GDNS
OSTERLEY VIEWS
WILLIAM CL
GRAND DR
LOCK CL
CHEVY RD
RIVER CL
NAVIGATOR DR
WINDMILL LA
Great Western Ind Pk
JACKSON WAY
DEAN WAY
ARMSTRONG WAY
Three Bridges Bsns Ctr
Ealing
Grand Union Canal Wlk
1 WATER LILY CL
2 COMER CRES
3 TULIP CL
WINDMILL BRIDGE
Glade Lane Canalside Park
YORK AVE
Schs
CONOLLY RD
LAWN GDNS
MYRTLE GDNS
LAUREL GDNS
HALFACRE RD
SPRINGFIELD RD
STATION RD
BALFOUR AVE
CLAIRVILLE GDNS
Liby
CHERINGTON RD
CHURCH RD
HOLLY PARK RD
NETHERAVON RD
BAKER HO
NIGHTINGALE RD
AZALEA CT
ZEALA CL
SHIRLEY GDNS
Cemy
BROADWAY
Hanwell
UXBRIDGE RD
A4001 BOSTON RD
HAYDON HO
FILANCO CT
MICHAEL GAYNOR CL
BARCHESTER CL
JESSAMINE RD
MONTAGUE AVE
ST GEORGE'S RD
City of Westminster Cemy
WALKER CL
WILMOT PL
LOWER BOSTON RD
ADELAIDE CT
A3002
MONTAGUE RD
DEAN'S RD
Sch
CAMBRIDGE RD
DENE CT
EDINBURGH RD
SOUTHFIELD COTTS
OAKLANDS RD
CUMBERLAND RD
MOUNT OLIVE CT
Capital Ring
GREEN LA
ST ANDREW'S RD
BISHOP'S RD
ST MARK'S RD
BOSTONTHORPE RD
ST DUNSTAN'S RD
ROSEBANK RD
OSTERLEY PARK VIEW RD
STUDLEY GRANGE RD
CARLTON CT
HUMES AVE
LAMBOURN CL
ST MARGARET'S RD
BILLETS HART CL
OAK COTTS
ROSEDALE CL
THE BEECHES
Bnstand
1 THORNWELL CT
2 ST MARK''S CT
3 DU BURSTOW TERR
4 CHURCHFIELD RD
5 MALLARD CL
6 QUEENS TERR COTTS
MURRAY CT
BELVEDERE
TRUMPERS WAY
TOLHOLM CRES
W7
Elthorne Park
Elthorne Park High Sch
Waterside Trad Ctr
Boston Bsns Pk
River Brent Bsns Pk
Pl Fld
UB2
WOLSEY CL
B454
Sports Gd
POPLAR AVE
TENTELOW LA
Allot Gdns
Sp Ctr
Pl Fld
The Aviary
WINDMILL LA
River Brent
Grand Union Canal
Osterley Lock
Trumper's Wood
M4
OSTERLEY LA
OSTERLEY LA
Hare & Hounds (PH)
Osterley Park Farm
TW7
Osterley Park
Osterley Park House
Tenn Cts
Bwg Gn
Sp Gd
Wyke Green
CH
B454 SYON LA
T Cts
OAKLANDS
Pav
Sp Gd

86
107
130

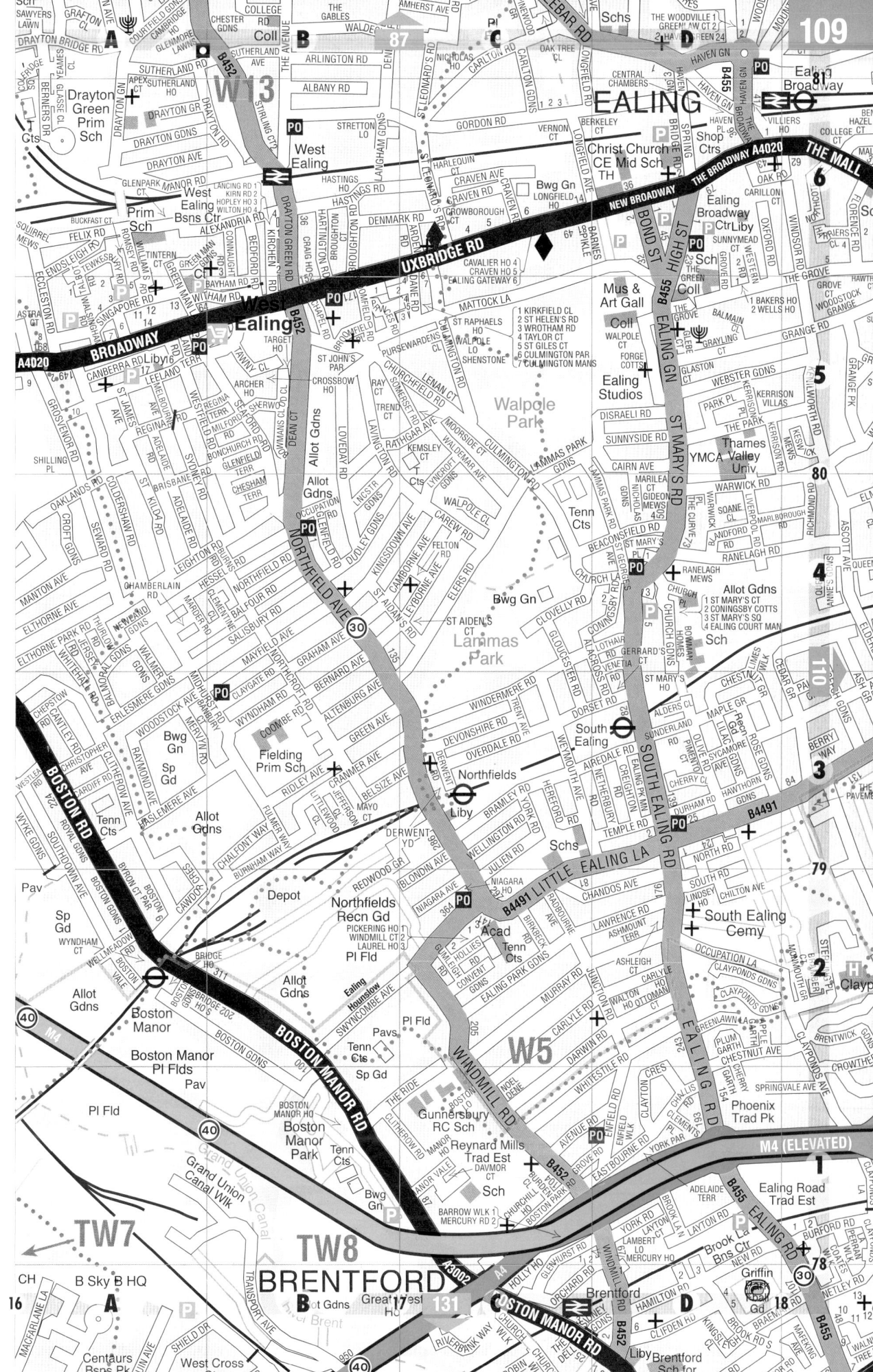

A
B
C
D
87
W13
EALING
Ealing Broadway
THE MALL
6
5
4
3
2
1
80
79
78
81
110
131
16
17
18
A4020
BROADWAY
West Ealing
UXBRIDGE RD
NEW BROADWAY
THE BROADWAY
B452
B455
B4491
DRAYTON BRIDGE RD
Drayton Green Prim Sch
DRAYTON GR
DRAYTON GDNS
DRAYTON AVE
SUTHERLAND RD
West Ealing
West Ealing Bsns Ctr
Prim Sch
ARLINGTON RD
ALBANY RD
GORDON RD
Christ Church CE Mid Sch
Shop Ctrs
Ealing Broadway Ctr
Mus & Art Gall
Coll
Ealing Studios
Walpole Park
Thames Valley Univ
YMCA
ST MARY'S RD
SOUTH EALING RD
EALING RD
HIGH ST
BOND ST
MATTOCK LA
NORTHFIELD AVE
Lammas Park
South Ealing
Northfields
LITTLE EALING LA
South Ealing Cemy
Northfields Recn Gd
Fielding Prim Sch
BOSTON RD
Boston Manor
Boston Manor Pl Flds
BOSTON MANOR RD
Boston Manor Park
M4
M4 (ELEVATED)
W5
WINDMILL RD
Gunnersbury RC Sch
Reynard Mills Trad Est
Phoenix Trad Pk
Ealing Road Trad Est
Grand Union Canal Wlk
TW7
TW8
BRENTFORD
B Sky B HQ
Centaurs Bsns Pk
West Cross
Brentford
Brook La Bsns Ctr
Griffin Park
A3002
A4
40
30
Allot Gdns
Depot
Pl Fld
Tenn Cts
Sp Gd
Bwg Gn
Pav

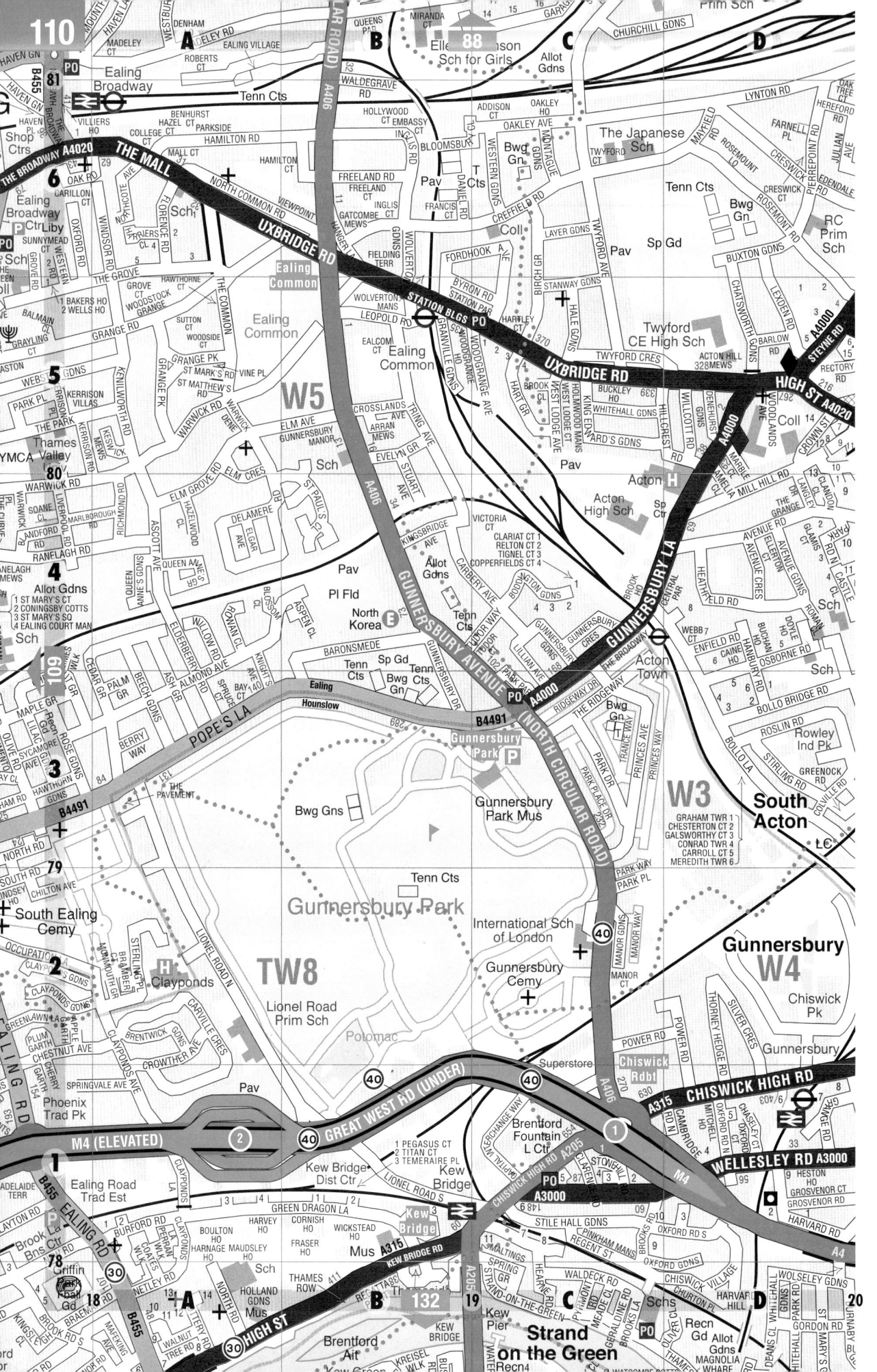
88
132
109
A
B
C
D
6
5
4
3
2
1
W5
W3
W4
TW8
Ealing Broadway
Ealing Common
Ealing Broadway Ctr
Shop Ctrs
Ellen Wilkinson Sch for Girls
The Japanese Sch
Twyford CE High Sch
Acton High Sch
Acton Town
South Acton
Gunnersbury
Gunnersbury Park
Gunnersbury Park Mus
Gunnersbury Cemy
International Sch of London
Chiswick Pk
North Korea
Thames Valley Univ
South Ealing Cemy
Claypond
Lionel Road Prim Sch
Potomac
Phoenix Trad Pk
Ealing Road Trad Est
Brook La Bns Ctr
Griffin Park Fball Gd
Kew Bridge Dist Ctr
Kew Bridge
Brentford Fountain L Ctr
Chiswick Rdbt
Superstore
Strand on the Green
Brentford Ait
Kew Pier
Rowley Ind Pk
Allot Gdns
Tenn Cts
Bwg Gn
Sp Gd
Pav
Pl Fld
Coll
Sch
THE MALL
UXBRIDGE RD
HIGH ST A4020
GUNNERSBURY LA
GUNNERSBURY AVENUE (NORTH CIRCULAR ROAD)
POPE'S LA
GREAT WEST RD (UNDER)
M4 (ELEVATED)
CHISWICK HIGH RD
WELLESLEY RD A3000
KEW BRIDGE RD
EALING RD
HIGH ST
THE BROADWAY A4020
NORTH COMMON RD
HANGER LA A406
WALDEGRAVE RD
LYNTON RD
CHURCHILL GDNS
OAKLEY AVE
CREFFIELD RD
TWYFORD AVE
TWYFORD CRES
WOODGRANGE AVE
GRANVILLE GDNS
THE GROVE
GRANGE RD
WARWICK RD
ELM GROVE RD
RICHMOND RD
KENILWORTH RD
ST MARK'S RD
ELM AVE
ST PAUL'S CL
CARBERY AVE
BODDINGTON GDNS
BOLLO BRIDGE RD
BOLLO LA
OSBORNE RD
MILL HILL RD
AVENUE RD
AVENUE GDNS
PRINCES AVE
PARK DR
THE RIDGEWAY
POWER RD
THORNEY HEDGE RD
SILVER CRES
STILE HALL GDNS
OXFORD RD S
CHISWICK VILLAGE
HARVARD RD
LIONEL ROAD N
LIONEL ROAD S
CARVILLE CRES
CLAYPONDS AVE
CHESTNUT AVE
GREEN DRAGON LA
NORTH RD
BRENTWICK GDNS
CROWTHER AVE
SPRINGVALE AVE
NETLEY RD
BURFORD RD
CHISWICK HIGH RD A205
STRAND-ON-THE-GREEN
GROSVENOR RD
WOLSELEY GDNS

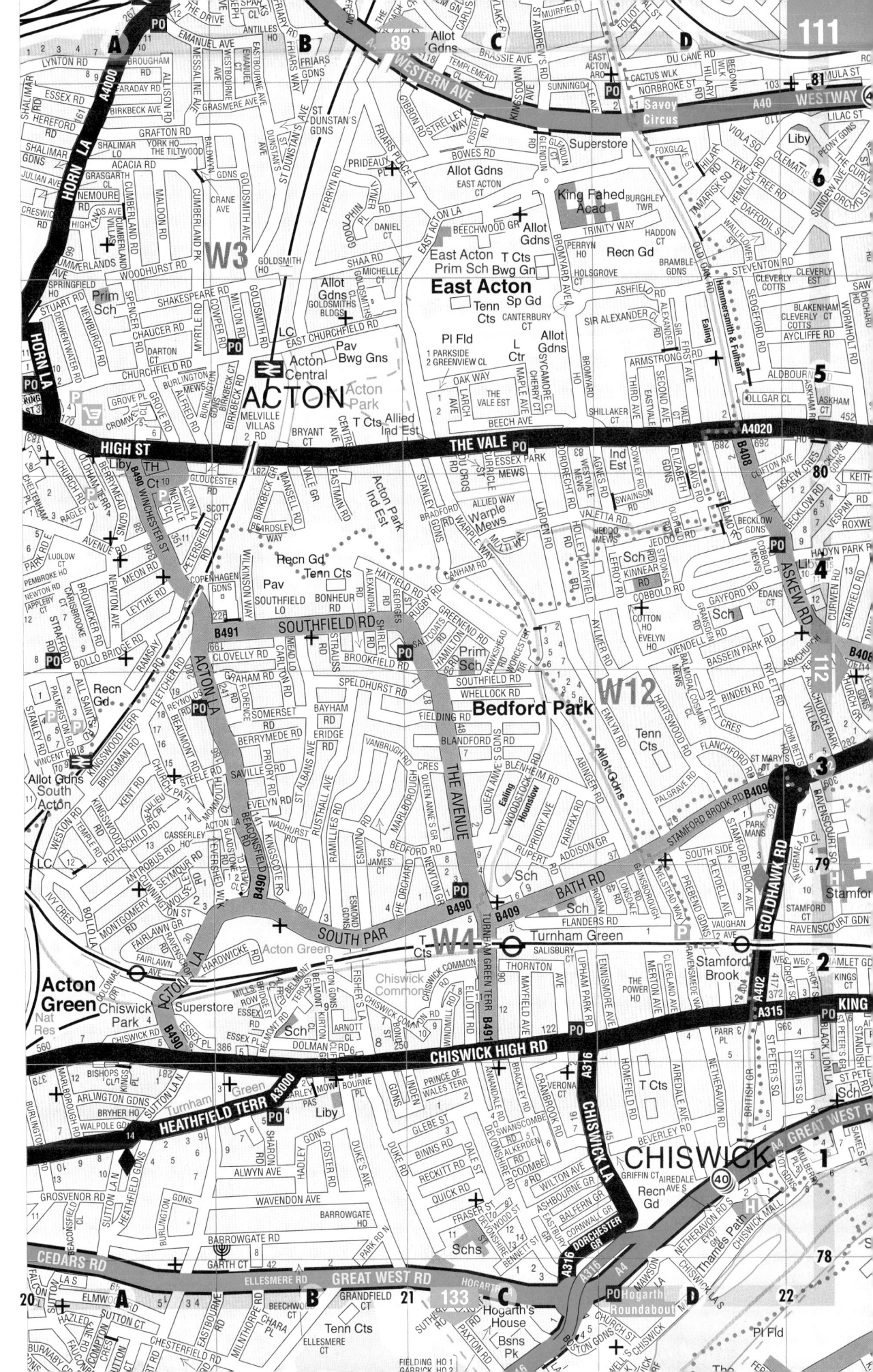

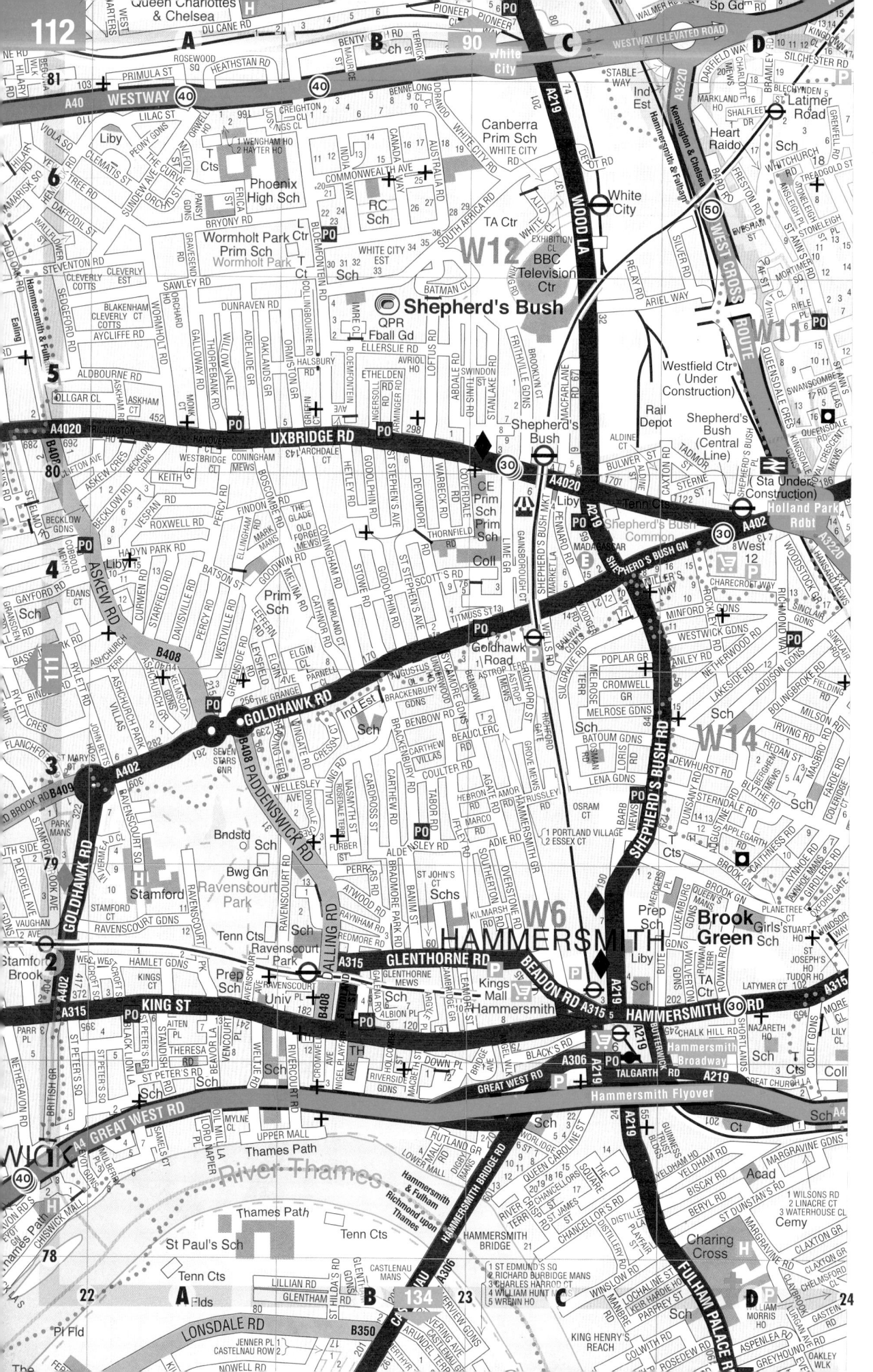
Queen Charlottes & Chelsea
DU CANE RD
PIONEER
90
White City
WESTWAY (ELEVATED ROAD)
81
WESTWAY
A40
40
PRIMULA ST
ROSEWOOD SQ
HEATHSTAN RD
BENTWORTH RD
Sch
WOOD LA
A219
Canberra Prim Sch
WHITE CITY RD
Ind Est
STABLE WAY
Latimer Road
SILCHESTER RD
Heart Raido
Kensington & Chelsea
Hammersmith & Fulham
A3220
Liby
Phoenix High Sch
T Cts
RC Sch
COMMONWEALTH AVE
WHITE CITY
White City
TA Ctr
W12
BBC Television Ctr
EXHIBITION CL
SOUTH AFRICA RD
Wormholt Park Prim Sch
Wormholt Park
BRYONY RD
WHITE CITY EST
Shepherd's Bush
QPR Fball Gd
ARIEL WAY
W11
50
WEST CROSS ROUTE
QUEENSDALE CRES
Westfield Ctr (Under Construction)
Rail Depot
6
5
4
3
2
1
STEVENTON RD
CLEVERLY COTTS
DUNRAVEN RD
SAWLEY RD
AYCLIFFE RD
ALDBOURNE RD
ELLERSLIE RD
OLLGAR CL
UXBRIDGE RD
A4020
Shepherd's Bush
Shepherd's Bush (Central Line)
(Sta Under Construction)
Holland Park Rdbt
30
A402
80
CE Prim Sch
Prim Sch
Coll
Shepherd's Bush Common
SHEPHERD'S BUSH GN
West 12
Liby
Tenn Cts
ASKEW RD
B408
Prim Sch
Goldhawk Road
GOLDHAWK RD
Ind Est
Sch
W14
BROOK GN
111
Sch
SHEPHERD'S BUSH RD
A402
GOLDHAWK RD
B409
79
PADDENSWICK RD
Bndstd
Sch
Bwg Gn
Ravenscourt Park
Stamford
RAVENSCOURT GDNS
Schs
W6
HAMMERSMITH
Prep Sch
Brook Green
Girls Sch
Tenn Cts
Ravenscourt Park
GLENTHORNE RD
A315
Kings Mall Hammersmith
BEADON RD
HAMMERSMITH RD
Stamford Brook
KING ST
Univ
Prep Sch
Sch
Liby
Sch
TA Ctr
Hammersmith Broadway
TALGARTH RD
A219
Hammersmith Flyover
GREAT WEST RD
A4
Sch
Ct
Coll
UPPER MALL
Thames Path
River Thames
40
78
Thames Path
St Paul's Sch
Tenn Cts
Hammersmith & Fulham
Richmond upon Thames
HAMMERSMITH BRIDGE RD
HAMMERSMITH BRIDGE
Acad
Charing Cross
Cemy
FULHAM PALACE RD
22
A
Flds
B
134
23
C
D
24
LONSDALE RD
B350
Pl Fld
KING HENRY'S REACH
Sch

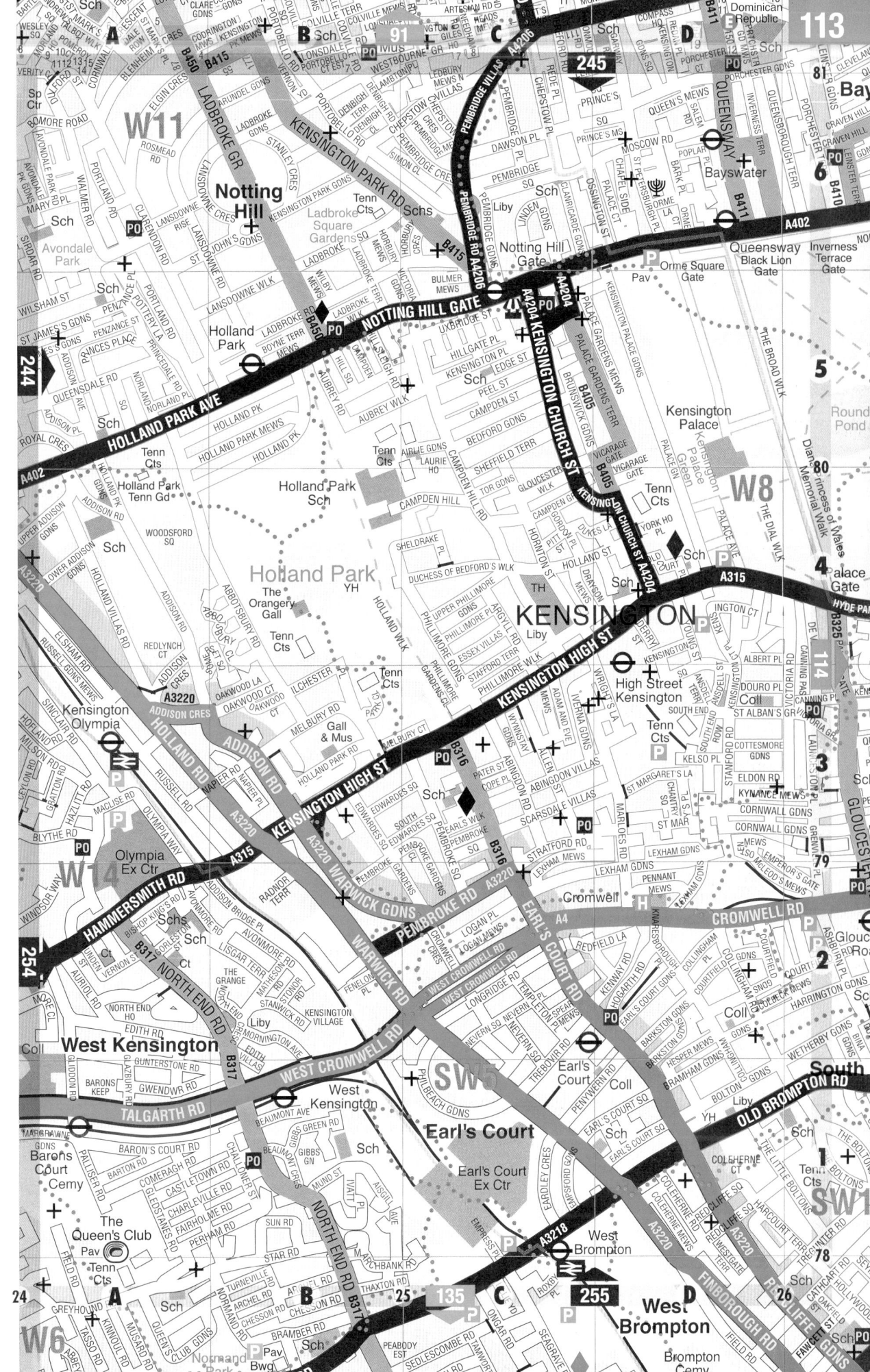

W11
Notting Hill
Ladbroke Square Gardens
Avondale Park
Holland Park
Notting Hill Gate
Queensway
Bayswater
Orme Square Gate
Queensway Black Lion Gate
Inverness Terrace Gate
Kensington Palace
Round Pond
W8
KENSINGTON
Holland Park
The Orangery Gall
Holland Park Sch
Holland Park Tenn Gd
High Street Kensington
Kensington Olympia
Olympia Ex Ctr
W14
West Kensington
SW5
Earl's Court
Earl's Court Ex Ctr
West Kensington
Cromwell
West Brompton
Barons Court Cemy
The Queen's Club
W6
Brompton Cemy
Palace Gate
Princess of Wales Memorial Walk
HOLLAND PARK AVE
NOTTING HILL GATE
KENSINGTON PARK RD
LADBROKE GR
PEMBRIDGE VILLAS
QUEENSWAY
KENSINGTON CHURCH ST
KENSINGTON HIGH ST
HAMMERSMITH RD
HOLLAND RD
ADDISON RD
WARWICK GDNS
PEMBROKE RD
WARWICK RD
EARL'S COURT RD
CROMWELL RD
WEST CROMWELL RD
TALGARTH RD
NORTH END RD
OLD BROMPTON RD
FINBOROUGH RD
REDCLIFFE GDNS
GLOUCESTER RD
HYDE PARK
THE BROAD WLK
A402
A4206
A4204
A315
A3220
A4
A3218
B450
B415
B405
B316
B317
B411
91
245
244
254
114
135
255

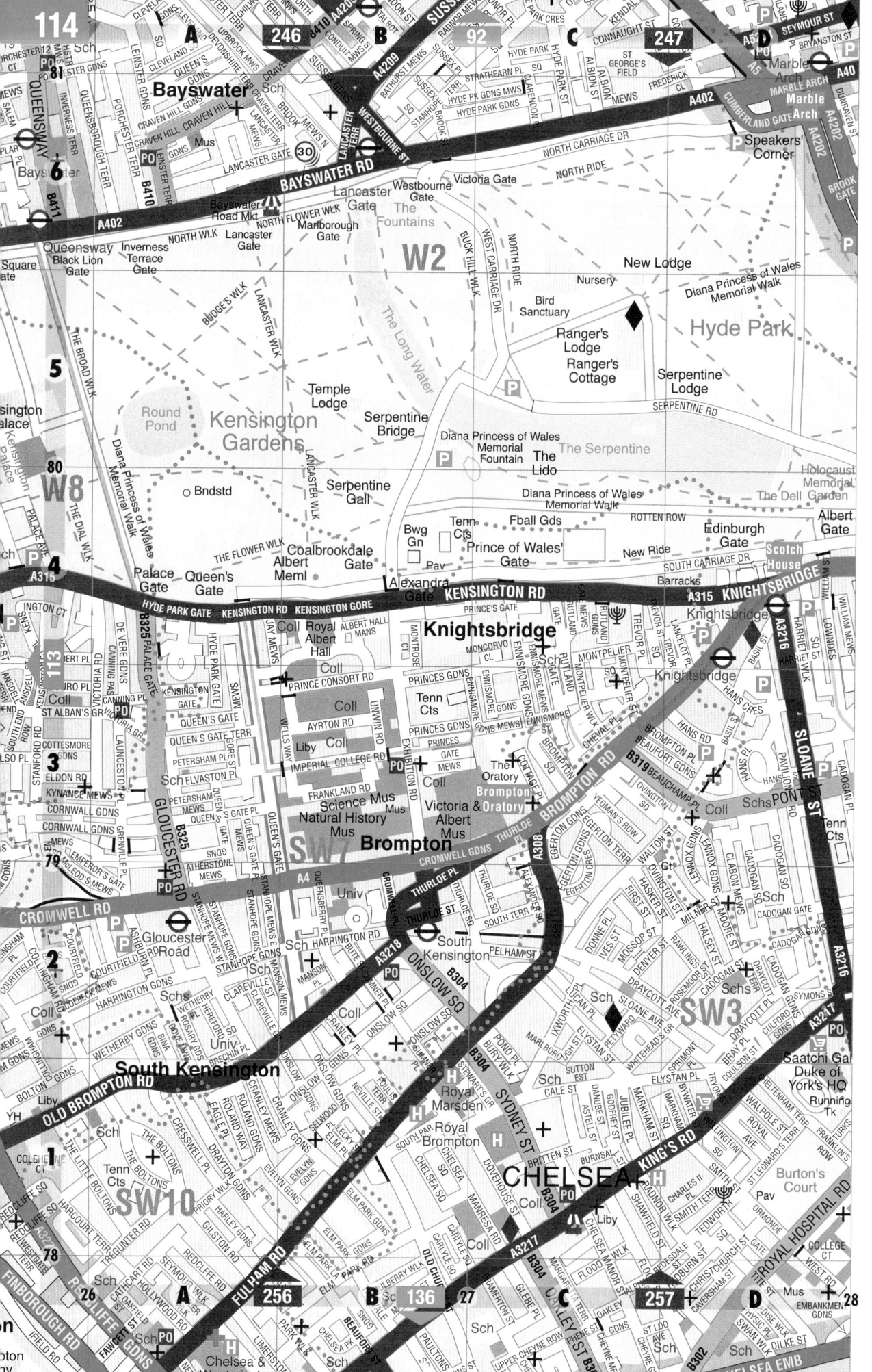
246
92
247
256
136
257
Bayswater
Queensway
Bayswater Rd
Kensington Gardens
Hyde Park
The Serpentine
The Long Water
Round Pond
Speakers' Corner
Marble Arch
W2
W8
SW7
SW3
SW10
Kensington Rd
Knightsbridge
Brompton
Brompton Rd
Cromwell Rd
Gloucester Road
South Kensington
Old Brompton Rd
Fulham Rd
King's Rd
Chelsea
Sloane St
Royal Albert Hall
Science Mus
Natural History Mus
Victoria & Albert Mus
Royal Marsden
Royal Brompton
Saatchi Gal
Duke of York's HQ
Royal Hospital Rd

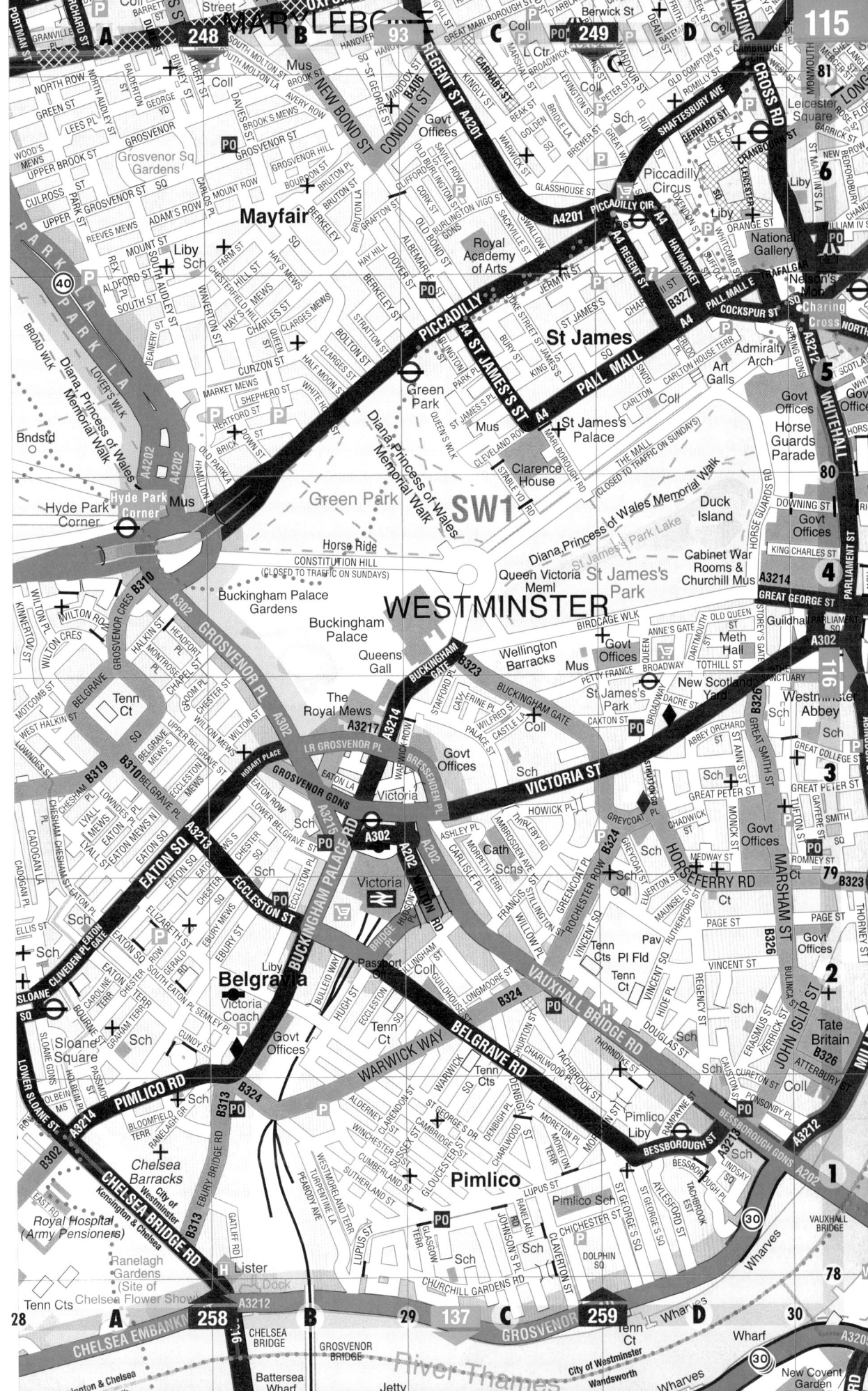
Mayfair
St James
Green Park
SW1
WESTMINSTER
Buckingham Palace
St James's Park
Belgravia
Pimlico
Victoria
Piccadilly Circus
Hyde Park Corner
Leicester Square
Charing Cross
National Gallery
Westminster Abbey
Tate Britain
Chelsea Barracks
Royal Hospital (Army Pensioners)
River Thames
PICCADILLY
PALL MALL
VICTORIA ST
BELGRAVE RD
VAUXHALL BRIDGE RD
WHITEHALL
GROSVENOR PL
BUCKINGHAM PALACE RD
CHELSEA BRIDGE RD
CHELSEA EMBANKMENT
248
93
249
258
137
259
116

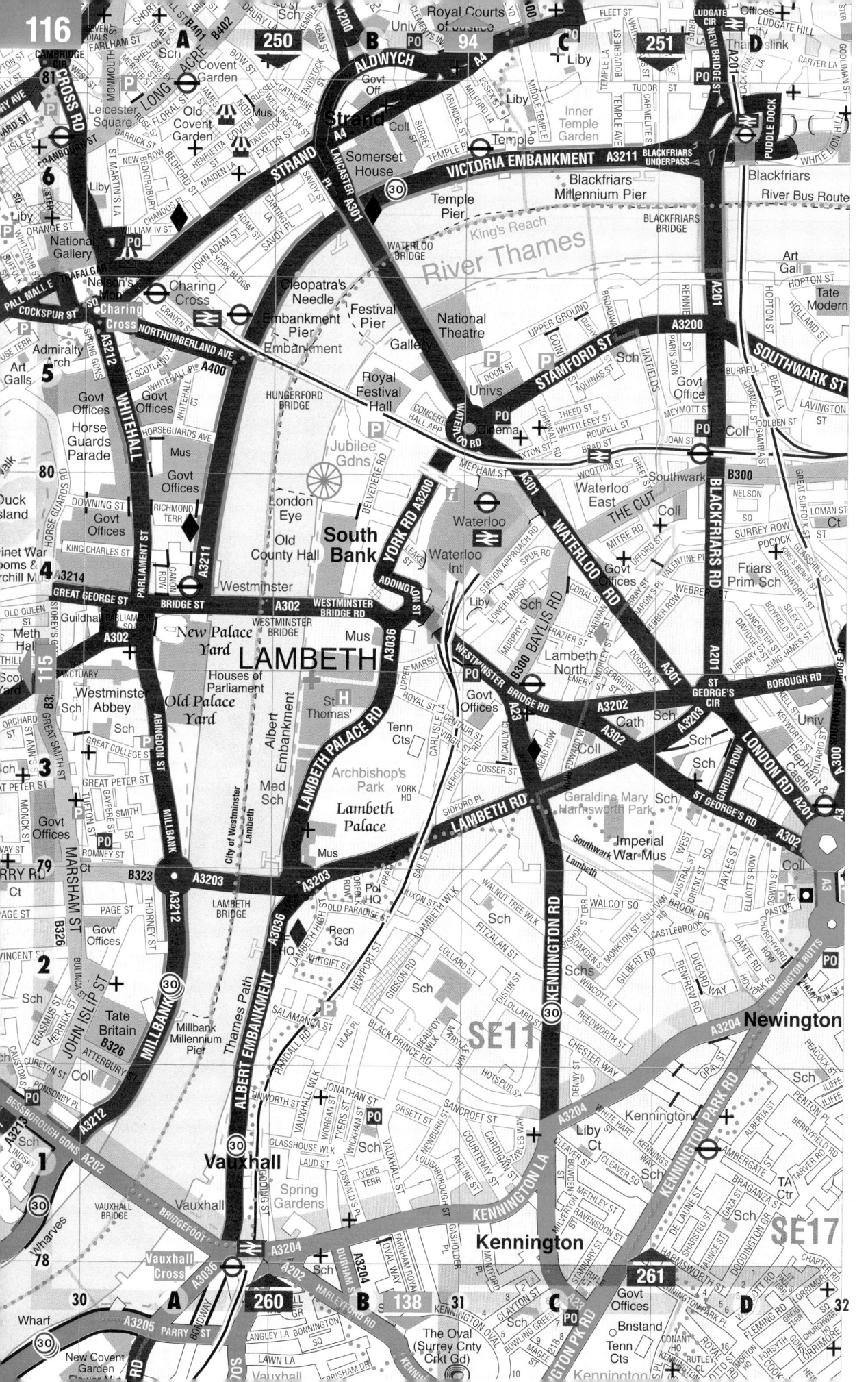

250
94
251
A
B
C
D
Royal Courts of Justice
Covent Garden
Long Acre
Old Covent Garden
Leicester Square
Cambridge Cir
Cross Rd
Aldwych
Strand
Somerset House
Lancaster Pl
Victoria Embankment
Temple
Inner Temple Garden
Blackfriars Underpass
Puddle Dock
Blackfriars
Blackfriars Millennium Pier
River Bus Route
Blackfriars Bridge
Temple Pier
King's Reach
River Thames
Waterloo Bridge
National Gallery
Trafalgar Sq
Nelson's Mon
Charing Cross
Cleopatra's Needle
Embankment Pier
Embankment
Festival Pier
National Theatre
Gallery
Royal Festival Hall
Hungerford Bridge
Northumberland Ave
Whitehall
Admiralty Arch
Art Galls
Govt Offices
Horse Guards Parade
Horse Guards Rd
Mus
Jubilee Gdns
London Eye
Old County Hall
South Bank
York Rd
Waterloo
Waterloo Int
Waterloo East
The Cut
Waterloo Rd
Stamford St
Southwark St
Southwark
Blackfriars Rd
Art Gall
Tate Modern
Friars Prim Sch
Downing St
King Charles St
Great George St
Parliament St
Bridge St
Westminster
Westminster Bridge Rd
Westminster Bridge
New Palace Yard
Lambeth
Houses of Parliament
Old Palace Yard
Westminster Abbey
Albert Embankment
St Thomas'
Lambeth Palace Rd
Archbishop's Park
Lambeth Palace
Baylis Rd
Lambeth North
St George's Cir
Borough Rd
London Rd
Elephant & Castle
St George's Rd
Geraldine Mary Harmsworth Park
Imperial War Mus
Lambeth Rd
Kennington Rd
Abingdon St
Millbank
Marsham St
Lambeth Bridge
Tate Britain
Millbank Millennium Pier
Thames Path
Albert Embankment
SE11
Newington
Newington Butts
Kennington
Kennington Park Rd
Kennington La
Bessborough Gdns
Vauxhall Bridge
Bridgefoot
Vauxhall
Vauxhall Cross
Spring Gardens
Wharves
Wharf
Parry St
New Covent Garden
The Oval (Surrey Cnty Crkt Gd)
SE17
115
260
138
261
30
31
32
78
79
80
81
1
2
3
4
5
6

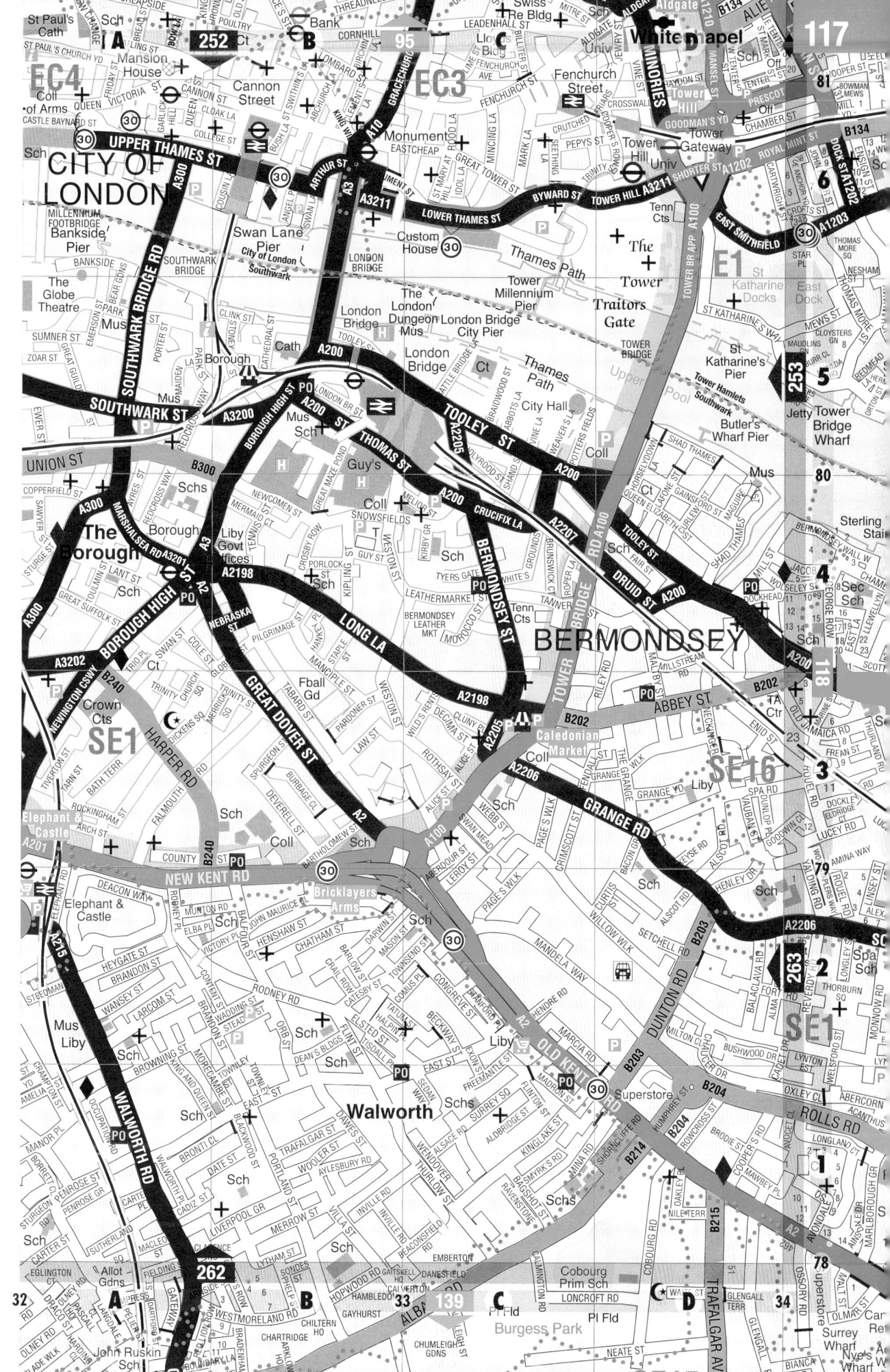
CITY OF LONDON
EC4
EC3
Whitechapel
Aldgate
St Paul's Cath
Mansion House
Cannon Street
Bank
Monument
Fenchurch Street
Tower Hill
Tower Gateway
UPPER THAMES ST
LOWER THAMES ST
Swan Lane Pier
Custom House
Millennium Footbridge
Bankside Pier
The Globe Theatre
Southwark Bridge
London Bridge
The London Dungeon Mus
London Bridge City Pier
Tower Millennium Pier
The Tower
Traitors Gate
Tower Bridge
Thames Path
St Katharine Docks
St Katharine's Pier
Butler's Wharf Pier
Tower Bridge Wharf
City Hall
E1
SOUTHWARK BRIDGE RD
SOUTHWARK ST
UNION ST
BOROUGH HIGH ST
TOOLEY ST
Guy's
The Borough
Borough
LONG LA
BERMONDSEY ST
BERMONDSEY
GREAT DOVER ST
TOWER BRIDGE RD
ABBEY ST
Caledonian Market
GRANGE RD
SE1
SE16
Elephant & Castle
NEW KENT RD
Bricklayers Arms
OLD KENT RD
DUNTON RD
Walworth
WALWORTH RD
ROLLS RD
Superstore
Cobourg Prim Sch
Burgess Park
TRAFALGAR AV
ALBANY RD
Surrey Wharf
252
95
253
118
263
262
139
32
33
34
81
80
79
78
A
B
C
D
1
2
3
4
5
6

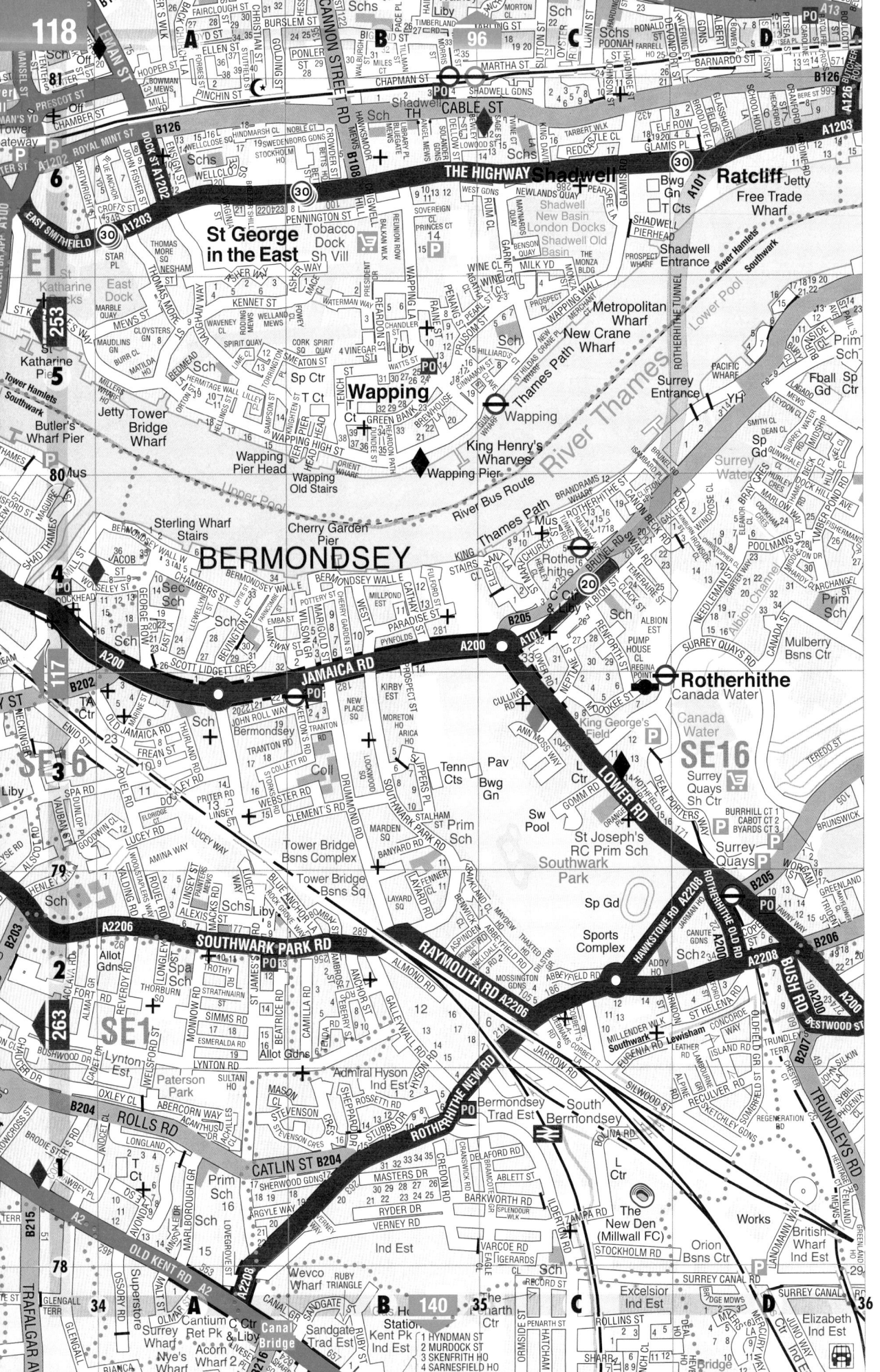

96
CANNON STREET RD
CABLE ST
Shadwell
THE HIGHWAY
Shadwell
Ratcliff
Free Trade Wharf
Shadwell New Basin
London Docks
Shadwell Old Basin
St George in the East
Tobacco Dock Sh Vill
E1
St Katharine Docks
East Dock
253
St Katharine Pier
Tower Hamlets
Southwark
Tower Bridge Wharf
Butler's Wharf Pier
Wapping
Wapping High St
Wapping Pier Head
Wapping Old Stairs
King Henry's Wharves
Wapping Pier
Metropolitan Wharf
New Crane Wharf
Thames Path
River Thames
River Bus Route
Upper Pool
Lower Pool
Shadwell Entrance
Surrey Entrance
ROTHERHITHE TUNNEL
Cherry Garden Pier
Sterling Wharf Stairs
BERMONDSEY
Rotherhithe
JAMAICA RD
117
SE16
Albion Channel
Surrey Water
Mulberry Bsns Ctr
Rotherhithe
Canada Water
Surrey Quays Sh Ctr
LOWER RD
King George's Field
Southwark Park
Sports Complex
St Joseph's RC Prim Sch
Tower Bridge Bsns Complex
Tower Bridge Bsns Sq
SOUTHWARK PARK RD
RAYMOUTH RD
ROTHERHITHE NEW RD
Bermondsey Trad Est
South Bermondsey
263
SE1
Paterson Park
Lynton Est
ROLLS RD
CATLIN ST
OLD KENT RD
Admiral Hyson Ind Est
The New Den (Millwall FC)
Orion Bsns Ctr
British Wharf Ind Est
Excelsior Ind Est
Elizabeth Ind Est
TRUNDLEYS RD
BUSH RD
Wevco Wharf
Canal Bridge
Cantium Ret Pk
Acorn Wharf
140
1 HYNDMAN ST
2 MURDOCK ST
3 SKENFRITH HO
4 SARNESFIELD HO

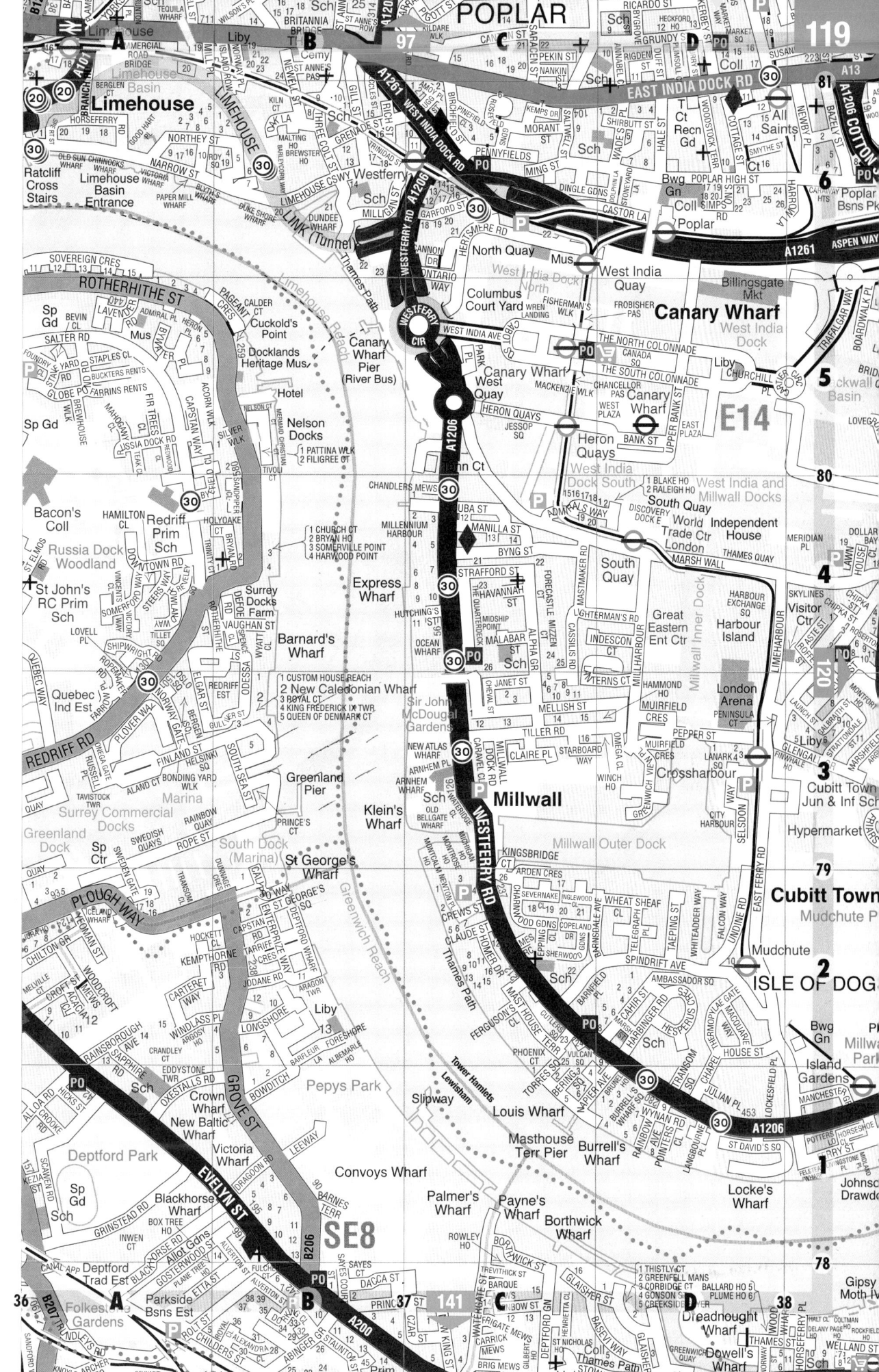
POPLAR
Limehouse
Ratcliff Cross Stairs
Limehouse Basin Entrance
LIMEHOUSE LINK (Tunnel)
EAST INDIA DOCK RD
WEST INDIA DOCK RD
Westferry
North Quay
West India Quay
Billingsgate Mkt
Canary Wharf
West India Dock
Columbus Court Yard
Cuckold's Point
Docklands Heritage Mus
Canary Wharf Pier (River Bus)
Nelson Docks
Heron Quays
E14
ROTHERHITHE ST
Bacon's Coll
Russia Dock Woodland
St John's RC Prim Sch
Redriff Prim Sch
Surrey Docks Farm
Barnard's Wharf
Express Wharf
South Quay
World Trade Ctr London
Independent House
Great Eastern Ent Ctr
Harbour Island
London Arena
Millwall Inner Dock
Quebec Ind Est
REDRIFF RD
Greenland Pier
Klein's Wharf
Millwall
Crossharbour
Cubitt Town Jun & Inf Sch
Hypermarket
Surrey Commercial Docks
Greenland Dock
South Dock (Marina)
St George's Wharf
Millwall Outer Dock
Cubitt Town
Mudchute
ISLE OF DOGS
PLOUGH WAY
WESTFERRY RD
Pepys Park
Slipway
Louis Wharf
Crown Wharf
New Baltic Wharf
Victoria Wharf
Deptford Park
Masthouse Terr Pier
Burrell's Wharf
Convoys Wharf
Palmer's Wharf
Payne's Wharf
Borthwick Wharf
Locke's Wharf
EVELYN ST
SE8
Deptford Trad Est
Parkside Bsns Est
Folkestone Gardens
Dreadnought Wharf
Dowell's Wharf
Thames Path
Greenwich Reach
Limehouse Reach
97
141
120

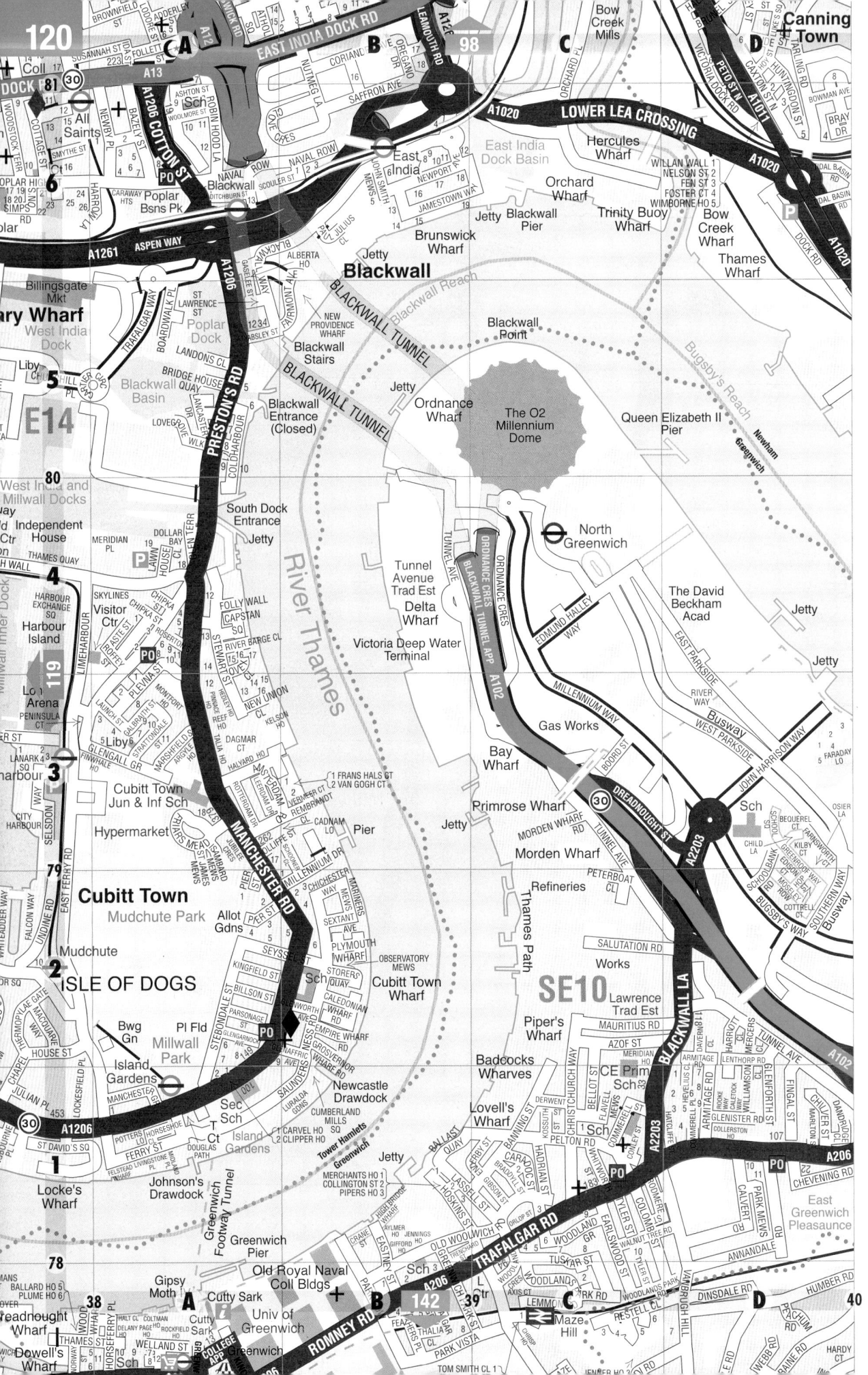

Blackwall
Cubitt Town
ISLE OF DOGS
SE10
E14
River Thames
The O2 Millennium Dome
North Greenwich
Canning Town
East India
Mudchute Park
Millwall Park
Island Gardens
Cutty Sark
Greenwich
Maze Hill
East Greenwich Pleasaunce
BLACKWALL TUNNEL
LOWER LEA CROSSING
EAST INDIA DOCK RD
PRESTON'S RD
MANCHESTER RD
BLACKWALL LA
TRAFALGAR RD
ROMNEY RD
ASPEN WAY
DREADNOUGHT ST
MILLENNIUM WAY

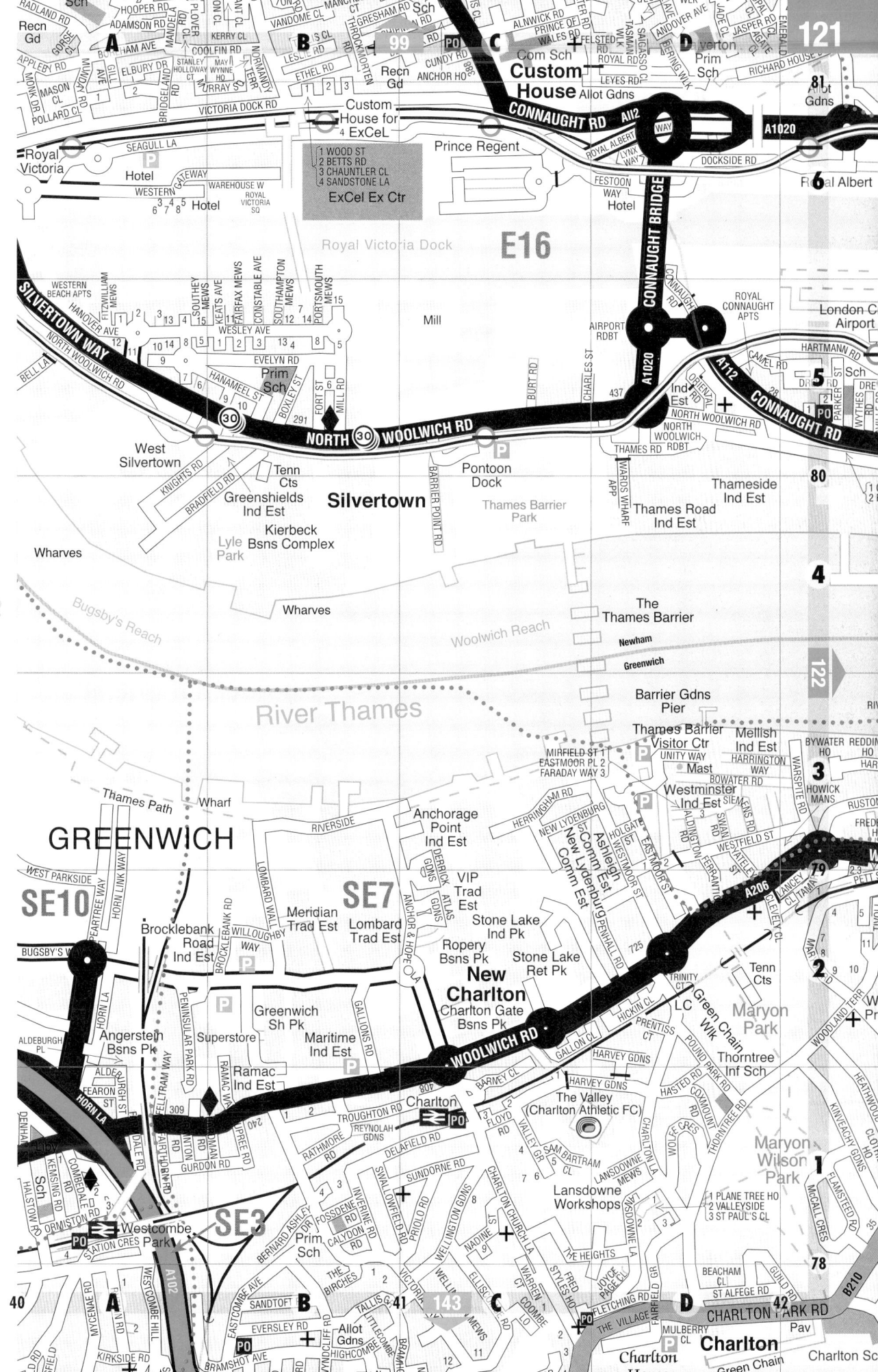
Custom House
Royal Victoria
Prince Regent
ExCel Ex Ctr
Royal Victoria Dock
E16
CONNAUGHT RD
CONNAUGHT BRIDGE
SILVERTOWN WAY
NORTH WOOLWICH RD
West Silvertown
Silvertown
Pontoon Dock
Thames Barrier Park
Thames Road Ind Est
Thameside Ind Est
London City Airport
Royal Albert
Bugsby's Reach
Woolwich Reach
The Thames Barrier
River Thames
Barrier Gdns Pier
Thames Barrier Visitor Ctr
GREENWICH
SE10
SE7
SE3
New Charlton
WOOLWICH RD
Charlton
Westcombe Park
The Valley (Charlton Athletic FC)
Maryon Park
Maryon Wilson Park
CHARLTON PARK RD
Charlton
Charlton House

99
122
143

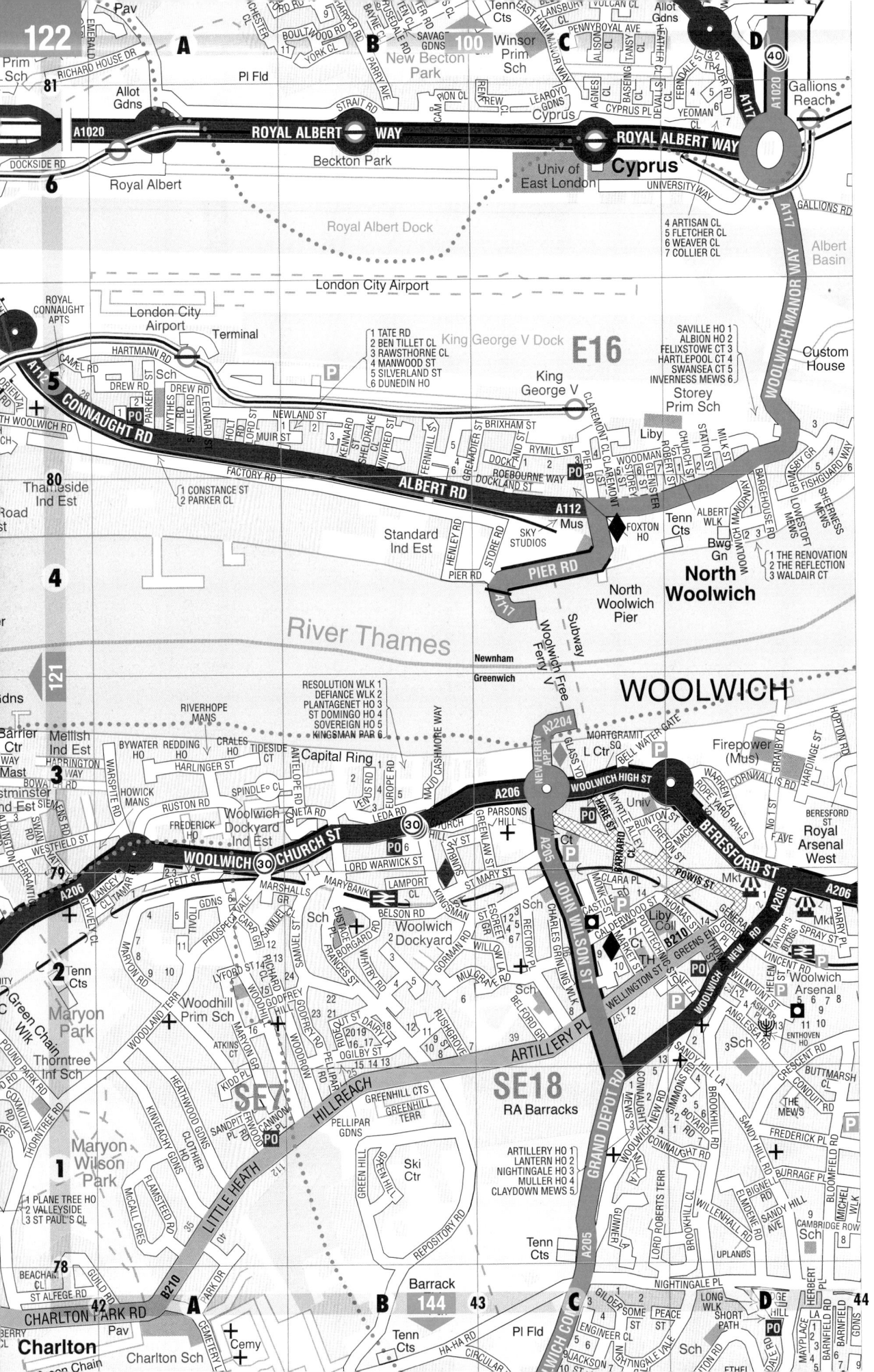
A
B
C
D
100
Pav
EMERALD
Prim Sch
RICHARD HOUSE DR
81
Allot Gdns
Pl Fld
BOULTWOOD RD
YORK CL
HARPER RD
BAYNE CL
SAVAGE GDNS
PARRY AVE
New Becton Park
Tenn Cts
Winsor Prim Sch
EAST HAM MANOR WAY
LANSBURY
VULCAN CL
PENNYROYAL AVE
ALISON CL
TANSY CL
HEATHER CL
Allot Gdns
FERNDALE ST
TRADER RD
YEOMAN CL
40
A1020
A117
Gallions Reach
STRAIT RD
PION CL
REW
LEAROYD GDNS
AGNES CL
BASING CL
DEVALLS CL
CYPRUS PL
Cyprus
A1020
ROYAL ALBERT
WAY
ROYAL ALBERT WAY
DOCKSIDE RD
6
Royal Albert
Beckton Park
Univ of East London
Cyprus
UNIVERSITY WAY
GALLIONS RD
Royal Albert Dock
4 ARTISAN CL
5 FLETCHER CL
6 WEAVER CL
7 COLLIER CL
Albert Basin
A117
WOOLWICH MANOR WAY
London City Airport
ROYAL CONNAUGHT APTS
London City Airport
Terminal
1 TATE RD
2 BEN TILLET CL
3 RAWSTHORNE CL
4 MANWOOD ST
5 SILVERLAND ST
6 DUNEDIN HO
King George V Dock
E16
SAVILLE HO 1
ALBION HO 2
FELIXSTOWE CT 3
HARTLEPOOL CT 4
SWANSEA CT 5
INVERNESS MEWS 6
Custom House
HARTMANN RD
CAMEL RD
A112
5
DREW RD
PARKER ST
Sch
PO
CONNAUGHT RD
WOOLWICH RD
WYTHES RD
SAVILLE RD
LEONARD ST
HOLT RD
LORD ST
NEWLAND ST
MUIR ST
KENNARD ST
SHELDRAKE CL
WINIFRED ST
FERNHILL ST
GRENADIER ST
BRIXHAM ST
King George V
CLAREMONT CL
Storey Prim Sch
Liby
RYMILL ST
DOCKLAND ST
ROEBOURNE WAY
PO
PIER RD
CLAREMONT ST
WOODMAN ST
STOREY ST
GLENISTER ST
ROBERT ST
CHURCH ST
STATION ST
MILK ST
GRIMSBY GR
FISHGUARD WAY
80
Thameside Ind Est
FACTORY RD
1 CONSTANCE ST
2 PARKER CL
ALBERT RD
A112
Mus
FOXTON HO
Tenn Cts
ALBERT WLK
WOOLWICH MANOR WAY
BARGEHOUSE RD
LOWESTOFT MEWS
SHEERNESS MEWS
Road
Standard Ind Est
HENLEY RD
STORE RD
SKY STUDIOS
PIER RD
Bwg Gn
1 THE RENOVATION
2 THE REFLECTION
3 WALDAIR CT
PIER RD
4
North Woolwich
North Woolwich Pier
A117
Subway
Woolwich Free Ferry
River Thames
Newnham
Greenwich
121
WOOLWICH
RESOLUTION WLK 1
DEFIANCE WLK 2
PLANTAGENET HO 3
ST DOMINGO HO 4
SOVEREIGN HO 5
KINGSMAN PAR 6
RIVERHOPE MANS
MAJD CASHMORE WAY
A2204
NEW FERRY APP
GLASS YD
MORTGRAMIT SQ
BELL WATER GATE
L Ctr
Firepower (Mus)
GRANBY RD
HARDINGE ST
HOPTON RD
Barrier Ctr
Mellish Ind Est
BYWATER HO
REDDING HO
CRALES HO
TIDESIDE CT
Capital Ring
HARRINGTON WAY
3
HARLINGER ST
WARSPITE RD
HOWICK MANS
SPINDLE CL
ANTELOPE RD
VENUS RD
EUROPE RD
RUSTON RD
BOWATER RD
SIEMENS RD
Woolwich Dockyard Ind Est
FREDERICK HO
BONETA RD
LEDA RD
A206
WOOLWICH HIGH ST
WARREN LA
ROPE YARD RAILS
CORNWALLIS RD
Univ
PO
HARE ST
MYRTLE ALLEY
BUNTON ST
CRETON ST
MACBEAN ST
BERESFORD ST
No 1 ST
F AVE
BERESFORD ST
Royal Arsenal West
WESTFIELD ST
WOOLWICH CHURCH ST
30
CHURCH HILL
PARSONS HILL
GREENLAW ST
A205
BARNARD CL
Ct
P
A206
79
TAMAR ST
PETT ST
MARSHALLS GR
LORD WARWICK ST
MARYBANK
LAMPORT CL
BELSON RD
KINGSMAN ST
ST MARY ST
JOHN WILSON ST
POWIS ST
CLARA PL
Mkt
A205
A206
CLEVELY CL
TIVOLI GDNS
PROSPECT VALE
CARR GR
SAMUEL CL
SAMUEL ST
Sch
EUSTACE PL
BORGARD RD
Woolwich Dockyard
ESCREET GR
RECTORY PL
Sch
CHARLES GRINLING WLK
MONK ST
CASTILE RD
CALDERWOOD ST
THOMAS ST
Liby
Coll
B210
Ct
TH
POLYTECHNIC ST
GREENS END
GENERAL GORDON PL
NEW RD
TAYLOR'S BLDGS
SPRAY ST
PARRY PL
Mkt
MARYON RD
FRANCES ST
WHITBY RD
GORMAN RD
WILLOW LA
MULGRAVE RD
MARKET ST
WELLINGTON ST
PO
LOVE LA
WOOLWICH NEW RD
VINCENT RD
HELEN ST
WILMOUNT ST
Woolwich Arsenal
2
Tenn Cts
LYFORD ST
RICHARD CL
GODFREY HILL
Woodhill Prim Sch
MARYON GR
WOODROW
GODFREY RD
RIDEOUT ST
DAIRY LA
OGILBY ST
PELLIPAR RD
RUSHGROVE ST
Sch
BELFORD GR
ARTILLERY PL
ASHLAR PL
ANGLESEA RD
ENTHOVEN HO
Green Chain Wlk
Maryon Park
WOODLAND TERR
ATKINS CT
KIDD PL
Thorntree Inf Sch
POUND PARK RD
COXMOUNT RD
THORNTREE RD
HEATHWOOD GDNS
CLOTHIER HO
SE7
SANDPIT PL
ERWOOD RD
CANNON PL
HILLREACH
GREENHILL CTS
GREENHILL TERR
PELLIPAR GDNS
SE18
RA Barracks
GRAND DEPOT RD
CONNAUGHT MEWS
Sch
SANDY HILL LA
SIMMONS RD
BROOKHILL RD
BOYARD RD
CRESCENT RD
BUTTMARSH CL
CONDUIT RD
THE MEWS
FREDERICK PL
Maryon Wilson Park
1
KINVEACHY GDNS
FLAMSTEED RD
McCALL CRES
LITTLE HEATH
PO
GREEN HILL
Ski Ctr
ARTILLERY HO 1
LANTERN HO 2
NIGHTINGALE HO 3
MULLER HO 4
CLAYDOWN MEWS 5
CONNAUGHT RD
SANDY HILL RD
BURRAGE PL
BIGNELL RD
ELMDENE RD
SANDY HILL AVE
BLOOMFIELD RD
MICHEL WLK
1 PLANE TREE HO
2 VALLEYSIDE
3 ST PAUL'S CL
REPOSITORY RD
GUNNER LA
LORD ROBERTS TERR
BROOKHILL CL
WILLENHALL RD
CAMBRIDGE ROW
Sch
Tenn Cts
A205
UPLANDS
78
BEACHAM CL
ST ALFEGE RD
GUILD RD
PARK DR
B210
42
CHARLTON PARK RD
A
Pav
Barrack
B
144
43
C
NIGHTINGALE PL
GILDERSOME ST
PEACE ST
ENGINEER CL
NIGHTINGALE VALE
LONG WLK
SHORT PATH
D
HERBERT PL
MAYPLACE LA
BARNFIELD RD
BARNFIELD GDNS
44
Charlton
Charlton Sch
Cemy
CEMETERY LA
Tenn Cts
HA-HA RD
CIRCULAR
Pl Fld
JACKSON
Sch
PO

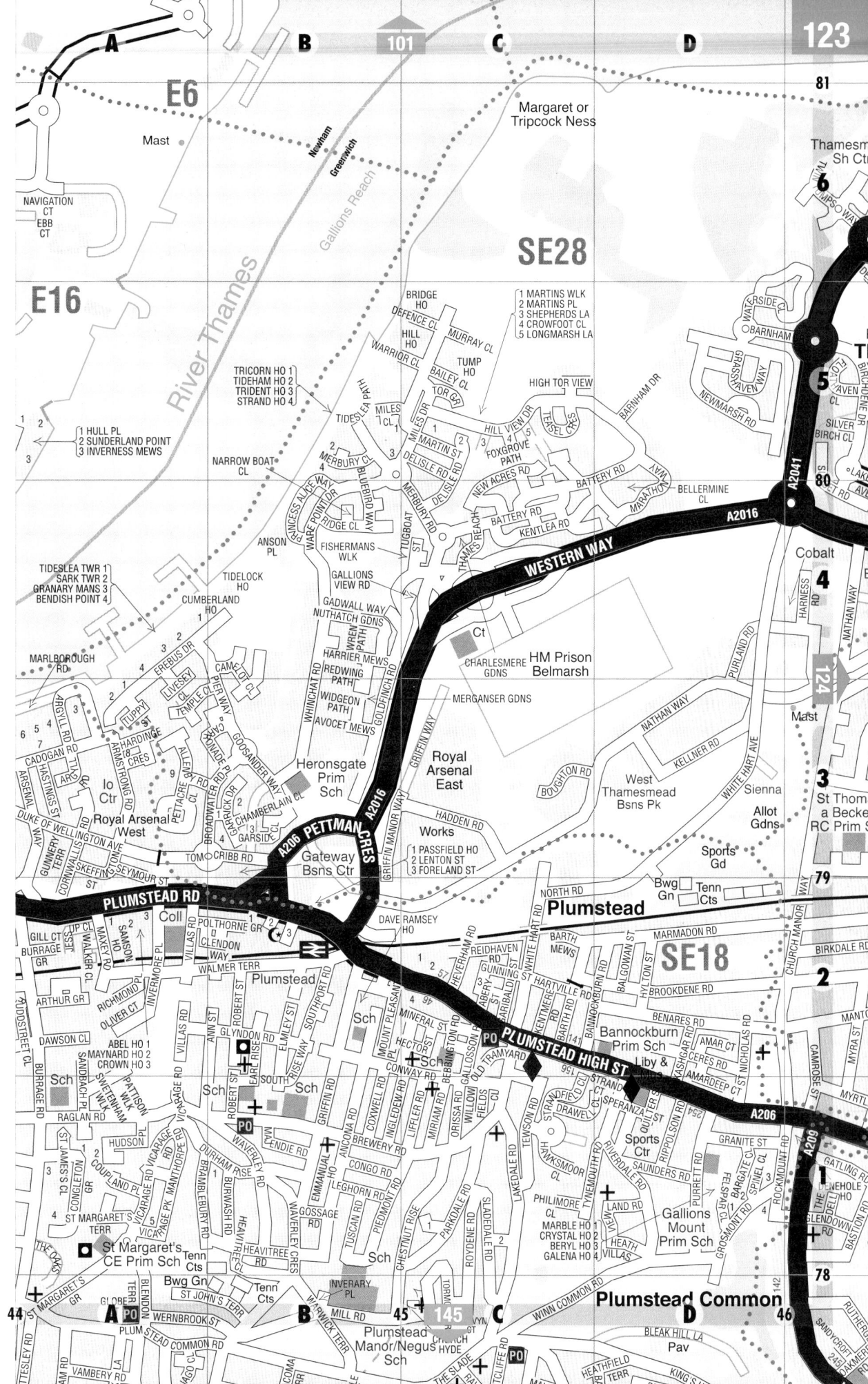

123
A
B
101
C
D
81
E6
Mast
Newham
Greenwich
Margaret or Tripcock Ness
Thamesmead Sh Ctr
6
NAVIGATION CT
EBB CT
Gallions Reach
SE28
E16
River Thames
BRIDGE HO
DEFENCE CL
HILL HO
MURRAY CL
WARRIOR CL
TUMP HO
BAILEY CL
TOR GR
1 MARTINS WLK
2 MARTINS PL
3 SHEPHERDS LA
4 CROWFOOT CL
5 LONGMARSH LA
HIGH TOR VIEW
BARNHAM DR
WATERSIDE CL
BARNHAM
GRASSHAVEN WAY
NEWMARSH RD
5
TRICORN HO 1
TIDEHAM HO 2
TRIDENT HO 3
STRAND HO 4
TIDESLEA PATH
MILES CL
MILES DR
MARTIN ST
DELISLE RD
HILL VIEW DR
TEASEL CRES
FOXGROVE PATH
1 HULL PL
2 SUNDERLAND POINT
3 INVERNESS MEWS
NARROW BOAT CL
MERBURY CL
BLUEBIRD WAY
NEW ACRES RD
BATTERY RD
MARATHON WAY
BELLERMINE CL
A2041
80
SILVER BIRCH CL
PRINCESS ALICE WAY
WARE POINT DR
RIDGE CL
MERBURY RD
TUGBOAT ST
THAMES REACH
BATTERY RD
KENTLEA RD
A2016
ANSON PL
FISHERMANS WLK
WESTERN WAY
Cobalt
4
HARNESS RD
NATHAN WAY
TIDESLEA TWR 1
SARK TWR 2
GRANARY MANS 3
BENDISH POINT 4
TIDELOCK HO
GALLIONS VIEW RD
CUMBERLAND HO
GADWALL WAY
NUTHATCH GDNS
WREN PATH
Ct
HM Prison Belmarsh
CHARLESMERE GDNS
PURLAND RD
124
MARLBOROUGH RD
EREBUS DR
LIVESEY CL
TEMPLE CL
PIER WAY
CAMELOT CL
HARRIER MEWS
REDWING PATH
WIDGEON PATH
AVOCET MEWS
WHINCHAT RD
GOLDFINCH RD
MERGANSER GDNS
NATHAN WAY
Mast
ARGYLL RD
TUPPY ST
HARDINGE CRES
CADOGAN RD
HASTINGS ST
ARSENAL WAY
ARMSTRONG RD
CARRONADE PL
GOOSANDER WAY
Heronsgate Prim Sch
GRIFFIN WAY
Royal Arsenal East
KELLNER RD
WHITE HART AVE
3
Io Ctr
ALLENBY RD
PETTACRE CL
BROADWATER RD
GARRICK DR
CHAMBERLAIN CL
GARSIDE CL
Royal Arsenal West
DUKE OF WELLINGTON AVE
BOUGHTON RD
West Thamesmead Bsns Pk
Sienna
Allot Gdns
St Thomas a Becket RC Prim Sch
A206
PETTMAN CRES
HADDEN RD
Works
GRIFFIN MANOR WAY
1 PASSFIELD HO
2 LENTON ST
3 FORELAND ST
GUNNERY TERR
CORNWALLIS RD
SKEFFINGTON ST
SEYMOUR ST
TOM CRIBB RD
Gateway Bsns Ctr
Sports Gd
79
PLUMSTEAD RD
Coll
POLTHORNE GR
DAVE RAMSEY HO
NORTH RD
Bwg Gn
Tenn Cts
Plumstead
CHURCH MANOR WAY
GILL CT
JESSUP CL
WALKER CL
MAXEY RD
SAMSON HO
INVERMORE PL
VILLAS RD
CLENDON WAY
BURRAGE GR
WALMER TERR
Plumstead
SOUTHPORT RD
HEVERHAM RD
REIDHAVEN RD
GUNNING ST
WHITE HART RD
BARTH MEWS
MARMADON RD
SE18
BIRKDALE RD
2
ARTHUR GR
RICHMOND PL
OLIVER CT
ROBERT ST
ELMLEY ST
RISE WAY
MOUNT PLEASANT PL
MINERAL ST
HARTVILLE RD
BANNOCKBURN RD
BALGOWAN ST
HYLTON ST
BROOKDENE RD
DAWSON CL
ABEL HO 1
MAYNARD HO 2
CROWN HO 3
SANDBACH PL
VILLAS RD
ANN ST
GLYNDON RD
EARL RISE
Sch
HECTOR ST
Sch
BEBBINGTON RD
PO
PLUMSTEAD HIGH ST
KENTMERE RD
BARTH RD
Bannockburn Prim Sch
BENARES RD
AMAR CT
CERES RD
AMARDEEP CT
ST NICHOLAS RD
MANTON RD
MYRA ST
BURRAGE RD
Sch
SWETENHAM WLK
PATTISON WLK
VICARAGE RD
Sch
SOUTH RISE
Sch
CONWAY RD
GALLOSSON RD
OLD TRAMYARD
Liby & Mus
KASHGAR RD
CAMROSE ST
MYRTLE
RAGLAN RD
ROBERT ST
PO
GRIFFIN RD
COXWELL RD
INGLEDEW RD
LIFFLER RD
MIRIAM RD
ORISSA RD
WILLOW FIELDS CL
STRANDFIELD CL
DRAWELL CL
SPERANZA ST
QUILTER ST
RIPPOLSON RD
A206
ST JAMES'S CL
CONGLETON GR
COUPLAND PL
HUDSON PL
VICARAGE RD
MANTHORPE RD
DURHAM RISE
WAVERLEY RD
MAJENDIE RD
BREWERY RD
EMMANUEL HO
ANCONA RD
CONGO RD
TEWSON RD
LAKEDALE RD
HAWKSMOOR CL
TYNEMOUTH RD
RIVERDALE RD
Sports Ctr
SAUNDERS RD
GRANITE ST
PURRETT RD
BARGATE CL
SPINEL CL
ROCKMOUNT RD
A209
GATLING RD
1
DENEHOLE HO
THE DELL
GLENDOWN RD
BASTION RD
BRAMBLEBURY RD
BURWASH RD
LEGHORN RD
PIEDMONT RD
PARKDALE RD
SLADEDALE RD
PHILIMORE CL
LAND RD
FELSPAR CL
GROSMONT RD
ST MARGARET'S TERR
VICARAGE PK
HEAVITREE RD
WAVERLEY CRES
GOSSAGE RD
TUSCAN RD
CHESTNUT RISE
ROYDENE RD
MARBLE HO 1
CRYSTAL HO 2
BERYL HO 3
GALENA HO 4
HEATH VILLAS
Gallions Mount Prim Sch
St Margaret's CE Prim Sch
Tenn Cts
THE OAKS
HEAVITREE CL
Sch
Bwg Gn
ST JOHN'S TERR
Tenn Cts
INVERARY PL
WINN COMMON RD
Plumstead Common
78
ST MARGARET'S GR
GLOBE TERR
44
A
PO
BLENDON TERR
WERNBROOK ST
B
MILL RD
45
145
C
D
46
PLUMSTEAD COMMON RD
WARWICK TERR
Plumstead Manor/Negus Sch
CHURCH HYDE
BLEAK HILL LA
Pav
SANDYCROFT
VAMBERY RD
THE SLADE
PO
HEATHFIELD TERR
KING'S
RUTHERGLEN RD
OAKMERE RD

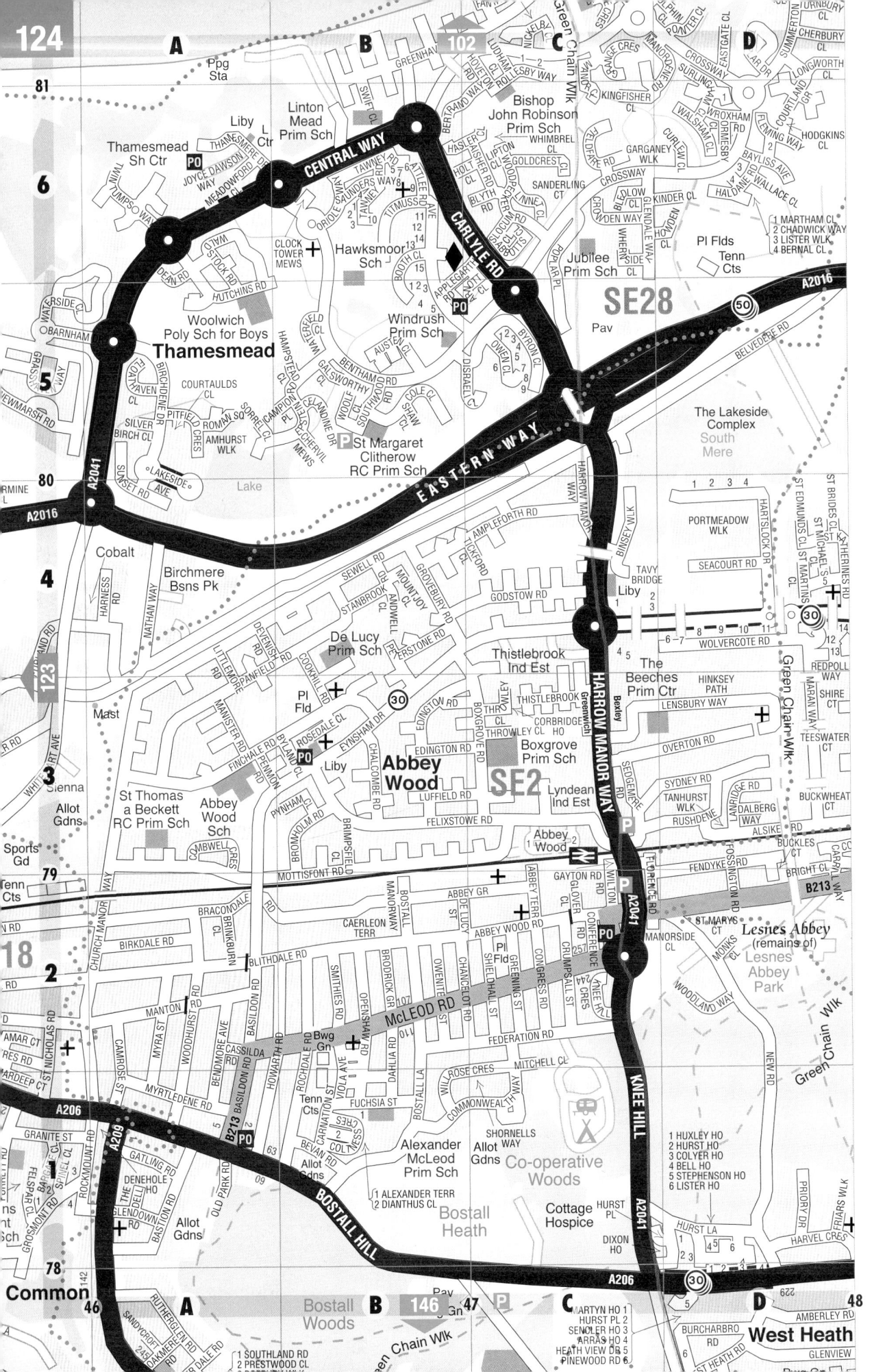

A
B
C
D
102
146
123
Thamesmead
Abbey Wood
SE28
SE2
West Heath
Common
Central Way
Carlyle Rd
Eastern Way
Harrow Manor Way
Knee Hill
Bostall Hill
McLeod Rd
Belvedere Rd
A2016
A2041
A206
A209
B213
Thamesmead Sh Ctr
Linton Mead Prim Sch
Bishop John Robinson Prim Sch
Hawksmoor Sch
Windrush Prim Sch
Woolwich Poly Sch for Boys
St Margaret Clitherow RC Prim Sch
Jubilee Prim Sch
The Lakeside Complex
South Mere
Birchmere Bsns Pk
De Lucy Prim Sch
Thistlebrook Ind Est
The Beeches Prim Ctr
Boxgrove Prim Sch
Lyndean Ind Est
St Thomas a Beckett RC Prim Sch
Abbey Wood Sch
Lesnes Abbey (remains of)
Lesnes Abbey Park
Alexander McLeod Prim Sch
Co-operative Woods
Bostall Heath
Bostall Woods
Cottage Hospice
Green Chain Wlk
1 MARTHAM CL
2 CHADWICK WAY
3 LISTER WLK
4 BERNAL CL
1 HUXLEY HO
2 HURST HO
3 COLYER HO
4 BELL HO
5 STEPHENSON HO
6 LISTER HO
1 ALEXANDER TERR
2 DIANTHUS CL
MARTYN HO 1
HURST PL 2
SENCLER HO 3
ARRAS HO 4
HEATH VIEW DR 5
PINEWOOD RD 6
1 SOUTHLAND RD
2 PRESTWOOD CL

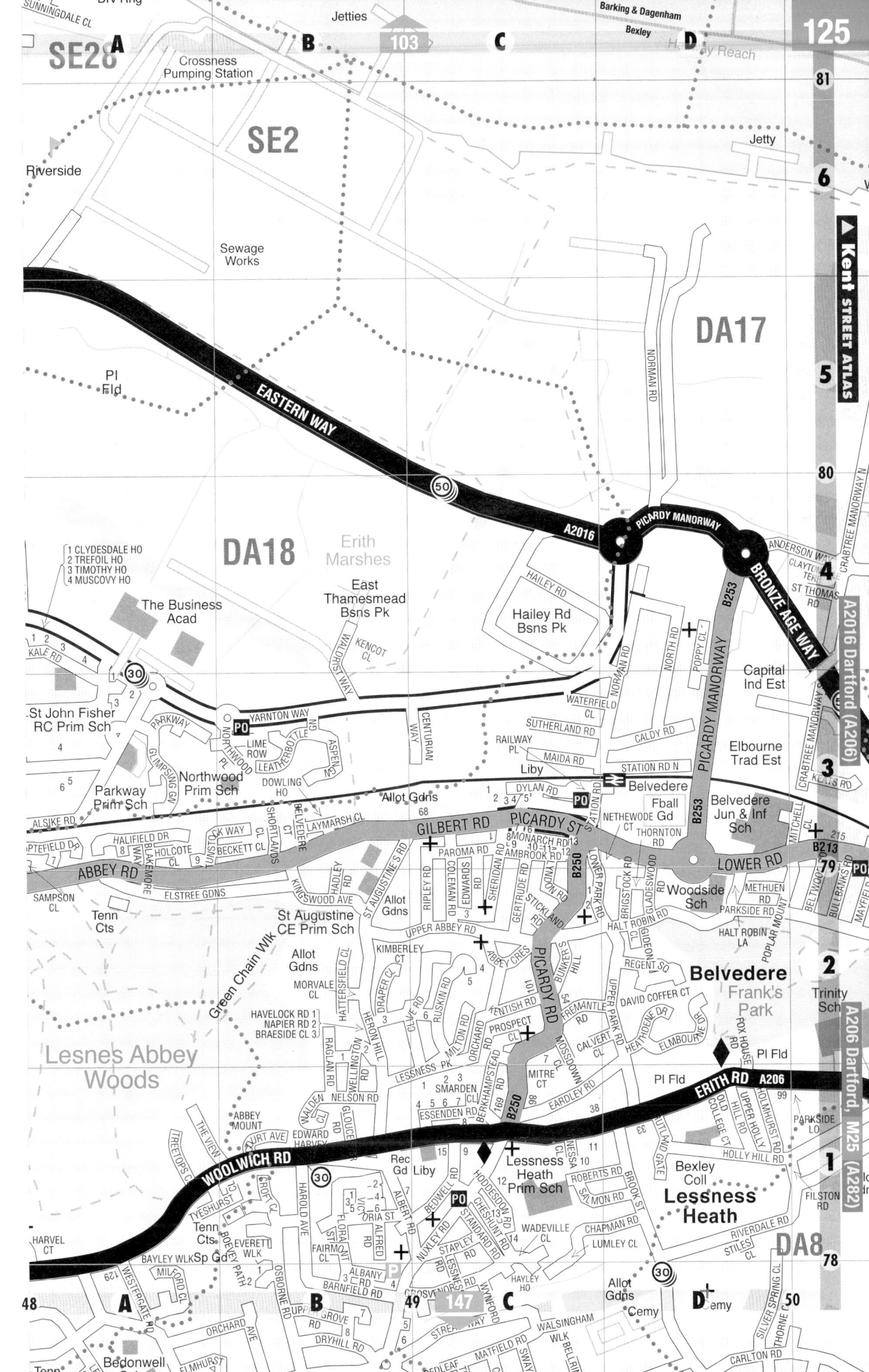
SE28
SE2
DA17
DA18
DA8
Riverside
Crossness Pumping Station
Sewage Works
Jetties
Jetty
Barking & Dagenham
Bexley
Erith Marshes
East Thamesmead Bsns Pk
Hailey Rd Bsns Pk
The Business Acad
Capital Ind Est
Elbourne Trad Est
EASTERN WAY
A2016
PICARDY MANORWAY
BRONZE AGE WAY
St John Fisher RC Prim Sch
Northwood Prim Sch
Parkway Prim Sch
YARNTON WAY
ABBEY RD
GILBERT RD
PICARDY ST
LOWER RD
Belvedere
Belvedere Jun & Inf Sch
Woodside Sch
St Augustine CE Prim Sch
Green Chain Wlk
Lesnes Abbey Woods
Frank's Park
PICARDY RD
ERITH RD
A206
WOOLWICH RD
Lessness Heath Prim Sch
Bexley Coll
Lessness Heath
Trinity Sch
Allot Gdns
Cemy
Bedonwell
1 CLYDESDALE HO
2 TREFOIL HO
3 TIMOTHY HO
4 MUSCOVY HO
HAVELOCK RD 1
NAPIER RD 2
BRAESIDE CL 3
Kent STREET ATLAS
A2016 Dartford (A206)
A206 Dartford, M25 (A282)

103
147

104

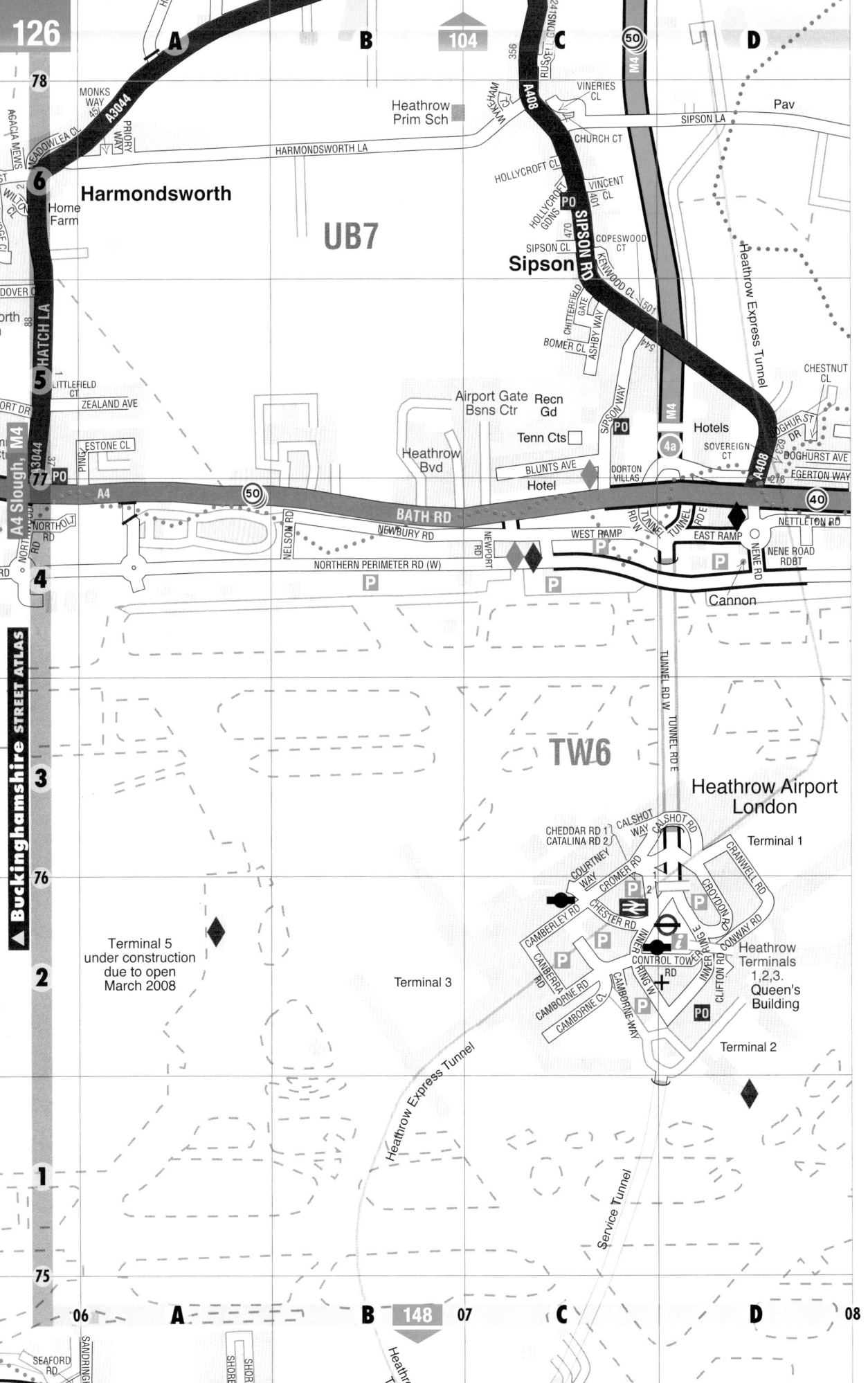
Harmondsworth
Home Farm
UB7
Heathrow Prim Sch
HARMONDSWORTH LA
MONKS WAY
PRIORY WAY
MEADOWLEA CL
ACACIA MEWS
A3044
HATCH LA
LITTLEFIELD CT
ZEALAND AVE
ESTONE CL
A4 Slough, M4
NORTHOLT RD
Sipson
SIPSON RD
A408
VINERIES CL
CHURCH CT
SIPSON LA
HOLLYCROFT CL
HOLLYCROFT GDNS
VINCENT CL
SIPSON CL
COPESWOOD CT
KENWOOD CL
CHITTERFIELD GATE
ASHBY WAY
BOMER CL
SIPSON WAY
Pav
Heathrow Express Tunnel
CHESTNUT CL
DOGHURST DR
DOGHURST AVE
SOVEREIGN CT
EGERTON WAY
Hotels
Airport Gate Bsns Ctr
Recn Gd
Tenn Cts
Heathrow Bvd
BLUNTS AVE
Hotel
DORTON VILLAS
BATH RD
A4
M4
NEWBURY RD
NELSON RD
NEWPORT RD
NORTHERN PERIMETER RD (W)
WEST RAMP
EAST RAMP
TUNNEL RD W
TUNNEL RD E
NETTLETON RD
NENE RD
NENE ROAD RDBT
Cannon
TW6
Heathrow Airport London
Terminal 1
CHEDDAR RD 1
CATALINA RD 2
CALSHOT WAY
CALSHOT RD
COURTNEY WAY
CROMER RD
CRANWELL RD
CROYDON RD
CHESTER RD
CAMBERLEY RD
CANBERRA RD
INNER RING W
INNER RING E
CONTROL TOWER RD
CONWAY RD
CLIFTON RD
CAMBORNE RD
CAMBORNE CL
CAMBORNE WAY
Heathrow Terminals 1,2,3. Queen's Building
Terminal 2
Terminal 3
Terminal 5 under construction due to open March 2008
Service Tunnel
SEAFORD RD
Buckinghamshire STREET ATLAS

148

Nine Elms Farm
Sports Gd
Pav
William Byrd Sch
Harlington
Hotel
Gravel Pits
Cranford Park
UB3
SIPSON LA
VICTORIA LA
BLETCHMORE CL
BRICKFIELD LA
HUDSON RD
HIGH ST
RICHARDS CL
FORGE CL
GOTHIC CT
FELLOWES CT
SHORTLANDS
ELBRIDGE CT
MANOR LA
PONDSIDE
MANSE CL
PROVIDENCE CT
PROVIDENCE LA
OAKLEY CT
THE CRESCENT
GILPIN WAY
CRANFORD LA
WEST END LA
HIGH STREET HARLINGTON
The White House
Poultry Farm
FIELD CL
RAYWOOD CL
TASKER CL
CROFT CL
HARLINGTON CL
GRAMPIAN CL
QUANTOCK CL
WARNER CL
LITTLE ELMS
ACORN GR
SAUNTON AVE
Sp Gd
GRAVES RD
BROWNING
PENNINE CL
PENNINE WAY
MARLBOROUGH CRES
DAVID CL
CAROLINE PL
VANTAGE CT
PENDELL AVE
STRATHEARN AVE
LANGLEY CRES
NEW RD
BRENDON CL
CHEVIOT CL
HALL LA
ETON RD
WINCHESTER RD
OXFORD AVE
BOLTON'S LA
MENDIP CL
HEATH CL
NOBEL DR
WINDSOR PARK RD
MONDIAL WAY
Hotel
Hotels
MALVERN RD
CRANESWATER
PARK LA
TRIUMPH CL
Harlington Cnr
Hotels
Hotel
The White Hart (PH)
BATH RD
A4
A437
40
Visitor Ctr
World Bsns Ctr
Hotel
NEWALL RD
HATTON RD N
NORTHROP RD
DUDSET
NEPTUNE RD
NORTHERN PERIMETER RD
P
CRANFORD LA
Hounslow
Hillingdon
London Loop
128
ENFIELD ROAD RDBT
ENFIELD RD
EPSOM SQ
EASTERN PERIMETER RD
TW6
ELY RD
ESHER CRES
ELGIN CRES
Eastern Bsns Pk
EASTCHURCH ROAD RDBT
EXETER WAY
VANGUARD WAY
EXETER RD
EASTCHURCH RD
TW6
EASTERN PERIMETER
ELECTRA AVE
EAGLE RD
ELMDON RD
CRANFORD LA
Hotel
HATTON CROSS RDBT
VISCOUNT WAY
EASTERN PERIMETER RD
A30
Hatton Cross
LITHGOW'S RD
DICK TURPIN WAY
STEAM FARM LA
GREAT SOUTH-WEST RD
SOUTHERN PERIMETER
DOCKWELL CL
GREEN MAN
HATTON RD
Radius Pk
ST THERESA RD
FAGG'S RD
Hatton
ST ANTHONY'S WAY
HATTON G
MYRTLE AVE
WELLINGTON RD
SOUTHERN PERIMETER RD
Tenn Cts
Fball Gd
Cemy
Playground
TW6
105
149
78
77
76
75
6
5
4
3
2
1
A
B
C
D
08
09
10

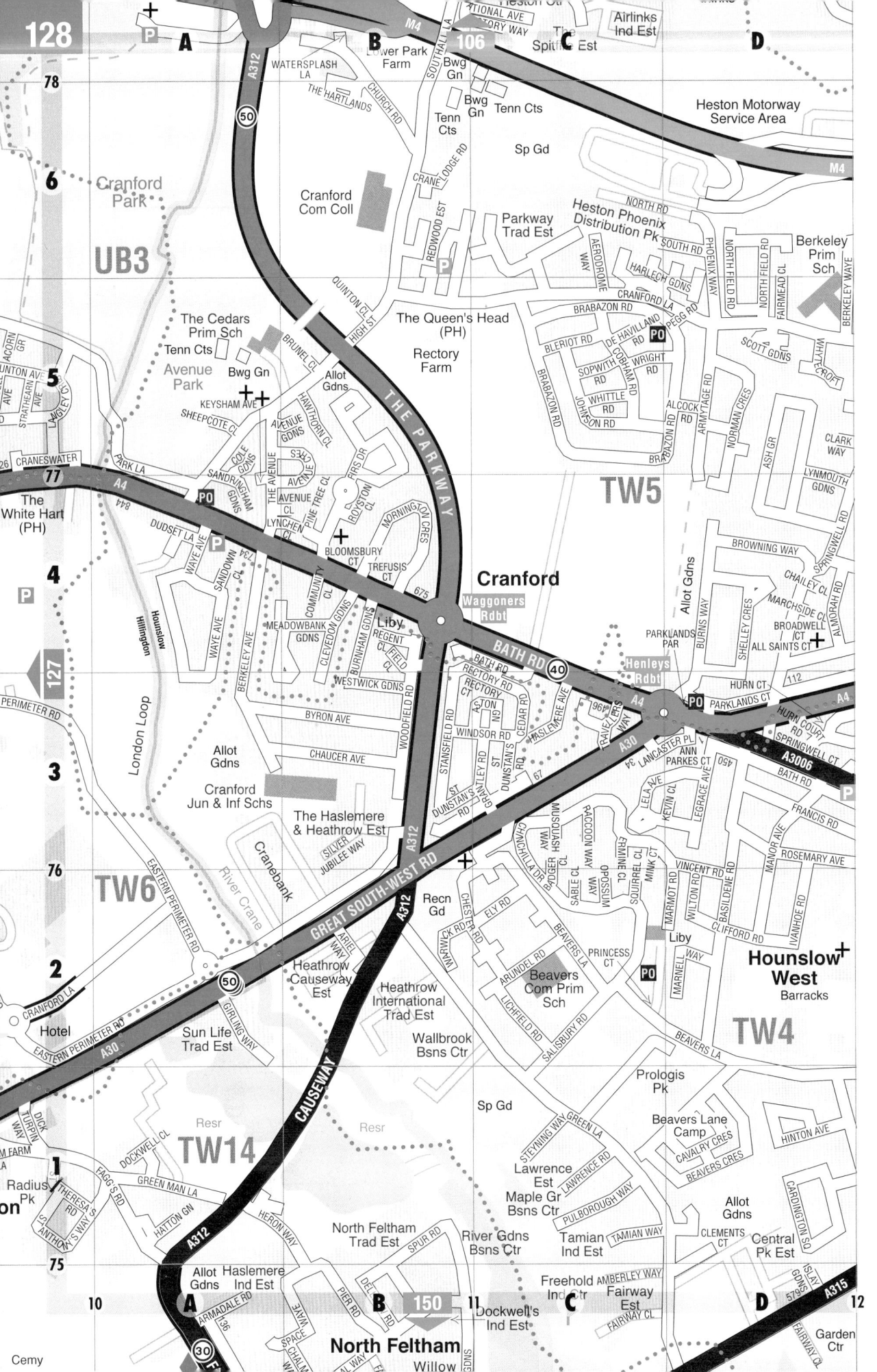

106
Cranford Park
UB3
Cranford Com Coll
Heston Motorway Service Area
Heston Phoenix Distribution Pk
Parkway Trad Est
Berkeley Prim Sch
The Cedars Prim Sch
Avenue Park
The Queen's Head (PH)
Rectory Farm
The White Hart (PH)
TW5
Cranford
Waggoners Rdbt
Henleys Rdbt
BATH RD
THE PARKWAY
127
Allot Gdns
Cranford Jun & Inf Schs
The Haslemere & Heathrow Est
London Loop
Cranebank
River Crane
TW6
GREAT SOUTH-WEST RD
Heathrow Causeway Est
Heathrow International Trad Est
Beavers Com Prim Sch
Hounslow West
Barracks
TW4
Sun Life Trad Est
Wallbrook Bsns Ctr
Prologis Pk
Beavers Lane Camp
TW14
Lawrence Est
Maple Gr Bsns Ctr
Tamian Ind Est
North Feltham Trad Est
River Gdns Bsns Ctr
Central Pk Est
Allot Gdns
Haslemere Ind Est
Freehold Ind Ctr
Fairway Est
150
Dockwell's Ind Est
North Feltham
Garden Ctr
Radius Pk
Hotel
Cemy

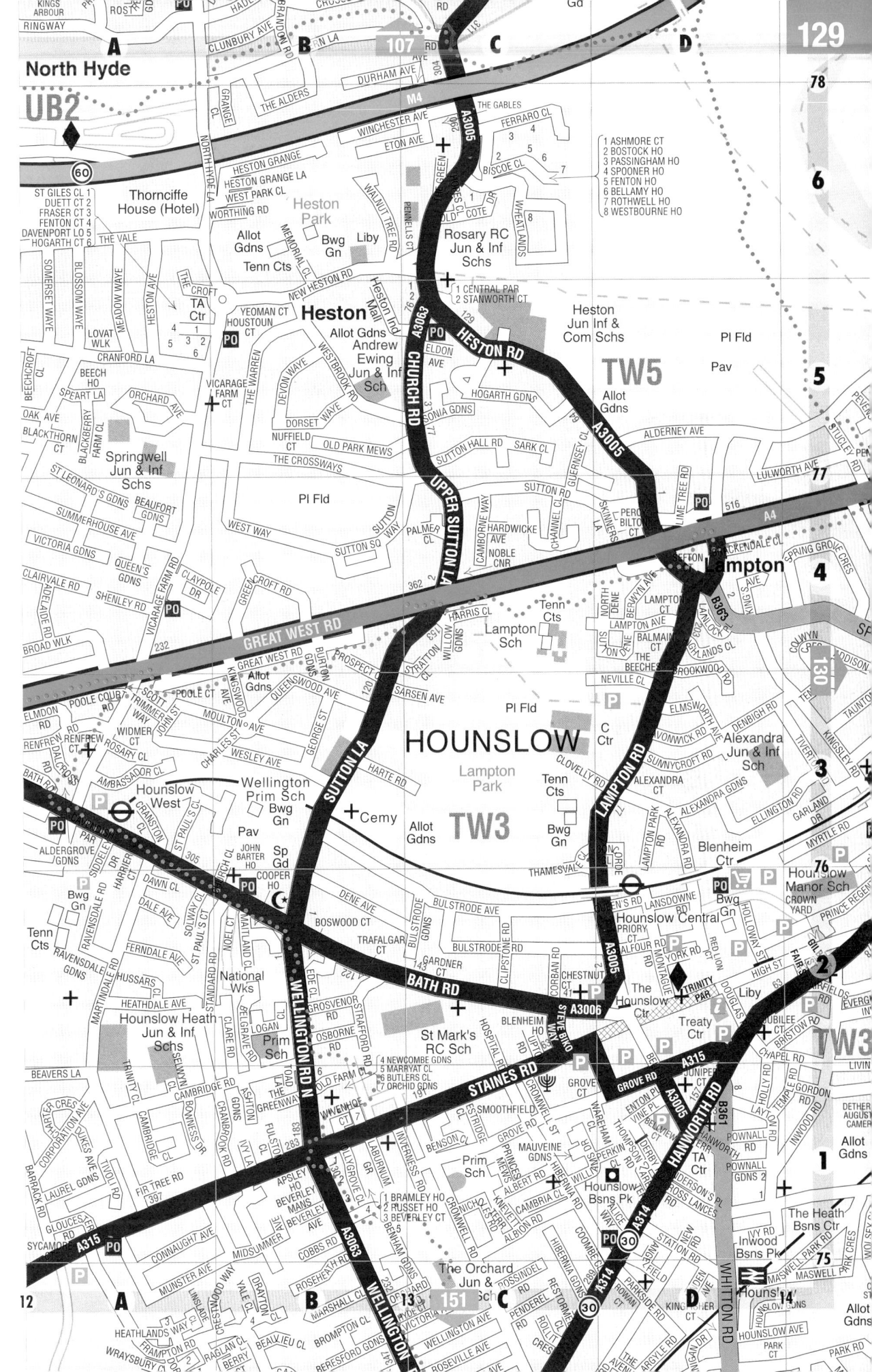
North Hyde
UB2
M4
Thorncliffe House (Hotel)
Heston Park
Allot Gdns
Tenn Cts
Bwg Gn
Liby
Rosary RC Jun & Inf Schs
Heston
Allot Gdns
Andrew Ewing Jun & Inf Sch
Heston Jun Inf & Com Schs
Pl Fld
Pav
TW5
Allot Gdns
Springwell Jun & Inf Schs
Pl Fld
GREAT WEST RD
Lampton
Tenn Cts
Lampton Sch
HOUNSLOW
Pl Fld
C Ctr
Lampton Park
Tenn Cts
TW3
Allot Gdns
Bwg Gn
Cemy
Alexandra Jun & Inf Sch
Hounslow West
Wellington Prim Sch
Bwg Gn
Pav
Sp Gd
Blenheim Ctr
Hounslow Manor Sch
Hounslow Central
Tenn Cts
Bwg Gn
National Wks
Hounslow Heath Jun & Inf Schs
Prim Sch
St Mark's RC Sch
The Hounslow Ctr
Treaty Ctr
Liby
Prim Sch
Hounslow Bsns Pk
TA Ctr
The Heath Bsns Ctr
Inwood Bsns Pk
Allot Gdns
The Orchard Jun & Inf Sch
Hounslow
Allot Gdns
BATH RD
STAINES RD
WELLINGTON RD N
HANWORTH RD
LAMPTON RD
CHURCH RD
UPPER SUTTON LA
SUTTON LA
HESTON RD
WHITTON RD
A3005
A3063
A3006
A315
A314
A4
B363
B361
1 ASHMORE CT
2 BOSTOCK HO
3 PASSINGHAM HO
4 SPOONER HO
5 FENTON HO
6 BELLAMY HO
7 ROTHWELL HO
8 WESTBOURNE HO
ST GILES CL 1
DUETT CT 2
FRASER CT 3
FENTON CT 4
DAVENPORT LO 5
HOGARTH CT 6
1 CENTRAL PAR
2 STANWORTH CT
4 NEWCOMBE GDNS
5 MARRYAT CL
6 BUTLERS CL
7 ORCHID GDNS
1 BRAMLEY HO
2 RUSSET HO
3 BEVERLEY CT
A
B
C
D
107
130
151
6
5
4
3
2
1
78
77
76
75
12
13
14

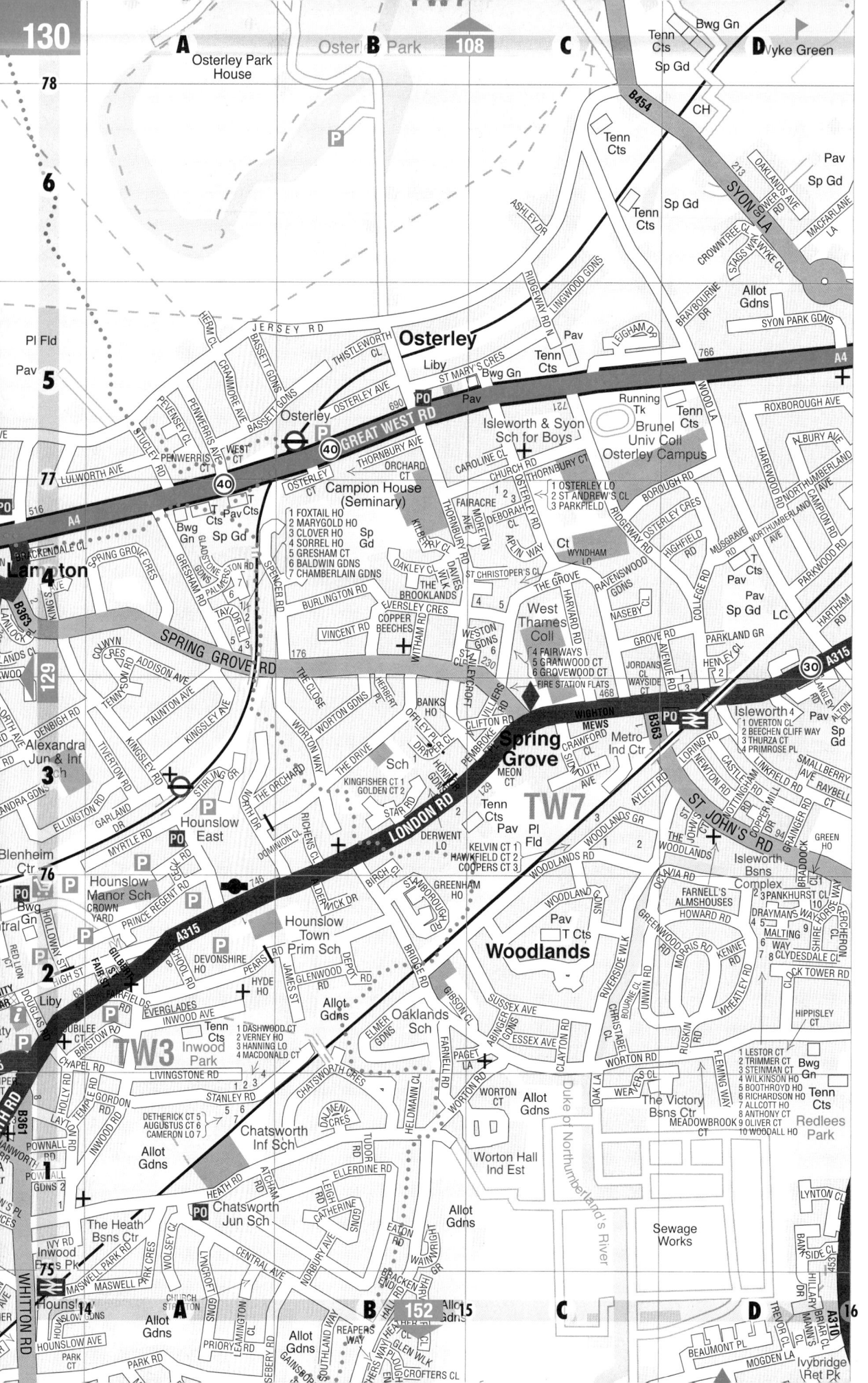

A
B
C
D
108
Osterley Park
Osterley Park House
Wyke Green
Bwg Gn
Tenn Cts
Sp Gd
CH
B454
SYON LA
OAKLANDS AVE
GOWER RD
MACFARLANE LA
CROWNTREE CL
STAGS WAY
WYKE CL
Allot Gdns
SYON PARK GDNS
BRAYBOURNE DR
ASHLEY DR
RIDGEWAY RD N
LINGWOOD GDNS
LEIGHAM DR
Pav
78
6
5
77
76
75
4
3
2
1
Pl Fld
JERSEY RD
HERM CL
BASSETT GDNS
THISTLEWORTH CL
Osterley
ST MARY'S CRES
Liby
766
A4
CRANMORE AVE
PEVENSEY CL
PENWERRIS AVE
STUCLEY RD
LULWORTH AVE
PENWERRIS CT
WEST CT
OSTERLEY AVE
690
PO
GREAT WEST RD
40
721
Running Tk
Brunel Univ Coll Osterley Campus
Isleworth & Syon Sch for Boys
ROXBOROUGH AVE
ALBURY AVE
NORTHUMBERLAND AVE
HAREWOOD RD
CAMPION RD
THORNBURY AVE
ORCHARD CT
OSTERLEY CT
Campion House (Seminary)
CAROLINE CL
CHURCH RD
THORNBURY CT
1 OSTERLEY LO
2 ST ANDREW'S CL
3 PARKFIELD
BOROUGH RD
OSTERLEY CRES
516
BRACKENDALE CL
Bwg Gn
Sp Gd
1 FOXTAIL HO
2 MARYGOLD HO
3 CLOVER HO
4 SORREL HO
5 GRESHAM CT
6 BALDWIN GDNS
7 CHAMBERLAIN GDNS
FAIRACRE
DEBORAH CL
THORNBURY RD
MORETON AVE
OSTERLEY RD
APLIN WAY
KILBERRY CL
Ct
WYNDHAM LO
RIDGEWAY RD
HIGHFIELD RD
MUSGRAVE RD
COLLEGE RD
PARKWOOD RD
Lampton
SPRING GROVE CRES
GRESHAM RD
GLADSTONE GDNS
PALMERSTON RD
SPENCER RD
OAKLEY CL
DAVIES WLK
THE BROOKLANDS
ST CHRISTOPHER'S CL
THE GROVE
RAVENSWOOD GDNS
NASEBY CL
LC
HARTHAM RD
B363
TAYLOR CL
BURLINGTON RD
EVERSLEY CRES
COPPER BEECHES
VINCENT RD
WITHAM RD
WESTON GDNS
West Thames Coll
HARVARD RD
GROVE RD
PARKLAND GR
HENLEY CL
129
SPRING GROVE RD
176
COLWYN CRES
ADDISON AVE
TENNYSON RD
TAUNTON AVE
KINGSLEY AVE
KINGSLEY RD
THE CLOSE
WORTON GDNS
HERBERT PL
STANLEYCROFT
230
4 FAIRWAYS
5 GRANWOOD CT
6 GROVEWOOD CT
FIRE STATION FLATS
468
JORDANS CL
WAYSIDE CT
AVENUE RD
30
A315
DENBIGH RD
Alexandra Jun & Inf Sch
TIVERTON RD
WORTON WAY
BANKS HO
OFFLEY PL
CLIFTON RD
VILLIERS RD
WIGHTON MEWS
Spring Grove
CRAWFORD CL
Metro Ind Ctr
Isleworth
1 OVERTON CL
2 BEECHEN CLIFF WAY
3 THURZA CT
4 PRIMROSE PL
Sp Gd
SMALLBERRY AVE
RAYBELL CT
ELLINGTON RD
GARLAND DR
STIRLING GR
Hounslow East
NORTH DR
THE ORCHARD
THE DRIVE
Sch
KINGFISHER CT 1
GOLDEN CT 2
DRAPER CL
HONNOR GDNS
PEMBROKE RD
MEON CT
SIDMOUTH AVE
TW7
AYLETT RD
LORING RD
NEWTON RD
CASTLE RD
NOTTINGHAM RD
LINKFIELD RD
COPPER MILL DR
GRAINGER RD
ST JOHN'S RD
Blenheim Ctr
MYRTLE RD
CECIL RD
DOMINION CL
RICHENS CL
STAR RD
LONDON RD
621
Tenn Cts
Pl Fld
DERWENT LO
KELVIN CT 1
HAWKFIELD CT 2
COOPERS CT 3
WOODLANDS GR
WOODLANDS RD
THE WOODLANDS
GREEN HO
Isleworth Bsns Complex
BRADDOCK CL
Hounslow Manor Sch
CROWN YARD
PRINCE REGENT RD
746
ALDERWICK DR
BIRCH CL
STANBOROUGH RD
GREENHAM HO
WOODLAND GDNS
OCTAVIA RD
FARNELL'S ALMSHOUSES
HOWARD RD
3 PANKHURST CL
DRAYMANS WAY
MALTING WAY
CLYDESDALE CL
SHIRE HORSE WAY
PERCHERON CL
Hounslow Town Prim Sch
HOLLOWAY ST
A315
SCHOOL RD
DEVONSHIRE HO
PEARS RD
JAMES ST
GLENWOOD RD
DEPOT RD
BRIDGE RD
Woodlands
GREENWOOD RD
MORRIS RD
KENNET RD
CLOCK TOWER RD
HIGH ST
FAIRFIELDS
GILBERT ST
FAIR ST
EVERGLADES
INWOOD AVE
HYDE HO
Allot Gdns
GIBSON CL
SUSSEX AVE
RIVERSIDE WLK
UNWIN RD
WHEATLEY RD
HIPPISLEY CT
RED LION CT
DOUGLAS RD
Liby
JUBILEE CT
BRISTOW RD
TW3
Inwood Park
1 DASHWOOD CT
2 VERNEY HO
3 HANNING LO
4 MACDONALD CT
Oaklands Sch
ELMER GDNS
FARNELL RD
ABINGER GDNS
ESSEX AVE
CLAYTON RD
BOURNE CL
CHRISTABEL CL
RUSKIN RD
FLEMING WAY
CHAPEL RD
LIVINGSTONE RD
CHATSWORTH CRES
PAGET LA
WORTON RD
1 LESTOR CT
2 TRIMMER CT
3 STEINMAN CT
4 WILKINSON HO
5 BOOTHROYD HO
6 RICHARDSON HO
7 ALLOTT HO
8 ANTHONY CT
9 OLIVER CT
10 WOODALL HO
Bwg Gn
Tenn Cts
Redlees Park
HOLLY RD
TEMPLE RD
GORDON RD
STANLEY RD
DALMENY CRES
HELDMANN CL
WORTON CT
OAK LA
WEAVER CL
The Victory Bsns Ctr
MEADOWBROOK CT
B361
LAYTON RD
INWOOD RD
DETHERICK CT 5
AUGUSTUS CT 6
CAMERON LO 7
Chatsworth Inf Sch
TUDOR RD
Duke of Northumberland's River
POWNALL RD
POWNALL GDNS
Allot Gdns
Worton Hall Ind Est
ELLERDINE RD
ATCHAM RD
LEIGH RD
CATHERINE GDNS
HEATH RD
Chatsworth Jun Sch
LYNTON CL
The Heath Bsns Ctr
IVY RD
Inwood Bsns Pk
WOLSEY CL
PARK CRES
LYNCROFT GDNS
CENTRAL AVE
NORBURY AVE
EATON RD
WAINWRIGHT GR
Sewage Works
BANKSIDE CL
453
MASWELL PARK RD
MASWELL PARK CRES
BRACKEN END
HARVEST LA
HILLARY DR
BRIAR CL
MANN'S CL
Hounslow
WHITTON RD
CHURCH STATION
14
LEAMINGTON CL
152
15
16
A310
Allot Gdns
HOUNSLOW AVE
PARK CT
PARK RD
PRIORY RD
SEBERY RD
SOUTHLAND WAY
REAPERS WAY
HALL RD
GLEN WLK
PLOUGH
CROFTERS CL
TREVOR CL
BEAUMONT PL
MOGDEN LA
Ivybridge Ret Pk

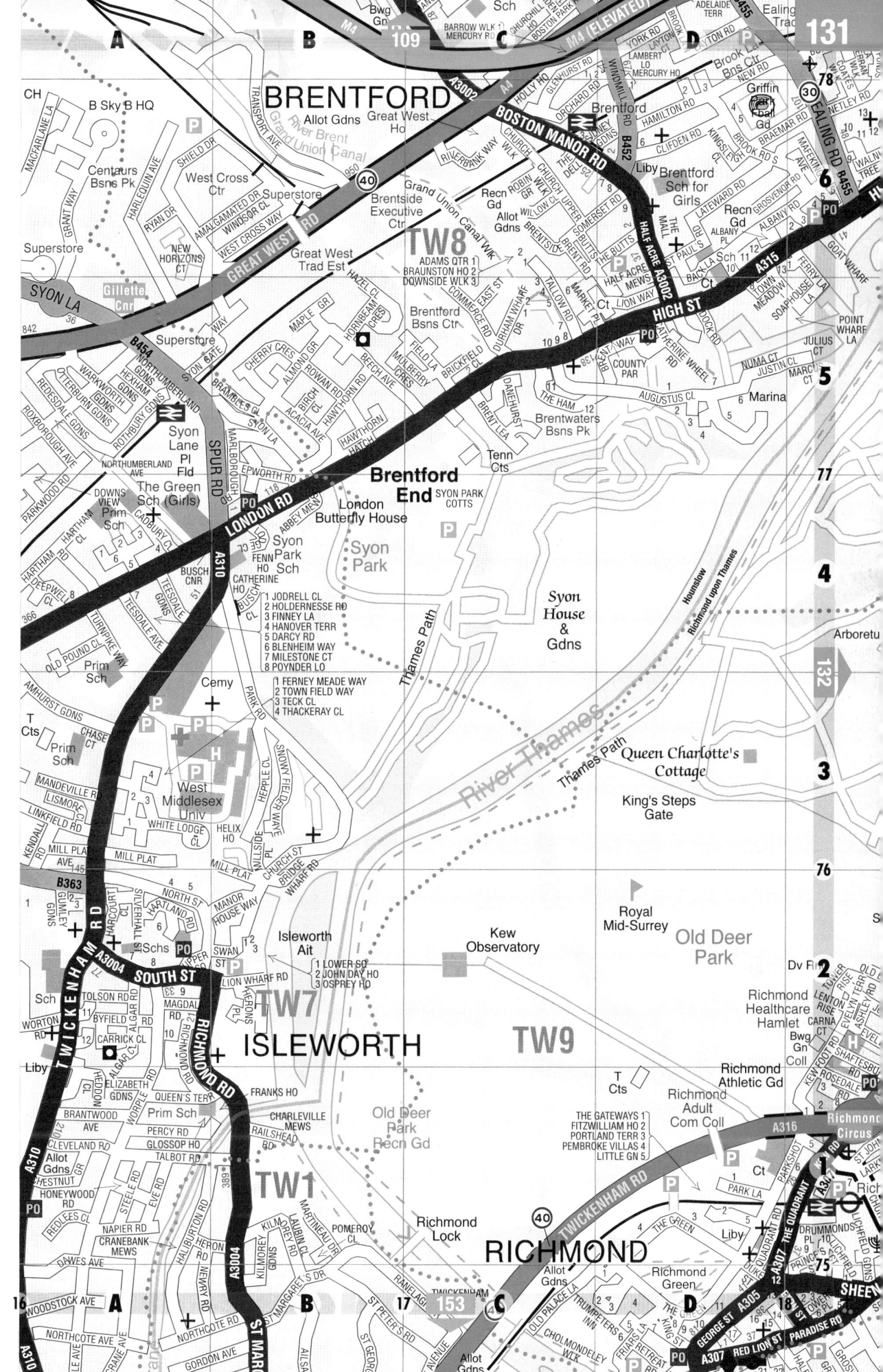
BRENTFORD
Brentford End
ISLEWORTH
RICHMOND
TW8
TW7
TW9
TW1
M4
M4 (ELEVATED)
A4
GREAT WEST RD
BOSTON MANOR RD
HIGH ST
LONDON RD
SPUR RD
TWICKENHAM RD
SOUTH ST
RICHMOND RD
SYON LA
HALF ACRE A3002
EALING RD
A316
A310
A3004
A315
B454
B363
B452
B455
River Thames
Grand Union Canal
River Brent
Thames Path
Syon Park
Syon House & Gdns
London Butterfly House
Queen Charlotte's Cottage
King's Steps Gate
Kew Observatory
Old Deer Park
Old Deer Park Recn Gd
Royal Mid-Surrey
Isleworth Ait
Richmond Lock
Richmond Green
Richmond Circus
Richmond Athletic Gd
Richmond Adult Com Coll
Richmond Healthcare Hamlet
West Middlesex Univ
Brentford Sch for Girls
Griffin Park Fball Gd
Brentwaters Bsns Pk
Brentford Bsns Ctr
Brentside Executive Ctr
Great West Trad Est
West Cross Ctr
Centaurs Bsns Pk
B Sky B HQ
Syon Lane
Gillette Cnr
Marina
Hounslow
Richmond upon Thames
109
132
153
Arboretu

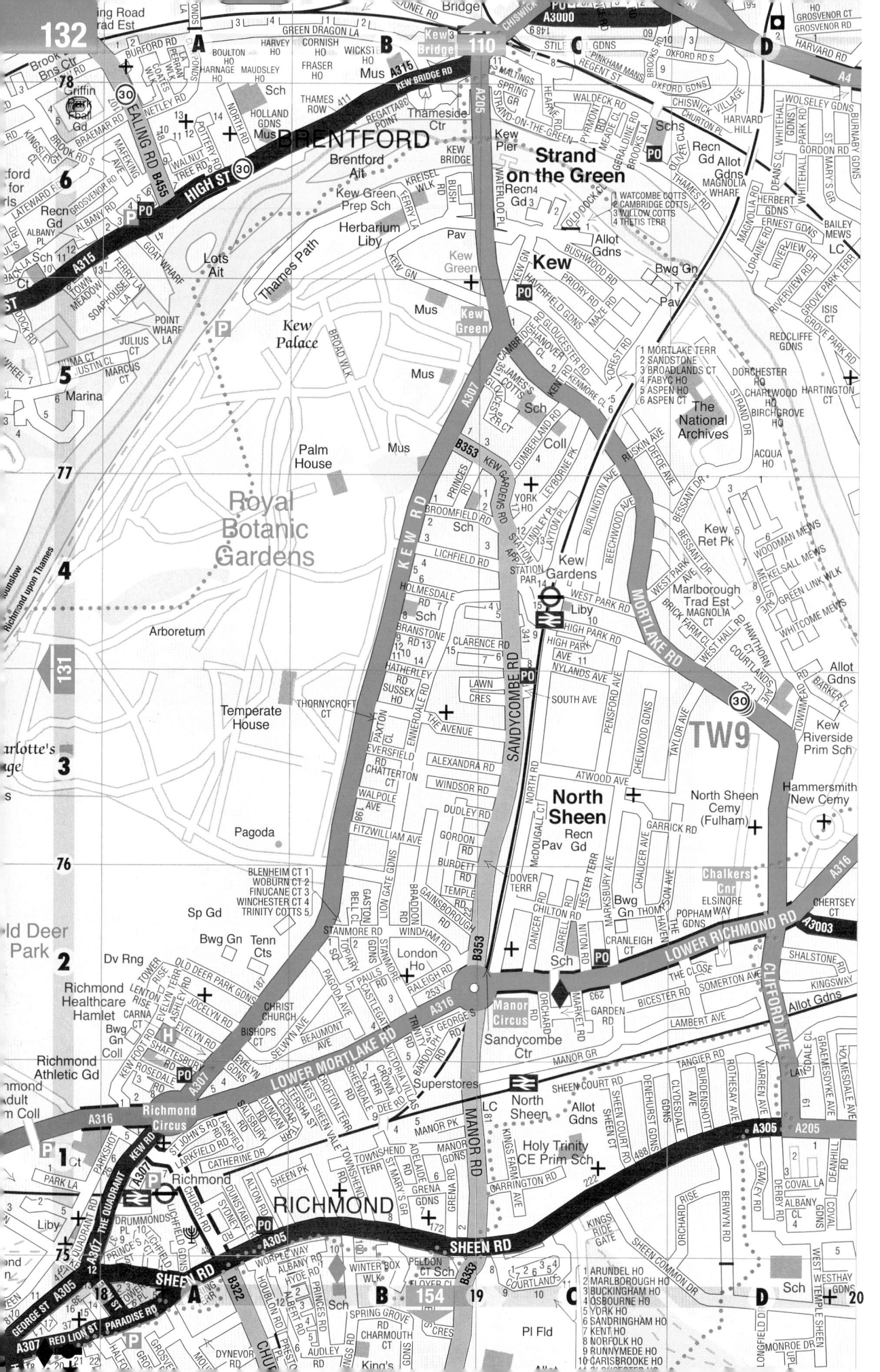
BRENTFORD
Strand on the Green
Kew
Royal Botanic Gardens
Kew Palace
Palm House
Temperate House
Pagoda
Arboretum
Brentford Ait
Lots Ait
Kew Gardens
North Sheen
RICHMOND
TW9
The National Archives
Kew Ret Pk
Marlborough Trad Est
North Sheen Cemy (Fulham)
Hammersmith New Cemy
Richmond Healthcare Hamlet
Richmond Athletic Gd
Old Deer Park
Manor Circus
Sandycombe Ctr
Richmond Circus
Chalkers Cnr
Holy Trinity CE Prim Sch
Kew Riverside Prim Sch
KEW RD
SANDYCOMBE RD
MORTLAKE RD
LOWER MORTLAKE RD
LOWER RICHMOND RD
SHEEN RD
MANOR RD
CLIFFORD AVE
HIGH ST
KEW BRIDGE RD
1 MORTLAKE TERR
2 SANDSTONE
3 BROADLANDS CT
4 FABYC HO
5 ASPEN HO
6 ASPEN CT
1 WATCOMBE COTTS
2 CAMBRIDGE COTTS
3 WILLOW COTTS
4 THETIS TERR
BLENHEIM CT 1
WOBURN CT 2
FINUCANE CT 3
WINCHESTER CT 4
TRINITY COTTS 5
1 ARUNDEL HO
2 MARLBOROUGH HO
3 BUCKINGHAM HO
4 OSBOURNE HO
5 YORK HO
6 SANDRINGHAM HO
7 KENT HO
8 NORFOLK HO
9 RUNNYMEDE HO
110
131
154

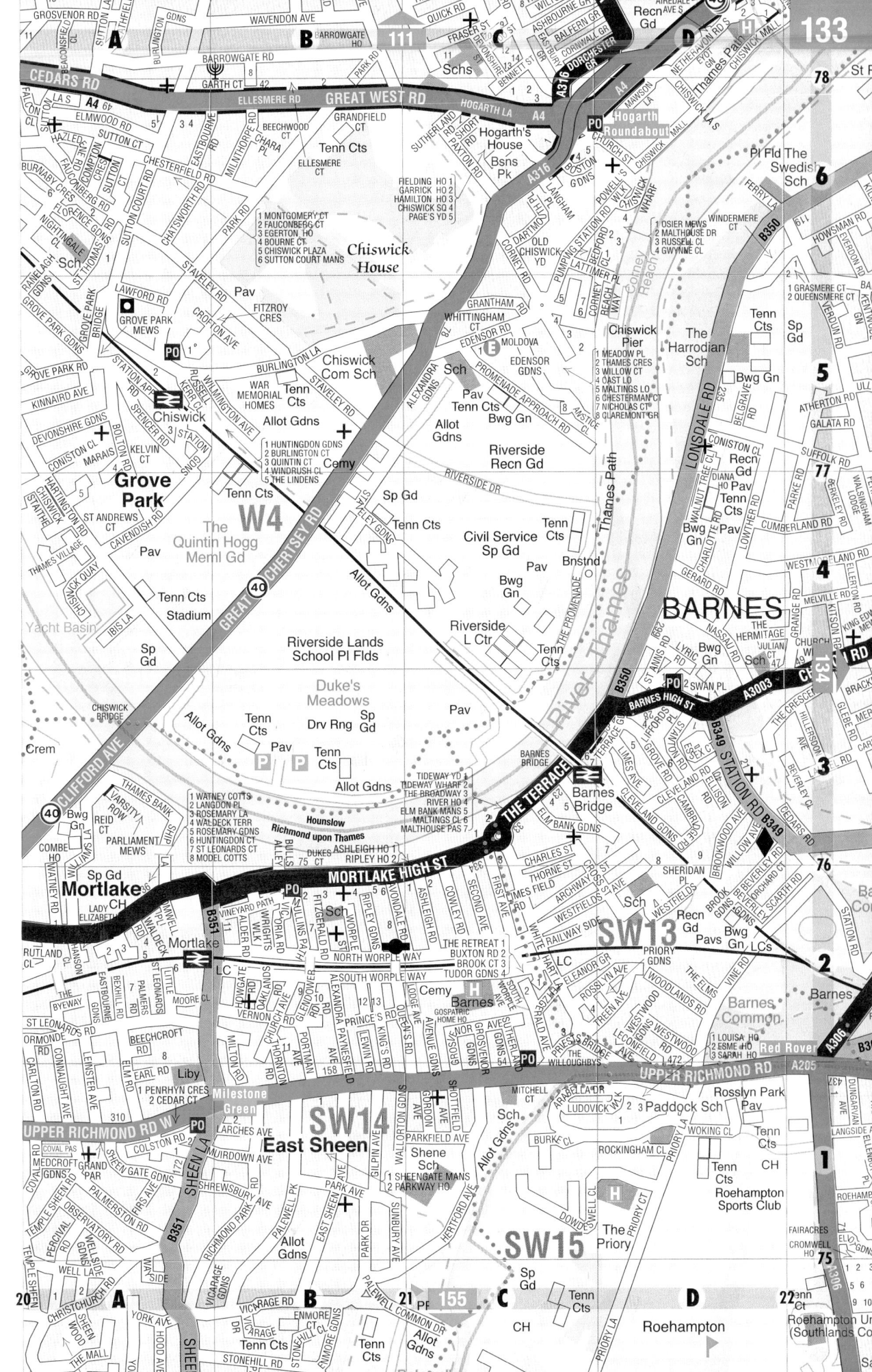
A
B
C
D
111
GROSVENOR RD
SUTTON LA
WAVENDON AVE
QUICK RD
BARROWGATE HO
BARROWGATE RD
GARTH CT
CEDARS RD
A4
GREAT WEST RD
ELLESMERE RD
HOGARTH LA
ELMWOOD RD
SUTTON CT
GRANDFIELD CT
BEECHWOOD CT
Tenn Cts
ELLESMERE CT
CHESTERFIELD RD
SUTTON COURT RD
CHATSWORTH RD
PARK RD
MILNTHORPE RD
EASTBOURNE RD
Hogarth's House
Bsns Pk
A316
DORCHESTER GR
Hogarth Roundabout
Schs
Recn Gd
Thames Path
CHISWICK MALL
CHISWICK LA S
CHURCH ST
78
6
Pl Fld The Swedish Sch
FERRY LA
1 MONTGOMERY CT
2 FAUCONBERG CT
3 EGERTON HO
4 BOURNE CT
5 CHISWICK PLAZA
6 SUTTON COURT MANS
Chiswick House
FIELDING HO 1
GARRICK HO 2
HAMILTON HO 3
CHISWICK SQ 4
PAGE'S YD 5
OLD CHISWICK YD
CORNEY RD
PUMPING STATION RD
LATTIMER PL
Corney Reach
1 OSIER MEWS
2 MALTHOUSE DR
3 RUSSELL CL
4 GWYNNE CL
WINDERMERE CT
B350
HOWSMAN RD
NIGHTINGALE CL
Sch
STAVELEY RD
LAWFORD RD
Pav
FITZROY CRES
GROVE PARK MEWS
GROVE PARK GDNS
CROFTON AVE
GRANTHAM RD
WHITTINGHAM CT
EDENSOR RD
MOLDOVA
EDENSOR GDNS
Chiswick Pier
1 MEADOW PL
2 THAMES CRES
3 WILLOW CT
4 OAST LO
5 MALTINGS LO
6 CHESTERMAN CT
7 NICHOLAS CT
8 CLAREMONT GR
The Harrodian Sch
Sp Gd
5
GROVE PARK RD
KINNAIRD AVE
STATION APP
BURLINGTON LA
Chiswick Com Sch
WAR MEMORIAL HOMES
ALEXANDRA GDNS
PROMENADE APPROACH RD
Bwg Gn
LONSDALE RD
BELGRAVE RD
ATHERTON RD
GALATA RD
DEVONSHIRE GDNS
Chiswick
WILMINGTON AVE
Allot Gdns
Riverside Recn Gd
CONISTON CL
SUFFOLK RD
Recn Gd
77
MARAIS
KELVIN CT
Grove Park
1 HUNTINGDON GDNS
2 BURLINGTON CT
3 QUINTIN CT
4 WINDRUSH CL
5 THE LINDENS
Cemy
RIVERSIDE DR
DIANA HO
ST ANDREWS CT
CAVENDISH RD
W4
The Quintin Hogg Meml Gd
Thames Path
Civil Service Sp Gd
CUMBERLAND RD
THAMES VILLAGE
CHISWICK QUAY
GREAT CHERTSEY RD
40
Allot Gdns
Bnstnd
WESTMORELAND RD
4
Yacht Basin
IBIS LA
Stadium
THE PROMENADE
River Thames
BARNES
Riverside Lands School Pl Flds
Riverside L Ctr
THE HERMITAGE
MELVILLE RD
Duke's Meadows
CHISWICK BRIDGE
Drv Rng
B350
BARNES HIGH ST
SWAN PL
A3003
134
Crem
Allot Gdns
BARNES BRIDGE
THE TERRACE
Barnes Bridge
B349
STATION RD
3
CLIFFORD AVE
THAMES BANK
1 WATNEY COTTS
2 LANGDON PL
3 ROSEMARY LA
4 WALDECK TERR
5 ROSEMARY GDNS
6 HUNTINGDON CT
7 ST LEONARDS CT
8 MODEL COTTS
TIDEWAY YD 1
TIDEWAY WHARF 2
THE BROADWAY 3
RIVER HO 4
ELM BANK MANS 5
MALTINGS CL 6
MALTHOUSE PAS 7
Hounslow
Richmond upon Thames
DUKES CT
ASHLEIGH HO 1
RIPLEY HO 2
PARLIAMENT MEWS
Mortlake
MORTLAKE HIGH ST
ELM BANK GDNS
CHARLES ST
THORNE ST
76
SHERIDAN PL
B351
Mortlake
NORTH WORPLE WAY
SOUTH WORPLE WAY
THE RETREAT 1
BUXTON RD 2
BROOK CT 3
TUDOR GDNS 4
SW13
PRIORY GDNS
2
Barnes Common
Barnes
Cemy
Barnes
GOSPATRIC HOME HO
A306
UPPER RICHMOND RD
1 LOUISA HO
2 ESME HO
3 SARAH HO
Red Rover
A205
Liby
1 PENRHYN CRES
2 CEDAR CT
Milestone Green
UPPER RICHMOND RD W
SW14
East Sheen
Rosslyn Park
Paddock Sch
Tenn Cts
CH
Roehampton Sports Club
1
Shene Sch
1 SHEENGATE MANS
2 PARKWAY HO
SHEEN LA
The Priory
SW15
75
20
A
B
21
155
C
D
22
Roehampton
Roehampton Univ (Southlands Col)
STONEHILL RD
THE MALL

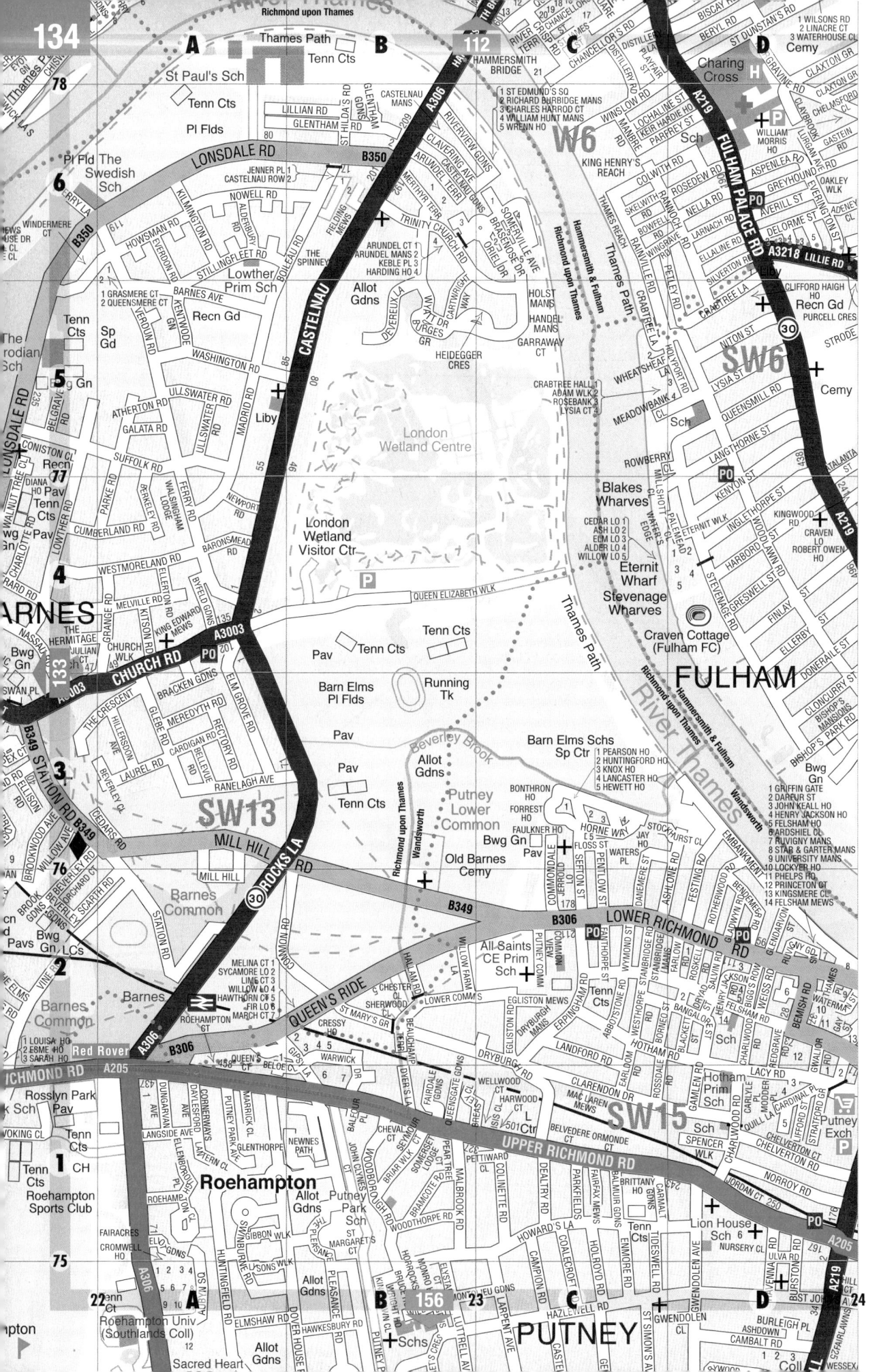
Richmond upon Thames
112
A
B
C
D
Thames Path
Tenn Cts
St Paul's Sch
Pl Flds
LILLIAN RD
GLENTHAM RD
HAMMERSMITH BRIDGE
CASTELNAU MANS
RIVERVIEW GDNS
LONSDALE RD
B350
The Swedish Sch
W6
Charing Cross
FULHAM PALACE RD
A219
CLAXTON GR
WILLIAM MORRIS HO
KING HENRY'S REACH
ASPENLEA RD
GREYHOUND RD
AVERILL ST
DELORME ST
A3218 LILLIE RD
Liby
CLIFFORD HAIGH HO
Recn Gd
PURCELL CRES
STRODE
Cemy
SW6
LYSIA ST
QUEENSMILL RD
LANGTHORNE ST
KENYON ST
INGLETHORPE ST
Thames Path
Hammersmith & Fulham
Richmond upon Thames
CASTELNAU
A306
TRINITY CHURCH RD
Lowther Prim Sch
BARNES AVE
Recn Gd
WASHINGTON RD
ULLSWATER RD
MADRID RD
Liby
Allot Gdns
THE SPINNEY
HOLST MANS
HANDEL MANS
GARRAWAY CT
HEIDEGGER CRES
London Wetland Centre
London Wetland Visitor Ctr
QUEEN ELIZABETH WLK
Blakes Wharves
Eternit Wharf
Stevenage Wharves
Craven Cottage (Fulham FC)
FULHAM
River Thames
BARNES
CHURCH RD
A3003
WESTMORELAND RD
CUMBERLAND RD
SUFFOLK RD
Tenn Cts
Pav
Running Tk
Barn Elms Pl Flds
Beverley Brook
Barn Elms Schs Sp Ctr
Allot Gdns
Putney Lower Common
Old Barnes Cemy
Bwg Gn
SW13
MILL HILL RD
ROCKS LA
B349
STATION RD
Barnes Common
Barnes
LOWER RICHMOND RD
B306
QUEEN'S RIDE
All Saints CE Prim Sch
Red Rover
RICHMOND RD
A205
UPPER RICHMOND RD
SW15
Roehampton
Rosslyn Park Pav
Roehampton Sports Club
Allot Gdns
Putney Park Sch
Hotham Prim Sch
Putney Exch
Lion House Sch
Roehampton Univ (Southlands Coll)
Sacred Heart
PUTNEY
156
133
22
23
24
1
2
3
4
5
6
75
76
77
78

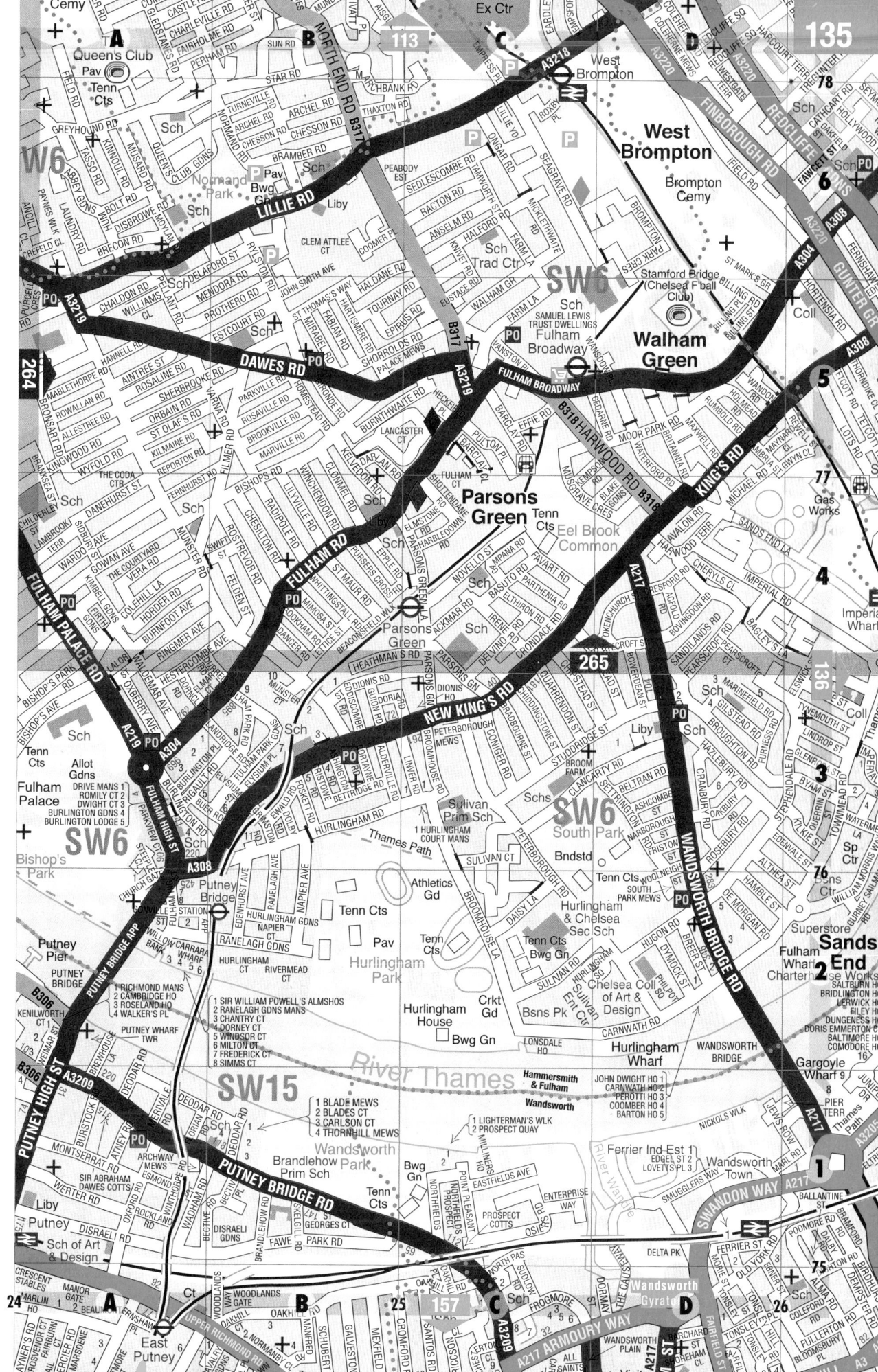
A
B
C
D
113
Queen's Club
Tenn Cts
West Brompton
Brompton Cemy
W6
LILLIE RD
NORTH END RD
B317
A3218
A3220
FINBOROUGH RD
REDCLIFFE GDNS
78
6
Normand Park
Stamford Bridge (Chelsea F'ball Club)
SW6
Walham Green
Fulham Broadway
FULHAM BROADWAY
DAWES RD
A3219
A3219
264
5
A308
GUNTER GR
HARWOOD RD
B318
KING'S RD
77
Gas Works
Parsons Green
Eel Brook Common
FULHAM RD
FULHAM PALACE RD
4
Imperial Wharf
A217
265
NEW KING'S RD
136
Fulham Palace
Bishop's Park
SW6
A219
A304
A308
FULHAM HIGH ST
3
SW6
South Park
Sulivan Prim Sch
Thames Path
Putney Bridge
Hurlingham Park
Athletics Gd
Hurlingham & Chelsea Sec Sch
WANDSWORTH BRIDGE RD
76
Sands End
2
Putney Pier
PUTNEY BRIDGE APP
B306
Hurlingham House
Hurlingham Wharf
WANDSWORTH BRIDGE
River Thames
Hammersmith & Fulham
Wandsworth
SW15
PUTNEY HIGH ST
A3209
Gargoyle Wharf
Wandsworth Park
Brandlehow Prim Sch
PUTNEY BRIDGE RD
River Wandle
Ferrier Ind Est
Wandsworth Town
SWANDON WAY
1
Putney
Sch of Art & Design
75
UPPER RICHMOND RD
East Putney
24
A
B
25
157
C
Wandsworth Gyratory
D
26
A3209
A217 ARMOURY WAY
WANDSWORTH PLAIN

SW10
A
B
C
D
114
CHELSEA
6
5
4
3
2
1
SW11
BATTERSEA
River Thames
Chelsea Reach
Battersea Reach
Sands End
Clapham Junction
Chelsea Harbour Pier
Cadogan Pier
Festival Pleasure Gardens
Chelsea & Westminster
Imperial Wharf
Old Ferry Wharf
Chelsea Wharf
Cremorne Wharf
Regent Wharf
Bridge Wharf
Gas Works
135
266
267
158
KING'S RD
FULHAM RD
CHEYNE WLK
CHELSEA EMB
ALBERT BRIDGE RD
BATTERSEA BRIDGE RD
BATTERSEA PARK RD
YORK RD
ST JOHN'S HILL
WANDSWORTH BRIDGE RD
SWANDON WAY
EAST HILL
BATTERSEA RISE
LOMBARD RD
VICARAGE CRES
WESTBRIDGE RD
FALCON RD
LATCHMERE RD
ELSPETH RD
OAKLEY ST
EDITH GR
GUNTER GR
REDCLIFFE GDNS
FINBOROUGH RD
ROYAL HOSPITAL RD

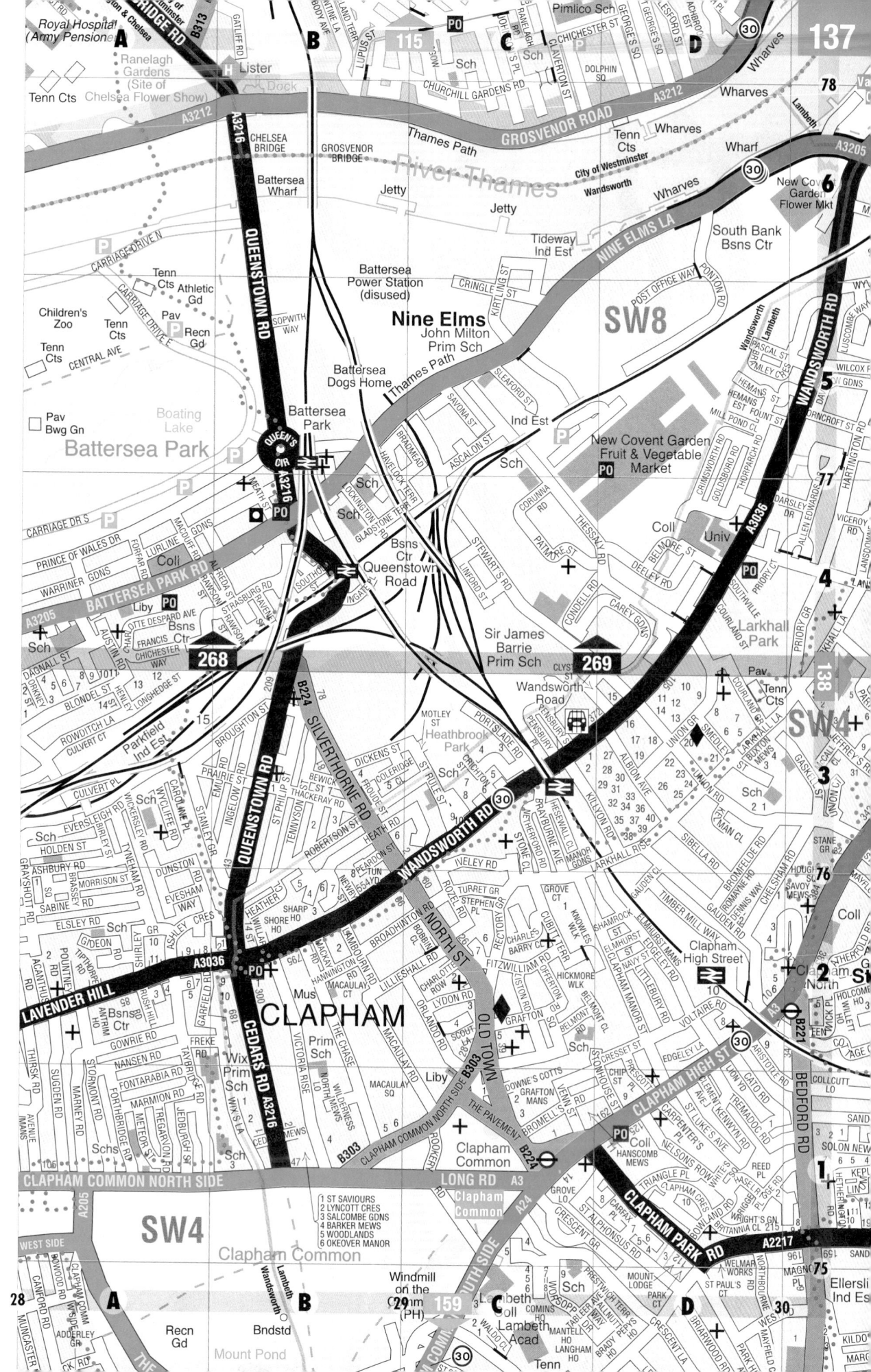
Royal Hospital (Army Pensioners)
Ranelagh Gardens (Site of Chelsea Flower Show)
Lister
Tenn Cts
GROSVENOR ROAD
CHELSEA BRIDGE
GROSVENOR BRIDGE
River Thames
Thames Path
City of Westminster
Wandsworth
Battersea Wharf
Jetty
NINE ELMS LA
Tideway Ind Est
South Bank Bsns Ctr
New Covent Garden Flower Mkt
Battersea Power Station (disused)
Nine Elms
John Milton Prim Sch
SW8
Children's Zoo
Athletic Gd
Recn Gd
CARRIAGE DRIVE N
CENTRAL AVE
Battersea Dogs Home
QUEENSTOWN RD
Boating Lake
Battersea Park
QUEEN'S CIR
New Covent Garden Fruit & Vegetable Market
WANDSWORTH RD
BATTERSEA PARK RD
PRINCE OF WALES DR
CARRIAGE DR S
Queenstown Road
Sir James Barrie Prim Sch
Wandsworth Road
Larkhall Park
Parkfield Ind Est
Heathbrook Park
SW4
LAVENDER HILL
CLAPHAM
CEDARS RD
SILVERTHORNE RD
NORTH ST
OLD TOWN
Clapham High Street
CLAPHAM HIGH ST
Clapham North
Wix Prim Sch
Clapham Common
CLAPHAM COMMON NORTH SIDE
LONG RD
CLAPHAM PARK RD
BEDFORD RD
1 ST SAVIOURS
2 LYNCOTT CRES
3 SALCOMBE GDNS
4 BARKER MEWS
5 WOODLANDS
6 OKEOVER MANOR
Clapham Common
Windmill on the Common (PH)
Lambeth Coll
Lambeth Acad
Recn Gd
Bndstd
Mount Pond
Ellerslie Ind Est
A
B
C
D
1
2
3
4
5
6
115
268
269
138
159
28
29
30
78
77
76
75

Vauxhall
VAUXHALL BRIDGE
Spring Gardens
Vauxhall Cross
Wharves
Wharf
New Covent Garden Flower Mkt
South Bank Bsns Ctr
Kennington
SE11
SE17
116
261
270
137
160
A3204
A3036
A3205
A202
A203
A3
A23
A2217
A204
B221
B223
KENNINGTON LA
HARLEYFORD RD
PARRY ST
BONDWAY
DURHAM ST
KENNINGTON OVAL
The Oval
Kennington Park
KENNINGTON PK RD
Govt Offices
Bnstnd
Tenn Cts
Fball Gd
Kennington Oval
Oval
Vauxhall Park
Bwg Gn
LAWN LA
MILES ST
WYVIL RD
RITA RD
FENTIMAN RD
COTTINGHAM RD
CAMBERWELL NEW RD
WANDSWORTH RD
SOUTH LAMBETH RD
CLAPHAM RD
BRIXTON RD
SW8
South Lambeth
Stockwell Park Sch
Stockwell
LANSDOWNE WAY
THORNE RD
HANDFORTH RD
CREWDSON RD
VASSALL RD
CRANMER RD
CAMBERWELL NEW RD
Larkhall Park
SW4
SW9
STOCKWELL RD
STOCKWELL PARK RD
STOCKWELL PARK CRES
Myatt's Fields Pk
Allot Gdns
Mostyn Gdns
YMCA
BRIXTON
Loughborough Junc
Stockwell
Clapham North
Clapham High Street
Lambeth
Coll
COLDHARBOUR LA
ATLANTIC RD
BRIXTON STATION RD
Brixton
ACRE LA
BEDFORD RD
SANDMERE RD
Ellerslie Ind Est
Works
EFFRA RD
Bsns Ctr
Ret Pk
MILKWOOD RD
LOUGHBOROUGH PK
Lambeth Coll
A
B
C
D
1
2
3
4
5
6
30
31
32
75
76
77
78

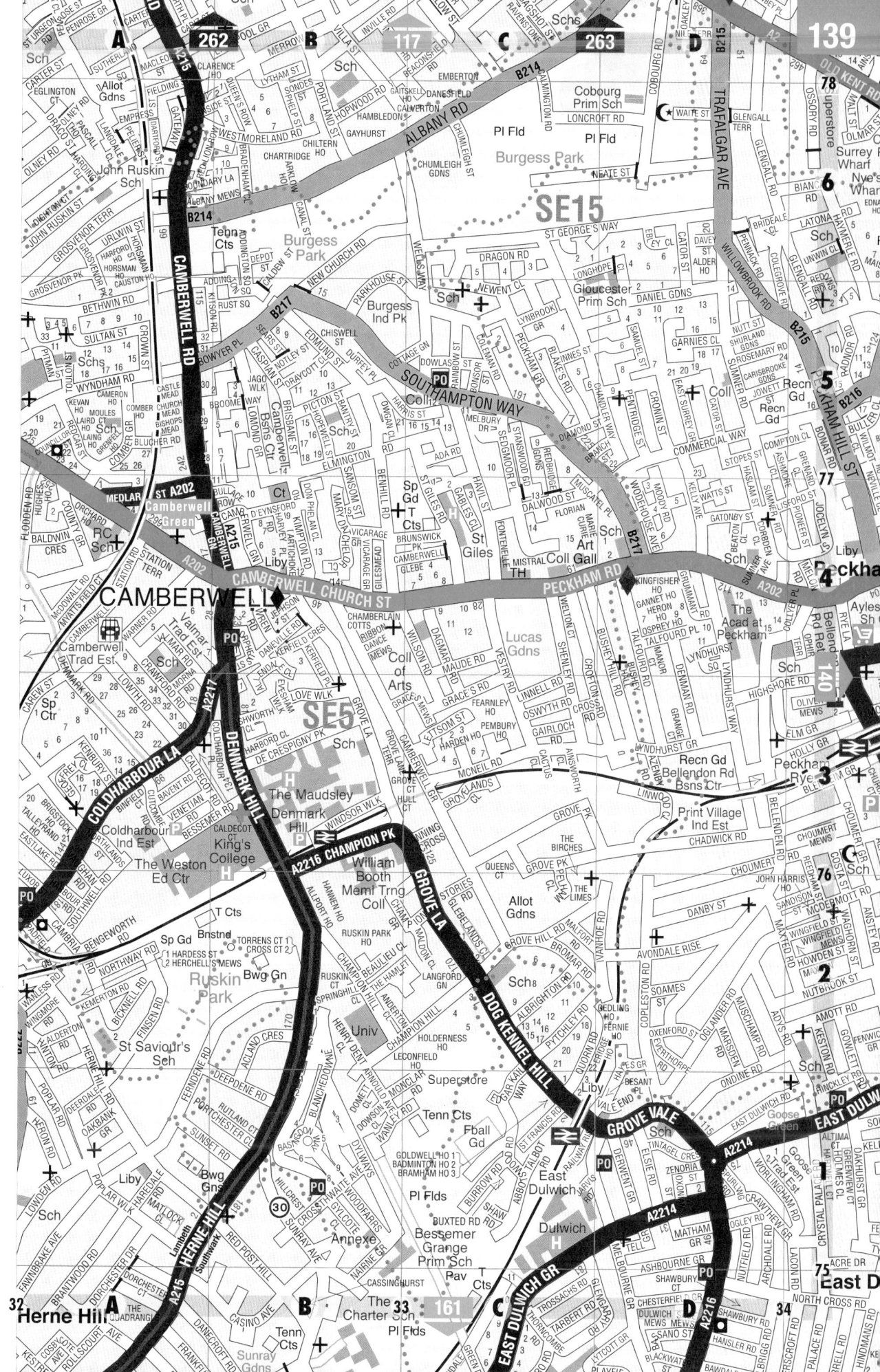

262
117
263
A
B
C
D
CAMBERWELL RD
CAMBERWELL
Camberwell Green
CAMBERWELL CHURCH ST
PECKHAM RD
SE15
SE5
Burgess Park
ALBANY RD
SOUTHAMPTON WAY
TRAFALGAR AVE
PECKHAM HILL ST
OLD KENT RD
COLDHARBOUR LA
DENMARK HILL
CHAMPION PK
GROVE LA
DOG KENNEL HILL
GROVE VALE
EAST DULWICH GR
HERNE HILL
Herne Hill
East Dulwich
Dulwich
The Maudsley
King's College
Denmark Hill
Ruskin Park
St Saviour's Sch
Lucas Gdns
Coll of Arts
Cobourg Prim Sch
Gloucester Prim Sch
John Ruskin Sch
The Acad at Peckham
Peckham Rye
Bellendon Rd Bsns Ctr
Print Village Ind Est
William Booth Meml Trng Coll
Camberwell Trad Est
Coldharbour Ind Est
The Weston Ed Ctr
Bessemer Grange Prim Sch
Burgess Ind Pk
Surrey Wharf
Goose Green
Superstore
140
161
32
33
34
1
2
3
4
5
6

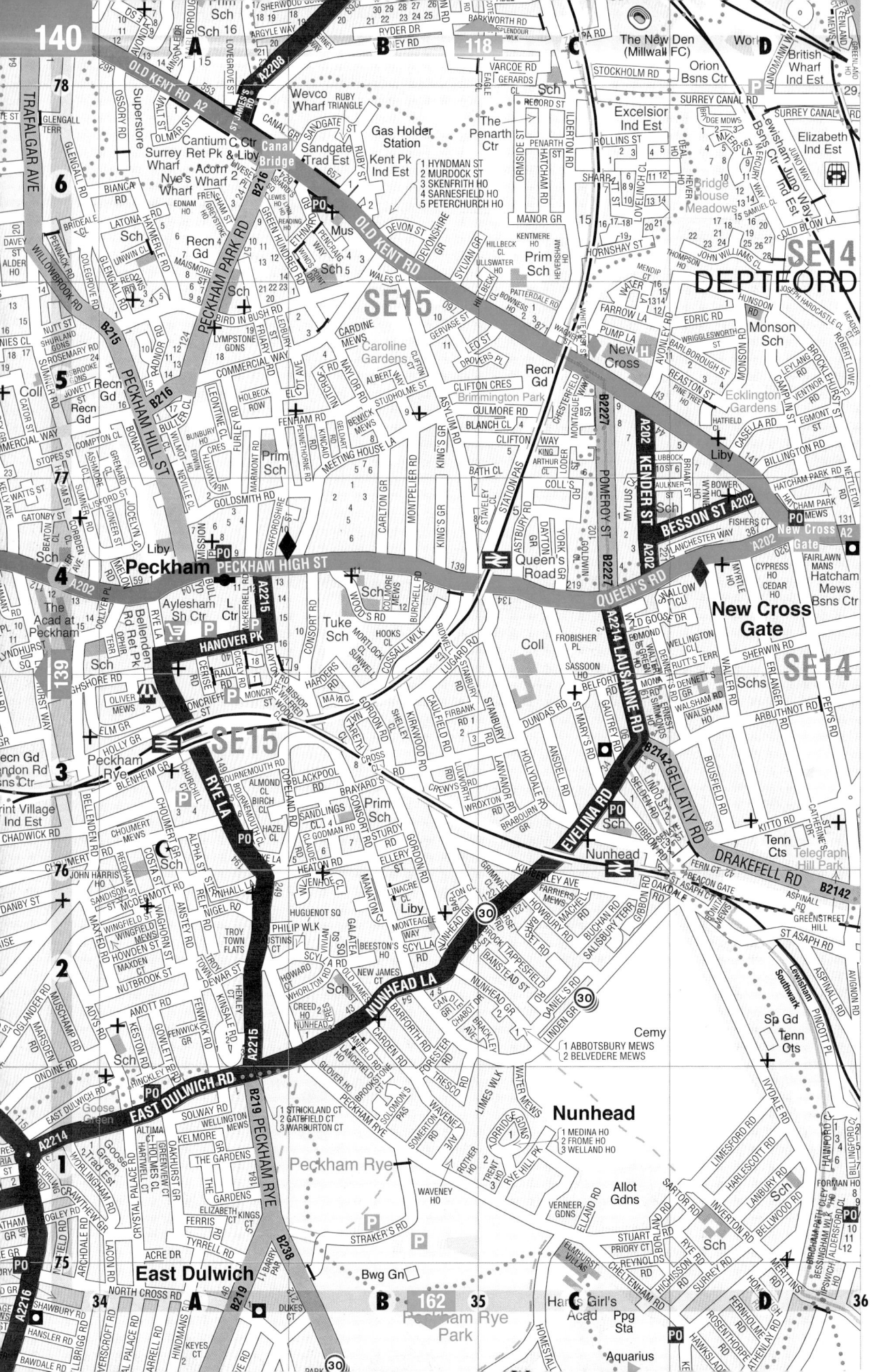
A
B
C
D
118
The New Den (Millwall FC)
Orion Bsns Ctr
British Wharf Ind Est
OLD KENT RD A2
A2208
Wevco Wharf
RUBY TRIANGLE
Gas Holder Station
Kent Pk Ind Est
Sandgate Trad Est
Canal Bridge
Cantium C Ctr & Liby
Surrey Ret Pk
Acorn Wharf
Nye's Wharf
Superstore
1 HYNDMAN ST
2 MURDOCK ST
3 SKENFRITH HO
4 SARNESFIELD HO
5 PETERCHURCH HO
The Penarth Ctr
Excelsior Ind Est
Lewisham Bsns Ctr
Elizabeth Ind Est
Juno Way Ind Est
Bridge House Meadows
SE14
DEPTFORD
SE15
Caroline Gardens
Brimmington Park
New Cross
Monson Sch
Ecklington Gardens
TRAFALGAR AVE
PECKHAM PARK RD
PECKHAM HILL ST
B216
B215
Peckham
PECKHAM HIGH ST
A202
QUEEN'S RD
KENDER ST
BESSON ST A202
New Cross Gate
Queen's Road
Aylesham Sh Ctr
Bellenden Rd Ret Pk
HANOVER PK
A2215
The Acad at Peckham
Tuke Sch
Coll
A2214 LAUSANNE RD
B2142 GELLATLY RD
DRAKEFELL RD
Telegraph Hill Park
New Cross Gate
Hatcham Mews Bsns Ctr
SE14
Peckham Rye
RYE LA
Print Village Ind Est
EVELINA RD
Nunhead
NUNHEAD LA
Lewisham
Southwark
Cemy
1 ABBOTSBURY MEWS
2 BELVEDERE MEWS
Nunhead
1 MEDINA HO
2 FROME HO
3 WELLAND HO
Allot Gdns
EAST DULWICH RD
A2214
Goose Green
Goose Green Trad Est
B219 PECKHAM RYE
1 STRICKLAND CT
2 GATEFIELD CT
3 WARBURTON CT
Peckham Rye
B238
Bwg Gn
East Dulwich
A2216
34
35
36
162
Peckham Rye Park
Harris Girl's Acad
Ppg Sta
Aquarius
139
78
77
76
75
6
5
4
3
2
1

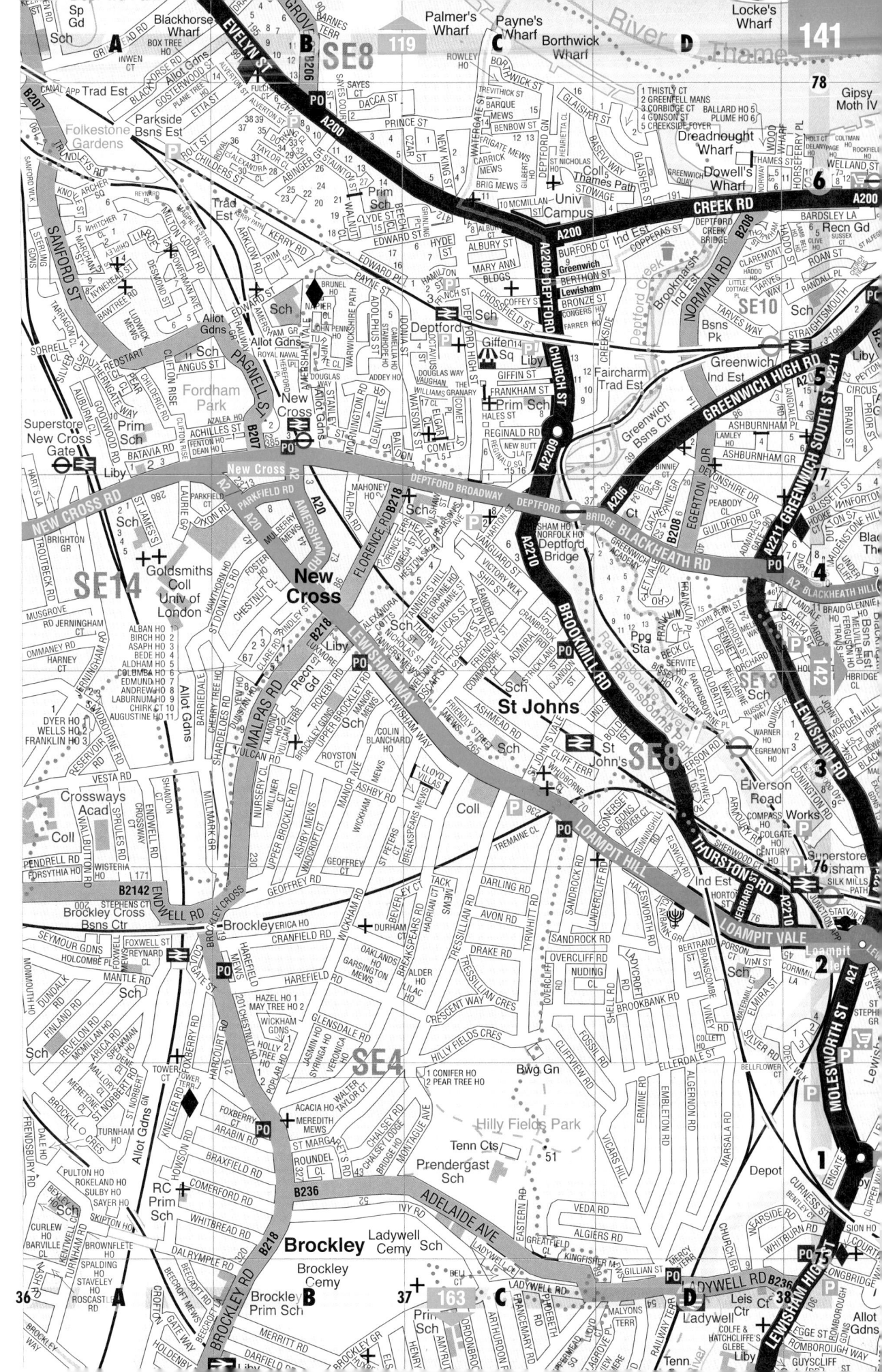
141
A
B
C
D
SE8
119
Palmer's Wharf
Payne's Wharf
Borthwick Wharf
Locke's Wharf
River Thames
78
Gipsy Moth IV
Blackhorse Wharf
EVELYN ST
GROVE ST
B206
A200
Trad Est
CANAL APP
B207
Folkestone Gardens
Parkside Bsns Est
TRUNDLEYS RD
SANFORD ST
PRINCE ST
CZAR ST
NEW KING ST
WATERGATE ST
BARQUE MEWS
BENBOW ST
FRIGATE MEWS
CARRICK MEWS
BRIG MEWS
DEPTFORD GN
Thames Path
STOWAGE
Univ Campus
GLAISHER ST
BASEVI WAY
1 THISTLY CT
2 GREENFELL MANS
3 CORBIDGE CT
4 GONSON ST
5 CREEKSIDE FOYER
BALLARD HO
PLUME HO
Dreadnought Wharf
Dowell's Wharf
THAMES ST
HORSEFERRY PL
WELLAND ST
CREEK RD
6
A200
ABINGER GR
STAUNTON ST
Prim Sch
LYDE ST
EDWARD ST
EDWARD PL
HYDE ST
ALBURY ST
MARY ANN BLDGS
COFFEY ST
CROSSFIELD ST
A2209
DEPTFORD CHURCH ST
Greenwich
Lewisham
BURFORD CT
Ind Est
COPPERAS ST
Deptford Creek
Brookmarsh Ind Est
NORMAN RD
B208
SE10
Bsns Pk
TARVES WAY
STRAIGHTSMOUTH
Recn Gd
BARDSLEY LA
ROAN ST
Sch
Trad Est
MILTON COURT RD
KERRY RD
TRIM ST
PAYNE ST
ARKLOW RD
EDWARD ST
Allot Gdns
Sch
REDSTART
PAGNELL ST
Fordham Park
New Cross
Deptford
Giffen Sq
Liby
GIFFIN ST
FRANKHAM ST
Prim Sch
DOUGLAS WAY
Faircharm Trad Est
Greenwich Ind Est
GREENWICH HIGH RD
GREENWICH SOUTH ST
A2211
5
Greenwich Bsns Ctr
ASHBURNHAM PL
ASHBURNHAM GR
Superstore New Cross Gate
Liby
NEW CROSS RD
New Cross
A2
PARKFIELD RD
A20
AMERSHAM RD
B218
FLORENCE RD
DEPTFORD BROADWAY
DEPTFORD BRIDGE
Deptford Bridge
A2210
BLACKHEATH RD
B208
A206
EGERTON DR
DEVONSHIRE DR
GUILDFORD GR
4
A2 BLACKHEATH HILL
SE14
Goldsmiths Coll Univ of London
New Cross
LEWISHAM WAY
Liby
Recn Gd
BROOKMILL RD
Ravensbourne River
Ravensbourne Park
Ppg Sta
SE13
Sch
LEWISHAM RD
142
Sch
St Johns
St John's
SE8
3
Elverson Road
Works
MALPAS RD
Allot Gdns
Crossways Acad
Coll
VESTA RD
RESERVOIR RD
ASHBY RD
LOAMPIT HILL
Coll
THURSTON RD
Ind Est
Superstore Lewisham
SILK MILLS PATH
Brockley Cross Bsns Ctr
B2142
ENDWELL RD
BROCKLEY CROSS
Brockley
CRANFIELD RD
LOAMPIT VALE
Loampit Vale
2
A21
MOLESWORTH ST
Sch
SE4
HARCOURT RD
HILLY FIELDS CRES
Bwg Gn
Hilly Fields Park
Tenn Cts
Prendergast Sch
VICARS HILL
ELLERDALE ST
1
Depot
B236
ADELAIDE AVE
Brockley
Ladywell Cemy
Brockley Cemy
Sch
RC Prim Sch
BROCKLEY RD
B218
36
A
B
37
163
C
D
38
Brockley Prim Sch
Prim Sch
LADYWELL RD
B236
Leis Ctr
Ladywell
LEWISHAM HIGH ST
Allot Gdns
Liby

A
B
C
D
120
GREENWICH
East Greenwich Pleasaunce
Greenwich Pier
Greenwich Footway Tunnel
Gipsy Moth IV
Cutty Sark
Old Royal Naval Coll Bldgs
Univ of Greenwich
Dreadnought Wharf
Dowells Wharf
TRAFALGAR RD
ROMNEY RD
CREEK RD
A206
A200
Maze Hill
National Maritime Mus
The Queen's House
Maze Hill House Gate
St Mary's Gate
One Tree Hill
Maze Hill Gate
National Fan Mus
The John Roan Sch
Flamsteed House
Meridian Building
The Royal Observatory
Tea House
SE10
Greenwich Park
Bndstd
Vanbrugh Park Gate
Blackheath
The Wilderness (Deer Park)
South Building
Croomshill Gate
Resr
Ranger's House (The Wernher Collection)
Blackheath Gate
GREENWICH HIGH RD
GREENWICH SOUTH ST
A2211
HYDE VALE
ROYAL HILL
CHARLTON WAY
SHOOTERS HILL RD
B210
A2
BLACKHEATH HILL
SE3
Blackheath The Point
Whitfield's Mound
Blackheath Vale
Blackheath Bsns Est
LEWISHAM RD
Elverson Road
Superstore
Lewisham
Works
Ind Est
THURSTON RD
LOAMPIT VALE
Loampit Vale
Sixth Form Coll
Blackheath RC Prim Sch
Acad
Pl Fld
LEE TERR
BELMONT HILL
B220
Blackheath
MOLESWORTH ST
A21
LEWISHAM HIGH ST
A20
Lewisham Ctr
SE13
LEWISHAM
LEE HIGH RD
Depot
Allot Gdns
Prim Sch
Liby
Lee Green
SE12
LEE RD
Kid Brook
Tenn Cts
Manor House Gardens
LADYWELL RD
Leis Ctr
Ladywell
141
164
A2212
ELTHAM RD
78
77
75
76
38
39
40

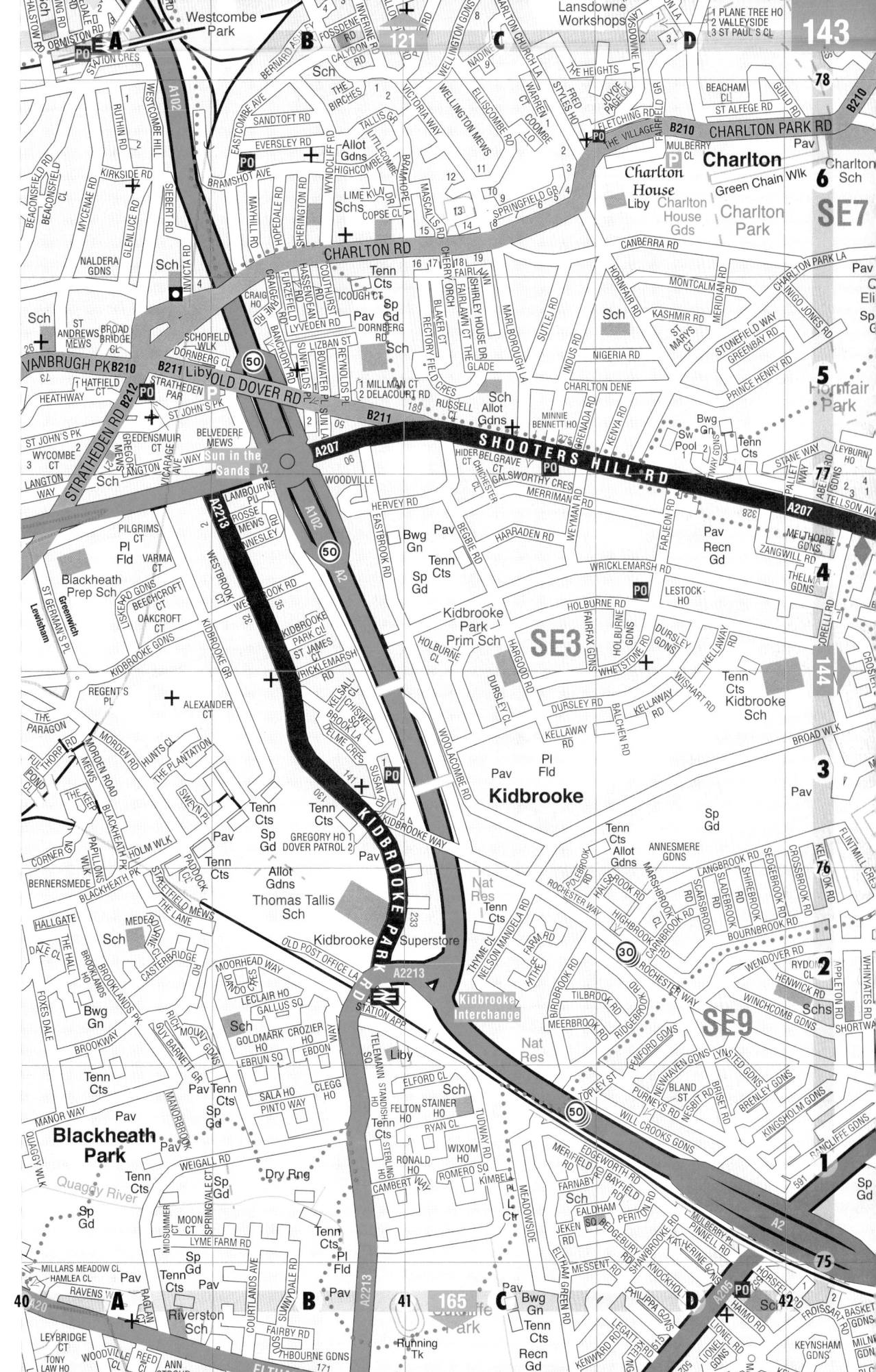

Westcombe Park
Lansdowne Workshops
1 PLANE TREE HO
2 VALLEYSIDE
3 ST PAUL'S CL
121
A
B
C
D
78
Charlton
Charlton House
Charlton House Gds
Charlton Park
Charlton Sch
SE7
CHARLTON PARK RD
B210
THE VILLAGE
Green Chain Wlk
CHARLTON RD
SPRINGFIELD GR
CANBERRA RD
CHARLTON PARK LA
MONTCALM RD
KASHMIR RD
STONEFIELD WAY
GREENBAY RD
PRINCE HENRY RD
INIGO JONES RD
NIGERIA RD
CHARLTON DENE
Hornfair Park
VANBRUGH PK
B211
OLD DOVER RD
STRATHEDEN RD
B212
Sun in the Sands
A2
A207
A102
SHOOTERS HILL RD
HERVEY RD
WOODVILLE
HARRADEN RD
WRICKLEMARSH RD
HOLBURNE RD
MERRIMAN RD
GALSWORTHY CRES
LESTOCK HO
Kidbrooke Park Prim Sch
SE3
A2213
WESTBROOK RD
KIDBROOKE GR
KIDBROOKE GDNS
Blackheath Prep Sch
Lewisham
Greenwich
ST GERMAN'S PL
REGENT'S PL
ALEXANDER CT
THE PARAGON
MORDEN RD
HUNTS CL
THE PLANTATION
Kidbrooke Sch
144
BROAD WLK
WOOLACOMBE RD
KELLAWAY RD
DURSLEY RD
Kidbrooke
KIDBROOKE WAY
KIDBROOKE PARK RD
Thomas Tallis Sch
Kidbrooke
Superstore
Kidbrooke Interchange
OLD POST OFFICE LA
STATION APP
BLACKHEATH PK
HOLM WLK
CORNER GN
BERNERSMEDE
HALLGATE
BROOKLANDS PK
ROCHESTER WAY
HIGHBROOK RD
ANNESMERE GDNS
LANGBROOK RD
BOURNBROOK RD
WENDOVER RD
HENWICK RD
WINCHCOMB GDNS
SE9
TILBROOK RD
BIRDBROOK RD
RIDGEBROOK RD
NELSON MANDELA RD
Nat Res
TOPLEY ST
WILL CROOKS GDNS
KINGSHOLM GDNS
RANCLIFFE GDNS
MANOR WAY
Blackheath Park
Quaggy River
WEIGALL RD
Dry Rng
LYME FARM RD
COURTLANDS AVE
SUNNYDALE RD
FAIRBY RD
ELTHAM GREEN RD
MEADOWSIDE
Running Tk
Sutcliffe Park
Riverston Sch
165
40
41
42
1
2
3
4
5
6
75
76
77
A20
A205

A
B
C
D
122
LITTLE HEATH
Mc CALL CRES
HAMSTEED RD
REPOSITORY RD
CLAYDOWN MEWS 5
Tenn Cts
GUNNER LA
LORD ROBERTS TER
BROOK HILL CL
WILLENHALL RD
BIGNELL RD
ELMDENE CL
SANDY HILL AVE
MICHEL WLK
CAMBRIDGE ROW
Sch
UPLANDS
78
BEACHAM CL
GUILD RD
ST ALFEGE RD
B210
CHARLTON PARK RD
PARK DR
CEMETERY LA
Cemy
Barrack Fld Pav
Tenn Cts
HA-HA RD
CIRCULAR WAY
Pl Fld
NIGHTINGALE PL
GILDERSOME ST
PEACE ST
ENGINEER CL
NIGHTINGALE VALE
JACKSON ST
KEMPT ST
RITTER ST
FENNELL ST
LONG WLK
SHORT PATH
EDGE HILL
PO
Sch
EGLINTON RD
WESTDALE RD
ETHEL BROOKS HO
COOPER CT
MAYPLACE LA
HERBERT PL
BARNFIELD RD
BARNFIELD GDNS
BARN FIELD RD
RIXON HO
KEEBLE CL
Charlton
Pav
Charlton Sch
6
Green Chain Wlk
Charlton Park
SE7
WOOLWICH COMM
A205
CHARLTON PARK LA
Pav
Queen Elizabeth Sports Gd
H
SHRAPNEL CL
STADIUM RD
Woolwich Stad
Woolwich Common
30
SE18
ORDNANCE RD
WOOLWICH COMM
LLANOVER RD
WHITWORTH RD
PAGET RISE
PAGET TERR
REEVES RD
RIPON RD
HERBERT RD
CANTWELL HO
CANTWELL RD
DALLIN RD
HIGHVIEW
SANTANA
BRENT RD
EGLINTON HILL
MAYPLACE LA
BRINKLOW CRES
ALMA RD
MERIDIAN RD
INIGO JONES RD
STONEFIELD WAY
GREENBAY RD
PRINCE HENRY RD
5
Hornfair Park
MANSERGH CL
ACADEMY RD
Pl Fld
DELVAN CL 1
KEEMOR CL 2
Green Chain Wlk
MATCHLESS DR
GARRISON CL
Pl Fld
GRAHAM HO
CONDOVER CRES
DOWNEND
BUSHMOOR CRES
Bwg Gn
Tenn Cts
PORTWAY GDNS
STANE WAY
LEYBURN HO
BAKER RD
GREENWICH HTS
77
PALLET WAY
ABERFORD GDNS
TELLSON AVE
PRINCE IMPERIAL RD
RED LION LA
DONALDSON RD
ANKERDINE CRES
MOORDOWN
OCCUPATION LA
RIVERVIEW HTS
THE OLD FIRE STATION
EAGLESFIELD RD
A207
328
GALTON HO 1
FLORENCE HO 2
SIDNEY HO 3
ROBERTSON HO 4
MENNIE HO 5
GODWIN HO 6
PANBRO HO 7
SUTHERLAND HO 8
SPRINGWATER CL
BARRINGTON VILLAS
Bwg Gn
Pav
Recn Gd
MELTHORPE GDNS
ZANGWILL RD
4
THELMA GDNS
SHOOTERS HILL RD
EDITH CAVELL WAY
BELL
CAIRNS MEWS
ELIZABETH FRY PL
KENDALL RD
BROOK SQ
BARLOW DR
HOWERD WAY
Tenn Cts
ACADEMY PL
CONSTITUTION RISE
CAMPBELL CL
RED LION PL
69
RAYLEAS CL
SHREWSBURY LA
FOXCROFT RD
CLEANTHUS RD
Recn Gd
THE CHESTNUTS
SHOOTERS HILL
VYVYAN HO
HILL END
145
CLEANTHUS CL
THE LEAS
LINKS VIEW
EAGLESFIELD RD
CORELLI RD
CROSIER CL
GILBERT CL
Tenn Cts
143
Kidbrooke Sch
Castlewood Day Sch
CRAIGHOLM
P
H
Mast
A207
178
Recn Gd
Eltham Common
Memorial
KENILWORTH GDNS
CROWN WOOD LA
BROAD WLK
MAYDAY GDNS
430
438
3
Pav
Cemy
Severndroog Castle
STONEY ALLEY
Green Chain Wlk
Jackwood
Sp Gd
WELL HALL RD
PO
HEATHERBANK
CASTLEWOOD DR
DUNBLANE RD
ALLENSWOOD RD
FLINTMILL CRES
LANGBROOK RD
76
SLADEBROOK RD
IREBROOK RD
SEDGEBROOK RD
CROSSBROOK RD
KELBROOK RD
BOURNBROOK RD
ARBROATH RD
MAUDSLAY RD
MARTIN BOWES RD
ARSENAL RD
GRANBY RD
CORNWALLIS WLK
LITTLECROFT
CROOKSTON RD
CROOKSTON RD
ROSS WAY
2
ENDOVER RD
RYDONS CL
HENWICK RD
PHINEAS PETT RD
FRANKLIN PAS
WHINYATES RD
APPLETON RD
DOWNMAN RD
LOVELACE GN
SHRAPNEL RD
BROME RD
GRANGEHILL PL
GARNETT CL
DAIRSIE RD
Deansfield Prim Sch
GLENBAR CL
GLENDAL CL
GLENHEAD CL
Tenn Cts
WINCHCOMB GDNS
Schs
SHORTWAY
DICKSON RD
125
SE9
A205
260
CONGREVE RD
ROCHESTER WAY
DUMBRECK RD
LYNSTED GDNS
BRISET RD
BRENLEY GDNS
COBBETT RD
A208
PRINCE RUPERT RD
ADMIRAL SEYMOUR RD
MORA RD
GRANGEHILL RD
WESTMOUNT RD
ELIBANK RD
SE9
BERRYHILL
BERRYHILL GDNS
Eltham Park North
KINGSHOLM GDNS
RANCLIFFE GDNS
687
ODEON PAR
TOM COOMBS CL
ELMBROOK GDNS
RICKYARD PATH
TUDOR PAR
PLEASAUNCE CT
CRANGTON RD
Sch
EARLSHALL RD
1
KIDBROOKE LA
591
Sp Gd
Pav
Tenn Cts
Well Hall Pleasaunce
GREENVALE RD
ELTHAM PARK GDNS
GLENESK RD
50
PO
A2
A2
WELL HALL PAR
DUNVEGAN RD
Eltham Park South
75
HORSFELD RD
Bwg Gns
PO
GLENLEA RD
GLENLYON RD
A205
PO
Sch
42
A
Eltham
B
166
43
C
Recn Gd
D
Tenn Cts
44
Green Chain Wlk
HAIMO RD
FROISSART RD
BASKET GDNS
PULLMAN PL
TATTERSALL CL
MILNE GDNS
KEYNSHAM GDNS
BLOXAM GDNS
EVEREST
WELL HALL
STRONGBOW RD
BALCASKIE RD
BEECHHILL RD
GLENHOUSE RD
GLENSHIEL RD
St Mary's RC Prim Sch
CONNIFFE CT
GLENURE RD
Eltham Warren

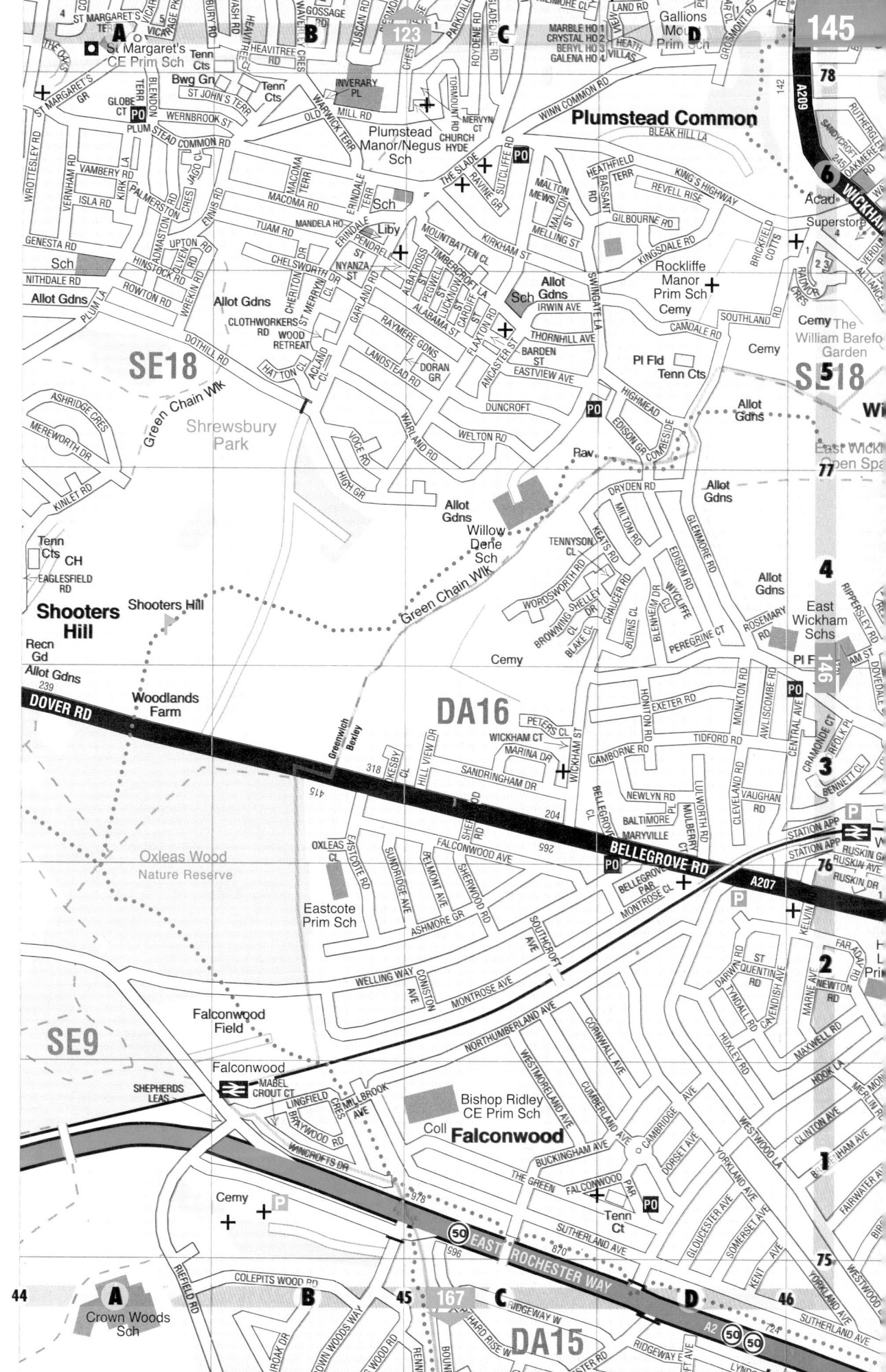

Plumstead Common
Plumstead Manor/Negus Sch
St Margaret's CE Prim Sch
Rockliffe Manor Prim Sch
SE18
Shrewsbury Park
Green Chain Wlk
Willow Dene Sch
Shooters Hill
Woodlands Farm
DOVER RD
DA16
BELLEGROVE RD
A207
East Wickham Schs
Oxleas Wood Nature Reserve
Eastcote Prim Sch
WELLING WAY
Falconwood Field
Falconwood
Bishop Ridley CE Prim Sch
Falconwood
SE9
EAST ROCHESTER WAY
A2
Crown Woods Sch
DA15
WINN COMMON RD
KING'S HIGHWAY
A209
NORTHUMBERLAND AVE
WESTWOOD LA
SUTHERLAND AVE
123
146
167
44
45
46
78
77
76
75

A
B
C
D
124
Bostall Heath
Co-operative Woods
Cottage Hospice
BOSTALL HILL
1 ALEXANDER TERR
2 DIANTHUS CL
HURST PL
DIXON HO
A2041
6 LISTER HO
HURST LA
PRIORY DR
FRIARS WLK
HARVEL CRES
A206
WOOLWICH RD
30
78
A209
Bostall Woods
Pav
Bwg Gn
Green Chain Wlk
MARTYN HO 1
HURST PL 2
SENCLER HO 3
ARRAS HO 4
HEATH VIEW DR 5
PINEWOOD RD 6
BURCHARBRO RD
West Heath
AMBERLEY RD
GLENVIEW
WEST HEATH RD
Bwg Gn
Pav
Recn Gd
HEATH AVE
CANBERRA RD
MARLEY AVE
POWYS CL
LESSNESS AVE
PO
ABBOTT'S WLK
BRAMPTON RD
Common
GLENDOWN RD
BASTION RD
OLD PARK
Allot Gdns
RUTHERGLEN RD
SANDYCROFT
OAKMERE RD
WATER DALE RD
1 SOUTHLAND RD
2 PRESTWOOD CL
3 DOEBURY WLK
4 CRAWFORD CT
Pl Fld
SE2
Goldie Leigh
Bostall Heath
LONGLEIGH LA
6
Acad
Superstore
WICKHAM LA
VERDUN RD
VILLACOURT RD
LITTLEDALE
STREAMDALE
WOODBROOK RD
ALLIANCE RD
GRASDENE RD
BRICKFIELD COTTS
RADNOR CRES
SOUTHLAND RD
BOURNEWOOD RD
PINECROFT
CEMETERY RD
Cemy
The William Barefoot Garden
Cemy
5
SE18
East Wickham
HIGHBANKS CL
PATRICIA CT
Allot Gdns
East Wickham Open Space
Greenwich
Bexley
LODGE HILL
ELMSTED CRES
LANGLEY RD
SANDGATE RD
HARTLEY RD
HADLOW RD
FIRST AVE
MADISON GDNS
LANSDOWNE AVE
DOWNE CL
DENTON RD
KESTON CL
HILLSGROVE CL
Hillsgrove Prim Sch
MADISON CRES
DA7
TOTNES RD
BIDEFORD RD
SIDMOUTH RD
SEATON RD
PLYMSTOCK RD
EXMOUTH RD
BUDLEIGH CRES
OKEHAMPTON CRES
QUADRANT
THE
BRAMPTON LO
77
Allot Gdns
CHALKSTONE CL
ELMFIELD CT
BRAMLEY CT
ST MICHAEL'S RISE
TEVIOT CL
STUART RD
TOR RD
AXMINSTER CRES
BURNS HO
SCOTTS HO
TENBY RD
COLYTON CL
BRIXHAM RD
BOGNOR RD
PRESTON DR
BERKELEY AVE
MAYFAIR AVE
BEAL CL
DARENTH RD
RIDLEY RD
ALICIA HO
BRUCE CL
DOUGLAS RD
LYME RD
CHARMOUTH RD
TAVISTOCK RD
SALTASH RD
Stevens Park
SELSEY CRES
4
Allot Gdns
RIPPERSLEY RD
YEWTREE CL
ANTHONY RD
LINTON CL
KAY ST
UPPER WICKHAM LA
BERWICK RD
Sch
ROSEMARY RD
East Wickham Schs
Welling Sch
WROTHAM RD
PO
TEIGNMOUTH RD
145
Pl Fld
WICKHAM ST
Allot Gdns
DOVEDALE CL
QUEEN'S RD
CHURCH RD
SWANLEY RD
NORMANHURST AVE
MONKTON RD
AWLISCOMBE RD
PO
CENTRAL AVE
MERTON CT
Victoria Bsns Ctr
EAST RD
DA16
FARNHAM RD
ELSA RD
GIPSY RD
WINCHESTER RD
ALEXANDER RD
Brampton Prim Sch
TIDFORD RD
CRAMONDE CT
NORFOLK PL
LOVEL AVE
BURNELL AVE
LEIGH PL
OLYFFE AVE
Dunstall Welling Est
BALLIOL RD
SOMERHILL RD
KENMERE RD
HAZELDENE RD
IVEDON RD
AVONDALE RD
SUTCLIFFE RD
HOLMESDALE RD
3
LULWORTH RD
CLEVELAND RD
VAUGHAN RD
BENNETT CL
Graves Est
Allot Gdns
LYNMERE RD
STEVEDALE RD
FAIRLAWN AVE
Barrington Prim Sch
BARRINGTON RD
P
STATION APP
RACKHAM CL
FOSTERS OLD SCH
NORTHDOWN RD
Welling
Sch
RUSKIN GR
RUSKIN AVE
RUSKIN DR
NEW RD
Foster's Prim Sch
FOX HOLLOW DR
MARLBOROUGH RD
PALMEIRA RD
76
A207
KELVIN RD
DEEPDENE RD
EDMUND RD
COTON RD
SPRINGFIELD RD
ORCHARD RD
CARLTON RD
WESTBROOKE RD
WESTBROOKE CRES
Welling
BULL ALLEY
CLIFTON RD
WARWICK RD
ELLARD CT
LEWIS RD
GRANVILLE RD
BETHEL RD
SOUTH GIPSY RD
Westbrooke Sch
LANGMORE CT 1
GAINSBOROUGH SQ 2
QUEEN ANNE GATE 3
HANOVER WAY
Liby
Hook Lane Prim Sch
FARADAY RD
CHURCHFIELD RD
WELLING HIGH ST
2
ST AUSTIN RD
CAVENDISH AVE
DARWIN RD
TYNDALL RD
MARNE AVE
NEWTON RD
MARWOOD CL
ST JOHN'S RD
ST MICHAEL'S RD
PENPOOL LA
McKINLAY CT
ROSEACRE RD
PARK VIEW RD
PO
PARK VIEW RD
Crook Log L Ctr
CROOK LOG
MAXWELL RD
HUXLEY RD
HOOK LA
MONMOUTH CL
PORTHKERRY AVE
LANCELOT RD
DANSON CRES
SELWYN CRES
PARK APP
Welling F.C Fball Gd
Tenn Cts
DANSON MEAD
Sw Pool
TURNPIKE CT 1
BRUNSWICK CL 2
A221
1 EMBASSY CT
2 NAG'S HEAD LA
3 SCHOOL LA
4 JOHN NEWTON CT
1 MOAT CROFT
2 DENHAM CL
3 SHARNBROOKE CL
4 STUART EVANS CL
Crook Log Prim Sch
DALLIN RD
ROBINA CL
MERLIN RD N
CLINTON AVE
WESTWOOD LA
DANSINGTON RD
DANSON LA
PP
Old English Garden
Bwg Gns
NORTH CL
BALCOMBE CL
THE GROVE
SYDNEY RD
1
YORKLAND AVE
BRADENHAM AVE
Danson Prim Sch
LAKEVIEW RD
FAIRWATER AVE
BIRCH GR
MERLIN RD
Tenn Cts
BEXLEY
Danson House
Danson Park
SOUTH CL
ASKERN CL
BEAN RD
LAUNTON DR
WATER VIEW CL
COBHAM PL
GLOUCESTER AVE
SOMERSET AVE
KENT AVE
75
WENDOVER WAY
COWPER CL
Bexley Gram Sch
Pl Fld
DA6
DANSON RD
IVERHURST CL
46
47
48
168
The Lake
Allot Gdns
YORKLAND AVE
SUTHERLAND AVE
INGLETON AVE
RADNOR AVE
DA16
A2
50
GROOMBRIDGE CL
Allot Gdns
ALERS RD
GREEN VALE

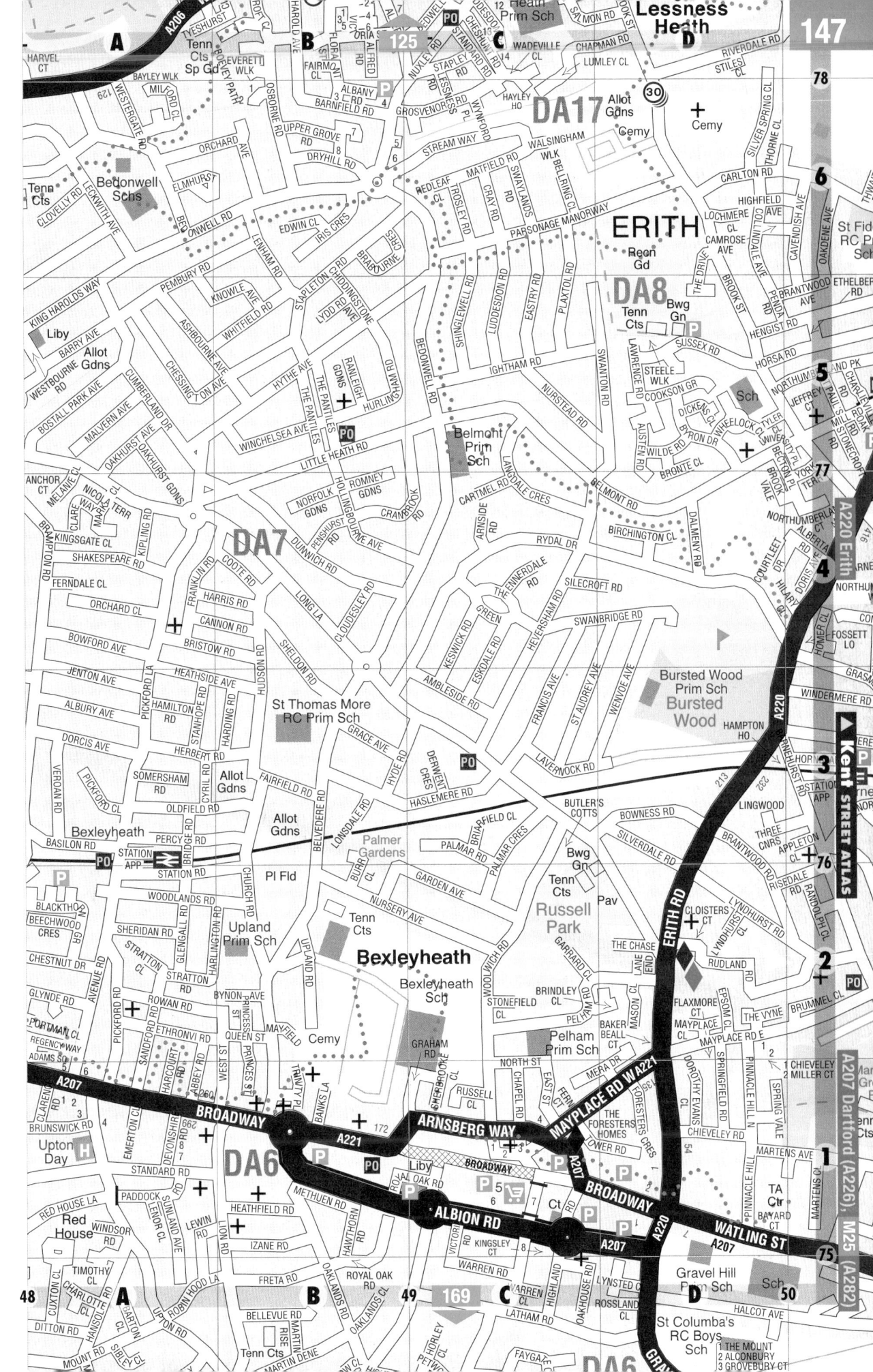

125
Lessness Heath
A
B
C
D
A206
DA17
Allot Gdns
Cemy
ERITH
Recn Gd
DA8
Bwg Gn
Tenn Cts
Bedonwell Schs
Liby
Allot Gdns
Belmont Prim Sch
DA7
St Thomas More RC Prim Sch
Bursted Wood Prim Sch
Bursted Wood
Allot Gdns
Bexleyheath
Palmer Gardens
Pl Fld
Upland Prim Sch
Tenn Cts
Bexleyheath
Bexleyheath Sch
Russell Park
Pav
Pelham Prim Sch
Cemy
DA6
Upton Day
Red House
Gravel Hill Prim Sch
St Columba's RC Boys Sch
A207
BROADWAY
A221
ARNSBERG WAY
ALBION RD
MAYPLACE RD W
WATLING ST
ERITH RD
A220
A220 Erith
Kent STREET ATLAS
A207 Dartford (A226), M25 (A282)
78
6
5
77
4
3
76
2
1
75
48
49
50
169
PARSONAGE MANORWAY
LITTLE HEATH RD
BEDONWELL RD
BELMONT RD
KING HAROLDS WAY
WESTBOURNE RD
BOSTALL PARK AVE
WINCHELSEA AVE
IGHTHAM RD
NURSTEAD RD
SWANTON RD
HEVERSHAM RD
SWANBRIDGE RD
RYDAL DR
LAVERNOCK RD
HASLEMERE RD
BUTLER'S COTTS
BOWNESS RD
SILVERDALE RD
BRANTWOOD RD
NURSERY AVE
GARDEN AVE
PALMAR RD
STATION RD
WOODLANDS RD
SHERIDAN RD
CHESTNUT DR
STANDARD RD
HEATHFIELD RD
IZANE RD
FRETA RD
ROYAL OAK RD
LATHAM RD
HALCOT AVE
1 THE MOUNT
2 ALCONBURY
3 GROVEBURY CT

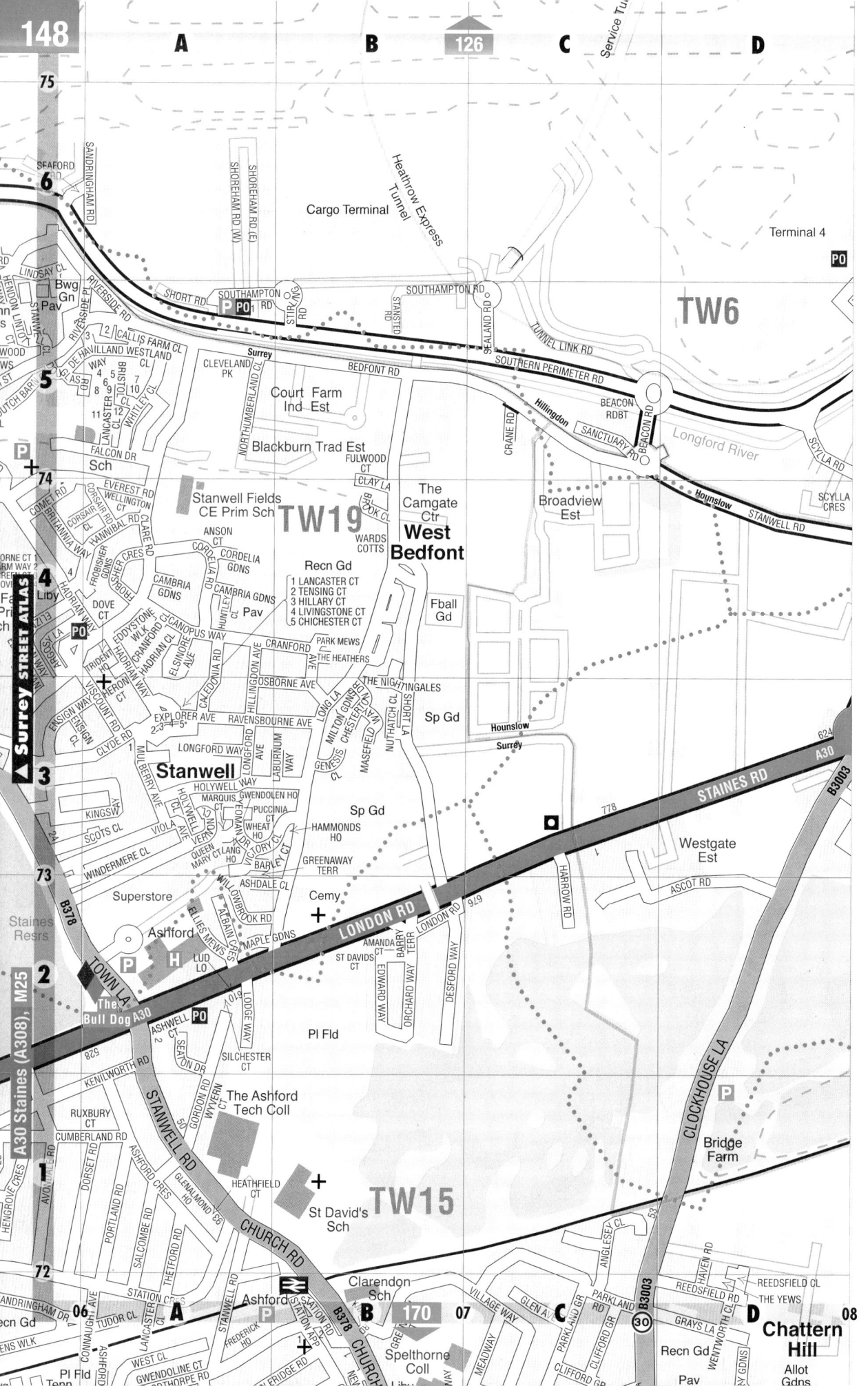

A
B
126
C
D
Cargo Terminal
Heathrow Express Tunnel
Terminal 4
TW6
SOUTHAMPTON RD
SOUTHERN PERIMETER RD
TUNNEL LINK RD
BEDFONT RD
Court Farm Ind Est
Blackburn Trad Est
Stanwell Fields CE Prim Sch
TW19
The Camgate Ctr
West Bedfont
Broadview Est
BEACON RDBT
Longford River
STANWELL RD
Recn Gd
1 LANCASTER CT
2 TENSING CT
3 HILLARY CT
4 LIVINGSTONE CT
5 CHICHESTER CT
Fball Gd
Sp Gd
Stanwell
STAINES RD
A30
Westgate Est
LONDON RD
Superstore
Ashford
Cemy
Staines Resrs
The Bull Dog
Pl Fld
The Ashford Tech Coll
St David's Sch
TW15
CLOCKHOUSE LA
Bridge Farm
STANWELL RD
CHURCH RD
Ashford
Clarendon Sch
Spelthorne Coll
170
Chattern Hill
Recn Gd
A30 Staines (A308), M25
Surrey STREET ATLAS
06
07
08

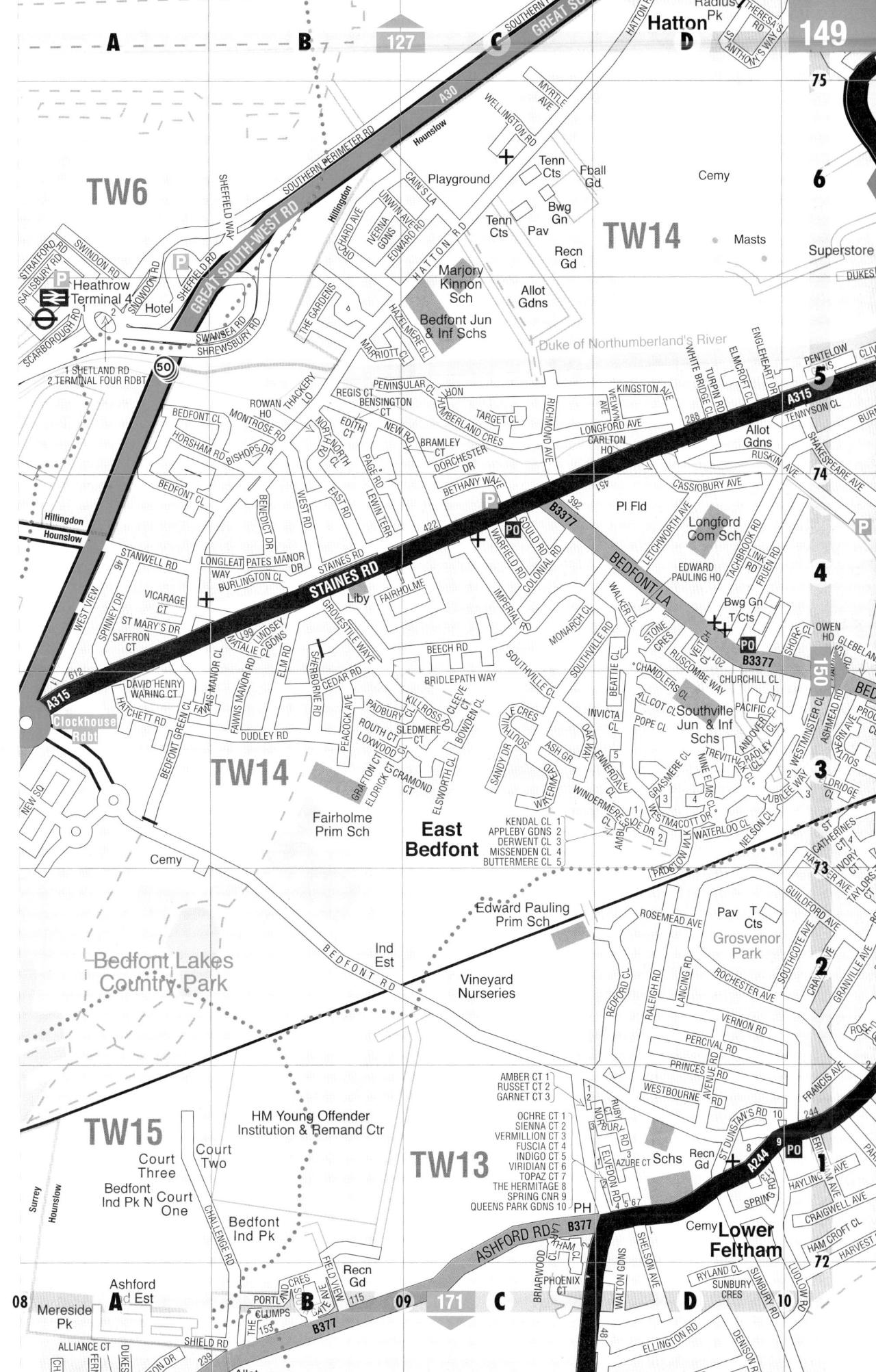
Hatton
TW6
TW14
TW15
TW13
Heathrow Terminal 4
East Bedfont
Lower Feltham
Bedfont Lakes Country Park
HM Young Offender Institution & Remand Ctr
Marjory Kinnon Sch
Bedfont Jun & Inf Schs
Longford Com Sch
Southville Jun & Inf Schs
Fairholme Prim Sch
Edward Pauling Prim Sch
Grosvenor Park
Vineyard Nurseries
Duke of Northumberland's River
GREAT SOUTH-WEST RD
STAINES RD
BEDFONT LA
BEDFONT RD
ASHFORD RD
1 SHETLAND RD
2 TERMINAL FOUR RDBT
KENDAL CL 1
APPLEBY GDNS 2
DERWENT CL 3
MISSENDEN CL 4
BUTTERMERE CL 5
AMBER CT 1
RUSSET CT 2
GARNET CT 3
OCHRE CT 1
SIENNA CT 2
VERMILLION CT 3
FUSCIA CT 4
INDIGO CT 5
VIRIDIAN CT 6
TOPAZ CT 7
THE HERMITAGE 8
SPRING CNR 9
QUEENS PARK GDNS 10
Clockhouse Rdbt
127
150
171

A
B
C
D
128
172
149
75
74
73
72
6
5
4
3
2
1
10
11
12
North Feltham Trad Est
Maple Gr Bsns Ctr
River Gdns Bsns Ctr
Tamian Ind Est
TAMIAN WAY
Allot Gdns
CLEMENTS CT
Central Pk Est
CARDINGTON SQ
HATTON GN
HERON WAY
A312
SPUR RD
BOROUGH WAY
Allot Gdns
Haslemere Ind Est
Freehold Ind Ctr
AMBERLEY WAY
Fairway Est
FAIRWAY CL
ISLAY GDNS
A315
ARMADALE RD
DELLBOW RD
PIER RD
SPACE WAYE
Dockwell's Ind Est
North Feltham
Garden Ctr
FAIRWAY CL
Cemy
FAGG'S RD
CHALMERS WAY
CENTRAL WAY
FALCON WAY
Willow Ho
RIVER GDNS
Mercury Ctr
Masts
Superstore
Duke of Northumberland's River
ROMAN CL
STAINES RD
CH
DUKES GREEN AVE
MILL WAY
BABER BRIDGE PAR
BABER BRIDGE
Griffin Ctr
THE VALE
A244
Hounslow Heath
River
ENGLEHEART DR
PENTELOW GDNS
CLIVE RD
MINIMAX CL
BYWARD AVE
BEESTON WAY
LANSBURY AVE
GARDNER PL
BABER DR
TURPIN RD
CHANDLER CT
PO
Allot Gdns
London Loop
A315
TENNYSON CL
BURNS AVE
ROSSLYN AVE
BUCKINGHAM AVE
BECKETTS CL
LAVENDER CT
FIELD RD
VIOLA AVE
Allot Gdns
Allot Gdns
RUSKIN AVE
Pl Fld
SHAKESPEARE AVE
SHAFTESBURY AVE
GLADSTONE AVE
HARLINGTON RD W
CARLTON AVE
Longford Com Sch
TACHBROOK RD
LINK WAY
FRUEN RD
1 FRANK TOWELL CT
2 BRASSEY CL
3 EASTLEIGH WAY
4 ORCHARD RD
5 PEACH RD
6 ALMOND CL
7 HAZEL GR
8 HUNTER HO
9 HAWTHORN RD
10 TILLEY RD
11 PLUM CL
12 ARCHER CT
13 MAGNOLIA CT
14 LEMON GR
15 BELVEDERE HO
16 QUINCE HO
17 CAMELLIA HO
THE DELL
MALSHAM RD
CHICHESTER WAY
DENHAM RD
FAREHAM RD
SPARROW FARM DR
HELEN AVE
CLYMPING DENE
HOUNSLOW RD
THE DRIVE
Sparrow Farm Schs
TW14
T Cts
Bwg Gn
Pl Fld
Feltham Arena
CAMBRIA CT
BRAINTON AVE
CENTRAL PAR
FINCH DR
CYGNET AVE
Bwg Gn
T Cts
OWEN HO
SHORE CL
NURSERY CL
FERN GR
PARK WAY
DURHAM RD
Pl Fld
GLEBELANDS RD
HAWKES RD
STATION PAR
STATION ESTATE RD
1 BERGENIA HO
2 AZALEA HO
3 HAMLYN HO
HARLINGTON RD E
NORFOLK RD
B377
BEDFONT LA
LOCOMOTIVE DR
MANOR PL
FELBRIDGE CT
NEW RD
Feltham
QUEEN'S RD
GLOUCESTER RD
HEREFORD RD
Tenn Cts
PACIFIC CL
ANDOVER CL
BRADLEY CL
WESTMINSTER CL
ASHMEAD RD
SOUTHERN AVE
PROCTORS CL
TYNAN CL
SANDYCOMBE RD
SYDNEY RD
LC
B3377
BEAUCLERK CL
CROMWELL RD
KINGS RD
SALISBURY RD
BOUNDARIES RD
Schs
TREVITHICK CL
NINE ELMS CL
JUBILEE WAY
ELDRIDGE CL
RAILWAY TERR
HANWORTH RD
LEIGH PL
Ct
Sch
CARDINAL RD
FLORENCE RD
BROOME RD
WYATT CL
Tenn Cts
WIGLEY RD
WATERLOO CL
NELSON CL
ST CATHERINES CT
The Centre
Liby
NEW CHAPEL SQ
ASHFIELD AVE
CAMDEN AVE
B3377
SLATTERY RD
ELTHORNE CT
WESTBURY
HANOVER AVE
IVORY CT
TAYLORS CT
HIGHFIELD RD
BOWSLEY CT
VICTORIA RD
Victoria Jun Sch
DANESBURY RD
ALFRED RD
LAFONE AVE
WIGLEY RD
AMESBURY RD
Pav
T Cts
Grosvenor Park
GUILDFORD AVE
WILTON PAR
THE GREEN
1 BROOKLYN CT
2 DEVONSHIRE CT
Sch
ASTRID HO
BROWELLS LA
MARLBOROUGH RD
EASTBOURNE
Superstore
AIR PARK WAY
Feltham Com Sch
UXBRIDGE RD
SOUTHCOTE AVE
CRAVAN AVE
GRANVILLE AVE
BROWELLS LA
Feltham Bsns Complex
ROCHESTER AVE
MANOR LA
MOSS GDNS
HIGH ST
CAVENDISH TERR
FELTHAM
Tenn Cts
A312
VERNON RD
PERCIVAL RD
1 PARKFIELD PAR
2 ROCHESTER PAR
3 THE VINEYARDS
4 CHERVIL CL
Tenn Cts
L Ctr
AVENUE RD
FRANCIS AVE
VINEYARD
ORDNANCE CL
Ind Est
MAPLE WAY
Sp Gd
FOREST RD
CHARLESTON CL
TAWNY CL
ELMWOOD AVE
ELMWOOD HO
OLAF PALME HO
SANDALWOOD RD
Feltham Corporate Ctr
Hanworth Park House
ST DUNSTAN'S RD
PARKFIELD RD
PARKFIELD AVE
POPLAR WAY
PINEWOOD RD
Hanworth Park
Pav
A314
A244
PO
PLANE TREE CRES
Felthambrook Ind Est
ASPEN WAY
CHESTNUT WAY
ROOKERIES CL
TW13
SPRING RD
HAYLING AVE
ERINGHAM AVE
PARKFIELD CRES
Lower Feltham
CRAIGWELL AVE
APRIL CL
SYCAMORE CL
BADGER CL
TANGLEWOOD WAY
CLIFTON AVE
HOUNSLOW RD
HAM CROFT CL
HARVEST RD
BROOKSIDE CL
FOXWOOD CL
Allot Gdns
ELMGATE AVE
PINKCOAT CL
CAMROSE AVE
Pav
RYLAND CL
SUNBURY CRES
SUNBURY RD
LUDLOW RD
DEERHURST CL
ROEBUCK CL
HUNTSMAN CL
CLIFTON PAR
RECTORY CT
1 BLAKEWOOD CL
2 SHAKESPEARE WAY
THE HOLLANDS
COTTINGTON RD
PARR CT
TUDOR HO
TUDOR CT
Hanworth
DENISON RD
SEYMOUR GDNS
ELIZABETH
CASTLE
Bwg Gn
T Cts

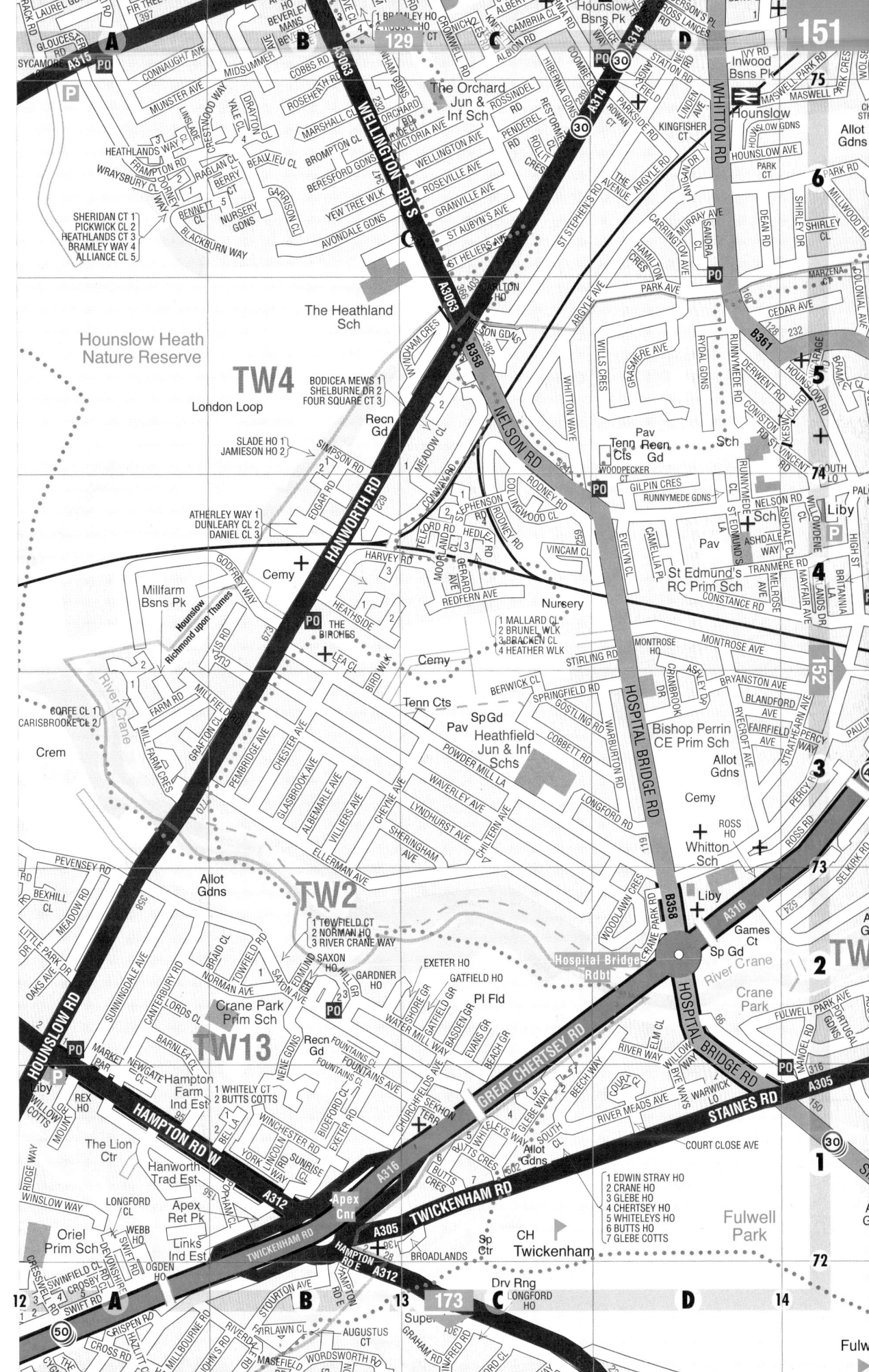
151
A
B
C
D
129
173
152
Hounslow Bsns Pk
Inwood Bsns Pk
Hounslow
Allot Gdns
The Orchard Jun & Inf Sch
The Heathland Sch
Hounslow Heath Nature Reserve
TW4
London Loop
Recn Gd
Tenn Cts
Pav
Recn Gd
Sch
Liby
St Edmund's RC Prim Sch
Millfarm Bsns Pk
Hounslow
Richmond upon Thames
Cemy
THE BIRCHES
Nursery
Cemy
Tenn Cts
Pav
Sp Gd
Heathfield Jun & Inf Schs
Bishop Perrin CE Prim Sch
Allot Gdns
Cemy
Whitton Sch
River Crane
Crem
Allot Gdns
TW2
Liby
Games Ct
Sp Gd
Crane Park
Hospital Bridge Rdbt
Crane Park Prim Sch
TW13
Recn Gd
Pl Fld
Hampton Farm Ind Est
The Lion Ctr
Hanworth Trad Est
Apex Ret Pk
Links Ind Est
Apex Cnr
Oriel Prim Sch
Sp Ctr
CH Twickenham
Drv Rng
Fulwell Park
Allot Gdns
WELLINGTON RD S
HANWORTH RD
NELSON RD
HOSPITAL BRIDGE RD
WHITTON RD
HOUNSLOW RD
HAMPTON RD W
GREAT CHERTSEY RD
TWICKENHAM RD
STAINES RD
HAMPTON RD E
A315
A3063
A314
B358
B361
A316
A312
A305
SHERIDAN CT 1
PICKWICK CL 2
HEATHLANDS CT 3
BRAMLEY WAY 4
ALLIANCE CL 5
BODICEA MEWS 1
SHELBURNE DR 2
FOUR SQUARE CT 3
SLADE HO 1
JAMIESON HO 2
ATHERLEY WAY 1
DUNLEARY CL 2
DANIEL CL 3
1 MALLARD CL
2 BRUNEL WLK
3 BRACKEN CL
4 HEATHER WLK
CORFE CL 1
CARISBROOKE CL 2
1 TOWFIELD CT
2 NORMAN HO
3 RIVER CRANE WAY
1 WHITELY CT
2 BUTTS COTTS
1 EDWIN STRAY HO
2 CRANE HO
3 GLEBE HO
4 CHERTSEY HO
5 WHITELEYS HO
6 BUTTS HO
7 GLEBE COTTS
75
74
73
72
6
5
4
3
2
1
12
13
14

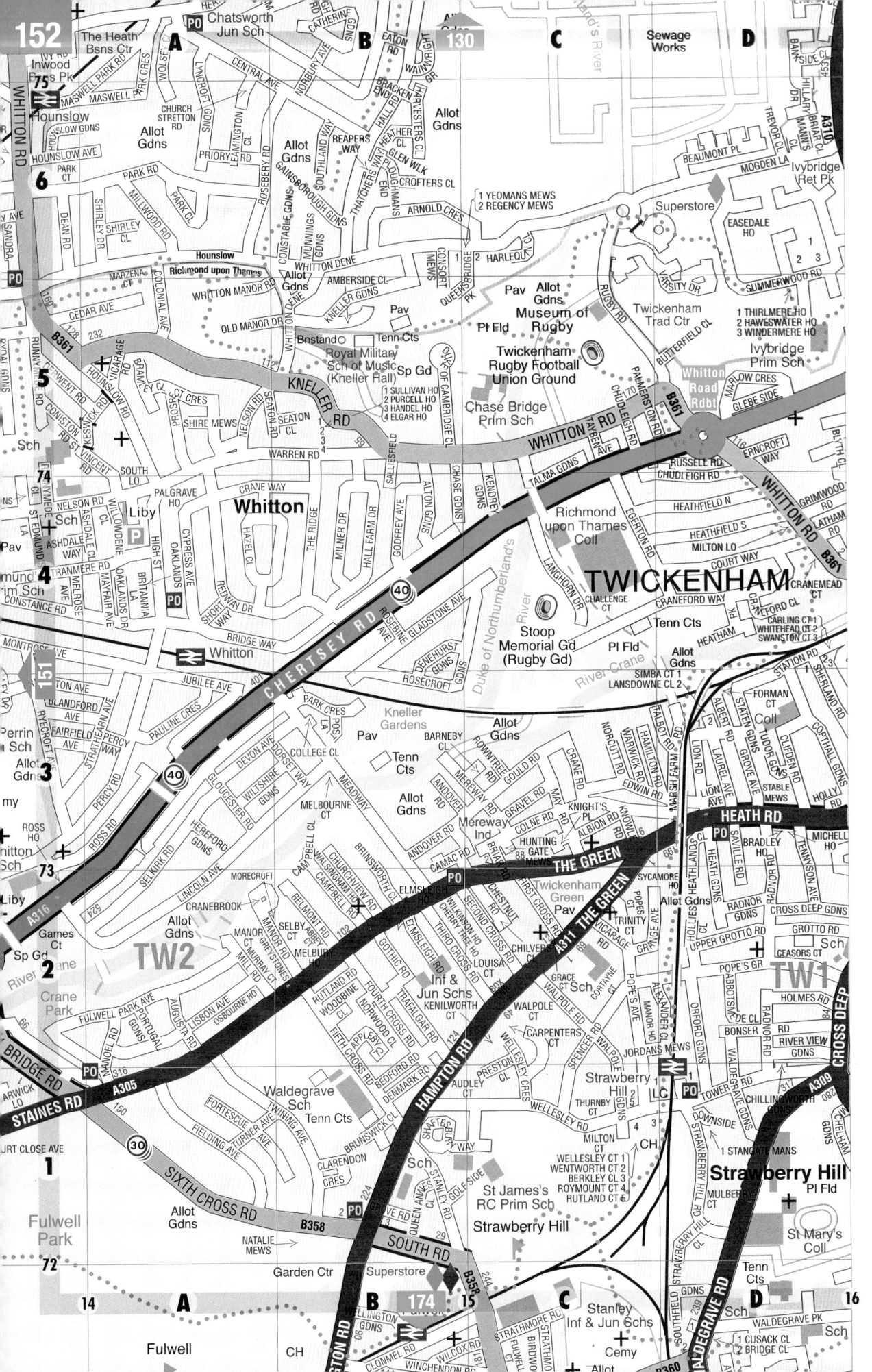

130
A
B
C
D
Chatsworth Jun Sch
The Heath Bsns Ctr
Inwood Bsns Pk
Hounslow
Sewage Works
Allot Gdns
WHITTON RD
MASWELL PARK RD
CENTRAL AVE
NORBURY AVE
CATHERINE GDNS
EATON RD
WAINWRIGHT GR
BRACKEN END
HALL RD
HARVESTERS CL
HEATHER CL
REAPERS WAY
SOUTHLAND WAY
GLEN WLK
PLOUGHMANS END
CROFTERS CL
THATCHERS WAY
GAINSBOROUGH GDNS
CONSTABLE GDNS
MUNNINGS GDNS
CHURCH STRETTON RD
LYNCROFT GDNS
LEAMINGTON CL
PRIORY RD
ROSEBERY RD
HOUNSLOW GDNS
HOUNSLOW AVE
PARK CT
PARK RD
MILLWOOD RD
PARK CL
SHIRLEY DR
SHIRLEY CL
DEAN RD
BEAUMONT PL
MOGDEN LA
Ivybridge Ret Pk
Superstore
EASEDALE HO
SUMMERWOOD RD
BANKSIDE CL
HILLARY DR
BRIAR CL
MANN'S CL
TREVOR CL
A310
1 YEOMANS MEWS
2 REGENCY MEWS
ARNOLD CRES
HARLEQUIN CL
CONSORT MEWS
QUEENSBRIDGE PK
WHITTON DENE
AMBERSIDE CL
KNELLER GDNS
Hounslow
Richmond upon Thames
MARZENA CT
WHITTON MANOR RD
COLONIAL AVE
CEDAR AVE
OLD MANOR DR
Pav
Museum of Rugby
Pl Fld
Twickenham Rugby Football Union Ground
Tenn Cts
Bnstand
Royal Military Sch of Music (Kneller Hall)
Sp Gd
DUKE OF CAMBRIDGE CL
1 SULLIVAN HO
2 PURCELL HO
3 HANDEL HO
4 ELGAR HO
Chase Bridge Prim Sch
RUGBY RD
VARSITY DR
Twickenham Trad Ctr
BUTTERFIELD CL
1 THIRLMERE HO
2 HAWESWATER HO
3 WINDERMERE HO
Ivybridge Prim Sch
Whitton Road Rdbt
MARLOW CRES
GLEBE SIDE
PALMERSTON RD
CHUDLEIGH RD
TAYBEN AVE
B361
KNELLER RD
WHITTON RD
HOUNSLOW RD
VICARAGE RD
BRAMLEY CL
PROSPECT CRES
SHIRE MEWS
NELSON RD
SEATON RD
SEATON CL
WARREN RD
SALLIESFIELD
CHASE GDNS
ALTON GDNS
KENDREY GDNS
TALMA GDNS
RUSSELL RD
CHUDLEIGH RD
ERNCROFT WAY
BLYTH CL
GRIMWOOD RD
LATHAM CL
HEATHFIELD N
HEATHFIELD S
MILTON LO
COURT WAY
CRANEMEAD CT
RUNNYMEDE RD
DERWENT RD
CONISTON RD
KESWICK AVE
ST VINCENT RD
SOUTH LO
PALGRAVE HO
CRANE WAY
Whitton
THE RIDGE
MILNER DR
HALL FARM DR
GODFREY AVE
HAZEL CL
Sch
Liby
NELSON RD
ASHDALE CL
WILLOWDENE CL
ASHDALE WAY
HIGH ST
OAKLANDS
CYPRESS AVE
ST EDMUND'S LA
TRANMERE RD
MELROSE AVE
MAYFAIR AVE
OAKLANDS DR
BRITANNIA LA
CONSTANCE RD
REDWAY DR
SHORT WAY
Richmond upon Thames Coll
TWICKENHAM
LANGHORN DR
CHALLENGE CT
CRANEFORD WAY
Tenn Cts
Pl Fld
HEATHAM PK
CRANEFORD CL
CARLING CT 1
WHITEHEAD CT 2
SWANSTON CT 3
Stoop Memorial Gd (Rugby Gd)
Duke of Northumberland's River
CHERTSEY RD
40
ROSEBINE AVE
GLADSTONE AVE
DENEHURST GDNS
ROSECROFT GDNS
BRIDGE WAY
Whitton
MONTROSE AVE
151
JUBILEE AVE
PAULINE CRES
BLANDFORD AVE
FAIRFIELD AVE
STRATHEARN AVE
PERCY WAY
RYECROFT AVE
Perrin Sch
PARK CRES
POST LA
COLLEGE CL
DEVON AVE
DORSET WAY
WILTSHIRE GDNS
GLOUCESTER RD
Kneller Gardens
River Crane
Allot Gdns
SIMBA CT 1
LANSDOWNE CL 2
STATION RD
SHERLAND RD
FORMAN CT
Coll
ALBERT RD
STATEN GDNS
TUDOR GDNS
CLIFDEN RD
COPTHALL GDNS
BARNEBY CL
ROWNTREE RD
GOULD RD
MEREWAY RD
ANDOVER RD
GRAVEL RD
CRANE RD
MAY RD
NORCUTT RD
WARWICK RD
HAMILTON RD
EDWIN RD
TALBOT RD
MARSH FARM RD
LION RD
LION AVE
LAUREL AVE
GROVE AVE
STABLE MEWS
HOLLY RD
PERCY RD
ROSS RD
ROSS HO
MEADWAY
MELBOURNE CT
HEREFORD GDNS
KNIGHT'S PL
ALBION RD
KNOWLE RD
COLNE RD
HUNTING GATE MEWS
Mereway Ind
BRIAR RD
CAMAC RD
HEATH RD
SAVILLE RD
BRADLEY HO
MICHELL HO
TENNYSON AVE
Whitton Sch
Liby
A316
SELKIRK RD
LINCOLN AVE
MORECROFT
CRANEBROOK
CAMPBELL CL
CHURCHVIEW RD
WALSINGHAM HO
CAMPBELL RD
BRINSWORTH CL
ELMSLEIGH HO
THE GREEN
Twickenham Green
SYCAMORE HO
HEATHLANDS CL
HEATH GDNS
RADNOR GDNS
CROSS DEEP GDNS
Games Ct
Sp Gd
River Crane
Crane Park
TW2
MANOR CT
GREYSTONES
MURRAY CT
MILL RD
MANOR RD
SELBY CT
ABBEY CT
BELMONT RD
MELBURY HO
GOTHIC RD
ELMSLEIGH RD
WILKINSON HO
CHERRY TREE HO
SECOND CROSS RD
THIRD CROSS RD
CHESTNUT RD
FIRST CROSS RD
POPES CT
TRINITY CT
GRANGE AVE
VICARAGE RD
A311 THE GREEN
CHILVERS CL
LOUISA CT
HOLLIES CL
UPPER GROTTO RD
GROTTO RD
CEASORS CT
POPE'S GR
TW1
FULWELL PARK AVE
PORTUGAL GDNS
AUGUSTA RD
LISBON AVE
OSBOURNE HO
RUTLAND RD
WOODBINE CL
FOURTH CROSS RD
NORWOOD CL
TRAFALGAR RD
Inf & Jun Schs
KENILWORTH CT
GRACE CT
Sch
CORTAYNE CT
WALPOLE RD
WALPOLE CT
POPE'S AVE
MANOR HO
ALEXANDER CL
ABBOTSMEDE CL
HOLMES RD
RADNOR RD
BONSER RD
RIVER VIEW GDNS
CROSS DEEP
BRIDGE RD
STAINES RD
A305
WARWICK LO
MANOEL RD
FIFTH CROSS RD
APPLEBY CL
BEDFORD RD
DENMARK RD
HAMPTON RD
AUDLEY CT
PRESTON CL
WELLESLEY CRES
CARPENTERS CT
SPENCER RD
WALPOLE GDNS
JORDANS MEWS
Strawberry Hill
THURNBY CT
WELLESLEY RD
LC
TOWER RD
WALDEGRAVE GDNS
CHILLINGWORTH GDNS
A309
CHELMSFORD
Waldegrave Sch
Tenn Cts
FORTESCUE AVE
TURNER AVE
TWINING AVE
FIELDING AVE
BRUNSWICK CL
SHAFTESBURY WAY
MILTON CT
WELLESLEY CT 1
WENTWORTH CT 2
BERKLEY CL 3
ROYMOUNT CT 4
RUTLAND CT 5
CH
DOWNSIDE
1 STANGATE MANS
COURT CLOSE AVE
30
SIXTH CROSS RD
CLARENDON CRES
Sch
QUEEN ANNES CL
STANLEY RD
GOLFSIDE
St James's RC Prim Sch
Strawberry Hill
STRAWBERRY HILL RD
STRAWBERRY HILL CL
MULBERRY CT
Pl Fld
St Mary's Coll
Fulwell Park
Allot Gdns
B358
GROVE RD
NATALIE MEWS
SOUTH RD
Garden Ctr
Superstore
Tenn Cts
14
A
B
174
15
C
D
16
Stanley Inf & Jun Schs
Cemy
WALDEGRAVE PK
1 CUSACK CL
2 BRIDGE CL
WALDEGRAVE RD
SOUTHFIELD GDNS
Sch
Fulwell
CH
WELLINGTON GDNS
CLONMEL RD
WILCOX RD
WINCHENDON RD
STRATHMORE RD
FULWELL RD
BIRDWOOD
B360
1
2
3
4
5
6
72
73
74
75

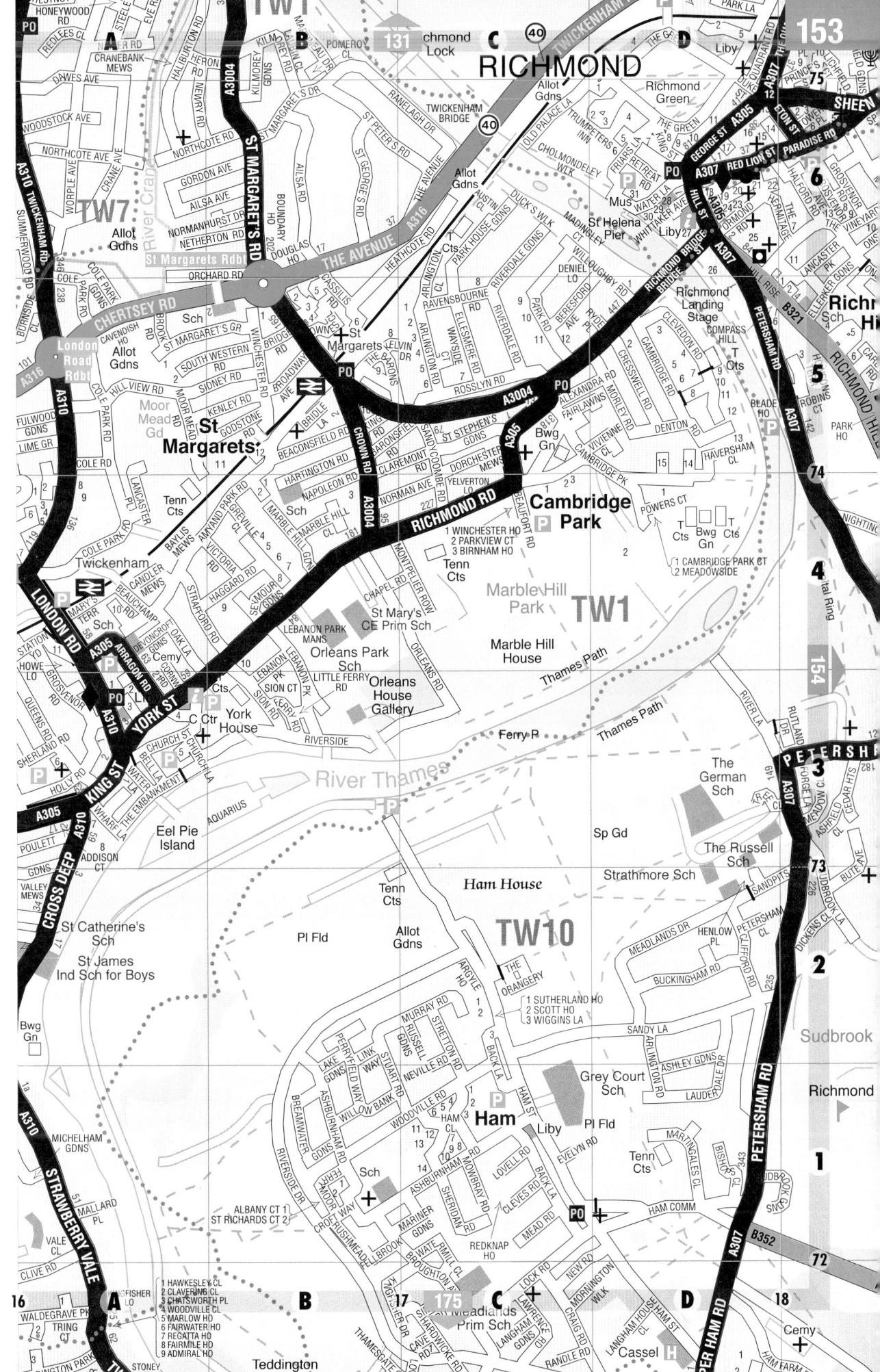
RICHMOND
TW7
TW1
TW10
St Margarets
Twickenham
Cambridge Park
Marble Hill Park
Marble Hill House
Ham House
Ham
River Thames
Eel Pie Island
Richmond Lock
Twickenham Bridge
St Helena Pier
Richmond Landing Stage
Orleans House Gallery
York House
St Mary's CE Prim Sch
Orleans Park Sch
St Catherine's Sch
St James Ind Sch for Boys
The German Sch
The Russell Sch
Strathmore Sch
Grey Court Sch
Meadlands Prim Sch
Sudbrook
Teddington
Cassel
131
154
175

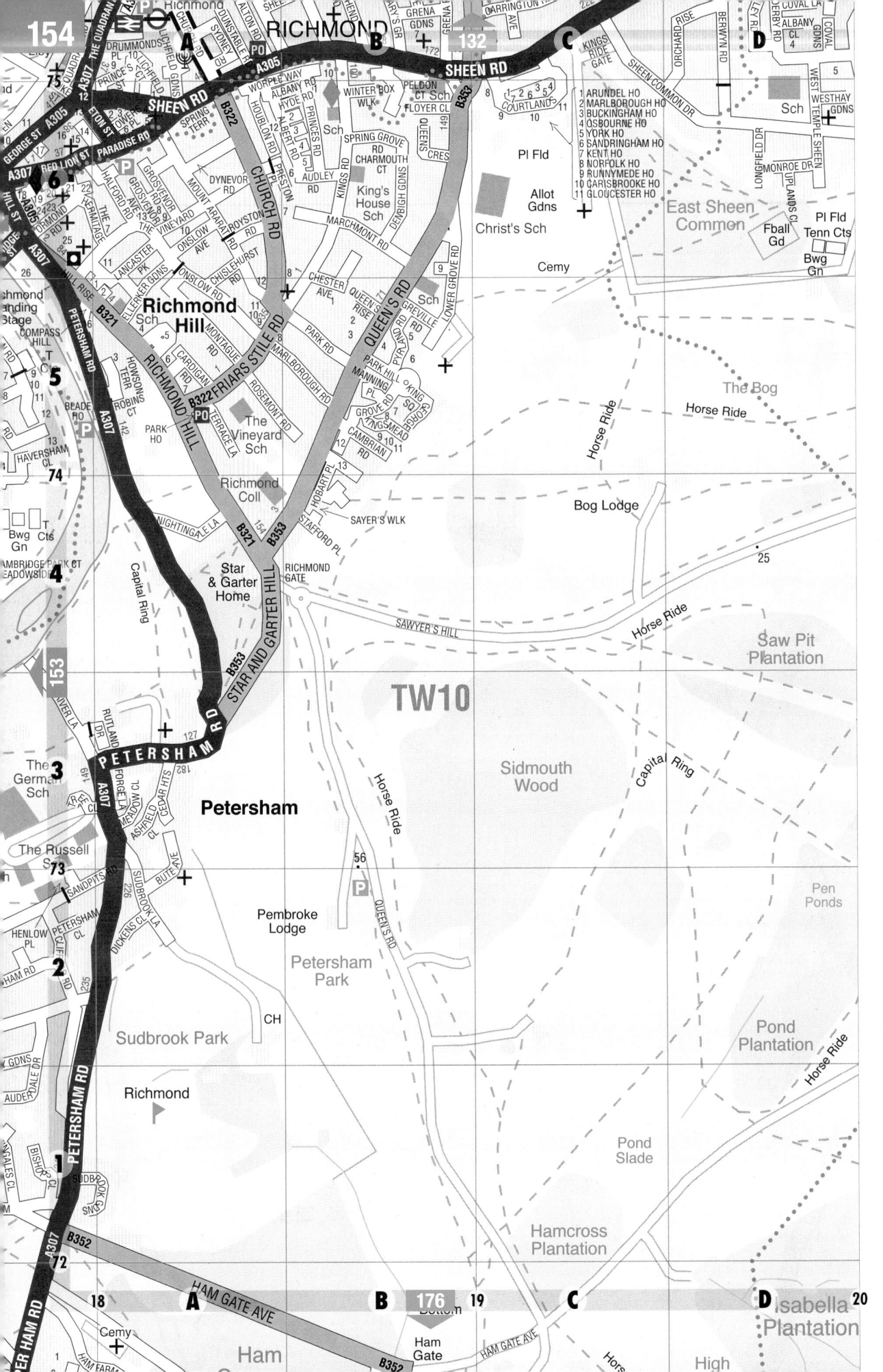
RICHMOND
132
SHEEN RD
A305
A307
B322
B353
B321
CHURCH RD
QUEEN'S RD
FRIARS STILE RD
RICHMOND HILL
PETERSHAM RD
STAR AND GARTER HILL
SHEEN COMMON DR
KINGS RIDE GATE
1 ARUNDEL HO
2 MARLBOROUGH HO
3 BUCKINGHAM HO
4 OSBOURNE HO
5 YORK HO
6 SANDRINGHAM HO
7 KENT HO
8 NORFOLK HO
9 RUNNYMEDE HO
10 CARISBROOKE HO
11 GLOUCESTER HO
Pl Fld
Allot Gdns
Christ's Sch
Cemy
East Sheen Common
Fball Gd
Tenn Cts
Bwg Gn
King's House Sch
Richmond Hill
The Vineyard Sch
Richmond Coll
Star & Garter Home
RICHMOND GATE
SAWYER'S HILL
Bog Lodge
The Bog
Horse Ride
Capital Ring
Saw Pit Plantation
TW10
Sidmouth Wood
Petersham
The German Sch
The Russell Sch
Pembroke Lodge
Petersham Park
Sudbrook Park
CH
Richmond
Pen Ponds
Pond Plantation
Pond Slade
Hamcross Plantation
Isabella Plantation
HAM GATE AVE
B352
176
Ham Gate
Ham
Cemy
153
18
19
20
A
B
C
D
1
2
3
4
5
6

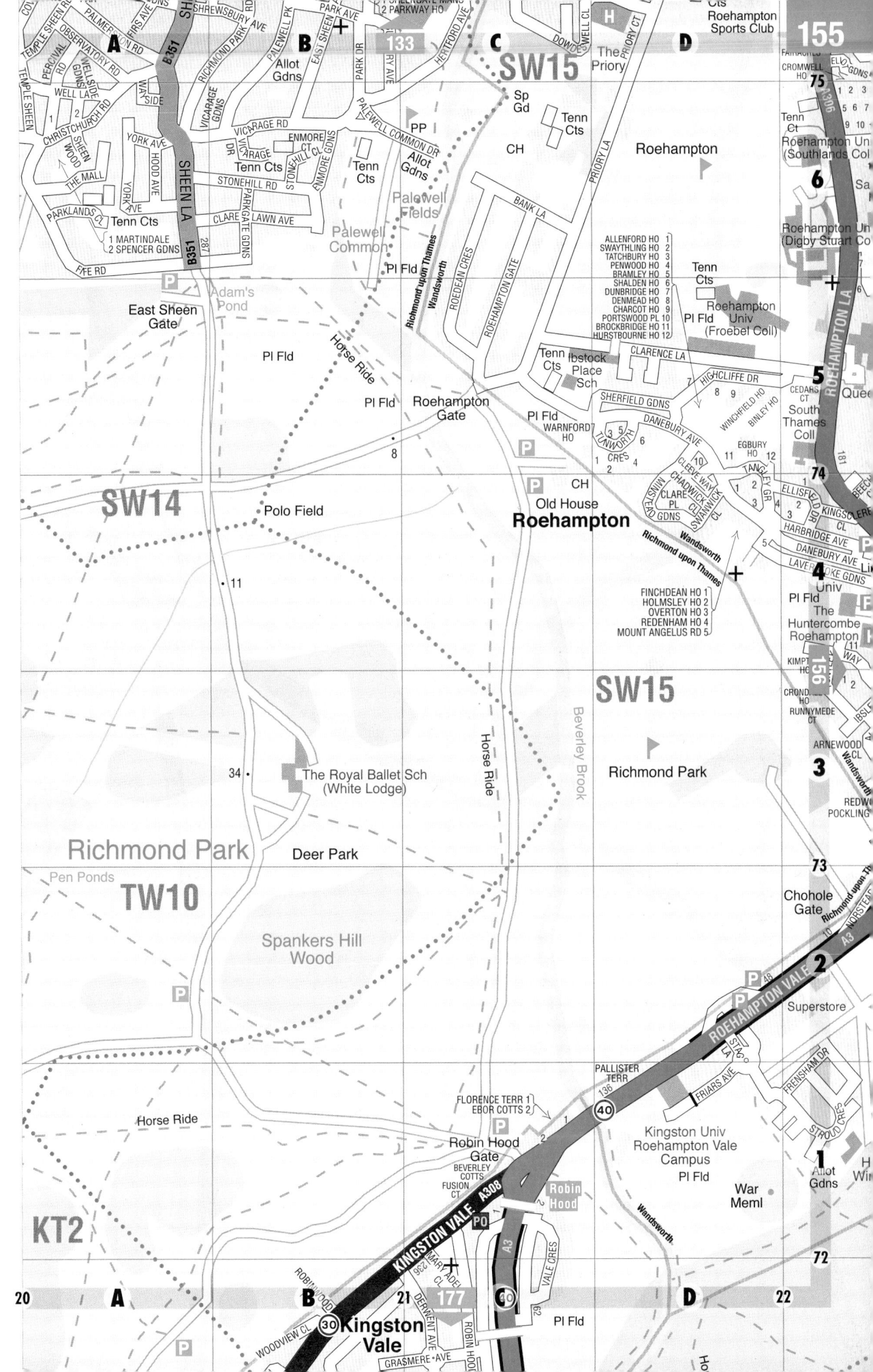
SW15
The Priory
Roehampton Sports Club
Roehampton
SW14
Polo Field
Roehampton Gate
East Sheen Gate
Adam's Pond
Palewell Common
Palewell Fields
Old House
Roehampton
The Royal Ballet Sch (White Lodge)
Richmond Park
Deer Park
Pen Ponds
TW10
Spankers Hill Wood
Beverley Brook
Horse Ride
Robin Hood Gate
Kingston Univ Roehampton Vale Campus
War Meml
Superstore
Chohole Gate
Roehampton Univ (Froebel Coll)
Ibstock Place Sch
South Thames Coll
The Huntercombe Roehampton
KT2
Kingston Vale
KINGSTON VALE
ROEHAMPTON VALE
ROEHAMPTON LA
SHEEN LA
Richmond upon Thames
Wandsworth
ALLENFORD HO 1
SWAYTHLING HO 2
TATCHBURY HO 3
PENWOOD HO 4
BRAMLEY HO 5
SHALDEN HO 6
DUNBRIDGE HO 7
DENMEAD HO 8
CHARCOT HO 9
PORTSWOOD PL 10
BROCKBRIDGE HO 11
HURSTBOURNE HO 12
FINCHDEAN HO 1
HOLMSLEY HO 2
OVERTON HO 3
REDENHAM HO 4
MOUNT ANGELUS RD 5
1 MARTINDALE
2 SPENCER GDNS
FLORENCE TERR 1
EBOR COTTS 2
20
21
22
133
156
177

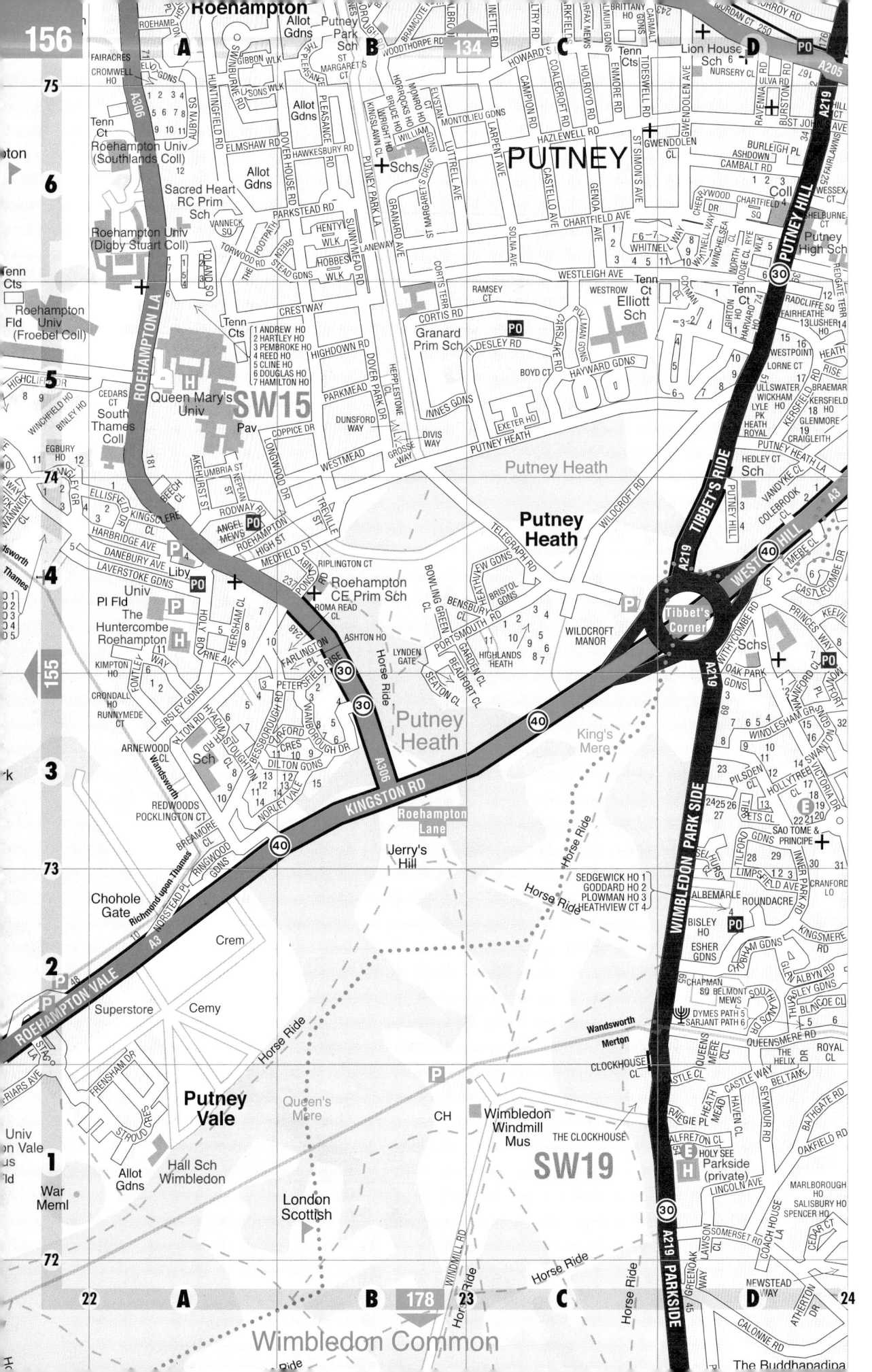
Roehampton
Allot Gdns
Putney Park Sch
134
A
B
C
D
75
6
5
74
4
3
73
2
1
72
PUTNEY
SW15
Putney Heath
Queen Mary's Univ
Roehampton Univ (Southlands Coll)
Roehampton Univ (Digby Stuart Coll)
Roehampton Univ (Froebel Coll)
Sacred Heart RC Prim Sch
Granard Prim Sch
Elliott Sch
Putney High Sch
Roehampton CE Prim Sch
The Huntercombe Roehampton
Tibbet's Corner
TIBBET'S RIDE
PUTNEY HILL
WEST HILL
WIMBLEDON PARK SIDE
PARKSIDE
KINGSTON RD
ROEHAMPTON LA
ROEHAMPTON VALE
Roehampton Lane
Jerry's Hill
King's Mere
Queen's Mere
Chohole Gate
Crem
Cemy
Superstore
Putney Vale
Hall Sch Wimbledon
Wimbledon Windmill Mus
London Scottish
SW19
Parkside (private)
Horse Ride
Wandsworth
Merton
Richmond upon Thames
155
22
23
24
178
Wimbledon Common
The Buddhapadipa

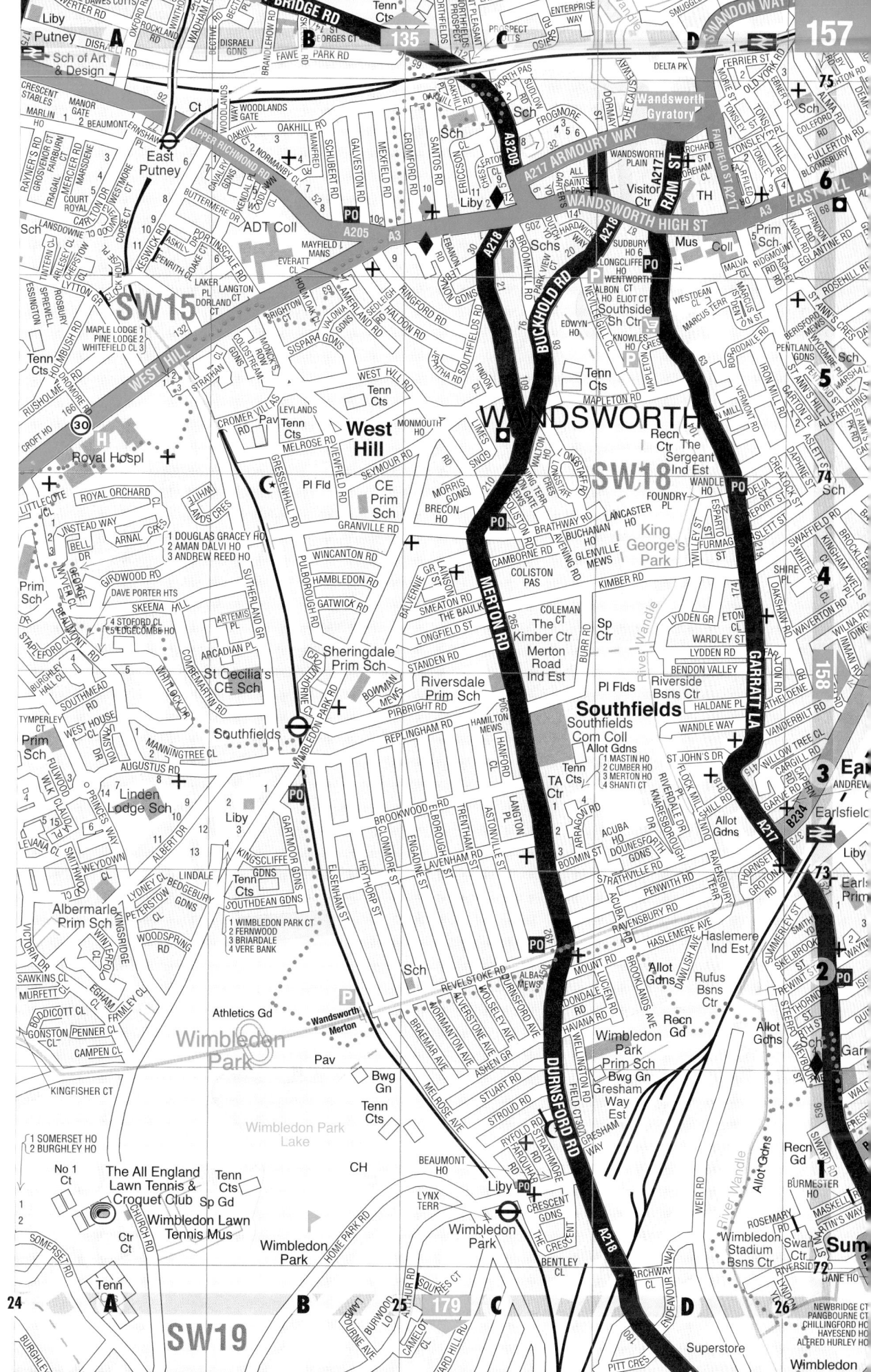

135
158
179
Putney
East Putney
SW15
West Hill
Royal Hospl
WANDSWORTH
SW18
Wandsworth Gyratory
WANDSWORTH HIGH ST
A217 ARMOURY WAY
UPPER RICHMOND RD
WEST HILL
BUCKHOLD RD
MERTON RD
GARRATT LA
DURNSFORD RD
WIMBLEDON PARK RD
Southside Sh Ctr
King George's Park
Southfields
Southfields Com Coll
Sheringdale Prim Sch
Riversdale Prim Sch
St Cecilia's CE Sch
Linden Lodge Sch
Albermarle Prim Sch
Wimbledon Park
Wimbledon Park Lake
Wimbledon Park Prim Sch
Athletics Gd
The All England Lawn Tennis & Croquet Club
Wimbledon Lawn Tennis Mus
Earlsfield
River Wandle
Haslemere Ind Est
Rufus Bsns Ctr
Gresham Way Est
Wimbledon Stadium Bsns Ctr
Riverside Bsns Ctr
Merton Road Ind Est
The Kimber Ctr
The Sergeant Ind Est
SW19
Superstore
Wimbledon

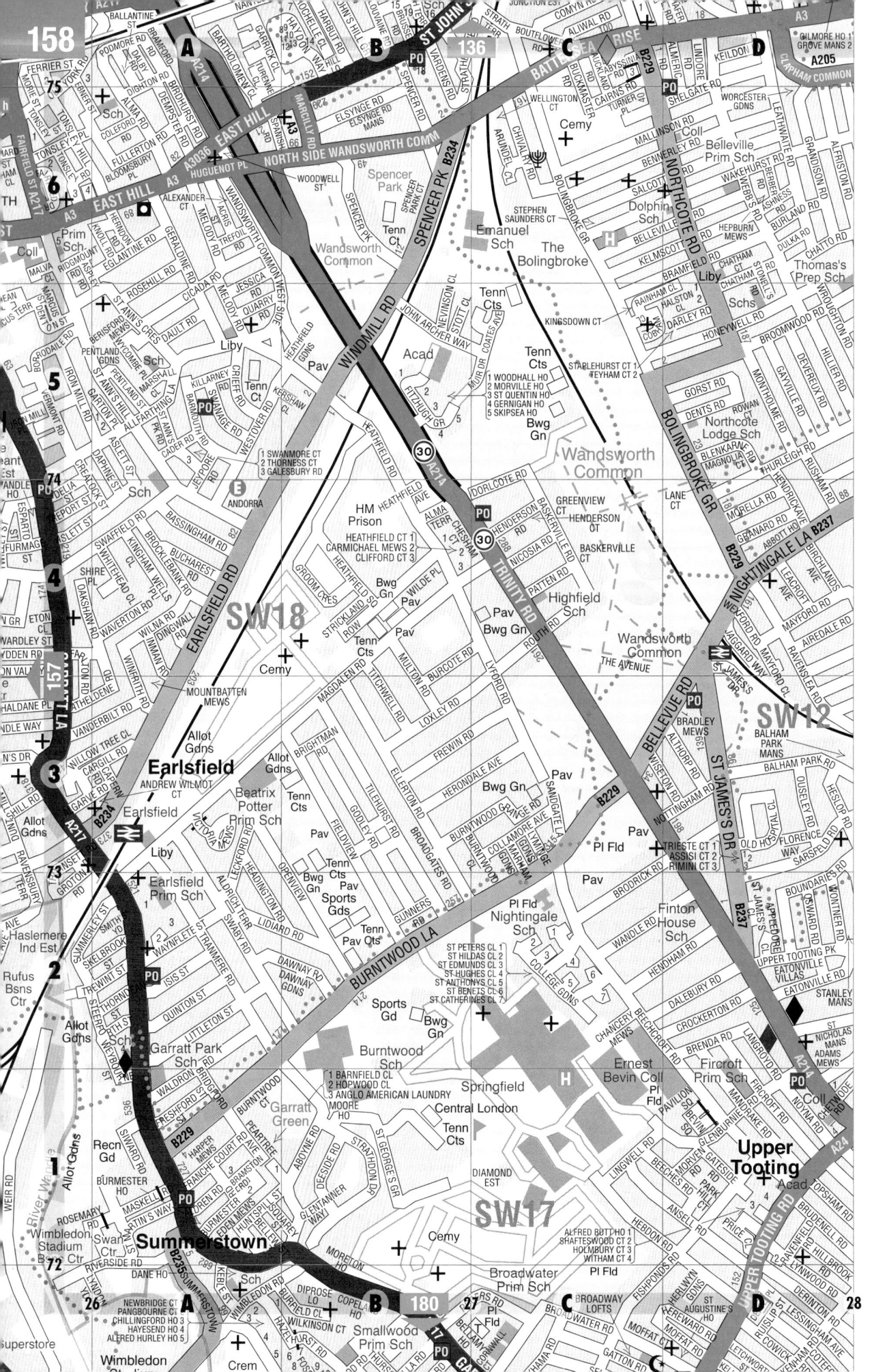
Earlsfield
SW18
SW12
SW17
Wandsworth Common
Upper Tooting
Summerstown
136
157
180
28
26
27
A
B
C
D

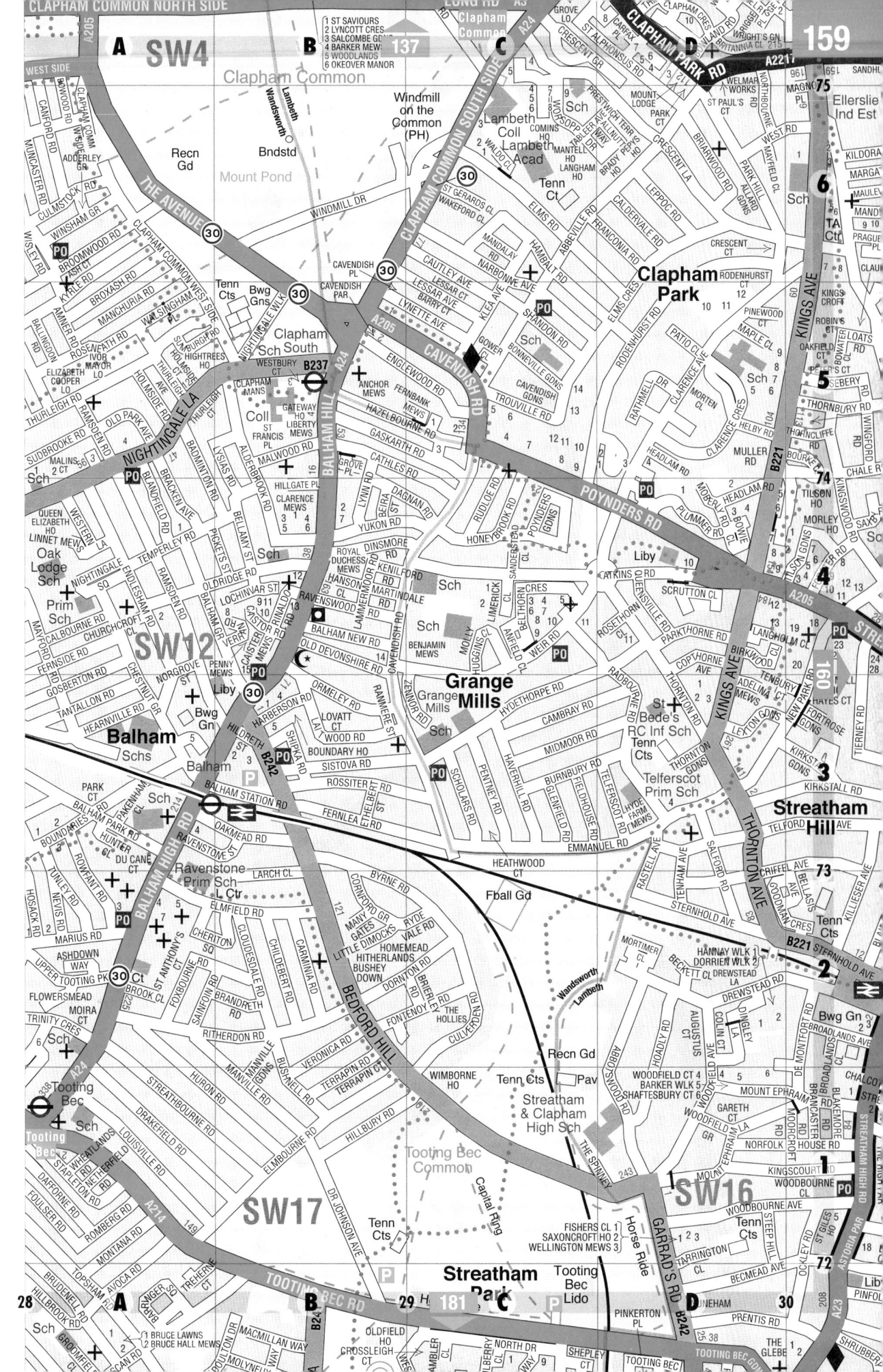
CLAPHAM COMMON NORTH SIDE
LONG RD
Clapham Common
SW4
A
B
C
D
137
1 ST SAVIOURS
2 LYNCOTT CRES
3 SALCOMBE GDNS
4 BARKER MEWS
5 WOODLANDS
6 OKEOVER MANOR
Clapham Common
Windmill on the Common (PH)
Lambeth
Wandsworth
Recn Gd
Bndstd
Mount Pond
WEST SIDE
THE AVENUE
WINDMILL DR
CLAPHAM COMMON SOUTH SIDE
CLAPHAM COMMON WEST SIDE
CLAPHAM PARK RD
A2217
CLAPHAM CRES
GROVE LO
CARFAX PL
ST ALPHONSUS RD
CRESCENT GR
ROWLAND RD
BRITANNIA CL
WRIGHT'S GN
SANDHURST
Lambeth Coll
Lambeth Acad
Sch
PRESTWICH TERR
TABLEER AVE
ALLNUTT WAY
BRADY HO
PEPYS HO
MANTELL HO
LANGHAM HO
COMINS HO
WALDO CL
Tenn Ct
MOUNT LODGE
PARK CT
ST PAUL'S CT
WELMAR WORKS
NORTHBOURNE RD
MAGNOLIA PL
Ellerslie Ind Est
CRESCENT LA
BRIARWOOD RD
PARK HILL
MAYFIELD CL
ALLARD GDNS
WEST RD
KILDORAN
MARGATE
MAULEVERER
MANDRELL
TA Ctr
PRAGUE PL
CLAUDIA
ST GERARDS CL
WAKEFORD CL
ELMS RD
ABBEVILLE RD
FRANCONIA RD
CALDERVALE RD
LEPPOC RD
MANDALAY RD
NARBONNE AVE
HAMBALT RD
KLEA AVE
CAUTLEY AVE
LESSAR CT
LESSAR AVE
BARRY CT
LYNETTE AVE
CRESCENT CT
RODENHURST CT
Clapham Park
ELMS CRES
RODENHURST RD
KINGS AVE
KINGS CROFT
ROBIN'S CT
LOATS RD
BOWATER CL
OAKFIELD CT
PETER'S CT
PINEWOOD CT
MAPLE CL
PATIO CL
CLARENCE AVE
MORTEN CL
CLARENCE CRES
HELBY RD
MULLER RD
RATHMELL DR
SHANDON RD
BONNEVILLE GDNS
CAVENDISH GDNS
TROUVILLE RD
GOWER CL
CAVENDISH RD
A205
CAVENDISH PL
CAVENDISH PAR
ENGLEWOOD RD
FERNBANK MEWS
HAZELBOURNE RD
GASKARTH RD
CATHLES RD
ANCHOR MEWS
Tenn Cts
Bwg Gns
Clapham South
Sch
WESTBURY CT
B237
CLAPHAM MANS
GATEWAY HO
LIBERTY MEWS
ST FRANCIS PL
Coll
NIGHTINGALE LA
NIGHTINGALE WLK
HIGHTREES HO
BURGH RD
HOLMSIDE RD
THURLEIGH AVE
THURLEIGH RD
THURLEIGH CT
WALSINGHAM PL
MANCHURIA RD
BROXASH RD
ROSENEATH RD
IVOR MAYOR LO
ELIZABETH COOPER LO
BALLINGDON RD
AMNER RD
KYRLE RD
BROOMWOOD RD
WINSHAM GR
CULMSTOCK RD
ADDERLEY GR
MUNCASTER RD
CANFORD RD
BOWOOD RD
WISLEY RD
RAMSDEN RD
OLD PARK AVE
SUDBROOKE RD
MALINS CT
Sch
QUEEN ELIZABETH HO
WESTERN LA
LINNET MEWS
Oak Lodge Sch
NIGHTINGALE SQ
Prim Sch
CALBOURNE RD
CHURCHCROFT CL
MAYFORD RD
FERNSIDE RD
GOSBERTON RD
TANTALLON RD
HEARNVILLE RD
CHESTNUT GR
ENDLESHAM RD
RAMSDEN RD
TEMPERLEY RD
BLANDFIELD RD
BRACKEN AVE
BADMINTON RD
LYSIAS RD
ALDERBROOK RD
MALWOOD RD
HILLGATE PL
CLARENCE MEWS
BELLAMY ST
PICKETS ST
OLDRIDGE RD
BALHAM GR
LOCHINVAR ST
CASTOR ST
RINALDO RD
CAISTER MEWS
PENNY MEWS
NORGROVE ST
SW12
Liby
Bwg Gn
Balham
Schs
BALHAM HILL
A24
GROVE PL
LYNN RD
BEIRA ST
DAGNAN RD
YUKON RD
ROYAL DUCHESS MEWS
DINSMORE RD
KENILFORD RD
HANSON CL
MARTINDALE
LAMMERMOOR RD
RAVENSWOOD RD
BALHAM NEW RD
OLD DEVONSHIRE RD
CAVENDISH RD
ORMELEY RD
LOVATT CT
WOOD RD
HARBERSON RD
HILDRETH ST
B242
SHIPKA RD
BOUNDARY HO
SISTOVA RD
ROSSITER RD
ETHELBERT ST
FERNLEA RD
RAMMERE ST
ZENNOR RD
Sch
BENJAMIN MEWS
MOLLY HUGGINS CL
LIMERICK CL
ANFIELD CL
BELTHORN CRES
WEIR RD
SANDERSTEAD CL
POYNDERS GDNS
HONEYBROOK RD
RUDLOE RD
POYNDERS RD
Grange Mills
HYDETHORPE RD
CAMBRAY RD
MIDMOOR RD
BURNBURY RD
GLENFIELD RD
FIELDHOUSE RD
TELFERSCOT RD
HYDE FARM MEWS
SCHOLARS RD
PENTNEY RD
HAVERHILL RD
ATKINS RD
QUEENSVILLE RD
SCRUTTON CL
ROSETHORN CL
RADBOURNE RD
PARKTHORNE RD
COPTHORNE AVE
THORNTON RD
St Bede's RC Inf Sch
Tenn Cts
Telferscot Prim Sch
THORNTON GDNS
THORNTON AVE
Liby
HEADLAM RD
MOBERLY RD
PLUMMER RD
BOWIE CL
B221
THORNBURY RD
THORNCLIFFE RD
BOURKE CL
TILSON HO
TILSON GDNS
MORLEY HO
KINGSWOOD RD
WINGFORD RD
CHALE RD
FOSTER RD
SEBERY
LANGHOLM CL
BIRKWOOD CL
ADELINA MEWS
TENBURY CT
NEW PARK RD
FORTROSE GDNS
HAYES CT
LEYTON GDNS
KIRKSTALL GDNS
KIRKSTALL RD
TIERNEY RD
160
Streatham Hill
TELFORD AVE
CRIFFEL AVE
BELLASIS AVE
GOODMAN CRES
KILLIESER AVE
Tenn Cts
STERNHOLD AVE
B221
HANNAY WLK
DORRIEN WLK
DREWSTEAD LA
DREWSTEAD RD
BECKETT CL
MORTIMER CL
STENHAM AVE
RASTELL AVE
SALFORD RD
EMMANUEL RD
HEATHWOOD CT
Fball Gd
PARK CT
BALHAM PARK RD
PAKENHAM CL
BALHAM STATION RD
BALHAM HIGH RD
BOUNDARIES RD
HUNTER CL
DU CANE CT
RAVENSTONE ST
OAKMEAD RD
Ravenstone Prim Sch
L Ctr
LARCH CL
ROWFANT RD
TUNLEY RD
NEVIS RD
HOSACK RD
MARIUS RD
ELMFIELD RD
CHERITON SQ
CLOUDESDALE RD
CHILDEBERT RD
CARMINIA RD
BYRNE RD
CORNFORD GR
MANY GATES
LITTLE DIMOCKS
RYDE VALE RD
HOMEMEAD
HITHERLANDS
BUSHEY DOWN
DORNTON RD
BRIERLEY RD
FONTENOY RD
THE HOLLIES
CULVERDEN RD
BEDFORD HILL
ASHDOWN WAY
UPPER TOOTING PK
FLOWERSMEAD
MOIRA CT
BROOK CL
ST ANTHONY'S CT
FOXBOURNE RD
SAINFOIN RD
BRANDRETH RD
RITHERDON RD
TRINITY CRES
HURON RD
MANVILLE GDNS
MANVILLE RD
BUSHNELL RD
VERONICA RD
TERRAPIN RD
TERRAPIN CT
WIMBORNE HO
HILLBURY RD
ELMBOURNE RD
STREATHBOURNE RD
DRAKEFIELD RD
LOUISVILLE RD
Tooting Bec
Sch
WHEATLANDS
STAPLETON RD
NETHERFIELD RD
DAFFORNE RD
FOULSER RD
ROMBERG RD
MONTANA RD
A214
SW17
Tooting Bec Common
Capital Ring
DR JOHNSON AVE
Tenn Cts
Wandsworth
Lambeth
Recn Gd
Tenn Cts
Pav
Streatham & Clapham High Sch
THE SPINNEY
ABBOTSWOOD RD
HOADLY RD
AUGUSTUS CT
COLIN CT
DINGLEY LA
WOODFIELD AVE
WOODFIELD CT 4
BARKER WLK 5
SHAFTESBURY CT 6
MOUNT EPHRAIM RD
GARETH CT
WOODFIELD GR
EPHRAIM LA
NORFOLK HOUSE RD
MOORCROFT RD
BRANCASTER RD
BLAKEMORE RD
DE MONTFORT RD
Bwg Gn
BROADLANDS AVE
CHALCOT
KINGSCOURT RD
WOODBOURNE CL
WOODBOURNE AVE
SW16
STREATHAM HIGH RD
ASTORIA PAR
Tenn Cts
STEEP HILL
ST GILES HO
OCKLEY RD
TARRINGTON CL
BECMEAD AVE
FISHERS CL 1
SAXONCROFT HO 2
WELLINGTON MEWS 3
Horse Ride
GARRAD'S RD
B242
Streatham Park
Tooting Bec Lido
TOOTING BEC RD
181
28
29
30
PINKERTON PL
PRENTIS RD
THE GLEBE
SHRUBBERY
A23
Lib
PINFOLD
HILLBROOK RD
BRUDENELL RD
TOPSHAM RD
AVOCA RD
TREHERNE CT
BARRINGER SQ
1 BRUCE LAWNS
2 BRUCE HALL MEWS
GROOMFIELD
Sch
OLDFIELD HO
CROSSLEIGH CT
MACMILLAN WAY
POULTON CL
MOLYNEUX
NORTH DR
SHEPLEY CT
TOOTING BEC GDNS
B241

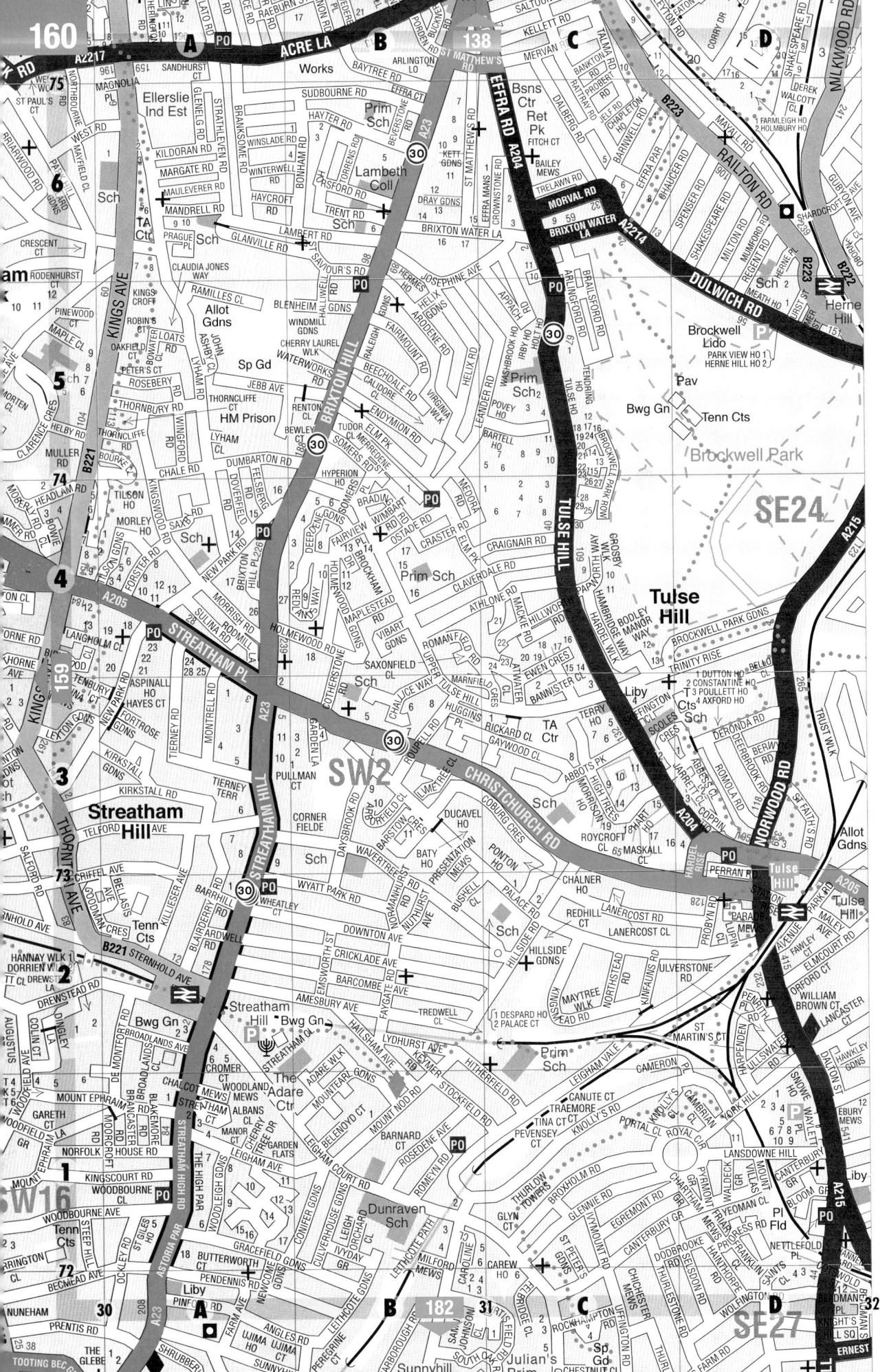

ACRE LA
A2217
138
EFFRA RD
A204
Ellerslie Ind Est
Works
Bsns Ctr Ret Pk
Lambeth Coll
BRIXTON HILL
A23
KINGS AVE
B221
MORVAL RD
BRIXTON WATER LA
A2214
DULWICH RD
RAILTON RD
B223
B222
MILKWOOD RD
Herne Hill
Brockwell Lido
Brockwell Park
SE24
Allot Gdns
Sp Gd
HM Prison
TULSE HILL
Tulse Hill
A215
NORWOOD RD
STREATHAM PL
A205
CHRISTCHURCH RD
SW2
Streatham Hill
STREATHAM HILL
THORNTON AVE
159
SW16
STREATHAM HIGH RD
Dunraven Sch
182
SE27
Sunnyhill

32

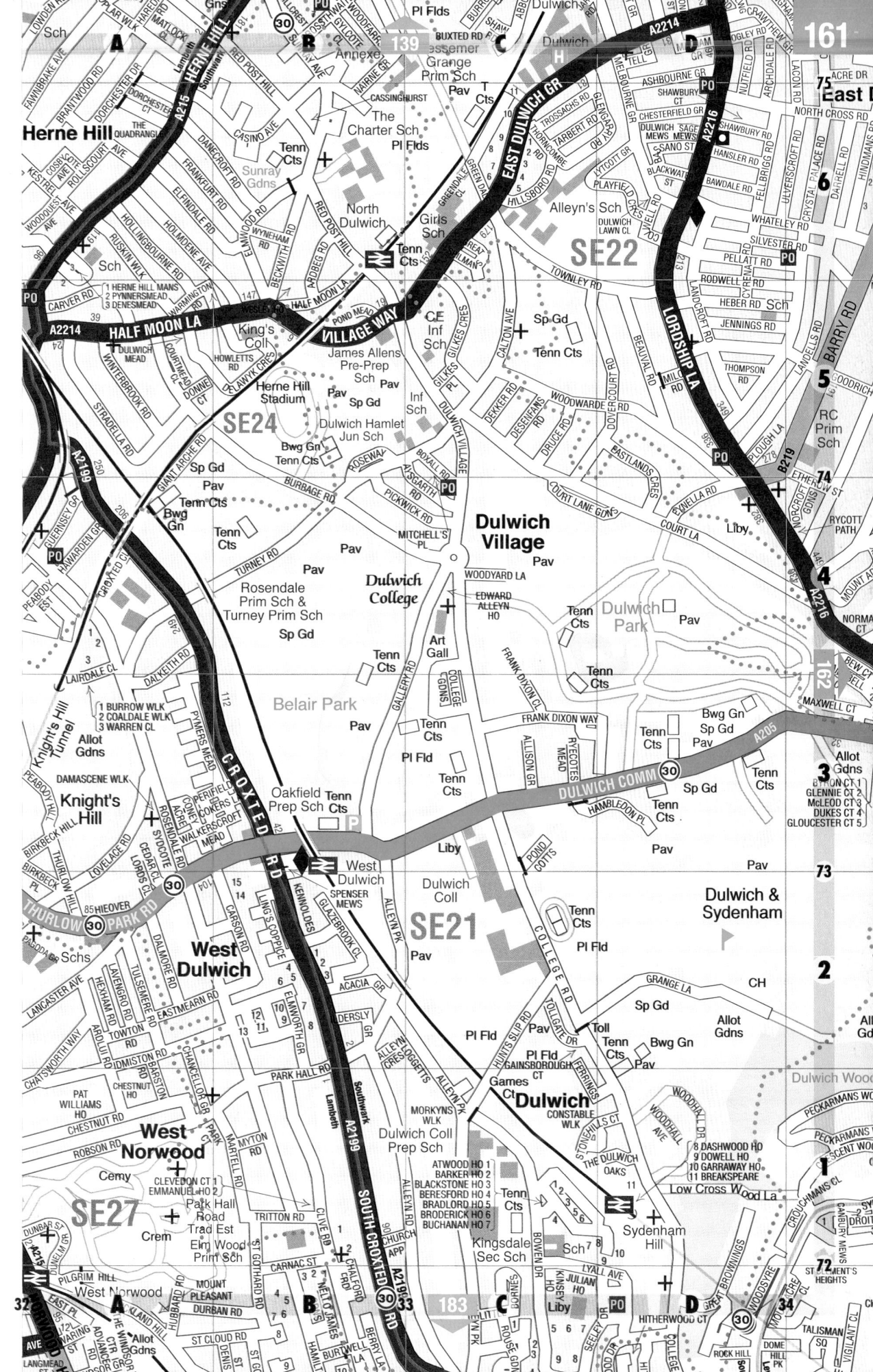
Herne Hill
SE24
SE22
SE21
SE27
Dulwich Village
Dulwich College
Dulwich Park
Belair Park
West Dulwich
West Norwood
Knight's Hill
Dulwich
Sydenham Hill
Dulwich & Sydenham
East Dulwich
Dulwich Wood
HALF MOON LA
VILLAGE WAY
EAST DULWICH GR
LORDSHIP LA
CROXTED RD
SOUTH CROXTED RD
DULWICH COMM
THURLOW PARK RD
COLLEGE RD
COURT LA
HERNE HILL
BARRY RD
Herne Hill Stadium
North Dulwich
Alleyn's Sch
Dulwich Coll Prep Sch
Kingsdale Sec Sch
Rosendale Prim Sch & Turney Prim Sch
Oakfield Prep Sch
Dulwich Hamlet Jun Sch
James Allens Pre-Prep Sch
The Charter Sch
Art Gall
139
162
183

A
B
C
D
140
161
184
East Dulwich
Peckham Rye Park
Honor Oak
SE22
SE23
SE26
Camberwell Old Cemetery
Brenchley Gardens
One Tree Hill (Recn Gd)
Honor Oak Park
Camberwell New Cemy
Harris Girl's Acad
Ppg Sta
Aquarius
Forest Hill
Dulwich & Sydenham
Dulwich Wood
Sydenham Hill Wood (Nat Res)
Horniman Mus
Horniman Sch
Fairlawn Prim Sch
Eliot Bank Prim Sch
Sydenham High Sch
Forest Hill Sec Sch
Forest Hill Ind Est
Forest Hill Bsns Ctr
Malham Road Ind Est
Dulwich Bsns Ctr
Willow Bsns Pk
Sydenham Wells Park
Mayow Park
RC Prim Sch
The Grove
Southwark
Lewisham
Nat Res
Bwg Gn
Allot Gdns
Tenn Cts
Sp Gd
Pl Fld
Liby
Sch
PO
B238
B219
A2216
A205
B227
LONDON RD
FOREST HILL RD
DARTMOUTH RD
BARRY RD
HONOR OAK PK
WALDRAM PARK RD
PERRY VALE
WELLS PARK RD
SYDENHAM HILL
NORTH CROSS RD
LORDSHIP LA
HONOR OAK RD
DEVONSHIRE RD
WOOD VALE
DUNSTAN'S RD
COLYTON RD
BRENCHLEY GDNS
DACRES RD
KIRKDALE
SYDENHAM PK
CRESCENT WOOD RD
PECKARMANS WOOD
COUNTISBURY HO
BYRON CT 1
GLENNIE CT 2
McLEOD CT 3
DUKES CT 4
GLOUCESTER CT 5
WELLS PARK CT 1
BRADFORD CL 2
PETER'S PATH 3
CHURCHLEY VILLAS 4
HOLLOW COMBE 5
DASHWOOD HO
DOWELL HO
GARRAWAY HO
BREAKSPEARE
Cross Wood La
75
73
72
74
30
34
35
36
1
2
3
4
5
6

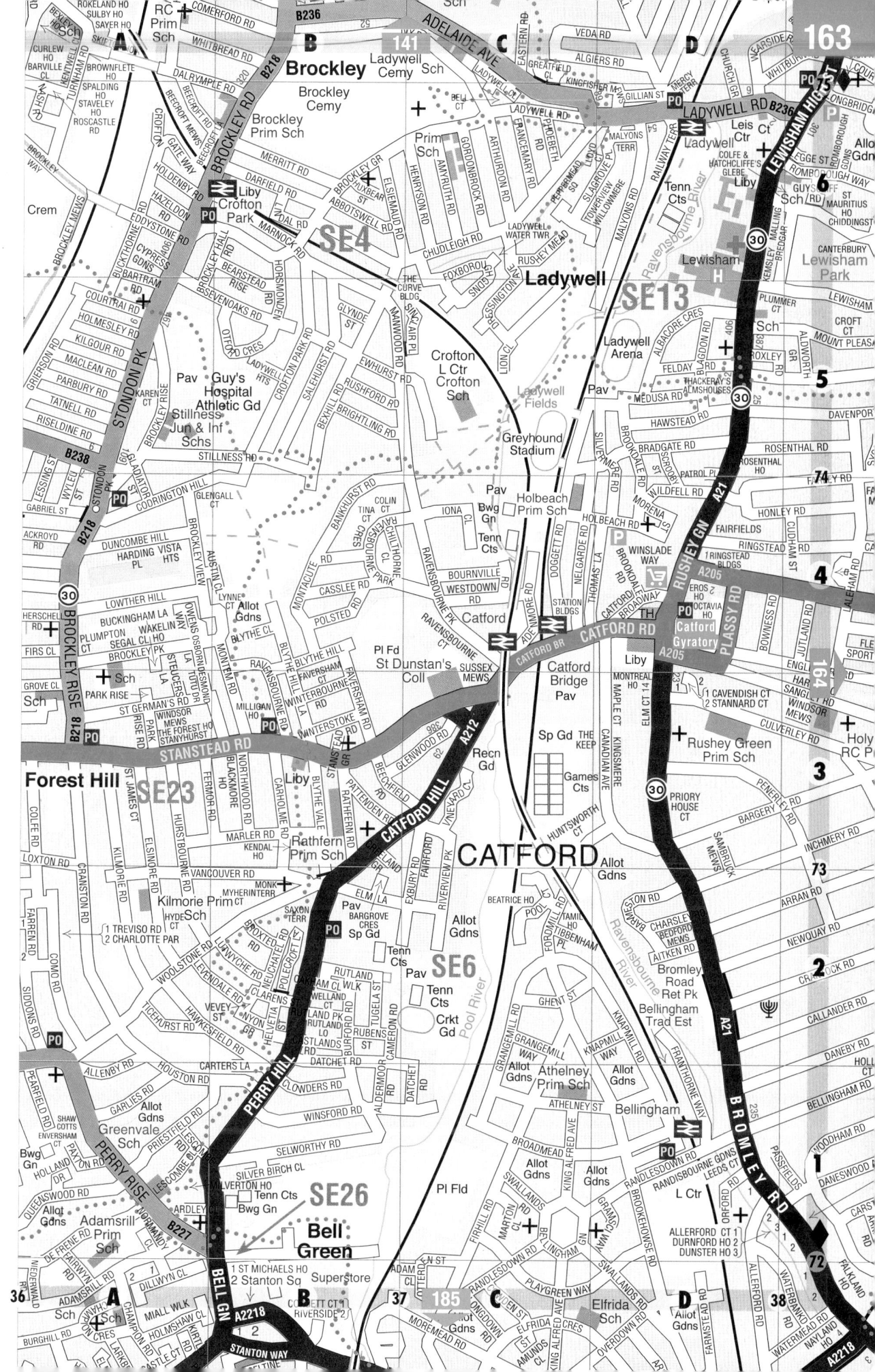
141
Brockley
Ladywell Cemy
Brockley Cemy
Brockley Prim Sch
Crofton Park
SE4
Ladywell
SE13
Lewisham
Lewisham Park
Ladywell Arena
Crofton L Ctr
Crofton Sch
Ladywell Fields
Greyhound Stadium
Holbeach Prim Sch
Guy's Hospital Athletic Gd
Stillness Jun & Inf Schs
Crem
Catford
Catford Gyratory
Catford Bridge
St Dunstan's Coll
Forest Hill
SE23
CATFORD
Rathfern Prim Sch
Kilmorie Prim Sch
SE6
Rushey Green Prim Sch
Bromley Road Ret Pk
Bellingham Trad Est
Athelney Prim Sch
Bellingham
Greenvale Sch
Adamsrill Prim Sch
SE26
Bell Green
Superstore
Elfrida Sch
164
185
36
37
38
A
B
C
D
1
2
3
4
5
6
72
73
74
75
B236
B218
B238
B227
A21
A205
A212
A2218
BROCKLEY RD
STONDON PK
BROCKLEY RISE
LADYWELL RD
ADELAIDE AVE
LEWISHAM HIGH ST
RUSHEY GN
CATFORD RD
CATFORD BR
STANSTEAD RD
CATFORD HILL
PERRY HILL
PERRY RISE
BROMLEY RD
BELL GN
STANTON WAY
PLASSY RD
LOWTHER HILL
DUNCOMBE HILL
CODRINGTON HILL
COURTRAI RD
HOLMESLEY RD
KILGOUR RD
MACLEAN RD
PARBURY RD
TATNELL RD
RISELDINE RD
MERRITT RD
DARFIELD RD
ABBOTSWELL RD
CHUDLEIGH RD
ELSIEMAUD RD
HENRYSON RD
GORDONBROCK RD
ARTHURDON RD
MALYONS RD
ALBACORE CRES
HAWSTEAD RD
BRADGATE RD
ROSENTHAL RD
HONLEY RD
RINGSTEAD RD
CULVERLEY RD
PENERLEY RD
BARGERY RD
INCHMERY RD
ARRAN RD
NEWQUAY RD
CALLANDER RD
DANEBY RD
BELLINGHAM RD
WOODHAM RD
DANESWOOD AVE
RANDLESDOWN RD
PLAYGREEN WAY
BROADMEAD
SILVER BIRCH CL
SELWORTHY RD
WINSFORD RD
CLOWDERS RD
HOUSTON RD
ALLENBY RD
QUEENSWOOD RD
WOOLSTONE RD
TICEHURST RD
VANCOUVER RD
MARLER RD
RUTLAND WLK
DATCHET RD
CARTERS LA
FIRS CL
GROVE CL
PARK RISE
ST GERMAN'S RD
MILLIGAN HO
CASSLEE RD
POLSTED RD
BLYTHE HILL
WINTERBOURNE RD
WINTERSTOKE RD
GLENWOOD RD
RAVENSBOURNE PK
BOURNVILLE RD
WESTDOWN RD
IONA CL
HOLBEACH RD
WINSLADE WAY
FAIRFIELDS
Pool River
Ravensbourne River

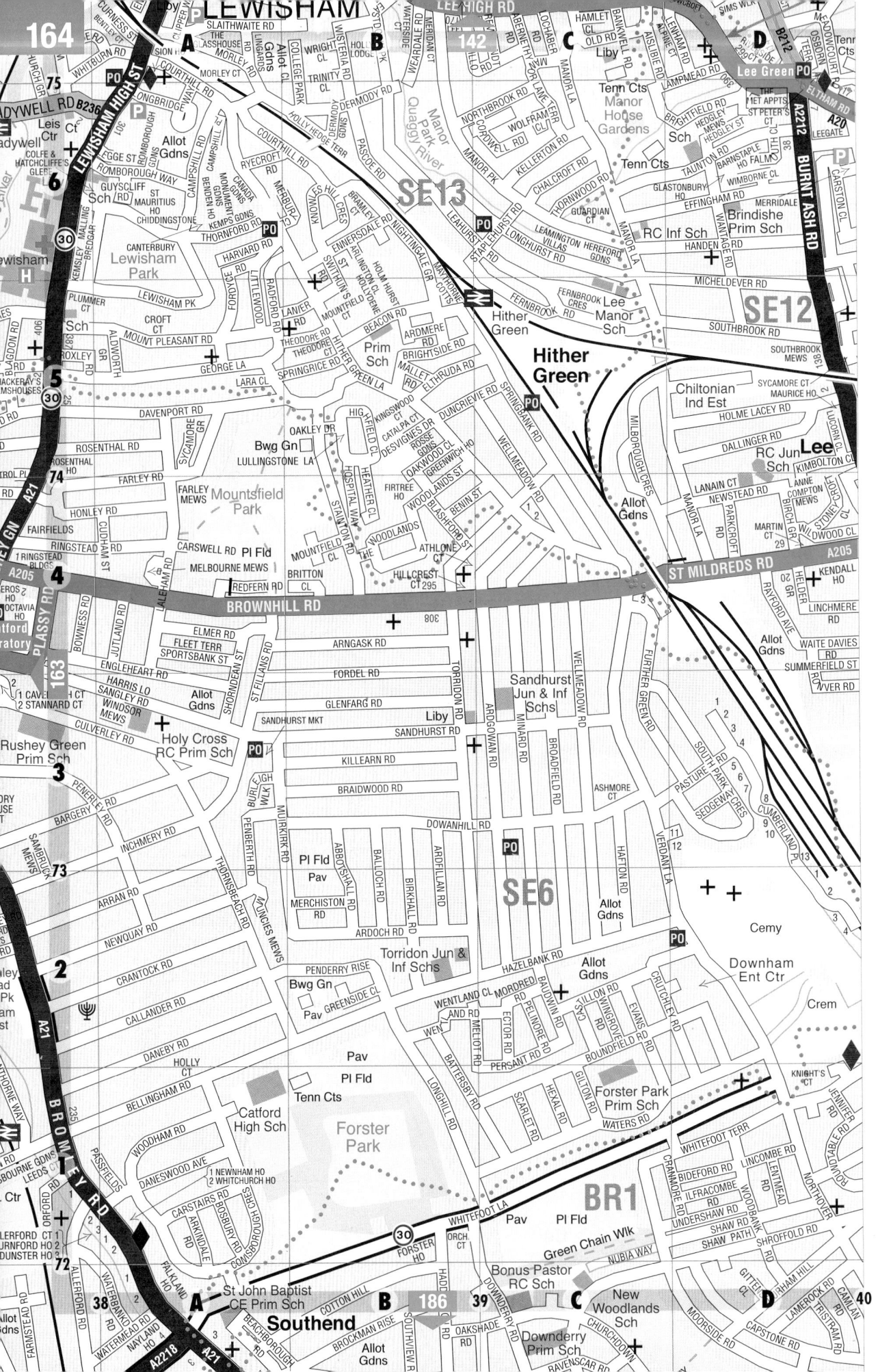

LEWISHAM
LEE HIGH RD
142
A
B
C
D
SLAITHWAITE RD
THE GLASSHOUSE
MORLEY RD
MORLEY CT
COURTHILL RD
WHITBURN RD
CURNESS ST
LADYWELL RD
B236
Ladywell
Leis Ctr
LEWISHAM HIGH ST
LONGBRIDGE WAY
ROMBOROUGH GDNS
ROMBOROUGH WAY
LEGGE ST
GUYSCLIFF RD
Sch
Allot Gdns
CAMPSHILL RD
CAMPSHILL CT
CANADA GDNS
MONUMENT GDNS
BENDEN HO
ST MAURITIUS HO
CHIDDINGSTONE
KEMPS GDNS
THORNFORD RD
RYECROFT RD
COURTHILL RD
HOLLY HEDGE TERR
MERBURY CL
KNOWLES HILL CRES
COLLEGE PARK
WRIGHT CL
TRINITY CT
WISTERIA RD
HOLLY LODGE
DERMODY RD
DERMODY GDNS
PASCOE RD
Allot Gdns
LINGARDS RD
WATERSIDE
WEARDALE RD
MERIDIAN CT
Manor Park
Quaggy River
SE13
ABERNETHY RD
MANOR LANE TERR
LOCHABER RD
MANOR LA
HAMLET CL
OLD RD
BANKWELL RD
Liby
AISLIBIE RD
LENHAM RD
LAMPMEAD RD
Tenn Cts
Manor House Gardens
Lee Green
PO
B212
ELTHAM RD
A20
A212
BURNT ASH RD
THE MET APPTS
ST PETER'S CT
LEEGATE
BRIGHTFIELD RD
HEDGLEY MEWS
HEDGLEY ST
Sch
TAUNTON RD
BARNSTAPLE HO
FALMOUTH CL
WIMBORNE CL
GLASTONBURY HO
EFFINGHAM RD
MERRIDALE
CARSTON CL
Brindishe Prim Sch
RC Inf Sch
HANDEN RD
WANTAGE RD
NORTHBROOK RD
CORDWELL RD
WOLFRAM CL
KELLERTON RD
CHALCROFT RD
THORNWOOD RD
MANOR PK
LEAHURST RD
STAPLEHURST RD
LONGHURST RD
LEAMINGTON VILLAS
HEREFORD GDNS
GUARDIAN CT
MANOR LA
MICHELDEVER RD
SE12
SOUTHBROOK RD
SOUTHBROOK MEWS
FERNBROOK RD
FERNBROOK CRES
Lee Manor Sch
Hither Green
Hither Green
LEWISHAM PARK
Lewisham Park
CANTERBURY
KEMSLEY
MALLING
BREDGAR
Lewisham
PLUMMER CT
CROFT CT
Sch
MOUNT PLEASANT RD
ALDWORTH GR
GEORGE LA
ROXLEY
LARA CL
HARVARD RD
FORDYCE RD
LITTLEWOOD
RADFORD RD
LANIER RD
THEODORE RD
THEODORE CT
SPRINGRICE RD
HITHER GREEN LA
ENNERSDALE RD
ARLINGTON CL
HOLLYDENE
ST SWITHUN'S RD
MOUNTFIELD CT
HOLM HURST
NIGHTINGALE GR
MAYTHORNE COTTS
BRAMLEY CT
BEACON RD
Prim Sch
ARDMERE RD
BRIGHTSIDE RD
MALLET RD
ETHRUDA RD
DUNCRIEVIE RD
SPRINGBANK RD
WELLMEADOW RD
Chiltonian Ind Est
SYCAMORE CT
MAURICE HO
HOLME LACEY RD
DALLINGER RD
RC Jun Sch
Lee
KIMBOLTON CL
LUCORN CL
MILBOROUGH CRES
LANAIN CT
NEWSTEAD RD
MANOR LA
PARKCROFT RD
ANNE COMPTON MEWS
BIRCH GR
STONEYCROFT CL
WILDWOOD CL
MARTIN CT
Allot Gdns
DAVENPORT RD
SYCAMORE GR
OAKLEY DR
Bwg Gn
LULLINGSTONE LA
HIGHFIELD CL
KINGSWOOD CT
CATALPA CT
DESVIGNES DR
ROSSE GDNS
OAKWOOD CL
GREENWICH HO
ROSENTHAL RD
ROSENTHAL HO
FARLEY RD
FARLEY MEWS
Mountsfield Park
HONLEY RD
FAIRFIELDS
CUDHAM ST
RINGSTEAD RD
1 RINGSTEAD BLDGS
CARSWELL RD
Pl Fld
MELBOURNE MEWS
LALEHAM RD
REDFERN RD
BRITTON CL
HOSPITAL WAY
HEATHER CL
FIRTREE HO
WOODLANDS ST
BLASHFORD ST
BENIN ST
STAINTON RD
MOUNTFIELD CL
THE WOODLANDS
ATHLONE CT
HILLCREST CT
A205
BROWNHILL RD
ST MILDREDS RD
KENDALL HO
RAYFORD AVE
HELDER GR
LINCHMERE RD
Allot Gdns
WAITE DAVIES RD
SUMMERFIELD ST
RONVER RD
PLASSY RD
163
BOWNESS RD
JUTLAND RD
ELMER RD
FLEET TERR
SPORTSBANK ST
ENGLEHEART RD
HARRIS LO
SANGLEY RD
WINDSOR MEWS
1 CAVELL CT
2 STANNARD CT
CULVERLEY RD
Allot Gdns
SHORNDEAN ST
ST FILLANS RD
ARNGASK RD
FORDEL RD
GLENFARG RD
SANDHURST MKT
SANDHURST RD
Liby
TORRIDON RD
Sandhurst Jun & Inf Schs
ARDGOWAN RD
MINARD RD
BROADFIELD RD
WELLMEADOW RD
FURTHER GREEN RD
SOUTH PARK CRES
PASTURE RD
SEDGEWAY
CUMBERLAND PL
Rushey Green Prim Sch
Holy Cross RC Prim Sch
KILLEARN RD
BRAIDWOOD RD
BURLEIGH WLK
PENERLEY RD
BARGERY RD
INCHMERY RD
SAMBRUCK MEWS
PENBERTH RD
MUIRKIRK RD
DOWANHILL RD
ASHMORE CT
VERDANT LA
Pl Fld
Pav
ABBOTSHALL RD
BALLOCH RD
BIRKHALL RD
ARDFILLAN RD
MERCHISTON RD
ARDOCH RD
SE6
HAFTON RD
Allot Gdns
Cemy
ARRAN RD
THORNSBEACH RD
MUNCIES MEWS
NEWQUAY RD
CRANTOCK RD
Torridon Jun & Inf Schs
PENDERRY RISE
HAZELBANK RD
Allot Gdns
Downham Ent Ctr
Crem
Bwg Gn
Pav
GREENSIDE CL
WENTLAND CL
WENTLAND RD
MORDRED RD
BAUDWIN RD
CASTILLON RD
WINGROVE RD
EVANS RD
CRUTCHLEY RD
CALLANDER RD
DANEBY RD
HOLLY CT
MELIOT RD
ECTOR RD
PELINORE RD
PERSANT RD
BOUNDFIELD RD
Pav
Pl Fld
BELLINGHAM RD
Tenn Cts
Catford High Sch
Forster Park
LONGHILL RD
BATTERSBY RD
SCARLET RD
HEXAL RD
GILTON RD
Forster Park Prim Sch
WATERS RD
KNIGHT'S CT
JENNIFER RD
ROUNDTABLE RD
A21
BROMLEY RD
WOODHAM RD
DANESWOOD AVE
PASSFIELDS
LEEDS CT
1 NEWNHAM HO
2 WHITCHURCH HO
CARSTAIRS RD
BOSBURY RD
ARKINDALE RD
CONISBOROUGH CRES
BR1
WHITEFOOT TERR
CRANMORE RD
BIDEFORD RD
ILFRACOMBE RD
UNDERSHAW RD
LINCOMBE RD
LENTMEAD RD
WOODBANK RD
NORTHOVER
SHAW RD
SHAW PATH
SHROFFOLD RD
WHITEFOOT LA
Pav
Pl Fld
Green Chain Wlk
NUBIA WAY
FORSTER HO
ORCHARD CT
FALKLAND HO
ORFORD RD
ALLERFORD RD
WATERBANK RD
FARMSTEAD RD
WATERMEAD RD
NAYLAND HO
A2218
St John Baptist CE Prim Sch
Southend
BEACHBOROUGH RD
COTTON HILL
BROCKMAN RISE
SOUTHVIEW RD
Allot Gdns
186
OAKSHADE RD
DOWNDERRY RD
Bonus Pastor RC Sch
Downderry Prim Sch
New Woodlands Sch
CHURCHDOWN
RAVENSCAR RD
MOORSIDE RD
GITTENS CL
DURHAM HILL
CAPSTONE RD
LAMEROCK RD
TRISTRAM RD
CAMLAN RD
38
39
40
72
73
74
75

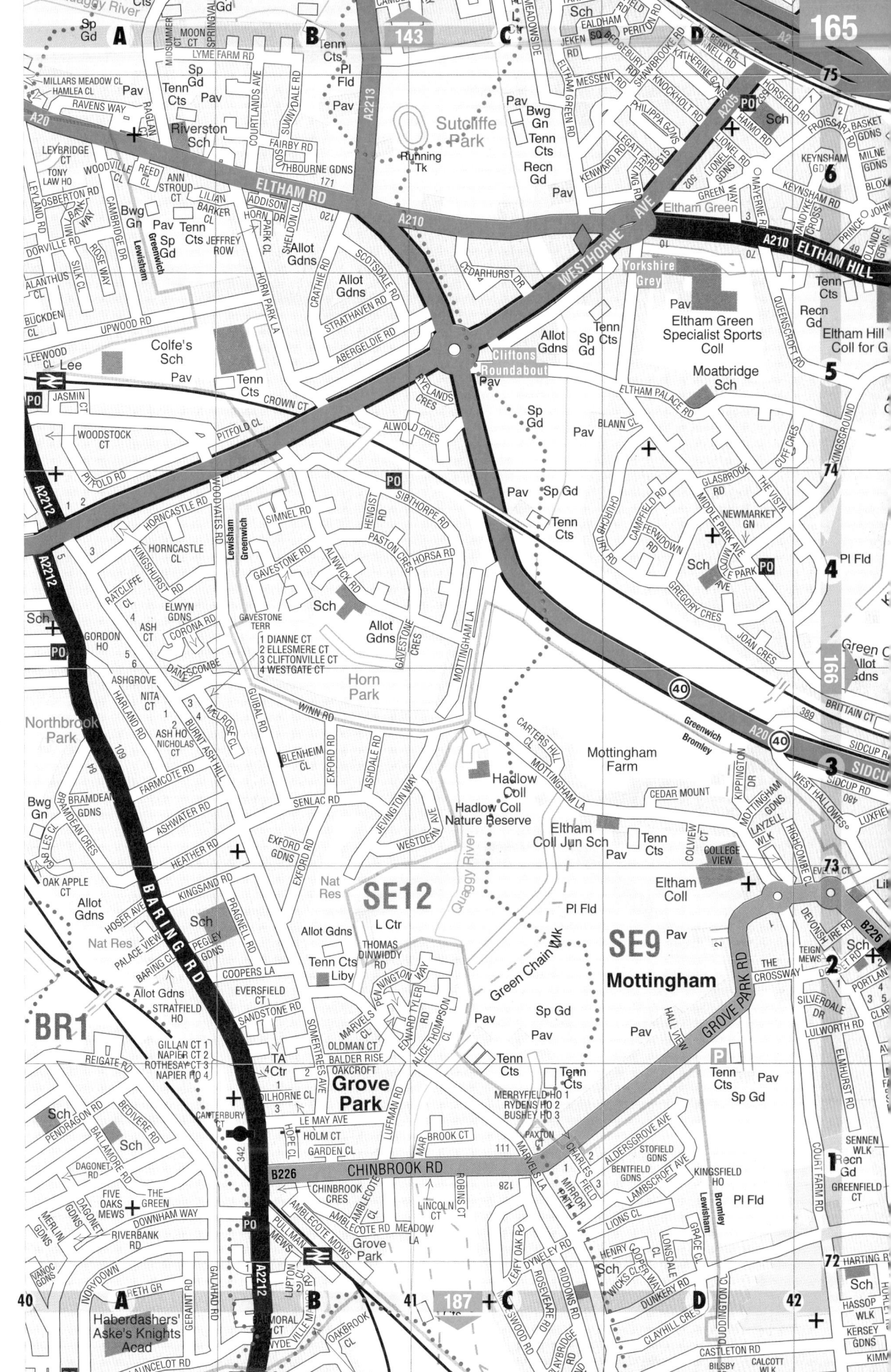
A
B
C
D
143
187
166
ELTHAM RD
ELTHAM HILL
A210
A20
A205
A2212
A2213
B226
WESTHORNE AVE
BARING RD
CHINBROOK RD
GROVE PARK RD
SIDCUP RD
Sutcliffe Park
Running Tk
Riverston Sch
Colfe's Sch
Lee
Eltham Green
Yorkshire Grey
Eltham Green Specialist Sports Coll
Eltham Hill Coll for G
Moatbridge Sch
Cliftons Roundabout
Horn Park
Northbrook Park
Hadlow Coll
Hadlow Coll Nature Reserve
Mottingham Farm
Eltham Coll Jun Sch
Eltham Coll
SE12
SE9
Mottingham
BR1
Grove Park
Green Chain Wk
Quaggy River
Haberdashers' Aske's Knights Acad
Lewisham
Greenwich
Bromley
ELTHAM PALACE RD
MOTTINGHAM LA
HORN PARK LA
SIBTHORPE RD
WINN RD
SENLAC RD
MARVELS LA
COURT FARM RD
LYME FARM RD
UPWOOD RD
CROWN CT
PITFOLD CL
WOODSTOCK CT
HORNCASTLE RD
KINGSHURST RD
ASHGROVE
BURNT ASH HILL
FARMCOTE RD
ASHWATER RD
HEATHER RD
KINGSAND RD
COOPERS LA
SANDSTONE RD
DOWNHAM WAY
RIVERBANK RD
AMBLECOTE RD
LUFFMAN RD
DUNKERY RD
CASTLETON RD
1 DIANNE CT
2 ELLESMERE CT
3 CLIFTONVILLE CT
4 WESTGATE CT
GILLAN CT 1
NAPIER CT 2
ROTHESAY CT 3
NAPIER HO 4
MERRYFIELD HO 1
RYDENS HO 2
BUSHEY HO 3
75
74
73
72
40
41
42
6
5
4
3
2
1

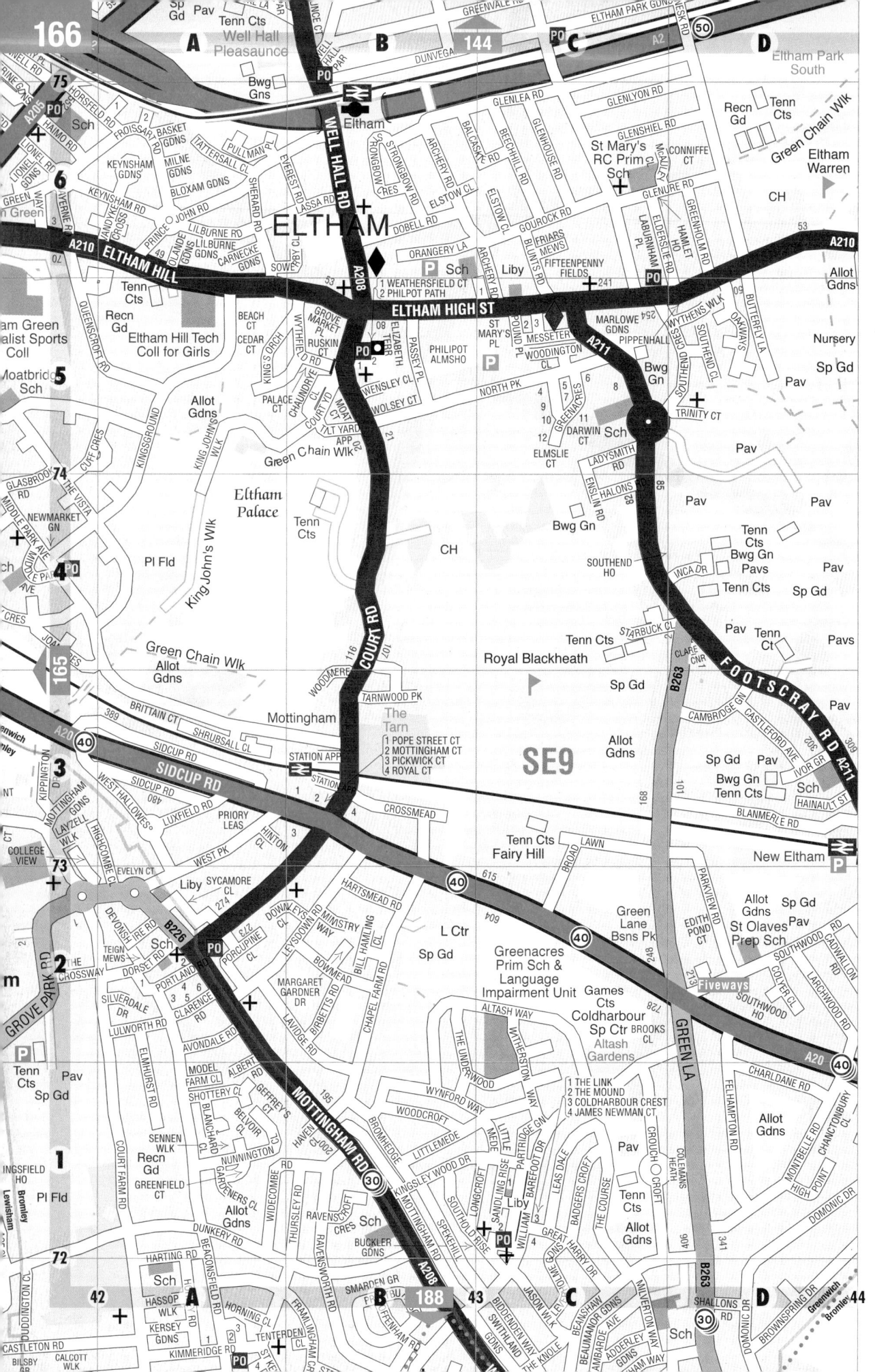
ELTHAM
Eltham
ELTHAM HIGH ST
ELTHAM HILL
WELL HALL RD
COURT RD
FOOTSCRAY RD
SIDCUP RD
MOTTINGHAM RD
GREEN LA
GROVE PARK RD
Eltham Palace
Royal Blackheath
Mottingham
SE9
New Eltham
Fairy Hill
Fiveways
Eltham Park South
Eltham Warren
Well Hall Pleasaunce
Eltham Hill Tech Coll for Girls
St Mary's RC Prim Sch
Greenacres Prim Sch & Language Impairment Unit
Coldharbour Sp Ctr
Altash Gardens
St Olaves Prep Sch
Green Lane Bsns Pk
Green Chain Wlk
King John's Wlk
The Tarn
1 POPE STREET CT
2 MOTTINGHAM CT
3 PICKWICK CT
4 ROYAL CT
1 WEATHERSFIELD CT
2 PHILPOT PATH
1 THE LINK
2 THE MOUND
3 COLDHARBOUR CREST
4 JAMES NEWMAN CT
144
165
188
A
B
C
D
6
5
4
3
2
1
42
43
44
72
73
74
75

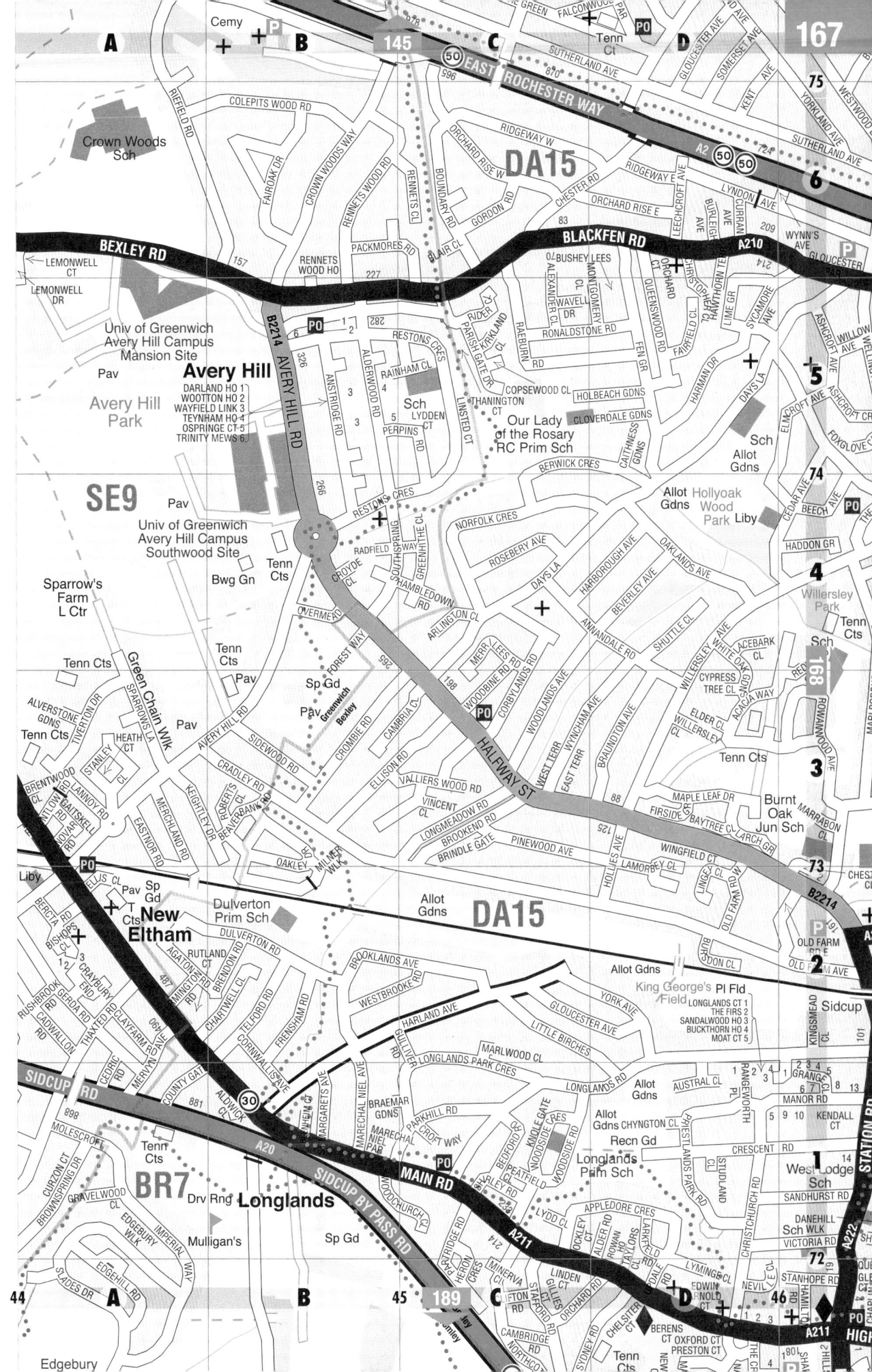

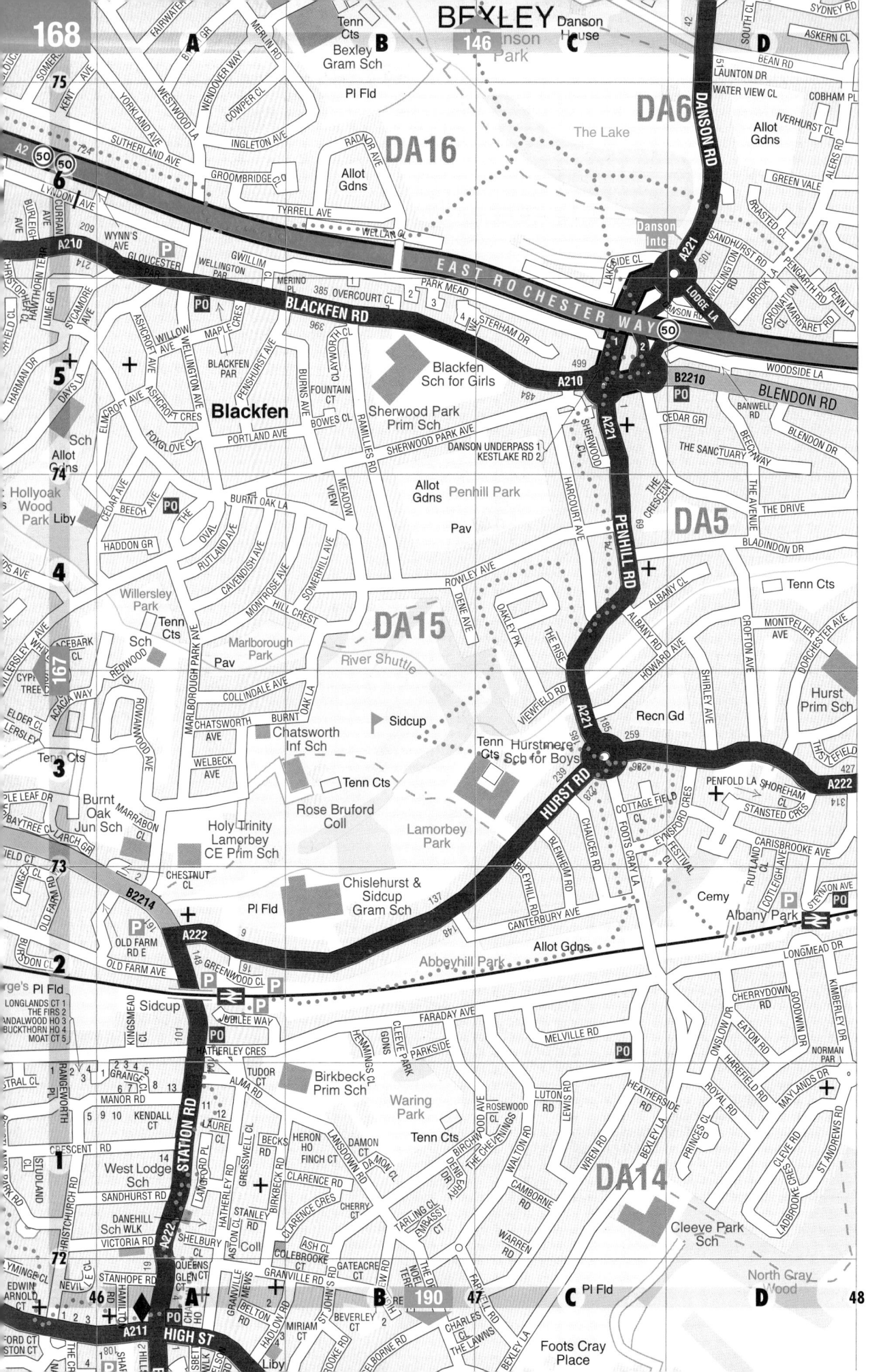
BEXLEY
146
Danson House
Danson Park
Bexley Gram Sch
Tenn Cts
Pl Fld
DA16
DA6
The Lake
DANSON RD
Allot Gdns
EAST ROCHESTER WAY
BLACKFEN RD
Blackfen
Blackfen Sch for Girls
Sherwood Park Prim Sch
Danson Intc
A2
A210
A221
B2210
BLENDON RD
DANSON UNDERPASS 1
KESTLAKE RD 2
Penhill Park
PENHILL RD
DA5
Hollyoak Wood Park
Willersley Park
Marlborough Park
DA15
River Shuttle
Sidcup
Chatsworth Inf Sch
Rose Bruford Coll
Hurstmere Sch for Boys
Recn Gd
Hurst Prim Sch
Holy Trinity Lamorbey CE Prim Sch
Lamorbey Park
Burnt Oak Jun Sch
Chislehurst & Sidcup Gram Sch
HURST RD
A222
B2214
Abbeyhill Park
Albany Park
Cemy
Allot Gdns
Birkbeck Prim Sch
Waring Park
West Lodge Sch
STATION RD
DA14
Cleeve Park Sch
North Cray Wood
Foots Cray Place
HIGH ST
A211
LONGLANDS CT 1
THE FIRS 2
SANDALWOOD HO 3
BUCKTHORN HO 4
MOAT CT 5
167
190
46
47
48
A
B
C
D
1
2
3
4
5
6
72
73
74
75

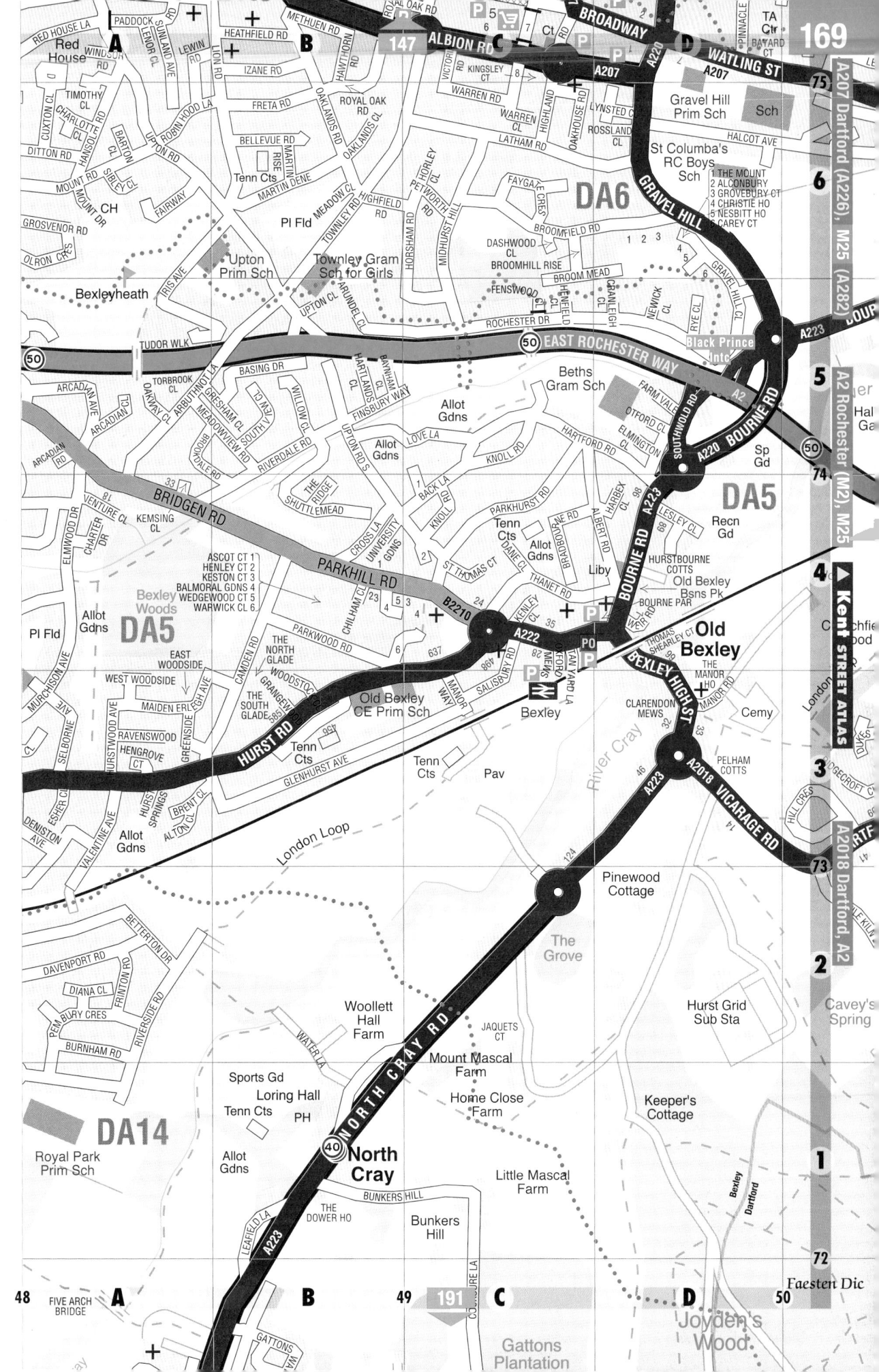

A207 Dartford (A226), M25 (A282)
A2 Rochester (M2), M25
A2018 Dartford, A2
Kent STREET ATLAS
DA6
DA5
DA14
BROADWAY
WATLING ST
ALBION RD
GRAVEL HILL
EAST ROCHESTER WAY
BOURNE RD
BRIDGEN RD
PARKHILL RD
HURST RD
BEXLEY HIGH ST
VICARAGE RD
NORTH CRAY RD
Bexleyheath
Old Bexley
North Cray
Bexley
Black Prince Intc
Red House
Upton Prim Sch
Townley Gram Sch for Girls
Gravel Hill Prim Sch
St Columba's RC Boys Sch
Beths Gram Sch
Old Bexley CE Prim Sch
Royal Park Prim Sch
Old Bexley Bsns Pk
Bexley Woods
London Loop
River Cray
Pinewood Cottage
The Grove
Woollett Hall Farm
Mount Mascal Farm
Home Close Farm
Little Mascal Farm
Loring Hall
Keeper's Cottage
Hurst Grid Sub Sta
Bunkers Hill
Joyden's Wood
Gattons Plantation
Cavey's Spring
1 THE MOUNT
2 ALCONBURY
3 GROVEBURY CT
4 CHRISTIE HO
5 NESBITT HO
6 CAREY CT
ASCOT CT 1
HENLEY CT 2
KESTON CT 3
BALMORAL GDNS 4
WEDGEWOOD CT 5
WARWICK CL 6
147
191

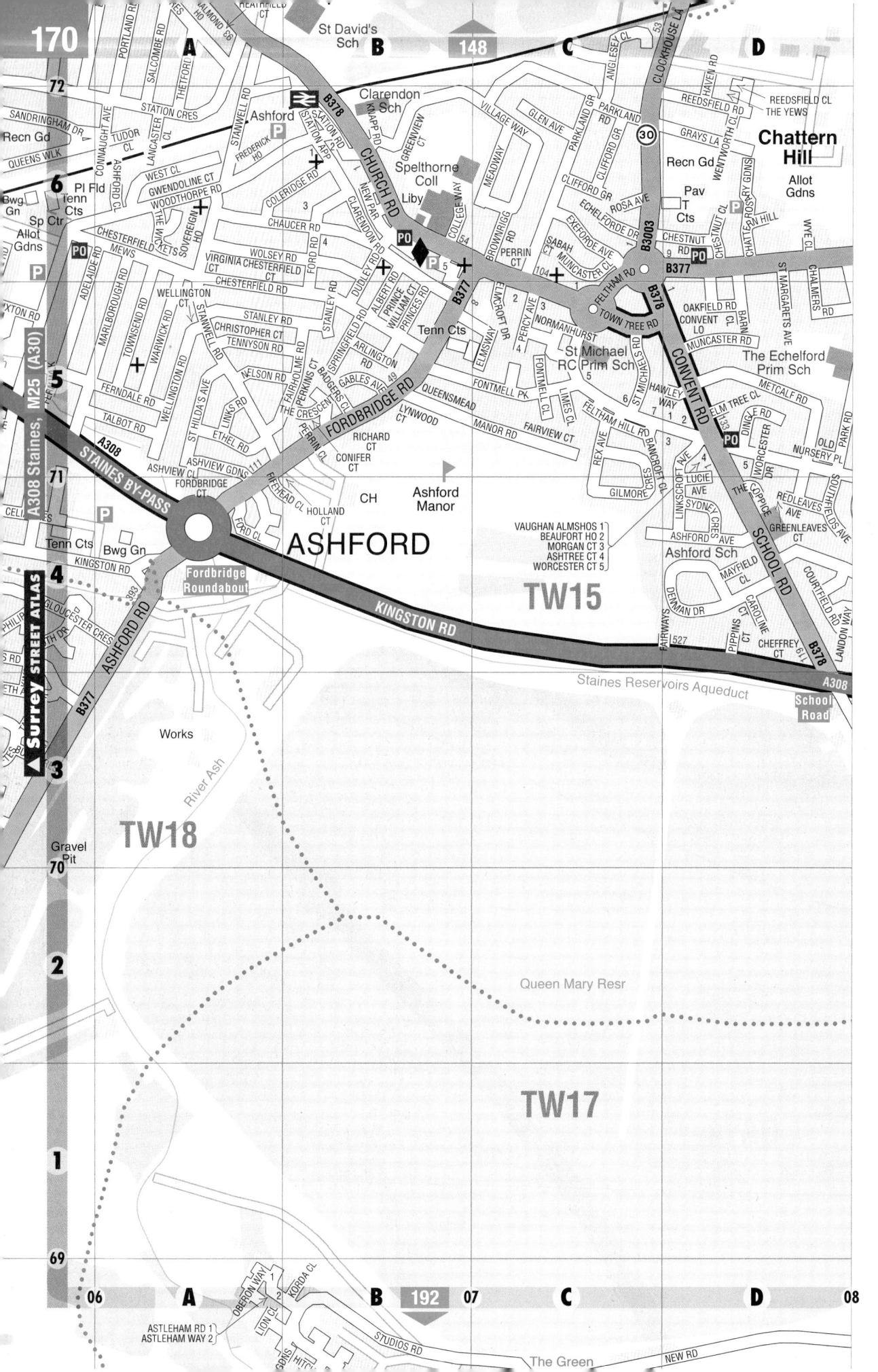

148
192
ASHFORD
TW15
TW18
TW17
Chattern Hill
Staines By-Pass
Kingston Rd
Church Rd
Fordbridge Rd
Ashford Rd
Convent Rd
School Rd
Clockhouse La
Feltham Hill Rd
Fordbridge Roundabout
Ashford Manor
Spelthorne Coll
St Michael RC Prim Sch
The Echelford Prim Sch
Ashford Sch
Clarendon Sch
St David's Sch
Staines Reservoirs Aqueduct
Queen Mary Resr
River Ash
Works
Gravel Pit
School Road
Studios Rd
The Green
New Rd
VAUGHAN ALMSHOS 1
BEAUFORT HO 2
MORGAN CT 3
ASHTREE CT 4
WORCESTER CT 5
ASTLEHAM RD 1
ASTLEHAM WAY 2
A308 Staines, M25 (A30)
Surrey STREET ATLAS

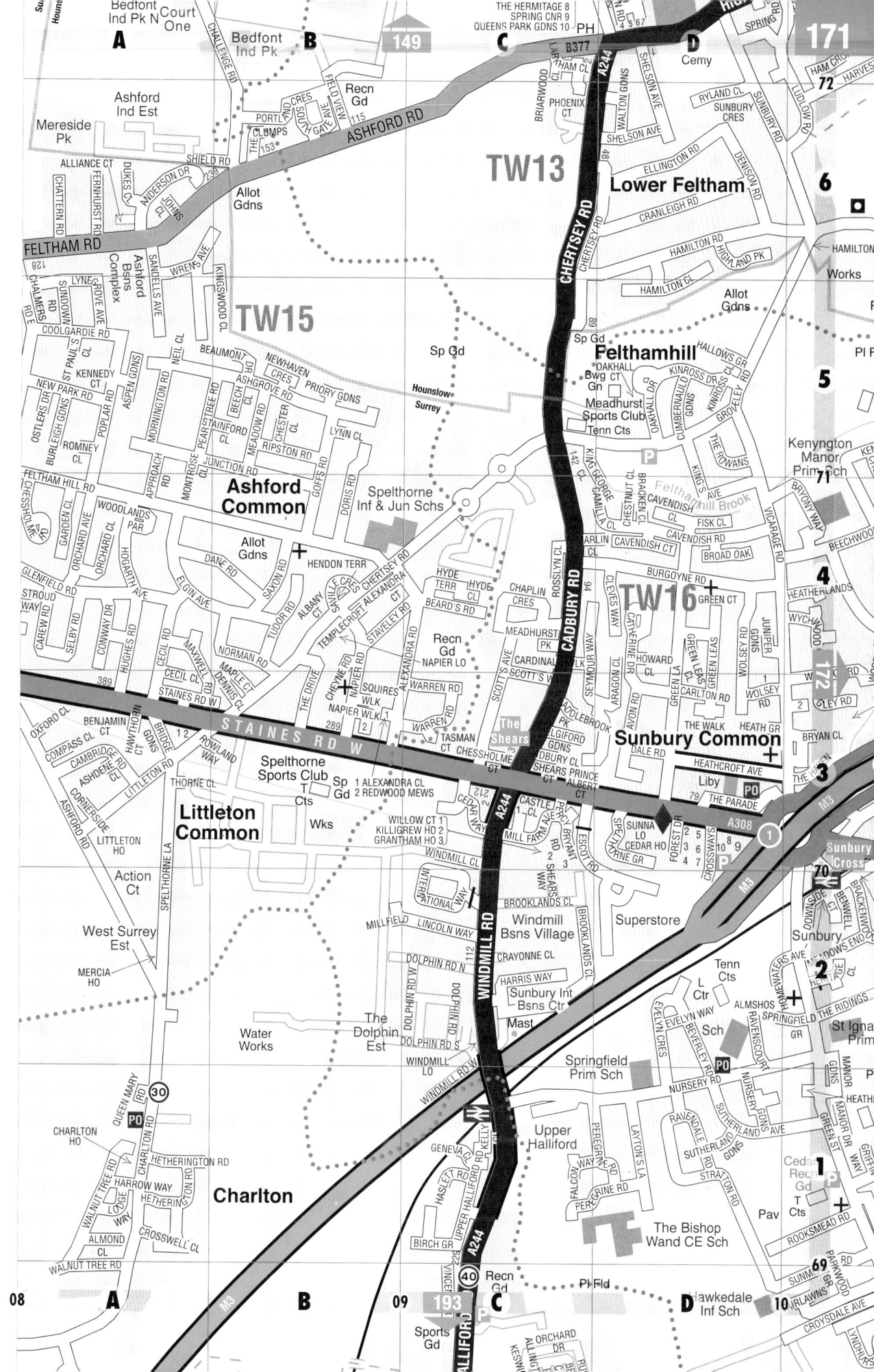

A
B
C
D
149
193
172
TW13
TW15
TW16
Lower Feltham
Felthamhill
Ashford Common
Sunbury Common
Littleton Common
Charlton
Upper Halliford
Bedfont Ind Pk N
Court One
Bedfont Ind Pk
Ashford Ind Est
Mereside Pk
ASHFORD RD
FELTHAM RD
CHERTSEY RD
CADBURY RD
STAINES RD W
WINDMILL RD
A244
A308
B377
M3
Sunbury Cross
Spelthorne Inf & Jun Schs
Spelthorne Sports Club
Meadhurst Sports Club
Kenyngton Manor Prim Sch
Springfield Prim Sch
The Bishop Wand CE Sch
Hawkedale Inf Sch
Windmill Bsns Village
Sunbury Int Bsns Ctr
The Dolphin Est
Water Works
West Surrey Est
Superstore
Hounslow
Surrey
08
09
10
1
2
3
4
5
6
69
70
71
72

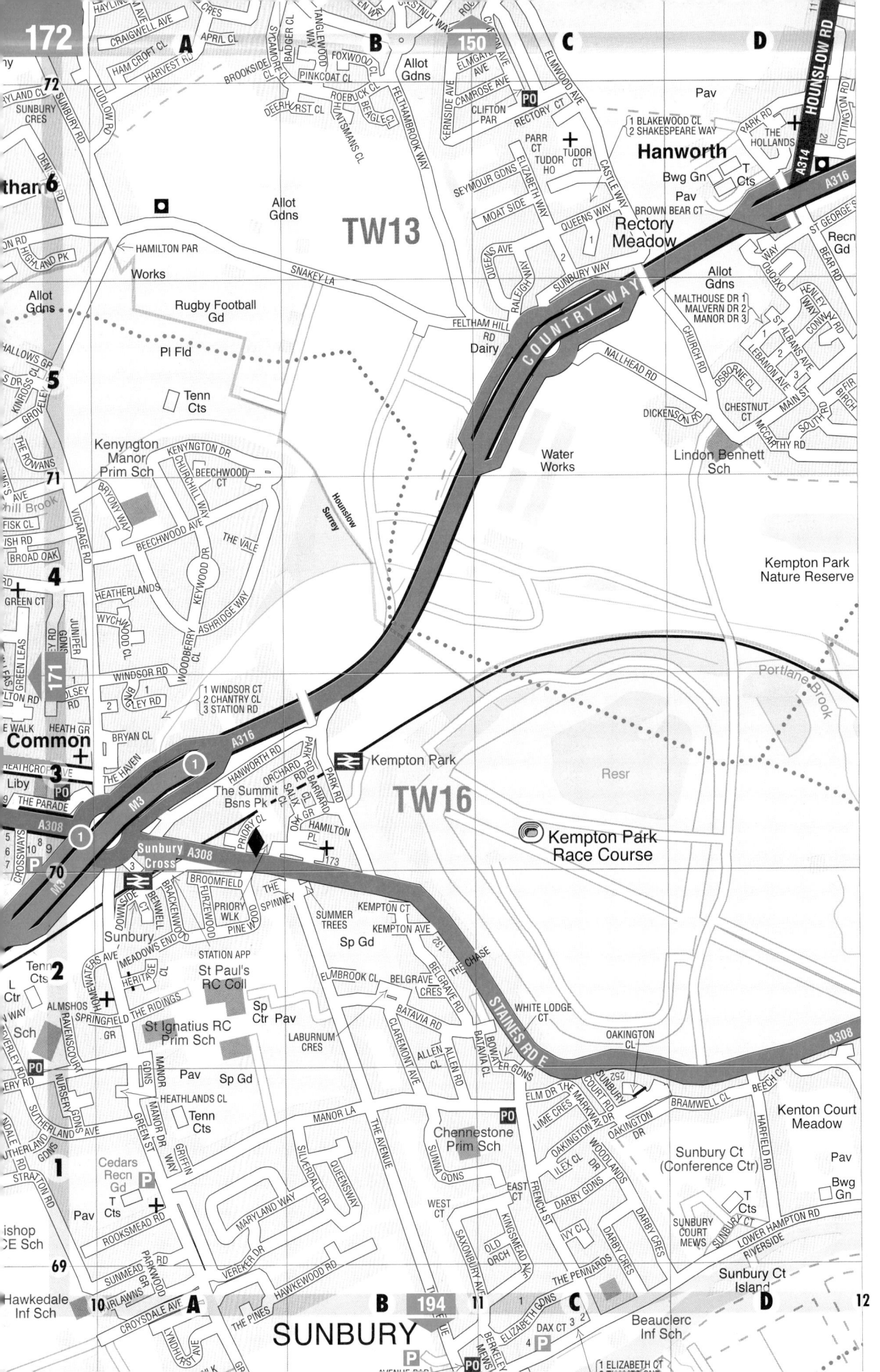
A
B
C
D
150
TW13
TW16
Hanworth
Rectory Meadow
Allot Gdns
Works
Rugby Football Gd
Pl Fld
Tenn Cts
Kenyngton Manor Prim Sch
Water Works
Lindon Bennett Sch
Kempton Park Nature Reserve
Portlane Brook
Resr
Kempton Park
Kempton Park Race Course
The Summit Bsns Pk
Common
Sunbury Cross
Sunbury
St Paul's RC Coll
St Ignatius RC Prim Sch
Sp Gd
Chennestone Prim Sch
Kenton Court Meadow
Sunbury Ct (Conference Ctr)
Sunbury Ct Island
Cedars Recn Gd
Hawkedale Inf Sch
Beauclerc Inf Sch
SUNBURY
194
171
COUNTRY WAY
STAINES RD E
HOUNSLOW RD
A316
A314
A308
M3
Hounslow
Surrey
1 BLAKEWOOD CL
2 SHAKESPEARE WAY
1 WINDSOR CT
2 CHANTRY CL
3 STATION RD
MALTHOUSE DR 1
MALVERN DR 2
MANOR DR 3
1 ELIZABETH CT

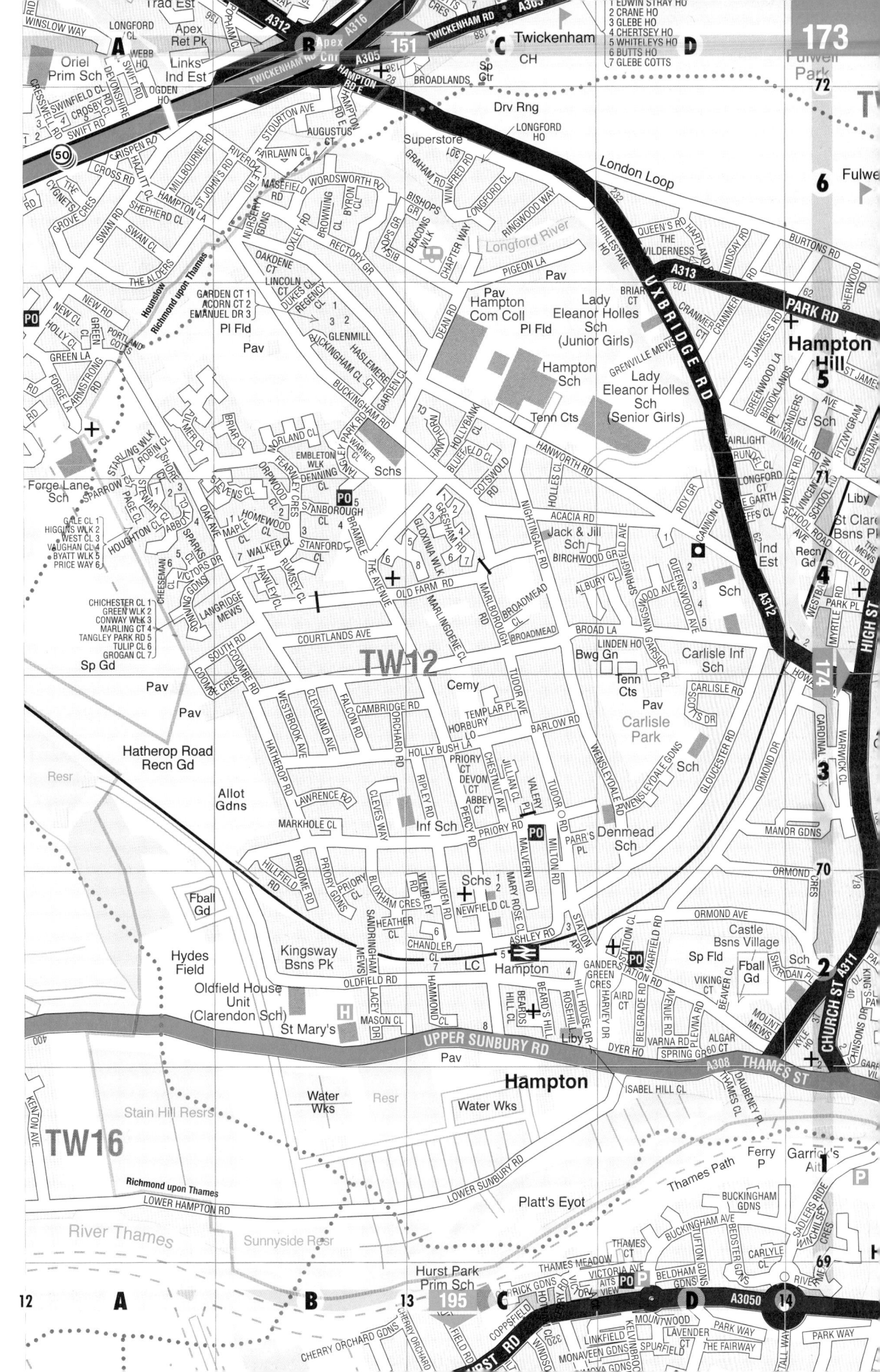

A
B
C
D
151
Twickenham
1 EDWIN STRAY HO
2 CRANE HO
3 GLEBE HO
4 CHERTSEY HO
5 WHITELEYS HO
6 BUTTS HO
7 GLEBE COTTS
Fulwell Park
72
Apex Ret Pk
Apex Cnr
Links Ind Est
Oriel Prim Sch
LONGFORD CL
WEBB HO
OGDEN HO
WINSLOW WAY
DEVONSHIRE
SWIFT RD
SWINFIELD CL
CROSBY RD
CRESSWELL RD
A312
A316
A305
TWICKENHAM RD
HAMPTON RD E
BROADLANDS
CH
Sp Ctr
Drv Rng
LONGFORD HO
Superstore
STOURTON AVE
AUGUSTUS CT
FAIRLAWN CL
CRISPEN RD
HAZLITT CL
CROSS RD
MILLBOURNE RD
ST JOHN'S RD
RIVERDALE RD
HAMPTON LA
SHEPHERD CL
THE CYGNETS
GROVE CRES
SWAN RD
SWAN CL
THE ALDERS
MASEFIELD RD
WORDSWORTH RD
BROWNING CL
BYRON CL
NURSERY GDNS
LOXLEY RD
RECTORY GR
GRAHAM RD
WINIFRED RD
BISHOPS GR
DEACONS WLK
CHAPTER WAY
LONGFORD CL
RINGWOOD WAY
Longford River
PIGEON LA
London Loop
6
Fulwell
THIRLESTANE HO
QUEEN'S RD
THE WILDERNESS
HARTLAND RD
LINDSAY RD
BURTONS RD
SHERWOOD RD
A313
PARK RD
UXBRIDGE RD
Hounslow
Richmond upon Thames
PO
NEW RD
NEW CL
HOLLY CL
GREEN CL
PORTLAND COTTS
GREEN LA
FORGE LA
ARMSTRONG RD
OAKDENE CT
LINCOLN CT
DUKES CL
REGENCY CL
GARDEN CT 1
ACORN CT 2
EMANUEL DR 3
Pl Fld
Pav
GLENMILL
HASLEMERE
BUCKINGHAM CL
BUCKINGHAM RD
GARDEN CL
DEAN RD
Hampton Com Coll
Lady Eleanor Holles Sch (Junior Girls)
Hampton Sch
Lady Eleanor Holles Sch (Senior Girls)
Tenn Cts
BRIAR CT
GRENVILLE MEWS
CRANMER CT
CRANMER
ST JAMES'S RD
Hampton Hill
5
GREENWOOD LA
BROOKLANDS PL
SANDERS CL
AVE
Sch
FITZWYGRAM CL
EASTBANK
WINDMILL RD
FAIRLIGHT
RUNDLE CL
LONGFORD CT
THE GARTH
JEFFS CL
WOLSEY RD
VINCENT RW
SCHOOL RD
SCHOOL RD AVE
71
Liby
St Clare Bsns Pk
THE MEWS
HOLLY RD
Recn Gd
Ind Est
4
WESTBANK RD
PARK PL
MYRTLE RD
HIGH ST
Forge Lane Sch
STARLING WLK
ROBIN CL
SPARROW CL
PAGE CL
STEWART CL
ABBOTT CL
SHORE CL
OAK AVE
SPARKS CL
GALE CL 1
HIGGINS WLK 2
WEST CL 3
VAUGHAN CL 4
BYATT WLK 5
PRICE WAY 6
HOUGHTON CL
CHEESEMAN CL
VICTORS DR
SONNING GDNS
LANGRIDGE MEWS
HAWLEY CL
RUMSEY CL
WALKER CL
MAPLE CL
HOMEWOOD CL
STEVENS CL
ORPWOOD CL
FEARNLEY CRES
DENNING CL
EMBLETON WLK
TANGLEY PARK RD
WARNER CL
NORLAND CL
BRIAR CL
LATIMER CL
STANBOROUGH CL
STANFORD CL
BRAMBLE LA
Schs
THE AVENUE
GLOXINIA WLK
GRESHAM RD
OLD FARM RD
MARLINGDENE CL
MARLBOROUGH RD
HAWTHORN CL
HOLLYBANK CL
BLUEFIELD CL
COTSWOLD RD
HANWORTH RD
HOLLES CL
NIGHTINGALE RD
ACACIA RD
Jack & Jill Sch
BIRCHWOOD GR
SPRINGFIELD AVE
ALBURY CL
ROY GR
CANNON CL
KINGSWOOD AVE
QUEENSWOOD AVE
Sch
A312
BROADMEAD CL
BROADMEAD
BROAD LA
CHICHESTER CL 1
GREEN WLK 2
CONWAY WLK 3
MARLING CT 4
TANGLEY PARK RD 5
TULIP CL 6
GROGAN CL 7
Sp Gd
COURTLANDS AVE
SOUTH RD
COOMBE RD
COOMBE CRES
TW12
LINDEN HO
Bwg Gn
GARSIDE CL
Carlisle Inf Sch
CARLISLE RD
SCOTTS DR
174
Pav
Hatherop Road Recn Gd
Resr
Allot Gdns
WESTBROOK AVE
CLEVELAND AVE
FALCON RD
CAMBRIDGE RD
ORCHARD RD
HATHEROP RD
Cemy
TEMPLAR PL
TUDOR AVE
HORBURY LO
BARLOW RD
HOLLY BUSH LA
PRIORY CT
DEVON CT
ABBEY CT
CHESTNUT AVE
JILLIAN CL
VALERY PL
WENSLEYDALE RD
WENSLEYDALE GDNS
Carlisle Park
GLOUCESTER RD
ORMOND DR
CARDINAL
WARWICK CL
3
LAWRENCE RD
CLEVES WAY
RIPLEY RD
PERCY RD
MARKHOLE CL
Inf Sch
PRIORY RD
TUDOR RD
MILTON RD
MALVERN RD
PARR'S PL
Denmead Sch
MANOR GDNS
ORMOND CRES
70
HILLFIELD RD
BROOME RD
PRIORY GDNS
PRIORY CL
BLOXHAM CRES
WEMBLEY RD
LINDEN RD
Schs
MARY ROSE CL
NEWFIELD CL
ASHLEY RD
STATION APP
ORMOND AVE
Castle Bsns Village
Fball Gd
HEATHER CL
SANDRINGHAM MEWS
CHANDLER CL
Hampton
LC
Kingsway Bsns Pk
Hydes Field
OLDFIELD RD
Oldfield House Unit (Clarendon Sch)
St Mary's
LACEY DR
MASON CL
HAMMOND CL
BEARDS HILL CL
BEARD'S HILL
ROSEHILL
HILL HOUSE DR
Liby
GANDERS GREEN CRES
HARVEY DR
STATION CL
STATION RD
WARFIELD RD
AIRD CT
BELGRADE RD
AVENUE RD
VARNA RD
PLEVNA RD
Sp Fld
VIKING CT
BEAVER CL
SHERIDAN PL
Sch
MOUNT MEWS
KYLE HO
2
CHURCH ST A311
KING'S
JOHNSONS DR
DYER HO
SPRING GR
ALGAR CT
UPPER SUNBURY RD
A308
THAMES ST
Pav
Hampton
ISABEL HILL CL
THAMES CL
DAUBENEY PL
KENTON AVE
Water Wks
Resr
Water Wks
Stain Hill Resrs
TW16
Ferry P
Garrick's Ait
1
Thames Path
Richmond upon Thames
LOWER SUNBURY RD
LOWER HAMPTON RD
Platt's Eyot
BUCKINGHAM GDNS
SADLERS RIDE
WINCHILSEA CRES
River Thames
Sunnyside Resr
BUCKINGHAM AVE
TUFTON GDNS
BEDSTER GDNS
THAMES CT
CARLYLE CL
THAMES MEADOW
VICTORIA AVE
Hurst Park Prim Sch
BELDHAM GDNS
69
RIVERMEAD
12
A
B
13
195
C
D
A3050
14
CHERRY ORCHARD GDNS
CHERRY ORCHARD
COPPSFIELD
MOUNTWOOD
PARK WAY
LAVENDER CT
LINKFIELD
MONAVEEN GDNS
SPURFIELD
THE FAIRWAY
PARK WAY

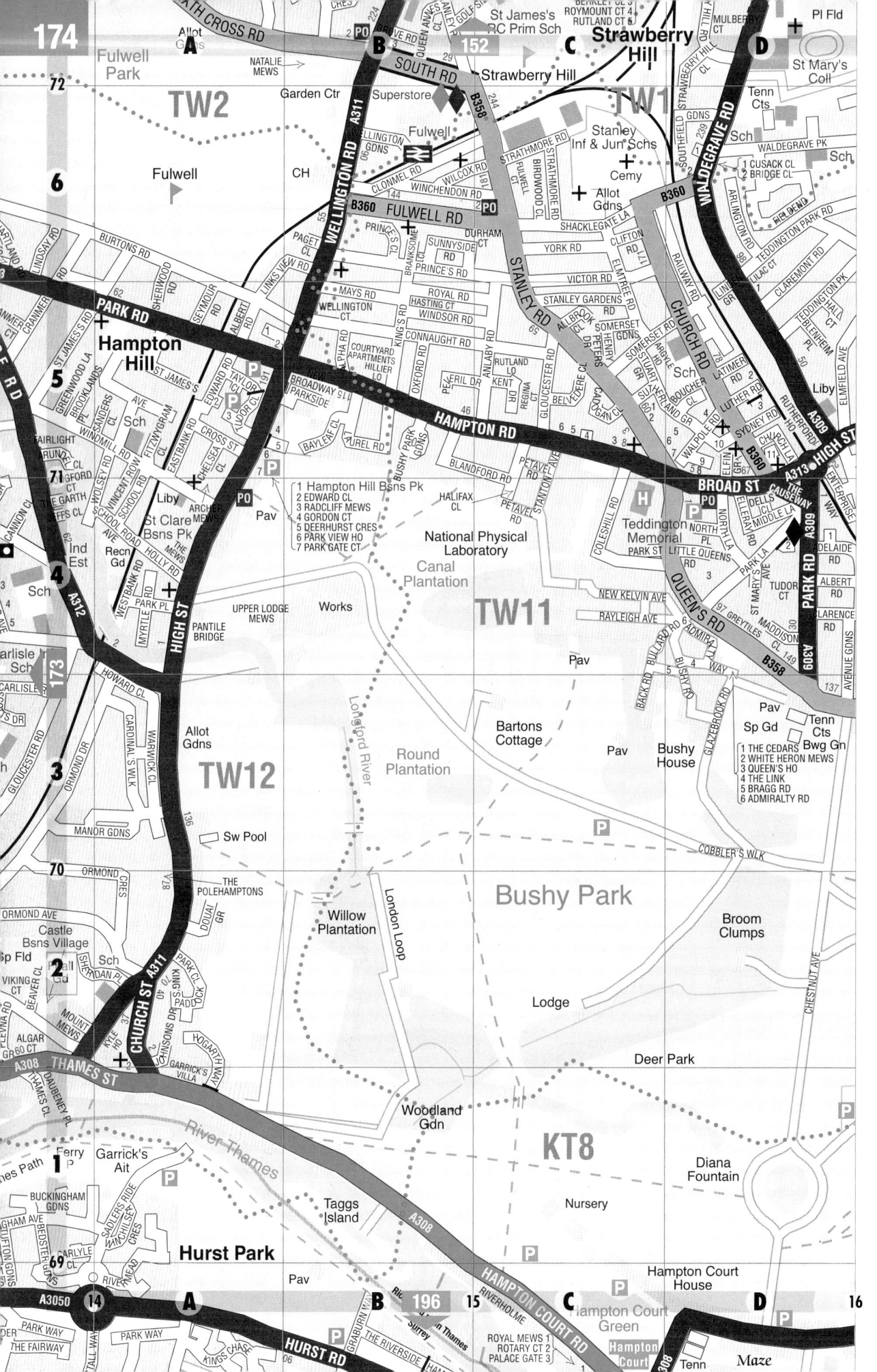
Fulwell Park
TW2
Fulwell
Strawberry Hill
TW1
St James's RC Prim Sch
Stanley Inf & Jun Schs
St Mary's Coll
Hampton Hill
St Clare Bsns Pk
1 Hampton Hill Bsns Pk
2 EDWARD CL
3 RADCLIFF MEWS
4 GORDON CT
5 DEERHURST CRES
6 PARK VIEW HO
7 PARK GATE CT
National Physical Laboratory
Canal Plantation
TW11
Teddington Memorial
TW12
Bartons Cottage
Round Plantation
Bushy House
1 THE CEDARS
2 WHITE HERON MEWS
3 QUEEN'S HO
4 THE LINK
5 BRAGG RD
6 ADMIRALTY RD
Bushy Park
Willow Plantation
London Loop
Broom Clumps
Lodge
Deer Park
Woodland Gdn
KT8
Diana Fountain
Garrick's Ait
River Thames
Taggs Island
Hurst Park
Nursery
Hampton Court House
Hampton Court Green
ROYAL MEWS 1
ROTARY CT 2
PALACE GATE 3
Maze
WELLINGTON RD
FULWELL RD
PARK RD
HAMPTON RD
BROAD ST
HIGH ST
STANLEY RD
CHURCH RD
WALDEGRAVE RD
QUEEN'S RD
THAMES ST
HAMPTON COURT RD
HURST RD
152
173
196
A
B
C
D
1
2
3
4
5
6
14
15
16
69
70
71
72

TEDDINGTON
Teddington Lock
Thames Path
Teddington Weir
Meadlands Prim Sch
Cassel
St George's Ind Est
Tiffin Girls' Sch
Fern Hill Prim Sch
Teddington Sch
Collis Prim Sch
Sacred Heart RC Prim Sch
Athletic Gd
Trowlock Island
River Thames
Hampton Wick
TW11
KT1
Warren Plantation
Cobbler's Wlk
Heron Pond
Oval Plantation
Boating Lake
The Royal Paddocks
Bushy Lodge
Hampton Wick Pond
Old Icehouse
KINGSTON UPON THAMES
The Griffin Ctr
Kingston Bridge
Richmond upon Thames
Kingston upon Thames
HIGH ST
KINGSTON RD
MANOR RD
TWICKENHAM RD
STRAWBERRY VALE
UPPER HAM RD
UPPER TEDDINGTON RD
HAMPTON COURT RD
PARK RD
SANDY LA
CHURCH GR
HORSE FAIR
WOOD ST
KINGSTON HALL RD
1 HAWKESLEY CL
2 CLAVERING CL
3 CHATSWORTH PL
4 WOODVILLE CL
5 MARLOW HO
6 FAIRWATER HO
7 REGATTA HO
8 FAIRMILE HO
9 ADMIRAL HO
WEEKS HO 1
TIDEWAY CL 2
HEADWAY CL 3
FISHERMAN CL 4
ANGLERS CL 5
1 BRAEMAR HO
2 QUAY WEST CT
1 DAVENPORT CL
2 REDLANDS
3 SHELDON HO
4 GROSVENOR CT
1 RIVERSIDE CT
2 BEECH CT
YORK CT 1
ULSTER CT 2
BRUNSWICK CT 3
1 MARINA WAY
2 CHERWELL CT
3 HAMBLE CT
4 RAEBURN CL
EISENHOWER HO 1
INGRAM HO 2
LINDLEY CT 3
TABARD HO 4
BUSHY CT 5
BEVERLEY RD 6
JUBILEE CL 7
SCHOOL LA 8
SCHOOL RD 9
BAYGROVE MEWS 10
CHURCH ST 1
MARKET PL 2
CROWN PAS 3
CROWN ARC 4
APPLE MKT 5
BATH PAS 6
TAGGS HO 7
RAVENS HO 8
STEVENS HO 9
GARRICKS HO 10

153
176
197

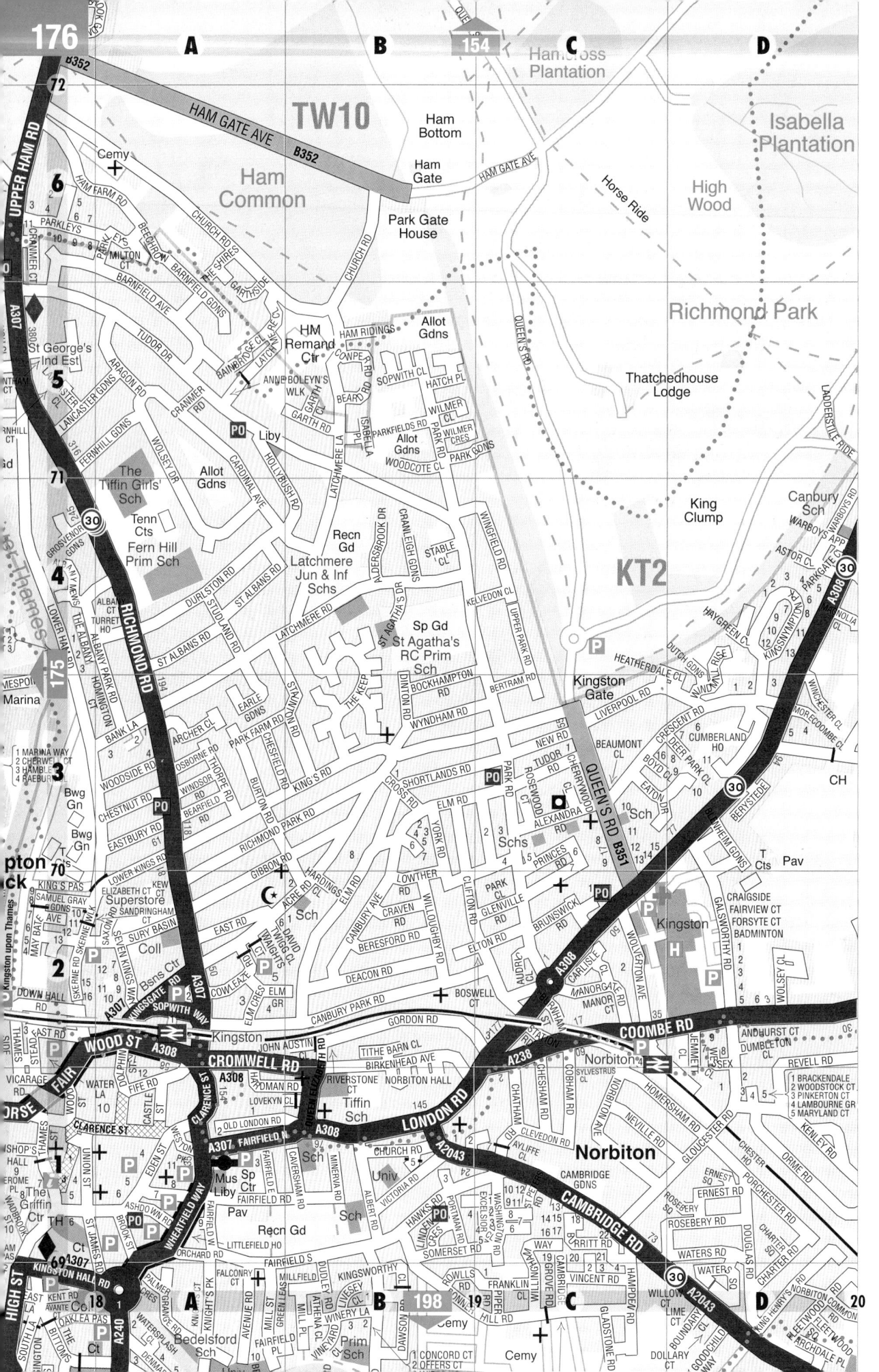
A
B
C
D
154
175
198
Hamcross Plantation
Isabella Plantation
TW10
Ham Bottom
Ham Gate
HAM GATE AVE
B352
Ham Common
Park Gate House
Horse Ride
High Wood
Richmond Park
Thatchedhouse Lodge
King Clump
KT2
Canbury Sch
Kingston Gate
UPPER HAM RD
RICHMOND RD
QUEEN'S RD
Cemy
HM Remand Ctr
Allot Gdns
St George's Ind Est
The Tiffin Girls' Sch
Tenn Cts
Fern Hill Prim Sch
Recn Gd
Latchmere Jun & Inf Schs
Sp Gd
St Agatha's RC Prim Sch
Marina
Bwg Gn
Superstore
Coll
Bsns Ctr
Kingston
Sch
Schs
Kingston
H
Norbiton
COOMBE RD
CROMWELL RD
WOOD ST
LONDON RD
CAMBRIDGE RD
Tiffin Sch
Univ
Mus Liby
Sp Ctr
Pav
Recn Gd
The Griffin Ctr
Bedelsford Sch
Prim Sch
Cemy
1 MARINA WAY
2 CHERWELL CT
3 HAMBLE ST
4 RAEBURN
1 BRACKENDALE
2 WOODSTOCK CT
3 PINKERTON CT
4 LAMBOURNE GR
5 MARYLAND CT
CRAIGSIDE
FAIRVIEW CT
FORSYTE CT
BADMINTON
1 CONCORD CT
2 OFFERS CT

KT2
A
B
155
C
D
Robin Hood
War Meml
Wandsworth
72
SW1
FUSION CT
KINGSTON VALE
A308
MARY ADELAIDE CL
ROBINWOOD PL
Kingston Vale
WOODVIEW CL
DERWENT AVE
GRASMERE AVE
ROBIN HOOD LA
VALE CRES
Pl Fld
SW15
6
Horse Ride
CEDAR CL
ULLSWATER CL
ULLSWATER CRES
KINGSTON HILL PL
WINDERMERE RD
ROBIN HOOD LA
Pav
Horse Ride
Richmond upon Thames
Kingston upon Thames
Coombehurst (Kingston University)
Kingston Univ
Sch
BOWNESS CRES
RYDAL GDNS
Tenn Cts
Merton
Kingston upon Thames
5
COOMBE PL
RANDOLPH CL
COOMBE WOOD RD
COOMBE PK
KESWICK AVE
ROBIN HOOD WAY
KINGSTON BY PASS
Allot Gdns
SW19
KINGSTON HILL
CORSCOMBE CL
COOMBE RIDINGS
PAGET PL
Pl Fld
Allot Gdns
71
Mill Corner
Warren House
KT2
FAIRLAWN CL
COTSWOLD CL
THE WATERGARDENS
Coombe Hill
4
WARREN PK
WARREN RD
SW20
178
Coombe Wood
RENFREW RD
HIGH COOMBE PL
WARREN CUTTING
THE LEIGH
GREENWOOD PK
Pl Fld
ELLERTON RD
Tenn Cts
Nat Res
STOKE RD
GEORGE RD
COOMBE NEVILLE
EDGECOOMBE CL
GOLF CLUB DR
CH
COOMBE HILL RD
HENLEY DR
3
COOMBE END
BEVERLEY CL
COOMBE HILL GLADE
Holy Cross Prep Sch
THE DRIVE
GATEHOUSE CL
Schs
Coombe
MOOR PARK GDNS
DEVEY CL
WARBANK LA
PRESTON RD
HOOD RD
BALLARD CL
LORD CHANCELLOR WLK
COOMBE LA WEST
B283
FITZGEORGE AVE
OAKCOMBE CL
COOMBE BANK
WONFORD CL
New Victoria
A3
BEVERLEY AVE
HOLLAND AVE
70
MELVILLE AVE
WARREN RISE
COOMBE HOUSE CHASE
NEVILLE AVE
THE FAIRWAY
THE CHESTERS
Coombe Lane
BURDETT AVE
COOMBE RISE
BROOK GDNS
ORCHARD RISE
WEST RD
SOUTHWOOD AVE
Coombe Hill Jun & Inf Schs
COOMBE LANE FLYOVER 1
BEVERLEY CT 2
Merton
COTTENHAM PARK RD
2
A238
CROWN RD
THE MOAT
BURGHLEY AVE
TRAPS LA
BEVERLEY WAY
KINGSTON BY PASS
WESTCOOMBE AVE
A238
ALBION RD
WOODLANDS AVE
MATLOCK WAY
CROMFORD WAY
SOAMES WLK
Pl Flds
BEECHCROFT AVE
CARDINAL CRES
BRANKSOME WAY
HIGH DR
BUXTON DR
BADGERS WLK
KT3
ARUNDEL RD
DICKERAGE RD
DARLEY DR
BAKEWELL WAY
Coombe Girls Sch
CH
Coombe Brook
Malden
ELY CL
OVERDALE AVE
OAK RD
LANGLEY GR
Tenn Cts
Sp Gd
1
Allot Gdns
OLIVER RD
CLARENCE AVE
ASH CL
BURBERRY CL
CARLTON RD
SELBORNE RD
GOLF SIDE CL
CH
ABOYNE DR
THE TRIANGLE
MYRTLE GR
THE CLOSE
LABURNUM GR
BARTON GN
WOODSIDE RD
DELL WLK
LINKSIDE
CAMBRIDGE AVE
1 PERTH CL
2 HUNTLEY WAY
DICKERAGE HILL
MUYBRIDGE RD
THE CRESCENT
Allot Gdns
POPLAR GDNS
LAWN CL
ROWAN CL
FORSYTH CT
ROSEBERY AVE
Allot Gdns
MIDDLETON RD
ASHCOMBE SQ
LONG WLK
THE GREEN
BEACONSFIELD RD
SYCAMORE GR
EDGAR CT
HOPPINGWOOD AVE
ORCHARD AVE
69
WARWICK RD
20
A
MOUNT PLEASANT RD
SALISBURY RD
B
21
199
C
COOMBE RD
Sch
LIME GR
D
22
DICKERAGE LA
LINCOLN AVE
ROSEMONT RD
Corpus Christi RC Prim Sch
MOUNT RD
BEECH GR
ELM RD
POPLAR GR
ST MARYS CT
CONCORD HO
ALRIC AVE
CRAMER CT
STAFFORD RD
CHESTNUT GR
CHESTNUT CT
GROVE CT
PHOENIX HO
VANFAME CT
New Malden
Beverley Park

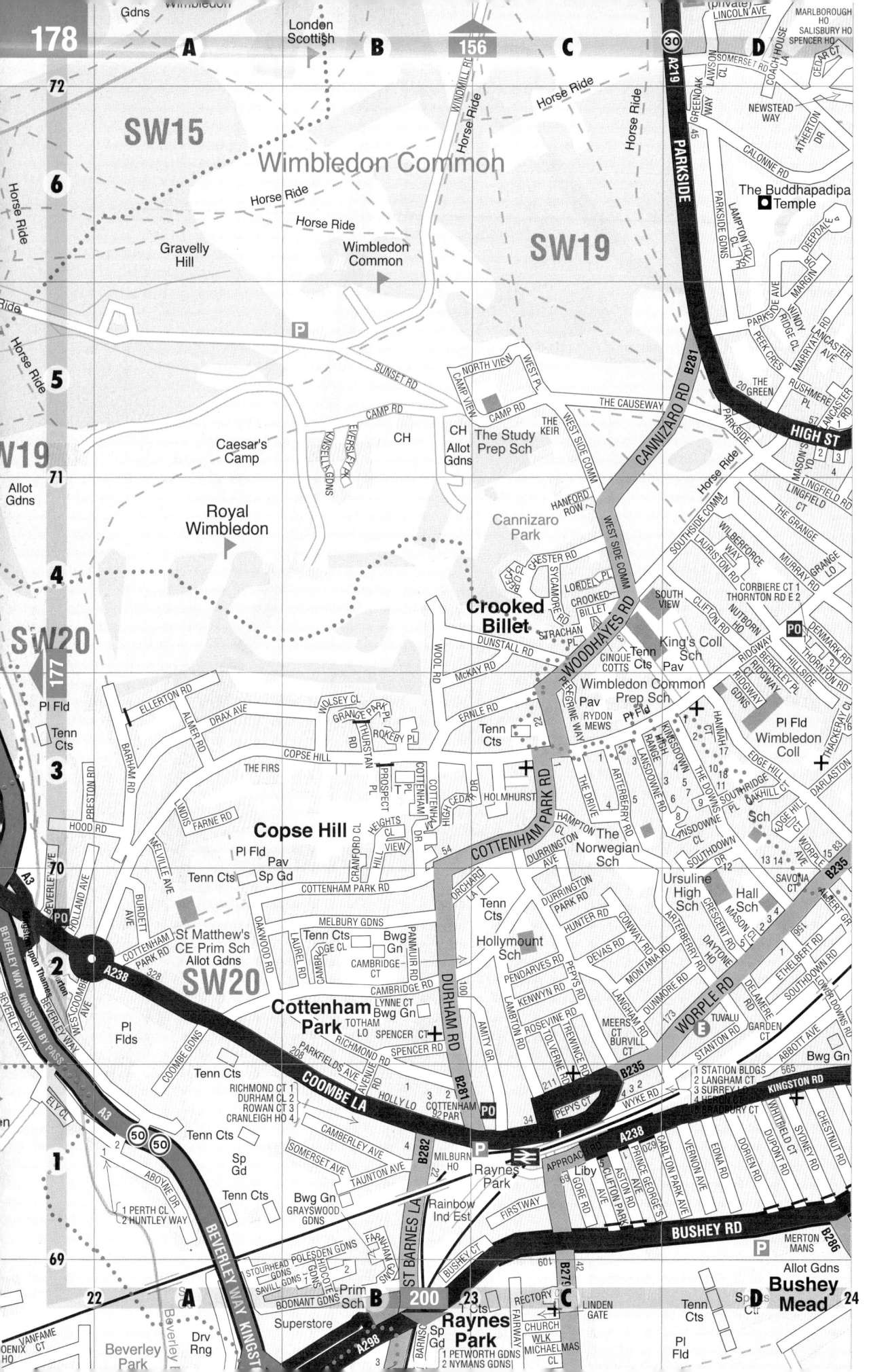
SW15
Wimbledon Common
SW19
SW20
London Scottish
Gravelly Hill
Wimbledon Common
Caesar's Camp
Royal Wimbledon
Horse Ride
PARKSIDE
The Buddhapadipa Temple
CANNIZARO RD
THE CAUSEWAY
HIGH ST
The Study Prep Sch
Cannizaro Park
Crooked Billet
WOODHAYES RD
WEST SIDE COMM
King's Coll Sch
Wimbledon Common Prep Sch
Wimbledon Coll
Copse Hill
COPSE HILL
COTTENHAM PARK RD
The Norwegian Sch
Ursuline High Sch
Hall Sch
Hollymount Sch
St Matthew's CE Prim Sch
Cottenham Park
DURHAM RD
COOMBE LA
WORPLE RD
KINGSTON RD
BUSHEY RD
Raynes Park
Rainbow Ind Est
BEVERLEY WAY
KINGSTON BY PASS
ST BARNES LA
Bushey Mead
Beverley Park
Superstore
A3
A238
A219
B281
B235
B282
A298
B279
B286
156
177
200
72
71
70
69
6
5
4
3
2
1
A
B
C
D
22
23
24

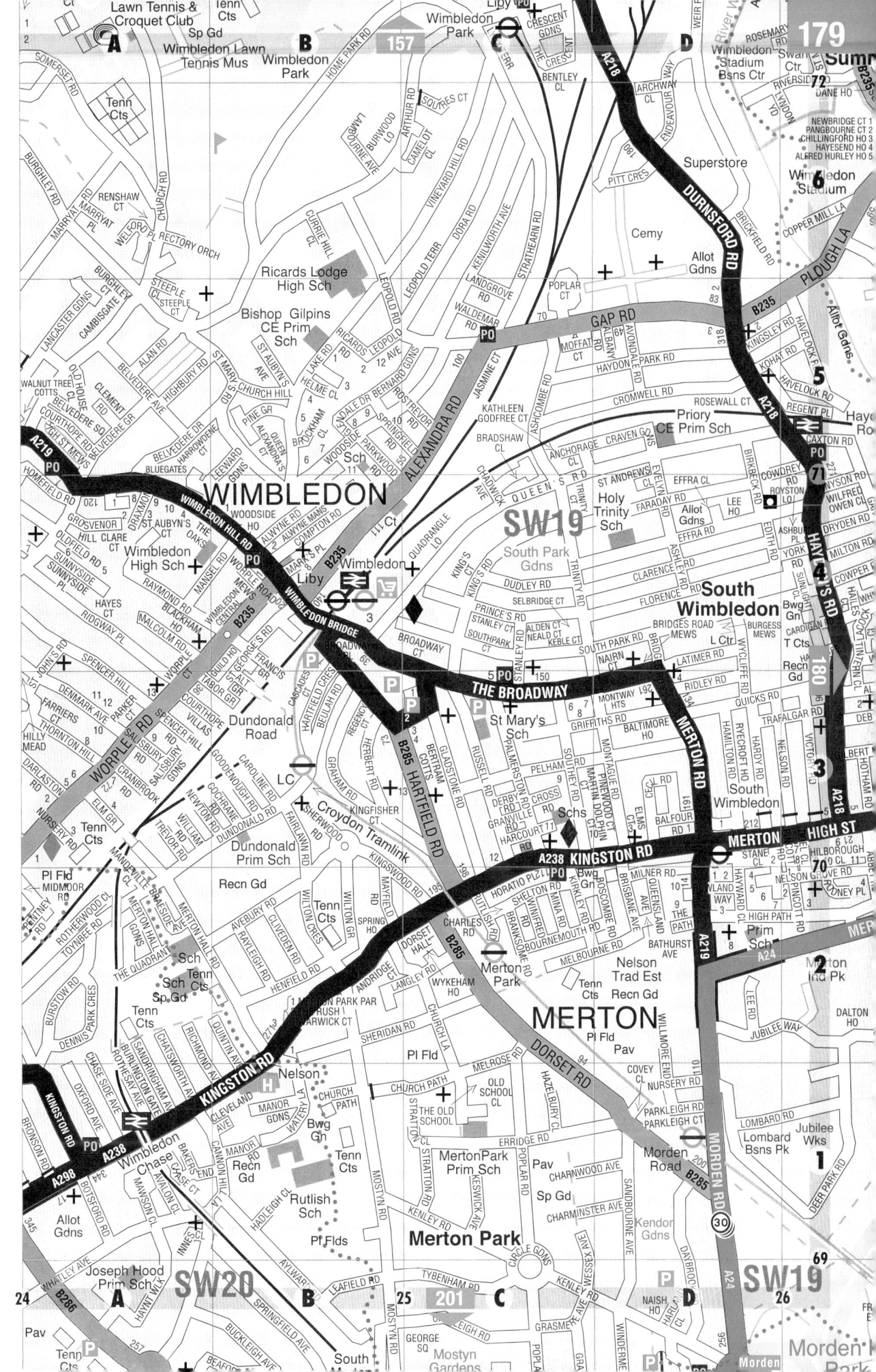

Lawn Tennis & Croquet Club
Wimbledon Lawn Tennis Mus
Wimbledon Park
157
Wimbledon Park
A
B
C
D
SOMERSET RD
HOME PARK RD
CRESCENT GDNS
THE CRESCENT
BENTLEY CL
A218
WEIR RD
ROSEMARY RD
Wimbledon Stadium Bsns Ctr
DANE HO
NEWBRIDGE CT
PANGBOURNE CT
CHILLINGFORD HO
HAYESEND HO
ALFRED HURLEY HO
ARCHWAY CL
ENDEAVOUR WAY
Superstore
Wimbledon Stadium
6
SQUIRES CT
ARTHUR RD
LAMBOURNE AVE
BURWOOD LO
CAMELOT CL
VINEYARD HILL RD
BURGHLEY RD
MARRYAT RD
MARRYAT PL
RENSHAW CT
WELFORD PL
CHURCH RD
RECTORY ORCH
PITT CRES
DURNSFORD RD
BRICKFIELD RD
COPPER MILL LA
PLOUGH LA
Cemy
Allot Gdns
CURRIE HILL CL
DORA RD
KENILWORTH AVE
STRATHEARN RD
Ricards Lodge High Sch
LEOPOLD RD
LEOPOLD TERR
LANDGROVE RD
POPLAR CT
Bishop Gilpins CE Prim Sch
WALDEMAR RD
GAP RD
B235
KINGSLEY RD
HAVELOCK RD
STEEPLE CL
STEEPLE CT
LANCASTER GDNS
CAMBISGATE
BURGHLEY CT
ALAN RD
HIGHBURY RD
ST MARY'S RD
ST AUBYN'S AVE
LAKE RD
RICARDS RD
LEOPOLD AVE
BERNARD GDNS
JASMINE CT
ALEXANDRA RD
MOFFAT CT
ALBANY RD
AVONDALE RD
HAYDON PARK RD
KOHAT RD
HAVELOCK RD
5
WALNUT TREE COTTS
OLD HOUSE CL
CLEMENT RD
BELVEDERE AVE
BELVEDERE SQ
BELVEDERE GR
CHURCH HILL
HELME CL
ROSTREVOR RD
ASHCOMBE RD
CROMWELL RD
ROSEWALL CT
REGENT PL
KATHLEEN GODFREE CT
Priory CE Prim Sch
CAXTON RD
COURTHOPE RD
HIGH ST MEWS
PINE GR
QUEEN ALEXANDRA'S CT
BROCKHAM CL
WOODSIDE
PARKWOOD RD
SPRINGFIELD RD
BRADSHAW CL
ANCHORAGE CL
CRAVEN GDNS
BELVEDERE DR
HARROWDENE CT
BLUEGATES
LEEWARD GDNS
Sch
A219
HOMEFIELD RD
WIMBLEDON
QUEEN'S RD
ST ANDREWS CL
EVELYN RD
EFFRA CL
COWDREY RD
ROYSTON LO
TYNSON RD
WILFRED OWEN CL
WIMBLEDON HILL RD
WOODSIDE HO
ALWYNE RD
ALWYNE MANS
COMPTON RD
CHADWICK AVE
TRINITY CT
Holy Trinity Sch
FARADAY RD
LEE HO
Allot Gdns
SW19
GROSVENOR HILL
CLARE CT
ST AUBYN'S CT
THE OAKS
Wimbledon High Sch
MANSEL RD
WORPLE RD
QUADRANGLE LO
KING'S CT
KING'S RD
South Park Gdns
EFFRA RD
EDITH RD
ASHBURN PL
YORK RD
HAYDONS RD
DRYDEN RD
MILTON RD
OLDFIELD RD
SUNNYSIDE
SUNNYSIDE PL
HAYES CT
RIDGWAY PL
RAYMOND RD
BLACKHAM HO
MALCOLM RD
WIMBLEDON CENTRAL
MARK'S PL
Wimbledon
Liby
WIMBLEDON BRIDGE
DUDLEY RD
SELBRIDGE CT
TRINITY RD
CLARENCE RD
FLORENCE RD
South Wimbledon
ASHLEY RD
SUNLIGHT CL
Bwg Gn
CARDIGAN RD
T Cts
COWPER RD
HAILES CL
4
PRINCE'S RD
STANLEY CT
SOUTHPARK CT
ALDEN CT
NEALD CT
KEBLE CT
BRIDGES ROAD MEWS
BURGESS MEWS
L Ctr
ST JOHN'S RD
SPENCER HILL
BROADWAY PL
BROADWAY CT
SOUTH PARK RD
NAIRN CT
LATIMER RD
WYCLIFFE RD
Recn Gd
TINTERN CL
DENMARK AVE
PARKER CT
FARRIERS CT
THORNTON HILL
GUILD HO
ST GEORGE'S RD
FRANCIS GR
TABOR GR
SALT GR
COURTHOPE VILLAS
CASCADES CT
HARTFIELD CRES
BEULAH RD
THE BROADWAY
MONTWAY HTS
RIDLEY RD
QUICKS RD
TRAFALGAR RD
180
HILLY MEAD
WORPLE RD
SPENCER RD
REGENCY CT
St Mary's Sch
GRIFFITHS RD
BALTIMORE HO
MERTON RD
HAMILTON RD
RYECROFT HO
HARDY RD
NELSON RD
VICTORY RD
GILBERT
HOTHAM RD
DARLASTON RD
SALISBURY RD
CRANBROOK RD
SALISBURY GDNS
Dundonald Road
CAROLINE RD
GOODENOUGH RD
HERBERT RD
B285 HARTFIELD RD
BERTRAM COTTS
GLADSTONE RD
RUSSELL RD
PALMERSTON RD
SOUTHEY RD
MONTAGUE RD
PINEWOOD CT
MARTIN DOLPHIN CT
PELHAM RD
CECIL RD
South Wimbledon
3
A218
NURSERY RD
ELM GR
Tenn Cts
WILLIAM RD
NEWTON RD
COCHRANE RD
DUNDONALD RD
LC
GRAHAM RD
KINGFISHER CT
DERBY RD
CROSS RD
GRANVILLE RD
HARCOURT RD
Schs
ELMS CT
BALFOUR RD
MERTON HIGH ST
HILBOROUGH CL
TREVOR RD
MANDEVILLE CL
Dundonald Prim Sch
FAIRLAWN RD
SHERWOOD RD
Croydon Tramlink
KINGSWOOD RD
A238 KINGSTON RD
STANE CL
NELSON GROVE RD
Pl Fld
MIDMOOR RD
PENTNEY RD
Recn Gd
HORATIO PL
SHELTON RD
KIRKLEY RD
MILNER RD
ROWLAND WAY
HAYWARD CL
RODNEY PL
ROTHERWOOD CL
TOYNBEE RD
MERTON HALL GDNS
BRAESIDE AVE
MERTON HALL RD
AVEBURY RD
RAYLEIGH RD
CLIVEDEN RD
WILTON CRES
Tenn Cts
WILTON GR
SPRING HO
MAYFIELD RD
CHARLES RD
RUTLISH RD
WINIFRED RD
MINA RD
ROSCOBE RD
BRISBANE AVE
QUEENSLAND AVE
THE PATH
HIGH PATH
PINCOTT RD
BATHURST AVE
Prim Sch
THE QUADRANT
Sch
Tenn Cts
Sp Gd
HENFIELD RD
DORSET HALL
ANDRIDGE CT
B285
Merton Park
BRANKSOME RD
BOURNEMOUTH RD
MELBOURNE RD
Nelson Trad Est
Tenn Cts
Recn Gd
A219
A24
Merton Ind Pk
2
BURSTOW RD
DENNIS PARK CRES
Tenn Cts
LANGLEY RD
WYKEHAM HO
MERTON PARK PAR
RUSH
WARWICK CT
SHERIDAN RD
CHURCH LA
MERTON
DORSET RD
Pl Fld
Pav
WILLMORE END
LEE RD
JUBILEE WAY
DALTON HO
SANDRINGHAM AVE
BURLINGTON GATE
ROTHESAY AVE
CHATSWORTH AVE
RICHMOND AVE
QUINTIN AVE
Pl Fld
MELROSE RD
COVEY CL
NURSERY RD
CHASE SIDE AVE
OXFORD AVE
KINGSTON RD
Nelson
H
CHURCH PATH
OLD SCHOOL CL
THE OLD SCHOOL
HAZELBURY CL
PARKLEIGH RD
PARKLEIGH CT
LOMBARD RD
Lombard Bsns Pk
Jubilee Wks
BRONSON RD
CLEVELAND AVE
MANOR GDNS
WATERY LA
Bwg Gn
Tenn Cts
STRATTON CL
ERRIDGE RD
MORDEN RD
Morden Road
1
A298
A238
Wimbledon Chase
BAKERS END
CHASE CT
MANOR RD
Recn Gd
MertonPark Prim Sch
Pav
CHARNWOOD AVE
Sp Gd
CHARMINSTER AVE
SANDBOURNE AVE
DEER PARK RD
BOTSFORD RD
MAWSON CL
AVALON CL
CANNON HILL LA
HADLEIGH CL
Rutlish Sch
MOSTYN RD
STRATTON RD
KEYNSHAM
KENLEY RD
KESWICK AVE
POPLAR RD
Kendor Gdns
30
Allot Gdns
INNES CL
Pl Flds
Merton Park
CIRCLE GDNS
WESSEX AVE
DAYBROOK RD
69
WHATLEY AVE
Joseph Hood Prim Sch
HAYNT WLK
SW20
AYLWARD RD
LEAFIELD RD
TYBENHAM RD
KENLEY RD
NAISH HO
HARLAND CL
SW19
24
B286
A
B
25
201
C
D
26
SPRINGFIELD AVE
GEORGE SQ
Mostyn Gardens
GRASMERE AVE
WINDERMERE
Pav
BUCKLEIGH RD
South Merton
Morden

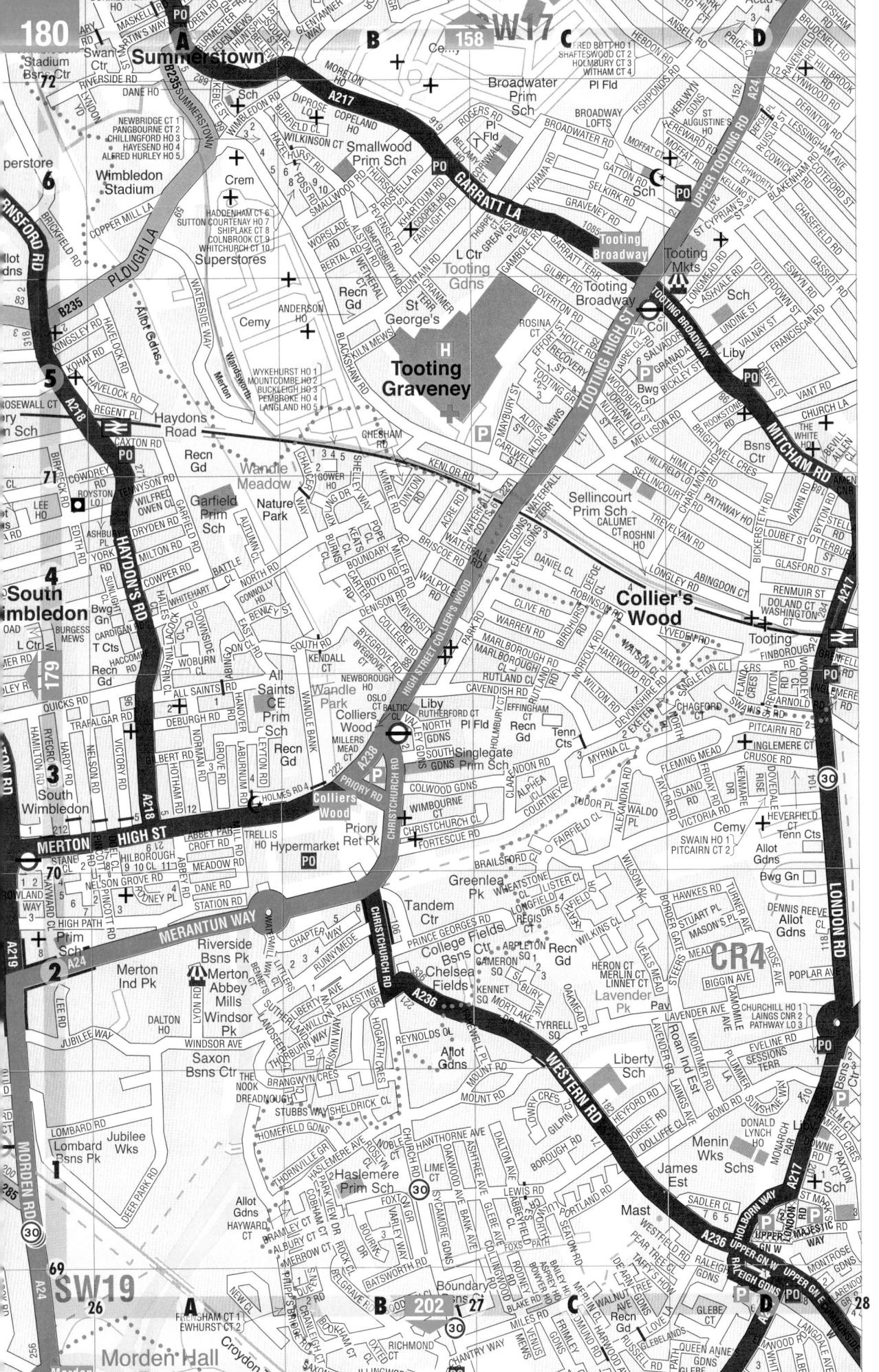
158
SW17
Summerstown
Wimbledon Stadium
Wimbledon Stadium Bsns Ctr
Superstores
Cemy
Crem
Smallwood Prim Sch
Broadwater Prim Sch
GARRATT LA
A217
Tooting Broadway
Tooting Mkts
Tooting Gdns
St George's
Tooting Graveney
TOOTING HIGH ST
UPPER TOOTING RD
TOOTING BROADWAY
MITCHAM RD
Haydons Road
Wandle Meadow Nature Park
Garfield Prim Sch
HAYDON'S RD
A218
PLOUGH LA
B235
South Wimbledon
Sellincourt Prim Sch
Collier's Wood
Tooting
HIGH STREET COLLIER'S WOOD
A238
Colliers Wood
All Saints CE Prim Sch
Wandle Park
Singlegate Prim Sch
Priory Ret Pk
Hypermarket
MERTON HIGH ST
MERANTUN WAY
A24
Merton Ind Pk
Merton Abbey Mills
Windsor Pk
Saxon Bsns Ctr
CHRISTCHURCH RD
College Fields Bsns Ctr
Chelsea Fields
Greenlea Pk
Tandem Ctr
Lavender Pk
CR4
A236
WESTERN RD
Liberty Sch
LONDON RD
Lombard Bsns Pk
Jubilee Wks
Haslemere Prim Sch
Menin Wks
James Est
Allot Gdns
MORDEN RD
SW19
Morden Hall
202
179
A
B
C
D
1
2
3
4
5
6

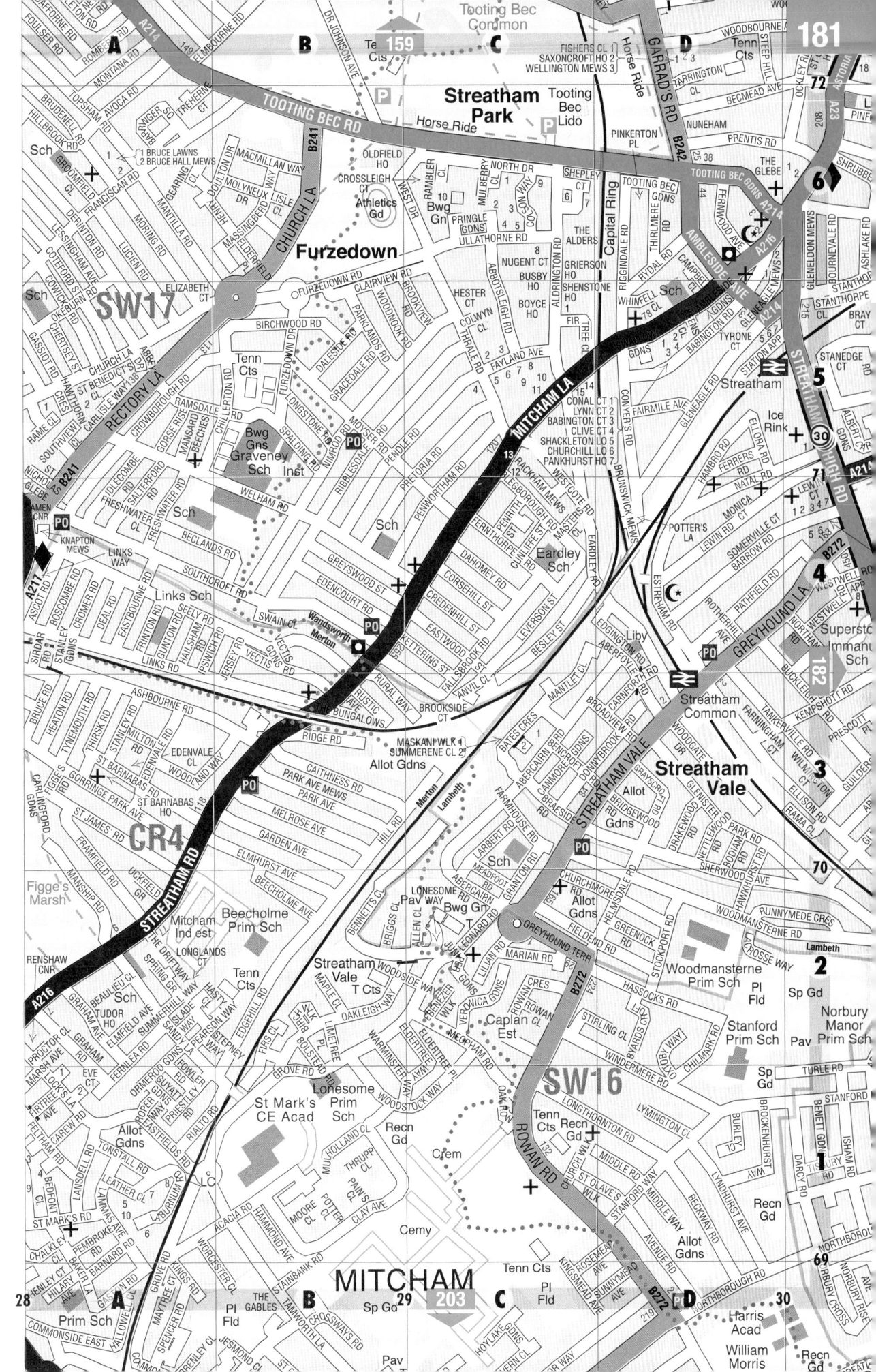
Tooting Bec Common
A
B
C
D
159
Streatham Park
Tooting Bec Lido
Horse Ride
TOOTING BEC RD
A214
B241
CHURCH LA
Furzedown
SW17
RECTORY LA
Athletics Gd
FISHERS CL 1
SAXONCROFT HO 2
WELLINGTON MEWS 3
GARRAD'S RD
B242
PINKERTON PL
TOOTING BEC GDNS
AMBLESIDE AVE
A216
Capital Ring
MITCHAM LA
Streatham
STREATHAM HIGH RD
A23
Ice Rink
CONAL CT 1
LYNN CT 2
BABINGTON CT 3
CLIVE CT 4
SHACKLETON LO 5
CHURCHILL LO 6
PANKHURST HO 7
Graveney Sch
Links Sch
Eardley Sch
Wandsworth
Merton
GREYHOUND LA
Streatham Common
Streatham Vale
STREATHAM VALE
B272
182
Lambeth
CR4
STREATHAM RD
A217
Figge's Marsh
Mitcham Ind est
Beecholme Prim Sch
Allot Gdns
Woodmansterne Prim Sch
Norbury Manor Prim Sch
Stanford Prim Sch
Caplan Est
SW16
ROWAN RD
St Mark's CE Acad
Lonesome Prim Sch
Crem
Cemy
MITCHAM
203
Harris Acad
William Morris
Prim Sch
28
29
30
1
2
3
4
5
6
69
70
71
72

A
B
C
D
160
181
204
SE27
STREATHAM
SW16
Norbury
Dunraven Sch
Liby
Sunnyhill Prim Sch
Julian's Prim Sch
Bishop Thomas Grant RC Sec Sch
St Andrews RC Prim Sch
Streatham Common
Capital Ring
Horse Ride
Crown Lane Prim Sch
St Joseph's RC Coll
Superstore
Immanuel Sch
Ice Rink
Streatham
Streatham Common
Streatham Vale
Norwood Grove
Norbury Park
Norbury Manor Bsns & Enterprise Coll for Girls
Norbury Manor Prim Sch
Stanford Prim Sch
Kensington Avenue Prim Sch
Norbury Trad Est
St James The Great RC Prim Sch
Harris Acad
William Morris
Allot Gdns
Tenn Cts
Bwg Gn
Pl Fld
Sp Gd
Recn Gd
Com Ctr
Pav
Lambeth
Croydon
STREATHAM COMMON N
CROWN LA
STREATHAM HIGH RD
LONDON RD
GREEN LA
KNIGHT'S HILL
STREATHAM COMMON S
GREYHOUND LA
GIBSON'S HILL
NORBURY HILL
WESTWELL ROAD
1 ELPHINSTONE CT
2 RIDLEY CT
3 BLADON CT
4 COMMONSIDE CT
5 SANDERS HO
6 BYRON CL
7 HAMBLY MANS
8 ST JOHNS HO
A23
A214
A215
A216
B272
B273
1
2
3
4
5
6
72
71
70
69
30
31
32

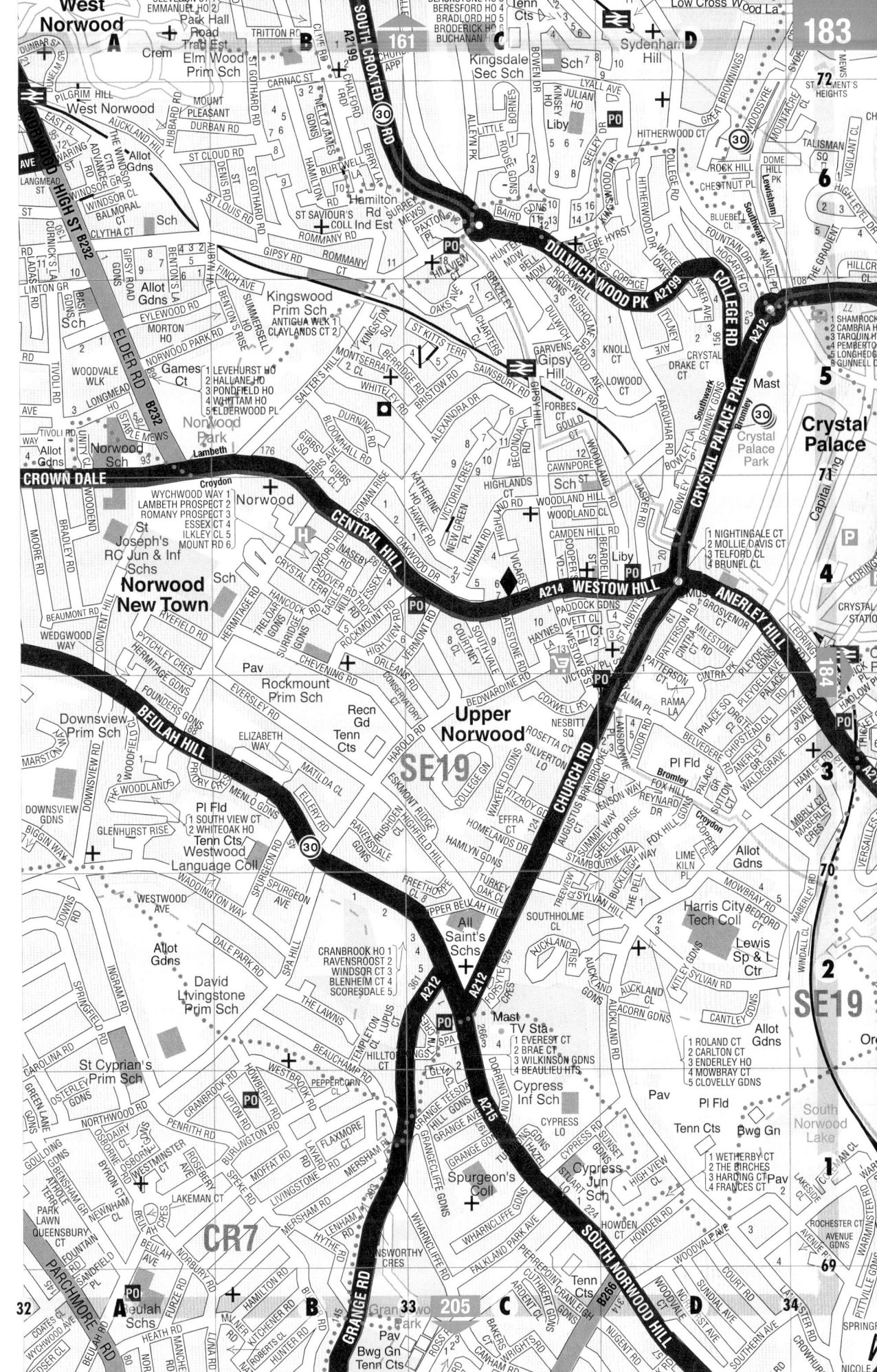
West Norwood
Upper Norwood
Norwood New Town
Crystal Palace
SE19
CR7
CROWN DALE
CENTRAL HILL
WESTOW HILL
BEULAH HILL
CHURCH RD
ANERLEY HILL
CRYSTAL PALACE PAR
COLLEGE RD
DULWICH WOOD PK
SOUTH CROXTED RD
SOUTH NORWOOD HILL
GRANGE RD
NORWOOD HIGH ST
ELDER RD
GIPSY HILL
Gipsy Hill
Sydenham Hill
Crystal Palace Park
Norwood Park
Kingswood Prim Sch
Rockmount Prim Sch
Downsview Prim Sch
David Livingstone Prim Sch
St Cyprian's Prim Sch
Harris City Tech Coll
Lewis Sp & L Ctr
Cypress Inf Sch
Cypress Jun Sch
Spurgeon's Coll
All Saint's Schs
Westwood Language Coll
St Joseph's RC Jun & Inf Schs
Kingsdale Sec Sch
Elm Wood Prim Sch
Beulah Schs
South Norwood Lake
161
184
205
32
33
34
A
B
C
D
1
2
3
4
5
6

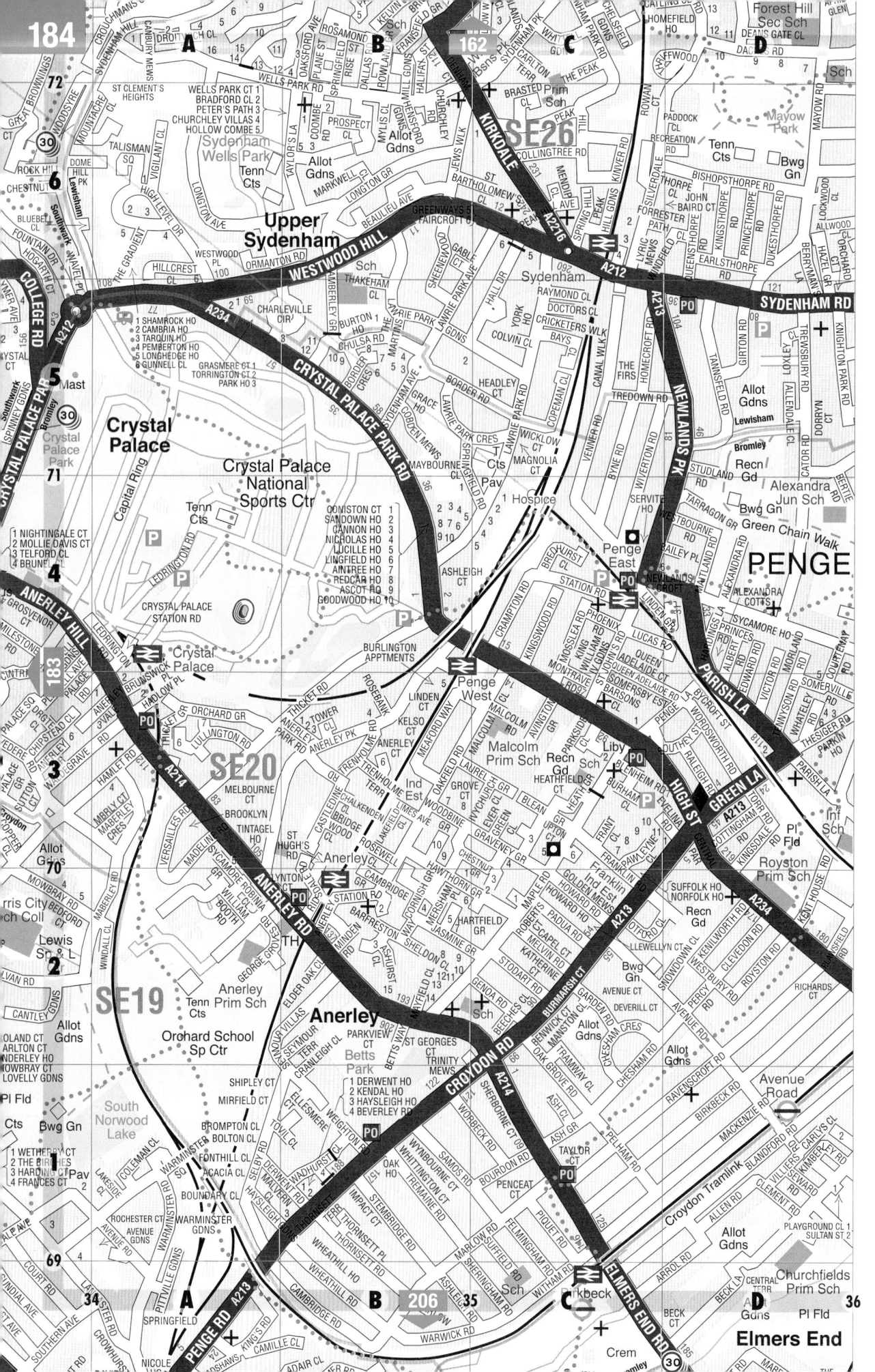
A
B
C
D
162
183
206
34
35
36
72
6
5
71
4
3
70
2
1
69
SE26
SE20
SE19
Upper Sydenham
Sydenham
Crystal Palace
Crystal Palace Park
Crystal Palace National Sports Ctr
Capital Ring
PENGE
Penge East
Penge West
Anerley
Birkbeck
Elmers End
Sydenham Wells Park
Forest Hill Sec Sch
Mayow Park
Alexandra Jun Sch
Green Chain Walk
Malcolm Prim Sch
Royston Prim Sch
Anerley Prim Sch
Orchard School Sp Ctr
South Norwood Lake
Betts Park
Churchfields Prim Sch
Avenue Road
Croydon Tramlink
Franklin Ind Est
Lewis Sp & L Ctr
Hospice
Crem
WESTWOOD HILL
SYDENHAM RD
CRYSTAL PALACE PARK RD
KIRKDALE
COLLEGE RD
CRYSTAL PALACE PAR
ANERLEY HILL
ANERLEY RD
CROYDON RD
HIGH ST
GREEN LA
PARISH LA
NEWLANDS PK
PENGE RD
ELMERS END RD
A212
A234
A213
A214
A2216
Lewisham
Southwark
Bromley
Croydon

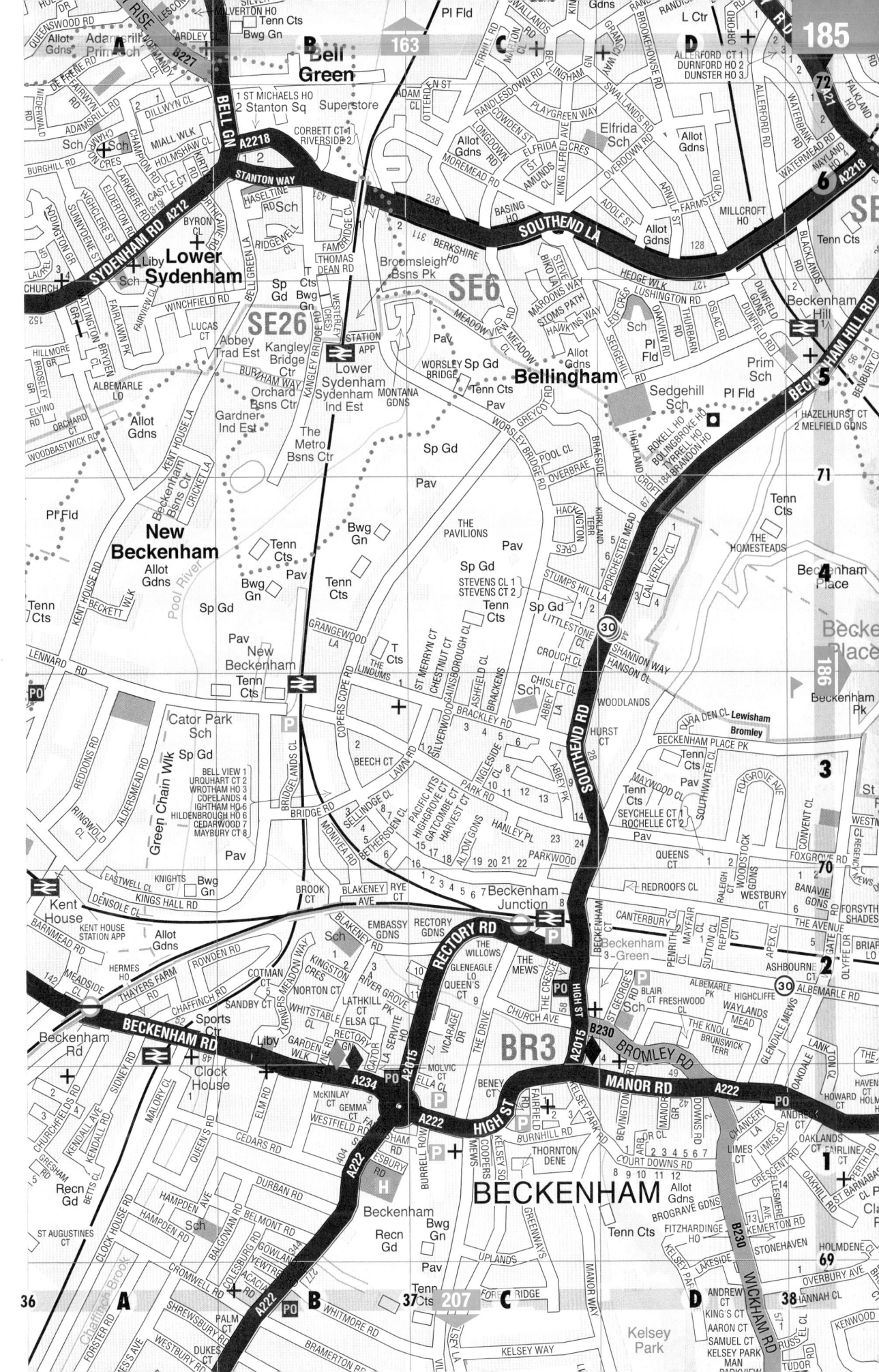
Bell Green
Lower Sydenham
SE26
SE6
Bellingham
New Beckenham
Kent House
Beckenham Junction
BR3
BECKENHAM
Beckenham Hill
Beckenham Place
Beckenham Pk
Lewisham
Bromley
SYDENHAM RD A212
BELL GN
A2218
STANTON WAY
SOUTHEND LA
BECKENHAM HILL RD
SOUTHEND RD
HIGH ST
A2015
RECTORY RD
BECKENHAM RD
A234
A222
MANOR RD
BROMLEY RD
B230
WICKHAM RD
B227
Superstore
Sedgehill Sch
Cator Park Sch
Green Chain Wlk
Pool River
Chaffinch Brook
Kelsey Park
Beckenham Place Pk
Lower Sydenham Ind Est
Kangley Bridge Ctr
Abbey Trad Est
Orchard Bsns Ctr
Gardner Ind Est
The Metro Bsns Ctr
Broomsleigh Bsns Pk
Beckenham Bsns Ctr
Clock House
Sports Ctr
Recn Gd
Allot Gdns
Tenn Cts
Sp Gd
Pav
Pl Fld
Bwg Gn
Sch
Liby
PO
163
186
207
36
37
38
A
B
C
D
1
2
3
4
5
6
69
70
71
72

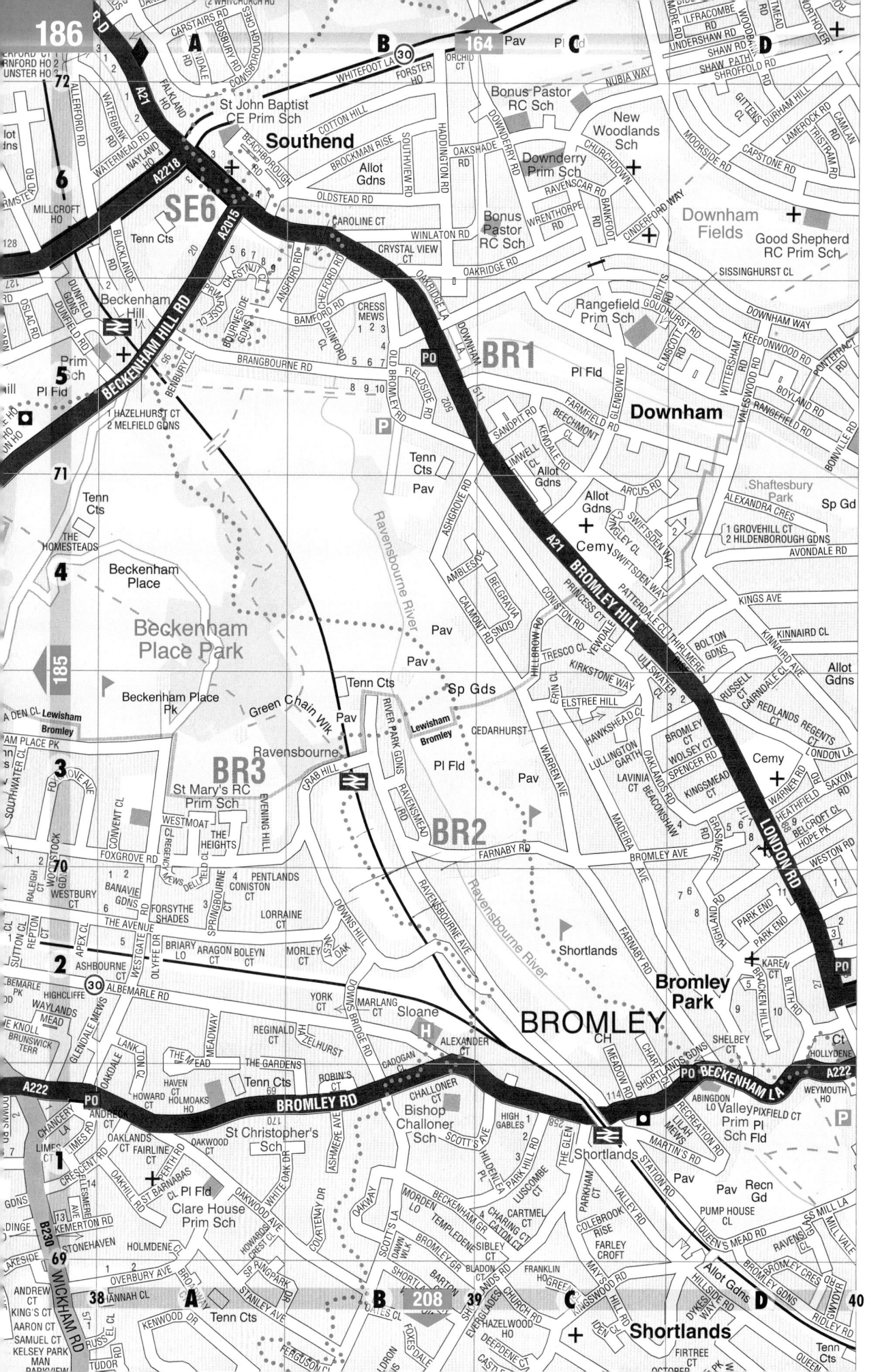

164
208
185
Southend
SE6
BR1
BR2
BR3
Downham
Downham Fields
Beckenham Place Park
Beckenham Place
Beckenham Hill
Ravensbourne
Shortlands
Bromley Park
BROMLEY
Sloane
A21
A2218
A2015
A222
B230
BECKENHAM HILL RD
BROMLEY HILL
LONDON RD
BROMLEY RD
BECKENHAM LA
WICKHAM RD
DOWNHAM WAY
WHITEFOOT LA
Ravensbourne River
Green Chain Wlk
St John Baptist CE Prim Sch
Bonus Pastor RC Sch
New Woodlands Sch
Downderry Prim Sch
Good Shepherd RC Prim Sch
Rangefield Prim Sch
St Mary's RC Prim Sch
Bishop Challoner Sch
St Christopher's Sch
Clare House Prim Sch
Valley Prim Sch
Shaftesbury Park

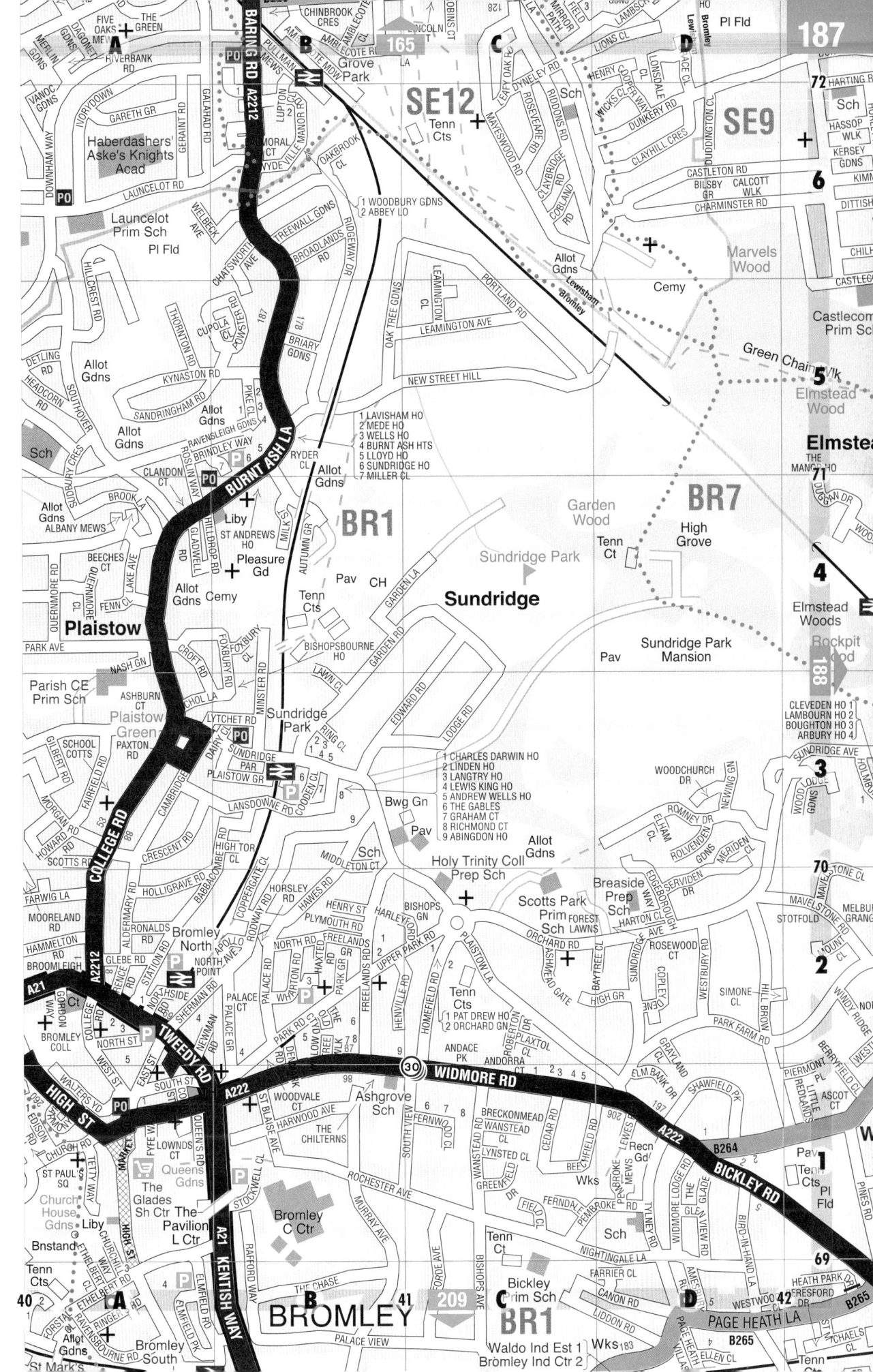

BARING RD
A2212
BURNT ASH LA
COLLEGE RD
SE12
SE9
BR1
BR7
Grove Park
Haberdashers' Aske's Knights Acad
Launcelot Prim Sch
Plaistow
Sundridge
Sundridge Park
Sundridge Park Mansion
Garden Wood
High Grove
Marvels Wood
Elmstead Wood
Elmstead Woods
Green Chain Wlk
Parish CE Prim Sch
Plaistow Green
Bromley North
Holy Trinity Coll Prep Sch
Scotts Park Prim Sch
Breaside Prep Sch
Ashgrove Sch
Bromley C Ctr
Bickley Prim Sch
The Glades Sh Ctr
The Pavilion L Ctr
Queens Gdns
Church House Gdns
Bromley South
WIDMORE RD
A222
BICKLEY RD
HIGH ST
TWEEDY RD
KENTISH WAY
A21
PAGE HEATH LA
BROMLEY
1 WOODBURY GDNS
2 ABBEY LO
1 LAVISHAM HO
2 MEDE HO
3 WELLS HO
4 BURNT ASH HTS
5 LLOYD HO
6 SUNDRIDGE HO
7 MILLER CL
1 CHARLES DARWIN HO
2 LINDEN HO
3 LANGTRY HO
4 LEWIS KING HO
5 ANDREW WELLS HO
6 THE GABLES
7 GRAHAM CT
8 RICHMOND CT
9 ABINGDON HO
CLEVEDEN HO 1
LAMBOURN HO 2
BOUGHTON HO 3
ARBURY HO 4
1 PAT DREW HO
2 ORCHARD GN
Waldo Ind Est 1
Bromley Ind Ctr 2
165
188
209

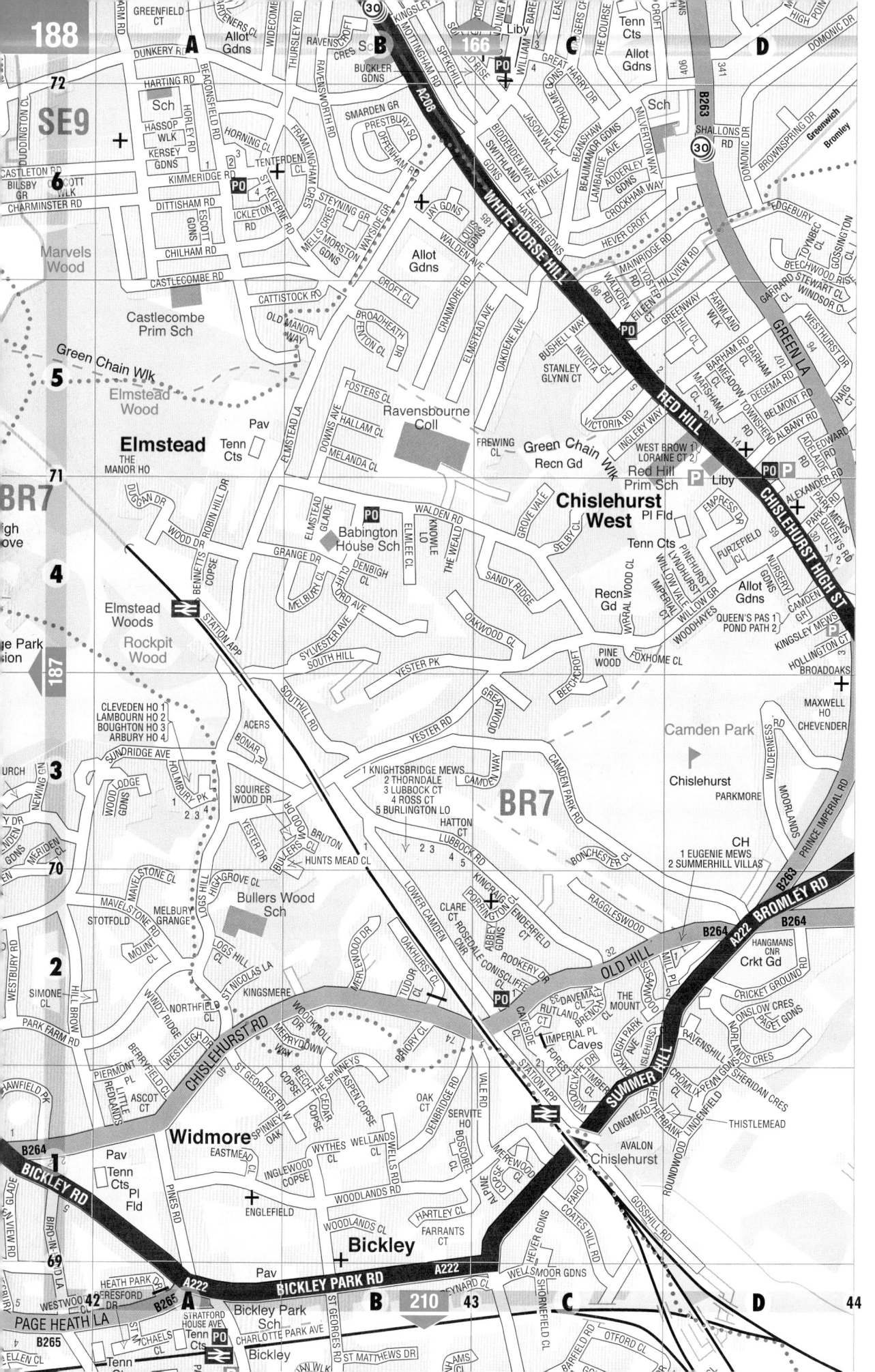

A
B
C
D
SE9
BR7
Elmstead
Chislehurst West
Widmore
Bickley
Chislehurst
Castlecombe Prim Sch
Ravensbourne Coll
Babington House Sch
Bullers Wood Sch
Red Hill Prim Sch
Bickley Park Sch
Elmstead Woods
Rockpit Wood
Elmstead Wood
Marvels Wood
Camden Park
Green Chain Wlk
WHITE HORSE HILL
RED HILL
CHISLEHURST HIGH ST
GREEN LA
CHISLEHURST RD
BICKLEY PARK RD
BICKLEY RD
BROMLEY RD
SUMMER HILL
OLD HILL
PAGE HEATH LA
MOTTINGHAM RD
STATION APP
SOUTHILL RD
YESTER RD
CAMDEN PARK RD
LOWER CAMDEN
WOODLANDS RD
ELMSTEAD LA
WALDEN RD
1 KNIGHTSBRIDGE MEWS
2 THORNDALE
3 LUBBOCK CT
4 ROSS CT
5 BURLINGTON LO
CLEVEDEN HO 1
LAMBOURN HO 2
BOUGHTON HO 3
ARBURY HO 4
1 EUGENIE MEWS
2 SUMMERHILL VILLAS
WEST BROW 1
LORAINE CT 2
QUEEN'S PAS 1
POND PATH 2
A208
A222
B263
B264
B265
166
187
210
72
71
70
69
42
43
44

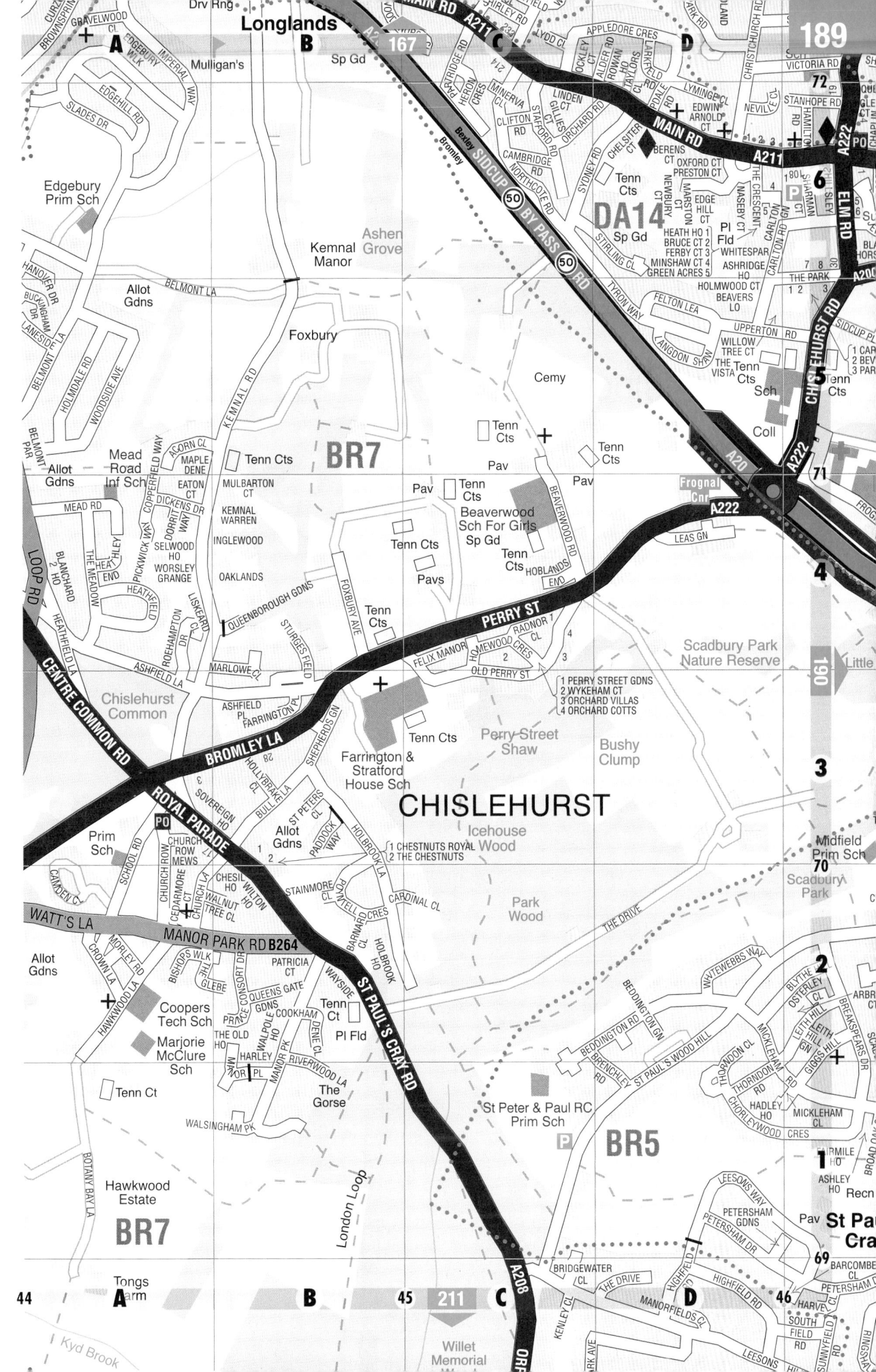
Longlands
Mulligan's
Sp Gd
Edgebury Prim Sch
Kemnal Manor
Ashen Grove
Allot Gdns
Foxbury
Cemy
BR7
DA14
SIDCUP BY PASS RD
MAIN RD
Mead Road Inf Sch
Beaverwood Sch For Girls
Frognal Cnr
PERRY ST
Scadbury Park Nature Reserve
Chislehurst Common
CENTRE COMMON RD
BROMLEY LA
ROYAL PARADE
Farrington & Stratford House Sch
Perry Street Shaw
Bushy Clump
CHISLEHURST
Icehouse Wood
1 PERRY STREET GDNS
2 WYKEHAM CT
3 ORCHARD VILLAS
4 ORCHARD COTTS
1 CHESTNUTS ROYAL
2 THE CHESTNUTS
Park Wood
Midfield Prim Sch
Scadbury Park
WATT'S LA
MANOR PARK RD B264
ST PAUL'S CRAY RD
Coopers Tech Sch
Marjorie McClure Sch
The Gorse
St Peter & Paul RC Prim Sch
BR5
Hawkwood Estate
London Loop
Tongs Farm
Kyd Brook
Willet Memorial

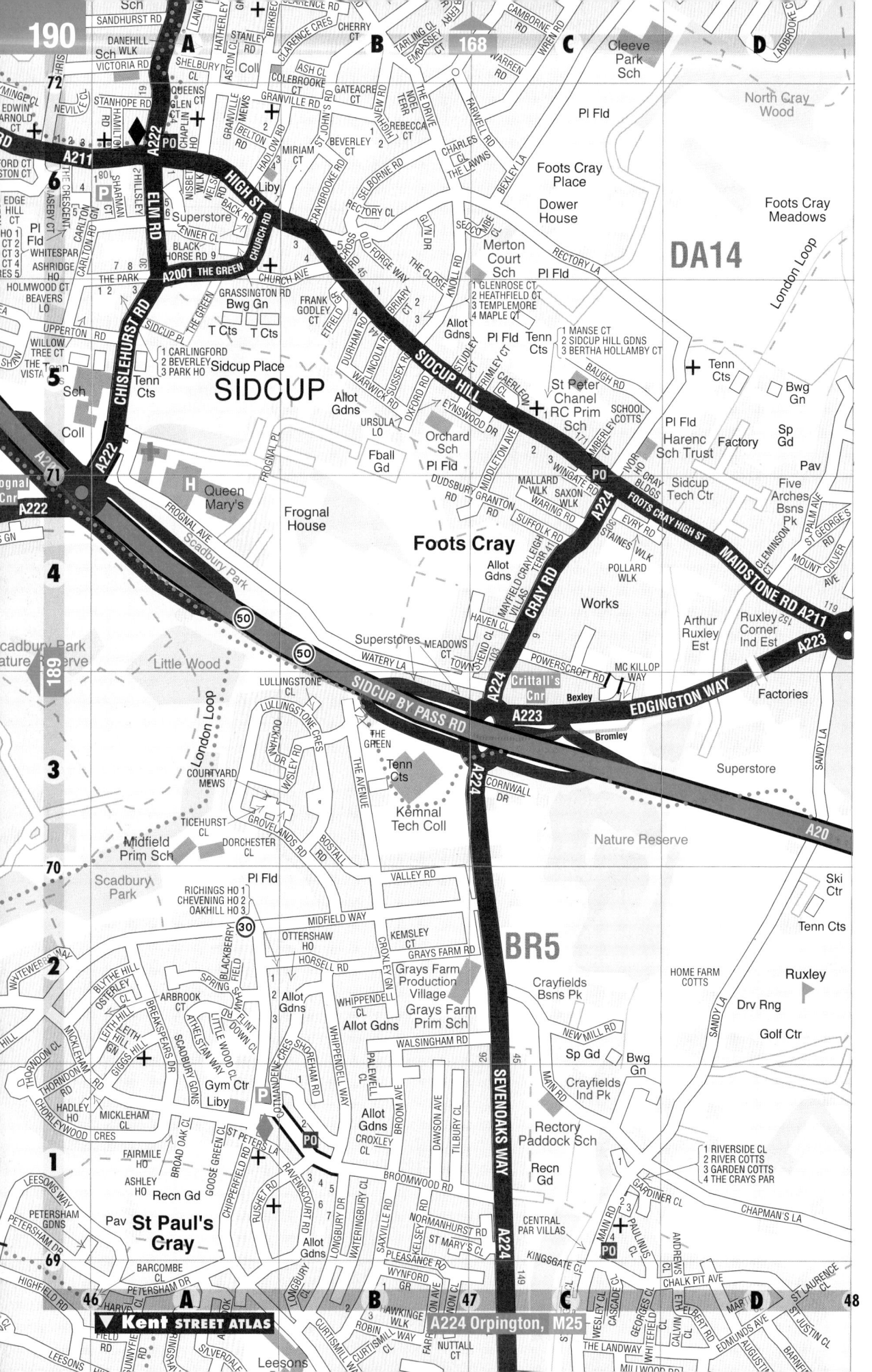
168
SIDCUP
Foots Cray
DA14
BR5
St Paul's Cray
Sidcup Place
Queen Mary's
Frognal House
Scadbury Park
Little Wood
Foots Cray Place
Dower House
Foots Cray Meadows
Merton Court Sch
Cleeve Park Sch
North Cray Wood
Kemnal Tech Coll
Grays Farm Production Village
Grays Farm Prim Sch
Crayfields Bsns Pk
Crayfields Ind Pk
Rectory Paddock Sch
Ruxley
Ruxley Corner Ind Est
Arthur Ruxley Est
Sidcup Tech Ctr
Harenc Sch Trust
St Peter Chanel RC Prim Sch
Orchard Sch
Midfield Prim Sch
Nature Reserve
Five Arches Bsns Pk
London Loop
A20
A211
A222
A223
A224
A2001
SIDCUP HILL
SIDCUP BY PASS RD
MAIDSTONE RD
EDGINGTON WAY
SEVENOAKS WAY
CRAY RD
FOOTS CRAY HIGH ST
HIGH ST
ELM RD
CHISLEHURST RD
Crittall's Cnr
Bexley
Bromley
189

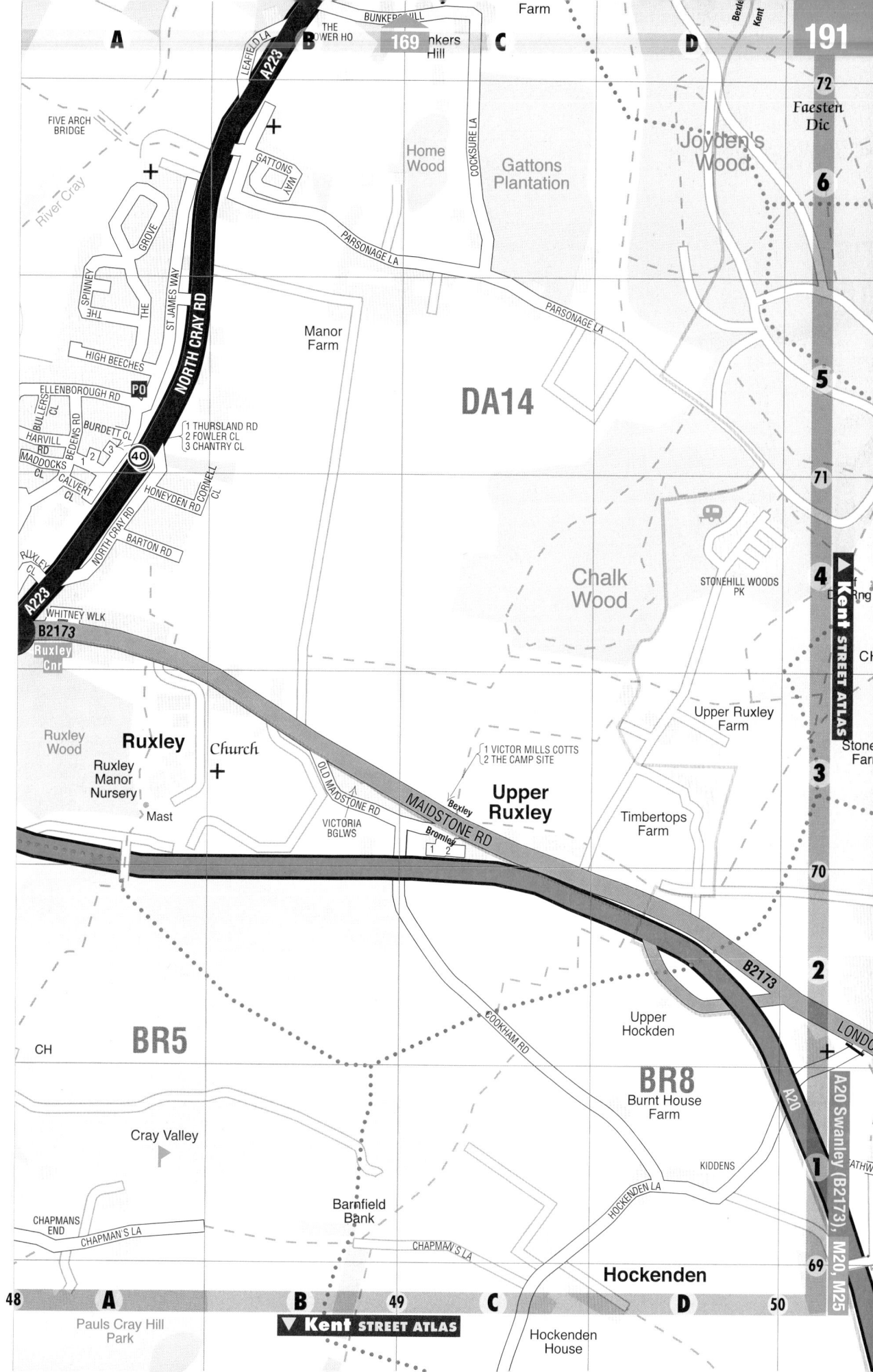

A   B   169   C   D

72

Faesten Dic

FIVE ARCH BRIDGE

Joyden's Wood

6

River Cray

BUNKERS HILL
THE TOWER HO

Bunkers Hill

COCKSURE LA

Home Wood

Gattons Plantation

GATTONS WAY

PARSONAGE LA

PARSONAGE LA

5

Manor Farm

DA14

71

THE SPINNEY
THE GROVE
ST JAMES WAY
HIGH BEECHES
NORTH CRAY RD

ELLENBOROUGH RD
BULLERS RD
BEDENS RD
BURDETT CL
HARVILL RD
MADDOCKS CL
CALVERT CL
PO
40

1 THURSLAND RD
2 FOWLER CL
3 CHANTRY CL

HONEYDEN RD
CORNELL CL

NORTH CRAY RD
BARTON RD

Chalk Wood

STONEHILL WOODS PK

4

RUXLEY CL
A223
B2173
WHITNEY WLK
Ruxley Cnr

Stone Far

Kent STREET ATLAS

Ruxley Wood

Ruxley

Church

Ruxley Manor Nursery

• Mast

OLD MAIDSTONE RD
VICTORIA BGLWS
MAIDSTONE RD

Bexley
Bromley
1 2

1 VICTOR MILLS COTTS
2 THE CAMP SITE

Upper Ruxley

Upper Ruxley Farm

Timbertops Farm

3

70

B2173

2

LONDO

BR5

CH

Cray Valley

COOKHAM RD

Upper Hockden

BR8

Burnt House Farm

A20

A20 Swanley (B2173), M20, M25

1

CHAPMANS END
CHAPMAN'S LA

Barnfield Bank

CHAPMAN'S LA

KIDDENS

HOCKENDEN LA

ATHW

69

48   A   B   49   C   D   50

Pauls Cray Hill Park

Hockenden

Hockenden House

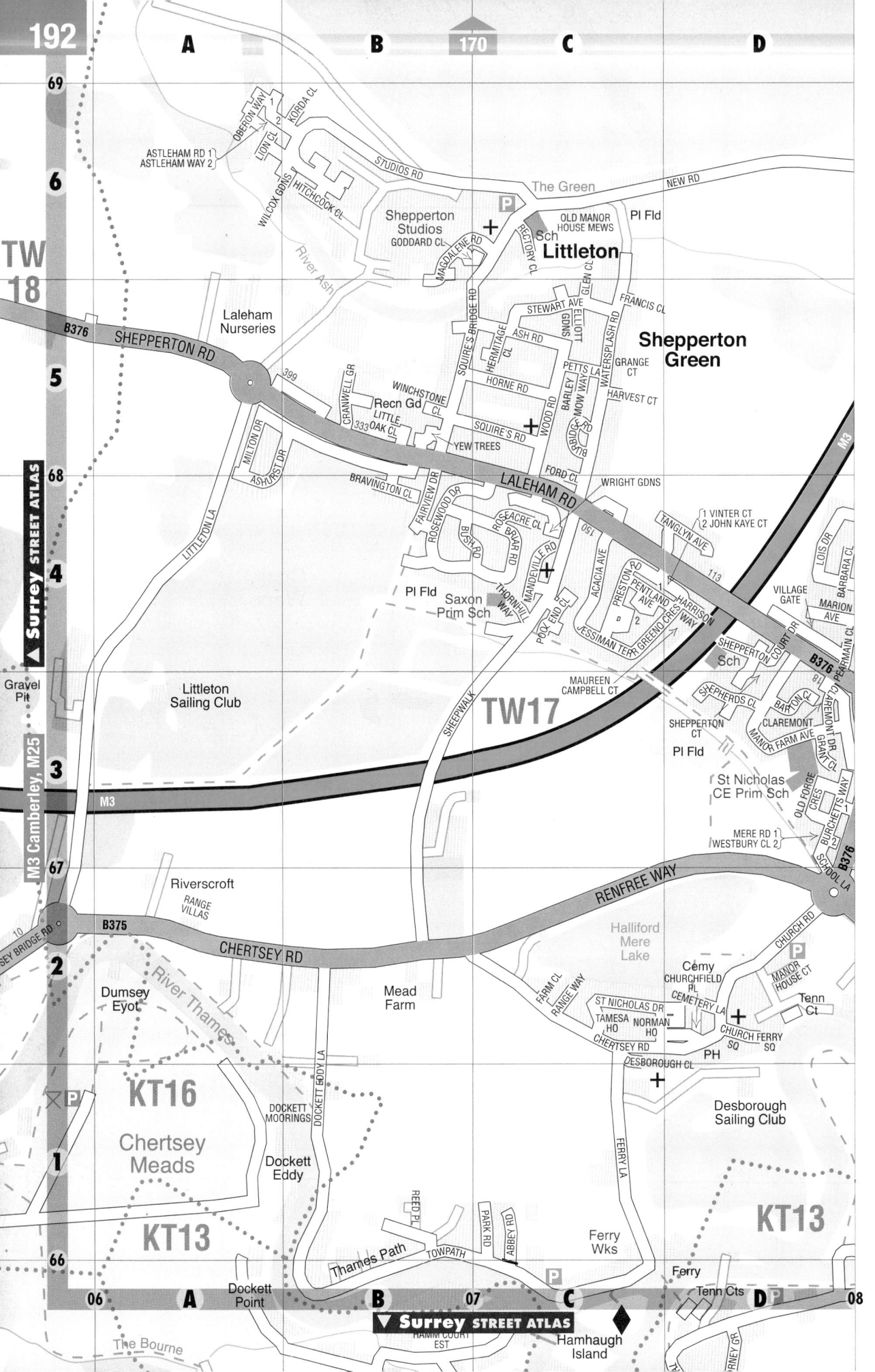
A
B
170
C
D
69
6
5
68
4
3
67
2
1
66
TW
18
Surrey STREET ATLAS
M3 Camberley, M25
OBERON WAY
KORDA CL
LION CL
ASTLEHAM RD 1
ASTLEHAM WAY 2
WILCOX GDNS
HITCHCOCK CL
STUDIOS RD
The Green
NEW RD
Shepperton Studios
GODDARD CL
MAGDALENE RD
RECTORY CL
OLD MANOR HOUSE MEWS
Pl Fld
Sch
Littleton
GLEN CL
River Ash
FRANCIS CL
STEWART AVE
ELLIOTT GDNS
SQUIRE'S BRIDGE RD
HERMITAGE CL
ASH RD
WATERSPLASH RD
Shepperton Green
B376
SHEPPERTON RD
Laleham Nurseries
GRANGE CT
PETTS LA
HORNE RD
399
CRANWELL GR
WINCHSTONE CL
Recn Gd
LITTLE OAK CL
333
BARLEY MOW WAY
HARVEST CT
BURBIDGE RD
WOOD RD
SQUIRE'S RD
YEW TREES
MILTON DR
ASHURST DR
BRAVINGTON CL
FORD CL
LALEHAM RD
WRIGHT GDNS
FAIRVIEW DR
ROSEWOOD DR
ROSEACRE CL
BUSH RD
BRIAR RD
MANDEVILLE RD
150
ACACIA AVE
1 VINTER CT
2 JOHN KAYE CT
TANGLYN AVE
113
M3
LOIS DR
BARBARA CL
LITTLETON LA
Pl Fld
Saxon Prim Sch
THORNHILL WAY
POOL END CL
PRESTON RD
PENTLAND AVE
HARRISON WAY
GREENO CRES
JESSIMAN TER
VILLAGE GATE
MARION AVE
PEARMAIN CL
SHEPPERTON COURT DR
Sch
MAUREEN CAMPBELL CT
Gravel Pit
Littleton Sailing Club
TW17
SHEPHERDS CL
BARTON CL
CLAREMONT DR
CLAREMONT
SHEPPERTON CT
MANOR FARM AVE
GRANT CL
SHEPPERWALK
Pl Fld
St Nicholas CE Prim Sch
OLD FORGE CRES
BURCHETTS WAY
MERE RD 1
WESTBURY CL 2
SCHOOL LA
M3
Riverscroft
RANGE VILLAS
RENFREE WAY
B375
CHERTSEY RD
Halliford Mere Lake
CHURCH RD
Cemy
CHURCHFIELD PL
MANOR HOUSE CT
Tenn Ct
FARM CL
RANGE WAY
ST NICHOLAS DR
CEMETERY LA
TAMESA HO
NORMAN HO
CHURCH SQ
FERRY SQ
CHERTSEY RD
DESBOROUGH CL
PH
Dumsey Eyot
River Thames
Mead Farm
DOCKETT EDDY LA
KT16
DOCKETT MOORINGS
Desborough Sailing Club
Chertsey Meads
Dockett Eddy
FERRY LA
REED PL
PARK RD
ABBEY RD
KT13
KT13
Ferry Wks
Thames Path
TOWPATH
Ferry
Tenn Cts
06
Dockett Point
07
08
Surrey STREET ATLAS
HAMM COURT EST
Hamhaugh Island
The Bourne
SEY BRIDGE RD
10

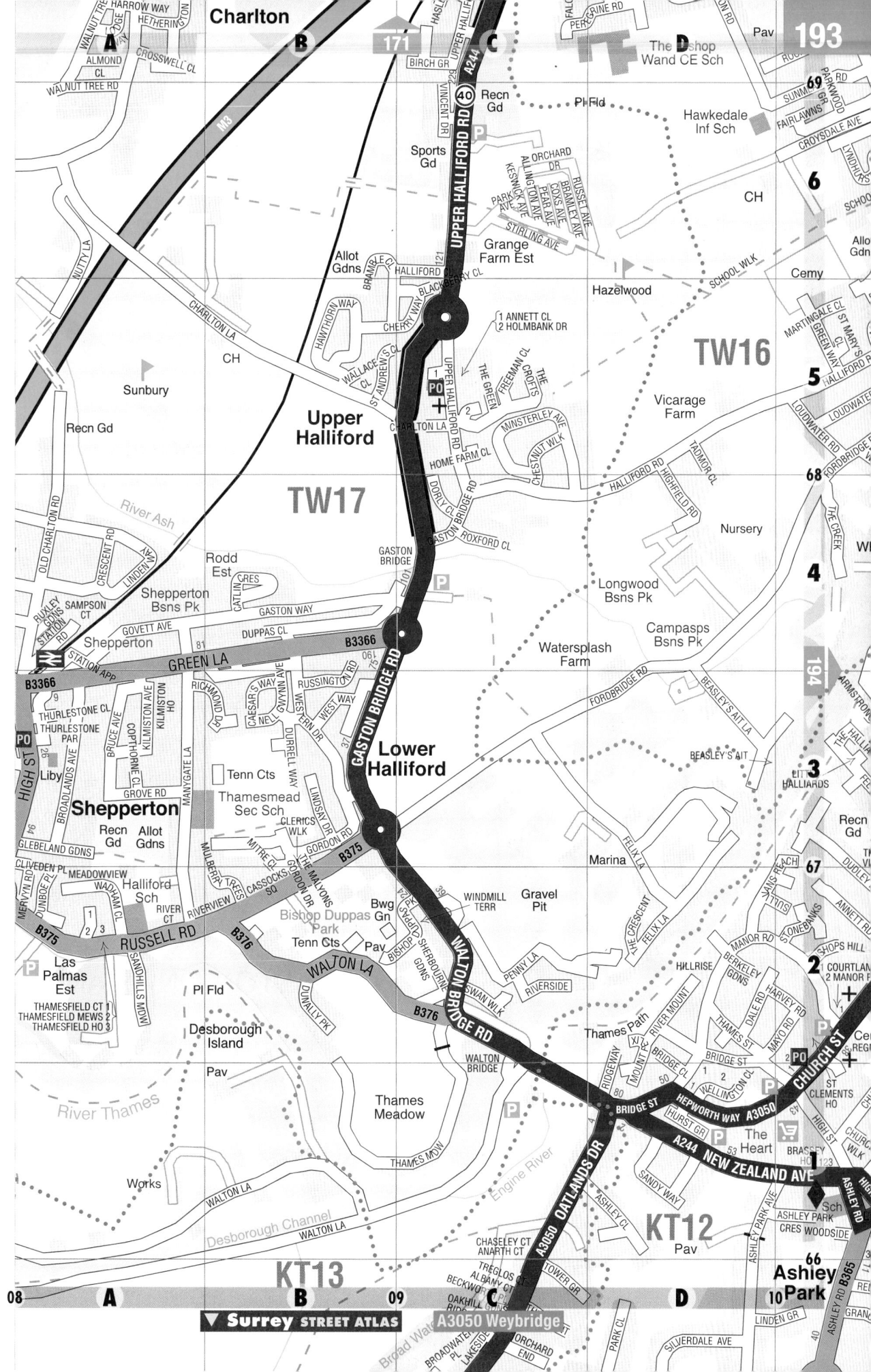
Charlton
171
Upper Halliford
TW17
TW16
Lower Halliford
Shepperton
KT12
KT13
Ashley Park
UPPER HALLIFORD RD
GASTON BRIDGE RD
WALTON BRIDGE RD
NEW ZEALAND AVE
OATLANDS DR
GREEN LA
RUSSELL RD
WALTON LA
CHARLTON LA
HALLIFORD RD
FORDBRIDGE RD
CHURCH ST
BRIDGE ST
HEPWORTH WAY
HIGH ST
M3
A244
A3050
B3366
B375
B376
B365
Sunbury
Hazelwood
Vicarage Farm
Watersplash Farm
Longwood Bsns Pk
Campasps Bsns Pk
Shepperton Bsns Pk
Grange Farm Est
Rodd Est
Las Palmas Est
Desborough Island
Thames Meadow
Thamesmead Sec Sch
Halliford Sch
Bishop Duppas Park
Hawkedale Inf Sch
The Bishop Wand CE Sch
River Thames
River Ash
Desborough Channel
Engine River
Marina
Gravel Pit
Nursery
194
1 ANNETT CL
2 HOLMBANK DR
THAMESFIELD CT 1
THAMESFIELD MEWS 2
THAMESFIELD HO 3
1 COURTLANDS
2 MANOR RD
A
B
C
D
1
2
3
4
5
6
08
09
10
66
67
68
69

A
B
C
D
172
SUNBURY
TW16
KT12
WALTON-ON-THAMES
River Thames
Thames Path
Sunbury Lock
Sunbury Ct Island
Beauclerc Inf Sch
Hawkedale Inf Sch
The Walled Garden
Tenn Cts
Cemy
Allot Gdns
Apps Court Farm
Knight Resr
Riverknook Farm
Bramble Hill Farm
Fball Gd
Leisure Ctr
Wheatley's Ait
Nursery
Thamesfield Farm
Recn Gd
Queen Elizabeth 2 Storage Resr
HURST RD
A3050
WALTON RD
B369
TERRACE RD
CHURCH ST
NEW ZEALAND AVE
HERSHAM RD
A244
B365
THAMES ST
1 ELIZABETH CT
2 THAMES CNR
3 RIVERMEAD HO
4 CASTLE WLK
1 LUSHINGTON HO
2 LYNDE HO
3 CROXALL HO
4 KIRBY WAY
1 COURTLANDS
2 MANOR PL
1 RYLTON HO
2 BLATCHFORD CT
3 ASHLEY PL
1 RODNEY CL
2 EDGEHILL CT
3 WORCESTER CT
4 DUNBAR CT
TELFORD DR
EMMELINE CT
VANBRUGH MEWS
Ashley Park
The Heart
193
69
6
5
68
4
3
67
2
1
66
10
11
12
A244 Esher
Surrey STREET ATLAS
Walton Comm

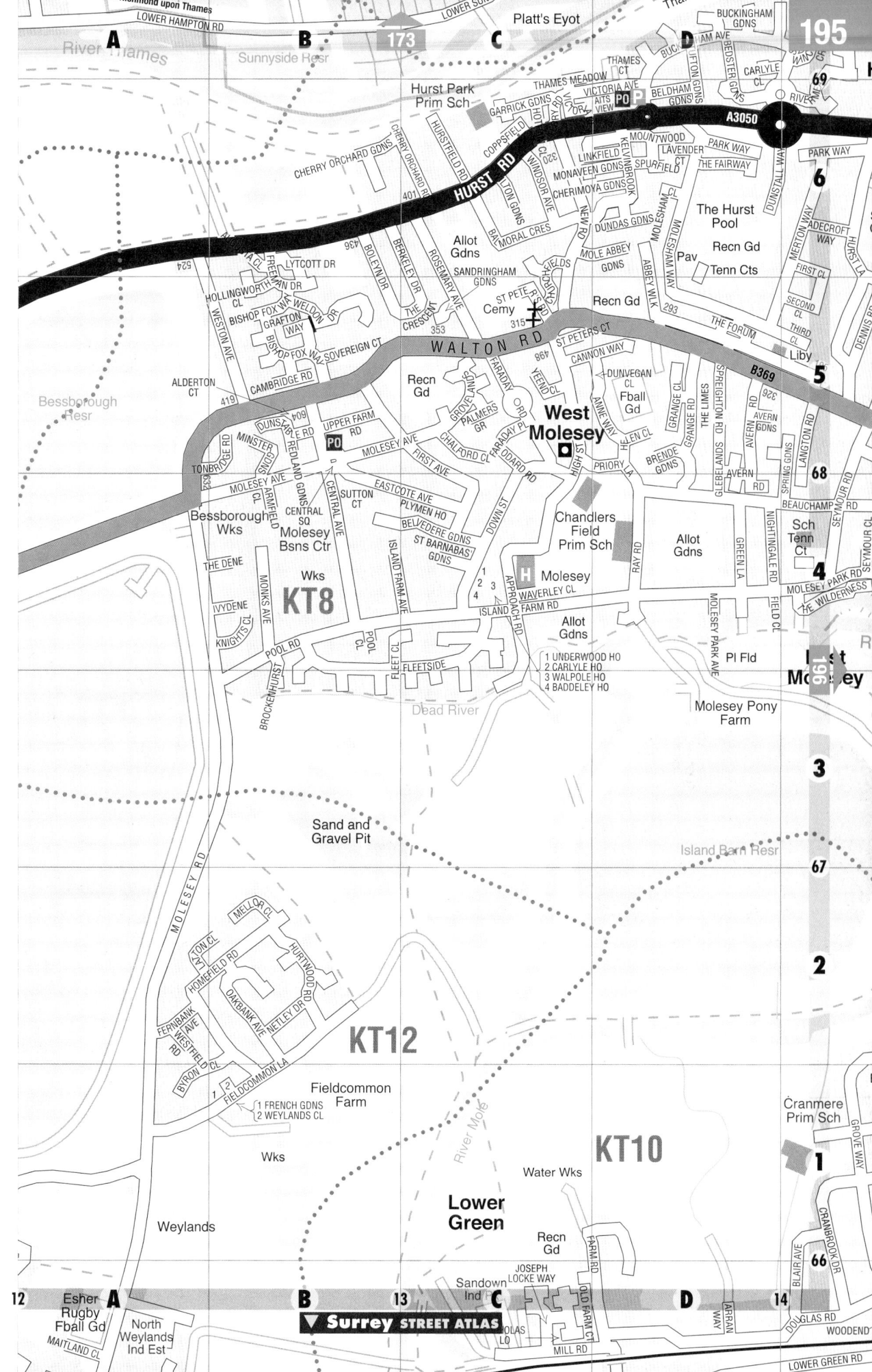
Richmond upon Thames
LOWER HAMPTON RD
173
Platt's Eyot
River Thames
Sunnyside Resr
Hurst Park
Prim Sch
BUCKINGHAM GDNS
THAMES CT
THAMES MEADOW
VICTORIA AVE
GARRICK GDNS
BELDHAM GDNS
CARLYLE CL
A3050
HURST RD
COPPSFIELD
CHERRY ORCHARD GDNS
CHERRY ORCHARD RD
HURSTFIELD RD
WINDSOR AVE
MOUNTWOOD
LAVENDER CT
PARK WAY
THE FAIRWAY
LINKFIELD
MONAVEEN GDNS
SPURFIELD
KELVINBROOK
CHERIMOYA GDNS
DUNSTALL WAY
The Hurst
Pool
Recn Gd
Pav
Tenn Cts
MOLESHAM CL
MOLESHAM WAY
DUNDAS GDNS
NEW RD
MOLE ABBEY GDNS
ABBEY WLK
BALMORAL CRES
Allot
Gdns
BOLEYN DR
BERKELEY DR
ROSEMARY AVE
SANDRINGHAM GDNS
LYTCOTT DR
FREEMAN DR
HOLLINGWORTH CL
BISHOP FOX WAY
WELDON DR
GRAFTON WAY
WESTON AVE
THE CRESCENT
Cemy
ST PETERS RD
Recn Gd
THE FORUM
ADECROFT WAY
MERTON WAY
FIRST CL
SECOND CL
THIRD CL
Liby
WALTON RD
SOVEREIGN CT
CAMBRIDGE RD
ST PETERS CT
CANNON WAY
B369
DUNVEGAN CL
Fball
Gd
ALDERTON CT
Bessborough
Resr
Recn
Gd
GROVELANDS
PALMERS GR
FARADAY RD
YEEND CL
West
Molesey
ANNE WAY
HELEN CL
GRANGE CL
GRANGE RD
THE LIMES
SPREIGHTON RD
AVERN RD
AVERN GDNS
LANGTON RD
DUNSTABLE RD
UPPER FARM RD
MINSTER GDNS
TONBRIDGE RD
REDLAND GDNS
MOLESEY AVE
FIRST AVE
CHALFORD CL
FARADAY PL
ODARD RD
HIGH ST
PRIORY LA
BRENDE GDNS
GLEBELANDS
SPRING GDNS
68
ARMFIELD CL
CENTRAL SQ
CENTRAL AVE
SUTTON CT
EASTCOTE AVE
PLYMEN HO
Chandlers
Field
Prim Sch
BEAUCHAMP RD
SEYMOUR RD
Bessborough
Wks
Molesey
Bsns Ctr
BELVEDERE GDNS
ST BARNABAS' GDNS
ISLAND FARM AVE
DOWN ST
RAY RD
Allot
Gdns
GREEN LA
NIGHTINGALE RD
Sch
Tenn
Ct
SEYMOUR CL
THE DENE
Wks
KT8
MONKS AVE
Molesey
APPROACH RD
WAVERLEY CL
ISLAND FARM RD
MOLESEY PARK RD
THE WILDERNESS
IVYDENE
KNIGHTS CL
POOL CL
MOLESEY PARK AVE
FIELD CL
Allot
Gdns
POOL RD
FLEET CL
FLEETSIDE
1 UNDERWOOD HO
2 CARLYLE HO
3 WALPOLE HO
4 BADDELEY HO
Pl Fld
East
Molesey
196
BROCKENHURST
Dead River
Molesey Pony
Farm
Sand and
Gravel Pit
Island Barn Resr
67
MOLESEY RD
MELLOR CL
LAYTON CL
HOMEFIELD RD
HURTWOOD RD
OAKBANK AVE
NETLEY DR
KT12
FERNBANK AVE
WESTFIELD RD
BYRON CL
FIELDCOMMON LA
1 FRENCH GDNS
2 WEYLANDS CL
Fieldcommon
Farm
Cranmere
Prim Sch
GROVE WAY
River Mole
KT10
Wks
Water Wks
Lower
Green
Weylands
Recn
Gd
FARM RD
CRANBROOK DR
BLAIR AVE
66
JOSEPH LOCKE WAY
Sandown
Ind Pk
OLD FARM CT
ARRAN WAY
Esher
Rugby
Fball Gd
North
Weylands
Ind Est
MAITLAND CL
MILL RD
DOUGLAS RD
WOODEND
LOWER GREEN RD
A B C D
12 13 14
6 5 4 3 2 1

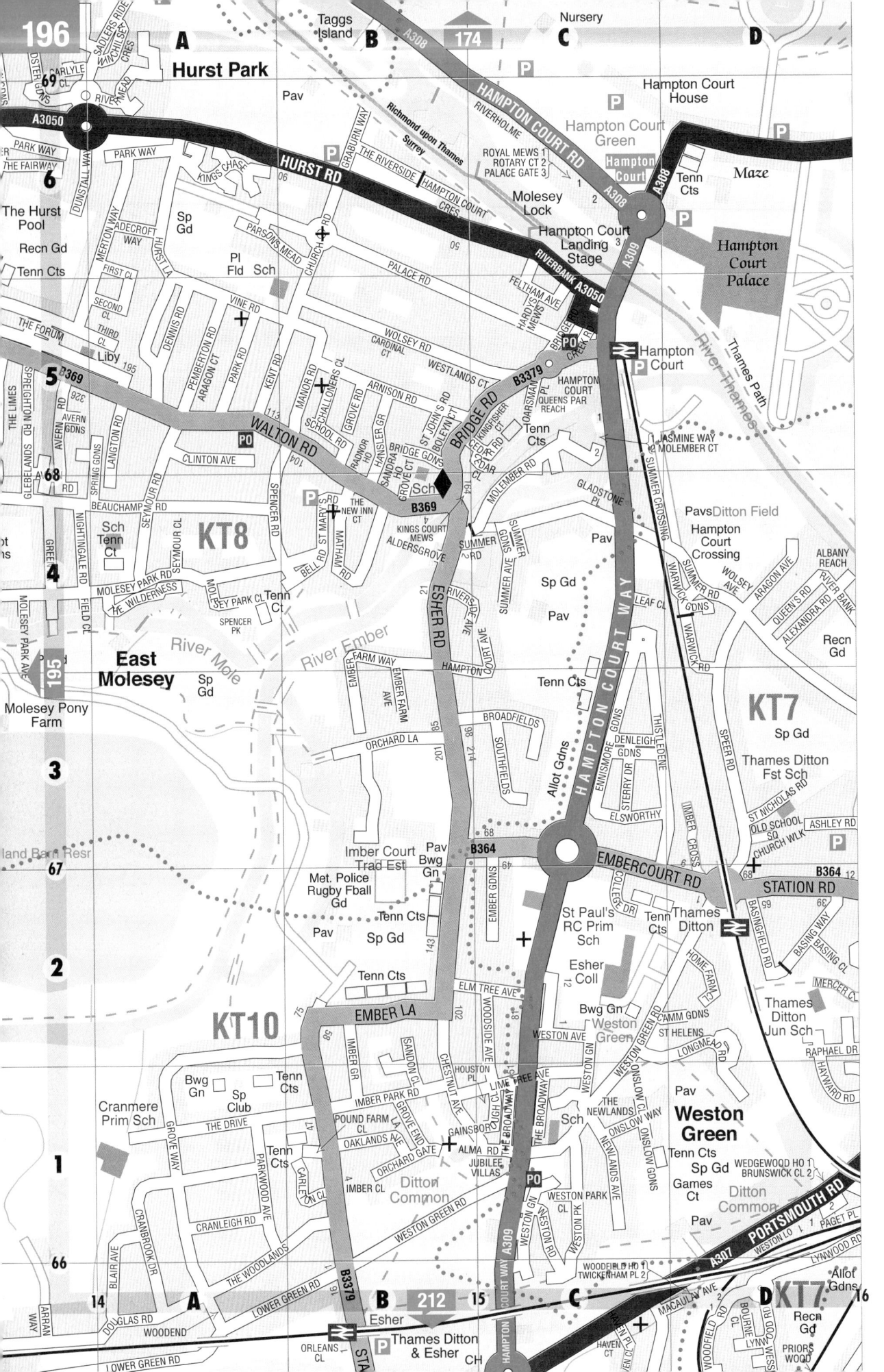
A
B
C
D
174
Taggs Island
Nursery
Hurst Park
Pav
A308
HAMPTON COURT RD
Hampton Court House
Hampton Court Green
Hampton Court
Maze
Tenn Cts
A3050
HURST RD
PARK WAY
THE FAIRWAY
KINGS CHASE
Richmond upon Thames
Surrey
THE RIVERSIDE
HAMPTON COURT CRES
RIVERHOLME
ROYAL MEWS 1
ROTARY CT 2
PALACE GATE 3
Molesey Lock
Hampton Court Landing Stage
RIVERBANK A3050
A309
Hampton Court Palace
The Hurst Pool
Recn Gd
Tenn Cts
DUNSTALL WAY
MERTON WAY
ADECROFT WAY
HURST LA
Sp Gd
Pl Fld
Sch
PARSONS MEAD
CHURCH RD
PALACE RD
FELTHAM AVE
HARDYS MEWS
BRIDGE RD
CREEK RD
FIRST CL
SECOND CL
THIRD CL
THE FORUM
Liby
VINE RD
DENNIS RD
WOLSEY RD
CARDINAL CT
WESTLANDS CT
B3379
Hampton Court
River Thames
Thames Path
B369
SPREIGHTON RD
THE LIMES
PEMBERTON RD
ARAGON CT
PARK RD
KENT RD
MANOR RD
CHALLONERS CL
GROVE RD
ARNISON RD
ST JOHN'S RD
BOLEYN CT
OARSMAN PL
HAMPTON COURT QUEENS PAR REACH
KINGFISHER CT
Tenn Cts
JASMINE WAY
MOLEMBER CT
AVERN RD
AVERN GDNS
LANGTON RD
WALTON RD
SCHOOL RD
RADNOR HO
HANSLER GR
SANDRA HO
BRIDGE GDNS
GROVE CT
CEDAR RD
MOLEMBER RD
GLADSTONE PL
SUMMER CROSSING
GLEBELANDS RD
SPRING GDNS
CLINTON AVE
SEYMOUR RD
SPENCER RD
Sch
THE NEW INN CT
KINGS COURT MEWS
ALDERSGROVE
SUMMER RD
SUMMER GDNS
SUMMER AVE
Pav
Pavs
Ditton Field
Hampton Court Crossing
ALBANY REACH
BEAUCHAMP RD
SEYMOUR CL
KT8
ST MARY'S RD
BELL RD
MATHAM RD
Sch
Tenn Ct
NIGHTINGALE RD
MOLESEY PARK RD
THE WILDERNESS
MOLESEY PARK CL
Tenn Ct
SPENCER PK
ESHER RD
RIVERSIDE AVE
Sp Gd
Pav
LEAF CL
WARWICK GDNS
WOLSEY AVE
ARAGON AVE
QUEEN'S RD
RIVER BANK
ALEXANDRA RD
Recn Gd
MOLESEY PARK AVE
FIELD CL
195
East Molesey
River Mole
River Ember
EMBER FARM WAY
EMBER FARM AVE
HAMPTON COURT AVE
Tenn Cts
HAMPTON COURT WAY
WARWICK RD
Sp Gd
Molesey Pony Farm
BROADFIELDS
ORCHARD LA
SOUTHFIELDS
Allot Gdns
ENNISMORE GDNS
DENLEIGH GDNS
STERRY DR
THISTLEDENE
ELSWORTHY
SPEER RD
KT7
Sp Gd
Thames Ditton Fst Sch
ST NICHOLAS RD
OLD SCHOOL SQ
ASHLEY RD
CHURCH WLK
Island Barn Resr
Imber Court Trad Est
Pav
Bwg Gn
B364
EMBERCOURT RD
IMBER CROSS
COLLEGE DR
B364
STATION RD
Met. Police Rugby Fball Gd
Tenn Cts
Pav
Sp Gd
EMBER GDNS
St Paul's RC Prim Sch
Tenn Cts
Thames Ditton
BASINGFIELD RD
BASING WAY
BASING CL
Tenn Cts
Esher Coll
HOME FARM CL
MERCER CL
ELM TREE AVE
WOODSIDE AVE
Bwg Gn
Weston Green
CAMM GDNS
ST HELENS
LONGMEAD RD
Thames Ditton Jun Sch
RAPHAEL DR
HAYWARD RD
KT10
EMBER LA
WESTON AVE
WESTON GN
WESTON GREEN RD
IMBER GR
SANDON CL
CHESTNUT AVE
HOUSTON PL
LIME TREE AVE
Bwg Gn
Sp Club
Tenn Cts
THE NEWLANDS
ONSLOW CL
ONSLOW WAY
ONSLOW GDNS
Pav
Weston Green
Cranmere Prim Sch
IMBER PARK RD
GROVE END LA
POUND FARM CL
OAKLANDS AVE
GAINSBOROUGH
THE BROADWAY
Sch
NEWLANDS AVE
THE DRIVE
GROVE WAY
Tenn Cts
ORCHARD GATE
ALMA RD
JUBILEE VILLAS
Tenn Cts
Sp Gd
Games Ct
WEDGEWOOD HO 1
BRUNSWICK CL 2
Ditton Common
PARKWOOD AVE
CARLETON CL
IMBER CL
PO
WESTON PARK CL
Ditton Common
PORTSMOUTH RD
PAGET PL
CRANBROOK DR
CRANLEIGH RD
WESTON GREEN RD
WESTON PK
Pav
A307
WESTON LO
LYNWOOD RD
BLAIR AVE
THE WOODLANDS
B3379
WOODFIELD HO 1
TWICKENHAM PL 2
MACAULAY AVE
Allot Gdns
14
A
LOWER GREEN RD
B
212
15
C
D
KT7
16
ARRAN WAY
DOUGLAS RD
WOODEND
Esher
Thames Ditton & Esher
ORLEANS CL
CH
HAVEN CT
HAVEN PL
WOODFIELD RD
BOURNE CL
LYNWOOD
Recn Gd
PRIORS WOOD
LOWER GREEN RD
6
5
4
3
2
1
69
68
67
66

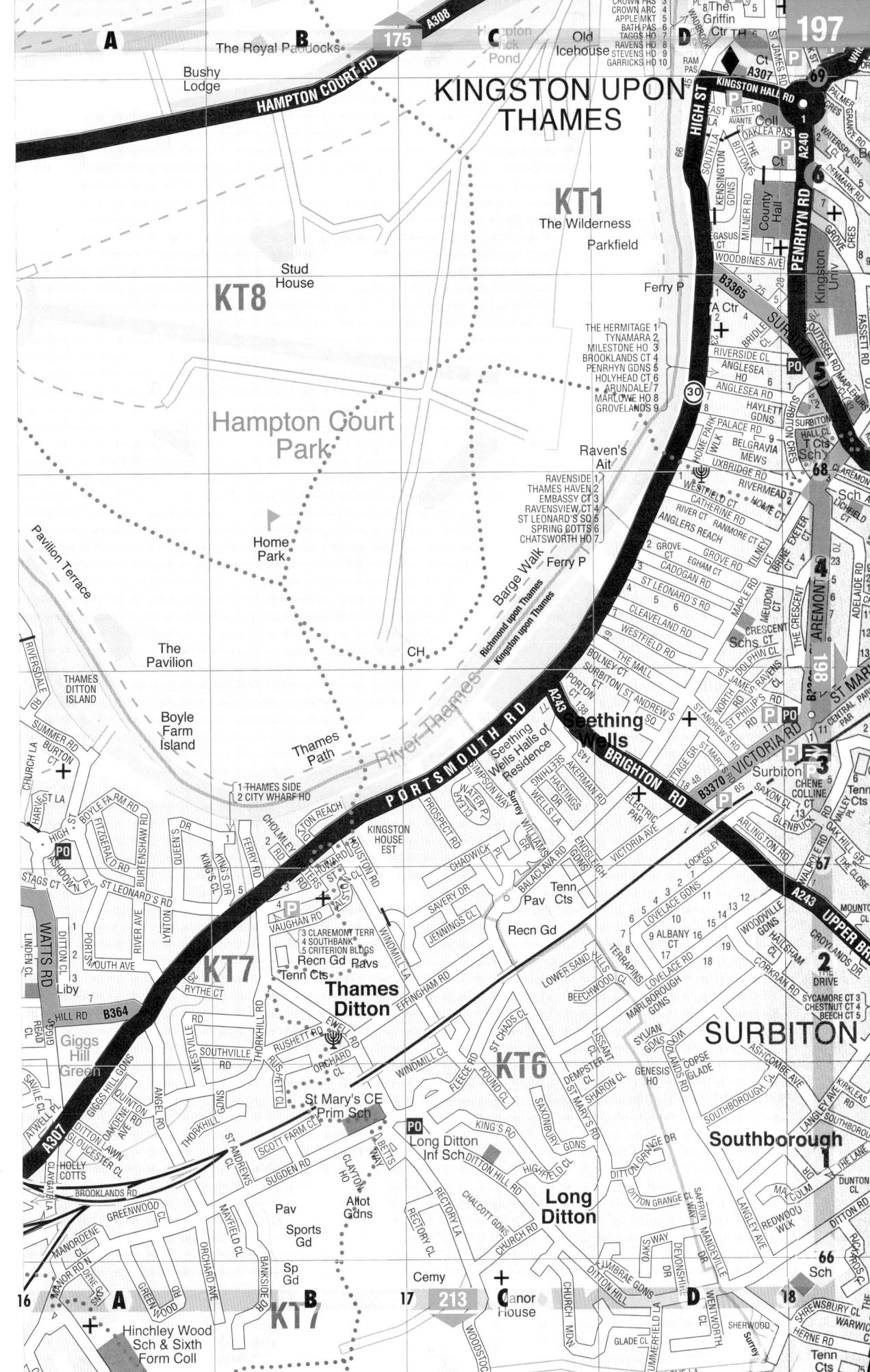

A
B
C
D
175
A308
The Royal Paddocks
Hampton Wick Pond
Old Icehouse
CROWN PAS 3
CROWN ARC 4
APPLE MKT 5
BATH PAS 6
TAGGS HO 7
RAVENS HO 8
STEVENS HO 9
GARRICKS HO 10
The Griffin Ctr
TH
Bushy Lodge
HAMPTON COURT RD
KINGSTON UPON THAMES
A307
KINGSTON HALL RD
HIGH ST
A240
PENRHYN RD
KT1
The Wilderness
Parkfield
County Hall
WOODBINES AVE
Kingston Univ
Stud House
KT8
Ferry P
B3365
SURBITON RD
TA Ctr
THE HERMITAGE 1
TYNAMARA 2
MILESTONE HO 3
BROOKLANDS CT 4
PENRHYN GDNS 5
HOLYHEAD CT 6
ARUNDALE 7
MARLOWE HO 8
GROVELANDS 9
RIVERSIDE CL
ANGLESEA HO
ANGLESEA RD
HAYLETT GDNS
PALACE RD
BELGRAVIA MEWS
UXBRIDGE RD
RIVERMEAD
Hampton Court Park
Raven's Ait
RAVENSIDE 1
THAMES HAVEN 2
EMBASSY CT 3
RAVENSVIEW CT 4
ST LEONARD'S SQ 5
SPRING COTTS 6
CHATSWORTH HO 7
Home Park
Pavilion Terrace
Barge Walk
Ferry P
Richmond upon Thames
Kingston upon Thames
CATHERINE RD
ANGLERS REACH
GROVE RD
CADOGAN RD
ST LEONARD'S RD
CLEAVELAND RD
WESTFIELD RD
MAPLE RD
THE CRESCENT
CLAREMONT RD
198
The Pavilion
CH
THAMES DITTON ISLAND
Boyle Farm Island
Thames Path
River Thames
PORTSMOUTH RD
A243
Seething Wells
Seething Wells Halls of Residence
BRIGHTON RD
VICTORIA RD
B3370
Surbiton
1 THAMES SIDE
2 CITY WHARF HO
KINGSTON HOUSE EST
VICTORIA AVE
ST MARK'S
Tenn Cts
Pav
Recn Gd
STAGS CT
ST LEONARD'S RD
WATTS RD
PORTSMOUTH AVE
KT7
3 CLAREMONT TERR
4 SOUTHBANK
5 CRITERION BLDGS
Recn Gd
Pavs
Tenn Cts
Thames Ditton
Liby
HILL RD
B364
Giggs Hill Green
LOVELACE GDNS
ALBANY CT
A243
UPPER BRIGHTON RD
SYCAMORE CT 3
CHESTNUT CT 4
BEECH CT 5
SURBITON
KT6
St Mary's CE Prim Sch
Long Ditton Inf Sch
Long Ditton
Southborough
A307
Pav
Sports Gd
Allot Gdns
Sp Gd
Cemy
Manor House
16
A
B
17
213
C
D
18
KT7
Hinchley Wood Sch & Sixth Form Coll
Sch

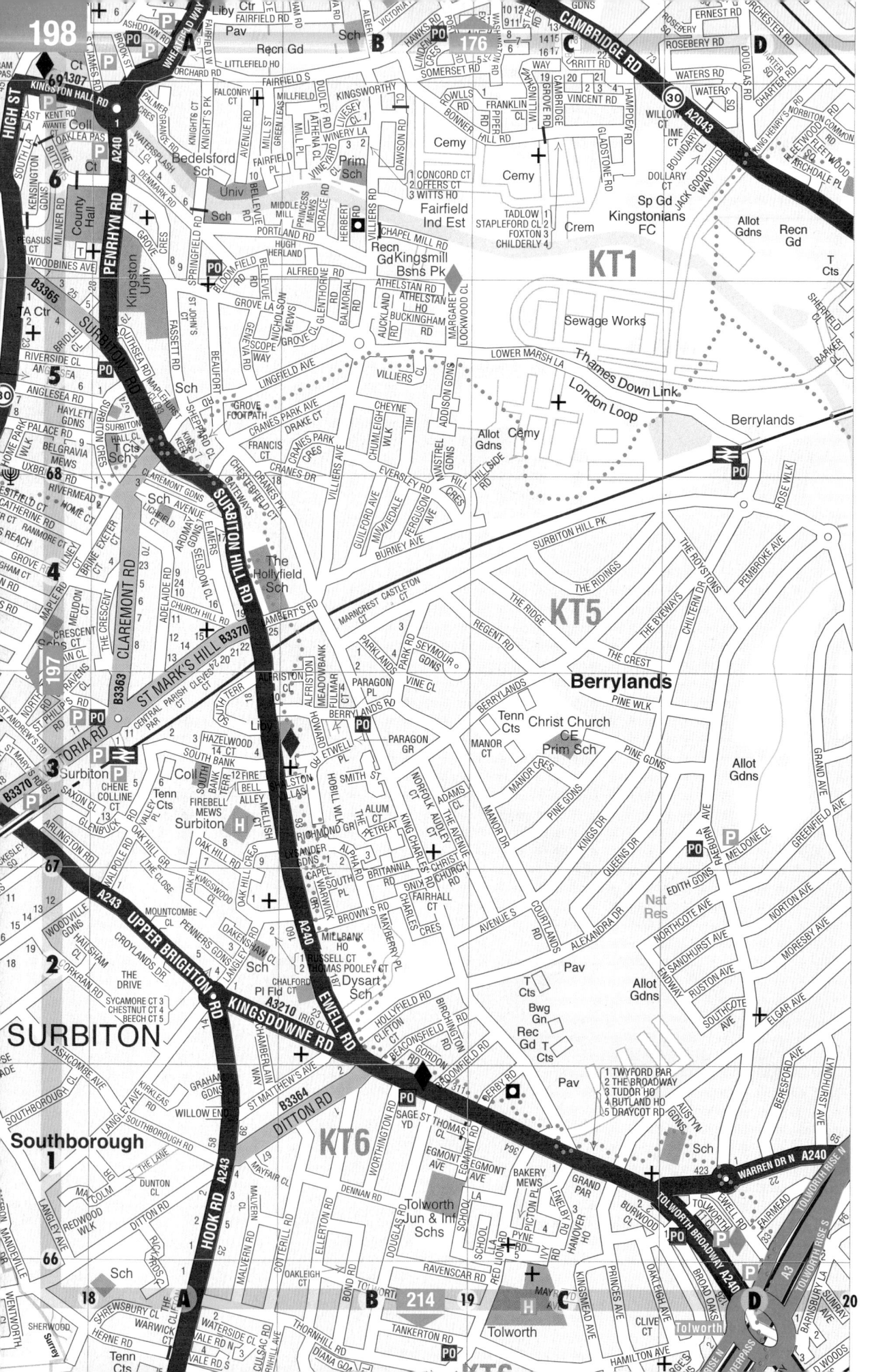
176
A
B
C
D
CAMBRIDGE RD
A2043
Recn Gd
Fairfield Rd
Kingston Hall Rd
High St
Penrhyn Rd
A240
County Hall
Kingston Univ
Bedelsford Sch
Univ
Fairfield Ind Est
Kingsmill Bsns Pk
Cemy
Crem
Kingstonians FC
Sp Gd
Allot Gdns
KT1
Sewage Works
Thames Down Link
London Loop
Lower Marsh La
Berrylands
Surbiton Rd
B3365
Surbiton Hill Rd
The Hollyfield Sch
Claremont Rd
St Mark's Hill
B3370
B3363
Victoria Rd
Surbiton
197
KT5
Surbiton Hill Pk
The Ridge
The Crest
Christ Church CE Prim Sch
Berrylands Rd
Kings Dr
Queens Dr
Alexandra Dr
Nat Res
Ewell Rd
Upper Brighton Rd
A243
Kingsdowne Rd
A3210
Dysart Sch
SURBITON
Southborough
Ditton Rd
B3364
Hook Rd
KT6
Tolworth Jun & Inf Schs
Tolworth Broadway
Warren Dr N
Tolworth
214
A3
Surrey
6
5
4
3
2
1
66
67
68
69
18
19
20

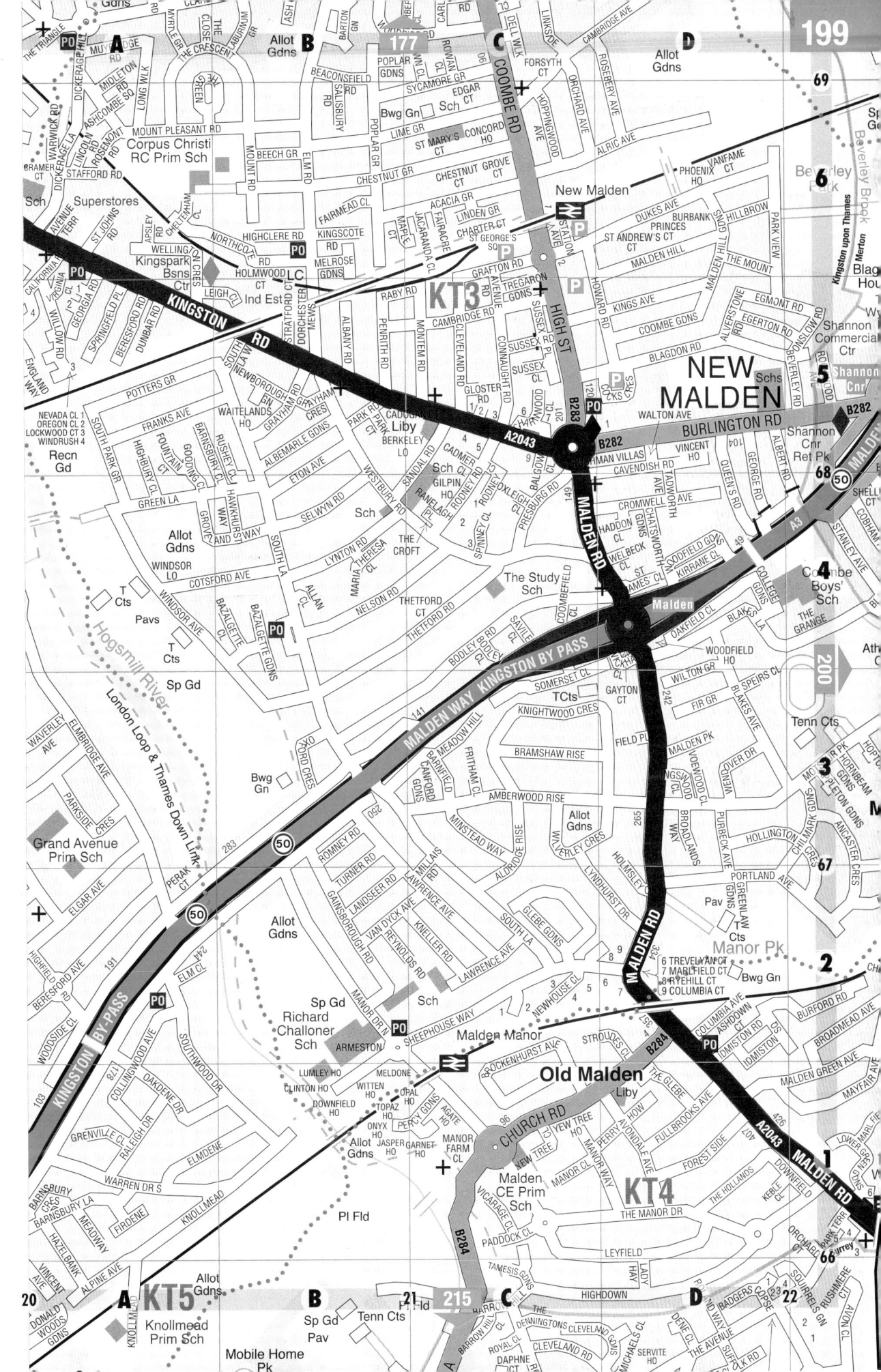

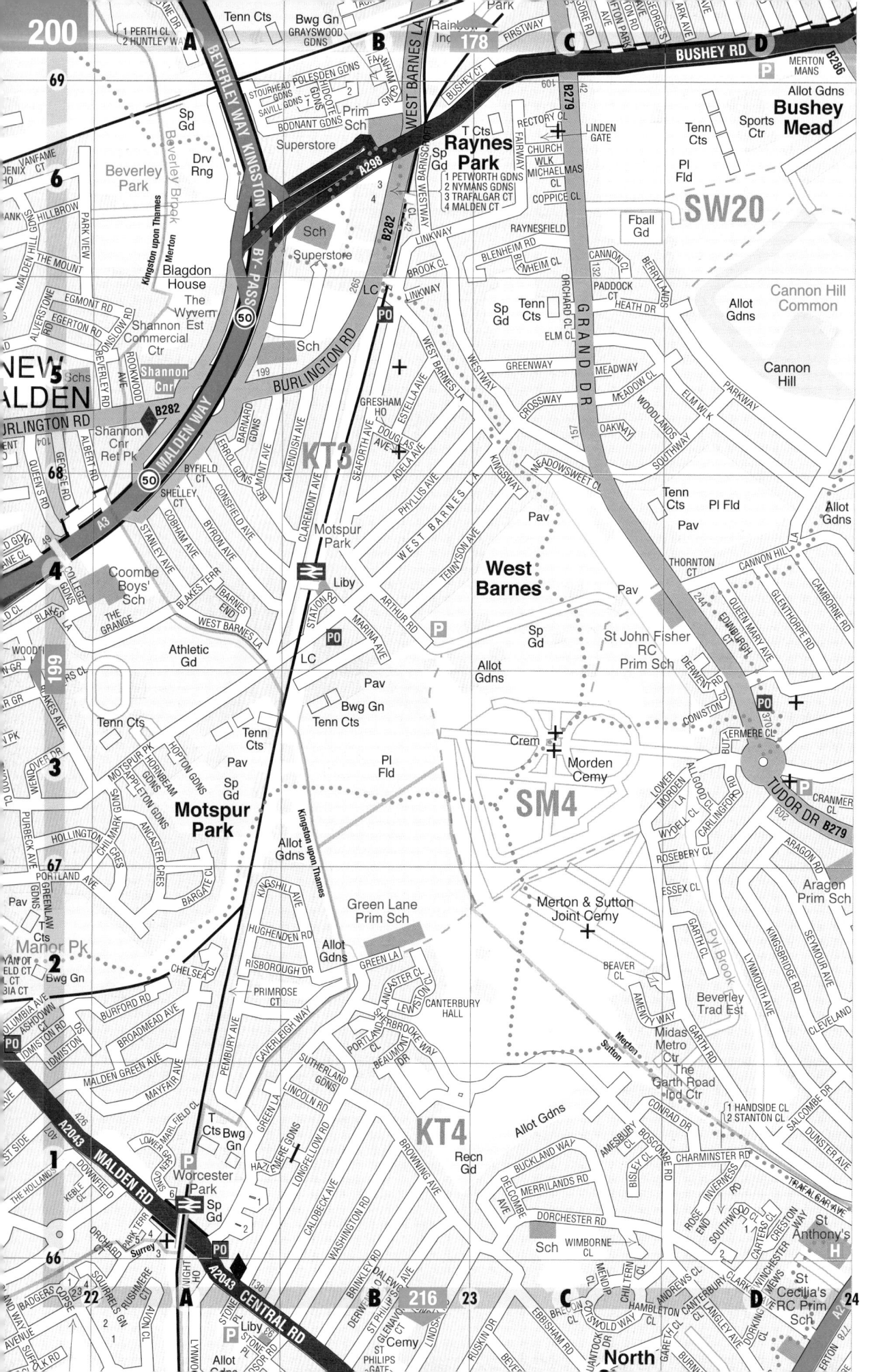
Raynes Park
West Barnes
Motspur Park
Bushey Mead
New Malden
SW20
KT3
SM4
KT4
Beverley Park
Cannon Hill Common
Cannon Hill
Morden Cemy
Merton & Sutton Joint Cemy
Green Lane Prim Sch
St John Fisher RC Prim Sch
Aragon Prim Sch
Coombe Boys' Sch
Worcester Park
Manor Pk
Blagdon House
The Wyvern Est
Shannon Commercial Ctr
Shannon Cnr Ret Pk
Beverley Trad Est
Midas Metro Ctr
The Garth Road Ind Ctr
St Anthony's
St Cecilia's RC Prim Sch
BEVERLEY WAY KINGSTON BY-PASS
MALDEN WAY
BURLINGTON RD
WEST BARNES LA
GRAND DR
BUSHEY RD
TUDOR DR
MALDEN RD
CENTRAL RD
178
199
216
North

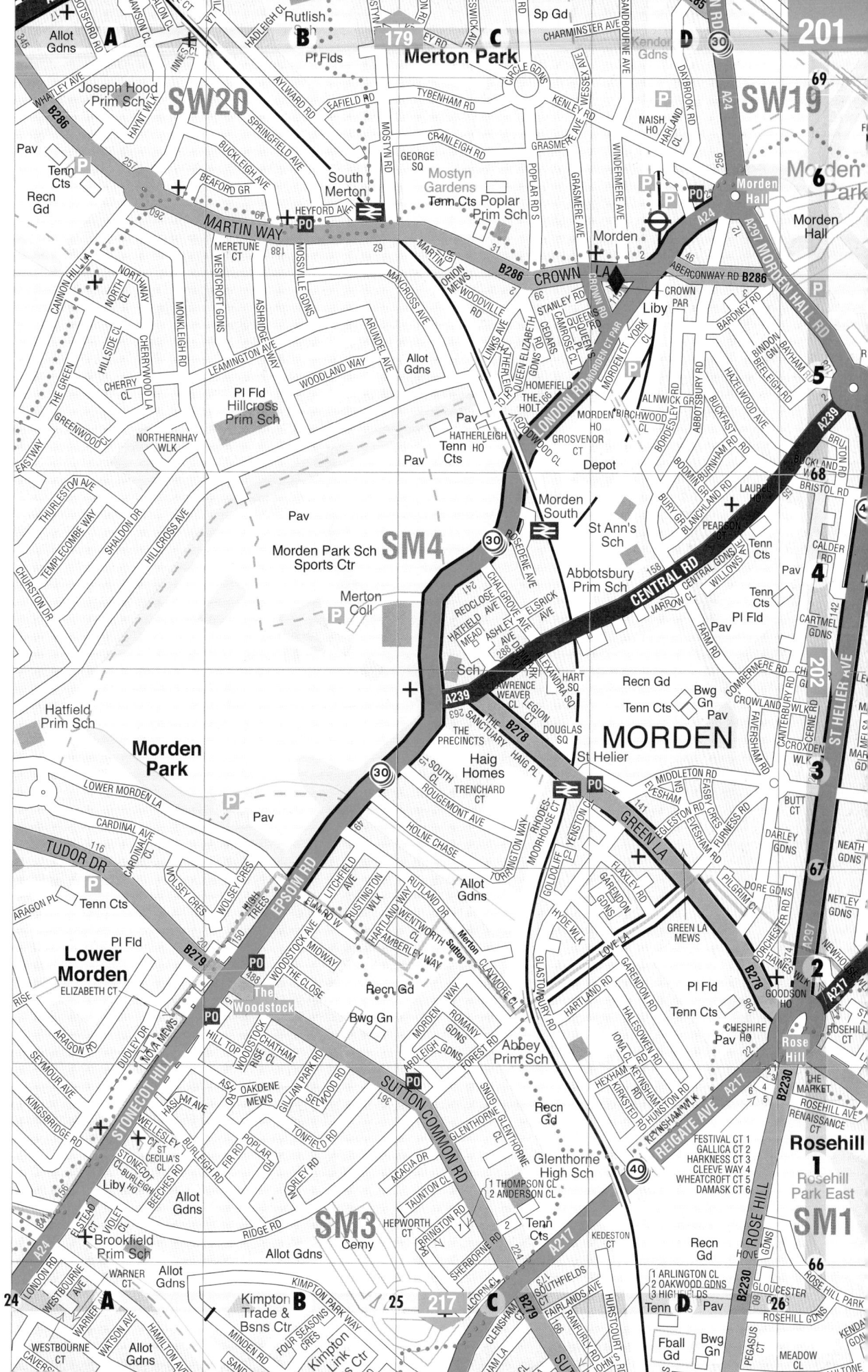

A
B
C
D
179
Merton Park
SW20
SW19
Rutlish Sch
Pl Flds
Allot Gdns
Joseph Hood Prim Sch
Kendor Gdns
Sp Gd
Pav
Tenn Cts
Recn Gd
South Merton
Mostyn Gardens
Tenn Cts Poplar Prim Sch
Morden
Morden Hall
Morden Park
Morden Hall
Liby
MARTIN WAY
CROWN LA
B286
A24
A297
MORDEN HALL RD
LONDON RD
Pl Fld Hillcross Prim Sch
Allot Gdns
Pav
Depot
Morden South
St Ann's Sch
Abbotsbury Prim Sch
SM4
Morden Park Sch Sports Ctr
Merton Coll
CENTRAL RD
A239
Sch
Hatfield Prim Sch
Morden Park
Haig Homes
MORDEN
St Helier
Recn Gd
Tenn Cts
Bwg Gn
Pav
Pl Fld
Tenn Cts
GREEN LA
EPSOM RD
TUDOR DR
B279
B278
Lower Morden
Allot Gdns
Recn Gd
Bwg Gn
The Woodstock
Abbey Prim Sch
Recn Gd
Glenthorne High Sch
SUTTON COMMON RD
STONECOT HILL
Liby
Allot Gdns
SM3
Cemy
Allot Gdns
Brookfield Prim Sch
Kimpton Trade & Bsns Ctr
Kimpton Link
REIGATE AVE
A217
Rose Hill
Rosehill
Rosehill Park East
SM1
ROSE HILL
B2230
ST HELIER AVE
Recn Gd
Tenn Cts
Pav
Fball Gd
Bwg Gn
FESTIVAL CT 1
GALLICA CT 2
HARKNESS CT 3
CLEEVE WAY 4
WHEATCROFT CT 5
DAMASK CT 6
1 THOMPSON CL
2 ANDERSON CL
1 ARLINGTON CL
2 OAKWOOD GDNS
3 HIGHFIELDS
202
217
24
25
26
69
68
67
66
6
5
4
3
2
1

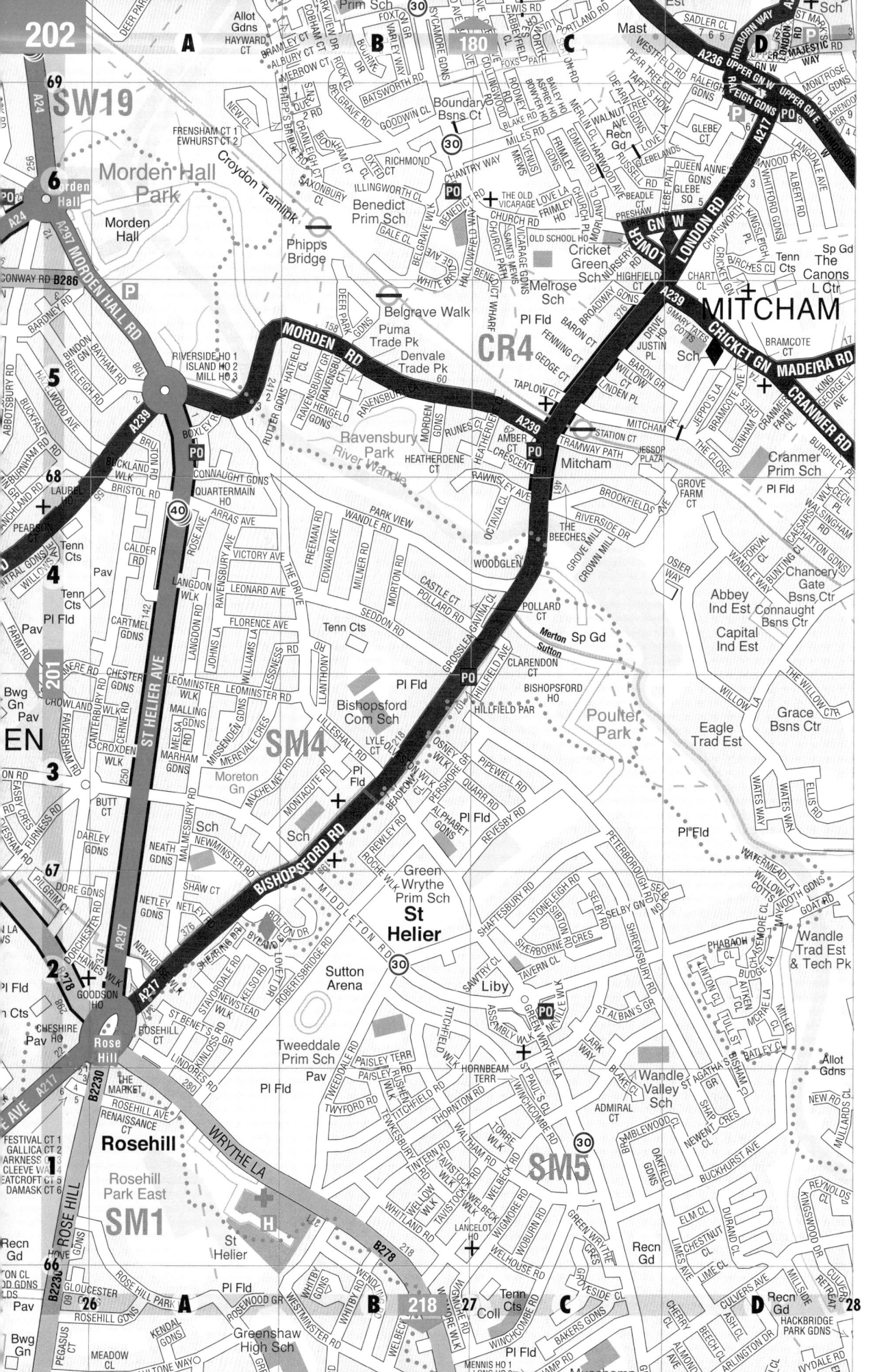
A
B
C
D
180
201
218
SW19
CR4
SM4
SM5
SM1
MITCHAM
St Helier
Rosehill
Morden Hall Park
Morden Hall
Croydon Tramlink
Phipps Bridge
Belgrave Walk
Puma Trade Pk
Denvale Trade Pk
Ravensbury Park
River Wandle
MORDEN RD
MORDEN HALL RD
A239
A297
A217
A236
A24
B286
B278
B2230
ST HELIER AVE
BISHOPSFORD RD
LONDON RD
CRICKET GN
MADEIRA RD
CRANMER RD
UPPER GN W
UPPER GN E
LOWER GN W
HOLBORN WAY
MAJESTIC WAY
COMMONSIDE
WRYTHE LA
ROSE HILL
MIDDLETON RD
CONWAY RD
Mitcham
Cricket Green Sch
Melrose Sch
Benedict Prim Sch
Boundary Bsns Ct
The Canons L Ctr
Cranmer Prim Sch
Abbey Ind Est
Capital Ind Est
Connaught Bsns Ctr
Chancery Gate Bsns Ctr
Grace Bsns Ctr
Eagle Trad Est
Wandle Trad Est & Tech Pk
Poulter Park
Bishopsford Com Sch
Green Wrythe Prim Sch
Sutton Arena
Tweeddale Prim Sch
Wandle Valley Sch
Greenshaw High Sch
Moreton Gn
Rosehill Park East
Merton
Sutton
Mast
Coll
Liby
Pl Fld
Tenn Cts
Recn Gd
Allot Gdns
Sch
Pav
Bwg Gn
Sp Gd

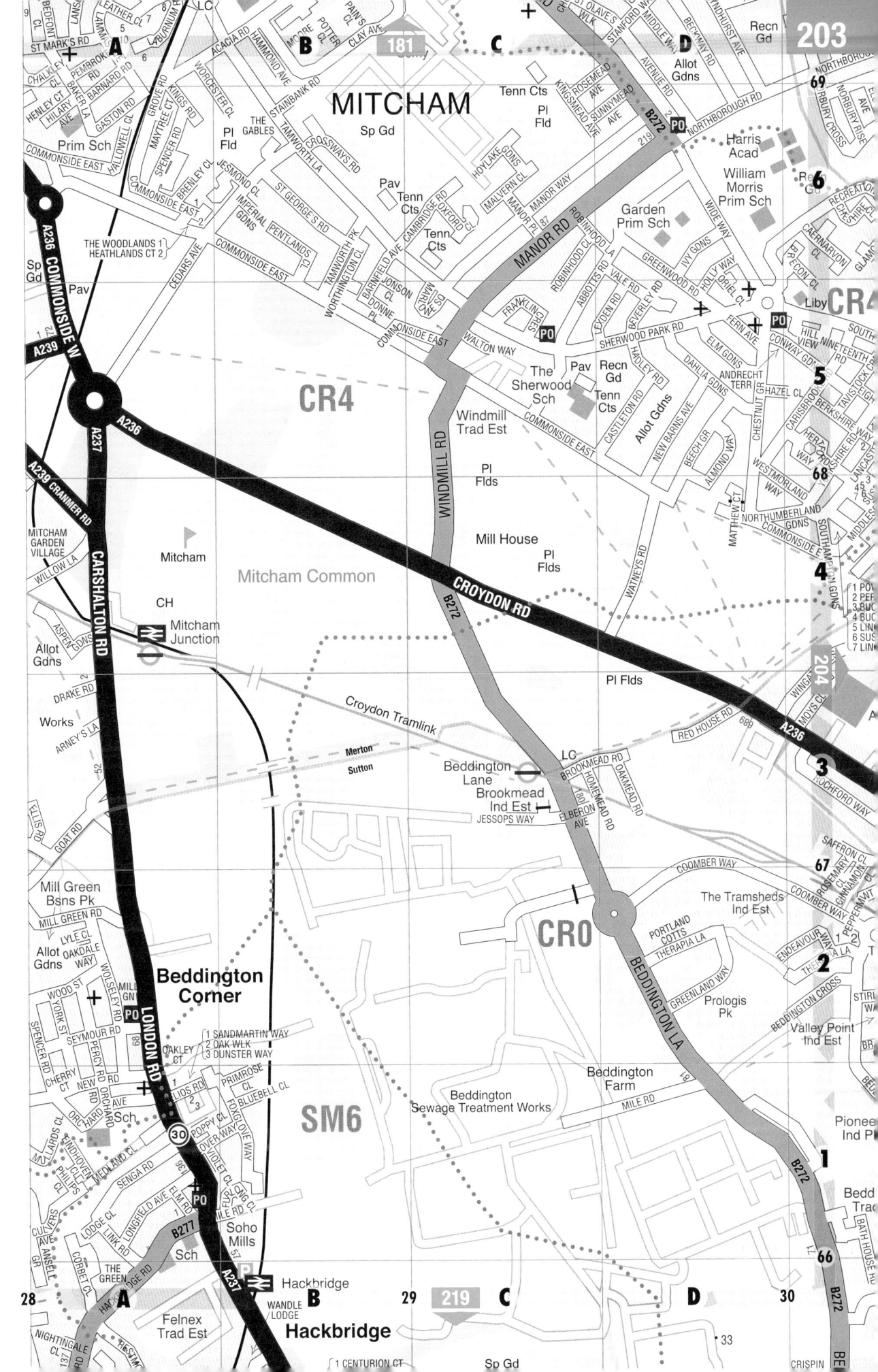

MITCHAM

CR4

CR4

CR0

SM6

Mitcham Common

Mitcham Junction

Beddington Corner

Croydon Tramlink

Beddington Lane

Brookmead Ind Est

Beddington Farm

Beddington Sewage Treatment Works

Hackbridge

Harris Acad

William Morris Prim Sch

The Sherwood Sch

The Tramsheds Ind Est

Portland Cotts

Prologis Pk

Valley Point Ind Est

Pioneer Ind Pk

69

6

5

4

3

2

1

68

67

66

204

181

219

28   29   30

Felnex Trad Est

Soho Mills

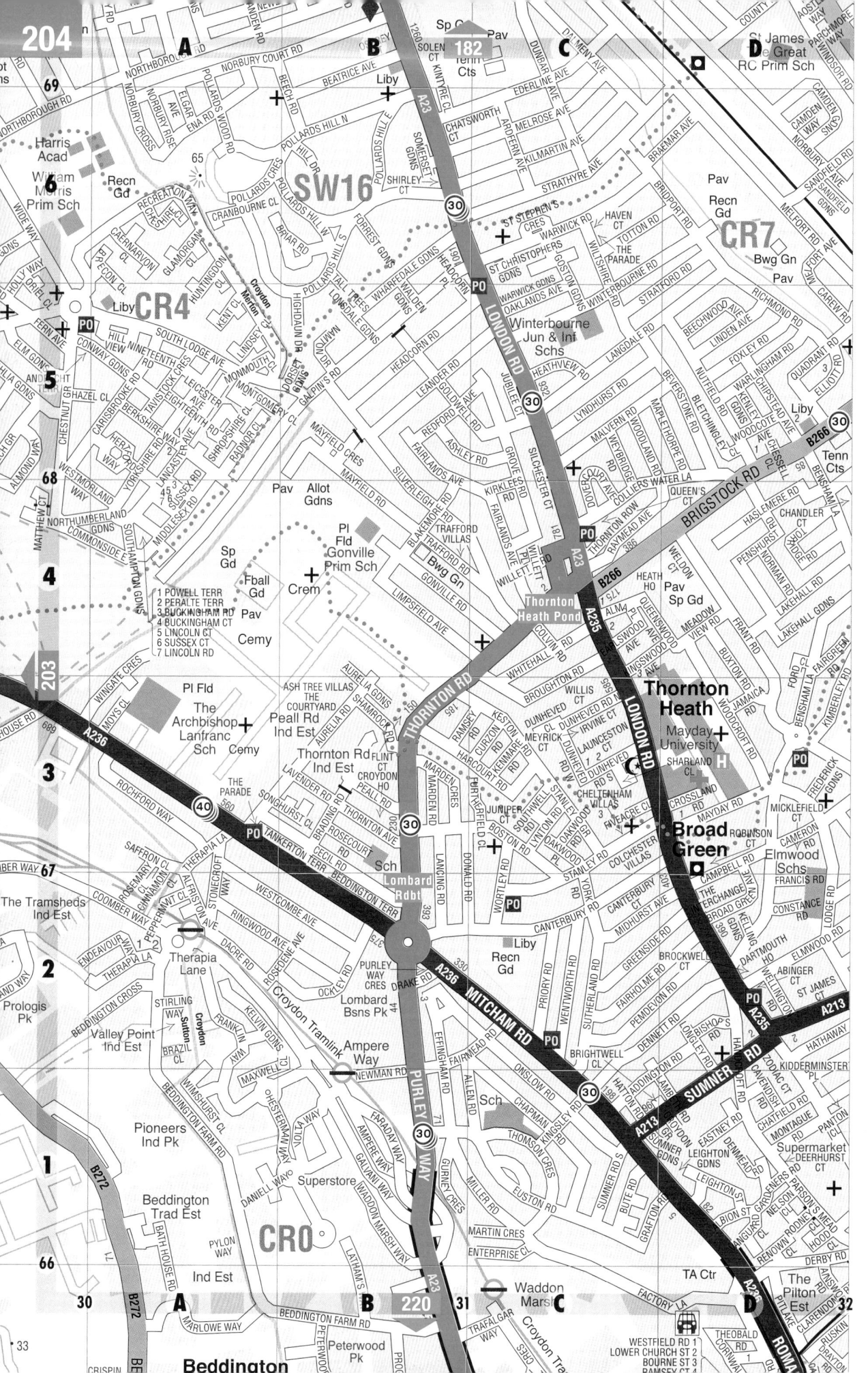

204
A
B
C
D
182
203
220
A
B
C
D
69
68
67
66
30
31
32
6
5
4
3
2
1
SW16
CR4
CR7
CR0
NORTHBOROUGH RD
NORBURY COURT RD
NORBURY CROSS
NORBURY RISE
ELGAR AVE
ENA RD
POLLARDS WOOD RD
BEATRICE AVE
BEECH RD
POLLARDS HILL N
POLLARDS HILL E
HILL DR
POLLARDS CRES
POLLARDS HILL W
POLLARDS HILL S
Liby
Harris Acad
William Morris Prim Sch
Recn Gd
65
RECREATION WAY
CHESHIRE CL
CAERNARVON CL
GLAMORGAN CL
BRECON CL
HUNTINGDON
CRANBOURNE CL
BRIAR RD
FORREST GDNS
SOMERSET GDNS
SHIRLEY CT
KINTYRE CL
SOLEN CT
Tenn Cts
Pav
CHATSWORTH CT
EDERLINE AVE
DUNBAR AVE
DALMENY AVE
MELROSE AVE
ARDFERN AVE
KILMARTIN AVE
STRATHYRE AVE
BRAEMAR AVE
St James the Great RC Prim Sch
CAMDEN WAY
NORBURY AVE
SANDFIELD GDNS
MELFORT RD
MELFORT AVE
CAREW RD
Recn Gd
Bwg Gn
ST STEPHEN'S CRES
WARWICK RD
HAVEN CT
TOTTON RD
THE PARADE
WILTSHIRE RD
ST CHRISTOPHERS GDNS
GOSTON GDNS
WARWICK GDNS
OAKLANDS AVE
WINTERBOURNE RD
STRATFORD RD
BRIDPORT RD
RICHMOND RD
BEECHWOOD AVE
LINDEN AVE
FOXLEY RD
WARLINGHAM RD
QUADRANT RD
ELLIOTT RD
HEADCORN PL
WHARFEDALE GDNS
WALDEN GDNS
LONSDALE GDNS
TALL TREES
HIGHDAUN DR
DORSET GDNS
HILL VIEW
NINETEENTH RD
SOUTH LODGE AVE
KENT CL
LINDSEY CL
MONMOUTH CL
MONTGOMERY CL
GALPIN'S RD
CONWAY GDNS
FERN AVE
ELM GDNS
Croydon
Merton
Winterbourne Jun & Inf Schs
HEATHVIEW RD
LANGDALE RD
LONDON RD
LEANDER RD
HEADCORN RD
GOLDWELL RD
REDFORD AVE
ASHLEY RD
JUBILEE CT
LYNDHURST RD
MALVERN RD
WEYBRIDGE RD
WOODLAND RD
MAPLETHORPE RD
BEVERSTONE RD
BLETCHINGLEY CL
NUTFIELD RD
KENLEY GDNS
CHIPSTEAD AVE
WOODCOTE AVE
CHESSELL CL
Liby
Tenn Cts
B266
BRIGSTOCK RD
BENSHAM LA
COLLIERS WATER LA
DOVERCOURT AVE
QUEEN'S CT
THORNTON ROW
RAYMEAD AVE
HASLEMERE RD
CHANDLER CT
PENSHURST RD
NORMAN RD
LAKEHALL RD
LAKEHALL GDNS
TAVISTOCK CRES
LEICESTER AVE
EIGHTEENTH RD
SHROPSHIRE CL
RADNOR CL
CARISBROOKE RD
BERKSHIRE WAY
HERTFORD WAY
YORKSHIRE RD
LANCASTER AVE
SUSSEX RD
MIDDLESEX RD
WESTMORLAND WAY
NORTHUMBERLAND GDNS
COMMONSIDE E
MATTHEW CT
HAZEL CL
CHESTNUT GR
ALMOND WAY
MAYFIELD CRES
MAYFIELD RD
SILVERLEIGH RD
FAIRLANDS AVE
BLAKEMORE RD
TRAFFORD VILLAS
TRAFFORD RD
KIRKLEES RD
GROVE RD
FAIRLANDS AVE
WILLETT PL
WILLETT RD
SILCHESTER CT
A23
Pav
Allot Gdns
Pl Fld
Gonville Prim Sch
Bwg Gn
GONVILLE RD
LIMPSFIELD AVE
Sp Gd
Fball Gd
Crem
Pav
Cemy
SOUTHAMPTON GDNS
1 POWELL TERR
2 PERALTE TERR
3 BUCKINGHAM RD
4 BUCKINGHAM CT
5 LINCOLN CT
6 SUSSEX CT
7 LINCOLN RD
Thornton Heath Pond
A235
HEATH HO
Pav
Sp Gd
WELDON CT
QUEENSWOOD AVE
MEADOW VIEW RD
FRANT RD
BUXTON RD
COLVIN RD
WHITEHALL RD
BROUGHTON RD
WILLIS CT
EARLSWOOD AVE
Thornton Heath
Mayday University
H
SHARLAND CL
JAMAICA RD
WOODCROFT RD
FORD CL
BENSHAM LA
FAIRGREEN RD
KIMBERLEY RD
FREDERICK GDNS
THORNTON RD
WINGATE CRES
MOYS CL
Pl Fld
The Archbishop Lanfranc Sch
Cemy
HOUSE RD
A236
ROCHFORD WAY
ASH TREE VILLAS
THE COURTYARD
AURELIA GDNS
SHAMROCK RD
AURELIA RD
Peall Rd Ind Est
Thornton Rd Ind Est
FLINT CT
CROYDON HO
PEALL RD
THORNTON AVE
LAVENDER RD
SONGHURST CL
BRADING RD
ROSECOURT RD
CECIL RD
TANKERTON TERR
BEDDINGTON TERR
THE PARADE
Sch
RAMSEY CT
CURZON RD
KESTON RD
KENMARE RD
HARCOURT RD
MARDEN CRES
MARDEN RD
FURTHERFIELD CL
DUNHEVED CL
DUNHEVED RD N
DUNHEVED RD W
DUNHEVED RD S
MEYRICK CT
IRVINE CT
LAUNCESTON CT
CHELTENHAM VILLAS
FIVEACRE CL
JUNIPER CT
SOUTHWELL RD
STANLEY GR
LYNTON RD
OAKWOOD RD
OAKWOOD PL
BOSTON RD
CROSSLAND RD
MAYDAY RD
MICKLEFIELD CT
ROBINSON CT
CAMERON RD
Broad Green
Elmwood Schs
FRANCIS RD
CONSTANCE RD
LODGE RD
Lombard Rdbt
LANSING RD
DONALD RD
WORTLEY RD
STANLEY RD
YORK RD
COLCHESTER VILLAS
CANTERBURY CT
CANTERBURY RD
MIDHURST AVE
CAMPBELL RD
THE INTERCHANGE
BROAD GREEN AVE
KELLING GDNS
DARTMOUTH HO
ELMWOOD RD
ABINGER CT
ST JAMES CT
WELLINGTON RD
SAFFRON CL
ROSEMARY CL
CINNAMON CL
PEPPERMINT CL
THERAPIA LA
ALFRISTON AVE
STONECROFT WAY
WESTCOMBE AVE
RINGWOOD AVE
ROSEDENE AVE
DACRE RD
OCKLEY RD
COOMBER WAY
The Tramsheds Ind Est
ENDEAVOUR WAY
THERAPIA LA
Therapia Lane
Prologis Pk
BEDDINGTON CROSS
STIRLING WAY
Croydon
Sutton
Valley Point Ind Est
BRAZIL CL
FRANKLIN WAY
KELVIN GDNS
MAXWELL CL
Croydon Tramlink
PURLEY WAY CRES
DRAKE RD
Lombard Bsns Pk
MITCHAM RD
Liby
Recn Gd
PRIORY RD
WENTWORTH RD
SUTHERLAND RD
GREENSIDE RD
FAIRHOLME RD
PEMDEVON RD
DENNETT RD
BROCKWELL CT
BISHOP'S RD
LONGLEY RD
HANDCROFT RD
BRIGHTWELL CL
A213
HATHAWAY RD
KIDDERMINSTER PL
ZODIAC CT
CAVENDISH RD
Ampere Way
NEWMAN RD
PURLEY WAY
EFFINGHAM RD
FAIRMEAD RD
ALLEN RD
ONSLOW RD
Sch
CHAPMAN RD
THOMSON CRES
KINGSLEY RD
ADDINGTON RD
HATTON RD
SUMNER RD
SUMNER GDNS
EASTNEY RD
DENMEAD RD
LEIGHTON GDNS
LEIGHTON ST
CHATFIELD RD
MONTAGUE RD
PANTON CL
Supermarket
DEERHURST CT
Pioneers Ind Pk
BEDDINGTON FARM RD
WIMSHURST CL
CHESTERMAN WAY
VOLTA WAY
FARADAY WAY
AMPERE WAY
GALVANI WAY
WADDON MARSH WAY
DANIELL WAY
Superstore
GURNEY CRES
MILLER RD
EUSTON RD
SUMNER RD S
BUTE RD
GRAFTON RD
ALBION ST
GARDENERS RD
NELSON CL
PARSON'S MEAD
RODNEY CL
HOOD CL
RENOWN CL
DERBY RD
B272
Beddington Trad Est
BATH HOUSE RD
PYLON WAY
Ind Est
LATHAM'S WAY
MARTIN CRES
ENTERPRISE CL
Waddon Marsh
FACTORY LA
TA Ctr
The Pilton Est
PITLAKE
CLARENDON RD
AINSWORTH RD
MARLOWE WAY
BEDDINGTON FARM RD
PETERWOOD WAY
Peterwood Pk
TRAFALGAR WAY
Croydon Tramlink
WESTFIELD RD 1
LOWER CHURCH ST 2
BOURNE ST 3
THEOBALD RD
RUSKIN
Beddington
CRISPIN
33

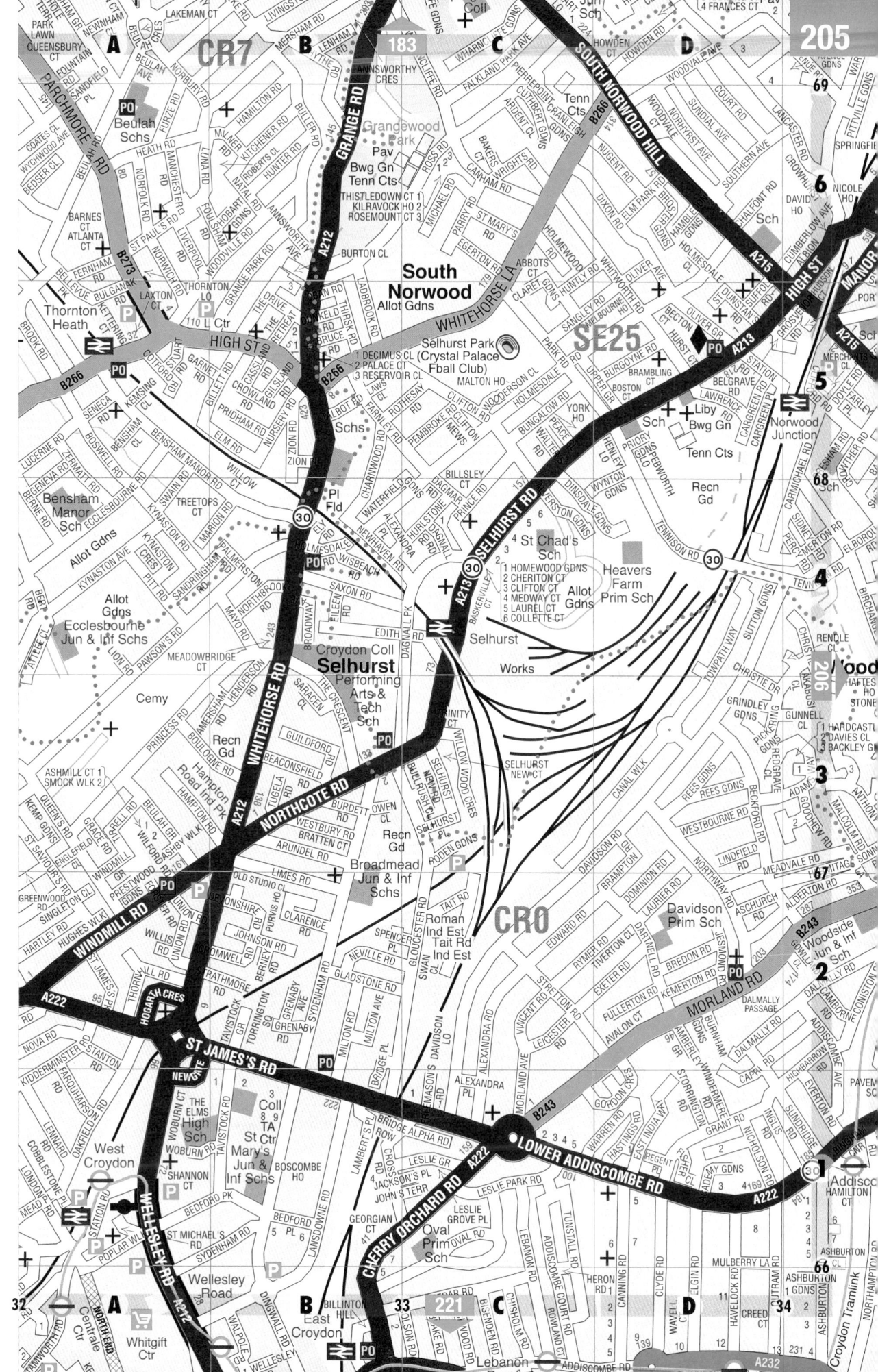
183
CR7
A
B
C
D
Thornton Heath
Beulah Schs
Grangewood Park
Pav
Bwg Gn
Tenn Cts
South Norwood
Allot Gdns
Selhurst Park (Crystal Palace Fball Club)
SE25
Norwood Junction
Bensham Manor Sch
Allot Gdns
Ecclesbourne Jun & Inf Schs
Cemy
Croydon Coll
Selhurst
Performing Arts & Tech Sch
St Chad's Sch
Heavers Farm Prim Sch
Selhurst Works
Recn Gd
Hampton Road Ind Pk
Broadmead Jun & Inf Schs
Roman Ind Est
Tait Rd Ind Est
CR0
Davidson Prim Sch
Woodside Jun & Inf Sch
West Croydon
The Elms High Sch
Coll
St Mary's Jun & Inf Schs
Oval Prim Sch
Wellesley Road
Whitgift Ctr
Centrale Ctr
East Croydon
Lebanon Road
Addiscombe
Croydon Tramlink
206
PARCHMORE RD
HIGH ST
GRANGE RD
WHITEHORSE LA
SOUTH NORWOOD HILL
SELHURST RD
WHITEHORSE RD
NORTHCOTE RD
WINDMILL RD
ST JAMES'S RD
LOWER ADDISCOMBE RD
CHERRY ORCHARD RD
WELLESLEY RD
MORLAND RD
A212
A213
A215
A222
A232
B243
B266
B273
32
33
34
221
66
67
68
69

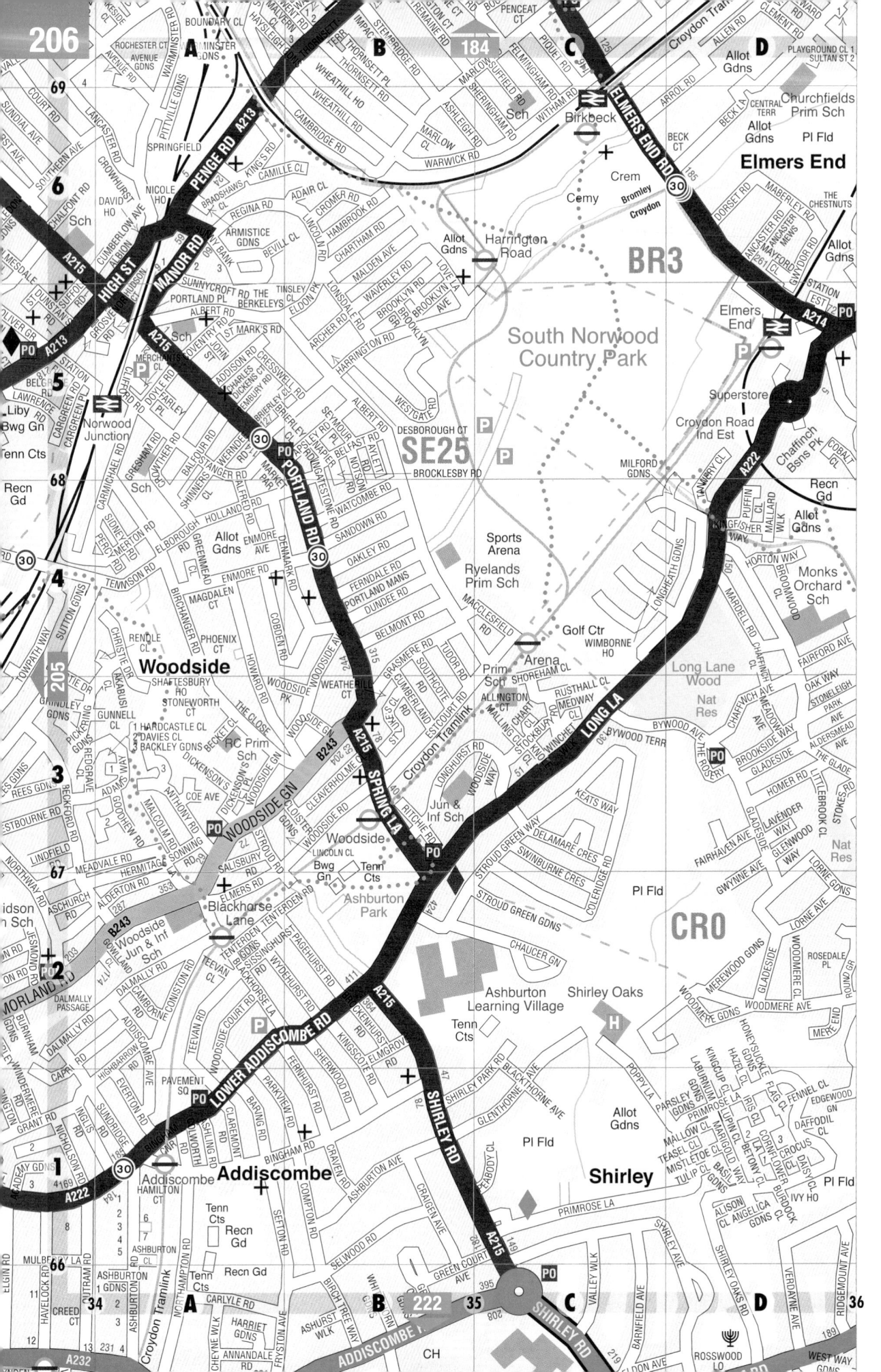
184
A
B
C
D
Elmers End
Churchfields Prim Sch
Birkbeck
ELMERS END RD
Croydon Tramlink
Crem
Cemy
Bromley
Croydon
BR3
Harrington Road
South Norwood Country Park
Elmers End
Superstore
Croydon Road Ind Est
Chaffinch Bsns Pk
SE25
PORTLAND RD
PENGE RD
HIGH ST
MANOR RD
Norwood Junction
Sports Arena
Ryelands Prim Sch
Golf Ctr
Arena
Monks Orchard Sch
Long Lane Wood
Nat Res
LONG LA
Woodside
WOODSIDE GN
SPRING LA
RC Prim Sch
Jun & Inf Sch
Woodside
Ashburton Park
Blackhorse Lane
Woodside Jun & Inf Sch
CR0
Ashburton Learning Village
Shirley Oaks
LOWER ADDISCOMBE RD
SHIRLEY RD
Addiscombe
Addiscombe
Shirley
PRIMROSE LA
SHIRLEY PARK RD
A215
A213
A222
A214
A232
B243
205
222
34
35
36
1
2
3
4
5
6
66
67
68
69

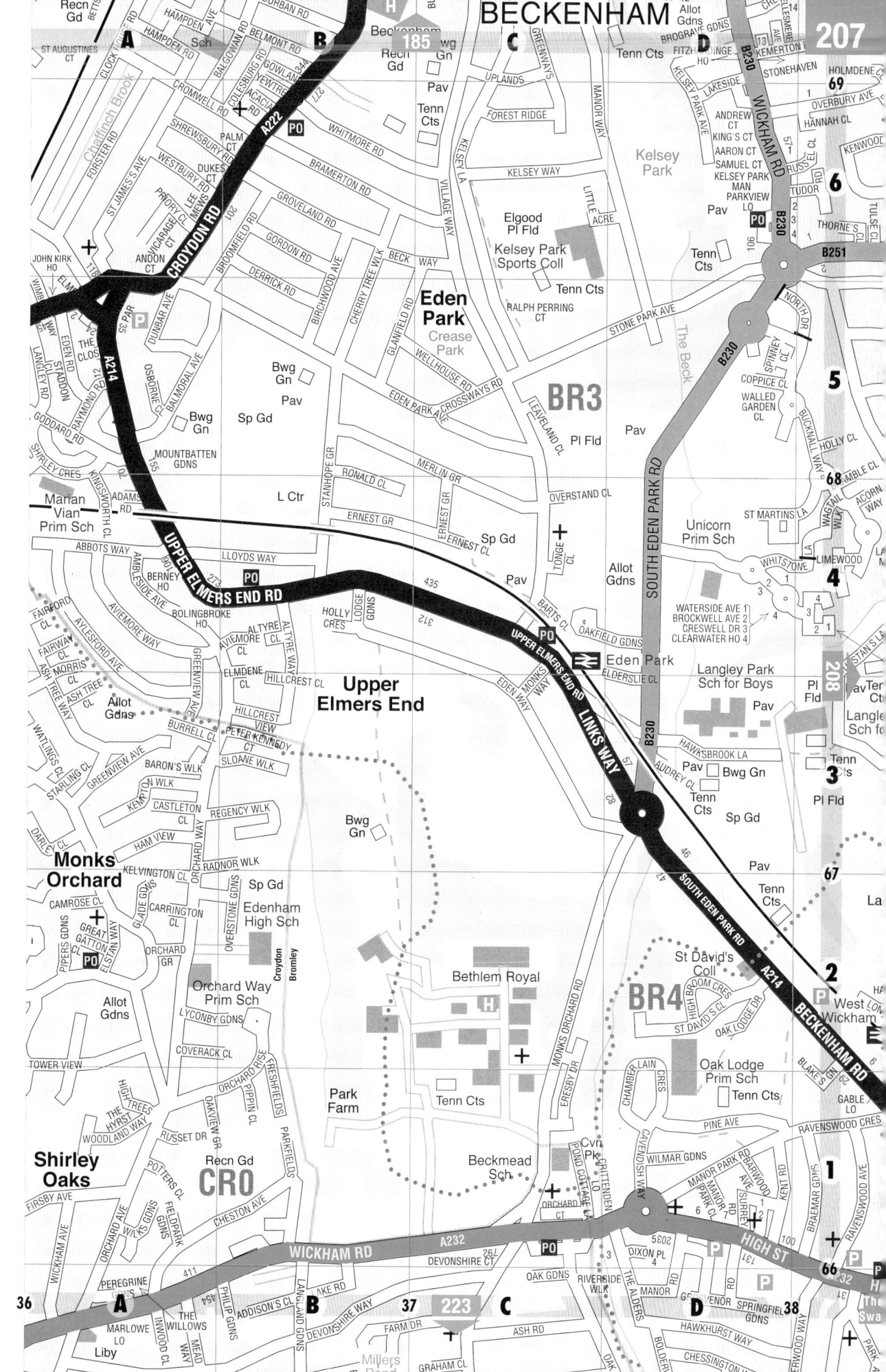
BECKENHAM
185
Eden Park
BR3
Upper Elmers End
Monks Orchard
Shirley Oaks
CR0
BR4
Kelsey Park
Elgood Pl Fld
Kelsey Park Sports Coll
Crease Park
Unicorn Prim Sch
Langley Park Sch for Boys
Edenham High Sch
Orchard Way Prim Sch
Bethlem Royal
Park Farm
Beckmead Sch
St David's Coll
Oak Lodge Prim Sch
Marian Vian Prim Sch
West Wickham
CROYDON RD
UPPER ELMERS END RD
LINKS WAY
SOUTH EDEN PARK RD
BECKENHAM RD
WICKHAM RD
HIGH ST
STONE PARK AVE
A222
A214
A232
B230
B251
208
223
36
37
38

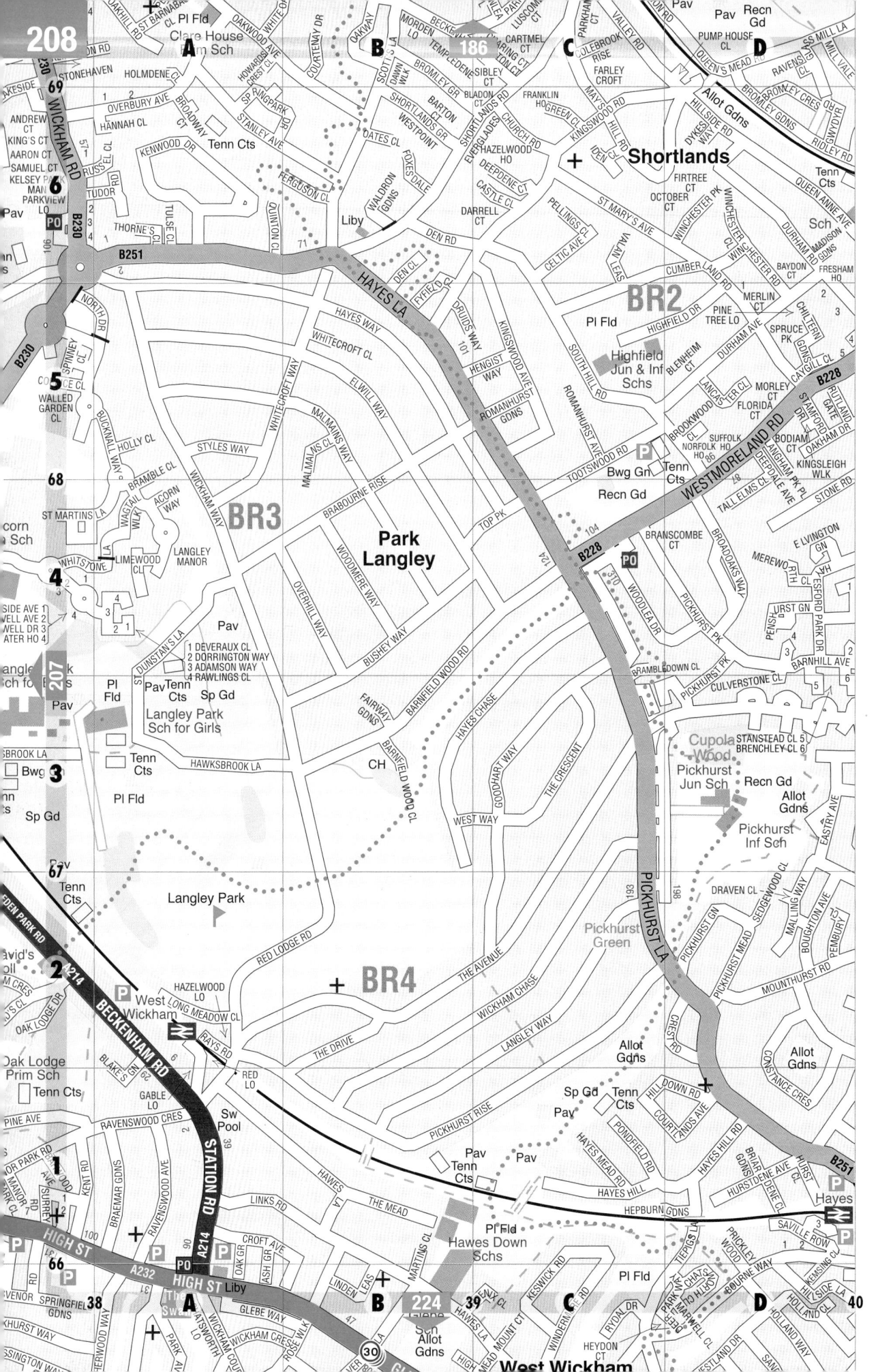

186
A
B
C
D
Shortlands
BR2
BR3
Park Langley
BR4
West Wickham
Hayes
Langley Park
Pickhurst Green
Cupola Wood
Clare House Prim Sch
Highfield Jun & Inf Schs
Langley Park Sch for Girls
Pickhurst Jun Sch
Pickhurst Inf Sch
Hawes Down Schs
Oak Lodge Prim Sch
HAYES LA
WESTMORELAND RD
PICKHURST LA
WICKHAM RD
BECKENHAM RD
STATION RD
HIGH ST
WICKHAM WAY
HAWKSBROOK LA
RED LODGE RD
THE AVENUE
WICKHAM CHASE
LANGLEY WAY
PICKHURST RISE
HAYES CHASE
BARNFIELD WOOD RD
BUSHEY WAY
BRABOURNE RISE
WHITECROFT WAY
HAYES WAY
WOODMERE WAY
OVERHILL WAY
TOOTSWOOD RD
ROMANHURST AVE
SOUTH HILL RD
KINGSWOOD AVE
HAWES LA
THE MEAD
LINKS RD
RAVENSWOOD CRES
1 DEVERAUX CL
2 DORRINGTON WAY
3 ADAMSON WAY
4 RAWLINGS CL
STANSTEAD CL 5
BRENCHLEY CL 6
207
224
B251
B228
B230
A214
A232
38
39
40
66
67
68
69

207
186
224

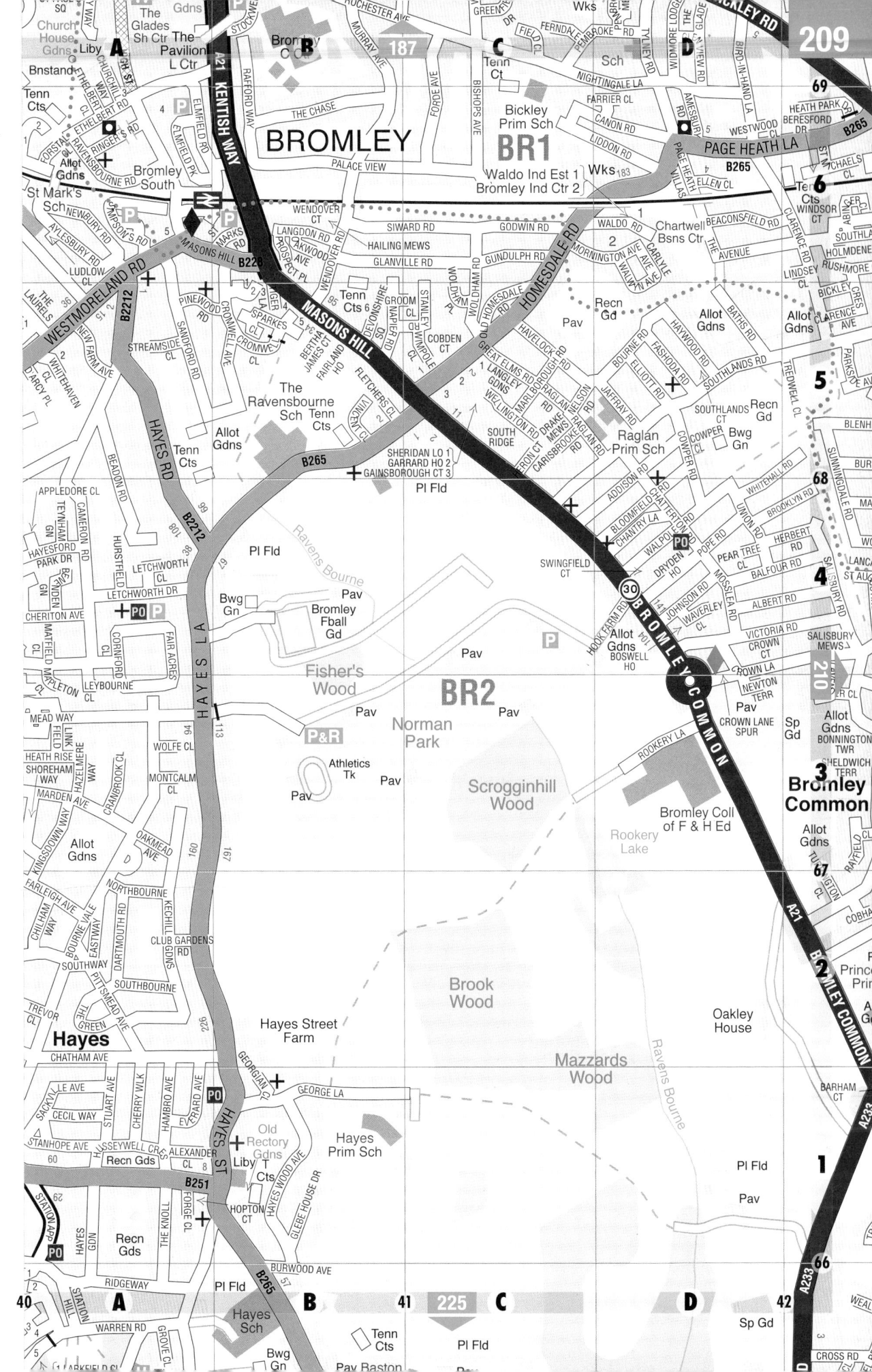
BROMLEY
BR1
BR2
Bromley South
Bromley Common
Hayes
Norman Park
Fisher's Wood
Scrogginhill Wood
Brook Wood
Mazzards Wood
Ravens Bourne
Rookery Lake
Hayes Street Farm
Oakley House
Bromley Coll of F & H Ed
The Ravensbourne Sch
Raglan Prim Sch
Bickley Prim Sch
Hayes Prim Sch
Bromley Fball Gd
Athletics Tk
KENTISH WAY
MASONS HILL
BROMLEY COMMON
HAYES LA
HAYES RD
HAYES ST
WESTMORELAND RD
HOMESDALE RD
PAGE HEATH LA
BURWOOD AVE
GEORGE LA
ROOKERY LA
A21
A233
B265
B2212
B251
B228
187
210
225
A
B
C
D
1
2
3
4
5
6
40
41
42
66
67
68
69

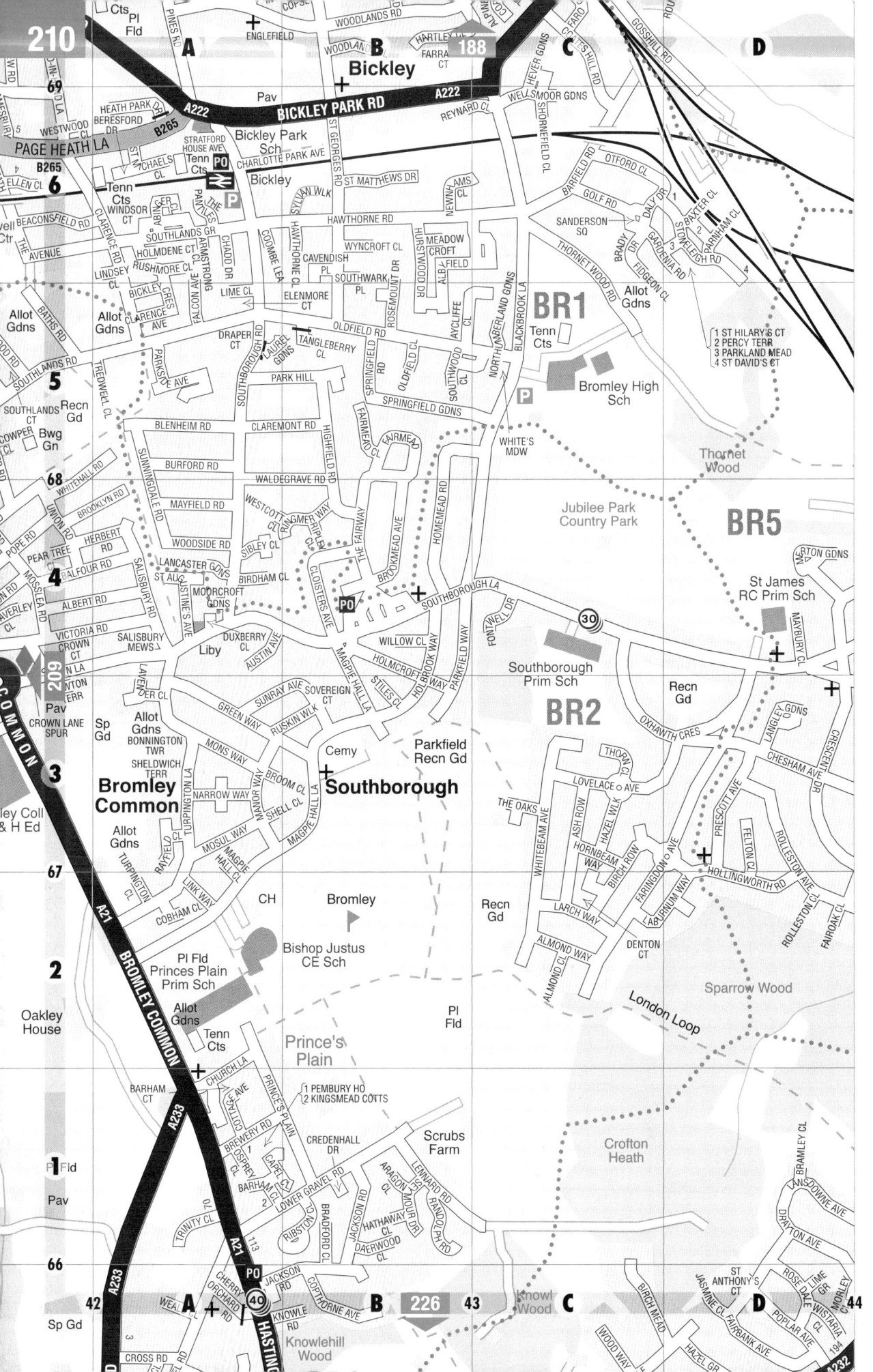
Bickley
BICKLEY PARK RD
A222
188
PAGE HEATH LA
B265
Bickley Park Sch
Bickley
BR1
Bromley High Sch
Thornet Wood
Jubilee Park Country Park
BR5
St James RC Prim Sch
SOUTHBOROUGH LA
Southborough Prim Sch
BR2
Parkfield Recn Gd
Southborough
Bromley Common
Bromley
Bishop Justus CE Sch
Princes Plain Prim Sch
Prince's Plain
Oakley House
Sparrow Wood
London Loop
Crofton Heath
Scrubs Farm
Knowlehill Wood
Knowl Wood
BROMLEY COMMON
A21
A233
209
226
1 ST HILARY'S CT
2 PERCY TERR
3 PARKLAND MEAD
4 ST DAVID'S CT
1 PEMBURY HO
2 KINGSMEAD COTTS
A
B
C
D
42
43
44
69
68
67
66
6
5
4
3
2
1

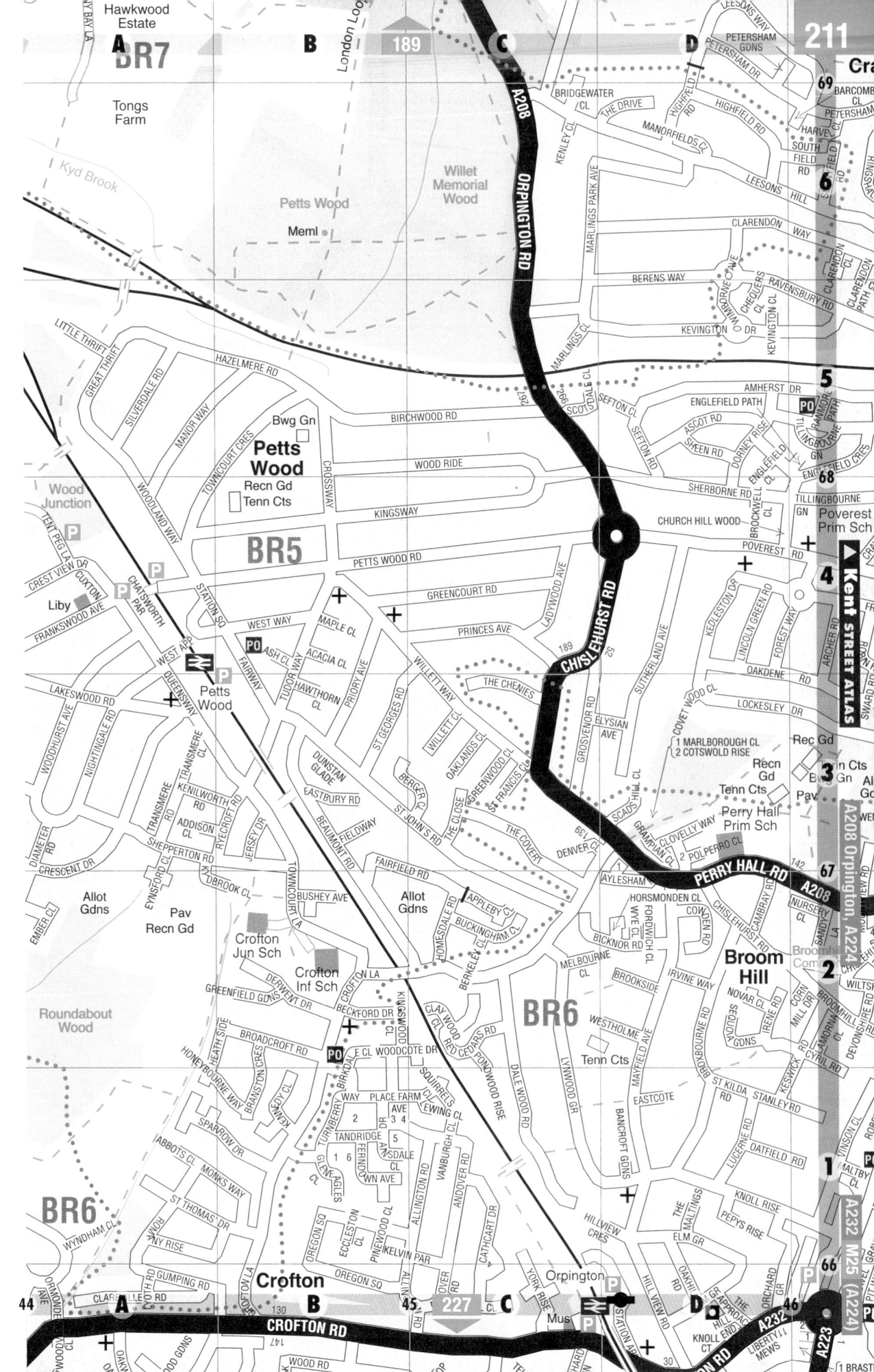
Hawkwood Estate
BR7
Tongs Farm
Kyd Brook
Petts Wood
Meml
Willet Memorial Wood
London Loop
189
A208
ORPINGTON RD
BRIDGEWATER CL
THE DRIVE
KENLEY CL
HIGHFIELD RD
MANORFIELDS CL
PETERSHAM GDNS
PETERSHAM DR
LEESONS WAY
LEESONS HILL
BARCOMBE CL
SOUTHFIELD RD
MARLINGS PARK AVE
CLARENDON WAY
BERENS WAY
RAVENSBURY RD
CHEQUERS CL
KEVINGTON CL
KEVINGTON DR
MARLINGS CL
LITTLE THRIFT
GREAT THRIFT
HAZELMERE RD
SILVERDALE RD
MANOR WAY
TOWNCOURT CRES
WOODLAND WAY
Bwg Gn
Petts Wood
Recn Gd
Tenn Cts
CROSSWAY
BIRCHWOOD RD
WOOD RIDE
KINGSWAY
SCOTSDALE CL
SEFTON CL
SEFTON RD
AMHERST DR
ENGLEFIELD PATH
ASCOT RD
SHEEN RD
DORNEY RISE
ENGLEFIELD CL
ENGLEFIELD CRES
TILLINGBOURNE GN
SHERBORNE RD
BROCKWELL CL
CHURCH HILL WOOD
Poverest Prim Sch
POVEREST RD
Kent STREET ATLAS
Wood Junction
TENT PEG LA
CREST VIEW DR
CUXTON
Liby
FRANKSWOOD AVE
CHATSWORTH PAR
BR5
PETTS WOOD RD
GREENCOURT RD
STATION SQ
WEST WAY
MAPLE CL
PRINCES AVE
LADYWOOD AVE
CHISLEHURST RD
SUTHERLAND AVE
KEDLESTON DR
LINCOLN GREEN RD
FOREST WAY
ARCHER RD
OAKDENE RD
LOCKESLEY DR
ASH CL
ACACIA CL
TUDOR WAY
HAWTHORN CL
PRIORY AVE
FAIRWAY
WEST APP
QUEENSWAY
Petts Wood
LAKESWOOD RD
WILLETT WAY
THE CHENIES
GROSVENOR RD
ELYSIAN AVE
COVET WOOD CL
1 MARLBOROUGH CL
2 COTSWOLD RISE
Rec Gd
Recn Gd
Tenn Cts
Pav
Perry Hall Prim Sch
WOODHURST AVE
NIGHTINGALE RD
TRANSMERE CL
TRANSMERE RD
KENILWORTH RD
ADDISON CL
RYECROFT RD
JERSEY DR
DUNSTAN GLADE
EASTBURY RD
BEAUMONT RD
FIELDWAY
ST GEORGES RD
BERGER CL
ST JOHN'S RD
WILLETT CL
OAKLANDS CL
GREENWOOD CL
THE CLOSE
ST FRANCIS CL
THE COVERT
SCADS HILL CL
GRAMPIAN CL
CLOVELLY WAY
2 POLPERRO CL
PERRY HALL RD
A208 Orpington, A224
DIAMETER RD
CRESCENT DR
SHEPPERTON RD
EYNSFORD CL
DBROOK CL
TOWNCOURT LA
BUSHEY AVE
FAIRFIELD RD
APPLEBY CL
DENVER CL
AYLESHAM
HORSMONDEN CL
WYE CL
FORDWICH CL
COWDEN RD
CHISLEHURST RD
CAMBRAY RD
NURSERY CL
SANDY LA
Allot Gdns
EMBER CL
Pav
Recn Gd
Crofton Jun Sch
Allot Gdns
HOMESDALE RD
BUCKINGHAM CL
BERKELEY CL
BICKNOR RD
MELBOURNE CL
BROOKSIDE
IRVINE WAY
Broom Hill
Crofton Inf Sch
CROFTON LA
Roundabout Wood
GREENFIELD GDNS
DERWENT DR
BECKFORD DR
KINGSWOOD CL
CLAY WOOD CL
RED CEDARS RD
BR6
WESTHOLME
NOVAR CL
IRENE RD
CORN MILL DR
SEQUOIA GDNS
BROOMHILL RD
LAMORNA CL
DEVONSHIRE RD
WILTSHIRE
HEATH SIDE
BROADCROFT RD
HONEYBOURNE WAY
BRANSTON CRES
KENNEDY CL
WOODCOTE DR
SQUIRRELS
PONDWOOD RISE
DALE WOOD RD
LYNWOOD GR
MAYFIELD AVE
Tenn Cts
BROXBOURNE RD
KESWICK RD
CYRIL RD
ST KILDA RD
STANLEY RD
SPARROW DR
ABBOTS CL
MONKS WAY
BIRKDALE
TURNBERRY WAY
PLACE FARM AVE
EWING CL
TANDRIDGE DR
ARMSDALE
FERNDOWN AVE
GLENEAGLES CL
VANBURGH CL
ANDOVER RD
ALLINGTON RD
EASTCOTE
BANCROFT GDNS
LUCERNE RD
OATFIELD RD
VINSON CL
MALTBY CL
KNOLL RISE
PEPYS RISE
BR6
WYNDHAM CL
ST THOMAS' DR
OREGON SQ
ECCLESTON CL
PINEWOOD CL
KELVIN PAR
CATHCART DR
HILLVIEW CRES
THE MALTINGS
ELM GR
A232
M25 (A224)
GUMPING RD
Crofton
Orpington
YORK RISE
HILL VIEW RD
ORCHARD GR
227
CROFTON RD
Mus
STATION APP
KNOLL CT
LIBERTY MEWS
STATION RD
A223
WOOD RD
44
45
46
A
B
C
D
1
2
3
4
5
6
66
67
68
69

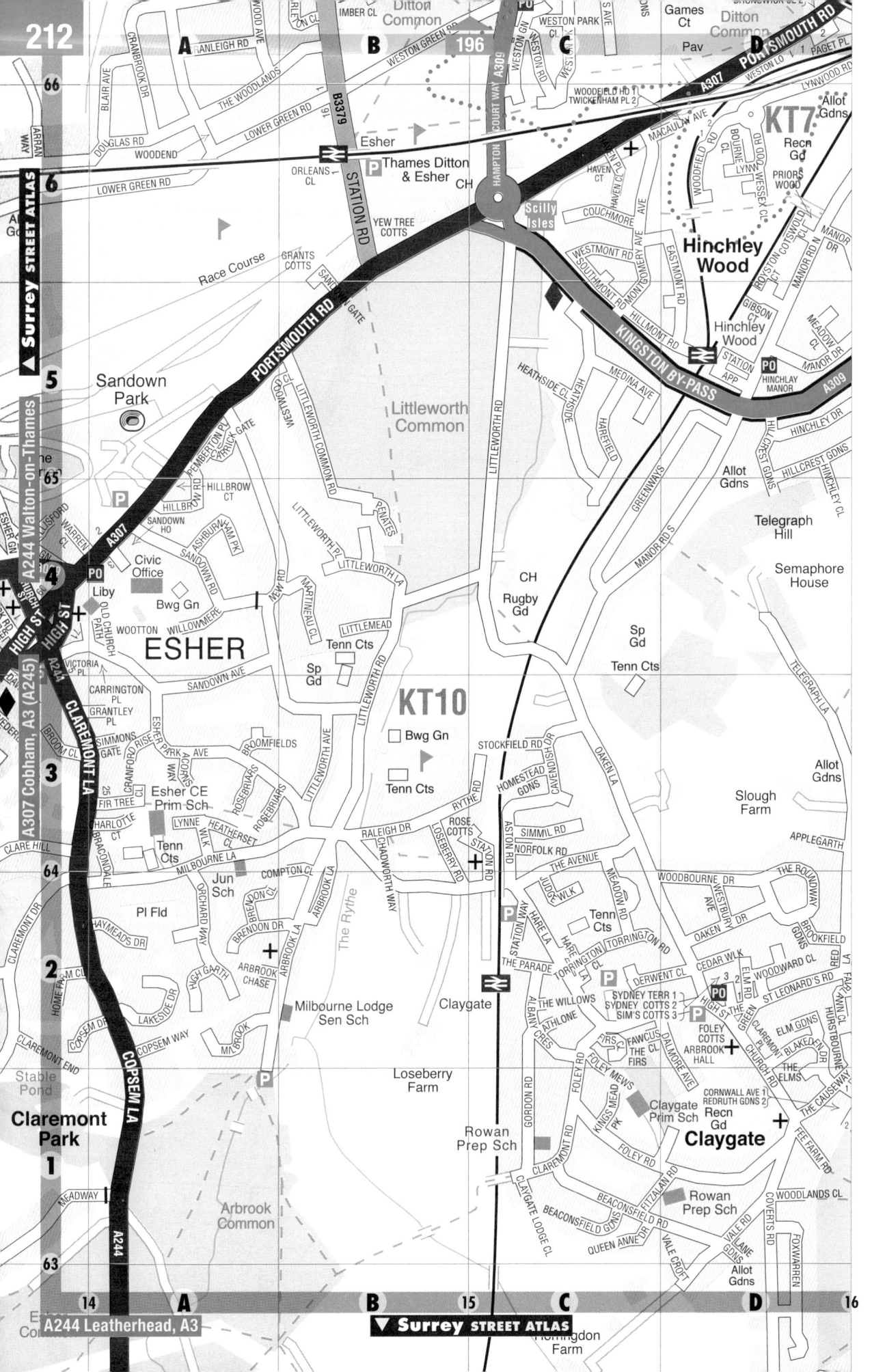

Surrey STREET ATLAS

A244 Walton-on-Thames

A307 Cobham, A3 (A245)

A244 Leatherhead, A3

▼ Surrey STREET ATLAS

ESHER

KT10

KT7

Hinchley Wood

Claygate

Claremont Park

Sandown Park

Littleworth Common

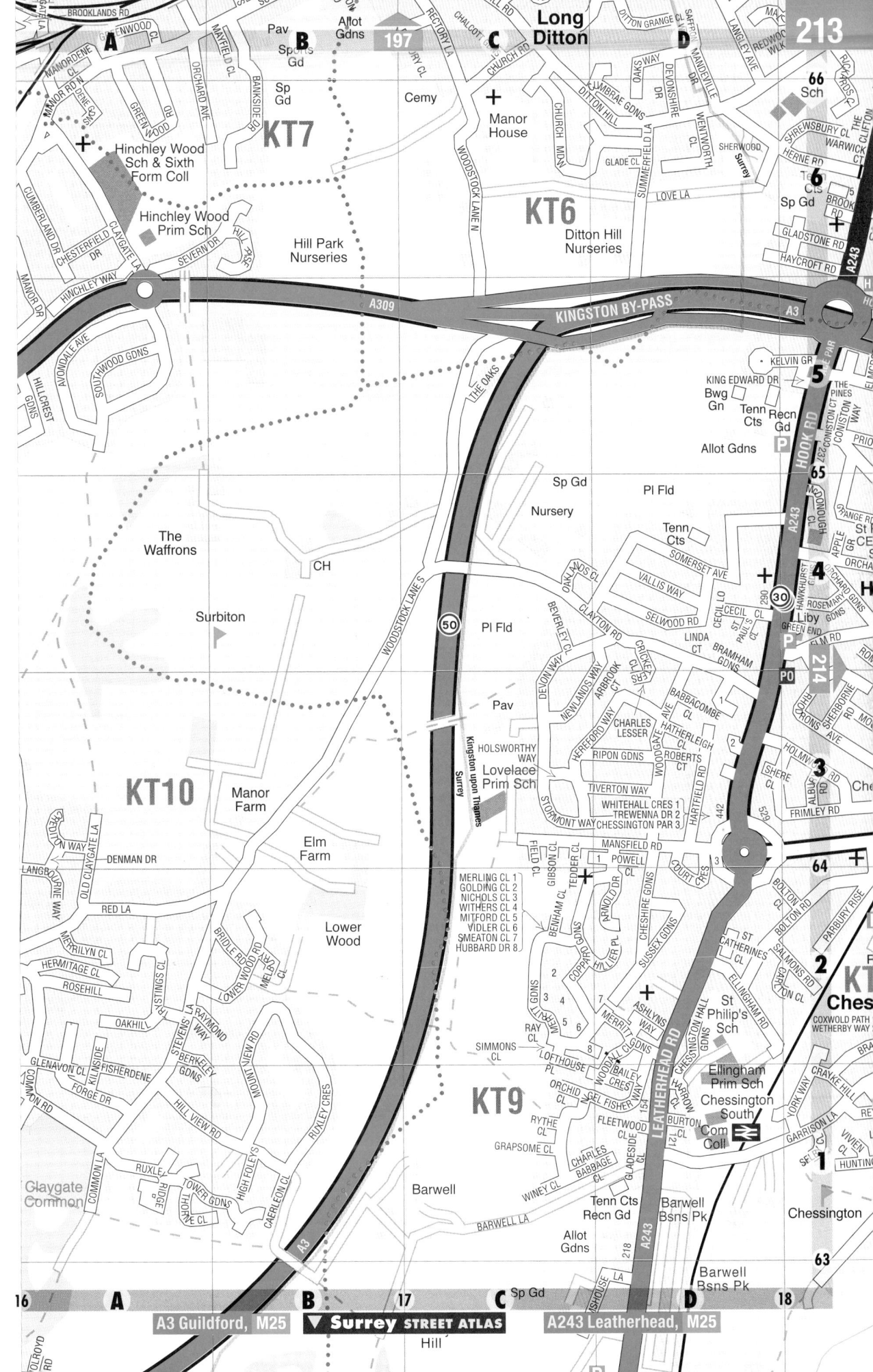

Long Ditton

Brooklands Rd

Greenwood

Pav Sports Gd

Allot Gdns

197

Chalcot

Rectory La

Church Rd

KT7

Cemy

Manor House

D

Sch 66

Warwick

Manordene Cl

Manor Rd N

Orchard Ave

Bankside Dr

Mayfield Cl

Greenwood Rd

Sp Gd

Woodstock Lane N

Cumbrae Gdns

Ditton Hill

Oaks Way

Devonshire Dr

Mandeville Cl

Langley Ave

Redwood Wlk

Shrewsbury Cl

Herne Rd

The Clifton

Hinchley Wood Sch & Sixth Form Coll

Claygate La

Chesterfield Dr

Cumberland Dr

Severn Dr

Hinchley Wood Prim Sch

Hill Rise

Hill Park Nurseries

Church Mdw

Glade Cl

Summerfield La

Love La

KT6

Ditton Hill Nurseries

Sherwood

Gladstone Rd

Haycroft Rd

Surrey

6

Brook Rd

Sp Gd 65

Hinchley Way

A309

Kingston By-Pass

A3

A243

Manor Dr

Avondale Ave

Southwood Gdns

Hillcrest Gdns

Kelvin Gr

King Edward Dr

Bwg Gn

Tenn Cts

Recn Gd

P

Allot Gdns

The Pines

Coniston Way

Hook Rd

5

The Waffrons

CH

Surbiton

Sp Gd

Nursery

Pl Fld

Tenn Cts

Oaklands Cl

Somerset Ave

Vallis Way

Selwood Rd

Cecil Lo

Cecil Rd

St Paul's Cl

Hawkhurst

30

Green End

Liby

Rosemary Gdns

Orchard Gdns

4

50

Pl Fld

Beverley Cl

Clayton Rd

Linda Ct

Bramham Gdns

Elm Rd

P

P0

214

KT10

Manor Farm

Elm Farm

Devon Way

Newlands Way

Hereford Rd

Arbrook Ct

Hatherleigh Cl

Ripon Gdns

Babbacombe Cl

Roberts Ct

Woodgate Ave

Hartfield Rd

Holmwood Rd

Shere Rd

Frimley Rd

Albury Rd

3

Che

Denman Dr

Old Claygate La

Clifton Way

Langbourne Way

Red La

Bridle Rd

Lower Wood Rd

Melton Cl

Lower Wood

Pav

Holsworthy Way

Lovelace Prim Sch

Charles Lesser

Tiverton Way

Whitehall Cres 1
Trewenna Dr 2
Chessington Par 3

Mansfield Rd

Powell Cl

Field Cl

Gibson Cl

Stormont Way

Tedder Cl

Arnold Dr

Cheshire Gdns

Court Cres

442

529

64

Bolton Rd

Parbury Rise

2

Merrilyn Cl

Hermitage Cl

Rosehill

Oakhill

Hastings Cl

Stevens La

Raymond Way

Berkeley Gdns

Mount View Rd

Ruxley Cres

MERLING CL 1
GOLDING CL 2
NICHOLS CL 3
WITHERS CL 4
MITFORD CL 5
VIDLER CL 6
SMEATON CL 7
HUBBARD DR 8

Benham Cl

Copford Gdns

Hillier Pl

Sussex Gdns

Ashlyns Way

Merritt Gdns

St Catherines Cl

Ellingham Rd

Carlton Rd

Bolton Cl

Salmons Rd

KT

Ches

Coxwold Path

Wetherby Way

Crayke Hill

Glenavon Cl

Common Rd

Kilnside

Fisherdene

Forge Dr

Hill View Rd

Ruxle

Lofthouse Pl

Simmons Cl

Ray Cl

Orchard

Nigel Fisher Way

Bailey Cres

Woodhall

Harrow Cl

Chessington Hall Gdns

St Philip's Sch

Ellingham Prim Sch

Chessington South Com Coll

York Way

Garrison La

Vivien Cl

Hunting

1

KT9

Rythe Cl

Fleetwood Cl

Burton Cl

Gladeside

Leatherhead Rd

Chessington South

Claygate Common

Common La

Tower Gdns

Thorne Cl

High Foleys Cl

Caerleon Cl

A3

Barwell

Winey Cl

Grapsome Cl

Charles Babbage Cl

Tenn Cts Recn Gd

Allot Gdns

218

A243

Barwell Bsns Pk

St Philip's Sch

Chessington

63

Nishouse La

Barwell La

Sp Gd

Barwell Bsns Pk

16

A

B

17

C

D

18

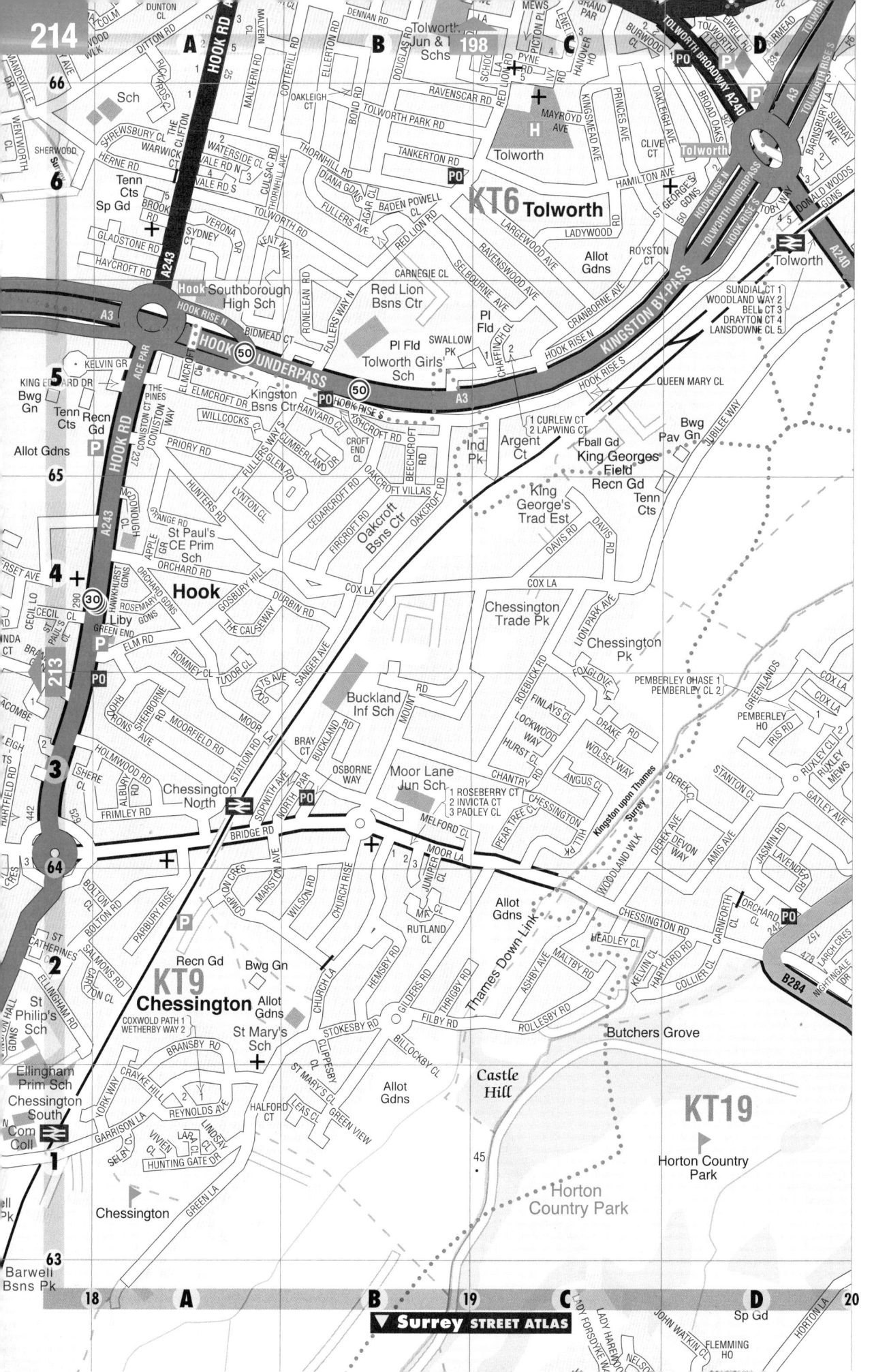

198
213
A
B
C
D
1
2
3
4
5
6
18
19
20
63
64
65
66
KT6
Tolworth
KT9
Chessington
KT19
Hook
HOOK RD
A243
A3
A240
HOOK UNDERPASS
KINGSTON BY-PASS
TOLWORTH BROADWAY
TOLWORTH UNDERPASS
HOOK RISE N
HOOK RISE S
TOLWORTH RISE S
Tolworth Jun & Inf Schs
Tolworth
Southborough High Sch
Red Lion Bsns Ctr
Pl Fld
Tolworth Girls' Sch
Kingston Bsns Ctr
Oakcroft Bsns Ctr
St Paul's CE Prim Sch
Liby
Allot Gdns
Tenn Cts
Sp Gd
Recn Gd
Bwg Gn
Ind Pk
Argent Ct
Fball Gd
King Georges Field
Recn Gd
Pav
King George's Trad Est
Chessington Trade Pk
Chessington Pk
Buckland Inf Sch
Moor Lane Jun Sch
Chessington North
St Philip's Sch
Ellingham Prim Sch
Chessington South
Com Coll
St Mary's Sch
Castle Hill
Butchers Grove
Horton Country Park
Thames Down Link
Kingston upon Thames
Surrey
Barwell Bsns Pk
TOLWORTH PARK RD
RAVENSCAR RD
TANKERTON RD
TOLWORTH RD
RED LION RD
ELMCROFT DR
PRIORY RD
HUNTERS RD
ORCHARD RD
GOSBURY HILL
DURBIN RD
ELM RD
COX LA
DAVIS RD
LION PARK AVE
ROEBUCK RD
MOOR LA
BRIDGE RD
CHURCH LA
GILDERS RD
FILBY RD
ROLLESBY RD
CHESSINGTON RD
GARRISON LA
GREEN LA
MOORFIELD RD
SANGER AVE
JUBILEE WAY
SUNDIAL CT 1
WOODLAND WAY 2
BELL CT 3
DRAYTON CT 4
LANSDOWNE CL 5
1 CURLEW CT
2 LAPWING CT
1 ROSEBERRY CT
2 INVICTA CT
3 PADLEY CL
PEMBERLEY CHASE 1
PEMBERLEY CL 2
COXWOLD PATH 1
WETHERBY WAY 2

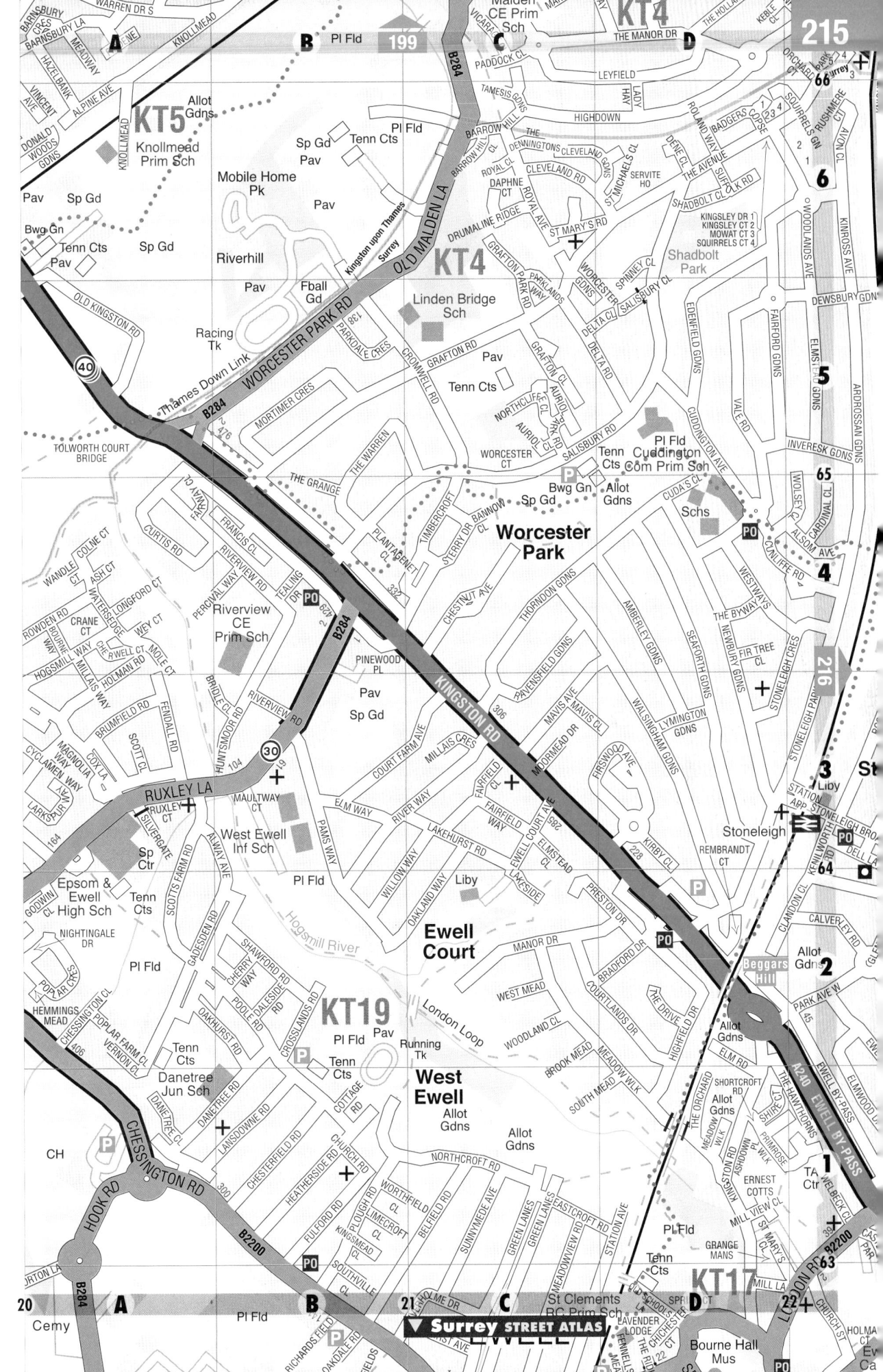
KT5
Knollmead Prim Sch
Allot Gdns
Mobile Home Pk
Riverhill
Racing Tk
Fball Gd
Pav
Sp Gd
Tenn Cts
Pl Fld
Bwg Gn
KT4
Linden Bridge Sch
Malden CE Prim Sch
THE MANOR DR
LEYFIELD
HIGHDOWN
Shadbolt Park
Cuddington Com Prim Sch
Worcester Park
Schs
Riverview CE Prim Sch
Pinewood Pl
KINGSTON RD
OLD MALDEN LA
WORCESTER PARK RD
Thames Down Link
TOLWORTH COURT BRIDGE
RUXLEY LA
West Ewell Inf Sch
Sp Ctr
Epsom & Ewell High Sch
Liby
Ewell Court
Hogsmill River
KT19
London Loop
Running Tk
West Ewell
Danetree Jun Sch
CHESSINGTON RD
HOOK RD
Stoneleigh
Beggars Hill
A240 EWELL BY-PASS
KT17
St Clements RC Prim Sch
Bourne Hall Mus
Cemy
CH
TA Ctr
Kingston upon Thames
Surrey
199
216
A
B
C
D
1
2
3
4
5
6
20
21
22
63
64
65
66

Worcester Park
A
B
C
D
200
North Cheam
KT4
Stoneleigh
SM3
Nonsuch Park
KT17
SM2
CENTRAL RD
CHEAM COMMON RD
MALDEN RD
LONDON RD
EWELL BY-PASS
THE AVENUE
CHEAM RD
EWELL RD
St Anthony's
St Cecilia's RC Prim Sch
Superstore
Recn Gd
Nonsuch Prim Sch
Nonsuch High Sch for Girls
Harefield Bridge
Cheam Park
Organ Crossroads
Ewell Castle
Bourne Hall Mus
215
66
6
5
65
4
3
64
2
1
63
22
23
24
A24 Epsom
A232 Epsom (A24)

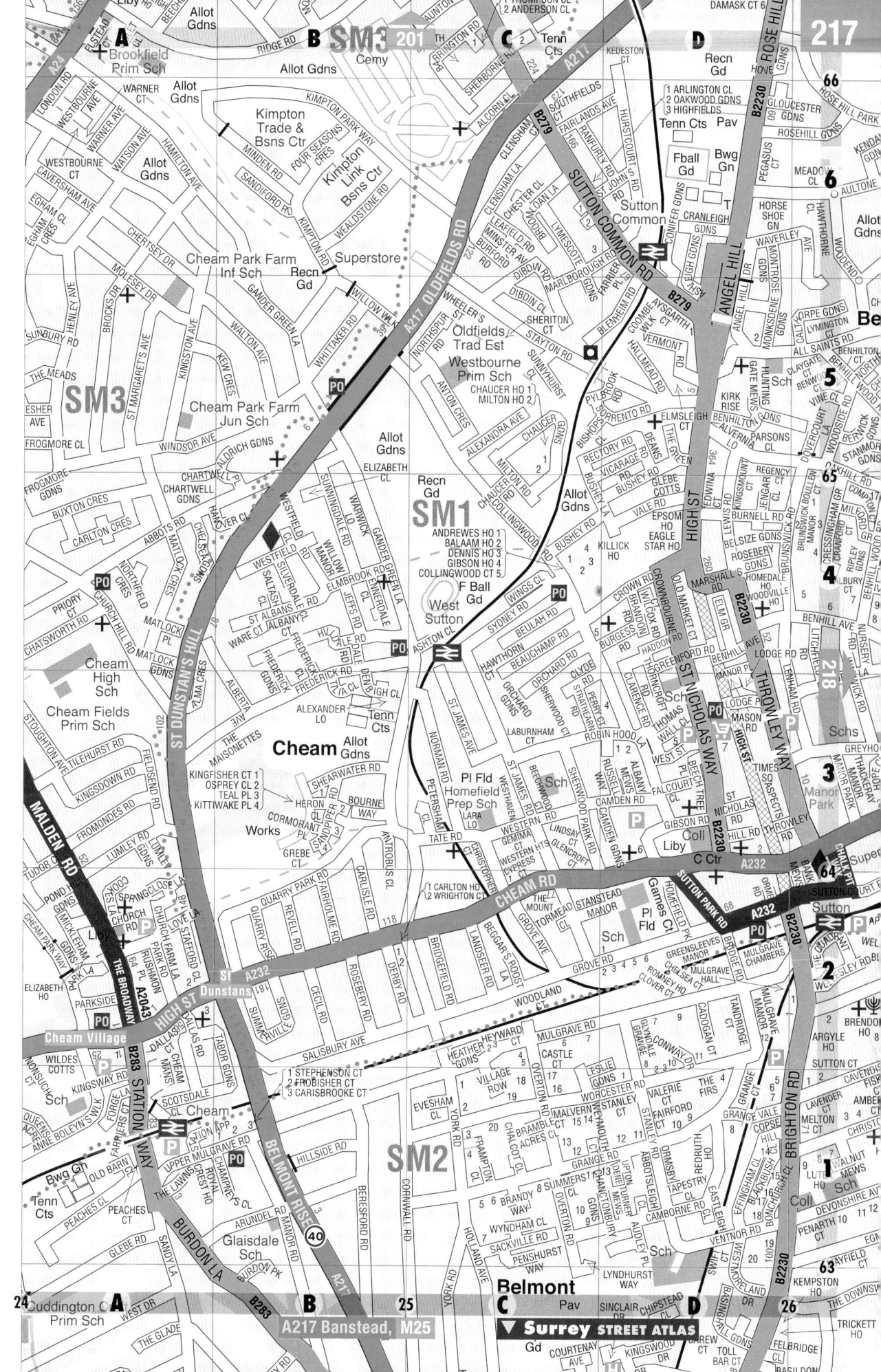
SM3
201
Brookfield Prim Sch
Allot Gdns
Cemy
Tenn Cts
Recn Gd
ROSE HILL
KIMPTON RD
Kimpton Trade & Bsns Ctr
Kimpton Link Bsns Ctr
Cheam Park Farm Inf Sch
Superstore
Cheam Park Farm Jun Sch
OLDFIELDS RD
A217
SUTTON COMMON RD
B279
Sutton Common
Oldfields Trad Est
Westbourne Prim Sch
Fball Gd
Bwg Gn
Pav
ANGEL HILL
B2230
HIGH ST
SM1
F Ball Gd
West Sutton
ST DUNSTAN'S HILL
ST NICHOLAS WAY
THROWLEY WAY
218
Schs
Manor Park
Cheam
Cheam High Sch
Cheam Fields Prim Sch
Pl Fld
Homefield Prep Sch
Works
MALDEN RD
CHEAM RD
A232
C Ctr
Coll
Liby
Games Ct
SUTTON PARK RD
Sutton
Cheam Village
THE BROADWAY
A2043
St Dunstans
B283
STATION WAY
BELMONT RISE
BRIGHTON RD
SM2
Glaisdale Sch
BURDON LA
Belmont
Cuddington Cft Prim Sch
A217 Banstead, M25
Surrey STREET ATLAS
24
25
26
66
6
5
4
3
2
1
65
64
63
A
B
C
D

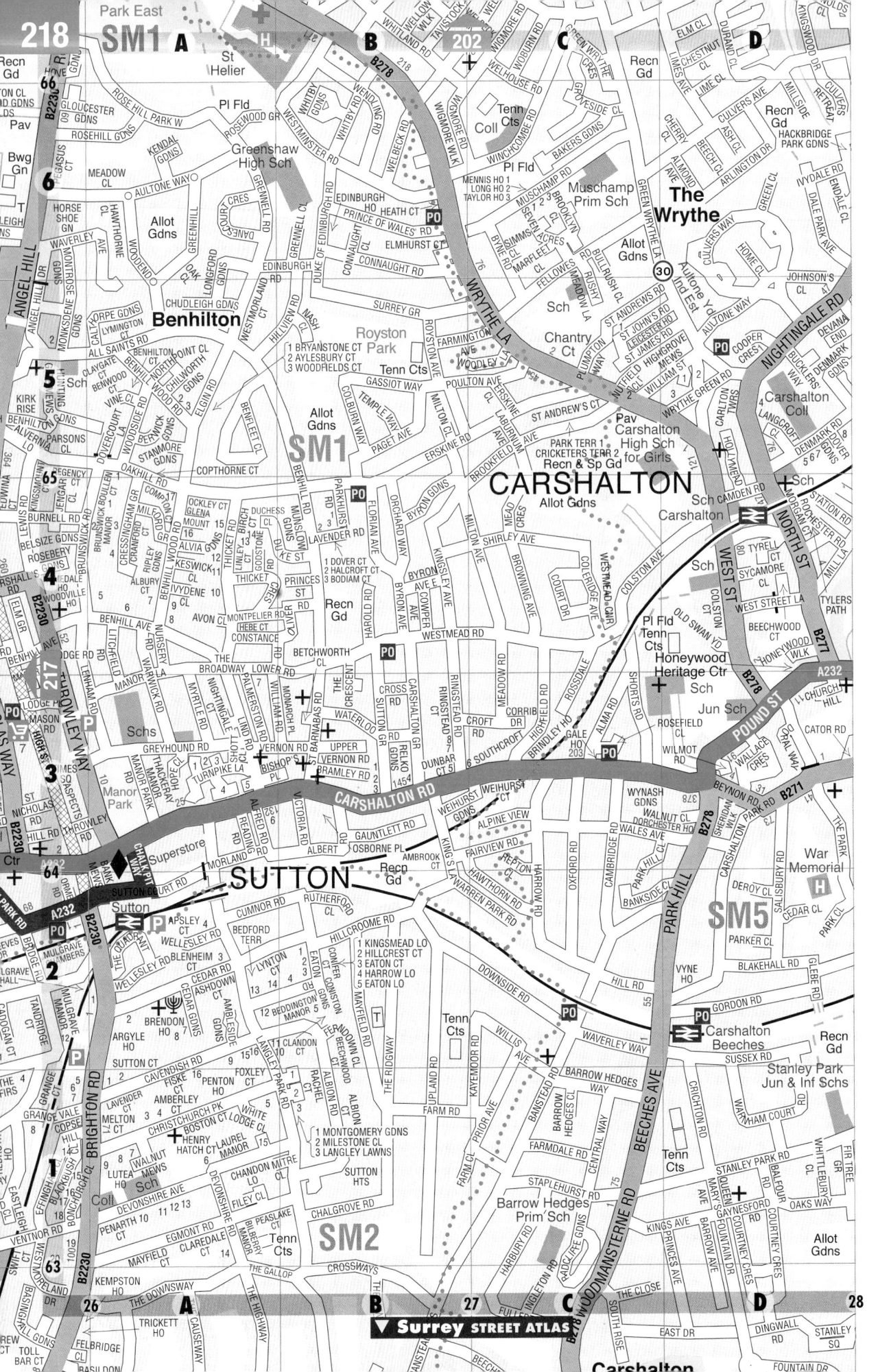
SM1
A
B
C
D
202
Park East
St Helier
Recn Gd
Pl Fld
Greenshaw High Sch
Benhilton
Royston Park
Allot Gdns
SM1
CARSHALTON
The Wrythe
Muschamp Prim Sch
Carshalton High Sch for Girls
Carshalton Coll
Carshalton
Honeywood Heritage Ctr
SUTTON
Sutton
SM5
SM2
Carshalton Beeches
Stanley Park Jun & Inf Schs
Barrow Hedges Prim Sch
War Memorial
Manor Park
Superstore
ANGEL HILL
WRYTHE LA
CARSHALTON RD
POUND ST
NIGHTINGALE RD
NORTH ST
WEST ST
PARK HILL
BEECHES AVE
WOODMANSTERNE RD
BRIGHTON RD
THROWLEY WAY
THE DOWNSWAY
DOWNSIDE RD
WAVERLEY WAY
CARSHALTON PARK RD
B278
B2230
B271
B277
A232
217
26
27
28
A
B
C
D
1
2
3
4
5
6
63
64
65
66
Carshalton

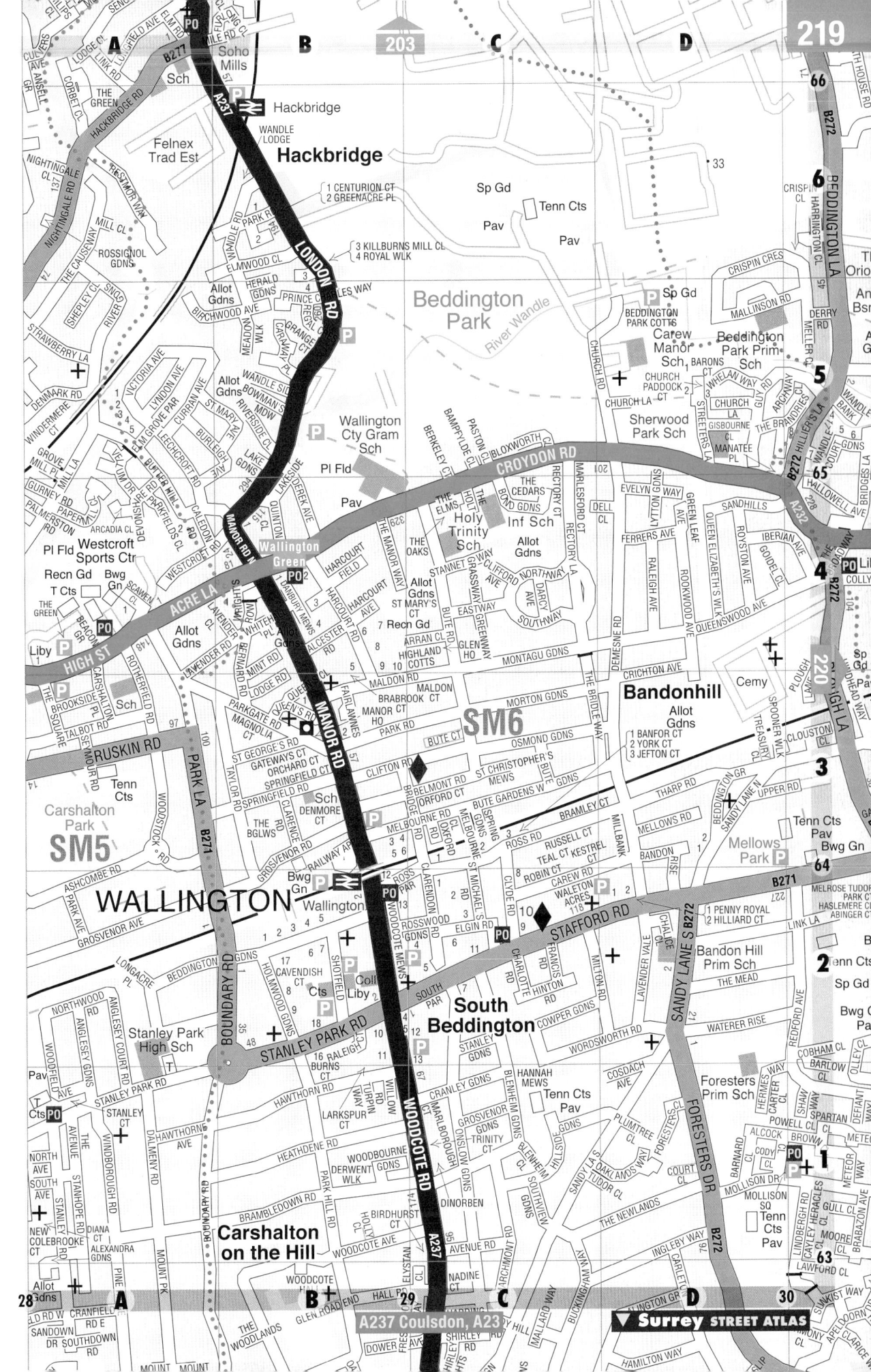
203
220
A
B
C
D
6
5
4
3
2
1
66
65
64
63
28
29
30
Hackbridge
Soho Mills
Felnex Trad Est
WANDLE LODGE
1 CENTURION CT
2 GREENACRE PL
3 KILLBURNS MILL CL
4 ROYAL WLK
LONDON RD
Sp Gd
Tenn Cts
Pav
Beddington Park
River Wandle
BEDDINGTON PARK COTTS
Carew Manor Sch
Beddington Park Prim Sch
Sherwood Park Sch
CHURCH PADDOCK CT
CHURCH LA
CRISPIN CRES
MALLINSON RD
BEDDINGTON LA
B272
Wallington Cty Gram Sch
Pl Fld
CROYDON RD
THE CEDARS
Holy Trinity Sch
Inf Sch
Allot Gdns
NIGHTINGALE RD
HACKBRIDGE RD
THE CAUSEWAY
MILL CL
ROSSIGNOL GDNS
SHEPLEY CL
RIVER GDNS
STRAWBERRY LA
DENMARK RD
WINDERMERE CT
VICTORIA AVE
LYNDON AVE
CURRAN AVE
ELM GROVE PAR
BIRCHWOOD AVE
ELMWOOD CL
PRINCE CHARLES WAY
Wallington Green
Westcroft Sports Ctr
Recn Gd
Bwg Gn
T Cts
Liby
HIGH ST
ACRE LA
MANOR RD
WESTCROFT RD
SM6
SM5
Bandonhill
Cemy
CRICHTON AVE
MORTON GDNS
OSMOND GDNS
QUEENSWOOD AVE
IBERIAN AVE
ROYSTON AVE
ROOKWOOD AVE
RALEIGH AVE
FERRERS AVE
1 BANFOR CT
2 YORK CT
3 JEFTON CT
RUSKIN RD
PARK LA
B271
Carshalton Park
WALLINGTON
Wallington
STAFFORD RD
1 PENNY ROYAL
2 HILLIARD CT
Bandon Hill Prim Sch
Mellows Park
South Beddington
STANLEY PARK RD
Stanley Park High Sch
BOUNDARY RD
SANDY LANE S
FORESTERS DR
Foresters Prim Sch
WOODCOTE RD
A237
Carshalton on the Hill
WOODCOTE AVE
BIRDHURST CT
ARCHMONT RD
BUCKINGHAM WAY
MALLARD WAY
THE NEWLANDS
COSDACH AVE
Tenn Cts Pav
Bwg Gn
GROSVENOR AVE
LONGACRE PL
BEDDINGTON GDNS
CAVENDISH CT
Coll
HAWTHORN RD
HEATHDENE RD
BRAMBLEDOWN RD
MOUNT PK
WINDBOROUGH RD
DALMENY RD

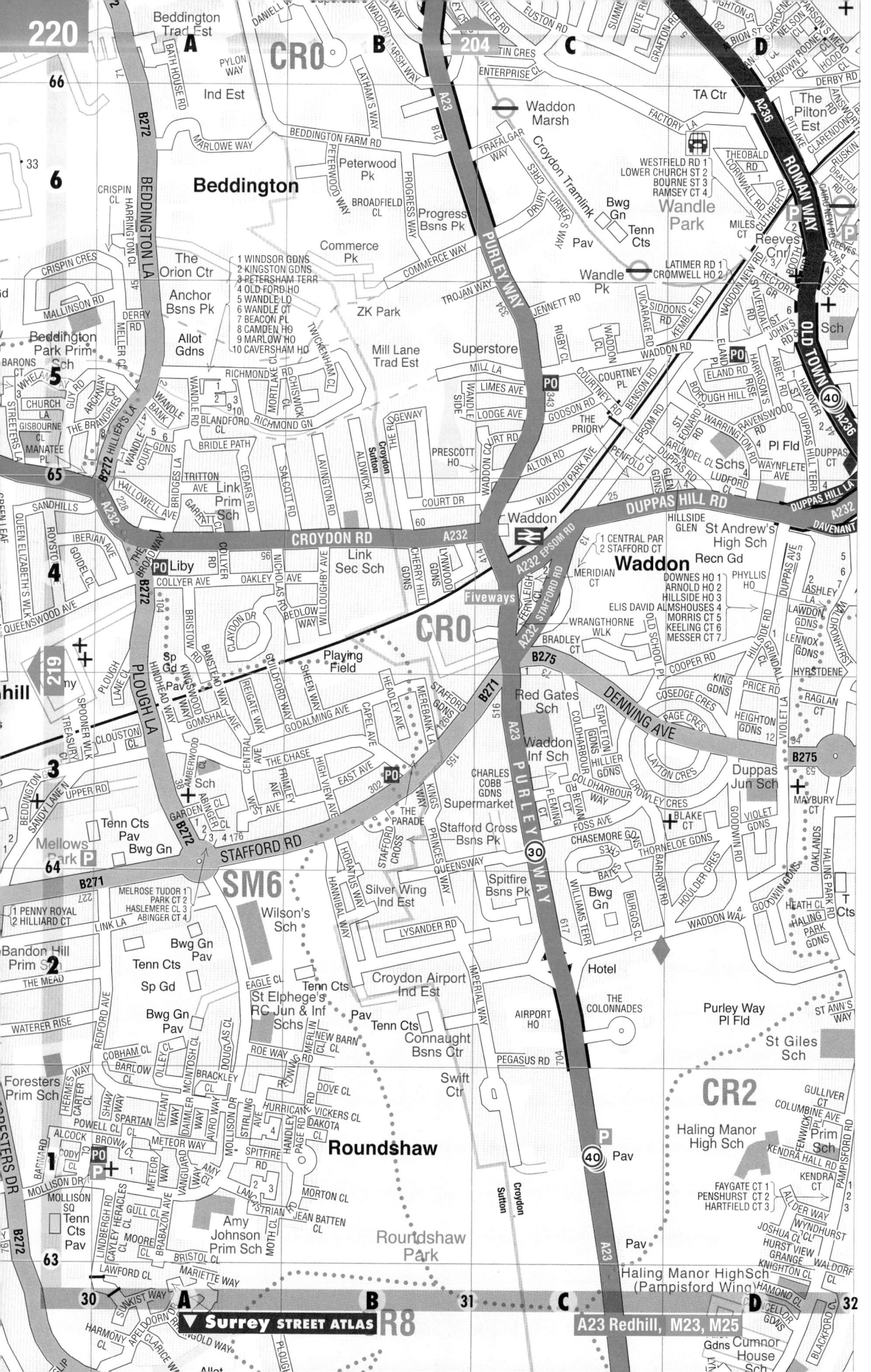
A
B
C
D
CR0
204
Beddington Trad Est
Pylon Way
Ind Est
Bath House Rd
Daniell Way
Waddon Marsh Way
Latham's Way
Euston Rd
Enterprise Cl
Waddon Marsh
TA Ctr
Factory La
The Pilton Est
Derby Rd
66
6
33
B272
Beddington La
Marlowe Way
Beddington Farm Rd
Peterwood Pk
Peterwood Way
Progress Way
A23
Trafalgar Way
Croydon Tramlink
Westfield Rd 1
Lower Church St 2
Bourne St 3
Ramsey Ct 4
Theobald Rd
Cornwall Rd
Cuthbert Rd
Roman Way
A236
Beddington
Crispin Cl
Harrington Cl
Broadfield Cl
Progress Bsns Pk
Bwg Gn
Tenn Cts
Wandle Park
Miles Ct
Reeves Cnr
Purley Way
Commerce Pk
Commerce Way
Pav
Wandle Pk
Latimer Rd 1
Cromwell Ho 2
Crispin Cres
The Orion Ctr
1 Windsor Gdns
2 Kingston Gdns
3 Petersham Terr
4 Old Ford Ho
5 Wandle Lo
6 Wandle Ct
7 Beacon Pl
8 Camden Ho
9 Marlow Ho
10 Caversham Ho
Anchor Bsns Pk
Trojan Way
Jennett Rd
Siddons Rd
Kemble Rd
Waddon New Rd
Rectory Gr
St John's Rd
Old Town
Sch
Mallinson Rd
Derry Rd
Meller Cl
ZK Park
Twickenham Cl
Allot Gdns
Mill Lane Trad Est
Superstore
Mill La
Rigby Cl
Waddon Cl
Vicarage Rd
Waddon Rd
Eland Pl
Eland Rd
Beddington Park Prim Sch
Barons Ct
Whelan Way
5
Church La
Gisbourne Cl
Manatee Pl
Streeters La
Guy Rd
Archway
The Brandries
Hillier's La
Richmond Rd
Mortlake Cl
Chiswick Cl
Richmond Gn
Blandford Cl
Wandle Rd
Wandle Bank
Wandle Ct Gdns
Limes Ave
Wandle Side
Lodge Ave
Courtney Pl
Benson Rd
Godson Rd
The Priory
Epsom Rd
St Leonard's Rd
Borough Hill
Harrison's Rise
Warrington Rd
Ravenswood Rd
Abbey Rd
Hanover St
Duppas Hill Terr
40
Bridle Path
The Ridgeway
Croydon
Sutton
Prescott Ho
Waddon Court Rd
Alton Rd
Waddon Park Ave
Penfold Cl
Arundel Cl
Duppas Rd
Schs
Pl Fld
Waynflete Ave
Duppas Ct
Ludford Cl
65
B272
Tritton Ave
Link Prim Sch
Hallowell Ave
Bridges La
Cedars Rd
Salcott Rd
Lavington Rd
Aldwick Rd
Court Dr
Duppas Hill Rd
Duppas Hill La
Davenant
Sandhills
A232
Queen Elizabeth's Wlk
Royston
Iberian Ave
Goidel Cl
The Broadway
Croydon Rd
Link Sec Sch
Cherry Hill Gdns
Lynwood Gdns
Waddon
1 Central Par
2 Stafford Ct
Hillside Glen
St Andrew's High Sch
Waddon
Recn Gd
4
PO
Liby
Collyer Ave
Collyer Rd
Oakley Ave
Nicholas Rd
Willoughby Ave
Fiveways
Fernleigh Cl
Stafford Rd
Meridian Ct
Downes Ho 1
Arnold Ho 2
Hillside Ho 3
Elis David Almshouses 4
Morris Ct 5
Keeling Ct 6
Messer Ct 7
Phyllis Ho
Ashley La
Lawdon Gdns
Lennox Gdns
Queenswood Ave
Bristow Rd
Claydon Dr
Bedlow Way
Wrangthorne Wlk
Old School Pl
Bradley Ct
Hillside Rd
Grindall Cl
Waldronhyrst
219
Sp Gd
Pav
Banstead Way
Kingswood Way
Playing Field
B275
Cooper Rd
Hyrstdene
Plough La
Hindhead Way
Guildford Way
Sheen Way
Stafford Gdns
Red Gates Sch
King Gdns
Price Rd
Raglan Ct
Spooner Wlk
Treasury Cl
Clouston Cl
Gomshall Ave
Reigate Way
Godalming Ave
Headley Ave
Merebank La
Capel Ave
B271
Denning Ave
Cosedge Cres
Page Cres
Heighton Gdns
Violet La
3
Amberwood
The Chase
Central Ave
Frimley Ave
High View Ave
Waddon Inf Sch
Coldharbour Rd
Stapleton Gdns
Hillier Gdns
Layton Cres
Duppas Jun Sch
Beddington
Sandy Lane N
Upper Rd
Sch
Abinger Cl
Garden Cl
West Ave
East Ave
The Parade
Kings Way
Charles Cobb Gdns
Supermarket
Coldharbour Way
Crowley Cres
Fleming Ct
Bevan Ct
Mayburg Ct
Tenn Cts Pav
Bwg Gn
Mellows Park
Stafford Rd
Stafford Cross
Princes Way
Stafford Cross Bsns Pk
Foss Ave
Chasemore Gdns
Blake Ct
Thorneloe Gdns
Violet Gdns
Goodwin Rd
Oaklands
Haling Park Rd
64
SM6
Queensway
30
Bates Cres
Barrow Rd
Houlder Cres
1 Penny Royal
2 Hilliard Ct
Melrose Tudor 1
Park Ct 2
Haslemere Cl 3
Abinger Ct 4
Link La
Wilson's Sch
Horatius Way
Hannibal Way
Silver Wing Ind Est
Spitfire Bsns Pk
Williams Terr
Bwg Gn
Burgos Cl
Goodwin Gdns
Heath Cl
Haling Park Gdns
T Cts
Bandon Hill Prim Sch
2
Bwg Gn Pav
Tenn Cts
Lysander Rd
Waddon Way
The Mead
Sp Gd
Eagle Cl
Tenn Cts
Croydon Airport Ind Est
Imperial Way
Hotel
St Elphege's RC Jun & Inf Schs
Pav
Tenn Cts
The Colonnades
Airport Ho
Purley Way Pl Fld
St Ann's Way
Waterer Rise
Bwg Gn Pav
Redford Ave
Connaught Bsns Ctr
St Giles Sch
Cobham Cl
Olley Cl
Mcintosh Cl
Douglas Cl
Roe Way
Merlin Cl
New Barn Cl
Pegasus Rd
Barlow Cl
Brackley Cl
Fowning Rd
Dove Cl
Swift Ctr
Foresters Prim Sch
Hermes Way
Carter Cl
Shaw Way
Spartan Cl
Defiant Way
Daimler Way
Avro Way
Mollison Dr
Stirling Ave
Hurricane Rd
Vickers Cl
Dakota Cl
CR2
Gulliver Ct
Columbine Ave
Powell Cl
Alcock Cl
Brown Cl
Meteor Way
Handley Page Rd
Haling Manor High Sch
Fenwick Pl
Prim Sch
Pampisford Rd
Cody Cl
Vanguard Way
Amy Cl
Spitfire Rd
Roundshaw
Kendra Hall Rd
Kendra Ct
1
Barnard Cl
Mollison Dr
Mollison Sq
Tenn Cts Pav
Lindbergh Rd
Cayley Cl
Heracles Cl
Gull Cl
Brabazon Ave
Moore Cl
Lancastrian Rd
Morton Cl
Jean Batten Cl
Moth Cl
Amy Johnson Prim Sch
Pav
Faygate Ct 1
Penshurst Ct 2
Hartfield Ct 3
Alder Way
Wyndhurst Cl
Joshua Cl
Hurst View Grange
Waldorf Cl
Foresters Dr
63
Bristol Cl
Roundshaw Park
Pav
Lawford Cl
Mariette Way
Haling Manor HighSch (Pampisford Wing)
Knighton Cl
Hamond Cl
30
Sunkist Way
A
B
31
C
D
32
Chancellor Gdns
Blackford Cl
Surrey STREET ATLAS
SR8
A23 Redhill, M23, M25
Harmony Cl
Apeldoorn Dr
Clarice Way
Ringold Way
Plough
Allot
Gdns
Cumnor House Sch

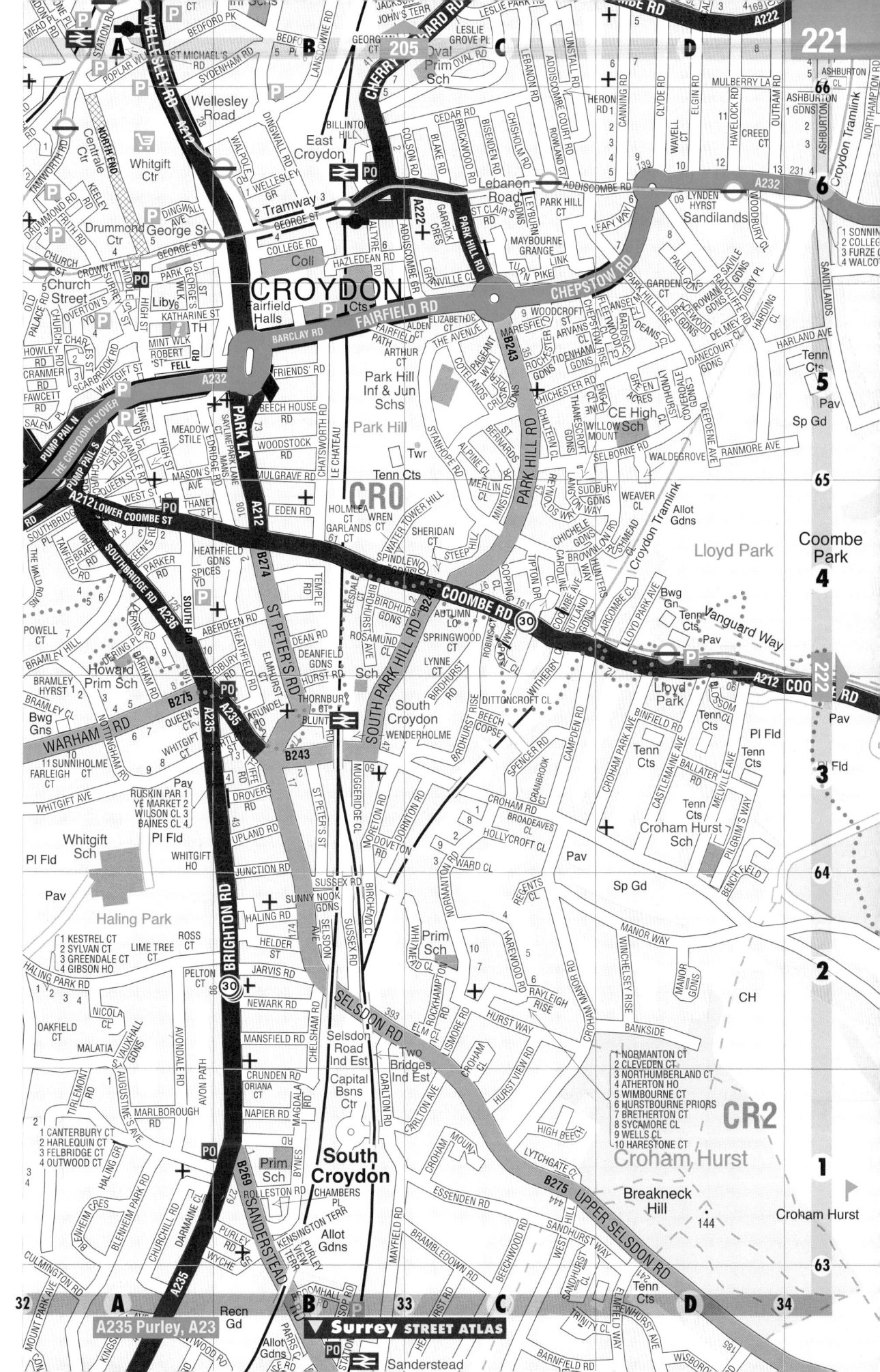
CROYDON
Wellesley Road
Whitgift Ctr
Centrale Ctr
East Croydon
Tramway
George St
Drummond Ctr
Church Street
Fairfield Halls
Coll
Liby
Lebanon Road
Sandilands
Park Hill Inf & Jun Schs
Park Hill
Twr
Tenn Cts
CR0
CE High Sch
Allot Gdns
Lloyd Park
Coombe Park
Vanguard Way
Croydon Tramlink
Howard Prim Sch
South Croydon
Croham Hurst Sch
Whitgift Sch
Haling Park
Prim Sch
Selsdon Road Ind Est
Two Bridges Ind Est
Capital Bsns Ctr
South Croydon
Allot Gdns
CR2
Croham Hurst
Breakneck Hill
144
Recn Gd
Sanderstead
WELLESLEY RD
CHERRY ORCHARD RD
ADDISCOMBE RD
FAIRFIELD RD
BARCLAY RD
CHEPSTOW RD
PARK HILL RD
PARK LA
COOMBE RD
LOWER COOMBE ST
SOUTHBRIDGE RD
ST PETER'S RD
SOUTH PARK HILL RD
WARHAM RD
BRIGHTON RD
SELSDON RD
UPPER SELSDON RD
SANDERSTEAD RD
A212
A222
A232
A235
A236
B243
B269
B274
B275
205
222
A
B
C
D
32
33
34
1
2
3
4
5
6
63
64
65
66
A235 Purley, A23
Surrey STREET ATLAS

Shirley
Tenn Cts
Recn Gd
ADDISCOMBE RD
SHIRLEY RD
WICKHAM RD
Trinity Sch
Shirley Park
Oaks Farm
Windmill (dis)
Coloma Convent Girls' Sch
Shirley High Sch
Upper Shirley
Coombe Park
Coombe Farm
Lloyd Park
CR0
Addington Hills
Vanguard Way
COOMBE RD
Croydon Tramlink
Hotel
Coombe Lane
COOMBE LA
Royal Russell Sch
Heathfield
Bramley Bank
Nat Res
London Loop
Selsdon High Sch
CR2
Croham Hurst
Littleheath Woods
Surrey STREET ATLAS
206
221

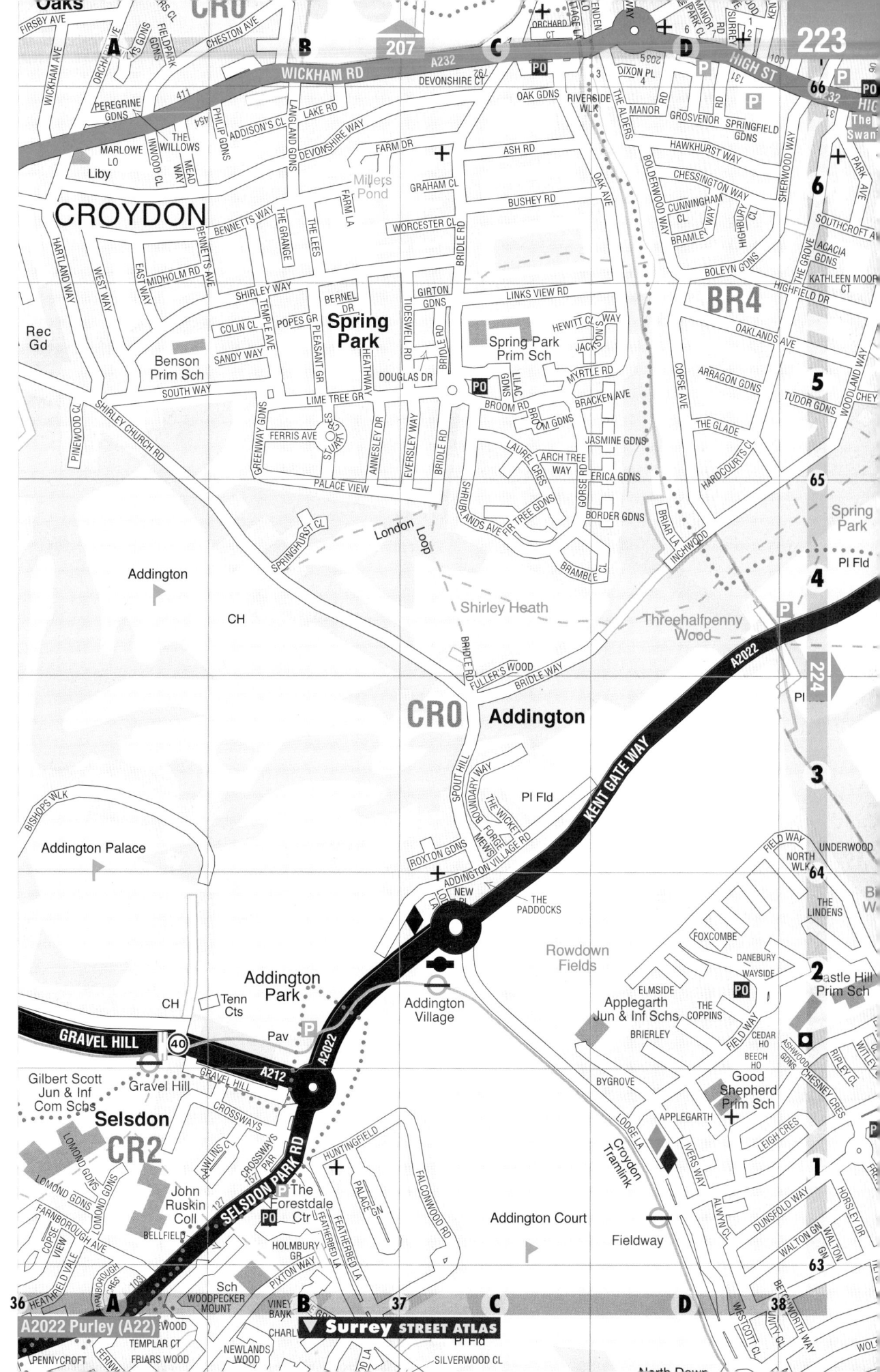
207
224
A
B
C
D
6
5
4
3
2
1
66
65
64
63
36
37
38
CROYDON
Spring Park
BR4
CR0
Addington
CR2
Selsdon
Oaks
WICKHAM RD
A232
HIGH ST
CHESTON AVE
FIRSBY AVE
WICKHAM AVE
ORCHARD AVE
FIELDPARK GDNS
PEREGRINE GDNS
MARLOWE LO
Liby
THE WILLOWS
INWOOD CL
MEAD WAY
PHILIP GDNS
ADDISON'S CL
LANGLAND GDNS
LAKE RD
DEVONSHIRE WAY
DEVONSHIRE CT
FARM DR
FARM LA
Millers Pond
GRAHAM CL
ASH RD
BUSHEY RD
WORCESTER CL
BRIDLE RD
OAK GDNS
RIVERSIDE WLK
ORCHARD CT
DIXON PL
MANOR RD
THE ALDERS
OAK AVE
GROSVENOR RD
SPRINGFIELD GDNS
HAWKHURST WAY
CHESSINGTON WAY
BOLDERWOOD WAY
CUNNINGHAM CL
BRAMLEY WAY
HIGHBURY CL
SHERWOOD WAY
PARK AVE
SOUTHCROFT AVE
ACACIA GDNS
KATHLEEN MOORE CT
HIGHFIELD DR
BOLEYN GDNS
THE GROVE
OAKLANDS AVE
ARRAGON GDNS
TUDOR GDNS
WOODLAND WAY
THE GLADE
HARDCOURTS CL
COPSE AVE
BENNETTS WAY
BENNETTS AVE
THE GRANGE
THE LEES
HARTLAND WAY
WEST WAY
EAST WAY
MIDHOLM RD
SHIRLEY WAY
TEMPLE AVE
COLIN CL
POPES GR
PLEASANT GR
BERNEL DR
HEATHWAY
TIDESWELL RD
GIRTON GDNS
LINKS VIEW RD
HEWITT CL
JACKSONS WAY
Spring Park Prim Sch
MYRTLE RD
LILAC GDNS
DOUGLAS DR
Rec Gd
Benson Prim Sch
SANDY WAY
SOUTH WAY
LIME TREE GR
BROOM RD
BROOM GDNS
BRACKEN AVE
JASMINE GDNS
LARCH TREE WAY
LAUREL CRES
ERICA GDNS
GORSE RD
PINEWOOD CL
SHIRLEY CHURCH RD
GREENWAY GDNS
FERRIS AVE
STUART CRES
ANNESLEY DR
EVERSLEY WAY
PALACE VIEW
SHRUBLANDS AVE
FIR TREE GDNS
BORDER GDNS
BRIAR LA
INCHWOOD
BRAMBLE CL
SPRINGHURST CL
London Loop
Addington
CH
Shirley Heath
Threehalfpenny Wood
Spring Park
Pl Fld
A2022
FULLER'S WOOD
BRIDLE WAY
KENT GATE WAY
SPOUT HILL
BOUNDARY WAY
THE WICKET
FORGE MEWS
ADDINGTON VILLAGE RD
ROXTON GDNS
NEW PL
THE PADDOCKS
BISHOPS WLK
Addington Palace
Rowdown Fields
FIELD WAY
NORTH WLK
UNDERWOOD
THE LINDENS
FOXCOMBE
DANEBURY
WAYSIDE
ELMSIDE
Applegarth Jun & Inf Schs
THE COPPINS
BRIERLEY
CEDAR HO
BEECH HO
Castle Hill Prim Sch
ASHWOOD GDNS
CHESNEY CRES
RIPLEY CL
Good Shepherd Prim Sch
BYGROVE
APPLEGARTH
LEIGH CRES
IVERS WAY
LODGE LA
Croydon Tramlink
ALWYN CL
DUNSFOLD WAY
WALTON GN
HORSLEY DR
Fieldway
Addington Court
WESTCOTT CL
BETCHWORTH WAY
Addington Park
Tenn Cts
Pav
Addington Village
GRAVEL HILL
A212
40
Gilbert Scott Jun & Inf Com Schs
Gravel Hill
CROSSWAYS
RAWLINS CL
CROSSWAYS PAR
SELSDON PARK RD
The Forestdale Ctr
HUNTINGFIELD
PALACE GN
FALCONWOOD RD
FEATHERBED LA
HOLMBURY GR
PIXTON WAY
LOMOND GDNS
John Ruskin Coll
BELLFIELD
FARNBOROUGH AVE
COPSE VIEW
HEATHFIELD VALE
FARNBOROUGH CRES
Sch
WOODPECKER MOUNT
VINEY BANK
TEMPLAR CT
FRIARS WOOD
PENNYCROFT
NEWLANDS WOOD
SILVERWOOD CL
Pl Fld
A2022 Purley (A22)

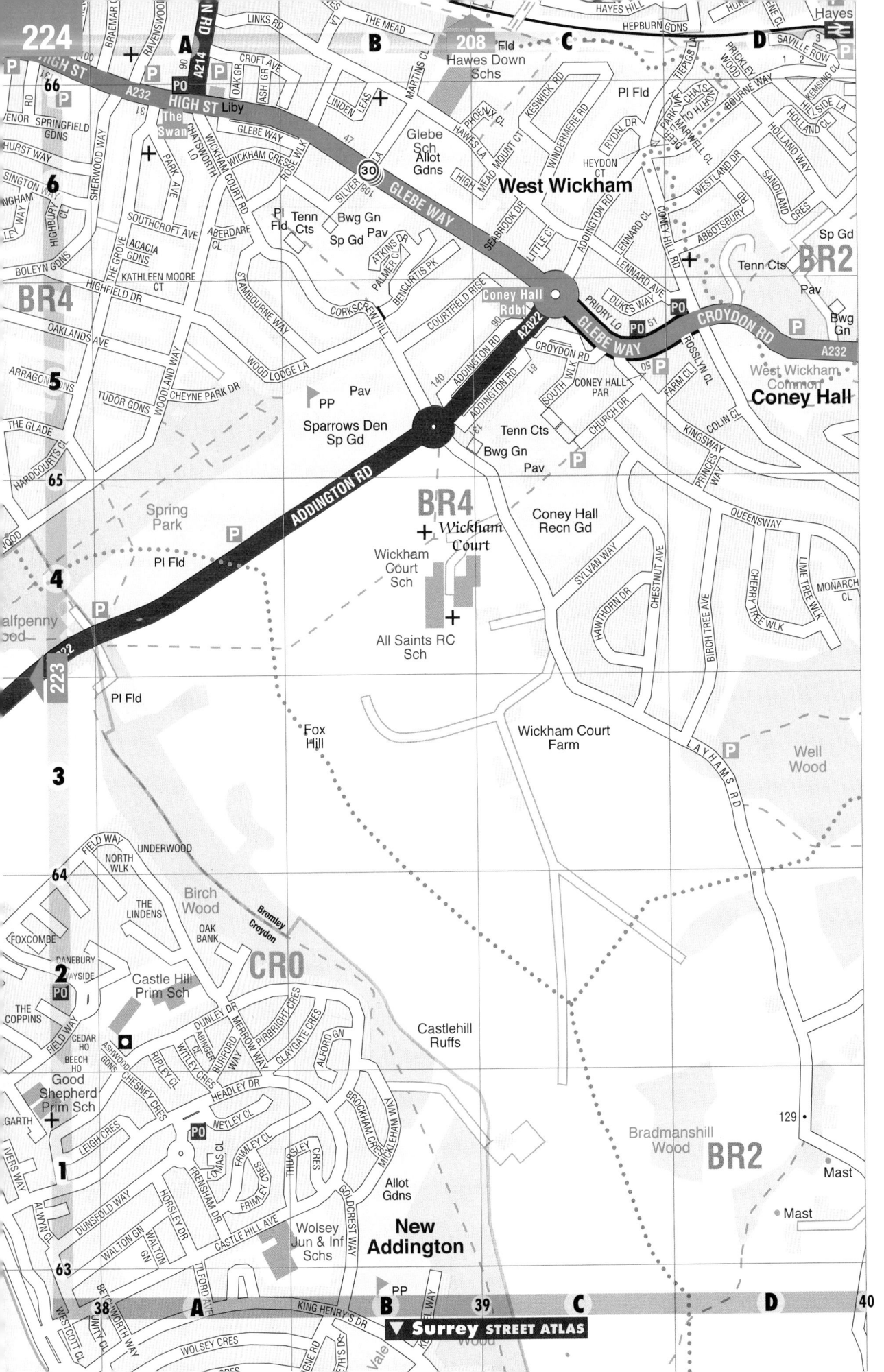
West Wickham
Coney Hall
New Addington
Wickham Court
Spring Park
Sparrows Den Sp Gd
Coney Hall Recn Gd
Wickham Court Farm
Fox Hill
Birch Wood
Castlehill Ruffs
Bradmanshill Wood
Well Wood
West Wickham Common
Hawes Down Schs
Glebe Sch
Wickham Court Sch
All Saints RC Sch
Castle Hill Prim Sch
Good Shepherd Prim Sch
Wolsey Jun & Inf Schs
HIGH ST
GLEBE WAY
ADDINGTON RD
CROYDON RD
LAYHAMS RD
KING HENRY'S DR
Coney Hall Rdbt
Hayes
BR4
BR2
CR0
208
223
Surrey STREET ATLAS

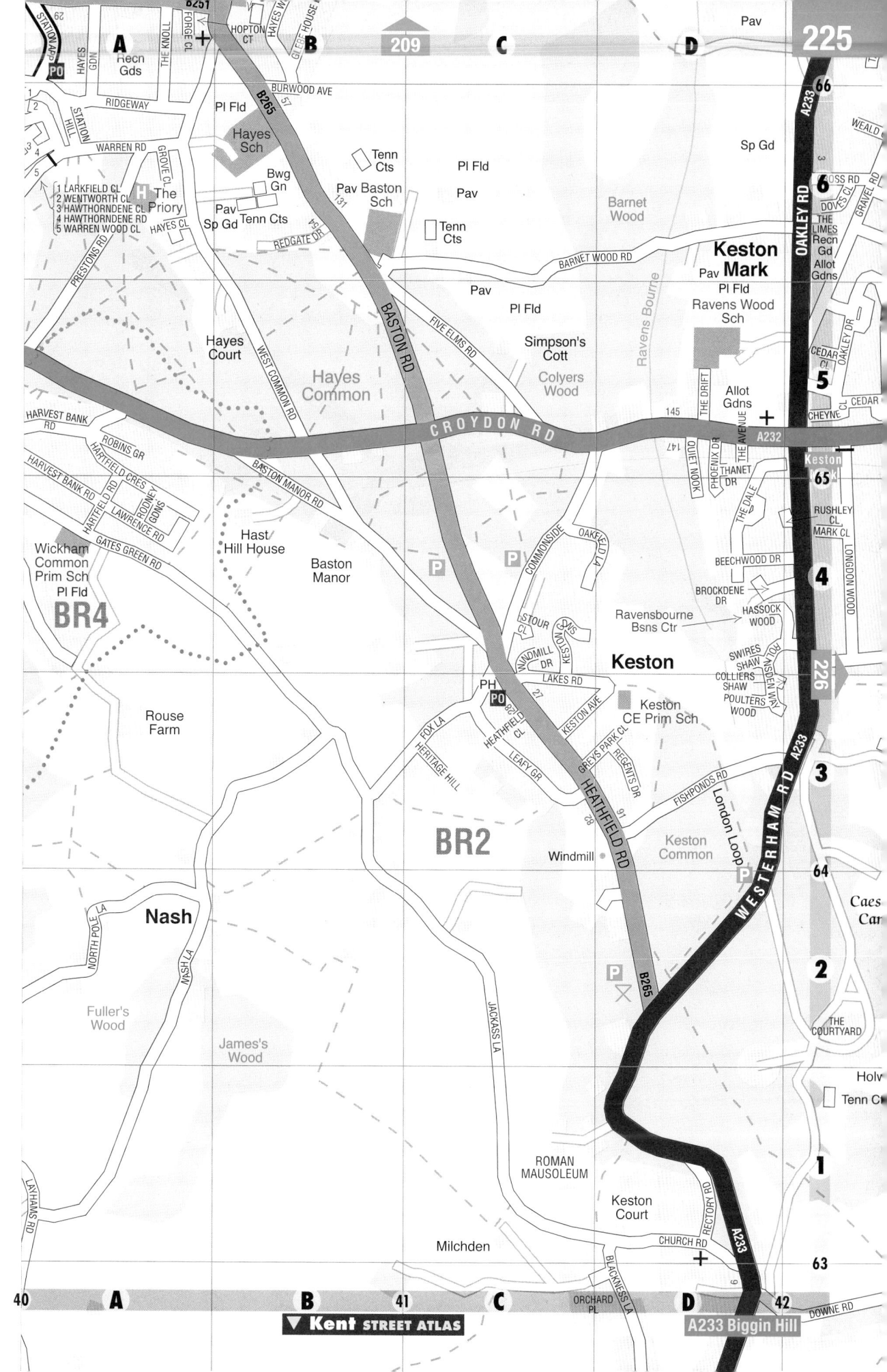

209
A
B
C
D
Recn Gds
HAYES GDN
THE KNOLL
FORGE CL
HOPTON CT
GLEBE HOUSE
STATION APP
PO
RIDGEWAY
STATION HILL
WARREN RD
GROVE CL
BURWOOD AVE
B265
Pl Fld
Hayes Sch
Bwg Gn
Tenn Cts
Pav Baston Sch
Pl Fld
Pav
Tenn Cts
Pav
Sp Gd
Pav Sp Gd
Tenn Cts
1 LARKFIELD CL
2 WENTWORTH CL
3 HAWTHORNDENE CL
4 HAWTHORNDENE RD
5 WARREN WOOD CL
The Priory
HAYES CL
REDGATE DR
PRESTONS RD
Barnet Wood
BARNET WOOD RD
Keston Mark
Pav
Pl Fld
Ravens Wood Sch
OAKLEY RD
A233
WEALD
CROSS RD
DOVES CL
GRAVEL RD
THE LIMES
Recn Gd
Allot Gdns
OAKLEY DR
CEDAR CL
CEDAR
CHEYNE CL
BASTON RD
FIVE ELMS RD
Pav
Pl Fld
Simpson's Cott
Colyers Wood
Ravens Bourne
THE DRIFT
Allot Gdns
Hayes Court
WEST COMMON RD
Hayes Common
HARVEST BANK RD
CROYDON RD
A232
THE AVENUE
QUIET NOOK
PHOENIX DR
THANET DR
Keston Mark
ROBINS GR
HARTFIELD CRES
HARVEST BANK RD
HARTFIELD RD
RODNEY GDNS
LAWRENCE RD
GATES GREEN RD
BASTON MANOR RD
THE DALE
RUSHLEY CL
MARK CL
LONGDON WOOD
Wickham Common Prim Sch
Pl Fld
BR4
Hast Hill House
Baston Manor
COMMONSIDE
OAKFIELD LA
BEECHWOOD DR
BROCKDENE DR
Ravensbourne Bsns Ctr
HASSOCK WOOD
STOUR CL
KESTON GDNS
WINDMILL DR
Keston
SWIRES SHAW
COLLIERS SHAW
POULTERS WOOD
ROUNSDEN WAY
226
LAKES RD
PH
PO
HEATHFIELD CL
KESTON AVE
Keston CE Prim Sch
Rouse Farm
FOX LA
HERITAGE HILL
LEAFY GR
GREYS PARK CL
REGENTS DR
FISHPONDS RD
London Loop
WESTERHAM RD
HEATHFIELD RD
BR2
Windmill
Keston Common
Nash
NORTH POLE LA
NASH LA
Fuller's Wood
James's Wood
JACKASS LA
THE COURTYARD
ROMAN MAUSOLEUM
Keston Court
RECTORY RD
CHURCH RD
Milchden
LAYHAMS RD
BLACKNESS LA
ORCHARD PL
DOWNE RD
A233 Biggin Hill

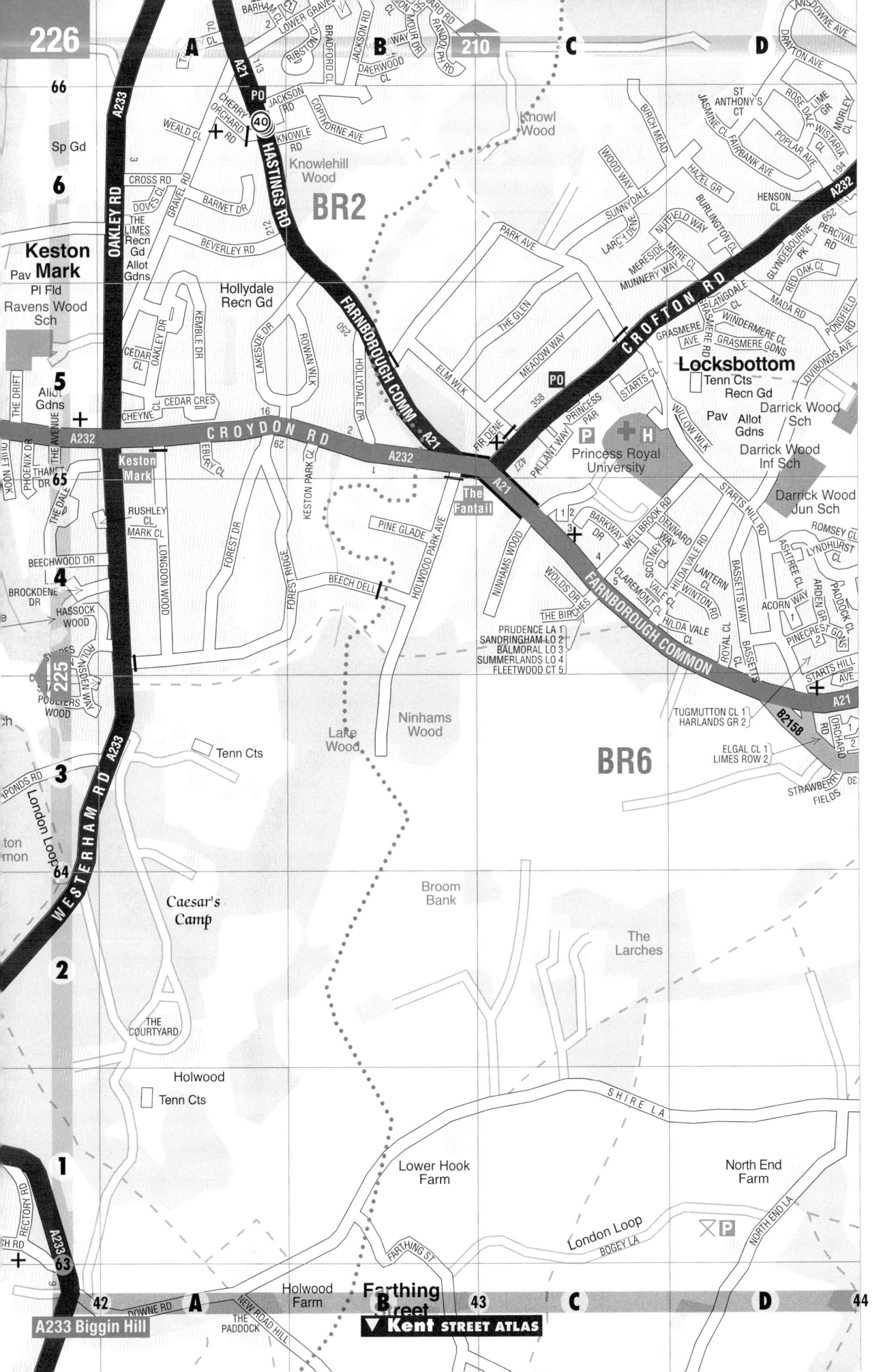

A21

210

D

66

Sp Gd

6

Keston Mark
Pav
Pl Fld

Ravens Wood
Sch

BR2

Knowl
Wood

ST
ANTHONY'S
CT

A232

Knowlehill
Wood

Hollydale
Recn Gd

The
Limes
Recn
Gd
Allot
Gdns

CROFTON RD

Locksbottom

Tenn Cts
Recn Gd

Pav

Allot
Gdns

Darrick Wood
Sch

Darrick Wood
Inf Sch

Darrick Wood
Jun Sch

5

Allot
Gdns

CROYDON RD   A232

A232

A21

Keston
Mark

The
Fantail

PO

Princess
Par

Princess Royal
University

H

65

Rushley
Cl
Mark Cl

Pine Glade

Beechwood Dr

4

Brockden
Dr

Hassock
Wood

Beech Dell

Ninhams Wood

The Birches

PRUDENCE LA 1
SANDRINGHAM LO 2
BALMORAL LO 3
SUMMERLANDS LO 4
FLEETWOOD CT 5

FARNBOROUGH COMMON

TUGMUTTON CL 1
HARLANDS GR 2

ELGAL CL 1
LIMES ROW 2

B2158

225

POOLERS
WOOD

Tenn Cts

Lake
Wood

Ninhams
Wood

BR6

STRAWBERRY
FIELDS

3

Ponds Rd

WESTERHAM RD   A233

London Loop

Caesar's
Camp

Broom
Bank

The
Larches

2

THE
COURTYARD

64

Holwood

Tenn Cts

SHIRE LA

1

Rectory Rd

Lower Hook
Farm

North End
Farm

London Loop

BOGEY LA

NORTH END LA

P

63

A233

42   A   DOWNE RD   43   C   D   44

NEW ROAD HILL

THE
PADDOCK

Holwood
Farm

FARTHING ST

Farthing
Street

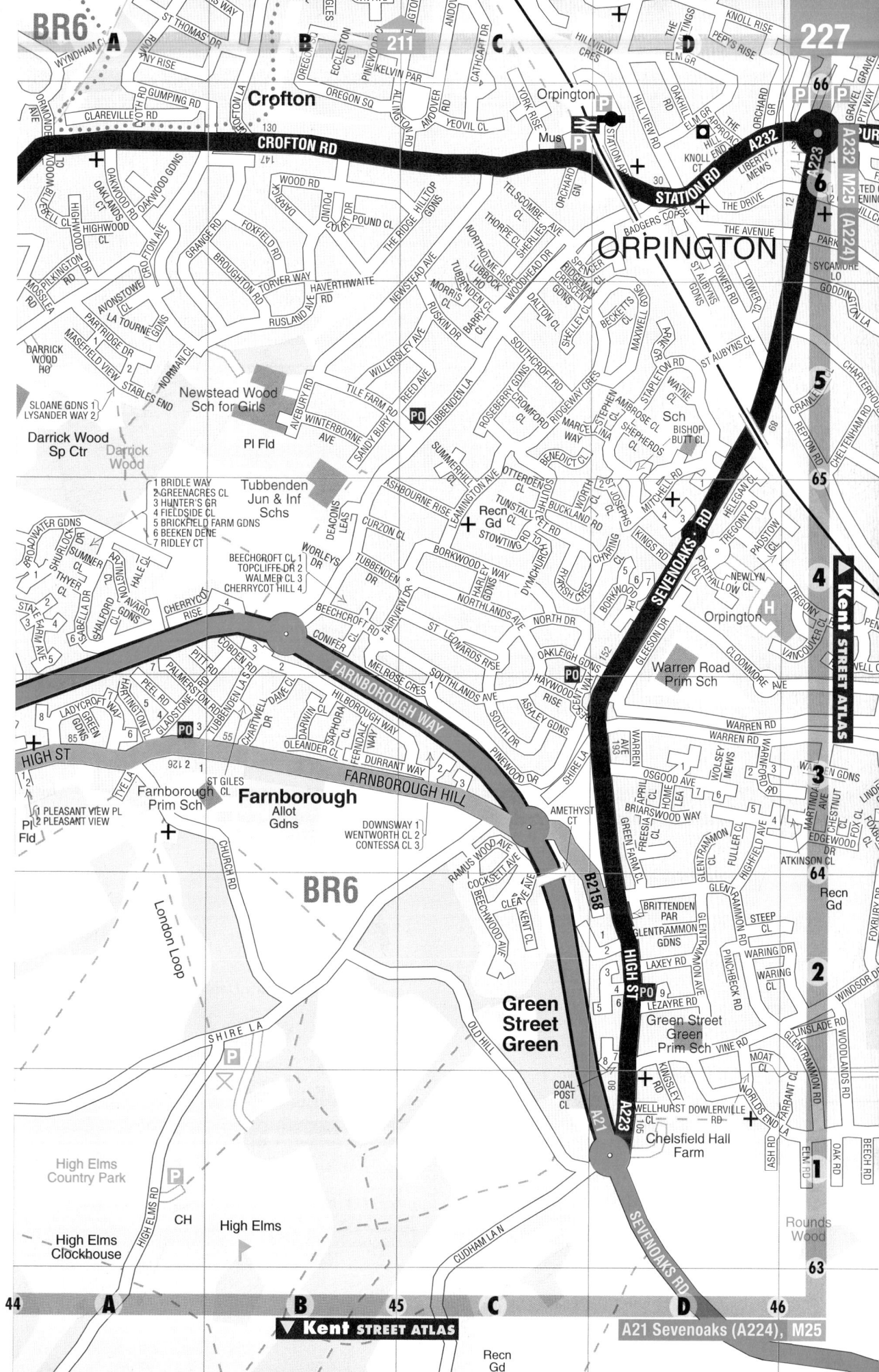

BR6
227
211
A
B
C
D
Crofton
CROFTON RD
Orpington
Mus
ORPINGTON
STATION RD
A232
A223
A232 M25 (A224)
ST THOMAS' DR
WYNDHAM CL
ORMONDE AVE
GUMPING RD
CLAREVILLE RD
CROFTON LA
ECCLESTON CL
OREGON SQ
PINEWOOD CT
KELVIN PAR
ALLINGTON RD
ANDOVER RD
CATHCART DR
YEOVIL CL
HILLVIEW CRES
YORK RISE
THE MALTINGS
KNOLL RISE
PEPYS RISE
ELM GR
HILL VIEW RD
OAKHILL RD
THE APPROACH
KNOLL CT
LIBERTY MEWS
THE DRIVE
THE AVENUE
ORCHARD GR
GRAVEL PIT WAY
SYCAMORE LO
GODDINGTON LA
CHARTERHOUSE RD
CRAMLEY
REPTON RD
CHELTENHAM RD
TOWER RD
TOWER CL
ST AUBYNS GDNS
ST AUBYNS CL
BADGERS COPSE
ORCHARD GN
STATION AP
WOOD RD
POUND CT DR
POUND CL
DARRICK
THE RIDGE
HILLTOP GDNS
TELSCOMBE CL
THORPE CL
SHERLIES AVE
NORTHOLME RISE
LUBBOCK HO
TUBBENDEN CL
WOODHEAD DR
MORRIS CL
BARRY CL
RUSKIN DR
NEWSTEAD AVE
GRANGE RD
FOXFIELD RD
BROUGHTON RD
TORVER WAY
HAVERTHWAITE RD
RUSLAND AVE
OAKWOOD RD
OAKWOOD GDNS
OAKLANDS CT
HIGHWOOD CL
HIGHWOOD DR
BLUEBELL CL
CROFTON AVE
PILKINGTON RD
MOSSLEA RD
AVONSTOWE CL
LA TOURNE GDNS
PARTRIDGE DR
MASEFIELD VIEW
NORMAN CL
STABLES END
DARRICK WOOD HO
SLOANE GDNS 1
LYSANDER WAY 2
Darrick Wood Sp Ctr
Darrick Wood
Newstead Wood Sch for Girls
Pl Fld
Tubbenden Jun & Inf Schs
1 BRIDLE WAY
2 GREENACRES CL
3 HUNTER'S GR
4 FIELDSIDE CL
5 BRICKFIELD FARM GDNS
6 BEEKEN DENE
7 RIDLEY CT
BEECHCROFT CL 1
TOPCLIFFE DR 2
WALMER CL 3
CHERRYCOT HILL 4
WILLERSLEY AVE
TILE FARM RD
REED AVE
AVEBURY RD
WINTERBORNE AVE
SANDY BURY
TUBBENDEN LA
PO
SOUTHCROFT RD
ROSEBERRY GDNS
CROMFORD
RIDGEWAY CRES
SPENCER CL
RIDGEWAY CRESCENT GDNS
DALTON CL
SHELLEY CL
BECKETTS CL
MAXWELL GDNS
ARNE GR
STAPLETON RD
WAYNE CL
STEPHEN CL
AMBROSE CL
SHEPHERDS CL
MARCELLINA WAY
Sch
BISHOP BUTT CL
BENEDICT CL
SUMMERHILL CL
LEAMINGTON AVE
OTTERDEN CL
SOUTHFLEET RD
WORTH CL
ST JOSEPHS
MITCHELL RD
BUCKLAND RD
TUNSTALL CL
Recn Gd
STOWTING RD
ASHBOURNE RISE
CURZON CL
DEACONS LEAS
WORLEYS DR
TUBBENDEN DR
BORKWOOD WAY
HARLEY GDNS
DYMCHURCH CL
RYARSH CRES
CHARING CL
BORKWOOD PK
NORTHLANDS AVE
KINGS RD
SEVENOAKS RD
HELEGAN CL
TREGONY RD
PADSTOW CL
PORTHALLOW CL
NEWLYN CL
Orpington
H
TREGONY
VANCOUVER CL
Kent STREET ATLAS
65
5
4
6
66
68
SHURLOCK DR
BROADWATER GDNS
SUMNER CL
ARTINGTON CL
HALE CL
THYER CL
AVARD GDNS
SABELLA DR
SHALFORD CL
STATE FARM AVE
CHERRYCOT RISE
FAIRVIEW DR
BEECHCROFT RD
CONIFER CL
ST LEONARDS RISE
NORTH DR
OAKLEIGH GDNS
GLEESON DR
Warren Road Prim Sch
CLOONMORE AVE
FARNBOROUGH WAY
MELROSE CRES
SOUTHLANDS AVE
HAYWOOD RISE
ASHLEY GDNS
SOUTH DR
CRESCENT WAY
PINEWOOD DR
SHIRE LA
152
PITT RD
COBDEN RD
PALMERSTON RD
PEEL RD
HARTINGTON CL
LADYCROFT WAY
GREEN GDNS
GLADSTONE RD
TUBBENDEN LA S
CHARTWELL DR
DAVIE CL
DARWIN CL
SAPHORA CL
HILBOROUGH WAY
FERNDALE WAY
OLEANDER CL
DURRANT WAY
HIGH ST
FARNBOROUGH HILL
ST GILES CL
Farnborough Prim Sch
Farnborough
Allot Gdns
TYE LA
1 PLEASANT VIEW PL
2 PLEASANT VIEW
Pl Fld
DOWNSWAY 1
WENTWORTH CL 2
CONTESSA CL 3
AMETHYST CT
WARREN RD
WARREN AVE
OSGOOD AVE
APRIL CL
HOME LEA
WOLSEY MEWS
WARNFORD RD
WARREN GDNS
BRIARSWOOD WAY
FREESIA CL
GREEN FARM CL
GLENTRAMMON CL
FULLER CL
HIGHFIELD AVE
MARTINDALE AVE
CHESTNUT AVE
FOX CL
EDGEWOOD DR
ATKINSON CL
64
3
Recn Gd
BR6
RAMUS WOOD AVE
COCKSETT AVE
BEECHWOOD AVE
CLEAVE AVE
KENT CL
B2158
BRITTENDEN PAR
GLENTRAMMON GDNS
GLENTRAMMON RD
GLENTRAMMON AVE
STEEP CL
WARING DR
WARING CL
PINCHBECK RD
LAXEY RD
LEZAYRE RD
HIGH ST
PO
CHURCH RD
London Loop
OLD HILL
Green Street Green
Green Street Green Prim Sch
VINE RD
MOAT CL
KINGSLEY RD
COAL POST CL
A21
A223
WELLHURST CL
DOWLERVILLE RD
WORLDS END LA
FARRANT CL
LINSLADE RD
GLENTRAMMON RD
WOODLANDS RD
WINDSOR DR
2
Chelsfield Hall Farm
ASH RD
ELM RD
OAK RD
BEECH RD
1
SHIRE LA
High Elms Country Park
HIGH ELMS RD
CH
High Elms
High Elms Clockhouse
CUDHAM LA N
SEVENOAKS RD
Rounds Wood
63
44
45
46
Kent STREET ATLAS
A21 Sevenoaks (A224), M25
Recn Gd

Key to enlarged map pages

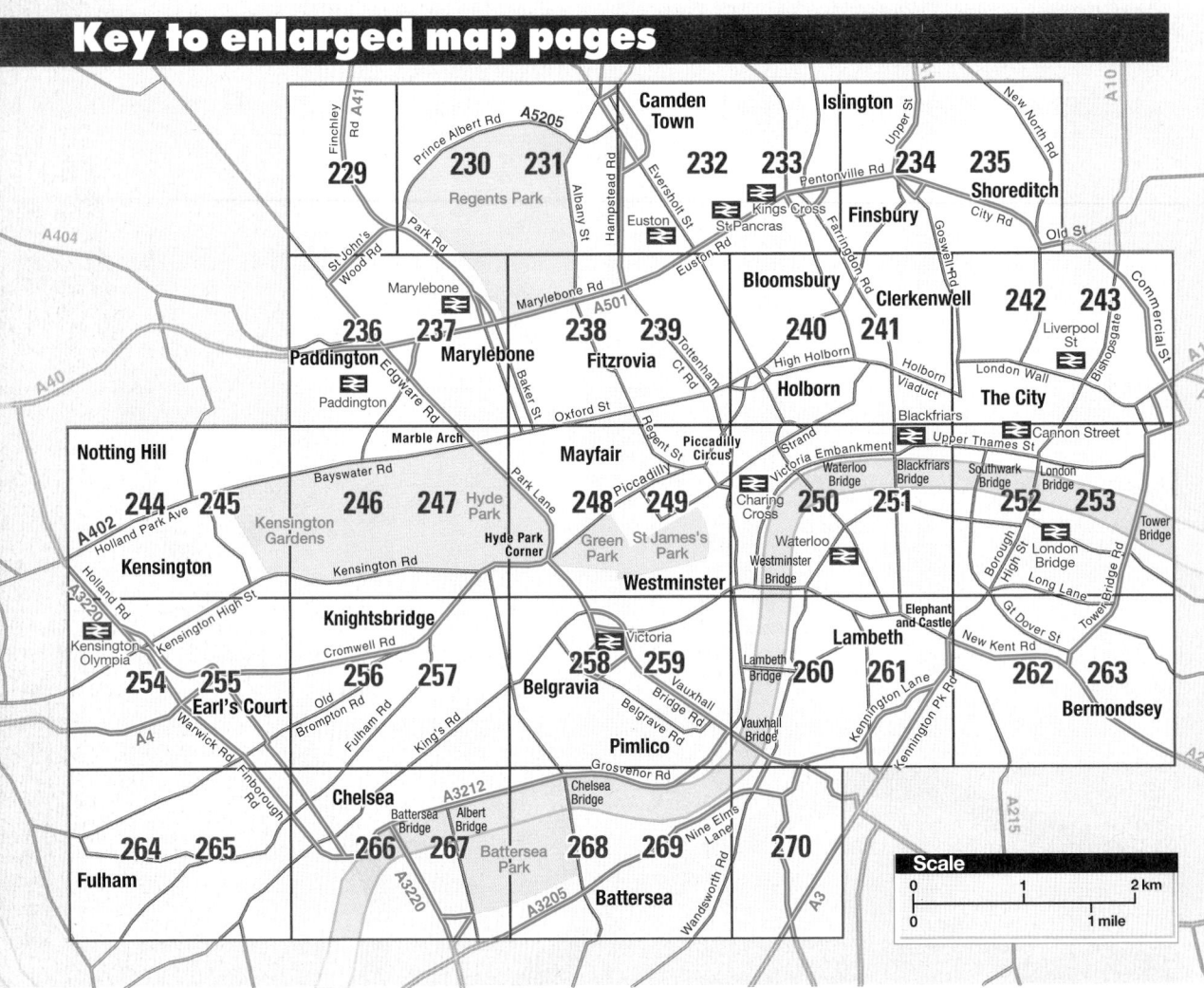

Additional symbols on enlarged maps

For all other symbols see page XXVIII

Primary route – single, dual carriageway	Public building
A road – single, dual carriageway	Railway or bus station building
B road	Place of interest
Through-route	ⓔ Embassy
Minor road	🎭 Theatre
One way street	🏛 Museum
No access in direction shown	

Congestion Charge Zone boundary
Roads within the zone are outlined in green – for further information call 0845 900 1234

Scale

9.67 inches to 1 mile   1 : 6 559

0	110yds	220yds	330yds	440 yards

0	125m	250m	325m	500 metres

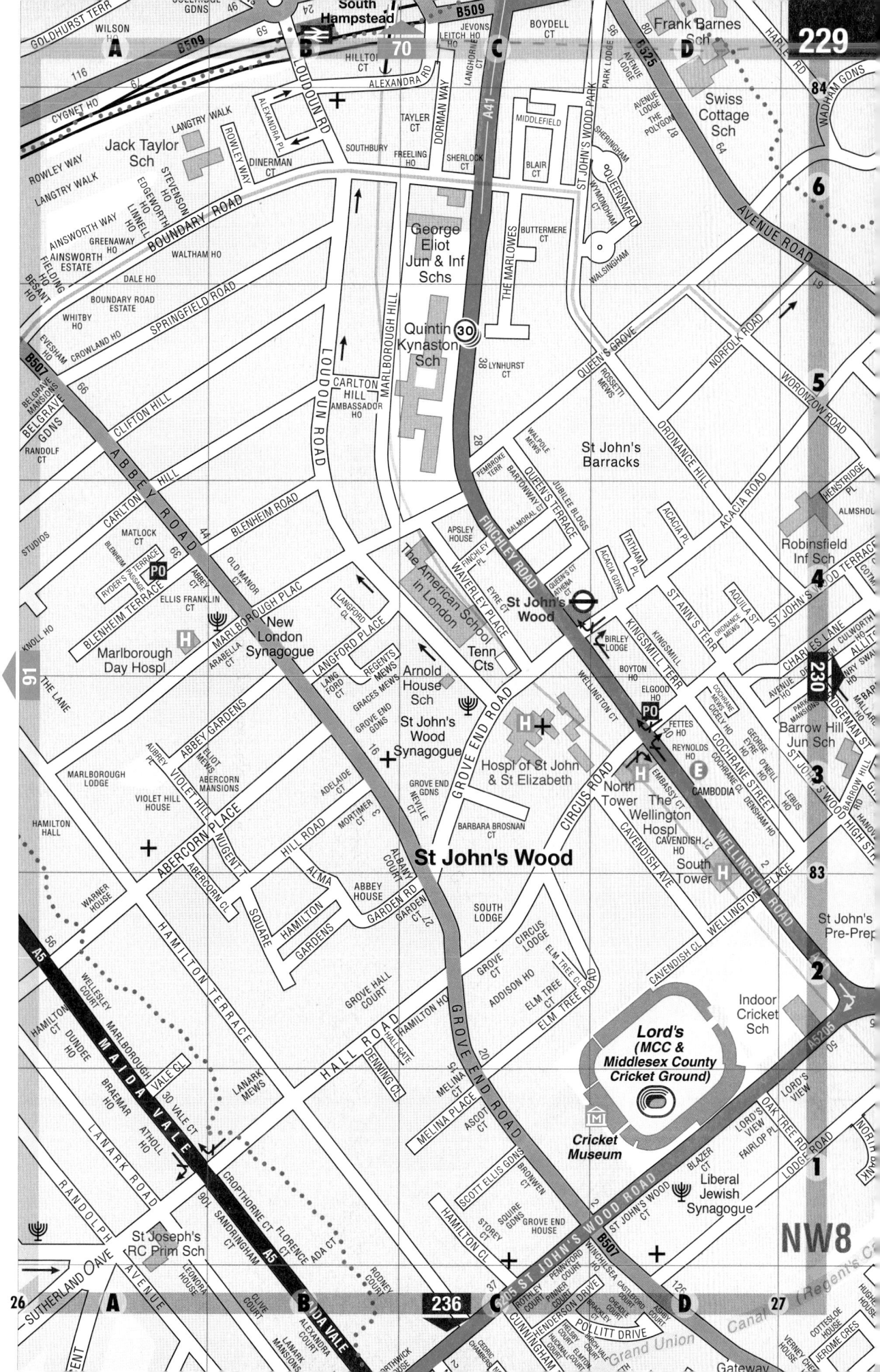

NW8

St John's Wood

South Hampstead

Swiss Cottage Sch

Frank Barnes Sch

Jack Taylor Sch

George Eliot Jun & Inf Schs

Quintin Kynaston Sch

St John's Barracks

CARLTON HILL

AMBASSADOR HO

The American School in London

St John's Wood

Robinsfield Inf Sch

New London Synagogue

Marlborough Day Hospl

Arnold House Sch

St John's Wood Synagogue

Barrow Hill Jun Sch

Hospl of St John & St Elizabeth

North Tower

The Wellington Hospl

South Tower

St John's Pre-Prep

Marlborough Lodge

Violet Hill House

Hamilton Hall

Warner House

ALBANY COURT

Abbey House

South Lodge

Circus Lodge

Grove Hall Court

Indoor Cricket Sch

Lord's (MCC & Middlesex County Cricket Ground)

Cricket Museum

Liberal Jewish Synagogue

Grove End House

St Joseph's RC Prim Sch

Grand Union Canal (Regent's C...)

Gateway

AVENUE ROAD

ABBEY ROAD

BOUNDARY ROAD

LOUDOUN ROAD

FINCHLEY ROAD

GROVE END ROAD

MAIDA VALE

HAMILTON TERRACE

ABERCORN PLACE

WELLINGTON ROAD

ST JOHN'S WOOD ROAD

CIRCUS ROAD

HALL ROAD

HILL ROAD

NORFOLK ROAD

ACACIA ROAD

ORDNANCE HILL

WORONZOW ROAD

CHARLES LANE

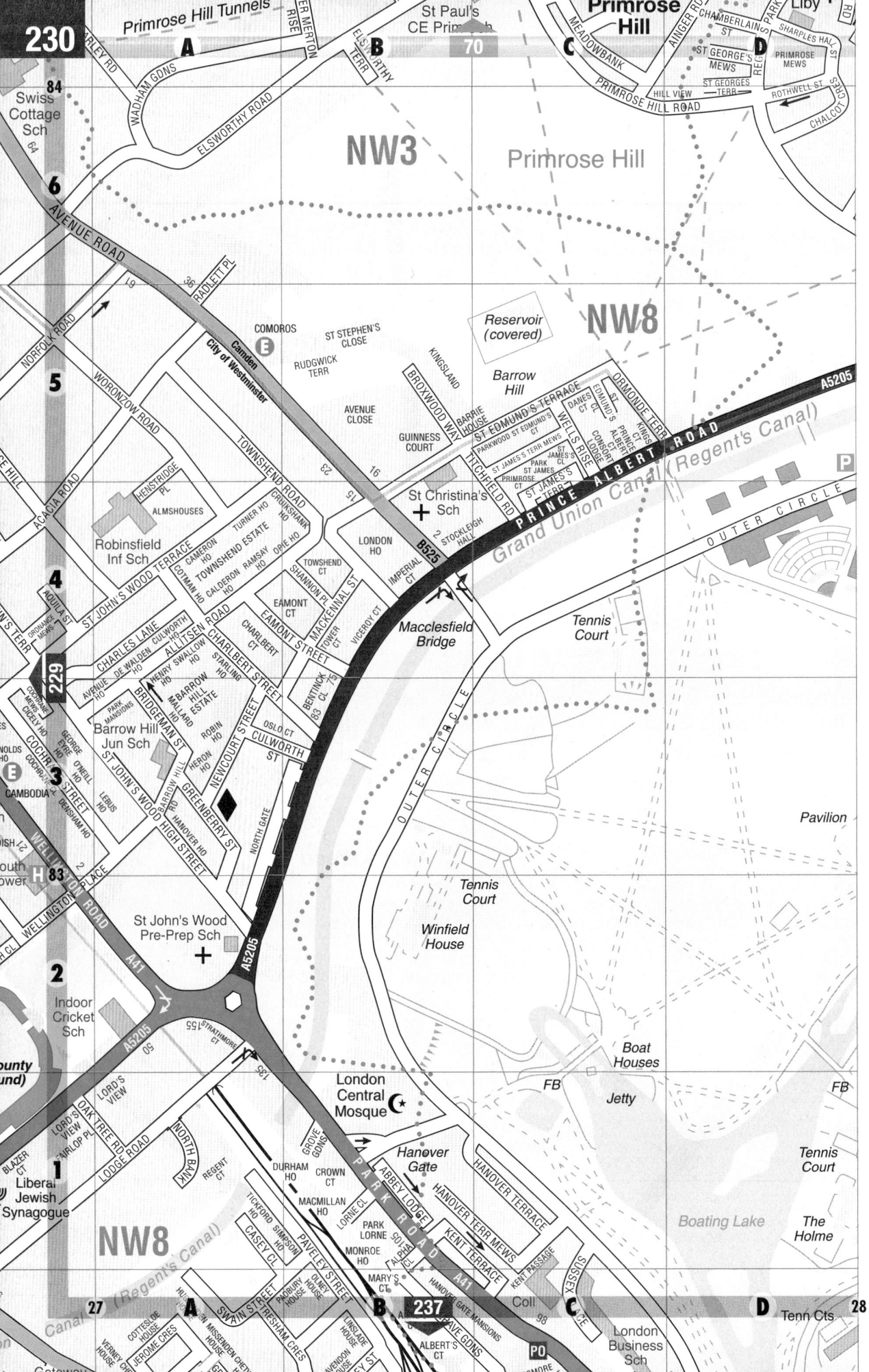

A B 70 C D

Primrose Hill Tunnels
St Paul's CE Prim Sch
Primrose Hill
CHAMBERLAIN ST
SHARPLES HALL ST
Liby
RD

AINGER RD
MEADOWBANK
ST GEORGE'S MEWS
ST GEORGES
HILL VIEW TERR
PRIMROSE MEWS
ROTHWELL ST
CHALCOT CRES

Swiss Cottage Sch
84
64

NW3
Primrose Hill
PRIMROSE HILL ROAD

6
AVENUE ROAD

NORFOLK ROAD
WORONZOW ROAD
RADLETT PL
36

Camden
City of Westminster
COMOROS
ST STEPHEN'S CLOSE
RUDGWICK TERR
Reservoir (covered)

NW8
A5205

5
AVENUE CLOSE
BROXWOOD WAY
GUINNESS COURT
KINGSLAND
BARRIE HOUSE
Barrow Hill
ST EDMUND'S TERRACE
ST JAMES'S TERR MEWS
PARKWOOD ST EDMUND'S CT
PARK ST JAMES PRIMROSE CT
ST JAMES'S TERR
KINGS CT
DANES CT
EDMUND'S ST
PRINCE ALBERT CT
CONSORT LODGE
WELLS RISE
ORMONDE TERR

ACACIA ROAD
TOWNSHEND ROAD
HENSTRIDGE PL
ALMSHOUSES
Robinsfield Inf Sch
St Christina's Sch
STOCKLEIGH HALL
B525
Grand Union Canal (Regent's Canal)
PRINCE ALBERT ROAD
OUTER CIRCLE
P

229
CHARLES LANE
ST JOHN'S WOOD TERRACE
TURNER HO
CRUIKSHANK HO
ORME HO
CAMERON HO
COTMAN HO
CALDERON HO
RAMSAY HO
TOWSHEND CT
London HO
Imperial CT
4
AQUILA ST
ORDNANCE MEWS
MINSTER TERR
ALLITSEN ROAD
EAMONT CT
CHARLBERT
EAMONT STREET
SHANNON PL
MACKENNAL ST
TOWER CT
VICEROY CT
Macclesfield Bridge
Tennis Court

CULWORTH
AVENUE
DE WALDEN HO
HENRY SWALLOW
MALLARD
STARLING HO
ROBIN HO
BARROW HILL ESTATE
BENTINCK CL
OSLO CT
E CAMBODIA
COCHRANE MEWS
CICELY HO
GEORGE EYRE HO
O'NEILL HO
LEBUS HO
BARROW HILL
HERON HO
PARK MANSIONS
BRIDGEMAN ST
NEWCOURT STREET
GREENBERRY ST
CULWORTH ST
OUTER CIRCLE

REYNOLDS HO
COCHR
Barrow Hill Jun Sch
3
ST JOHN'S WOOD HIGH STREET
HANOVER HO
NORTH GATE
Pavilion

DISH
South Tower
H 83
WELLINGTON PLACE
WELLINGTON ROAD
Tennis Court
Winfield House

CL
2
Indoor Cricket Sch
A41
St John's Wood Pre-Prep Sch
A5205
STRATHMORE CT
55
135
Boat Houses

County (Ground)
LORD'S VIEW
OAK TREE RD
LODGE ROAD
NORTH BANK
REGENT CT
GROVE GDNS
DURHAM HO
CROWN CT
London Central Mosque
Jetty
FB
FB

1
BLAZER CT
Liberal Jewish Synagogue
LORD'S VIEW
PARLOP PL
TICKFORD SIMPSON HO
CASEY CL
MACMILLAN HO
MONROE HO
PARK LORNE
MARY'S CT
Hanover Gate
HANOVER TERR MEWS
HANOVER GATE MANSIONS
KENT TERRACE
KENT PASSAGE
HANOVER TERRACE
PARK ROAD
ABBEY LODGE
Boating Lake
Tennis Court
The Holme

Gateway
NW8
(Regent's Canal)
SWAIN STREET
HUTTON
COTTESLOE HOUSE
JEROME CRES
VERNEY HOUSE
PAVELEY STREET
MISSENDEN
RESHAM CRES
PORBURY HOUSE
AVENDON
LINSLADE
TINSLADE
ALBERT'S CT
237
PO
GRAVE GDNS
Coll
98
London Business Sch
SUSSEX
Tenn Cts

27 A B C D 28

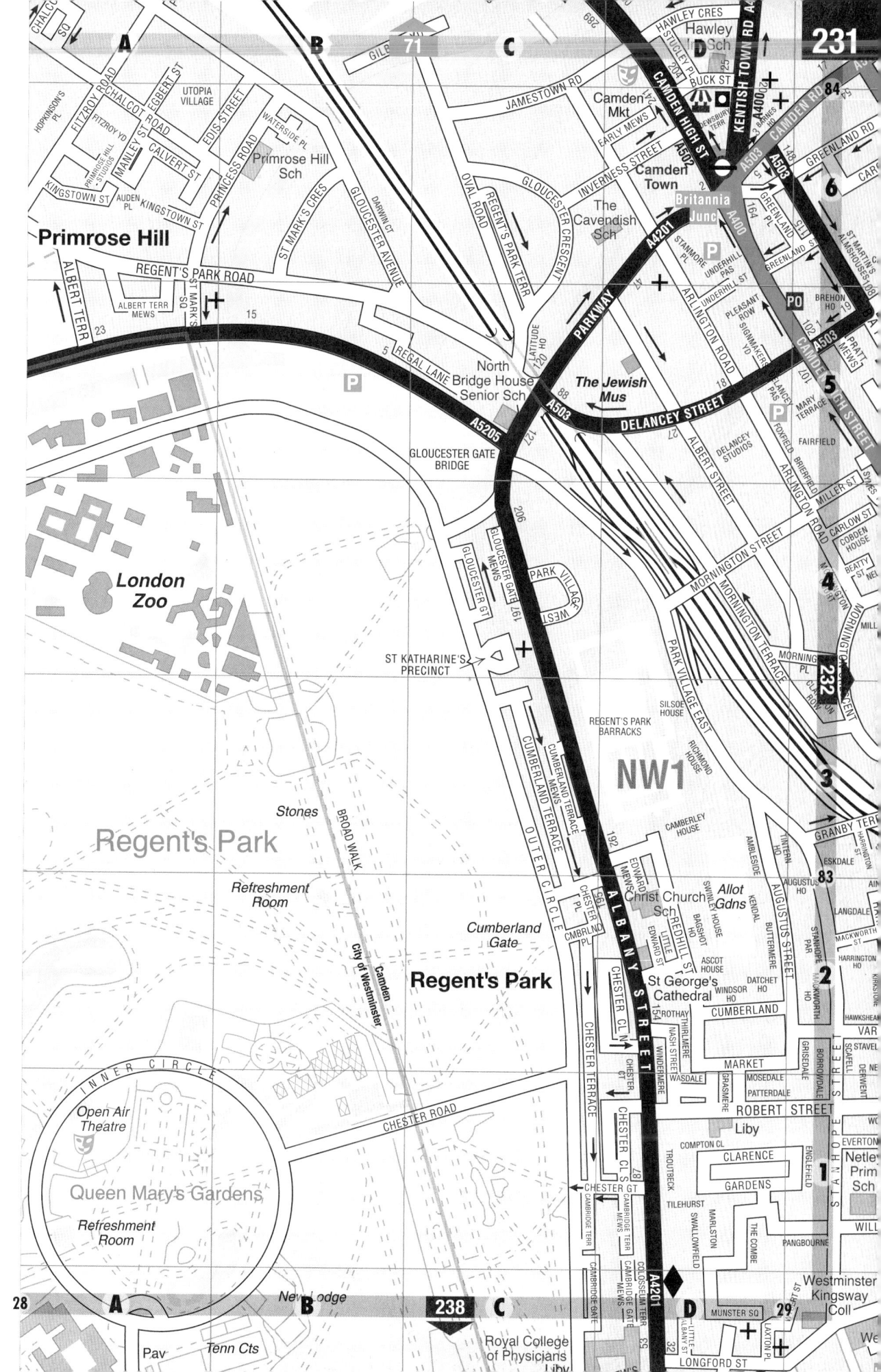

A
B
C
D
71
Primrose Hill
Primrose Hill Sch
UTOPIA VILLAGE
FITZROY ROAD
CHALCOT ROAD
EGBERT ST
EDIS STREET
CALVERT ST
MANLEY ST
KINGSTOWN ST
AUDEN PL
PRINCESS ROAD
WATERSIDE PL
ST MARK'S CRES
GLOUCESTER AVENUE
DARWIN CT
REGENT'S PARK ROAD
ALBERT TERR
ALBERT TERR MEWS
ST MARK'S SQ
JAMESTOWN RD
OVAL ROAD
REGENT'S PARK TERR
GLOUCESTER CRESCENT
INVERNESS STREET
EARLY MEWS
Camden Mkt
HAWLEY CRES
Hawley Inf Sch
BUCK ST
CAMDEN HIGH ST
KENTISH TOWN RD
CAMDEN RD
GREENLAND RD
Camden Town
Britannia Junc
The Cavendish Sch
PARKWAY
A4201
A503
A502
A400
A5205
REGAL LANE
North Bridge House Senior Sch
The Jewish Mus
DELANCEY STREET
ARLINGTON ROAD
ALBERT STREET
GLOUCESTER GATE BRIDGE
London Zoo
GLOUCESTER GATE MEWS
GLOUCESTER GT
PARK VILLAGE WEST
ST KATHARINE'S PRECINCT
MORNINGTON STREET
MORNINGTON TERRACE
MORNINGTON CRESCENT
PARK VILLAGE EAST
REGENT'S PARK BARRACKS
NW1
CUMBERLAND TERRACE
CUMBERLAND TERRACE MEWS
OUTER CIRCLE
Stones
BROAD WALK
Regent's Park
Refreshment Room
Cumberland Gate
ALBANY STREET
Christ Church Sch
Allot Gdns
St George's Cathedral
AUGUSTUS STREET
GRANBY TERR
CHESTER TERRACE
CHESTER ROAD
City of Westminster
Camden
INNER CIRCLE
Open Air Theatre
Queen Mary's Gardens
Refreshment Room
ROBERT STREET
Liby
CLARENCE GARDENS
STANHOPE STREET
Netley Prim Sch
Westminster Kingsway Coll
CHESTER GT
New Lodge
238
28
29
Pav
Tenn Cts
Royal College of Physicians
MUNSTER SQ
LONGFORD ST

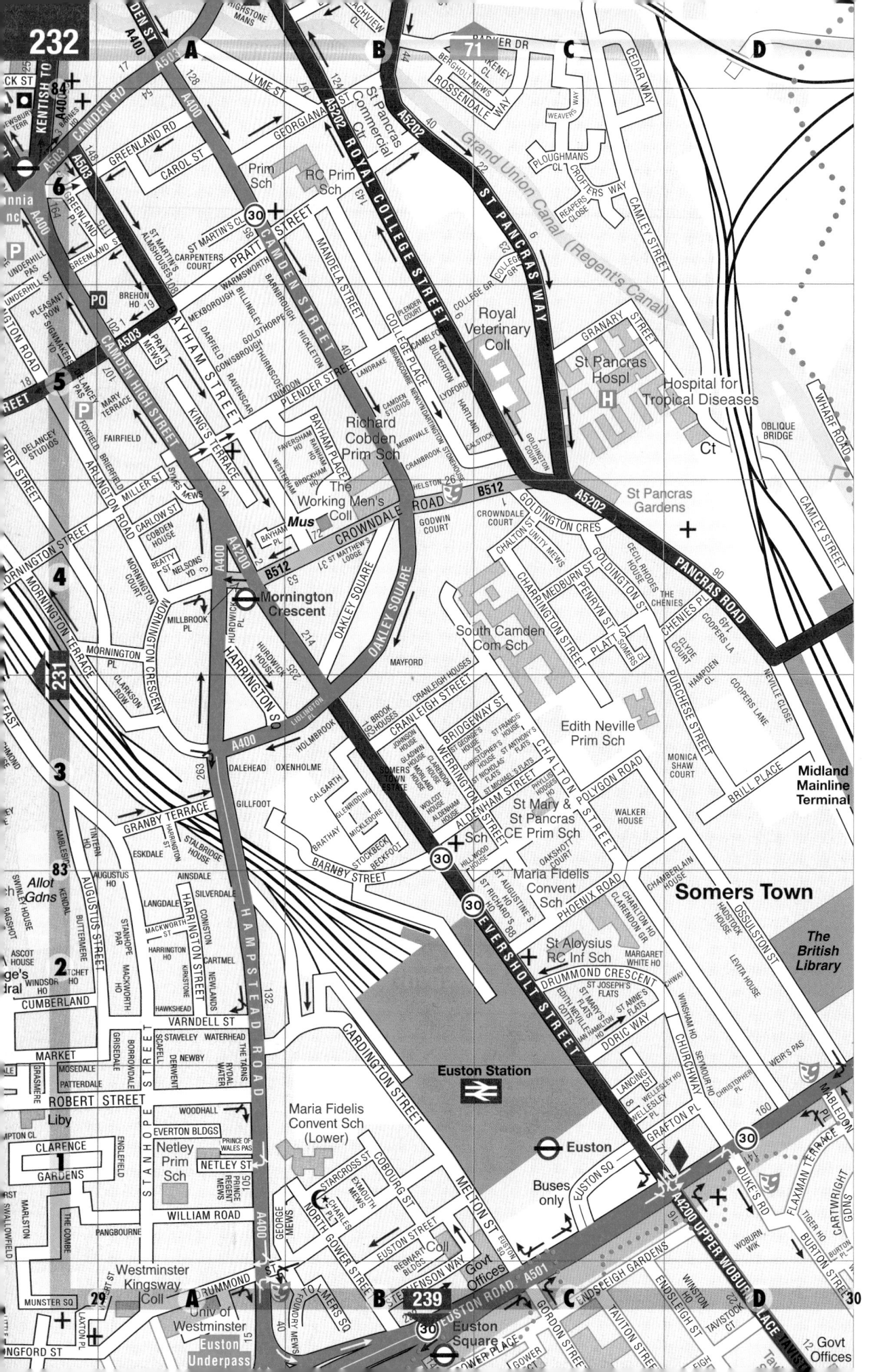
A
B
C
D
71
KENTISH TOWN RD
CAMDEN RD
GREENLAND RD
CAROL ST
LYME ST
GEORGIANA ST
St Pancras Commercial Ctr
BARKER DR
BERGHOLT MEWS
ROSSENDALE WAY
CEDAR WAY
WEAVERS WAY
PLOUGHMANS CL
CROFTERS WAY
REAPERS CLOSE
CAMLEY STREET
Grand Union Canal (Regent's Canal)
A5202 ROYAL COLLEGE STREET
ST PANCRAS WAY
Prim Sch
RC Prim Sch
MANDELA STREET
PRATT STREET
CAMDEN STREET
ST MARTIN'S CL
ST MARTIN'S ALMSHOUSES
CARPENTERS COURT
GREENLAND PL
GREENLAND ST
UNDERHILL PAS
UNDERHILL ST
PLEASANT ROW
SIGNMAKERS YD
DELANCEY PAS
BREHON HO
BAYHAM STREET
PRATT MEWS
CAMDEN HIGH STREET
KING'S TERRACE
PLENDER STREET
COLLEGE PLACE
COLLEGE GR
Royal Veterinary Coll
GRANARY STREET
St Pancras Hospl
Hospital for Tropical Diseases
OBLIQUE BRIDGE
WHARF ROAD
Richard Cobden Prim Sch
The Working Men's Coll
Mus
CROWNDALE ROAD
B512
A5202
St Pancras Gardens
PANCRAS ROAD
GOLDINGTON CRES
GOLDINGTON ST
CROWNDALE COURT
GODWIN COURT
MARY TERRACE
FAIRFIELD
DELANCEY STUDIOS
ARLINGTON ROAD
MILLER ST
CARLOW ST
COBDEN HOUSE
MORNINGTON STREET
MORNINGTON TERRACE
MORNINGTON CRESCENT
MORNINGTON PL
Mornington Crescent
MILLBROOK PL
HARRINGTON SQ
OAKLEY SQUARE
South Camden Com Sch
CHARRINGTON STREET
MEDBURN ST
PENRYN ST
PLATT ST
THE CHENIES
CHENIES PL
COOPERS LA
COOPERS LANE
NEVILLE CLOSE
PURCHESE STREET
Edith Neville Prim Sch
MONICA SHAW COURT
BRILL PLACE
Midland Mainline Terminal
231
A400
A4200
HAMPSTEAD ROAD
GRANBY TERRACE
CRANLEIGH STREET
BRIDGEWAY ST
WERRINGTON STREET
ALDENHAM STREET
CHALTON STREET
POLYGON ROAD
WALKER HOUSE
St Mary & St Pancras CE Prim Sch
Maria Fidelis Convent Sch
PHOENIX ROAD
Somers Town
OSSULSTON ST
The British Library
BARNBY STREET
EVERSHOLT STREET
St Aloysius RC Inf Sch
DRUMMOND CRESCENT
DORIC WAY
CHURCHWAY
Euston Station
Euston
Buses only
EUSTON SQ
GRAFTON PL
LANCING ST
WEIR'S PAS
MABLEDON PL
DUKE'S RD
FLAXMAN TERRACE
CARTWRIGHT GDNS
BURTON STREET
A4200 UPPER WOBURN PLACE
ENDSLEIGH GARDENS
ENDSLEIGH ST
TAVITON STREET
GORDON STREET
EUSTON ROAD
A501
239
Euston Square
Govt Offices
Allot Gdns
AUGUSTUS STREET
HARRINGTON STREET
CUMBERLAND
MARKET
VARNDELL ST
ROBERT STREET
Liby
CLARENCE GARDENS
STANHOPE STREET
Netley Prim Sch
NETLEY ST
WILLIAM ROAD
Westminster Kingsway Coll
DRUMMOND ST
Univ of Westminster
Euston Underpass
MUNSTER SQ
CARDINGTON STREET
Maria Fidelis Convent Sch (Lower)
COBOURG ST
MELTON ST
EUSTON STREET
NORTH GOWER STREET
STEPHENSON WAY
TOLMERS SQ
Coll
Govt Offices
1
2
3
4
5
6
30

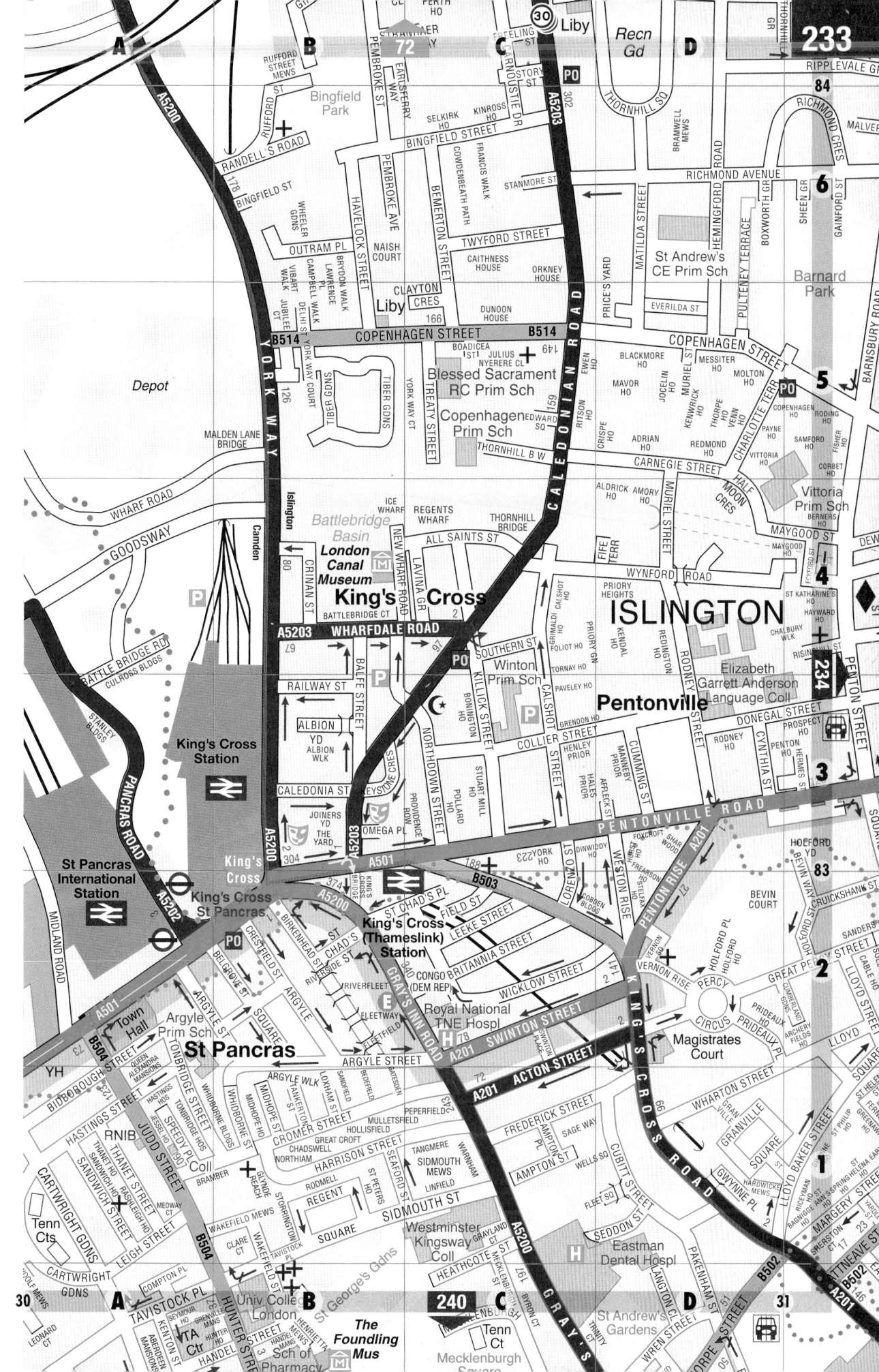
72
Liby
Recn Gd
RIPPLEVALE GR
84
RUFFORD STREET MEWS
RUFFORD ST
Bingfield Park
PEMBROKE ST
EARLSFERRY WAY
CARNOUSTIE DR
STORY ST
PO
THORNHILL SQ
RICHMOND CRES
MALVERN
SELKIRK HO
KINROSS HO
BINGFIELD STREET
RANDELL'S ROAD
A5200
A5203
COWDENBEATH PATH
FRANCIS WALK
BRAMWELL MEWS
HEMINGFORD ROAD
RICHMOND AVENUE
BINGFIELD ST
STANMORE ST
6
WHEELER GDNS
HAVELOCK STREET
PEMBROKE AVE
BEMERTON STREET
MATILDA STREET
SHEEN GR
GAINFORD ST
BOXWORTH GR
PULTENEY TERRACE
TWYFORD STREET
OUTRAM PL
NAISH COURT
CAITHNESS HOUSE
ORKNEY HOUSE
PRICE'S YARD
St Andrew's CE Prim Sch
Barnard Park
VIBART WALK
BRYDON WALK
LAWRENCE PL
CAMPBELL WALK
DELHI ST
JUBILEE CT
CLAYTON CRES
Liby
DUNOON HOUSE
EVERILDA ST
BARNSBURY
B514
COPENHAGEN STREET
B514
YORK WAY
CALEDONIAN ROAD
BOADICEA ST
JULIUS NYERERE CL
EWEN HO
BLACKMORE HO
MESSITER HO
COPENHAGEN STREET
MOLTON HO
PO
5
Depot
TIBER GDNS
YORK WAY COURT
YORK WAY CT
TREATY STREET
Blessed Sacrament RC Prim Sch
Copenhagen Prim Sch
EDWARD SQ
MAVOR HO
JOCELIN HO
MURIEL ST
KENWRICK HO
THORPE HO
VENN HO
CHARLOTTE TERR
COPENHAGEN HO
RODING HO
PAYNE HO
SAMFORD HO
FISHER HO
MALDEN LANE BRIDGE
RITSON HO
CRISPE HO
ADRIAN HO
REDMOND HO
VITTORIA HO
THORNHILL B W
CARNEGIE STREET
CORBET HO
ALDRICK HO
AMORY HO
MURIEL STREET
HALF MOON CRES
Vittoria Prim Sch
BERNERS HO
WHARF ROAD
Islington
Camden
ICE WHARF
REGENTS WHARF
THORNHILL BRIDGE
GOODSWAY
Battlebridge Basin
ALL SAINTS ST
FIFE TERR
MAYGOOD ST
MAYGOOD HO
London Canal Museum
NEW WHARF ROAD
LAVINA GR
CRINAN ST
WYNFORD ROAD
FOXFORD ST
4
P
King's Cross
CALSHOT HO
PRIORY HEIGHTS
ISLINGTON
ST KATHARINE'S HO
BATTLEBRIDGE CT
A5203
WHARFDALE ROAD
HAYWARD HO
CHALBURY WLK
GRIMALDI HO
FOLIOT HO
PRIORY GN
KENDAL HO
REDINGTON HO
RISINGHILL ST
234
BATTLE BRIDGE RD
CULROSS BLDGS
SOUTHERN ST
PO
Winton Prim Sch
TORNAY HO
Elizabeth Garrett Anderson Language Coll
PENTON STREET
RAILWAY ST
BALFE STREET
KILLICK STREET
CALSHOT STREET
PAVELEY HO
Pentonville
STANLEY BLDGS
ALBION YD
ALBION WLK
BONINGTON HO
GRENDON HO
RODNEY STREET
DONEGAL STREET
PROSPECT HO
King's Cross Station
KEYSTONE CRES
NORTHDOWN STREET
COLLIER STREET
RODNEY HO
CYNTHIA ST
PENTON HO
HERMES ST
HENLEY PRIOR
MANNEBY PRIOR
CUMMING ST
3
PANCRAS ROAD
CALEDONIA ST
STUART MILL HO
POLLARD HO
PROVIDENCE ROW
HALES PRIOR
AFFLECK ST
JOINERS YD
THE YARD
OMEGA PL
PENTONVILLE ROAD
FOXCROFT
SHARWOOD
SQUARE
St Pancras International Station
A5200
King's Cross
304
A501
188
YORK HO
LORENZO ST
DINWIDDY HO
WESTON RISE
HURST HO
FREARSON HO
A201
PENTON RISE
HOLFORD YD
BEVIN WAY
83
A5202
King's Cross St Pancras
374
A5200
KING'S CROSS BRIDGE
ST CHAD'S PL
B503
COBDEN BLDGS
BEVIN COURT
CRUICKSHANK ST
MIDLAND ROAD
BIRKENHEAD ST
ST CHAD'S ST
King's Cross (Thameslink) Station
FIELD ST
LEEKE STREET
BRITANNIA STREET
VERNON SQ
HOLFORD PL
HOLFORD HO
HOLFORD ST
SANDERS HO
GREAT PERCY STREET
CABLE HO
2
PO
BELGROVE ST
CRESTFIELD ST
ARGYLE
RIVERSIDE CT
RIVERFLEET
GRAY'S INN ROAD
CONGO (DEM REP)
WICKLOW STREET
VERNON RISE
PERCY CIRCUS
CUMBERLAND GDNS
PRIDEAUX HO
PRIDEAUX PL
LLOYD STREET
ARCHERY FIELDS HO
A501
Town Hall
Argyle Prim Sch
ARGYLE ST
SQUARE
FLEETWAY
FLEETFIELD
Royal National TNE Hospl
SWINTON STREET
SWINTON PLACE
Magistrates Court
LLOYD
St Pancras
B504
QUEEN ALEXANDRA MANSIONS
ARGYLE STREET
A201
ACTON STREET
YH
BIDBOROUGH STREET
TONBRIDGE STREET
WHIDBORNE STREET
WHIDBORNE BLDGS
ARGYLE WLK
LOXHAM ST
SANDFIELD
BEDEFIELD
BATESDEN
WHARTON STREET
GRANVILLE SQUARE
HASTINGS STREET
HASTINGS HO
TONBRIDGE HOS
MIDHOPE ST
MIDHOPE HO
TANKERTON ST
CROMER STREET
PEPPERFIELD
MULLETSFIELD
HOLLISFIELD
FREDERICK STREET
SAGE WAY
AMPTON PL
LLOYD BAKER STREET
1
RNIB
THANET STREET
JUDD STREET
SPEEDY PL
GREAT CROFT
CHADSWELL
NORTHIAM
HARRISON STREET
SEAFORD ST
TANGMERE
SIDMOUTH MEWS
WARNHAM
AMPTON ST
WELLS SQ
CUBITT STREET
GWYNNE PL
HARDWICKE MEWS
CARTWRIGHT GDNS
THANET HO
SANDWICH HO
SANDWICH STREET
RASHLEIGH HO
Coll
BRAMBER
GLYNDE REACH
RODMELL
REGENT
ST PETERS HO
LINFIELD
SIDMOUTH ST
FLEET SQ
MEDWAY CT
Tenn Cts
WAKEFIELD MEWS
STORRINGTON
SQUARE
Westminster Kingsway Coll
GRAYLAND
SEDDON ST
Eastman Dental Hospl
MARGERY STREET
LEIGH STREET
CLARE CT
WAKEFIELD ST
TAVISTOCK PL
St George's Gdns
HEATHCOTE ST
MECKLENBURGH ST
A5200
PAKENHAM ST
LANGTON CL
B502
SHERSTON CT
ATTNEAVE ST
B502
A201
CARTWRIGHT GDNS
COMPTON PL
B504
30
A
TAVISTOCK PL
B
Univ College London
240
C
BYRON CT
D
31
St Andrew's Gardens
SEYMOUR HO
GRENVILLE MANS
HUNTER HO
KENTON ST
ABERDEEN MANSIONS
TA Ctr
HANDEL
HUNTER ST
HANDEL MEWS
HENRIETTA MEWS
Sch of Pharmacy
The Foundling Mus
MECKLENBURGH
Tenn Ct
Mecklenburgh Square
GRAY'S
TRINITY CT
WREN STREET
THORPE STREET
LEONARD CT

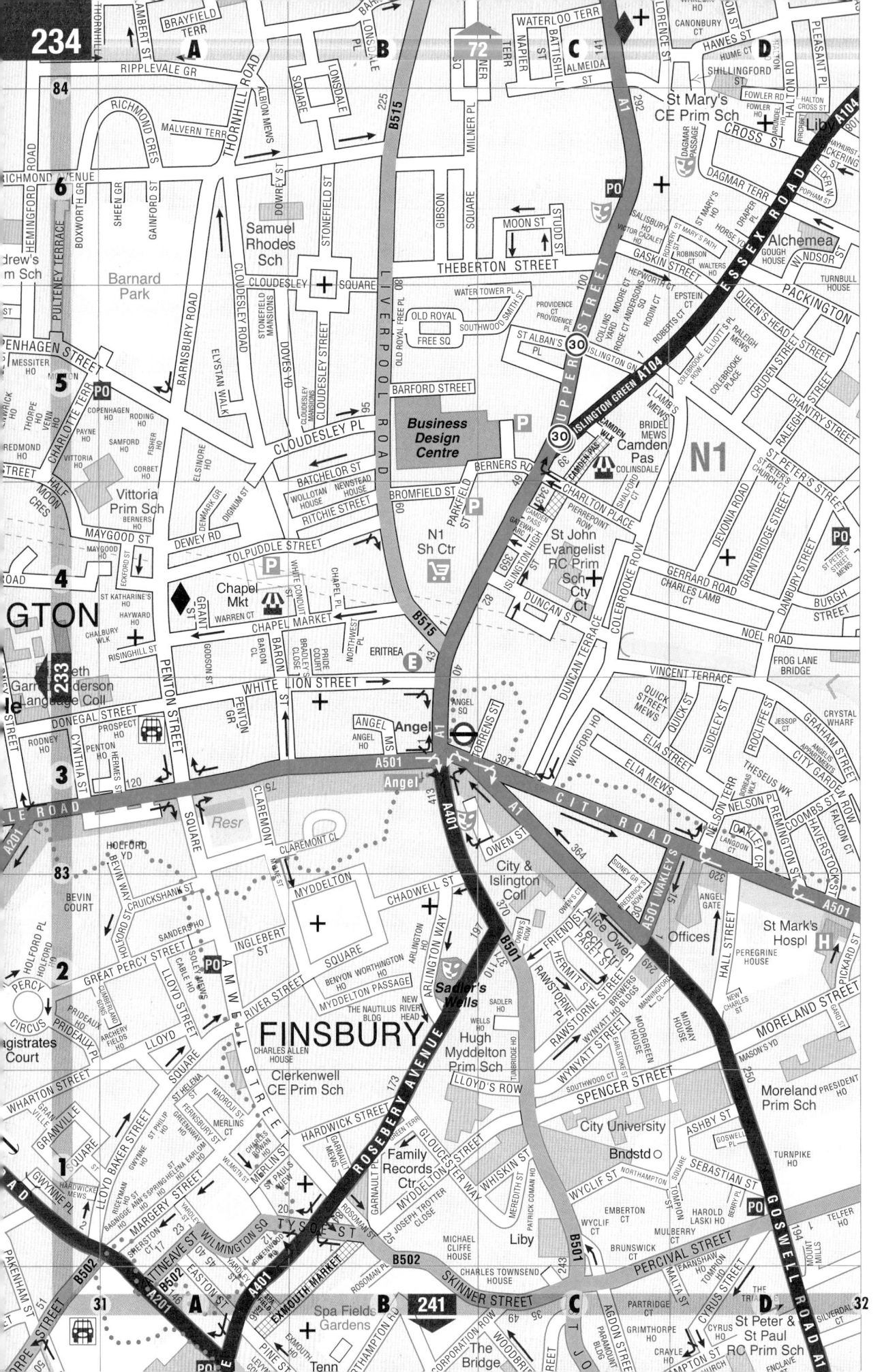
A
B
C
D
72
84
6
5
4
3
2
1
83
31
32
241
233
BRAYFIELD TERR
RIPPLEVALE GR
RICHMOND CRES
MALVERN TERR
THORNHILL ROAD
ALBION MEWS
SQUARE
LONSDALE
B515
WATERLOO TERR
NAPIER TERR
BATTISHILL ST
ALMEIDA ST
LORENCE ST
CANONBURY CT
HAWES ST
HUME CT
SHILLINGFORD ST
HALTON RD
PLEASANT PL
FOWLER RD
St Mary's CE Prim Sch
CROSS ST
DAGMAR PASSAGE
DAGMAR TERR
Liby
A104
ESSEX ROAD
RICHMOND AVENUE
HEMINGFORD ROAD
BOXWORTH GR
SHEEN GR
GAINFORD ST
DOWREY ST
STONEFIELD ST
GIBSON SQUARE
MILNER PL
MILNER SQUARE
MOON ST
STUDD ST
PO
Samuel Rhodes Sch
Barnard Park
PULTENEY TERRACE
CLOUDESLEY SQUARE
THEBERTON STREET
LIVERPOOL ROAD
WATER TOWER PL
OLD ROYAL FREE SQ
OLD ROYAL FREE PL
SOUTHWOOD SMITH ST
PROVIDENCE CT
ST ALBAN'S PL
UPPER STREET
A1
ISLINGTON GREEN A104
SALISBURY HO
VICTOR CAZALET HO
GASKIN STREET
HEPWORTH CT
COLLINS YARD
MOORE CT
ROSE CT
ANDERSONS SQ
RODIN CT
ROBERTS CT
EPSTEIN CT
WALTERS HO
ROBINSON CT
ST MARY'S PATH
Alchemea
GOUGH HOUSE
WINDSOR ST
TURNBULL HOUSE
PACKINGTON
QUEEN'S HEAD STREET
RALEIGH MEWS
ELLIOTT'S PL
COLEBROOKE PLACE
CRUDEN STREET
CHANTRY STREET
RALEIGH STREET
COPENHAGEN STREET
MESSITER HO
CHARLOTTE TERR
COPENHAGEN HO
RODING HO
PAYNE HO
SAMFORD HO
FISHER HO
VITTORIA HO
CORBET HO
REDMOND HO
BARNSBURY ROAD
CLOUDESLEY ROAD
ELYSTAN WALK
STONEFIELD MANSIONS
DOVES YD
CLOUDESLEY MANSIONS
CLOUDESLEY STREET
CLOUDESLEY PL
BARFORD STREET
Business Design Centre
P
ISLINGTON GN
LAMB'S MEWS
BRIDEL MEWS
Camden Pas
CAMDEN WLK
CAMDEN PAS
COLINSDALE
N1
ST PETER'S STREET
ST PETER'S CHURCH CT
DEVONIA ROAD
HALF MOON CRES
Vittoria Prim Sch
BERNERS HO
ELSINORE HO
DENMARK GR
DIGNUM ST
BATCHELOR ST
WOLLOTAN HOUSE
NEWSTEAD HOUSE
RITCHIE STREET
BROMFIELD ST
PARKFIELD ST
BERNERS RD
CHARLTON PLACE
PIERREPOINT ROW
SHALFORD CT
GRANTBRIDGE STREET
MAYGOOD ST
MAYGOOD HO
DEWEY RD
TOLPUDDLE STREET
N1 Sh Ctr
CAMDEN PASS
GATEWAY ARC
ISLINGTON HIGH ST
St John Evangelist RC Prim Sch
Cty Ct
COLEBROOKE ROW
GERRARD ROAD
CHARLES LAMB CT
DANBURY STREET
ST PETER'S STREET MEWS
BURGH STREET
ECKFORD ST
ST KATHARINE'S HO
HAYWARD HO
GTON
Chapel Mkt
GRANT ST
WARREN CT
WHITE CONDUIT ST
CHAPEL PL
CHAPEL MARKET
NORTHWEST PL
DUNCAN ST
DUNCAN TERRACE
NOEL ROAD
CHALBURY WLK
RISINGHILL ST
PENTON STREET
GODSON ST
BARON CL
BARON ST
BRADLEY'S CLOSE
PRIDE COURT
ERITREA
E
B515
FROG LANE BRIDGE
VINCENT TERRACE
Garrett Anderson Language Coll
DONEGAL STREET
PROSPECT HO
WHITE LION STREET
PENTON GR
ANGEL SQ
TORRENS ST
WIDFORD HO
QUICK STREET MEWS
QUICK ST
SUDELEY ST
ROCLIFFE ST
JESSOP CT
GRAHAM STREET
CRYSTAL WHARF
RODNEY HO
CYNTHIA ST
PENTON HO
HERMES ST
ANGEL MS
ANGEL HO
Angel
A501
ELIA STREET
ELIA MEWS
ANGELIS APPARTMENTS
CITY GARDEN ROW
THESEUS WK
NELSON TERR
BOREAS WLK
NELSON PL
REMINGTON ST
COOMBS ST
HAVERSTOCK ST
FALCON CT
OAKLEY CR
LANGDON CT
CITY ROAD
A201
Resr
CLAREMONT SQUARE
CLAREMONT CL
A401
OWEN ST
City & Islington Coll
HOLFORD YD
BEVIN WAY
BEVIN COURT
CRUICKSHANK ST
MYDDELTON SQUARE
MYDDELTON
CHADWELL ST
SIDNEY GR
FREDERICK'S ROW
A501 WAKLEY ST
ANGEL GATE
Offices
St Mark's Hospl
H
PEREGRINE HOUSE
HALL STREET
PICKARD ST
HOLFORD ST
SANDERS HO
INGLEBERT ST
OWEN'S ROW
OWEN'S CT
FRIEND ST
Alice Owen Tech Ctr
PAGET ST
HOLFORD PL
GREAT PERCY STREET
CABLE HO
SOLEY MEWS
AMWELL STREET
BENYON HO
WORTHINGTON HO
ARLINGTON HO
ARLINGTON WAY
B501
HERMIT ST
RAWSTORNE PL
RAWSTORNE STREET
BREWERS BLDGS
MANNINGFORD CL
NEW CHARLES ST
MORELAND STREET
GARD ST
PERCY CIRCUS
PRIDEAUX PL
CUMBERLAND GDNS
ARCHERY FIELDS HO
LLOYD STREET
RIVER STREET
MYDDELTON PASSAGE
THE NAUTILUS BLDG
NEW RIVER HEAD
Sadler's Wells
SADLER HO
WELLS HO
WYNYATT HO
WYNYATT STREET
EARLSTOKE ST
MOORGREEN HOUSE
MIDWAY HOUSE
MASON'S YD
agistrates Court
LLOYD SQUARE
FINSBURY
CHARLES ALLEN HOUSE
Clerkenwell CE Prim Sch
Hugh Myddelton Prim Sch
TUNBRIDGE HO
LLOYD'S ROW
SOUTHWOOD CT
SPENCER STREET
Moreland Prim Sch
PRESIDENT HO
WHARTON STREET
GRANVILLE SQUARE
LLOYD BAKER STREET
ST HELENA ST
NAOROJI ST
MERLINS CT
FERNSBURY ST
GREENAWAY HO
ST PHILIP HO
GWYNNE HO
CHARLES ROWAN HO
MERLIN ST
HARDWICK STREET
GARNAULT MEWS
GREEN TERR
ROSEBERY AVENUE
Family Records Ctr
GLOUCESTER WAY
MYDDELTON STREET
City University
ASHBY ST
GOSWELL PL
Bndstd
TURNPIKE HO
WHISKIN ST
MEREDITH ST
PATRICK COMAN HO
WYCLIF ST
NORTHAMPTON SQUARE
SEBASTIAN ST
BERRY PL
GWYNNE PL
HARDWICKE MEWS
RICEYMAN HO
MARGERY STREET
SPRING HO
EARLOM HO
WILMGTN ST
ST PAULS VIEW
GARNAULT PL
ROSOMAN ST
JOSEPH TROTTER CLOSE
MICHAEL CLIFFE HOUSE
Liby
EMBERTON CT
WYCLIF CT
TOMPION ST
HAROLD LASKI HO
MULBERRY CT
BRUNSWICK CT
TELFER HO
GOSWELL ROAD A1
MOUNT MILLS
PAKENHAM ST
B502
CUBITT HO
WILMINGTON SQ
TYSOE ST
EXMOUTH MARKET
CHARLES TOWNSEND HOUSE
SKINNER STREET
PERCIVAL STREET
EARNSHAW HO
TOMPION HO
MALTA ST
CYRUS STREET
THE TRIANGLE
YARDLEY ST
ATTNEAVE ST
EASTON ST
Spa Fields Gardens
ROSOMAN PL
NORTHAMPTON RD
CORPORATION ROW
WOODBRIDGE
The Bridge
Tenn
EXMOUTH HO
PINE ST
AGDON STREET
PARAMOUNT BLDG
PARTRIDGE CT
GRIMTHORPE HO
CRAYLE HO
CYRUS HO
St Peter & St Paul RC Prim Sch
SILVERDALE CT
ENCLAVE

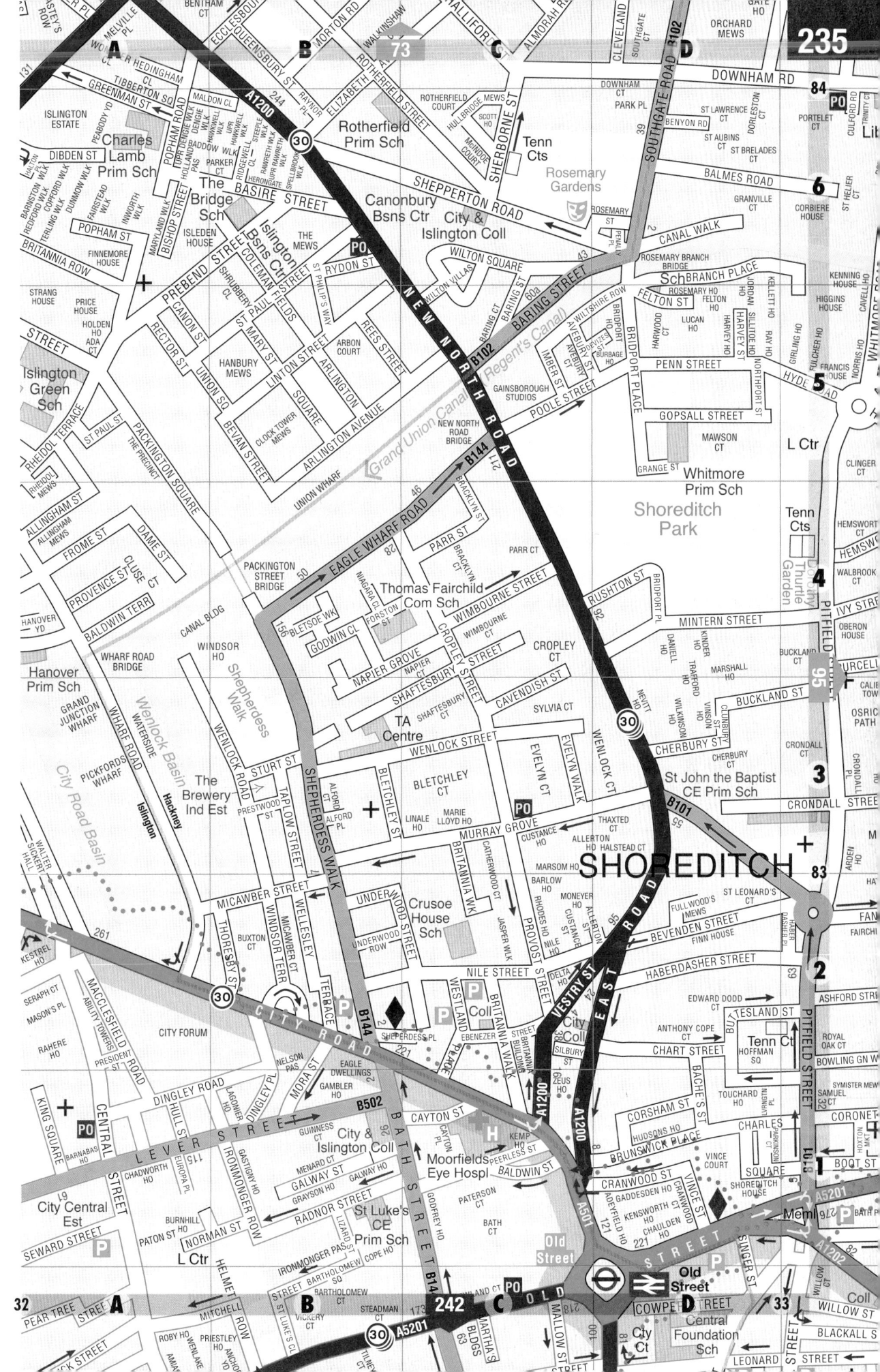
A
B
C
D
73
SHOREDITCH
NEW NORTH ROAD
EAST ROAD
CITY ROAD
LEVER STREET
BATH STREET
OLD STREET
PITFIELD STREET
SOUTHGATE ROAD
DOWNHAM RD
Grand Union Canal (Regent's Canal)
Rotherfield Prim Sch
Charles Lamb Prim Sch
The Bridge Sch
Islington Bsns Ctr
Canonbury Bsns Ctr
City & Islington Coll
Rosemary Gardens
Tenn Cts
Islington Green Sch
Hanover Prim Sch
Thomas Fairchild Com Sch
TA Centre
The Brewery Ind Est
Whitmore Prim Sch
Shoreditch Park
St John the Baptist CE Prim Sch
Crusoe House Sch
City Forum
Moorfields Eye Hospl
St Luke's CE Prim Sch
City Central Est
Central Foundation Sch
Old Street
Wenlock Basin
City Road Basin
Shepherdess Walk
Dorothy Thurtle Garden
Islington
Hackney
BASIRE STREET
SHEPPERTON ROAD
BARING STREET
CANAL WALK
WILTON SQUARE
PREBEND STREET
EAGLE WHARF ROAD
WENLOCK STREET
MURRAY GROVE
MICAWBER STREET
NILE STREET
HABERDASHER STREET
BEVENDEN STREET
CHART STREET
MINTERN STREET
PENN STREET
GOPSALL STREET
BUCKLAND ST
CHERBURY ST
CRONDALL STREET
DINGLEY ROAD
CENTRAL STREET
RADNOR STREET
GALWAY ST
SEWARD STREET
ARLINGTON AVENUE
PACKINGTON SQUARE
WHARF ROAD
WIMBOURNE STREET
SHAFTESBURY STREET
CAVENDISH ST
NAPIER GROVE
A1200
A5201
A501
A1202
B102
B144
B101
B502
242
95
32
33
83
84
1
2
3
4
5
6

229
246
91
26
27
A
B
C
D
1
2
3
4
5
6
PADDINGTON
W2
W9
Little Venice
Bayswater
Warwick Avenue
Paddington
Paddington (Hammersmith & City)
Heathrow Express Terminal
Paddington Station
Paddington Basin
Grand Union Canal
Grand Union Canal Wlk
Canal (Paddington Branch)
Alexander Fleming Laboratory Mus
St Mary's Hospl
Medical Sch
Hilton London Paddington Hotel
Paddington Acad
Paddington Green Prim Sch
St Mary's Gardens
City of Westminster Coll
Hallfield Jun & Inf Schs
St Joseph's RC Prim Sch
Gateway Prim Sch
Liberal Jewish Synagogue
HARROW ROAD
A404
A40
WESTWAY (ELEVATED)
HARROW RD (UNDER)
MAIDA VALE
A5
ST JOHN'S WOOD ROAD
A5205
B507
CLIFTON ROAD
B413
CLIFTON GARDENS
WARWICK AVENUE
BLOMFIELD ROAD
MAIDA AVENUE
EDGWARE ROAD
BISHOP'S BRIDGE ROAD
A4206
EASTBOURNE TERRACE
A4205
PRAED STREET
SUSSEX GARDENS
A4209
CRAVEN ROAD
B410
WESTBOURNE TERRACE
GLOUCESTER TERRACE
CLEVELAND SQUARE
NORTH WHARF ROAD
SOUTH WHARF ROAD
HARBET ROAD
RANELAGH BRIDGE
WESTBOURNE BRIDGE
BISHOP'S ROAD BRIDGE
SHELDON SQ
WARRINGTON CRESCENT
RANDOLPH CRESCENT
RANDOLPH AVENUE
RANDOLPH ROAD
SUTHERLAND AVE
FORMOSA STREET
WARWICK CRESCENT
WARWICK PLACE
DELAMERE TERRACE
BLOMFIELD VILLAS
WESTBOURNE TERRACE RD
HOWLEY PLACE
PARK PLACE VILLAS
CLARENDON GDNS
RANDOLPH MEWS
CROMPTON STREET
HALL PLACE
ADPAR STREET
CHURCH STREET
PENFOLD STREET
FISHERTON STREET
FRAMPTON STREET
LUTON STREET
CAPLAND STREET
LYONS PLACE
ABERDEEN PLACE
NORTHWICK TERR
CUNNINGHAM PL
HENDERSON DRIVE
POLLITT DRIVE
HERMITAGE ST
DUDLEY ST
WINSLAND STREET
LONDON ST
NORFOLK PLACE
NORFOLK SQUARE
SPRING ST
CONDUIT PL
TALBOT SQUARE
SUSSEX PLACE
HYDE PARK
CRAVEN HILL
CRAVEN HILL GDNS
QUEEN'S GARDENS
LEINSTER GARDENS
CLEVELAND GDNS
CLEVELAND SQUARE
ORSETT TERRACE
PORCHESTER TERRACE N
PORCHESTER SQUARE
CHILWORTH STREET
CHILWORTH MEWS
GLOUCESTER MEWS
UPBROOK MEWS
DEVONSHIRE TERR
BATHURST MEWS
SUSSEX GDNS
ST MARY'S TERR
ST MARY'S SQ
NEWCASTLE PL
PADDINGTON GREEN

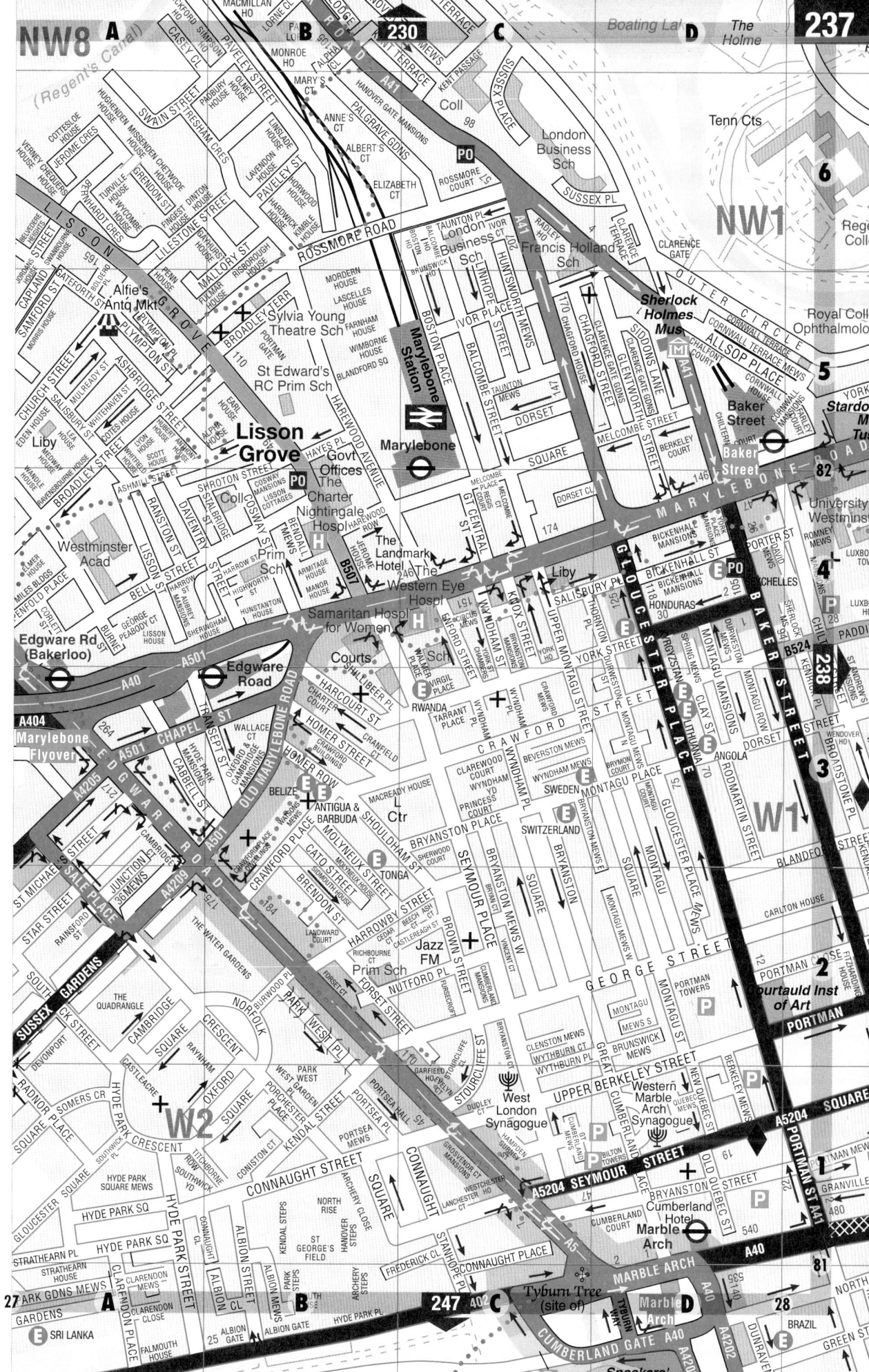

NW8
A
B
C
D
(Regent's Canal)
Boating Lake
The Holme
Tenn Cts
NW1
Regent's College
London Business Sch
Sussex Place
Sussex Pl
Clarence Gate
Outer Circle
Cornwall Terrace
Allsop Place
Royal Coll of Ophthalmologists
York Terrace
Kent Terrace
Kent Passage
Hanover Gate Mansions
Palgrave Gdns
Coll
PO
Rossmore Court
Rossmore Road
Elizabeth Ct
Albert's Ct
Anne's Ct
Mary's Ct
Monroe Ho
Macmillan Ho
Lorne Cl
Alpha Cl
Casey Cl
Paveley Street
Swain Street
Tresham Cres
Paveley St
Lilestone Street
Mallory St
Fulmar House
Penn House
Risborough House
Broadley Terr
Alfie's Antq Mkt
Plympton St
Plympton Pl
Ashbridge Street
Church Street
Salisbury St
Mulready St
Whitehaven St
Cotes House
Capland St
Gateforth St
Samford St
Jerome Cres
Lisson Grove
Broadley Street
Ashmill Street
Ranston St
Daventry St
Stalbridge St
Cosway St
Shroton Street
Bendall Mews
Bell Street
Lisson St
Penfold Place
Corlett St
Burne St
George Peabody Ct
Westminster Acad
Liby
Edgware Rd (Bakerloo)
Edgware Road
A501
A40
A404
Marylebone Flyover
Chapel St
Transept St
Cabbell St
Old Marylebone Road
Edgware Road
A4205
A4209
Sale Place
St Michael's Street
Junction Mews
Star Street
Rainsford St
Sussex Gardens
The Water Gardens
The Quadrangle
Cambridge Square
Norfolk Crescent
Oxford Square
Hyde Park Crescent
Somers Cr
Radnor Place
Hyde Park Square Mews
Hyde Park Sq
Gloucester Square
Strathearn Pl
Hyde Park Street
Clarendon Place
Clarendon Close
Albion Street
Albion Mews
Albion Gate
Albion Cl
Kendal Steps
Park Steps
St George's Field
Hanover Steps
Archery Steps
Archery Close
North Rise
Connaught Street
Connaught Square
Connaught
Connaught Place
Stanhope Pl
Frederick Cl
Kendal Street
Porchester Place
Portsea Pl
Portsea Mews
Portsea Hall
Park West Pl
Forset Street
Burwood Pl
Nutford Pl
Brown Street
Seymour Place
Harrowby Street
Brendon St
Cato Street
Molyneux Street
Crawford Place
Shouldham St
Homer Row
Homer Street
Harcourt St
Shillibeer Pl
Cranfield Ct
Belize
Antigua & Barbuda
Macready House
L Ctr
Tonga
Richbourne Ct
Prim Sch
Jazz FM
Sylvia Young Theatre Sch
St Edward's RC Prim Sch
Portman Gate
Harewood Avenue
Harewood Row
Hayes Pl
Govt Offices
The Charter Nightingale Hospl
Lisson Grove
Coll
Prim Sch
The Landmark Hotel
The Western Eye Hospl
Samaritan Hospl for Women
Courts
Sch
B507
Marylebone Station
Marylebone
Boston Place
Balcombe Street
Ivor Place
Huntsworth Mews
Linhope St
Taunton Pl
Taunton Mews
Dorset Square
London Business Sch
Francis Holland Sch
Chagford Street
Clarence Gate Gdns
Glentworth Street
Siddons Lane
Melcombe Street
Berkeley Court
Sherlock Holmes Mus
Baker Street
Baker Street
Marylebone Road
82
University of Westminster
Bickenhall Mansions
Bickenhall St
York Street
Gloucester Place
Salisbury Pl
Thornton Pl
Upper Montagu Street
Knox Street
Wyndham Street
Enford Street
Wyndham Pl
Crawford Street
Bryanston Place
Bryanston Square
Bryanston Mews W
Bryanston Mews E
Montagu Square
Montagu Place
Montagu Mansions
Montagu Row
Montagu Mews N
Montagu Mews W
Montagu Mews S
Montagu St
George Street
Gloucester Place Mews
Rodmartin Street
Dorset Street
Durweston Mews
Clay St
Kyrgyzstan
Lithuania
Angola
Sweden
Switzerland
Rwanda
Honduras
Seychelles
Liby
B524
238
Baker Street
Portman Close
Portman Towers
Courtauld Inst of Art
Portman Square
Portman St
A5204
Seymour Street
Upper Berkeley Street
Great Cumberland Place
Brunswick Mews
Clenston Mews
Wythburn Ct
Wythburn Pl
Berkeley Mews
New Quebec St
Old Quebec St
Western Marble Arch Synagogue
West London Synagogue
Stourcliffe St
Bryanston Street
Cumberland Hotel
Cumberland Court
Marble Arch
Marble Arch
Cumberland Gate
A40
A5
Tyburn Tree (site of)
Tyburn Way
Speakers'
Sri Lanka
Brazil
Granville Pl
North Row
Green St
Dunraven
Blandford Street
Broadstone Pl
Carlton House
W1
W2
A41
1
2
3
4
5
6
247
230
27
28
81

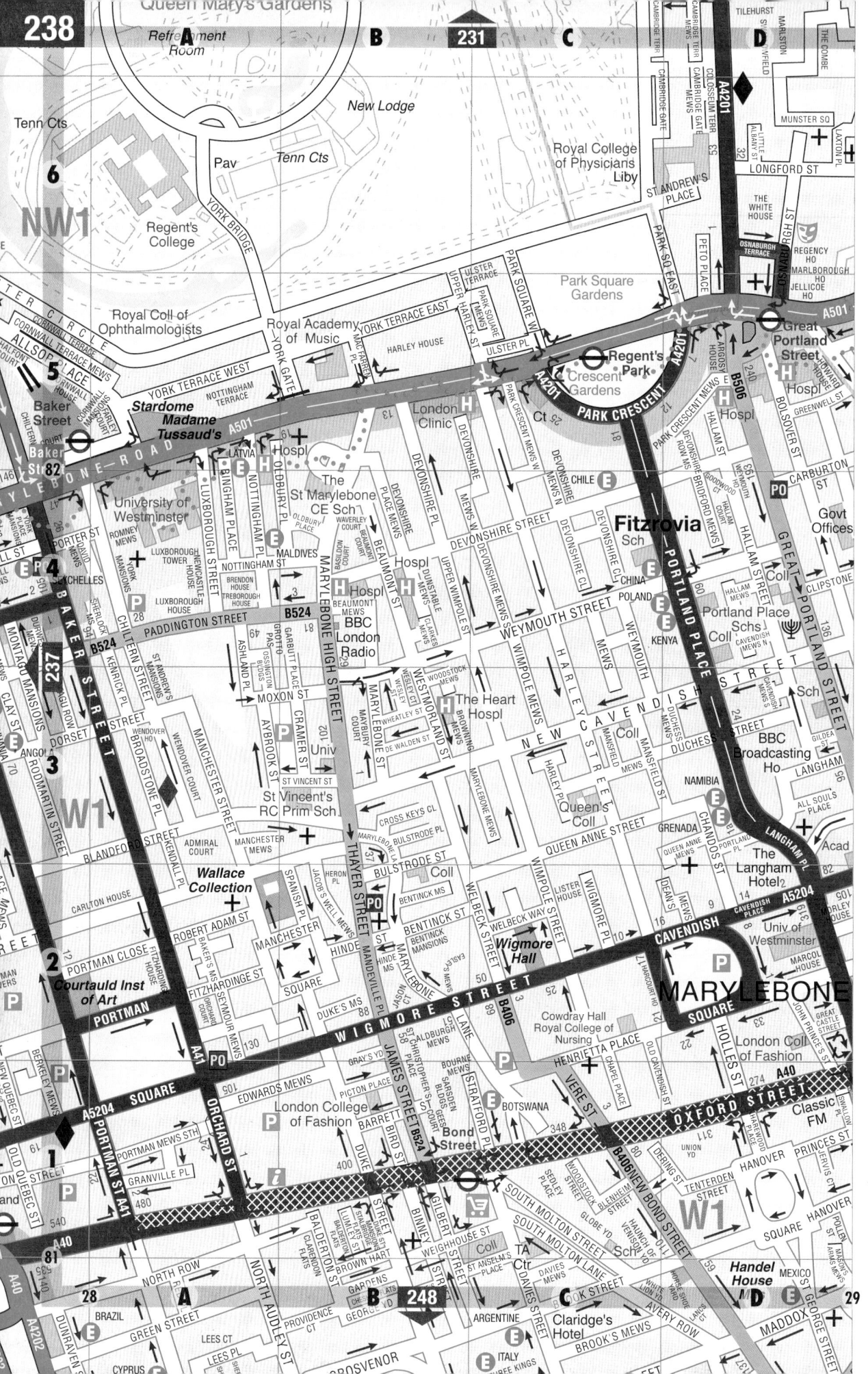

231
248
A
B
C
D
6
5
4
3
2
1
28
29
NW1
W1
Queen Marys Gardens
Refreshment Room
New Lodge
Tenn Cts
Pav
Regent's College
York Bridge
Royal College of Physicians Liby
St Andrew's Place
Park Square Gardens
Park Square East
Royal Coll of Ophthalmologists
Royal Academy of Music
York Terrace East
York Terrace West
York Gate
Harley House
Ulster Terrace
Ulster Pl
Park Square West
Regent's Park
Crescent Gardens
Park Crescent
Great Portland Street
Baker Street
Stardome
Madame Tussaud's
Marylebone Road
A501
A4201
B506
A5204
A40
A41
B524
B406
London Clinic
Hospl
The St Marylebone CE Sch
University of Westminster
Luxborough Street
Bingham Place
Nottingham Pl
Oldbury Pl
Devonshire Pl
Devonshire Street
Fitzrovia
Portland Place
Hallam St
Bolsover St
Carburton St
Govt Offices
Clipstone St
Paddington Street
Marylebone High Street
BBC London Radio
Beaumont St
Weymouth Street
Upper Wimpole St
Wimpole Mews
Harley Street
New Cavendish Street
Portland Place Schs
The Heart Hospl
Chiltern Street
Baker Street
Moxon St
Aybrook St
Cramer St
Univ
Manchester Street
Broadstone Pl
Dorset St
Rodmartin Street
Montagu Mansions
St Vincent's RC Prim Sch
Cross Keys Cl
Bulstrode St
Marylebone Mews
Queen Anne Street
Queen's Coll
Chandos St
BBC Broadcasting Ho
Langham Pl
The Langham Hotel
Acad
Blandford Street
Wallace Collection
Manchester Square
Spanish Pl
Thayer Street
Bentinck St
Welbeck Street
Wimpole Street
Wigmore Hall
Wigmore Pl
Cavendish Square
Univ of Westminster
Marylebone
Portman Close
Courtauld Inst of Art
Portman Square
Wigmore Street
Mandeville Pl
James Street
Marylebone Lane
Cowdray Hall Royal College of Nursing
Henrietta Place
Holles St
London Coll of Fashion
Orchard St
Edwards Mews
Vere St
Oxford Street
Classic FM
Portman St
Bond Street
Stratford Pl
New Bond Street
Hanover Square
Princes St
Duke Street
Gilbert St
South Molton Street
South Molton Lane
North Audley St
North Row
Green Street
Brook Street
Claridge's Hotel
Brook's Mews
Avery Row
Handel House
Maddox St
St George Street
Davies Street
Grosvenor

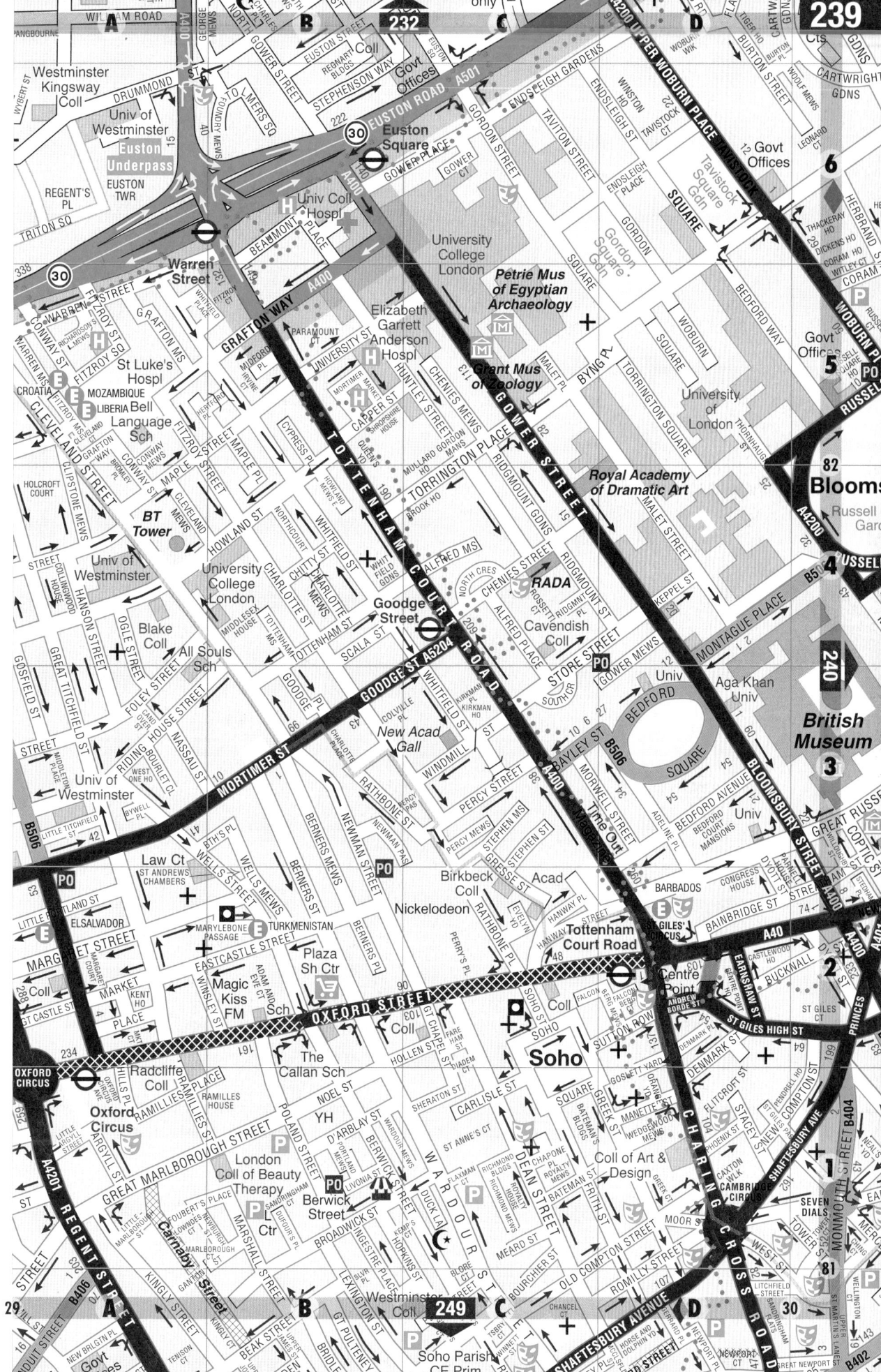

232
249
240
A
B
C
D
6
5
4
3
2
1
29
30
WILLIAM ROAD
Westminster Kingsway Coll
DRUMMOND ST
Univ of Westminster
Euston Underpass
EUSTON TWR
REGENT'S PL
TRITON SQ
Warren Street
EUSTON ROAD A501
Euston Square
GOWER PLACE
GOWER STREET
EUSTON STREET
STEPHENSON WAY
Govt Offices
Coll
Univ Coll Hospl
BEAUMONT PLACE
GRAFTON WAY
University College London
Petrie Mus of Egyptian Archaeology
Grant Mus of Zoology
Elizabeth Garrett Anderson Hospl
UNIVERSITY ST
HUNTLEY STREET
CHENIES MEWS
GORDON STREET
ENDSLEIGH GARDENS
TAVITON STREET
ENDSLEIGH PLACE
GORDON SQUARE
Gordon Square Gdn
Tavistock Square Gdn
TAVISTOCK SQUARE
UPPER WOBURN PLACE
WOBURN PLACE
BEDFORD WAY
WOBURN SQUARE
TORRINGTON SQUARE
University of London
Royal Academy of Dramatic Art
MALET STREET
MALET PL
BYNG PL
Govt Offices
CARTWRIGHT GDNS
BURTON STREET
Bloomsbury
Russell Square Gardens
RUSSELL SQUARE
WARREN STREET
FITZROY SQ
FITZROY ST
CONWAY ST
GRAFTON MS
St Luke's Hospl
CROATIA
MOZAMBIQUE
LIBERIA
Bell Language Sch
CLEVELAND STREET
CLIPSTONE MEWS
HOLCROFT COURT
MAPLE STREET
FITZROY STREET
BT Tower
HOWLAND ST
TORRINGTON PLACE
RIDGMOUNT GDNS
TOTTENHAM COURT ROAD
Univ of Westminster
University College London
CHARLOTTE ST
WHITFIELD ST
Goodge Street
ALFRED MS
CHENIES STREET
RADA
Cavendish Coll
ALFRED PLACE
STORE STREET
GOWER MEWS
MONTAGUE PLACE
KEPPEL ST
Univ
BEDFORD SQUARE
Aga Khan Univ
British Museum
Blake Coll
All Souls Sch
HANSON STREET
OGLE STREET
GREAT TITCHFIELD ST
GOSFIELD ST
FOLEY STREET
RIDING HOUSE STREET
NASSAU ST
GOODGE ST A5204
MORTIMER ST
SCALA ST
New Acad Gall
WINDMILL ST
PERCY STREET
RATHBONE ST
BAYLEY ST
MORWELL STREET
Time Out Magazine
BLOOMSBURY STREET
BEDFORD AVENUE
GREAT RUSSELL ST
Univ of Westminster
LITTLE TITCHFIELD ST
Law Ct
WELLS STREET
WELLS MEWS
BERNERS MEWS
BERNERS ST
NEWMAN STREET
Birkbeck Coll
Acad
Nickelodeon
RATHBONE PL
HANWAY ST
Tottenham Court Road
ST GILES' CIRCUS
Centre Point
BAINBRIDGE ST
BUCKNALL ST
ST GILES HIGH ST
BARBADOS
LITTLE PORTLAND ST
EL SALVADOR
TURKMENISTAN
MARGARET STREET
EASTCASTLE STREET
Plaza Sh Ctr
Magic Kiss FM
Sch
OXFORD STREET
MARKET PLACE
Coll
Radcliffe Coll
OXFORD CIRCUS
Oxford Circus
RAMILLIES PLACE
NOEL ST
YH
The Callan Sch
HOLLEN ST
SOHO ST
Soho
SOHO SQUARE
SUTTON ROW
CHARING CROSS ROAD
DENMARK ST
FLITCROFT ST
SHAFTESBURY AVE
NEW COMPTON ST
MONMOUTH STREET
SEVEN DIALS
CAMBRIDGE CIRCUS
GREAT MARLBOROUGH STREET
London Coll of Beauty Therapy
POLAND STREET
D'ARBLAY ST
BERWICK STREET
WARDOUR ST
CARLISLE ST
DEAN STREET
GREEK ST
FRITH ST
Coll of Art & Design
Berwick Street
ARGYLL ST
A4201 REGENT STREET
Carnaby Street
KINGLY STREET
MARSHALL STREET
BROADWICK ST
OLD COMPTON STREET
ROMILLY STREET
MOOR ST
WEST ST
Westminster Coll
SHAFTESBURY AVENUE
Govt Offices
Soho Parish CE Prim
BEAK STREET
LEXINGTON ST

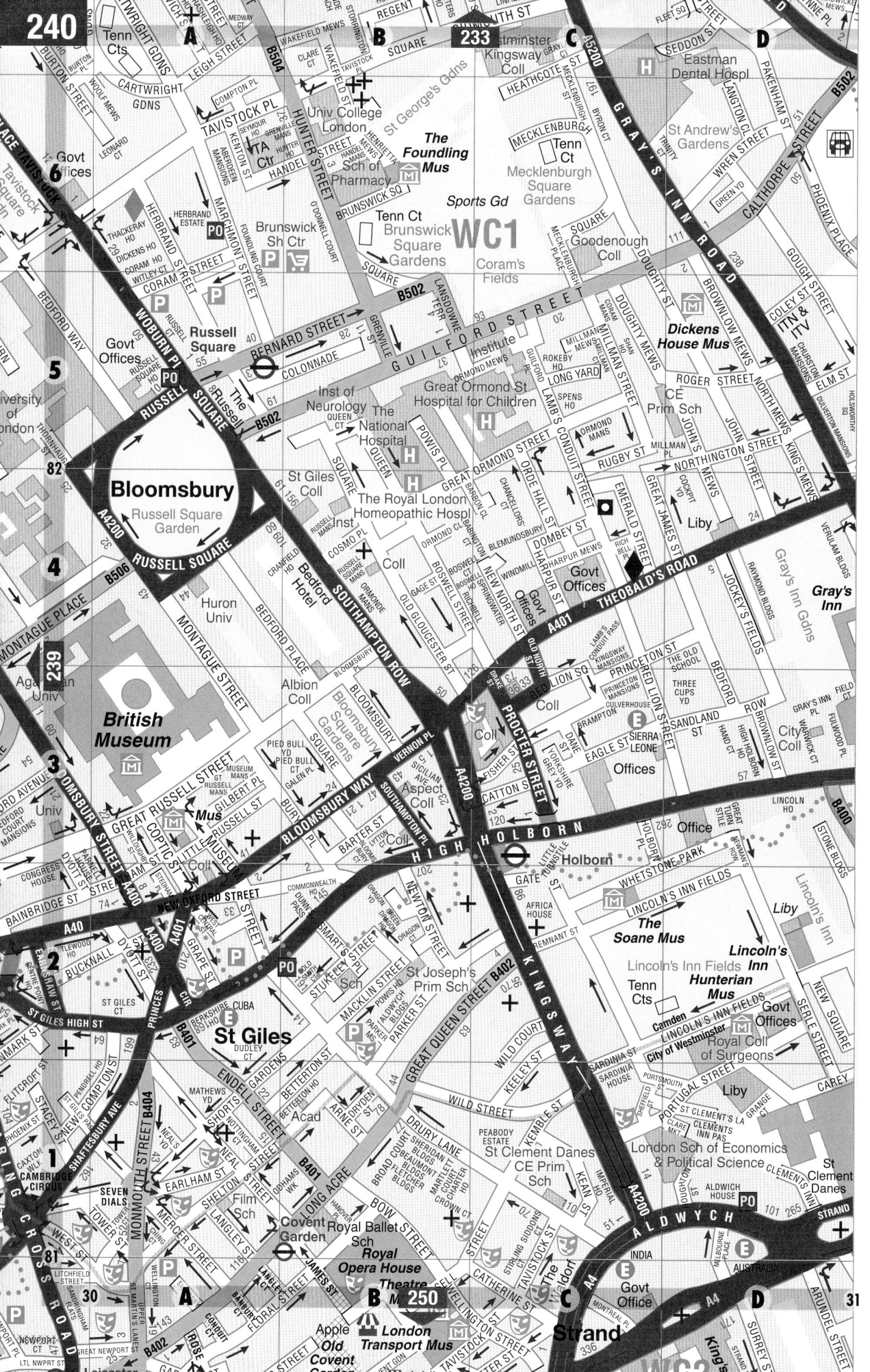

A
B
C
D
233
250
239
6
5
4
3
2
1
30
31
WC1
Bloomsbury
Russell Square Garden
RUSSELL SQUARE
Russell Square
British Museum
Mus
The Foundling Mus
Sports Gd
Brunswick Square Gardens
Brunswick Sh Ctr
Coram's Fields
Mecklenburgh Square Gardens
Goodenough Coll
Univ College London
Sch of Pharmacy
St George's Gdns
Kingsway Coll
Eastman Dental Hospl
St Andrew's Gardens
Dickens House Mus
ITN & ITV
Great Ormond St Hospital for Children
The National Hospital
The Royal London Homeopathic Hospl
Inst of Neurology
Bedford Hotel
Huron Univ
Albion Coll
Bloomsbury Square Gardens
Aspect Coll
Govt Offices
Gray's Inn Gdns
Gray's Inn
City Coll
Holborn
The Soane Mus
Lincoln's Inn Fields
Lincoln's Inn
Hunterian Mus
Royal Coll of Surgeons
London Sch of Economics & Political Science
St Clement Danes
St Clement Danes CE Prim Sch
St Joseph's Prim Sch
St Giles
Covent Garden
Royal Ballet Sch
Royal Opera House
London Transport Mus
Old Covent Garden
Strand
The Waldorf
Camden
City of Westminster
WOBURN PL
SOUTHAMPTON ROW
GUILFORD STREET
THEOBALD'S ROAD
GRAY'S INN ROAD
HIGH HOLBORN
KINGSWAY
NEW OXFORD STREET
BLOOMSBURY WAY
GREAT RUSSELL STREET
SHAFTESBURY AVE
CHARING CROSS ROAD
LONG ACRE
DRURY LANE
GREAT QUEEN STREET
BOW STREET
ALDWYCH
STRAND
MONTAGUE PLACE
MONTAGUE STREET
BEDFORD PLACE
BERNARD STREET
HUNTER STREET
MARCHMONT STREET
LAMB'S CONDUIT STREET
PROCTER STREET
RED LION STREET
ENDELL STREET
MONMOUTH STREET
SEVEN DIALS
CAMBRIDGE CIRCUS
A4200
A401
A400
A40
B502
B504
B506
B401
B402
B404
B400
A4

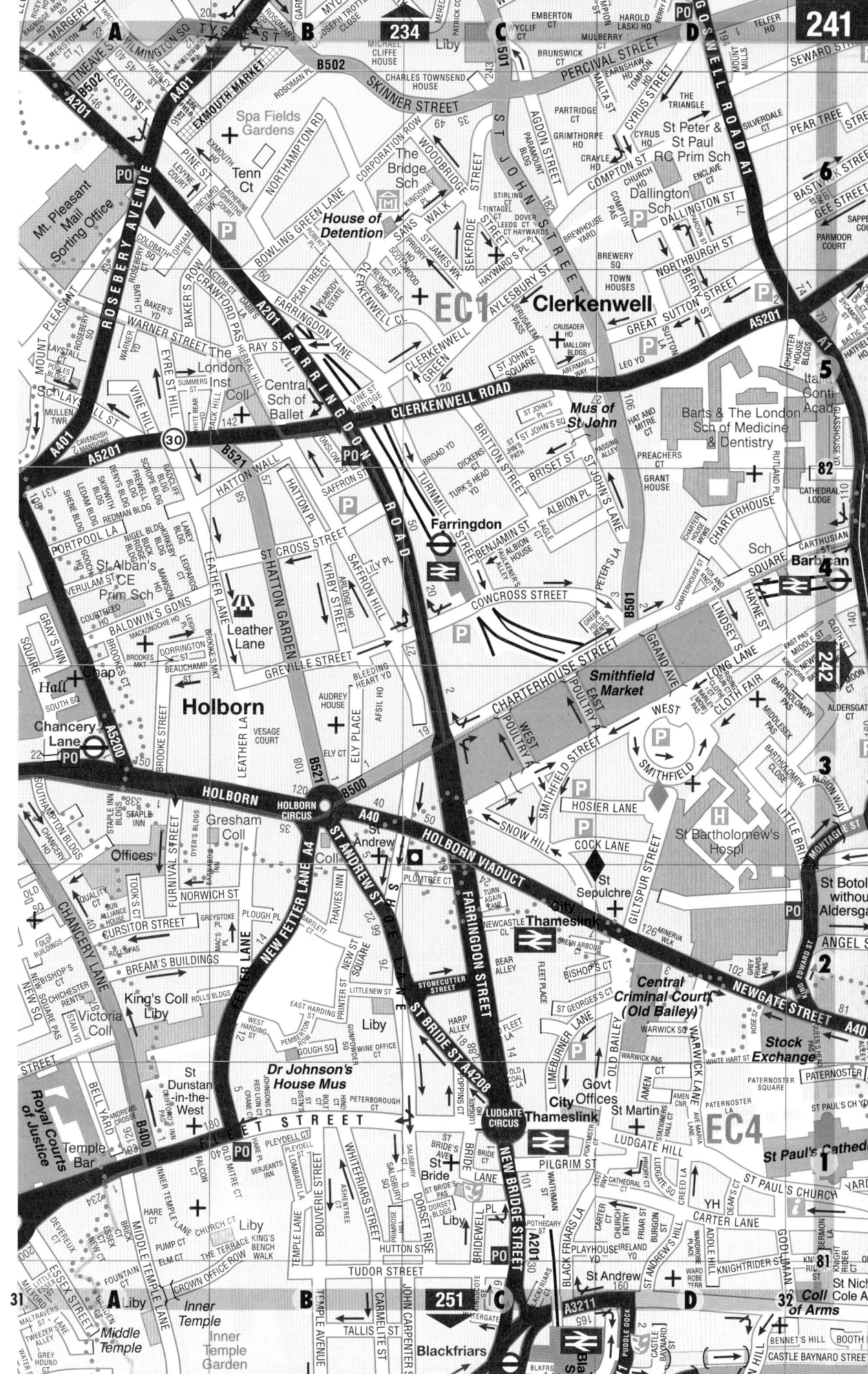
234
251
242
EC1
Clerkenwell
EC4
Holborn
Smithfield Market
Central Criminal Court (Old Bailey)
St Paul's Cathedral
Farringdon
Barbican
City Thameslink
Blackfriars
Chancery Lane
Holborn Circus
Ludgate Circus
Clerkenwell Road
Farringdon Road
Farringdon Street
Holborn Viaduct
Fleet Street
Charterhouse Street
Goswell Road A1
Rosebery Avenue
Skinner Street
New Fetter Lane
St John Street
Newgate Street
Hatton Garden
Leather Lane
Chancery Lane
Mt. Pleasant Mail Sorting Office
House of Detention
Mus of St John
Barts & The London Sch of Medicine & Dentistry
St Bartholomew's Hospl
Dr Johnson's House Mus
Royal Courts of Justice
Inner Temple
Middle Temple
Temple Bar
Spa Fields Gardens
Stock Exchange
Govt Offices

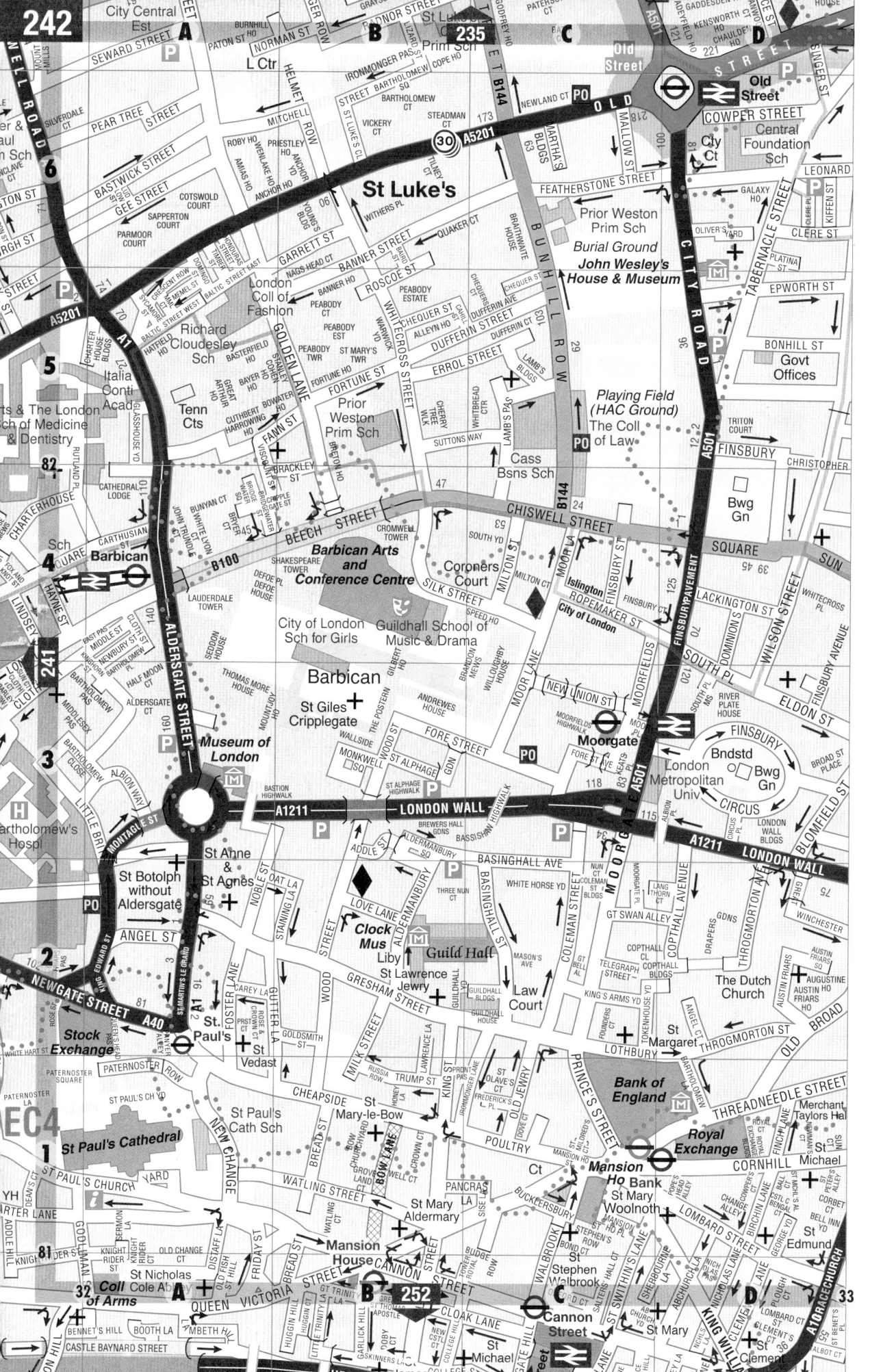

A
B
C
D
235
City Central Est
Seward Street
Paton St
Burnhill Ho
Norman St
Radnor Street
St Luke's C of E Prim Sch
Godfrey Ho
Paterson Ct
Gaddesden Ho
Kensworth Ct
Chaulden Ho
L Ctr
Helmet Row
Ironmonger Pas
Bartholomew Sq
Bartholomew Ct
Old Street
Old Street
Cowper Street
City Ct
Central Foundation Sch
Silverdale Ct
Pear Tree Street
Mitchell Ct
Vickery Ct
Steadman Ct
Newland Ct
PO
B144
A5201
6
Roby Ho
Priestley Ho
Bastwick Street
Gee Street
Cotswold Court
Sapperton Court
Parmoor Court
Featherstone Street
Galaxy Ho
Leonard
Clere Pl
Kiffen St
St Luke's
Withers Pl
Quaker Ct
Prior Weston Prim Sch
Burial Ground
John Wesley's House & Museum
Oliver's Yard
Clere St
Tabernacle Street
Platina St
Epworth St
Garrett St
Nags Head Ct
Banner Street
Roscoe St
Braithwaite House
Bunhill Row
City Road
London Coll of Fashion
Banner Ho
Peabody Estate
Chequer St
Dufferin Ave
Dufferin Street
Crescent Row
Memel St
Baltic Street East
Baltic Street West
Sycamore St
A5201
A1
Richard Cloudesley Sch
Golden Lane
Peabody Ct
Peabody Est
Peabody Twr
St Mary's Twr
Fortune Ho
Fortune St
Errol Street
Lamb's Bldgs
Bonhill St
Govt Offices
5
Italia Conti Acad
Tenn Cts
Basterfield Ho
Bayer Ho
Great Arthur Ho
Cuthbert Harrowing Ho
Bowater Ho
Fann St
Prior Weston Prim Sch
Whitecross Street
Cherry Tree Wlk
Whitbread Ctr
Lamb's Pas
Suttons Way
Playing Field (HAC Ground)
The Coll of Law
Triton Court
Finsbury
Christopher
A501
Arts & The London Sch of Medicine & Dentistry
Glasshouse Yd
Rutland Pl
Cathedral Lodge
Charterhouse
Brackley St
Cass Bsns Sch
Bwg Gn
Chiswell Street
Bunyan Ct
John Trundle Ct
White Lyon Ct
Bryer Ct
Cripplegate St
Beech Street
Cromwell Tower
South Yd
Milton St
Moor La
Finsbury St
Square
Sun
4
Sch
Carthusian St
Square
Barbican
B100
Shakespeare Tower
Barbican Arts and Conference Centre
Corporners Court
Milton Ct
Islington
City of London
Finsbury Ct
Ropemaker St
Lackington St
Whitecross Pl
Lindsey St
Hayne St
Lauderdale Tower
Defoe Pl
Defoe House
Silk Street
Speed Ho
Finsburypavement
Dominion St
Wilson Street
Finsbury Avenue
241
Middle St
Newbury St
Cloth St
East Pas
Half Moon Ct
Aldersgate Street
Seddon House
City of London Sch for Girls
Guildhall School of Music & Drama
Gilbert Ho
Brandon Mews
Willoughby House
Moorfields
South Pl
Eldon St
Bartholomew Pl
Thomas More House
Barbican
Moor Lane
New Union St
Aldersgate Ct
Middlesex Pas
Mountjoy Ho
St Giles Cripplegate
Andrewes House
Moorfields Highwalk
Moorgate
River Plate House
Finsbury
Bartholomew Close
Museum of London
Wallside
Wood St
Fore Street
Fore St Ave
Bndstd
Broad St Place
3
Albion Way
Monkwell Sq
St Alphage Gdn
PO
London Metropolitan Univ
Bwg Gn
Circus
Blomfield St
Bastion Highwalk
St Alphage Highwalk
A1211
London Wall
A1211
London Wall
Montague St
Little Britain
Bartholomew's Hospl
Brewers Hall Gdns
Bassishaw Highwalk
Albion Pl
Circus Pl
London Wall Bldgs
Addle St
Aldermanbury Sq
Basinghall Ave
St Anne & St Agnes
St Botolph without Aldersgate
Noble St
Oat La
White Horse Yd
Three Nun Ct
Basinghall St
Coleman Street
Nun Ct
Coleman St Bldgs
Moorgate
Moorgate Pl
Lang Thorn Ct
Copthall Avenue
Throgmorton Ave
Great Winchester St
Winchester
PO
Angel St
Staining La
Love Lane
Aldermanbury
Clock Mus
Guild Hall
Mason's Ave
GT Swan Alley
Drapers Gdns
2
King Edward St
Liby
St Lawrence Jewry
Gresham Street
Gutter La
Wood
Street
Copthall Cl
Telegraph Street
Copthall Bldgs
Austin Friars Sq
Austin Friars
The Dutch Church
Augustine Ho
Austin Friars Ho
Newgate Street
A40
St Martin's Le Grand
Foster Lane
Carey La
Rose & Crown Ct
Guildhall Bldgs
Guildhall House
Law Court
King's Arms Yd
Tokenhouse Yd
Founders Ct
Angel Ct
Old Broad
Stock Exchange
St. Paul's
St Vedast
Goldsmith St
Milk Street
Lawrence La
Lothbury
St Margaret
Throgmorton St
White Hart St
Paternoster Square
Paternoster Row
Russia Row
Trump St
King St
Ironmonger Lane
St Olave's Ct
Old Jewry
Prince's Street
Bank of England
Bartholomew La
Threadneedle Street
Merchant Taylors Hall
St Paul's Ch Yd
Cheapside
St Mary-le-Bow
Frederick's Pl
Dove Ct
EC4
St Pauls Cath Sch
New Change
Bread St
Bow Lane
Crown Ct
Poultry
Royal Exchange
Finch Lane
St Michael
Cornhill
1
St Paul's Cathedral
St Paul's Church Yard
Watling Street
Groveland Ct
Well Ct
Pancras La
Sise La
Mansion Ho Bank
St Mary Woolnoth
Lombard Street
Birchin Lane
Change Alley
Bell Inn
St Edmund
Carter Lane
Watling Ct
St Mary Aldermary
Bucklersbury
Walbrook
St Stephen Walbrook
Mansion Ho Pl
St Swithin's Lane
Sherbourne La
Abchurch La
Nicholas Lane
Clements Lane
George Yd
Addle Hill
Godliman St
Knightrider St
Sermon La
Distaff La
Old Fish St Hill
Friday St
Bread St
Mansion House
Cannon Street
Budge Row
Bond Ct
Salters Hall Ct
St Nicholas Cole Abbey
Coll of Arms
Queen Victoria Street
Gt Trinity La
252
Cloak Lane
Cannon Street
St Mary
King William
Plough Ct
Gracechurch
A10
33
32
Bennet's Hill
Booth La
Lambeth Hill
Castle Baynard Street
Huggin Hill
Little Trinity La
Garlick Hill
Skinners La
New Cstl Ct
College Hill
St Michael
College St
Abchurch Yd
Lombard Ct
St Clement's Ct
St Clement
St Benet's Pl
Talbot Ct

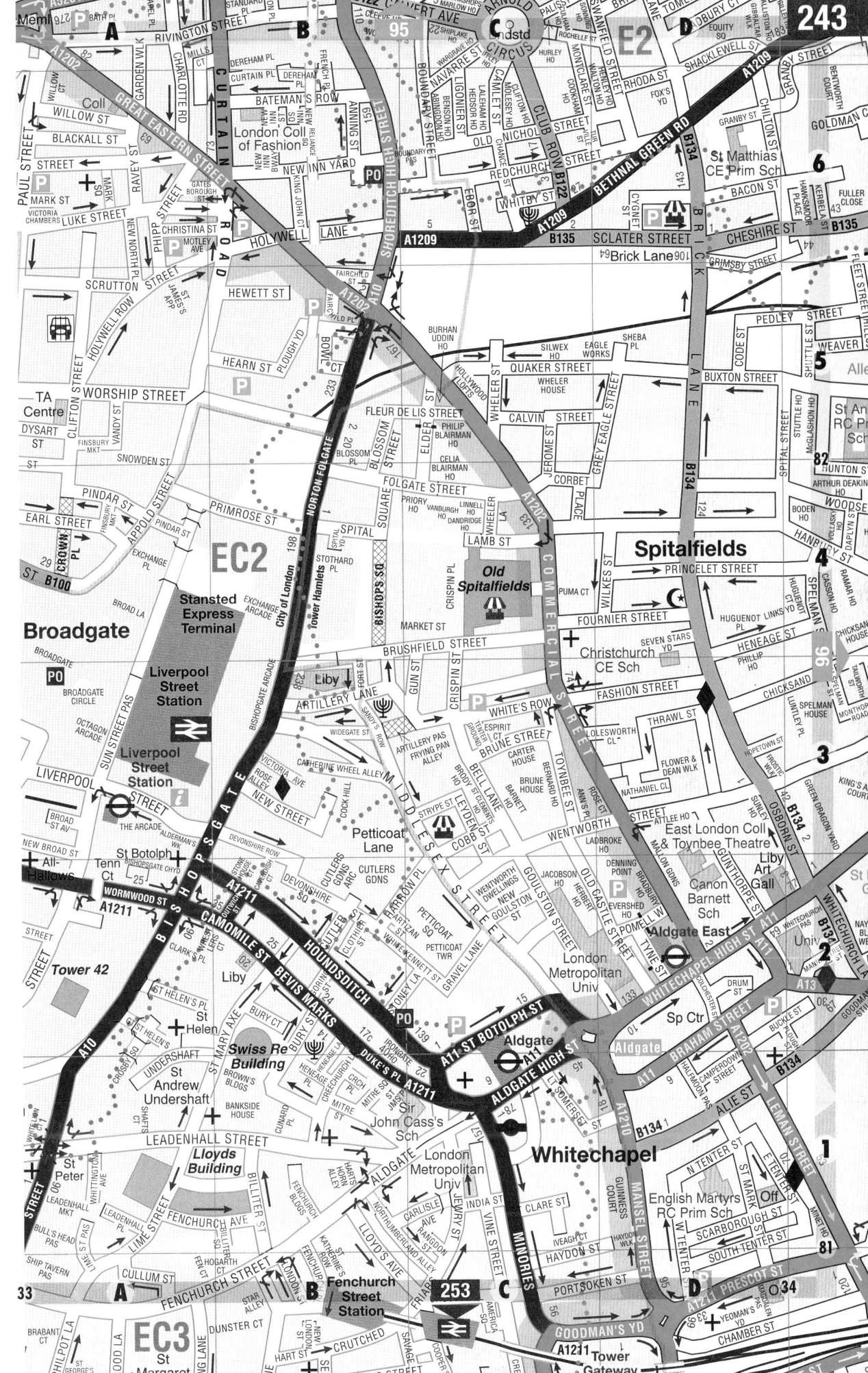

A
B
C
D
E2
95
253
6
5
4
3
2
1
96
EC2
EC3
Broadgate
Spitalfields
Whitechapel
Aldgate
Aldgate East
Liverpool Street Station
Stansted Express Terminal
Fenchurch Street Station
Tower Gateway
Old Spitalfields
Petticoat Lane
Swiss Re Building
Lloyds Building
Tower 42
London Coll of Fashion
St Matthias CE Prim Sch
Christchurch CE Sch
East London Coll & Toynbee Theatre
Canon Barnett Sch
London Metropolitan Univ
English Martyrs RC Prim Sch
Sir John Cass's Sch
St Andrew Undershaft
St Botolph
St Helen
St Peter
Brick Lane
ARNOLD CIRCUS
GREAT EASTERN STREET
CURTAIN ROAD
SHOREDITCH HIGH STREET
BETHNAL GREEN RD
SCLATER STREET
CHESHIRE ST
QUAKER STREET
BUXTON STREET
HANBURY ST
PRINCELET STREET
FOURNIER STREET
BRUSHFIELD STREET
FOLGATE STREET
NORTON FOLGATE
BISHOPSGATE
COMMERCIAL STREET
MIDDLESEX STREET
HOUNDSDITCH
CAMOMILE ST
BEVIS MARKS
ST BOTOLPH ST
ALDGATE HIGH ST
WHITECHAPEL HIGH ST
MINORIES
LEMAN STREET
MANSEL STREET
ALIE ST
PRESCOT ST
LEADENHALL STREET
FENCHURCH STREET
FENCHURCH AVE
WORSHIP STREET
LIVERPOOL STREET
WORMWOOD ST
HOLYWELL LANE
REDCHURCH STREET
OLD NICHOL STREET
RIVINGTON STREET
WENTWORTH STREET
OSBORN ST
GOODMAN'S YD
PORTSOKEN ST

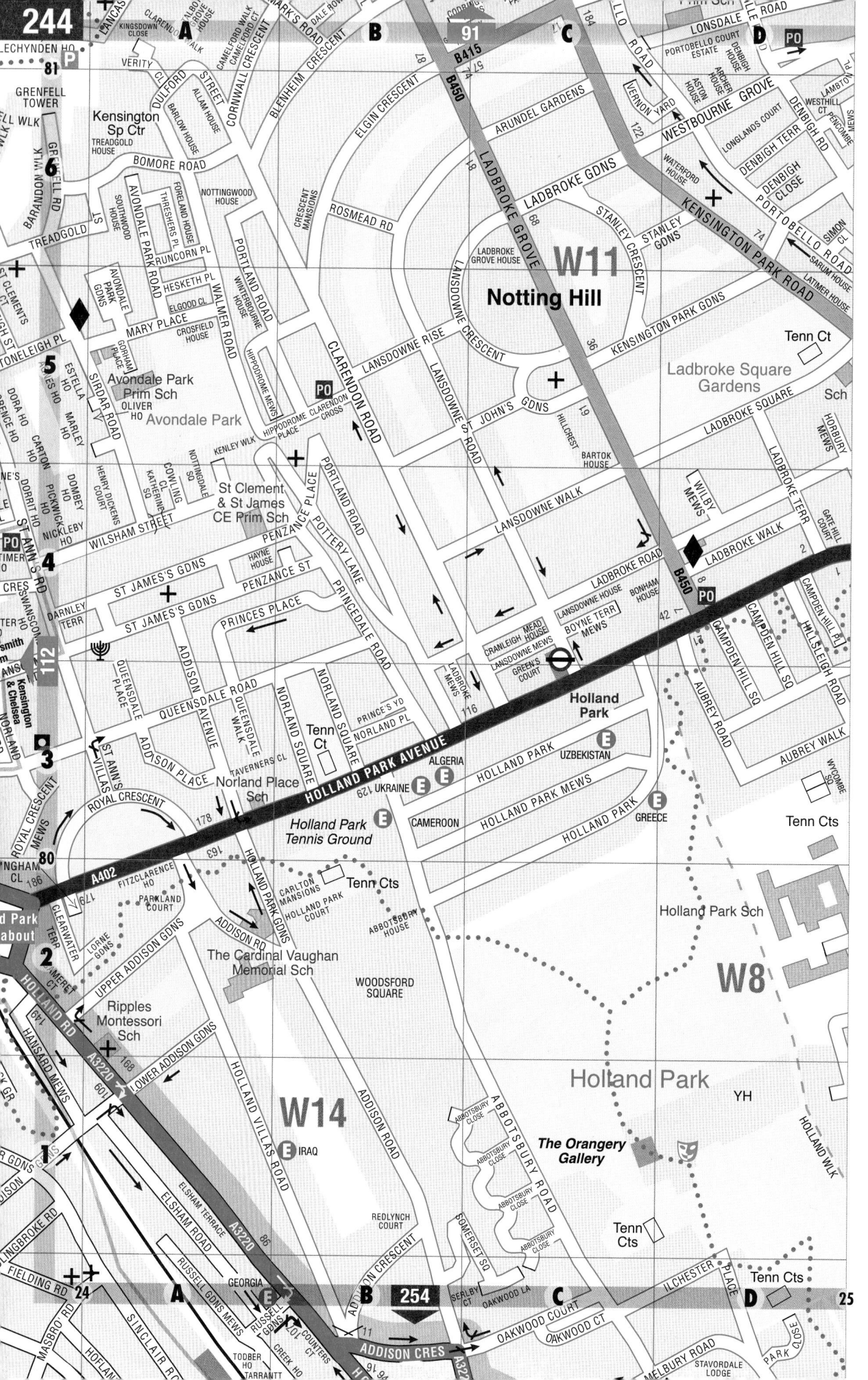
A
B
C
D
91
254
112
W11
Notting Hill
W14
W8
Holland Park
Holland Park Avenue
Ladbroke Grove
Clarendon Road
Kensington Park Road
Westbourne Grove
Ladbroke Square Gardens
Avondale Park
Avondale Park Prim Sch
St Clement & St James CE Prim Sch
Norland Place Sch
Holland Park Tennis Ground
The Cardinal Vaughan Memorial Sch
Ripples Montessori Sch
Holland Park Sch
The Orangery Gallery
Kensington Sp Ctr
Grenfell Tower
Woodsford Square
Holland Rd
Addison Road
Abbotsbury Road
Holland Villas Road
Holland Park Gdns
Royal Crescent
Addison Cres
Lansdowne Crescent
Lansdowne Rise
Ladbroke Square
Ladbroke Road
Portland Road
Pottery Lane
Princedale Road
Queensdale Road
St Ann's Villas
Elsham Road
Melbury Road
Ilchester Place
Holland Wlk
Aubrey Road
Campden Hill Sq
Hillsleigh Road
Walmer Road
Bomore Road
Portobello Road
Elgin Crescent
Blenheim Crescent
Arundel Gardens
Ladbroke Gdns
Stanley Crescent
Kensington Park Gdns
St John's Gdns
Lansdowne Walk
Ladbroke Walk
Ladbroke Terr
Holland Park Mews
Upper Addison Gdns
Lower Addison Gdns
Addison Place
Addison Avenue
Norland Square
St James's Gdns
Penzance Place
Wilsham Street
Tenn Ct
Tenn Cts
YH
A402
A3220
B450
B415
Algeria
Ukraine
Uzbekistan
Cameroon
Greece
Iraq
Georgia
80
81
24
25
1
2
3
4
5
6

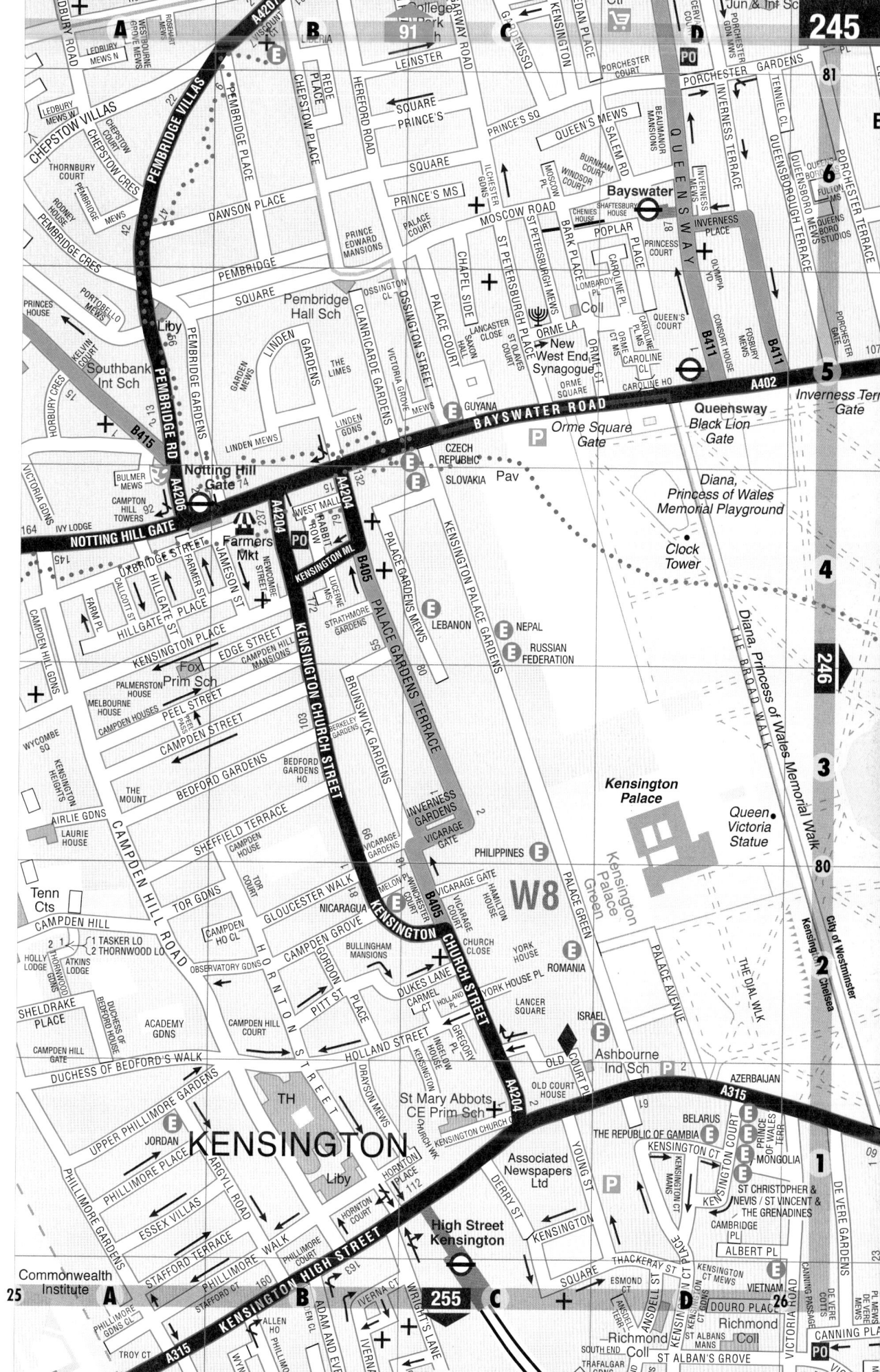
245
91
A
B
C
D
LEDBURY ROAD
LEDBURY MEWS N
LEDBURY MEWS W
WESTBOURNE GROVE MEWS
ROSEHART MEWS
A4207
VISCOUNT CT
LIBERIA
College Park Sch
GARWAY ROAD
LEINSTER SQUARE
GARDENS SQ
KENSINGTON
LEDAN PLACE
PORCHESTER COURT
PORCHESTER GDN MEWS
PORCHESTER GARDENS
Jun & Inf Sch
PO
81
CHEPSTOW VILLAS
CHEPSTOW COURT
CHEPSTOW CRES
PEMBRIDGE VILLAS
PEMBRIDGE PLACE
REDE PLACE
CHEPSTOW PLACE
HEREFORD ROAD
PRINCE'S SQUARE
PRINCE'S SQ
QUEEN'S MEWS
SALEM RD
BEAUMANOR MANSIONS
QUEENSWAY
INVERNESS TERRACE
TENNIEL CL
QUEENSBOROUGH TERRACE
PORCHESTER TERRACE
THORNBURY COURT
RODNEY HOUSE
PEMBRIDGE MEWS
PEMBRIDGE CRES
DAWSON PLACE
PRINCE'S MS
ILCHESTER GDNS
BURNHAM COURT
MOSCOW PL
WINDSOR COURT
Bayswater
INVERNESS MEWS
QUEENSBOROUGH MEWS
FULTON MS
QUEENS BORO STUDIOS
6
MOSCOW ROAD
CHENIES HOUSE
SHAFTESBURY HOUSE
INVERNESS PLACE
PRINCE EDWARD MANSIONS
PALACE COURT
POPLAR PLACE
PRINCESS COURT
OLYMPIA YD
PEMBRIDGE SQUARE
CHAPEL SIDE
ST PETERSBURGH PLACE
ST PETERSBURGH MEWS
BARK PLACE
LOMBARDY PL
CAROLINE PL
PRINCES HOUSE
PORTOBELLO MEWS
OSSINGTON CL
OSSINGTON STREET
Pembridge Hall Sch
Coll
QUEEN'S COURT
CONSORT HOUSE
FOSBURY MEWS
B411
PORCHESTER GATE
107
Liby
KELVIN COURT
Southbank Int Sch
HORBURY CRES
PEMBRIDGE GARDENS
PEMBRIDGE RD
GARDEN MEWS
LINDEN GARDENS
THE LIMES
CLANRICARDE GARDENS
VICTORIA GROVE MEWS
LANCASTER CLOSE
SAXON HALL
ST OLAVES COURT
ORME LA
New West End Synagogue
ORME CT
ORME CT MS
CAROLINE PL MS
CAROLINE CL
CAROLINE HO
ORME SQUARE
5
A402
Inverness Terr Gate
B415
LINDEN MEWS
LINDEN GDNS
GUYANA
BAYSWATER ROAD
Orme Square Gate
Queensway Black Lion Gate
Notting Hill Gate
CZECH REPUBLIC
SLOVAKIA
Pav
Diana, Princess of Wales Memorial Playground
VICTORIA GDNS
BULMER MEWS
CAMPTON HILL TOWERS
A4206
IVY LODGE
NOTTING HILL GATE
WEST MALL
RABBIT ROW
A4204
PO
Farmers Mkt
Clock Tower
4
UXBRIDGE STREET
FARMER ST
JAMESON ST
NEWCOMBE STREET
KENSINGTON ML
B405
LUCERNE MS
CAMPDEN HILL GDNS
FARM PL
CALLCOTT ST
HILLGATE ST
HILLGATE PLACE
KENSINGTON PLACE
STRATHMORE GARDENS
PALACE GARDENS MEWS
LEBANON
KENSINGTON PALACE GARDENS
NEPAL
RUSSIAN FEDERATION
THE BROAD WALK
Diana, Princess of Wales Memorial Walk
246
EDGE STREET
CAMPDEN HILL MANSIONS
Fox Prim Sch
PALMERSTON HOUSE
MELBOURNE HOUSE
CAMPDEN HOUSES
PEEL STREET
PEEL PASS
CAMPDEN STREET
KENSINGTON CHURCH STREET
BRUNSWICK GARDENS
PALACE GARDENS TERRACE
BERKELEY GARDENS
WYCOMBE SQ
KENSINGTON HEIGHTS
THE MOUNT
BEDFORD GARDENS
BEDFORD GARDENS HO
3
Kensington Palace
AIRLIE GDNS
LAURIE HOUSE
SHEFFIELD TERRACE
CAMPDEN HOUSE
INVERNESS GARDENS
VICARAGE GATE
VICARAGE GARDENS
Queen Victoria Statue
PHILIPPINES
CAMPDEN HILL ROAD
TOR COURT
GLOUCESTER WALK
MELON PL
WINCHESTER COURT
VICARAGE GATE
HAMILTON HOUSE
W8
Kensington Palace Green
PALACE GREEN
80
Tenn Cts
CAMPDEN HILL
TOR GDNS
CAMPDEN HO CL
NICARAGUA
VICARAGE COURT
1 TASKER LO
2 THORNWOOD LO
HOLLY LODGE
ATKINS LODGE
THORNWOOD GDNS
OBSERVATORY GDNS
CAMPDEN GROVE
BULLINGHAM MANSIONS
CHURCH CLOSE
YORK HOUSE
ROMANIA
PALACE AVENUE
THE DIAL WLK
2
City of Westminster
Kensington & Chelsea
SHELDRAKE PLACE
DUCHESS OF BEDFORD HOUSE
ACADEMY GDNS
HORNTON STREET
GORDON PLACE
PITT ST
DUKES LANE
CARMEL CT
HOLLAND PL
YORK HOUSE PL
LANCER SQUARE
ISRAEL
CAMPDEN HILL GATE
CAMPDEN HILL COURT
HOLLAND STREET
KENSINGTON HOUSE
INGELOW HOUSE
GREGORY PL
Ashbourne Ind Sch
OLD COURT PL
P
DUCHESS OF BEDFORD'S WALK
TH
DRAYSON MEWS
OLD COURT HOUSE
AZERBAIJAN
A315
UPPER PHILLIMORE GARDENS
JORDAN
KENSINGTON
St Mary Abbots CE Prim Sch
CHURCH WK
KENSINGTON CHURCH CT
BELARUS
THE REPUBLIC OF GAMBIA
KENSINGTON COURT
PRINCE OF WALES TERR
KENSINGTON CT
MONGOLIA
1
PHILLIMORE PLACE
ARGYLL ROAD
Liby
HORNTON PLACE
Associated Newspapers Ltd
DERRY ST
YOUNG ST
KENSINGTON CT MANS
ST CHRISTOPHER & NEVIS / ST VINCENT & THE GRENADINES
DE VERE GARDENS
PHILLIMORE GARDENS
ESSEX VILLAS
HORNTON COURT
High Street Kensington
KENSINGTON SQUARE
CAMBRIDGE PL
ALBERT PL
STAFFORD TERRACE
PHILLIMORE WALK
PHILLIMORE COURT
THACKERAY ST
KENSINGTON CT PLACE
KENSINGTON CT MEWS
VIETNAM
CANNING PASSAGE
Commonwealth Institute
25
STAFFORD CT
KENSINGTON HIGH STREET
255
ESMOND CT
ANSDELL ST
ANSDELL TERR
KENSINGTON CT GDNS
DOURO PLACE
26
DE VERE COTTS
DE VERE MEWS
PL MEWS
PHILLIMORE GDNS CL
IVERNA CT
WRIGHTS LANE
ADAM AND EVE
ALLEN HO
Richmond Coll
SOUTH END
ST ALBANS MANS
TRAFALGAR GDNS
ST ALBAN'S GROVE
VICTORIA ROAD
CANNING PLACE
TROY CT
ARMENIA

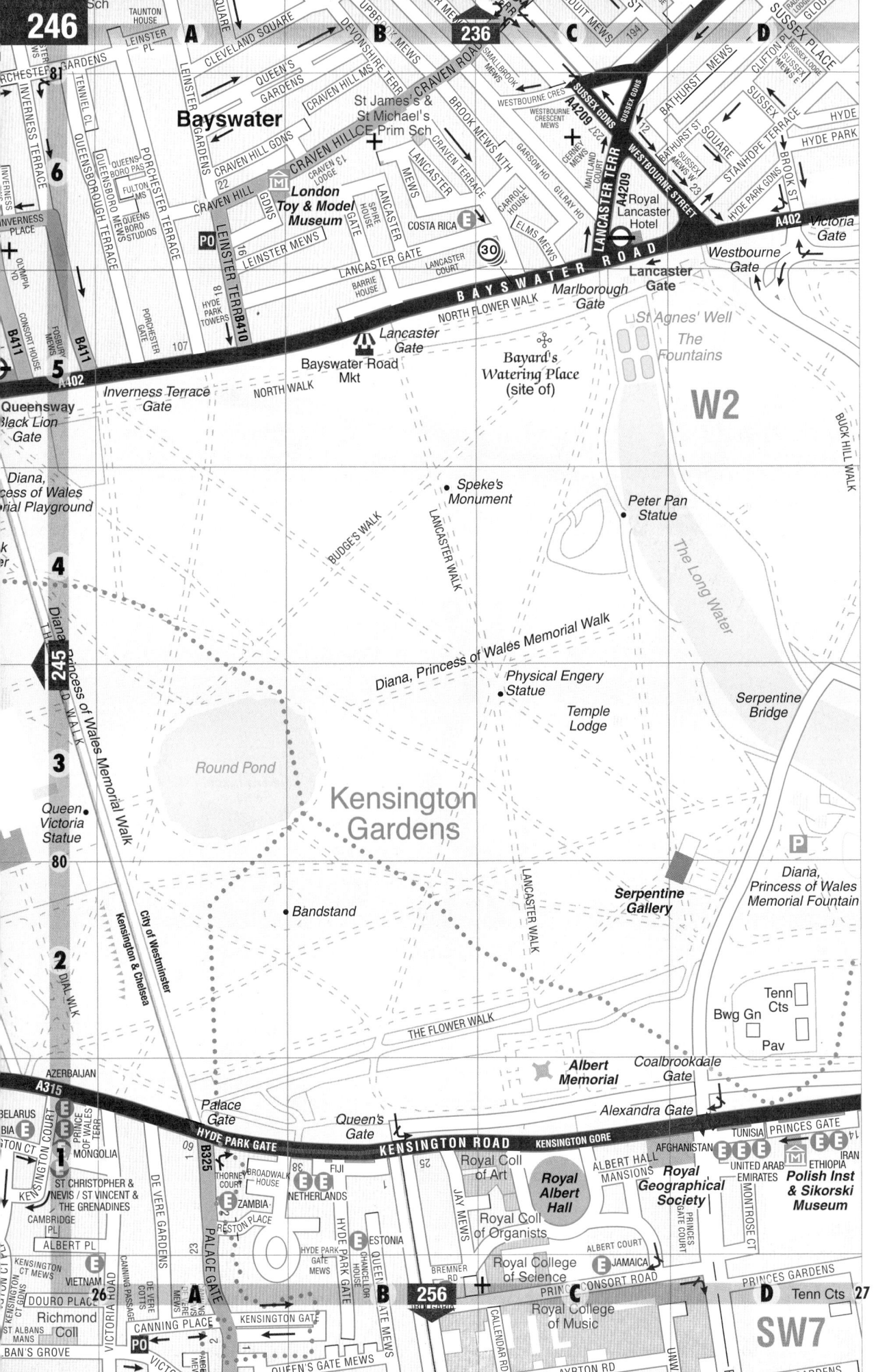

A · 236 · B · C · D · SUSSEX PLACE

Bayswater

St James's & St Michael's CE Prim Sch

London Toy & Model Museum

Costa Rica E

Royal Lancaster Hotel

BAYSWATER ROAD A402 Victoria Gate

Lancaster Gate Westbourne Gate

Bayswater Road Mkt

Lancaster Gate

NORTH FLOWER WALK Marlborough Gate

St Agnes' Well The Fountains

Queensway Black Lion Gate

Inverness Terrace Gate NORTH WALK Bayard's Watering Place (site of)

W2

Diana, Princess of Wales Memorial Playground

Speke's Monument

Peter Pan Statue

BUDGE'S WALK LANCASTER WALK

The Long Water

Diana, Princess of Wales Memorial Walk

Physical Engery Statue

Serpentine Bridge

Temple Lodge

Round Pond

Kensington Gardens

Queen Victoria Statue

Bandstand

Serpentine Gallery

Diana, Princess of Wales Memorial Fountain

LANCASTER WALK

City of Westminster Kensington & Chelsea

Tenn Cts

Bwg Gn

Pav

THE FLOWER WALK

Albert Memorial

Coalbrookdale Gate

AZERBAIJAN

A315

BELARUS E

Palace Gate

Queen's Gate

Alexandra Gate

TUNISIA PRINCES GATE

MONGOLIA

ST CHRISTOPHER & NEVIS / ST VINCENT & THE GRENADINES

HYDE PARK GATE B325

KENSINGTON ROAD KENSINGTON GORE

AFGHANISTAN

UNITED ARAB EMIRATES

ETHIOPIA

IRAN

Royal Coll of Art

Royal Albert Hall

ALBERT HALL MANSIONS

Royal Geographical Society

Polish Inst & Sikorski Museum

FIJI

ZAMBIA

NETHERLANDS

Royal Coll of Organists

ESTONIA

Royal College of Science

JAMAICA

VIETNAM

Richmond Coll

26 A

B 256 C

Royal College of Music

D 27

SW7

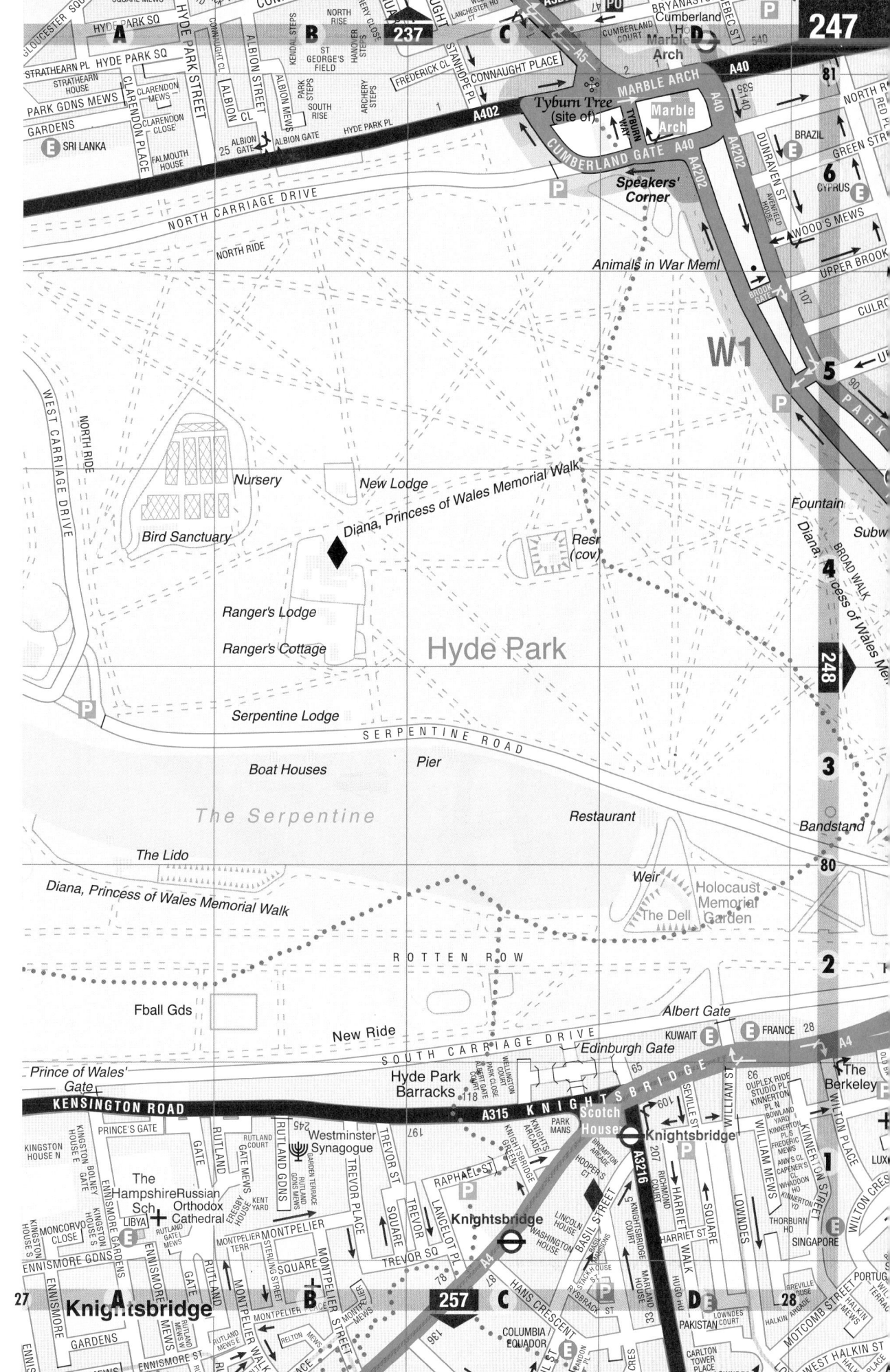
Hyde Park
The Serpentine
Marble Arch
Tyburn Tree (site of)
Speakers' Corner
Cumberland Gate
North Carriage Drive
North Ride
Animals in War Meml
W1
West Carriage Drive
Nursery
New Lodge
Diana, Princess of Wales Memorial Walk
Bird Sanctuary
Ranger's Lodge
Ranger's Cottage
Resr (cov)
Serpentine Lodge
Serpentine Road
Boat Houses
Pier
Restaurant
Bandstand
The Lido
Weir
Holocaust Memorial Garden
The Dell
Rotten Row
Fball Gds
New Ride
Albert Gate
South Carriage Drive
Edinburgh Gate
Prince of Wales' Gate
Hyde Park Barracks
Kensington Road
Knightsbridge
Scotch House
Westminster Synagogue
The Hampshire Sch
Russian Orthodox Cathedral
Fountain
Broad Walk
Park Lane
Connaught Place
Hyde Park Sq
Hyde Park Street
Albion Street
Clarendon Place
Sri Lanka
Kuwait
France
Libya
Singapore
Cyprus
Brazil
Columbia Equador
Pakistan
The Berkeley
Wilton Place
Lowndes Square
Basil Street
Hans Crescent
Montpelier Square
Trevor Square
Ennismore Gardens
Motcomb Street
West Halkin St
237
248
257
27
28

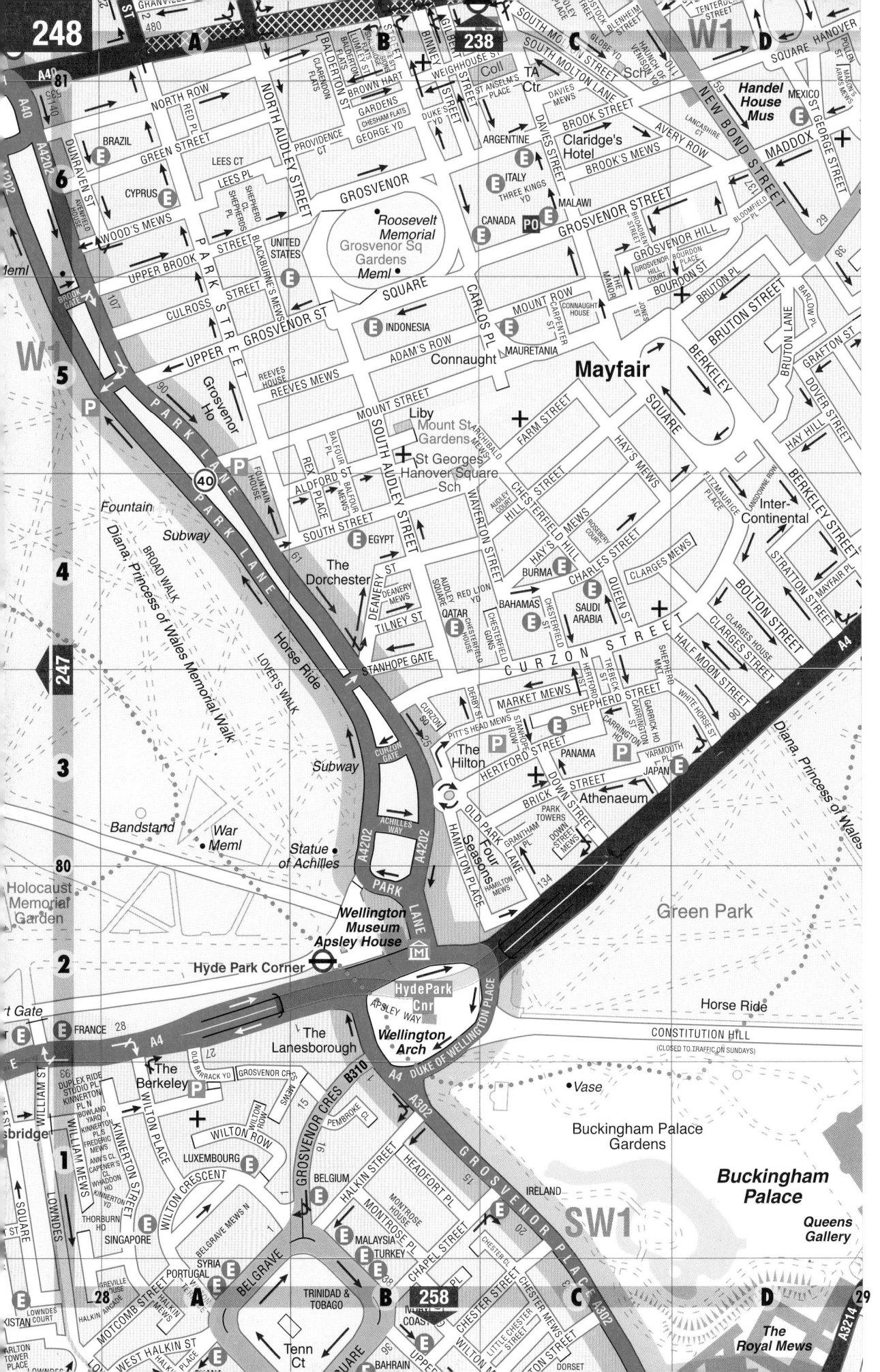
A
B
238
C
D
W1
North Row
Red Pl
North Audley Street
Balderton St
Brown Hart Gardens
Chesham Flats
George Yd
Binney Street
Weighhouse St
Gilbert Street
Duke's Yd
Coll
St Anselm's Place
TA Ctr
South Molton Lane
South Molton Street
Davies Mews
Brook Street
Avery Row
Argentine
Davies Street
Claridge's Hotel
Brook's Mews
New Bond Street
Lancashire Ct
Handel House Mus
Mexico
St George Street
Maddox
Hanover Square
Brazil
Green Street
Providence Ct
Lees Ct
Lees Pl
Dunraven St
Cyprus
Shepherds Pl
Grosvenor
Roosevelt Memorial
Grosvenor Sq Gardens
Meml
Italy
Three Kings Yd
Malawi
Canada
PO
Grosvenor Street
Grosvenor Hill
Bourdon Place
Bourdon St
Bloomfield Pl
Wood's Mews
Upper Brook Street
Park Street
United States
Blackburne's Mews
Culross Street
Brook Gate
Square
Upper Grosvenor St
Indonesia
Carlos Pl
Mount Row
Connaught House
Carpenter St
Jones St
The Manor
Bruton Pl
Bruton Street
Bruton Lane
Barlow Pl
W1
5
6
Upper
Reeves House
Reeves Mews
Adam's Row
Connaught
Mauretania
Mayfair
Berkeley Square
Grafton St
Dover Street
Hay Hill
Park Lane
Grosvenor Ho
Mount Street
Liby
Mount St Gardens
Farm Street
Archibald Mews
Hay's Mews
Balfour Pl
Rex Place
Alford St
Balfour Mews
South Audley Street
St Georges Hanover Square Sch
Fountain House
40
Fountain
Subway
Diana, Princess of Wales Memorial Walk
Broad Walk
South Street
Egypt
Audley Court
Hill Street
Chesterfield Hill
Waverton Street
Hay's Mews
Rosebery Court
Fitzmaurice Place
Lansdowne Row
Inter-Continental
Berkeley Street
4
The Dorchester
Deanery St
Deanery Mews
Tilney St
Audley Square
Red Lion Yd
Qatar
Chesterfield House
Chesterfield Gdns
Burma
Bahamas
Charles Street
Saudi Arabia
Queen St
Clarges Mews
Stratton Street
Mayfair Pl
Bolton Street
Clarges House
Clarges Street
Half Moon Street
A4
247
Horse Ride
Lover's Walk
Stanhope Gate
Curzon Street
Derby St
Hertford St
Trebeck St
Shepherd Mkt
Market Mews
Shepherd Street
Carrington St
Carrington Ho
Garrick Ho
White Horse St
Curzon Sq
Curzon Gate
Pitt's Head Mews
Stanhope Row
The Hilton
Hertford Street
Panama
Yarmouth Pl
Japan
3
Subway
Brick Street
Athenaeum
Achilles Way
A4202
Old Park Lane
Hamilton Place
Four Seasons
Park Towers
Grantham Pl
Down Street
Down Street Mews
Hamilton Mews
Bandstand
War Meml
Statue of Achilles
80
Holocaust Memorial Garden
Green Park
Diana, Princess of Wales
Wellington Museum
Apsley House
2
Hyde Park Corner
Hyde Park Cnr
Apsley Way
Wellington Arch
Duke of Wellington Place
Horse Ride
Constitution Hill
(Closed to traffic on Sundays)
France
The Lanesborough
The Berkeley
Old Barrack Yd
Grosvenor Cres Mews
B310
A302
Vase
William St
Duplex Ride
Studio Pl
Kinnerton Pl N
Bowland Yard
Kinnerton Pl S
Frederic Mews
Ann's Cl
Capener's Cl
Whaddon Ho
Kinnerton Yd
Wilton Place
Wilton Row
Pembroke Cl
Grosvenor Cres
Buckingham Palace Gardens
1
William Mews
Kinnerton Street
Luxembourg
Wilton Crescent
Belgium
Halkin Street
Headfort Pl
Montrose House
Montrose Pl
Grosvenor Place
Ireland
Buckingham Palace
Queens Gallery
SW1
Lowndes Square
Thorburn Ho
Singapore
Belgrave Mews N
Syria
Malaysia
Turkey
Chapel Street
Chester Cl
Portugal
Greville House
Belgrave
Trinidad & Tobago
258
Chester Street
Chester Mews
28
A
B
C
D
29
Motcomb Street
Halkin Arcade
Halkin Mews
Lowndes Court
West Halkin St
Tenn Ct
Little Chester Street
Wilton Mews
Bahrain
Dorset
The Royal Mews
A3214

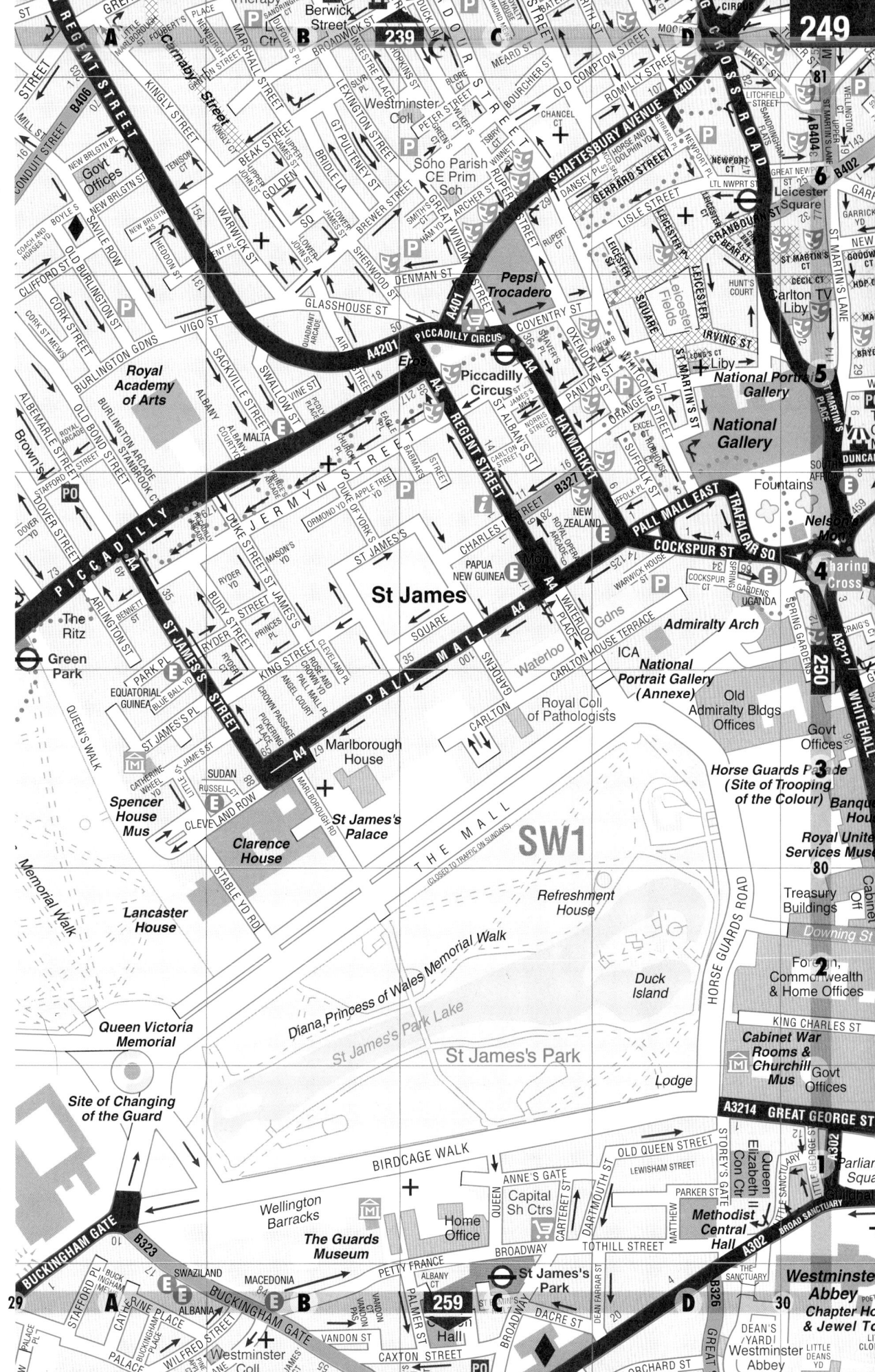

Regent Street
Carnaby Street
Kingly Street
Marshall Street
Broadwick St
Berwick Street
Wardour Street
Dean Street
Frith St
Old Compton Street
Romilly Street
Charing Cross Road
Shaftesbury Avenue
A401
Gerrard Street
Lisle Street
Leicester Square
Leicester Fields
Cranbourn St
Irving St
Westminster Coll
Soho Parish CE Prim Sch
Golden Sq
Beak Street
Lexington Street
Gt Pulteney St
Brewer Street
Bridle La
Great Windmill St
Rupert St
Denman St
Glasshouse St
Sherwood St
Pepsi Trocadero
Coventry St
Piccadilly Circus
A4201
Eros
Haymarket
Oxendon St
Whitcomb Street
Panton St
Orange St
Suffolk St
National Portrait Gallery
National Gallery
Fountains
Trafalgar Sq
Nelson's Mon
Charing Cross
Pall Mall East
Cockspur St
Govt Offices
New Burlington Pl
Savile Row
Old Burlington St
Cork Street
Clifford St
Burlington Gdns
Vigo St
Sackville Street
Swallow St
Vine St
Royal Academy of Arts
Albany
Malta
Albemarle Street
Old Bond Street
Burlington Arcade
Stafford St
Dover Street
Brown's
PO
Piccadilly
Jermyn Street
Duke Street St James's
Ryder Yd
Bury Street
Ryder Street
Mason's Yd
St James's
St James Square
St James's Street
King Street
Arlington St
Bennett St
The Ritz
Green Park
Park Pl
Blue Ball Yd
Equatorial Guinea
St James's Pl
Charles II Street
Papua New Guinea
New Zealand
Waterloo Place
Waterloo Gdns
Carlton House Terrace
Carlton Gardens
Pall Mall
Marlborough House
Uganda
Admiralty Arch
ICA
National Portrait Gallery (Annexe)
Old Admiralty Bldgs Offices
Royal Coll of Pathologists
Horse Guards Parade (Site of Trooping of the Colour)
Whitehall
Banqueting Hous
Royal United Services Mus
Treasury Buildings
Cabinet Off
Downing St
Foreign, Commonwealth & Home Offices
King Charles St
Cabinet War Rooms & Churchill Mus
Govt Offices
Great George St
A3214
Parliament Squ
Queen's Walk
Catherine Wheel Yd
Sudan
Russell Ct
Cleveland Row
Spencer House Mus
Clarence House
St James's Palace
Marlborough Rd
Stable Yd Rd
Lancaster House
The Mall (closed to traffic on Sundays)
SW1
Refreshment House
Memorial Walk
Diana, Princess of Wales Memorial Walk
Duck Island
Horse Guards Road
St James's Park Lake
St James's Park
Lodge
Queen Victoria Memorial
Site of Changing of the Guard
Birdcage Walk
Old Queen Street
Lewisham Street
Queen Elizabeth II Con Ctr
Methodist Central Hall
Storey's Gate
Parker St
Matthew Parker St
Queen Anne's Gate
Capital Sh Ctrs
Carteret St
Dartmouth St
Tothill Street
Broadway
Wellington Barracks
The Guards Museum
Home Office
Buckingham Gate
B323
Petty France
Palmer St
Vandon St
Caxton Street
Caxton Hall
St James's Park
Dacre St
Westminster Abbey
Chapter House & Jewel Tower
Broad Sanctuary
A302
Dean's Yard
Great Smith St
Swaziland
Macedonia
Albania
Stafford Pl
Catherine Place
Wilfred Street
Westminster Coll
Little Deans Yd
239
259
250

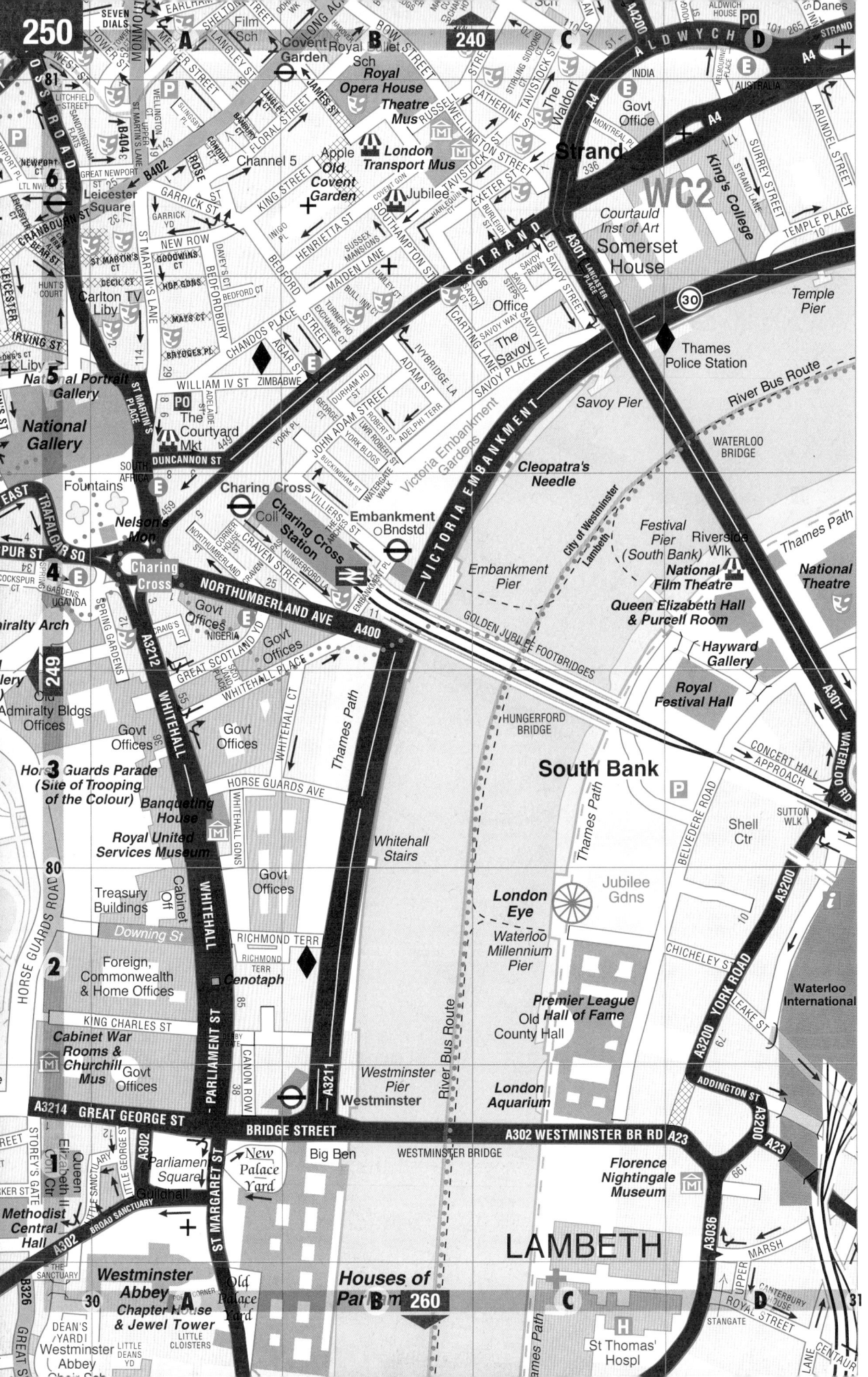

240
260
249
Covent Garden
Royal Ballet Sch
Royal Opera House
Theatre Mus
London Transport Mus
Apple
Old Covent Garden
Jubilee
Channel 5
Leicester Square
Carlton TV Liby
National Portrait Gallery
National Gallery
The Courtyard Mkt
Fountains
Nelson's Mon
Charing Cross
Charing Cross Station
Embankment
Bndstd
The Waldorf
Strand
Aldwych
India
Australia
Govt Office
WC2
King's College
Courtauld Inst of Art
Somerset House
Temple Pier
Thames Police Station
The Savoy
Savoy Pier
River Bus Route
Waterloo Bridge
Cleopatra's Needle
Victoria Embankment Gardens
Victoria Embankment
Embankment Pier
Festival Pier (South Bank)
Riverside Wlk
National Film Theatre
National Theatre
Queen Elizabeth Hall & Purcell Room
Hayward Gallery
Royal Festival Hall
Golden Jubilee Footbridges
Hungerford Bridge
South Bank
Thames Path
Shell Ctr
Jubilee Gdns
London Eye
Waterloo Millennium Pier
Premier League Hall of Fame
Old County Hall
London Aquarium
Waterloo International
Admiralty Arch
Old Admiralty Bldgs Offices
Govt Offices
Horse Guards Parade (Site of Trooping of the Colour)
Banqueting House
Royal United Services Museum
Treasury Buildings
Cabinet Off
Downing St
Foreign, Commonwealth & Home Offices
Cenotaph
Cabinet War Rooms & Churchill Mus
Whitehall Stairs
Westminster Pier
Westminster
Big Ben
Westminster Bridge
New Palace Yard
Parliament Square
Guildhall
Queen Elizabeth II Con Ctr
Methodist Central Hall
Westminster Abbey
Chapter House & Jewel Tower
Old Palace Yard
Houses of Parliament
Westminster Abbey Choir Sch
Florence Nightingale Museum
LAMBETH
St Thomas' Hospl
Whitehall
Parliament St
St Margaret St
Great George St
Bridge Street
A302 Westminster Br Rd
Northumberland Ave
Trafalgar Sq
Charing Cross Road
St Martin's Lane
York Road
Waterloo Rd
Belvedere Road
Concert Hall Approach
Horse Guards Road
Horse Guards Ave
Whitehall Place
Great Scotland Yd
Duncannon St
William IV St
Chandos Place
Bedford St
Southampton St
Wellington St
Savoy Street
Lancaster Place
Surrey Street
Arundel Street
Temple Place
Villiers St
Craven Street
John Adam Street
Adam St
King Street
Garrick St
Floral Street
Long Acre
Bow Street
Tavistock St
Exeter St
Henrietta St
Maiden Lane
Richmond Terr
King Charles St
Canon Row
Broad Sanctuary
Storey's Gate
Chicheley St
Addington St
Leake St
Upper Marsh
Royal Street
Stangate

RIVER THAMES
King's Reach
CITY OF LONDON
Blackfriars Station
Blackfriars Millennium Pier
BLACKFRIARS BRIDGE
BLACKFRIARS UNDERPASS
Inner Temple
Middle Temple
Temple
HQS Wellington
Chrysanthemum
President
Oxo Tower
Bankside Art Gal
Tate Modern
Mermaid Theatre
STAMFORD STREET
BLACKFRIARS ROAD
UPPER GROUND
THE CUT
WATERLOO ROAD
Waterloo Station
Waterloo East
Southwark
Lambeth North
BFI London Imax Cinema
King's Coll Univ
Schiller Int Univ
The London Nautical Sch
EF Int Language Sch
Govt Office
Southwark Coll
Friars Prim Sch
London Amb Service HQ
St George's Cathedral RC J & I Sch
Crown Court
Grand Vitesse Ind Est
GMTV
UNION ST
BOROUGH ROAD
WESTMINSTER BRIDGE ROAD
ST GEORGE'S CIRCUS
SE1
241
252
261

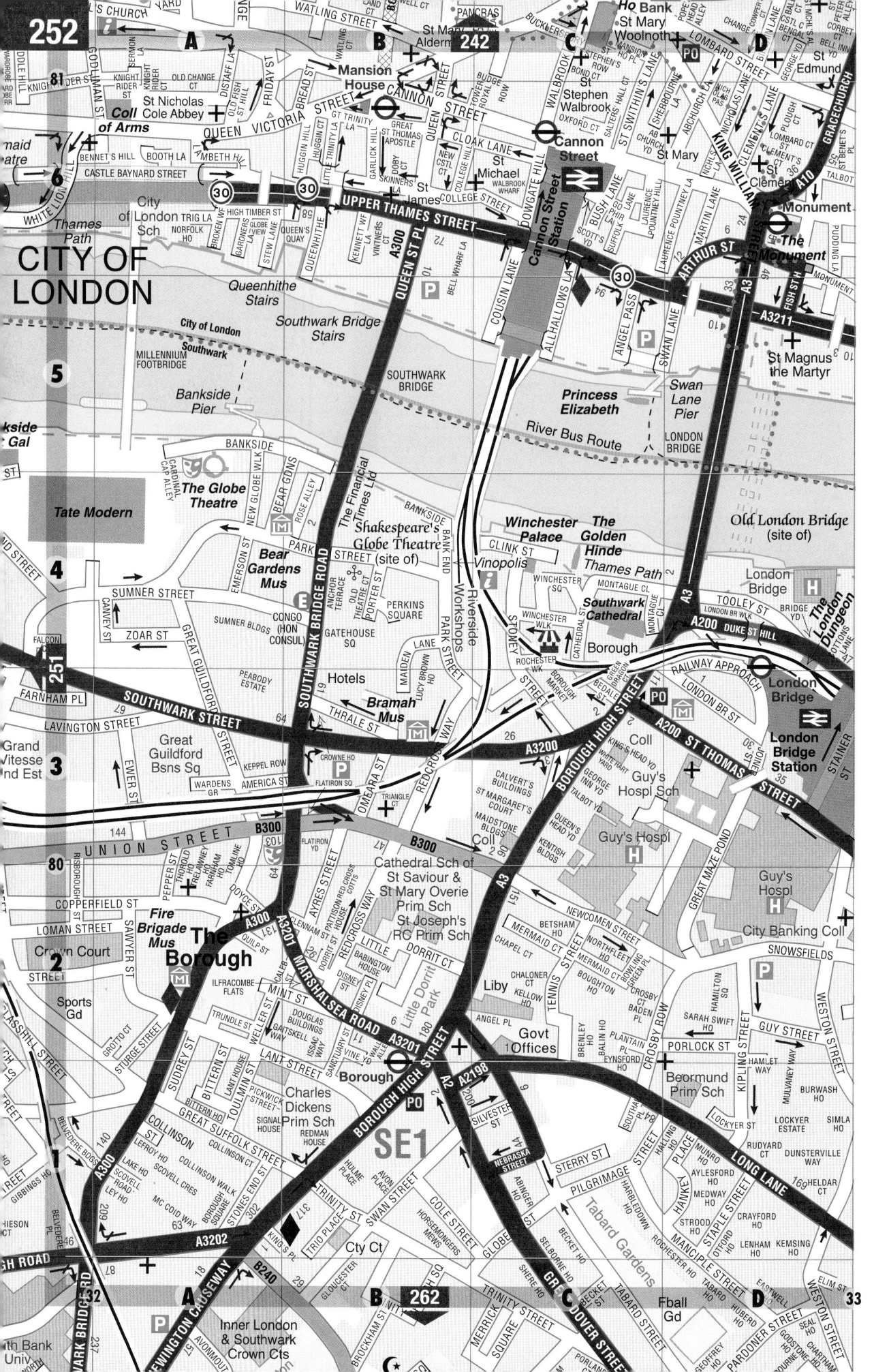
242
262
251
CITY OF LONDON
SE1
A
B
C
D
6
5
4
3
2
1
81
80
32
33
Watling Street
St Mary Aldermary
Bank
St Mary Woolnoth
Lombard Street
St Edmund
Gracechurch
Mansion House
Cannon Street
Queen Victoria Street
St Nicholas Cole Abbey
Coll of Arms
Queen Street
Cloak Lane
St Stephen Walbrook
Walbrook
Cannon Street
Cannon Street Station
St Michael
St James
Upper Thames Street
St Swithin's Lane
Abchurch La
St Mary
Nicholas Lane
King William Street
Clement's Lane
St Clement
Monument
The Monument
Fish St H
Pudding La
Arthur St
Castle Baynard Street
Bennet's Hill
Booth La
Lambeth Hill
White Lion Hill
Thames Path
City of London Sch
High Timber St
Queenhithe
Queenhithe Stairs
Southwark Bridge Stairs
Queen St Pl
A300
A3
A3211
A10
Cousin Lane
Allhallows La
Angel Pass
Swan Lane
St Magnus the Martyr
City of London
Southwark
Millennium Footbridge
Bankside Pier
Southwark Bridge
Princess Elizabeth
River Bus Route
Swan Lane Pier
London Bridge
Bankside
The Globe Theatre
Tate Modern
New Globe Wlk
Bear Gdns
Rose Alley
The Financial Times Ltd
Shakespeare's Globe Theatre (site of)
Winchester Palace
The Golden Hinde
Old London Bridge (site of)
Clink St
Vinopolis
Thames Path
Park Street
Bear Gardens Mus
Emerson St
Sumner Street
Southwark Bridge Road
Riverside Workshops
Winchester Sq
Montague Cl
Southwark Cathedral
Borough
London Bridge
Tooley St
The London Dungeon
Duke St Hill
A200
Sumner Bldgs
Congo (Hon Consul)
Gatehouse Sq
Perkins Square
Anchor Terrace
Old Theatre Ct
Porter St
Canvey St
Zoar St
Great Guildford Street
Peabody Estate
Hotels
Maiden Lane
Lucy Brown Ho
Stoney Street
Rochester Wk
Borough Market
Green Dragon Ct
Bedale St
Railway Approach
London Br St
London Bridge Station
Stainer St
Farnham Pl
Southwark Street
Lavington Street
Thrale St
Bramah Mus
Redcross Way
A3200
Borough High Street
Coll
King's Head Yd
White Hart Yard
George Inn Yd
Talbot Yd
St Thomas Street
Guy's Hospl Sch
Joiner St
Grand Vitesse Ind Est
Great Guildford Bsns Sq
Ewer St
Keppel Row
Wardens Gr
America St
Crowne Ho
Flatiron Sq
Omeara St
Triangle Ct
Calvert's Buildings
St Margaret's Court
Maidstone Bldgs
Queen's Head Yd
Kentish Bldgs
Guy's Hospl
Great Maze Pond
Union Street
B300
Flatiron Yd
Cathedral Sch of St Saviour & St Mary Overie Prim Sch
St Joseph's RC Prim Sch
Risborough St
Pepper St
Copperfield St
Loman Street
Sawyer St
Crown Court
Fire Brigade Mus
The Borough
Doyce St
Quilp St
A3201
Marshalsea Road
Ayres Street
Redcross Way
Little Dorrit Ct
Little Dorrit Park
Newcomen Street
Betsham Ho
Mermaid Ct
Chapel Ct
Tennis Street
Bowling Green Pl
Snowsfields
City Banking Coll
Sports Gd
Ilfracombe Flats
Mint St
Douglas Buildings
Disney Pl
Liby
Chaloner Ct
Kellow Ho
Angel Pl
Govt Offices
Crosby Row
Sarah Swift Ho
Hamilton Sq
Guy Street
Weston Street
Porlock St
Kipling Street
Mulvaney Way
Hamlet Way
Burwash Ho
Trundle St
Weller St
Lant Street
Sudrey St
Bittern St
Toulmin St
Pickwick Street
Charles Dickens Prim Sch
Borough
Sturge Street
Grotto Ct
Gaitskell Way
Issac Way
Sanctuary St
Vine Yd
A2198
A2
Silvester St
Beormund Prim Sch
Lockyer St
Lockyer Estate
Simla Ho
Rudyard Ct
Dunsterville Way
Heldar Ct
Long Lane
Great Suffolk Street
Collinson St
Collinson Walk
Collinson Ct
Scovell Cres
Scovell Road
Lefroy Ho
Lake Ho
Ley Ho
Mc Coid Way
Borough Square
Stones End St
Signal House
Redman House
Nebraska Street
Sterry St
Pilgrimage Street
Harbledown Ho
Hankey Place
Munro Ho
Aylesford Ho
Medway Ho
Strood Ho
Staple Street
Crayford Ho
Otford Ho
Lenham Ho
Kemsing Ho
Rochester Ho
Mancipe Street
Tabard Gardens
Abinger Ho
Selborne Ho
Becket Ho
Hulme Place
Avon Place
Swan Street
Cole Street
Horsemongers Mews
Trinity St
Trio Place
King's Pl
A3202
City Ct
Belvedere Bdgs
Belvedere Pl
Gibbings Ho
B240
Newington Causeway
Southwark Bridge Rd
Globe St
Great Dover Street
Trinity Street
Merrick Square
Becket St
Tabard Street
Fball Gd
Hubert Ho
Tabard Ho
Eastwell Ho
Pardoner Street
Weston Street
Elim St
Inner London & Southwark Crown Cts
Gloucester Ct
Brockham St
Avonmouth
South Bank Univ
Lambeth Hill
Old Change Ct
Godliman St
Knightrider St
Distaff La
Friday St
Bread St
Huggin Hill
Little Trinity La
Garlick Hill
Great St Thomas Apostle
Dowgate Hill
College Street
College Hill
Bush Lane
Suffolk Lane
Laurence Pountney Hill
Martin Lane
Skinners La
Kennet Wf La
Vintners Pl
Bell Wharf La
Broken Wf
Trig La
Stew Lane
Queenhithe
Norfolk Ho
Lombard Ct
Plough Ct
Talbot Yd
Monument St
Farnham Ho
Tomline Ho
Thorold Ho
Trelawney Ho
Caleb St
Dorrit St
Pattison Ho
Babington House
Little Dorrit Ct
Northfleet Ho
Boughton Ho
Crosby Ct
Baden Pl
Brenley Ho
Balin Ho
Eynsford Ho
Plantain Pl
Southall Pl
Falcon Cl
Glasshill Street
Hieson Ct

243
Metropolitan Univ
INDIA ST
CLARE ST
MINORIES
GUINNESS COURT
MANSEL STREET
English Martyrs RC Prim Sch
SCARBOROUGH ST
SOUTH TENTER ST
W TENTER ST
81
LEADENHALL MKT
FENCHURCH AV
BILLITER ST
LIME STREET
LLOYD'S AVE
JEWRY ST
VINE STREET
HAYDON ST
IVERGH CT
HAYDON WLK
PORTSOKEN ST
BULL'S HEAD PAS
SHIP TAVERN PAS
CULLUM ST
FENCHURCH STREET
LONDON ST
FENCHURCH PL
Fenchurch Street Station
FRIARS
CROSSWALL
AMERICA SQ
GOODMAN'S YD
PRESCOT ST
YEOMAN'S YD
CHAMBER ST
EC3
BRABANT CT
PHILPOT LA
ROOD LA
St Margaret Pattens
PLANTATION LA
MINCING LANE
DUNSTER CT
STAR ALLEY
HART ST
CRUTCHED
SAVAGE GARDENS
COOPER'S ROW
PEPYS STREET
St Olave's
SEETHING LANE
MARK LANE
MINSTER CT
EASTCHEAP
PO
St Mary -at-Hill
BOTOLPH LA
BOTOLPH ALLEY
LOVAT LA
ST MARY AT HILL
IDOL LA
GREAT TOWER STREET
ST DUNSTAN'S ALLEY
ST DUNSTAN'S HILL
ST DUNSTAN'S LA
Tower Hill
London Wall
CRESCENT
HAMMETT ST
Tower Gateway
Tower Hill
SHORTER ST
A1211
A1202
ROYAL MINT ST
CARTWRIGHT ST
ST MARY GRACES COURT
ROYAL MINT PL
BLUE ANCHOR YARD
JOHN FISHER ST
PEABODY ESTATE
SWAN PASSAGE
6
MUSCOVY ST
TRINITY SQUARE
Trinity Sq Gdns
TRINITY PL
Univ
BYWARD ST
TOWER HILL A3211
100
30
LOWER THAMES ST
All-Hallows
TOWER PL W
TOWER PL E
GLOUCESTER CT
TOWER HILL
Custom House
OLD BILLINGSGATE WLK
Tenn Ct
St Peter ad Vincula
Royal Fusiliers Mus
The Tower
The Royal Armouries
St John's Chapel
A1203
EAST SMITHFIELD
CROFTS ST
VICTORIA COURT
5
COMMODITY QUAY
E1
West Dock
ST KATHARINE'S WAY
TOWER BR APPROACH
A100
City of London
Tower Hamlets
PETTY WALES
Pontoon
RIVER THAMES
Tower Stairs
Tower Millennium Pier
Traitors Gate
Thames Path
London Bridge City Pier
River Bus Route
HMS Belfast
TOWER BRIDGE
IVORY HOUSE
St Katharine Docks
East Dock
MEWS ST
4
MAUDLINS GREEN
Jetty
St Katharine's Pier
Dock Entrance
Upper Pool
Hay's Galleria
HAY'S LANE
COUNTER ST
BATTLE BRIDGE LANE
ENGLISH GROUNDS
Crown Court
Thames Path
City Hall
Britain at War Experience
West India Dock Pier 4km
London City Airport 11km
Greenwich Pier 5km
MILLERS WHARF HO
118
Jetty
Horselydown Old Stairs
London Bridge City Park
3
Butler's Wharf Pier
BOILERHOUSE
MALT MILL
BUTLER'S WHARF W
SHAD THAMES
WESTON ST
SHIPWRIGHT YD
A2205
TOOLEY STREET
OXFORD DR
BRAIDWOOD ST
ABBOTS LANE
BURSAR ST
MAGDALEN ST
GIBBON'S RENTS
HOLYROOD STREET
VINE LANE
173
WEAVER'S LANE
POTTERS FIELDS
Lambeth Tertiary Coll (Tower Bridge Centre)
TOWER BRIDGE RD
226
HORSELYDOWN LANE
ADMIRALS CT
COMPASS COURT
TOWER BR PIAZZA
KNOT HOUSE
BREWERY SQUARE
COPPERAGE CT
EAGLE WHARF
ASSAM
JASMIN
COPPER ROW
LAPSANG
PEKOE
SPICE QUAY HEIGHTS
Jetty
Wharves
80
A200
SHAND STREET
BARNHAM STREET
DEVON MANSIONS
LEWES HOUSE
DRUID ST
A2207
ST OLAVE'S ESTATE
GREAT YD
185
A100 TOWER BRIDGE RD
204
Ct
CANDISHE HO
KNIGHTS HO
TOWER BRIDGE SQ
WHITSTERS HO
STREET
HORSELYDOWN MANS
RAYNE CT
WHELDON CT
ALUMNI CT
WOLESON CT
STREET
GAINSFORD ST
THAMES HTS
MAGUIRE ST
Design Museum
CORIANDER CT
CINNAMON WHARF
2
BERMONDSEY
MELIOR ST
FENNING ST
VINEGAR YD
MELIOR PL
A200
CRUCIFIX LANE
35
20
Glass House
HARDWIDGE ST
SHIP AND MERMAID ROW
GUINNESS TRUST BLDGS
KIRBY GR
Snowsfields Prim Sch
CARMARTHEN PL
BLACK SWAN YD
TYER'S ESTATE
WHITE'S GROUNDS ESTATE
WHITE'S GROUNDS
CHERRY TREE TERR
BRUNSWICK CT
A2207
BOSS ST
BOSS HO
LAFONE ST
QUEEN ELIZABETH ST
RAVEN WHARF
TRIANGLE HOUSE
THREE OAK LA
JUBILEE YD
CURLEW
THE CIRCLE
BUTLERS & COLONIAL WHARF
SAFFRON WHARF
JAVA WHARF
SHAD THAMES
ST ANDREW'S WHARF
St Saviour's Dock
NEW CONCORDIA WHARF
ST SAVIOUR'S WHARF
VOGANS MILL
PROVIDENCE SQ
FAIR STREET
TOOLEY STREET
A100
Tower Bridge Prim Sch
COOPERS LODGE
TOWER WHARF
MILLENNIUM SQ
DOCKHEAD WHARF
MILL STREET
HOBB'S CT
FARTHING ALLEY
JACOB ST
PETER BUTLER HO
Leathermarket Com Park
TYERS GATE
BERMONDSEY STREET
The Fashion & Design Museum
MALTINGS PL
ROPER LA
ST JOHN'S ESTATE
COXSON WAY
DEVON MANS
287
SCOTT'S SUFFERANCE WHARF
WOLSELEY ST
DOMBEY HO
Leathermarket Gdns
PO
TANNER HO
LEATHERMARKET ST
A2207
A200
132
DOCKHEAD
PO
TAPLEY HO
COPPERFIELD HO
PARKERS ROW
St Joseph's RC Jun & Inf Sch
LEATHERMARKET COURT
MOROCCO STREET
Tenn Cts
TANNER
ARCHIE ST
163
STREET
DRUID STREET
DEVON MANSIONS
PHOENIX WHARF RD
SWEENEY CRES
JAMAICA ROAD
PARKER'S ROW
WADE HO
NICKLEBY HO
BARDELL HO
1
BERMONDSEY LEATHER MKT
LAMB WLK
142
HATCHERS MEWS
FLORIN CT
POPE ST
VESTA CT
HESTIA HO
ANTONINE HTS
CITY WLK
ATHENA CT
ROYAL OAK YD
BELL YARD MEWS
COLOUR HO
NEWHAM'S ROW
PURBROOK ESTATE
RILEY ROAD
MALTBY STREET
MILLSTREAM RD
WHARTON HO
STANWORTH ST
GEDLING PL
ARNOLD ESTATE
NECKINGER ST
LUPIN PT
DARNAY HOUSE
33
ELIM ESTATE
208
A
BLUE LION PL
MARKET YD MEWS
255
Caledonian Market
B
BRIDGE ROAD
PURBROOK ST
ST LAWRENCE HOUSE
263
C
PRESTON HOUSE
MARLOW HOUSE
RUFUS HOUSE
D
B202
168
34
CARTON HOUSE
GILES HOUSE
ELIM ST
ARCHDALE HO
A2198
B202
STEVENS ST
CHARLES HO
ATTILBURGH HOUSE
BROMLEIGH HOUSE
PO
ABBEY STREET
BRETON HO
TA Ctr
MARINE ST

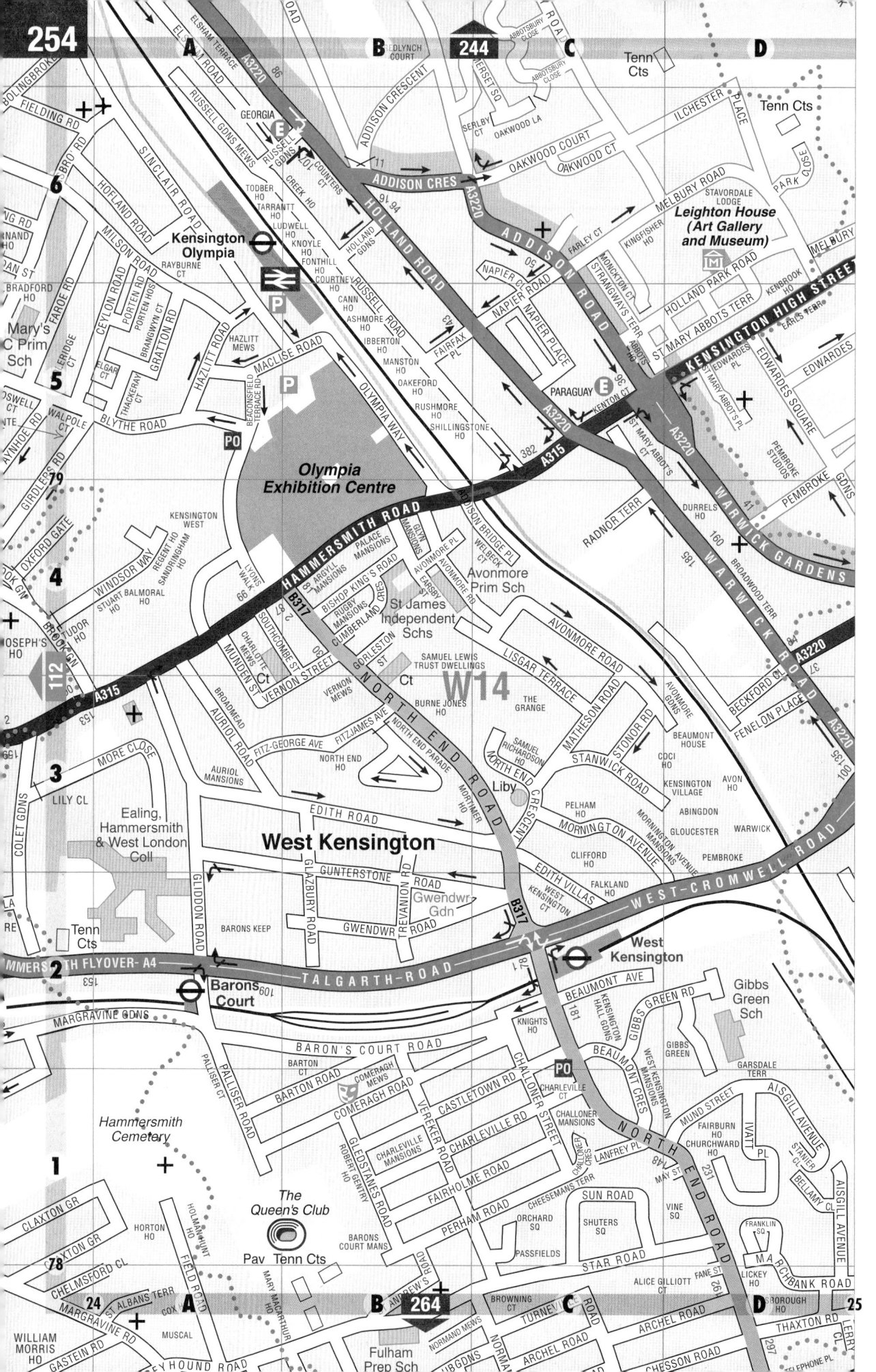
A
B
C
D
244
264
112
1
2
3
4
5
6
Kensington Olympia
Olympia Exhibition Centre
Leighton House (Art Gallery and Museum)
West Kensington
W14
Ealing, Hammersmith & West London Coll
Avonmore Prim Sch
St James Independent Schs
Gibbs Green Sch
Mary's C Prim Sch
The Queen's Club
Hammersmith Cemetery
Fulham Prep Sch
Barons Court
West Kensington
HAMMERSMITH ROAD
HOLLAND ROAD
ADDISON ROAD
ADDISON CRES
ADDISON CRESCENT
KENSINGTON HIGH STREET
WARWICK ROAD
WARWICK GARDENS
NORTH END ROAD
WEST CROMWELL ROAD
TALGARTH ROAD
HAMMERSMITH FLYOVER A4
RUSSELL ROAD
OLYMPIA WAY
MACLISE ROAD
BLYTHE ROAD
SINCLAIR ROAD
HOFLAND ROAD
MILSON ROAD
CEYLON ROAD
GRATTON RD
HAZLITT ROAD
AVONMORE ROAD
LISGAR TERRACE
MATHESON ROAD
STANWICK ROAD
EDITH ROAD
GUNTERSTONE ROAD
GWENDWR ROAD
GLAZBURY ROAD
GLIDDON ROAD
BARON'S COURT ROAD
COMERAGH ROAD
CHARLEVILLE RD
CHALLONER STREET
FAIRHOLME ROAD
PERHAM ROAD
STAR ROAD
SUN ROAD
MARGRAVINE GDNS
MARGRAVINE RD
PALLISER ROAD
EDWARDES SQUARE
MELBURY ROAD
ILCHESTER PLACE
OAKWOOD COURT
HOLLAND PARK ROAD
ST MARY ABBOTS TERR
PEMBROKE GDNS
BEAUMONT AVE
BEAUMONT CRES
GIBBS GREEN RD
AISGILL AVENUE
MARCHBANK ROAD
ARCHEL ROAD
CHESSON ROAD
A3220
A315
B317
A4

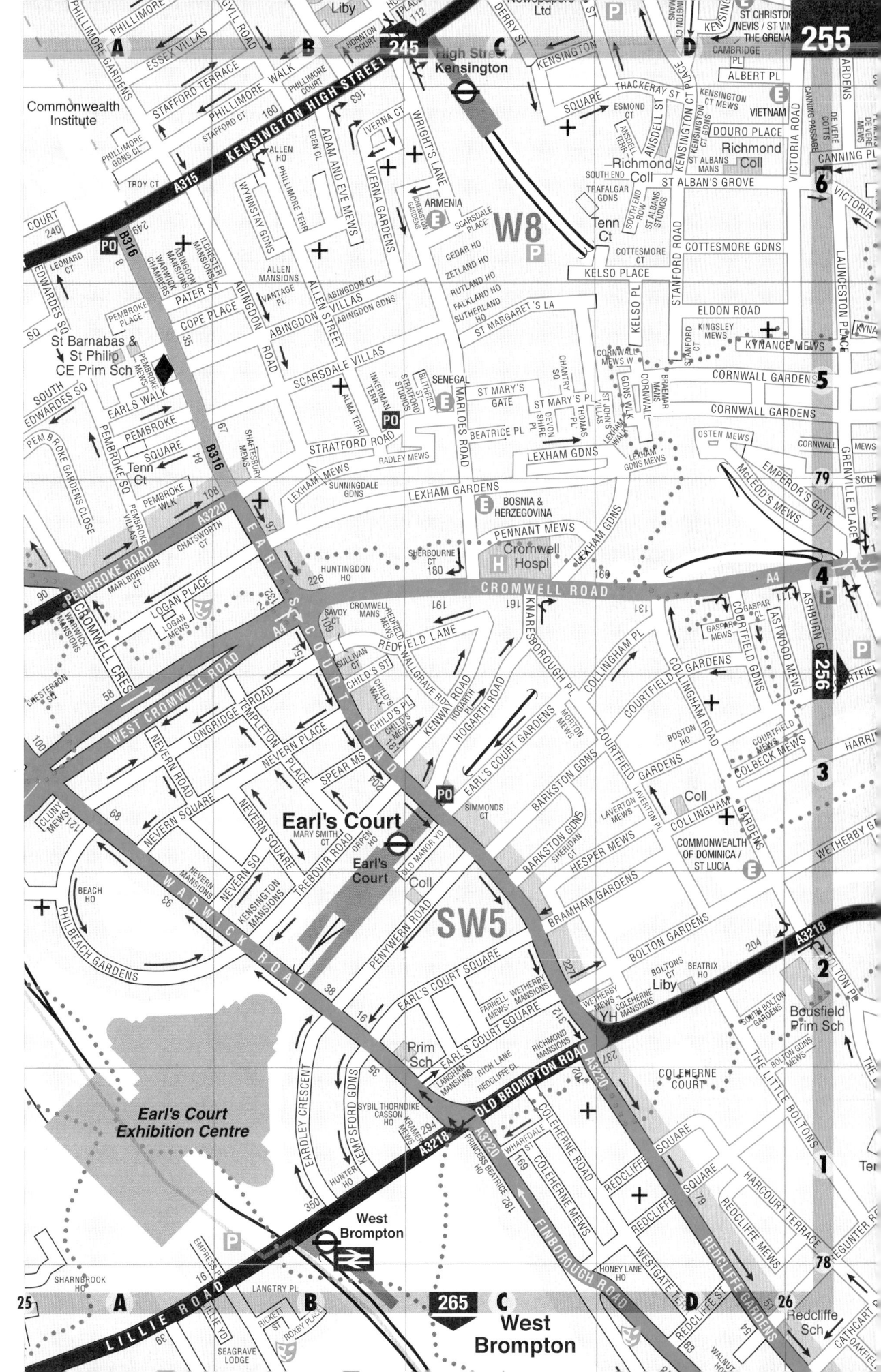
A
B
C
D
245
High Street Kensington
Commonwealth Institute
KENSINGTON HIGH STREET
A315
PHILLIMORE GARDENS
PHILLIMORE WALK
ESSEX VILLAS
STAFFORD TERRACE
STAFFORD CT
PHILLIMORE COURT
HORNTON COURT
PHILLIMORE GDNS CL
TROY CT
ALLEN HO
PHILLIMORE TERR
WYNNSTAY GDNS
ADAM AND EVE MEWS
IVERNA CT
IVERNA GARDENS
EDEN CL
WRIGHT'S LANE
ARMENIA
CHENISTON GARDENS
SCARSDALE PLACE
W8
KENSINGTON SQUARE
THACKERAY ST
ESMOND CT
ANSDELL ST
ANSDELL TERR
KENSINGTON CT PLACE
KENSINGTON CT MEWS
VIETNAM
DOURO PLACE
Richmond Coll
ALBERT PL
CAMBRIDGE PL
VICTORIA ROAD
CANNING PASSAGE
DE VERE COTTS
CANNING PL
ST ALBANS MANS
ST ALBAN'S GROVE
SOUTH END
TRAFALGAR GDNS
SOUTH END ROW
ST ALBANS STUDIOS
Tenn Ct
COTTESMORE CT
COTTESMORE GDNS
STANFORD ROAD
KELSO PLACE
KELSO PL
ELDON ROAD
KINGSLEY MEWS
STANFORD CT
KYNANCE MEWS
LAUNCESTON PLACE
COURT
LEONARD CT
EDWARDES SQ
B316
ABINGDON MANSIONS
WARWICK CHAMBERS
ILCHESTER MANSIONS
PATER ST
ALLEN MANSIONS
VANTAGE PL
ABINGDON CT
ABINGDON VILLAS
ABINGDON GDNS
ABINGDON ROAD
ALLEN STREET
PEMBROKE PLACE
COPE PLACE
CEDAR HO
ZETLAND HO
RUTLAND HO
FALKLAND HO
SUTHERLAND HO
ST MARGARET'S LA
St Barnabas & St Philip CE Prim Sch
PEMBROKE MEWS
EARLS WALK
SOUTH EDWARDES SQ
SCARSDALE VILLAS
INKERMAN TERR
STRATFORD STUDIOS
BLITHFIELD ST
SENEGAL
MARLOES ROAD
ST MARY'S GATE
CHANTRY SQ
ST MARY'S PL
DEVONSHIRE PL
THOMAS PL
ST JOHN'S VILLAS
CORNWALL MEWS W
GDNS WLK
CORNWALL
BRAEMAR MANS
CORNWALL GARDENS
PEMBROKE SQUARE
PEMBROKE SQ
PEMBROKE GARDENS CLOSE
SHAFTESBURY MEWS
ALMA TERR
STRATFORD ROAD
RADLEY MEWS
BEATRICE PL
LEXHAM GDNS
LEXHAM WALK
LEXHAM GDNS MEWS
OSTEN MEWS
MCLEOD'S MEWS
EMPEROR'S GATE
GRENVILLE PLACE
PEMBROKE WLK
PEMBROKE VILLAS
LEXHAM MEWS
SUNNINGDALE GDNS
LEXHAM GARDENS
BOSNIA & HERZEGOVINA
PENNANT MEWS
A3220
CHATSWORTH CT
PEMBROKE ROAD
MARLBOROUGH CT
HUNTINGDON HO
SHERBOURNE CT
Cromwell Hospl
CROMWELL ROAD
A4
EARL'S COURT ROAD
LOGAN PLACE
LOGAN MEWS
CROMWELL CRES
WARWICK MANSIONS
SAVOY CT
CROMWELL MANS
REDFIELD MEWS
REDFIELD LANE
KNARESBOROUGH PL
COLLINGHAM PL
COURTFIELD GDNS
GASPAR CL
GASPAR MEWS
ASTWOOD MEWS
ASHBURN G
256
WEST CROMWELL ROAD
CHESTERTON SQ
SULLIVAN CT
CHILD'S ST
CHILD'S WALK
CHILD'S PL
CHILD'S MEWS
WALLGRAVE RD
KENWAY ROAD
HOGARTH PL
HOGARTH ROAD
EARL'S COURT GARDENS
MORTON MEWS
COURTFIELD GARDENS
COLLINGHAM GARDENS
COLLINGHAM ROAD
BOSTON HO
COURTFIELD MEWS
COLBECK MEWS
LONGRIDGE ROAD
TEMPLETON PLACE
NEVERN ROAD
NEVERN PLACE
SPEAR MS
BARKSTON GDNS
SIMMONDS CT
LAVERTON MEWS
LAVERTON PL
Coll
COLLINGHAM GARDENS
WETHERBY GDNS
CLUNY MEWS
NEVERN SQUARE
NEVERN SQ
Earl's Court
MARY SMITH CT
TREBOVIR ROAD
ORPEN HO
OLD MANOR YD
SHERIDAN CT
HESPER MEWS
COMMONWEALTH OF DOMINICA / ST LUCIA
BEACH HO
NEVERN MANSIONS
KENSINGTON MANSIONS
WARWICK ROAD
PHILBEACH GARDENS
PENYWERN ROAD
SW5
BRAMHAM GARDENS
BOLTON GARDENS
A3218
BOLTON PL
EARL'S COURT SQUARE
FARNELL MEWS
WETHERBY MANSIONS
WETHERBY PL
COLEHERNE MANSIONS
YH
BOLTONS CT
BEATRIX HO
Liby
SOUTH BOLTON GARDENS
Bousfield Prim Sch
Prim Sch
LANGHAM MANSIONS
RICH LANE
REDCLIFFE CL
RICHMOND MANSIONS
OLD BROMPTON ROAD
BOLTON GDNS MEWS
COLEHERNE COURT
THE LITTLE BOLTONS
Earl's Court Exhibition Centre
EARDLEY CRESCENT
KEMPSFORD GDNS
SYBIL THORNDIKE CASSON HO
KRAMER MEWS
PRINCESS BEATRICE HO
WHARFDALE ST
COLEHERNE ROAD
REDCLIFFE SQUARE
HARCOURT TERRACE
HUNTER HO
COLEHERNE MEWS
FINBOROUGH ROAD
REDCLIFFE MEWS
West Brompton
EMPRESS PL
SHARNBROOK HO
HONEY LANE HO
WESTGATE TER
REDCLIFFE GARDENS
LILLIE ROAD
LILLIE YD
LANGTRY PL
RICKETT ST
ROXBY PLACE
265
REDCLIFFE ST
Redcliffe Sch
CATHCART R
SEAGRAVE LODGE
1
2
3
4
5
6

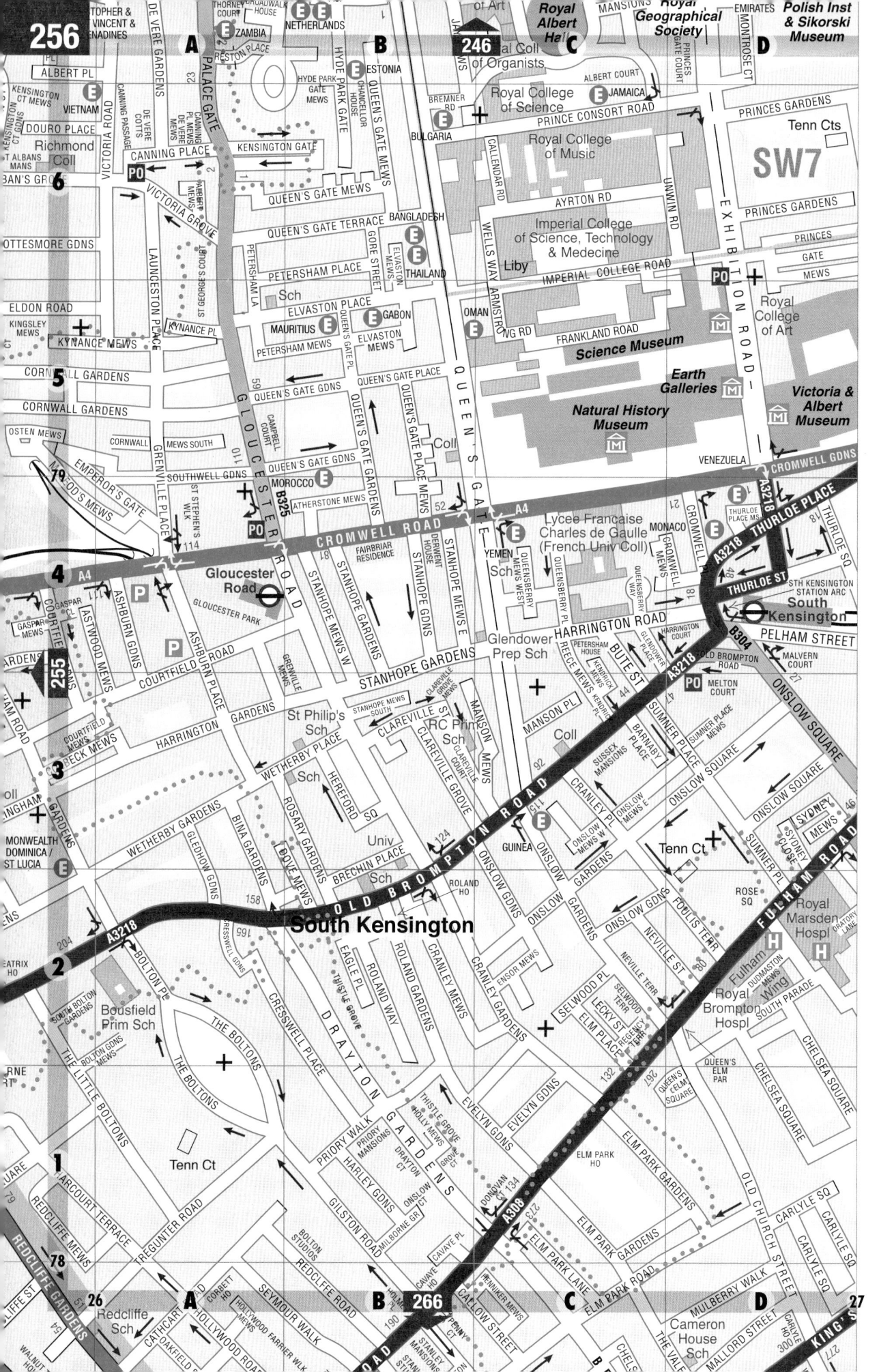

246
255
266
Royal Albert Hall
Royal Geographical Society
Polish Inst & Sikorski Museum
Royal College of Science
Royal College of Music
Imperial College of Science, Technology & Medecine
SW7
Science Museum
Earth Galleries
Natural History Museum
Victoria & Albert Museum
Royal College of Art
CROMWELL ROAD
Lycee Francaise Charles de Gaulle (French Univ Coll)
Gloucester Road
South Kensington
OLD BROMPTON ROAD
FULHAM ROAD
Royal Marsden Hospl
Royal Brompton Hospl
Richmond Coll
PALACE GATE
GLOUCESTER ROAD
QUEEN'S GATE
EXHIBITION ROAD
PRINCE CONSORT ROAD
IMPERIAL COLLEGE ROAD
HARRINGTON ROAD
THURLOE PLACE
PELHAM STREET
ONSLOW SQUARE
THE BOLTONS
DRAYTON GARDENS
ELM PARK GARDENS
REDCLIFFE GARDENS
CORNWALL GARDENS
STANHOPE GARDENS
Bousfield Prim Sch
Glendower Prep Sch
Cameron House Sch
Redcliffe Sch

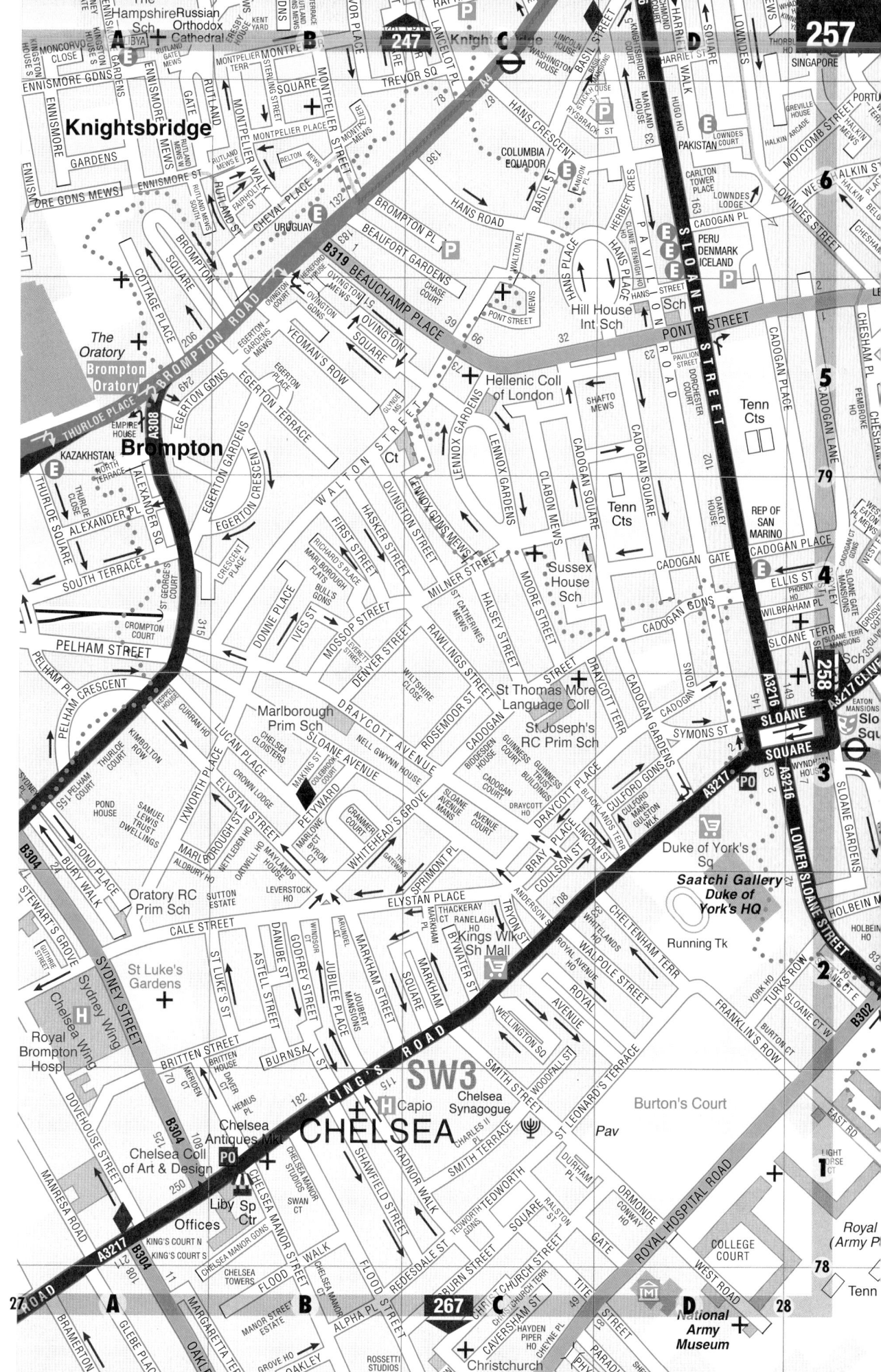
A
B
C
D
247
Knightsbridge
Knightsbridge
Brompton
CHELSEA
SW3
The Hampshire Sch
Russian Orthodox Cathedral
LIBYA
ENNISMORE GDNS
ENNISMORE GARDENS
ENNISMORE GDNS MEWS
ENNISMORE ST
ENNISMORE MEWS
RUTLAND GATE
RUTLAND MEWS
MONTPELIER PLACE
MONTPELIER SQUARE
MONTPELIER STREET
MONTPELIER WALK
MONTPELIER TERR
MONTPELIER MEWS
STERLING STREET
TREVOR SQ
LANCELOT PL
FAIRHOLT ST
CHEVAL PLACE
RUTLAND ST
URUGUAY
BROMPTON SQUARE
BROMPTON ROAD
COTTAGE PLACE
The Oratory
Brompton Oratory
THURLOE PLACE
EMPIRE HOUSE
KAZAKHSTAN
THURLOE SQUARE
THURLOE CLOSE
ALEXANDER PL
ALEXANDER SQ
NORTH TERRACE
SOUTH TERRACE
EGERTON GDNS
EGERTON GARDENS
EGERTON CRESCENT
EGERTON TERRACE
EGERTON PLACE
EGERTON GARDENS MEWS
CRESCENT PLACE
ST GEORGE'S COURT
CROMPTON COURT
PELHAM STREET
PELHAM CRESCENT
PELHAM PL
OVINGTON SQUARE
OVINGTON MEWS
OVINGTON GDNS
OVINGTON COURT
OVINGTON STREET
YEOMAN'S ROW
BEAUCHAMP PLACE
B319
BEAUFORT GARDENS
BROMPTON PL
CHASE COURT
HANS ROAD
HANS CRESCENT
HANS PLACE
HANS ST
COLUMBIA / EQUADOR
BASIL ST
BASIL STREET
WALTON PL
WALTON STREET
PONT STREET
PONT STREET MEWS
HERBERT CRES
Hill House Int Sch
Sch
PAVILION ROAD
SLOANE STREET
A3216
A4
PAKISTAN
LOWNDES COURT
CARLTON TOWER PLACE
LOWNDES LODGE
CADOGAN PL
PERU
DENMARK
ICELAND
SINGAPORE
HARRIET ST
HARRIET WALK
LOWNDES SQUARE
LOWNDES STREET
MOTCOMB STREET
HALKIN ST
HALKIN ARCADE
CHESHAM PL
CADOGAN LANE
CADOGAN PLACE
Tenn Cts
REP OF SAN MARINO
OAKLEY HOUSE
DORCHESTER COURT
PAVILION STREET
Hellenic Coll of London
SHAFTO MEWS
LENNOX GARDENS
LENNOX GDNS MEWS
CADOGAN SQUARE
CLABON MEWS
CADOGAN GATE
CADOGAN GDNS
CADOGAN GARDENS
Sussex House Sch
MOORE STREET
HALSEY STREET
MILNER STREET
ST CATHERINES MEWS
OVINGTON STREET
HASKER STREET
FIRST STREET
RICHARD'S PLACE
MARLBOROUGH FLATS
BULL'S GDNS
DONNE PLACE
IVES ST
MOSSOP STREET
LEVERETT STREET
DENYER STREET
RAWLINGS STREET
WILTSHIRE CLOSE
ROSEMOOR ST
DRAYCOTT AVENUE
DRAYCOTT PLACE
DRAYCOTT TERR
St Thomas More Language Coll
St Joseph's RC Prim Sch
SYMONS ST
ELLIS ST
WILBRAHAM PL
SLOANE TERR
SLOANE SQUARE
258
A3217
Marlborough Prim Sch
SLOANE AVENUE
NELL GWYNN HOUSE
CHELSEA CLOISTERS
MAKINS ST
PETYWARD
CRANMER COURT
MARLOWE CT
BYRON CT
WHITEHEAD'S GROVE
CULFORD GDNS
BLACKLANDS TERR
LINCOLN ST
BRAY PLACE
COULSON ST
ANDERSON ST
Duke of York's Sq
Saatchi Gallery Duke of York's HQ
Running Tk
LOWER SLOANE STREET
SLOANE GARDENS
HOLBEIN MEWS
TURKS ROW
FRANKLIN'S ROW
B302
LUCAN PLACE
IXWORTH PLACE
ELYSTAN STREET
ELYSTAN PLACE
MARLBOROUGH ST
POND PLACE
BURY WALK
B304
Oratory RC Prim Sch
CALE STREET
St Luke's Gardens
ST LUKE'S ST
SYDNEY STREET
Royal Brompton Hospl
Chelsea Wing
Sydney Wing
DANUBE ST
ASTELL STREET
GODFREY STREET
JUBILEE PLACE
MARKHAM STREET
MARKHAM SQUARE
Kings Wlk Sh Mall
BYWATER ST
TRYON ST
WALPOLE STREET
CHELTENHAM TERR
ROYAL AVENUE
WELLINGTON SQ
KING'S ROAD
SMITH STREET
WOODFALL ST
ST LEONARD'S TERRACE
Burton's Court
Pav
BRITTEN STREET
Capio
Chelsea Synagogue
Chelsea Antiques Mkt
Chelsea Coll of Art & Design
Liby
Sp Ctr
Offices
CHELSEA MANOR STREET
SHAWFIELD STREET
RADNOR WALK
SMITH TERRACE
TEDWORTH SQUARE
ROYAL HOSPITAL ROAD
COLLEGE COURT
WEST ROAD
Royal Army P
National Army Museum
DOVEHOUSE STREET
MANRESA ROAD
KING'S COURT N
KING'S COURT S
FLOOD WALK
FLOOD STREET
REDESDALE ST
CHRISTCHURCH STREET
CAVERSHAM ST
TITE STREET
267
Christchurch
OAKLEY
GLEBE PLACE
BRAMERTON
27
28
1
2
3
4
5
6
78
79

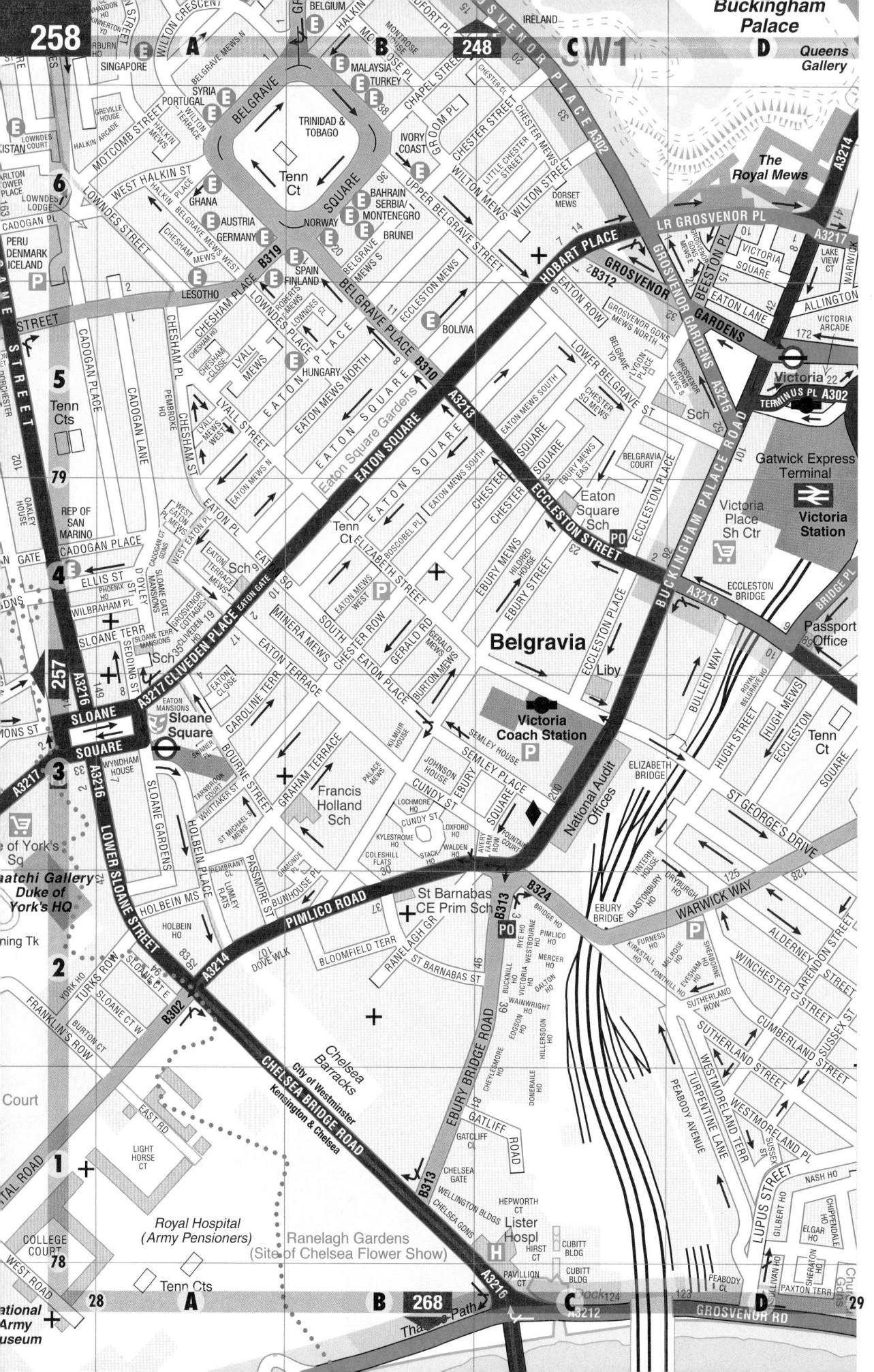

248
SW1
Buckingham Palace
Queens Gallery
The Royal Mews
Belgrave Square
Tenn Ct
Trinidad & Tobago
Eaton Square
Eaton Square Gardens
Belgravia
Victoria Coach Station
Victoria Station
Gatwick Express Terminal
Victoria Place Sh Ctr
Passport Office
National Audit Offices
Francis Holland Sch
Eaton Square Sch
St Barnabas CE Prim Sch
Sloane Square
Chelsea Barracks
Royal Hospital (Army Pensioners)
Ranelagh Gardens (Site of Chelsea Flower Show)
Lister Hospl
National Army Museum
Duke of York's HQ
Grosvenor Place
Hobart Place
Grosvenor Gardens
Buckingham Palace Road
Eccleston Street
Lower Belgrave St
Ebury Street
Elizabeth Street
Pimlico Road
Lower Sloane Street
Chelsea Bridge Road
Ebury Bridge Road
Warwick Way
St George's Drive
Grosvenor Rd
Lupus Street
Cliveden Place
Sloane Street
Chesham Place
Lowndes Street
Cadogan Place
Eaton Place
Eaton Terrace
Bourne Street
Holbein Place
Sloane Gardens
Westmoreland Terr
Peabody Avenue
Turpentine Lane
Sutherland Street
Cumberland Street
Alderney Street
Clarendon Street
Winchester Street
Thames Path
City of Westminster
Kensington & Chelsea
257
268

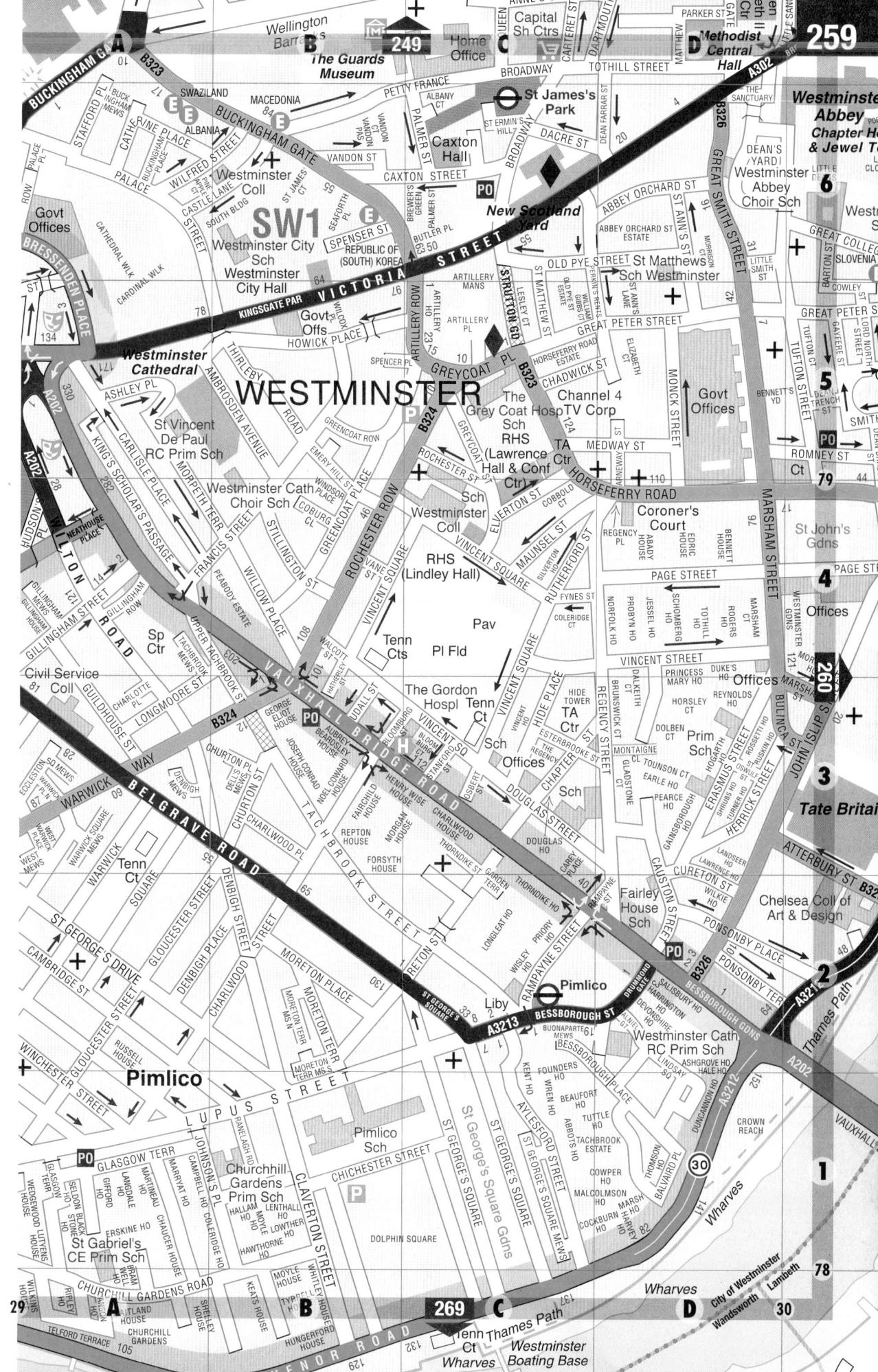

249
260
269
A
B
C
D
1
2
3
4
5
6
78
79
WESTMINSTER
SW1
Pimlico
Wellington Barracks
The Guards Museum
Home Office
Capital Sh Ctrs
Methodist Central Hall
Westminster Abbey
Chapter Ho & Jewel Tower
Westminster Abbey Choir Sch
St James's Park
Caxton Hall
New Scotland Yard
Westminster Coll
Westminster City Sch
Westminster City Hall
REPUBLIC OF (SOUTH) KOREA
Govt Offices
Govt Offs
Westminster Cathedral
St Vincent De Paul RC Prim Sch
Westminster Cath Choir Sch
The Grey Coat Hosp Sch
RHS (Lawrence Hall & Conf Ctr)
Channel 4 TV Corp
TA Ctr
Coroner's Court
St John's Gdns
St Matthews Sch Westminster
RHS (Lindley Hall)
Pav
Pl Fld
Tenn Cts
The Gordon Hospl
Tenn Ct
Sch
Offices
Sp Ctr
Civil Service Coll
Prim Sch
Tate Britain
Chelsea Coll of Art & Design
Fairley House Sch
Liby
Westminster Cath RC Prim Sch
Pimlico Sch
Churchhill Gardens Prim Sch
St Gabriel's CE Prim Sch
St George's Square Gdns
DOLPHIN SQUARE
CROWN REACH
Wharves
Thames Path
Westminster Boating Base
City of Westminster
Wandsworth
Lambeth
BUCKINGHAM GATE
PETTY FRANCE
BROADWAY
TOTHILL STREET
CAXTON STREET
VICTORIA STREET
KINGSGATE PAR
ABBEY ORCHARD ST
OLD PYE STREET
GREAT PETER STREET
GREAT SMITH STREET
GREAT COLLEGE ST
BRESSENDEN PLACE
CATHEDRAL WLK
HOWICK PLACE
GREYCOAT PL
ARTILLERY ROW
ROCHESTER ROW
HORSEFERRY ROAD
MARSHAM STREET
MONCK STREET
PAGE STREET
VINCENT SQUARE
VINCENT STREET
ASHLEY PL
AMBROSDEN AVENUE
THIRLEBY ROAD
CARLISLE PLACE
MORPETH TERR
FRANCIS STREET
KING'S SCHOLAR'S PASSAGE
VAUXHALL BRIDGE ROAD
WILTON ROAD
GILLINGHAM STREET
BELGRAVE ROAD
WARWICK WAY
WARWICK SQUARE
ST GEORGE'S DRIVE
GLOUCESTER STREET
DENBIGH STREET
TACHBROOK STREET
CHURTON ST
MORETON PLACE
MORETON TERR
LUPUS STREET
BESSBOROUGH ST
BESSBOROUGH GDNS
BESSBOROUGH PLACE
ST GEORGE'S SQUARE
AYLESFORD STREET
CHICHESTER STREET
CLAVERTON STREET
GLASGOW TERR
CHURCHILL GARDENS ROAD
GROSVENOR ROAD
JOHN ISLIP ST
ATTERBURY ST
PONSONBY PLACE
PONSONBY TER
ERASMUS STREET
HERRICK STREET
BULINCA ST
DOUGLAS STREET
REGENCY STREET
RAMPAYNE STREET
CAUSTON STREET
A302
A202
A3213
A3212
A321
B323
B324
B326

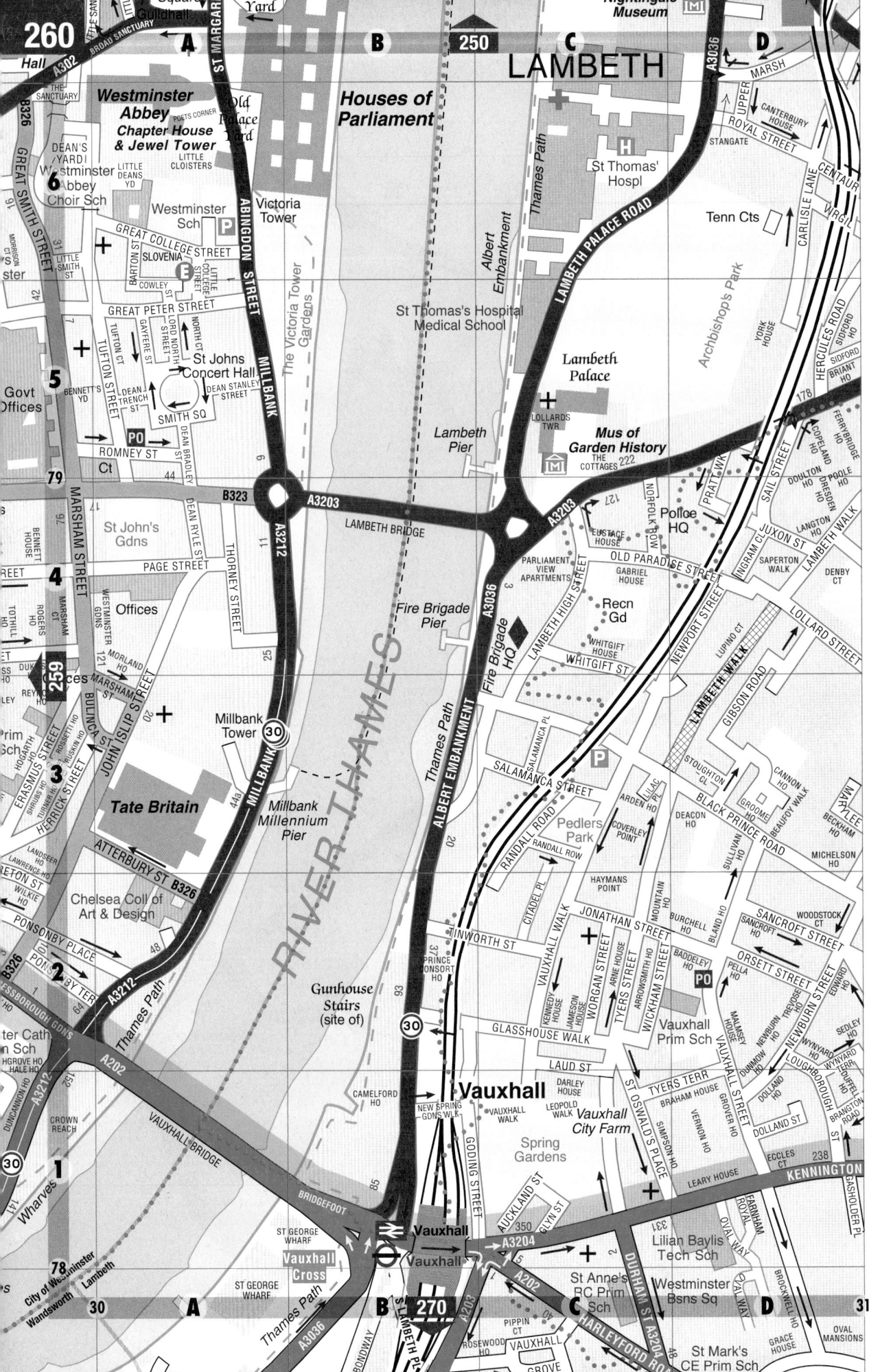

Hall

THE SANCTUARY

B326

GREAT SMITH STREET

Westminster Abbey
Chapter House & Jewel Tower

DEAN'S YARD
Westminster Abbey Choir Sch

Westminster Sch

P

Victoria Tower

Houses of Parliament

A302

ST MARGARET

Square

Guildhall

Yard

Old Palace Yard

LITTLE CLOISTERS

POETS CORNER

LITTLE DEANS YD

GREAT COLLEGE STREET

ABINGDON STREET

Slovenia

E

Barton St

Cowley St

LITTLE COLLEGE ST

NORTH CT

GREAT PETER STREET

MILLBANK

TUFTON CT

GAYFERE ST

LORD NORTH STREET

TUFTON STREET

St Johns Concert Hall

DEAN TRENCH ST

DEAN STANLEY STREET

SMITH SQ

Govt Offices

BENNETT'S YD

PO

ROMNEY ST

DEAN BRADLEY ST

Ct

MARSHAM STREET

St John's Gdns

DEAN RYLE ST

PAGE STREET

THORNEY STREET

B323

A3212

A3203

LAMBETH BRIDGE

St Thomas's Hospital Medical School

Albert Embankment

Thames Path

250

LAMBETH

A3036

UPPER MARSH

ROYAL STREET

CANTERBURY HOUSE

MARSH

STANGATE

CARLISLE LANE

CENTAUR

VIRGIL

Tenn Cts

HERCULES ROAD

178

York House

Archbishop's Park

St Thomas' Hospl

H

LAMBETH PALACE ROAD

Lambeth Palace

LOLLARDS TWR

Mus of Garden History

THE COTTAGES

222

SIDFORD HO

BRIANT HO

SIDFORD HO

COPELAND HO

DRESDEN HO

POOLE HO

DOULTON HO

SAIL STREET

PRATT WK

Polloc HQ

EUSTACE HOUSE

NORFOLK ROW

127

OLD PARADISE STREET

GABRIEL HOUSE

Recn Gd

WHITGIFT HOUSE

WHITGIFT ST

NEWPORT STREET

JUXON ST

LANGTON

INGRAM CL

SAPERTON WALK

LAMBETH WALK

DENBY CT

LOLLARD STREET

LUPINO CT

GIBSON ROAD

STOUGHTON CL

LILAC HO

ARDEN HO

DEACON HO

BLACK PRINCE ROAD

CANNON HO

GROOME

BEAUFOY WALK

P

MAR LEE

BECKHAM HO

MICHELSON HO

SULLIVAN HO

BLAND HO

SANCROFT STREET

WOODSTOCK CT

ORSETT STREET

PO

SEDLEY PL

EDWARD

4

259

BULINGA STREET

JOHN ISLIP STREET

MARSHAM ST

MORLAND HO

121

Offices

Millbank Tower

30

Tate Britain

Millbank Millennium Pier

ATTERBURY ST B326

Chelsea Coll of Art & Design

PONSONBY PLACE

B326

PONSONBY TER

2

A3212

Thames Path

RIVER THAMES

ALBERT EMBANKMENT

A3036

Thames Path

Fire Brigade Pier

A3203

Parliament View Apartments

Fire Brigade HQ

LAMBETH HIGH STREET

SALAMANCA PL

SALAMANCA STREET

P

RANDALL ROAD

RANDALL ROW

Pedlers Park

COVERLEY POINT

HAYMANS POINT

TINWORTH ST

CITADEL PL

VAUXHALL WALK

PRINCE CONSORT HO

JONATHAN STREET

WORGAN STREET

ARNE HOUSE

KENNEDY HOUSE

JAMESON HOUSE

TYERS STREET

WICKHAM STREET

MOUNTAIN HO

ARROWSMITH HO

BADDELEY HO

BURCHELL HO

PELLA

Lambeth Pier

Mus of Garden History

Crown Reach

A3212

30

Wharves

1

78

City of Westminster

Lambeth

30

Wandsworth

VAUXHALL BRIDGE

BRIDGEFOOT

ST GEORGE WHARF

Vauxhall Cross

ST GEORGE WHARF

Thames Path

Gunhouse Stairs (site of)

GODING STREET

30

CAMELFORD HO

NEW SPRING GDNS WLK

Vauxhall Walk

GLASSHOUSE WALK

LAUD ST

DARLEY HOUSE

LEOPOLD WALK

Vauxhall

Spring Gardens

Vauxhall City Farm

BRAHAM HOUSE

ST OSWALD'S PLACE

SIMPSON HO

VERNON HO

LEARY HOUSE

DUNWOOD

TYERS TERR

VAUXHALL STREET

GROVER HO

DOLAND HO

DOLAND ST

NEWBURN ST

MALMSEY HOUSE

WYNYARD TERR

LOUGHBOROUGH STREET

BRANGTON ROAD

TREVOSE HO

ECCLES CT

OVAL WAY

238

KENNINGTON

GASHOLDER PL

Vauxhall Prim Sch

Vauxhall

Vauxhall

270

A3204

Lilian Baylis Tech Sch

St Anne's RC Prim Sch

Westminster Bsns Sq

DURHAM ST

A3204

HARLEYFORD ROAD

BROCKWELL HO

FARNHAM ROYAL

OVAL MANSIONS

St Mark's CE Prim Sch

GRACE HOUSE

A202

AUCKLAND ST

GLYN ST

350

331

2

PIPPIN CT

BONDWAY

ROSEWOOD ST

VAUXHALL GROVE

ST LAMBETH PL

PINFOLD

31

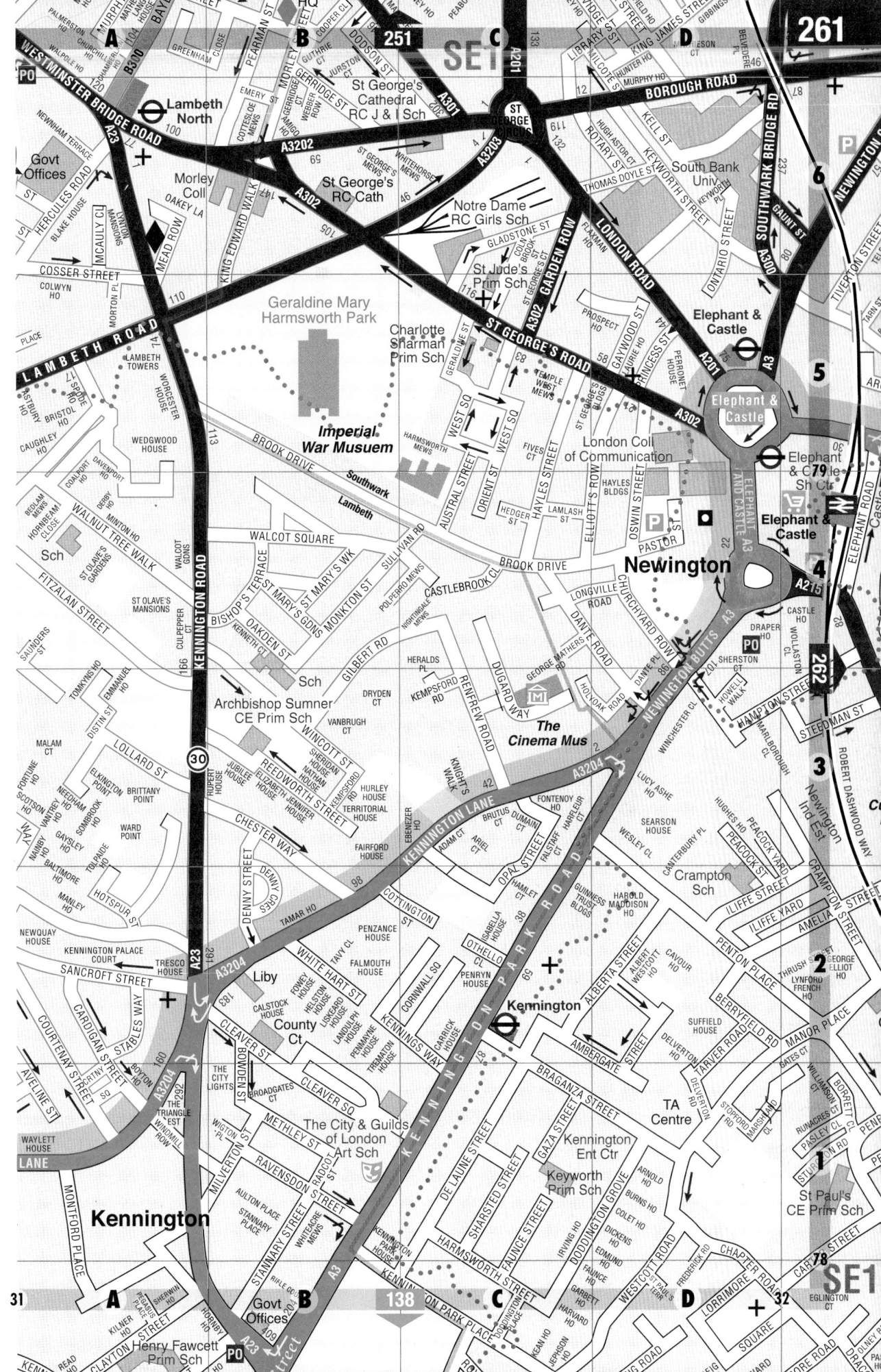

261
251
138
262
A
B
C
D
SE1
Westminster Bridge Road
Lambeth North
Govt Offices
Morley Coll
St George's Cathedral RC J & I Sch
St George's RC Cath
St George Circus
Borough Road
South Bank Univ
Notre Dame RC Girls Sch
St Jude's Prim Sch
London Road
Southwark Bridge Rd
Newington Causeway
Elephant & Castle
Geraldine Mary Harmsworth Park
Imperial War Musuem
Charlotte Sharman Prim Sch
St George's Road
Lambeth Road
Kennington Road
Cosser Street
London Coll of Communication
Elephant & Castle Sh Ctr
Newington
Brook Drive
Walcot Square
Southwark
Lambeth
Archbishop Sumner CE Prim Sch
The Cinema Mus
Newington Butts
Kennington Lane
Kennington Park Road
Kennington
Crampton Sch
TA Centre
Kennington Ent Ctr
Keyworth Prim Sch
The City & Guilds of London Art Sch
County Ct
Liby
St Paul's CE Prim Sch
Henry Fawcett Prim Sch
Newington Ind Est
Robert Dashwood Way
Walnut Tree Walk
Fitzalan Street
Lollard St
Chester Way
Reedworth Street
Cleaver St
Cleaver Sq
Ravensdon Street
Montford Place
Sancroft Street
Braganza Street
Doddington Grove
Manor Place
Penton Place
Crampton Street
Harmsworth Street
Kennington Park Place
Chapter Road

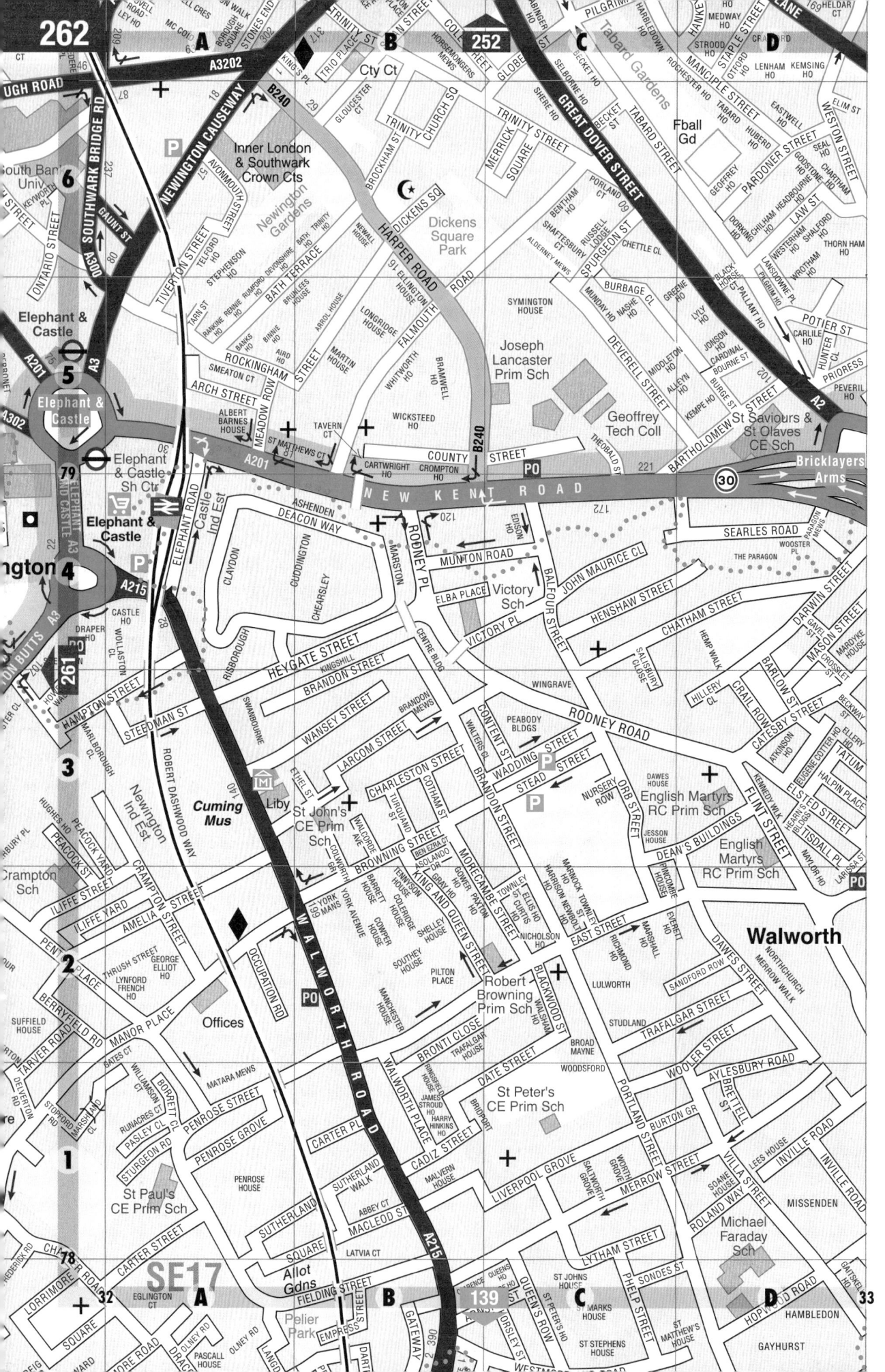
A
B
C
D
252
A3202
B240
Trinity St
Trio Place
King's Pl
Cty Ct
Gloucester Ct
Trinity Church Sq
Brockham St
Horsemongers Mews
Globe St
Great Dover Street
Becket Ho
Selborne Ho
Shere Ho
Trinity Street
Merrick Square
Tabard Gardens
Tabard Street
Fball Gd
Harbledown Ho
Rochester Ho
Manciple Street
Staple Street
Tabard Ho
Huberd Ho
Pardoner Street
Medway Ho
Strood Ho
Lenham Ho
Kemsing Ho
Eastwell Ho
Weston Street
Elim St
Heldar Ct
Pilgrim
Mc Coid
Borough Square
Stones End
Newington Causeway
Inner London & Southwark Crown Cts
Newington Gardens
Avonmouth Street
Southwark Bridge Rd
South Bank Univ
Gaunt St
A300
Ontario Street
Keyworth Pl
Harper Road
Dickens Sq
Dickens Square Park
Newall House
Ellington House
Falmouth Road
Bath Terrace
Tiverton Street
Telford Ho
Stephenson Ho
Rumford Ho
Devonshire Ho
Bath Ho
Trinity Ho
Brunlees House
Arrol House
Longridge House
Whitworth Ho
Bramwell Ho
Wicksteed Ho
Symington House
Joseph Lancaster Prim Sch
Portland Ct
Bentham Ho
Shaftesbury Ct
Russell Lodge
Spurgeon St
Chettle Cl
Alderney Mews
Burbage Cl
Munday Ho
Nashe Ho
Greene Ho
Lyly Ho
Deverell Street
Middleton Ho
Alleyn Ho
Jonson Ho
Cardinal Bourne St
Burge St
Kempe Ho
Black Horse Ct
Pallant Ho
Lansdowne Pl
Pilgrim Ho
Potier St
Carlile Ho
Hunter Cl
Prioress
Peveril Ho
Geoffrey Tech Coll
Bartholomew Street
St Saviours & St Olaves CE Sch
A2
Bricklayers Arms
Theobald St
Elephant & Castle
Tarn St
Rankine Ho
Rennie Ho
Banks Ho
Binnie Ho
Aird Ho
Martin House
Rockingham Street
Smeaton Ct
Arch Street
Meadow Row
Albert Barnes House
St Matthews Ct
Tavern Ct
Cartwright Ho
Crompton Ho
County Street
PO
New Kent Road
A201
A3
A302
Elephant & Castle Sh Ctr
Elephant Road
Castle Ind Est
Ashenden
Deacon Way
Claydon
Cuddington
Chearsley
Marston
Rodney Pl
Munton Road
Edison Ho
Elba Place
Victory Sch
Victory Pl
Balfour Street
John Maurice Cl
Searles Road
Paragon Mews
Wooster Pl
The Paragon
Henshaw Street
Chatham Street
Darwin Street
Hemp Walk
Salisbury Close
Wingrave
Rodney Road
Content St
Walters Cl
Peabody Bldgs
Wadding Street
Stead Street
Nursery Row
Orb Street
Dawes House
English Martyrs RC Prim Sch
Jesson House
Dean's Buildings
Pincombe House
Flint Street
Kennedy Wlk
Hillery Cl
Crail Row
Barlow St
Catesby Street
Atkinson Ho
Eugene Cotter Ho
Tatum
Ellery
Beckway St
Mason Street
Gavel St
Mardyke House
Crosslet St
Elsted Street
Halpin Place
Tisdall Pl
Hearn's Bldgs
Naylor Ho
Larissa St
Ngton
A215
Castle Ho
Wollaston Cl
Draper Ho
261
Risborough
Heygate Street
Kingshill
Brandon Street
Centre Bldg
Swanbourne
Wansey Street
Brandon Mews
Larcom Street
Hampton Street
Steedman St
Marlborough Cl
Robert Dashwood Way
Ethel St
Charleston Street
Cotham St
Turquand St
Brandon Street
Morecambe Street
Townley St
Curtis Ho
Ellis Ho
Harrison Ho
Marnock Ho
Newbolt Ho
Townley St
Cuming Mus
Liby
St John's CE Prim Sch
Walcorde Ave
Colworth Gro
Browning Street
Ben Ezra Ct
Asolando Dr
Gray Ho
Gower Ho
Paxton Ho
King and Queen Street
Barrett House
Tennyson House
Coleridge House
Shelley House
York Mans
York Avenue
Cowper House
Southey House
Nicholson Ho
East Street
Richmond Ho
Marshall Ho
Everett Ho
Walworth
Dawes Street
Northchurch
Merrow Walk
Newington Ind Est
Hughes Ho
Peacock Yard
Peacock St
Crampton Street
Crampton Sch
Iliffe Street
Iliffe Yard
Amelia Street
Penton Place
Thrush Street
George Elliot Ho
Lynford French Ho
Occupation Rd
Walworth Road
Pilton Place
Manchester House
Robert Browning Prim Sch
Blackwood St
Walsham Ho
Lulworth
Sandford Row
Trafalgar Street
Studland
Suffield House
Berryfield Rd
Manor Place
Offices
Tarver Road
Deverton Rd
Gates Ct
Williamson Ct
Borrett Cl
Matara Mews
Penrose Street
Penrose Grove
Runacres Ct
Stopford Rd
Marshland Cl
Pasley Cl
Sturgeon Rd
Bronti Close
Trafalgar House
Ringsfield House
James Stroud Ho
Harry Hinkins Ho
Date Street
Bridport
Broad Mayne
Woodsford
St Peter's CE Prim Sch
Portland Street
Wooler Street
Aylesbury Road
Brettell St
Burton Gr
Carter Pl
Cadiz Street
Walworth Place
Liverpool Grove
Saltworth Grove
Worth Grove
Merrow Street
Villa Street
Soane House
Lees House
Inville Road
Penrose House
St Paul's CE Prim Sch
Sutherland Walk
Malvern House
Abbey Ct
Macleod St
Sutherland Square
Latvia Ct
Roland Way
Missenden
Michael Faraday Sch
Lytham Street
Sondes St
Charter Road
Carter Street
Lorrimore Square
SE17
Eglinton Ct
Allot Gdns
Fielding Street
Queens Ho
Clarence Ho
St Johns House
St Marks House
Phelp Street
St Matthew's House
Hopwood Road
Gaitskell Ho
Hambledon
139
Pelier Park
Empress Street
Gateway
Queen's Row
St Peter's Ho
St Stephens House
Gayhurst
Pascall House
Olney Rd
32
33
1
2
3
4
5
6

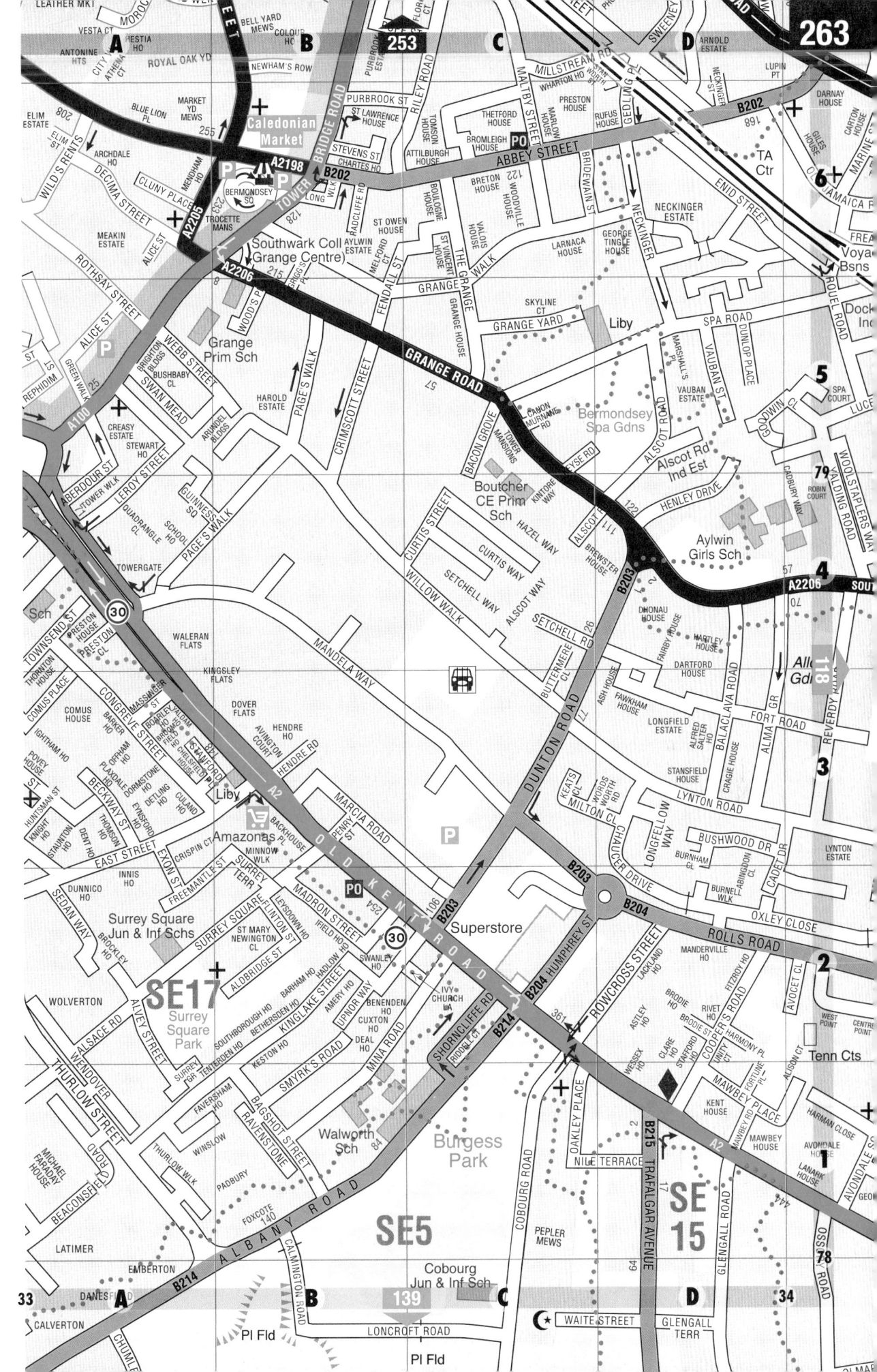
253
139
118
SE17
SE5
SE 15
Caledonian Market
Bermondsey Sq
Southwark Coll Grange Centre
Grange Prim Sch
Bermondsey Spa Gdns
Boutcher CE Prim Sch
Aylwin Girls Sch
Surrey Square Jun & Inf Schs
Surrey Square Park
Walworth Sch
Burgess Park
Cobourg Jun & Inf Sch
Superstore
Amazonas
Tenn Cts
Tower Bridge Road
Abbey Street
Grange Road
Old Kent Road
Albany Road
Dunton Road
Rolls Road
Mandela Way
Willow Walk
Spa Road
Enid Street
Neckinger
Lynton Road
Fort Road
Trafalgar Avenue
Cobourg Road
Rowcross Street
Thurlow Street
East Street
Surrey Square
Decima Street
Rothsay Street
Page's Walk
Crimscott Street
Longfield Estate
Neckinger Estate
Meakin Estate
Lynton Estate
Pl Fld

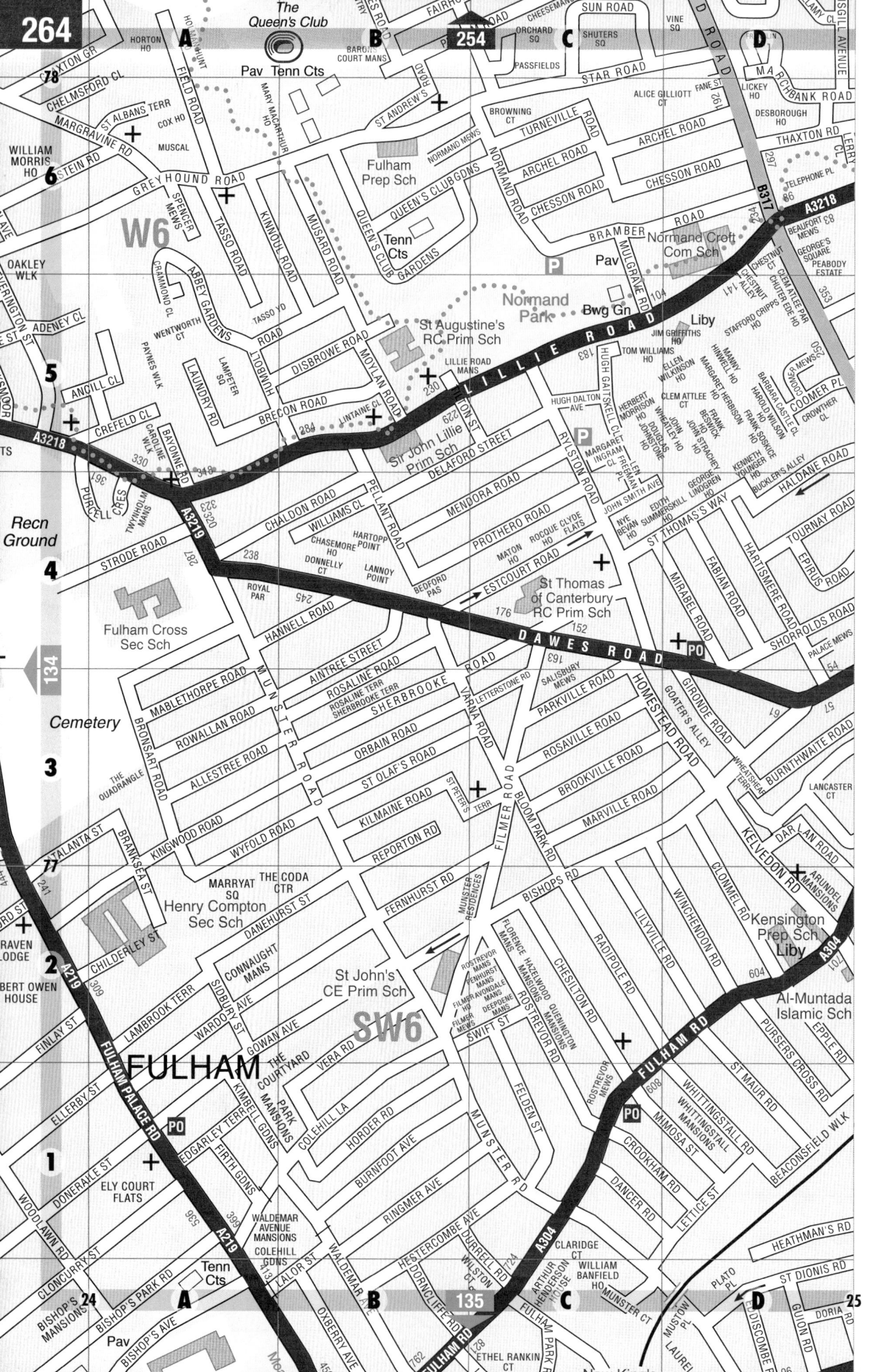

The Queen's Club
Pav Tenn Cts
254
134
135
W6
SW6
FULHAM
Recn Ground
Cemetery
A3218
A3219
A219
A304
B317
LILLIE ROAD
DAWES ROAD
FULHAM PALACE RD
FULHAM RD
GREYHOUND ROAD
MARGRAVINE RD
CHELMSFORD CL
ST ALBANS TERR
STEIN RD
WILLIAM MORRIS HO
COX HO
MUSCAL
HORTON HO
FIELD ROAD
MARY MACARTHUR HO
ST ANDREW'S ROAD
BARONS COURT MANS
CHEESEMAN
SUN ROAD
ORCHARD SQ
PASSFIELDS
SHUTERS SQ
VINE SQ
STAR ROAD
BROWNING CT
TURNEVILLE ROAD
ALICE GILLIOTT CT
FANE ST
LICKEY HO
DESBOROUGH HO
MARCHBANK ROAD
THAXTON RD
ARCHEL ROAD
CHESSON ROAD
NORMAND MEWS
NORMAND ROAD
QUEEN'S CLUB GDNS
QUEEN'S CLUB GARDENS
Fulham Prep Sch
Tenn Cts
TELEPHONE PL
BEAUFORT MEWS
GEORGE'S SQUARE
PEABODY ESTATE
BRAMBER ROAD
Normand Croft Com Sch
MULGRAVE RD
Pav
Normand Park
Bwg Gn
Liby
SPENCER MEWS
TASSO ROAD
KINNOUL ROAD
MUSARD ROAD
CRAMMOND CL
ABBEY GARDENS
TASSO YD
WENTWORTH CT
OAKLEY WLK
ADENEY CL
PAYNES WLK
LAMPETER SQ
LAUNDRY RD
HIGHGATE?
DISBROWE ROAD
MOYLAN ROAD
BRECON ROAD
LINTAINE CL
St Augustine's RC Prim Sch
LILLIE ROAD MANS
TILTON ST
Sir John Lillie Prim Sch
HUGH GAITSKELL CL
JIM GRIFFITHS HO
TOM WILLIAMS HO
HUGH DALTON AVE
ELLEN WILKINSON HO
CLEM ATTLEE CT
HERBERT MORRISON HO
MARGARET HERBISON HO
MANNY HINWELL HO
STAFFORD CRIPPS HO
CHESTNUT CT
CHESTNUT ALLEY
CLEM ATTLEE PAR
CHUTER EDE HO
BARBARA CASTLE CL
HAROLD WILSON HO
FRANK SOSKICE HO
COOMER MEWS
COOMER PL
CROWTHER CL
ANCILL CL
CREFELD CL
CAROLINE WLK
BAYONNE RD
PURCELL CRES
TWYNHOLM MANS
DELAFORD STREET
RYLSTON ROAD
MARGARET INGRAM CL
FREEMAN PL
JOHN SMITH AVE
KENNETH YOUNGER HO
BUCKLER'S ALLEY
HALDANE ROAD
CHALDON ROAD
WILLIAMS CL
PELLANT ROAD
MENDORA ROAD
PROTHERO ROAD
HARTOPP POINT
CHASEMORE HO
DONNELLY CT
LANNOY POINT
MATON HO
ROCQUE HO
CLYDE FLATS
NYE BEVAN HO
EDITH SUMMERSKILL HO
GEORGE LINDGREN HO
ST THOMAS'S WAY
TOURNAY ROAD
EPIRUS ROAD
STRODE ROAD
ROYAL PAR
BEDFORD PAS
ESTCOURT ROAD
St Thomas of Canterbury RC Prim Sch
MIRABEL ROAD
FABIAN ROAD
HARTISMERE ROAD
SHORROLDS ROAD
PALACE MEWS
Fulham Cross Sec Sch
HANNELL ROAD
AINTREE STREET
ROSALINE ROAD
ROSALINE TERR
SHERBROOKE TERR
SHERBROOKE
MABLETHORPE ROAD
MUNSTER ROAD
LETTERSTONE RD
SALISBURY MEWS
PARKVILLE ROAD
HOMESTEAD ROAD
GOATER'S ALLEY
GIRONDE ROAD
PO
BRONSART ROAD
ROWALLAN ROAD
VARNA ROAD
ORBAIN ROAD
ROSAVILLE ROAD
BURNTHWAITE ROAD
THE QUADRANGLE
ALLESTREE ROAD
ST OLAF'S ROAD
BROOKVILLE ROAD
WHEATSHEAF TERR
LANCASTER CT
ST PETER'S TERR
FILMER ROAD
BLOOM PARK RD
MARVILLE ROAD
KILMAINE ROAD
DARLAN ROAD
KINGWOOD ROAD
WYFOLD ROAD
REPORTON RD
KELVEDON RD
ARUNDEL MANSIONS
TALANTA ST
BRANKSEA ST
MARRYAT SQ
THE CODA CTR
FERNHURST RD
MUNSTER RESIDENCES
BISHOPS RD
CLONMEL RD
LILYVILLE RD
WINCHENDON RD
Henry Compton Sec Sch
DANEHURST ST
CHILDERLEY ST
FLORENCE MANS
HAZELWOOD MANSIONS
CHESILTON RD
RADIPOLE RD
Kensington Prep Sch
CRAVEN LODGE
BERT OWEN HOUSE
CONNAUGHT MANS
St John's CE Prim Sch
ROSTREVOR MANS
PENHURST MANS
AVONDALE MANS
DEEPDENE MANS
FILMER HO
FILMER MEWS
QUENINGTON MANSIONS
Al-Muntada Islamic Sch
EPPLE RD
LAMBROOK TERR
SIDBURY ST
WARDO AVE
GOWAN AVE
SWIFT ST
ROSTREVOR RD
PURSERS CROSS RD
FINLAY ST
THE COURTYARD
VERA RD
FELDEN ST
ROSTREVOR MEWS
ST MAUR RD
WHITTINGSTALL RD
WHITTINGSTALL MANSIONS
ELLERBY ST
KIMBELL GDNS
PARK MANSIONS
COLEHILL LA
HORDER RD
MIMOSA ST
CROOKHAM RD
BEACONSFIELD WLK
DONERAILE ST
EDGARLEY TERR
FIRTH GDNS
BURNFOOT AVE
DANCER RD
LETTICE ST
ELY COURT FLATS
WOODLAWN RD
WALDEMAR AVENUE MANSIONS
COLEHILL GDNS
RINGMER AVE
HESTERCOMBE AVE
HEATHMAN'S RD
CLONCURRY ST
LALOR ST
WALDEMAR AVE
DURRELL RD
CLARIDGE CT
WILLIAM BANFIELD HO
ARTHUR HENDERSON HOUSE
WILSTON CT
PLATO PL
ST DIONIS RD
BISHOP'S MANSIONS
BISHOP'S PARK RD
BISHOP'S AVE
OXBERRY AVE
DORNCLIFFE RD
FULHAM PARK RD
MUNSTER CT
MUSTOW PL
EDDISCOMBE RD
GUION RD
DORIA RD
LAUREL
ETHEL RANKIN CT
A
B
C
D
1
2
3
4
5
6
77
78
24
25

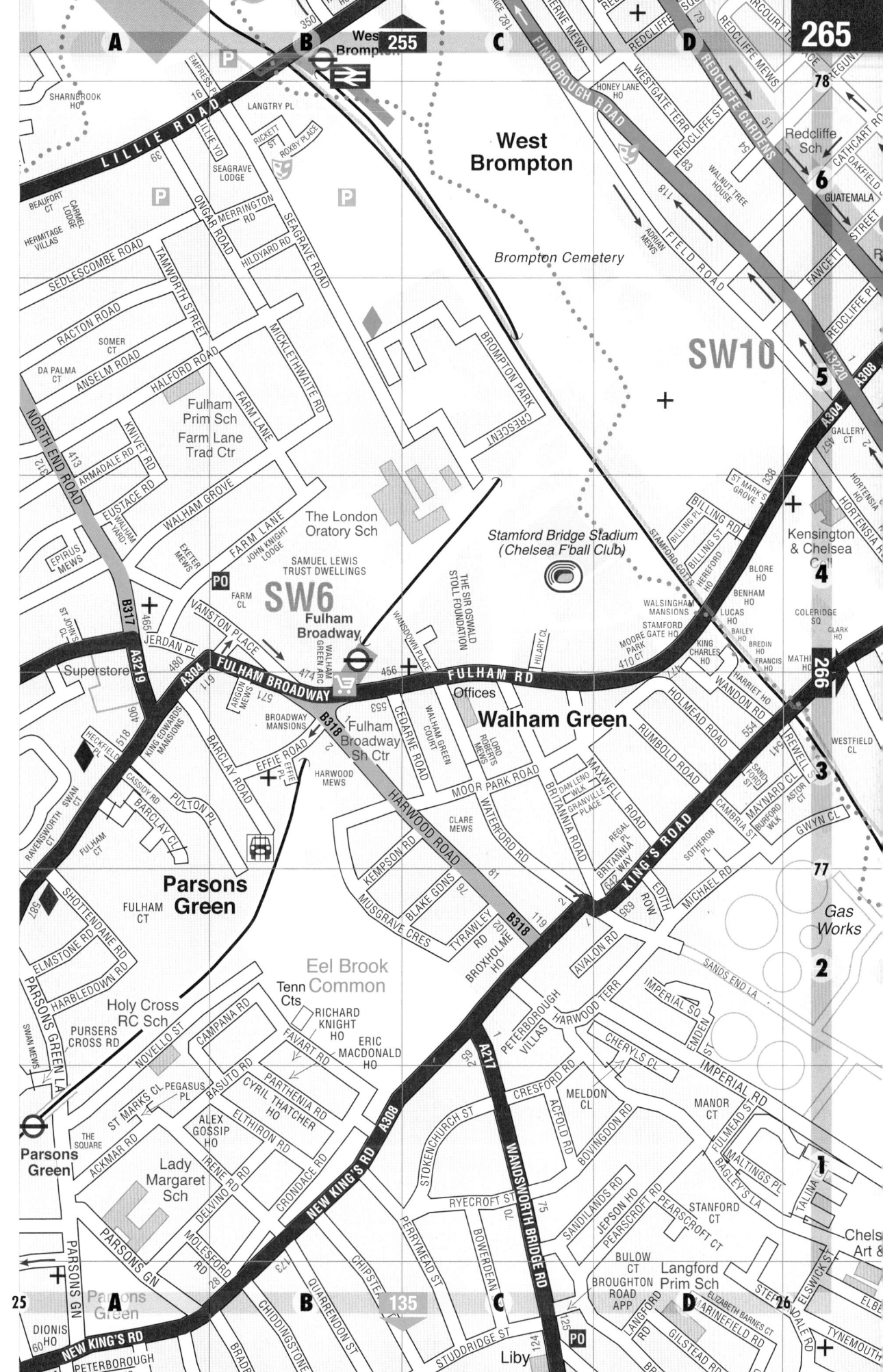
A
B
C
D
255
West Brompton
Fulham Broadway
SHARNBROOK HO
LILLIE ROAD
EMPRESS PL
LILLIE YD
LANGTRY PL
RICKETT ST
ROXBY PLACE
SEAGRAVE LODGE
BEAUFORT CT
CARMEL LODGE
HERMITAGE VILLAS
ONGAR ROAD
MERRINGTON RD
HILDYARD RD
SEAGRAVE ROAD
SEDLESCOMBE ROAD
TAMWORTH STREET
RACTON ROAD
SOMER CT
DA PALMA CT
ANSELM ROAD
HALFORD ROAD
MICKLETHWAITE RD
FARM LANE
Fulham Prim Sch
Farm Lane Trad Ctr
NORTH END ROAD
KNIVET RD
ARMADALE RD
EUSTACE RD
WALHAM YARD
WALHAM GROVE
EPIRUS MEWS
EXETER MEWS
JOHN KNIGHT LODGE
The London Oratory Sch
SAMUEL LEWIS TRUST DWELLINGS
PO
FARM CL
SW6
ST JOHN'S CL
B317
A3219
JERDAN PL
VANSTON PLACE
A304
FULHAM BROADWAY
WALHAM GREEN ARC
Superstore
ARGON MEWS
BROADWAY MANSIONS
B318
EFFIE ROAD
EFFIE PL
HARWOOD MEWS
Fulham Broadway Sh Ctr
KING EDWARDS MANSIONS
BARCLAY ROAD
HECKFIELD PL
CASSIDY RD
BARCLAY CL
PULTON PL
RAVENSWORTH CT
SWAN CT
FULHAM CT
Parsons Green
SHOTTENDANE RD
ELMSTONE RD
HARBLEDOWN RD
PARSONS GREEN LA
SWAN MEWS
Holy Cross RC Sch
PURSERS CROSS RD
NOVELLO ST
CAMPANA RD
Tenn Cts
Eel Brook Common
RICHARD KNIGHT HO
ERIC MACDONALD HO
FAVART RD
PARTHENIA RD
BASUTO RD
CYRIL THATCHER HO
PEGASUS PL
ST MARKS CL
ALEX GOSSIP HO
ELTHIRON RD
THE SQUARE
ACKMAR RD
Lady Margaret Sch
IRENE RD
DELVINO RD
CRONDACE RD
MOLESFORD RD
PARSONS GN
NEW KING'S RD
A308
CHIDDINGSTONE
QUARRENDON ST
CHIPSTEAD
PERRYMEAD ST
135
PETERBOROUGH
DIONIS HO
West Brompton
FINBOROUGH ROAD
HONEY LANE HO
WESTGATE TERR
REDCLIFFE ST
REDCLIFFE GARDENS
REDCLIFFE MEWS
HARCOURT TERRACE
Redcliffe Sch
CATHCART RD
OAKFIELD
GUATEMALA
STREET
WALNUT TREE HOUSE
ADRIAN MEWS
IFIELD ROAD
Brompton Cemetery
FAWCETT
REDCLIFFE PL
SW10
A3220
A308
GALLERY CT
BROMPTON PARK CRESCENT
THE SIR OSWALD STOLL FOUNDATION
Stamford Bridge Stadium (Chelsea F'ball Club)
STAMFORD COTTS
ST MARK'S GROVE
BILLING PL
BILLING RD
BILLING ST
HEREFORD HO
HORTENSIA HO
HORTENSIA RD
Kensington & Chelsea Coll
BLORE HO
BENHAM HO
WALSINGHAM MANSIONS
STAMFORD GATE HO
MOORE PARK CT
LUCAS HO
BAILEY HO
BREDIN HO
FRANCIS HO
COLERIDGE SQ
CLARK HO
MATHIE HO
HILARY CL
KING CHARLES HO
WANSDOWN PLACE
FULHAM RD
Offices
Walham Green
266
HARRIET HO
WANDON RD
HOLMEAD ROAD
RUMBOLD ROAD
CEDARNE ROAD
WALHAM GREEN COURT
LORD ROBERTS MEWS
MOOR PARK ROAD
DAN LENO WLK
GRANVILLE PLACE
MAXWELL ROAD
BRITANNIA ROAD
REGAL PL
BRITANNIA WAY
CLARE MEWS
WATERFORD RD
KEMPSON RD
HARWOOD ROAD
BLAKE GDNS
MUSGRAVE CRES
TYRAWLEY RD
BROXHOLME HO
KING'S ROAD
EDITH ROW
SOTHERON PL
MICHAEL RD
CAMBRIA ST
SANDFORD ST
REWELL ST
MAYNARD CL
BURFORD WLK
ASTOR CT
GWYN CL
WESTFIELD CL
Gas Works
AVALON RD
SANDS END LA
IMPERIAL SQ
EMDEN ST
PETERBOROUGH VILLAS
HARWOOD TERR
CHERYLS CL
IMPERIAL RD
A217
CRESFORD RD
MELDON CL
ACFOLD RD
BOVINGDON RD
MANOR CT
FULMEAD ST
MALTINGS PL
BAGLEY'S LA
TALINA
STOKENCHURCH ST
WANDSWORTH BRIDGE RD
RYECROFT ST
BOWERDEAN
SANDILANDS RD
JEPSON HO
PEARSCROFT RD
PEARSCROFT CT
STANFORD CT
BULOW CT
BROUGHTON ROAD APP
Langford Prim Sch
ELIZABETH BARNES CT
MARINEFIELD RD
LANGFORD RD
GILSTEAD RD
STEPHENDALE RD
ELSWICK ST
Chelsea Art &
TYNEMOUTH
ELBE
STUDDRIDGE ST
Liby
BRADBOURNE
25
26
1
2
3
4
5
6
77
78

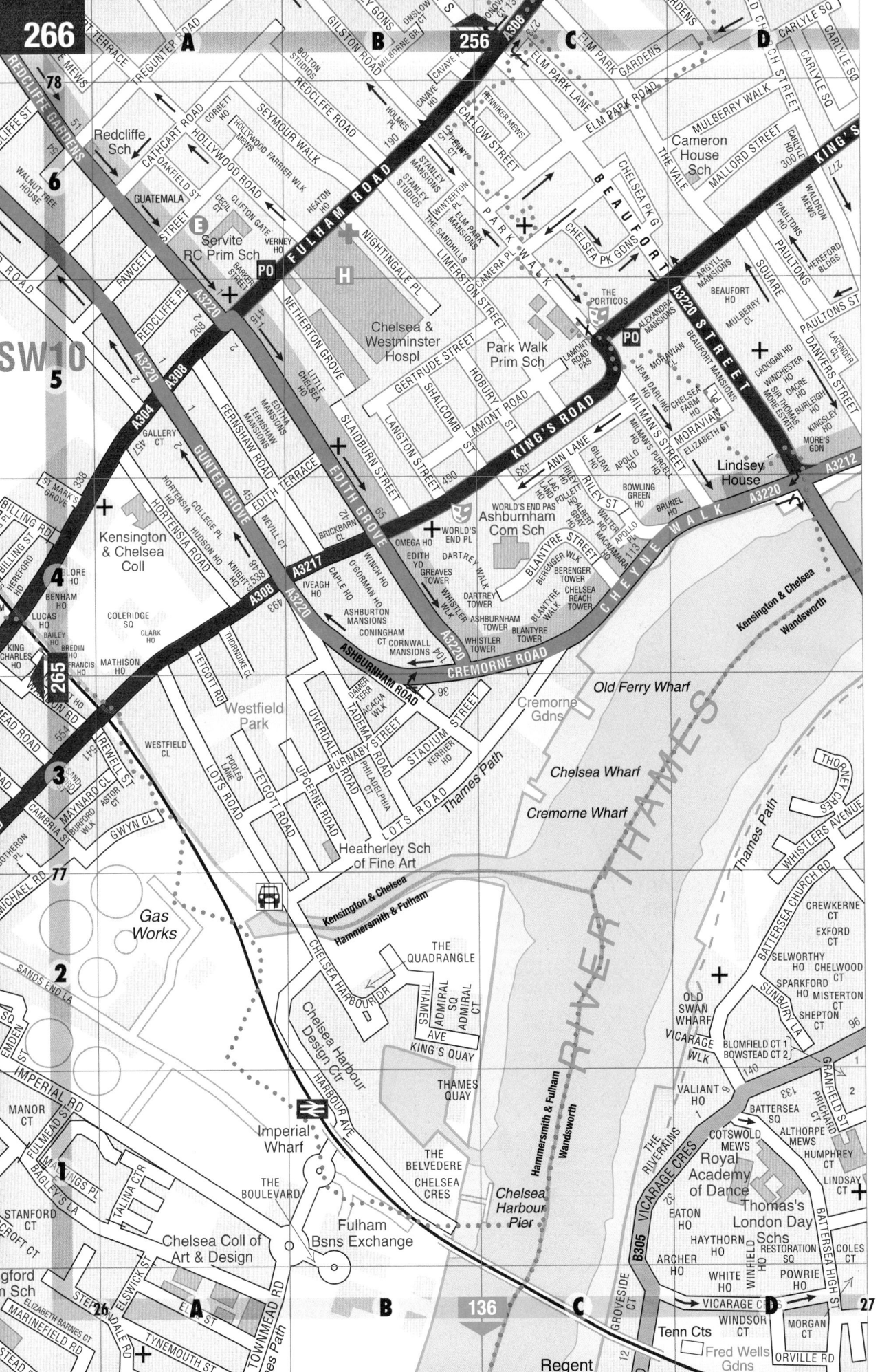

SW10
Redcliffe Gardens
Fulham Road
King's Road
Gunter Grove
Edith Grove
Cheyne Walk
Cremorne Road
Lots Road
Chelsea & Westminster Hospl
Park Walk Prim Sch
Ashburnham Com Sch
Kensington & Chelsea Coll
Servite RC Prim Sch
Redcliffe Sch
Cameron House Sch
Lindsey House
Westfield Park
Heatherley Sch of Fine Art
Gas Works
Imperial Wharf
Chelsea Harbour Design Ctr
Chelsea Coll of Art & Design
Fulham Bsns Exchange
Chelsea Harbour Pier
Old Ferry Wharf
Chelsea Wharf
Cremorne Wharf
Cremorne Gdns
River Thames
Thames Path
Royal Academy of Dance
Thomas's London Day Schs
Kensington & Chelsea
Hammersmith & Fulham
Wandsworth
Old Swan Wharf
Battersea Church Rd
Vicarage Cres
Battersea High St
Tenn Cts
Fred Wells Gdns
Regent

256
265
136
267

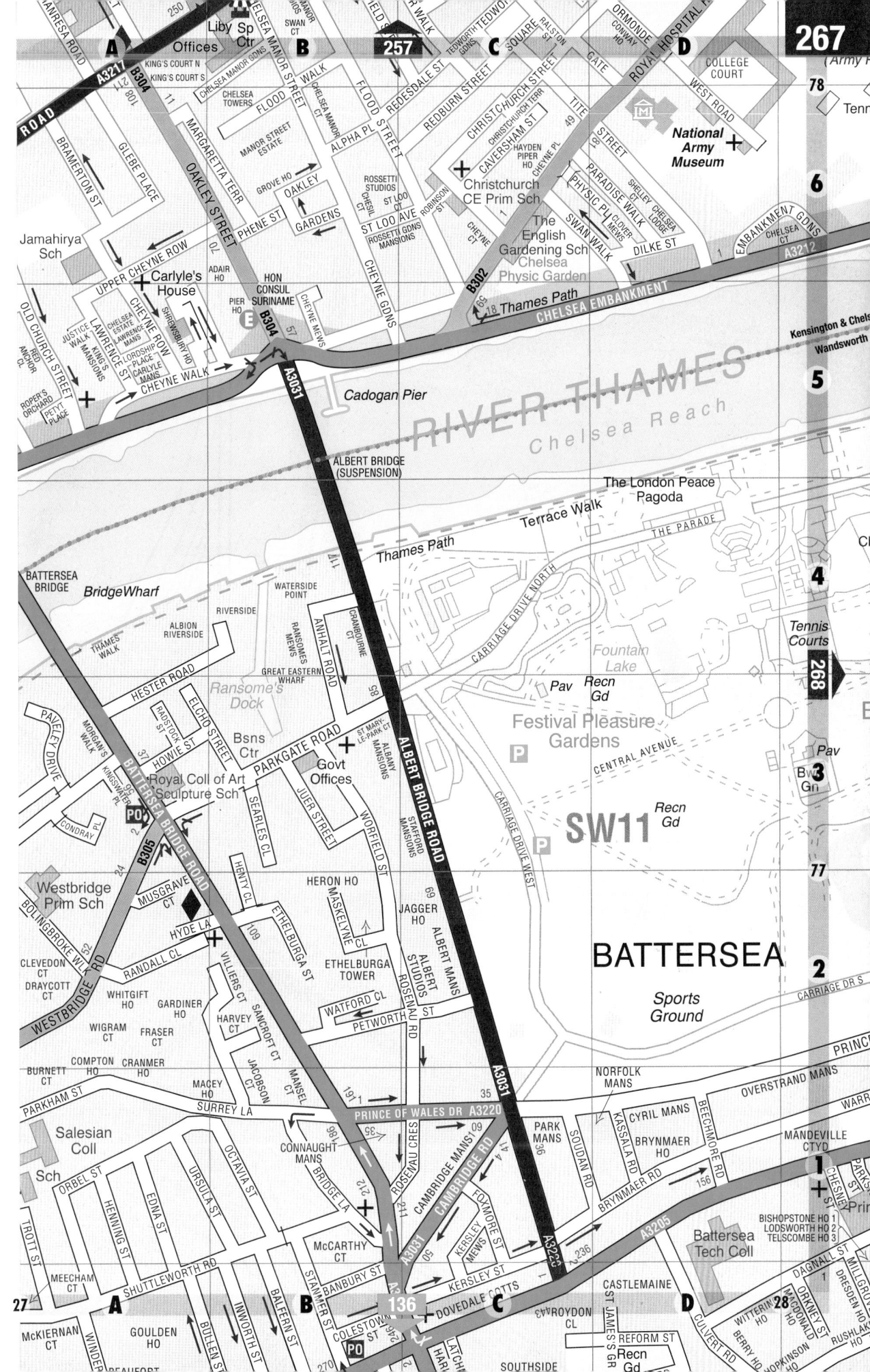

RIVER THAMES
Chelsea Reach
Cadogan Pier
ALBERT BRIDGE (SUSPENSION)
BATTERSEA BRIDGE
BATTERSEA
SW11
Festival Pleasure Gardens
Sports Ground
The London Peace Pagoda
Terrace Walk
Thames Path
Fountain Lake
National Army Museum
Carlyle's House
Chelsea Physic Garden
The English Gardening Sch
Christchurch CE Prim Sch
Jamahirya Sch
Westbridge Prim Sch
Salesian Coll
Battersea Tech Coll
Royal Coll of Art Sculpture Sch
Govt Offices
Bsns Ctr
Ransome's Dock
CHELSEA EMBANKMENT
ALBERT BRIDGE ROAD
BATTERSEA BRIDGE ROAD
OAKLEY STREET
CHEYNE WALK
PRINCE OF WALES DR A3220
PARKGATE ROAD
CARRIAGE DRIVE NORTH
CENTRAL AVENUE
CARRIAGE DRIVE WEST
ROYAL HOSPITAL ROAD
Kensington & Chelsea
Wandsworth

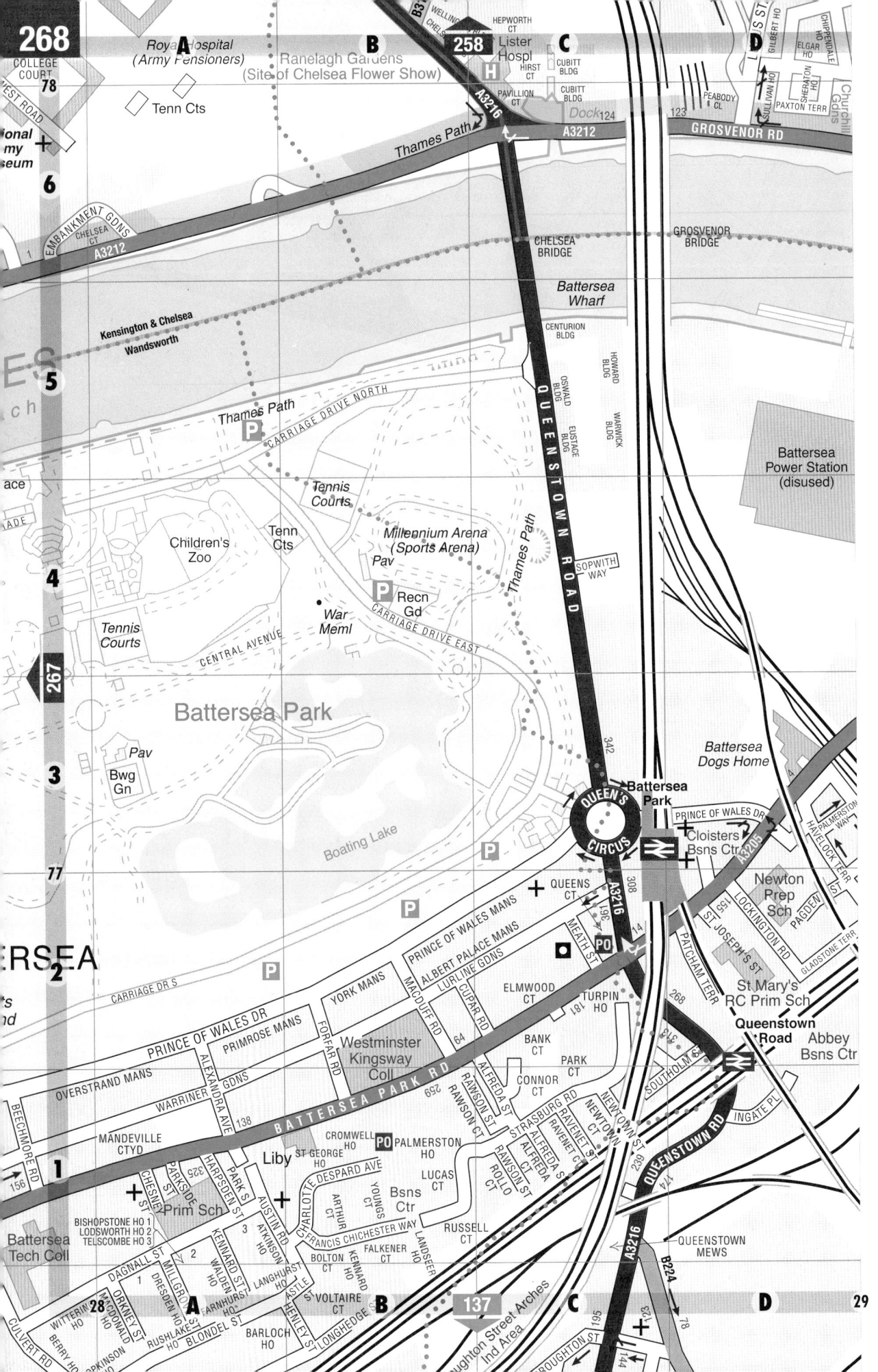

Royal Hospital (Army Pensioners)
Ranelagh Gardens (Site of Chelsea Flower Show)
Lister Hospl
HEPWORTH CT
HIRST CT
CUBITT BLDG
PAVILLION CT
Dock
Tenn Cts
Thames Path
A3216
A3212
GROSVENOR RD
PEABODY CL
PAXTON TERR
SULLIVAN HO
SHERATON HO
ELGAR HO
CHIPPENDALE HO
GILBERT HO
Churchill Gdns
COLLEGE COURT
EMBANKMENT GDNS
CHELSEA CT
CHELSEA BRIDGE
GROSVENOR BRIDGE
Battersea Wharf
Kensington & Chelsea
Wandsworth
CENTURION BLDG
OSWALD BLDG
HOWARD BLDG
EUSTACE BLDG
WARWICK BLDG
QUEENSTOWN ROAD
CARRIAGE DRIVE NORTH
Battersea Power Station (disused)
Tennis Courts
Tenn Cts
Children's Zoo
Millennium Arena (Sports Arena)
Pav
SOPWITH WAY
Recn Gd
War Meml
CARRIAGE DRIVE EAST
CENTRAL AVENUE
Tennis Courts
Battersea Park
Pav
Bwg Gn
Boating Lake
Battersea Dogs Home
QUEEN'S CIRCUS
Battersea Park
PRINCE OF WALES DR
Cloisters Bsns Ctr
A3205
PALMERSTON WAY
HAVELOCK TERR
QUEENS CT
Newton Prep Sch
PRINCE OF WALES MANS
ALBERT PALACE MANS
LURLINE GDNS
MEATH ST
PO
ST JOSEPH'S ST
LOCKINGTON RD
PAGDEN ST
GLADSTONE TERR
PATCHAM TERR
CARRIAGE DR S
YORK MANS
MACDUFF RD
CUPAR RD
ELMWOOD CT
TURPIN HO
St Mary's RC Prim Sch
Queenstown Road
Abbey Bsns Ctr
PRINCE OF WALES DR
PRIMROSE MANS
FORFAR RD
Westminster Kingsway Coll
BANK CT
PARK CT
ALFREDA ST
RAWSON ST
CONNOR CT
SOUTHOLM ST
OVERSTRAND MANS
ALEXANDRA AVE
WARRINER GDNS
BATTERSEA PARK RD
RAWSON CT
STRASBURG RD
RAVENET ST
RAVENET CT
NEWTOWN CT
NEWTOWN ST
QUEENSTOWN RD
INGATE PL
BEECHMORE RD
MANDEVILLE CTYD
CROMWELL HO
PO
PALMERSTON HO
ST GEORGE HO
Liby
PARK ST
HARPSDEN ST
PARKSIDE ST
CHESNEY ST
Prim Sch
AUSTIN RD
CHARLOTTE DESPARD AVE
LUCAS CT
ARTHUR CT
YOUNGS CT
Bsns Ctr
ALFREDA CT
ROLLO CT
RAWSON ST
BISHOPSTONE HO 1
LODSWORTH HO 2
TELSCOMBE HO 3
Battersea Tech Coll
FRANCIS CHICHESTER WAY
RUSSELL CT
LANDSEER HO
QUEENSTOWN MEWS
DAGNALL ST
KENNARD ST
WALDEN HO
ATKINSON HO
BOLTON CT
KENNARD HO
FALKENER CT
B224
MILLGROVE ST
DRESDEN HO
ORKNEY ST
MACDONALD HO
WITTERING HO
FARNHURST HO
LANGHURST HO
ASTLE ST
VOLTAIRE CT
HENLEY ST
LONGHEDGE ST
Stewart's Rd / Broughton Street Arches Ind Area
BROUGHTON ST
RUSHLAKE HO
BLONDEL ST
BARLOCH HO
CULVERT RD
BERRY HO
HOPKINSON
258
137
267
A B C D
1 2 3 4 5 6
77 78 28 29

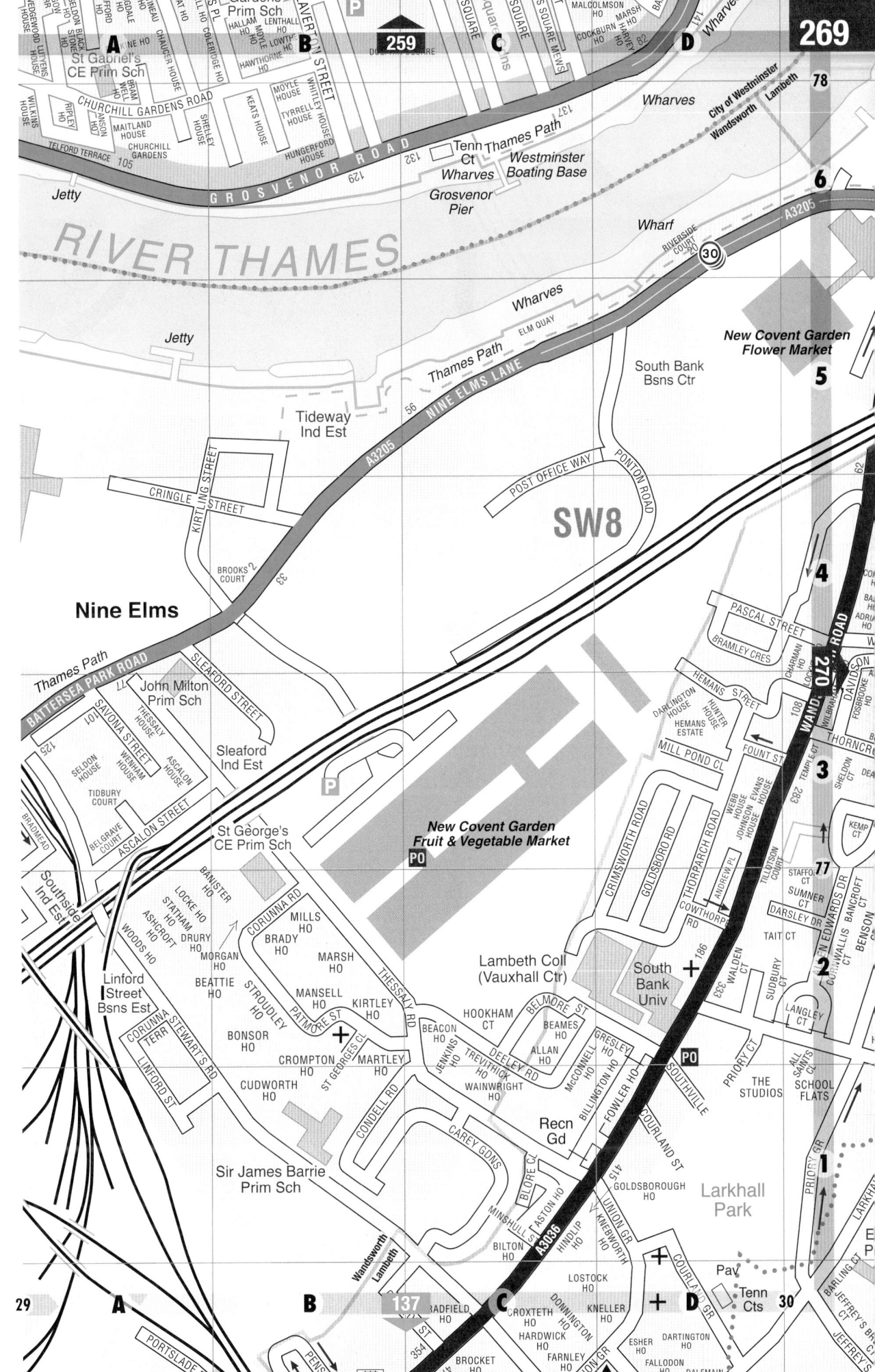

RIVER THAMES

SW8

Nine Elms

New Covent Garden
Flower Market

New Covent Garden
Fruit & Vegetable Market

Larkhall
Park

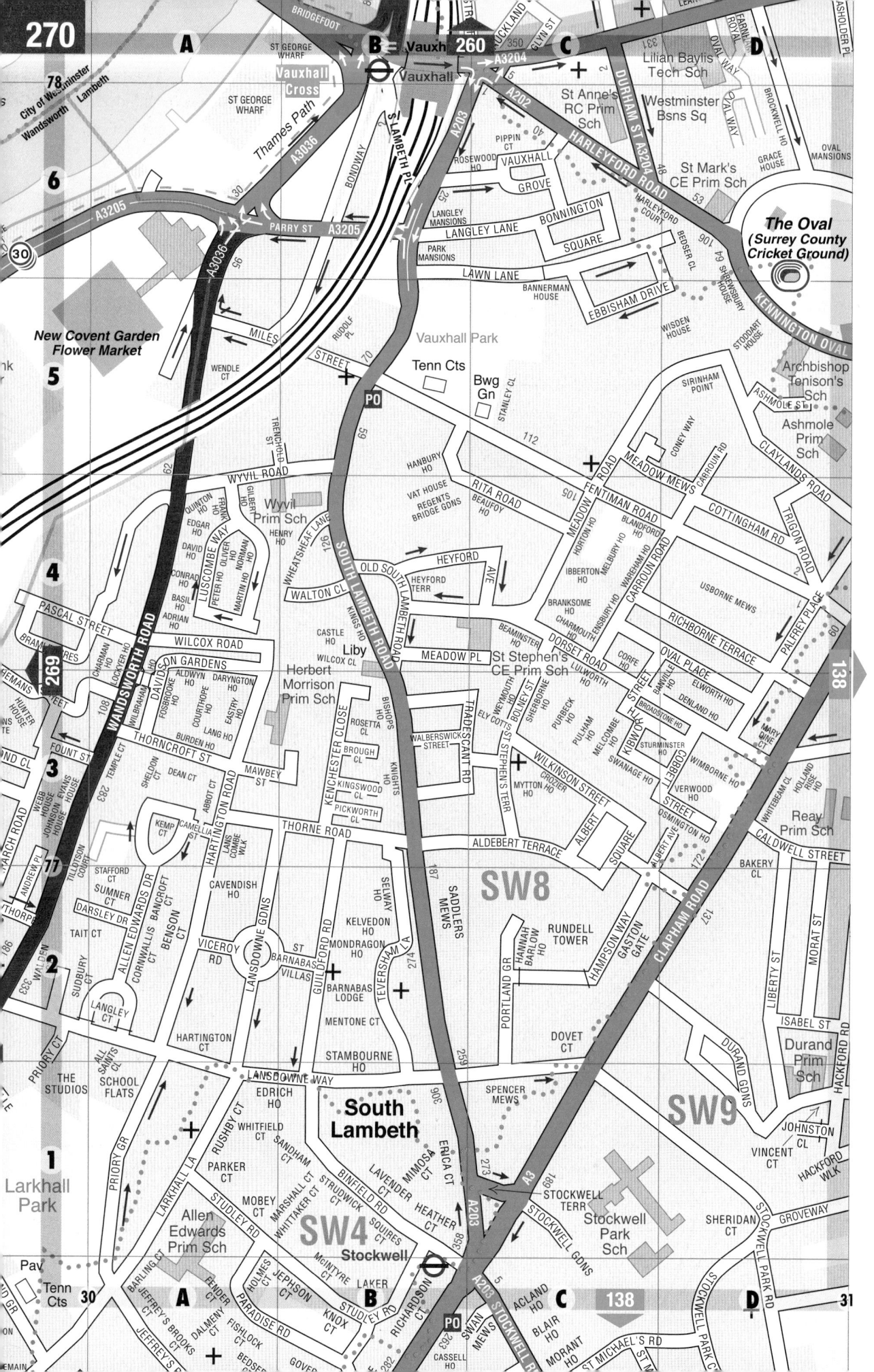
A
B
C
D
260
Vauxhall
Vauxhall Cross
BRIDGEFOOT
ST GEORGE WHARF
Thames Path
A3036
A3205
PARRY ST
A3204
A202
A203
City of Westminster
Lambeth
Wandsworth
78
6
5
4
3
2
1
30
New Covent Garden Flower Market
BONDWAY
S LAMBETH PL
HARLEYFORD ROAD
DURHAM ST A3204
Lilian Baylis Tech Sch
Westminster Bsns Sq
St Anne's RC Prim Sch
St Mark's CE Prim Sch
The Oval (Surrey County Cricket Ground)
OVAL MANSIONS
GRACE HOUSE
BROCKWELL HO
OVAL WAY
FARNHAM ROYAL
ASHOLDER PL
GLYN ST
PIPPIN CT
ROSEWOOD HO
VAUXHALL GROVE
BONNINGTON SQUARE
LANGLEY MANSIONS
LANGLEY LANE
PARK MANSIONS
LAWN LANE
BANNERMAN HOUSE
HARLEYFORD COURT
BEDSER CL
SHREWSBURY HOUSE
EBBISHAM DRIVE
WISDEN HOUSE
STODDART HOUSE
KENNINGTON OVAL
Vauxhall Park
Tenn Cts
Bwg Gn
STANLEY CL
MILES ST
RUDOLF PL
WENDLE CT
TRENCHOLD ST
PO
Archbishop Tenison's Sch
ASHMOLE ST
Ashmole Prim Sch
SIRINHAM POINT
CONEY WAY
CARROUN RD
MEADOW MEWS
CLAYLANDS ROAD
HANBURY HO
WYVIL ROAD
VAT HOUSE
REGENTS BRIDGE GDNS
BEAUFOY HO
RITA ROAD
MEADOW ROAD
FENTIMAN ROAD
COTTINGHAM RD
TRIGON ROAD
Wyvil Prim Sch
HENRY HO
QUINTON HO
FRANK HO
GILBERT HO
EDGAR HO
DAVID HO
LUSCOMBE WAY
OLIVER HO
NORMAN HO
CONRAD HO
PETER HO
MARTIN HO
BASIL HO
ADRIAN HO
WHEATSHEAF LANE
SOUTH LAMBETH ROAD
OLD SOUTH LAMBETH ROAD
HEYFORD AVE
HEYFORD TERR
WALTON CL
KINGS HO
HORTON HO
BLANDFORD HO
MELBURY HO
WAREHAM HO
CARROUN ROAD
IBBERTON HO
USBORNE MEWS
BRANKSOME HO
CHARMOUTH HO
ENSBURY HO
RICHBORNE TERRACE
PALFREY PLACE
PASCAL STREET
WILCOX ROAD
WANDSWORTH ROAD
BRAMLEY CRES
DAVIDSON GARDENS
CHARMAN HO
LOCKYER HO
WILBRAHAM HO
ALDWYN HO
DARYNGTON HO
FOSBROOKE HO
COURTHOPE HO
EASTRY HO
LANG HO
BURDEN HO
THORNCROFT ST
269
HEMANS STREET
HUNTER HOUSE
FOUNT ST
TEMPLE CT
CASTLE HO
WILCOX CL
Liby
MEADOW PL
BEAMINSTER HO
St Stephen's CE Prim Sch
DORSET ROAD
CORFE HO
OVAL PLACE
ELWORTH HO
DENLAND HO
Herbert Morrison Prim Sch
ROSETTA CL
BISHOPS HO
BROUGH CL
KINGSWOOD CL
PICKWORTH CL
KNIGHTS HO
KENCHESTER CLOSE
WALBERSWICK STREET
TRADESCANT RD
ELY COTTS
WEYMOUTH HO
BOLNEY ST
SHERBORNE HO
LULWORTH HO
PURBECK HO
PULHAM HO
MELCOMBE HO
KIBWORTH ST
BROADSTONE HO
STURMINSTER HO
BANVILLE HO
COBBETT STREET
WIMBORNE HO
SWANAGE HO
VERWOOD HO
OSMINGTON HO
MARY DINE CT
138
ST STEPHEN'S TERR
MYTTON HO
CROZIER HO
WILKINSON STREET
ALBERT SQUARE
ALBERT AVE
WHITEBEAM CL
HOLLAND RISE HO
Reay Prim Sch
CALDWELL STREET
BAKERY CL
SHELDON CT
DEAN CT
MAWBEY ST
ABBOT CT
HARTINGTON ROAD
THORNE ROAD
ALDEBERT TERRACE
KEMP CT
CAMELLIA ST
LANSCOMBE WLK
CAVENDISH HO
SELWAY HO
SW8
SADDLERS MEWS
WEBB HOUSE
JOHNSON HOUSE
EVANS HOUSE
TILLOTSON COURT
ANDREW PL
77
STAFFORD CT
SUMNER CT
DARSLEY DR
ALLEN EDWARDS DR
BANCROFT CT
BENSON CT
CORNWALLIS CT
TAIT CT
VICEROY RD
LANSDOWNE GDNS
ST BARNABAS VILLAS
GUILDFORD RD
KELVEDON HO
MONDRAGON HO
TEVERSHAM LA
ST BARNABAS LODGE
RUNDELL TOWER
HANNAH BARLOW HO
HAMPSON WAY
GASTON GATE
CLAPHAM ROAD
PORTLAND GR
LIBERTY ST
MORAT ST
ISABEL ST
HACKFORD RD
WALDEN HO
SUDBURY CT
LANGLEY CT
HARTINGTON CT
MENTONE CT
STAMBOURNE HO
DOVET CT
Durand Prim Sch
DURAND GDNS
PRIORY CT
ALL SAINTS CL
THE STUDIOS
SCHOOL FLATS
LANSDOWNE WAY
EDRICH HO
South Lambeth
SPENCER MEWS
SW9
JOHNSTON CL
VINCENT CT
HACKFORD WLK
RUSHBY CT
WHITFIELD CT
SANDHAM CT
PARKER CT
Larkhall Park
PRIORY GR
LARKHALL LA
MOBEY CT
MARSHALL CT
WHITTAKER CT
STRUDWICK CT
BINFIELD RD
LAVENDER CT
MIMOSA CT
ERICA CT
HEATHER CT
A3
STOCKWELL TERR
STOCKWELL GDNS
Stockwell Park Sch
SHERIDAN CT
GROVEWAY
STOCKWELL PARK RD
Allen Edwards Prim Sch
STUDLEY RD
SW4
SQUIRES CT
Stockwell
McINTYRE CT
LAKER CT
STUDLEY RD
Pav
Tenn Cts
BARLING CT
FENDER CT
HOLMES CT
JEPHSON CT
KNOX CT
PARADISE RD
JEFFREY'S RD
BROOKS CT
DALMENY CT
FISHLOCK CT
RICHARDSON CT
SWAN MEWS
CASSELL HO
STOCKWELL RD
ACLAND HO
BLAIR HO
MORANT HO
ST MICHAEL'S RD
STOCKWELL PARK CRES
31

Index

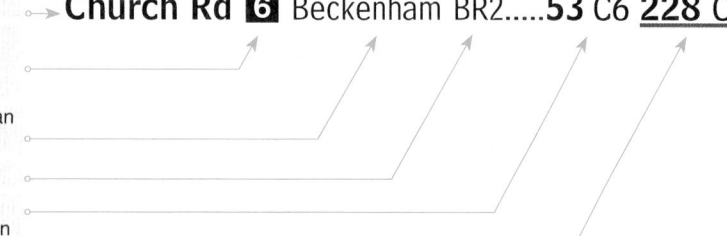

Place name May be abbreviated on the map

Location number Present when a number indicates the place's position in a crowded area of mapping

Locality, town or village Shown when more than one place has the same name

Postcode district District for the indexed place

Standard-scale reference Page number and grid reference for the standard-scale mapping on pages 1–227

Large-scale reference Page number and grid reference for the large-scale central London mapping on pages 229–270, underlined in red

Cities, towns and villages are listed in **CAPITAL LETTERS** **Public and commercial buildings** are highlighted in **magenta**
Places of interest are highlighted in blue with a star★

Abbreviations used in the index

Acad	**Academy**	Comm	**Common**	Gd	**Ground**	L	**Leisure**	Prom	**Promenade**
App	**Approach**	Cott	**Cottage**	Gdn	**Garden**	La	**Lane**	Rd	**Road**
Arc	**Arcade**	Cres	**Crescent**	Gn	**Green**	Liby	**Library**	Recn	**Recreation**
Ave	**Avenue**	Cswy	**Causeway**	Gr	**Grove**	Mdw	**Meadow**	Ret	**Retail**
Bglw	**Bungalow**	Ct	**Court**	H	**Hall**	Meml	**Memorial**	Sh	**Shopping**
Bldg	**Building**	Ctr	**Centre**	Ho	**House**	Mkt	**Market**	Sq	**Square**
Bsns, Bus	**Business**	Ctry	**Country**	Hospl	**Hospital**	Mus	**Museum**	St	**Street**
Bvd	**Boulevard**	Cty	**County**	HQ	**Headquarters**	Orch	**Orchard**	Sta	**Station**
Cath	**Cathedral**	Dr	**Drive**	Hts	**Heights**	Pal	**Palace**	Terr	**Terrace**
Cir	**Circus**	Dro	**Drove**	Ind	**Industrial**	Par	**Parade**	TH	**Town Hall**
Cl	**Close**	Ed	**Education**	Inst	**Institute**	Pas	**Passage**	Univ	**University**
Cnr	**Corner**	Emb	**Embankment**	Int	**International**	Pk	**Park**	Wk, Wlk	**Walk**
Coll	**College**	Est	**Estate**	Intc	**Interchange**	Pl	**Place**	Wr	**Water**
Com	**Community**	Ex	**Exhibition**	Junc	**Junction**	Prec	**Precinct**	Yd	**Yard**

Index of towns, villages, streets, hospitals, industrial estates, railway stations, schools, shopping centres, universities and places of interest

A

Aaron Ct BR3 . . . 207 D6
Aaron Hill Rd E6 . . . 100 C2
Abady Ho SW1 . . . 259 D4
Abberley Mews [9] SW8 . . . 137 B2
Abberton IG8 . . . 37 C5
Abbess Cl
[11] Newham E6 . . . 100 A2
Streatham SW2 . . . 160 D3
Abbeville Mews [3] SW4 . . . 137 D1
Abbeville Rd
Clapham Pk SW4 . . . 159 C6
Hornsey N8 . . . 49 D5
Abbey Ave HA0 . . . 88 A5
Abbey Bsns Ctr SW8 . . . 137 B4 268 D2
Abbey Cl Hayes UB3 . . . 106 B5
Northolt UB5 . . . 85 B4
Pinner HA5 . . . 40 C6
Abbey Cres DA17 . . . 125 C2
Abbey Ct
[6] Bedford Pk W12 . . . 111 C3
Camberwell SE17 . . . 262 B1
Church End N3 . . . 47 C6
[5] Edgware HA8 . . . 26 D5
Hampton TW12 . . . 173 C3
St John's Wood NW8 . . . 229 A4
Twickenham TW2 . . . 152 B2
Abbeydale Rd HA0 . . . 88 C6
Abbey Dr SW17 . . . 181 A5
Abbeyfield Cl CR4 . . . 180 C1
Abbeyfield Rd SE16 . . . 118 C2
Abbeyfields Cl NW10 . . . 88 C5
Abbey Gdns
[10] Bermondsey SE16 . . . 118 A2
Chislehurst BR7 . . . 188 C2
St John's Wood NW8 . . . 92 A5 229 B3
West Kensington W6 . . . 135 A6 264 A5
Abbey Gr SE2 . . . 124 B2
Abbeyhill Rd DA15 . . . 168 C2
Abbey Ho Newham E15 . . . 98 C5
St John's Wood NW8 . . . 229 B2
Abbey Ind Est CR4 . . . 202 D4
Abbey La
Beckenham BR3 . . . 185 C3
Mill Meads E15 . . . 98 B5
Abbey Lane Commercial Est [1] E15 . . . 98 C5
Abbey Lo Bromley SE12 . . . 187 B6
[1] Ealing W5 . . . 109 C6
Lisson Gr NW8 . . . 230 B1
Abbey Manufacturing Est HA0 . . . 88 B6
Abbey Mews
Brentford TW7 . . . 131 B4
Walthamstow E17 . . . 53 C4
Abbey Mount DA17 . . . 125 B1
Abbey Orchard St SW1 . . . 115 D3 259 D6
Abbey Orchard Street Est SW1 . . . 259 D6
Abbey Par Ealing NW10 . . . 88 B4
Merton SW19 . . . 180 A3
Abbey Park Ind Est IG11 . . . 101 A6
Abbey Pk BR3 . . . 185 C3
Abbey Prim Sch SM4 . . . 201 C2
Abbey Rd Barking IG11 . . . 100 D6
Bexley DA7 . . . 147 A1
Croydon CR0 . . . 220 D5
Enfield EN1 . . . 17 C6
Erith DA17 . . . 125 A3
Ilford IG2 . . . 57 B4
Lower Halliford TW17 . . . 192 C1
Merton SW19 . . . 180 A2
Newham E15 . . . 98 C5
St John's Wood NW8 . . . 92 A5 229 A4
Wembley NW10 . . . 88 D5
Abbey Rd Motorist Ctr [4] NW6 . . . 91 D6
Abbey St
Bermondsey SE1 . . . 117 D3 263 C6
Newham E13 . . . 99 A3
Abbey Terr SE2 . . . 124 C2
Abbey Trad Est SE26 . . . 185 B5
Abbey View NW7 . . . 11 D1
Abbey Wlk KT8 . . . 195 D5
ABBEY WOOD . . . 124 B3
Abbey Wood Rd SE2 . . . 124 C2
Abbey Wood Sch SE2 . . . 124 A3
Abbey Wood Sta SE2 . . . 124 C3
Abbot Cl HA4 . . . 62 D5
Abbot Ct SW8 . . . 270 A3
Abbot Ho [14] E14 . . . 119 D6
Abbotsbury Cl
Kensington W14 . . . 113 B4 244 C1
Mill Meads E15 . . . 98 A5
Abbotsbury Gdns HA5 . . . 40 C3
Abbotsbury Ho W14 . . . 244 B2
Abbotsbury Mews SE15 . . . 140 C2
Abbotsbury Prim Sch SM4 . . . 201 D4
Abbotsbury Rd
Coney Hall BR2, BR4 . . . 224 D6
Kensington W14 . . . 113 B4 244 C1
Morden SM4 . . . 201 D5
Abbots Cl BR5 . . . 211 A1
Abbots Ct SE25 . . . 205 C6
Abbots Dr HA2 . . . 63 C6
Abbotsfield Sch UB10 . . . 82 D5
Abbotsford Ave N15 . . . 51 A5
Abbotsford Gdns IG8 . . . 37 A3
Abbotsford Rd IG3 . . . 80 B6
Abbots Gdns N2 . . . 48 B5
Abbots Gn CR0, CR2 . . . 222 D2
Abbots Green CR2 . . . 222 D2
Abbotshade Rd [15] SE16 . . . 118 D5
Abbotshall Ave N14 . . . 15 C1
Abbotshall Rd SE6 . . . 164 B2
Abbots Ho
Kensington W14 . . . 254 C5
Pimlico SW1 . . . 259 C1
Walthamstow E17 . . . 35 B1
Abbots La SE1 . . . 117 C5 253 B3
Abbotsleigh Cl SM2 . . . 217 D1
Abbotsleigh Rd SW16 . . . 181 C5
Abbotsmede Cl TW1 . . . 152 D2
Abbots Pk SW2 . . . 160 C3
Abbot's Pl NW6 . . . 91 D6
Abbots Rd
Burnt Oak HA8 . . . 27 B3
Cheam SM3 . . . 217 A4
Abbots Rd *continued* .
Newham E6 . . . 99 D6
Abbot St E8 . . . 73 D2
Abbots Terr N8 . . . 50 A3
Abbotstone Ho [4] E5 . . . 74 A6
Abbotstone Rd SW15 . . . 134 C2
Abbotsview Ct NW7 . . . 12 A1
Abbots Way BR3 . . . 207 A4
Abbotswell Rd SE4 . . . 163 B6
Abbotswood Cl [7] DA17 . . . 125 A3
Abbotswood Gdns IG5 . . . 56 B6
Abbotswood Rd
London SE22 . . . 139 C1
Streatham SW16 . . . 159 D1
Abbotswood Way UB3 . . . 106 B5
Abbott Ave SW20 . . . 178 D2
Abbott Cl
Hampton TW12 . . . 173 A4
Northolt UB5 . . . 63 B2
Abbott Ho SW12 . . . 158 D4
Abbott Rd E14 . . . 98 B1
Abbotts Cl
Canonbury N1 . . . 73 A2
Romford RM7 . . . 59 D6
Woolwich SE28 . . . 124 C6
Abbotts Cres
Chingford E4 . . . 36 B6
Enfield EN2 . . . 4 D3
Abbotts Ct HA2 . . . 64 B6
Abbotts Dr HA0 . . . 65 B6
Abbotts Park Rd E10 . . . 54 A2
Abbotts Rd Barnet EN5 . . . 1 D1
Mitcham CR4 . . . 203 C5
Southall UB1 . . . 107 A5
Abbotts Wharf [4] E14 . . . 97 C1
Abbott's Wlk DA7 . . . 146 D5
Abchurch La EC2, EC4 . . . 117 B6 252 D6
Abchurch Yd EC4 . . . 252 C6
Abdale Rd W12 . . . 112 B5
Abel Ho
[7] Kennington SE11 . . . 138 C6
Woolwich SE18 . . . 123 A2
Abenglen Ind Est UB3 . . . 105 B4
Aberavon Rd E3 . . . 97 A4
Abercairn Rd SW16 . . . 181 C3
Aberconway Rd SM4 . . . 201 D5
Abercorn Cl
Finchley NW7 . . . 29 A3
St John's Wood NW8 . . . 92 A4 229 A2
Abercorn Cres HA2 . . . 41 D1
Abercorn Gdns
Harrow HA3 . . . 43 D2
Ilford RM6 . . . 58 B3
Abercorn Gr HA4 . . . 39 B5
Abercorn Mans NW8 . . . 229 B3
Abercorn Mews [10] TW10 . . . 132 B1
Abercorn Pl NW8 . . . 92 A5 229 A3
Abercorn Rd
Finchley NW7 . . . 29 A3
Stanmore HA7 . . . 25 C3
Abercorn Trad Est HA0 . . . 87 D6
Abercorn Way SE1 . . . 118 A1
Abercrombie Dr EN1 . . . 6 A4
Abercrombie Ho [1] W12 . . . 112 B6
Abercrombie St SW11 . . . 136 C3
Aberdale Ct [22] SE16 . . . 118 D4
Aberdare Cl BR4 . . . 224 A6
Aberdare Gdns
Finchley NW7 . . . 28 D3
South Hampstead NW6 . . . 69 D1
Aberdare Rd EN3 . . . 6 C1
Aberdeen Cotts HA7 . . . 25 C3
Aberdeen Ct
Canonbury N5 . . . 73 A3
Paddington W2 . . . 236 C5
Aberdeen Ctr N5 . . . 73 A3
Aberdeen La N5 . . . 73 A3
Aberdeen Mans WC1 . . . 240 A6
Aberdeen Par N18 . . . 34 B5
Aberdeen Pk N5 . . . 73 A3
Aberdeen Pl NW8 . . . 92 B3 236 C6
Aberdeen Rd
Canonbury N5 . . . 73 A4
Croydon CR0 . . . 221 B4
Dudden Hill NW10 . . . 67 D3
Edmonton N18 . . . 34 B5
Harrow HA3 . . . 24 D1
Aberdeen Terr SE3 . . . 142 B3
Aberdour Rd IG3 . . . 80 B6

Aberdour St SE1 . . . 117 C2 263 A4
Aberfeldy Ho SE5 . . . 138 D5
Aberfeldy St E14 . . . 98 A1
Aberford Gdns SE18 . . . 144 A4
Aberfoyle Rd SW16 . . . 181 D4
Abergeldie Rd SE12 . . . 165 B5
Abernethy Rd SE13 . . . 142 C1
Abersham Rd E8 . . . 73 D3
Abery St SE18 . . . 123 C2
Ability Plaza [8] E8 . . . 73 D1
Ability Twrs EC1 . . . 235 A2
Abingdon W14 . . . 254 D3
Abingdon Cl
Fulham SE1 . . . 263 D2
Hillingdon UB10 . . . 82 B6
Kentish Town NW1 . . . 71 D2
Wimbledon SW19 . . . 180 A4
Abingdon Ct
Earl's Ct W8 . . . 255 B5
Edgware HA8 . . . 26 A6
Upper Tooting SW17 . . . 180 D4
Abingdon Gdns W8 . . . 255 B5
Abingdon Ho
Bromley BR1 . . . 187 B3
Spitalfields E2 . . . 243 C6
Abingdon Lo
[2] Barnet EN5 . . . 1 A1
Bromley BR2 . . . 186 D1
Abingdon Mans W8 . . . 255 A6
Abingdon Rd
Finchley N3 . . . 30 A1
Kensington W8 . . . 113 C3 255 B5
Thornton Heath SW16 . . . 182 A2
Abingdon St SW1 . . . 116 A3 260 A6
Abingdon Villas W8 . . . 113 C3 255 B5
Abinger Cl Barking IG11 . . . 80 A4
Bickley BR1 . . . 210 A6
New Addington CR0 . . . 224 A2
Wallington SM6 . . . 220 A3
Abinger Ct
[3] Ealing W5 . . . 109 C6
Thornton Heath CR0 . . . 204 D2

Abinger Ct continued
Wallington SM6 . . . . . . 220 A3
Abinger Gdns TW7 . . . . 130 C2
Abinger Gr SE8 . . . . . . 141 B6
Abinger Ho
Borough The SE1 . . . . . 252 A1
2 Kingston u T KT2 . . . 176 D3
Abinger Mews W9 . . . . 91 C3
Abinger Rd W4 . . . . . . 111 C3
Abington Ho NW11 . . . . 48 A3
Ablett St SE16 . . . . 118 C1
Abney Gdns 5 N16 . . . 73 D6
Abney Park Cemetery★
N16 . . . . 73 C6
Abney Park Ct N16 . . . . 73 D6
Aborfield 6 NW5 . . . . . 71 C3
Aboyne Dr SW20 . . . . . 178 A1
Aboyne Ho
Neasden NW10 . . . . . . 67 C5
Wandsworth SW17 . . . . 158 B1
Abraham Cl W20 . . . . . 22 B6
Abraham Cohen Ct IG1 . 56 C3
Abraham Fisher Ho 2
E12 . . . . 78 C3
Abridge Way IG11 . . . . 102 B5
Abyssinia Cl SW11 . . . . 136 C1
Abyssinia Rd SW11 . . . . 136 C1
Acacia Ave
Brentford TW8 . . . . . . 131 B5
East Finchley N2 . . . . . 47 D6
Hayes UB3 . . . . 83 D1
Littleton TW17 . . . . . . 192 C4
Ruislip HA4 . . . . 40 B2
Tottenham N17 . . . . . . 33 B3
Wembley HA9 . . . . 66 A3
Yiewsley UB7 . . . . 104 B6
Acacia Bsns Ctr 1 E11 . 76 C5
Acacia Cl
Petts Wood BR5 . . . . . 211 B4
Rotherhithe SE8 . . . . . 119 A2
Stanmore HA7 . . . . . . 24 C4
Acacia Ct Harrow HA1 . . 41 D3
5 West Norwood
SW16 . . . . 182 C5
Acacia Dr SM3 . . . . . . 201 C1
Acacia Gdns
St John's Wood NW8 . . 229 D4
West Wickham BR4 . . . 224 A6
Acacia Gdns Dulwich SE21 161 B2
Kingston u T KT3 . . . . 199 C6
Acacia Ho Brockley SE4 . 141 B1
1 New Malden KT3 . . . 199 C5
Stoke Newington N16 . . 73 B6
Wood Green N22 . . . . . 32 C2
Acacia Lo 6 N3 . . . . . . 29 B1
Acacia Pl NW8 . . . 92 B5 229 D4
Acacia Rd Acton W3 . . . 111 A6
Beckenham BR3 . . . . . 207 B6
Enfield EN2 . . . . 5 B4
Hampton TW12 . . . . . 173 C4
Leyton E11 . . . . 76 C6
Mitcham CR4 . . . . 181 B1
St John's Wood
NW8 . . . . 92 B5 229 D4
Thornton Heath SW16 . . 182 A2
Walthamstow E17 . . . . 53 A3
Wood Green N22 . . . . . 32 C2
Acacias The EN4 . . . . . 14 B6
Acacia Way HA15 . . . . . 167 D3
Acacia Wlk SW10 . . . . . 266 B3
Acad at Peckham The
SE15 . . . . 139 D4
Academy Ct 13 E2 . . . . 96 C4
Academy Gdns
Croydon CR0 . . . . 205 D1
Kensington W8 . . . . . . 245 A2
Northolt UB5 . . . . 84 D5
Academy Pl SE18 . . . . . 144 C4
Academy Rd SE18 . . . . 144 C4
Academy Sch The NW3 . 70 B4
Academy The 2 N19 . . . 49 C1
Acad of Live & Recorded
Arts The SW18 . . . . . . 158 B5
Acanthus Dr SE1 . . . . . 118 A1
Acanthus Rd SW11 . . . . 137 A2
Accadia Ct NW9 . . . . . . 67 A6
Accommodation Rd
NW11 . . . . 47 B1
Ace Par KT9 . . . . 214 A6
Acer Ave UB4 . . . . 85 A2
Acer Ct
2 Cricklewood NW2 . . 68 D4
3 Enfield EN3 . . . . . . 7 A2
Acers BR7 . . . . 188 A3
Acfold Rd SW6 . . . . . . 265 C1
Achilles Cl SE1 . . . . . . 118 A1
Achilles Ho 16 E2 . . . . . 96 B5
Achilles Rd NW6 . . . . . 69 C3
Achilles Way W1 . . . . . 248 B3
Acklam Rd W10 . . . . . . 91 B2
Acklington Dr NW9 . . . . 27 C2
Ackmar Rd
SW6 . . . . 135 C4 265 A1
Ackroyd Dr E3 . . . . 97 C2
Ackroyd Rd SE23 . . . . . 163 A4
Acland Burghley Sch
NW5 . . . . 71 B4
Acland Cl SE18 . . . . . . 145 B5
Acland Cres SE5 . . . . . 139 B2
Acland Ho SW9 . . . . . . 138 B3
Acland Rd NW2 . . . . . . 68 B2
Acock Gr UB5 . . . . 64 A4
Acol Cres HA4 . . . . 62 B3
Acol Ct 3 NW6 . . . . . . 69 C1
Acol Rd NW6 . . . . 69 D1

Aconbury Rd RM9 . . . . 102 B6
Acorn Cl Chingford E4 . . 35 D5
Chislehurst BR7 . . . . . 189 A5
Enfield EN2 . . . . 4 D4
1 Hampton TW12 . . . . 173 D4
Acorn Ct 5 Bow E3 . . . . 97 C5
Hampton TW12 . . . . . 173 B5
Ilford IG2 . . . . 57 C4
Upton Pk E6 . . . . 78 A1
Wood Green N11 . . . . 31 D4
Acorn Gdns
North Acton W3 . . . . . 89 B2
South Norwood SE19 . . 183 D2
Acorn Gr
Harlington UB3 . . . . . 127 D5
Ruislip HA4 . . . . 61 D4
Acorn Par 7 SE15 . . . . 140 B5
Acorn Production Ctr
N7 . . . . 72 A1
Acorns The 21 SW19 . . . 156 D3
Acorns Way KT10 . . . . . 212 A3
Acorn Way
Beckenham BR3 . . . . . 208 A4
Forest Hill SE23 . . . . . 162 D1
Orpington BR6 . . . . . . 226 D4
Acorn Wharf SE15 . . . . 140 A6
Acorn Wlk SE16 . . . . . . 119 A5
Acqua Ho TW9 . . . . . . 132 D5
Acrefield Ho 4 NW4 . . . 46 D5
Acre La Brixton SW2 . . . 138 B1
Wallington SM5 . . . . . 219 A4
Acre Path UB5 . . . . 63 A2
Acre Rd
Dagenham RM10 . . . . 81 D1
Kingston u T KT2 . . . . 176 B2
Mitcham SW19 . . . . . . 180 B4
Acre Way HA6 . . . . 22 A2
Acris St SW18 . . . . 158 A6
ACS Hillingdon
International Sch
UB10 . . . . 82 B6
Action Ct TW15 . . . . . . 171 A2
ACTON 110 D5
Acton Bsns Ctr NW10 . . 89 B3
Acton Central Ind Est 4
W3 . . . . 110 D5
Acton Central Sta W3 . . 111 B5
Acton Cl N9 . . . . 18 A2
Acton Green W4 . . . . . 110 D5
Acton High Sch W3 . . . 110 D5
Acton Hill Mews W3 . . . 110 D5
Acton Ho 5 Acton W3 . . 89 A1
16 Haggerston E8 . . . . 95 D6
Acton Hospl W3 . . . . . 110 C4
Acton La
Acton Green W4 . . . . . 111 A4
Acton W3 . . . . 111 A4
Harlesden NW10 . . . . . 89 B5
Acton Main Line Sta
W3 . . . . 89 A1
Acton Mews E8 . . . . . . 95 D6
Acton Park Ind Est
W3 . . . . 111 B4
Acton St WC1 . . . 94 B4 233 C1
Acton Town Sta W3 . . . 110 C4
Acton Vale Ind Pk W3 . . 111 D5
Acuba Ho SW18 . . . . . . 157 D3
Acuba Rd SW18 . . . . . . 157 D2
Acworth Cl N9 . . . . 18 C4
Acworth Ho 1 SE18 . . . 144 D6
Ada Ct Islington N1 . . . . 235 A5
St John's Wood
W9 . . . . 92 A4 229 B1
Ada Gdns Plaistow E15 . 98 D6
South Bromley E14 . . . 98 B1
Ada Ho 28 E2 . . . . 96 A6
Adair Cl SE25 . . . . 206 B6
Adair Ho SW3 . . . . 267 B6
Adair Rd W10 . . . . 91 A3
Adair Twr 7 W10 . . . . . 91 A3
Ada Kennedy Ct 6
SE10 . . . . 142 A5
Ada Lewis Ho HA9 . . . . 66 B4
Adam Cl SE6 . . . . 185 C4
Adam Ct
Newington SE11 . . . . . 261 C3
15 Sutton SM1 . . . . . 218 A4
Adam & Eve Ct W1 . . . . 239 B2
Adam & Eve Mews
W8 . . . . 113 C3 255 B6
Adamfields NW3 . . . . . 70 B1
Adam Lo N21 . . . . 16 B6
Adam Rd E4 . . . . 35 B4
Adams Bridge Bsns Ctr
HA9 . . . . 66 D3
Adams Cl Finchley N3 . . 29 C3
Surbiton KT5 . . . . 198 B3
Wembley Pk NW9 . . . . 66 C2
Adams Ct E17 . . . . 53 A3
Adams Gardens Est 5
SE16 . . . . 118 C4
Adams Ho
3 South Bromley E14 . 98 B1
3 Streatham SW16 . . . 181 C5
Adams Mews
Upper Tooting SW17 . . 158 D2
Wood Green N22 . . . . . 32 B3
Adamson Ct N2 . . . . . . 48 C6
Adamson Rd
Hampstead NW3 . . . . . 70 B1
Newham E16 . . . . 99 A1
Adamson Way BR3 . . . . 208 A4
Adams Pl N7 . . . . 72 B3
Adams Qtr RM8 . . . . . . 131 C6
Adams Rd
Beckenham BR3 . . . . . 207 A4
Tottenham N17 . . . . . . 33 B4
Adamsrill Cl EN1 . . . . . 17 B5

Adamsrill Prim Sch
SE26 . . . . 163 A1
Adamsrill Rd SE26 . . . . 185 A6
Adam's Row
W1 . . . . 115 A6 248 B5
Adams Sq DA6 . . . . . . 147 A2
Adam St WC2 . . . 116 A6 250 B5
Adams Way CR0 . . . . . . 206 A3
Adams Wlk 1 KT1 . . . . 176 A1
Ada Pl E2 . . . . 96 A6
Ada Rd Camberwell SE5 . 139 C5
Wembley HA0, HA9 . . . 65 D5
Adare Ctr The SW16 . . . 160 A1
Adare Wlk SW16, SW2 . 160 B3
Ada St E8 . . . . 96 B6
Adcot Wlk 8 BR6 . . . . . 227 D4
Adderley Gdns SE9 . . . 188 C6
Adderley Gr SW11 . . . . 159 A6
Adderley Rd HA3 . . . . . 24 D2
Adderley St E14 . . . . . . 98 A1
Addey Ho 9 SE8 . . . . . 141 B5
Addey & Stanhope Sch
SE14 . . . . 141 C4
ADDINGTON 223 C3
Addington Ct 7
SW14 . . . . 133 B2
Addington Dr N12 . . . . 30 B4
Addington Gr SE26 . . . . 185 A6
Addington Ho 18 SW9 . . 138 B3
Addington Rd Bow E3 . . 97 C4
Newham E16 . . . . 98 C3
Stroud Green N4 . . . . . 50 C3
Thornton Heath CR0 . . 204 C1
West Wickham BR4 . . . 224 C6
West Wickham BR4,
CR0 . . . . 224 B4
Addington Sq SE5 . . . . 139 B5
Addington St
SE1 . . . . 116 B4 250 D1
Addington Village Rd
CR0 . . . . 223 C3
Addington Village Sta
CR0 . . . . 223 C2
Addis Cl EN3 . . . . 6 D4
ADDISCOMBE 206 A1
Addiscombe Ave CR0 . . 206 A1
Addiscombe Cl HA3 . . . 43 C4
Addiscombe Court Rd
CR0 . . . . 221 C6
Addiscombe Rd CR0 . . . 222 B6
Addiscombe Sta CR0 . . 206 A1
Addis Ho 13 E1 . . . . . . 96 C2
Addison Ave
Hounslow TW3 . . . . . . 130 A4
Notting Hill
W11 . . . . 113 A5 244 A3
Southgate N14 . . . . . . 15 C5
Addison Bridge Pl
W14 . . . . 113 B2 254 C4
Addison Cl
Northwood HA6 . . . . . 22 A2
Orpington BR5 . . . . . . 211 A3
Addison Cres
W14 . . . . 113 A3 254 B6
Addison Ct
3 Belmont SM2 . . . . . 217 D1
Ealing W5 . . . . 110 C6
Twickenham TW1 . . . . 153 A3
Addison Dr SE12 . . . . . 165 B6
Addison Gdns
Hammersmith W14 . . . 112 D3
Kingston u T KT5 . . . . 198 B5
Addison Gr W4 . . . . . . 111 C3
Addison Ho
NW8 . . . . 92 B4 229 C2
Addison Park Mans 12
W14 . . . . 112 D4
Addison Pl
Notting Hill
W11 . . . . 113 A5 244 A3
Southall UB1 . . . . 107 C6
Addison Prim Sch
W14 . . . . 112 D3
Addison Rd
Bromley BR2 . . . . 209 D4
Croydon SE25 . . . . . . 206 A5
Enfield EN3 . . . . 6 D4
Kensington
W14 . . . . 113 B3 254 C6
Teddington TW11 . . . . 175 B4
Walthamstow E17 . . . . 54 A4
Wanstead E11 . . . . . . 55 A3
Addison's Cl CR0 . . . . . 223 B6
Addison Way
Hampstead Garden Suburb
NW11 . . . . 47 C5
Hayes UB3 . . . . 84 A1
Northwood HA6 . . . . . 22 A2
Addle Hill EC4 . . . . 241 D1
Addle St EC2 . . . . 242 B3
Addlestone Ho 4 W10 . . 90 C2
Addy Ho SE16 . . . . 118 C2
Adecroft Way KT8 . . . . 196 A6
Adela Ave KT3 . . . . 200 B5
Adela Ho 9 W6 . . . . . . 112 C1
Adelaide Ave SE4 . . . . . 141 C1
Adelaide Cl
Brixton SW9 . . . . 138 C1
Enfield EN1 . . . . 5 C5
Stanmore HA7 . . . . . . 25 A6
Adelaide Ct
15 Beckenham BR3 . . . 185 C3
Hackney E5 . . . . 75 A3
Hanwell W7 . . . . 108 A4
St John's Wood NW8 . . 229 B3
Adelaide Gdns RM6 . . . 59 C2
Adelaide Gr W12 . . . . . 112 A5
Adelaide Ho E17 . . . . . 53 B6

Adelaide Rd
Ashford TW15 . . . . . . 170 A6
Chislehurst BR7 . . . . . 188 D5
Ealing W13 . . . . 109 A4
Heston TW5 . . . . 129 A4
Ilford IG1 . . . . 78 D6
Kingston u T KT6 . . . . 198 A4
Leyton E10 . . . . 76 A5
Primrose Hill NW3 . . . . 70 C1
Richmond TW9 . . . . . . 132 B1
Southall UB2 . . . . 107 A2
Teddington TW11 . . . . 174 D4
2 Wandsworth SW18 . 157 C6
Adelaide St WC2 . . . . . 250 A5
Adelaide Terr TW8 . . . . 109 D1
Adela St W10 . . . . 91 A3
Adelina Gr E1 . . . . 96 C2
Adelina Mews SW12 . . . 159 B3
Adeline Pl WC1 . . 93 D2 239 D3
Adelphi Cres UB4 . . . . . 83 D4
Adelphi Ct
19 Finchley N12 . . . . . 30 B1
20 Rotherhithe SE16 . . 118 D4
Adelphi Terr WC2 . . . . . 250 B5
Adelphi Way UB4 . . . . . 83 D4
Adeney Cl W6 . . . . 134 D6
Aden Gr N16 . . . . 73 B4
Aden Ho 16 E1 . . . . . . 96 D2
Aden Lo N16 . . . . 73 B4
Adenmore Rd SE6 . . . . 163 C4
Aden Rd Enfield EN3 . . . 7 A1
Ilford IG1 . . . . 57 A2
Adeyfield Ho EC1 . . . . . 235 D1
Adhara Rd HA6 . . . . . . 22 A5
Adie Rd W6 . . . . 112 C3
Adine Rd E13 . . . . 99 B3
Adisham Ho 4 E5 . . . . . 74 B3
Adler Ind Est UB3 . . . . 105 B4
Adler St E1 . . . . 96 A1
Adley St E5 . . . . 75 A3
Adlington Cl N18 . . . . . 33 C5
Admaston Rd SE18 . . . . 145 A6
Admiral Ct
Barking IG11 . . . . 102 C5
Carshalton SM5 . . . . . 202 C1
Chelsea SW10 . . . 136 A4 266 B2
Dollis Hill NW2 . . . . . . 68 A5
Hendon NW4 . . . . 46 A4
Marylebone W1 . . . . . 238 A3
Admiral Ho TW1 . . . . . 175 A6
Admiral Hyson Ind Est
SE16 . . . . 118 B1
Admiral Mews W10 . . . 90 D3
Admiral Pl Harringay N8 . 50 D5
Rotherhithe SE16 . . . . 119 A5
Admirals Cl E18 . . . . . . 55 B5
Admirals Ct
Bermondsey SE1 . . . . . 253 C3
3 Newham E6 . . . . . . 100 D1
32 Putney SW19 . . . . 156 D3
Admiral Seymour Rd
SE9 . . . . 144 B1
Admirals Gate SE10 . . . 141 D4
Admiral Sq
SW10 . . . . 136 A4 266 B2
Admiral St SE8 . . . . . . 141 C4
Admirals Way E14 . . . . 119 C4
Admiral's Wlk NW3 . . . . 70 A5
Admiralty Arch★ SW1 . 249 D4
Admiralty Cl 1 SE8 . . . 141 C4
Admiralty Rd TW11 . . . 174 D4
Admiralty Way TW11 . . 174 D4
Admiral Wlk W9 . . . . . . 91 C2
Adolf St SE6 . . . . 185 D6
Adolphus Rd N4 . . . . . . 50 D1
Adolphus St SE8 . . . . . 141 B5
Adomar Rd RM8 . . . . . . 81 A5
Adpar St W2 . . . 92 B2 236 C4
Adrian Ave NW2 . . . . . . 46 B1
Adrian Bolt Ho 2 E2 . . . 96 B4
Adrian Ct EN5 . . . . 12 C5
Adrian Ho Islington N1 . 233 D5
South Lambeth SW8 . . 270 A4
Stratford E15 . . . . 76 B1
Adrian Mews SW10 . . . 265 C6
Adriatic Bldg 18 E14 . . . 119 A6
Adriatic Ho 18 E1 . . . . . 96 D3
Adrienne Ave UB1 . . . . 85 B4
Adron Ho 13 SE16 . . . . 118 C2
Adstock Ho 5 N1 . . . . . 72 D1
ADT Coll SW15 . . . . . . 157 B6
Advance Rd SE27 . . . . . 183 A6
Advent Ct IG8 . . . . 36 D5
Adventurers Ct 17
E14 . . . . 120 B6
Advent Way N18 . . . . . 34 D5
Adyar Ct 7 SW19 . . . . . 179 A3
Adys Lawn NW2 . . . . . . 68 B3
Adys Rd SE15 . . . . 139 D2
Aegean Apts 7 E16 . . . . 121 A6
Aegon Ho 8 E14 . . . . . . 119 D3
Aerodrome Rd NW4,
NW9 . . . . 45 D6
Aerodrome Way TW5 . . 128 C6
Aeroville NW9 . . . . 27 C6
Affleck St N1 . . . . 233 D3
Afghan Rd SW11 . . . . . 136 C3
Africa Ho WC2 . . . . 240 C2
Afsil Ho EC1 . . . . 241 B3
Aga Khan Univ WC1 . . . 239 D3
Agamemnon Rd NW6 . . 69 B3
Agar Cl KT6 . . . . 214 B6
Agar Gr NW1 . . . . 71 D1
Agar Pl NW1 . . . . 71 C1
Agar St WC2 . . . . 250 B5
Agate Cl E16 . . . . 99 D1
Agate Ho
New Malden KT4 . . . . . 199 C1
12 Penge SE26 . . . . . 184 B5
Agate Rd W6 . . . . 112 C3

Agatha Cl E1 . . . . 118 C5
Agaton Rd SE9 . . . . . . 167 A2
Agave Rd NW2 . . . . 68 C4
Agdon St EC1 . . . 94 C3 241 C6
Agincourt E11 . . . . 54 D3
Agincourt Rd NW3 . . . . 70 D4
Agnes Ave IG1 . . . . 78 A4
Agnes Cl E6 . . . . 122 C6
Agnes Ct 11 SW18 . . . . 136 B1
Agnes Gdns RM8 . . . . . 80 D4
Agnes Ho 13 W11 . . . . 112 D6
Agnes Rd W3 . . . . 111 D4
2 Wandsworth SW18 . 157 C6
Agnes St E14 . . . . 97 B1
Agnesfield Cl N12 . . . . 30 C4
Agnew Rd SE23 . . . . . . 162 D4
Agricola Pl EN1 . . . . . . 17 C6
Aidan Cl RM8 . . . . 81 A4
Aidans Ct N12 . . . . 30 C5
Aigburth Mans 5
SW9 . . . . 138 C5
Ailantus Ct HA8 . . . . . . 26 B5
Aileen Wlk E15 . . . . . . 76 D1
Ailsa Ave TW1 . . . . 153 B6
Ailsa Rd TW1 . . . . 153 B6
Ailsa St E14 . . . . 98 A2
Ainger Rd NW3 . . . . . . 70 D1
Ainsdale NW1 . . . . 232 A2
Ainsdale Cl BR6 . . . . . . 211 B1
Ainsdale Cres HA5 . . . . 41 C6
Ainsdale Dr SE1 . . . . . . 118 A1
Ainsdale Rd W5 . . . . . . 87 D3
Ainsley Ave RM7 . . . . . 59 D3
Ainsley Cl N9 . . . . 17 C3
Ainsley St 2 E2 . . . . . . 96 B4
Ainslie Ct 2 HA0 . . . . . 88 A5
Ainslie Ho 1 E4 . . . . . . 35 C5
Ainslie Wlk 8 SW12 . . . 159 B4
Ainslie Wood Cres E4 . . 35 D5
Ainslie Wood Gdns E4 . 35 D5
Ainslie Wood Prim Sch
E4 . . . . 35 D5
Ainslie Wood Rd E4 . . . 35 D5
Ainsty St 20 SE16 . . . . 118 C4
Ainsworth Cl
Camberwell SE5 . . . . . 139 C3
Hendon NW4 . . . . 46 A4
Ainsworth Est
NW8 . . . . 92 A6 229 A6
Ainsworth Ho NW8 . . . . 91 D6
Ainsworth Rd
Croydon CR0 . . . . 220 D6
Hackney E9 . . . . 74 C1
Ainsworth Way
NW8 . . . . 92 A6 229 A6
Aintree Ave E6 . . . . 100 A6
Aintree Cl UB8 . . . . 82 D2
Aintree Ho SE26 . . . . . 184 B4
Aintree Rd UB6 . . . . . . 87 B5
Aintree St SW6 . 135 A5 264 B4
Airborne Ho 10 SM6 . . . 219 B4
Aird Ct TW12 . . . . 173 D2
Aird Ho SE1 . . . . 262 A5
Airdrie Cl Barnsbury N1 . 72 B1
Hayes UB4 . . . . 85 A2
Airedale Ave W4 . . . . . 111 D1
Airedale Ave S W4 . . . . 111 D1
Airedale Rd
Balham SW12 . . . . . . 158 D4
Ealing W5 . . . . 109 D3
Airlie Gdns Ilford IG1 . . 56 D1
Kensington W8 . . 113 C5 245 A3
Airlinks Ind Est TW5 . . . 106 C1
Air Park Way TW13 . . . 150 B2
Airport Gate Bsns Ctr
UB7 . . . . 126 C5
Airport Ho CR0 . . . . . . 220 C2
Airport Rdbt E16 . . . . . 121 D5
Air St W1 . . . . 249 B5
Airthrie Rd IG3 . . . . . . 80 B6
Aisgill Ave
SW5 . . . . 113 B1 254 D1
Aisher Rd SE28 . . . . . . 124 C6
Aislabie Ho N21 . . . . . . 17 B5
Aislibie Rd SE12 . . . . . 142 C1
Aiten Pl W6 . . . . 112 A2
Aithan Ho 16 E14 . . . . . 97 B1
Aitken Cl
Carshalton CR4 . . . . . 202 D2
Hackney E8 . . . . 96 A6
Aitken Rd Barnet EN5 . . 12 C6
Catford SE6 . . . . 163 D2
Aits View KT8 . . . . 195 D6
Ajax Ave NW9 . . . . 45 C6
Ajax Ct NW9 . . . . 45 C6
Ajax Ho 16 E2 . . . . 96 B5
Ajax Rd NW6 . . . . 69 C3
Akabusi Cl SE25 . . . . . 206 A3
Akbar Ho 7 E14 . . . . . . 119 D2
Akehurst St SW15 . . . . 156 A4
Akenside Ct 3 NW3 . . . 70 B3
Akenside Rd NW3 . . . . . 70 B3
Akerman Rd
Brixton SW9 . . . . 138 D4
Kingston u T KT6 . . . . 197 C3
Akintaro Ho 7 SE8 . . . . 141 B6
Akiva Sch N3 . . . . 29 D1
Alabama St SE18 . . . . . 145 C5
Alacross Rd W5 . . . . . . 109 D4
Aladdin Workspace
UB6 . . . . 85 D6
Alamaro Lo 5 SE10 . . . . 120 D3
Alandale Dr HA5 . . . . . 22 B2
Aland Ct SE16 . . . . 119 A3
Alander Mews E17 . . . . 54 A5
Alan Dr EN5 . . . . 13 A5
Alan Gdns RM7 . . . . . . 59 C2
Alan Hocken Way E15 . . 98 C5
Alan Lo N3 . . . . 29 C2
Alan Preece Ct NW6 . . . 68 D1
Alan Rd SW19 . . . . 179 A5

Alanthus Cl SE12 . . . . . 165 A5
Alaska Bldg 12 SE13 . . . 141 D4
Alaska St SE1 . . . . 251 A3
Alastor Ho 10 E14 . . . . 120 A3
Alba Cl UB4 . . . . 84 C3
Albacore Cres SE13 . . . 163 D5
Alba Gdns NW11 . . . . . 47 A3
Albain Cres TW15 . . . . . 148 A5
Alba Mews SW18,
SW19 . . . . 157 C2
Alban Ho
Hampstead NW3 . . . . . 70 A2
New Cross SE14 . . . . . 141 B4
Albans Cl SW16 . . . . . . 160 A1
Albany W1 . . . . 249 A5
Albany Bushey WD23 . . 8 B5
Ickenham UB10 . . . . . 60 C3
Mortlake SW14 . . . . . . 132 D1
Sidcup DA5 . . . . 168 D4
West Green N15 . . . . . 51 A5
Albany Coll NW4 . . . . . 46 C4
Albany Coll Hendry Ho
NW4 . . . . 46 B4
Albany Cres
Claygate KT10 . . . . . . 212 C2
Edgware HA8 . . . . 26 C3
Albany Ct
Ashford TW15 . . . . . . 171 B4
Cheam SM1 . . . . 217 B4
Chingford E4 . . . . 19 D5
College Pk NW10 . . . . 90 B4
Finchley N12 . . . . 29 D4
Grahame Pk HA8 . . . . 27 B2
Kingston u T KT2 . . . . 176 A4
NW8 . . . . 229 C3
Richmond TW10 . . . . . 153 B1
Surbiton KT6 . . . . 197 D2
Walthamstow E10 . . . . 53 C2
Westminster SW1 . . . . 259 C6
8 Whitechapel E1 . . . . 96 A1
Albany Ctyd W1 . . . . . . 249 B5
Albany Ho
6 Brentford TW8 . . . . 132 A6
Edgware HA8 . . . . 26 C3
Upper Clapton E5 . . . . 74 C6
Albany Mans SW11 . . . 267 B3
Albany Mews
Camberwell SE5 . . . . . 139 A6
Islington N1 . . . . 72 C1
Kingston u T KT2 . . . . 175 D4
Plaistow BR1 . . . . 187 A4
Sutton SM1 . . . . 217 D4
Albany Par 4 TW8 . . . . 132 A6
Albany Park Ave EN3 . . 6 C6
Albany Park Rd KT2 . . . 176 A4
Albany Park Sta DA14 . . 168 D2
Albany Pas 7 TW10 . . . 154 A6
Albany Pl TW8 . . . . 131 D6
Albany Rd
Brentford TW8 . . . . . . 131 D6
Camberwell SE5 . . . . . 139 C6
Chislehurst BR7 . . . . . 188 D5
Dagenham RM6 . . . . . 59 B3
Ealing W13 . . . . 109 B6
Enfield EN3 . . . . 6 D5
Erith DA17 . . . . 147 B6
Leyton E10 . . . . 53 C2
Manor Pk E12 . . . . . . 77 D4
New Malden KT3 . . . . . 199 B5
Richmond TW10 . . . . . 154 A6
Sidcup DA5 . . . . 168 C4
Stroud Green N4 . . . . . 50 C3
Upper Edmonton N18 . 34 C5
Walthamstow E17 . . . . 53 A3
Wimbledon SW19 . . . . 179 D5
Albany Reach KT7 . . . . 196 D4
Albany St NW1 . . 93 B4 231 D2
Albany Terr 6 TW10 . . . 154 B6
Albany The
Kingston u T KT2 . . . . 175 D4
Woodford IG8 . . . . 36 D6
Albany View IG9 . . . . . 21 A3
Albany Wlk N15 . . . . . . 50 D5
Alba Pl W11 . . . . 91 B1
Albatross 51 NW9 . . . . 27 D1
Albatross Cl E6 . . . . . . 100 D3
Albatross St SE18 . . . . 145 C5
Albemarle SW19 . . . . . 156 D2
Albemarle App IG2 . . . . 56 D3
Albemarle Ave TW2 . . . 151 B3
Albemarle Gdns
Ilford IG2 . . . . 56 D3
New Malden KT3 . . . . . 199 B5
Albemarle Ho
2 Brixton SW9 . . . . . . 138 C2
Rotherhithe SE16 . . . . 119 B2
Albemarle Lo SE26 . . . . 185 A5
Albemarle Mans NW3 . . 69 D4
Albemarle Pk
Beckenham BR3 . . . . . 185 D2
Stanmore HA7 . . . . . . 25 C5
Albemarle Prim Sch
SW19 . . . . 157 A2
Albemarle Rd
Beckenham BR2, BR3 . . 186 A2
East Barnet EN4 . . . . . 14 C4
Albemarle St
W1 . . . . 115 C6 249 A5
Albemarle Way EC1 . . . 241 C5
Alberon Gdns NW11 . . . 47 B5
Alberta Ct 1 TW10 . . . . 154 B6
Alberta Ho
Blackwall E14 . . . . 120 A5
Hayes UB4 . . . . 84 B4
Alberta Rd EN1 . . . . . . 18 A5
Alberta St
SE17 . . . . 116 D1 261 D2
Albert Ave Chingford E4 . 35 C6

Albert Ave continued
South Lambeth SW8 ... 270 C3
Albert Barnes Ho SE1 . 262 A5
Albert Bigg Point E15 .. 98 A6
Albert Bridge Rd
SW11 ... 136 D5 267 C3
Albert Carr Gdns
SW16 ... 182 A5
Albert Cl 11 Hackney E9 .. 96 B6
Wood Green N22 ... 31 D2
Albert Cotts 2 E1 ... 96 A2
Albert Cres E4 ... 35 C6
Albert Ct
Knightsbridge SW7 ... 246 C1
9 Putney SW19 ... 157 A3
Albert Dr SW19 ... 157 A3
Albert Emb
SE1 ... 116 A2 260 B3
Albert Gate Ct SW1 ... 247 C1
Albert Gdns E1 ... 96 D1
Albert Gr SW20 ... 178 D2
Albert Gray Ho SW10 .. 266 C4
Albert Hall Mans
SW7 ... 114 B4 246 C1
Albert Ho Stanmore HA7 .. 25 B5
5 Wanstead E18 ... 55 B6
2 Woolwich SE28 ... 123 A3
Albert Mans
Battersea SW11 ... 267 C2
Hornsey N8 ... 50 A2
Albert Meml*
SW7 ... 114 B4 246 C1
Albert Mews W8 ... 256 A6
Albert Palace Mans
SW11 ... 268 B2
Albert Pl Finchley N3 ... 29 C2
Kensington
W8 ... 113 D4 245 D1
Albert Rd
Ashford TW15 ... 170 B5
Bromley Comm BR2 ... 209 D4
Buckhurst Hill IG9 ... 21 D2
Chislehurst SE9 ... 166 A1
Croydon SE25 ... 206 B5
Dagenham RM8 ... 59 C1
Ealing W5 ... 87 B3
East Barnet EN4 ... 2 A1
Erith DA17 ... 125 B1
Finsbury Pk N4 ... 50 B2
Hampton TW12 ... 174 A5
Harrow HA2 ... 42 A6
Hayes UB3 ... 105 C3
Hendon NW4 ... 46 D5
Hounslow TW3 ... 129 C1
Ilford IG1 ... 79 A5
Kilburn NW6 ... 91 B5
Kingston u T KT1 ... 176 B1
Leyton E10 ... 54 A1
Mill Hill NW7 ... 27 D5
Mitcham CR4 ... 202 D6
Newham E16 ... 122 B4
New Malden KT3 ... 199 D5
Penge SE20 ... 184 D4
Richmond TW10 ... 154 B6
Sidcup DA5 ... 169 D4
Southall UB2 ... 106 D3
South Tottenham N15 ... 51 C3
Sutton SM1 ... 218 B3
Teddington TW11 ... 174 D4
Twickenham TW1 ... 152 D3
Walthamstow E17 ... 53 C4
4 Wanstead E18 ... 55 B6
Wood Green N22 ... 31 C2
Yiewsley UB7 ... 104 A5
Albert's Ct NW1 ... 237 B6
Albert Sleet Ct N9 ... 18 B1
Albert Sq Leyton E15 ... 76 C3
South Lambeth
SW8 ... 138 B5 270 C3
Albert St
Camden Town
NW1 ... 93 B6 231 D5
North Finchley N12 ... 30 A5
Albert Starr Ho 7
SE8 ... 118 D2
Albert Studios SW11 .. 267 C2
Albert Terr
Buckhurst Hill IG9 ... 21 D2
Camden Town
NW1 ... 93 A6 231 A5
Stonebridge NW10 ... 89 A6
Albert Terr Mews
NW1 ... 231 A5
Albert Victoria Ho N22 .. 32 C2
Albert Way SE15 ... 140 B5
Albert Westcott Ho
SE17 ... 261 D2
Albert Whicher Ho 3
E17 ... 54 A5
Albert Wlk E16 ... 122 D4
Albion Ave
Clapham SW8 ... 137 D3
Muswell Hill N10 ... 31 A2
Albion Cl W2 ... 247 B6
Albion Coll WC1 94 A2 240 B3
Albion Ct
7 Hammersmith W6 ... 112 B2
Sutton SM2 ... 218 B1
2 Woolwich SE7 ... 122 A2
Albion Dr E8 ... 74 A1
Albion Est SE16 ... 118 C4
Albion Gate W2 ... 247 B6
Albion Gdns 1 W6 ... 112 B2
Albion Gr N16 ... 73 C4
Albion Hill IG10 ... 21 D6
Albion Ho
17 Deptford SE8 ... 141 C5
EC1 ... 241 C4
Newham E16 ... 122 D5
Albion Mews
Bayswater
W2 ... 114 C6 247 B6
8 Hammersmith W6 ... 112 B2
Islington N1 ... 234 A6
Albion Pk IG10 ... 21 D6
Albion Pl
Broadgate EC2 ... 242 D3
Clerkenwell EC1 ... 241 C4
Hammersmith W6 ... 112 B2
South Norwood SE25 ... 206 A6
Albion Prim Sch SE16 .. 118 C4
Albion Rd Bexley DA6 ... 147 C1
Dagenham RM10 ... 81 B3
Hayes UB3 ... 83 C1
Hounslow TW3 ... 129 C1
Kingston u T KT2 ... 177 A2
Stoke Newington N16 ... 73 B4
Sutton SM2 ... 218 B1
Tottenham N17 ... 34 A1
Twickenham TW2 ... 152 C3
Walthamstow E17 ... 54 A6
Albion Riverside SW11 267 A4
Albion Sq E8 ... 73 D1
Albion St
Bayswater
W2 ... 114 C6 247 B6
Rotherhithe SE16 ... 118 C4
Thornton Heath CR0 ... 204 D1
Albion Terr Hackney E8 .. 73 D1
Sewardstone E4 ... 7 D1
Albion Villas Rd SE23,
SE26 ... 162 C1
Albion Way
Barbican EC1 ... 242 A3
Lewisham SE13 ... 142 A1
Wembley HA9 ... 66 C5
Albion Wlk N1 ... 233 B3
Albion Works Studios 14
E8 ... 74 A3
Albion Yd N1 ... 233 B3
Albon Ho SW18 ... 157 D5
Albrighton Rd SE5,
SE22 ... 139 C2
Albuhera Cl EN2 ... 4 C4
Albury Ave
Bexleyheath DA7 ... 147 A3
Hounslow TW7 ... 130 D5
Albury Bldgs SE1 ... 251 D1
Albury Cl TW12 ... 173 D4
Albury Ct
4 Croydon CR0 ... 221 A4
Deptford SE8 ... 141 C6
Mitcham CR4 ... 180 B1
6 Northolt UB5 ... 84 C4
Ruislip HA4 ... 62 C3
Sutton SM1 ... 218 A4
Albury Dr HA5 ... 22 D3
Albury Lo 7 SW2 ... 160 B4
Albury Mews E12 ... 77 C6
Albury Rd KT9 ... 214 A3
Albury St SE8 ... 141 C6
Albyfield BR1 ... 210 B6
Albyn Rd SE8 ... 141 C4
Alcester Cres E5 ... 74 B6
Alcester Ct 4 SM6 ... 219 B4
Alcester Rd SM6 ... 219 B4
Alchemea Coll of Audio
Engineering
N1 ... 94 D6 234 D6
Alcock Cl SM6 ... 219 D1
Alcock Rd TW5 ... 128 D5
Alconbury DA6 ... 169 D6
Alconbury Rd E5 ... 74 A6
Alcorn Cl SM3 ... 217 C6
Alcott Cl W7 ... 86 D2
Aldborough Ct
Chingford E4 ... 19 D1
Ilford IG2 ... 57 D4
ALDBOROUGH HATCH
... 57 C5
Aldborough Rd IG2 ... 57 D6
Aldborough Rd N IG2 ... 57 D4
Aldborough Rd S IG3 ... 57 C2
Aldbourne Rd W12 ... 112 A5
Aldbridge St
SE17 ... 117 C1 263 B2
Aldburgh Mews W1 ... 238 B2
Aldbury Ave HA9 ... 66 D1
Aldbury Ho SW3 ... 257 A3
Aldbury Mews N9 ... 17 B4
Aldebert Terr
SW8 ... 138 B5 270 C3
Aldeburgh Cl 16 E5 ... 74 B6
Aldeburgh Pl
Greenwich SE10 ... 121 A2
Woodford IG8 ... 37 A6
Aldeburgh St SE10 ... 121 A1
Alden Ave E15 ... 98 D4
Alden Ct
South Croydon CR0 ... 221 C5
Wimbledon SW19 ... 179 C4
Aldenham Ctry Pk WD6 .. 9 B6
Aldenham Dr UB8 ... 82 D3
Aldenham Ho NW1 ... 232 B3
Aldenham Rd WD6 ... 9 C6
Aldenham St
NW1 ... 93 D5 232 C3
Alden Ho E8 ... 96 B6
Aldensley Rd W6 ... 112 B3
Alderbrook Prim Sch
SW12 ... 159 B4
Alderbrook Rd SW12 ... 159 B5
Alderbury Rd SW13 ... 134 A6
Alder Ct East Finchley N2 . 48 B6
3 West Norwood
SW16 ... 182 C5
Alder Gr NW2 ... 68 B6
Aldergrove Gdns TW4 .. 129 A3
Aldergrove Ho 3 E5 ... 74 A6
Alder Ho
Camberwell SE15 ... 139 D6
1 Maitland Pk NW3 ... 70 D2
St Johns SE4 ... 141 C2
Alderley Ho 36 SW8 ... 137 D3
Alder Lo SW6 ... 134 D4
Alder Lodge N9 ... 17 C3
Alderman Ave IG11 ... 102 A4
Aldermanbury
EC2 ... 95 A1 242 B2
Aldermanbury Sq EC2 . 242 B3
Alderman Ct 13 N11 ... 30 D5
Alderman Judge Mall 6
KT1 ... 176 A1
Alderman's Hill N13 ... 32 B6
Alderman's Wlk EC2 .. 243 A3
Aldermary Rd BR1 ... 187 A2
Aldermead 2 TW3 ... 129 D1
Alder Mews 12 N19 ... 71 C6
Aldermoor Rd SE6 ... 163 B1
Alderney Ave TW5 ... 129 D5
Alderney Gdns UB5 ... 63 B1
Alderney Ho
20 Canonbury N1 ... 73 A2
Enfield EN3 ... 6 D5
Alderney Mews SE1 ... 262 C6
Alderney Rd E1 ... 96 D3
Alderney St
SW1 ... 115 B1 258 D2
Alder Rd
Mortlake SW14 ... 133 B2
Sidcup DA14 ... 167 D1
Alders Ave IG8 ... 36 C4
ALDERSBROOK ... 77 C6
Aldersbrook Ave EN1 ... 5 C3
Aldersbrook Dr KT2 ... 176 B4
Aldersbrook La E12 ... 78 B5
Aldersbrook Prim Sch
E12 ... 77 C6
Aldersbrook Rd E11,
E12 ... 77 C6
Alders Cl Ealing W5 ... 109 D3
Edgware HA8 ... 27 A5
Wanstead E11 ... 77 B6
Alders Ct N17 ... 52 B5
Aldersey Gdns IG11 ... 79 B2
Aldersford Cl SE4 ... 140 D1
Aldersgate Ct EC1 ... 242 A3
Aldersgate St
EC1 ... 95 A2 242 A3
Aldersgrove KT8 ... 196 B4
Aldersgrove Ave SE9,
SE12 ... 165 D1
Aldershot Rd NW6 ... 91 B6
Aldersmead Ave CR0 ... 206 D3
Aldersmead Rd BR3 ... 185 A3
Alderson Pl UB2 ... 108 A5
Alderson St W10 ... 91 A3
Alders Rd HA8 ... 27 A5
Alders The
Feltham TW13 ... 173 A6
Heston TW5 ... 129 B6
Southgate N21 ... 16 C5
Streatham SW16 ... 181 C6
West Wickham BR4 ... 223 D6
Alderton 9 KT2 ... 176 D2
Alderton Cl NW10 ... 67 B5
Alderton Cres NW4 ... 46 B4
Alderton Ct KT8 ... 195 B5
Alderton Rd
Croydon CR0 ... 206 A2
Herne Hill SE24 ... 139 A2
Alderton Way NW4 ... 46 B4
Alderville Rd SW6 ... 135 B3
Alderwick Ct N7 ... 72 B2
Alderwick Dr TW3 ... 130 B2
Alder Wlk IG11 ... 79 A2
Alderwood Mews EN4 ... 2 A5
Alderwood Prim Sch
SE9 ... 167 C5
Alderwood Rd SE9 ... 167 B5
Aldford St W1 .. 115 A5 248 B4
Aldgate EC3 ... 95 C1 243 B1
Aldgate East Sta
E1 ... 95 D1 243 D2
Aldgate High St
EC3 ... 95 D1 243 C1
Aldgate Sta EC3 .95 D1 243 C1
Aldham Hall 1 E11 ... 55 A3
Aldham Ho SE4 ... 141 B4
Aldine Ct W12 ... 112 C5
Aldine St W12 ... 112 C4
Aldington Cl RM8 ... 58 C1
Aldington Ct 1 E8 ... 74 A1
Aldington Rd SE18 ... 121 D3
Aldis Mews
3 Holdbrook EN3 ... 7 C6
Upper Tooting SW17 ... 180 C5
Aldis St SW17 ... 180 C5
Aldred Rd NW6 ... 69 C3
Aldren Rd SW17 ... 158 A1
Aldriche Way E4 ... 36 A4
Aldrich Gdns SM3 ... 217 B5
Aldrich Terr SW18 ... 158 A2
Aldrick Ho N1 ... 233 D4
Aldridge Ave
Edgware HA8 ... 10 D1
Holdbrook EN3 ... 7 C5
Ruislip HA4 ... 62 D6
Stanmore HA7 ... 26 A2
Aldridge Ct W11 ... 91 B2
Aldridge Rd Villas W11 .. 91 B2
Aldridge Rise KT3 ... 199 C3
Aldridge Wlk N14 ... 16 A4
Aldrington Rd SW16 ... 181 C6
Aldsworth Cl W9 ... 91 D3
Aldwich Ho WC2 ... 240 D1
Aldwick Cl SE9 ... 167 B1
Aldwick Ct N12 ... 30 A6
Aldwick Rd CR0 ... 220 B4
Aldworth Gr SE13 ... 164 A5
Aldworth Rd E15 ... 76 C1
Aldwych WC2 ... 94 B1 240 D1
Aldwych Ave IG6 ... 57 A5
Aldwych Bldgs WC2 ... 240 B2
Aldwyn Ho SW8 ... 270 A3
Alers Rd DA6 ... 168 D6
Alesia Cl N22 ... 32 A3
Alestan Beck Rd E16 ... 99 D1
Alexa Ct 4 SM2 ... 217 C2
Alexander Ave NW10 ... 68 B1
Alexander Cl Barnet EN4 .. 2 B1
Hayes BR2 ... 209 A1
Sidcup DA15 ... 167 C5
Southall UB2 ... 108 A5
Twickenham TW2 ... 152 D2
Alexander Ct
Beckenham BR3 ... 186 B2
Greenwich SE3 ... 143 B3
Stanmore HA7 ... 44 B6
14 Surbiton KT6 ... 197 D2
Wandsworth SW18 ... 158 A6
Alexander Evans Mews
SE23 ... 162 D2
Alexander Fleming
Laboratory Mus*
W2 ... 236 D2
Alexander Ho
8 Kingston u T KT2 ... 176 A2
15 Millwall E14 ... 119 C3
16 Sutton SM2 ... 218 A2
Alexander Lo SM1 ... 217 B3
Alexander McLeod Prim
Sch SE2 ... 124 B1
Alexander Mews 2
W2 ... 91 D1
Alexander Pl SW7 ... 257 A4
Alexander Rd
Bexley DA7 ... 146 D3
Chislehurst BR7 ... 188 D5
Upper Holloway N19 ... 72 A6
Alexander Sq
SW3 ... 114 C2 257 A4
Alexander St W2 ... 91 C1
Alexander Terr SE2 ... 124 B1
Alexandra Ave
Battersea SW11 ... 268 A1
Harrow HA2 ... 63 C5
Southall UB1 ... 107 B6
Sutton SM1 ... 217 C5
Wood Green N22 ... 31 D2
Alexandra Bsns Ctr EN3 .. 6 D1
Alexandra Cl
Ashford TW15 ... 171 B3
Deptford SE8 ... 141 B6
Harrow HA2 ... 63 D5
Alexandra Cotts
New Cross SE14 ... 141 B4
Penge SE20 ... 184 D4
Alexandra Cres BR1 ... 186 D4
Alexandra Ct
Ashford TW15 ... 171 B4
Ealing W5 ... 87 C2
Greenford UB6 ... 85 D5
Hounslow TW3 ... 129 D3
Paddington W9 ... 236 B6
4 Shacklewell N16 ... 73 D4
5 Shepherd's Bush
W12 ... 112 A4
Southgate N14 ... 15 C6
Wembley HA9 ... 66 B4
Alexandra Dr
Surbiton KT5 ... 198 C2
West Norwood SE19 ... 183 C5
Alexandra Gdns
Chiswick W4 ... 133 C5
Cranley Gdns N10 ... 49 B5
Hounslow TW3 ... 129 D3
Wallington SM5 ... 219 A1
Alexandra Gr
Finchley N12 ... 29 D4
Finsbury Pk N4 ... 50 D1
Alexandra Ho 13 W6 ... 112 C1
Alexandra Inf Sch
Kingston u T KT2 ... 176 C3
Penge BR3 ... 184 D3
Alexandra Jun & Inf Sch
TW3 ... 129 D3
Alexandra Jun Sch
SE26 ... 184 D4
Alexandra Mans
Chelsea SW3 ... 266 C5
Cricklewood NW2 ... 68 D3
6 Hampstead NW6 ... 69 C3
9 Shepherd's Bush
W12 ... 112 C5
Alexandra Mews N2 ... 48 D6
Alexandra National Ho
N4 ... 72 D6
Alexandra Pal* N22 ... 31 D1
Alexandra Palace Sta
N22 ... 32 A1
Alexandra Palace Way
N10 ... 49 C6
Alexandra Park Rd N10,
N22 ... 31 D2
Alexandra Park Sch
N11 ... 31 C2
Alexandra Pl
Croydon CR0 ... 205 C1
South Norwood SE25 ... 205 B4
St John's Wood
NW8 ... 92 A6 229 B6
Alexandra Prim Sch
N22 ... 32 B1
Alexandra Rd
Acton W4 ... 111 B4
Ashford TW15 ... 171 C4
10 Brentford TW8 ... 131 D6
Croydon CR0 ... 205 C2
Alexandra Rd continued
Dagenham RM6 ... 59 A3
Edmonton N9 ... 18 B4
Enfield EN3 ... 6 D1
Hampstead NW8 ... 70 B1
Hendon NW4 ... 46 D5
Hornsey N8, N22 ... 50 C6
Hounslow TW3 ... 129 D3
Kingston u T KT2 ... 176 C3
Leyton E10 ... 76 A5
Mitcham SW19 ... 180 C3
Mortlake SW14 ... 133 B2
Muswell Hill N10 ... 31 B3
Penge SE26 ... 184 D4
Richmond TW9 ... 132 B3
Thames Ditton KT7 ... 196 D4
Tottenham N15 ... 51 B4
Twickenham TW1 ... 153 C5
Wallend E6 ... 100 C4
Walthamstow E17 ... 53 B2
Wanstead E18 ... 55 B6
Wimbledon SW19 ... 179 C5
Alexandra Sch HA2 ... 63 C6
Alexandra Sq SM4 ... 201 C4
Alexandra St
5 Deptford SE14 ... 141 A5
Newham E16 ... 99 A2
Alexandra Wlk 8
SE19 ... 183 C5
Alexandria Rd W13 ... 109 B6
Alex Gossip Ho SW6 .. 265 A1
Alexis St SE16 ... 118 A2
Alfearn Rd E5 ... 74 C4
Alford Ct
18 Belmont SM2 ... 217 D1
Shoreditch N1 ... 235 B3
Alford Gn CR0 ... 224 B2
Alford Ho Crouch End N6 .. 49 C3
6 Woolwich SE18 ... 144 D6
Alford Pl N1 ... 235 B3
Alfoxton Ave N8, N15 ... 50 D5
Alfreda Ct SW11 ... 268 C1
Alfreda St
SW11 ... 137 B4 268 C1
Alfred Butt Ho SW17 ... 158 D1
Alfred Cl W4 ... 111 B2
Alfred Findley Ho N22 .. 32 D1
Alfred Gdns UB1 ... 107 A6
Alfred Ho E9 ... 75 A3
Alfred Hurley Ho
SW17 ... 180 A6
Alfred Mews W1, WC1 . 239 C4
Alfred Nunn Ho NW10 ... 89 D6
Alfred Pl WC1 ... 93 D2 239 C4
Alfred Prior Ho 7 E12 .. 78 C4
Alfred Rd Acton W3 ... 111 A5
Buckhurst Hill IG9 ... 21 D2
Croydon SE25 ... 206 A4
Erith DA17 ... 125 B1
Feltham TW13 ... 150 C2
Kingston u T KT1 ... 198 B6
Leyton E15 ... 76 D3
Paddington W2 ... 91 C2
Sutton SM1 ... 218 A3
Alfred Salter Ho SE1 .. 263 D3
Alfred Salter Prim Sch
SE16 ... 118 D4
Alfred's Gdns IG11 ... 101 C5
Alfred St E3 ... 97 B4
Alfred's Way (East Ham &
Barking By-Pass)
IG11 ... 101 B5
Alfred's Way Ind Est
IG11 ... 102 A6
Alfred Villas 9 E17 ... 54 A5
Alfreton Cl SW19 ... 156 D1
Alfriston KT5 ... 198 B3
Alfriston Ave
Harrow HA2 ... 41 C2
Thornton Heath CR0 ... 204 A2
Alfriston Cl KT5 ... 198 B3
Alfriston Rd SW11 ... 158 D6
Algar Cl Isleworth TW7 .. 131 A2
Stanmore HA7 ... 24 D5
Algar Ct TW12 ... 173 D2
Algar Ho SE1 ... 251 C1
Algar Rd TW7 ... 131 A2
Algarve Rd SW18 ... 157 D3
Algernon Rd
Hendon NW4 ... 46 A3
Kilburn NW6 ... 91 C6
Lewisham SE13 ... 141 D1
Algers Cl IG10 ... 21 D6
Algers Rd IG10 ... 21 D6
Alghers Mead IG10 ... 21 D6
Algiers Rd SE13 ... 141 C1
Alguin Ct HA7 ... 25 C3
Alibon Gdns RM10 ... 81 C3
Alibon Rd RM10 ... 81 C3
Alice Cl 13 EN5 ... 2 A1
Alice Ct 10 N3 ... 29 C2
Alice Gilliott Ct W14 .. 264 D6
Alice La E3 ... 97 B6
Alice Mews 3 TW11 ... 174 D5
Alice Owen Tech Ctr
EC1 ... 234 C2
Alice Shepherd Ho 12
E14 ... 120 A4
Alice St SE1 ... 117 C3 263 A5
Alice Thompson Cl
SE12 ... 165 C2
Alice Walker Cl 8
SE24 ... 138 D1
Alice Way TW3 ... 129 D1
Alicia Ave HA3 ... 43 C5
Alicia Cl HA3 ... 43 C5
Alicia Gdns HA3 ... 43 C5
Alicia Ho DA16 ... 146 B4
Alie St E1 ... 95 D1 243 D1
Alington Cres NW9 ... 45 A1
Alison Cl Croydon CR0 ... 206 D1
Newham E6 ... 100 C1
Alison Ct HA8 ... 26 D5
Aliwal Rd SW11 ... 136 C1
Alkerden Rd W4 ... 111 C1
Alkham Rd N16 ... 73 D6
Allam Ho W11 ... 244 A6
Allan Barclay Cl N15 ... 51 D3
Allanbridge N16 ... 51 C2
Allan Cl KT3 ... 199 B4
Allandale Ave N3 ... 47 B6
Allan Ho SW8 ... 269 C2
Allanson Ct E10 ... 75 C6
Allan Way W3 ... 89 A2
Allard Cres WD23 ... 8 A2
Allard Gdns SW4 ... 159 D6
Allardyce St SW4, SW9 .. 138 B1
Allbrook Cl TW11 ... 174 C5
Allbrook Ho 4 SW15 ... 156 A4
Allcot Cl TW14 ... 149 D3
Allcott Ho TW7 ... 130 D2
Allcroft Rd NW5 ... 71 A2
Allder Way CR2 ... 220 D1
Allenby Cl UB6 ... 85 C4
Allenby Prim Sch UB1 .. 85 C1
Allenby Rd
Forest Hill SE23 ... 163 A1
Southall UB1 ... 85 C3
Woolwich SE28 ... 123 A3
Allen Cl Streatham CR4 .. 181 C2
Sunbury TW16 ... 172 B2
Allen Ct Greenford UB6 ... 64 D3
Walthamstow E17 ... 53 C3
Allendale Ave UB1 ... 85 C1
Allendale Cl
Camberwell SE5 ... 139 B4
Forest Hill SE26 ... 184 D5
Allendale Rd UB6 ... 65 B2
Allen Edwards Dr
SW8 ... 138 A4 270 A2
Allen Edwards Prim Sch
SW4 ... 138 A4 270 A1
Allenford Ho SW15 ... 155 D5
All England Lawn Tennis &
Croquet Club The
SW19 ... 157 A1
Allen Ho W8 ... 255 B6
Allen Mans W8 ... 255 B6
Allen Rd Old Ford E3 ... 97 B5
Penge BR3 ... 184 D1
Stoke Newington N16 ... 73 C4
Sunbury TW16 ... 172 B1
Thornton Heath CR0 ... 204 C1
Allensbury Pl
7 Camden Town NW1 ... 71 D1
Camden Town NW1 ... 72 A1
Allens Rd EN3 ... 18 C6
Allen St W8 ... 113 C3 255 B5
Allenswood 12 SW19 ... 157 A3
Allenswood Rd SE9 ... 144 B3
Allerdale Ho 7 N4 ... 51 B2
Allerford Ct
Catford SE6 ... 163 D1
Harrow HA2 ... 42 A4
Allerford Rd SE6 ... 185 D6
Allerton Ct
5 Hendon NW4 ... 28 D1
North Cheam SM3 ... 216 D6
Allerton Ho
4 Merton SW19 ... 180 A3
Shoreditch N1 ... 235 D3
Allerton Rd N16 ... 73 A6
Allerton St N1 ... 235 D2
Allerton Wlk 11 N7 ... 72 B6
Allestree Rd
SW6 ... 135 A5 264 A3
Alleyn Cres SE21 ... 161 B2
Alleyndale Rd RM8 ... 80 C6
Alleyn Ho
Bermondsey SE1 ... 262 C5
St Luke's EC1 ... 242 B5
Alleyn Pk Dulwich SE21 .. 161 C1
Southall UB2 ... 107 C1
Alleyn Rd SE21 ... 161 C1
Alleyn's Sch SE22 ... 161 C6
Allfarthing La SW18 ... 158 A5
Allfarthing Prim Sch
SW18 ... 158 A5
Allgood Cl SM4 ... 200 D3
Allgood St 10 E2 ... 95 D5
Allhallows La EC4 ... 252 C5
Allhallows Rd E6 ... 100 A1
All Hallows Rd N17 ... 33 C2
Alliance Cl
Twickenham TW4 ... 151 B6
Wembley HA0 ... 65 D4
Alliance Ct Acton W3 ... 88 B2
Ashford TW15 ... 171 A6
Alliance Rd Acton W3 ... 88 D3
East Wickham SE18 ... 146 A5
1 Newham E16 ... 99 C2
Allied Ind Est W3 ... 111 C5
Allied Way W3 ... 111 C4
Allingham Cl W7 ... 108 D6
Allingham Ct NW3 ... 70 C3
Allingham Mews N1 .. 235 A4
Allingham St
N1 ... 95 A5 235 A4
Allington Ave
Tottenham N17 ... 33 C4
Upper Halliford TW17 ... 193 C6
Allington Cl
Greenford UB6 ... 64 A1
3 Wimbledon SW19 ... 178 D5
Allington Ct
6 Clapham SW8 ... 137 C3
Croydon CR0 ... 206 C3

Allington Ct *continued*
Enfield EN3 . . . 18 D6
Allington Rd
Harrow HA2 . . . 42 A4
Hendon NW4 . . . 46 B3
Kensal Rise W10 . . . 91 A5
Orpington BR6 . . . 211 C1
Allington St SW1 . . . 258 D5
Allison Cl SE10 . . . 142 A4
Allison Gr SE21 . . . 161 C3
Allison Rd Acton W3 . . . 111 A6
Harringay N8 . . . 50 D4
Alliston Ho 27 E2 . . . 95 D4
Allitsen Rd NW8 . 92 C5 230 A4
All Nations Ho 10 E8 . . . 74 B1
Allnutt Way SW4 . . . 159 D6
Alloa Ct N14 . . . 15 C2
Alloa Rd IG3 . . . 80 A6
Allom Ct 11 SW4 . . . 138 A3
Allonby Dr HA4 . . . 38 D2
Allonby Gdns HA9 . . . 43 C1
Allonby Ho E14 . . . 97 A2
Alloway Rd E3 . . . 97 A4
Allport Ho SE5 . . . 139 B2
Allport Mews 4 E1 . . . 96 C3
All Saints' Benhilton CE Prim Sch SM1 . . . 217 D5
All Saint's CE Jun Sch SE19 . . . 183 C2
All Saints CE Prim Sch
Merton SW19 . . . 180 A3
Putney SW15 . . . 134 C2
All Saints' CE Prim Sch
Blackheath Vale SE3 . . . 142 C3
Child's Hill NW2 . . . 69 B5
East Barnet N20 . . . 14 B2
Wallington SM5 . . . 219 A3
All Saints Church 9 N19 . . . 71 D5
All Saints' Cl N9 . . . 18 A2
All Saints Ct
Heston TW5 . . . 128 D4
Lower Clapton E5 . . . 74 C4
10 Shadwell E1 . . . 118 C6
All Saints Dr SE3 . . . 142 D3
All Saints Ho 2 W11 . . . 91 B2
All Saint's Inf Sch SE19 . . . 183 C2
All Saints Mews HA3 . . . 24 C4
All Saints Pas SW18 . . . 157 C6
All Saints RC Sch BR4 . . 224 B4
All Saints RC Sch & Tech Coll RM8 . . . 59 C1
All Saints Rd
Merton SW19 . . . 180 A3
Notting Hill W11 . . . 91 B1
Sutton SM1 . . . 218 A5
All Saints' Rd W3 . . . 111 A3
All Saints St N1 . . 94 B5 233 C4
All Saints Sta E14 . . . 119 D6
All Saints Twr 19 E10 . . . 53 D2
Allsop Pl NW1 . . . 92 D3 237 D5
All Souls' Ave NW10 . . . 90 B6
All Souls CE Prim Sch W1 . . . 93 C2 239 A4
All Souls Pl W1 . . . 238 D3
Allum La WD6 . . . 10 A6
Allum Way N20 . . . 14 A3
Allwood Cl SE26 . . . 184 D6
Alma Ave E4 . . . 36 A3
Alma Birk Ho 1 NW6 . . . 69 B1
Almack Rd E5 . . . 74 C4
Alma Cl N10 . . . 31 B2
Alma Cres SM1 . . . 217 A3
Alma Gr SE1 . . . 117 D2 263 D3
Alma Ho
7 Brentford TW8 . . . 132 A6
2 Edmonton N9 . . . 34 A6
Alma Pl College Pk NW10 . 90 B4
Penge SE19 . . . 183 D3
Thornton Heath CR7 . . . 204 C4
Alma Prim Sch
Bermondsey SE16 . . . 118 A2
Enfield EN3 . . . 18 D6
Alma Rd
Carshalton SM5 . . . 218 C3
Enfield EN3 . . . 7 A1
Muswell Hill N10 . . . 31 B3
Sidcup DA14 . . . 168 A1
Southall UB1 . . . 107 A6
Thames Ditton KT10, KT7 . . . 196 C1
Wandsworth SW18 . . . 158 A6
Alma Row HA3 . . . 24 B2
Alma Sq NW8 . . . 92 A4 229 B2
Alma St
Camden Town NW5 . . . 71 B2
Stratford New Town E15 . . 76 B2
Alma Terr Earl's Ct W8 . 255 B5
Wandsworth SW18 . . . 158 B4
Almeida St 10 N1 . . . 72 D1
Almeric Rd SW11 . . . 136 D1
Almer Rd SW20 . . . 178 A3
Almington St N4 . . . 50 B1
Almond Ave
Carshalton SM5 . . . 218 D6
Ealing W5 . . . 110 A3
Uxbridge UB10 . . . 60 D5
West Drayton UB7 . . . 104 C3
Almond Cl
Bromley BR2 . . . 210 C2
Charlton TW17 . . . 171 A1
Feltham TW14 . . . 150 A3
Hayes UB3 . . . 105 C6
Peckham SE15 . . . 140 A3
Ruislip HA4 . . . 61 D5
Almond Gr TW8 . . . 131 B5
Almond Ho SE4 . . . 141 B3
Almond Rd
Bermondsey SE16 . . . 118 B2
Tottenham N17 . . . 34 A3
Almonds Ave IG9 . . . 21 A2
Almond Way
Bromley BR2 . . . 210 C2
Harrow HA2 . . . 24 A1
Mitcham CR4 . . . 203 D5
Almorah Rd
De Beauvoir Town N1 . . . 73 B1
Heston TW5 . . . 128 D4
Almshouse La EN1 . . . 6 B6
Almshouses
Edmonton N9 . . . 17 D2
Leyton E10 . . . 75 D6
Southall UB1 . . . 85 C1
Sunbury TW16 . . . 171 D2
Almshouses The IG11 . . . 79 A2
Al-Muntada Islamic Sch SW6 . . . 135 B4 264 D2
Alnmouth Ct 10 UB1 . . . 86 A1
Al-Noor Muslim Prim Sch IG3 . . . 58 B1
Alnwick 8 N17 . . . 34 B3
Alnwick Gr SM4 . . . 201 D5
Alnwick Rd
Eltham SE12 . . . 165 B4
Newham E16 . . . 99 C1
Alonso Ho 4 DA17 . . . 125 C1
ALPERTON . . . 88 A6
Alperton Com Sch HA0 . . 66 B1
Alperton La UB6 . . . 87 D5
Alperton Lower Sch HA0 . . . 87 D6
Alperton St W10 . . . 91 B3
Alperton Sta HA0 . . . 88 A6
Alphabet Gdns SM5 . . . 202 B3
Alphabet Sq E3 . . . 97 C2
Alpha Bsns Ctr E17 . . . 53 B4
Alpha Cl NW8 . . . 92 C4 230 B1
Alpha Ct 6 NW5 . . . 71 B2
Alpha Est The UB3 . . . 105 C4
Alpha Gr E14 . . . 119 C4
Alpha Ho
19 Brixton SW4 . . . 138 B1
Kilburn NW6 . . . 91 C5
Lisson Gr NW8 . . . 237 B5
Alpha Pl
Chelsea SW3 . . . 136 C6 267 B6
Kilburn NW6 . . . 91 C5
Alpha Rd Chingford E4 . . . 19 D1
Croydon CR0 . . . 205 C1
Edmonton N18 . . . 34 A4
Enfield EN3 . . . 7 A1
Hillingdon UB10 . . . 82 D3
New Cross SE14 . . . 141 B4
Surbiton KT5 . . . 198 B3
Teddington TW12 . . . 174 B5
Alpha St SE15 . . . 140 A3
Alphea Cl SW19 . . . 180 C3
Alpine Ave KT5 . . . 215 A6
Alpine Bsns Ctr E6 . . . 100 C2
Alpine Cl CR0 . . . 221 C5
Alpine Copse BR1 . . . 188 C1
Alpine Ct SE12 . . . 142 D1
Alpine Gr 37 E9 . . . 74 C1
Alpine Rd
Deptford SE16 . . . 118 D1
Leyton E10 . . . 75 D6
Walton-on-T KT12 . . . 194 A2
Alpine View SM5 . . . 218 C3
Alpine Way E6 . . . 100 C2
Alpine Wlk HA7 . . . 8 C2
Alric Ave
Kingston u T KT3 . . . 199 D6
Willesden NW10 . . . 67 B1
Alroy Rd N4 . . . 50 C2
Alsace Rd SE17 . . . 117 C1 263 A2
Al Sadiq & Al Zahra Schs NW6 . . . 91 A6
Alscot Rd SE1 . . 117 D3 263 D5
Alscot Road Ind Est SE1 . . . 263 D5
Alscot Way SE1 . . . 263 C4
Alsike Rd DA18 . . . 125 A3
Alsom Ave KT19, KT4 . . 216 A4
Alston Cl KT7 . . . 197 B2
Alston Ct 2 EN5 . . . 1 A2
Alstone Ct N9 . . . 18 A2
Alston Rd Edmonton N18 . . 34 B5
High Barnet EN5 . . . 1 A2
Upper Tooting SW17 . . . 180 B6
Altair Cl N17 . . . 33 D4
Altair Ct N1 . . . 73 B2
Altash Way SE9 . . . 166 C2
Altenburg Ave W13 . . . 109 B3
Altenburg Gdns SW11 . . 136 D1
Alt Gr SW19 . . . 179 B3
Altham Gdns WD19 . . . 22 D6
Altham Rd HA5 . . . 23 A3
Althea St SW6 . . . 135 D2
Althorne Gdns E18 . . . 54 D5
Althorne Way RM10 . . . 81 C6
Althorp Cl EN5 . . . 12 A4
Althorpe Mews SW11 . 266 D1
Althorpe Rd HA1 . . . 42 A4
Althorp Rd SW17 . . . 158 D3
Altima Ct SE22 . . . 140 A1
Altior Ct N6 . . . 49 C3
Altmore Ave E6 . . . 100 B6
Altmore Inf Sch E6 . . . 100 B6
Alton Ave HA7 . . . 24 D3
Alton Cl Isleworth TW7 . . 130 D3
Sidcup DA5 . . . 169 A3
Alton Ct 18 BR3 . . . 185 C3
Alton Gdns
Beckenham BR3 . . . 185 C3
Twickenham TW2 . . . 152 B4
Alton Ho 3 E3 . . . 97 D4
Alton Rd Croydon CR0 . . . 220 C5
Richmond TW10, TW9 . . . 132 A1
Roehampton SW15 . . . 156 A3
Tottenham N17 . . . 51 B6
Alton St E14 . . . 97 D2
Altyre Cl BR3 . . . 207 B4
Altyre Rd CR0 . . . 221 B6
Altyre Way BR3 . . . 207 B4
Alum Ct KT5 . . . 198 B3
Alumni Ct SE1 . . . 253 D2
Alvanley Ct NW3 . . . 69 D3
Alvanley Gdns NW6 . . . 69 D3
Alvanley Ho 14 SW9 . . . 138 C4
Alvernia Lo SM1 . . . 217 D5
Alverstone Ave
East Barnet EN4 . . . 14 C4
Wimbledon SW18, SW19 . . . 157 C2
Alverstone Gdns SE9 . . . 167 A3
Alverstone Ho 11 SE11 . . . 138 C6
Alverstone Rd
Little Ilford E12 . . . 78 C4
New Malden KT3 . . . 199 D5
Wembley HA9 . . . 44 B1
Willesden NW2 . . . 68 C1
Alverston Gdns SE25 . . . 205 C4
Alverton St SE8 . . . 141 B6
Alveston Ave HA3 . . . 43 B6
Alveston Sq 5 E18 . . . 37 A1
Alvey St SE17 . . . 263 A2
Alvia Gdns SM1 . . . 218 A4
Alvington Cres E8 . . . 73 D3
Alway Ave KT19 . . . 215 B3
Alwen Cotts CR0 . . . 222 D4
Alwold Cres SE12 . . . 165 C5
Alwyn Ave W4 . . . 111 B1
Alwyn Cl
Borehamwood WD6 . . . 10 B5
New Addington CR0 . . . 223 D1
Alwyne La N1 . . . 72 D1
Alwyne Mans SW19 . . . 179 B4
Alwyne Pl N1 . . . 73 A1
Alwyne Rd
Canonbury N1 . . . 73 A1
Ealing W7 . . . 108 C6
Wimbledon SW19 . . . 179 B4
Alwyne Sq N1 . . . 73 A2
Alwyne Villas N1 . . . 72 D1
Alwyn Gdns Acton W3 . . . 88 D1
Hendon NW9 . . . 46 A5
Alyn Ct N8 . . . 49 D3
Alyth Gdns NW11 . . . 47 C3
Alzette Ho 11 E2 . . . 96 D5
Amalgamated Dr TW8 . . 131 B6
Amanda Ct
Ashford TW15 . . . 148 B2
Chingford E4 . . . 36 C4
Aman Dalvi Ho SW18 . . . 157 A4
Amar Ct SE18 . . . 123 D2
Amardeep Ct SE18 . . . 123 D1
Amazon Apartments N8 . . . 50 B6
Amazonas SE1 . . 117 C2 263 B3
Amazon St E1 . . . 96 B1
Ambassador Cl TW3 . . . 129 A3
Ambassador Ct
9 Hampstead NW6 . . . 69 C3
Hendon NW4 . . . 46 D4
Ambassador Gdns E6 . . 100 B2
Ambassador Ho
Harrow HA3 . . . 42 C6
St John's Wood NW8 . . . 229 B5
Ambassador Sq E14 . . . 119 D2
Amber Ave E17 . . . 35 A2
Amber Ct
Feltham TW13 . . . 149 C1
Islington N7 . . . 72 C2
Mitcham CR4 . . . 202 C5
Southall UB1 . . . 107 D5
Amberden Ave N3 . . . 47 C6
Amberdene HA7 . . . 24 D4
Ambergate St SE17 . . . 116 D1 261 D2
Amber Gr NW2 . . . 46 D1
Amber Ho HA7 . . . 25 D3
Amberley Cl
2 Orpington BR6 . . . 227 D3
Pinner HA5 . . . 41 B6
Amberley Ct
2 Brixton SW9 . . . 138 D2
Sidcup DA14 . . . 190 C5
Sutton SM2 . . . 218 A1
Amberley Gdns
Enfield EN1 . . . 17 C4
Worcester Pk KT19 . . . 215 D4
Amberley Gr
Croydon CR0 . . . 205 D2
Penge SE26 . . . 184 B5
Amberley Ho
8 Barnet EN5 . . . 1 D1
7 Ealing W7 . . . 108 C5
Amberley Rd
Buckhurst Hill IG9 . . . 21 C3
Enfield EN1 . . . 17 D5
Palmers Green N13 . . . 16 B2
Walthamstow E10 . . . 53 D2
Westbourne Green W9 . . 91 C2
West Heath SE2 . . . 146 D6
Amberley Way
Heston TW4 . . . 150 C6
Morden SM4 . . . 201 B2
Romford RM7 . . . 59 D5
Uxbridge UB10 . . . 82 A5
Amberside Cl TW2 . . . 152 B5
Amber Wharf 29 E2 . . . 95 D6
Amberwood Cl SM6 . . . 220 A3
Amberwood Rise KT3 . . 199 C3
Amblecote Cl SE12 . . . 165 B1
Amblecote Mdws SE12 . . . 165 B1
Amblecote Rd SE12 . . . 165 B1
Ambler Prim Sch N4 . . . 72 D6
Ambler Rd N4 . . . 72 D5
Ambleside Catford BR1 . . 186 B4
13 Putney SW19 . . . 157 A3
Regent's Pk NW1 . . . 231 D3
Ambleside Ave
Beckenham BR3 . . . 207 A4
Streatham SW16 . . . 181 D6
Walton-on-T KT12 . . . 194 C1
Ambleside Cl
Lower Clapton E9 . . . 74 C3
5 Tottenham N17 . . . 51 D6
Walthamstow E10 . . . 53 D2
Ambleside Cres EN3 . . . 6 D2
Ambleside Dr TW14 . . . 149 D3
Ambleside Gdns
Redbridge IG4 . . . 56 A4
Streatham SW16 . . . 181 D5
Sutton SM2 . . . 218 A2
Wembley HA9 . . . 43 D1
Ambleside Ho HA8 . . . 27 A5
Ambleside Point 1 SE15 . . . 140 C5
Ambleside Rd
Bexleyheath DA7 . . . 147 C3
Willesden NW10 . . . 67 D1
Ambrook Ct SM1 . . . 218 B3
Ambrook Rd DA17 . . . 125 C3
Ambrosden Ave SW1 . . . 115 C3 259 B5
Ambrose Ave NW11 . . . 47 B3
Ambrose Cl
6 Newham E6 . . . 100 B2
Orpington BR6 . . . 227 D5
Ambrose Ho 9 E14 . . . 97 C2
Ambrose Mews 2 SW11 . . . 136 D3
Ambrose St SE16 . . . 118 B2
Ambrose Wlk E3 . . . 97 C5
AMC Bsns Ctr NW10 . . . 88 D4
Amelia Cl W3 . . . 110 D4
Amelia Ho 5 W6 . . . 112 C1
Amelia St SE17 . 117 A1 262 A2
Amen Cnr Holborn EC4 . 241 D1
Streatham SW17 . . . 181 A4
Amen Ct EC4 . . . 94 D1 241 D1
Amenity Way SM4 . . . 200 C2
American Intercontinental Univ W1 . . . 93 A2 238 B3
American Sch in London The NW8 . . . 92 B5 229 C4
American Univ in London The N7 . . . 72 B5
America Sq EC3 . . . 253 C6
America St SE1 . . . 252 A3
Amerland Rd SW18 . . . 157 B5
Amersham Ave N18 . . . 33 B4
Amersham Gr SE14 . . . 141 B5
Amersham Rd
New Cross SE14 . . . 141 B4
Thornton Heath CR0 . . . 205 B3
Amersham Vale SE14, SE8 . . . 141 B5
Amery Gdns NW10 . . . 90 B6
Amery Ho SE17 . . . 263 B2
Amery Rd HA1 . . . 65 A6
Amesbury Ave SW2 . . . 160 B2
Amesbury Cl KT4 . . . 200 C1
Amesbury Ct EN2 . . . 4 C3
Amesbury Dr E4 . . . 19 D5
Amesbury Rd
Bromley BR1 . . . 209 D6
Dagenham RM9 . . . 80 D1
Feltham TW13 . . . 150 D2
Amesbury Twr 4 SW8 . . . 137 C3
Ames Cotts 12 E3 . . . 97 A2
Ames Ho 10 E2 . . . 96 D5
Amethyst Ct 1 EN3 . . . 7 A2
Amethyst Cl N11 . . . 31 D3
Amethyst Ct BR6 . . . 227 C3
Amethyst Rd E15 . . . 76 B4
Amherst Ave W13 . . . 87 C1
Amherst Dr BR5 . . . 211 D5
Amherst Gdns 2 W13 . . . 87 C1
Amherst Rd W13 . . . 87 C1
Amhurst Ct N4 . . . 51 B2
Amhurst Gdns TW7 . . . 131 A3
Amhurst Par N16 . . . 51 D2
Amhurst Pk N4, N16 . . . 51 C2
Amhurst Rd E8, N16 . . . 74 A4
Amhurst Terr E8 . . . 74 A4
Amhurst Wlk SE28 . . . 124 A5
Amias Ho EC1 . . . 242 A6
Amidas Gdns RM8 . . . 80 B4
Amiel St 15 E1 . . . 96 C3
Amies St SW11 . . . 136 D2
Amigo Ho SE1 . . . 261 B6
Amina Way SE16 . . . 118 A3
Amis Ave KT19 . . . 214 D3
Amity Gr SW20 . . . 178 C2
Amity Rd E15 . . . 76 D1
Ammanford Gn NW9 . . . 45 C3
Ammonite Ho 3 E15 . . . 76 D1
Amner Rd SW11 . . . 159 A5
Amora 8 HA7 . . . 25 C6
Amor Rd W6 . . . 112 C3
Amory Ho N1 . . . 233 D4
Amott Rd SE15 . . . 140 A2
Amoy Pl E14 . . . 119 C6
Ampere Way CR0 . . . 204 B1
Ampleforth Rd SE2 . . . 124 C4
Ampton Pl WC1 . . . 233 C1
Ampton St WC1 . . 94 B4 233 C1
Amroth Cl SE23 . . . 162 B3
Amroth Gn NW9 . . . 45 C3
Amstel Ct 12 SE15 . . . 139 D5
Amsterdam Rd E14 . . . 120 A3
Amundsen Ct 7 E14 . . . 119 C1
Amundsen Ho 6 NW10 . . 67 B1
Amwell Cl EN2 . . . 17 B6
Amwell St EC1 . . 94 C4 234 A2
Amyand Cotts 12 TW1 . . 153 B5
Amyand Park Gdns 2 TW1 . . . 153 B4
Amyand Park Rd TW1 . . 153 B4
Amy Cl SM6 . . . 220 A1
Amy Johnson Ct HA8 . . . 26 D1
Amy Johnson Prim Sch SM6 . . . 220 A1
Amyruth Rd SE4 . . . 163 C6
Amy Warne Cl E6 . . . 100 A3
Anarth Ct KT13 . . . 193 C1
Anatola Rd N19 . . . 71 C6
Ancaster Cres KT3 . . . 200 A3
Ancaster Mews CR0 . . . 206 D6
Ancaster Rd BR3 . . . 206 D6
Ancaster St SE18 . . . 145 C5
Anchorage Cl SW19 . . . 179 C5
Anchorage Point 1 E14 . . . 119 C4
Anchorage Point Ind Est SE7 . . . 121 C3
Anchor Bsns Pk CR0, SM6 . . . 220 A5
Anchor Cl IG11 . . . 102 B4
Anchor Ct Bexley DA7 . . . 147 A4
5 Enfield EN1 . . . 17 C6
Anchor Ho Ilford IG3 . . . 80 A5
Newham E16 . . . 99 C1
St Luke's EC1 . . . 242 A6
Anchor & Hope La SE7 . . . 121 C2
Anchor Mews SW12 . . . 159 B5
Anchor Ret Pk E1 . . . 96 C3
Anchor St SE16 . . . 118 B2
Anchor Terr SE1 . . . 252 B4
Anchor Yd EC1 . . . 242 B6
Ancill Cl W6 . . . 135 A6 264 A5
Ancona Rd
Plumstead SE18 . . . 123 B1
Willesden Green NW10 . . 90 A5
Andace Pk BR1 . . . 187 C2
Andalus Rd SW9 . . . 138 A2
Andaman Ho 3 E1 . . . 97 A2
Ander Cl HA0 . . . 65 D4
Andersens Wharf 9 E14 . . . 97 B1
Anderson Cl
Morden SM3 . . . 201 C1
North Acton W3 . . . 89 B1
Southgate N21 . . . 16 B6
Anderson Ct NW2 . . . 46 C2
Anderson Dr TW15 . . . 171 A6
Anderson Ho
1 Barking IG11 . . . 101 B5
10 Blackwall E14 . . . 120 A6
Upper Tooting SW17 . . . 180 B5
Anderson Rd
Homerton E9 . . . 74 D2
Redbridge IG8 . . . 55 D6
Anderson's Pl TW3 . . . 129 D1
Andersons Sq N1 . . . 234 C5
Anderson St SW3 . . . 257 C2
Anderson Way
Erith DA17 . . . 125 D4
Erith DA17 . . . 125 D4
Anderton Cl SE5 . . . 139 B2
Anderton Ct N22 . . . 31 D1
Andhurst Ct KT2 . . . 176 D2
Andmark Ct UB1 . . . 107 B5
Andon Ct BR3 . . . 207 A6
Andorra Ct BR1 . . . 187 C2
Andover Ave E16 . . . 99 D1
Andover Cl
East Bedfont TW14 . . . 149 D3
Greenford UB6 . . . 85 D3
Andover Ho 5 N7 . . . 72 B6
Andover Pl NW6 . . . 91 D5
Andover Rd
Finsbury Pk N7 . . . 72 B6
Orpington BR6 . . . 211 C1
Twickenham TW2 . . . 152 B3
Andoversford Ct 2 SE15 . . . 139 C6
Andrecht Terr CR4 . . . 203 D5
Andreck Ct BR3 . . . 186 A1
Andre Malraux Sch W7 . 86 C2
Andre St E8 . . . 74 A3
Andrew Borde St WC2 239 D2
Andrew Ct
Beckenham BR3 . . . 207 D6
2 Forest Hill SE23 . . . 162 D2
Andrewes Ct 2 W7 . . . 108 C5
Andrewes Gdns E6 . . . 100 A1
Andrewes Ho
Barbican EC2 . . . 242 B3
Sutton SM1 . . . 217 C4
Andrew Ewing Jun & Inf Sch TW5 . . . 129 B5
Andrew Ho Enfield EN3 . . . 18 C6
New Cross SE4 . . . 141 B3
Putney SW15 . . . 156 A6
Andrew Logan's Glass Ho* SE1 . . . 253 A2
Andrew Marvell Ho 12 N16 . . . 73 C4
Andrew Pl SW8 . . . 269 D2
Andrew Reed Ho SW18 . . . 157 A4
Andrews Cl
Buckhurst Hill IG9 . . . 21 C2
Harrow HA1 . . . 42 B2
North Cheam KT4 . . . 216 D6
Sidcup BR5 . . . 190 D1
Andrews Crosse WC2 . 241 A1
Andrew's Rd E8 . . . 96 B6
Andrew St E14 . . . 98 A1
Andrews Wharf 14 E8 . . . 96 B6
Andrews Wlk SE17 . . . 138 D6
Andrew Wells Ho BR1 . . 187 B3
Andrew Wilmot Ct SW18 . . . 158 A3
Andridge Ct SW19 . . . 179 B2
Andringham Lo 4 BR1 . . . 187 B2
Andrula Ct N22 . . . 32 D2
Andwell Cl SE2 . . . 124 B4
ANERLEY . . . 184 B2
Anerley Ct SE20 . . . 184 B3
Anerley Gr SE19 . . . 183 D3
Anerley Hill SE19 . . . 183 D4
Anerley Park Rd SE20 . . 184 B3
Anerley Pk SE20 . . . 184 B3
Anerley Rd SE20 . . . 184 B2
Anerley Sta SE20 . . . 184 B2
Anerley Station Rd SE20 . . . 184 B2
Anerley Vale SE19 . . . 184 A3
Aneurin Bevan Ct NW2 . . 68 B6
Aneurin Bevan Ho N11 . . 31 D3
Anfield Cl SW12 . . . 159 C4
Angel EC1 . . . 94 D5 234 D3
Angela Ct 2 SE23 . . . 162 C3
Angela Davis Ind Est 20 SW9 . . . 138 D1
Angel Cl N18 . . . 34 A6
Angel Corner Par 6 N18 . . . 34 A6
Angel Ct Broadgate EC2 242 D2
St James SW1 . . . 249 B3
5 Willesden NW2 . . . 68 A2
Angel Edmonton N18 . . . 34 A5
Angelfield TW3 . . . 151 D6
Angel Gate EC1 . . . 234 D2
Angel Hill SM1 . . . 217 D5
Angel Hill Dr SM1 . . . 217 D5
Angel Ho N1 . . . 234 B3
Angelica Cl UB7 . . . 82 B1
Angelica Dr E6 . . . 100 C2
Angelica Gdns CR0 . . . 206 D1
Angelina Ho 2 SE15 . . . 140 A4
Angelis Appartments N1 . . . 234 D3
Angel La Hayes UB3 . . . 83 B2
Stratford E15 . . . 76 B2
Angell Park Gdns 4 SW9 . . . 138 C2
Angell Rd SW9 . . . 138 D2
Angel Mews
Finsbury N1 . . . 234 B3
Putney SW15 . . . 156 A4
Stepney E1 . . . 118 B6
Angel Pas EC4 . . 117 B6 252 C5
Angel Pl
Borough The SE1 . . . 252 C2
1 Edmonton N18 . . . 34 A5
Angel Rd Harrow HA1 . . . 42 C3
Thames Ditton KT7 . . . 197 A1
Angel Rd (North Circular Rd) N18 . . . 34 B5
Angel Rd Works N18 . . . 34 C5
Angel Road Sta N18 . . . 34 C5
Angel Sq N1 . . . 234 B3
Angel St EC1 . . . 95 A1 242 A2
Angel Sta EC1 . . . 94 C5 234 B3
Angel Wlk W6 . . . 112 C2
Angerstein Bsns Pk SE10 . . . 121 A2
Angerstein La SE3 . . . 142 D4
Anglebury 5 W2 . . . 91 C1
Angle Cl UB10 . . . 82 C6
Angle Gn RM8 . . . 58 C1
Anglers Cl TW10 . . . 175 C6
Anglers La NW5 . . . 71 B2
Anglers Reach KT6 . . . 197 D4
Anglesea Ave 4 SE18 . . 122 D2
Anglesea Ho KT1 . . . 197 D5
Anglesea Mews 12 SE18 . . . 122 D2
Anglesea Rd
Kingston u T KT1 . . . 197 D5
Woolwich SE18 . . . 122 D2
Anglesey Cl TW15 . . . 148 C1
Anglesey Court Rd SM5 . . . 219 A2
Anglesey Ct W7 . . . 86 D3
Anglesey Gdns SM5 . . . 219 A2
Anglesey Ho 13 E14 . . . 97 C1
Anglesey Rd Enfield EN3 . . . 6 B1
South Oxhey WD19 . . . 22 C5
Anglesmede Cres HA5 . . 41 C6
Anglesmede Way HA5 . . . 41 C6
Angles Rd SW16 . . . 182 A6
Anglia Cl N17 . . . 34 B3
Anglia Ct RM8 . . . 58 D1
Anglia Ho 13 E14 . . . 97 A1
Anglian Ind Est IG11 . . . 101 D2
Anglian Rd E11 . . . 76 B5
Anglia Wlk E6 . . . 100 C6
Anglo American Laundry SW17 . . . 158 A1
Anglo Rd 16 E3 . . . 97 B5
Angrave Ct 4 E8 . . . 95 D6
Angrave Pas 5 E8 . . . 95 D6
Angus Cl KT9 . . . 214 C3
Angus Dr HA4 . . . 62 C4
Angus Gdns NW9 . . . 27 B2
Angus Ho 12 SW12 . . . 159 D4
Angus Rd E13 . . . 99 C4
Angus St SE14 . . . 141 A5
Anhalt Rd SW11 . . . 136 C5 267 B4
Animals in War Meml* W1 . . . 247 D6
Ankerdine Cres SE18 . . . 144 D4
Anlaby Rd TW11 . . . 174 C5

Anley Rd W14 112 D4
Anmersh Gr HA7 25 D2
Annabel Cl E14 97 D1
Anna Cl E8 95 D6
Annadale N22 32 B5
Annandale Gr UB10 61 A5
Annandale Rd
Chiswick W4 111 C1
Croydon CR0 222 A6
Greenwich SE10 120 D1
Sidcup DA15 167 D4
Anna Neagle Cl 2 E7 77 A4
Anne Boleyn's Wlk
Belmont SM3 217 A1
Kingston u T KT2 176 A5
Anne Compton Mews
SE12 164 D4
Anne Goodman Ho 3
E1 96 C1
Anne Kerr Ct 18 SW15 156 D5
Annemount Sch N2 48 B3
Anne's Ct NW8 237 B6
Annesley Ave NW9 45 B6
Annesley Cl NW10 67 C5
Annesley Dr CR0 223 B5
Annesley Ho
31 Brixton SW9 138 C4
15 Kennington SW9 138 C5
Annesley Rd SE3 143 B4
Annesley Wlk N19 71 C6
Annesmere Gdns SE3 143 D2
Anne St E13 99 A3
Annett Cl TW17 193 C5
Annette Cl HA3 24 C1
Annette Cres 16 N1 73 A1
Annette Ct N7 72 B5
Annette Rd N7 72 B4
Annette White Lo 20
N2 30 B1
Annett Rd KT12 194 A2
Anne Way KT8 195 D5
Annie Besant Cl E3 97 B6
Annie Taylor Ho 2 E12 78 C4
Anning St E2 243 B6
Annington Rd N2 48 D6
Annis Rd E9 75 A2
Ann La SW10 136 B6 266 C5
Ann Moss Way SE16 118 C3
Ann Parkes Ct TW5 128 D3
Ann's Cl SW1 248 A1
Ann's Pl E1 243 C3
Ann St SE18 123 B2
Ann Stroud Ct SE12 165 A6
Annsworthy Ave CR7 205 B6
Annsworthy Cres CR7 183 B1
Annunciation RC Inf Sch
The HA8 27 B2
Annunciation RC Jun Sch
The HA8 27 B4
Ansar Gdns E17 53 B4
Ansdell Rd SE15 140 C3
Ansdell St W8 113 D3 255 D6
Ansdell Terr
W8 113 D3 255 D6
Ansell Gr SM5 203 A1
Ansell Ho E1 96 C2
Ansell Rd SW17 158 D1
Anselm Cl CR0 221 D5
Anselm Rd
Hatch End HA5 23 B3
West Brompton
SW6 135 C6 265 A5
Ansford Rd BR1, SE6 186 B6
Ansleigh Pl W11 112 D6
Anson 30 NW9 27 D1
Anson Ct TW19 148 A4
Anson Ho Pimlico SW1 269 A6
6 Tower Hamlets E1 97 A3
Anson Pl SE28 123 B4
Anson Prim Sch NW2 68 D3
Anson Rd
Cricklewood NW2 68 C3
Tufnell Pk N7 71 D4
Anson Terr UB5 63 D2
Anstey Ct 6 W3 110 D4
Anstey Ho 7 E9 96 C6
Anstey Lo EN1 17 C5
Anstey Rd SE15 140 A2
Anstey Wlk N15 51 A5
Anstice Cl W4 133 C5
Anstridge Rd SE9 167 B5
Antelope Rd SE18 122 B3
Antenor Ho 11 E2 96 B5
Anthony Cl NW7 27 C6
Anthony Cope Ct N1 235 D2
Anthony Ct Harrow HA1 42 B2
Isleworth TW7 130 D2
Anthony Ho NW8 237 A5
Anthony Kendal Ho 4
E5 74 B5
Anthony Rd
Croydon SE25 206 A3
East Wickham DA16 146 A4
Greenford UB6 86 C4
Anthony St E1 96 B1
Antigua Wlk SE19 183 B5
Antilles Bay 19 E14 120 A4
Antilles Ho W3 89 B1
Antill Rd Mile End E3 97 A4
Tottenham Hale N15 52 A5
Antill Terr 5 E1 96 D1
Antlers Hill E4 19 D6
Anton Cres SM1 217 C5
Antoneys Cl HA5 22 D1
Antonine Hts SE1 253 A1
Anton Pl HA9 66 D5
Anton St E8 74 A3
Antony Ho
4 Deptford SE14 140 D5
2 Rotherhithe SE16 118 C2
Antrim Gr NW3 70 D2
Antrim Ho SW11 137 A2
Antrim Mans NW3 70 D2
Antrim Rd NW3 70 D2
Antrobus Cl SM1 217 B3
Antrobus Rd W4 111 A3
Anvil Cl SW16 181 C3
Anvil Ho 10 N9 18 A1
Anvil Rd TW16 194 A6
Anworth Cl IG8 37 B4
Apex Cl BR3 185 D2
Apex Cnr Edgware NW7 27 B6
Twickenham TW13 151 B1
Apex Ct W13 87 A1
Apex Ind Est NW10 89 D3
Apex Lo 10 EN5 14 A6
Apex Ret Pk TW13 151 B1
Aphrodite Ct 11 E14 119 C2
Aplin Ct 4 SM1 217 D2
Aplin Way TW7 130 C4
Apollo Ave
Bromley BR1 187 B2
Loughton HA6 22 A5
Apollo Bldg 2 E14 119 C2
Apollo Ho
Chelsea SW10 266 C5
32 Hackney E2 96 B5
Highgate N6 48 D2
Apollo Ind Bsns Ctr 29
SE8 140 D6
Apollo Pl Chelsea SW10 266 C4
6 Leyton E11 76 C5
Apollo Studios 18 NW5 71 D3
Apollo Way 1 SE18 123 B3
Apostle Way CR7 182 D1
Apothecary St EC4 241 C1
Appach Rd SW2 160 C5
Appin Ct HA1 42 C2
Appleby Cl Chingford E4 36 A4
Hayes UB3, UB8 83 A1
Orpington BR5 211 C2
Twickenham TW2 152 B2
West Green N15 51 B4
Appleby Ct W3 111 A4
Appleby Gdns TW14 149 D3
Appleby Rd Hackney E8 74 A1
Newham E16 99 A1
Appleby St E2 95 D5
Appledore Ave HA4 62 C5
Appledore Cl
Bromley BR2 209 A4
Edgware HA8 26 C2
Upper Tooting SW12,
SW17 158 D2
Appledore Cres DA14 167 D1
Appledore Way NW7 28 D3
Appleford 8 NW5 71 C3
Appleford Ho 6 W10 91 A3
Appleford Rd W10 91 A3
Applegarth
Claygate KT10 212 D3
New Addington CR0 223 D1
Apple Garth TW8 109 D2
Applegarth Dr IG2 57 D5
Applegarth Ho
Borough The SE1 251 D2
9 Camberwell SE15 140 A5
Applegarth Inf Sch
CR0 223 D2
Applegarth Jun Sch
CR0 223 D2
Applegarth Rd
Hammersmith W14 112 D3
Woolwich SE28 124 C6
Apple Gr
Chessington KT9 214 A4
Enfield EN1 5 C2
Apple Lo HA0 65 C5
Apple Mkt KT1 175 D1
Apple Mkt WC2 250 B6
Apple Rd E11 76 C5
Appleshaw Ho 4 SE5 139 C2
Appleton Ct 30 E8 74 B3
Appleton Gdns KT3 200 A3
Appleton Rd SE9 144 A2
Appleton Sq CR4 180 C2
Apple Tree Ave UB7 82 B1
Appletree Cl 5 SE20 184 B2
Appletree Ct
Lewisham SE13 142 B1
Northolt UB5 85 A4
Appletree Gdns EN4 2 C1
Apple Tree Yd SW1 249 B4
Applewood Cl
Dollis Hill NW2 68 B5
Ickenham UB10 60 A4
Oakleigh Pk N20 14 C3
Applewood Dr E13 99 B3
Appold St EC2 95 C2 243 A4
Apollo Ct 7 SW9 138 C4
Apprentice Gdns UB5 85 B4
Apprentice Way 5 E5 74 B4
Approach Cl N16 73 C4
Approach La NW7 29 A5
Approach Rd
Ashford TW15 171 A4
Bethnal Green E2 96 C5
East Molesey KT8 195 C4
Edgware HA8 26 C4
Merton SW20 178 C1
New Barnet EN4, EN5 2 B1
Approach The Acton W3 89 B1
Enfield EN1 6 B3
Hendon NW4 46 D4
Orpington BR6 227 D6
Aprey Gdns NW4 46 C5
April Cl Ealing W7 108 C6
Feltham TW13 150 A1
Orpington BR6 227 D3
April Ct 20 E2 96 A5
April Glen SE23 162 D1
April St E8 73 D4
Apsley Cl HA2 42 A4
Apsley Ct SM2 218 A2
Apsley Ctr The NW2 68 A6
Apsley Ho Enfield EN1 17 C5
Hounslow TW4 129 B1
Stepney E1 96 C2
St John's Wood NW8 229 C4
Apsley Rd
Croydon SE25 206 B5
Kingston u T KT3 199 A6
Apsley Way
Dollis Hill NW2 68 A6
Mayfair W1 248 B2
Aquarius TW1 153 B3
Aquarius Bsns Pk NW2 46 A1
Aquarius Way HA6 22 A6
Aquila St NW8 92 B5 229 D4
Aquinas St SE1 116 C5 251 B3
Arabella Ct NW8 229 B4
Arabella Dr SW15 133 C1
Arabia Cl E4 20 B4
Arabian Ho 3 E1 97 A3
Arabin Rd SE4 141 B1
Aragon Ave KT7 196 D4
Aragon Cl
Ashford TW16 171 D3
Bromley BR2 210 B1
Enfield EN2 4 B5
Aragon Ct
Beckenham BR3 186 A2
East Molesey KT8 196 A5
Aragon Dr HA4 40 D1
Aragon Pl SM4 201 A2
Aragon Prim Sch
SM4 200 D2
Aragon Rd
Kingston u T KT2 176 A5
West Barnes SM4 201 A2
Aragon Twr SE8 119 B2
Arakan Ho 4 N16 73 B4
Aral Ho 14 E1 96 D3
Arandora Cres RM6 58 B2
Aranya Ct 3 E17 35 A1
Arapiles Ho 6 E14 98 B1
Arbery Rd E3 97 A5
Arbon Ct N1 235 B5
Arbor Cl BR3 185 D1
Arbor Ct N16 73 B6
Arborfield Cl SW2 160 B3
Arborfield Ho 7 E14 119 C6
Arbor Rd E4 20 B1
Arbour Ho 3 E1 96 D1
Arbour Rd EN3 6 D2
Arbour Sq E1 96 D1
Arbroath Rd SE9 144 A2
Arbrook Chase KT10 212 A2
Arbrook Ct
Chessington KT9 213 D3
St Paul's Cray BR5 190 A2
Arbrook Hall KT10 212 D2
Arbrook La KT10 212 B2
Arbury Ho BR1 188 A3
Arbury Terr 3 SE26 162 B1
Arbuthnot La DA5 169 A5
Arbuthnot Rd SE14 140 D3
Arbutus St E8 95 D6
Arcade Ho 7 NW11 47 B4
Arcade The
Broadgate EC2 243 A3
2 Eltham SE9 166 C5
1 Tufnell Pk N7 72 A4
Walthamstow E17 53 C5
Arcadia Ave N3 29 C2
Arcadia Centre The
W5 109 D6
Arcadia Cl SM5 219 A4
Arcadian Ave DA5 169 A5
Arcadian Cl DA5 169 A5
Arcadian Gdns N22 32 C3
Arcadian Ho SW6 136 A3
Arcadian Pl SW18 157 B4
Arcadian Rd DA5 169 A5
Arcadia St E14 97 C1
Archangel St SE16 118 D4
Archbishop Coggan Ho
SE13 142 B1
Archbishop Lanfranc Sch
The CR0 204 A3
Archbishop Michael
Ramsey Tech Coll
SE5 138 D5
Archbishop's Pl 1
SW2 160 B4
Archbishop Sumner CE
Prim Sch
SE11 116 C2 261 B3
Archbishop Tenison's CE
High Sch CR0 221 D5
Archbishop Tenison's Sch
SE11 138 B6 270 D5
Archdale Bsns Ctr HA2 64 A6
Archdale Ct W12 112 B5
Archdale Ho SE1 263 A6
Archdale Pl KT3 198 D6
Archdale Rd SE22 139 D1
Archdeacon Cambridge's
CE Prim Sch TW2 152 C2
Archel Rd W14 135 B6 264 C6
Archer Cl KT2 176 A3
Archer Ct TW13 150 A3
Archer Ho
1 Battersea SW11 136 B3
Ealing W13 109 B5
24 Hoxton N1 95 C6
1 New Cross SE14 141 A4
Notting Hill W11 244 D6
Archer Mews TW12 174 A4
Archer Rd SE25 206 B5
Archers Ct 3 CR2 221 A3
Archers Dr EN3 6 C3
Archers Lo 22 SE16 118 A1
Archer Sq SE14 141 A6
Archer St W1 249 C6
Archer Terr UB7 104 A6
Archery Cl Harrow HA3 42 D6
Paddington W2 237 B1
Archery Fields Ho
WC1 234 A2
Archery Rd SE9 166 B6
Archery Stps W2 247 B6
Arches Bsns Ctr The
UB2 107 B4
Arches The Harrow HA2 63 D6
Strand WC2 250 B4
Archgate Bsns Ctr 1
N12 30 A5
Archibald Mews W1 248 C5
Archibald Rd N7 71 D4
Archibald St E3 97 C4
Archie Cl UB7 104 C4
Archie St SE1 253 B1
Arch St SE1 117 A3 262 A5
Archway N19 71 C6
Archway Bsns Ctr 5
N19 71 D5
Archway Cl
North Kensington W10 90 D2
2 Upper Holloway N19 71 C6
Wallington SM6 220 A5
Wimbledon SW19 179 D6
Archway Hts 5 N19 49 C1
Archway Mews SW15 135 A1
Archway Rd N6 49 B2
Archway St SW13,
SW14 133 C2
Archway Sta N19 71 C6
Arcola St E8 73 D3
Arcon Dr UB5 85 A3
Arctic St NW5 71 B3
Arcus Rd BR1 186 C4
Ardbeg Rd SE24 161 B6
Arden 17 SW19 156 D3
Arden Cl
Bushey Heath WD23 8 D4
Erith SE28 102 D1
Harrow HA1 64 B5
Arden Court Gdns N2 48 B3
Arden Cres
Dagenham RM9 80 D1
Millwall E14 119 C2
Arden Gr BR6 226 D4
Arden Grange N12 30 A6
Arden Ho 21 Hoxton N1 95 C5
29 Stockwell SW9 138 A3
Vauxhall SE11 260 C3
Arden Mews E17 53 D4
Arden Mhor HA5 40 B5
Arden Rd Ealing W13 109 C6
Finchley N3 47 B6
Ardent Cl SE25 205 C6
Ardent Ho 30 E3 97 A5
Ardfern Ave SW16 204 C6
Ardfillan Rd SE6 164 B2
Ardgowan Rd SE6 164 C3
Ardilaun Rd N5 73 A4
Ardingly Cl CR0 222 D5
Ardleigh Gdns SM3 201 C2
Ardleigh Ho 5 IG11 101 A6
Ardleigh Rd
Kingsland N1 73 C2
Walthamstow E17 35 B2
Ardleigh Terr E17 35 B2
Ardley Cl
Forest Hill SE6 163 A1
Neasden NW10 67 C5
Ruislip HA4 39 A2
Ardlui Rd SE27 161 A2
Ardmay Gdns KT6 198 A4
Ardmere Rd SE13 164 B5
Ardmore La IG9 21 B4
Ardmore Pl IG9 21 B4
Ardoch Rd SE6 164 B2
Ardra Rd N9 18 D1
Ardrossan Gdns KT4 216 A5
Ardshiel Cl SW15 134 D2
Ardwell Ave IG6 57 A4
Ardwell Rd SW2 160 A2
Ardwick Rd NW2 69 C4
Arena Bsns Ctr N4 51 A3
Arena Est N4 50 D3
Arena Sta SE25 206 C4
Arena The EN3 7 B5
Ares Ct 16 E14 119 C2
Arethusa Ho 8 E14 119 D2
Argali Ho 3 DA18 125 A3
Argall Ave E10 52 D1
Argall Way E10 53 A1
Argenta Way NW10 66 D1
Argent Ct KT6 214 C5
Argent Ctr The UB3 106 A4
Argent Ho HA5 23 B4
Argo Bsns Ctr 7 NW6 91 C4
Argon Mews SW6 265 B3
Argon Rd N18 34 D5
Argos Ct 5 SW9 138 C4
Argos Ho 8 E2 96 B5
Argosy Ho Fitzrovia W1 238 D5
Rotherhithe SE8 119 A2
Argus Way UB5 85 A4
Argyle Cl W13 87 A3
Argyle Ho
Cubitt Town E14 120 A3
Richmond TW10 153 C2
Sutton SM2 218 A2
Teddington TW11 174 C5
Argyle Mans 4 NW2 68 D4
Argyle Pl W6 112 B2
Argyle Prim Sch
WC1 94 A4 233 A2
Argyle Rd Ealing W13 87 A2
Edmonton N18 34 A6
Harrow HA2 41 D3
Hounslow TW3 151 D6
Ilford IG1 78 C6
Leyton E15 76 C4
Newham E16 99 B1
Stepney E1 96 D3
Tottenham N17 34 A2
Woodside Pk N12 29 C5
Argyle Sq WC1 94 A4 233 B2
Argyle St WC1 94 A4 233 B2
Argyle Way SE16 118 A1
Argyle Wlk WC1 233 B1
Argyll Ave UB1 107 D5
Argyll Cl SW9 138 B2
Argyll Ct 15 SW2 160 A4
Argyll Gdns HA8 26 D2
Argyll Mans
Chelsea SW3 266 D6
West Kensington W14 254 B4
Argyll Rd
Kensington
W8 113 C4 245 B1
Woolwich SE18 123 A3
Argyll St W1 93 C1 239 A1
Aria Ct IG2 57 A3
Arica Ho SE16 118 B3
Arica Rd SE4 141 A2
Ariel Ct
5 Belvedere DA17 125 C1
5 Hammersmith W12 112 A3
Newington SE11 261 C3
Ariel Rd NW6 69 C2
Ariel Way
Hounslow TW4 128 B2
Shepherd's Bush W12 112 C5
Aristotle Rd SW4 137 D2
Arizona Bldg 10 SE13 141 D4
Arkansas Ho 21 N19 49 D2
Ark Ct N16 73 D6
Arkell Gr SW16 182 D3
Arkindale Rd SE6 164 A1
Arklay Cl UB8 82 B3
ARKLEY 12 A6
Arkley Cres E17 53 B4
Arkley Dr EN5 12 B6
Arkley Pk EN5 11 B5
Arkley Rd E17 53 B4
Arklow Ho SE17 139 B6
Arklow Mews 4 KT6 214 A6
Arklow Rd SE14 141 B6
Arklow Road Trad Est
SE14 141 B6
Arkwright Ho 23 SW2 160 A4
Arkwright Mans NW3 70 A3
Arkwright Rd NW3 70 A3
Arlesey Cl SW15 157 A6
Arlesford Rd SW9 138 A2
Arless Ho 8 HA1 42 D4
Arlidge Ho EC1 241 B4
Arlingford Rd SW2 160 C5
Arlington N12 13 C1
Arlington Ave
N1 95 A6 235 B5
Arlington Cl
Lewisham SE13 164 B6
Sidcup DA15 167 C4
Sutton SM1 217 C6
Twickenham TW1 153 C5
Arlington Ct
13 Acton W3 110 D5
Highgate N6 49 A3
4 Twickenham TW1 153 C5
Arlington Dr
Carshalton SM5 218 D6
Ruislip HA4 39 B3
Arlington Gdns
Acton Green W4 111 A1
Ilford IG1 56 C1
Arlington Gn NW7 28 D3
Arlington Ho
3 Deptford SE8 141 B6
Finsbury EC1 234 B2
1 Shepherd's Bush
W12 112 B5
Arlington Lo SW2 138 B1
Arlington Park Mans 1
W4 111 A1
Arlington Pl 7 SE10 142 A5
Arlington Rd
Ashford TW15 170 B5
Camden Town
NW1 93 B6 231 D5
Ealing W13 87 B1
Osidge N14 15 C3
Richmond TW10 153 D2
Surbiton KT6 197 D3
Teddington TW11 174 D6
Twickenham TW1 153 C5
Woodford IG8 37 B3
Arlington Sq N1 95 A6 235 B5
Arlington St
SW1 115 C5 249 A4
Arlington Way
EC1 94 C4 234 B2
Arliss Way UB5 84 C6
Arlow Rd N21 16 C3
Armada Ct 11 SE8 141 C6
Armadale Cl N17 52 B5
Armadale Rd
Feltham TW14 150 A6
West Brompton SW6 265 A5
Armada St 10 SE8 141 C6
Armada Way E6 101 B1
Armagh Rd E3 97 B6
Armeston KT3 199 B2
Armfield Cl KT8 195 B4
Armfield Cotts 3
SW19 180 D1
Armfield Cres CR4 180 D1
Armfield Rd EN2 5 B4
Arminger Rd W12 112 B5
Armistice Gdns SE25 206 A6
Armitage Ho
NW1 92 C2 237 B4
Armitage Rd
Golders Green NW11 47 B1
Greenwich SE10 120 D1
Armour Cl N7 72 B2
Armoury Ho E3 97 A6
Armoury Rd SE8 141 D3
Armoury Way SW18 157 C6
Armsby Ho 17 E1 96 C2
Armstead Wlk RM10 81 C1
Armstrong Ave IG8 36 C4
Armstrong Cl
Bickley BR1 210 A6
Dagenham RM8 58 D2
Newham E6 100 B1
Pinner HA5 40 A3
Walton-on-T KT12 194 A3
Armstrong Cres EN4 2 B2
Armstrong Ho 8
SW15 156 D5
Armstrong Rd
East Acton W3 111 D5
Feltham TW13 173 A5
Knightsbridge SW7 256 C5
Woolwich SE18 123 A3
Armstrong Way UB2 107 D4
Armytage Rd TW5 128 D5
Arnal Cres SW18 157 A4
Arncliffe NW6 91 D6
Arncliffe Cl N11 31 A4
Arncroft Ct IG11 102 B4
Arndale Wlk 6 SW18 157 D6
Arndell Ho 16 SM1 218 A4
Arne Gr BR6 227 D5
Arne Ho SE11 260 C2
Arne St WC2 94 A1 240 B1
Arnett Sq E4 35 B4
Arneways Ave RM6 58 D6
Arneway St SW1 259 D5
Arne Wlk SE3 142 D1
Arnewood Cl SW15 156 A3
Arney's La CR4 203 A3
Arngask Rd SE6 164 B4
Arnhem Pl E14 119 C3
Arnhem Way 3 SE22 161 C6
Arnhem Wharf E14 119 C3
Arnhem Wharf Prim Sch
E14 119 C3
Arnison Rd KT8 196 B5
Arnold Ave E EN3 7 C5
Arnold Ave W EN3 7 B5
Arnold Cir E2 95 D4
Arnold Cl HA3 44 B2
Arnold Cres TW7 152 B6
Arnold Ct E18 36 D2
Arnold Dr KT9 213 D2
Arnold Est SE1 253 D1
Arnold Gdns N13 32 D5
Arnold Ho
Croydon CR0 220 D4
Newington SE17 261 D1
9 Stoke Newington N16 73 C5
Arnold House Sch
NW8 92 B5 229 C3
Arnold Rd Bow E3 97 C4
Dagenham RM10 81 C1
Mitcham SW17 180 D3
Northolt UB5 63 A2
Tottenham N15 51 D6
Arnos Gr N14 15 D1
Arnos Grove Ct 4 N11 31 C5
Arnos Grove Sta N11 31 C6
Arnos Rd N11 31 C6
Arnot Ho 27 SE5 139 A5
Arnott Cl
Acton Green W4 111 B2
Thamesmead SE28 124 C5
Arnould Ave SE5 139 B1
Arnsberg Way DA6,
DA7 147 C1
Arnside Gdns HA9 43 D1
Arnside Ho 2 SE17 139 B6
Arnside Rd DA7 147 C4
Arnside St SE17 139 A6
Arnulf St SE6 185 D6
Arnull's Rd SW16 182 D4
Arodene Rd SW2 160 B5
Arosa Rd 8 TW1 153 D5
Arragon Gdns
Streatham SW16 182 A3
West Wickham BR4 223 D5
Arragon Rd Newham E6 99 D6
4 Twickenham TW1 153 A3
Wandsworth SW18 157 C3
Arran Cl SM6 219 C4
Arran Ct Edgware HA8 10 D2
32 Hendon NW9 27 D1
Neasden NW10 67 B5
Arrandene Ho 3 BR5 190 B1
Arran Dr Stanmore HA7 25 C6
Wanstead E12 77 D6
Arran Ho
5 Canary Wharf E14 120 A5
Stoke Newington N16 51 D1
Arran Mews W5 110 B5
Arran Rd SE6 164 A2
Arran Wlk N1 73 A1
Arras Ave SM4 202 A4
Arras Ho SE2 146 D6
Arrol Ho SE1 262 B5

Arrol Rd BR3 206 D6
Arrowe Ct 6 E5 74 B4
Arrow Ho 23 N1 95 C6
Arrow Rd E3 97 D4
Arrow Scout Wlk UB5 85 A4
Arrowsmith Ho SE11 260 C2
Arsenal Rd SE9 144 B2
Arsenal Sta N5 72 C5
Arsenal Way SE18 123 A3
Arta Ho 26 E1 96 C1
Artemis Ct 14 E14 119 C2
Artemis Pl SW18 157 B4
Arterberry Rd SW20, SW19 178 D2
Artesian Cl NW10 67 B1
Artesian Gr EN5 2 A1
Artesian Rd W2 91 C1
Artesian Wlk 4 E11 76 C5
Arthingworth St E15 98 C6
Arthur Ct
Battersea SW11 268 B1
10 North Kensington W10 90 D1
Paddington W2 91 D1
South Croydon CR0 221 B5
Arthur Deakin Ho 1 E1 96 A2
Arthurdon Rd SE4 163 C6
Arthur Gr SE18 123 A2
Arthur Henderson Ho
9 Crouch End N19 49 D2
9 Fulham SW6 135 B3
Arthur Newton Ho 20 SW11 136 B2
Arthur Rd
Dagenham RM6 58 D3
Edmonton N9 17 D2
6 Kingston u T KT2 176 C3
Lower Holloway N7 72 B4
Newham E6 100 B5
West Barnes KT3 200 B4
Wimbledon SW19 179 C6
Arthur Ruxley Est DA14 190 D4
Arthur St EC4 117 B6 252 D6
Arthur Wade Ho 7 E2 95 D4
Arthur Walls Ho 3 E12 78 C5
Artichoke Hill 8 E1 118 B6
Artichoke Mews 5 SE5 139 B4
Artichoke Pl SE5 139 B4
Artillery Cl IG2 57 A3
Artillery Ho Bow E3 97 A6
Westminster SW1 259 C5
Woolwich SE18 122 C1
Artillery La
Broadgate E1 95 C2 243 B3
North Kensington W12 90 A1
Artillery Pas E1 243 B3
Artillery Pl
Harrow Weald HA3 24 A3
Westminster SW1 259 C5
Woolwich SE18 122 C2
Artillery Row SW1 259 C5
Artington Cl BR6 227 A4
Artisan Cl E16 122 D6
Artisan Ct E8 74 A2
Artisan Mews 9 NW10 90 D4
Artisan Quarter 10 NW10 90 D4
Artizan St E1 243 B2
Arton Wilson Ho 12 SW15 156 A6
Arts Educational Sch The W4 111 C2
Arundale KT1 197 D5
Arundel Ave SM4 201 B5
Arundel Bldgs SE1 263 B5
Arundel Cl
Croydon CR0 220 D5
Hampton TW12 173 D5
Leyton E15 76 C4
Sidcup DA5 169 B5
Wandsworth SW11 158 C6
Arundel Ct
Barnes SW13 134 B6
4 Beckenham BR2 186 C1
2 Bexley DA6 147 A1
Chelsea SW3 257 B2
Colney Hatch N12 30 C4
3 Croydon CR0 220 D5
Harrow HA2 63 C4
Putney SW15 156 D6
Tottenham N17 34 A2
Arundel Dr
Borehamwood WD6 11 A6
Harrow HA2 63 C4
Woodford IG8 37 A3
Arundel Gdns
Burnt Oak HA8 27 B3
Ilford IG3 80 A6
Notting Hill W11 113 B6 244 C6
Southgate N21 16 C3
Arundel Gr N16 73 C3
Arundel Ho
Croydon CR0 221 B3
Islington N1 94 D6 234 D6
Richmond TW10 154 C6
3 South Acton W3 110 D4
Arundel Lo
Church End N3 29 B1
9 Upper Holloway N19 72 A6
Arundel Mans
Barnes SW13 134 B6
Fulham SW6 264 D2
Arundel Pl N1, N7 72 C2
Arundel Rd
Belmont SM2 217 B1
Cockfosters EN4 2 C2
Hounslow TW4 128 C2
Kingston u T KT1 177 A1
Thornton Heath CR0 205 B3
Arundel Sq N7 72 C2
Arundel St WC2 116 B6 250 D6
Arundel Terr SW13 134 B6
Arun Ho 5 KT2 175 D2
Arvon Rd N5 72 C3
Asa Ct UB3 105 D3
Asaph Ho SE14 141 B4
Asbaston Terr IG11 79 A2
Asbury Ct N21 16 A6
Ascalon Ct 16 SW2 160 B4
Ascalon Ho SW8 269 A3
Ascalon St SW8 137 C5 269 A3
Ascham Dr E4 35 C3
Ascham End E17 35 A2
Ascham St NW5 71 C3
Aschurch Rd CR0 205 D2
Ascot Cl
Borehamwood WD6 10 C6
Northolt UB5 63 C3
Ascot Ct
8 Brixton SW4 138 A1
Bromley BR1 188 A1
Old Bexley DA5 169 B4
St John's Wood NW8 229 C1
Ascot Gdns Enfield EN3 6 C6
Southall UB1 85 C2
Ascot Ho
6 Acton Green W4 111 A1
1 Paddington W9 91 C2
Penge SE26 184 B4
Regent's Pk NW1 231 D2
Ascot Lo Enfield EN1 17 B6
Paddington NW6 91 D5
Ascot Par 9 SW4 138 A1
Ascot Pl 12 HA7 25 C5
Ascot Rd
East Bedfont TW14 148 D2
Edmonton N18 34 A6
Newham E6 100 B4
Orpington BR5 211 D5
Streatham SW17 181 A4
Tottenham N15 51 B4
Ascott Ave W5 110 A4
Ascott Ct HA5 40 A5
Ashbourne Ave
East Barnet N20 14 D2
Erith DA7 147 A5
Harrow HA2 64 B6
Temple Fortune NW11 47 B4
Wanstead E18 55 B5
Ashbourne Cl Ealing W5 88 C2
18 Woodside Pk N12 29 D6
Ashbourne Ct
Beckenham BR3 186 A2
Clapton Pk E5 75 A4
13 Woodside Pk N12 29 D6
Ashbourne Gr
Chiswick W4 111 C1
East Dulwich SE22 139 D1
Edgware NW7 27 B5
Ashbourne Ind Sch W8 113 D4 245 C1
Ashbourne Lo 2 N13 32 C6
Ashbourne Par 2 NW11 47 B5
Ashbourne Rd
Ealing W5 88 B3
Mitcham CR4 181 A3
Ashbourne Rise BR6 227 C4
Ashbourne Terr 1 SW19 179 C3
Ashbourne Way NW11 47 B4
Ashbridge Ct 3 W6 112 B3
Ashbridge Rd E11 54 D2
Ashbridge St NW8 92 C3 237 A5
Ashbrook HA8 26 B4
Ashbrook Rd
Dagenham RM10 81 D5
Upper Holloway N19 71 D6
Ashburn Ct BR1 187 A3
Ashburn Gdns SW7 256 A4
Ashburnham Ave HA1 42 D3
Ashburnham Cl N2 48 B5
Ashburnham Com Sch SW10 266 C4
Ashburnham Gdns HA1 42 D3
Ashburnham Gr SE10 141 D5
Ashburnham Pk KT10 212 A4
Ashburnham Pl SE10 141 D5
Ashburnham Rd
Chelsea SW10 136 A5 266 B3
Kensal Rise NW10 90 C5
Richmond TW10 153 B1
Ashburnham Retreat 4 SE10 141 D5
Ashburnham Twr SW10 266 C4
Ashburn Pl SW7 114 A2 256 A3
Ashburton Ave
Croydon CR0 206 B1
Ilford IG3 79 D4
Ashburton Cl CR0 206 A1
Ashburton Ct 1 HA5 40 D6
Ashburton Gdns CR0 222 A6
Ashburton Ho
Enfield EN3 6 D2
2 Wallington SM6 219 D3
Ashburton Jun & Inf Sch CR0 206 B3
Ashburton Learning Village CR9 206 B2
Ashburton Mans SW10 266 B4
Ashburton Rd
Croydon CR0 222 A6
Newham E16 99 A1
Ruislip HA4 62 A6
Ashburton Terr 2 E13 99 A5
Ashbury Dr UB10 60 D5
Ashbury Gdns RM6 58 D4
Ashbury Pl SW19 180 A4
Ashbury Rd SW11 137 A2
Ashby Ave KT19, KT9 214 C2
Ashby Ct NW8 236 D6
Ashby Gr N1 73 A1
Ashby Grange 7 SM6 219 C2
Ashby Ho
6 Brixton SW9 138 D3
17 Islington N1 73 A1
3 Northolt UB5 85 B3
14 Surbiton KT6 198 A3
Ashby Mews
10 Clapham Pk SW2 160 A6
New Cross SE4 141 B3
Ashby Rd
New Cross SE4 141 B3
South Tottenham N15 52 A4
Ashby St EC1 94 D4 234 D1
Ashby Way UB7 126 C5
Ashby Wlk CR0 205 A3
Ashchurch Ct 2 W12 112 A3
Ashchurch Gr W12 112 A3
Ashchurch Park Villas W12 112 A3
Ashchurch Terr W12 112 A3
Ash Cl Carshalton SM5 218 D6
Edgware HA8 27 A6
Kingston u T KT3 177 B1
Penge SE20 184 C1
Petts Wood BR5 211 B4
Sidcup DA14 168 B1
Stanmore HA7 25 A4
Ashcombe Ave KT6 197 D2
Ashcombe Ct 4 SW15 157 A6
Ashcombe Gdns HA8 26 C6
Ashcombe Ho 39 E3 97 D4
Ashcombe Pk NW2 67 C5
Ashcombe Rd
Wallington SM5 219 A2
Wimbledon SW19 179 C5
Ashcombe Sq KT3 199 A6
Ashcombe St SW6 135 D3
Ashcroft Hatch End HA5 23 C4
Osidge N14 15 D2
Ashcroft Ave DA15 168 A5
Ashcroft Cres DA15 168 A5
Ashcroft Ct
5 Eltham SE9 166 C5
Wembley HA0 65 A4
3 Whetstone N20 14 B2
Ashcroft Ho SW8 269 A2
Ashcroft Rd Bow E3 97 A4
Chessington KT9 214 B5
Ashcroft Sq 8 W6 112 C2
Ash Ct Chingford E4 20 B4
Clapham SW11 159 A6
Lee SE12 165 A4
Marylebone W1 237 C2
Romford RM7 59 D3
6 Rotherhithe SE16 119 A5
Upper Holloway N19 71 C6
West Ewell KT19 215 A4
2 West Norwood SW16 182 C5
9 Wimbledon SW19 179 A3
Woodford E18 37 C2
Ashdale Cl
Stanwell TW19 148 A2
Twickenham TW2 152 A4
Ashdale Gr HA7 24 D4
Ashdale Ho N4 51 B2
Ashdale Rd SE12 165 B3
Ashdale Way TW2 151 D4
Ashdene
6 Deptford SE15 140 B5
Pinner HA5 40 C6
Ashdene Cl TW15 171 A3
Ashdon Cl IG8 37 B4
Ashdon Rd NW10 89 D6
Ashdown Ealing W13 87 B2
Putney SW15 156 D6
Ashdown Cl 13 BR3 185 D1
Ashdown Cres NW5 71 A3
Ashdown Ct
Dulwich SE22 162 A3
Ilford IG1 78 D2
New Malden KT4 199 D2
Sutton SM2 218 A2
Ashdowne Ct N17 34 A2
Ashdown Ho 7 E5 74 A6
Ashdown Pl
Ewell KT17 215 D1
Thames Ditton KT7 197 A2
Ashdown Rd Enfield EN3 6 C3
Hillingdon UB10 82 C5
Kingston u T KT1 176 A1
Ashdown Way SW17 159 A2
Ashdown Wlk 20 E14 119 C2
Ashe Ho 9 TW1 153 D5
Ashen E6 100 C1
Ashenden SE17 262 B4
Ashenden Rd E5 75 A3
Ashen Gr SW19 157 C2
Ashentree Ct EC4 241 B1
Asher Loftus Way N11 30 D4
Asher Way E1 118 A6
Ashfield Ave
Bushey WD23 8 A4
Feltham TW13 150 B3
Ashfield Cl
Beckenham BR3 185 C3
Richmond TW10 154 A3
Ashfield Ct SW9 138 A3
Ashfield Ho 5 N5 73 A3
Ashfield La BR7 189 A3
Ashfield Par N14 15 D3
Ashfield Pl BR7 189 B3
Ashfield Rd
East Acton W3 111 D5
New Southgate N14 15 C1
Tottenham N4 51 A3
Ashfield St E1 96 C2
Ashfield Yd 21 E1 96 C2
ASHFORD 170 B4
Ashford Ave
Ashford TW15 170 D4
Hayes UB4 84 D1
Hornsey N8 50 A5
Ashford Bsns Complex TW15 171 A6
Ashford CE Prim Sch TW15 170 D4
Ashford Cl
Ashford TW15 170 A6
Walthamstow E17 53 B3
ASHFORD COMMON 171 B4
Ashford Cres EN3 6 C3
Ashford Ct
Cricklewood NW2 68 D4
Edgware HA8 10 D1
Ashford Gn WD19 22 D5
Ashford Ho
14 Brixton SW9 138 D1
11 Deptford SE8 141 B6
Ashford Hospl TW15 148 A2
Ashford Ind Est TW15 171 A6
Ashford Mews N17 34 A2
Ashford Rd
Cricklewood NW2 68 D4
Feltham TW13, TW15 171 B6
Littleton TW15, TW17 171 A3
Staines TW18 170 A4
Wallend E6 78 C1
Woodford E18 37 B1
Ashford St N1 95 C4
Ash Gr Cricklewood NW2 69 A4
Ealing W5 110 A3
East Bedfont TW14 149 C3
Edmonton N13 17 A1
Enfield EN1 17 C4
Hackney E8 96 B6
Hayes UB3 105 B6
Heston TW5 128 D5
Penge SE20 184 C1
Southall UB1 85 C2
Wembley HA0 65 A4
West Wickham BR4 208 A1
Yiewsley UB7 104 B6
Ashgrove SE12 165 A3
Ashgrove Ct 2 W9 91 C2
Ashgrove Ho SW1 259 D2
Ashgrove Rd
Ashford TW15 171 B5
Catford BR1 186 B4
Ashgrove Sch BR1 187 B1
Ash Hill Dr HA5 40 C6
Ash Ho
3 Canary Wharf E14 120 A4
Fulham SE1 263 D3
Kenton NW9 45 A6
Lewisham SE12 165 A3
2 Teddington TW11 175 C3
Ashingdon Cl E4 20 A1
Ashington 1 NW5 71 B2
Ashington Ho 16 E1 96 B3
Ashington Rd SW6 135 B3
Ashlake Rd SW16 182 A6
Ashland Pl W1 238 A4
Ashlar Ct N2 48 C6
Ashlar Pl SE18 122 D2
Ashleigh Commercial Est SE7 121 D3
Ashleigh Ct Ealing W5 109 D2
Osidge N14 15 C4
Penge SE26 184 B4
Ashleigh Gdns SM1 217 D6
Ashleigh Ho
Mortlake SW14 133 C2
1 Streatham SW16 182 B6
Ashleigh Point 8 SE26 162 D1
Ashleigh Rd
Mortlake SW14 133 C2
Penge SE20 206 B6
Ashley Ave SM4 201 C4
Ashley CE Prim Sch KT12 194 A1
Ashley Cl Hendon NW4 28 C1
Oatlands Pk KT12, KT13 193 D1
Pinner Green HA5 22 B1
Ashley Cres
Clapham SW11 137 A2
Wood Green N22 32 C1
Ashley Ct
Hampstead NW3 69 D3
Hendon NW4 28 C1
19 Kingsland N16 73 C3
New Barnet EN5 14 A6
Northolt UB5 85 A6
Stanmore HA7 25 B1
Yiewsley UB7 104 A5
Ashley Dr
Borehamwood WD6 11 B6
Hounslow TW7 130 C6
Twickenham TW2 151 D3
Ashley Gdns
Edmonton N13 33 A6
Orpington BR6 227 C3
Ashley Gdns *continued*
Richmond TW10 153 D2
Wembley HA9 66 A6
Ashley Ho BR5 190 A1
Ashley La Croydon CR0 220 D4
Edgware NW7 28 D3
Hendon NW4 28 C1
Ashley Park Ave KT12 193 D1
Ashley Park Cres KT12 194 A1
Ashley Pl
Walton-on-T KT12 194 A1
Westminster SW1 115 C3 259 A5
Ashley Rd Chingford E4 35 C4
Enfield EN3 6 C3
Hampton TW12 173 C2
Hornsey N19 50 A2
Richmond TW9 132 A2
Thames Ditton KT7 196 D3
Thornton Heath CR7 204 B5
Tottenham Hale N17 52 A6
Upton E7 77 C1
Walton-on-T KT12 194 A1
Wimbledon SW19 179 D4
Ashleys Alley N15 51 A5
Ashley Wlk NW7 28 D3
Ashling Ho 2 N17 33 D1
Ashling Rd CR0 206 A1
Ashlin Rd E15 76 B4
Ash Lo
2 Ashford TW16 171 D3
Fulham SW6 134 D4
Ashlone Rd SW15 134 D2
Ashlyns Way KT9 213 D2
Ashmead 4 N14 15 C6
Ashmead Bsns Ctr 2 E16 98 B3
Ashmead Gate BR1 187 C2
Ashmead Ho E9 75 A3
Ashmead Prim Sch SE8 141 C3
Ashmead Rd
East Bedfont TW14 150 A3
St Johns SE8 141 C3
Ashmere Ave BR3 186 B1
Ashmere Cl SM3 216 D3
Ashmere Gr 11 SW2, SW4 138 A1
Ashmere Ho 10 SW2 138 A1
Ashmill Ct CR0 205 A3
Ashmill St NW8 92 C2 237 A4
Ashmole Prim Sch SW8 138 B6 270 D5
Ashmole Sch N14 15 C3
Ashmole St SW8 138 B6 270 D5
Ashmoor Lo NW7 27 B4
Ashmore NW1 71 D1
Ashmore Cl SE15 139 D5
Ashmore Ct
Catford SE6 164 C3
Colney Hatch N11 30 D4
Heston TW5 129 C6
Ashmore Gr DA16 145 C2
Ashmore Ho W14 254 B5
Ashmore Rd W9 91 B4
Ashmount Prim Sch N19 49 C2
Ashmount Rd
Crouch End N19 49 D2
South Tottenham N15 51 D4
Ashmount Terr W5 109 D2
Ashneal Gdns HA1 64 B5
Ashness Gdns UB6 65 B2
Ashness Rd SW11 158 D6
Ashpark Ho 4 E14 97 B1
Ash Rd Cheam SM3 201 B1
Croydon CR0 223 C6
Littleton TW17 192 C5
Orpington BR6 227 D1
Plashet E15 76 D3
Ashridge Cl HA3 43 C3
Ashridge Cres SE18 145 A5
Ashridge Ct
Southall UB1 108 A6
Southgate N14 15 C6
Ashridge Dr WD19 22 C5
Ashridge Gdns
Bowes Pk N13 32 A5
Pinner HA5 41 A5
Ashridge Ho DA14 189 D6
Ashridge Way
Ashford TW16 172 A4
Merton SM4 201 B5
Ash Row BR2 210 C3
Ashtead Ct 15 SW19 156 D3
Ashtead Rd E5 52 A2
Ash Tech Coll The TW15 148 A1
Ashton Cl SM1 217 C4
Ashton Ct
1 Beckenham BR3 185 B2
Chingford E4 20 C1
Harrow HA1 64 D5
Ashton Gdns
Dagenham RM6 59 A3
Hounslow TW4 129 B1
Ashton Ho
13 Kennington SW9 138 C5
Roehampton SW15 156 B4
Ashton Rd E15 76 B3
Ashton St E14 120 A6
Ashtree Ave CR4 180 B1
Ashtree Cl BR6 226 D4
Ash Tree Cl
Croydon CR0 207 A3
1 Surbiton KT6 198 A1
Ashtree Ct TW15 170 D5
Ash Tree Dell NW9 45 B4
Ash Tree Villas CR0 204 B3
Ash Tree Way CR0 207 A3
Ashurst Cl SE20 184 B2
Ashurst Dr
Ilford IG2, IG6 57 A4
Littleton TW17 192 A4
Ashurst Lo 4 N5 72 D3
Ashurst Rd
Cockfosters EN4 14 D6
Colney Hatch N12 30 C5
Ashurst Wlk CR0 222 B6
Ashvale Rd SW17 180 D5
Ashview Cl TW15 170 A5
Ashview Gdns TW15 170 A5
Ashville Rd E11 76 B6
Ashwater Rd SE12 165 A3
Ashway Ctr 5 KT2 176 A2
Ashwell Cl 8 E6 100 A1
Ashwell Ct TW15 148 A2
Ashwin St E8 73 D2
Ash Wlk HA0 65 C4
Ashwood Ave UB8 82 C1
Ashwood Ct HA9 66 B4
Ashwood Gdns
Hayes UB3 105 D2
New Addington CR0 224 A2
Ashwood Ho 10 NW4 46 C5
Ashwood Lo
9 New Barnet EN5 13 D6
Southgate N21 16 B5
Ashwood Pk 6 SM2 217 C1
Ashwood Rd E4 20 B1
Ashworth Cl SE5 139 B3
Ashworth Mans W9 91 D4
Ashworth Rd W9 91 D4
Aske Ho 2 N1 95 C4
Asker Ho N7 72 A4
Askern Cl DA6 146 D1
Aske St N1 95 C4
Askew Cres W12 112 A4
Askew Mans 14 W12 112 A4
Askew Rd W12 112 A4
Askham Ct W12 112 A5
Askham Lo 5 SE12 165 A4
Askham Rd W12 112 A5
Askill Dr SW15 157 A6
Asland Rd E15 98 B6
Aslett St SW18 158 A4
Asmara Rd NW2 69 A3
Asmuns Hill NW11 47 C4
Asmuns Pl NW11 47 B4
Asolando Dr SE17 262 B3
Aspect Coll WC1 94 A2 240 B3
Aspect Ho 7 E14 120 A4
Aspects SM1 217 D3
Aspen Cl Ealing W5 110 B4
13 Upper Holloway N19 71 C6
Yiewsley UB7 104 B5
Aspen Copse BR1 188 B1
Aspen Ct 10 Acton W3 89 A1
12 Hackney E8 74 A3
Redbridge IG5 56 A6
Richmond TW9 132 C5
Aspen Dr HA0 65 A5
Aspen Gdns
Ashford TW15 171 A5
2 Hammersmith W6 112 B1
Mitcham CR4 203 A4
Aspen Gn DA18 125 B3
Aspen Gr HA5 39 D6
Aspen Ho
8 Deptford SE15 140 C6
4 Maitland Pk NW3 70 D2
Richmond TW9 132 C5
2 Sidcup DA15 168 A1
Southgate N21 16 B6
Aspen La UB5 85 A4
Aspenlea Rd W6 134 D6
Aspen Lo 1 SW19 179 B4
Aspen Way
Canary Wharf E14 120 A6
Feltham TW13 150 B1
Aspern Gr NW3 70 C3
Aspinall Ho SW12 160 A3
Aspinall Rd SE4 140 D2
Aspinden Rd SE16 118 B2
Aspire Bld 10 SW15 157 B6
Aspley Rd SW18 157 D6
Asplins Rd N17 34 B2
Asprey Ho CR4 202 C6
Asquith Cl RM8 58 C1
Assam SE1 253 D3
Assam St E1 96 A1
Assata Mews N1 72 D2
Assembly Pas E1 96 C2
Assembly Wlk SM5 202 C2
Assheton-Bennett Ho 15 KT6 198 A4
Ass House La HA3 23 D6
Assisi Ct
Upper Tooting SW12 158 D3
Wembley HA0 64 D5
Astall Cl HA3 24 C2
Astbury Bsns Pk 5 SE15 140 C4
Astbury Ho SE11 261 A5
Astbury Rd SE15 140 C4
Astell St SW3 114 C1 257 B2
Aster Ct 3 HA8 27 A6
Aster Ho 3 SE13 142 A3
Aste St E14 120 A4
Astey's Row 1 N1 73 A1
Asthall Gdns IG6 57 A5
Astins Ho 4 E17 53 D5
Astleham Rd TW17 192 A6
Astleham Way TW17 192 A6
Astle St SW11 137 A3
Astley Ave NW2 68 C3
Astley Ho Fulham SE1 263 D2

Astley Ho *continued*
39 Paddington W2 ... 91 C2
8 West Norwood SE27 ... 183 A6
Aston Ave HA3 ... 43 C2
Aston Cl Bushey WD23 ... 8 A5
Sidcup DA14 ... 168 A1
Aston Ct
Stoke Newington N4 ... 73 A6
3 Wimbledon SW19 ... 178 C3
10 Woodford IG8 ... 37 A4
Aston Gn TW5 ... 128 C3
Aston Ho
Notting Hill W11 ... 244 D6
South Lambeth SW8 ... 269 C1
Aston House Sch W5 ... 87 D1
Aston Mews RM6 ... 58 C2
Aston Pl SW16 ... 182 D4
Aston Rd
Claygate KT10 ... 212 C3
Ealing W5 ... 87 D1
Merton SW20 ... 178 C1
Aston St E14 ... 97 A2
Astonville St SW18 ... 157 C3
Astor Ave RM7 ... 59 D3
Astor Cl KT2 ... 176 D4
Astor Ct
Colney Hatch N12 ... 30 C4
Newham E16 ... 99 C1
Walham Green SW6 ... 266 A3
Astoria Mans 18 SW16 ... 160 A1
Astoria Par SW16 ... 160 A1
Astoria Wlk SW9 ... 138 C2
Astra Ct W13 ... 109 A5
Astra Ho 4 Bow E3 ... 97 B4
Hornsey N4 ... 50 B2
Astrid Ho TW13 ... 150 C2
Astrop Mews W6 ... 112 C3
Astrop Terr W6 ... 112 C4
Astwood Mews SW7 ... 256 A4
Asylum Rd SE15 ... 140 B5
Atalanta St SW6 ... 134 D5 264 A3
Atbara Ct TW11 ... 175 B4
Atbara Rd TW11 ... 175 B4
Atcham Rd TW3 ... 130 A1
Atcost Rd IG11 ... 102 A2
Atheldene Rd SW18 ... 158 A3
Athelney Prim Sch SE6 ... 163 C1
Athelney St SE6 ... 163 C1
Athelstan Ct E6 ... 100 C5
Athelstane Gr E3 ... 97 B5
Athelstane Mews N4 ... 50 C1
Athelstan Gdns 8 NW6 ... 69 A1
Athelstan Ho
Hackney Wick E9 ... 75 B3
Kingston u T KT1 ... 198 B5
Stoke Newington N16 ... 73 C4
Athelstan House Sch TW12 ... 173 C2
Athelstan Rd KT1 ... 198 B5
Athelstan Way BR5 ... 190 A2
Athelstone Rd HA3 ... 24 B1
Athena Cl Harrow HA2 ... 64 C6
Kingston u T KT1 ... 198 B6
Athena Ct
Bermondsey SE1 ... 253 A1
St John's Wood NW8 ... 229 C4
Athenaeum Pl 3 N10 ... 49 B6
Athenaeum Rd N20 ... 14 B3
Athenia Ho 7 E14 ... 98 B1
Athenlay Rd SE15 ... 162 D6
Athenoeum Ct N5 ... 73 A4
Athens Gdns W9 ... 91 C3
Atherden Rd E5 ... 74 C4
Atherfield Ct SW18 ... 157 D5
Atherfold Rd SW9 ... 138 A2
Atherley Way TW4 ... 151 B4
Atherstone Ct W2 ... 91 D2
Atherstone Mews SW7 ... 114 A2 256 B4
Atherton Dr SW19 ... 178 D6
Atherton Ho CR2 ... 221 C2
Atherton Hts HA0 ... 65 C2
Atherton Mews E7 ... 77 A2
Atherton Pl Harrow HA2 ... 42 B6
Southall UB1 ... 107 C6
Atherton Rd
Barnes SW13 ... 134 A5
Stratford E7 ... 76 D2
Atherton St SW11 ... 136 C3
Athlone KT10 ... 212 C2
Athlone Cl 24 E5 ... 74 B3
Athlone Ct
Lewisham SE6 ... 164 B4
Upper Walthamstow E17 ... 54 B6
Athlone Ho
16 Camden Town NW5 ... 71 A2
9 Stepney E1 ... 96 C1
Athlone House N6 ... 48 D1
Athlone Rd SW2 ... 160 C4
Athlone St NW5 ... 71 A2
Athlon Ind Est HA0 ... 87 D5
Athlon Rd HA0 ... 87 D5
Athol Cl HA5 ... 22 B2
Athol Ct 15 N4 ... 72 B6
Athole Gdns EN1 ... 17 C6
Athole Terr CR7 ... 183 A1
Athol Gdns HA5 ... 22 B2
Atholl Ho W9 ... 229 A1
Atholl Rd IG3 ... 58 A2
Athol Sq E14 ... 98 A1
Athol Way UB10 ... 82 C4
Atkins Ct 13 Old Ford E3 ... 97 B6
Woolwich SE7 ... 122 A2
Atkins Dr BR4 ... 224 B6
Atkins Lo W8 ... 245 A2
Atkinson Ct 3 E10 ... 53 D2
Atkinson Ho
11 Battersea SW11 ... 137 A3
Battersea SW11 ... 268 A1
15 Hackney E2 ... 96 A5
Newham E13 ... 98 D3
Walworth SE17 ... 262 D3
Atkinson Rd E16 ... 99 C2
Atkinson's Almshouses HA8 ... 26 B5
Atkins Rd
Streatham SW4, SW12 ... 159 D4
Walthamstow E10 ... 53 D3
Atlanta Bldg 8 SE13 ... 141 D4
Atlanta Ct CR7 ... 205 A6
Atlantic Ct 19 E14 ... 120 B6
Atlantic Ho
5 Putney SW15 ... 157 B6
4 Tower Hamlets E1 ... 97 A2
Atlantic Rd SW2, SW9, SE24 ... 138 C1
Atlantis Cl IG11 ... 102 B4
Atlas Bsns Ctr NW2 ... 68 B6
Atlas Gdns SE7 ... 121 C2
Atlas Mews Dalston E8 ... 73 D2
Islington N7 ... 72 B2
Atlas Rd
Friern Barnet N11 ... 31 A4
Newham E13 ... 99 A5
North Acton NW10 ... 89 C4
Wembley HA9 ... 67 A4
Atley Rd E3 ... 97 C6
Atlip Rd HA0 ... 88 A6
Atney Rd SW15 ... 135 A1
Atria Rd HA6 ... 22 A5
Atrium 9 IG9 ... 21 D2
Atterbury Rd N4 ... 50 D3
Atterbury St SW1 ... 116 A2 260 A3
Attewood Ave NW10 ... 67 C5
Attewood Rd UB5 ... 63 A2
Attfield Cl N20 ... 14 B2
Attilburgh Ho SE1 ... 263 C6
Attleborough Ct 4 SE21 ... 162 B2
Attle Cl UB10 ... 82 C5
Attlee Cl Hayes UB4 ... 84 B4
Thornton Heath CR7 ... 205 A4
Attlee Ct UB4 ... 84 B4
Attlee Ho E1 ... 243 D3
Attlee Rd Hayes UB4 ... 84 B4
Thamesmead SE28 ... 124 B6
Attlee Terr 3 E17 ... 53 D5
Attneave St WC1 ... 234 A1
Atwater Cl SW2 ... 160 C3
Atwell Cl E10 ... 53 D3
Atwell Pl KT7 ... 197 A1
Atwell Rd 6 SE15 ... 140 A3
Atwood Ave TW9 ... 132 C3
Atwood Ho SE21 ... 161 C1
Atwood Rd W6 ... 112 B2
Aubert Ct N5 ... 72 D4
Aubert Pk N5 ... 72 D4
Aubert Rd N5 ... 72 D4
Aubrey Beardsley Ho SW1 ... 259 B3
Aubrey Mans NW1 ... 237 A4
Aubrey Moore Point E15 ... 98 A5
Aubrey Pl NW8 ... 229 A3
Aubrey Rd Hornsey N8 ... 50 A4
Kensington W14 ... 113 B5 244 D3
Walthamstow E17 ... 53 D6
Aubrey Wlk W14 ... 113 B5 244 D3
Auburn Cl SE14 ... 141 A5
Aubyn Hill SE27 ... 183 B6
Aubyn Sq SW15 ... 156 A6
Auckland Cl Enfield EN1 ... 6 B6
South Norwood SE19 ... 183 D2
Auckland Ct UB4 ... 84 C3
Auckland Gdns SE19 ... 183 D2
Auckland Hill SE27 ... 183 A6
Auckland Ho 11 W12 ... 112 B6
Auckland Rd
Clapham SW11 ... 136 C1
Ilford IG1 ... 57 A2
Kingston u T KT1 ... 198 B5
Leyton E10 ... 75 D5
South Norwood SE19 ... 183 D2
Auckland Rise SE19 ... 183 C2
Auckland St SE11 ... 260 C1
Audax 28 NW9 ... 27 D1
Auden Dr WD6 ... 10 C6
Auden Pl NW1 ... 231 A6
Audley Cl
8 Clapham SW11 ... 137 A2
Muswell Hill N10 ... 31 B3
Audley Ct Ealing W5 ... 88 C2
Mayfair W1 ... 248 C4
Northolt UB5 ... 84 C4
Pinner Green HA5 ... 22 C1
Snaresbrook E11, E18 ... 54 D5
Surbiton KT5 ... 198 B3
Twickenham TW2 ... 152 B1
Audley Dr 3 E16 ... 121 B5
Audley Gdns IG3 ... 79 D6
Audley Ho N8 ... 50 A5
Audley Pl SM2 ... 217 D1
Audley Rd Ealing W5 ... 88 B2
Enfield EN2 ... 4 D3
Hendon NW4 ... 46 B3
Richmond TW10 ... 154 B6
Audley Sq W1 ... 248 B4
Audrey Cl BR3 ... 207 D3
Audrey Gdns HA0 ... 65 B6
Audrey Ho EC1 ... 241 B3
Audrey Rd IG1 ... 78 D5
Audrey St E2 ... 96 A5
Audric Cl KT2 ... 176 C2
Augurs La 3 E13 ... 99 B4
Augusta Cl KT8 ... 195 B6
Augusta Ct NW4 ... 28 C1
Augusta Rd TW2 ... 152 A2
Augusta St E14 ... 97 D1
Augustine Ho
Broadgate EC2 ... 242 D2
New Cross SE4 ... 141 B4
Augustine Rd
Hammersmith W14 ... 112 D3
Harrow Weald HA3 ... 24 A2
Augustines Ct E9 ... 74 C3
Augustus Cl
Brentford TW8 ... 131 D5
Hammersmith W12 ... 112 B3
Stanmore HA7 ... 9 D1
Augustus Ct
Feltham TW13 ... 173 B6
Isleworth TW3 ... 130 A1
8 Putney SW19 ... 157 A3
South Norwood SE19 ... 183 C3
Streatham SW16 ... 159 D2
Augustus Ho NW1 ... 232 A2
Augustus Rd SW19 ... 157 A3
Augustus St NW1 ... 93 B4 231 D2
Aulay Lawrence Ct N9 ... 18 B1
Aultone Way
Carshalton SM5 ... 218 D5
Sutton SM1 ... 218 A6
Aultone Yd Ind Est SM5 ... 218 D5
Aulton Pl SE11 ... 261 B1
Aura Ho 3 TW9 ... 132 D4
Aurelia Gdns CR0 ... 204 B3
Aurelia Rd CR0 ... 204 B3
Auriga Mews N1 ... 73 B3
Auriol Cl KT4 ... 215 C5
Auriol Dr Greenford UB6 ... 64 B1
Hillingdon UB10 ... 60 D2
Auriol Jun Sch KT19 ... 215 D4
Auriol Mans W14 ... 254 A3
Auriol Park Rd KT4 ... 215 C5
Auriol Rd W14 ... 113 A2 254 A3
Aurora Bldg 4 E14 ... 120 A5
Aurora Ct IG8 ... 36 D6
Aurora Ho E14 ... 97 D1
Austell Gdns NW7 ... 11 C1
Austell Hts NW7 ... 11 C1
Austen Cl SE28 ... 124 B5
Austen Ho 5 NW6 ... 91 C4
Austen Rd Erith DA8 ... 147 D5
Harrow HA2 ... 63 D6
Austin Ave BR1, BR2 ... 210 A4
Austin Cl
Forest Hill SE23 ... 163 B4
Twickenham TW1 ... 153 C6
Austin Ct 9 Enfield EN1 ... 17 C6
9 Newham E6 ... 99 C6
Austin Friars EC2 ... 242 D2
Austin Friars Ho EC2 ... 242 D2
Austin Friars Sq EC2 ... 242 D2
Austin Ho
6 Brixton SW2 ... 160 B6
19 Kingston u T KT6 ... 198 A4
1 New Cross SE14 ... 141 B5
Austin Rd
Battersea SW11 ... 137 A4 268 A1
Hayes UB3 ... 105 D4
Austins Ct SE15 ... 140 A2
Austin's La UB10 ... 61 A5
Austin St E2 ... 95 D4
Austral Cl DA15 ... 167 D1
Australia Rd W12 ... 112 B6
Austral St SE11 ... 116 D2 261 C4
Austyn Gdns KT5 ... 198 D1
Autumn Cl Enfield EN1 ... 6 A4
Wimbledon SW19 ... 180 A4
Autumn Gr BR1 ... 187 B4
Autumn Lo CR2 ... 221 C4
Autumn Rise 9 W4 ... 111 B1
Autumn St E3 ... 97 C6
Avalon BR7 ... 188 C1
Avalon Cl Ealing W13 ... 87 A2
Enfield EN2 ... 4 C3
Merton SW20 ... 179 A1
Avalon Ct CR0 ... 205 D2
Avalon Rd Ealing W13 ... 87 A3
Parsons Green SW6 ... 135 D4 265 C2
Avante Ct KT1 ... 197 D6
Avard Gdns BR6 ... 227 A4
Avarn Rd SW17 ... 180 D4
Avebury Ct N1 ... 235 C5
Avebury Rd
Leytonstone E11 ... 54 B1
Merton SW19 ... 179 B2
Orpington BR6 ... 227 B5
Avebury St N1 ... 235 C5
Aveley Ct 15 E5 ... 74 B6
Aveley Mans 1 IG11 ... 78 D1
Aveline St SE11 ... 116 C1 261 A1
Aveling Ho 12 N19 ... 71 C5
Aveling Park Rd E17 ... 35 C1
Aveling Park Sch E17 ... 35 C1
Ave Maria La EC4 ... 241 D1
Avenell Mans N5 ... 72 D4
Avenell Rd N5 ... 72 D5
Avenfield Ho W1 ... 247 D6
Avening Rd SW18 ... 157 C4
Avening Terr SW18 ... 157 C4
Avenons Rd E13 ... 99 A3
Avenue Cl
Cranford TW5 ... 128 B4
Avenue Cl *continued*
Primrose Hill NW8 ... 92 C6 230 B5
Southgate N14 ... 15 C5
Avenue Cres
Cranford TW5 ... 128 B5
South Acton W3 ... 110 D4
Avenue Ct Chelsea SW3 ... 257 C3
Cricklewood NW2 ... 69 A5
Ealing W5 ... 87 D2
Penge SE20 ... 184 C2
Redbridge IG5 ... 56 A6
Southgate N14 ... 15 C5
Avenue Elmers KT6 ... 198 A4
Avenue Gate IG10 ... 21 C5
Avenue Gdns
Cranford TW5 ... 128 B5
Mortlake SW14 ... 133 C2
South Acton W3 ... 110 D4
South Norwood SE25 ... 184 A1
Teddington TW11 ... 174 D4
Avenue Hall N6 ... 49 D3
Avenue Ho
St John's Wood NW8 ... 230 A3
Upper Clapton N16 ... 74 A6
Willesden Green NW10 ... 90 B5
Avenue Ind Est E4 ... 35 B4
Avenue Lo 12 NW8 ... 70 B1
Avenue Mans Barnet EN5 ... 1 B1
Clapham SW11 ... 137 A1
Hampstead NW3 ... 69 D3
Muswell Hill N10 ... 31 C1
Willesden NW2 ... 68 B2
Avenue Mews N10 ... 49 B6
Avenue Par
Southgate N21 ... 17 B4
Sunbury TW16 ... 194 B6
Avenue Park Rd SE21, SE27 ... 160 D2
Avenue Prim Sch E12 ... 78 A3
Avenue Rd
Bexley DA6, DA7 ... 147 A2
Brentford TW8 ... 109 C1
Crouch End N6 ... 49 D2
Feltham TW13 ... 149 D1
Forest Gate E7 ... 77 B4
Hampton TW12 ... 173 D2
Harlesden NW10 ... 89 D5
Hounslow TW7 ... 130 D4
Ilford RM6 ... 58 C2
Kingston u T KT1 ... 198 A6
Mitcham SW16 ... 181 D1
New Malden KT3 ... 199 C5
North Finchley N12 ... 30 A6
Penge BR3, SE20 ... 184 D2
Pinner HA5 ... 41 A6
Primrose Hill NW8 ... 92 C6 230 A6
South Acton W3 ... 110 D4
Southall UB1 ... 107 B5
Southgate N14 ... 15 C5
South Norwood SE25 ... 184 A1
Teddington TW11 ... 175 A4
Tottenham N15 ... 51 B4
Wallington SM6 ... 219 C1
Wimbledon SW20 ... 178 B1
Woodford IG8 ... 37 C4
Avenue Road Sta BR3 ... 184 D1
Avenue S KT5 ... 198 C2
Avenue Sch The NW6 ... 69 A1
Avenue Terr Ilford IG2 ... 57 C3
Kingston u T KT3 ... 199 A6
Avenue The Barnet EN5 ... 1 A2
Beckenham BR3 ... 186 A2
Bedford Pk W4 ... 111 C3
Bromley BR1 ... 209 D6
Brondesbury Pk NW6 ... 91 A6
8 Buckhurst Hill IG9 ... 21 C2
Chingford E4 ... 36 B5
Clapham SW4 ... 159 A6
Claygate KT10 ... 212 C3
Cranford TW5 ... 128 A4
Ealing W13 ... 87 B1
Finchley N3 ... 29 C1
Friern Barnet N11 ... 31 B5
Greenwich SE10 ... 142 B5
Hampton TW12 ... 173 B4
Harrow HA3 ... 24 D2
Hatch End HA5 ... 23 B4
Hornsey N8 ... 50 C6
Hounslow TW3 ... 151 D6
Isleworth TW1 ... 153 B6
Keston Mark BR2 ... 225 D5
Loughton IG10 ... 21 D5
Muswell Hill N10 ... 31 C1
4 New Malden KT4 ... 200 A1
Orpington BR6 ... 227 D6
Pinner HA5 ... 41 B3
Richmond TW9 ... 132 B3
Sidcup DA5 ... 168 D4
South Croydon CR0 ... 221 C5
Stoneleigh KT17, SM3 ... 216 C1
St Paul's Cray BR5 ... 190 B3
Sunbury TW16 ... 172 B1
Surbiton KT5 ... 198 B3
Tottenham N17 ... 33 C1
Uxbridge UB10 ... 60 D5
Wallington SM5 ... 219 A1
Wandsworth SW18, SW12 ... 158 C4
Wanstead E11 ... 55 B4
Wembley HA9 ... 44 B1
West Wickham BR4 ... 208 C2
Worcester Pk KT4 ... 215 D6
Averil Gr SW16 ... 182 D4
Averill St W6 ... 134 D6
Avern Gdns KT8 ... 195 D5
Avern Rd KT8 ... 195 D5
Avery Ct 1 SE20 ... 184 B3
Avery Farm Row SW1 ... 258 C3
Avery Gdns IG2 ... 56 B4
AVERY HILL ... 167 B5
Avery Hill Coll (Mile End Annexe) E3 ... 97 B3
Avery Hill Rd SE9 ... 167 B3
Avery Row W1 ... 115 B6 248 D6
Aviary Cl E16 ... 98 D2
Aviemore Cl BR3 ... 207 B4
Aviemore Way BR3 ... 207 A4
Avignon Rd SE4 ... 140 D2
Avingdor Ct 10 W3 ... 111 A5
Avington Ct SE1 ... 263 B3
Avington Gr SE20 ... 184 C3
Avion Cres NW7, NW9 ... 28 A2
Avis Sq E1 ... 96 D1
Avoca Rd SW17 ... 181 A6
Avocet Cl SE1 ... 118 A1
Avocet Mews SE28 ... 123 B3
Avon Cl Hayes UB4 ... 84 C3
Sutton SM1 ... 218 A4
Worcester Pk KT4 ... 216 A6
Avon Ct 1 Acton W3 ... 89 A1
13 Chingford E4 ... 20 A3
Greenford UB6 ... 85 D3
North Finchley N12 ... 29 D5
11 Putney SW15 ... 157 A6
Wembley HA0 ... 65 A4
Avondale N22 ... 32 A3
Avondale Ave
Barnet EN4 ... 14 D3
Finchley N12 ... 29 D5
Hinchley Wood KT10 ... 213 A5
Neasden NW2 ... 67 C5
New Malden KT4 ... 199 D1
Avondale Cres
Enfield EN3 ... 7 A2
Redbridge IG4 ... 55 D4
Avondale Ct
Canning Town E16 ... 98 C2
Leytonstone E11 ... 54 C1
9 Sutton SM2 ... 218 A1
Woodford E18 ... 37 B2
Avondale Dr UB3 ... 106 B5
Avondale Gdns TW4 ... 151 B6
Avondale Ho
11 Bermondsey SE1 ... 118 A1
6 Mortlake SW14 ... 133 B2
Avondale Mans SW6 ... 264 C2
Avondale Park Gdns W11 ... 113 A6 244 A5
Avondale Park Prim Sch W11 ... 113 A6 244 A5
Avondale Park Rd W11 ... 113 A6 244 A6
Avondale Pavement 7 SE1 ... 118 A1
Avondale Rd
Bexley DA16 ... 146 C3
Bromley BR1 ... 186 D4
Chislehurst SE9 ... 166 A2
Finchley N3 ... 30 A2
Harringay N15 ... 50 D4
Harrow HA3 ... 42 D6
Mortlake SW14 ... 133 B2
Newham E16 ... 98 C2
South Croydon CR2 ... 221 A2
Southgate N13 ... 16 C2
Walthamstow E17 ... 53 C2
Wimbledon SW19 ... 179 D5
Avondale Rise SE15 ... 139 D2
Avondale Sq SE1 ... 118 A1
Avonfield Ct E17 ... 54 B6
Avon Ho 2 Islington N1 ... 72 C1
7 Kingston u T KT2 ... 175 D2
Northolt UB5 ... 85 A3
Southgate N21 ... 16 B6
14 Stoke Newington N16 ... 73 B4
West Kensington W14 ... 254 D3
Avon House Sch IG8 ... 37 A6
Avonhurst Ho NW6 ... 69 A1
Avonley Rd SE14 ... 140 C5
Avon Mews HA5 ... 23 B2
Avonmore Gdns W14 ... 254 D3
Avonmore Pl W14 ... 254 B4
Avonmore Prim Sch W14 ... 113 A2 254 B4
Avonmore Rd W14 ... 113 B2 254 C4
Avonmouth St SE1 ... 262 A6
Avon Path CR0 ... 221 A1
Avon Pl SE1 ... 252 B1
Avon Rd Ashford TW16 ... 171 D3
Greenford UB6 ... 85 D3
St Johns SE4 ... 141 C2
Upper Walthamstow E17 ... 54 B6
Avonstowe Cl BR6 ... 227 A5
Avon Way E18 ... 55 A6
Avonwick Rd TW3 ... 129 D3
Avril Way E4 ... 36 A5
Avriol Ho W12 ... 112 B5
Avro Ct E9 ... 75 A3
Avro Way SM6 ... 220 A1
Awlfield Ave N17 ... 33 B2
Awliscombe Rd DA16 ... 145 D3
Axeholm Ave HA8 ... 26 D2
Axe St IG11 ... 101 A6
Axford Ho SW2 ... 160 D3
Axiom Apartments 5 BR2 ... 209 B5
Axis Bsns Ctr E15 ... 97 D6
Axis Ct
7 Bermondsey SE16 ... 118 A4
Greenwich SE10 ... 142 C6
Axminster Cres DA16 ... 146 C4
Axminster Rd N7 ... 72 B5
Axon Pl 5 IG1 ... 79 A6
Aybrook St W1 ... 93 A2 238 A3
Aycliffe Cl BR1 ... 210 B5
Aycliffe Rd W12 ... 112 A5
Ayerst Ct 1 E10 ... 54 A2
Aylands Cl HA9 ... 66 A6
Aylesbury Cl E7 ... 76 D2
Aylesbury Ct SM1 ... 218 A5
Aylesbury Ho 13 SE15 ... 140 A6
Aylesbury Rd
Bromley BR2 ... 209 A6
Walworth SE17 ... 117 B1 262 D1
Aylesbury St
Clerkenwell EC1 ... 94 D3 241 C5
Neasden NW10 ... 67 B5
Ayles Ct UB4 ... 84 B4
Aylesford Ave BR3 ... 207 A4
Aylesford Ho SE1 ... 252 D1
Aylesford St SW1 ... 115 D1 259 C1
Aylesham Cl NW7 ... 28 A3
Aylesham Rd BR6 ... 211 D2
Aylesham Sh Ctr SE15 ... 140 A4
Ayles Rd UB4 ... 84 B4
Aylestone Ave NW6 ... 90 D6
Aylestone Ct 10 HA0 ... 66 A2
Aylett Rd Croydon SE25 ... 206 B5
Isleworth TW7 ... 130 C3
Ayley Croft EN1 ... 18 A6
Ayliffe Cl KT1 ... 176 C1
Aylmer Cl HA7 ... 25 A6
Aylmer Ct N2 ... 48 D4
Aylmer Dr HA7 ... 25 A6
Aylmer Ho SE10 ... 120 B1
Aylmer Par N2 ... 48 D4
Aylmer Rd Acton W12 ... 111 D4
Dagenham RM8 ... 81 A5
East Finchley N2 ... 48 C4
Leytonstone E11 ... 54 D1
Ayloffe Rd RM9 ... 81 B2
Aylsham Dr UB10 ... 61 A6
Aylton Est 23 SE16 ... 118 C4
Aylward Fst & Mid Schs HA7 ... 25 D5
Aylward Rd
Forest Hill SE23 ... 162 D2
Merton SW20 ... 201 B6
Aylward Sch N18 ... 33 B6
Aylwards Rise HA7 ... 25 A6
Aylward St E1 ... 96 D1
Aylwin Est SE1 ... 263 B6
Aylwin Girls Sch SE1 ... 117 D2 263 D4
Aynhoe Mans W14 ... 112 D2
Aynhoe Rd W14 ... 112 D3
Ayr Ct W3 ... 88 C2
Ayres Cl E13 ... 99 A4
Ayres Cres NW10 ... 67 B1
Ayres St SE1 ... 117 A4 252 B2
Ayrsome Rd N16 ... 73 C5
Ayrton Gould Ho 9 E2 ... 96 D4
Ayrton Ho HA9 ... 65 D6
Ayrton Rd SW7 ... 114 B3 256 C6
Aysgarth Ct SM1 ... 217 D5
Aysgarth Rd SE21 ... 161 C4
Ayshford Ho E1 ... 96 B4
Ayston Ho 19 SE8 ... 118 D2
Aytoun Ct 17 SW9 ... 138 B3
Aytoun Pl SW9 ... 138 B3
Aytoun Rd SW9 ... 138 B3
Azalea Cl Ealing W7 ... 108 D5
Ilford IG1 ... 78 D3
Azalea Ct Chingford IG8 ... 36 C3
Ealing W7 ... 108 D5
Azalea Ho
Feltham TW13 ... 150 B3
New Cross SE14 ... 141 B5
Azalea Wlk HA5 ... 40 B3
Azania Mews NW5 ... 71 B2
Azenby Rd SE15 ... 139 D3
Azhar Acad E7 ... 77 A2
Azof St SE10 ... 120 C2
Azov Ho 10 E1 ... 97 A3
Aztec Ct 8 N16 ... 73 C2
Azure Appartments HA3 ... 24 B3
Azure Ct TW13 ... 149 D1
Azure Ho 28 E2 ... 96 A4

B

Baalbec Rd N5 ... 72 D3
Babbacombe Cl KT9 ... 213 D3
Babbacombe Gdns IG4 ... 56 A5
Babbacombe Rd BR1 ... 187 A2
Baber Bridge Par TW14 ... 150 C5
Baber Dr TW14 ... 150 C5
Babington Ct
Bloomsbury WC1 ... 240 B4
Streatham SW16 ... 181 D5
Babington Ho SE1 ... 252 B2
Babington House Sch BR7 ... 188 B4
Babington Rd
Dagenham RM8 ... 80 C4
Hendon NW4 ... 46 B5
Streatham SW16 ... 181 D5
Babington Rise HA9 ... 66 C2
Babmaes St SW1 ... 249 C5
Bacchus Wlk 12 N1 ... 95 C5
Bache's St N1 ... 95 B4 235 D1
Back Church La E1 ... 96 A1
Back Hill EC1 ... 241 B5
Backhouse Pl SE1 ... 263 B3
Back La Brentford TW8 ... 131 D6
Buckhurst Hill IG9 ... 21 D2
Burnt Oak HA8 ... 27 A2
Dagenham RM6 ... 59 A2

Back La continued
Hampstead NW3 . . . . .70 A4
Hornsey N8 . . . . .50 A4
Richmond TW10 . . . . .153 C2
Sidcup DA5 . . . . .169 C4
Backley Gdns SE25 . . . . . .206 A3
Back Rd Sidcup DA14 . . . .190 A6
Teddington TW11 . . . . . . .174 C3
Bacon Gr SE1 . . .117 D3 263 C5
Bacon La Edgware HA8 . . .26 C2
Queensbury NW9 . . . . .44 D5
Bacon's Coll SE16 . . . . . .119 A4
Bacon's La N6 . . . . .49 A1
Bacon St E2 . . . . .95 D3 243 D6
Bacon Terr RM8 . . . . .80 B3
Bacton St E2 . . . . .96 C4
Baddeley Cl 11 EN3 . . . . . .7 C6
Baddeley Ho
East Molesey KT8 . . . . . .195 C4
Vauxhall SE11 . . . . 260 D2
Baddow Cl
Dagenham RM10 . . . . . . .103 C6
Woodford IG8 . . . . .37 D4
Baddow Wlk N1 . . . . 235 A6
Baden Ct N11 . . . . .31 D3
Baden Pl SE1 . . . . 252 C2
Baden Powell Cl
Dagenham RM9 . . . . .103 A6
Surbiton KT6 . . . . .214 B6
Baden Powell Ho 11
DA17 . . . . .125 C3
Baden Powell Sch E5 . . . .74 B5
Baden Rd Hornsey N8 . . . .49 D5
Ilford IG1 . . . . .78 D3
Badger Cl
Feltham TW13 . . . . .150 B1
Hounslow TW4 . . . . .128 C2
Ilford IG2 . . . . .57 A2
Badger Ct Chingford E4 . . .36 B6
Dollis Hill NW2 . . . . .68 C5
Badgers Cl
Ashford TW15 . . . . .170 B5
Enfield EN2 . . . . .4 D2
Harrow HA1 . . . . .42 B3
Hayes UB3 . . . . .105 C6
Badgers Copse
Orpington BR6 . . . . .227 D6
Worcester Pk KT4 . . . . . .215 D6
Badgers Croft
Barnet N20 . . . . .13 A3
Chislehurst SE9 . . . . .166 C1
Badgers Hole CR0 . . . . . .222 D4
Badgers Wlk KT3 . . . . . . .177 C1
Badlis Rd E17 . . . . .53 C6
Badma Cl N9 . . . . .18 C1
Badminton KT2 . . . . .176 D2
Badminton Cl
Harrow HA1 . . . . .42 C5
Northolt UB5 . . . . .63 C2
Badminton Ct 9 N4 . . . . . .51 A2
Badminton Ho SE22 . . . . .139 C1
Badminton Mews 9
E16 . . . . .121 A5
Badminton Rd SW12 . . . . .159 A5
Badric Ct SW11 . . . . .136 B3
Badsworth Rd 3 SE5 . . . .139 A4
Bagley Cl UB7 . . . . .104 A4
Bagley's La
SW6 . . . . .135 D4 265 D1
Bagleys Spring RM6 . . . . .59 A5
Bagnigge Ho WC1 . . . . . . 234 A1
Bagshot Ho NW1 . . . . . . 231 D2
Bagshot Rd EN1 . . . . .17 D5
Bagshot St
SE17 . . . . .117 C1 263 B1
Baildon 27 E2 . . . . .96 C5
Baildon St SE8 . . . . .141 B5
Bailey Cl Chingford E4 . . . .36 A6
Wood Green N11 . . . . .31 D3
Woolwich SE28 . . . . .123 C5
Bailey Cres KT9 . . . . .213 D1
Bailey Ct
4 Chingford E4 . . . . .36 B5
9 Shepherd's Bush
W12 . . . . .112 A4
Bailey Ho Mitcham CR4 . .202 C6
11 Penge SE26 . . . . .184 B5
Walham Green SW10 . . 265 D4
Bailey Mews
Brixton SW2 . . . . .160 C6
Chiswick W4 . . . . .132 D6
Bailey Pl SE26 . . . . .184 D4
Bainbridge cl KT2 . . . . . .176 A5
Bainbridge Rd RM9 . . . . .81 B4
Bainbridge St WC1 . . . . . 239 D2
Baines Cl CR2 . . . . .221 B3
Bain Ho 28 SW9 . . . . . . .138 A3
Baird Ave UB1 . . . . .108 A6
Baird Cl Kingsbury NW9 . .45 A3
Walthamstow E10 . . . . . . .53 C1
Baird Gdns SE19 . . . . . . .183 C4
Baird Ho
12 Belvedere DA17 . . . . .125 C3
26 Shepherd's Bush
W12 . . . . .112 B6
Baird Rd EN1 . . . . .6 B1
Baird St EC1 . . . . 242 B6
Bairny Wood App IG8 . . . .37 B4
Baizdon Rd SE3 . . . . .142 C3
Baker Beall Ct DA7 . . . . .147 D2
Baker Ct E15 . . . . .76 B5
Baker Ho 12 Bromley E3 . .97 D4
Ealing W7 . . . . .108 D5
Baker La CR4 . . . . .203 A6
Baker Rd
Harlesden NW10 . . . . .89 C6

Baker Rd continued
Kidbrooke SE18 . . . . .144 A4
Bakers' Almshouses
E10 . . . . .53 D3
Bakers Ave E17 . . . . .53 D3
Bakers Ct RM8 . . . . .59 B2
Bakers Ct SE25 . . . . .205 C6
Bakers Field N7 . . . . .72 A4
Bakers Gdns SM5 . . . . . .218 C6
Bakers Hall EC3 . . . . . . 253 B5
Bakers Hill Barnet EN5 . . .1 D3
Upper Clapton E5 . . . . . . .52 C1
Bakers Ho W5 . . . . .109 D5
Bakers Mews 9 BR6 . . . .227 D2
Baker's La N6 . . . . .48 D3
Baker's Mews W1 . . . . . 238 A2
Bakers Pas 20 NW3 . . . . .70 A4
Bakers Rents 13 E2 . . . . .95 D4
Bakers Row E15 . . . . .98 C5
Baker's Row
EC1 . . . . .94 C3 241 A5
Baker St Enfield EN1 . . . . .5 B4
Marylebone W1 . . . .92 B2 237 D4
Baker Street
W1 . . . . .92 B2 237 D4
Baker Street Sta
NW1 . . . . .92 B3 237 D4
Bakery Cl SW9 . . . . 270 D3
Bakery Mews KT6 . . . . . .198 C1
Bakewell Way KT3 . . . . . .177 C1
Balaam Ho SM1 . . . . .217 C4
Balaams La N14 . . . . .15 D2
Balaam St E13 . . . . .99 B4
Balaclava Rd
Bermondsey
SE1 . . . . .117 D2 263 D3
Kingston u T KT6 . . . . . . .197 D2
Bala Gn NW9 . . . . .45 C3
Balcaskie Rd SE9 . . . . . .166 B6
Balchen Rd SE3 . . . . .143 D3
Balchier Rd SE22 . . . . . .162 B5
Balcombe Cl DA6 . . . . . . .146 D1
Balcombe Ho
Lisson Gr NW1 . . . . 237 C6
3 Streatham SW2 . . . . . .160 B3
Balcombe St
NW1 . . . . .92 B3 237 C5
Balcon Ct W5 . . . . .88 B1
Balcorne St E9 . . . . .74 C1
Balder Rise SE12 . . . . . . .165 B2
Balderton Flats W1 . . . . 238 B1
Balderton St
W1 . . . . .93 A1 238 B1
Baldewyne Ct N17 . . . . . . .34 A2
Baldock Ho 31 SE5 . . . . .139 A3
Baldock St E3 . . . . .97 D5
Baldrey Ho 1 SE10 . . . . .120 D1
Baldry Gdns SW16 . . . . . .182 B4
Baldwin Cres SE5 . . . . . .139 A4
Baldwin Gdns TW3 . . . . . .130 A4
Baldwin Ho
15 Streatham SW2 . . . . .160 C3
Wallend E13 . . . . .78 C1
Baldwin's Gdns
EC1 . . . . .94 C2 241 A4
Baldwin St EC1 . . . . 235 C1
Baldwin Terr
N1 . . . . .95 A5 235 A4
Baldwyn Gdns W3 . . . . . .111 B6
Balearic Apts 3 E16 . . . .121 A6
Bale Rd E1 . . . . .97 A2
Bales Coll W10 . . . . .90 D4
Balfern Gr W4 . . . . .111 C1
Balfern St SW11 . . . . . . .136 C3
Balfe St N1 . . . . . .94 A5 233 B1
Balfour Ave W7 . . . . .108 D5
Balfour Bsns Ctr UB2 . . .106 D3
Balfour Gr N20 . . . . .14 D1
Balfour Ho W10 . . . . .90 D2
Balfour Mews
Edmonton N9 . . . . .18 A1
Mayfair W1 . . . . 248 B4
Kingston u T KT1 . . . . . . .198 B5
Putney SW15 . . . . .134 B1
Balfour Rd
Bromley Comm BR2 . . . . .209 D4
Croydon SE25 . . . . .206 A5
Ealing W13 . . . . .109 B4
Harrow HA1 . . . . .42 B4
Highbury N5 . . . . .73 A4
Hounslow TW3 . . . . .129 D2
Ilford IG1 . . . . .57 A1
Merton SW19 . . . . .179 D3
North Acton W3 . . . . .89 A2
Southall UB2 . . . . .106 C4
Wallington SM5 . . . . .218 D1
Balfour St
SE17 . . . . .117 B2 262 C4
Balfron Twr 4 E14 . . . . . .98 A1
Balgonie Rd E4 . . . . .20 B3
Balgowan Cl KT3 . . . . . . .199 C5
Balgowan Prim Sch
BR3 . . . . .185 A1
Balgowan Rd BR3 . . . . . .185 B1
Balgowan St SE18 . . . . . .123 D2
Balham High Rd SW12,
SW17 . . . . .159 A3
Balham Hill SW12 . . . . . .159 B5
Balham New Rd SW12 . . .159 B4
Balham Park Mans
SW12 . . . . .158 D3
Balham Park Rd SW12,
SW17 . . . . .159 A3
Balham Rd N9 . . . . .18 A2
Balham Sta SW12 . . . . . .159 B3

Balham Station Rd
SW12 . . . . .159 B3
Balin Ho SE1 . . . . 252 C2
Balkan Wlk E1 . . . . .118 B6
Balladier Wlk E14 . . . . . . .97 D2
Ballamore Rd BR1 . . . . . .165 A1
Ballance Rd E9 . . . . .75 A2
Ballantine St SW18 . . . . .136 A1
Ballantrae Ho NW2 . . . . . .69 B4
Ballard Cl KT2 . . . . .177 B3
Ballard Ho SE10 . . . . .141 D6
Ballards Cl RM10 . . . . . . .103 D6
Ballards Farm Rd CR0,
CR2 . . . . .222 A2
Ballards La N3 . . . . .29 D3
Ballards Mews HA8 . . . . . .26 C4
Ballards Rd
Dagenham RM10 . . . . . . .103 D6
Dollis Hill NW2 . . . . .68 A6
Ballards Rise CR2 . . . . . .222 A2
Ballards Way CR0, CR2 . .222 B2
Ballast Quay SE10 . . . . . .120 B1
Ballater Cl WD19 . . . . . . .22 C6
Ballater Rd
Brixton SW2, SW4 . . . . . .138 A1
South Croydon CR2 . . . . .221 D3
Ball Ct EC3 . . . . 242 C2
Ballentyne Ct N21 . . . . . . .16 B6
Ballina St SE23 . . . . .162 D4
Ballin Ct 14 E14 . . . . . . .120 A4
Ballingdon Rd SW11 . . . . .159 A5
Ballinger Point 18 E3 . . . . .97 D4
Ballinger Way UB5 . . . . . . .85 A3
Balliol Ave E4 . . . . .36 C6
Balliol Ho 11 SW15 . . . . .156 D5
Balliol Rd Bexley DA16 . . .146 B3
North Kensington W10 . . . .90 D1
Tottenham N17 . . . . .33 C2
Balloch Rd SE6 . . . . .164 B2
Ballogie Ave NW10 . . . . . .67 C4
Ballow Cl 15 SE5 . . . . . . .139 C5
Ball's Pond Pl 3 N1 . . . . .73 B2
Ball's Pond Rd N1 . . . . . . .73 C2
Balmain Cl W5 . . . . .109 D5
Balmaïn Ct TW3 . . . . . . .129 D4
Balman Ho 3 SE16 . . . . . .118 D2
Balmer Rd E3 . . . . .97 B5
Balmes Rd N1 . . .95 B6 235 D6
Balmoral Ave
Beckenham BR3 . . . . . . .207 A5
Friern Barnet N11 . . . . .31 B5
Balmoral Cl 1 SW15 . . . .156 D5
Balmoral Cres KT8 . . . . . .195 C6
Balmoral Ct
18 Belmont SM2 . . . . . . .217 C1
Ealing W5 . . . . .87 D1
Edgware HA8 . . . . .26 C6
Grove Pk SE12 . . . . .187 B6
North Cheam KT4 . . . . . .216 B6
21 Rotherhithe SE16 . . . .118 C5
St John's Wood NW8 . . . 229 C4
Wembley HA9 . . . . .66 B5
West Norwood SE27 . . . . .183 A6
Balmoral Dr
Borehamwood WD6 . . . . . .11 B6
Hayes UB4 . . . . .83 D3
Southall UB1 . . . . .85 B3
Balmoral Gdns
Ealing W13 . . . . .109 A3
Ilford IG3 . . . . .57 D1
Old Bexley DA5 . . . . .169 B4
Balmoral Gr N7 . . . . .72 B2
Balmoral Ho
2 Isle Of Dogs E14 . . . . .119 D3
Stanmore HA7 . . . . .26 A1
Stoke Newington N4 . . . . .51 A1
Walthamstow E17 . . . . . . .35 B1
West Kensington W14 . . . 254 A4
Balmoral Lo BR6 . . . . . . .226 C4
Balmoral Mews W12 . . . .111 D3
Balmoral Rd
Forest Gate E7 . . . . .77 C3
Harrow HA2 . . . . .63 C4
Kingston u T KT1 . . . . . . .198 B5
Leyton E10 . . . . .75 D6
North Cheam KT4 . . . . . .216 B6
Willesden NW2 . . . . .68 B2
Balmoral Trad Est
IG11 . . . . .101 D2
Balmore Cl E14 . . . . .98 A1
Balmore Cres EN4 . . . . . . .15 A4
Balmore St N19 . . . . .71 B6
Balmuir Gdns SW15 . . . . .134 C1
Balnacraig Ave NW10 . . . .67 C4
Balniel Gate SW1 . . . . . . 259 D2
Balsam Ho 9 E14 . . . . . . .119 D6
Baltic Apts 5 E16 . . . . . .121 A6
Baltic Ct SW15 . . . . .180 B3
Baltic Ho 7 SE5 . . . . . . .139 A3
Baltic St E EC1 . . . .95 A3 242 A5
Baltic St W EC1 . . .95 A3 242 A5
Baltimore Ho
Clapham SW18 . . . . .136 A1
Kennington SE11 . . . . . . 261 A2
Merton SW19 . . . . .179 D3
Baltimore Pl DA16 . . . . . .145 D3
Balvaird Pl SW1 . . . . 259 D1
Balvernie Gr SW18 . . . . . .157 C4
Bamber Ho IG11 . . . . .101 A6
Bamber Rd 5 SE15 . . . . .139 D4
Bamborough Gdns 12
W12 . . . . .112 C4
Bamburgh 9 N17 . . . . . . .34 B3
Bamford Ave HA0 . . . . . . .88 B5
Bamford Ct E15 . . . . .75 D3
Bamford Rd
Barking IG11 . . . . .79 A2
Catford BR1 . . . . .186 B5
Bampfylde Cl SM6 . . . . . .219 C5
Bampton Ct W5 . . . . .87 D1

Bampton Dr NW7 . . . . . . .28 A3
Bampton Rd SE23 . . . . . .162 D1
Banavie Gdns BR3 . . . . . .186 A2
Banbury Ct EN2 . . . . .4 D4
Banbury Ct
11 Belmont SM2 . . . . . . .217 C1
Ealing W13 . . . . .109 A3
Strand WC2 . . . . 250 A6
Banbury Ho 5 E9 . . . . . . .74 D1
Banbury Rd
Higham Hill E17 . . . . .35 A3
Homerton E9 . . . . .74 D1
Banbury St SW11 . . . . . . .136 C3
Banbury Wlk UB5 . . . . . . .85 C5
Banchory Rd SE3 . . . . . . .143 B5
Bancroft Ave
East Finchley N2 . . . . .48 C4
Woodford IG9 . . . . .21 A2
Bancroft Ct TW15 . . . . . .170 C5
Bancroft Ct
Northolt UB5 . . . . .84 C6
South Lambeth SW8 . . . . 270 A2
Bancroft Gdns
Harrow Weald HA3 . . . . . .24 A2
Orpington BR6 . . . . .211 D1
Bancroft Ho 11 E1 . . . . . . .96 C3
Bancroft Rd
Bethnal Green E1 . . . . .96 D3
Harrow Weald HA3 . . . . . .24 A1
Bancrofts Sch IG8 . . . . . . .21 A1
Bandon Cl UB10 . . . . .82 B5
BANDONHILL 219 D3
Bandon Hill Prim Sch
SM6 . . . . .219 D2
Bandon Rise SM6 . . . . . . .219 D3
Banff Ho 1 NW3 . . . . .70 C2
Banfield Rd SE15 . . . . . . .140 B2
Banfor Ct SM6 . . . . .219 C3
Bangabandhu Prim Sch
E2 . . . . .96 C4
Bangalore St SW15 . . . . .134 D2
Bangor Cl UB5 . . . . .63 D3
Banim St W6 . . . . .112 B2
Banister Ho Hackney E9 . .74 D3
Nine Elms SW8 . . . . 269 B2
9 West Kilburn W10 . . . . .91 A4
Banister Rd W10 . . . . .90 D4
Bank Ave CR4 . . . . .180 B1
Bank Bldgs 13 SW16 . . . .181 C5
Bank Ct SW11 . . . . 268 C2
Bank End SE1 . . . . 252 B4
Bankfoot Rd BR1 . . . . . . .186 C6
Bankhurst Rd SE6 . . . . . .163 B4
Bank La
Kingston u T KT2 . . . . . . .176 A3
Roehampton SW15 . . . . . .155 C6
Bank Mews SM1 . . . . . . .218 A2
Bank of England*
EC2 . . . . .95 B1 242 C1
Bank of England Mus*
EC2 . . . . .95 B1 242 C1
Bank Par N11 . . . . .31 B5
Banks Ho
Isleworth TW7 . . . . .130 C3
Newington SE1 . . . . 262 A5
Banksia Rd N18 . . . . .34 D5
Bankside
Borough The
SE1 . . . . .117 A6 252 A5
Borough The SE1 . . . . . . 252 B4
Enfield EN2 . . . . .4 D4
Southall UB1 . . . . .106 D5
South Croydon CR2 . . . . .221 D2
Bankside Art Gal*
SE1 . . . . .116 A6 251 D5
Bankside Ave
1 Lewisham SE13 . . . . . .142 A2
Northolt UB5 . . . . .84 A5
Bankside Cl
Carshalton SM5 . . . . .218 C2
Isleworth TW7 . . . . .130 D1
Bankside Dr KT7 . . . . . . .213 B6
Bankside Ho EC3 . . . . . . 243 B1
Bankside Pier
SE1 . . . . .117 A6 252 A5
Bankside Pk IG11 . . . . . . .102 A4
Bankside Rd IG1 . . . . .79 B3
Bankside Way 6
SE19 . . . . .183 C4
Banks La DA6 . . . . .147 B1
Bank St E14 . . . . .119 C5
Bank Sta EC3 . . . .95 B1 242 D1
Banks Way E12 . . . . .78 C4
Bankton Rd SW2 . . . . . . .138 C1
Bankwell Rd SE13 . . . . . .142 C1
Banner Ct 5 SE16 . . . . . .118 C2
Banner Ho EC1 . . . . 242 B5
Bannerman Ho SW8 . . . . 270 C5
Banner St EC1 . . .95 A3 242 B6
Banning Ho 4 SW19 . . . . .156 D3
Banning St SE10 . . . . . . .120 C1
Bannister Cl
Greenford UB6 . . . . .64 B3
Streatham SW2 . . . . .160 C3
Bannister Ho
28 Deptford SE14 . . . . . .140 D6
Harrow HA3 . . . . .42 C6
Bannister Sports Ctr The
HA3 . . . . .24 A4
Bannockburn Prim Sch
SE18 . . . . .123 D2
Bannockburn Rd
SE18 . . . . .123 D2
Bannow Cl KT19 . . . . . . .215 C4
Banqueting Ho* SW1 . . . 250 A3
Banstead Ct
Stoke Newington N4 . . . . .51 A1
Walthamstow E10 . . . . . . .53 D1
Banstead Gdns N9 . . . . . . .17 C1

Banstead Rd SM5 . . . . . .218 C1
Banstead St SE15 . . . . . .140 C2
Banstead Way SM6 . . . . .220 A3
Banstock Rd HA8 . . . . . . .26 C4
Banting Dr N21 . . . . .16 B6
Banting Ho 6 NW2 . . . . . .68 A5
Bantock Ho 3 W10 . . . . . .91 A4
Banton Cl EN1 . . . . .6 B3
Bantry Ho 18 E1 . . . . .96 D3
Bantry St SE5 . . . . .139 B5
Banville Ho SW8 . . . . 270 D3
Banwell Rd DA5 . . . . .168 D5
Banyan Ho 8 NW3 . . . . . . .69 D2
Banyard Ho SE16 . . . . . . .118 B3
Baptist Gdns NW5 . . . . . . .71 A2
Barandon Wlk 6
W11 . . . . .112 D6
Barbanel Ho 28 E1 . . . . . . .96 C3
Barbara Brosnan Ct
NW8 . . . . 229 C3
Barbara Castle Cl SW6 . 264 D5
Barbara Ct TW17 . . . . . . .192 D4
Barbara Hucklesbury Cl
N22 . . . . .32 C1
Barbara Martin Ho 1
N11 . . . . .31 C5
Barbara Rudolph Ct 5
N19 . . . . .50 A4
Barbara Ward Ct 3
E1 . . . . .76 C6
Barbauld Rd N16 . . . . .73 C5
Barber Beaumont Ho 21
E1 . . . . .96 D4
Barber Cl N21 . . . . .16 C4
Barberry Cl E15 . . . . .76 C2
Barbers Alley 1 E13 . . . . .99 B4
Barbers Rd E15 . . . . .97 D5
BARBICAN 95 A2 242 A4
Barbican* EC2 . . . .95 A2 242 B3
Barbican Arts & Con Ctr*
EC2 . . . . .95 A2 242 B4
Barbican Rd UB1 . . . . .85 D1
Barbican Sta
EC1 . . . . .95 A2 242 A4
Barb Mews W6 . . . . .112 C3
Barbon Cl WC1 . . . . 240 C4
Barbot Cl N9 . . . . .18 A1
Barbrook Ho E9 . . . . .74 C2
Barchard St SW18 . . . . . .137 D6
Barchester Cl W7 . . . . . . .108 D5
Barchester Lo N12 . . . . . . .29 D6
Barchester Rd HA3 . . . . . .24 B1
Barchester St E14 . . . . . . .97 D2
Barclay Cl
SW6 . . . . .135 C5 265 A3
Barclay Ct N12 . . . . .30 A5
Barclay Ho 21 E9 . . . . . . .74 C1
Barclay Prim Sch E10 . . . .54 B3
Barclay Rd
Edmonton N18 . . . . .33 B4
Leyton E11 . . . . .54 D1
Newham E13 . . . . .99 C4
Parsons Green
SW6 . . . . .135 C5 265 B3
South Croydon CR0 . . . . .221 B5
Walthamstow E17 . . . . . . .54 A4
Barcombe Ave SW2 . . . . .160 B2
Barcom Trad Est 1
CR0 . . . . .204 A2
Bardell Ho 17 SE1 . . . . . .118 A4
Barden St SE18 . . . . .145 C5
Bardfield Ave RM6 . . . . . . .58 D6
Bardney Rd SM4 . . . . .201 B5
Bardolph Rd
Richmond TW9 . . . . .132 B2
Tufnell Pk N7 . . . . .72 A4
Bard Rd W10 . . . . .112 D6
Bardsey Pl 41 E1 . . . . . . .96 C3
Bardsey Wlk 5 N1 . . . . . . .73 A2
Bardsley Cl CR0 . . . . .221 D5
Bardsley Ho 5 SE10 . . . . .142 A6
Bardsley La SE10 . . . . . . .142 A6
Barents Ho 10 E1 . . . . . . .96 D3
Barfett St W10 . . . . .91 B3
Barfield Ave N20 . . . . .14 D2
Barfield Rd
Bromley BR1, BR7 . . . . . .210 C6
Leytonstone E11 . . . . .54 D1
Barfleur La SE8 . . . . .119 B2
Barford Cl NW4 . . . . .28 A2
Barford Ho 23 E3 . . . . . . .97 B5
Barford St N1 . . . .94 C6 234 B5
Barforth Rd SE15 . . . . . . .140 B2
Barfreston Way SE20 . . . .184 B2
Bargate Cl
New Malden KT3 . . . . . . .200 A2
Plumstead Comm SE18 . .123 D1
Bargehouse Rd E16 . . . . .122 D4
Barge House St SE1 . . . . 251 B4
Barge La 10 E3 . . . . .97 B6
Bargery Rd SE6 . . . . .163 D3
Bargrove Cl 8 SE20 . . . . .184 A3
Bargrove Cres SE6 . . . . . .163 B2
Barham Cl
Chislehurst BR7 . . . . .188 D5
Keston Mark BR2 . . . . . . .210 A1
Wembley HA0 . . . . .65 C2
Barham Ct
8 Croydon CR2 . . . . .221 A4
Keston Mark BR2 . . . . . . .210 A1
Wembley HA0 . . . . .65 C2
Woodside Pk N12 . . . . . . .29 B5
Barham Ho SE17 . . . . 263 B2
Barham Prim Sch HA0 . . . .65 C2
Barham Rd
Chislehurst BR7 . . . . .188 D5
Croydon CR2 . . . . .221 A3
Wimbledon SW20 . . . . . . .178 A3

Baring Cl SE12 . . . . .165 A2
Baring Ho 31 N1 . . . . . . 235 C5
Baring Ho 18 E14 . . . . . . .97 C1
Baring Prim Sch SE12 . . .165 A4
Baring Rd Barnet EN4 . . . .2 B2
Croydon CR0 . . . . .206 A1
Grove Pk SE12 . . . . .165 A2
Baring St N1 . . . . .95 B6 235 C5
Barker Cl
Kingston u T KT3 . . . . . . .198 D5
Richmond TW9 . . . . .132 D3
Barker Dr NW1 . . . . .71 D1
Barker Ho
Dulwich SE21 . . . . .161 C1
3 Harringay N15 . . . . .50 D5
Walthamstow E17 . . . . . . .53 B2
Walworth SE17 . . . . 263 A3
Barker Mews SW4 . . . . . .137 B1
Barker St SW10 . . . . .266 A6
Barker Wlk SW16 . . . . . . .159 D1
Barkham Rd N17 . . . . .33 C3
BARKING 79 B1
Barking Abbey Comp Sch
(Sports & Humanities
Coll)) IG11 . . . . .79 C1
Barking Abbey Sch (Sports
& Humanities Coll)
IG11 . . . . .79 D2
Barking Bsns Ctr
IG11 . . . . .102 A4
Barking Flyover IG11 . . . . .78 D1
Barking Hospl IG11 . . . . . .79 D1
Barking Ind Pk IG11 . . . . .102 A4
Barking Rd
East Ham E6 . . . . .100 B6
Plaistow E13 . . . . .99 B4
BARKINGSIDE 57 A6
Barkingside Sta IG6 . . . . . .57 B6
Barking Sta IG11 . . . . .79 A1
Bark Pl W2 . . . . . .113 D6 245 C6
Barkston Gdns
SW5 . . . . .113 D2 255 C3
Barkway Cl BR6 . . . . .226 C4
Barkway Ct N4 . . . . .73 A6
Barkwith Ho 27 SE14 . . . .140 D6
Barkworth Rd SE16 . . . . .118 C1
Barlborough St SE14 . . . .140 D5
Barlby Gdns W10 . . . . .90 D3
Barlby Prim Sch W10 . . . . .90 D3
Barlby Rd W10 . . . . .90 D2
Barley Cl WD23 . . . . .8 A6
Barleycorn Way E14 . . . . .119 B6
Barley Ct Ilford IG3 . . . . . .58 B4
Stanwell TW19 . . . . .148 A3
Barleyfields Cl RM6 . . . . . .58 C2
Barley La IG3 . . . . .58 B3
Barley Lane Prim Sch
RM6 . . . . .58 B2
Barley Mow Pas
Chiswick W4 . . . . .111 B1
Clerkenwell EC1 . . . . . . 241 D3
Barley Mow Way
TW17 . . . . .192 C3
Barley Shotts Bsns Pk
W10 . . . . .91 B2
Barling 6 NW1 . . . . .71 B1
Barling Ct 1 SW4 . . . . . . .138 A3
Barlings Ho 2 SE4 . . . . . .140 D1
Barloch Ho 14 SW11 . . . . .137 A2
Barlow Cl SM6 . . . . .220 A1
Barlow Dr SE18 . . . . .144 A4
Barlow Ho
14 Bermondsey SE16 . . .118 B2
Notting Hill W11 . . . . . . 244 A6
Shoreditch N1 . . . . 235 C2
Barlow Pl W1 . . . . 248 D5
Barlow Rd Acton W3 . . . . .110 D5
Brondesbury NW6 . . . . . . .69 B2
Hampton TW12 . . . . .173 C3
Barlow St
SE17 . . . . .117 B2 262 D3
Barmeston Rd SE6 . . . . . .163 D2
Barmor Cl HA2 . . . . .23 D1
Barmouth Ave UB6 . . . . . . .86 D5
Barmouth Ho 6 N7 . . . . . .72 B6
Barmouth Rd
Croydon CR0 . . . . .222 D6
Wandsworth SW18 . . . . . .158 A5
Barnabas Ct N21 . . . . .16 C6
Barnabas Ho EC1 . . . . . 235 A1
Barnabas Lo SW8 . . . . . . 270 B2
Barnabas Rd E9 . . . . .74 D3
Barnaby Cl HA2 . . . . .64 A6
Barnaby Ct NW9 . . . . .45 C6
Barnaby Pl SW7 . . . . 256 C3
Barnard Cl
Chislehurst BR7 . . . . .189 B2
Sunbury TW16 . . . . .172 B3
Wallington SM6 . . . . .219 D1
Woolwich SE18 . . . . .122 C3
Barnard Ct SW16 . . . . . . .160 B1
Barnard Gdns
Hayes UB4 . . . . .84 B3
West Barnes KT3 . . . . . . .200 A5
Barnard Hill N10 . . . . .31 B2
Barnard Ho 17 E2 . . . . . . .96 B4
Barnard Lo
New Barnet EN5 . . . . .2 A1
10 Paddington W9 . . . . . .91 C2
Barnard Mews SW11 . . . .136 C1
Barnardo Gdns 1 E1 . . . .118 D6
Barnardo St E1 . . . . .96 D1
Barnard Rd
Clapham SW11 . . . . .136 C1
Enfield EN1 . . . . .6 B3
Mitcham CR4 . . . . .181 A1
Barnard's Inn EC4 . . . . . 241 B2
Barnbrough NW1 . . . . . . 232 A5

Barnby Sq 1 E15 ..98 C6
Barnby St
Somers Town
NW1..93 C4 232 B2
2 West Ham E15..98 C6
Barn Cl Ashford TW15 ..170 D5
19 Kentish Town NW5 ..71 D3
Northolt UB5..84 C5
Barn Cres HA7..25 C4
Barncroft Cl UB8 ..82 D2
Barn Croft Prim Sch
E17..53 A3
Barneby Cl TW2 ..152 C3
Barnehurst Rd DA7 ..147 D3
Barnersbury Ho N7 ..72 A4
BARNES ..133 D4
Barnes Ave
Barnes SW13 ..134 A5
Southall UB2..107 B2
Barnes Bridge Sta
SW13..133 C3
Barnes Cl E12 ..77 D4
Barnes Common*
SW13..134 A2
Barnes Ct Barnet EN5 ..1 D1
Islington N1 ..72 C1
3 Newham E16 ..99 C2
South Norwood CR7 ..205 A6
Woodford IG8..37 D5
Wood Green N22..32 A3
Barnes End KT3..200 A4
Barnes High St SW13 ..133 D3
Barnes Ho
8 Barking IG11..101 B6
14 Bethnal Green E2 ..96 C5
Camden Town NW1.. 231 D6
26 Deptford SE14..140 D6
Hornsey N19..50 A2
Barnes Hospl SW14..133 C2
Barnes Prim Sch
SW13..133 D2
Barnes Qtr 6 TW8..131 C5
Barnes Rd
Edmonton N18..34 C6
Ilford IG1..79 A3
Barnes St E14 ..97 A1
Barnes Sta SW13 ..134 A2
Barnes Terr SE8 ..119 B1
Barnes Wallis Ct HA9 ..67 A5
BARNET ..13 B6
Barnet By-Pass WD6..11 C6
Barnet Coll EN5 ..1 B1
Barnet Coll (Grahame
Park Ctr) NW9 ..27 D2
Barnet Coll (Montagu Rd)
NW4..46 A3
Barnet Dr BR2..226 A6
BARNET GATE ..11 C5
Barnet Gate La EN5..11 D4
Barnet Gr E2 ..96 A4
Barnet Hill EN5..1 C1
Barnet Hill JMI Sch
EN5..13 B6
Barnet Ho 35 SE5 ..139 A3
Barnet La
Barnet EN5, N20..13 B4
Borehamwood WD6 ..10 B5
Barnet Mus* EN5..1 A1
Barnet Rd Barnet EN5..1 B5
Edgware EN5..11 C5
Barnett Ho E1 .. 243 C3
Barnett Homestead
NW11..47 C5
Barnet Trad Est EN5..1 B2
Barnetts Ct HA2 ..63 D5
Barnett St 18 E1..96 B1
Barnet Way (Barnet By-
Pass) EN5, NW7, WD6..11 B3
Barnet Wood Rd BR2..225 C6
Barney Cl SE7 ..121 C1
Barnfield KT3..199 C3
Barn Field NW3..70 D3
Barnfield Ave
Croydon CR0..222 C6
Kingston u T KT2..176 A5
Mitcham CR4..203 B6
Barnfield Cl London N4..50 A2
Wandsworth SW17..158 A1
Barnfield Gdns
Kingston u T KT2..176 A5
Shooters Hill SE18 ..144 D6
Barnfield Pl E14 ..119 C2
Barnfield Prim Sch
HA8..27 A2
Barnfield Rd
Burnt Oak HA8 ..27 A2
Ealing W5 ..87 C3
Erith DA17..147 B6
Shooters Hill SE18 ..144 D6
Barnfield Wood Cl
BR3..208 B3
Barnfield Wood Rd
BR3..208 B3
Barnham Dr SE28..123 D5
Barnham Rd UB6 ..86 A4
Barnham St SE1 .. 253 B2
Barnhill HA5..40 C4
Barn Hill HA9..44 D1
Barnhill Ave BR2..208 D4
Barnhill Com High Sch
UB4..84 C4
Barnhill Ct UB4..84 B4
Barnhill La UB4..84 B3
Barnhill Rd Hayes UB4 ..84 C3
Wembley HA9..67 A5
Barnhurst Path WD19 ..22 C5
Barningham Way NW9 ..45 B3
Barnlea Cl TW13..151 A2
Barnmead Ct RM9 ..81 B3
Barnmead Gdns RM9..81 B3
Barnmead Rd
Dagenham RM9..81 B3
Penge BR3..185 A2
Barn Rise HA9..66 C6
BARNSBURY ..72 A1
Barnsbury Cl KT3 ..199 A5
Barnsbury Cres KT5..199 A1
Barnsbury Gr N7..72 B1
Barnsbury Ho 12 SW4 ..159 D5
Barnsbury La KT5..199 A1
Barnsbury Pk N1 ..72 C1
Barnsbury Rd
N1..94 C6 234 A5
Barnsbury Sq N1 ..72 C1
Barnsbury St N1..72 C1
Barnsbury Terr N1..72 B1
Barnscroft SW20..200 B6
Barnsdale Ave E14..119 C2
Barnsdale Rd W9..91 B3
Barnsley St E1..96 B3
Barn St N16 ..73 C6
Barnstaple Ho SE12..164 D6
Barnstaple La SE13 ..142 A1
Barnstaple Rd HA4..62 C5
Barnston Wlk N1 .. 235 A6
Barnview Lo HA3 ..24 C2
Barn Way HA9..66 C6
Barnwell Ho 1 SE5 ..139 C4
Barnwell Rd SW2 ..160 C6
Barnwood Cl
Barnet N20 ..13 B3
Ruislip HA4..61 B6
Westbourne Green W9..91 D3
Baron Cl
Friern Barnet N11..31 B5
Islington N1 .. 234 A4
Baron Ct Barnet EN5 ..1 D1
Mitcham CR4..202 C5
Baroness Rd 5 E2..95 D4
Baronet Gr N17..34 A2
Baronet Rd N17 ..34 A2
Baron Gdns IG6 ..57 A6
Baron Gr CR4..202 C5
Baron Ho 6 SW19 ..180 B2
Baron Rd RM8 ..58 D1
Barons 14 BR3..185 D1
Barons Court Mans
W14.. 254 B1
Baron's Court Rd
W14..113 A1 254 B2
Barons Court Sta
W14 ..113 A1 254 A2
Barons Ct Ilford IG1 ..79 B6
Kingsbury NW9..45 B3
Wallington SM6..219 D5
Baronsfield Rd TW1..153 B5
Barons Gate
East Barnet EN4 ..14 C5
13 South Acton W4..111 A3
Barons Keep
W14..113 A1 254 A2
Barons Lo 9 E14 ..120 A2
Barons Mead HA1..42 C5
Baronsmead Rd SW13..134 A4
Baronsmede W5..110 B4
Baronsmere Ct 9 EN5 ..1 A1
Baronsmere Rd N2 ..48 C5
Baron's Pl SE1..116 C4 251 B1
Baron St N1..94 C5 234 A4
Barons The TW1..153 B5
Baron's Wlk CR0..207 A3
Baron Wlk E16 ..98 D2
Barque Mews SE8 ..141 C6
Barrack Rd TW4 ..129 A1
Barradell Ho 15 W14..112 D3
Barra Hall Cir UB3 ..83 C1
Barra Hall Rd UB3 ..105 C6
Barrass Cl 7 EN3..7 C6
Barratt Ave N22 ..32 B1
Barratt Ho 15 N1..72 D1
Barratt Ind Pk Poplar E3 . 98 A3
Southall UB1..107 C5
Barratt Way HA3..42 B6
Barr Beacon SE23..162 C4
Barrenger Rd N10 ..30 D1
Barret Ho NW6 ..91 C6
Barrett Ct 2 NW10 ..89 C5
Barrett Rd E17..54 A5
Barrett's Gr N16 ..73 C3
Barrett's Green Rd
NW10..89 B5
Barrett St W1 ..93 A1 238 B1
Barrhill Rd SW2 ..160 A2
Barrie Ct EN5..14 A6
Barriedale SE14 ..141 A3
Barrie Ho Acton W3..111 A4
Bayswater W2.. 246 B5
Edmonton N9..18 B4
Primrose Hill NW8 .. 230 B5
8 Stoke Newington N16 . 73 C5
Barrier Gdns Pier
SE18..121 D3
Barrier Point Rd E16..121 C4
Barringers Ct HA4 ..39 B2
Barringer Sq SW17 ..181 A6
Barrington N20..14 B3
Barrington Cl NW5..71 A3
Barrington Ct
9 Acton W3..110 D4
Kentish Town NW5 ..71 A3
4 Muswell Hill N10..31 B1
31 South Lambeth SW9 . 138 A3
Barrington Prim Sch
DA7..146 D3
Barrington Rd
Bexley DA7 ..146 D3
Brixton SW9 ..138 D2
Cheam SM3..201 C1
Hornsey N8..49 D4
Little Ilford E12..78 C2
Barrington Villas
SE18..144 C4
Barrington Wlk 9
SE19..183 C4
Barrow Ave SM5..218 D1
Barrow Cl N21..16 D2
Barrow Ct 6 SE6 ..164 D3
Barrowdene Cl HA5..23 A1
Barrowell Gn N21..17 A2
Barrowfield Cl N9 ..18 C1
Barrowgate Ho W4 ..111 B1
Barrowgate Rd W4 ..111 B1
Barrow Hedges Cl
SM5..218 C1
Barrow Hedges Prim Sch
SM5..218 C1
Barrow Hedges Way
SM5..218 C1
Barrow Hill KT4..215 C6
Barrow Hill Cl KT4 ..215 C6
Barrow Hill Est
NW8 ..92 C5 230 A3
Barrow Hill Jun Sch
NW8..92 C5 230 A3
Barrow Hill Rd NW8.. 230 A3
Barrow Point Ave HA5 ..23 A1
Barrow Point La HA5..23 A1
Barrow Rd
Croydon CR0..220 C3
Streatham SW16..181 D4
Barrow Wlk TW8..109 C1
Barrs Rd NW10 ..67 B1
Barry Ave Erith DA7..147 A5
South Tottenham N15 ..51 D3
Barry Cl BR6..227 C5
Barry Ct SW4 ..159 C5
Barrydene N20 ..14 B2
Barrydene Ct EN2..4 D2
Barry Ho 4 SE16 ..118 B1
Barry Lo N4 ..50 B2
Barrymore N12 ..30 A3
Barry Par SE22 ..140 A1
Barry Rd London SE22 ..162 A6
Newham E6..100 A1
Willesden NW10..67 A1
Barry Terr TW15 ..148 B2
Barset Rd SE15 ..140 C2
Barsons Cl SE20 ..184 C3
Barston Rd SE27..161 A1
Barstow Cres SW2..160 B3
Bartell Ho SW2 ..160 C5
Barter St WC1 ..94 A2 240 B3
Barters Wlk HA5..41 A6
Barth Mews SE18 ..123 C2
Bartholomew Cl
Barbican EC1.. 242 A3
Wandsworth SW18..136 A1
Bartholomew Ct
16 Blackwall E14 ..120 B6
Edgware HA8 ..25 D3
St Luke's EC1 .. 242 B6
Bartholomew Ho
22 Camberwell SE5..139 A3
Enfield EN3 ..7 A6
Bartholomew La EC2.. 242 D1
Bartholomew Pas EC1 241 D3
Bartholomew Pl EC1.. 242 A3
Bartholomew Rd NW5 ..71 C2
Bartholomew Sq
18 Bethnal Green E1 ..96 B3
St Luke's EC1 .. 242 B6
Bartholomew St
SE1 ..117 B3 262 D5
Bartholomew Villas
NW5..71 C2
Barth Rd SE18 ..123 C2
Bartle Ave E6..100 A5
Bartle Rd W11..91 A1
Bartlett Cl E14..97 C1
Bartlett Ct EC4 .. 241 B2
Bartletts Cotts 4 EN5..1 A2
Bartletts Ho 10 RM10..81 D2
Bartlett St CR2 ..221 B3
Bartok Ho W11 .. 244 C5
Barton Ave RM7 ..59 D1
Barton Cl Bexley DA6 ..169 A6
Hackney E9 ..74 C3
Hendon NW4..46 A5
2 Newham E6..100 B1
Peckham SE15..140 B2
Shepperton TW17 ..192 D3
Barton Ct
Beckenham BR2 ..208 B6
10 South Lambeth SW4 . 138 A3
3 Sutton SM1 ..217 D2
West Kensington W14.. 254 B2
Barton Gn KT3..177 B1
Barton Ho
8 Bromley E3 ..97 D4
Islington N1 ..72 D1
Sands End SW6..135 D2
Barton Mdws IG6..57 A5
Barton Rd Sidcup DA14 ..191 A4
West Kensington
W14..113 A1 254 B1
Barton St SW1.. 260 A6
Bartons The WD6 ..9 D5
Bartonway NW8 .. 229 C4
Bartram Cl UB8 ..82 D3
Bartram Ct RM9 ..80 B2
Bartram Rd SE4 ..163 A5
Bartrams La EN4..2 A5
Bartrip St E9 ..75 B2
Barts Cl BR3..207 C4
Barts & The London Sch of
Medicine & Dentistry
EC1..94 D3 241 D5
Barville Cl SE4..141 A1
Barwell Bsns Pk KT9..213 D1
Barwell Ho 7 E2 ..96 A3
Barwell La KT9 ..213 C1
Barwick Dr UB8..82 D2
Barwick Ho 7 W3 ..111 A4
Barwick Rd E7..77 B4
Barwood Ave BR4..207 D1
Bascome St 13 SW2..160 C5
Basden Gr TW13..151 C2
Base Apartments 8
N1..73 A1
Basedale Rd RM9..80 B1
Baseing Cl E6 ..122 C6
Baseline Business Studios
18 W11 ..112 D6
Basevi Way SE8..141 D6
Bashley Rd NW10 ..89 B3
Basil Ave E6..100 A4
Basil Ct 11 EN5 ..2 A1
Basildene Rd TW4,
TW5..128 D2
Basildon Ct W1.. 238 B4
Basildon Rd SE2..124 A1
Basil Gdns
Croydon CR0 ..206 D1
West Norwood SE27..183 A5
Basil Ho
South Lambeth SW8.. 270 A4
22 Whitechapel E1 ..96 A1
Basil Mans SW1 .. 247 C1
Basilon Rd DA7 ..147 A3
Basil Spence Ho N22..32 B2
Basil St
Knightsbridge
SW1.. 114 D4 247 C1
Knightsbridge SW1,
SW3.. 114 D3 257 C6
Basin App 20 E14 ..97 A1
Basing Cl KT7 ..196 D2
Basing Ct 13 SE15..139 D4
Basingdon Way SE5..139 B1
Basing Dr DA5..169 B5
Basingfield Rd KT7 ..196 D2
Basinghall Ave
EC2 ..95 B1 242 C2
Basinghall St
EC2 ..95 B1 242 C2
Basing Hill
London NW11 ..47 B1
Wembley HA9 ..44 C1
Basing Ho
7 Barking IG11..101 B6
Catford SE6..185 C6
Basing House Yd 22 E2.. 95 C4
Basing Pl E2 ..95 C4
Basing St W11..91 B1
Basing Way London N3..47 D6
Thames Ditton KT7 ..196 D2
Basire St N1..95 A6 235 B6
Baskerville Ct
South Norwood SE25 ..205 C4
Wandsworth SW18..158 C4
Baskerville Gdns NW10.. 67 C4
Baskerville Rd SW18..158 C4
Basket Gdns SE9..166 A6
Basle Ho 3 E15 ..76 C3
Baslow Cl HA3..24 B2
Baslow Wlk E5 ..74 D4
Basnett Rd 9 SW11..137 A2
Basque Ct 21 SE16 ..118 D4
Bassano St SE22..161 D6
Bassant Rd SE18..145 D6
Bassein Park Rd W12 ..111 D4
Bassett Gdns TW7 ..130 A5
Bassett Ho RM9..102 B6
Bassett Rd W10..90 D1
Bassetts Cl BR6..226 D4
Bassett St NW5..71 A2
Bassetts Way BR6..226 D4
Bassett Way UB1 ..85 D1
Bassingbourn Ho 3
N1..72 D1
Bassingham Rd
Wandsworth SW18..158 A4
Wembley HA0 ..65 D2
Bassishaw Highwalk
EC2 .. 242 C3
Basswood Cl 5 SE15..140 B2
Bastable Ave IG11..102 A5
Basterfield Ho EC1.. 242 A5
Bastion Highwalk EC2. 242 A3
Bastion Rd SE18, SE2 ..124 A1
Baston Manor Rd BR2,
BR4..225 B4
Baston Rd BR2..225 B5
Baston Sch BR2 ..225 B6
Bastwick St EC1 . 95 A3 242 A6
Basuto Rd
SW6..135 C4 265 B1
Batavia Cl TW16 ..172 C2
Batavia Ho 1 SE14..141 A5
Batavia Mews 3 SE14..141 A5
Batavia Rd
Deptford SE14..141 A5
Sunbury TW16..172 B2
Batchelor St N1 . 94 C6 234 B5
Bateman Cl IG11..79 A2
Bateman Ho 8 SE17 ..138 D6
Bateman Rd E4..35 C4
Bateman's Bldgs W1.. 239 C1
Bateman's Row
EC2 ..95 C3 243 B6
Bateman St W1.. 93 D1 239 C1
Bates Cres
Croydon CR0..220 C3
Streatham SW16..181 C3
Bateson St 3 SE18..123 C2
Bate St 10 E14..119 B6
Bath Cl SE15..140 B5
Bath Ct Finsbury EC1.. 235 C1
3 Forest Hill SE26..162 A1
Holborn EC1 .. 241 A5
Bathgate Ho 8 SW9 ..138 D4
Bathgate Rd SW19 ..156 D1
Bath Gr E2 ..96 A5
Bath Ho
Bethnal Green E2 ..96 A3
Borough The SE1.. 262 B6
Bath House Rd CR0 ..204 A1
Bath Pas KT1..175 D1
Bath Pl Barnet EN5 ..1 B2
14 Hammersmith W6 ..112 C1
11 Shoreditch EC2 ..95 C4
Bath Rd Acton W4 ..111 C2
Cranford TW3, TW4,
TW5..128 C4
Dagenham RM6..59 A3
Harlington TW6, UB7,
TW5..127 B4
Harmondsworth TW6,
UB7 ..126 B4
Lower Edmonton N9 ..18 C2
Upton E7 ..77 D2
Baths Rd BR1, BR2..209 D5
Bath St EC1 ..95 B4 235 C1
Bath Terr SE1 ..117 A3 262 A6
Bathurst Ave SW19 ..179 D2
Bathurst Gdns NW10..90 B5
Bathurst Ho 2 W12..112 B6
Bathurst Mews
W2..114 B6 246 D6
Bathurst Rd IG1 ..56 D1
Bathurst St W2 .. 246 D6
Bathway 11 SE18..122 C2
Batley Cl CR4..202 D2
Batley Pl 3 N16 ..73 D5
Batley Rd Enfield EN2 ..5 B4
Shacklewell N16 ..73 D5
Batman Cl W12 ..112 B5
Batoum Gdns W6..112 C3
Batson Ho 29 E1..96 A1
Batson St W12..112 A4
Batsworth Rd CR4 ..202 B6
Battenburg Wlk 10
SE19..183 C5
Batten Cl E6..100 B1
Batten Ho
7 London SW4..159 C6
8 Walthamstow E17 ..53 D6
10 West Kilburn W10 ..91 A4
Batten St SW11 ..136 C2
Battersby Rd SE6 ..164 B1
BATTERSEA ..136 D4
Battersea Bridge Rd
SW11..136 C5 267 A3
Battersea Bsns Ctr
SW11..137 A2
Battersea Church Rd
SW11..136 B4 266 D2
Battersea Dogs Home
SW8 ..137 B5 268 D3
Battersea High St
SW11..136 B3
Battersea Hts SW11..136 D2
Battersea Park*
SW11.. 137 A5 268 A3
Battersea Park Rd SW11,
SW8.. 267 D1
Battersea Park Sta
SW8 ..137 B5 268 C3
Battersea Power
Station(dis)
SW8 ..137 B6 268 D6
Battersea Rise SW11..136 C1
Battersea Sq SW11.. 266 D1
Battery Rd SE28 ..123 C4
Battishill St 9 N1 ..72 D1
Battlebridge Ct NW1.. 233 B4
Battle Bridge La
SE1 ..117 C5 253 A3
Battle Bridge Rd
NW1 ..94 A5 233 A4
Battle Cl SW19..180 A4
Battledean Rd N5..72 D3
Battle Ho 8 SE15 ..140 A6
Battle House Mews 7
EN5 ..2 A1
Battle of Britain Mus*
NW9..27 D1
Batty St E1 ..96 A1
Baty Ho SW2 ..160 B3
Baudwin Rd SE6 ..164 C2
Baugh Rd DA14 ..190 C5
Baulk The SW18 ..157 C4
Bavant Rd SW16 ..182 B1
Bavaria Rd N19..72 A6
Bavdene Mews NW4 ..46 B5
Bavent Rd SE5..139 A3
Bawdale Rd SE22 ..161 D6
Bawdsey Ave IG2..57 D5
Bawtree Rd SE14 ..141 A5
Bawtry Rd N20 ..14 D1
Baxendale N20 ..14 A2
Baxendale St E2..96 A4
Baxter Cl Bromley BR1 ..210 D6
Hillingdon UB10 ..82 D4
Southall UB2..107 D3
Baxter Ho 11 E3 ..97 D4
Baxter Rd Edmonton N18.. 34 B6
Ilford IG1 ..78 D3
Islington N1 ..73 B2
Newham E16..99 C1
Bayard Ct DA7..147 D1
Baycliffe Ho 8 E9 ..74 D2
Baycroft Cl HA5 ..40 C6
Bay Ct Ealing W5 ..110 A3
7 Stepney E1..96 D3
Baydon Ct BR2 ..208 D6
Bayer Ho EC1.. 242 A5
Bayes Ct NW3 ..70 D1
Bayeux Ho 10 SE7..143 C6
Bayfield Ho 3 SE4..140 D1
Bayfield Rd SE9..143 D1
Bayford Lodge HA5 ..23 B2
Bayford Rd NW10..90 D4
Bayford St Ind Ctr 4
E8..74 B1
Bayford St 5 E8..74 B1
Baygrove Mews KT1 ..175 C2
Bayham Pl NW1 . 93 C6 232 B5
Bayham Rd Acton W4 ..111 B3
Ealing W13 ..109 B5
Morden SM4 ..202 A5
Bayham St NW1 . 93 C6 232 A5
Bay Ho UB10 ..60 C4
Bayhurst Ho N4..51 A2
Bayhurst Wood
Countryside Park
UB9..38 B4
Bayleaf Cl TW12 ..174 B5
Bayley St WC1.. 239 C3
Bayley Wlk SE2..125 A1
Baylis Mews TW1..153 A4
Baylis Rd SE1..116 C4 251 A1
Bayliss Ave SE28..124 D6
Bayliss Cl
4 Southall UB1 ..85 D1
Southgate N21 ..16 A6
Bayne Cl E6 ..100 B1
Baynes Cl EN1 ..6 A4
Baynes Mews 2 NW3 ..70 B2
Baynes St NW1 ..71 C1
Baynham Cl DA5..169 B5
Bayon Ho 27 N19 ..49 D2
Bayonne Rd W6 .. 264 A5
Bays Cl SE26..184 C5
Bays Ct HA8 ..26 D5
Bayshill Rise UB5..63 D2
Bayston Rd N16..73 D5
BAYSWATER ..114 A6
Bayswater Rd
W2..114 B6 246 C5
Bayswater Sta
W2 .. 113 D6 245 D6
Bayton Ct 2 E8..74 A1
Baytree Cl
Bromley BR1..187 D2
Sidcup DA15 ..167 D3
Baytree Ho E4..19 D4
Baytree Rd SW2..138 B1
Bazalgette Cl KT3..199 B4
Bazalgette Gdns KT3..199 B4
Bazalgette Ho NW8 .. 236 D6
Bazeley Ho SE1 .. 251 C1
Bazely St E14..120 A6
Bazile Rd N21 ..16 C5
BBC Television Ctr
W12..112 C5
Beacham Cl SE7 ..143 D6
Beachborough Rd
BR1..186 A6
Beachcroft Ave UB1..107 B5
Beachcroft Rd E11..76 C5
Beach Ct SE9..166 A5
Beach Gr TW13 ..151 C2
Beach Ho SW5.. 255 A2
Beachy Rd E3 ..75 C1
Beaconfield Terrace Rd
W14.. 254 A5
Beacon Gate SE14 ..140 D2
Beacon Gr SM5..219 A4
Beacon Hill N7 ..72 A3
Beacon Ho
11 Camberwell SE5..139 C5
7 Isle Of Dogs E14 ..119 D1
10 Penge SE26 ..184 B5
South Lambeth SW8 .. 269 C2
Beacon House Sch
W5..110 B5
Beacon Pl CR0..220 A5
Beacon Rd
Harlington TW19,
TW6..148 C5
Hither Green SE13 ..164 B5
Beacon Rdbt TW6..148 C5
Beacons Cl 10 E6 ..100 A2
Beaconsfield Cl
Acton Green W4 ..111 A1
Friern Barnet N11..31 A5
Greenwich SE3 ..143 A6
Beaconsfield Ct N11 ..31 A5
Beaconsfield Gdns
KT10..212 C1
Beaconsfield Par 1
SE9..188 A6
Beaconsfield Prim Sch
UB2..107 A5
Beaconsfield Rd
Acton W4..111 B3
Bromley BR1..209 D6
Claygate KT10..212 C1
Ealing W5 ..109 D4
Edmonton N9..18 A1
Elmstead SE9..188 A6
Enfield EN3 ..6 D6
Friern Barnet N11..31 A6
Greenwich SE3 ..143 A5
Hayes UB4..106 C5
Kingston u T KT3..177 B1
Leyton E10..76 A5
Newham E16..98 D3
Southall UB1..107 A5
South Tottenham N15 ..51 C5
Surbiton KT5 ..198 B2
Thornton Heath CR0 ..205 B3
Twickenham TW1..153 B5
Walthamstow E17 ..53 B3
Walworth
SE17.. 117 C1 263 A1

Beaconsfield Rd *continued*
Willesden NW10 . . . . 67 D2
Beaconsfield Wlk
SW6 . . . . 135 B4 264 D1
Beaconshaw BR1 . . . . . . 186 C3
Beacontree Ave E17 . . . . 36 B1
Beacontree Rd E11 . . . . . 54 D2
Beadle Ct CR4 . . . . 202 C6
Beadlow Cl SM4 . . . . 202 B3
Beadman Pl SE27 . . . . . . 182 D6
Beadman St SE27 . . . . . . 182 D6
Beadnell Rd SE23 . . . . . . 162 D3
Beadon Rd
Bromley BR2 . . . . 209 A4
Hammersmith W6 . . . . . . 112 C2
Beaford Gr SW20 . . . . . . 201 B6
Beagle Cl TW13 . . . . 172 B6
Beak St W1 . . . . 115 C6 249 B6
Beal Cl DA16 . . . . 146 A4
Beale Cl N13 . . . . 32 D5
Beale Ho 7 SW9 . . . . 138 B3
Beale Pl E3 . . . . 97 B5
Beale Rd E3 . . . . 97 B6
Beal High Sch IG5 . . . . . . 56 A5
Beal Rd IG1 . . . . 78 C6
Beam Ave RM10 . . . . 103 D6
Beames Ho SW8 . . . . . . 269 C2
Beames Rd NW10 . . . . 89 B6
Beaminster Ct N15 . . . . . . 51 B4
Beaminster Gdns IG6 . . . 56 D6
Beaminster Ho SW8 . . 270 C4
Beamish Dr WD23 . . . . 8 A3
Beamish Ho 7 SE16 . . . 118 C2
Beamish Rd N9 . . . . 18 A3
Beanacre Cl E9 . . . . 75 B2
Bean Rd DA6 . . . . 146 D1
Beanshaw SE9 . . . . 188 C6
Beansland Gr RM6 . . . . . . 59 A6
Bear Alley EC4 . . . . 241 C2
Bear Cl RM7 . . . . 59 D3
Bear Croft Ho 6 SW6 . . 135 B3
Beardell St SE19 . . . . 183 D4
Beardow Gr N14 . . . . 15 C5
Beard Rd KT2 . . . . 176 B5
Beardsfield E13 . . . . 99 A5
Beard's Hill TW12 . . . . . . 173 C2
Beards Hill Cl TW12 . . . . 173 C2
Beardsley Terr RM8 . . . . . 80 B3
Beardsley Way W3 . . . . . 111 B4
Beard's Rd TW15,
TW16 . . . . 171 C4
Bearfield Rd KT2 . . . . . . 176 A3
Bear Gardens Mus*
SE1 . . . . 117 A5 252 A4
Bear Gdns SE1 . . 117 A5 252 A4
Bear La SE1 . . . . 116 D5 251 D3
Bear Rd TW13 . . . . 172 D6
Bear St WC2 . . . . 249 D6
Bearstead Rise SE4 . . . . 163 B6
Bearsted Terr 7 BR3 . . 185 C2
Beasley's Ait TW17 . . . . . 193 D3
Beasley's Ait La TW16,
TW17 . . . . 193 D3
Beaton Cl SE15 . . . . 139 D4
Beatrice Ave
Thornton Heath
SW16 . . . . 182 B1
Wembley HA9 . . . . 66 A3
Beatrice Cl Newham E13 . 99 A3
Pinner HA5 . . . . 40 A5
Beatrice Ct
Buckhurst Hill IG9 . . . . 21 D2
Hendon NW4 . . . . 46 C4
Beatrice Ho
1 Brixton SW2 . . . . 160 B6
Forest Hill SE6 . . . . 163 C2
4 Hammersmith W6 . . . 112 C1
2 Stepney E1 . . . . 96 D2
Beatrice Lo 3 N12 . . . . . . 30 A4
Beatrice Pl W8 . . . . 255 C5
Beatrice Rd
Bermondsey SE1 . . . . 118 A2
Edmonton N9 . . . . 18 C4
Finsbury Pk N4 . . . . 50 C2
2 Richmond TW10 . . . . . 154 B6
Southall UB1 . . . . 107 B5
Walthamstow E17 . . . . 53 C4
Beatrice Tate Sch E2 . . . . 96 B4
Beatrice Webb Ho 4
E3 . . . . 97 A5
Beatrix Ho SW5 . . . . 255 D2
Beatrix Potter Prim Sch
SW18 . . . . 158 A3
Beatson Wlk 23 SE16 . . . 118 D5
Beattie Cl TW14 . . . . 149 D3
Beattie Ho SW8 . . . . 269 B2
Beattock Rise N10 . . . . . . 49 B5
Beatty Ho 16 E14 . . . . . . 119 C4
Beatty Rd Stanmore HA7 . . 25 C4
Stoke Newington N16 . . . . 73 C4
Beatty St NW1 . . . . 232 A4
Beattyville Gdns IG6 . . . . 56 D5
Beauchamp Cl 17 W4 . . . 111 A3
Beauchamp Ct HA7 . . . . . 25 C5
Beauchamp Pl
SW3 . . . . 114 C3 257 B5
Beauchamp Rd
Clapham SW11 . . . . 136 D1
East Molesey KT8 . . . . . . 196 A4
South Norwood SE19 . . . 183 B2
Sutton SM1 . . . . 217 C4
Twickenham TW1 . . . . 153 A4
Upton E7 . . . . 77 B1
Beauchamp St EC1 . . . . 241 A3
Beauchamp Terr
SW15 . . . . 134 B2
Beauclerc Inf Sch
TW16 . . . . 194 C6
Beauclerc Rd W6 . . . . . . 112 B3
Beauclere Ho 1 SM2 . . 218 A1
Beauclerk Cl TW13 . . . . . 150 B3
Beauclerk Ho 10
SW16 . . . . 160 A1
Beaudesert Mews
UB7 . . . . 104 A4
Beaufort E6 . . . . 100 C2
Beaufort Ave HA3 . . . . 43 B6
Beaufort Cl
Chingford E4 . . . . 35 D4
Ealing W5 . . . . 88 B2
Putney SW19 . . . . 156 B4
Beaufort Ct
Friern Barnet N11 . . . . 31 B5
Harrow HA3 . . . . 43 A3
3 New Barnet EN5 . . . . . 14 A6
Richmond TW10 . . . . 175 C6
West Brompton SW6 . . . 265 A6
Beaufort Dr NW11 . . . . . . 47 C5
Beaufort Gdns
Hendon NW4 . . . . 46 C3
Heston TW5 . . . . 129 A4
Ilford IG1 . . . . 56 C1
Knightsbridge
SW3 . . . . 114 C3 257 B6
South Norwood SW16 . . . 182 B3
Beaufort Ho
Ashford TW15 . . . . 170 D5
Battersea SW11 . . . . 136 C3
Chelsea SW3 . . . . 266 D5
Hampstead Garden Suburb
NW11 . . . . 48 A3
20 Millwall E14 . . . . 119 C4
Pimlico SW1 . . . . 259 C1
8 South Tottenham N15 . 51 D5
1 Wimbledon SW20 . . . 178 D2
Beaufort Mans SW3 . . . 266 D5
Beaufort Mews SW6 . . 264 D6
Beaufort Pk NW11 . . . . . . 47 C5
Beaufort Rd Ealing W5 . . . 88 B2
Kingston u T KT1, KT5,
KT6 . . . . 198 A5
Richmond TW10 . . . . 175 C6
Ruislip HA4 . . . . 61 B6
Twickenham TW1 . . . . 153 C4
Beaufort St
SW3 . . . . 136 B6 266 C6
Beaufort Way KT17 . . . . 216 A1
Beaufoy Ho
South Lambeth SW8 . . . 270 C4
3 West Norwood
SE27 . . . . 160 D1
Beaufoy Rd
11 London SW8 . . . . 137 B2
Tottenham N17 . . . . 33 C3
Beaufoy Wlk
SE11 . . . . 116 B2 260 D3
Beaulieu Ave
Forest Hill SE26 . . . . 184 B6
1 Newham E16 . . . . 121 B5
Beaulieu Cl
Camberwell SE5 . . . . 139 B2
Colindale NW9 . . . . 45 C5
Hounslow TW4 . . . . 151 B6
Mitcham CR4 . . . . 181 A2
14 Twickenham TW1 . . . . 153 D5
Beaulieu Ct W5 . . . . 88 A2
Beaulieu Dr HA5 . . . . 40 D2
Beaulieu Gdns N21 . . . . . 17 A4
Beaulieu Ho 6 NW4 . . . . 28 D1
Beaulieu Hts CR7 . . . . . . 183 C2
Beaulieu Pl W4 . . . . 111 A3
Beaumanor Gdns SE9 . . 188 C6
Beaumanor Mans W2 . . 245 D6
Beaumaris 5 N11 . . . . . . 32 A4
Beaumaris Dr IG8 . . . . . . 37 D3
Beaumaris Gn NW9 . . . . . 45 C3
Beaumaris Twr 2
W3 . . . . 110 D4
Beaumont SW15 . . . . 157 A6
Beaumont Ave
Harrow HA2 . . . . 41 D3
Richmond TW9 . . . . 132 B2
Wembley HA0 . . . . 65 C4
West Kensington
W14 . . . . 113 B1 254 C2
Beaumont Bldgs WC2 . 240 B1
Beaumont Cl KT2 . . . . . . 176 C3
Beaumont Cres
W14 . . . . 113 B1 254 C1
Beaumont Ct
10 Acton Green W4 . . . . 111 A1
16 Hendon NW9 . . . . 27 D1
Lower Clapton E5 . . . . 74 B5
Marylebone W1 . . . . 238 B4
7 Mile End E1 . . . . 97 A4
6 Mitcham CR4 . . . . 181 A1
Wembley HA0 . . . . 65 C3
17 Wimbledon SW19 . . . 178 D3
Beaumont Dr
Ashford TW15 . . . . 171 B5
New Malden KT4 . . . . . . 200 B2
Beaumont Gdns NW3 . . . 69 C5
Beaumont Gr E1 . . . . 96 D3
Beaumont Ho
12 Leyton E10 . . . . 53 D2
1 Streatham SW2 . . . . . 160 A3
West Kensington W14 . . 254 D3
Wimbledon SW19 . . . . . . 157 C1
Beaumont Lo E8 . . . . 74 A2
Beaumont Pl Barnet EN5 . . 1 B4
Fitzrovia NW1, WC1,
W1 . . . . 93 C3 239 B6
Isleworth TW7 . . . . 152 D6
Beaumont Rd
Leyton E10 . . . . 53 D2
Newham E13 . . . . 99 B4
Beaumont Rd *continued*
Orpington BR5 . . . . 211 B3
Putney SW15, SW19 . . . 157 A4
South Acton W4 . . . . 111 A3
South Norwood SE19 . . . 183 A4
Beaumont Rise N19 . . . . . 49 D1
Beaumont Sch The
E10 . . . . 53 D1
Beaumont Sq E1 . . . . 96 D2
Beaumont St W1 . . . . . 238 B4
Beaumont Terr 1
SE13 . . . . 164 C4
Beaumont Wlk NW3 . . . . 70 D1
Beauvais Terr UB5 . . . . . . 84 D4
Beauvale 6 NW1 . . . . 71 A1
Beauval Rd SE22 . . . . . . 161 D5
Beaverbank Rd SE9 . . . . 167 B3
Beaver Cl
Hampton TW12 . . . . 173 D2
9 Penge SE20 . . . . 184 A3
West Barnes SM4 . . . . . . 200 C2
Beaver Ctr The RM8 . . . . . 59 A2
Beaver Gr UB5 . . . . 85 A4
Beavers Com Prim Sch
TW4 . . . . 128 C2
Beavers Cres TW4 . . . . . 128 D1
Beavers La TW4 . . . . 128 C2
Beavers Lo DA14 . . . . . . 189 D5
Beaverwood Rd BR7 . . . 189 C4
Beaverwood Sch for Girls
BR7 . . . . 189 C4
Beavis Ho N16 . . . . 73 C5
Beavor La W6 . . . . 112 A1
Bebbington Rd SE18 . . . 123 C2
Beblets Cl 4 BR6 . . . . . 227 D3
Bec Cl HA4 . . . . 62 D5
Beccles Dr IG11 . . . . 79 D2
Beccles St E14 . . . . 119 B6
Bechervaise Ct 2 E10 . . 53 D1
Beck Cl SE13 . . . . 141 D4
Beck Ct BR3 . . . . 206 D6
BECKENHAM 185 C1
Beckenham Bsns Ctr
BR3 . . . . 185 A4
Beckenham Ct BR3 . . . . 185 C2
Beckenham Gdns N9 . . . . 17 C1
Beckenham Gr BR2 . . . . 186 B1
Beckenham Hill Rd BR3,
SE6 . . . . 186 A5
Beckenham Hill Sta
SE6 . . . . 186 A5
Beckenham Hospl
BR3 . . . . 185 B1
Beckenham Junction Sta
BR3 . . . . 185 C2
Beckenham La BR1,
BR2 . . . . 186 D1
Beckenham Place Pk
BR3 . . . . 185 D3
Beckenham Rd
Penge BR3 . . . . 185 A2
West Wickham BR3,
BR4 . . . . 208 A2
Beckenham Rd Sta
BR3 . . . . 185 A2
Beckers The N16 . . . . 74 A4
Becket Ave E6 . . . . 100 C4
Becket Cl
Croydon SE25 . . . . 206 A3
2 Merton SW19 . . . . 179 D2
Becket Fold 10 HA1 . . . . . 42 D4
Becket Ho SE1 . . . . 252 C1
Becket Rd N18 . . . . 34 C6
Becket St SE1 . . . . 262 C6
Beckett Cl
Abbey Wood DA17 . . . . . 125 B3
Streatham SW16 . . . . 159 D2
Willesden NW10 . . . . 67 C2
Beckett Ho
28 London SW9 . . . . 138 A3
15 Stepney E1 . . . . 96 C2
Becketts Cl
Feltham TW14 . . . . 150 B5
Orpington BR6 . . . . 227 D5
Becketts Pl KT1 . . . . 175 D2
Beckett Wlk BR3 . . . . 185 A4
Beckfoot NW1 . . . . 232 B3
Beckford Cl W14 . . . . . 254 D3
Beckford Dr BR5 . . . . 211 B2
Beckford Ho 18 N16 . . . . . 73 C3
Beckford Prim Sch
NW6 . . . . 69 B3
Beckford Rd CR0 . . . . . . 205 D3
Beckham Ho SE11 . . . . 260 D3
Beck Ho
4 Edmonton N18 . . . . 34 A5
Stoke Newington N16 . . . . 73 C5
Beckington 18 NW5 . . . . . 71 A2
Beck La BR3 . . . . 206 D6
Beckley Ho E3 . . . . 97 B3
Becklow Gdns
Chiswick W12 . . . . 111 D4
1 Shepherd's Bush
W12 . . . . 112 A4
Becklow Mews 7
W12 . . . . 112 A4
Becklow Rd W12 . . . . 112 A4
Beckmead Sch BR3 . . . . 207 C1
Beck Rd E8 . . . . 96 B6
Beck River Pk 10 BR3 . . 185 C2
Becks Rd DA14 . . . . 168 A1
BECKTON 100 D2
Beckton Alps E6 . . . . 100 C3
Beckton Alps Ski Ctr
E6 . . . . 100 C3
Beckton Park Sta E6 . . . 122 B6
Beckton Rd E16 . . . . 98 D2
Beckton Ret Pk E6 . . . . . 100 C2
Beckton Sta E6 . . . . 100 C2
Beckton Triangle Ret Pk
E6 . . . . 100 D3
Beck Way BR3 . . . . 207 B6
Beckway Rd SW16 . . . . . 181 D1
Beckway St
SE17 . . . . 117 C2 263 A3
Beckwith Ho 22 E2 . . . . . . 96 B5
Beckwith Rd SE24 . . . . . 161 B6
Beclands Rd SW17 . . . . 181 A4
Becmead Ave
Harrow HA3 . . . . 43 B4
Streatham SW16 . . . . 181 D6
Becondale Rd SE19 . . . . 183 C5
BECONTREE 81 A4
Becontree Ave RM8 . . . . . 80 C5
Becontree Day Hospl
RM8 . . . . 81 A6
Becontree Prim Sch
RM8 . . . . 80 B5
Becontree Sta RM9 . . . . . 80 D2
Bective Pl SW15 . . . . 135 B1
Bective Rd
Forest Gate E7 . . . . 77 A4
Putney SW15 . . . . 135 B1
Becton Pl DA8 . . . . 147 D5
Bedale Rd EN2 . . . . 5 A5
Bedale St SE1 . . . . 252 C3
Beddan Ct HA8 . . . . 26 C4
BEDDINGTON 220 A6
BEDDINGTON CORNER
. . . . 203 A2
Beddington Cross
CR0 . . . . 204 A2
Beddington Farm Rd
CR0 . . . . 204 A1
Beddington Gdns SM5,
SM6 . . . . 219 A2
Beddington Gn BR5 . . . . 189 D2
Beddington Gr SM6 . . . . 219 D3
Beddington Inf Sch
SM6 . . . . 219 C4
Beddington La
Wallington CR0 . . . . 203 D2
Wallington CR0 . . . . 220 A6
Beddington Lane Sta
CR0 . . . . 203 C3
Beddington Manor
SM2 . . . . 218 B2
Beddington Park Cotts
SM6 . . . . 219 D5
Beddington Park Prim Sch
CR0 . . . . 219 D5
Beddington Rd
Ilford IG3 . . . . 57 D2
St Paul's Cray BR5 . . . . . 189 D2
Beddington Terr CR0 . . 204 B2
Beddington Trad Est
CR0 . . . . 204 A1
Bede Cl HA5 . . . . 22 D2
Bedefield WC1 . . . . 233 B1
Bede Ho London SE14 . . 141 B4
5 Putney SW15 . . . . 156 D5
Bedelsford Sch KT1 . . . . 198 A6
Bedens Rd DA14 . . . . . . 191 A5
Bede Rd RM6 . . . . 58 C3
Bedevere Rd N9 . . . . 18 A1
Bedfont Cl
East Bedfont TW14 . . . . . 149 A5
Mitcham CR4 . . . . 181 A1
Bedfont Green Cl
TW14 . . . . 149 A3
Bedfont Ind Pk TW15 . . 149 B1
Bedfont Ind Pk N
TW15 . . . . 149 A1
Bedfont Jun & Inf Schs
TW14 . . . . 149 C5
Bedfont La TW14,
TW13 . . . . 149 D4
Bedfont Lakes Ctry Pk
TW14 . . . . 149 A2
Bedfont Rd
East Bedfont TW13,
TW14 . . . . 149 B2
Stanwell TW19 . . . . 148 B5
Bedford Ave Barnet EN5 . . 13 B6
Bloomsbury
WC1 . . . . 93 D2 239 D3
Hayes UB4 . . . . 84 B1
Bedfordbury
WC2 . . . . 116 A6 250 A5
Bedford Cl
Chiswick W4 . . . . 133 D6
Muswell Hill N10 . . . . 31 A3
Bedford Cnr 3 W4 . . . . 111 C2
Bedford Court Mans
WC1 . . . . 239 D3
Bedford Ct
6 Richmond TW9 . . . . . . 132 B1
South Norwood SE19 . . . 183 D2
St James WC2 . . . . 250 A5
Wembley HA0 . . . . 65 D4
Bedford Gardens Ho
W8 . . . . 245 B3
Bedford Gdns
W8 . . . . 113 C5 245 B3
Bedford Hill SW12 . . . . . 159 B2
Bedford Ho
2 Acton W4 . . . . 111 C2
Edgware HA8 . . . . 26 B3
7 Stockwell SW4 . . . . . 138 A1
Bedford Mews SE6 . . . . 163 D2
BEDFORD PARK 111 C3
Bedford Park Cnr 5
W4 . . . . 111 C2
Bedford Park Mans 4
W4 . . . . 111 B2
Bedford Pas SW6 . . . . . 264 B4
Bedford Pk CR0 . . . . 205 A1
Bedford Pl
Bloomsbury
WC1 . . . . 94 A2 240 A4
Croydon CR0 . . . . 205 B1
Bedford Rd Acton W4 . . . 111 C3
Barking E6 . . . . 100 C6
Crouch End N8 . . . . 49 D3
Ealing W13 . . . . 109 B6
East Finchley N2 . . . . 48 C6
Edgware NW7 . . . . 11 C1
Edmonton N9 . . . . 18 B4
Harrow HA1 . . . . 42 A3
Ilford IG1 . . . . 78 D5
North Cheam KT4 . . . . . . 216 C6
Ruislip HA4 . . . . 61 D4
Sidcup DA15 . . . . 167 C1
South Tottenham N15 . . . . 51 C5
Stockwell SW2, SW4 . . . . 138 A1
Twickenham TW2 . . . . . . 152 B1
Walthamstow E17 . . . . 53 C6
Woodford E18 . . . . 37 A1
Wood Green N22 . . . . 32 A1
Bedford Row
WC1 . . . . 94 B2 240 D3
Bedford Sq
WC1 . . . . 93 D2 239 D3
Bedford St
WC2 . . . . 116 A6 250 B5
Bedford Terr SM2 . . . . . . 218 A2
Bedford Villas 3 SM5 . . 218 D5
Bedford Way
WC1 . . . . 93 D3 239 D5
Bedgebury Gdns
SW19 . . . . 157 A2
Bedgebury Rd SE9 . . . . . 143 D1
Bedivere Rd BR1 . . . . . . 165 A1
Bedlam Mews SE11 . . . 261 A4
Bedlow Cl NW8 . . . . 236 D5
Bedlow Way CR0 . . . . . . 220 B4
Bedonwell Inf Sch
DA17 . . . . 147 A6
Bedonwell Jun Sch
DA17 . . . . 147 A6
Bedonwell Rd
Bexley DA17 . . . . 147 A6
Erith DA7 . . . . 147 C5
Bedser Cl
Kennington SE11 . . . . . . 270 D6
South Norwood CR7 . . . . 205 A6
Bedser Ct 7 SW4 . . . . . 138 A3
Bedser Dr UB6 . . . . 64 B3
Bedster Gdns KT8 . . . . . 195 D6
Bedwardine Rd SE19 . . . 183 C3
Bedwell Ct 4 RM6 . . . . . . 58 D2
Bedwell Gdns UB3 . . . . . 105 C2
Bedwell Ho 18 SW9 . . . 138 C3
Bedwell Rd
Belvedere DA17 . . . . 125 C1
Tottenham N17 . . . . 33 C2
Beeby Rd E16 . . . . 99 B2
Beech Ave Acton W3 . . . . 111 C5
Brentford TW8 . . . . 131 B5
4 Chigwell IG9 . . . . 21 B2
East Barnet N20 . . . . 14 C3
Ruislip HA4 . . . . 40 B1
Sidcup DA15 . . . . 168 A4
Beech Cl Ashford TW15 . . 171 B5
Carshalton SM5 . . . . 218 D6
Deptford SE8 . . . . 141 B6
Enfield N9 . . . . 18 B5
Putney SW15 . . . . 156 A4
Sunbury TW16 . . . . 172 D1
West Drayton UB7 . . . . . 104 C3
Wimbledon SW19 . . . . . . 178 C4
Beech Copse
Bickley BR1 . . . . 188 B1
South Croydon CR2 . . . . 221 C3
Beechcroft
Chislehurst West
BR7 . . . . 188 C3
3 Kingston u T KT2 . . . . 176 D2
Beechcroft Ave
Golders Green NW11 . . . . 47 B2
Harrow HA2 . . . . 41 C2
Kingston u T KT1, KT3 . . 177 A1
Beechcroft Cl
Heston TW5 . . . . 129 A5
Orpington BR6 . . . . 227 B4
Streatham SW16 . . . . 182 B5
Beechcroft Ct
3 Golders Green
NW11 . . . . 47 B2
Greenwich SE3 . . . . 143 A4
8 Woodside Pk N12 . . . . 29 D6
Beech Croft Ct N5 . . . . . . 72 D4
Beechcroft Gdns HA9 . . . 66 B5
Beechcroft Ho W5 . . . . . . 88 A2
Beechcroft Lo 6 SM2 . . 218 A1
Beechcroft Mans
SW16 . . . . 182 B5
Beechcroft Rd
Chessington KT9 . . . . 214 B5
Mortlake SW14 . . . . 133 A2
Orpington BR6 . . . . 227 B4
Upper Tooting SW17 . . . . 158 C2
Woodford E18 . . . . 37 B1
Beechcroft Way N19 . . . . 49 D1
Beech Ct
Beckenham BR3 . . . . 185 B3
3 Buckhurst Hill IG9 . . . . 21 D2
Child's Hill NW2 . . . . 69 B6
Hayes UB3 . . . . 105 D5
6 Ilford E12 . . . . 78 C5
Marylebone W1 . . . . 237 C2
Northolt UB5 . . . . 85 A6
43 Notting Hill W2 . . . . . . 91 C2
7 Rotherhithe SE16 . . . 119 A5
Surbiton KT6 . . . . 198 A2
Teddington TW11 . . . . . . 175 C4
Walthamstow E17 . . . . 54 B6
Beech Ct *continued*
4 West Norwood
SW16 . . . . 182 C5
Beechdale N21 . . . . 16 B2
Beechdale Rd SW2 . . . . . 160 B5
Beech Dell BR2, BR6 . . . 226 B4
Beechdene 4 SE15 . . . . 140 B4
Beech Dr N2 . . . . 48 D6
Beechen Cliff Way
TW7 . . . . 130 D3
Beechengrove HA5 . . . . . 41 B6
Beechen Pl SE23 . . . . . . 162 C2
Beeches Ave SM5 . . . . . . 218 C1
Beeches Cl SE20 . . . . . . 184 C2
Beeches Ct BR1 . . . . 187 A4
Beeches Prim Ctr The
SE2 . . . . 124 C3
Beeches Rd
Cheam SM3 . . . . 201 A1
Upper Tooting SW17 . . . . 158 D1
Beeches The
Ealing W7 . . . . 108 D4
East Barnet N20 . . . . 14 C2
East Ham E12 . . . . 78 B1
Hounslow TW3 . . . . 129 D4
Mitcham CR4 . . . . 202 C4
1 Upper Holloway N19 . . 50 A1
Beechey Ho 30 E1 . . . . . 118 B5
Beech Farm Cotts IG8 . . 36 B3
Beechfield Cotts 5
BR1 . . . . 187 C1
Beechfield Ct 7 CR2 . . . 221 A4
Beechfield Rd
Bromley BR1 . . . . 187 C1
Forest Hill SE6 . . . . 163 B3
Harringay N4 . . . . 51 A3
Beech Gdns
Dagenham RM10 . . . . 81 D1
Ealing W5 . . . . 110 A3
Beech Gr
Kingston u T KT3 . . . . 199 B6
Mitcham CR4 . . . . 203 D5
Beech Hall Cres E4 . . . . . 36 B3
Beech Hall Rd E4 . . . . 36 B3
Beech Hill EN4 . . . . 2 C5
Beech Hill Ave EN4 . . . . . . 2 B4
Beechhill Rd SE9 . . . . . . 166 C6
Beech Ho Chingford E4 . . . 35 C6
Hayes UB4 . . . . 84 D2
Heston TW5 . . . . 129 A5
6 Maitland Pk NW3 . . . . . 70 D2
New Addington CR0 . . . . 223 D2
22 Rotherhithe SE16 . . . . 118 C4
7 Sidcup DA15 . . . . 168 A1
5 Stoke Newington N16 . 73 B6
12 Wallington SM6 . . . . . 219 C2
Beech House Rd CR0 . . . 221 B5
Beech La IG9 . . . . 21 B2
Beech Lawns N12 . . . . 30 B5
Beechmont Cl BR1 . . . . . 186 C5
Beechmore Gdns
SM3 . . . . 216 D6
Beechmore Rd
SW11 . . . . 136 D4 267 D1
Beechmount Ave W7 . . . . 86 C2
Beecholme 15 N12 . . . . . . 29 D6
Beecholme Ave CR4 . . . . 181 B2
Beecholme Est E5 . . . . . . 74 B5
Beecholme Prim Sch
CR4 . . . . 181 B2
Beech Rd Bowes Pk N11 . . 32 A4
East Bedfont TW14 . . . . . 149 C4
Thornton Heath SW16 . . . 204 B6
Beechrow KT2 . . . . 176 A6
Beech St EC2 . . . . . 95 A2 242 B4
Beech Tree Cl
Islington N1 . . . . 72 C1
Stanmore HA7 . . . . 25 C5
Beech Tree Glade E4 . . . 20 D3
Beech Tree Pl SM1 . . . . . 217 D3
Beechvale Cl N12 . . . . 30 C5
Beechway DA5 . . . . 168 D5
Beech Way
Twickenham TW2 . . . . . . 151 C1
Willesden NW10 . . . . 67 B1
Beech Wlk NW7 . . . . 27 C4
Beechwood Ave
Ashford TW16 . . . . 172 A4
East Finchley N3 . . . . 47 C6
Greenford UB6 . . . . 85 D4
Harrow HA2 . . . . 63 D5
Hayes UB3 . . . . 105 B6
Hillingdon UB8 . . . . 82 C1
Orpington BR6 . . . . 227 C2
Richmond TW9 . . . . 132 C4
Ruislip HA4 . . . . 61 D6
Thornton Heath CR7 . . . . 204 D5
Beechwood Circ HA2 . . . 63 D5
Beechwood Cl
Edgware NW7 . . . . 27 C5
Fortis Green N2 . . . . 48 D5
Surbiton KT6 . . . . 197 D2
Beechwood Cres DA7 . . 147 A2
Beechwood Ct
Ashford TW16 . . . . 172 A5
Carshalton SM5 . . . . 218 D4
Cheam SM1 . . . . 217 C3
Chiswick W4 . . . . 133 B6
Stamford Hill N16 . . . . 51 C2
Sutton SM2 . . . . 218 B2
Beechwood Dr
Keston BR2 . . . . 225 D4
Woodford IG8 . . . . 36 D5
Beechwood Gdns
Ealing NW10 . . . . 88 B4
Harrow HA2 . . . . 63 D5
Ilford IG5 . . . . 56 C5
Beechwood Gr W3 . . . . . 111 C6
Beechwood Hall N3 . . . . . 47 B6
Beechwood Ho 23 E2 . . . 96 A5

Beechwood Mews 2 N9 18 A2
Beechwood Pk E18 55 A6
Beechwood Rd
Dalston E8 73 D2
London N8 50 A5
South Croydon CR2 221 C1
Beechwood Rise BR7 188 D6
Beechwoods Ct 5 SE19 183 D5
Beechworth Cl NW3 69 C6
Beecroft La SE4 163 A6
Beecroft Mews SE4 163 A6
Beecroft Rd SE4 163 A6
Beehive Cl Dalston E8 73 D1
Elstree WD6 9 D5
Hillingdon UB10 60 B1
Beehive Ct IG1 56 B3
Beehive La IG1 56 B3
Beehive Pl SW9 138 C2
Beehive Prep Sch IG4 56 B4
Beeken Dene BR6 227 A4
Beeleigh Rd SM4 201 D5
Beemans Row 1 SW18 158 A2
Beeston Cl
5 Dalston E8 74 A3
South Oxhey WD19 22 D6
Beeston Pl SW1 258 D6
Beeston Rd EN4 14 B5
Beeston's Ho SE15 140 B2
Beeston Way TW14 150 C5
Beethoven Rd WD6 9 D5
Beethoven St W10 91 A4
Beeton Cl HA5 23 C3
Begbie Ho SW9 138 B3
Begbie Rd SE3 143 C4
Beggars Hill KT17 215 D2
Beggar's Roost La SM1 217 C2
Begonia Cl E6 100 B3
Begonia Pl 1 TW12 173 C4
Begonia Wlk W12 89 D1
Beira St SW12 159 B4
Beis Chinuch Lebonos Girls Sch N4 51 A2
Beis Rochel d'Satmar Girls Sch N16 51 C2
Beis Soroh Schneirer (Sch) NW4 46 A3
Beis Yaakov Prim Sch NW9 45 B6
Bekesbourne St 17 E14 97 A1
Belcroft Cl BR1 186 D3
Beldanes Lo NW10 68 A1
Beldham Gdns KT8 195 D6
Belenoyd Ct SW16 160 B1
Belfairs Dr RM6 58 C2
Belfairs Gn WD19 22 D5
Belfast Rd
Croydon SE25 206 B5
Stoke Newington N16 73 D6
Belfield Rd KT19 215 C1
Belfont Wlk N7 72 A4
Belford Gr SE18 122 C2
Belford Ho 7 E8 95 D6
Belfort Rd SE15 140 C3
Belfry Cl 33 SE16 118 B1
Belgrade Ho N16 73 C4
Belgrade Rd
Hampton TW12 173 D2
Stoke Newington N16 73 C4
Belgrave Cl
1 Acton W3 111 A4
Burnt Oak NW7 27 B5
Southgate N14 15 C6
Belgrave Cres TW16 172 B2
Belgrave Ct
8 Acton Green W4 111 A1
Charlton SE3 143 C5
22 Limehouse E14 119 B6
Newham E13 99 C3
Nine Elms SW8 269 A3
Belgrave Gdns
Kilburn NW8 91 D6
Southgate N14 3 D1
1 Stanmore HA7 25 C5
St John's Wood NW8 229 A5
Belgrave Ho SW9 138 C5
Belgrave Hts E11 55 A1
Belgrave Mans NW8 229 A5
Belgrave Market IG1 78 C6
Belgrave Mews N SW1 248 A1
Belgrave Mews S SW1 115 A3 258 B6
Belgrave Mews W SW1 258 A6
Belgrave Pl SW1 115 A3 258 B5
Belgrave Rd
Barnes SW13 133 D5
Hounslow TW4 129 B2
Leyton E10 54 A1
Mitcham CR4 202 B6
Newham E13 99 C3
Redbridge IG1 56 B1
South Norwood SE25 205 D5
Sunbury TW16 172 B2
Walthamstow E17 53 C3
Wanstead E11 55 A1
Westminster SW1 115 C2 259 A3
Belgrave Sq SW1 115 A3 258 A6
Belgrave St E1 96 D1
Belgrave Terr IG8 21 A3
Belgrave Wlk CR4 202 B6
Belgrave Wlk Sta CR4 202 B5
Belgrave Yd SW1 258 C5
BELGRAVIA 115 B2
Belgravia Cl EN5 1 B2
Belgravia Ct SW1 258 C5
Belgravia Gdns BR1 186 C4
Belgravia Ho
11 London SW4 159 D5
1 Teddington TW11 175 C3
Belgravia Lo N21 16 D6
Belgravia Mews KT1 197 D5
Belgrove St WC1 233 B2
Belham Wlk 13 SE5 139 B4
Belinda Rd 8 SW9 138 D2
Belitha Villas N1 72 C1
Bel La TW13 151 B1
Bellamy Cl Edgware HA8 11 A1
13 Millwall E14 119 C4
Uxbridge UB10 60 C5
West Kensington SW5 254 D1
Bellamy Ct HA7 25 B2
Bellamy Dr HA7 25 B2
Bellamy Ho Harrow HA3 44 A2
Heston TW5 129 C6
Upper Tooting SW17 180 B6
Bellamy Rd Chingford E4 35 D4
Enfield EN2 5 B3
Bellamy's Ct 16 SE16 118 D5
Bellamy St SW12 159 B4
Bellasis Ave SW2 160 A2
Bell Ave UB7 104 B3
Bell Cl Pinner HA5 40 C6
Ruislip HA4 61 D5
Bellclose Rd UB7 104 A4
Bell Ct Hendon NW4 46 C5
Ladywell SE13 163 C6
Tolworth KT5 214 D6
Bell Dr SW18 157 A4
Bellefields Rd SW9 138 B2
Bellegrove Cl DA16 145 D3
Bellegrove Par DA16 145 D2
Bellegrove Rd DA16 145 D3
Bellenden Prim Sch SE15 140 A3
Bellenden Rd SE15 139 D3
Bellenden Rd Ret Pk SE15 140 A4
Bellendon Road Bsns Ctr SE15 139 D3
Bellerbys Coll SE8 141 C6
Bellermine Cl SE28 123 D4
Belle Staines Pleasaunce E4 19 C2
Belleville Prim Sch SW11 158 D6
Belleville Rd SW11 158 D6
Belle Vue UB6 86 B6
Belle Vue Gdns SW9 138 A3
Belle Vue La WD23 8 B3
Bellevue Mews N11 31 A5
Bellevue Pk CR7 205 A5
Bellevue Pl E1 96 C3
Bellevue Rd
Barnes SW13 134 A3
Bexley DA6 169 B6
Ealing W13 87 B3
Friern Barnet N11 31 A5
Kingston u T KT1 198 A6
Upper Tooting SW17 158 D3
Belle Vue Rd
Chingford E17 36 B1
8 Hendon NW4 46 C5
Bellew St SW17 158 A1
Bellfield CR0 223 B1
Bellfield Ave HA3 24 B4
Bell Flats 4 NW2 68 A2
Bellflower Cl 2 E6 100 A2
Bellflower Ct SE13 141 D1
Bellgate Mews NW5 71 B5
Bell Gn SE26 185 B6
Bellgrave Lo 9 W4 110 D1
BELL GREEN 163 B1
Bell Green La SE26 185 B6
Bell Ho
6 Dagenham RM10 81 D2
Greenwich SE10 142 A6
15 Streatham SW2 160 C4
Wembley HA9 66 A5
West Heath SE2 124 D1
Bellina Mews NW5 71 C4
Bell Ind Est 2 W4 111 A2
BELLINGHAM 185 C5
Bellingham 10 N17 34 B3
Bellingham Ct IG11 102 B4
Bellingham Gn SE6 163 C1
Bellingham Rd SE6 164 A1
Bellingham Sta SE6 163 D1
Bellingham Trad Est SE6 163 D2
Bell Inn Yd EC3 242 D1
Bell La Enfield EN3 6 D5
Hendon NW4 46 D5
Newham E16 121 A5
Spitalfields E1 95 D2 243 C3
Twickenham TW1 153 A3
Wembley HA9 65 D6
Bell Lane Prim Sch NW4 46 D5
Bell Language Sch W1 93 C3 239 A5
Bellmaker Ct 13 E3 97 C2
Bell Mdw SE19 183 C6
Bell Moor NW3 70 A5
Bellmore Ct 5 CR0 205 D1
Bello Cl SE24, SW2 160 D3
Bellot Gdns 1 SE10 120 C1
Bellot St SE10 120 C1
Bell Rd
East Molesey KT8 196 B4
Enfield EN1 5 B4
Hounslow TW3 129 D1
Bellring Cl DA17 147 C6
Bell's Coll IG3 58 A1
Bells Hill EN5 12 D6
Bell St Kidbrooke SE18 144 A4
Paddington NW1 92 C2 237 A4
Bell The E17 53 C6
Bell View BR3 185 B3
Bellview Ct TW3 129 D1
Bell View Manor HA4 39 C2
Bell Water Gate SE18 122 C3
Bell Wharf La EC4 252 B6
Bellwood Rd SE15 140 D1
Bell Yard Mews SE1 253 B1
Bell Yd WC2 94 C1 241 A1
BELMONT 25 B2
Belmont Ave
Bowes Pk N13 32 B5
Cockfosters EN4 14 D6
Edmonton N9 18 A3
Falconwood DA16 145 C2
Southall UB2 107 A3
Tottenham N17 51 A6
Wembley HA0 88 B6
West Barnes KT3 200 A5
Belmont Circ HA3 25 B2
Belmont Cl Chingford E4 36 B5
Clapham SW4 137 C2
Cockfosters EN4 2 D1
Totteridge N20 13 D3
Uxbridge UB8 60 A2
Woodford IG8 37 B6
Belmont Ct Highbury N5 73 A4
6 Stamford Hill N16 51 C1
Temple Fortune NW11 47 B4
1 Whetstone N20 14 A1
Wood Green N11 31 D3
Belmont Fst & Mid Schs HA3 24 D1
Belmont Gr
Chiswick W4 111 B2
Lewisham SE13 142 B2
Belmont Hall Ct SE13 142 B2
Belmont Hill SE13 142 B2
Belmont Jun & Inf Schs N22 51 A6
Belmont La
Chislehurst BR7 189 A5
Stanmore HA7 25 C3
Belmont Lo Harrow HA3 24 B3
Stanmore HA7 25 C6
Belmont Mews SW19 156 D2
Belmont Mill Hill Jun Sch NW7 12 A1
Belmont Par
Chislehurst BR7 189 A5
2 Temple Fortune NW11 47 B4
Belmont Park Cl SE13 142 C1
Belmont Park Rd E10 53 D3
Belmont Pk SE13 142 C1
Belmont Pk Sch E10 54 A3
Belmont Prim Sch
Chiswick W4 111 B2
Erith DA8 147 C5
Belmont Rd
Beckenham BR3 185 B1
Chislehurst BR7 188 D5
Clapham SW4 137 C2
Croydon SE25 206 B4
Erith DA8 147 D4
Harrow HA3 43 A6
Ilford IG1 79 A5
London W4 111 B2
Twickenham TW2 152 B2
Uxbridge UB8 60 A2
Wallington SM6 219 C3
West Green N15, N17 51 A5
Belmont Rise SM1, SM2 217 B1
Belmont St NW1 71 A1
Belmont Terr W4 111 B2
Belmor WD6 10 C5
Belmore Ave UB4 84 A1
Belmore Ho N7 71 D3
Belmore La N7 71 D3
Belmore Prim Sch UB4 84 B4
Belmore St SW8 137 D4 269 C2
Beloe Cl SW15 134 A1
Belper Ct 11 E5 74 D4
Belsham St E9 74 C2
Belsize Ave
Bowes Pk N13 32 B4
Ealing W13 109 B3
Maitland Pk NW3 70 C3
Belsize Court Garages 1 NW3 70 B3
Belsize Cres NW3 70 B2
Belsize Ct NW3 70 B3
Belsize Gdns SM1 217 D4
Belsize Gr NW3 70 C2
Belsize La NW3 70 B3
Belsize Mews NW3 70 B2
Belsize Park Gdns NW3 70 C2
Belsize Park Mews 1 NW3 70 B2
Belsize Park Sta NW3 70 C3
Belsize Pk NW3 70 B2
Belsize Pl NW3 70 B3
Belsize Rd Harrow HA3 24 B3
Kilburn NW6 91 D6
Belsize Sq NW3 70 B2
Belsize Terr NW3 70 B2
Belson Rd SE18 122 B2
Beltane Dr SW19 156 D1
Belthorn Cres SW12 159 C4
Belton Rd Leyton E11 76 C4
Sidcup DA14 190 A6
Tottenham N17 51 C6
Upton E7 77 B1
Willesden NW2 68 A2
Belton Way E3 97 C2
Beltran Rd SW6 135 D3
BELVEDERE 125 D2
Belvedere Ave SW19 179 A5
Belvedere Bldgs SE1 251 D1
Belvedere Cl TW11 174 C5
Belvedere Ct
Abbey Wood DA17 125 B3
Brondesbury NW2 68 D2
7 Clapham Pk SW4 159 D5
East Finchley N2 48 B4
8 Kingston u T KT2 176 C3
Putney SW15 134 C1
33 Shoreditch N1 95 C6
Southall UB1 107 D6
Southgate N21 16 C4
Belvedere Dr SW19 179 A5
Belvedere Gdns KT8 195 C4
Belvedere Gr SW19 179 A5
Belvedere Ho TW14 150 A3
Belvedere Htss NW8 237 A6
Belvedere Jun & Inf Sch DA17 125 D3
Belvedere Mews
Greenwich SE3 143 B5
Nunhead SE15 140 C2
Belvedere Pl
Brixton SW2 138 B1
Lambeth SE1 251 D1
Belvedere Rd
Bexleyheath DA7 147 B3
Erith SE2, SE28 124 D5
Hanwell W7 108 D3
Lambeth SE1 116 B5 250 D3
Penge SE19 183 D3
Walthamstow E10 53 A1
Belvedere Sq SW19 179 A5
Belvedere Sta DA17 125 D3
Belvedere Strand NW9 27 D1
Belvedere The SW10 266 B1
Belvedere Way HA3 44 A3
Belvoir Cl SE9 166 A1
Belvoir Ct HA3 43 A3
Belvoir Lo SE22 162 A4
Belvoir Rd SE22 162 A4
Belvue Bsns Ctr UB5 63 D1
Belvue Cl UB5 63 C1
Belvue Rd UB5 63 C1
Belvue Sch UB5 85 C6
Bembridge Cl NW6 69 A1
Bembridge Gdns HA4 61 B6
Bembridge Ho
9 Deptford SE8 119 B2
Wandsworth SW18 157 D5
Bemersyde Point 6 E13 99 B4
Bemerton St N1 94 B6 233 C6
Bemish Rd SW15 134 D2
Bempton Dr HA4 62 B5
Bemsted Rd E17 53 B6
Benabo Ct 6 E8 74 A3
Benares Rd SE18, SE2 123 D2
Benbow Ct W6 112 B3
Benbow Ho 12 SE8 141 C6
Benbow Rd W6 112 B3
Benbow St SE8 141 C6
Benbury Cl BR1 186 A5
Bence Ho 13 SE8 119 A2
Bench Field CR2 221 D3
Bencroft Rd SW16 181 C3
Bencurtis Pk BR4 224 B6
Bendall Mews NW1 237 B4
Bendemeer Rd SW15 134 D2
Benden Ho SE13 164 A6
Bendish Point SE28 123 A4
Bendish Rd E6 78 A1
Bendmore Ave SE2 124 A2
Bendon Valley SW18 157 D4
Benedict Cl
9 Erith DA17 125 A3
Orpington BR6 227 C5
Benedict Ct
Dagenham RM9 59 B3
Pinner HA5 23 B2
Benedict Dr TW14 149 B4
Benedict House Prep Sch DA15 168 A1
Benedict Prim Sch CR4 202 B6
Benedict Rd
London SW9 138 B2
Mitcham CR4 202 B6
Benedict Way N2 48 A6
Benedict Wharf CR4 202 C6
Benenden Gn BR2 209 A4
Benenden Ho SE17 263 B2
Benett Gdns SW16 182 A1
Beney Ct BR3 185 C1
Ben Ezra Ct SE17 262 B3
Benfleet Cl SM1 218 A5
Benfleet Ct 6 E8 95 D6
Benfleet Way N11 15 A2
Bengal Ct EC3 242 D1
Bengal Ho E1 96 D2
Bengal Rd IG1 78 D5
Bengarth Dr HA3 24 B1
Bengarth Rd UB5 85 A6
Bengeo Gdns RM6 58 C3
Bengeworth Rd
Camberwell SE5 139 A2
Harrow HA1 65 A5
Ben Hale Cl HA7 25 B5
Benham Cl
1 Battersea SW11 136 B2
Chessington KT9 213 C2
Benham Gdns TW3, TW4 151 B6
Benham Ho SW10 265 D4
Benham Rd W7 86 C2
Benham's Pl 11 NW3 70 A4
Benhill Ave SM1 218 A4
Benhill Rd London SE5 139 B4
Sutton SM1 218 B4
Benhill Wood Rd SM1 218 A4
BENHILTON 218 A5
Benhilton Ct SM1 218 A5
Benhilton Gdns SM1 217 D5
Benhurst Ct Ealing W5 110 A6
12 Penge SE20 184 B2
West Norwood SW16 182 C5
Benhurst La SW16 182 C5
Benington Ct N4 73 A6
Benin St SE13 164 B4
Benjafield Cl N18 34 B6
Benjamin Cl E8 96 A6
Benjamin Ct
4 Ealing W7 108 C5
4 Erith DA17 147 B6
Littleton TW15 171 A3
Benjamin Ho 12 W3 110 D5
Benjamin Mews SW12 159 C4
Benjamin St EC1 241 C4
Ben Jonson Ct 30 N1 95 C5
Ben Jonson Prim Sch E1 97 A3
Ben Jonson Rd E1 97 A2
Benledi Rd E14 98 B1
Bennelong Cl W12 90 B1
Bennerley Rd SW11 158 D6
Bennet Cl KT1 175 C2
Bennets Ct SW19 180 A2
Bennetsfield Rd UB11 104 D5
Bennet's Hill EC4 251 D6
Bennets Lo EN2 5 A2
Bennett Cl
Twickenham TW4 151 A6
Welling DA16 146 A3
Bennett Ct
Hampstead NW6 69 D2
Lower Holloway N7 72 B5
7 South Acton W3 110 D4
Bennett Gr SE13 141 D4
Bennett Ho
2 Streatham SW4 159 D4
Westminster SW1 259 D4
Bennett Pk SE3 142 D2
Bennett Rd
Brixton SW9 138 C3
Dagenham RM6 59 A2
Newham E13 99 C3
Bennetts Ave
Croydon CR0 223 A6
Greenford UB6 86 C6
Bennett's Castle La RM8 80 D5
Bennetts Cl
Mitcham CR4, SW16 181 B2
Tottenham N17 33 D4
Bennetts Copse BR7 188 A4
Bennett St
Chiswick W4 111 C1
St James SW1 249 A4
Bennetts Way CR0 223 B6
Bennett's Yd SW1 259 D5
Benn Ho
Bethnal Green E2 96 A4
7 Greenwich SE7 121 C1
Benningholme Rd HA8 27 C4
Bennington Rd
Chingford IG8 36 C3
Tottenham N17 33 C2
Benn St E9 75 A2
Benns Wlk 8 TW9 132 A1
Bensbury Cl SW15 156 C4
Bensham Cl CR7 205 A5
Bensham Gr CR7 183 A1
Bensham La CR0, CR7 204 D3
Bensham Manor Rd CR7 205 A5
Bensham Manor Sch CR7 205 A4
Bensington Ct TW14 149 B5
Bensley Cl 7 N11 30 D5
Ben Smith Way 21 SE16 118 A3
Benson Ave E13, E6 99 D5
Benson Cl
Hillingdon UB8 82 A2
Hounslow TW3 129 C1
Benson Ct Holdbrook EN3 7 C5
South Lambeth SW8 270 A2
1 Tufnell Pk N19 71 C4
Benson Ho
Lambeth SE1 251 B3
1 Richmond TW10 153 C1
Shoreditch E2 243 C6
Benson Prim sch CR0 223 A5
Benson Quay E1 118 C6
Benson Rd
Croydon CR0 220 C5
Forest Hill SE23 162 C3
Bentall Sh Ctr The 10 KT1 176 A1
Bentfield Gdns SE9 165 D1
Benthal Ct N16 74 A5
Benthal Prim Sch N16 74 A5
Benthal Rd N16 74 A5
Bentham Ct 11 N1 73 A1
Bentham Ho SE1 262 C6
Bentham Rd
Homerton E9 74 D2
Woolwich SE28 124 B5
Bentham Wlk NW10 67 A3
Ben Tillet Cl E16 122 B5
Ben Tillet Ho N15 50 D6
Bentinck Cl NW8 230 B3
Bentinck Ho
4 Richmond TW10 153 C1
4 Shepherd's Bush W12 112 B6
Bentinck Mans W1 238 B2
Bentinck Mews W1 238 B2
Bentinck Rd UB7 104 A5
Bentinck St W1 93 A1 238 B2
Bentley Cl SW19 157 C1
Bentley Ct SE13 142 A1
Bentley Dr IG2 57 A3
Bentley Ho 6 Bow E3 97 C3
4 Camberwell SE5 139 C4
Bentley Lo WD23 8 C2
Bentley Mews EN1 17 B5
Bentley Rd N1 73 C2
Bentley Way
Stanmore HA7 25 A5
Woodford IG8 21 A1
Bentley Wood High Sch HA7 24 D5
Benton Rd
Ilford IG1, IG2 57 B1
South Oxhey WD19 22 D5
Benton's La SE27 183 A6
Benton's Rise SE27 183 B5
Bentry Cl RM8 81 A6
Bentry Rd RM8 81 B6
Bentworth Ct 1 E2 96 A3
Bentworth Prim Sch W12 90 B1
Bentworth Rd W12 90 B1
Benwell Ct TW16 172 A2
Benwell Rd N7 72 C3
Benwick Cl SE16 118 B2
Benwick Ct SE20 184 C2
Benwood Ct SM1 218 A5
Benworth St E3 97 B4
Benyon Ho EC1 234 B2
Benyon Rd N1 95 B6 235 D6
Benyon Wharf 31 E8 95 C6
Beormund Prim Sch SE1 117 B4 252 D1
Bequerel Ct SE10 120 D3
Berberis Ct IG1 78 D2
Berberis Ho 17 E3 97 C2
Berberis Wlk UB7 104 A2
Berber Pl 2 E14 119 C6
Berber Rd SW11 158 D6
Berberry Cl 5 HA8 27 A6
Bercta Rd SE9 167 A2
Berebinder Ho 21 E3 97 B5
Berengers Pl RM9 80 B2
Berenger Twr SW10 266 C4
Berenger Wlk SW10 266 C4
Berens Ct DA14 189 D6
Berens Rd NW10 90 D4
Berens Way BR5, BR7 211 D6
Beresford Ave
Ealing W7 86 C2
Friern Barnet N20 14 D2
Tolworth KT5 199 A2
Twickenham TW1 153 C5
Wembley HA0 88 C6
Beresford Ct
Homerton E9 75 A3
11 Twickenham TW1 153 C5
Beresford Dr
Bickley BR1 210 A6
Woodford IG8 37 C6
Beresford Gdns
Dagenham RM6 59 A4
Enfield EN1 5 C1
Hounslow TW4 151 B6
Beresford Ho
Dulwich SE21 161 C1
15 Stockwell SW4 138 A1
Beresford Lo N4 73 B3
Beresford Rd
Belmont SM2 217 B1
Canonbury N5 73 B3
Chingford E4 20 C3
East Finchley N2 48 C6
Harringay N8 50 D4
Harrow HA1 42 B4
Kingston u T KT2 176 B2
New Malden KT3 199 A5
Southall UB1 106 D5
Walthamstow E17 35 D2
Beresford Sq 1 SE18 122 D2
Beresford Square Mkt SE18 122 D2
Beresford St SE18 122 D3
Beresford Terr 3 N5 73 A3
Bere St E1 118 D6
Berestede Rd 4 W6 111 D1
Bergen Ho 1 SE5 139 A3
Bergenia Ho TW13 150 B3
Bergen Sq SE16 119 A3
Berger Cl BR5 211 C3
Berger Prim Sch E9 74 D2
Berger Rd E9 74 D2
Berghem Mews W14 112 D3
Bergholt Ave IG4 56 A4
Bergholt Cres N16 51 C2
Bergholt Mews 4 NW1 71 D1
Berglen Ct E14 119 A6
Berica Ct IG6 57 A6
Bering Sq E14 119 C1
Bering Wlk E16 99 D1
Berisford Mews SW18 158 A5
Berkeley Ave
Cranford TW4 128 A3
Erith DA16 146 D4
Northolt UB6 64 C2
Berkeley Cl
Borehamwood WD6 10 C6
Broom Hill BR5 211 C2
2 Kingston u T KT2 176 A3
Ruislip HA4 62 A5

Berkeley Cres EN4 14 B6
Berkeley Ct Ealing W5 109 C6
Edgware HA8 26 D5
Finchley N3 29 D2
1 Golders Green NW11 47 B2
Marylebone NW1 237 D5
Southgate N14 15 C5
Wallington SM6 219 C4
Willesden NW10 67 C4
Berkeley Dr KT8 195 C6
Berkeley Gdns
Claygate KT10 213 A2
Kensington W8 245 B3
Southgate N21 17 B4
Walton-on-T KT12 193 D2
Berkeley Ho 17 Bow E3 97 C4
11 Brentford TW8 131 D6
8 Deptford SE8 119 B1
Berkeley Lo Enfield EN2 4 C2
New Malden KT3 199 C5
Berkeley Mews
Marylebone W1 237 D1
Sunbury TW16 194 C6
Berkeley Pl SW19 178 D4
Berkeley Prim Sch
TW5 128 D5
Berkeley Rd
Barnes SW13 134 A4
Crouch End N8 49 D3
Hillingdon UB10 61 A1
Manor Pk E12 78 A3
Queensbury NW9 44 C4
Stamford Hill N15 51 B3
Berkeley Sq
W1 115 B6 248 D5
Berkeley St
W1 115 B5 248 D4
Berkeleys The SE25 206 A5
Berkeley The NW11 47 D2
Berkeley Waye TW5 128 D5
Berkeley Wlk 1 N7 72 B6
Berkhampstead Rd
DA17 125 C1
Berkhamsted Ave HA9 66 C2
Berkley Cl TW2 152 C1
Berkley Ct 8 TW1 153 A4
Berkley Gr NW1 71 A1
Berkley Rd NW1 70 D1
Berkshire Ct 1 W7 86 D3
Berkshire Gdns
Bowes Pk N13 32 C4
Upper Edmonton N18 34 B5
Berkshire Ho
Catford SE6 185 C6
St Giles WC2 240 A2
Berkshire Rd E9 75 B2
Berkshire Way CR4 204 A5
Bermans Way NW10 67 D4
BERMONDSEY 118 A4
Bermondsey Leather Mkt
SE1 253 A1
Bermondsey Mkt*
SE1 117 C3 263 B6
Bermondsey Sq SE1 263 B6
Bermondsey St
SE1 117 C4 253 A1
Bermondsey Trad Est
SE16 118 C1
Bermondsey Wall E
SE16 118 B4
Bermondsey Wall W SE1,
SE16 118 A4
Bermuda Ho HA1 64 B5
Bernal Cl SE28 124 D6
Bernard Angell Ho 4
SE10 142 B6
Bernard Ashley Dr
SE7 121 B1
Bernard Ave W13 109 B3
Bernard Cassidy St 2
E16 98 D2
Bernard Gdns SW19 179 B5
Bernard Ho E1 243 C3
Bernard Rd
South Tottenham N15 51 D4
Wallington SM5, SM6 219 B4
Bernard Shaw Ct 5
NW1 71 C1
Bernard Shaw Ho 2
NW10 89 B6
Bernard St WC1 94 A3 240 B5
Bernays Cl HA7 25 C4
Bernay's Gr SW9 138 B1
Bernel Dr CR0 223 B5
Berne Rd CR7 205 A4
Berners Dr W13 109 A6
Berners Ho N1 234 A4
Bernersmede SE3 143 A2
Berners Mews
W1 93 C2 239 B3
Berners Pl W1 239 B2
Berners Rd Islington N1 234 C5
Wood Green N22 32 C1
Berners St W1 93 C1 239 B2
Berner Terr 27 E1 96 A1
Berney Ho BR3 207 A4
Berney Rd CR0 205 B2
Bernhard Baron Ho 23
E1 96 A1
Bernhardt Cres NW8 237 A6
Bernhart Cl HA8 27 A3
Bernie Grant Ho 40 E9 74 C1
Bernwell Rd E4 20 C1
Bernwood Ho 6 N4 51 B2
Berridge Gn HA8 26 C3
Berridge Mews NW6 69 C3
Berridge Rd SE19 183 C5
Berriman Rd N7 72 B5
Berrite Works UB7 104 C4
Berriton Rd HA2 41 B1
Berrybank Cl 4 E4 20 A2
Berry Cl
Dagenham RM10 81 C3
Southgate N21 16 D3
Berry Cotts 2 E14 97 A1
Berry Ct TW4 151 B6
Berrydale Rd UB4 85 A3
Berryfield Cl BR1 188 A1
Berry Field Cl 8 E17 53 D5
Berryfield Rd
SE17 116 D1 261 D2
Berryhill SE9 144 D1
Berry Hill HA7 25 D6
Berryhill Gdns SE9 144 D1
Berry Ho
10 Battersea SW11 136 D3
25 Bethnal Green E1 96 B3
Berry La SE21 183 B6
BERRYLANDS 198 C3
Berrylands
Surbiton KT5 198 C3
West Barnes SW20 200 C5
Berrylands Ct 16 SM2 217 D1
Berrylands Rd KT5 198 B3
Berrylands Sta KT5 198 D5
Berryman Cl RM8 80 C5
Berryman's La SE26 184 D6
Berrymead Gdns W3 111 A4
Berrymede Inf Sch
W3 110 D4
Berrymede Jun Sch
W3 110 D4
Berrymede Rd W4 111 B3
Berry Pl EC1 234 D1
Berry St EC1 241 D5
Berry Way W5 110 A3
Bertal Rd SW17 180 B6
Bertha Hollamby Ct
DA14 190 C5
Bertha James Ct BR2 209 B5
Bertha Neubergh Ho 1
SE5 139 A4
Berthan Gdns E17 54 B4
Berthon St SE8 141 C6
Bertie Rd Penge SE26 184 D4
Willesden NW10 68 A2
Bertram Cotts SW19 179 C3
Bertram Rd Enfield EN1 6 A1
Hendon NW4 46 A3
Kingston u T KT2 176 C3
Bertram St N19 71 B6
Bertrand Ho 11 SW16 160 A1
Bertrand St SE13 141 D2
Bertrand Way SE28 124 C6
Bert Rd CR7 205 A4
Bert Reilly Ho 1 SE18 123 B1
Bertrum House Sch
SW17 159 A2
Bert Way EN1 5 D1
Berwick Ave UB4 106 D6
Berwick Cl Harrow HA7 24 D4
Twickenham TW2 151 C3
Berwick Cres DA15 167 C5
Berwick Ct 8 BR3 185 C2
Berwick Gdns SM1 218 A5
Berwick Ho 10 N2 30 B1
Berwick Rd
Newham E16 99 C1
Tottenham N22 32 D2
Welling DA16 146 B4
Berwick St W1 93 C1 239 B1
Berwyn Ave TW3 129 D4
Berwyn Ho 3 N16 51 D1
Berwyn Rd
Mortlake SW14,
TW10 132 D1
Streatham SE24 160 D3
Beryl Ave E6 100 A2
Beryl Harding Ho 3
SW19 178 D3
Beryl Ho SE18 123 D1
Beryl Rd W6 112 D1
Berystede KT2 176 D3
Besant Cl NW2 69 A5
Besant Ct Canonbury N1 73 B3
15 Thamesmead SE28 124 B6
Besant Ho NW8 229 A5
Besant Pl SE22 139 D1
Besant Rd NW2 69 A4
Besant Way NW10 67 A3
Besant Wlk N7 72 B6
Besford Ho 26 E2 96 A5
Besley St SW16 181 C4
Bessant Dr TW9 132 D4
Bessborough Gdns
SW1 115 D1 259 D2
Bessborough Pl
SW1 115 D1 259 D2
Bessborough Rd
Harrow HA1 42 B1
Roehampton SW15 156 A3
Bessborough St
SW1 115 D1 259 C2
Bessborough Wks
KT8 195 B4
Bessemer Ct 7 NW1 71 C1
Bessemer Grange Prim
Sch SE5 139 C1
Bessemer Park Ind Est 3
SE24 138 D1
Bessemer Rd SE5 139 A3
Bessie Lansbury Cl
E6 100 C1
Bessingby Rd HA4 62 B6
Bessingham Wlk SE4 162 D6
Besson St SE14 140 D4
Bessy St E2 96 C4
Bestwood St SE8 118 D2
Beswick Mews 1 NW6 69 D2
Betam Rd UB3 105 B4
Beta Pl 20 SW4 138 B1
Betchworth Cl SM1 218 B3
Betchworth Ho 8 N7 71 D3
Betchworth Rd IG3 79 C5
Betham Rd UB6 86 B4
Bethany Ct 8 DA6 147 A1
Bethany Waye TW14 149 C4
Bethecar Rd HA1 42 C4
Bethel Cl NW4 46 D4
Bethell Ave Ilford IG1 56 C2
Newham E13, E16 98 D3
Bethel Lo N11 31 C5
Bethel Rd DA16 146 C2
Bethersden Cl BR3 185 B3
Bethersden Ho SE17 263 B2
Bethesda Ct 5 SE20 184 C3
Beth Jacob Gram Sch
NW4 46 D5
Bethlehem Ho 13 E14 119 B6
Bethlem Royal Hospl
BR3 207 C2
BETHNAL GREEN 96 B4
Bethnal Green Rd
Bethnal Green E2 96 A4
Shoreditch E1,
E2 95 D3 243 D6
Bethnal Green Sta
Bethnal Green E1 96 B3
Bethnal Green E2 96 C4
Bethnal Green Tech Coll
E2 95 D4
Beths Gram Sch DA5 169 D5
Bethune Ave N11 30 D6
Bethune Rd
North Acton NW10 89 B3
Stamford Hill N16 51 C2
Bethwin Rd SE5 139 A5
Betjeman Cl HA5 41 C5
Betjeman Ct EN4 15 A6
Betony Cl CR0 206 D1
Betoyne Ave E4 36 C6
Betsham Ho SE1 252 C2
Betspath Ho 6 N11 31 C5
Betstyle Circus N11 31 B6
Betstyle Ho 2 N10 31 A3
Betstyle Rd N11 31 B6
Betterton Dr DA14 169 A2
Betterton Ho WC2 240 B1
Betterton St
WC2 94 A1 240 B1
Bettons Pk E15 98 C6
Bettridge Rd SW6 135 B3
Betts Cl BR3 185 A1
Betts Ho E1 118 B6
Betts Mews E17 53 B3
Betts Rd E16 121 B6
Betts St E1 118 B6
Betts Way
Long Ditton KT6 197 B1
Penge SE20 184 B2
Bettswood Ct 15 SE20 184 B2
Betty Brooks Ho E11 76 B5
Betty Layward Prim Sch
N16 73 B5
Betty May Gray Ho 2
E14 120 A2
Beulah Ave CR7 183 A1
Beulah Cl HA8 10 D1
Beulah Cres CR7 183 A1
Beulah Gr CR0 205 A3
Beulah Hill SE19 183 A3
Beulah Inf Sch CR7 205 A6
Beulah Jun Sch CR7 205 A6
Beulah Rd
Merton SW19 179 B3
South Norwood CR7 205 A6
Sutton SM1 217 C4
Walthamstow E17 53 D4
Beuleigh Ct E17 54 B4
Bevan Ave IG11 80 A1
Bevan Ct Croydon CR0 220 C3
10 Twickenham TW1 153 D5
Bevan Ho IG11 80 B1
Bevan Rd Cockfosters EN4 2 D1
Plumstead Comm SE2 124 B1
Bevan St N1 95 A6 235 B5
Bev Callender Cl 4
SW8 137 B2
Bevenden St N1 95 B4 235 D2
Bevercote Wlk 1
DA17 147 B6
Beveridge Ct
Southgate N21 16 A6
1 Thamesmead SE28 124 B6
Beveridge Rd 1 NW10 67 C1
Beverley DA14 190 A5
Beverley Ave
Hounslow TW4 129 B1
Sidcup DA15 167 D4
Wimbledon SW20 177 D2
Beverley Cl
Barnes SW13 134 A3
Chessington KT9 213 C4
Edmonton N21 17 A3
Enfield EN1 5 C1
6 Wandsworth SW11 136 B1
Beverley Cotts SW15 155 C1
Beverley Cres IG8 37 B2
Beverley Ct
9 Acton Green W4 111 A1
5 Acton W12 111 C4
Brockley SE4 141 B2
6 Cheam SM2 217 C2
Chingford Hatch E4 35 B6
Fortis Green N2 48 D5
Harrow HA2 42 B6
Hounslow TW4 129 B1
Beverley Ct continued
Islington N5 72 D2
Northolt UB5 84 C5
Oakleigh Pk N20 14 A4
Oakwood N14 15 C4
Sidcup DA14 190 B6
Wimbledon SW20 177 D2
Beverley Dr HA8 44 C6
Beverley Gdns
Barnes SW13 133 D2
Hendon NW11 47 A2
2 New Malden KT4 200 A1
Stanmore HA7 25 A2
Wembley HA9 44 C1
Beverley Ho 5 BR1 186 B5
Beverley Hyrst 10 CR0 221 D6
Beverley La KT2 177 C3
Beverley Lo 6 TW10 154 A6
Beverley Mans TW4 129 B1
Beverley Path 9
SW13 133 D3
Beverley Rd
Barnes SW13 133 D2
Chingford E4 36 B4
Chiswick W4 111 D1
Dagenham RM9 81 A4
Keston Mark BR2 226 A6
Mitcham CR4 203 D5
Newham E6 99 D4
North Cheam KT4 216 C6
Penge SE20 184 B1
Ruislip HA4 62 B6
Southall UB2 107 A3
Sunbury TW16 171 D2
Teddington KT1 175 C2
West Barnes KT3 200 A5
Beverley Trad Est
SM4 200 D2
Beverley Way KT3, SW20,
KT2 177 D2
Beverley Way (Kingston By
Pass) KT3, SW20 200 A6
Beverly Ct HA3 43 C5
Beversbrook Rd N19 71 D5
Beverstone Rd
London SW2 160 B6
Thornton Heath CR7 204 D5
Beverston Mews NW1 237 C3
Bevill Allen Cl SW17 180 D5
Bevill Cl SE25 206 A6
Bevin Cl SE16 119 A5
Bevin Ct WC1 233 D2
Bevington Prim Sch
W10 91 A2
Bevington Rd
Beckenham BR3 185 D1
Kensal Town W10 91 A2
Bevington St SE16 118 A4
Bevin Ho
35 Bethnal Green E2 96 C4
8 Bow E3 97 C4
Bevin Rd UB4 84 B4
Bevin Sq SW17 158 D1
Bevin Way WC1 234 A2
Bevis Marks
EC3 95 C1 243 B2
Bewcastle Gdns EN2 4 A1
Bew Ct SE21 162 A4
Bewdley Ho N4 51 A2
Bewdley St N1 72 C1
Bewick Mews SE15 140 B5
Bewick St SW8 137 B3
Bewley Ct SW2 160 B5
Bewley Ho 7 E1 118 B6
Bewley St Stepney E1 118 B6
Wimbledon SW19 180 A4
Bewlys Rd SE27 182 D5
Bexhill Cl TW13 151 A2
Bexhill Rd Catford SE4 163 B5
Mortlake SW14 133 A2
Wood Green N11 31 D5
Bexhill Wlk 6 E15 98 C6
BEXLEY 146 B1
Bexley Coll (Erith Rd
Campus) DA17 125 D1
Bexley Gdns
Edmonton N9 17 B1
Ilford RM6 58 B4
Bexley Gram Sch
DA16 146 B1
BEXLEYHEATH 147 B2
Bexleyheath Sch DA6 147 C2
Bexleyheath Sta DA7 147 A3
Bexley High St DA5 169 D3
Bexley Ho SE4 141 A1
Bexley La DA14 168 C1
Bexley Rd SE9 167 A6
Bexley Sta DA5 169 C3
Beynon Rd SM5 218 D3
BFI London Imax Cinema
SE1 116 C5 251 A3
Bglws The SM6 219 B3
Bianca Rd SE1, SE15 140 A6
Bibsworth Lo N3 29 B1
Bibsworth Rd N3 29 B1
Bicester Rd TW9 132 D2
Bickenhall Mans W1 237 D4
Bickenhall St
W1 92 D2 237 D4
Bickersteth Rd SW17 180 D4
Bickerton Rd N19 71 C6
BICKLEY 188 B1
Bickley Cres BR1 210 A5
Bickley Ct
10 Merton SW19 179 C3
1 Stanmore HA7 25 C6
Bickley Park Rd BR1,
BR7 210 B6
Bickley Park Sch BR1 210 A6
Bickley Prim Sch BR1 209 C6
Bickley Rd
Bromley BR1 187 D1
Leyton E10 53 D2
Bickley St SW17 180 D5
Bickley Sta BR1 210 A6
Bicknell Ho 34 E1 96 A1
Bicknell Rd SE5 139 A2
Bicknoller Rd EN1 5 D4
Bicknor Ho 2 E5 74 B3
Bicknor Rd BR6 211 D2
Bidborough Cl 3 BR2 208 D4
Bidborough St N1,
WC1 94 A4 233 A1
Biddenden Way SE9 188 C6
Biddenham Ho 18
SE16 118 D2
Bidder St E16 98 C2
Biddesden Ho SW3 257 C3
Biddestone Rd N7 72 B4
Biddulph Ho 22 SE18 122 B2
Biddulph Mans W9 91 D4
Biddulph Rd W9 91 D4
Bideford Ave UB6 87 B5
Bideford Cl
Edgware HA8 26 C2
Twickenham TW13 151 B1
Bideford Gdns EN1 17 C4
Bideford Rd
Catford BR1 164 D1
East Wickham DA16 146 B5
Enfield EN3 7 B5
Ruislip HA4 62 B5
Bidmead Ct KT6 214 A5
Bidwell Gdns N11 31 C3
Bidwell Ho
Southall UB2 107 A2
3 Willesden NW2 68 A5
Bidwell St SE15 140 B4
Big Ben* SW1 250 B1
Bigbury Cl N17 33 C3
Biggerstaff Rd E15 98 A6
Biggerstaff St N4 72 C6
Biggin Ave CR4 180 D2
Biggin Hill SE19 182 D3
Biggin Hill Cl KT2 175 C5
Biggin Way SE19 183 A3
Bigginwood Rd SW16 182 D3
Bigg's Row SW15 134 D2
Big Hill E5 52 B1
Bigland Green Prim Sch
E1 96 B1
Bigland St E1 96 B1
Bignell Rd SE18 122 D1
Bignold Rd E7 77 A4
Bigwood Ct NW11 47 D4
Bigwood Rd NW11 47 D3
Biko Ho 1 NW10 67 B1
Bilberry Ho 18 E3 97 C2
Bilberry Manor SM2 218 A1
Billet Rd Ilford RM6 58 C6
Walthamstow E17 35 B2
Billetts Hart Cl W7 108 C4
Bill Hamling Cl SE9 166 B2
Billie Holiday Ct NW10 89 B5
Billingford Cl SE4 140 D1
Billing Ho 7 E1 96 D1
Billingley NW1 232 A5
Billing Pl
SW10 135 D5 265 D4
Billing Rd
SW10 135 D5 265 D4
Billings Cl RM9 80 C1
Billingsgate Mkt E14 119 D5
Billing St
SW10 135 D5 265 D4
Billington Ho SW8 269 D1
Billington Rd SE14 140 D5
Billinton Hill CR0 221 B6
Billiter Sq EC3 243 B1
Billiter St EC3 95 C1 243 B1
Bill Nicholson Way
N17 33 D3
Billockby Cl KT9 214 B2
Billsley Ct SE25 205 C5
Billson St E14 120 A2
Bilsby Gr SE9 187 D6
Bilton Ho SW8 269 C1
Bilton Rd UB6 87 B6
Bilton Twrs W1 237 D1
Bilton Way Enfield EN3 7 B5
Hayes UB3 106 B4
Bina Gdns
SW5 114 A2 256 A3
Binbrook Ho 13 W10 90 C2
Bincote Rd EN2 4 B2
Binden Rd W12 111 D3
Bindon Gn SM4 201 D5
Binfield Ct SE5 139 A3
Binfield Rd
London SW4 138 A4 270 B1
South Croydon CR2 221 D3
Bingfield St N1 94 B6 233 C6
Bingham Cnr CR0 206 A1
Bingham Pl W1 93 A2 238 A4
Bingham Point 11
SE18 122 D2
Bingham Rd CR0 206 B1
Bingham St N1 73 B2
Bingley Rd
Ashford TW16 172 A3
Newham E16 99 C1
Southall UB6 86 A2
Binley Ho SW15 155 D5
Binney St W1 93 A1 238 B1
Binnie Ct SE10 141 D5
Binnie Ho SE1 262 A5
Binns Rd W4 111 C1
Binns Terr 3 W4 111 C1
Binsey Wlk 1 SE2 124 C4
Binstead Cl UB4 85 A2
Binstead Ho SW18 157 D5
Binyon Cres HA7 24 D5
Binyon Ho 8 N16 73 C4
Birbeck Ho 4 N19 49 D1
Birbetts Rd SE9 166 B2
Bircham Path SE4 140 D1
Birchanger Rd SE25 206 A4
Birch Ave Edmonton N13 17 A1
Hillingdon UB7 82 B1
Birch Cl Brentford TW8 131 B5
Buckhurst Hill IG9 21 D1
Hounslow TW3 130 B3
Newham E16 98 C2
Peckham SE15 140 A3
Romford RM7 59 D6
Teddington TW11 175 A5
Upper Holloway N19 71 C6
Birch Cres UB10 82 B6
Birch Ct Chingford E4 35 D4
Forest Gate E7 76 D4
Ilford RM6 58 C3
Sutton SM1 218 A4
9 Wallington SM6 219 B4
7 Woodside Pk N12 29 D6
Birchdale Gdns RM6 58 D2
Birchdale Rd E7 77 C3
Birchdene Dr SE28 124 A5
Birchdown Ho 32 E3 97 D4
Birchen Cl NW9 67 B6
Birchend Cl CR2 221 B2
Birchen Gr NW9 67 B6
Birches Cl
Mitcham CR4 202 D6
Pinner HA5 41 A4
Birches The
2 Beckenham BR2 208 D5
Bushey WD23 8 A6
Camberwell SE5 139 C3
Greenwich SE7 143 B6
Manor Pk E12 78 A4
Orpington BR6 226 C4
Southgate N21 16 B5
South Norwood SE25 183 D1
Twickenham TW4 151 B4
Birchfield Ho 3 E14 119 C6
Birchfield St E14 119 C6
Birch Gn NW9 27 C3
Birch Gr Acton W3 110 C6
Bexley DA16 146 A1
Lewisham SE12 164 D4
Leyton E11 76 C5
Upper Halliford TW17 171 C1
Birchgrove Ho TW9 132 D5
Birch Hill CR0 222 D3
Birch Ho
New Cross Gate SE14 141 B4
Teddington TW11 175 C3
8 Tulse Hill SW2 160 C5
Birchington Cl DA7 147 D4
Birchington Ct
Crouch End N8 49 D3
2 Kilburn NW6 91 D6
Birchington Ho 1 E5 74 B3
Birchington Rd
Crouch End N8 49 D3
Kilburn NW6 91 C6
Surbiton KT5 198 B2
Birchin La EC3 242 D1
Birchlands Ave SW12 158 D4
Birch Mead BR2, BR6 226 C6
Birchmead Ave HA5 40 C5
Birchmere Bsns Pk
SE2 124 A4
Birchmere Lo 18 SE16 118 B1
Birchmere Row SE3 142 D3
Birchmore Wlk N5 73 A5
Birch Pk HA3 24 A3
Birch Rd Feltham TW13 172 D5
Romford RM7 59 D6
Birch Row BR2 210 C3
Birch Tree Ave BR4 224 D4
Birch Tree Ho 16 SE7 143 C6
Birch Tree Way CR0 222 B6
Birch Vale Ct NW8 236 D6
Birchway UB3 106 A5
Birch Wlk CR4 181 B2
Birchwood Ave
Beckenham BR3 207 B5
Hackbridge SM5, SM6 219 B5
Muswell Hill N10 49 A6
Sidcup DA14 168 C1
Birchwood Cl SM4 201 D5
Birchwood Ct
Burnt Oak HA8 27 A1
Edmonton N13 32 D5
Birchwood Dr NW3 69 D5
Birchwood Gr TW12 173 C4
Birchwood Rd
Orpington BR5 211 C5
Streatham SW17 181 B5
Birdbrook Rd SE3 143 C2
Birdcage Wlk
SW1 115 D4 249 C1
Bird Coll DA14 168 A1
Birdham Cl BR1 210 A4
Birdhurst Ave CR2 221 B4
Birdhurst Ct SM6 219 C1
Birdhurst Gdns CR2 221 B4
Birdhurst Rd
London SW18 158 A6
Mitcham SW19 180 C4
South Croydon CR2 221 C3
Birdhurst Rise CR2 221 C3
Bird In Bush Rd SE15 140 A5
Bird-in-Hand La BR1 187 D1
Bird-in-Hand Pas
SE23 162 C2
Bird In Hand Yd 24
NW3 70 A4
Birdsall Ho 5 SE5 139 C2

Birdsfield La [12] E3 97 B6
Bird St W1 238 B1
Bird Wlk TW2 151 B3
Birdwood Cl TW11 174 C6
Birkbeck Ave
 Acton W3 111 A6
 Greenford UB6 86 A6
Birkbeck Coll
 W1 93 D1 239 C2
Birkbeck Ct W3 111 B5
Birkbeck Gdns IG8 21 A2
Birkbeck Gr W3 111 B4
Birkbeck Hill SE21 160 D3
Birkbeck Mews [5] E8 73 D3
Birkbeck Pl SE21 161 A2
Birkbeck Prim Sch
 DA14 168 B1
Birkbeck Rd Acton W3 111 B5
 Dalston E8 73 D3
 Ealing W5 109 C2
 Edgware NW7 27 D5
 Enfield EN2 5 B5
 Hornsey N8 50 A5
 Ilford IG2 57 B4
 North Finchley N12 30 A5
 Penge BR3 184 D1
 Sidcup DA14 168 A1
 Tottenham N17 33 D2
 Wimbledon SW19 179 D4
Birkbeck St E2 96 B4
Birkbeck Sta SE20 206 C6
Birkbeck Way UB6 86 B6
Birkdale Ave HA5 41 C6
Birkdale Cl
 [30] Bermondsey SE16 118 B1
 Crofton BR6 211 B2
 Erith SE28 102 D1
Birkdale Ct [3] UB1 86 A1
Birkdale Gdns CR0 222 D4
Birkdale Rd
 Abbey Wood SE2 124 A2
 Ealing W5 88 A3
Birkenhead Ave KT2 176 B2
Birkenhead Ho [11] N7 72 C3
Birkenhead St
 WC1 94 A4 233 B2
Birkhall Rd SE6 164 B2
Birkwood Cl SW12 159 D4
Birley Lo NW8 229 D4
Birley Rd N20 14 A2
Birley St SW11 137 A3
Birnam Rd N4 72 B6
Birnbeck Ct NW11 47 B4
Birnham Ho TW1 153 C4
Birrell Ho [9] SW9 138 B3
Birse Cres NW10 67 C4
Birstal Gn WD19 22 D6
Birstall Rd N15 51 C4
Birtwhistle Ho [5] E3 97 B6
Biscay Ho [11] E1 96 D3
Biscay Rd W6 112 D1
Biscoe Cl TW5 129 C6
Biscoe Ho UB2 107 D2
Biscoe Way SE13 142 B2
Biscott Ho [3] E3 97 D3
Bisenden Rd CR0 221 C6
Bisham Cl CR4 202 D1
Bisham Gdns N6 49 A1
Bishop Butt Cl BR6 227 D5
Bishop Challoner
 Collegiate Sch E1 96 C1
Bishop Challoner Sch
 BR2 186 B1
Bishop Ct [20] SW2 160 C5
Bishop Douglass RC High
 Sch N2 48 A6
Bishop Duppa's
 Almshouses [7]
 TW10 154 A6
Bishop Duppas Pk
 TW17 193 C2
Bishop Fox Way KT8 195 B5
Bishop Gilpins CE Prim
 Sch SW19 179 B5
Bishop John Robinson CE
 Prim Sch SE28 124 C6
Bishop Justus CE Sch
 BR2 210 A2
Bishop Ken Rd HA3 24 D2
Bishop King's Rd
 W14 113 A2 254 B4
Bishop Perrin CE Prim Sch
 TW2 151 D3
Bishop Ramsey CE Sch
 HA4 40 A2
Bishop Ramsey CE Sch
 (Annexe) HA4 39 D2
Bishop Rd N14 15 B4
Bishop Ridley CE Prim Sch
 DA16 145 C1
Bishops Ave
 Borehamwood WD6 10 B6
 Bromley BR1 209 C6
 Ilford RM6 58 C3
 Newham E13 99 B6
Bishop's Ave SW6 135 A3
Bishops Ave The N2 48 B3
Bishopsbourne Ho
 BR1 187 B3
Bishop's Bridge Rd
 W2 92 A1 236 A2
Bishops Cl
 Acton Green W4 111 A1
 Barnet EN5 12 D5
 Enfield EN1 6 B3
 New Eltham SE9 167 A2
 Richmond TW10 153 D1
 Sutton SM1 217 C5
Bishop's Cl
 Dartmouth Pk N19 71 C5
Bishop's Cl *continued*
 Hillingdon UB10 82 C5
 Walthamstow E17 53 D5
Bishopscourt [8] CR0 221 D6
Bishops Ct
 [1] Ashford TW16 171 D3
 [18] Bayswater W2 91 D1
 East Finchley N2 48 C5
 Richmond TW9 132 A2
 Romford RM7 59 D5
 Wembley HA0 65 B4
Bishop's Ct Holborn EC4 241 C2
 Holborn WC2 241 A2
Bishopsdale Ho [8]
 NW6 91 C6
Bishops Dr
 East Bedfont TW14 149 B5
 Northolt UB5 85 A6
Bishopsford Com Sch
 SM4 202 B3
Bishopsford Ho SM4 202 C3
Bishopsford Rd SM4 202 B3
Bishopsgate
 EC2 95 C1 243 A2
Bishopsgate Arc E1 243 B3
Bishopsgate Churchyard
 EC2 243 A2
Bishops Gn BR1 187 C2
Bishops Gr
 East Finchley N2 48 C3
 Feltham TW12 173 B6
Bishop's Hall KT1 175 D1
Bishopshalt Sch UB8 82 B4
Bishops Hill KT12 194 A2
Bishops Ho SW8 270 B3
Bishop's Mans SW6 134 D3
Bishops Mead SE5 139 A5
Bishops Park Rd
 SW16 182 A2
Bishop's Park Rd SW6 134 D3
Bishop's Pl SM1 218 A3
Bishops Rd
 Fulham SW6 135 B4 264 C2
 Highgate N6 49 A3
Bishop's Rd
 Hanwell W7 108 C4
 Hayes UB3 83 A1
 Thornton Heath CR0 204 D2
Bishops Sq E1 243 B4
Bishop St N1 95 A6 235 A6
Bishop's Terr
 SE11 116 C2 261 B4
Bishopsthorpe Rd
 SE26 184 D6
Bishopstone Ho [4]
 SW11 137 A3
Bishop Stopford's Sch
 EN1 6 B3
Bishops View Ct N10 49 B5
Bishop's Way E2 96 C5
Bishops Wlk
 Chislehurst BR7 189 A2
 South Croydon CR0,
 CR9 223 A3
Bishopswood Rd N6 48 D2
Bishop Thomas Grant RC
 Sec Sch SW16 182 B5
Bishop Wand CE Sch The
 TW16 171 D1
Bishop Way NW10 67 C1
Bishop Wilfred Wood Cl
 SE15 140 A3
Bishop Wilfred Wood Ct
 [3] E13 99 C5
Bishop Winnington-
 Ingram CE Prim Sch
 HA4 39 B2
Bisley Cl KT4 200 C1
Bisley Ho SW19 156 D2
Bispham Rd NW10 88 B4
Bissextile Ho SE13 141 D3
Bisson Rd E15 98 A5
Bisterne Ave E17 54 B6
Bittacy Bsns Ctr NW7 29 A3
Bittacy Cl NW7 28 D4
Bittacy Ct NW7 29 A3
Bittacy Hill NW7 28 D4
Bittacy Park Ave NW7 28 D5
Bittacy Rd NW7 28 D4
Bittacy Rise NW7 28 D4
Bittern Cl UB4 84 D2
Bittern Ct Chingford E4 20 B4
 [7] Deptford SE8 141 C6
 Hendon NW9 27 C1
Bittern Ho SE1 252 A1
Bittern St SE1 252 A1
Bittoms The KT1 197 D6
Bixley Cl UB2 107 B2
Blackall St EC2 243 A6
Blackberry Cl TW17 193 C5
Blackberry Farm Cl
 TW5 129 A5
Blackberry Field BR5 190 A2
Blackbird Ct NW9 67 B5
Blackbird Hill NW9 67 B5
Blackborne Rd RM10 81 D2
Black Boy La N15 51 A4
Blackbrook La BR1,
 BR2 210 C5
Blackburn [28] NW9 27 D1
Blackburn Ct [21] SW2 160 C5
Blackburne's Mews
 W1 248 A5
Blackburn Rd NW6 69 D2
Blackburn Trad Est
 TW19 148 B5
Blackburn Way TW4 151 A6
Blackbush Ave RM6 58 D4
Blackbush Cl SM2 217 D1
Blackcap Ct NW9 27 C1
Blackdown Cl N2 30 A1
Blackdown Ho E8 74 A4
Blackett St SW15 134 D2
Black Fan Cl EN2 5 A4
BLACKFEN 168 A5
Blackfen Par DA15 168 A5
Blackfen Rd DA15 168 B5
Blackfen Sch for Girls
 DA15 168 B5
Blackford Rd WD19 22 D5
Blackfriars Bridge EC4 251 C5
Blackfriars Ct EC4 251 C6
Black Friars La
 EC4 94 D1 241 C1
Blackfriars Pas EC4 251 C6
Blackfriars Pier EC4 251 C6
Blackfriars Rd
 SE1 116 D5 251 C3
Blackfriars Sta
 EC4 116 D6 251 C6
Blackfriars Underpass
 EC4 116 C6 251 B6
Blackham Ho SW19 179 A4
BLACKHEATH 142 C2
Blackheath* SE3 142 C4
Blackheath Ave SE3 142 C5
Blackheath Bluecoat CE
 Sec Sch SE3 143 B5
Blackheath Bsns Est
 SE10 142 A4
Blackheath Gr SE3 142 D3
Blackheath High Sch
 Blackheath SE3 142 D3
 Greenwich SE3 143 A5
Blackheath Hill SE10 142 A4
Blackheath Hospl SE3 142 C2
BLACKHEATH PARK 143 A1
Blackheath Pk SE3 143 A2
Blackheath Prep Sch
 SE3 143 A4
Blackheath Rd SE10 141 D4
Blackheath Rise SE13 142 A3
Blackheath Sta SE3 142 D2
BLACKHEATH VALE 142 D3
Blackheath Vale SE3 142 C3
Blackheath Village
 SE3 142 D3
Black Horse Ct SE1 262 D6
Blackhorse La
 Croydon CR0 206 A2
 Higham Hill E17 34 D1
Blackhorse La Sta
 CR0 206 A2
Blackhorse Mews E17 52 D6
Black Horse Par HA5 40 B4
Blackhorse Rd
 Deptford SE8 141 A6
 Walthamstow E17 53 A5
Black Horse Rd DA14 190 A6
Blackhorse Road E17 52 D5
Blackhorse Road Sta
 E17 52 D5
Blacklands Dr UB4 83 A3
Blacklands Rd SE6 186 A6
Blacklands Terr SW3 257 D3
Black Lion La W6 112 A2
Black Lion Mews [4]
 W6 112 A2
Blackmore Ave UB1 108 B5
Blackmore Dr NW10 66 D1
Blackmore Ho
 Forest Hill SE23 163 B3
 Islington N1 233 D5
 [2] Wandsworth SW18 157 D6
Blackmore's Gr TW11 175 A4
Blackmore Twr [1]
 W3 111 A3
Blackness La BR2 225 D1
Blackpool Gdns UB4 83 C3
Blackpool Rd SE15 140 B3
Black Prince Intc DA6 169 D5
Black Prince Rd SE1,
 SE11 116 B2 260 D3
Black Rod Cl UB3 105 D3
Black Roof Ho [9] SE5 138 D4
Blackshaw Rd SW17 180 B5
Blacksmith Cl RM6 58 C3
Blacksmiths Ho [7] E17 53 C5
Black's Rd W6 112 C2
Blackstock Ho [2] N5 72 D5
Blackstock Mews N4 72 D5
Blackstock Rd N4, N5 72 D6
Blackstone Ho
 Dulwich SE21 161 C1
 Pimlico SW1 259 A1
Blackstone Rd NW2 68 C4
Black Swan Yd SE1 253 A2
Blackthorn Ave UB7 104 C3
Blackthorn Ct
 [20] Camberwell SE15 139 D5
 Heston TW5 129 A5
 [4] Leyton E15 76 B4
 [6] West Norwood
 SW16 182 C5
Blackthorne Ave CR0 206 C1
Blackthorne Ct
 [2] Littleton TW15 171 A3
 Southall UB1 107 D5
Blackthorne Dr E4 36 B6
Blackthorn Gr DA7 147 A2
Blackthorn Rd IG1 79 B3
Blackthorn St E3 97 C3
Blacktree Mews [11]
 SW9 138 C2
BLACKWALL 120 B6
Blackwall Sta E14 120 A6
Blackwall Trad Est E14 98 B2
Blackwall Tunnel E14,
 SE10 120 B5
Blackwall Tunnel App
 SE10 120 C4
Blackwall Tunnel Northern
 Approach E14, E3 98 A3
Blackwall Way E14 120 A6
Blackwater Cl E7 76 D4
Blackwater Ho NW8 236 D4
Blackwater St SE22 161 D6
Blackwell Cl
 [10] Clapton Pk E5 74 D4
 Harrow HA3 24 B3
Blackwell Gdns HA8 10 C1
Blackwell Ho [3] SW4 159 D5
Blackwood Ho [11] E1 96 B3
Blackwood St
 SE17 117 B1 262 C2
Blade Ho TW1 153 D5
Blade Mews SW15 135 B1
Bladen Ho [4] E1 96 D1
Blades Ct
 [4] Hammersmith W6 112 B1
 Putney SW15 135 B1
Blades Ho [12] SE11 138 C6
Blades Lo [16] SW2 160 C5
Bladindon Dr DA5 168 D4
Bladon Ct
 Beckenham BR2 208 C6
 Streatham SW16 182 A4
Bladon Gdns HA2 41 D3
Blagden's Cl N14 15 D2
Blagden's La N14 15 D2
Blagdon Ct W7 108 C6
Blagdon Rd
 London SE13 163 D5
 New Malden KT3 199 D5
Blagdon Wlk TW11 175 C4
Blagrove Rd [1] W10 91 B2
Blair Ave London NW9 45 C2
 Thames Ditton KT10 212 A6
Blair Cl Avery Hill DA15 167 C6
 Canonbury N1 73 A2
 Hayes UB3 106 A2
Blair Ct
 Beckenham BR3 185 D2
 [8] Carshalton SM5 218 D5
 [7] Catford SE6 164 D3
 St John's Wood NW8 229 C6
Blairderry Rd SW2 160 A2
Blairgowrie Ct [13] E14 98 B1
Blair Ho SW9 138 B3
Blair Peach Prim Sch
 UB1 106 D5
Blair St E14 98 B1
Blake Apartments N8 50 B6
Blake Ave IG11 101 D6
Blake Cl Bexley DA16 145 C4
 Carshalton SM5 202 C1
Blake Coll W1 93 C2 239 A4
Blake Ct
 [8] Bermondsey SE16 118 B1
 [9] Clapham SW8 137 C3
 Croydon CR2 220 D3
 Kilburn NW6 91 C4
 Southgate N21 16 B6
Blakeden Dr KT10 212 D2
Blake Gdns
 SW6 135 D4 265 C2
Blake Hall Cres E11 55 A1
Blakehall Rd SM5 218 D2
Blake Hall Rd E11 55 A2
Blake Ho
 [6] Beckenham BR3 185 D4
 [2] Deptford SE8 141 C6
 Harrow HA1 64 C6
 Isle Of Dogs E14 119 D4
 [1] Kentish Town N19 71 D3
 Lambeth SE1 261 A6
 [14] Stoke Newington N16 73 C4
Blake Lo N3 29 B1
Blake Mews [15] TW9 132 C4
Blakemore Rd
 Streatham SW16 160 A1
 Thornton Heath CR7 204 B4
Blakemore Way DA17 125 A3
Blakeney Ave BR3 185 B2
Blakeney Cl
 [5] Camden Town NW1 71 D1
 [4] Dalston E8 74 A3
 Whetstone N20 14 A3
Blakeney Ct EN2 17 B6
Blakeney Rd BR3 185 B2
Blakenham Ct W12 112 A5
Blakenham Rd SW17 180 D6
Blaker Ct SE7 143 C5
Blake Rd Croydon CR0 221 C6
 Mitcham CR4 202 C6
 Newham E16 98 D3
 Wood Green N11 31 C3
Blaker Rd E15 98 A6
Blakes Ave KT3 199 D3
Blakes Cl W10 90 C2
Blake's Gn BR4 208 A1
Blakes La KT3 199 D4
Blakesley Ave W5 87 C1
Blakesley Ct W5 87 C1
Blakesley Ho [4] E12 78 C5
Blake's Rd SE15 139 C5
Blakes Terr KT3 200 A4
Blakesware Gdns N9 17 B4
Blakewood Cl TW13 172 C6
Blakewood Ct [5] SE20 184 B3
Blanca Ho [16] N1 95 C5
Blanchard Cl SE9 166 A1
Blanchard Gr EN3 7 D5
Blanchard Ho
 Chislehurst BR7 189 A4
 [7] Twickenham TW1 153 D5
Blanchard Way E8 74 A2
Blanch Cl SE15 140 C5
Blanchedowne SE5 139 B1
Blanche Nevile Sch
 N10 31 A1
Blanche St E16 98 D3
Blanchland Rd SM4 201 D4
Blandfield Rd SW12 159 A4
Blandford Ave
 [2] Beckenham BR3 185 A1
 Twickenham TW2 151 D3
Blandford Cl London N2 48 A5
 Romford RM7 59 D5
 Wallington CR0 220 A5
Blandford Cres E4 20 A4
Blandford Ct
 Brondesbury Pk NW6 69 A1
 [6] De Beauvoir Town N1 73 C1
Blandford Ho SW8 270 C4
Blandford Rd
 Acton W4 111 C3
 Ealing W5 109 D4
 Penge BR3 184 D1
 Southall UB2 107 C2
 Teddington TW11 174 C5
Blandford Sq NW1 237 B5
Blandford St
 W1 93 A2 238 A3
Blandford Waye UB4 84 C1
Bland Ho SE11 260 D2
Bland St SE9 143 D1
Blaney Cres E6 100 D4
Blanmerle Rd SE9 166 D3
Blann Cl SE9 165 D5
Blantyre St
 SW10 136 B5 266 C4
Blantyre Twr SW10 266 C4
Blantyre Wlk
 SW10 136 B5 266 C4
Blashford NW3 70 D1
Blashford St SE13 164 B4
Blasker Wlk [8] E14 119 D1
Blatchford Ct KT12 194 A1
Blatchford Ho [8] RM10 81 C5
Blawith Rd HA1 42 D5
Blaxland Ho [12] W12 112 B6
Blaydon Cl HA4 39 C2
Blaydon Ct [4] UB5 63 C2
Blaydon Wlk N17 34 B3
Blazer Ct NW8 229 D1
Bleak Hill La SE18 145 D6
Blean Gr SE20 184 C3
Bleasdale Ave UB6 87 A5
Blechynden Ho [17] W10 90 D1
Blechynden St W10 112 D6
Bledlow Cl SE28 124 C6
Bledlow Rise UB6 86 A5
Bleeding Heart Yd
 EC1 241 B3
Blegborough Rd
 SW16 181 C4
Blemundsbury WC1 240 C4
Blendon Dr DA5 168 D5
Blendon Path [9] BR1 186 D3
Blendon Rd DA5 168 D5
Blendon Terr SE18 145 A6
Blendworth Point [4]
 SW15 156 B3
Blenheim [26] SW19 156 D3
Blenheim Ave IG2 56 C3
Blenheim Bsns Ctr
 CR4 180 D1
Blenheim Centre [7]
 SE20 184 D3
Blenheim Cl
 Edmonton N21 17 A3
 Eltham SE12 165 B3
 Greenford UB6 86 B5
 Wallington SM6 219 C1
 West Barnes SW20 200 C6
Blenheim Cres
 Notting Hill W11 91 A1
 Notting Hill W11 244 B6
 Ruislip HA4 61 B6
 South Croydon CR2 221 A1
Blenheim Ct
 Barnsbury N7 72 A2
 Beckenham BR2 208 D5
 [5] Hampton TW12 173 C2
 Harrow HA3 43 A3
 Hendon NW4 46 D5
 Longlands DA14 167 B1
 Richmond TW9 132 B2
 [17] Rotherhithe SE16 118 D5
 South Norwood SE19 183 C2
 Sutton SM2 218 A2
 Upper Holloway N19 72 A6
 Woodford IG8 37 B3
Blenheim Ctr TW3 129 D2
Blenheim Dr DA16 145 D4
Blenheim Gdns
 Clapham Pk SW2 160 B5
 Dollis Hill NW2 68 C3
 Kingston u T KT2 176 D3
 Wallington SM6 219 C1
 Wembley HA9 66 A5
Blenheim Gr SE15 140 A3
Blenheim Ho
 [6] Edmonton N9 18 A1
 Hounslow TW3 129 C2
 [8] Woolwich SE18 123 A3
Blenheim Par [2] UB10 82 D3
Blenheim Park Rd
 CR2 221 A1
Blenheim Pas NW8 229 A4
Blenheim Pl TW11 174 D5
Blenheim Rd
 Acton W4 111 C3
 Bromley BR1, BR2 210 A5
 Harrow HA2 41 D3
 Leyton E15 76 C4
 Newham E6 99 D4
 Northolt UB5 63 D2
Blenheim Rd *continued*
 Penge SE20 184 C3
 Sidcup DA15 168 C3
 St John's Wood
 NW8 92 A5 229 B4
 Sutton SM1 217 D5
 Walthamstow E17 53 A6
 West Barnes SW20 200 C6
Blenheim Rise N15 51 D5
Blenheim St W1 238 C1
Blenheim Terr
 NW8 92 A5 229 A4
Blenheim Way TW7 131 A4
Blenkarne Rd SW11 158 D5
Bleriot [27] NW9 27 D1
Bleriot Rd TW5 128 C5
Blessbury Rd HA8 27 A2
Blessed Dominic RC Sch
 NW9 27 D1
Blessed Sacrament RC
 Prim Sch N1 94 B6 233 C5
Blessington Cl SE13 142 B2
Blessington Rd SE13 142 B1
Blessing Way IG11 102 C5
Bletchingley Cl CR7 204 D5
Bletchington Ct [2]
 DA17 125 C2
Bletchley Ct N1 235 C3
Bletchley St N1 95 A5 235 B3
Bletchmore Cl UB3 105 B1
Bletsoe Wlk N1 235 B4
Blewbury Ho [3] SE2 124 C4
Blick Ho [1] SE16 118 C3
Bligh Ho [4] SE27 183 A6
Blincoe Cl SW19 156 D2
Blissett St SE10 142 A4
Blissland Ct [5] N12 30 A4
Bliss Mews [14] W10 91 A4
Blisworth Cl UB4 85 A3
Blisworth Ho [12] E2 96 A6
Blithbury Rd RM9 80 B2
Blithdale Rd SE2 124 A2
Blithfield St W8 255 C5
Blockley Rd HA0 65 B6
Bloemfontein Ave
 W12 112 B5
Bloemfontein Rd W12 112 B6
Blomfield Ct
 Battersea SW11 266 D2
 Paddington W9 236 B6
Blomfield Ho [4] E14 119 D6
Blomfield Mans [3]
 W12 112 C5
Blomfield Rd
 W9 92 A2 236 A4
Blomfield St
 EC2 95 B2 242 D3
Blomfield Villas W9 236 A4
Blomville Rd RM8 81 A5
Blondel St SW11 137 A3
Blondin Ave W5 109 C3
Blondin St E3 97 C5
Bloomburg St SW1 259 B3
Bloomfield Cres IG2 56 D3
Bloomfield Ct N6 49 A3
Bloomfield Ho [19] E1 96 A2
Bloomfield Pl W1 248 D6
Bloomfield Rd
 Bromley Comm BR2 209 D4
 Highgate N6 49 A3
 Kingston u T KT1 198 A6
 Woolwich SE18 122 D1
Bloomfield Terr
 SW1 115 A1 258 B2
Bloom Gr SE27 160 D1
Bloomhall Rd SE19 183 B5
Bloom Park Rd SW6 264 C3
BLOOMSBURY 93 D2
Bloomsbury Cl
 Ealing W5 110 B6
 Edgware NW7 28 A3
Bloomsbury Ct
 Cranford TW5 128 B4
 Leytonstone E11 54 B1
 Pinner HA5 41 B6
 St Giles WC1 240 B3
Bloomsbury Ho [10]
 SW4 159 D5
Bloomsbury Pl
 London SW18 158 A6
 St Giles WC1 240 B3
Bloomsbury Sq
 WC1 94 A2 240 B3
Bloomsbury St
 WC1 93 D2 239 D3
Bloomsbury Way
 WC1 94 A2 240 B3
Blore Cl SW8 269 C1
Blore Ct W1 249 C6
Blore Ho SW10 265 D4
Blossom Cl
 Dagenham RM9 103 B6
 Ealing W5 110 A4
 South Croydon CR2 221 D3
Blossom La EN2 5 A4
Blossom Pl E1 243 B5
Blossom St E1 95 C3 243 B5
Blossom Way
 Hillingdon UB10 60 B1
 West Drayton UB7 104 C2
Blossom Waye TW5 129 A5
Blount St E14 97 A1
Bloxam Gdns SE9 166 A6
Bloxhall Rd E10 53 B1
Bloxham Cres TW12 173 B2
Bloxworth Cl SM6 219 C5
Blucher Rd SE5 139 A5

Blue Anchor Alley 4 TW9 132 A1
Blue Anchor La SE16 118 B2
Blue Anchor Yd E1 118 A6
Blue Ball Yd SW1 249 A3
Bluebell Ave E12 78 A3
Bluebell Cl
Forest Hill SE26 183 D6
Hackbridge SM6 203 B1
10 Hackney E9 96 C6
Northolt UB5 63 B2
Orpington BR6 227 A6
Bluebell Ct 4 N12 14 A1
Bluebell Way IG1 78 D2
Blueberry Cl IG8 37 A4
Blueberry Ct
Edgware HA8 27 A5
3 Enfield EN2 4 D3
Bluebird La RM10 81 C1
Bluebird Way SE28 123 B4
Bluefield Cl TW12 173 C5
Blue Gate Fields Jun & Inf Schs E1 118 C6
Bluegate Mews E1 118 B6
Bluegates
Stoneleigh KT17 216 A1
Wimbledon SW19 179 A5
Bluehouse Rd E4 20 C1
Blue Lion Pl SE1 263 A6
Blue Point Ct 2 HA1 42 D4
Blueprint Apartments 15 SW12 159 B4
Blue Sch The TW7 131 A2
Blundell Cl E8 74 A4
Blundell Rd HA8 27 C3
Blundell St N7 72 A2
Blunden Cl RM8 58 C1
Blunt Rd CR0 221 B3
Blunts Ave UB7 126 C5
Blunts Rd SE9 166 C6
Blurton Rd E5 74 D4
Blydon Ct N21 16 B6
Blyth Cl
4 Cubitt Town E14 120 B2
Twickenham TW1 152 D5
Blythe Cl SE23 163 B4
Blythe Hill
Forest Hill SE6 163 B4
St Paul's Cray BR5 190 A2
Blythe Hill La SE6 163 B3
Blythe Ho 8 SE11 138 C6
Blythe Mews 2 W14 112 D3
Blythendale Ho 34 E2 96 A5
Blythe Rd W14 113 A3 254 A5
Blythe St E2 96 B4
Blytheswood Pl 4 SW16 182 B6
Blythe Vale SE6 163 B3
Blythewood 5 SM1 218 B3
Blyth Rd Bromley BR1 186 D2
Hayes UB3 105 C4
Walthamstow E17 53 B2
Woolwich SE28 124 C6
Blyth's Wharf E14 119 A6
Blythswood Rd IG3 58 A2
Blythwood Pk 10 BR1 186 D2
Blythwood Rd
London N4 50 A2
Pinner HA5 22 D2
Bnois Jerusalem Sch N16 51 B2
Boades Mews 3 NW3 70 B4
Boadicea St N1 233 C5
Boardman Ave E4 19 D6
Boardman Cl EN5 13 A6
Boardwalk Pl E14 120 A5
Boarhound 25 NW9 27 D2
Boarley Ho SE17 263 A3
Boatemah Wlk 21 SW9 138 C3
Boathouse Ctr The W10 90 D3
Boathouse Wlk 24 SE15 139 D5
Boat Lifter Way 19 SE16 119 A2
Bob Anker Cl 1 E13 99 A4
Bobbin Cl SW4 137 C2
Bobby Moore Bridge The HA9 66 C5
Bob Marley Way 11 SE24 138 C1
Bob Thompson Ct HA9 66 D5
Bockhampton Rd KT2 176 B3
Bocking St E8 96 B6
Boddicott Cl SW19 157 A2
Boddington Gdns W3 110 C4
Boddington Ho 2 SE14 140 C4
Bodeney Ho 10 SE5 139 C4
Boden Ho 4 E1 96 A2
Bodiam Cl EN1 5 C3
Bodiam Ct
Beckenham BR2 208 D5
Sutton SM1 218 B4
Bodiam Rd SW16 181 D3
Bodiam Way NW10 88 B4
Bodicea Mews TW4 151 C5
Bodington Ct 2 W12 112 D4
Bodley Cl KT3 199 C4
Bodley Manor Way SE24 160 C4
Bodley Rd KT3 199 C4
Bodmin 26 NW9 27 D1
Bodmin Cl HA2 63 B5
Bodmin Gr SM4 201 D1
Bodmin St SW18 157 C3
Bodnant Gdns SW20 200 B6
Bodney Rd E5, E8 74 B3
Boeing Way UB2 106 B3
Boevey Path DA17 125 B1
Bogart Ct 13 E14 119 C6
Bognor Gdns WD19 22 C5
Bognor Rd DA16 146 D4
Bohemia Pl 1 E8 74 B2
Bohn Rd E1 97 A2
Bohun Gr EN4 14 D5
Boileau Par W5 88 B1
Boileau Rd
Barnes SW13 134 B6
Ealing W5 88 B1
Boilerhouse SE1 253 C3
Boisseau Ho 31 E1 96 C2
Bolden St SE8 141 D3
Boldero Pl NW8 237 A5
Bolderwood Way BR4 223 D6
Boldmere Rd HA5 40 C2
Boleyn Ave EN1 6 B4
Boleyn Ct
Beckenham BR3 186 A2
Buckhurst Hill IG9 21 B3
East Molesey KT8 196 B5
Hayes UB3 105 D4
Walthamstow E17 53 C5
Boleyn Dr
East Molesey KT8 195 B6
Ruislip HA4 62 D6
Boleyn Gdns BR4 223 D6
Boleyn Ground(Upton Park) (West Ham Utd FC) E13, E6 99 D5
Boleyn Rd Newham E6 99 D5
Stoke Newington N16 73 C3
Upton E7 77 B1
Boleyn Way EN5 2 A2
Bolina Rd SE16 118 C1
Bolingbroke Gr SW11 158 D5
Bolingbroke Ho
Beckenham BR3 207 A4
Catford BR3 185 D5
Bolingbroke Hospl The SW11 158 C6
Bolingbroke Rd W14 112 D3
Bolingbroke Way UB3, UB11 105 B5
Bolingbroke Wlk SW11 136 C4 267 A2
Bollo Bridge Rd W3 111 A4
Bollo Ct 2 W3 111 A3
Bollo La W3 110 D3
Bolney Ct KT6 197 D4
Bolney Gate SW7 247 A1
Bolney St SW8 138 B5 270 C3
Bolsover St W1 93 B3 238 D5
Bolstead Rd CR4 181 B2
Bolster Gr N22 31 D2
Bolt Ct EC4 241 B1
Boltmore Cl NW4 46 D6
Bolton Cl
Chessington KT9 214 A2
Penge SE20 184 A1
Bolton Cres SE5 138 D5
Bolton Ct SW11 268 B1
Bolton Dr SM4 202 B2
Bolton Gdns
Bromley BR1 186 D4
Kensal Rise NW10 90 D5
South Kensington SW5 113 D1 255 D2
Teddington TW11 175 A4
Bolton Gdns Mews SW10 256 A2
Bolton Ho 4 SE10 120 C1
Bolton Pl SW5 256 A2
Bolton Rd
Chessington KT9 214 A2
Chiswick W4 133 A5
Edmonton N18 33 D5
Harlesden NW10 89 C6
Harrow HA1 42 B5
Kilburn NW8 91 D6
Stratford E15 76 D2
Boltons Ct SW5 255 D2
Bolton's La TW6, UB7 127 A5
Bolton St W1 115 B5 248 D4
Boltons The
Harrow HA1 42 A5
South Kensington SW10 114 A1 256 A2
6 Stratford E15 76 D2
Wembley HA0 64 D4
Woodford IG8 37 A6
Bolton Studios SW10 256 B1
Bolton Wlk N7 72 B6
Bombay Ct 8 SE16 118 C4
Bombay St SE16 118 B2
Bomer Cl UB7 126 C5
Bomore Rd W11 113 A6 244 A6
Bonar Pl BR7 188 A3
Bonar Rd SE15 140 A5
Bonchester Cl BR7 188 C3
Bonchurch Cl SM2 217 D1
Bonchurch Rd
Ealing W13 109 B5
Kensal Town W10 91 A2
Bond Cl UB7 82 B1
Bond Ct EC4 242 C1
Bondfield Ave UB4 84 A4
Bondfield Rd 4 E6 100 B2
Bond Gdns SM6 219 C4
Bond Ho 4 NW6 91 B5
Bonding Yard Wlk SE16 119 A3
Bond Prim Sch CR4 180 D1
Bond Rd Mitcham CR4 180 D1
Surbiton KT6 214 B6
Bond St Chiswick W4 111 B2
Ealing W5 109 D6
Stratford E15 76 C3
Bond Street Sta W1 93 A1 238 B1
Bondway SW8 138 A6 270 B6
Boneta Rd SE18 122 B3
Bonfield Rd SE13 142 A1
Bonham Gdns RM8 80 D6
Bonham Ho W11 244 C4
Bonham Rd
Brixton SW2 160 B6
Dagenham RM8 80 D5
Bonheur Rd W4 111 B4
Bonhill St EC2 95 B3 242 D5
Boniface Gdns HA3 23 D3
Boniface Rd UB10 60 D5
Boniface Wlk HA3 23 D3
Bonington Ho
Enfield EN1 18 A6
Pentonville N1 233 C3
Bonita Mews SE15 140 D2
Bonne Marche Terr Mews 18 SE27 183 C6
Bonner Hill Rd KT1 198 C6
Bonner Ho 3 SW15 156 A6
Bonner Prim Sch E2 96 C4
Bonner Rd E2 96 C5
Bonnersfield Cl HA1 43 A3
Bonnersfield La
Greenhill HA1 42 D3
Kenton HA1, HA3 43 A3
Bonner St E2 96 C5
Bonneville Gdns SW4 159 C5
Bonneville Prim Sch SW4 159 C5
Bonnington Ct 14 UB5 84 D5
Bonnington Ho 9 SM2 217 D2
Bonnington Sq SW8 138 B6 270 C6
Bonnington Twr BR2 210 A3
Bonny St NW1 71 C1
Bonser Rd TW1 152 D2
Bonsor Ho SW8 269 B2
Bonsor St SE5 139 C5
Bonthron Ho SW15 134 C3
Bonus Pastor RC Sch BR1 186 C6
Bonville Gdns 17 NW4 46 A5
Bonville Rd BR1 186 D5
Bookbinder Cotts N20 14 D1
Booker Cl 11 E3 97 B2
Booker Rd 5 N18 34 A5
Bookham Ct CR4 202 B6
Boone Ct N9 18 C1
Boones Rd SE13 142 C1
Boone St SE13 142 C1
Boord St SE10 120 C3
Boothby Ct E4 20 A1
Boothby Ho 2 SW16 181 C5
Boothby Rd N19 71 D6
Booth Cl 10 Hackney E9 96 B6
Thamesmead SE28 124 B6
Booth Ho
9 Brentford TW8 131 C5
2 Streatham SW2 160 C4
Booth La EC4 252 A6
Boothman Ho HA3 43 D6
Booth Rd Croydon CR0 220 D6
Hendon NW9 27 C1
Boothroyd Ho TW7 130 D2
Booth's Pl W1 239 B3
Boot Par HA8 26 C4
Boot St N1 95 C4
Bordars Rd W7 86 D2
Bordars Wlk W7 86 C2
Bordeaux Ho 1 E15 76 C3
Borden Ave EN1 17 B5
Border Cres SE26 184 B5
Border Gate CR4 180 D2
Border Gdns CR0 223 D4
Border Rd SE26 184 B5
Bordesley Rd SM4 201 D5
Bordeston Ct 11 TW8 131 C5
Bordley Ct 4 N20 14 D2
Bordon Wlk 5 SW15 156 A4
Boreas Wlk N1 234 D3
Boreham Ave E16 99 A1
Boreham Cl E11 54 A1
Boreham Rd N22 33 A1
BOREHAMWOOD 11 A5
Boreman Ho 11 SE10 142 A6
Borgard Rd SE18 122 B2
Borkwood Pk BR6 227 D4
Borkwood Way BR6 227 C4
Borland Rd
London SE15 140 C1
Teddington TW11 175 B3
Borneo St SW15 134 C2
Borough High St SE1 117 B5 252 C4
Borough Hill CR0 220 D5
Borough Mkt* SE1 252 C3
Borough Rd
Hounslow TW7 130 D4
7 Kingston u T KT2 176 C3
Lambeth SE1 116 D3 261 D6
Mitcham CR4 180 C1
Borough Sq SE1 252 A1
Borough Sta SE1 117 A4 252 B1
BOROUGH THE 117 A4
Borrett Cl SE17 117 A1 262 A1
Borrodaile Rd SW18 157 D5
Borrowdale NW1 232 A1
Borrowdale Ave HA3 25 A1
Borrowdale Cl IG4 56 A5
Borrowdale Ct EN2 5 A4
Borthwick Mews E15 76 C4
Borthwick Rd
Leyton E15 76 C4
London NW9 45 D3
Borthwick St SE8 119 C1
Borwick Ave E17 53 B6
Bosbury Rd SE6 164 A1
Boscastle Rd NW5 71 B5
Boscobel Cl BR1 188 B1
Boscobel Ho 4 E8 74 B2
Boscobel Pl SW1 258 B4
Boscobel St NW8 92 B3 236 D5
Boscombe Ave E10 54 B2
Boscombe Circus NW9 27 B1
Boscombe Cl E5 75 A3
Boscombe Gdns SW16 182 A4
Boscombe Ho CR0 205 B1
Boscombe Rd
Merton SW19 179 D2
North Cheam KT4 200 D1
Shepherd's Bush W12 112 A4
Streatham SW17 181 A4
Bose Cl N3 29 A2
Bosgrove E4 20 A2
Boss Ho SE1 253 C2
Boss St SE1 253 C2
Bostall Hill SE2 124 B1
Bostall La SE2 124 B1
Bostall Manorway SE2 124 B2
Bostall Park Ave DA7 147 A5
Bostall Rd BR5 190 B3
Bostock Ho TW5 129 C6
Boston Bsns Pk W7 108 C3
Boston Ct
South Norwood SE25 205 D5
Sutton SM2 218 A1
Boston Gdns
Brentford TW8 109 B2
Chiswick W4 133 C6
Boston Gr HA4 39 A3
Boston Ho
24 Camberwell SE5 139 A3
Earl's Ct SW5 255 D3
Lisson Gr NW1 237 C6
Boston Lo W13 109 C1
Boston Manor Ho TW8 109 B1
Boston Manor Rd TW8 109 B1
Boston Manor Sta TW8 109 A2
Boston Par W7 109 A2
Boston Park Rd TW8 109 C1
Boston Pl NW1 92 D3 237 C5
Boston Rd
Burnt Oak HA8 27 A3
Ealing W7 109 A3
Newham E6 100 A4
Thornton Heath CR0 204 C3
Bostonthorpe Rd W7 108 C4
Boston Vale W7 109 A2
Bosun Cl 22 E14 119 C4
Boswell Ct
Bloomsbury WC1 240 B4
9 Hammersmith W14 112 D3
Kingston u T KT2 176 C2
Boswell Ho
Bloomsbury WC1 240 B4
Bromley Comm BR2 209 D4
5 Streatham SW16 181 C5
Boswell Rd CR7 205 A5
Boswell St WC1 94 A2 240 B4
Boswood Ct TW4 129 B2
Bosworth Cl E17 35 B2
Bosworth Ho 4 W10 91 A3
Bosworth Rd Barnet EN5 1 C2
Dagenham RM10 81 C5
Kensal Town W10 91 A3
Wood Green N11 31 D4
Botany Bay La BR7 189 A1
Botany Cl EN4 2 C1
Boteley Cl E4 20 B2
Botham Cl 6 HA8 27 A3
Botha Rd E13 99 C2
Bothwell Cl E16 98 D2
Bothwell St 4 W6 134 D6
Botolph Alley EC3 253 A6
Botolph La EC3 253 A6
Botsford Rd SW20 179 A1
Bott's Mews W2 91 C1
Botwell Common Rd UB3 105 C6
Botwell Cres UB3 83 C1
Botwell House RC Prim Sch UB3 105 D4
Botwell La UB3 105 C6
Boucher Cl TW11 174 D5
Bouchier Ho 6 N2 30 B1
Bough Beech Ct EN3 6 D6
Boughton Ave BR2 208 D2
Boughton Ho
Borough The SE1 252 C2
Bromley BR1 188 A3
Boughton Rd SE28 123 C3
Boulcott St E1 96 D1
Boulevard The
Chelsea SW6 266 B1
4 Upper Tooting SW17 159 A2
Boullen Ct SM1 218 A4
Boulogne Ho SE1 263 C6
Boulogne Rd CR0 205 A3
Boulter Ho 4 SE14 140 C4
Boulters Ct HA0 65 A4
Boulton Ho TW8 110 A1
Boulton Rd RM8 81 B6
Boultwood Rd E6 100 B1
Bounces La N9 18 B2
Bounces Rd N9 18 C2
Boundaries Mans 3 SW12 159 A3
Boundaries Rd
Feltham TW13 150 C3
Upper Tooting SW12 159 A3
Boundary Ave E17 53 B2
Boundary Bsns Ct CR4 202 B6
Boundary Cl Barnet EN5 1 B4
Ilford IG3 79 C4
Kingston u T KT1 198 D6
Penge SE20 184 A1
Southall UB2 107 C1
Boundary Ct
3 Edmonton N18 33 D4
9 New Southgate N11 31 B6
Boundary Ho
Balham SW12 159 B3
1 Camberwell SE5 139 A5
Edgware HA8 44 B6
Isleworth TW1 153 B6
15 Notting Hill W11 112 D5
Boundary La
Camberwell SE17 139 A6
Newham E13, E6 99 D3
Boundary Pas E2 243 C6
Boundary Rd
Avery Hill DA15 167 C6
Barking IG11 101 A5
London N2 30 B2
Mitcham SW19 180 B4
Newham E13 99 D4
Pinner HA5 40 D2
Ponders End N9 18 C5
St John's Wood NW8 92 A6 229 B6
Tottenham N22 33 A1
Wallington SM5, SM6 219 A1
Walthamstow E17 53 C3
Boundary Road Est NW8 92 A6 229 A5
Boundary Row SE1 251 C2
Boundary St E2 95 D3 243 C6
Boundary Way CR0 223 C3
Boundfield Rd SE6 164 C2
Bounds Green Ct N11 31 D4
Bounds Green Ind Est N11 31 C4
Bounds Green Jun & Inf Schs N11 32 A3
Bounds Green Rd
London N11 31 D4
Wood Green N22 32 A3
Bounds Green Sta N11 31 D3
Bourbon Ho 9 SE6 186 A6
Bourchier St W1 249 C6
Bourdillon Ct 2 SE9 166 A2
Bourdon Pl W1 248 D6
Bourdon Rd SE20 184 C1
Bourdon St W1 115 B6 248 D5
Bourke Cl London SW4 160 A5
Willesden NW10 67 C2
Bourlet Cl W1 239 A3
Bourn Ave
Hillingdon UB8 82 C3
New Barnet EN4 14 B6
West Green N15 51 B5
Bournbrook Rd SE3, SE9 143 D2
Bourne Ave Hayes UB3 105 B3
Palmers Green N14 16 A2
Ruislip HA4 62 C3
Bourne Cir UB3 105 A3
Bourne Cl
Hinchley Wood KT7 212 D6
Isleworth TW7 130 C2
Bourne Ct Chiswick W4 133 A6
Ruislip HA4 62 B3
Wanstead E11 55 A4
Woodford IG8 37 D1
Bourne Dr CR4 180 B1
Bourne Gdns E4 35 D6
Bourne Hill N13 16 B2
Bourne Ho
4 Ashford TW15 170 C5
3 Buckhurst Hill IG9 21 D1
5 Clapham SW4 137 C1
1 Dollis Hill NW2 68 A5
Bourne Mans N13 32 C5
Bournemead Ave UB5 84 A5
Bournemead Cl UB5 84 A4
Bournemead Way UB5 84 B5
Bourne Mews W1 238 B1
Bournemouth Cl SE15 140 A3
Bournemouth Ct 6 SM1 218 A3
Bournemouth Rd
London SE15 140 A3
Merton SW19 179 C2
Bourne Par DA5 169 D4
Bourne Pl W4 111 B1
Bourne Prim Sch HA4 62 C2
Bourne Rd Bexley DA5 169 D5
Bromley BR2 209 D5
Hornsey N8 50 A3
Leyton E7, E11 76 D5
Bournes Ho 4 N15 51 C3
Bourneside 5 N14 15 D3
Bourneside Cres 6 N14 15 D3
Bourneside Gdns SE6 186 A5
Bourne St
Belgravia SW1 115 A2 258 A3
Croydon CR0 220 D6
Bourne Terr W2 91 D2
Bourne The N14 16 A3
Bourne Vale BR2 209 A2
Bournevale Rd SW16 182 A6
Bourne View UB6 64 D3
Bourne Way
Cheam SM1 217 B3
Coney Hall BR2, BR4 224 D6
West Ewell KT19 215 A4
Bournewood Rd SE18 146 A5
Bournville Rd SE6 163 C4
Bournwell Cl EN4 2 D3
Bourton Cl UB3 106 A5
Bousfield Prim Sch SW10 114 A1 256 A2
Bousfield Rd SE14 140 D3
Boutcher CE Prim Sch SE1 117 D2 263 C4
Boutflower Rd SW11 136 C1
Bouverie Ct 4 SW16 182 A5
Bouverie Gdns HA3 43 D3
Bouverie Mews N16 73 C6
Bouverie Pl W2 236 D2
Bouverie Rd
Harrow HA1 42 A3
Stoke Newington N16 73 C6
Bouverie St EC4 94 C1 241 B1
Bouvier Rd EN3 6 C5
Boveney Rd SE23 162 D4
Bovill Rd SE23 162 D4
Bovingdon Ave HA9 66 C2
Bovingdon Cl 4 N19 71 C6
Bovingdon La NW9 27 C2
Bovingdon Rd SW6 135 D4 265 D1
Bovril Ho EN1 5 C2
BOW 97 B5
Bowater Cl
Clapham Pk SW2 160 A5
Kingsbury NW9 45 B4
Bowater Gdns TW16 172 C2
Bowater Ho EC1 242 B5
Bowater Pl SE3 143 B5
Bowater Rd
Greenwich SE18 121 D3
Wembley HA9 66 D5
Bow Brook The 20 E2 96 D5
Bow Church Sta E3 97 C4
BOW COMMON 97 D2
Bow Common La E3 97 B3
Bowden Cl TW14 149 C3
Bowden Ct HA4 62 C3
Bowden Ho 29 E3 97 D4
Bowden House Hospl (Private) HA1 64 C6
Bowden St SE11 116 C1 261 B1
Bowditch SE8 119 B1
Bowdon Rd E17 53 C2
Bowen Ct 2 N5 72 D4
Bowen Dr SE21 161 C1
Bowen Rd HA1 42 A2
Bowen St E14 97 D1
Bower Ave SE3 142 C5
Bower Cl UB5 84 C5
Bowerdean St SW6 135 D3
Bower Ho SE14 140 D4
Bowerman Ave SE14 141 A6
Bowerman Ct 1 N19 71 D6
Bowers Ho 5 IG11 78 D1
Bower St E1 96 D1
Bowers Wlk 1 E6 100 B1
Bowery Ct 16 RM10 81 D2
Bowes Cl DA15 168 B5
Bowes Ho N13 32 B5
Bowes-Lyon Hall 13 E16 121 A5
Bowes Lyon Ho 2 TW10 153 C1
BOWES PARK 32 A4
Bowes Park Sta N22 32 A3
Bowes Prim Sch N11 31 D5
Bowes Rd Acton W3 111 C6
Dagenham RM8 80 C4
New Southgate N11 31 C5
Walton-on-T KT12 194 B1
Bowes Rd (North Circular Rd) N13 32 A5
Bowfell Rd W6 134 C6
Bowford Ave DA7 147 A4
Bowhill Cl SW9 138 C5
Bow Ho 1 E3 97 C4
Bowie Cl SW4 159 D4
Bow Ind Pk E15 75 C1
Bow La
Barbican EC2, EC4 95 A1 242 B1
Finchley N12 30 A3
Bowland Ho N4 51 A2
Bowland Rd
London SW4 137 D1
Woodford IG8 37 C4
Bowland Yd SW1 247 D1
Bowl Ct EC2 243 B5
Bowles Ct Finchley N12 30 C3
Harrow HA3 43 A3
Bowles Rd 1 SE1 140 A6
Bowley Cl SE19 183 D4
Bowley Ho 6 SE16 118 A3
Bowley La SE19 183 D5
Bowling Cl UB10 82 B6
Bowling Green Cl SW19 156 B4
Bowling Green Ct HA9 66 B6
Bowling Green Ho SW10 266 C4
Bowling Green La EC1 94 C3 241 B6
Bowling Green Pl SE1 252 C2
Bowling Green Row 1 SE18 122 B2

Bowling Green St SE11 ... 138 C6
Bowling Green Wlk N1 .. 95 C4
Bowls Cl HA7 ... 25 B5
Bowman Ave E16 ... 120 D6
Bowman Homes W5 ... 109 D4
Bowman Mews
St George in t East E1 ... 118 A6
Wandsworth SW18 ... 157 B3
Bowmans Cl W13 ... 109 B5
Bowmans Lea SE23 ... 162 C4
Bowman's Meadow SM6 ... 219 B5
Bowman's Mews N7 ... 72 A5
Bowman's Pl N7 ... 72 A5
Bowman Trad Est NW9 .. 44 C5
Bowmar Lo 13 EN5 ... 1 D1
Bowmead SE9 ... 166 B2
Bowmore Wlk NW1 ... 71 D1
Bowness Cl 5 E8 ... 73 D2
Bowness Cres KT2, SW15 ... 177 C5
Bowness Dr TW4 ... 129 A1
Bowness Ho SE15 ... 140 C5
Bowness Rd
Catford SE6 ... 163 D4
Erith DA7 ... 147 D3
Bowood Rd
Clapham SW11 ... 159 A6
Enfield EN3 ... 6 D3
Bow Rd E3 ... 97 C4
Bowring Gn WD19 ... 22 C5
Bow Road Sta E3 ... 97 C4
Bowrons Ave HA0 ... 65 D1
Bowry Ho 14 E14 ... 97 B2
Bow Sch E3 ... 97 C4
Bowsley Ct TW13 ... 150 A2
Bowsprit Point 1 E14 ... 119 C3
Bow St
St Giles WC2 ... 94 A1 240 B1
Stratford E15 ... 76 C3
Bowstead Ct SW11 ... 266 D1
Bow Triangle Bsns Ctr 17 E3 ... 97 C3
Bowyer Cl E6 ... 100 B2
Bowyer Ct 4 E4 ... 20 A3
Bowyer Ho
Mitcham CR4 ... 202 C6
27 Shoreditch N1 ... 95 C6
Wandsworth SW18 ... 157 D5
Bowyer Pl SE5 ... 139 A5
Bowyer St 15 SE5 ... 139 A5
Boxall Rd SE21 ... 161 C5
Box Cnr TW2 ... 152 C2
Box Elder Cl HA8 ... 27 A5
Boxgrove Prim Sch SE2 ... 124 C3
Boxgrove Rd SE2 ... 124 C3
Box La IG11 ... 102 C5
Boxley Ho 3 E5 ... 74 B3
Boxley Rd SM4 ... 202 A5
Boxley St E16 ... 121 B5
Boxmoor Ho
16 Hackney E2 ... 96 A6
9 Shepherd's Bush W11 ... 112 D5
Boxmoor Rd HA3 ... 43 B5
Boxoll Rd RM9 ... 81 B5
Boxshall Ho 7 SE18 ... 144 D6
Box Tree Ho SE8 ... 119 A1
Boxtree La HA3 ... 24 B3
Boxtree Rd HA3 ... 24 B3
Boxwood Cl UB7 ... 104 B4
Boxworth Cl N12 ... 30 B5
Boxworth Gr N1 .. 94 B6 233 D6
Boyard Rd SE18 ... 122 D1
Boyce Ho
Streatham SW16 ... 181 C5
1 West Kilburn W10 ... 91 B4
Boyce Way E13 ... 99 A3
Boycroft Ave NW9 ... 45 A3
Boyd Ave UB1 ... 107 B5
Boyd Cl KT2 ... 176 C3
Boyd Ct SW15 ... 156 C5
Boydell Ct NW8 ... 70 B1
Boyden Ho 8 E17 ... 54 A6
Boyd Rd SW19 ... 180 B4
Boyd St E1 ... 96 A1
Boyfield St SE1 ... 116 D4 251 D1
Boyland Rd BR1 ... 186 D5
Boyle Ave HA7 ... 25 A4
Boyle Cl UB10 ... 82 B5
Boyle Farm Rd KT7 ... 197 A3
Boyle Ho
13 Belvedere DA17 ... 125 C3
Wembley HA9 ... 66 D5
Boyle St W1 ... 249 A6
Boyne Ave NW4 ... 46 D5
Boyne Ct NW10 ... 68 A1
Boyne Ho 10 E5 ... 74 B6
Boyne Rd
Dagenham RM10 ... 81 C5
Lewisham SE13 ... 142 B2
Boyne Terr Mews W11 ... 113 B5 244 C4
Boyson Rd 10 SE17 ... 139 B6
Boyton Cl London N8 ... 50 A6
Stepney E1 ... 96 D3
Boyton Ho
Kennington SE11 ... 261 A1
St John's Wood NW8 .. 229 D4
Boyton Rd N8 ... 50 A6
Brabant Ct EC3 ... 253 A6
Brabant Rd N22 ... 32 B1
Brabazon Ave SM6 ... 220 A1
Brabazon Rd
Heston TW5 ... 128 D5

Brabazon Rd *continued*
Northolt UB5 ... 85 C5
Brabazon St E14 ... 97 D2
Brabner Ho 3 E2 ... 96 A4
Brabourne Cl 7 SE19 .. 183 C5
Brabourne Cres DA7 .. 147 B6
Brabourne Hts NW7 ... 11 C1
Brabourne Rise BR3 ... 208 B4
Brabourn Gr SE15 ... 140 C3
Brabrook Ct SM6 ... 219 B3
Brabstone Ho 2 UB6 ... 86 D5
Bracer Ho 1 N1 ... 95 C5
Bracewell Ave UB6 ... 65 A2
Bracewell Rd W10 ... 90 C2
Bracewood Gdns CR0 .. 221 D5
Bracey Mews 1 N4 ... 72 A6
Bracey St N4 ... 72 A6
Bracken Ave
Balham SW12 ... 159 A4
Croydon CR0 ... 223 C5
Brackenbridge Dr HA4 .. 62 D5
Brackenbury N4 ... 50 B1
Brackenbury Gdns W6 ... 112 B3
Brackenbury Prim Sch W6 ... 112 B3
Brackenbury Rd
East Finchley N2 ... 48 A6
Hammersmith W6 ... 112 B3
Bracken Cl
Ashford TW16 ... 171 D4
Newham E6 ... 100 B2
Twickenham TW4 ... 151 C4
Brackendale
Kingston u T KT1 ... 176 D1
Southgate N21 ... 16 B2
Brackendale Cl TW5 ... 129 D4
Brackendale Ct 2 BR3 ... 185 C3
Bracken End TW7 ... 152 B6
Brackenfield Cl E5 ... 74 B5
Bracken Gdns SW13 ... 134 A3
Brackenhill HA4 ... 63 A4
Bracken Hill Cl 5 BR1 ... 186 D2
Bracken Hill La BR1 ... 186 D2
Bracken Ho 15 E3 ... 97 C2
Bracken Mews
Chingford E4 ... 20 A3
Romford RM7 ... 59 D3
Brackens BR3 ... 185 C3
Brackens The EN1 ... 17 C4
Bracken The E4 ... 20 A2
Brackenwood TW16 ... 172 A2
Brackenwood Lo EN5 ... 1 C1
Brackley Ave SE15 ... 140 C2
Brackley Cl SM6 ... 220 A1
Brackley Ct NW8 ... 236 D6
Brackley Rd
Beckenham BR3 ... 185 C3
Chiswick W4 ... 111 C1
Brackley Sq IG8 ... 37 D3
Brackley St EC1 ... 242 B4
Brackley Terr 6 W4 ... 111 C1
Bracklyn Ct N1 ... 235 C4
Bracklyn St N1 ... 235 C4
Bracknell Cl N22 ... 32 C2
Bracknell Gate NW3 ... 69 D3
Bracknell Gdns NW3 ... 69 D4
Bracknell Way NW3 ... 69 D4
Bracondale KT10 ... 212 A3
Bracondale Rd SE2 ... 124 A2
Braconhyrst HA1 ... 42 C2
Bradbeer Ho 24 E2 ... 96 C4
Bradbourne Ct 11 SM2 ... 217 D2
Bradbourne Rd DA5 ... 169 C4
Bradbourne St SW6 ... 135 C3
Bradbury Cl UB2 ... 107 B2
Bradbury Ct
4 Barnet EN5 ... 1 D1
2 Greenwich SE3 ... 143 A5
Merton SW20 ... 178 C1
Bradbury Ho E1 ... 243 D2
Bradbury St 28 N16 ... 73 C3
Bradby Ho NW8 ... 91 D5
Braddock Cl TW7 ... 130 D3
Braddon Rd TW9 ... 132 B2
Braddyll St SE10 ... 120 C1
Bradenham 11 SE17 ... 139 B6
Bradenham Ave DA16 .. 146 A1
Bradenham Cl SE17 ... 139 B6
Bradenham Rd
Harrow HA3 ... 43 B5
Hayes UB4 ... 83 C4
Braden St W9 ... 91 D3
Bradfield Ct 14 NW1 ... 71 B1
Bradfield Dr IG11 ... 80 A3
Bradfield Ho 15 SW8 ... 137 D3
Bradfield Rd
Newham E16 ... 121 B4
Ruislip HA4 ... 63 A3
Bradford Cl
Bromley BR2 ... 210 B1
Forest Hill SE26 ... 184 B6
Tottenham N17 ... 33 D4
Bradford Dr KT19 ... 215 D2
Bradford Ho 4 W14 ... 112 D3
Bradford Rd Acton W3 .. 111 C4
Ilford IG1 ... 57 C1
Bradgate Rd SE6 ... 163 D5
Brading Cres E11 ... 77 B6
Brading Rd
Streatham SW2 ... 160 B4
Thornton Heath CR0 ... 204 B3
Brading Terr W12 ... 112 A3
Bradiston Rd W9 ... 91 B4
Bradley Cl N7 ... 72 B2
Bradley Ct CR0 ... 220 C4
Bradley Gdns W13 ... 87 B1

Bradley Ho
Bermondsey SE16 ... 118 B2
1 Bromley E3 ... 97 D4
Twickenham TW1 ... 152 D3
Woodford IG8 ... 37 A3
Bradley Mews SW12 ... 158 D3
Bradley Rd Enfield EN3 ... 7 A6
South Norwood SE19 ... 183 A4
Wood Green N22 ... 32 B1
Bradley's Cl N1 ... 234 B4
Bradley Stone Rd E6 ... 100 B2
Bradlord Ho SE21 ... 161 C1
Bradman Row 7 HA8 ... 27 A3
Bradmead SW8 ... 137 C5 269 A3
Bradmore Ct 2 EN3 ... 7 A2
Bradmore Park Rd W6 ... 112 B2
Bradon 24 NW9 ... 27 D1
Bradshaw Cl SW19 ... 179 C4
Bradshaw Dr NW7 ... 28 D3
Bradshawe Waye UB8 ... 82 B2
Bradshaws Cl SE25 ... 206 A6
Bradsole Ho 13 BR3 ... 185 C3
Brad St SE1 ... 116 C5 251 B3
Bradstock Ho E9 ... 75 A1
Bradstock Rd
Homerton E9 ... 74 D2
Stoneleigh KT17 ... 216 B3
Bradwell Ave RM10 ... 81 C6
Bradwell Cl E18 ... 54 D5
Bradwell Ho
8 Kilburn NW6 ... 91 D6
9 Walthamstow E17 ... 53 D6
Bradwell Mews 5 N18 .. 34 A6
Brady Ct RM8 ... 58 D1
Brady Dr BR1 ... 210 C6
Brady Ho London SW4 ... 159 D6
South Lambeth SW8 ... 269 B2
Bradymead E6 ... 100 D1
Brady St E1 ... 96 B3
Braeburn Ct 1 EN4 ... 2 C1
Brae Ct
2 Kingston u T KT2 ... 176 C2
South Norwood SE25 ... 183 C2
Braefoot Ct SW15 ... 156 D6
Braemar SW15 ... 156 D5
Braemar Ave
Thornton Heath CR7 ... 204 D6
Welsh Harp NW10 ... 67 B6
Wembley HA0 ... 66 A1
Wimbledon SW18, SW19 ... 157 C2
Wood Green N22 ... 32 A2
Braemar Ct
4 Brentford TW8 ... 131 D6
5 Catford SE6 ... 164 D3
Braemar Gdns
Hendon NW9 ... 27 B2
Longlands DA15 ... 167 B1
West Wickham BR4 ... 208 A1
Braemar Ho
Richmond TW11 ... 175 B5
St John's Wood W9 ... 229 A1
Braemar Mans W8 ... 255 D5
Braemar Rd
Brentford TW8 ... 131 D6
Newham E13 ... 98 D3
North Cheam KT4 ... 216 B5
South Tottenham N15 ... 51 C4
Braemore Ct EN4 ... 3 A1
Braeside BR3 ... 185 D5
Braeside Ave SW19 ... 179 A2
Braeside Cl HA5 ... 23 C3
Braeside Rd SW16 ... 181 C3
Braeside Sch
Buckhurst Hill IG9 ... 21 B3
Buckhurst Hill IG9 ... 21 C2
Braes St N1 ... 72 D1
Braesyde Cl DA17 ... 125 B2
Brafferton Rd CR0 ... 221 A4
Braganza St SE17 ... 116 D1 261 C1
Bragg Cl RM8 ... 80 B2
Bragg Rd TW11 ... 174 D4
Braham Ho SE11 ... 260 D1
Braham St E1 ... 243 D2
Brahma Kumaris World Spiritual Univ NW10 ... 68 A1
Braid Ave W3 ... 89 C1
Braid Cl TW13 ... 151 B2
Braid Ho SE10 ... 142 A4
Braidwood Ho 2 CR7 .. 204 D5
Braidwood Rd SE6 ... 164 B3
Braidwood St SE1 ... 117 C5 253 A3
Braikenridge Ho N21 ... 17 B5
Brailsford Cl SW19 ... 180 C3
Brailsford Rd SW2 ... 160 C5
Braintcroft Prim Sch NW2 ... 67 D5
Brainton Ave TW14 ... 150 C4
Braintree Ave IG4 ... 56 A5
Braintree Ho 6 E1 ... 96 C3
Braintree Ind Est HA4 ... 62 B4
Braintree Rd
Dagenham RM10 ... 81 C5
Ruislip HA4 ... 62 B4
Braintree St E2 ... 96 C4
Braithwaite Ave RM7 ... 59 C2
Braithwaite Gdns HA7 ... 25 C2
Braithwaite Ho EC1 ... 242 C6
Braithwaite Rd EN3 ... 7 B2
Braithwaite Twr W2 .. 236 C4
Brake Shear Ho 1 EN5 ... 1 B2
Bramah Gn SW9 ... 138 C4
Bramah Mus of Tea & Coffee* SE1 ... 252 B3
Bramalea Cl N6 ... 49 A3
Bramall Cl E15 ... 76 D3

Bramall Ct N7 ... 72 B2
Bramber WC1 ... 233 A1
Bramber Ct TW8 ... 110 A2
Bramber Ho 9 KT2 ... 176 A2
Bramber Rd
Colney Hatch N12 ... 30 C5
Fulham W14 ... 135 B6 264 C6
Bramble Acres Cl SM2 ... 217 C1
Bramblebury Rd SE18 .. 123 A1
Bramble Cl
Beckenham BR3 ... 208 A4
Croydon CR0 ... 223 D4
Hillingdon UB8 ... 82 B3
South Tottenham N15 ... 52 A5
Stanmore HA7 ... 25 D3
Upper Halliford TW17 ... 193 B6
Brambledown 8 N4 ... 50 A2
Brambledown Cl BR2, BR4 ... 208 C4
Brambledown Rd
South Croydon CR2 ... 221 C1
Wallington SM5, SM6 ... 219 B1
Bramble Gdns W12 ... 111 D6
Bramble Ho 16 E3 ... 97 C2
Bramble La TW12 ... 173 B4
Brambles Cl TW7, TW8 .. 131 B5
Brambles Farm Dr UB10 ... 82 C4
Brambles The
West Drayton UB7 ... 104 A2
8 Wimbledon SW19 ... 179 B5
Bramblewood Cl SM5 .. 202 C1
Brambling Ct
25 Deptford SE8 ... 141 B6
South Norwood SE25 ... 205 D5
Bramblings The E4 ... 36 B6
Bramcote Ave CR4 ... 202 D5
Bramcote Ct CR4 ... 202 D5
Bramcote Gr SE16 ... 118 C1
Bramcote Rd SW15 ... 134 B1
Bramdean Cres SE12 ... 165 A3
Bramdean Gdns SE12 .. 165 A3
Bramerton NW6 ... 68 D1
Bramerton Rd BR3 ... 207 B6
Bramerton St SW3 ... 136 C6 267 A6
Bramfield Ct N4 ... 73 A6
Bramfield Rd SW11 ... 158 D6
Bramford Ct N14 ... 15 D2
Bramford Rd SW18 ... 136 A1
Bramham Gdns
Chessington KT9 ... 213 D4
South Kensington SW5 ... 113 D1 255 D2
Bramham Ho SE22 ... 139 C1
Bramhope La SE7 ... 143 B6
Bramlands Cl SW11 ... 136 C2
Bramley Ave TW17 ... 193 C6
Bramley Cl
Croydon CR2 ... 221 A3
East Barnet N14 ... 15 B6
Hayes UB3 ... 106 A6
Higham Hill E17 ... 35 A1
Orpington BR6 ... 210 D1
Pinner HA5 ... 39 D6
Twickenham TW2 ... 152 A5
Woodford IG8 ... 37 C3
Bramley Cres Ilford IG2 .. 56 C3
Nine Elms SW8 ... 137 D5 269 D4
Bramley Ct 2 Barnet EN4 . 2 C1
9 Chingford E4 ... 20 A3
Dollis Hill NW2 ... 68 B5
Feltham TW14 ... 149 C5
Hither Green SE13 ... 164 B6
Mitcham CR4 ... 180 B1
Southall UB1 ... 108 A6
Wallington SM6 ... 219 C3
Welling DA16 ... 146 B4
Bramley Gdns WD19 ... 22 C5
Bramley Hill CR2 ... 221 A4
Bramley Ho
Hounslow TW3 ... 129 B1
Ilford IG2 ... 56 C3
1 Kingston u T KT2 ... 176 D3
19 North Kensington W10 ... 90 D1
Roehampton SW15 ... 155 D5
Bramley House Ct EN2 ... 5 B6
Bramleyhyrst CR2 ... 221 A3
Bramley Lo HA0 ... 65 D4
Bramley Rd Ealing W5 ... 109 C3
North Kensington W10 ... 90 D1
Southgate N14 ... 15 C6
Sutton SM1 ... 218 B3
Bramley Way
Hounslow TW4 ... 151 B6
West Wickham BR4 ... 223 D6
Brampton WC1 ... 240 C3
Brampton Cl 14 E5 ... 74 B6
Brampton Coll NW4 ... 46 C5
Brampton Ct NW4 ... 46 B5
Brampton Gr
Harrow HA3 ... 43 B5
Hendon NW4 ... 46 C5
Wembley HA9 ... 44 C1
Brampton La 6 NW4 ... 46 C5
Brampton Lo DA7 ... 146 D5
Brampton Manor Sch E6 ... 99 D3
Brampton Park Rd N22 .. 50 C6
Brampton Prim Sch
Bexley DA7 ... 146 D3
Newham E6 ... 100 A4
Brampton Rd
Bexleyheath DA7 ... 147 A4
Croydon CR0 ... 205 D3
Harringay N15 ... 51 A4
Hillingdon UB10 ... 82 D5

Brampton Rd *continued*
Newham E6 ... 99 D4
Queensbury NW9 ... 44 C5
Bramshaw Gdns WD19 .. 22 D5
Bramshaw Rd E9 ... 74 D2
Bramshaw Rise KT3 ... 199 C3
Bramshill Gdns NW5 ... 71 B5
Bramshill Rd NW10 ... 89 D5
Bramshot Ave SE7 ... 143 B6
Bramshott Ct 3 KT6 ... 198 A3
Bramshurst NW8 ... 91 D6
Bramston Rd
Harlesden NW10 ... 90 A5
Wandsworth SW17 ... 158 A1
Bramwell Cl TW16 ... 172 D1
Bramwell Ho
Borough The SE1 ... 262 B5
Chelsea SW1 ... 269 A6
Bramwell Mews N1 ... 233 D6
Brancaster Dr NW7 ... 28 A3
Brancaster Ho
22 Globe Town E1 ... 96 D4
Islington N5 ... 72 D3
Brancaster Rd
Ilford E12 ... 78 B4
Newbury Pk IG2 ... 57 C3
Streatham SW16 ... 160 A1
Brancepeth Gdns IG9 ... 21 A2
Branch Hill NW3 ... 70 A5
Branch Ho 13 SM1 ... 218 A4
Branch Pl N1 ... 95 B6 235 D6
Branch Rd E14 ... 119 A6
Branch St SE15 ... 139 C5
Brancker Rd HA3 ... 43 D6
Brancroft Way EN3 ... 7 B4
Brandan Ho 11 HA1 ... 42 D4
Brand Cl N4 ... 50 D1
Branden Lo 13 W4 ... 111 A1
Brandlehow Rd SW15 .. 135 B1
Brandon Ho BR3 ... 185 D5
Brandon Mews
Barbican EC2 ... 242 C4
Walworth SE17 ... 262 B3
Brandon Pl N8 ... 50 B5
Brandon Rd
Barnsbury N7 ... 72 A1
Southall UB2 ... 107 B1
Sutton SM1 ... 217 D4
Walthamstow E17 ... 54 A6
Brandon St SE17 ... 117 A2 262 B3
Brandram Rd SE13 ... 142 C1
Brandrams Wharf SE16 ... 118 C4
Brandreth Ct HA1 ... 42 D3
Brandreth Rd
Newham E6 ... 100 B1
Upper Tooting SW17 ... 159 B2
Brandries The SM6 ... 219 D5
Brand St SE10 ... 142 A5
Brandville Gdns IG6 ... 56 D5
Brandville Rd UB7 ... 104 A4
Brandy Way SM2 ... 217 C1
Brangbourne Rd BR1 .. 186 A5
Brangton Rd SE11 ... 260 D1
Brangwyn Cres SW19 .. 180 B1
Brangwyn Ct W14 ... 254 A5
Branham Ho 11 SE18 ... 122 D1
Branksea St SW6 ... 135 A5 264 A3
Branksome Ave N18 ... 33 D5
Branksome Cl
Teddington TW11 ... 174 B6
Walton-on-T KT12 ... 194 D1
Branksome Ct 6 N2 ... 48 A6
Branksome Ho SW8 ... 270 C4
Branksome Rd
London SW2 ... 160 A6
Merton SW19 ... 179 C2
Branksome Way
Harrow HA3 ... 44 B3
Kingston u T KT3 ... 177 B2
Bransby Ct 4 N16 ... 73 C4
Bransby Rd KT9 ... 214 A2
Branscombe NW1 ... 232 B5
Branscombe Ct BR2 ... 208 C4
Branscombe Gdns N21 .. 16 C4
Branscombe St SE13 ... 141 D2
Bransdale Cl NW6 ... 91 C6
Bransgrove Rd HA8 ... 26 B3
Branston Cres BR5 ... 211 B1
Branstone Ct 9 TW9 ... 132 B4
Branstone Rd TW9 ... 132 B4
Branston Ho N7 ... 72 C3
Brants Wlk W7 ... 86 C3
Brantwood Ave
Erith DA8 ... 147 D5
Isleworth TW7 ... 131 A1
Brantwood Cl E17 ... 53 D6
Brantwood Gdns
Enfield EN2 ... 16 A6
Redbridge IG4 ... 56 A5
Brantwood Ho 9 SE5 ... 139 A5
Brantwood Rd
Erith DA7 ... 147 D3
Herne Hill SE24 ... 161 A6
Tottenham N17 ... 34 A4
Brasenose Dr SW13 ... 134 C6
Brasher Cl UB6 ... 64 B3
Brashley Road Cvn Site NW10 ... 89 C4
Brassett Point 3 E15 ... 98 C6
Brassey Cl TW14 ... 150 A3
Brassey Ho
1 Millwall E14 ... 119 D2
Walton-on-T KT12 ... 194 A1
Brassey Rd NW6 ... 69 B2
Brassey Sq SW11 ... 137 A2
Brassie Ave W3 ... 89 C1

Brass Talley Alley 31 SE16 ... 118 D4
Brasted Cl Bexley DA6 ... 168 D6
Forest Hill SE26 ... 184 C6
Brasted Lo 11 BR3 ... 185 C3
Brathay NW1 ... 232 B3
Brathway Rd SW18 ... 157 C4
Bratley St 11 E1 ... 96 A3
Bratten Ct CR0 ... 205 B3
Braund Ave UB6 ... 85 D3
Braundton Ave DA15 ... 167 D3
Braunston Dr UB4 ... 85 A3
Braunston Ho TW8 ... 131 C6
Bravington Cl TW17 ... 192 B4
Bravington Pl W9 ... 91 B3
Bravington Rd W9 ... 91 B4
Brawne Ho 12 SE17 ... 138 D6
Braxfield Rd SE4 ... 141 B1
Braxted Pk SW16 ... 182 B4
Bray NW3 ... 70 C1
Brayard's Rd SE15 ... 140 B3
Braybourne Dr TW7 ... 130 D5
Braybrooke Gdns SE19 ... 183 C3
Braybrook St W12 ... 89 D1
Brayburne Ave SW4 ... 137 C3
Braycourt Ave KT12 ... 194 C2
Bray Cres SE16 ... 118 D4
Bray Ct
Chessington KT9 ... 214 B3
Streatham SW16 ... 182 A5
Braydon Rd N16 ... 52 A1
Bray Dr E16 ... 120 D6
Brayfield Terr N1 ... 72 C1
Brayford Sq 12 E1 ... 96 C1
Bray Pl SW3 ... 114 D2 257 C3
Bray Rd NW7 ... 28 D4
Brayton Gdns EN2 ... 3 D1
Braywick Ct 9 KT2 ... 176 C3
Braywood Rd SE9 ... 145 B1
Brazier Cres UB5 ... 85 B3
Brazil Cl CR0 ... 204 A2
Breach La RM9 ... 103 C4
Bread St EC2, EC4 ... 242 B1
Breakspeare SE21 ... 161 D1
Breakspear Jun & Inf Schs UB10 ... 60 C6
Breakspear Rd HA4, UB9 ... 38 D3
Breakspear Rd N UB9 ... 38 B5
Breakspear Rd S UB9, UB10 ... 38 C1
Breakspears Dr BR5 ... 190 A2
Breakspears Mews SE4 ... 141 C3
Breakspears Rd SE4 ... 141 C2
Breakwell Ct 16 W10 ... 91 A3
Bream Cl N17 ... 52 B5
Bream Gdns E6 ... 100 C4
Breamore Cl SW15 ... 156 A3
Breamore Ct IG3 ... 80 A6
Breamore Ho 21 SE15 ... 140 A5
Breamore Rd IG3 ... 79 D6
Bream's Bldgs EC4 ... 94 C1 241 A2
Bream St E3 ... 75 C1
Breamwater Gdns TW10 ... 153 B1
Brearley Cl
Burnt Oak HA8 ... 27 A3
Uxbridge UB8 ... 60 A2
Breaside Prep Sch BR1 ... 187 D2
Breasley Cl SW15 ... 134 B1
Brechin Pl SW7 ... 114 A2 256 B3
Brecknock Prim Sch N7 ... 71 D2
Brecknock Rd N19 ... 71 D3
Breckonmead BR1 ... 187 C1
Brecon Cl Mitcham CR4 .. 204 A6
North Cheam KT4 ... 216 C6
Brecon Ct
7 Eltham SE9 ... 166 C5
Whetstone N12 ... 14 A1
Brecon Gn NW9 ... 45 C3
Brecon Ho
Stamford Hill N16 ... 51 D1
Wandsworth SW18 ... 157 C4
Brecon Rd Enfield EN3 ... 6 C1
Fulham W6 ... 135 A6 264 B5
Brede Cl E6 ... 100 C4
Bredel Ho 1 E14 ... 97 C2
Bredgar SE13 ... 163 D6
Bredgar Rd N19 ... 71 C6
Bredhurst Cl SE20 ... 184 C4
Bredinghurst SE22 ... 162 A4
Bredinghurst Sch SE15 ... 140 D1
Bredin Ho SW10 ... 265 D4
Bredo Ho IG11 ... 102 B4
Bredon Ct HA8 ... 26 B6
Bredon Rd CR0 ... 205 D2
Breer St SW6 ... 135 D2
Breezer's Ct 22 E1 ... 118 A6
Breezer's Hill E1 ... 118 A6
Brehon Ho NW1 ... 232 A5
Brember Rd HA2 ... 64 A6
Bremer Mews E17 ... 53 D5
Bremner Rd SW7 ... 256 B6
Brenchley Cl
Chislehurst BR7 ... 188 C2
Hayes BR2 ... 208 D3
Brenchley Gdns SE15, SE22, SE23 ... 162 D5
Brenchley Rd BR5 ... 189 D1
Bren Ct 27 EN3 ... 7 C6

Brenda Rd SW17..........158 D2
Brende Gdns KT8.......195 D5
Brendon Ave NW10.......67 C4
Brendon Cl Esher KT10..212 A2
  Harlington UB7.........127 A5
Brendon Ct
  3 London N20.........14 C2
  Southall UB1..........107 D2
Brendon Dr KT10.......212 A2
Brendon Gdns
  Harrow HA2............63 D4
  Ilford IG2............57 C4
Brendon Gr N2...........30 A1
Brendon Ho
  Marylebone W1........**238** A4
  Sutton SM2...........218 A4
Brendon Rd
  Dagenham RM8........59 C1
  New Eltham SE9......167 B2
Brendon St W1..92 C1 **237** B2
Brendon Villas N21.....17 A3
Brendon Way EN1.......11 C7
Brenley Cl CR4.........203 A6
Brenley Gdns SE9......143 D1
Brenley Ho SE1........**252** C2
Brennands Ct **14** N19....71 C5
Brent Adult Comm
  Education Service Coll
  NW10.................89 B6
Brent Cl DA5..........169 A3
Brentcot Cl W13........87 B3
Brent Cres NW10........88 B5
Brent Cross Flyover NW2,
  NW4.................46 D2
Brent Cross Gdns NW4..46 D3
Brent Cross Interchange
  NW2, NW4............46 D2
Brent Cross Sh Ctr
  NW4.................46 C2
Brent Cross Sta NW11..46 D2
Brent Ct **5** Acton W12..111 C3
  Ealing W7............108 B6
  Hendon NW11..........46 D2
Brentfield NW10........66 D1
Brentfield Cl NW10.....67 B2
Brentfield Gdns NW2....46 D2
Brentfield Ho **7** NW10..67 B1
Brentfield Prim Sch
  NW10.................67 B2
Brentfield Rd NW10.....67 B2
BRENTFORD..........131 B6
Brentford Bsns Ctr
  TW8.................131 C5
Brentford Cl UB4.......84 D3
BRENTFORD END......131 C4
Brentford Fountain L Ctr
  W4..................110 C1
Brentford Ho **6** TW1..153 B4
Brentford Sch for Girls
  TW8.................131 D6
Brentford Sta TW8.....131 C6
Brent Gn NW4..........46 D4
Brentham Way W5.......87 D3
Brent Ho
  3 Catford BR1......186 B5
  16 Hackney E9.......74 C2
  Wembley HA9..........66 B3
Brenthouse Rd E9......74 C2
Brenthurst Rd NW10....67 B2
Brent Knoll Sch SE26..162 D1
Brent Lea TW8.........131 C5
Brent Mans NW4........46 C4
Brentmead Cl W7......108 C6
Brentmead Gdns NW10..88 B5
Brentmead Pl NW11....46 D3
Brent Mus* NW10.......68 B2
Brent New Ent Ctr
  NW10.................67 D2
Brenton Ct E9..........75 A3
Brenton St E14.........97 A1
Brent Park Ind Est
  UB2.................106 C3
Brent Park Rd NW4.....46 B2
Brent Pl EN5...........13 B6
Brent Rd
  Brentford TW8.......131 C4
  Newham E16...........99 A2
  Southall UB2.........106 C3
  Woolwich SE18.......144 D5
Brentside TW8.........131 C6
Brentside Cl W13.......87 A3
Brentside Executive Ctr
  TW8.................131 B6
Brentside High Sch
  W7..................86 C3
Brentside Prim Sch
  W7..................86 C3
Brent St NW4..........46 C4
Brent Trad Est NW10...67 C3
Brentvale Ave
  Southall UB1........108 B5
  Wembley HA0..........88 B6
Brent View Rd NW9.....46 A2
Brentwaters Bsns Pk
  TW8.................131 C5
Brent Way
  Brentford TW8.......131 D5
  Finchley N3..........29 C4
  Wembley HA9..........66 D2
Brentwick Gdns TW8..110 A2
Brentwood Cl SE9.....167 A3
Brentwood Ho **2**
  SE18................143 D1
Brentwood Lo NW4.....46 D4
Brereton Ho **4** SW2...160 C4
Brereton Rd N17........33 D3

Bressenden Pl
  SW1.........115 C3 **259** A6
Bressey Ave EN1.........6 A4
Bressey Gr E18.........36 D1
Bretherton Ct CR2.....221 C2
Breton Ho
  Bermondsey SE1.....**263** D4
  St Luke's EC2........**242** B5
Brett Cl **15** Northolt UB5..84 D4
  Stoke Newington N16..73 C4
Brett Cres NW10........89 B6
Brett Ct N9............18 C2
Brettell St SE17.......**262** D1
Brettenham Ave E17....35 C2
Brettenham Prim Sch
  N18.................34 A6
Brettenham Rd
  Edmonton N18.........34 A6
  Walthamstow E17......35 C2
Brett Ho **1** SW15......156 D4
Brett House Cl **2**
  SW15................156 D4
Brettinghurst **8** SE1..118 A1
Bretton Ho N19.........50 A1
Brett Pas **8** E8........74 B3
Brett Rd Barnet EN5....12 C5
  Hackney E8...........74 B3
Brewers Bldgs EC1....**234** C2
Brewers Ct W2........**236** A2
Brewer's Gn SW1.....**259** C6
Brewers Hall Gdns
  EC2.................**242** A3
Brewers La **11** TW9....153 D6
Brewer St W1...115 C6 **249** B6
Brewery Cl HA0.........65 A4
Brewery Ind Est The
  N1..................**235** B3
Brewery Mews Bsns Ctr **1**
  TW7................131 A2
Brewery Rd Islington N7..72 A2
  Keston Mark BR2.....210 A1
  Plumstead SE18......123 B1
Brewery Sq
  Bermondsey SE1.....**253** C3
  Clerkenwell EC1.....**241** D6
Brewhouse La
  Putney SW15.........135 A2
  Wapping E1..........118 B5
Brewhouse Rd **3**
  SE18................122 B2
Brewhouse Wlk SE16...119 A5
Brewhouse Yd EC1....**241** C6
Brewood Rd RM8........80 B2
Brewster Gdns W10.....90 C2
Brewster Ho
  Bermondsey SE1.....**263** D4
  Poplar E14..........119 B6
Brewster Rd E10........53 D1
Brian Ct N10...........31 B2
Brian Rd RM6..........58 C4
Briant Ho SE1........**260** D5
Briants Cl HA5.........23 B1
Briant St SE14........140 D5
Briar Ave SW16........182 B3
Briarbank Rd W13......87 A1
Briar Cl
  Buckhurst Hill IG9...21 D2
  Edmonton N13.........17 A1
  Finchley N2..........30 A1
  Hampton TW12.......173 B5
  Isleworth TW7.......152 D6
Briar Cres UB5.........63 D2
Briar Ct **7** Bow E3.....97 C5
  Cheam SM3..........216 C4
  Dalston E8...........73 D1
  Hampton TW12.......173 D5
  Leytonstone E11......54 B2
Briardale Edgware HA8...27 B6
  Wandsworth SW19....157 B3
Briardale Gdns NW3....69 C5
Briarfield Ho **12** N16..51 C1
Briarfield Ave N3......29 D1
Briarfield Cl DA7.....147 C3
Briar Gdns BR2........208 D1
Briaris Cl **1** N17.......34 B3
Briar La CR0..........223 D4
Briar Lo E18...........37 C2
Briar Rd
  Cricklewood NW2......68 C4
  Harrow HA3...........43 C4
  Littleton TW17......192 C4
  Thornton Heath SW16..204 B6
  Twickenham TW2......152 C3
Briars The WD23........8 C4
Briarswood Way BR6..227 D3
Briar The **11** SM1......218 A4
Briarview Ct E4........36 B4
Briar Way UB7.........104 C4
Briar Wlk Burnt Oak HA8..27 A3
  Putney SW15.........134 B1
  West Kilburn W10.....91 A3
Briarwood Cl
  Feltham TW13........149 C1
  Kingsbury NW9........45 A3
Briarwood Ct **5** KT4..200 A1
Briarwood Dr HA6......22 A1
Briarwood Rd
  London SW4.........159 D6
  Stoneleigh KT17.....216 A2
Briary Cl **1** NW3.......70 C1
Briary Ct
  10 Canning Town E16..98 D1
  Sidcup DA14.........190 B5
Briary Gdns BR1.......187 B5
Briary Gr HA8..........26 D1
Briary La N9............17 D1
Briary Lo BR3.........186 A2
Brickbarn Cl SW10....**266** B4
Brick Ct EC4..........**241** A1
Brickett Cl HA4........39 A4

Brick Farm Cl TW9....132 D4
Brickfield Cl TW8.....131 C5
Brickfield Cotts SE18..145 D6
Brickfield Farm Gdns
  BR6................227 A4
Brickfield La
  Edgware EN5..........11 D5
  Harlington UB3......127 B6
Brickfield Rd
  South Norwood CR7,
  SW16...............182 D2
  Wimbledon SW19.....179 D6
Brickfields HA2.......64 B6
Brickfields Way UB7..104 B3
Brick La Enfield EN1....6 B3
  Northolt UB5.........85 B4
  Shoreditch E2........95 D4
  Spitalfields E1..95 D3 **243** D5
  Stanmore HA7.........25 D3
Bricklayers Arms SE1..**262** D5
Brick St W1....115 B5 **248** C3
Brickwall La HA4.......39 D1
Brickwood Cl SE26....162 B1
Brickwood Rd CR0....221 C6
Brickworth Ho **26**
  SW9................138 C4
Brideale Cl SE15......139 D6
Bride Ct EC4..........**241** C1
Bride La EC4...94 D1 **241** C1
Bridel Mews N1.......**234** C5
Bride St N7............72 B2
Bridewain St SE1.....**263** C6
Bridewell Pl
  Holborn EC4.........**241** C1
  20 Wapping E1......118 B5
Bridford Mews W1.....**238** D4
Bridge App NW3........71 A1
Bridge Ave Ealing W7...86 B2
  Hammersmith W6.....112 C1
Bridge Avenue Mans **1**
  W6.................112 C1
Bridge Bsns Ctr The
  UB2................107 C4
Bridge Cl Enfield EN1...6 B3
  13 North Kensington
  W10.................90 D1
  Teddington TW11.....174 D6
  Walton-on-T KT12...193 D1
Bridge Ct
  9 Blackwall E14....120 B6
  Leyton E10...........53 B2
  7 Walton-on-T KT12..193 D1
  7 Willesden NW10...67 C1
Bridge Dr N13..........32 B6
Bridge End E17.........36 A2
Bridge Field Ho **7** W2..91 D1
Bridgefield Rd SM1....217 C2
Bridgefoot SE1..116 A1 **260** B1
Bridge Gate N21........17 A4
Bridge Gdns
  Canonbury N16........73 B4
  East Molesey KT8....196 B5
  Littleton TW15......171 A3
Bridge Ho Brockley SE4..141 B1
  1 Camden Town NW1..71 A1
  Ealing TW8..........109 A2
  Homerton E9..........74 D3
  Woolwich SE28.......123 C5
Bridge Ho S **17** SE8....119 A2
Bridge House Quay
  E14................120 A5
Bridge La
  Battersea
  SW11.........136 C4 **267** B1
  Temple Fortune NW11..47 B4
Bridgeland Rd E16....121 A6
Bridgelands Cl BR3....185 B3
Bridgeman Ho **19** E9...74 C1
Bridgeman Rd
  Islington N1.........72 B1
  Teddington TW11.....175 A4
Bridgeman St
  NW8.........92 C5 **230** A3
Bridge Meadows
  SE14...............140 D6
Bridgend Rd SW18....136 A1
Bridgenhall Rd EN1.....5 D4
Bridgen Ho **9** E1......96 B1
Bridgen Rd DA5.......169 A4
Bridge Par
  7 Croydon CR0.....220 D5
  Edmonton N21.........17 A4
Bridge Pk
  7 London SW18....157 C6
  Wembley HA0.........66 D1
Bridge Pl
  Belgravia
  SW1.........115 B2 **258** D4
  Croydon CR0.........205 B1
Bridgepoint Lofts **2**
  E7..................77 C1
Bridgeport Pl **4** E1...118 A5
Bridge Rd
  Beckenham BR3.......185 B3
  Bexleyheath DA7.....147 A3
  Chessington KT9.....214 A3
  East Ham E6..........78 B1
  East Molesey KT8....196 D5
  Isleworth TW3, TW7..130 B2
  Southall UB2........107 C4
  Stratford Marsh E15..98 B6
  Sutton SM2..........217 D2
  Twickenham TW1.....153 B5
  Wallington SM6......219 C3
  Walthamstow E17......53 B2
  Wembley HA9..........66 C5
  Willesden NW10.......67 C2
  Wood Green N22......32 A2
Bridge Row CR0.......205 B1

Bridge Sch The
  Clerkenwell
  EC1............94 D3 **241** C6
  Shoreditch N1...95 A6 **235** B6
Bridges Ct SW11......136 B3
Bridges Ho **16** SE5...139 B5
Bridges La CR0........220 A4
Bridges Rd
  Stanmore HA7.........24 D5
  Wimbledon SW19.....179 D4
Bridges Road Mews
  SW19...............179 D4
Bridge St Chiswick W4..111 B3
  Pinner HA5...........41 A6
  Richmond TW10.......153 D6
  Walton-on-T KT12...193 D2
  Westminster
  SW1.........116 A4 **250** B1
Bridges The NW4.......46 A6
Bridge Terr E15........76 B1
Bridge The HA3........42 D5
Bridgetown Cl **5**
  SE19...............183 C5
Bridgeview **2** W6....112 C1
Bridgewater Cl BR7...211 C6
Bridgewater Ct HA0....65 C2
Bridgewater Gdns HA8..26 B1
Bridgewater Ho UB5....85 A3
Bridgewater Rd
  Ruislip HA4..........62 B4
  Stratford Marsh E15..98 A6
  Wembley HA0..........65 C1
Bridgewater Sq EC2..**242** A4
Bridgewater St EC2...**242** A4
Bridgeway Barking IG11..79 D1
  Wembley HA0..........66 B1
Bridgeway St
  NW1.........93 C5 **232** B3
Bridge Wharf **1** E2....96 D5
Bridge Wharf Rd TW7..131 B2
Bridgewood Cl SE20..184 B3
Bridgewood Rd
  North Cheam KT17,
  KT4................216 A4
  Streatham SW16.....181 D3
Bridge Yd SE1........**252** D4
Bridgford St SW17,
  SW18...............158 A1
Bridgman Rd W4.......111 A3
Bridgnorth Ho **10**
  SE15...............140 A6
Bridgwater Ho W2....**236** A2
Bridle Cl Enfield EN3...7 B6
  Kingston u T KT1....197 D5
  Sunbury TW16.......194 A6
  West Ewell KT19....215 B3
Bridle La
  Marylebone
  W1.........115 C6 **249** B6
  Twickenham TW1.....153 B5
Bridle Path CR0.......220 A5
Bridle Path The IG6...36 C3
Bridlepath Way TW14..149 C3
Bridle Rd
  Addington CR0.......223 C4
  Claygate KT10.......213 B2
  Croydon CR0.........223 C6
  Pinner HA5...........40 C4
Bridle Way
  Addington CR0.......223 C3
  Orpington BR6.......227 A4
Bridle Way The SM6...219 C3
Bridlington Ho **8**
  SW18...............136 A1
Bridlington Rd N9......18 B4
Bridport SE17........**262** B1
Bridport Ave RM7......59 D3
Bridport Ho
  6 Edmonton N18...34 A5
  Shoreditch N1.......95 B6
Bridport Pl N1...95 B6 **235** D5
Bridport Rd
  Edmonton N18........33 D5
  Greenford UB6........85 D6
  Thornton Heath CR7..204 A6
Bridstow Pl W2.........91 C1
Brief St SE5..........138 D4
Brierfield NW1.......**232** A5
Brierley CR0..........223 D2
Brierley Ave N9........18 C3
Brierley Cl SE25......206 A5
Brierley Ct W7........108 C6
Brierley Rd Leyton E11..76 B4
  Upper Tooting SW12..159 C2
Brierly Gdns E2........96 C5
Brigade Cl HA2........64 B6
Brigade St SE3.......142 D3
Brigadier Ave EN2......5 A4
Brigadier Hill EN2.....5 A5
Briggeford Cl **5** E5...74 A6
Briggs Cl CR4.........181 B2
Briggs Ho **20** E2......95 D4
Bright Cl DA17........124 D2
Bright Ct **8** SE28....124 C5
Brightfield Rd SE12...164 D6
Brightling Rd SE4....163 B5
Brightlingsea Pl **5**
  E14................119 B6
Brightman Rd SW18...158 B3
Brighton Ave E17......53 B4
Brighton Cl UB10......60 D1
Brighton Ct SW15.....157 B5
Brighton Dr **3** UB5...63 C2
Brighton Gr SE14.....141 A4
Brighton Ho **7** SE5...139 B4

Brighton Rd
  Belmont SM2.........217 D1
  Finchley N2..........30 A1
  South Croydon CR2...221 B2
  Stoke Newington N16..73 C4
  Surbiton KT6........197 D3
  Sutton SM2..........218 A1
  Wallend E6..........100 C4
Brighton Terr SW9....138 B1
Brightside Rd SE13...164 B5
Brightside The EN3.....7 A4
Bright St E14..........97 D2
Brightwell Cl CR0....204 C1
Brightwell Cres SW17..180 D5
Brightwell Ct N7......72 B2
Brightwells **1** SW6...135 D3
Brig Mews SE8........141 C6
Brigstock Ho SE5......139 A3
Brigstock Par **1** CR7..204 C4
Brigstock Rd
  Belvedere DA17......125 D2
  Thornton Heath CR7..204 D4
Brill Ho NW10.........67 B5
Brill Pl NW1....93 D5 **232** D3
Brim Hill N2...........48 B5
Brimpsfield Cl SE2...124 B3
BRIMSDOWN...........7 B3
Brimsdown Ave EN3.....7 A4
Brimsdown Ho **8** E3...98 A3
Brimsdown Jun & Inf Sch
  EN3.................6 D2
Brimsdown Sta EN3.....7 A3
Brimstone Ho **4** E15..76 C1
Brindishe Prim Sch
  SE12...............164 D6
Brindle Gate DA15....167 C3
Brindley Cl
  Bexleyheath DA7.....147 D2
  Wembley HA0..........87 D6
Brindley Ho
  Bromley BR1.........187 B5
  Southall UB1........107 D6
Brindwood Rd E4.......19 C1
Brine Ct KT6..........197 D4
Brine Ho **11** E3.......97 A5
Brinkburn Cl
  Abbey Wood SE2.....124 A2
  Edgware HA8.........44 D6
Brinkburn Gdns HA8....44 C6
Brinkley **18** KT1.....176 C1
Brinkley Rd KT4......216 B6
Brinklow Cres SE18...144 D5
Brinklow Ho W2........91 D2
Brinkworth Rd IG5.....56 A6
Brinkworth Way E9.....75 B2
Brinsdale Rd NW4......46 D6
Brinsley Ho **7** E1.....96 C1
Brinsley Rd HA3........24 B1
Brinsley St **35** E1.....96 B1
Brinsworth Ct TW2....152 B2
Brinton Wlk SE1......**251** C3
Brion Pl E14...........98 A2
Brisbane Ave SW19...179 D2
Brisbane Ct N10........31 B3
Brisbane Ho **3** W12...112 B6
Brisbane Rd
  Ealing W13..........109 A4
  Ilford IG1...........57 A1
  Leyton E10...........75 D6
Brisbane St SE5.......139 B5
Briscoe Cl E11.........76 D6
Briscoe Rd SW19......180 B4
Briset Rd SE9.........143 D1
Briset St EC1...94 D3 **241** C5
Briset Way N7..........72 B6
Bristol Cl
  Stanwell TW19.......148 A5
  Wallington SM6......220 A1
Bristol Ct **11** TW19...148 A5
Bristol Gdns
  Putney SW15.........156 C4
  Westbourne Green W9..91 D3
Bristol Ho
  1 Barking IG11.....80 A1
  SE11...............**261** A5
Bristol Mews W9.......91 D3
Bristol Park Rd **1** E17..53 A5
Bristol Rd
  Greenford UB6........85 D6
  Morden SM4.........202 A4
  Upton E7............77 D2
Briston Gr N8..........50 A3
Briston Mews NW7......28 A3
Bristowe Cl **24** SW2..160 C5
Bristow Rd
  Bexleyheath DA7.....147 A4
  Hounslow TW3........130 A2
  Wallington CR0......220 A4
  West Norwood SE19..183 C5
Britain at War
  Experience*
  SE1................**253** A3
Britannia Building N1..**235** C2
Britannia Cl
  London SW4.........137 D1
  Northolt UB5.........84 D4
Britannia Gate **11** E16..121 A5
Britannia Ho N20......14 A1
Britannia Junc NW1...**231** D6
Britannia La TW2......152 A4
Britannia Rd Ilford IG1..78 D1

Britannia Rd continued
  Whetstone N12........14 A1
Britannia Row
  N1..........95 A6 **235** A6
Britannia St
  WC1.........94 B4 **233** C2
Britannia Village Prim Sch
  E16................121 B5
Britannia Way NW10....88 D2
Britannia Wlk N1.....**235** C2
British Coll of Osteopathic
  Medicine NW3........70 A2
British Gr W4.........111 D1
British Grove Pas **2**
  W4.................111 D1
British Grove S **3**
  W4.................111 D1
British Home & Hospl for
  Incurables SE27.....182 D5
British Legion Rd E4...20 D2
British Library (Newspaper
  Library) NW9........45 C6
British Library The*
  WC1..........93 D4 **232** D2
British Mus*
  WC1..........94 A2 **240** A3
British St E3..........97 B4
British Wharf Ind Est
  SE14...............140 D6
Britley Ho **16** E14....97 B1
Brittain Ct SE9.......166 A3
Brittain Rd RM8........81 B5
Brittany Ho SW15.....134 C1
Brittany Point SE11...**261** A3
Britten Cl Elstree WD6...9 D5
  Golders Green NW11...47 D1
Brittenden Cl **1** BR6..227 D2
Brittenden Par BR6...227 D2
Britten Dr UB1.........85 C1
Britten Ho SW3.......**257** B2
Britten St SW3..114 C1 **257** A2
Britton Cl SE6........164 B4
Britton St EC1...94 D3 **241** C5
Brixham Cres HA4......40 A1
Brixham Gdns IG3......79 C3
Brixham Rd DA16.....146 D4
Brixham St E16.......122 C5
BRIXTON.............138 C2
Brixton Day Coll SW9..138 A2
Brixton Hill SW2......160 B5
Brixton Hill Ct **5** SW2..160 B4
Brixton Hill Pl SW2...160 A4
Brixton Mkt SW9......138 C1
Brixton Oval **7** SW2..138 C1
Brixton Rd SW9.......138 C4
Brixton Sta SW9......138 C1
Brixton Station Rd
  SW9................138 C2
Brixton Water La SW2..160 B6
Broadacre Cl UB10.....60 D5
Broadbent Cl N6.......49 B1
Broadbent St W1.....**248** C6
Broadberry Ct N18.....34 B5
Broadbridge Cl SE3...143 A5
Broad Common Est
  N16.................52 A1
Broadcoombe CR2.....222 D1
Broadcroft Ave HA7....25 D1
Broadcroft Rd BR5....211 B2
Broad Ct WC2........**240** B1
Broadeaves Cl CR2....221 C3
Broadfield NW6........69 D2
Broadfield Cl
  Croydon CR0........220 B6
  Dollis Hill NW2......68 C5
Broadfield Ct
  Bushey WD23..........8 C2
  Edgware HA8.........10 D1
Broadfield La NW1.....72 A1
Broadfield Rd SE6....164 C3
Broadfields Harrow HA2..23 D1
  Thames Ditton KT8...196 C4
Broadfields Ave
  Edgware HA8.........10 C1
  Southgate N21........16 C4
Broadfields Hts **1** HA8..26 D6
Broadfields Prim Sch
  HA8................10 C2
Broadfield Sq EN1......6 B3
Broadfields Way NW10..67 D3
Broadfield Way IG9....21 C1
Broadford Ho **12** E1...97 A3
BROADGATE..........95 C2
Broadgate EC2..95 C2 **243** A4
Broadgate Circ
  EC2..........95 C2 **243** A4
Broadgate Rd E16......99 D1
Broadgates Ave EN4....1 D4
Broadgates Ct SE11...**261** B3
Broadgates Rd SW18..158 B3
BROAD GREEN.......204 D2
Broad Green Ave CR0..204 D2
Broadhead Strand
  NW9................27 D2
Broadheath Dr BR7...188 B5
Broadhinton Rd SW4..137 C2
Broadhurst Ave
  Edgware HA8.........26 D6
  Ilford IG3...........79 D4
Broadhurst Cl
  Hampstead NW6.......70 A2
  9 Richmond TW10..154 B1
Broadhurst Gdns
  Hampstead NW6.......69 D2
  Ruislip HA4..........62 D2
Broadhurst Mans NW6..69 D2
Broad La Broadgate EC2 **243** A4
  Hampton TW12.......173 C4
  Hornsey Vale N8......50 B4
  South Tottenham N15..51 B5

Broad La continued
South Tottenham N15 . . . . 52 A5
Broadlands
Feltham TW13 . . . . 151 C1
Highgate N6 . . . . 49 A2
Broadlands Ave
Enfield EN3 . . . . 6 B2
Shepperton TW17 . . . . . . 193 A3
Streatham SW16 . . . . 160 A2
Broadlands Cl
Enfield EN3 . . . . 6 C2
Highgate N6 . . . . 49 A2
Streatham SW16 . . . . 160 A2
Broadlands Ct TW9 . . . . 132 C5
Broadlands Lo N6 . . . . 48 D2
Broadlands Mans 2
SW16 . . . . 160 A2
Broadlands Rd
Grove Pk BR1 . . . . 187 B6
Highgate N6 . . . . 48 D2
Broadlands Way KT3 . . . 199 D3
Broad Lawn SE9 . . . . 166 C3
Broadlawns Ct HA3 . . . . . 24 D2
Broadley St
NW8 . . . . 92 C2 237 A4
Broadley Terr
NW1 . . . . 92 C3 237 B5
Broadmayne SE17 . . . . 262 C2
Broadmead
Catford SE6 . . . . 163 C1
Hampton TW12 . . . . 173 C4
West Kensington W14 . . 254 A3
Broadmead Ave KT4 . . . 200 A2
Broadmead Cl
Hampton TW12 . . . . 173 C4
Pinner HA5 . . . . 23 A3
Broadmead Ct 6 IG8 . . . 37 A4
Broadmead Inf Sch
CR0 . . . . 205 B2
Broadmead Jun Sch
CR0 . . . . 205 B3
Broadmead Rd
Northolt UB5 . . . . 85 A3
Woodford IG8 . . . . 37 B3
Broad Oak
Ashford TW16 . . . . 171 D4
Woodford IG8 . . . . 37 B5
Broad Oak Cl
Chingford E4 . . . . 35 C5
St Paul's Cray BR5 . . . . . 190 A1
Broadoak Ct 8 SW9 . . . 138 C2
Broadoak Ho 11 NW6 . . . 91 D6
Broadoaks BR7 . . . . 188 D4
Broad Oaks KT6 . . . . 214 D6
Broadoaks Way BR2 . . . 208 D4
Broad St Ave EC2 . . . . . 243 A3
Broad Sanctuary SW1. 250 A1
Broad St
Dagenham RM10 . . . . 81 C1
Teddington TW11 . . . . . . 174 D4
Broadstone Ho SW8 . . 270 C3
Broadstone Pl W1 . . . . 238 A3
Broad Street Health Ctr
RM10 . . . . 103 C6
Broad Street Pl EC2 . . 242 D3
Broadview NW9 . . . . 44 C3
Broadview Est TW19 . . . 148 C4
Broadview Ho RM8 . . . . . 58 D1
Broadview Rd SW16 . . . 181 D3
Broadwalk Harrow HA2 . . 41 D4
Snaresbrook E18 . . . . 54 D6
Broadwalk Ho SW7 . . . 246 A1
Broadwalk La NW11 . . . . . 47 B2
Broadwalk Sh Ctr The
HA8 . . . . 26 D4
Broadwall SE1 . . 116 C5 251 B4
Broadwater Farm Prim
Sch N17 . . . . 33 B1
Broadwater Gdns BR6 . . 227 A4
Broadwater Prim Sch
SW17 . . . . 180 C6
Broadwater Rd
Plumstead SE18 . . . . 123 B3
Tottenham N17 . . . . 33 C1
Upper Tooting SW17 . . . . 180 C6
Broadway
Barking IG11 . . . . 101 A6
Bexley DA6 . . . . 147 C1
Bexleyheath DA6 . . . . . . 147 B1
Hanwell W7 . . . . 108 C5
Stratford E15 . . . . 76 B1
West Ealing W13 . . . . 109 A5
Westminster
SW1 . . . . 115 D3 259 C6
Broadway Arc 3 W6 . . . 112 C2
Broadway Ave
Thornton Heath CR0 . . . . 205 B4
Twickenham TW1 . . . . 153 B5
Broadway Bldgs 5
W7 . . . . 108 C5
Broadway Cl IG8 . . . . 37 B4
Broadway Ct
Beckenham BR3 . . . . 208 A6
Wimbledon SW19 . . . . . . 179 C4
Broadway Ctr The 6
W6 . . . . 112 C2
Broadway Gdns
Mitcham CR4 . . . . 202 C5
Woodford IG8 . . . . 37 B4
Broadway Ho 2 E8 . . . . . 96 B6
Broadway Ho 5
SW19 . . . . 179 C3
Broadway Lofts SW17 . . 180 C6
Broadway Mans SW6 . . 265 B3
Broadway Market E8 . . . . 96 B6
Broadway Market Mews 21
E8 . . . . 96 A6
Broadway Mews
Bowes Pk N13 . . . . 32 B5
Southgate N21 . . . . 16 D3
Broadway Mews continued
Stamford Hill E5 . . . . 51 D2
Broadway Par
Chingford E4 . . . . 36 A4
Hayes UB3 . . . . 106 A5
Hornsey N8 . . . . 50 A3
West Drayton UB7 . . . . . 104 A4
Broadway Pl SW19 . . . . . 179 B4
Broadway Ret Pk NW2 . . 68 D4
Broadway Sh Ctr 5
DA6 . . . . 147 C1
Broadway The
Barnes SW13 . . . . 133 C3
Cheam SM3 . . . . 217 A2
Chingford E4 . . . . 36 B4
Dagenham RM8 . . . . 81 C6
Ealing W5 . . . . 109 D6
Edgware NW7 . . . . 27 D5
Edmonton N9 . . . . 18 A1
Friern Barnet N11 . . . . 31 A5
Greenford UB6 . . . . 86 A3
Harrow HA3 . . . . 24 D1
Hornsey N8 . . . . 50 A3
Merton SW19 . . . . 179 C3
Newham E13 . . . . 99 B5
Pinner HA5 . . . . 23 B3
South Acton W3 . . . . 110 C4
Southall UB1 . . . . 107 A6
2 Southgate N14 . . . . 15 D3
Stanmore HA7 . . . . 25 C5
Sutton SM1 . . . . 218 A4
Thames Ditton KT10 . . . . 196 C1
Tolworth KT6 . . . . 198 C1
Wallington SM6 . . . . 220 A4
Wembley HA9 . . . . 66 A5
Woodford IG8 . . . . 37 B4
Wood Green N22 . . . . 32 C1
Broadway Wlk 4 E14 . . 119 C3
Broadwell Ct TW5 . . . . . 128 D4
Broadwick St
W1 . . . . 93 C1 239 B1
Broad Wlk
Eltham SE3, SE18 . . . . . . 144 A3
Heston TW5 . . . . 129 A4
Mayfair W1 . . . 115 A5 248 A4
Regent's Pk
NW1 . . . . 93 A5 231 B3
Richmond TW9 . . . . 132 B5
Southgate N21 . . . . 16 B3
Broad Wlk The
W8 . . . . 113 D5 245 D3
Broadwood Ave HA4 . . . . 39 C3
Broadwood Terr W14 . 254 D4
Broad Yd EC1 . . . . 241 C5
Brocade Ct NW9 . . . . 45 D5
Brocas Cl NW3 . . . . 70 C1
Brockbridge Ho
SW15 . . . . 155 D5
Brockdene Dr BR2 . . . . . 225 D4
Brockdish Ave IG11 . . . . . 79 D3
Brockelbank Lo RM8 . . . . 80 D6
Brockenhurst KT8 . . . . . 195 B3
Brockenhurst Ave
KT4 . . . . 199 C1
Brockenhurst Gdns
Edgware NW7 . . . . 27 C5
Ilford IG1 . . . . 79 A3
Brockenhurst Mews 9
N18 . . . . 34 A6
Brockenhurst Rd CR0 . . 206 B2
Brockenhurst Way
SW16 . . . . 181 D1
Brocket Ho 16 SW8 . . . . 137 D3
Brockham Cl SW19 . . . . 179 B5
Brockham Cres CR0 . . . . 224 B1
Brockham Ct
17 Belmont SM2 . . . . 217 D1
8 South Croydon CR2 . . 221 A3
Brockham Dr Ilford IG2 . . 57 A4
Streatham SW2 . . . . 160 B4
Brockham Ho
Camden Town NW1 . . . . 232 B5
11 Streatham SW2 . . . . . . 160 B4
Brockham St SE1 . . . . . 262 B6
Brockhurst Cl HA7 . . . . . . 24 D4
Brockhurst Ho N4 . . . . . . 51 B2
Brockill Cres SE4 . . . . . . 141 A1
Brocklebank Ho 7
E16 . . . . 122 C5
Brocklebank Rd
Greenwich SE7 . . . . 121 B2
Wandsworth SW18 . . . . . 158 A4
Brocklebank Road Ind Est
SE7 . . . . 121 A2
Brocklehurst St SE14 . . . 140 D5
Brocklesby Rd SE25 . . . . 206 B5
BROCKLEY 141 B1
Brockley Ave HA7 . . . . 10 A1
Brockley Cl HA7 . . . . 26 A6
Brockley Cross SE4 . . . . 141 B2
Brockley Cross Bsns Ctr
SE4 . . . . 141 A2
Brockley Gdns SE4 . . . . . 141 B3
Brockley Gr SE4 . . . . 163 B6
Brockley Hall Rd SE4 . . 163 A6
Brockley Hill HA7, HA8 . . . . 9 D2
Brockley Hill Ho HA7 . . . . . 9 C3
Brockley Ho SE17 . . . . . 263 A2
Brockley Mews SE4 . . . . 163 A6
Brockley Pk SE23 . . . . . . 163 A4
Brockley Prim Sch
SE4 . . . . 163 B6
Brockley Rd SE4 . . . . 163 B6
Brockley Rise SE23 . . . . 163 A4
Brockleyside HA7 . . . . 26 A6
Brockley Sta SE4 . . . . . . 141 A2
Brockley View SE23 . . . . 163 A4
Brockley Way SE4 . . . . . 163 A6
Brockman Rise BR1 . . . . 186 B6
Brockmer Ho 5 E1 . . . . . 118 B6
Brock Pl E3 . . . . 97 D3
Brock Rd E13 . . . . 99 B2
Brocks Dr SM3 . . . . 217 A5
Brockshot Cl 11 TW8 . . . 131 D6
Brock St SE15 . . . . 140 C2
Brockway Cl E11 . . . . 76 C6
Brockweir 23 E2 . . . . 96 C5
Brockwell Ave BR3 . . . . . 207 D4
Brockwell Cl BR5 . . . . . . 211 D4
Brockwell Ct
2 London SW2 . . . . 160 C6
Thornton Heath CR0 . . . . 204 D2
Brockwell Ho SE11 . . . . 270 D6
Brockwell Park*
SE24 . . . . 160 D5
Brockwell Park Gdns
SE24 . . . . 160 D4
Brockwell Park Row
SW2 . . . . 160 C5
Brockworth 8 KT2 . . . . 176 D2
Broderick Ho SE21 . . . . . 161 C1
Brodia Rd N16 . . . . 73 C5
Brodick Ho 12 E3 . . . . 97 B5
Brodie Ct E10 . . . . 54 B1
Brodie Ho
Bermondsey SE1 . . . . . . 263 D2
7 Wallington SM6 . . . . . . 219 B4
Brodie Rd Chingford E4 . . 20 A2
Enfield EN2 . . . . 5 A5
Brodie St SE1 . . . 117 D1 263 D2
Brodlove La E1 . . . . 118 D6
Brodrick Gr SE2 . . . . 124 B2
Brodrick Rd SW17 . . . . . 158 C2
Brody Ho E1 . . . . 243 C3
Brograve Gdns BR3 . . . . 185 D1
Broken Wharf EC4 . . . . 252 A6
Brokesley St E3 . . . . 97 B4
Broke Wlk Hackney E8 . . . 95 D6
1 Hackney E8 . . . . 96 A6
Bromar Rd SE5 . . . . 139 C2
Bromborough Gn
WD19 . . . . 22 C5
Bromefield HA7 . . . . 25 C2
Bromehead St 8 E1 . . . . 96 C1
Bromell's Rd SW4 . . . . . 137 C1
Brome Rd SE9 . . . . 144 B2
Bromfelde Rd SW4 . . . . . 137 D3
Bromfield Ct 20 SE16 . . . 118 A3
Bromfield St N1 . . . . . . 234 B4
Bromhall Rd RM8 . . . . 80 B3
Bromhedge SE9 . . . . 166 B1
Bromholm Rd SE2 . . . . . 124 B3
Bromleigh Ct 1 SE21,
SE22 . . . . 162 B2
Bromleigh Ho SE1 . . . . 263 C6
BROMLEY BR1 . . . . 186 C2
E3 . . . . 97 D4
Bromley Ave BR1 . . . . . . 186 C3
Bromley-by-Bow Sta
E3 . . . . 98 A4
Bromley Coll BR1 . . . . . . 187 A2
Bromley Coll of F & H Ed
BR2 . . . . 209 D3
Bromley Comm BR2 . . . 209 D4
BROMLEY COMMON . . 210 A3
Bromley Cres
Beckenham BR2 . . . . 208 D6
Ruislip HA4 . . . . 61 D4
Bromley Ct BR1 . . . . 186 D3
Bromley Gdns BR2 . . . . . 208 D6
Bromley Gr BR2 . . . . 186 B1
Bromley Hall Rd E14 . . . . 98 A2
Bromley High Sch
BR1 . . . . 210 C5
Bromley High St E3 . . . . . 97 D4
Bromley Hill BR1 . . . . . . 186 C4
Bromley Ho 5 BR1 . . . . . 187 A2
Bromley Ind Ctr BR1 . . . 209 D6
Bromley La BR7 . . . . 189 B3
Bromley Lo 2 W3 . . . . . . 89 A1
Bromley Manor Mans 3
BR1 . . . . 209 A6
Bromley North Sta
BR1 . . . . 187 A2
BROMLEY PARK 186 D2
Bromley Pk 11 BR1 . . . . . 186 D2
Bromley Pl W1 . . . . 239 A4
Bromley Rd
Beckenham BR3 . . . . 185 D2
Bromley BR2, BR3 . . . . . 186 B1
Catford SE6 . . . . 163 D1
Chislehurst BR7 . . . . 188 D2
Edmonton N18 . . . . 17 B1
Leyton E10 . . . . 53 D3
Tottenham N17 . . . . 34 A2
Walthamstow E17 . . . . 53 C6
Bromley Road Inf Sch
BR3 . . . . 185 D2
Bromley Road Ret Pk
SE6 . . . . 163 D2
Bromley South Sta
BR2 . . . . 209 A6
Bromley St E1 . . . . 96 D1
BROMPTON 114 B3
Brompton Arc SW1 . . . 247 D1
Brompton Cl
Hounslow TW4 . . . . 151 B6
Penge SE20 . . . . 184 A1
Brompton Ct 4 HA7 . . . . 25 C6
Brompton Gr N2 . . . . 48 C5
Brompton Ho 3 N9 . . . . . 34 A6
Brompton Oratory
SW3 . . . . 114 C3 257 A5
Brompton Park Cres
SW6 . . . . 135 D6 265 C5
Brompton Pl
SW3 . . . . 114 C3 257 B6
Brompton Rd
SW3 . . . . 114 C3 257 A5
Brompton Sq
SW3 . . . . 114 C3 257 A6
Bromstone Ho 10
SW9 . . . . 138 C4
Bromwich Ave N6 . . . . 71 A6
Bromwich Ho 3
TW10 . . . . 154 A5
Bromyard Ave W3 . . . . . 111 C6
Bromyard Ho
Acton W3 . . . . 111 C5
3 Peckham SE15 . . . . 140 B5
Bron Ct NW6 . . . . 91 C6
BRONDESBURY 69 A2
Brondesbury Coll for Boys
NW6 . . . . 69 A1
Brondesbury Ct NW2 . . . . 68 D2
Brondesbury Mews 11
NW6 . . . . 69 C1
BRONDESBURY PARK . . 90 D6
Brondesbury Park Sta
NW6 . . . . 91 A6
Brondesbury Pk NW2 . . . 68 D1
Brondesbury Rd NW6 . . . 91 C5
Brondesbury Sta NW6 . . 69 B1
Brondesbury Villas
NW6 . . . . 91 C5
Bronhill Terr N17 . . . . 34 A2
Bronsart Rd
SW6 . . . . 135 A5 264 A3
Bronson Rd SW20 . . . . . . 179 A1
Bronte Cl Erith DA8 . . . . 147 D5
1 Forest Gate E7 . . . . 77 A4
Ilford IG2 . . . . 56 C5
Bronte Ct 8 W14 . . . . . . 112 D3
Bronte Ho Kilburn NW6 . . . 91 C4
6 Stoke Newington N16 . 73 C3
Bronti Cl SE17 . . 117 A1 262 B2
Bronwen Ct NW8 . . . . . 229 C1
Bronze Age Way
DA17 . . . . 125 D4
Bronze St SE8 . . . . 141 C5
Brook Ave
Dagenham RM10 . . . . 81 D1
Edgware HA8 . . . . 26 D4
Wembley HA9 . . . . 66 C5
Brook Bank EN1 . . . . 6 B6
Brookbank Ave W7 . . . . . . 86 B2
Brookbank Rd SE13 . . . . 141 D2
Brook Cl Acton W3 . . . . . 110 C5
Finchley N12 . . . . 29 A3
Ruislip HA4 . . . . 39 C2
Stanwell TW19 . . . . 148 B4
Upper Tooting SW17 . . . . 159 A2
West Barnes SW20 . . . . . 200 B6
Brook Com Prim Sch
E8 . . . . 74 A3
Brook Cres Chingford E4 . . 35 D6
Edmonton N9 . . . . 34 B6
Brook Ct Barking IG11 . . . 101 D6
Beckenham BR3 . . . . 185 B2
5 Brentford TW8 . . . . 131 D6
Cheam SM3 . . . . 216 C4
Edgware HA8 . . . . 26 D5
2 Leyton E11 . . . . 76 C5
Mortlake SW14 . . . . 133 C2
Stratford New Town E15 . . 76 A3
Walthamstow E17 . . . . 53 A6
Brookdale N11 . . . . 31 C6
Brookdale Rd
Catford SE6 . . . . 163 D4
Lewisham SE6 . . . . 163 D5
Sidcup DA5 . . . . 169 A5
Walthamstow E17 . . . . 53 C6
Brookdales The NW4 . . . . 47 A5
Brookdene N12 . . . . 29 D6
Brookdene Rd SE18,
SE2 . . . . 123 D2
Brook Dr Harrow HA1 . . . . 42 A5
Newington
SE11 . . . . 116 D2 261 C4
Ruislip HA4 . . . . 39 C2
Brooke Ave HA2 . . . . 64 A5
Brooke Cl WD23 . . . . 8 A4
Brooke Ct Kilburn W10 . . . 91 A5
7 Kingston u T KT2 . . . . . 175 D6
Brooke Ho Bushey WD23 . . 8 A4
4 New Cross Gate
SE14 . . . . 141 A4
Brookehowse Rd SE6 . . 163 D1
Brookend Rd DA15 . . . . . 167 C3
Brooke Rd
Shacklewell E5, N16 . . . . . 74 A5
Walthamstow E17 . . . . 54 A5
Brookes Ct EC1 . . . . 241 A4
Brooke's Mkt EC1 . . . . . 241 B4
Brooke St EC1 . . . 94 C2 241 A3
Brooke Way WD23 . . . . 8 A4
Brookfield
Dartmouth Pk N6 . . . . 71 A5
1 Finsbury Pk N4 . . . . 72 C6
Brookfield Ave
Carshalton SM1, SM5 . . . 218 C5
Ealing W5 . . . . 87 D3
Mill Hill NW7 . . . . 28 B4
Walthamstow E17 . . . . 54 A5
Brookfield Cl NW7 . . . . . . 28 B4
Brookfield Cres
Harrow HA3 . . . . 44 A4
Mill Hill NW7 . . . . 28 B4
Brookfield Ct
Greenford UB6 . . . . 86 A4
1 London N12 . . . . 29 D6
Brookfield Gdns KT10 . . 212 D2
Brookfield Ho 23 E2 . . . . 96 B5
Brookfield House Sch
IG8 . . . . 36 C4
Brookfield Path IG8 . . . . . 36 C4
Brookfield Pk NW5 . . . . . 71 B5
Brookfield Prim Sch
Cheam SM3 . . . . 201 A1
Brookfield Prim Sch
continued
Dartmouth Pk N19 . . . . . . 71 B6
Brookfield Rd
Acton W4 . . . . 111 B4
Edmonton N9 . . . . 18 B1
Homerton E9 . . . . 75 A2
Brookfields EN3 . . . . 6 D1
Brookfields Ave CR4 . . . 202 C4
Brookgate N16 . . . . 73 B6
Brook Gate
W1 . . . . 114 D6 247 D5
Brook Gdns
Barnes SW13 . . . . 133 D2
Chingford E4 . . . . 35 D6
Kingston u T KT2 . . . . . . 177 A2
Brook Gn W6 . . . . 112 D2
BROOK GREEN 112 D2
Brook Green Flats 11
W14 . . . . 112 D3
Brookhill Cl
East Barnet EN4 . . . . 14 C6
Woolwich SE18 . . . . 122 D1
Brookhill Ct 2 EN4 . . . . . 14 C5
Brookhill Rd
East Barnet EN4 . . . . 14 C6
Woolwich SE18 . . . . 122 D1
Brook Ho
3 Clapham Pk SW4 . . . . 159 C6
Ealing W3 . . . . 110 C4
3 Edmonton N9 . . . . 18 A1
4 Hammersmith W6 . . . 112 C2
Marylebone WC1 . . . . . . 239 C4
4 Twickenham TW1 . . . . 153 A4
Brook Hos NW1 . . . . 232 B3
Brookhouse Gdns E4 . . . . 36 C6
Brook House Sixth Form
Coll E5 . . . . 74 B5
Brook Ind Est UB4 . . . . . 106 C5
Brooking Cl RM8 . . . . 80 C5
Brooking Rd E7 . . . . 77 A3
Brook La Bexley DA5 . . . . 168 D5
Greenwich SE3 . . . . 143 A3
Plaistow BR1 . . . . 187 A4
Brook La N 3 TW8 . . . . . 131 D6
Brookland Cl NW11 . . . . . 47 C5
Brookland Garth NW11 . . 47 D5
Brookland Hill NW11 . . . . 47 D5
Brookland Jun & Inf Schs
NW11 . . . . 47 D5
Brookland Rise NW11 . . . 47 C5
Brooklands Ave
New Eltham DA15 . . . . . 167 B2
Wandsworth SW18 . . . . . 157 D2
Brooklands Cl TW16 . . . 171 C2
Brooklands Court
Apartments 3 NW6 . . . 69 B1
Brooklands Ct
10 Clapham SW8 . . . . . . 137 C3
Enfield N21 . . . . 17 B6
Kingston u T KT1 . . . . 197 D5
2 London NW6 . . . . 69 B1
2 Mitcham CR4 . . . . 180 B1
Brooklands Dr UB6 . . . . . 87 D6
Brooklands Ho SE3 . . . . 143 A2
Brooklands Pk SE3 . . . . . 143 A2
Brooklands Pl TW12 . . . . 173 D5
Brooklands Prim Sch
SE3 . . . . 143 A2
Brooklands Rd KT7 . . . . . 197 A1
Brooklands The TW7 . . . 130 B4
Brook Lane Bns Ctr
TW8 . . . . 109 D1
Brooklea Cl NW9 . . . . 27 C2
Brook Lo Crouch End N8 . . 49 D3
Edgware HA8 . . . . 26 D4
Hendon NW4 . . . . 46 D4
Brooklyn SE20 . . . . 184 A3
Brooklyn Ave SE25 . . . . 206 B5
Brooklyn Cl SM5 . . . . 218 C6
Brooklyn Ct
Feltham TW13 . . . . 150 B2
Shepherd's Bush W12 . . . 112 C5
Brooklyn Gr SE25 . . . . . . 206 B5
Brooklyn Rd
Bromley BR2 . . . . 210 A4
Croydon SE25 . . . . 206 B5
Brookmarsh Ind Est
SE10 . . . . 141 D5
Brook Mdw N12 . . . . 13 D1
Brook Mead KT19 . . . . . . 215 C2
Brookmead Ave BR1,
BR2 . . . . 210 B4
Brookmead Ct N20 . . . . . 14 A2
Brookmead Ind Est
CR4 . . . . 203 C3
Brook Meadow Cl IG8 . . . 36 C4
Brookmead Rd CR0 . . . . 203 C3
Brook Mews N
W2 . . . . 114 A6 246 B6
Brookmill Rd SE8 . . . . . . 141 C4
Brook Park Cl N21 . . . . . . 16 D6
Brook Pl EN5 . . . . 13 C6
Brook Rd
Buckhurst Hill IG9 . . . . . . 21 A3
Dollis Hill NW2 . . . . 68 A6
Finchley N12 . . . . 30 C3
Hornsey N8 . . . . 50 A5
Ilford IG2 . . . . 57 C3
South Norwood CR7 . . . . 205 A5
Surbiton KT6 . . . . 214 A6
Twickenham TW1 . . . . 153 A5
Wood Green N22 . . . . 50 B6
Brook Rd S TW8 . . . . 131 D6
Brook Ret Pk HA4 . . . . 62 D3
Brooks Ave E6 . . . . 100 B3
Brooksbank Ho 7 E9 . . . . 74 C2
Brooksbank St 9 E9 . . . . 74 C2
Brooksby Ho 9 N1 . . . . . . 72 C1
Brooksby Mews N1 . . . . . 72 C1
Brooksby St N1 . . . . 72 C1
Brooksby's Wlk E9 . . . . . . 74 D3
Brooks Cl SE9 . . . . 166 C2
Brookscroft E17 . . . . 53 D6
Brookscroft Rd E17 . . . . . 35 D2
Brooks Ct
3 London SW4 . . . . 138 A3
Nine Elms SW8 . . . . 269 B4
Brookshill HA3 . . . . 24 B5
Brookshill Ave HA3 . . . . . 24 C5
Brookshill Dr HA3 . . . . . . 24 B5
Brookshill Gate HA3 . . . . 24 B5
Brooks Ho 6 SW2 . . . . . 160 C3
Brookside
Broom Hill BR6 . . . . 211 D2
East Barnet EN4 . . . . 14 C5
Hillingdon UB10 . . . . 60 B1
Southgate N21 . . . . 16 B5
Wallington SM5 . . . . 219 A3
Brookside Cl
Barnet EN5 . . . . 13 A5
Feltham TW13 . . . . 150 A1
Harrow HA3 . . . . 43 D4
South Harrow HA2, HA4 . . 63 A4
Brookside Cres 1
KT4 . . . . 200 A1
Brookside Ct SW16 . . . . 181 C3
Brookside Gdns EN1 . . . . . 6 C6
Brookside Ho N17 . . . . . . 33 C1
Brookside Prim Sch
UB4 . . . . 84 C4
Brookside Rd
Edmonton N9 . . . . 34 B6
Hayes UB4 . . . . 106 C6
Temple Fortune NW11 . . . 47 B3
Upper Holloway N19 . . . . 71 C6
Brookside S EN4 . . . . 15 A4
Brookside Way CR0 . . . . 206 D3
Brooks La W4 . . . . 132 C6
Brook's Mans 5 IG3 . . . . 58 B1
Brook's Mews
W1 . . . . 115 B6 248 C6
Brook's Par 6 IG3 . . . . . . 58 B1
Brook Sq SE18 . . . . 144 A4
Brooks Rd W4 . . . . 110 C1
Brook's Rd E13 . . . . 99 A6
Brook St
Bayswater
W2 . . . . 114 B6 246 D6
Erith DA8 . . . . 147 D5
Kingston u T KT1 . . . . 176 A1
Mayfair W1 . . . . 115 B6 248 C6
7 Tottenham N17 . . . . 33 D1
Brookstone Ct SE15 . . . . 140 B1
Brooksville Ave NW6 . . . . 91 A6
Brook Vale DA8 . . . . 147 D4
Brookview Ct 11 EN1 . . . . 17 C6
Brookview Rd SW16 . . . 181 C5
Brookville Rd
SW6 . . . . 135 B5 264 C3
Brookway SE3 . . . . 143 A2
Brook Wlk
Burnt Oak HA8 . . . . 27 B4
Finchley N2 . . . . 30 B2
Brookwood Ave SW13 . . 133 D3
Brookwood Cl BR2 . . . . . 208 D5
Brookwood Ho SE1 . . . 251 D1
Brookwood Rd
Hounslow TW3 . . . . 129 D4
Wandsworth SW18 . . . . . 157 C3
Broom Ave BR5 . . . . 190 B1
Broom Cl
Bromley Comm BR2 . . . . 210 A3
Teddington KT1, TW11 . . 175 D3
Broomcroft Ave UB5 . . . . 84 C4
Broome Ct 3 TW9 . . . . . 132 C4
Broome Ho 7 E5 . . . . 74 B3
Broome Rd TW12 . . . . . . 173 B2
Broome Way SE5 . . . . . . 139 B5
Broom Farm SW6 . . . . . . 135 C3
Broomfield
7 Camden Town NW1 . . . 71 A1
Sunbury TW16 . . . . 172 A2
Walthamstow E17 . . . . 53 B2
Broomfield Ave N13 . . . . 32 B5
Broomfield Cotts N13 . . . 32 A5
Broomfield Ct N13 . . . . . 32 A5
Broomfield Ho
Stanmore HA7 . . . . 9 A1
4 St Paul's Cray BR5 . . . 190 B1
Walworth SE17 . . . . 263 A3
Broomfield House Sch
TW9 . . . . 132 B4
Broomfield La N13 . . . . . 32 B6
Broomfield Pl W13 . . . . . 109 B5
Broomfield Rd
Beckenham BR3 . . . . 207 B6
Bexley DA6 . . . . 169 C6
Bowes Pk N13 . . . . 32 A5
Dagenham RM6 . . . . 58 D2
Ealing W13 . . . . 109 B5
Richmond TW9 . . . . 132 B4
Surbiton KT5 . . . . 198 B1
Teddington TW11 . . . . . . 175 C4
Broomfields KT10 . . . . . . 212 A3
Broomfield Sch N14 . . . . 31 D5
Broomfield St E14 . . . . . . 97 D2
Broom Gdns CR0 . . . . . . 223 C5
Broomgrove Gdns HA8 . . 26 C2
Broomgrove Rd SW9 . . . 138 B3
BROOM HILL 211 D2
Broomhill Ct 2 IG8 . . . . . 37 A4
Broomhill Rd
Broom Hill BR6 . . . . 211 D2
Ilford IG3 . . . . 80 A6
Wandsworth SW18 . . . . . 157 C6
Woodford IG8 . . . . 37 A4

Broomhill Rise DA6 .....169 C6
Broomhill Wlk IG8.....36 C3
Broomhouse La SW6....135 C2
Broomhouse Rd SW6 ....135 C3
Broomleigh BR1.......187 A2
Broomloan La SM1....217 C6
Broom Lock TW11 .....175 C4
Broom Mead DA6.......169 C6
Broom Pk KT1.........175 D3
Broom Rd Croydon CR0...223 C5
  Teddington TW11.......175 C4
Broomsleigh Bsns Pk
  SE26..................185 B5
Broomsleigh St NW6.....69 B3
Broom Water TW11......175 C5
Broom Water W
  TW11.................175 C5
Broomwood Cl CR0....206 D4
Broomwood Hall Sch
  SW12................159 A4
Broomwood Rd
  London SW11 ....159 A6
  St Paul's Cray BR5.....190 B1
Broseley Gr SE26 ......185 A5
Broster Gdns SE25......205 D6
Brougham Rd Acton W3...89 A1
  Hackney E8............96 A6
Brougham St SW11 ....136 D3
Brough Cl
  Kingston u T KT2......175 D5
  South Lambeth SW8.....270 B3
Broughton Ave
  London N3............47 A6
  Richmond TW10 ......175 C6
Broughton Ct W13......109 B6
Broughton Dr 19 SW9..138 D1
Broughton Gdns N6.....49 C3
Broughton Ho 10
  SW19................179 A3
Broughton Rd
  Ealing W13...........109 B6
  Orpington BR6........227 B6
  Sands End SW6........135 D3
  Thornton Heath CR7....204 C3
Broughton Road App 2
  SW6.................135 D3
Broughton St SW8......137 B3
Brouncker Rd W3......111 A4
Browells La TW13......150 B2
Brown Bear Ct TW13...172 D6
Brown Cl SM6.........220 A1
Browne Ho
  13 Deptford SE8......141 C5
  9 Penge SE26........184 B5
Brownfield St E14.......98 A1
Brownflete Ho SE4.....141 A4
Browngraves Rd UB7...127 A5
Brown Hart Gdns W1...248 B6
Brownhill Rd SE6......164 A4
Browning Ave
  Carshalton SM1......218 C4
  Ealing W7.............86 D1
  North Cheam KT4.....200 B1
Browning Cl
  Bexley DA16..........145 C4
  Feltham TW12........173 B6
  Paddington W9 ......236 B5
  Walthamstow E17......54 A5
Browning Ct W14......264 C6
Browning Ho
  2 London SE14......141 A4
  7 Shepherd's Bush
  W12.................90 C1
  10 Stoke Newington N16..73 C4
Browning Mews W1 ...238 B3
Browning Rd Enfield EN2..5 B5
  Leytonstone E11.......54 D2
  Plashet E12...........78 B2
Browning St
  SE17.........117 A2 262 B3
Browning Way TW5....128 C4
Brownlea Gdns IG3.....80 A6
Brownlow Cl EN4.......14 B6
Brownlow Ct
  2 Bowes Pk N11.......32 A4
  Hampstead Garden Suburb
  N2...................48 A4
Brownlow Ho 10 SE16..118 A4
Brownlow Lo 1 N11....32 A4
Brownlow Mews
  WC1..........94 B3 240 D5
Brownlow Rd
  Bowes Pk N11.........32 A4
  6 Ealing W13.........109 A5
  Finchley N3...........29 D3
  3 Forest Gate E7.......77 A4
  Hackney E8............96 A6
  South Croydon CR0....221 D4
  Willesden NW10........67 C1
Brownlow St
  WC1..........94 B2 240 D3
Brownrigg Rd TW15....170 C6
Brown's Bldgs EC3.....243 B1
Brownsea Wlk NW7.....28 D4
Brownspring Dr SE9 ...166 D1
Brown's Rd
  Surbiton KT5, KT6.....198 B2
  Walthamstow E17......53 C6
Brown St W1....92 D1 237 C2
Brownswell Rd N2......30 B1
Brownswood Rd N4.....73 A6
Broxash Rd SW11......159 A5
Broxbourne Ave E18.....55 B5
Broxbourne Ho 1 E3...97 D3
Broxbourne Rd

Broxholme Ho SW6 ....265 C2
Broxholm Rd SE27,
  SW16................160 C1
Broxted Rd SE6........163 B2
Broxwood Way
  NW8........92 C6 230 B5
Bruce Ave TW17......193 A3
Bruce Castle Ct N17 ....33 C2
Bruce Castle Mus ★
  N17..................33 C2
Bruce Castle Rd N17...33 D2
Bruce Cl
  North Kensington W10...90 D2
  Welling DA16.........146 B4
Bruce Ct DA15........189 D6
Bruce Gdns N20........14 D1
Bruce Glasier Ho 13
  N19..................49 D2
Bruce Gr N17..........33 D1
Bruce Grove N17.......33 D1
Bruce Grove Prim Sch
  N17..................33 D1
Bruce Grove Sta N17...33 D1
Bruce Hall Mews
  SW17................181 A6
Bruce Ho
  4 Clapham Pk SW4...159 D5
  5 Greenhill HA1.......42 A4
  North Kensington W10...90 D2
  Preston HA3...........44 A2
  Putney SW15.........156 B6
Bruce Lawns SW17.....181 A6
Bruce Rd Barnet EN5......1 A2
  Bromley E3............97 D4
  Harrow HA3...........24 C1
  Mitcham CR4.........181 A3
  South Norwood SE25...205 B5
  Willesden NW10........67 B1
Bruckner St W10.......91 B4
Brudenell Rd SW17....181 A6
Bruffs Meadow UB5.....63 A2
Bruges Pl 16 NW1......71 C1
Brumfield Rd KT19....215 A3
Brune Ho E1...........243 C3
Brunei Gallery ★
  WC1.........94 A3 240 B6
Brunel Cl
  Cranford TW5........128 B5
  Northolt UB5...........85 B4
  Penge SE19..........183 D4
Brunel Ct 8 SW13.....133 D3
Brunel Engine House
Rotherhithe ★ SE16.....118 C4
Brunel Est 2 W2.......91 C2
Brunel Ho
  Chelsea SW10........266 D4
  4 Gospel Oak NW5.....71 B4
  Hayes UB3...........105 C3
  Millwall E14..........119 D1
  New Cross SE8.......141 B5
  25 Streatham SW2....160 A4
Brunel Mews NW10.....90 D4
Brunel Pl 7 UB1........85 D1
Brunel Rd Acton W3...89 C2
  Walthamstow E17......53 A3
  Wapping SE16........118 C5
Brunel Science Pk UB8..82 A4
Brunel St E16..........98 D1
Brunel Univ Coll Osterley
  Campus TW7.........130 D5
Brunel Wlk
  South Tottenham N15...51 C2
  Twickenham TW4......151 C4
Brune St E1.....95 D2 243 C3
Brunlees Ho SE1.......262 B5
Brunner Cl NW11......48 A4
Brunner Ho 6 SE6.....186 A6
Brunner Rd Ealing W5...87 D3
  Walthamstow E17......53 B4
Bruno Ct 5 E8..........74 A2
Bruno Pl NW9..........67 A6
Brunswick Ave N11 ....15 A1

Brunswick Pl
  Penge SE19..........184 A3
  Shoreditch N1...95 B4 235 D1
Brunswick Quay SE16..118 D3
Brunswick Rd
  Bexley DA6..........147 A1
  Ealing W5.............88 A4
  Holdbrook EN3.........7 C5
  Kingston u T KT2.....176 C2
  Leyton E10............54 A1
  Poplar E14............98 A1
  South Tottenham N15...51 C4
  South Tottenham N15...51 C5
  Sutton SM1..........217 D3
Brunswick Sh Ctr
  WC1.........94 A3 240 B6
Brunswick Sq
  St Pancras
  WC1.........94 A3 240 B6
  Tottenham N17........33 D4
Brunswick St E17.......54 A4
Brunswick Terr BR3....185 D2
Brunswick Villas 2
  SE5.................139 C4
Brunswick Way N11.....31 B6
Brunton Pl E14.........97 A1
Brushfield St
  E1...........95 D2 243 C4
Brushwood Lo 1
  DA17................125 C2
Brussels Ct N18........33 C5
Brussels Rd SW11.....136 B1
Bruton Cl BR7.........188 B3
Bruton La W1..115 B6 248 D5
Bruton Pl W1...115 B6 248 D5
Bruton Rd SM4........202 A5
Bruton St W1...115 B6 248 D5
Bruton Way W13........87 A2
Brutus Ct SE11........261 C3
Bryan Ave NW10........68 B1
Bryan Cl TW16........172 A3
Bryan Ct W1..........237 C2
Bryan Ho SE16........119 B4
Bryan Rd SE16........119 B4
Bryanston Ave TW2...151 B3
Bryanston Cl UB2.....107 B2
Bryanston Ct W1......237 C2
Bryanstone Rd N8.....49 D4
Bryanston Ho 12 SE15..139 D4
Bryanston Mans W1...237 C4
Bryanston Mews E W1..237 C3
Bryanston Mews W
  W1.................237 C2
Bryanston Pl
  W1..........92 D2 237 C3
Bryanston Sq
  W1..........92 D1 237 C2
Bryanston St
  W1..........92 D1 237 D1
Bryant Cl EN5..........13 B6
Bryant Ct Acton W3....111 B5
  Haggerston E2..........95 D5
Bryant Rd UB5..........84 C4
Bryant St E15..........76 C1
Bryantwood Rd N5, N7..72 C3
Brycedale Cres N14.....15 D1
Bryce Ho 25 SE14......140 D6
Bryce Rd RM8..........80 C4
Brydale Ho 2 SE16....118 D2
Bryden St SE26.......185 A5
Brydges Pl WC2.......250 A5
Brydges Rd E15.........76 B3
Brydon Wlk N1.........233 B6
Bryer Ct EC2..........242 A4
Bryett Rd N7...........72 A5
Bryher Ho W4.........111 A1
Brymay Cl E3...........97 C5
Brymon Ct W1........237 D3
Brynmaer Ho SW11....267 D1
Brynmaer Rd
  SW11.........136 D4 267 D1
Bryn-y-Mawr Rd EN1....5 D1
Bryony Cl UB8..........82 B2
Bryony Rd W12........112 A6
Bryony Way TW16.....172 A4
B Sky B Hq TW7......131 A6
BT Telecom Twr ★
  W1...........93 C2 239 A4
Buccleuch Ho E5........52 A2
Buchanan Cl N21......16 B6
Buchanan Ct 18 SE16...118 D2
Buchanan Gdns NW10...90 B5
Buchanan Ho
  Dulwich SE21........161 C1
  Wandsworth SW18.....157 C4
Buchan Ho W3........110 D4
Buchan Rd SE15.......140 C2
Bucharest Rd SW18....158 A4
Buckden Cl
  Fortis Green N2........48 D5
  Lee SE12.............165 A5
Buckfast Ct W13......109 A6
Buckfast Ho N14........15 C6
Buckfast Rd SM4......201 D5
Buckfast St E2..........96 A4
Buck Hill Wlk
  W2...........114 B6 246 B6
Buckhold Rd SW18....157 C5
Buckhurst Ave CR4,
  SM5................218 A4
Buckhurst Ct 7 IG9.....21 D2
BUCKHURST HILL......21 C2
Buckhurst Hill Sch 3
  IG9..................21 B2
Buckhurst Hill Sta IG9...21 A2
Buckhurst Ho 15 N7.....71 D3
Buckhurst St E1.........96 B3
Buckhurst Way IG9.....21 D1

Buckingham Ave
  East Molesey KT8.....173 D1
  Falconwood DA16.....145 C1
  Feltham TW14........150 B5
  Oakleigh Pk N20.......14 B4
  South Norwood CR7...182 C2
  Wembley UB6..........87 A6
Buckingham Cl
  Broom Hill BR5......211 C2
  Ealing W5.............87 C2
  Enfield EN1.............5 C3
  Hampton TW12........173 B5
Buckingham College Sch
  HA1.................42 C4
Buckingham Ct
  2 Ealing W7...........86 D3
  Hendon NW4...........46 A6
  Mitcham CR4.........204 A4
  Northolt UB5...........85 A6
  Wembley HA0..........65 A2
Buckingham Dr BR7...189 A5
Buckingham Gate
  SW1.........115 C3 259 B6
Buckingham Gdns
  East Molesey KT8.....173 D1
  Edgware HA8...........26 B3
  South Norwood CR7...182 C1
Buckingham Gr UB10...82 C5
Buckingham Ho
  1 Acton W3...........88 C1
  Finsbury Pk N4........51 A1
  Richmond TW10 ......154 C6
Buckingham La SE23...163 A4
Buckingham Lo N10.....49 C5
Buckingham Mans
  NW6.................69 D3
Buckingham Mews
  Harlesden NW10.......89 D5
  7 Kingsland N1.......73 C2
  Westminster SW1.....259 A6
Buckingham Pal ★
  SW1.........115 C4 249 A1
Buckingham Palace Rd
  SW1.........115 B2 258 D6
Buckingham Par 19
  HA7.................25 C5
Buckingham Pl SW1...259 A6
Buckingham Prim Sch
  TW12................173 B5
Buckingham Rd
  Edgware HA8..........26 B3
  Hampton TW12, TW13...173 B5
  Harlesden NW10.......89 D5
  Harrow HA1............42 B4
  Ilford IG1.............79 B6
  Kingsland N1..........73 C2
  Kingston u T KT1.....198 B5
  Leyton E10............75 D5
  Mitcham CR4.........204 A4
  Richmond TW10 ......153 D2
  Stratford E15..........76 D3
  Wanstead E11.........55 C4
  Woodford E18..........36 D2
Buckingham St WC2...250 B5
Buckingham Way
  SM6.................219 C1
Buckingham Yd NW10...89 D5
Buck La NW9...........45 B4
Buckland Cl NW7.......28 A6
Buckland Cres NW3....70 B2
Buckland Ct
  6 Shoreditch N1.......95 C5
  Uxbridge UB10........61 A6
Buckland Ho 3 N1.....72 C1
Buckland Inf Sch KT9..214 B3
Buckland Rd
  Chessington KT9.....214 B3
  Leyton E10............76 A6
  Orpington BR6........227 C4
Buckland Rise HA5.....22 D2
Bucklands Rd TW11....175 C4
Buckland St N1...95 B5 235 D3
Buckland Way KT4....200 C1
Buckland Wlk
  2 Acton W3..........111 A4
  Morden SM4.........202 A5
Buckle Ct HA8.........27 A3
Buckleigh Ave SW20...201 B6
Buckleigh Ho SW17...180 B5
Buckleigh Rd SW16...182 A3
Buckleigh Way SE19...183 D3
Buckler Gdns SE9.....166 B1
Buckler's Alley SW6...264 D4
Bucklersbury EC2, EC4..242 C1
Buckler's Way SM5....218 D5
Buckles Ct DA17......124 D2
Buckle St
  15 Whitechapel E1......96 A1
  Whitechapel E1.......243 D2
Buckley Cl SE23......162 B4
Buckley Ct
  5 Brondesbury NW6...69 B1
  London N8............49 D4
Buckley Ho W3........110 C5
Buckley Rd NW6........69 B1
Buckmaster Cl 1
  SW9................138 C2
Buckmaster Ho 1 N7...72 B4
Buckmaster Rd SW11..136 C1
Bucknall St WC1.......240 A2
Bucknall Way BR3.....208 A5
Bucknell Cl SW2......138 B1
Buckner Rd SW2......138 B1
Buckrell Rd E4..........20 B2
Buckridge Bldg EC1....241 A4
Buckshead Ho 19 W2...91 C2
Buck St NW1...........71 B1
Buckstone Cl SE23....162 C5
Buckstone Rd N18......34 A5

Buckters Rents SE16...119 A5
Buckthorne Rd SE4....163 A6
Buckthorn Ho DA15...167 D1
Buckwheat Ct DA18...124 D3
Budd Cl N12...........29 C6
Buddings Circ HA9.....67 A5
Bude Cl E17............53 B4
Budge La CR4.........202 D2
Budge Row EC4.......242 C1
Budge's Wlk
  W2..........114 A5 246 B4
Budleigh Cres DA16....146 C4
Budleigh Ho 10 SE15....140 A5
Budoch Ct IG3.........80 A6
Budoch Dr IG3.........80 A6
Buer RC SW6..........135 A3
Bugsby's Way SE10...120 D2
Buick Ho 8 E3..........97 C3
Building 36 7 SE18.....123 A3
Building 47 6 SE18.....123 A3
Building 48 5 SE18.....123 A3
Building 49 4 SE18.....123 A3
Building 50 3 SE18.....123 A3
Bulbarrow NW8.........91 D6
Bulganak Rd CR7......205 A5
Bulinca St
  SW1.........115 D2 259 D3
Bullace Row SE5.......139 B4
Bull Alley DA16.......146 B2
Bullard Rd TW11......174 D4
Bullards Pl 13 E2........96 D4
Bull Dog The (Juct)
  TW15................148 A2
Bulleid Way
  SW1.........115 B2 258 D3
Bullen Ho 13 E1.........96 B3
Bullen St SW11........136 C3
Buller Cl SE15..........140 A5
Buller Rd Barking IG11...79 C1
  Kensal Green NW10....90 D4
  South Norwood CR7...205 B6
  Tottenham N17.........34 A1
  Wood Green N22.......32 C1
Bullers Cl DA14.......191 A5
Bullers Wood Dr BR7..188 B3
Bullers Wood Sch
  BR7.................188 A2
Bullescroft Rd HA8.....10 D1
Bullfinch Ct 4 SE21....161 B2
Bullingham Mans W8...245 B2
Bull Inn Ct WC2.......250 B5
Bullivant St 9 E14.....120 A6
Bull La Chislehurst BR7..189 B3
  Dagenham RM10........81 D5
  Edmonton N18.........33 C5
Bull Rd E15............98 D5
Bullrush Cl
  Carshalton SM5.......218 C6
  Thornton Heath CR0...205 C4
Bulls Alley SW14......133 B3
Bulls Bridge Ind Est
  UB2.................106 B2
Bulls Bridge Rd UB2..106 B2
Bullsbrook Rd UB4....106 C5
Bull's Cross EN1, EN2....6 A6
Bull's Gdns SW3......257 B4
Bulls Head Pas EC3...243 A1
Bull Yd SE15..........140 A4
Bulmer Gdns HA3......43 D2
Bulmer Mews
  W11.........113 C5 245 A4
Bulow Ct 3 SW6.......135 D3
Bulstrode Ave TW3...129 C2
Bulstrode Gdns TW3...129 C2
Bulstrode Pl W1......238 B3
Bulstrode Rd TW3....129 C2
Bulstrode St
  W1..........93 A1 238 B2
Bulwer Court Rd E11....54 B1
Bulwer Ct E11..........54 B1
Bulwer Gdns EN5........2 A1
Bulwer Rd
  Edmonton N18.........33 C6
  Leytonstone E11.......54 B1
  New Barnet EN5........2 A1
Bulwer St W12........112 C5
Bunbury Ho SE15.....140 A5
Bunces La IG8..........36 D3
Bungalow Rd SE25....205 C5
Bungalows The
  Leyton E10............54 A3
  Mitcham SW16.......181 B3
Bunhill Row
  EC1..........95 B3 242 C5
Bunhouse Pl SW1.....258 B2
Bunkers Hill
  London NW11..........48 A2
  North Cray DA14.....169 B1
Bunker's Hill DA17....125 C2
Bunning Ho N7.........72 A4
Bunning Way N7........72 B1
Bunn's La NW7..........27 D4
Bunsen Ho 2 E3........97 A5
Bunsen St 3 E3.........97 A5
Buntingbridge Rd IG2...57 B4
Bunting Cl London N9...18 D3
  Mitcham CR4.........202 D4
Bunton Ct NW9.........27 C1
Bunton St SE18.......122 C3
Bunyan Ct EC2.......242 A4
Bunyan Rd E17.........53 A6
Buonaparte Mews
  SW1.................259 C2

Burbage Ho
  16 Deptford SE14.....140 D6
  Shoreditch N1........235 D5
Burbage Rd SE21,
  SE24................161 B4
Burbage Sch N1........95 C5
Burbank KT3..........199 D6
Burberry Cl KT3......177 C1
Burberry Ct 8 N3.......29 D3
Burbidge Rd TW17....192 C5
Burbridge Way N17......34 A1
Burcham St E14.........98 A1
Burcharbro Rd SE2....146 D6
Burchell Ct WD23........8 A4
Burchell Ho SE11......260 D2
Burchell Rd Leyton E10...53 D1
  London SE15.........140 B4
Burcher Gale Gr 5
  SE15................139 D5
Burchetts Way TW17...192 D3
Burchett Way RM6......59 B3
Burcote Rd SW18.....158 B4
Burden Cl TW8.........109 C1
Burden Ho SW8.......270 A3
Burdenshott Ave
  TW10................132 C3
Burden Way E11........77 B6
Burder Cl N1...........73 C2
Burder Rd N1...........73 C2
Burdett Ave SW20....178 A2
Burdett Cl
  2 Ealing W7..........108 C5
  Sidcup DA14.........191 A5
Burdett Coutts &
Townshend CE Prim Sch
  SW1.........115 D2 259 D3
Burdett Mews 4 W2...91 D1
Burdett Rd
  Richmond TW9.......132 B2
  Thornton Heath CR0...205 B3
  Tower Hamlets E3.....97 B2
Burdetts Rd RM9.....103 B6
Burdock Cl CR0.......206 D1
Burdock Rd N17.......52 A6
Burdon Ct 3 E8........74 A2
Burdon La SM2........217 A1
Bure Ct 17 EN5.........13 D6
Burfield Cl SW17.....180 B6
Burford Cl
  Dagenham RM8........80 C5
  Ickenham UB10........60 A4
  Ilford IG6.............57 A5
Burford Ct SE8.......141 C6
Burford Gdns N13......16 B3
Burford Ho
  1 Brentford TW8......110 A1
  11 South Lambeth SW9..138 B3
Burford Rd
  Brentford TW8........110 A1
  Bromley BR1.........210 A5
  Forest Hill SE6.......163 B2
  Newham E6...........100 A4
  New Malden KT4.....200 A4
  5 Stratford Marsh E15...98 B6
  Sutton SM1..........217 C6
Burford Way CR0.....224 C2
Burford Wlk SW6.....265 D3
Burgate Ct 9 SW9.....138 C2
Burges Gr SW13......134 B5
Burges Rd E6..........78 B4
Burgess Ave NW9......45 B3
Burgess Cl 4 TW13...173 A6
Burgess Ct
  2 London N20.........14 D2
  3 Southall UB1........85 D1
  Wallend E12..........78 C1
Burgess Hill NW2......69 C4
Burgess Ho 3 SE5....139 A5
Burgess Ind Pk SE5...139 B5
Burgess Mews SW19...179 D4
Burgess Park Mans
  NW6.................69 C4
Burgess Rd Leyton E15...76 C4
  Sutton SM1..........217 D4
Burgess St E14.........97 C2
Burge St SE1..........262 D5
Burghill Rd SE26......185 B4
Burghley Ave
  Borehamwood WD6......11 A6
  Kingston u T KT3.....177 B2
Burghley Ct SW19....179 A5
Burghley Hall Cl
  SW19................157 A3
Burghley Ho SW19....157 A1
Burghley Pl CR4......202 D5
Burghley Rd
  Camden Town NW5....71 B4
  Leytonstone E11.......54 C1
  London N8.............50 C6
  Wimbledon SW19......179 A6
Burghley Twr W3......111 D5
Burgh St N1.....94 D3 234 D4
Burgon St EC4........241 D1
Burgos Cl CR0........220 C2
Burgos Gr SE10......141 D4
Burgoyne Rd
  Ashford TW16........171 D4
  Brixton SW9.........138 C2
  Harringay N4...........50 D3
  South Norwood SE25...205 D5
Burham Cl SE20......184 C3
Burhan Uddin Ho E1...243 C5
Burhill Gr HA5.........23 A1
Buriton Ho 9 SW15...156 B3
Burke Cl SW15........133 C4
Burke Ho 1 SW11.....136 B1
Burke Lodge E13.......99 B4
Burke St E16...........98 C2
Burket Cl UB2........107 B2
Burland Rd SW11.....158 D6

Burleigh Ave
Bexley DA15 167 D6
Hackbridge SM6 219 B5
Burleigh Ct N17 34 A4
Burleigh Gdns
Ashford TW15 171 A5
Osidge N14 15 C3
Burleigh Ho
Cheam SM3 201 A1
Chelsea SW3 266 D5
North Kensington W10 90 D2
Burleigh Lo 3 SW19 179 D3
Burleigh Par N14 15 D3
Burleigh Pl SW15 156 D6
Burleigh Rd
Cheam SM3 201 A1
Enfield EN1 5 C1
Hillingdon UB10 82 D6
Burleigh St WC2 250 C6
Burleigh Way EN2 5 B2
Burleigh Wlk SE6 164 A3
Burley Cl Chingford E4 35 C5
Mitcham SW16 181 D1
Burley Ho E1 96 D1
Burley Rd E16 99 C2
Burlington Apartments
SE20 184 B3
Burlington Arc W1 249 A5
Burlington Ave
Richmond TW9 132 C4
Romford RM7 59 D3
Burlington Cl
East Bedfont TW14 149 B4
5 Newham E6 100 A1
Orpington BR6 226 D6
Paddington W9 91 C3
Pinner HA5 40 B6
Burlington Ct
Chiswick W4 133 A5
Highgate N6 49 A1
Burlington Danes Sch
W12 90 B1
Burlington Gate
SW20 179 A1
Burlington Gdns
Acton Green W4 111 A1
Acton W3 111 A5
Dagenham RM6 59 A2
Fulham SW6 135 A3
Marylebone
W1 115 C6 249 A5
Burlington Ho NW3 70 B3
Burlington Inf Sch
KT3 199 D5
Burlington Jun Sch
KT3 199 D5
Burlington La W4 133 B5
Burlington Lo BR7 188 B3
Burlington Mews
Acton W3 111 A5
2 Putney SW15 157 B6
Burlington Park Ho 6
HA7 25 C6
Burlington Pl
Fulham SW6 135 A3
Woodford IG8 21 A1
Burlington Rd
Acton Green W4 111 A1
Enfield EN2 5 B4
Fulham SW6 135 A3
Hounslow TW7 130 B4
Muswell Hill N10 49 A6
New Malden KT3 199 D5
South Norwood CR7 183 B1
Tottenham N17 34 A2
Burlington Rise EN4 14 D4
Burma Rd N16 73 B4
Burmarsh 6 NW5 71 A2
Burmarsh Ct SE20 184 C2
Burma Terr 11 SE19 183 C5
Burmester Ho SW17 158 A1
Burmester Rd SW17 158 A1
Burnaby Cres W4 133 A6
Burnaby Ct 31 SE16 118 A4
Burnaby Gdns W4 132 D6
Burnaby St
SW10 136 A5 266 B3
Burnand Ho 3 W14 112 D3
Burnbrae Cl N12 29 D4
Burnbury Rd SW12 159 C3
Burncroft Ave EN3 6 C3
Burndell Way UB4 84 D2
Burne Jones Ho W14 254 B3
Burnell Ave
Richmond TW10 175 C5
Welling DA16 146 A3
Burnell Gdns HA7 25 D1
Burnell Ho 18 SW2 160 C3
Burnell Rd SM1 217 D4
Burnell Wlk SE1 263 D2
Burnels Ave E6 100 C4
Burness Cl N7 72 B2
Burne St NW1 237 A4
Burnett Cl E9 74 C3
Burnett Ct SW11 267 A1
Burnett Ho 6 SE13 142 A3
Burney Ave KT5 198 B4
Burney Ho 4 SW16 181 C5
Burney St SE10 142 A5
Burnfoot Ave
SW6 135 A4 264 B1
Burnham NW3 70 C1
Burnham Ave UB10 61 A4
Burnham Cl
Bermondsey SE1 263 D3
Enfield EN1 5 C5
Harrow HA3 43 A5
Hendon NW7 28 A3
Burnham Cres E11 55 C5
Burnham Ct
Bayswater W2 245 D6
Hendon NW4 46 C5
18 Stanmore HA7 25 C5
Burnham Dr KT4 216 D6
Burnham Est 8 E2 96 C4
Burnham Gdns
Cranford TW4 128 B4
Croydon CR0 205 D2
Hayes UB3 105 B3
Burnham Rd
Chingford Hatch E4 35 B5
Dagenham RM9 102 B6
Morden SM4 201 D5
Sidcup DA14 169 A2
Burnham St
Bethnal Green E2 96 C4
Kingston u T KT2 176 C2
Burnham Way
Ealing W13 109 B3
Penge SE26 185 B5
Burnhill Ho EC1 235 A1
Burnhill Rd BR3 185 C1
Burnley Cl WD19 22 C5
Burnley Rd
London SW9 138 B3
Willesden NW10 68 A3
Burnsall St
SW3 114 C1 257 B2
Burns Ave
Blackfen DA15 168 B5
Feltham TW14 150 A5
Ilford RM6 58 C2
Southall UB1 107 C6
Burns Cl Bexley DA16 145 D4
Hayes UB4 84 A2
Mitcham SW17 180 B4
Walthamstow E17 54 A5
Burns Ct Tottenham N17 34 B3
Wallington SM6 219 B1
Burns Ho
18 Bethnal Green E2 96 C4
Bexley DA16 146 C4
1 Islington N7 72 B2
Kennington SE17 261 D1
11 Stoke Newington N16 73 C4
Burn's Ho NW10 89 C6
Burnside Ave E4 35 B4
Burnside Cl Barnet EN5 1 C2
Rotherhithe SE16 118 D5
Twickenham TW1 153 A5
Burnside Cres HA0 87 D6
Burnside Ct 1 SM6 219 A5
Burnside Rd RM8 58 D1
Burns Rd
Battersea SW11 136 D3
Ealing W13 109 B4
Wembley HA0 88 A5
Burn's Rd NW10 89 D6
Burns Way TW5 128 D4
Burnt Ash Hill
Lee SE12 164 D5
Lewisham SE12 165 A3
Burnt Ash Hts BR1 187 B5
Burnt Ash La BR1,
SE12 187 B5
Burnt Ash Prim Sch
BR1 187 A5
Burnt Ash Rd SE12 164 D6
Burnthwaite Rd
SW6 135 B5 264 D3
BURNT OAK 27 B3
Burnt Oak Broadway
HA8 26 D2
Burnt Oak Fields HA8 27 A2
Burnt Oak Jun Sch
DA15 168 A3
Burnt Oak La DA15 168 B3
Burnt Oak Sta HA8 27 A2
Burntwood Cl SW18 158 C3
Burntwood Ct SW17 158 A1
Burntwood Grange Rd
SW18 158 C3
Burntwood La SW17 158 B2
Burntwood Sch SW17 158 B2
Burntwood View 6
SE19 183 D5
Buross St E1 96 B1
Burpham Cl UB4 84 D2
Burrage Ct 17 SE16 118 D2
Burrage Gr SE18 123 A2
Burrage Pl SE18 122 D1
Burrage Rd SE18 123 A1
Burrard Ho 11 E2 96 C5
Burrard Rd Newham E16 99 B1
West Hampstead NW6 69 C4
Burr Cl
Bexleyheath DA7 147 B2
St George in t East E1 118 A5
Burrell Cl Croydon CR0 207 A3
Edgware HA8 10 D2
Burrell Ct HA1 42 B2
Burrell Ho 4 TW1 153 B4
Burrell Row BR3 185 C1
Burrells 9 BR3 185 D1
Burrell St SE1 116 D5 251 C4
Burrell's Wharf Sq
E14 119 D1
Burrell Twrs E10 53 C2
Burrhill Ct SE16 118 D3
Burritt Rd KT1 176 C1
Burrmead Ct NW2 67 D5
Burroughs Gdns NW4 46 B5
Burroughs The NW4 46 B5
Burrow Ho 19 SW9 138 B3
Burrow Rd SE22 139 C1
Burrows Mews SE1 251 C2
Burrows Rd NW10 90 C4
Burrow Wlk SE21 161 A4
Burr Rd SW18 157 C4
Bursar St SE1 253 A3
Bursdon Cl DA15 167 D2
Bursland Rd EN3 6 D1
Burslem St E1 96 A1
Bursted Wood Prim Sch
DA7 147 D3
Burstock Rd SW15 135 A1
Burston Rd SW15 156 D6
Burstow Rd SW20 179 A2
Burtenshaw Rd KT7 197 A3
Burtley Cl N4 51 A1
Burton Bank N1 73 B1
Burton Cl
Chessington KT9 213 D1
South Norwood CR7 205 B6
Burton Ct Chelsea SW3 257 D2
10 Friern Barnet N11 30 D5
Thames Ditton KT7 197 A3
Burton Dr EN3 7 C6
Burton Gdns TW5 129 B4
Burton Gr SE17 262 C1
Burton Ho
8 Bermondsey SE16 118 B4
Brixton SE5 138 D4
Penge SE26 184 B5
Burtonhole Cl NW7 28 D6
Burtonhole La
Finchley NW7 29 A6
Mill Hill NW7 28 D6
Burton La 3 SW9 138 C3
Burton Lo 6 SW15 157 B6
Burton Mews SW1 258 B3
Burton Pl WC1 232 D1
Burton Rd
7 Brixton SW9 138 C3
Brixton SW9 138 D3
Brondesbury NW6 69 B1
Kingston u T KT2 176 A3
Wanstead E18 55 B6
Burtons Ct E15 76 B1
Burtons Rd TW12 174 A6
Burton St WC1 93 D3 239 D6
Burtonwood Ho N4 51 B2
Burt Rd E16 121 C5
Burtt Ho 6 N1 95 C4
Burtwell La SE21, SE27 183 B6
Burvill Ct SW20 178 C2
Burwash Ho SE1 252 D1
Burwash Rd SE18 123 B1
Burwell 2 KT1 176 C1
Burwell Ave UB6 64 C2
Burwell Cl 27 E1 96 B1
Burwell Rd E10 53 A1
Burwell Wlk 14 E3 97 C3
Burwood Ave
Hayes BR2 225 B6
Pinner HA5 40 C4
Burwood Cl KT6 198 C1
Burwood Ct SE23 162 C4
Burwood Ho 11 SW9 138 D1
Burwood Lo SW19 179 B6
Burwood Pl Barnet EN4 2 A4
Paddington W2 237 B2
Bury Ave Hayes UB4 83 C5
Ruislip HA4 39 A3
Bury Cl SE16 118 D5
Bury Ct EC3 243 B2
Buryfield Ct 23 SE8 118 D2
Bury Gr SM4 201 D4
Bury Hall Villas N9 17 D4
Bury Pl WC1 94 A2 240 B3
Bury Rd Chingford E4 20 C6
Dagenham RM10 81 D3
Hornsey N22 50 C6
Bury St W N9 17 C4
Buryside Cl IG2 57 D5
Bury St Edmonton N9 18 A3
Ruislip HA4 39 B3
St James SW1 115 C5 249 B4
Whitechapel EC3 95 C1 243 B2
Bury Wlk SW3 114 C1 257 A2
Burywood Ct EN3 6 C3
Busbridge Ho 24 E14 97 C2
Busby Ho SW16 181 C6
Busby Mews 5 NW1 71 D2
Busby Pl NW5 71 D2
Busch Cl TW7 131 B4
Busch Cnr TW7 131 B4
Bushbaby Cl SE1 263 A5
Bushberry Rd E9 75 A2
Bush Cl IG2 57 B4
Bush Cotts 12 SW18 157 C6
Bush Ct London N14 15 C3
7 Shepherd's Bush
W12 112 D4
Bushell Cl SW2 160 B2
Bushell Gn WD23 8 B2
Bushell Ho 3 SE27 183 A6
Bushell Way BR7 188 C5
BUSHEY 8 A2
Bushey Ave
Crofton BR5 211 B2
Snaresbrook E18 54 D6
Bushey Cl Chingford E4 20 A1
Ickenham UB10 60 C6
Bushey Ct SW20 178 B1
Bushey Down SW12 159 B2
Bushey Hall SE5 139 D4
BUSHEY HEATH 8 C4
Bushey Heath Prim Sch
WD23 8 B3
Bushey Hill Rd SE5 139 D4
Bushey Ho SE12 165 C1
Bushey La SM1 217 C4
Bushey Lees DA15 167 D5
BUSHEY MEAD 200 D6
Bushey Meads Sch
WD23 8 A6
Bushey Rd
Croydon CR0 223 C6
Bushey Rd *continued*
Hayes UB3 105 C2
Ickenham UB10 60 C6
Newham E13 99 C5
South Tottenham N15 51 C3
Sutton SM1 217 C4
West Barnes SW20 178 D1
Bushey Way BR3 208 B4
Bush Fair Ct N14 15 B5
Bushfield Cl HA8 10 D2
Bushfield Cres HA8 10 D2
Bushfield Ho N5 73 A3
Bush Gr London NW9 45 A2
Stanmore HA7 25 D2
Bushgrove Rd RM8 80 D5
BUSH HILL 17 B5
Bush Hill N21 17 A5
Bush Hill Par EN1 17 B4
BUSH HILL PARK 17 C5
Bush Hill Park Prim Sch
EN1 18 A6
Bush Hill Park Sta EN1 17 D5
Bush Hill Rd Enfield N21 17 B5
Harrow HA3 44 B3
Bush Ind Est NW10 89 B3
Bush La EC4 117 B6 252 C6
Bushmead Cl 7 N15 51 D5
Bushmoor Cres SE18 144 D5
Bushnell Rd SW17 159 B1
Bush Rd
Bermondsey SE8 118 D2
Hackney E8 96 B6
Littleton TW17 192 B4
Richmond TW9 132 B6
Wanstead E11 55 A2
Woodford IG9 37 D6
Bushway RM8 80 D5
Bushwood E11 55 A1
Bushwood Dr
SE1 117 D2 263 D3
Bushwood Rd TW9 132 C6
Bushy Ct KT1 175 C2
Bushy Park Gdns
TW12 174 B5
Bushy Park Rd TW11 175 B3
Bushy Rd TW11 174 D3
Business Acad Bexley The
DA18 125 A4
Business Design Ctr*
N1 94 C6 234 B5
Buspace Studios 3
W10 91 A3
Butcher Row E1 96 D1
Butchers Rd E16 99 A1
Bute Ave TW10 154 A2
Bute Ct SM6 219 C3
Bute Gardens W SM6 219 C3
Bute Gdns
Hammersmith W6 112 D2
Wallington SM6 219 C3
Bute House Prep Sch
W6 112 D2
Bute Mews NW11 48 A4
Bute Rd Ilford IG6 56 D4
Thornton Heath CR0 204 C1
Wallington SM6 219 C4
Bute St SW7 114 B2 256 C4
Bute Wlk 18 N1 73 B2
Butfield Ho 6 E9 74 C2
Butler Ave HA1 42 B2
Butler Cl HA8 26 D1
Butler Ct Dagenham RM8 81 C6
Wembley HA0 65 A4
Butler Ho
32 Bethnal Green E2 96 C4
5 Brixton SW9 138 D4
11 Poplar E14 97 B1
Butler Pl SW1 259 C6
Butler Rd
Dagenham RM8 80 B4
Harrow HA1 42 A2
Willesden NW10 67 D1
Butlers Cl TW3 129 B1
Butlers & Colonial Wharf
SE1 253 D2
Butler's Cotts DA7 147 C3
Butler St
33 Bethnal Green E2 96 C4
Hillingdon UB10 82 D3
Butler's Wharf W SE1 253 C3
Butley Ct 8 E3 97 A5
Butt Ct SM4 202 A3
Buttercup Cl UB5 63 B2
Butterfield Cl
1 Bermondsey SE16 118 B4
Tottenham N17 33 A4
Twickenham TW1 152 D5
Butterfield Ho 4 EN2 4 D3
Butterfields E17 54 A4
Butterfield Sq 10 E6 100 B1
Butterfly Ct E6 100 B4
Butterfly La SE9 166 D5
Butterfly Wlk 2 SE5 139 B4
Butter Hill SM5, SM6 219 A4
Butteridges Cl RM9 103 B6
Buttermere NW1 231 D2
Buttermere Cl
Bermondsey SE1 263 C3
East Bedfont TW14 149 D3
Leyton E11 76 B4
West Barnes SM4 200 D3
Buttermere Ct NW8 229 C6
Buttermere Dr SW15 157 A6
Buttermere Ho
London N12 30 C5
13 Tower Hamlets E3 97 B4
Buttermere Wlk 9 E8 73 D2
Butterwick W6 112 C2
Butterworth Ct SW16 160 A1
Butterworth Gdns IG8 37 A5
Buttesland St
N1 95 B4 235 D2
Buttfield Cl RM10 81 D2
Buttmarsh Cl SE18 122 D1
Buttsbury Rd IG1 79 A3
Butts Cotts TW13 151 B1
Butts Cres TW13 151 C1
Butts Ho TW13 151 C1
Butts Piece UB5 84 B5
Butts Rd BR1 186 C5
Butts The TW8 131 D6
Buxhall Cres E9 75 B2
Buxlow Prep Sch HA9 66 A5
Buxted Rd
Camberwell SE22 139 C1
Colney Hatch N12 30 C5
Dalston E8 73 D1
Buxton Cl London N9 18 C2
Woodford IG8 37 D4
Buxton Cres SM3 217 A4
Buxton Ct 1 Leyton E11 54 D2
Shoreditch N1 235 B2
Buxton Dr
Kingston u T KT3 177 B1
Leytonstone E11 54 C5
Buxton Gdns W3 110 D6
Buxton Ho
Leytonstone E11 54 C5
3 London SW11 136 B1
Buxton Lo E11 77 B6
Buxton Mews SW4 137 D3
Buxton Rd Chingford E4 20 B4
Ilford IG2 57 C3
Mortlake SW14 133 C2
Newham E6 100 A4
Stratford E15 76 C3
Thornton Heath CR7 204 D4
Upper Holloway N19 49 D1
Walthamstow E17 53 A5
Willesden NW2 68 B2
Buxton St E1 95 D3 243 D5
Buzzard Creek Ind Est
IG11 102 A2
Byam Shaw Sch of Art
N19 71 D6
Byam St SW6 136 A3
Byards Croft SW16 181 D2
Byards Ct SE16 118 D3
Byas Ho 6 E3 97 B4
Byatt Wlk TW12 173 A4
Bychurch End 11
TW11 174 D5
Bycroft Rd UB1 85 C3
Bycroft St SE20 184 D3
Bycullah Ave EN2 4 D3
Bycullah Ct EN2 4 D2
Bycullah Rd EN2 4 D3
Byefield Cl SE16 119 A4
Byegrove Ct SW19 180 B4
Byegrove Rd SW19 180 B4
Byelands Cl 12 SE16 118 D5
Bye The W3 89 C1
Bye Ways TW2 151 D1
Byeways The KT5 198 D4
Byeway The SW14 133 A2
Bye Way The HA3 24 D2
Byfeld Gdns SW13 134 A4
Byfield Ct KT3 200 A5
Byfield Rd TW7 131 A2
Byford Cl E15 76 C1
Bygrove CR0 223 D1
Bygrove Prim Sch E14 97 D1
Bygrove St E14 97 D1
Byland Cl
Abbey Wood SE2 124 B3
Carshalton SM4 202 B2
Southgate N21 16 B4
Byne Rd
Carshalton SM5 218 C6
Forest Hill SE26 184 C5
Bynes Rd CR2 221 B1
Byng Pl WC1 93 D3 239 C5
Byng St E14 119 C4
Bynon Ave DA7 147 B2
Byre Rd N14 15 B5
Byrne Ho 11 SW2 160 B6
Byrne Rd SW12 159 B2
Byron Ave
Borehamwood WD6 10 C6
Cranford TW4 128 B3
Plashet E12 78 A2
Queensbury NW9 44 D6
Sutton SM1 218 B4
West Barnes KT3 200 A4
Woodford E18 36 D1
Byron Ave E SM1 218 B4
Byron Cl Feltham TW12 173 B6
Forest Hill SE26 185 A6
Hackney E8 96 A6
Streatham SW16 182 A4
Thamesmead SE28 124 C5
Walton-on-T KT12 195 A1
Byron Court Prim Sch
HA0 65 C6
Byron Ct Chelsea SW3 257 B3
Dulwich SE21 162 A3
Ealing W7 109 A2
Enfield EN2 4 D3
3 Hampstead NW6 70 A1
Harrow HA1 42 C3
4 New Barnet EN5 2 A1
Paddington W9 91 C3
1 Richmond TW10 175 D6
South Norwood CR7 183 A1
St Pancras WC1 240 C6
11 Wanstead E11 55 A5
Woodford E18 37 B2
Byron Dr
East Finchley N2 48 B3
Erith DA8 147 D5
Byron Gdns SM1 218 B4
Byron Hill Rd HA1, HA2 64 C6
Byron Ho 5 BR3 185 D4
Byron Mews
Hampstead NW3 70 C4
2 Maida Vale W9 91 C3
Byron Par UB10 83 A3
Byron Rd Dollis Hill NW2 68 B6
Ealing W5 110 B5
Edgware NW7 28 A5
Harrow HA1 42 C3
Leyton E10 53 D1
Walthamstow E17 53 C6
Wealdstone HA3 24 D1
Wembley HA0 65 C5
Byron St E14 98 A1
Byron Way Hayes UB4 83 D3
Northolt UB5 85 A4
West Drayton UB7 104 B2
Bysouth Cl N15 51 B5
Bythorn St SW9 138 B1
Byton Rd SW17 180 D4
Byward Ave TW14 150 C5
Byward St EC3 117 C6 253 B5
Bywater Ho SE18 122 A3
Bywater Pl SE16 119 A5
Bywater St
SW3 114 D1 257 C2
Byway The KT19 215 D4
Bywell Pl W1 239 A3
Bywood Ave CR0 206 D3
Bywood Terr CR0 206 C3
Byworth Ho HA7 25 C4
Byworth Wlk N19 50 A1

C

Cabbell St NW1 92 C2 237 A3
Cabinet Off SW1 250 A2
Cabinet War Rooms & Churchill Mus*
SW1 115 D4 249 D2
Cabinet Way E4 35 B4
Cable Ho WC1 234 A2
Cable Pl SE10 142 A4
Cable St E1 118 B6
Cabot Ct SE16 118 D3
Cabot Sq E14 119 C5
Cabot Way 3 E6 99 D6
Cabul Rd SW11 136 C3
Cactus Cl SE5 139 C3
Cactus Wlk W12 89 D1
Cadbury Cl
Ashford TW16 171 C3
Isleworth TW7 131 A4
Cadbury Rd TW16 171 C4
Cadbury Way 1 SE16 118 A2
Caddington Cl EN4 14 C6
Caddington Rd NW2 69 A5
Caddis Cl HA7 24 D3
Cadell Cl E2 95 D5
Cadell Ho 10 E2 95 D5
Cade Rd SE10 142 B4
Cader Rd SW18 158 A5
Cadet Dr SE1 117 D1 263 D2
Cade Tyler Ho 10
SE10 142 A4
Cadiz St SE17 117 A1 262 B1
Cadley Terr SE23 162 C2
Cadman Cl SW9 138 D5
Cadmer Cl KT3 199 C5
Cadmore Ho 4 N1 72 D1
Cadmus Cl 9 SW4 137 D2
Cadmus Ct 6 SW9 138 C4
Cadnam Lo E14 120 B3
Cadnam Point 15
SW15 156 B3
Cadogan Cl
Beckenham BR3 186 B1
Hackney Wick E9 75 B1
Harrow HA2 63 D4
Teddington TW11 174 C5
Cadogan Ct
Chelsea SW3 257 C3
New Malden KT3 199 C5
Sutton SM2 217 D2
Cadogan Ct Gdns SW1 258 A4
Cadogan Gate
SW1 114 D2 257 D4
Cadogan Gdns
Chelsea
SW3 114 D2 257 D3
Finchley N3 29 D2
Southgate N21 16 C6
Wanstead E18 55 B6
Cadogan Ho SW3 266 D5
Cadogan La
SW1 115 A3 258 A5
Cadogan Pl
SW1 114 D3 257 D5
Cadogan Rd
Kingston u T KT6 197 D4
Woolwich SE18 123 A3
Cadogan Sq
SW1 114 D3 257 D5
Cadogan St
SW3 114 D2 257 C3
Cadogan Terr E9 75 B1
Cadoxton Ave 3 N15 51 D3
Cadwallon Rd SE9 167 A2
Caedmon Rd N7 72 B4
Caerleon Cl
Claygate KT10 213 B1
Sidcup DA14 190 C5
Caerleon Terr SE2 124 B2
Caernafon Ho HA7 25 A5

Caernarvon Cl CR4 204 A6
Caernarvon Ct 3 KT5 198 B4
Caernarvon Ho W2 236 A2
Caesar Ct 25 E2 96 D5
Caesar's Way TW17 193 B3
Caesars Wlk CR4 202 D4
Cahill St EC1 242 B5
Cahir St E14 119 D2
Cain Ct 2 W5 87 C2
Caine Ho W3 110 D4
Cain's La TW14 149 C6
Caird St W10 91 B4
Cairn Ave W5 109 D5
Cairndale Cl BR1 186 D3
Cairnfield Ave NW2 67 D5
Cairnfield Ct NW2 67 C5
Cairngorm Cl 3 TW11 175 A5
Cairn Ho 3 SW19 180 C3
Cairns Ho 3 N7 72 B4
Cairns Mews SE18 144 A4
Cairns Rd SW11 158 C6
Cairn Way HA7 24 D4
Cairo New Rd CR0 220 D6
Cairo Rd E17 53 C5
Caister Ho N7 72 B2
Caistor Ho
 10 Balham SW12 159 B4
 5 West Ham E15 98 D6
Caistor Mews SW12 159 B4
Caistor Park Rd E15 98 D6
Caistor Rd SW12 159 B4
Caithness Gdns DA15 167 D5
Caithness Ho N1 233 C6
Caithness Rd
 Hammersmith W14 112 D3
 Mitcham CR4 181 B3
Calabria Rd N5 72 D3
Calais Gate SE5 138 D4
Calais St SE5 138 D4
Calbourne Rd SW12 159 A4
Calcott Wlk SE9 187 D6
Calcraft Ho 10 E2 96 C5
Caldbeck Ave KT4 200 B1
Caldecot Ct SE5 139 A3
Caldecote 3 KT1 176 C1
Caldecote Gdns WD23 8 C4
Caldecote La WD23 8 D5
Caldecot Rd SE5 139 A3
Caldecott Way E5 74 D5
Calder Ave UB6 86 D5
Calder Cl EN1 5 C2
Calder Ct SE16 119 B5
Calder Gdns HA8 44 C6
Calder Ho UB5 85 A6
Calderon Ho NW8 230 A4
Calderon Pl 20 W10 90 C2
Calderon Rd E11 76 B5
Calder Rd SM4 202 A4
Caldervale Rd SW4 159 D6
Calderwood St SE18 122 C2
Caldew Ct NW7 28 A3
Caldew St SE5 139 B5
Caldicote Gn NW9 45 C3
Caldon Ho 2 UB5 85 B3
Caldwell Rd WD19 22 D6
Caldwell St SW9 138 B5 270 D3
Caldy Rd DA17 125 D3
Caldy Wlk 19 N1 73 A2
Caleb St SE1 252 B2
Caledonia Ct
 Barking IG11 102 C5
 Hendon NW4 28 C1
Caledonia Ho 15 E14 97 A1
Caledonian Cl 1 IG3 58 B1
Caledonian Ct UB5 85 A3
Caledonian Market SE1 117 C3 263 B6
Caledonian Rd
 Islington N1 94 B6 233 C5
 Lower Holloway N7 72 B2
Caledonian Road & Barnsbury Sta N7 72 B1
Caledonian Road Sta N7 72 B2
Caledonian Sq 6 NW1 71 D2
Caledonian Wharf Rd E14 120 B2
Caledonia Rd TW19 148 A3
Caledonia St N1 233 B3
Caledon Rd East Ham E6 78 B1
 Hackbridge SM5, SM6 219 A4
Cale St SW3 114 C1 257 A2
Caletock Way SE10 120 D1
Calgarth NW1 232 B3
Calgary Ct 30 SE16 118 C4
Caliban Twr 9 N1 95 C5
Calico Ho 4 SW11 136 A2
Calico Row 5 SW11 136 A2
Calidore Cl SW2 160 B5
California Bldg 2 SE13 141 D4
California La WD23 8 B3
California Rd KT3 199 A6
Callaby Terr 11 N1 73 B2
Callaghan Cl SE13 142 C1
Callahan Cotts 8 E1 96 C2
Callander Rd SE6 164 A2
Callanders The WD23 8 C3
Callan Sch The W1 93 C1 239 B2
Callard Ave N13 32 D6
Callcott Ct NW6 69 B1
Callcott Rd NW6 69 B1
Callcott St W8 245 A4
Callendar Rd SW7 256 C6
Callingham Cl 13 E14 97 B2
Callingham Ho 1 SW4 138 A2
Callis Farm Cl TW19 148 A5
Callis Rd E17 53 B3
Callonfield 3 E17 53 A5
Callow St SW3 136 B6 266 C6
Calmington Rd SE5 139 C6
Calmont Rd BR1 186 C4
Calonne Rd SW19 178 D6
Calshot Ho N1 233 C4
Calshot Rd TW6 126 D3
Calshot St N1 94 B5 233 C3
Calshot Way Enfield EN2 4 D2
 Harlington TW6 126 C3
Calstock NW1 232 C5
Calstock Ho SE11 261 B2
Calthorpe Gdns
 Edgware HA8 26 B5
 Sutton SM1 218 A5
Calthorpe St WC1 94 B3 240 D6
Calton Ave SE21 161 C5
Calton Rd EN5 14 B5
Calumet Ct SW17 180 C4
Calver 18 NW5 71 B4
Calver Ct E17 54 B6
Calverley Cl BR3 185 D4
Calverley Cres RM10 81 C6
Calverley Gdns HA3 43 D2
Calverley Gr N19 49 D1
Calverley Rd KT17 216 A2
Calvert Ave E2 95 D4
Calvert Cl
 Belvedere DA17 125 D2
 Sidcup DA14 191 A4
Calvert Ct
 1 London N19 49 C1
 5 Richmond TW9 132 B1
Calvert Ho 9 W12 112 B6
Calverton SE5 139 C6
Calverton Prim Sch E16 99 D1
Calverton Rd E6 100 C6
Calvert Rd SE10 120 D1
Calvert's Bldgs SE1 252 C3
Calvert St NW1 93 A6 231 A6
Calvin St E1 95 D3 243 C5
Calydon Rd SE7 121 B1
Calypso Cres 6 SE15 139 D5
Calypso Way SE8, SE16 119 B2
Camac Rd TW2 152 B3
Camarthen Gn NW9 45 C3
Cambalt Ho 3 SW15 156 D6
Cambalt Rd SW15 156 D6
Cambay Ho 7 E1 97 A3
Cambell Jun & Inf Schs RM9 80 D1
Camber Ho 4 SE15 140 C6
Camberley Ave
 Enfield EN1 5 C1
 Wimbledon SW20 178 B1
Camberley Cl SM3 216 D5
Camberley Ct 15 SM2 217 D1
Camberley Ho NW1 231 D3
Camberley Rd TW6 126 C2
Cambert Way SE9 143 B1
CAMBERWELL 139 A4
Camberwell Bsns Ctr SE5 139 B5
Camberwell Church St SE5 139 B4
Camberwell Coll of Arts
 Camberwell SE5 139 C4
 Camberwell SE15 139 D5
Camberwell Glebe SE5 139 C4
Camberwell Gn SE5 139 B4
Camberwell Gr SE5 139 C3
Camberwell Green SE5 139 A4
Camberwell New Rd SW9 138 D5
Camberwell Rd SE5 139 A5
Camberwell Station Rd SE5 139 A4
Camberwell Trad Est SE5 139 A4
Cambeys Rd RM10 81 D3
Cambisgate SW19 179 A5
Camborne Ave W13 109 C4
Camborne Cl TW6 126 C2
Camborne Rd
 Belmont SM2 217 D1
 Bexley DA16 145 D3
 Croydon CR0 206 A2
 Harmondsworth TW6 126 C2
 Sidcup DA14 168 C1
 Wandsworth SW18 157 C4
 West Barnes SM4 200 D4
Camborne Way
 Harlington TW6 126 C2
 Heston TW5 129 C4
Cambourne Ave N9 18 D4
Cambourne Mews 6 W11 91 A1
Cambrai Ct N13 32 A6
Cambray Rd
 Broom Hill BR6 211 D2
 Streatham SW12 159 C3
Cambria 6 BR3 185 D1
Cambria Cl
 Hounslow TW3 129 C1
 Sidcup DA15 167 C3
Cambria Ct TW14 150 B4
Cambria Gdns TW19 148 A4
Cambria Ho
 Forest Hill SE26 184 A6
 14 Limehouse E14 97 A1
Cambria Lo 3 SW15 157 B6
Cambrian Ave IG2 57 C4
Cambrian Cl SE27 160 D1
Cambrian Ct UB2 107 D2
Cambrian Gn NW9 45 C4
Cambrian Rd Leyton E10 53 C1
 Richmond TW10 154 B5
Cambria Rd SE5 139 A2
Cambria St SW6 135 D5 265 D3
Cambridge Ave
 Falconwood DA16 145 D1
 Greenford UB6 64 D3
 Kilburn NW6 91 C5
 Kingston u T KT3, SW20 177 D1
Cambridge Barracks Rd 11 SE18 122 B2
Cambridge Cir WC2 93 D1 239 D1
Cambridge Cl
 Hounslow TW4 129 A1
 Walthamstow E17 53 B3
 Willesden NW10 67 A5
 Wimbledon SW20 178 B2
 Wood Green N22 32 C2
Cambridge Cotts TW9 132 C6
Cambridge Cres
 20 Bethnal Green E2 96 B5
 Teddington TW11 175 A5
Cambridge Ct
 4 Barnet EN5 1 B2
 26 Bethnal Green E2 96 B5
 7 Hammersmith W6 112 C2
 2 Kilburn NW6 91 C5
 Marylebone W2 237 A3
 Stamford Hill N16 51 C2
 Wembley HA0 65 D4
 Wimbledon SW20 178 B1
Cambridge Dr
 Lee SE12 165 A6
 Ruislip HA4 62 D6
Cambridge Gate NW1 238 C6
Cambridge Gate Mews NW1 238 D6
Cambridge Gdns
 Enfield EN1 6 A3
 Kilburn NW6 91 C5
 Kingston u T KT1 176 C1
 Muswell Hill N10 31 B2
 North Kensington W10 91 A1
 Southgate N21 17 B4
 Tottenham N17 33 B3
Cambridge Gn SE9 166 D3
Cambridge Gr
 Hammersmith W6 112 B2
 Penge SE20 184 B2
Cambridge Grove Rd
 13 Kingston u T KT1 176 C1
 Kingston u T KT1 198 C6
Cambridge Heath Rd E1, E2 96 B4
Cambridge Heath Sta E2 96 B5
Cambridge Ho
 Barking IG11 79 A1
 Ealing W13 87 A1
 Fulham SW6 135 A2
 2 Teddington TW11 175 A5
 8 Woolwich SE18 122 B2
Cambridge Mans SW11 267 C1
Cambridge Par EN1 6 A4
CAMBRIDGE PARK 153 C4
Cambridge Park Ct TW1 153 D4
Cambridge Park Rd E11 55 A2
Cambridge Pas 9 E9 74 C1
Cambridge Pk
 Twickenham TW1 153 D5
 Wanstead E11 55 A3
Cambridge Pl W8 245 D1
Cambridge Rd
 Barking IG11 79 A1
 Barnes SW13 133 D3
 Battersea SW11 136 D4 267 C1
 Carshalton SM5 218 C3
 3 Chingford E4 20 B3
 East Molesey KT8 195 B5
 Hampton TW12 173 B3
 Hanwell W7 108 D4
 Harrow HA2 41 C4
 Hounslow TW4 129 A1
 Ilford IG3 57 C1
 Kilburn NW6 91 C4
 Kilburn NW6 91 C5
 Kingston u T KT1 176 C1
 Leytonstone E11 54 D3
 Littleton TW15 171 A3
 Mitcham CR4 203 C6
 New Malden KT3 199 C5
 Penge SE20 206 B6
 Plaistow BR1 187 A3
 Richmond TW9 132 C5
 Sidcup DA14 189 C6
 Southall UB1 107 B5
 Teddington TW11 175 A5
 Twickenham TW1 153 D5
 Walton-on-T KT12 194 B3
 Wimbledon SW20 178 B2
Cambridge Rd N W4 110 D1
Cambridge Rd S 3 W4 110 D1
Cambridge Row SE18 122 D1
Cambridge Sch W6 112 B2
Cambridge Sq W2 92 C1 237 A2
Cambridge St SW1 115 C1 259 A2
Cambridge Terr
 Edmonton N9 17 D4
 Regent's Pk NW1 231 C1
Cambridge Terr Mews NW1 231 D1
Cambstone Cl N11 15 A2
Cambus Cl UB4 85 A2
Cambus Rd E16 99 A2
Cam Ct 2 SE15 139 D6
Camdale Rd SE18 145 D5
Camden Ave
 Feltham TW13 150 C3
 Hayes UB4 106 D6
Camden Cl BR7 189 A2
Camden Coll of English NW1 71 A1
Camden Ct 9 DA17 125 C1
Camden Gdns
 Camden Town NW1 71 B1
 Sutton SM1 217 D3
 Thornton Heath CR7 204 D6
Camden Gr BR7 188 D4
Camden High St NW1 93 C6 232 A5
Camden Hill Rd SE19 183 C4
Camden Ho
 6 Deptford SE8 119 B1
 Wallington CR6 220 A5
Camdenhurst St E14 97 A1
Camden Jun Sch SM5 218 D4
Camden Lock Pl NW1 71 B1
Camden Mews NW1 71 D2
Camden Mkt* NW1 93 B6 231 D6
Camden Park Rd
 Camden Town NW1 71 D2
 Chislehurst West BR7 188 C3
Camden Pas N1 94 D6 234 C5
Camden Rd
 Camden Town NW1 93 B6 231 D6
 Carshalton SM5 218 D3
 Old Bexley DA5 169 B4
 Sutton SM1 217 D3
 Walthamstow E17 53 B3
 Wanstead E11 55 B3
Camden Road Sta NW1 71 C1
Camden Row SE3 142 C3
Camden Sch for Girls The NW5 71 C2
Camden Sq NW1 71 D2
Camden St NW1 93 C6 232 B5
Camden Studios NW1 232 B5
Camden Terr 17 NW1 71 D2
CAMDEN TOWN 71 B1
Camden Town Sta NW1 93 B6 231 D6
Camden Way
 Chislehurst West BR7 188 C3
 Thornton Heath CR7 204 D6
Camden Wlk N1 234 C5
Cameford Ct 20 SW12 160 A4
Camelford NW1 232 B5
Camelford Ct 15 W11 91 A1
Camelford Ho SE1 260 B1
Camelford Wlk 13 W11 91 A1
Camel Gr KT2 175 D5
Camelia Ct IG8 36 C4
Camellia Ct 20 BR3 185 C3
Camellia Ho
 Feltham TW13 150 A3
 New Cross SE8 141 B5
Camellia Pl TW2 151 D4
Camellia St SW8 270 A3
Camelot Cl
 Plumstead SE18 123 B4
 Wimbledon SW19 179 C6
Camelot Ho 15 NW1 71 D2
Camelot Prim Sch SE15 140 B6
Camel Rd E16 121 D5
Camera Pl SW10 266 C6
Cameret Ct 6 W11 112 D4
Cameron Cl
 East Barnet N20 14 C2
 Edmonton N18 34 B5
Cameron Ct 3 SW19 157 A3
Cameron Ho
 8 Bromley BR1 186 D2
 Camberwell SE5 139 A5
 St John's Wood NW8 230 A4
Cameron House Sch SW10 266 D6
Cameron Lo TW3 130 A1
Cameron Pl SW16 160 C2
Cameron Rd
 Bromley BR2 209 A4
 Forest Hill SE6 163 B2
 Ilford IG3 57 C1
 Thornton Heath CR0 204 D3
Cameron Sq CR4 180 C2
Camerton Cl 8 E8 73 D2
Camfrey Ct N8 50 A5
Camgate Ctr The TW19 148 B4
Camilla Cl TW16 171 D4
Camilla Ct 12 SM2 217 C1
Camilla Rd SE16 118 B2
Camille Cl SE25 206 A6
Camlan Rd BR1 186 D6
Camlet St E2 243 C6
Camlet Way EN4 1 D4
Camley St NW1 93 D5 232 D4
Camm 23 NW9 27 D1
Camm Gdns
 5 Kingston u T KT1 176 B1
 Thames Ditton KT7 196 D2
Camomile Ave CR4 180 D2
Camomile St EC3 95 C1 243 B2
Camomile Way UB7 82 A1
Campaign Ct W9 91 B3
Campana Rd SW6 135 C4 265 B2
Campasps Bsns Pk TW16 193 D4
Campbell Ave IG6 57 A5
Campbell Cl Ruislip HA4 40 A3
 Shooters Hill SE18 144 C4
 Streatham SW16 181 D6
 Twickenham TW2 152 B3
Campbell Croft HA8 26 C5
Campbell Ct
 Dulwich SE21 162 A3
 Ealing W7 108 C6
 Kingsbury NW9 45 A3
 South Kensington SW7 256 A5
 Tottenham N17 33 D2
Campbell Gordon Way NW2 68 B4
Campbell Ho
 Paddington W2 236 C5
 Pimlico SW1 259 A1
 30 Shepherd's Bush W12 112 B6
 6 Wallington SM6 219 B4
Campbell Rd Bow E3 97 C4
 Ealing W7 108 C6
 Newham E6 100 A6
 Stratford E15 76 D4
 Thornton Heath CR0 204 D3
 Tottenham N17 34 A2
 Twickenham TW2 152 B2
 Walthamstow E17 53 B5
Campbell Wlk N1 233 B6
Campdale Rd N7 71 D5
Campden Cres
 Dagenham RM8 80 C4
 Wembley HA0 65 B5
Campden Gr W8 113 C4 245 B2
Campden Hill W8 113 C4 245 A2
Campden Hill Ct W8 245 B2
Campden Hill Gate W8 245 A2
Campden Hill Gdns W8 245 A4
Campden Hill Mans W8 245 B4
Campden Hill Pl W14 244 D4
Campden Hill Rd W8 113 C4 245 A2
Campden Hill Sq W14 113 B5 244 D4
Campden Ho 4 NW6 70 B1
Campden Hos W8 245 A3
Campden House Cl W8 245 B2
Campden Rd
 Ickenham UB10 60 B4
 South Croydon CR2 221 C3
Campden St W8 113 C5 245 A3
Campden Way RM8 80 B4
Campe Ho 1 N10 31 A3
Campen Cl SW19 157 A2
Camperdown St E1 243 D1
Campfield Rd SE9 165 D4
Campion Cl Harrow HA3 44 B3
 Hillingdon UB8 82 B2
 Newham E6 122 B6
 South Croydon CR2 221 C4
Campion Ct London N12 30 C4
 10 Wembley HA0 88 A5
Campion Gdns IG8 37 A5
Campion Ho 15 N16 73 C3
Campion House (Seminary) TW7 130 B4
Campion Pl SE28 124 B5
Campion Rd
 Hounslow TW7 130 D4
 Putney SW15 156 C6
Campion Terr NW2 68 D5
Campion Way HA8 27 A6
Camplin Rd HA3 44 A4
Camplin St SE14 140 D5
Camp Rd SW19 178 C5
Campsbourne Ho 3 N8 50 A5
Campsbourne Jun & Inf Schs N8 50 A6
Campsbourne Rd
 Hornsey N8 50 A5
 Hornsey N8 50 A6
Campsbourne The N8 50 A5
Campsey Gdns RM9 80 B1
Campsey Rd RM9 80 B1
Campsfield Ho N8 50 A6
Campsfield Rd N8 50 A6
Campshill Pl SE13 164 A6
Campshill Rd SE13 164 A6
Camp Site The BR8 191 C3
Campton Hill Twrs W8 245 A4
Campus Rd E17 53 B3
Camp View SW19 178 B5
Cam Rd E15 98 B6
Camrose Ave
 Edgware HA8 26 B2
 Erith DA8 147 D6
 Feltham TW13 172 C6
Camrose Cl
 Croydon CR0 207 A2
 Morden SM4 201 C5
Camrose St SE2 124 A2
Camsey Ho 8 SW2 160 B6
Canada Ave N18 33 A4
Canada Cres W3 89 A3
Canada Gdns SE13 164 A6
Canada Rd W3 89 A2
Canada Sq E14 119 D5
Canada St SE16 118 D4
Canada Water Sta SE16 118 D3
Canada Way W12 112 B6
Canadian Ave SE6 163 D3
Canal App SE8 141 A6
Canal Bldg N1 235 A4
Canal Bridge SE15 140 A6
Canal Bvd 7 NW1 71 D2
Canal Cl Mile End E1 97 A3
 North Kensington W10 90 D3
Canal Gr SE15 140 B6
Canal Head Public Sq 1 SE15 140 A4
Canal Path 22 E2 95 D6
Canalside Studios 29 N1 95 C6
Canal St SE5 139 B6
Canal Way W10 90 D3
Canal Wlk
 Croydon CR0 205 D3
 Forest Hill SE26 184 C5
 Shoreditch N1 95 B6 235 D6
CANARY WHARF 119 D5
Canary Wharf* E14 119 D5
Canary Wharf Pier (River Bus) E14 119 B5
Canary Wharf Sta E14 119 D5
Canary Wharf Sta (DLR) E14 119 C5
Canberra Cl NW4 46 A6
Canberra Dr UB4 84 C4
Canberra Ho 7 HA4 40 C1
Canberra Prim Sch W12 112 B6
Canberra Rd
 Charlton SE7 143 D6
 Ealing W13 109 A5
 Erith DA7 146 D6
 Harlington TW6 126 C2
 Newham E6 100 B6
Canbury Ave KT2 176 B2
Canbury Bsns Pk 3 KT2 176 A2
Canbury Ct 3 KT2 176 A3
Canbury Mews SE26 162 A1
Canbury Park Rd KT2 176 B2
Canbury Sch KT2 176 D4
Cancell Rd SW9 138 C4
Candahar Rd SW11 136 C3
Candida Ct 9 NW1 71 B1
Candishe Ho SE1 253 C2
Candle Gr SE15 140 B2
Candlelight Ct 5 E15 76 D2
Candlemakers 25 SW11 136 B2
Candler Mews TW1 153 A4
Candler St N15 51 B3
Candover St W1 239 A3
Candy St E3 97 B6
Caney Mews NW2 68 D6
Canfield Dr HA4 62 B3
Canfield Gdns NW6 69 D1
Canfield Ho N15 51 C3
Canfield Pl NW6 70 A2
Canford Ave UB5 85 A6
Canford Cl EN2 4 C3
Canford Gdns KT3 199 C3
Canford Pl TW11 175 C4
Canford Rd SW11 159 A6
Canham Rd Acton W3 111 C4
 South Norwood SE25 205 C6
Canmore Gdns SW16 181 C3
Cann Hall Prim Sch E11 76 D5
Cann Hall Rd E11 76 D4
Cann Ho W14 254 B5
Canning Cres N22 32 B2
Canning Cross SE5 139 C3
Canning Ct N22 32 B2
Canning Ho 23 W12 112 B6
Canning Pas W8 114 A3 256 A6
Canning Pl W8 114 A3 256 A6
Canning Pl Mews W8 256 A6
Canning Rd
 Croydon CR0 221 D6
 Harrow HA3 42 D6
 Highbury N5 72 D5
 Walthamstow E17 53 A6
 West Ham E15 98 C5
Cannington 14 NW5 71 A2
Cannington Rd RM9 80 C2
CANNING TOWN 99 B2
Canning Town E16 98 C1
Canning Town Sta E16 98 C1
Cannizaro Rd SW19 178 D5
Cannock Ho N4 51 B2
Cannock Lo EN1 17 C5
Cannonbury Ave HA5 40 D3
Cannon Cl
 Hampton TW12 173 D4
 West Barnes SW20 200 C6
Cannon Dr 21 E14 119 C6
Cannon Hill
 Palmers Green N14 16 A1
 West Hampstead NW6 69 C3
Cannon Hill La SM4, SW20 201 A5
Cannon Hill Mews N14 16 A1
Cannon Ho
 Lambeth SE11 260 D3
 Penge SE26 184 B4
Cannon La
 Hampstead NW3 70 B5
 Pinner HA5 41 A3

Cannon Lane Fst & Mid Schs HA5 ... 40 D3
Cannon Pl
Hampstead NW3 ... 70 B5
Woolwich SE7 ... 122 A1
Cannon Rd Erith DA7 ... 147 B4
Palmers Green N14 ... 16 A1
Cannon St EC4 . 117 A6 252 B6
Cannon Street Rd E1 ... 96 B1
Cannon Street Sta EC4 ... 117 B6 252 C6
Cannon Trad Est HA9 ... 66 D4
Cannon Way KT8 ... 195 D5
Cannon (W End of General Roy's Base Line)* TW6 ... 126 D4
Cannon Wharf Bsns Ctr 12 SE8 ... 119 A2
Canon Ave RM6 ... 58 C4
Canon Barnett Prim Sch E1 ... 95 D1 243 D2
Canon Beck Rd SE16 ... 118 C4
Canonbie Rd SE23 ... 162 C4
CANONBURY ... 73 A2
Canonbury Bsns Ctr N1 ... 235 B6
Canonbury Cres N1 ... 73 A1
Canonbury Ct 21 N1 ... 72 D1
Canonbury Gr N1 ... 73 A1
Canonbury Hts 6 N1 ... 73 B2
Canonbury La N1 ... 72 D1
Canonbury Pk N N1 ... 73 A2
Canonbury Pk S N1 ... 73 A2
Canonbury Pl N1 ... 72 D2
Canonbury Prim Sch N1 ... 72 D2
Canonbury Rd
Enfield EN1 ... 5 C4
Islington N1 ... 72 D1
Canonbury Sq N1 ... 72 D1
Canonbury St N1 ... 73 A1
Canonbury Sta N1, N5 ... 73 A3
Canonbury Villas N1 ... 72 D1
Canon Mohan Cl N14 ... 15 B5
Canon Murnane Rd SE1 ... 263 C5
Canon Palmer RC Sch IG3 ... 57 C1
Canon Rd BR1 ... 209 D6
Canon Row SW1 ... 116 A4 250 A1
Canons Cl
East Finchley N2 ... 48 B2
Edgware HA8 ... 26 B4
Canons Cnr HA8 ... 26 A6
Canons Ct Edgware HA8 . 26 B4
Leyton E15 ... 76 C4
Canons Dr HA8 ... 26 B4
Canons High Sch HA8 ... 26 B1
Canons L Ctr The CR4 ... 202 D5
Canonsleigh Rd RM9 ... 80 B1
CANONS PARK ... 26 A3
Canons Park Cl HA8 ... 26 A4
Canons Park Sta HA8 ... 26 A3
Canon St N1 ... 95 A6 235 A5
Canon's Wlk CR0 ... 222 D5
Canopus Way
Northwood HA6 ... 22 A6
Stanwell TW19 ... 148 A4
Canrobert St E2 ... 96 B4
Cantelowes Ho EN5 ... 12 D6
Cantelowes Rd NW1 ... 71 D2
Canterbury SE13 ... 164 A6
Canterbury Ave
Redbridge IG1 ... 56 A2
Sidcup DA15 ... 168 C2
Canterbury Cl
Beckenham BR3 ... 185 D2
16 Camberwell SE5 ... 139 A3
7 Newham E6 ... 100 B1
North Cheam KT4 ... 216 D6
Southall UB6 ... 85 D2
Canterbury Cres SW9 ... 138 C2
Canterbury Ct
Acton W3 ... 111 C5
4 Ashford TW15 ... 170 B6
Eltham SE12 ... 165 B1
15 Hendon NW9 ... 27 D1
Kilburn NW6 ... 91 C5
South Croydon CR2 ... 221 A1
Thornton Heath CR0 ... 204 C2
Canterbury Gr SE27, SW16 ... 160 C1
Canterbury Hall KT4 ... 200 B2
Canterbury Ho
2 Barking IG11 ... 80 A1
6 Bromley E3 ... 97 D4
Lambeth SE1 ... 260 D6
Canterbury Ind Pk 15 SE15 ... 140 C6
Canterbury Mans NW6 ... 69 D2
Canterbury Pl SE17 ... 261 D3
Canterbury Rd
Feltham TW13 ... 151 A2
Harrow HA1, HA2 ... 42 A4
Kilburn NW6 ... 91 C5
Leyton E10 ... 54 A3
Morden SM4 ... 202 A3
Thornton Heath CR0 ... 204 C2
Canterbury Terr NW6 ... 91 C5
Cantium Ret Pk SE1 ... 140 A6
Cantley Gdns Ilford IG2 ... 57 A3
South Norwood SE19 ... 183 D2
Cantley Rd W7 ... 109 A3
Canton St E14 ... 97 C1
Cantrell Rd E3 ... 97 C3
Cantwell Ho SE18 ... 144 D5
Cantwell Rd SE18 ... 144 D5
Canute Ct SW16 ... 160 C1
Canute Gdns SE16 ... 118 D2
Canute Ho 1 TW8 ... 131 C5
Canvey St SE1 ... 252 A4
Cape Cl IG11 ... 78 D1
Cape Henry Ct 15 E14 ... 120 B6
Capel KT5 ... 198 B2
Capel Ave SM6 ... 220 B3
Capel Cl
Keston Mark BR2 ... 210 A1
Whetstone N20 ... 14 A1
Capel Ct SE20 ... 184 C2
Capel Gdns Ilford IG3 ... 79 D4
Pinner HA5 ... 41 B5
Capel Ho 17 Hackney E9 ... 74 C1
South Oxhey WD19 ... 22 D6
Capella Ho 1 SE7 ... 143 B6
Capel Lo
5 Richmond TW9 ... 132 B4
12 Streatham SW2 ... 160 B4
Capel Point E7 ... 77 B4
Capel Rd
East Barnet EN4 ... 14 C5
Forest Gate E7, E12 ... 77 C4
Capener's Cl SW1 ... 248 A1
Cape Rd N17 ... 52 A6
Capern Rd SW18 ... 158 A3
Cape Yd 6 E1 ... 118 A5
Capio Nightingale Hospl SW3 ... 257 B1
Capital Bsns Ctr
South Croydon CR0 ... 221 B1
Wembley HA0 ... 87 D5
Capital City Acad NW10 ... 90 B6
Capital East Apts 8 E16 ... 121 A6
Capital Ind Est
Belvedere DA17 ... 125 D3
Mitcham CR4 ... 202 D4
Capital Interchange Way TW8 ... 110 C1
Capital Sh Ctrs SW1 ... 249 C1
Capital Wharf 15 E1 ... 118 A5
Capitol Ind Pk NW9 ... 45 A6
Capitol Way NW9 ... 45 A6
Capland Ho NW8 ... 236 D6
Capland St NW8 . 92 B3 236 D6
Caplan Est CR4 ... 181 C2
Caple Ho SW10 ... 266 B4
Caple Rd NW10 ... 89 D5
Capper St WC1 ... 93 C3 239 B5
Caprea Cl UB4 ... 84 D2
Capricorn Ctr RM8 ... 59 B2
Capri Ho E17 ... 35 B1
Capri Rd CR0 ... 205 D2
Capstan Cl RM6 ... 58 B3
Capstan Ho 6 E14 ... 120 A2
Capstan Rd SE8 ... 119 B2
Capstan Ride EN2 ... 4 C3
Capstan Sq E14 ... 120 A4
Capstan Way SE16 ... 119 A5
Capstone Rd BR1 ... 186 D6
Capthorne Ave HA2 ... 41 B1
Capuchin Cl HA7 ... 25 B4
Capulet Mews 1 E16 ... 121 A5
Capworth St E10 ... 53 D2
Caradoc Cl W2 ... 91 C1
Caradoc Evans Cl N11 ... 31 B5
Caradoc St SE10 ... 120 C1
Caradon Cl 4 E11 ... 76 C6
Caradon Ct 7 TW1 ... 153 C5
Caradon Way N15 ... 51 B5
Cara Ho 10 N1 ... 72 C1
Caranday Villas 5 W11 ... 112 D5
Caravel Cl E14 ... 119 C3
Caravelle Gdns 1 UB5 ... 84 D4
Caravel Mews 14 SE8 ... 141 C6
Caraway Cl E13 ... 99 B2
Caraway Hts E14 ... 120 A6
Caraway Pl SM6 ... 219 B5
Carberry Rd 12 SE19 ... 183 C4
Carbery Ave W3 ... 110 B4
Carbis Cl E4 ... 20 B3
Carbis Rd E14 ... 97 B1
Carbroke Ho 9 E9 ... 96 C6
Carburton St W1 ... 93 B3 238 D5
Cardale St 1 E14 ... 120 A3
Cardamom Ct 1 E12 ... 78 C4
Carden Rd SE15 ... 140 B2
Cardiff Ho 9 SE15 ... 140 A6
Cardiff Rd Ealing W7 ... 109 A3
Enfield EN3 ... 6 B1
Cardiff St SE18 ... 145 C5
Cardigan Ct 3 W7 ... 86 D3
Cardigan Gdns IG3 ... 80 A6
Cardigan Rd
Barnes SW13 ... 134 A3
Bow E3 ... 97 B5
Richmond TW10 ... 154 A5
Wimbledon SW19 ... 180 A4
Cardigan St SE11 ... 116 C1 261 A2
Cardigan Wlk 19 N1 ... 73 A1
Cardinal Ave
Kingston u T KT2 ... 176 A4
West Barnes SM4 ... 201 A3
Cardinal Bourne St SE1 ... 262 D5
Cardinal Cap Alley SE1 ... 252 A5
Cardinal Cl
Burnt Oak HA8 ... 27 B3
Chislehurst BR7 ... 189 B2
West Barnes SM4 ... 201 A3
Worcester Pk KT19, KT4 ... 216 A4
Cardinal Cres KT3 ... 177 A1
Cardinal Ct KT8 ... 196 B5
Cardinal Dr KT12 ... 194 D1
Cardinal Hinsey Cl NW10 ... 90 A5
Cardinal Hinsley RC High Sch (Boys) NW10 ... 90 A6
Cardinal Pl SW15 ... 134 D1
Cardinal Pole RC Sch
London E9 ... 74 D1
London E9 ... 75 A3
Cardinal Rd
Feltham TW13 ... 150 B3
Ruislip HA4 ... 40 D1
Cardinal Road Inf Sch TW13 ... 150 B3
Cardinals Way N19 ... 49 D1
Cardinal's Wlk
Ashford TW16 ... 171 C4
Hampton TW12 ... 174 A3
Cardinal Vaughan Meml Sch The W14 ... 244 A2
Cardinal Way HA3 ... 42 C6
Cardinal Wiseman RC Sch The UB6 ... 86 A2
Cardinal Wlk SW1 ... 259 A5
Cardine Mews SE15 ... 140 B5
Cardington Sq TW4 ... 128 D1
Cardington St NW1 ... 93 C4 232 B1
Cardozo Rd N7 ... 72 A3
Cardrew Ave N12 ... 30 B5
Cardrew Cl N12 ... 30 B5
Cardrew Ct 8 N12 ... 30 B5
Cardross St W6 ... 112 B3
Cardwell Prim Sch SE18 ... 122 B2
Cardwell Rd 3 N7 ... 72 A4
Career Ct 11 SE16 ... 118 D4
Carew Cl N7 ... 72 B6
Carew Ct
15 Deptford SE14 ... 140 D6
Ilford RM6 ... 58 B3
Carew Ho
West Norwood SW16 ... 160 C1
23 Woolwich SE18 ... 122 B2
Carew Manor Sch SM6 ... 219 D5
Carew Rd
Ashford TW15 ... 171 A4
Ealing W13 ... 109 C4
Mitcham CR4 ... 181 A1
Thornton Heath CR7 ... 204 D5
Tottenham N17 ... 34 A1
Wallington SM6 ... 219 C2
Carew St SE5 ... 139 A3
Carey Ct Bexley DA6 ... 169 D6
20 Camberwell SE5 ... 139 A5
Carey Gdns SW8 ... 137 D4 269 C1
Carey Ho E5 ... 74 B5
Carey La EC2 ... 242 A2
Carey Pl SW1 ... 259 C3
Carey Rd RM9 ... 81 A4
Carey St WC2 ... 94 B1 240 D1
Carey Way HA9 ... 66 D4
Carfax Pl SW4 ... 137 D1
Carfax Rd UB3 ... 106 A2
Carfree Cl 5 N1 ... 72 C1
Cargill Rd SW18 ... 158 A3
Cargreen Pl SE25 ... 205 D5
Cargreen Rd SE25 ... 205 D5
Cargrey Ho 9 HA7 ... 25 C5
Carholme Rd SE23 ... 163 B3
Carillon Ct W5 ... 109 D6
Carinthia Ct 5 SE8 ... 119 A2
Carisbrook 2 N10 ... 31 B1
Carisbrook Cl EN1 ... 5 D4
Carisbrooke Ave DA5 ... 168 D3
Carisbrooke Cl
Stanmore HA7 ... 25 D1
Twickenham TW4 ... 151 A4
Carisbrooke Ct
Acton W3 ... 111 A4
Belmont SM2 ... 217 B1
Northolt UB5 ... 85 B6
1 Streatham SW16 ... 160 B1
Carisbrooke Gdns SE15 ... 139 D5
Carisbrooke Ho
10 Kingston u T KT2 ... 176 A2
Richmond TW10 ... 154 C6
Carisbrooke Rd
Bromley BR2 ... 209 C5
Mitcham CR4 ... 204 A5
Walthamstow E17 ... 53 A4
Carleton Ave SM6 ... 219 D1
Carleton Cl KT10 ... 196 B1
Carleton Gdns N19 ... 71 C3
Carleton Ho 4 N8 ... 50 A4
Carleton Rd N7 ... 71 D4
Carley Ct 6 N12 ... 30 B5
Carlile Cl E3 ... 97 B5
Carlile Ho SE1 ... 262 D5
Carlina Gdns IG8 ... 37 B5
Carling Ct TW1 ... 152 D4
Carlingford DA14 ... 190 A5
Carlingford Gdns CR4 ... 181 A3
Carlingford Rd
Hampstead NW3 ... 70 B4
London N15 ... 50 D6
West Barnes SM4 ... 200 D3
Carlisle Ave Acton W3 ... 89 C1
Whitechapel EC3 ... 243 C1
Carlisle Cl
Kingston u T KT2 ... 176 C2
Pinner HA5 ... 41 A2
Carlisle Gdns
Harrow HA3 ... 43 D2
Redbridge IG1 ... 56 A3
Carlisle Ho
6 Dartmouth Pk NW5 ... 71 C5
Redbridge IG1 ... 56 A3
Carlisle Inf Sch TW12 ... 173 D4
Carlisle La SE1 . 116 B3 260 D6
Carlisle Lo 1 N3 ... 29 B1
Carlisle Pl London N11 ... 31 B6
Westminster SW1 ... 115 C3 259 A5
Carlisle Rd Cheam SM1 ... 217 B2
Finsbury Pk N4 ... 50 C2
Hampton TW12 ... 173 D3
Hendon NW9 ... 45 A6
Kilburn NW6 ... 91 A6
Leyton E10 ... 53 C1
Carlisle St W1 ... 93 D1 239 C1
Carlisle Way SW17 ... 181 A5
Carlisle Wlk 6 E8 ... 73 D2
Carlos Pl W1 ... 115 B6 248 C5
Carlow St NW1 ... 232 A4
Carlson Ct SW15 ... 135 B1
Carlton Ave
Feltham TW14 ... 150 C5
Harrow HA3 ... 43 B4
Hayes UB3 ... 105 C2
South Croydon CR2 ... 221 C1
Southgate N14 ... 15 D6
Carlton Ave E HA9 ... 65 D6
Carlton Ave W HA0 ... 65 B6
Carlton Cl
Chessington KT9 ... 213 D2
Child's Hill NW3 ... 69 C6
Edgware HA8 ... 26 C5
Northolt UB5 ... 64 A3
Carlton Cres SM3 ... 217 A4
Carlton Ct Brixton SW9 ... 138 D4
Ealing W7 ... 108 D4
Finchley N3 ... 29 C3
Ilford IG6 ... 57 B6
Kilburn NW6 ... 91 D5
11 Penge SE20 ... 184 B2
South Norwood SE19 ... 183 D2
8 Willesden NW2 ... 68 C2
Carlton Dr Ilford IG6 ... 57 B6
Putney SW15 ... 157 A6
Carlton Gdns
Ealing W5 ... 109 C6
St James SW1 . 115 D5 249 C3
Carlton Gn DA14 ... 189 D6
Carlton Gr SE15 ... 140 B4
Carlton Hill NW8 ... 92 A5 229 A4
Carlton Ho Cheam SM1 ... 217 B2
Edmonton N21 ... 17 A3
Feltham TW14 ... 149 D5
Hounslow TW4 ... 151 C5
8 Kilburn NW6 ... 91 B5
Kilburn NW6 ... 91 C5
Marylebone W1 ... 237 D2
Carlton House Terr SW1 ... 115 D5 249 D4
Carlton Lo N4 ... 50 C2
Carlton Mans
Brixton SW9 ... 138 C1
Cricklewood NW2 ... 68 D3
Kensington W14 ... 244 B2
Maida Vale W9 ... 91 D4
7 South Hampstead NW6 ... 69 C1
Stamford Hill N16 ... 51 D1
Carlton Par HA9 ... 44 A1
Carlton Park Ave SW20 ... 178 D1
Carlton Prim Sch NW5 ... 71 A3
Carlton Rd Acton W4 ... 111 B4
Ashford TW16 ... 171 D3
Ealing W5 ... 87 C1
Erith DA8 ... 147 D6
Finsbury Pk N4 ... 50 C2
Friern Barnet N11 ... 31 A5
Higham Hill E17 ... 35 A2
Kingston u T KT3 ... 177 C1
Leytonstone E11 ... 54 D1
Manor Pk E12 ... 77 D4
Mortlake SW14 ... 133 A1
Sidcup DA14 ... 189 D6
South Croydon CR2 ... 221 B1
Walton-on-T KT12 ... 194 B2
Welling DA16 ... 146 B2
Carlton Sq E1 ... 96 D3
Carlton St SW1 ... 249 C5
Carltons The 5 SW15 ... 157 A6
Carlton Terr
Edmonton N18 ... 33 B6
Forest Hill SE26 ... 162 C1
Upton E7 ... 77 C1
Wanstead E11 ... 55 B4
Carlton Tower Pl SW1 257 D6
Carlton Twrs SM5 ... 218 D5
Carlton Vale NW6 ... 91 C5
Carlton Vale Inf Sch NW6 ... 91 B4
Carlwell St SW17 ... 180 C5
Carlyle Ave
Bromley BR1 ... 209 D6
Southall UB1 ... 107 B6
Carlyle Cl
East Molesey KT8 ... 173 D1
Hampstead Garden Suburb N2 ... 48 A3
Carlyle Gdns UB1 ... 107 B6
Carlyle Ho
4 Camberwell SE5 ... 139 A5
Chelsea SW3 ... 266 D6
Ealing W5 ... 109 D2
East Molesey KT8 ... 195 C4
12 Stoke Newington N16 . 73 C5
Carlyle Lo 6 EN5 ... 14 A6
Carlyle Mans SW3 ... 267 A5
Carlyle Mews 24 E1 ... 96 D3
Carlyle Pl SW15 ... 134 D1
Carlyle Rd
Croydon CR0 ... 222 A6
Carlyle Rd *continued*
Ealing W5 ... 109 C2
Manor Pk E12 ... 78 A4
1 Stonebridge NW10 ... 89 B6
Woolwich SE28 ... 124 C6
Carlyle's Ho* SW3 ... 267 A5
Carlyle Sq SW3 ... 114 B1 256 D1
Carlyon Ave HA2 ... 63 C4
Carlyon Cl HA0 ... 88 A6
Carlyon Ct HA0 ... 88 B6
Carlyon Mans 1 HA0 ... 88 A5
Carlyon Rd Hayes UB4 ... 84 C2
Wembley HA0 ... 88 A6
Carlys Cl BR3 ... 184 D1
Carmalt Gdns SW15 ... 134 C1
Carmarthen Ct 4 W7 ... 86 D3
Carmarthen Ho 8 SW15 ... 156 C4
Carmarthen Pl SE1 ... 253 A2
Carmel Ct
Kensington W8 ... 245 C2
Wembley Pk HA9 ... 66 D6
Carmelite Cl HA3 ... 24 A2
Carmelite Rd HA3 ... 24 A1
Carmelite St EC4 ... 116 C6 251 B6
Carmelite Way HA3 ... 24 A1
Carmelite Wlk HA3 ... 24 A2
Carmel Lo SW6 ... 265 A6
Carmen St E14 ... 97 D1
Carmichael Cl
9 London SW11 ... 136 B2
Ruislip HA4 ... 62 A4
Carmichael Ct 5 SW13 ... 133 D3
Carmichael Ho
17 Dulwich SE21 ... 183 C6
6 Poplar E14 ... 120 A6
Carmichael Mews SW18 ... 158 B4
Carmichael Rd SE25 ... 206 A5
Carminia Rd SW17 ... 159 B2
Carnaby St* W1 ... 93 C1 239 A1
Carnac St SE21, SE27 ... 161 B1
Carna Ct TW9 ... 132 A2
Carnanton Rd E17 ... 36 B2
Carnarvon Ave EN1 ... 5 D3
Carnarvon Dr UB3 ... 105 A3
Carnarvon Rd Barnet EN5 . 1 A2
Leyton E10 ... 54 A4
Stratford E15 ... 76 D2
Woodford E18 ... 36 D2
Carnation St SE2 ... 124 B1
Carnbrook Rd SE3 ... 143 D2
Carnecke Gdns SE9 ... 166 A6
Carnegie Cl
Holdbrook EN3 ... 7 D5
Surbiton KT6 ... 214 B6
Carnegie Ho NW3 ... 70 B5
Carnegie Pl SW19 ... 156 D1
Carnegie St N1 ... 94 B6 233 D5
Carnforth Cl KT19 ... 214 D2
Carnforth Rd SW16 ... 181 D3
Carnicot Ho 9 SE15 ... 140 B4
Carnoustie Cl SE28 ... 102 D1
Carnoustie Dr N1 ... 72 B1
Carnwath Ho SW6 ... 135 D2
Carnwath Rd SW6 ... 135 D2
Caroe Ct N9 ... 18 B3
Carol Cl NW4 ... 46 D5
Carole Ho 13 SE20 ... 184 B2
Carolina Cl E15 ... 76 C3
Carolina Rd CR7 ... 183 A2
Caroline Cl
Bayswater W2 ... 245 D5
Hounslow TW7 ... 130 C5
Muswell Hill N10 ... 31 B1
South Croydon CR0 ... 221 C4
Streatham SW16 ... 160 B1
Caroline Ct
Ashford TW15 ... 170 D4
Catford SE6 ... 186 B6
Stanmore HA7 ... 25 A4
17 Surbiton KT6 ... 197 D2
23 Woodside Pk N12 ... 29 D6
Caroline Gdns E2 ... 95 C4
Caroline Ho
Bayswater W2 ... 245 D5
20 Hammersmith W6 ... 112 C1
Caroline Martyn Ho 8 N19 ... 49 D2
Caroline Pl
Bayswater W2 ... 245 D5
Clapham SW11 ... 137 A3
Harlington UB3 ... 127 C5
Caroline Pl Mews W2 . 245 D5
Caroline Rd SW19 ... 179 B3
Caroline St E1 ... 96 D1
Caroline Terr SW1 ... 115 A2 258 A3
Caroline Wlk W6 ... 264 A5
Carol St NW1 ... 93 C6 232 A6
Carolyn Ho IG3 ... 58 A1
Caronia Ct 4 SE16 ... 119 A2
Carpenter Gdns N21 ... 16 D2
Carpenter Ho
London NW11 ... 48 A3
11 Tower Hamlets E14 ... 97 C2
5 Tufnell Pk N19 ... 71 D4
Carpenters Bsns Pk E15 ... 75 D1
Carpenters Cl EN5 ... 13 D5
Carpenters Ct
Camden Town NW1 ... 232 A6
5 Dagenham RM10 ... 81 D2
Twickenham TW2 ... 152 C2
Carpenter's Pl SW4 ... 137 D1
Carpenters Prim Sch E15 ... 98 A6
Carpenter's Rd E15 ... 75 D1
Carpenter St W1 ... 248 C5
Carradale Ho 2 E14 ... 98 A1
Carrara Cl 18 SW9 ... 138 D1
Carrara Wharf SW6 ... 135 A2
Carr Cl HA7 ... 25 A4
Carr Gr SE18 ... 122 A2
Carriage Dr E SW11 ... 137 A5 268 B4
Carriage Drive E SW11 ... 137 A5 268 B4
Carriage Drive N SW11, SW8 ... 137 A6 268 B5
Carriage Dr N
Battersea SW8, SW11 ... 136 D5 267 C4
Battersea SW8, SW11 ... 137 A6 268 B5
Carriage Dr S SW11 ... 137 A4 268 A2
Carriage Dr W SW11 ... 136 D5 267 C3
Carriage Mews IG1 ... 79 A6
Carriage Pl 14 SW16 ... 181 C5
Carrick Cl TW7 ... 131 A2
Carrick Gate KT10 ... 212 A5
Carrick Gdns N17 ... 33 C3
Carrick Ho Islington N7 ... 72 B2
Kennington SE11 ... 261 C2
Carrick Mews SE8 ... 141 C6
Carrill Way DA17 ... 124 D3
Carrington Ave
Borehamwood WD6 ... 10 D6
Hounslow TW3 ... 151 D6
Carrington Cl
Barnet EN5 ... 12 A6
Borehamwood WD6 ... 11 A6
Croydon CR0 ... 207 A2
Carrington Ct
London SW11 ... 136 C1
3 New Malden KT3 ... 199 C5
Southgate N21 ... 16 D5
Carrington Gdns 4 E7 ... 77 A4
Carrington Ho
Mayfair W1 ... 248 C3
7 Merton SW19 ... 179 C3
Carrington Lo
3 Richmond TW10 ... 154 A6
Wembley HA9 ... 66 B5
Carrington Pl KT10 ... 212 A4
Carrington Rd TW10 ... 132 C1
Carrington Sq HA3 ... 24 A3
Carrington St W1 ... 248 C3
Carrol Cl NW5 ... 71 B4
Carroll Cl E15 ... 76 D3
Carroll Ct Acton W3 ... 110 D3
4 Shacklewell E5 ... 74 A5
Carroll Ho W2 ... 246 C6
Carronade Pl SE18 ... 123 B3
Carron Cl E14 ... 97 D1
Carroun Rd SW8 ... 138 B5 270 C4
Carroway La UB6 ... 86 B4
Carrow Rd RM9 ... 80 B1
Carr Rd Northolt UB5 ... 64 A1
Walthamstow E17 ... 35 C1
Carrs La N21 ... 17 B6
Carr St 5 E14 ... 97 A1
CARSHALTON ... 218 C4
Carshalton, Beddington & Wallington War Meml Hospl SM5 ... 218 D2
Carshalton Beeches Sta SM5 ... 218 D2
Carshalton Boys Sports Coll SM5 ... 218 C6
Carshalton Coll SM5 ... 218 D5
Carshalton Gr SM1 ... 218 B3
Carshalton High Sch for Girls SM5 ... 218 C5
CARSHALTON ON THE HILL ... 219 B1
Carshalton Park Rd SM5 ... 218 D3
Carshalton Pl SM5 ... 219 A3
Carshalton Rd
Mitcham CR4 ... 203 A4
Sutton SM1, SM5 ... 218 B3
Carshalton Sta SM5 ... 218 D4
Carslake Rd SW15 ... 156 C5
Carson Rd
Cockfosters EN4 ... 2 D1
Dulwich SE21 ... 161 B2
Newham E16 ... 99 A2
Carstairs Rd SE6 ... 164 A1
Carston Cl SE12 ... 164 D6
Carswell Cl IG4 ... 55 D5
Carswell Rd SE6 ... 164 A4
Carter Cl Kenton NW9 ... 45 B3
Wallington SM6 ... 219 D1
Carter Ct EC4 ... 241 D1
Carteret Ho 8 W12 ... 112 B6
Carteret St SW1 ... 249 C1
Carteret Way SE8 ... 119 A2
Carterhatch Jun & Inf Schs EN1 ... 6 B4
Carterhatch La EN1 ... 6 A4
Carterhatch Rd EN3 ... 6 D4
Carter Ho
11 London SW2 ... 160 C6
Spitalfields E1 ... 243 C3
Carter La EC4 ... 94 D1 241 D1
Carter Pl SE17 ... 117 A1 262 B1
Carter Rd
Mitcham SW19 ... 180 B4

Carter Rd *continued*
Newham E13 ... 99 B6
Carters Cl
10 Kentish Town NW5 ... 71 D2
North Cheam KT4 ... 200 D1
Carters Hill Cl SE9 ... 165 C3
Carters La SE23 ... 163 B1
Carters Rd N2 ... 30 C3
Carter St SE17 .. 117 A1 262 A1
Carter's Yd SW18 ... 157 C6
Carthew Rd W6 ... 112 B3
Carthew Villas W6 ... 112 B3
Carthusian St EC1 ... 242 A4
Cartier Circ E14 ... 120 A5
Carting La WC2 ... 116 A6 250 B5
Cart La E4 ... 20 C3
Cartmel NW1 ... 232 A2
Cartmel Cl N17 ... 34 B3
Cartmel Ct
Beckenham BR2 ... 186 C1
Northolt UB5 ... 63 A2
Cartmel Gdns SM4 ... 202 A4
Cartmel Rd DA7 ... 147 C4
Carton Ho
4 Bermondsey SE16 ... 118 A3
2 Dollis Hill NW2 ... 68 A5
12 Shepherd's Bush W11 ... 112 D6
Cartoon Mus The★ WC1 ... 94 A2 240 A3
Cartwright Gdns WC1 ... 94 A4 233 A1
Cartwright Ho SE1 ... 262 B5
Cartwright Rd RM9 ... 81 B1
Cartwright St E1 ... 117 D6 253 D5
Cartwright Way SW13 .. 134 B5
Carvel Ho E14 ... 120 A1
Carver Cl 15 W4 ... 111 A3
Carver Rd SE24 ... 161 A5
Carville Cres TW8 ... 110 A2
Caryl Ho 6 SW19 ... 156 D3
Cary Rd E11 ... 76 C5
Carysfort Rd
Canonbury N16 ... 73 B4
London N8 ... 49 D4
Casby Ho 7 SE16 ... 118 A3
Cascade Ave N10 ... 49 C5
Cascade Cl IG9 ... 21 D2
Cascade Rd IG9 ... 21 D2
Cascadia Ho 22 KT1 ... 176 C1
Casella Rd SE14 ... 140 D5
Casewick Rd SE27 ... 182 D6
Casey Cl NW8 ... 92 C4 230 B1
Casimir Rd E5 ... 74 C5
Casino Ave SE24 ... 161 B6
Caspian Ho 10 E1 ... 96 D2
Caspian St SE5 ... 139 B5
Caspian Wlk E16 ... 99 D1
Cassandra Cl UB5 ... 64 B4
Cassandra Ct 7 NW2 ... 68 C2
Cass Bsns Sch EC1 ... 95 B3 242 C5
Casselden Rd NW10 ... 67 B1
Cassel Hospl TW10 ... 175 D6
Cassell Ho 21 SW9 ... 138 A3
Casserley Ho W4 ... 111 B3
Cass Ho 23 E9 ... 74 D2
Cassidy Rd SW6 ... 265 A3
Cassilda Rd SE2 ... 124 A2
Cassilis Rd
Millwall E14 ... 119 C4
Twickenham TW1 ... 153 B5
Cassinghurst SE24 ... 161 B6
Cassiobury Ave TW14 .. 149 D4
Cassiobury Rd E17 ... 53 A4
Cassland Rd
Homerton E9 ... 74 D2
South Norwood CR7 ... 205 B5
Casslee Rd SE6 ... 163 B4
Cassocks Sq TW17 ... 193 B2
Casson Ho 11 E1 ... 96 A2
Casson St E1 ... 96 A2
Castalia Sq 6 E14 ... 120 A4
Castellain Mans W9 ... 91 D3
Castellain Rd W9 ... 91 D3
Castellane Cl HA7 ... 24 D3
Castell Ho 11 SE8 ... 141 C5
Castello Ave SW15 ... 156 C6
Castelnau SW13 ... 134 B5
Castelnau Gdns SW13 .. 134 B6
Castelnau Mans SW13 .. 134 B6
Castelnau Row SW13 .. 134 B6
Casterbridge
Kilburn NW6 ... 91 D6
3 Notting Hill W11 ... 91 C1
Casterbridge Rd SE3 ... 143 A2
Casterton St E8 ... 74 B2
Castile Rd SE18 ... 122 C2
Castilion Prim Sch SE28 ... 102 C1
Castillon Rd SE6 ... 164 C2
Castlands Rd SE6 ... 163 B2
Castleacre W2 ... 237 A1
Castle Ave Chingford E4 .. 36 B5
Yiewsley UB7 ... 104 B6
Castlebar Ct 5 W5 ... 87 C2
Castlebar Hill W5 ... 87 C2
Castlebar Mews W5 ... 87 C2
Castle Bar Park Sta W7 ... 86 D2
Castlebar Pk W5 ... 87 B2
Castlebar Rd W5 ... 87 C1
Castlebar Sch W13 ... 87 A2
Castle Baynard St EC4 ... 117 A6 252 A6
Castlebrook Cl SE11 ... 116 D2 261 C4
Castle Bsns Village TW12 ... 173 D2
Castle Cl 12 Acton W3 ... 111 A4
Ashford TW16 ... 171 C3
Beckenham BR2 ... 208 C6
Homerton E9 ... 75 A3
South Acton W3 ... 110 D4
Wimbledon SW19 ... 156 D1
Castlecombe Dr SW19 ... 156 D4
Castlecombe Prim Sch SE9 ... 188 A5
Castlecombe Rd SE9 ... 188 A6
Castle Ct Belmont SM2 .. 217 C2
City of London EC3 ... 242 D1
Dagenham RM9 ... 103 A6
Forest Hill SE26 ... 185 A6
Morden SM4 ... 202 B4
Castleden Ho NW6 ... 70 B1
Castledine Rd SE20 ... 184 B3
Castle Dr IG4 ... 56 A3
Castleford Ave SE9 ... 166 D3
Castleford Cl N17 ... 33 D4
Castleford Ct NW8 ... 236 D6
Castlefrank Ho 20 N1 ... 95 C4
Castlegate TW9 ... 132 B2
CASTLE GREEN ... 102 C6
Castleham Ct HA8 ... 26 C4
Castlehaven Rd NW1 ... 71 B1
Castle Hill Ave CR0 ... 224 A1
Castle Hill Prim Sch CR0 ... 224 A1
Castle Ho
17 Belmont SM2 ... 217 C1
3 Chingford E4 ... 36 B5
Newington SE1 ... 262 A4
South Lambeth SW8 ... 270 B4
Castle Hts RM9 ... 102 B6
Castle Ind Est SE17 ... 262 A4
Castle La SW1 .. 115 C3 259 A6
Castleleigh Ct EN2 ... 17 B6
Castlemaine 8 SW11 .. 136 D3
Castlemaine Ave CR2 .. 221 D3
Castlemaine St 2 E1 ... 96 B2
Castle Mead SE5 ... 139 A5
Castle Mews
Camden Town NW1 ... 71 B2
North Finchley N12 ... 30 A5
Castle Par KT17 ... 216 A1
Castle Pl 8 Acton W4 ... 111 C2
Camden Town NW1 ... 71 B2
Castle Point 4 E13 ... 99 C5
Castle Rd
Camden Town NW1 ... 71 B2
Dagenham RM9 ... 102 B6
Enfield EN3 ... 7 A5
Isleworth TW7 ... 130 D3
North Finchley N12 ... 30 B5
Northolt UB5 ... 63 D1
Southall UB2 ... 107 B3
Castlereagh Ho HA7 ... 25 B4
Castlereagh St W1 ... 237 C2
Castle St
Kingston u T KT2 ... 176 A1
Newham E6 ... 99 C5
Castleton Ave HA9 ... 66 A4
Castleton Cl CR0 ... 207 A3
Castleton Ct KT5 ... 198 B4
Castleton Gdns HA9 ... 66 A5
Castleton Ho 3 E14 ... 120 A2
Castleton Rd
Chingford E17 ... 36 B1
Ilford IG3 ... 58 B1
Mitcham CR4 ... 203 D5
Mottingham SE12, SE9 .. 187 D6
Ruislip HA4 ... 40 D1
Castletown Rd W14 ... 113 A1 254 B1
Castleview Cl N4 ... 73 A6
Castleview Gdns IG1 ... 56 B3
Castle Way
Feltham TW13 ... 172 C6
Wimbledon SW19 ... 156 D1
Castle Wlk TW16 ... 194 C6
Castlewood Day Hospl SE18 ... 144 C4
Castlewood Dr SE9 ... 144 B3
Castlewood Ho WC1 ... 239 D2
Castlewood Rd
Barnet EN4 ... 2 B2
Stamford Hill N16 ... 52 A3
Castle Yd Highgate N6 ... 49 A2
Lambeth SE1 ... 251 D4
18 Richmond TW10 ... 153 D6
Castor La E14 ... 119 D6
Catalina Rd TW6 ... 126 C2
Catalpa Ct SE13 ... 164 B5
Caterham Rd SE13 ... 142 B2
Catesby Ho 25 E9 ... 74 C1
Catesby St SE17 ... 117 B2 262 D3
CATFORD ... 163 C3
Catford Br SE6 ... 163 C4
Catford Bridge Sta SE6 ... 163 C4
Catford Broadway SE6 ... 163 D4
Catford Gyratory SE6 .. 163 D4
Catford High Sch SE6 .. 164 A1
Catford Hill SE6 ... 163 C3
Catford Rd SE6 ... 163 C4
Catford Sh Ctr SE6 ... 163 D4
Catford Sta SE6 ... 163 C4
Cathall Rd E11 ... 76 B5
Cathay Ho SE16 ... 118 B4
Cathay St 12 SE16 ... 118 B4
Cathay Wlk UB5 ... 85 C5
Cathcart Dr BR6 ... 211 C1
Cathcart Hill N19 ... 71 C5
Cathcart Rd SW10 ... 136 A6 266 A6
Cathcart St NW5 ... 71 B2
Cathedral Ct EC4 ... 241 D1
Cathedral Lo EC1 ... 242 A4
Cathedral Sch of St Saviour & St Mary Overie Prim Sch SE1 ... 117 A4 252 B2
Cathedral St SE1 ... 117 B5 252 C4
Cathedral Wlk SW1 ... 259 A6
Catherall Rd N5, N16 ... 73 A5
Catherine Baird Ct 12 SW12 ... 159 B4
Catherine Ct Barnet EN5 .. 1 D2
1 Ilford IG2 ... 57 A3
2 Southgate N14 ... 15 C6
3 Wimbledon SW19 ... 179 B5
Catherine Dr
Ashford TW16 ... 171 D4
Richmond TW9 ... 132 A1
Catherine Gdns TW3 ... 130 B1
Catherine Godfrey Ho RM9 ... 103 B6
Catherine Gr SE10 ... 141 D4
Catherine Griffiths Ct EC1 ... 241 B6
Catherine Ho
Isleworth TW7 ... 131 B4
16 Shoreditch N1 ... 95 C6
Catherine Lo E18 ... 37 C2
Catherine Pl
Harrow HA1 ... 42 D4
Westminster SW1 ... 115 C3 259 A6
Catherine Rd Enfield EN3 .. 7 A6
Kingston u T KT6 ... 197 D4
Catherine St WC2 ... 116 B6 250 C6
Catherine Wheel Alley E1 ... 243 B3
Catherine Wheel Rd TW8 ... 131 D5
Catherine Wheel Yd SW1 ... 249 A3
Catherwood Ct N1 ... 235 C3
Cat Hill EN4 ... 14 D6
Cathles Rd SW12 ... 159 B5
Cathnor Rd W12 ... 112 B4
Catisfield Rd EN3 ... 7 A6
Catlin Cres TW17 ... 193 B4
Catling Cl SE23 ... 162 D1
Catlin's La HA5 ... 40 B5
Catlin St SE16 ... 118 B1
Catman Ho N4 ... 50 B1
Caton Ct BR2 ... 186 C1
Cato Rd SW4 ... 137 D1
Cator La BR3 ... 185 B2
Cator Park Sch BR3 ... 185 A3
Cator Rd
Penge SE20, SE26 ... 184 D5
Wallington SM5 ... 218 D3
Cator St
Camberwell SE15 ... 139 D5
Camberwell SE15 ... 139 D6
Cato St W1 ... 92 C1 237 B2
Catsey La WD23 ... 8 A4
Catsey Wood WD23 ... 8 A4
Catterick Cl N11 ... 31 A4
Cattistock Rd SE9 ... 188 B5
Cattley Cl EN5 ... 1 A1
Catton St WC1 ... 240 C3
Caughley Ho SE11 ... 261 A5
Caulfield Ct 15 NW1 ... 71 C1
Caulfield Rd
East Ham E6 ... 78 B1
London SE15 ... 140 B3
Causeway TW14, TW4 ... 128 B1
Causeway The
Carshalton SM5 ... 219 A6
Chessington KT9 ... 214 A4
Claygate KT10 ... 212 D1
East Finchley N2 ... 48 C5
Teddington TW11 ... 174 D4
Wandsworth SW18 ... 157 D6
Wimbledon SW19 ... 178 C5
Causeyware Rd N9 ... 18 C4
Causton Cotts 3 E14 ... 97 A1
Causton Ho SE5 ... 139 A5
Causton Rd N6 ... 49 B2
Causton Sq RM10 ... 81 C1
Causton St SW1 ... 115 D1 259 D2
Cautley Ave SW4 ... 159 C6
Cavalier Cl RM6 ... 58 D5
Cavalier Gdns UB3 ... 83 B1
Cavalier Ho W5 ... 109 C6
Cavalry Cres TW4 ... 128 D1
Cavalry Gdns SW15 ... 157 B6
Cavan Pl HA5 ... 23 B2
Cavaye Ho SW10 ... 266 B6
Cavaye Pl SW10 ... 256 B1
Cavell Ct 5 N19 ... 71 C6
Cavell Dr EN2 ... 4 C3
Cavell Ho 8 N1 ... 95 C6
Cavell Rd N17 ... 33 B3
Cavell St E1 ... 96 B2
Cavendish Ave
Ealing W13 ... 87 A1
Falconwood DA16 ... 145 D2
Finchley N3 ... 29 C1
Harrow HA1 ... 64 C4
Ruislip HA4 ... 62 B3
Sidcup DA15 ... 168 A4
St John's Wood NW8 ... 92 B5 229 D3
West Barnes KT3 ... 200 B5
Woodford IG8 ... 37 B3
Cavendish Cl
Ashford TW16 ... 171 D4
Brondesbury NW6 ... 69 B2
Edmonton N18 ... 34 B5
Hayes UB4 ... 83 C2
3 Putney SW15 ... 157 A6
St John's Wood NW8 ... 92 B4 229 D2
Cavendish Coll WC1 ... 93 D2 239 C4
Cavendish Cres WD6 ... 10 C6
Cavendish Ct
Ashford TW16 ... 171 D4
Catford SE6 ... 163 D3
5 Chingford E4 ... 20 C4
Wallington SM6 ... 219 B2
Wembley HA0 ... 65 D3
Whitechapel EC2 ... 243 B2
Cavendish Dr
Claygate KT10 ... 212 C3
Edgware HA8 ... 26 B4
Leytonstone E11 ... 54 B1
Cavendish Gdns
Barking IG11 ... 79 D3
Clapham Pk SW4 ... 159 C5
Dagenham RM6 ... 59 A4
Ilford IG1 ... 56 C1
Cavendish Ho
London N12 ... 30 A6
5 Muswell Hill N10 ... 31 A3
3 Richmond TW10 ... 153 C1
South Lambeth SW8 ... 270 A2
St John's Wood NW8 ... 229 D3
Twickenham TW1 ... 153 A5
Cavendish Mans
2 Clapham Pk SW12 ... 159 C5
Hackney E5 ... 74 C3
Holborn EC1 ... 241 A5
8 West Hampstead NW6 ... 69 C3
Cavendish Mews N W1 ... 238 D4
Cavendish Mews S W1 ... 238 D3
Cavendish Par
Balham SW12 ... 159 B5
Hounslow TW4 ... 129 A3
Cavendish Pl
Balham SW4 ... 159 B5
Bromley BR1 ... 210 B6
Brondesbury NW2 ... 68 D2
Marylebone W1 ... 238 D2
Cavendish Prim Sch W4 ... 133 C5
Cavendish Rd
Ashford TW16 ... 171 D4
Brondesbury NW6 ... 69 B1
Chingford E4 ... 36 A4
Chiswick W4 ... 133 A4
Clapham Pk SW12 ... 159 C5
Edmonton N18 ... 34 B5
Harringay N4 ... 50 D3
Mitcham SW19 ... 180 C3
New Malden KT3 ... 199 D5
Sutton SM2 ... 218 A1
Thornton Heath CR0 ... 204 D1
Cavendish Sch The NW1 ... 93 B6 231 D6
Cavendish Sq W1 ... 93 B1 238 D2
Cavendish St N1 ... 95 B5 235 C3
Cavendish Terr
Feltham TW13 ... 150 A2
11 Tower Hamlets E3 ... 97 B4
Cavendish The NW11 ... 47 D2
Cavendish Way BR4 ... 207 D1
Cavenham Gdns IG1 ... 79 B5
Cave Rd Newham E13 ... 99 B4
Richmond TW10 ... 175 C6
Caverleigh Way KT4 ... 200 B2
Caversham Ave
Cheam SM3 ... 217 A6
Palmers Green N13 ... 16 C1
Caversham Ct N11 ... 15 A1
Caversham Ho
8 Kingston u T KT1 ... 176 A1
7 Peckham SE15 ... 140 A6
Wallington CR0 ... 220 A5
West Green N15 ... 51 A5
Caversham Lo N10 ... 31 C1
Caversham Rd
Kentish Town NW5 ... 71 C2
Kingston u T KT1 ... 176 B1
West Green N15 ... 51 A5
Caversham St SW3 ... 136 D6 267 C6
Caverswall St W12 ... 90 C1
Caveside Cl BR7 ... 188 C2
Cavour Ho SE17 ... 261 D2
Cawdor Cres W7 ... 109 A2
Cawnpore St SE19 ... 183 C5
Cawston Ct 8 BR1 ... 186 D3
Caxton Gr E3 ... 97 C4
Caxton Hall★ SW1 ... 259 C6
Caxton Rd
Shepherd's Bush W12 ... 112 D4
Southall UB2 ... 106 D3
Wimbledon SW19 ... 180 A5
Wood Green N22 ... 32 B1
Caxton St N E16 ... 98 D1
Caxton St SW1 .. 115 D3 259 C6
Caxton Trad Est UB3 ... 105 C5
Caxton Wlk WC2 ... 239 D1
Cayford Ho 1 NW3 ... 70 D3
Caygill Cl BR2 ... 208 D5
Cayley Cl SM6 ... 220 A1
Cayley Prim Sch E14 ... 97 A1
Cayley Rd UB2 ... 107 D3
Cayton Pl EC1 ... 235 C1
Cayton Rd UB6 ... 86 C5
Cayton St EC1 ... 235 C1
Cazenove Mans 1 N16 .. 74 A6
Cazenove Rd
Stoke Newington N16 ... 74 A6
Walthamstow E17 ... 35 C2
Cearns Ho E6 ... 99 D6
Ceasors Ct TW1 ... 152 D2
Cecil Ave Barking IG11 ... 79 B1
Enfield EN1 ... 5 D1
Wembley HA9 ... 66 B3
Cecil Cl
Chessington KT9 ... 213 D4
Ealing W5 ... 87 D2
Littleton TW15 ... 171 A3
Cecil Ct Chelsea SW10 .. 266 A6
12 Croydon CR0 ... 221 D6
Ealing W5 ... 87 D2
South Hampstead NW6 .. 69 D1
St James WC2 ... 250 A5
Cecile Pk N8 ... 50 A3
Cecil Ho E17 ... 35 C2
Cecilia Cl N2 ... 48 A6
Cecilia Rd E8 ... 74 A3
Cecil Lo KT9 ... 213 D4
Cecil Mans 2 SW17 ... 159 A2
Cecil Pk HA5 ... 41 A5
Cecil Pl CR4 ... 202 D4
Cecil Rd Acton W3 ... 89 A2
Ashford TW15 ... 171 A4
Cheam SM1, SM2 ... 217 B2
Colindale NW9 ... 45 C6
Dagenham RM6 ... 58 D2
Enfield EN2 ... 5 B1
Harlesden NW10 ... 89 C6
Harrow HA3 ... 42 C6
Hounslow TW3 ... 130 A3
Ilford IG1 ... 78 D4
Leyton E11 ... 76 C5
Merton SW19 ... 179 D3
Muswell Hill N10 ... 31 B1
Newham E13 ... 99 A6
Osidge N14 ... 15 C3
Thornton Heath CR0 ... 204 B3
Walthamstow E17 ... 35 C2
Cecil Rhodes Ho NW1 ... 232 C4
Cecil Rosen Ct HA0 ... 65 B5
Cecil Way BR2 ... 209 A1
Cedar Ave
Dagenham RM6 ... 59 A4
East Barnet EN4 ... 14 C4
Enfield EN3 ... 6 C3
Hayes UB3 ... 84 A1
Ruislip HA4 ... 62 C3
Sidcup DA15 ... 168 A4
Twickenham TW2 ... 152 A5
Yiewsley UB7 ... 104 B6
Cedar Cl
Buckhurst Hill IG9 ... 21 D2
East Molesey KT8 ... 196 C5
Keston Mark BR2 ... 226 A5
Kingston u T KT2 ... 177 B6
Old Ford E3 ... 97 B6
Wallington SM5 ... 218 D2
West Norwood SE21 ... 161 A2
Cedar Copse BR1 ... 188 B1
Cedar Cres BR2 ... 226 A5
Cedarcroft Rd KT9 ... 214 B4
Cedar Ct
7 Brentford TW8 ... 131 D6
19 Charlton SE7 ... 143 C6
Edgware HA8 ... 11 A1
Eltham SE9 ... 166 A5
Finchley N3 ... 29 C3
Islington N1 ... 73 A1
Marylebone W1 ... 237 B2
Mortlake SW14 ... 133 A1
1 Muswell Hill N10 ... 31 B1
5 New Southgate N11 ... 31 C5
Oakleigh Pk N20 ... 14 B3
Stoneleigh KT17 ... 216 A1
3 Sutton SM2 ... 218 A2
6 Wanstead E11 ... 55 B4
Wembley HA0 ... 65 B4
Wimbledon SW19 ... 156 D1
5 Woodford E18 ... 37 A2
Cedar Dr London N2 ... 48 C5
Pinner HA5 ... 23 C4
Cedar Gdns SM2 ... 218 A2
Cedar Gr Ealing W5 ... 110 A3
Sidcup DA5 ... 168 D5
Southall UB1 ... 85 C2
Cedar Grange 10 EN1 ... 17 C6
Cedar Ho
Ashford TW16 ... 171 D3
5 Cubitt Town E14 ... 120 A4
Hayes UB4 ... 84 C3
Kensington W8 ... 255 C6
New Addington CR0 ... 223 D2
New Cross Gate SE14 ... 140 D4
5 Richmond TW9 ... 132 D4
16 Rotherhithe SE16 ... 118 D4
Wood Green N22 ... 32 C2
Cedar Hts TW10 ... 154 A3
Cedarhurst BR1 ... 186 C3
Cedarhurst Dr SE9 ... 165 C6
Cedar Lawn Ave EN5 ... 13 A6
Cedar Lo
Brondesbury NW2 ... 69 B2
Fulham SW6 ... 134 D4
Cedarmore Ct BR7 ... 189 A2
Cedar Mount SE9 ... 165 D3
Cedarne Rd SW6 ... 135 D5 265 C3
Cedar Park Gdns RM6 ... 58 D2
Cedar Park Rd EN2 ... 5 A5
Cedar Pl 3 SE7 ... 121 C1
Cedar Rd Bromley BR1 .. 187 C1
Cedar Rd *continued*
Cranford TW5 ... 128 C3
Cricklewood NW2 ... 68 C4
Croydon CR0 ... 221 C6
East Bedfont TW14 ... 149 B3
East Molesey KT8 ... 196 C5
Enfield EN2 ... 5 A5
Sutton SM2 ... 218 A2
Teddington TW11 ... 175 A5
Tottenham N17 ... 33 D2
Cedar Rise N14 ... 15 A4
Cedars Ave
Mitcham CR4 ... 203 A6
Walthamstow E17 ... 53 C4
Cedars Cl Hendon NW4 ... 46 D6
Lewisham SE13 ... 142 B2
Cedars Ct Edmonton N9 .. 17 D2
Putney SW15 ... 156 A5
Cedars Dr UB10 ... 82 C5
Cedars Fst & Mid Schs HA3 ... 24 A2
Cedars Ho
21 London SW2 ... 138 B1
15 Walthamstow E17 ... 53 D6
5 West Norwood SW27 ... 182 D5
Cedars Mews SW4 ... 137 B1
Cedars Prim Sch The TW5 ... 128 A5
Cedars Rd
Barnes SW13 ... 134 A3
Beckenham BR3 ... 185 B1
Clapham SW4 ... 137 B1
4 Lower Edmonton N9 .. 18 A2
Morden SM4 ... 201 C5
Stratford E15 ... 76 C2
Teddington KT8 ... 175 C2
Wallington CR0 ... 220 A4
Winchmore Hill N21 ... 16 D2
Cedars The
Buckhurst Hill IG9 ... 21 A3
Ealing W13 ... 87 C1
Hackney E9 ... 74 D1
4 Kingston u T KT2 ... 176 D2
Teddington TW11 ... 174 D4
Wallington SM6 ... 219 C4
Cedar Terr
9 Dagenham RM8 ... 58 D2
Richmond TW9 ... 132 A1
Cedar Tree Gr SE27 ... 182 D5
Cedarville Gdns SW16 .. 182 B4
Cedar Way
Ashford TW16 ... 171 C3
Camden Town NW1 ... 93 D6 232 C6
Cedar Wlk KT10 ... 212 D2
Cedarwood BR3 ... 185 B3
Cedarwood Ho EN2 ... 4 D3
Cedarwood Lo HA8 ... 26 B5
Cedra Ct N16 ... 52 A1
Cedric Chambers NW8 236 C6
Cedric Rd SE9 ... 167 A1
Celadon Cl EN3 ... 7 A2
Celandine Cl E3, E14 ... 97 C2
Celandine Ct E4 ... 19 D1
Celandine Dr
Dalston E8 ... 73 D1
Woolwich SE28 ... 124 B5
Celandine Gr N14 ... 15 C6
Celandine Way E15 ... 98 C4
Celbridge Mews W2 ... 91 D1
Celestial Gdns SE13 ... 142 B1
Celia Blairman Ho E1 . 243 C4
Celia Ct 7 TW9 ... 132 B4
Celia Ho 10 N1 ... 95 C5
Celia Rd N19 ... 71 C4
Celtic Ave BR2 ... 208 C6
Celtic St E14 ... 97 D2
Cemetery La
Lower Halliford TW17 ... 192 D2
Woolwich SE7 ... 144 A6
Cemetery Rd
East Wickham SE2 ... 146 B5
Forest Gate E7 ... 76 D4
Tottenham N17 ... 33 C3
Cenacle Cl NW3 ... 69 C5
Cenotaph★ SW1 ... 250 A2
Centaur Ct 3 TW8 ... 110 A1
Centaurs Bsns Pk TW7 ... 131 A6
Centaur St SE1 . 116 B3 260 D6
Centenary Rd EN3 ... 7 B1
Centennial Ave WD6 ... 9 C4
Centennial Ct WD6 ... 9 C4
Centennial Pk HA7, WD6 .. 9 C4
Central Ave
Battersea SW11 ... 136 D5 267 D3
East Finchley N2 ... 47 D6
East Molesey KT8 ... 195 B4
Edmonton N9 ... 17 D1
Enfield EN1 ... 6 B3
Finchley N2 ... 30 B1
Hayes UB3 ... 106 A6
Isleworth TW3, TW7 ... 131 A1
Leyton E11 ... 76 B6
Pinner HA5 ... 41 B2
Wallington SM6 ... 220 A3
Welling DA16 ... 146 A3
Central Bsns Ctr NW10 .. 67 C3
Central Chambers W5 ... 109 D6
Central Cir NW4 ... 46 B4
Central Criminal Court (Old Bailey)★ EC4 ... 94 D1 241 D2
Central Ct 2 SE18 ... 122 D2
Centrale Ctr CR0 ... 221 A6

Central Foundation Boys' Sch EC2 ... 95 B3 242 D6
Central Foundation Lower Girls Sch The E3 ... 97 A4
Central Foundation Upper Girls Sch The E3 ... 97 B4
Central Gdns SM4 ... 201 D4
Central Hill SE19 ... 183 B4
Central Ho Barking IG11 .. 79 A1
Mill Meads E15 ... 98 A5
Central Mans
8 London NW4 ... 46 B4
1 Streatham SW16 ... 182 A6
Central Middlesex Hospl NW10 ... 89 A4
Central Par
Croydon CR0 ... 220 C4
Ealing UB6 ... 87 A4
Enfield EN3 ... 6 C3
Feltham TW14 ... 150 C4
Harrow HA1 ... 42 D4
Heston TW5 ... 129 C5
Ilford IG2 ... 57 B3
Penge SE20 ... 184 D3
South Acton W3 ... 110 D4
2 Streatham SW16 ... 182 A6
Surbiton KT6 ... 198 A3
8 Walthamstow E17 ... 53 C5
Central Park Ave RM10 .. 81 D5
Central Park Prim Sch E6 ... 99 D5
Central Park Rd E6 ... 99 D5
Central Par Villas BR5 ... 190 C1
Central Pk Est TW4 ... 128 D1
Central Public Health Laboratories NW9 ... 45 C6
Central Rd
Morden SM4 ... 201 D4
Wembley HA0 ... 65 B3
Worcester Pk KT4 ... 216 A6
Central St Martins Coll EC1 ... 94 C3 241 B5
Central St Martin's Coll of Art & Design W1 ... 93 D1 239 D1
Central St Martins Coll of Art & Design (The London Inst) WC1 ... 94 B2 240 C3
Central Sch of Ballet EC1 ... 94 C3 241 B5
Central Sch of Speech & Drama The NW3 ... 70 B1
Central Sq
East Molesey KT8 ... 195 B5
Hampstead Garden Suburb NW11 ... 47 D3
4 Wembley HA9 ... 66 A3
Central St EC1 ... 95 A4 235 A1
Central Terr BR3 ... 206 D6
Central Way
Feltham TW14 ... 150 B6
Lower Place NW10 ... 89 A4
Sutton SM5 ... 218 C1
Thamesmead SE28 ... 124 B6
Centre Ave Acton W3 ... 111 B5
Finchley N2 ... 30 C1
Centre Bldg SE17 ... 262 B4
Centre Common Rd BR7 ... 189 A3
Centre Court Sh Ctr 3 SW19 ... 179 B4
Centre Ct N20 ... 14 B2
Centre Dr E7 ... 77 C4
Centre Hts 5 NW3 ... 70 B1
Centre Point 3 SE1 ... 118 A1
Centre Point Ho WC2 . 239 D2
Centre Rd
Dagenham RM10 ... 103 D5
Wanstead E7, E11 ... 77 A6
Centre St E2 ... 96 B5
Centre The TW13 ... 150 B3
Centreway 4 IG1 ... 79 A6
Centre Way N9 ... 18 D2
Centro Ct E11 ... 54 C1
Centurian Way DA18 ... 125 C3
Centurion Bldg SW8 .. 268 C5
Centurion Cl N7 ... 72 B1
Centurion Ct
Hackbridge SM6 ... 219 B6
7 Woolwich SE18 ... 122 B2
Centurion La E3 ... 97 B5
Centurion Lodge 2 RM10 ... 81 D2
Century Cl NW4 ... 46 D4
Century Ho
Edgware HA8 ... 26 C3
Harrow HA3 ... 42 C6
Lewisham SE13 ... 141 D3
Wembley HA9 ... 66 B6
Century Rd E17 ... 53 A6
Century Yd SE23 ... 162 C2
Cephas Ave E1 ... 96 C3
Cephas Ho 9 E1 ... 96 C3
Cephas St E1 ... 96 C3
Ceres Ct 12 KT1 ... 176 A1
Ceres Rd SE18 ... 123 D2
Cerise Rd SE15 ... 140 A4
Cerne Cl UB4 ... 106 C6
Cerne Rd SM4 ... 202 A3
Cerney Mews W2 ... 246 C6
Cervantes Ct 12 W2 ... 91 D1
Cester St E2 ... 96 A6
Ceylon Rd
6 Hammersmith W14 ... 112 D3
Kensington W14 ... 254 A5
Chabot Dr SE15 ... 140 B2
Chace Com Sch EN1 ... 5 C4
Chadacre Ave IG5 ... 56 B6
Chadacre Ct E15 ... 99 A6
Chadacre Ho 10 SW9 ... 138 D1
Chadacre Rd KT17 ... 216 B3
Chadbourn St E14 ... 97 D2
Chadbury Ct NW7 ... 28 A2
Chad Cres N9 ... 18 C1
Chadd Dr BR1 ... 210 A6
Chadd Gn E13 ... 99 A6
Chaddlewood EN4 ... 3 A1
Chadston Ho 17 N1 ... 72 D1
Chadswell WC1 ... 233 B1
Chadview Ct 2 RM6 ... 58 D2
Chadville Gdns RM6 ... 58 D4
Chadway RM8 ... 58 C1
Chadwell Ave RM6 ... 58 B2
CHADWELL HEATH ... 58 D4
Chadwell Heath Foundation Sch The RM6 ... 58 B3
Chadwell Heath Hospl RM6 ... 58 B4
Chadwell Heath Ind Pk RM8 ... 58 D1
Chadwell Heath La RM6 ... 58 C3
Chadwell Heath Sta RM6 ... 58 D2
Chadwell Prim Sch RM6 ... 58 C2
Chadwell St EC1 . 94 C4 234 B2
Chadwick Ave
Chingford E4 ... 36 B6
Enfield N21 ... 4 B1
Wimbledon SW19 ... 179 C4
Chadwick Cl
12 Ealing W7 ... 86 D2
Roehampton SW15 ... 155 D4
Teddington TW11 ... 175 A4
Chadwick Ct 4 SE28 ... 124 B5
Chadwick Pl KT6 ... 197 C3
Chadwick Rd
Harlesden NW10 ... 89 D6
Ilford IG1 ... 78 D5
Leytonstone E11 ... 54 D3
Peckham SE15 ... 139 D3
Chadwick St SW1 ... 115 D3 259 C5
Chadwick Way SE28 ... 124 D6
Chadwin Rd E13 ... 99 B2
Chadworth Ho
Finsbury EC1 ... 235 A1
Finsbury Pk N4 ... 51 A1
Chadworth Way KT10 .. 212 B3
Chaffey Ho 6 SE7 ... 121 C1
Chaffinch Ave CR0 ... 206 D3
Chaffinch Bsns Pk CR0 ... 206 D5
Chaffinch Cl
Croydon CR0 ... 206 D3
Edmonton N9 ... 18 D3
Tolworth KT6 ... 214 C5
Chaffinch Rd BR3 ... 185 A2
Chafford Way RM6 ... 58 C5
Chagford Ct SW19 ... 180 C3
Chagford Ho
38 Bromley E3 ... 97 D4
Marylebone NW1 ... 237 C5
Chagford St NW1 ... 92 D3 237 D5
Chailey Ave EN1 ... 5 D3
Chailey Cl TW5 ... 128 D4
Chailey Ind Est UB3 ... 106 A4
Chailey St E5 ... 74 C5
Chalbury Ho 8 SW9 ... 138 B1
Chalbury Wlk N1 ... 234 A4
Chalcombe Rd SE2 ... 124 B3
Chalcot Cl SM2 ... 217 C1
Chalcot Cres NW1 ... 92 D6 230 D6
Chalcot Gdns NW3 ... 70 D2
Chalcot Mews SW16 ... 160 A1
Chalcot Rd NW1 . 93 A6 231 A6
Chalcot Sch NW1 ... 71 B1
Chalcot Sq NW1 ... 71 A1
Chalcott Gdns KT6 ... 197 C1
Chalcroft Rd SE13 ... 164 C6
Chaldon Rd SW6 ... 135 A5 264 B4
Chale Rd SW2 ... 160 A5
Chalfont Ave HA9 ... 66 D2
Chalfont Ct
3 Belvedere DA17 ... 125 C1
12 Harrow HA1 ... 42 D3
Hendon NW9 ... 45 D6
Marylebone NW1 ... 237 D5
Chalfont Gn N9 ... 17 C1
Chalfont Ho
2 Bermondsey SE16 ... 118 B3
Willesden NW10 ... 67 B5
Chalfont Rd
Edmonton N9 ... 17 D1
Hayes UB3 ... 106 A4
South Norwood SE25 ... 205 D6
Chalfont Way W13 ... 109 B3
Chalfont Wlk 5 HA5 ... 22 C1
Chalford 7 NW3 ... 70 A2
Chalford Cl KT8 ... 195 C5
Chalford Ct Ilford IG2 ... 56 D4
15 Putney SW15 ... 156 D5
Surbiton KT6 ... 198 B2
Chalford Rd SE21 ... 183 B6
Chalford Wlk IG8 ... 37 D3
Chalgrove Ave SM4 ... 201 C4
Chalgrove Gdns N3 ... 47 A6
Chalgrove Prim Sch N3 ... 47 A6
Chalgrove Rd
Sutton SM2 ... 218 B1
Tottenham N17 ... 34 B2
Chalice Cl SM6 ... 219 D2
Chalice Ct N2 ... 48 C5
Chalkenden Cl SE20 ... 184 B3
Chalkers Cnr TW9 ... 132 D2
Chalk Farm Sta NW3 ... 71 A1
Chalkhill Prim Sch HA9 ... 66 D5
Chalkhill Rd HA9 ... 67 A5
Chalk Hill Rd W6 ... 112 D2
Chalk La EN4 ... 2 D1
Chalklands HA9 ... 67 A5
Chalkley Cl CR4 ... 181 A1
Chalkmill Dr EN1 ... 6 B2
Chalk Pit Ave BR5 ... 190 C1
Chalk Pit Way SM1 ... 218 A3
Chalk Rd E13 ... 99 C2
Chalkstone Cl DA16 ... 146 A4
Chalkwell Ho 10 E1 ... 96 D1
Chalkwell Park Ave EN1 .. 5 C1
Challenge Cl NW10 ... 89 C6
Challenge Ct TW2 ... 152 C4
Challenge Rd TW15 ... 149 B1
Challenger Ho 7 E14 .. 119 A6
Challice Way SW2 ... 160 B3
Challiner Ct HA1 ... 43 A4
Challin St 1 SE20 ... 184 C2
Challis Rd TW8 ... 109 D1
Challoner Cl N2 ... 30 B1
Challoner Cres W14 .. 254 C1
Challoner Ct BR2 ... 186 B1
Challoner Mans W14 .. 254 C1
Challoners Cl KT8 ... 196 B5
Challoner St W14 ... 113 B1 254 C1
Chalmers Ho
13 London SW11 ... 136 A2
Walthamstow E17 ... 53 D4
Chalmers Rd TW15 ... 170 D5
Chalmers Rd E TW15 ... 171 A5
Chalmers Way TW14 ... 150 B6
Chalmer's Wlk 14 SE17 ... 138 D6
Chalner Ho SW2 ... 160 C3
Chaloner Ct SE1 ... 252 C2
Chalsey Lodge SE4 ... 141 B1
Chalsey Rd SE4 ... 141 B1
Chalton Dr N2 ... 48 B3
Chalton St NW1 .. 93 D5 232 C3
Chamberlain Cl
Ilford IG1 ... 79 A5
Plumstead SE18 ... 123 B3
Chamberlain Cotts SE5 ... 139 B4
Chamberlain Cres BR4 ... 207 D1
Chamberlain Gdns TW3 ... 130 A4
Chamberlain Ho 6 E1 ... 118 C6
Chamberlain La HA5 ... 40 A5
Chamberlain Pl E17 ... 53 A6
Chamberlain Rd
Ealing W13 ... 109 A4
Finchley N2 ... 30 A1
Chamberlain St 7 NW1 ... 70 D1
Chamberlain Way
Pinner HA5 ... 40 B6
Surbiton KT6 ... 198 A2
Chamberlain Wlk 5 TW13 ... 173 A6
Chamberlayne Ave HA9 ... 66 A6
Chamberlayne Mans 3 NW10 ... 90 D4
Chamberlayne Rd NW10 ... 90 C6
Chambers Gdns N2 ... 30 B2
Chambers Ho 2 SW16 ... 181 C6
Chambers La NW10 ... 68 C1
Chambers Pl CR2 ... 221 B1
Chambers Rd N7 ... 72 A4
Chambers St SE16 ... 118 A4
Chamber St E1 ... 117 D6 253 D6
Chambers Walk HA7 ... 25 B5
Chambon Pl 7 W6 ... 112 A2
Chambord Ho 24 E2 ... 95 D4
Chambord St E2 ... 95 D4
Chamomile Ct E17 ... 53 C3
Champa Cl N17 ... 33 D1
Champion Cres SE26 ... 185 A6
Champion Gr SE5 ... 139 B2
Champion Hill SE5 ... 139 B2
Champion Pk SE5 ... 139 B3
Champion Rd SE26 ... 185 A6
Champlain Ho 26 W12 .. 112 B6
Champness Cl 9 SE27 ... 183 B6
Champness Rd IG11 ... 79 D1
Champneys Cl SM2 ... 217 B1
Champneys Ct N21 ... 16 A6
Chancel Ct W1 ... 249 C6
Chancellor Gr SE21 ... 161 A1
Chancellor Ho
South Kensington SW7 ... 256 B6
29 Wapping E1 ... 118 B5
Chancellor Pas E14 ... 119 C5
Chancellor Pl NW9 ... 27 D1
Chancellors' Ct WC1 .. 240 C4
Chancellors Loft N8 ... 50 A3
Chancellor's Rd W6 ... 112 C1
Chancellors St W6 ... 112 C1
Chancellors Wharf 21 W6 ... 112 C1
Chancelot Rd SE2 ... 124 B2
Chancel St SE1 ... 116 D5 251 C3
Chancery Bldgs 14 E1 .. 118 C6
Chancerygate Bsns Ctr HA4 ... 63 A3
Chancery Gate Bsns Ctr CR4 ... 202 D4
Chancery Ho WC2 ... 241 A3
Chancery La
Beckenham BR3 ... 185 D1
Holborn EC4 ... 94 C1 241 A2
Chancery Lane Sta WC1 ... 94 C2 241 A3
Chancery Mews SW17 .. 158 C2
Chance St E2 ... 243 C6
Chanctonbury Cl SE9 .. 166 D1
Chanctonbury Gdns SM2 ... 217 D1
Chanctonbury Way N12 ... 29 C6
Chanderia Ct 5 CR0 ... 221 A5
Chand Ho 7 N12 ... 30 A5
Chandler Ave E16 ... 99 A2
Chandler Cl TW12 ... 173 C2
Chandler Ct
Feltham TW14 ... 150 A5
Thornton Heath CR7 ... 204 D4
2 Tolworth KT5 ... 198 D1
8 Wallington SM6 ... 219 B2
Chandlers Cl TW14 ... 149 D4
Chandlers Field Prim Sch KT8 ... 195 C4
Chandlers Mews E14 ... 119 C4
Chandler St E1 ... 118 B5
Chandlers Way 11 SE24 ... 160 C4
Chandler Way SE15 ... 139 D5
Chandlery Ho 26 E1 ... 96 A1
Chandon Lo SM2 ... 218 A1
Chandos Ave
Ealing W5 ... 109 D2
New Southgate N14 ... 15 C1
Oakleigh Pk N20 ... 14 B3
Walthamstow E17 ... 35 C1
Chandos Bsns Ctr 11 SM6 ... 219 C2
Chandos Cl IG9 ... 21 B2
Chandos Cres HA8 ... 26 C3
Chandos Ct
Edgware HA8 ... 26 B3
Palmers Green N14 ... 15 D2
Stanmore HA7 ... 25 B4
Chandos Pl WC2 ... 116 A6 250 A5
Chandos Rd
Cricklewood NW2 ... 68 C3
Finchley N2 ... 30 C1
Harrow HA1 ... 42 A4
Old Oak Comm NW10 ... 89 C3
Pinner HA5 ... 40 D2
Stratford New Town E15 .. 76 B3
Tottenham N17 ... 33 C1
Chandos St W1 .. 93 B2 238 D3
Chandos Way NW11 ... 47 D1
Change Alley EC3 ... 242 D1
Channel Cl TW5 ... 129 C4
Channel Gate Rd NW10 .. 89 C4
Channel Ho E14 ... 97 A2
Channelsea Bsns Ctr E15 ... 98 B5
Channelsea Rd E15 ... 98 B6
Channing Sch N6 ... 49 B1
Channon Ct 3 KT6 ... 198 A4
Chantrey Rd SW9 ... 138 B2
Chantries The HA7 ... 25 A5
Chantry Cl
2 Abbey Wood SE2 ... 124 C3
Edgware NW7 ... 11 D4
Enfield EN2 ... 5 A5
Harrow HA3 ... 44 B4
Sidcup DA14 ... 191 A5
Sunbury TW16 ... 172 A3
West Kilburn W9 ... 91 B3
Chantry Cres NW10 ... 67 D2
Chantry Ct SM5 ... 218 C5
Chantry Ct SW6 ... 135 A2
Chantry La BR2 ... 209 D4
Chantry Pl HA3 ... 23 D2
Chantry Rd
Chessington KT9 ... 214 C3
Harrow HA3 ... 23 D2
Chantry Sch UB7 ... 104 A6
Chantry Sq W8 ... 113 D3 255 C5
Chantry St N1 ... 94 D6 234 D5
Chantry The
3 Chingford E4 ... 20 A3
Hillingdon UB8 ... 82 B4
Chantry Way CR4 ... 202 B6
Chant Sq E15 ... 76 B1
Chant St E15 ... 76 B1
Chapel Cl NW10 ... 67 D2
Chapel Ct
Borough The SE1 ... 252 C2
East Finchley N2 ... 48 C6
Hayes UB3 ... 105 D6
Chapel End Ho E17 ... 35 D2
Chapel End Inf Sch E17 ... 35 D2
Chapel End Jun Sch E17 ... 35 D2
Chapel Farm Rd SE9 ... 166 B2
Chapel Hill N2 ... 30 C1
Chapel House St E14 ... 119 D2
Chapel La
5 Dagenham RM6 ... 58 D2
Hillingdon UB8 ... 82 C1
Pinner HA5 ... 40 D6
Chapel Market N1 ... 94 C5 234 A4
Chapel Mill Rd KT1 ... 198 B6
Chapel Pl Islington N1 . 234 B4
Chapel Pl *continued*
Marylebone W1 ... 238 C1
12 Shoreditch EC2 ... 95 C4
Tottenham N17 ... 33 D3
Chapel Rd
Bexleyheath DA7 ... 147 C1
Ealing W13 ... 109 B5
Hounslow TW3 ... 129 D2
Ilford IG1 ... 78 D5
Twickenham TW1 ... 153 B4
West Norwood SE27 ... 182 D6
Chapel Side W2 ... 113 D6 245 C5
Chapel St Enfield EN2 ... 5 B2
Paddington NW1 92 C2 237 A3
Westminster SW1 ... 115 A4 248 B1
Chapel View CR2 ... 222 C1
Chapel Wlk NW4 ... 46 C5
Chapleton Ho SW2 ... 160 C6
Chaplin Cl Lambeth SE1 251 C2
Wembley HA0 ... 65 D2
Chaplin Cres TW16 ... 171 C4
Chaplin Ho
6 London SW9 ... 138 C1
Sidcup DA14 ... 190 A6
Chaplin Rd
Dagenham RM9 ... 81 A1
3 Tottenham N17 ... 51 D6
Wembley HA0 ... 65 D2
West Ham E15 ... 98 D6
Willesden NW2 ... 68 A2
Chaplow Cl SW6 ... 136 A3
Chapman Cl UB7 ... 104 B3
Chapman Cres HA3 ... 44 B4
Chapman Gn N22 ... 32 C2
Chapman Ho
28 Stepney E1 ... 96 B1
2 West Norwood SE27 ... 160 D1
Chapman Rd
Belvedere DA17 ... 125 D1
Hackney Wick E9 ... 75 B2
Thornton Heath CR0 ... 204 C1
Chapmans End BR5 ... 191 A1
Chapman's La BR5 ... 190 D1
Chapmans Park Ind Est NW10 ... 67 D2
Chapman Sq SW19 ... 156 D2
Chapman St E1 ... 118 B6
Chapone Pl W1 ... 239 C1
Chapter Cl
Hillingdon UB10 ... 60 B1
16 South Acton W4 ... 111 A3
Chapter House & Jewel Twr* SW1 ... 260 A6
Chapter Rd
Kennington SE17 ... 116 D1 261 D1
Willesden NW2 ... 68 A3
Chapter St SW1 ... 259 C3
Chapter Way
Hampton TW12 ... 173 C6
Mitcham SW19 ... 180 B2
Chara Pl W4 ... 133 B6
Charcot Ho SW15 ... 155 D5
Charcroft Ct 11 W14 ... 112 D4
Charcroft Gdns EN3 ... 6 D1
Chard Ho 7 N7 ... 72 B6
Chardin Ho 30 SW9 ... 138 C4
Chardin Rd 11 W4 ... 111 C2
Chardmore Rd N16 ... 52 A1
Chardwell Cl E6 ... 100 B1
Charecroft Way W12 ... 112 D4
Charfield Ct W9 ... 91 D3
Charford Rd E16 ... 99 A2
Chargeable La E13 ... 99 A3
Chargeable St E16 ... 98 D3
Chargrove Cl 24 SE16 ... 118 D4
Charing Cl BR6 ... 227 D4
Charing Cross SW1 ... 116 A5 250 A4
Charing Cross Hospl W6 ... 112 D1
Charing Cross Rd WC2 ... 93 D1 239 D1
Charing Cross Sta WC2 ... 116 A5 250 B4
Charing Ct BR2 ... 186 C1
Charing Ho SE1 ... 251 B2
Chariot Cl 8 E3 ... 97 C6
Charlbert Ct NW8 ... 230 A4
Charlbert St NW8 ... 92 C5 230 A4
Charlbury Ave HA7 ... 25 D5
Charlbury Gdns IG3 ... 79 D6
Charlbury Gr W5 ... 87 C1
Charlbury Ho 1 E12 ... 78 C5
Charlbury Rd UB10 ... 60 B5
Charldane Rd SE9 ... 166 D1
Charlecote Gr SE26 ... 162 B1
Charlecote Rd RM8 ... 81 A5
Charlemont Rd E6 ... 100 C4
Charles Allen Ho EC1 . 234 A2
Charles Auffray Ho 30 E1 ... 96 C2
Charles Babbage Cl KT9 ... 213 C1
Charles Barry Cl SW4 .. 137 C2
Charles Bradlaugh Ho 2 N17 ... 34 B3
Charles Burton Ct E5 ... 75 A4
Charles Cl DA14 ... 190 B6
Charles Cobb Gdns CR0 ... 220 C3
Charles Coveney Rd 4 SE15 ... 139 D4
Charles Cres HA1 ... 42 B2
Charles Ct 5 TW11 ... 174 C5
Charles Darwin Ho
8 Bethnal Green E2 ... 96 B4
Bromley BR1 ... 187 B3
Charles Dickens Ct SE25 ... 206 A5
Charles Dickens Ho 1 E2 ... 96 B4
Charles Dickens Prim Sch SE1 ... 117 A4 252 A1
Charles Edward Brooke Sch SW9 ... 138 D4
Charles Edward Brooke Sch (Dennen Site) SE5 ... 138 D4
Charlesfield SE12 ... 165 C1
Charles Flemwell Mews 7 E16 ... 121 A5
Charles Goddard Ho 3 HA0 ... 65 D3
Charles Gr N14 ... 15 C3
Charles Grinling Wlk SE18 ... 122 C2
Charles Haller St 25 SW2 ... 160 C4
Charles Harrod Ct SW13 ... 134 C6
Charles Ho
Southall UB2 ... 107 C4
1 Tottenham N17 ... 33 D3
Charles Hobson Ho 4 NW10 ... 67 C1
Charles Hocking Ho 8 W3 ... 111 A4
Charles II Pl SW3 ... 114 D1 257 C1
Charles II St SW1 ... 115 D5 249 C4
Charles La NW8 . 92 C5 230 A4
Charles Lamb Ct N1 .. 234 D4
Charles Lamb Prim Sch N1 ... 95 A6 235 A6
Charles Lesser KT9 ... 213 D3
Charles Mackenzie Ho 7 SE16 ... 118 A2
Charlesmere Gdns SE28 ... 123 C4
Charles Mills Ct SW16 .. 182 A4
Charles Pl NW1 ... 232 B1
Charles Rd
Dagenham RM6 ... 58 D3
Ealing W13 ... 87 A1
Merton SW19 ... 179 C2
Upton E7 ... 77 C1
Charles Rowan Ho WC1 ... 234 A1
Charles Sevright Dr NW7 ... 28 D5
Charles Sq N1 ... 95 B4 235 D1
Charles St
Barnes SW13 ... 133 C3
Croydon CR0 ... 221 A5
Enfield EN1 ... 17 D6
Hillingdon UB10 ... 82 D3
Hounslow TW3 ... 129 B3
Mayfair W1 ... 115 B5 248 C4
Newham E16 ... 121 C5
Charles Staunton Ho 3 SE27 ... 183 B6
Charleston Cl TW13 ... 150 A1
Charleston St SE17 ... 262 B3
Charles Townsend Ho EC1 ... 241 C6
Charles Utton Ct E8 ... 74 A4
Charles Whincup Rd 2 E16 ... 121 B5
Charlesworth Ho 6 E14 ... 97 C1
Charleville Cir SE26 ... 184 A5
Charleville Ct SW5 ... 254 C1
Charleville Mans W14. 254 B1
Charleville Mews TW7 ... 131 B1
Charleville Rd W14 ... 113 B1 254 C1
Charlie Browns Rdbt E18 ... 37 C1
Charlmont Rd SW17 ... 180 D4
Charlotte Cl DA6 ... 169 A6
Charlotte Ct
Crouch End N8 ... 49 D3
Esher KT10 ... 212 A3
10 Hammersmith W6 ... 112 A2
Ilford IG2 ... 56 C3
11 Wembley HA0 ... 66 A2
Charlotte Despard Ave SW11 ... 137 A4 268 B1
Charlotte Ho 12 W6 ... 112 C1
Charlotte Mews
Marylebone W1 ... 239 B4
North Kensington W10 ... 90 D1
West Kensington W14 .. 254 A4
Charlotte Par SE23 ... 163 A2
Charlotte Park Ave BR1 ... 210 A6
Charlotte Pl
Kenton NW9 ... 45 A4
Marylebone W1 ... 239 B3
Westminster SW1 ... 259 A3
Charlotte Rd
Barnes SW13 ... 133 D4
Dagenham RM10 ... 81 D2
Shoreditch EC2 .. 95 C3 243 A6
Wallington SM6 ... 219 C2
Charlotte Row SW4 ... 137 C2
Charlotte Sharman Prim Sch SE11 ... 116 D3 261 C5
Charlotte Sq 5 TW10 ... 154 B5

Charlotte St W1 . 93 C2 239 B4
Charlotte Terr
N1 ... 94 B6 233 D5
CHARLTON ... 143 D6
171 B1
Charlton Church La
SE7 ... 121 C1
Charlton Cl UB10 ... 60 D6
Charlton Cres IG11 ... 101 D5
Charlton Ct Finchley N3 .. 29 A1
25 Hackney E2 ... 95 D6
17 Kentish Town N7 ... 71 D3
Newham E6 ... 100 B4
Charlton Dene SE7 ... 143 D5
Charlton Gate Bsns Pk
SE7 ... 121 C2
Charlton Ho
5 Brentford TW8 ... 132 A6
Charlton TW17 ... 171 A1
Somers Town NW1 ... 232 C2
Charlton King's Rd
NW5 ... 71 D3
Charlton La
Greenwich SE7 ... 121 D1
Upper Halliford TW17 ... 193 B5
Upper Halliford TW17 ... 193 C5
Charlton Lo 1 NW11 ... 47 B3
Charlton Manor Prim Sch
SE7 ... 143 D5
Charlton Park La SE7 ... 144 A6
Charlton Park Rd SE7 ... 143 D6
Charlton Pl N1 .. 94 D5 234 C4
Charlton Rd
Charlton TW17 ... 171 A1
Edmonton N9 ... 18 D4
Greenwich SE3, SE7 ... 143 B6
Harlesden NW10 ... 89 C6
Harrow HA3 ... 43 D5
Wembley HA9 ... 44 B1
Charlton Sch SE7 ... 144 A6
Charlton Way SE10,
SE3 ... 142 C4
Charlwood Cl HA3 ... 24 C4
Charlwood Ho
Richmond TW9 ... 132 D5
1 Streatham SW2 ... 160 B3
Westminster SW1 ... 259 C3
Charlwood Pl
SW1 ... 115 C2 259 B3
Charlwood Rd SW15 ... 134 D1
Charlwood St
SW1 ... 115 C1 259 B2
Charlwood Terr 5
SW15 ... 134 D1
Charman Ho
18 London SW2 ... 160 C5
South Lambeth SW8 ... 270 A4
Charmian Ave HA7 ... 25 D1
Charmian Ho 19 N1 ... 95 C5
Charminster Ave
SW19 ... 179 D1
Charminster Ct 3
KT6 ... 197 D2
Charminster Rd
Mottingham SE12,
SE9 ... 187 D6
North Cheam KT4 ... 200 D1
Charmouth Ct TW10 ... 154 B6
Charmouth Ho SW8 ... 270 C4
Charmouth Rd DA16 ... 146 C4
Charnock Ho 22 W12 ... 112 B6
Charnock Rd E5 ... 74 B5
Charnwood Ave SW19 ... 179 D1
Charnwood Cl KT3 ... 199 C5
Charnwood Dr E18 ... 55 B5
Charnwood Gdns E14 ... 119 C2
Charnwood Ho 9 E5 ... 74 B6
Charnwood Pl N20 ... 14 A1
Charnwood Rd
Hillingdon UB10 ... 82 C5
South Norwood SE25 ... 205 B5
Charnwood St E5 ... 74 B6
Charolais Ho UB4 ... 83 B2
Charrington Ho 42 E1 ... 96 C3
Charrington Rd 2
CR0 ... 221 A6
Charrington St
NW1 ... 93 D5 232 C4
Charsley Rd SE6 ... 163 D2
Chart Cl Bromley BR2 ... 186 C2
Croydon CR0 ... 206 C3
Mitcham CR4 ... 202 D5
Charter Ave IG2 ... 57 B2
Charter Bldgs 14
SE10 ... 141 D4
Charter Cres TW4 ... 129 A1
Charter Ct
Finsbury Pk N4 ... 50 C1
Kingston u T KT3 ... 199 C6
Marylebone W1 ... 237 B3
Southall UB1 ... 107 C5
Wood Green N22 ... 31 D2
Charter Dr DA5 ... 169 A4
Charter Ho WC2 ... 240 B1
Charterhouse Ave HA0 .. 65 C3
Charterhouse Bldgs
EC1 ... 242 A5
Charterhouse Mews
EC1 ... 241 D4
Charterhouse Rd E8 ... 74 A3
Charterhouse Sq
EC1 ... 94 D2 241 D4
Charterhouse Square Sch
EC1 ... 94 D2 241 D4
Charterhouse St EC1 .. 241 C3
Charterhouse Works
SW18 ... 136 A1
Charteris Rd
Finsbury Pk N4 ... 50 C1
Kilburn NW6 ... 91 B6
Woodford IG8 ... 37 B4
Charter Nightingale Hospl
The NW1 ... 92 C2 237 B4
Charter Rd KT1 ... 198 D6
Charter Rd The IG8 ... 36 D4
Charter Sch The SE24 .. 161 B6
Charters Cl SE19 ... 183 C5
Charter Sq KT1 ... 176 D1
Charter Way
London NW3 ... 47 B5
Southgate N14 ... 15 D5
Chartes Ho SE1 ... 263 B6
Chartfield Ave SW15 ... 156 C6
Chartfield Sch SW15 ... 156 B6
Chartfield Sq SW15 ... 156 D6
Chartham Ct 12 SW9 ... 138 C2
Chartham Gr SE27 ... 160 D1
Chartham Ho SE1 ... 262 D6
Chartham Rd SE25 ... 206 B6
Chart Hills Cl SE28 ... 103 A1
Chart Ho 17 SW19 ... 180 D1
Chart House The 5
E14 ... 119 D1
Chartley Ave
Harrow HA7 ... 24 D4
Neasden NW2 ... 67 C5
Charton Cl 5 DA17 ... 147 B6
Chartres Ct UB6 ... 86 B5
Chartridge SE17 ... 139 B6
Chartridge Cl
Barnet EN5 ... 12 A6
Bushey WD23 ... 8 A5
Chartridge Ct 6 HA7 ... 25 C5
Chart St N1 ... 95 B4 235 D2
Chartwell 25 SW19 ... 156 D3
Chartwell Bsns Ctr
BR1 ... 209 D6
Chartwell Cl
2 Croydon CR0 ... 205 B1
Greenford UB6 ... 85 D6
Sidcup SE9 ... 167 B2
Chartwell Ct
10 Barnet EN5 ... 1 A1
Dollis Hill NW2 ... 68 A5
2 Woodford IG8 ... 37 A3
Chartwell Dr BR6 ... 227 B3
Chartwell Gdns SM3 ... 217 A4
Chartwell Lo 5 BR3 ... 185 C3
Chartwell Pl
Cheam SM3 ... 217 B4
Harrow HA2 ... 64 B6
Chartwell Way 3
SE20 ... 184 B2
Charville Ct 8 HA1 ... 42 D3
Charville La UB4 ... 83 C5
Charville La W UB10 ... 82 D4
Charville Prim Sch
UB4 ... 83 C5
Charwood SW16 ... 182 C6
Chase Bridge Prim Sch
TW2 ... 152 C5
Chase Court Gdns EN2 ... 5 A2
Chase Ct Chelsea SW3 . 257 C5
Isleworth TW7 ... 131 A3
Merton SW20 ... 179 A1
Southgate N14 ... 15 C5
Wembley HA0 ... 65 D2
Chase Ctr The NW10 ... 89 B4
Chase Farm Hospl EN2 ... 4 C5
Chasefield Rd SW17 ... 180 D6
Chase Gdns
Chingford E4 ... 35 C6
Twickenham TW2 ... 152 B4
Chase Gn EN2 ... 5 A2
Chase Green Ave EN2 ... 5 A3
Chase Hill EN2 ... 5 A2
Chase La IG6 ... 57 B4
Chase Lane Inf Sch E4 .. 35 B6
Chase Lane Jun Sch
E4 ... 35 B6
Chaseley Ct
Gunnersbury W4 ... 110 D1
Oatlands Pk KT13 ... 193 C1
Chaseley St E14 ... 97 A1
Chasemore Cl CR4 ... 202 D2
Chasemore Gdns CR0 ... 220 C3
Chasemore Ho SW6 ... 264 B4
Chase Rd
North Acton NW10 ... 89 B3
Southgate N14 ... 15 D5
Chase Ridings EN2 ... 4 C3
Chase Road Trad Est
NW10 ... 89 B3
Chase Side
East Barnet N14 ... 15 B4
Enfield EN2 ... 5 A3
Chase Side Ave
Enfield EN2 ... 5 A3
Merton SW20 ... 179 A1
Chase Side Cres EN2 ... 5 A4
Chase Side Pl EN2 ... 5 A3
Chase Side Prim Sch
EN2 ... 5 A3
Chase Side Works N14 .. 15 D4
Chase The
Bromley BR1 ... 209 B6
Clapham SW4 ... 137 B2
Dagenham RM6 ... 59 A3
Eastcote HA5 ... 40 C3
Edgware HA8 ... 26 D2
Erith DA7 ... 147 D2
Ickenham UB10 ... 60 C3
Loughton IG10 ... 21 D4
Manor Pk E12 ... 77 D4
Pinner HA5 ... 41 B5
South Norwood SW16 .. 182 C3
Stanmore HA7 ... 25 A4
Chase The *continued*
Sunbury TW16 ... 172 B2
Wallington CR0, SM6 ... 220 B3
Chaseville Par N21 ... 16 B6
Chaseville Park Rd N21 . 16 B6
Chase Way N14 ... 15 C3
Chasewood Ave EN2 ... 4 D3
Chasewood Ct 4 NW7 .. 27 B5
Chasewood Pk HA1 ... 64 C5
Chateau The 4 SM5 ... 218 D5
Chatelain Ho NW7 ... 28 C6
Chater Ho 6 E2 ... 96 D4
Chatfield Rd
London SW11 ... 136 A2
Thornton Heath CR0 ... 204 D1
Chatham Ave BR2 ... 209 A2
Chatham Cl
Cheam SM3 ... 201 B2
Hampstead Garden Suburb
NW11 ... 47 C4
Chatham Ct SW11 ... 158 D6
Chatham Ho
7 London SE5 ... 139 C3
6 Wallington SM6 ... 219 B3
21 Woolwich SE18 ... 122 B2
Chatham Pl E9 ... 74 C2
Chatham Rd
Clapham SW11 ... 158 D6
Kingston u T KT1, KT2 ... 176 C1
Walthamstow E17 ... 53 A6
1 Woodford E18 ... 36 D1
Chatham St
SE17 ... 117 B2 262 D4
Chatsfield Pl W5 ... 88 A1
Chatsworth Ave
Grove Pk BR1 ... 187 B6
Hendon NW4 ... 28 C1
Merton SW20 ... 179 A1
Sidcup DA15 ... 168 A3
Wembley HA9 ... 66 B3
Chatsworth Cl
Coney Hall BR2, BR4 ... 224 D6
Hendon NW4 ... 28 C1
Chatsworth Cres TW3,
TW7 ... 130 B2
Chatsworth Ct
Brondesbury NW2 ... 68 D2
Clapton Pk E5 ... 74 D4
Earl's Ct W8 ... 255 A4
5 Stanmore HA7 ... 25 C5
Thornton Heath SW16 ... 204 B6
Chatsworth Dr EN1 ... 18 A5
Chatsworth Est E5 ... 74 D4
Chatsworth Gdns
Acton W3 ... 110 D5
Harrow HA2 ... 41 D1
New Malden KT3 ... 199 D4
Chatsworth Ho
2 Bromley BR2 ... 209 A5
Kingston u T KT6 ... 197 D4
Chatsworth Inf Sch
Isleworth TW3 ... 130 A1
Sidcup DA15 ... 168 A3
Chatsworth Jun Sch
TW3 ... 130 A1
Chatsworth Lo
1 Chiswick W4 ... 111 B1
West Wickham BR4 ... 224 A6
Chatsworth Par BR5 ... 211 A4
Chatsworth Pl
Mitcham CR4 ... 202 D6
Teddington TW11 ... 175 A6
Chatsworth Rd
Brondesbury NW2 ... 68 D2
Cheam SM3 ... 217 A4
Chiswick W4 ... 133 A6
Clapton Pk E5 ... 74 D4
Ealing W5 ... 88 B3
Hayes UB4 ... 84 B3
South Croydon CR0 ... 221 B5
Stratford E15 ... 76 D3
Chatsworth Rise W5 ... 88 B3
Chatsworth Way SE27 .. 161 A1
Chattenden Ho 8 N4 ... 51 B2
Chatteris Ct NW4 ... 46 D6
CHATTERN HILL ... 170 D6
Chattern Hill TW15 ... 170 D6
Chattern Rd TW15 ... 171 A6
Chatterton Ct TW9 ... 132 B3
Chatterton Rd
Bromley Comm BR2 ... 209 D4
Highbury N4 ... 72 D5
Chatton Ct 5 NW9 ... 46 A5
Chatto Rd SW11 ... 158 D6
Chaucer Ave
Cranford TW4 ... 128 B3
Hayes UB4 ... 84 A2
Richmond TW9 ... 132 C3
Chaucer Cl N11 ... 31 D5
Chaucer Ct
14 New Barnet EN5 ... 13 D6
17 Stoke Newington N16 . 73 C4
Chaucer Dr
SE1 ... 117 D2 263 D3
Chaucer Gdns SM1 ... 217 C5
Chaucer Gn CR0 ... 206 C2
Chaucer Ho
Harrow HA2 ... 41 D4
Pimlico SW1 ... 259 A1
Sutton SM1 ... 217 C5
2 West Norwood
SE27 ... 183 A6
Chaucer Rd Acton W3 ... 111 A5
Ashford TW15 ... 170 B6
Bexley DA16 ... 145 D4
Chingford E17 ... 36 A1
Herne Hill SE24 ... 160 D6
Sidcup DA15 ... 168 C3
Sutton SM1 ... 217 C4
Upton E7 ... 77 A2
Chaucer Rd *continued*
Wanstead E11 ... 55 A3
Chaucer Way SW17 ... 180 B5
Chaulden Ho EC1 ... 235 D1
Chauncey Cl N9 ... 18 A1
Chaundrye Cl SE9 ... 166 B5
Chauntler Cl E16 ... 121 B6
Chaville Ct N11 ... 31 A6
Cheadle Ct NW8 ... 236 D6
Cheadle Ho 17 E14 ... 97 B1
CHEAM ... 217 B3
Cheam Common Inf Sch
KT4 ... 216 B6
Cheam Common Jun Sch
KT4 ... 216 B6
Cheam Common Rd
KT4 ... 216 C5
Cheam Court Flats 1
SM3 ... 217 A2
Cheam Fields Prim Sch
SM3 ... 217 A3
Cheam High Sch SM3 .. 217 A4
Cheam Mans SM3 ... 217 A1
Cheam Park Farm Inf Sch
SM3 ... 217 A5
Cheam Park Farm Jun Sch
SM3 ... 217 A5
Cheam Park Way SM3 .. 217 A2
Cheam Rd
Belmont SM2, SM3 ... 216 D1
Cheam SM1 ... 217 C2
Cheam St 6 SE15 ... 140 B2
Cheam Sta SM2 ... 217 A1
Cheam Village SM3 ... 217 A2
Cheapside
Barbican EC2 ... 95 A1 242 B1
Edmonton N13 ... 33 A6
Chearsley SE17 ... 262 B4
Cheddar Cl 1 N11 ... 31 A4
Cheddar Rd TW6 ... 126 C3
Cheddar Waye UB4 ... 84 B1
Cheddington Ho 9 E2 .. 96 A6
Cheddington Rd N18 ... 33 C6
Chedworth Cl E16 ... 98 D1
Chedworth Ho
London N15 ... 51 B5
2 Stoke Newington E5 .. 74 A6
Cheeseman Cl TW12 ... 173 A4
Cheeseman Ct UB1 ... 107 D6
Cheesemans Terr W14 254 C1
Cheffrey Ct TW15 ... 170 D4
Cheldon Ave NW7 ... 28 D3
Chelford Rd BR1 ... 186 B5
Chelmer Cres IG11 ... 102 B5
Chelmer Ct E18 ... 37 B2
Chelmer Rd E9 ... 74 D3
Chelmsford Cl
Fulham W6 ... 134 D6
Newham E6 ... 100 B1
Chelmsford Ct N14 ... 15 D4
Chelmsford Gdns IG1 ... 56 B2
Chelmsford Ho 5 N7 ... 72 B4
Chelmsford Rd
Leytonstone E11 ... 54 B1
London N14 ... 15 C4
Walthamstow E17 ... 53 C3
Woodford E18 ... 36 D2
Chelmsford Sq NW10 ... 90 C6
CHELSEA ... 114 C1
Chelsea Barracks*
SW1 ... 115 A1 258 B1
Chelsea Bridge
SW1 ... 137 B6 268 C6
Chelsea Bridge Rd
SW1 ... 115 A1 258 B1
Chelsea Cl Edgware HA8 .. 26 C1
Hampton TW12 ... 174 A5
New Malden KT4 ... 200 A2
Stonebridge NW10 ... 89 B6
Chelsea Cloisters SW3 257 B3
Chelsea Coll of Art &
Design
Chelsea SW3 .. 114 C1 257 A1
Pimlico SW1 .. 116 A1 260 A2
Chelsea Cres
Brondesbury NW2 ... 69 B2
Chelsea SW10 ... 266 B1
Chelsea Ct
Chelsea SW3 ... 268 A6
8 Chingford E4 ... 20 A3
Sutton SM2 ... 217 D2
Chelsea Emb
SW3 ... 136 D6 267 C5
Chelsea Est SW3 ... 267 A5
Chelsea Farm Ho
SW10 ... 266 D5
Chelsea Fields SW19 ... 180 B2
Chelsea Gate SW1 ... 258 B1
Chelsea Gdns
Cheam SM3 ... 217 A4
Chelsea SW1 ... 258 B1
Ealing W13 ... 86 D2
Chelsea Harbour Design
Ctr SW10 ... 266 B2
Chelsea Harbour Dr
SW10 ... 136 A4 266 B2
Chelsea Harbour Pier
SW10 ... 266 C1
Chelsea Lo SW3 ... 267 D6
Chelsea Manor Ct
SW3 ... 267 B6
Chelsea Manor Gdns
SW3 ... 257 B1
Chelsea Manor St
SW3 ... 114 C1 257 B1
Chelsea Manor Studios
SW3 ... 257 B1
Chelsea Park Gdns
SW3 ... 136 B6 266 C6
Chelsea Physic Gdn*
SW1 ... 267 C6
Chelsea Reach Twr
SW10 ... 266 C4
Chelsea Sq
SW3 ... 114 B1 256 D1
Chelsea Twrs SW3 ... 267 B6
Chelsea & Westminster
Hospl SW10 ... 136 A6 266 B5
Chelsfield Ave N9 ... 18 D4
Chelsfield Gdns SE26 .. 162 C1
Chelsfield Gn N9 ... 18 D4
Chelsfield Ho SE17 ... 263 A3
Chelsfield Point 3 E9 .. 74 D1
Chelsham Ho 1 SW4 .. 137 D2
Chelsham Rd
London SW4 ... 137 D2
South Croydon CR2 ... 221 B2
Chelsiter Ct DA14 ... 189 D6
Chelston App HA4 ... 62 A6
Chelston Ct 2 E11 ... 55 B4
Chelston Rd HA4 ... 40 A1
Chelsworth Dr SE18 ... 145 B6
Cheltenham Ave 10
TW1 ... 153 A4
Cheltenham Cl
Kingston u T KT3 ... 199 A6
Northolt UB5 ... 63 D2
Cheltenham Ct 8 HA7 .. 25 C5
Cheltenham Gdns E6 .. 100 A5
Cheltenham Ho UB3 ... 105 A3
Cheltenham Pl
10 Acton W3 ... 110 D5
Acton W3 ... 111 A4
Harrow HA3 ... 44 A5
1 South Acton W3 ... 110 D4
Cheltenham Rd
Leyton E10 ... 54 A3
London SE15 ... 162 C6
Cheltenham Terr
SW3 ... 114 D1 257 D2
Cheltenham Villas
CR7 ... 204 C3
Chelverton Ct SW15 ... 134 D1
Chelverton Rd SW15 ... 134 D1
Chelwood
Gospel Oak NW5 ... 71 A3
London N20 ... 14 B2
Chelwood Cl E4 ... 19 D5
Chelwood Ct
Battersea SW11 ... 266 D2
9 South Croydon CR2 .. 221 A3
Chelwood Gdns TW9 ... 132 C3
Chelwood Ho W2 ... 236 D1
Chelwood Lo N12 ... 30 A4
Chenappa Cl E13 ... 99 A4
Chenduit Way HA7 ... 24 D5
Chene Colline Ct KT6 .. 198 A3
Cheney Ct SE23 ... 162 D3
Cheney Row E17 ... 35 B2
Cheneys Rd E11 ... 76 C5
Cheney St HA5 ... 40 C4
Chenies Ho W2 ... 245 C6
Chenies Mews WC1 ... 239 C5
Chenies Pl NW1 ... 232 D4
Chenies St WC1 . 93 D2 239 C4
Chenies The
Orpington BR6 ... 211 C3
Somers Town NW1 ... 232 D4
Cheniston Gdns W8 ... 255 C6
Chennestone Prim Sch
TW16 ... 172 B1
Chepstow Cl SW15 ... 157 A6
Chepstow Cres
Ilford IG3 ... 57 C3
Notting Hill
W11 ... 113 C6 245 A6
Chepstow Ct W11 ... 245 A6
Chepstow Gdns UB1 ... 85 B1
Chepstow Pl
W2 ... 113 C6 245 B6
Chepstow Rd
Croydon CR0 ... 221 D6
Ealing W7 ... 109 A3
Paddington W2 ... 91 C1
Chepstow Rise CR0 ... 221 C5
Chepstow Villas
W11 ... 113 C6 245 A6
Chequers IG9 ... 21 B3
Chequers Cl
London NW9 ... 45 C6
Orpington BR5 ... 211 D5
Chequers Ct
7 Croydon CR0 ... 205 D1
St Luke's EC1 ... 242 C5
Chequers Ho NW8 ... 237 A6
Chequers La RM9 ... 103 C5
Chequers Par
Dagenham RM9 ... 103 C6
Edmonton N13 ... 33 A5
Chequer St EC1 .. 95 A3 242 B5
Chequers The HA5 ... 40 D6
Chequers Way N13 ... 32 D5
Cherbury Cl SE28 ... 102 D1
Cherbury Ct N1 ... 235 D3
Cherbury St N1 .. 95 B5 235 D3
Cherchefells Mews
HA7 ... 25 B5
Cherimoya Gdns KT8 ... 195 D6
Cherington Rd W7 ... 108 D5
Cheriton Ave BR2 ... 209 A4
Cheriton Cl
Cockfosters EN4 ... 2 D1
10 Ealing W5 ... 87 C2
Cheriton Ct
4 Lee SE12 ... 165 A4
South Norwood SE25 ... 205 C4
Walton-on-T KT12 ... 194 C1
Cheriton Dr SE18 ... 145 B6
Cheriton Ho 9 E5 ... 74 B3
Cheriton Sq SW17 ... 159 A2
Cherry Ave UB1 ... 106 D5
Cherry Blossom Cl N13 .. 32 D5
Cherry Cl
Carshalton SM5 ... 218 D6
Ealing W5 ... 109 D3
Merton SM4 ... 201 A5
Ruislip HA4 ... 61 D5
7 Streatham SW2 ... 160 C4
Walthamstow E17 ... 53 D4
Cherrycot Hill BR6 ... 227 B4
Cherrycot Rise BR6 ... 227 A4
Cherry Cres TW8 ... 131 B5
Cherry Croft Gdns 3
HA5 ... 23 B3
Cherry Ct Acton W3 ... 111 C5
Hackbridge CR4 ... 203 A1
Ilford IG6 ... 56 D6
Pinner HA5 ... 22 D2
5 Rotherhithe SE16 ... 119 A5
Sidcup DA14 ... 168 B1
Cherrydeal Ct E11 ... 54 B2
Cherrydown Ave E4 ... 19 C1
Cherrydown Cl E4 ... 19 C1
Cherrydown Rd DA14 .. 168 D2
Cherry Garden Ho 7
SE16 ... 118 B4
Cherry Garden Sch
SE16 ... 118 A2
Cherry Garden St
SE16 ... 118 B4
Cherry Garth TW8 ... 109 D1
Cherry Gdns
Dagenham RM9 ... 81 B3
Northolt UB5 ... 63 D1
Cherry Gr Hayes UB3 ... 106 B5
Hillingdon UB8 ... 83 A2
Cherry Hill
New Barnet EN5 ... 13 D5
Stanmore HA3 ... 24 C4
Cherry Hill Gdns CR0 .. 220 B4
Cherry Hills WD19 ... 23 A5
Cherry La UB7 ... 104 C2
Cherrylands Cl NW9 ... 67 A6
Cherry Lane Prim Sch
UB7 ... 104 B2
Cherry Laurel Wlk
SW2 ... 160 B5
Cherry Orch
Charlton SE7 ... 143 C6
West Drayton UB7 ... 104 A4
Cherry Orchard Gdns
7 Croydon CR0 ... 205 B1
East Molesey KT8 ... 195 B6
5 South Croydon CR0 ... 221 B6
Cherry Orchard Prim Sch
SE7 ... 143 C5
Cherry Orchard Rd
Croydon CR0 ... 205 C1
East Molesey KT8 ... 195 C6
Keston Mark BR2 ... 226 A6
Cherry Rd EN3 ... 6 C5
Cherry Tree Ave UB7 ... 82 B1
Cherry Tree Cl
11 Hackney E9 ... 96 C6
Wembley HA0 ... 65 A4
Cherry Tree Ct
1 Camden Town NW1 ... 71 C1
17 Charlton SE7 ... 143 C6
Kingsbury NW9 ... 45 A5
11 Peckham SE15 ... 140 B4
3 Woodford E18 ... 36 D1
Cherry Tree Dr SW16 ... 160 A1
Cherry Tree Hill N6 ... 48 D4
Cherrytree Ho 8 W10 ... 90 D4
Cherry Tree Ho
London SE14 ... 141 B3
Ruislip HA4 ... 39 C1
Twickenham TW2 ... 152 B2
Wood Green N22 ... 32 A3
Cherry Tree Rd
London N2 ... 48 D5
Stratford E15 ... 76 C3
Cherry Tree Rise IG9 ... 37 D6
Cherry Trees Sch The
E3 ... 97 C4
Cherry Tree Terr SE1 . 253 B2
Cherry Tree Way HA7 ... 25 B4
Cherry Tree Wlk
Beckenham BR3 ... 207 B5
Coney Hall BR4 ... 224 D4
St Luke's EC1 ... 242 B5
Cherry Way
Upper Halliford
TW17 ... 193 C5
West Ewell KT19 ... 215 B2
Cherry Wlk BR2 ... 209 A1
Cherrywood Cl Bow E3 .. 97 A4
Kingston u T KT2 ... 176 C3
Cherrywood Ct 1
TW11 ... 175 A5
Cherrywood Dr SW15 .. 156 D6
Cherrywood La SM4,
SW20 ... 201 A5
Cherry Wood Way W5 ... 88 C2
Chertsey Ct SW14 ... 132 D2
Chertsey Dr SM3 ... 217 A6
Chertsey Ho
Feltham TW13 ... 151 C1
37 Shoreditch E2 ... 95 D4
Chertsey Rd
Ashford TW15, TW16 ... 171 B4
Feltham TW13, TW16 ... 171 C6
Ilford IG1 ... 79 B4
Leyton E11 ... 76 B6
Lower Halliford TW17 ... 192 C2
Shepperton TW17 ... 192 A2
Twickenham TW2 ... 152 B4
Chertsey St SW17 ... 181 A5
Chervil Cl TW13 ... 150 A1

Chervil Mews SE28 124 B5
Cherwell Ct
Teddington KT1 175 D3
West Ewell KT19 215 A4
Cherwell Ho NW8 236 D5
Cherwell Way HA4 39 A3
Cheryls Cl
SW6 135 D4 265 D2
Cheseman St SE26 162 B1
Chesfield Rd KT2 176 A3
Chesham Ave BR2,
BR5 210 D3
Chesham Cl SW1 258 A5
Chesham Cres SE20 184 C2
Chesham Ct SW18 158 B4
Chesham Flats W1 248 B6
Chesham Ho SW1 258 A5
Chesham Mews SW1 258 A6
Chesham Pl
SW1 115 A3 258 A5
Chesham Rd
Kingston u T KT1,
KT2 176 C1
Mitcham SW19 180 B4
Penge SE20 184 C2
Chesham St
Westminster
SW1 115 A3 258 A5
Willesden NW10 67 B5
Chesham Terr W13 109 B4
Cheshire Cl
Chingford E17 35 D2
Mitcham CR4, SW16 204 A6
Cheshire Gdns KT9 213 D2
Cheshire Ho SM4 201 D2
Cheshire Rd N22 32 B4
Cheshire St E2 95 D3 243 D6
Cheshir Ho NW4 46 C5
Chesholm Rd N16 73 C5
Cheshunt Ho
Hendon NW4 46 C6
9 Kilburn NW6 91 D6
Cheshunt Rd
Belvedere DA17 125 C1
Upton E7 77 B2
Chesil Ct
17 Bethnal Green E2 96 C5
Chelsea SW3 267 B6
Chesil Ho BR7 189 B2
Chesilton Rd
SW6 135 B4 264 C2
Chesil Way UB4 83 D4
Chesley Gdns E6 100 A4
Chesney Cres CR0 224 A1
Chesney Ct W9 91 C3
Chesney Ho SE13 142 B1
Chesney St SW11 268 A1
Chesnut Gr N17 51 D6
Chesnut Rd N17 51 D6
Chessell Cl CR7 204 D5
Chessholme Ct TW16 171 C3
Chessholme Rd TW15 171 A4
Chessing Ct N2 48 D6
CHESSINGTON 214 A2
Chessington Ave
Church End N3 47 B6
Erith DA7 147 A5
Chessington Cl KT19 215 A2
Chessington Com Coll
KT9 213 D1
Chessington Ct
London N3 47 B6
Pinner HA5 41 B5
Chessington Hall Gdns
KT9 213 D1
Chessington Hill Pk
KT9 214 C3
Chessington Ho 19
SW8 137 D3
Chessington Lo N3 47 B6
Chessington Mans
Leyton E10 53 C2
Leytonstone E11 54 C2
Chessington North Sta
KT9 214 A3
Chessington Par KT9 213 D3
Chessington Pk KT9 214 C4
Chessington Rd KT19 215 B1
Chessington South Sta
KT9 213 D1
Chessington Trade Pk
KT9 214 C4
Chessington Way BR4 223 D6
Chesson Rd
W14 135 B6 264 D6
Chessum Ho E8 74 A2
Chesswood Way HA5 22 D1
Chestbrook Ct 12 EN1 17 C6
Chester Ave
Richmond TW10 154 B5
Twickenham TW2 151 B3
Chester Cl
Ashford TW15 171 B5
Barnes SW13 134 B2
Hayes UB8 82 D1
Knightsbridge SW1 248 C1
1 Richmond TW10 154 B5
Sutton SM1 217 C6
Chester Close N NW1 231 D2
Chester Close S NW1 231 D1
Chester Cres E8 73 D3
Chester Ct 2 Acton W3 88 C1
Bermondsey SE8 118 D1
4 Camberwell SE5 139 B5
Gospel Oak NW5 71 A4
Harrow HA1 42 D3
Regent's Pk NW1 231 D1
Chester Dr HA2 41 C3
Chesterfield Ct
Ashford TW15 170 A6
Chesterfield Ct *continued*
Kingston u T KT6 198 A4
Lewisham SE13 142 A2
Chesterfield Dr KT10 213 A6
Chesterfield Flats EN5 12 D6
Chesterfield Gdns
Greenwich SE10 142 B5
Harringay N4 50 D4
Mayfair W1 248 C4
Chesterfield Gr SE22 161 D6
Chesterfield Hill
W1 115 B5 248 C4
Chesterfield Ho
Highgate N6 49 A1
Mayfair W1 248 B4
6 Streatham SW16 181 C5
Chesterfield Lo N21 16 B4
Chesterfield Mews
Ashford TW15 170 A6
Harringay N4 50 D4
Chesterfield Rd
Ashford TW15 170 A5
Barnet EN5 12 D6
Chiswick W4 133 A6
Enfield EN3 7 A6
Finchley N3 29 C4
Leyton E10 54 A3
West Ewell KT19 215 B1
Chesterfield Sch EN3 7 A6
Chesterfield St W1 248 C4
Chesterfield Way
Hayes UB3 106 A4
Peckham SE15 140 C5
Chesterford Gdns NW3 69 D4
Chesterford Ho 4
SE18 143 D5
Chesterford Rd E12 78 B3
Chester Gate NW1 231 D1
Chester Gdns
Ealing W13 87 B1
Enfield EN3 18 B5
Morden SM4 202 A3
Chester Ho
5 Barnet EN5 1 D1
Dartmouth Pk N19 71 B6
1 Deptford SE8 141 B6
Kingston u T KT1 176 D1
Chesterman Ct W4 133 C5
Chester Mews
Belgravia SW1 258 C6
Walthamstow E17 35 C1
Chester Pl NW1 231 C2
Chester Rd
Avery Hill DA15 167 C6
Dartmouth Pk N19 71 B6
Edmonton N9 18 B3
Harlington TW6 126 C2
Hounslow TW4 128 B2
Ilford IG3 57 D2
Newham E16 98 C3
Regent's Pk
NW1 93 B4 231 C2
Tottenham N17 51 C6
Upton E7 77 D1
Walthamstow E17 52 D4
Wanstead E11 55 B3
Wimbledon SW19,
SW20 178 C4
Chester Row
SW1 115 A2 258 B4
Chester Sq
SW1 115 B2 258 C4
Chester Sq Mews SW1 258 C5
Chester St
Bethnal Green E2 96 A3
Westminster
SW1 115 A3 258 B6
Chesters The KT3 177 C2
Chester Terr
NW1 93 B4 231 C2
Chesterton Cl
Greenford UB6 85 D5
Wandsworth SW18 157 C6
Chesterton Ct W3 110 D3
Chesterton Dr TW19 148 B3
Chesterton Ho
21 Battersea SW11 136 B2
3 Kensal Town W10 91 A2
3 Sutton SM1 218 A4
Chesterton Prim Sch
SW11 137 A4 268 A1
Chesterton Rd
Kensal Town W10 91 A2
Newham E13 99 A4
Chesterton Sq W8 255 A3
Chesterton Terr
6 Kingston u T KT1 176 C1
Newham E13 99 A4
Chester Way
SE11 116 C2 261 B3
Chesthunte Rd N17 33 A2
Chestnut Alley SW6 264 D5
Chestnut Ave
Brentford TW8 109 D2
Buckhurst Hill IG9 21 D1
Coney Hall BR4 224 C4
Edgware HA8 26 B4
Forest Gate E7 77 B4
Hampton TW12 173 C3
Hornsey N8 50 A4
Kingston u T KT8, KT11 174 D2
11 Mortlake SW14 133 B2
Thames Ditton KT10 196 B1
Wembley HA0 65 B3
Worcester Pk KT19 215 C4
Yiewsley UB7 104 B6
Chestnut Ave N E17 54 B5
Chestnut Ave S E17 54 B4
Chestnut Cl
Buckhurst Hill IG9 21 D2
Chestnut Cl *continued*
Carshalton SM5 202 D1
Catford SE6 186 A6
Chattern Hill TW15 170 D6
Harlington UB7 126 D5
Hayes UB3 105 C6
New Cross Gate SE14 141 B4
Sidcup DA15 168 A2
Southgate N14 15 D6
1 Stoke Newington N16 73 B6
Sunbury Comm TW16 171 D4
West Norwood SW16 182 C6
Chestnut Ct
Beckenham BR3 185 C3
7 Cheam SM2 217 C2
5 Croydon CR0 221 A4
Feltham TW13 172 D5
Harrow HA1 42 C2
Hornsey N8 50 A4
Hounslow TW3 129 C2
Kingston u T KT3 199 C6
Surbiton KT6 198 A2
Wembley HA0 65 B3
West Brompton SW6 264 D6
Chestnut Dr
Bexley DA7 147 A2
Harrow HA3 24 D2
Pinner HA5 41 A3
Wanstead E11 55 A3
Chestnut Gr
Cockfosters EN4 14 D6
Ealing W5 109 D3
Isleworth TW7 131 A1
Kingston u T KT3 199 B6
Mitcham CR4 203 D5
Penge SE20 184 C3
South Croydon CR2 222 B1
Upper Tooting SW12 159 A3
Wembley HA0 65 B3
Chestnut Grove Sch
SW12 159 A3
Chestnut Ho
1 Acton W4 111 C2
Brockley SE4 141 B2
7 Maitland Pk NW3 70 D2
West Norwood SE27 161 A1
Chestnut La N20 13 A3
Chestnut Pl SE19 183 D6
Chestnut Rd
Ashford TW15 170 D6
Kingston u T KT2 176 A3
Twickenham TW2 152 C2
West Barnes SW20 178 D1
West Norwood SE21,
SE27 161 A1
Chestnut Rise SE18 123 C1
Chestnut Row N3 29 C3
Chestnuts Ct 3 E17 54 A6
Chestnuts Prim Sch
N15 51 A4
Chestnuts Royal BR7 189 B3
Chestnuts The
Chislehurst BR7 189 B3
Colindale NW9 45 C6
East Finchley N2 48 D4
7 Erith DA17 125 B1
1 Highbury N5 72 D4
Penge BR3 206 D6
8 Pinner HA5 23 B3
Shooters Hill SE18 144 D4
Uxbridge UB10 60 A1
Walton-on-T KT12 194 B1
Chestnut Way TW13 150 B1
Chestnut Wlk
Upper Halliford
TW17 193 C5
Woodford IG8 37 A5
Cheston Ave CR0 207 B1
Chestwood Gr UB10 60 B1
Chettle Cl SE1 262 C6
Chettle Ct N8 50 C3
Chetwode Ho NW8 237 A6
Chetwode Rd SW17 158 D1
Chetwood Wlk 13 E6 100 A2
Chetwynd Ave EN4 14 D3
Chetwynd Dr UB10 82 B5
Chetwynd Rd NW5 71 B5
Cheval Ct SW15 134 B1
Chevalier Cl HA7 26 A6
Cheval Pl SW7 114 C3 257 B6
Cheval St E14 119 C3
Chevender BR7 188 D3
Cheveney Wlk 2 BR2 209 A6
Chevening Ho BR5 190 A2
Chevening Rd
Cubitt Town SE10 120 D1
Kilburn NW6 91 A6
South Norwood SE19 183 B4
Chevenings The DA14 168 C1
Cheverell Ho 25 E2 96 A5
Cheverton Rd N19 49 D1
Chevet St E9 75 A3
Chevington NW2 69 B2
Cheviot 4 N17 34 B3
Cheviot Cl Bushey WD23 8 A5
Enfield EN1 5 B3
Harlington UB3 127 B5
Cheviot Ct
16 Deptford SE14 140 C5
Enfield EN2 5 B3
Southall UB2 107 D2
Cheviot Gate NW2 69 A6
Cheviot Gdns
Cricklewood NW2 69 A6
West Norwood SE27 182 D6
Cheviot Ho N16 51 D1
Cheviot Rd SE27 182 D5
Cheviots Hostel EN1 5 B3
Cheviot Way IG2 57 C5
Chevron Cl E16 99 A1
Chevy Rd UB2 108 A4
Chewton Rd E17 53 A5
Cheylesmore Ho SW1 258 C2
Cheyne Ave
Snaresbrook E18 54 D6
Twickenham TW2 151 B3
Cheyne Cl
6 Hendon NW4 46 B4
Keston Mark BR2 226 A5
Cheyne Ct Chelsea SW3 267 C6
1 Croydon CR0 221 D6
Ruislip HA4 39 C1
4 Wallington SM6 219 B2
Cheyne Gdns
SW3 136 C6 267 B5
Cheyne Hill KT5 198 B5
Cheyne Mews
SW3 136 C6 267 B5
Cheyne Park Dr BR4 224 A5
Cheyne Path W7 86 D1
Cheyne Pl SW3 267 C6
Cheyne Rd TW15 171 B4
Cheyne Row
SW3 136 C6 267 A5
Cheyne Wlk
Chelsea
SW10 136 B5 266 C4
Croydon CR0 222 A6
Hendon NW4 46 C3
Southgate N21 16 D6
Cheyney Ho 2 E9 74 D2
Cheyneys Ave HA8 25 D4
Chichele Gdns CR0 221 C4
Chichele Ho HA8 26 B6
Chichele Mans NW2 68 D3
Chichele Rd NW2 68 D3
Chicheley Gdns HA3 24 A3
Chicheley Rd HA3 24 A3
Chicheley St SE1 250 D2
Chichester Ave HA4 61 B6
Chichester Cl
Hampton TW12 173 B4
Kidbrooke SE3 143 C4
Newham E6 100 A1
Chichester Ct Barnet EN4 2 B1
2 Camden Town NW1 71 C1
Edgware HA8 26 C4
Harrow HA2 41 B1
Northolt UB5 85 A6
3 Sidcup DA5 169 C4
Stanmore HA7 44 A6
Stanwell TW19 148 A3
Chichester Gdns IG1 56 B2
Chichester Ho
Kilburn NW6 91 C5
2 Kingston u T KT2 176 D2
Chichester Mews
SE27 182 C6
Chichester Rd
Bayswater W2 91 D2
Edmonton N9 18 A3
Kilburn NW6 91 C5
Leyton E11 76 C5
South Croydon CR0 221 C5
Chichester Rents WC2 241 A2
Chichester St
SW1 115 C1 259 B1
Chichester Way
Cubitt Town E14 120 B2
Feltham TW14 150 C4
Chicksand Ho 14 E1 96 A2
Chicksand St
E1 95 D2 243 D3
Chicksand Street E1 96 A2
Chiddingfold N12 13 C1
Chiddingstone SE13 164 A6
Chiddingstone Ave
DA7 147 B5
Chiddingstone St
SW6 135 C3
Chieveley Par DA7 147 D2
Chieveley Rd DA7 147 D1
Chignell Pl 7 W13 109 A5
Chigwell Ct 1 E9 75 A2
Chigwell Hill E1 118 B6
Chigwell Hurst Ct HA5 40 D6
Chigwell Rd
Wanstead E18 55 B6
Woodford IG8 37 D3
Chiham Ho 5 SE15 140 C6
Chilchester Ct 3 BR3 207 D6
Chilcombe Ho 6
SW15 156 A4
Chilcot Cl 13 E14 97 D1
Chilcott Cl HA0 65 C4
Child Ct E11 54 B2
Childebert Rd SW17 159 B2
Childeric Prim Sch
SE14 141 A5
Childeric Rd SE14 141 A5
Childerley St
SW6 135 A4 264 A2
Childerly KT1 198 C6
Childers St SE8 141 B6
Chlld La SE10 120 D3
Childs Ct UB3 106 A6
CHILD'S HILL 69 C6
Child's Hill Prim Sch
NW2 69 A5
Childs La 11 SE19 183 C4
Child's Mews SW5 255 B3
Child's Pl SW5 255 B3
Child's St SW5 255 B3
Childs Way NW11 47 B4
Child's Wlk SW5 255 B3
Chilham Cl
Old Bexley DA5 169 B4
Wembley UB6 87 A5
Chilham Ct 13 SW9 138 C2
Chilham Ho SE1 262 D6
Chilham Rd SE9 188 A6
Chilham Way BR2 209 A2
Chillerton Rd SW17 181 B5
Chillingford Ho SW17 180 A6
Chillington Dr SW11 136 B1
Chillingworth Gdns
TW1 152 D1
Chillingworth Rd N7 72 C3
Chilmark Gdns KT3 200 A3
Chilmark Rd SW16 181 D2
Chiltern Ave
Bushey WD23 8 A5
Twickenham TW2 151 C3
Chiltern Cl Bus WD23 8 A5
Ickenham UB10 60 C6
North Cheam KT4 216 C6
South Croydon CR0 221 C5
Chiltern Ct
15 Deptford SE14 140 C5
6 East Barnet N20 14 C2
11 Eltham SE9 166 C5
Harrow HA1 42 B4
Hillingdon UB8 82 D3
Marylebone NW1 237 D5
Muswell Hill N10 31 A1
1 New Barnet EN5 14 A6
Chiltern Dene EN2 4 B1
Chiltern Dr KT5 198 D4
Chiltern Gdns
Beckenham BR2 208 D5
Cricklewood NW2 68 D5
Chiltern Ho
Camberwell SE17 139 B6
Ealing W5 88 A2
5 Edmonton N9 18 A1
Harrow HA1 42 C1
4 Kensal Town W10 91 A2
5 Stamford Hill N16 51 D1
Chiltern Rd Bow E3 97 C3
Ilford IG2 57 C4
Pinner HA5 40 C4
Chiltern St W1 93 A2 238 A4
Chilterns The BR1 187 B1
Chiltern Way IG8 21 A1
Chilthorne Cl SE6 163 B4
Chilton Ave W5 109 D2
Chilton Gr SE8 119 A2
Chiltonian Ind Est
SE12 164 D5
Chilton Rd Edgware HA8 26 C4
Richmond TW9 132 C2
Chilton St E2 95 D3 243 D6
Chiltons The 1 E18 37 A1
Chilvers Cl TW2 152 C2
Chilver St SE10 120 D1
Chilwell Gdns WD19 22 C6
Chilworth Ct 8 SW19 156 D3
Chilworth Gdns SM1 218 A5
Chilworth Mews
W2 92 B1 236 C1
Chilworth St
W2 92 A1 236 B1
Chimes Ave N13 32 D6
Chimney Ct 23 E1 118 B5
Chimneys Ct 2 SW19 178 C3
China Ct 1 E1 118 B5
China Hall Mews 16
SE16 118 C3
China Mews 17 SW2 160 B4
Chinbrook Cres SE12 165 B1
Chinbrook Rd SE12 165 B1
Chinchilla Dr TW4 128 C3
Chindit Ho 11 N16 73 B4
Chine The London N10 49 C5
Southgate N21 16 D6
Wembley HA0 65 B3
Ching Ct Chingford E4 20 C1
St Giles WC2 240 A1
Chingdale Rd E4 20 C1
CHINGFORD 20 C3
Chingford Ave E4 19 D2
Chingford CE Inf Sch
E4 20 B3
Chingford CE Jun Sch
E4 20 B3
Chingford Foundation Sch
E4 19 D3
CHINGFORD GREEN 20 A4
Chingford Hall Com Prim
Sch E4 35 B4
CHINGFORD HATCH 36 B6
Chingford Hospl E4 20 A1
Chingford Ind Ctr E4 35 A5
Chingford La IG8 36 D5
Chingford Mount Rd
E4 35 C5
Chingford Rd
Highams Pk E4 35 C3
Walthamstow E17 35 D1
Chingford Sta E4 20 C4
Chingley Cl BR1 186 C4
Ching Way E4 35 B4
Chinnery Cl EN1 5 D4
Chinnocks Wharf E14 119 A6
Chinnor Cres UB6 86 A5
Chipka St E14 120 A4
Chipley St SE14 141 A6
Chipmunk Gr UB5 85 A4
Chippendale Ho SW1 258 D1
Chippendale St E5 74 D5
Chippenham 4 KT1 176 B1
Chippenham Ave HA9 66 D3
Chippenham Cl HA5 39 D5
Chippenham Gdns
NW6 91 C4
Chippenham Mews W9 91 C3
Chippenham Rd W9 91 C3
Chipperfield Rd BR5 190 A1
CHIPPING BARNET 1 B1
Chipping Cl EN5 1 A2
Chip St SW4 137 D1
Chipstead Ave CR7 204 D5
Chipstead Cl SE19 183 D3
Chipstead Gdns NW2 68 B6
Chipstead Ho 4 SW2 160 A3
Chipstead St SW6 135 C3
Chirk Cl UB4 85 A3
Chirk Ct SE4 141 B3
Chisenhale Prim Sch
E3 97 A5
Chisenhale Rd E3 97 A5
Chisholm Ct 1 W6 112 A1
Chisholm Rd
Croydon CR0 221 C6
13 Richmond TW10 154 B5
Chisledon Wlk E9 75 B2
CHISLEHURST 189 C3
Chislehurst Ave N12 30 A3
Chislehurst High St
BR7 188 D4
Chislehurst Rd
Bromley BR1, BR7 188 A2
Broom Hill BR6 211 D2
Orpington BR5, BR6,
BR7 211 C4
Richmond TW10 154 A6
Sidcup DA14 190 A5
Chislehurst St Nicholas CE
Prim Sch BR7 189 A3
Chislehurst & Sidcup
Gram Sch DA15 168 B2
Chislehurst Sta BR7 188 C1
CHISLEHURST WEST 188 C4
Chislet 5 NW5 71 A2
Chislet Cl BR3 185 C3
Chisley Rd 5 N15 51 C3
Chiswell Sq SE3 143 B3
Chiswell St
Barbican EC1 95 B2 242 C4
Camberwell SE5 139 B5
CHISWICK 111 D1
Chiswick & Bedford Park
Prep Sch W4 111 C2
Chiswick Cl CR0 220 B5
Chiswick Common Rd
W4 111 B2
Chiswick Com Sch
W4 133 B5
Chiswick Ct HA5 41 B6
Chiswick Green Studios 1
W4 111 A2
Chiswick High Rd W4 111 C2
Chiswick High Road
(North Circular Rd)
W4 110 C1
Chiswick Ho* W4 133 B6
Chiswick La W4 111 C1
Chiswick La S W4 133 D6
Chiswick Mall W4 111 D1
Chiswick Maternity Hospl
W4 111 D1
Chiswick Park Sta
W4 111 A2
Chiswick Pier W4 133 D5
Chiswick Pk W4 110 D2
Chiswick Plaza W4 133 A6
Chiswick Quay W4 133 A4
Chiswick Rd Acton W4 111 A2
Edmonton N9 18 A2
Chiswick Rdbt W4 110 C1
Chiswick Sq W4 133 C6
Chiswick Sta W4 133 A5
Chiswick Staithe W4 133 A4
Chiswick Terr 6 W4 111 A2
Chiswick Village W4 132 D6
Chiswick Wharf W4 133 D6
Chitterfield Gate UB7 126 C5
Chitty's La RM8 80 D6
Chitty St W1 93 C2 239 B4
Chivalry Rd SW11 158 C6
Chivelston 27 SW19 156 D3
Chivenor Gr KT2 175 D5
Chivers Rd E4 35 D6
Chivins Ct N3 29 C3
Choats Manor Way
RM9 103 B4
Choats Rd IG11 102 D4
Chobham Gdns SW19 156 D2
Chobham Rd E15 76 B3
Cholmeley Cres N6 49 B2
Cholmeley Ct N12 30 A6
Cholmeley Lo N6 49 B1
Cholmeley Pk N6 49 B2
Cholmley Gdns NW6 69 C3
Cholmley Rd KT7 197 B3
Cholmondeley Ave
NW10 90 A5
Cholmondeley Wlk
TW9 153 C6
Chopin's Ct 8 E1 118 B5
Chopwell Cl E15 76 B1
Chorleywood Cres
BR5 190 A1
Choumert Gr SE15 140 A3
Choumert Mews SE15 140 A3
Choumert Rd SE15 139 D3
Choumert Sq 4 SE15 140 A3
Chow Sq 2 E8 73 D3
Chrisp Ho SE10 142 C6
Chrisp St E14 97 D1
Christabel Cl TW7 130 C2
Christ Church TW9 132 A2
Christchurch Ave
Brondesbury Pk NW6 69 A1
Finchley N12 30 A4
Harrow HA3 42 D5
Harrow HA3 43 A5

Christchurch Ave *continued*
5 Teddington TW11....175 A5
Wembley HA0..........66 A2
Christ Church Bentinck CE Prim Sch NW1 . 92 C2 237 B4
Christ Church CE Mid Sch W5..................109 D6
Christchurch CE Prim Sch SW3......... 136 D6 267 C6
Christ Church CE Prim Sch
Battersea SW11.......136 C2
Brondesbury NW6.......69 B1
Camberwell SW9.......138 C4
Cubitt Town SE10......120 C1
Forest Hill SE23.......162 D2
Shooters Hill SE18.....144 C4
Surbiton KT5..........198 C3
Christchurch CE Sch E1.............95 D2 243 D3
Christchurch Cl
Enfield EN2.............5 A3
Finchley N12...........30 B3
Mitcham SW19........180 B3
Christchurch Ct UB4....84 C3
Christ Church Ct
1 Brondesbury Pk NW6...............69 A1
Harlesden NW10........89 C6
Christchurch Gdns HA3.................43 A5
Christchurch Gn HA0...66 A2
Christchurch Hill NW3..70 B4
Christchurch Ho 2 SW2................160 A3
Christ Church La EN5....1 A3
Christchurch Lo EN4.....2 D1
Christ Church New Malden CE Prim Sch KT3.....199 C6
Christchurch Pas NW3..70 A5
Christchurch Pk SM2..218 A1
Christchurch Prim Sch IG1..................57 A1
Christ Church Prim Sch, Hampstead NW3......70 B5
Christchurch Rd
Ilford IG1.............57 A1
Mitcham SW19........180 B3
Mortlake SW14........155 A6
Sidcup DA15..........167 D1
Streatham SW2........160 C3
Christ Church Rd
1 Beckenham BR3.....185 C1
Hornsey N8............50 A3
Surbiton KT5..........198 B3
Christ Church Sch NW1...........93 B4 231 D2
Christchurch Sq 2 E9..96 C6
Christchurch St SW3..........136 D6 267 C6
Christ Church Streatham CE Prim Sch SW2....160 B3
Christchurch Terr SW3.................267 C6
Christchurch Way SE10................120 C1
Christian Ct SE16......119 B5
Christian Fields SW16..182 C3
Christian St E1.........96 A1
Christie Ct
Maitland Pk NW3.......70 C3
2 Upper Holloway N19..72 A6
Christie Dr SE25.......206 A4
Christie Gdns RM6......58 B2
Christie Ho Bexley DA6..169 D6
2 Cubitt Town SE10....120 D1
Harrow HA3............42 D6
4 West Wickham BR4..207 D1
Christie Rd E9..........75 A2
Christina Sq N4........50 D1
Christina St EC2......243 A6
Christine Worsley Cl N21..................16 D3
Christopher Ave W7...109 A3
Christopher Boone's Almshouses SE13....142 B1
Christopher Cl
Bexley DA15..........167 D6
Rotherhithe SE16......118 D4
Christopher Ct
Ashford TW15.........170 A5
12 Barnet EN5...........1 D1
6 Croydon CR0.......206 A1
Hendon NW4...........28 C1
23 Surbiton KT6........198 A4
Sutton SM1...........217 C3
Christopher France Ho 6 E1..................97 A4
Christopher Gdns RM9..80 D3
Christopher Hatton Prim Sch EC1........94 C3 241 A5
Christopher Lo 2 N6...49 D2
Christopher Pl NW1...232 D1
Christopher Rd UB2....106 B2
Christopher St EC2...........95 B3 242 D5
Christ's Coll Finchley NW11..................47 D6
Christ's Coll Upper Sch N3....................29 B1
Christ's Sch TW10.....154 C6
Christ the King RC Fst Sch TW19..................148 A5
Christ the King RC Prim Sch N4..............72 B6
Christ the King Sixth Form Coll SE13............142 B2
Chryssell Rd SW9......138 C5
Chubworthy St 5 SE14................141 A6
Chudleigh 1 DA14.....190 B6
Chudleigh Cres IG3.....79 C4
Chudleigh Gdns SM1...218 A5
Chudleigh Rd
Hampstead NW6........68 D1
London SE4...........163 C6
Twickenham TW1, TW2..152 D4
Chudleigh St E1........96 D1
Chudleigh Way HA4.....40 A1
Chulsa Rd SE26........184 B5
Chumleigh Gdns SE5...139 C6
Chumleigh St SE5......139 C6
Chumleigh Wlk KT5....198 B5
Church App SE21.......161 B1
Church Ave
Beckenham BR3.......185 C2
Camden Town NW1......71 B2
Chingford E4...........36 B4
Finchley N2............30 B2
Mortlake SW14........133 B2
Northolt UB5...........63 B1
Pinner HA5.............41 B3
Ruislip HA4............39 B1
Sidcup DA14..........190 B5
Southall UB2..........107 A3
Churchbank E17........53 C5
Churchbury Cl EN1......5 C3
Churchbury La EN1......5 C3
Churchbury Rd
Eltham SE9...........165 D4
Enfield EN1.............5 C3
Church Cl Edgware HA8..27 A5
Friern Barnet N20.......14 C1
Hayes UB4.............83 B2
Hounslow TW4........129 B3
Kensington W8.......245 C2
West Drayton UB7.....104 A3
Church Cres
Church End N3.........29 B2
Cranley Gdns N10.......49 B5
Friern Barnet N20.......14 C1
Hackney E9............74 D1
Churchcroft Cl SW12...159 A4
Church Ct
East Finchley N2........48 B6
Forest Hill SE26.......185 A5
Harmondsworth UB7....126 C6
Holborn EC4..........241 B1
16 Richmond TW10.....153 D6
Rotherhithe SE16......119 B4
Ruislip HA4............62 D5
5 West Norwood SE27................182 D6
Churchdale Ct 1 W4..110 D1
Churchdown BR1......186 C6
Church Dr
Coney Hall BR4........224 C5
Harrow HA2............41 C3
Welsh Harp NW9........45 B1
Church Elm La RM10....81 C2
Church End NW4.......46 B6
CHURCH END N3.......29 C1
NW10..................67 D3
Church End E17........53 D5
Church Entry EC4.....241 D1
Church Estate Almshouses
8 TW9...............132 B1
Church Farm House Mus★ NW4..................46 B6
Church Farm La SM3...217 A2
Churchfield Ave N12....30 B4
Churchfield Cl
Harrow HA2............42 A5
Hayes UB3............105 D6
Churchfield Ho W2....236 C5
Churchfield Mans 5 SW6..................135 B3
Churchfield Pl TW17...192 D2
Churchfield Prim Sch N9....................17 D3
Churchfield Rd
Acton W3.............111 A5
Ealing W13...........109 C5
Hanwell W7...........108 C4
Walton-on-T KT12......194 A1
Welling DA16..........146 A2
Churchfields
East Molesey KT8......195 C6
Greenwich SE10.......142 A6
Woodford E18..........37 A2
Churchfields Ave TW13.................151 C1
Churchfields Jun & Inf Sch E18...................37 A2
Churchfields Prim Sch BR3..................206 D6
Churchfields Rd BR3...185 A1
Churchfield Way N12....30 A4
Church Garth 4 N19....71 D6
Church Gate SW6......135 A2
Church Gdns
Ealing W5............109 D4
Wembley HA0..........65 A4
Church Gn
4 Brixton SW9........138 C3
Hayes UB3.............83 D1
Church Gr
London SE13..........163 D6
Teddington KT1........175 C1
Church Hill Harrow HA1..42 C1
Southgate N21..........16 C4
Wallington SM5........218 D3
Walthamstow E17.......53 D5
Wimbledon SW19......179 B5
Woolwich SE18........122 B3
Churchhill Gardens Prim Sch SW1......115 C1 259 B1
Church Hill Rd
Cheam SM1, SM3......217 A4
East Barnet EN4........14 D4
Kingston u T KT6......198 A4
Walthamstow E17.......53 D5
Church Hill Sch EN4....14 D4
Church Hill Wood BR5.................211 D4
Church Ho EC1........241 D6
Church Hyde SE18.....145 C6
Churchill Ave
Harrow HA3............43 B3
Hillingdon UB10........82 D4
Churchill Cl
East Bedfont TW14.....149 D3
Hillingdon UB10........82 D4
Churchill Ct Ealing W5...88 B3
Edmonton N9...........17 B3
4 Farnborough BR6....227 A3
Finsbury Pk N4.........50 C2
Harrow HA2............41 D4
7 Ilford IG1............78 D5
Northolt UB5...........63 C3
Peckham SE15.........140 A3
Willesden NW2.........68 B3
9 Woolwich SE18.....122 B2
Churchill Gdns
Acton W3..............88 C1
Pimlico SW1..137 C6 269 A6
Churchill Gdns Rd SW1...........137 C6 269 A6
Churchill Ho
Brentford TW8........109 C1
Mitcham CR4..........180 D2
Churchill Lo
Streatham SW16.......181 D5
Woodford IG8...........36 D4
Churchill Lodge IG6....57 A5
Churchill Mews IG8.....36 D4
Churchill Pl
Canary Wharf E14......119 D5
Harrow HA1............42 C5
Churchill Rd
Edgware HA8...........26 C4
Gospel Oak NW5........71 B4
Newham E16............99 C1
South Croydon CR2.....221 A1
Willesden NW2.........68 B2
Churchill Terr E4.......19 C1
Churchill Way
Ashford TW16.........172 A4
Bromley BR1..........187 A1
Churchill Wlk E9........74 C3
Church La
Chessington KT9.......214 B2
Chislehurst BR7.......189 A2
Dagenham RM10........81 D1
Ealing W5............109 D4
East Finchley N2........48 B6
Edmonton N9...........18 A2
Enfield EN1..............5 B2
Harrow HA3............24 D2
Hornsey N8............50 B5
Keston Mark BR2......210 A1
Kingsbury NW9.........45 B2
Leytonstone E11........54 C1
Merton SW19..........179 C2
Pinner HA5.............41 B6
Teddington TW11......174 D5
Thames Ditton KT7.....197 A3
Tottenham N17.........33 C2
Twickenham TW1.......153 A3
Upper Tooting SW17....181 A5
Wallington SM6........219 D5
Walthamstow E17.......53 D5
Churchley Rd SE26.....184 B6
Churchley Villas SE26..184 B6
Church Lo UB5.........63 B1
Church Manor Way SE18, SE2..................124 A2
Church Mdw KT6......213 C6
Church Mead SE5......139 A5
Churchmead Cl EN4....14 C5
Church Mead Inf Sch E10....................53 C1
Churchmead Rd NW10..68 A2
Churchmore Rd SW16..181 D2
Church Mount N2.......48 B4
Church Paddock Ct SM6.................219 D5
Church Par
5 Ashford TW15......170 B6
Harrow HA3............42 C6
Church Path
Merton SW19..........179 C1
Mitcham CR4..........202 C6
South Acton W4........111 A3
Walthamstow E17.......53 D5
Wanstead E11..........55 A4
Church Pl Ealing W5....109 D4
Mitcham CR4..........202 C6
St James SW1..........249 B5
Uxbridge UB10..........61 A5
Church Rd Acton W3....111 A4
Ashford TW15..........170 B6
Barking IG11...........79 A2
Barnes SW13..........134 A4
Beckenham BR2........208 C6
Bexleyheath DA7.......147 B2
Bromley BR1, BR2.....187 A1
Buckhurst Hill IG9.......21 B3
24 Canonbury N1.......73 A2
Cheam SM3............217 A2
Claygate KT10.........212 D1
Cranford TW5..........128 B6
Croydon CR0..........221 A5
Ealing W7.............108 C6
East Molesey KT8......196 B6
Enfield EN3............18 C6
Farnborough BR6......227 B3
Church Rd *continued*
Feltham TW13.........172 D5
Hayes UB3............105 D6
Hendon NW4............46 C5
Heston TW5...........129 C5
Higham Hill E17.........35 A1
Highgate N6............49 A3
Hillingdon UB8.........82 A3
Hounslow TW7.........130 C5
Ilford IG2..............57 C3
Keston BR2...........225 D1
Kingston u T KT1.......176 B1
Leyton E10.............75 C6
Long Ditton KT6.......197 C1
Lower Halliford TW17...192 D2
Manor Pk E12...........78 A3
Mitcham CR4..........202 C6
Mitcham CR4, SW19....180 B1
New Malden KT4.......199 C1
Northolt UB5...........85 A6
Richmond TW10........176 A6
Richmond TW10, TW9...154 A6
Sidcup DA14..........190 A6
Southall UB2..........107 B3
South Norwood SE19...183 C3
Stanmore HA7..........25 B5
Teddington TW11......174 D5
Tottenham N17.........33 D3
Wallington SM6........219 D5
Welling DA16..........146 B3
West Drayton UB7.....104 A3
West Ewell KT19.......215 B1
Willesden NW10........67 C1
Wimbledon SW19......179 A6
Church Rd N N2........30 B2
Church Rd S N2........30 B2
Church Rise
Chessington KT9.......214 B2
Forest Hill SE23.......162 D2
Church Row
Chislehurst BR7.......189 A2
Hampstead NW3........70 A4
Church Row Mews BR7..................189 A3
Church St N E15........98 C6
Church St Sta CR0.....221 A6
Church Sq TW17.......192 D2
Church St Chiswick W4..133 D6
Croydon CR0..........220 D6
Croydon CR0..........221 A6
Dagenham RM10........81 D2
Edmonton N9...........17 C2
Enfield EN2.............5 B2
Hampton TW12.........174 A2
Isleworth TW7.........131 B3
Kingston u T KT1.......175 D1
Lisson Gr NW8..92 C3 237 A5
Newham E16...........122 D5
Sunbury TW16.........194 B6
Twickenham TW1.......153 A3
Walton-on-T KT12......194 A2
West Ham E15..........98 D6
Church Street Est NW8.................236 D5
Church Stretton Rd TW3..................152 A6
Church Studios 16 NW1..................71 D2
Church Terr
Hendon NW4............46 B6
Lewisham SE13........142 C2
21 Richmond TW10.....153 D6
Church Vale
Forest Hill SE23.......162 D2
Muswell Hill N2.........48 D6
Churchview Rd TW2...152 B2
Church Villa TW16.....194 B6
Churchward Ho
Camberwell SE17......138 D6
West Kensington SW5 .254 D1
Churchway NW1.......232 D2
Church Way
Cockfosters EN4.........2 D1
Friern Barnet N20.......14 C1
Church Wlk
Barnes SW13..........134 A4
Brentford TW8.........131 C6
Canonbury N16.........73 B4
Child's Hill NW2........69 B5
Dartmouth Pk N6........71 A5
Hayes UB3.............83 D1
Mitcham SW16.........181 C1
15 Richmond TW10.....153 D6
Thames Ditton KT7.....196 D3
Walton-on-T KT12......194 A1
Welsh Harp NW9........67 B6
West Barnes SW20......200 C6
Churchwood Gdns IG8..37 A6
Churchyard Row SE11........116 D2 261 D4
Churnfield 2 N4.......72 C6
Churston Ave E13.......99 B6
Churston Cl 16 SW2....160 C3
Churston Dr SM4......201 A4
Churston Gdns N11.....31 C4
Churston Mans WC1...240 D5
Churton Pl
Brentford W4..........132 D6
Pimlico SW1..........259 B3
Churton St SW1.........115 C2 259 B3
Chute Ho 17 SW9......138 C3
Chuter Ede Ho SW6....264 D5
Chyngton Cl DA15.....167 D1
Chyngton Ct HA1.......64 C6
Cibber Rd SE23........162 D2
Cicada Rd SW18.......158 A6
Cicely Ho NW8........229 D3
Cicely Rd SE15........140 A4
Cinderford Way BR1...186 C6
Cinema Mus The★ SE11................261 C3
Cinema Par RM8........81 B6
Cinnabar Wharf Central 17 E1....................118 A5
Cinnabar Wharf East 16 E1....................118 A5
Cinnabar Wharf West 18 E1....................118 A5
Cinnamon Cl
8 Camberwell SE15....139 D5
Thornton Heath CR0....204 A2
Cinnamon Row 3 SW11................136 A2
Cinnamon St E1........118 B5
Cinnamon Wharf SE1.253 D2
Cinque Cotts SW19....178 C4
Cintra Ct SE19.........183 D4
Cintra Pk SE19.........183 D3
Circle Ct HA0...........65 D4
Circle Gdns SW19......179 C1
Circle Ho 14 E14........98 B1
Circle The
Bermondsey SE1......253 D2
Burnt Oak NW7..........27 B4
Neasden NW2...........67 C5
Circuits The HA5........40 C5
Circular Rd London N2...30 B2
Tottenham N17.........51 D6
Circular Way SE18.....144 C6
Circus Lo NW8.........229 C2
Circus Mews W1......237 C4
Circus Pl EC2.........242 D3
Circus Rd NW8..92 B5 229 C3
Circus St SE10.........142 A5
Cirencester St W2......91 D2
Cirrus 17 NW9..........27 D1
Cirrus Cl 4 SM6.......220 A1
Cissbury Ho 6 SE26...162 A1
Cissbury Rd N15........51 B4
Cissbury Ring N N12....29 C5
Cissbury Ring S N12....29 B5
Citadel Pl SE11.......260 C2
Citizen Ho N7..........72 C4
Citizen Rd N7..........72 C4
Citron Terr 4 SE15....140 B2
Citrus Ho 14 SE8.......119 B1
City Banking Coll SE1.........117 B4 252 D2
City Bsns Ctr 33 SE16..118 C4
City Central Est EC1..235 A1
City Coll N1...........235 C2
City Coll of London The WC1................240 D3
City Forum EC1..95 A4 235 A2
City Garden Row N1...........94 D5 234 D3
City Gate E1............96 C3
City & Guilds of London Art Sch The SE11.........116 C1 261 B1
City Harbour E14......119 D3
City & Islington 6th Form Coll EC1.......94 D4 234 C2
City & Islington Coll
Finsbury Pk N4.........72 D6
Lower Holloway N7......72 A4
Lower Holloway N7......72 B4
Shoreditch EC1..95 A4 235 B1
Shoreditch N1...95 B6 235 C6
City Lights The SE11...261 B1
CITY OF LONDON.....117 A6
City of London Sch EC4..........117 A6 252 A6
City of London Sch for Girls EC2.......95 A2 242 B4
City of Westminster Coll
Paddington NW1........92 C2 237 B4
Paddington W2..92 B2 236 C4
City of Westminster Coll, Maida Vale Ctr W9.....91 D4
City of Westminster Coll, Queens Park Ctr W9...91 C4
City Prospect 5 SE19..183 C4
City Rd EC1.......95 A4 235 B2
City Thameslink Sta EC4..........94 D1 241 C1
City University EC1............94 D4 234 C1
City View 3 IG1........79 A6
City Wharf Ho KT7.....197 B3
City Wlk SE1.........253 A1
Civic Way Ilford IG6.....57 A5
Ruislip HA4............62 D3
Civil Service Coll SW1..........115 C2 259 A3
Clabon Mews SW1.........114 D2 257 C4
Clack St SE16..........118 C4
Clacton Rd Newham E6...99 A4
Tottenham N17.........33 D1
Walthamstow E17.......53 A3
Claigmar Gdns N3......29 D2
Claire Ct
Brondesbury NW2.......69 A2
Bushey WD23............8 B3
4 Pinner HA5...........23 B3
Whetstone N12..........14 A1
Claire Gdns HA7........25 C5
Claire Pl E14..........119 C3
Clairvale Rd TW5......129 A4
Clairview Rd SW16.....181 B5
Clairville Gdns W7.....108 C5
Clairville Point 12 SE23.................162 D1
Clamp Hill HA7.........24 C5
Clancarty Rd SW6.....135 C3
Clandon Cl
South Acton W3........110 D4
Clandon Cl *continued*
Stoneleigh KT17.......216 A2
Clandon Ct
Plaistow BR1..........187 A4
Sutton SM2...........218 B2
Clandon Gdns N3.......47 C6
Clandon Ho
East Finchley N3........47 C6
12 Kingston u T KT2....176 D4
Clandon Rd IG3.........79 C6
Clandon St SE8........141 C3
Clanfield Ho 12 SW15..156 A3
Clanricarde Gdns W2..........113 C6 245 B5
CLAPHAM.............137 B2
Clapham Common★ SW4.................137 B1
Clapham Common North Side SW4.............137 A1
Clapham Common South Side SW4...........159 C6
Clapham Common Sta SW4.................137 C1
Clapham Common West Side
Clapham SW4, SW11...136 D1
Clapham SW11.........159 A6
Clapham Computer & Secretarial Coll SW11.................158 D6
Clapham Court Terr 2 SW4.................160 A6
Clapham Cres SW4.....137 D1
Clapham Ct 3 SW4....160 A6
Clapham High St SW4.................137 D1
Clapham High Street Sta SW4.................137 D2
Clapham Junction Est SW11................136 C1
Clapham Junction Sta SW11................136 C1
Clapham Manor Ct 1 SW4.................137 C2
Clapham Manor Prim Sch SW4.................137 C2
Clapham Manor St SW4.................137 D2
Clapham Mans SW4....159 B5
Clapham North Bsns Ctr 10 SW4..............137 D2
Clapham North Sta SW4.................138 A2
CLAPHAM PARK......159 D6
Clapham Park Rd SW4.................137 D1
Clapham Park Terr 4 SW2.................160 A6
Clapham Rd SW9..........138 B5 270 D4
Clapham South Sta SW4.................159 B5
Claps Gate La E6......100 D3
Clapton Comm E5......52 A2
Clapton Girls Tec Coll E5....................74 C4
CLAPTON PARK.......74 D4
Clapton Pas E5.........74 C3
Clapton Sq E5..........74 C3
Clapton Sta E5.........74 B6
Clapton Terr E5........52 A1
Clapton Way E5........74 A4
Clara Grant Ho 10 E14...................119 C3
Clara Grant Prim Sch The E3....................97 C3
Clara Pl SE18..........122 C2
Clare Cl
Borehamwood WD6.....10 B5
East Finchley N2........48 A6
Clare Cnr SE9.........166 D4
Clare Ct
Chislehurst BR7.......188 B2
St Pancras WC1.......233 B1
Wimbledon SW19......179 A4
Claredale Ct SM2......218 A1
Claredale Ho 3 E2.....96 B5
Claredale St E2.........96 A5
Clare Gdns Barking IG11.80 A1
Forest Gate E7.........77 A4
Notting Hill W11........91 A1
Clare Ho
Bermondsey SE1.......263 D2
4 Burnt Oak HA8.......27 A1
5 Ealing W7...........108 D5
6 Old Ford E3..........97 B6
Clare House Prim Sch BR3..................186 A1
Clare La N1.............73 A1
Clare Lawn Ave SW14..155 B6
Clare Mews SW6.......265 C3
Clare Mkt WC2........240 D1
Claremont
1 Putney SW15........157 A6
Shepperton TW17......192 D3
Claremont Ave
Harrow HA3............44 A4
Sunbury TW16.........172 B2
West Barnes KT3......200 B4
Claremont Cl
Finsbury N1.....94 C5 234 B3
Newham E16..........122 C5
Orpington BR6.........226 C4
4 Streatham SW2......160 B3
Claremont Ct 1 W9....91 B5
Claremont Dr TW17....192 D3
Claremont Gdns
Ilford IG3..............79 C6
Kingston u T KT6.......198 A4

Claremont Gr
Chiswick W4 ... 133 C5
Woodford IG8 ... 37 C4
Claremont High Sch
HA3 ... 44 A4
Claremont Ho 15 SM2 .. 217 C1
Claremont Hts EN2 ... 4 D1
Claremont La KT10 ... 212 A3
Claremont Lo 12
SW19 ... 178 D3
Claremont Pk N3 ... 29 A2
Claremont Pl KT10 ... 212 D2
Claremont Prim Sch
NW2 ... 68 D6
Claremont Rd
Bromley BR1 ... 210 B5
Claygate KT10 ... 212 C1
Croydon CR0 ... 206 A1
Ealing W13 ... 87 A2
Forest Gate E7 ... 77 C3
Hadley Wood EN4 ... 2 B6
Harrow HA3 ... 24 C1
Hendon NW2 ... 68 D6
Higham Hill E17 ... 35 A1
Highgate N6 ... 49 C2
Kingston u T KT6 ... 198 A4
Leyton E7 ... 76 B5
Teddington TW11 ... 174 D6
Twickenham TW1 ... 153 C5
West Kilburn W9 ... 91 B5
Claremont Sq
N1 ... 94 C5 234 A3
Claremont St
Edmonton N18 ... 34 A4
Greenwich SE10 ... 141 D6
Newham E16 ... 122 C4
Claremont Terr KT7 ... 197 B2
Claremont Way NW2 ... 46 C1
Claremont Way Ind Est
NW2 ... 46 C1
Clarence Ave
Bromley BR1, BR2 ... 210 A5
Clapham Pk SW4 ... 159 D5
Ilford IG2 ... 56 C3
Kingston u T KT3 ... 177 B1
Clarence Cl Bushey WD23 . 8 D4
New Barnet EN4 ... 14 B6
Clarence Cres
Clapham Pk SW4 ... 159 D5
Sidcup DA14 ... 168 B1
Clarence Ct
Edgware NW7 ... 27 D5
10 Hammersmith W6 ... 112 B2
5 North Finchley N12 ... 30 B5
Clarence Gate NW1 ... 237 D6
Clarence Gate Gdns
NW1 ... 237 D5
Clarence Gdns
NW1 ... 93 B4 231 D1
Clarence Ho SE17 ... 139 A6
Clarence Ho*
SW1 ... 115 C5 249 B3
Clarence La SW15 ... 155 D5
Clarence Mews
Balham SW12 ... 159 B4
Hackney E5 ... 74 B3
1 Rotherhithe SE16 ... 118 D5
Clarence Pl 25 E5 ... 74 B3
Clarence Rd
Bexley DA6 ... 147 A1
Brentford W4 ... 110 C1
Bromley BR1, BR2 ... 210 A6
Brondesbury NW6 ... 69 B1
Chislehurst SE9 ... 166 A2
Enfield EN3 ... 18 C6
Harringay N15 ... 51 A4
Higham Hill E17 ... 34 D1
Lower Clapton E5 ... 74 B4
Manor Pk E12 ... 77 D3
Newham E16 ... 98 C3
Richmond TW9 ... 132 C4
Sidcup DA14 ... 168 B1
Sutton SM1 ... 217 D3
Teddington TW11 ... 175 A4
Thornton Heath CR0 ... 205 B2
Wallington SM6 ... 219 B3
Wimbledon SW19 ... 179 D4
Wood Green N22 ... 32 A3
Clarence St
Kingston u T KT1,
KT2 ... 176 A1
5 Richmond TW9 ... 132 A1
Southall UB2 ... 106 D3
Clarence Terr
Hounslow TW3 ... 129 D1
Lisson Gr NW1 ... 237 D6
Clarence Way NW1 ... 71 B1
Clarence Wlk 9 SW4 .. 138 A3
Clarendon Cl
Bayswater W2 ... 247 A6
38 Hackney E9 ... 74 C1
Clarendon Cres TW2 ... 152 B1
Clarendon Cross W11 . 244 B5
Clarendon Ct
London NW11 ... 47 B5
Mitcham SM4 ... 202 C4
Paddington W9 ... 236 B6
1 Richmond TW9 ... 132 C4
Willesden NW2 ... 68 C1
Clarendon Dr SW15 ... 134 C1
Clarendon Flats W1 ... 238 B1
Clarendon Gdns
Hendon NW4 ... 46 B6
Paddington W9 .. 92 A3 236 B5
Redbridge IG1 ... 56 B2
Wembley HA9 ... 66 A4
Clarendon Gr
Mitcham CR4 ... 202 D6
Somers Town NW1 ... 232 C2
Clarendon Ho
Harrow HA2 ... 42 B6
North Finchley N12 ... 30 A5
Somers Town NW1 ... 232 B3
South Oxhey WD19 ... 22 D5
Clarendon Mews
Bayswater W2 ... 247 A6
Old Bexley DA5 ... 169 D3
Clarendon Pl
W2 ... 114 C6 247 A6
Clarendon Prim Sch
TW15 ... 170 B6
Clarendon Rd
Ashford TW15 ... 170 B6
Croydon CR0 ... 220 D6
Ealing W5 ... 88 A3
Edmonton N18 ... 34 A5
Harrow HA1 ... 42 C3
Hayes UB3 ... 105 D4
Hornsey N8 ... 50 B6
Leytonstone E11 ... 54 B1
Mitcham SW19 ... 180 C3
Notting Hill
W11 ... 113 A6 244 B5
Wallington SM6 ... 219 C2
Walthamstow E17 ... 53 D3
Wanstead E18 ... 55 A6
West Green N15 ... 51 A5
Wood Green N22 ... 32 B1
Clarendon Rise SE13 ... 142 A1
Clarendon Sch TW12 ... 173 D4
Clarendon St
SW1 ... 115 B1 258 D2
Clarendon Terr W9 ... 236 B6
Clarendon Way
Enfield N21 ... 17 A5
Orpington BR5, BR7 ... 211 D6
Clarendon Wlk 11 W11 .. 91 A1
Clarens St SE6 ... 163 B2
Clare Pl SW15 ... 155 D4
Clare Point NW2 ... 46 D1
Clare Rd
Hounslow TW4 ... 129 B2
Leytonstone E11 ... 54 B3
New Cross Gate SE14 ... 141 B4
Northolt UB6 ... 64 B2
Stanwell TW19 ... 148 A4
Willesden NW10 ... 68 A1
Clare St E2 ... 96 B5
Claret Gdns SE25 ... 205 C5
Clareville Ct SW7 ... 256 B3
Clareville Gr
SW7 ... 114 A2 256 B3
Clareville Grove Mews
SW7 ... 256 B3
Clareville Rd BR5 ... 227 A6
Clareville St
SW7 ... 114 A2 256 B3
Clare Way DA7 ... 147 A4
Clarewood Ct W1 ... 237 C3
Clarewood Wlk SW9 ... 138 C1
Clarges Ho W1 ... 248 D4
Clarges Mews
W1 ... 115 B5 248 C4
Clarges St W1 .. 115 B5 248 D4
Clariat Ct W3 ... 110 C4
Claribel Rd SW9 ... 138 D3
Clarice Ct NW4 ... 46 B6
Claridge Ct SW6 ... 264 C1
Claridge Rd RM8 ... 58 D1
Clarinet Ct HA8 ... 26 D3
Clarissa Ho 7 E14 ... 97 D1
Clarissa Rd RM6 ... 58 D2
Clarissa St E8 ... 95 D6
Clark Ct 17 NW10 ... 67 B1
Clarke Ho
2 London SW4 ... 137 C2
5 Richmond TW10 ... 153 C1
Clarke Mans 9 IG11 ... 79 D1
Clarke Mews N9 ... 18 B1
Clarke Path N16 ... 52 A1
Clarke's Ave KT4, SM3 .. 216 D6
Clarkes Dr UB8 ... 82 A2
Clarkes Mews W1 ... 238 B4
Clark Ho SW10 ... 266 A4
Clark Lawrence Ct 11
SW11 ... 136 B2
Clarks Mead WD23 ... 8 B4
Clarkson Rd E16 ... 98 D1
Clarkson Row NW1 ... 232 A3
Clarkson St E2 ... 96 B4
Clarksons The IG11 ... 101 A5
Clark's Pl EC2 ... 243 A2
Clark's Rd IG1 ... 79 B6
Clark St E1 ... 96 C2
Clark Way TW5 ... 128 D5
Classic Mans 33 E9 ... 74 C1
Classinghall Ho 14
SW15 ... 156 D5
Classon Cl UB7 ... 104 A4
Claude Rd Leyton E10 ... 54 A1
London SE15 ... 140 B3
Newham E13 ... 99 B6
Claude St E14 ... 119 C2
Claudia Jones Way
SW2 ... 160 A5
Claudia Pl SW19 ... 157 A3
Claudius Cl HA7 ... 9 D1
Claughton Rd E13 ... 99 C5
Clauson Ave UB5 ... 64 A3
Clavell St 8 SE10 ... 142 A6
Claverdale Rd SW2 ... 160 C4
Clavering Ave SW13 ... 134 B6
Clavering Cl TW1 ... 175 A6
Clavering Ho SE13 ... 142 B1
Clavering Rd E12 ... 77 D6
Claverings Ind Est N9 ... 18 C2
Claverley Gr N3 ... 29 D2
Claverley Villas N3 ... 29 D3
Claverton St
SW1 ... 115 C1 259 B1
Clave St E1 ... 118 C5
Claxton Gr W6 .. 112 D1 254 A1
Clay Ave CR4 ... 181 B1
Claybank Gr SE13 ... 141 D2
Claybee Ct N22 ... 32 B5
Claybourne Mews 2
SE19 ... 183 D3
Claybridge Rd SE12 ... 187 C6
Claybrook Cl N2 ... 48 B6
Claybrook Rd W6 ... 134 D6
Claybury Broadway
IG5 ... 56 A6
Clay Ct E17 ... 54 B6
Claydon SE17 ... 262 A4
Claydon Dr CR0 ... 220 A4
Claydon Ho NW4 ... 28 D1
Claydown Mews SE18 .. 122 C1
Clayfarm Rd SE9 ... 167 A2
CLAYGATE ... 212 D1
Claygate Cres CR0 ... 224 B2
Claygate Ct SM1 ... 218 A5
Claygate La
Hinchley Wood KT10 ... 213 A6
Thames Ditton KT7 ... 197 A1
Claygate Lodge Cl
KT10 ... 212 C1
Claygate Prim Sch
KT10 ... 212 C1
Claygate Rd W13 ... 109 B3
Claygate Sta KT10 ... 212 C2
CLAYHALL ... 56 B6
Clayhall Ct 20 E3 ... 97 B5
CLAY HILL ... 5 A6
Clay Hill EN2 ... 5 B6
Clayhill Cres SE12,
SE9 ... 187 D6
Clay La Bushey WD23 ... 8 C4
Stanwell TW19 ... 148 B4
Claylands Ct SE19 ... 183 B5
Claylands Pl SW8 ... 138 C5
Claylands Rd
SW8 ... 138 B6 270 D5
Claymill Ho 2 SE18 ... 123 A1
Claymore Cl SM3, SM4 .. 201 C2
Claymore Ct 4 E17 ... 35 A2
Claypole Ct E17 ... 53 C4
Claypole Dr TW5 ... 129 A4
Claypole Rd E15 ... 98 A5
Clayponds Ave TW8 ... 110 A2
Clayponds Gdns W5 ... 109 D2
Clayponds Hospl & Day
Treatment Ctr TW8 ... 110 A2
Clayponds La TW8 ... 110 A1
Clays Ct N16 ... 51 D1
Clays La E15 ... 75 D3
Clays Lane Cl E15 ... 75 D3
Clays Lane Cvn Site
E15 ... 76 A3
Clay St W1 ... 92 D2 237 D3
Clayton 22 NW9 ... 27 D1
Clayton Ave HA0 ... 66 A1
Clayton Bsns Ctr UB3 .. 105 C4
Clayton Cl 3 E6 ... 100 B1
Clayton Cres
Brentford TW8 ... 109 D1
Islington N1 ... 233 C5
Clayton Ct
1 Higham Hill E17 ... 35 A1
Stamford Hill N16 ... 52 A2
Clayton Field NW9 ... 27 C2
Clayton Ho
22 Hackney E9 ... 74 C1
Long Ditton KT7 ... 197 B1
Clayton Mews SE10 ... 142 B4
Clayton Rd
Chessington KT10,
KT9 ... 213 D4
Hayes UB3 ... 105 C4
Isleworth TW7 ... 130 C2
Peckham SE15 ... 140 A4
Clayton St SE11 ... 138 C6
Clayton Terr UB4 ... 84 D2
Claytonville Terr
DA17 ... 125 D4
Clay Wood Cl BR6 ... 211 C2
Clayworth Cl DA15 ... 168 B5
Cleanthus Cl SE18 ... 144 D4
Cleanthus Rd SE18 ... 144 D4
Clearbrook Way 13 E1 .. 96 C1
Clearmont Ho UB2 ... 107 C3
Clearwater Ho BR3 ... 207 D4
Clear Water Ho 9
TW10 ... 154 A6
Clearwater Pl KT6 ... 197 C3
Clearwater Terr 4
W11 ... 112 D4
Clearwell Dr W9 ... 91 D3
Cleave Ave Hayes UB3 .. 105 C2
Orpington BR6 ... 227 C2
Cleaveland Rd KT6 ... 197 D4
Cleaver Ho 6 NW3 ... 70 D1
Cleaverholme Cl SE25 .. 206 B3
Cleaver Sq
SE11 ... 116 C1 261 B1
Cleaver St
SE11 ... 116 C1 261 B2
Cleave's Almshos 1
KT2 ... 176 A1
Cleeve Ct
East Bedfont TW14 ... 149 C3
Muswell Hill N10 ... 31 B3
Cleeve Hill SE23 ... 162 B3
Cleeve Ho 15 E2 ... 95 C4
Cleeve Park Gdns
DA14 ... 168 B2
Cleeve Park Sch DA14 . 168 C1
Cleeve Way
Cheam SM1 ... 201 D1
Cleeve Way *continued*
Roehampton SW15 ... 155 D4
Cleeve Workshops 14
E2 ... 95 C4
Clegg Ho SE3 ... 143 B1
Clegg St Newham E13 ... 99 A5
16 Wapping E1 ... 118 B5
Cleland Ho 19 E2 ... 96 C5
Clematis Gdns IG8 ... 37 A5
Clematis St W12 ... 112 A6
Clem Atlee Par SW6 .. 264 D5
Clem Attlee Ct
SW6 ... 135 B6 264 D5
Clemence St E14 ... 97 B2
Clement Attlee Ho
NW10 ... 67 D1
Clement Ave SW4 ... 137 D1
Clement Cl Acton W4 ... 111 B2
Hampstead NW6 ... 68 C1
Clement Danes Ho 2
W12 ... 90 B1
Clement Gdns UB3 ... 105 C2
Clement Ho
14 Deptford SE8 ... 119 A2
17 North Kensington
W10 ... 90 C2
Clementhorpe Rd RM9 .. 80 C2
Clementina Rd E10 ... 53 B1
Clementine Churchill
Hospl The HA1 ... 64 D5
Clementine Cl W13 ... 109 B4
Clementine Wlk 4 IG8 .. 37 A3
Clement Rd Penge BR3 .. 184 D1
Wimbledon SW19 ... 179 A5
Clements Ave 1 E16 ... 121 A6
Clements Cl 19 N12 ... 29 D6
Clements Ct
Hounslow TW4 ... 128 D1
5 Ilford IG1 ... 78 D5
Clements Ho N17 ... 34 A2
Clements Inn
WC2 ... 94 B1 240 D1
Clements Inn Pas
WC2 ... 240 D1
Clements La IG1 ... 78 D5
Clement's La EC2,
EC4 ... 117 B6 252 D6
Clements Pl TW8 ... 109 D1
Clements Rd
East Ham E6 ... 78 B1
Ilford IG1 ... 78 D5
Clement's Rd SE16 ... 118 B3
Cleminson Ct DA14 ... 190 D4
Clemson Ho 9 E8 ... 95 D6
Clendon Way SE18 ... 123 B2
Clennam St SE1 ... 252 B2
Clensham Ct SM3 ... 217 C6
Clensham La SM1 ... 217 C6
Clenston Mews W1 ... 237 C2
Clent Ho 4 N16 ... 51 D1
Cleopatra's Needle*
WC2 ... 116 B6 250 C5
Clephane Rd 13 N1 ... 73 A2
Clephane Rd N N1 ... 73 A2
Clephane Rd S N1 ... 73 B2
Clere Pl EC2 ... 242 D6
Clere St EC2 ... 95 B3 242 D6
Clerics Wlk TW17 ... 193 B3
CLERKENWELL ... 94 D3
Clerkenwell Cl
EC1 ... 94 C3 241 B5
Clerkenwell Gn
EC1 ... 94 D3 241 C5
Clerkenwell Parochial CE
Prim Sch EC1 .. 94 C4 234 A1
Clerkenwell Rd
EC1 ... 94 D3 241 C5
Clermont Rd E9 ... 96 C6
Cleveden Ct CR2 ... 221 C3
Cleveden Ho BR1 ... 188 A3
Clevedon Ct
Battersea SW11 ... 267 A2
Dulwich SE21 ... 161 B1
Clevedon Gdns
Cranford TW5 ... 128 B4
Hayes UB3 ... 105 B3
Clevedon Ho 4 SM1 ... 218 A4
Clevedon Mans NW5 ... 71 A4
Clevedon Rd
Kingston u T KT1 ... 176 C1
Penge SE20 ... 184 D2
Twickenham TW1 ... 153 D5
Cleve Ho NW6 ... 69 D1
Cleveland Ave
Chiswick W4 ... 111 D2
Hampton TW12 ... 173 B3
Merton SW20 ... 179 B1
Cleveland Cres WD6 ... 11 A6
Cleveland Ct Ealing W13 . 87 B2
Marylebone W1 ... 239 B5
Southall UB2 ... 107 D2
Cleveland Gdns
Barnes SW13 ... 133 D3
Harringay N4, N15 ... 51 A4
Hendon NW2 ... 68 D6
Paddington W2 .. 92 A1 236 A1
Worcester Pk KT4 ... 215 D6
Cleveland Gr 39 E1 ... 96 C3
Cleveland Ho 7 N2 ... 30 B1
Cleveland Inf Sch IG1 .. 78 D5
Cleveland Jun Sch IG1 .. 78 D5
Cleveland Mans
8 Brixton SW9 ... 138 C5
4 Brondesbury NW6 ... 69 B1
Paddington W9 ... 91 C3
Cleveland Mews W1 .. 239 A4
Cleveland Park Ave
E17 ... 53 C5
Cleveland Park Cres
E17 ... 53 C5
Cleveland Pk TW19 ... 148 A5
Cleveland Pl SW1 ... 249 B4
Cleveland Rd
Barnes SW13 ... 133 D3
Bexley DA16 ... 145 D3
Ealing W13 ... 87 B2
Edmonton N9 ... 18 B4
Ilford IG1 ... 78 D5
Isleworth TW7 ... 131 A1
Islington N1 ... 73 B1
New Malden KT3 ... 199 C5
12 South Acton W4 ... 111 A3
Wanstead E18 ... 55 A6
Worcester Pk KT4 ... 215 C6
Cleveland Rise SM4 ... 200 D2
Cleveland Row
SW1 ... 115 C5 249 B3
Cleveland Sq
W2 ... 92 A1 236 A1
Cleveland St
W1 ... 93 C3 239 A5
Cleveland Terr
W2 ... 92 A1 236 B2
Cleveland Way E1 ... 96 C3
Cleveley Cres W5 ... 88 B5
Cleveleys Rd E5 ... 74 B5
Clevely Cl SE7 ... 121 D2
Clevendon Cl N16 ... 73 D5
Cleve Rd Sidcup DA14 ... 168 D1
South Hampstead NW6 .. 69 D1
Cleverly Cotts W12 ... 111 D5
Cleverly Est W12 ... 112 A6
Cleves Ct KT6 ... 198 A3
Cleves Prim Sch E6 ... 99 D6
Cleves Rd Newham E6 ... 99 D5
Richmond TW10 ... 153 C1
Cleves Way
Ashford TW16 ... 171 D4
Hampton TW12 ... 173 B3
Ruislip HA4 ... 40 D1
Clewer Cres HA3 ... 24 B2
Clewer Ct 2 E10 ... 53 C1
Clewer Ho 6 SE2 ... 124 D4
Cley Ho SE4 ... 140 D1
Clichy Ho 32 E1 ... 96 C2
Clifden Centre (Richmond
Adult & Com Coll)
TW1 ... 152 D3
Clifden Ho 6 TW8 ... 131 D6
Clifden Mews E5 ... 74 D3
Clifden Rd
Brentford TW8 ... 131 D6
Homerton E5 ... 74 D3
Twickenham TW1 ... 152 D3
Cliff Ct 14 NW1 ... 71 D2
Cliffe Ho 4 SE10 ... 120 D1
Cliffe Rd CR2 ... 221 B3
Cliffe Wlk 2 SM1 ... 218 A3
Clifford Ave
Elmstead BR7 ... 188 B4
Mortlake SW14 ... 133 A3
Mortlake SW14, TW9 .. 132 D2
Wallington SM6 ... 219 C4
Clifford Cl UB5 ... 85 A6
Clifford Ct
Bayswater W2 ... 91 D2
Wandsworth SW18 ... 158 B4
Willesden NW10 ... 67 C4
Clifford Dr SW9 ... 138 D1
Clifford Gdns
Hayes UB3 ... 105 B2
Kensal Green NW10 ... 90 C5
Clifford Gr TW15 ... 170 C6
Clifford Haigh Ho
SW6 ... 134 D5
Clifford Ho
2 Beckenham BR3 ... 185 D4
West Kensington W14 .. 254 C3
Clifford Lo 5 N3 ... 29 B1
Clifford Rd Barnet EN5 ... 1 D2
Chingford E17 ... 36 A1
Croydon SE25 ... 206 A5
Hounslow TW4 ... 128 D2
Newham E16 ... 98 D3
Ponders End N9 ... 18 C5
Richmond TW10 ... 153 D2
Wembley HA0 ... 87 D6
Clifford's Inn Pas EC4 . 241 A1
Clifford St W1 .. 115 C6 249 A5
Clifford Way NW10 ... 67 D4
Cliff Rd NW1 ... 71 D2
Cliff Road Studios 13
NW1 ... 71 D2
Cliffsend Ho 23 SW9 ... 138 C4
Cliff Terr SE8 ... 141 C3
Cliffview Rd SE13 ... 141 C2
Cliff Villas NW1 ... 71 D2
Cliff Wlk E16 ... 98 D2
Clifton Ave
Church End N3 ... 29 B2
Feltham TW13 ... 150 C1
Shepherd's Bush W12 ... 111 D5
Stanmore HA7 ... 25 B1
Walthamstow E17 ... 52 D6
Wembley HA9 ... 66 B2
Clifton Cl 18 BR6 ... 227 A3
Clifton Cres SE15 ... 140 B5
Clifton Ct
1 Beckenham BR3 ... 185 D2
Finsbury Pk N4 ... 72 C6
Paddington NW8 ... 236 C6
Peckham SE15 ... 140 B5
Putney SW15 ... 156 D6
South Norwood SE25 ... 205 C4
9 Stanwell TW19 ... 148 A5
Surbiton KT5 ... 198 B2
3 Woodford IG8 ... 37 A4
Clifton Gate SW10 ... 266 A6
Clifton Gdns
Chiswick W4 ... 111 B2
Clifton Gdns *continued*
Enfield EN2 ... 16 A6
Hillingdon UB10 ... 82 D5
Paddington W9 .. 92 A3 236 A5
South Tottenham N15 ... 51 D3
2 Temple Fortune
NW11 ... 47 B3
Clifton Gr E8 ... 74 A2
Clifton Hill NW8 . 92 A6 229 A5
Clifton Ho Leyton E11 ... 76 C6
Shoreditch E2 ... 243 C6
Clifton Mans 4 SW9 ... 138 C1
Clifton Mews SE25 ... 205 C5
Clifton Par TW13 ... 172 C6
Clifton Park Ave
SW20 ... 178 C1
Clifton Pl
Paddington W2 ... 236 D1
Rotherhithe SE16 ... 118 C4
Clifton Prim Sch UB2 .. 107 A2
Clifton Rd Bexley DA16 .. 146 C2
Crouch End N8 ... 49 D3
Finchley N3 ... 30 A2
Greenford UB6 ... 86 B3
Harlesden NW10 ... 90 A5
Harlington TW6 ... 126 D2
Harrow HA3 ... 44 B4
Ilford IG2 ... 57 B3
Isleworth TW7 ... 130 C3
Kingston u T KT2 ... 176 B2
Newham E16 ... 98 C2
Paddington W9 .. 92 A3 236 B6
Sidcup DA14 ... 189 C6
Southall UB2 ... 107 A2
South Norwood SE25 ... 205 C5
Teddington TW11 ... 174 C6
Upton E7 ... 77 D2
Wallington SM6 ... 219 B3
Wimbledon SW19 ... 178 D4
Wood Green N22 ... 31 C2
Clifton Rise SE14 ... 141 A5
Cliftons Roundabout SE9,
SE12 ... 165 C5
Clifton St EC2 ... 95 C3 243 A5
Clifton Terr N4 ... 72 C6
Clifton The KT6 ... 214 A6
Clifton Villas
W9 ... 92 A2 236 A4
Cliftonville Ct SE12 ... 165 A3
Clifton Way
Peckham SE15 ... 140 C5
Wembley HA0 ... 88 A6
Climsland Ho SE1 ... 251 B4
Clinch Ct 11 E16 ... 99 A2
Cline Ho SW15 ... 156 A6
Cline Rd N11 ... 31 C4
Clinger Ct N1 ... 95 C6
Clink St SE1 ... 117 B5 252 C4
Clinton Ave
Bexley DA16 ... 146 A1
East Molesey KT8 ... 196 A5
Clinton Ho
New Malden KT3 ... 199 B1
6 Surbiton KT6 ... 197 D2
Clinton Rd Bow E3 ... 97 A4
Forest Gate E7 ... 77 A4
West Green N15 ... 51 B5
Clipper Appts 12 SE10 .. 142 A6
Clipper Cl 3 SE16 ... 118 D4
Clipper Ho E14 ... 120 A1
Clipper Way SE13 ... 142 A1
Clippesby Cl KT9 ... 214 B2
Clipstone Ho 10 SW15 .. 156 A6
Clipstone Mews W1 ... 239 A4
Clipstone Rd TW3 ... 129 C2
Clipstone St W1 . 93 C2 239 A4
Clissold Cl N2 ... 48 D6
Clissold Cres N16 ... 73 B4
Clissold Ct N4 ... 73 A6
Clissold Ho 4 N16 ... 73 B6
Clissold Rd N16 ... 73 B5
Clitheroe Ave HA2 ... 41 C1
Clitheroe Rd SW9 ... 138 A3
Clitherow Ave W7 ... 109 A3
Clitherow Rd TW8 ... 109 C1
Clitterhouse Cres NW2 .. 46 C1
Clitterhouse Rd NW2 ... 46 C1
Clive Ave N18 ... 34 A4
Clive Ct Paddington W9 . 236 B6
Streatham SW16 ... 181 D5
Tolworth KT6 ... 214 C6
Cliveden Cl N12 ... 30 A6
Cliveden Ho SW1 ... 258 A4
Cliveden Pl
Belgravia
SW1 ... 115 A2 258 A4
Shepperton TW17 ... 193 A3
Cliveden Rd SW19 ... 179 B2
Clivedon Ct Ealing W13 .. 87 B2
6 New Barnet EN5 ... 2 A1
Clivedon Rd E4 ... 36 C5
Clive Ho
18 Clapham SW8 ... 137 D3
3 Croydon CR0 ... 205 D1
Greenwich SE10 ... 142 A6
Clive Lloyd Ho N15 ... 51 A4
Clive Lo NW4 ... 46 D3
Clive Rd
Belvedere DA17 ... 125 C2
Enfield EN1 ... 6 A1
Feltham TW14 ... 150 A5
Mitcham SW19 ... 180 C4
Teddington TW1 ... 175 A6
West Norwood SE21,
SE27 ... 161 B1
Clivesdale Dr UB3 ... 106 B5
Clive Way EN1 ... 6 A1

Cloak La EC4 . . . . . . .117 B6 252 C6
Clochar Ct NW10 . . . . .89 D6
Clock Ct 2 E11 . . . . .55 B5
Clock Ho
　Stamford Hill N16 . . . . . . .51 D2
　Walthamstow E17 . . . . . .54 B5
Clock Ho The EN2 . . . . .5 D6
Clockhouse Ave IG11 . .101 A6
Clockhouse Cl SW19 . .156 C2
Clock House Ct 1
　BR3 . . . . .185 A1
Clockhouse Junc N13 . .32 C5
Clockhouse La TW14,
　TW15 . . . . .148 D2
Clockhouse Mans N13 . .32 C5
Clockhouse Par N13 . . .32 C5
Clock House Par E11 . . .55 B3
Clockhouse Pl SW15 . .157 A5
Clock House Rd BR3 . .185 A1
Clockhouse Rdbt
　TW14 . . . . .149 A3
Clock House Sta BR3 . .185 A2
Clockhouse The
　SW19 . . . . .156 C1
Clock Mus*
　EC2 . . . . .95 A1 242 B2
Clocktower Mews 6
　W7 . . . . .108 C5
Clock Tower Mews
　Islington N1 . . . . .235 B3
　Thamesmead SE28 . . .124 B6
Clock Tower Pl N7 . . . . .72 A2
Clock Tower Rd TW7. .130 D2
Cloister Cl TW11 . . . . .175 B5
Cloister Gdns
　Croydon SE25 . . . . . .206 B3
　Edgware HA8 . . . . .27 A5
Cloister Rd Acton W3 . . .89 A2
　Child's Hill NW2 . . . . . . .69 B6
Cloisters Ave BR1, BR2. .210 B4
Cloisters Ct Erith DA7. .147 D2
　Highgate N6 . . . . .49 B1
Cloisters Ho 8 SW19 . .179 C3
Cloisters The 22 SW9 . .138 C4
Clonard Way HA5 . . . . . .23 C4
Clonbrock Rd N16 . . . . .73 C4
Cloncurry St SW6 . . . .134 D3
Clone Ct 4 W12 . . . . . .111 C3
Clone The 5 KT2 . . . . .176 D3
Clonmel Cl HA2 . . . . .42 B1
Clonmell Rd N17 . . . . . .51 B6
Clonmel Rd
　Fulham SW6 . . .135 B4 264 D2
　Teddington TW11 . . . .174 B6
Clonmore St SW18 . . .157 B3
Cloonmore Ave BR6 . .227 D4
Clorane Gdns NW3 . . . .69 C5
Close The
　Beckenham BR3 . . . . .207 A5
　Cheam SM3 . . . . .201 B2
　Chingford E4 . . . . .36 A3
　Cockfosters EN4 . . . . . .14 D6
　Croydon SE25 . . . . . .206 A3
　Dagenham RM6 . . . . . . .59 A3
　Eastcote HA5 . . . . .40 C2
　Harrow HA2 . . . . .24 A1
　Hillingdon UB10 . . . . . .82 C6
　Hounslow TW7 . . . . . .130 B3
　Ilford IG2 . . . . .57 C3
　Kingston u T KT3 . . . .177 A1
　Lewisham SE3 . . . . . .142 B3
　Mitcham CR4 . . . . . . .202 D5
　Mortlake TW9 . . . . . . .132 D2
　Muswell Hill N10 . . . . . .31 B1
　1 Old Bexley DA5 . . . .169 C4
　Palmers Green N14 . . . .15 D2
　Petts Wood BR5 . . . . .211 C3
　Rayners La HA5 . . . . . .41 B2
　Sidcup DA14 . . . . . . .190 B5
　Surbiton KT6 . . . . . . .198 A3
　Totteridge N20 . . . . . . .13 B2
　Wembley HA0 . . . . .66 A2
　Wembley Pk HA9 . . . . . .67 A5
Cloth Ct EC1 . . . . .241 D3
Cloth Fair EC1 . . .94 D2 241 D3
Clothier Ho SE7 . . . . . .122 A1
Clothier St E1 . . . . . . .243 B2
Cloth St EC1 . . . . .95 A2 242 A4
Clothworkers Rd SE18 .145 B5
Cloudesdale Rd SW17 .159 B2
Cloudesley Mans N1. .234 B5
Cloudesley Pl
　N1 . . . . .94 C6 234 B5
Cloudesley Rd
　Erith DA7 . . . . .147 B4
　Islington N1 . . .94 C6 234 A5
Cloudesley Sq
　N1 . . . . .94 C6 234 B6
Cloudesley St
　N1 . . . . .94 C6 234 B5
Clouston Cl SM6 . . . . . .220 A3
Clova Rd E7 . . . . .77 A3
Clove Cres E14 . . . . . .120 B6
Clovelly Ave
　London NW9 . . . . .45 D5
　Uxbridge UB10 . . . . . . .61 A4
Clovelly Cl Pinner HA5 . .40 C6
　Uxbridge UB10 . . . . . . .61 A4
Clovelly Ct NW2 . . . . . .68 C3
Clovelly Gdns
　Enfield EN1 . . . . .17 C4
　South Norwood SE19 . .183 D2
Clovelly Ho W2 . . . . . .100 A2
Clovelly Rd Acton W4 . .111 B4
　Ealing W5 . . . . .109 C4
　Erith DA7 . . . . .147 A6
　Hornsey N8 . . . . .49 D5

Clovelly Rd continued
　Hounslow TW3 . . . . . .129 C3
Clovelly Way
　Harrow HA2 . . . . .63 B6
　Orpington BR6 . . . . . .211 D3
　Stepney E1 . . . . .96 C1
Clover Cl E11 . . . . .76 B6
Clover Ct Enfield EN3 . . . .7 A1
　Sutton SM2 . . . . .217 D2
Cloverdale Gdns
　DA15 . . . . .167 D5
Clover Ho
　Hounslow TW3 . . . . . .130 A4
　Southgate N21 . . . . . . .16 B6
Cloverleys IG10. . . . . . . .21 D6
Clover Mews SW3 . . . .267 D6
Clove St 9 E13 . . . . .99 A3
Clowders Rd SE6 . . . . .163 B1
Clowes Ho 3 SW4 . . . .138 A1
Clowser Cl 4 SM1 . . . .218 A3
Cloysters Gn E1 . . . . . .118 A5
Cloyster Wood HA8 . . . .25 D4
Club Gardens Rd BR2 . .209 A2
Club Row E2 . . .95 D3 243 C6
Clumps The TW15 . . . .171 B6
Clunbury Ave SE21 . . .161 C5
Clunbury St N1 . . . . . . .235 D3
Clunie Ho SW1 . . . . . . .257 D6
Cluny Mews SW5 . . . . .255 A3
Cluny Pl SE1 . . . .117 C3 263 A6
Cluse Ct N1 . . . . .235 A4
Clutton St E14 . . . . .97 D2
Clydach Rd EN1 . . . . .5 D1
Clyde Cir N15 . . . . .51 C5
Clyde Ct NW1 . . . . .232 D4
Clyde Flats SW6 . . . . .264 C4
Clyde Ho 9 KT2 . . . . . .175 D2
Clyde Rd Croydon CR0. .221 D6
　South Tottenham N15 . . .51 C5
　Stanwell TW19 . . . . . .148 A3
　Sutton SM1 . . . . .217 C3
　Wallington SM6 . . . . . .219 C2
　Wood Green N22 . . . . . .31 D2
Clydesdale EN3 . . . . .6 D1
Clydesdale Ave HA7 . . . .43 D6
Clydesdale Cl
　Borehamwood WD6 . . . .11 B6
　Isleworth TW7 . . . . . .130 D2
Clydesdale Ct N20 . . . .14 B3
Clydesdale Gdns
　TW10 . . . . .132 D1
Clydesdale Ho
　Abbey Wood DA18 . . . .125 A4
　4 Notting Hill W11 . . . .91 B1
Clydesdale Path WD6 . . .11 B6
Clydesdale Rd W11 . . . .91 B1
Clyde St SE8 . . . . .141 B6
Clyde Terr SE23 . . . . . .162 C2
Clyde Vale SE23 . . . . . .162 C2
Clyde Works 10 SW6 . .219 C2
Clyfford Rd HA4 . . . . . . .61 D4
Clymping Dene TW14 . .150 B4
Clynes Ho
　6 Dagenham RM10 . . . .81 C5
　3 Globe Town E2 . . . . .96 D4
　Hayes UB4 . . . . .84 A4
Clyro Ct N4 . . . . .50 B1
Clyston St SW8 . . . . . .137 C3
Clytha Ct SE27 . . . . . . .183 A6
Coach Ho NW10 . . . . . . .67 A1
Coach & Horses Yd
　W1 . . . . .249 A6
Coach House La
　Highbury N5 . . . . .72 C4
　Wimbledon SW19 . . . .156 D1
Coach House Mews
　SE23 . . . . .162 D5
Coach House Yd 5
　NW3 . . . . .70 B4
Coachmaker Mews 5
　SW9. . . . . .138 A2
Coachman Lo N12 . . . . .30 A5
Coalbrook Mans 3
　SW12. . . . . .159 B3
Coaldale Wlk SE21 . . . .161 A4
Coalecroft Rd SW15. . .156 C6
Coalport Ho SE11 . . . . .261 A4
Coal Post Cl BR6. . . . . .227 D2
Coatbridge Ho 8 N1 . .72 B1
Coates Ave SW18 . . . .158 C5
Coates Cl CR7 . . . . . . .205 A4
Coates Ct NW3 . . . . . . .70 C3
Coates Hill Rd BR1. . . .188 C1
Coates Rd WD6 . . . . .9 D4
Coate St E2 . . . . .96 A5
Coates Wlk TW8 . . . . .110 A1
Cobalt SE2 . . . . .124 A4
Cobalt Cl CR0. . . . . . . .206 D5
Cobbett Rd
　Kidbrooke SE9 . . . . . .144 A2
　Twickenham TW2 . . . .151 C3
Cobbett St
　SW8. . . . . .138 B5 270 D3
Cobble La N1 . . . . .72 D1
Cobble Mews N4, N5 . . .73 A5
Cobbler's Wlk TW11 . .174 D3
Cobblestone Pl CR0. . .205 A1
Cobbold Ct SW1 . . . . .259 C4
Cobbold Ind Est NW10 . .67 D2
Cobbold Mews W12. . .111 D4
Cobbold Rd
　Bedford Pk W12 . . . . .111 D4
　Leyton E11 . . . . .76 D5
　Willesden NW10 . . . . . .67 D3
Cobb's Hall 1 SW6 . .134 D6
Cobbs Rd TW4 . . . . . . .129 B1

Cobb St E1 . . . . .243 C1
Cobden Bldgs WC1 . . .233 C2
Cobden Ct
　Bromley BR2 . . . . .209 C5
　9 Thamesmead SE28 . .124 C5
Cobden Ho
　1 Bethnal Green E2 . . . .96 A4
　Regent's Pk NW1 . . . .232 A4
Cobden Mews SE26 . . .184 B5
Cobden Rd
　Croydon SE25 . . . . . .206 A4
　Leyton E11 . . . . .76 C6
　Orpington BR6. . . . . . .227 B4
Cobham 21 NW9 . . . . . .27 D1
Cobham Ave KT3 . . . . .200 A4
Cobham Cl
　2 Blackfen DA15 . . . . .168 B5
　Bromley BR2 . . . . .210 A2
　Clapham SW11 . . . . . .158 C5
　Edgware HA8 . . . . .26 D1
　Enfield EN1 . . . . .6 A2
　Wallington SM6. . . . . .220 A2
Cobham Ct CR4. . . . . . .180 B1
Cobham Ho IG11 . . . . . .101 A6
Cobham Mews 3 NW1. .71 D1
Cobham Pl DA6. . . . . . .168 D6
Cobham Rd
　Chingford E17 . . . . .36 A2
　Harringay N22. . . . . . . .50 D6
　Heston TW5. . . . . .128 C5
　Ilford IG3 . . . . .79 C5
　Kingston u T KT1, KT2. .176 C1
Cobland Rd SE12 . . . . .187 C6
Coborn Mews 9 E3. . . .97 B4
Coborn Rd E3 . . . . .97 B4
Coborn St E3 . . . . .97 B4
Cobourg Prim Sch
　SE5 . . . . .139 D6
Cobourg Rd SE5 . . . . . .139 D6
Cobourg St
　NW1 . . . . .93 C4 232 B1
Coburg Cl SW1 . . . . . . .259 B4
Coburg Cres SW2. . . . .160 C3
Coburg Dwellings 11
　E1 . . . . .118 C6
Coburg Gdns IG5 . . . . . .37 D1
Coburg Rd N22 . . . . . . .32 B1
Cochrane Cl NW8 . . . . .229 D3
Cochrane Ct 3 E10 . . . .53 C1
Cochrane Ho 15 E14 . . .119 C4
Cochrane Mews
　NW8 . . . . .92 B5 229 D3
Cochrane Rd SW19 . . .179 B3
Cochrane St
　NW8 . . . . .92 B5 229 D3
Coci Ho W14 . . . . .254 D3
Cockburn Ho SW1 . . . .259 D1
Cockerell Rd E17 . . . . . .53 A3
COCKFOSTERS 2 D1
Cockfosters Par EN4 . . .3 A1
Cockfosters Rd EN4 . . . .2 D3
Cockfosters Sta EN4 . . .3 A1
Cock Hill E1 . . . . .243 B3
Cock La EC1 . . . .94 D2 241 D3
Cockpit Yd WC1 . . . . . .240 D4
Cocks Cres KT3. . . . . . .199 D5
Cocksett Ave BR6. . . . .227 C2
Cockspur Ct SW1 . . . . .249 D4
Cockspur St
　SW1. . . . . . . .115 D5 249 D4
Cocksure La DA14 . . . .191 C6
Coda Ctr The
　SW6. . . . . . . .135 A4 264 B2
Code St E1 . . . . .95 D3 243 D5
Codicote Ho 22 SE8 . . .118 D2
Codicote Terr N4 . . . . . .73 A6
Codling Cl 15 E1 . . . . . .118 A5
Codling Way HA0 . . . . . .65 D4
Codrington Ct 3
　SE16 . . . . .119 A5
Codrington Hill SE23 . .163 A4
Codrington Ho 7 E1. . . .96 B3
Codrington Mews W11. .91 A1
Cody Cl Harrow HA3 . . . .43 D6
　Wallington SM6. . . . . .219 D1
Cody Rd E16. . . . . .98 B3
Coe Ave SE25 . . . . .206 A3
Coe's Alley N5 . . . . .1 A1
Coffey St SE8 . . . . .141 C5
Cogan Ave E17 . . . . .35 A2
Cohen Ho NW7 . . . . .28 A6
Cohen Lo E5 . . . . .75 A3
Coin St SE1 . . . .116 C5 251 A4
Coity Rd NW5 . . . . .71 A2
Cokers La SE21 . . . . . .161 B3
Coke St E1 . . . . .96 A1
Colab Ct N22 . . . . .32 C2
Colas Mews 7 NW6 . . . .91 C6
Colbeck Mews
　SW5. . . . . . . .113 D2 255 D3
Colbeck Rd HA1 . . . . . . .42 A2
Colberg Pl N16 . . . . .51 D2
Colbert 1 SE5. . . . . . .139 D4
Colborne Ct 8 SW19 . .179 D2
Colborne Ho 8 E14 . . . .119 C6
Colborne Way KT4. . . . .216 C6
Colbrook Ave UB3 . . . .105 B3
Colbrook Cl UB3 . . . . . .105 B3
Colburn Ave HA5 . . . . . .23 A4
Colburn Way SM1. . . . .218 B5
Colby Rd
　Walton-on-T KT12 . . . .194 A1
　West Norwood SE19 . .183 C5
Colchester Ave E12 . . . .78 B5
Colchester Dr HA5 . . . .40 C4
Colchester Ho 17
　SW8. . . . . .137 D3
Colchester Rd
　Burnt Oak HA8 . . . . . . .27 A3
　Leyton E10 . . . . .54 A2

Colchester Rd continued
　Pinner HA6 . . . . .22 A1
　Walthamstow E17 . . . . . .53 C3
Colchester St E1 . . . . . .243 D2
Colchester Villas CR7 . .204 C3
Coldbath Sq EC1. . . . . .241 A6
Coldbath St SE13 . . . . .141 D3
Cold Blow La SE14 . . . .140 D6
Coldershaw Rd W13 . . .109 A4
Coldfall Ave N10 . . . . . .31 A1
Coldfall Prim Sch N10 . .30 D1
Coldham Ct N22 . . . . . . .32 D2
Coldham Gr EN3 . . . . . . .7 A6
Coldharbour E14 . . . . .120 A5
Coldharbour Crest
　SE9 . . . . .166 C1
Coldharbour Ind Est
　SE5. . . . . .139 A3
Coldharbour La
　Brixton SW9 . . . . .138 D2
　Bushey WD23 . . . . .8 A6
　Hayes UB3. . . . . .106 A5
Coldharbour Lane Ho
　UB3 . . . . .106 A5
Coldharbour Pl SE5 . . .139 B3
Coldharbour Rd CR0. . .220 C3
Coldharbour Sports Ctr
　SE9. . . . . .166 C2
Coldharbour Way CR0. .220 C3
Coldstream Gdns
　SW18 . . . . .157 B5
Colebeck Mews N1 . . . .72 C2
Colebert Ave E1 . . . . . . .96 C3
Colebert Ho 21 E1 . . . . .96 C3
Colebrook Cl
　Edgware NW7 . . . . .28 D3
　Putney SW19 . . . . . . .156 D2
Colebrook Ct SW3 . . . .257 B3
Colebrooke Ave W13. . . .87 B1
Colebrooke Ct DA14 . . .190 B6
Colebrooke Dr E11 . . . . .55 C2
Colebrooke Pl N1. . . . . .234 D5
Colebrooke Row
　Islington N1 . . .94 D5 234 D5
　Islington N1 . . . . .234 D5
Colebrook Ho 1 E14. . . .97 D1
Colebrook Rd SW16. . . .182 A2
Colebrook Rise BR2. . .186 C1
Colebrook Way N11. . . . .31 B5
Coleby Path 21 SE5 . . .139 B5
Colechurch Ho 9
　SE1 . . . . .118 A1
Cole Cl SE28. . . . . .124 B5
Cole Court Lo 9 TW1. .153 A4
Coledale Dr HA7. . . . . . .25 C2
Colefax Bldg 12 E1. . . . .96 A1
Coleford Rd SW18 . . . .158 A6
Cole Gdns TW5 . . . . . .128 A5
Colegrave Prim Sch
　E15. . . . . .76 B3
Colegrave Rd E15. . . . . .76 B3
Colegrove Rd SE15. . . .139 D6
Coleherne Ct
　SW10. . . . . . . .113 D1 255 D1
Coleherne Mans SW5 . .255 D2
Coleherne Mews
　SW10. . . . . . . .113 D1 255 C1
Coleherne Rd
　SW10. . . . . . . .113 D1 255 C1
Colehill Gdns SW6 . . . .264 A1
Colehill La
　SW6. . . . . . . .135 A4 264 B1
Cole Ho SE1 . . . . .251 B1
Coleman Cl SE25 . . . . .184 A1
Coleman Ct SW18. . . . .157 C4
Coleman Fields
　N1 . . . . .95 A6 235 B6
Coleman Mans N19 . . . .50 A2
Coleman Rd
　Belvedere DA17 . . . . . .125 C2
　Camberwell SE5 . . . . .139 C5
　Dagenham RM9. . . . . . .81 A2
Colemans Heath SE9. .166 D1
Coleman St EC2 .95 B1 242 C2
Coleman Street Bldgs
　EC2 . . . . .242 C2
Colenso Dr NW7 . . . . . .28 A3
Colenso Rd Ilford IG2. . . .57 C2
　Lower Clapton E5 . . . . . .74 C4
Cole Park Gdns TW1 . .153 A5
Cole Park Rd TW1 . . . .153 A5
Cole Park View 2
　TW1. . . . . .153 A5
Colepits Wood Rd
　SE9 . . . . .167 B6
Coleraine Park Prim Sch
　N17. . . . . .34 B2
Coleraine Rd
　Greenwich SE3 . . . . . .142 D6
　Hornsey N8, N22. . . . . . .50 C5
Cole Rd TW1 . . . . .153 A5
Coleridge Ave
　Carshalton SM1. . . . . .218 A4
　Plashet E12. . . . . .78 A2
Coleridge Cl SW8 . . . . .137 B3
Coleridge Ct
　Hammersmith W14. . . .112 D3
　15 New Barnet EN5 . . . .13 D6
　2 Richmond TW10. . . . .175 D6
Coleridge Gdns NW6. . . .70 D1
Coleridge Ho
　Pimlico SW1 . . . . .259 B1
　Walworth SE17 . . . . . .262 B2
　Wembley HA9 . . . . .65 D6
Coleridge Prim Sch N8 . .49 D2
Coleridge Rd
　Ashford TW15 . . . . . . .170 B6
　Crouch End N8 . . . . .49 D3
　Croydon CR0 . . . . .206 C2
　Finsbury Pk N4, N7 . . . .72 C5

Coleridge Rd continued
　North Finchley N12 . . . .30 A5
　Walthamstow E17. . . . . .53 B5
Coleridge Sq
　Chelsea SW10 . . . . . . .266 A4
　Ealing W13 . . . . .87 A1
Coleridge Way
　Borehamwood WD6 . . . .10 C6
　Hayes UB4. . . . . .84 A1
　West Drayton UB7 . . . .104 B2
Coleridge Wlk NW11. . . .47 C5
Colerne Ct NW4 . . . . . . .29 A1
Colesburg Rd BR3 . . . .185 B1
Coles Cres HA2 . . . . . . .63 D6
Coles Ct SW11 . . . . . . .266 D1
Coles Gn WD23 . . . . .8 A3
Coles Green Ct NW2 . . .68 A6
Coles Green Rd NW2. . . .68 B6
Coleshill Flats SW1 . . .258 B3
Coleshill Rd TW11 . . . .174 C6
Colestown St 4
　SW11. . . . . .136 C3
Coleswood N20. . . . . . . .14 C3
Colesworth Ho 1 HA8 . .27 A1
Colet Cl N13. . . . . .32 D4
Colet Gdns W14 . . . . . .112 D2
Colet Ho SE17 . . . . .261 D1
Colette Ct 5 SE16 . . . .118 D4
Coley St WC1 . . .94 B3 240 D5
Colfe & Hatchcliffe's Glebe
　SE13 . . . . .163 D6
Colfe Rd SE23 . . . . . . .163 B3
Colfe's Sch SE12. . . . . .165 A5
Colgate Ct EN5 . . . . . . .13 A6
Colgate Ho 13 SE13 . . .141 D3
Colgate Pl 10 EN3. . . . . .7 C6
Colham Ave UB7 . . . . .104 A5
COLHAM GREEN 82 C2
Colham Green Rd UB8. .82 C2
Colham Manor Prim Sch
　UB8. . . . . .82 C1
Colham Rd UB8. . . . . . .82 B3
Colina Mews N8, N15. . .50 D5
Colina Rd N8, N15. . . . .50 D4
Colin Blanchard Ho
　SE4 . . . . .141 C3
Colin Cl Colindale NW9 . . .45 C5
　Coney Hall BR4 . . . . . .224 D5
　Croydon CR0 . . . . .223 B5
Colin Cres NW9 . . . . . . .45 D5
Colin Ct Forest Hill SE6 . .163 B4
　Hendon NW9 . . . . .45 D5
　Streatham SW16 . . . . .159 D2
COLINDALE 45 C6
Colindale Ave NW9 . . . .45 C6
Colindale Bsns Pk
　NW9 . . . . .45 A6
Colindale Hospl NW9. . .45 C6
Colindale Prim Sch
　NW9 . . . . .45 D5
Colindale Sta NW9. . . . .45 C6
Colindeep Gdns NW4 . .46 A5
Colindeep La NW9,
　NW4 . . . . .45 D5
Colin Dr NW9. . . . . .45 D5
Colinette Rd SW15. . . .134 C1
Colin Gdns NW9 . . . . . .45 D5
Colin Par NW9. . . . . . . .45 C6
Colin Park Rd NW9 . . . .45 C5
Colin Pond Ct RM6. . . . .58 D6
Colin Rd NW10 . . . . . . .68 A2
Colinsdale N1 . . . . .234 C5
Colinton Rd IG3 . . . . . . .80 B6
Colin Winter Ho 45 E1 . .96 C3
Coliseum Apartments
　N8 . . . . .50 B4
Coliston Pas SW18. . . .157 C4
Coliston Rd SW18. . . . .157 C4
Collamore Ave SW18. . .158 C3
Collapit Cl HA1 . . . . .41 D3
Collard Pl NW1 . . . . . . .71 B1
Collard's Almshouses 1
　E17. . . . . .54 A4
Collcutt Lo SW4 . . . . . .138 A1
Collection Point N8. . . .50 A3
College App SE10. . . . .142 A6
College Ave HA3 . . . . . .24 C2
College Cl
　Edmonton N18. . . . . . . .33 D5
　Hackney E5 . . . . .74 C3
　Harrow HA3 . . . . .24 C3
　Twickenham TW2 . . . .152 B3
College Cres NW3 . . . .70 B2
College Cross N1 . . . . . .72 C1
College Ct
　Chelsea
　SW3. . . . . . . .114 D1 257 D1
　Croydon CR0 . . . . .222 A6
　Ealing W5 . . . . .110 A6
　Enfield EN3 . . . . .18 C6
　3 Hammersmith W6 . . .112 C1
　Hampstead NW3 . . . . . .70 B2
College Dr Ruislip HA4 . . .40 A2
　Thames Ditton KT7 . . . .196 C2
College Fields Bsns Ctr
　SW19 . . . . .180 B2
College Gdns
　Chingford E4 . . . . .20 A3
　Dulwich SE21 . . . . . . .161 C3
　Edmonton N18. . . . . . . .34 A5
　Enfield EN2 . . . . .5 B4
　New Malden KT3. . . . . .199 D4
　Redbridge IG4. . . . . . . .56 A4
　Upper Tooting SW17 . . .158 C2
College Gn SE19 . . . . .183 C3
College Gr NW1 . . . . . .232 C6
College Hill EC4 . . . . . .252 B6

College Hill Rd HA3. . . . .24 C3
College La NW5 . . . . . . .71 B4
College Mews 6
　SW18. . . . . .157 D6
COLLEGE PARK 90 B4
College Park Cl SE13. .142 B1
College Park Rd N17. . .33 D4
College Park Sch W2 . .91 D1
College Pl
　Camden Town
　NW1. . . . . .93 C6 232 B5
　Chelsea SW10 . . . . . . .266 A4
　Walthamstow E17 . . . . . .54 C5
College Pt 3 E15 . . . . . .76 D2
College Rd
　Dulwich SE19, SE21 . . .161 C2
　Ealing W13 . . . . .87 B1
　Enfield EN2 . . . . .5 B3
　Harrow HA1 . . . . .42 C3
　Harrow Weald HA3. . . . .24 C2
　Hounslow TW7 . . . . . .130 D4
　Kensal Green NW10 . . . .90 C5
　Mitcham SW19 . . . . . .180 A6
　Plaistow BR1. . . . . . . .187 A3
　South Croydon CR0 . . . .221 B6
　Southgate N21 . . . . . . .16 C2
　Tottenham N17 . . . . . . .33 D4
　Walthamstow E17. . . . . .54 A4
　Wembley HA9 . . . . .43 D1
College Rdbt 1 KT1. . .198 A2
College St EC4 . .117 A6 252 B6
College Terr Bow E3. . . .97 B4
　Church End N3 . . . . .29 B1
College View SE9 . . . . .165 D3
College Way
　Ashford TW15 . . . . . . .170 B6
　Hayes UB3. . . . . .106 A6
College Wlk 10 KT1 . . .198 A6
Collent Ho 12 E9. . . . . . .74 C2
Collent St E9 . . . . .74 C2
Collerston Ho SE10 . . .120 D1
Colless Rd N15 . . . . . . .51 D4
Collette Ct SE25 . . . . . .205 C4
Collette Ho N16 . . . . . . .51 D1
Collett Ho SE13 . . . . . .141 D2
Collett Rd SE16 . . . . . .118 A3
Collett Way UB2 . . . . . .107 D4
Colley Ho 12 N7 . . . . . . .71 D3
Collier Cl Newham E16 . .122 D6
　West Ewell KT19 . . . . . .214 D2
Collier Dr HA8 . . . . .26 C1
Colliers Shaw BR2 . . . .225 D3
Collier St N1 . . . . .95 B5 233 C3
Colliers Water La CR7. .204 C4
Colliers Wood SW19 . .180 B3
COLLIER'S WOOD 180 C4
Collier's Wood Sta
　SW19 . . . . .180 B3
Collindale Ave
　Erith DA8. . . . . .147 D6
　Sidcup DA15 . . . . .168 A3
Collingbourne Rd
　W12. . . . . .112 B5
Collingham Gdns
　SW5. . . . . . . .113 D2 255 D3
Collingham Pl
　SW5. . . . . . . .113 D2 255 D3
Collingham Rd
　SW5. . . . . . . .113 D2 255 D3
Collingham Sixth Form
　Coll SW5 . . . . .113 D2 255 D3
Collings Cl N22 . . . . . . .32 B4
Collington Ho 2 SE7. . .143 B6
Collington St SE10. . . .120 B1
Collingtree Rd SE26. . .184 C6
Collingwood Ave
　London N10. . . . . .49 A5
　Tolworth KT5 . . . . .199 A1
Collingwood Cl
　2 Penge SE20 . . . . . . .184 B2
　Twickenham TW2, TW4 . .151 C4
Collingwood Ct
　London NW4 . . . . .46 C4
　New Barnet EN5 . . . . . .13 D6
　Sutton SM1 . . . . .217 C4
Collingwood Ho
　27 Bethnal Green E1 . . . .96 B3
　Marylebone W1 . . . . . .239 A4
Collingwood Rd
　Hillingdon UB8 . . . . . . .82 D3
　Mitcham CR4. . . . . . . .202 C6
　South Tottenham N15 . . .51 C5
　Sutton SM1 . . . . .217 C4
Collingwood Sch SM6. .219 B3
Collingwood St E1. . . . .96 B3
Collins Ave HA7 . . . . . . .26 A1
Collins Ct Dalston E8. . . .74 A2
　3 Loughton IG10. . . . . . .21 D6
Collins Dr HA4 . . . . .62 C6
Collins Ho
　8 Barking IG11 . . . . . . .78 D1
　16 Cubitt Town SE10. . .120 D1
　4 Poplar E14. . . . . . . .120 A6
Collinson Ct
　Borough The SE1. . . . .252 A1
　Edgware HA8 . . . . .26 B6
Collinson Ho 14 SE15. .140 A5
Collinson St SE1 . . . . . .252 A1
Collinson Wlk SE1 . . . .252 A1
Collins Rd N5, N16 . . . . .73 A4
Collins Sq SE3 . . . . . . .142 D3
Collins St SE3 . . . . .142 C3
Collins'Yd N1 . . . . .234 C5
Collinwood Ave EN3 . . . .6 C2
Collinwood Gdns IG5 . . .56 C5
Collison Pl N16. . . . . . . .51 C1
Collis Prim Sch TW11. .175 B4
Coll of Arms*
　EC4. . . . . .117 A6 252 A6

Coll of Central London
The EC2 243 A6
Coll of Law The
EC1 95 B3 242 C5
Coll of North East London
The N15 51 D5
Coll of NW London
NW6 91 C6
Coll of NW London
(Willesden Centre)
NW10 67 D3
Coll of Optometrists The
SW1 250 A4
Coll Sharp Ct 42 E2 95 D4
Coll's Rd SE15 140 C4
Collyer Ave CR0 220 A4
Collyer Pl SE15 140 A4
Collyer Rd CR0 220 A4
Colman Ct London N12 30 A4
Stanmore HA7 25 B4
Colman Rd E16 99 C2
Colmans Wharf 5 E14 97 D2
Colmar Cl 3 E1 96 D3
Colmer Pl HA3 24 B3
Colmer Rd SW16 182 A3
Colmore Ct NW4 46 A6
Colmore Mews SE15 140 B4
Colmore Rd EN3 6 C1
Colnbrook Ct SW17 180 B6
Colnbrook St SE1 261 C6
Colne Ct Ealing W7 86 B1
West Ewell KT19 215 A4
Colne Ho Barking IG11 78 D2
Paddington NW8 236 D5
Colne Rd Clapton Pk E5 75 A4
Southgate N21 17 B4
Twickenham TW1, TW2 152 C3
Colne St E13 99 A4
COLNEY HATCH 30 C4
Colney Hatch N10 31 A3
Colney Hatch La N10 31 A3
Cologne Rd SW11 136 B1
Coloma Convent Girls Sch
CR0 222 D5
Colombo Rd IG1 57 A2
Colombo St SE1 251 C3
Colomb St SE10 120 C1
Colonades The 4 SE5 139 B4
Colonels Wlk EN2 4 D2
Colonial Ave TW2 152 A5
Colonial Dr W4 111 A2
Colonial Rd TW14 149 C4
Colonnade WC1 240 B5
Colonnade Ho SE3 142 D3
Colonnades The
Croydon CR0 220 C2
6 Hackney E8 74 B2
Colonnade The 12
SE8 119 B2
Colorado Bldg 9
SE13 141 D4
Colosseum Ct N3 29 B1
Colosseum Ret Pk EN1 6 A1
Colosseum Terr NW1 238 D6
Colour Ho SE1 253 B1
Colroy Ct NW4 47 A4
Colson Rd CR0 221 C6
Colson Way SW16 181 C6
Colstead Ho 22 E1 96 B1
Colsterworth Rd N15 51 D5
Colston Ave SM1, SM5 218 C4
Colston Ct SM5 218 D4
Colston Rd
Mortlake SW14 133 A1
Upton E7 77 D2
Colthurst Cres N4 73 A6
Colthurst Dr N9 18 B1
Coltman Ho SE10 142 A6
Coltman St E14 97 A2
Colt Mews 5 EN3 7 C6
Coltness Cres SE2 124 B1
Colton Gdns N17 51 A6
Colton Rd HA1 42 C4
Coltsfoot Dr UB7 82 A1
Coltswood Ct N14 15 D3
Colts Yd E11 54 D2
Columba Ho SE14 141 B4
Columbas Dr NW3 48 B1
Columbia Ave
Edgware HA8 26 D2
New Malden KT4 199 D2
Ruislip HA4 40 B1
Columbia Ct
Edgware HA8 26 D2
New Malden KT3 199 D2
Columbia Ho 18 E3 97 C4
Columbia Point 7
SE16 118 C3
Columbia Prim Sch E2 95 D4
Columbia Rd
9 Hackney E2 96 A5
Newham E13 98 D3
Shoreditch E2 95 D4
Columbia Road Mkt E2 95 D4
Columbine Ave
Croydon CR2 220 D1
Newham E6 100 A2
Columbus Gdns HA6 22 A2
Colveiw Ct SE9 165 D3
Colverson Ho 14 E1 96 C2
Colvestone Cres E8 73 D3
Colvestone Prim Sch
E8 73 D3
Colville Gdns W11 91 B1
Colville Ho
32 Bethnal Green E2 96 C5
Notting Hill W11 91 B1
Colville Mews W11 91 B1
Colville Pl W1 239 B3
Colville Prim Sch W11 91 B1
Colville Rd Edmonton N9 18 B3
Higham Hill E17 35 A1
Leyton E11 76 A5
Notting Hill W11 91 B1
South Acton W3 110 D3
Colville Sq W11 91 B1
Colville Terr W11 91 B1
Colvin Cl SE26 184 C5
Colvin Gdns
Chingford E4 20 A1
Wanstead E11 55 B5
Colvin Rd
Thornton Heath CR7 204 C4
Upton Pk E6 78 A1
Colwall Gdns IG8 37 A5
Colwall Ho 18 SW9 138 B3
Colwell Rd SE22 161 D6
Colwick Cl N6 49 D2
Colwith Rd W6 134 C6
Colwood Gdns SW19 180 B3
Colworth Gr SE17 262 B3
Colworth Rd
Croydon CR0 206 A1
Leytonstone E11 54 C2
Colwyn Ave UB6 86 D5
Colwyn Cl SW16 181 C5
Colwyn Cres TW3 130 A4
Colwyn Gn NW9 45 C3
Colwyn Ho SE1 261 A5
Colwyn Rd NW2 68 B5
Colyer Cl SE9 166 D2
Colyer Ho SE2 124 D1
Colyton Cl Erith DA16 146 D4
Wembley HA0 65 C2
Colyton La 14 SW16 182 C5
Colyton Rd SE22 162 B6
Colyton Way N18 34 A5
Combe Ave SE3 142 D5
Combedale Rd SE10 121 A1
Combe Ho
Mortlake SW14 133 A3
20 Paddington W2 91 C2
Combe Lane Sta CR0 222 C5
Combemartin Rd
SW18 157 A3
Combe Mews 4 SE3 142 D5
Comber Cl NW2 68 B6
Comber Gr SE5 139 A5
Comber Grove Prim Sch
SE5 139 A5
Comber Ho SE5 139 A5
Combermere Rd
London SW9 138 B2
Morden SM4 201 D4
Comberton 10 KT1 176 C1
Comberton Rd E5 74 B6
Combeside SE18 145 D5
Combes Rd RM9 81 B1
Combe The NW1 231 D1
Combwell Cres SE2 124 A3
Com Coll Hackney The
E8 96 B6
Comely Bank Rd E17 54 A4
Comeragh Mews W14 254 B1
Comeragh Rd
W14 113 A1 254 B1
Comer Cres UB2 108 A4
Comerford Rd SE4 141 B1
Comer Ho 10 EN5 2 A1
Comet Cl E12 77 D4
Comet Pl SE8 141 C5
Comet St SE8 141 C5
Comins Ho SW4 159 C6
Commerce Est E18 37 C1
Commerce Pk CR0 220 B6
Commerce Rd
Brentford TW8 131 C5
Wood Green N22 32 B2
Commerce Way CR0 220 B6
Commercial Rd
Edmonton N18 33 C4
Stepney E1 96 C1
Whitechapel E1 96 A1
Commercial St
E1 95 D2 243 C4
Commercial Way
Peckham SE15 140 A5
Wembley NW10 88 D5
Commerell Pl SE10 120 D1
Commerell St SE10 120 C1
Commodity Quay E1 253 D5
Commodore Ct SE8 141 C4
Commodore Ho 7
E14 120 A6
Commodore St E1 97 A3
Commondale SW15 134 C2
Common La KT10 213 A1
Common Rd
Barnes SW13 134 A2
Claygate KT10 213 A1
Stanmore HA7 8 C1
Commonside BR2 225 C4
Commonside Ct SW16 182 A4
Commonside E CR4 203 B6
Commonside W CR4 203 A6
Common The
Ealing W5 110 A5
Southall UB2 106 D2
Stanmore HA7 8 D2
1 Stratford E15 76 D2
Common View SW15 134 C2
Commonwealth Ave
Hayes UB3 83 B1
21 Shepherd's Bush
W12 112 B6
25 Shepherd's Bush
W12 112 B6
Commonwealth Ho
WC1 240 B2
Commonwealth Rd
N17 34 A3
Commonwealth Way
SE2 124 C1
Community Cl
Cranford TW5 128 B4
Uxbridge UB10 61 A5
Community Rd
Greenford UB6 86 A6
Stratford New Town E15 76 B3
Comodore Ho SW18 136 A1
Como Rd SE23 163 A2
Compania Bldg 12 E1 118 D6
Compass Cl
Edgware HA8 26 B6
Littleton TW15 171 A3
Compass Ct SE1 253 C3
Compass Hill TW10 153 D5
Compass Ho
Bayswater W2 91 D1
London SE8 141 D3
Compass Point 10
E14 119 C6
Compayne Gdns NW6 69 D1
Compton Ave
Islington N1 72 D2
London N6 48 C2
Newham E6 99 D5
Wembley HA0 65 C4
Compton Cl
5 Burnt Oak HA8 27 A3
Camberwell SE15 139 D5
Cricklewood NW11 68 D5
Ealing W13 87 A1
Esher KT10 212 B3
Regent's Pk NW1 231 D1
Compton Cres
Chessington KT9 214 A2
Chiswick W4 133 A6
Northolt UB5 84 D6
Tottenham N17 33 A3
Compton Ct London N12 30 A2
Sutton SM1 218 A4
9 West Norwood
SE19 183 C5
Compton Ho SW11 267 A2
Compton Lo N21 16 D3
Compton Pas EC1 241 D6
Compton Pl
Bloomsbury WC1 240 A6
South Oxhey WD19 23 A6
Compton Rd
Croydon CR0 206 B1
Hayes UB3 105 D6
Islington N1 72 D2
Kensal Green NW10 90 D4
Southgate N21 16 D3
Wimbledon SW19 179 B4
Compton Rise HA5 41 B4
Compton Sch The N12 30 C4
Compton St
EC1 94 D3 241 D6
Compton Terr
Islington N1 72 D2
Southgate N21 16 C3
Comreddy Cl EN2 4 D4
Comus Ho SE17 263 A3
Comus Pl SE17 117 C2 263 A3
Comyn Rd SW11 136 C1
Comyns Cl E16 98 D2
Comyns Rd RM9 81 C1
Comyns The WD23 8 A3
Conal Ct SW16 181 D5
Conant Ho SE11 138 D6
Conant Mews 1 E1 118 A6
Concanon Rd SW2,
SW4 138 B1
Concert Hall App
SE1 116 B5 250 D3
Concord Bsns Ctr W3 88 D2
Concord Cl UB5 85 A4
Concord Ct KT1 198 B6
Concorde Cl
Hounslow TW3 129 D3
Uxbridge UB10 82 A5
Concorde Dr E6 100 B2
Concorde Way SE16 118 D2
Concord Ho
Kingston u T KT3 199 C6
5 Tottenham N17 33 D3
Concordia Wharf 10
E14 120 A5
Concord Rd Acton W3 88 D3
Enfield EN3 18 C6
Concord Terr HA2 63 D6
Concourse The
32 Edgware NW9 27 D2
7 Edmonton N9 18 A2
Condell Rd
SW8 137 C4 269 B1
Conder St E14 97 A1
Condor Path UB5 85 C5
Condover Cres SE18 144 D5
Condray Pl SW11 267 A3
Conduit Ct WC2 250 A6
Conduit Ho SE10 142 B4
Conduit La London N18 34 C5
South Croydon CR0 222 A3
Conduit Mews
W2 92 B1 236 C1
Conduit Pas W2 236 C1
Conduit Pl W2 236 C1
Conduit Rd SE18 122 D1
Conduit St W1 115 C6 249 A6
Conduit Way NW10 67 A1
Conewood St N5 72 D5
Coney Acre SE21 161 A3
Coney Burrows E4 20 C2
Coney Gr UB8 82 C4
Coneygrove Path UB5 63 A2
CONEY HALL 224 D5
Coney Hall Par BR4 224 C5
Coney Hall Rdbt BR4 224 C5
Coney Hill Rd BR4 224 D6
Coney Way SW8 270 D5
Conference Cl 3 E4 20 A2
Conference Ho UB8 83 A1
Conference Rd SE2 124 C2
Congers Ho SE8 141 C5
Congleton Gr SE18 123 A1
Congo Dr N9 18 C1
Congo Rd SE18 123 B1
Congress Ho WC1 239 D2
Congress Rd SE2 124 C2
Congreve Ho 10 N16 73 C3
Congreve Rd SE9 144 B2
Congreve St
SE17 117 C2 263 A3
Congreve Wlk 6 E16 99 D2
Conical Cnr EN2 5 A3
Conifer Cl BR6 227 B4
Conifer Ct
Ashford TW15 170 B5
Hendon NW4 28 C1
Ilford IG1 78 D2
23 Putney SW19 156 D3
Sutton SM2 218 B2
Conifer Gdns
Enfield EN1 17 C5
Streatham SW16 160 B1
Sutton SM1 217 D6
Conifer Ho SE4 141 B1
Conifers Cl TW11 175 C3
Conifer Way
Hayes UB3 106 A6
Wembley HA0 65 C5
Coniger Rd SW6 135 C3
Coningham Ct SW10 266 B4
Coningham Mews
W12 112 A5
Coningham Rd W12 112 B4
Coningsby Ave NW9 27 C1
Coningsby Cotts W5 109 D4
Coningsby Ct 4 CR4 181 A1
Coningsby Gdns E4 35 D4
Coningsby Rd
Ealing W5 109 D4
Harringay N4 50 D2
Conington Rd SE13 142 A3
Conisbee Ct 3 N14 15 C6
Conisborough Cres
SE6 164 A1
Conisbrough NW1 232 A5
Coniscliffe Cl BR7 188 C2
Coniscliffe Rd N13 17 A1
Coniston NW1 232 A2
Coniston Ave
Barking IG11 79 C1
Ealing UB6 87 B4
Falconwood DA16 145 C2
Coniston Cl
Barking IG11 79 C1
Barnes SW13 133 D5
Chiswick W4 133 A5
West Barnes SM4 200 D3
Whetstone N20 14 A1
Coniston Ct
Beckenham BR3 186 A2
Chessington KT9 214 A5
Edgware HA8 26 B5
4 Finchley NW7 29 A3
Marylebone W2 237 B1
Penge SE26 184 B4
6 Rotherhithe SE16 118 D4
3 Wallington SM6 219 B4
Conistone Way N7 72 A1
Coniston Gdns
Edmonton N9 18 C3
Kingsbury NW9 45 B4
Pinner HA5 40 A5
Redbridge IG4 56 A5
Sutton SM2 218 B2
Wembley HA9 43 C1
Coniston Ho 14 Bow E3 97 B4
18 Camberwell SE5 139 A5
Coniston Rd
Catford BR1 186 C4
Croydon CR0 206 A2
Muswell Hill N10 31 B1
Tottenham N17 34 A4
Twickenham TW2 151 D5
Coniston Way KT9 214 A5
Coniston Wlk E9 74 C3
Conlan St W10 91 A3
Conley Rd NW10 67 C2
Conley St SE10 120 C1
Connaught Ave
Ashford TW15 170 A6
Barnet EN4 14 D3
Chingford E4 20 B4
Enfield EN1 5 C3
Hounslow TW4 129 A1
Mortlake SW14 133 A1
Connaught Bridge
E16 121 D6
Connaught Bsns Ctr
London NW9 45 D4
Mitcham CR4 202 D4
Wallington CR0 220 B2
Connaught Cl
Carshalton SM1 218 B6
Enfield EN1 5 C3
Hillingdon UB8 83 A3
Lea Bridge E10 75 A6
Marylebone W2 237 B1
Connaught Ct
1 Chingford E4 20 C4
9 Walthamstow E17 53 D5
Connaught Day Hospl
E11 54 C3
Connaught Dr NW11 47 C5
Connaught Gdns
Cranley Gdns N10 49 B4
Edmonton N13 32 D6
Morden SM4 202 A5
Connaught Grange
N13 32 D6
Connaught Ho
College Pk NW10 90 B4
London N10 49 B4
Mayfair W1 248 C5
Connaught Hts UB10 83 A3
Connaught La IG1 79 B6
Connaught Lo N4 50 C2
Connaught Mans
Battersea SW11 267 B1
3 Brixton SW9 138 C1
15 Canonbury N16 73 B4
Fulham SW6 264 A2
Connaught Mews
Ilford IG1 79 B6
Woolwich SE18 122 C1
Connaught Pl W2 237 C1
Connaught Rd
Barnet EN5 12 D5
Carshalton SM1 218 B6
Chingford E4 20 C3
Ealing W13 109 B6
Finsbury Pk N4 50 C2
Harlesden NW10 89 C5
Harrow HA3 24 D2
Ilford IG1 79 B6
Leytonstone E11 54 B1
Newham E16 121 D5
New Malden KT3 199 C5
5 Richmond TW10 154 B6
Teddington TW11,
TW12 174 B5
Walthamstow E17 53 C4
Woolwich SE18 122 D1
Connaught Sch for Girls
E11 54 C1
Connaught Sch for Girls
(Annexe) E11 76 C6
Connaught Sq
W2 92 D1 237 C1
Connaught St
W2 92 C1 237 B1
Connaught Way N13 32 D6
Connaught Works E3 97 A6
Connections Ho N2 30 B2
Connell Cres W5 88 B3
Connell Ct 6 SE14 140 D6
Connell Ho 6 SM6 219 C2
Connemara Cl WD6 11 B5
Conniffe Ct SE9 166 D6
Connington 5 KT1 176 C1
Connington Cres E4 20 B1
Connolly Ho SW19 180 A4
Connoly Ct NW2 68 B5
Connop Rd EN3 6 D5
Connor Cl E11 54 C2
Connor Ct SW11 268 C1
Connor Rd RM9 81 B4
Connor St E9 96 D6
Conolly Rd W7 108 C5
Conrad Dr KT4 200 D1
Conrad Ho
8 Limehouse SE16 119 A6
South Lambeth SW8 270 A4
12 Stoke Newington N16 73 C3
Conrad Twr W3 110 D3
Conroy Ct 6 DA14 190 A6
Conservatory Ct SE19 183 C3
Consfield Ave KT3 200 A4
Consort Ho
Bayswater W2 245 D5
Edgware NW7 27 D5
Consort Lo NW8 230 C5
Consort Mews TW7 152 B6
Consort Rd SE15 140 B3
Cons St SE1 251 B2
Constable Ave E16 121 B5
Constable Cl
12 Friern Barnet N11 30 D5
Hampstead Garden Suburb
NW11 47 D3
Hayes UB4 83 A5
Constable Cres N15 52 A4
Constable Ct 11 SE16 118 B1
Constable Gdns
Edgware HA8 26 C1
Isleworth TW7 152 B6
Constable Ho
Enfield EN1 18 A6
25 Millwall E14 119 C4
13 Northolt UB5 84 D5
Primrose Hill NW3 70 D1
Constable Mews RM8 80 B4
Constable Wlk SE21 161 C1
Constance Cres BR2 208 D1
Constance Ct N10 31 B3
Constance Rd
Enfield EN1 17 C5
Sutton SM1 218 A4
Thornton Heath CR0 204 D2
Twickenham TW2 151 D4
Constance St E16 122 A5
Constant Ho 26 E14 119 D6
Constantine Ho SW2 160 D3
Constantine Pl UB10 82 B6
Constantine Rd NW3 70 C4
Constitution Hill SW1,
W1 115 B4 248 D2
Constitution Rise
SE18 144 C4
Consul Ho 5 E3 97 C3
Content St
SE17 117 B2 262 C3
Contessa Cl BR6 227 C3
Control Tower Rd
TW6 126 D2
Convair Wlk 11 UB5 84 D4
Convent Cl BR3 186 A3
Convent Gdns
Ealing W5 109 C2
Notting Hill W11 91 B1
Convent Hill SE19 183 A4
Convent Lo TW15 170 D5
Convent of Jesus & Mary
Language Coll NW10 89 D6
Convent of Jesus & Mary
RC Inf Sch NW2 68 C2
Convent Rd TW15 170 D5
Convent Way UB2 106 D2
Conway Cl HA7 25 A4
Conway Cres
Dagenham RM6 58 C3
Greenford UB6 86 C5
Conway Dr
Ashford TW15 171 A4
Hayes UB3 105 A3
Sutton SM2 217 D2
Conway Gdns Enfield EN2 5 C5
Mitcham CR4 204 A5
Wembley HA9 43 C2
Conway Gr W3 89 B2
Conway Ho
Chelsea SW3 257 D1
5 Millwall E14 119 D2
6 Streatham SW2 160 A3
Conway Mews W1 239 A5
Conway Prim Sch
SE18 123 C2
Conway Rd
Dollis Hill NW2 68 C6
Feltham TW13 172 D5
Harlington TW6 126 D2
Harringay N15 51 A4
Palmers Green N14 16 A1
Plumstead SE18 123 C2
Twickenham TW4 151 C4
Wimbledon SW20 178 C2
Conway St W1 93 C3 239 A5
Conway Wlk TW12 173 B4
Conybeare NW3 70 C1
Conyers Cl IG8 36 C4
Conyer's Rd SW16 181 D5
Conyer St 21 E3 97 A5
Cooden Cl BR1 187 B3
Cookes Cl E11 76 D6
Cookes La SM3 217 A2
Cooke St 3 IG11 101 A6
Cookham Cl UB2 107 D4
Cookham Cres SE16 118 D4
Cookham Dene Cl
BR7 189 B2
Cookham Ho E2 243 C6
Cookham Rd BR8,
DA14 191 C2
Cookhill Rd SE2 124 B3
Cooks Ferry N18 34 D5
Cook's Hole Rd EN2 5 A5
Cookson Gr DA8 147 D5
Cook's Rd
Camberwell SE17 138 D6
Stratford Marsh E15 97 D5
Coolfin Rd E16 99 B1
Coolgardie Ave E4 36 B5
Coolgardie Rd TW15 171 A5
Coolhurst Rd N8 49 D3
Cool Oak La NW9 45 D2
Coomassie Rd W9 91 B3
COOMBE 177 B3
Coombe Ave CR0 221 C4
Coombe Bank KT2,
KT3 177 C2
Coombe Boys' Sch
KT3 200 A4
Coombe Cl
Edgware HA8 26 B1
Hounslow TW3 129 C1
Coombe Cnr N21 16 D3
Coombe Cres TW12 173 A3
Coombe Ct 2 BR3 185 B2
Coombe Dr HA4 40 B1
Coombe End KT2 177 B3
Coombefield Cl KT3 199 C4
Coombe Gdns
New Malden KT3 199 D5
Wimbledon SW20 178 A2
Coombe Girls Sch
KT3 177 B1
Coombe Hill Glade
KT2 177 C3
Coombe Hill Inf Sch
KT2 177 B2
Coombe Hill Jun Sch
KT2 177 B2
Coombe Hill Rd KT2 177 C3
Coombe Ho 18 N7 71 D3
Coombe House Chase
KT3 177 B2
Coombehurst Cl EN4 2 D3
Coombehurst (Kingston
University) KT2 177 A5
Coombe La CR0 222 B3
Coombe Lane Flyover
SW20 177 D2
Coombe La W KT2 177 B2
Coombe Lea BR1 210 A6
Coombe Lo SE7 143 C6
Coombe Neville KT2 177 B3
Coombe Pk KT2 177 B5
Coombe Pl KT2 177 A5
Coombe Rd Bushey WD23 8 B4
Chiswick W4 111 C1

Coombe Rd *continued*
Ealing W13 109 B3
Forest Hill SE26 184 B6
Hampton TW12 173 B4
New Malden KT3 199 C6
Norbiton KT2 176 C2
South Croydon CR0, CR2 221 C4
Willesden NW10 67 B5
Wood Green N22 32 C2
Coomber Ho SW6 135 D2
Coombe Ridings KT2 177 A5
Coombe Rise KT2 177 A2
Coomber Way CR0 203 D3
Coombes Rd RM9 103 B6
Coombe Wlk SM1 217 D5
Coombewood Dr RM6 59 B3
Coombe Wood Rd KT2 177 A5
Coombs St N1 234 D3
Coomer Mews SW6 264 D5
Coomer Pl SW6 135 B6 264 D5
Cooms Wlk HA8 27 A2
Cooperage Cl 5 N17 33 D4
Cooperage The SE1 253 C3
Cooper Ave E17 35 A2
Cooper Cl SE1 251 B1
Cooper Cres SM5 218 D5
Cooper Ct
Shooters Hill SE18 144 D6
Stratford New Town E15 76 A3
Cooper Ho
Hounslow TW4 129 B2
Paddington NW8 236 C5
Upper Tooting SW17 180 B6
7 West Norwood SE27 182 D5
Cooper Rd
Croydon CR0, CR9 220 D4
Hendon NW4 46 D3
Willesden NW10 68 A3
Coopersale Cl 3 IG8 37 C3
Coopersale Rd E9 74 D3
Coopers Cl
Bethnal Green E1 96 C3
Dagenham RM10 81 D2
Coopers Ct
9 Acton W3 111 A5
4 Friern Barnet N20 14 D1
Isleworth TW7 130 D3
Tower Hamlets E3 97 B3
Coopers La
Grove Pk SE12 165 B2
Somers Town NW1 232 D3
Cooper's La E10 54 A1
Cooper's Lane Prim Sch SE12 165 B2
Coopers Lo SE1 253 C2
Coopers Mews BR3 185 C1
Cooper's Rd SE1 117 D1 263 D2
Cooper's Row EC3 117 D6 253 C6
Cooper St 10 E16 98 D2
Coopers Tech Sch BR7 189 A2
Coopers Yd N1 72 D1
Cooper's Yd SE19 183 C4
Coote Gdns RM8 81 B5
Coote Rd
Dagenham RM8 81 B5
Erith DA7 147 B4
Cope Ho EC1 235 B1
Copeland Dr E14 119 C2
Copeland Ho
Lambeth SE11 260 D5
Upper Tooting SW17 180 B6
Copeland Rd
London SE15 140 B3
Walthamstow E17 53 D3
Copelands BR3 185 B3
Copeman Cl SE26 184 C5
Copenhagen Gdns W4 111 B4
Copenhagen Ho N1 234 A5
Copenhagen Pl E14 97 B1
Copenhagen Prim Sch N1 94 B6 233 C5
Copenhagen St N1 94 B6 233 C5
Cope Pl W8 113 C3 255 A5
Copers Cope Rd BR3 185 B3
Cope St SE16 118 D2
Copeswood Ct UB7 126 C5
Copford Wlk N1 235 A6
Copgate Path SW16 182 C4
Copinger Wlk HA8 26 D2
Copland Ave HA0 65 D3
Copland Cl HA0 65 C3
Copland Com Sch & Tech Ctr HA9 66 B3
Copland Ho UB1 107 B4
Copland Mews 8 HA0 66 A2
Copland Rd HA0 66 A2
Copleston Rd SE15 139 D2
Copley Cl
15 Camberwell SE17 138 D6
Ealing W7 86 D2
Copley Dene BR1 187 D2
Copley Pk SW16 182 B4
Copley Rd HA7 25 C5
Coppard Gdns KT9 213 C2
Coppedhall 2 SE21 161 B2
Coppelia Rd SE3 142 D1
Coppen Rd RM8 59 B2
Copperas St SE8 141 D6
Copper Beech N6 49 A2
Copperbeech Cl NW3 70 B3
Copper Beech Ct N20 14 A1
Copper Beeches TW7 130 B4
Copper Cl Penge SE19 183 D3
Tottenham N17 34 B3
Copperdale Rd UB3 106 A4
Copperfield Ave UB8 82 C3
Copperfield Ct
Blackheath SE3 142 D2
Ilford IG6 57 A6
Copperfield Dr N15 51 D5
Copperfield Ho 12 SE1 118 A4
Copperfield Mews N18 33 C5
Copperfield Rd
Stepney E3 97 A2
Thamesmead SE28 102 C1
Copperfields
5 Beckenham BR3 186 A2
Harrow HA1 42 C2
Copperfields Ct W3 110 C4
Copperfield St SE1 117 A4 252 A2
Copperfield Way
Chislehurst BR7 189 A4
Pinner HA5 41 B5
Coppergate Cl BR1 187 B2
Coppermead Cl NW2 68 C5
Copper Mews 15 W4 111 A3
Copper Mill Dr TW7 130 D3
Coppermill La E17 52 D4
Copper Mill La SW17 180 A6
Coppermill Prim Sch E17 52 D4
Copper Row SE1 253 C3
Copperwood Lo EN2 4 D3
Coppetts Cl N12 30 D3
Coppetts Ctr N12 30 D3
Coppetts Rd N10 30 D2
Coppetts Wood Hospl N10 30 D2
Coppetts Wood Prim Sch N10 31 A2
Coppice Cl
Beckenham BR3 207 D5
Harrow HA7 24 D4
Ruislip HA4 39 B3
West Barnes SW20 200 C6
Coppice Dr SW15 156 B5
Coppice The
Ashford TW15 170 D4
Enfield EN2 4 D1
Hillingdon UB7 82 A1
New Barnet EN5 13 D5
Coppice Way E18 54 D6
Coppice Wlk N20 13 C1
Coppies Gr N11 31 B6
Copping Cl CR0 221 C4
Coppin Ho SW2 160 D3
Coppins The
2 Ilford RM6 58 B2
New Addington CR0 223 D2
Stanmore HA3 24 C4
Coppock Cl SW11 136 C3
Coppsfield KT8 195 C6
Copse Ave BR4 223 D5
Copse Cl SE7 143 B6
Copse Ct SW15 157 A6
Copse Glade KT6 197 D1
COPSE HILL 178 B3
Copse Hill
Belmont SM2 217 D1
Wimbledon SW20 178 B3
Copsem Dr KT10 212 A2
Copsem La KT10 212 A1
Copsem Way KT10 212 A2
Copse The Chingford E4 20 D3
Muswell Hill N2 48 D6
Copse View CR2 223 A1
Copsewood Cl DA15 167 C5
Coptefield Dr DA17 125 A3
Copthall Ave EC2 95 B1 242 D2
Copthall Bldgs EC2 242 D2
Copthall Cl EC2 242 C2
Copthall Dr NW7 28 A4
Copthall Gdns
Hendon NW7 28 A3
Twickenham TW1 152 D3
Copthall Rd E UB10 60 C5
Copthall Rd W UB10 60 C6
Copthall Sch NW7 28 B3
Copthall Sports Ctr NW4 28 B2
Copthorne Ave
Bromley BR2 226 B6
Streatham SW12 159 D4
Copthorne Chase 3 TW15 170 B6
Copthorne Cl TW17 193 A3
Copthorne Ct SM1 218 A5
Copthorne Mews UB3 105 C2
Coptic St WC1 94 A2 240 A3
Copton Cl E3 97 C2
Copwood Cl N12 30 B6
Coral Apts 6 E16 121 A6
Coral Cl RM6 58 C6
Coral Ho 5 E1 97 A3
Coraline Cl UB1 85 B4
Coralline Wlk 4 SE2 124 C4
Coral Row 14 SW11 136 A2
Coral St SE1 116 C4 251 B1
Coram Ho
Bloomsbury WC1 240 A6
8 Chiswick W4 111 C1
Coram Mans WC1 240 C5
Coram St WC1 94 A3 240 A5
Coran Cl N9 18 D4
Corban Rd TW3 129 C2
Corbar Cl EN4 2 B4
Corbden Cl SE15 139 D4
Corbet Cl CR4, SM6 219 A6
Corbet Ct EC3 242 D1
Corbet Ho N1 234 A5
Corbet Pl E1 95 D2 243 C4
Corbett Ct SE26 185 B6
Corbett Gr N22 32 A3
Corbett Ho SW10 266 A6
Corbett Rd
Walthamstow E17 54 A6
Wanstead E11 55 C3
Corbett's La SE16 118 C2
Corbetts Pas 8 SE16 118 C2
Corbett Villas RM8 58 C1
Corbicum E11 54 C2
Corbidge Ct SE8 141 D6
Corbiere Ct SW19 178 D4
Corbiere Ho 5 N1 95 C6
Corbin Ho 7 E3 97 D4
Corbin's La HA2 63 D5
Corbridge 5 N17 34 B3
Corbridge Cres E2 96 B5
Corbridge Ho SE2 124 C3
Corby Cres EN2 4 A1
Corbylands Rd DA15 167 C3
Corbyn St N4, N19 50 A1
Corby Rd NW10 89 B5
Corby Way E3 97 C3
Cordelia Cl SE24 138 D1
Cordelia Gdns TW19 148 A4
Cordelia Ho 28 N1 95 C5
Cordelia Rd TW19 148 A4
Cordelia St E14 97 D1
Cordell Ho N15 51 D4
Cordingley Rd HA4 61 B6
Cording St E14 97 D2
Cordwainers Ct 18 E9 74 C1
Cordwainers Wlk 9 E13 99 A5
Cordwain Ho 7 N18 34 A5
Cordwell Rd SE13 164 C6
Corefield Cl N11 15 A2
Corelli Rd SE3 144 A4
Corfe Ave HA2 63 C4
Corfe Cl Hayes UB4 84 C1
Twickenham TW4 151 A3
Corfe Ho SW8 270 C4
Corfe Lodge 15 SE21 161 B2
Corfe Twr 6 W3 111 A4
Corfield Rd N21 16 B6
Corfield St E2 96 B4
Corfton Lo W5 88 A2
Corfton Rd W5 88 A2
Coriander Ave E14 98 B1
Coriander Ct SE1 253 D2
Cories Cl RM8 80 D6
Corigan Ct 6 E11 76 C6
Corinium Cl HA9 66 B4
Corinne Rd N19 71 C4
Corinth Ho IG3 58 A2
Cork St Mews W1 249 A5
Corkscrew Hill BR4 224 B5
Cork Sq E1 118 B5
Cork St W1 115 C6 249 A5
Cork Tree Ho 3 SE27 182 D5
Cork Tree Ret Pk N18 35 A4
Cork Tree Way E4 35 A5
Corlett St NW1 237 A4
Cormont Rd SE5 138 D4
Cormorant Cl E17 35 A3
Cormorant Ct
36 Deptford SE8 141 B6
13 Dulwich SE21 161 B2
Cormorant Ho EN3 18 D6
Cormorant Pl SM1 217 B3
Cormorant Rd E7 76 D3
Cornbury Ho 5 SE8 141 B6
Cornbury Rd HA8 25 D3
Cornel Ho 4 DA15 168 A1
Cornelia Dr UB4 84 C3
Cornelia St N7 72 B2
Cornelion Cotts 1 SM6 219 B3
Cornelius Ct 4 N12 30 A5
Cornell Bldg 9 E1 96 A1
Cornell Cl DA14 191 A4
Cornell Ct 4 EN3 7 A2
Cornell Ho HA2 63 B5
Corner Fielde SW2 160 B3
Corner Gn SE3 143 A3
Corner House St WC2 250 A4
Corner Mead NW9 27 D2
Cornerside TW15 171 A3
Cornerstone Ct 13 E1 96 A3
Cornerways Harrow HA1 65 A5
Putney SW15 134 A1
Corney Rd W4 133 C6
Corney Reach Way W4 133 C5
Cornflower La CR0 206 D1
Cornflower Terr SE22 162 B5
Cornford Cl BR2 209 A4
Cornford Gr SW12 159 B2
Cornhill EC3 95 B1 242 D1
Cornhill Dr EN3 7 A6
Cornick Ho 7 SE16 118 B3
Cornish Ct N9 18 B4
Cornish Gr SE20 184 B2
Cornish Ho
Brentford TW8 110 B1
7 Camberwell SE17 138 D6
Cornmill La SE13 142 A2
Cornmow Dr NW10 68 A3
Cornshaw Rd RM8 58 D1
Cornthwaite Rd E5 74 C5
Cornwall Ave
Bethnal Green E2 96 C4
Claygate KT10 212 D1
Cornwall Ave *continued*
Falconwood DA16 145 D2
Finchley N3 29 C3
Southall UB1 85 C2
Wood Green N22 32 A2
Cornwall Cl IG11 79 D2
Cornwall Cres W11 91 A1
Cornwall Ct
5 Ealing W7 86 D3
5 Pinner HA5 23 B3
Upper Tooting SW17 180 C6
Cornwall Dr BR5 190 C3
Cornwall Flats SE1 251 B2
Cornwall Gdns
Kensington SW7 113 D3 255 D5
Willesden NW10 68 B2
Cornwall Gdns Wlk SW7 255 D5
Cornwall Gr W4 111 C1
Cornwall Ho
Marylebone NW1 237 D5
3 Putney SW15 156 C4
Cornwallis Ave
London N9 18 C2
New Eltham SE9 167 B2
Cornwallis Ct SW8 270 A2
Cornwallis Gr N9 18 C2
Cornwallis Ho 24 W12 112 B6
Cornwallis Rd
Dagenham RM9 81 A4
Edmonton N9 18 B2
Upper Holloway N19 72 A6
Walthamstow E17 52 D5
Woolwich SE18 122 D3
Woolwich SE18 123 A3
Cornwallis Sq N19 72 A6
Cornwallis Wlk SE9 144 B2
Cornwall Mans
Chelsea SW10 266 B4
Marylebone NW1 237 D5
Cornwall Mews S SW7 256 A5
Cornwall Mews W SW7 255 D5
Cornwall Rd
Belmont SM2 217 B1
Croydon CR0 220 D6
Edmonton N18 34 A5
Finsbury Pk N4 50 C2
Harrow HA1 42 A3
Lambeth SE1 116 C4 251 B2
Pinner HA5 23 B3
Ruislip HA4 61 D6
Twickenham TW1 153 A3
West Green N15 51 B4
Cornwall Sq SE11 261 C2
Cornwall St 4 E1 118 B6
Cornwall Terr NW1 237 D5
Cornwall Terrace Mews NW1 237 D5
Corn Way E11 76 C5
Cornwood Cl N2 48 B5
Cornwood Dr E1 96 C1
Cornworthy Rd RM8 80 C3
Corona Rd SE12 165 A4
Coronation Ave 1 N16 73 D4
Coronation Cl
Bexley DA5 168 D5
Ilford IG6 57 A5
Coronation Ct
19 North Kensington W10 90 C2
Stratford E15 76 D2
Coronation Rd
Acton NW10 88 C3
Hayes UB3 105 D2
Newham E13 99 C4
Coronet Ho HA7 24 D4
Coronet Par 9 HA0 66 A2
Coronet St N1 95 C4
Corporation Ave TW4 129 A1
Corporation Row EC1 241 B6
Corporation St
Lower Holloway N7 72 A3
West Ham E15 98 D5
Corpus Christi RC Prim Sch
Brixton SW2 160 B6
Kingston u T KT3 199 A6
Corrance Rd SW2, SW4 138 A1
Corri Ave N14 31 D6
Corrib Ct N13 16 B1
Corrib Dr SM1 218 C3
Corrib Hts N8 49 D3
Corrigan Cl NW4 46 C6
Corringham Ct NW11 47 C2
Corringham Ho 11 E1 96 D1
Corringham Rd
London NW11 47 C2
Wembley HA9 66 C6
Corringway Ealing W5 88 C2
Golders Green NW11 47 D2
Corris Gn NW9 45 C3
Corry Dr SW9 138 D1
Corry Ho 2 E14 119 D6
Corsair Cl TW19 148 A4
Corsair Rd TW19 148 A4
Corscombe Cl KT2 177 A5
Corsehill St SW16 181 C4
Corsell Ho 5 TW8 131 C5
Corsham Ho HA9 66 C2
Corsham St N1 95 B4 235 D1
Corsica St N5 72 D2
Corsley Way E9 75 B2
Cortayne Ct TW2 152 C2
Cortayne Rd SW6 135 B3
Cortis Rd SW15 156 B5
Cortis Terr SW15 156 B5
Corunna Rd SW8 137 C4 269 B2
Corunna Terr SW8 269 A2
Corvette Sq 5 SE10 142 B6
Corwell Gdns UB8 83 A1
Corwell La UB8 83 A1
Coryton Path W9 91 B3
Cosbycote Ave SE24 161 A6
Cosdach Ave SM6 219 D1
Cosedge Cres CR0, CR9 220 D3
Cosgrove Cl
Edmonton N21 17 A2
Hayes UB4 84 D3
Cosgrove Ho 11 E2 96 A6
Cosmo Pl WC1 240 B4
Cosmur Cl W12 111 D3
Cossall Wlk SE15 140 B4
Cossar Mews 10 SW2 160 C6
Cosser St SE1 116 C3 261 A6
Costa St SE15 140 A3
Coston Prim Sch UB6 86 A4
Costons Ave UB6 86 B4
Costons La UB6 86 B4
Coston Wlk 4 SE4 140 D1
Cosway Ho NW11 48 A3
Cosway Mans NW1 237 B4
Cosway St NW1 92 C2 237 B4
Cotall St E14 97 C2
Coteford Cl HA5 40 A4
Coteford Inf Sch HA5 40 A3
Coteford Jun Sch HA5 39 D4
Coteford St SW17 181 A6
Cotelands CR0 221 C5
Cotesbach Rd E5 74 C5
Cotes Ho NW8 237 A5
Cotesmore Gdns RM8 80 C4
Cotford Rd CR7 205 A5
Cotham St SE17 262 B3
Cotherstone Rd SW2 160 B3
Cotleigh Ave DA5 168 D2
Cotleigh Rd NW6 69 C1
Cotman Cl London NW11 48 A3
Putney SW15 156 D6
Cotman Ct BR3 185 B2
Cotmandene Cres BR5 190 A1
Cotman Gdns HA8 26 C1
Cotman Ho
5 Northolt UB5 84 D5
St John's Wood NW8 230 A4
Cotman Mews RM8 80 C3
Cotmans Cl UB3 106 A5
Coton Rd DA16 146 A2
Cotrill Gdns E8 74 B2
Cotsford Ave KT3 199 B4
Cotswold Ave WD23 8 A5
Cotswold Cl
Hinchley Wood KT10 212 D6
Kingston u T KT2 177 A4
Cotswold Ct London N11 31 A6
St Luke's EC1 242 A6
3 Wembley UB6 86 D5
Cotswold Gate NW2 47 A1
Cotswold Gdns
Hendon NW2 68 D6
Ilford IG2 57 B2
Newham E6 99 D5
Cotswold Gn EN2 4 B1
Cotswold Ho N16 51 D1
Cotswold Mews SW11 266 D1
Cotswold Rd TW12 173 C4
Cotswold Rise BR6 211 D3
Cotswold St SE27 182 D6
Cotswold Way
Enfield EN2 4 B2
North Cheam KT4 216 C6
Cottage Ave BR2 210 A1
Cottage Cl Harrow HA2 64 C6
Ruislip HA4 39 B1
Cottage Field Cl DA14 168 C3
Cottage Gn SE5 139 B5
Cottage Gr
London SW9 138 A2
Surbiton KT6 197 D3
Cottage Pl SW3 114 C3 257 A5
Cottage Rd KT19 215 B1
Cottage St E14 119 D6
Cottages The
Ickenham UB10 60 A6
Lambeth SE1 260 C5
Uxbridge UB10 60 D5
Cottage Wlk 2 N16 73 D5
Cottenham Dr
London NW9 45 D6
Wimbledon SW20 178 B3
Cottenham Ho 5 N19 72 A6
Cottenham Par SW20 178 B1
COTTENHAM PARK 178 B2
Cottenham Park Rd SW20 178 C3
Cottenham Pl SW20 178 B3
Cottenham Rd E17 53 B5
Cotterill Rd KT6 198 B1
Cottesbrook St 9 SE14 141 A5
Cottesloe Ho NW8 237 A6
Cottesloe Mews SE1 261 B6
Cottesmore Ct W8 255 D6
Cottesmore Gdns W8 113 D3 255 D6
Cottimore Ave KT12 194 B1
Cottimore Cres KT12 194 B2
Cottimore La KT12 194 B2
Cottimore Terr KT12 194 B2
Cottingham Chase HA4 62 A5
Cottingham Rd
Penge SE20 184 D3
Cottingham Rd *continued*
South Lambeth SW8 138 B5 270 D4
Cottington Rd TW13 172 D6
Cottington St SE11 261 C2
Cotton Ave W3 89 B1
Cotton Cl
Dagenham RM9 80 C1
12 Leyton E11 76 C6
Cottongrass Cl 1 CR0 206 D1
Cotton Hill BR1 186 B6
Cotton Ho
Bedford Pk W12 111 D4
18 Streatham SW12 160 A4
Cotton Row SW11 136 B2
Cotton's Gdns E2 95 C4
Cottons La SE1 252 D4
Cotton St E14 120 A6
Cottrell Ct SE10 120 D2
Cotts Cl 13 W7 86 D2
Couchman Ho 8 SW4 159 C5
Couchmore Ave KT10 212 C6
Coulgate St SE4 141 A2
Coulsdon Ct 4 N8 49 D4
Coulsdon Ho 5 SW2 160 A3
Coulson Cl RM8 58 C1
Coulson St SW3 114 D1 257 C2
Coulter Cl UB4 85 A3
Coulter Rd W6 112 B3
Coulthurst Ct SW16 182 A3
Coults Cres NW5 71 A5
Councillor St SE5 139 A5
Counters Ct W14 254 B6
Counter St SE1 253 A3
Countess Rd NW5 71 C3
Countisbury Ave EN1 17 D4
Countisbury Ho SE26 162 A1
Country Way TW13, TW16 172 C5
County Gate
Longlands SE9 167 A1
New Barnet EN5 13 D5
County Gr SE5 139 A4
County Ho
22 Herne Hill SE24 138 D1
9 South Lambeth SW9 138 C4
County Par TW8 131 D5
County Rd Newham E6 100 D2
South Norwood CR7 182 D1
County St SE1 117 A3 262 B5
Coupland Pl SE18 123 A1
Courcy Rd N8, N22 50 C6
Courier Ho 17 SW2 160 C4
Courland Gr SW8 137 D3
Courland St SW8 137 D4 269 D1
Course The SE9 166 C1
Courtauld Ho 12 E2 96 A5
Courtauld Inst of Art*
Marylebone W1 237 D2
Strand WC2 250 C6
Courtauld Rd N19 50 A1
Courtaulds Cl SE28 124 A5
Court Ave DA17 125 B1
Court Cl Harrow HA3 44 A6
Twickenham TW13, TW2 151 D1
Wallington SM6 219 D1
Court Close Ave TW13, TW2 151 D1
Court Cres KT9 213 D2
Court Downs Rd BR3 185 D1
Court Dr
Carshalton SM1 218 C4
Edgware HA7 26 A6
Hillingdon UB10 82 C6
Wallington CR0 220 B4
Courtenay Ave
Harrow HA3 24 A2
Highgate N6 48 C2
Courtenay Dr BR3 186 B1
Courtenay Gdns HA3 24 A1
Courtenay Mews E17 53 A4
Courtenay Pl E17 53 A4
Courtenay Rd
Leyton E11 76 D5
North Cheam KT4, SM3 216 C5
Penge BR3, SE20 184 D4
Walthamstow E17 52 D5
Courtenay Rd HA9 65 D5
Courtenay Sq SE11 261 A1
Courtenay St SE11 116 C1 261 A2
Courtens Mews HA7 25 C3
Court Farm Ave KT19 215 B3
Court Farm Ind Est TW19 148 B5
Court Farm Rd
Chislehurst SE9 166 A1
Northolt UB5 63 C1
Courtfield W13 87 C2
Courtfield Ave HA1 42 D4
Courtfield Cres HA1 42 D4
Courtfield Gdns
Ealing W13 87 A1
Ruislip HA4 61 D6
South Kensington SW5 113 D2 255 D3
Courtfield Ho EC1 241 A4
Courtfield Mews SW7 255 D3
Courtfield Rd
Ashford TW15 170 D4
South Kensington SW7 114 A2 256 A3
Courtfield Rise BR4 224 B5
Courtgate Cl NW7 27 D4
Court Gdns N7 72 C2

Courthill Rd SE13......142 A1
Courthope Ho
14 Rotherhithe SE16....118 C3
South Lambeth SW8... 270 A3
Courthope Rd
Gospel Oak NW3........70 D4
Greenford UB6.........86 B5
Wimbledon SW19......179 A5
Courthope Villas
SW19...............179 A3
Court House Gdns N3...29 C4
Court House Rd N12....29 D4
Court La SE21.........161 D4
Courtland Ave
Chingford E4..........20 D2
Edgware NW7..........11 C1
Redbridge IG1.........78 B6
South Norwood SW16...182 B3
Courtland Gr SE28.....124 D6
Courtland Rd E6.......100 A6
Courtlands
11 Beckenham BR3.....185 D1
8 Belmont SM2.......217 D1
Ealing W5.............87 C2
Richmond TW10.......154 C6
5 Upper Clapton E5.....52 B1
Walton-on-T KT12......194 A2
Courtlands Ave
Hampton TW12........173 B4
Hayes BR2............208 D1
Lee SE12.............165 B6
Richmond TW9........132 D3
Courtland Sch NW7.....11 C2
Courtlands Cl HA4.....39 D2
Courtlands Dr KT19....215 D2
Courtlands Rd KT5.....198 C2
Court Lane Gdns
SE21................161 C4
Courtleet Dr DA8......147 D4
Courtleigh 6 NW11......47 B4
Courtleigh Ave EN4......2 B5
Courtleigh Gdns NW11..47 A5
Court Lo 11 DA17......125 C1
Courtman Rd N17.......33 A3
Court Mans 8 W6.....112 A2
Court Mead UB5........85 B4
Courtmead Cl SE24....161 A5
Courtnell St W2........91 C1
Courtney Cl SE19......183 C4
Courtney Cres SM5....218 D1
Courtney Ct N7.........72 C3
Courtney Ho
1 Hendon NW4........46 C5
Kensington W14...... 254 B6
Courtney Pl CR0.......220 C5
Courtney Rd
Croydon CR0..........220 C5
Islington N7...........72 C3
Mitcham SW19........180 C3
Courtney Twrs IG2......57 B3
Courtney Way TW6.....126 C2
Court One TW15.......149 A1
Court Par HA0..........65 B5
Courtrai Rd SE23......163 A5
Court Rd Eltham SE9....166 B4
Southall UB2.........107 B1
South Norwood SE25...205 D6
Uxbridge UB10.........60 D4
Court Royal SW15......157 A6
Courtside Crouch End N8.49 D3
Forest Hill SE23.......162 C1
Court St Bromley BR1...187 A1
3 Stepney E1..........96 B2
Court The London N10....49 C5
Ruislip HA4............63 A4
Court Three TW15......149 A1
Court Two TW15.......149 A1
Courtville Ho 12 W10....91 A4
Courtway IG8...........37 C5
Court Way Acton W3.....89 B2
Colindale NW9.........45 C5
Ilford IG6.............57 A6
Twickenham TW1, TW2..152 D4
Courtyard Apartments
TW11................174 B5
Courtyard Mews BR5...190 A3
Courtyard The
Fulham SW6.. 135 A4 264 A1
Islington N1...........72 B1
Keston BR2...........226 A2
Thornton Heath CR0....204 B3
13 Wandsworth SW18..136 B1
Court Yd SE9..........166 B5
Cousin La EC4..117 B6 252 C5
Cousins Cl 2 UB7......104 A6
Cousins Ct 2 NW9.......46 A5
Couthurst Rd SE3......143 B5
Coutts Ave KT9........214 A3
Couzens Ho 8 E3.......97 B2
Coval Gdns SW14......132 D1
Coval La SW14.........132 D1
Coval Pas SW14.......133 A1
Coval Rd SW14........133 A1
Covardale Ct EN3........7 A6
Covelees Wall E6......100 C1
Covell Ct 16 SE8.......141 C5
Covent Garden Sta
WC2..........94 A1 240 B1
Covent Gdn*
WC2..........116 A6 250 B6
Coventry Cl Kilburn NW6.91 C6
9 Newham E6.........100 B1
Coventry Rd
Bethnal Green E1.......96 B3
Croydon SE25.........206 A5
Ilford IG1.............56 D1
Coventry St W1....... 249 C5
Coverack Cl
Croydon CR0..........207 A2
Southgate N14.........15 C5
Coverdale Cl HA7.......25 B5
Coverdale Gdns CR0...221 D5
Coverdale Rd
Brondesbury NW2.......69 A2
Friern Barnet N11.......31 A4
Hammersmith W12......112 B4
Hampstead NW6........68 D1
Coverdales The IG11...101 B5
Coverham Ho 5 SE4...140 D1
Coverley Cl E1.........96 A2
Coverley Point SE11.. 260 C3
Coverton Rd SW17.....180 C5
Coverts Rd KT10.......212 D1
Covert The BR6........211 C3
Covert Way EN4.........2 A3
Covet Wood Cl BR5....211 D3
Covey Cl SW19.........179 D1
Covington Gdns
SW16................182 D3
Covington Way
South Norwood
SW16.............182 C3
South Norwood SW16...182 D3
Cowan Cl E6..........100 A2
Cowan Ct 14 NW10......67 B1
Cowan Lo 6 IG8.......37 C4
Cowbridge La IG11.....78 D1
Cowbridge Rd HA3......44 B5
Cowcross St
EC1...........94 D2 241 C4
Cowdenbeath Path N1 233 C6
Cowden Rd BR6........211 D2
Cowden St SE6........185 C6
Cowdray Hall Royal Coll of
Nursing W1....93 B1 238 C2
Cowdray Ho 22 SE22...139 C2
Cowdray Rd UB10.......83 A6
Cowdrey Cl EN1.........5 C3
Cowdrey Rd SW19.....180 A5
Cowdry Rd E9...........75 B2
Cowell Lo E4...........36 D5
Cowen Ave HA2.........64 B6
Cowen Ho 4 SE18......144 D6
Cowgate Rd UB6........86 B4
Cowick Rd SW17.......180 D6
Cowings Mead UB5......63 A2
Cowland Ave EN3........6 C1
Cow Leaze E6.........100 C1
Cowleaze Rd KT2......176 A2
Cowley Ct 8 E18.......37 A1
Cowley La E11..........76 C5
COWLEY PEACHY........82 A2
Cowley Pl NW4.........46 C4
Cowley Rd
Brixton SW9..........138 C4
East Acton W3.........111 D5
16 Kennington SW9....138 C5
Mortlake SW14........133 C2
Redbridge IG1..........56 B2
Wanstead E11..........55 B4
Cowley St SW1....... 260 A5
Cowling Cl W11...... 244 A4
Cowper Ave
Sutton SM1...........218 B4
Upton Pk E6...........78 A1
Cowper Cl Bexley DA16..168 A6
Bromley BR2..........209 D5
Cowper Gdns
Southgate N14.........15 C5
Wallington SM6.......219 C2
Cowper Ho
Pimlico SW1......... 259 D1
Walworth SE17....... 262 B2
Cowper Rd Acton W3....111 B5
6 Belvedere DA17.....125 C2
Bromley BR2..........209 D5
Ealing W7............108 D6
East Barnet N14........15 B3
Edmonton N18..........34 A5
Kingston u T KT2......176 B5
Stoke Newington N16....73 C4
Wimbledon SW19......180 A4
Cowper's Ct EC3...... 242 D1
Cowper St EC1,
EC2...........95 B3 242 D6
Cowper Terr W10.......90 D2
Cowslip Cl UB10........60 A1
Cowslip Rd E18.........37 B1
Cowthorpe Rd SW8... 269 D2
Cox Ct 3 EN4...........2 C1
Coxe Pl HA3............43 A5
Cox Ho W6........... 264 A6
Cox La Chessington KT9..214 B4
West Ewell KT19.......215 A3
Coxmount Rd SE7......121 D1
Coxs Ave TW17........193 C6
Coxson Way SE1...... 253 C1
Coxwell Rd
Plumstead SE18.......123 B1
South Norwood SE19...183 C3
Coxwold Path KT9.....214 A1
Coysh Ct 8 SW15......157 A6
Crabbs Croft Cl 7
BR6..................227 A3
Crab Hill BR3.........186 B3
Crabtree Ave
Dagenham RM6.........58 D5
Wembley HA0...........88 B5
Crabtree Cl E2.........95 D5
Crabtree Ct Barnet EN5...1 D1
Temple Mills E15.......75 D3
Crabtree Hall SW6.....134 C5
Crabtree La SW6......134 D5
Cracknell Cl EN1........6 B6
Craddock Rd EN1........5 D2
Craddock St NW5.......71 A2
Cradley Rd SE9........167 B3
Cragie Ho SE1....... 263 D3
Craig Dr UB8...........82 D1
Craigen Ave CR0.......206 B1
Craigerne Rd SE3......143 B5
Craig Gdns E18.........36 D1
Craig Ho Ealing W13....109 B6
Greenwich SE3........143 B5
Craigholm SE18.......144 C4
Craigie Lea N10........31 B1
Craigleith SW15.......156 D5
Craigmuir Pk HA0......88 B6
Craignair Rd SW2......160 C4
Craignish Ave SW16....182 B1
Craig Park Rd N18......34 B6
Craig Rd TW10.........175 C6
Craig's Ct SW1....... 250 A4
Craigside KT2.........176 D2
Craigton Rd SE9.......144 B1
Craigweil Cl HA7.......25 D5
Craigweil Dr HA7.......25 D5
Craigwell Ave TW13....150 A1
Craik Ct NW6...........91 B5
Crail Row SE17.117 B2 262 D3
Crales Ho SE18........122 A3
Cramer Ct KT3.........199 A6
Cramer St W1...93 A2 238 B3
Cramhurst Ho 3 SM1..218 B3
Crammond Cl W6...... 264 A5
Cramond Ct TW14.....149 C3
Cramonde Ct DA16.....146 A3
Crampton Rd SE20.....184 C4
Crampton Sch
SE17.........116 D1 261 D2
Crampton St
SE17.........117 A1 262 A2
Cranberry Cl 2 UB5....84 D5
Cranberry La E16.......98 C3
Cranborne Ave
Southall UB2..........107 C2
Tolworth KT6, KT9.....214 C5
Cranborne Rd IG11.....101 B6
Cranborne Waye
Hayes UB4.............84 B1
Hayes UB4............106 C6
Cranbourn Alley WC2. 249 D6
Cranbourne Cl SW16...204 A6
Cranbourne Ct
East Finchley N2........47 D6
2 Edgware HA8.........26 D5
Finchley NW7..........29 A3
SW11............... 267 B4
Walton-on-T KT12......194 B2
Wanstead E18..........55 B5
Cranbourne Dr HA5.....40 D4
Cranbourne Gdns
Ilford IG6..............57 A6
Temple Fortune NW11...47 B4
Cranbourne Rd
Leyton E15.............76 A4
London N10............31 B1
Manor Pk E12..........78 A3
Northwood HA6.........39 D6
Cranbourn Ho 6
SE16................118 B4
Cranbourn Pas 5
SE16................118 B4
Cranbourn St
WC2.........115 D6 249 D6
CRANBROOK..........56 C1
Cranbrook NW1...... 232 B5
Cranbrook Cl BR2.....209 A3
Cranbrook Coll (Boys)
IG1..................78 C6
Cranbrook Ct
8 Brentford TW8......131 D6
South Croydon CR2.....221 C3
Cranbrook Dr
Thames Ditton KT10....196 A1
Twickenham TW2.......151 D3
Cranbrook Ho
5 Hackney E5..........74 B3
South Norwood SE19...183 B2
Cranbrook La N11.......31 B6
Cranbrook Mews E17...53 B4
Cranbrook Pk N22.......32 C2
Cranbrook Rd
Chiswick W4..........111 C1
Erith DA7.............147 B4
Hounslow TW4.........129 B1
Ilford IG1, IG2.........56 C3
New Barnet EN4........14 B5
South Norwood CR7....183 A1
St Johns SE8..........141 C4
Wimbledon SW19......179 A3
Cranbrook Rise IG1.....56 B2
Cranbrook St E2........96 D5
Cranbury Rd SW6......135 D3
Crandale Ho 18 E5......74 B3
Crandley Ct SE8.......119 A2
Crane Ave Acton W3....111 A6
Isleworth TW7.........153 A6
Cranebank TW4........128 B2
Cranebank Mews
TW1.................131 A1
Cranebrook TW2.......152 A2
Crane Cl
Dagenham RM10........81 C2
Harrow HA2............64 A5
Crane Ct 7 Acton W12..111 C4
Holborn EC4......... 241 B1
West Ewell KT19.......215 A4
Craneford Cl TW2......152 D4
Craneford Way TW2....152 D4
Crane Gdns UB3.......105 D2
Crane Gr N7...........72 C2
Crane Ho 24 Bow E3.....97 A5
9 Catford BR1.........186 B5
Feltham TW13.........151 C1
10 Peckham SE15......139 D4
Crane Lodge Rd TW5...128 B6
Crane Mead SE16......118 D2
Crane Mead Ct TW1....152 D4
Crane Park Prim Sch
TW13................151 B2
Crane Park Rd TW2....151 D2
Crane Rd
Stanwell TW19........148 C5
Twickenham TW2.......152 C3
Cranesbill Cl NW9......45 B6
Cranes Dr KT5.........198 B5
Cranes Park Ave KT5,
KT6..................198 B5
Cranes Park Cres KT5..198 B5
Cranes Pk KT5, KT6.....198 A4
Crane St
Greenwich SE10.......120 B1
6 Peckham SE15.......139 D4
Craneswater TW6......127 D5
Craneswater Pk UB2...107 B1
Cranes Way WD6.......11 A6
Crane Way TW2........152 A4
Cranfield Ct
Marylebone NW1..... 237 B3
2 Woodford IG8........37 A6
Cranfield Dr NW9.......27 C3
Cranfield Ho WC1..... 240 B4
Cranfield Rd SE4......141 B2
CRANFORD............128 C4
Cranford Ave
Bowes Pk N13..........32 A5
Stanwell TW19........148 B4
Cranford Cl
Stanwell TW19........148 A4
Wimbledon SW20......178 B3
Cranford Com Coll
TW5.................128 B6
Cranford Cotts 8 E1...118 D6
Cranford Ct SM1.......218 A4
Cranford Dr UB3.......105 D2
Cranford Jun & Inf Schs
TW4.................128 B3
Cranford La
Harlington TW6........127 D4
Harlington UB3........127 C5
Hatton TW6...........127 D2
Heston TW5...........128 C5
Cranford Lo SW19.....156 D2
Cranford Park Prim Sch
UB3.................105 D2
Cranford Park Rd
UB3.................105 D2
Cranford Rise KT10....212 A3
Cranford St E1........118 D6
Cranford Way N8.......50 C4
Cranhurst Rd NW2......68 C3
Cranleigh W11....... 244 C4
Cranleigh Cl
Bexley DA5...........169 D5
Penge SE20...........184 B1
Cranleigh Ct
1 Barnet EN5...........1 D1
Mitcham CR4..........202 B6
Richmond TW9.........132 C2
Southall UB1...........85 B1
4 Stamford Hill N16....51 C1
Cranleigh Gardens Ind Est
UB1..................85 B2
Cranleigh Gdns
Barking IG11...........79 B2
Harrow HA3............44 A4
Kingston u T KT2.......176 B4
Southall UB1...........85 B1
Southgate N21..........16 C6
South Norwood SE25...205 C6
Sutton SM1...........217 D6
Cranleigh Ho SW20....178 B1
Cranleigh Hos NW1... 232 B3
Cranleigh Mews
SW11................136 D3
Cranleigh Rd
Feltham TW13.........171 D6
Harringay N15..........51 A4
Merton SW19..........201 C6
Thames Ditton KT10....196 A1
Cranleigh St
NW1..........93 C5 232 B3
Cranley Dene Ct N10....49 B5
Cranley Dr Ilford IG2....57 A2
Ruislip HA4............61 D6
CRANLEY GARDENS ...49 B5
Cranley Gdns
London N10............49 B5
Palmers Green N13......16 B1
South Kensington
SW7........114 B1 256 C2
Wallington SM6........219 C1
Cranley Mews
SW7..........114 A1 256 B2
Cranley Par 2 SE9.....188 A6
Cranley Pl
SW7..........114 B2 256 C3
Cranley Rd Ilford IG2....57 A2
Newham E13............99 B2
Cranmer Ave W13......109 B3
Cranmer Cl Ruislip HA4..40 D1
Stanmore HA7..........25 C3
West Barnes SM4......200 D3
Cranmer Ct
Chelsea SW3......... 257 B3
Church End N3..........29 A1
Hampton TW12.........173 D5
Kingston u T KT2......175 D6
Cranmere Prim Sch
KT10................196 A1
Cranmer Farm Cl CR4..202 D5
Cranmer Ho SW11.... 267 A2
Cranmer Prim Sch
CR4.................202 D5
Cranmer Rd
Brixton SW9..........138 C5
Croydon CR0..........221 A5
Edgware HA8...........10 D1
Cranmer Rd *continued*
Forest Gate E7.........77 B4
Hampton TW12.........173 D5
Hayes UB3.............83 B1
Kingston u T KT2.......176 A5
Mitcham CR4..........202 B5
Cranmer Terr SW17....180 B5
Cranmore Ave TW7.....130 A5
Cranmore Rd
Catford BR1..........164 D1
Elmstead BR7.........188 B5
Cranmore Way N10.....49 C5
Cranston Cl
Hounslow TW3, TW4....129 A3
Uxbridge UB10.........61 B6
Cranston Ct 6 N20.....14 D2
Cranston Gdns E4......35 D4
Cranston Rd SE23......163 A2
Cranswick Rd SE16....118 B1
Crantock Rd SE6.......164 A2
Cranwell Cl E3.........97 D3
Cranwell Ct
Croydon CR0..........222 D6
6 Hendon NW9.........27 D3
Cranwell Gr TW17.....192 B5
Cranwell Rd TW6......126 D3
Cranwich Ave N21......17 B4
Cranwich Rd N16.......51 C2
Cranwood Ct EC1..... 235 D1
Cranwood St
EC1...........95 B4 235 D1
Cranworth Cres 7 E4...20 B3
Cranworth Gdns SW9..138 C4
Cranworth Ho 6 N7....72 B4
Craster Rd SW2........160 B4
Craston Ho 2 SE5.....139 C3
Crathie Rd SE12.......165 B5
Crathorne Ho N2........30 B1
Cravan Ave TW13......150 A2
Craven Ave Ealing W5...109 C6
Southall UB1...........85 B2
Craven Cl Hayes UB4.....84 A1
Stamford Hill N16.......52 A2
Craven Cottage (Fulham
FC) SW6.............134 D4
Craven Ct
Dagenham RM6.........59 A3
Edgware HA8...........26 B6
Harlesden NW10........89 C6
Southall UB1..........107 D5
Craven Gdns
Barking IG11..........101 C5
Ilford IG6.............57 B6
Wimbledon SW19......179 D5
Craven Hill W2 .114 A6 246 B6
Craven Hill Gdns
W2...........114 A6 246 A6
Craven Hill Mews W2. 246 B6
Craven Ho Ealing W5....109 C6
16 Finchley N2.........30 B1
2 Mortlake SW14......133 B2
Craven Lo
Bayswater W2........ 246 B6
Fulham SW6..........134 D4
Craven Mews 6
SW11................137 A2
Craven Park Mews
NW10.................89 C6
Craven Park Rd
Harlesden NW10........89 C6
South Tottenham N15...52 A3
Craven Pas WC2...... 250 A4
Craven Pk NW10........89 C6
Craven Rd Croydon CR0.206 B1
Ealing W5............109 C6
Kingston u T KT2......176 B2
Paddington W2..92 A1 236 B1
Stonebridge NW10......89 B6
Craven St WC2.116 A5 250 A4
Craven Terr
W2...........114 A6 246 B6
Craven Wlk E5, N16.....52 A2
Crawford Ave HA0......65 D3
Crawford Bldgs NW1.. 237 B3
Crawford Cl TW7......130 C3
Crawford Ct SE18......146 A6
Crawford Gdns
Edmonton N13..........16 D1
Northolt UB5...........85 B4
Crawford Mews W1... 237 C3
Crawford Pas EC1..... 241 B5
Crawford Pl W1. 92 C2 237 B3
Crawford Place Dwellings
NW1................ 237 B3
Crawford Point 4 E16..98 D1
Crawford Prim Sch
SE5.................139 A4
Crawford Rd SE5......139 A3
Crawford St
Marylebone
W1...........92 D2 237 C3
16 Willesden NW10.....67 B1
Crawley Rd Enfield EN1...17 D4
Leyton E10.............53 D1
Tottenham N22.........33 A1
Crawshay Ct SW9......138 C4
Crawshay Ho 18 N16....73 B4
Crawthew Gr SE22.....139 D1
Cray Bldgs DA14.......190 C4
Craybrooke Rd DA14...190 B6
Craybury End SE9......167 A2
Crayfields Bsns Pk
BR5..................190 C2
Crayfields Ind Pk BR5..190 C1
Crayford Cl E6........100 A1
Crayford Ho
Bermondsey SE1..... 252 D1
5 Lower Holloway N7...72 A4
Crayford Rd N7.........72 A4
Crayke Hill KT9.......214 A1
Crayle Ho EC1........ 241 D6
Crayleigh Terr DA14...190 C4
Crayonne Cl TW16.....171 C2
Cray Rd Erith DA17.....147 C6
Sidcup DA14..........190 C4
Crays Par The BR5.....190 C1
Crealock Gr IG8........36 D5
Crealock St SW18......157 D5
Creasy Est SE1....... 263 A5
Crebor St SE22........162 A5
Credenhall Dr BR2.....210 B1
Credenhill Ho 2 SE15..140 B5
Credenhill St SW16....181 C4
Crediton Hill NW6......69 D3
Crediton Ho EN3.........6 D2
Crediton Rd
Brondesbury Pk NW10...90 D6
Newham E16............99 A1
Crediton Way KT10....213 A3
Credon Rd
Bermondsey SE16......118 B1
Newham E13............99 C5
Creechurch La EC3... 243 B1
Creechurch Pl EC3.... 243 B1
Creed Ct 5 E1.........97 A4
Creed Ho SE15.........140 B2
Creed La EC4........ 241 D1
Creek Ho W14....... 254 B6
CREEKMOUTH........101 D2
Creekmouth Ind Pk
IG11.................101 D3
Creek Rd Barking IG11..101 D4
East Molesey KT8......196 C5
Greenwich SE10, SE8...141 D6
Creek Road Ind Est
SE8..................141 D6
Creekside SE8.........141 D5
Creekside Foyer SE8...141 D6
Creek The TW16.......194 A4
Creeland Gr SE6.......163 B3
Crefeld Cl W6..135 A6 264 A5
Creffield Rd W3, W5....110 C6
Creighton Ave
London N2, N10.........30 D1
Newham E6.............99 D5
Creighton Cl W12......112 B6
Creighton Ho N2........48 C6
Creighton Rd
Ealing W5............109 D3
Kensal Rise NW6.......90 D5
Tottenham N17.........33 C3
Cremer Bsns Ctr 8 E2..95 D5
Cremer Ho 9 SE8.....141 C5
Cremer St E2...........95 D5
Cremorne Rd
SW10.........136 B5 266 C4
Creon Ct 3 SW9.......138 C4
Crescent EC3........ 253 C6
Crescent Arc 1 SE10..142 A6
Crescent Court Bsns Ctr
1 E16.................98 B3
Crescent Ct
Clapham Pk SW4.......159 D6
Crouch End N8..........49 D3
Kingston u T KT6......197 D4
14 Sidcup DA15.......168 A1
Crescent Dr BR5.......211 A3
Crescent E EN4..........2 A5
Crescent Gdns
Ruislip HA4............40 B2
Wimbledon SW19......157 C1
Crescent Gr
London SW4..........137 C1
Mitcham CR4..........202 C5
Crescent Ho
London SE13..........141 D3
5 Wimbledon SW20...178 D2
Crescent La SW4......159 D6
Crescent Mans
Islington N5...........72 D3
Notting Hill W11...... 244 B6
Crescent Par UB10.....82 C4
Crescent Pl SW3...... 257 B4
Crescent Rd
Beckenham BR3.......185 D1
Chingford E4...........20 C4
Church End N3..........29 B2
Crouch End N8..........49 D3
Dagenham RM10........81 D5
East Barnet EN4........14 C6
Edmonton N9...........18 A3
Enfield EN2.............4 D1
Friern Barnet N11......30 D6
Harringay N15..........50 D6
Kingston u T KT2......176 D3
Leyton E10.............75 D6
Plaistow BR1..........187 A3
Shepperton TW17......193 A4
Sidcup DA15..........167 D1
Upton Pk E6............99 C6
West Ham E13..........99 A6
Wimbledon SW20......178 D2
Woodford E18..........37 C2
Wood Green N22........31 D2
Woolwich SE18........122 D2
Crescent Rise
East Barnet EN4........14 C6
3 Finchley N3.........29 C2
Wood Green N22........31 D2
Crescent Row EC1.... 242 A5
Crescent St N1.........72 B1
Crescent Stables
SW15.................157 A6
Crescent The Acton W3..89 C1
Ashford TW15.........170 B5
Barnes SW13..........134 A3
Barnet EN5..............1 D3

Crescent The continued
Beckenham BR3 . . . .**185** C2
Bexley DA5 . . . .**168** C4
Coombe KT3 . . . .**177** A1
Dollis Hill NW2 . . . .**68** B5
East Finchley N2 . . . .**47** D6
East Molesey KT8 . . . . . .**195** C5
Friern Barnet N11 . . . .**31** A4
Harlington UB7 . . . .**127** B5
Harrow HA2 . . . .**42** A1
Ilford IG2 . . . .**56** C3
Loughton IG10 . . . .**21** D5
Lower Halliford TW17 . . .**193** D2
Sidcup DA14 . . . .**189** D6
Southall UB1 . . . .**107** A4
Surbiton KT6 . . . .**198** A4
Sutton SM1 . . . .**218** B3
Thornton Heath CR0 . . . .**205** B3
Walthamstow E17 . . . .**53** A4
Wembley HA0 . . . .**65** B6
West Wickham BR4 . . . . .**208** C3
Wimbledon SW19 . . . . . .**157** C1
Crescent View IG10 . . . . .**21** D6
Crescent W EN4 . . . .**2** A5
Crescentway N12 . . . .**30** C4
Crescent Way
London SE4 . . . .**141** C5
Orpington BR6 . . . .**227** C3
South Norwood SW16 . . .**182** C3
Crescent Wood Rd SE21,
SE26 . . . .**162** A1
Cresford Rd
SW6 . . . . . . **135** D4 **265** C1
Crespigny Rd NW4 . . . . . .**46** B3
Cressage Cl UB1 . . . .**85** C3
Cressage Ho [9] TW8 . . . .**132** A6
Cressall Ho [14] E14 . . . . .**119** C3
Cresset Ho [8] E9 . . . .**74** C2
Cresset Rd E9 . . . .**74** C2
Cresset St SW4 . . . .**137** D2
Cressida Rd N19 . . . .**49** D1
Cressingham Ct [1]
DA17 . . . .**125** C3
Cressingham Gr SM1 . . .**218** A4
Cressingham Rd
Burnt Oak NW7 . . . .**27** B3
Lewisham SE13 . . . .**142** A2
Cressington Cl [4] N16 . .**73** C3
Cress Mews BR1 . . . .**186** B5
Cresswell Gdns SW5 . .**256** A4
Cresswell Ho HA4 . . . . . .**66** A5
Cresswell Pk SE3 . . . . . .**142** D2
Cresswell Pl
SW10 . . . . . .**114** A1 **256** B2
Cresswell Rd
Croydon SE25 . . . .**206** A4
Feltham TW13 . . . .**173** A6
Twickenham TW1 . . . . . .**153** D5
Cresswell Way N21 . . . . .**16** C4
Cressy Ct
Hammersmith W6 . . . . . .**112** B3
[6] Stepney E1 . . . .**96** C2
Cressy Ho SW13 . . . .**134** B2
Cressy Hos [7] E1 . . . . . .**96** C2
Cressy Pl E1 . . . .**96** C2
Cressy Rd NW3 . . . .**70** D4
Cresta Ct W5 . . . .**88** B3
Cresta Ho [1] Bow E3 . . . .**97** C3
Hampstead NW6 . . . .**70** B1
Crestbrook Ave N13 . . . . .**16** D1
Crestbrook Pl N13 . . . . . .**16** D1
Crest Cl NW4 . . . .**46** C4
Crest Dr EN3 . . . .**6** C5
Crestfield St N1, WC1. .**233** B2
Crest Gdns HA4 . . . .**62** C5
Crest Ho [3] TW9 . . . .**170** C5
Creston Way KT4 . . . .**200** D1
Crest Rd Dollis Hill NW2 . .**68** A6
Hayes BR2 . . . .**208** D2
South Croydon CR2 . . . . .**222** B1
Crest The Edmonton N13 . .**32** C6
Finchley N12 . . . .**29** D4
Hendon NW4 . . . .**46** C4
Surbiton KT5 . . . .**198** A4
[10] West Norwood
SW27 . . . .**182** D5
Crestview NW5 . . . .**71** B5
Crest View HA5 . . . .**40** D5
Crest View Dr BR5 . . . . . .**211** A4
Crestway SW15 . . . .**156** B5
Crestwood Way TW4 . . . .**151** A4
Creswell Dr BR3 . . . .**207** D4
Creswick Ct W3 . . . .**110** C6
Creswick Rd W3 . . . .**110** C6
Creswick Wlk
[7] Bow E3 . . . .**97** C4
Temple Fortune NW11 . . . .**47** B5
Creton St SE18 . . . .**122** C3
Crewdson Rd SW9 . . . . . .**138** C5
Crewe Pl NW10 . . . .**89** D4
Crewkerne Ct SW11. . . .**266** D2
Crews St E14 . . . .**119** C2
Crewys Rd
Child's Hill NW2 . . . .**69** B6
London SE15 . . . .**140** B3
Crichton Ave SM6 . . . . . .**219** D4
Crichton Rd SM5 . . . .**218** D1
Crichton St SW8 . . . .**137** C3
Cricket Ct E6 . . . .**100** B4
Cricketers Arms Rd EN2. . .**5** A3
Cricketers Cl
Chessington KT9 . . . .**213** C4
Oakwood N14 . . . .**15** C4
Cricketers Mews [4]
SW18 . . . .**157** D6
Cricketers Terr SM5 . . . .**218** C5

Cricketers Wlk SE26 . . . .**184** C5
Cricketfield Rd E5 . . . .**74** B4
Cricket Gn CR4 . . . .**202** D5
Cricket Green Sch
CR4 . . . .**202** C6
Cricket Ground Rd
BR7 . . . .**188** D2
Cricket La BR3 . . . .**185** A4
Cricket Row N2 . . . .**48** B6
Cricklade Ave SW2 . . . . .**160** B2
CRICKLEWOOD **68** C4
Cricklewood Broadway
NW2 . . . .**68** D4
Cricklewood La NW2 . . . . .**69** B5
Cricklewood Sta NW2. . . .**68** D4
Cridland St E15 . . . .**98** D6
Crieff Ct [3] TW11 . . . . . .**175** C3
Crieff Rd SW18 . . . .**158** A5
Criffel Ave SW2 . . . .**159** D3
Crimscott St
SE1 . . . . **117** C3 **263** B5
Crimsworth Rd
SW8 . . . .**137** D5 **269** D3
Crinan St N1 . . . **94** A5 **233** B4
Cringle St
SW8 . . . .**137** C5 **269** A4
Cripplegate St EC1. . . . .**242** B4
Cripps Gn UB4 . . . .**84** B3
Crispe Ho
[4] Barking IG11. . . . . .**101** B5
Islington N1 . . . .**233** D5
Crispen Rd TW13 . . . . . .**173** A6
Crispian Cl NW10 . . . .**67** C4
Crispin Cl SM6 . . . .**219** D6
Crispin Ct SE17 . . . .**263** A3
Crispin Pl E1 . . . .**243** C4
Crispin Rd HA8 . . . .**27** A4
Crispin St E1 . . . **95** D2 **243** C4
Crispin Way UB8. . . . .**82** B3
Crisp Rd W6 . . . .**112** C1
Cristowe Rd SW6 . . . . . .**135** B3
Criterion Bldgs KT7 . . . .**197** B2
Criterion Mews N19. . . . . .**71** B6
Crittall's Cnr DA14. . . . . .**190** C3
Crittenden Lo BR4 . . . . . .**207** C1
Crockerton Rd SW17. . . .**158** C2
Crockham Way SE9 . . . . .**188** C6
Crocus Cl CR0 . . . .**206** D1
Crocus Field EN5 . . . .**13** B5
Croft Ave BR4 . . . .**208** A4
Croft Cl Edgware NW7 . . . .**11** C1
Elmstead BR7 . . . .**188** B5
Erith DA17 . . . .**125** C1
Harlington UB7 . . . .**127** A5
Hillingdon UB10 . . . .**60** C1
Croft Ct London SE13 . . . .**164** A5
Ruislip HA4 . . . .**39** C1
Croftdown Rd NW5 . . . . . .**71** B5
Croft End Cl KT9. . . . .**214** B5
Crofters Cl TW7 . . . .**152** B6
Crofters Ct [8] SE8 . . . . .**119** A2
Crofters Way
NW1 . . . .**93** D6 **232** C6
Croft Gdns Ealing W7 . . . .**109** A4
Ruislip HA4 . . . .**39** D1
Croft Ho Putney SW15. . . .**157** A5
[11] West Kilburn W10 . . .**91** A4
Croft Lodge Cl IG8. . . . . . .**37** B4
Croft Mews [3] IG2. . . . . . .**14** A1
CROFTON **227** B6
Crofton Ave
Chiswick W4 . . . .**133** B5
Orpington BR6. . . . .**227** A6
Sidcup DA5 . . . .**168** A4
Crofton Gate Way
SE4 . . . .**163** A6
Crofton Gr E4 . . . .**36** B6
Crofton Inf Sch BR5. . . . .**211** B4
Crofton Jun Sch BR5. . . .**211** B4
Crofton La BR5, BR6 . . . .**211** B2
Crofton L Ctr SE4. . . . . . .**163** C4
Crofton Park Rd SE4 . . . .**163** B5
Crofton Park Sta SE4 . . .**163** A6
Crofton Rd
Camberwell SE5 . . . .**139** C4
Locksbottom BR6 . . . . . .**226** C5
Newham E13 . . . .**99** B3
Crofton Roman Villa ✱
BR6 . . . .**227** C6
Crofton Sch SE4 . . . .**163** C5
Crofton Terr
Homerton E5 . . . .**75** D4
Richmond TW9 . . . .**132** B1
Crofton Way Enfield EN2 . . .**4** C3
New Barnet EN5 . . . .**13** D5
Croft Rd
Carshalton SM1. . . . .**218** C4
Enfield EN3 . . . .**7** A4
Merton SW19 . . . .**180** A3
Plaistow E13 . . . .**187** A4
South Norwood SW16 . . .**182** C3
Crofts Ho [21] E2. . . . .**96** A5
Croftside The [3] SE25. .**206** A6
Crofts La N22. . . . .**32** C3
Crofts Rd HA1 . . . .**43** A4
Crofts St E1 . . . .**118** A6
Croft St SE8 . . . .**119** A2
Crofts The TW17 . . . .**193** C5
Croft The Barnet EN5 . . . . . .**1** A1
Chingford E4 . . . .**20** C2
Ealing W5 . . . .**88** A2
Edgware HA8 . . . .**26** D3
Harlesden NW10 . . . .**89** D5
Heston TW5. . . . .**129** A5
New Malden KT3. . . . . . .**199** C4
Pinner HA5 . . . .**41** B2
Ruislip HA4 . . . .**62** C4
Wembley HA0 . . . .**65** C3
Croft Villas HA1 . . . .**43** A3

Croft Way
Richmond TW10 . . . .**153** B1
Sidcup DA15 . . . .**167** C1
Crogsland Rd NW1. . . . . . .**71** A1
Croham Cl CR2 . . . .**221** C1
Croham Hurst Sch
CR2 . . . .**221** D3
Croham Manor Rd
CR2 . . . .**221** D3
Croham Mount CR2 . . . . .**221** C1
Croham Park Ave
CR2 . . . .**221** D3
Croham Rd CR2. . . . .**221** D2
Croham Valley Rd
CR2 . . . .**222** B1
Croindene Rd SW16. . . . .**182** A2
Crokesley Ho [2] HA8. . . .**27** A1
Cromartie Rd N19 . . . .**49** D2
Cromarty Ct [7] BR1. . . . .**187** C1
Cromarty Ho [8] E1. . . . . . .**97** A2
Cromarty Rd HA8 . . . .**10** C1
Cromberdale Ct N17 . . . . .**34** A2
Crombie Cl IG4. . . . .**56** B4
Crombie Mews [5]
SW11 . . . .**136** C3
Crombie Rd DA15 . . . . . .**167** B3
Cromdale Ct N16 . . . .**51** D2
Crome Ho N5 . . . .**85** A5
Crome Rd NW10 . . . .**67** C2
Cromer Cl UB8 . . . .**83** A1
Cromer Ct
Streatham SW16 . . . .**160** A1
Wandsworth SW18 . . . . .**157** B5
Cromer Mans [6] SM1 . .**217** D3
Cromer Pl [5] BR6. . . . . . .**211** B1
Cromer Rd Barnet EN5 . . . .**2** A2
Croydon SE25 . . . .**206** B6
Dagenham RM6. . . . .**59** A3
Harlington TW6. . . . .**126** C3
Leyton E10. . . . .**54** B2
Streatham SW17. . . . . . .**181** A4
Tottenham N17 . . . .**34** A1
Woodford IG8 . . . .**37** A6
Cromer Road Prim Sch
EN5. . . . .**2** A2
Cromer St WC1 . . **94** A4 **233** B1
Cromer Terr Dalston E8. . .**74** A3
[3] Ilford RM6. . . . .**58** B4
Cromer Villas Rd
SW18 . . . .**157** B5
Cromford Cl BR6. . . . .**227** C5
Cromford Path [1] E5. . . . .**74** D4
Cromford Rd SW18 . . . . .**157** C6
Cromford Way KT3. . . . . .**177** B2
Cromlix Cl BR7 . . . .**188** D1
Crompton Ct SW3 . . . . . .**257** A4
Crompton Ho
Borough The SE1. . . . . .**262** B5
Paddington W2 . . . .**236** C5
South Lambeth SW8 . . . .**269** B1
Crompton Pl EN3 . . . .**7** C5
Crompton St
W2. . . . .**92** B3 **236** C5
Cromwell Ave
Bromley BR2. . . . .**209** B5
Hammersmith W6 . . . . . .**112** B2
Highgate N6 . . . .**49** B1
New Malden KT3. . . . . . .**199** D4
Cromwell Cl Acton W3 . . .**111** A5
Bromley BR2. . . . .**209** B5
East Finchley N2 . . . .**48** B5
[2] Gunnersbury W4 . . . .**110** D1
Walton-on-T KT12 . . . . . .**194** B1
Cromwell Cres
SW5 . . . .**113** C2 **255** A4
Cromwell Ct Enfield EN3. .**18** D6
[15] Kingston u T KT2 . . .**176** C3
Wembley HA0 . . . .**88** A3
Cromwell Ctr
Barking IG11 . . . .**102** A4
North Acton NW10 . . . . . .**89** B4
Cromwell Ctr The RM8. . .**59** B2
Cromwell Est E10. . . . .**53** A1
Cromwell Gdns
SW7 . . . .**114** B3 **256** D5
Cromwell Gr W6. . . . .**112** C3
Cromwell Ho
Battersea SW11 . . . .**268** B1
[2] Croydon CR0 . . . . . .**220** D5
Muswell Hill N10 . . . .**31** B3
Putney SW15. . . . .**134** A1
Cromwell Hospl
SW5 . . . .**113** D2 **255** C4
Cromwell Lo
Barking IG11 . . . .**79** C3
[40] Bethnal Green E1 . . .**96** C3
Cromwell Mans SW5. . . .**255** B4
Cromwell Mews SW7. . . .**256** C4
Cromwell Pl
[5] Acton W3 . . . .**111** A5
Highgate N6 . . . .**49** B1
Mortlake SW14 . . . .**133** A2
South Kensington
SW7 . . . . **114** B2 **256** D4
Cromwell Rd
Beckenham BR3 . . . .**207** A6
Brixton SW9 . . . .**138** C4
Feltham TW13 . . . .**150** B3
Finchley N3 . . . .**30** A2
Hayes UB3. . . . .**83** B1
Hounslow TW5 . . . .**129** C1
Kingston u T KT2 . . . .**176** A2
Muswell Hill N10 . . . .**31** A3
South Kensington SW7 . .**256** B4
Teddington TW11 . . . . . .**175** A4
Thornton Heath CR0 . . . .**205** B2
Upton E7 . . . .**77** C1
Walthamstow E17 . . . .**54** A4
Walton-on-T KT12 . . . . . .**194** B1
Wembley HA0 . . . .**88** A5

Cromwell Rd continued
Wimbledon SW19 . . . . . .**179** D5
Worcester Pk KT4 . . . . . .**215** C5
Cromwell St TW3 . . . .**129** C1
Cromwell Trad Ctr
IG11 . . . .**101** C4
Cromwell Twr EC2. . . . . .**242** B4
Crondace Rd
SW6 . . . .**135** C4 **265** B1
Crondall Ct [7] N1. . . . .**95** C5
Crondall Ho SW15 . . . . . .**156** A3
Crondall Pl [15] N1. . . . . . .**95** C5
Crondall St N1 . . . .**95** C5
Crone Ct [5] NW6 . . . .**91** B5
Cronin St SE15 . . . .**139** D5
CROOKED BILLET **178** C4
Crooked Billet
Chingford E4 . . . .**35** C3
Wimbledon SW19 . . . . . .**178** C4
Crooked Billet Yd [18]
E2. . . . .**95** C4
Crooked Usage N3. . . . . . .**47** A6
Crooke Rd SE8 . . . .**119** A1
Crookham Rd
SW6 . . . .**135** B4 **264** C1
Crook Log DA6 . . . .**146** B3
Crook Log L Ctr DA7. . . . .**146** D2
Crook Log Prim Sch
DA6. . . . .**146** D1
Crookston Rd SE9 . . . . . .**144** C2
Croombs Rd E16. . . . .**99** C2
Croom's Hill SE10 . . . . . .**142** A5
Croom's Hill Gr SE10. . . .**142** A5
Cropley Ct N1 . . . .**235** C4
Cropley St N1 . . . **95** B5 **235** C4
Croppath Rd RM10. . . . . . .**81** C4
Cropthorne Ct W9 . . . . . .**229** B1
Crosbie [10] NW9. . . . .**27** D1
Crosbie Ho [20] E17 . . . . .**53** B6
Crosby Cl TW13 . . . .**173** A6
Crosby Ct
Borough The SE1. . . . . .**252** C2
East Finchley N2 . . . .**48** A5
[7] New Southgate N11. . .**31** B6
Crosby Ho
[18] Cubitt Town E14. . . .**120** A3
Forest Gate E7 . . . .**77** A2
Crosby Rd
Dagenham RM10 . . . .**103** D6
Upton E7 . . . .**77** A2
Crosby Row
SE1 . . . . **117** B4 **252** C2
Crosby Sq EC3. . . . .**243** A4
Crosby Wlk
[3] Dalston E8 . . . .**73** D2
Streatham SE24 . . . .**160** C4
Crosfield Ct [3] W10. . . . . .**90** D1
Crosfield Ho W11. . . . . . .**244** A5
Crosier Cl SE3 . . . .**144** A3
Crosier Rd UB10 . . . .**61** A4
Crosier Way HA4 . . . .**61** C5
Crosland Pl [5] SW11. . . .**137** A2
Crossbow Ho
Ealing W13 . . . .**109** B5
[15] Shoreditch N1 . . . . . .**95** C6
Crossbrook Rd SE3 . . . . .**144** A2
Cross Cl SE15. . . . .**140** B3
Cross Ct London SE5 . . . .**139** B2
[11] Thamesmead SE28 . .**124** B6
Cross Deep TW1 . . . .**153** A2
Cross Deep Gdns
TW1 . . . .**152** D2
Crossfield Rd
Hampstead NW3 . . . .**70** B2
London N17. . . . .**51** A6
Crossfield St SE8 . . . . . .**141** C5
Crossford St SW9. . . . . . .**138** B3
Crossgate Edgware HA8 . .**10** C1
Wembley UB6 . . . .**65** B2
Crossharbour Sta E14. .**119** D3
Cross Ho N8. . . . .**50** B5
Cross Keys Cl
[5] Edmonton N9 . . . .**18** A2
Marylebone W1. . . . .**238** B3
Cross La
City of London EC3 . . . . .**253** A5
Hornsey N8 . . . .**50** B5
Old Bexley DA5 . . . .**169** B4
Cross Lances Rd TW3 . . .**129** D1
Crossland Rd CR7. . . . . . .**204** D3
Crosslands Ave
Ealing W5 . . . .**110** B5
Southall UB2 . . . .**107** A1
Crosslands Rd KT19. . . . .**215** B2
Crossleigh Ct
[3] New Cross SE14 . . . .**141** B5
Streatham SW16 . . . .**181** B6
Crosslet St SE17 . . . .**262** D4
Crosslet Vale SE10. . . . . .**141** D4
Crossley St N7. . . . .**72** C2
Crossman Hos [19]
SW12 . . . .**160** A4
Crossmead SE9 . . . .**166** B3
Crossmead Ave UB6 . . . . .**85** C4
Crossmount Ho [13]
SE5 . . . .**139** A5
Crossness Rd IG11. . . . . .**101** D4
Cross Rd Belmont HA3. . . . .**25** A1
Camberwell SE5 . . . .**139** C3
Chingford E4 . . . .**20** C3
Croydon CR0 . . . .**205** B1
Enfield EN1 . . . .**5** C1
Feltham TW13 . . . .**173** A6
Finchley N2 . . . .**30** C1
Friern Barnet N11 . . . .**31** B1
Harrow HA1 . . . .**42** C1
Ilford RM6. . . . .**58** C2
Keston Mark BR2, BR4, ...
Kingston u T KT2 . . . .**176** B3
Merton SW19 . . . .**179** C3

Cross Rd continued
Romford RM7 . . . .**59** C6
Sidcup DA14 . . . .**190** B6
South Harrow HA2 . . . . . .**63** D5
Sutton SM1 . . . .**218** B3
Wood Green N22. . . . .**32** C3
Cross St
[2] Edmonton N18. . . . . . .**34** A5
Hampton TW12 . . . .**174** A5
Islington N1 . . **94** D6 **234** D6
Mortlake SW13 . . . .**133** C2
Crossthwaite Ave SE5,
SE24 . . . .**163** C3
Crosstrees Ho [7] E14. .**119** C3
Crosswall EC3 . **117** D6 **253** C6
Crossway
Dagenham RM8. . . . .**80** C5
Ealing W13 . . . .**87** A3
Enfield EN1 . . . .**17** C1
Finchley N12 . . . .**30** B4
Hayes UB3. . . . .**106** A5
Hendon NW9. . . . .**45** D5
Kingsland E8, N16 . . . .**73** C3
Petts Wood BR5 . . . .**211** B4
Pinner HA5 . . . .**22** B1
Ruislip HA4 . . . .**62** C4
West Barnes KT3, ...
SW20 . . . .**200** C5
Woodford IG8 . . . .**37** C6
Crossway Ct SE4. . . . . . .**141** A3
Crossway Par N22 . . . .**32** C3
Crossways
Ashford TW16. . . . .**171** D3
South Croydon CR2. . . . .**223** B1
Sutton SM2 . . . .**218** B1
Crossways Acad SE4. . . .**141** A3
Crossways Par CR2 . . . . .**223** B1
Crossways Rd
Beckenham BR3 . . . .**207** C6
Mitcham CR4. . . . .**203** B6
Crossways The
Heston TW5. . . . .**129** B5
[1] Wembley HA9 . . . .**66** C6
Crossway The
Chislehurst SE9. . . . .**165** D2
Hillingdon UB10 . . . .**82** B5
Tottenham N22 . . . .**32** D3
Cross Way The HA3. . . . . .**24** C1
Crosswell Cl TW17 . . . . . .**171** A1
Croston St E8 . . . .**96** A6
Crothall Cl N13 . . . .**16** B1
Crouch Cl BR3 . . . .**185** C6
Crouch Cl London SE5 . . .**139** B2
[11] Thamesmead SE28 . .**124** B6
Cross Deep TW1 . . . .**153** A2
Crouch Croft SE9 . . . . . .**166** C1
CROUCH END **49** D3
Crouch End Hill N8 . . . . . .**49** D2
Crouch Hall Ct N19 . . . . . .**50** A1
Crouch Hall Rd N8. . . . . . .**49** D3
Crouch Hill N4, N8, N19 . .**50** A2
Crouch Hill Sta N4 . . . . . .**50** B2
Crouchmans Cl SE21,
SE26 . . . .**162** A1
Crouch Rd NW10 . . . .**67** B1
Crowborough Ct W13 . . .**109** A5
Crowborough Path
WD19 . . . .**22** D6
Crowborough Rd
SW17. . . . .**181** A5
Crowden Way SE28 . . . . .**124** C6
Crowder Cl N12 . . . .**30** A3
Crowder St E1. . . . .**118** B6
Crowfield Ho N5. . . . .**73** A4
Crowfoot Cl
Hackney Wick E9. . . . .**75** B3
Woolwich SE28 . . . .**123** C5
Crowhurst SE25 . . . .**206** A6
Crowhurst Cl SW9 . . . . . .**138** C3
Crowhurst Cl N17. . . . .**34** B2
Crowhurst Ho [2] SW9. . .**138** B3
Crow La RM7, RM8. . . . . . .**59** D2
Crowland Ave UB3 . . . . . .**105** D2
Crowland Gdns N14. . . . . .**16** A4
Crowland Ho NW8 . . . . . .**229** A5
Crowland Prim Sch
N15. . . . .**52** A4
Crowland Rd
South Norwood CR7 . . . .**205** B5
South Tottenham N15 . . . .**51** A4
Crowlands Ave RM7. . . . . .**59** D3
Crowland Terr N1 . . . .**73** B1
Crowland Wlk SM4 . . . . . .**202** A3
Crowley Cres CR0. . . . . . .**220** C3
Crowline Wlk [1] N1. . . . . .**73** C2
Crowmarsh Gdns
SE23 . . . .**162** C4
Crown Arc KT1 . . . .**175** C1
Crown Bldgs [4] E4. . . . . .**20** B3
Crownbourne Ct SM1 . . .**217** D4
Crown Cl Bow E3 . . . .**97** C6
Edgware NW7 . . . .**11** D2
Hampstead NW6 . . . .**69** D2
Hayes UB3. . . . .**105** D4
Walton-on-T KT12 . . . . . .**194** C2
Wood Green N22. . . . .**32** C3
Crown Close Bsns Ctr [12]
E3 . . . .**97** C6
Crown Ct Bromley BR1 . . .**209** D4
City of London EC4 . . . . .**242** B1
Harrow HA2 . . . .**42** C1
Lee SE12 . . . .**165** B5
[11] Muswell Hill N10 . . . .**31** A3
[4] Putney SW15. . . . . . .**134** D1
St Giles WC2. . . . .**240** B1
St John's Wood NW8 . . . .**230** B1
[3] Twickenham TW1. . . .**153** B4
Crown Dale SE19 . . . .**183** A5
Crowndale Ct NW1. . . . . .**232** C2
Crowndale Rd
NW1 . . . .**93** C5 **232** B4

Crowne Ho SE1. . . . .**252** B3
Crownfield Ave IG2. . . . . . .**57** C4
Crownfield Rd E15. . . . . . .**76** B4
Crowngate Ho [13] E3 . . . .**97** B5
Crown Hill CR0 . . . .**221** A5
Crownhill Rd NW10 . . . . . .**89** D6
Crown Ho Ruislip HA4. . . . .**40** A1
Wembley HA9 . . . .**66** B3
Woolwich SE18 . . . .**123** A2
Crown La
Bromley Comm BR2 . . . .**209** D4
Chislehurst BR7 . . . .**189** A2
Merton SM4 . . . .**201** C6
Osidge N14 . . . .**15** C3
South Norwood SE19,
SW16. . . . .**182** C5
Crown Lane Gdns
SE27 . . . .**182** C5
Crown Lane Prim Sch
SE27 . . . .**182** D5
Crown Lane Spur BR2. . .**209** D3
Crownleigh Ct SW2 . . . . .**160** C6
Crown Lo Chelsea SW3 . .**257** B3
Finchley N3 . . . .**29** B1
Crownmead Way RM7. . . .**59** D5
Crown Mews
[2] Newham E13 . . . .**99** C6
[9] Stepney E1. . . . .**96** D2
Crown Mill CR4. . . . .**202** C4
Crown Office Row EC4 . .**251** A6
Crown Par London N14. . . .**15** C3
Morden SM4 . . . .**201** C5
Crown Pas
Kingston u T KT1. . . . . . .**175** C1
St James SW1. . . . .**249** B3
Crown Pl
Broadgate EC2 . . . .**243** A4
Kentish Town NW5 . . . . . .**71** B2
Crown Point Par SE19. . .**182** D4
Crown Rd Enfield EN1 . . . . . .**6** B2
Ilford IG6 . . . .**57** B5
Kingston u T KT3 . . . .**177** A2
Morden SM4 . . . .**201** D5
Muswell Hill N10. . . . .**31** A3
Ruislip HA4 . . . .**62** D3
Sutton SM1 . . . .**217** D4
Twickenham TW1. . . . . . .**153** B5
Crown Reach SW1 . . . . . .**259** D1
Crown St Acton W3 . . . . . .**110** C5
Camberwell SE5 . . . .**139** A5
Dagenham RM10. . . . .**81** D2
Harrow HA2 . . . .**42** C1
Crownstone Ct [1]
SW2 . . . .**160** C6
Crownstone Rd SW2 . . . .**160** C6
Crown Terr TW9 . . . .**132** B1
Crown Trad Ctr UB3. . . . .**105** C4
Crowntree Cl TW7 . . . . . .**130** D6
Crown Way UB7 . . . .**104** B5
Crown Wlk HA9. . . . .**66** B5
Crown Wood La SE18 . . . .**144** D3
Crown Woods Sch
SE9 . . . .**167** A6
Crown Woods Way
SE9 . . . .**167** B6
Crown Yard TW3 . . . .**130** A2
Crowshott Ave HA7 . . . . . .**25** D2
Crows Rd Barking IG11. . . .**78** D2
Mill Meads E15 . . . .**98** B4
Crowther Ave TW8. . . . . .**110** A2
Crowther Cl
SW6. . . . .**135** B6 **264** D5
Crowther Rd SE25 . . . . . .**206** A5
Crowthorne Cl SW18 . . .**157** B3
Crowthorne Rd W10 . . . . .**90** D1
Croxall Ho KT12 . . . .**194** C3
Croxden Cl HA8 . . . .**44** C6
Croxden Wlk SM4. . . . . . .**202** A3
Croxford Gdns N22 . . . . . .**32** D3
Croxley Cl BR5. . . . .**190** B2
Croxley Gn BR5 . . . .**190** B2
Croxley Rd W9 . . . .**91** B4
Croxted Cl SE21 . . . .**161** A4
Croxted Rd SE21, SE24 . .**161** A3
Croxteth Ho [11] SW8. . . .**137** D3
Croxton [7] KT1 . . . .**176** C1
Croyde Ave
Greenford UB6 . . . .**86** A4
Hayes UB3. . . . .**105** C2
Croyde Cl DA15 . . . .**167** B4
Croyden Ct HA0 . . . .**65** D2
CROYDON **221** B5
Croydon N17. . . . .**33** B1
Croydon Airport Ind Est
CR0. . . . .**220** B2
Croydon Coll CR0 . . . . . .**221** B5
Croydon Coll Annexe
CR0. . . . .**205** B2
Croydon Coll (Selhurst
Tertiary Ctr) SE25 . . . .**205** B4
Croydon Flyover The
CR0 . . . .**221** A5
Croydon Gr CR0 . . . .**204** D1
Croydon Ho
Lambeth SE1. . . . .**251** B1
Thornton Heath CR0 . . . .**204** B3
Croydon Rd
Bandonhill CR0, SM5,
SM6 . . . .**219** C5
Beckenham BR3 . . . .**207** A6
Coney Hall BR2, BR4 . . .**224** D5
Harlington TW6 . . . .**126** D2
Keston Mark BR2, BR4,
RM6. . . . .**225** C5
Mitcham CR0, CR4. . . . . .**203** C4
Newham E13 . . . .**98** D3
Penge SE20 . . . .**184** C2
Waddon CR0 . . . .**220** B4
Croydon Rd Ind Est
BR3. . . . .**206** D5

Croydon Valley Trade Pk
2 CR0..........204 A2
Croyland Rd N9.........18 A3
Croylands Dr KT6......198 A2
Croysdale Ave TW16...194 A6
Crozier Ho
  Blackheath Pk SE3......143 B2
  South Lambeth SW8....270 C3
Crozier Terr E9.........74 D3
Crucible Cl RM6.........58 B3
Crucifix La
  SE1.........117 C4 253 A2
Cruden Ho 15 Bow E3.....97 B3
  11 Camberwell SE17...138 D6
Cruden St N1....94 D6 234 D5
Cruikshank Ho SW18.....157 C3
Cruikshank St WC1......234 A2
Cruikshank Rd E15.......76 C3
Crummock Gdns NW9.....45 C4
Crumpsall St SE2......124 C2
Crundale Ave NW9.......44 C4
Crunden Rd CR2........221 B1
Crusader Gdns CR0.....221 B1
Crusader Ho EC1.......241 C5
Crusader Ind Est N4....51 A3
Crusoe Ct E11..........76 D5
Crusoe House Sch
  N1..........95 B4 235 C2
Crusoe Mews N16........73 B6
Crusoe Rd CR4.........180 D3
Crutched Friars
  EC3.........117 C6 253 B6
Crutchfield La KT12....194 B1
Crutchley Rd SE6......164 C2
Crystal Ct SE19........183 D6
Crystal Ctr The 1 HA1..42 D4
Crystal Ho SE18.......123 D1
CRYSTAL PALACE........184 A5
Crystal Palace Mus*
  SE19.......183 D4
Crystal Palace National
  Sports Ctr SE19......184 A4
Crystal Palace Par
  SE19........183 D5
Crystal Palace Park Rd
  SE26........184 B5
Crystal Palace Rd
  SE22........162 A6
Crystal Palace Sta
  SE19........184 A4
Crystal Palace Station Rd
  SE19........184 A4
Crystal Terr SE19......183 B4
Crystal View Ct BR1...186 B6
Crystal Way
  Dagenham RM8........58 C1
  Harrow HA1..........42 D4
Crystal Wharf N1......234 D3
Cuba Dr EN3...........6 C3
Cuba St E14..........119 C4
Cubitt Bldg SW1......258 C1
Cubitt Ho 4 SW4......159 C5
Cubitt Sq UB2.........108 A5
Cubitt St WC1....94 B4 233 D1
Cubitt Terr SW4......137 C2
CUBITT TOWN.........120 A2
Cubitt Town Jun & Inf Sch
  E14..........120 A3
Cuckoo Ave W7.........86 C3
Cuckoo Dene W7........86 B2
Cuckoo Hall La N9.......18 D4
Cuckoo Hall Prim Sch
  N9..........18 C4
Cuckoo Hill HA5.......40 C6
Cuckoo Hill Dr HA5.....40 C6
Cuckoo Hill Rd HA5.....40 D5
Cuckoo La W7.........108 C6
Cuda's Cl KT19.......215 D4
Cuddington Ho 7......262 B4
Cuddington Ave KT19,
  KT4..........215 D5
Cuddington Com Prim Sch
  KT4..........215 D5
Cudham La N BR6......227 C1
Cudham St SE6.........164 A4
Cudworth Ho SW8......269 B1
Cudworth St E1.........96 B3
Cuff Cres SE9.........165 D5
Cuffley Ho 3 W10......90 C2
Cuff Point 12 E2.......95 D4
Culand Ho SE17........263 A3
Culford Gdns
  SW3.........114 D2 257 D3
Culford Gr N1..........73 C2
Culford Mans SW3.....257 D3
Culford Mews N1........73 C2
Culford Rd Kingsland N1..73 C2
  Shoreditch N1.........95 C6
Culgaith Gdns EN2......4 A1
Culham Ho
  21 Paddington W2.....91 C2
  33 Shoreditch E2......95 D4
Cullen Ho W9..........91 B5
Cullen Way NW10.......89 A3
Culling Rd SE16.......118 C3
Cullington Cl HA3......43 A5
Cullingworth Rd NW10..68 B3
Culloden Cl 21 SE16...118 A1
Culloden Prim Sch E14..98 A1
Culloden Rd EN2.......4 D3
Cullum St EC3.......253 A6
Culmington Mans
  W13.........109 C6
Culmington Par W13...109 C6
Culmington Rd
  Ealing W13, W5......109 C5
  South Croydon CR2...221 B1
Culmore Rd SE15.....140 C5
Culmstock Rd SW11....159 A6
Culpepper Cl N18.......34 B5

Culpepper Ct SE11.....261 A4
Culross Bldgs NW1....233 A4
Culross Cl N15.........51 A5
Culross St W1...115 A6 248 A5
Culsac Rd KT6.........214 A6
Culver Ct SW18........157 D5
Culverden Rd SW12....159 C2
Culver Gr HA7.........25 C1
Culverhouse WC1......240 C3
Culverhouse Gdns
  SW16........160 B1
Culverin Ct 1 N7.......72 B3
Culverlands Cl HA7.....26 B6
Culverlands Ct N20.....14 B3
Culverley Rd SE6......164 A3
Culvers Ave SM5......218 C6
Culvers House Prim Sch
  CR4.........203 A1
Culvers Retreat SM5...218 C6
Culverstone Cl BR2....208 D4
Culvers Way SM5......218 C6
Culvert Ct SW11.......137 A3
Culverton Ct 8 DA14..190 A6
Culvert Pl SW11.......137 A3
Culvert Rd
  London SW11.........136 D3
  South Tottenham N15...51 C4
Culworth Ho NW8......230 A4
Culworth St NW8......230 A3
Cumber Ho SW18.......157 C3
Cumberland Ave
  Falconwood DA16.....145 D1
  Wembley NW10........88 B4
Cumberland Bsns Pk
  NW10........88 B4
Cumberland Cl
  Dalston E8...........73 D2
  2 Twickenham TW1...153 B5
  8 Wimbledon SW20...178 D3
Cumberland Cres W14..254 B1
Cumberland Ct
  4 Croydon CR0.......205 B1
  7 Finchley N3........29 B1
  Harrow HA1..........42 C4
  Marylebone W1.......237 D1
  Woodford IG8........37 B3
Cumberland Dr
  Chessington KT9.....214 B5
  Erith DA7...........147 A5
  Hinchley Wood KT10..213 A6
Cumberland Gate
  W1..........114 D6 247 D6
Cumberland Gdns
  Church End NW4.......29 A1
  Finsbury WC1.......234 A2
Cumberland Ho
  Edmonton N9.........18 C3
  Kingston u T KT2.....176 D3
  Paddington W9......236 A5
  1 Putney SW15.......156 C4
  Woolwich SE28.......123 B4
Cumberland Mans
  Marylebone W1......237 C2
  7 West Hampstead
  NW6..........69 C3
Cumberland Market
  NW1..........93 B4 231 D2
Cumberland Mills Sq
  E14..........120 B1
Cumberland Park Ind Est
  NW10........90 A4
Cumberland Pk W3....111 A6
Cumberland Pl
  Catford SE6.........164 D3
  Regent's Pk NW1.....231 C2
  Sunbury TW16.......194 A5
Cumberland Rd
  Acton W3...........111 A6
  Ashford TW15.......148 A1
  Barnes SW13.........134 A4
  Beckenham BR2......208 D6
  Croydon SE25.......206 B3
  Edmonton N9.........18 C3
  Hanwell W7..........108 D4
  Harrow HA1..........41 D4
  Higham Hill E17.......35 A1
  Manor Pk E12.........77 D4
  Newham E13..........99 B3
  Richmond TW9.......132 C5
  Stanmore HA7, HA8....44 B6
  Wood Green N22.......32 B1
Cumberland Sch E13...99 C3
Cumberland St
  SW1.........115 B1 258 D2
Cumberland Terr NW1..231 C3
Cumberland Terrace
  Mews NW1.........231 C3
Cumberland Villas
  W3..........111 A6
Cumberland Wharf 12
  SE16........118 C4
Cumberlow Ave SE25...206 A6
Cumbernauld Gdns
  TW16........171 D5
Cumberton Rd N17......33 B2
Cumbrae Gdns KT6....213 D6
Cumbrian Gdns NW2....69 A6
Cumming St N1.......233 D3
Cumnor Cl 28 SW9.....138 B3
Cumnor Gdns KT17...216 A2
Cumnor Rd SM2......218 A2
Cunard Cres N21.......17 B5
Cunard Pl EC3.......243 B1
Cunard Rd NW10........89 B4
Cunard Wlk 3 SE16...119 A2
Cundy Rd E16..........99 C1
Cundy St SW1...115 A2 258 B3
Cunliffe Rd KT19.....215 D4
Cunliffe St SW16.....181 C4

Cunningham Cl
  Dagenham RM6........58 C4
  West Wickham BR4...223 D6
Cunningham Ct
  Harrow HA1..........42 B4
  Paddington W2......236 C5
Cunningham Ho 16
  SE5..........139 B5
Cunningham Pk HA1.....42 B4
Cunningham Pl
  NW8.........92 B3 236 C6
Cunningham Rd N15.....52 A5
Cunnington St W4......111 A2
Cupar Rd SW11.......268 B2
Cupola Cl BR1.........187 B5
Cureton St
  SW1.........115 D2 259 D3
Curie Gdns NW9........27 C1
Curie Ho 1 HA9........67 A5
Curlew Cl SE28.......124 D6
Curlew Ct KT6........214 C5
Curlew Ho
  Brockley SE4........141 A1
  Enfield EN3..........18 D6
  7 Peckham SE15......139 D4
Curlew St SE1...117 D4 253 D2
Curlew Way UB4........84 D2
Curness St SE13......142 A1
Curnick's La SE27....183 A6
Curran Ave
  Bexley DA15.........167 D6
  Hackbridge SM6.....219 A5
Curran Ho SW3........257 A3
Currey Rd UB6.........64 B2
Curricle St W3........111 C5
Currie Hill Cl SW19...179 B6
Currie Ho 13 SW12....159 D4
Curry Rise NW7.........28 D4
Cursitor St EC4....94 C1 241 A2
Curtain Pl EC2.......243 B6
Curtain Rd EC2...95 C3 243 B6
Curthwaite Gdns EN2...15 D6
Curtis Dr W3..........111 A6
Curtis Field Rd SW16..182 C6
Curtis Ho 7 London N11..31 C5
  Walworth SE17......262 C2
Curtis La HA0..........66 A3
Curtis Rd
  Twickenham TW4.....151 B4
  West Ewell KT19.....215 A1
Curtis St SE1...117 D2 263 C4
Curtis Way
  Bermondsey SE1.....263 C4
  7 Thamesmead SE28..124 D6
Curtlington Ho 3 HA8..27 A1
Curve Bldg The SE4....163 B6
Curve The Ealing W5..109 D4
  Shepherd's Bush W12..112 A6
Curwen Ave E7.........77 B4
Curwen & New Acad Gall*
  W1..........239 C3
Curwen Prim Sch E13...99 B5
Curwen Rd W12.......112 A4
Curzon Ave Enfield EN3..18 D6
  Stanmore HA7........25 A2
Curzon Cl BR6........227 B4
Curzon Cres
  Barking IG11........101 C4
  Willesden NW10......67 C1
Curzon Ct SE9........167 A1
Curzon Gate W1......248 B3
Curzon Ho W5.........87 B3
Curzon Pl HA5.........40 C4
Curzon Rd Ealing W5...87 B3
  Muswell Hill N10......31 B1
  Thornton Heath CR7...204 C3
Curzon Sq W1........248 B3
Curzon St W1...115 B5 248 C4
Cusack Cl TW1........174 D6
Custance Ho N1......235 C3
Custance St N1.......235 C2
CUSTOM HOUSE.......121 C4
Custom House
  EC3.........117 C6 253 A6
Custom House for ExCeL
  Sta E16...........121 B4
Custom House Reach
  SE16........119 B3
Cutbush Ho N7.........71 D3
Cutcombe Rd SE5.....139 A3
Cuthberga Cl IG11......79 A1
Cuthbert Gdns SE25...205 C6
Cuthbert Harrowing Ho
  EC1.........242 A5
Cuthbert Ho W2......236 C4
Cuthbert Rd
  Croydon CR0........220 D6
  8 Edmonton N18......34 A4
  Walthamstow E17.....54 A6
Cuthbert St W2......236 C5
Cuthill Wlk 3 SE5....139 B4
Cutlers Gdns EC2....243 B2
Cutlers Gdns Arc EC2..243 B2
Cutlers Sq E14.......119 C2
Cutler St EC2.......243 B2
Cut The E14...116 C4 251 B2
Cutty Sark* SE10....142 A6
Cutty Sark Ho 10 E14..119 D2
Cutty Sark Ret
  Development SE10...142 A6
Cutty Sark Sta SE10..142 A6
Cuxton BR5..........211 A4
Cuxton Cl DA6.......169 A6
Cuxton Ho SE17......263 B2
Cyclamen Cl 4 TW12..173 C4
Cyclamen Way KT19...215 A3
Cyclops Mews 12 E14..119 C2
Cygnet Ave TW14.....150 D4
Cygnet Cl NW10........67 B3
Cygnet Ct EN3.........7 A1

Cygnet Ho Harrow HA7...24 D4
  St John's Wood NW8...229 A6
Cygnet House N 15 E14..97 D1
Cygnet House S 16 E14..97 D1
Cygnets The TW13.....178 A1
Cygnet St E1.........243 D6
Cygnet Way UB4........84 D2
Cymbeline Ct 6 HA1....42 D3
Cyna Ct 5 E11.........55 A3
Cynthia St N1.......233 D3
Cyntra Pl 8 E8........74 B1
Cypress Ave London N2..29 A1
  Twickenham TW2.....152 A4
Cypress Cl 9 E5.......74 A6
Cypress Cl Cheam SM1..217 C2
  5 Leyton E11.........76 B4
  7 West Norwood
  SW16........182 C5
Cypress Gdns SE4.....163 A6
Cypress Ho SE14......140 D4
Cypress Inf Sch SE25..183 C1
Cypress Jun Sch SE25..183 C1
Cypress Lo SE25......183 C1
Cypress Pl W1.......239 B5
Cypress Rd Harrow HA3..24 B1
  South Norwood SE25..183 C1
Cypress Tree Cl DA15..167 D3
CYPRUS..............122 C6
Cyprus Ave N3.........29 B1
Cyprus Cl N4..........50 C3
Cyprus Ct 9 N3........29 B1
Cyprus Gdns N3........29 A1
Cyprus Ho 10 N3.......29 B1
Cyprus Pl
  23 Bethnal Green E2...96 C5
  Newham E6..........122 C6
Cyprus Rd
  Church End N3........29 B1
  Edmonton N9.........17 D2
Cyprus St E2.........96 C5
Cyprus Sta E6........122 C6
Cyrena Rd SE22.......161 D6
Cyril Jackson Prim Sch
  (North Bldg) E14......119 B6
Cyril Jackson Prim Sch
  (South Bldg) E14......119 B6
Cyril Lo 2 DA14.......190 A6
Cyril Mans SW11.....267 D1
Cyril Rd DA7.........147 A3
Cyril Smith Ho N13.....32 B5
Cyril Thatcher Ho
  SW6.........265 B1
Cyrus Ho EC1.......241 D6
Cyrus St EC1....94 D3 241 D6
Czar St SE8..........141 C6

D

Dabbs Hill La UB5......63 C3
Dabb's La EC1.......241 B5
Dabin Cres SE10......142 A4
Dacca St SE8.........141 B6
Dace Rd E3...........97 C6
Dacre Ave
  Borehamwood WD6...11 B6
  Lewisham SE13......142 C1
Dacre Ho SW3........266 D5
Dacre Pk SE13........142 C2
Dacre Pl SE13........142 C2
Dacre Rd
  Leytonstone E11......54 D1
  Newham E13..........99 B6
  Thornton Heath CR0..204 A2
Dacres Rd SE23......162 D1
Dacre St SW1...115 D3 259 C6
Dade Way UB2........107 B3
Daerwood Cl BR2.....210 B1
Daffodil Cl CR0.......206 D1
Daffodil Gdns IG1......78 D3
Daffodil Pl 7 TW12...173 C4
Daffodil St W12......111 D6
Dafforne Rd SW17....159 A1
DAGENHAM...........81 D1
Dagenham Ave
  Dagenham RM9.......81 B1
  Dagenham RM9......103 A6
Dagenham Dock Sta
  RM9.........103 B5
Dagenham East Sta
  RM10........81 D3
Dagenham Heathway Sta
  RM9.........81 B2
Dagenham Park Com Sch
  RM10........103 D6
Dagenham Rd
  Dagenham RM10......81 D3
  London E10..........53 B1
Dagger La WD23.......9 A6
Dagmar Ave HA9........66 B4
Dagmar Ct
  Cubitt Town E14......120 A3
  South Tottenham N15...51 B5
Dagmar Gdns NW10....90 D5
Dagmar Mews UB2....107 A3
Dagmar Pas N1.......234 D6
Dagmar Rd
  Camberwell SE5......139 C4
  Finsbury Pk N4.......50 C2
  4 Kingston u T KT2...176 D3
  Southall UB2........107 A3
  South Norwood SE25..205 C4
  West Green N15.......51 B5
  Wood Green N22.......31 D2
Dagmar Terr
  N1..........94 D6 234 D6
Dagnall Pk SE25......205 C4
Dagnall Rd SE25......205 C4

Cro-Dan 303

Dagnall St
  SW11.......137 A4 268 A4
Dagnan Rd SW12.....159 C4
Dagobert Ho 27 E1....96 C2
Dagonet Gdns BR1....165 A1
Dagonet Rd BR1......165 A1
Dahlia Gdns Ilford IG1..78 D2
  Mitcham CR4.......203 D5
Dahlia Rd SE2........124 B2
Dahomey Rd SW16....181 C4
Daiglen Sch The IG9...21 C2
Daimler Ho 8 E3......97 C3
Daimler Way SM6......220 A1
Daines Cl E12.........78 B5
Dainford Cl BR1......186 B5
Dainton Cl 1 BR1.....187 B2
Dainton Ho 22 W2.....91 C2
Daintry Cl HA3........43 A5
Daintry Way E9........75 B2
Dairsie Ct 3 BR1......187 C1
Dairsie Rd SE9.......144 C2
Dairy Cl Bromley BR1..187 B3
  South Norwood CR7...183 A1
  Willesden NW10......90 A6
Dairy La SE18.........122 B2
Dairyman Cl NW2......69 A5
Dairy Meadow Prim Sch
  UB2.........107 B3
Daisy Cl CR0.........206 D1
Daisy Dormer Ct 11
  SW9.........138 B3
Daisy Ho GI3..........58 A1
Daisy La SW6.........135 C2
Daisy Rd Newham E16...98 C3
  Woodford E18.........37 B1
Dakin Pl 5 E1..........97 A2
Dakota bldg 6 SE13...141 D4
Dakota Cl SM6........220 B1
Dakota Gdns
  Newham E6..........100 A3
  Northolt UB5.........85 A4
Dalberg Rd SW2......160 C6
Dalberg Way SE2......124 D3
Dalbury Ho 6 SW9....138 B1
Dalby Rd SW18.......136 A1
Dalbys Cres N17.......33 C4
Dalby St NW5..........71 B2
Dalcross Rd TW4, TW5.129 A3
Dale Ave Edgware HA8..26 B1
  Hounslow TW4......129 A2
Dalebury Rd SW17....158 D2
Dale Cl
  Blackheath Pk SE3...143 A2
  New Barnet EN5......13 D5
  Pinner HA5..........22 B2
Dale Croft N4.........73 A5
Dale Ct Cranleigh Gdns N8..49 C5
  3 Kingston u T KT2...176 B3
  Northolt UB5.........63 B1
  Wembley HA0.........65 D4
  Woodford E18.........37 A1
Dale Dr UB4...........83 D4
Dalefield IG9..........21 D3
Dale Gdns IG8..........37 B6
Dale Gr N12...........30 A5
Dale Green Rd N11.....15 B1
Dalehead NW1.......232 A3
Daleham Dr UB8........82 D1
Daleham Gdns NW3.....70 B2
Daleham Mews NW3....70 B2
Dale Ho London SE4...141 A1
  St John's Wood NW8..229 A6
Dale Lo N6...........49 C3
Dalemain Ho 5 SW8...137 D3
Dalemain Mews 12
  E16.........121 A5
Dale Park Ave SM5....218 D6
Dale Park Rd SE19...183 B2
Dale Rd Ashford TW16..171 D3
  Camberwell SE17.....138 D6
  Cheam SM1.........217 B4
  Gospel Oak NW5......71 A3
  Southall UB2.........85 D2
  Walton-on-T KT12...193 D2
Dale Row W11.........91 A1
Daleside Rd
  Streatham SW17.....181 B5
  West Ewell KT19.....215 B2
Dales Path WD6........11 B6
Dales Rd WD6.........11 B6
Dale St W4..........111 C1
Dale The BR2........225 D4
Dale View Ave E4......20 A2
Dale View Cres E4.....20 A1
Dale View Gdns E4.....20 B1
Daleview Rd N15.......51 C3
Dalewood Gdns KT4...216 B6
Dale Wood Rd BR6....211 C1
Daley Ho 6 W12........90 B1
Daley St E9...........74 D2
Daley Thompson Way 7
  SW8.........137 B2
Dalgarno Gdns W10....90 C2
Dalgarno Way W10.....90 C3
Daling Way E3.........97 A5
Dalkeith Ct SW1......259 D3
Dalkeith Gr HA7.......26 A5
Dalkeith Ho 5 SW9....138 D4
Dalkeith Rd Ilford IG1..79 A5
  West Norwood SE21...161 A4
Dallas Ct SM3.......217 A2
Dallas Rd Cheam SM3..217 A2
  Ealing W5...........88 B2
  Forest Hill SE26.....162 B1
  Hendon NW4..........46 A2
Dallas Terr UB3.......105 D3
Dallega Cl UB3.......105 A6
Dallinger Rd SE12....164 D5
Dalling Rd W6.........112 B2

Cro-Dan 303

Dallington Sch
  EC1.........94 D3 241 D6
Dallington St
  EC1.........94 D3 241 D6
Dallin Rd Bexley DA6..146 D1
  Woolwich SE18......144 D5
Dalmain Prim Sch
  SE23........163 A3
Dalmain Rd SE23.....162 D3
Dalmally Pas CR0.....205 D2
Dalmally Passage
  CR0.........205 D2
Dalmally Rd CR0......206 D2
Dalmeny Ave
  Thornton Heath
  SW16........182 C1
  Tufnell Pk N7.........71 D4
Dalmeny Avenue Est 3
  N7..........71 D4
Dalmeny Cl HA0........65 C2
Dalmeny Cres TW3....130 B1
Dalmeny Ct 4 SW4....138 A3
Dalmeny Rd Erith DA8..147 B3
  New Barnet EN5......14 A5
  North Cheam KT4....216 B5
  Tufnell Pk N7.........71 D4
  Wallington SM5.....219 A1
Dalmeyer Rd NW10.....67 D2
Dalmore Ave KT10....212 D2
Dalmore Rd SE21.....161 A2
Dalrymple Cl N14......15 D4
Dalrymple Rd SE4.....141 A1
DALSTON............74 A2
Dalston Gdns HA7......26 A1
Dalston Jct E8........73 D2
Dalston Kingsland Sta
  E8..........73 D3
Dalston La E8.........74 A3
Dalton Ave CR4......180 C5
Dalton Cl Hayes UB4...83 B3
  Orpington BR6......227 C5
Dalton Ho
  7 Balham SW12.....159 B4
  10 Bow E3..........97 A5
  19 Deptford SE14...140 D6
  Merton SW19.......180 A2
  Stanmore HA7.......25 B5
Dalton St SE27.......160 D1
Daltry Ho HA1.........42 D5
Dalwood St SE5......139 C4
Daly Ct E15...........76 A3
Daly Dr BR1..........210 C6
Dalyell Rd SW9.......138 B2
Damascene Wlk SE21..161 A3
Damask Cres E16......98 C3
Damask Ct SM1.......201 D1
Damer Ho 9 TW10....154 B5
Damer Terr SW10.....266 B3
Dames Rd E7..........77 A5
Dame St N1......95 A5 235 A4
Damien Ct 12 E1.......96 B1
Damien St E1..........96 B1
Damon Cl DA14.......168 B1
Damon Ct DA14.......168 B1
Damory Ho 1 SE16...118 C2
Damsel Ct DA14.......168 B1
Damson Dr UB3......106 A6
Damsonwood Rd NW2..107 C3
Danbrook Rd SW16...182 A3
Dan Bryant Ho 5
  SW12........159 C4
Danbury Cl RM6........58 C4
Danbury Mans IG11...78 D1
Danbury Mews SM5,
  SM6.........219 B4
Danbury St N1...94 D5 234 D4
Danbury Way IG8......37 C4
Danby Ct EN2.........5 A2
Danby Ho
  22 Hackney E9........74 C1
  3 West Kilburn W10...91 B4
Danby St SE15.......139 D2
Dancastle Ct 7 N3....29 C2
Dancer Rd
  Fulham SW6.....135 B4 264 C1
  Richmond TW9......132 C2
Dando Cres SE3......143 B2
Dandridge Cl SE10...120 D1
Dandridge Ho E1.....243 C4
Danebury
  New Addington CR0...223 D2
  18 North Kensington
  W10.........90 C2
Danebury Ave SW15...155 D5
Daneby Rd SE6......164 A2
Dane Ct
  Farnborough BR6...227 B3
  Sidcup DA5.........169 C4
Danecourt Gdns CR0..221 D5
Danecroft Rd SE24...161 B6
Daneglen Ct 18 HA7...25 C5
Danegrove Prim Sch
  EN4.........14 C5
Danegrove Sch EN4...14 D5
Danehill Wlk DA14...168 A1
Dane Ho
  15 London SE5......139 A3
  Upper Tooting SW17..180 A6
Danehurst TW8......131 C4
Danehurst Gdns IG4...56 B4
Danehurst St
  SW6.........135 A4 264 C2
Daneland EN4........14 D5
Danemead Gr UB5......63 D3
Danemere St SW15...134 C2
Dane Pl E3...........97 B5
Dane Rd Ashford TW15..171 B4

Dane Rd *continued*
Ealing W13 ... 109 C5
Ilford IG1 ... 79 A3
Lower Edmonton N18 ... 18 C1
Merton SW19 ... 180 A2
Southall UB1 ... 107 A6
Danesbury Rd TW13 ... 150 B3
Danescombe SE12 ... 165 A3
Danescourt Cres SM1 ... 218 A6
Danescroft Hendon NW4 ... 46 D4
3 North Finchley N12 ... 30 A5
Danescroft Ave NW4 ... 46 D4
Danescroft Gdns NW4 ... 46 D4
Danes Ct
Primrose Hill NW8 ... 230 C5
Wembley HA9 ... 66 D5
Danesdale Rd E9 ... 75 A2
Danesfield SE5 ... 139 C6
Danes Gate HA1 ... 42 C6
Danes Ho 10 W10 ... 90 C2
Dane St WC1 ... 240 C3
Daneswood Ave SE6 ... 164 A1
Danethorpe Rd HA0 ... 65 D2
Danetree Cl KT19 ... 215 A1
Danetree Jun Sch
KT19 ... 215 A1
Danetree Rd KT19 ... 215 A1
Danette Gdns RM8 ... 81 B6
Daneville Rd SE5 ... 139 B4
Danford Ho 9 N11 ... 31 C5
Dangan Rd E11 ... 55 A3
Daniel Almshouse NW4 ... 46 B5
Daniel Bolt Cl E14 ... 97 D2
Daniel Cl London N18 ... 34 C6
Twickenham TW4 ... 151 B4
Upper Tooting SW17 ... 180 C4
Daniel Ct Acton W3 ... 111 C6
3 Beckenham BR3 ... 185 C3
7 Edgware HA8 ... 26 D5
10 Hendon NW9 ... 27 C2
Daniel Gdns SE15 ... 139 D5
Daniel Ho 1 HA5 ... 22 C1
Daniell Ho N1 ... 235 D4
Daniell Way CR0 ... 204 B1
Daniel Pl NW4 ... 46 B2
Daniel Rd W5 ... 110 B6
Daniel's Rd SE15 ... 140 C2
Dan Leno Wlk SW6 ... 265 C3
Dansey Pl W1 ... 249 C6
Dansington Rd DA16 ... 146 A1
Danson Cres DA16 ... 146 B2
Danson House★ DA6 ... 146 C1
Danson Intc DA5 ... 168 C5
Danson La DA16 ... 146 B1
Danson Mead DA16 ... 146 C2
Danson Prim Sch
DA16 ... 146 A1
Danson Rd DA5 ... 168 D6
Danson Underpass
DA5 ... 168 C5
Dante Pl SE11 ... 261 D3
Dante Rd SE11 .. 116 D2 261 C4
Danube Ct 13 SE15 ... 139 D5
Danube St
SW3 ... 114 C1 257 B2
Danvers Ho 35 E1 ... 96 A1
Danvers Rd N8 ... 49 D5
Danvers St
SW3 ... 136 B6 266 D5
Da Palma Ct SW6 ... 265 A5
Daphne Ct Ealing W5 ... 87 C1
Wembley HA0 ... 65 D3
Worcester Pk KT4 ... 215 C6
Daphne Gdns E4 ... 20 A1
Daphne Ho N22 ... 32 C2
Daphne St SW18 ... 158 A5
Daplyn St 6 E1 ... 96 A2
D'arblay St W1 .. 93 C1 239 B1
Darby Cres TW16 ... 172 C1
Darby Gdns TW16 ... 172 C1
Darcy Ave SM6 ... 219 C4
Darcy Cl N20 ... 14 B2
D'arcy Dr HA3 ... 43 D5
D'arcy Gdns
Dagenham RM9 ... 103 B6
Harrow HA3 ... 44 A5
Darcy Ho E8 ... 96 B6
D'arcy Pl BR2 ... 209 A5
Darcy Rd
Isleworth TW7 ... 131 A4
Thornton Heath SW16 ... 182 A1
D'arcy Rd SM3 ... 216 D4
Dare Ct 2 E10 ... 54 A2
Dare Gdns RM8 ... 81 A5
Darell Prim Sch TW9 ... 132 C2
Darell Rd TW9 ... 132 C2
Daren Ct N7 ... 72 A4
Darent Ho
4 Catford BR1 ... 186 B5
Lisson Gr NW8 ... 236 D4
Darenth Rd
Stamford Hill N16 ... 51 D1
Welling DA16 ... 146 A4
Darfield NW1 ... 232 A5
Darfield Rd SE4 ... 163 B6
Darfield Way W10 ... 90 D1
Darfur St SW15 ... 134 D2
Dargate Cl SE19 ... 183 D3
Darien Ho
17 London SW11 ... 136 B2
11 Stepney E1 ... 96 D2
Darien Rd SW11 ... 136 B2
Daring Ho 23 E3 ... 97 A5
Darland Ho SE9 ... 167 B5
Darlands Dr EN5 ... 12 D6
Darlan Rd SW6 . 135 B5 264 D3
Darlaston Rd SW19 ... 179 A3
Darley Cl CR0 ... 207 A3
Darley Dr KT3 ... 177 B1
Darley Gdns SM4 ... 201 D3
Darley Ho SE11 ... 260 C1
Darley Rd
Clapham SW11 ... 158 D5
Edmonton N9 ... 17 D3
Darling Ho 12 TW1 ... 153 D5
Darling Rd SE4 ... 141 C2
Darling Row E1 ... 96 B3
Darlington Ct 8 SE6 ... 164 D3
Darlington Ho
South Lambeth SW8 ... 269 D3
2 Surbiton KT6 ... 197 D2
Darlington Rd SE27 ... 182 D5
Darmaine Cl CR2 ... 221 A1
Darnall Ho 4 SE10 ... 142 A4
Darnay Ho 3 SE16 ... 118 A3
Darndale Cl E17 ... 35 B1
Darnell Ho 9 SE10 ... 142 A5
Darnley Ho 7 E14 ... 97 A1
Darnley Rd Hackney E9 ... 74 C2
Woodford IG8 ... 37 B2
Darnley Terr 12 W11 ... 112 D5
Darrell Ct BR2 ... 208 C6
Darrell Rd SE22 ... 162 A6
Darren Cl N4 ... 50 B2
Darrick Wood Ho BR6 .. 227 A5
Darrick Wood Inf Sch
BR6 ... 226 D5
Darrick Wood Jun Sch
BR6 ... 226 D4
Darrick Wood Rd BR6 .. 227 B6
Darrick Wood Sch
BR6 ... 226 D5
Darrick Wood Sports Ctr
BR6 ... 227 A5
Darris Cl UB4 ... 85 A3
Darsley Dr
SW8 ... 138 A4 270 A2
Dartford Ave N9 ... 18 D5
Dartford Gdns RM6 ... 58 B4
Dartford Ho SE1 ... 263 D4
Dartford St SE17 ... 139 A6
Dartington NW1 ... 232 B5
Dartington Ho
Bayswater W2 ... 91 D2
7 London SW8 ... 137 D3
Dartle Ct 23 SE16 ... 118 A4
Dartmoor Wlk 18 E14 .. 119 C2
Dartmouth Cl W11 ... 91 C1
Dartmouth Ct SE10 ... 142 A4
Dartmouth Gr SE10 ... 142 A4
Dartmouth Hill SE10 ... 142 A4
Dartmouth Ho
Dartmouth Pk N19 ... 71 B6
11 Kingston u T KT2 ... 176 A2
Lewisham SE10 ... 142 A3
Thornton Heath CR0 ... 204 D2
DARTMOUTH PARK ... 71 B5
Dartmouth Park Ave
NW5 ... 71 B5
Dartmouth Park Hill
N19 ... 71 B6
Dartmouth Park Rd
NW5 ... 71 B5
Dartmouth Pl
Chiswick W4 ... 133 C6
Forest Hill SE23 ... 162 C2
Dartmouth Rd
Brondesbury NW2 ... 68 D2
Forest Hill SE23, SE26 .. 162 C1
Hayes BR2 ... 209 A2
Hendon NW4 ... 46 A3
Ruislip HA4 ... 62 A5
Dartmouth Row SE10 .. 142 A4
Dartmouth St
SW1 ... 115 D4 249 D1
Dartmouth Terr SE10 .. 142 B4
Dartnell Rd CR0 ... 205 D2
Darton Ct W3 ... 111 A5
Dartrey Twr SW10 ... 266 C4
Dartrey Wlk
SW10 ... 136 A5 266 B4
Dart St W10 ... 91 B4
Darville Rd N16 ... 73 D5
Darwell Cl E6 ... 100 C5
Darwen Pl E2 ... 96 B6
Darwin Cl
Farnborough BR6 ... 227 B3
New Southgate N11 ... 15 B1
Darwin Ct Eltham SE9 ... 166 C5
Newham E13 ... 99 B4
Primrose Hill NW1 ... 231 B6
Darwin Dr UB1 ... 85 D1
Darwin Gdns WD19 ... 22 C5
Darwin Ho
8 London SE13 ... 142 A3
2 Wembley HA9 ... 67 A5
Darwin Rd Ealing W5 ... 109 C2
Falconwood DA16 ... 145 D2
Tottenham N22 ... 32 D1
Darwin St
SE17 ... 117 B2 262 D4
Daryngton Dr UB6 ... 86 C5
Daryngton Ho SW8 ... 270 A3
Dashwood Cl DA6 ... 169 C6
Dashwood Ct TW3 ... 130 A1
Dashwood Ho SE21 ... 161 D1
Dashwood Rd N8 ... 50 B3
Dassett Rd SE27 ... 182 D5
Data Point Bsns Ctr
E16 ... 98 B3
Datchelor Pl 14 SE5 ... 139 B4
Datchet Ho NW1 ... 231 D2
Datchet Rd SE6 ... 163 B2
Datchett Ho 40 E2 ... 95 D4
Datchwood Ct N4 ... 73 A5
Datchworth Ct 7 EN1 ... 17 C6
Datchworth Ho 8 N1 ... 72 D1
Date St SE17 ... 117 B1 262 C1
Daubeney Gdns N17 ... 33 A3
Daubeney Pl TW12 ... 173 D1
Daubeney Prim Sch E5 . 75 A4
Daubeney Rd
Clapton Pk E5 ... 75 A4
Tottenham N17 ... 33 A3
Daubeney Twr 2 SE8 .. 119 B1
Dault Rd SW18 ... 158 A5
Dauney Ho SE1 ... 251 C1
Dauphine Ct HA3 ... 24 C1
Dave Adams Ho 8 E3 ... 97 B5
Davenant Ho 20 E1 ... 96 A2
Davenant Rd
Croydon CR0, CR9 ... 220 D4
Upper Holloway N19 ... 71 D6
Davenant St E1 ... 96 A2
Davenport Cl TW11 ... 175 A4
Davenport Ctr IG11 ... 102 B5
Davenport Ho SE11 ... 261 A5
Davenport Lo TW3 ... 129 A5
Davenport Mews 6
W12 ... 112 B5
Davenport Rd
London SE6 ... 164 A5
Sidcup DA14 ... 169 A2
Daventer Dr HA7 ... 24 D3
Daventry Ave E17 ... 53 C3
Daventry St
NW1 ... 92 C2 237 A4
Dave Porter Hts
SW19 ... 157 A4
Dave Ramsey Ho SE18 .. 123 B2
Daver Ct Chelsea SW3 .. 257 B1
Ealing W5 ... 87 D3
Davern Cl SE10 ... 120 D2
Davey Cl Bowes Pk N13 ... 32 B5
Islington N7 ... 72 B2
Davey Ho HA9 ... 67 A6
Davey Rd E9 ... 75 C1
Davey's Ct WC2 ... 250 A6
Davey St SE15 ... 139 D6
David Ave UB6 ... 86 C5
David Beckham Acad The
SE10 ... 120 D4
David Cl UB3 ... 127 C5
David Coffer Ct DA17 .. 125 D2
David Ct N20 ... 14 A1
David Devine Ho 7 E8 .. 74 A3
David Game Coll SW7 . 256 C3
Davidge Ho SE1 ... 251 B1
Davidge St
SE1 ... 116 D4 251 D1
David Henry Waring Ct
TW14 ... 149 A3
David Hewitt Ho 2 E3 .. 97 D2
David Ho
8 Putney SW15 ... 156 A6
South Lambeth SW8 ... 270 A4
South Norwood SE25 ... 206 A6
David Lee Point 4 E15 .. 98 C6
David Livingstone Prim
Sch CR7 ... 183 A2
David Mews W1 ... 237 D4
David Rd RM8 ... 81 A6
Davidson Gdns
SW8 ... 138 A5 270 A4
Davidson Ho 7 N19 ... 71 C4
Davidson Lo CR0 ... 205 C2
Davidson Prim Sch
CR0 ... 205 D2
Davidson Rd CR0 ... 205 D3
Davidson Terrs E7 ... 77 B3
David's Rd SE23 ... 162 C3
David St E15 ... 76 B3
David Twigg Cl KT2 ... 176 A2
Davies Cl CR0 ... 206 A3
Davies La E11 ... 76 D6
Davies Laing & Dick Coll
W1 ... 93 A1 238 B2
Davies Lane Prim Sch
E11 ... 76 D6
Davies Mews W1 ... 248 C6
Davies St W1 ... 115 B6 248 C6
Davies Walk TW7 ... 130 B4
Davina Ho
Brondesbury NW2 ... 69 B2
14 Hackney E5 ... 74 B3
Da Vinci Ct 12 SE16 ... 118 B1
Davington Ct 19 SM2 ... 217 C1
Davington Gdns RM8 ... 80 B3
Davington Rd RM8 ... 80 B3
Davis Ct 1 N20 ... 14 B2
Davis Ho 35 W12 ... 112 B6
Davis Rd
Bedford Pk W3 ... 111 D4
Chessington KT9 ... 214 C4
Davis Sch The E10 ... 53 D1
Davis St E13 ... 99 B5
Davisville Rd W12 ... 112 A4
Davmor Ct TW8 ... 109 C1
Dawes Ave TW7 ... 131 A1
Dawe's Cl UB10 ... 82 A5
Dawes Ho SE17 ... 262 C3
Dawes Rd SW6 . 135 B5 264 C4
Dawe's Rd UB10 ... 82 A5
Dawes St SE17 .. 117 B1 262 D2
Dawley Ave UB8 ... 83 A1
Dawley Par UB3 ... 105 A6
Dawley Rd
Harlington UB3 ... 105 C2
Hayes UB3 ... 105 B6
Dawlish Ave
Bowes Pk N13 ... 32 A5
Wandsworth SW18 ... 157 D2
Wembley UB6 ... 87 A5
Dawlish Dr Ilford IG3 ... 79 D4
Pinner HA5 ... 41 A3
Ruislip HA4 ... 62 B6
Dawlish Prim Sch E10 ... 54 A1
Dawlish Rd
Brondesbury NW2 ... 68 D2
Leyton E10 ... 76 A6
Tottenham Hale N17 ... 52 A6
Dawnay Gdns SW18 ... 158 B2
Dawnay Rd SW17,
SW18 ... 158 B2
Dawn Cl TW4 ... 129 A2
Dawn Cres E15 ... 98 B6
Dawn Wlk BR2 ... 186 B1
Dawpool Rd NW2 ... 67 D6
Daws La NW7 ... 28 A5
Dawson Ave
Barking IG11 ... 79 D1
St Paul's Cray BR5 ... 190 B1
Dawson Cl Hayes UB3 ... 83 B2
Woolwich SE18 ... 123 A2
Dawson Gdns 10 IG11 ... 79 D1
Dawson Ho
23 Bethnal Green E2 ... 96 C4
5 Camberwell SE5 ... 139 C4
Dawson Pl W2 .. 113 C6 245 B6
Dawson Rd
Cricklewood NW2 ... 68 C4
Kingston u T KT1 ... 198 B6
Dawson St E2 ... 95 D5
Dawson Terr N9 ... 18 C4
Dax Ct TW16 ... 194 C6
Daybrook Rd SW19 ... 201 D6
Day Ho 2 SE5 ... 139 A5
Daylesford Ave SW15 .. 134 A1
Daymer Gdns HA5 ... 40 C5
Daynor Ho 4 NW6 ... 91 C6
Day's Armhouses HA8 ... 26 B5
Daysbrook Rd SW2 ... 160 B3
Days La DA15 ... 167 C4
Days Lane Prim Sch
DA15 ... 167 D5
Daytone Ho SW20 ... 178 D2
Dayton Gr SE15 ... 140 C4
Deaconess Ct 5 N15 ... 51 D5
Deacon Ho SE11 ... 260 D3
Deacon Mews N1 ... 73 B1
Deacon Rd
Kingston u T KT2 ... 176 B2
Willesden NW2 ... 68 A2
Deacons Cl HA5 ... 22 B1
DEACONS HILL ... 10 C5
Deacon's Hill Rd WD6 ... 10 C6
Deacons Hts WD6 ... 10 C5
Deacons Leas BR6 ... 227 B4
Deacons Rise N2 ... 48 B4
Deacons Wlk TW12 ... 173 C6
Deacon Way
SE17 ... 117 A2 262 B4
Deal Ct 13 Hendon NW9 .. 27 D1
7 Southall UB1 ... 86 A1
Deal Ho Deptford SE15 .. 140 D6
Walworth SE17 ... 263 B2
Deal Porters Way
SE16 ... 118 D3
Deal Rd SW17 ... 181 A4
Deal St E1 ... 96 A2
Dealtry Rd SW15 ... 134 C1
Deal Wlk 3 SW9 ... 138 C5
Dean Bradley St SW1 . 260 A5
Dean Cl Hackney E9 ... 74 C3
Hillingdon UB10 ... 60 B1
Rotherhithe SE16 ... 118 D5
Dean Coll of London
N7 ... 72 B5
Deancross St E1 ... 96 C1
Dean Ct Acton W3 ... 89 B1
Ealing W13 ... 109 B5
10 Kingston u T KT2 ... 176 C3
South Lambeth SW8 ... 270 A3
Wembley HA0 ... 65 B5
Dean Dr HA7 ... 26 A1
Deane Ave HA4 ... 62 C3
Deane Croft Rd HA5 ... 40 C3
Deanery Cl N2 ... 48 C5
Deanery Mews W1 ... 248 B4
Deanery Rd E15 ... 76 C2
Deanery St W1 . 115 A5 248 B4
Deanesfield Prim HA4 .. 62 D4
Deane Way HA4 ... 40 B3
Dean Farrar St SW1 ... 259 D6
Deanfield Gdns CR0 ... 221 B4
Dean Gdns E17 ... 54 B5
Deanhill Ct 2 SW14 ... 132 D1
Deanhill Rd SW14 ... 132 D1
Dean Ho London N4 ... 51 A2
New Cross SE14 ... 141 B5
Ruislip HA4 ... 39 B1
Stamford Hill N16 ... 51 D1
18 Stepney E1 ... 96 C1
Dean Rd Croydon CR0 ... 221 B4
Hampton TW12 ... 173 C5
Hounslow TW3 ... 151 D6
Thamesmead SE28 ... 124 A6
Willesden NW2 ... 68 C2
Dean Ryle St SW1 ... 260 A4
Dean's Bldgs
SE17 ... 117 B2 262 D3
Deansbrook Cl HA8 ... 27 A3
Deansbrook Jun & Inf
Schs NW7 ... 27 A4
Deansbrook Rd
Burnt Oak HA8 ... 27 B4
Edgware HA8 ... 26 D3
Deans Cl Burnt Oak HA8 .. 27 A4
Chiswick W4 ... 132 D6
South Croydon CR0 ... 221 D5
Deanscroft Ave NW9 ... 45 A1
Deans Ct HA8 ... 26 D4
Dean's Ct EC4 ... 241 D1
Deans Dr N13 ... 32 D4
Dean's Dr HA8 ... 27 B5
Deansfield Prim Sch
Eltham SE9 ... 144 C2
Deansfield Prim Sch
continued
Ruislip HA4 ... 62 D4
Deans Gate Cl SE23 ... 162 D1
Deanshanger Ho 21
SE8 ... 118 D2
Dean's La HA8 ... 27 A4
Dean's Mews W1 ... 238 D2
Deans Rd SM1 ... 217 D5
Dean's Rd W7 ... 108 D4
Dean St Forest Gate E7 ... 77 A3
Soho W1 ... 93 D1 239 C1
Dean Stanley St SW1 .. 260 A5
Deansway
East Finchley N2 ... 48 B5
Edmonton N9 ... 17 C1
Deans Way HA8 ... 27 A5
Deanswood N11 ... 31 D4
Dean's Yd SW1 ... 259 D6
Dean Trench St SW1 .. 260 A5
Dean Way UB2 ... 107 D4
Dean Wlk HA8 ... 27 B3
Deanwood Ct N14 ... 15 C3
Dearmer Ho 6 SW2 ... 160 C4
Dearne Cl HA7 ... 25 A5
De'arn Gdns CR4 ... 202 C6
Dearsley Rd EN1 ... 6 A2
Deason St E15 ... 98 A6
Deauville Ct
14 London SW4 ... 159 C5
4 Rotherhithe SE16 ... 118 D4
Deauville Mans 13
SW4 ... 159 C5
De Barowe Mews 1
N5 ... 72 D3
Debdale Ho 20 E2 ... 96 A6
Debden N17 ... 33 B1
Debden Cl
7 Edgware NW9 ... 27 C2
Kingston u T KT2 ... 175 D5
Woodford IG8 ... 37 D3
De Beauvoir Cres N1 ... 95 C6
De Beauvoir Ct N1 ... 73 B1
De Beauvoir Pl 5 N1 ... 73 C2
De Beauvoir Prim Sch
N1 ... 73 C2
De Beauvoir Rd N1 ... 73 C1
De Beauvoir Sq N1 ... 73 C1
DE BEAUVOIR TOWN ... 73 C1
Debenham Ct
Barnet EN5 ... 12 C6
Hackney E8 ... 96 A6
Debham Ct NW2 ... 68 C5
Debnams Rd SE16 ... 118 C2
De Bohun Ave N14 ... 15 B5
De Bohun Prim Sch
N14 ... 15 B6
Deborah Cl TW7 ... 130 C4
Deborah Cres HA4 ... 39 B2
Deborah Ct 7 E18 ... 55 B6
Deborah Lo HA8 ... 26 D2
De Broome Rd TW13 ... 150 C3
De Burgh Ho 10 SW19 .. 180 A3
Deburgh Rd SW19 ... 180 A3
Debussy 9 NW9 ... 27 D1
Decimal Ctr UB2 ... 107 C4
Decima St SE1 .. 117 C3 263 A6
Decimus Cl CR7 ... 205 B5
Deck Cl SE16 ... 118 D5
Decoy Ave NW11 ... 47 A5
De Crespigny Pk SE5 ... 139 B3
Dedham Ho 1 SE6 ... 186 A6
Dee Ct W7 ... 86 B1
Deeley Rd
SW8 ... 137 D4 269 C2
Deena Cl W3 ... 88 B1
Deepdale Highbury N4 ... 72 D5
Wimbledon SW19 ... 178 D6
Deepdale Ave BR2 ... 208 D5
Deepdale Cl N11 ... 31 A4
Deepdene N12 ... 30 C6
Deepdene Ave CR0 ... 221 D5
Deepdene Cl E11 ... 55 A5
Deepdene Ct
Beckenham BR2 ... 208 C6
Southgate N21 ... 16 D5
Deepdene Gdns SW2 ... 160 B4
Deepdene Ho N16 ... 51 B1
Deepdene Lo 5 SW2 ... 160 B4
Deepdene Mans SW6 ... 264 C2
Deepdene Point 9
SE26 ... 162 D1
Deepdene Rd
London SE5, SE24 ... 139 B1
Welling DA16 ... 146 A2
Deepwell Cl TW7 ... 131 A4
Deepwood La UB6 ... 86 B4
Deerbrook Rd SE24,
SW2 ... 160 D3
Dee Rd TW9 ... 132 B1
Deerdale Rd SE24 ... 139 A1
Deerfield Cl NW9 ... 45 D4
Deerhurst
7 Kingston u T KT2 ... 176 D2
5 Streatham SW16 ... 182 A5
Deerhurst Cl TW13 ... 172 B6
Deerhurst Cres TW12 ... 174 A5
Deerhurst Ct CR0 ... 204 D1
Deerhurst Ho 6 SE15 .. 140 A6
Deerhurst Rd
Brondesbury NW2 ... 68 D2
Streatham SW16 ... 182 B5
Deerings Ct 2 N20 ... 14 B2
Deerings Dr HA5 ... 40 A4
Deerleap Gr E4 ... 19 D6
Deer Lo SW6 ... 135 A2
Deer Park Cl KT2 ... 176 D3
Deer Park Gdns CR4 ... 202 B5
Deer Park Rd SW19 ... 180 A1
Deer Park Way BR4 ... 224 D6
Deesdale Ct CR2 ... 221 B4
Deeside Rd SW17 ... 158 B1
Dee St E14 ... 98 A1
Defence Cl SE28 ... 123 C5
Defiance Wlk SE18 ... 122 B3
Defiant 18 NW9 ... 27 D1
Defiant Way SM6 ... 220 A1
Defoe Ave TW9 ... 132 C5
Defoe Cl SW17 ... 180 C4
Defoe Ho Barbican EC2 . 242 A4
5 Stoke Newington N16 . 73 C5
Defoe Pl Barbican EC2 .. 242 A4
Upper Tooting SW17 ... 180 D6
Defoe Rd
Rotherhithe SE16 ... 119 B4
Stoke Newington N16 ... 73 C5
De Frene Rd SE26 ... 163 A1
De Gama Pl 3 E14 ... 119 C1
Degema Rd BR7 ... 188 D5
Dehar Cres NW9 ... 46 A2
De Haviland Dr 8
SE18 ... 122 D1
Dehavilland Cl UB5 ... 84 D4
De Havilland Rd
Edgware HA8 ... 26 D1
Heston TW5 ... 128 C5
De Havilland Sq IG1 ... 57 B1
Dehavilland Studios E5 . 74 C6
De Havilland Way
TW19 ... 148 A5
Dekker Ho 19 SE5 ... 139 B5
Dekker Rd SE21 ... 161 C5
Delacourt Rd SE3 ... 143 B5
Delafield Ho 25 E1 ... 96 A1
Delafield Rd SE7 ... 121 C1
Delaford Rd SE16 ... 118 B1
Delaford St
SW6 ... 135 A6 264 B5
Delamare Cres CR0 ... 206 C3
Delamere Gdns NW7 ... 27 B4
Delamere Ho 4 N4 ... 51 B2
Delamere Rd
Ealing W5 ... 110 A4
Hayes UB4 ... 106 D6
Wimbledon SW20 ... 178 D2
Delamere St W2 ... 236 A3
Delamere Terr W2 ... 91 D2
Delancey Pas NW1 ... 231 D5
Delancey St
NW1 ... 93 B6 231 D5
Delancey Studios
NW1 ... 231 D5
Delany Ho SE10 ... 142 A6
Delarch Ho SE1 ... 251 C1
De Laune St
SE17 ... 116 D1 261 C1
Delaware Rd W9 ... 91 D3
Delawyk Cres SE24 ... 161 B5
Delcombe Ave KT4 ... 200 C1
Delft Ho 8 KT2 ... 176 B3
Delft Way 2 SE22 ... 161 C6
Delhi Rd EN1 ... 17 D4
Delhi St N1 ... 94 A6 233 B5
Delia St SW18 ... 157 D4
Delisle Rd SE28 ... 123 C5
Delius Cl WD6 ... 9 C5
Delius Gr E15 ... 98 A5
Dellafield N4 ... 72 C6
Della Path E5 ... 74 B5
Dellbow Rd TW14 ... 150 B6
Dell Cl
Stratford Marsh E15 ... 98 B6
Wallington SM6 ... 219 D4
Woodford IG8 ... 21 B1
Dellfield Cl BR3 ... 186 A2
Dell La KT17 ... 216 A3
Dellors Cl EN5 ... 12 D6
Dellow Cl IG2 ... 57 B2
Dellow Ho 6 E1 ... 118 B6
Dellow St E1 ... 118 B6
Dell Rd Enfield EN3 ... 6 C5
Stoneleigh KT17 ... 216 A2
West Drayton UB7 ... 104 B3
Dells Cl Chingford E4 ... 19 D4
Teddington TW11 ... 174 D4
Dell's Mews SW1 ... 259 B3
Dell The Brentford TW8 .. 131 C6
Feltham TW14 ... 150 B4
Pinner HA5 ... 22 D1
Plumstead Comm SE2 ... 124 A1
South Norwood SE19 ... 183 D2
Wembley HA0 ... 65 B3
Woodford IG8 ... 21 B1
Dell Way W13 ... 87 C1
Dell Wlk KT3 ... 177 C1
Dellwood Gdns IG5 ... 56 C6
Delme Cres SE3 ... 143 B3
Delmey Cl CR0 ... 221 D5
Deloraine Ho SE8 ... 141 C4
Deloraine St SE8 ... 141 C4
Delorme St W6 ... 134 D6
Delphian Ct 5 SW16 ... 182 C6
Delroy Ct N20 ... 14 A4
Delta Bldg 7 E14 ... 98 A1
Delta Cl KT4 ... 215 D5
Delta Ct NW2 ... 68 A6
Delta Gr UB5 ... 84 D4
Delta Ho N1 ... 235 C2
Delta Pk SW18 ... 135 D1
Delta Pk Ind Est EN3 ... 7 B3
Delta Point 5 E2 ... 96 A4
Delta Rd KT4 ... 215 C5
Delta St 4 E2 ... 96 A4
De Lucy Prim Sch SE2 . 124 B4
De Lucy St SE2 ... 124 B2
Delvan Cl SE18 ... 144 C5
Delverton Ho SE17 ... 261 D2
Delverton Rd SE17 ... 261 D1
Delvino Rd
SW6 ... 135 C4 265 B1

De Mandeville Gate EN1 . 6 B1
Demesne Rd SM6 219 D4
Demeta Cl HA9 67 A5
De Montfort Ct 1
SW16 160 A1
De Montfort Rd SW16 160 A2
De Morgan Rd SW6 135 D2
Dempster Cl KT6 197 C1
Dempster Rd SW18 158 A6
Denberry Dr DA14 168 B1
Denbigh Cl
Cheam SM1 217 B3
Elmstead BR7 188 B4
Notting Hill
W11 113 B6 244 D6
Ruislip HA4 61 D6
Southall UB1 85 B1
Willesden NW10 67 C1
Denbigh Ct
1 Ealing W7 86 D2
Newham E6 99 D4
Denbigh Dr UB3 105 A4
Denbigh Gdns TW10 154 B6
Denbigh Ho
Knightsbridge SW1 257 D6
7 Notting Hill W11 91 B1
Notting Hill W11 244 D6
Denbigh Mews SW1 259 A3
Denbigh Pl
SW1 115 C1 259 A2
Denbigh Rd Ealing W13 87 B1
Hounslow TW3 129 D3
Newham E6 99 D4
Notting Hill
W11 113 B6 244 D6
Southall UB1 85 B1
Denbigh St
SW1 115 C1 259 B2
Denbigh Terr
W11 113 B6 244 D6
Denbridge Rd BR1,
BR7 188 B1
Denbury Ho 48 E3 97 D4
Denby Ct Barnet EN5 1 D2
Lambeth SE11 260 D4
Dence Ho 15 E2 96 A4
Denchworth Ho 14
SW9 138 C3
Den Cl BR2, BR3 208 B6
Dencliffe 2 TW15 170 C5
Dencora Centre The
EN3 7 A2
Dendridge Cl EN1 6 B6
Dene Ave
Blackfen DA15 168 B4
Hounslow TW3 129 B2
Dene Cl Brockley SE4 141 A1
Hayes BR2 208 D1
Worcester Pk KT4 215 D6
Denecroft Cres UB10 82 D6
Dene Ct Ealing W5 87 C2
Hanwell W7 108 D4
Dene Gdns
Hinchley Wood KT7 213 A6
Stanmore HA7 25 C5
Dene Ho N14 15 D4
Denehole Ho SE18 124 A1
Denehurst Gdns
Acton W3 110 D5
Hendon NW4 46 C3
Richmond TW10 132 C1
Twickenham TW2 152 B4
Woodford IG8 37 B6
Dene Mans 1 NW6 69 C2
Dene Rd
Buckhurst Hill IG9 21 D3
Friern Barnet N11 14 D2
Denesmead SE24 161 A6
Dene The Ealing W13 87 B2
East Molesey KT12,
KT8 195 B4
South Croydon CR0 222 D4
Wembley HA9 66 A4
Denewood EN5 14 A6
Denewood Ho 6 SM1 218 A4
Denewood Rd N6 48 D2
Dengie Wlk N1 235 A6
Denham Cl DA16 146 C2
Denham Cres CR4 202 D5
Denham Ct
Forest Hill SE26 162 B1
Southall UB1 108 A6
Denham Dr IG2 57 A3
Denham Ho 32 W12 112 B6
Denham Lo W5 88 A1
Denham Rd
Feltham TW14 150 C4
Friern Barnet N20 14 D1
Denham St SE10 121 A1
Denham Way IG11 101 D6
Denholme Rd W9 91 B4
Deniel Lo TW9 153 C6
Denise Ct HA0 65 C4
Denison Cl N2 48 A6
Denison Rd Ealing W5 87 C3
Feltham TW13 171 D6
Mitcham SW19 180 B4
Deniston Ave DA5 169 A3
Denland Ho SW8 270 D3
Denleigh Ct N14 15 D4
Denleigh Gdns
Southgate N21 16 C4
Thames Ditton KT7 196 C3
Denman Dr
Ashford TW15 170 D4
Claygate KT10 213 A3
Hampstead Garden Suburb
NW11 47 C4
Denman Dr N NW11 47 C4
Denman Dr S NW11 47 C4
Denman Ho N16 73 C6
Denman Rd SE15 139 D3
Denman St W1 249 C5
Denmark Ave SW19 179 A3
Denmark Ct SM4 201 C4
Denmark Gdns SM5 218 D5
Denmark Gr N1 234 A4
Denmark Hill SE5 139 B3
Denmark Hill Dr NW9 46 A6
Denmark Hill Sta SE5 139 B3
Denmark Ho 9 SE7 122 A2
Denmark Mans 14
SE5 139 A3
Denmark Pl
2 Bromley E3 97 C4
Soho WC2 239 D2
Denmark Rd
Bromley BR1 187 B2
Camberwell SE5 139 A3
Carshalton SM5 218 D5
Croydon SE25 206 B4
Ealing W13 109 B6
Hornsey N8 50 C5
Kilburn NW6 91 B5
Kingston u T KT1 198 A6
Twickenham TW2 152 B1
Wimbledon SW19 178 D4
Denmark St
8 Leyton E11 76 C5
Newham E13 99 B2
Soho WC2 239 D2
Tottenham N17 34 B3
Denmark Terr NW2 48 D6
Denmead Ho SW15 155 D5
Denmead Rd CR0 204 D1
Denmead Sch TW12 173 D3
Denmead Upper Sch
TW12 173 D3
Denmore Ct SM6 219 B3
Dennan Rd KT6 198 B1
Dennard Way BR6 226 C4
Denner Rd E4 19 C2
Denne Terr E8 95 D6
Dennett Rd CR0 204 C2
Dennett's Gr SE14 140 D3
Dennett's Rd SE14 140 C4
Denning Ave CR0 220 C3
Denning Cl
Hampton TW12 173 B5
St John's Wood
NW8 92 A4 229 B1
Denning Point E1 243 D2
Denning Rd NW3 70 B4
Dennington Cl 17 E5 74 B6
Dennington Park
Mansions 12 NW6 69 C3
Dennington Park Rd
NW6 69 C2
Denningtons The KT4 215 C6
Dennis Ave HA9 66 B3
Dennis Cl TW15 171 B3
Dennis Ct Chingford E17 36 B1
Greenford UB6 86 A1
Lewisham SE10 142 A4
Dennis Gdns HA7 25 C5
Dennis Ho 4 Bow E3 97 B5
Sutton SM1 217 C4
Dennis La HA7 25 B6
Dennison Point E15 76 A1
Dennis Par 1 N14 15 D3
Dennis Park Cres
SW20 179 A2
Dennis Rd KT8 196 A5
Dennis Reeve Cl CR4 180 D2
Dennis Way SW4 137 D2
Denny Cl 15 E6 100 A2
Denny Cres SE11 261 B2
Denny Gdns RM9 80 B1
Denny Rd N9 18 B3
Denny St SE11 116 C1 261 B2
Den Rd BR2 208 B6
Densham Ho NW8 229 D3
Densham Rd E15 98 C6
Densole Cl BR3 185 A2
Denstone Ho 5 SE15 140 A6
Densworth Gr N9 18 C2
Dent Ho SE17 263 A3
Denton NW1 71 A2
Denton Cl EN5 12 C6
Denton Ct BR2 210 C2
Denton Ho N1 72 D1
Denton Rd
Bexley DA16 146 C5
Edmonton N18 33 C6
Hornsey N8 50 B3
Twickenham TW1 153 D5
Denton St SW18 157 D5
Denton Way E5 74 D5
Dents Rd SW11 158 D5
Denvale Trade Pk
CR4 202 B5
Denver Cl BR6 211 C3
Denver Ct UB1 107 B5
Denver Rd N16 51 C2
Denwood SE23 162 D1
Denyer Ho 1 NW5 71 B4
Denyer St SW3 114 C2 257 B4
Denys Bldg EC1 241 A4
Denziloe Ave UB10 82 D4
Denzil Rd NW10 67 D3
Deodar Rd SW15 135 A1
Deodara Cl N20 14 D1
Depot App NW2 68 D4
Depot Rd
Isleworth TW3, TW7 130 B2
Shepherd's Bush W12 112 C6
Depot St SE5 139 B6
DEPTFORD 140 D6
Deptford Bridge SE8 141 C4
Deptford Bridge Sta
SE8 141 C4
Deptford Broadway SE8,
SE14 141 C4
Deptford Church St
SE8 141 C5
Deptford Ferry Rd 24
E14 119 C2
Deptford Gn SE8 141 C6
Deptford Green Sch
SE14 141 B5
Deptford Green Sch
(Annex) SE14 141 A5
Deptford High St SE8 141 C5
Deptford Park Prim Sch
SE8 119 A1
Deptford Sta SE8 141 C5
Deptford Trad Est
SE8 141 A6
Deptford Wharf SE8 119 B2
Dept of Transport &
Environment SW1 259 D5
De Quincey Mews 3
E16 121 A5
De Quincey Rd N17 33 B2
Derby Ave Harrow HA3 24 B2
North Finchley N12 30 A5
Romford RM7 59 D3
Derby Ct
8 Clapton Pk E5 74 D4
Woodford E18 36 D2
Derby Gate SW1 250 A2
Derby Hill SE23 162 C2
Derby Hill Cres SE23 162 C2
Derby Ho Hendon NW4 46 C6
Lambeth SE11 261 A4
Pinner HA5 22 D1
4 Wallington SM6 219 B3
Derby Lo N3 29 B1
Derby Rd
Cheam SM1, SM2 217 B2
Edmonton N18 34 C5
Enfield EN3 18 C6
Greenford UB6 85 D6
Hounslow TW3 129 D1
Merton SW19 179 C3
Mortlake SW14 132 D1
South Hackney E9 96 D6
Surbiton KT5, KT6 198 C1
Thornton Heath CR0 204 D1
Upton E7 77 D1
Woodford E18 36 D2
Derbyshire St E2 96 A4
Derby St W1 248 B3
Dereham Ho 7 SE4 140 D1
Dereham Pl EC2 243 B6
Dereham Rd IG11 79 D3
Derek Ave
Chessington KT19 214 D3
Wallington SM6 219 B4
Wembley HA9 66 D1
Derek Cl KT19 214 D3
Derek Walcott Cl
SE24 160 D6
Dericote St E8 96 B6
Deri Dene Cl 2 TW19 148 A5
Derifall Cl E6 100 B2
Dering Pl CR0 221 A4
Dering Rd CR0 221 A4
Dering St W1 238 D1
Derinton Rd SW17 181 A6
Derley Rd UB2 106 D3
Dermody Gdns SE13 164 B6
Dermody Rd SE13 164 B6
Deronda Rd SE24,
SW2 160 D3
Deroy Cl SM5 218 D2
Derrick Gdns SE7 121 C2
Derrick Ho 13 SW2 160 C3
Derrick Rd BR3 207 B5
Derrycombe Ho 18 W2 91 C2
Derry Rd CR0, SM6 220 A5
Derry St W8 113 D4 245 C1
Dersingham Ave E12 78 C4
Dersingham Inf Sch
E12 78 C3
Dersingham Rd NW2 69 A5
Derwent NW1 232 A1
Derwent Ave
Barnet EN4 14 D3
Burnt Oak NW7 27 B4
Edmonton N18 33 B5
Hyde The NW9 45 C4
Kingston u T SW15 177 C6
Pinner HA5 23 A4
Uxbridge UB10 60 C5
Derwent Cl
Claygate KT10 212 D2
East Bedfont TW14 149 D3
Derwent Cres
Bexleyheath DA7 147 C3
Stanmore HA7 25 C1
Whetstone N20 14 A1
Derwent Ct
2 Hammersmith W6 112 A2
Hornsey N8 50 A3
8 Rotherhithe SE16 118 D4
Derwent Dr
Crofton BR5 211 B2
Hayes UB4 83 C2
Derwent Gdns
Redbridge IG4 56 A5
Wembley HA9 43 C2
Derwent Gr SE22 139 D1
Derwent Ho
Penge SE20 184 B1
South Kensington SW7 256 B4
Tower Hamlets E3 97 B3
Derwent Lo
Hounslow TW7 130 B3
Derwent Lo *continued*
North Cheam KT4 216 B6
Derwent Rd Ealing W5 109 C3
Palmers Green N13 16 B1
Penge SE20 184 B1
Southall UB1 85 B1
Twickenham TW2 151 D5
West Barnes SM4 200 D3
Derwent Rise NW9 45 C3
Derwent St SE10 120 C1
Derwentwater Mans 2
W3 111 A5
Derwentwater Prim Sch
W3 111 A5
Derwentwater Rd W3 111 A5
Derwent Wlk SM6 219 B1
Derwent Yd W5 109 C3
De Salis Rd UB10 83 A3
Desborough Cl
Bayswater W2 91 D2
Lower Halliford TW17 192 C2
Desborough Ct SE25 206 B5
Desborough Ho W14 264 D6
Desenfans Rd SE21 161 C5
Deseret Ho 6 CR4 202 D6
Desford Rd E16 98 C3
Desford Way TW15 148 B2
Desmond Ho 4 EN4 14 C5
Desmond St SE14 141 A6
Desmond Tutu Dr
SE23 163 A3
Despard Ho SW2 160 C2
Despard Rd N19 49 C1
Dessouter 19 NW9 27 D1
Desvignes Dr SE13 164 B5
Detherick Ct TW3 130 A1
Dethick Ct E3 97 A6
Detling Ho SE17 263 A3
Detling Rd BR1 187 A5
Detmold Rd E5 74 C6
Devalls Cl E6 122 C6
Devana End SM5 218 D5
Devas Rd SW20 178 C2
Devas St E3 97 D3
Devema Cl BR7 188 C2
Devenay Rd E15 76 D1
Devenish Rd SE2 124 A4
Deventer Cres 8
SE22 161 C6
Deveraux Cl BR3 208 A4
De Vere Cotts W8 256 A6
De Vere Ct 1 E5 74 B5
De Vere Gdns
Kensington
W8 114 A4 246 A1
Redbridge IG1 56 B1
Deverell St
SE1 117 B3 262 C5
De Vere Mews W8 256 A6
Devereux Ct WC2 241 A1
Devereux Ho 7 SW15 156 A6
Devereux La SW13 134 B5
Devereux Rd SW11 158 D5
Deverill Ct SE20 184 C2
Devey Cl KT2 177 B5
Devitt Ho 5 E14 119 D6
Devizes St N1 235 D5
Devon Ave TW2 152 A3
Devon Cl Chigwell IG9 21 B2
Tottenham N17 51 D6
Wembley UB6 87 C6
Devoncroft Gdns TW1 153 A4
Devon Ct 3 Acton W3 88 C1
2 Ealing W7 86 D2
Hampton TW12 173 C3
Devon Gdns N4 50 D3
Devon Ho
9 Penge SE20 184 B3
Walthamstow E17 35 B1
6 Wanstead E11 55 A4
Devonhurst Pl 4 W4 111 B1
Devonia Gdns N18 33 A4
Devonia Rd N1 94 D5 234 D4
Devon Mans SE1 253 B2
Devon Par HA3 43 C4
Devonport W2 237 A2
Devonport Gdns IG1 56 B3
Devonport Ho
Greenwich SE10 142 A6
23 Paddington W2 91 C2
Devonport Rd W12 112 B4
Devonport St E1 96 D1
Devon Rd IG11 101 C6
Devon Rise N2 48 B5
Devonshire Ave SM2 218 A1
Devonshire Cl
Edmonton N13 32 C6
Leyton E15 76 C4
Marylebone W1 238 C4
Devonshire Cres NW7 28 D3
Devonshire Ct
14 Balham SW12 159 B4
Croydon CR0 207 C1
Feltham TW13 150 B2
Pinner HA5 23 B2
6 Richmond TW9 132 B4
Tottenham N17 33 A4
Devonshire Dr
London SE10 141 D4
Long Ditton KT6 213 D6
Devonshire Gdns
Chiswick W4 133 A5
Edmonton N21 17 A4
Tottenham N17 33 A4
Devonshire Gr SE15 140 B6
Devonshire Hall 15 E9 74 C2
Devonshire Hill La N17 33 A4
Devonshire Hill Prim Sch
N17 33 B4
Devonshire Ho
Brondesbury NW6 69 B2
Hounslow TW3 130 A2
Newington SE1 262 A6
Paddington W2 236 D4
2 Putney SW15 156 C4
10 Sutton SM2 218 A1
Westminster SW1 259 D2
Whetstone N12 14 A1
Devonshire Hospl
W1 93 A2 238 B4
Devonshire House Prep
Sch NW3 70 B3
Devonshire House Sch
NW3 70 A3
Devonshire Mews 2
W4 111 C1
Devonshire Mews N
W1 238 C4
Devonshire Mews S
W1 238 C4
Devonshire Mews W
W1 238 B4
Devonshire Pl
Child's Hill NW2 69 C5
Kensington W8 255 C5
Marylebone W1 93 A2 238 B4
Devonshire Place Mews
W1 238 B4
Devonshire Prim Sch
SM2 218 A1
Devonshire Rd
Bexley DA6 147 A1
Chislehurst SE9 166 A2
Chiswick W4 111 C1
Ealing W5 109 C3
Eastcote HA5 40 C2
Edmonton N9 18 C3
Feltham TW13 173 A6
Forest Hill SE23 162 C4
Hackbridge SM5, SM6 219 A4
Harrow HA1 42 B3
Hatch End HA5 23 B2
Ilford IG2 57 C2
Mill Hill NW7 28 D3
Mitcham SW19 180 C3
Newham E16 99 B1
Palmers Green N13 32 C6
Southall UB1 85 C2
Sutton SM2 218 A1
Thornton Heath CR0 205 B2
Tottenham N17 33 A4
Walthamstow E17 53 C3
Devonshire Row EC2 243 B3
Devonshire Row Mews
W1 238 D5
Devonshire Sq
Bromley BR2 209 B5
Whitechapel EC2 95 C1 243 B2
Devonshire St
Chiswick W4 111 C1
Marylebone W1 93 B2 238 C4
Devonshire Terr
W2 92 A1 236 B1
Devonshire Way
Croydon CR0, CR9 223 B6
Hayes UB4 84 B1
Devons Rd E3 97 D3
Devons Road Sta E3 97 D3
Devon St SE15 140 B6
Devon Way
Chessington KT9 213 C3
Ewell KT19 214 D3
Hillingdon UB10 82 B5
Devon Waye TW5 129 B5
De Walden Ho NW8 230 A4
De Walden St W1 238 B3
Dewar Ho 2 SW17 180 C5
Dewar St SE15 140 A2
Dewberry Gdns E6 100 A2
Dewberry St E14 98 A2
Dewey Rd
Dagenham RM10 81 D2
Islington N1 94 C5 234 A4
Dewey St SW17 180 D5
Dewhurst Rd W14 112 D3
Dewlands Ct 7 NW4 28 D1
Dewsbury Cl HA5 41 A3
Dewsbury Ct 5 W4 111 A2
Dewsbury Gdns KT4 216 A5
Dewsbury Rd NW10 68 A3
Dewsbury Terr NW1 231 D6
Dexter Ho 2 DA18 125 A3
Dexter Rd EN5 12 D5
Deyncourt Rd N17 33 A2
Deynecourt Gdns E11 55 C5
D'eynsford Rd SE5 139 B4
Dhonau Ho SE16 263 D4
Diadem Ct W1 239 C2
Dial Wlk The
W8 113 D4 245 D2
Diameter Rd BR5 211 A3
Diamond Cl RM8 58 C1
Diamond Ct 8 W7 108 C5
Diamond Est SW17 158 C1
Diamond Ho 22 E3 97 A5
Diamond Rd HA4 63 A4
Diamond St
18 London NW10 67 B1
SE15 139 C5
Diamond Terr SE10 142 A4
Diana Cl
27 Deptford SE8 141 B6
Sidcup DA14 169 A2
Woodford E18 37 B2
Diana Ct SM5 219 A1
Diana Gdns KT6 214 B6
Diana Ho Barnes SW13 133 D4
4 Brixton SW2 160 B6
Diana, Princess of Wales
Mml Wlk W2 114 A5 246 A3
Diana Rd E17 53 B6
Dianne Ct SE12 165 A3
Dianne Way EN4 2 C1
Dianthus Cl SE2 124 B1
Dias Ho UB5 85 A6
Dibden Ho 8 SE5 139 C5
Dibden St N1 95 A6 235 A6
Dibdin Cl SM1 217 C5
Dibdin Ho W9 91 D5
Dibdin Rd SM1 217 C6
Dicey Ave NW2 68 C4
Dickens Ave Finchley N3 30 A2
Hayes UB8 82 D1
Dickens Cl Erith DA8 147 D5
Hayes UB3 105 C2
Richmond TW10 154 A2
Dickens Ct
Clerkenwell EC1 241 C5
10 Wanstead E11 55 A5
Wembley HA0 65 C5
Dickens Dr BR7 189 A4
Dickens Ho
Bloomsbury WC1 240 A6
3 Erith DA17 125 B1
Hayes UB3 105 C2
Kennington SE17 261 D1
Kilburn NW6 91 C4
Paddington NW8 236 D6
Dickens House Mus*
WC1 94 B3 240 D5
Dickens La N18 33 C5
Dickenson Cl N9 18 A3
Dickenson Ho N8 50 B3
Dickenson Rd
Feltham TW13 172 D5
Hornsey N8 50 A2
Dickenson's La SE25 206 A3
Dickenson's Pl SE25 206 A3
Dickens Rd E6 99 D5
Dickens Sq
SE1 117 A3 262 B6
Dickens St SW8 137 B3
Dickenswood Cl SE19 182 D3
Dickerage Hill
Kingston u T KT3 177 A1
Kingston u T KT3 199 A6
Dickerage La KT3 199 A6
Dickerage Rd KT1, KT2,
KT3 177 A1
Dickinson Ho 18 E2 96 A4
Dicksee Ho NW8 236 C5
Dick Shepherd Ct 17
SW2 160 C5
Dickson Fold HA5 40 D5
Dickson Ho
3 Charlton SE18 144 A4
4 Stepney E1 96 B1
Dickson Rd SE9 144 A2
Dick Turpin Way
TW14 127 D1
Didbin Ho N7 72 B6
Didsbury Cl E6 100 B6
Digby Bsns Ctr E9 74 D2
Digby Cres N4 73 A6
Digby Gdns RM10 103 C6
Digby Mans W6 112 C1
Digby Pl CR0 221 D5
Digby Rd Barking IG11 79 D1
Homerton E9 74 D2
Digby St E2 96 C4
Diggon St E1 96 D2
Dighton Ct SE17 139 A6
Dighton Rd SW18 136 A1
Dignum St N1 234 A4
Digswell St N7 72 C2
Dilhorne Cl SE12 165 B1
Dilke St SW3 136 D6 267 D6
Dilloway Yd UB2 107 A4
Dillwyn Cl SE26 185 A6
Dilston Cl 1 UB5 84 C4
Dilston Gr SE16 118 C2
Dilton Gdns SW15 156 B3
Dilwyn Ct E17 35 A1
Dimes Pl 9 W6 112 B2
Dimmock Dr UB6 64 B3
Dimond Cl E7 77 A4
Dimsdale Dr Enfield EN1 18 A5
Welsh Harp NW9 45 A1
Dimsdale Wlk 4 E13 99 A5
Dimson Cres E3 97 C4
Dinerman Ct NW8 229 B6
Dingle Cl EN5 11 D5
Dingle Ct 16 HA7 25 C5
Dingle Gdns E14 119 C6
Dingle Rd TW15 170 D5
Dingles Ct HA5 22 D1
Dingle The UB10 82 D4
Dingley La SW16 159 D2
Dingley Pl EC1 95 A4 235 B1
Dingley Rd EC1 95 A4 235 A1
Dingwall Ave CR0 221 A6
Dingwall Gdns NW11 47 C3
Dingwall Rd
South Croydon CR0 221 B6
Wandsworth SW18 158 A4
Dinmont Ho 27 E2 96 A5
Dinmont St 1 E2 96 B5
Dinmore Ho 6 E9 96 C6
Dinnington Ho 17 E1 96 B3
Dinorben SM6 219 C1
Dinsdale Ct EN5 13 D6
Dinsdale Gdns
New Barnet EN5 13 D6
South Norwood SE25 205 C4
Dinsdale Rd SE3 142 D6

Dinsmore Rd SW12 . . . . 159 B4
Dinton Ho NW8 . . . . 237 A6
Dinton Rd
Kingston u T KT2 . . . . 176 B3
Mitcham SW19 . . . . 180 B4
Dinwiddy Ho N1 . . . . . . 233 C3
Dionis Ho SW6 . . . . 135 C3
Diploma Ave N2 . . . . 48 C5
Diploma Ct N2 . . . . 48 C5
Diprose Lo SW17 . . . . . . 180 B6
Dirleton Rd E15 . . . . 98 D6
Disbrowe Rd
W6 . . . . 135 A6 264 B5
Discovery Bsns Pk 13
SE16 . . . . 118 A3
Discovery Dock E E14 . . 119 D4
Discovery Ho 1 E14 . . . 120 A6
Dishforth La NW9 . . . . 27 C2
Disley Ct 2 UB1 . . . . 85 D1
Disney Pl SE1 . . . . 252 B2
Disney St SE1 . . . . 252 B2
Dison Cl EN3 . . . . 6 D4
Disraeli Cl
1 Acton W4 . . . . 111 B2
Thamesmead SE28 . . . . . 124 C5
Disraeli Gdns SW15 . . . . 135 B1
Disraeli Rd Acton NW10 . . 89 B5
Ealing W5 . . . . 109 D5
Putney SW15 . . . . 135 A1
Upton E7 . . . . 77 A2
Diss St E2 . . . . 95 D4
Distaff La EC4 . . . . 252 A6
Distillery La W6 . . . . 112 C1
Distillery Rd W6 . . . . 112 C1
Distillery Wlk 14 TW8 . . 132 A6
Distin Ct 3 SM1 . . . . 217 D3
Distin St SE11 . . 116 C2 261 A3
District Rd HA0 . . . . 65 B3
Ditchburn St E14 . . . . . . 120 A6
Ditchfield Rd UB4 . . . . 85 A3
Ditchley Ct W7 . . . . 86 D2
Dittisham Rd SE9 . . . . . . 188 A6
Ditton Cl KT7 . . . . 197 A2
Dittoncroft Cl CR0 . . . . . 221 C4
Ditton Grange Cl KT6 . . 197 D1
Ditton Grange Dr KT6 . . 197 D1
Ditton Hill KT6 . . . . 213 D6
Ditton Hill Rd KT6 . . . . . 197 C1
Ditton Ho 10 E5 . . . . 74 B3
Ditton Lawn KT7 . . . . 197 A1
Ditton Pl 6 SE20 . . . . . . 184 B2
Ditton Rd Bexley DA6 . . . 169 A6
Southall UB2 . . . . 107 B1
Surbiton KT6 . . . . 198 B1
Ditton Reach KT7 . . . . . . 197 B3
Divis Way SW15 . . . . 156 B5
Dixon Cl 4 E6 . . . . 100 B1
Dixon Clark Ct N1 . . . . . . 72 D2
Dixon Ct N4 . . . . 50 C3
Dixon Ho
20 North Kensington
NW10 . . . . 90 D1
West Heath SE2 . . . . 124 C1
Dixon Pl BR4 . . . . 207 D1
Dixon Rd London SE14 . . . 141 A4
South Norwood SE25 . . . 205 D6
Dixon's Alley 10 SE16 . . 118 B4
Dobbin Cl HA3 . . . . 25 A1
Dobell Rd SE9 . . . . 166 B6
Dobree Ave NW10 . . . . 68 B1
Dobson Cl NW6 . . . . 70 B1
Dobson Ho 18 SE14 . . . . 140 D6
Doby Ct EC4 . . . . 252 B6
Dockers Tanner Rd 26
E14 . . . . 119 C2
Dockett Eddy La KT16,
TW17 . . . . 192 B1
Dockett Moorings
KT16 . . . . 192 B1
Dockhead SE1 . . 117 D4 253 D1
Dockhead Wharf SE1 . 253 D2
Dock Hill Ave SE16 . . . . . 118 D4
Docklands Ct 20 E14 . . . . 97 B1
Docklands Heritage Mus*
SE16 . . . . 119 B5
Dockland St E16 . . . . 122 C5
Dockley Rd SE16 . . . . 118 A3
Dockley Road Ind Est 11
SE16 . . . . 118 A3
Dock Offices 12 SE16 . . . 118 C3
Dock Rd
Brentford TW8 . . . . 131 D5
Canning Town E16 . . . . . 120 D6
Dockside Rd E16 . . . . 121 D6
Dock St E1 . . . . 118 A6
Dockwell Cl TW14 . . . . . 128 A1
Dockwell's Ind Est
TW14 . . . . 150 B6
Doctor Johnson Ho 2
SW16 . . . . 181 D6
Doctors Cl SE26 . . . . 184 C5
Doctor Spurstowe
Almshouses 9 E8 . . . . . 74 B2
Docura Ho N7 . . . . 72 B6
Docwras Bldgs N1 . . . . . . 73 C2
Dodbrooke Rd SE27 . . . . 160 D1
Dodd Ho 18 SE16 . . . . . . 118 B2
Doddington Gr
SE17 . . . . 116 D1 261 D1
Doddington Pl 4
SE17 . . . . 138 D6
Dodsley Pl N9 . . . . 18 C1
Dodson St SE1 . . 116 C4 251 B1
Dod St E14 . . . . 97 C1
Doebury Wlk SE18 . . . . . 146 A6
Doel Cl SW19 . . . . 180 A3
Doggett Rd SE6 . . . . 163 C4
Doggetts Ct EN4 . . . . 14 C6
Doghurst Ave UB3 . . . . . 126 D5
Doghurst Dr UB7 . . . . . . 126 D5
Dog Kennel Hill SE22 . . 139 C2
Dog Kennel Hill Sch
SE22 . . . . 139 C2
Dog La NW10 . . . . 67 C4
Dogrose Ct 14 NW9 . . . . . 46 A5
Doherty Rd E13 . . . . 99 A3
Dokal Ind Est UB2 . . . . . 107 A4
Doland Ct SW17 . . . . 180 D4
Dolben Ct SW1 . . . . 259 D3
Dolben St SE1 . . 116 D5 251 D3
Dolby Rd SW6 . . . . 135 B3
Doleman Ho 19 SE10 . . . 141 D4
Dolland Ho SE11 . . . . 260 D1
Dolland St SE11 . . . . 260 D1
Dollar Bay E14 . . . . 120 A4
Dollary Ct KT3 . . . . 198 D6
Dolliffe Cl CR4 . . . . 180 D1
Dollis Ave N3 . . . . 29 B2
Dollis Brook Wlk EN5 . . . 13 A5
Dollis Cres HA4 . . . . 40 C1
Dolliscroft NW7 . . . . 29 A3
Dollis Ct N3 . . . . 29 B2
DOLLIS HILL 68 B5
Dollis Hill Ave NW2 . . . . . 68 B5
Dollis Hill Est NW2 . . . . . 68 A5
Dollis Hill La NW2 . . . . . . 68 A5
Dollis Hill Sta NW2 . . . . . 68 A3
Dollis Hts NW2 . . . . 68 B5
Dollis Jun & Inf Schs
NW7 . . . . 28 C3
Dollis Mews N3 . . . . 29 C2
Dollis Pk N3 . . . . 29 B2
Dollis Rd N3, NW7 . . . . . . 29 B3
Dollis Valley Dr EN5 . . . . 13 B6
Dollis Valley Way EN5 . . . 13 B5
Dolman Cl N3 . . . . 30 A1
Dolman Rd W4 . . . . 111 B2
Dolman St SW4 . . . . 138 B1
Dolphin Cl
Kingston u T KT6 . . . . . . 197 D4
2 Rotherhithe SE16 . . . 118 D4
Thamesmead SE28 . . . . . 102 D1
Dolphin Ct
London NW11 . . . . 47 A3
Merton SW19 . . . . 179 C3
Tufnell Pk N7 . . . . 71 D4
2 Wallington SM6 . . . . . 219 B2
Dolphin Est The TW16 . . 171 B2
Dolphin La E14 . . . . 119 D6
Dolphin Rd
Charlton TW16 . . . . 171 C2
Northolt UB5 . . . . 85 B5
Dolphin Rd N TW16 . . . . 171 C2
Dolphin Rd S TW16 . . . . 171 C2
Dolphin Rd W TW16 . . . . 171 C2
Dolphin Sch SW11 . . . . . 158 D6
Dolphin Sq
SW1 . . . . 115 C1 259 B1
Dolphin St KT2 . . . . 176 A2
Dolphin Twr 21 SE8 . . . . 141 B6
Dombey Ho
18 Bermondsey SE1 . . . . 118 A4
4 Shepherd's Bush
W11 . . . . 112 D5
Dombey St WC1 . . . . 240 C4
Dome Hill Pk SE26 . . . . . 183 D6
Domelton Ho SW18 . . . . 157 D5
Domett Cl SE5 . . . . 139 B1
Domfe Pl E5 . . . . 74 C4
Domingo St EC1 . . . . 242 A5
Dominica Cl 6 E6 . . . . 99 D5
Dominion Bsns Pk N9 . . . 18 D2
Dominion Cl TW3 . . . . . . 130 B3
Dominion Ind Est UB2 . . 107 A4
Dominion Par HA1 . . . . . . 42 D4
Dominion Rd
Croydon CR0 . . . . 205 D2
Southall UB2 . . . . 107 A3
Dominion St
EC2 . . . . 95 B2 242 D4
Dominion Wks RM8 . . . . . 59 A1
Domonic Dr SE9 . . . . 166 D1
Domville Cl N20 . . . . 14 B2
Donaghue Cotts 11 E14 . 97 A2
Donald Dr RM6 . . . . 58 C4
Donald Lynch Ho CR4 . . 180 D1
Donald Rd Newham E13 . . 99 B6
Thornton Heath CR0 . . . . 204 B2
Donaldson Rd
Kilburn NW6 . . . . 91 B6
Shooters Hill SE18 . . . . . 144 C4
Donald Woods Gdns
KT5 . . . . 215 A6
Doncaster Dr UB5 . . . . . . 63 B3
Doncaster Gdns
London N4 . . . . 51 A3
Northolt UB5 . . . . 63 B3
Doncaster Gn WD19 . . . . 22 C5
Doncaster Rd N9 . . . . 18 B4
Doncel Ct E4 . . . . 20 B4
Donegal Ho 2 E1 . . . . 96 C3
Donegal St N1 . . . 94 B5 233 D3
Doneraile Ho SW1 . . . . . 258 C1
Doneraile St SW6 . . . . . . 134 D4
Dongola Rd
Newham E13 . . . . 99 B4
Tottenham N17 . . . . 51 C6
Tower Hamlets E1 . . . . 97 A2
Dongola Rd W 5 E13 . . . . 99 B4
Don Gratton Ho 23 E1 . . . 96 A2
Donington Ave IG6 . . . . . 57 A4
Donkey Alley SE22 . . . . . 162 A5
Donkey La EN1 . . . . 6 A3
Donkin Ho 15 SE16 . . . . . 118 B2
Donne Ct SE24 . . . . 161 A5
Donnefield Ave HA8 . . . . 26 A3
Donne Ho
18 Canonbury N16 . . . . . . 73 B4
14 Deptford SE14 . . . . . 140 D6
11 Poplar E14 . . . . 97 C1
Donnelly Ct SW6 . . . . 264 B4
Donne Pl
Chelsea SW3 . . . 114 C2 257 B4
Mitcham CR4 . . . . 203 B5
Donne Rd RM8 . . . . 80 C6
Donnington Ct
11 Camden Town NW1 . . . 71 B1
Willesden NW10 . . . . 68 B1
Donnington Ho 12
SW8 . . . . 137 D3
Donnington Prim Sch
NW10 . . . . 90 B6
Donnington Rd
Harrow HA3 . . . . 43 D3
Willesden Green NW10 . . . 90 B6
Worcester Pk KT4 . . . . . . 216 A6
Donnybrook Rd SW16 . . 181 D3
Donoghue Bsns Pk
NW2 . . . . 68 D5
Donovan Ave N10 . . . . 31 C1
Donovan Ct SW7 . . . . 256 C1
Donovan Ho 4 E1 . . . . . . 118 C6
Donovan Pl N21 . . . . 16 B6
Don Phelan Cl SE5 . . . . . 139 B4
Doone Cl TW11 . . . . 175 A4
Doon St SE1 . . . . 116 C5 251 A4
Doradus Ct 20 SW19 . . . 156 D3
Dora Ho
11 Shepherd's Bush
W11 . . . . 112 D6
1 Tower Hamlets E14 . . . 97 B1
Doral Way SM5 . . . . 218 D3
Doran Ct E6 . . . . 100 B5
Dorando Cl W12 . . . . 112 B6
Doran Gr SE18 . . . . 145 C5
Doran Manor N2 . . . . 48 D4
Doran Wlk Stratford E15 . . 76 A1
Stratford Marsh E15 . . . . 98 A6
Dora Rd SW19 . . . . 179 C6
Dora St E14 . . . . 97 B1
Dora Way SW9 . . . . 138 C3
Dorcas Ct 9 SW18 . . . . . 136 B1
Dorchester Ave
Edmonton N13 . . . . 33 A6
Harrow HA2 . . . . 42 A3
Sidcup DA5 . . . . 168 D4
Dorchester Cl
Northolt UB5 . . . . 63 D3
St Paul's Cray BR5 . . . . . 190 B3
Dorchester Ct
Cricklewood NW2 . . . . 68 D5
1 De Beauvoir Town N1 . 73 C1
East Barnet N14 . . . . 15 B4
Herne Hill SE24 . . . . 161 A6
Knightsbridge SW1 . . . . . 257 D5
1 Muswell Hill N10 . . . . . 49 B6
5 Streatham SW16 . . . . 160 A2
2 Woodford E18 . . . . 36 D2
Dorchester Dr
Feltham TW14 . . . . 149 C5
Herne Hill SE24 . . . . 161 A6
Dorchester Gdns
Chingford E4 . . . . 35 C6
East Finchley NW11 . . . . . 47 C5
Dorchester Gr W4 . . . . . . 111 D1
Dorchester Ho
Richmond TW9 . . . . 132 D5
Wallington SM5 . . . . 218 D3
Dorchester Mews
New Malden KT3 . . . . 199 B5
Twickenham TW1 . . . . . . 153 C5
Dorchester Prim Sch
KT4 . . . . 200 C1
Dorchester Rd
Cheam SM4 . . . . 202 A2
North Cheam KT4 . . . . . . 200 C1
Northolt UB5 . . . . 63 D3
Dorchester Way HA3 . . . . 44 B3
Dorchester Waye
Hayes UB4 . . . . 84 B1
Hayes UB4 . . . . 84 C1
Dorcis Ave DA7 . . . . 147 A3
Dordrecht Rd W3 . . . . . . 111 C5
Dore Ave E12 . . . . 78 C3
Doreen Ave NW9 . . . . 45 B1
Doreen Capstan Ho 5
E11 . . . . 76 C5
Dore Gdns SM4 . . . . 201 D2
Dorell Cl UB1 . . . . 85 B2
Dorey Ho 7 TW8 . . . . 131 C5
Doria Rd SW6 . . . . 135 B3
Doric Ho 7 E2 . . . . 96 D5
Doric Way NW1 . . 93 D4 232 C2
Dorie Mews N12 . . . . 29 D6
Dorien Rd SW20 . . . . 178 D1
Doris Emmerton Ct
SW18 . . . . 136 A1
Doris Rd Ashford TW15 . . 171 B4
Upton E7 . . . . 77 A1
Dorking Cl
Deptford SE8 . . . . 141 B6
North Cheam KT4 . . . . . . 216 D6
Dorking Ct N17 . . . . 34 A2
Dorking Ho SE1 . . . . 262 D6
Dorland Ct SW15 . . . . 157 B5
Dorlcote Rd SW18 . . . . . 158 C4
Dorleston Ct N1 . . . . 235 D6
Dorly Cl TW17 . . . . 193 C4
Dorman Pl 6 N9 . . . . 18 A2
Dorman Way
NW8 . . . . 92 B6 229 C6
Dorman Wlk NW10 . . . . . . 67 B2
Dorma Trad Pk E10 . . . . . 52 D1
Dormay St SW18 . . . . 157 D6
Dormer Cl Barnet EN5 . . . 12 D6
Stratford E15 . . . . 76 D2
Dormer's Ave UB1 . . . . . . 85 C1
Dormers Lo EN4 . . . . 2 D3
Dormers Rise UB1 . . . . . . 85 D1
DORMER'S WELLS 107 C6
Dormer's Wells High Sch
UB1 . . . . 85 C1
Dormers Wells Ho UB4 . . 84 C2
Dormer's Wells Inf Sch
UB1 . . . . 107 D6
Dormer's Wells Jun Sch
UB1 . . . . 107 D6
Dormer's Wells La
UB1 . . . . 107 C5
Dormstone Ho SE17 . . . . 263 A3
Dormywood HA4 . . . . 39 D4
Dornberg Cl SE3 . . . . 143 A5
Dornberg Rd SE3 . . . . . . 143 B5
Dorncliffe Rd SW6 . . . . . 135 A3
Dorney NW3 . . . . 70 C1
Dorney Ct SW6 . . . . 135 A2
Dorney Rise BR5 . . . . 211 D5
Dorney Way TW4 . . . . . . 151 A6
Dornfell St NW6 . . . . 69 B3
Dornoch Ho 26 E3 . . . . 97 B5
Dornton Rd
South Croydon CR2 . . . . . 221 C3
Upper Tooting SW12,
SW17 . . . . 159 C2
Dorothy Ave HA0 . . . . 66 A1
Dorothy Barley Schs
RM8 . . . . 80 B3
Dorothy Charrington Ho
1 SE22 . . . . 162 A6
Dorothy Evans Cl DA7 . . 147 D1
Dorothy Gdns RM8 . . . . . . 80 B4
Dorothy Pettingel Ho 1
SM1 . . . . 217 D5
Dorothy Rd SW11 . . . . . . 136 D2
Dorothy Villas UB1 . . . . . 107 C5
Dorrien Wlk SW16 . . . . . 159 D2
Dorrington Ct SE25 . . . . 183 C1
Dorrington Point 20 E3 . . 97 D4
Dorrington St EC1 . . . . . 241 A4
Dorrington Way BR3 . . . 208 A4
Dorrit Ho 2 W11 . . . . 112 D5
Dorrit Mews N18 . . . . 33 C5
Dorrit St SE1 . . . . 252 B2
Dorrit Way BR7 . . . . 189 A4
Dorryn Ct SE26 . . . . 184 D5
Dors Cl NW9 . . . . 45 B1
Dorset Ave
Falconwood DA16 . . . . . . 145 D1
Hayes UB4 . . . . 83 C4
Southall UB2 . . . . 107 C2
Dorset Bldgs EC4 . . . . . . 241 C1
Dorset Cl Hayes UB4 . . . . 83 C4
Marylebone NW1 . . . . . . 237 C4
Dorset Ct 3 Ealing W7 . . . 86 D2
3 London N1 . . . . 73 C1
4 Northolt UB5 . . . . 85 B4
Dorset Dr HA8 . . . . 26 B4
Dorset Gdns SW16 . . . . . 204 B5
Dorset Hall SW19 . . . . . . 179 C2
Dorset Ho 1 SE20 . . . . . . 184 B2
Dorset Mans 2 W6 . . . . . 134 D6
Dorset Mews
Belgravia SW1 . . . . 258 C6
Finchley N3 . . . . 29 C2
Dorset Pl E15 . . . . 76 B2
Dorset Rd
Ashford TW15 . . . . 148 A1
Chislehurst SE9 . . . . 166 A2
Ealing W5 . . . . 109 D3
Harrow HA1 . . . . 42 A3
Merton SW19 . . . . 179 C1
Mitcham CR4 . . . . 180 C1
Penge BR3 . . . . 206 D6
South Lambeth
SW8 . . . . 138 B5 270 C4
Upton E7 . . . . 77 C1
West Green N15 . . . . 51 B5
Wood Green N22 . . . . 32 A2
Dorset Rise EC4 . . 94 D1 241 C1
Dorset Road Inf Sch
SE9 . . . . 166 A2
Dorset Sq NW1 . . 92 D3 237 C5
Dorset St W1 . . . . 92 D2 237 D3
Dorset Way
Hillingdon UB10 . . . . 82 B5
Twickenham TW2 . . . . . . 152 B3
Dorset Waye TW5 . . . . . . 129 B5
Dorton Cl 6 SE15 . . . . . . 139 C5
Dorton Villas UB7 . . . . . 126 C4
Dorville Cres W6 . . . . . . 112 B3
Dorville Rd SE12 . . . . 165 A6
Dothill Rd SE18 . . . . 145 A5
Douai Gr TW12 . . . . 174 A2
Douay Martyrs RC Sch
(Annexe) The UB10 . . . . 60 D3
Douay Martyrs RC Sch The
UB10 . . . . 60 D4
Doughty Ct 11 E1 . . . . . . 118 B5
Doughty Mews
WC1 . . . . 94 B3 240 C5
Doughty St WC1 . 94 B3 240 C5
Douglas 20 NW9 . . . . 27 D1
Douglas Ave
Walthamstow E17 . . . . 35 C2
Wembley HA0 . . . . 66 A1
West Barnes KT3 . . . . 200 B5
Douglas Bader Ho N3 . . . 29 D4
Douglas Bldgs SE1 . . . . . 252 B2
Douglas Cl
Stanmore HA7 . . . . 25 A5
Wallington SM6 . . . . 220 A2
Douglas Cres UB4 . . . . . . 84 D3
Douglas Ct London N3 . . . 29 D1
5 South Hampstead
NW6 . . . . 69 C1
Douglas Ct continued
1 Upper Tooting
SW17 . . . . 180 C4
Douglas Dr CR0 . . . . 223 C5
Douglas Gracey Ho
SW18 . . . . 157 A4
Douglas Ho
Isleworth TW1 . . . . 153 B6
Putney SW15 . . . . 156 A5
Westminster SW1 . . . . . . 259 C3
Douglas Johnstone Ho
SW6 . . . . 264 C5
Douglas Mews NW2 . . . . . 69 A5
Douglas Path E14 . . . . . . 120 A1
Douglas Rd
Chingford E4 . . . . 20 C3
Hounslow TW3 . . . . 129 D2
Ilford IG3 . . . . 58 A3
Islington N1 . . . . 73 A1
Kilburn NW6 . . . . 91 B6
Kingston u T KT1 . . . . 176 D1
5 Newham E16 . . . . 99 A2
Stanwell TW19 . . . . 148 A5
Surbiton KT6 . . . . 198 B1
Thames Ditton KT10 . . . . 212 A6
Welling DA16 . . . . 146 B4
Wood Green N22 . . . . 32 C2
Douglas Rd N N1 . . . . 73 A2
Douglas Rd S N1 . . . . 73 A2
Douglas Robinson Ct
SW16 . . . . 182 A3
Douglas Sq SM4 . . . . 201 C3
Douglas St
SW1 . . . . 115 D2 259 C3
Douglas Terr E17 . . . . 35 B2
Douglas Waite Ho
NW6 . . . . 69 D1
Douglas Way SE8 . . . . . . 141 B5
Doulton Ho SE11 . . . . 260 D4
Doulton Mews 4 NW6 . . 69 D2
Dounesforth Gdns
SW18 . . . . 157 D3
Douro Pl W8 . . . 113 D3 255 D6
Douro St E3 . . . . 97 C5
Douthwaite Sq 12 E1 . . . 118 A5
Dove App E6 . . . . 100 A2
Dove Cl Hendon NW7 . . . . 27 D3
Northolt UB5 . . . . 84 D3
Wallington SM6 . . . . 220 B1
Dovecot Cl HA5 . . . . 40 C4
Dovecote Gdns 8
SW14 . . . . 133 B2
Dove Ct
City of London EC2 . . . . . 242 C1
Enfield EN3 . . . . 18 B6
Stanwell TW19 . . . . 148 A4
Dovedale Ave HA3 . . . . . . 43 C3
Dovedale Cl DA16 . . . . . . 146 A3
Dovedale Cotts 6
SW11 . . . . 136 D3
Dovedale Ho N16 . . . . 51 B2
Dovedale Rd SE22 . . . . . 162 B5
Dovedale Rise CR4 . . . . . 180 D3
Dovedon Cl N14 . . . . 16 A2
Dove House Gdns E4 . . . . 19 C2
Dovehouse Mead
IG11 . . . . 101 B5
Dovehouse St
SW3 . . . . 114 C1 257 A1
Dove Mews
SW7 . . . . 114 A1 256 B2
Dove Pk HA5 . . . . 23 C3
Dover Cl NW2 . . . . 68 D6
Dovercourt Ave CR7 . . . 204 C5
Dovercourt Gdns HA7 . . . 26 A5
Dovercourt La SM1 . . . . . 218 A5
Dovercourt Rd SE22 . . . . 161 D5
Dover Ct
Clerkenwell EC1 . . . . 241 C6
17 Greenwich SE10 . . . . 141 D4
Sutton SM1 . . . . 218 B4
Dove Rd N1 . . . . 73 B2
Doverfield Rd SW2 . . . . . 160 A4
Dover Flats SE1 . . . . 263 B3
Dover Gdns SM5 . . . . 218 D5
Dover Ho
7 Beckenham BR3 . . . . . 185 C3
Brixton SE5 . . . . 138 D4
11 Deptford SE15 . . . . . . 140 C6
Edgware HA8 . . . . 26 B3
14 Penge SE20 . . . . 184 B2
Dover House Rd
SW15 . . . . 156 B6
Doveridge Gdns N13 . . . . 32 D6
Dover Mans 16 SW9 . . . . 138 C2
Dove Row E2 . . . . 96 A6
Dover Park Dr SW15 . . . 156 B5
Dover Patrol SE3 . . . . . . 143 C3
Dover Rd
Dagenham RM6 . . . . 59 A3
Lower Edmonton N9 . . . . . 18 C2
South Norwood SE19 . . . 183 B4
Wanstead E12 . . . . 77 C6
Woolwich SE18 . . . . 145 A3
Dover St W1 . . . . 115 C5 249 A4
Dover Terr TW9 . . . . 132 C3
Dover Yd W1 . . . . 249 A4
Doves Cl BR2 . . . . 226 A6
Doves Yd N1 . . . . 94 C6 234 A5
Dovet Ct SW8 . . . . 270 C2
Doveton Ho 7 E1 . . . . 96 C3
Doveton Rd CR2 . . . . 221 B3
Doveton St 8 E1 . . . . 96 C3
Dove Wlk SW1 . . . . 258 A2
Dovey Lo 4 N1 . . . . 72 C1
Dowanhill Rd SE6 . . . . . . 164 B3
Dowd Cl N11 . . . . 15 A2
Dowdeny Cl 12 NW5 . . . . 71 C3
Dowdeswell Cl SW15 . . . 133 C1
Dowding Ho N6 . . . . 49 A2
Dowding Pl HA7 . . . . 25 A4
Dowding Rd UB10 . . . . 60 B1
Dowe Ho SE3 . . . . 142 C2
Dowell Ho SE21 . . . . 161 D1
Dower Ho The DA14 . . . . 169 B1
Dowes Ho 13 SW16 . . . . 160 A1
Dowgate Hill EC4 . . . . . . 252 C6
Dowland Ho EN1 . . . . 5 D5
Dowland St W10 . . . . 91 A4
Dowlas St SE5 . . . . 139 C5
Dowlen Ct 14 E14 . . . . . . 119 C4
Dowler Ct 2 KT2 . . . . 176 B2
Dowler Ho 32 E1 . . . . 96 A1
Dowlerville Rd BR6 . . . . . 227 D2
Dowling Ho DA17 . . . . . . 125 B3
Dowman Cl 2 SW19 . . . . 179 D3
Downage NW4 . . . . 46 C6
Downalong WD23 . . . . 8 B3
Down Barns Rd HA4 . . . . 62 D5
Downbarton Ho 11
SW9 . . . . 138 C4
Downbury Mews 13
SW18 . . . . 157 C6
Down Cl UB5 . . . . 84 B5
Downderry Prim Sch
BR1 . . . . 186 C6
Downderry Rd BR1 . . . . . 186 C6
Downe Cl DA16 . . . . 146 C5
Downe Ho 9 SE7 . . . . . . 143 C6
Downe Manor Prim Sch
UB5 . . . . 84 B4
Downend SE18 . . . . 144 D5
Downend Ct 1 SE15 . . . . 139 C6
Downe Rd CR4 . . . . 180 D1
Downer's Cotts SW4 . . . 137 C1
Downes Cl TW1 . . . . 153 B5
Downes Ct N21 . . . . 16 C3
Downes Ho CR0 . . . . 220 D4
Downey Ho 6 E1 . . . . 96 D3
Downfield KT4 . . . . 200 A1
Downfield Cl W9 . . . . 91 D3
Downfield Ho KT3 . . . . . 199 B1
Down Hall Rd KT2 . . . . . 175 D2
DOWNHAM 186 C5
Downham Ct 1 N1 . . . . . . 73 B1
Downham Ent Ctr
SE6 . . . . 164 D2
Downham La BR1 . . . . . . 186 B5
Downham Rd N1 . . . . 73 B1
Downham Way BR1 . . . . 186 C6
Downhills Ave N17 . . . . . . 51 B6
Downhills Park Rd N17 . . 51 A6
Downhills Prim Sch
N15 . . . . 51 B5
Downhills Way N17 . . . . . 33 A1
Downhurst Ave NW7 . . . . 27 B5
Downhurst Ct NW4 . . . . . . 46 C6
Downing Cl HA2 . . . . 42 A6
Downing Ct N12 . . . . 29 D5
Downing Dr UB6 . . . . 86 C6
Downing Ho
9 Merton SW19 . . . . 179 C3
2 North Kensington
W10 . . . . 90 D1
4 Putney SW15 . . . . 156 A6
Downing Rd RM9 . . . . 81 B1
Downings E6 . . . . 100 C1
Downing St*
SW1 . . . . 116 A4 250 A2
Downland Cl N20 . . . . 14 A3
Downland Ct E11 . . . . 76 C6
Downleys Cl SE9 . . . . 166 B2
Downman Rd SE9 . . . . . . 144 A2
Down Pl W6 . . . . 112 B1
Down Rd TW11 . . . . 175 B4
Down St Mews W1 . . . . . 248 C3
Downs Ave
Elmstead BR7 . . . . 188 B5
Pinner HA5 . . . . 41 B2
Downs Bridge Rd BR3 . . 186 B2
Downs Ct 16 Hackney E8 . . 74 B3
13 Wimbledon SW19 . . . 178 D3
Downsell Prim Sch E15 . 76 B4
Downsell Rd E15 . . . . 76 B4
Downsfield Rd E17 . . . . . . 53 A3
Downshall Ave IG3 . . . . . . 57 C3
Downshall Ct IG3 . . . . 57 C3
Downshall Prim Sch
IG3 . . . . 57 C2
Downs Hill BR2, BR3 . . . 186 B2
Downshire Hill NW3 . . . . 70 B4
Downside
2 Putney SW15 . . . . 157 A6
Sunbury TW16 . . . . 172 A2
Twickenham TW1 . . . . . . 152 D1
Downside Cl SW19 . . . . . 180 A4
Downside Cres
Ealing W13 . . . . 87 A3
Maitland Pk NW3 . . . . 70 C3
Downside Rd SM2 . . . . . 218 C2
Downside Wlk UB5 . . . . . 85 B4
Downs La 2 E5 . . . . 74 B4
Downs Park Rd E5, E8 . . . 74 A3
Downs Rd
Beckenham BR3 . . . . 185 D1
Enfield EN1 . . . . 5 C1
Shacklewell E5, N16 . . . . . 74 A4
South Norwood CR7 . . . . 183 A2
Down St
East Molesey KT8 . . . . . . 195 C4
Mayfair W1 . . . . 115 B5 248 C3
Downs The SW19,
SW20 . . . . 178 D3
Downs View TW7 . . . . . . 131 A4
Downsview Gdns
SE19 . . . . 183 A3
Downs View Lo 9
KT6 . . . . 198 A3
Downsview Prim Sch
SE19 . . . . 183 A3

Downsview Rd SE19 183 A3
Downsview Sch E5 74 B4
Downsway BR6 227 C3
Downton Ave SW2 160 B2
Downtown Rd SE16 119 A4
Downway N12 30 C3
Down Way UB5 84 B4
Dowrey St N1 234 A6
Dowsett Rd N17 34 A1
Dowson Cl SE5 139 B1
Dowson Ct SE13 142 B2
Dowson Ho 8 E1 96 D1
Doyce St SE1 252 A2
Doyle Gdns NW10 90 B6
Doyle Ho W3 110 D4
Doyle Rd SE25 206 A5
D'Oyley St SW1 258 A4
Doynton St N19 71 B6
Draco St SE17 139 A6
Dragon Ct WC2 240 B2
Dragonfly Cl E13 99 B4
Dragon Rd SE15 139 C6
Dragon Yd WC1 240 B2
Dragoon Rd SE8 119 B1
Dragor Rd NW10 89 A3
Drake Cl 30 SE16 118 D4
Drake Cres SE28 102 C1
Drake Croft N16 73 B6
Drake Ct Dulwich SE19 183 D5
5 Hammersmith W12 112 B4
Kingston u T KT5 198 B5
Drakefell Rd SE4,
SE14 140 D2
Drakefield Rd SW17 159 A1
Drake Hall 13 E16 121 B5
Drake Ho
2 Limehouse E14 119 A6
20 Stepney E1 96 C2
Drakeley Ct N5 72 D4
Drake Mews BR2 209 C5
Drake Rd Brockley SE4 141 C2
Chessington KT9 214 C3
Harrow HA2 63 B6
Mitcham CR4 203 A3
Thornton Heath CR0 204 B2
Drakes Ct SE23 162 C3
Drakes Ctyd NW6 69 B1
Drake St Enfield EN2 5 B4
Holborn WC1 240 C3
Drakes Wlk E6 100 B6
Drakewood Rd SW16 181 D3
Draper Cl
Belvedere DA17 125 B2
Hounslow TW7 130 B3
Draper Ct BR1 210 A5
Draper Ho SE1 261 D4
Draper Pl N1 234 D6
Drapers Almhouses 5
E3 97 C4
Draper's Cottage Homes
NW7 28 A6
Drapers Gdns EC2 242 D2
Drapers Rd Enfield EN2 4 D4
Leyton E15 76 B4
Tottenham N17 51 D6
Drappers Way 8
SE16 118 A2
Draven Cl BR2 208 D2
Drawell Cl SE18 123 C1
Drax Ave SW20 178 A3
Draxmont SW19 179 A4
Draycot Rd
Tolworth KT6 198 C1
Wanstead E11 55 B2
Draycott Ave
Chelsea SW3 114 C2 257 B3
Harrow HA3 43 C3
Draycott Cl
Camberwell SE5 139 B5
Cricklewood NW2 68 D5
Harrow HA3 43 B3
Draycott Ct SW11 267 A2
Draycott Ho SW3 257 C3
Draycott Pl
SW3 114 D2 257 C3
Draycott Terr
SW3 114 D2 257 D3
Drayford Cl W9 91 B3
Dray Gdns SW2 160 B6
Draymans Ct 4 SW9 138 B2
Draymans Way TW7 130 D2
Drayside Mews UB2 107 B4
Drayson Mews
W8 113 C4 245 B1
Drayton Ave
Ealing W13 109 A6
Orpington BR6 210 D1
Drayton Bridge Rd
Ealing W7, W13 108 D6
Ealing W13 87 A1
Drayton Cl
Hounslow TW4 151 B6
Ilford IG1 57 B1
Drayton Ct
South Kensington
SW10 256 B1
Tolworth KT5 214 D6
West Drayton UB7 104 B2
Drayton Gdns
Ealing W13 109 A6
Southgate N21 16 D4
South Kensington
SW10 114 A1 256 B1
West Drayton UB7 104 A4
Drayton Gn W13 109 A6
Drayton Gr W13 109 A6
Drayton Green Prim Sch
W13 109 A6
Drayton Green Rd
W13 109 B6
Drayton Green Sta W7 86 D1
Drayton Ho
14 Camberwell SE5 139 B5
Leytonstone E11 54 B1
Drayton Lo E17 35 D1
Drayton Manor High Sch
W7 86 D1
Drayton Park Mews 12
N5 72 C3
Drayton Park Prim Sch
N5 72 C3
Drayton Park Sta N5 72 C3
Drayton Pk N5, N7 72 C4
Drayton Rd
Croydon CR0 220 D6
Ealing W13 109 B6
Harlesden NW10 89 D6
Leytonstone E11 54 B1
Tottenham N17 33 C1
Drayton Waye HA3 43 B3
Dreadnought Cl SW19 180 B1
Dreadnought St SE10 120 C3
Drenon Sq UB3 105 D6
Dresden Cl NW6 69 D2
Dresden Ho
5 Clapham SW11 137 A3
Lambeth SE11 260 D4
Dresden Rd N19 49 D1
Dressington Ave SE4 163 C5
Drew Ave NW7 29 A4
Drewery Ct SE3 142 C2
Drewett Ho 31 E1 96 A1
Drew Gdns UB6 64 D2
Drew Ho 12 SW16 160 A1
Drew Prim Sch E16 122 A5
Drew Rd E16 122 A5
Drewstead La SW16 159 D2
Drewstead Rd SW16 159 D2
Driberg Ct RM9 80 B2
Driffield Ct 4 NW9 27 C2
Driffield Rd E3 97 A5
Drift The BR2 225 D5
Driftway Ho 19 E3 97 B5
Driftway The CR4 181 A2
Drinkwater Ho 11 SE5 139 B5
Drinkwater Rd HA2 63 D6
Drive Ct HA8 26 C5
Drive Ho CR4 202 C5
Drive Mans SW6 135 A3
Drive The Acton W3 89 A1
Ashford TW15 171 B3
Barking IG11 79 D1
Barking IG11 80 A2
Barnet EN5 1 A2
Beckenham BR3 185 C2
Bexley DA5 168 D4
Buckhurst Hill IG9 21 C4
Chingford E4 20 B4
Chislehurst BR7 189 D2
Edgware HA8 26 C5
Enfield EN2 5 B4
Erith DA8 147 D6
Feltham TW14 150 C4
Finchley N3 29 C3
Fortis Green N6 48 D4
Harlesden NW10 89 D6
Harrow HA2 41 C2
Hendon NW11 47 A2
Hounslow TW3, TW7 130 B3
Ickenham UB10 60 A5
Islington N7 72 B2
Kingston u T KT2 177 A3
Morden SM4 202 B4
New Barnet EN5 14 A5
Orpington BR6 227 D6
Redbridge IG1 56 B2
Sidcup DA14 190 B6
South Norwood CR7 205 B5
St Paul's Cray BR7 211 D6
Surbiton KT6 198 A2
Thames Ditton KT10 196 A1
Walthamstow E17 53 D6
Wanstead E18 55 A6
Wembley Pk HA9 67 A6
West Ewell KT19 215 D2
West Wickham BR4 208 B2
Wimbledon SW19,
SW20 178 C3
Wood Green N11 31 D4
Dr Johnson Ave SW17 159 B1
Dr Johnson's House Mus*
EC4 241 B1
Droitwich Cl SE26 162 A1
Dromey Gdns HA3 24 D3
Dromore Rd SW15 157 A5
Dronfield Gdns RM8 80 C3
Dron Ho E1 96 C2
Droop St W10 91 A3
Drovers Ct
3 Kingston u T KT1 176 A1
Lewisham SE13 142 A2
Drovers Pl SE15 140 B5
Drovers Rd CR2 221 B3
Dr Triplett's CE Prim Sch
UB3 83 D1
Druce Rd SE21 161 C5
Druid St SE1 117 D4 253 C1
Druids Way BR2 208 B5
Drumaline Ridge KT4 215 C6
Drummer Lo N7 72 B5
Drummond Castle Ct
E7 76 D4
Drummond Cres
NW1 93 D4 232 C2
Drummond Ct
Finchley N12 30 C3
Harrow HA1 42 C2
Drummond Ctr CR0 221 A6
Drummond Dr HA7 24 D3
Drummond Gate SW1 259 D2
Drummond Ho
13 Bethnal Green E2 96 A5
Finchley N2 30 A1
Drummond Rd
Bermondsey SE16 118 B3
Croydon CR0 221 A6
Wanstead E11 55 C3
Drummonds Pl TW9 132 A1
Drummond St
NW1 93 C3 239 A6
Drummonds The IG9 21 B2
Drum St E1 243 D2
Drury Cres CR0 220 C6
Drury Ho SW8 269 A2
Drury La WC2 94 A1 240 B1
Drury Rd HA1 42 A2
Drury Way NW10 67 B3
Drury Way Ind Est
NW10 67 B3
Dryad St SW15 134 D2
Dryburgh Gdns NW9 44 C6
Dryburgh Ho SW1 258 D2
Dryburgh Mans SW15 134 C2
Dryburgh Rd SW15 134 C2
Dryden Ave W7 86 D1
Dryden Bldg 10 E1 96 A1
Dryden Ct
Lambeth SE11 261 B3
11 Richmond TW10 175 D6
Dryden Ho
Bromley Comm BR2 209 D4
6 Camberwell SE5 139 C4
16 Stoke Newington N16 73 C5
Dryden Rd
Bexley DA16 145 D4
Enfield EN1 17 D5
Harrow HA3 24 D2
Wimbledon SW19 180 A4
Dryden St WC2 240 B1
Dryer Ct 21 EN3 7 C6
Dryfield Cl NW10 67 A2
Dryfield Rd HA8 27 A4
Dryfield Wlk 1 SE8 141 C6
Dryhill Rd DA17 147 B6
Dryland Ave 5 BR6 227 D4
Drylands Rd N8 50 A3
Drysdale Ave E4 19 D5
Drysdale Flats 3 E8 73 D3
Drysdale Ho 19 E2 95 C4
Drysdale Pl N1 95 C4
Drysdale St N1 95 C4
Dublin Ave E8 96 A6
Du Burstow Terr W7 108 C4
Ducal St 25 E2 95 D4
Ducane Cl 6 W12 90 C1
Du Cane Ct SW12 159 A3
Du Cane Rd W12 90 A1
Ducavel Ho SW2 160 B3
Duchess Cl London N11 31 B5
Sutton SM1 218 A4
Duchess Gr IG9 21 B2
Duchess Mews W1 238 D3
Duchess of Bedford Ho
W8 245 A2
Duchess of Bedford's Wlk
W8 113 C4 245 A1
Duchess St W1 93 B2 238 D3
Duchy Rd EN4 2 B5
Duchy St SE1 116 C5 251 B4
Ducie Ho
8 Charlton SE7 143 C6
2 Putney SW15 156 C6
Ducie St SW4 138 B1
Duckett Mews N4 50 D3
Duckett Rd N4 50 D3
Duckett St E1 97 A2
Duck La W1 239 C1
Duck Lees La EN3 7 A1
Ducks Hill Rd HA4, HA6 39 A5
DUCKS ISLAND 12 D5
Duck's Wlk TW1 153 C6
Du Cros Dr HA7 25 D4
Du Cros Rd W3 111 C5
DUDDEN HILL 68 A3
Dudden Hill La NW10 67 D3
Duddington Cl SE9 187 D6
Dudley Ave HA3 43 C6
Dudley Ct
Colney Hatch N12 30 C5
Marylebone W1 237 C1
St Giles WC2 240 A2
Temple Fortune NW11 47 B5
14 Wanstead E11 55 A4
Wembley HA0 65 D3
Dudley Dr Ruislip HA4 62 B3
West Barnes SM4 201 A2
Dudley Gdns
Ealing W13 109 B4
Harrow HA2 42 B1
Dudley Ho
13 Brixton SW9 138 C3
Edgware HA8 26 B3
Paddington W2 236 C3
Dudley Mews 14 SW2 160 C5
Dudley Pl UB3 105 B2
Dudley Rd
Ashford TW15 170 B6
East Bedfont TW14 149 B3
Finchley N3 29 D1
Harrow HA2 64 A6
Ilford IG1 78 D4
Kilburn NW6 91 B5
Kingston u T KT1 198 B6
Richmond TW9 132 B3
Southall UB2 106 D3
Walthamstow E17 35 C1
Walton-on-T KT12 194 A2
Wimbledon SW19 179 C4
Dudley St W2 236 C3
Dudlington Rd E5 74 C6
Dudmaston Mews
SW3 256 D2
Dudsbury Rd DA14 190 B4
Dudset La TW5 128 A4
Duett Ct TW3 129 A5
Duffell Ho SE11 260 D1
Dufferin Ave EC1 242 C5
Dufferin Ct EC1 242 C5
Dufferin St EC1 95 A3 242 B5
Duffield Cl HA1 42 D4
Duffield Dr N15 51 D5
Duffield Ho N4 51 A2
Duff St E14 97 D1
Dufour's Pl W1 239 B1
Dugard Way
SE11 116 D2 261 C3
Dugdale Ho 10 N7 71 D3
Duggan Dr BR7 188 A4
Dugolly Ave HA9 66 D5
Duke Gdns IG6 57 B5
Duke Humphrey Rd
SE3 142 C3
Duke Of Cambridge Cl
TW2 152 B5
Duke Of Edinburgh Rd
SM1 218 B6
Duke Of Wellington Ave
SE18 123 A3
Duke of Wellington Pl SW1,
W1 248 B2
Duke of York's Sq
SW3 114 D2 257 D3
Duke of York St SW1 249 B4
Duke Rd Chiswick W4 111 B1
Ilford IG6 57 B5
Duke St Hill SE1 252 D4
Duke St St James's
SW1 115 C5 249 B4
Dukes Ave Edgware HA8 26 B5
Finchley N3 29 D2
Hornsey N10 49 C6
Hounslow TW4 129 A1
Kingston u T KT3 199 D6
Northolt UB5 63 A1
Rayners La HA2, HA5 41 B3
Richmond KT2, TW10 175 D6
Wealdstone HA1 42 C5
Duke's Ave W4 111 B1
Dukes Cl Ashford TW15 171 A6
Hampton TW12 173 B5
Dukes Ct Barking E6 100 C6
Beckenham BR3 207 A6
Dulwich SE22 162 A3
Ealing W13 87 B2
East Dulwich SE22 162 B6
Lewisham SE13 142 A3
Mortlake SW14 133 B3
Dukes Gate 4 W4 111 A2
Dukes Green Ave
TW14 150 A6
Dukes Head Yd N6 49 B1
Duke's Ho SW1 259 D4
Duke Shore Wharf
E14 119 B6
Dukes La W8 113 D4 245 C2
Dukes Mews N10 49 B6
Duke's Mews W1 238 B2
Duke's Pl EC3 95 C1 243 B1
Dukes Point N6 49 B1
Dukes Rd Acton W3 88 C3
Barking E6 100 C6
Duke's Rd WC1 93 D4 232 D1
Dukes Ride UB10 60 A4
Duke St
Marylebone
W1 93 A1 238 B1
Richmond TW10, TW9 153 D6
Sutton SM1 218 B4
Dukesthorpe Rd SE26 184 D6
Duke Street Mans W1 238 B1
Dukes Way BR4 224 C5
Duke's Yd W1 248 B6
Dulas St N4 50 B1
Dulford St
W11 113 A6 244 A6
Dulka Rd SW11 158 D6
Dulverton NW1 232 B5
Dulverton Ct 12 KT6 198 A4
Dulverton Mans WC1 240 D5
Dulverton Prim Sch
SE9 167 B2
Dulverton Rd
New Eltham SE9 167 B2
Ruislip HA4 62 A6
DULWICH 161 C1
Dulwich Bsns Ctr
SE23 162 D3
Dulwich Coll SE21 161 C2
Dulwich Coll Picture
Gall* SE21 161 C4
Dulwich Coll Prep Sch
SE21 161 C1
Dulwich Comm SE21 161 C3
Dulwich Ct SE22 162 B3
Dulwich Hamlet Jun Sch
SE21 161 B5
Dulwich Hospl SE22 139 C1
Dulwich Lawn Cl
SE22 161 D6
Dulwich Mead SE24 161 A5
Dulwich Mews
1 East Dulwich
SE22 139 D1
East Dulwich SE22 161 D6
Dulwich Oaks The
SE21 161 D1
Dulwich Rd SE24 160 D5
DULWICH VILLAGE 161 C4
Dulwich Village SE21 161 C5
Dulwich Village CE Inf Sch
SE21 161 C5
Dulwich Wood Ave
SE19 183 C5
Dulwich Wood Pk
SE19 183 C6
Dumain Ct SE11 261 C3
Du Maurier Ho 2 NW3 70 D3
Dumbarton Ct 16
SW2 160 A4
Dumbarton Rd SW2 160 A5
Dumbleton Cl KT2 176 D2
Dumbreck Rd SE9 144 C2
Dumont Rd N16 73 C5
Dumphreys Ho 5
SW4 159 D4
Dumpton Pl NW1 71 A1
Dunally Pk TW17 193 B2
Dunbar Ave
Beckenham BR3 207 A5
Dagenham RM10 81 C5
Thornton Heath SW16 182 C1
Dunbar Cl UB4 84 A2
Dunbar Ct
3 London N12 29 D6
Sutton SM1 218 B3
Walton-on-T KT12 194 C1
Dunbar Gdns RM10 81 D3
Dunbar Rd
New Malden KT3 199 A5
Tottenham N22 32 D2
Upton E7 77 A2
Dunbar St SE27 161 A1
Dunbar Wharf 20 E14 119 B6
Dunblane Cl HA8 10 D2
Dunblane Rd SE9 144 A3
Dunboe Pl TW17 193 A2
Dunboyne Rd NW3 70 D3
Dunbridge Ho SW15 155 D5
Dunbridge St
Bethnal Green E2
Bethnal Green E2 96 B3
Duncan Cl EN5 2 A1
Duncan Ct
5 London N12 29 D5
3 Poplar E14 98 A2
Southgate N21 16 D3
Duncan Gr W3 89 C1
Duncan Ho Harrow HA2 64 A5
3 Primrose Hill NW3 70 D1
Duncannon Ho SW1 259 D1
Duncannon St WC2 250 A5
Duncan Rd Hackney E8 96 B6
Richmond TW9 132 A1
Duncan St N1 94 D5 234 C4
Duncan Terr N1 94 D5 234 C4
Dunch St 33 E1 96 B1
Dunchurch Ho RM10 81 C1
Duncombe Hill SE23 163 A4
Duncombe Ho 7
SW19 156 D3
Duncombe Prim Sch
N19 50 A1
Duncombe Rd N19 49 D1
Duncrievie Rd SE13 164 B5
Duncroft SE18 145 C5
Dundalk Ho 2 E1 96 C1
Dundalk Rd SE4 141 A2
Dundas Gdns KT8 195 D6
Dundas Ho 12 E2 96 C5
Dundas Mews 4 EN3 7 C6
Dundas Rd SE15 140 C3
Dundee Ct 36 E1 118 B5
Dundee Ho W9 229 A2
Dundee Rd
Croydon SE25 206 B4
Newham E13 99 B5
Dundee St E1 118 B5
Dundee Way EN3 7 A2
Dundee Wharf E14 119 B6
Dundela Gdns KT17,
KT4 216 B4
Dundonald Cl 6 E6 100 A1
Dundonald Prim Sch
SW19 179 B3
Dundonald Rd
Brondesbury Pk NW10 90 D6
Merton SW19 179 B3
Dundonald Road Sta
SW19 179 B3
Dundry Ho 8 SE26 162 A1
Duneaves HA1 64 C5
Dunedin Ho E16 122 B5
Dunedin Rd Ilford IG1 57 A1
Leyton E10 75 D5
Dunedin Way UB4 84 C3
Dunelm Gr SE27 161 A1
Dunelm St E1 96 D1
Dunfield Gdns SE6 185 D5
Dunfield Rd SE6 185 D5
Dunford Ct 9 HA5 23 B3
Dunford Rd N7 72 B4
Dungarvan Ave SW15 134 A1
Dungeness Ho SW18 136 A1
Dunheved Cl CR7 204 C3
Dunheved Ct 2 CR7 204 C3
Dunheved Rd N CR7 204 C3
Dunheved Rd S CR7 204 C3
Dunheved Rd W CR7 204 C3
Dunhill Point 12
SW15 156 B3
Dunholme Gn N9 17 D1
Dunholme La N9 17 D1
Dunholme Rd N9 17 D1
Dunkeld Ho 15 E14 98 B1
Dunkeld Rd
Dagenham RM8 80 C6
South Norwood SE25 205 B5
Dunkery Rd SE9 166 A1
Dunkirk St 12 SE27 183 A6
Dunlace Rd E5 74 D4
Dunleary Cl TW4 151 B4
Dunley Dr CR0 224 A2
Dunlin Ct 12 SE21 161 B2
Dunlin Ho 18 SE16 118 D2
Dunloe Ave N17 51 B6
Dunloe Ct 7 E2 95 D5
Dunloe St E2 95 D5
Dunlop Pl
SE16 117 D3 263 D5
Dunmore Point 15 E2 95 D4
Dunmore Rd
Kilburn NW6 91 A6
Wimbledon SW20 178 D2
Dunmow Cl
Dagenham RM6 58 C4
3 Feltham TW13 173 A6
Dunmow Ho
Dagenham RM9 102 B6
Vauxhall SE11 260 D2
Dunmow Rd E15 76 B4
Dunmow Wlk N1 235 A6
Dunnage Cres SE16 119 A2
Dunne Mews 11 NW5 71 C3
Dunnet Ho 27 E3 97 B5
Dunnico Ho SE17 263 A2
Dunn Mead NW9 27 D3
Dunnock Cl N9 18 D3
Dunnock Ct 11 SE21 161 B2
Dunnock Rd E6 100 A1
Dunn's Pas WC1 240 B2
Dunn St E8 73 D3
Dunollie Pl NW5 71 C3
Dunollie Rd NW5 71 C3
Dunoon Gdns SE23 162 D4
Dunoon Ho N1 233 C5
Dunoon Rd SE23 162 C4
Dunraven Dr EN2 4 C3
Dunraven Ho 12 TW9 132 B4
Dunraven Rd W12 112 A5
Dunraven Sch SW16 160 B1
Dunraven St
W1 114 D6 247 D6
Dunrobin Ct NW3 69 D3
Dunsany Rd W14 112 D3
Dunsfold Ct 14 SM2 217 D1
Dunsfold Ho
10 Kingston u T KT2 176 D4
4 Streatham SW2 160 B4
Dunsfold Way CR0 223 D1
Dunsford Way SW15 156 B5
Dunsmore Cl
Bushey WD23 8 B5
Hayes UB4 85 A3
Dunsmore Rd KT12 194 B3
Dunsmore Way WD23 8 B5
Dunsmure Rd N16 51 C1
Dunstable Ct 3 SE3 143 A5
Dunstable Mews W1 238 B4
Dunstable Rd
East Molesey KT8 195 B5
Richmond TW10, TW9 132 A1
Dunstall Ho 9 SE15 140 A4
Dunstall Rd SW19,
SW20 178 C4
Dunstall Way KT8 195 D6
Dunstall Welling Est
DA16 146 B3
Dunstan Cl 2 N2 48 A6
Dunstan Glade BR5 211 B3
Dunstan Ho SE4 141 B3
Dunstan Hos 5 E1 96 C2
Dunstan Rd NW11 47 C1
Dunstan's Gr SE22 162 B5
Dunstan's Rd SE22 162 A5
Dunster Ave SM4 200 D1
Dunster Ct EC3 253 B6
Dunster Dr NW9 45 A1
Dunster Gdns NW6 69 B1
Dunster Ho SE6 163 D1
Dunsterville Way SE1 252 D1
Dunster Way
Carshalton CR4 203 A1
Harrow HA2 63 A5
Dunston Rd
Clapham SW11 137 A3
Hackney E8 95 D6
Dunston St E8 95 D6
Dunton Cl KT6 198 A1
Dunton Ct 5 SE26 162 B2
Dunton Ho 14 SW16 160 A1
Dunton Rd
Bermondsey
SE1 117 D2 263 C3
Leyton E10 53 D2
Duntshill Rd SW18 157 D3
Dunvegan Cl KT8 195 D5
Dunvegan Rd SE9 144 B1
Dunwich Ct 2 RM6 58 B4
Dunwich Rd DA7 147 B4
Dunworth Mews W11 91 B1
Duplex Ride SW1 247 D1
Dupont Rd SW20 178 D1
Duppas Ave CR0 220 D4
Duppas Cl TW17 193 B4
Duppas Ct CR0 220 D5
Duppas Hill La CR0 220 D4
Duppas Hill Rd CR0 220 D4
Duppas Hill Terr CR0 220 D5
Duppas Jun Sch CR0 220 D3
Duppas Rd CR0 220 D5
Dupree Rd SE7 121 B1
Dura Den Cl BR3 185 D3
Durand Cl SM5 202 D1
Durand Gdns
SW9 138 B4 270 D1

Durand Prim Sch
SW9 138 B4 270 D2
Durand Way NW10 67 A1
Durants Lo EN3 6 D2
Durants Park Ave EN3 6 D1
Durants Rd EN3 6 D1
Durants Sch EN3 6 C4
Durant St E2 96 A4
Durban Ct E7 77 D1
Durban Ho 28 W12 112 B6
Durban Rd
Beckenham BR3 185 B1
Ilford IG2 57 C1
Newham E15 98 C4
Tottenham N17 33 D4
Walthamstow E17 35 B2
West Norwood SE27 183 B6
Durbin Ho 13 N9 18 A1
Durbin Rd KT9 214 B4
Durdan Cotts UB5 85 B1
Durdans Ho 3 NW1 71 C1
Durdans Park Prim Sch
UB1 85 B2
Durdans Rd UB1 85 B1
Durell Gdns RM9 80 D3
Durell Rd RM9 80 D3
Durfey Pl SE5 139 B5
Durford Cres SW15 156 B3
Durham Ave
Beckenham BR2 208 D5
Hounslow TW5 107 B1
Woodford IG8 37 D5
Durham Cl SW20 178 B1
Durham Ct 2 Barnet EN5 1 B2
Brockley SE4 141 C2
4 Kilburn NW6 91 C5
Teddington TW11 174 C6
Durham Hill BR1 186 D6
Durham Ho
3 Barking IG11 80 A1
7 Dartmouth Pk NW5 71 C5
Edgware HA8 26 B3
Lisson Gr NW8 230 B1
Durham House St
WC2 250 B5
Durham Pl
Chelsea SW3 257 C1
Ilford IG1 79 A4
Durham Rd
Beckenham BR2 208 D6
Ealing W5 109 D3
Edmonton N9 18 A2
Feltham TW14 150 C4
Harrow HA1 41 D4
Lower Holloway N4, N7 72 B6
Manor Pk E12 77 D4
Muswell Hill N2 48 D6
Newham E16 98 C3
Sidcup DA14 190 B5
Wimbledon SW20 178 B2
Durham Rise SE18 123 B1
Durham Row E1 97 A2
Durham St
SE11 138 B6 270 C6
Durham Terr W2 91 D1
Durham Wharf Dr
TW8 131 C5
Durley Ave HA5 41 A3
Durley Rd N16 51 C2
Durlock Ho 16 SW9 138 C4
Durlston Rd
Kingston u T KT2 176 A4
Stoke Newington E5 74 A6
Durnford Ho SE6 163 D1
Durnford St
4 Greenwich SE10 142 A6
South Tottenham N15 51 C4
Durning Rd SE19 183 B5
Durnsford Ave SW18,
SW19 157 C2
Durnsford Ct 5 EN3 7 A2
Durnsford Rd
London N11 31 D3
Wimbledon SW18,
SW19 157 C1
Durnston Ct 2 SM1 217 D2
Durrant Ct HA3 24 C2
Durrant Way BR6 227 B3
Durrell Rd SW6 264 C1
Durrell Way TW17 193 B3
Durrels Ho W14 254 D4
Durrington Ave SW20 178 C3
Durrington Park Rd
SW20 178 C2
Durrington Rd E5 75 A4
Durrington Twr 3
SW8 137 C3
Durrisdeer Ho NW2 69 B4
Dursley Cl SE3 143 C3
Dursley Gdns SE3 143 D4
Dursley Rd SE3 143 C3
Durston NW5 71 A3
Durston House
Middleton's Sch W5 87 D1
Durston House Prep Sch
W5 87 D1
Durward St E1 96 B2
Durweston Mews W1 237 D4
Durweston St W1 237 D3
Dury Rd EN5 1 B3
Dutch Gdns KT2 176 D4
Dutch Yd SW18 157 C6
Dutton Ho SW2 160 D3
Dutton St SE10 142 A4
Duxberry Cl BR2 210 A4
Duxford 21 KT1 176 C1
Duxford Ho 10 SE2 124 D4
Dwight Ct SW6 135 A3
Dycer Ho 19 E9 74 D2
Dye House La E3 97 C6
Dyer Ho
Hampton TW12 173 D2
New Cross SE4 141 A3
Dyer's Bldgs EC1 241 A3
Dyers Hall Rd
Leyton E11 76 B6
Leytonstone E11 54 C1
Dyer's La SW15 134 B1
Dykes Ct 11 SW2 160 B3
Dykes Way BR2 208 D6
Dylan Cl WD6 9 D4
Dylan Rd
Belvedere DA17 125 C3
2 Brixton SE24 138 D1
Dylways SE5 139 B1
Dymchurch Cl
Ilford IG5 56 C6
Orpington BR6 227 C4
Dymchurch Ho 12 E5 74 B3
Dymes Path SW19 156 D2
Dymock St SW6 135 D2
Dyneley Rd SE12 165 C1
Dyne Rd NW6 69 B1
Dynevor Rd
Richmond TW10 154 A6
Shacklewell N16 73 D5
Dynham Rd NW6 69 C1
Dyott St Soho WC1 239 D2
St Giles WC1,
WC2 94 A1 240 A2
Dysart Ave KT2, TW10 175 C6
Dysart Sch KT6 198 B2
Dysart St EC2 95 C3 243 A5
Dyson Ct London NW2 46 C2
Wembley HA0 65 A4
Dyson Ho 3 SE10 120 D1
Dyson Rd
Leytonstone E11 54 C3
Stratford E15 76 D2
Dyson's Rd N18 34 B4

E

Eade Rd N4 51 A2
Eagans Cl N2 48 B6
Eagle Ave RM6 59 A3
Eagle Cl
Bermondsey SE16 118 C1
Enfield EN3 6 C1
Wallington SM6 220 A2
Eagle Ct
10 Dulwich SE21 161 B2
Edmonton N18 33 D4
Holborn EC1 241 C4
6 Wanstead E11 55 A5
Eagle Dr NW9 27 C1
Eagle Dwellings EC1 235 B2
Eagle Hill SE19 183 B4
Eagle Ho
22 Bethnal Green E1 96 B3
Finsbury Pk N7 72 B5
Eagle House Sch CR4 180 D1
Eagle Hts 10 SW11 136 C2
Eagle La E11 55 A5
Eagle Lo
Leytonstone E11 54 D5
London NW11 47 B2
Eagle Mans N16 73 D3
Eagle Mews N1 73 C2
Eagle Pl
South Kensington
SW7 114 A1 256 B2
St James SW1 249 B5
Eagle Rd Hatton TW6 127 D2
Wembley HA0 65 D1
Eaglesfield Rd SE18 144 D4
Eagle St WC1 94 B2 240 C3
Eagle Star Ho SM1 217 D4
Eagle Terr IG8 37 B3
Eagle Trad Est CR4 202 D3
Eagle Wharf SE1 253 C3
Eagle Wharf Rd
N1 95 A5 235 B4
Eagle Works E1 243 D5
Eagling Cl E3 97 C4
Ealcom Ct W5 110 B5
Ealdham Prim Sch
SE9 143 C1
Ealdham Sq SE9 143 C1
EALING 109 D6
Ealing Broadway Ctr
W5 109 D6
Ealing Broadway Sta
W5 109 D6
Ealing Coll W13 87 B1
Ealing Coll of Higher Ed
W5 109 D5
Ealing Common W5 110 B6
Ealing Common Sta
W5 110 B5
Ealing Court Man W5 109 D4
Ealing Gateway W5 109 C6
Ealing Gn W5 109 D5
Ealing, Hammersmith &
West London Coll
W14 113 A1 254 A2
Ealing Hospl UB1, UB2 108 B4
Ealing Park Gdns W5 109 C2
Ealing Park Lo UB6 87 A5
Ealing Park Mans W5 109 D3
Ealing Rd
Brentford TW8 109 D2
Northolt UB5 63 C1
Wembley HA0 66 A1
Ealing Road Trad Est
TW8 109 D1
Ealing Tertiary Coll
W3 110 D5
Ealing Village W5 88 A1
Ealing & West London Coll
W5 109 D5
Eamann Casey Ho 34
SW9 138 C4
Eamont Cl HA4 38 D2
Eamont Ct NW8 230 B4
Eamont St NW8 92 C5 230 B4
Eardley Cres
SW5 113 C1 255 B1
Eardley Point 9 SE18 122 D2
Eardley Rd
Belvedere DA17 125 C1
Streatham SW16 181 C4
Eardley Sch SW16 181 C4
Earl Cl N11 31 B5
Earldom Rd SW15 134 C1
Earle Gdns KT2 176 A3
Earle Ho SW1 259 D3
Earlham Gr
Forest Gate E7 77 A3
Wood Green N22 32 B3
Earlham Prim Sch
Stratford E7 76 D3
Wood Green N22 32 C3
Earlham St WC2 94 A1 240 A1
Earl Ho NW1 237 B5
Earlom Ho WC1 234 A1
Earl Rd SW14 133 A1
Earl Rise SE18 123 B2
EARL'S COURT 113 C1
Earl's Court Ex Ctr*
SW5 113 C1 255 A1
Earl's Court Gdns
SW5 113 D2 255 C3
Earl's Court Rd SW5,
W8 113 C2 255 B4
Earl's Court Sq
SW5 113 D1 255 C2
Earl's Court Sta
SW5 113 C2 255 B3
Earls Cres HA1 42 C5
Earlsdown Ho 6 IG11 101 B5
Earlsferry Way N1 72 A1
EARLSFIELD 158 A3
Earlsfield Ho 16 KT2 175 D2
Earlsfield Prim Sch
SW18 158 A2
Earlsfield Rd SW18 158 A4
Earlsfield Sta SW18 158 A3
Earlshall Rd SE9 144 C1
Earlsmead HA2 63 B4
Earlsmead Fst & Mid Sch
HA2 63 B4
Earlsmead Prim Sch
N15 51 D5
Earlsmead Rd
Kensal Green NW10 90 C4
South Tottenham N15 51 D4
Earl St EC2 95 C2 243 A4
Earls Terr W8 254 D5
Earlsthorpe Mews 3
SW12 159 A5
Earlsthorpe Rd SE26 184 D6
Earlstoke St EC1 234 C2
Earlston Gr E9 96 B6
Earls Wlk
Dagenham RM8 80 B4
Kensington W8 113 C3 255 A5
Earlswood Ave CR7 204 C4
Earlswood Cl 10 SE10 120 C1
Earlswood Gdns IG5 56 C6
Earlswood Ho 2 SW2 160 B3
Earlswood St SE10 120 C1
Early Mews NW1 231 D6
Earnshaw Ho EC1 234 D1
Earnshaw St WC1, WC2 239 D2
Earsby St W14 254 B4
Earth Galleries*
SW7 114 B3 256 D5
Easby Cres SM4 201 D3
Easebourne Rd RM8 80 C3
Easedale Ho TW7 152 D6
Eashing Point 5
SW15 156 B3
Easleys Mews W1 238 B2
East 10 Ent Pk E10 53 A1
EAST ACTON 111 C5
East Acton Arc W3 89 D1
East Acton Ct W3 111 C6
East Acton La W3 111 C6
East Acton Prim Sch
W3 111 C6
East Acton Sta W12 89 D1
East Arbour St E1 96 D1
East Ave Croydon CR0 220 B3
East Finchley NW2 48 A6
Hayes UB3 106 A5
Plashet E12 78 A1
Southall UB1 107 B6
Walthamstow E17 53 D5
East Bank N16 51 C2
Eastbank Rd TW12 174 A5
EAST BARNET 14 D4
East Barnet Rd EN4 2 B1
East Barnet Sch
Barnet EN4 2 B2
East Barnet EN4 14 D5
East Beckton District Ctr
E6 100 B2
EAST BEDFONT 149 C3
East Block 5 E1 118 D6
Eastbourne Ave W3 89 B1
Eastbourne Gdns
SW14 133 A2
Eastbourne Mews
W2 92 A1 236 B2
Eastbourne Rd
Brentford TW8 109 D1
Chiswick W4 133 A6
Feltham TW13 150 D2
South Tottenham N15 51 C3
Streatham SW17 181 A4
Wallend E6 100 C4
West Ham E15 98 C6
Eastbourne Terr
W2 92 A1 236 B2
Eastbournia Ave N9 18 B1
Eastbrook Ave N9 18 C4
Eastbrook Rd SE3 143 B4
EASTBURY 22 A5
Eastbury Ave
Barking IG11 101 C6
Enfield EN1 5 D4
Mo Pk HA6 22 A5
Eastbury Comp Sch
IG11 79 C2
Eastbury Ct
Barking IG11 101 C6
New Barnet EN5 14 A6
Eastbury Gr W4 111 C1
Eastbury Inf Sch IG11 79 D1
Eastbury Rd
Kingston u T KT2 176 A3
Newham E6 100 C3
Orpington BR5 211 B3
Eastbury Sq IG11 101 D6
Eastbury Terr E1 96 D3
Eastcastle St
W1 93 C1 239 B2
Eastcheap EC3 117 C6 253 A6
East Churchfield Rd
W3 111 B5
Eastchurch Rd TW6 127 C2
Eastchurch Road Rdbt
TW6 127 C3
East Cl Cockfosters EN4 3 A1
Ealing W5 88 C3
Greenford UB6 86 A5
Eastcombe Ave SE7 143 B6
EASTCOTE 40 C3
Eastcote BR6 211 D1
Eastcote Ave
East Molesey KT8 195 C4
Harrow HA2 64 A6
Wembley UB6 65 A3
Eastcote Ind Est HA4 40 C2
Eastcote La Harrow HA2 63 C5
Northolt UB5 63 B2
Eastcote La N UB5 63 C2
Eastcote Pl HA5 40 B3
Eastcote Prim Sch
DA16 145 B2
Eastcote Rd
Bexley DA16 145 B3
Harrow HA2 64 A5
Pinner HA5 40 D4
Ruislip HA4 40 A3
Eastcote St SW9 138 B3
Eastcote Sta HA5 40 C2
Eastcote View HA5 40 C5
EASTCOTE VILLAGE 40 B4
Eastcourt Ind Sch IG3 58 A1
East Cres Enfield EN1 17 D6
Friern Barnet N11 30 D6
Eastcroft Rd KT19 215 C1
East Cross Ctr E15 75 C2
East Cross Route
Bow E3 97 C6
Hackney Wick E9 75 B3
East Croydon Sta CR0 221 B6
East Ct Sunbury TW16 172 C1
Wembley HA0 65 C6
Eastdown Ho E8 74 A4
Eastdown Pk SE13 142 B1
East Duck Lees La EN3 7 B1
EAST DULWICH 162 A6
East Dulwich Gr SE22 161 C6
East Dulwich Rd SE15,
SE22 140 A1
East Dulwich Sta
SE22 139 C1
East End Rd
East Finchley N2, N3 48 A6
Finchley N3 29 C1
East End Way HA5 41 A6
East Entrance RM10 103 D5
Eastern Ave
Gants Hill IG1, IG2,
IG4 56 C3
Newbury Pk IG2 57 B3
Pinner HA5 40 D2
Wanstead E11 55 C3
Eastern Avenue W RM7 59 C5
Eastern Bsns Pk
TW16 127 D3
Eastern Perimeter Rd
TW14 127 D3
Eastern Quay 15 E16 121 B5
Eastern Rd
Brockley SE4 141 C1
Fortis Green N2 48 D5
Newham E13 99 B5
Walthamstow E17 54 A4
Wood Green N22 32 A2
Easternville Gdns IG2 57 A3
Eastern Way SE28 124 B4
East Ferry Rd E14 119 D2
Eastfield Gdns RM10 81 C4
Eastfield Prim Sch EN3 6 D5
Eastfield Rd
Dagenham RM9 81 B4
Dagenham RM10 81 C4
Enfield EN3 6 D5
Hornsey N8 50 A6
Walthamstow E17 53 C5
Eastfields HA5 40 C4
Eastfields Ave SW18 135 C1
Eastfields Rd Acton W3 89 A2
Mitcham CR4 181 A1
Eastfield St E14 97 A2
EAST FINCHLEY 48 B5
East Finchley Sta N2 48 C5
Eastgate Bsns Pk E10 53 A1
Eastgate Cl SE28 102 D1
Eastgate Ct N3 29 C1
East Gdns SW17 180 C4
Eastglade HA5 41 B6
EAST HAM 100 A5
Eastham Cl EN5 13 B6
East Ham Ind Est E6 100 A2
East Ham Manor Way
E6 100 C1
East Ham Meml Hospl
E7 77 D1
East Ham Sta E6 78 A1
East Harding St EC4 241 B2
East Heath Rd NW3 70 B5
East Hill London SW18 158 A6
Wembley HA9 44 C1
Eastholm NW11 47 D5
Eastholme UB3 106 A5
East India Bldgs 9
E14 119 C6
East India Ct 7 SE16 118 C4
East India Dock Basin*
E14 120 C6
East India Dock Rd
E14 119 D6
East India Dock Road
Tunnel 18 E14 98 B1
East India Sta E14 120 B6
East India Way CR0 205 D1
East La
5 Bermondsey SE16 118 A4
Bermondsey SE16 118 A4
Kingston u T KT1 197 D6
Wembley HA0, HA9 65 D5
Eastlake Ho NW8 236 D5
Eastlake Rd SE5 139 A3
Eastland Ct 2 BR1 187 C1
Eastlands Cres SE21 161 D5
East Lane Bsns Pk HA9 65 D5
Eastlea Com Sch E16 98 C3
Eastlea Mews E16 98 C3
Eastleigh Ave HA2 63 D6
Eastleigh Cl
Belmont SM2 217 D1
Neasden NW2 67 C5
Eastleigh Rd E17 35 B1
Eastleigh Way TW14 150 A3
Eastleigh Wlk 9
SW15 156 A4
East London Coll E11 76 C6
East London Coll &
Toynbee Theatre
E1 95 D2 243 D3
East London Stad E3 97 B2
Eastman Dental Hospl
WC1 94 B3 240 C6
Eastman Ho 7 SW4 159 C5
Eastman Rd W3 111 B4
East Mascalls 15 SE7 143 C6
Eastmead IG3 58 A2
East Mead HA4 62 D5
Eastmead Ave UB6 85 D4
Eastmead Cl BR1 188 A1
Eastmearn Rd SE21,
SE27 161 A2
EAST MOLESEY 196 A4
Eastmont Rd KT10 212 D6
Eastmoor Pl SE7 121 D3
Eastmoor St SE7 121 D3
East Mount St E1 96 B2
Eastney Rd CR0 204 D1
Eastney St SE10 120 B1
Eastnor Rd SE9 167 A3
Easton Ho 4 SE27 160 D1
Easton St WC1 241 A6
East Park Cl RM6 59 A4
East Parkside SE10 120 D4
East Pas EC1 242 A4
East Pl SE27 183 A6
East Plaza E14 119 D5
East Point 4 SE1 118 A1
Eastpole Cotts N14 3 D1
East Poultry Ave EC1 241 C3
East Putney Sta SW15 157 A6
East Ramp TW6 126 D4
East Rd Burnt Oak HA8 27 A2
Chelsea SW1 115 A1 258 A1
Dagenham RM6 59 A4
East Barnet EN4 15 A3
East Bedfont TW14 149 B4
Enfield EN3 6 C5
Finchley N2 30 C2
Kingston u T KT2 176 A2
Newham E15 99 A6
Shoreditch N1 95 B4 235 D2
Welling DA16 146 B3
West Drayton UB7 104 C2
Wimbledon SW19 180 A4
East Rochester Way DA5,
DA15, SE9 168 C5
East Row
Kensal Town W10 91 A3
Wanstead E11 55 A3
Eastry Ave BR2 208 D3
Eastry Ho SW8 270 A3
Eastry Rd DA8 147 C5
EAST SHEEN 133 B1
East Sheen Ave SW14 133 B1
East Sheen Prim Sch
SW14 133 C1
Eastside Rd NW11 47 B5
East Smithfield
E1 117 D6 253 D5
East St Barking IG11 79 A1
Bexleyheath DA7 147 C1
Brentford TW8 131 C5
Bromley BR1 187 A1
Walworth SE17 117 B1 262 C2
East Surrey Gr SE15 139 D5
East Tenter St
E1 95 D1 243 D1
East Terr DA15 167 C3
East Thamesmead Bsns Pk
DA18 125 B4
East Towers HA5 40 D3
Eastvale W3 111 D5
East View Barnet EN5 1 B2
Chingford E4 36 A5
Hampstead NW3 70 B6
Eastview Ave SE18 145 C5
East View Ho 13 N2 30 B1
Eastville Ave NW11 47 B3
Eastway Hayes BR2 209 A2
Merton SM4, SW20 201 A5
South Hackney E3, E9 97 A6
Temple Mills E9, E10 75 C4
Wallington SM6 219 C4
Wanstead E11 55 B4
East Way Croydon CR0 223 A5
Hayes UB3 106 A5
Ruislip HA4 40 A1
Eastway Cres HA2 63 D6
Eastwell Cl BR3 185 A2
Eastwell Ho SE1 262 D6
Eastwick Ct 2 SW19 156 D3
EAST WICKHAM 146 A5
East Wickham Inf Sch
DA16 145 D4
East Wickham Jun Sch
DA16 146 A4
East Wlk
East Barnet EN4 15 A3
Hayes UB3 106 A5
Eastwood Cl
2 Islington N7 72 C3
7 Tottenham N17 34 B3
Woodford E18 37 A1
Eastwood Rd Ilford IG3 58 A2
Muswell Hill N10 31 A1
West Drayton UB7 104 C4
Woodford E18 37 A1
East Woodside DA5 169 A3
Eastwood St SW16 181 C4
Eatington Rd E10 54 B4
Eaton Cl Belgravia SW1 258 A3
Stanmore HA7 25 B6
Eaton Ct
Chislehurst BR7 189 A4
Ealing W5 87 D1
Edgware HA8 26 C6
Southall UB1 107 B6
Sutton SM2 218 B2
6 Woodford E18 37 A1
Eaton Dr Brixton SW9 138 D1
Kingston u T KT2 176 C3
Eaton Gate
SW1 115 A2 258 A4
Eaton Gdns RM9 81 A1
Eaton Ho
Battersea SW11 266 D1
Ealing W5 87 D1
23 Limehouse E14 119 B6
Eaton House Sch
SW1 115 A2 258 A4
Eaton House The Manor
Sch SW4 137 B1
Eaton La SW1 115 B3 258 D5
Eaton Lo SM2 218 B2
Eaton Mans SW1 258 A3
Eaton Mews N
SW1 115 A3 258 B5
Eaton Mews S
SW1 115 B3 258 C5
Eaton Mews W SW1 258 B4
Eaton Park Rd N13 16 D2
Eaton Pl SW1 115 A3 258 B5
Eaton Rd Enfield EN1 5 C1
Hendon NW4 46 C4
Isleworth TW3, TW7 130 B1
Sidcup DA14 168 D2
Sutton SM2 218 B1
Eaton Rise Ealing W5 87 D1
Wanstead E11 55 C4
Eaton Row
SW1 115 B3 258 C5
Eatons Mead E4 19 C2
Eaton Sq SW1 115 A3 258 B5
Eaton Square Sch
SW1 115 B2 258 C4
Eaton Terr
Belgravia
SW1 115 A2 258 B4
Bow E3 97 A4
Eaton Terr Mews SW1 258 A4
Eatonville Rd SW17 158 D2
Eatonville Villas
SW17 158 D2
Ebb Ct E16 123 A6
Ebbisham Dr
SW8 138 B6 270 C5
Ebbisham Rd KT4 216 C6
Ebbsfleet Rd NW2 69 A4
Ebdon Way SE3 143 B2
Ebenezer Ho SE11 261 C3
Ebenezer Mussel Ho 5
E2 96 C5
Ebenezer St N1 235 C2
Ebenezer Wlk CR4 181 C2
Ebley Cl SE15 139 D6
Ebner St SW18 157 D6
Ebony Ct NW10 67 D2
Ebony Ho
27 Bethnal Green E2 96 A4

Ebony Ho *continued*
10 West Hampstead NW3 . . . 69 D2
Ebor Cotts SW15 . . . 155 C1
Ebor St E1, E2 . . . 243 C6
Ebrington Rd HA3 . . . 43 D3
Ebsworth St SE23 . . . 162 D4
Eburne Rd N7 . . . 72 A5
Ebury Bridge Rd SW1 . . . 115 A1 258 B1
Ebury Cl BR2 . . . 226 A5
Ebury Mews
Belgravia SW1 . . . 115 B2 258 C4
West Norwood SE27 . . . 160 D1
Ebury Mews E SW1 . . . 258 C5
Ebury Sq SW1 . . . 258 B3
Ebury St SW1 . . . 115 B2 258 C4
Ecclesbourne Cl N13 . . . 32 C5
Ecclesbourne Gdns N13 . . . 32 C5
Ecclesbourne Inf Sch CR7 . . . 205 A4
Ecclesbourne Jun Sch CR7 . . . 205 A4
Ecclesbourne Rd
Islington N1 . . . 73 A1
Thornton Heath CR7 . . . 205 A4
Eccles Ct SE11 . . . 260 D1
Eccleshill 3 BR2 . . . 208 D5
Eccles Rd SW11 . . . 136 D1
Eccleston Cl
Cockfosters EN4 . . . 2 D1
Crofton BR6 . . . 211 B1
Eccleston Cres RM6 . . . 58 B2
Ecclestone Ct HA9 . . . 66 A3
Ecclestone Mews HA9 . . . 66 A3
Ecclestone Pl HA9 . . . 66 B3
Eccleston Ho 1 SW2 . . . 160 C5
Eccleston Mews SW1 . . . 115 A3 258 B5
Eccleston Pl SW1 . . . 115 B2 258 C4
Eccleston Rd W13 . . . 109 A5
Eccleston Sq SW1 . . . 115 B2 258 D3
Eccleston Sq Mews SW1 . . . 259 A3
Eccleston St SW1 . . . 115 B2 258 C4
Echelforde Dr TW15 . . . 170 C6
Echelford Prim Sch The TW15 . . . 170 D5
Echo Hts E4 . . . 19 D3
Eckford St N1 . . . 234 A4
Eckington Ho N15 . . . 51 B3
Eckstein Rd SW11 . . . 136 C1
Eclipse Ho N22 . . . 32 B1
Eclipse Rd E13 . . . 99 B2
Ector Rd SE6 . . . 164 C2
Edam Ct 11 DA14 . . . 168 A1
Edans Ct W12 . . . 111 D4
Edbrooke Rd W9 . . . 91 C3
Eddisbury Ho 7 SE26 . . . 162 A1
Eddiscombe Rd SW6 . . . 135 B3
Eddison Ct N19 . . . 72 A6
Eddy Cl RM7 . . . 59 D3
Eddystone Rd SE4 . . . 163 A6
Eddystone Twr SE8 . . . 119 A1
Eddystone Wlk TW19 . . . 148 A4
Ede Cl TW4 . . . 129 B2
Edenbridge Cl 29 SE16 . . . 118 B1
Edenbridge Rd
Enfield EN1 . . . 17 C5
Hackney E9 . . . 74 D1
Eden Cl Child's Hill NW3 . . . 69 C6
Enfield EN3 . . . 7 C5
Kensington W8 . . . 255 B6
Wembley HA0 . . . 87 D6
Edencourt W5 . . . 88 B1
Edencourt Rd SW16 . . . 181 B4
Eden Ct 3 N3 . . . 29 B1
Edendale W3 . . . 110 D6
Edenfield Gdns KT4 . . . 215 D5
Eden Gr Islington N7 . . . 72 B3
Walthamstow E17 . . . 53 D4
Edenham High Sch CR0 . . . 207 B2
Edenham Way W10 . . . 91 B2
Eden Ho
15 Battersea SW11 . . . 136 C2
Lisson Gr NW8 . . . 237 A5
Edenhurst Ave SW6 . . . 135 B2
Eden Lodge NW6 . . . 68 D1
Eden Mews SW17 . . . 158 A1
EDEN PARK . . . 207 C5
Eden Park Ave BR3 . . . 207 C4
Eden Park Sta BR3 . . . 207 C4
Eden Rd Croydon CR0 . . . 221 B4
Penge BR3 . . . 185 A2
Walthamstow E17 . . . 53 D4
West Norwood SE27 . . . 182 D5
Edensmuir Ct SE3 . . . 143 A5
Edensor Gdns W4 . . . 133 C5
Edensor Rd W4 . . . 133 C5
Eden St KT1, KT2 . . . 176 A1
Edenvale Cl CR4 . . . 181 A3
Edenvale Rd CR4 . . . 181 A3
Edenvale St SW6 . . . 136 A3
Eden Way
Beckenham BR3 . . . 207 C3
Bow E3 . . . 97 B6
Eden Wlk 5 KT1 . . . 176 A1
Ederline Ave SW16 . . . 182 C1
Edgar Ct KT3 . . . 199 C6
Edgar Ho Homerton E9 . . . 75 A3
South Lambeth SW8 . . . 270 A4
Wanstead E11 . . . 55 A2
Edgar Kail Way SE22 . . . 139 C1
Edgarley Terr SW6 . . . 264 A1
Edgar Rd Bromley E3 . . . 97 D4
Dagenham RM6 . . . 58 D2
Twickenham TW4 . . . 151 B4
Yiewsley UB7 . . . 104 A5
Edgar Wallace Cl 4 SE15 . . . 139 C5
Edgbury Ct NW9 . . . 45 A5
Edgcott Ho 2 W10 . . . 90 C2
Edgeborough Way BR1 . . . 187 D2
Edge Bsns Ctr The NW2 . . . 68 B6
Edgebury BR7, SE9 . . . 188 D6
Edgebury Prim Sch BR7 . . . 189 A6
Edgebury Wlk BR7 . . . 167 A1
Edgecombe Ho
4 London SE5 . . . 139 C3
Putney SW19 . . . 157 A4
Edgecoombe CR2 . . . 222 C1
Edgecoombe Cl KT2 . . . 177 B3
Edgecote Cl 7 W3 . . . 111 A5
Edgecot Gr N15 . . . 51 C4
Edgecumbe Ct 2 CR0 . . . 206 A1
Edgefield Ave IG11 . . . 79 D1
Edgefield Ct 3 IG11 . . . 79 D1
Edge Hill
Shooters Hill SE18 . . . 144 D6
Wimbledon SW19 . . . 178 D3
Edge Hill Ave N3 . . . 47 C5
Edgehill Ct KT12 . . . 194 C1
Edge Hill Ct
Sidcup DA14 . . . 189 D6
Wimbledon SW19 . . . 178 D3
Edgehill Gdns RM10 . . . 81 C4
Edgehill Ho 4 SW9 . . . 138 D3
Edgehill Rd Ealing W13 . . . 87 C2
Longlands BR7 . . . 189 A6
Mitcham CR4 . . . 181 B2
Edgeley La SW4 . . . 137 D2
Edgeley Rd SW4 . . . 137 D2
Edgel St SW18 . . . 135 D1
Edge Point Cl SE27 . . . 182 D5
Edge St W8 . . . 113 C5 245 B4
Edgewood Dr BR6 . . . 227 D3
Edgewood Gn CR0 . . . 206 D1
Edgeworth Ave NW4 . . . 46 A4
Edgeworth Cl NW4 . . . 46 A4
Edgeworth Cres NW4 . . . 46 A4
Edgeworth Ct 10 EN4 . . . 2 C1
Edgeworth Ho NW8 . . . 229 A6
Edgeworth Rd
Barnet EN4 . . . 2 C1
Eltham SE9 . . . 143 D1
Edgington Rd SW16 . . . 181 D4
Edgington Way DA14 . . . 190 D3
Edgson Ho SW1 . . . 258 C2
EDGWARE . . . 26 C6
Edgware Acad WC2 . . . 240 B1
EDGWARE BURY . . . 10 B3
Edgwarebury Ct HA8 . . . 26 C5
Edgwarebury Gdns HA8 . . . 26 C5
Edgwarebury La
Edgware Bury HA8 . . . 10 C2
Edgware HA8 . . . 26 C5
Edgware Community Hospl HA8 . . . 26 D3
Edgware Ct HA8 . . . 26 C4
Edgware Jun & Inf Schs HA8 . . . 26 C4
Edgware Rd
Dollis Hill NW2 . . . 68 C6
Paddington W1, W2, NW1, NW8 . . . 92 C2 237 A3
Edgware Rd Burnt Oak Broadway HA8 . . . 26 D3
Edgware Rd High St HA8 . . . 26 C4
Edgware Road Sta (Bakerloo) NW1 . . . 92 C2 237 A3
Edgware Road Sta (Met, Distr, Circle) NW1 . . . 237 B3
Edgware Road The Hyde NW9 . . . 45 C5
Edgware Road West Hendon Broadway NW9 . . . 46 A2
Edgware Sta HA8 . . . 26 D4
Edgware Way (Watford By-Pass) HA8 . . . 27 A6
Edinburgh Cl
7 Bethnal Green E2 . . . 96 C5
Pinner HA5 . . . 41 A2
Uxbridge UB10 . . . 60 D4
Edinburgh Ct
1 Catford SE6 . . . 164 D3
2 Kingston u T KT1 . . . 198 A6
Newham E13 . . . 99 B5
10 Rotherhithe SE16 . . . 118 D5
West Barnes SM4 . . . 200 D4
Edinburgh Dr UB10 . . . 60 D4
Edinburgh Ho
3 Acton W3 . . . 89 B1
Carshalton SM1 . . . 218 B6
Hendon NW4 . . . 46 C6
Maida Vale W9 . . . 91 D4
Edinburgh Prim Sch E17 . . . 53 B4
Edinburgh Rd
Carshalton SM1 . . . 218 B6
Edmonton N18 . . . 34 A5
Hanwell W7 . . . 108 D4
Newham E13 . . . 99 B5
Walthamstow E17 . . . 53 C4
Edington 20 NW5 . . . 71 A2
Edington Rd
Abbey Wood SE2 . . . 124 B3
Edington Rd *continued*
Enfield EN3 . . . 6 C3
Edison Bldg 7 E14 . . . 119 C4
Edison Cl
Walthamstow E17 . . . 53 C4
West Drayton UB7 . . . 104 B4
Edison Ct SE10 . . . 120 D3
Edison Dr Southall UB1 . . . 85 D1
Wembley HA9 . . . 66 A6
Edison Gr SE18 . . . 145 D5
Edison Ho
Walworth SE1 . . . 262 C4
7 Wembley HA9 . . . 67 A5
Edison Rd Bexley DA16 . . . 145 D4
Brimsdown EN3 . . . 7 B3
Bromley BR2 . . . 187 A1
Crouch End N8 . . . 49 D3
Edis St NW1 . . . 93 A6 231 B6
Editha Mans SW10 . . . 266 A5
Edith Cavell Cl 2 N19 . . . 50 A2
Edith Cavell Way SE18 . . . 144 A4
Edith Ct TW14 . . . 149 B5
Edith Gdns KT5 . . . 198 D2
Edith Gr SW10 . . . 136 A5 266 B4
Edith Ho 6 W6 . . . 112 C1
Edithna St SW9 . . . 138 A2
Edith Neville Cotts NW1 . . . 232 C2
Edith Neville Prim Sch NW1 . . . 93 D5 232 C3
Edith Pond Ct SE9 . . . 166 D2
Edith Ramsay Ho 2 E1 . . . 97 A2
Edith Rd Dagenham RM6 . . . 58 D2
South Norwood SE25 . . . 205 B4
Stratford New Town E15 . . . 76 B3
Upton Pk E6 . . . 77 D1
West Kensington W14 . . . 113 A2 254 B3
Wimbledon SW19 . . . 179 D4
Wood Green N11 . . . 31 D3
Edith Row SW6 . . . 265 D2
Edith St E2 . . . 96 A5
Edith Summerskill Ho SW6 . . . 264 C4
Edith Terr SW10 . . . 136 A5 266 A4
Edith Villas W14 . . . 113 B1 254 C2
Edith Yd SW10 . . . 266 B4
Edmansons' Cl N17 . . . 33 D2
Edmeston Cl E9 . . . 75 A2
Edmond Ct SE14 . . . 140 C4
Edmonscote W13 . . . 87 A2
EDMONTON . . . 33 D6
Edmonton Ct 5 SE16 . . . 118 C3
Edmonton Cty Lower Sch N9 . . . 17 C3
Edmonton Cty Upper Sch EN1 . . . 17 D4
Edmonton Green Sh Ctr N9 . . . 18 B2
Edmonton Green Sta N9 . . . 18 A2
Edmonton Wharf N18 . . . 34 D4
Edmund Gr TW13 . . . 151 B2
Edmund Halley Way SE10 . . . 120 C4
Edmund Ho
Kennington SE17 . . . 261 D1
New Cross Gate SE14 . . . 141 B4
Edmund Hurst Dr E6 . . . 100 D2
Edmund Rd
Mitcham CR4 . . . 202 C6
Welling DA16 . . . 146 A2
Edmundsbury Ct Est 16 SW9 . . . 138 B1
Edmunds Cl UB4 . . . 84 C2
Edmund St SE5 . . . 139 B5
Edmunds Wlk N2 . . . 48 C5
Edmund Waller Prim Sch SE14 . . . 140 D3
Ednam Ho SE15 . . . 140 A6
Edna Rd SW20 . . . 178 D1
Edna St SW11 . . . 136 C4 267 A1
Edred Ho E9 . . . 75 A4
Edrich Ho SW4 . . . 270 A1
Edric Ho SW1 . . . 259 D4
Edrick Rd HA8 . . . 27 A4
Edrick Wlk HA8 . . . 27 A4
Edric Rd SE14 . . . 140 D5
Edridge Cl WD23 . . . 8 A6
Edridge Ho 9 SE27 . . . 160 D1
Edridge Rd CR0 . . . 221 B5
Edward Alleyn Ho SE21 . . . 161 C4
Edward Ave
Chingford E4 . . . 35 D4
Morden SM4 . . . 202 B4
Edward Betham CE Prim Sch UB6 . . . 86 A5
Edward Cl Edmonton N9 . . . 17 D4
Hampton TW12 . . . 174 A5
Edward Ct 2 Ealing W5 . . . 87 B3
Harrow HA1 . . . 64 C6
2 Newham E16 . . . 99 A2
Edward Dodd Ct N1 . . . 235 D2
Edward Edward's Ho SE1 . . . 251 C3
Edwardes Pl W8 . . . 254 D5
Edwardes Sq W8 . . . 113 B3 254 D5
Edward Friend Ho 6 N16 . . . 73 C5
Edward Gr EN4 . . . 14 B6
Edward Harvey Ct DA17 . . . 125 B1
Edward Ho
Paddington W2 . . . 236 C5
Vauxhall SE11 . . . 260 D2
Edward Kennedy Ho 18 W10 . . . 91 A3
Edward Mann Cl 13 E1 . . . 96 D1
Edward Mans 8 IG11 . . . 79 D1
Edward Mews NW1 . . . 231 D3
Edward Pauling Ho TW14 . . . 149 D4
Edward Pauling Prim Sch TW13 . . . 149 C2
Edward Pinner Ct 5 KT6 . . . 214 A6
Edward Pl SE8 . . . 141 B6
Edward Rd
Bromley BR1 . . . 187 C3
Chislehurst BR7 . . . 188 D5
Croydon CR0 . . . 205 C2
Dagenham RM6 . . . 59 A3
Hampton TW12 . . . 174 A5
Harrow HA2 . . . 42 A6
Hatton TW14 . . . 149 C6
New Barnet EN4 . . . 14 B6
Northolt UB5 . . . 84 C5
Penge SE20 . . . 184 D4
Walthamstow E17 . . . 52 D4
Edward Robinson Ho 3 SE14 . . . 140 D5
Edward's Ave HA4 . . . 62 C2
Edwards Cl KT4 . . . 216 D6
Edward's Cotts 11 N1 . . . 72 D1
Edwards Dr N11 . . . 31 D3
Edwards Ho 7 TW10 . . . 153 C1
Edward's La N16 . . . 73 C6
Edwards Language Sch W5 . . . 110 A6
Edwards Mews
Islington N1 . . . 72 C1
Marylebone W1 . . . 93 A1 238 A1
Edward Sq Islington N1 . . . 233 C5
1 Rotherhithe SE16 . . . 119 A5
Edwards Rd DA17 . . . 125 C2
Edward St
New Cross SE14 . . . 141 B5
10 Newham E16 . . . 99 A3
Edward Temme Ave E15 . . . 76 D1
Edward Tyler Rd SE12 . . . 165 C2
Edward VII Mans NW10 . . . 90 D4
Edward Way TW15 . . . 148 B2
Edward Wilson Prim Sch W2 . . . 91 D2
Edwina Ct SM1 . . . 217 D4
Edwina Gdns IG4 . . . 56 A4
Edwin Arnold Ct DA15 . . . 189 D6
Edwin Ave E6 . . . 100 C5
Edwin Cl DA7 . . . 147 B6
Edwin Ho SE15 . . . 140 A5
Edwin Rd Burnt Oak HA8 . . . 27 B4
Twickenham TW1, TW2 . . . 152 C3
Edwin's Mead E9 . . . 75 A4
Edwin St
Bethnal Green E1 . . . 96 C3
Newham E16 . . . 99 A2
Edwin Stray Ho TW13 . . . 151 C1
Edwin Ware Ct 4 HA5 . . . 22 C1
Edwy Ho E9 . . . 75 B4
Edwyn Cl EN5 . . . 12 D5
Edwyn Ho SW18 . . . 157 D5
Eel Pie Island* TW1 . . . 153 A3
Effie Pl SW6 . . . 265 B3
Effie Rd SW6 . . . 135 C5 265 B3
Effingham Cl SM2 . . . 217 D1
Effingham Ct SW19 . . . 180 C3
Effingham Ho
37 Clapham SW8 . . . 137 D3
9 Kingston u T KT2 . . . 176 D4
Effingham Lo 1 KT6 . . . 198 A4
Effingham Rd
Hornsey N8 . . . 50 C5
Lewisham SE12 . . . 164 D6
Thames Ditton KT6, KT7 . . . 197 C2
Thornton Heath CR0 . . . 204 B2
Effort St SW17 . . . 180 C5
Effra Cl SW19 . . . 179 D4
Effra Ct London SW2 . . . 160 B6
South Norwood SE19 . . . 183 C3
Effra Mans SW2 . . . 160 C6
Effra Par SW2 . . . 160 C6
Effra Rd London SW2 . . . 160 C6
Wimbledon SW19 . . . 179 D4
Effra Road Ret Pk SW2 . . . 160 C6
EF International Language Sch SE1 . . . 251 B3
Egan Way UB3 . . . 105 C6
Egbert Ho E9 . . . 75 A3
Egbert St NW1 . . . 93 A6 231 A6
Egbury Ho SW15 . . . 155 D5
Egerton Cl HA5 . . . 40 A5
Egerton Cres SW3 . . . 114 C2 257 B4
Egerton Ct
Leytonstone E11 . . . 54 B2
5 Richmond TW10 . . . 154 A6
Egerton Dr SE10 . . . 141 D4
Egerton Gdns
Ealing W13 . . . 87 B1
Hendon NW4 . . . 46 B5
Ilford IG3 . . . 79 D5
Knightsbridge SW3 . . . 114 C3 257 A5
Willesden NW10 . . . 90 C6
Egerton Gdns Mews SW3 . . . 257 B5
Egerton Ho W4 . . . 133 A6
Egerton Pl SW3 . . . 257 B5
Egerton Rd
New Malden KT3 . . . 199 D5
South Norwood SE25 . . . 205 C6
Egerton Rd *continued*
Stamford Hill N16 . . . 51 D2
Twickenham TW2 . . . 152 C4
Wembley HA0 . . . 66 B1
Egerton Terr SW3 . . . 114 C3 257 B5
Egerton Way UB3 . . . 126 D5
Eggardon Ct UB5 . . . 64 A2
Egham Cl Cheam SM3 . . . 217 A6
Putney SW19 . . . 157 A2
Egham Cres SM3 . . . 217 A6
Egham Ct KT6 . . . 197 D4
Egham Rd E13 . . . 99 B2
Eglantine Rd SW18 . . . 158 A6
Egleston Rd SM4 . . . 201 D3
Eglington Ct SE17 . . . 139 A6
Eglington Rd E4 . . . 20 B4
Eglinton Hill SE18 . . . 144 D5
Eglinton Prim Sch SE18 . . . 144 C6
Eglinton Rd SE18 . . . 144 D6
Egliston Mews SW15 . . . 134 C2
Egliston Rd SW15 . . . 134 C2
Egmont Ave KT6 . . . 198 B1
Egmont Rd
New Malden KT3 . . . 199 D5
Sutton SM2 . . . 218 A1
Tolworth KT6 . . . 198 C1
Walton-on-T KT12 . . . 194 B2
Egmont St SE14 . . . 140 D5
Egremont Ho SE13 . . . 141 D3
Egremont Rd SE27 . . . 160 C1
Egret Ho 11 SE16 . . . 118 D2
Egret Way UB4 . . . 84 D2
Eider Cl Hayes UB4 . . . 84 D2
Stratford E7 . . . 76 D3
Eider Ct 38 SE8 . . . 141 B6
Eighteenth Rd CR4 . . . 204 A5
Eighth Ave Hayes UB3 . . . 106 A5
Ilford E12 . . . 78 B4
Eileen Ct BR7 . . . 188 C5
Eileen Rd SE25 . . . 205 B4
Eindhoven Cl SM5 . . . 203 A1
Einstein Ho HA9 . . . 67 A5
Eisenhower Dr E6 . . . 100 A2
Eisenhower Ho KT8 . . . 175 C2
Elaine Ct 13 NW3 . . . 70 D2
Elaine Gr NW5 . . . 71 A3
Elaine Ho N4 . . . 50 A1
Elam Cl SE5 . . . 138 D3
Elam St SE5 . . . 138 D3
Elan Ct E1 . . . 96 B2
Eland Pl CR0 . . . 220 D5
Eland Rd
Clapham SW11 . . . 136 D2
Croydon CR0 . . . 220 D5
Elba Pl SE17 . . . 117 A2 262 B4
Elberon Ave CR0 . . . 203 C3
Elbe St SW6 . . . 136 A3
Elborough Rd SE25 . . . 206 A4
Elborough St SW18 . . . 157 C3
Elbourne Trad Est DA17 . . . 125 D3
Elbury Dr E16 . . . 99 A1
Elcho St SW11 . . . 136 C5 267 B3
Elcot Ave SE15 . . . 140 B5
Elder Ave N8 . . . 50 A4
Elderberry Ct 2 EN2 . . . 4 D3
Elderberry Gr 10 SE27 . . . 183 A6
Elderberry Rd W5 . . . 110 A4
Elderberry Way E6 . . . 100 B4
Elder Cl Barnet N20 . . . 13 D3
Sidcup DA15 . . . 167 D3
Yiewsley UB7 . . . 104 A6
Elder Ct WD23 . . . 8 C2
Elderfield Ho 4 E14 . . . 119 C6
Elderfield Pl SW17 . . . 181 B6
Elderfield Rd E5 . . . 74 C4
Elderfield Wlk E11 . . . 55 B4
Elderflower Way E15 . . . 76 C1
Elder Gdns 9 SE27 . . . 183 A6
Elder Oak Cl SE20 . . . 184 B2
Elder Rd SE27 . . . 183 A5
Elderslie Cl BR3 . . . 207 D3
Elderslie Rd SE9 . . . 166 C6
Elder St E1 . . . 95 D3 243 C5
Elderton Rd SE26 . . . 185 A6
Eldertree Pl CR4 . . . 181 C2
Eldertree Way CR4 . . . 181 C2
Elder Wlk Islington N1 . . . 234 D6
2 Lewisham SE13 . . . 142 A2
Elderwood Pl SE27 . . . 183 A5
Eldon Ave Croydon CR0 . . . 222 C6
Heston TW5 . . . 129 C5
Eldon Ct NW6 . . . 91 C6
Eldon Gr NW3 . . . 70 B3
Eldon Ho SW9 . . . 138 D2
Eldon Jun & Inf Schs N9 . . . 18 C3
Eldon Pk SE25 . . . 206 B5
Eldon Rd Edmonton N9 . . . 18 C3
Kensington W8 . . . 113 D3 255 D5
Tottenham N22 . . . 32 D2
Walthamstow E17 . . . 53 B5
Eldon St EC2 . . . 95 B2 242 D3
Eldonwall Est RM8 . . . 59 B1
Eldon Way NW10 . . . 88 D5
Eldred Rd IG11 . . . 101 C6
Eldrick Ct TW14 . . . 149 B3
Eldridge Cl TW14 . . . 150 A3
Eldridge Ct
Bermondsey SE16 . . . 118 A3
14 Dagenham RM10 . . . 81 D2
Eleanor Cl
Rotherhithe SE16 . . . 118 D4
South Tottenham N15 . . . 51 D6
Eleanor Cres NW7 . . . 28 D6
Eleanor Ct 18 E2 . . . 96 A6
Eleanor Gdns
Barnet EN5 . . . 12 D6
Dagenham RM8 . . . 81 B6
Eleanor Gr
Mortlake SW13 . . . 133 C2
Uxbridge UB10 . . . 60 D5
Eleanor Ho
18 Hammersmith W6 . . . 112 C1
1 Kentish Town NW5 . . . 71 C3
6 Merton SW19 . . . 179 D2
Eleanor Palmer Prim Sch NW5 . . . 71 C4
Eleanor Rathbone Ho 1 N6 . . . 49 D2
Eleanor Rd
Bowes Pk N11 . . . 32 A4
Hackney E8 . . . 74 B1
Stratford E15 . . . 76 D2
Eleanor Smith Sch E13 . . . 99 B5
Eleanor Smith Sch (West Beckton Site) E16 . . . 99 C2
Eleanor St E3 . . . 97 C4
Eleanor Wlk 24 SE18 . . . 122 B2
Electra Ave TW6 . . . 127 D2
Electra Ct 6 NW2 . . . 68 C2
Electric Ave SW9 . . . 138 C1
Electric Ho 13 Bow E3 . . . 97 C4
Walthamstow E17 . . . 53 C5
Electric La 2 SW9 . . . 138 C1
Electric Mans 1 SW9 . . . 138 C1
Electric Par Ilford IG3 . . . 57 D1
Surbiton KT6 . . . 197 D3
Woodford E18 . . . 37 A1
Elenmore Ct BR1 . . . 210 A5
Elephant & Castle
Newington SE1 . . . 116 D3 261 D5
Newington SE1 . . . 261 D4
Elephant & Castle Sh Ctr SE1 . . . 117 A2 262 A4
Elephant & Castle Sta
Lambeth SE1 . . . 116 D3 261 D5
Newington SE17 . . . 117 A2 262 A4
Elephant La SE16 . . . 118 C4
Elephant Rd SE17 . . . 117 A2 262 A4
Elers Rd Ealing W13 . . . 109 C4
Hayes UB3 . . . 105 B2
Eley Rd N18 . . . 34 D5
Eley's Est N18 . . . 34 D6
Elfindale Rd SE24 . . . 161 A6
Elfin Gr TW11 . . . 174 D5
Elford Cl SE9 . . . 143 C1
Elfort Rd N5 . . . 72 C4
Elfrida Cres SE6 . . . 185 C6
Elfrida Prim Sch SE6 . . . 185 C6
Elf Row E1 . . . 118 C6
Elfwine Rd W7 . . . 86 C2
Elgal Cl BR6 . . . 226 D3
Elgar N8 . . . 50 A6
Elgar Ave Ealing W5 . . . 110 A4
Thornton Heath SW16 . . . 204 A6
Tolworth KT5, KT6 . . . 198 D2
Willesden NW10 . . . 67 B2
Elgar Cl
Buckhurst Hill IG9 . . . 21 D2
Deptford SE8 . . . 141 C5
Elstree WD6 . . . 9 D4
Ickenham UB10 . . . 60 C6
Newham E13 . . . 99 C5
Elgar Ct W14 . . . 254 A5
Elgar Ho Hayes UB4 . . . 84 C2
Isleworth TW2 . . . 152 B5
Pimlico SW1 . . . 258 D1
Southall UB1 . . . 85 C1
South Hampstead NW6 . . . 70 A1
Elgar St SE16 . . . 119 A3
Elgin Ave
Ashford TW15 . . . 171 A4
Hammersmith W12 . . . 112 B3
Harrow HA3 . . . 25 B1
Westbourne Green W9 . . . 91 D3
Elgin Cl W12 . . . 112 B4
Elgin Cres Hatton TW6 . . . 127 C3
Notting Hill W11 . . . 113 A6 244 B6
Elgin Ct
6 Croydon CR0 . . . 221 A4
Westbourne Green W9 . . . 91 D3
Elgin Ho Northolt UB5 . . . 84 B5
8 Poplar E14 . . . 97 D1
Elgin Mans W9 . . . 91 D4
Elgin Mews W11 . . . 91 A1
Elgin Mews N W9 . . . 91 D4
Elgin Mews S W9 . . . 91 D4
Elgin Rd Croydon CR0 . . . 221 D6
Ilford IG3 . . . 57 C2
Sutton SM1 . . . 218 A5
Wallington SM6 . . . 219 C2
Wood Green N22 . . . 31 C1
Elgood Ave HA6 . . . 22 A3
Elgood Cl W11 . . . 244 A3
Elgood Ho NW8 . . . 229 D3
Elham Cl BR1 . . . 187 D3
Elham Ho 13 E5 . . . 74 B3
Elia Mews N1 . . . 94 D5 234 C3
Elias Pl SW8 . . . 138 C6
Elia St N1 . . . 94 D5 234 C3
Elibank Rd SE9 . . . 144 C1
Elim Est SE1 . . . 263 A6
Elim St SE1 . . . 263 A6
Elim Way E13 . . . 98 D4
Eliot Bank SE23, SE26 . . . 162 B2
Eliot Bank Prim Sch SE26 . . . 162 B2
Eliot Cotts SE3 . . . 142 C3

Eliot Ct SW18 157 D5
Eliot Dr HA2 63 D6
Eliot Gdns SW15 134 A1
Eliot Hill SE13 142 A3
Eliot Ho [10] TW10 154 B5
Eliot Mews NW8 229 A3
Eliot Pk SE13 142 A3
Eliot Pl SE3 142 C3
Eliot Rd RM9 80 D4
Eliot Vale SE3 142 B3
Elis David Almshouses CR0 220 D4
Elizabethan Ct N3 47 A6
Elizabeth Ave Enfield EN2 4 D2
Ilford IG1 79 B6
Islington N1 73 B1
Shoreditch N1 95 A6 235 B6
Elizabeth Barnes Ct [5] SW6 135 D3
Elizabeth Blackwell Ho N22 32 C2
Elizabeth Blount Ct [4] E14 97 A1
Elizabeth Cl
Cheam SM1 217 B4
Paddington W9 236 B5
[12] Poplar E14 97 D1
Elizabeth Clyde Cl N15 51 C5
Elizabeth Cooper Lo SW12 159 A5
Elizabeth Cotts [5] TW9 132 C4
Elizabeth Ct
Buckhurst Hill IG9 21 B3
Chelsea SW10 266 D5
East Dulwich SE22 140 A1
Kingston u T KT2 176 A2
Marylebone NW8 237 B6
South Croydon CR0 221 C5
Sunbury TW16 194 C6
[3] Teddington TW11 174 C6
Upper Tooting SW17 181 A5
West Barnes SM4 201 A2
Westminster SW1 259 D5
[6] Woodford Green E18 37 A2
[2] Woodford Green IG8 37 C3
[10] Woolwich SE18 122 B2
Elizabeth Finn Ho [1] W12 112 A3
Elizabeth Fry Ho UB3 105 D2
Elizabeth Fry Pl SE18 144 A4
Elizabeth Garrett Anderson Ho [9] DA17 125 C3
Elizabeth Garrett Anderson Hospl NW1 93 C3 239 B5
Elizabeth Garrett Anderson Language Coll N1 94 B5 233 D3
Elizabeth Gdns
East Acton W3 111 D5
Isleworth TW7 131 A1
Stanmore HA7 25 C5
Sunbury TW16 194 C6
Elizabeth Ho
Cheam SM3 217 A2
Friern Barnet N20 14 D1
[15] Hammersmith W6 112 C1
Lambeth SE11 261 B3
Stanmore HA7 26 A1
Wembley HA9 66 B3
Elizabeth Ind Est SE14 140 D6
Elizabeth Kenny Ho N1 73 A2
Elizabeth Mews
[28] Hackney E2 96 A5
Maitland Pk NW3 70 D2
Elizabeth Pl N15 51 B5
Elizabeth Rd
Newham E6 99 D6
South Tottenham N15 51 C4
Elizabeth Ride N9 18 B4
Elizabeth Selby Inf Sch E2 96 A4
Elizabeth Sq [13] SE16 119 A6
Elizabeth St SW1 115 A2 258 B4
Elizabeth Terr SE9 166 B5
Elizabeth Way
Feltham TW13 172 C6
South Norwood SE19 183 B3
Elkanette Mews N20 14 A2
Elkington Point SE11 261 A3
Elkington Rd E13 99 B3
Elkstone Rd W10 91 B2
Ella Cl BR3 185 C1
Ellacombe Ho [1] SW2 160 C4
Ellaline Rd W6 134 D6
Ella Mews NW3 70 D4
Ellanby Cres N18 34 B5
Elland Ho [18] E14 97 B1
Elland Rd SE15 140 C1
Ella Rd N4, N8 50 A2
Ellard Ct DA16 146 C2
Elle Ct N12 29 D5
Ellement Cl HA5 40 D4
Ellena Ct N14 16 A1
Ellenborough Ct N22 32 D2
Ellenborough Ho [5] W12 112 B6
Ellenborough Pl SW15 134 A1
Ellenborough Rd
Sidcup DA14 191 A5
Tottenham N22 33 A2
Ellen Cl BR1 209 D6
Ellen Ct [6] Chingford E4 20 A3
Lower Edmonton N9 18 C2
Ellen Miller Ho [2] E17 54 A4
Ellen St E1 96 A1
Ellen Webb Dr HA3 42 C6
Ellen Wilkinson Ho
[12] Dagenham RM10 81 C5
[7] Globe Town E2 96 D4
West Brompton SW6 264 D5
Ellen Wilkinson Prim Sch E6 100 A2
Ellen Wilkinson Sch for Girls W3 88 B1
Elleray Rd TW11 174 D4
Ellerby St SW6 134 D4
Ellerdale Cl [15] NW3 70 A4
Ellerdale Rd NW3 70 A3
Ellerdale St SE13 141 D2
Ellerdine Rd TW3 130 B1
Ellerker Gdns TW10 154 A5
Ellerman Ave TW2, TW4 151 B3
Ellerslie Ct [6] SM6 219 B2
Ellerslie Gdns NW10 90 A6
Ellerslie Ind Est SW2 160 A6
Ellerslie Rd W12 112 B5
Ellerton Ct W3 110 D4
Ellerton Gdns RM9 80 C1
Ellerton Lo N3 29 C1
Ellerton Rd
Barnes SW13 134 A4
Dagenham RM9 80 C1
Surbiton KT6 198 B1
Wandsworth SW17, SW18 158 B3
Wimbledon SW20 178 A3
Ellery Cl [5] NW10 89 D5
Ellery Ho SE17 262 D3
Ellery Rd SE19 183 B3
Ellery St SE15 140 B3
Ellesborough Cl WD19 22 C5
Ellesmere Ave
Beckenham BR3 185 D1
Edgware NW7 11 B1
Ellesmere Cl
Leytonstone E11 54 D4
Ruislip HA4 39 A2
Ellesmere Ct
Chiswick W4 133 B6
Lewisham SE12 165 A3
Penge SE20 184 B1
Ellesmere Gdns IG4 56 A3
Ellesmere Gr EN5 13 B6
Ellesmere Rd Bow E3 97 A5
Chiswick W4 133 B6
Greenford UB6 86 A3
Twickenham TW1 153 C5
Willesden NW10 68 A3
Ellesmere St E14 97 D1
Ellies Mews TW15 148 A2
Ellingfort Rd E8 74 B1
Ellingham Prim Sch KT9 213 D1
Ellingham Rd
Chessington KT9 213 D2
Leyton E15 76 B4
Shepherd's Bush W12 112 A4
Ellington Ct N14 15 D2
Ellington Ho SE1 262 B5
Ellington Rd
Cranley Gdns N10 49 B5
Feltham TW13 171 D6
Hounslow TW3 129 D3
Ellington St N7 72 C2
Elliot Cl Stratford E15 76 C1
Wembley HA9 66 C5
Woodford IG8 37 D4
Elliot Ct [6] N15 51 D5
Elliot Rd NW4 46 B3
Elliott Ave HA4 62 B6
Elliott Gdns TW17 192 C5
Elliott Ho [3] CR7 204 D5
Elliott Rd Acton W4 111 C2
Brixton SW9 138 D4
Bromley BR2 209 D5
Camberwell SW9 138 D4
Stanmore HA7 25 A4
Thornton Heath CR7 204 D5
Elliott Sch SW15 156 C5
Elliott's Pl N1 234 D5
Elliott Sq NW3 70 C1
Elliott's Row SE11 116 D2 261 D4
Ellis Cl Burnt Oak HA8 27 C4
New Eltham SE9 167 A2
Willesden NW10 68 C2
Elliscombe Mount [11] SE7 143 C6
Elliscombe Rd SE7 143 C6
Ellis Ct W7 86 D2
Ellisfield Dr SW15 156 A4
Ellis Franklin Ct NW8 229 A4
Ellis Ho
Walthamstow E17 54 A4
Walworth SE17 262 C2
Ellison Gdns UB2 107 B2
Ellison Ho [1] SE13 142 A3
Ellison Rd
Barnes SW13 133 D3
New Eltham DA15 167 B3
Streatham SW16 182 A3
Ellis Rd Mitcham CR4 202 D3
Southall UB2 108 A5
Ellis St SW1 115 A2 258 A4
Elliston Ho [8] SE18 122 C2
Ellora Rd SW16 181 D5
Ellswood Ct [18] KT6 197 D2
Ellsworth St E2 96 B4
Ellwood Ct [1] W9 91 D3
Elmar Ct SW6 135 A3
Elmar Rd N15 51 B5
Elm Ave Ealing W5 110 B5
Ruislip HA4 40 B2
Elmbank N14 16 A4
Elm Bank Dr BR1 187 D1
Elm Bank Gdns SW13 133 C3
Elm Bank Mans SW13 133 C3
Elmbank Way W7 86 B2
Elmbourne Dr DA17 125 D2
Elmbourne Rd SW17 159 B1
Elmbridge Ave KT5 199 A3
Elmbridge Cl HA4 40 A3
Elmbridge Dr HA4 40 A3
Elmbridge Wlk E8 74 A1
Elmbrook [3] E18 55 A6
Elmbrook Cl TW16 172 B2
Elmbrook Gdns SE9 144 A1
Elmbrook Rd SM1 217 B4
Elm Cl Buckhurst Hill IG9 21 D2
Carshalton SM5 202 D1
Harrow HA2 41 D3
Hayes UB3 84 A1
Hendon NW4 46 D4
South Croydon CR2 221 C2
Tolworth KT5 199 A2
Twickenham TW13, TW2 151 D2
Upper Holloway N19 71 C6
Wanstead E11 55 B3
West Barnes SW20 200 C5
Elmcote HA5 22 D1
Elmcourt Rd SE21, SE27 160 D2
Elm Court Sch SE27 161 A2
Elm Cres Ealing W5 110 A4
Kingston u T KT2 176 A2
Elmcroft Highgate N6 49 C2
Hornsey Vale N8 50 B4
Elmcroft Ave
Blackfen DA15 168 A5
Enfield N9 18 B5
Golders Green NW11 47 B2
Wanstead E11 55 B5
Elmcroft Cl
Chessington KT9 214 A5
Ealing W5 87 D1
Feltham TW14 149 D5
Wanstead E11 55 B5
Elmcroft Cres
Harrow HA2 41 C6
Hendon NW11 47 A2
Elmcroft Dr
Ashford TW15 170 C5
Chessington KT9 214 A5
Elmcroft Gdns NW9 44 C4
Elmcroft St E5 74 C4
Elmcroft Terr UB8 82 C1
Elm Ct
[5] Ashford TW16 171 D3
Brixton SW9 138 C4
Catford SE6 163 D3
Chingford E4 36 A4
[4] Finchley N3 29 C2
Lewisham SE13 142 B2
Mitcham CR4 180 D1
[42] Notting Hill W2 91 C2
Strand EC4 251 A6
Elmdale Rd N13 32 B5
Elmdene KT5 199 A1
Elmdene Cl BR3 207 B4
Elmdene Rd SE18 122 D1
Elmdon Rd
Hatton TW6 127 D2
Hounslow TW5 129 A3
Elm Dr Harrow HA2 41 D3
Sunbury TW16 172 C1
Elmer Cl EN2 4 B2
Elmer Ct HA1 42 D3
Elmer Gdns
Edgware HA8 26 D3
Isleworth TW7 130 B2
Elmer Ho NW1 237 A4
Elmer Rd SE6 164 A4
Elmer's Dr TW11 175 B4
ELMERS END 206 D6
Elmers End Rd BR3, SE20 206 C6
Elmers End Sta BR3 206 D5
Elmerside Rd BR3 207 A5
Elmers Rd SE25 206 A2
Elmfield Ave London N8 50 A4
Mitcham CR4 181 A2
Teddington TW11 174 D5
Elmfield Cl HA1 64 C6
Elmfield Ct DA16 146 B4
Elmfield Ho
[6] Canonbury N5 73 A3
[22] London N2 30 B1
Paddington W9 91 C3
Elmfield Mans [5] SW17 159 A2
Elmfield Pk BR1 209 A6
Elmfield Rd
Bromley BR1 209 A6
Chingford E4 20 B2
East Finchley N2 48 B6
Southall UB2 107 A3
Upper Tooting SW17 159 B2
Walthamstow E17 52 D3
Elmfield Way
Paddington W9 91 C2
South Croydon CR2 221 D1
Elm Friars Wlk NW1 71 D1
Elmgate Ave TW13 150 C1
Elmgate Ct HA8 27 A5
Elmgate Gdns HA8 27 B6
Elm Gdns
Claygate KT10 212 D2
East Finchley N2 48 A6
Enfield EN2 5 B5
Elm Gdns *continued*
Mitcham CR4 203 D5
Elm Gn W3 89 C1
Elm Gr Cricklewood NW2 68 D4
Harrow HA2 41 C2
Hornsey N8 50 A3
Kingston u T KT2 176 A2
Orpington BR6 211 D1
Peckham SE15 140 A3
Sutton SM1 217 D4
Wimbledon SW19 179 A3
Woodford IG8 36 D5
Yiewsley UB7 104 B6
Elmgreen Cl [8] E15 98 C6
Elmgrove Cres HA1 43 A4
Elmgrove Fst & Mid Schs HA3 43 A5
Elmgrove Gdns HA1 43 A4
Elm Grove Par SM6 219 A5
Elmgrove Rd
Croydon CR0 206 B2
Harrow HA1 42 D4
Elm Grove Rd
Barnes SW13 134 A3
Ealing W5 110 A4
Elm Hall Gdns E11 55 B3
Elm Hatch HA5 23 B3
Elm Ho
[4] Cubitt Town E14 120 A4
[2] Kingston u T KT2 176 B3
Teddington TW11 175 C3
Elmhurst DA17 147 A6
Elmhurst Ave London N2 48 B6
Mitcham CR4 181 B3
Elmhurst Cres N2 48 B5
Elmhurst Ct
Carshalton SM5 218 B6
Croydon CR0 221 B3
Elmhurst Dr E18 37 A1
Elmhurst Lo [3] SM2 218 A1
Elmhurst Mans SW4 137 D2
Elmhurst Prim Sch E7 77 B1
Elmhurst Rd
Chislehurst SE9 166 A1
Enfield EN3 6 C6
Tottenham N17 33 D1
Upton E7 77 B1
Elmhurst Sch CR2 221 B3
Elmhurst St SW4 137 D2
Elmhurst Villas SE15 140 C1
Elmington Cl DA5 169 D5
Elmington Rd SE5 139 B5
Elmira St SE13 141 D2
Elm La SE6 163 B2
Elm Lawn Cl UB8 60 A1
Elmlea Dr UB3 83 D2
Elm Lea Trad Est N17 34 B4
Elmlee Cl BR7 188 B4
Elmley Cl [12] E6 100 A2
Elmley St SE18 123 B2
Elm Lo SW6 134 D4
Elmore Cl HA0 88 A5
Elmore Ho SW9 138 D3
Elmore Rd Enfield EN3 6 D5
Leyton E11 76 B5
Elmore St N1 73 B1
Elm Park Ave N15 52 A3
Elm Park Ct HA5 40 C6
Elm Park Gdns
Chelsea SW10 114 B1 256 C1
Hendon NW4 46 D4
Elm Park Ho SW10 256 C1
Elm Park La SW3 114 B1 256 C1
Elm Park Mans SW10 266 B6
Elm Park Rd
Chelsea SW3 136 B6 266 C6
Edmonton N21 17 A4
Finchley N3 29 B3
Pinner HA5 40 D6
South Norwood SE25 205 D6
Walthamstow E10 53 A1
Elm Pk Stanmore HA7 25 C5
Streatham SW2 160 B4
Elm Pl SW7 114 B1 256 C2
Elm Quay SW8 269 C5
Elm Rd Barnet EN5 1 B1
Beckenham BR3 185 B1
Chessington KT9 214 A4
Claygate KT10 212 D2
East Bedfont TW14 149 B4
Hackbridge SM6 203 A1
Kingston u T KT2 176 B2
Leyton E11 76 B6
Mortlake SW14 133 A1
New Malden KT3 199 B6
Sidcup DA14 190 A6
South Norwood CR7 205 B5
Stoneleigh KT17 215 D2
Stratford E7 76 D2
Tottenham N22 32 D2
Walthamstow E17 54 A4
Wembley HA9 66 A3
Elm Rd W SM4 201 B2
Elm Row NW3 70 A5
Elms Ave Hendon NW4 46 D4
Muswell Hill N10 49 B6
Elmscott Gdns N21 17 A5
Elmscott Rd BR1 186 D5
Elms Cotts [1] CR4 180 D1
Elms Cres SW4 159 D5
Elms Ct Merton SW19 179 D3
Wembley HA0 65 A4
Elmsdale Rd E17 53 B5
Elms Gdns
Dagenham RM9 81 B4
Wembley HA0 65 A4
Elmshaw Rd SW15 156 A6
Elmside CR0 223 D2
Elmside Rd HA9 66 C5
Elms La HA0 65 A5
Elmsleigh Ave HA3 43 C5
Elmsleigh Ct SM1 217 D5
Elmsleigh Ho TW2 152 B2
Elmsleigh Rd TW2 152 B2
Elmslie Ct SE9 166 C5
Elmslie Point [2] E3 97 B2
Elms Mews W2 246 C6
Elms Park Ave HA0 65 A4
Elms Rd
Clapham Pk SW4 159 C6
Harrow HA3 24 C3
Elm St WC1 94 B3 240 D5
ELMSTEAD 188 A5
Elmstead Ave
Elmstead BR7 188 B5
Wembley HA9 66 B6
Elmstead Cl
Totteridge N20 13 C2
West Ewell KT19 215 C3
Elmstead Ct HA9 44 B1
Elmstead Gdns KT4 216 A5
Elmstead Glade BR7 188 B4
Elmstead La BR7 188 B5
Elmstead Rd IG3 79 D6
Elmstead Woods Sta BR7 188 A4
Elmsted Cres DA16 146 C6
Elms The
[5] Ashford TW15 170 C5
Barnes SW13 133 D2
Claygate KT10 212 D1
Croydon CR0 205 A1
[3] Harlesden NW10 89 C5
Kingsbury NW9 45 A3
Plashet E12 78 A2
Wallington SM6 219 C4
Elmstone Rd SW6 265 A2
Elmsway TW15 170 C5
Elmsworth Ave TW3 129 D3
Elm Terr Child's Hill NW2 69 C5
[3] Eltham SE9 166 C5
Harrow HA3 24 B2
Elmton Ct NW8 236 C6
Elm Tree Ave KT10 196 C2
Elm Tree Cl
Ashford TW15 170 D5
Northolt UB5 85 B5
St John's Wood NW8 92 B4 229 C2
Elmtree Ct HA4 40 A1
Elm Tree Ct
[5] Camberwell SE5 139 A4
[18] Charlton SE7 143 C6
St John's Wood NW8 229 C2
Elmtree Rd TW11 174 C5
Elm Tree Rd NW8 92 B4 229 C2
Elm View Ct UB2 107 C2
Elm Way London N11 31 A4
North Cheam KT4 216 C5
West Ewell KT19 215 B3
Willesden NW10 67 C4
Elm Wlk Child's Hill NW3 69 C6
Orpington BR6 226 B5
West Barnes SW20 200 D5
Elmwood Ave
Bowes Pk N13 32 A5
Feltham TW13 150 B1
Harrow HA3 43 B3
Elmwood Cl
Hackbridge SM6 219 B6
Stoneleigh KT17 216 A1
Elmwood Cres NW9 45 A5
Elmwood Ct
Battersea SW11 268 C2
Walthamstow E10 53 C1
Wembley HA0 65 A5
Elmwood Dr
Sidcup DA5 169 A4
Stoneleigh KT17 216 A1
Elmwood Gdns W7 86 C1
Elmwood Ho Enfield EN2 4 D1
Feltham TW13 150 B1
Elmwood Inf Sch CR0 204 D3
Elmwood Jun Sch CR0 204 D2
Elm Wood Prim Sch SE27 161 B1
Elmwood Rd
Chiswick W4 133 A6
Herne Hill SE24 161 B6
Mitcham CR4 202 D6
Thornton Heath CR0 204 D2
Elmworth Gr SE21 161 B2
Elnathan Mews W9 91 D3
Elphinstone Ct SW16 182 A4
Elphinstone Rd E17 35 B1
Elphinstone St N5 72 D4
Elrington Rd Dalston E8 74 A2
Woodford IG8 37 A5
Elsa Ct BR3 185 B2
Elsa Rd DA16 146 C3
Elsa St E1 97 A2
Elsdale Ho [14] E9 74 C2
Elsdale St E9 74 C1
Elsden Mews E2 96 C5
Elsden Rd N17 33 D2
Elsenham Rd E12 78 C3
Elsenham St SW18, SW19 157 B2
Elsfield NW5 71 B3
Elsham Rd
Kensington W14 113 A4 244 A1
Leyton E11 76 C4
Elsham Terr W14 244 A1
Elsiedene Rd N21 17 A4
Elsie Lane Ct W2 91 D2
Elsiemaud Rd SE4 163 B6
Elsie Rd SE22 139 D1
Elsinge Rd EN1 6 B6
Elsinore Ave TW19 148 A4
Elsinore Gdns NW2 69 A5
Elsinore Ho
[12] Camberwell SE5 139 A3
Islington N1 234 A5
[7] Woolwich SE7 122 A2
Elsinore Rd SE23 163 A3
Elsinore Way TW9 132 D2
Elsley Ct HA9 66 D2
Elsley Prim Sch HA9 66 B2
Elsley Rd SW11 137 A2
Elsley Sch SW11 137 A2
Elspeth Rd
London SW11 136 D1
Wembley HA0 66 A3
Elsrick Ave SM4 201 C4
Elstan Way CR0 207 A2
Elstead Ct SM3 201 A1
Elstead Ho [9] SW2 160 B4
Elsted St SE17 117 B2 262 D3
Elstow Cl Eltham SE9 166 B6
Ruislip HA4 40 D2
Elstow Gdns RM9 103 A6
Elstow Grange NW6 68 D1
Elstow Rd RM9 103 A6
ELSTREE 10 A5
Elstree Gdns
Abbey Wood DA17 125 A2
Edmonton N9 18 B3
Ilford IG1 79 A3
Elstree Hill BR1 186 C3
Elstree Hill N WD6 9 D6
Elstree Hill S WD6 9 D4
Elstree Ho [3] HA7 25 C6
Elstree Pk WD6 11 B5
Elstree Rd Bushey WD23 8 C4
Elstree WD6 9 A5
Elswick Rd SE13 141 D3
Elswick St SW6 136 A3
Elsworth Cl TW14 149 C3
Elsworthy KT7 196 C3
Elsworthy Rd NW3 92 C6 230 A6
Elsworthy Rise NW3 70 C1
Elsworthy Terr NW3 70 C1
Elsynge Rd SW18 158 B6
Elsynge Road Mans SW18 158 B6
ELTHAM 166 B6
Eltham CE Prim Sch SE9 166 B6
Eltham Coll SE9 165 D2
Eltham Coll Jun Sch SE9 165 D3
Eltham Green Rd SE9 165 C6
Eltham Green Specialist Sports Coll SE9 165 D5
Eltham High St SE9 166 B5
Eltham Hill SE9 166 A6
Eltham Hill Tech Coll for Girls SE9 166 A5
Eltham Pal* SE9 166 A4
Eltham Palace Rd SE9 165 D5
Eltham Park Gdns SE9 144 C1
Eltham Rd SE9, SE12 165 B6
Eltham Sta SE9 166 B6
Elthiron Rd SW6 135 C4 265 B1
Elthorne Ave W7 109 A4
Elthorne Ct
Feltham TW13 150 C3
Kingsbury NW9 45 B3
Elthorne Park High Sch W7 108 D3
Elthorne Park Rd W7 109 A4
Elthorne Rd
London NW9 45 B2
Upper Holloway N19 71 D6
Elthorne Way NW9 45 B3
Elthruda Rd SE13 164 B5
Eltisley Rd IG1 78 D4
Elton Ave Barnet EN5 13 B6
Wembley HA0 65 B3
Wembley UB6 64 D2
Elton Cl KT1 175 C3
Elton Ho [3] E3 97 B6
Elton Lo [4] W5 110 A6
Elton Pl N16 73 C3
Elton Rd KT2 176 C2
Elton St [11] N16 73 C3
Eltringham St SW18 136 A1
Elvaston Ct EN5 12 C6
Elvaston Mews SW7 256 B6
Elvaston Pl SW7 114 A3 256 B5
Elveden Ho [17] SW9 138 D1
Elveden Pl NW10 88 C5
Elveden Rd NW10 88 C5
Elvedon Rd TW13 149 D1
Elvendon Rd N13 32 A4
Elver Gdns [10] E2 96 A4
Elverson Rd SE8 141 D3
Elverson Rd Sta SE8 141 D3
Elverton St SW1 115 D2 259 C4
Elvin Ct NW9 45 A2
Elvington Gn BR2 208 D4
Elvington La NW9 27 C2
Elvin Ho [2] E9 74 C2
Elvino Rd SE26 185 A5
Elvis Rd NW2 68 C2
Elwill Way BR3 208 B5
Elwin St E2 96 A4
Elwood Ho N5 72 D5
Elwood St N4, N5 72 D5

Elworth Ho SW8 270 D3
Elwyn Gdns SE12 165 A4
Ely Cl SW20 177 D1
Ely Cotts SW8 270 C3
Ely Court Flats SW6 264 A1
Ely Ct Holborn EC1 241 B3
3 Maida Vale NW6 91 C5
Ely Gdns
Borehamwood WD6 11 B6
Redbridge IG1 56 A2
Ely Ho Barnet EN4 2 C1
Northolt UB5 85 A6
22 Peckham SE15 140 A5
Elyne Rd N4 50 C3
Ely Pl EC1 94 C2 241 B3
Ely Rd Hatton TW6 127 D3
Hounslow TW4 128 C2
Leyton E10 54 A2
Thornton Heath CR0 205 B4
Elysian Ave BR5 211 D3
Elysium Gate 7 SW6 135 B3
Elysium Pl SW6 135 B3
Elysium St SW6 135 B3
Elystan Bsns Ctr UB4 106 C6
Elystan Ct SW15 156 B6
Elystan Pl SW3 114 D1 257 C2
Elystan St SW3 114 C2 257 B3
Elystan Wlk N1 234 A5
Emanuel Ave W3 89 A1
Emanuel Ct Acton W3 89 B1
10 Leyton E10 53 D2
Emanuel Dr TW12 173 B5
Emanuel Sch SW11 158 C6
Embankment SW15 134 D3
Embankment Gdns
SW3 136 D6 267 D6
Embankment Pier
WC2 116 A5 250 B4
Embankment Pl WC2 250 B4
Embankment Sta
WC2 116 A5 250 B4
Embankment The
TW1 153 A3
Embassy Ct Ealing W5 110 B6
Kingston u T KT6 197 D4
Sidcup DA14 168 B1
St John's Wood NW8 229 D3
7 Wallington SM6 219 B2
8 Wanstead E18 55 A6
Welling DA16 146 B2
Wood Green N11 31 D4
Embassy Gdns BR3 185 B2
Embassy Ho 2 NW6 69 C1
Embassy Lo N3 29 B1
Emba St SE16 118 A4
Ember Cl BR5 211 A2
Embercourt Rd KT10, KT7,
KT8 196 C3
Ember Ct
2 Acton W12 111 C3
14 Hendon NW9 27 D1
Ember Farm Ave KT8 196 B3
Ember Farm Way KT8 196 B4
Ember Gdns KT10, KT8 196 C2
Ember Ho 8 BR1 186 B5
Ember La KT10, KT8 196 B2
Emberson Ho 7 E17 54 A5
Emberton SE5 139 C6
Emberton Ct EC1 234 C1
Embleton Rd SE13 141 D1
Embleton Wlk TW12 173 B5
Embry Cl HA7 25 A6
Embry Dr HA7 25 A4
Embry Way HA7 25 A6
Emden Cl UB7 104 C4
Emden St SW6 265 D2
Emerald Cl E16 100 A1
Emerald Ct N12 30 A6
Emerald Gdns RM8 59 C1
Emerald Rd NW10 89 B6
Emerald Sq UB2 106 D3
Emerald St WC1 94 B2 240 C4
Emerson Apartments
N8 50 B6
Emerson Ct 8 SW19 179 A4
Emerson Gdns HA3 44 B3
Emerson Ho N16 73 C3
Emerson Rd IG1 56 C2
Emerson St
SE1 117 A5 252 A4
Emerton Cl DA6 147 A1
Emery Hill St SW1 259 B5
Emery St SE1 116 C3 261 B6
Emilia Cl EN3 18 B6
Emily St 7 E16 98 D1
Emirates Stad (Arsenal
FC) N7 72 C4
Emlyn Gdns 3 W12 111 C3
Emlyn Rd W12 111 D3
Emmanual Ho SE18 123 B1
Emmanuel CE Prim Sch
NW6 69 C3
Emmanuel Ct 3 EN4 14 D3
Emmanuel Ho
Dulwich SE21 161 B1
Lambeth SE11 261 A3
Emmanuel Rd
Northwood HA6 22 A3
Streatham SW12 159 D3
Emma Rd E13 98 D5
Emma St E2 96 B5
Emmeline Ct KT12 194 C2
Emminster NW6 91 D6
Emmott Ave IG6 57 A4
Emmott Cl
London NW11 48 A3
Mile End E1 97 A3
Emperor's Gate
SW7 114 A2 256 A4
Empingham Ho 20
SE8 118 D2
Empire Ave N18 33 A4
Empire Ct HA9 66 D5
Empire Ho
Brompton SW3 257 A5
Edmonton N18 33 B4
Empire Par
Edmonton N18 33 B4
Wembley HA9 66 C5
Empire Rd UB6 65 C1
Empire Sq N19 72 A5
Empire Way HA9 66 C4
Empire Wharf E3 97 A6
Empire Wharf Rd E14 120 B2
Empress Ave
Chingford E4 35 D3
Ilford IG1 78 C6
Wanstead E12 77 D6
Woodford IG8 36 D3
Empress Dr BR7 188 D4
Empress Mews 36
SE5 139 A3
Empress Par E4 35 C3
Empress Pl
SW5 113 C1 255 A1
Empress St SE17 139 A6
Empson St E3 97 D3
Emsworth Cl N9 18 C3
Emsworth St SW2 160 B2
Emu Rd SW8 137 B3
Ena Rd SW16 204 A6
Enard Ho 28 E3 97 B5
Enbrook St W10 91 A4
Enclave Ct EC1 241 D6
Endale Cl SM5 218 D6
Endeavour Way
Barking IG11 102 A5
Thornton Heath CR0 204 A2
Wimbledon SW19 179 D6
Endell St WC2 94 A1 240 A1
Enderby St SE10 120 C1
Enderfield Ct BR7 188 C2
Enderley Cl HA3 24 C2
Enderley Ho SE19 183 D2
Enderley Rd HA3 24 C2
Endersby Rd EN5 12 C6
Endersleigh Gdns NW4 46 A5
Endlebury Ct E4 20 B2
Endlebury Rd E4 20 A2
Endlesham Ct 2
SW12 159 A4
Endlesham Rd SW12 159 A4
Endsleigh Gdns
Bloomsbury
WC1 93 D3 239 C6
Ilford IG1 56 D1
Kingston u T KT6 197 C3
Endsleigh Ind Est UB2 107 B2
Endsleigh Mans 4
SW16 160 A1
Endsleigh Pl WC1 239 D6
Endsleigh Rd
Ealing W13 109 A6
Southall UB2 107 A2
Endsleigh St
WC1 93 D3 239 D6
Endway KT5 198 D2
Endwell Rd SE4 141 A3
Endymion Rd
Harringay N4 50 D2
Tulse Hill SW2 160 B5
Energen Cl NW10 67 C2
ENFIELD 6 B2
Enfield Chase Sta EN2 5 A2
Enfield Cloisters 7 N1 95 C4
Enfield Coll EN3 6 C2
Enfield Gram Sch EN2 5 B2
Enfield Gram Sch Lower
EN1 5 B3
ENFIELD HIGHWAY 6 C3
Enfield Ho 24 SW9 138 A3
ENFIELD LOCK 7 B6
Enfield Lock Sta EN3 7 A6
Enfield Rd
Brentford TW8 109 D1
De Beauvoir Town E8,
N1 73 C1
Enfield EN2 4 A2
Hatton TW6 127 C3
South Acton W3 110 D4
Enfield Ret Pk EN1 6 A2
Enfield Road Rdbt
TW6 127 C3
Enfield Sec Tuition Ctr
PRU N9 18 C3
ENFIELD TOWN 5 B1
Enfield Town Sta EN1 5 B2
ENFIELD WASH 6 D5
Enfield Wlk TW8 109 D1
Enford St W1 92 D2 237 C4
Engadine Cl CR0 221 D5
Engadine St SW18 157 C3
Engate St SE13 142 A1
Engel Pk NW7 28 C4
Engineer Cl SE18 144 C6
Engineers Way HA9 66 C4
England's La NW3 70 D2
England Way KT3 199 A5
Englefield
Bromley BR1 188 A1
Regent's Pk NW1 232 A1
Englefield Cl Enfield EN2 4 C3
Orpington BR5 211 D5
Thornton Heath CR0 205 A3
Englefield Path BR5 211 D5
Englefield Rd N1 73 C1
Engleheart Dr TW14 149 D5
Engleheart Rd SE6 164 A4
Englewood Rd SW12 159 C5
English Gardening Sch
The SW3 136 D6 267 C6
English Grounds SE1 253 A3
English Martyrs RC Prim
Sch E1 95 D1 243 D1
English St E3 97 B3
Enid St SE16 117 D3 263 D6
Enid Stacy Ho 11 N19 49 D2
Enmore Ave SE25 206 A4
Enmore Ct SW14 155 B6
Enmore Gdns SW14 155 B6
Enmore Rd
Croydon SE25 206 A4
Putney SW15 156 C6
Southall UB1 85 C3
Ennerdale Ave HA3,
HA7 43 C6
Ennerdale Cl
Cheam SM1 217 B4
East Bedfont TW14 149 D3
Ennerdale Ct E11 55 A2
Ennerdale Dr NW9 45 C4
Ennerdale Gdns HA9 43 C1
Ennerdale Ho 3 N4 51 B2
Ennerdale Rd
Erith DA7 147 C4
Richmond TW9 132 B3
Ennersdale Rd SE13 164 B6
Ennis Ho 16 E14 97 D1
Ennismore Ave
Chiswick W4 111 D2
Greenford UB6 64 C3
Ennismore Gdns
Knightsbridge
SW7 114 C3 257 A6
Thames Ditton KT7 196 C3
Ennismore Gdns Mews
SW7 114 C3 257 A6
Ennismore Mews
SW7 114 C3 257 A6
Ennismore St
SW7 114 C3 257 A6
Ennis Rd London N4 50 C1
Shooters Hill SE18 145 A6
Ennor Ct KT4 216 C4
Ensbury Ho SW8 270 C4
Ensign Cl TW19 148 A3
Ensign Ct 12 E1 118 A6
Ensign Dr N13 17 A1
Ensign Ho 19 E14 119 C4
Ensign St E1 118 A6
Ensign Way
Stanwell TW19 148 A3
2 Wallington SM6 220 A1
Enslin Rd SE9 166 C4
Ensor Mews SW7 256 C2
Enstone Rd Enfield EN3 7 A2
Ickenham UB10 60 B5
Enterprise Cl CR0 204 C1
Enterprise Ho IG11 101 D4
Enterprise Ho E4 20 A4
Enterprise Ho
36 Hackney E9 74 C1
Walton-on-T KT12 194 B2
Enterprise Row N15 51 D4
Enterprise Way
College Pk NW10 90 A4
Teddington TW11 174 D4
Wandsworth SW18 135 C1
Enterprise Works EN3 7 B4
Enterprize Way SE8 119 B2
Enthoven Ho SE18 122 D2
Enton Pl TW3 129 D1
Enversham Ct SE23 163 A1
Epirus Mews SW6 265 A4
Epirus Rd SW6 135 B5 264 D4
Epping Cl Millwall E14 119 C2
Romford RM7 59 D6
Epping Forest* IG10 21 B6
Epping Glade E4 20 A5
Epping Ho 8 E5 74 A6
Epping New Rd IG9 21 B5
Epping Pl N1 72 C2
Epping Way E4 19 D5
Epple Rd SW6 135 B4 264 D2
Epsom Cl Erith DA7 147 D2
Northolt UB5 63 B3
Epsom & Ewell High Sch
KT19 215 A3
Epsom Ho SM1 217 D4
Epsom Rd Croydon CR0 220 C4
Ilford IG3 57 D3
Leyton E10 54 A3
Morden SM3, SM4 201 B2
Epsom Sq TW6 127 D3
Epstein Ct N1 234 D5
Epstein Rd SE28 124 B5
Epworth Rd TW7, TW8 131 B5
Epworth St EC2 95 B3 242 D5
Equity Sq 29 E2 95 D4
Erasmus St
SW1 115 D2 259 D3
Erconwald St W12 89 D1
Erebus Dr SE28 123 B4
Eresby Dr BR3 207 C1
Eresby Ho SW7 247 B1
Eresby Pl NW6 69 C1
Erica Ct SW4 270 B1
Erica Gdns CR0 223 D5
Erica Ho London SE4 141 B2
6 Wimbledon SW19 179 A3
Wood Green N22 32 C2
Erica St W12 112 A6
Eric Cl E7 77 A4
Eric Clarke La IG11 101 A4
Ericcson Cl SW18 157 C6
Eric Fletcher Ct 15 N1 73 A1
Eric Macdonald Ho
SW6 265 B1
Eric Rd Dagenham RM6 58 D2
Forest Gate E7 77 A4
Willesden NW10 67 D2
Eric Shipman Terr 2
E13 99 A3
Ericson Ho
London SE13 142 B1
Stamford Hill N16 51 D1
Eric St E3 97 B3
Eric Wilkins Ho 14
SE1 118 A1
Eridge Ho SE22 139 D2
Eridge Rd W4 111 B3
Erin Cl Bromley BR1 186 C3
Ilford IG3 58 A3
Erin Ct NW2 68 C2
Erindale SE18 145 B6
Erindale Ct 1 BR3 185 C2
Erindale Terr SE18 145 B6
ERITH 147 D6
Erith Rd
Belvedere DA17 125 D1
Erith DA7 147 D2
Erlanger Rd SE14 140 D3
Erlesmere Gdns W13 109 A3
Ermine Cl TW4 128 C3
Ermine Ho 3 N17 33 D3
Ermine Rd
London SE13 141 D1
South Tottenham N15 51 D3
Ermine Side EN1 18 A6
Ermington Rd SE9 167 A2
Ernald Ave E6 100 A5
Erncroft Way TW1 152 D5
Ernest Ave SE27 182 D6
Ernest Bevin Coll
SW17 158 C2
Ernest Cl BR3 207 C4
Ernest Cotts KT17 215 D1
Ernest Gdns W4 132 D6
Ernest Gr BR3 207 B4
Ernest Rd KT1 176 D1
Ernest Richards Twr
E17 53 B3
Ernest Simmonds Ho
SE14 140 C3
Ernest Sq KT1 176 D1
Ernest St E1 96 D3
Ernle Rd SW20 178 C3
Ernshaw Pl SW15 157 A6
Eros Ho SE6 163 D4
Eros (Shaftesbury Meml)*
W1 115 D6 249 C5
Erpingham Rd SW15 134 C2
Erridge Rd SW19 179 C1
Errington Manor 6
SM5 218 D5
Errington Rd W9 91 B3
Errol Gdns Hayes UB4 84 B3
West Barnes KT3 200 A5
Errol St EC1 95 A3 242 B5
Erskine Cl SM1 218 C5
Erskine Cres N17 52 B5
Erskine Hill NW11 47 C4
Erskine Ho
7 Charlton SE7 143 C6
Pimlico SW1 259 A1
Erskine Rd
Carshalton SM1 218 B5
Primrose Hill NW3 70 D1
Walthamstow E17 53 B5
Erwood Rd SE7 122 A1
Esam Way SW16 182 C5
Escot Rd TW16 171 C3
Escott Gdns SE9 188 A6
Escot Way EN5 12 C6
Escreet Gr SE18 122 C2
Escuan Lo N5 73 A3
ESHER 212 A4
Esher Ave Cheam SM3 216 D5
Walton-on-T KT12 194 A1
Esher CE Prim Sch
KT10 212 A3
Esher Cl DA5 169 A3
Esher Coll KT7 196 C2
Esher Cres TW6 127 D3
Esher Gdns SW19 156 D2
Esher Ho 8 SW8 137 D3
Esher Mews 4 CR4 202 D6
Esher Park Ave KT10 212 A3
Esher Rd
East Molesey KT8 196 B4
Ilford IG3 79 C5
Esher Sta KT10 212 B6
Eskdale Enfield EN1 17 C6
Regent's Pk NW1 232 A3
Eskdale Ave UB5 85 B6
Eskdale Cl HA9 65 D6
Eskdale Rd DA7 147 C4
Esk Ho E3 97 B3
Eskmont Ridge SE19 183 C3
Esk Rd E13 99 B3
Esmar Cres NW9 46 A2
Esme Ho SW15 133 D1
Esmeralda Rd SE1 118 A2
Esmond Ct Barnet EN5 1 C1
Kensington W8 255 D6
Esmond Gdns W4 111 B2
Esmond Rd Acton W4 111 B3
Kilburn NW6 91 B6
Esmond St SW15 135 A1
Esparto St SW18 157 D4
Espirit Ct E1 243 C3
Espirit Ho 6 SW15 157 A6
Essan Ho W13 87 B2
Essence Ct HA9 66 B6
Essenden Rd
Belvedere DA17 125 C1
South Croydon CR2 221 C1
Essendine Mans W9 91 C4
Essendine Prim Sch
W9 91 C4
Essendine Rd W9 91 C4
Essex Ave TW7 130 C2
Essex Cl Romford RM7 59 D5
Ruislip HA4 40 D1
Walthamstow E17 53 A5
West Barnes SM4 200 D2
Essex Ct Barnes SW13 133 D3
Hammersmith W6 112 C3
Holborn EC4 241 A1
South Norwood SE19 183 B4
Essex Gdns N4 50 D3
Essex Gr SE19 183 B4
Essex Ho 4 Acton W3 88 C1
2 Poplar E14 97 D1
Essex Lo 5 N10 31 B1
Essex Mans E11 54 B2
Essex Park Mews W3 111 C5
Essex Pk N3 29 D4
Essex Pl W4 111 A2
Essex Place Sq 5 W4 111 B2
Essex Prim Sch E12 78 A3
Essex Rd Acton W3 111 A6
Barking IG11 79 B1
Chingford E4 20 C3
Chiswick W4 111 B2
Enfield EN2 5 B1
Ilford RM6 58 C2
Islington N1 94 D6 234 D6
Leyton E10 54 A3
Plashet E12 78 A2
Romford RM7 59 D5
Walthamstow E17 53 A3
Willesden NW10 67 C1
Woodford E18 37 B1
Essex Rd S E11 54 B2
Essex Road Sta N1 73 A1
Essex St Forest Gate E7 77 A3
Strand WC2 116 C6 251 A6
Essex Twr 4 SE20 184 B2
Essex Villas
W8 113 C4 245 A1
Essian St E1 97 A2
Essington SW15 157 A5
Essoldo Way HA8 44 B6
Estate Way E10 53 B1
Estcourt Rd
Croydon SE25 206 B3
Fulham SW6 135 B5 264 C4
Estella Ave KT3 200 B5
Estella Ho 15 W11 112 D6
Estelle Rd NW3 70 D4
Esterbrooke St SW1 259 C3
Este Rd SW11 136 C2
Esther Cl N21 16 C4
Esther Doe Lo N21 16 C4
Esther Rd E11 54 C2
Estoria Cl 22 SW2 160 C4
Estreham Rd SW16 181 D4
Estridge Cl TW3 129 C1
Estuary Cl IG11 102 B4
Eswyn Rd SW17 180 D5
Etal Ho N1 72 D1
Etchingham Ct N12 30 A3
Etchingham Park Rd
N3 29 D3
Etchingham Rd E15 76 A4
Eternit Wlk SW6 134 D4
Etfield Gr DA14 190 B5
Ethelbert Cl BR1 209 A6
Ethelbert Gdns IG2 56 C4
Ethelbert Ho E9 75 A4
Ethelbert Rd
Bromley BR1, BR2 209 A6
Wimbledon SW20 178 D2
Ethelbert St SW12 159 B3
Ethel Brooks Ho SE18 144 D6
Ethelburga St
SW11 136 C4 267 B2
Ethelburga Twr SW11 267 B2
Ethel Cotts RM6 58 D6
Etheldene Ave N10 49 C5
Ethelden Rd W12 112 B5
Ethel Rankin Ct 8
SW6 135 B3
Ethel Rd Ashford TW15 170 A5
Newham E16 99 B1
Ethel St SE17 262 B3
Ethelworth Ct 4 SW2 160 C3
Etheridge Rd NW2 46 C2
Etherley Rd N15 51 A4
Etherow St SE22 162 A4
Etherstone Gn SW16 182 C6
Etherstone Rd SW16 182 C6
Ethnard Rd SE15 140 B6
Ethronvi Rd DA7 147 A2
Etienne Ho NW7 28 C6
Etloe Ho E10 53 C1
Etloe Rd E10 75 C6
Eton Ave
East Barnet EN4 14 C5
Finchley N12 30 A3
Heston TW5 129 C6
New Malden KT3 199 B5
Primrose Hill NW3 70 C1
Wembley HA0 65 C4
Eton Cl SW18 157 D4
Eton College Rd NW3 70 D2
Eton Ct Hampstead NW3 70 B1
Highgate N6 49 B3
Wembley HA0 65 C4
Eton Garages 11 NW3 70 C2
Eton Gr Lewisham SE13 142 C2
Queensbury NW9 44 C5
Eton Hall NW3 70 D2
Eton Ho Hackney E9 75 B2
Highbury N5 72 D4
Eton Manor Ct E10 75 C6
Eton Pl NW1 71 A1
Eton Rd Harlington UB3 127 D5
Ilford IG1 79 B4
Maitland Pk NW3 70 D2
Eton Rise NW3 70 D2
Eton St TW10 154 A6
Eton Villas NW3 70 D2
Etta St SE8 141 A6
Ettrick Ho 8 E5 74 B6
Ettrick St E14 98 A1
Etwell Pl KT5 198 B3
Euesden Cl N9 18 B1
Eugene Cotter Ho
SE17 262 D3
Eugenia Rd SE16 118 C2
Eugenie Mews BR7 188 D2
Eureka Rd 8 KT1 176 C1
Euro Bsns Ctr 3 E15 98 D6
Euro Cl NW10 68 A2
Eurolink Bsns Ctr
SW2 160 C6
Europa Pl EC1 235 A1
Europe Rd SE18 122 B3
Eustace Bldg SW8 268 C5
Eustace Ho SE11 260 C4
Eustace Pl SE18 122 B2
Eustace Rd
Dagenham RM6 58 D2
Newham E6 100 A4
Walham Green
SW6 135 C5 265 A4
Euston Ct 5 HA0 66 A2
Euston Rd
Fitzrovia NW1 93 C3 239 B6
Thornton Heath CR0 204 C1
Euston Sq NW1 232 C1
Euston Square Sta
WC1 93 C3 239 B6
Euston St NW1 93 C4 232 B1
Euston Sta NW1 93 D4 232 C1
Euston Underpass
NW1 239 A6
Evandale Rd SW9 138 C3
Evangelist Rd NW5 71 B4
Evans Cl E8 73 D2
Evans Gr TW13 151 C2
Evans Ho
34 Shepherd's Bush
W12 112 B6
South Lambeth SW8 269 D3
Evans Rd SE6 164 C2
Evanston Ave E4 36 A3
Evanston Gdns IG4 56 A3
Eva Rd RM6 58 D2
Eve Ct CR4 181 A1
Evelina Mans 9 SE5 139 B5
Evelina Rd
London SE15 140 C3
Penge SE20 184 D3
Eveline Ct N10 49 B4
Eveline Lowe Prim Sch
SE1 118 A1
Eveline Rd CR4 180 D2
Evelyn Ave London NW9 45 B5
Ruislip HA4 39 D2
Evelyn Cl TW2 151 D4
Evelyn Cres TW16 171 D2
Evelyn Ct
Chislehurst SE9 166 A2
Marylebone W1 237 C1
Shacklewell E8 74 A4
Shoreditch N1 235 C3
Evelyn Denington Ct 2
N1 72 D1
Evelyn Denington Rd
E6 100 A3
Evelyn Dr HA5 22 D3
Evelyn Fox Ct W10 90 C2
Evelyn Gdns
Richmond TW9 132 A1
South Kensington
SW7 114 B1 256 C1
Evelyn Gr Ealing W5 110 B5
Southall UB1 85 B1
Evelyn Ho
Bedford Pk W12 111 D4
3 Brixton SW2 160 B6
Harrow HA1 42 B4
18 Spitalfields E1 96 A2
Evelyn Rd Acton W4 111 B3
Cockfosters EN4 2 D1
Ham TW10 153 C1
Newham E16 121 B5
Richmond TW9 132 A2
Walthamstow E17 54 A5
Wimbledon SW19 179 D4
Evelyns Cl UB8 82 C1
Evelyn St SE8 119 A1
Evelyn Terr TW9 132 A2
Evelyn Way
Sunbury TW16 171 D2
Wallington SM6 219 D4
Evelyn Wlk N1 95 B5 235 C3
Evelyn Yd W1 239 C2
Evening Hill BR3 186 A3
Evenlode Ho 5 SE2 124 C4
Evenwood Cl SW15 157 A6
Everard Ave BR2 209 A1
Everard Ct N13 16 B1
Everard Ho 33 E1 96 A1
Everard Way HA9 66 A5
Everatt Cl SW18 157 B6
Eve Rd Isleworth TW7 131 A1
Leyton E11 76 C4
Tottenham N17 51 C6
West Ham E15 98 C5
Everdale Ct N2 48 C5
Everdon Rd SW13 134 A6

Everest Ct
6 Chislehurst SE9 166 A2
South Norwood SE19 183 C2
Everest Pl E14 98 A2
Everest Rd Eltham SE9 166 B6
Stanwell TW19 148 A4
Everett Cl Bushey WD23 8 C3
Pinner HA5 39 D6
Everett Ho Islington N7 72 C4
Walworth SE17 262 C2
Everett Wlk DA17 125 B1
Everglade Ho E17 35 B1
Everglades
Beckenham BR2 208 C6
Hounslow TW3 130 A2
Everglade Strand NW9 27 D2
Evergreen Cl SE20 184 C3
Evergreen Ct 6 SM2 218 A2
Evergreen Sq 3 E8 73 D1
Evergreen Way UB3 105 D6
Everilda St N1 233 D5
Evering Rd E5, N16 74 A5
Everington Rd N10 30 D1
Everington St W6 134 D6
Everitt Rd NW10 89 B4
Everleigh St N4 50 B1
Eversfield Ct SE12 165 B2
Eversfield Gdns HA8, NW7 27 C3
Eversfield Rd TW9 132 B3
Evershed Ho E1 243 D2
Evershed Wlk W4 111 B2
Eversholt Ct EN5 14 A6
Eversholt St NW1 93 D4 232 C2
Evershot Rd N4 50 B1
Eversleigh Ct N3 29 C3
Eversleigh Rd
Clapham SW11 137 A3
Finchley N3 29 B3
New Barnet EN5 14 A6
Newham E6 99 D6
Eversley Ave HA9 66 C6
Eversley Cl N21 16 B5
Eversley Cres
Hounslow TW7 130 B4
Ruislip HA4 61 D6
Southgate N21 16 C5
Eversley Ho 12 E2 96 A4
Eversley Mount N21 16 B5
Eversley Park Rd N21 16 B5
Eversley Pk SW19 178 B5
Eversley Prim Sch N21 16 B5
Eversley Rd
Greenwich SE7 143 B6
Kingston u T KT5 198 B4
South Norwood SE19 183 B3
Eversley Way CR0 223 C5
Everthorpe Rd SE15 139 D2
Everton Bldgs NW1 232 A1
Everton Ct HA0 65 D4
Everton Dr HA7 44 A6
Everton Rd CR0 206 A1
Evesham Ave E17 35 C1
Evesham Cl
Belmont SM2 217 C1
Greenford UB6 85 D5
Evesham Ct
2 Ealing W13 109 A5
2 Richmond TW10 154 B5
Evesham Gn SM4 201 D3
Evesham Ho
1 Bethnal Green E2 96 C5
Pimlico SW1 258 D2
St John's Wood NW8 229 A5
Evesham Rd
London N11 31 D5
Morden SM4 201 D3
Stratford E15 76 D1
Evesham St W11 112 D6
Evesham Way
Clapham SW11 137 A2
Ilford IG5 56 C6
Evesham Wlk
Brixton SW9 138 C3
Camberwell SE5 139 B3
Evry Rd DA14 190 C4
Ewald Rd SW6 135 B3
Ewanrigg Terr IG8 37 C5
Ewart Gr N22 32 C2
Ewart Pl 13 E3 97 B5
Ewart Rd SE23 162 D4
Ewe Cl N7 72 A2
EWELL 215 C1
Ewell By-Pass KT17 216 A1
EWELL COURT 215 C2
Ewell Court Ave KT19 215 C3
Ewell Park Gdns KT17 216 A1
Ewell Park Way KT17 216 A1
Ewell Rd
Cheam SM2, SM3 216 D2
Surbiton KT6 198 B2
Thames Ditton KT6, KT7 197 B2
Tolworth KT6 198 D1
Ewelme Rd SE23 162 C3
Ewen Cres SW2 160 C4
Ewen Henderson Ct 10 SE14 141 A5
Ewen Ho N1 233 C5
Ewer St SE1 117 A5 252 A3
Ewhurst 19 SW15 156 D5
Ewhurst Cl E1 96 C2
Ewhurst Ct CR4 202 B6
Ewhurst Rd SE4 163 B5
Exbury Ho Hackney E9 74 C2
4 London SW9 138 B1
Exbury Rd SE6 163 C2
Excel Ct WC2 249 D5
Excel Ex Ctr E16 121 B6
Excelsior Cl KT1 176 C1
Excelsior Gdns SE13 142 A3
Excelsior Ind Est SE16 140 C6
Exchange Apartments 4 BR2 209 B5
Exchange Arc EC2 243 B4
Exchange Cl N11 15 A2
Exchange Ct WC2 250 B5
Exchange Mans 2 NW11 47 B2
Exchange Pl EC2 243 A4
Exchange The IG1 78 D6
Exchange Wlk HA5 41 A2
Exeforde Ave TW15 170 C6
Exeter Cl E6 100 B1
Exeter Ct Kilburn NW6 91 C5
Kingston u T KT6 198 A4
Mitcham SW19 180 C3
Exeter Gdns IG1 56 B1
Exeter Ho
7 Barking IG11 80 A1
Feltham TW13 151 C2
Paddington W2 236 A2
11 Peckham SE15 140 A6
Putney SW15 156 C5
Exeter Mans NW2 69 A2
Exeter Mews
Fulham SW6 265 A4
12 Hampstead NW6 69 D2
Exeter Rd Bexley DA16 145 D3
Brondesbury NW2 69 A2
Croydon CR0 205 D2
Dagenham RM10 81 D2
East Barnet N14 15 B4
Enfield EN3 6 D2
Harrow HA2 63 A6
Hatton TW6 127 C2
Lower Edmonton N9 18 C2
Newham E16 99 A2
Twickenham TW13 151 B1
Walthamstow E17 53 C4
Exeter St WC2 116 B6 250 C6
Exeter Way
Hatton TW6 127 C3
2 New Cross SE14 141 B5
Exford Ct SW11 266 D2
Exford Gdns SE12 165 B3
Exford Rd SE12 165 B3
Exhibition Cl W12 112 C6
Exhibition Rd SW7 114 B3 256 D6
Exit Rd N2 30 B1
Exmoor Ho 25 E3 97 A5
Exmoor St W10 90 D2
Exmouth Ho
Clerkenwell EC1 241 B6
6 Millwall E14 119 D2
Exmouth Market EC1 94 C3 241 B6
Exmouth Mews NW1 232 B1
Exmouth Pl E8 74 B1
Exmouth Rd
Bexley DA16 146 C5
Hayes UB4 83 C4
Ruislip HA4 62 C5
Walthamstow E17 53 B4
Exmouth St E1 96 C1
Exning Rd E16 98 D3
Exonbury NW8 91 D6
Exon St SE17 117 C2 263 A3
Explorer Ave TW19 148 A3
Explorers Ct 6 E14 120 B6
Express Dr IG3 58 B1
Express Wharf 10 E14 119 C4
Exton Cres NW10 67 A1
Exton Gdns RM8 80 C3
Exton Rd NW10 67 A1
Exton St SE1 116 C5 251 A3
Eyebright Cl 3 CR0 206 D1
Eyhurst Cl NW2 68 A6
Eylewood Rd SE27 183 A5
Eynella Rd SE21 161 D4
Eynham Rd W12 90 C1
Eynsford Cl BR5 211 A3
Eynsford Cres DA5 168 D3
Eynsford Ho
Borough The SE1 252 C2
12 Deptford SE15 140 C6
Walworth SE17 263 A3
Eynsford Rd IG3 79 C6
Eynsford Terr UB7 82 B1
Eynsham Dr SE2 124 B3
Eynswood Dr DA14 190 C5
Eyot Gdns W6 111 D1
Eyot Gn W4 111 D1
Eyre Ct NW8 229 C4
Eyre St Hill EC1 94 C3 241 A5
Eysham Ct 12 EN5 13 D6
Eythorne Rd SW9 138 C4
Ezra St E2 95 D4

F

Faber Gdns NW4 46 A4
Fabian Rd SW6 135 B5 264 D4
Fabian St E6 100 B3
Fabyc Ho TW9 132 C5
Factory La
Croydon CR0 220 D6
Tottenham N17 33 D1
Factory Rd E16 122 A5
Factory Yd W7 108 C5
Fagg's Rd TW14 150 A6
Fairacre Hounslow TW7 130 B4
Kingston u T KT3 199 C6
Fairacre *continued*
Pinner HA5 40 A5
Fairacres Putney SW15 134 A1
Ruislip HA4 39 D2
Fair Acres BR2 209 A4
Fairbairn Gn 1 SW9 138 D4
Fairbairn Hall E13 99 A3
Fairbank Ave BR6 226 D6
Fairbanks Rd N17 52 A6
Fairbourne Ho UB3 105 A3
Fairbourne Rd N17 51 C6
Fairbriar Residence SW7 256 B4
Fairbridge Rd N19 71 D6
Fairbrook Cl N13 32 C5
Fairbrook Rd N13 32 C4
Fairburn Ct SW15 157 A6
Fairburn Ho
9 Stamford Hill N16 51 C1
West Kensington SW5 254 D1
Fairby Ho SE1 263 D4
Fairby Rd SE12 165 B6
Faircharm Trad Est SE8 141 D5
Fairchild Cl 6 SW11 136 B3
Fairchild Ho
13 Hackney E9 74 C1
Pimlico SW1 259 B3
5 Shoreditch N1 95 C4
Fairchild Pl EC2 243 B5
Fairchild St EC2 243 B5
Fairclough Cl UB5 85 B3
Fairclough St E1 96 A1
Faircourt 14 NW3 70 D2
Faircroft
6 Forest Hill SE26 184 C6
Stoke Newington N16 51 B1
FAIR CROSS 79 D3
Fair Cross IG11 79 C3
Faircross Ave IG11 79 A2
Faircross Par IG11 79 C3
Fairdale Gdns
Hayes UB3 106 A4
Putney SW15 134 B1
Fairdene Ct N7 72 A3
Fairey Ave UB3 105 D3
Fairfax Cl KT12 194 B1
Fairfax Gdns SE3 143 C4
Fairfax Ho
11 Brixton SW9 138 C3
5 Ealing W5 88 A4
6 Putney SW15 156 A6
Fairfax Mews
London N8 50 D5
Newham E16 121 B5
Putney SW15 134 C1
Fairfax Pl
Kensington W14 254 B5
South Hampstead NW6 70 A1
Fairfax Rd Acton W4 111 C3
Hornsey N8 50 C5
South Hampstead NW6 70 A1
Teddington TW11 175 B3
Fairfax Way N10 31 A3
Fairfield
Camden Town NW1 232 A5
Oakleigh Pk N20 14 B4
Pinner HA6 22 A1
Walthamstow E17 53 B4
4 Stepney E1 96 C2
Fairfield Ave
Edgware HA8 26 D3
Hendon NW4 46 B3
Ruislip HA4 39 A2
Twickenham TW2 151 D3
Fairfield Cl
Blackfen DA15 167 D5
Enfield EN3 7 A1
Mitcham SW19 180 C3
North Finchley N12 30 A6
West Ewell KT19 215 C3
Fairfield Cres HA8 26 D4
Fairfield Ct
Harlesden NW10 90 A6
1 London SW18 157 D6
Ruislip HA4 39 B1
8 Woodford IG8 37 A4
Fairfield Dr Harrow HA2 42 A6
Wandsworth SW18 157 D6
Wembley UB6 87 C6
Fairfield E KT1 176 A1
Fairfield Gdns N8 50 A4
Fairfield Gr SE7 143 D6
Fairfield Ind Est KT1 198 B6
Fairfield N KT1, KT2 176 A1
Fairfield Path CR0 221 B5
Fairfield Pl KT1 198 A6
Fairfield Rd
Beckenham BR3 185 C1
Bexleyheath DA7 147 B3
Bow E3 97 C5
Edmonton N18 34 A6
Higham Hill E17 35 A1
Hornsey N8 50 A4
Ilford IG1 78 D2
Kingston u T KT1 176 A1
Petts Wood BR5 211 B3
Plaistow BR1 187 A3
Southall UB1 85 B1
South Croydon CR0 221 C5
Woodford IG8 37 A4
Yiewsley UB7 104 A6
Fairfields SE6 163 D4
Fairfield S KT1 176 B1
Fairfields Cl NW9 45 A4
Fairfields Cres NW9 45 A4
Fairfields Rd TW3 130 A2
Fairfield St SW18 157 D6
Fairfield W KT1 176 A1
Fairfield Way
Barnet EN5 13 C6
Fairfield Way *continued*
West Ewell KT19 215 C3
Fairfoot Rd E3 97 C3
Fairford SE6 163 C3
Fairford Ave CR0 206 D4
Fairford Cl CR0 207 A4
Fairford Ct SM2 217 D1
Fairford Gdns KT4 215 D5
Fairford Ho SE11 261 B3
Fairgreen EN4 2 D2
Fairgreen Ct EN4 2 D2
Fair Green Ct 1 CR4 202 D6
Fairgreen E EN4 2 D2
Fairgreen Rd CR7 204 D4
Fairhall Ct KT6 198 B2
Fairhaven Ave CR0 206 D3
Fairhaven Ct 7 CR2 221 A3
Fairhazel Gdns NW6 70 A1
Fairheathe SW15 156 D5
Fairholme TW14 149 C4
Fairholme Cl N3 47 A5
Fairholme Cres UB4 84 A3
Fairholme Gdns N3 47 A5
Fairholme Ho 4 KT3 199 C5
Fairholme Prim Sch TW14 149 B3
Fairholme Rd
Ashford TW15 170 B5
Cheam SM1 217 B2
Harrow HA1 42 D4
Ilford IG1 56 C2
Thornton Heath CR0 204 C2
West Kensington W14 113 A1 254 B1
Fairholt Cl N16 51 C1
Fairholt Rd N16 51 B1
Fairholt St SW7 257 B6
Fairhurst 4 NW6 70 A2
Fairland Ho BR2 209 B5
Fairland Rd E15 76 D1
Fairlands Ave
Sutton SM1 217 C6
Thornton Heath CR7 204 C4
Woodford IG9 21 A2
Fairlands Ct 6 SE9 166 C5
Fairlawn SE7 143 C6
Fairlawn Ave
Acton W4 111 A2
Bexley DA7 146 D3
East Finchley N2 48 C5
Fairlawn Cl
Claygate KT10 212 D2
Feltham TW13 173 B6
Kingston u T KT2 177 A4
Southgate N14 15 D5
Fairlawn Ct
3 Acton W4 111 A2
Charlton SE7 143 C5
Fairlawn Dr IG8 37 A3
Fairlawnes SM6 219 B3
Fairlawn Gdns UB1 107 B6
Fairlawn Gr W4 111 A2
Fairlawn Mans SE14 140 D4
Fairlawn Pk SE26 185 A5
Fairlawn Prim Sch SE23 162 C4
Fairlawn Prim Sch (Annexe) SE23 162 C3
Fairlawn Rd SW19 179 B3
Fairlawns
4 Bowes Pk N11 32 A4
10 Chingford E4 20 A2
Pinner HA5 22 D1
Putney SW15 156 D6
Sunbury TW16 194 A6
Twickenham TW1 153 C5
Fairlead Ho 6 E14 119 C3
Fairlea Pl W5 87 D3
Fair Lea Pl W5 87 C2
Fairleas 12 BR3 185 D1
Fairley Ct HA0 65 D3
Fairley House Sch SW1 259 D2
Fairlie Ct 22 Bromley E3 97 D4
1 Tufnell Pk N7 71 D4
Fairlie Gdns SE23 162 C4
Fairlight TW12 173 D5
Fairlight Ave
Chingford E4 20 B2
Harlesden NW10 89 C5
Woodford IG8 37 A4
Fairlight Cl Cheam KT4 216 C4
Chingford E4 20 B2
Fairlight Ct
Greenford UB6 86 B5
4 Harlesden NW10 89 C5
Fairlight Rd SW17 180 B6
Fairline Ct BR3 186 A1
Fairlop Ct E11 54 C1
Fairlop Pl NW8 229 D1
Fairlop Rd E11 54 B2
Fairmark Cl UB10 60 C2
Fairmead Bromley BR1 210 B5
Tolworth KT5, KT6 198 D1
Fairmead Cl
Bromley BR1 210 B5
Heston TW5 128 D5
Kingston u T KT3 199 B6
Fairmead Cres HA8 11 A1
Fairmead Ct
3 Chingford E4 20 C4
Oakleigh Pk N20 14 A4
Fairmead Gdns IG4 56 A4
Fairmead Ho E9 75 A4
Fairmead Rd
Lower Holloway N7, N19 72 A5
Thornton Heath CR0 204 C2
Fairmeadside IG10 21 C6
Fairmile Ave SW16 181 D5
Fairmile Ho
St Paul's Cray BR5 190 A1
Teddington TW11 175 A6
Fairmont Ave E14 120 B5
Fairmont Cl DA17 125 B1
Fairmont Ho 1 E3 97 C3
Fairmount Rd SW2 160 B5
Fairoak Cl BR5 210 D2
Fairoak Dr SE9 167 B6
Fairoaks Gr EN3 6 D6
Fairseat Cl WD23 8 C2
Fair St
Bermondsey SE1 117 D4 253 C2
Hounslow TW3 130 A2
Fairstead Lo 4 IG8 37 A4
Fairstead Wlk N1 235 A6
Fairthorn Rd SE7, SE10 121 A1
Fairview Ave HA0 65 D2
Fairview Cl SE26 185 A5
Fair View Cl E17 35 A2
Fairview Cres HA2 41 C1
Fairview Ct
Ashford TW15 170 C5
Hendon NW4 28 D1
Kingston u T KT2 176 D2
Fairview Dr
Littleton TW17 192 B4
Orpington BR6 227 B4
Fairview Gdns IG8 37 B2
Fairview Ho 14 SW2 160 B4
Fairview Pl SW2 160 B4
Fairview Rd
Carshalton SM1, SM5 218 C3
Enfield EN2 4 C4
South Tottenham N15 51 D3
Thornton Heath SW16 182 B2
Fairview Way HA8 26 C6
Fairwall Ho 9 SE5 139 C4
Fairwater Ave DA16 146 A1
Fairwater Ho TW11 175 A6
Fairway Bexley DA6 169 A6
Petts Wood BR5 211 B4
West Barnes SW20 200 C6
Woodford IG8 37 C5
Fairway Ave NW9 44 D6
Fairway Cl
Croydon CR0 207 A4
Heston TW4 150 C6
Hounslow TW4 150 D6
North End NW11 48 A2
West Ewell KT19 215 A4
Fairway Ct
Edgware NW7 11 B1
12 Eltham SE9 166 C5
New Barnet EN5 13 D5
13 Rotherhithe SE16 118 D4
Fairway Dr Erith SE28 103 A1
Greenford UB6 63 D1
Fairway Est TW4 150 C6
Fairway Gdns Ilford IG1 79 A3
West Wickham BR3 208 B3
Fairway Prim Sch NW7 11 B2
Fairways Ashford TW15 170 D4
12 Chingford E4 20 A3
4 Hounslow TW7 130 C4
Stanmore HA7 26 A1
Teddington TW11 175 D3
Walthamstow E17 54 A5
Fairways Bsns Pk E10 75 A6
Fairway The Acton W3 89 C1
Bromley BR1, BR2 210 B4
East Molesey KT8 195 D6
Edgware NW7 11 B1
Edmonton N13 17 B1
Hillingdon UB10 82 B5
Kingston u T KT3 177 B2
New Barnet EN5 13 D5
Northolt UB5 64 A2
Ruislip HA4 62 D5
Southgate N14 15 C5
Wembley HA0 65 B6
Fairweather Cl N15 51 C5
Fairweather Ct N13 32 B6
Fairweather Ho N7 72 A4
Fairweather Rd N16 52 A3
Fairwood Ct E11 54 B2
Fairwyn Rd SE26 185 A6
Faith Ct NW2 68 B2
Faithfull Ho N5 73 A3
Fakenham Cl
Hendon NW7 28 A3
5 Northolt UB5 63 C2
Fakruddin St E1 96 A3
Falcon Ave BR1 210 A5
Falconberg Ct W1 239 D2
Falconberg Mews W1 239 D2
Falconbrook Prim Sch SW11 136 B2
Falcon Cl Chiswick W4 133 A6
Lambeth SE1 251 D4
Falcon Cres EN3 18 D6
Falcon Ct
9 Dulwich SE21 161 B2
Holborn EC4 241 A1
Islington N1 234 D3
New Barnet EN5 2 A1
Ruislip HA4 61 C6
6 Wanstead E18 55 B6
Falcon Dr TW19 148 A5
Falconer Ct N17 33 A3
Falconer Wlk 12 N7 72 B6
Falcon Gr SW11 136 C2
Falcon Ho
11 London SE15 139 D4
9 Merton SW19 179 D2
Falconhurst 4 KT6 198 A4
Falcon La SW11 136 C2
Falcon Lo
11 Paddington W9 91 C2
West Hampstead NW3 69 D4
Falcon Pk Ind Est NW10 67 C3
Falcon Point SE1 251 D5
Falcon Rd
Battersea SW11 136 C2
Enfield EN3 18 D6
Hampton TW12 173 B3
Falconry Ct KT1 198 A6
Falcon St E13 99 A3
Falcon Terr SW11 136 C2
Falcon Way
Feltham TW14 150 B6
Harrow HA3 44 A3
Hendon NW9 27 C1
Millwall E14 119 D2
Sunbury TW16 171 C1
Wanstead E11 55 A5
FALCONWOOD 145 C1
Falconwood Ave DA16 145 C3
Falconwood Ct SE3 142 D3
Falconwood Par DA16 145 D1
Falconwood Rd CR0 223 C1
Falconwood Sta SE9 145 B1
Falcourt Cl SM1 217 D3
Falkener Ct SW11 268 B1
Falkirk Ct 11 SE16 118 D5
Falkirk Gdns WD19 22 D5
Falkirk Ho W9 91 D4
Falkirk St N1 95 C5
Falkland Ave
Finchley N3 29 C3
Friern Barnet N11 31 B6
Falkland Ho
Catford SE6 186 A6
Kensington W8 255 C5
West Kensington W14 254 C2
Falkland Park Ave SE25 183 C1
Falkland Pl 2 NW5 71 C3
Falkland Rd Barnet EN5 1 A3
Hornsey N8 50 C5
Kentish Town NW5 71 C3
Falkner House Sch SW7 256 B2
Fallaize Ave IG1 78 D4
Falling La UB7 104 A6
Falloden Ct NW11 47 C5
Falloden Way NW11 47 C5
Fallodon Ho
6 London SW8 137 D3
Paddington W11 91 B2
Fallow Court Ave N12 30 A4
Fallow Ct 20 SE16 118 A1
Fallowfield
Lower Holloway N4 72 B6
Stanmore HA7 9 A1
Fallowfield Ct HA7 9 A1
Fallow Fields IG10 21 C4
Fallowfields Dr N12 30 C4
Fallows Cl N2 30 B1
Fallsbrook Rd SW16 181 C4
Falman Cl N9 18 A3
Falmer Rd Enfield EN1 5 C1
Walthamstow E17 53 D6
West Green N15 51 B4
Falmouth Ave E4 36 C5
Falmouth Cl
London SE12 164 D6
Wood Green N22 32 B3
Falmouth Gdns IG4 55 D5
Falmouth Ho
Bayswater W2 247 A6
Kennington SE11 261 B2
15 Kingston u T KT2 175 D2
6 Pinner HA5 23 B3
Falmouth Rd SE1 117 A3 262 B5
Falmouth St E15 76 B3
Falmouth Way E17 53 B4
Falstaff Ct SE11 261 C3
Falstaff Ho 18 N1 95 C5
Fambridge Cl SE26 185 B6
Fambridge Rd RM8 59 C1
Fane St W14 264 D6
Fann St EC1 95 A3 242 B5
Fanshawe Ave IG11 79 A2
Fanshawe Cres RM9 81 B3
Fanshawe Rd TW10 175 C6
Fanshaw Ho 6 E17 53 D6
Fanshaw St N1 95 C4
Fantail Cl SE28 102 C1
Fantail The BR6 226 B5
Fanthorpe St SW15 134 C2
Faraday Ave DA14 168 B2
Faraday Cl N7 72 B2
Faraday Ho
2 Balham SW12 159 B4
4 Belvedere DA17 125 C3
6 Gospel Oak NW5 71 B4
5 Hampton TW12 173 D4
Kensal Town W10 91 A2
6 Poplar E14 119 B6
Wembley HA9 67 A5
Faraday Lo SE10 120 D3
Faraday Pl KT8 195 C5
Faraday Rd Acton W3 111 A6
East Molesey KT8 195 C5
Kensal Town W10 91 A2
Southall UB1 107 D6
Stratford E15 76 D2
Welling DA16 146 A2
Wimbledon SW19 179 D4
Faraday Way
Greenwich SE18 121 D3
Thornton Heath CR0 204 B1

Fareham Ho 13 SW15 156 A3
Fareham Rd TW14 150 C4
Fareham St W1 239 C2
Farendon Ho 15 SM2 218 A2
Farewell Pl CR4 180 C2
Faringdon Ave BR2 210 C3
Faringford Rd E15 76 C1
Farjeon Ho NW6 70 B1
Farjeon Rd SE3 143 D4
Farleigh Ave BR2 209 A2
Farleigh Ct CR2 221 A3
Farleigh Ho 7 KT2 176 D4
Farleigh Pl N16 73 D4
Farleigh Rd N16 73 D4
Farleycroft 1 CR0 206 A1
Farley Croft BR2 186 C1
Farley Ct
Kensington W14 254 C6
Marylebone NW1 238 A5
Farley Dr IG3 57 C1
Farley Ho SE26 162 B1
Farley Mews SE6 164 A4
Farley Pl SE25 206 A5
Farley Rd Catford SE6 164 A4
South Croydon CR2 222 B1
Farlington Pl SW15 156 B4
Farlow Rd SW15 134 D2
Farlton Rd SW18 157 D4
Farman Gr 2 UB5 84 D4
Farman Terr HA3 43 D5
Farm Ave
Child's Hill NW2 69 B5
Harrow HA2, HA5 41 C3
Streatham SW16 182 A6
Wembley HA0 65 C2
Farmborough Cl HA1 42 B2
Farm Cl Barnet EN5 12 C6
Buckhurst Hill IG9 21 C1
Coney Hall BR4 224 D5
Lower Halliford TW17 192 C2
Southall UB1 107 D6
Sutton SM2 218 B1
Uxbridge UB10 60 D6
Walham Green SW6 265 B4
Farmcote Rd SE12 165 A3
Farm Cotts E17 53 A3
Farm Ct NW4 46 A6
Farmdale Rd
Greenwich SE10 121 A1
Sutton SM5 218 C1
Farm Dr CR0 223 B6
Farm End E4 20 C6
Farmer Ho 4 SE16 118 B3
Farmer Rd E10 53 D1
Farmers Rd SE5 138 D5
Farmer St W8 245 A4
Farmfield Rd BR1 186 C5
Farm House Ct NW7 28 A3
Farmhouse Rd SW16 181 C3
Farmilo Rd E17 53 C2
Farmington Ave SM1 218 B5
Farm La Croydon CR0 223 B6
East Barnet N14 15 B5
Walham Green SW6 135 C5 265 B4
Farmlands Enfield EN2 4 C4
Pinner HA5 40 A5
Farmlands The UB5 63 C2
Farmland Wlk BR7 188 D5
Farm Lane Trad Ctr SW6 135 C6 265 B5
Farmleigh N14 15 C4
Farmleigh Ho SW9 160 D6
Farm Pl W8 245 A4
Farm Rd Edgware HA8 27 A5
Edmonton N21 17 A3
Morden SM4 201 D4
Stonebridge NW10 89 B6
Sutton SM2 218 B1
Thames Ditton KT10 195 C1
Twickenham TW4 151 A3
Farm St W1 115 B6 248 C5
Farmstead Ct 3 SM6 219 B3
Farmstead Rd
Catford SE6 185 D6
Harrow HA3 24 B1
Farm Vale DA5 169 D5
Farm View N3 47 B6
Farmway RM8 80 C5
Farm Way
Buckhurst Hill IG9 37 C6
North Cheam KT4 216 C5
Farm Wlk NW11 47 C4
Farnaby Ho 2 W10 91 B4
Farnaby Rd
Bromley BR1, BR2 186 C2
Kidbrooke SE9 143 C1
Farnan Ave E17 53 D6
Farnan Hall 6 SW16 182 A5
Farnan Rd SW16 182 A5
FARNBOROUGH 227 B3
Farnborough Ave
South Croydon CR2 223 A1
Walthamstow E17 53 A6
Farnborough Cl HA9 66 D6
Farnborough Comm
Keston Mark BR2, BR6 226 B5
Orpington BR6 226 C4
Farnborough Cres
3 Hayes BR2 208 D1
South Croydon CR2 223 A1
Farnborough Ct 2 BR6 227 A3
Farnborough Hill BR6 227 C3
Farnborough Ho 1 SW15 156 A3
Farnborough Prim Sch BR6 227 A3
Farnborough Way BR6 227 B3
Farncombe St SE16 118 A4
Farndale Ave N13 17 A1
Farndale Cres UB6 86 A4
Farndale Ho 3 NW6 91 D6
Farnell Mews SW5 255 C2
Farnell Pl W3 110 D6
Farnell Rd TW7 130 B2
Farnell's Almshouses TW7 130 D3
Farnfield Ho 12 SW2 160 B6
Farnham Cl N20 14 A4
Farnham Ct
2 Cheam SM3 217 A2
1 Southall UB1 86 A1
2 Stamford Hill N16 51 C1
Farnham Gdns SW20 178 B1
Farnham Green Prim Sch IG3 58 A3
Farnham Ho
Borough The SE1 252 A3
Marylebone NW1 237 B5
Farnham Pl SE1 251 D3
Farnham Rd
Bexley DA16 146 C3
Ilford IG3 57 D2
Farnham Royal SE11 116 B1 260 D1
Farnhurst Ho 7 SW11 137 A3
Farningham Ct SW16 181 D3
Farningham Ho 9 N4 51 B2
Farningham Rd N17 34 A3
Farnley Ho 13 SW8 137 D3
Farnley Rd Chingford E4 20 C4
South Norwood SE25 205 B5
Farnsworth Ct SE10 120 D3
Farnsworth Ho 8 SW27 182 D5
Farnworth Ho 5 E14 120 B2
Faro Cl BR1 188 C1
Faroe Rd W14 112 D3
Farorna Wlk EN2 4 C4
Farquhar Rd
Dulwich SE19 183 D5
Wimbledon SW19 157 C1
Farquharson Rd CR0 205 A1
Farrance Rd RM6 59 A2
Farrance St E14 97 C1
Farrans Ct HA3 43 B2
Farrant Ave N22 32 D1
Farrant Cl BR6 227 D1
Farrant Ho 15 SW11 136 B2
Farrants Ct BR1 188 B1
Farr Ave IG11 102 A5
Farrell Ho E1 96 C1
Farren Rd SE23 163 A2
Farrer Ho SE8 141 C5
Farrer Mews N8 49 C5
Farrer Rd Harrow HA3 44 A5
Hornsey N8 49 D5
Farrer's Pl CR0 222 D4
Farrier Cl Bromley BR1 209 D6
Hillingdon UB8 82 C1
Sunbury TW16 194 A5
Farrier Pl SM1 217 D6
Farrier Rd UB5 85 C5
Farriers Ct
Belmont SM2 217 A1
Wimbledon SW19 179 A3
Farriers Mews SE15 140 C2
Farrier St NW1 71 C1
Farriers Way WD6 11 B6
Farrier Wlk SW10 136 A6 266 A6
Farringdon La EC1 94 C3 241 B5
Farringdon Rd EC1 94 C3 241 B5
Farringdon St EC4 94 D1 241 C2
Farringdon Sta EC1 94 D2 241 C4
Farrington Pl BR7 189 B3
Farrington & Stratford House Sch BR7 189 B3
Farrins Rents SE16 119 A5
Farrow La SE14 140 C5
Farrow Pl SE16 119 A3
Farr Rd EN2 5 B4
Farthingale Wlk E15 76 B1
Farthing Alley 8 SE1 118 A4
Farthing Ct 3 NW7 29 A3
Farthing Fields 8 E1 118 B5
Farthings Cl
Chingford E4 20 C1
Pinner HA5 40 B3
Farthing St BR6 226 B1
Farthings The 1 KT2 176 C2
FARTHING STREET 226 B1
Farwell Rd DA14 190 C6
Farwig La BR1 187 A2
Fashion & Design Mus The* SE1 253 A2
Fashion Retail Acad The W1 239 C2
Fashion St E1 95 D2 243 D3
Fashoda Rd BR2 209 D5
Fassett Rd Dalston E8 74 A2
Kingston u T KT1 198 A5
Fassett Sq E8 74 A2
Fauconberg Ct W4 133 A6
Fauconberg Rd W4 133 A6
Faulkner Cl 6 RM8 58 D2
Faulkner Ho SW15 134 C3
Faulkner's Alley EC1 241 C4
Faulkner St SE14 140 C4
Fauna Cl Dagenham RM6 58 C3
Stanmore HA7 25 D6
Faunce Ho 1 SE17 138 D6
Faunce St SE17 116 D1 261 C1
Favart Rd SW6 135 C4 265 B2
F Ave SE18 122 D3
Faversham Ave
Chingford E4 20 D3
Enfield EN1 17 B5
Faversham Ct SE6 163 B3
Faversham Ho
Camden Town NW1 232 B5
Walworth SE17 263 A1
Faversham Rd
Beckenham BR3 185 B1
Forest Hill SE6 163 B3
Morden SM4 201 D3
Fawcett Cl
London SW11 136 B3
West Norwood SW16 182 C6
Fawcett Est E5 52 A1
Fawcett Ho 25 SW9 138 A3
Fawcett Rd
Croydon CR0 221 A5
Willesden NW10 67 D1
Fawcett St SW10 136 A6 266 A6
Fawcus Cl KT10 212 C2
Fawe Park Rd SW15 135 B1
Fawe St E14 97 D2
Fawkham Ho SE1 263 D3
Fawley Ct SE27 160 D2
Fawley Lo 2 E14 120 B2
Fawley Rd NW6 69 D3
Fawnbrake Ave SE24 161 A6
Fawn Rd E13 99 C5
Fawns Manor Cl TW14 149 A3
Fawns Manor Rd TW14 149 B3
Fawood Ave NW10 67 B1
Fayetville Ho 28 N19 49 D2
Faygate Cres DA6 169 C6
Faygate Ct CR2 220 D1
Faygate Rd SW2 160 B2
Fayland Ave SW16 181 C5
Fazal Laj IG1 79 A6
Fazerley Ct 49 W2 91 C2
Fearnley Cres TW12 173 B4
Fearnley Ho SE5 139 C3
Fearon St SE10 121 A1
Featherbed La CR0 223 B1
Feathers Pl SE10 142 B6
Featherstone Ave 4 SE23 162 C2
Featherstone Ct NW7 28 A3
Featherstone High Sch UB2 107 A3
Featherstone Ho UB4 84 C2
Featherstone Ind Est UB2 107 A3
Featherstone Prim Sch UB2 106 C2
Featherstone Rd
Mill Hill NW7 28 B4
Southall UB2 107 A3
Featherstone St EC1 95 B3 242 C6
Featherstone Terr UB2 107 A3
Featley Rd SW9 138 D2
Federal Rd UB6 87 C5
Federation Rd SE2 124 C2
Fee Farm Rd KT10 212 D1
Felbridge Ave HA7 25 B2
Felbridge Cl SW16 182 C6
Felbridge Ct
Croydon CR2 221 A1
Feltham TW13 150 B3
Harlington UB3 127 B6
Felbridge Ho 21 SE22 139 C2
Felbrigge Rd IG3 57 D1
Felday Rd SE13 163 D5
Felden Cl HA5 23 A3
Felden St SW6 135 B4 264 C1
Feldman Cl N16 52 A1
Feldspar Ct 6 EN3 7 A2
Felgate Mews 4 W6 112 B2
Felhampton Rd SE9 166 D1
Felhurst Cres RM10 81 D4
Feline Ct 1 EN4 14 C5
Felix Ave N8 50 A3
Felix Ct E17 53 D4
Felix La TW17 193 D3
Felix Manor BR7 189 C4
Felix Neubergh Ct EN1 5 C1
Felix Rd Ealing W13 109 A6
Walton-on-T KT12 194 A3
Felix St 19 E2 96 B5
Felixstowe Ct E16 122 D5
Felixstowe Rd
Abbey Wood SE2 124 B3
College Pk NW10 90 B4
Edmonton N9 34 A6
Tottenham N17 51 D6
Fellbrigg Rd SE22 161 D6
Fellbrigg St 21 E1 96 B3
Fellbrook TW10 153 B1
Fell Ho 11 N19 71 C5
Fellmongers Yd 1 CR0 221 A5
Fellowes Cl UB4 84 D3
Fellowes Ct UB3 127 B6
Fellowes Rd SM5 218 C6
Fellows Ct E2 95 D5
Fellows Rd NW3 70 C1
Fell Rd CR0 221 A5
Fells Haugh 6 W3 89 A1
Felltram Way SE7 121 A1
Fell Wlk HA8 26 D2
Felmersham Cl 2 SW4 137 D1
Felmingham Rd SE20 184 C1
Felnex Trad Est SM6 219 A6
Felpham Ct HA9 65 D4
Felsberg Rd SW2 160 A4
Fels Cl RM10 81 D5
Felsham Ho SW15 134 D2
Felsham Mews SW15 134 D2
Felsham Rd SW15 134 D2
Felspar Cl SE18 123 D1
Felstead Cl N13 32 C5
Felstead Rd E11 55 A2
Felstead St E9 75 B2
Felstead Wharf E14 120 A1
Felsted Rd E16 99 D1
FELTHAM 150 B2
Feltham Ave KT8 196 C5
Felthambrook Ind Est TW13 150 B1
Felthambrook Way TW13 172 B6
Feltham Bsns Complex TW13 150 B2
Feltham Com Sch TW13 150 C2
Feltham Corporate Ctr TW13 150 B1
FELTHAMHILL 171 D5
Feltham Hill Jun & Inf Schs TW13 149 D1
Feltham Hill Rd
Ashford TW15 171 A4
Feltham TW13 172 C5
Feltham Rd
Ashford TW15 171 A6
Mitcham CR4 181 A1
Feltham Sta TW13 150 B3
Felton Cl BR5 210 D3
Felton Gdns IG11 101 C5
Felton Ho
Kidbrooke SE9 143 C1
Shoreditch N1 235 D5
Felton Lea DA14 189 D5
Felton Rd Barking IG11 101 C5
Ealing W13 109 C4
Felton St N1 95 B6 235 D5
Fenchurch Ave EC3 95 C1 243 A1
Fenchurch Bldgs EC3 243 B1
Fenchurch Pl EC3 253 B6
Fenchurch St EC3 117 C6 253 B6
Fenchurch Street Sta EC3 117 C6 253 B6
Fen Ct EC3 253 A6
Fendall Rd KT19 215 A3
Fendall St SE1 117 C3 263 B5
Fender Ct 5 SW4 138 A3
Fendt Cl 8 E16 98 D1
Fendyke Rd SE2, DA17 124 D3
Fenelon Pl W14 113 B2 254 D3
Fen Gr DA15 167 D5
Fenham Rd SE15 140 B5
Fenman Ct N17 34 B2
Fenman Gdns IG3 58 B1
Fenn Cl BR1 187 A4
Fenn Ct HA1 43 A4
Fennel Cl Croydon CR0 206 D1
Newham E16 98 C3
Fennell St SE18 144 C6
Fenner Cl SE16 118 B2
Fenner Ho 25 E1 118 B5
Fenner Sq 10 SW11 136 B2
Fenn Ho TW7 131 B4
Fenning Ct CR4 202 C5
Fenning St SE1 253 A2
Fenn St E9 74 C3
Fen St E16 120 D6
Fenstanton 3 N4 50 B1
Fenstanton Ave N12 30 B5
Fenstanton Prim Sch SW2 160 C3
Fenswood Cl DA5 169 C5
Fentiman Rd SW8 138 B5 270 C4
Fentiman Way HA2 63 D6
Fenton Cl Dalston E8 73 D2
Elmstead BR7 188 B5
South Lambeth SW9 138 B3
Fenton Ct TW3 129 A5
Fenton Ho
Deptford SE14 141 A5
Heston TW5 129 C6
Fenton House* NW3 70 A5
Fenton Rd N17 33 A3
Fentons SE3 142 D5
Fenton's Ave E13 99 B5
Fenton St E1 96 B1
Fenwick Cl 16 SE18 144 C6
Fenwick Gr SE15 140 A2
Fenwick Pl
Croydon CR2 220 D1
Stockwell SW9 138 A2
Fenwick Rd SE15 140 A2
Ferby Ct DA15 189 D6
Ferdinand Ho 1 NW1 71 B1
Ferdinand Pl NW1 71 A1
Ferdinand St NW1 71 A1
Ferguson Ave KT5 198 B4
Ferguson Cl BR2, BR3 208 B6
Ferguson Dr W3 89 B1
Ferguson Ho SE10 142 A4
Ferguson's Cl E14 119 C2
Fergus Rd N5 72 D3
Fermain Ct E N1 95 C6
Fermain Ct N N1 95 C6
Fermain Ct W N1 95 C6
Ferme Park Rd N4, N8 50 B3
Fermor Rd SE23 163 A3
Fermoy Rd
Greenford UB6 85 D3
West Kilburn W9 91 B3
Fern Ave CR4 203 D5
Fernbank IG9 21 B3
Fernbank Ave
Walton-on-T KT12 195 A2
Wembley HA0 64 D3
Fernbank Mews SW12 159 C5
Fernbrook Cres SE13 164 C5
Fernbrook Dr HA2 41 D2
Fernbrook Rd SE13 164 C5
Fern Cl 3 N1 95 C5
Ferncliff Rd E8 74 A3
Ferncroft Ave
London N12 30 D4
Ruislip HA4 62 C6
West Hampstead NW3 69 C4
Fern Ct
Bexleyheath DA7 147 C1
Chingford E4 36 A4
New Cross Gate SE14 140 D3
Ferndale BR1 187 C1
Ferndale Ave
Hounslow TW4 129 A2
Walthamstow E17 54 B4
Ferndale Cl DA7 147 A4
Ferndale Ct 3 SE3 142 D5
Ferndale Ho N16 51 B1
Ferndale Rd
Ashford TW15 170 A5
Brixton SW4, SW9 138 B1
Croydon SE25 206 B4
Enfield EN3 7 A6
Leyton E11 76 D6
South Tottenham N15 51 D4
Upton E7 77 B1
Ferndale St E6 100 D1
Ferndale Way BR6 227 B3
Ferndene NW9 45 A4
Fern Dene W13 87 B2
Ferndene Rd SE24 139 A1
Fernden Way RM7 59 D3
Ferndown
5 Kingston u T KT6 198 A4
Pinner HA6 22 A1
7 Wanstead E18 55 A6
Ferndown Ave BR6 211 B1
Ferndown Cl
Pinner HA5 23 A3
Sutton SM2 218 B2
Ferndown Ct 6 UB1 86 A1
Ferndown Lo 17 E14 120 A3
Ferndown Rd
Eltham SE9 165 D4
South Oxhey WD19 22 C6
Ferney Meade Way TW7 131 A3
Ferney Rd EN4 15 A3
Fern Gr TW14 150 B4
Fernhall N12 30 C5
Fernhall Dr IG4 55 D4
Fernham Rd CR7 205 A6
Fernhead 12 SM1 218 A4
Fernhead Rd W9 91 B4
Fernhill Ct
Chingford E17 36 B1
Kingston u T KT2 175 D5
Fernhill Gdns KT2 176 A5
Fernhill Ho E5 74 A6
Fern Hill Pl 3 BR6 227 A3
Fern Hill Prim Sch KT2 176 A4
Fernhill St E16 122 B5
Fern Ho HA7 24 D4
Fernholme Rd SE15 162 D6
Fernhurst Gdns HA8 26 C4
Fernhurst Rd
Ashford TW15 171 A6
Croydon CR0 206 B1
Fulham SW6 135 A4 264 B2
Fernie Ho SE22 139 D2
Fern La TW5 107 B1
Fernlea Ho NW10 88 B4
Fernlea Rd
Balham SW12 159 B3
Mitcham CR4 181 A2
Fernleigh Cl
Croydon CR0 220 C4
West Kilburn W9 91 B4
Fernleigh Ct
Harrow HA2 23 D1
Wembley HA9 44 A1
Fernleigh Rd N21 16 D2
Fern Lo 13 SW16 182 C5
Fernly Cl HA5 40 A5
Fernsbury St WC1 234 A1
Fernshaw Mans SW10 266 A5
Fernshaw Rd SW10 136 A6 266 A5
Fernside
Buckhurst Hill IG9 21 B3
Golders Green NW11 47 C1
Fernside Ave
Edgware NW7 11 B1
Feltham TW13 172 B6
Fernside Ct NW4 28 D1
Fernside Rd SW12 159 A4
Ferns Rd E15 76 D2
Fern St E3 97 C3
Fernthorpe Rd SW16 181 C4
Ferntower Rd N5 73 B3
Fernways IG1 78 D4
Fern Wlk 18 SE16 118 A1
Fernwood
Wandsworth SW19 157 B3
Wood Green N22 32 A3
Fernwood Ave
Streatham SW16 181 D6
Fernwood Ave *continued*
Wembley HA0 65 C2
Fernwood Cl BR1 187 C1
Fernwood Cres N20 14 D1
Fernwood Ct N14 15 D3
Ferny Hill EN4 3 A5
Ferranti Cl SE18 121 D3
Ferraro Cl TW5 129 C6
Ferrers Ave
Wallington SM6 219 D4
West Drayton UB7 104 A4
Ferrers Rd SW16 181 D5
Ferrestone Rd N8 50 B5
Ferrey Mews 19 SW9 138 C3
Ferriby Cl N1 72 C1
Ferrier Ind Est SW18 135 D1
Ferrier Point 6 E16 99 A2
Ferrier St SW18 135 D1
Ferring Cl HA2 42 A1
Ferrings SE21 161 C1
Ferris Ave CR0 223 B5
Ferris Rd SE22 140 A1
Ferron Rd E5 74 B5
Ferrour Ct N2 48 B6
Ferrybridge Ho SE11 260 D5
Ferrydale Lo 4 NW4 46 C5
Ferry Ho E5 52 B1
Ferry Island Ret Pk N17 52 A6
Ferry La Barnes SW13 133 D6
Brentford TW8 132 A6
Lower Halliford TW17 192 C1
Richmond TW9 132 B6
Tottenham Hale N17 52 B5
Ferry Lane Ind Est E17 52 D5
Ferry Lane Prim Sch N17 52 B5
Ferrymead Ave UB6 85 C5
Ferrymead Dr UB6 85 C5
Ferrymead Gdns UB6 86 A5
Ferrymoor TW10 153 B1
Ferry Quays Ctyd 13 TW8 131 D6
Ferry Rd Barnes SW13 134 A4
East Molesey KT8 195 C6
Richmond TW11 175 B5
Thames Ditton KT7 197 B3
Twickenham TW1 153 B3
Ferry Sq
1 Brentford TW8 132 A6
Lower Halliford TW17 192 D2
Ferry St E14 120 A1
Ferry Wks TW17 192 C1
Festing Rd SW15 134 D2
Festival Cl
Hillingdon UB10 82 D6
Sidcup DA5 168 D3
Festival Ct Cheam SM1 201 D1
5 Dalston E8 73 D1
Festival Pier SE1 116 B5 250 C4
Festival Pleasure Gdns SW11 136 D5 267 C3
Festoon Way E16 121 D6
Fetherston Ct RM6 59 B3
Fetter La EC4 94 C1 241 B2
Fettes Ho NW8 229 D3
Fews Lodge RM6 58 D5
Ffinch St SE8 141 C5
Fidgeon Cl BR1 210 C6
Field Cl Bromley BR1 187 C1
Buckhurst Hill IG9 21 C1
Chessington KT9 213 C3
Chingford E4 35 D4
Cranford TW4 128 B4
East Molesey KT8 195 D4
Harlington UB7 127 A5
Ruislip HA4 39 A1
Uxbridge UB10 60 D6
Willesden NW2 68 A6
Fieldcommon La KT12 195 B1
Field Ct Hampstead NW3 70 A3
Holborn WC1 240 D3
Lower Holloway N7 72 A3
Wimbledon SW19 157 C1
Fieldend TW11 174 D6
Field End HA4 62 C2
Field End Jun & Inf Schs HA4 62 D6
Fieldend Rd SW16 181 C2
Field End Rd HA5, HA4 40 C1
Fielders Cl 2 Enfield EN1 5 C1
Harrow HA2 42 A1
Fieldfare Rd SE28 124 C6
Fieldgate Mans 25 E1 96 A2
Fieldgate St E1 96 A2
Field Ho
4 Edmonton N9 34 A6
Kensal Green NW10 90 D4
8 Richmond TW10 153 C1
Fieldhouse Cl E18 37 B2
Fieldhouse Rd SW12 159 C3
Fielding Ave TW2 152 A1
Fielding Ho
Chiswick W4 133 C6
6 Kilburn NW6 91 C4
St John's Wood NW8 229 A6
Fielding Mews SW13 134 B6
Fielding Prim Sch W13 109 B3
Fielding Rd Acton W4 111 C3
Hammersmith W14 112 D3
Fielding St SE17 139 A6
Fieldings The SE23 162 C3
Fielding Terr W5 110 B6
Field La Brentford TW8 131 C5
Teddington TW11 175 A5

Field Lo NW10 . . . . .67 D2
Field Mead NW9, NW7 . . . .27 D3
Fieldpark Gdns CR0 . . . .207 A1
Field Pl KT3 . . . . .199 D3
Field Point E7 . . . . .77 A4
Field Rd Feltham TW14 . .150 B5
Forest Gate E7 . . . . .77 A4
Fulham W6 . . . 135 A6 **262** A6
Tottenham N17 . . . . .51 C6
Fieldsend Rd SM3 . . . . . .217 A3
Fields Est E8 . . . . .74 A1
Fieldside Cl BR6 . . . . .227 A4
Fieldside Rd BR1 . . . . . . .186 B5
Fields Park Cres RM6 . . . .58 D4
Field St WC1 . . . . **233** C2
Fieldsway Ho N5 . . . . .72 C3
Fieldview SW17, SW18 . .158 B3
Field View TW13 . . . . . . .171 B6
Field View RM7 . . . . .59 C6
Fieldview Ct
2 Islington N5 . . . . .72 C3
London NW9 . . . . .44 C3
Fieldway Dagenham RM8 .80 C4
Petts Wood BR5 . . . . . .211 B3
Field Way
Greenford UB6 . . . . . . .85 D6
New Addington CR0 . . . .223 D2
Ruislip HA4 . . . . .39 A1
Willesden NW10 . . . . . .67 A1
Fieldway Cres N5, N7 . . . .72 C3
Fieldway Sta CR0 . . . . . . .223 D1
Fieldwick Ho **14** E9 . . . . . . .74 D2
Fiennes Cl RM8 . . . . .58 C1
Fife Ct 5 W3 . . . . .88 C1
Fifehead Cl TW15 . . . . . .170 A4
Fife Rd
Kingston u T KT2 . . . . . .176 A1
Mortlake SW14 . . . . . . .155 A6
Newham E16 . . . . .99 A2
Tottenham N22 . . . . . . .32 D3
Fife Terr N1 . . . . **233** D4
Fifield Path SE23 . . . . . . .162 D1
Fifteenpenny Fields
SE9 . . . . .166 C6
Fifth Ave Hayes UB3 . . . .105 D5
Ilford E12 . . . . .78 B4
West Kilburn W10 . . . . .91 A4
Fifth Cross Rd TW2 . . . . .152 B2
Fifth Way HA9 . . . . .66 D4
Figge's Rd CR4 . . . . .181 A3
Fig Tree Cl NW10 . . . . . . .89 C6
Filanco Ct W7 . . . . .108 D5
Filby Rd KT9 . . . . .214 B2
Filey Ave N16 . . . . .52 A1
Filey Cl SM2 . . . . .218 A1
Filey Ho SW18 . . . . .136 A1
Filey Waye HA4 . . . . .62 B6
Filigree Ct SE16 . . . . .119 B5
Fillebrook Ave EN1 . . . . . . .5 D3
Fillebrook Rd E11 . . . . . . .54 C1
Filmer Ho SW6 . . . . **264** B2
Filmer Mews SW6 . . . . **264** B2
Filmer Rd SW6 . .135 B5 **264** C3
Filston Rd DA8 . . . . .125 D1
Filton Cl E14 . . . . .140 C5
Finborough Rd
Upper Tooting SW17 . . .180 D4
West Brompton
SW10 . . . . . .135 D6 **265** D6
Finchale Rd SE2 . . . . .124 A3
Fincham Cl UB10 . . . . .61 A5
Finch Ave SE27 . . . . .183 B6
Finch Cl Barnet EN5 . . . . .13 C6
Willesden NW10 . . . . . .67 B2
Finch Ct DA14 . . . . .168 B1
Finchdean Ho SW15 . . . .155 D4
Finch Dr TW14 . . . . .150 D4
Finch Gdns E4 . . . . .35 C5
Finch Ho **1** SE8 . . . . .141 D5
Finchingfield Ave IG8 . . . .37 C3
Finch La EC2, EC3 . . . . . **242** D1
FINCHLEY 29 D3
Finchley Cath High Sch
N12 . . . . .13 D1
Finchley Central Sta
N3 . . . . .29 C2
Finchley Ct N3 . . . . .29 D4
Finchley La NW4 . . . . .46 D5
Finchley Lo N12 . . . . .29 D5
Finchley Meml Hospl
N12 . . . . .30 A3
Finchley Pk N12 . . . . .30 B6
Finchley Pl NW8 . . . . . . **229** C4
Finchley Rd
Hampstead NW3 . . . . . .70 A2
London NW11 . . . . .47 B3
St John's Wood NW8 . **229** C4
Finchley Road & Frognal
Sta NW3 . . . . .70 A3
Finchley Road Sta
NW3 . . . . .70 A2
Finchley Way N3 . . . . .29 C3
Finch Lo **15** W9 . . . . .91 C2
Finch Mews **3** SE15 . . . .139 D4
Finch's Ct **10** E14 . . . . . .119 D6
Finden Rd E7 . . . . .77 C3
Findhorn Ave UB4 . . . . . . .84 B2
Findhorn St **8** E14 . . . . . .98 A1
Findon Cl Harrow HA2 . . . .63 D5
Wandsworth SW18 . . . .157 C5
Findon Rd Edmonton N9 . .18 B3
Shepherd's Bush W12 . .112 A4
Fine Bush La HA4 . . . . .38 D3
Fineran Ct **8** SW11 . . . . .136 B1
Fingal St SE10 . . . . .120 D1
Fingest Ho NW8 . . . . . **237** A6

Finians Cl UB10 . . . . .60 B1
Finland Rd SE4 . . . . .141 A2
Finland St SE16 . . . . .119 A3
Finlays Cl KT9 . . . . .214 C3
Finlay St SW6 . . . . .134 D4
Finley Ct **21** SE5 . . . . . . .139 A5
Finmere Ho **1** N4 . . . . . . .51 A2
Finnemore Ho N1 . . . . . **235** A6
Finney La TW7 . . . . .131 A4
Finn Ho N1 . . . . **235** D2
Finnis St E2 . . . . .96 B3
Finnymore Rd RM9 . . . . . .81 A1
FINSBURY 94 C4
Finsbury Ave EC2 . . . . . **242** D3
Finsbury Cir
EC2 . . . . .95 B2 **242** D3
Finsbury Coll N4 . . . . .72 C6
Finsbury Cotts N22 . . . . . .32 A3
Finsbury Ct EC2 . . . . . . **242** C4
Finsbury Ho N22 . . . . .32 A2
Finsbury Market EC2 . . . **243** A4
Finsbury Mkt EC2 . . . . . **243** A5
FINSBURY PARK 72 C6
Finsbury Park Ave N4 . . . .51 A3
Finsbury Park Rd N4,
N5 . . . . .72 D6
Finsbury Park Sta N4 . . . .72 C6
Finsbury Pavement
EC2 . . . . .95 B2 **242** D4
Finsbury Rd N22 . . . . .32 B2
Finsbury Sq EC2 .95 B2 **242** D4
Finsbury St EC2 . . . . . . **242** C4
Finsbury Way DA5 . . . . . .169 B5
Finsen Rd SE5 . . . . .139 A2
Finstock Rd W10 . . . . .90 D1
Finton House Sch
SW17 . . . . .158 D2
Finucane Ct TW9 . . . . . . .132 B2
Finucane Rise WD23 . . . . . .8 A2
Finwhale Ho E14 . . . . . . .119 D3
Fiona Ct Enfield EN2 . . . . . .4 D2
9 Kilburn NW6 . . . . . . .91 B5
Firbank Cl Enfield EN2 . . . . .5 A1
Newham E16 . . . . .99 D2
Firbank Rd SE15 . . . . . . .140 B3
Fir Cl KT12 . . . . .194 A2
Fircroft N1 . . . .94 D6 **234** D6
Fircroft Gdns HA1 . . . . . . .64 C5
Fircroft Prim Sch
SW17 . . . . .158 D1
Fircroft Rd
Chessington KT9 . . . . . .214 B4
Upper Tooting SW17 . . .158 D1
Firdene KT5 . . . . .199 A1
Fir Dene BR6 . . . . .226 C5
Fire Bell Alley KT6 . . . . . .198 A3
Firebell Mews KT6 . . . . . .198 A3
Fire Brigade Cotts HA5. . . .41 C5
Fire Brigade Pier SE1 . . . **260** B4
Firecrest Dr NW3 . . . . .69 D5
Firefly **7** NW9 . . . . .27 D1
Firefly Gdns E6 . . . . .100 A3
Firemans Cotts N10 . . . . . .49 A6
Fireman's Flats N22 . . . .32 A2
Fireman's Firepower (The Royal
Artillery Mus)*
SE18 . . . . .122 D3
Fire Station Alley EN5 . . . . .1 A3
Fire Station Flats
TW7 . . . . .130 C3
Fire Station Mews 4
BR3 . . . . .185 D2
Firethorn Cl **4** HA8 . . . . . .27 A6
Fir Gr KT3 . . . . .199 D3
Fir Grove Rd **23** SW9 . . . .138 C3
Firhill Rd SE6 . . . . .163 C1
Fir Island NW7 . . . . .28 C5
Firle Ho **7** W10 . . . . .90 C2
Fir Lo SW15 . . . . .134 B1
Firmans Ct E17 . . . . .54 B5
Firmston Ho **9** SW14 . . . .133 B2
Fir Rd Cheam SM3 . . . . . .201 B4
Feltham TW13 . . . . .172 D5
Firs Ave
Fortis Green N10 . . . . . .49 A5
Friern Barnet N11 . . . . . .31 A4
Mortlake SW14 . . . . . . .133 A1
Firsby Ave CR0 . . . . .207 A1
Firsby Rd N16 . . . . .52 A1
Firs Cl Claygate KT10 . . . .212 C2
Forest Hill SE23 . . . . . .163 A4
Mitcham CR4 . . . . .181 B2
Muswell Hill N10 . . . . . .49 A6
Firscroft N13 . . . . .17 A1
Firs Dr TW5 . . . . .128 B5
Firs Farm Prim Sch
N13 . . . . .17 B1
Firs Ho N22 . . . . .32 C2
Firside Gr DA15 . . . . .167 D3
Firs La N21, N13 . . . . .17 A2
Firs Park Ave N21 . . . . . . .17 B3
Firs Park Gdns N21 . . . . . .17 B3
First Ave Bexley DA7 . . . .146 C5
Chadwell Heath RM6 . . . .58 C4
Dagenham RM10 . . . . .103 D5
East Acton W3 . . . . . . .111 D5
East Molesey KT8 . . . . .195 C5
Edmonton N18 . . . . .34 C6
Enfield EN1 . . . . .17 D1
Hayes UB3 . . . . .105 D5
Hendon NW4 . . . . .46 C5
Manor Pk E12 . . . . .78 A4
Mortlake SW14 . . . . . . .133 C2
Newham E13 . . . . .99 A4
Walthamstow E17 . . . . . .53 D4
Walton-on-T KT12 . . . .194 B3
Wembley HA9 . . . . .65 D6
West Kilburn W10 . . . . .91 B3
First Cl KT8 . . . . .196 A6
First Cross Rd TW2 . . . . .152 C2

First Dr NW10 . . . . .67 A1
Firs The Belmont SM2 . . .217 D1
Claygate KT10 . . . . . . .212 C2
Ealing W5 . . . . .87 D2
Forest Hill SE26 . . . . . .184 C5
Oakleigh Pk N20 . . . . . .14 B3
2 Penge SE26 . . . . . . .184 B5
Sidcup DA15 . . . . .167 D1
Upton Pk E6 . . . . .78 A1
Wimbledon SW20 . . . . .178 A3
Woodford IG8 . . . . .37 C3
First St SW3 . . . .114 C2 **257** B4
Firstway SW20 . . . . .178 C1
First Way HA9 . . . . .66 D4
Firs Wlk IG8 . . . . .37 A5
Firswood Ave KT19 . . . . .215 D3
Firth Gdns
SW6 . . . . .135 A4 **264** A5
Firtree Ave CR4 . . . . .181 A1
Fir Tree Ave SE7 . . . . . . .104 C3
Fir Tree Cl Ealing W5 . . . . .88 A1
Esher KT10 . . . . .212 A3
5 Orpington BR6 . . . . .227 D3
Streatham SW16 . . . . .181 C5
Worcester Pk KT19 . . . .215 D4
Fir Tree Gdns CR0 . . . . . .223 C4
Fir Tree Gr SM5 . . . . .218 D1
Firtree Ho SE13 . . . . .164 B4
Fir Tree Ho **11** SE14 . . . .140 C5
Firtree Lodge N21 . . . . . . .17 A2
Fir Tree Rd TW4 . . . . .129 A1
Fir Trees Cl SE16 . . . . . . .119 A5
Fir Tree Wlk EN1 . . . . .5 B2
Fir Wlk KT17, SM3 . . . . . .216 D2
Fisher Cl Croydon CR0 . . .205 D1
Holdbrook EN3 . . . . .7 C6
Southall UB1 . . . . .85 C4
Fisherdene KT10 . . . . . . .213 A1
Fisher Ho Islington N1 . **234** A5
1 Shadwell E1 . . . . . . .118 C6
2 Tufnell Pk N19 . . . . . .71 C5
Fisherman Cl TW10 . . . . .175 C6
Fishermans Dr SE16 . . . . .118 D4
Fishermans Wlk SE28 . . .123 C4
Fisherman's Wlk E14 . . . .119 C5
Fisher Rd HA3 . . . . .24 D1
Fishers Cl SW16 . . . . .159 D1
Fishers Ct London SE14 . .140 D4
6 Teddington TW11 . . .174 D5
Fisher's La W4 . . . . .111 B2
Fisher St Holborn WC1 . **240** C3
Newham E16 . . . . .99 A2
Fisherton St
NW8 . . . . .92 B3 **236** D6
Fisherton Street Est
NW8 . . . . .92 B3 **236** D5
Fishguard Way E16 . . . . .122 D5
Fishlock Ct **6** SW4 . . . . .138 A3
Fishponds Rd
Keston BR2 . . . . .225 D3
Upper Tooting SW17 . . .180 C6
Fish St Hill EC3 . . . . . . **252** D5
Fisk Cl TW16 . . . . .171 D4
Fiske Ct Barking IG11 . . . .101 B5
1 Merton SW19 . . . . . .180 A3
Sutton SM2 . . . . .218 A1
Tottenham N17 . . . . . . .34 A2
Fitch Ct London SW2 . . . .160 C6
8 Mitcham CR4 . . . . . .181 A1
Fitzalan Rd
Church End N3 . . . . .47 B6
Claygate KT10 . . . . . . .212 C1
Fitzalan St
SE11 . . . . . . .116 C2 **261** A4
Fitzclarence Ho **11** . . . **244** A2
Fitzgeorge Ave KT2,
KT3 . . . . .177 B2
Fitz-George Ave W14 . . **254** A3
Fitzgerald Ave SW14 . . . .133 C2
Fitzgerald Ct **1** E10 . . . . .53 D1
Fitzgerald Ho
15 Brixton SW9 . . . . . .138 C3
Hayes UB3 . . . . .106 A5
14 Poplar E14 . . . . . . .97 D1
Fitzgerald Rd
Mortlake SW14 . . . . . . .133 B2
Thames Ditton KT7 . . . .197 A3
Wanstead E11 . . . . .55 A4
Fitzhardinge Ho
Beckenham BR3 . . . . . .185 D1
Marylebone W1 . . . . . **238** A2
Fitzhardinge St W1 . . . **238** A2
Fitzherbert Ho 11
TW10 . . . . .154 B5
Fitzhugh Gr SW18 . . . . . .158 B5
Fitzjames Ave
Croydon CR0 . . . . .222 A6
West Kensington W14 . **254** B3
Fitzjohn Ave EN5 . . . . .1 B1
Fitzjohn's Ave NW3 . . . . . .70 B3
Fitzjohns Mans NW3 . . . . .70 A2
Fitzjohns Prim Sch
NW3 . . . . .70 B3
Fitzmaurice Ho 17
SE16 . . . . .118 B2
Fitzmaurice Pl W1 . . . . **248** A4
Fitzneal St W12 . . . . .89 D1
FITZROVIA 93 C2
Fitzroy Cl N6 . . . . .48 D1
Fitzroy Cres W4 . . . . .133 B5
Fitzroy Ct London N6 . . . . .49 C3
Marylebone W1 . . . . . **239** B5
Fitzroy Gdns SE19 . . . . . .183 C3
Fitzroy Ho
Bermondsey SE1 . . . . . **263** D2
12 Tower Hamlets E14 . . .97 B1
Fitzroy Lo N21 . . . . .16 D6
Fitzroy Mews W1 . . . . . **239** A5
Fitzroy Pk N6 . . . . .48 D1

Fitzroy Rd NW1. .93 A6 **231** A6
Fitzroy Sq W1 . . . . **239** A5
Fitzroy St W1 . . .93 C3 **239** A5
Fitzroy Yd NW1 . . . . **231** A6
Fitzstephen Rd RM8 . . . . .80 C3
Fitzwarren Gdns N19 . . . . .49 C1
Fitzwilliam Ave TW9 . . . .132 B3
Fitzwilliam Ho
4 Higham Hill E17 . . . . .35 A1
Richmond TW9 . . . . . . .131 D1
Fitzwilliam Hts 1
SE23 . . . . .162 C2
Fitzwilliam Mews E16. . . .121 A5
Fitzwilliam Rd SW4 . . . . .137 C2
Fitzwygram Cl TW12 . . . .174 A5
Five Acre NW9 . . . . .27 D1
Fiveacre Cl CR7 . . . . .204 C3
Five Arch Bridge
DA14 . . . . .191 A6
Five Arches Bsns Pk
DA14 . . . . .190 D4
Five Elms Prim Sch
RM8 . . . . .81 B5
Five Elms Rd
Dagenham RM9 . . . . . . .81 B5
Keston Mark BR2 . . . . .225 C5
Five Oaks Mews BR1. . . . .165 A1
Fives Ct SE11 . . . . **261** C5
Fiveways
Chislehurst SE9 . . . . . .166 D2
Croydon CR0 . . . . .220 C4
Ruislip HA4 . . . . .39 B1
Fiveways Rd SW9 . . . . . .138 C3
Five Ways Cnr NW4 . . . . . .28 A2
Five Ways Cnr NW4 . . . . . .28 A2
Flack Ct **15** E10 . . . . .53 D2
Fladbury Rd N15 . . . . .51 B3
Fladgate Rd E11 . . . . .54 C3
Flag Cl CR0 . . . . .206 D1
Flag Wlk HA5 . . . . .40 A3
Flambard Rd HA1, HA3. . . .43 A3
Flamborough Ho 12
SE15 . . . . .140 A4
Flamborough Rd HA4 . . . . .62 A5
Flamborough St E14 . . . . .97 A1
Flamingo Ct **2** SE8 . . . . .141 C5
Flamingo Gdns UB5 . . . . . .85 A4
Flamstead Gdns RM9 . . . . .80 C1
Flamstead Rd RM9 . . . . . .80 C1
Flamsteed Ave HA9 . . . . . .66 C3
Flamsteed Ho **17** SE10 . . .143 D4
Flamsteed Rd SE7 . . . . . .122 A1
Flanchford Rd W12 . . . . . .111 D3
Flanders Cres SW17. . . . .180 D4
Flanders Ct E17 . . . . .53 A3
Flanders Ho N16 . . . . .73 C5
Flanders Mans **1** W4 . . .111 D2
Flanders Rd Acton W4 . . .111 C2
Wallend E6 . . . . .100 C5
Flanders Way E9 . . . . .74 D2
Flandrian Cl EN3 . . . . .7 D5
Flank St **1** E1 . . . . .118 A3
Flansham Ho **2** E14 . . . . .97 B1
Flash La EN2 . . . . .5 A4
Flask Cotts **4** NW3 . . . . . .70 B4
Flask Wlk NW3 . . . . .70 B4
Flatford Ho **2** SE6 . . . . . .186 A6
Flather Cl **12** SW16. . . . .181 C5
Flatiron Sq SE1 . . . . . . **252** B3
Flatiron Yd SE1 . . . . . . **252** B3
Flavell Mews SE10 . . . . . .120 C1
Flaxen Cl E4 . . . . .19 D1
Flaxen Rd E4 . . . . .19 D1
Flaxley Rd SM4 . . . . .201 D2
Flaxman Ct
12 Belvedere DA17. . . . .125 C1
Soho W1 . . . . **239** C1
Flaxman Ho
10 Chiswick W4 . . . . . .111 C1
Newington SE1 . . . . . **261** D6
Flaxman Rd SE5 . . . . . . .138 C3
Flaxman Terr
WC1 . . . . .93 D4 **232** D1
Flaxmore Cl Erith DA7 . . .147 D2
South Norwood CR7 . . .187 B1
Flaxton Rd SE18 . . . . . . .145 C5
Flecker Cl HA7 . . . . .24 D5
Flecker Ho **6** SE5 . . . . . .139 B5
Fleece Dr N9 . . . . .34 A4
Fleecefield Prim Sch
N18 . . . . .34 A6
Fleece Rd KT6 . . . . .197 C1
Fleece Wlk N7 . . . . .72 A2
Fleeming Cl E17 . . . . .35 B1
Fleeming Rd E17 . . . . .35 B1
Fleet Cl
East Molesey KT8 . . . . .195 B4
Ruislip HA4 . . . . .39 A3
Fleet Ct **1** W12. . . . . . . .111 C3
Fleetfield WC1 . . . . **233** B2
Fleet Ho
6 Brixton SW2 . . . . . .160 C6
4 Limehouse E14 . . . . .119 A6
Fleet Pl EC4 . . . . **241** C2
Fleet Prim Sch NW3 . . . . .70 D3
Fleet Rd NW3 . . . . .70 D3
Fleetside KT8 . . . . .195 C4
Fleet Sq WC1 . . . . **233** D1
Fleet St EC4 . . . .94 C1 **241** B1
Fleet Street Hill **10** E1. . . .96 A4
Fleet Terr 164 A4
Fleetway WC1 . . . . **233** B2
Fleetway West Bsns Pk
UB6 . . . . .87 B5
Fleet Wood **6** N16. . . . . . .73 D6
Fleetwood Cl
Chessington KT9 . . . . . .213 D1
Newham E16 . . . . .99 D1
South Croydon CR0 . . . .221 D5

Fleetwood Ct
1 Newham E6 . . . . . . .100 B2
Orpington BR6 . . . . . . .226 C4
8 Stanwell TW19 . . . . .148 A5
Fleetwood Rd
Kingston u T KT3 . . . . .198 D6
Willesden NW10 . . . . . .68 A3
Fleetwood Sq KT3 . . . . . .198 D6
Fleetwood St N16. . . . . . . .73 C6
Fleetwood Way WD19. . . . .22 C6
Fleming Cl **4** W9 . . . . . . .91 C3
Fleming Ct
Croydon CR0 . . . . .220 C3
Paddington W2 . . . . . **236** C4
Fleming Dr N21. . . . . .16 B6
Fleming Ho
14 Bermondsey SE16 . .118 A4
Finsbury Pk N4 . . . . . . .51 A1
5 Wembley HA9 . . . . . .67 A5
Fleming Mead CR4. . . . . .180 D3
Camberwell SE17 . . . . .138 D6
Southall UB1 . . . . .86 A1
Fleming Way
Isleworth TW7 . . . . . . .130 D1
Thamesmead SE28 . . . .124 D6
Fleming Wlk NW9 . . . . . . .27 C1
Flemming Ave HA4 . . . . . .62 B6
Flempton Rd E10 . . . . .53 A1
Fletcher Bldgs WC2. . . . **240** B1
Fletcher Cl E16 . . . . .122 D6
Fletcher Ct **9** NW5 . . . . . .71 B4
Fletcher Ho **16** N16 . . . . . .73 C4
Fletcher La E10 . . . . .54 A2
Fletcher Path **7** SE8. . . . .141 C5
Fletcher Rd W4 . . . . .111 A3
Fletchers Cl BR2. . . . . . . .209 B5
Fletcher St **16** E1 . . . . . . .118 A6
Fletching Rd
Charlton SE7 . . . . .143 D6
Lower Clapton E5 . . . . . .74 C5
Fletton Rd N11 . . . . .32 A3
Fleur De Lis St E1 . . . . **243** C5
Fleur Gates **7** SW19 . . . .156 D4
Flexmere Rd N17 . . . . .33 C2
Flimwell Cl BR1 . . . . .186 C5
Flinders Ho **28** E1. . . . . . .118 B5
Flint Cl
8 Green Street Green
BR6 . . . . .227 D2
1 Stratford E15. . . . . . . .76 D1
Flint Ct CR0 . . . . .204 B3
Flint Down Cl BR5 . . . . . .190 A2
Flintmill Cres SE3, SE9. . .144 A3
Flinton St SE17 . .117 C2 **263** B2
Flint St SE17. . . .117 B2 **262** D3
Flitcroft St WC2 . . . . . . **239** D1
Flitton Ho **7** N1 . . . . .72 D1
Floathaven Cl SE28 . . . . .124 A5
Flock Mill Pl SW18. . . . . .157 D3
Flockton St
20 Bermondsey SE16 . .118 A4
2 Bermondsey SE16 . . .118 A4
Flodden Rd SE5. . . . . . . .139 A4
Flood La **5** TW1. . . . . . . .153 A3
Flood St SW3 . . .136 C6 **267** B6
Flood Wlk
SW3. . . . . . . .136 C6 **267** B6
Flora Cl E14 . . . . .97 D1
Flora Gardens Prim Sch
W6 . . . . .112 B2
Flora Gdns
Dagenham RM6. . . . . . . .58 C3
2 Hammersmith W6 . . .112 B2
Floral St WC2. . .116 A6 **250** A6
Flora St DA17. . . . . .125 B1
Florence Ave Enfield EN2. . .5 A2
Morden SM4 . . . . .202 A4
Florence Cl KT12 . . . . . . .194 B2
Florence Ct
18 New Barnet EN5 . . . .13 D6
St John's Wood W9 . . **229** B1
Wanstead E11. . . . . .55 C5
5 Wimbledon SW19 . . .179 A4
Florence Dr EN2 . . . . .5 A2
Florence Elson Cl E12. . . . .78 C4
Florence Gdns
Chiswick W4 . . . . .133 A6
Ilford RM6. . . . . .58 C2
Florence Ho
20 Bermondsey SE16 . .118 B1
2 Brixton SW2 . . . . . . .160 B6
Kidbrooke SE18. . . . . . .144 B4
10 Kingston u T KT2 . . .176 B3
10 Shepherd's Bush
W11 . . . . .112 D6
7 Wandsworth SW18 . .136 B1
Florence Mans
Fulham SW6 . . . . **264** C2
4 Hendon NW4 . . . . . . .46 B4
Florence Nightingale Ho
14 N1 . . . . .73 A2
Florence Nightingale
Mus* SE1 . . . . **250** D1
Florence Rd
Abbey Wood SE2 . . . . .124 C2
Acton W4. . . . . .111 B3
5 Beckenham BR3. . . . .185 A1
Bromley BR1. . . . . .187 A2
Ealing W5 . . . . .110 A6
Feltham TW13 . . . . . . .150 B3
Finsbury Pk N4 . . . . . . .50 C2
6 Kingston u T KT2 . . .176 B3
New Cross Gate SE14. . .141 B4
Southall UB2 . . . . .106 D3
7 Upton Pk E6 . . . . .99 C6
Walton-on-T KT12. . . . .194 B2
West Ham E13 . . . . .99 A5
Wimbledon SW19 . . . .179 D4

Florence Root Ho 3
IG4 . . . . .56 B4
Florence St Islington N1. . .72 C1
London NW4 . . . . .46 C5
Newham E16 . . . . .98 D3
Florence Terr
Kingston u T SW15 . . . .155 C1
New Cross Gate SE14. . .141 B4
Florence Way SW12. . . . .158 D3
Florence White Ct **9** 18 B1
Florentine Ho **3** IG1. . . . . .78 D6
Flores Ho **13** E1. . . . . .96 D2
Florey Sq N21 . . . . .16 B6
Florfield Rd E8 . . . . .74 B2
Florian Ct SE5 . . . . .139 C4
Florian Ave SM1 . . . . .218 B4
Florian Rd SW15 . . . . . . .135 A1
Florida Cl WD23 . . . . .8 B2
Florida Ct BR2. . . . . .208 D5
Florida Rd CR7 . . . . .182 D2
Florida St E2 . . . . .96 A4
Florida State Univ
WC1. . . . . .93 D2 **239** D3
Florin Ct
Bermondsey SE1 . . . . **253** C1
Edmonton N18. . . . . . . .33 C6
8 St George in t East
SE1. . . . . .118 A6
Floris Pl **7** SW4 . . . . . . .137 C2
Floriston Ave UB10 . . . . . .61 A1
Floriston Cl HA7. . . . . .25 B2
Floriston Ct UB5. . . . . .63 D3
Floriston Gdns HA7 . . . . . .25 B2
Florys Ct **7** SW19. . . . . .157 A3
Floss St SW15 . . . . .134 C3
Flower & Dean Wlk
E1. . . . . **243** D3
Flower La NW7 . . . . .27 D4
Flower Mews NW11. . . . . .47 A3
Flower Pot Cl N15 . . . . . . .51 D3
Flowers Cl NW2 . . . . .68 A5
Flowersmead SW17. . . . .159 A2
Flowers Mews **1** N19. . . . .71 C6
Flower Wlk The
SW7. . . . . . . .114 A4 **246** B2
Floyd Rd SE7 . . . . .121 C1
Floyer Cl TW10 . . . . .154 B6
Fludyer St SE13. . . . . . . .142 C1
Flynn Ct **19** E14. . . . . . . .119 C3
Fogerty Cl EN3 . . . . .7 D6
Foley Cotts KT10. . . . . . .212 D2
Foley Ct N12 . . . . .30 A5
Foley Ho **19** E1 . . . . .96 C1
Foley Mews KT10 . . . . . .212 C2
Foley Rd KT10 . . . . .212 C1
Foley St W1 . . . .93 C2 **239** A3
Folgate St E1 . . .95 D2 **243** C4
Foliot Ho N1 . . . . **233** C4
Foliot St W12. . . . . .89 D1
Folkestone Ct UB5 . . . . . . .63 D3
Folkestone Rd
Edmonton N18. . . . . . . .34 A4
Wallend E6 . . . . .100 C4
Walthamstow E17. . . . . .53 D5
Folkingham La **6** NW9 . . .27 C2
Folkington Cnr N12 . . . . . .29 B5
Folland **6** NW9. . . . . .27 D1
Follett Ho SW10 . . . . . . **266** C4
Follett St E14. . . . . .98 A1
Folly La Higham Hill E17 . .35 A4
Walthamstow E4 . . . . . . .35 B3
Folly Wall E14. . . . . .120 A4
Fonda Ct **14** E14 . . . . . . .119 C6
Fontaine Ct
3 Beckenham BR3. . . . .185 B2
Southgate N14 . . . . . . .15 C3
Fontaine Rd SW16 . . . . . .182 B3
Fontarabia Rd SW11 . . . .137 A1
Fontenelle SE5. . . . . .139 C4
Fontenoy Ho SE11 . . . . **261** C3
Fontenoy Rd SW12,
SW17 . . . . .159 C2
Fonteyne Gdns IG8 . . . . . .37 D1
Fonthill Cl SE20. . . . . . . .184 A1
Fonthill Ct SE23 . . . . . . .162 C4
Fonthill Ho
Kensington W14 . . . . **254** B6
Pimlico SW1 . . . . **258** D2
Fonthill Mews N4. . . . . . . .72 B6
Fonthill Rd N4. . . . . .72 C6
Font Hills N2 . . . . .30 A1
Fontley Way SW15 . . . . .156 A4
Fontmell Cl TW15. . . . . . .170 C5
Fontmell Pk TW15 . . . . . .170 C5
Fontwell Cl Harrow HA3. . .24 C3
Northolt UB5 . . . . .63 C2
Fontwell Dr BR2. . . . . . . .210 C4
Football La HA1 . . . . .42 C1
Footpath The SW15. . . . .156 A6
FOOTS CRAY 190 B4
Foots Cray High St
DA14. . . . . .190 D4
Foots Cray La DA14. . . . .168 C3
Footscray Rd SE9 . . . . . .166 C4
Forber Ho **25** E2 . . . . .96 C4
Forbes Cl NW2 . . . . .68 A5
Forbes Ct SE19 . . . . .183 C5
Forbes Ho **2** W4. . . . . . .110 C1
Forbes St **1** E1. . . . . .96 A1
Forbes Way HA4 . . . . .62 B6
Forburg Rd N16 . . . . .52 A1
Fordbridge Ct TW15 . . . .170 A4
Fordbridge Rd
Ashford TW15. . . . . . . .170 B5
Lower Halliford TW16,
TW17 . . . . .193 D3
Sunbury TW16. . . . . . . .194 A5
Fordbridge Rdbt
TW15. . . . . .170 A4
Ford Cl Ashford TW15 . . .170 A4

Ford Cl *continued*
12 Bow E3 97 A5
Harrow HA1 42 B2
Littleton TW17 192 C4
Thornton Heath CR7 204 D4
Fordcombe 13 NW5 71 A2
Forde Ave BR1 209 C6
Fordel Rd SE6 164 B3
Ford End IG8 37 B4
Fordham 4 KT1 176 C1
Fordham Cl EN4 2 C2
Fordham Ho 11 SE14 141 A5
Fordham Rd EN4 2 C2
Fordham St 13 E1 96 A1
Ford Ho
2 New Barnet EN5 13 D6
2 Woolwich SE18 122 D1
Fordhook Ave W5 110 C6
Fordingley Rd W9 91 B4
Fordington Ho 2
SE26 162 B1
Fordington Rd N6 48 D5
Fordmill Rd SE6 163 C2
Ford Rd Ashford TW15 170 B6
Bow E3 97 B5
Dagenham RM10 81 C1
Ford's Gr N21 17 A3
Fords Park Rd E16 99 A1
Ford Sq E1 96 B2
Ford St Bow E3 97 A5
Canning Town E16 98 D1
Fordwich Cl BR6 211 D2
Fordwych Ct NW2 69 A2
Fordwych Rd NW2 69 A3
Fordyce Ho 3 SW16 181 C6
Fordyce Rd SE13 164 A6
Fordyke Rd RM8 81 B6
Forecastle Ct E14 119 C4
Foreign, Commonwealth & Home Offices SW1 250 A2
Foreland Ct NW4 29 A2
Foreland Ho W11 244 A6
Foreland St SE18 123 B2
Foreshore SE8 119 B2
Fore St
Barbican EC2 95 A2 242 B3
Edmonton N18 34 A6
Pinner HA5 40 A4
Forest App Chingford E4 20 C4
Woodford IG8 37 A3
Forest Ave E4 20 C4
Forest Bsns Pk E17 52 D2
Forest Cl
Brondesbury NW6 69 A1
Chislehurst BR7 188 C2
Wanstead E11 55 A4
Woodford IG8 37 B6
Forest Croft SE23 162 B2
Forest Ct Chingford E4 20 D3
Leytonstone E11 54 C5
14 Woodside Pk N12 29 D6
Forestdale N14 31 D6
Forestdale Ctr The
CR0 223 B1
Forest Dene Ct 2
SM2 218 A2
Forest Dr
Ashford TW16 171 D3
Chingford IG8 36 C3
Keston Mark BR2 226 A4
Wanstead E12 77 D5
Forest Dr E E11 54 B3
Forest Dr W E11 54 B2
Forest Edge IG9 21 D1
Forester Rd SE15 140 B2
Foresters Cl SM6 219 D1
Foresters Cres DA7 147 D1
Foresters Dr
Wallington SM6 219 D1
Walthamstow E17 54 B5
Foresters Homes The
DA7 147 D1
Foresters Prim Sch
SM6 219 D1
FOREST GATE 77 A3
Forest Gate NW9 45 C4
Forest Gate Com Sch
E7 77 A3
Forest Gate Sta E7 77 A3
Forest Gdns N17 33 D1
Forest Glade
Chingford E4 36 C5
Leytonstone E11 54 C3
Forest Gr E8 73 D2
FOREST HILL 163 A3
Forest Hill SE23 162 C3
Forest Hill Bsns Ctr
SE23 162 C2
Forest Hill Ct 6 SE26 162 B1
Forest Hill Ind Est
SE23 162 C2
Forest Hill Rd SE22 162 B5
Forest Hill Sec Sch
SE23 162 D1
Forest Hill Sta SE23 162 C2
Forest Ho 9 E4 20 C4
Forestholme Cl SE23 162 C2
Forest Ho The SE23 163 A3
Forest Hts IG9 21 A2
Forest La E7, E15 76 D3
Forest Lawns BR1 187 C2
Forest Lea 3 E11 54 D2
Forest Lo 1 SE23 162 C1
Forest Mount Rd IG8 36 B3
Forest Point E7 77 B3
Forest Rd Dalston E8 73 D2
Edmonton N9 18 B3
Feltham TW13 150 C1
Forest Gate E7 77 A4
Leytonstone E11 54 B2

Forest Rd *continued*
Morden SM3, SM4 201 C2
Richmond TW9 132 C5
Romford RM7 59 D6
Walthamstow E17 53 C6
Woodford IG8 21 A1
Fore Street Ave EC2 242 C3
Forest Ridge
Beckenham BR3 207 C6
Bromley BR2 226 B4
Forest Rise E17 54 B5
Forest Sch E17 54 C5
Forest Side
Buckhurst Hill IG9 21 C3
Chingford E4 20 D3
Forest Gate E7 77 B4
New Malden KT4 199 D1
Forest St E7 77 A3
Forest The E11 54 C5
Forest Trad Est E17 52 D6
Forest View
Chingford E4 20 B4
Leytonstone E11 54 D2
Forest View Ave E10 54 B4
Forest View Rd
Chingford E17 36 A2
Manor Pk E12 78 A4
Forest Way
Orpington BR5 211 D4
Sidcup DA15 167 B4
9 Upper Holloway N19 71 C6
Woodford IG8 37 B6
Forest Wlk N10 31 B2
Forfar Rd
London
SW11 137 A4 268 B2
Tottenham N22 32 D2
Forge Cl
Harlington UB3 127 B6
Hayes BR2 209 A1
Forge Cotts W5 109 D5
Forge Dr KT10 213 A1
Forge La Belmont SM3 217 A1
Feltham TW13 173 A5
Richmond TW10 154 A3
Sunbury TW16 194 A6
Forge Lane Prim Sch
TW13 173 A5
Forge Lo 2 TW7 131 A2
Forge Mews
Addington CR0 223 C3
Sunbury TW16 194 A6
Forge Pl NW1 71 A2
Forlong Path UB5 63 A2
Forman Ct TW1 152 D3
Forman Ho SE4 140 D1
Forman Pl N16 73 D4
Formby Ave HA3, HA7 43 C6
Formby Ct 9 N7 72 C3
Formosa Ho 1 E1 97 A3
Formosa St W9 91 D3
Formunt Cl E16 98 D2
Forres Gdns NW11 47 C3
Forrest Ct N7 72 C2
Forrester Path SE26 184 C6
Forresters The HA5 40 B3
Forrest Gdns SW16 204 B6
Forrest Ho SW15 134 C3
Forris Ave UB3 105 D5
Forset Ct W1 237 B2
Forset St W1 92 C1 237 B2
Forstal Cl BR2 209 A6
Forster Cl IG8 36 B3
Forster Ho SE6 164 B1
Forster Park Prim Sch
SE6 164 C1
Forster Rd
Beckenham BR3 207 A6
Streatham SW2 160 A4
Thornton Heath CR0 205 A2
Tottenham N17 51 D6
Walthamstow E17 53 A3
Forsters Cl RM6 59 B3
Forsters Way UB4 84 B1
Forston St N1 95 A5 235 B4
Forsyte Cres SE19 183 C2
Forsyte Ct KT2 176 D2
Forsyth Ct
13 Dagenham RM10 81 D2
Harrow HA1 42 B3
Kingston u T KT3 177 C1
Forsythe Shades BR3 186 A2
Forsyth Gdns SE17 138 D6
Forsyth Ho
14 Hackney E9 74 C1
Pimlico SW1 259 B3
Forsythia Cl IG1 78 D3
Forsythia Ho SE4 141 A2
Forsyth Pl EN1 17 C6
Forterie Gdns IG3 80 A4
Fortescue Ave
1 Hackney E8 74 B1
Twickenham TW2 152 A1
Fortescue Rd
Burnt Oak HA8 27 B3
Mitcham SW19 180 B3
Fortess Gr NW5 71 C3
Fortess Rd NW5 71 C4
Fortess Wlk NW5 71 B3
Forthbridge Rd SW11 137 A1
Forth Ho 30 E3 97 B5
Forties The 9 NW5 71 C3
Fortior Ct N6 49 C2
Fortis Cl E16 99 C1
Fortis Ct N10 49 A6
Fortis Gn N2, N10 48 D6
FORTIS GREEN 48 D5
Fortis Green Ave N2 48 D5
Fortis Green Cotts N2 48 D6
Fortismere Ave N10 49 A6

Fortismere Sch N10 30 D1
Fortismere Sch (South Wing) N10 49 A6
Fortnam Rd N19 71 D6
Fortnums Acre HA7 24 D4
Fort Rd
Bermondsey
SE1 117 D2 263 D3
Northolt UB5 63 C1
Fortrose Cl E14 98 B1
Fortrose Gdns SW12,
SW2 160 A3
Fort St Broadgate E1 243 B3
Newham E16 121 B5
Fortuna Cl N7 72 B2
Fortune Ct
Barking IG11 102 B5
6 Dalston E8 73 D1
Fortune Gate Rd NW10 89 C6
Fortune Green Rd NW6 69 C4
Fortune Ho
Lambeth SE11 261 A3
St Luke's EC1 242 B5
Fortune La WD6 9 D5
Fortunes Mead UB5 63 A2
Fortune St EC1 95 A3 242 B5
Fortune Way NW10 90 A4
Fortune Wlk 4 SE28 123 B3
Forty Acre La E16 99 A2
Forty Ave HA9 66 B6
Forty Cl HA9 66 B5
Forty Hall* EN2 5 D6
FORTY HILL 5 D4
Forty Hill EN2 5 D5
Forty Hill CE Prim Sch
EN2 6 A6
Forty Hill Ho EN1 5 D5
Forty La HA9 66 D6
Forum Cl 7 E3 97 C6
Forumside HA8 26 C4
Forum The KT8 195 D5
Forum Way HA8 26 C4
Forval Cl CR4 202 D4
Forward Bsns Ctr The 3
E16 98 B3
Forward Dr HA3 42 D5
Fosbrooke Ho SW8 270 A3
Fosbury Ho 7 SW9 138 B1
Fosbury Mews W2 245 D5
Foscote Mews W9 91 C2
Foscote Rd NW4 46 B3
Foskett Ho 21 N2 30 B1
Foskett Rd SW6 135 B3
Foss Ave CR0, CR9 220 C3
Fossdene Prim Sch
SE7 121 B1
Fossdene Rd SE7 121 B1
Fossdyke Cl UB4 85 A2
Fosse Way W13 87 A2
Fossil Rd SE13 141 C2
Fossington Rd DA17 124 D2
Foss Rd SW17 180 B6
Fossway RM8 80 C6
Foster Ct
6 Camden Town NW1 71 C1
Canning Town E16 120 D6
Hendon NW4 46 C5
Foster Ho SE14 141 B4
Foster La EC2 95 A1 242 A2
Foster Rd Acton W3 111 C6
Chiswick W4 111 B1
Newham E13 99 A3
Fosters Cl
Elmstead BR7 188 B5
Woodford E18 37 B2
Fosters Old Sch DA16 146 B3
Foster's Prim Sch
DA16 146 C2
Foster St NW4 46 C5
Foster Wlk NW4 46 C5
Fothergill Cl E13 99 A5
Fothergill Dr N21 16 A6
Fotheringham Ct EN1 5 D1
Fotheringham Rd EN1 5 D1
Foubert's Pl W1 239 A1
Foulden Rd N16 73 D4
Foulden Terr N16 73 D4
Foulis Terr
SW7 114 B1 256 D2
Foulser Rd SW17 159 A1
Foulsham Rd CR7 205 B6
Foundary Ho 6 E14 97 D2
Founder Cl 2 E6 100 D1
Founders Cl UB5 85 B4
Founders Ct EC2 242 C2
Founders Gdns SE19 183 A3
Founders Ho SW1 259 C2
Foundling Ct WC1 240 A6
Foundling Mus The*
WC1 94 A3 240 B6
Foundry Cl SE16 119 A5
Foundry Mews NW1 239 B6
Foundry Pl Stepney E1 96 C2
Wandsworth SW18 157 D4
Fountain Cl UB8 83 A2
Fountain Ct
Belgravia SW1 258 C3
Blackfen DA15 168 B5
New Malden KT3 199 A5
5 Penge SE26 184 C4
14 Shepherd's Bush
W11 112 D4
Strand EC4 251 A6
Fountain Dr
Dulwich SE19 183 D6
Wallington SM5 218 D1
Fountain Green Sq 34
SE16 118 A4
Fountain Ho
33 Bermondsey SE16 118 A4

Fountain Ho *continued*
3 Brondesbury Pk NW6 69 A1
Mayfair W1 248 A4
5 Mitcham SW19 180 D1
Fountain Mews
1 Highbury N5 73 A4
Maitland Pk NW3 70 D2
Fountain Pl SW9 138 C4
Fountain Rd
South Norwood CR7 183 A1
Upper Tooting SW17 180 B6
Fountains Ave TW13 151 B1
Fountains Cl TW13 151 B1
Fountains Cres N14 16 A4
Fountains The
London N3 29 D3
Loughton IG10 21 D4
Fountayne Bsns Ctr
N15 52 A5
Fountayne Rd
South Tottenham N15 52 A5
Stoke Newington N16 74 A6
Fount St SW8 137 D5 269 D3
Fouracres EN3 7 A4
Four Acres N12 29 D6
Fourland Wlk HA8 27 A4
Fournier St E1 95 D2 243 D4
Fourscore Mans E8 74 A1
Four Seasons Cl E3 97 C5
Four Seasons Cres
SM3 217 B6
Four Square Ct TW4 151 C5
Fourth Ave Hayes UB3 105 D5
Ilford E12 78 B4
West Kilburn W10 91 A4
Fourth Cross Rd TW2 152 B2
Fourth Way
Wembley HA9 66 D4
Wembley HA9 67 A4
Four Tubs The WD23 8 B4
Fourways 2 CR0 221 D6
Four Wents The E4 20 B2
Fovant Ct 5 SW8 137 C3
Fowey Ave IG4 55 D4
Fowey Cl E1 118 B5
Fowey Ho SE11 261 B2
Fowler Cl
London SW11 136 B2
Sidcup DA14 191 A5
Fowler Ho
5 Camberwell SE5 139 C3
Islington N1 94 D6 234 D6
South Lambeth SW8 269 D1
West Green N15 51 B4
Fowler Rd
Forest Gate E7 77 A4
Islington N1 94 D6 234 D6
Mitcham CR4 181 A1
Fowler's Wlk W5 87 D3
Fownes St SW11 136 C2
Fox and Knot St EC1 241 D4
Foxberry Ct SE4 141 B1
Foxberry Rd SE4 141 A2
Foxborough Gdns
SE4 163 C6
Foxbourne Rd SW17 159 A2
Foxbury Ave BR7 189 B4
Foxbury Cl BR1 187 B4
Foxbury Rd BR1 187 B4
Fox Cl Bethnal Green E1 96 C3
Elstree WD6 9 D5
Newham E16 99 A2
Foxcombe CR0 223 D2
Foxcombe Cl 1 E6 99 D5
Foxcombe Rd 6
SW15 156 A3
Foxcote SE5 263 B1
Foxcroft N1 233 D3
Foxcroft Rd SE18 144 D4
Foxes Dale
Beckenham BR2 208 B6
Blackheath Pk SE3 143 A2
Foxfield NW1 231 D5
Foxfield Prim Sch
SE18 123 A1
Foxfield Rd BR6 227 B6
Foxglove Cl
Bexley DA15 168 A5
Edmonton N9 18 C3
Southall UB1 107 A6
Foxglove Ct 11 HA0 88 A5
Foxglove Gdns E11 55 C5
Foxglove La KT9 214 C4
Foxglove Path SE28 123 C5
Foxglove St W12 111 D6
Foxglove Way SM6 203 B1
Fox Gr KT12 194 B2
Foxgrove N14 16 A1
Foxgrove Ave BR3 185 D3
Foxgrove Path WD19 22 D5
Foxgrove Rd BR3 186 A3
Foxham Rd N19 71 D5
Fox Hill SE19 183 D3
Fox Hill Gdns SE19 183 D3
Fox Ho
2 London SW11 136 B1
Northolt UB5 85 A6
Foxhole Rd 2 SE9 166 A6
Fox Hollow Cl 1
SE18 123 C1
Fox Hollow Dr DA7 146 D2
Foxholt Gdns NW10 67 A1
Foxhome Cl BR7 188 C4
Fox House Rd DA17 125 D1
Fox La Ealing W5 88 A3
Keston BR2 225 C3
Palmers Green N13 16 B1
Foxlees HA0 65 A4
Foxley Cl E8 74 A3
Foxley Ct SM2 218 A1

Foxley Ho 4 E3 97 D4
Foxley Rd
Camberwell SW9 138 D5
Thornton Heath CR7 204 D5
Foxley Sq 3 SW9 138 D4
Foxmead Cl EN2 4 B2
Foxmore St SW11 267 C1
Fox Prim Sch
W8 113 C5 245 A3
Fox Rd E16 98 D2
Foxs Path CR4 180 C1
Fox's Yd E2 243 D6
Foxtail Ho TW3 130 A4
Foxton KT1 198 C6
Foxton Gr CR4 180 B1
Foxton Ho E16 122 C4
Foxwarren KT10 212 D1
Foxwell Mews SE4 141 A2
Foxwell St SE4 141 A2
Foxwood Cl
Edgware NW7 27 C6
Feltham TW13 150 B1
Foxwood Green Cl EN1 17 C5
Foxwood Rd SE3 142 D1
Foyle Rd
Greenwich SE3 142 D6
Tottenham N17 34 A2
Fradel Lo N16 51 B1
Framfield Cl N12 13 C1
Framfield Ct EN1 17 C5
Framfield Rd Ealing W7 86 D1
Islington N5 72 D3
Mitcham CR4 181 A3
Framlingham Cl 2 E5 74 C6
Framlingham Cres
SE9 188 B6
Framlingham Ct 5
RM6 58 B4
Frampton NW1 71 D1
Frampton Cl SM2 217 C1
Frampton Ct 3 W3 111 A4
Frampton Ho NW8 236 D5
Frampton Park Rd E9 74 C1
Frampton Rd TW4 151 A6
Frampton St
NW8 92 B3 236 D5
Francemary Rd SE4 163 C6
Frances Ct
South Norwood SE25 183 D1
Walthamstow E17 53 C3
Frances & Dick James Ct
2 NW7 29 A3
Frances Rd E4 35 C4
Frances St SE18 122 B2
Franche Court Rd
SW17 158 A1
Francis Ave
Bexleyheath DA7 147 C3
Feltham TW13 150 A1
Ilford IG1 79 B6
Francis Barber Cl
SW16 182 B6
Franciscan Prim Sch
SW17 181 A5
Franciscan Rd SW17 181 A6
Francis Chichester Way
SW11 137 A4 268 B1
Francis Cl
6 Cubitt Town E14 120 B2
Littleton TW17 192 C5
West Ewell KT19 215 B4
Francis Ct
12 Deptford SE14 140 D6
Ealing W5 110 B6
Edgware NW7 27 D5
Kingston u T KT5 198 A5
Francis Gr SW19 179 B4
Francis Ho
Harlesden NW10 89 D6
11 Shoreditch N1 95 C6
Walham Green SW10 265 D4
Francis Holland Sch
Belgravia
SW1 115 A2 258 B3
Marylebone
NW1 92 D3 237 C6
Francis Rd
Fortis Green N2 48 D5
Harrow HA1 43 A4
Hounslow TW4 128 D3
Ilford IG1 79 B6
Leyton E10 76 A6
Pinner HA5 40 C4
Thornton Heath CR0 204 D2
Wallington SM6 219 C2
Wembley UB6 87 C6
Francis Snary Lo 11
SW18 157 C6
Francis St Ilford IG1 79 B6
Stratford E15 76 C3
Westminster
SW1 115 C2 259 B4
Francis Terr N19 71 C5
Francis Terrace Mews 16
N19 71 C5
Francis Wlk N1 233 C6
Francklyn Gdns HA8 10 C1
Franconia Rd SW4 159 D6
Frank Bailey Wlk E12 78 C2
Frank Barnes Sch NW3 70 B1
Frank Beswick Ho
SW6 264 D5
Frank Burton Cl 4
SE7 121 B1
Frank Dixon Cl SE21 161 C3
Frank Dixon Way
SE21 161 C3
Frankfurt Rd SE24 161 A6
Frank Godley Ct DA14 190 B5
Frankham Ho 8 SE8 141 C5

Frankham St SE8 141 C5
Frank Ho SW8 270 A4
Frankland Cl
Bermondsey SE16 118 B2
Woodford IG8 37 C5
Frankland Ho 4
SW12 159 B4
Frankland Rd
Brompton
SW7 114 B3 256 C5
Chingford E4 35 C5
Franklin Bldg 5 E14 119 C4
Franklin Cl
Greenwich SE13 141 D4
Kingston u T KT1 198 C6
Oakleigh Pk N20 14 A4
West Norwood SE27 160 D1
Franklin Cres CR4 203 C5
Franklin Ho
Beckenham BR2 208 C6
New Cross SE4 141 A3
28 Wapping E1 118 B5
West Hendon NW9 45 D2
Franklin Ind Est SE20 184 C2
Franklin Pas SE9 144 A2
Franklin Pl SE13 141 D4
Franklin Rd
Bexleyheath DA7 147 A4
Penge SE20 184 C3
Walton-on-T KT12 194 A3
Franklins Mews HA2 64 A6
Franklin Sq SW5 254 D1
Franklin's Row
SW3 114 D1 257 D2
Franklin St
43 Bromley E3 97 D4
South Tottenham N15 51 C3
Franklin Way CR0 204 A2
Franklyn Rd
Walton-on-T KT12 194 B3
Willesden NW10 67 D2
Franks Ave KT3 199 A5
Franks Ho TW7 131 B1
Frank Slater Ho 4 IG3 58 B1
Frank Soskice Ho
SW6 264 D5
Frank St 5 E13 99 A3
Frankswood Ave
Hillingdon UB7 82 B1
Petts Wood BR2, BR5 211 A4
Frank Towell Ct TW14 150 A3
Frank Welch Ct HA5 40 C5
Frank Whymark Ho 4
SE16 118 C4
Franlaw Cres N13 33 A6
Frans Ct HA4 40 A1
Fransfield Gr SE26 162 B1
Frans Hals Ct E14 120 B3
Franshams WD23 8 C2
Frant Cl SE20 184 C3
Franthorne Way SE6 163 D1
Frant Rd CR7 204 D4
Fraserburgh Ho 29 E3 97 B5
Fraser Cl 3 E6 100 A1
Fraser Ct
Battersea SW11 267 A2
Heston TW3 129 A5
Fraser Ho
Brentford TW8 110 B1
40 Clapham SW8 137 D3
3 Woolwich SE18 122 C2
Fraser Rd Edmonton N9 18 B1
Walthamstow E17 53 D3
Wembley UB6 87 C6
Fraser Regnart Ct 12
NW5 70 D3
Fraser St W4 111 C1
Frating Cres IG8 37 B4
Frazer Ave HA4 62 C3
Frazier St SE1 116 C4 251 A1
Freame Ho N21 17 B5
Frean St SE16 118 A3
Frearson Ho WC1 233 D2
Freda Corbett Cl 10
SE15 140 A5
Frederica Rd E4 20 B4
Frederica St 4 N7 72 B1
Frederick Blg N1 73 C2
Frederick Charrington Ho
4 E1 96 C3
Frederick Cl
Cheam SM1 217 B3
Marylebone
W2 114 D6 247 C6
Frederick Cres
Camberwell SW9 138 D5
Enfield EN3 6 C3
Frederick Ct SW6 135 A2
Frederick Gdns
Cheam SM1 217 B3
Thornton Heath CR0 204 D3
Frederick Ho
Ashford TW15 170 A6
Southall UB1 107 B6
Woolwich SE7 122 A3
Frederick Pl SE18 122 D1
Frederick Rd SM1 217 B3
Frederick's Pl
City of London EC2 242 C1
North Finchley N12 30 A6
Frederick Sq 11 SE16 119 A6
Frederick's Row EC1 234 C2
Frederick St
WC1 94 B4 233 C1
Frederick Terr E8 73 D1
Frederic Mews SW1 248 A1
Frederic St E17 53 A4

Fredora Ave UB4 83 D3
Fred Styles Ho SE7 143 C6
Fred Tibble Ct RM9 81 A4
Fred Wigg Twr E11 76 D6
Freedom Cl E17 53 A5
Freedom St SW11 136 D3
Freegrove Rd N7 72 A3
Freehold Ind Ctr TW4 150 C6
Freeland Ct Ealing W5 110 B6
15 Sidcup DA14 168 A1
Freeland Pk N3 29 A1
Freeland Rd W5 110 B6
Freelands Ave CR2 222 D1
Freelands Gr BR1 187 B2
Freelands Rd BR1 187 B2
Freeling Ho NW8 229 C6
Freeling St 7 N1 72 B1
Freeman Cl
Northolt UB5 63 A1
Upper Halliford TW17 193 C5
Freeman Ct SW16 182 A1
Freeman Dr KT8 195 B5
Freeman Ho 13 SW2 160 A4
Freeman Rd SM4 202 B4
Freemans La UB3 105 C6
Freemantle Ave EN3 18 D6
Freemantle St
SE17 117 C1 263 A2
Freemasons Rd E16 99 B1
Freemason's Rd CR0 205 C1
Freemens Hos 1
SW9 138 B1
Freesia Cl BR6 227 D3
Freethorpe Cl SE19 183 C2
Freezeland Way UB10 60 D2
Freke Rd SW11 137 A2
Fremantle Ho 14 E1 96 B3
Fremantle Rd
Belvedere DA17 125 C2
Ilford IG6 57 A6
Fremont St E9 96 C6
French Gdns KT12 195 B1
French Pl E1 243 B6
French St TW16 172 C1
Frendsbury Rd SE4 141 A1
Frensham Cl UB1 85 B4
Frensham Ct
Canonbury N5 73 A3
4 London NW9 46 A5
Mitcham CR4 202 B6
Frensham Dr
New Addington CR0 224 A1
Roehampton SW15 156 A2
Frensham Ho 7 KT6 198 A4
Frensham Rd SE9 167 B2
Frensham St SE15 140 A6
Frere St 6 SW11 136 C3
Fresham Ho BR2 208 D6
Freshfield Ave E8 73 D1
Freshfield Cl SE13 142 B1
Freshfield Dr N14 15 B4
Freshfields CR0 207 B1
Freshford St SW17,
SW18 158 A1
Freshwater Cl SW17 181 A4
Freshwater Ct UB1 85 C4
Freshwater Rd
Dagenham RM8 59 A1
Streatham SW17 181 A4
Freshwell Ave RM6 58 C5
Fresh Wharf Est IG11 100 D6
Fresh Wharf Rd IG11 100 D5
Freshwood Cl BR3 185 D2
Freston Gdns EN4 15 A6
Freston Pk N3 29 B1
Freston Rd W10, W11 112 D6
Freswick Ho 6 SE8 119 A2
Freta Rd DA6 169 B6
Freud Mus The★ NW3 70 A2
Frewell Bldg EC1 241 A4
Frewing Cl BR7 188 C5
Frewin Rd SW18 158 B3
Friar Mews SE27 160 D1
Friar Rd UB4 84 D3
Friars Ave London N20 30 C6
Roehampton SW15 155 D1
Friars Cl Chingford E4 20 A1
Ilford IG1 57 B1
Lambeth SE1 251 D3
16 Northolt UB5 84 D4
Friars Ct
5 Wallington SM6 219 B4
Walthamstow E17 35 B2
Friars Gate Cl IG8 37 A6
Friars Gdns W3 89 B1
Friars La TW9 153 D6
Friars Mead E14 120 A3
Friars Mews SE9 166 C6
Friars Place La W3 111 B6
Friars Prim Sch
SE1 116 D4 251 D1
Friar's Rd E6 99 D6
Friars Stile Pl 9
TW10 154 A5
Friars Stile Rd TW10 154 A5
Friar St EC4 241 D1
Friars Way W3 89 B1
Friars Wlk London N14 15 B4
West Heath SE2 124 D1
Friary Cl N12 30 C5
Friary La IG8 37 A6
Friary Park Ct 12 W3 89 A1
Friary Rd Acton W3 89 B1
London N12 30 C6
Peckham SE15 140 A5
Friary Way N12 30 C6
Friday Grove Mews 11
SW12 159 C4
FRIDAY HILL 20 C1
Friday Hill E4 20 C1
Friday Hill E E4 20 C1
Friday Hill W E4 20 C2
Friday Rd CR4 180 D3
Friday St EC4 117 A6 252 A6
Frideswide Pl NW5 71 C3
Friendly Pl 16 SE13 141 D4
Friendly St SE8 141 C4
Friendly Street Mews
SE8 141 C3
Friendship Way E15 98 A6
Friendship Wlk UB5 84 D4
Friends' Rd CR0 221 B5
Friend St EC1 94 D4 234 C2
FRIERN BARNET 31 A6
Friern Barnet La N20 30 C6
Friern Barnet Rd N11 31 A5
Friern Barnet Sch N11 30 D5
Friern Bridge Ret Pk
N11 31 B4
Friern Ct N20 14 B1
Friern Mount Dr N20 14 A4
Friern Pk N12 30 B5
Friern Rd SE22 162 A5
Friern Watch Ave N12 30 B6
Frigate Ho 7 E14 120 A2
Frigate Mews SE8 141 C6
Frimley Ave SM6 220 B3
Frimley Cl
New Addington CR0 224 A1
Putney SW19 157 A2
Frimley Cres CR0 224 A1
Frimley Ct DA14 190 C5
Frimley Gdns CR4 202 C6
Frimley Ho CR4 202 C6
Frimley Rd
Chessington KT9 214 A3
Ilford IG3 79 C5
Frimley Way E1 96 D3
Frinstead Ho 1 W10 112 D6
Frinton Ct W13 87 B2
Frinton Dr IG8 36 B3
Frinton Mews IG2 56 C3
Frinton Rd Newham E6 99 D4
Sidcup DA14 169 A2
South Tottenham N15 51 C3
Streatham SW17 181 A4
Friston St SW6 135 D3
Friswell Pl 1 DA6 147 C1
Fritham Cl KT3 199 C3
Frith Ct NW7 29 A3
Frith Ho
Bethnal Green E2 96 A4
Paddington NW8 236 D5
Frith La NW7 29 A4
Frith Manor Cotts N12 29 B5
Frith Manor Prim Sch
N12 29 B5
Frith Rd Croydon CR0 221 A6
Leyton E11 76 B4
Frith St W1 93 D1 239 C1
Frithville Ct 2 W12 112 C5
Frithville Gdns W12 112 C5
Frizlands La RM10 81 D5
Frobisher Cl HA5 40 D2
Frobisher Cres TW19 148 A4
Frobisher Ct
Belmont SM2 217 B1
6 Forest Hill SE23 162 B2
1 Greenwich SE10 142 B6
Hendon NW9 27 C1
3 Shepherd's Bush
W12 112 C4
Frobisher Gdns TW19 148 A4
Frobisher Ho
3 Ealing W5 88 A4
27 Wapping E1 118 B5
Frobisher Mews EN2 5 B1
Frobisher Pas E14 119 C5
Frobisher Pl SE14 140 C4
Frobisher Rd London N8 50 C5
Newham E6 100 B1
Frobisher St SE10 142 C6
Froghall Cotts EN5 11 B5
Frogley Rd SE22 139 D1
Frogmore SW18 157 C6
Frogmore Ave UB4 83 C3
Frogmore Cl SM3 217 A5
Frogmore Ct UB2 107 B2
Frogmore Est NW10 89 A4
Frogmore Gdns
Cheam SM3 217 A4
Hayes UB4 83 C3
Frogmore Ind Est
Hayes UB3 105 D4
Highbury N5 73 A4
Frognal NW3 70 A3
Frognal Ave
Harrow HA1 42 D5
Sidcup DA14 190 A4
Frognal Cl NW3 70 A3
Frognal Cnr BR7 189 D4
Frognal Ct NW3 70 A2
Frognal Gdns NW3 70 A4
Frognal La NW3 69 D3
Frognal Par NW3 70 A2
Frognal Pl DA14 190 A5
Frognal Rise NW3 70 A4
Frognal Way NW3 70 A4
Froissart Rd SE9 166 A6
Frome Ho SE15 140 C1
Frome Rd N22 50 D6
Frome St N1 95 A5 235 A4
Fromondes Rd SM3 217 A3
Fromow's Cnr 14 W4 111 A1
Frontenac NW10 68 B1
Frontier Works N17 33 C4
Frosbery Ct 23 EN3 7 C6
Frostic Wlk E1 243 D3
Froude St SW8 137 B3
Fruen Rd TW14 149 D4
Fryatt Rd N17 33 B3
Frye Ct 5 E3 97 B4
Fryent Cl NW9 44 C3
Fryent Cres NW9 45 C3
Fryent Ctry Park HA3, HA9,
NW9 44 C2
Fryent Fields NW9 45 C3
Fryent Gr NW9 45 C3
Fryent Prim Sch NW9 45 A2
Fryent Way HA9, NW9 44 D2
Fry Ho E6 77 C1
Frying Pan Alley E1 243 C3
Fry Rd Harlesden NW10 89 D6
Upton Pk E6 77 D1
Fryston Ave CR0 222 A6
Fuchsia St SE2 124 B1
Fulbeck Dr NW9 27 C2
Fulbeck Ho N7 72 B2
Fulbeck Way HA2 24 A1
Fulbourn 9 KT1 176 C1
Fulbourne Rd E17 36 A1
Fulbourne St E1 96 B2
Fulbrook Rd N19 71 C4
Fulcher Ct SE8 141 B6
Fulcher Ho
13 Deptford SE8 119 B1
10 Shoreditch N1 95 C6
Fulford Mans 3 N19 72 A5
Fulford Rd KT19 215 B1
Fulford St SE16 118 B4
FULHAM 134 D3
Fulham Broadway
SW6 135 C5 265 B3
Fulham Broadway Sh Ctr
SW6 265 B3
Fulham Broadway Sta
SW6 135 C5 265 B4
Fulham Bsns Exchange
SW6 266 B1
Fulham Cl UB10 83 A3
Fulham Cross Sec Sch
SW6 135 A5 264 A3
Fulham Ct
SW6 135 C4 265 A2
Fulham High St SW6 135 A3
Fulham Pal★ SW6 135 A3
Fulham Palace Rd SW6,
W6 134 D6
Fulham Park Gdns
SW6 135 B3
Fulham Park Rd SW6 135 B3
Fulham Prep Sch
Fulham SW6 135 A3
Fulham W14 135 A6 264 B6
Fulham Prim Sch
SW6 135 C6 265 A5
Fulham Rd
Chelsea
SW10 136 A6 266 B6
Fulham SW6 135 B4 264 D2
Fulke Ho E5 74 B5
Fullbrooks Ave KT4 199 D1
Fuller Cl
4 Bethnal Green E2 96 A3
Bushey WD23 8 B4
Orpington BR6 227 D3
Fuller Rd RM8 80 C4
Fullers Ave KT6 214 B6
Fuller's Ave IG8 36 D3
Fullers Ho 6 SW18 157 C6
Fuller's Rd E18 36 D3
Fuller St NW4 46 C5
Fullers Way N KT6 214 B5
Fullers Way S KT9 214 A5
Fuller's Wood CR0 223 C3
Fuller Terr IG1 79 B3
Fullerton Ct TW11 175 A4
Fullerton Rd
Croydon CR0 205 D2
Wandsworth SW18 158 A6
Fuller Way UB3 105 D1
Fullwood Prim Sch
IG6 57 A5
Fullwood's Mews N1 235 D2
Fulmar Ct
6 Dulwich SE21 161 B2
10 Ealing W13 86 D3
Surbiton KT5 198 B3
Fulmar Ho
12 Bermondsey SE16 118 D2
Marylebone NW8 237 B5
Fulmead St SW6 265 D1
Fulmer Cl TW12 173 A5
Fulmer Rd E16 99 D2
Fulmer Way W13 109 B3
Fulneck 1 E1 96 C2
Fulready Rd E10 54 B4
Fulstone Cl TW4 129 B1
Fulthorp Rd SE3 143 A3
Fulton Ct EN3 7 C5
Fulton Mews W2 246 A6
Fulton Rd HA9 66 C5
Fulwell Ct Southall UB1 108 A6
Teddington TW11 174 C6
Fulwell Park Ave TW2 152 A2
Fulwell Rd TW11,
TW12 174 B6
Fulwell Sta TW11 174 B6
Fulwood Ave HA0 88 B5
Fulwood Cl UB3 83 D1
Fulwood Ct Harrow HA3 43 A3
Stanwell TW19 148 B5
Fulwood Gdns TW1 153 A5
Fulwood Pl WC1 240 D3
Fulwood Wlk SW19 157 A3
Furber St W6 112 B3
Furham Field HA5 23 C3
Furley Ho 7 SE15 140 A5
Furley Rd SE15 140 A5
Furlong Cl SM6 203 B1
Furlong Rd N7 72 C2
Furmage St SW18 157 D4
Furneaux Ave SE27 182 D5
Furness Ho SW1 258 C2
Furness Lo 4 SW14 132 D1
Furness Prim Sch The
NW10 90 A5
Furness Rd
Harlesden NW10 90 A5
Harrow HA2 41 D1
Morden SM4 201 D3
Sands End SW6 135 D3
Furnival St EC4 94 C1 241 A2
Furrow La E9 74 C3
Furrows The KT12 194 C1
Fursby Ave N3 29 C4
Fursecroft W1 237 C2
Further Acre NW9 27 D1
Furtherfield Cl CR0 204 C3
Further Green Rd SE6 164 C3
Furze Cl WD19 22 C5
Furze Ct CR0 222 A6
FURZEDOWN 181 B6
Furzedown Dr SW17 181 B5
Furzedown Prim Sch
SW17 181 A4
Furzedown Rd SW17 181 B5
Furzefield Cl BR7 188 D4
Furzefield Rd SE3 143 B5
Furzeground Way
UB11 105 A5
Furzeham Rd UB7 104 A4
Furzehill Rd WD6 11 A6
Furze Inf Sch RM6 59 A3
Furzeland Ho 2 KT3 199 C2
Furze Rd CR7 205 A6
Furze St E3 97 C2
Furzewood TW16 172 A2
Fuschia Ct IG8 36 C4
Fuscia Ct TW13 149 D1
Fusion Ct SW15 155 C1
Futters Ct 1 NW10 89 C5
Fyfe Way BR1 187 A1
Fyfield N4 72 C6
Fyfield Cl BR2, BR3 208 B5
Fyfield Ct E7 77 A2
Fyfield Ho RM9 80 B1
Fyfield Rd
5 Brixton SW9 138 C2
Enfield EN1 5 C2
Walthamstow E17 54 B6
Woodford IG8 37 C3
Fynes St SW1 259 C4

G

Gable Cl HA5 23 C3
Gable Ct SE26 184 B6
Gable Ho 12 W4 111 C2
Gable Lo
Hadley Wood EN4 2 A5
5 North Finchley N12 30 A5
West Wickham BR4 208 A1
Gables Ave TW15 170 B5
Gables Cl
Camberwell SE5 139 C4
Lewisham SE12 165 A3
Gables The
Barking IG11 79 A2
Bromley BR1 187 B3
3 Clapham SW4 137 C2
Ealing W13 87 B1
Hampstead NW3 70 B6
Heston TW5 129 C6
Mitcham CR4 203 B6
Muswell Hill N10 49 A6
North Finchley N12 29 D5
Wembley HA9 66 B5
Gabriel Cl 1 TW13 173 A6
Gabriel Ho SE11 260 C4
Gabrielle Cl HA9 66 B5
Gabrielle Ct NW3 70 B2
Gabriel Mews NW2 69 B6
Gabriel St SE23 163 A4
Gabriel's Wharf SE1 251 A4
Gad Cl E13 99 B4
Gaddesden Ave HA9 66 B2
Gaddesden Ho EC1 235 D1
Gade Cl UB3 106 B5
Gadesden Rd KT19 215 A2
Gadsbury Cl NW9 45 D3
Gadsden Ho
6 Homerton E9 74 D2
8 Kensal Town W10 91 A3
Gadwall Cl E16 99 B1
Gadwall Way SE28 123 B4
Gagarin Ho SW11 136 B2
Gage Rd E16 98 C2
Gage St WC1 240 B4
Gainford Ho 18 E2 96 B4
Gainford St N1 94 C6 234 A6
Gainsboro Gdns UB6 64 D3
Gainsborough Ave E12 78 C3
Gainsborough Cl
Beckenham BR3 185 C3
Thames Ditton KT10 196 C1
Gainsborough Ct
11 Barnet EN5 1 D1
6 Bermondsey SE16 118 B1
Bromley BR2 209 C5
Dulwich SE21 161 C2
North Finchley N12 29 D5
Shepherd's Bush W12 112 C4
Gainsborough Gdns
Edgware HA8 26 C1
Gainsborough Gdns
continued
Golders Green NW11 47 B2
Hampstead NW3 70 B5
Isleworth TW7 152 B6
Gainsborough Ho
Dagenham RM8 80 B4
Enfield EN1 18 A6
Finsbury Pk N4 50 B1
3 Hampstead NW3 70 A4
5 Limehouse E14 119 A6
Westminster SW1 259 D3
Gainsborough Lodge
HA1 42 C4
Gainsborough Mews 5
SE26 162 B1
Gainsborough Prim Sch
Hackney Wick E9 75 C2
Newham E15 98 C4
Gainsborough Rd
Bedford Pk W4 111 D2
Dagenham RM8 80 B5
Hayes UB4 83 B5
Leytonstone E11 54 C2
Newham E15 98 C4
New Malden KT3 199 B2
North Finchley N12 29 D5
Richmond TW9 132 B2
Gainsborough Sq
DA6 146 D2
Gainsborough St 3 E9 75 B2
Gainsborough Studios
N1 235 C5
Gainsborough Twr 7
UB5 84 D5
Gainsfield Ct 3 E11 76 C5
Gainsford Rd E17 53 B5
Gainsford St
SE1 117 D4 253 D2
Gairloch Ho 2 NW1 71 D1
Gairloch Rd SE5 139 C3
Gaisford St NW5 71 C2
Gaitskell Ct SW11 136 C3
Gaitskell Ho
Camberwell SE17 139 B6
2 Newham E6 99 D6
3 Walthamstow E17 53 D6
Gaitskell Rd SE9 167 A3
Gaitskell Way SE1 252 A2
Galahad Rd
Edmonton N9 18 A1
Grove Pk BR1 187 A6
Galata Rd SW13 134 A5
Galatea Sq SE15 140 B2
Galaxy Bldg 6 E14 119 C2
Galaxy Ho EC2 242 D6
Galba Ct 1 TW8 131 D5
Galbraith St E14 120 A3
Galdana Ave EN5 2 A2
Galeborough Ave IG8 36 B3
Gale Cl Hampton TW12 173 A4
Mitcham CR4 202 B6
Gale Ho
10 Brixton SW2 160 B6
Carshalton SM5 218 C3
Galena Ho
5 Hammersmith W6 112 B2
Plumstead Comm SE18 123 D1
Galena Rd W6 112 B2
Galen Pl WC1 240 B3
Galesbury Rd SW18 158 A5
Gales Gdns E2 96 B4
Gale St Dagenham RM9 80 D1
Tower Hamlets E3 97 C2
Galgate Cl 4 SW19 157 A3
Gallants Farm Rd EN4 14 C3
Galleon Cl SE16 118 D4
Galleon Ho 8 E14 120 A2
Galleons Dr IG11 102 A4
Gallery Ct SW10 266 A5
Gallery Gdns UB5 84 D5
Gallery Rd SE21 161 B3
Galleywall Rd SE16 118 B2
Galleywall Road Trad Est
12 SE16 118 B2
Galleywood Ho 1 W10 90 C2
Gallia Rd N5 72 D3
Galliard Cl N9 18 C5
Galliard Ct N9 18 A5
Galliard Prim Sch N9 18 A4
Galliard Rd N9 18 A5
Gallica Ct SM1 201 D1
Gallions Cl IG11 102 A4
Gallions Mount Prim Sch
SE18 123 D1
Gallions Prim Sch E6 100 D1
Gallions Rd E16 122 D6
Gallions Reach Shp Pk
IG11 101 A2
Gallions Reach Sta
E16 122 D6
Gallions View Rd
SE28 123 C4
Gallon Cl SE7 121 C2
Gallop The
South Croydon CR2 222 B1
Sutton SM2 218 A1
Gallosson Rd SE18 123 C2
Galloway Rd W12 112 A5
Gallus Cl N21 16 B5
Gallus Sq SE3 143 B2
Galpin's Rd CR4, CR7 204 B5
Galsworthy Ave
Ilford RM6 58 B2
Tower Hamlets E14 97 A2
Galsworthy Cl SE28 124 B5
Galsworthy Cres SE3 143 C4
Galsworthy Ct W3 110 D3
Galsworthy Ho 4 W11 91 A1
Galsworthy Rd
Cricklewood NW2 69 A4
Kingston u T KT2 176 D2
Galton Ho SE18 144 B4
Galton St W10 91 A4
Galva Cl EN4 3 A1
Galvani Way CR0 204 B1
Galveston Ho 2 E1 97 A3
Galveston Rd SW15 157 B6
Galway Cl 23 SE16 118 B1
Galway Ho Finsbury EC1 235 B1
7 Stepney E1 96 D2
Galway St EC1 95 A4 235 B1
Galy 5 NW9 27 D1
Gambetta St 3 SW8 137 B3
Gambia St SE1 116 D5 251 D3
Gambler Ho EC1 235 B1
Gambole Rd SW17 180 C6
Games Ho 6 SE7 143 C6
Games Rd EN4 2 D2
Gamlen Rd SW15 134 D1
Gamma Ct 9 CR0 205 B1
Gamuel Cl E17 53 C3
Gander Green Cres
TW12 173 C2
Gander Green La KT4, SM1,
SM3 217 B5
Gandhi Cl E17 53 C3
Gandolfi St 5 SE15 139 C6
Ganley Ct 10 SW11 136 B2
Gannet Ct 5 SE21 161 B2
Gannet Ho SE15 139 D4
Ganton St W1 239 B1
Ganton Wlk WD19 22 D6
GANTS HILL 56 C3
Gants Hill IG2 56 C3
Gantshill Cres IG2 56 C4
Gants Hill Sta IG2 56 C3
Gap Rd SW19 179 D5
Garage Rd W3 88 C1
Garand Ct 2 N7 72 B3
Garbett Ho 2 SE17 138 D6
Garbutt Pl W1 238 B3
Garden Ave
Bexleyheath DA7 147 C2
Mitcham CR4 181 B3
Garden City HA8 26 C4
Garden Cl
Ashford TW15 171 A4
Chingford E4 35 C5
Grove Pk SE12 165 B1
Hampton TW12 173 B5
Northolt UB5 85 A6
Roehampton SW15 156 B4
Ruislip HA4 61 D6
Wallington SM6 220 A3
Garden Cotts BR5 190 C1
Garden Ct
5 Belmont SM2 217 C1
10 Eltham SE9 166 C5
Hampton TW12 173 B5
North Finchley N12 29 D5
4 Richmond TW9 132 B4
12 South Acton W4 111 A3
South Croydon CR0 221 D5
4 Stanmore HA7 25 C5
St John's Wood NW8 229 C2
Strand EC4 251 A6
Wembley HA0 65 C5
Wimbledon SW20 178 D2
Gardeners Cl SE9 166 A1
Gardeners Rd CR0 204 D1
Garden Flats SW16 160 A1
Garden Ho
2 Finchley N2 30 B1
12 South Lambeth SW9 138 A3
Garden Hospl The
NW4 46 C6
Gardenia Ct 1 BR3 185 C3
Gardenia Rd
Bromley BR1 210 C6
Enfield EN1 17 C5
Gardenia Way IG8 37 A5
Garden La Bromley BR1 187 B4
Streatham SW2 160 B3
Garden Lodge Ct N2 48 B6
Garden Mews W2 245 B5
Garden Pl 23 E2 95 D6
Garden Prim Sch CR4 203 D6
Garden Rd
Bromley BR1 187 B4
Penge SE20 184 C2
Richmond TW9 132 C2
St John's Wood
NW8 92 A4 229 B2
Walton-on-T KT12 194 B2
Garden Row
SE1 116 D3 261 C6
Garden Royal 16
SW15 156 D5
Garden St E1 96 D2
Gardens The
Beckenham BR3 186 A2
East Bedfont TW14 149 B5
East Dulwich SE22 140 A1
Harrow HA1, HA2 42 A3
Pinner HA5 41 B3
Stamford Hill N16 51 D2
Garden Suburb Jun & Inf
Schs NW11 47 B4
Garden Terr
Knightsbridge SW7 247 B1
Pimlico SW1 259 C2
Garden Way NW10 67 A2
Garden Wlk
Beckenham BR3 185 B2
Shoreditch EC2 95 C3 243 A6
Gardiner Ave NW2 68 C3
Gardiner Cl
Chislehurst BR5 190 C1

Gardiner Cl *continued*
Dagenham RM8 . . . . 80 D4
Enfield EN3 . . . . 18 D5
Gardiner Ct NW10 . . . . 89 B6
Gardiner Ho SW11 . . . . 267 A2
Gardner Cl E11 . . . . 55 B3
Gardner Ct Highbury N5 . . 73 A4
Hounslow TW3 . . . . 129 C2
Tottenham N22 . . . . 32 D1
Gardner Ho
Feltham TW13 . . . . 151 B2
Southall UB1 . . . . 106 D6
Gardner Ind Est SE26 . . 185 B5
Gardner Pl TW14 . . . . 150 B5
Gardner Rd E13 . . . . 99 B3
Gardners Cl N11 . . . . 15 A2
Gardners La EC4 . . . . 252 A6
Gardnor Mans 14 NW3 . . 70 A4
Gardnor Rd NW3 . . . . 70 B4
Gard St EC1 . . . . 234 D2
Garendon Gdns SM4 . . . 201 D2
Garendon Rd SM4 . . . . 201 D2
Garenne Ct 10 E4 . . . . 20 A3
Gareth Cl KT4 . . . . 216 D6
Gareth Ct SW16 . . . . 159 D1
Gareth Gr BR1 . . . . 187 A6
Garfield Edmonton N9 . . . 18 B3
Enfield EN2 . . . . 17 B6
Garfield Ho W2 . . . . 237 C1
Garfield Mews 7
SW11 . . . . 137 A2
Garfield Prim Sch
London N11 . . . . 31 C5
Wimbledon SW19 . . . . 180 A4
Garfield Rd Chingford E4 . 20 B3
Clapham SW11 . . . . 137 A2
Enfield EN3 . . . . 6 C1
Newham E13 . . . . 98 D3
3 Twickenham TW1 . . . 153 A3
Wimbledon SW19 . . . . 180 A4
Garford St E14 . . . . 119 C6
Garganey Ct NW10 . . . . 67 B2
Garganey Wlk SE28 . . . 124 C6
Garibaldi St SE18 . . . . 123 C2
Garland Ct 12 E14 . . . . 119 C6
Garland Dr TW3 . . . . 130 A3
Garland Ho
12 Kingston u T KT2 . . . 176 A2
Stoke Newington N16 . . . 73 B5
Garland Rd
Plumstead Comm
SE18 . . . . 145 B5
Stanmore HA7 . . . . 26 A2
Garlands Ct CR0 . . . . 221 B4
Garlands Ho NW8 . . . . 91 D5
Garlands La HA1 . . . . 42 D1
Garlands The HA1 . . . . 42 D2
Garlick Hill
EC4 . . . . 117 A6 252 B6
Garlies Rd SE23 . . . . 163 A1
Garlinge Ho 12 SW9 . . . 138 C4
Garlinge Rd NW2 . . . . 69 B2
Garman Cl N18 . . . . 33 B5
Garman Rd N17 . . . . 34 C3
Garnault Mews EC1 . . . 234 B1
Garnault Pl EC1 . . . . 234 B1
Garnault Rd EN1 . . . . 5 D5
Garner Cl RM8 . . . . 58 D1
Garner Rd E17 . . . . 36 A2
Garner St E2 . . . . 96 A5
Garnet Ct TW13 . . . . 149 C1
Garnet Ho KT4 . . . . 199 B1
Garnet Rd
South Norwood CR7 . . . 205 B5
Willesden NW10 . . . . 67 C2
Garnet St E1 . . . . 118 C6
Garnett Cl SE9 . . . . 144 B2
Garnett Ho 5 NW3 . . . . 70 D3
Garnett Rd NW3 . . . . 70 D3
Garnett Way 3 E17 . . . 35 A2
Garnet Wlk 3 E6 . . . . 100 A2
Garnham Cl 2 N16 . . . 73 D6
Garnham St 1 N16 . . . 73 D6
Garnies Cl SE15 . . . . 139 D5
Garrad's Rd SW16 . . . . 159 D1
Garrard Cl
Bexleyheath DA7 . . . . 147 C2
Chislehurst BR7 . . . . 188 D5
Garrard Ho BR2 . . . . 209 C5
Garrard Wlk NW10 . . . . 67 C2
Garratt Cl CR0 . . . . 220 A4
Garratt Ho 8 N16 . . . . 51 C1
Garratt La
Upper Tooting SW17,
SW18 . . . . 180 C6
Wandsworth SW18 . . . . 157 D3
Garratt Park Sch
SW18 . . . . 158 A1
Garratt Rd HA8 . . . . 26 C3
Garratts Rd WD23 . . . . 8 A4
Garratt Terr SW17 . . . . 180 C6
Garraway Ct SW13 . . . . 134 C5
Garraway Ho SE21 . . . . 161 D1
Garrett Cl W3 . . . . 89 B2
Garrett Ho
8 Shepherd's Bush
W12 . . . . 90 B1
Teddington TW11 . . . . 175 B4
Garrett St EC1 . . . 95 A3 242 B6
Garrick Ave NW11 . . . . 47 A3
Garrick Cl Ealing W5 . . . . 88 A3
1 Richmond TW9 . . . . 153 D6
Wandsworth SW18 . . . . 136 A1
Garrick Cres CR0 . . . . 221 C6
Garrick Ct HA8 . . . . 26 B6
Garrick Dr Hendon NW4 . . 28 C1
Plumstead SE18 . . . . 123 B3
Garrick Gdns KT8 . . . . 195 C6
Garrick Ho
Chiswick W4 . . . . 133 C6
Garrick Ho *continued*
2 Kingston u T KT1 . . . 198 A5
Mayfair W1 . . . . 248 C3
7 Streatham SW16 . . . 181 C5
Garrick Ind Ctr NW9 . . . 45 D4
Garrick Pk NW4 . . . . 28 D1
Garrick Rd
Greenford UB6 . . . . 85 D3
Richmond TW9 . . . . 132 C3
West Hendon NW9 . . . . 45 D3
Garrick's Ait KT8 . . . . 174 A1
Garricks Ho KT1 . . . . 175 D1
Garrick St
WC2 . . . . 116 A6 250 A6
Garrick's Villa TW12 . . . 174 A1
Garrick Way NW4 . . . . 46 D5
Garrick Yd WC2 . . . . 250 A6
Garrison Cl
Hounslow TW4 . . . . 151 B6
Shooters Hill SE18 . . . . 144 C5
Garrison La KT9 . . . . 214 A1
Garrowsfield EN5 . . . . 13 B6
Garsdale Cl N11 . . . . 31 A4
Garsdale Terr SW5 . . . . 254 D2
Garside Cl
Hampton TW12 . . . . 173 D4
Plumstead SE28 . . . . 123 B3
Garside Ct 5 N20 . . . . 14 D2
Garsington Mews SE4 . . 141 B2
Garson Ho W2 . . . . 246 C6
Garston Ho 6 N1 . . . . 72 D1
Garter Way SE16 . . . . 118 D4
Garth Cl
Kingston u T KT2 . . . . 176 B5
Ruislip HA4 . . . . 40 D1
West Barnes SM4 . . . . 200 D2
Garth Ct Chiswick W4 . . 133 B6
11 Harrow HA1 . . . . 42 D3
Garth Dr N9 . . . . 18 A2
Garth Ho NW2 . . . . 69 B6
Garthland Dr EN5 . . . . 12 C6
Garth Mews W5 . . . . 88 A3
Garthorne Rd SE23 . . . . 162 D4
Garth Rd Child's Hill NW2 . 69 B6
8 Chiswick W4 . . . . 111 B1
Kingston u T KT2 . . . . 176 B5
West Barnes SM4 . . . . 200 D2
Garth Road Ind Ctr The
SM4 . . . . 200 D1
Garthside TW10 . . . . 176 A5
Garth The
Hampton TW12 . . . . 173 D4
Harrow HA3 . . . . 44 B3
North Finchley N12 . . . . 29 D5
Garthway N12 . . . . 30 C4
Gartmoor Gdns SW19 . . 157 B3
Gartmore Rd IG3 . . . . 79 D6
Garton Ho 6 N6 . . . . 49 D2
Garton Pl SW18 . . . . 158 A5
Gartons Cl EN3 . . . . 6 C1
Gartons Way SW11 . . . . 136 A2
Garvary Rd E16 . . . . 99 B1
Garvens SE19 . . . . 183 C5
Garway Rd W2 . . . . 91 D1
Garwood Cl N17 . . . . 34 B2
Garwood Lo N22 . . . . 32 B3
Gascoigne Gdns IG8 . . . 36 C3
Gascoigne Pl 17 E2 . . . . 95 D4
Gascoigne Prim Sch
IG11 . . . . 101 A6
Gascoigne Rd IG11 . . . . 101 A5
Gascony Ave NW6 . . . . 69 C1
Gascoyne Ho 2 E9 . . . . 74 D1
Gascoyne Rd E9 . . . . 74 D1
Gaselee St E14 . . . . 120 A6
Gasholder Pl
SE11 . . . . 116 B1 260 D1
Gaskarth Rd
Balham SW12 . . . . 159 B5
Burnt Oak HA8 . . . . 27 A1
Gaskell Rd N6 . . . . 48 D3
Gaskell St SW4 . . . . 138 A3
Gaskin Ho N16 . . . . 73 B5
Gaskin St N1 . . . 94 D6 234 C6
Gaspar Cl SW7 . . . . 255 D4
Gaspar Mews SW5 . . . . 255 D4
Gassiot Rd SW17 . . . . 180 D6
Gassiot Way SM1 . . . . 218 B5
Gasson Ho 24 SE14 . . . . 140 D6
Gastein Rd W6 . . . . 134 D6
Gastigny Ho EC1 . . . . 235 B1
Gaston Bell Cl TW9 . . . . 132 B2
Gaston Bridge Rd
TW17 . . . . 193 B3
Gaston Gate SW8 . . . . 270 C2
Gaston Rd CR4 . . . . 203 A6
Gaston Way TW17 . . . . 193 B4
Gataker Ho 5 SE16 . . . . 118 B3
Gataker St 6 SE16 . . . . 118 B3
Gatcliff Cl SW1 . . . . 258 B1
Gatcombe Ct BR3 . . . . 185 C3
Gatcombe Ho 20 SE22 . . 139 C2
Gatcombe Mews W5 . . . 110 B6
Gatcombe Rd
8 Newham E16 . . . . 121 A5
Tufnell Pk N19 . . . . 71 D5
Gatcombe Way EN4 . . . . 2 D2
Gateacre Ct DA14 . . . . 190 B6
Gate End HA6 . . . . 22 A3
Gatefield Ct SE15 . . . . 140 A2
Gateforth St NW8 . . . . 237 A5
Gate Hill Ct W11 . . . . 244 D4
Gatehill Rd HA6 . . . . 22 A3
Gate Ho 4 KT6 . . . . 198 A1
Gatehouse Cl KT2 . . . . 177 A3
Gatehouse Sch E2 . . . . 96 D5
Gatehouse Sq SE1 . . . . 252 B4
Gateley Ho 6 SE4 . . . . 140 D1
Gateley Rd SW9 . . . . 138 B2
Gate Mews
SW7 . . . . 114 C4 247 B1
Gater Dr EN2 . . . . 5 B4
Gates 4 NW9 . . . . 27 D1
Gatesborough St EC2 . . 243 A6
Gates Ct SE17 . . . . 262 A2
Gatesden WC1 . . . . 233 B1
Gates Green Rd BR2,
BR4 . . . . 225 A4
Gateside Rd SW17 . . . . 158 D1
Gate St WC2 . . . 94 B1 240 C2
Gatestone Ct 10 SE19 . . 183 C4
Gatestone Rd SE19 . . . . 183 C4
Gateway SE17 . . . . 139 A6
Gateway Arc N1 . . . . 234 C4
Gateway Bsns Ctr
SE28 . . . . 123 B3
Gateway Ho
Balham SW12 . . . . 159 B5
4 Barking IG11 . . . . 101 A6
3 Upper Tooting
SW17 . . . . 180 C4
Gateway Mews 4 E8 . . . 73 D3
Gateway Prim Sch
NW8 . . . . 92 B3 236 D6
Gateway Ret Pk E6 . . . . 100 D3
Gateways KT6 . . . . 198 A4
Gateways Ct SM6 . . . . 219 B3
Gateways The
Chelsea SW3 . . . . 257 B3
Richmond TW9 . . . . 131 D1
Gateway Trad Est
NW10 . . . . 89 D4
Gatfield Gr TW13 . . . . 151 C2
Gatfield Ho TW13 . . . . 151 C2
Gathorne Rd N22 . . . . 32 C2
Gathorne St 19 E2 . . . . 96 D5
Gatley Ave KT19 . . . . 214 D3
Gatliff Rd SW1 . . 115 B1 258 C1
Gatling Rd SE18, SE2 . . . 124 A1
Gatonby St SE15 . . . . 139 D4
Gatting Cl HA8 . . . . 27 A3
Gatting Way UB8 . . . . 60 A2
Gatton Prim Sch
SW17 . . . . 180 C6
Gatton Rd SW17 . . . . 180 C6
Gattons Way DA14 . . . . 191 B6
Gatward Cl N21 . . . . 16 D5
Gatward Gn N9 . . . . 17 D2
Gatwick Ho 3 E14 . . . . 97 B1
Gatwick Rd SW18 . . . . 157 B4
Gauden Cl SW4 . . . . 137 D2
Gauden Rd SW4 . . . . 137 D2
Gaugin Ct 13 SE16 . . . . 118 B1
Gauntlet 1 NW9 . . . . 27 D1
Gauntlet Cl UB5 . . . . 63 A1
Gauntlett Ct HA0 . . . . 65 B3
Gauntlett Rd SM1 . . . . 218 B3
Gaunt St SE1 . . . . 262 A6
Gautrey Rd SE15 . . . . 140 C3
Gautrey Sq 5 E6 . . . . 100 B1
Gavel St SE17 . . . . 262 D4
Gaven Ho N17 . . . . 33 C1
Gaverick Mews 3
E14 . . . . 119 C2
Gavestone Cres SE12 . . . 165 B4
Gavestone Rd SE12 . . . 165 B4
Gavestone Terr SE12 . . . 165 B4
Gaviller Pl 3 E5 . . . . 74 B4
Gavina Cl SM4 . . . . 202 C4
Gavin Ho 1 SE18 . . . . 123 C2
Gawain Wlk N9 . . . . 18 A1
Gawber St E2 . . . . 96 C4
Gawsworth Cl E15 . . . . 76 D3
Gawthorne Ave NW7 . . . 29 A5
Gawthorne Ct E3 . . . . 97 C5
Gay Cl NW2 . . . . 68 B3
Gaydon Ho W2 . . . . 91 D2
Gaydon La NW9 . . . . 27 C2
Gayfere Rd
Redbridge IG5 . . . . 56 B6
Stoneleigh KT17 . . . . 216 A3
Gayfere St
SW1 . . . . 116 A3 260 A5
Gayford Rd W12 . . . . 111 D4
Gay Ho N16 . . . . 73 C3
Gayhurst SE17 . . . . 139 B6
Gayhurst Ct 9 UB5 . . . . 84 C4
Gayhurst Ho NW8 . . . . 237 B6
Gayhurst Prim Sch E8 . . 74 A1
Gayhurst Rd E8 . . . . 74 A1
Gaylor Rd UB5 . . . . 63 B3
Gaymead NW8 . . . . 91 D6
Gaynesford Rd
Forest Hill SE23 . . . . 162 D2
Wallington SM5 . . . . 218 D1
Gay Rd E15 . . . . 98 B5
Gaysham Ave IG2 . . . . 56 D4
Gaysham Hall IG5 . . . . 56 D6
Gaysley Ho SE11 . . . . 261 A3
Gay St SW15 . . . . 134 D2
Gayton Cres NW3 . . . . 70 B4
Gayton Ct
3 Harrow HA1 . . . . 42 D3
New Malden KT3 . . . . 199 D4
Gayton Ho E3 . . . . 97 C3
Gayton Rd
Abbey Wood SE2 . . . . 124 C3
Hampstead NW3 . . . . 70 B4
Harrow HA1 . . . . 43 A3
Gayville Rd SW11 . . . . 158 D5
Gaywood Cl SW2 . . . . 160 C3
Gaywood Rd E17 . . . . 53 C6
Gaywood St SE1 . . . . 261 D5
Gaza St SE17 . . . 116 D1 261 C1
Gaze Ho 11 E14 . . . . 98 B1
Gean Ct 3 E11 . . . . 76 B4
Gearies Inf Sch IG2 . . . . 56 D4
Gearies Jun Sch IG2 . . . 56 D4
Geariesville Gdns IG6 . . . 56 D5
Gearing Cl SW17 . . . . 181 A6
Geary Ho N7 . . . . 72 B3
Geary Rd NW10 . . . . 68 A3
Geary St N7 . . . . 72 B3
GEC Est HA9 . . . . 65 D6
Geddes Pl 3 DA6 . . . . 147 C1
Gedeney Rd N17 . . . . 33 A2
Gedge Ct CR4 . . . . 202 C5
Gedling Ho SE22 . . . . 139 D2
Gedling Pl SE1 . . . . 263 D6
Geere Rd E15 . . . . 98 D6
Gees Ct W1 . . . . 238 B1
Gee St EC1 . . . 95 A3 242 A6
Geffrey's Ct SE9 . . . . 166 A1
Geffrye Ct N1 . . . . 95 C5
Geffrye Mus* E2 . . . . 95 D5
Geffrye St E2 . . . . 95 D5
Geldart Rd SE15 . . . . 140 B5
Geldeston Rd E5 . . . . 74 A6
Gellatly Rd SE14 . . . . 140 D3
Gell Cl UB10 . . . . 60 B5
Gemima Ct SM1 . . . . 217 C3
Gemini Bsns Ctr E16 . . . 98 B3
Gemini Gr UB5 . . . . 85 A4
Gemini Ho 11 E3 . . . . 97 C6
Gemma Ct BR3 . . . . 185 B1
General Gordon Pl
SE18 . . . . 122 D2
Generals Wlk The EN3 . . . 7 A6
General Wolfe Rd
SE10 . . . . 142 B4
Genesis Bsns Pk NW10 . . 88 D5
Genesis Cl TW19 . . . . 148 B3
Genesis Ho KT6 . . . . 197 D1
Genesta Rd SE18 . . . . 145 A6
Geneva Cl TW17 . . . . 171 C1
Geneva Ct Hendon NW9 . . 45 D4
1 Putney SW15 . . . . 156 D6
Stoke Newington N16 . . . 51 B1
Geneva Dr SW9 . . . . 138 C1
Geneva Gdns RM6 . . . . 59 A4
Geneva Rd
Kingston u T KT1 . . . . 198 A5
Thornton Heath CR7 . . . 205 A4
Genever Cl E4 . . . . 35 C5
Genista Rd N18 . . . . 34 B5
Genoa Ave SW15 . . . . 156 C6
Genoa Ho 19 E1 . . . . 96 D3
Genoa Rd SE20 . . . . 184 C2
Genotin Rd EN1 . . . . 5 B2
Genotin Terr EN1 . . . . 5 B2
Gentleman's Row EN2 . . . 5 A2
Gentry Gdns E13 . . . . 99 A4
Geoffrey Chaucer Tech
Coll SE1 . . . 117 B3 262 D5
Geoffrey Cl SE5 . . . . 139 A3
Geoffrey Ct SE4 . . . . 141 B2
Geoffrey Gdns E6 . . . . 100 A5
Geoffrey Ho SE1 . . . . 262 D6
Geoffrey Jones Ct
NW10 . . . . 90 A6
Geoffrey Rd SE4 . . . . 141 B2
George Akass Ho 5
SE18 . . . . 123 A1
George Beard Rd 11
SE8 . . . . 119 B2
George Beare Lo 9
SW4 . . . . 159 C6
George Belt Ho 8 E2 . . . 96 D4
George Carver Ho E7 . . . 77 A3
George Comberton Wlk 4
E12 . . . . 78 C3
George Cres N10 . . . . 31 A3
George Ct
Buckhurst Hill IG9 . . . . 21 D2
St James WC2 . . . . 250 B5
George Davies Lodge
IG6 . . . . 57 A4
George Downing Est
N16 . . . . 73 D6
George Eliot Ho SW1 . . . 259 B3
George Eliot Jun & Inf
Schs NW8 . . . 92 B6 229 C6
George Elliot Ho SE17 . . 262 A2
George Elliston Ho 13
SE1 . . . . 118 A1
George Eyre Ho NW8 . . . 229 D3
George Gange Way
HA3 . . . . 42 D6
George Green's Sec Sch
E14 . . . . 120 A1
George Groves Rd
SE20 . . . . 184 A2
George Ho 8 SE26 . . . . 184 B5
George Inn Yd SE1 . . . . 252 C3
George La Hayes BR2 . . . 209 B1
Lewisham SE13 . . . . 164 A5
Wanstead E18 . . . . 55 B6
Woodford E18 . . . . 37 A1
George Lansbury Ho
7 Bow E3 . . . . 97 B4
3 Willesden NW10 . . . . 67 C1
Wood Green N22 . . . . 32 C2
George Lashwood Ct 12
SW9 . . . . 138 B1
George Leybourne Ho 15
E1 . . . . 118 A6
George Lindgren Ho
SW6 . . . . 264 D4
George Loveless Ho 4
E2 . . . . 95 D4
George Lovell Dr EN3 . . . 7 C6
George Mathers Rd
SE11 . . . . 261 C4
George Mews NW1 . . . . 232 A1
George Mitchell Sch
E10 . . . . 53 D1
George Parr Ho N21 . . . . 16 D4
George Peabody Ct
NW1 . . . . 237 A4
George Rd Chingford E4 . . 35 C4
Kingston u T KT2 . . . . 177 A3
New Malden KT3 . . . . 199 D4
George Row SE16 . . . . 118 A4
Georges Mead WD6 . . . . 10 A5
George Spicer Prim Sch
EN1 . . . . 5 D2
George Sq SW19 . . . . 201 C6
George's Rd N7 . . . . 72 B3
George's Sq SW6 . . . . 264 D6
George St Barking IG11 . . 79 A1
6 Canning Town E16 . . . 98 D1
Ealing W7 . . . . 108 C5
Hounslow TW3, TW5 . . . 129 B3
Marylebone W1 . 92 D1 237 D2
Richmond TW10 . . . . 153 D6
Southall UB2 . . . . 107 A2
South Croydon CR0 . . . . 221 B6
George Street Sta
CR0 . . . . 221 A6
George Taylor CT N9 . . . 18 B1
George Tingle Ho SE1 . . 263 D6
George Tomlinson Prim
Sch E11 . . . . 54 C1
Georgetown Cl 4
SE19 . . . . 183 C5
Georgette Pl SE10 . . . . 142 A5
George Vale Ho 35 E2 . . . 96 A5
George V Ave HA2, HA5 . . 41 C6
Georgeville Gdns IG6 . . . 56 D5
George V Way UB6 . . . . 87 B6
George Walter Ho 11
SE16 . . . . 118 C2
George Wyver Cl
SW18 . . . . 157 A4
George Yd
City of London EC3 . . . . 242 D1
Mayfair W1 . . . 115 A6 248 B6
Georgiana St
NW1 . . . . 93 C6 232 B6
Georgian Cl Hayes BR2 . . 209 B1
Ickenham UB10 . . . . 60 A4
Stanmore HA7 . . . . 25 A3
Georgian Ct
Croydon CR0 . . . . 205 B1
12 Hackney E9 . . . . 96 C6
3 Hendon NW4 . . . . 46 B4
Wembley HA9 . . . . 66 D2
Georgian Ho HA0 . . . . 65 A5
Georgian Lo HA5 . . . . 40 B4
Georgian Village The
E17 . . . . 54 A6
Georgian Way HA1 . . . . 64 B6
Georgia Rd
New Malden KT3 . . . . 199 A5
South Norwood CR7 . . . . 182 D2
Georgina Ct 5 TW1 . . . . 153 C5
Georgina Gdns 10 E2 . . . 95 D4
Geraint Rd BR1 . . . . 187 A6
Geraldine Ct 6 NW9 . . . 46 A5
Geraldine Rd
Brentford W4 . . . . 132 C6
Wandsworth SW18 . . . . 158 A6
Geraldine St SE11 . . . . 261 C5
Gerald Mews SW1 . . . . 258 B4
Gerald Rd
Belgravia
SW1 . . . 115 A2 258 B4
Dagenham RM8 . . . . 59 B1
Newham E16 . . . . 98 D3
Gerard Ave TW4 . . . . 151 C4
Gerard Ct NW2 . . . . 68 D3
Gerard Rd
Barnes SW13 . . . . 133 D4
Harrow HA1 . . . . 43 A3
Gerards Cl SE16 . . . . 118 C1
Gerboa Ct 6 E4 . . . . 36 B5
Gerda Rd SE9 . . . . 167 A2
Germander Way E15 . . . 98 C4
German Sch The
TW10 . . . . 153 D3
Gernigan Ho SW18 . . . . 158 B5
Gernon Rd E3 . . . . 97 A5
Geron Way NW2 . . . . 68 C6
Gerrard Gdns HA5 . . . . 40 A4
Gerrard Ho 5 SE14 . . . . 140 D5
Gerrard Pl W1 . . . . 249 D6
Gerrard Rd N1 . . . 94 D5 234 D4
Gerrards Cl N14 . . . . 15 C6
Gerrard's Ct W5 . . . . 109 D3
Gerrard St W1 . . 115 D6 249 D6
Gerridge Ct SE1 . . . . 261 B6
Gerridge St
SE1 . . . 116 C3 261 B6
Gerry Raffles Sq E15 . . . 76 B2
Gertrude Rd DA17 . . . . 125 C2
Gertrude St
SW10 . . . 136 A6 266 B5
Gervase Cl HA9 . . . . 67 A5
Gervase Rd HA8 . . . . 27 B2
Gervase St SE15 . . . . 140 B5
Getters Talmud Torah
N16 . . . . 51 B2
Ghent St SE6 . . . . 163 C2
Ghent Way E8 . . . . 73 D2
Giant Arches Rd SE24 . . 161 A5
Giant Tree Hill WD23 . . . 8 B3
Gibbards Cott 1 IG11 . . . 79 D1
Gibbfield Cl RM6 . . . . 59 A6
Gibbings Ho SE1 . . . . 251 D1
Gibbins Rd E15 . . . . 76 A1
Gibbon Ho NW8 . . . . 236 D5
Gibbon Rd Acton W3 . . . 111 C6
Kingston u T KT2 . . . . 176 A3
Nunhead SE15 . . . . 140 C3
Gibbons Mews NW11 . . . 47 B4
Gibbons Rd NW10 . . . . 67 C2
Gibbon's Rents SE1 . . . 253 A3
Gibbon Wlk SW15 . . . . 134 A1
Gibbs Ave SE19 . . . . 183 B5
Gibbs Cl SE19 . . . . 183 B5
Gibbs Gn Edgware HA8 . . . 27 A6
West Kensington
W14 . . . . 113 B1 254 D2
Gibbs Green Rd
W14 . . . . 113 B1 254 C2
Gibbs Green Sch
W14 . . . . 113 B1 254 D2
Gibbs Ho
6 Balham SW12 . . . . 159 B4
2 Bromley BR1 . . . . 186 D2
Gibbs Rd N18 . . . . 34 C6
Gibbs Sq SE19 . . . . 183 B5
Gibraltar Ho NW10 . . . . 89 C5
Gibraltar Wlk 28 E2 . . . . 95 D4
Gibson Bsns Ctr 10
N17 . . . . 33 D3
Gibson Cl
Bethnal Green E1 . . . . 96 C3
Chessington KT9 . . . . 213 C3
Isleworth TW7 . . . . 130 B2
Southgate N21 . . . . 16 C5
Gibson Ct
9 Friern Barnet N11 . . . 30 D5
Hinchley Wood KT10 . . . 212 D5
Gibson Gdns N16 . . . . 73 D6
Gibson Ho
South Croydon CR2 . . . . 221 A2
Sutton SM1 . . . . 217 C4
Gibson Rd
Dagenham RM8 . . . . 58 C1
Ickenham UB10 . . . . 60 B4
Lambeth SE11 . . . . 260 D3
Sutton SM1 . . . . 217 D3
Gibson's Hill SW16 . . . . 182 C3
Gibson Sq N1 . . . 94 C6 234 B6
Gibson St SE10 . . . . 120 C1
Gideon Cl DA17 . . . . 125 D2
Gideon Mews W5 . . . . 109 D4
Gideon Rd SW11 . . . . 137 A2
Giesbach Rd N19 . . . . 71 D6
Giffard Rd N18 . . . . 33 C4
Giffen Square Mkt
SE8 . . . . 141 C5
Giffin St SE8 . . . . 141 C5
Gifford Gdns W7 . . . . 86 C2
Gifford Ho
5 Clapham SW4 . . . . 137 D1
Greenwich SE10 . . . . 120 B1
Pimlico SW1 . . . . 259 A1
Gifford Prim Sch UB5 . . . 85 B5
Gifford St N1 . . . . 72 A1
Gift La E15 . . . . 98 D6
Giggs Hill BR5 . . . . 190 A2
Giggs Hill Gdns KT7 . . . 197 A1
Giggs Hill Rd KT7 . . . . 197 A2
Gilbert Cl
Kidbrooke SE18 . . . . 144 B4
1 Merton SW19 . . . . 179 D2
Gilbert Ct W5 . . . . 88 B1
Gilbert Gr HA8 . . . . 27 B2
Gilbert Ho Barbican EC2 . 242 B3
Deptford SE8 . . . . 141 C6
5 Globe Town E2 . . . . 96 D4
Pimlico SW1 . . . . 258 D1
South Lambeth SW8 . . . 270 A4
5 Walthamstow E17 . . . 54 A6
Gilbert Pl WC1 . . 94 A2 240 A3
Gilbert Rd
Belvedere DA17 . . . . 125 C3
Lambeth SE11 . . 116 C2 261 B4
Merton SW19 . . . . 180 A3
Pinner HA5 . . . . 40 D5
Plaistow BR1 . . . . 187 A3
Gilbert Scott Inf Com Sch
CR2 . . . . 223 A1
Gilbert Scott Jun Com Sch
CR2 . . . . 223 A1
Gilbert Sheldon Ho
W2 . . . . 236 D4
Gilbertson Ho 11 E14 . . . 119 C3
Gilbert St Enfield EN3 . . . 6 C6
Hounslow TW3 . . . . 130 A2
Leyton E15 . . . . 76 C4
Marylebone W1 . . 93 A1 238 B1
Gilbey Cl UB10 . . . . 60 D4
Gilbey Rd SW17 . . . . 180 C5
Gilbeys Yd NW1 . . . . 71 A1
Gilbourne Rd SE18 . . . . 145 D6
Gilby Ho 5 E9 . . . . 74 D2
Gilda Ave EN3 . . . . 19 A6
Gilda Cres N16 . . . . 52 A1
Gilda Ct NW7 . . . . 28 A2
Gildea Cl HA5 . . . . 23 C3
Gildea St W1 . . . . 238 D3
Gilden Cres NW5 . . . . 71 A3
Gildersome St SE18 . . . . 144 C6
Gilders Rd KT9 . . . . 214 B2
Giles Coppice SE19 . . . . 183 D6
Giles Ho
5 Bermondsey SE16 . . . 118 A3
Notting Hill W11 . . . . 91 C1
Gilesmead SE5 . . . . 139 B4
Gilfrid Cl UB8 . . . . 82 D1
Gilkes Cres SE21 . . . . 161 C5
Gilkes Pl SE21 . . . . 161 C5
Gillam Ho 9 SE16 . . . . 118 C2
Gillan Ct SE12 . . . . 165 B1
Gillan Gn WD23 . . . . 8 A2
Gillards Mews 6 E17 . . . 53 C5
Gillards Way E17 . . . . 53 C5
Gill Ave E16 . . . . 99 A1
Gill Ct SE18 . . . . 123 A2
Gillender St E3 . . . . 98 A3
Gillespie Prim Sch N5 . . 72 D5
Gillespie Rd N4, N5 . . . . 72 D5
Gillett Ave E6 . . . . 100 A5

Gillette Cnr TW7...........131 A5
Gillett Ho N8............50 A6
Gillett Pl 27 E8.........73 C3
Gillett St CR7..........205 B5
Gillett St E8, N16.......73 C3
Gillfoot NW1.............232 A3
Gillham Terr N17.........34 A3
Gillian Ho HA3...........24 C4
Gillian Park Rd SM3....201 B1
Gillian St SE13........163 D6
Gillies Ct Sidcup DA14...189 C6
Southgate N21...........16 B6
Gillies St NW5..........71 A3
Gilling Ct 5 NW3........70 C2
Gillingham Ho SW1......259 A4
Gillingham Mews SW1....259 A4
Gillingham Rd NW2.......69 A5
Gillingham Row NW2.....259 A4
Gillingham St
SW1.........115 C2 259 A4
Gillings Ct EN5.........1 A1
Gillison Wlk 19 SE16....118 A3
Gillman Dr E15..........98 D6
Gillman Ho 24 E2........96 A5
Gillray Ho
Chelsea SW10..........266 C5
2 Sutton SM1..........218 B3
Gills Ct 2 EN5..........14 A6
Gill St E14............119 B6
Gillum Cl EN4...........14 D3
Gilmore Cl UB10.........60 C5
Gilmore Cres TW15......170 C4
Gilmore Ct N11..........30 D5
Gilmore Ho SW4.........136 D1
Gilmore Rd SE13........142 B1
Gilpin Ave SW14........133 B1
Gilpin Cl Mitcham CR4...180 C1
Paddington W2..........236 B4
Gilpin Cres
Edmonton N18...........33 D5
Twickenham TW2.........151 D4
Gilpin Ho
9 Edmonton N9..........18 A1
New Malden KT3........199 C4
Gilpin Rd E5............75 A4
Gilpin Way UB3.........127 B5
Gilray Ho W2...........246 C6
Gilsland Rd CR7........205 B5
Gilstead Ho IG11.......102 B5
Gilstead Rd SW6........135 D3
Gilston Rd
SW10........114 A1 256 B1
Gilton Rd SE6..........164 C1
Giltspur St EC1...94 D1 241 D2
Gilwell Cl E4...........7 D1
Gilwell Ct 7 E5.........74 B4
Gippeswyck Cl HA5......22 D2
Gipsy Cnr W3...........89 B2
Gipsy Hill SE19........183 C5
Gipsy Hill Sta SE19....183 C5
Gipsy La SW15.........134 B2
Gipsy Moth IV* SE10...142 A6
Gipsy Rd Bexley DA16...146 D3
West Norwood SE27.....183 B6
Gipsy Road Gdns
SE27.................183 A6
Giralda Cl E16.........99 D2
Giraud St E14..........97 D1
Girdlers Rd W14.......112 D2
Girdlestone Wlk N19....71 C6
Girdwood Rd SW18,
SW19................157 A4
Girling Ho 9 N1........95 C6
Girling Way TW14.....128 A2
Gironde Rd
SW6.........135 B5 264 D3
Girtin Ho
6 Belmont SM2........217 D1
4 Northolt UB5........84 D5
Girton Ave NW9........44 C6
Girton Cl UB5..........64 A2
Girton Gdns CR0.......223 C5
Girton Ho SW15........156 C5
Girton Rd
Forest Hill SE26......184 D5
Northolt UB5...........64 A2
Girton Villas 6 W10....90 D1
Gisbourne Cl SM6......219 D5
Gisburn Ho 23 SE15....140 A5
Gisburn Rd N8..........50 B5
Gissing Wlk N1.........72 C1
Gittens Ct BR1........186 D6
Given-Wilson Wlk E13...98 C5
Glacier Way HA0........87 D5
Gladbeck Way EN2........4 D1
Gladding Rd E12........77 D4
Gladebury Ct 2 SW19..179 B4
Glade Cl KT6..........213 D6
Glade Gdns CR0........207 A2
Glade La UB2..........107 D4
Gladeside Croydon CR0..206 D3
Southgate N21..........16 B4
Gladeside Cl KT9......213 D1
Gladesmore Com Sch
N15..................52 A4
Gladesmore Rd N15......51 D3
Glades Sh Ctr The
BR1.................187 A1
Gladeswood Rd DA17...125 D2
Glade The
Bromley BR1..........187 D1
Charlton SE7.........143 C5
Croydon CR0..........206 D3
Enfield EN2.............4 C3
Hammersmith W12......112 B4
Southgate N21..........16 B4

Glade The continued
Stoneleigh KT17......216 A2
West Wickham BR4.....223 D5
Woodford IG8..........21 B1
Gladiator St SE23.....163 A4
Glading Terr N16.......73 D5
Gladioli Cl 6 TW12...173 C4
Gladsdale Dr HA5.......40 B5
Gladsmuir Rd Barnet EN5..1 A3
Upper Holloway N19....49 C1
Gladstone Ave
Feltham TW14.........150 B5
Plashet E12...........78 A1
Tottenham N22.........32 D1
Twickenham TW2.......152 B4
Gladstone Ct
12 Merton SW19.......179 C3
Ruislip HA4...........61 C6
Westminster SW1.....259 D3
Willesden NW2.........68 B3
Gladstone Ho
6 Mitcham SW19......180 D1
16 Poplar E14.........97 C1
Gladstone Mews
5 Penge SE20.........184 C3
Wood Green N22........32 C1
Gladstone Par NW2......68 C5
Gladstone Park Gdns
NW2..................68 B5
Gladstone Park Sch
NW10.................68 B3
Gladstone Pl KT8.....196 C4
Gladstone Rd
Acton W4.............111 B3
Buckhurst Hill IG9....21 C3
Farnborough BR6......227 A3
Kingston u T KT1.....198 C6
Merton SW19..........179 C3
Southall UB2.........107 A4
Surbiton KT6.........214 A6
Thornton Heath CR0...205 B2
Gladstone St SE1.....261 C6
Gladstone Terr
SW8.........137 B4 268 D2
Gladstone Way HA3......42 C6
Gladwell Rd London N8...50 B3
Plaistow BR1.........187 A4
Gladwin Ho NW1.......232 B3
Gladwyn Rd SW15......134 D2
Gladys Dimson Ho E7...76 D3
Gladys Rd NW6..........69 C1
Glaisdale Sch SM2....217 B1
Glaisher St SE8.......141 D6
Glamis Cres UB3.......105 A3
Glamis Ct W3..........110 D4
Glamis Est 3 E1......118 D6
Glamis Pl E1.........118 C6
Glamis Rd E1.........118 C6
Glamis Way UB5........64 A2
Glamorgan Cl CR4,
SW16................204 A6
Glamorgan Ct 4 W7....86 D2
Glamorgan Rd KT1.....175 C3
Glandford Way RM6.....58 B4
Glanfield Rd BR3.....207 B5
Glanleam Rd HA7........25 D6
Glanville Ho 4 SW12..159 C4
Glanville Mews HA7....25 A5
Glanville Rd
Bromley BR2..........209 B6
Clapham Pk SW2.......160 A6
Glasbrook Ave TW2....151 B3
Glasbrook Rd SE9......165 D4
Glasbury Ho 5 SW9....138 B1
Glaserton Rd N16......51 C2
Glasford St SW17.....180 D4
Glasfryn Ct HA2........64 B6
Glasgow Ho W9.........91 D5
Glasgow Rd
Edmonton N18..........34 B5
Newham E13............99 B5
Glasgow Terr
SW1.........115 C1 259 A1
Glasier Ct 6 E15......76 C1
Glasse Cl W13.........109 A6
Glasshill St
SE1.........116 D4 251 D2
Glasshouse Cl UB8.....82 D2
Glasshouse Fields E1..118 D6
Glasshouse St
W1.........115 C6 249 B5
Glasshouse The SE13..142 A1
Glasshouse Wlk
SE11.......116 B1 260 C2
Glasshouse Yd EC1...242 A5
Glasslyn Rd N8.........49 D4
Glassmill La BR2.....186 D1
Glass St 4 E2..........96 B3
Glass Yd SE18........122 C3
Glastonbury Ave IG8...37 D4
Glastonbury Ct
12 Deptford SE14....140 C5
1 Ealing W13.........109 A5
Glastonbury Ho
London SE12..........164 D6
Pimlico SW1..........258 C2
Glastonbury Pl 22 E1..96 C1
Glastonbury Rd
Edmonton N9...........18 A3
Morden SM4..........201 C2
Glastonbury St NW6....69 B3
Glaston Ct W5........109 D5
Glaucus St E3..........97 D2
Glazbury Rd
W14........113 A1 254 B1
Glazebrook Cl SE21...161 B2
Glazebrook Rd TW11...174 D3
Gleave Ct 7 N20.......14 D2
Glebe Ave Enfield EN2...4 D2

Glebe Ave continued
Harrow HA3............44 A6
Mitcham CR4..........180 C1
Ruislip HA4...........62 B2
Uxbridge UB10.........61 A4
Woodford IG8..........37 A4
Glebe Cl
1 Chiswick W4.......111 C1
Uxbridge UB10.........61 A4
Glebe Cotts
Feltham TW13.........151 C1
Sutton SM1...........217 D4
Glebe Cres Harrow HA3..44 A6
Hendon NW4............46 C5
Glebe Ct 15 Bromley E3...97 D4
Ealing W5............109 D5
Hanwell W7...........108 B6
Lewisham SE3.........142 C2
Mitcham CR4..........202 D6
Palmers Green N13.....16 C1
Ruislip HA4...........39 B2
Stanmore HA7..........25 C5
Glebe House Dr BR2...209 B1
Glebehyrst SE19......183 C6
Glebe La Barnet EN5....12 A5
Harrow HA3............44 A6
Glebeland Gdns TW17..193 A3
Glebelands
East Molesey KT8.....195 D5
Leyton E10............75 D6
Mitcham CR4..........202 C6
Glebelands Ave
Ilford IG2............57 B2
Woodford E18..........37 A1
Glebelands Cl
Camberwell SE5.......139 C2
Finchley N2...........30 B2
Glebelands Rd TW14...150 A4
Glebe Path CR4.......202 D6
Glebe Pl SW3...136 C6 267 A6
Glebe Prim Sch UB10...61 B4
Glebe Rd Barnes SW13..134 A3
Belmont SM2..........217 A1
Bromley BR1..........187 A2
Dagenham RM10.........81 D2
Dalston E8............73 D1
Finchley N3...........30 A2
Hayes UB3............105 D5
Hornsey N8............50 B5
Stanmore HA7..........25 C5
Wallington SM5.......218 D2
Willesden NW10........68 A2
Glebe Sch BR4........224 B6
Glebe Side TW1.......152 D5
Glebe Sq CR4.........202 D6
Glebe St W4..........111 C1
Glebe The
Chislehurst BR7......189 A2
Lewisham SE3.........142 C2
New Malden KT4.......199 D1
Streatham SW16.......181 D6
West Drayton UB7.....104 B2
Shepperd IG8..........37 C5
Glebe Way
Feltham TW13.........151 C1
West Wickham BR4.....224 B6
Gledhow Gdns SW5.....256 A3
Gledstanes Rd
W14........113 A1 254 B1
Gledwood Ave UB4......84 A2
Gledwood Cres UB4.....83 D2
Gledwood Ct UB4.......83 D2
Gledwood Dr UB4.......83 D2
Gledwood Gdns UB4.....84 A2
Gleed Ave WD23.........8 B2
Gleeson Dr BR6.......227 D4
Glegg Pl 3 SW15......134 D1
Glenaffric Ave E14...120 B2
Glenalla Rd HA4.......39 D2
Glenalmond Ho
Ashford TW15.........148 A1
2 Putney SW15.......156 C5
Glenalvon Way 5
SE7.................122 A2
Glena Mount SM1......218 A4
Glenarm Coll IG1......78 D6
Glenarm Rd E5.........74 D4
Glen Ave TW15........170 C6
Glenavon Cl KT10.....213 A1
Glenavon Ct KT4......216 B6
Glenavon Rd E15.......76 C1
Glenbarr Cl SE9......144 D2
Glenbow Rd BR1.......186 C5
Glenbrook N EN2........4 B1
Glenbrook Prim Sch
SW4.................159 D5
Glenbrook Rd NW6......69 C3
Glenbrook S EN2........4 B1
Glenbuck Ct 6 KT6....198 A3
Glenbuck Rd KT6......198 A3
Glenburnie Rd SW17...158 D1
Glencairn Dr W5.......87 C3
Glencairne Cl E16.....99 D2
Glencairn Rd SW16....182 A3
Glen Cl TW17.........192 C5
Glencoe Ave IG2.......57 C2
Glencoe Dr RM10.......81 C4
Glencoe Mans 6
SW9.................138 C5
Glencoe Rd UB4........84 D3

Glencorse Gn WD19......22 D6
Glen Cres IG8..........37 B4
Glencroft Ct SM1.....217 C3
Glen Ct
6 Bromley BR1.......186 D3
6 Penge SE20........184 B2
Sidcup DA14..........190 A6
Glendale Ave
Edgware HA8...........26 C6
Ilford RM6............58 C2
Wood Green N22........32 C3
Glendale Cl SE9......144 C2
Glendale Dr SW19.....179 B5
Glendale Gdns HA9.....44 A1
Glendale Mews BR3....185 D2
Glendale Way SE28....124 C6
Glendall St SW9......138 B1
Glendarvon St SW15...134 D2
Glendevon Cl HA8......10 D1
Glendish Rd N17.......34 B2
Glendor Gdns NW7......27 B6
Glendower Gdns 10
SW14................133 B2
Glendower Pl SW7....256 C4
Glendower Prep Sch
SW7.........114 B2 256 C4
Glendower Rd
Chingford E4..........20 B3
Mortlake SW14........133 B2
Glendown Ho 2 E8.....74 A3
Glendown Rd SE2......124 A1
Glendun Ct W3........111 C6
Glendun Rd W3........111 C6
Gleneagle Lo BR3.....185 C2
Gleneagle Mews
SW16................181 D5
Gleneagle Rd SW16....181 D5
Gleneagles Ealing W13...87 B2
Stanmore HA7..........25 B4
Gleneagles Cl
21 Bermondsey SE16..118 B1
Crofton BR6..........211 B1
South Wimbledon SW19..22 D6
Gleneagles Ct 4
TW11................175 A5
Gleneagles Gn 1 BR6..211 B1
Gleneagles Twr 2 UB1..86 A1
Gleneldon Mews
SW16................182 A6
Gleneldon Rd SW16....182 A6
Glenelg Rd SW2.......160 A6
Glenesk Rd SE9.......144 D1
Glenfarg Rd SE6......164 B3
Glenfield Cres HA4....39 B2
Glenfield Ho
Ashford TW15.........171 A4
Ealing W13...........109 B4
Streatham SW12......159 C3
Glenfield Terr W13...109 A4
Glenfinlas Way SE5...138 D5
Glenforth St SE10....120 D1
Glengall Gr E14......120 A3
Glengall Pass 2 NW6..91 C6
Glengall Rd
Bexley DA7...........147 A2
Camberwell SE15......139 D6
Edgware HA8...........10 D1
Kilburn NW6...........91 B6
Woodford IG8..........37 B4
Glengall Terr SE15...139 D6
Glengarnock Ave E14..120 A2
Glengarry Rd SE22....161 D6
Glen Gdns CR0........220 C4
Glenham Dr IG2........56 D4
Glenhead Cl SE9......144 D2
Glenhill Cl N3.........29 C1
Glen Ho
6 Newham E16........122 C5
Wallington SM6.......219 C4
Glenhouse Rd SE9.....166 C6
Glenhurst 4 BR3......186 A2
Glenhurst Ave
Gospel Oak NW5........71 A4
Ruislip HA4...........39 A1
Sidcup DA5...........169 B3
Glenhurst Ct 1 SE19..183 D5
Glenhurst Rd
Brentford TW8........109 C1
North Finchley N12....30 B5
Glenhurst Rise SE19..183 A3
Glenilla Rd NW3.......70 C2
Glenister Ho UB3.....106 B5
Glenister Park Rd
SW16................181 D3
Glenister Rd SE10....120 D1
Glenister St E16.....122 C5
Glenkerry Ho 1 E14...98 A1
Glenlea Rd SE9.......166 C6
Glenloch Ct 2 NW3....70 C2
Glenloch Rd Enfield EN3..6 C3
Maitland Pk NW3.......70 C3
Glenluce Rd SE3......143 A6
Glenlyon Rd SE9......166 C6
Glenmead IG9..........21 C3
Glenmere Ave NW7.....28 A4
Glenmill TW12........173 B5
Glenmore SW15........156 D5
Glenmore Ho 6
TW10................154 A5
Glenmore Lawns W13...87 A1
Glenmore Rd
Bexley DA16..........145 D4
Maitland Pk NW3.......70 C3
Glenmore Way IG11....102 A5
Glenmount Path 1
SE18................123 A1
Glennie Ho SE10......142 A4
Glennie Rd SE27......162 A3

Glennie Rd SE27,
SW16................160 C1
Glenny Rd IG11........79 A2
Glenorchy Cl UB4......85 A2
Glenpark Ct W13......109 A6
Glenparke Rd E7.......77 B2
Glen Rd
Chessington KT9.....214 A5
Newham E13............99 C3
Walthamstow E17.......53 B4
Glenridding NW1......232 B3
Glen Rise IG8.........37 B4
Glenrosa St SW6......136 A3
Glenrose Ct DA14.....190 B5
Glenrose Ho 9 SM1....218 A4
Glenroy St W12........90 C1
Glensdale Rd SE4.....141 B2
Glenshaw Mans 7
SW9.................138 C5
Glenshiel Rd SE9.....166 C6
Glentanner Way
SW17................158 B1
Glen Terr E14........120 A4
Glentham Gdns SW13...134 B6
Glentham Rd SW13.....134 B6
Glen The
Beckenham BR2........186 C1
Eastcote Village HA5..40 B4
Enfield EN2............4 D1
Lockesbottom BR6.....226 C5
Rayners La HA5........41 A2
Southall UB2.........107 B1
South Croydon CR0....222 D5
Wembley HA9...........65 D2
Glenthorne Ave CR0...206 C1
Glenthorne Cl SM3....201 C1
Glenthorne Gdns
Cheam SM3............201 C1
Ilford IG6............56 D5
Glenthorne High Sch
SM3.................201 C1
Glenthorne Mews W6...112 B2
Glenthorne Rd
Friern Barnet N11.....31 A5
Hammersmith W6.......112 B2
Kingston u T KT1.....198 B5
Walthamstow E17.......53 A4
Glenthorpe SW15......134 A1
Glenthorpe Rd SM4....200 D4
Glenton Rd SE13......142 C1
Glentrammon Ave
BR6.................227 D2
Glentrammon Cl BR6...227 D3
Glentrammon Gdns
BR6.................227 D2
Glentrammon Rd BR6...227 D2
Glentworth Ct HA8....26 B5
Glentworth St
NW1.........92 D3 237 D5
Glenure Rd SE9.......166 C6
Glenview SE2.........146 D6
Glen View Rd BR1.....187 D1
Glenville Ave EN2......5 A5
Glenville Gr SE8.....141 B5
Glenville Mews SW18..157 C4
Glenville Rd KT2.....176 C2
Glen Wlk TW7.........152 B6
Glenwood Ave NW9.....45 C1
Glenwood Cl HA1.......42 D4
Glenwood Ct
7 Sidcup DA14.......190 A6
6 Wanstead E18.......55 A6
Glenwood Gdns IG2.....56 C4
Glenwood Gr NW9.......45 A1
Glenwood Ho 3 EN5....13 D6
Glenwood Rd
Edgware NW7...........11 C1
Forest Hill SE6......163 C3
Harringay N15.........50 D4
Hounslow TW3.........130 B2
Stoneleigh KT17......216 A2
Glenwood Way CR0.....206 D3
Glenworth Ave E14....120 B2
Gliddon Dr E5.........74 B4
Gliddon Rd
W14........113 A1 254 A2
Glimpsing Gn DA18....125 A3
Glisson Rd UB10.......82 C5
Globe Ct SE18........145 A6
Globe Pond Rd SE16...119 A5
Globe Prim Sch E2.....96 C4
Globe Rd
Bethnal Green E1, E2..96 C3
Stratford E15.........76 D3
Woodford IG8..........37 C4
Globe St SE1...117 B4 252 C1
Globe Terr 9 E2.......96 C4
Globe Theatre The*
SE1.................252 A5
GLOBE TOWN............96 D4
Globe View EC4.......252 A6
Globe Yd W1..........238 C1
Glossop Ho TW7.......131 A1
Gloster Rd KT3.......199 C5
Gloucester W14.......254 D3
Gloucester Ave
Camden Town
NW1.........93 A6 231 B6
Falconwood DA16......145 D1
Sidcup DA15..........167 C2
Gloucester Cir SE10..142 A5
Gloucester Cl
Thames Ditton KT7...197 A1
Willesden NW10........67 B1
Gloucester Cres
Camden Town
NW1.........93 B6 231 C6
Staines TW18.........170 A4
Gloucester Ct
6 Acton W3...........88 C1

Gloucester Ct continued
10 Belmont SM2.......217 C1
Borough The SE1......262 B6
City of London EC3...253 B5
Dulwich SE22.........162 A3
5 Ealing W7..........86 D2
Golders Green NW11....47 B2
Harrow HA1............42 C6
Redbridge IG1.........56 B2
Richmond TW9.........132 C5
8 Surbiton KT6......197 D2
Gloucester Dr
Finsbury Pk N4........72 D6
London NW11...........47 C5
Gloucester Gate NW1..231 C4
Gloucester Gate Mews
NW1.................231 C4
Gloucester Gdns
Cockfosters EN4......15 A6
Golders Green NW11....47 B2
Paddington W2........236 A2
Redbridge IG1.........56 A2
Sutton SM1...........217 D6
Gloucester Gr HA8.....27 B2
Gloucester Ho
Kilburn NW6...........91 C5
Richmond TW10........154 C6
Gloucester Lo 9 CR0..221 D6
Gloucester Mews
Paddington W2........236 B1
Walthamstow E17.......53 C2
Gloucester Mews W
W2..................236 B1
Gloucester Par
Bexley DA15..........168 A6
Hayes UB3............105 A3
Gloucester Pk SW7....256 A4
Gloucester Pl
W1.........92 D2 237 D4
Gloucester Pl Mews
W1.........92 D2 237 D3
Gloucester Prim Sch
SE15................139 C5
Gloucester Rd
Acton W3.............111 A4
Croydon CR0..........205 C2
Ealing W5............109 C4
Edmonton N18..........33 D5
Enfield EN2............5 A5
Erith DA17...........125 B1
Feltham TW13.........150 C3
Hampton TW12.........173 D3
Harrow HA1............41 C4
Higham Hill E17.......34 C1
Hounslow TW4.........129 A1
Ilford E12............78 B4
Kingston u T KT1, KT2..176 D1
Leyton E10............53 C2
New Barnet EN5........14 A6
Richmond TW9.........132 C5
South Kensington
SW7.........114 A2 256 A4
Teddington TW11......174 C1
Tottenham N17.........51 B6
Twickenham TW2.......152 A3
Wanstead E11..........55 C4
Gloucester Road Sta
SW7.........114 A2 256 A4
Gloucester Sq
6 Hackney E2.........96 A6
Paddington W2...92 C1 237 A1
Gloucester St
SW1.........115 C1 259 A2
Gloucester Terr
W2.........92 A1 236 B1
Gloucester Way EC1...234 B1
Gloucester Wlk
W8.........113 C4 245 B4
Glover Cl SE2........124 C2
Glover Dr N18.........34 C4
Glover Ho London SE15..140 B1
2 South Hampstead
NW6.................70 A1
Glover Rd HA5.........40 D3
Glovers Gr HA4........38 D2
Glovers Lo 24 TW10...153 D6
Glowhill Ct N12.......30 A3
Gloxinia Wlk TW12....173 C4
Glycena Rd SW11......136 D2
Glyn Ave EN4...........2 B1
Glyn Cl SE25.........183 C2
Glyn Ct Stanmore HA7...25 B4
West Norwood SE27....160 C1
Glyndale Grange SM2..217 D3
Glyndebourne Ct 5
UB5.................84 C4
Glyndebourne Pk BR6..226 C6
Glynde Mews SW3.....257 B5
Glynde Rd DA7........147 A2
Glynde Reach WC1....233 B1
Glynde St SE4........163 B5
Glyndon Rd SE18......123 B2
Glyn Dr DA14.........190 B6
Glynfield Rd NW10.....67 C1
Glyn Mans W14........254 B4
Glynne Rd N22.........32 C1
Glyn Rd Clapton Pk E5..74 D4
Enfield EN3............6 C1
North Cheam KT4, SM3..216 B4
Glyn St SE11.........260 C1
Glynwood Ct 7 SE23..162 C2
Goaters' Alley SW6...264 D3
Goat La EN1............5 D5
Goat Rd CR4..........202 D2
Goat Wharf TW8.......132 A6
Godalming Ave SM6....220 B3
Godalming Rd E14......97 D2
Godbold Rd E15........98 C4
Goddard Cl TW17......192 B6
Goddard Ct HA3........25 A1

Goddard Ho SW19 ... 156 D2
Goddard Pl N19 ... 71 C5
Goddard Rd BR3 ... 207 A5
Goddards Way IG1 ... 57 B1
Goddarts Ho E17 ... 53 C6
Godfrey Ave
Northolt UB5 ... 85 A6
Twickenham TW2 ... 152 B4
Godfrey Hill SE18 ... 122 A2
Godfrey Ho EC1 ... 235 C1
Godfrey Rd SE18 ... 122 B2
Godfrey St
Chelsea SW3 ... 114 C1 257 B2
Mill Meads E15 ... 98 A5
Godfrey Way TW4 ... 151 B4
Goding St
SE11 ... 116 A1 260 B1
Godley Rd SW18 ... 158 B3
Godliman St EC4 ... 252 A6
Godman Rd SE15 ... 140 B3
Godolphin Cl N13 ... 32 D4
Godolphin Ho
Primrose Hill NW3 ... 70 C1
7 Streatham SW2 ... 160 C3
Godolphin & Latymer Sch
W6 ... 112 B2
Godolphin Pl W3 ... 111 B6
Godolphin Rd W12 ... 112 B4
Godson Rd CR0 ... 220 C5
Godson St N1 ... 234 A4
Godstone Ct 1 N16 ... 51 C1
Godstone Ho
Borough The SE1 ... 262 D6
1 Kingston u T KT2 ... 176 D4
Godstone Rd
Sutton SM1 ... 218 A4
Twickenham TW1 ... 153 B5
Godstow Rd SE2 ... 124 C4
Godwin Cl
Shoreditch N1 ... 235 B4
West Ewell KT19 ... 215 A2
Godwin Ct NW1 ... 232 B4
Godwin Ho
2 Haggerston E2 ... 95 D5
Kidbrooke SE18 ... 144 B4
Kilburn NW6 ... 91 D5
Godwin Jun Sch E7 ... 77 B4
Godwin Prim Sch RM9 ... 81 A1
Godwin Rd
Bromley BR1, BR2 ... 209 C6
Forest Gate E7 ... 77 B4
Godwyn Ho 13 KT6 ... 198 A3
Goffers Ho SE3 ... 142 C3
Goffers Rd SE3, SE13 ... 142 C3
Goffs Rd TW15 ... 171 B4
Goffton Ho 14 SW9 ... 138 B3
Goidel Cl SM6 ... 219 D4
Golborne Gdns
5 Kensal Town W10 ... 91 A3
West Kilburn W10 ... 91 B3
Golborne Mews 9
W10 ... 91 A2
Golborne Rd W10 ... 91 A2
Golda Cl EN5 ... 12 D5
Golda Ct N3 ... 29 B1
Goldbeaters Gr HA8 ... 27 C3
Goldbeaters Prim Sch
HA8 ... 27 B2
Goldcliff Cl SM4 ... 201 C2
Goldcrest Cl
Newham E16 ... 99 D2
Woolwich SE28 ... 124 C6
Goldcrest Mews W5 ... 87 D2
Goldcrest Way
Bushey WD23 ... 8 A3
New Addington CR0 ... 224 B1
Golden Cres UB3 ... 105 D5
Golden Cross Mews 2
W11 ... 91 B1
Golden Ct 4 Barnet EN4 ... 2 C1
Ealing W7 ... 108 C6
Hounslow TW3 ... 130 B3
10 Richmond TW9 ... 153 D6
Golden Hinde The*
SE1 ... 252 C4
Golden Hind Pl 5
SE8 ... 119 B2
Golden La EC1 ... 95 A3 242 B5
Golden Manor W7 ... 108 C6
Golden Mews SE20 ... 184 C2
Golden Par 2 E17 ... 54 A6
Golden Plover Cl E16 ... 99 A1
Golden Sq W1 ... 115 C6 249 B6
Golders Cl HA8 ... 26 D5
Golders Ct NW11 ... 47 B2
Golders Gdns NW11 ... 47 B2
GOLDERS GREEN ... 47 B2
Golders Green Coll
NW11 ... 47 C1
Golders Green Cres
NW11 ... 47 C2
Golders Green Rd
NW11 ... 47 A2
Golders Green Sta
NW11 ... 47 C1
Golders Hill Sch NW11 ... 47 C2
Goldersleа NW11 ... 47 C1
Golders Manor Dr
NW11 ... 47 A3
Golders Park Cl NW11 ... 47 C1
Golders Rise NW4 ... 46 D4
Golders Way NW11 ... 47 B2
Golderton 2 NW4 ... 46 C5
Goldfinch Rd SE28 ... 123 B3
Goldhawk Ind Est The
W6 ... 112 B3
Goldhawk Mews 2
W12 ... 112 B4
Goldhawk Rd W12 ... 112 A3
Goldhawk Road Sta
W12 ... 112 C4
Goldhaze Cl IG8 ... 37 D3
Gold Hill HA8 ... 27 B4
Goldhurst Terr NW6 ... 70 A1
Goldie Ho N19 ... 49 D2
Goldie Leigh Hospl
SE2 ... 146 C6
Golding Cl KT9 ... 213 C2
Golding Ct 7 IG1 ... 78 C5
Golding St E1 ... 96 A1
Goldington Cres NW1 ... 232 C4
Goldington Ct NW1 ... 232 C5
Goldington St
NW1 ... 93 D5 232 C4
Gold La HA8 ... 27 B4
Goldman Cl E2 ... 96 A3
Goldmark Ho SE3 ... 143 B2
Goldney Rd W9 ... 91 C3
Goldrill Dr N11 ... 15 A2
Goldsboro Rd
SW8 ... 137 D5 269 D3
Goldsborough Cres E4 ... 20 A2
Goldsborough Ho
SW8 ... 269 D1
Goldsdown Cl EN3 ... 7 A3
Goldsdown Rd EN3 ... 7 A3
Goldsmid St 2 SE18 ... 123 C1
Goldsmith Ave
Acton W3 ... 111 B6
Dagenham RM7 ... 59 C2
Hyde The NW9 ... 45 C3
Plashet E12 ... 78 A2
Goldsmith Cl HA2 ... 41 D1
Goldsmith Ct
Edgware HA8 ... 26 B6
St Giles WC1 ... 240 B2
Goldsmith Ho W3 ... 111 B6
Goldsmith La NW9 ... 45 A5
Goldsmith Rd
Acton W3 ... 111 B5
Friern Barnet N11 ... 30 D5
Higham Hill E17 ... 34 D1
Leyton E10 ... 53 D1
Peckham SE15 ... 140 A4
Goldsmiths Bldgs W3 ... 111 B5
Goldsmiths Cl W3 ... 111 B5
Goldsmiths Coll, Univ of
London SE14 ... 141 A4
Goldsmith's Ct N6 ... 49 B3
Goldsmith's Pl 6 NW6 ... 91 D6
Goldsmith's Row E2 ... 96 A5
Goldsmith's Sq 17 E2 ... 96 A5
Goldsmith St EC2 ... 242 B2
Goldthorpe NW1 ... 232 A5
Goldwell Ho SE22 ... 139 C1
Goldwell Rd CR7 ... 204 B5
Goldwin Cl SE14 ... 140 C4
Goldwing Cl E16 ... 99 A1
Golf Cl
South Norwood
SW16 ... 182 C2
Stanmore HA7 ... 25 C3
Golf Club Dr KT2 ... 177 B3
Golfe Ho IG1 ... 79 B5
Golfe Rd IG1 ... 79 B5
Golfers View N12 ... 30 B6
Golf Rd Bromley BR1 ... 210 C6
Ealing W5 ... 88 B1
Golf Side TW2 ... 152 B1
Golfside Cl N20 ... 14 C1
Golf Side Cl KT3 ... 177 C1
Gollogly Terr 9 SE7 ... 121 C1
Gomer Gdns TW11 ... 175 A4
Gomer Pl TW11 ... 175 A4
Gomm Rd SE16 ... 118 C3
Gomshall Ave SM6 ... 220 A3
Gondar Gdns NW6 ... 69 B3
Gondar Mans NW6 ... 69 B3
Gonson St SE8 ... 141 D6
Gonston Cl SW19 ... 157 A2
Gonville Cres UB5 ... 63 D2
Gonville Ct 6 EN4 ... 14 D3
Gonville Ho 6 SW15 ... 156 D5
Gonville Prim Sch
CR7 ... 204 B4
Gonville Rd CR7 ... 204 B4
Gonville St SW6 ... 135 A2
Gooch Ho Holborn EC1 ... 241 A4
Lower Clapton E5 ... 74 B5
Goodall Ho 10 SE4 ... 140 D1
Goodall Rd E11 ... 76 A5
Goodbehere Ho 7
SE27 ... 183 A6
Gooden Ct HA1 ... 64 C5
Goodenough Coll
WC1 ... 94 B3 240 C6
Goodenough Rd
SW19 ... 179 B3
Goodey Rd IG11 ... 79 D1
Goodfaith Ho 18 E14 ... 119 D6
Goodge Pl W1 ... 239 B3
Goodge St W1 ... 93 C2 239 B3
Goodge Street Sta
W1 ... 93 D2 239 C4
Goodhall Cl HA7 ... 25 B4
Goodhall St NW10 ... 89 D4
Good Hart Pl E14 ... 119 A6
Goodhart Way BR4 ... 208 C3
Goodhew Rd CR0 ... 206 A3
Goodhope Ho 17 E14 ... 119 D6
Gooding Cl KT3 ... 199 A4
Goodinge Cl N7 ... 72 A2
Goodinge Rd N7 ... 72 A2
Gooding Ho 4 SE7 ... 121 C1
Goodison Cl WD23 ... 8 A6
Goodland Ho 1 KT3 ... 199 C2
Goodman Cres SW2 ... 159 D2
Goodman Rd E10 ... 54 A2
Goodmans Ct HA0 ... 65 D4
Goodman's Stile 17 E1 ... 96 A1
Goodman's Yd E1,
EC3 ... 117 D6 253 C6
GOODMAYES ... 58 B1
Goodmayes Ave IG3 ... 58 A1
Goodmayes Hospl IG3 ... 58 A4
Goodmayes La IG3 ... 80 A5
Goodmayes Lodge
RM8 ... 80 A4
Goodmayes Prim Sch
IG3 ... 58 B1
Goodmayes Rd IG3 ... 58 A1
Goodmayes Ret Pk
RM6 ... 58 B2
Goodmayes Sta IG3 ... 58 A1
Goodrich Com Sch
SE22 ... 162 A5
Goodrich Ct 9 W10 ... 90 D1
Goodrich Ho
20 Bethnal Green E2 ... 96 C5
Stamford Hill N16 ... 51 C2
Goodrich Rd SE22 ... 162 A5
Goodridge Ho E17 ... 36 A3
Good Shepherd RC Prim
Sch
Catford BR1 ... 186 D6
New Addington CR0 ... 223 D1
Good Shepherd RC Prim
Sch The W12 ... 111 D4
Goodson Ho SM4 ... 202 A2
Goodson Rd NW10 ... 67 C1
Goodspeed Ho 20 E14 ... 119 D6
Goodsway NW1 ... 94 A5 233 A4
Goodway Gdns E14 ... 98 B1
Goodwill Ho 22 E14 ... 119 D6
Goodwin Cl
Bermondsey
SE16 ... 117 D3 263 D5
Mitcham CR4 ... 202 B6
Goodwin Ct
East Barnet EN4 ... 14 C5
Hornsey N8 ... 50 A6
2 Mitcham SW19 ... 180 C3
Goodwin Dr DA14 ... 168 D2
Goodwin Gdns CR0,
CR2 ... 220 D2
Goodwin Ho
Edmonton N9 ... 18 C3
2 Peckham SE15 ... 140 B2
Goodwin Rd
Croydon CR0 ... 220 D3
Edmonton N9 ... 18 D3
Shepherd's Bush W12 ... 112 A4
Goodwins Ct WC2 ... 250 A6
Goodwin St N4 ... 72 C6
Goodwood Ave EN3 ... 6 C6
Goodwood Cl
Morden SM4 ... 201 C5
11 Stanmore HA7 ... 25 C5
Goodwood Ct W1 ... 238 D4
Goodwood Dr UB5 ... 63 C2
Goodwood Ho
3 Acton Green W4 ... 111 A1
Penge SE26 ... 184 B4
Goodwood Lo 1 SM6 ... 219 D5
Goodwood Mans 3
SW9 ... 138 C2
Goodwood Par BR3 ... 207 A5
Goodwood Rd SE14 ... 141 A5
Goodwyn Ave NW7 ... 27 C5
Goodwyn Sch NW7 ... 28 A5
Goodwyn's Vale N10 ... 31 B2
Goodyear Ho 8 N2 ... 30 B1
Goodyers Gdns NW4 ... 46 D4
Goosander Ct 34 NW9 ... 27 D1
Goosander Way SE18,
SE28 ... 123 B3
Gooseacre La HA3 ... 43 D4
Goose Green Cl BR5 ... 190 A1
Goose Green Prim Sch
SE22 ... 139 D1
Goose Green Trad Est
SE22 ... 140 A1
Gooseley La E6 ... 100 C4
Goose Sq 8 E6 ... 100 B1
Goossens Cl 1 SM1 ... 218 A3
Gophir La EC4 ... 252 C6
Gopsall St N1 ... 95 B6 235 D5
Gordon Ave
Chingford E4 ... 36 C4
Isleworth TW1 ... 153 B6
Mortlake SW14 ... 133 C1
Stanmore HA7 ... 25 A4
Gordonbrock Prim Sch
SE4 ... 163 C6
Gordonbrock Rd SE4 ... 163 C6
Gordon Cl E17 ... 53 C3
Gordon Cres
Croydon CR0 ... 205 D1
Hayes UB3 ... 106 A2
Gordon Ct Edgware HA8 ... 26 B5
Hampton TW12 ... 174 A5
5 Shepherd's Bush
W12 ... 90 C1
18 Wimbledon SW20 ... 178 D3
Gordondale Rd SW18,
SW19 ... 157 C2
Gordon Dr TW17 ... 193 B2
Gordon Gdns HA8 ... 26 D1
Gordon Gr SE5 ... 138 D3
Gordon Hill EN2 ... 5 A4
Gordon Hill Sta EN2 ... 4 D4
Gordon Ho
2 Ealing W5 ... 88 A4
Lee SE12 ... 165 A4
17 Shadwell E1 ... 118 C6
Gordon Hospl The
SW1 ... 115 D2 259 C3
Gordon House Rd NW5 ... 71 A4
Gordon Inf Sch IG1 ... 79 B5
Gordon Lo N16 ... 51 B1
Gordon Mans
3 Barnet EN5 ... 1 B1
Marylebone WC1 ... 239 C5
Gordon Pl W8 ... 113 C4 245 B2
Gordon Prim Sch SE9 ... 144 B1
Gordon Rd
Ashford TW15 ... 148 A1
Avery Hill DA15 ... 167 C6
Barking IG11 ... 101 C6
Beckenham BR3 ... 207 B6
Chingford E4 ... 20 C4
Chiswick W4 ... 132 D6
Claygate KT10 ... 212 C1
Dagenham RM6 ... 59 B3
Ealing W13 ... 109 C6
Edmonton N9 ... 18 B2
Enfield EN2 ... 5 B3
Finchley N3 ... 29 B3
Harrow HA3 ... 42 C6
Ilford IG1 ... 79 B5
Isleworth TW3 ... 130 A1
Kingston u T KT2 ... 176 B2
Leyton E15 ... 76 A4
Peckham SE15 ... 140 B3
Richmond TW9 ... 132 B3
Shepperton TW17 ... 193 B3
Southall UB2 ... 107 A2
Surbiton KT5 ... 198 B2
Wallington SM5 ... 218 D2
Wanstead E11 ... 55 A3
Woodford E18 ... 37 B2
Wood Green N11 ... 31 D3
Yiewsley UB7 ... 104 A6
Gordon Sq WC1 ... 93 D3 239 D6
Gordon St
Bloomsbury
WC1 ... 93 D3 239 C6
Newham E13 ... 99 A4
Gordon Way Barnet EN5 ... 1 B1
Bromley BR1 ... 187 A2
Gore Ct NW9 ... 44 C4
Gorefield Ho NW6 ... 91 C5
Gorefield Pl NW6 ... 91 C5
Gore Rd Hackney E9 ... 96 C6
Merton SW20 ... 178 C1
Goresbrook Rd RM9 ... 102 D6
Gore St SW7 ... 114 A3 256 B6
Gorham Ho 12 SW4 ... 159 C5
Gorham Pl W11 ... 244 A5
Goring Gdns RM8 ... 80 C4
Goring Rd N11 ... 32 A4
Goring St EC3 ... 243 B2
Goring Way UB6 ... 86 A5
Gorleston Rd N15 ... 51 B4
Gorleston St
W14 ... 113 A2 254 B4
Gorman Rd SE18 ... 122 B2
Gorringe Park Ave
CR4 ... 181 A3
Gorringe Park Prim Sch
CR4 ... 181 A2
Gorse Cl E16 ... 99 A1
Gorsefield Ho 6 E14 ... 119 C6
Gorse Rd CR0 ... 223 C5
Gorse Rise SW17 ... 181 A5
Gorse Wlk UB7 ... 82 A1
Gorst Rd London SW11 ... 158 D5
North Acton NW10 ... 89 B3
Gorsuch Pl 1 E2 ... 95 D4
Gorsuch St E2 ... 95 D4
Gosberton Rd SW12 ... 159 A3
Gosbury Hill KT9 ... 214 A4
Gosfield Rd RM8 ... 59 C1
Gosfield St W1 ... 93 C2 239 A3
Gosford Gdns IG4 ... 56 B4
Gosford Ho 25 E3 ... 97 B5
Goshawk Gdns UB4 ... 83 C5
Goslett Yd WC2 ... 239 D2
Gosling Cl UB6 ... 85 C4
Gosling Ho 2 E1 ... 118 C6
Gosling Way SW9 ... 138 C4
Gosmore Ct N9 ... 18 B2
Gospatric Home Ho
SW14 ... 133 C2
Gospatrick Rd N17 ... 33 A2
GOSPEL OAK ... 71 A4
Gospel Oak Prim Sch
NW5 ... 71 A4
Gospel Oak Sta NW5 ... 71 A4
Gosport Ho 9 SW15 ... 156 A3
Gosport Rd E17 ... 53 B4
Gosport Wlk N17 ... 52 B5
Gossage Rd
Hillingdon UB10 ... 60 B1
Plumstead SE18 ... 123 B1
Gosset St E2 ... 96 A4
Gosshill Rd BR7 ... 188 C1
Gossington Cl BR7 ... 188 D6
Gosterwood St SE8 ... 141 A6
Gostling Rd TW2 ... 151 C3
Goston Gdns CR7 ... 204 C6
Goswell Pl EC1 ... 234 D1
Goswell Rd EC1 ... 94 D4 234 D2
Gothic Ct
17 Camberwell SE5 ... 139 A5
Harlington UB3 ... 127 B6
Gothic Rd TW2 ... 152 B2
Gottfried Mews NW5 ... 71 C4
Goudhurst Ho 7
SE20 ... 184 C3
Goudhurst Rd BR1 ... 186 D5
Gough Ho Islington N1 ... 234 D6
4 Kingston u T KT1 ... 176 A1
Gough Rd Enfield EN1 ... 6 B3
Stratford E15 ... 76 D4
Gough Sq EC4 ... 94 C1 241 B2
Gough St WC1 ... 94 B3 240 D5
Gough Wlk 14 E14 ... 97 C1
Gould Ct SE19 ... 183 C5
Goulden Ho SW11 ... 136 C3
Goulding Gdns CR7 ... 183 A1
Gouldman Ho 33 E1 ... 96 C3
Gould Rd
East Bedfont TW14 ... 149 C4
Twickenham TW2 ... 152 C3
Gould's Gn UB8 ... 104 D6
Gould Terr 26 E8 ... 74 B3
Goulston St E1 ... 95 D1 243 C2
Goulton Rd E5 ... 74 B4
Gourley Pl N15 ... 51 C4
Gourley St N15 ... 51 C4
Gourock Rd SE9 ... 166 C6
Govan St E2 ... 96 A6
Gover Ct 8 SW4 ... 138 A3
Government Row EN3 ... 7 C6
Govett Ave TW17 ... 193 A4
Govier Cl E15 ... 76 C1
Gowan Ave
SW6 ... 135 A4 264 A2
Gowan Ho 22 E2 ... 95 D4
Gowan Lea 4 E18 ... 55 A5
Gowan Rd NW10 ... 68 B2
Gower Cl SW4 ... 159 C5
Gower Ct WC1 ... 239 C6
Gower Ho Barking IG11 ... 79 A1
Hayes UB3 ... 105 C6
Upper Tooting SW17 ... 180 B4
12 Walthamstow E17 ... 53 D6
Walworth SE17 ... 262 B2
Gower House Sch NW9 ... 67 A6
Gower Mews WC1 ... 239 D4
Gower Pl NW1,
WC1 ... 93 D3 239 C6
Gower Rd
Hounslow TW7 ... 130 D6
Upton E7 ... 77 A2
Gower Sch The N7 ... 72 A2
Gower St WC1 ... 93 D3 239 C5
Gower's Wlk E1 ... 96 A1
Gowland Pl BR3 ... 185 B1
Gowlett Rd SE15 ... 140 A2
Gowlland Cl CR0 ... 206 A2
Gowrie Rd SW11 ... 137 A2
Graburn Way KT8 ... 196 B6
Grace Ave DA7 ... 147 B3
Grace Bsns Ctr CR4 ... 202 D3
Gracechurch St EC2,
EC4 ... 252 D6
Grace Cl Burnt Oak HA8 ... 27 A3
Mottingham SE9 ... 165 D1
Grace Ct
5 Croydon CR0 ... 220 D5
Twickenham TW2 ... 152 C2
Gracedale Rd SW16 ... 181 B5
Gracedyer Ho N22 ... 32 A3
Gracefield Gdns
SW16 ... 160 A1
Gracehill 2 E1 ... 96 C2
Grace Ho
Kennington SE11 ... 270 D6
Penge SE26 ... 184 B5
Grace Jones Cl E8 ... 74 A2
Grace Path 2 SE26 ... 184 C6
Grace Pl E3 ... 97 D4
Grace Rd CR0 ... 205 A3
Graces Alley 14 SE1 ... 118 A6
Graces Mews NW8 ... 229 B3
Grace's Mews SE5 ... 139 C3
Grace's Rd SE5 ... 139 C3
Grace St E3 ... 97 D4
Gradient The SE26 ... 184 A6
Graeme Ct UB6 ... 85 D4
Graeme Rd EN1 ... 5 C3
Graemesdyke Ave
SW14 ... 132 D1
Grafton Cl Ealing W13 ... 87 A1
Twickenham TW4 ... 151 B3
Worcester Pk KT4 ... 215 C5
Grafton Cres NW1 ... 71 B2
Grafton Ct
10 Dalston E8 ... 74 A3
East Bedfont TW14 ... 149 B3
Grafton Gdns
Dagenham RM8 ... 81 A6
Harringay N4 ... 51 A3
Grafton Ho 16 Bow E3 ... 97 C4
12 Deptford SE8 ... 119 B1
Grafton Jun & Inf Schs
RM8 ... 81 B6
Grafton Mans SW4 ... 137 C1
Grafton Mews W1 ... 239 A5
Grafton Park Rd KT4 ... 215 C6
Grafton Pl NW1 ... 93 D4 232 D1
Grafton Prim Sch N7 ... 72 A5
Grafton Rd Acton W3 ... 111 A6
Dagenham RM8 ... 81 A6
Enfield EN2 ... 4 B2
Gospel Oak NW5 ... 71 A3
Harrow HA1 ... 42 A4
Kingston u T KT3 ... 199 C6
Thornton Heath CR0 ... 204 C1
Worcester Pk KT4 ... 215 C5
Grafton Sq SW4 ... 137 C2
Grafton St W1 ... 115 B6 248 D5
Grafton Terr NW5 ... 71 A3
Grafton Way
East Molesey KT8 ... 195 B5
Marylebone W1 ... 239 B5
Grafton Yd NW5 ... 71 B2
Graham Ave
Ealing W13 ... 109 B4
Mitcham CR4 ... 181 A2
Graham Cl CR0 ... 223 C6
Graham Ct
Bromley BR1 ... 187 B3
5 Deptford SE14 ... 140 D6
Northolt UB5 ... 63 B3
GRAHAME PARK ... 27 C2
Grahame Park Way NW7,
NW9 ... 27 D2
Grahame White Ho
HA3 ... 43 D6
Graham Gdns KT6 ... 198 A1
Graham Ho
5 Balham SW12 ... 159 B4
6 Barnet EN5 ... 1 D1
Edmonton N9 ... 18 C3
6 Tufnell Pk N19 ... 71 D4
Woolwich SE18 ... 144 D5
Graham Lo Edgware HA8 ... 26 B4
Hendon NW4 ... 46 B3
Graham Mans
11 Barking IG11 ... 80 A1
2 Hackney E8 ... 74 B2
Graham Rd Acton W4 ... 111 B3
Bexleyheath DA6 ... 147 C1
Dalston E8 ... 74 A2
Hampton TW12 ... 173 C6
Harringay N15 ... 50 D6
Harrow HA3 ... 42 C6
Hendon NW4 ... 46 B3
Merton SW19 ... 179 B3
Mitcham CR4 ... 181 A2
Newham E13 ... 99 A3
Graham St N1 ... 94 D5 234 D3
Graham Terr
SW1 ... 115 A2 258 B3
Graham Twr W3 ... 110 D3
Grainger Cl UB5 ... 64 A3
Grainger Ct 22 SE5 ... 139 A5
Grainger Rd
Isleworth TW7 ... 130 D3
Tottenham N22 ... 33 A2
Gramer Cl E11 ... 76 B6
Grampian Cl
Harlington UB3 ... 127 B5
Orpington BR6 ... 211 D3
15 Sutton SM2 ... 218 A1
Grampian Gdns NW2 ... 47 A1
Grampians The 10
W14 ... 112 D4
Gramsci Way SE6 ... 163 D1
Granada St SW17 ... 180 D5
Granard Ave SW15 ... 156 B6
Granard Bsns Ctr NW7 ... 27 C4
Granard Ho 20 E9 ... 74 D2
Granard Prim Sch
SW15 ... 156 B5
Granard Rd SW11,
SW12 ... 158 D4
Granary Cl N9 ... 18 C4
Granary Ct 3 RM6 ... 58 D2
Granary Mans SE28 ... 123 A4
Granary Rd E1 ... 96 B3
Granary Sq N1 ... 72 C2
Granary St NW1 ... 93 D6 232 C5
Granary The SE8 ... 141 C5
Granby Ho 18 SE18 ... 122 B2
Granby Pl SE1 ... 251 A1
Granby Rd Eltham SE9 ... 144 B2
Woolwich SE18 ... 122 D3
Granby St
Bethnal Green E2 ... 96 A3
Shoreditch E2 ... 243 D6
Granby Terr
NW1 ... 93 C5 232 A3
Grand Arc N12 ... 30 A5
Grand Ave
Clerkenwell EC1 ... 241 D4
Fortis Green N10 ... 49 A5
Tolworth KT5 ... 198 D3
Wembley HA9 ... 66 C3
Grand Ave E HA9 ... 66 D3
Grand Avenue Prim Sch
KT5 ... 199 A3
Grand Ct RM8 ... 81 A5
Grand Depot Rd SE18 ... 122 C1
Grand Dr Southall UB2 ... 108 A4
West Barnes SM4,
SW20 ... 200 C5
Granden Rd SW16 ... 182 A1
Grandfield Ct W4 ... 133 B6
Grandison Rd
London SW11 ... 158 D6
North Cheam KT4 ... 216 C5
Grand Junction Wharf
N1 ... 235 A3
Grand Par London N4 ... 50 D3
Mortlake SW14 ... 133 A1
Tolworth KT6 ... 198 C1
Wembley HA9 ... 66 C6
Grand Union Cl W9 ... 91 B2
Grand Union Cres E8 ... 96 A6
Grand Union Ind Est
NW10 ... 88 D5
Grand Union Way
UB2 ... 107 C4
Grand Vitesse Ind Est
SE1 ... 251 D3
Granfield St SW11 ... 266 D1
Grange Ave
East Barnet EN4 ... 14 D3
North Finchley N12 ... 30 A5
South Norwood SE25 ... 183 C1
Stanmore HA7 ... 25 C1
Totteridge N20 ... 13 A4
Twickenham TW2 ... 152 C2
Woodford IG8 ... 37 A3
Grange Cl
East Molesey KT8 ... 195 D5
Edgware HA8 ... 27 A5
Hayes UB3 ... 83 C2
Heston TW5 ... 129 B6
Sidcup DA15 ... 168 A1
Woodford IG8 ... 37 A3

Grangecliffe Gdns
SE25 ... 183 C1
Grangecourt Rd N16 ... 51 C1
Grange Cres SE28 ... 102 C1
Grange Ct
Belmont SM2 ... 217 D1
4 Finchley N12 ... 30 A4
Hackbridge SM6 ... 219 B5
Harrow HA1 ... 64 D5
Ilford IG6 ... 57 A6
Littleton TW17 ... 192 C5
Loughton IG10 ... 21 D6
Northolt UB5 ... 84 C5
Peckham SE15 ... 139 D3
Pinner HA5 ... 41 A6
Strand WC2 ... 240 D1
Wembley HA0 ... 65 C3
1 Willesden NW10 ... 67 C4
Grange Dr BR7 ... 188 B4
Grange Farm Cl HA2 ... 64 A6
Grange Farm Est
TW17 ... 193 C6
Grangefield NW1 ... 72 A1
Grange Fst & Mid Schs
HA2 ... 41 D1
Grange Gdns
London N14 ... 15 D3
Pinner HA5 ... 41 A5
South Norwood SE25 ... 183 C1
West Hampstead NW3 ... 69 D5
Grange Gr N1 ... 73 A2
Grange Hill
Edgware HA8 ... 27 A5
South Norwood SE25 ... 183 C1
Grangehill Pl SE9 ... 144 B2
Grangehill Rd SE9 ... 144 B1
Grange Ho
6 Barking IG11 ... 101 B6
Bermondsey SE1 ... 263 C5
Willesden NW10 ... 68 B1
Grange La SE21 ... 161 D2
Grange Lo SW19 ... 178 D4
Grange Mans KT17 ... 215 D1
Grangemill 11 NW5 ... 71 B4
Grangemill Rd SE6 ... 163 C2
GRANGE MILLS ... 113 C3
Grange Mills SW12 ... 159 C3
Grangemill Way SE6 ... 163 C2
GRANGE PARK ... 16 C6
Grange Park Ave N21 ... 17 A5
Grange Park Jun & Inf
Schs UB4 ... 83 D3
Grange Park Pl SW20 ... 178 B3
Grange Park Prep Sch
N21 ... 16 D5
Grange Park Prim Sch
N21 ... 4 C1
Grange Park Rd
Leyton E10 ... 53 D1
South Norwood CR7 ... 205 B6
Grange Park Sta N21 ... 16 D5
Grange Pk W5 ... 110 A5
Grange Pl NW6 ... 69 C1
Grange Prim Sch
Bermondsey
SE1 ... 117 C3 263 A5
Ealing W5 ... 109 D4
Newham E13 ... 98 D4
Grange Rd
Barnes SW13 ... 134 A4
Belmont SM2 ... 217 C1
Bermondsey
SE1 ... 117 D3 263 C5
Borehamwood WD6 ... 10 B6
Burnt Oak HA8 ... 27 B4
Chessington KT9 ... 214 A4
Ealing W5 ... 110 A5
East Molesey KT8 ... 195 D5
Greenhill HA1 ... 43 A4
Gunnersbury W4 ... 110 D1
Hayes UB3 ... 83 C1
Highgate N6 ... 49 A3
Ilford IG1 ... 79 A4
Kingston u T KT1 ... 198 A6
Leyton E10 ... 53 C1
Newham E13 ... 98 D4
Orpington BR6 ... 227 A6
Roxeth HA2 ... 64 B6
Southall UB1 ... 107 A4
South Norwood SE19,
SE25 ... 183 B1
Tottenham N17 ... 34 A4
Walthamstow E17 ... 53 A4
Willesden NW10 ... 68 B2
Grange St N1 ... 235 D5
Grange The
Bermondsey
SE1 ... 117 D3 263 C5
Cockfosters EN4 ... 2 D2
Croydon CR0 ... 223 B6
Ealing W13 ... 87 C2
7 Gunnersbury W4 ... 110 D1
Hammersmith W12 ... 112 B3
19 Maitland Pk NW3 ... 70 D2
South Acton W3 ... 110 D4
3 Walthamstow E17 ... 53 A4
4 Wanstead E18 ... 55 A6
Wembley HA0 ... 66 C1
West Barnes KT3 ... 200 A4
West Ewell KT19 ... 215 B4
West Kensington
W14 ... 113 B2 254 C3
Wimbledon SW19 ... 178 D4
Grange Vale SM2 ... 217 D1
Grange View Rd N20 ... 14 A3
Grangeway London N12 ... 29 D6
Grangeway *continued*
South Hampstead NW6 ... 69 C1
Woodford IG8 ... 37 C6
Grangeway Gdns IG4 ... 56 A4
Grangeway The N21 ... 16 D5
Grange Wlk
SE1 ... 117 D3 263 C5
Grangewood DA5 ... 169 B3
Grangewood Cl HA5 ... 40 A4
Grangewood Ind Sch
E7 ... 77 D1
Grangewood La BR3 ... 185 B4
Grangewood Sch HA5 ... 39 D4
Grangewood St E6 ... 99 D6
Grange Yd SE1 ... 117 D3 263 C5
Granham Gdns N9 ... 17 D2
Granite Apts E15 ... 76 B2
Granite St SE18 ... 123 D1
Granleigh Rd E11 ... 76 C6
Grannary The 12 SE16 ... 118 C4
Gransden Ave E8 ... 74 B1
Gransden Ho 1 SE8 ... 119 B1
Gransden Rd W12 ... 111 D4
Grantbridge St
N1 ... 94 D5 234 D4
Grantchester 12 KT1 ... 176 C1
Grantchester Cl HA1 ... 64 D5
Grant Cl London N14 ... 15 C4
Shepperton TW17 ... 192 D3
Tottenham N17 ... 33 C1
Grant Ct 2 Chingford E4 ... 20 A3
11 Hendon NW9 ... 27 D1
Grantham Cl HA8 ... 10 A1
Grantham Ct
Dagenham RM6 ... 59 B2
Kingston u T KT2 ... 175 D5
9 Rotherhithe SE16 ... 118 D4
Grantham Gdns RM6 ... 59 B2
Grantham Gn WD6 ... 11 A6
Grantham Ho
Ashford TW16 ... 171 C3
12 Peckham SE15 ... 140 A6
Grantham Pl W1 ... 248 C3
Grantham Rd
Chiswick W4 ... 133 C5
Little Ilford E12 ... 78 C4
South Lambeth SW9 ... 138 A3
Grant Ho
38 Clapham SW8 ... 137 D3
Clerkenwell EC1 ... 241 D4
Grantley Ho
2 Deptford SE14 ... 140 D6
5 Putney SW19 ... 156 D3
Grantley Pl KT10 ... 212 A3
Grantley Rd TW4, TW5 ... 128 C3
Grantley St E1 ... 96 D3
Grant Mus of Zoology &
Comparative Anatomy*
WC1 ... 93 D3 239 C5
Grantock Rd E17 ... 36 B2
Granton Prim Sch
SW16 ... 181 C3
Granton Rd Ilford IG3 ... 58 A1
Sidcup DA14 ... 190 C4
Streatham SW16 ... 181 C2
Grant Pl 2 CR0 ... 205 D1
Grant Rd
Battersea SW11 ... 136 C2
Croydon CR0 ... 205 D1
Harrow HA3 ... 42 D6
Grants Cl NW7 ... 28 D3
Grants Cotts KT10 ... 212 B6
Grant St Islington N1 ... 234 A4
Newham E13 ... 99 A4
Grantully Rd W9 ... 91 D4
Grant Way TW7 ... 131 A6
Granville Ave
Feltham TW13 ... 150 A2
Hounslow TW3, TW4 ... 151 C6
Lower Edmonton N9 ... 18 C1
Granville Cl CR0 ... 221 C6
Granville Ct
8 Deptford SE14 ... 141 A5
Hornsey N4 ... 50 B3
Shoreditch N1 ... 235 D6
Granville Gdns
Ealing W5 ... 110 B5
South Norwood SW16 ... 182 B3
Granville Gr SE13 ... 142 A2
Granville Ho 18 E14 ... 97 C1
Granville Ind Est NW2 ... 69 B6
Granville Mans 8
W12 ... 112 C4
Granville Mews DA14 ... 190 A6
Granville Pk SE13 ... 142 B2
Granville Pl London N12 ... 30 A3
Marylebone W1 ... 93 A1 238 A1
Pinner HA5 ... 40 D6
Walham Green SW6 ... 265 C3
Granville Point NW2 ... 69 B6
Granville Rd
Bexley DA16 ... 146 C2
Bowes Pk N13 ... 32 B4
Child's Hill NW2 ... 69 B6
Finchley N12 ... 30 A3
Hayes UB3 ... 105 D2
Hillingdon UB10 ... 60 D2
Hornsey N4, N8 ... 50 B3
Ilford IG1 ... 78 D6
Kilburn NW6 ... 91 C5
Merton SW19 ... 179 C3
Sidcup DA14 ... 190 B6
Tottenham N22 ... 32 D2
Walthamstow E17 ... 53 D3
Wandsworth SW18 ... 157 B4
Woodford E18 ... 37 B1
Granville Sq
3 Camberwell SE15 ... 139 C5
Finsbury WC1 ... 94 B4 233 D1
Granville St WC1 ... 233 D1
Granwood Ct 5 TW7 ... 130 C4
Grape St WC2 ... 240 A2
Grapsome Cl KT9 ... 213 C1
Grasdene Rd SE18 ... 146 A5
Grasgarth Cl W3 ... 111 A6
Grasmere NW1 ... 231 D1
Grasmere Ave
Acton W3 ... 111 B6
Kingston u T SW15 ... 177 C6
Locksbottom BR6 ... 226 D5
Merton SW19 ... 201 C6
Ruislip HA4 ... 39 A2
Twickenham TW3 ... 151 D5
Wembley HA9 ... 43 D1
Grasmere Cl TW14 ... 149 D3
Grasmere Ct
Barnes SW13 ... 134 A6
Bowes Pk N22 ... 32 B4
Forest Hill SE26 ... 184 A5
7 Sutton SM2 ... 218 A2
Grasmere Gdns
Harrow HA3 ... 25 A1
Locksbottom BR6 ... 226 D5
Redbridge IG4 ... 56 B4
Grasmere Ho 20 N16 ... 73 B4
Grasmere Point 2
SE15 ... 140 C5
Grasmere Prim Sch
N16 ... 73 B4
Grasmere Rd
Bromley BR1 ... 186 D3
Croydon SE25 ... 206 B4
Locksbottom BR6 ... 226 D5
Muswell Hill N10 ... 31 B2
3 Newham E13 ... 99 A5
Streatham SW16 ... 182 B5
Tottenham N17 ... 34 A4
Grasshaven Way SE28 ... 123 D5
Grassington Cl N11 ... 31 A4
Grassington Rd DA14 ... 190 A6
Grassmere Ct 6 EN1 ... 17 C6
Grassmount SE23 ... 162 B2
Grass Pk N3 ... 29 B2
Grassway SM6 ... 219 C4
Grasvenor Ave EN5 ... 13 C5
Grasvenor Avenue Inf Sch
EN5 ... 13 C5
Grateley Ho 10 SW15 ... 156 B3
Gratton Rd
W14 ... 113 A3 254 A5
Gratton Terr NW2 ... 68 D5
Graveley 16 KT1 ... 176 C1
Graveley Ave WD6 ... 11 A6
Graveley Ho 7 SE8 ... 119 A2
Gravel Hill Bexley DA6 ... 169 D6
Church End N3 ... 29 B1
South Croydon CR0,
CR2 ... 223 B1
Gravel Hill Cl DA6 ... 169 D5
Gravel Hill Prim Sch
DA6 ... 169 D6
Gravel Hill Sta CR0 ... 223 A2
Gravel La E1 ... 95 D1 243 C2
Gravel Rd
Keston Mark BR2 ... 226 A6
Twickenham TW2 ... 152 C3
Gravelwood Cl BR7 ... 167 A1
Gravenel Gdns 5
SW17 ... 180 C5
Graveney Gr SE20 ... 184 C3
Graveney Rd SW17 ... 180 C6
Graveney Sch SW17 ... 181 B5
Gravesend Rd W12 ... 112 A6
Graves Est DA16 ... 146 B3
Gray Ave RM8 ... 59 B1
Gray Ct 8 KT2 ... 175 D6
Grayfriars Pas EC1 ... 241 D2
Grayham Cres KT3 ... 199 B5
Grayham Rd KT3 ... 199 B5
Gray Ho SE17 ... 262 B2
Grayland Cl BR1 ... 187 D2
Grayland Ct WC1 ... 233 C1
Grayling Cl E16 ... 98 C3
Grayling Ct Ealing W5 ... 109 D5
Tottenham Hale N17 ... 52 B5
Grayling Rd N16 ... 73 B6
Grayling Sq E2 ... 96 A4
Grays Cotts UB9 ... 38 C1
Grays Court Hospl
RM10 ... 81 D1
Grayscroft Rd SW16 ... 181 D3
Grays Farm Prim Sch
BR5 ... 190 B2
Grays Farm Production
Village BR5 ... 190 B2
Grays Farm Rd BR5 ... 190 B2
Grayshott Ct 10 SM2 ... 217 D1
Grayshott Rd SW11 ... 137 A2
Gray's Inn*
WC1 ... 94 B2 240 D4
Gray's Inn Pl WC1 ... 240 D3
Gray's Inn Rd
WC1 ... 94 B3 240 D6
Gray's Inn Sq
WC1 ... 94 C2 241 A4
Grays La TW15 ... 170 D6
Grayson Ho EC1 ... 235 B1
Gray's Rd UB10 ... 60 A1
Gray St SE1 ... 116 C4 251 B1
Grayswood Gdns
SW20 ... 178 B1
Grayswood Point 14
SW15 ... 156 A3
Gray's Yd W1 ... 238 B2
Graywood Ct N12 ... 30 A3
Grazebrook Prim Sch
N16 ... 73 C6
Grazebrook Rd N16 ... 73 B6
Grazeley Ct SE19 ... 183 C5
Great Arthur Ho EC1 ... 242 A5
Great Bell Alley EC2 ... 242 C2
Great Benty UB7 ... 104 A2
Great Brownings
SE21 ... 183 D6
Great Bushey Dr N20 ... 13 D3
Great Cambridge Ind Est
EN1 ... 18 B6
Great Cambridge Junction
N13, N18 ... 33 B6
Great Cambridge Rd
Edmonton N9, N18 ... 17 C3
Enfield EN1 ... 6 A3
Great Castle St W1 ... 239 A2
Great Central Ave HA4 ... 62 C3
Great Central St
NW1 ... 92 D2 237 C4
Great Central Way
NW10 ... 67 B4
Great Chapel St
W1 ... 93 D1 239 C2
Great Chart St SW11 ... 136 A1
Great Chertsey Rd
Chiswick SW14, W4 ... 133 B4
Feltham TW13, TW2 ... 151 C1
Great Church La W6 ... 112 D1
Great College St
SW1 ... 116 A3 260 A6
Great Croft WC1 ... 233 B1
Great Cross Ave SE3 ... 142 C5
Great Cumberland Mews
W1 ... 237 C1
Great Cumberland Pl
W1 ... 92 D1 237 D1
Great Dover St
SE1 ... 117 B3 262 C6
Greatdown Rd W7 ... 86 D2
Great Eastern Bldgs 10
E8 ... 74 B2
Great Eastern Ent Ctr
E14 ... 119 D4
Great Eastern Pier
E14 ... 119 C1
Great Eastern Rd E15 ... 76 B2
Great Eastern St
EC2 ... 95 C3 243 A6
Great Eastern Wharf
SW11 ... 267 B3
Great Elms Rd BR2 ... 209 C5
Great Field
Hendon NW9 ... 27 D2
7 Kentish Town NW5 ... 71 C3
Greatfield Ave E6 ... 100 B3
Greatfield Cl
London SE4 ... 141 C1
4 Tufnell Pk N19 ... 71 C4
Greatfields Dr UB8 ... 82 C2
Greatfields Rd IG11 ... 101 B5
Great Fleete Way
IG11 ... 102 C5
Great Galley Cl IG11 ... 102 C4
Great Gatton Cl CR0 ... 207 A2
Great George St
SW1 ... 116 A4 250 A1
Great Guildford Bsns Sq
SE1 ... 252 A3
Great Guildford St
SE1 ... 117 A5 252 A3
Great Hall The 1 E11 ... 55 B5
Greatham Wlk 8
SW15 ... 156 A3
Great Harry Dr SE9 ... 166 C1
Great James St WC1 ... 240 C4
Great Marlborough St
W1 ... 93 C1 239 A1
Great Maze Pond
SE1 ... 117 B4 252 D2
Great Newport St WC2 ... 250 A6
Great North Rd
Barnet EN5 ... 1 A2
East Finchley N2 ... 48 C5
New Barnet EN5 ... 13 D6
Great North Way (Barnet
By-Pass) NW4 ... 46 D6
Greatorex Ho 13 E1 ... 96 A2
Greatorex St E1 ... 96 A2
Great Ormond St Hospl for
Children WC1 ... 94 B3 240 C5
Great Ormond St
WC1 ... 94 B3 240 C5
Great Percy St
WC1 ... 94 C4 234 A2
Great Peter St
SW1 ... 115 D3 259 D5
Great Portland St
W1 ... 93 B2 238 D4
Great Portland Street Sta
W1 ... 93 B3 238 D5
Great Pulteney St W1 ... 249 B6
Great Queen St
WC2 ... 94 A1 240 B2
Great Russell Mans
WC1 ... 240 A3
Great Russell St
WC1 ... 94 A2 240 A3
Great St Helen's EC3 ... 243 A2
Great St Thomas Apostle
EC4 ... 252 B6
Great Scotland Yd SW1,
WC2 ... 116 A5 250 A4
Great Smith St
SW1 ... 115 D3 259 D6
Great South West Rd TW6,
TW14, TW4 ... 148 B6
Great South-West Rd
TW5 ... 128 B2
Great Spilmans SE22 ... 161 C6
Greatstone Ho 10
SE20 ... 184 C3
Great Strand NW9 ... 27 D1
Great Suffolk St
SE1 ... 116 D5 251 D3
Great Sutton St
EC1 ... 94 D3 241 D5
Great Swan Alley EC2 ... 242 C2
Great Thrift BR5 ... 211 A5
Great Titchfield St
W1 ... 93 C2 239 A3
Great Tower St
EC3 ... 117 C6 253 A6
Great Trinity La EC4 ... 252 B6
Great Turnstile WC2 ... 240 D3
Great Western Ind Pk
UB2 ... 108 A4
Great Western Rd W2,
W9 ... 91 B2
Great West Ho TW8 ... 131 C6
Great West Rd
Brentford TW7, TW8 ... 131 B6
Chiswick W4, W6 ... 133 B6
Heston TW5, TW7 ... 129 B4
Hounslow TW5, TW7 ... 130 B5
Great West Road Cedars
Rd W4 ... 133 A6
Great West Road Hogarth
La W4 ... 133 C6
Great West Trad Est
TW8 ... 131 B6
Great Winchester St
EC2 ... 95 B1 242 D2
Great Windmill St
W1 ... 115 D6 249 C6
Greatwood BR7 ... 188 C3
Great Yd SE1 ... 253 B2
Greaves Cl IG11 ... 79 C1
Greaves Cotts 10 E14 ... 97 A2
Greaves Ct N8 ... 50 C5
Greaves Pl SW17 ... 180 C6
Greaves Twr SW10 ... 266 B4
Grebe 3 NW9 ... 27 D1
Grebe Ave UB4 ... 84 D1
Grebe Cl Barking IG11 ... 102 A3
Higham Hill E17 ... 35 A3
Stratford E7 ... 76 D3
Grebe Ct Cheam SM1 ... 217 B3
16 Cubitt Town E14 ... 120 A4
Grebe Terr 4 KT1 ... 198 A6
Grecian Cres SE19 ... 182 D4
Greek Ct W1 ... 239 D1
Greek St W1 ... 93 D1 239 D1
Greenacre Cl Barnet EN5 ... 1 B5
Northolt UB5 ... 63 B3
Greenacre Ct E8 ... 74 A3
Greenacre Gdns E17 ... 54 A5
Greenacre Pl SM6 ... 219 B6
Greenacres Bushey WD23 ... 8 B2
Church End N3 ... 29 A1
Eltham SE9 ... 166 C5
Green Acres Hayes UB4 ... 84 B3
Sidcup DA14 ... 189 D6
South Croydon CR0 ... 221 D5
Greenacres Ave UB10 ... 60 C5
Greenacres Cl BR6 ... 227 A4
Greenacres Dr HA7 ... 25 B3
Greenacres Prim Sch
SE9 ... 166 C2
Greenacre Sq 26 SE16 ... 118 D4
Greenacre Wlk N14 ... 15 D1
Green Arbour Ct EC1 ... 241 C2
Green Ave Ealing W13 ... 109 B3
Edgware NW7 ... 27 C6
Greenaway Gdns NW3 ... 69 D4
Greenaway Ho
Finsbury WC1 ... 234 A1
St John's Wood NW8 ... 229 A6
Greenaway Terr
TW19 ... 148 A3
Green Bank London N12 ... 29 D6
Wapping E1 ... 118 B5
Greenbank Ave HA0 ... 65 A3
Greenbank Cl E4 ... 20 A2
Greenbank Cres NW4 ... 47 A5
Greenbank Lo 2 BR7 ... 188 C2
Greenbanks HA1 ... 64 C4
Greenbay Rd SE7 ... 143 D5
Greenberry St NW8 ... 230 A3
Greenbrook Ave EN4 ... 2 A4
Green CE Prim Sch The
N17 ... 51 D6
Green CE Sch Holy Trinity
(Inf Annexe) The N15 ... 51 D5
Green Cl
Beckenham BR2 ... 208 C6
Carshalton SM5 ... 218 D6
Feltham TW13 ... 173 A5
Kingsbury NW9 ... 45 A3
North End NW11 ... 48 A2
Greencoat Pl
SW1 ... 115 C2 259 B4
Greencoat Row SW1 ... 259 B5
Greencourt Ave HA8 ... 26 D2
Green Court Ave CR0 ... 222 B6
Green Court Gdns
CR0 ... 222 B6
Greencourt Ho 25 E1 ... 96 D3
Greencourt Rd BR5 ... 211 C4
Greencroft HA8 ... 27 A5
Greencroft Ave HA4 ... 62 C6
Greencroft Cl E16 ... 99 D2
Greencroft Gdns
Enfield EN1 ... 5 C2
South Hampstead NW6 ... 70 A1
Greencroft Rd TW5 ... 129 B4
Green Ct Ashford TW16 ... 171 D4
2 Willesden NW10 ... 67 C4
Greendale NW7 ... 27 C6
Green Dale SE22 ... 161 C6
Greendale Cl SE22 ... 161 C6
Greendale Ct CR2 ... 221 A2
Green Dr UB1 ... 107 C5
Green Dragon Ct SE1 ... 252 C3
Green Dragon Ho
WC1 ... 240 B2
Green Dragon La
Brentford TW8 ... 110 B1
Southgate N21 ... 16 D5
Green Dragon Prim Sch
TW8 ... 132 A6
Green Dragon Yd 24
E1 ... 96 A2
Greene Ct 20 SE14 ... 140 D6
Greene Ho SE1 ... 262 C5
Green Elms IG6 ... 57 A6
Green End
Chessington KT9 ... 214 A4
Edmonton N21 ... 16 D2
Greenend Rd W4 ... 111 C4
Greener Ct 26 EN3 ... 7 C6
Greener Ho 3 SW4 ... 137 D2
Green Farm Cl BR6 ... 227 D3
Greenfell Mans SE8 ... 141 D6
Greenfield Ave KT5 ... 198 D3
Greenfield Ct SE9 ... 166 A1
Greenfield Dr
Bromley BR1 ... 187 C1
Fortis Green N2 ... 48 D5
Greenfield Gdns
Cricklewood NW2 ... 69 A5
Crofton BR5 ... 211 B2
Dagenham RM9 ... 102 D6
Greenfield Ho 28
SW19 ... 156 D3
Greenfield Rd
Dagenham RM9 ... 102 C6
South Tottenham N15 ... 51 C4
Whitechapel E1 ... 96 A1
Greenfields UB1 ... 85 C1
Greenfields Prim Sch
WD19 ... 22 C5
Greenfield Way HA2 ... 41 D6
GREENFORD ... 86 A4
Greenford Ave
Ealing W7 ... 86 C1
Southall UB1 ... 107 B6
Greenford Gdns UB6 ... 86 A4
Greenford High Sch
UB6 ... 85 C4
Greenford Rd
Greenford UB6 ... 86 A3
Sudbury HA1, UB6 ... 64 C3
Sutton SM1 ... 217 D4
Greenford Rdbt UB6 ... 86 B5
Greenford Sta UB6 ... 86 B6
Greengate UB6 ... 65 B2
Greengate St E13 ... 99 B4
Green Gdns BR6 ... 227 A3
Greenhalgh Wlk N2 ... 48 A5
Greenham Cl SE1 ... 251 A1
Greenham Cres E4 ... 35 B4
Greenham Ho
5 Hackney E9 ... 96 C6
Isleworth TW7 ... 130 B2
Greenham Rd N10 ... 31 A1
Greenhaven Dr SE28 ... 102 B1
Greenheath Bsns Ctr 3
E2 ... 96 B3
Green Hedges 8
TW1 ... 153 C5
Greenheys Dr E18 ... 54 D6
GREENHILL ... 42 D4
Greenhill
Buckhurst Hill IG9 ... 21 C3
Hampstead NW3 ... 70 B4
Sutton SM1 ... 218 A6
Wembley Pk HA9 ... 66 D6
Green Hill SE18 ... 122 B1
Greenhill Cts SE7 ... 122 B1
Greenhill Gdns UB5 ... 85 B5
Greenhill Gr E12 ... 78 A4
Greenhill Par EN5 ... 13 D6
Greenhill Pk
Harlesden NW10 ... 89 C6
New Barnet EN5 ... 13 D6
Greenhill Rd
Harlesden NW10 ... 89 C6
Harrow HA1 ... 42 C3
Greenhill's Rents EC1 ... 241 C4
Greenhills Terr 16 N1 ... 73 B2
Greenhill Terr
Northolt UB5 ... 85 B5
Woolwich SE18 ... 122 B1
Greenhill Way
Harrow HA1 ... 42 C3
Wembley Pk HA9 ... 66 D6
Greenhithe Cl DA15 ... 167 C4
Green Ho TW7 ... 130 D3
Greenholm Rd SE9 ... 166 D6
Green Ho The 5
SW19 ... 157 A3
Green Hundred Rd
SE15 ... 140 A6
Greenhurst Rd SE27 ... 182 C5
Greening Ho SE13 ... 142 B1
Greening St SE2 ... 124 C2
Green La
Ashford TW16 ... 171 D4
Chessington KT9 ... 214 A1
Chislehurst SE9 ... 166 D1
Dagenham RM8 ... 81 B6
East Molesey KT8 ... 195 D4
Edgware HA8 ... 26 C5
Feltham TW13 ... 173 A5
Hanwell W7 ... 108 C4
Hendon NW4 ... 46 D4
Hillingdon UB8 ... 83 A2
Hounslow TW4 ... 128 C1
Ilford IG1, IG3 ... 79 C6
Morden SM4 ... 201 D3
New Malden KT3 ... 199 A4
New Malden KT4 ... 200 A1

Green La continued
Penge SE20 . . . 184 D3
Shepperton TW17 . . . 193 A4
South Norwood CR7, SW16 . . . 182 C2
Stanmore HA7 . . . 25 B5
Greenland Cres UB2 . . . 106 D3
Greenland Ho
Bermondsey SE8 . . . 118 D1
4 Mile End E1 . . . 97 A3
Greenland Mews SE8 . . 118 D1
Greenland Pl NW1 . . . 231 D6
Greenland Quay SE16 . . 118 D2
Greenland Rd
Barnet EN5 . . . 12 C5
Camden Town NW1 . . . 93 C6 232 A6
Greenlands
Borehamwood WD6 . . . 11 B5
Chessington KT19 . . . 214 D3
Greenland St NW1 . . . 231 D6
Greenland Way CR0 . . . 203 D2
Green Lane Bsns Pk SE9 . . . 166 C2
Green Lane Cotts HA7 . . . 25 B6
Green Lane Gdns CR7 . . 183 A1
Green Lane Mews SM4 . . . 201 D3
Green Lane Prim Sch KT4 . . . 200 B2
Green Lanes
London N4, N8, N15 . . . 50 D2
Palmers Green N13 . . . 16 C1
West Ewell KT19 . . . 215 C1
Greenlaw Ct W5 . . . 87 D1
Greenlaw Gdns KT3 . . . 199 D2
Greenlawn La TW8 . . . 109 D2
Greenlawns N12 . . . 29 D4
Green Lawns
Ruislip HA4 . . . 40 C1
8 Woolwich SE18 . . . 122 D2
Greenlaw St SE18 . . . 122 C3
Green Leaf Ave SM6 . . 219 D4
Greenleaf Cl 8 SW2 . . . 160 C4
Greenleaf Ct N20 . . . 14 B3
Greenleafe Dr IG6 . . . 56 D6
Greenleaf Prim Sch E17 . . . 53 B6
Greenleaf Rd
5 Newham E6 . . . 99 C6
Walthamstow E17 . . . 53 B6
Greenleaf Way HA3 . . . 42 D6
Greenlea Pk SW19 . . . 180 C2
Green Leas
Ashford TW16 . . . 171 D4
Kingston u T KT1 . . . 198 A6
Green Leas Cl TW16 . . . 171 D4
Greenleaves Ct TW15 . . 170 D4
Green Link Wlk TW9 . . . 132 D4
Green Man Gdns W13 . . 109 A6
Green Man Intc E11 . . . 54 D2
Green Man La
Ealing W13 . . . 109 A5
Hatton TW14 . . . 128 A1
Greenman St N1 . . . 95 A6 235 A6
Greenmead Cl SE25 . . . 206 A4
Greenmead Sch SW15 . 156 B6
Green Moor Link N21 . . 16 D4
Greenmoor Rd EN3 . . . 6 C3
Greenoak Pl EN4 . . . 2 D3
Green Oaks UB2 . . . 106 D2
Greenoak Way SW19 . . . 178 D6
Greenock Rd
Mitcham SW16 . . . 181 D2
11 South Acton W3 . . . 111 A3
Greeno Cres TW17 . . . 192 C4
Green Park* SW1, W1 . . . 115 B4 248 D2
Greenpark Ct HA0 . . . 65 C1
Green Park Sta W1 . . . 115 C5 249 A4
Green Park Way UB6 . . . 86 C6
Green Pond Cl E17 . . . 53 B6
Green Pond Rd E17 . . . 53 A6
Green Pt E15 . . . 76 C2
Green Rd
East Barnet N14 . . . 15 B5
Whetstone N20 . . . 14 A1
Green Ride IG10, E4 . . . 21 A6
Greenroof Way SE10 . . 120 D3
Green Sch (Girls) The TW7 . . . 131 A4
Greens Ct Soho W1 . . . 249 C6
Wembley HA9 . . . 65 D5
Green's Ct W11 . . . 244 C3
Greens End SE18 . . . 122 D2
Greenshank Cl E17 . . . 35 A3
Greenshaw High Sch SM1 . . . 218 A6
Greenshields Ind Est E16 . . . 121 B5
Greenside
Dagenham RM8 . . . 58 C1
Sidcup DA5 . . . 169 A3
Greenside Cl
Catford SE6 . . . 164 B2
Whetstone N20 . . . 14 B2
Greenside Prim Sch W12 . . . 112 A4
Greenside Rd
Shepherd's Bush W12 . . . 112 A4
Thornton Heath CR0 . . . 204 C2
Greenslade Prim Sch SE18 . . . 145 B6
Greenslade Rd IG11 . . . 79 B1
Greensleeves Ho UB2 . . 107 D2
Greensleeves Manor SM2 . . . 217 D2
Green St Enfield EN3 . . . 6 D3
Mayfair W1 . . . 115 A6 248 A6
Newham E13 . . . 99 C6
Sunbury TW16 . . . 172 A1
Upton E7 . . . 77 C1
Greenstead Ave IG8 . . . 37 C4
Greenstead Cl IG8 . . . 37 C4
Greenstead Gdns
Putney SW15 . . . 156 B6
Woodford IG8 . . . 37 C4
Greenstone Mews E11 . . 55 A3
GREEN STREET GREEN . . . 227 C2
Green Street Green Prim Sch BR6 . . . 227 D2
Greenstreet Hill SE4 . . . 140 D2
Greensward Ho SW6 . . . 136 A3
Green Terr EC1 . . . 234 B1
Green The Acton W3 . . . 89 C1
Buckhurst Hill IG9 . . . 21 B3
Chingford E4 . . . 20 B3
Claygate KT10 . . . 212 D2
Ealing W5 . . . 109 D6
Edmonton N9 . . . 18 A2
Erith DA7 . . . 147 C4
Falconwood DA16 . . . 145 C1
Feltham TW13 . . . 150 B2
Grove Pk BR1 . . . 165 A1
Hackbridge SM6 . . . 219 A6
Hayes BR2 . . . 209 A2
Heston TW5 . . . 129 C6
Kingston u T KT3 . . . 177 A1
Merton SM4 . . . 201 A5
Palmers Green N14 . . . 15 D1
Richmond TW9 . . . 131 D1
7 Richmond TW9 . . . 153 D6
Sidcup DA14 . . . 190 A5
Southall UB2 . . . 107 B4
Southgate N21 . . . 16 C4
St Paul's Cray BR5 . . . 190 B3
Stratford E15 . . . 76 D2
Sutton SM1 . . . 217 D5
Tottenham N17 . . . 33 A4
Twickenham TW2 . . . 152 C2
Upper Halliford TW17 . . . 193 C5
Uxbridge UB10 . . . 61 A6
Wallington SM5 . . . 219 A4
Wanstead E11 . . . 55 B3
Wembley HA0 . . . 65 A6
Wimbledon SW19 . . . 178 D5
Woodford IG8 . . . 37 A5
Green Vale Bexley DA6 . . 168 D6
Ealing W5 . . . 88 B1
Greenvale Rd SE9 . . . 144 C1
Greenvale Sch SE23 . . . 163 A1
Green Verges HA7 . . . 25 D3
Green View KT9 . . . 214 B1
Greenview Ave CR0 . . . 207 A3
Greenview Cl W3 . . . 111 C5
Greenview Ct
Ashford TW15 . . . 170 B6
East Dulwich SE22 . . . 140 A1
Oakleigh Pk N20 . . . 14 A4
Wandsworth SW18 . . . 158 C4
Greenway
Chislehurst BR7 . . . 188 D5
Dagenham RM8 . . . 58 C1
Harrow HA3 . . . 44 A4
Hayes UB4 . . . 84 B3
Palmers Green N14 . . . 16 A2
Pinner HA5 . . . 22 B1
Totteridge N20 . . . 13 C2
Wallington SM6 . . . 219 C4
West Barnes SW20 . . . 200 C5
Woodford IG8 . . . 37 C5
Green Way
Bromley Comm BR2 . . . 210 A3
Eltham SE9 . . . 165 D6
Sunbury TW16 . . . 194 A5
Greenway Ave E17 . . . 54 B5
Greenway Cl
Finsbury Pk N4 . . . 73 A6
Friern Barnet N11 . . . 31 A4
Hendon NW9 . . . 27 B1
2 South Tottenham N15 . 51 D5
Totteridge N20 . . . 13 C2
Greenway Ct Hayes UB4 . . 84 B3
Ilford IG1 . . . 56 D1
2 Newham E15 . . . 98 C5
Greenway Gdns
Croydon CR0 . . . 223 B5
Greenford UB6 . . . 85 D4
Hendon NW9 . . . 27 B1
Green Way Gdns HA3 . . . 24 C1
Greenways
Beckenham BR3 . . . 185 C1
5 Forest Hill SE26 . . . 184 C6
Hinchley Wood KT10 . . . 212 C4
Greenways The 1 TW1 . . . 153 A5
Greenway The
Harrow HA3 . . . 24 C2
Hendon NW9 . . . 27 B1
Hounslow TW4 . . . 129 B1
Pinner HA5 . . . 41 B3
Uxbridge UB8 . . . 82 A5
West Ruislip UB10 . . . 61 A6
Greenwell St W1 . . . 238 D5
GREENWICH . . . 142 C6
Greenwich Acad SE10 . . 141 D4
Greenwich Borough Mus* SE18 . . . 123 D1
Greenwich Bsns Ctr SE10 . . . 141 D5
Greenwich Bsns Pk SE10 . . . 141 D5
Greenwich Church St SE10 . . . 142 A6
Greenwich Coll SE10 . . . 142 A5
Greenwich Com Coll Plumstead Ctr SE18 . . 123 A2
Greenwich Cres E6 . . . 100 A2
Greenwich Ct 11 E1 . . . 96 B1
Greenwich High Rd SE10 . . . 141 D5
Greenwich Ho SE13 . . . 164 B5
Greenwich Hts SE18 . . . 144 A5
Greenwich Ind Est SE10 . . . 141 D5
Greenwich London Coll SE18 . . . 122 D2
Greenwich Mkt SE10 . . . 142 A6
Greenwich Mkt 2 SE10 . . . 142 A6
Greenwich Park* SE10 . . . 142 C5
Greenwich Park St SE10 . . . 142 B6
Greenwich Quay SE8 . . . 141 D6
Greenwich Sh Pk SE7 . . . 121 B2
Greenwich South St SE10 . . . 142 A4
Greenwich Sta SE10 . . . 141 D5
Greenwich View Pl E14 . . . 119 D3
Green Wlk
Bermondsey SE1 . . . 263 A5
Hampton TW12 . . . 173 B4
Hendon NW4 . . . 46 D4
Ruislip HA4 . . . 39 D1
Southall UB2 . . . 107 C1
Green Wlk The E4 . . . 20 B3
Greenwood
8 Putney SW19 . . . 156 D4
3 Woodford IG8 . . . 37 A3
Green Wood NW5 . . . 71 C3
Greenwood Ave
Dagenham RM10 . . . 81 D4
Enfield EN3 . . . 7 A4
Greenwood Cl
Bushey WD23 . . . 8 C3
Merton SM4 . . . 201 A5
Orpington BR5 . . . 211 C3
Sidcup DA15 . . . 168 A2
Thames Ditton KT7 . . . 197 A1
Greenwood Dr E4 . . . 36 B5
Greenwood Gdns N13 . . . 16 D1
Greenwood Ho
Finsbury WC1 . . . 234 A1
8 Nunhead SE4 . . . 140 D1
Wood Green N22 . . . 32 C2
Greenwood La TW12 . . . 173 D5
Greenwood Mans 9 IG11 . . . 80 A1
Greenwood Pk KT2 . . . 177 C3
Greenwood Pl NW5 . . . 71 B3
Greenwood Prim Sch UB5 . . . 64 A3
Greenwood Rd
Dalston E8 . . . 74 A2
Hinchley Wood KT7 . . . 213 A6
Isleworth TW7 . . . 130 D2
Mitcham CR4 . . . 203 D6
Thornton Heath CR0 . . . 205 A2
West Ham E13 . . . 98 D5
Greenwoods The HA2 . . 64 A5
Greenwood Terr NW10 . . 89 B5
Green Wrythe Cres SM5 . . . 202 C1
Green Wrythe La SM5 . . 202 C2
Green Wrythe Prim Sch SM5 . . . 202 B3
Green Yd WC1 . . . 240 D6
Greer Rd HA3 . . . 24 A2
Greet Ho SE1 . . . 251 B1
Greet St SE1 . . . 116 C5 251 B3
Greg Cl E10 . . . 54 A3
Gregor Mews SE3 . . . 143 A5
Gregory Cres SE9 . . . 165 D4
Gregory Ho SE3 . . . 143 B3
Gregory Pl W8 . . . 245 C2
Gregory Rd
Dagenham RM6 . . . 58 D5
Southall UB2 . . . 107 C3
Greig City Acad N8 . . . 50 A5
Greig Cl N8 . . . 50 A4
Greig Ho 9 TW10 . . . 153 C1
Greig Terr SE17 . . . 138 D6
Grenaby Ave CR0 . . . 205 B2
Grenaby Rd CR0 . . . 205 B2
Grenada Ho 18 E14 . . . 119 B6
Grenada Rd SE7 . . . 143 C5
Grenade St E14 . . . 119 B6
Grenadier St E16 . . . 122 C5
Grena Gdns TW9 . . . 132 B1
Grena Rd TW10, TW9 . . . 132 B1
Grenard Cl SE15 . . . 140 A5
Grendon Gdns HA9 . . . 66 C6
Grendon Ho
29 Hackney E9 . . . 74 C1
Pentonville N1 . . . 233 C3
Grendon St NW8 . . . 92 C3 237 A6
Grenfell Ct NW7 . . . 28 B4
Grenfell Gdns
Harrow HA3 . . . 44 A2
Ilford IG2 . . . 57 D4
Grenfell Ho SE5 . . . 139 A5
Grenfell Rd
Mitcham CR4, SW17 . . . 180 D4
Shepherd's Bush W11 . . . 112 D6
Grenfell Twr 5 W11 . . . 112 D6
Grenfell Wlk 4 W11 . . . 112 D6
Grengate Lodge 2 E13 . 99 B4
Grenier Apartments 11 SE15 . . . 140 B5
Grennell Cl SM1 . . . 218 B6
Grennell Rd SM1 . . . 218 A6
Grenoble Gdns N13 . . . 32 C4
Grenville Cl
Church End N3 . . . 29 B2
Tolworth KT5 . . . 199 A1
Grenville Ct
3 Dulwich SE19 . . . 183 D5
Ealing W13 . . . 87 B2
Edgware HA8 . . . 26 D6
Grenville Gdns IG8 . . . 37 C3
Grenville Ho 26 Bow E3 . . 97 A5
4 Deptford SE8 . . . 141 C6
Grenville Lo N6 . . . 49 C2
Grenville Mans WC1 . . 240 A6
Grenville Mews
Hampton TW12 . . . 173 D5
South Kensington SW7 . 256 A3
Grenville Pl
Burnt Oak NW7 . . . 27 B5
South Kensington SW7 . . . 114 A2 256 A4
Grenville Rd N19 . . . 50 A1
Grenville St WC1 . . . 240 B5
Gresham Almshouses 3 SW9 . . . 138 B1
Gresham Ave N20 . . . 30 D6
Gresham Cl Enfield EN2 . . 5 A2
Sidcup DA5 . . . 169 B5
Gresham Coll EC1 . . . 94 C2 241 B3
Gresham Ct TW3 . . . 130 A4
Gresham Dr RM6 . . . 58 B3
Gresham Gdns NW11 . . . 47 A1
Gresham Ho
4 Teddington TW11 . . . 174 D5
3 Thames Ditton KT7 . . 197 A2
West Barnes KT3 . . . 200 B5
Gresham Lo E17 . . . 53 D4
Gresham Pl 2 N19 . . . 71 D6
Gresham Rd
Beckenham BR3 . . . 185 A1
Brixton SW9 . . . 138 C2
Canning Town E16 . . . 99 B1
Croydon SE25 . . . 206 A5
East Ham E6 . . . 100 B5
Edgware HA8 . . . 26 B4
Hampton TW12 . . . 173 C4
Hillingdon UB10 . . . 82 C5
Hounslow TW3, TW5 . . . 130 A4
Willesden NW10 . . . 67 B3
Gresham St EC2 . 95 A1 242 B2
Gresham Way SW19 . . . 157 C1
Gresham Way Est SW19 . . . 157 D1
Gresley Cl London N15 . . . 51 B5
Walthamstow E17 . . . 53 A3
Gresley Ho SW8 . . . 269 D2
Gresley Rd N19 . . . 49 C2
Gressenhall Rd SW18 . . 157 B4
Gressenham Ct 7 HA7 . . 25 C6
Gresse St W1 . . . 93 D1 239 C2
Gresswell Cl DA14 . . . 168 A1
Greswell St SW6 . . . 134 D4
Greta Ho SE3 . . . 142 D6
Gretton Ho 2 E2 . . . 96 C4
Gretton Rd N17 . . . 33 D3
Greville Cl TW1 . . . 153 B4
Greville Ct Harrow HA1 . . 64 C4
3 Lower Clapton E5 . . . 74 B5
Greville Hall NW6 . . . 91 D5
Greville Ho Harrow HA2 . . 42 B1
Knightsbridge SW1 . . . 258 A6
Putney SW15 . . . 134 D2
Greville Lo
5 Bayswater W2 . . . 91 D1
16 London N12 . . . 29 D6
Greville Mews 5 NW6 . . 91 D6
Greville Pl W9 . . . 91 D5
Greville Rd Kilburn NW6 . . 91 D5
Richmond TW10 . . . 154 B5
Walthamstow E17 . . . 54 A5
Greville St EC1 . . 94 C2 241 B4
Grey Cl NW11 . . . 48 A3
Grey Coat Hospital Sch (St Michaels) The SW1 . . . 115 D2 259 C3
Grey Coat Hospital Sch The SW1 . . . 115 D3 259 C5
Greycoat Pl SW1 . . . 115 D3 259 C5
Greycoat St SW1 . . . 115 D3 259 C5
Greycot Rd BR3 . . . 185 C5
Grey Court Sch TW10 . . 153 C1
Grey Eagle St E1 . . . 95 D3 243 D5
Greyfell Cl HA7 . . . 25 B5
Greyfriars 16 SE26 . . . 162 A1
Greyfriars Ho SE3 . . . 142 D6
Grey Ho 27 W12 . . . 112 B6
Greyhound Ct WC2 . . . 251 A6
Greyhound Hill NW4 . . . 46 B6
Greyhound La SW16 . . . 181 D4
Greyhound Rd
College Pk NW10 . . . 90 B4
Fulham W6 . . 135 A6 264 A6
Sutton SM1 . . . 218 A3
Tottenham N17 . . . 51 C6
Greyhound Terr SW16 . . 181 C2
Greyladies Gdns SE10 . . 142 A3
Greys Park Cl BR2 . . . 225 D3
Greystead Rd SE23 . . . 162 C4
Greystoke Ave HA5 . . . 41 C6
Greystoke Ct W5 . . . 88 B3
Greystoke Dr HA4 . . . 38 D3
Greystoke Gdns
Ealing W5 . . . 88 B3
Enfield EN2 . . . 3 D1
Greystoke Ho Ealing W5 . . 88 A3
Peckham SE15 . . . 140 A6
Greystoke Lo W5 . . . 88 B3
Greystoke Park Terr W5 . . . 88 A4
Greystoke Pl EC4 . . . 241 B2
Greystone Gdns HA3 . . . 43 C3
Greystones TW2 . . . 152 A2
Greyswood St SW16 . . . 181 B4
Greytiles TW11 . . . 174 D4
Grey Turner Ho W12 . . . 90 A1
Grice Ct N1 . . . 73 A2
Grierson Ho SW16 . . . 181 C6
Grierson Rd
Forest Hill SE23 . . . 162 D4
Forest Hill SE23 . . . 163 A5
Griffin Cl NW10 . . . 68 B3
Griffin Ct
8 Brentford TW8 . . . 132 A6
Chiswick W4 . . . 111 D1
Shepherd's Bush W12 . . . 112 B5
Griffin Ctr TW14 . . . 150 B5
Griffin Ctr The KT1 . . . 175 D1
Griffin Gate SW15 . . . 134 D2
Griffin Lo N12 . . . 30 A6
Griffin Manor Way SE28 . . . 123 B3
Griffin Park (Brentford FC) TW8 . . . 131 D6
Griffin Rd
Plumstead SE18 . . . 123 B1
Tottenham N17 . . . 33 C1
Griffins Cl N21 . . . 17 B4
Griffin Way
Sunbury TW16 . . . 172 A1
Woolwich SE28 . . . 123 C3
Griffith Cl RM8 . . . 58 C1
Griffiths Cl KT4 . . . 216 B6
Griffiths Ho 2 SE18 . . . 144 D6
Griffiths Rd SW19 . . . 179 D3
Griffon Ho 3 SW11 . . . 136 C2
Griggs App IG1 . . . 79 A6
Grigg's Pl SE1 . . . 263 B5
Griggs Rd E10 . . . 54 A3
Grilse Cl N9 . . . 34 B6
Grimaldi Ho N1 . . . 233 C4
Grimsby Gr E16 . . . 122 D5
Grimsby St
8 Bethnal Green E2 . . . 96 A3
Shoreditch E2 . . . 243 D6
Grimsdyke Fst & Mid Sch HA5 . . . 23 B4
Grimsdyke Rd HA5 . . . 23 A3
Grimsel Path SE5 . . . 138 D5
Grimshaw Cl N6 . . . 49 A2
Grimston Rd SW6 . . . 135 B3
Grimthorpe Ho EC1 . . . 241 C6
Grimwade Ave CR0 . . . 222 A5
Grimwade Cl SE15 . . . 140 C2
Grimwood Rd TW1 . . . 152 D4
Grindall Cl CR0 . . . 220 D4
Grindall Ho 26 E1 . . . 96 B3
Grindal St SE1 . . . 251 A1
Grindleford Ave N11 . . . 15 A2
Grindley Gdns CR0 . . . 205 D3
Grindley Ho 3 E3 . . . 97 B2
Grinling Gibbons Prim Sch SE8 . . . 141 B6
Grinling Ho 6 SE18 . . . 122 C2
Grinling Pl SE8 . . . 141 C6
Grinstead Rd SE8 . . . 119 A1
Grisedale NW1 . . . 232 A2
Grittleton Ave HA9 . . . 66 D2
Grittleton Rd W9 . . . 91 C3
Grizedale Terr 8 SE23 . . . 162 B2
Grogan Cl TW12 . . . 173 B4
Groombridge Cl DA16 . . 168 A6
Groombridge Ho 1 SE20 . . . 184 D3
Groombridge Rd E9 . . . 74 D1
Groom Cl BR2 . . . 209 B5
Groom Cres SW18 . . . 158 B4
Groome Ho SE11 . . . 260 D3
Groomfield Cl SW17 . . . 181 A6
Groom Pl SW1 . . 115 A3 258 B6
Grooms Dr HA5 . . . 40 A4
Grosmont Rd SE18 . . . 123 D1
Grosse Way SW15 . . . 156 B5
Grosslea SM4 . . . 202 B4
Grosvenor Ave
Canonbury N5 . . . 73 A3
Harrow HA2 . . . 41 D3
Hayes UB4 . . . 83 D5
Mortlake SW14 . . . 133 C2
Richmond TW10 . . . 154 A6
Wallington SM5, SM6 . . . 219 A2
Grosvenor Bridge SW1 . . . 137 B6 268 D6
Grosvenor Cotts SW1 . . 258 A4
Grosvenor Court Mans W2 . . . 237 C1
Grosvenor Cres
Hillingdon UB10 . . . 82 D6
Queensbury NW9 . . . 44 C5
Westminster SW1 . . . 115 A4 248 B1
Grosvenor Cres Mews SW1 . . . 248 A1
Grosvenor Ct
4 Acton W3 . . . 110 C5
Brondesbury Pk NW6 . . . 90 D6
3 Ealing W5 . . . 110 A6
3 Edgware NW7 . . . 27 B5
Gunnersbury W4 . . . 110 D1
Leyton E10 . . . 53 D1
Morden SM4 . . . 201 C5
Oakwood N14 . . . 15 C4
Penge SE19 . . . 183 D4
22 Poplar E14 . . . 97 B1
Putney SW15 . . . 157 A6
1 Sutton SM2 . . . 218 A2
Teddington TW11 . . . 175 A4
Grosvenor Ct continued
3 Wanstead E11 . . . 55 B4
2 Wimbledon SW19 . . . 179 A4
Grosvenor Gdns
Cricklewood NW2 . . . 68 C3
Hornsey N10 . . . 49 C6
Kingston u T KT2 . . . 175 D4
Mortlake SW14 . . . 133 C2
Newham E6 . . . 99 D4
Southgate N14 . . . 15 D6
Temple Fortune NW11 . . . 47 B4
Wallington SM6 . . . 219 C1
Westminster SW1 . . . 115 B3 258 D5
Woodford IG8 . . . 37 B4
Grosvenor Gdns Mews E SW1 . . . 258 D6
Grosvenor Gdns Mews N SW1 . . . 258 C5
Grosvenor Gdns Mews S SW1 . . . 258 D5
Grosvenor Hill
Mayfair W1 . . . 115 B6 248 C6
Wimbledon SW19 . . . 179 A4
Grosvenor Hill Ct W1 . 248 C6
Grosvenor Ho
5 Sutton SM1 . . . 217 D3
Upper Clapton E5 . . . 52 A1
Grosvenor Hts E4 . . . 20 C4
Grosvenor Lo
London N20 . . . 14 A1
4 Woodford E18 . . . 36 D1
Grosvenor Par 1 W5 . . 110 C5
Grosvenor Park SE5 . . . 139 A5
Grosvenor Park Rd E17 . . . 53 D4
Grosvenor Pier SW1 . . 269 C6
Grosvenor Pk SE5 . . . 139 A6
Grosvenor Pl SW1 . . . 115 B4 248 C1
Grosvenor Rd
Acton Green W4 . . . 111 A1
Bexley DA6 . . . 169 A6
Brentford TW8 . . . 131 D6
Croydon SE25 . . . 206 A5
Dagenham RM8 . . . 59 B1
Ealing W7 . . . 109 A5
Edmonton N9 . . . 18 B3
Erith DA17 . . . 147 C6
Finchley N3 . . . 29 C3
Hounslow TW3, TW4 . . . 129 B2
Ilford IG1 . . . 79 A5
Leyton E10 . . . 54 A1
Muswell Hill N10 . . . 31 B2
Newham E6 . . . 99 D6
Orpington BR6 . . . 211 C3
Pimlico SW1 . . 137 C6 269 B6
Richmond TW10 . . . 154 A6
Southall UB2 . . . 107 B3
Twickenham TW1 . . . 153 A3
Upton E7 . . . 77 B2
Wallington SM6 . . . 219 B3
Wanstead E11 . . . 55 B4
West Wickham BR4 . . . 223 D6
Grosvenor Residences 1 W14 . . . 112 D3
Grosvenor Rise E E17 . . 53 D4
Grosvenor Sq W1 . . . 115 A6 248 B6
Grosvenor St W1 . . . 115 B6 248 C6
Grosvenor Terr SE5 . . . 139 A6
Grosvenor The NW11 . . . 47 D2
Grosvenor Vale HA4 . . . 61 D6
Grosvenor Way E5 . . . 74 C6
Grosvernor Wharf Rd E14 . . . 120 B2
Grote's Bldgs SE3 . . . 142 C3
Grote's Pl SE3 . . . 142 C3
Groton Rd SW18 . . . 157 D2
Grotto Ct SE1 . . . 252 A2
Grotto Pas W1 . . . 238 A4
Grotto Rd TW1 . . . 152 D2
Grove Ave Cheam SM1 . . 217 C2
Ealing W7 . . . 86 C1
Finchley N3 . . . 29 C3
Pinner HA5 . . . 41 A5
Twickenham TW1 . . . 152 D3
Wood Green N10 . . . 31 C1
Grovebury Ct
Bexley DA6 . . . 169 D6
Southgate N14 . . . 15 D4
Grovebury Rd SE2 . . . 124 B4
Grove Cl East Barnet N14 . 15 B4
Forest Hill SE23 . . . 163 A3
Hayes BR2 . . . 225 A6
Ickenham UB10 . . . 60 C3
Kingston u T KT1 . . . 198 B5
Grove Cres
Feltham TW13 . . . 173 A6
Kingsbury NW9 . . . 45 B5
Kingston u T KT1 . . . 198 A6
Walton-on-T KT12 . . . 194 B2
Woodford E18 . . . 36 D1
Grove Crescent Rd E15 . . 76 B2
Grove Ct Barnet EN5 . . . 1 B2
Camberwell SE5 . . . 139 C3
Clapham SW4 . . . 137 C2
Ealing W5 . . . 110 A5
East Molesey KT8 . . . 196 B4
3 Forest Hill SE26 . . . 185 A6
Hounslow TW3 . . . 129 C1
8 Kingston u T KT1 . . . 198 A6
New Malden KT3 . . . 199 C6
Penge SE20 . . . 184 B3
Seething Wells KT6 . . . 197 D4
South Kensington SW10 . 256 B1

Grove Ct *continued*
St John's Wood NW8 .. 229 C2
Grovedale Rd N19 ...... 71 D6
Grove Dwellings E1 ..... 96 C2
Grove End
Gospel Oak NW5 .... 71 B4
Woodford E18 .... 36 D1
Grove End Gdns NW8 . 229 B3
Grove End Ho NW8 ... 229 C1
Grove End La KT10 ..... 196 B1
Grove End Rd
NW8 .... 92 B4 229 C1
Grove Farm Ct CR4 .... 202 D4
Grovefield 6 N11 .... 31 B6
Grove Footpath KT5 ... 198 A5
Grove Gdns Enfield EN3 ... 6 D5
Hendon NW4 .... 46 A5
Lisson Gr NW8 .. 92 C4 230 B1
Teddington TW11 ...... 175 A6
Grove Glade Shop Hall
W13 .... 109 A5
Grove Green Rd E11 .... 76 B6
Grove Hall Ct Bow E3 .... 97 C5
St John's Wood
NW8 .... 92 A4 229 B2
Grove Hill Harrow HA1 ... 42 C2
Woodford E18 .... 36 D1
Grovehill Ct BR1 .... 186 D4
Grove Hill Rd
Camberwell SE5 .... 139 C2
Harrow HA1 .... 42 D2
Grove Ho
Blackheath SE3 .... 142 D3
Chelsea SW3 .... 267 B6
Hendon N3 .... 46 D6
Grove House Rd N8 ..... 50 A5
Grove La
Camberwell SE5 .... 139 C2
Hillingdon UB8 .... 82 B3
Kingston u T KT1 .... 198 A5
Groveland Ave SW16 ... 182 B3
Groveland Ct EC4 ..... 242 B1
Groveland Rd BR3 ..... 207 B6
Grovelands
East Molesey KT8 ...... 195 C5
Kingston u T KT1 .... 197 D5
Grovelands Cl
Camberwell SE5 .... 139 C3
Harrow HA2 .... 63 D5
Grovelands Ct N14 ...... 15 D4
Grovelands Inf Sch
KT12 .... 194 B3
Grovelands Priory (Private
Hospl) N14 .... 16 A3
Grovelands Rd
Palmers Green N13 ...... 16 B1
South Tottenham N15 .... 52 A3
St Paul's Cray BR5 ..... 190 A3
Groveland Way KT3 .... 199 B4
Grove Lane Terr SE5 ... 139 B3
Groveley Ho 7 N4 ...... 51 A2
Groveley Rd TW13,
TW16 .... 171 D5
Grove Lo Clapham SW4 . 137 C1
Cranley Gdns N10 .... 49 C5
Grove Mans
London SW4 .... 136 D1
2 Shepherd's Bush
W6 .... 112 C4
3 Stamford Hill N16 .... 52 A1
Grove Market Pl SE9 ... 166 B5
Grove Mews W6 .... 112 C3
Grove Mill CR4 .... 202 C4
Grove Mill Pl SM5 ...... 219 A5
GROVE PARK SE9 ...... 165 B1
W4 .... 133 A4
Grove Park Ave E4 ...... 35 D3
Grove Park Bridge
W4 .... 133 A5
Grove Park Gdns W4 ... 133 A5
Grove Park Mews W4 . 133 A5
Grove Park Prim Sch
W4 .... 133 A6
Grove Park Rd
Chiswick W4 .... 132 D5
Mottingham SE9, SE12 . 165 D2
South Tottenham N15 .... 51 C5
Grove Park Sch NW9 .... 45 A5
Grove Park Sta SE12 ... 165 B1
Grove Park Terr W4 ... 132 D6
Grove Pk
Camberwell SE5 .... 139 C3
Kingsbury NW9 .... 45 B5
Wanstead E11 .... 55 B4
Grove Pl Acton W3 ..... 111 A5
Balham SW12 .... 159 B5
Hampstead NW3 .... 70 B5
Grove Prim Sch RM6 .... 58 C4
Grover Ct SE13 .... 141 D3
Grove Rd Acton W3 .... 111 A5
Barnes SW13 .... 133 D3
Belmont SM2 .... 217 C2
Bow E3 .... 97 A5
Brentford TW8 .... 109 C1
Chingford E4 .... 20 A1
Cockfosters EN4 .... 2 C2
Dagenham RM6 .... 58 C3
Ealing W5 .... 109 D6
East Molesey KT8 ...... 196 B5
Edgware HA8 .... 26 C4
8 Erith DA17 .... 147 B6
Friern Barnet N11 .... 31 B5
Hounslow TW3 .... 129 C1
Kingston u T KT6 .... 197 D4
Leytonstone E11 .... 54 D2
Merton SW19 .... 180 A3
Mitcham CR4 .... 181 B1
Grove Rd *continued*
North Finchley N12 ...... 30 B5
Pinner HA5 .... 41 B4
Richmond TW10 .... 154 B5
Shepperton TW17 ..... 193 A3
South Tottenham N15 .... 51 C4
Spring Gr TW7 .... 130 C4
Thornton Heath CR7 ... 204 C5
Twickenham TW2 ...... 152 B1
Uxbridge UB8 .... 60 A1
Walthamstow E17 .... 53 D4
Willesden NW2 .... 68 C2
Woodford E18 .... 36 D1
Grove Rd Prim Sch
TW3 .... 129 C1
Grove Rd W EN3 .... 6 C6
Grover Ho
4 London SW4 .... 159 C6
Vauxhall SE11 .... 260 D1
Groves Ho UB4 .... 84 B4
Groveside Cl Acton W3 ... 88 C1
Carshalton SM5 .... 218 C6
Groveside Ct SW11 .... 136 B3
Groveside Rd E4 .... 20 C1
Grove St Deptford SE8 ... 119 B1
Edmonton N18 .... 33 D4
Grovestile Waye
TW14 .... 149 B4
Grove Terr
Gospel Oak NW5 .... 71 B4
Southall UB1 .... 107 C6
Teddington TW11 ...... 175 A6
Grove Terrace Mews
NW5 .... 71 B5
Grove The Bexley DA6 ... 146 D1
Dulwich SE21 .... 162 A3
Ealing W5 .... 110 A5
Edgware HA8 .... 26 D6
Edmonton N13 .... 32 C6
Enfield EN2 .... 4 C3
Finchley N3 .... 29 C3
Hendon NW11 .... 47 A2
Highgate N6 .... 49 A1
Hornsey N8 .... 49 D4
Hounslow TW7 .... 130 C4
Ickenham UB10 .... 60 C3
Kingsbury NW9 .... 45 B4
Sidcup DA14 .... 191 A6
Southall UB6 .... 86 A1
Stratford E15 .... 76 C2
Stroud Green N4 .... 50 B2
Teddington TW11 ...... 175 A6
1 Twickenham TW1 .... 153 B5
Walton-on-T KT12 ..... 194 B2
West Wickham BR4 .... 224 A6
Grove Vale
Chislehurst West
BR7 .... 188 C4
East Dulwich SE22 ..... 139 D1
Groveway
Dagenham RM8 .... 80 D4
South Lambeth
SW9 .... 138 B4 270 D1
Grove Way
Thames Ditton KT10 .... 196 A1
Wembley HA9 .... 67 A3
Grovewood 9 TW9 .... 132 C4
Grovewood Ct 6
TW7 .... 130 C4
Grovewood Ho NW2 .... 69 B6
Grummant Rd SE15 .... 139 D4
Grundy St E14 .... 97 D1
Gruneisen Rd N3 .... 29 D3
Guardian Angels RC Prim
Sch E3 .... 97 A4
Guardian Ct SE12 ..... 164 C6
Guards Mus The*
SW1 .... 115 C4 249 B1
Gubyon Ave SE24 ..... 160 D6
Guerin Sq E3 .... 97 B4
Guernsey Cl TW5 ..... 129 C5
Guernsey Gr SE24 ..... 161 A4
Guernsey Ho
10 Canonbury N1 .... 73 A2
Enfield EN3 .... 6 D5
Guernsey Rd
11 Canonbury N1 .... 73 A2
Leytonstone E11 .... 54 B1
Guibal Rd SE12 .... 165 B3
Guildersfield Rd
SW16 .... 182 A3
Guildford Ave TW13 .... 150 A2
Guildford Gr SE10 ..... 141 D4
Guildford Ho 23 SE5 ... 139 A3
Guildford Rd
Chingford E17 .... 36 A2
Ilford IG3 .... 79 C6
Newham E6 .... 100 B1
South Lambeth
SW8 .... 138 A4 270 B2
Thornton Heath CR0 .... 205 B3
Guildford Way SM6 .... 220 A3
Guild Hall* EC2 . 95 A1 242 B2
Guildhall Bldgs EC2 ... 242 C2
Guildhall Ho EC2 ..... 242 C2
Guildhall Sch Music &
Drama EC2 .... 95 A2 242 B4
Guildhall Yd EC2 ...... 242 B2
Guild Ho SW19 .... 179 B4
Guildhouse St
SW1 .... 115 C2 259 A3
Guildown Ave N12 ...... 29 D6
Guild Rd SE7 .... 143 D6
Guildsway E17 .... 35 B2
Guilford Ave KT5 ...... 198 B4
Guilford Pl WC1 ...... 240 C5
Guilford St WC1 . 94 A3 240 B5
Guilfoyle 2 NW9 .... 27 D1
Guillemot Ct 28 SE8 .... 141 B6
Guilsborough Cl NW10 .. 67 C1
Guinness Cl Hayes UB3 . 105 B3
Homerton E9 .... 75 A1
Guinness Ct
Chelsea SW3 .... 257 C3
6 Croydon CR0 .... 221 D6
Finsbury EC1 .... 235 B1
Primrose Hill NW8 .... 230 B5
Whitechapel E1 .... 243 D1
Guinness Sq SE1 ...... 263 A4
Guinness Trust Bldgs
Bermondsey SE1 ...... 253 A2
7 Bethnal Green E2 .... 96 A5
Chelsea SW3 .... 257 C3
Hammersmith W6 ..... 112 C1
Kennington SE11 ..... 261 C2
Guion Rd SW6 .... 135 B3
Gujarat Ho 1 N16 ...... 73 C5
Gulland Cl WD23 .... 8 A6
Gulland Wlk 21 N1 ...... 73 A2
Gullane Ho 24 E3 .... 97 B5
Gull Cl SM6 .... 220 A1
Gulliver Cl UB5 .... 85 B6
Gulliver Ct CR2 .... 220 D1
Gulliver Rd DA15 ..... 167 C2
Gulliver St SE16 ...... 119 B3
Gulston Wlk SW3 ..... 257 D3
Gumleigh Rd W5 ...... 109 C2
Gumley Gdns TW7 ..... 131 A2
Gumley House RC Convent
Sch (Girls) TW7 ..... 131 A2
Gumping Rd BR5 ...... 227 A6
Gundulph Rd BR2 ..... 209 C6
Gunmakers La E3 .... 97 A6
Gunnel Cl SE20 .... 184 A6
Gunnell Cl SE25 ...... 206 A3
Gunnell Ct 3 CR4 ..... 180 C2
Gunnels Ct & Hastingwood
Ct 6 IG9 .... 21 C2
Gunner Dr 9 EN3 .... 7 C6
Gunner La SE18 .... 122 C1
GUNNERSBURY 110 D2
Gunnersbury Avenue
(North Circular Rd)
W3 .... 110 C3
Gunnersbury Cl 8
W4 .... 110 D1
Gunnersbury Cres
W3 .... 110 C4
Gunnersbury Ct 8
W3 .... 110 D4
Gunnersbury Dr W5 .... 110 B4
Gunnersbury Gdns
W3 .... 110 C4
Gunnersbury La W3 .... 110 C4
Gunnersbury Manor
W5 .... 110 B5
Gunnersbury Mews 6
W4 .... 110 D1
Gunnersbury Park
W3 .... 110 C3
Gunnersbury Park Mus*
W3 .... 110 C3
Gunnersbury RC Sch
TW8 .... 109 C1
Gunnersbury Sta W4 ... 110 D1
Gunners Gr E4 .... 20 A1
Gunners Rd SW18 ..... 158 B2
Gunnery Terr SE18 .... 123 A3
Gunning St SE18 ...... 123 C2
Gunpowder Sq EC4 .... 241 B2
Gun St E1 .... 243 C3
Gunstor Rd N16 .... 73 C4
Gunter Gr
Chelsea SW6 .. 136 A5 266 A4
Hendon HA8 .... 27 B2
Gunterstone Rd
W14 .... 113 A1 254 B2
Gunthorpe St
E1 .... 95 D1 243 D2
Gunton Rd
Streatham SW17 ...... 181 A4
Upper Clapton E5 .... 74 B6
Gunwhale Cl SE16 ..... 118 D5
Gun Wharf Old Ford E3 ... 97 A6
Wapping E1 .... 118 C5
Gurdon Ho 7 E14 ...... 97 C1
Gurdon Rd SE7 .... 121 A1
Gurnell Gr W13 .... 86 D3
Gurney Cl Barking IG11 .. 78 D2
Higham Hill E17 .... 34 D2
Stratford E15 .... 76 C3
Gurney Cres CR0 ...... 204 B1
Gurney Dr N2 .... 48 A5
Gurney Ho
3 Bayswater W2 .... 91 D1
14 Bethnal Green E2 .... 96 A5
Hayes UB3 .... 105 C2
Gurney Rd
London SW6 .... 136 A2
Northolt UB5 .... 84 C4
Stratford E15 .... 76 C3
Wallington SM5 ...... 219 A4
Guru Nanak Sikh Prim &
Sec Schs UB4 .... 106 C5
Guthrie Ct SE1 .... 251 B1
Guthrie St SW3 .... 257 A2
Gutter La EC2 ... 95 A1 242 A2
Guyatt Gdns CR4 ..... 181 A1
Guy Barnett Gr SE3 ... 143 A2
Guy Rd SM6 .... 219 D5
Guyscliff Rd SE13 ..... 164 A6
Guy's Hospl
SE1 .... 117 B4 252 D2
Guy's Hospl Sch
SE1 .... 117 B5 252 D3
Guy's Retreat IG9 ...... 21 C4
Guy St SE1 ..... 117 B4 252 D2
Gwalior Ho N14 .... 15 C5
Gwalior Rd SW15 ..... 134 D2
Gwendolen Ave SW15 .. 156 D6
Gwendolen Cl SW15 ... 156 D6
Gwendolen Ho TW19 ... 148 A3
Gwendoline Ave E13 .... 99 B6
Gwendoline Ct TW15 ... 170 A6
Gwendwr Rd
W14 .... 113 A1 254 B2
Gwent Ct 18 SE16 ..... 118 D5
Gwillim Cl DA15 .... 168 A6
Gwilym Maries Ho 11
E2 .... 96 B4
Gwydor Rd BR3 .... 206 D6
Gwydyr Rd BR2 .... 208 D6
Gwyn Cl SW6 ... 136 A5 266 A3
Gwyn Jones Prim Sch
E11 .... 54 B2
Gwynne Ave CR0 ...... 206 D2
Gwynne Cl W4 .... 133 D6
Gwynne Ho
Finsbury WC1 .... 234 A1
6 Streatham SW2 ..... 160 B3
3 Wanstead E11 .... 55 A4
Whitechapel E1 .... 96 B2
Gwynne Pl WC1 ...... 233 D1
Gwynne Rd SW11 ..... 136 B3
Gye Ho 2 SW4 .... 138 A1
Gylcote Cl SE5 .... 139 B1
Gyles Pk HA7 .... 25 C2
Gyllyngdune Gdns IG3 .. 79 D5

H

Haarlem Rd 12 W14 .... 112 D3
Haberdasher Pl 4 N1 ... 95 C4
Haberdashers' Aske's
Hatcham Coll SE4 .... 141 A3
Haberdashers' Aske's
Knights Acad BR1 .... 187 A6
Haberdasher St
N1 .... 95 B4 235 D2
Haccombe Rd SW19 .... 180 A4
HACKBRIDGE 219 B6
Hackbridge Park Gdns
SM5 .... 218 D6
Hackbridge Prim Sch
SM5 .... 203 A1
Hackbridge Rd SM5,
SM6 .... 219 A6
Hackbridge Sta SM6 ... 219 B6
Hackford Rd
SW9 .... 138 B4 270 D2
Hackford Wlk SW9 .... 138 C4
Hackforth Cl EN5 .... 12 B6
Hackington Cres BR3 .. 185 C4
HACKNEY 74 B2
Hackney Central Sta
E8 .... 74 B2
Hackney Cl WD6 .... 11 B6
Hackney Coll (Poplar Ctr)
E3 .... 97 D3
Hackney Com Coll N1 ... 95 C4
Hackney Downs Sta E8 . 74 B3
Hackney Free & Parochial
CE Sec Sch E9 .... 74 C2
Hackney Gr E8 .... 74 B2
Hackney Hospl E9 .... 75 A3
Hackney Rd E2 .... 96 A5
Hackney Stadium Mkt*
E15 .... 75 C2
HACKNEY WICK 75 C2
Hackney Wick E9 .... 75 B2
Hackney Wick Sta E9 ... 75 C2
Hackworth Point 24 E3 .. 97 D4
Hacon Sq 12 E8 .... 74 B1
Hadar Cl N20 .... 13 D3
Haddenham Ct SW17 ... 180 B6
Hadden Rd SE28 ...... 123 C3
Hadden Way UB6 .... 64 B2
Haddington Rd BR1 .... 186 B6
Haddo Ho
Gospel Oak NW5 .... 71 B4
Greenwich SE10 ...... 141 D6
Haddon Cl Enfield EN1 ... 18 A5
New Malden KT3 ..... 199 D4
Haddon Ct
East Acton W3 .... 111 D6
Hendon NW4 .... 46 C6
Haddon Gr DA15 ...... 168 A4
Haddon Rd SM1 .... 217 D4
Haddo St SE10 .... 142 A6
Haden Ct N4 .... 72 C6
Hadfield Cl UB1 .... 85 B4
Hadfield Ho
Edgware NW7 .... 28 C6
37 Whitechapel E1 ...... 96 A1
Hadleigh Cl
17 Bethnal Green E1 .... 96 C3
Merton SW20 .... 179 B1
Hadleigh Ct 8 E4 .... 20 C4
Hadleigh Ho 16 E1 ...... 96 C3
Hadleigh Lo 5 IG8 ...... 37 A4
Hadleigh Rd N9 .... 18 B4
Hadleigh St E2 .... 96 C4
Hadleigh Wlk 1 E6 .... 100 A1
HADLEY 1 B2
Hadley Cl
Borehamwood WD6 ..... 10 B5
Southgate N21 .... 16 C5
Hadley Ct 1 London N3 .. 29 D3
Stamford Hill N16 .... 52 A1
Hadley Gdns
Chiswick W4 .... 111 B1
Southall UB2 .... 107 B1
Hadley Gn EN5 .... 1 B3
Hadley Gn W EN5 .... 1 B3
Hadley Gr EN5 .... 1 A3
Hadley Green Rd EN5 .... 1 B3
Hadley Hall N21 .... 16 C3
Hadley Highstone EN5 ... 1 B4
Hadley Ho BR5 .... 189 D1
Hadley Hts EN5 .... 1 D3
Hadley Rd Barnet EN5 ..... 1 D2
Belvedere DA17 ...... 125 B2
Enfield EN2 .... 4 A5
Mitcham CR4 .... 203 D5
Hadley Ridge EN5 .... 1 B2
Hadley St NW1 .... 71 B2
Hadleyvale Ct EN5 .... 1 D2
Hadley View 9 EN5 ...... 1 D1
Hadley Way N21 .... 16 C5
HADLEY WOOD 2 B5
Hadley Wood Prim Sch
EN4 .... 2 A5
Hadley Wood Rd
Barnet EN4 .... 2 A3
Barnet EN5 .... 1 C3
Hadley Wood Sta EN4 .... 2 A5
Hadlow Coll (Mottingham
Ctr) SE12 .... 165 C3
Hadlow Coll Nature
Reserve* SE12 .... 165 C3
Hadlow Ho SE17 ...... 263 B2
Hadlow Pl SE19 .... 184 A3
Hadlow Rd
Bexley DA16 .... 146 C5
Sidcup DA14 .... 190 A6
Hadrian Cl
5 Old Ford E3 .... 97 C6
Stanwell TW19 .... 148 A4
Hadrian Ct Barnet EN5 .... 1 D1
11 Belmont SM2 ...... 217 D1
Brockley SE4 .... 141 C2
Hadrian Est 33 E2 ...... 96 A5
Hadrian's Ride EN1 ..... 17 D6
Hadrian St SE10 ...... 120 C1
Hadrian Way TW19 .... 148 A4
Hadstock Ho NW1 ..... 232 D2
Hadyn Park Ct 13
W12 .... 112 A4
Hadyn Park Rd W12 ... 112 A4
Hafer Rd SW11 .... 136 D1
Hafton Rd SE6 .... 164 C2
Haggard Rd TW1 ...... 153 B4
Hagger Ct E17 .... 54 B6
HAGGERSTON 95 D5
Haggerston Rd E8 ...... 95 D6
Haggerston Sch E2 ..... 95 D5
Haggerston Studios 30
E8 .... 95 D6
Hague Prim Sch E2 ..... 96 B3
Hague St 30 E2 .... 96 A4
Ha-Ha Rd SE7, SE18 .... 144 B6
Haig Ct BR7 .... 188 D5
Haig Ho 4 E2 .... 96 A5
Haig Pl SM4 .... 201 C3
Haig Rd Hillingdon UB8 ... 83 A2
Stanmore HA7 .... 25 C5
Haig Rd E E13 .... 99 C5
Haig Rd W E13 .... 99 C4
Haigville Gdns IG6 ...... 56 D5
Hailes Cl SW19 .... 180 A4
Haileybury Ave EN1 ..... 17 D5
Hailey Rd DA18 .... 125 C4
Hailey Rd Bsns Pk
DA18 .... 125 C4
Hailing Mews BR2 ..... 209 B6
Hailsham Ave SW2 .... 160 B2
Hailsham Cl KT6 ...... 197 D2
Hailsham Dr HA1 .... 42 B6
Hailsham Rd SW17 .... 181 A4
Hailsham Terr N18 ...... 33 B5
Haimo Prim Sch SE9 ... 165 D6
Haimo Rd SE9 .... 165 D6
Hainault Bldgs E10 ..... 54 A1
Hainault Bridge Par 5
IG1 .... 78 D6
Hainault Ct E17 .... 54 B5
Hainault Gore RM6 ..... 59 A4
Hainault Rd
Dagenham RM6 .... 59 B3
Ilford RM6 .... 58 B6
Leytonstone E11 .... 54 B2
Hainault St Ilford IG1 .... 78 D6
New Eltham SE9 ...... 166 D3
Haines Wlk SM4 ...... 201 D2
Hainford Cl SE4 ...... 140 D1
Haining Cl 3 W4 ..... 110 C1
Hainthorpe Rd SE27 ... 182 D6
Hainton Cl E1 .... 96 B1
Halberd Mews E5 .... 74 B6
Halbutt Gdns RM9 ...... 81 B5
Halbutt St RM9 .... 81 B4
Halcomb St N1 .... 95 C6
Halcot Ave DA6 ...... 169 D6
Halcroft Ct SM1 ...... 218 B4
Halcrow St E1 .... 96 B2
Halcyon Ho 3 EN1 ...... 17 C6
Halcyon Wharf 19 E1 ... 118 A5
Haldane Cl
Holdbrook EN3 .... 7 D5
Muswell Hill N10 .... 31 B3
Haldane Pl SW18 ..... 157 D3
Haldane Rd
Fulham SW6 .. 135 B6 264 D5
Newham E6 .... 100 A4
Southall UB1 .... 86 A1
Thamesmead SE28 .... 124 D6
Haldan Rd E4 .... 36 A4
Haldon Rd SW18 ...... 157 B5
Hale Cl Chingford E4 ..... 20 A1
Edgware HA8 .... 27 A5
Orpington BR6 .... 227 A4
Hale Ct HA8 .... 27 A5
Hale Dr NW7 .... 27 B4
HALE END 36 C4
Hale End Cl HA4 .... 40 A3
Hale End Rd E17 .... 36 B2
Halefield Rd N17 .... 34 B2
Hale Gdns Acton W3 ... 110 C5
Tottenham Hale N17 ..... 52 A6
Hale Grove Gdns NW7 ... 27 C5
Hale Ho Enfield EN3 ...... 6 D6
Westminster SW1 ..... 259 D2
Hale La NW7, HA8 ...... 27 B5
Hale Lo HA1 .... 42 C2
Hale Rd Newham E6 .... 100 A3
Tottenham Hale N17 ..... 52 A6
Hales Ct 6 TW11 ..... 175 A5
Hales Ho 3 SW12 .... 159 B4
Halesowen Rd SM4 .... 201 D2
Hales Prior N1 .... 233 C3
Hales St SE8 .... 141 C5
Hale St E14 .... 119 D6
Halesworth Cl 3 E5 ..... 74 C6
Halesworth Rd SE13 ... 141 D2
Hale The Chingford E4 ... 36 B3
Tottenham Hale N17 ..... 52 A6
Hale Wlk W7 .... 86 C2
Haley Rd NW4 .... 46 C3
Halfacre 11 HA7 .... 25 C5
Half Acre
Brentford TW8 .... 131 D6
2 Wanstead E18 .... 55 A6
Half Acre Mews TW8 ... 131 D6
Half Acre Rd W7 ...... 108 C5
Half Moon Cres N1 ... 233 D4
Half Moon Ct EC1 .... 242 A3
Half Moon La SE24 .... 161 A5
Halfmoon Pas E1 ..... 243 D1
Half Moon St
W1 .... 115 B5 248 D3
Halford Cl HA8 .... 26 D1
Halford Ct KT9 .... 214 A1
Halford Ho 9 SW15 ... 156 D6
Halford Rd
Ickenham UB10 .... 60 C3
Leyton E10 .... 54 B4
Richmond TW10 ...... 154 A6
West Brompton
SW6 .... 135 C6 265 A5
Halfway St DA15 ...... 167 C3
Haliburton Rd TW1,
TW7 .... 131 A1
Haliday Ho N1 .... 73 B2
Haliday Wlk 4 N1 ...... 73 B2
Halidon Cl E9 .... 74 C3
Halifax 8 NW9 .... 27 D1
Halifax Cl TW11 ...... 174 C4
Halifax Rd Enfield EN2 .... 5 B3
Greenford UB6 .... 85 D6
Halifax St SE26 .... 162 B1
Halifield Dr DA17 ..... 125 A3
Haling Gr CR2 .... 221 A1
Haling Manor High Sch
CR2 .... 220 D1
Haling Park Gdns
CR2 .... 220 D2
Haling Park Rd
Croydon CR2 .... 220 D3
South Croydon CR2 .... 221 A2
Haling Rd CR2 .... 221 B2
Haliwell Ho 10 NW6 .... 91 D6
Halkett Ho 1 E2 .... 96 C6
Halkin Arc
SW1 .... 114 D3 257 D6
Halkin Mews SW1 .... 258 A6
Halkin Pl SW1 .... 258 A6
Halkin St SW1 .. 115 A4 248 B1
Hallam Cl BR7 .... 188 B5
Hallam Ct W1 .... 238 D4
Hallam Gdns HA5 .... 23 A3
Hallam Ho
17 London SW9 .... 138 C4
Pimlico SW1 .... 259 B1
Hallam Mews W1 ..... 238 D4
Hallam Rd
Barnes SW13 .... 134 B2
Harringay N15 .... 50 D5
Hallam St W1 ... 93 B2 238 D4
Hallane Ho SE27 ..... 183 A5
Hall Cl W5 .... 88 A2
Hall Ct TW11 .... 174 D5
Hall Dr Ealing W7 ...... 86 C1
Forest Hill SE26 ...... 184 C5
Halley Gdns SE13 ..... 142 B1
Halley Ho
16 Bethnal Green E2 .... 96 A5
8 Cubitt Town SE10 .... 120 D1
Halley Prim Sch E14 .... 97 A2
Halley Rd E7, E12 ...... 77 D2
Halley St E14 .... 97 A2
Hall Farm Cl HA7 ...... 25 B6
Hall Farm Dr TW2 .... 152 B4
Hallfield Jun & Inf Schs
W2 .... 91 D1
Hallgate SE3 .... 143 A2
Hall Gate NW8 .. 92 A4 229 B2
Hall Gdns E4 .... 35 B6
Halliards The KT12 .... 194 A3
Halliday Ho 40 E1 ...... 96 A1
Halliday Sq UB2 ...... 108 B5
Halliford Cl TW17 ..... 193 C6
Halliford Rd
Sunbury TW16 .... 194 A5
Upper Halliford TW16,
TW17 .... 193 D5
Halliford Sch TW17 ... 193 A2
Halliford St N1 .... 73 B1
Hallingbury Ct 1 E17 ... 53 D6
Halling Ho SE1 ...... 252 D1
Hallings Wharf Studios 2
E15 .... 98 B6
Halliwell Ct 4 SE22 ... 162 A6
Halliwell Rd SW2 ..... 160 B5
Halliwick Court Par 2
N12 .... 30 D5
Halliwick Ct 1 N12 ..... 30 D5
Halliwick Ho N21 .... 17 B5
Halliwick Rd N10 .... 31 A2

Hall La
  Chingford Hatch E4 . . . . .35 B5
  Harlington UB3 . . . . .127 B5
  Hendon NW4 . . . . .28 A1
Hallmark Trad Ctr HA9 . . .67 A4
Hallmead Rd SM1 . . . . . . .217 D5
Hall Oak Wlk NW6 . . . . . . .69 B2
Hallowell Ave CR0 . . . . . .220 A4
Hallowell Cl CR4 . . . . . . .203 A6
Hallowfield Way CR4 . . . .202 C6
Hallows Gr TW16 . . . . . . .171 D5
Hall Pl W2 . . . . . .92 B3 236 C5
Hall Rd Dagenham RM6 . . . .58 D3
  Isleworth TW7 . . . . .152 B6
  Leyton E15 . . . . .76 B4
  Newham E6 . . . . .100 B6
  St John's Wood
  NW8 . . . . .92 A4 229 B2
Halls Bsns Ctr UB3 . . . . .106 A4
Hall Sch The NW3 . . . . . . .70 B2
Hall Sch SW20 . . . . .178 D2
Hall Sch Wimbledon
  SW15 . . . . .156 A1
Hall St
  Finsbury EC1 . . .94 D4 234 D2
  North Finchley N12 . . . . . . .30 A5
Halls Terr UB10 . . . . .82 D3
Hallside Rd EN1 . . . . .5 D5
Hallsville Prim Sch E16 . .99 A1
Hallsville Rd E16 . . . . .98 D1
Hallswelle Par 1
  NW11 . . . . .47 B4
Hallswelle Rd NW11 . . . . . .47 B4
Hall The SE3 . . . . .143 A2
Hall Twr W2 . . . . .236 D4
Hall View SE9 . . . . .165 D2
Hallywell Cres E6 . . . . . . .100 B2
Halons Rd SE9 . . . . .166 C4
Halpin Pl SE17 . .117 B2 262 D3
Halsbrook Rd SE3 . . . . . .143 D2
Halsbury Cl HA7 . . . . .25 B6
Halsbury Ct HA7 . . . . .25 B6
Halsbury Ho 4 N7 . . . . . . .72 B4
Halsbury Rd W12 . . . . . . .112 B5
Halsbury Rd E UB5 . . . . . . .64 A4
Halsbury Rd W UB5 . . . . . .63 D3
Halsend UB3 . . . . .106 B5
Halsey St SW3 . .114 D2 257 C4
Halsham Cres IG11 . . . . . . .79 D3
Halstead Cl 2 CR0 . . . . . .221 A5
Halstead Ct
  Shoreditch N1 . . . . .235 D3
  Walthamstow E17 . . . . .53 B2
Halstead Gdns N21 . . . . . . .17 B3
Halstead Rd
  Edmonton N21 . . . . .17 B3
  Enfield EN1 . . . . .5 C1
  Wanstead E11 . . . . .55 B4
Halston Cl SW11 . . . . .158 D5
Halstow 12 NW5 . . . . .71 A2
Halstow Prim Sch
  SE10 . . . . .121 A1
Halstow Rd
  Greenwich SE3, SE10 . . . .121 A1
  Kensal Green NW10 . . . . . . .90 D4
Halsway UB3 . . . . .106 A5
Halter Cl WD6 . . . . .11 B6
Halton Cl N11 . . . . .30 C4
Halton Cross St
  N1 . . . . .94 D6 234 D6
Haltone Ho 1 SW4 . . . . .137 D3
Halton Ho 22 N1 . . . . .72 D1
Halton Mans N1 . . . . .72 D1
Halton Pl N1 . . . . .235 A6
Halton Rd N1 . . . .94 D6 234 D6
Halt Robin La DA17 . . . . .125 D2
Halt Robin Rd DA17 . . . . .125 D2
Halyard Ho E14 . . . . .120 A3
HAM 153 C1
Hamara Ghar 4 E13 . . . . .99 C6
Hambalt Rd SW4 . . . . . . .159 C6
Hamble Cl HA4 . . . . .61 C6
Hamble Ct KT1 . . . . .175 D3
Hambledon SE17 . . . . . . .139 B6
Hambledon Chase N4 . . . . .50 A2
Hambledon Cl UB8 . . . . . . .82 D3
Hambledon Ct
  5 Ealing W5 . . . . .110 A6
  9 Wallington SM6 . . . . . .219 B2
Hambledon Gdns
  SE25 . . . . .205 D6
Hambledon Ho
  2 Kingston u T KT2 . . . .176 D4
  Lower Clapton E5 . . . . .74 B4
Hambledon Pl SE21 . . . . .161 D3
Hambledon Rd SW18 . . . .157 B4
Hambledown Rd
  DA15 . . . . .167 C4
Hamble St SW6 . . . . .135 D2
Hambleton Cl KT4 . . . . . .216 C6
Hamble Wlk UB5 . . . . .85 C5
Hambley Ho 5 SE16 . . . . .118 B2
Hamblyn Ct N16 . . . . .51 D2
Hambridge Way SW2 . . . .160 C4
Hambro Ave BR2 . . . . .209 A1
Hambrook Ct 12 NW5 . . .71 B4
Hambrook Rd SE25 . . . . . .206 B6
Hambro Rd SW16 . . . . . . .181 D5
Hambrough Prim Sch
  UB1 . . . . .107 B5
Hambrough Rd UB1 . . . . . .107 A5
Ham Cl TW10 . . . . .153 C1
Ham Comm TW10 . . . . . . .153 D1
Ham Croft Cl TW13 . . . . . .150 A1
Ham Ct 12 NW9 . . . . .27 D1

Hamden Cres RM10 . . . . . .81 D5
Hamel Cl HA3 . . . . .43 D5
Hamers Ho 19 SW2 . . . . .160 C4
Hameway E6 . . . . .100 C3
Ham Farm Rd KT2,
  TW10 . . . . .176 A6
Hamfrith Rd E15 . . . . .76 D2
Ham Gate Ave TW10 . . . .176 A6
Ham Ho* TW10 . . . . .153 C2
Hamilton Ave
  Cheam SM3 . . . . .217 A6
  Edmonton N9 . . . . .18 A4
  Ilford IG6 . . . . .57 A4
  Tolworth KT6, SM3 . . . . . .214 C6
Hamilton Cl
  Ashford TW13 . . . . .171 D5
  Cockfosters EN4 . . . . .2 D1
  Rotherhithe SE16 . . . . . . .119 A4
  St John's Wood
  NW8 . . . . .92 B4 229 C1
  Teddington TW11 . . . . . . .175 B4
  Tottenham N17 . . . . .51 D6
Hamilton Ct
  9 Catford SE6 . . . . .164 D3
  Croydon CR0 . . . . .206 A1
  Ealing W5 . . . . .110 B6
  St John's Wood W9 . . . . .229 A2
Hamilton Cres
  Edmonton N13 . . . . .32 C6
  Harrow HA2 . . . . .63 B5
  Hounslow TW3 . . . . .151 D6
Hamilton Ct
  Harrow HA1 . . . . .42 A5
  10 Muswell Hill N10 . . . . .31 A3
Hamilton Gdns
  NW8 . . . . .92 A4 229 B2
Hamilton Hall
  NW8 . . . . .92 A5 229 A3
Hamilton Ho 28 Bow E3 . .97 B4
  Chiswick W4 . . . . .133 C4
  Kensington W8 . . . . .245 C2
  Oakleigh Pk N20 . . . . .14 A4
  1 Poplar E14 . . . . .119 B6
  Putney SW15 . . . . .156 A6
  10 Richmond TW9 . . . . . .132 C4
  St John's Wood NW8 . . . .229 C2
Hamilton La N5 . . . . .72 C4
Hamilton Lo 37 E1 . . . . . . .96 C3
Hamilton Mews W1 . . . . . .248 C2
Hamilton Par TW13 . . . . . .172 A6
Hamilton Pk N5 . . . . .72 C4
Hamilton Pk W N5 . . . . . . .72 C4
Hamilton Pl
  Mayfair W1 . . . .115 A5 248 B3
  Sunbury TW16 . . . . .172 B3
  Tottenham N17 . . . . .33 D1
Hamilton Rd Acton W4 . . .111 C4
  Barnet EN4 . . . . .2 C1
  Bexleyheath DA7 . . . . .147 A3
  Brentford TW8 . . . . .131 D6
  East Finchley N2 . . . . .48 A6
  Edmonton N9 . . . . .18 A4
  Feltham TW13 . . . . .171 D6
  Harrow HA1 . . . . .42 C4
  Hayes UB3 . . . . .106 B6
  Hendon NW11 . . . . .47 A2
  Higham Hill E17 . . . . .35 A1
  Ilford IG1 . . . . .78 D4
  Merton SW19 . . . . .179 D5
  Newham E15 . . . . .98 C4
  Sidcup DA15 . . . . .190 A6
  South Norwood CR7 . . . . .205 B6
  Twickenham TW2 . . . . . . .152 C3
  West Norwood SE27 . . . . .183 B6
  Willesden NW10 . . . . .68 A3
Hamilton Road Ind Est
  SE27 . . . . .183 B6
Hamilton Road Mews 1
  SW19 . . . . .179 D3
Hamilton Sq
  Bermondsey SE1 . . . . . . .252 C2
  Finchley N12 . . . . .30 A4
Hamilton St SE8 . . . . .141 C6
Hamilton Terr
  NW8 . . . . .92 A4 229 B4
Hamilton Way
  Edmonton N13 . . . . .32 D6
  Finchley N3 . . . . .29 C4
Hamlea Cl SE12 . . . . .165 A6
Hamlet Cl SE13 . . . . .142 C1
Hamlet Ct
  14 Enfield EN1 . . . . .17 C6
  1 Hammersmith W6 . . . .112 A2
  Kennington SE11 . . . . . . .261 C2
Hamlet Gdns W6 . . . . .112 A2
Hamlet Ho SE9 . . . . .166 C6
Hamlet Ind Est E9 . . . . . . .75 C1
Hamleton Terr RM9 . . . . . .80 C1
Hamlet Rd SE19 . . . . .184 A3
Hamlet Sq NW2 . . . . .69 A5
Hamlets Way E3 . . . . .97 B3
Hamlet The SE5 . . . . .139 B2
Hamlet Way SE1 . . . . .252 D2
Hamlin Cres HA5 . . . . .40 C4
Hamlyn Cl HA8 . . . . .10 A1
Hamlyn Gdns SE19 . . . . . .183 C3
Hamlyn Ho TW13 . . . . . . .150 A1
Hammelton Ct 4 BR1 . . . .186 D2
Hammelton Gn 2
  SW9 . . . . .138 D4
Hammelton Rd BR1 . . . . . .187 A2
Hammers La NW7 . . . . .28 A4
Hammersley Ho 8
  SE14 . . . . .140 C5
HAMMERSMITH 112 C2
Hammersmith Bridge Rd
  W6, SW13 . . . . .112 C1
Hammersmith Broadway
  Hammersmith W6 . . . . . . .112 C1
  5 Hammersmith W6 . . . .112 C2

Hammersmith Flyover
  W6 . . . . .112 C1
Hammersmith Gr W6 . . . .112 C3
Hammersmith Hospl
  W12 . . . . .90 B1
Hammersmith Rd
  Hammersmith W6 . . . . . . .112 D2
  Kensington W14 . . . . .254 B4
Hammersmith Sta
  W6 . . . . .112 C2
Hammersmith Terr 6
  W6 . . . . .112 A1
Hammet Cl UB4 . . . . .84 D2
Hammett St EC3 . . . . .253 C6
Hammond Ave CR4 . . . . . .181 B1
Hammond Cl
  Barnet EN5 . . . . .13 B6
  Greenford UB6 . . . . .64 B3
  Hampton TW12 . . . . .173 C2
Hammond Ct
  1 Leyton E10 . . . . .75 D6
  1 Walthamstow E17 . . . . .53 A4
Hammond Ho
  10 Deptford SE14 . . . . . .140 C5
  Millwall E14 . . . . .119 D3
Hammond Lo 6 W9 . . . . . . .91 C2
Hammond Rd Enfield EN1 . .6 B3
  Southall UB2 . . . . .107 A3
Hammonds Cl RM8 . . . . . . .80 C5
Hammonds Ho TW19 . . . .148 B3
Hammond St NW5 . . . . . . .71 C2
Hammond Way 2
  SE28 . . . . .124 B6
Hamonde Cl HA8 . . . . .10 D2
Hamond Sq N1 . . . . .95 C5
Hampden Ave BR3 . . . . . .185 A1
Hampden Cl NW1 . . . . . . .232 D4
Hampden Ct
  Harrow HA1 . . . . .42 A5
  10 Muswell Hill N10 . . . . .31 A3
Hampden Gurney CE Prim
  Sch W1 . . . . . .92 C1 237 B2
Hampden Gurney St
  W1 . . . . .237 C1
Hampden La N17 . . . . .34 A2
Hampden Rd
  Beckenham BR3 . . . . .185 A1
  Harrow HA3 . . . . .24 A1
  Hornsey N8 . . . . .50 C5
  Kingston u T KT1 . . . . . . .198 C6
  Muswell Hill N10 . . . . .31 A3
  Tottenham N17 . . . . .34 A2
  Upper Holloway N19 . . . . . .71 D6
Hampden Sq N14 . . . . .15 B3
Hampden Way N14 . . . . . . .15 B2
Hampshire Cl N18 . . . . .34 B5
Hampshire Ct
  6 Barnes SW13 . . . . . . .133 D3
  Hendon NW4 . . . . .46 D4
Hampshire Ho HA8 . . . . . . .26 B3
  3 Hammersmith W6 . . . .112 B1
  11 Hammersmith W6 . . .112 B2
Hampshire Rd N22 . . . . . . .32 B3
Hampshire Sch The
  SW7 . . . . .114 C4 247 A1
Hampshire St 8 NW5 . . . . .71 D2
Hampson Way
  SW8 . . . . .138 B4 270 C2
HAMPSTEAD 70 A3
Hampstead Cl SE28 . . . . .124 B5
Hampstead Coll of Fine
  Arts & Humanities
  NW3 . . . . .70 C4
HAMPSTEAD GARDEN
  SUBURB 47 D4
Hampstead Garden
  Suburb Inst NW11 . . . . . . .47 D4
Hampstead Gate NW3 . . . .70 A3
Hampstead Gdns NW11 . . .47 D3
Hampstead Gn NW3 . . . . . .70 C3
Hampstead Gr NW3 . . . . . .70 A3
Hampstead Heath* 70 B6
Hampstead Heath Sta
  NW3 . . . . .70 C4
Hampstead High St
  NW3 . . . . .70 B4
Hampstead Hill Gdns
  NW3 . . . . .70 C4
Hampstead Hill Sch
  NW3 . . . . .70 C3
Hampstead Hts N2 . . . . . . .48 A6
Hampstead La N6 . . . . .48 C2
Hampstead Parochial CE
  Prim Sch NW3 . . . . .70 A4
Hampstead Rd
  NW1 . . . . .93 C4 232 A2
Hampstead Sch NW2 . . . . .69 A4
Hampstead Sq 1 NW3 . . . .70 A4
Hampstead Station NW3 . . .70 A4
Hampstead Way NW11 . . . .47 A3
Hampstead West 4
  NW6 . . . . .69 C2
Hampstead Wlk 1 E3 . . . . .97 B6
HAMPTON 173 C1
Hampton Cl
  Borehamwood WD6 . . . . . .11 A6
  Friern Barnet N11 . . . . .31 B5
  Kilburn NW6 . . . . .91 C4
  Wimbledon SW20 . . . . . . .178 C1
Hampton Com Coll
  TW12 . . . . .173 C4
Hampton Court Ave
  KT8 . . . . .196 C3
Hampton Court Cres
  KT8 . . . . .196 B6
Hampton Court Landing
  Stage KT8 . . . . .196 D5

Hampton Court Pal*
  KT8 . . . . .196 D6
Hampton Court Par
  KT8 . . . . .196 C5
Hampton Court Rd KT1,
  KT8 . . . . .197 B6
Hampton Court Sta
  KT8 . . . . .196 C5
Hampton Court Way KT10,
  KT7, KT8 . . . . .196 C3
Hampton Ct
  Hampton KT8 . . . . .196 C6
  1 Islington N1 . . . . .72 D2
  19 Rotherhithe SE16 . . . .118 D5
  Wood Green N22 . . . . .31 C2
Hampton Farm Ind Est
  TW13 . . . . .151 A1
HAMPTON HILL 174 A5
Hampton Hill Bsns Pk
  TW12 . . . . .174 A5
Hampton Hill Jun Sch
  TW12 . . . . .174 A5
Hampton Ho DA7 . . . . . . .147 D3
Hampton Inf Sch
  TW12 . . . . .173 C3
Hampton Jun Sch
  TW12 . . . . .173 C3
Hampton La TW13 . . . . . . .173 A6
Hampton Rd
  Chingford Hatch E4 . . . . . .35 B5
  Forest Gate E7 . . . . .77 C3
  Ilford IG1 . . . . .79 A4
  Leytonstone E11 . . . . .54 B1
  North Cheam KT4 . . . . . . .216 B6
  Teddington TW11,
  TW12 . . . . .174 C5
  Thornton Heath CR0 . . . . .205 A3
  Twickenham TW2 . . . . . . .152 B1
Hampton Rd E TW13 . . . .151 B1
Hampton Rd W TW13 . . . .151 A1
Hampton Rise HA3 . . . . . . .44 A3
Hampton Road Ind Pk
  CR0 . . . . .205 A3
Hampton Sch TW12 . . . . .173 C5
Hampton St
  SE1 . . . . .116 D2 261 D3
Hampton Sta TW12 . . . . . .173 C2
HAMPTON WICK 175 D3
Hampton Wick Inf Sch
  TW11 . . . . .175 D3
Hampton Wick Sta
  KT1 . . . . .175 C2
Ham Ridings TW10 . . . . . .176 B5
Ham Shades Cl 1
  DA15 . . . . .168 A1
Hamson Ct HA2 . . . . .64 B6
Ham St TW10 . . . . .153 C1
Hamstead Gates 11
  NW5 . . . . .71 B2
Ham The TW8 . . . . .131 C5
Ham View CR0 . . . . .207 A3
Ham Yd W1 . . . . .249 C6
Hanameel St E16 . . . . .121 B5
Hana Mews E5 . . . . .74 B4
Hanbury Cl NW4 . . . . .46 C6
Hanbury Ct HA1 . . . . .42 D1
Hanbury Dr
  2 Leyton E11 . . . . .54 D2
  Southgate N21 . . . . .16 B6
Hanbury Ho
  8 Bethnal Green E1 . . . . .96 A2
  South Lambeth SW8 . . . . .270 B5
Hanbury Mews N1 . . . . . . .235 B5
Hanbury Rd
  South Acton W3 . . . . .110 D4
  Tottenham N17 . . . . .34 B1
Hanbury St E1 . . .95 D2 243 D4
Hancocke Ho 4 E1 . . . . . . .53 D6
Hancock Rd Bromley E3 . . .98 A4
  South Norwood SE19 . . . .183 B4
Handa Wlk 3 N1 . . . . .73 A2
Handcroft Rd CR0 . . . . . . .204 D1
Hand Ct WC1 . . . . .240 D3
Handel Cl HA8 . . . . .26 B4
Handel Ho NW2 . . . . .152 B5
Handel Mans
  Barnes SW13 . . . . .134 C5
  Bloomsbury WC1 . . . . . . .240 B6
Handel Par HA8 . . . . .26 C3
Handel Pl NW10 . . . . .67 B2
Handel St WC1 . . .94 A3 240 B6
Handel Way HA8 . . . . .26 C2
Handen Rd SE12 . . . . .164 D6
Handforth Rd
  Brixton SW9 . . . . .138 C5
  6 Ilford IG1 . . . . .78 D5
Handley Gr NW2 . . . . .68 D5
Handley Page Rd SM6 . . .220 B1
Handley Rd E9 . . . . .96 C6
Handowe Cl NW4 . . . . .46 A5
Handside Cl KT4 . . . . .200 D1
Hands Wlk E16 . . . . .99 A1
Handsworth Ave E4 . . . . . .36 B4
Handsworth Prim Sch
  E4 . . . . .36 B4
Handsworth Rd N17 . . . . . .51 B6
Handtrough Way
  IG11 . . . . .100 D5
Hanford Cl SW18 . . . . .157 D3
Hanford Row SW19 . . . . . .178 C4
Hanger Ct W5 . . . . .88 C3
Hanger Gn W5 . . . . .88 C3
Hanger Lane Sta W5 . . . . .88 A4
Hanger La (North Circular
  Rd) W5 . . . . .88 A2
Hanger Vale La W5 . . . . . . .88 B1
Hanger View Way W3 . . . . .88 C2
Hangmans Cnr BR7 . . . . . .188 D2

Hankey Pl SE1 . . .117 B4 252 D1
Hankins La NW7 . . . . .11 C1
Hanley Ct N4 . . . . .50 B1
Hanley Gdns N4 . . . . .50 B1
Hanley Pl BR3 . . . . .185 C3
Hanmer Wlk N7 . . . . .72 B6
Hannah Cl
  Beckenham BR3 . . . . .208 A6
  Wembley NW10 . . . . .67 A4
Hannah Ct
  Palmers Green N13 . . . . . .16 B2
  5 Sutton SM1 . . . . .217 D2
  19 Wimbledon SW19 . . . .178 D3
Hannah Mary Way 17
  SE1 . . . . .118 A2
Hannah Mews SM6 . . . . . .219 C1
Hannay La N8 . . . . .49 D2
Hannay La SW16 . . . . .159 D2
Hannell Rd
  SW6 . . . . .135 A5 264 B4
Hannen Ho SE5 . . . . .139 B2
Hannen Rd SE27 . . . . .160 D1
Hannibal Rd
  Stanwell TW19 . . . . .148 A4
  Stepney E1 . . . . .96 C2
Hannibal Way CR0 . . . . . .220 B2
Hanning Lo TW3 . . . . .130 A1
Hannington Rd SW4 . . . . .137 B2
Hanover Ave
  Feltham TW13 . . . . .150 A2
  Newham E16 . . . . .121 A5
Hanover Circ UB3 . . . . .83 B1
Hanover Ct Cheam SM3 . .217 B4
  Richmond TW9 . . . . .132 C5
Hanover Ct
  Colindale NW9 . . . . .45 C6
  Harrow HA1 . . . . .42 B2
  11 Penge SE19 . . . . .184 A3
  11 Pinner HA5 . . . . .23 B3
  Shepherd's Bush W12 . . . .112 A5
  Stamford Hill N16 . . . . .51 D2
Hanover Dr BR7 . . . . .189 A6
Hanover Gate Mans
  NW1 . . . . .237 B6
Hanover Gdns SE11 . . . . .138 C6
Hanover Ho
  1 New Barnet EN5 . . . . . . .2 A1
  St John's Wood NW8 . . . .230 A3
  Tolworth KT6 . . . . .198 C1
Hanover Lo N21 . . . . .16 D6
Hanover Mans 5
  SW2 . . . . .160 C6
Hanover Mead NW11 . . . . .47 A3
Hanover Pk SE15 . . . . .140 A4
Hanover Pl 16 Bow E3 . . . .97 B4
  St Giles WC2 . . . . .240 B1
Hanover Prim Sch
  N1 . . . . .95 A5 235 A4
Hanover Rd
  Merton SW19 . . . . .180 A3
  South Tottenham N15 . . . . .51 D5
  Willesden NW10 . . . . .90 C6
Hanover Sq W1 . .93 B1 238 D1
Hanover St
  Croydon CR0 . . . . .220 D5
  Marylebone W1 . . .93 B1 238 D1
Hanover Stps W2 . . . . . . .237 B1
Hanover Terr
  Isleworth TW7 . . . . .131 A4
  Lisson Gr NW1 . .92 D4 230 C1
Hanover Terrace Mews
  NW1 . . . . .92 C4 230 B1
Hanover Way DA6 . . . . . . .146 D2
Hanover West Ind Est
  NW10 . . . . .89 B4
Hanover Yd N1 . . . . .235 A4
Hansard Mews W14 . . . . .112 D4
Hansart Way EN2 . . . . .4 C1
Hanscomb Mews
  SW4 . . . . .137 C1
Hans Cres
  SW1 . . . . .114 D3 257 C6
Hanselin Cl HA7 . . . . .24 D5
Hansen Dr N21 . . . . .16 B6
Hanshaw Dr HA8 . . . . .27 B2
Hansler Ct 14 SW19 . . . . .157 A3
Hansler Gr KT8 . . . . .196 B5
Hansler Rd SE22 . . . . .161 D6
Hansol Rd DA6 . . . . .169 A6
Hanson Cl
  Balham SW12 . . . . .159 B4
  Beckenham BR3 . . . . .185 D4
  Mortlake SW14 . . . . .133 A2
  West Drayton UB7 . . . . . . .104 B3
Hanson Ct E17 . . . . .53 D3
Hanson Gdns UB1 . . . . . . .107 A4
Hanson Ho 2 E1 . . . . .118 A6
Hanson St W1 . . .93 C2 239 A4
Hans Pl SW1 . . . .114 D3 257 C6
Hans Rd SW3 . . . .114 D3 257 C6
Hans St SW1 . . . .114 D3 257 D5
Hanway Ho 25 SW9 . . . . .138 C4
Hanway Pl W1 . . . . .239 C2
Hanway Rd W7 . . . . .86 C1
Hanway St W1 . . . . .239 C2
HANWELL 108 D5
Hanwell Sta W7 . . . . .108 C6
HANWORTH 172 D6
Hanworth Rd
  Ashford TW16 . . . . .172 A3
  Feltham TW13 . . . . .150 B3
  Hampton TW12 . . . . .173 C5
  Hounslow TW3, TW4 . . . .129 D1
  Twickenham TW4 . . . . . . .151 B4
Hanworth Terr TW3 . . . . . .129 D1
Hanworth Trad Est
  TW13 . . . . .151 A1

Harben Rd NW6 . . . . .70 A1
Harberson Rd
  Balham SW12 . . . . .159 B3
  West Ham E15 . . . . .98 D6
Harberton Rd N19 . . . . .49 C1
Harbet Rd
  Highams Pk N18 . . . . .35 A4
  Paddington W2 . . .92 B2 236 D3
Harbex Cl DA5 . . . . .169 D4
Harbinger Prim Sch
  E14 . . . . .119 D2
Harbinger Rd E14 . . . . . . .119 D2
Harbin Ho 5 SW2 . . . . . . .160 C3
Harbledown Ho 6 SE1 . . .252 C1
Harbledown Rd SW6 . . . . .265 A2
Harbord Cl SE5 . . . . .139 B3
Harbord Ho 6 SE16 . . . . .118 D2
Harbord St SW6 . . . . .134 D4
Harborne Cl WD19 . . . . . . .22 C5
Harborough Ave
  DA15 . . . . .167 C4
Harborough Rd SW16 . . . .182 B6
Harborough Sch N19 . . . . .71 D6
Harbour Ave
  SW10 . . . . .136 A4 266 B1
Harbour Exchange Sq
  E14 . . . . .119 D4
Harbour Rd SE5 . . . . .139 A2
Harbridge Ave SW15 . . . . .156 A4
Harbury Rd SM5 . . . . .218 C1
Harbut Rd SW11 . . . . .136 B1
Harcombe Rd N16 . . . . . . .73 C5
Harcourt Ave
  Edgware HA8 . . . . .11 A1
  Little Ilford E12 . . . . .78 B3
  Sidcup DA15 . . . . .168 C4
  Wallington SM6 . . . . .219 B4
Harcourt Cl TW7 . . . . .131 A2
Harcourt Field SM6 . . . . . .219 B4
Harcourt Ho
  5 Chingford E4 . . . . .36 B5
  27 Clapham SW8 . . . . . .137 D3
  Marylebone W1 . . . . .238 C2
  4 Willesden NW10 . . . . . .68 C2
Harcourt Lo 2 SM6 . . . . . .219 B4
Harcourt Rd
  Bexley DA6 . . . . .147 A4
  Brockley SE4 . . . . .141 B2
  Bushey WD23 . . . . .8 A6
  Merton SW19 . . . . .179 C3
  Thornton Heath CR7 . . . . .204 C3
  Wallington SM6 . . . . .219 B4
  West Ham E15 . . . . .98 D5
  Wood Green N22 . . . . .31 D2
Harcourt St W1 . .92 C2 237 B3
Harcourt Terr
  SW10 . . . . .113 D1 255 D1
Hardcastle Cl SE25 . . . . . .206 A3
Hardcastle Ho
  3 New Cross Gate
  SE14 . . . . .141 A4
  8 Peckham SE15 . . . . . .140 A4
Hardcourts Cl BR4 . . . . . . .223 D5
Hard Ct IG8 . . . . .37 C4
Hardel Rise SW2 . . . . .160 D3
Hardel Wlk SE24, SW2 . . .160 C4
Harden Ct 1 SE7 . . . . .122 A2
Harden Ho 5 SE5 . . . . . . .139 C3
Harders Rd SE15 . . . . .140 B3
Hardess St SE24 . . . . .139 A2
Hardham Ho 5 SW2 . . . . .160 C4
Hardie Cl NW10 . . . . .67 B3
Harding Cl
  Camberwell SE17 . . . . . . .139 A6
  South Croydon CR0 . . . . . .221 D5
Harding Ct SE25 . . . . .183 D1
Hardinge Cl UB8 . . . . .82 D1
Hardinge Cres SE18 . . . . .123 A3
Hardinge Rd
  Edmonton N18 . . . . .33 C4
  Willesden NW10 . . . . .90 C6
Hardinge St Stepney E1 . . .96 C1
  Woolwich SE18 . . . . .122 D3
Harding Ho
  Barnes SW13 . . . . .134 B6
  Hayes UB3 . . . . .84 B1
  14 Woolwich SE18 . . . . .122 D3
Harding Rd DA7 . . . . .147 B3
Hardings Cl KT2 . . . . .176 B2
Hardings La SE20 . . . . . . .184 D4
Hardington 2 NW1 . . . . . . .71 A1
Hardman Rd
  Greenwich SE7 . . . . .121 D1
  Kingston u T KT2 . . . . . . .176 A1
Hardwick Cl 7 HA7 . . . . . .25 C5
Hardwick Ct 8 E11 . . . . . .55 A3
Hardwicke Ave 5 NW5 . . .129 C4
Hardwicke Ho 14 E3 . . . . .97 D4
Hardwicke Mews WC1 . . . .233 D1
Hardwicke Rd
  Acton W4 . . . . .111 B2
  Bowes Pk N13 . . . . .32 A4
  Richmond TW10 . . . . .175 C6
Hardwick St IG11 . . . . . . .101 A6
Hardwick Gn W13 . . . . .87 B2
Hardwick Ho
  14 London SW8 . . . . .137 D3
  Marylebone NW8 . . . . . . .237 B6
Hardwick St
  EC1 . . . . .94 C4 234 B1
Hardwick's Way SW18 . . .157 C6
Hardwidge St SE1 . . . . . . .253 A2
Hardy Ave
  4 Newham E16 . . . . .121 A5
  Ruislip HA4 . . . . .62 B3
Hardy Cl Barnet EN5 . . . . .13 A6

Hardy Cl *continued*
Pinner HA5 40 D2
Rotherhithe SE16 118 D4
Hardy Cotts 2 SE10 142 B6
Hardy Ct
Greenwich SE3 142 D6
9 Wanstead E11 55 A5
Hardyng Ho 4 E17 53 A5
Hardy Pas N22 32 C1
Hardy Rd
Greenwich SE3 142 D6
Merton SW19 179 D3
Walthamstow E4 35 B4
Hardys Mews KT8 196 C5
Hardy Way EN2 4 C4
Hare and Billet Rd
SE3 142 B3
Harebell Dr E6 100 C2
Harecastle Cl UB4 85 A3
Harecourt Rd N1 73 A2
Hare Ct EC4 241 A1
Haredale Ho 24 SE16 118 A4
Haredale Rd SE24 139 A1
Haredon Cl SE23 162 D4
Harefield KT10 212 C5
Harefield Cl EN2 4 C4
Harefield Ct 4 SW19 179 C3
Harefield Mews SE4 141 B2
Harefield Rd
Brockley SE4 141 B2
Hornsey N8 49 D4
Sidcup DA14 168 D1
South Norwood SW16 182 B3
Uxbridge UB8 60 A3
Hare La KT10 212 C2
Hare Marsh E2 96 A3
Harenc Sch Trust
DA14 190 C5
Hare Pl EC4 241 B1
Hare Row E2 96 B5
Haresfield Rd RM10 81 C2
Hare St SE18 122 C3
Harestone Ct CR2 221 C2
Hare Wlk N1 95 C5
Harewood Ave
Lisson Gr
NW1 92 C3 237 B5
Northolt UB5 63 B1
Harewood Cl UB5 63 B1
Harewood Ct HA3 24 C2
Harewood Pl W1 238 D1
Harewood Rd
Hounslow TW7 130 D4
Mitcham SW19 180 C4
South Croydon CR2 221 C2
Harewood Row NW1 237 B4
Harewood Terr UB2 107 B2
Harfield Gdns 1 SE5 139 C2
Harfield Rd TW16 172 D1
Harfleur Ct SE11 261 C3
Harford Cl E4 19 D4
Harford Ho
Camberwell SE5 139 A6
Notting Hill W11 91 B2
Harford Mews 6 N19 71 D5
Harford Rd E4 19 D4
Harford St E1 97 A3
Harford Wlk N2 48 B5
Hargood Cl HA3 44 A3
Hargood Rd SE3 143 C4
Hargrave Mans 3 N19 71 D6
Hargrave Park Prim Sch
N19 71 C6
Hargrave Pk N19 71 C6
Hargrave Pl N7 71 D3
Hargrave Rd N19 71 C6
Hargraves Ho 14 W12 112 B6
Hargwyne St SW9 138 B2
Haringey Pk N8 50 A3
Haringey Rd N8 50 A5
Harington Terr N18 17 B1
Harkett Cl HA3 24 D1
Harkett Ct HA3 24 D1
Harkness Ct SM1 201 D1
Harkness Ho 30 E1 96 A1
Harland Ave
Sidcup DA15 167 C2
South Croydon CR0 222 A5
Harland Cl SW19 201 D6
Harland Rd SE12 165 A3
Harlands Gr BR6 226 D4
Harlech Ct 1 SE23 162 C3
Harlech Gdns TW5 128 C5
Harlech Rd N14 16 A1
Harlech Twr 5 W3 111 A4
Harlequin Ave TW8 131 A6
Harlequin Cl Hayes UB4 84 D2
Isleworth TW7 152 C6
Harlequin Ct
Croydon CR2 221 A1
Ealing W5 109 C6
Willesden NW10 67 B2
Harlequin Ho 1 DA18 125 A3
Harlequin Rd TW11 175 B3
Harlescott Rd SE15 140 D1
HARLESDEN 89 D6
Harlesden Gdns NW10 89 D6
Harlesden Plaza 2
NW10 89 D5
Harlesden Prim Sch
NW10 89 C5
Harlesden Rd NW10 90 A6
Harlesden Sta NW10 89 B5
Harleston Cl 4 E5 74 C6
Harley BR7 189 B2
Harley Cl HA0 65 D2
Harley Cres HA1 42 B5
Harley Ct Harrow HA1 42 B5
Wanstead E11 55 A2
Whetstone N20 14 A1
Harleyford BR1 187 C2
Harleyford Ct
Kennington SW8 270 C6
Wembley HA0 65 A4
Harleyford Manor 8
W3 111 A5
Harleyford Rd
SE11 138 B6 270 C6
Harleyford St SE11 138 C6
Harley Gdns
Orpington BR6 227 C4
South Kensington
SW10 114 A1 256 B1
Harley Gr E3 97 B4
Harley Ho
Leytonstone E11 54 B2
Marylebone NW1 238 B5
Harley Pl W1 93 B2 238 C3
Harley Rd
Hampstead NW3 70 B1
Harlesden NW10 89 C5
Harrow HA1 42 B5
Harley St W1 93 B2 238 C3
Harley Villas NW10 89 C5
Harling Ct 3 SW11 136 D3
Harlinger St SE18 122 A3
HARLINGTON 127 A6
Harlington Cl UB7 127 A5
Harlington Cnr UB3 127 B4
Harlington Com Sch
UB3 105 B2
Harlington Rd
Bexley DA7 147 A2
Hillingdon UB8 82 C3
Harlington Rd E TW13,
TW14 150 C3
Harlington Rd W
TW14 150 B5
Harlowe Ho 13 E8 95 D6
Harlow Mans 2 IG11 78 D1
Harlow Rd N13 17 B1
Harlyn Dr HA5 40 B6
Harlyn Prim Sch HA5 40 B6
Harlynwood 19 SE5 139 A5
Harman Ave IG8 36 D4
Harman Cl
10 Bermondsey SE1 118 A1
Chingford E4 36 B6
Cricklewood NW2 69 A5
Harman Dr
Blackfen DA15 167 D5
Cricklewood NW2 69 A4
Harman Rd EN1 17 D6
HARMONDSWORTH 126 A6
Harmondsworth La
UB7 126 B6
Harmondsworth Rd
UB7 104 A2
Harmon Ho 7 SE8 119 B2
Harmony Cl NW11 47 A4
Harmony Way
Bromley BR1 187 A1
Hendon NW4 46 C5
Harmood Gr NW1 71 B1
Harmood Ho 2 NW1 71 B1
Harmood St NW1 71 B1
Harmsworth St
SE17 116 D1 261 C1
Harmsworth Way N20 13 C3
Harnage Ho TW8 110 A1
Harness Rd SE28 124 A4
Harney Ct SE14 141 A4
Harold Ave Erith DA17 125 B1
Hayes UB3 105 D3
Harold Ct
14 Rotherhithe SE16 118 D4
6 Teddington TW11 174 C5
Harold Est SE1 263 B5
Harold Gibbons Ct 12
SE7 143 C6
Harold Ho 16 E2 96 D5
Harold Laski Ho EC1 234 D1
Harold Maddison Ho
SE17 261 D2
Harold Rd Chingford E4 20 A1
Hornsey N8 50 B5
Leytonstone E11 54 C1
Newham E13 99 B6
North Acton NW10 89 B4
South Norwood SE19 183 B3
South Tottenham N15 51 D4
Sutton SM1 218 B4
Woodford IG8 37 A2
Haroldstone Rd E17 53 A4
Harold Wilson Ho
SW6 264 D5
Haronton Ct E10 76 A6
Harp Alley EC4 241 C2
Harp Bsns Ctr The
NW2 68 A6
Harpenden Rd
Wanstead E12 77 C6
West Norwood SE27,
SW16 160 D2
Harpenmead Point
NW2 69 B6
Harper Cl N14 15 C6
Harper Ho 3 SW9 138 D2
Harper Mews SW17 158 A1
Harper Rd
Bermondsey
SE1 117 A3 262 B6
Newham E6 100 B1
Harper's Yd N17 33 D2
Harp Island Cl NW10 67 B6
Harp La EC3 253 A5
Harpley Sq E1 96 D3
Harpour Rd IG11 79 A2
Harp Rd W7 86 D3
Harpsden St SW11 268 A1
Harpur Mews WC1 240 C4
Harpur St WC1 94 B2 240 C4
Harraden Rd SE3 143 C4
Harrier Ave E11 55 B3
Harrier Ct TW4 129 A3
Harrier Ho 9 SW11 136 C2
Harrier Mews SE28 123 B4
Harrier Rd NW9 27 C1
Harriers Cl W5 110 A6
Harrier Way E6 100 B2
Harries Rd UB4 84 C3
Harriet Cl E8 96 A6
Harriet Gdns CR0 222 A6
Harriet Ho
Walham Green SW6 265 D3
Walthamstow E17 53 D4
Harriet St
SW1 114 D4 247 D1
Harriet Tubman Cl 21
SW2 160 C4
Harriet Way WD23 8 B4
Harriet Wlk
SW1 114 D4 247 D1
HARRINGAY 50 D4
Harringay Gdns N8 50 D5
Harringay Green Lanes Sta
N4 50 D3
Harringay Rd N15 50 D5
Harringay Sta N4 50 C3
Harrington Cl
Wallington CR0 220 A6
Willesden NW10 67 B5
Harrington Ct
6 South Croydon
CR0 221 B6
South Kensington SW7 256 D4
9 West Kilburn W9 91 B4
Harrington Gdns
SW7 114 A2 256 A3
Harrington Hill E5 52 B1
Harrington Hill Prim Sch
E5 52 B1
Harrington Ho
2 Bromley BR1 187 A2
Regent's Pk NW1 232 A2
Upper Clapton E5 52 C1
Westminster SW1 259 D2
Harrington Rd
Croydon SE25 206 B5
Leytonstone E11 54 C1
South Kensington
SW7 114 B2 256 C4
Harrington Road Sta
SE25 206 C6
Harrington Sq
NW1 93 C5 232 A3
Harrington St
NW1 93 C4 232 A2
Harrington Way SE18 121 D3
Harriott Cl SE10 120 D2
Harriott Ho 11 E1 96 C1
Harris Acad CR4 203 D6
Harris City Tech Coll
SE19 183 D2
Harris Cl Enfield EN2 4 D4
Heston TW5 129 C4
Harris Cotts 1 E15 98 D6
Harris Ct HA9 66 B5
Harris Girl's Acad
SE15 162 C6
Harris Ho 11 Bow E3 97 C4
7 Brixton SW9 138 C2
Harris Lo SE6 164 A3
Harrison Cl N20 14 C3
Harrison Ho SE17 262 C2
Harrison Rd
Dagenham RM10 81 D2
Stonebridge NW10 89 B6
Harrisons Ct 1 SE14 140 D6
Harrison's Rise CR0 220 D5
Harrison St
WC1 94 A4 233 B1
Harrison Way TW17 192 D4
Harris Rd
Dagenham RM9 81 B3
Erith DA7 147 B4
Harris St
Camberwell SE5 139 B5
Walthamstow E17 53 B2
Harris Way TW16 171 C2
Harrodian Sch The
SW13 133 D5
Harrogate Ct
2 Forest Hill SE26 162 A1
9 New Southgate N11 31 A4
Harrold Ho 1 NW3 70 A1
Harrold Rd RM8 80 B3
HARROW 42 B3
Harrow Ave EN1 17 D5
Harroway Rd SW11 136 B3
Harrowby St
W1 92 C1 237 B2
Harrow Cl KT9 213 D1
Harrow Coll HA1 42 C2
Harrow Coll (Harrow
Weald Campus) HA3 24 C4
Harrowdene Cl HA0 65 D4
Harrowdene Ct SW19 179 A5
Harrowdene Gdns
TW11 175 A3
Harrowdene Rd HA0 65 D4
Harrow Dr N9 17 D3
Harrowes Meade HA8 10 C1
Harrow Fields Gdns
HA1 64 C5
Harrowgate Ho 22 E9 74 D2
Harrowgate Rd E9 75 A1
Harrow Gn E11 76 C5
Harrow High Sch & Sports
Coll HA1 43 A3
Harrow La E14 120 A6
Harrow Lo SM2 218 B2
Harrow Manor Way
SE2 124 C3
Harrow Mus & Her Ctr*
HA2 42 A6
HARROW ON THE HILL
42 C1
Harrow-on-the-Hill Sta
HA1 42 C3
Harrow Pk HA1 64 C6
Harrow Pl E1 95 C1 243 B2
Harrow Rd
Ashford TW15 148 C2
Barking IG11 101 C6
Carshalton SM5 218 C2
Ilford IG1 79 A4
Leyton E11 76 D5
Little Venice W2 92 A2 236 B3
2 Newham E6 100 A6
Sudbury HA0 65 A4
Tokyngton HA9 66 C2
Wembley HA0 65 D3
Westbourne Green W2,
W9 91 C3
Harrow Sch HA1 42 C1
Harrow St NW1 237 A4
Harrow View
Harrow HA1, HA2 42 B5
Hayes UB3 84 A1
Hillingdon UB10 83 A4
Harrow View Rd W5 87 B3
Harrow Way
Charlton TW17 171 A1
South Oxhey WD19 23 A6
HARROW WEALD 24 B2
Harrow Weald Pk HA3 24 B4
Harrow & Wealdstone Sta
HA1 42 C5
Harry Ct 15 NW9 46 A5
Harry Gosling Prim Sch
E1 96 A1
Harry Hinkins Ho SE17 262 B1
Harry Lambourn Ho 10
SE15 140 B5
Harston 13 KT1 176 C1
Harston Dr EN3 7 C5
Hart Ct E12 78 C1
Harte Rd TW3 129 B3
Hartfield Ave
Borehamwood WD6 10 C6
Northolt UB5 84 B5
Hartfield Cl WD6 10 C6
Hartfield Cres
Coney Hall BR4 225 A5
Merton SW19 179 B3
Hartfield Ct CR2 220 D1
Hartfield Gr SE20 184 C2
Hartfield Ho UB5 84 B5
Hartfield Rd
Chessington KT9 213 D3
Hayes BR4 225 A4
Merton SW19 179 C3
Hartfield Terr E3 97 C5
Hartford Ave HA3 43 B6
Hartford Rd
Old Bexley DA5 169 C5
West Ewell KT19 214 D2
Hart Gr Ealing W5 110 C5
Southall UB1 85 C2
Hartgrove Ct NW9 45 A5
Hart Grove Ct 3 W5 110 C5
Hartham Cl
Isleworth TW7 131 A4
Lower Holloway N7 72 A3
Hartham Rd
Isleworth TW7 131 A4
Lower Holloway N7 72 A3
Tottenham N17 33 D1
Hart Ho Hayes UB4 83 B2
Streatham SW2 160 C3
Harting Rd SE9 166 A1
Hartington Cl
Farnborough BR6 227 A3
Harrow HA1 64 C4
Hartington Ct
Chiswick W4 132 D5
South Lambeth SW8 270 A2
Hartington Rd
Chiswick W4 133 A4
Ealing W13 109 B6
Newham E16 99 B1
Southall UB2 107 A3
South Lambeth
SW8 138 A5 270 A3
Twickenham TW1 153 B5
Walthamstow E17 53 A3
Hartismere Rd
SW6 135 B5 264 D4
Hartlake Rd E9 75 A2
Hartland NW1 232 B5
Hartland Cl
Edgware HA8 10 C2
Enfield N21 17 A5
Hartland Ct 5 N11 30 D5
Hartland Dr
Edgware HA8 10 C2
Ruislip HA4 62 B4
Hartland Rd
Camden Town NW1 71 B1
Cheam SM4 201 D2
Friern Barnet N11 30 D5
Hampton TW12 173 D6
Isleworth TW7 131 A2
Kilburn NW6 91 B6
Stratford E15 76 D1
Hartlands Cl DA5 169 B5
Hartlands The TW5 128 B6
Hartland Way
Croydon CR0 223 A6
Morden SM4 201 B2
Hartlepool Ct E16 122 D5
Hartley Ave
Edgware NW7 27 D5
Newham E6 100 A6
Hartley Cl Bickley BR1 188 B1
Edgware NW7 27 D5
Hartley Ct Ealing W5 110 C5
5 Mitcham CR4 180 C2
Hartley Ho
Bermondsey SE1 263 D4
Finchley N3 29 D4
Putney SW15 156 A6
Hartley Prim Sch E6 100 A6
Hartley Rd
Bexley DA16 146 C5
Leytonstone E11 54 D1
Thornton Heath CR0 205 A2
Hartley St E2 96 C4
Hart Lo EN5 1 A2
Hartmann Rd E16 122 A5
Hartmoor Mews EN3 6 D6
Hartnoll Ho 4 N7 72 C3
Hartnoll St N7 72 B3
Harton Cl BR1 187 D2
Harton Lodge 2 SE8 141 C4
Harton Rd N9 18 B2
Harton St SE8 141 C4
Hartopp Ct 20 N16 73 C5
Hartopp Point SW6 264 B4
Hartsbourne Ave WD23 8 B2
Hartsbourne Cl WD23 8 B2
Hartsbourne Ct 5 UB1 86 A1
Hartsbourne Pk WD23 8 C2
Hartsbourne Prim Sch
WD23 8 B2
Hartsbourne Rd WD23 8 B2
Harts Gr IG8 37 A5
Hartshill Cl UB10 60 D2
Hartshorn Alley EC3 243 B1
Hartshorn Gdns E6 100 C3
Harts La IG11 78 D2
Hart's La SE14 141 A4
Hartslock Dr SE2 124 D4
Hartsmead Rd SE9 166 B2
Hart Sq SM4 201 C3
Hart St EC3 253 B6
Hartsway EN3 6 C1
Hartswood Gn WD23 8 B2
Hartswood Ho 10
SW2 160 A3
Hartswood Rd W12 111 D3
Hartsworth Cl E13 98 D5
Hartville Rd SE18 123 C2
Hartwell Ct SE22 140 A1
Hartwell Dr E4 36 A4
Hartwell Ho 2 SE7 121 B1
Hartwell St E8 73 D2
Harvard Ct
9 Eltham SE9 166 C5
West Hampstead NW6 69 D3
Harvard Hill W4 132 D6
Harvard Ho
3 Camberwell SE17 138 D6
Putney SW15 156 D5
Harvard Mans 18
SW11 136 B1
Harvard Rd
11 Acton Green W4 111 A1
Gunnersbury W4 110 D1
Hounslow TW7 130 C4
Lewisham SE13 164 A6
Harvel Cres SE2 124 D1
Harvel Ct SE2 125 A1
Harvest Bank Rd BR4 225 A5
Harvest Ct
Beckenham BR3 185 C3
Littleton TW17 192 C5
Harvesters Cl TW7 152 B6
Harvest La
Loughton IG10 21 D4
Thames Ditton KT7 197 A3
Harvest Rd TW13 150 A1
Harvey Ct
Battersea SW11 267 B2
Walthamstow E17 53 C4
Harvey Dr TW12 173 C2
Harvey Gdns
Greenwich SE7 121 C1
Leytonstone E11 54 D1
Harvey Ho Barking IG11 79 A1
10 Bethnal Green E1 96 B3
Brentford TW8 110 A1
Dagenham RM6 58 D5
Hornsey N8 50 A6
Pimlico SW1 259 D1
Shoreditch N1 235 D5
Wembley Pk HA9 66 D6
Harvey Lo 8 W9 91 C2
Harvey Mews N8 50 B4
Harvey Point 7 E16 99 A2
Harvey Rd
15 Camberwell SE5 139 B4
Hillingdon UB10 82 C5
Hornsey Vale N8 50 B4
Ilford IG1 78 D3
Leytonstone E11 54 D1
Ruislip UB5 62 C1
Twickenham TW4 151 B4
Walton-on-T KT12 194 A2
Harvey St N1 235 D5
Harvill Rd
Newyears Green UB9 38 A2
Sidcup DA14 191 A5
Harvil Rd UB9, UB10 38 A2
Harvington Sch W5 87 D1
Harvington Wlk E8 74 A1
Harvist Rd NW6 91 A5
Harwell Cl HA4 39 B1
Harwood Ave
Bromley BR1 187 B1
Mitcham CR4 202 C6
Harwood Cl London N12 30 C4
Wembley HA0 65 D4
Harwood Ct
Putney SW15 134 C1
Shoreditch N1 235 D5
Harwood Dr UB10 82 B6
Harwood Point SE16 119 B4
Harwood Rd
SW6 135 D5 265 C3
Harwoods Yd N21 16 C4
Harwood Terr
SW6 135 D4 265 C2
Hascombe Ho 11
SW15 156 B3
Hascombe Terr 2
SE5 139 B3
Haselbury Rd N9 17 C1
Haseley End SE23 162 C4
Haselrigge Rd SW4 137 D1
Haseltine Prim Sch
SE26 185 B6
Haseltine Rd SE26 185 B6
Haselwood Dr EN2 4 D1
Haskard Rd RM9 80 D4
Hasker St SW3 114 C2 257 B4
Haslam Ave SM3 201 A1
Haslam Cl Islington N1 72 C1
Uxbridge UB10 61 A6
Haslam Ct N11 31 B6
Haslam Ho 12 N1 73 A1
Haslam St SE15 139 D4
Haslemere Ave
Barnet EN4 14 D3
Cranford TW5 128 C3
Ealing W13 109 A3
Hendon NW4 46 D3
Mitcham CR4, SW19 180 B1
Wandsworth SW18 157 D2
Haslemere Bsns Ctr
EN1 18 B6
Haslemere Cl
Hampton TW12 173 B5
Wallington SM6 220 A3
Haslemere Ct 5 N16 51 C1
Haslemere Gdns N3 47 B5
Haslemere & Heathrow
Est The TW4 128 B3
Haslemere Ind Est
Feltham TW14 150 A6
Wandsworth SW18 157 D2
Haslemere Prim Sch
CR4 180 B1
Haslemere Rd
Bexleyheath DA7 147 C3
Hornsey N8 50 A2
Ilford IG3 79 D6
Southgate N21 16 D3
Thornton Heath CR7 204 D4
Hasler Cl SE28 124 C6
Hasler Ct E12 78 A4
Haslett Rd TW17 171 C1
Hasluck Gdns EN5 14 A5
Hasmonean High Sch
(Boys) NW4 28 D1
Hasmonean High Sch
(Girls) NW7 28 A2
Hasmonean Prim Sch
NW4 46 D4
Hassard St E2 95 D5
Hassendean Rd SE3 143 B5
Hassett Rd E9 75 A2
Hassocks Cl SE23,
SE26 162 B1
Hassocks Rd SW16 181 D2
Hassock Wood BR2 225 D4
Hassop Rd NW2 68 D4
Hassop Wlk SE9 188 A6
Hasted Rd SE7 121 D1
Hasting Ct TW11 174 B5
Hastings Ave IG6 57 A5
Hastings Cl
New Barnet EN5 2 A1
17 Peckham SE15 140 A5
Wembley HA0 65 C4
Hastings Dr KT6 197 C3
Hastings Ho
Ealing W13 109 B6
Enfield EN3 6 C3
18 Shepherd's Bush
W12 112 B6
Tottenham N17 34 A2
6 Woolwich SE18 122 B2
Hastings Hos WC1 233 A1
Hastings Pl 1 CR0 205 D1
Hastings Rd
Croydon CR0 205 D1
Ealing W13 109 B6
Keston Mark BR2 226 A6
Tottenham N17 51 B6
Wood Green N11 31 D5
Hastings St
St Pancras
WC1 94 A4 233 A1
Woolwich SE18 123 A3
Hastingwood Ct
Newham E6 100 B5
Walthamstow E17 53 D4
Hastingwood Trad Est
N18 35 A4
Hastoe Cl UB4 85 A3
Hasty Cl CR4 181 A2
Hatcham Mews Bsns Ctr
SE14 140 D4
Hatcham Park Mews
SE14 140 D4

Hatcham Park Rd
SE14 140 D4
Hatcham Rd SE15 140 C6
Hatchard Rd N19 72 A6
Hatchcroft NW4 46 B6
HATCH END 23 A3
Hatch End High Sch
HA3 23 D2
Hatch End Sta HA5 23 C3
Hatchers Mews SE1 253 B1
Hatchett Rd TW14 149 A3
Hatchfield Ho 8 N15 51 C3
Hatch Gr RM6 59 A5
Hatch Ho
9 Muswell Hill N10 31 A3
14 Richmond TW10 153 C1
Hatch La E4 20 C1
Hatch Pl KT2 176 B5
Hatch Rd SW16 182 A1
Hatch The EN3 6 D4
Hatchwoods IG8 36 D6
Hatcliffe Almshouses 8
SE10 120 C1
Hatcliffe Cl SE3 142 D2
Hatcliffe St SE10 120 D1
Hatfield Cl
Deptford SE14 140 D5
Ilford IG6 56 D6
Mitcham CR4 202 B5
Hatfield Ct
Greenwich SE3 143 A5
8 Northolt UB5 84 C4
Hatfield Ho
16 Kingston u T KT6 198 A4
Leytonstone E11 54 D2
St Luke's EC1 242 A5
Hatfield Mead SM4 201 C4
Hatfield Mews RM9 81 A1
Hatfield Prim Sch
SM4 201 A3
Hatfield Rd Acton W4 111 B4
Dagenham RM9 81 A1
10 Ealing W13, W7 109 A5
Stratford E15 76 C3
Hatfields SE1 116 C5 251 B4
Hathaway Cl
Bromley BR2 210 B1
Ruislip HA4 61 D4
Stanmore HA7 25 A5
Hathaway Cres E12 78 C2
Hathaway Gdns
Ealing W13 87 A2
Ilford RM6 58 D4
Hathaway Ho 3 N1 95 C4
Hathaway Prim Sch
W13 86 D2
Hathaway Rd CR0 204 D2
Hatherleigh Cl
Barnet EN4 1 D4
Chessington KT9 213 D3
Edgware NW7 28 D3
Morden SM4 201 C5
Hatherleigh Ho SM4 201 C5
Hatherleigh Rd HA4 62 A6
Hatherley Cres DA14 168 A2
Hatherley Ct 6 W2 91 D1
Hatherley Gdns
London N8 50 A3
Newham E6 99 D4
Hatherley Gr W2 91 D1
Hatherley Ho 2 E17 53 C5
Hatherley Mews E17 53 C5
Hatherley Rd
Richmond TW9 132 B4
Sidcup DA14 168 A1
Walthamstow E17 53 C5
Hatherley St SW1 259 B3
Hathern Gdns SE9 188 C6
Hatherop Rd TW12 173 B3
Hathersage Ct N1 73 B3
Hathersley Ho 3
SW2 160 C4
Hathorne Cl 3 SE15 140 B3
Hathway Ho 3 SE15 140 C3
Hathway St 4 SE15 140 C3
Hatley Ave IG6 57 A5
Hatley Cl N11 30 D5
Hatley Rd N4, N7 72 B6
Hat & Mitre Ct EC1 241 D5
Hatstone Ct NW3 70 A3
Hatteraick St 6 SE16 118 C4
Hattersfield Cl DA17 125 B2
HATTON 127 D1
Hatton Cl SE18 145 B5
Hatton Cross Rdbt
TW6 127 D2
Hatton Cross Sta TW6 127 D1
Hatton Ct BR7 188 B3
Hatton Gdn EC1 94 C2 241 B4
Hatton Gdns CR4 202 D4
Hatton Gn TW14 128 A1
Hatton Ho 17 E1 118 A6
Hatton Pl EC1 241 B4
Hatton Rd
Hatton TW14, TW6 149 C6
Thornton Heath CR0 204 C1
Hatton Rd N TW6 127 B4
Hatton Row NW8 236 D5
Hatton Sch IG8 55 D6
Hatton St NW8 236 D5
Hatton Wall EC1 94 C2 241 B4
Haughmond 4 N12 29 D6
Haunch of Venison Yd
W1 238 C1
Hauteville Court Gdns 2
W6 111 D3
Havana Rd SW18,
SW19 157 C2
Havannah St E14 119 C4
Havant Rd E17 54 A6
Havelock Cl 13 W12 112 B6
Havelock Ct
8 Peckham SE15 140 B5
Southall UB2 107 B3
Havelock Hall 8 CR0 205 D1
Havelock Ho
4 Croydon CR0 205 D1
Forest Hill SE23 162 C3
Havelock Pl HA1 42 C3
Havelock Prim Sch
UB2 107 B3
Havelock Rd
Belvedere DA17 125 B2
Bromley BR2 209 C5
Croydon CR0 221 D6
Harrow HA3 42 C6
Southall UB2 107 C3
Tottenham N17 34 A1
Wimbledon SW19 180 A5
Havelock St Ilford IG1 78 D6
Islington N1 94 A6 233 B6
Havelock Terr
SW8 137 B5 268 D3
Havelock Wlk SE23 162 C2
Haven Cl
Chislehurst SE9 166 B1
Hayes UB4 83 C3
Hinchley Wood KT10 212 C6
Sidcup DA14 190 C4
Wimbledon SW19 156 D1
Haven Ct
Beckenham BR3 186 A1
Hinchley Wood KT10 212 C6
Thornton Heath CR7 204 C6
Haven Gn W5 87 D1
Haven Green Ct W5 87 D1
Havenhurst Rise EN2 4 C3
Haven La W5 88 A1
Haven Lo 16 Enfield EN1 17 C6
Temple Fortune NW11 47 B4
7 Woolwich SE18 122 D2
Haven Pl Ealing W5 109 D6
Hinchley Wood KT10 212 C6
Havenpool NW8 91 D6
Haven Rd TW15 148 D1
Haven St 18 NW1 71 B1
Haven The
Ashford TW16 172 A3
East Barnet N14 15 B5
Richmond TW9 132 C2
Havenwood HA9 66 D5
Havercourt 3 NW3 70 C2
Haverfield Gdns TW9 132 C5
Haverfield Rd E3 97 A4
Haverford Way HA8 26 B2
Havergal Villas N15 50 D6
Haverhill Rd
Chingford E4 20 A3
Streatham SW12 159 C3
Havering 8 NW1 71 B1
Havering Gdns RM6 58 D4
Havering Ho N4 51 A2
Havering St E1 96 D1
Havering Way IG11 102 B4
Haverley 15 SW20 178 D3
Haversham Cl TW1 153 D5
Haversham Ct UB6 64 D2
Haversham Lo NW2 68 D3
Haversham Pl N6 70 D6
Haverstock Ct 2 BR5 190 B1
Haverstock Hill NW3 70 D2
Haverstock Rd NW5 71 A3
Haverstock Sch NW1 71 A2
Haverstock St
N1 94 D5 234 D3
Haverthwaite Rd BR6 227 B5
Havilland Ct HA8 26 B6
Havil St SE5 139 C4
Havisham Ho 25 SE16 118 A4
Havisham Pl SW16 182 D3
Hawarden Gr SE24 161 A4
Hawarden Hill NW2 68 A5
Hawarden Rd E17 52 D5
Hawberry Lo N7 72 A2
Hawbridge Rd E11 54 B1
Hawes Down Inf Sch
BR4 208 B1
Hawes Down Jun Sch
BR4 208 B1
Hawes La BR4 224 C6
Hawes Rd Bromley BR1 187 B2
Edmonton N18 34 B4
Hawes St N1 72 D1
Haweswater Ho TW1 152 D6
Hawfinch 29 NW9 27 D2
Hawgood St E3 97 C2
Hawkdene E4 20 A5
Hawke Ct UB4 84 C3
Hawkedale Inf Sch
TW16 193 D6
Hawke Ho 20 E1 96 D3
Hawke Park Rd N22 50 D6
Hawke Pl 29 SE16 118 D4
Hawker 28 NW9 27 D2
Hawker Ct 14 KT2 176 C3
Hawke Rd SE19 183 C4
Hawkesbury Rd SW15 156 B6
Hawkesfield Rd SE23 163 B2
Hawkesley Cl TW1 175 A6
Hawkes Rd
Feltham TW14 150 A4
Mitcham CR4 180 D2
Hawkesworth Ho 5
SW4 159 C5
Hawke Twr 4 SE14 141 A6
Hawkewood Rd TW16 194 A6
Hawkfield Ct TW7 130 C3
Hawk Ho 7 SW11 136 C2
Hawkhurst Gdns KT9 214 A4
Hawkhurst Rd SW16 181 D2
Hawkhurst Way
New Malden KT3 199 B4
West Wickham BR4 223 D6
Hawkinge N17 33 B1
Hawkins Cl
Burnt Oak NW7 27 B5
Harrow HA1 42 B2
Hawkins Ho
3 Deptford SE8 141 C6
10 Richmond TW10 153 C1
Hawkins Rd
Teddington TW11 175 B4
Willesden NW10 67 C1
Hawkins Way SE6 185 C5
Hawkley Gdns SE27 160 D2
Hawkridge 19 NW5 71 A2
Hawkridge Cl RM6 58 C3
Hawksbrook La BR3 208 A3
Hawkshaw Cl 28 SW2 160 A4
Hawkshead NW1 232 A2
Hawkshead Cl BR1 186 C3
Hawkshead Rd
Acton W4 111 C4
Willesden NW10 67 D1
Hawkslade Rd SE15 162 D6
Hawksley Rd N16 73 C5
Hawks Mews 10 SE10 142 A5
Hawksmoor Cl
2 Newham E6 100 A1
Plumstead Comm SE18 123 C1
Hawksmoor Mews E1 118 B6
Hawksmoor Pl 2 E2 96 A3
Hawksmoor Sch SE28 124 B6
Hawksmoor St 5 W6 134 D6
Hawksmouth E4 20 A4
Hawks Rd KT1 176 B1
Hawkstone Rd SE16 118 C2
Hawkwell Ct E4 20 A1
Hawkwell Ho RM8 81 C6
Hawkwell Wlk N1 235 B6
Hawkwood Cres E4 19 D5
Hawkwood La BR7 189 A2
Hawkwood Mount 1
E5 52 B1
Hawlands Dr HA5 41 A2
Hawley Cl TW12 173 B4
Hawley Cres NW1 71 B1
Hawley Inf Sch NW1 71 B1
Hawley Mews 4 NW1 71 B1
Hawley Rd
3 Camden Town NW1 71 B1
London N18 34 D5
Hawley St NW1 71 B1
Hawley Way TW15 170 D5
Haworth Ho 7 SW2 160 C5
Hawstead Rd SE6 163 D5
Hawsted IG9 21 B4
Hawthorn Ave
Bowes Pk N13 32 A5
Old Ford E3 97 B6
South Norwood CR7 182 D2
Hawthorn Cl
Cranford TW5 128 B5
Hampton TW12 173 C5
Petts Wood BR5 211 B3
Hawthorn Cres SW17 181 A5
Hawthorn Ct
Littleton TW15 171 A3
2 Pinner HA5 22 C1
Putney SW15 134 B2
Redbridge IG5 56 B6
Richmond TW9 132 D4
Sutton SM1 217 C4
8 West Norwood
SW16 182 C5
Hawthorn Ctr HA1 43 A4
Hawthornden Cl N12 30 C4
Hawthorndene Cl BR2 225 A6
Hawthorndene Rd
BR2 225 A6
Hawthorn Dr
Coney Hall BR4 224 C4
Harrow HA2 41 C3
Hawthorne Ave
Harrow HA3 43 A3
Mitcham CR4 180 B1
Ruislip HA4 40 B2
Wallington SM5 219 A1
Hawthorne Cl
Bickley BR1 210 B6
Kingsland N1 73 C2
Sutton SM1 218 A6
Hawthorne Cres UB7 104 B4
Hawthorne Ct
Chingford E4 35 D4
Ealing W5 110 A5
Pinner HA6 22 A1
Hawthorne Gr NW9 45 A2
Hawthorne Ho SW1 259 B1
Hawthorne Mews UB6 86 A1
Hawthorne Rd
Bickley BR1 210 B6
Edmonton N18 33 D5
Walthamstow E17 53 C6
Hawthorne Way N9 17 D2
Hawthorn Farm Ave
UB5 85 A6
Hawthorn Gdns W5 109 D3
Hawthorn Gr
Edgware EN5 11 D5
Enfield EN2 5 B5
Penge SE20 184 B2
Hawthorn Hatch TW8 131 B5
Hawthorn Ho SE14 141 B4
Hawthorn Mews NW7 29 A2
Hawthorn Pl UB3 105 D6
Hawthorn Rd
Bexleyheath DA6 147 B1
Brentford TW8 131 B5
Carshalton SM1 218 C2
Hawthorn Rd continued
Feltham TW14 150 A3
Hornsey N8 50 A6
Wallington SM5, SM6 219 B1
Willesden NW10 68 A1
Woodford IG9 37 D6
Hawthorns IG8 21 A1
Hawthorns The
2 Cheam SM2 217 C2
Edgware NW7 27 B4
Stoneleigh KT17 216 A1
Hawthorn Terr DA15 167 D6
Hawthorn Way TW17 193 B5
Hawthorn Wlk W10 91 A3
Hawtrey Ave UB5 84 D5
Hawtrey Dr HA4 40 A2
Hawtrey Rd NW3 70 C1
Haxted Rd BR1 187 B2
Haybridge Ho 1 E5 74 C6
Hay Cl E15 76 D1
Haycroft Gdns NW10 90 B6
Haycroft Mans NW10 90 A6
Haycroft Rd
London SW2 160 A6
Surbiton KT6 214 A6
Hay Currie St E14 97 D1
Hayday Rd E16 99 A2
Hayden Piper Ho SW3 267 C6
Hayden's Pl W11 91 B1
Haydock Ave UB5 63 C2
Haydock Gn UB5 63 C2
Haydock Green Flats 2
UB5 63 C2
Haydock Lo 2 SM6 219 D5
Haydon Cl Enfield EN1 17 C6
Kingsbury NW9 45 A5
Haydon Ct NW9 45 A5
Haydon Dr HA5 40 A5
Haydon Ho W7 108 D5
Haydon Park Rd
SW19 179 D5
Haydon Rd RM8 80 C6
Haydon Sch HA5 39 D6
Haydon's Rd SW19 180 A4
Haydons Road Sta
SW19 180 A5
Haydon St E1,
EC3 117 D6 253 C6
Haydon Way SW11 136 B1
Haydon Wlk E1 243 D1
HAYES BR2 209 A2
UB3 83 C1
Hayes Bridge Ret Pk
UB4 106 D6
Hayes Chase BR4 208 C3
Hayes Cl BR2 225 A6
Hayes Cres
Cheam SM3 216 D4
Temple Fortune NW11 47 B4
Hayes Ct
23 Camberwell SE5 139 A5
Streatham SW12 160 A3
Wimbledon SW19 179 A4
HAYES END 83 B3
Hayes End Cl UB4 83 B2
Hayes End Dr UB4 83 B3
Hayesend Ho SW17 180 A6
Hayes End Rd UB4 83 B3
Hayesford Park Dr
BR2 208 D4
Hayes Gdn BR2 209 A1
Hayes Gr SE15, SE22 139 D1
Hayes & Harlington Sta
UB3 105 D3
Hayes Hill BR2 208 C1
Hayes Hill Rd BR2 208 D1
Hayes La
Beckenham BR2, BR3 208 B5
Hayes BR2 209 A4
Hayes Mead Rd BR2 208 C1
Hayes Park Sch UB4 83 D3
Hayes Pl NW1 237 B5
Hayes Prim Sch BR2 209 B1
Hayes Rd Bromley BR2 209 A5
Southall UB2 106 B2
Hayes Sch BR2 225 B6
Hayes St BR2 209 B1
Hayes Sta BR2 208 D1
HAYES TOWN 106 B5
Hayes Way BR3 208 B5
Hayes Wood Ave BR2 209 B1
Hayfield Pas E1 96 C3
Hayfield Yd 43 E1 96 C3
Hayford Ct NW2 68 D5
Haygarth Pl 2 SW19 178 D5
Haygreen Cl KT2 176 D4
Hay Hill W1 115 B6 248 D5
Hayhurst N1 234 D6
Hay La NW9 45 B5
Hayland Cl NW9 45 B5
Hay Lane Sch NW9 45 A5
Hayles Bldgs SE11 261 D4
Hayles St SE11 116 D2 261 C4
Haylett Gdns KT1 197 D5
Hayley Ho DA17 147 C6
Hayling Ave TW13 150 A1
Hayling Cl 20 N16 73 C3
Hayling Ct SM3 216 C4
Haymaker Cl UB10 60 B1
Hayman Cres UB4 83 B5
Haymans Point SE11 260 C2
Haymarket
SW1 115 D6 249 C5
Haymeads Dr KT10 212 A2
Haymer Gdns KT4 216 A5
Haymerle Ho 6 SE15 140 A5
Haymerle Rd SE15 140 A6
Haymerle Sch SE15 140 A6
Haymill Cl UB6 86 D4
Haymills Ct W5 88 B3
Hayne Ho W11 244 A4
Hayne Rd BR3 185 B2
Haynes Cl
Friern Barnet N11 15 A1
Lewisham SE3 142 C2
Tottenham N17 34 B3
Haynes Dr N9 18 B1
Haynes Ho 3 E9 74 D2
Haynes La SE19 183 C4
Haynes Rd HA0 66 A1
Hayne St EC1 94 D2 241 D4
Haynt Wlk SW20 201 A6
Hay's Galleria* SE1 253 A4
Hay's La SE1 253 A4
Haysleigh Gdns SE20 184 A1
Haysleigh Ho SE20 184 B1
Hay's Mews
W1 115 B5 248 C4
Hay St E2 96 A6
Haystall Cl UB4 83 C5
Hayter Ct E11 77 B6
Hayter Ho W12 112 A6
Hayter Rd SW2 160 B6
Haythorn Ho
SW11 136 B4 266 D1
Hayton Cl 11 E8 73 D2
Hayward Cl SW19 179 D2
Hayward Ct
14 London SW4 138 A3
Mitcham CR4 180 B1
Hayward Gallery*
SE1 116 B5 250 D4
Hayward Gdns SW15 156 C5
Hayward Ho
Islington N1 234 A4
Lower Clapton E5 74 B5
Hayward Rd London N20 14 A2
Thames Ditton KT7 196 D1
Haywards Cl RM6 58 C4
Haywards Pl EC1 241 C6
Hayward's Pl EC1 241 C6
Haywood Cl HA5 22 D1
Haywood Ct N11 31 D4
Haywood Lo 23 N7 71 D3
Haywood Rd BR2 209 D5
Haywood Rise BR6 227 C3
Hazel Ave UB7 104 C3
Hazelbank KT5 199 A1
Hazel Bank SE25 183 C1
Hazelbank Rd SE6 164 C2
Hazelbourne Rd SW12 159 B5
Hazelbury Cl SW19 179 C1
Hazelbury Gn N9 17 C1
Hazelbury Inf Sch N9 17 C1
Hazelbury Jun Sch N9 17 C1
Hazelbury La N9 17 C1
Hazel Cl Brentford TW8 131 B5
Croydon CR0 206 D1
Edmonton N13 17 B1
Hendon NW9 27 D1
Mitcham CR4 203 D5
Peckham SE15 140 A3
Twickenham TW2 152 A4
Upper Holloway N19 71 C6
Hazelcroft HA5 23 D4
Hazelcroft Cl UB10 60 B1
Hazel Ct Ealing W5 110 A6
8 Rotherhithe SE16 119 A5
9 West Norwood
SW16 182 C5
Hazeldean Rd NW10 67 B1
Hazeldene Dr HA5 40 C6
Hazeldene Gdns UB10 83 A6
Hazeldene Rd
Bexley DA16 146 C3
Ilford IG3 80 B6
Hazeldon Rd SE4 163 A6
Hazel Gdns HA8 26 D6
Hazel Gr Dagenham RM6 59 A6
Enfield EN1 18 A5
Feltham TW14 150 A3
Forest Hill SE26 184 D6
Orpington BR6 226 D6
Wembley HA0 88 A6
Hazelgreen Cl N21 16 D3
Hazel Ho London SE4 141 B2
12 Maitland Pk NW3 70 D2
Hazelhurst BR3 186 B2
Hazelhurst Ct SE6 186 A5
Hazelhurst Rd SW17 180 B6
Hazellville Rd N19 49 D1
Hazel Mead EN5 12 B6
Hazelmere Cl
Feltham TW14 149 C5
Northolt UB5 85 B5
Hazelmere Ct 10 SW2 160 B3
Hazelmere Dr UB5 85 B5
Hazelmere Rd
Kilburn NW6 91 B6
Northolt UB5 85 B5
Petts Wood BR5 211 B5
Hazelmere Way BR2 209 A3
Hazelmere Wlk UB5 85 B5
Hazel Rd
Kensal Green NW10 90 C4
Stratford E15 76 C3
Hazeltree La UB5 85 A4
Hazel Way
Bermondsey SE1 263 C4
Walthamstow E4 35 B4
Hazel Wlk BR2 210 C3
Hazelwood IG10 21 D6
Hazelwood Ave SM4 201 D5
Hazelwood Cl
Clapton Pk E5 75 A5
Ealing W5 110 A4
Harrow HA2 41 D5
Hazelwood Cres N13 32 C6
Hazelwood Ct
1 Edmonton N13 32 C6
Hazelwood Ct continued
Surbiton KT6 198 A3
1 Willesden NW10 67 C5
Hazelwood Dr HA5 22 B1
Hazelwood Ho
Beckenham BR2 208 C6
Chingford E4 20 B4
11 Deptford SE8 119 A2
Edmonton N13 32 D6
2 Sutton SM1 218 A4
Hazelwood Jun & Inf Schs
N13 32 C6
Hazelwood La N13 32 C6
Hazelwood Lo BR4 208 A2
Hazelwood Mans SW6 264 C2
Hazelwood Rd
Enfield EN1 17 D5
Walthamstow E17 53 A4
Hazlebury Rd SW6 135 D3
Hazledean Rd CR0 221 B6
Hazledene Rd W4 133 A6
Hazlemere 3 DA14 190 A6
Hazlemere Gdns KT4 200 A1
Hazlewell Rd SW15 156 C6
Hazlewood Cres W10 91 A3
Hazlewood Twr W10 91 B3
Hazlitt Cl TW13 173 A6
Hazlitt Ct 4 SE28 124 C5
Hazlitt Mews W14 254 A5
Hazlitt Rd W14 113 A3 254 A5
Heacham Ave UB10 61 A5
Headbourne Ho SE1 262 D6
Headcorn 10 NW5 71 A2
Headcorn Pl CR7 204 B5
Headcorn Rd
Plaistow BR1 187 A5
Thornton Heath CR7 204 B5
Tottenham N17 33 D3
Headfort Pl
SW1 115 A4 248 B1
Headington Rd SW18 158 A2
Headlam Rd SW4 159 D4
Headlam St E1 96 B3
Headley App IG2 56 D4
Headley Ave CR0, SM6 220 B3
Headley Cl KT19 214 C2
Headley Ct SE26 184 C5
Headley Dr Ilford IG2 56 D3
New Addington CR0 224 A1
Headley Ho 5 BR5 190 B1
Heads Mews W11 91 C1
Head St E1 96 D1
Headstart Montessori Sch
SW17 180 A6
HEADSTONE 41 D5
Headstone Dr HA1, HA3 42 C6
Headstone Gdns HA2 42 A5
Headstone La
Harrow HA2, HA3 23 D2
Headstone HA2 41 D5
Headstone Lane Sta
HA3 23 D2
Headstone Rd HA1 42 C3
Headway Cl TW10 175 C6
Heald St SE8, SE14 141 C4
Healey Ho RM6 59 A5
Healey St NW1 71 B2
Healy Ct EN5 12 D5
Healy Dr 1 BR6 227 D4
Healy Ho
12 Kennington SW9 138 C5
2 Tower Hamlets E3 97 C3
Heanor Ct 4 E5 74 D4
Hearne Rd W4 132 C6
Hearn Rise UB5 84 D6
Hearn's Bldgs SE17 262 D3
Hearnshaw St 1 E14 97 A1
Hearn St EC2 95 C3 243 B5
Hearnville Rd SW12 159 A3
Heart Hospl The
W1 93 A2 238 B3
Heart Raido W11 112 D6
Heart The KT12 193 D1
Heatham Pk TW2 152 D4
Heath Ave DA7 146 D6
Heathbourne Rd WD23 8 D3
Heathbrook Prim Sch
SW4 137 C3
Heath Brow NW3 70 A5
Heath Bsns Ctr The
TW3 130 A1
Heath Cl Croydon CR2 220 D2
Ealing W5 88 B3
Golders Green NW11 47 D2
Harlington UB3 127 B5
Heathcote Gr E4 20 A2
Heathcote Point 25 E9 74 D2
Heathcote Rd TW1 153 B6
Heathcote Sch E4 20 C2
Heathcote St
WC1 94 B4 233 C1
Heathcroft Ealing W5 88 B3
Golders Green NW11 47 D1
Heathcroft Ave TW16 171 D3
Heathcroft Gdns E4 36 B2
Heath Ct
Carshalton SM5 218 B6
Eltham SE9 167 A3
2 Hampstead NW3 70 A2
Leytonstone E11 54 D3
Stoke Newington N16 51 B1
Uxbridge UB8 60 A1
Heathdale Ave TW4 129 A2
Heathdene N14 15 C4
Heathdene Dr DA17 125 D2

Heathdene Rd
South Norwood SW16 182 B3
Wallington SM5, SM6 219 B1
Heath Dr SW20 200 C5
Heathedge SE23, SE26 162 B2
Heath End Ct WD23 8 C2
Heatherbank
Chislehurst BR7 188 C1
Eltham SE9 144 B3
Heather Cl
Clapham SW8 137 B2
Hampton TW12 173 B2
Hillingdon UB8 82 B2
Hither Green SE13 164 B4
Isleworth TW7 152 B6
Newham E6 100 C1
Heather Ct
South Lambeth SW4 270 B1
6 West Norwood SW16 182 C6
Heatherdale Cl KT2 176 D3
Heatherdene Cl
London N12 30 A2
Mitcham CR4 202 C5
Heatherdene Ct CR4 202 B5
Heatherdene Mans 2 TW1 153 D5
Heather Dr EN2 4 D3
Heatherfold Way HA5, HA6 39 D6
Heather Gdns
Belmont SM2 217 C2
Hendon NW11 47 A3
Heather Ho 11 E14 98 A1
Heather La UB7 82 A1
Heatherlands TW16 172 A4
Heatherley Ct N16 74 A5
Heatherley Dr IG5 56 B6
Heatherley Sch of Fine Art SW10 266 B3
Heather Lo N16 51 C1
Heather Park Dr HA0 66 C1
Heather Park Par HA0 66 B1
Heather Rd
Dollis Hill NW2 67 D6
Lewisham SE12 165 A3
Walthamstow E4 35 B4
Heatherset Cl KT10 212 A3
Heatherset Gdns SW16 182 B3
Heatherside Rd
Sidcup DA14 168 C1
West Ewell KT19 215 B1
Heathers The TW19 148 B4
Heather Way HA7 24 D4
Heather Wlk
Edgware HA8 26 D5
Twickenham TW4 151 C4
West Kilburn W10 91 A3
Heatherwood Cl E12 77 C6
Heatherwood Dr UB4 83 B5
Heathfield Chingford E4 20 A1
Chislehurst BR7 189 A4
Heathfield Ave SW18 158 B4
Heathfield Cl
Keston BR2 225 C3
Newham E16 99 D2
Heathfield Ct
Ashford TW15 148 A1
3 Bow E3 97 C5
5 Chiswick W4 111 B1
Penge SE20 184 C3
Sidcup DA14 190 B5
8 Sutton SM2 218 A2
Wandsworth SW18 158 B4
Heathfield Dr CR4 180 C2
Heathfielde N2 48 A4
Heathfield Gdns
Acton Green W4 111 A1
Blackheath SE3 142 C3
Croydon CR0 221 B4
Hendon NW11 46 D3
Wandsworth SW18 158 B5
Heathfield Ho SE3 142 C3
Heathfield Inf Sch TW2 151 C3
Heathfield Jun Sch TW2 151 C3
Heathfield La BR7 189 A4
Heathfield N TW1, TW2 152 D4
Heathfield Park Dr RM6 58 B4
Heathfield Pk NW2 68 C2
Heathfield Rd
Bexleyheath DA6 147 B1
Bromley BR1 186 D3
Croydon CR0 221 B4
Keston BR2 225 D3
South Acton W3 110 D4
Wandsworth SW18 158 B5
Heathfield Rise HA4 39 A2
Heathfield S TW1, TW2 152 D4
Heathfield Sch HA5 40 D2
Heathfield Sq SW18 158 B4
Heathfield Terr
Chiswick W4 111 B1
Plumstead Comm SE18 145 D6
Heathfield Vale CR2 223 A1
Heathgate NW11 47 D3
Heathgate Pl NW3 70 D4
Heath Gdns TW1 152 D2
Heath Gr
Ashford TW16 171 D3
Penge SE20 184 C3
Heath Ho Sidcup DA15 189 D6
Thornton Heath CR7 204 C4
Uxbridge UB10 60 D4
Heath Hurst Rd NW3 70 C4
Heath La SE3 142 B3
Heathland Rd N16 51 C1
Heathland Sch The TW4 151 B5
Heathlands Cl
Sunbury TW16 172 A1
Twickenham TW1 152 D3
Heathlands Ct
Hounslow TW4 151 A6
Mitcham CR4 203 A6
Heathlands Way TW4 151 A6
Heathlee Rd SE3 142 D1
Heathley End BR7 189 A4
Heath Lo WD23 8 B3
Heath Mans
5 Hampstead NW3 70 A4
Putney SW15 156 D5
Heathman's Rd SW6 135 B4 264 D1
Heath Mead SW19 156 D1
Heathmere Prim Sch SW15 156 A3
Heath Park Dr BR1 210 A6
Heath Park Gdns NW3 69 D5
Heath Park Ind Est RM8 59 A1
Heathpool Ct 8 E1 96 B3
Heath Rd Clapham SW8 137 B3
Dagenham RM6 59 A2
Harrow HA1 42 A2
Hillingdon UB10 83 A3
Isleworth TW3, TW7 130 A1
South Norwood CR7 205 A6
Twickenham TW1 152 D3
Heath Rise Hayes BR2 209 A3
Putney SW15 156 D5
Heathrow Airport London TW6 126 D3
Heathrow Bvd UB7 126 B5
Heathrow Causeway Est TW4 128 B2
Heathrow International Trad Est TW4 128 B2
Heathrow Prim Sch UB7 126 B6
Heathrow Terminal 4 Sta TW6 149 A5
Heathrow Terminals 1, 2, 3 TW6 126 D2
Heath Royal SW15 156 D5
Heath's Cl EN1 5 C3
Heathshott 8 TW10 154 A5
Heathside
Hampstead NW3 70 B4
Hinchley Wood KT10 212 C5
Twickenham TW4 151 B4
Heath Side BR5 211 A2
Heathside Ave DA7 147 A3
Heathside Cl
Hinchley Wood KT10 212 C5
Ilford IG2 57 B4
Heathside Prep Sch NW3 70 A4
Heath St NW3 70 A5
Heathstan Rd W12 90 A1
Heath Terr RM6 58 D2
Heath The W7 108 C5
Heath View
Gospel Oak NW5 71 A4
London N2 48 A5
Heath View Cl N2 48 A5
Heathview Ct SW19 156 D2
Heath View Dr SE2 146 D6
Heathview Gdns SW15 156 C4
Heathview Rd CR7 204 C5
Heath Villas
Hampstead NW3 70 B5
Plumstead Comm SE18 123 D1
Heathville Rd N4, N19 50 A2
Heathwall St SW11 136 D2
Heathway Croydon CR0 223 B5
Dagenham RM10 81 C2
Dagenham RM10 103 C6
Greenwich SE3 143 A5
Woodford IG8 37 C5
Heathway Ct NW3 69 C6
Heathway Ind Est RM10 81 D4
Heathwood Ct
1 Hounslow TW3 129 D1
Streatham SW12 159 C3
Heathwood Gdns SE7 122 A1
Heathwood Point 7 SE26 162 D1
Heaton Cl E4 20 A1
Heaton Ct 3 N20 14 D2
Heaton Ho
Chelsea SW10 266 B6
6 Peckham SE15 140 B3
Heaton Rd
London SE15 140 B3
Mitcham CR4 181 A3
Heaven Tree Cl N1 73 A3
Heaver Rd 24 SW11 136 B2
Heavers Farm Prim Sch SE25 205 D4
Heavitree Cl SE18 123 B1
Heavitree Ct E17 35 D2
Heavitree Rd SE18 123 B1
Hebble Ho UB5 85 A6
Hebden Ct 24 E2 95 D6
Hebden Terr N17 33 C4
Hebdon Rd SW17 158 C1
Hebe Ct SM1 218 A4
Heber Prim Sch SE22 161 D5
Heber Rd
Cricklewood NW2 68 D4
East Dulwich SE22 161 D5
Hebron Rd W6 112 B3
Hecham Cl E17 35 A2
Heckfield Pl SW6 135 C5 265 A3
Heckford Ho E14 97 D1
Heckford St E1 118 D6
Hector 31 NW9 27 D2
Hector Ct
1 London SW9 138 C4
Putney SW15 156 D6
Hector Ho 14 E2 96 B5
Hector St SE18 123 C2
Heddington Gr N7 72 B3
Heddon Cl TW7 131 A1
Heddon Court Ave EN4 14 D6
Heddon Court Par EN4 15 A6
Heddon Ct EN4 15 A6
Heddon Rd EN4 14 D6
Heddon St W1 249 A6
Hedge Hill EN2 4 D4
Hedge La N13 17 A1
Hedgeley IG4 56 B5
Hedgemans Rd RM9 81 A1
Hedgemans Way RM9 81 A2
Hedgemoor Ct 1 E4 36 B5
Hedgerley Gdns UB6 86 A5
Hedgerow La EN5 12 B6
Hedger's Gr E9 75 A2
Hedger St SE11 261 C4
Hedge Wlk SE6 185 D6
Hedgewood Gdns IG5 56 C4
Hedgewood Specl Sch UB4 83 C4
Hedgley Mews SE12 164 D6
Hedgley St SE12 164 D6
Hedingham Cl 6 N1 73 A1
Hedingham Ho 7 KT2 176 A2
Hedingham Rd RM8 80 B3
Hedley Ct SW15 156 D5
Hedley Ho E14 120 A3
Hedley Rd TW4 151 C4
Hedley Row N5, N16 73 B3
Hedsor Ho E2 243 C6
Heenan Cl IG11 79 A2
Heene Rd EN2 5 B4
Heidegger Cres SW13 134 B5
Heigham Rd E6 78 A1
Heighton Gdns CR0 220 D3
Heights Cl SW20 178 B3
Heights The
Beckenham BR3 186 A3
Greenwich SE7 121 C1
Hampstead NW3 70 A4
Northolt UB5 63 C3
Stroud Green N4 50 C3
Heiron St SE17 138 D6
Helby Rd SW4 159 D5
Heldar Ct SE1 252 D1
Helder Gr SE12 164 D4
Helder St CR2 221 B2
Heldmann Cl TW7 130 B1
Helegan Cl BR6 227 D4
Helena Cl EN4 2 B5
Helena Ct W5 87 D2
Helena Pl 3 E9 96 C6
Helena Rd Ealing W5 87 D2
Newham E13 99 A5
Walthamstow E17 53 C4
Willesden NW10 68 B3
Helena Sq 12 SE16 119 A6
Helen Ave TW14 150 B4
Helen Cl
East Finchley N2 48 A6
East Molesey KT8 195 D5
Helen Clare Ct EN2 4 D2
Helen Ct N3 47 A6
Helen Gladstone Ho SE1 251 C2
Helen Ho 9 E2 96 B5
Helen Mackay Ho 10 E14 98 B1
Helen Peele Cotts 10 SE16 118 C3
Helenslea Ave NW11 47 C1
Helen's Pl E2 96 C4
Helen St SE18 122 D2
Helen Taylor Ho 5 SE16 118 A2
Helford Cl HA4 61 C6
Helgiford Gdns TW16 171 C3
Helios Rd CR4 203 A1
Heliport Est The SW11 136 B3
Helix Ct 17 W11 112 D5
Helix Gdns SW2 160 B5
Helix Ho TW7 131 B3
Helix Rd SW2 160 B5
Helix The SW19 156 D2
Hellenic Coll of London SW1 114 D3 257 C5
Hellen Way WD19 22 D6
Hellings St E1 118 A5
Helme Cl SW19 179 B5
Helmet Row EC1 242 B6
Helmore Rd IG11 79 D1
Helmsdale Cl UB4 85 A3
Helmsdale Ho NW6 91 D5
Helmsdale Rd SW16 181 D2
Helmsley 11 E18 55 A6
Helmsley Pl E8 74 B1
Helmsley St 7 E8 74 B1
Helperby Rd NW10 67 C1
Helsby Ct NW8 236 C6
Helsinki Sq SE16 119 A3
Helston NW1 232 B4
Helston Cl HA5 23 B3
Helston Ct N15 51 C4
Helston Ho SE11 261 B2
Helvetia St SE6 163 B2
Helwys Ct E4 36 A4
Hemans Est SW8 137 D5 269 D3
Hemans St SW8 137 D5 269 D3
Hemberton Rd SW9 138 A2
Hemery Rd UB6 64 B3
Hemingford Cl N12 30 B5
Hemingford Rd
Cheam SM3 216 C4
Islington N1 94 B6 233 D6
Heming Rd HA8 26 D3
Hemington Ave N11 30 D5
Hemlock Rd W12 111 D6
Hemmen La UB3 83 D1
Hemming Cl 6 TW12 173 C2
Hemmings Cl DA14 168 B2
Hemmings Ct HA8 27 A3
Hemmings Mead KT19 215 A2
Hemming St E1 96 A3
Hemmingway Cl NW5 71 A4
Hempstead Cl IG9 21 A2
Hempstead Rd E17 36 B1
Hemp Wlk SE17 262 D4
Hemsby Rd KT9 214 B2
Hemstal Rd NW6 69 C1
Hemswell Dr NW9 27 C2
Hemsworth Ct N1 95 C5
Hemsworth St N1 95 C5
Hemus Pl SW3 257 B1
Henchman St W12 89 D1
Hendale Ave NW4 46 B6
Hendale Ho 13 E5 74 B6
Henderson Cl NW10 67 A2
Henderson Ct
8 Deptford SE14 140 D6
Hampstead NW3 70 B3
Wandsworth SW18 158 C4
Woodside Pk N12 29 D6
Henderson Dr NW8 92 B3 236 C6
Henderson Ho 7 RM10 81 C5
Henderson Rd
Edmonton N9 18 B3
Forest Gate E7 77 C2
Hayes UB4 84 A4
Thornton Heath CR0 205 B3
Wandsworth SW18 158 C4
Hendfield Ct 5 SM6 219 B2
Hendham Rd SW17 158 D2
HENDON 46 C3
Hendon Ave N3 29 A2
Hendon Central NW4 46 B4
Hendon Central Sta NW4 46 B4
Hendon Hall Ct NW4 46 D6
Hendon Ho NW4 46 D4
Hendon La N3 29 B1
Hendon Lo NW4 46 B6
Hendon Park Mans NW4 46 C4
Hendon Park Row NW11 47 B3
Hendon Pk Cotts NW7 11 D2
Hendon Prep Sch NW4 46 D6
Hendon Rd N9 18 A2
Hendon Sch NW4 46 D4
Hendon Sta NW4 46 A3
Hendon Terr TW15 171 B4
Hendon Way NW2, NW4 46 C3
Hendon Wood La NW7 12 A3
Hendre Ho SE1 263 B3
Hendren Cl UB6 64 B3
Hendre Rd SE1 117 C2 263 B3
Hendrick Ave SW12 158 D4
Heneage La EC3 243 B1
Heneage Pl EC3 243 B1
Heneage St E1 95 D2 243 D4
Henfield Cl London N19 49 C1
Old Bexley DA5 169 C5
Henfield Rd SW19 179 B2
Hengelo Gdns CR4 202 B5
Hengist Rd
Eltham SE12 165 B4
Erith DA8 147 D5
Hengist Way BR2, BR3 208 C5
Hengrave Rd SE23 162 D4
Hengrove Ct DA5 169 A3
Henley Ave SM3 217 A5
Henley Cl Greenford UB6 86 A5
Hounslow TW7 130 D4
Rotherhithe SE16 118 C4
Henley Ct
Brondesbury NW2 68 D2
Hendon NW4 46 A6
Ilford IG1 78 D4
Mitcham CR4 203 A6
Oakwood N14 15 C4
Peckham SE15 140 A2
Sidcup DA5 169 B4
Henley Dr
Bermondsey SE1 117 D2 263 D4
Kingston u T KT2 177 D3
Henley Gdns
Dagenham RM6 59 A4
Pinner HA5 40 B6
Henley Ho London N12 30 B5
Shoreditch E2 243 D6
Henley Lo
South Norwood SE25 205 D5
Walthamstow E17 53 B4
Henley Prior N1 233 C3
Henley Rd
Edmonton N18 33 C6
Ilford IG1 79 B4
Henley Rd *continued*
Newham E16 122 B4
Willesden NW10 90 C6
Henleys Cnr NW11 47 B5
Henleys Rdbt TW5 128 C3
Henley St SW11 137 A3
Henley Way TW13 172 D5
Henlow Pl TW10 153 D2
Hennel Cl SE23 162 C1
Hennessy Rd N9 18 C2
Henniker Gdns E6 100 A4
Henniker Mews SW3 266 C6
Henniker Point E15 76 C3
Henniker Rd E15 76 B3
Henningham Rd N17 33 B2
Henning St SW11 136 C4 267 A1
Henrietta Barnett Sch NW11 47 D3
Henrietta Cl SE8 141 C6
Henrietta Ho
11 Hammersmith W6 112 C1
3 New Barnet EN5 2 A1
3 South Tottenham N15 51 C3
Henrietta Mews WC1 240 B6
Henrietta Pl W1 93 B1 238 C2
Henrietta St
Strand WC2 116 A6 250 B6
Stratford New Town E15 76 A3
Henriques St E1 96 A1
Henry Addlington Cl E6 100 D2
Henry Cavendish Prim Sch SW12 159 C3
Henry Cl EN2 5 C5
Henry Compton Sec Sch SW6 135 A4 264 A2
Henry Cooper Way SE12 187 D6
Henry Darlot Dr NW7 29 A5
Henry Dent Cl SE5 139 B2
Henry Dickens Ct W11 244 A4
Henry Doulton Dr SW17 181 B6
Henry Fawcett Prim Sch SE11 138 C6
Henry Green Prim Sch RM8 80 D6
Henry Hatch Ct SM2 218 A1
Henry Ho Lambeth SE1 251 B3
South Lambeth SW8 270 A4
St John's Wood NW8 230 A4
Henry Jackson Ho SW15 134 D2
Henry Jackson Rd SW15 134 D2
Henry Macaulay Ave 13 KT2 175 D2
Henry Maynard Inf Sch E17 54 A4
Henry Maynard Jun Sch E17 54 A4
Henry Peters Dr TW11 174 C5
Henry Rd London N4 51 A1
New Barnet EN4 14 B6
Newham E6 100 A5
Henry's Ave IG8 36 D5
Henryson Rd SE4 163 C6
Henry St BR1 187 B2
Henry Tate Mews SW16 182 C5
Henry Wise Ho SW1 259 B3
Hensford Gdns SE26 184 B6
Henshall Point 19 E3 97 D4
Henshall St N1 73 B2
Henshawe Rd RM8 80 D5
Henshaw St SE17 117 B2 262 C4
Hensley Point 28 E9 74 D2
Henslowe Rd SE22 162 A6
Henslow Ho 12 SE15 140 A5
Henson Ave NW2 68 C3
Henson Cl BR6 226 D6
Henson Ct 3 N5 73 A4
Henson Path HA3 43 D6
Henson Pl UB5 84 C6
Henstridge Pl NW8 230 A5
Henty Cl SW11 136 C4 267 B2
Henty Wlk SW15 156 B6
Henville Rd BR1 187 B2
Henwick Prim Sch SE9 144 A2
Henwick Rd SE9 144 A2
Hepburn Gdns BR2 208 D1
Hepburn Mews SW11 158 D6
Hepple Cl TW7 131 B3
Hepplestone Cl SW15 156 B5
Hepscott Rd E9 75 C1
Hepworth Ct
Barking IG11 80 A3
Cheam SM3 201 C1
Chelsea SW1 258 C1
Islington N1 234 C6
Hepworth Gdns IG11 80 A3
Hepworth Ho IG8 21 A1
Hepworth Rd SW16 182 A3
Hepworth Way KT12 193 D1
Heracles 30 NW9 27 D2
Heracles Cl SM6 220 A1
Hera Ct 15 E14 119 C2
Herald Gdns SM6 219 B5
Heralds Pl SE11 261 C4
Herald St 5 E2 96 B3
Herbal Hill EC1 241 B5
Herbert Chapman Ct N5 72 D4
Herbert Cres SW1 257 D6
Herbert Ct 4 KT5 198 B3
Herbert Gdns
Chiswick W4 132 D6
Dagenham RM6 58 D2
Willesden Green NW10 90 B5
Herbert Ho E1 243 C2
Herbert Mews 15 SW2 160 C5
Herbert Morrison Ho SW6 264 C5
Herbert Morrison Prim Sch SW8 138 A5 270 A3
Herbert Pl
Hounslow TW3 130 B3
Shooters Hill SE18 144 D6
Herbert Rd
Bexleyheath DA7 147 A3
Bromley BR2 210 A4
Hendon NW9 46 A3
Ilford IG3 79 C6
Kingston u T KT1 198 B6
Manor Pk E12 78 A4
Merton SW19 179 B3
Shooters Hill SE18 144 D6
Southall UB1 107 B5
South Tottenham N15 51 D4
Walthamstow E17 53 B2
Wood Green N11 32 A3
Herbert St
Camden Town NW5 71 A2
Newham E13 99 A5
Herbrand Est WC1 94 A3 240 A6
Herbrand St WC1 94 A3 240 A6
Hercies Rd UB10 60 C2
Hercules Ct 7 SE14 141 A6
Hercules Pl N7 72 A5
Hercules Rd SE1 116 B3 260 D5
Hercules St N7 72 A5
Hereford Ave EN4 14 D3
Hereford Bldgs SW3 266 D6
Hereford Ct
20 Belmont SM2 217 C1
6 Croydon CR0 205 D1
6 Ealing W7 86 D2
Harrow HA1 42 C6
Hereford Gdns
London SE13 164 C6
Pinner HA5 41 A4
Redbridge IG1 56 A2
Twickenham TW2 152 A3
Hereford Ho
7 Acton W3 88 C1
5 Brixton SW2 138 C1
25 Camberwell SE5 139 A3
Edgware HA8 26 B3
Knightsbridge SW3 257 B6
Walham Green SW10 265 D4
Hereford Mans 10 W2 91 C1
Hereford Mews 11 W2 91 C1
Hereford Pl SE14 141 B5
Hereford Rd Acton W3 111 A6
Bayswater W2 113 C6 245 B6
Ealing W5 109 C3
Feltham TW13 150 C3
Wanstead E11 55 B4
Hereford Retreat 5 SE15 140 A5
Hereford Sq SW7 114 A2 256 B3
Hereford St E2 96 A3
Hereford Way KT9 213 D3
Herent Dr IG5 56 B6
Hereward Gdns N13 32 C5
Hereward House Sch NW3 70 B2
Hereward Rd SW17 180 D6
Herga Ct HA1 64 C6
Herga Rd HA3 42 D5
Heriot Ave E4 19 C2
Heriot Rd NW4 46 C4
Heriots Cl HA7 25 A6
Heritage Cl
London SW9 138 D2
Sunbury TW16 172 A2
Heritage Ct SE8 118 D1
Heritage Hill BR2 225 C3
Heritage Ho
22 Putney SW19 156 D3
3 Twickenham TW1 153 A4
Heritage View HA1 64 D5
Herlwyn Ave HA4 61 C5
Herlwyn Gdns SW17 180 D6
Herm Cl TW7 130 A5
Hermes Cl 5 W9 91 C3
Hermes Ct 4 SW9 138 C4
Hermes Ho BR3 185 A2
Hermes St N1 234 A3
Hermes Way SM6 219 D1
Hermes Wlk UB5 85 C5
Herm Ho EN3 6 D5
Hermiston Ave N8 50 A4
Hermiston Ct
3 Hornsey N8 50 A4
7 North Finchley N12 30 B5
Hermitage Cl
1 Abbey Wood SE2 124 C3
Claygate KT10 213 A2
Enfield EN2 4 D3
Littleton TW17 192 C5
Snaresbrook E18 54 D5
Hermitage Ct
2 Child's Hill NW2 69 C5
Colney Hatch N11 30 D4
3 Wanstead E18 55 A5
14 Wapping E1 118 A5
Hermitage Gdns
Child's Hill NW2 69 C5
South Norwood SE19 183 A3

Her–Hig 327

Hermitage La
Child's Hill NW2 . . . . 69 C5
Croydon CR0 . . . . 206 A3
South Norwood SW16 . . . 182 B3
Hermitage Prim Sch
E1 . . . . 118 A5
Hermitage Rd
London N4, N15 . . . . 51 A3
South Norwood SE19 . . . 183 B4
Hermitage Row 9 E8 . . . 74 A3
Hermitage St W2 . . . . . 236 C3
Hermitage The
Barnes SW13 . . . . 133 D4
Feltham TW13 . . . . 149 D1
Forest Hill SE23 . . . . . . 162 C3
Kingston u T KT1 . . . . . . 197 D5
Richmond TW10 . . . . . . 154 A6
Uxbridge UB8 . . . . 60 A2
Hermitage Villas SW6. 265 A6
Hermitage Wall E1 . . . . 118 A5
Hermitage Way HA7 . . . . 25 A2
Hermitage Wlk E18 . . . . . 54 D5
Hermit Pl NW6 . . . . 91 D6
Hermit Rd E16 . . . . 98 D3
Hermit St EC1 . . . . 234 C2
Hermon Gr UB3 . . . . 106 A5
Hermon Hill E11 . . . . 55 A5
Herndon Rd SW18 . . . . 158 A6
Herne Cl Hayes UB3 . . . . 83 D1
Willesden NW10 . . . . 67 B3
Herne Ct WD23 . . . . 8 A4
HERNE HILL 161 A6
Herne Hill SE24 . . . . 139 A1
Herne Hill Ho SE24 . . . . 160 D5
Herne Hill Mans SE24 . . 161 A5
Herne Hill Rd SE24 . . . . 139 A1
Herne Hill Sch SE24 . . . 161 A6
Herne Hill Sta SE24 . . . 160 D5
Herne Hill Stad SE24 . . . 161 B5
Herne Mews N18 . . . . 34 A6
Herne Pl SE24 . . . . 160 D6
Herne Rd KT6 . . . . 214 A6
Heron Cl
Buckhurst Hill IG9 . . . . 21 A3
Cheam SM1 . . . . 217 B3
Walthamstow E17 . . . . 35 B1
Willesden NW10 . . . . 67 C2
Heron Cres DA14 . . . . . . 189 C6
Heron Ct Bromley BR2 . . 209 C5
16 Cubitt Town E14 . . . . . 120 A3
7 Dulwich SE21 . . . . 161 B2
9 Forest Hill SE23 . . . . . . 162 C3
Ilford IG1 . . . . 78 D6
5 Kingston u T KT1 . . . . . 198 A6
Merton SW20 . . . . 178 C1
Mitcham CR4 . . . . 180 C2
Ruislip HA4 . . . . 61 B6
Stanwell TW19 . . . . 148 A3
Herondale Ave SW18 . . . 158 C3
Heron Dr N4 . . . . 73 A6
Herongate N1 . . . . 235 B6
Herongate Rd E12 . . . . . . 77 C6
Heron Hill DA17 . . . . 125 B2
Heron Ho
Battersea SW11 . . . . . . 267 B2
Ealing W13 . . . . 87 A3
Peckham SE15 . . . . 139 D4
Sidcup DA14 . . . . 168 B1
St John's Wood NW8 . . 230 A3
Teddington KT1 . . . . 175 C2
Heron Ind Est E15 . . . . . . 97 D5
Heron Mead EN3 . . . . 7 C5
Heron Mews IG1 . . . . 78 D6
Heron Pl
Marylebone W1 . . . . 238 B2
Rotherhithe SE16 . . . . . . 119 A5
Heron Quays E14 . . . . . . 119 C5
Heron Quays Sta E14 . . 119 C5
Heron Rd Croydon CR0 . . 221 C6
Herne Hill SE24 . . . . 139 A1
Isleworth TW1 . . . . 131 B1
Heronsforde W13 . . . . 87 C1
Heronsgate HA8 . . . . 26 C5
Heronsgate Prim Sch
SE28 . . . . 123 B3
Heron's Lea N6 . . . . 48 D3
Heronslea Dr HA7 . . . . . . 26 A5
Herons Pl TW7 . . . . 131 B2
Heron Sq 27 TW10 . . . . . 153 D6
Herons Rise EN4 . . . . 2 C1
Herons The E11 . . . . 54 D3
Heron Trad Est W3 . . . . . . 88 D2
Heronway IG8 . . . . 37 C6
Heron Way TW14 . . . . . . 128 A1
Herrick Ct 4 TW10 . . . . . 175 D6
Herrick Ho
18 Camberwell SE5 . . . . . 139 B5
17 Canonbury N16 . . . . . . 73 B4
Herrick Rd N5 . . . . 73 A5
Herrick St
SW1 . . . . 115 D2 259 D3
Herries St W10 . . . . 91 A5
Herringham Rd SE7 . . . . 121 C3
Herrongate Cl EN1 . . . . 5 D3
Hersant Cl NW10 . . . . 90 A6
Herschell Rd SE23 . . . . . 163 A4
Herschell's Mews SE5 . . 139 A2
Hersham Cl SW15 . . . . . . 156 A4
Hersham Rd KT12 . . . . . . 194 A1
Hershell Ct 1 SW14 . . . . 132 D1
Hertford Ave SW14 . . . . 133 C1
Hertford Cl EN4 . . . . 2 B2
Hertford Ct
16 London SW11 . . . . 136 C2
Newham E6 . . . . 100 B4
Palmers Green N13 . . . . . . 16 C1
Hertford Ho 5 UB5 . . . . . 85 B3
Hertford Lo 10 SW19 . . . 157 A3
Hertford Pl W1 . . . . 239 B5
Hertford Rd
Barking IG11 . . . . 78 D1
Barnet EN4 . . . . 2 A2
East Finchley N2 . . . . 48 C6
Edmonton N9 . . . . 18 B3
Enfield EN3 . . . . 6 C5
Ilford IG2 . . . . 57 C3
Shoreditch N1 . . . . 95 C6
Hertford Rd High St
EN3 . . . . 18 C6
Hertford St
W1 . . . . 115 B5 248 C3
Hertford Way CR4 . . . . . 204 A5
Hertford Wlk 13 DA17 . . . 125 C1
Hertmitage The 5
SE13 . . . . 142 A3
Hertslet Rd N7 . . . . 72 B5
Hertsmere Rd E14 . . . . . 119 C6
Hertswood Ct 1 EN5 . . . . . 1 A1
Hervey Cl N3 . . . . 29 C2
Hervey Park Rd E17 . . . . . 53 A5
Hervey Rd SE3 . . . . 143 B4
Hesa Rd UB3 . . . . 106 A6
Hesewall Cl SW4 . . . . . . 137 C3
Hesketh Pl W11 . . . . 244 A5
Hesketh Rd E7 . . . . 77 A5
Heslop Ct 1 SW12 . . . . . 159 A3
Heslop Rd SW12 . . . . 158 D3
Hesper Mews
SW5 . . . . 113 D2 255 C3
Hesperus Cres E14 . . . . . 119 D2
Hessel Rd W13 . . . . 109 B4
Hessel St E1 . . . . 96 B1
Hestercombe Ave
SW6 . . . . 135 A4 264 B1
Hester Ct SW16 . . . . 181 C5
Hesterman Way CR0 . . . 204 B1
Hester Rd
Battersea
SW11 . . . . . . 136 C5 267 A3
Edmonton N18 . . . . 34 A5
Hester Terr TW9 . . . . 132 C2
Hestia Ho SE1 . . . . 253 A1
HESTON 129 B5
Heston Ave TW5 . . . . 129 A5
Heston Com Sch TW5 . . 129 C5
Heston Ctr The TW5 . . . 106 C1
Heston Grange TW5 . . . . 129 B6
Heston Grange La
TW5 . . . . 129 B6
Heston Ho
Gunnersbury W4 . . . . 110 D1
5 St Johns SE8 . . . . 141 C4
Heston Ind Mall TW5 . . . 129 B5
Heston Inf Sch TW5 . . . . 129 C5
Heston Jun Sch TW5 . . . 129 C5
Heston Phoenix
Distribution Pk TW5 . . 128 C6
Heston Rd TW5 . . . . 129 C5
Heston St SE14 . . . . 141 C4
Hetherington Rd
Charlton TW17 . . . . 171 A1
Stockwell SW2, SW4 . . . . 138 A1
Hetherington Way
UB10 . . . . 60 A4
Hethpool Ho W2 . . . . 236 C5
Hetley Gdns 1 SE19 . . . 183 D3
Hetley Rd W12 . . . . 112 B4
Heton Gdns NW4 . . . . 46 A5
Hetty Rees Ct 6 N19 . . . . 50 A2
Hevelius Cl SE10 . . . . 120 D1
Hever Croft SE9 . . . . 188 C6
Heverfield Ct CR4 . . . . . . 180 D3
Hever Gdns BR1 . . . . 188 C1
Heverham Rd SE18 . . . . . 123 C2
Hever Ho SE15 . . . . 140 D6
Heversham Ho SE15 . . . . 140 C6
Heversham Rd DA7 . . . . . 147 C4
Hevingham Dr RM6 . . . . . 58 C4
Heward Ct SE13 . . . . 142 A3
Hewens Rd UB4 . . . . 83 A3
Hewer Ho 6 SW4 . . . . . . 159 C6
Hewer St W10 . . . . 90 D2
Hewes Ho E17 . . . . 52 D5
Hewett Cl HA7 . . . . 25 B6
Hewett Ho
Putney SW15 . . . . 134 C3
7 Woolwich SE18 . . . . . . 122 D1
Hewett Rd RM8 . . . . 80 D4
Hewetts Quay 7 IG11 . . 101 A6
Hewett St EC2 . . . 95 C3 243 B5
Hewish Rd N18 . . . . 33 C6
Hewison St E3 . . . . 97 B5
Hewitt Ave N22 . . . . 32 D1
Hewitt Cl CR0 . . . . 223 C5
Hewitt Ho 2 E4 . . . . 36 B5
Hewitt Rd N8 . . . . 50 D4
Hewlett Rd E3 . . . . 97 A5
Hewling Ho 1 N16 . . . . . 73 C3
Hexagon Bsns Ctr
UB4 . . . . 106 C6
Hexagon The N6 . . . . 48 D1
Hexal Rd SE6 . . . . 164 C1
Hexham Gdns TW7 . . . . . 131 A5
Hexham Rd Barnet EN5 . . . . 1 D1
Cheam SM4 . . . . 201 D1
West Norwood SE27 . . . . 161 A2
Hexton Ct N4 . . . . 73 A6
Heybourne Rd N17 . . . . . . 34 B3
Heybridge 9 NW1 . . . . . . 71 B2
Heybridge Ave SW16 . . . 182 B4
Heybridge Dr IG6 . . . . 57 B6
Heybridge Way E10 . . . . . 53 B1
Heydon Ct BR4 . . . . 224 C6
Heydon Ho 3 SE14 . . . . 140 C4
Heyford Ave
Merton SW20 . . . . 201 B6
South Lambeth
SW8 . . . . 138 A5 270 B4
Heyford Rd CR4 . . . . 180 C1
Heyford Terr SW8 . . . . 270 B4
Heygate St
SE17 . . . . 117 A2 262 B4
Heylyn Sq E3 . . . . 97 B4
Heynes Rd RM8 . . . . 80 C4
Heysham Dr WD19 . . . . . . 22 D5
Heysham La NW3 . . . . 69 D5
Heysham Rd N15 . . . . 51 B3
Heythorp St SW18 . . . . 157 B2
Heythrop Dr UB10 . . . . . . 60 B4
Heyward Ct SM2 . . . . . . 217 C2
Heywood Ave NW9 . . . . . . 27 C2
Heywood Ct 2 HA7 . . . . . 25 C5
Heywood Ho
11 Deptford SE14 . . . . . 140 D6
6 Tulse Hill SW2 . . . . . . 160 C5
Heyworth Rd
Lower Clapton E5 . . . . . . 74 B4
Stratford E15 . . . . 76 D4
Hibbert Ho 13 E14 . . . . 119 C3
Hibbert Rd Harrow HA3 . . 24 D1
Walthamstow E17 . . . . . . 53 B2
Hibbert St SW11 . . . . . . 136 B2
Hibernia Gdns TW3 . . . 151 C6
Hibernia Point 9 SE2 . . 124 D4
Hibernia Rd TW3 . . . . . 129 C1
Hibiscus Cl 6 HA8 . . . . . 27 A6
Hibiscus Lo 5 E15 . . . . . 76 C1
Hichisson Rd SE15 . . . . 162 C6
Hickes Ho 6 NW6 . . . . . . 70 B1
Hickey's Almshouses 7
TW9 . . . . 132 B1
Hickin Cl SE7 . . . . 121 D2
Hickin St 2 E14 . . . . . . 120 A3
Hickleton NW1 . . . . 232 B5
Hickling Ho 10 SE16 . . . 118 B3
Hickling Rd IG1 . . . . 78 D3
Hickman Ave E4 . . . . 36 A4
Hickman Cl E16 . . . . 99 D2
Hickman Rd RM6 . . . . 58 C2
Hickmore Wlk SW4 . . . . 137 C2
Hickory Cl N9 . . . . 18 A4
Hicks Ave UB6 . . . . 86 C4
Hicks Cl SW11 . . . . 136 C2
Hicks Ct RM10 . . . . 81 D5
Hicks St SE8 . . . . 119 A1
Hidaburn Ct 7 SW16 . . . 181 C6
Hidcote Gdns SW20 . . . 200 B6
Hidcote Ho 11 SM2 . . . . 218 A1
Hide E6 . . . . 100 C1
Hide Pl SW1 . . . . 115 D2 259 C3
Hider Ct SE3 . . . . 143 C5
Hide Rd HA1 . . . . 42 B5
Hide Twr SW1 . . . . 259 C3
Hieover SE21 . . . . 161 A2
Higgins Ho 7 N1 . . . . 95 C6
Higginson Ho 2 NW3 . . . 70 D1
Higgins Wlk TW12 . . . . . 173 A4
Higgs Ind Est 9 SE24 . . 138 D2
High Acre EN2 . . . . 4 D2
Higham Ct 9 IG8 . . . . 37 A4
HIGHAM HILL 35 A2
Higham Hill Ho E17 . . . . . 34 D2
Higham Hill Rd E17 . . . . . 35 A1
Higham Ho E4 . . . . 35 C4
Higham Mews UB5 . . . . . . 85 B3
Higham Pl E17 . . . . 53 A6
Higham Rd
Tottenham N17 . . . . 51 B6
Woodford IG8 . . . . 37 A4
Highams Lodge Bsns Ctr
E17 . . . . 52 D6
HIGHAMS PARK 36 A3
Highams Park Sch E4 . . . 36 B4
Highams Park Sta E4 . . . 36 B4
Higham St E17 . . . . 53 A6
Higham Station Ave E4 . 35 D4
Highams The E17 . . . . 36 A2
High Ashton 11 KT2 . . . 176 D3
Highbanks Cl DA16 . . . . 146 B5
Highbanks Rd HA5 . . . . . . 23 D4
Highbank Way N8 . . . . 50 C3
HIGH BARNET 1 B2
High Barnet Sta EN5 . . . . . 1 C1
Highbarrow Rd CR0 . . . . 206 A1
High Beech
South Croydon CR2 . . . . 221 C1
Southgate N21 . . . . 16 B5
High Beeches DA14 . . . . 191 A5
High Birch Ct 7 EN4 . . . . . 2 C1
Highbridge Ct 13
SE14 . . . . 140 C5
Highbridge Rd IG11 . . . . 100 D6
High Bridge Wharf
SE10 . . . . 120 B1
Highbrook Rd SE3 . . . . . 143 D2
High Broom Cres BR4 . . 207 D2
Highburty Mans 24 N1 . . 72 D1
HIGHBURY 72 D4
Highbury Ave CR7 . . . . . 182 D1
Highbury Cl
New Malden KT3 . . . . . . 199 A4
West Wickham BR4 . . . . 223 D6
Highbury Cnr N5 . . . . 72 D2
Highbury Corner N5 . . . . 72 D2
Highbury Cres N5 . . . . . . 72 C3
Highbury Fields Sch
N5 . . . . 72 D3
Highbury Gdns IG3 . . . . . 79 C6
Highbury Gr N5 . . . . 72 D3
Highbury Grange N5 . . . . 73 A4
Highbury Grove Ct N5 . . . 72 D2
Highbury Grove Sch
N5 . . . . 73 A3
Highbury Hill N5 . . . . 72 D4
Highbury & Islington Sta
N1 . . . . 72 D2
Highbury New Pk N5 . . . . 73 A4
Highbury Pk N5 . . . . 72 D4
Highbury Pl N5 . . . . 72 D3
Highbury Quadrant N5 . . 73 A5
Highbury Quadrant Prim
Sch N5 . . . . 73 A4
Highbury Rd SW19 . . . . . 179 A5
Highbury Sq N14 . . . . 15 C3
Highbury Station Rd
N1 . . . . 72 C2
Highbury Terr N5 . . . . 72 D3
Highbury Terrace Mews
N5 . . . . 72 D3
High Cedar Dr SW20 . . . 178 B3
Highclears 6 IG9 . . . . 21 B2
Highclere Rd KT3 . . . . . . 199 B6
Highclere St SE26 . . . . . 185 A6
Highcliffe
Beckenham BR3 . . . . 185 D2
Ealing W13 . . . . 87 B2
Highcliffe Dr SW15 . . . . 155 D5
Highcliffe Gdns IG4 . . . . . 56 A4
Highcombe SE7 . . . . 143 B6
Highcombe Cl SE9 . . . . . 166 A3
High Coombe Pl KT2 . . . 177 B3
Highcroft Highgate N6 . . . 49 A3
Hyde The NW9 . . . . 45 C4
2 Kingston u T KT5 . . . . 198 B4
Highcroft Ave HA0 . . . . . . 88 C6
Highcroft Gdns NW11 . . . 47 B3
Highcroft Point E17 . . . . . 35 D2
Highcroft Rd N19 . . . . 50 A2
High Cross Ctr The
N15 . . . . 52 A5
High Cross Rd N17 . . . . . . 52 A6
Highcross Way 4
SW15 . . . . 156 A3
Highdaun Dr SW16 . . . . . 204 B5
High Dene EN2 . . . . 4 D2
Highdown KT4 . . . . 215 D6
Highdown Rd SW15 . . . . 156 B5
High Dr KT2, KT3 . . . . 177 A1
High Elms IG8 . . . . 37 A5
High Elms Ctry Pk*
BR6 . . . . 227 A1
High Elms Rd BR6 . . . . . . 227 A1
Highfield WD23 . . . . 8 C2
Highfield Ave
Erith DA8 . . . . 147 D6
Greenford UB6 . . . . 64 D3
Hendon NW11 . . . . 47 A2
Kingsbury NW9 . . . . 45 A4
Orpington BR6 . . . . 227 D3
Pinner HA5 . . . . 41 B4
Wembley HA9 . . . . 66 B5
Highfield Cl
Hither Green SE13 . . . . . 164 B5
Kingsbury NW9 . . . . 45 A4
Long Ditton KT6 . . . . 197 C1
Wood Green N22 . . . . 32 C2
Highfield Ct
7 Barnet EN5 . . . . 1 D1
Hendon NW11 . . . . 47 A3
Mitcham CR4 . . . . 202 C5
Southgate N14 . . . . 15 C5
Wanstead E12 . . . . 77 C6
Highfield Dr
Beckenham BR2 . . . . 208 D5
Ickenham UB10 . . . . 60 A5
West Ewell KT19 . . . . 215 D2
West Wickham BR4 . . . . 224 A5
Highfield Gdns NW11 . . . 47 A3
Highfield Hill SE19 . . . . 183 C3
Highfield Ho N21 . . . . 16 D3
Highfield Inf Sch BR2 . . 208 C5
Highfield Jun Sch
BR2 . . . . 208 C5
Highfield Mews NW6 . . . . 69 D1
Highfield Prim Sch
Edmonton N21 . . . . 17 A3
Hillingdon UB10 . . . . 82 D4
Highfield Rd Acton W3 . . . 89 A2
Bexley DA6 . . . . 169 B6
Bromley BR1 . . . . 210 B5
Carshalton SM1 . . . . 218 C3
Edmonton N21 . . . . 16 D2
Feltham TW13 . . . . 150 A2
Hendon NW11 . . . . 47 A3
Hounslow TW7 . . . . 130 D4
Orpington BR5, BR7 . . . . 211 D6
St Paul's Cray BR5, BR7 . 211 D6
Tolworth KT5 . . . . 199 A2
Upper Halliford TW16 . . . 193 D4
Walton-on-T KT12 . . . . . . 194 A1
Highfields SM1 . . . . 217 C6
Highfield Sch SW18 . . . . 158 C4
Highfields Gr N6 . . . . 48 D1
High Foleys KT10 . . . . . . 213 B1
High Gables
Beckenham BR2 . . . . 186 C1
Loughton IG10 . . . . 21 D6
High Garth KT10 . . . . 212 A2
HIGHGATE 49 A2
Highgate Archway N6 . . . 49 C1
Highgate Ave N6 . . . . 49 B2
Highgate Ballet Sch
NW11 . . . . 47 D5
Highgate Cemetery*
N19 . . . . 71 B6
Highgate Cl N6 . . . . 49 A2
High Gate Edge N2 . . . . . 48 C4
Highgate High St N6 . . . . 49 B1
Highgate Hill N19 . . . . . . 49 C1
Highgate Ho 11 SE26 . . . 162 A1
Highgate Hts N6 . . . . 49 C3
Highgate Prim Sch N6 . . 48 D3
Highgate Private Hospl
N6 . . . . 48 D3
Highgate Rd NW5 . . . . . . 71 B4
Highgate Sch
Highgate N6 . . . . 48 D2
Highgate N6 . . . . 49 A2
Highgate Spinney N8 . . . 49 D3
Highgate Sta N6 . . . . 49 B3
Highgate West Hill N6 . . 71 A6
Highgate Wlk SE23 . . . . 162 C2
Highgate Wood Sec Sch
N8 . . . . 49 C4
High Gr Bromley BR1 . . . . 187 D2
Woolwich SE18 . . . . 145 B4
Highgrove Cl
London N11 . . . . 31 A5
Widmore BR7 . . . . 188 A2
Highgrove Ct BR3 . . . . . 185 C3
Highgrove Ho HA4 . . . . . . 40 A3
Highgrove Mews SM5 . . 218 D5
Highgrove Point 2
NW3 . . . . 70 A4
Highgrove Rd RM8 . . . . . . 80 C4
Highgrove Way HA4 . . . . . 40 A2
High Hill Ferry 3 E5 . . . . 52 B1
High Holborn
WC1 . . . . 94 B2 240 C3
High Holborn Ho WC1 . 240 D3
High La W7 . . . . 86 B1
Highland Ave W7 . . . . 86 C1
Highland Cotts SM6 . . . . 219 C4
Highland Croft BR3 . . . . 185 D4
Highland Ct E18 . . . . 37 B2
Highland Dr WD23 . . . . 8 A4
Highland Lo 3 SE19 . . . 183 D3
Highland Pk TW13 . . . . . 171 D6
Highland Rd
Bexley DA6 . . . . 147 C1
Bromley BR1 . . . . 186 D2
Pinner HA6 . . . . 22 A1
West Norwood SE19 . . . . 183 C4
Highlands N20 . . . . 14 B2
Highlands Ave
Acton W3 . . . . 111 A6
Southgate N21 . . . . 16 B6
Highlands Cl
Hornsey N4 . . . . 50 A2
Hounslow TW3 . . . . 129 D4
Highlands Ct SE19 . . . . . 183 C4
Highlands Gdns IG1 . . . . 56 B1
Highlands Heath
SW15 . . . . 156 C4
Highlands Prim Sch
IG1 . . . . 56 B1
Highlands Rd EN5 . . . . . . 13 C6
Highlands Sch N21 . . . . . . 4 C1
Highlands The
Barnet EN5 . . . . 1 D1
Edgware HA8 . . . . 26 D1
Highlawn Hall HA1 . . . . . 64 C5
Highlea Cl NW9 . . . . 27 C2
High Level Dr SE26 . . . . 184 A6
Highlever Rd W10 . . . . . . 90 C2
High Limes 2 SE19 . . . . 183 C4
High London 5 N6 . . . . . 49 D2
Highmead
9 Edmonton N18 . . . . 34 A5
Plumstead Comm SE18 . 145 D5
High Mead Harrow HA1 . . 42 D4
West Wickham BR4 . . . . . 224 C6
Highmead Cres HA0 . . . . 66 B1
High Meadow Cl HA5 . . . 40 C5
High Meadow Cres
NW9 . . . . 45 B4
High Meads Rd E16 . . . . . 99 D1
Highmore Rd SE3 . . . . . 142 C5
High Mount
Hendon NW4 . . . . 46 A3
11 Hornsey N4 . . . . 50 A2
High Oaks EN2 . . . . 4 B5
High Oaks Lo 9 E18 . . . . 37 A1
High Park Ave TW9 . . . . 132 C4
High Park Rd TW9 . . . . . 132 C4
High Par The SW16 . . . . 160 A1
High Path SW19 . . . . 180 A2
Highpoint EN5 . . . . 14 A6
High Point
Chislehurst SE9 . . . . 166 D1
Highgate N6 . . . . 49 A2
High Range SW20 . . . . . . 178 C3
High Rd
Buckhurst Hill IG9,
IG10 . . . . 21 C5
Bushey WD23 . . . . 8 B3
Chadwell Heath RM6 . . . . 58 C2
East Finchley N2 . . . . 48 C6
Finchley N2, N12 . . . . 30 A3
Friern Barnet N11 . . . . 31 B5
Harrow HA3 . . . . 24 C3
Ilford IG1 . . . . 78 D6
Leyton E10 . . . . 53 D3
Oakleigh Pk N20 . . . . 14 A4
Seven Kings IG1, IG3 . . . . 79 C6
South Tottenham N15,
N17 . . . . 51 D5
Tottenham N17 . . . . 33 D2
Wembley HA0, HA9 . . . . . . 66 A3
Willesden NW10 . . . . 68 A2
Woodford E18 . . . . 37 A2
Wood Green N22 . . . . 32 B3
High Ridge N10 . . . . 31 B2
Highridge Pl EN2 . . . . 4 B5
High Road Buckhurst Hill
5 IG9 . . . . 21 B2
High Road Eastcote
HA5 . . . . 40 B4
High Road, Ickenham
UB10 . . . . 61 A6
High Road Leyton E10 . . . 75 D6
High Road Leytonstone
E11 . . . . 76 C6
High Road Woodford Gn
IG8 . . . . 37 A6
High St Mews SW19 . . . . 179 A5
High St N Newham E6 . . . 100 A6
Plashet E12 . . . . 78 A2
High St S E6 . . . . 100 B4
High Sheldon N6 . . . . 48 D3
Highshore Rd SE15 . . . . 139 D3
Highshore Sch SE15 . . . 139 D4
High Silver IG10 . . . . 21 D6
High St Acton W3 . . . . 110 D5
Barnet EN5 . . . . 1 B1
Beckenham BR3 . . . . 185 C1
Brentford TW8 . . . . 132 A6
Bromley BR1 . . . . 187 A1
Cheam SM1, KT17 . . . . . . 217 A2
Claygate KT10 . . . . 212 D2
Cranford TW5 . . . . 128 B5
Croydon CR0 . . . . 221 A5
Ealing W5 . . . . 109 D6
East Molesey KT8 . . . . . . 195 C5
Elstree WD6 . . . . 9 D5
Farnborough BR6 . . . . . . 227 A3
Feltham TW13 . . . . 150 A2
Green Street Green
BR6 . . . . 227 D2
Hampton TW12 . . . . 174 A4
Harlington UB3 . . . . 127 B6
Harrow on t H HA1 . . . . . . 42 C1
Hornsey N8 . . . . 50 B5
Hounslow TW3 . . . . 129 D2
Ilford IG6 . . . . 57 A6
Kingston u T KT1 . . . . 175 D2
Kingston u T KT1 . . . . 197 D6
Mill Hill NW7 . . . . 28 B5
Newham E13 . . . . 99 A5
New Malden KT3 . . . . 199 C5
Palmers Green N14 . . . . . . 15 D2
Penge SE20 . . . . 184 D3
Pinner HA5 . . . . 41 A6
Ruislip HA4 . . . . 39 C1
Shepperton TW17 . . . . . . 193 A3
Sidcup DA14 . . . . 190 A6
Southall UB1 . . . . 107 B5
South Norwood CR7 . . . . 205 B5
South Norwood SE25 . . . 206 A5
Stratford Marsh E15 . . . . . 98 A6
Sutton SM1 . . . . 217 D4
Sutton SM1, SM2 . . . . 217 D3
Teddington TW11 . . . . . . 175 A5
Thames Ditton KT7 . . . . . 197 A3
Twickenham TW2 . . . . . . 152 A4
Wallington SM5 . . . . 219 A4
Walthamstow E17 . . . . 53 B5
Walton-on-T KT12 . . . . . . 194 A1
Wanstead E11 . . . . 55 A4
Wealdstone HA3 . . . . 24 C1
Wealdstone HA3 . . . . 42 C6
Wembley HA9 . . . . 66 B4
West Wickham BR4 . . . . . 207 D1
Wimbledon SW19 . . . . . . 178 D5
Yiewsley UB7 . . . . 104 A6
Highstone Ave E11 . . . . . 55 A3
Highstone Ct E11 . . . . 54 D3
High Street Collier's Wood
SW17, SW19 . . . . 180 B4
High Street Harlesden
NW10 . . . . 89 D5
High Street Harlington
TW6 . . . . 127 B5
High Street Kensington
Sta W8 . . . . . . 113 D4 245 C1
High The SW16 . . . . 160 A1
High Timber St EC4 . . . . 252 A6
High Tor Cl BR1 . . . . 187 B3
High Tor View SE28 . . . . 123 C5
High Trees Cheam SM3 . . 201 B2
Croydon CR0 . . . . 207 A1
East Barnet EN4 . . . . 14 C6
Streatham SW2 . . . . 160 C3
Uxbridge UB10 . . . . 61 A6
Whetstone N20 . . . . 14 A1
Hightrees Ct W7 . . . . 108 C6
Hightrees Ho SW12 . . . . 159 A5
Highview Crouch End N6 . . 49 C3
Hornsey N8 . . . . 50 A2
Northolt UB5 . . . . 85 A4
Woolwich SE18 . . . . 144 D5
High View
6 Penge SE19 . . . . 183 D3
Pinner HA5 . . . . 40 C6
Highview Ave HA8 . . . . . . 27 A6
High View Ave CR0,
SM6 . . . . 220 B3
High View Cl
Loughton IG10 . . . . 21 C6
South Norwood SE19 . . . 183 D1
Highview Ct
2 Loughton IG10 . . . . 21 D6
2 Putney SW19 . . . . 157 A3
High View Ct HA3 . . . . . . 24 C3
Highview Gdns
Edgware HA8 . . . . 27 A6
Hendon N3 . . . . 47 A6
New Southgate N11 . . . . . 31 C5
Highview Ho
2 Buckhurst Hill IG9 . . . . 21 D1
1 Buckhurst Hill IG9 . . . . 21 D1
High View Ho RM6 . . . . . . 59 A5
High View Par 1 IG4 . . . 56 B4
High View Prim Sch
London SW11 . . . . 136 B1
Wallington SM6 . . . . 220 A3
Highview Rd Ealing W13 . 87 A1
Sidcup DA14 . . . . 190 B6
High View Rd
London N10 . . . . 30 D2
Snaresbrook E18 . . . . 54 D6
South Norwood SE19 . . . 183 B4
Highway Bsns Pk The 7
E1 . . . . 118 D6
Highway The
Shadwell E1 . . . . 118 C6

Highway The *continued*
Stanmore HA7 ... 25 A3
Highway Trad Ctr The 6
E1 ... 118 D6
High Wigsell TW11 ... 175 A5
Highwood IG8 ... 36 D6
Highwood Ave N12 ... 30 A6
Highwood Cl
Dulwich SE22 ... 162 A3
Orpington BR6 ... 227 A6
Highwood Ct
Barnet EN5 ... 13 C6
Whetstone N12 ... 14 A1
Highwood Dr BR6 ... 227 A6
Highwood Gdns IG5 ... 56 B5
Highwood Gr NW7 ... 27 B5
Highwood Hill NW7 ... 11 D2
Highwood Rd N19 ... 72 A5
High Worple HA2 ... 41 B1
Highworth Rd N11 ... 31 D5
Highworth St NW1 ... 237 B4
Hilary Ave CR4 ... 203 A6
Hilary Cl Bexley DA8 ... 147 D4
Walham Green SW6 ... 265 C4
Hilary Ct N9 ... 18 D3
Hilary Rd W12 ... 111 D6
Hilbert Rd SM3 ... 216 D5
Hilborough Cl SW19 ... 180 A3
Hilborough Ct 1 E8 ... 95 D6
Hilborough Rd 1 E8 ... 73 D1
Hilborough Way BR6 ... 227 B3
Hilda Lockert Wlk
SW9 ... 138 D3
Hilda Rd Newham E16 ... 98 C3
Upton Pk E6 ... 77 D1
Hilda Terr 2 SW9 ... 138 C3
Hilda Vale Cl BR6 ... 226 D4
Hilda Vale Rd BR6 ... 226 D4
Hildenborough Gdns
BR1 ... 186 D4
Hildenbrough Ho BR3 ... 185 B3
Hildenlea Pl BR2 ... 186 C1
Hilditch Ho 7 TW10 ... 154 B5
Hildred Ho SW1 ... 258 C4
Hildreth St SW12 ... 159 B3
Hildreth Street Mews 2
SW12 ... 159 B3
Hildyard Rd SW6 ... 265 B6
Hiley Rd NW10 ... 90 C4
Hilfield La WD23 ... 8 C6
Hilgrove Rd NW6 ... 70 A1
Hiliary Gdns HA7 ... 25 C1
Hillary Cres KT12 ... 194 C1
Hillary Ct
3 Chislehurst SE9 ... 166 A2
13 Shepherd's Bush
W12 ... 112 C4
Stanwell TW19 ... 148 A3
Hillary Dr TW7 ... 152 D6
Hillary Rd UB2 ... 107 C3
Hillary Rise EN5 ... 1 C1
Hillbeck Cl
Deptford SE15 ... 140 C5
Deptford SE15 ... 140 C6
Hillbeck Way UB6 ... 86 B6
Hillborne Cl UB3 ... 106 A1
Hillboro Ct
Leytonstone E11 ... 54 B2
1 Woodford E18 ... 36 D2
Hillborough Ct HA1 ... 42 C2
Hillbrook Rd SW17 ... 181 A6
Hillbrook Sch SW17 ... 181 A6
Hillbrow
Kingston u T KT3 ... 199 D6
7 Richmond TW10 ... 154 A5
Hill Brow BR1 ... 187 D2
Hillbrow Ct KT10 ... 212 A4
Hillbrow Rd
Catford BR1 ... 186 C4
Esher KT10 ... 212 A4
Hill Bunker's DA17 ... 125 C2
Hillbury Ave HA3 ... 43 B4
Hillbury Rd SW17 ... 159 B1
Hill Cl Barnet EN5 ... 12 C6
Chislehurst BR7 ... 188 D5
Dollis Hill NW2 ... 68 B5
Hampstead Garden Suburb
NW11 ... 47 C3
Harrow HA1 ... 64 C5
Stanmore HA7 ... 25 B6
Hillcote Ave SW16 ... 182 C3
Hillcourt N6 ... 49 C3
Hillcourt Ave N12 ... 29 D4
Hillcourt Rd SE22 ... 162 B5
Hill Cres Harrow HA1 ... 43 A4
Kingston u T KT5 ... 198 B4
North Cheam KT4 ... 216 C6
Totteridge N20 ... 13 D2
Hillcrest
Camberwell SE24 ... 139 B1
Highgate N6 ... 49 A2
Notting Hill W11 ... 244 C5
Southgate N21 ... 16 C4
Hill Crest DA15 ... 168 B4
Hillcrest Ave
Edgware HA8 ... 26 D6
Pinner HA5 ... 40 D5
Temple Fortune NW11 ... 47 B4
Hillcrest Cl
Beckenham BR3 ... 207 B3
Forest Hill SE26 ... 184 A6
Hillcrest Ct
Brondesbury NW2 ... 69 A3
8 Edgware HA8 ... 26 D5
Lewisham SE6 ... 164 B4
Sutton SM2 ... 218 B2
Hillcrest Gdns
Dollis Hill NW2 ... 68 A5
Hendon N3 ... 47 A5
Hinchley Wood KT10 ... 212 D5
Hillcrest Hts W5 ... 88 A3
Hillcrest Rd Acton W3 ... 110 D5
Chingford E17 ... 36 B1
Ealing W5 ... 88 A2
Grove Pk BR1 ... 187 A6
Loughton IG10 ... 21 D5
Woodford E18 ... 37 A1
Hillcrest View BR3 ... 207 B3
Hillcroft Ave HA5 ... 41 B3
Hillcroft Coll KT6 ... 198 A3
Hillcroft Cres Ealing W5 ... 87 D1
Ruislip HA4 ... 62 D5
Wembley HA9 ... 66 B4
Hillcroft Rd E6 ... 100 D2
Hillcroome Rd SM2 ... 218 B2
Hillcross Ave SM4 ... 201 A4
Hillcross Prim Sch
SM4 ... 201 B5
Hill Ct Barnet EN4 ... 2 C1
Ealing W5 ... 88 B3
Hampstead NW3 ... 70 C4
8 Norbiton KT2 ... 176 D3
Northolt UB5 ... 63 C3
Putney SW15 ... 156 D6
14 Surbiton KT6 ... 198 A4
Wembley HA0 ... 65 A4
9 Wimbledon SW19 ... 179 A4
Hilldale Rd SM1 ... 217 B4
Hilldown Ct SW16 ... 182 A3
Hilldown Rd
Hayes BR2 ... 208 D1
South Norwood SW16 ... 182 B3
Hill Dr London NW9 ... 45 A1
Thornton Heath SW16 ... 204 B6
Hilldrop Cres N7 ... 71 D3
Hilldrop La N7 ... 71 D3
Hilldrop Rd
Bromley BR1 ... 187 B4
Kentish Town N7 ... 71 D3
Hill End Orpington BR6 ... 227 D6
Shooters Hill SE18 ... 144 C4
Hillersdon Ave
Barnes SW13 ... 134 A3
Edgware HA8 ... 26 B5
Hillersdon Ho SW1 ... 258 C2
Hillery Cl SE17 ... 262 D3
Hill Farm Rd W10 ... 90 D2
Hillfield Ave
Colindale NW9 ... 45 C5
Hornsey N8 ... 50 A5
Mitcham SM4 ... 202 C4
Wembley HA0 ... 66 B1
Hillfield Cl HA2 ... 42 A5
Hillfield Ct NW3 ... 70 C3
Hillfield Ho N5 ... 73 A3
Hillfield La S WD23 ... 8 D5
Hillfield Lo SW17 ... 180 D5
Hillfield Mans NW3 ... 70 C3
Hillfield Par SM4 ... 202 B3
Hillfield Park Mews
N10 ... 49 B5
Hillfield Pk London N10 ... 49 B5
Southgate N21 ... 16 C2
Hillfield Rd
Hampton TW12 ... 173 B2
West Hampstead NW6 ... 69 C3
Hillgate Pl
Balham SW12 ... 159 B4
Kensington W8 113 C5 245 A4
Hillgate St W8 ... 245 A4
Hill Gate Wlk N6 ... 49 C3
Hill Gr TW13 ... 151 B2
Hill Ho Southall UB1 ... 85 C1
Stanmore HA7 ... 9 A1
Upper Clapton E5 ... 52 B1
Woolwich SE28 ... 123 C5
Hill House Ave HA7 ... 24 D3
Hill House Cl N21 ... 16 C4
Hill House Dr TW12 ... 173 C2
Hill House Rd SW16 ... 182 B5
Hill House Sch
SW1 ... 114 D3 257 D5
Hilliard Ct SM6 ... 219 D2
Hilliard Ho 15 E1 ... 118 B5
Hilliard's Ct E1 ... 118 C5
Hillier Cl EN5 ... 13 D5
Hillier Gdns CR0 ... 220 C3
Hillier Ho 1 NW1 ... 71 D1
Hillier Lo TW12 ... 174 B5
Hillier Pl KT9 ... 213 D2
Hillier Rd SW11 ... 158 D5
Hilliers Ave UB8 ... 82 C4
Hillier's La CR0, SM6 ... 220 A5
HILLINGDON ... 82 D5
Hillingdon Ave TW19 ... 148 A3
Hillingdon Circus UB10 ... 60 D2
HILLINGDON HEATH ... 82 D2
Hillingdon Hill UB10 ... 82 B4
Hillingdon Hospl UB8 ... 82 B2
Hillingdon Manor Sch
UB8 ... 82 D2
Hillingdon Par 6 UB10 ... 82 D3
Hillingdon Prim Sch
UB10 ... 82 D4
Hillingdon Rd UB10 ... 82 A5
Hillingdon St SE17 ... 138 D6
Hillingdon Sta UB10 ... 60 D3
Hillington Gdns IG8 ... 37 D1
Hill La HA4 ... 39 A1
Hill Lo SW11 ... 136 B1
Hillman Cl UB8 ... 60 A3
Hillman Dr 12 NW10 ... 90 C3
Hillman St E8 ... 74 B2
Hillmarton Rd N7 ... 72 A3
Hillmead Dr SW9 ... 138 D1
Hill Mead Prim Sch
SW9 ... 138 D1
Hillmont Rd KT10 ... 212 C5
Hillmore Ct SE13 ... 142 B2
Hillmore Gr SE26 ... 185 A5
Hill Rd Carshalton SM5 ... 218 C2
Finchley N10 ... 30 D2
Harrow HA1 ... 43 A4
Mitcham CR4 ... 181 B3
Pinner HA5 ... 41 A3
St John's Wood
NW8 ... 92 A5 229 B3
Sutton SM1 ... 217 D3
Wembley HA0 ... 65 B5
Hillreach SE7, SE18 ... 122 B1
Hillrise KT12 ... 193 D2
Hill Rise
East Finchley NW11 ... 47 D5
Enfield N9 ... 18 B5
Forest Hill SE23 ... 162 B3
Greenford UB6 ... 86 A6
Hinchley Wood KT10 ... 213 B6
Richmond TW10 ... 153 D6
Ruislip HA4 ... 39 B1
Hillrise Mans N19 ... 50 A2
Hillrise Rd N19 ... 50 A2
Hillsboro Rd SE22 ... 161 C6
Hillsborough Ct 13
NW6 ... 91 D6
Hillsde 6 SM1 ... 218 B3
Hillsgrove Cl DA16 ... 146 C5
Hillsgrove Prim Sch
DA16 ... 146 C5
Hillside Barnet EN5 ... 14 A6
Crouch End N8 ... 49 D3
Greenwich SE10 ... 142 B5
Kingsbury NW9 ... 45 B5
Stonebridge NW10 ... 89 B6
Wimbledon SW19 ... 178 D4
Hill Side EN5 ... 14 A6
Hillside Ave London N11 ... 30 D4
Wembley HA9 ... 66 B4
Woodford IG8 ... 37 C5
Hillside Cl Merton SM4 ... 201 A5
St John's Wood NW8 ... 91 D5
Woodford IG8 ... 37 C5
Hillside Cres Enfield EN2 ... 5 B5
Harrow HA2 ... 42 A1
Northwood HA6 ... 22 A2
Hillside Ct
Hampstead NW3 ... 69 D3
7 Kingston u T KT2 ... 176 D3
Hillside Dr HA8 ... 26 C5
Hillside Gdns
Chipping Barnet EN5 ... 1 A1
Edgware HA8 ... 26 B6
Friern Barnet N11 ... 31 C4
Harrow HA3 ... 44 A2
Highgate N6 ... 49 B3
Northwood HA6 ... 22 B2
Streatham SW2 ... 160 C2
Wallington SM6 ... 219 C1
Walthamstow E17 ... 54 B6
Hillside Glen CR0 ... 220 D4
Hillside Gr Hendon NW7 ... 28 A3
Southgate N14 ... 15 D4
Hillside Ho CR0 ... 220 D4
Hillside Jun & Inf Schs
HA6 ... 22 A3
Hillside La BR2 ... 224 D6
Hillside Mans EN5 ... 1 B1
Hillside Rd
Beckenham BR2 ... 208 D6
Belmont SM2 ... 217 B1
Croydon CR0 ... 220 D4
Ealing W5 ... 88 A2
Northwood HA6, HA5 ... 22 B3
Southall UB1 ... 85 C3
South Tottenham N15 ... 51 C3
Streatham SW2 ... 160 C2
Surbiton KT5 ... 198 C4
Hillside Rise HA6 ... 22 A3
Hillsleigh Rd
W14 ... 113 B5 244 D4
Hillsley DA14 ... 190 A6
Hills Mews 2 W5 ... 110 A6
Hills Pl W1 ... 239 A1
Hills Rd IG9 ... 21 B3
Hill St
Mayfair W1 ... 115 B5 248 C4
Richmond TW10 ... 153 D6
Hillstone Ct 5 E3 ... 97 D3
Hillstowe St E5 ... 74 C5
Hilltop 2 E17 ... 53 D6
Hill Top Cheam SM3 ... 201 B2
East Finchley NW11 ... 47 D5
Hilltop Ave NW10 ... 67 A1
Hilltop Ct
12 London SW18 ... 136 B1
South Hampstead NW8 ... 70 A1
South Norwood SE19 ... 183 B2
Hilltop Gdns
Hendon NW4 ... 28 B1
Orpington BR6 ... 227 C6
Hilltop Ho 7 N6 ... 49 D2
Hilltop Rd NW6 ... 69 C1
Hilltop Way HA7 ... 9 A1
Hillview SW20 ... 178 B3
Hill View Mitcham CR4 ... 204 A5
Primrose Hill NW1 ... 230 D6
Hillview Ave HA3 ... 44 A4
Hillview Cl Pinner HA5 ... 23 B4
Wembley HA9 ... 66 B6
Hillview Cres
Orpington BR6 ... 211 D1
Redbridge IG1 ... 56 B3
Hillview Ct SE19 ... 183 C6
Hill View Dr
Bexley DA16 ... 145 C3
Woolwich SE28 ... 123 C5
Hillview Gdns
Harrow HA2 ... 41 C5
Hendon NW4 ... 46 D5
Hill View Gdns NW9 ... 45 B4
Hillview Rd
Carshalton SM1 ... 218 B5
Chislehurst BR7 ... 188 D6
Mill Hill NW7 ... 28 D6
Pinner HA5 ... 23 B4
Hill View Rd
Claygate KT10 ... 213 A1
Orpington BR6 ... 227 D6
Twickenham TW1 ... 153 A5
Hillway Highgate N6 ... 71 A6
London NW9 ... 45 C1
Hill Wood Ho NW1 ... 232 C3
Hillworth 7 BR3 ... 185 D1
Hillworth Rd SW2 ... 160 C4
Hillyard Rd W7 ... 86 C2
Hillyard St SW9 ... 138 C4
Hillyfield E17 ... 35 A1
Hillyfield Cl E9 ... 75 A3
Hillyfield Prim Sch E17 ... 53 A6
Hilly Fields Cres SE4 ... 141 C2
Hilly Mead SW19 ... 179 A3
Hilsea Point 7 SW15 ... 156 B3
Hilsea St E5 ... 74 C4
Hilton Ave N12 ... 30 B5
Hilton Ho 4 Ealing W13 ... 87 C1
12 Finchley N2 ... 30 B1
Lower Holloway N7 ... 72 A4
9 Nunhead SE4 ... 140 D1
Hilversum Cres 10
SE22 ... 161 C6
Himley Rd SW17 ... 180 D4
Hinchlay Manor KT10 ... 212 D5
Hinchley Cl KT10 ... 212 D5
Hinchley Dr KT10 ... 212 D5
Hinchley Way KT10 ... 213 A5
HINCHLEY WOOD ... 212 D6
Hinchley Wood Prim Sch
KT10 ... 213 A6
Hinchley Wood Sch &
Sixth Form Ctr KT10 ... 213 A6
Hinchley Wood Sta
KT10 ... 212 D5
Hinckley Rd SE15 ... 140 A1
Hind Ct EC4 ... 241 B1
Hinde Mews W1 ... 238 B2
Hindes Rd HA1 ... 42 C4
Hinde St W1 ... 93 A1 238 B2
Hind Gr E14 ... 97 C1
Hindhead Cl UB8 ... 82 D2
Hindhead Gdns UB5 ... 85 A6
Hindhead Gn WD19 ... 22 C5
Hindhead Point 6
SW15 ... 156 B3
Hindhead Way SM6 ... 220 A3
Hind Ho
13 Deptford SE14 ... 140 D6
Islington N7 ... 72 C4
Hindhurst Ct NW9 ... 45 A5
Hindle Ho E8 ... 73 D3
Hindley Ho N7 ... 72 B5
Hindlip Ho SW8 ... 269 C1
Hindmans Rd SE22 ... 162 A6
Hindmans Way RM9 ... 103 B3
Hindmarsh Cl E1 ... 118 A6
Hindrey Rd E5 ... 74 B3
Hindsley's Pl SE23 ... 162 C2
Hines Ct HA1 ... 43 A4
Hinkler Rd HA3 ... 43 D6
Hinksey Path SE2 ... 124 D3
Hinstock NW6 ... 91 D6
Hinstock Rd SE18 ... 145 A5
Hinton Ave TW4 ... 128 D1
Hinton Cl SE9 ... 166 A3
Hinton Ct 3 E10 ... 75 D6
Hinton Rd Brixton SE24 ... 138 D2
Edmonton N18 ... 33 C6
Wallington SM6 ... 219 C2
Hippisley Ct TW7 ... 130 D2
Hippodrome Mews
W11 ... 244 A5
Hippodrome Pl W11 ... 244 B5
Hirst Cres HA9 ... 66 A5
Hirst Ct SW1 ... 258 C1
Hispano Mews 17 EN3 ... 7 C6
Hitcham Rd E17 ... 53 B2
Hitchcock Cl TW17 ... 192 B6
Hitchin Sq E3 ... 97 A5
Hithe Gr 15 SE16 ... 118 C3
Hitherbroom Rd UB3 ... 106 A6
Hither Farm Rd SE3 ... 143 C2
Hitherfield Prim Sch
SW16 ... 160 C2
Hitherfield Rd
Dagenham RM8 ... 81 A6
Streatham SW16,
SW27 ... 160 C1
HITHER GREEN ... 164 C5
Hither Green La SE13 ... 164 B5
Hither Green Prim Sch
SE13 ... 164 B5
Hither Green Sta
SE13 ... 164 C5
Hitherlands SW12 ... 159 B2
Hitherwell Dr HA3 ... 24 B2
Hitherwood Ct SE21 ... 183 D6
Hitherwood Dr SE19 ... 183 D6
Hive Cl WD23 ... 8 B2
Hive Rd WD23 ... 8 C2
Hive Wood Ho E7 ... 77 A2
HM Prison Wormwood
Scrubs W12 ... 90 A1
HMS Belfast* SE1 ... 253 B4
Hoadly Rd SW16 ... 159 D2
Hobart Cl
East Barnet N20 ... 14 C2
Hayes UB4 ... 84 D3
Hobart Ct Harrow HA1 ... 42 C2
Woodford IG8 ... 36 D6
Hobart Dr UB4 ... 84 D3
Hobart Gdns CR7 ... 205 B6
Hobart Ho 24 KT6 ... 198 A4
Hobart La UB4 ... 84 D3
Hobart Pl
Richmond TW10 ... 154 B4
Westminster
SW1 ... 115 B3 258 C6
Hobart Rd
Dagenham RM9 ... 80 D4
Hayes UB4 ... 84 D3
North Cheam KT4 ... 216 B5
Hobbayne Prim Sch
W7 ... 86 D1
Hobbayne Rd W7 ... 86 B1
Hobbes Wlk SW15 ... 156 B6
Hobb's Ct SE1 ... 253 D2
Hobbs Gn N2 ... 48 A6
Hobbs Mews IG3 ... 79 D6
Hobbs' Pl N1 ... 95 C6
Hobbs Rd 5 SE27 ... 183 A6
Hobby St EN3 ... 18 D6
Hobday St E14 ... 97 D1
Hobhouse Ct SW1 ... 249 D5
Hobill Wlk KT5 ... 198 B3
Hoblands End BR7 ... 189 C4
Hobsons Pl 7 E1 ... 96 A2
Hobury St
SW10 ... 136 B6 266 C5
Hockenden La BR5,
BR8 ... 191 D1
Hocker St 41 E2 ... 95 D4
Hockett Cl SE8 ... 119 B2
Hockington Ct 7 EN5 ... 13 D6
Hockley Ave E6 ... 100 A5
Hockley Ct 2 E18 ... 37 A2
Hockley Ho 4 E9 ... 74 C2
Hockley Mews IG11 ... 101 C5
Hockliffe Ho 5 W10 ... 90 C2
Hockney Ct 1 SE16 ... 118 B1
Hockworth Ho 7 N16 ... 51 C1
Hocroft Ave NW2 ... 69 B5
Hocroft Ct NW2 ... 69 B5
Hocroft Rd NW2 ... 69 B5
Hocroft Wlk NW2 ... 69 B5
Hodder Dr UB6 ... 86 D5
Hoddesdon Rd DA17 ... 125 C1
Hodford Lo NW11 ... 69 C6
Hodford Rd NW11 ... 47 B1
Hodgkins Cl SE28 ... 124 D6
Hodgkins Mews HA7 ... 25 B5
Hodister Cl 26 SE5 ... 139 A5
Hodson Cl HA2 ... 63 B5
Hodson Pl EN3 ... 7 C5
Hoecroft Ct EN3 ... 6 C5
Hoe La EN1 ... 6 B5
Hoe St E17 ... 53 C4
Hoffman Gdns CR2 ... 222 B1
Hoffman Sq N1 ... 235 D2
Hofland Rd
W14 ... 113 A3 254 A6
Hogan Mews W2 ... 236 C4
Hogan Way E5 ... 74 A6
Hogarth Ave TW15 ... 171 A4
Hogarth Bsns Pk W4 ... 133 C6
Hogarth Cl Ealing W5 ... 88 A2
Newham E16 ... 99 D2
Hogarth Cres
Mitcham SW19 ... 180 B2
Thornton Heath CR0 ... 205 A2
Hogarth Ct
8 Camden Town NW1 ... 71 C1
City of London EC3 ... 253 B6
Dulwich SE19 ... 183 D6
Heston TW5 ... 129 A5
24 Whitechapel E1 ... 96 A1
Hogarth Gdns TW5 ... 129 C5
Hogarth Hill NW11 ... 47 B5
Hogarth Ho Enfield EN1 ... 18 A6
12 Northolt UB5 ... 84 D5
1 Sutton SM1 ... 218 B3
Westminster SW1 ... 259 D3
6 West Norwood
SE27 ... 183 A6
Hogarth Ind Est NW10 ... 90 A3
Hogarth La W4 ... 133 C6
Hogarth Pl SW5 ... 255 C3
Hogarth Rd Barking RM8 ... 80 B3
Earl's Ct SW5 ... 113 D2 255 C3
Edgware HA8 ... 26 C1
Hogarth Roundabout
W4 ... 133 C6
Hogarth's House*
W4 ... 133 C6
Hogarth Way TW12 ... 174 A2
Hogsmill Way KT19 ... 215 A4
Holbeach Cl 8 NW9 ... 27 C2
Holbeach Gdns DA15 ... 167 D5
Holbeach Mews 1
SW12 ... 159 B3
Holbeach Prim Sch
SE6 ... 163 C4
Holbeach Rd SE6 ... 163 D4
Holbeck Row SE15 ... 140 A5
Holbein Ho
Chelsea SW1 ... 258 A2
10 Stanmore HA7 ... 25 C5
Holbein Mews
SW1 ... 115 A1 258 A2
Holbein Pl
SW1 ... 115 A2 258 A3
Holberry Ho 5 SE21 ... 183 C6
Holberton Gdns NW10 ... 90 B4
HOLBORN ... 94 C2
Holborn EC1 ... 94 C2 241 B3
Holborn Cir EC1 ... 94 C2 241 B3
Holborn Ho 1 W12 ... 90 B1
Holborn Pl WC1 ... 240 C3
Holborn Rd E13 ... 99 B3
Holborn Sta
WC1 ... 94 B2 240 C3
Holborn Viaduct
EC1 ... 94 D2 241 C3
Holborn Way CR4 ... 180 D1
Holbrook Cl Enfield EN1 ... 6 A5
Highgate N19 ... 49 B1
Holbrook Ct W7 ... 108 C6
Holbrooke Ct N7 ... 72 A4
Holbrooke Pl 25
TW10 ... 153 D6
Holbrook Ho Acton W3 ... 89 B2
Chislehurst BR7 ... 189 B2
5 Streatham SW2 ... 160 B3
Holbrook La BR7 ... 189 B3
Holbrook Rd E15 ... 98 D5
Holbrook Way BR2 ... 210 B4
Holburne Cl SE3 ... 143 C4
Holburne Gdns SE3 ... 143 D4
Holburne Rd SE3 ... 143 D4
Holcombe Hill NW7 ... 12 A1
Holcombe Ho SW9 ... 138 A2
Holcombe Pl SE4 ... 141 A2
Holcombe Rd Ilford IG1 ... 56 C2
Tottenham Hale N17 ... 52 A6
1 Tottenham N17 ... 51 D6
Holcombe St W6 ... 112 B2
Holcote Cl DA17 ... 125 A3
Holcroft Ct W1 ... 239 A4
Holcroft Ho
Battersea SW11 ... 136 B2
Lewisham SE10 ... 142 A4
Holcroft Rd E9 ... 74 C1
Holden Ave
North Finchley N12 ... 29 D5
Welsh Harp NW9 ... 45 A1
Holdenby Rd SE4 ... 163 A6
Holden Cl RM8 ... 80 B5
Holden Ho
12 Deptford SE8 ... 141 C5
Islington N1 ... 235 A5
Holden Hts N12 ... 13 D1
Holdenhurst Ave N12 ... 30 A3
Holden Lo N11 ... 31 C5
Holden Point E15 ... 76 B2
Holden Rd N12 ... 29 D6
Holden St SW11 ... 137 A3
Holdernesse Rd
Isleworth TW7 ... 131 A4
6 Upper Tooting
SW17 ... 159 A2
Holderness Ho SE5 ... 139 C2
Holderness Way SE27 ... 182 D5
Holders Hill Ave NW4 ... 46 D6
Holders Hill Cres NW4 ... 28 D1
Holders Hill Dr NW4 ... 28 D1
Holders Hill Gdns NW4 ... 29 A1
Holders Hill Par NW7 ... 29 A2
Holders Hill Rd
Church End NW4, NW7 ... 29 A2
Hendon NW4 ... 28 D1
Holdsworth Ho 5
SW2 ... 160 C4
Holford Ho
6 Bermondsey SE16 ... 118 B2
Finsbury WC1 ... 233 D2
Holford Pl WC1 ... 233 D2
Holford Rd NW3 ... 70 A5
Holford St WC1 ... 234 A2
Holford Yd WC1 ... 234 A3
Holgate Ave SW11 ... 136 B2
Holgate Ct HA8 ... 26 B6
Holgate Gdns RM10 ... 81 C2
Holgate Rd RM10 ... 81 C3
Holgate St SE7 ... 121 D3
Holkham Ho 6 EN5 ... 1 A2
Hollam Ho N8 ... 50 B5
Holland Ave
Belmont SM2 ... 217 C1
Wimbledon SW20 ... 177 D2
Holland Cl
Coney Hall BR2 ... 224 D6
New Barnet EN5 ... 14 B4
Stanmore HA7 ... 25 B5
Holland Ct
Ashford TW15 ... 170 B4
Hendon NW7 ... 28 A4
6 Walthamstow E17 ... 54 A5
Holland Dr SE23 ... 163 A1
Holland Gdns
Brentford TW8 ... 132 A6
Kensington W14 ... 254 B6
Holland Gr SW9 ... 138 C5
Holland Ho E4 ... 36 A6
Holland House Sch
HA8 ... 26 D6
Holland Park
W11 ... 113 B5 244 C3
Holland Park Ave
Ilford IG3 ... 57 D4
Notting Hill
W11 ... 113 A5 244 B3
Holland Park Ct W14 ... 244 B2
Holland Park Gdns
W14 ... 113 A4 244 A2
Holland Park Mews
W11 ... 113 B5 244 C3
Holland Park Rd
W14 ... 113 B3 254 D5
Holland Park Rdbt
W12 ... 112 D4
Holland Park Sch
W8 ... 113 B4 244 D2
Holland Park Sta
W11 ... 113 B5 244 C3
Holland Pas N1 ... 235 A6
Holland Pl W8 ... 245 C2
Holland Rd
Croydon SE25 ... 206 A4

Holland Rd continued
Newham E15 98 C4
Wallend E6 78 C1
Wembley HA0 65 D2
West Kensington
W14 113 A3 254 B6
Willesden Green NW10 90 B5
Holland Rise Ho SW9 270 D3
Holland St
Kensington
W8 113 C4 245 B2
Lambeth SE1 116 D5 251 D4
Hollands The
Feltham TW13 172 D6
New Malden KT4 199 D1
Holland Villas Rd
W14 113 A4 244 A1
Holland Way BR2 224 D6
Holland Wlk
Kensington
W14 113 B4 244 D1
Stanmore HA7 25 A5
Upper Holloway N19 49 D1
Hollar Rd N16 73 D5
Hollen St W1 239 C2
Holles Cl TW12 173 C5
Holles Ho 8 SW9 138 C3
Holles St W1 93 B1 238 D2
Holley Rd W3 111 C4
Hollickwood Ave N12 30 D4
Hollickwood Prim Sch
N10 31 B3
Holliday Sq 7 SW11 136 B2
Hollidge Way RM10 81 D1
Hollies Ave DA15 167 D3
Hollies Cl
South Norwood
SW16 182 C4
Twickenham TW1 152 D2
Hollies End NW7 28 B5
Hollies Rd W5 109 C2
Hollies The Harrow HA3 43 A5
Oakleigh Pk N20 14 B3
Upper Tooting SW12 159 C2
9 Wanstead E11 55 A4
Wood Green N11 31 D4
Hollies Way 1 SW12 159 A4
Holligrave Rd BR1 187 A2
Hollingbourne Ave
DA7 147 B4
Hollingbourne Gdns
W13 87 B2
Hollingbourne Rd
SE24 161 A6
Hollingsworth Ct 7
KT6 197 D2
Hollingsworth Rd CR0 222 B2
Hollington Cres KT3 199 D3
Hollington Ct BR7 188 D4
Hollington Rd
Newham E6 100 B4
Tottenham N17 34 A1
Hollingworth Cl KT8 195 B5
Hollingworth Rd BR2,
BR5 210 D2
Hollins Ho N7 72 A4
Hollisfield WC1 233 B1
Hollman Gdns SW16 182 D4
Holloway Cl UB7 104 A1
Holloway La UB7 104 B1
Holloway Rd Leyton E11 76 B5
Lower Holloway N7 72 B4
Newham E6 100 B4
Upper Holloway N19 71 D6
Holloway Road Sta N7 72 B3
Holloway Sch N7 71 D3
Holloway St TW3 129 D2
Hollow Combe SE20 184 B6
Hollowfield Wlk UB5 63 A2
Hollow The IG8 36 D6
Holly Ave London N2 47 D6
Stanmore HA7 26 A1
Walton-on-T KT12 194 D1
Hollybank Cl TW12 173 C5
Holly Berry La 8 NW3 70 A4
Hollybrake Cl BR7 189 B3
Hollybush Cl
Harrow HA3 24 C2
Wanstead E11 55 A4
Hollybush Gdns E2 96 B4
Hollybush Hill E11 54 D3
Holly Bush Hill 4 NW3 70 A4
Hollybush Ho 23 E2 96 B4
Holly Bush La TW12 173 C3
Hollybush Pl E2 96 B4
Hollybush Rd KT2 176 A4
Hollybush St E13 99 B4
Holly Bush Steps 6
NW3 70 A4
Holly Bush Vale 10
NW3 70 A4
Holly Cl
Beckenham BR3 208 A5
Buckhurst Hill IG9 21 D1
Feltham TW13 173 A5
Wallington SM6 219 B1
Holly Cottage Mews
UB8 82 C2
Holly Cotts KT7 197 A1
Holly Cres
Beckenham BR3 207 B4
Chingford IG8 36 B3
Hollycroft Ave
Child's Hill NW3 69 C5
Wembley HA9 66 B5
Hollycroft Cl
Harmondsworth UB7 126 C6
South Croydon CR2 221 C3
Hollycroft Gdns UB7 126 C6
Holly Ct
16 Belmont SM2 217 C1
Catford SE6 164 A1
4 Sidcup DA14 190 B6
South Tottenham N15 51 C5
Hollydale Cl UB5 63 D4
Hollydale Dr BR2 226 B5
Hollydale Prim Sch
SE15 140 C3
Hollydale Rd SE15 140 C3
Hollydene
Bromley BR1 186 D2
Hither Green SE13 164 B5
5 Peckham SE15 140 B4
Hollydown Way E11 76 B5
Holly Dr E4 19 D4
Holly Farm Rd UB2 107 A1
Hollyfield Ave N11 30 D5
Hollyfield Rd KT5 198 B2
Hollyfield Sch & Sixth
Form Ctr The KT6 198 A4
Holly Gdns UB7 104 B4
Holly Gr Kingsbury NW9 45 A2
Peckham SE15 140 A3
Pinner HA5 23 A2
Hollygrove WD23 8 B4
Hollygrove Cl TW3 129 B1
Hollyhedge Ho SE3 142 B3
Holly Hedge Terr
SE13 164 B6
Holly Hill
Hampstead NW3 70 A4
Southgate N21 16 B5
Holly Hill Rd DA8,
DA17 125 D1
Holly Ho
Brentford TW8 131 C6
Ilford IG3 58 A1
Holly House Hospl IG9 21 B2
Holly Lo
Cottenham Pk SW20 178 B1
Harrow HA1 42 B4
Kensington W8 245 A2
Southgate N21 16 C3
4 Wimbledon SW19 179 A4
Holly Lodge
Lewisham SE13 142 B1
Southall UB2 107 B2
Holly Lodge Gdns N6 49 A1
Holly Lodge Mans N6 71 A6
Hollymead SM5 218 D5
Holly Mews SW10 256 B1
Holly Mount NW3 70 A4
Hollymount Cl 9
SE10 142 A4
Hollymount Sch
SW20 178 C2
Holly Park Est N4 50 B2
Holly Park Gdns N3 47 C6
Holly Park Prim Sch
N11 31 A5
Holly Park Rd
Ealing W7 108 D5
Friern Barnet N11 31 A5
Holly Pk East Finchley N3 47 C6
Hornsey N4 50 B2
Holly Pl NW3 70 A4
Holly Rd
6 Chiswick W4 111 B2
Hampton TW12 174 A4
Hounslow TW3 129 D1
Leytonstone E11 54 D2
Twickenham TW1 153 A3
Holly St E8 73 D1
Holly Terr N6 49 A1
Hollytree Cl SW19 156 D3
Holly Tree Ho SE4 141 B2
Holly Tree Lo EN2 4 D3
Hollyview Cl NW4 46 A3
Holly Village N6 71 B6
Holly Way CR4 203 D6
Holly Wlk Enfield EN2 5 B2
Hampstead NW3 70 A4
Hollywood Ct W5 110 B6
Hollywood Gdns UB4 84 B1
Hollywood Lofts E1 243 C5
Hollywood Mews
SW10 266 A6
Hollywood Rd
Chelsea
SW10 136 A6 266 A6
Highams Pk E4 35 A5
Hollywood Way IG8 36 B4
Holman Ho 2 E2 96 D4
Holman Hunt Ho W14 254 A1
Holman Rd
London SW11 136 B3
West Ewell KT19 215 A3
Holmbank Dr TW17 193 C5
Holmbridge Gdns EN3 6 D1
Holmbrook NW1 232 B3
Holmbrook Dr NW4 46 D4
Holmbury Cl WD23 8 C2
Holmbury Ct
Mitcham SW19 180 C3
Upper Tooting SW17 158 D1
Holmbury Gdns UB3 105 D5
Holmbury Gr CR0 223 B1
Holmbury Ho SW9 160 D6
Holmbury Manor 9
DA14 190 A6
Holmbury Pk BR7 188 A3
Holmbury View 2 E5 52 B1
Holmbush Ct NW4 46 D4
Holmbush Rd SW15 157 A5
Holmcote Gdns N5 73 A3
Holmcroft Ho 10 E17 53 D5
Holmcroft Way BR2 210 B4
Holm Ct SE12 165 B1
Holmdale Gdns NW4 46 D4
Holmdale Rd
Chislehurst BR7 189 A5
South Hampstead NW6 69 C3
Holmdale Terr N15 51 C3
Holmdene N12 29 D5
Holmdene Ave
Harrow HA2 41 D6
Hendon NW7 28 A4
Herne Hill SE24 161 A6
Holmdene Cl BR3 186 A1
Holmdene Ct BR1 210 A6
Holmead Rd
SW6 135 D5 265 D3
Holme Ct 12 TW7 131 A2
Holmefield Ct 4 NW3 70 C2
Holmefield Ho W10 91 A3
Holme Lacey Rd SE12 164 D5
Holmeleigh Ct EN3 6 C1
Holme Rd E6 100 A6
Holmes Ave
Mill Hill NW7 29 A5
Walthamstow E17 53 B6
Holmes Cl SE22 140 A1
Holmes Ct Chingford E4 20 B2
18 South Acton W4 111 A3
18 South Lambeth SW4 138 A3
Holmesdale Ave
SW14 132 D1
Holmesdale Cl SE25 205 D6
Holmesdale Ho 12
NW6 91 C6
Holmesdale Rd
Bexley DA7 146 D3
Highgate N6 49 B2
Richmond TW9 132 B4
South Norwood SE25 205 C5
Teddington TW11 175 C4
Thornton Heath CR0 205 B4
Holmesley Rd SE23 163 A5
Holmes Pl SW10 266 B6
Holmes Rd
Kentish Town NW5 71 B3
Merton SW19 180 A3
Twickenham TW1 152 D2
Holmes Terr SE1 251 A2
Holmeswood 1 SM2 217 D1
Holmeswood Ct 3 N22 32 C1
Holme Way HA7 24 D4
Holmewood Gdns
SW2 160 B4
Holmewood Rd
South Norwood SE25 205 C6
Streatham SW2 160 B4
Holmfield Ave NW4 46 D4
Holmfield Ho E17 54 B5
Holm Gr UB10 60 C1
Holmhurst
London SE13 164 B5
Wimbledon SW19 178 C3
Holmhurst Rd DA17 125 D1
Holmlea Ct CR0 221 B4
Holmleigh Prim Sch
N16 51 C1
Holmleigh Rd N16 51 C1
Holm Oak Cl SW15 157 B5
Holmoaks Ho BR3 186 A1
Holmsbury Ho 6 N7 71 D3
Holmsdale Ho
6 London N11 31 B6
24 Poplar E14 119 D6
Holmshaw Cl SE26 185 A6
Holmside Ct SW12 159 A5
Holmside Rd SW12 159 A5
Holmsley Cl KT3 199 D2
Holmsley Ho SW15 155 D4
Holmstall Ave HA8 27 A1
Holmstall Par HA8 27 A1
Holm Wlk SE3 143 A3
Holmwood 2 KT5 198 B3
Holmwood Cl
Cheam SM2 216 D1
Harrow HA2 42 A6
Northolt UB5 63 D2
Holmwood Ct
Kingston u T KT3 199 B6
Sidcup DA14 189 D5
3 Stamford Hill N16 51 D2
Holmwood Gdns
London N3 29 C1
Wallington SM6 219 B2
Holmwood Gr NW7 27 B5
Holmwood Mans W3 110 C5
Holmwood Rd
Chessington KT9 214 A3
Ilford IG3 79 C6
Holne Chase London N2 48 A3
Morden SM4 201 C3
Holne Lo N6 49 C3
Holness Rd E15 76 D2
Holocaust Meml Gdn*
W2 114 D4 247 D2
Holroyd Rd SW15 156 C6
Holsgrove Ct W3 111 C5
Holstein Way 6 DA18 125 A3
Holst Mans SW13 134 C5
Holstock Rd IG1 79 A6
Holsworth Cl HA2 42 A4
Holsworthy Ho 49 E3 97 D4
Holsworthy Sq WC1 240 D5
Holsworthy Way KT9 213 C3
Holt Cl London N10 49 A5
Woolwich SE28 124 C6
Holt Ct Greenwich SE10 142 A6
Stratford New Town E15 76 A3
Holt Ho SW2 160 C5
Holtoake Ct 1 W5 87 C3
Holtoake Ho 3 W5 87 C3
Holton St E1 96 D3
Holt Rd Newham E16 122 A5
Wembley HA0 65 C5
Holt The Morden SM4 201 C5
Wallington SM6 219 C4
Holtwhite Ave EN2 5 A3
Holtwhite's Hill EN2 4 D4
Holwell Pl HA5 41 A5
Holwood Park Ave BR2,
BR6 226 B4
Holwood Pl 7 SW4 137 D1
Holybourne Ave
SW15 156 A4
Holy Cross Prep Sch
KT2 177 A3
Holy Cross RC Prim Sch
SE6 164 A3
Holy Cross RC Sch
SW6 135 C4 265 A2
Holy Cross Sch The
KT3 199 C4
Holy Family RC Coll The
Walthamstow E17 54 A5
Walthamstow E17 54 A6
Holy Family RC Prim Sch
Kidbrooke SE9 143 C1
Poplar E14 119 C6
Holy Ghost RC Prim Sch
SW12 159 A4
Holyhead Cl Bow E3 97 C4
3 Newham E6 100 B2
Holyhead Ct KT1 197 D5
Holy Innocents RC Prim
Sch BR6 227 D5
Holyoake Ct SE16 119 B4
Holyoake Wlk
Ealing W5 87 C3
East Finchley N2 48 A6
Holyoak Rd
SE11 116 D2 261 D3
Holyport Rd SW6 134 D5
Holyrood Ave HA2 63 B4
Holyrood Gdns HA8 26 D1
Holyrood Ho N4 51 A1
Holyrood Mews 10
E16 121 A5
Holyrood Rd EN5 14 B5
Holyrood St
SE1 117 C5 253 A3
Holy Trinity CE Jun Sch
SM6 219 C4
Holy Trinity CE Prim Sch
Belgravia
SW1 115 A2 258 A4
Dalston E8 73 D2
East Finchley N2 48 B6
Forest Hill SE26 162 C2
Hampstead NW3 70 A2
Richmond TW10 132 C1
Streatham SW2 160 B4
Wimbledon SW19 179 D4
Holy Trinity Coll Prep Sch
BR1 187 C2
Holy Trinity Lamorbey CE
Prim Sch DA15 168 A3
Holy Trinity & Saint Silas
CE Prim Sch NW1 71 B1
Holywell Cl
35 Bermondsey SE16 118 B1
2 Greenwich SE3 143 A6
Stanwell TW19 148 A3
Holywell La EC2 243 B6
Holywell Lo EN2 4 B5
Holywell Row
EC2 95 C3 243 A5
Holywell Way TW19 148 A3
Homan Ct N12 30 A6
Homan Ho 6 SW4 159 D4
Homebush Ho E4 19 D4
Homecedars Ho WD23 8 B3
Homecherry Ho 5
IG10 21 D6
Home Cl
Carshalton SM5 218 D6
Northolt UB5 85 B4
Homecoppice Ho 1
BR1 186 D3
Homecroft Rd
Forest Hill SE26 184 C5
Tottenham N22 33 A2
Homecross Ho 7 W4 111 B2
Home Ct KT6 197 D4
Homedale Ho SM1 217 D4
Home Farm Cl
Thames Ditton KT7 196 D2
Upper Halliford TW17 193 C5
Home Farm Cotts
BR5 190 D2
Homefarm Rd W7 86 D1
Homefield SM4 201 C5
Home Field EN5 13 B6
Homefield Ave IG2 57 C4
Homefield Cl
Hayes UB4 84 D3
Willesden NW10 67 A2
Homefield Ct NW4 46 C5
Homefield Gdns
London N2 48 B6
Mitcham CR4, SW19 180 B1
Homefield Ho SE23 162 D1
Homefield Pk SM1,
SM2 217 D2
Homefield Pl 4
SW19 178 D5
Homefield Prep Sch
SM1 217 C3
Homefield Rd
Bromley BR1 187 C2
Burnt Oak HA8 27 B4
Chiswick W4 111 D1
Walton-on-T KT12 195 A2
Homefield Rd continued
Wembley HA0 65 B4
Wimbledon SW19 179 A4
Homefield St 14 N1 95 C5
Homefirs Ho HA9 66 B5
Homeheather Ho 5
IG4 56 B4
Homelands Dr SE19 183 C3
Home Lea BR6 227 D3
Homeleigh Ct 8
SW16 160 A1
Homeleigh Rd SE15 162 D6
Homemead SW12 159 B2
Home Mead HA7 25 C2
Homemead Rd
Bromley BR2 210 B4
Wallington CR0 203 C3
Home Office SW1 249 C1
Home Park Rd SW19 157 B1
Home Park Terr KT1 175 D1
Home Park Wlk KT1 197 D5
Home Rd SW11 136 C3
Homer Dr E14 119 C2
Homer Rd
Croydon CR0 206 D3
Homerton E9 75 A2
Homer Row W1 237 B3
Homersham Rd KT1 176 D1
Homer St W1 92 C2 237 B3
HOMERTON 74 D1
Homerton Coll of
Technology E9 74 C3
Homerton Ct 2 EN4 14 D3
Homerton Gr E9 74 D3
Homerton High St E9 74 D3
Homerton Rd E9 75 B3
Homerton Row E9 74 C3
Homerton Sta E9 74 D2
Homerton Terr E9 74 C2
Homerton University
Hospl E9 74 D3
Homesdale Cl E11 55 A4
Homesdale Rd
Bromley BR1, BR2 209 C6
Orpington BR5 211 C2
Homesfield NW11 47 C4
Homes Of Rest (CE
Temperance Society)
IG1 79 B5
Homestall Rd SE22 162 C6
Homestead Ct EN5 13 C6
Homestead Gdns
KT10 212 C3
Homestead Paddock
N14 15 B6
Homestead Pk NW2 67 D5
Homestead Rd
Dagenham RM8 81 B6
Fulham SW6 135 B5 264 D3
Homesteads The BR3 185 D4
Homestead The N11 31 B6
Homewalk Ho 1
SE26 184 C6
Homewaters Ave
TW16 171 D2
Homewillow Cl N21 16 D5
Homewood Cl TW12 173 B4
Homewood Cres BR7 189 C4
Homewood Gdns
SE25 205 C4
Homewoods 2 SW12 159 C4
Homildon Ho 10 SE26 162 A1
Homington Ct KT2 176 A3
Honduras St EC1 242 A6
Honeybourne Rd NW6 69 D3
Honeybourne Way
BR5 211 B1
Honeybrook Rd SW12,
SW4 159 C4
Honey Cl RM10 81 D2
Honeycroft Hill UB10 60 A1
Honeyden Rd DA14 191 A4
Honeyfield N4 72 C6
Honey Hill UB10 60 B1
Honey La EC2 242 B1
Honey Lane Ho SW10 265 D6
Honeyman Cl NW6 68 D1
Honeypot Bsns Ctr
HA7 26 A2
Honeypot Cl NW9 44 B5
Honeypot La HA3, HA7,
NW9 44 B6
Honeysett Rd 3 N17 33 D1
Honeysuckle Cl UB1 107 A6
Honeysuckle Ct
Ilford IG1 78 D2
2 Lee SE12 165 A4
6 Sutton SM2 217 D2
Honeysuckle Gdns
CR0 206 D1
Honeywell Jun & Inf Schs
SW11 158 D5
Honeywell Rd SW11 158 D5
Honeywood Heritage Ctr*
SM5 218 D4
Honeywood Ho 5
SE15 140 A4
Honeywood Rd
Harlesden NW10 89 D5
Isleworth TW7 131 A1
Honeywood Wlk SM5 218 D4
Honister Cl HA7 25 B2
Honister Gdns HA7 25 B2
Honister Pl HA7 25 B2
Honiton Gdns
Edgware NW7 28 D3
1 Nunhead SE15 140 C3
Honiton Ho 23 SE5 139 A3
Honiton Rd
Bexley DA16 145 D3
Honiton Rd continued
Kilburn NW6 91 B5
Honley Rd SE6 163 D4
Honnor Gdns TW7 130 B3
HONOR OAK 162 C6
Honor Oak Park Sta
SE23 162 D5
Honor Oak Pk SE23 162 D5
Honor Oak Rd SE23 162 C4
Honor Oak Rise SE23 162 C5
Honwell Ho 24 W2 91 C2
Hood Ave
East Barnet N14 15 B5
Mortlake SW14 155 A6
Hood Cl CR0 204 D1
Hoodcote Gdns N21 16 D4
Hood Ct N7 72 B5
Hood Ho 17 SE5 139 B5
Hood Lo E11 77 B6
Hood Rd SW20 177 D3
HOOK 214 A4
Hook KT6 214 A5
Hooke Ct SE10 142 A4
Hooke Ho 32 E3 97 A5
Hooker's Rd E17 52 D6
Hook Farm Rd BR2 209 D4
Hookham Ct SW8 269 C2
Hook Ho 9 SW27 182 D5
Hooking Gn HA2 41 D4
Hook La DA16 146 A1
Hook Lane Prim Sch
DA16 146 A2
Hook Rd KT19, KT17 215 A1
Hook Rise N
Surbiton KT6 214 A5
Tolworth KT6 214 D6
Hook Rise S KT6, KT9 214 D6
Hook Rise South KT6 214 A5
Hook Rise South Ind Pk
KT6 214 C5
Hooks Cl SE15 140 B4
Hookstone Way IG8 37 D3
Hook The EN5 14 B5
Hook Underpass KT6 214 A5
Hook Wlk HA8 27 A4
Hooper Dr UB8 82 D2
Hooper Ho 9 SW18 157 B6
Hooper Rd E16 99 A1
Hooper's Ct SW1 247 C1
Hooper's Mews 4
W3 111 A5
Hooper St E1 96 A1
Hoop La NW11 47 C2
Hoover Ho 5 SE6 186 A6
Hope Cl
2 Brentford TW8 110 A1
Canonbury N1 73 A2
Dagenham RM6 58 D5
Grove Pk SE12 165 B1
Sutton SM1 218 A3
1 Woodford IG8 37 C4
Hope Ct 1 SE1 118 A1
Hopedale Rd SE7 143 B6
Hopefield 3 W7 108 D5
Hopefield Ave NW6 91 A5
Hope Gdns 10 W3 110 D4
Hope Pk BR1 186 D3
Hopes Cl TW5 129 C6
Hope St SW11 136 B2
Hopetown St E1 243 D3
Hopewell St SE5 139 B5
Hop Gdns WC2 250 A5
Hopgood St 5 W12 112 C5
Hopkins Cl N10 31 A3
Hopkins Ho 17 E14 97 C1
Hopkins Mews E15 98 D6
Hopkinson Ho 1
SW11 137 A3
Hopkinson's Pl NW1 231 A6
Hopkins St W1 93 D1 239 C1
Hopley Ho W13 109 B6
Hoppers Rd N21 16 C2
Hoppett Rd E4 20 C2
Hopping La N1 72 D2
Hoppingwood Ave
KT3 199 C6
Hoppner Rd UB4 83 B5
Hop St SE10 120 D2
Hopton Ct BR2 209 A1
Hopton Gdns KT3 200 A3
Hopton Ho 5 SW9 138 D3
Hopton Par 2 SW16 182 A5
Hopton Rd
Streatham SW16 182 A5
Woolwich SE18 122 D3
Hopton's Gdns SE1 251 D4
Hopton St SE1 116 D5 251 D4
Hoptree Cl N12 29 D6
Hopwood Cl SW17 158 A1
Hopwood Rd SE17 139 B6
Hopwood Wlk E8 74 A1
Horace Rd
Forest Gate E7 77 B4
Ilford IG6 57 A4
Kingston u T KT1 198 B6
Horatio Ho
13 Haggerston E2 95 D5
4 Merton SW19 179 D3
Horatio Pl
9 Canary Wharf E14 120 A5
Merton SW19 179 C2
Horatio St 11 E2 95 D5
Horatius Way CR0 220 B2
Horbury Cres
W11 113 C6 245 A5
Horbury Lo TW12 173 C3

Horbury Mews W11 113 B6 244 D5
Horder Rd SW6 135 A4 264 B1
Hordle Prom E 15 SE15 139 D5
Hordle Prom N 4 SE15 139 D5
Hordle Prom S 7 SE15 139 D5
Horizon Bldg 22 E14 119 C6
Horizon Sch N16 73 C4
Horle Wlk SE5 138 D3
Horley Cl DA6 169 C6
Horley Rd SE9 188 A6
Hormead Rd W9 91 B3
Hornbeam Cl
Barking IG11 102 B3
Buckhurst Hill IG9 21 D1
Edgware NW7 11 D1
Ilford IG1 79 B3
Lambeth SE11 261 A4
Northolt UB5 63 B3
Hornbeam Cres TW8 131 B5
Hornbeam Gdns KT3 200 A3
Hornbeam Gr E4 20 D1
Hornbeam Ho
1 Buckhurst Hill IG9 21 D1
2 Maitland Pk NW3 70 D2
6 Penge SE20 184 D3
6 Sidcup DA15 168 A1
Hornbeam La E4 20 C6
Hornbeam Rd
Buckhurst Hill IG9 21 D1
Hayes UB4 84 C2
Hornbeam Sq 8 E3 97 B6
Hornbeams Rise N11 31 A4
Hornbeam Terr SM5 202 C1
Hornbeam Way BR2 210 C3
Hornblower Cl 2 SE16 119 A2
Hornbuckle Cl HA2 64 B6
Hornby Cl NW3 70 B1
Hornby Ho
6 Kennington SE11 138 C6
13 Richmond TW10 153 C1
Horncastle Cl SE12 165 A4
Horncastle Rd SE12 165 A4
Hornchurch N17 33 B1
Hornchurch Cl KT2 175 D6
Horndean Cl 3 SW15 156 A3
Horne Ho 4 SE18 144 A4
Horner Ct E11 76 B5
Horne Rd TW17 192 C5
Horner Hos 18 N1 95 C6
Horner La 3 CR4 180 B1
Horne Way SW15 134 C3
Hornfair Rd SE7 143 D5
Horniman Dr SE23 162 C4
Horniman Grange 7 SE23 162 C3
Horniman Mus & Gdns* SE23 162 B3
Horniman Sch SE23 162 B3
Horning Cl SE9 188 A6
Horn La Acton W3 89 A1
Greenwich SE10 121 A2
Woodford IG8 37 A3
Horn Link Way SE10 121 A2
Horn Park Cl SE12 165 B6
Horn Park La SE12 165 B5
Horn Park Prim Sch SE12 165 B4
Hornsby House Sch SW12 159 A3
Horns Croft IG11 79 C1
Horns End Pl HA5 40 C4
HORNSEY 50 A5
Hornsey Central Hospl N8 49 D4
Hornsey La N6 49 C2
Hornsey Lane Gdns N6 49 C2
Hornsey Park Rd N8 50 B6
Hornsey Rd N7, N19 72 B6
Hornsey Rise Gdns N19 50 A2
Hornsey Sch for Girls N8 50 B4
Hornsey St N7 72 B3
Hornsey Sta N8 50 B5
HORNSEY VALE 50 B4
Hornshay St SE15 140 C6
Horns Rd IG2, IG6 57 A4
Hornton Ct W8 245 B1
Hornton Pl W8 245 B1
Hornton St W8 113 C4 245 B2
Horrocks Ho SW15 156 B6
Horsa Rd Eltham SE12 165 C4
Erith DA8 147 D5
Horsebridge Cl RM9 103 A6
Horsecroft Rd HA8 27 B3
Horse & Dolphin Yd W1 249 D6
Horse Fair KT1 175 D1
Horseferry Pl SE10 142 A6
Horseferry Rd
Limehouse E14 119 A6
Westminster SW1 115 D2 259 D4
Horseferry Rd Est SW1 259 C5
Horse Guards Ave SW1 116 A5 250 A3
Horse Guards Par* SW1 115 D5 249 D3
Horse Guards Rd SW1 115 D4 249 D2
Horse Leaze E6 100 C1
Horsell Rd Islington N5 72 C3
St Paul's Cray BR5 190 B2
Horselydown La SE1 117 D5 253 C3
Horselydown Mans SE1 253 C2
Horsemongers Mews SE1 252 B1
Horsenden Ave UB6 64 D3
Horsenden Cres UB6 64 D3
Horsenden La N UB6 64 D1
Horsenden La S UB6 87 A6
Horsenden Prim Sch UB6 64 C2
Horsendon Ho 11 N7 71 D3
Horseshoe Cl
Cubitt Town E14 120 A1
Dollis Hill NW2 68 B6
Horse Shoe Cres UB5 85 C5
Horseshoe Dr UB8 82 C1
Horse Shoe Gn SM1 217 D6
Horseshoe La
Barnet N20 12 D3
Enfield EN2 5 A2
Horse Yd N1 234 D6
Horsfeld Gdns 1 SE9 166 A6
Horsfeld Rd SE9 165 D6
Horsfield Ho 13 N1 73 A1
Horsford Rd SW2 160 B6
Horsham Ave N12 30 C5
Horsham Ct N17 34 A2
Horsham Rd
Bexley DA6 169 C6
East Bedfont TW14 149 A5
Horsley Ct SW1 259 D3
Horsley Dr
Kingston u T KT2 175 D5
New Addington CR0 224 A1
Horsley Ho 11 SE4 140 D1
Horsley Rd
Bromley BR1 187 B2
Chingford E4 20 A2
Horsley St 3 SE17 139 B6
Horsman Ho SE5 139 A6
Horsman St SE5 139 A6
Horsmonden Cl BR6 211 D2
Horsmonden Rd SE4 163 B5
Horston Ho N4 51 A2
Hortensia Ho SW10 266 A4
Hortensia Rd SW10 136 A5 266 A4
Horticultural Pl 6 W4 111 B1
Horton Ave NW2 69 A4
Horton Bridge Rd UB7 104 B5
Horton Cl UB7 104 B5
Horton Ctry Pk KT19 214 C1
Horton Ho
13 Deptford SE15 140 C6
South Lambeth SW8 270 C4
West Kensington W14 254 A1
Horton Ind Pk UB7 104 B5
Horton La KT19 215 A1
Horton Par UB7 104 A5
Horton Rd Hackney E8 74 B2
Yiewsley UB7 104 B5
Horton Road Ind Est UB7 104 B5
Horton St SE13 141 D2
Horton Way CR0 206 D4
Hortus Rd Chingford E4 20 A2
Southall UB2 107 B4
Horwood Ho
24 Bethnal Green E2 96 B4
Marylebone NW8 237 B6
Hosack Rd SW12, SW17 159 A2
Hoser Ave SE12 165 A2
Hosier La EC1 94 D2 241 D3
Hoskins Cl UB3 105 D1
Hoskin's Cl E16 99 C1
Hoskins St SE10 120 B1
Hospital Bridge Rd TW2 151 D3
Hospital Bridge Rdbt TW2 151 D2
Hospital of the Holy Trinity (Almshouses) 5 CR0 221 A6
Hospital Rd TW3 129 C2
Hospital Way SE13 164 B4
Hospl for Tropical Diseases
Fitzrovia WC1 93 C3 239 B5
Somers Town NW1 232 D5
Hospl of St John & St Elizabeth NW8 92 B5 229 C3
Hotham Cl KT8 195 C6
Hotham Prim Sch SW15 134 D1
Hotham Rd
Merton SW19 180 A3
Putney SW15 134 C2
Hotham Road Mews 12 SW19 180 A3
Hotham St E15 98 C6
Hothfield Pl SE16 118 C3
Hotspur Ind Est N17 34 B4
Hotspur Rd UB5 85 C5
Hotspur St SE11 116 C1 261 A2
Houblon Rd TW10 154 A6
Houghton Cl
10 Dalston E8 73 D2
Hampton TW12 173 A4
Houghton Rd N15 51 D5
Houghton Sq SW9 138 A2
Houghton St WC2 240 D1
Houlder Cres CR0 220 D2
Houndsden Rd N21 16 C5
Houndsditch EC3 95 C1 243 B2
Houndsfield Prim Sch N9 18 B4
Houndsfield Rd N9 18 B4
HOUNSLOW 129 C3
Hounslow Ave TW3 151 D6
Hounslow Bsns Pk TW3 129 D1
Hounslow Central Sta TW3 129 D2
Hounslow Ctr The TW3 129 D2
Hounslow East Sta TW3 130 A3
Hounslow Gdns TW3 151 D6
Hounslow Heath Jun & Inf Schs TW4 129 A2
Hounslow Heath Nature Reserve TW4 151 A5
Hounslow Manor Sch TW3 130 A2
Hounslow Rd
Feltham TW14 150 B4
Hanworth TW13 151 A2
Twickenham TW2, TW3 152 A5
Hounslow Sta TW3 151 D6
Hounslow Town Prim Sch TW3 130 B2
HOUNSLOW WEST 128 D2
Hounslow West Sta TW3 129 A3
Houseman Way 20 SE5 139 B5
House of Detention* EC1 94 C3 241 B6
Houses of Parliament* SW1 116 A3 260 B6
Houston Ct 3 CR0 205 C1
Houston Pl KT10 196 C1
Houston Rd
Forest Hill SE23 163 A1
Thames Ditton KT6 197 B3
Houstoun Ct TW5 129 B5
Hove Ave E17 53 B4
Hoveden Rd NW2 69 A3
Hove Gdns SM1 201 D1
Hovenden Ho 6 SE21 183 C6
Hoveton Rd SE28 102 C1
Howard Ave DA5 168 C4
Howard Bldg SW8 268 C5
Howard Cl Acton W3 88 D1
Ashford TW16 171 D4
Brunswick Pk N11 15 A2
Bushey WD23 8 C4
Cricklewood NW2 69 A4
Hampton TW12 174 A4
Howard Ct
12 Barking IG11 101 B6
Beckenham BR3 186 A1
Lewisham SE10 142 A4
Peckham SE15 140 A2
Howard Ho
6 Brixton SW9 138 C2
14 Deptford SE8 141 B6
Fitzrovia W1 238 D5
Penge SE20 184 C2
6 Upper Clapton E5 74 C6
Howard Mans E17 53 D6
Howard Mews N5 72 D4
Howard Prim Sch CR0 221 A4
Howard Rd
Barking IG11 101 B6
Canonbury N16 73 B4
Cricklewood NW2 68 D4
Croydon SE25 206 A3
Ilford IG1 78 D4
Isleworth TW7 130 D2
Leyton E11 76 C5
Newham E6 100 B5
New Malden KT3 199 D5
Penge SE20 184 C2
Plaistow BR1 187 A3
Southall UB1 85 D1
South Tottenham N15 51 C3
Surbiton KT5 198 B3
Walthamstow E17 53 D6
Howards Cl HA5 22 B1
Howards Crest Cl BR3 186 A1
Howard's La SW15 134 C1
Howard's Rd E13 99 A4
Howard St KT7 197 B3
Howard Way EN5 12 D6
Howard Wlk N2 48 B5
Howarth Ct E15 76 A3
Howarth Rd SE2 124 A2
Howberry Cl HA8 25 D4
Howberry Rd
South Norwood CR7 183 B1
Stanmore HA7, H8 25 D4
Howbury Rd SE15 140 C2
Howcroft Cres N3 29 C3
Howcroft Ho 3 E3 97 B4
Howcroft La UB6 86 B4
Howden Cl SE28 124 D6
Howden Ct SE25 183 D1
Howden Rd SE25 183 D1
Howden St SE15 140 A2
Howell Cl RM6 58 D4
Howell Ct 2 E10 53 D2
Howell Ho 5 N7 71 D3
Howell Wlk SE1 261 D3
Howe Lo TW1 153 A4
Howerd Way SE18 144 A4
Howes Cl N3 47 C6
Howeth Ct 7 N11 31 A4
Howfield Pl N17 51 D6
Howgate Rd SW14 133 B2
Howick Mans SE18 122 A3
Howick Pl SW1 115 C3 259 B5
Howie St SW11 136 C5 267 A3
Howitt Cl
6 Maitland Pk NW3 70 C2
Stoke Newington N16 73 C4
Howitt Rd NW3 70 C2
Howland Ho 9 SW16 160 A1
Howland Mews E W1 239 B4
Howland St W1 93 C2 239 B4
Howland Way SE16 119 A4
Howletts La HA4 39 A3
Howletts Rd SE24 161 A5
Howley Pl W2 92 A2 236 B4
Howley Rd CR0 221 A5
Howmic Ct 1 TW1 153 C5
Howsman Rd SW13 134 A6
Howson Rd SE4 141 A1
Howson Terr TW10 154 A5
How's St E2 95 D5
Howton Pl WD23 8 B3
HOXTON 95 C5
Hoxton Mkt 10 N1 95 C4
Hoxton Point EC1 95 C4
Hoxton Sq N1 95 C4
Hoxton St N1 95 C5
Hoylake Cres UB10 60 D6
Hoylake Gdns
Mitcham CR4 203 C6
Ruislip HA4 40 B1
South Oxhey WD19 22 D6
Hoylake Rd W3 89 C1
Hoyland Cl 4 SE15 140 B5
Hoyle Rd SW17 180 C5
Hoy St E16 98 D1
Hubbard Dr KT9 213 D2
Hubbard Rd SE27 183 A6
Hubbards Cl UB8 82 D1
Hubbard St E15 98 C6
Hub Buildings The 4 SW12 159 B3
Huberd Ho SE1 262 D6
Hubert Gr SW9 138 A2
Hubert Ho NW8 237 A5
Hubert Rd E6 99 D4
Hucknall Ct NW8 236 C6
Huddart St 6 E3 97 B2
Huddleston Cl E2 96 C5
Huddlestone Rd
Forest Gate E7 76 D4
Willesden NW2 68 B2
Huddleston Rd N7 71 C4
Hudson 27 NW9 27 D2
Hudson Cl Newham E15 99 A6
15 Shepherd's Bush W12 112 B6
Hudson Ct
Croydon SE25 206 A5
1 Isle Of Dogs E14 119 C1
4 Merton SW19 179 D2
Hudson Ho
Chelsea SW10 266 A4
5 Notting Hill W11 91 A1
Hudson Pl SE18 123 A1
Hudson Rd Erith DA7 147 B4
Harlington UB7 127 B6
Hudsons Ho N1 235 D1
Hudson's Pl SW1 115 C2 259 A4
Hudson Way N9 18 C2
Huggin Ct EC4 252 B6
Huggin Hill EC4 252 B6
Huggins Ho 9 E3 97 C4
Huggins Pl SW2 160 B3
Hughan Rd E15 76 B3
Hugh Astor Ct SE1 261 D6
Hugh Clark Ho 13 W13 109 A5
Hugh Dalton Ave SW6 264 C5
Hughenden Ave HA3 43 B4
Hughenden Gdns UB5 84 C4
Hughenden Ho NW8 237 A6
Hughenden Rd KT4 200 A2
Hughendon EN5 1 D1
Hughendon Terr E15 76 A4
Hughes Cl N12 30 A5
Hughes Ho
26 Bethnal Green E2 96 C4
Camberwell SE5 139 A4
15 Deptford SE8 141 C6
Newington SE17 261 D3
Hughes Mans E1 96 A3
Hughes Rd
Ashford TW15 171 A4
Hayes UB3 106 B6
Hughes Terr 6 E16 98 D2
Hughes Wlk CR0 205 A2
Hugh Gaitskell Cl SW6 264 C5
Hugh Gaitskell Ho
Stoke Newington N16 73 D6
Willesden NW10 67 D1
Hugh Herland KT1 198 A6
Hugh Mews SW1 258 D3
Hugh Morgan Ho 5 SW4 137 D2
Hugh Myddelton Prim Sch EC1 94 C4 234 B1
Hugh Platt Ho 29 E2 96 B5
Hugh St SW1 115 B2 258 D3
Hugo Ho SW1 257 D6
Hugon Rd SW6 135 D2
Hugo Rd N19 71 C4
Huguenot Ct 9 E1 96 A2
Huguenot Pl
London SW18 158 A6
Spitalfields E1 243 D4
Huguenot Sq SE15 140 B2
Hullbridge Mews N1 235 C6
Hull Cl SE16 118 D5
Hull Ct SE5 139 B3
Hull Pl E16 123 A5
Hull St EC1 235 A1
Hulme Pl SE1 252 B1
Hulse Ave IG11 79 C2
Humber Ct W7 86 B1
Humber Dr W10 90 D3
Humber Rd
Dollis Hill NW2 68 B6
Greenwich SE3 142 D6
Humberstone Rd E13 99 C4
Humberton Cl E9 75 A3
Humber Trad Est NW2 68 B6
Humbolt Rd W6 135 A6 264 A5
Hume Ct N1 72 D1
Hume Ho 14 W11 112 D5
Humes Ave W7 108 D4
Hume Terr E16 99 B1
Hume Way HA4 40 A3
Humphrey Ct SW11 266 D1
Humphrey St SE1 117 D1 263 C2
Humphries Cl RM9 81 B4
Humphry Ho 10 SW15 156 D6
Hundred Acre NW9 27 D1
Hungerdown E4 20 A3
Hungerford Bridge WC2 250 C4
Hungerford Ho SW1 269 B6
Hungerford La WC2 250 B4
Hungerford Prim Sch N7 71 D2
Hungerford Rd
12 Camden Town N7 71 D2
Lower Holloway N7 72 A3
Hungerford St 21 E1 96 B1
Hunsdon Cl RM9 81 A2
Hunsdon Ho E5 74 B5
Hunsdon Rd SE14 140 D5
Hunslett St 26 E2 96 C5
Hunstanton Ho NW1 237 B4
Hunston Rd SM4 201 D1
Hunt Cl W11 112 D5
Hunt Ct London N14 15 B4
10 Northolt UB5 84 D5
Hunter Cl
Borehamwood WD6 11 A6
Borough The SE1 262 D5
Upper Tooting SW12 159 A3
3 Wallington SM6 220 A1
Huntercombe Roehampton Hospl The SW15 156 A4
Huntercrombe Gdns WD19 22 C5
Hunter Ct
8 London SE5 139 B1
27 Streatham SW2 160 C4
11 Wanstead E11 55 A4
Hunter Ho
Bloomsbury WC1 240 B6
Feltham TW14 150 A3
Lambeth SE1 251 D1
South Lambeth SW8 269 D3
1 Tufnell Pk N19 71 C5
West Brompton SW5 255 B1
Hunterian Mus* WC2 94 B1 240 D2
Hunter Lo 9 W9 91 C2
Hunter Rd
South Norwood CR7 205 B6
Wimbledon SW20 178 C2
Hunters Ct 5 TW9 153 D6
Hunters Gr Harrow HA3 43 C5
Hayes UB3 106 A4
Hunter's Gr BR6 227 A4
Hunters Hall Prim Sch RM10 81 D3
Hunters Hall Rd RM10 81 C3
Hunters Hill HA4 62 D5
Hunters Lo
9 Edgware HA8 26 D5
10 Sidcup DA15 168 A1
Hunters Mdw SE19 183 C6
Hunters Rd
Chessington KT9 214 A4
Ilford IG1 78 D3
Hunters Sq RM10 81 C4
Hunter St WC1 94 A3 240 B6
Hunters The 2 BR3 186 A2
Hunters Way Enfield EN2 4 C4
South Croydon CR0 221 C4
Hunter Wlk
Borehamwood WD6 11 B6
Newham E13 99 A5
Huntingdon Cl
Mitcham CR4, SW16 204 A5
Northolt UB5 63 C2
Huntingdon Ct
3 Barnet EN5 1 B2
Mortlake SW14 133 A2
Huntingdon Gdns
Chiswick W4 133 A5
North Cheam KT4 216 C5
Huntingdon Ho SW5 255 B4
Huntingdon Rd
East Finchley N2 48 C6
Edmonton N9 18 C3
Huntingdon St
Canning Town E16 98 D1
Islington N1 72 B1
Huntingfield CR0 223 B1
Huntingfield Rd SW15 156 A6
Huntingford Ho SW15 134 C3
Hunting Gate Cl EN2 4 C2
Hunting Gate Dr KT9 214 A1
Hunting Gate Mews
Sutton SM1 217 D5
Twickenham TW2 152 C3
Huntings Farm IG1 79 C6
Huntings Rd RM10 81 C2
Huntington Ho NW2 68 C2
Huntley Cl TW19 148 A4
Huntley Ho 12 SE21 183 C6
Huntley St WC1 93 D3 239 C5
Huntley Way SW20 178 A1
Huntly Dr N3 29 C4
Huntly Rd SE25 205 C5
Hunton St E1 96 A2
Hunt Rd UB2 107 C3
Hunts Cl SE3 143 A3
Hunt's Ct WC2 249 D5
Huntshaw Ho 37 E3 97 D4
Hunt's La E15 98 A5
Huntsmans Cl TW13 172 B6
Huntsman St SE17 263 A3
Hunts Mead EN3 6 D2
Hunts Mead Cl BR7 188 B3
Huntsmoor Rd KT19 215 B3
Huntspill St SW17 158 A1
Hunts Slip Rd SE21 161 C2
Huntsworth Ct SE6 163 C3
Huntsworth Mews NW1 92 D3 237 C5
Huon Ct N20 14 C2
Hurdwick Ho NW1 232 A4
Hurdwick Pl NW1 232 A4
Hurleston Ho 11 SE8 119 B1
Hurley Cres SE16 118 D4
Hurley Ct 1 W5 87 C1
Hurley Ho
Lambeth SE11 261 B3
34 Shoreditch E2 95 D4
Hurley Lo SE22 162 C5
Hurley Rd UB6 85 D2
Hurlingham Bsns Pk SW6 135 C2
Hurlingham & Chelsea Sec Sch SW6 135 C2
Hurlingham Court Mans SW6 135 C3
Hurlingham Ct SW6 135 B2
Hurlingham Gdns SW6 135 B2
Hurlingham Rd
Erith DA7 147 B5
Fulham SW6 135 B3
Hurlingham Sch SW15 135 B1
Hurlingham Sq SW6 135 D2
Hurlock Ho 1 N5 72 D5
Hurlock St N5 72 D5
Hurlstone Rd SE25 205 C4
Hurn Court Rd TW5 128 D3
Hurn Ct TW5 128 D3
Huron Cl 5 BR6 227 D2
Huron Rd SW17 159 A1
Huron Univ WC1 94 A2 240 A4
Hurren Cl SE3 142 C2
Hurricane Rd SM6 220 B1
Hurricane Trad Ctr NW9 28 A2
Hurry Cl E15 76 C1
Hursley Ct 11 KT6 197 D2
Hurst Ave Chingford E4 19 C1
Highgate N6 49 C3
Hurstbourne KT10 212 D2
Hurstbourne Cotts DA5 169 D4
Hurstbourne Gdns IG11 79 C2
Hurstbourne Ho SW15 155 D5
Hurstbourne Priors CR2 221 C2
Hurstbourne Rd SE23 163 A3
Hurst Cl
Chessington KT9 214 C3
Chingford E4 19 C1
Hampstead Garden Suburb NW11 47 D3
Hayes BR2 208 D1
Northolt UB5 63 B3
Hurstcombe IG9 21 A2
Hurstcourt Rd SM1 217 D6
Hurst Ct
Beckenham BR3 185 C3
Newham E6 99 D2
South Norwood SE25 205 D5
Woodford IG8 37 B4
Hurstdene Ave BR2 208 D1
Hurstdene Gdns N15 51 C2
Hurstfield BR2 209 A4
Hurstfield Cres UB4 83 C2
Hurstfield Rd KT8 195 C6
Hurst Gr KT12 193 D1
Hurst Ho
7 Penge SE26 184 B5
Pentonville N1 233 D3
West Heath SE2 124 D1
Hurst La
East Molesey KT8 196 A6
West Heath SE2 124 D1
Hurst Lo London N8 49 D3
Wembley HA0 66 B1
Hurstmead Ct HA8 26 D6
Hurstmere Foundation Sch for Boys DA15 168 C3
HURST PARK 174 A1
Hurst Park Prim Sch KT8 195 C6
Hurst Pl Erith SE2 146 D6
Woolwich SE2 124 C1
Hurst Prim Sch DA5 168 D3

Hurst Rd
Buckhurst Hill IG9 ... 21 D3
Croydon CR0 ... 221 B3
East Molesey KT8, KT12 ... 195 C6
Sidcup DA5, DA15 ... 168 C3
Southgate N21 ... 16 C3
Walthamstow E17 ... 53 D6
Walton-on-T KT8&KT12 .. 194 D5
Hurst Rise EN5 ... 1 C2
Hurst Springs DA5 ... 169 A3
Hurst St SE24 ... 160 D5
Hurst View Grange CR2 ... 220 D1
Hurst View Rd CR2 ... 221 C1
Hurst Way CR2 ... 221 C2
Hurstway Wlk 2 W11 .. 112 D6
Hurstwood Ave
Sidcup DA5 ... 169 A3
Wanstead E18 ... 55 B5
Hurstwood Ct
Colney Hatch N12 ... 30 C4
Temple Fortune NW11 ... 47 B5
Hurstwood Dr BR1 ... 210 B6
Hurstwood Rd NW11 ... 47 B5
Hurtwood Rd KT12 ... 195 B2
Husbourne Ho 8 SE8 .. 119 A2
Huson Cl NW3 ... 70 C1
Hussain Cl HA1 ... 64 D4
Hussars Cl TW4 ... 129 A2
Husseywell Cres BR2 .. 209 A1
Hutching's St E14 ... 119 C4
Hutching's Wharf 11 E14 ... 119 C4
Hutchings Wlk NW11 ... 47 D5
Hutchins Cl E15 ... 76 A1
Hutchins Ho 8 SW4 ... 159 D4
Hutchinson Ct RM6 ... 58 D5
Hutchinson Ho 9 SE14 ... 140 C5
Hutchinson Terr HA9 ... 65 D5
Hutchins Rd SE28 ... 124 A5
Hutton Cl Greenford UB6 . 64 B3
Woodford IG8 ... 37 B4
Hutton Ct 1 Ealing W5 .. 87 C2
Edmonton N9 ... 18 C4
4 Finsbury Pk N4 ... 50 B1
Hutton Gdns HA3 ... 24 A3
Hutton Gr N12 ... 29 D5
Hutton Ho 19 E2 ... 96 A4
Hutton La HA3 ... 24 A3
Hutton Row 4 HA8 ... 27 A3
Hutton St EC4 ... 241 B1
Hutton Wlk HA3 ... 24 A3
Huxbear St SE4 ... 163 B6
Huxley Cl UB5 ... 85 A6
Huxley Dr RM6 ... 58 B2
Huxley Gdns NW10 ... 88 B5
Huxley Ho
4 London SW9 ... 138 B3
Paddington NW8 ... 236 D5
West Heath SE2 ... 124 D1
Huxley Par N18 ... 33 B5
Huxley Pl N13 ... 16 D1
Huxley Rd
Edmonton N18 ... 33 C6
Falconwood DA16 ... 145 D2
Leyton E10 ... 76 A6
Huxley Sayze N18 ... 33 B5
Huxley South N18 ... 33 B5
Huxley St W10 ... 91 A4
Hyacinth Cl
3 Hampton TW12 ... 173 C4
Ilford IG1 ... 78 D2
Hyacinth Ct 2 HA5 ... 40 C6
Hyacinth Dr UB10 ... 60 A1
Hyacinth Rd SW15 ... 156 A3
Hyde Cl Ashford TW16 .. 171 C4
Barnet EN5 ... 1 B2
Newham E13 ... 99 A5
Hyde Cres NW9 ... 45 C4
Hyde Ct
Forest Hill SE23 ... 163 A2
Hounslow TW4 ... 151 B6
Kingsbury NW9 ... 45 B2
Whetstone N20 ... 14 B1
Hyde Estate Rd NW9 ... 45 D4
Hyde Farm Mews SW12 ... 159 D3
Hydefield Cl N21 ... 17 B3
Hydefield Ct N9 ... 17 C2
Hyde Ho 12 Ealing W13 .. 109 A5
Hounslow TW3 ... 130 A2
Hyde Ind Est The NW9 .. 45 D4
Hyde La SW11 .. 136 C4 267 A2
Hyde Park* W2 ... 114 D5 247 C3
Hyde Park Ave N21 ... 17 B3
Hyde Park Cnr SW1 ... 248 B2
Hyde Park Corner Sta SW1 ... 115 A4 248 B2
Hyde Park Cres W2 ... 92 C1 237 A1
Hyde Park Gate Mews SW7 ... 246 B1
Hyde Park Gdns
Bayswater W2 ... 114 B6 246 D6
Edmonton N21 ... 17 A3
Hyde Park Gdns Mews W2 ... 114 C6 247 A6
Hyde Park Mans NW1 .. 237 A3
Hyde Park Pl W2 ... 247 B6
Hyde Park Sq W2 ... 92 C1 237 A1
Hyde Park Square Mews W2 ... 237 A1
Hyde Park St W2 ... 92 C1 237 A1
Hyde Park Twrs W2 ... 246 A5
Hyderabad Way E15 ... 76 C1
Hyde Rd
Bexleyheath DA7 ... 147 B3
Richmond TW10 ... 154 B6
Shoreditch N1 ... 95 C6
Hyde Sch The NW9 ... 45 D4
Hydeside Gdns N9 ... 17 D2
Hyde's Pl 12 N1 ... 72 D1
Hyde St SE8 ... 141 C6
Hyde Terr TW15, TW16 .. 171 C4
HYDE THE ... 45 D4
Hydethorpe Ave N9 ... 17 D2
Hydethorpe Rd SW12 .. 159 C3
Hyde Vale SE10 ... 142 A5
Hyde Way Edmonton N9 .. 17 D2
Hayes UB3 ... 105 D2
Hyde Wlk SM4 ... 201 C2
Hydon Ct N11 ... 30 D5
Hyh Ho E17 ... 35 D2
Hyland House Sch E17 .. 36 B1
Hylands Rd E17 ... 36 B1
Hylda Ct NW5 ... 71 A5
Hylton St SE18 ... 123 D2
Hyndewood 14 SE23 ... 162 D1
Hyndman Ho
5 Dagenham RM10 ... 81 C5
4 Tufnell Pk N19 ... 71 D4
Hyndman St SE15 ... 140 B6
Hynton Rd RM8 ... 80 C6
Hyperion Ho 27 Bow E3 .. 97 A5
Streatham SW2 ... 160 B4
Hyrstdene CR0 ... 220 D4
Hyrst The CR0 ... 207 A1
Hyson Rd SE16 ... 118 B1
Hythe Ave DA7 ... 147 B5
Hythe Cl N18 ... 34 A6
Hythe Ho 14 SE16 ... 118 C4
Hythe Rd
College Pk NW10 ... 90 A3
South Norwood CR7 ... 183 B1
Hythe Road Ind Est NW10 ... 90 A3
Hyver Hill NW7 ... 11 B4

I

Ian Ct SE23 ... 162 C2
Ian Hamilton Ho NW1 . 232 C2
Ian Mikardo Sch E3 ... 97 D4
Ian Sq EN3 ... 6 D4
Ibberton Ho
Kensington W14 ... 254 B5
South Lambeth SW8 ... 270 C4
Ibbotson Ave E16 ... 98 D1
Ibbott St 22 E1 ... 96 C3
Iberia Ho 17 N19 ... 49 D2
Iberian Ave CR0, SM6 .. 220 A4
Ibex Ho E15 ... 76 C3
Ibis Ct 16 SE8 ... 141 B6
Ibis Ho E12 ... 78 B4
Ibis La W4 ... 133 A4
Ibis Way UB4 ... 84 D1
Ibrox Ct 3 IG9 ... 21 C2
Ibsley Gdns SW15 ... 156 A3
Ibsley Way EN4 ... 2 C1
Ibstock Place Sch SW15 ... 155 C5
Icarus Ho 21 E3 ... 97 B4
Iceland Rd E3 ... 97 C6
Iceland Wharf SE16 ... 119 A2
Iceni Ct 23 Bow E3 ... 97 B6
Buckhurst Hill IG9 ... 21 B3
Ice Wharf NW1 ... 233 B4
Ickburgh Est E5 ... 74 B6
Ickburgh Rd E5 ... 74 B5
Ickburgh Sch E5 ... 74 B5
ICKENHAM ... 60 C4
Ickenham Cl HA4 ... 61 B6
Ickenham Rd HA4 ... 39 B1
Ickenham Sta UB10 ... 61 A4
Ickleton Rd SE9 ... 188 A6
Icknield Dr IG2 ... 56 D4
Ickworth Park Rd E17 ... 53 A5
Icough Ct SE3 ... 143 B5
Idaho Bldg 7 SE13 ... 141 D4
Ida Rd N15 ... 51 B5
Ida St E14 ... 98 A1
Iden Cl BR2 ... 208 C6
Idlecombe Rd SW17 ... 181 A4
Idmiston Rd
New Malden KT4 ... 199 D2
Stratford E15 ... 76 D3
West Norwood SE21, SE27 ... 161 A2
Idmiston Sq KT4 ... 199 D2
Idol La EC3 ... 117 C6 253 A5
Idonia St SE8 ... 141 C5
Iffley Ho 47 E2 ... 95 D4
Iffley Rd W6 ... 112 B3
Ifield Ho SE17 ... 263 B2
Ifield Rd SW10 . 135 D6 265 D6
Ifor Evans Pl E1 ... 96 D3
Ightham Ho
Beckenham BR3 ... 185 B3
Walworth SE17 ... 263 A3
Ightham Rd DA8 ... 147 C5
Ikon Ho 21 E1 ... 118 C6
Ikra Prim Sch N16 ... 73 D4
Ilbert St W10 ... 91 A4
Ilchester Gdns W2 ... 245 C6
Ilchester Mans W8 ... 255 A6
Ilchester Pl W14 ... 113 B3 254 D6
Ilchester Rd RM8 ... 80 C3
Ildersly Gr SE21 ... 161 B2
Ilderton Prim Sch SE16 ... 118 C1
Ilderton Rd SE15, SE16 .. 140 C6
Ilex Cl TW16 ... 172 C1
Ilex Rd NW10 ... 67 D2
Ilex Way SW16 ... 182 C5
ILFORD ... 78 D6
Ilford Chambers 10 IG1 ... 78 D5
Ilford Hill IG1 ... 78 C5
Ilford Ho 14 N1 ... 73 B2
Ilford Interchange IG1 .. 78 C5
Ilford Jewish Prim Sch IG6 ... 57 B6
Ilford La IG1 ... 78 D4
Ilford Prep Sch IG3 ... 58 A1
Ilford Ret Pk IG1 ... 79 A6
Ilford Sta IG1 ... 78 D6
Ilford Ursuline High Sch IG1 ... 78 D6
Ilfracombe Flats SE1 .. 252 B2
Ilfracombe Gdns RM6 ... 58 B2
Ilfracombe Rd BR1 ... 164 D1
Iliffe St SE17 ... 116 D1 261 D2
Iliffe Yd SE17 ... 116 D1 261 D2
Ilkeston Ct 7 E5 ... 74 D4
Ilkley Cl SE19 ... 183 B4
Ilkley Ct N11 ... 31 A4
Ilkley Rd Newham E16 ... 99 C2
South Oxhey WD19 ... 22 D5
Illingworth Cl CR4 ... 202 B6
Illingworth Way EN1 ... 17 C6
Ilmington Rd HA3 ... 43 D3
Ilminster Gdns SW11 .. 136 C1
Ilsley Ct 8 SW8 ... 137 C3
Imber Cl London N14 ... 15 C4
Thames Ditton KT7 ... 196 B1
Imber Court Trad Est KT8 ... 196 B3
Imber Cross KT7 ... 196 D3
Imber Ct 4 SE9 ... 166 C5
Imber Gr KT10 ... 196 B2
Imber Park Rd KT10 ... 196 B1
Imber St N1 ... 235 C5
Immanuel Coll WD23 ... 8 C4
Immanuel & St Andrew CE Prim Sch SW16 ... 182 A4
Impact Ct SE20 ... 184 B1
Imperial Ave 5 N16 ... 73 C4
Imperial Cl HA2 ... 41 C3
Imperial College Rd SW7 ... 114 B3 256 C6
Imperial Coll of Science, Technology & Medicine SW7 ... 114 B3 256 C6
Imperial Cres SW6 ... 136 A3
Imperial Ct
Chislehurst BR7 ... 188 D4
Harrow HA2 ... 41 C2
St John's Wood NW8 .. 230 B4
Wembley HA9 ... 66 C5
Whetstone N20 ... 14 A1
Imperial Dr HA2 ... 41 C3
Imperial Gdns CR4 ... 203 B6
Imperial Ho 1 Bow E3 .. 97 A4
2 Poplar E14 ... 119 B6
Strand WC2 ... 240 C1
Imperial Mews 5 E6 ... 99 D5
Imperial Pl BR7 ... 188 C2
Imperial Rd
East Bedfont TW14 ... 149 C4
Walham Green SW6 ... 265 D1
Wood Green N22 ... 32 A2
Imperial Sq SW6 ... 265 D2
Imperial St E3 ... 98 A4
Imperial Twrs 3 NW3 ... 70 A2
Imperial War Mus* SE1, SE11 ... 116 C3 261 B5
Imperial Way
Croydon CR0, CR9 ... 220 C2
Harrow HA3 ... 44 A3
Longlands BR7 ... 167 A1
Imperial Wharf Sta SW10 ... 136 A4 266 B1
Impington 19 KT1 ... 176 C1
Imre Cl W12 ... 112 B5
Inca Dr SE9 ... 166 D4
Ince Terr 3 N15 ... 50 D6
Inchmery Rd SE6 ... 164 A3
Inchwood BR4, CR0 ... 223 D4
Independant Jewish Day Sch NW4 ... 46 D4
Independence Ho 4 SW19 ... 180 B2
Independent Ind Est UB7 ... 104 C5
Independent Pl E8 ... 73 D3
Independents Rd SE3 .. 142 D2
Inderwick Rd N8 ... 50 B4
Indescon Ct E14 ... 119 D4
Indiana Bldg 7 SE8 ... 141 C4
India St EC3 ... 243 C1
India Way W12 ... 112 B6
Indigo Ct TW13 ... 149 D1
Indigo Mews N16 ... 73 B5
Indus Ct 16 SE15 ... 139 D5
Indus Rd SE7 ... 143 C5
Ingal Rd E13 ... 99 A3
Ingate Pl SW8 .. 137 B4 268 D1
Ingatestone Rd
Croydon SE25 ... 206 B5
Wanstead E12 ... 55 C1
Woodford IG8 ... 37 B3
Ingelow Ho W8 ... 245 C2
Ingelow Rd SW8 ... 137 B3
Ingersoll Rd Enfield EN3 ... 6 C5
Shepherd's Bush W12 ... 112 B5
Ingestre Pl W1 ... 239 B1
Ingestre Rd
Forest Gate E7 ... 77 A4
Gospel Oak NW5 ... 71 B4
Ingham Rd NW6 ... 69 C4
Inglebert St EC1 . 94 C4 234 A2
Ingleborough EN2 ... 4 C3
Ingleborough St SW9 .. 138 C3
Ingleby Ct N21 ... 16 D3
Ingleby Dr HA1 ... 64 B5
Ingleby Rd
Dagenham RM10 ... 81 D2
Ilford IG1 ... 56 D1
Lower Holloway N7 ... 72 A5
Ingleby Way
Chislehurst West BR7 ... 188 C5
Wallington SM6 ... 219 D1
Ingle Cl HA5 ... 41 B6
Ingledew Rd SE18 ... 123 B1
Inglefield Sq 12 E1 ... 118 B5
Ingle Ho 3 SW12 ... 159 D3
Inglehurst Gdns IG4 ... 56 B4
Inglemere Ct CR4, SW17 ... 180 D3
Inglemere Rd
Forest Hill SE23 ... 162 D1
Mitcham CR4, SW17 .. 180 D3
Inglesham Wlk E9 ... 75 B2
Ingleside Cl BR3 ... 185 C3
Ingleside Gr SE3 ... 142 D6
Inglethorpe Ho 6 E5 ... 74 A6
Inglethorpe St SW6 ... 134 D4
Ingleton Ave DA16 ... 168 A6
Ingleton Rd N18 ... 34 A4
Ingleton St SW9 ... 138 C3
Ingleway N12 ... 30 C4
Inglewood BR7 ... 189 B4
Inglewood Cl E14 ... 119 C2
Inglewood Copse BR1 .. 188 B1
Inglewood Ct 4 BR1 ... 186 D3
Inglewood Mans 11 NW6 ... 69 C3
Inglewood Rd NW6 ... 69 C3
Inglis Ct W5 ... 110 B6
Inglis Ho 1 SW15 ... 156 C6
Inglis Rd Croydon CR0 ... 205 D1
Ealing W5 ... 110 B6
Inglis St SE5 ... 138 D4
Ingram Ave NW11 ... 48 A2
Ingram Cl
Lambeth SE11 ... 260 D4
Stanmore HA7 ... 25 C5
Ingram Ct EN1 ... 17 D5
Ingram Ho
7 Harrow HA1 ... 42 D4
Old Ford E3 ... 97 A6
Teddington KT8 ... 175 C2
Ingram Lo 8 SW4 ... 159 D5
Ingram Rd London N2 ... 48 C5
South Norwood CR7 ... 183 A2
Ingram Way UB6 ... 86 B6
Ingrave Ho RM9 ... 102 B6
Ingrave St SW11 ... 136 C2
Ingrebourne Ct E4 ... 19 D2
Ingrebourne Ho
2 Catford BR1 ... 186 B5
Lisson Gr NW8 ... 236 D4
Ingress St 4 W4 ... 111 C1
Inigo Jones Rd SE7 ... 144 A5
Inigo Pl WC2 ... 250 A6
Inkerman Rd NW5 ... 71 B2
Inkerman Terr W8 ... 255 B5
Inks Gn E4 ... 36 A5
Inkster Ho 8 SW11 ... 136 C2
Inkwell Cl N12 ... 14 A1
Inman Rd
Harlesden NW10 ... 89 C6
Wandsworth SW18 ... 158 A4
Inmans Row IG8 ... 37 A6
Inner Circ NW1 .. 93 A4 231 A2
Inner Park Rd SW19 ... 156 D2
Inner Ring E TW6 ... 126 D2
Inner Ring W TW6 ... 126 C2
Inner Temple* EC4 ... 251 A6
Inner Temple La EC4 .. 241 A1
Innes Cl SW20 ... 179 A1
Innes Gdns SW15 ... 156 B5
Innes Lo SE23 ... 162 D1
Innes Yd CR0 ... 221 A5
Innisfree Ho NW2 ... 68 D2
Innis Ho SE17 ... 263 A2
Inniskilling Rd E13 ... 99 C5
Innova Bsns Pk EN3 ... 7 B3
Innovation Cl HA0 ... 88 A6
Inskip Cl E10 ... 75 D6
Inskip Rd RM8 ... 58 D1
Insley Ho 13 E3 ... 97 D4
Inst for Child Health WC1 ... 94 B3 240 C5
Institute Pl E8 ... 74 B3
Instituto Espanol Vicente Canada Blanch W10 ... 91 A2
Inst of Neurology
Bloomsbury WC1 ... 94 A2 240 B4
St Pancras WC1 . 94 A3 240 B5
Int Coll of Accountancy The SW17 ... 158 D1
Integer Gdns E11 ... 54 B2
Interchange The
Kentish Town NW5 ... 71 B3
Thornton Heath CR0 ... 204 D2
International Ave TW5 ... 106 C1
International House Language Sch WC2 ... 94 A1 240 B2
International Sch of London W3 ... 110 C2
International Trad Est UB2 ... 106 B3
International Way TW16 ... 171 C2
Inverary Pl SE18 ... 145 B6
Inver Cl E5 ... 74 C6
Inverclyde Gdns RM6 ... 58 D5
Inver Ct
11 Bayswater W2 ... 91 D1
4 Hammersmith W6 ... 112 A3
Inveresk Gdns KT4 ... 216 A5
Inverey Ho 2 N12 ... 29 D5
Inverforth Cl NW3 ... 70 A6
Inverforth Ho NW3 ... 70 A6
Inverforth Rd N11 ... 31 B5
Invergarry Ct 11 EN5 ... 13 D6
Invergarry Ho NW6 ... 91 D5
Inverine Rd SE7 ... 121 B1
Invermead Cl W6 ... 112 A2
Invermore Pl SE18 ... 123 A2
Inverness Ave EN1 ... 5 C4
Inverness Ct
8 Acton W3 ... 88 C1
10 Catford SE6 ... 164 D3
Inverness Gdns W8 ... 245 C3
Inverness Mews
Bayswater W2 ... 245 D6
Newham E16 ... 122 D5
North Woolwich E16 ... 123 A5
Inverness Pl W2 ... 245 D6
Inverness Rd
Edmonton N18 ... 34 B5
Hounslow TW3 ... 129 C1
North Cheam KT4 ... 200 D1
Southall UB2 ... 107 A2
Inverness St NW1 ... 231 D6
Inverness Terr W2 ... 113 D6 245 D6
Inverton Rd SE15 ... 140 D1
Invicta Cl
Chislehurst West BR7 ... 188 C5
East Bedfont TW14 ... 149 D3
21 Tower Hamlets E3 ... 97 C2
Invicta Ct KT9 ... 214 B3
Invicta Ctr The IG11 ... 102 A6
Invicta Gr UB5 ... 85 B4
Invicta Plaza SE1 ... 251 C4
Invicta Prim Sch SE3 ... 143 A5
Invicta Rd SE3, SE7 ... 143 A6
Inville Rd SE17 .. 117 B1 262 D1
Inwen Ct SE8 ... 119 A1
Inwood Ave TW3 ... 130 A2
Inwood Bsns Pk TW3 .. 129 D1
Inwood Cl CR0 ... 223 A6
Inwood Ct 12 NW1 ... 71 C1
Inwood Ho 19 SE22 ... 139 C2
Inwood Rd TW3 ... 130 A1
Inworth St SW11 ... 136 C3
Inworth Wlk N1 ... 235 A6
Io Ctr Barking IG11 ... 101 D3
Woolwich SE18 ... 123 A3
Iona Cl Catford SE6 ... 163 C4
Morden SM4 ... 201 D2
Ion Ct 8 E2 ... 96 A5
Ionian Bldg 19 E14 ... 119 A6
Ionian Ho 22 E1 ... 96 D3
Ipsden Bldgs SE1 ... 251 B2
Ipswich Ho SE4 ... 162 D6
Ipswich Rd SW17 ... 181 A4
Irby Ho SW2 ... 160 C5
Ireland Cl E6 ... 100 B2
Ireland Pl N22 ... 32 A3
Ireland Yd EC4 ... 241 D1
Irene Rd
Broom Hill BR6 ... 211 D2
Parsons Green SW6 ... 135 C4 265 B1
Ireton Cl N10 ... 31 A3
Ireton Ho 22 SW9 ... 138 C3
Ireton St 12 E3 ... 97 C3
Iris Ave DA5 ... 169 A5
Iris Cl Croydon CR0 ... 206 D1
Newham E6 ... 100 A3
Surbiton KT6 ... 198 B2
Iris Cres DA7 ... 147 B6
Iris Ct Dagenham IG11 ... 80 B1
8 Peckham SE15 ... 140 B3
4 Pinner HA5 ... 40 C6
Iris Rd KT19 ... 214 D3
Iris Way E4 ... 35 B4
Iris Wlk 1 HA8 ... 27 A6
Irkdale Ave EN1 ... 5 D4
Iroko Ho 7 NW3 ... 69 D2
Iron Bridge Cl
Southall UB2 ... 108 A5
Willesden NW10 ... 67 C3
Iron Bridge Ho NW3 ... 70 D1
Iron Bridge Rd N UB11 ... 104 C5
Iron Bridge Rd S UB7 .. 104 C4
Irongate Ho EC3 ... 243 B2
Iron Mill Pl SW18 ... 157 D5
Iron Mill Rd SW18 ... 157 D5
Ironmonger La EC2 ... 95 B1 242 C1
Ironmonger Pas EC1 .. 235 B1
Ironmonger Row EC1 ... 95 A4 235 B1
Ironmonger's Pl 22 E14 ... 119 C2
Ironside Cl SE16 ... 118 D4
Ironside Ho E9 ... 75 A4
Ironworks 1 E3 ... 97 C6
Irvine Ave HA3 ... 43 B6
Irvine Cl N20 ... 14 C2
Irvine Ct
Marylebone W1 ... 239 B5
Thornton Heath CR7 ... 204 C3
Irvine Ho N7 ... 72 B2
Irvine Way BR6 ... 211 D2
Irving Ave UB5 ... 84 D6
Irving Ct N22 ... 32 D2
Irving Gr SW9 ... 138 B3
Irving Ho SE17 ... 261 C1
Irving Mews N1 ... 73 A2
Irving Rd W14 ... 112 D3
Irving St WC2 ... 249 D5
Irwell Ct W7 ... 86 B1
Irwell Est 31 SE16 ... 118 C4
Irwin Ave SE18 ... 145 C5
Irwin Cl UB10 ... 60 C5
Irwin Gdns NW10 ... 90 B6
Isabel Hill Cl TW12 ... 173 C2
Isabella Cl N14 ... 15 C4
Isabella Ct 8 TW10 ... 154 B5
Isabella Dr BR6 ... 227 A4
Isabella Ho
19 Hammersmith W6 ... 112 C1
Kennington SE11 ... 261 C2
Isabella Pl KT2 ... 176 B5
Isabella Rd E9 ... 74 C3
Isabella St SE1 ... 251 C3
Isabel St SW9 ... 270 D2
Isambard Mews E14 ... 120 A3
Isambard Pl SE16 ... 118 C5
Iseldon Ct N7 ... 72 A4
Isel Way 4 SE22 ... 161 C6
Isham Rd SW16 ... 182 A1
Isis Cl Putney SW15 ... 134 C1
Ruislip HA4 ... 39 A3
Isis Ct W4 ... 132 D5
Isis Ho 2 Edmonton N18 .. 33 D4
Paddington NW8 ... 236 D5
Isis St SW18 ... 158 A2
Islamia Girls' High Sch NW6 ... 91 A6
Islamia Prim Sch NW6 .. 91 A6
Islamic Coll for Advanced Studies NW10 ... 68 B2
Island Centre Way 16 EN3 ... 7 C6
Island Farm Ave KT8 ... 195 B4
Island Farm Rd KT8 ... 195 C4
Island Gardens Sta E14 ... 120 A1
Island Ho Bromley E14 ... 98 A4
Morden SW19 ... 202 A5
Island Rd
Deptford SE16 ... 118 D2
Mitcham CR4 ... 180 D3
Island Row E14 ... 97 B1
Isla Rd SE18 ... 145 A6
Islay Gdns TW4 ... 150 D6
Islay Wlk 17 N1 ... 73 A2
Isleden Ho N1 ... 235 A6
Isledon Rd N4, N7 ... 72 C5
Islehurst Cl BR7 ... 188 C2
ISLE OF DOGS ... 120 A2
ISLEWORTH ... 131 B2
Isleworth Bsns Complex TW7 ... 130 D3
Isleworth Sta TW7 ... 130 D3
Isleworth & Syon Sch for Boys TW7 ... 130 C5
Isleworth Town Prim Sch TW7 ... 131 A3
ISLINGTON ... 72 D2
Islington Arts & Media Sch N4 ... 50 B1
Islington Bsns Ctr N1 . 235 B6
Islington Est N1 . 95 A6 235 A6
Islington Gn N1 .. 94 D6 234 C5
Islington Green Sch N1 ... 95 A6 235 A5
Islington High St N1 ... 94 D5 234 C4
Islington Park Mews 1 N1 ... 72 D1
Islington Park St N1 ... 72 D1
Islington Sixth Form Ctr N7 ... 72 C4
Islip Gdns Burnt Oak HA8 . 27 B3
Northolt UB5 ... 63 A1
Islip Manor Rd UB5 ... 63 A1
Islip St NW5 ... 71 C3
Ismailia Rd E7 ... 77 B1
Isobel Ho
10 Ashford TW16 ... 171 D3
Harrow HA1 ... 42 D4
Isokon Flats 3 NW3 ... 70 D3
Isom Cl E13 ... 99 B4
Issac Way SE1 ... 252 B2
Italia Conti Acad of Theatre Arts EC1 ... 242 A5
Ithell Ct HA0 ... 65 D3
Ivanhoe Dr HA3 ... 25 B1
Ivanhoe Ho
11 Balham SW12 ... 159 B4
34 Bow E3 ... 97 A5
Ivanhoe Rd
Hounslow TW4 ... 128 D2
Peckham SE5 ... 139 D2
Ivatt Pl W14 ... 113 B1 254 D1
Ivatt Way N17 ... 50 D6
Iveagh Ave NW10 ... 88 C5
Iveagh Cl Ealing NW10 ... 88 C5
South Hackney E9 ... 96 D6
Iveagh Ct
4 Beckenham BR3 ... 207 D6
Whitechapel EC3 ... 243 C1
Iveagh Ho
2 Brixton SW9 ... 138 D3
Chelsea SW10 ... 266 B4
Ivebury Ct 9 W10 ... 90 C1
Ivedon Rd DA16 ... 146 C3
Ive Farm Cl E10 ... 75 C6
Ive Farm La E10 ... 75 C6
Iveley Rd SW4 ... 137 C3
Iver Ct N1 ... 73 A2
Ivere Dr EN5 ... 13 D5
Iverhurst Cl DA6 ... 168 D6
Iverna Ct W8 ... 255 B6

Iverna Gdns
Hatton TW14 . . . . 149 B6
Kensington W8 . 113 C3 255 B6
Iverson Rd NW6 . . . . 69 C2
Ivers Way CR0 . . . . 223 D1
Ives Rd E16 . . . . 98 C2
Ives St SW3 . . . . 114 C2 257 B4
Ivestor Terr SE23 . . . . 162 C4
Ivimey St E2 . . . . 96 A4
Ivinghoe Cl EN1 . . . . 5 C4
Ivinghoe Ho 14 N7 . . . . 71 D3
Ivinghoe Rd
Barking RM8 . . . . 80 B3
Bushey WD23 . . . . 8 B4
Ivor Ct Hendon N3 . . . . 47 A6
Hornsey N8 . . . . 50 A3
Lisson Gr NW1 . . . . 237 C6
Ivor Gr SE9 . . . . 166 D3
Ivor Ho DA14 . . . . 190 C5
Ivories The N1 . . . . 73 A1
Ivor Mayor Lo SW12 . . . . 159 A5
Ivor Pl NW1 . . . . 92 D3 237 C5
Ivor St NW1 . . . . 71 C1
Ivory Ct TW13 . . . . 150 A3
Ivorydown BR1 . . . . 187 A6
Ivory Ho
9 London SW11 . . . . 136 A2
St George in t East E1 . . 253 D4
Ivory Sq 15 SW18 . . . . 136 A2
Ivybridge Cl
2 Twickenham TW1 . . . . 153 A4
Uxbridge UB8 . . . . 82 A4
Ivybridge Ct 1 BR7 . . . . 188 C2
Ivybridge Ho 18 SE22 . . . 139 C2
Ivybridge La WC2 . . . . 250 B5
Ivybridge Prim Sch
TW1 . . . . 152 D5
Ivybridge Ret Pk TW7 . . 152 D6
Ivychurch Cl SE20 . . . . 184 C3
Ivy Church La SE1,
SE17 . . . . 263 C2
Ivy Cl Harrow HA2 . . . . 63 B4
Pinner HA5 . . . . 40 C2
Sunbury TW16 . . . . 172 C1
Ivy Cotts UB10 . . . . 82 C4
Ivy Cres W4 . . . . 111 A2
Ivy Ct
19 Bermondsey SE16 . . . 118 A1
Lewisham SE3 . . . . 142 D1
Ivydale Prim Sch
SE15 . . . . 140 D1
Ivydale Rd
Carshalton SM5 . . . . 218 D6
Nunhead SE15 . . . . 140 D1
Ivyday Gr SW16 . . . . 160 B1
Ivydene KT12, KT8 . . . . 195 B4
Ivydene Cl SM1 . . . . 218 A4
Ivy Gdns London N8 . . . . 50 A3
Mitcham CR4 . . . . 203 D6
Ivy Ho Croydon CR0 . . . . 206 D1
6 Upper Clapton E5 . . . . 52 B1
Ivyhouse Rd RM9 . . . . 81 A2
Ivy House Rd UB10 . . . . 60 D5
Ivy La TW4 . . . . 129 B1
Ivy Lo W8 . . . . 245 A4
Ivymount Rd SE27 . . . . 160 C1
Ivy Rd Brockley SE4 . . . . 141 C1
Cricklewood NW2 . . . . 68 C4
Hounslow TW3 . . . . 129 D1
Newham E16 . . . . 99 A1
Southgate N14 . . . . 15 D4
Tolworth KT6 . . . . 198 C1
Upper Tooting SW17 . . . . 180 C5
Walthamstow E17 . . . . 53 C3
Ivy St N1 . . . . 95 C5
Ivy Terr 3 IG2 . . . . 57 A3
Ivy Wlk RM9 . . . . 81 A2
Ixworth Pl
SW3 . . . . 114 C2 257 A3
Izane Rd DA6 . . . . 147 B1

J

Jacaranda Cl KT3 . . . . 199 C6
Jacaranda Gr E8 . . . . 73 D1
Jack Ashley Ct 5 NW9 . . 27 C2
Jackass La BR2 . . . . 225 C2
Jack Barnett Way N22 . . 32 B1
Jack Clow Rd E15 . . . . 98 C5
Jack Cook Ho 9 IG11 . . . 78 D1
Jack Cornwell St E12 . . . 78 C4
Jack Goodchild Way
KT3 . . . . 198 D6
Jack & Jill Sch TW12 . . 173 C4
Jacklin Gn IG8 . . . . 37 A6
Jackman Ho 24 E1 . . . . 118 B5
Jackman Mews NW2 . . . . 67 C5
Jackman St E8 . . . . 96 B6
Jackson Cl Hackney E9 . . 74 D1
Uxbridge UB10 . . . . 60 A1
Jackson Ct
Forest Gate E7 . . . . 77 B2
Wanstead E11 . . . . 55 B1
Jackson Ho
16 London SW11 . . . . 136 B2
13 New Southgate N11 . . 31 C5
Jackson Rd
Barking IG11 . . . . 101 B6
Bromley BR2 . . . . 226 B6
East Barnet EN4 . . . . 14 C5
Lower Holloway N7 . . . . 72 B4
Uxbridge UB10 . . . . 60 A1
Jackson's La N6 . . . . 49 B2
Jackson's Pl CR0 . . . . 205 C1
Jackson St SE18 . . . . 144 C6
Jackson's Way CR0 . . . . 223 C5
Jackson Way UB2 . . . . 107 D4
Jack Taylor Sch
NW8 . . . . 92 A6 229 A6
Jack Tizard Sch W12 . . . 112 B5
Jack Walker Ct N5 . . . . 72 D4
Jacob Ct 24 EN3 . . . . 7 C6
Jacob Ho 14 DA18 . . . . 124 D4
Jacobin Lo N7 . . . . 72 A3
Jacob Mans 15 E1 . . . . 96 B1
Jacobs Cl RM10 . . . . 81 D4
Jacobs Ho E13 . . . . 99 C4
Jacobson Ct SW11 . . . . 267 B1
Jacobson Ho E1 . . . . 243 C2
Jacob St SE1 . . . . 118 A4
Jacob's Well Mews
W1 . . . . 238 B2
Jacotts Ho W10 . . . . 90 C3
Jacqueline Cl UB5 . . . . 85 A6
Jacqueline Ho 8 E1 . . . . 96 D2
Jade Cl Dagenham RM8 . . . 58 C1
Hendon NW2 . . . . 46 D2
Newham E16 . . . . 99 D1
Jaffe Rd IG1 . . . . 57 B1
Jaffray Rd BR2 . . . . 209 D5
Jaggard Way SW12 . . . . 158 D4
Jagger Ho SW11 . . . . 267 C2
Jago Cl SE18 . . . . 145 A6
Jago Wlk SE5 . . . . 139 B5
Jamahirya Sch
SW3 . . . . 136 C6 267 A6
Jamaica Rd
Bermondsey SE1 . . . . 253 D1
Bermondsey SE16 . . . . 118 B3
Thornton Heath CR7 . . . . 204 D3
Jamaica St E1 . . . . 96 C2
James Allen's Girls' Sch
SE22 . . . . 161 C6
James Allens Pre-Prep
Sch SE21 . . . . 161 B5
James Anderson Ct 29
E2 . . . . 95 C5
James Ave
Cricklewood NW2 . . . . 68 C3
Dagenham RM8 . . . . 59 B1
James Bedford Cl HA5 . . 22 C1
James Boswell Cl 1
SW16 . . . . 182 C6
James Brine Ho 6 E2 . . . 95 D4
James Campbell Ho 2
E2 . . . . 96 C5
James Cl London NW11 . . . 47 A3
8 Newham E13 . . . . 99 A5
James Collins Cl W9 . . . 91 B3
James Ct Chingford E4 . . . 20 B2
Finchley N12 . . . . 30 C3
Hendon NW9 . . . . 27 C1
Northolt UB5 . . . . 85 A5
3 Woodford E18 . . . . 37 B1
James Dixon Prim Sch
SE20 . . . . 184 B3
James Docherty Ho 4
E2 . . . . 96 C5
James Dudson Ct
NW10 . . . . 67 A1
James Est CR4 . . . . 180 D1
James Gdns N22 . . . . 32 D3
James Hammett Ho 9
E2 . . . . 95 D5
James Ho Mile End E1 . . . 97 A3
33 Rotherhithe SE16 . . . 118 D4
James Joyce Wlk 7
SE24 . . . . 138 D1
James La E10, E11 . . . . 54 B3
James Lee Sq EN3 . . . . 7 C5
James Leicester Hall of
Residence N7 . . . . 72 A2
James Lind Ho 6 SE8 . . 119 B2
James Middleton Ho 20
E2 . . . . 96 B4
James Newman Ct
SE9 . . . . 166 C1
Jameson Ct 6 E2 . . . . 96 C5
Jameson Ho SE11 . . . . 260 C2
Jameson Lo N6 . . . . 49 C3
Jameson Pl 11 W3 . . . . 111 A4
Jameson St W8 . . . . 245 B4
James Pl N17 . . . . 33 D2
James's Cotts TW9 . . . . 132 C5
James St Barking IG11 . . . 79 A1
Enfield EN1 . . . . 17 D6
Hounslow TW3 . . . . 130 B2
Marylebone W1 . . 93 A1 238 B1
Strand WC2 . . . . 116 A6 250 B6
James Stewart Ho
NW6 . . . . 69 B1
James Stroud Ho SE17 262 B1
Jamestown Rd
NW1 . . . . 93 B6 231 C6
Jamestown Way E14 . . . 120 B6
James Way WD19 . . . . 22 D6
James Wolfe Prim Sch
SE10 . . . . 142 A5
Jamieson Ho TW4 . . . . 151 B5
Jamuna Cl E14 . . . . 97 A2
Jane Austen Hall 14
E16 . . . . 121 B5
Jane St E1 . . . . 96 B1
Janet Ct
4 Bexleyheath DA7 . . . 147 C1
Wood Green N22 . . . . 32 B2
Janet St E14 . . . . 119 C3
Janeway Pl 2 SE16 . . . . 118 B4
Janeway St SE16 . . . . 118 A4
Janice Mews 3 IG1 . . . . 78 D5
Jansen Ho 5 SW15 . . . . 156 A6
Jansen Wlk SW11 . . . . 136 B1
Janson Cl Stratford E15 . . 76 C3
Willesden NW10 . . . . 67 C5
Janson Rd E15 . . . . 76 C3
Jansons Rd N15 . . . . 51 C6
Japan Cres N4 . . . . 50 B1
Japanese Sch The
W3 . . . . 110 C6
Japan Rd RM6 . . . . 58 D3
Jaquets Ct DA5 . . . . 169 C2
Jardine Ho HA1 . . . . 42 C2
Jardine Rd E1 . . . . 118 D6
Jarman Ho
Bermondsey SE16 . . . . 118 D2
16 Stepney E1 . . . . 96 C2
Jarrett Cl SW2 . . . . 160 D3
Jarrow Cl SM4 . . . . 201 D4
Jarrow Rd
Bermondsey SE16 . . . . 118 C1
Dagenham RM6 . . . . 58 C3
Tottenham Hale N17 . . . . 52 B5
Jarrow Way E9 . . . . 75 A4
Jarvis Cl
1 Barking IG11 . . . . 101 B6
Barnet EN5 . . . . 12 D6
Jarvis Ho 3 SE15 . . . . 140 A4
Jarvis Rd London SE22 . . 139 C1
South Croydon CR2 . . . . 221 B2
Jasmin SE1 . . . . 253 D3
Jasmine Cl Ilford IG1 . . . . 78 D3
Orpington BR6 . . . . 226 D6
Southall UB1 . . . . 107 A6
Jasmine Ct Lee SE12 . . . 165 A5
11 Wallington SM6 . . . . 219 B2
Wimbledon SW19 . . . . 179 C5
Jasmine Gdns
Harrow HA2 . . . . 63 C6
West Wickham CR0 . . . . 223 D5
Jasmine Gr SE20 . . . . 184 B2
Jasmine Sq 15 E3 . . . . 97 B6
Jasmine Terr UB7 . . . . 104 C4
Jasmine Way KT7 . . . . 196 C5
Jasmin Ho SE4 . . . . 141 B2
Jasmin Lo 17 SE16 . . . . 118 B1
Jasmin Rd KT19 . . . . 214 D3
Jason Ct
2 London SW9 . . . . 138 C4
Marylebone W1 . . . . 238 B2
Jason Ho UB5 . . . . 84 B4
Jason Wlk SE9 . . . . 188 C6
Jasper Cl EN3 . . . . 6 C5
Jasper Ho KT4 . . . . 199 B1
Jasper Rd Newham E16 . . 99 D1
Penge SE19 . . . . 183 D4
Jasper Wlk N1 . . . . 235 C2
Java Wharf SE1 . . . . 253 D2
Javelin Ct HA7 . . . . 25 B5
Javelin Way UB5 . . . . 84 D4
Jawahar Bagh SW16 . . . 182 D4
Jaycroft EN2 . . . . 4 C4
Jay Gdns BR7 . . . . 188 B6
Jay Ho SW15 . . . . 134 C3
Jay Mews SW7 . 114 A4 246 B1
Jayson Ct 7 CR0 . . . . 206 A1
Jazzfern Terr HA0 . . . . 65 A3
Jean Batten Cl SM6 . . . 220 B1
Jean Darling Ho SW10 266 C5
Jean Ho 3 SW17 . . . . 180 C5
Jean Humbert Ho 2
SE27 . . . . 183 B6
Jean Pardies Ho 23 E1 . . 96 C2
Jebb Ave SW2 . . . . 160 A5
Jebb St E3 . . . . 97 C5
Jedburgh Rd E13 . . . . 99 C4
Jedburgh St SW11 . . . . 137 A1
Jeddo Mews W12 . . . . 111 D4
Jeddo Rd W12 . . . . 111 D4
Jefferies Ho 13 NW10 . . . 67 B1
Jefferson Bldg 3 E14 . . 119 C4
Jefferson Cl
Ealing W13 . . . . 109 B3
Ilford IG2 . . . . 56 D4
Jefferson Wlk 13
SE18 . . . . 144 C6
Jeffrey Row SE12 . . . . 165 B6
Jeffrey's Ct 2 SW4 . . . . 138 A3
Jeffrey's Pl NW1 . . . . 71 C1
Jeffreys Rd EN3 . . . . 7 B1
Jeffrey's Rd SW4 . . . . 138 A3
Jeffrey's St NW1 . . . . 71 C1
Jeffs Cl TW12 . . . . 173 D4
Jeffs Rd SM1 . . . . 217 B4
Jeff Wooller Coll
WC1 . . . . 94 A2 240 B4
Jefton Ct SM6 . . . . 219 C3
Jeger Ave E2 . . . . 95 D6
Jeken Rd SE9 . . . . 143 C1
Jelf Rd SW2 . . . . 160 C6
Jellicoe Ct E4 . . . . 36 B4
Jellicoe Gdns HA7 . . . . 25 A4
Jellicoe Ho
5 Bethnal Green E2 . . . . 96 A5
Fitzrovia NW1 . . . . 238 D5
11 Putney SW15 . . . . 156 D6
Jellicoe Rd
4 Newham E13 . . . . 99 A3
Tottenham N17 . . . . 33 B3
Jemmett Cl KT2 . . . . 176 D2
Jemotts Ct 3 SE14 . . . . 140 D6
Jem Paterson Ct HA1 . . . 64 C4
Jengar Cl SM1 . . . . 217 D4
Jenkins Ho SW8 . . . . 269 C2
Jenkins La IG11 . . . . 101 A4
Jenkinson Ho 12 E2 . . . . 96 D4
Jenkins Rd E13 . . . . 99 B3
Jenner Ave W3 . . . . 89 B2
Jenner Cl DA14 . . . . 190 A6
Jenner Ct N21 . . . . 16 A6
Jenner Ho
5 Belvedere DA17 . . . . 125 C3
Greenwich SE3 . . . . 142 C6
Jenner Pl SW13 . . . . 134 B6
Jenner Rd N16 . . . . 73 D5
Jennett Rd CR0 . . . . 220 C5
Jennifer Ho SE11 . . . . 261 B3
Jennifer Rd BR1 . . . . 164 D1
Jennings Cl KT6 . . . . 197 C2
Jennings Ho SE10 . . . . 120 B1
Jennings Rd SE22 . . . . 161 D5
Jenny Hammond Cl
E11 . . . . 76 D5
Jenny Hammond Prim Sch
E11 . . . . 76 C4
Jensen Ho 10 E3 . . . . 97 C3
Jenson Way SE19 . . . . 183 D3
Jenton Ave DA7 . . . . 147 A3
Jephson Ct 17 SW4 . . . . 138 A3
Jephson Ho 6 SE17 . . . 138 D6
Jephson Rd E7 . . . . 77 C1
Jephson St SE5 . . . . 139 B4
Jephtha Rd SW18 . . . . 157 C5
Jeppo's La CR4 . . . . 202 D5
Jerdan Pl SW6 . . . . 265 A4
Jeremiah St 11 E14 . . . . 97 D1
Jeremy Bentham Ho 24
E2 . . . . 96 A4
Jeremy's Gn N18 . . . . 34 C6
Jermyn St
SW1 . . . . 115 C5 249 B4
Jerningham Ct SE14 . . . 141 A4
Jerningham Rd SE14 . . . 141 A4
Jerome Cres
NW8 . . . . 92 C3 237 A6
Jerome Ct 2 N11 . . . . 31 C5
Jerome Ho
Kingston u T KT1 . . . . 175 D1
Lisson Gr NW1 . . . . 237 B4
Jerome Pl KT1 . . . . 175 D1
Jerome St E1 . . . . 95 D3 243 C5
Jerome Twr 5 W3 . . . . 110 D4
Jerrard St SE13 . . . . 141 D2
Jerrold Lo SW15 . . . . 134 C2
Jerrold St 24 N1 . . . . 95 C5
Jersey Ave HA7 . . . . 25 C1
Jersey Ct UB2 . . . . 107 B3
Jersey Dr BR5 . . . . 211 B3
Jersey Ho
15 Canonbury N1 . . . . 73 A2
Enfield EN3 . . . . 6 D5
Jersey Rd Canonbury N1 . . 73 A2
Ealing W7 . . . . 109 A4
Hounslow TW5, TW7 . . . . 130 B5
Ilford IG1 . . . . 78 D4
Leytonstone E11 . . . . 54 B1
Mitcham SW17 . . . . 181 B4
Newham E16 . . . . 99 C1
Jersey St E2 . . . . 96 B4
Jerusalem Pas EC1 . . . . 241 C5
Jervis Bay Ho 9 E14 . . . 98 B1
Jervis Ct
9 Dagenham RM10 . . . . 81 D2
2 Greenwich SE10 . . . . 142 A4
Marylebone W1 . . . . 238 D1
Jerviston Gdns SW16 . . 182 C4
Jesmond Ave HA9 . . . . 66 B2
Jesmond Cl CR4 . . . . 203 B6
Jesmond Ct HA9 . . . . 66 C2
Jesmond Rd CR0 . . . . 205 D2
Jesmond Way HA7 . . . . 26 A5
Jessam Ave E5 . . . . 52 B1
Jessamine Rd W7 . . . . 108 D5
Jessel Ho
St Pancras WC1 . . . . 233 A1
Westminster SW1 . . . . 259 D4
Jesse Rd E10 . . . . 54 A1
Jessica Rd SW18 . . . . 158 A6
Jessie Blythe La 4
N19 . . . . 50 A2
Jessie Duffett Ho 11
SE5 . . . . 139 A5
Jessie's Cotts E17 . . . . 53 A3
Jessiman Terr TW17 . . . 192 C4
Jesson Ho SE17 . . . . 262 C3
Jessop Ave UB2 . . . . 107 B2
Jessop Ct N1 . . . . 234 D3
Jessop Ho 9 W4 . . . . 111 B2
Jessop Pl CR4 . . . . 202 C5
Jessop Prim Sch
SE24 . . . . 139 A1
Jessop Sq E14 . . . . 119 C5
Jessops Way CR0 . . . . 203 C3
Jessops Wharf 4
TW8 . . . . 131 C5
Jessup Cl SE18 . . . . 123 A2
Jeston Ho 10 SE27 . . . . 160 D1
Jethou Ho 16 N1 . . . . 73 A2
Jetstar Way UB5 . . . . 85 A4
Jevington Way SE12 . . . 165 B3
Jevons Ho 9 NW8 . . . . 70 B1
Jewell Ho 3 SW12 . . . . 159 C4
Jewel Rd E17 . . . . 53 C6
Jewish Mus The*
Camden Town
NW1 . . . . 93 B6 231 D5
Finchley N3 . . . . 29 D1
Jewry St EC3 . . . . 95 D1 243 C1
Jews Row SW18 . . . . 136 A1
Jews Wlk SE26 . . . . 184 B6
Jeymer Ave NW2 . . . . 68 C3
Jeymer Dr UB6 . . . . 86 A6
Jeypore Rd SW18 . . . . 158 A5
JFS Sch HA3 . . . . 44 C3
Jillian Cl TW12 . . . . 173 C3
Jim Bradley Cl 10
SE18 . . . . 122 C2
Jim Griffiths Ho SW6 . 264 D5
Joan Cres SE9 . . . . 165 D4
Joan Gdns RM8 . . . . 81 A6
Joanna Ho 7 W6 . . . . 112 C1
Joanne Ct EN1 . . . . 17 C5
Joan Player Ho EN3 . . . . 6 D6
Joan Rd RM8 . . . . 81 A6
Joan St SE1 . . . 116 D5 251 C3
Joan Villas IG2 . . . . 57 A2
Jocelin Ho N1 . . . . 233 D5
Jocelyn Rd TW9 . . . . 132 A2
Jocelyn St SE15 . . . . 140 A4
Jockey's Fields
WC1 . . . . 94 B2 240 D4
Jodane Rd SE8 . . . . 119 B2
Jodrell Cl TW7 . . . . 131 A4
Jodrell Rd E3 . . . . 75 B1
Joe Hunte Ct 2
SW27 . . . . 182 D5
Joel St HA5, HA6 . . . . 40 A5
Johanna Prim Sch
SE1 . . . . 116 C4 251 A1
Johanna St SE1 . . . . 251 A1
John Adam St
WC2 . . . . 116 A6 250 B5
John Aird Ct
W2 . . . . 92 A2 236 B4
John Aldis Ho N22 . . . . 32 B1
John Archer Way
SW18 . . . . 158 B5
John Ashby Cl SW2 . . . . 160 A5
John Austin Cl KT2 . . . . 176 B2
John Baird Ct SE26 . . . . 184 D6
John Baird Ho 11
SE20 . . . . 184 C3
John Ball Prim Sch
SE3 . . . . 142 C3
John Barker Ct NW6 . . . . 69 A1
John Barker Ho IG1 . . . . 79 B6
John Barnes Wlk E15 . . . 76 D2
John Barter Ho TW3 . . . 129 B3
John Betts' Ho W12 . . . . 112 A3
John Betts Prim Sch
W6 . . . . 112 B3
John Bond Ho 2 E3 . . . . 97 B5
John Bradshaw Rd
N14 . . . . 15 D3
John Brent Ho 8 SE8 . . 118 D2
John Buck Ho NW10 . . . . 89 D6
John Burns Dr IG11 . . . . 79 C1
John Burns Prim Sch
SW11 . . . . 137 A3
Johnby Cl EN3 . . . . 7 A6
John Campbell Rd 26
N16 . . . . 73 C3
John Carpenter St
EC4 . . . . 251 C6
John Cartwright Ho 7
E2 . . . . 96 B4
John Chilton Sch UB5 . . 63 A1
John Clifford Ho N8 . . . . 50 A3
John Clynes Ct SW15 . . 134 B1
John Conwey Ho 23
SW2 . . . . 160 C5
John Cornwell VC Ho 6
E12 . . . . 78 C4
John Day Ho TW7 . . . . 131 B2
John Dee Ho 3 SW14 . . 133 B2
John Donne Prim Sch
SE15 . . . . 140 B4
John Drinkwater Cl
E11 . . . . 54 D2
John Dwight Ho SW6 . . 135 D2
John Fearon Wlk 5
W10 . . . . 91 A4
John Felton Rd 19
SE16 . . . . 118 A4
John Fielden Ho 10 E2 . . 96 B4
John Fisher St E1 . . . . 118 A6
John F. Kennedy Specl
Sch E15 . . . . 98 B6
John Gooch Dr EN2 . . . . 4 D4
John Harris Ho SE15 . . . 140 A2
John Harrison Way
SE10 . . . . 120 D3
John Hunt Ct 5 SE9 . . . 166 A2
John Islip St
SW1 . . . . 116 A2 260 A3
John Kaye Ct TW17 . . . 192 C4
John Keall Ho SW15 . . . 134 D2
John Keats Ho N22 . . . . 32 B2
John Keats Lo EN2 . . . . 5 B4
John Keble CE Prim Sch
NW10 . . . . 89 D6
John Kelly Tech Colls
NW2 . . . . 67 D5
John Kennedy Ct 1
N1 . . . . 73 B2
John Kennedy Ho 1
SE16 . . . . 118 D2
John Kennedy Lo 2
N1 . . . . 73 B2
John King Ct 5 N19 . . . . 71 D6
John Kirk Ho
22 Battersea SW11 . . . 136 B2
Beckenham BR3 . . . . 207 A5
5 Streatham SW16 . . . . 160 A1
John Knight Lo SW6 . . . 265 B4
John Lamb Ct HA3 . . . . 24 C2
John Loughborough Sch
N17 . . . . 33 D1
John Lyon Sch The
HA2 . . . . 42 B1
John McDonald Ho 3
E14 . . . . 120 A3
John McKenna Wlk 17
SE16 . . . . 118 A3
John & Mary Sch NW5 . . 71 D3
John Masefield Ho N15 . 51 B3
John Maurice Cl
SE17 . . . . 117 B2 262 C4
John Milton Prim Sch
SW8 . . . . 137 C5 269 A3
John Nettleford Ho 14
E2 . . . . 96 B4
John Newton Ct DA16 . . 146 B2
John Orwell Sports Ctr
E1 . . . . 118 B5
John Parker Cl RM10 . . . 81 D1
John Parker Sq 8
SW11 . . . . 136 B2
John Parry Ct 28 N1 . . . . 95 C5
John Paul II Sch
SW19 . . . . 156 D4
John Penn Ho SE8 . . . . 141 B5
John Penn St SE13 . . . . 141 D4
John Perrin Pl HA3 . . . . 44 A2
John Perryn Prim Sch
W3 . . . . 89 C1
John Prince's St W1 . . . 238 D2
John Pritchard Ho 16
E1 . . . . 96 A3
John Ratcliffe Ho 8
NW6 . . . . 91 C4
John Rennie Wlk 1
E1 . . . . 118 C5
John Roan Sch The
SE3 . . . . 142 C5
John Roll Way SE16 . . . 118 A3
John Ruskin Coll CR2 . . 223 A1
John Ruskin Prim Sch
SE5 . . . . 139 A6
John Ruskin St SE5 . . . 139 A6
John's Ave NW4 . . . . 46 C5
Johns Cl TW15 . . . . 171 A6
John Scurr Ho 18 E14 . . . 97 A1
John Scurr Prim Sch
E1 . . . . 96 C3
John Silkin La SE8 . . . . 118 D1
Johns La SM4 . . . . 202 A4
John's Mews
WC1 . . . . 94 B3 240 D5
John Smith Ave
SW6 . . . . 135 B5 264 C4
John Smith Mews
E14 . . . . 120 B6
Johnson Cl E8 . . . . 96 A6
Johnson Ct
Hendon NW4 . . . . 46 A6
10 Wandsworth SW18 . . 136 B1
Johnson Ho
Belgravia SW1 . . . . 258 B3
23 Bethnal Green E2 . . . . 96 A4
Somers Town NW1 . . . . 232 B3
South Lambeth SW8 . . . 269 D3
Johnson Lo 12 W9 . . . . 91 C2
Johnson Rd
Bromley Comm BR2 . . . . 209 D4
Heston TW5 . . . . 128 C5
Stonebridge NW10 . . . . 89 B6
Thornton Heath CR0 . . . . 205 B2
Johnson's Cl SM5 . . . . 218 D5
Johnsons Ct EC4 . . . . 241 B1
Johnsons Dr TW12 . . . . 174 A2
Johnson's Ind Est
UB3 . . . . 106 A3
Johnson's Pl
SW1 . . . . 115 C1 259 A1
Johnson St
Southall UB2 . . . . 106 D3
Stepney E1 . . . . 96 C1
Johnsons Way NW10 . . . . 88 D3
John Spencer Sq N1 . . . . 72 D2
John's Pl E1 . . . . 96 B1
John St Croydon SE25 . . . 206 A5
Enfield EN1 . . . . 17 D6
Finsbury WC1 . . 94 B3 240 D5
Hounslow TW3, TW5 . . . 129 A3
West Ham E15 . . . . 98 D6
John Stainer Com Prim
Sch SE4 . . . . 141 A2
John's Terr CR0 . . . . 205 C1
Johnston Cl SW9 . . . . 270 D1
Johnstone Ho SE13 . . . . 142 B2
Johnstone Rd E6 . . . . 100 B4
Johnston Rd IG8 . . . . 37 A5
Johnston Terr NW2 . . . . 68 D5
John Strachey Ho
SW6 . . . . 264 D5
John Strype Ct E10 . . . . 53 D1
John Trundle Ct EC2 . . . 242 A4
John Tucker Ho 3
E14 . . . . 119 C3
John Walsh Twr E11 . . . . 76 D6
John Wesley Ct 6
TW1 . . . . 153 A3
John Wesley's House &
Mus* EC1 . . . . 242 D6
John Wheatley Ho
14 London N19 . . . . 49 D2
West Brompton SW6 . . . 264 D5
John William Cl 12
KT2 . . . . 175 D2
John Williams Cl
SE14 . . . . 140 D6
John Wilson St SE18 . . . 122 C2
John Wooley Cl SE13 . . 142 C1
Joiners Arms Yd 1
SE5 . . . . 139 B4
Joiners Ct 5 N20 . . . . 14 D1
Joiner St SE1 . . . . 252 D3
Joiners Yd N1 . . . . 233 B3
Joint Rd N10 . . . . 30 C2
Jolles Ho 9 E3 . . . . 97 D4
Jollys La Harrow HA2 . . . . 42 B1
Hayes UB4 . . . . 84 D2
Jonathan Ct 9 W4 . . . . 111 C2
Jonathan St
SE11 . . . . 116 B1 260 C2
Jones Ho
4 South Bromley E14 . . . 98 B1
Stamford Hill N16 . . . . 51 C1
Jones Rd E13 . . . . 99 B3
Jones St W1 . . . . 248 C5
Jones Wlk 6 TW10 . . . . 154 B5
Jonquil Gdns 5
TW12 . . . . 173 C4
Jonson Cl Hayes UB4 . . . 84 A2
Mitcham CR4 . . . . 203 B6

Jonson Ho
Borough The SE1 262 D5
16 Canonbury N16 73 B4
Jordan Cl HA2 63 B5
Jordan Ct SW15 134 D1
Jordan Hill N10 30 C2
Jordan Ho
12 London SE4 140 D1
Shoreditch N1 235 D5
Jordan Lo SW17 180 C5
Jordan Rd UB6 87 C6
Jordans Cl
Dagenham RM10 81 D4
Hounslow TW7 130 C4
Jordans Ho NW8 237 A5
Jordans Mews TW11 152 C2
Jo Richardson Comm Sch RM9 102 D6
Jo Richardson Com Sch RM9 80 C2
Joscoyne Ho 5 E1 96 B1
Josef Perrin Ho 1 SE27 183 B6
Joseph Ave W3 89 B1
Joseph Clarke Sch E4 36 B4
Joseph Conrad Ho SW1 259 B3
Joseph Ct N16 51 C2
Joseph Hardcastle Cl SE14 140 D5
Joseph Hood Prim Sch SW20 201 A6
Josephine Ave SW2 160 B6
Joseph Irwin Ho 11 E14 119 B6
Joseph Lancaster Prim Sch SE1 117 B3 262 C5
Joseph Lister Ct E7 77 A1
Joseph Lister Lo E11 55 B1
Joseph Powell Cl 1 SW12 159 C5
Joseph Priestley Ho 12 E2 96 B4
Joseph Ray Rd E11 76 C6
Joseph St E3 97 B3
Joseph Trotter Cl EC1 234 B1
Joshua Cl Croydon CR2 220 D1
Muswell Hill N10 31 B3
Joshua St E14 98 A1
Joslings Cl W12 112 A6
Joslyn Cl EN3 7 C5
Josseline Ct 9 E3 97 A5
Joubert Mans SW3 257 B2
Joubert St SW11 136 D3
Jowett Ho 27 SW9 138 A3
Jowett St SE15 139 D5
Joyce Ave N18 33 D5
Joyce Butler Ho N22 32 B2
Joyce Dawson Way SE28 124 A6
Joyce Lattimore Ct N9 18 B1
Joyce Page Cl SE7 143 D6
Joy Ct NW2 68 D5
Joydon Dr RM6 58 B3
Joyner Ct UB1 107 B6
Joyners Cl RM9 81 B4
Joystone Ct 8 EN4 2 C1
Jubb Powell Ho N15 51 C3
Jubet Ho 9 N16 73 B4
Jubilee Ave
Chingford E4 36 A4
Romford RM7 59 D4
Twickenham TW2 152 A3
Jubilee Bldgs NW8 229 C4
Jubilee Cl
4 Harlesden NW10 89 D5
Kingsbury NW9 45 B3
Pinner HA5 22 C1
Romford RM7 59 D4
Teddington KT1 175 C2
Jubilee Cres
Cubitt Town E14 120 A3
Edmonton N9 18 A3
Jubilee Ct Harrow HA3 44 A2
Hounslow TW3 129 D2
Islington N1 233 B6
Muswell Hill N10 49 A6
12 Sutton SM2 218 A2
Thornton Heath CR7 204 C5
Jubilee Dr HA4 63 A4
Jubilee Gdns UB1 85 C1
Jubilee Ho
3 Hampton TW12 173 C2
Lambeth SE11 261 B3
Jubilee Hts NW2 69 B2
Jubilee Lo HA7 25 A5
Jubilee Mans 10 E1 96 C1
Jubilee Mkt WC2 250 B6
Jubilee Par IG8 37 C4
Jubilee Park Ctry Pk BR2 210 C4
Jubilee Pl SW3 114 C1 257 B2
Jubilee Prim Sch
London SW2 160 C5
Stamford Hill N16 52 A1
Woolwich SE28 124 C6
Jubilee Rd Cheam SM3 216 D1
Wembley UB6 87 B6
Jubilee St E1 96 C2
Jubilee The 2 SE10 141 D5
Jubilee Villas KT10 196 C1
Jubilee Way
East Bedfont TW14 150 A3
Merton SW19 179 D2
Sidcup DA14 168 A2
Tolworth KT4, KT9 214 D5
Jubilee Wks SW19 180 A1
Jubilee Wlk WD19 22 B6
Jubilee Yd SE1 253 C2
Judd St WC1 94 A4 233 A1
Jude St E16 98 D1
Judge Heath La UB3 83 B1
Judges' Wlk NW3 70 A5
Judge Wlk KT10 212 C2
Juer St SW11 136 C5 267 B3
Jules Thorn Ave EN1 6 A1
Julia Ct E17 53 D4
Julia Garfield Mews 4 E16 121 B5
Julia Gdns IG11 102 D5
Juliana Cl N2 48 A6
Julian Ave W3 110 D6
Julian Cl EN5 1 D2
Julian Ct SW13 133 D4
Julian Hill HA1 64 C6
Julian Ho SE21 183 C6
Julian Pl E14 119 D1
Julian's Prim Sch SW16 182 C6
Julian Taylor Path 7 SE23 162 B2
Julia St NW5 71 A3
Julien Rd W5 109 C3
Juliet Ho 11 N1 95 C5
Juliette Rd E13 99 A5
Julius Caesar Way HA7 9 D1
Julius Ct TW8 132 A5
Julius Ho 8 E14 98 B1
Julius Nyerere Cl N1 233 C5
Junction App
Battersea SW11 136 C2
Lewisham SE13 142 A2
Junction Mews W2 237 A2
Junction Pl W2 236 D2
Junction Rd
Ashford TW15 171 B5
Brentford TW8 109 D2
Croydon CR2 221 B3
Dartmouth Pk N19 71 C5
Edmonton N9 18 A3
Harrow HA1 42 C3
Newham E13 99 B5
Tottenham Hale N17 52 A6
Junction Rd E RM6 59 A2
Junction Rd W RM6 59 A2
Junction Wembley Ret Pk The HA9 66 D4
Juniper Cl Barnet EN5 12 D6
Chessington KT9 214 B3
Wembley HA9 66 C3
Juniper Cres NW1 71 A1
Juniper Ct
Dagenham RM6 58 C3
Harrow HA3 24 D2
Hounslow TW3 129 D1
Stoke Newington N16 73 B6
Thornton Heath CR0 204 C3
Juniper Dr SW18 136 A1
Juniper Gdns
Ashford TW16 171 D4
Streatham CR4 181 C2
Juniper Ho
12 Ealing W5 87 C2
6 Peckham SE14, SE15 140 C5
9 Richmond TW9 132 D4
Juniper La E6 100 A2
Juniper Rd IG1 78 D4
Juniper St 16 E1 118 C6
Juniper Way UB3 105 C6
Juno Ct 11 SW9 138 C5
Juno Ho 2 E3 97 C6
Juno Way SE14 140 D6
Juno Way Ind Est SE14 140 D6
Jupiter Ct
10 Brixton SW9 138 C5
8 Northolt UB5 84 D4
Jupiter Hts UB10 82 B6
Jupiter Way N7 72 B2
Jupp Rd E15 76 B1
Jupp Rd W E15 98 B6
Jura Ho SE16 119 A2
Jurston Ct SE1 251 B1
Justice Wlk SW3 267 A5
Justin Cl TW8 131 D5
Justin Ct 3 CR7 204 C4
Justines Pl E2 96 D4
Justin Plaza CR4 202 C5
Justin Rd E4 35 B4
Jute La EN3 7 A2
Jutland Cl N19 50 A1
Jutland Ho
4 London SE5 139 A3
10 Woolwich SE7 122 A2
Jutland Rd Catford SE6 164 A4
Newham E13 99 A3
Jutsums Ave RM7 59 D3
Jutsums Ct RM7 59 D3
Jutsums La RM7 59 D2
Juxon Cl HA3 23 D2
Juxon St SE11 116 B2 260 D4
JVC Bsns Pk NW2 46 A1

K

Kaduna Cl HA5 40 B4
Kaizen Prim Sch E13 99 B3
Kale Rd DA18 125 A4
Kambala Rd SW11 136 B2
Kangley Bridge Ctr SE26 185 B5
Kangley Bridge Rd SE26 185 B5
Kaplan Dr N21 16 B6
Karachi Ho E15 76 C2
Kara Way NW2 68 D4
Karen Ct Bromley BR1 186 D2
2 Camberwell SE5 139 C2
Karen Ct *continued*
Forest Hill SE23 163 A5
Karen Ho 7 N16 73 B4
Karens Ct EN3 6 D6
Karen Terr Ilford IG2 57 B4
Leyton E11 76 D6
Karenza Ct HA9 43 C2
Kariba Cl N9 18 C1
Karman Ct HA3 42 C6
Karma Way HA2 41 C1
Karoline Gdns UB6 86 B5
Karyatis Ct EN1 17 D6
Kashgar Rd SE18 123 D2
Kashmir Rd SE7 143 D5
Kasmin Ct NW10 68 A1
Kassala Rd SW11 136 D4 267 D1
Katella Trad Est IG11 101 C4
Kates Cl EN5 12 A6
Katharine Rd 1 TW1 153 A3
Katharine St CR0 221 A5
Katherine Cl 3 SE16 118 D5
Katherine Ct
10 Forest Hill SE23 162 C3
Penge SE20 184 C2
Katherine Gdns SE9 143 D1
Katherine Ho
15 Kensal Town W10 91 A3
6 South Croydon CR0 221 A5
South Norwood SE19 183 C4
Katherine Rd E6, E7 77 C1
Katherine Sq W11 244 A4
Kathleen Ave Acton W3 89 A2
Wembley HA0 66 A1
Kathleen Ferrier Ct 4 N17 33 D3
Kathleen Godfree Ct SW19 179 C5
Kathleen Moore Ct BR4 224 A6
Kathleen Rd SW11 136 D2
Katrine Ct NW2 68 C5
Kayemoor Rd SM2 218 C2
Kay Rd SW9 138 B3
Kays Ct EN3 6 D1
Kay St Bethnal Green E2 96 A5
Welling DA16 146 B4
Keadby Ho 2 UB5 85 B4
Kean Ho 5 SE17 138 D6
Kean St WC2 94 B1 240 C1
Keates Est N16 73 D6
Keatley Gn E4 35 B4
Keats Ave E16 121 B5
Keats Cl
Bermondsey SE1 263 C3
Enfield EN3 18 D6
Hampstead NW3 70 C4
Hayes UB4 84 A2
Mitcham SW19 180 B4
Wanstead E11 55 B4
Keats Ct HA0 65 C5
Keats Gr NW3 70 C4
Keats Ho
7 Beckenham BR3 185 D4
22 Bethnal Green E2 96 C4
30 Camberwell SE5 139 A5
Chelsea SW1 269 B6
Harrow HA2 64 C6
Keats House Mus* NW3 70 C4
Keats Par 3 N9 18 A2
Keats Pl EC2 242 C3
Keats Rd DA16 145 D4
Keats Way
Croydon CR0 206 C3
Southall UB6 85 D2
West Drayton UB7 104 B2
Kebbell Terr E7 77 B3
Keble Cl
New Malden KT4 199 D1
Northolt UB5 64 A3
Keble Ct SW19 179 C4
Keble Ho 4 SW15 156 D5
Keble Pl SW13 134 B6
Keble Prep Sch N21 16 C4
Keble St SW17 180 A6
Kechill Gdns BR2 209 A2
Kedelston Ct E5 75 A4
Kedeston Ct SM1 201 D1
Kedge Ho 16 E14 119 C3
Kedleston Dr BR5 211 D4
Kedleston Wlk 21 E2 96 B4
Kedyngton Ho 5 HA8 27 A1
Keeble Cl SE18 144 D6
Keedonwood Rd BR1 186 D5
Keel Cl Barking IG11 102 C5
Rotherhithe SE16 118 D5
Keel Ct 8 E14 120 B6
Keeley Rd CR0 221 A6
Keeley St WC2 94 B1 240 C1
Keeling 2 TW11 174 C5
Keeling Ct CR0 220 D4
Keeling Ho 4 E2 96 B5
Keeling Rd SE9 165 D6
Keelson Ho 9 E14 119 C3
Keely Cl EN4 14 C6
Keemor Cl SE18 144 C5
Keens Cl SW16 181 D5
Keen's Rd CR0 221 A4
Keen's Yd N1 72 D2
Keepers Ct 4 CR2 221 A3
Keepers Mews TW11 175 C4
Keeper Wharf E1 118 D6
Keepier Wharf 15 E1 118 D6
Keep The
Forest Hill SE6 163 C3
Kidbrooke SE3 143 A3
Kingston u T KT2 176 B3
Keeton's Rd SE16 118 B3
Keevil Dr SW19 157 A4
Keighley Cl N7 72 A4
Keightley Dr SE9 167 A3
Keilder Cl UB10 82 C5
Keildon Rd SW11 136 D1
Keir Hardie Est E5 52 B1
Keir Hardie Ho
6 Belvedere DA17 125 C3
Fulham W6 134 D6
15 Upper Holloway N19 49 D2
Willesden NW10 67 D1
Keir Hardie Way
Barking IG11 80 A1
Hayes UB4 84 A4
Keir Hardy Prim Sch E16 99 A2
Keir The SW19 178 C5
Keith Connor Cl 5 SW8 137 B2
Keith Gr W12 112 A5
Keith Ho NW6 91 D5
Keith Park Rd UB10 60 B1
Keith Rd Barking IG11 101 B5
Hayes UB3 105 C3
Walthamstow E17 35 B2
Keith Sutton Ho 3 SE9 167 A2
Kelbrook Rd SE3 144 A2
Kelby Ho N7 72 B2
Kelceda Cl NW2 68 A6
Kelf Gr UB3 83 D1
Kelfield Ct 1 W10 90 D1
Kelfield Gdns W10 90 D1
Kelfield Mews W10 90 D1
Kelham Ho 10 SE18 144 D6
Kelland Cl 1 N8 49 D4
Kelland Rd E13 99 A3
Kellaway Rd SE3 143 D3
Keller Cres E12 77 D4
Kellerton Rd SE13 164 C6
Kellett Ho N1 235 D5
Kellett Rd SW2 138 C1
Kelling Gdns CR0 204 D2
Kellino St SW17 180 D6
Kellner Rd SE28 123 D3
Kellow Ho SE1 252 C2
Kell St SE1 116 D3 261 D6
Kelly Ave SE15 139 D4
Kelly Cl
Upper Halliford TW17 171 C1
Willesden NW10 67 B5
Kelly Ct 18 E14 119 C6
Kelly Mews 4 W9 91 B3
Kelly Rd NW7 29 A4
Kelly St NW1 71 B2
Kelly Way RM6 59 A3
Kelman Cl SW4 137 D3
Kelmore Gr SE22 140 A1
Kelmscott 5 SE23 162 D1
Kelmscott Cl E17 35 B2
Kelmscott Ct 2 HA7 25 C6
Kelmscott Gdns W12 112 A3
Kelmscott L Ctr E17 53 B3
Kelmscott Rd SW11 158 D6
Kelmscott Sch E17 53 B3
Kelross Rd N5 73 A4
Kelsall Cl SE3 143 B3
Kelsall Mews TW9 132 D4
Kelsey Gate 8 BR3 185 D1
Kelsey La BR3 207 C6
Kelsey Park Ave BR3 185 D1
Kelsey Park Man BR3 207 D6
Kelsey Park Rd BR3 185 C1
Kelsey Park Sp Coll BR3 207 C6
Kelsey Rd BR5 190 B1
Kelsey Sq BR3 185 C1
Kelsey St E2 96 A3
Kelsey Way BR3 207 C6
Kelshall Ct N4 73 A6
Kelso Ct SE20 184 B3
Kelso Lo E18 37 B1
Kelson Ho E14 120 A3
Kelso Pl W8 113 D3 255 D6
Kelso Rd SM5 202 A2
Kelvedon Cl KT2 176 C4
Kelvedon Ct HA4 62 C4
Kelvedon Ho SW8 270 B2
Kelvedon Rd SW6 135 B5 264 D3
Kelvin Ave N13 32 B4
Kelvinbrook KT8 195 D6
Kelvin Cl KT19 214 C2
Kelvin Cres HA3 24 C3
Kelvin Ct Chiswick W4 133 A5
Harrow HA2 42 A1
Isleworth TW7 130 C3
Notting Hill W11 245 A5
7 Penge SE20 184 B2
8 Twickenham TW1 153 B5
Kelvin Dr TW1 153 B5
Kelvin Gdns
Southall UB1 85 C1
Thornton Heath CR0 204 A2
Kelvin Gr
Forest Hill SE26 162 B1
Surbiton KT6 214 A5
Kelvin Grove Prim Sch SE26 162 B1
Kelvington Cl CR0 207 A2
Kelvington Rd SE15 162 D6
Kelvin Ho 3 DA17 125 C3
Kelvin Par BR6 211 C1
Kelvin Rd Highbury N5 73 A4
Welling DA16 146 A2
Kelyway Ho 20 SW2 160 C4
Kember St N1 72 B1
Kemble Dr BR2 226 A5
Kemble Ho
London SW9 138 D2
Kemble Ho *continued*
Stanmore HA7 24 D5
Kemble Rd
Croydon CR0 220 D5
Forest Hill SE23 162 D3
Tottenham N17 34 A2
Kemble St WC2 94 B1 240 C1
Kemerton Rd
Beckenham BR3 185 D1
Camberwell SE5 139 A2
Croydon CR0 205 D2
Kemey's St E9 75 A3
Kemnal Rd BR7 189 B5
Kemnal Tech Coll DA14 190 B3
Kemnal Warren BR7 189 B4
Kemp 24 NW9 27 D2
Kemp Ct SW8 270 A3
Kempe Ho SE1 262 D5
Kempe Rd NW6 90 D5
Kemp Gdns CR0 205 A3
Kemp Ho Finsbury EC1 235 C1
1 Globe Town E2 96 D5
Wallend E6 78 C2
Kempis Way 5 SE22 161 C6
Kemplay Rd NW3 70 B4
Kemp Rd RM8 58 D1
Kemps Ct NW2 68 D5
Kemp's Ct W1 239 C1
Kemps Dr E14 119 C6
Kempsford Gdns SW5 113 C1 255 B1
Kempsford Rd
Lambeth SE11 261 B3
Newington SE11 261 C3
Kemps Gdns SE13 164 A6
Kempshott Rd SW16 182 A3
Kempson Rd SW6 135 C5 265 B3
Kempthorne Rd SE8 119 B2
Kempton Ave
Northolt UB5 63 C3
Sunbury TW16 172 B2
Kempton Cl UB10 61 A4
Kempton Ct Stepney E1 96 B2
Sunbury TW16 172 B2
Kempton Ho 13 N1 95 C6
Kempton Lo 3 SM6 219 D5
Kempton Park Race Course TW16 172 C3
Kempton Park Sta TW16 172 B3
Kempton Rd E6 100 B6
Kempton Wlk CR0 207 A3
Kempt St SE18 144 C6
Kemsing Cl
Coney Hall BR2 224 D6
Sidcup DA5 169 A4
South Norwood CR7 205 A5
Kemsing Ho SE1 252 D1
Kemsing Rd SE10 121 A1
Kemsley SE13 163 D6
Kemsley Ct Ealing W13 109 C5
St Paul's Cray BR5 190 B2
Kenbrook Ho
Kensington W14 254 D5
5 Kentish Town NW5 71 C3
Kenbury Cl UB10 60 C5
Kenbury Gdns 10 SE5 139 A3
Kenbury Mans 18 SE5 139 A3
Kenbury St SE5 139 A3
Kenchester Cl SW8 138 A5 270 B3
Kencot Cl DA18 125 B4
Kendal NW1 231 D2
Kendal Ave Acton W3 88 D2
Barking IG11 101 C6
Edmonton N18 33 B6
Kendal Cl
Camberwell SE5 138 D5
East Bedfont TW14 149 D3
Hayes UB4 83 C5
Woodford IG8 20 D2
Kendal Ct Acton W3 88 C2
Brondesbury NW2 69 A3
11 Chingford E4 20 A3
Kendale Rd BR1 186 C5
Kendal Gdns
Edmonton N18 33 B6
Sutton SM1 218 A6
Kendal Ho Edgware HA8 27 A6
Forest Hill SE23 163 B3
32 Hackney E9 74 C1
Islington N1 233 D4
Penge SE20 184 B1
Kendall Ave BR3 185 A1
Kendall Ct
3 London SE22 162 A6
Mitcham SW19 180 B4
5 Penge SE19 183 D3
Sidcup DA15 168 A1
Kendall Ho SE12 164 D4
Kendall Lo 5 BR1 187 B2
Kendall Pl W1 238 A3
Kendall Rd
Beckenham BR3 185 A1
Isleworth TW7 131 A3
Kidbrooke SE18 144 A4
Kendalmere Cl N10 31 B2
Kendal Par N18 33 B6
Kendal Pl SW15 157 B6
Kendal Rd NW10 68 A4
Kendal St W2 92 C1 237 B1
Kendal Stps W2 237 B1
Kender Prim Sch SE14 140 C4
Kender St SE14 140 C4
Kendoa Rd 1 SW4 137 D1
Kendon Cl E11 55 B4
Kendon Ho E15 76 B1
Kendra Ct CR2 220 D1
Kendra Hall Rd CR2 220 D1
Kendrey Gdns TW2 152 C4
Kendrick Ct 12 SE15 140 B4
Kendrick Mews SW7 256 C3
Kendrick Pl SW7 256 C3
Kenelm Cl HA1 65 A5
Kenerne Dr EN5 13 A6
Kenilford Rd SW12 159 B4
Kenilworth Ave
Harrow HA2 63 B4
Walthamstow E17 53 C6
Wimbledon SW19 179 C6
Kenilworth Cres EN1 5 C4
Kenilworth Ct
7 Chingford E4 20 A2
Fulham SW6 135 A2
Twickenham TW2 152 C2
Kenilworth Gdns
Hayes UB4 83 D2
Ilford IG3 79 D6
Southall UB1 85 B4
South Oxhey WD19 22 C5
Woolwich SE18 144 D3
Kenilworth Ho HA7 25 B3
Kenilworth Rd
Ashford TW15, TW19 148 A1
Bow E3 97 A5
Ealing W5 110 A5
Edgware HA8 11 A1
Kilburn NW6 91 B6
Orpington BR5 211 A3
Penge SE20 184 D2
Stoneleigh KT17 216 A3
Kenilworth Terr 3 SM2 217 C1
Kenley N17 33 B1
Kenley Ave NW9 27 C2
Kenley Cl Barnet EN4 2 C1
Sidcup DA5 169 C4
St Paul's Cray BR7 211 C6
Kenley Gdns CR7 204 D5
Kenley Ho
5 Croydon CR0 206 A1
6 St Paul's Cray BR5 190 B1
Kenley Rd
Kingston u T KT1, KT3 176 D1
Merton SW19 201 C6
Twickenham TW1 153 B5
Kenley Wlk
Cheam SM3 216 D4
Notting Hill W11 244 A5
Kenlor Ct 6 HA8 26 D5
Kenlor Rd SW17 180 B5
Kenmare Ct 5 HA7 25 C6
Kenmare Dr
Mitcham CR4 180 D3
1 Tottenham N17 33 D1
Kenmare Gdns N13 33 A6
Kenmare Rd CR7 204 C3
Kenmere Gdns HA0 88 C6
Kenmere Rd DA16 146 C3
Kenmont Gdns NW10 90 B4
Kenmont Prim Sch NW10 90 B4
Kenmore Ave HA3 43 A6
Kenmore Cl TW9 132 C5
Kenmore Cres UB4 83 D4
Kenmore Ct NW6 69 C1
Kenmore Gdns HA8 26 D1
Kenmore Park Fst & Mid Schs HA3 44 A6
Kenmore Rd HA3 43 D5
Kenmure Mans W5 87 C3
Kenmure Rd E8 74 B3
Kenmure Yd E8 74 B3
Kennacraig Cl 6 E16 121 A5
Kennard Ho 12 SW11 137 A3
Kennard Mans 6 N11 30 D5
Kennard Rd London N11 30 D5
Stratford E15 76 B1
Kennard St
9 London SW11 137 A3
Newham E16 122 B5
Kennedy Ave EN3 18 C5
Kennedy Cl
Crofton BR5 211 B1
1 Mitcham CR4 181 A1
Newham E13 99 A5
Pinner HA5 23 B4
Kennedy Cox Ho 9 E16 98 D2
Kennedy Ct
Ashford TW15 171 A5
Bushey WD23 8 B2
Kennedy Ho SE11 260 C2
Kennedy Path W7 86 D3
Kennedy Rd
Barking IG11 101 C6
Ealing W7 86 C2
Kennedy Wlk SE17 262 D3
Kennet Cl SW11 136 B1
Kennet Ct 47 W2 91 C2
Kennet Dr UB4 85 A2
Kenneth Ave IG1 78 D4
Kenneth Campbell Ho NW8 236 D6
Kenneth Cres NW2 68 B3
Kenneth Ct SE11 261 B4
Kenneth Gdns HA7 25 A4
Kenneth More Rd 4 IG1 78 D5
Kennet Ho NW8 236 D5
Kenneth Rd RM6 59 A2
Kenneth Robbins Ho 1 N17 34 B3

Kenneth Younger Ho
  SW6. . . . . **264** D5
Kennet Rd
  Isleworth TW7 . . . . . .**130** D2
  West Kilburn W9 . . . . . .**91** B3
Kennet Sq CR4 . . . . . . **180** C2
Kennet St E1 . . . .**118** A5
Kennett Ho HA1 . . . . . .**64** D6
Kennett Wharf La EC4 . .**252** B6
Kenninghall N18 . . . . . **34** C5
Kenninghall Rd
  London N18 . . . .**34** C5
  Lower Clapton E5 . . . . **74** B5
Kenning Ho **6** N1 . . . .**95** C6
Kenning St SE16 . . . . .**118** C4
Kennings Way
  SE11 . . . . . . **116** C1 **261** B2
KENNINGTON. **116** C1
Kennington Ent Ctr
  SE17 . . . . **261** C1
Kennington La
  SE11 . . . . . . **116** B1 **260** D1
Kennington Oval
  SE11 . . . . . **138** B6 **270** C1
Kennington Palace Ct
  SE11 . . . . **261** A2
Kennington Park Gdns
  SE17 . . . .**138** D6
Kennington Park Ho
  SE11 . . . . **261** B1
Kennington Park Pl
  SE11 . . . .**138** D6
Kennington Park Rd
  SE11 . . . . . . **116** C2 **261** C2
Kennington Rd
  SE11 . . . . . . **116** C2 **261** A3
Kennington Sta
  SE17 . . . . . **116** D1 **261** C2
Kennoldes SE21 . . . . .**161** B2
Kennyland Ct NW4 . . . .**46** B3
Kenny Rd NW7 . . . .**29** A5
Kenrick Pl W1 . . . .**238** A3
KENSAL GREEN **90** C4
Kensal Green Cemy (All
  Souls)* NW10 . . . . . .**90** C4
Kensal Green Sta
  NW10 . . . .**90** C4
Kensal Ho W10 . . . . . .**90** D3
Kensal Rd W10 . . . . . . **91** A3
KENSAL RISE **90** D5
Kensal Rise Prim Sch
  NW6 . . . .**90** C4
Kensal Rise Sta NW10. .**90** D5
KENSAL TOWN **91** A3
KENSINGTON **113** C4
Kensington Ave
  Plashet E7 . . . .**78** B2
  South Norwood CR7 . . . .**182** C2
Kensington Avenue Prim
  Sch CR7 . . . .**182** C2
Kensington & Chelsea
  Coll
  Chelsea
  SW10 . . . . . . **136** A5 **266** A4
  Kensal Town W10 . . . . . .**91** A2
Kensington Church Ct
  W8 . . . . **245** C1
Kensington Church St
  W8 . . . . **113** C4 **245** B3
Kensington Church Wlk
  W8 . . . . **245** C1
Kensington Cl N11 . . . .**31** A4
Kensington Court Mans
  W8 . . . . **245** D1
Kensington Court Mews
  W8 . . . . **255** D6
Kensington Court Pl
  W8 . . . . **113** D3 **255** D6
Kensington Ct
  2 Burnt Oak NW7 . . . .**27** B5
  Enfield EN2 . . . .**5** C1
  Hendon NW4 . . . .**28** C1
  Kensington
  W8 . . . . **113** D4 **245** D1
Kensington Ct Gdns
  W8 . . . . **255** D6
Kensington Dr IG8. . . . .**37** D1
Kensington Gardens*
  W2 . . . . **114** A5 **246** B3
Kensington Gate
  W8 . . . . **114** A3 **256** A6
Kensington Gdns
  Kingston u T KT1. . . . . .**197** C6
  Redbridge IG1. . . . .**56** B1
Kensington Gdns Sq
  W2 . . . .**91** D1
Kensington Gore
  SW7 . . . . **114** B4 **246** C1
Kensington Hall Gdns
  W14 . . . . **254** C2
Kensington High St
  W8 . . . . **113** C3 **255** B6
Kensington Ho **3** NW5. .**71** C3
Kensington Hts
  Harrow HA1 . . . .**42** D3
  Kensington W8 . . . .**113** B2
Kensington Lodge UB5. .**85** C5
Kensington Mall W8 . . .**245** B4
Kensington Mans SW5 . .**255** B2
Kensington Olympia Sta
  W14 . . . . **113** A3 **254** A6
Kensington Pal*
  W8 . . . . **113** D5 **245** D3
Kensington Palace Gdns
  W8 . . . . **113** D5 **245** D3
Kensington Park Gdns
  W11 . . . . **113** B6 **244** D5

Kensington Park Mews
  W11 . . . .**91** B1
Kensington Park Rd
  W11 . . . . **113** B6 **244** D6
Kensington Pl
  W8 . . . . **113** C5 **245** A4
Kensington Prep Sch
  SW6 . . . . **135** B4 **264** D2
Kensington Prim Sch
  E12 . . . .**78** B2
Kensington Rd
  Kensington
  SW7 . . . . **114** A4 **246** B1
  Northolt UB5 . . . .**85** C5
Kensington Sports Ctr
  W11 . . . . **244** A6
Kensington Sq
  W8 . . . . **113** D4 **245** C1
Kensington Terr CR2. . .**221** B1
Kensington Village
  W14 . . . . **113** B2 **254** D3
Kensington W W14 . . . .**254** A4
Kensit Meml Coll N3. . . .**29** A1
Kensworth Ho EC1. . . . .**235** D1
Kent Ave Bexley DA16 . .**167** D6
  Dagenham RM9. . . . . . .**103** C3
  Ealing W13 . . . .**87** B2
Kent Cl
  Mitcham CR4, SW16 . . . .**204** A5
  Orpington BR6. . . . .**227** C2
Kent Ct Acton W3. . . . . .**88** B1
  3 Haggerston E2. . . . . .**95** D5
  Hendon NW9. . . . .**27** C1
Kent Dr Cockfosters EN4 . .**15** A6
  Teddington TW11 . . . . . .**174** C5
Kentford Way UB5 . . . . .**85** A6
Kent Gate Way CR0 . . . .**223** D3
Kent Gdns Ealing W13. . .**87** B2
  Ruislip HA4 . . . .**40** B3
Kent Ho
  Camberwell SE1 . . . . . . **263** D1
  13 Chiswick W4 . . . . . .**111** C1
  Edgware HA8 . . . .**26** B3
  Marylebone W1 . . . .**239** A2
  Pimlico SW1 . . . . **259** C1
  Richmond TW10 . . . .**154** C6
Kent House La BR3 . . . .**185** A5
Kent House Rd BR3 . . . .**185** A4
Kent House Sta BR3 . . .**185** A2
Kent House Station App
  BR3 . . . . **184** D2
Kentish Bldgs SE1 . . . . **252** C3
Kentish Rd DA17. . . . . .**125** C2
KENTISH TOWN **71** C3
Kentish Town CE Prim Sch
  NW5 . . . .**71** C3
Kentish Town Rd NW1 . .**71** B2
Kentish Town Sta NW5 . .**71** C3
Kentish Town West Sta
  NW5 . . . .**71** B2
Kentish Way BR1, BR2. .**209** B6
Kentlea Rd SE28 . . . . .**123** C4
Kent Lo **9** SW19. . . . .**156** D3
Kentmere Ho SE15 . . . .**140** C6
Kentmere Rd SE18 . . . .**123** C2
KENTON **43** C3
Kenton Ave Harrow HA1. .**42** D2
  Southall UB1 . . . .**107** C6
  Sunbury TW16 . . . .**173** A1
Kenton Ct
  2 Forest Hill SE26 . . . .**185** A6
  Harrow HA3 . . . .**43** B3
  3 Richmond TW10 . . . .**153** D5
  West Kensington W14 . . .**254** C5
Kenton Gdns HA3 . . . . .**43** C4
Kenton Grove Ho HA3 . .**44** B4
Kenton Ho
  20 Globe Town E1. . . . .**96** C3
  Highbury N5 . . . .**72** C5
  Kenton HA3 . . . .**43** A3
Kenton La Harrow HA3 . .**24** D3
  Kenton HA3 . . . .**43** A3
Kenton Park Ave HA3 . . .**43** C5
Kenton Park Cl HA3. . . .**43** C4
Kenton Park Cres HA3 . .**43** C5
Kenton Park Mans HA3. .**43** C4
Kenton Park Par HA3. . . .**43** C5
Kenton Park Rd HA3 . . .**43** C5
Kenton Rd Harrow HA3. . .**43** C4
  Homerton E9 . . . .**74** D2
Kenton St WC1 . . . .**240** A6
Kenton Sta HA3. . . . . . .**43** B3
Kenton Way UB4. . . . . . .**83** C4
Kent Pas NW1 . . . .**237** C6
Kent Pk Ind Est SE15 . .**140** B6
Kent Rd
  Dagenham RM10. . . . . . .**81** D3
  East Molesey KT8 . . . . . .**196** A5
  Kingston u T KT1 . . . . . .**197** C6
  Richmond TW9 . . . .**132** C5
  South Acton W4. . . . . . .**111** A3
  Southgate N21 . . . .**17** B4
  West Wickham BR4 . . . . .**207** D1
Kent St Haggerston E2. . .**95** D5
  Newham E13 . . . .**99** B4
Kent Terr NW1 . . **92** C4 **230** B1
Kent Twr SE20 . . . .**184** B3
Kent View Gdns IG3 . . . .**79** C6
Kent Way KT6 . . . .**214** B6
Kentwell Cl SE4 . . . . . .**141** A1
Kentwins N14 . . . .**15** B6
Kentwode Gn SW13. . . .**134** A5
Kent Yard SW7 . . . .**247** B1
Kenver Ave N12 . . . .**30** B4
Kenward Rd SE9. . . . . .**165** D6
Ken Way HA9. . . . .**67** A5
Kenway Rd
  SW5. . . . . **113** D2 **255** C3
Ken Wilson Ho **16** E2. . .**96** A5
Kenwood Ave N14 . . . . .**15** D6

Kenwood Cl
  North End NW3 . . . .**48** B1
  Sipson UB7 . . . .**126** C6
Kenwood Ct NW9 . . . . . .**45** A5
Kenwood Dr BR3 . . . . . .**208** A6
Kenwood Gdns
  Ilford IG2 . . . .**56** C4
  2 Wanstead E18 . . . . . .**55** B6
Kenwood Ho
  16 Brixton SW9. . . . . .**138** D1
  Enfield EN1 . . . .**17** C5
Kenwood Ho* NW3. . . . .**48** C1
Kenwood Rd
  Edmonton N9. . . . .**18** A3
  Highgate N6 . . . .**48** D3
Kenworthy Rd E9 . . . . . .**75** A2
Kenwrick Ho N1. . . . . . .**233** D5
Kenwyn Dr NW2 . . . .**67** D3
Kenwyn Rd
  Clapham SW4 . . . .**137** D1
  Wimbledon SW20 . . . . . .**178** C2
Kenya Rd SE7 . . . .**143** D5
Kenyngton Dr TW16. . . .**172** A5
Kenyngton Manor Prim
  Sch TW16 . . . .**172** A4
Kenyngton Pl HA3 . . . . .**43** C4
Kenyon Ho **31** SE5 . . . .**139** A5
Kenyon St SW6 . . . .**134** D4
Keogh Rd E15 . . . .**76** D2
Kepler Ho **9** SE10 . . . .**120** D1
Kepler Rd SW2, SW4. . .**138** A1
Keppel Ho
  Brompton SW3 . . . .**257** A3
  2 Deptford SE8 . . . . . .**119** B1
Keppel Rd
  Dagenham RM9. . . . . . .**81** A4
  Newham E6 . . . .**100** B6
Keppel Row SE1 . . . . . .**252** B2
Keppel St WC1 . . . .**239** D4
Kerala Ct N17 . . . .**33** D2
Kerbela St E2. . . . .**96** A3
Kerbey St E14 . . . .**97** D1
Kerem Sch N2 . . . .**48** B4
Kerfield Cres SE5 . . . . .**139** B4
Kerfield Pl SE5 . . . .**139** B4
Kerridge Ct N1 . . . .**73** C2
Kerrier Ho SW10. . . . . .**266** B3
Kerrington Ct **7** W12 . .**112** C4
Kerrison Pl W5 . . . .**109** D5
Kerrison Rd
  Battersea SW11 . . . . . .**136** C2
  Ealing W5 . . . .**109** D5
  Mill Meads E15 . . . .**98** B6
Kerrison Villas W5. . . . .**109** D5
Kerry N7 . . . .**72** A2
Kerry Ave HA7 . . . .**25** D6
Kerry Ct **1** Newham E16 . . .**99** B1
  Palmers Green N13. . . . . .**16** B2
Kerry Ct HA7 . . . .**25** D6
Kerry Ho **6** E1 . . . .**96** C1
Kerry Path SE8 . . . .**141** B6
Kerry Rd SE8 . . . .**141** B6
Kerscott Ho **30** E3. . . . .**97** D4
Kersey Gdns SE9 . . . . .**188** A6
Kersfield Ho SW15 . . . .**156** D5
Kersfield Rd SW15 . . . .**156** D5
Kershaw Cl SW18 . . . . .**158** B5
Kershaw Ho **7** SE27 . .**160** D1
Kershaw Rd RM10 . . . . .**81** C5
Kersley Mews SW11 . . .**267** C1
Kersley Rd N16 . . . .**73** C5
Kersley St SW11 . . . . . .**136** D3
Kerstin Cl UB3. . . . .**105** D6
Kerswell Cl N15 . . . .**51** C4
Kerwick Cl **1** N7 . . . . . .**72** B1
Keslake Mans NW10 . . . .**90** D5
Keslake Rd NW6 . . . .**90** D5
Kessock Cl N17 . . . .**52** B4
Kestlake Rd DA5. . . . . .**168** C5
KESTON **225** D4
Keston Ave BR2. . . . . . .**225** C3
Keston CE Prim Sch
  BR2. . . . .**225** D3
Keston Cl Bexley DA16 . .**146** C5
  Edmonton N18. . . . .**17** B1
Keston Ct DA5. . . . .**169** B4
Keston Gdns BR2. . . . . .**225** C3
Keston Ho SE17. . . . . . .**263** B2
Keston Mark BR2 . . . . .**226** A5
Keston Park Cl BR2 . . . .**226** B5
Keston Rd
  East Dulwich SE15 . . . . .**140** A2
  Thornton Heath CR7. . . .**204** C3
  West Green N17 . . . .**51** B5
Kestrel Ave
  East Ham E6 . . . .**100** A2
  Herne Hill SE24. . . . . . .**161** A6
Kestrel Cl
  Grahame Pk NW9 . . . . . .**27** C1
  Kingston u T KT2 . . . . . .**175** D4
  Neasden NW10 . . . .**67** B3
Kestrel Ct
  Higham Hill E17. . . . .**34** D1
  Ruislip HA4 . . . .**61** B6
  South Croydon CR2 . . . . .**221** A2
  Wallington SM6. . . . . . .**219** C3
Kestrel Ho
  4 Battersea SW11 . . . .**136** C2
  Enfield EN3 . . . .**19** A6
  Finsbury EC1. . . . .**235** A2
Kestrel Pl SE14 . . . . . .**141** A6
Kestrel Way UB3. . . . . .**105** B4
Keswick Apartments **4**
  N17 . . . .**51** D6
Keswick Ave
  Kingston u T KT2,
  SW15. . . . .**177** C5
  Merton SW19 . . . .**179** C1
  Upper Halliford TW17. . . .**193** C4

Keswick Broadway **1**
  SW15. . . . .**157** B6
Keswick Cl SM1. . . . . . .**218** A4
Keswick Ct
  13 Catford SE6. . . . . . .**164** D3
  2 East Dulwich SE22 . .**162** A6
Keswick Dr EN3 . . . .**6** C1
Keswick Gdns
  Redbridge IG4. . . . .**56** A5
  Ruislip HA4 . . . .**39** B3
  Wembley HA9 . . . .**66** A4
Keswick Ho **8** SE5. . . .**139** A4
Keswick Hts **9** SW15 . .**157** A6
Keswick Lo E8. . . . .**73** D2
Keswick Mews W5. . . . .**110** A5
Keswick Rd
  Bexleyheath DA7. . . . . .**147** C4
  Broom Hill BR6 . . . .**211** D1
  Putney SW15. . . . .**157** A6
  Twickenham TW2. . . . . .**152** A5
  West Wickham BR4. . . . .**224** C6
Kettering Ct CR7. . . . . .**205** A5
Kettering Rd EN3 . . . . . .**6** D6
Kettering St SW16 . . . .**181** C4
Kett Gdns SW2 . . . .**160** B6
Kettleby Ho SW9 . . . . . .**138** D2
Kettlebaston Rd E10 . . .**53** B1
Kettlewell Cl N11. . . . . . .**31** A4
Ketton Ho **11** W10 . . . . .**90** C3
Kevan Ct **6** E17 . . . . . .**53** D5
Kevan Ho SE5 . . . .**139** A5
Kevelioc Rd N17 . . . .**33** A2
Kevin Cl TW4 . . . .**128** D3
Kevington Cl BR5. . . . . .**211** D5
Kevington Dr BR5,
  BR7 . . . .**211** D5
KEW **132** C6
Kew Bridge TW8 . . . . . .**110** B1
Kew Bridge Ct **8** W4 . .**110** C1
Kew Bridge Distribution
  Ctr TW8. . . . .**110** B1
Kew Bridge Rd TW8. . . .**110** B1
Kew Bridge Sta TW8. . .**110** B1
Kew Bridge Steam Mus*
  TW8 . . . .**110** B1
Kew Coll TW9 . . . .**132** C5
Kew Cres SM3 . . . .**217** B5
Kew Ct KT2. . . . .**176** A2
Kew Foot Rd TW9. . . . .**132** A2
Kew Gardens Rd TW9. . .**132** C4
Kew Gardens (Royal
  Botanic)* TW9 . . . . . .**132** A4
Kew Gardens Sta
  TW9 . . . .**132** C5
Kew Gn TW9 . . . .**132** B6
Kew Green TW9 . . . . . .**132** B6
Kew Green Prep Sch
  TW9 . . . .**132** B6
Kew Lo **11** TW9 . . . . . .**132** B4
Kew Montessori Sch
  TW9 . . . .**132** C4
Kew Obsy* TW9 . . . . . .**131** C2
Kew Pal* TW9 . . . .**132** A5
Kew Pier TW9 . . . .**132** C6
Kew Rd Finchley N2 . . . . .**30** C2
  Richmond TW9, W4. . . . .**132** B4
Kew Ret Pk TW9. . . . . .**132** C4
Kew Riverside Prim Sch
  TW9 . . . .**132** D3
Key Cl E1 . . . .**96** B3
Keyes Ct SE22 . . . .**162** A6
Keyes Rd NW2. . . . .**68** D3
Keyham Ho **31** W2 . . . .**91** C2
Key Ho **9** SE11 . . . . . .**138** C6
Keymer Rd SW2 . . . . . .**160** B2
Keynes Cl N2. . . . .**48** D6
Keynes Ct **9** SE28 . . . .**124** B6
Keynsham Ave IG8. . . . .**36** C6
Keynsham Gdns SE9 . . .**166** A6
Keynsham Ho **2** N4 . . . .**51** A2
Keynsham Rd
  Cheam SM4. . . . .**201** D1
  Eltham SE9 . . . .**166** A6
Keynsham Wlk SM4. . . .**201** D1
Keyse Rd SE1. . . .**117** D3 **263** C5
Keysham Ave TW5 . . . . .**128** A4
Keysham Ct HA9 . . . . . .**66** A6
Keystone Cres N1. . . . .**233** B3
Keywood Dr TW16 . . . . .**172** A4
Keyworth Cl E5. . . . .**75** A4
Keyworth Pl SE1. . . . . .**261** D6
Keyworth Prim Sch
  SE17 . . . . . . **116** D1 **261** C2
Keyworth St
  SE1 . . . . **116** D3 **261** D6
Kezia St SE8 . . . .**119** A1
Khalsa Ct N22 . . . .**32** D2
Khama Rd SW17 . . . . . .**180** C6
Khartoum Rd Ilford IG1. .**78** D3
  Newham E13 . . . .**99** B4
  Upper Tooting SW17. . . .**180** B6
Khyber Rd SW11. . . . . .**136** C3
Kibworth St
  SW8. . . . . **138** B5 **270** C5
KIDBROOKE **143** C2
Kidbrooke Gdns SE3 . . .**143** A4
Kidbrooke Gr SE3 . . . . .**143** B4
Kidbrooke Interchange
  SE3 . . . .**143** B2
Kidbrooke La SE9. . . . .**144** A1
Kidbrooke Park Cl
  SE3 . . . .**143** B4
Kidbrooke Park Prim Sch
  SE3 . . . .**143** B4
Kidbrooke Park Rd SE12,
  SE3 . . . .**143** B2
Kidbrooke Sch SE3 . . . .**143** D3
Kidbrooke Sta SE3 . . . .**143** A3
Kidbrooke Way SE3. . . .**143** B3
Kiddens BR8. . . . .**191** D1

Kidderminster Pl CR0. . .**204** D1
Kidderminster Rd
  CR0. . . . .**205** A2
Kidderpore Ave NW3. . . .**69** C4
Kidderpore Gdns NW3 . .**69** C4
Kidd Ho RM9 . . . .**81** B4
Kidd Pl SE7. . . . .**122** A1
Kidlington Way NW9 . . . .**27** C2
Kierbeck Bsns Complex
  E16. . . . .**121** B4
Kiffen St EC2 . . . .**242** D6
Kilberry Cl TW7. . . . . . .**130** B4
Kilbrennan Ho **9** E14. . .**98** A1
KILBURN **91** C6
Kilburn Bridge **14** NW6. .**91** C6
Kilburn Gate NW6 . . . . .**91** D6
Kilburn High Rd NW6 . . .**91** C6
Kilburn High Road Sta
  NW6. . . . .**91** B6
Kilburn Ho **11** W9 . . . . .**91** B4
Kilburn La W10 . . . .**91** A5
Kilburn Park Foundation
  Sch The NW6. . . . .**91** B5
Kilburn Park Rd NW6. . .**91** C4
Kilburn Park Sta NW6. . .**91** C5
Kilburn Pl NW6 . . . .**91** C6
Kilburn Priory NW6 . . . .**91** C6
Kilburn Sq NW6 . . . . . .**91** C6
Kilburn Sta NW2. . . . . . .**69** B2
Kilburn Vale NW6 . . . . .**91** C6
Kilburn Vale Est **13**
  NW6 . . . .**91** C6
Kilby Ct SE10 . . . .**120** D3
Kildare Cl HA4. . . . .**40** C1
Kildare Ct W2 . . . .**91** C1
Kildare Gdns W2 . . . . . .**91** C1
Kildare Rd E16 . . . .**99** A2
Kildare Terr W2 . . . .**91** C1
Kildare Wlk E14 . . . .**97** C1
Kildoran Rd SW2 . . . . . .**160** A6
Kildowan Rd IG3 . . . . . .**58** A1
Kilgour Rd SE23 . . . . . .**163** A5
Kilkie St SW6. . . . .**136** A3
Killarney Rd SW18 . . . .**158** A5
Killearn Rd SE6. . . . . . .**164** B3
Killester Gdns KT17,
  KT4 . . . .**216** B4
Killick St N1. . . . **94** B5 **233** C3
Killieser Ave SW2 . . . . .**160** A2
Killigrew Ho TW16. . . . .**171** C3
Killip Cl E16 . . . .**98** D1
Killoran Ho **9** E14. . . . .**120** A3
Killowen Ave UB5. . . . . .**64** A3
Killowen Rd E9 . . . .**74** D2
Killyon Rd SW8. . . . . . .**137** C3
Kilmaine Rd
  SW6. . . . . **135** A5 **264** B3
Kilmarnock Gdns RM8 . .**80** C5
Kilmarnock Rd WD19 . . .**22** D6
Kilmarsh Rd W6 . . . . . .**112** C2
Kilmartin Ave SW16. . . .**204** C6
Kilmartin Rd IG3 . . . . . .**80** A6
Kilmington Rd SW13 . . .**134** A6
Kilmiston Ave TW17. . . .**193** A3
Kilmiston Ho TW17 . . . .**193** A3
Kilmore Ho **17** E14 . . . . .**97** D1
Kilmorey Gdns TW1. . . .**131** B1
Kilmorey Rd TW1 . . . . .**131** B1
Kilmorie Prim Sch
  SE23. . . . .**163** A2
Kilmorie Rd SE23 . . . . .**163** A2
Kilmuir Ho SW1 . . . . . .**258** B3
Kiln Cl UB3 . . . .**127** B6
Kiln Ct E14 . . . .**119** B6
Kilner Ho **3** SE11. . . . .**138** C4
Kilner St E14 . . . .**97** C2
Kiln Mews SW17 . . . . . .**180** B5
Kiln Pl NW5 . . . .**71** A3
Kilnsey Ct **8** N11 . . . . . .**31** A4
Kilnside KT10. . . . .**213** A1
Kiloh Ct **1** SW11 . . . . .**136** C2
Kilpatrick Ct N16 . . . . . .**51** D1
Kilpatrick Way UB4. . . . .**85** A2
Kilpeck Ho **9** N4 . . . . . .**51** A2
Kilravock Ho SE25 . . . .**205** C6
Kilravock St W10 . . . . . .**91** A4
Kilronan **5** W3 . . . .**89** B1
Kilross Rd TW14 . . . . . .**149** C3
Kilsby Wlk RM9 . . . .**80** B2
Kilsha Rd KT12. . . . . . .**194** C3
Kilvinton Dr EN2. . . . . . .**5** B4
Kimball Gdns
  SW6. . . . . **135** A4 **264** A1
Kimbell Pl SE9. . . . .**143** C1
Kimber Ctr The SW18 . .**157** C4
Kimber Ho **11** SE18. . . .**144** D6
Kimberley Ave
  Ilford IG2 . . . .**57** C2
  Newham E6 . . . .**100** A5
  Nunhead SE15. . . . .**140** C2
Kimberley Ct
  Belvedere DA17 . . . .**125** B2
  Kilburn NW6 . . . .**91** A6
Kimberley Dr DA14. . . .**168** D2
Kimberley Gate **3**
  BR1 . . . .**186** D3
Kimberley Gdns
  Enfield EN1 . . . .**5** D2
  Harringay N4. . . . .**50** D4
Kimberley Ho **7** E14. . .**120** A3
Kimberley Ind Est E17 . .**35** B2
Kimberley Rd
  Chingford E4. . . . .**20** C3
  Edmonton N18. . . . .**34** B4
  Kilburn NW6 . . . .**91** A6
  Leyton E11. . . . .**76** B6
  Newham E16. . . . .**98** D3
  Penge BR3. . . . .**184** D1

Kimberley Rd continued
  Stockwell SW9 . . . .**138** A2
  Thornton Heath CR0 . . . .**204** D3
  Tottenham N17 . . . .**34** A1
  Walthamstow E17. . . . . .**35** B2
Kimberley Way E4 . . . . .**20** C3
Kimberley Wlk KT12 . . .**194** B2
Kimber Rd SW18. . . . . .**157** D4
Kimble Cres WD23 . . . . .**8** A4
Kimble Ho
  Lisson Gr NW8 . . . .**237** B6
  1 Lower Holloway N7 . . .**72** A1
Kimble Rd SW17 . . . . . .**180** B4
Kimbolton Cl SE12. . . . .**164** D5
Kimbolton Row SW3 . . .**257** A3
Kimmeridge Gdns **3**
  SE9 . . . .**188** A6
Kimmeridge Rd SE9. . . .**188** A6
Kimm Ho **16** E17 . . . . . .**53** D6
Kimpton Ct **1** SE5 . . . .**139** B4
Kimpton Ho SW15 . . . . .**156** A4
Kimpton Link Bsns Ctr
  SM3 . . . .**217** B6
Kimpton Park Way
  SM3. . . . .**217** B6
Kimpton Rd
  Camberwell SE5 . . . . . .**139** B4
  Cheam SM3. . . . .**217** B6
Kimpton Trade & Bsns Ctr
  SM3 . . . .**217** B6
Kinburn St SE16. . . . . .**118** D4
Kincaid Rd SE15 . . . . . .**140** B5
Kincardine Gdns W9. . . .**91** C3
Kinch Gr HA3, HA9. . . . .**44** B2
Kincraig BR7 . . . .**188** C2
Kindell Ho **4** SW14 . . .**133** B2
Kinder Cl SE28. . . . . . .**124** D6
Kinder Ho N1. . . . .**235** D4
Kindersley Ho **38** E1 . . .**96** A1
Kinder St **15** E1 . . . . . .**96** B1
Kinderton Cl N14 . . . . . .**15** C2
Kinefold Ho N7 . . . .**72** A2
Kinfauns Rd Ilford IG3. . .**58** B1
  Streatham SW2 . . . .**160** C2
King Alfred Ave
  Catford SE6. . . . .**163** C1
  Catford SE6. . . . .**185** C6
King Alfred Sch NW11 . .**47** D1
King Arthur Cl SE15 . . . .**140** C5
King Athelstan Prim Sch
  KT1. . . . .**198** B6
King Charles Cres
  KT5 . . . .**198** B1
King Charles Ct **16**
  SE17 . . . .**138** C6
King Charles Ho SW6 . .**265** D4
King Charles' Rd KT5,
  KT6 . . . .**198** B3
King Charles St
  SW1. . . . . **116** A4 **250** A2
King Charles Terr **11**
  E1 . . . .**118** B6
King Charles Wlk **6**
  SW19. . . . .**157** A3
King Ct **16** E10 . . . .**53** D2
Kingcup Cl CR0. . . . . . .**206** D1
King David La E1 . . . . . .**118** C6
Kingdon Ho **8** E14. . . .**120** A4
Kingdon Rd NW6 . . . . . .**69** C2
Kingdown Cl W10. . . . . .**90** D1
King Edward Dr KT6 . . .**214** A5
King Edward Mans **12**
  E8 . . . .**96** B6
King Edward Mews
  SW13. . . . .**134** A4
King Edward Rd
  Barnet EN5 . . . .**1** D1
  Leytonstone E10 . . . .**54** A1
  Walthamstow E17 . . . . . .**53** A6
King Edward's Gdns
  W3. . . . .**110** C5
King Edward's Gr
  TW11 . . . .**175** C4
King Edwards Mans
  SW6. . . . .**265** A3
King Edward's Rd
  Barking IG11. . . . .**101** B5
  Edmonton N9. . . . .**18** A4
  Enfield EN3 . . . .**6** D1
  Ruislip HA4 . . . .**39** B1
  South Hackney E9 . . . . . .**96** C6
King Edward St EC1. . . .**242** A2
King Edward The Third
  Mews **11** SE16. . . . . .**118** B4
King Edward VII Hospl-
  Sister Agnes
  W1 . . . .**93** A2 **238** A4
King Edward Wlk
  SE1 . . . . **116** C3 **261** B6
King Fahad Acad The
  W5 . . . .**109** C2
King Fahed Acad W3 . .**111** D6
Kingfield Rd W5 . . . .**87** D3
Kingfield St E14 . . . . . .**120** A2
Kingfisher Ave E11 . . . . .**55** B3
Kingfisher Cl
  Harrow HA3 . . . .**24** D3
  Woolwich SE28 . . . .**124** C6
Kingfisher Ct
  11 Battersea SW11 . . .**136** C2
  Cheam SM1. . . . .**217** B3
  17 Cubitt Town E14. . . .**120** A4
  East Molesey KT8 . . . . . .**196** A6
  Enfield EN2 . . . .**4** B5
  Hounslow TW3 . . . .**151** A4
  Merton SW19 . . . .**179** B3
  Putney SW19. . . . .**157** A2
  Spring Gr TW3. . . . .**130** B3
Kingfisher Dr TW10 . . . .**175** B6

Kingfisher Ho
16 Battersea SW18 ....136 A2
Peckham SE15 ....139 D4
West Kensington W14 .. 254 C6
Kingfisher Lo TW11 ....175 A6
Kingfisher Mews
SE13 ....163 D6
Kingfisher Sq 19 SE8 ...141 B6
Kingfisher St E6 ....100 A2
Kingfisher Way
Croydon CR0 ....206 D4
Neasden NW10 ....67 B3
Kingfisher Wlk NW9 ....27 C1
King Frederick IX Twr
SE16 ....119 B3
King Garth Mews
SE23 ....162 C2
King Gdns CR0 ....220 D3
King George Ave
Ilford IG2 ....57 B3
Newham E16 ....99 D1
Walton-on-T KT12 ....194 D1
King George Cl TW16 ..171 C5
King George Hospl IG3 ..58 A4
King George Sq TW10 ..154 B5
King George St SE10 ...142 A5
King George's Trad Est
KT9 ....214 C4
King George VI Ave
CR4 ....202 D5
King George V Sta
E16 ....122 C5
Kingham Cl
3 Shepherd's Bush
W11 ....112 D4
Wandsworth SW18 ....158 A4
Kingham Ind Est NW10 ..89 B4
King Harolds Way
DA7 ....147 A5
King Henry Mews
Harrow HA2 ....42 C1
7 Orpington BR6 ....227 D3
King Henry's Mews EN3 ..7 C6
King Henry's Rd
Kingston u T KT1,
KT3 ....198 D6
Primrose Hill NW3 ....70 C1
King Henry's Reach
W6 ....134 C6
King Henry St N16 ....73 C3
King Henry's Wlk N1 ....73 C2
King Henry's Yd 5 N16 .73 C3
King Henry Terr 10
E1 ....118 B6
King Ho 5 W12 ....90 B1
Kinghorn St EC1 .... 242 A3
King James St
SE1 ....116 D4 251 D1
King John Ct EC2 .... 243 B6
King John St E1 ....96 D2
King John's Wlk SE9 ...166 A5
Kinglake St
SE17 ....117 C1 263 B2
Kinglet Cl E7 ....77 A2
Kingly Ct W1 .... 249 B6
Kingly St W1 ...115 C6 249 A6
King & Queen Cl 4
SE9 ....188 A6
King & Queen St
SE17 ....117 A1 262 B2
Kingsand Rd SE12 ....165 A2
Kings Arbour UB2 ....107 A1
King's Arms Ct E1 ....96 A2
King's Arms Yd EC2 ... 242 C2
Kingsash Dr UB4 ....85 A3
Kings Ave Bromley BR1 ..186 D4
Clapham Pk SW4 ....160 A5
Dagenham RM6 ....59 B3
Ealing W5 ....87 D1
Muswell Hill N10 ....49 A6
New Malden KT3 ....199 D5
Wallington SM5 ....218 D1
King's Ave
Ashford TW16 ....171 D4
Buckhurst Hill IG9 ....21 D2
Hounslow TW3, TW5 ....129 D4
Southall UB1 ....85 D1
Southgate N21 ....16 D3
Woodford IG8 ....37 C5
Kings Avenue Sch
SW4 ....160 A6
King's Bench St
SE1 ....116 D4 251 D2
King's Bench Wlk EC4. 241 B1
Kingsbridge N16 ....51 B1
Kingsbridge Ave W3 ...110 B4
Kingsbridge Cres UB1 ..85 B2
Kingsbridge Ct
Edmonton N21 ....16 D2
Millwall E14 ....119 C2
Kingsbridge Dr NW7 ....28 D3
Kingsbridge Ho 10
SE20 ....184 B2
Kingsbridge Ind Est
IG11 ....101 C4
Kingsbridge Rd
Barking IG11 ....101 B5
North Kensington W10 ...90 C1
Southall UB2 ....107 B2
Walton-on-T KT12 ....194 B2
West Barnes SM4 ....200 D2
Kingsbridge Way UB4 ...83 C4
KINGSBURY 45 B3
Kingsbury Green Prim Sch
NW9 ....44 D4
Kingsbury High Sch
(Lower Sch) NW9 ....45 A5
Kingsbury High Sch
(Upper Sch) NW9 ....44 D5
Kingsbury Hospl NW9 ...44 C5
Kingsbury Rd
Kingsbury NW9 ....44 D4
Kingsland N1 ....73 C2
Kingsbury Sta NW9 ....44 C4
Kingsbury Terr N1 ....73 C2
Kingsbury Trad Est
NW9 ....45 B3
Kings Chase KT8 ....196 A6
Kings Chase View EN2 ...4 C3
Kings Cl Hendon NW4 ....46 D5
Walton-on-T KT12 ....194 B1
King's Cl
Thames Ditton KT7 ....197 A2
Walthamstow E10 ....53 D2
Kingsclere Cl SW15 ....156 A4
Kingsclere Ct
Colney Hatch N12 ....30 C5
New Barnet EN5 ....14 A6
Kingsclere Pl EN2 ....5 A3
Kingscliffe Gdns
SW19 ....157 B3
King's Coll
Dulwich Village SE24 ....161 B5
Strand WC2 ... 116 B6 250 D6
Kings College Ct NW3 ...70 C1
King's College Hospl
SE5 ....139 B3
Kings College Rd
Primrose Hill NW3 ....70 B1
Ruislip HA4 ....39 D3
King's Coll London
(Hampstead) NW3 ....69 C4
King's Coll Sch SW19 ..178 D4
King's Coll Univ
SE1 ....116 C5 251 A3
Kingscote NW11 ....47 B1
Kingscote Rd
Bedford Pk W4 ....111 B3
Croydon CR0 ....206 B2
Kingston u T KT3 ....199 B6
Kingscote St EC4 .... 251 C6
Kings Court Mews
KT8 ....196 B4
King's Court N SW3 ... 257 A1
Kingscourt Rd SW16 ...160 A1
King's Court S SW3 ... 257 A1
King's Cres N4, N5 ....73 A5
Kingscroft SW4 ....160 A5
Kingscroft Rd NW2 ....69 B2
KING'S CROSS 94 A5
King's Cross
WC1 ....94 A4 233 B2
King's Cross Bridge
WC1 .... 233 B2
King's Cross Rd
WC1 ....94 B4 233 D1
King's Cross, St Pancras
N1 ....94 A4 233 A2
King's Cross Sta
N1 ....94 A5 233 B3
King's Cross (Thames
Link) Sta WC1 ..94 A4 233 B2
Kings Ct
6 Barnsbury N7 ....72 B1
2 Buckhurst Hill IG9 ....21 D2
Chiswick W6 ....112 A2
East Dulwich SE22 ....140 A1
16 Kingston u T KT2 ....176 C3
Newham E13 ....99 B6
Primrose Hill NW8 .... 230 C5
10 Putney SW15 ....156 A4
3 Wallington SM6 ....219 B2
Wembley Pk HA9 ....66 D6
King's Ct
Beckenham BR3 ....207 D6
9 Ealing W5 ....87 C2
Wimbledon SW19 ....179 C4
Kingsdale Ct EN4 ....2 D3
Kingsdale Gdns W11 ...112 D5
Kingsdale Rd
Penge SE20 ....184 D3
Plumstead Comm SE18 ..145 D6
Kingsdale Sec Sch
SE21 ....161 C1
Kingsdown SW19 ....178 D3
Kingsdown Ave
East Acton W3 ....111 C6
West Ealing W13 ....109 B4
Kingsdown Cl
26 Deptford SE16 ....118 B1
8 Notting Hill W11 ....91 A1
Kingsdown Ct SW11 ...158 C5
Kingsdowne Rd KT6 ...198 B2
Kingsdown Ho 1 E8 ....74 A3
Kingsdown Rd
Cheam SM3 ....217 A3
Leyton E11 ....76 C5
4 Upper Holloway N19 ..72 A6
Kingsdown Way BR2 ...209 A3
Kings Dr Edgware HA8 ...26 B6
Surbiton KT5 ....198 C3
Wembley Pk HA9 ....66 D6
King's Dr KT7 ....197 B2
Kingsend HA4 ....39 C1
Kingsend Ct HA4 ....39 C1
Kings Farm E17 ....35 D2
Kings Farm Ave TW10 ..132 C1
Kingsfield Ave HA1,
HA2 ....42 A4
Kingsfield Ct HA1 ....42 B2
Kingsfield Ho
Mottingham SE9 ....165 D1
7 Muswell Hill N10 ....31 A3
18 Stoke Newington N16 .73 C5
Kingsfield Rd HA1 ....42 B2
Kingsford Com Sch
E6 ....100 B1
Kingsford St NW5 ....70 D3
Kingsford Way E6 ....100 B2
Kingsgate HA9 ....67 A5
Kingsgate Ave N3 ....47 C6
Kingsgate Bsns Ctr
KT2 ....176 A2
Kingsgate Cl Erith DA7 ..147 A4
Sidcup BR5 ....190 C1
Kingsgate Est N1 ....73 C2
Kingsgate Ho 23 SW9 ..138 C4
Kingsgate Par SW1 ... 259 B5
Kingsgate Pl NW6 ....69 C1
Kingsgate Prim Sch
NW6 ....69 C1
Kingsgate Rd
Hampstead NW6 ....69 C1
Kingston u T KT2 ....176 A2
Kings Gdns IG1 ....57 B1
King's Gdns 6 NW6 ....69 C1
King's Gr
Peckham SE15 ....140 B4
Peckham SE15 ....140 B5
Kings Grange HA4 ....39 D1
Kingsground SE9 ....166 A5
Kingshall Mews SE13 ..142 A2
Kings Hall Rd BR3 ....185 A2
Kings Head Hill E4 ....19 D4
King's Head Yd SE1 ... 252 C3
King's Highway SE18 ...145 D6
Kingshill SE17 .... 262 B4
Kingshill Ave
Harrow HA3 ....43 B5
Hayes UB4 ....83 D4
New Malden KT4 ....200 B2
Northolt UB5 ....84 B4
Kingshill Cl UB4, UB5 ....84 A4
Kingshill Ct 8 EN5 ....1 A1
Kingshill Dr HA3 ....43 B6
Kings Ho
19 Limehouse E14 ....119 B6
South Lambeth SW8 ... 270 B4
Kingshold Rd E9 ....74 C1
Kingsholm Gdns SE9 ...144 A1
King's House Sch
TW10 ....154 B6
King's House Sch (Jun)
TW10 ....154 B6
Kingshurst Rd SE12 ....165 A4
Kings Keep KT6 ....198 A5
King's Keep 6 SW15 ...156 D6
King's La SM1 ....218 B3
KINGSLAND 73 C2
Kingsland NW8 ...92 C6 230 B5
Kingsland Gn 1 E8, N1 ..73 C2
Kingsland High St E8 ...73 D3
Kingsland Pas 2 E8 ....73 C2
Kingsland Rd Hoxton E2 ..95 C5
Newham E13 ....99 C4
Kingsland Sh Ctr 12 E8 ..73 D2
Kingslawn Cl SW15 ....156 B6
Kingslee Ct 4 SM2 ....217 D1
Kingsleigh Cl TW8 ....131 D6
Kingsleigh Pl CR4 ....202 D6
Kingsleigh Wlk BR2 ...208 D5
Kingsley Ave
Ealing W13 ....87 A1
Hounslow TW3 ....130 A3
Southall UB1 ....107 C6
Sutton SM1 ....218 B4
Kingsley Cl
Dagenham RM10 ....81 D4
East Finchley N2 ....48 A4
Kingsley Ct Bexley DA6 ..147 C1
Edgware HA8 ....10 D2
Snaresbrook E11 ....54 D3
1 Thamesmead SE28 ..124 C5
Willesden NW2 ....68 B2
Wood Green N22 ....32 B3
Worcester Pk KT4 ....215 D6
Kingsley Dr KT4 ....215 D6
Kingsley Flats SE1 .... 263 B3
Kingsley Gdns E4 ....35 C5
Kingsley Grange 1
E11 ....55 A4
Kingsley High Sch HA3 ..24 A3
Kingsley Ho
Chelsea SW3 .... 266 D5
3 Clapham SW4 ....137 D3
East Finchley NW11 ....48 A3
8 Kingston u T KT6 ....198 A4
Kingsley Mews
Chislehurst West
BR7 ....188 D4
Dagenham RM9 ....80 D4
4 Ilford IG1 ....78 D6
Kensington W8 .... 255 D5
15 St George in t East
E1 ....118 B6
Kingsley Pl N6 ....49 A2
Kingsley Prim Sch
CR9 ....204 C1
Kingsley Rd
Chingford E17 ....36 A1
Edmonton N13 ....32 D6
Harrow HA2 ....64 A5
Hounslow TW3 ....130 A3
Kilburn NW6 ....91 B6
Orpington BR6 ....227 D1
Pinner HA5 ....41 B5
Thornton Heath CR0 ....204 C1
Upton E7 ....77 A1
Wimbledon SW19 ....179 D5
Kingsley St SW11 ....136 D2
Kingsley Way N2 ....48 A4
Kingsley Wood Dr
SE9 ....166 B1
Kings Lo HA4 ....39 C1
Kingslyn Cres SE19 ....183 C2
Kings Mall Sh Ctr W6 ..112 C2
Kingsman Par SE18 ....122 B3
King's Mans SW3 .... 267 A5
Kingsman St SE18 ....122 B2
Kingsmead Barnet EN5 ....1 C1
Kingsmead continued
Richmond TW10 ....154 B5
Kingsmead Ave
Edmonton N9 ....18 B3
Kingsbury NW9 ....45 B2
Mitcham CR4 ....203 C6
North Cheam KT4 ....216 B5
Sunbury TW16 ....172 C1
Tolworth KT6 ....214 C6
Kingsmead Cl
Sidcup DA15 ....168 A2
Teddington TW11 ....175 B4
West Ewell KT19 ....215 B1
Kingsmead Cotts BR2 ..210 A1
Kingsmead Ct
Bromley BR1 ....186 D3
Crouch End N6 ....49 D2
Kingsmead Dr UB5 ....63 B1
Kingsmead Ho E9 ....75 A4
Kingsmead Lo
9 Chingford E4 ....20 A2
Sutton SM2 ....218 B2
Kings Mead Pk KT10 ...212 C1
Kingsmead Prim Sch
E9 ....75 A4
Kingsmead Rd SW2 ....160 C2
Kingsmead Sch EN1 ....6 A2
King's Mead Way E5,
E9 ....75 A4
Kingsmere Catford SE6 ..163 D3
Widmore BR7 ....188 A2
Kingsmere Cl SW15 ....134 D2
Kingsmere Ct NW9 ....44 D1
Kingsmere Pk NW9 ....45 A1
Kingsmere Pl N16 ....51 B1
Kingsmere Rd SW19 ...156 D2
King's Mews
1 Clapham Pk SW4 ....160 A6
Gray's Inn WC1 ..94 B3 240 D5
Kingsmill NW8 ...92 B5 229 D4
Kingsmill Bsns Pk
KT1 ....198 B6
Kingsmill Gdns RM9 ....81 B3
Kingsmill Rd RM9 ....81 B3
Kingsmill Terr
NW8 ....92 B5 229 D4
Kingsmount Ct SM1 ...217 D4
Kingsnorth Ho 12 W10 ..90 D1
Kingsnympton Pk
KT2 ....176 D4
Kings Oak RM7 ....59 C6
Kings Oak Hospl (Private)
The EN2 ....4 C5
King's Orch SE9 ....166 A5
King's Paddock TW12 ..174 A2
King's Par
3 Hammersmith
W12 ....112 A3
Willesden NW10 ....90 C6
Kingspark Bsns Ctr
KT3 ....199 A6
Kingspark Ct E18 ....55 A6
King's Pas KT2 ....175 D2
King's Penny Ho 4
KT2 ....176 A3
Kings Pl
Acton Green W4 ....111 A2
Buckhurst Hill IG9 ....21 D2
Loughton IG10 ....21 D4
King's Pl SE1 .... 252 A1
King Sq EC1 ....95 A4 235 A1
King's Quay SW10 .... 266 B2
Kings Rd Ealing W5 ....87 D2
Feltham TW13 ....150 C3
Harrow HA2 ....63 B6
Mitcham CR4 ....203 A6
Orpington BR6 ....227 D4
Richmond TW10, TW9 ..154 B6
Walton-on-T KT12 ....194 B1
West Drayton UB7 ....104 B4
Willesden NW10 ....68 B1
Wood Green N22 ....32 B2
King's Rd Barking IG11 ...79 A1
Chelsea SW3 .... 257 B1
Chelsea SW10 ..136 B6 266 C5
Chingford E4 ....20 B3
Edmonton N18 ....34 A6
Kingston u T KT2 ....176 B3
Leytonstone E11 ....54 C2
Long Ditton KT6 ....197 C1
Mortlake SW14 ....133 B2
Newham E6 ....99 C6
South Norwood SE25 ...206 A6
Teddington TW11,
TW12 ....174 B5
Tottenham N17 ....33 D2
Twickenham TW1 ....153 B5
Wimbledon SW19 ....179 C4
Kings Ride Gate
TW10 ....132 C1
Kingsridge SW19 ....157 A2
Kings Road Bglws HA2 ..63 B5
King's Scholars' Pas
SW1 .... 259 A4
King St Acton W3 ....111 A5
East Finchley N2 ....48 B6
Hammersmith W6 ....112 A2
Newham E13 ....98 D3
Newham E13 ....99 A3
Richmond TW9 ....153 D6
Southall UB2 ....107 A3
St James SW1 ..115 C5 249 B4
Strand WC2 .... 250 A6
Tottenham N17 ....33 D2
Twickenham TW1 ....153 A3
Whitechapel EC2 95 A1 242 B1
King Stairs Cl SE16 ....118 B4
King's Terr
Camden Town
NW1 ....93 C6 232 A5
King's Terr continued
10 Isleworth TW7 ....131 A2
Kingsthorpe Rd SE26 ...184 D6
Kingston Ave
Cheam SM3 ....217 A5
Feltham TW14 ....149 D5
Yiewsley UB7 ....104 B6
Kingston Bsns Ctr
KT9 ....214 B5
Kingston By-Pass KT6, KT7,
KT9 ....213 C5
Kingston By - Pass
KT6 ....214 C5
Kingston Cl
Dagenham RM6 ....59 A6
Northolt UB5 ....85 B6
Teddington TW11 ....175 B4
Kingston Coll of F Ed
KT1 ....197 D6
Kingston Coll of F Ed (M V
Annex) KT2 ....176 A2
Kingston Cres BR3 ....185 B2
Kingston Ct HA3 ....44 B4
Kingston Gdns CR0 ....220 A5
Kingston Gram Sch
KT2 ....176 B1
Kingston Hall Rd KT1 ..197 D6
Kingston Hill KT2 ....177 A5
Kingston Hill Ave RM6 ..59 A6
Kingston Hill Pl KT2,
TW10 ....177 A6
Kingston Ho 4 NW6 ....69 A1
Kingston Ho E SW7 ... 247 A1
Kingston Ho N SW7 ... 247 A1
Kingston Ho S SW7 ... 247 A1
Kingston Hospl KT2 ....176 D2
Kingston House Est
KT6 ....197 B3
Kingston La
Teddington TW11 ....175 B4
Uxbridge UB8 ....82 A4
West Drayton UB7 ....104 B4
Kingston Lo 2 KT3 ....199 C5
Kingston Mus* KT1 ....176 A1
Kingston Pl HA3 ....24 D3
Kingston Rd
Ashford TW15 ....170 A4
Ashford TW15 ....170 B4
Edmonton N9 ....18 A2
Ewell KT17 ....215 D1
Ilford IG1 ....79 A4
Kingston u T KT1, KT3 ...199 A5
Merton SW19, SW20 ....179 B1
New Barnet EN4 ....14 B6
Roehampton SW15,
SW19 ....156 B3
Southall UB2 ....107 B4
Teddington TW11 ....175 B4
Kingston Sq SE19 ....183 B5
Kingston Sta KT2 ....176 A2
Kingston Univ
Kingston u T KT1 ....198 A6
Kingston Vale KT2 ....177 B5
Kingston Univ Annex
KT1 ....176 B1
Kingston Univ
Roehampton Vale
Campus SW15 ....155 D1
KINGSTON UPON THAMES
....197 C6
KINGSTON VALE 177 B6
Kingston Vale SW15 ...155 C1
Kingstown St
NW1 ....93 A6 231 A6
King Street Cloisters 8
W6 ....112 B2
King Street Coll W12 ..112 C4
King Street Par 7
TW1 ....153 A3
Kings View Ct 1
SW20 ....178 D3
Kingswater Pl SW11 .. 267 A3
Kingsway
Coney Hall BR4 ....224 D5
Enfield EN3 ....18 B6
Hayes UB3 ....83 A2
Mortlake SW14, TW9 ...132 D2
North Finchley N12 ....30 A4
Petts Wood BR5 ....211 B4
Stanwell TW19 ....148 A3
St Giles WC2 ....94 B1 240 C2
Wembley HA9 ....66 A4
West Barnes KT3 ....200 C4
Woodford IG8 ....37 C5
Kings Way
Croydon CR0 ....220 B3
Harrow HA1 ....42 C5
Kingsway Bsns Pk
TW12 ....173 B2
Kingsway Coll NW5 ....71 B2
Kingsway Cres HA2 ....42 A5
Kingsway Est N18 ....34 D4
Kingsway Mans WC1 .. 240 C4
Kingsway Pl EC1 .... 241 C6
Kingsway Rd SM3 ....217 A1
Kingswear Ho 5
SE23 ....162 C2
Kingswear Rd
Dartmouth Pk NW5 ....71 B5
Ruislip HA4 ....62 A6
Kings Well 25 NW3 ....70 A4
Kings Wlk Sh Mall
SW3 .... 114 D1 257 C2
Kingswood 31 E2 ....96 C5
Kingswood Ave
Beckenham BR2, BR3 ...208 C5
Belvedere DA17 ....125 B2
Hampton TW12 ....173 D4
Hounslow TW3, TW5 ....129 B3
Kensal Rise NW6 ....91 A5
Kingswood Ave continued
Thornton Heath CR7 ....204 C4
Kingswood Cl
Ashford TW15 ....171 B5
Crofton BR6 ....211 B2
East Barnet N20 ....14 A4
Enfield EN1 ....17 D6
New Malden KT3 ....199 D3
South Lambeth SW8 ... 270 B3
Surbiton KT6 ....198 A2
Kingswood Ct
Chingford E4 ....35 C5
Hither Green SE13 ....164 B5
7 Richmond TW10 ....154 B6
Kings Wood Ct 4 NW6 ..69 C1
Kingswood Dr
Carshalton SM5 ....202 D1
Dulwich SE19, SE21 ....183 D6
Kingswood Ho 3 KT2 ..176 D4
Kingswood Mans 14
SM2 ....217 C1
Kingswood Pk N3 ....29 B1
Kingswood Pl SE13 ....142 C1
Kingswood Prim Sch
SE27 ....183 B5
Kingswood Rd
Beckenham BR2 ....208 C6
Ilford IG3 ....58 A2
Leytonstone E11 ....54 C2
Merton SW19 ....179 B2
Penge SE20 ....184 C4
South Acton W4 ....111 A3
Streatham SW2 ....160 A4
Wembley HA9 ....66 C5
Kingswood Terr W4 ....111 A3
Kingswood Way SM6 ..220 A3
Kingsworth Cl BR3 ....207 A4
Kingsworthy Cl KT1 ....198 B6
Kings Yd E15 ....75 C2
Kingthorpe Rd NW10 ....67 B1
Kingthorpe Terr 2
NW10 ....67 B1
Kington Ho 18 NW6 ....91 D6
Kingward Ho E1 ....96 A2
Kingwell Rd EN4 ....2 B5
Kingweston Cl NW2 ....69 A5
King William IV Gdns
SE20 ....184 C4
King William La 3
SE10 ....120 C1
King William St
EC4 ....117 B6 252 D6
King William Wlk
SE10 ....142 A6
Kingwood Rd
SW6 ....135 A5 264 A3
Kinlet Rd SE18 ....145 A4
Kinloch Dr NW9 ....45 C2
Kinloch St N7 ....72 B5
Kinloss Ct NW3 ....47 B5
Kinloss Gdns NW3 ....47 B5
Kinloss Rd SM5 ....202 A2
Kinnaird Ave
Bromley BR1 ....186 D4
Chiswick W4 ....133 A5
Kinnaird Cl BR1 ....186 D4
Kinnear Ct 2 SW20 ....178 D2
Kinnear Rd W12 ....111 D4
Kinnerton Pl N SW1 ... 247 D1
Kinnerton Pl S SW1 ... 247 D1
Kinnerton St
SW1 ....115 A4 248 A1
Kinnerton Yd SW1 .... 248 A1
Kinnoull Mans 10 E5 ....74 B4
Kinnoul Rd
W6 ....135 A6 264 A6
Kinross Ave KT4 ....216 A6
Kinross Cl
Ashford TW16 ....171 D5
Edgware HA8 ....10 D2
Harrow HA3 ....44 B4
Kinross Ct 1 SE6 ....164 D2
Kinross Dr TW16 ....171 D5
Kinross Ho N1 .... 233 C6
Kinross Terr E17 ....35 B1
Kinsale Grange 10
SM2 ....218 A2
Kinsale Rd SE15 ....140 A2
Kinsella Gdns SW19 ....178 B5
Kinsey Ho SE21 ....183 C6
Kinsham Ho 5 E2 ....96 A3
Kintore Way SE1 .... 263 C4
Kintyre Cl SW16 ....204 B6
Kintyre Ct 17 SW2 ....160 A4
Kintyre Ho 6 E14 ....120 A5
Kinveachy Gdns SE7 ...122 A1
Kinver Ho N4 ....51 B2
Kinver Rd SE26 ....184 C6
Kipling Ct W7 ....108 D6
Kipling Dr SW17 ....180 B4
Kipling Ho 29 SE5 ....139 A5
Kipling Pl HA7 ....24 D4
Kipling Rd DA7 ....147 A4
Kipling St SE1 ..117 B4 252 D2
Kipling Terr N9 ....17 B2
Kipling Twr 3 W3 ....111 A3
Kippington Dr SE9 ....165 D3
Kirby Cl KT19 ....215 D3
Kirby Est SE16 ....118 B3
Kirby Gr SE1 ...117 C4 253 A2
Kirby St EC1 ....94 C2 241 B4
Kirby Way
Hillingdon UB8 ....82 B3
Walton-on-T KT12 ....194 C3
Kirchen Rd W13 ....109 B6
Kirkby Cl N11 ....31 A4
Kirkdale SE26 ....162 B1

Kirkdale Rd E11 54 C2
Kirkeby Bldg EC1 241 A4
Kirkfield Cl W13 109 B5
Kirkham Rd E6 100 A1
Kirkham St SE18 145 C6
Kirk Ho HA9 66 A5
Kirk La SE18 145 A6
Kirkland Cl DA15 167 C5
Kirkland Dr EN2 5 A4
Kirkland Terr BR3 185 C4
Kirkland Wlk 4 E8 73 D2
Kirkleas Rd KT6 198 A1
Kirklees Rd
Dagenham RM8 80 C3
Thornton Heath CR7 204 C4
Kirkley Ho N16 51 C1
Kirkley Rd SW19 179 C2
Kirkman Ho W1 239 C3
Kirkman Pl W1 239 C3
Kirkmichael Rd E14 98 A1
Kirk Rd E17 53 B3
Kirk Rise SM1 217 D5
Kirkside Rd SE3 143 A6
Kirkstall Ave N17 51 B5
Kirkstall Gdns SW2 160 A3
Kirkstall Ho SW1 258 C2
Kirkstall Rd SW2 160 A3
Kirkstead Ct E5 75 A4
Kirksted Rd SM4 201 D1
Kirkstone NW1 232 A2
Kirkstone Way BR1 186 C3
Kirkton Rd N15 51 C5
Kirkwall Pl E2 96 C4
Kirkwood Rd SE15 140 B3
Kirn Rd W13 109 B6
Kirrane Cl KT3 199 D4
Kirtley Ho SW8 269 B2
Kirtley Rd SE26 185 A6
Kirtling St
SW8 137 C5 269 A4
Kirton Cl W4 111 B2
Kirton Gdns 23 E2 95 D4
Kirton Rd E13 99 C5
Kirton Wlk HA8 27 A3
Kirwin Way SE5 138 D5
Kisharon Day Sch
NW11 47 B3
Kitcat Terr E3 97 C4
Kitchener Rd
Dagenham RM10 81 D2
East Finchley N2 48 C6
South Norwood CR7 205 B6
Tottenham N17 51 C6
Upton E7 77 B2
Walthamstow E17 35 D2
Kite Ho 5 SW11 136 C2
Kite Pl 9 E2 96 A4
Kitley Gdns SE19 183 D2
Kitson Rd
Barnes SW13 134 A4
Camberwell SE5 139 A5
Kittiwake Ct 26 SE8 141 B6
Kittiwake Pl SM1 217 B3
Kittiwake Rd UB5 84 D4
Kittiwake Way UB4 84 D2
Kitto Rd SE14 140 D3
KITTS END 1 A5
Kitt's End Rd EN5 1 A6
Kiver Rd N19 72 A6
Klea Ave SW4 159 C5
Kleffens Ct 2 SE3 142 D5
Kleine Wharf 30 N1 95 C6
Knaggs Ho 1 TW11 174 C5
Knapdale Cl SE23 162 B2
Knapmill Rd SE6 163 D2
Knapmill Way SE6 163 D2
Knapp Cl NW10 67 C2
Knapp Rd
Ashford TW15 170 B6
Bow E3 97 C3
Knapton Mews SW17 181 A4
Knaresborough Dr
SW18 157 D3
Knaresborough Ho 4
N4 51 A2
Knaresborough Pl
SW5 113 D2 255 C4
Knatchbull Rd
Brixton SE5 138 D4
Stonebridge NW10 89 B6
Knebworth Ave E17 35 C2
Knebworth Ho
South Lambeth SW8 269 D1
2 Stoke Newington N16 73 C4
Walthamstow E17 35 C2
Knebworth Rd 3 N16 73 C4
Knee Hill SE2 124 C1
Knee Hill Cres SE2 124 C2
Kneller Gdns TW7 152 B5
Kneller Ho 9 SW8 137 D3
Kneller Rd
Brockley SE4 141 A1
Isleworth TW2 152 B5
New Malden KT3 199 C2
Knevett Terr TW3 129 C1
Knight Cl RM8 80 C6
Knight Ct
1 Chingford E4 20 A3
Stamford Hill N15 51 C4
Knighten St E1 118 B5
Knighthead Point 26
E14 119 C4
Knight Ho
Walworth SE17 263 A3
Worcester Pk KT4 216 A6
Knightland Ho E5 74 B6
Knightland Rd E5 74 B6
Knightleas Ct NW2 68 C2
Knightleys Ct E10 53 A1
Knighton Cl
Croydon CR2 220 D1
Woodford IG8 37 B6
Knighton Dr IG8 37 B6
Knighton Gn IG9 21 B2
Knighton La IG9 21 B2
Knighton Park Rd
SE26 184 D5
Knighton Rd E7 77 A4
Knightrider Ct EC4 252 A6
Knightrider St EC4 251 D6
Knights Arc SW1 247 C1
Knight's Ave W5 110 A4
KNIGHTSBRIDGE 114 C4
Knightsbridge SW1,
SW7 114 D4 247 C1
Knightsbridge Ct SW1 247 D1
Knightsbridge Gn SW1 247 C1
Knightsbridge Mews
BR7 188 B3
Knightsbridge Under Sch
SW7 256 B3
Knights Cl
East Molesey KT8 195 B4
Lower Clapton E9 74 C3
Knights Ct Bushey WD23 8 B3
11 Friern Barnet N11 30 D5
Kingston u T KT1 198 A6
Penge BR3 185 A2
Knight's Ct BR1 164 D1
Knightshayes Ho 8
NW4 28 D1
Knight's Hill SE19,
SE27 182 D6
Knight's Hill Sq SE27 182 D6
Knights Ho
Bermondsey SE1 253 C2
South Lambeth SW8 270 B3
West Kensington SW5 254 C2
Knight's Ho SW10 266 A4
Knight's Pk KT1 198 A6
Knight's Pl TW2 152 C3
Knights Rd
Newham E16 121 A4
Stanmore HA7 25 C6
Knight's Wlk SE11 261 C3
Knightswood Cl HA8 11 A2
Knightswood Ct N6 49 D2
Knightswood Ho N12 30 A4
Knightwood Cres KT3 199 C3
Knivet Rd SW6 135 C6 265 A5
Knobs Hill Rd E15 97 D6
Knockholt Rd SE9 165 D6
Knole Cl CR0 206 C3
Knole Ct UB5 84 C4
Knole Gate DA15 167 C1
Knole The SE9 188 C6
Knoll Ct Dulwich SE19 183 D5
Orpington BR6 227 D6
Knoll Dr N14 15 A4
Knoll Ho NW8 229 A4
Knoll Lo EN5 14 A6
Knollmead KT4, KT5 199 A1
Knollmead Prim Sch
KT5 215 A6
Knoll Rd Bexley DA5 169 C5
Sidcup DA14 190 B6
Wandsworth SW18 158 A6
Knoll Rise BR6 211 D1
Knolls Cl KT4 216 B5
Knoll The
Beckenham BR3 185 D2
Ealing W13 87 C2
Hayes BR2 209 A1
Knolly's Cl SE27, SW16 160 C1
Knolly's Rd SE27,
SW16 160 C1
Knot Ho SE1 253 C3
Knottisford St E2 96 C4
Knotts Green Mews
E10 54 A3
Knotts Green Rd E10 54 A3
Knowlden Ho 5 E1 118 C6
Knowle Ave DA7 147 B5
Knowle Cl SW9 138 C2
Knowledge Point Sch
N7 72 B2
Knowle Lo BR7 188 B4
Knowle Rd
Bromley BR2 226 A6
Twickenham TW2 152 C3
Knowles Cl UB7 104 A5
Knowles Ct 7 HA1 42 D3
Knowles Hill Cres
SE13 164 B6
Knowles Ho
Wandsworth SW18 157 D5
Willesden Green NW10 90 A6
Knowles Wlk SW4 137 C2
Knowl Pk WD6 10 A6
Knowlton Gn 1 BR2 208 D4
Knowlton Ho 32 SW9 138 C4
Knowl Way WD6 10 B6
Knowsley Ave UB1 107 D5
Knowsley Rd SW11 136 D3
Knox Ct 16 SW4 138 A3
Knox Ho SW15 134 C3
Knox Rd E7 77 A2
Knox St W1 92 D2 237 C4
Knoyle Ho W14 254 B6
Knoyle St SE14 141 A6
Kobi Nazrul Prim Sch
E1 96 A1
Koblenz Ho N8 50 A6
Kohat Rd SW19 179 D5
Korda Cl TW17 192 B6
Kossuth St SE10 120 C1
Kotree Way 16 SE1 118 A2
Kramer Mews SW5 255 C1
Kreedman Wlk 8 E8 74 A3
Kreisel Wlk TW9 132 B6
Kristina Ct 5 SM2 217 C2
Kuala Gdns SW16 182 B2
Kubrick Bsns Est E7 77 B4
Kuhn Way E7 77 A3
Kwesi Johnson Ct 4
N22 32 C1
Kydbrook Cl BR5 211 A2
Kyle Ho TW12 174 A2
Kylemore Cl 3 E6 99 D5
Kylemore Ct 4 W12 112 A4
Kylemore Rd NW6 69 C1
Kylestrome Ho SW1 258 B3
Kymberley Rd HA1 42 C3
Kynance Gdns HA7 25 C2
Kynance Mews
SW7 113 D3 255 D5
Kynance Pl SW7 256 A5
Kynaston Ave CR7 205 A4
Kynaston Cl HA3 24 B3
Kynaston Cres CR7 205 A4
Kynaston Ho 7 SW2 160 B3
Kynaston Rd Enfield EN2 5 B4
Plaistow BR1 187 A5
Stoke Newington N16 73 C5
Thornton Heath CR7 205 A4
Kynaston Wood HA3 24 B3
Kynersley Cl 1 SM5 218 D5
Kynoch Rd N18 34 D6
Kyrle Rd SW11 159 A5
Kyverdale Rd N16 51 D1

L

Laburnam Ct 12 SW16 182 C5
Laburnham Cl HA0 88 C6
Laburnham Ct
Child's Hill NW2 69 B6
Sutton SM1 217 C3
Laburnham Pl SE9 166 C6
Laburnum Ave
Carshalton SM1 218 C5
Edmonton N9 17 D2
Tottenham N17 33 B3
Yiewsley UB7 104 B6
Laburnum Cl
Friern Barnet N11 31 A4
5 Nunhead SE15 140 C5
Walthamstow E4 35 B4
Laburnum Cres TW16 172 B2
Laburnum Ct
26 Haggerston E2 95 D6
Harrow HA1 41 D3
5 Mitcham CR4 181 A1
Stanmore HA7 25 C6
Laburnum Gdns
Croydon CR0 206 D1
Edmonton N21 17 A2
Laburnum Gr
Edmonton N21 17 A2
Hounslow TW3 129 B1
Kingsbury NW9 45 A2
Kingston u T KT3 177 B1
Ruislip HA4 39 B3
Southall UB1 85 B3
Laburnum Ho
Dagenham RM10 81 C6
New Cross SE4 141 B3
6 Stoke Newington N16 73 B6
Laburnum JMI Sch E2 95 D6
Laburnum Lo 2 N3 29 B1
Laburnum Rd
Hayes UB3 105 D2
Merton SW19 180 A3
Mitcham CR4 181 A1
Laburnum St E2 95 D6
Laburnums The E6 100 A3
Laburnum Way
Southborough BR2 210 D2
Stanwell TW19 148 B3
Lacebark Cl DA15 167 D4
Lacewing Cl E13 99 A4
Lacey Cl N9 18 A2
Lacey Dr Dagenham RM8 80 C5
Edgware HA8 26 B6
Hampton TW12 173 B2
Lacey Ho 7 SE13 142 A3
Lacine Ct 12 SE16 118 D4
Lackington St EC2 242 D4
Lackland Ho SE1 263 D2
Lacland Ho SW10 266 C4
Lacock Cl SW19 180 A4
Lacock Ct 3 W13 109 A5
Lacon Rd SE22 140 A1
Lacrosse Way SW16 181 D2
Lacy Rd SW15 134 D1
Ladas Rd SE27 183 A5
Ladbroke Cres W11 91 A1
Ladbroke Gdns
W11 113 B6 244 C6
Ladbroke Gr
Kensal Town W10 91 A2
Notting Hill
W11 113 B6 244 C6
Ladbroke Grove Ho
W11 244 C6
Ladbroke Grove Sta
W10 91 A1
Ladbroke Ho E1 243 D3
Ladbroke Mews W11 244 B3
Ladbroke Rd
Enfield EN1 17 D5
Notting Hill
W11 113 B5 244 C4
Ladbroke Sq
W11 113 B6 244 D5
Ladbroke Terr
W11 113 B5 244 D4
Ladbroke Wlk
W11 113 B5 244 D4
Ladbrook Cl HA5 41 B4
Ladbrooke Cres DA14 168 D1
Ladbrook Rd SE25 205 B5
Ladderstile Ride KT2,
TW10 176 D5
Ladderswood Way N11 31 C5
Ladlands SE22 162 A4
Lady Alesford Ave HA7 25 B5
Lady Bankes Jun & Inf
Schs HA4 62 A6
Lady Booth Rd 7 KT1 176 A1
Ladybower Ct 6 E5 74 D4
Ladycroft Gdns 6
BR6 227 A3
Ladycroft Rd SE13 141 D2
Ladycroft Way BR6 227 A3
Ladycroft Wlk HA7 25 D1
Lady Eleanor Holles Sch
The (Jun Girls)
TW12 173 D5
Lady Eleanor Holles Sch
The (Senior Girls)
TW12 173 D5
Lady Elizabeth Ho
SW14 133 A2
Ladyfern Ho 19 E3 97 C2
Lady Florence Ctyd 15
SE8 141 C5
Ladygate La HA4 39 A3
Lady Hay KT4 215 D6
Lady Helen Seymour Ho 14
E13 99 A5
Lady Margaret Prim Sch
UB1 85 B2
Lady Margaret Rd
Kentish Town NW5 71 C3
Southall UB1 85 B2
Lady Margaret Sch
SW6 135 C4 265 A1
Lady Shaw Ct N13 16 B1
Ladysmith Ave
Ilford IG2 57 C2
Newham E6 100 A5
Ladysmith Cl NW7 28 A3
Ladysmith Rd
Edmonton N18 34 B5
Eltham SE9 166 C5
Enfield EN1 5 D3
Harrow HA3 24 C1
Newham E16 98 D4
Tottenham N17 34 A1
Lady Somerset Rd
NW5 71 B4
LADYWELL 163 C6
Ladywell Cl SE4 141 C1
Ladywell Ho 7 BR5 190 B1
Ladywell Hts SE4 163 B5
Ladywell Rd SE13 163 D6
Ladywell St 4 E15 98 D6
Ladywell Sta SE13 163 D6
Ladywell Water Twr
SE4 163 C6
Ladywood Ave BR5 211 C4
Ladywood Rd KT6 214 C6
Lafitte Ho 22 N19 49 D2
Lafone Ave TW13 150 C2
Lafone Ho 11 SW2 160 A4
Lafone St SE1 117 D4 253 C2
Lagado Mews SE16 118 D5
Lagonda Ho 11 E3 97 C3
Lagonier Ho EC1 235 B1
Laidlaw Dr N21 16 B6
Laindon Ho 6 N16 51 D1
Laing Dean UB5 84 C6
Laing Ho SE5 139 A5
Laings Ave CR4 180 D1
Laings Cnr CR4 180 D2
Lainlock Pl TW3 129 D4
Lainson St SW18 157 C4
Lairdale Cl SE21 161 A4
Laird Ho SE5 139 A5
Lairs Cl N7 72 A2
Lait Ho 3 BR3 185 D2
Laitwood Rd SW12 159 B3
Lakanal 14 SE5 139 C4
Lake Ave BR1 187 A4
Lake Bsns Ctr N17 34 A3
Lake Cl Dagenham RM8 80 D5
6 Wimbledon SW19 179 B5
Lakedale Ct IG11 102 A3
Lakedale Rd SE18 123 C1
Lake Dr WD23 8 B2
Lake Farm Ctry Pk
UB3 105 C5
Lakefield Cl SE20 184 B3
Lakefield Rd N22 32 D1
Lake Gdns
Dagenham RM10 81 C3
Hackbridge SM6 219 B5
Richmond TW10 153 B2
Lakehall Gdns CR7 204 D4
Lakehall Rd CR7 204 D4
Lake Ho
Borough The SE1 252 A1
4 West Norwood
SW27 182 D5
Lake House Rd E11 77 A6
Lakehurst Rd KT19 215 C3
Lakeland Cl HA3 24 B4
Lakeman Ct CR7 183 A1
Lakenheath N14 15 D6
Laker Ct SW4 138 A3
Lake Rd Croydon CR0 223 B6
Dagenham RM6 58 D5
Wimbledon SW19 179 B5
Laker Pl SW15 157 A5
Lakeside
Beckenham BR3 207 D6
Deacons Hill WD6 10 C6
Ealing W13 87 C1
Enfield EN2 3 D1
Finchley N3 29 D1
10 Kingston u T KT2 176 D3
Wallington SM6 219 B4
West Ewell KT19 215 C2
Lakeside Ave
Redbridge IG4 55 D5
Thamesmead SE28 124 A5
Lakeside Cl Ruislip HA4 39 B5
Sidcup DA15 168 C6
South Norwood SE25 184 A1
Lakeside Complex The
SE2 124 D5
Lakeside Cres EN4 14 D6
Lakeside Ct N4 51 A1
Lakeside Dr Acton NW10 88 B4
Esher KT10 212 A2
Keston Mark BR2 226 A5
Lakeside Lo NW4 47 A5
Lakeside Rd
Brook Green W14 112 D3
Palmers Green N13 16 B1
Lakeside Way HA9 66 C4
Lakes Rd BR2 225 C3
Lakeswood Rd BR5 211 A3
Lake The WD23 8 B3
Lakeview 23 E3 96 D5
Lake View HA8 26 B5
Lakeview Ct E4 36 B4
Lake View Ct SW1 258 D6
Lakeview Rd
Bexley DA16 146 B1
West Norwood SE27 182 D5
Lake View Terr N18 33 D6
Lakis Cl NW3 70 A4
Laleham Ave NW7 11 B1
Laleham Ho E2 243 C6
Laleham Rd
Catford SE6 164 A4
Littleton TW17 192 C4
Lalor St SW6 135 A3
Lambarde Ave SE9 188 C6
Lambard Ho 4 SE10 142 A5
Lamb Cl UB5 85 A4
Lamb Ct 16 E14 119 A6
Lamberhurst Ho 14
SE15 140 C6
Lamberhurst Rd
Dagenham RM8 59 B1
West Norwood SE27 182 C5
Lambert Ave TW9 132 D2
Lambert Ho
16 Brixton SW9 138 C3
19 Crouch End N19 49 D2
Lambert Lo TW8 109 D1
Lambert Rd
Clapham Pk SW2 160 B6
Newham E16 99 B1
North Finchley N12 30 B5
Lambert's Pl CR0 205 B1
Lambert's Rd KT6 198 B4
Lambert St N1 72 C1
Lambert Way N12 30 A5
Lambert Wlk HA9 65 D5
LAMBETH 116 B4
Lambeth Acad SW4 159 C6
Lambeth Coll (Brixton Ctr)
SW2 160 B6
Lambeth Coll (Clapham
Ctr) SW4 159 C6
Lambeth Coll (Tower
Bridge Ctr)
SE1 117 C5 253 B3
Lambeth Coll (Vauxhall
Ctr) SW8 137 D4 269 C2
Lambeth Ct 8 SW18 157 C6
Lambeth High St
SE1 116 B2 260 C4
Lambeth Hill EC4 252 A6
Lambeth Hospl SW9 138 B2
Lambeth North Sta
SE1 116 C3 261 A6
Lambeth Pal*
SE1 116 B3 260 C5
Lambeth Palace Rd
SE1 116 B3 260 C6
Lambeth Pier SE1 260 B5
Lambeth Prospect
SE19 183 B4
Lambeth Rd
Lambeth SE1 116 C3 261 B5
Thornton Heath CR0 204 D1
Lambeth Twrs SE11 261 A5
Lambeth Wlk
SE11 116 B2 260 D4
Lambfold Ho N7 72 A2
Lamb Ho
28 Camberwell SE5 139 A5
11 Camberwell SE5 139 B4
Greenwich SE10 142 A6
Lamb La E8 74 B1
Lamble St NW5 71 A4
Lambley Rd RM9 80 B2
Lambolle Pl NW3 70 C2
Lambolle Rd NW3 70 C2
Lambourn Cl
Hanwell W7 108 D4
9 Kentish Town NW5 71 C4
Lambourne Ave SW19 179 B6
Lambourne Ct 5 IG8 37 C3
Lambourne Gdns
5 Barking IG11 79 D1
Chingford E4 19 C2
Enfield EN1 5 D3
Lambourne Gr
Deptford SE16 118 D1
Lambourne Gr *continued*
Kingston u T KT1 176 D1
Lambourne Ho NW8 236 D4
Lambourne Pl SE3 143 B4
Lambourne Rd
Barking IG11 79 D1
Ilford IG3 79 C6
Leytonstone E11 54 A2
Lambourn Ho BR1 188 A3
Lambourn Rd SW4 137 B2
Lambrook Ho 18 SE15 140 A4
Lambrook Terr
SW6 135 A4 264 A2
Lamb's Bldgs EC1 242 C5
Lamb's Cl N9 18 A2
Lamb's Conduit Pas
WC1 240 C4
Lamb's Conduit St
WC1 94 B3 240 C5
Lambscroft Ave SE9,
SE12 165 D1
Lambs Mdw IG8 37 D1
Lamb's Mews N1 234 C5
Lamb's Pas EC1 95 B3 242 C5
Lamb St E1 95 D2 243 C4
Lamb's Terr N9 17 B2
Lambs Wlk EN2 5 A3
Lambton Ct 2 N19 50 A1
Lambton Mews 4 N19 50 A1
Lambton Pl W11 244 D6
Lambton Rd
Finsbury Pk N19 50 A1
Wimbledon SW20 178 C2
Lamb Wlk SE1 253 A1
Lamerock Rd BR1 186 D6
Lamerton Lo 10 TW9 132 B4
Lamerton St 8 SE8 141 C6
Lamford Cl N17 33 B3
Lamington St 3 W6 112 B2
Lamlash St SE11 261 C4
Lamley Ho SE10 141 D5
Lammas Ave CR4 181 A1
Lammas Gn SE26 162 B1
Lammas Park Gdns
W5 109 C5
Lammas Park Rd W5 109 D4
Lammas Rd
Homerton E9 74 D1
Richmond TW10 175 C6
Walthamstow E10 53 A1
Lammas Sch The E10 53 B1
Lammermoor Rd
SW12 159 B4
Lamont Rd
SW10 136 B6 266 C5
Lamont Rd Pas SW10 266 C5
Lamorbey Cl DA15 167 D2
Lamorna Cl E17 36 A2
Lamorna Gr HA7 25 D1
Lampard Gr N16 51 D1
Lampern Sq 8 E2 96 A4
Lampeter Cl NW9 45 C3
Lampeter Sq W6 264 A5
Lamplighter Cl 34 E1 96 C3
Lampmead Rd SE12 142 D1
Lamport Cl SE18 122 B2
Lampson Ho 6 N19 71 C4
LAMPTON 129 D4
Lampton Ave TW5 129 D4
Lampton Ct TW5 129 D4
Lampton House Cl
SW19 178 D6
Lampton Park Rd
TW3 129 D3
Lampton Rd TW3,
TW5 129 D3
Lampton Sch TW5 129 C4
Lanacre Ave NW9 27 C2
Lanain Ct SE12 164 D4
Lanark Cl W5 87 C2
Lanark Ct UB5 63 C3
Lanark Ho 12 SE1 118 A1
Lanark Mans
Paddington W9 236 B6
15 Shepherd's Bush
W12 112 C4
Lanark Mews NW8 229 B1
Lanark Pl W9 92 A3 236 B6
Lanark Rd W9 92 A4 229 A1
Lanark Sq E14 119 D3
Lanata Wlk UB4 84 D3
Lanbury Rd SE15 140 D1
Lancashire Ct W1 248 D6
Lancaster Ave
Barking IG11 101 C6
Croydon CR4 204 A5
Hadley Wood EN4 2 B5
Wanstead E18 55 B5
West Norwood SE21,
SE27 161 A2
Wimbledon SW19 178 D5
Lancaster Cl
Ashford TW15 170 A6
Beckenham BR2 208 D5
10 De Beauvoir Town N1 73 C1
Grahame Pk NW9 27 D3
Kensington W2 245 C5
Kingston u T KT2 175 D5
New Malden KT4 200 B2
Stanwell TW19 148 A5
Tottenham N17 34 A3
Lancaster Cotts 1
TW10 154 A5
Lancaster Ct
Bayswater W2 246 B6
1 Belmont SM2 217 C1
Parsons Green SW6 264 D3
Stanwell TW19 148 A3
Walton-on-T KT12 194 B2
West Norwood SE27 160 D2

Lancaster Dr
Canary Wharf E14 120 A5
Maitland Pk NW3 70 C2
Lancaster Gate
W2 114 A6 246 B6
Lancaster Gate Sta
W2 114 B6 246 C6
Lancaster Gdns
Bromley BR1 210 A4
Kingston u T KT2 175 D5
West Ealing W13 109 B4
Wimbledon SW19 179 A5
Lancaster Gr NW3 70 C2
Lancaster hall 14 E16 121 A5
Lancaster Ho Enfield EN2 5 B4
Putney SW15 134 C3
Stanmore HA7 9 A1
Lancaster Ho SW1 249 A2
Lancaster Ho SW18 157 D4
Lancasterian Prim Sch
N17 33 D2
Lancaster Lo 2 W11 91 A1
Lancaster Mews
Bayswater
W2 114 A6 246 B6
2 Richmond TW10 154 A5
3 Wandsworth SW18 157 D6
Lancaster Pk TW10 154 A6
Lancaster Pl
Hounslow TW5 128 D3
Ilford IG1 79 A4
Strand WC2 116 B6 250 C5
Twickenham TW1 153 A4
1 Wimbledon SW19 178 D5
Lancaster Rd
Bowes Pk N11 31 D4
Dudden Hill NW10 68 A3
Edmonton N18 33 D5
Enfield EN2 5 B4
Finsbury Pk N4 50 C2
Harrow HA2 41 C4
Higham Hill E17 34 D1
Leytonstone E11 76 C6
New Barnet EN4 14 B6
Northolt UB5 64 A2
Notting Hill W11 91 A1
Southall UB1 107 A6
South Norwood SE25 206 A6
Upton E7 77 A1
Wimbledon SW19 178 D5
Lancaster Road Ind Est 2
EN4 14 B6
Lancaster St
SE1 116 D4 251 D1
Lancaster Stables 10
NW3 70 C2
Lancaster Terr
W2 114 B6 246 C6
Lancaster Wlk
Hayes UB3 83 A1
Knightsbridge
W2 114 A5 246 B4
Lancastrian Rd SM6 220 B1
Lancefield Ho SE15 140 B2
Lancefield St W10 91 B4
Lancell St N16 73 C6
Lancelot Ave HA0 65 D4
Lancelot Cres HA0 65 D4
Lancelot Gdns EN4 15 A4
Lancelot Ho SM5 202 C1
Lancelot Pl
SW7 114 D4 247 C1
Lancelot Rd
Welling DA16 146 A2
Wembley HA0 65 D3
Lance Rd HA1 42 A2
Lancer Sq W8 245 C2
Lancey Cl SE7 122 A2
Lanchester Ct W2 237 C1
Lanchester Rd N6 48 D4
Lanchester Way SE14 140 D4
Lancing Gdns N9 17 D3
Lancing Rd Ealing W13 109 B6
Feltham TW13 149 D2
Ilford IG2 57 B2
Thornton Heath CR0 204 B2
Lancing St NW1 232 C1
Lancresse Ct N1 95 C6
Landale Ct SE10 142 A4
Landale Ho 13 SE16 118 C3
Landau Ct 11 CR2 221 A3
Landcroft Rd SE22 161 D5
Landells Rd SE22 162 A5
Lander Ct EN5 14 A6
Landford Rd SW15 134 C2
Landgrove Rd SW19 179 C5
Landin Ho 1 E14 97 C1
Landleys Field 21 N7 71 D3
Landmann Ho 16 SE16 118 B2
Landmann Way SE14 118 D1
Landmark Commercial Ctr
N18 33 C4
Landmark Hts E5 75 A4
Landon Pl SW1 257 C6
Landons Cl E14 120 A5
Landon Way TW15 170 D4
Landon Wlk 16 E14 119 D6
Landor Ct N16 73 C3
Landor Ho 7 SE5 139 B5
Landor Rd SW9 138 A2
Landor Wlk 11 W12 112 A4
Landra Gdns N21 16 D5
Landrake NW1 232 B5
Landridge Dr EN1 6 B5
Landridge Rd SW6 135 B3
Landrock Rd N8 50 B3
Landscape Rd IG8 37 B3
Landsdown Cl 9 EN5 2 A1
Landseer Ave E12 78 C3
Landseer Cl
Edgware HA8 26 C1
Mitcham SW19 180 B2
Landseer Ct Hayes UB4 83 B5
10 Upper Holloway N19 72 A6
Landseer Ho
Battersea SW11 268 B1
16 Northolt UB5 84 D5
Paddington NW8 236 D6
Westminster SW1 259 D3
Landseer Rd
Cheam SM1 217 C2
Enfield EN1 18 A6
New Malden KT3 199 B2
Upper Holloway N19 72 A6
Lands' End WD6 9 D5
Landstead Rd SE18 145 B5
Landulph Ho SE11 261 B2
Landward Ct W1 237 B2
Lane Cl NW2 68 B5
Lane Ct SW11 158 D4
Lane End DA7 147 D2
Lane Gdns
Bushey Heath WD23 8 C4
Claygate KT10 212 D1
Lane Mews E12 78 B5
Lanercost Cl SW2 160 C2
Lanercost Gdns N14 16 A4
Lanercost Rd SW2 160 C2
Laneside
Chislehurst BR7 189 A5
Edgware HA8 27 A5
Laneside Ave RM8 59 B2
Lane The
Blackheath Pk SE3 143 A2
St John's Wood
NW8 92 A5 229 A3
Laneway SW15 156 B6
Laney Bldg EC1 241 A4
Lanfranc Ct HA1 64 D5
Lanfranc Rd E3 97 A5
Lanfrey Pl W14 254 C1
Langbourn Ct E17 53 A3
Langbourne Ave N6 71 A6
Langbourne Ho 7
SW2 160 C6
Langbourne Mans N6 71 A6
Langbourne Pl E14 119 D1
Langbourne Prim Sch
SE21 161 C1
Langbourne Way
KT10 213 A2
Langbrook Rd SE3 143 D3
Langcroft Cl SM5 218 D5
Langdale NW1 232 A2
Langdale Ave CR4 202 D6
Langdale Cl
Camberwell SE17 139 A6
Dagenham RM8 58 C1
Locksbottom BR6 226 D5
Mortlake SW14 132 D1
Langdale Cres DA7 147 C4
Langdale Ct
3 Ealing W5 87 C2
9 Ilford IG1 78 D5
Ruislip HA4 62 B3
Langdale Dr UB4 83 C5
Langdale Gdns UB6 87 B4
Langdale Ho SW1 259 A1
Langdale Par 8 CR4 202 D6
Langdale Rd
Greenwich SE10 142 A5
Thornton Heath CR7 204 C5
Langdale St 25 E1 96 B1
Langdon Cres E6 100 C5
Langdon Ct
Finsbury EC1 234 D3
Harlesden NW10 89 C6
Langdon Dr NW9 45 A1
Langdon Ho 3 E14 98 A1
Langdon Park Rd N6 49 C2
Langdon Park Sec Sch
E14 98 A1
Langdon Pk TW11 175 C3
Langdon Pl SW14 133 A2
Langdon Rd
Barking E6 100 C6
Bromley BR2 209 B6
Morden SM4 202 A4
Langdon Sch E6 100 D6
Langdons Ct UB2 107 C3
Langdon Shaw DA14 189 D5
Langdon Way 18 SE1 118 A2
Langdon Wlk SM4 202 A4
Langford Cl
Shacklewell E8 74 A3
7 South Tottenham N15 51 C3
St John's Wood NW8 229 B4
Langford Cres EN4 2 D1
Langford Ct NW8 229 B3
Langford Gn SE5 139 C2
Langford Ho 5 SE8 141 C6
Langford Pl
Sidcup DA14 168 A1
St John's Wood
NW8 92 A5 229 B4
Langford Prim Sch
SW6 135 D3
Langford Rd
Cockfosters EN4 2 D1
4 Sands End SW6 135 D3
Woodford IG8 37 C4
Langfords IG9 21 D2
Langham Cl 1 N15 50 D6
Langham Ct
Hendon NW4 46 D4
Merton SW20 178 C1
4 Putney SW15 156 D6
Ruislip HA4 62 B3
12 Twickenham TW1 153 C5
Langham Dr RM6 58 B3
Langham Gdns
Burnt Oak HA8 27 A3
Ealing W13 109 B6
Richmond TW10 175 C6
Southgate N21 16 D6
Wembley HA0 65 C6
Langham Ho
Clapham Pk SW4 159 C6
3 Wanstead E11 55 B5
Langham House Cl
TW10 175 D6
Langham Mans SW5 255 C1
Langham Park Pl BR2 208 D5
Langham Pl
Chiswick W4 133 C6
Fitzrovia W1 93 B2 238 D3
Noel Pk N15 50 D6
Langham Rd
Burnt Oak HA8 27 A4
Teddington TW11 175 B4
West Green N15 51 A6
Wimbledon SW20 178 C2
Langham St W1 93 B2 238 D3
Langhedge Cl N18 33 D4
Langhedge La N18 33 D4
Langhedge Lane Ind Est
N18 33 D4
Lang Ho
South Lambeth SW8 270 A3
Stanwell TW19 148 A3
3 Tufnell Pk N19 71 C5
Langholm Cl SW12 159 D4
Langholme WD23 8 A3
Langhorn Dr TW2 152 C4
Langhorne Ct 10 NW8 70 B1
Langhorne Ho 5 SE7 143 C6
Langhorne Rd RM10 81 C1
Langhurst Ho 10
SW11 137 A3
Langland Cres HA7 25 D1
Langland Dr HA5 23 A3
Langland Gdns
Croydon CR0 223 B6
West Hampstead NW3 69 D3
Langland Ho 10 SE5 139 B5
Upper Tooting SW17 180 B5
Langland Mans NW3 69 D3
Langler Rd NW10 90 C5
Langley Ave
North Cheam KT4,
SM3 216 D6
Ruislip HA4 62 B6
Surbiton KT6 198 A1
Langley Cres
Dagenham RM9 80 D1
Edgware HA8 11 A1
Harlington UB3 127 D5
Wanstead E11 55 C2
Langley Ct
South Lambeth SW8 270 A2
Strand WC2 250 A6
13 Sutton SM2 218 A2
Langley Dr
South Acton W3 110 D4
Wanstead E11 55 B2
Langley Gdns
Bromley BR2 209 C5
Dagenham RM9 80 D1
Southborough BR5 210 D3
Langley Gr KT3 177 C1
Langley Ho
11 Lower Clapton E5 74 B3
36 Paddington W2 91 C2
Langley La
SW8 138 A6 270 B6
Langley Lawns SM2 218 B1
Langley Manor BR3 208 A4
Langley Mans SW8 270 B6
Langley Park Rd SM1,
SM2 218 A1
Langley Park Sch for Boys
BR3 207 D3
Langley Park Sch for Girls
BR3 208 A3
Langley Pk NW7 27 C4
Langley Rd
Beckenham BR3 207 A5
Isleworth TW7 130 D3
Merton SW19 179 C2
Surbiton KT6 198 A2
West Heath DA16 146 C6
Langley Row EN5 1 B4
Langley St WC2 94 A1 240 A1
Langley Way BR4 208 C2
Langmead Dr WD23 8 B3
Langmead Ho 34 E3 97 D4
Langmead St SE27 183 A6
Langmore Ct DA6 146 D2
Langmore Ho 39 E1 96 A1
Langport Ct KT12 194 C1
Langport Ho 1 SW9 138 D3
Langridge 15 NW5 71 A2
Langridge Mews
TW12 173 B4
Langroyd Rd SW17 158 D2
Langside Ave SW15 134 A1
Langside Cres N14 15 D1
Lang St E1 96 C3
Langstone Way NW7 28 D3
Langston Hughes Cl 5
SE24 138 D1
Langthorn Ct EC2 242 D2
Langthorne Ct 3 SE6 186 A6
Langthorne Ho UB3 105 C2
Langthorne Hospl E11 76 B5
Langthorne Lo 30
SW2 160 C4
Langthorne Rd E11 76 B5
Langthorne St SW6 134 D5
Langton Ave
Oakleigh Pk N20 14 B4
Wallend E6 100 C4
Langton Cl WC1 94 B3 240 D6
Langton Ct SW15 157 B5
Langton Ho Harrow HA2 64 C6
Lambeth SE11 260 D4
5 Streatham SW16 181 C6
Langton Pl SW18 157 C3
Langton Rd
Camberwell SW9 138 D5
Cricklewood NW2 68 C5
East Molesey KT8 196 A5
Harrow Weald HA3 24 A3
Langton Rise SE22,
SE23 162 B4
Langton St
SW10 136 A6 266 B5
Langton Way
Greenwich SE3 143 A5
South Croydon CR0 221 C4
Langtry Ho BR1 187 B3
Langtry Pl SW6 265 B6
Langtry Rd Northolt UB5 84 D5
Paddington NW8 91 D6
Langtry Wlk
NW8 92 A6 229 A6
Langwood Chase
TW11 175 C4
Langworth Dr UB4 84 B1
Langworthy HA5 23 C4
Lanherne Ho 7 SW19 178 D3
Lanhill Rd W9 91 C3
Lanier Rd SE13 164 B5
Lanigan Dr TW3 151 D6
Lankaster Gdns N2 30 B2
Lankers Dr HA2 41 B3
Lankton Cl BR3 186 A2
Lanner Ho 2 SW11 136 C2
Lannock Ct 2 SW17 180 C4
Lannock Rd UB3 105 D5
Lannoy Point SW6 264 B4
Lannoy Rd SE9 167 A3
Lanrick Rd E14 98 C1
Lanridge Rd SE2 124 D3
Lansan Ct E11 76 D6
Lansbury Ave
Barking IG11 80 A1
Dagenham RM6 59 A4
Edmonton N18 33 C5
Feltham TW14 150 B5
Lansbury Cl NW10 67 A3
Lansbury Ct 4 SE28 124 B6
Lansbury Dr UB4 83 D3
Lansbury Gdns 1 E14 98 B1
Lansbury Ho 5 DA17 125 B1
Lansbury Lawrence Prim
Sch E14 97 D1
Lansbury Rd EN3 6 D4
Lansbury Way N18 33 C5
Lanscombe Wlk SW8 270 A3
Lansdell Ho 9 SW2 160 C5
Lansdell Rd CR4 181 A1
Lansdown Cl KT12 194 C1
Lansdowne Ave
Orpington BR6 210 D1
West Heath DA7 146 D5
Lansdowne Cl
Tolworth KT5 214 D6
Twickenham TW1 152 D3
Wimbledon SW20 178 D3
Lansdowne Coll W2 245 C5
Lansdowne Copse 1
KT4 216 A6
Lansdowne Cres
W11 113 A6 244 B5
Lansdowne Ct
Redbridge IG5 56 A6
2 Worcester Pk KT4 216 A6
Lansdowne Dr E8 74 A1
Lansdowne Gdns
SW8 138 A4 270 A2
Lansdowne Gr NW10 67 C4
Lansdowne Hill SE27 160 D1
Lansdowne Ho
19 Belmont SM2 217 D1
Enfield EN2 4 C3
Notting Hill W11 244 C4
Lansdowne Int Coll Ltd
SW7 256 B5
Lansdowne La SE7 121 D1
Lansdowne Mews
Greenwich SE7 121 D1
Notting Hill W11 244 C4
Lansdowne Pl
Borough The SE1 262 D6
Penge SE19 183 D3
Lansdowne Rd
Chingford E4 19 C2
Croydon CR0 205 B1
Finchley N3 29 C3
Harrow HA1 42 C2
Hayes UB8 83 A1
Hounslow TW3 129 D2
Ilford IG3 57 D2
Leytonstone E11 76 D6
Muswell Hill N10 31 C1
Notting Hill
W11 113 A6 244 B5
Stanmore HA7 25 C4
Sundridge BR1 187 B3
Tottenham N17 34 A2
Walthamstow E17 53 C3
Wanstead E18 55 A6
West Ewell KT19 215 B1
Wimbledon SW19,
SW20 178 C3
Lansdowne Rise
W11 113 A6 244 B5
Lansdowne Row W1 248 D4
Lansdowne Sch SW9 138 B2
Lansdowne Terr WC1 240 B5
Lansdowne Way SW4,
SW8 138 A4 270 B1
Lansdowne Wlk
W11 113 B5 244 C4
Lansdowne Wood Cl 11
SE27 160 D1
Lansdowne Workshops
SE7 121 D1
Lansdown Ho 28 SE5 139 A3
Lansdown Rd
Sidcup DA14 168 B1
Upton E7 77 C1
Lansfield Ave N18 34 A6
Lanson Ho HA8 26 C4
Lantern Cl
Orpington BR6 226 D4
Putney SW15 134 A1
Wembley HA0 65 D3
Lantern Ct
Southgate N14 15 D3
4 Wimbledon SW20 178 D2
Lantern Ho
Millwall E14 119 C4
Woolwich SE18 122 C1
Lanterns Ct E14 119 C3
Lanterns The N12 29 D4
Lantern Way UB7 104 B4
Lant Ho SE1 252 A1
Lantry Ct 1 W3 110 D5
Lant St SE1 117 A4 252 B1
Lanvanor Rd SE15 140 C3
Lanyard Ho 4 SE8 119 B2
Lapford Cl W9 91 B3
Lapponum Wlk UB4 84 D2
Lapsang SE1 253 D3
Lapse Wood Wlk SE22 162 B3
Lapstone Gdns HA3 43 C3
Lapwing Ct
Grahame Pk NW9 27 C1
Tolworth KT6 214 C5
Lapwing Terr E7 77 D3
Lapwing Twr 31 SE8 141 B6
Lapwing Way UB4 84 D1
Lapworth 2 N11 31 B6
Lapworth Ct W2 91 D2
Lara Cl
Chessington KT9 214 A1
Lewisham SE13 164 A5
Lara Lo SM1 217 C3
Larbert Rd SW16 181 C3
Larch Ave W3 111 C5
Larch Cl Balham SW12 159 B2
Colney Hatch N11 31 A3
15 Deptford SE8 141 B6
Newham E13 99 C3
10 Upper Holloway N19 71 C6
Larch Cres Hayes UB4 84 D2
West Ewell KT19 214 D2
Larch Ct 41 W2 91 C2
Larch Dene BR6 226 C6
Larches Ave SW14 133 B1
Larches The
Edmonton N13 17 A1
Hillingdon UB10 82 D5
Larchfield Ho 2 N5 73 A3
Larch Gn NW9 27 C2
Larch Gr DA15 167 D3
Larch Ho Hayes UB4 84 C2
23 Rotherhithe SE16 118 C4
Larchmont HA4 39 B2
Larchmore Ct N19 72 A6
Larch Rd
Criclewood NW2 68 C4
Leyton E10 75 C6
Larch Tree Way CR0 223 C5
Larchvale Ct 20 SM2 217 D1
Larch Way BR2 210 C2
Larchwood Rd SE9 166 D2
Larcombe Cl CR0 221 D4
Larcom St
SE17 117 A2 262 B3
Larden Rd W3 111 C4
La Retraite RC Girls Sch
SW12 159 C4
Largewood Ave KT6 214 C6
Larissa St SE17 262 D3
Larix Ct NW10 90 A6
Larkbere Rd SE26 185 A6
Larken Cl WD23 8 A3
Larken Dr WD23 8 A3
Larkfield Ave HA3 43 B6
Larkfield Cl BR2 225 A6
Larkfield Rd
Longlands DA14 167 D1
Richmond TW9 132 A1
Larkhall La
SW4 138 A4 270 A1
Lark Hall Prim Sch
SW4 137 D3
Larkhall Rise SW4 137 D3
Larkham Cl TW13 149 C1
Lark Row E2 96 C6
Larksfield Gr EN1 6 B4
Larks Gr IG11 79 C1
Larkshall Bsns Ctr E4 20 B2
Larkshall Cres E4 36 A6
Larkshall Ct E4 36 A5
Larkshall Rd E4 36 B6
Larkspur Cl
Kingsbury NW9 44 D4
4 Newham E6 100 A2
Ruislip HA4 39 A2
Tottenham N17 33 B3
Larkspur Ct SM6 219 B1
Larkspur Gr HA8 27 A6
Larkspur Way KT19 215 A3
Larkswood Ct E4 36 B5
Larkswood Prim Sch
E4 35 D6
Larkswood Rd E4 35 D6
Larkswood Rise HA5 40 C5
Lark Way SM5 202 C2
Larkway Cl NW9 45 B5
Larmenier & Sacred Heart
RC Prim Sch W6 112 D2
Larnaca Ho SE1 263 C6
Larnach Rd W6 134 D6
Larne Rd HA4 39 D2
Larpent Ave SW15 156 C6
Larwood Cl UB6 64 B3
La Saint Union RC Sec Sch
NW5 71 A5
Lascelles Ave HA1 42 B2
Lascelles Cl E11 76 B6
Lascelles Ho NW1 237 B5
Lascott's Rd N22 32 B4
Laseron Ho 1 N15 51 D5
Lashford Ho HA8 27 A4
Lassa Rd SE9 166 B6
Lassell St SE10 120 B1
Lasseter Pl SE3 142 D6
Latchett Rd E18 37 B2
Latchingdon Ct E17 52 D5
Latchmere Cl KT2,
TW10 176 A5
Latchmere Jun & Inf Schs
KT2 176 B4
Latchmere La KT2,
TW10 176 B5
Latchmere Rd
Battersea SW11 136 D3
Kingston u T KT2 176 B4
Latchmere St 5
SW11 136 D3
Lateward Rd TW8 131 D6
Latham Cl Newham E6 100 A1
6 Twickenham TW1 153 A4
Latham Ct
3 Bowes Pk N11 32 A4
7 Northolt UB5 84 D4
Latham Ho Stepney E1 96 D1
18 Walthamstow E17 53 D6
Latham Rd
Bexleyheath DA6 169 C6
Twickenham TW1 152 D4
Latham's Way CR0 220 B6
Lathkill Cl EN1 18 A4
Lathkill Ct BR3 185 B2
Lathom Jun Sch E6 78 A1
Lathom Rd E6 78 B1
Lathwood Ho 6 SE26 184 B5
Latimer SE17 263 A1
Latimer Ave E6 100 B6
Latimer Cl
North Cheam KT4 216 B4
Pinner Green HA5 22 C2
Latimer Gdns HA5 22 C2
Latimer Ho
11 Homerton E9 74 D2
Notting Hill W11 244 D5
Latimer Ind Est 1
NW10 90 C1
Latimer Pl W10 90 C1
Latimer Rd Barnet EN5 1 D2
1 Croydon CR0 220 D5
Forest Gate E7 77 B4
North Kensington W10 90 C1
South Tottenham N15 51 C3
Teddington TW11 174 D5
Wimbledon SW19 179 D4
Latimer Road Sta
W10 112 D6
Latitude Ho NW1 231 C5
Latona Rd SE15 140 A6
La Tourne Gdns BR6 227 A5
Lattimer Pl W4 133 C6
Latton Cl KT12 195 A2
Latvia Ct SE17 262 B1
Latymer All Saints CE Prim
Sch N9 17 D2
Latymer Ct W6 112 D2
Latymer Rd N9 17 D3
Latymer Sch The N9 17 C2
Latymer Upper Sch
W6 112 A1
Latymer Way N9 17 C2
Laubin Cl TW1 131 B1
Lauder Cl UB5 84 D5
Lauder Ct N14 16 A4
Lauderdale Dr TW10 153 D1
Lauderdale Mans W9 91 D4
Lauderdale Rd W9 91 D4
Lauderdale Twr EC2 242 A4
Laud St Croydon CR0 221 A5
Vauxhall SE11 116 B1 260 C2
Laughton Ho 11 SW2 160 C5
Laughton Rd UB5 84 D6
Launcelot Prim Sch
BR1 187 A6
Launcelot Rd BR1,
SE12 187 A6
Launcelot St SE1 251 A1
Launceston Ct CR7 204 C3
Launceston Gdns UB6 65 C1
Launceston Pl
W8 114 A3 256 A5
Launceston Rd UB6 87 C6
Launch St E14 120 A3
Laundress La N16 74 A5
Laundry La 7 N1 73 A1
Laundry Mews SE23 162 D4
Laundry Rd
W6 135 A6 264 A5
Launton Dr DA6 146 D1

Laura Cl Enfield EN1 . . . . . 17 C6
Wanstead E11 . . . . 55 C4
Laura Ct HA2 . . . . 24 A1
Lauradale Rd N2 . . . . 48 D5
Laura Pl E5 . . . . 74 C4
Laurel Ave TW1 . . . . 152 D3
Laurel Bank Gdns 3
SW6 . . . . 135 B3
Laurel Bank Rd EN2 . . . . . . 5 B4
Laurel Cl Sidcup DA14 . . . 168 A1
8 Upper Holloway N19 . . 71 C6
Upper Tooting SW17 . . . . 180 C5
Laurel Cres CR0 . . . . 223 C5
Laurel Ct Dalston E8 . . . . . 73 D1
2 Putney SW15 . . . . 156 D6
9 Rotherhithe SE16 . . . . 119 A5
South Norwood SE25 . . . 205 C4
8 Wembley HA0 . . . . 88 A5
Laurel Dr N21 . . . . 16 C4
Laurel Gdns
Bromley BR1 . . . . 210 A5
Chingford E4 . . . . 19 D4
Ealing W7 . . . . 108 C5
Edgware NW7 . . . . 11 B1
Hounslow TW4 . . . . 129 A1
Laurel Gr
Forest Hill SE26 . . . . 185 A6
Penge SE20 . . . . 184 C3
Laurel Ho
Brentford W5 . . . . 109 C2
9 Deptford SE8 . . . . 141 B6
5 Hamstead NW3 . . . . 69 D2
Morden SM4 . . . . 201 D4
Laurel La UB7 . . . . 104 A2
Laurel Manor SM2 . . . . . 218 A1
Laurel Mead Ct 8 E18 . . 37 A2
Laurel Pk HA3 . . . . 24 D3
Laurel Rd
Barnes SW13 . . . . 134 A3
Teddington TW12 . . . . . . 174 B5
Wimbledon SW20 . . . . . . 178 B2
Laurel St E8 . . . . 73 D2
Laurels The
8 Belvedere DA17 . . . . . 125 C1
2 Buckhurst Hill IG9 . . . . 21 C3
Bushey WD23 . . . . 8 C2
Finchley N3 . . . . 29 D4
Shortlands BR2 . . . . 209 A5
9 Sundridge BR1 . . . . . . 187 B2
Laurel View N12 . . . . 13 D1
Laurel Way
Snaresbrook E18 . . . . 54 D5
Woodside Pk N20 . . . . 13 C1
Laurence Ct E10 . . . . 53 D2
Laurence Mews 12
W12 . . . . 112 A4
Laurence Pountney Hill
EC4 . . . . 252 C6
Laurence Pountney La
EC4 . . . . 252 D6
Laurie Gr SE14 . . . . 141 A4
Laurie Ho
Newington SE1 . . . . 261 D5
Notting Hill W8 113 C5 245 A3
Laurie Rd W7 . . . . 86 C2
Laurier Rd
Croydon CR0 . . . . 205 D2
Dartmouth Pk NW5 . . . . . . 71 B5
Laurimel Cl HA7 . . . . 25 B4
Laurino Pl WD23 . . . . 8 A2
Lauriston Apartments 6
N17 . . . . 51 D6
Lauriston Ho 6 E9 . . . . . . 74 D1
Lauriston Lo NW6 . . . . 69 B2
Lauriston Rd
Homerton E9 . . . . 74 D1
Wimbledon SW19 . . . . . . 178 D4
Lauriston Sch E9 . . . . 96 D6
Lausanne Rd
Hornsey N8 . . . . 50 C5
St Johns SE15 . . . . 140 C4
Lavehham Ho E17 . . . . 35 D2
Lavell St N16 . . . . 73 B4
Lavender Ave
Mitcham CR4 . . . . 180 D2
North Cheam KT4, SM3 . . 216 C5
Welsh Harp NW9 . . . . 45 A1
Lavender Cl
Bromley Comm BR2 . . . . 210 A3
South Kensington SW3 . 266 D5
Wallington SM5 . . . . 219 B4
Lavender Ct
Colney Hatch N12 . . . . 30 C4
East Molesey KT8 . . . . . . 195 D6
Edgware HA8 . . . . 27 A5
Feltham TW14 . . . . 150 B5
South Lambeth SW4 . . . 270 B1
Sutton SM2 . . . . 218 A1
Lavender Gdns
Clapham SW11 . . . . 136 D1
Enfield EN2 . . . . 4 D4
Stanmore HA3 . . . . 24 C4
Lavender Gr Dalston E8 . . 74 A1
Mitcham CR4 . . . . 180 C2
Lavender Hill
Clapham SW11 . . . . 137 A2
Enfield EN2 . . . . 4 D4
Lavender Ho
8 Richmond TW9 . . . . . . 132 D4
14 Rotherhithe SE16 . . . . 118 D5
Lavender Pl IG1 . . . . 78 D3
Lavender Prim Sch EN2 . . 5 C5
Lavender Rd
Battersea SW11 . . . . 136 B2
Enfield EN2 . . . . 5 B4
Hillingdon UB8 . . . . 82 B2
Rotherhithe SE16 . . . . . . 119 A5
Lavender Rd continued
Sutton SM1 . . . . 218 B4
Thornton Heath CR0 . . . . 204 B3
Wallington SM5 . . . . 219 A4
West Ewell KT19 . . . . 214 D2
Lavender Rise UB7 . . . . . 104 C4
Lavender St E15 . . . . 76 C2
Lavender Sweep
SW11 . . . . 136 D1
Lavender Terr 12
SW11 . . . . 136 C2
Lavender Vale SM6 . . . . 219 D2
Lavender Way CR0 . . . . . 206 D3
Lavender Wlk SW11 . . . . 136 D1
Lavendon Ho NW8 . . . . . 237 B6
Lavengro Rd SE27 . . . . . 161 A2
Lavenham Rd SW18 . . . . 157 C3
Lavernock Rd DA7 . . . . . 147 C3
Lavers Rd N16 . . . . 73 C5
Laverstoke Gdns
SW15 . . . . 156 A4
Laverton Mews SW5 . . 255 D3
Laverton Pl SW5 . . . . . . 255 D3
Lavidge Rd SE9 . . . . 166 B2
Lavina Gr N1 . . . . 233 C4
Lavington Cl E9 . . . . 75 B2
Lavington Rd
Ealing W13 . . . . 109 B5
Wallington CR0 . . . . 220 B4
Lavington St
SE1 . . . . 116 D5 251 D3
Lavinia Ct BR1 . . . . 186 C3
Lavisham Ho BR1 . . . . . . 187 B5
Lawdale Jun Sch E2 . . . . 96 A4
Lawdon Gdns CR0 . . . . . 220 D4
Lawford Rd
Chiswick W4 . . . . 133 A5
De Beauvoir Town N1 . . . . 73 C1
Kentish Town NW5 . . . . . . 71 C2
Lawfords Wharf 18
NW1 . . . . 71 C1
Law Ho IG11 . . . . 102 A5
Lawless Ho 5 E14 . . . . . 120 A6
Lawless St 12 E14 . . . . . 119 D6
Lawley Ho 11 TW1 . . . . . 153 D5
Lawley Rd N14 . . . . 15 B4
Lawley St E5 . . . . 74 C4
Lawman Ct 2 TW9 . . . . . 132 B4
Lawn Cl Edmonton N9 . . . 17 D4
Kingston u T KT3 . . . . . . 177 C1
Ruislip HA4 . . . . 61 D5
Sundridge BR1 . . . . 187 B3
Lawn Cres TW9 . . . . 132 C3
Lawn Farm Gr RM6 . . . . . 59 A5
Lawnfield Ct NW6 . . . . . . 68 D1
Lawn Gdns W7 . . . . 108 C5
Lawn House Cl E14 . . . . 120 A4
Lawn La SW8 . . . 138 B6 270 C6
Lawn Mans EN5 . . . . 1 B1
Lawn Rd
Beckenham BR3 . . . . 185 B3
Maitland Pk NW3 . . . . 70 D3
Lawns Ct HA9 . . . . 66 C6
Lawnside SE3 . . . . 142 D1
Lawns The
Belmont SM2 . . . . 217 A1
Blackheath SE3 . . . . 142 D2
Chingford E4 . . . . 35 C5
Harrow HA5 . . . . 23 D3
Sidcup DA14 . . . . 190 B6
South Norwood SE19 . . . 183 B2
Stoke Newington N16 . . . . 73 C3
1 Wimbledon SW19 . . . 179 B5
Lawn Terr SE3 . . . . 142 C2
Lawn The UB2 . . . . 107 C1
Lawn Vale HA5 . . . . 23 A1
Lawrence Ave
Edmonton N13 . . . . 32 D6
Higham Hill E17 . . . . 34 D2
Little Ilford E12 . . . . 78 C4
Mill Hill NW7 . . . . 27 D6
New Malden KT3 . . . . 199 C2
Stonebridge NW10 . . . . . . 89 B6
Lawrence Bldgs 1
N16 . . . . 73 D5
Lawrence Camp Cl N20 . 14 B1
Lawrence Cl Bow E3 . . . . . 97 C5
6 Shepherd's Bush
W12 . . . . 112 B6
West Green N15 . . . . 51 C5
Lawrence Cres
Dagenham RM10 . . . . 81 D5
Edgware HA8 . . . . 26 C1
Lawrence Ct
Hornsey N10 . . . . 49 C6
Mill Hill NW7 . . . . 27 C5
4 South Acton W3 . . . . . 111 A3
Stoke Newington N16 . . . . 73 C5
5 Woodford IG8 . . . . 37 C4
Lawrence Dr UB10 . . . . . . 61 A4
Lawrence Est TW4 . . . . . 128 C1
Lawrence Gdns NW7 . . . . 11 D1
Lawrence Hall E13 . . . . . . 99 B3
Lawrence Hill E4 . . . . 19 C2
Lawrence Ho
Bowes Pk N22 . . . . 32 B4
20 Camden Town NW1 . . . 71 B1
Westminster SW1 . . . . . 259 D3
Lawrence La EC2 . . . . . . 242 B2
Lawrence Mans SW3 . . 267 A5
Lawrence Pl N1 . . . . 233 B6
Lawrence Rd
Coney Hall BR4 . . . . 225 A4
Ealing W5 . . . . 109 D2
Edmonton N18 . . . . 34 B6
Erith DA8 . . . . 147 D5
Hampton TW12 . . . . 173 B3
Hillingdon UB4 . . . . 83 A5
Hounslow TW4 . . . . 128 C1
Pinner HA5 . . . . 40 D4
Lawrence Rd continued
Richmond TW10 . . . . 175 C6
South Norwood SE25 . . . 205 D5
Tottenham N15 . . . . 51 C5
Upton Pk E6 . . . . 100 A6
West Ham E13 . . . . 99 B6
Lawrence St
Canning Town E16 . . . . . . 98 D2
Chelsea SW3 . . 136 C6 267 A5
Mill Hill NW7 . . . . 27 D6
Lawrence Trad Est
SE10 . . . . 120 C2
Lawrence Univ SW7 . . . 256 B3
Lawrence Way NW10 . . . . 67 B5
Lawrence Weaver Cl
SM4 . . . . 201 C3
Lawrence Yd N15 . . . . 51 C5
Lawrie Ct HA3 . . . . 24 D3
Lawrie Park Ave SE26 . . 184 B5
Lawrie Park Cres
SE26 . . . . 184 B5
Lawrie Park Gdns
SE26 . . . . 184 B5
Lawrie Park Rd SE26 . . . 184 C5
Laws Cl SE25 . . . . 205 B5
Lawson Cl Ilford IG1 . . . . . 79 B3
Newham E16 . . . . 99 C2
Wimbledon SW19 . . . . . . 156 D1
Lawson Ct
1 Finsbury Pk N4 . . . . . . 50 B1
13 Surbiton KT6 . . . . 197 D2
Lawson Gdns HA5 . . . . . . 40 B6
Lawson Ho
17 Shepherd's Bush
W12 . . . . 112 B6
1 Woolwich SE18 . . . . . 144 C6
Lawson Rd Enfield EN3 . . . . 6 C4
Southall UB1 . . . . 85 C3
Law St SE1 . . . . . 117 B3 262 D6
Lawton Rd Barnet EN4 . . . . 2 B2
Bow E3 . . . . 97 A4
Leytonstone E10 . . . . 54 A1
Laxcon Cl NW10 . . . . 67 B3
Laxey Rd BR6 . . . . 227 D2
Laxfield Ct E8 . . . . 96 A6
Laxley Cl SE5 . . . . 138 D5
Laxmi Ct N3 . . . . 29 B2
Laxton Ct CR7 . . . . 205 A5
Laxton Path 1 SE4 . . . . 140 D1
Laxton Pl NW1 . . . . 238 D6
Layard Rd Enfield EN1 . . . . 5 D4
Rotherhithe SE16 . . . . . . 118 B2
South Norwood CR7 . . . . 183 B1
Layard Sq SE16 . . . . 118 B2
Laybourne Ho 18 E14 . . 119 C4
Laycock Prim Sch N1 . . . 72 D2
Laycock St N1 . . . . 72 C2
Layer Gdns W3 . . . . 110 C6
Layfield Cl NW4 . . . . 46 B2
Layfield Cres NW4 . . . . . . 46 B2
Layfield Ho 1 SE10 . . . . 121 A1
Layfield Rd NW4 . . . . 46 B2
Laymarsh Cl DA17 . . . . . 125 B3
Laymead Cl UB5 . . . . 63 A2
Laystall Ct EC1 . . . . 241 A5
Laystall St EC1 . . . . 241 A5
Layton Cres CR0 . . . . 220 D3
Layton Ct TW8 . . . . 109 D1
Layton Pl TW9 . . . . 132 C4
Layton Rd
Brentford TW8 . . . . 109 D1
Hounslow TW3 . . . . 129 D1
Layton's La TW16 . . . . . . 171 D1
Layzell Wlk SE9 . . . . 165 D3
Lazar Wlk 2 N7 . . . . 72 B6
Leabank Cl HA1 . . . . 64 C5
Leabank Sq E9 . . . . 75 C2
Leabank View N15 . . . . . . 52 A3
Leabourne Rd N16 . . . . . . 52 A2
LEA BRIDGE 74 D5
Lea Bridge Rd E10 . . . . . . 53 C2
Lea Cl TW2 . . . . 151 B4
Lea Cotts 10 CR4 . . . . . . 181 A1
Lea Cres HA4 . . . . 61 D4
Leacroft Ave SW12 . . . . . 158 D4
Leacroft Cl
Southgate N21 . . . . 16 D2
3 Yiewsley UB7 . . . . . . 104 A6
Lea Ct
3 Bedford Pk W12 . . . . . 111 C4
1 Chingford E4 . . . . 20 A2
3 Hillingdon UB10 . . . . . 82 D3
2 Newham E13 . . . . 99 A4
Leadale Ave E4 . . . . 19 C2
Leadale Rd N16 . . . . 52 A3
Leadbeaters Cl 8 N11 . . 30 D5
Leadbetter Ct 12 NW10 . . 67 B1
Leadenhall Mkt EC3 . . . 243 A1
Leadenhall Pl EC3 . . . . 243 A1
Leadenhall St
EC3 . . . . 95 C1 243 A1
Leadenham Ct 15 E3 . . . . 97 C3
Leader Ave E12 . . . . 78 C3
Leadings The HA9 . . . . . . 67 A5
Leaf Cl KT7, KT8 . . . . 196 C4
Leaf Gr SE27 . . . . 182 C5
Leaf Ho Barnet EN5 . . . . . . 1 D1
9 Harrow HA1 . . . . 42 D4
Leafield Cl SW16 . . . . . . 182 D4
Leafield La DA14 . . . . . . 169 B1
Leafield Rd
Merton SW19, SW20 . . . 201 B6
Sutton SM1 . . . . 217 C6
Leafy Gr BR2 . . . . 225 C3
Leafy Oak Rd SE12 . . . . . 165 C1
Leafy Way CR0 . . . . 221 D6
Lea Gdns HA9 . . . . 66 B4
Leagrave St E5 . . . . 74 C5
Lea Hall Gdns E10 . . . . . . 53 C1
Lea Hall Rd E10 . . . . 53 C1
Lea Ho 2 Edmonton N9 . . . 18 A1
Lisson Gr NW8 . . . . 237 A5
Upper Clapton E5 . . . . 52 C1
Leaholme Waye HA4 . . . . 39 A3
Leahurst Rd SE13 . . . . . . 164 B6
Lea Int E9 . . . . 75 C3
Leake St Lambeth SE1 . . 251 A1
South Bank
SE1 . . . . 116 B4 250 D2
Lealand Rd N15 . . . . 51 D3
Leamington Ave
Bromley BR1 . . . . 187 C5
Farnborough BR6 . . . . . . 227 C4
Merton SM4 . . . . 201 B5
Walthamstow E17 . . . . 53 C4
Leamington Cl
Bromley BR1 . . . . 187 C5
Hounslow TW3 . . . . 152 A6
Plashet E12 . . . . 78 A3
Leamington Cres HA2 . . . 63 B5
Leamington Ct
4 Forest Hill SE26 . . . . . 162 A1
North Acton W3 . . . . 89 B2
Leamington Gdns IG3 . . . 79 D6
Leamington Ho
Edgware HA8 . . . . 26 B5
4 Kensal Town W11 . . . . . 91 B2
Leamington Pk W3 . . . . . . 89 B2
Leamington Pl UB4 . . . . . 83 D3
Leamington Rd UB2 . . . . 106 D2
Leamington Rd Villas
W11 . . . . 91 B2
Leamington Villas
SE13 . . . . 164 C6
Leamore St W6 . . . . 112 C2
Leamouth Rd
Newham E6 . . . . 100 A2
South Bromley E14 . . . . . . 98 B1
Leander Ct
11 Edgware NW9 . . . . 27 C2
27 Hackney E9 . . . . 74 C1
St Johns SE8 . . . . 141 C4
5 Surbiton KT6 . . . . 197 D2
Leander Rd
Northolt UB5 . . . . 85 C5
Thornton Heath CR7 . . . . 204 B5
Tulse Hill SW2 . . . . 160 C5
Lea Park Trad Est E10 . . . 53 B1
Lea Rd
2 Beckenham BR3 . . . . . 185 C1
Enfield EN2 . . . . 5 B4
Southall UB2 . . . . 107 A2
Learner Dr HA2 . . . . 63 C6
Learoyd Gdns E6 . . . . . . 122 C6
Leary Ho SE11 . . . . 260 D1
Leas Cl KT9 . . . . 214 B1
Leas Dale SE9 . . . . 166 C1
Leas Gn BR7 . . . . 189 D4
Leaside Ave N10 . . . . 49 A5
Leaside Bsns Ctr EN3 . . . . 7 B3
Leaside Ct UB10 . . . . 82 D4
Leaside Ho 4 E5 . . . . 52 B1
Leaside Mans N10 . . . . . . 49 A6
Leaside Rd E5 . . . . 52 C1
Leasowes Rd E10 . . . . 53 C1
Lea Sq 22 E3 . . . . 97 B6
Leas The SE18 . . . . 144 D4
Leatherbottle Gn
DA18 . . . . 125 B3
Leather Cl CR4 . . . . 181 A1
Leatherdale St
32 Bethnal Green E1 . . . . 96 C3
19 Globe Town E1 . . . . . . 96 D4
Leather Gdns E15 . . . . 98 C6
Leatherhead Cl N16 . . . . . 51 D1
Leatherhead Rd KT9 . . . 213 D1
Leather La EC1 . . 94 C2 241 B4
Leathermarket Ct SE1 . 253 A1
Leathermarket St
SE1 . . . . 117 C4 253 A1
Leather Rd SE16 . . . . 118 D2
Leathersellers Cl 5 EN5 . 1 A2
Leathsale Rd HA2 . . . . . . 63 D5
Leathwaite Rd SW11 . . . 158 D6
Leathwell Rd SE8 . . . . . . 141 D3
Lea Valley Prim Sch
N17 . . . . 34 A3
Lea Valley Rd EN3 . . . . . . 19 B5
Lea Valley Technopark
N17 . . . . 52 A6
Lea Valley Trad Est
N18 . . . . 34 D5
Leaveland Cl BR3 . . . . . . 207 C5
Leaver Gdns UB6 . . . . 86 C5
Leavesden Rd HA7 . . . . . . 25 A4
Lea View Ho E5 . . . . 52 B1
Lebanon Ave TW13 . . . . 172 D5
Lebanon Ct 10 TW1 . . . . 153 B4
Lebanon Gdns SW18 . . . 157 C5
Lebanon Park Mans
TW1 . . . . 153 B4
Lebanon Pk TW1 . . . . . . 153 B4
Lebanon Rd
Croydon CR0 . . . . 205 C1
Wandsworth SW18 . . . . . 157 C6
Lebanon Road Sta
CR0 . . . . 221 C6
Lebrun Sq SE3 . . . . 143 B2
Lebus Ho NW8 . . . . 230 A3
Le Chateau CR0 . . . . 221 B5
Lechmere App IG8 . . . . . . 37 D1
Lechmere Ave IG8 . . . . . . 37 D1
Lechmere Rd NW2 . . . . . . 68 B2
Leckford Rd SW18 . . . . . 158 A3
Leckhampton Pl 23
SW2 . . . . 160 C4
Leckwith Ave DA7 . . . . . 147 A6
Lecky Ho NW2 . . . . 68 B4
Lecky St SW7 . . . 114 B1 256 C2
Leclair Ho SE3 . . . . 143 B2
L'Ecole des Petits Sch
SW6 . . . . 135 D3
Leconfield Ave SW13,
SW15 . . . . 133 D2
Leconfield Ho SE5 . . . . . 139 C2
Leconfield Rd N5 . . . . 73 B4
Lector Ct EC1 . . . . 241 B5
Leda Ave EN3 . . . . 6 D5
Leda Ct 9 SW9 . . . . 138 C5
Ledalle Ho NW2 . . . . 68 B5
Ledam Bldg EC1 . . . . . . 241 A4
Leda Rd SE18 . . . . 122 B3
Ledbury Ho 12 SE22 . . . . 139 C2
Ledbury Mews N W11 . . . 91 C1
Ledbury Mews W W11 . 245 A6
Ledbury Pl 10 CR0 . . . . . 221 A4
Ledbury Rd
Croydon CR0 . . . . 221 B4
Kensington W11 . . . . 91 C1
Ledbury St SE15 . . . . 140 A5
Ledo Ho 1 N16 . . . . 73 B4
Ledrington Rd SE19 . . . . 184 A4
Ledway Dr HA9 . . . . 44 B2
LEE 164 D5
Lee Ave RM6 . . . . 59 A3
Leechcroft Ave DA15 . . . 167 D6
Leechcroft Rd SM6 . . . . 219 A5
Lee Church St SE13 . . . . 142 C1
Lee Cl Higham Hill E17 . . . . 34 D2
New Barnet EN5 . . . . 2 A1
Lee Conservancy Rd
E9 . . . . 75 B3
Leecroft Rd EN5 . . . . 1 A1
Lee Ct SE13 . . . . 142 B1
Leeds Ct
7 Carshalton SM5 . . . . . 218 D5
Catford SE6 . . . . 163 D1
Clerkenwell EC1 . . . . . . 241 C6
Leeds Rd IG1 . . . . 57 B1
Leeds St N18 . . . . 34 A5
Leegate SE12 . . . . 164 D6
Lee Green SE12 . . . . 142 D1
Lee High Rd SE12,
SE13 . . . . 142 C1
Lee Ho
3 Kentish Town N19 . . . . 71 D3
Wimbledon SW19 . . . . . . 179 D4
Leeke St WC1 . . . 94 B4 233 C2
Leeland Mans 15 W13 . . 109 A5
Leeland Rd W13 . . . . 109 A5
Leeland Terr W13 . . . . . . 109 A5
Leeland Way NW10 . . . . . 67 D4
Lee Manor Sch SE13 . . . 164 C5
Lee Mews BR3 . . . . 207 A6
Lee Park Way N9, N18 . . . 19 A1
Lee Pk SE3 . . . . 142 D2
Lee Rd Enfield EN1 . . . . 18 A5
Lewisham SE3 . . . . 142 D1
Merton SW19 . . . . 179 D2
Mill Hill NW7 . . . . 28 D3
Wembley UB6 . . . . 87 C6
Leerdam Dr E14 . . . . 120 A3
Lees Ct W1 . . . . 248 A6
Lees Ho SE17 . . . . 262 D1
Leeside EN5 . . . . 13 A5
Leeside Cres NW11 . . . . . 47 C3
Leeside Ind Est N17 . . . . . 34 B3
Leeside Rd N17 . . . . 34 B4
Leeside Trad Est N17 . . . . 34 C3
Leeside Works N17 . . . . . 34 C3
Leeson Ho 7 TW1 . . . . . 153 B4
Leeson Rd 12 SE24 . . . . 138 C1
Leesons Hill BR5, BR7 . . 211 D6
Leesons Way BR5 . . . . . . 189 D1
Lees Par UB10 . . . . 82 D3
Lees Pl W1 . . . . . 115 A6 248 A6
Lees Rd UB8 . . . . 82 D3
Lee St E8 . . . . 95 D6
Lee Sta SE12 . . . . 165 A5
Lees The CR0 . . . . 223 B6
Leet Ct N16 . . . . 73 B4
Lee Terr SE3 . . . . 142 C2
Lee Valley Country Pk
EN3 . . . . 7 C4
Lee Valley L Ctr N9 . . . . . 19 A3
Lee Valley Riding Ctr
E10 . . . . 52 D1
Lee Valley Sp Ctr E10 . . . 75 D4
Leeve Ho 7 W9 . . . . 91 B4
Lee View EN2 . . . . 4 D4
Leeview Ct 7 E4 . . . . 20 A3
Leeward Ct 3 E1 . . . . . . 118 A5
Leeward Gdns SW19 . . . 179 B5
Leeway SE8 . . . . 119 B1
Leeway Cl HA5 . . . . 23 B3
Leewood Cl SE12 . . . . . . 165 A5
Lefevre Wlk E3 . . . . 97 C6
Leffern Rd W12 . . . . 112 A4
Leff Ho 9 NW6 . . . . 69 A1
Lefroy Ho SE1 . . . . 252 A1
Lefroy Rd W12 . . . . 111 D4
Legard Rd N5 . . . . 72 D5
Legat Ct N4 . . . . 51 A4
Legatt Rd SE9 . . . . 165 D6
Leggatt Rd E15 . . . . 98 A5
Legge St SE13 . . . . 164 A6
Leghorn Rd
Plumstead SE18 . . . . 123 B1
Willesden Green NW10 . . . 90 A5
Legion Cl N1 . . . . 72 C1
Legion Ct SM4 . . . . 201 C3
Legion Rd UB6 . . . . 86 A5
Legion Terr E3 . . . . 97 C6
Legion Way N12 . . . . 30 C3
Legrace Ave TW4,
TW5 . . . . 128 D3
Leicester Ave CR4 . . . . . 204 A5
Leicester Cl KT4 . . . . . . 216 C4
Leicester Ct
46 Paddington W2 . . . . . . 91 C2
Leicester Ct continued
St James WC2 . . . . 249 D6
5 Twickenham TW1 . . . . 153 D5
Leicester Gdns IG3 . . . . . 57 C2
Leicester Ho
4 Brixton SW9 . . . . 138 D2
Carshalton SM5 . . . . 218 C5
5 Putney SW15 . . . . 156 C4
2 Thames Ditton KT7 . . 197 A2
Leicester Mews N2 . . . . . 48 C6
Leicester Pl WC2 . . . . . 249 D6
Leicester Rd Barnet EN5 . . 1 D1
Croydon CR0 . . . . 205 C2
East Finchley N2 . . . . 48 C6
Stonebridge NW10 . . . . . . 67 B1
Wanstead E11 . . . . 55 B4
Leicester Sq*
WC2 . . . . 115 D6 249 D5
Leicester Square Sta
WC2 . . . . 115 D6 249 D6
Leicester St WC2 . . . . . 249 D6
Leigham Ave SW16 . . . . 160 A1
Leigham Cl
Streatham SW16 . . . . 182 B6
9 Wallington SM6 . . . . . 219 C2
Leigham Court Rd
SW16 . . . . 182 C6
Leigham Dr TW7 . . . . 130 C5
Leigham Hall 3
SW16 . . . . 160 A1
Leigham Hall Par 2
SW16 . . . . 160 A1
Leigham Vale SE27, SW16,
SW2 . . . . 160 C2
Leigh Ave IG4 . . . . 55 D5
Leigh Cl KT3 . . . . 199 B5
Leigh Close Ind Est
KT3 . . . . 199 B5
Leigh Cres CR0 . . . . 223 D1
Leigh Ct Harrow HA2 . . . . . 42 C1
22 Tulse Hill SW2 . . . . . . 160 C5
3 Woodford E18 . . . . 37 A1
Leighfield Ho 5 N4 . . . . . 51 A2
Leigh Gdns NW10 . . . . 90 C5
Leigh Ho
4 Kingston u T KT2 . . . . 176 D4
9 Putney SW15 . . . . 156 A6
Leigh Hunt Dr N14 . . . . . . 15 D3
Leigh Orchard Cl
SW16 . . . . 160 B1
Leigh Pl Feltham TW13 . . 150 C3
Holborn EC1 . . . . 241 A4
Welling DA16 . . . . 146 A3
Leigh Rd Highbury N5 . . . . 72 D4
Isleworth TW3 . . . . 130 B1
Leytonstone E10 . . . . 54 A2
Wallend E6 . . . . 78 C2
Leigh St WC1 . . . . 94 A4 233 A1
Leigh The KT2 . . . . 177 C3
Leighton Ave
Little Ilford E12 . . . . 78 C3
Pinner HA5 . . . . 41 A6
Leighton Cl HA8 . . . . 26 C1
Leighton Cres NW5 . . . . . 71 C3
Leighton Ct NW7 . . . . 28 D3
Leighton Gdns
Thornton Heath CR0 . . . . 204 D1
Willesden Green NW10 . . 90 C5
Leighton Gr NW5 . . . . 71 C3
Leighton Ho 7 KT6 . . . . 198 A3
Leighton House (Art Gall
& Mus)* W14 . . . . 254 D6
Leighton Pl NW5 . . . . 71 C3
Leighton Rd
Ealing W13 . . . . 109 A4
Enfield EN1 . . . . 18 A6
Harrow HA3 . . . . 24 B1
Kentish Town NW5 . . . . . . 71 C3
Leighton St CR0 . . . . 204 D1
Leila Parnell Pl 14
SE7 . . . . 143 C6
Leinster Ave SW14 . . . . . 133 A1
Leinster Gdns
W2 . . . . 114 A6 246 A6
Leinster Mews
7 Barnet EN5 . . . . 1 A2
Bayswater W2 . . . . 246 A6
Leinster Pl W2 . . . . 236 A1
Leinster Rd N10 . . . . 49 B5
Leinster Sq W2 . . . . 91 D1
Leinster Terr W2 . . . . . . 246 A6
Leisure Way N12 . . . . 30 B3
Leitch Ho 8 NW8 . . . . 70 B1
Leith Cl NW9 . . . . 45 B1
Leithcote Gdns SW16 . . 182 B6
Leithcote Path SW16 . . . 160 B1
Leith Hill BR5 . . . . 190 A2
Leith Hill Gn BR5 . . . . . . 190 A2
Leith Ho
7 Kentish Town N7 . . . . . 71 D3
13 Streatham SW2 . . . . . 160 B4
Leith Mans W9 . . . . 91 D4
Leith Rd N22 . . . . 32 D2
Leith Towers 7 SM2 . . . 217 D1
Leith Yd 3 NW6 . . . . 91 C6
Lela Ave TW4, TW5 . . . . 128 C3
Lelitia Cl E8 . . . . 96 A6
Lely Ho 3 UB5 . . . . 84 D5
Leman St E1 . . . . 96 A1
Lemark Cl HA7 . . . . 25 C4
Le May Ave SE12 . . . . . . 165 B1
Lemmon Rd SE10 . . . . . . 142 C6
Lemna Ct E11 . . . . 54 C2
Lemna Rd E11 . . . . 54 C2
Le Moal Ho 28 E1 . . . . . . 96 C2
Lemon Gr TW14 . . . . 150 A3
Lemonwell Ct SE9 . . . . . 167 A6
Lemonwell Dr SE9 . . . . . 167 A6
Lemsford Cl N15 . . . . 52 A4
Lemsford Ct N4 . . . . 73 A6

Lena Cres N9 ... 18 C2
Lena Gardens Prim Sch
W6 ... 112 C3
Lena Gdns W6 ... 112 C3
Lena Kennedy Cl E4 ... 36 A4
Lenan Ct W13 ... 109 C5
Len Clifton Ho 12
SE18 ... 122 B2
Lendal Terr 7 SW4 ... 137 D2
Lenelby Rd KT6 ... 198 C1
Len Freeman Pl SW6 ... 264 C5
Lenham 11 NW5 ... 71 A2
Lenham Ho SE1 ... 252 D1
Lenham Rd Erith DA7 ... 147 B6
Lewisham SE12 ... 142 D1
South Norwood CR7 ... 183 B1
Sutton SM1 ... 218 A3
Lennard Ave BR4 ... 224 C6
Lennard Cl BR4 ... 224 C6
Lennard Rd
Bromley BR2 ... 210 B1
Croydon CR0 ... 205 A1
Penge BR3 ... 185 A4
Lennon Rd NW2 ... 68 C2
Lennox Gdns
Croydon CR0 ... 220 D4
Knightsbridge
SW1 ... 114 D3 257 C5
Redbridge IG1 ... 56 B1
Willesden NW10 ... 67 D4
Lennox Gdns Mews
SW1 ... 257 C4
Lennox Ho
7 Belvedere DA17 ... 125 C3
10 Hackney E9 ... 74 C2
4 Twickenham TW1 ... 153 D5
Lennox Rd
Finsbury Pk N4, N7 ... 72 C6
Walthamstow E17 ... 53 C3
Lenor Cl DA6 ... 147 A1
Lensbury Way SE2 ... 124 D3
Lens Rd E7 ... 77 C1
Lenthall Ho SW1 ... 259 B1
Lenthall Rd E8 ... 74 A1
Lenthorp Rd SE10 ... 120 D2
Lentmead Rd BR1 ... 164 D1
Lenton Rise TW9 ... 132 A2
Lenton St SE18 ... 123 B2
Len Williams Ct NW6 ... 91 C5
Leo Ct 4 TW8 ... 131 D5
Leof Cres SE6 ... 185 D5
Leominster Rd SM4 ... 202 A3
Leominster Wlk SM4 ... 202 A3
Leonard Ave SM4 ... 202 A4
Leonard Ct
Bloomsbury WC1 ... 240 A6
Harrow HA3 ... 24 C3
Kensington W8 ... 255 A6
Leonard Day Ho 3
NW5 ... 71 B2
Leonard Ho 10 E17 ... 54 A5
Leonard Pl 6 N16 ... 73 C4
Leonard Rd
Chingford E4 ... 35 C4
Edmonton N9 ... 18 A1
Forest Gate E7 ... 77 A4
Mitcham CR4, SW16 ... 181 C2
Southall UB2 ... 106 D2
Leonard Robbins Path 3
SE28 ... 124 B6
Leonard St
Broadgate
EC2 ... 95 B3 242 D6
Newham E16 ... 122 A5
Leonora Ho W9 ... 236 A6
Leontine Cl SE15 ... 140 A5
Leopards Ct EC1 ... 241 A4
Leopold Ave SW19 ... 179 B5
Leopold Bldgs 14 E2 ... 95 D4
Leopold Ct 12 SW19 ... 179 B5
Leopold Mews E9 ... 96 C6
Leopold Prim Sch
NW10 ... 67 D1
Leopold Rd Ealing W5 ... 110 B5
East Finchley N2 ... 48 B6
Edmonton N18 ... 34 B5
Walthamstow E17 ... 53 C4
Willesden NW10 ... 67 C1
Wimbledon SW19 ... 179 B5
Leopold St E3 ... 97 B2
Leopold Terr SW19 ... 179 C5
Leopold Wlk SE11 ... 260 C1
Leo St SE15 ... 140 B5
Leo Yd EC1 ... 241 D5
Leppoc Rd SW4 ... 159 D6
Leroy St SE1 ... 117 C2 263 A4
Lerry Cl W14 ... 264 D6
Lerwick Ct 4 EN1 ... 17 C6
Lerwick Ho SW18 ... 136 A1
Lescombe Cl SE23 ... 163 A1
Lescombe Rd SE23,
SE6 ... 163 A1
Lesley Cl DA5 ... 169 D4
Lesley Ct
8 Wallington SM6 ... 219 B4
Westminster SW1 ... 259 C5
Leslie Gdns SM2 ... 217 C1
Leslie Gr CR0 ... 205 C1
Leslie Grove Pl CR0 ... 205 C1
Leslie Park Rd CR0 ... 205 C1
Leslie Prince Ct 8
SE5 ... 139 B5
Leslie Rd
East Finchley N2 ... 48 B6
Leyton E11 ... 76 B4
Newham E16 ... 99 B1
Leslie Smith Sq 7
SE18 ... 144 C6
Lessar Ave SW4 ... 159 C5
Lessar Ct SW4 ... 159 C5
Lessingham Ave
Ilford IG5 ... 56 C6
Upper Tooting SW17 ... 181 A6
Lessing St SE23 ... 163 A4
Lessness Ave DA7 ... 146 D5
LESSNESS HEATH ... 125 D1
Lessness Heath Prim Sch
DA17 ... 125 C1
Lessness Pk DA17 ... 125 C1
Lessness Rd
Belvedere DA17 ... 125 C1
Morden SM4 ... 202 A4
Lester Ave E16 ... 98 C3
Lester Ct 42 E3 ... 97 D4
Lester Ho IG8 ... 36 B3
Lestock Cl 2 SE25 ... 206 A6
Lestock Ho SE3 ... 143 D4
Lestor Ct TW7 ... 130 D2
Leswin Pl N16 ... 73 D5
Leswin Rd N16 ... 73 D5
Letchford Gdns NW10 ... 90 A4
Letchford Mews NW10 ... 90 A4
Letchmore Ho 7 W10 ... 90 C3
Letchworth Ave TW14 ... 149 D4
Letchworth Cl
Bromley BR2 ... 209 A4
South Oxhey WD19 ... 22 D5
Letchworth Dr BR2 ... 209 A4
Letchworth St SW17 ... 180 D6
Lethaby Ho 15 SW4 ... 138 B2
Lethbridge Cl SE13 ... 142 A3
Letterstone Rd SW6 ... 264 C3
Lettice St SW6 ... 135 B4 264 D1
Lett Rd E15 ... 76 B1
Lettsom St SE5 ... 139 C3
Lettsom Wlk 1 E13 ... 99 A5
Leucha Rd E17 ... 53 A4
Levana Cl SW19 ... 157 A3
Levant Ho 17 E1 ... 96 D3
Levehurst Ho SE27 ... 183 A5
Levehurst Way SW4,
SW9 ... 138 A3
Leven Cl WD19 ... 22 D5
Levendale Rd SE23 ... 163 B2
Leven Rd E14 ... 98 B1
Leven Way UB3 ... 83 C1
Lever Ct 15 E9 ... 74 D2
Leverett St SW3 ... 257 B4
Leverholme Gdns SE9 ... 188 C6
Leverington Pl N1 ... 235 D1
Leverson St SW16 ... 181 C4
Lever St EC1 ... 95 A4 235 A1
Leverstock Ho SW3 ... 257 B2
Leverton Pl NW5 ... 71 C3
Leverton St NW5 ... 71 C3
Levett Gdns IG3 ... 80 A5
Levett Ho 8 SW16 ... 181 C5
Levett Rd IG11 ... 79 C2
Levine Gdns IG11 ... 102 D5
Levison Way 2 N19 ... 49 D1
Levita Ho NW1 ... 232 D2
Levyne Ct EC1 ... 241 A6
Lewes Cl UB5 ... 63 C2
Lewes Ct 3 CR4 ... 202 D6
Lewesdon Cl 13 SW19 ... 156 D3
Lewes Ho
Bermondsey SE1 ... 253 B2
Peckham SE15 ... 140 A6
Lewes Rd Bromley BR1 ... 187 D1
Colney Hatch N12 ... 30 C5
Leweston Pl N16 ... 51 D2
Lewey Ho E3 ... 97 B3
Lewgars Ave NW9 ... 45 A3
Lewin Ct
4 Plumstead SE18 ... 123 C2
Streatham SW16 ... 182 A4
Lewing Cl BR6 ... 211 C1
Lewington Ct EN3 ... 6 D6
Lewin Rd Bexley DA6 ... 147 A1
Mortlake SW14 ... 133 B2
Streatham SW16 ... 181 D4
Lewin Terr TW14 ... 149 B4
Lewis Ave E17 ... 35 C2
Lewis Cl N14 ... 15 C4
Lewis Cres NW10 ... 67 B3
Lewis Ct 5 SE16 ... 118 B1
Lewis Gdns N2 ... 30 B1
Lewis Gr SE13 ... 142 A2
LEWISHAM ... 142 A1
Lewisham Bridge Prim
Sch SE13 ... 141 D2
Lewisham Bsns Ctr
SE14 ... 140 D6
Lewisham Coll SE4 ... 141 C3
Lewisham Ct EN3 ... 7 C5
Lewisham Ctr SE13 ... 142 A2
Lewisham High St
SE13 ... 163 D6
Lewisham Hill SE13 ... 142 A3
Lewisham Hospl SE13 ... 163 D6
Lewisham Pk SE13 ... 164 A5
Lewisham Rd SE13 ... 142 A3
Lewisham St SW1 ... 249 D1
Lewisham Sta SE13 ... 142 A2
Lewisham Way SE4,
SE14 ... 141 B4
Lewis Ho 2 E4 ... 35 C5
Lewis King Ho BR1 ... 187 B3
Lewis Pl E8 ... 74 A3
Lewis Rd Bexley DA16 ... 146 C2
Mitcham CR4 ... 180 C1
19 Richmond TW10 ... 153 D6
Sidcup DA14 ... 168 C1
Southall UB1 ... 107 A4
Sutton SM1 ... 217 D4
Lewis Silkin Ho 9
SE15 ... 140 C6
Lewis Sports & L Ctr
SE19 ... 183 D2
Lewis St NW1 ... 71 B2
Lewiston Cl KT4 ... 200 B2
Lewis Way RM10 ... 81 D2
Lexden Dr RM6 ... 58 B3
Lexden Rd Acton W3 ... 110 D5
Mitcham CR4 ... 203 D5
Lexdon Ct RM6 ... 58 B3
Lexfield Ho N5 ... 73 A4
Lexham Ct UB6 ... 86 B6
Lexham Gardens Mews
W8 ... 255 D5
Lexham Gdns
W8 ... 113 D2 255 C4
Lexham Ho 9 IG11 ... 101 B6
Lexham Mews
W8 ... 113 C2 255 B4
Lexham Wlk W8 ... 255 D5
Lexington Pl KT1 ... 175 D2
Lexington St
W1 ... 115 C6 249 B6
Lexton Gdns SW12 ... 159 D3
Leyborne Ave W13 ... 109 C4
Leyborne Pk TW9 ... 132 C4
Leybourne Cl BR2 ... 209 A3
Leybourne Ct 1 SE25 ... 206 A6
Leybourne Ho 20
SE15 ... 140 C6
Leybourne Rd
17 Camden Town NW1 ... 71 B1
Hillingdon UB10 ... 83 A6
Leytonstone E11 ... 54 D1
Queensbury NW9 ... 44 C4
Leybourne St 5 NW1 ... 71 B1
Leybridge Ct SE12 ... 165 A6
Leyburn Cl E17 ... 53 D5
Leyburn Gdns CR0 ... 221 C6
Leyburn Gr N18 ... 34 A4
Leyburn Ho SE18 ... 144 A5
Leyburn Rd N18 ... 34 B4
Leyden Mans 7 N19 ... 50 A2
Leyden St E1 ... 95 D2 243 C3
Leydon Cl SE16 ... 118 D5
Leyes Rd E16 ... 99 D1
Leyfield KT4 ... 199 D1
Ley Ho SE1 ... 252 A1
Leyland Ave EN3 ... 7 A3
Leyland Ct 8 N11 ... 31 B6
Leyland Gdns IG8 ... 37 C5
Leyland Ho
6 Canary Wharf
E14 ... 119 D6
12 Richmond TW10 ... 153 C1
Leyland Rd SE12 ... 165 A6
Leylands SW18 ... 157 B5
Leylang Rd SE14 ... 140 D5
Leys Cl Finchley N12 ... 30 C3
Harrow HA1 ... 42 B4
Leys Ct 9 SW9 ... 138 C3
Leysdown 9 NW5 ... 71 A2
Leysdown Ho SE17 ... 263 B2
Leysdown Rd SE9 ... 166 B2
Leysfield Rd W12 ... 112 A4
Leys Gdns EN4 ... 15 A6
Leyspring Rd E11 ... 54 D1
Leys Rd E EN3 ... 7 A4
Leys Rd W EN3 ... 7 A4
Ley St Ilford IG1 ... 78 D6
Newbury Pk IG1, IG2 ... 57 B1
Leys The
East Finchley N2 ... 48 A5
Harrow HA3 ... 44 B3
Leyswood Dr IG2 ... 57 C4
Leythe Rd W3 ... 111 A4
LEYTON ... 76 B5
Leyton Bsns Ctr E10 ... 75 C6
Leyton Ct SE23 ... 162 C3
Leyton Grange E10 ... 53 C1
Leyton Green Rd E10 ... 54 A3
Leyton Green Twrs E10 ... 54 A3
Leyton Ind Village E10 ... 52 D2
Leyton Link Est E10 ... 53 A2
Leyton Midland Road Sta
E10 ... 54 A1
Leyton Mills E10 ... 76 A4
Leyton Park Rd E10 ... 76 A5
Leyton Rd
Merton SW19 ... 180 A3
Stratford E15 ... 76 B2
Leyton Sixth Form Coll
E10 ... 54 B3
Leyton Sta E11 ... 76 A5
Leyton Stadium (Leyton
Orient FC) E10 ... 75 D5
LEYTONSTONE ... 54 D1
Leytonstone Bsns & Spec
Sch E11 ... 54 C3
Leytonstone High Road
Sta E11 ... 76 C6
Leytonstone Rd E15 ... 76 C3
Leytonstone Sta E11 ... 54 C1
Leyton Town Ctr E10 ... 76 A5
Leywick St E15 ... 98 C5
Lezayre Rd BR6 ... 227 D2
Liardet St SE14 ... 141 A6
Liberia Rd N5 ... 72 D2
Libert Cl N18 ... 33 D6
Liberty Ave SW19 ... 180 B2
Liberty Ct IG11 ... 102 C5
Liberty Ctr HA0 ... 88 B6
Liberty Ho 11 E1 ... 118 A6
Liberty Mews
Balham SW12 ... 159 B5
Orpington BR6 ... 227 D6
Liberty Sch CR4 ... 180 C1
Liberty St SW9 ... 138 B4 270 D2
Libra Rd 7 Bow E3 ... 97 B5
Newham E13 ... 99 A5
Library Ct N17 ... 51 D6
Library Mans 4 W12 ... 112 C4
Library Par NW10 ... 89 C6
Library Pl E1 ... 118 B6
Library St SE1 ... 116 D4 251 D1
Libro Ct E4 ... 35 C6
Lichen Ct IG6 ... 56 D6
Lichfield Cl EN4 ... 2 D2
Lichfield Ct
Kingston u T KT6 ... 198 A4
Richmond TW9 ... 132 A1
Lichfield Gdns TW10,
TW9 ... 154 A6
Lichfield Gr N3 ... 29 C1
Lichfield Ho 27 SE5 ... 139 A3
Lichfield Rd
Dagenham RM8 ... 80 C5
Edmonton N9 ... 18 A2
Hounslow TW4 ... 128 C2
Mile End E3 ... 97 A4
Newham E6 ... 99 D4
Northwood HA6 ... 40 A6
Richmond TW9 ... 132 B4
West Hampstead NW2 ... 69 A4
Woodford IG8 ... 36 C6
Lichfield Terr 1 TW9 ... 154 A6
Lichlade Cl 7 BR6 ... 227 D4
Lichport Ct N4 ... 50 D1
Lickey Ho W14 ... 264 D6
Lidbury Rd NW7 ... 29 A4
Lidcote Gdns 22 SW9 ... 138 B3
Liddall Way UB7 ... 104 B5
Liddell Cl HA3 ... 43 D6
Liddell Gdns NW10 ... 90 C5
Liddell Rd NW6 ... 69 C2
Lidding Rd HA3 ... 43 D4
Liddington Rd E15 ... 98 D6
Liddlesdale Ho E 6
KT2 ... 176 D2
Liddlesdale Ho W 5
KT2 ... 176 D2
Liddon Rd
Bromley BR1 ... 209 D6
Newham E13 ... 99 B4
Liden Cl E10, E17 ... 53 B1
Lidfield Rd N16 ... 73 B4
Lidgate Rd 22 SE15 ... 139 D5
Lidiard Rd SW18 ... 158 A2
Lidlington Pl NW1 ... 232 B3
Lido Sq N17 ... 33 B1
Lidyard Rd N19 ... 49 C1
Liffey Ct Edmonton N9 ... 18 C1
Willesden NW10 ... 68 A1
Liffler Rd SE18 ... 123 C1
Liffords Pl SW13 ... 133 D3
Lifford St SW15 ... 134 D1
Lightcliffe Rd N13 ... 16 C1
Lighter Cl 16 SE16 ... 119 A2
Lighterman Mews 15
E1 ... 96 D1
Lighterman's Rd E14 ... 119 D4
Lighterman's Wlk
SW18 ... 135 C1
Lightfoot Rd N8 ... 50 A4
Light Horse Ct SW1 ... 258 A1
Lightley Cl HA0 ... 88 B6
Ligonier St E2 ... 243 C6
Lilac Cl E4 ... 35 B4
Lilac Ct
Colney Hatch N12 ... 30 C4
3 Newham E13 ... 99 C6
Teddington TW11 ... 174 D6
Lilac Gdns
Croydon CR0 ... 223 C5
Ealing W5 ... 109 D3
Hayes UB3 ... 83 C1
Lilac Ho SE4 ... 141 B2
Lilac Pl
Vauxhall
SE11 ... 116 B2 260 C3
Yiewsley UB7 ... 104 B6
Lilac St W12 ... 112 A6
Lilah Mews BR2 ... 186 D1
Lilburne Gdns SE9 ... 166 A6
Lilburne Rd SE9 ... 166 A6
Lilburne Wlk NW10 ... 67 A2
Lile Cres W7 ... 86 C2
Lilestone Est NW8 ... 236 D5
Lilestone Ho NW8 ... 236 D6
Lilestone St
NW8 ... 92 C3 237 A6
Lilford Ho 21 SE5 ... 139 A3
Lilford Rd SE5 ... 138 D3
Lilian Barker Cl SE12 ... 165 A6
Lilian Baylis Ho N1 ... 73 A2
Lilian Baylis Tech Sch
SE11 ... 116 B1 260 D1
Lilian Board Way UB6 ... 64 B3
Lilian Gdns IG8 ... 37 B2
Lilian Rd SW16 ... 181 C2
Lilian Rolfe Ho 5
SE27 ... 183 B6
Lillechurch Rd RM8 ... 80 C2
Lilleshall Rd SM4 ... 202 B3
Lilley Cl E1 ... 118 A5
Lillian Ave W3 ... 110 C4
Lillian Cl 14 N16 ... 73 C5
Lillian Rd SW13 ... 134 B6
Lillie Ho N5 ... 72 C3
Lillie Rd SW6 ... 135 B6 264 C5
Lillie Road Mans SW6 ... 264 B5
Lillieshall Rd SW4 ... 137 C2
Lillie Yd SW6 ... 135 C6 265 A6
Lillingston Ho N7 ... 72 C4
Lilliput Ave UB5 ... 85 B6
Lillywhite 21 NW9 ... 27 D2
Lily Albon Ct RM9 ... 81 B4
Lily Cl W14 ... 112 D2
Lily Gdns HA0 ... 87 C5
Lily Ho 7 HA9 ... 66 A3
Lily Pl EC1 ... 241 B4
Lily Rd E17 ... 53 C3
Lilyville Rd
SW6 ... 135 B4 264 C2
Limavady Ho 12 SE18 ... 122 C2
Limborough Ho 5 E14 ... 97 C2
Limbourne Ave RM8 ... 59 B2
Limburg Rd SW11 ... 136 C1
Lime Ave UB7 ... 104 B6
Limeburner La
EC4 ... 94 D1 241 C2
Lime Cl Bromley BR1 ... 210 A5
Buckhurst Hill IG9 ... 21 D2
Carshalton SM5 ... 218 D6
Harrow HA3 ... 25 A1
Pinner HA5 ... 39 D6
Wapping E1 ... 118 A5
Lime Cres TW16 ... 172 C1
Limecroft Cl KT19 ... 215 B1
Lime Ct 9 Harrow HA1 ... 42 D3
Hendon NW4 ... 28 C1
Kingston u T KT3 ... 198 D6
9 Leyton E11 ... 76 C6
Mitcham CR4 ... 180 B1
Putney SW15 ... 134 B2
Limedene Cl HA5 ... 22 D2
Lime Gr Barnet N20 ... 13 B3
Blackfen DA15 ... 167 D5
Hayes UB3 ... 105 B6
Kingston u T KT3 ... 199 C6
Orpington BR6 ... 226 D6
Ruislip HA4 ... 40 B2
Shepherd's Bush W12 ... 112 C4
Twickenham TW1 ... 153 A5
Walthamstow E4 ... 35 B4
Limeharbour E14 ... 119 D4
Lime Ho 7 TW9 ... 132 D4
LIMEHOUSE ... 119 A6
Limehouse Cswy E14 ... 119 B6
Limehouse Ct 5 E14 ... 97 C1
Limehouse Ct 23 E14 ... 97 B1
Limehouse Cut 4 E14 ... 97 D2
Limehouse Fields Est 14
E14 ... 97 A2
Limehouse Link (Tunnel)
E14 ... 119 B6
Limehouse Sta E14 ... 97 A1
Lime Kiln Dr SE7 ... 143 B6
Limekiln Pl SE19 ... 183 D3
Limekiln Wharf 21
E14 ... 119 B6
Limeleaf Ct HA8 ... 27 A6
Lime Lo 3 TW16 ... 171 D3
Limerick Cl SW12 ... 159 C4
Limerick Ct 1 SW12 ... 159 C4
Lime Row DA18 ... 125 B3
Limerston St
SW10 ... 136 A6 266 B5
Lime St Pas EC3 ... 253 A6
Limes Ave
Barnes SW13 ... 133 D3
Carshalton SM5 ... 202 D1
Croydon CR0 ... 220 C5
Edgware NW7 ... 27 C4
Golders Green NW11 ... 47 A2
North Finchley N12 ... 30 A6
Penge SE20 ... 184 B3
Wanstead E11 ... 55 B5
Limes Ave The N11 ... 31 C5
Limes Cl Ashford TW15 ... 170 C5
3 Friern Barnet N11 ... 31 C5
Limes Ct
Beckenham BR3 ... 185 D1
Willesden NW6 ... 68 D1
Limesdale Gdns HA8 ... 27 A1
Limes Field Rd SW14 ... 133 C2
Limesford Rd SE15 ... 140 D1
Limes Gdns SW18 ... 157 C5
Limes Gr SE13 ... 142 A1
Limes Rd
Beckenham BR3 ... 185 D1
Thornton Heath CR0 ... 205 B2
Limes Row BR6 ... 226 D3
Lime St
Walthamstow E17 ... 53 A5
Whitechapel
EC3 ... 95 C1 243 A1
Limes The
Camberwell SE5 ... 139 C2
3 Cheam SM2 ... 217 C2
East Molesey KT8 ... 195 D5
Kensington W2 ... 245 B5
Keston Mark BR2 ... 226 A6
Stanmore HA7 ... 9 B2
Limestone Wlk 12
DA18 ... 124 D4
Limes Wlk Ealing W5 ... 109 D4
Nunhead SE15 ... 140 C1
Lime Terr W7 ... 108 C6
Lime Tree Ave KT10,
KT7 ... 196 C1
Limetree Cl SW2 ... 160 B3
Lime Tree Cl E11 ... 55 C5
Limetree Ct HA5 ... 23 C3
Lime Tree Ct
East Barnet EN4 ... 14 C6
East Finchley N2 ... 47 D6
14 Poplar E3 ... 97 C2
South Croydon CR2 ... 221 A2
Lime Tree Gr CR0 ... 223 B5
Limetree Pl CR4 ... 181 B2
Lime Tree Rd TW5 ... 129 D4
Limetree Wlk 2
SW17 ... 181 A5
Lime Tree Wlk
Bushey WD23 ... 8 C2
Coney Hall BR4 ... 224 D4
Enfield EN2 ... 5 A5
Lime Wlk 11 E15 ... 98 C6
Limewood Cl
Beckenham BR3 ... 208 A4
Ealing W13 ... 87 B1
Walthamstow E17 ... 53 B5
Limewood Ct IG4 ... 56 B4
Limpsfield Ave
Putney SW19 ... 156 D2
Thornton Heath CR7 ... 204 B4
Limscott Ho 35 E3 ... 97 D4
Linacre Cl SE15 ... 140 B2
Linacre Ct W6 ... 112 D1
Linacre Rd NW2 ... 68 B2
Linale Ho N1 ... 235 C3
Linberry Wlk 3 SE8 ... 119 B2
Linchmere Rd SE12 ... 164 D4
Lincoln Ave Osidge N14 ... 15 C2
Twickenham TW2 ... 152 A2
Wimbledon SW19 ... 156 D1
Lincoln Cl
Croydon SE25 ... 206 B3
Greenford UB6 ... 86 A6
Harrow HA2 ... 41 B4
Lincoln Cres EN1 ... 17 D6
Lincoln Ct
Borehamwood WD6 ... 11 B6
Enfield EN2 ... 5 B1
Grove Pk SE12 ... 165 C1
Hampton TW12 ... 173 B5
Hendon NW4 ... 46 B5
2 Ilford IG2 ... 57 A3
Mitcham CR4 ... 204 A4
Redbridge IG1 ... 56 B2
5 South Croydon CR2 ... 221 A3
Stoke Newington N16 ... 51 B2
Lincoln Gdns IG1 ... 56 A2
Lincoln Green Rd BR5 ... 211 D4
Lincoln Ho
Bloomsbury WC1 ... 240 D3
9 Dartmouth Pk NW5 ... 71 C5
2 Islington N1 ... 73 A1
Knightsbridge SW1 ... 247 C1
10 Putney SW15 ... 157 A6
Lincoln Lo 10 BR3 ... 185 D1
Lincoln Mews NW6 ... 91 B6
Lincoln Rd
Croydon SE25 ... 206 B6
East Finchley N2 ... 48 C6
Enfield EN1, EN3 ... 18 B6
Harrow HA2, HA5 ... 41 B4
Kingston u T KT3 ... 199 A6
Mitcham CR4 ... 204 A4
Newham E13 ... 99 B3
North Cheam KT4 ... 200 B1
Northwood HA6 ... 39 D6
Plashet E7 ... 77 D2
Sidcup DA14 ... 190 B5
Twickenham TW13 ... 151 B1
Wembley HA0 ... 65 D2
Woodford IG8 ... 37 A2
Lincoln's Inn*
WC2 ... 94 B1 240 D2
Lincoln's Inn Fields
WC2 ... 94 B1 240 D2
Lincoln St Chelsea SW3 ... 257 C3
Leyton E11 ... 76 C6
Lincolns The NW7 ... 11 D1
Lincoln Terr 4 SM2 ... 217 C1
Lincoln Way
Charlton TW16 ... 171 C2
Enfield EN1 ... 18 B6
Lincombe Rd BR1 ... 164 D1
Linda Ct KT9 ... 213 D4
Lindal Cres EN2 ... 4 B1
Lindal Ct 1 E18 ... 37 A2
Lindale SW19 ... 157 A2
Lindales The N17 ... 33 D4
Lindal Rd SE4 ... 163 B6
Lindbergh Rd SM6 ... 220 A1
Linden Ave Enfield EN1 ... 6 A4
Hounslow TW3 ... 151 D6
Kensal Rise NW10 ... 90 D5
Ruislip HA4 ... 40 A1
Thornton Heath CR7 ... 204 D5
Wembley HA9 ... 66 B3
Linden Bridge Sch
KT4 ... 215 C5
Linden Cl Ruislip HA4 ... 40 A1
Southgate N14 ... 15 C5
Stanmore HA7 ... 25 B5
Thames Ditton KT7 ... 197 A2
Linden Cotts 6 SW19 ... 179 A4
Linden Cres
Kingston u T KT1 ... 176 B1
Wembley UB6 ... 64 D2
Woodford IG8 ... 37 B4
Linden Ct
8 Battersea SW18 ... 136 B1
1 Beckenham BR3 ... 207 D6
2 Bromley BR1 ... 186 D3
Edgware NW7 ... 27 B5
Penge SE20 ... 184 B3
1 Shepherd's Bush
W12 ... 112 C5
Sidcup DA14 ... 189 C6
11 Sutton SM2 ... 218 A2
Lindenfield BR7 ... 188 D1
Linden Gate SW20 ... 200 C6
Linden Gdns
Chiswick W4 ... 111 B1
Enfield EN1 ... 6 A4
Notting Hill W2 ... 113 C6 245 B5
Linden Gr
Kingston u T KT3 ... 199 C6
Nunhead SE15 ... 140 C2
Penge SE20 ... 184 C4
Teddington TW11 ... 174 D5
Linden Ho Bromley BR1 ... 187 B3
10 Deptford SE8 ... 141 B6
Hampton TW12 ... 173 D4
Walthamstow E17 ... 35 B1
Linden Lawns HA9 ... 66 B4
Linden Lea N2 ... 48 A4

Lindenlea Ct E17 53 B5
Linden Leas BR4 224 B6
Linden Lo N21 16 B4
Linden Lodge Sch
SW19 157 A3
Linden Mans N6 49 B1
Linden Mews
Kensington W2 245 B5
Stoke Newington N1 73 B3
Linden Pl CR4 202 C5
Linden Rd
Brunswick Pk N11 15 A2
Cranley Gdns N10 49 B5
Hampton TW12 173 C2
Tottenham N15 51 A5
Lindens The
Chiswick W4 133 A4
New Addington CR0 224 A2
North Finchley N12 30 B5
5 Walthamstow E17 53 D5
Linden Way
Shepperton TW17 193 A4
Southgate N14 15 C5
Lindeth Cl HA7 25 B4
Lindfield Gdns NW3 70 A3
Lindfield Hts NW3 70 A3
Lindfield Rd
Croydon CR0 205 D3
Ealing W5 87 C3
Lindfield St E14 97 C1
Lindford Christie Stadium
The W12 90 B2
Lindhill Cl EN3 6 D3
Lindholme Ct 3 NW9 27 C2
Lindisfarne Rd
Dagenham RM8 80 C5
Wimbledon SW20 178 A3
Lindisfarne Way E9 75 A4
Lindley Ct KT1 175 C2
Lindley Ho
13 Peckham SE15 140 A5
9 Stepney E1 96 C2
Lindley Pl TW9 132 C4
Lindley Rd E10 76 A6
Lindley St E1 96 C2
Lindon Bennett Sch
TW13 172 D5
Lindop Ho 8 E1 97 A3
Lindore Rd SW11 136 D1
Lindores Rd SM5 202 A1
Lindo St SE15 140 C3
Lind Rd SM1 218 A3
Lindrop St SW6 136 A3
Lindsay Cl KT9 214 A1
Lindsay Ct
Battersea SW11 266 D1
Sutton SM1 217 C3
Lindsay Dr Harrow HA3 44 B4
Shepperton TW17 193 B3
Lindsay Ho 2 SE18 122 C2
Lindsay Rd
Hampton TW12 173 D6
North Cheam KT4 216 B6
Lindsay Sq
SW1 115 D1 259 D2
Lindsell St 6 SE10 142 A4
Lindsey Cl Bickley BR1 210 A6
Mitcham CR4, SW16 204 A5
Lindsey Ct N13 16 C1
Lindsey Gdns TW14 149 B4
Lindsey Ho W5 109 D2
Lindsey Ho* SW10 266 D4
Lindsey Mews 18 N1 73 A1
Lindsey Rd RM8 80 C5
Lindsey St EC1 94 D2 241 D4
Lind St SE8 141 D3
Lindum Rd TW11 175 C3
Lindums The BR3 185 B4
Lindway SE27 182 D5
Lindwood Cl 8 E6 100 B2
Linear View HA9 66 D6
Linfield WC1 233 C1
Linfield Cl NW4 46 C5
Linford Ct 1 CR4 180 C2
Linford Ho 17 E2 96 A6
Linford Rd E17 54 A6
Linford St SW8 137 C4 269 A1
Linford Street Bsns Est
SW8 269 A2
Lingard Ho 11 E14 120 A3
Lingards Rd SE13 142 A1
Lingey Cl DA15 167 D2
Lingfield Ave KT1, KT5 198 B5
Lingfield Cl EN1 17 C5
Lingfield Cres SE9 145 B1
Lingfield Ct
Northolt UB5 85 C5
Wimbledon SW19 178 D4
Lingfield Gdns N9 18 B4
Lingfield Ho
5 Acton Green W4 111 A1
Lambeth SE1 251 D1
Penge SE26 184 B4
Lingfield Rd
North Cheam KT4 216 C5
Wimbledon SW19 178 D4
Lingham St SW9 138 B3
Lingholm Way EN5 12 D6
Ling Rd E16 99 A2
Lingrove Gdns IG9 21 B2
Ling's Coppice SE21 161 B2
Lingwell Rd SW17 158 C1
Lingwood DA7 147 D3
Lingwood Gdns TW7 130 C5
Lingwood Rd E5 52 A2
Linhope St NW1 92 D3 237 C5
Linkenholt Mans 8
W6 111 D2
Linkfield KT8 195 D6
Link Field BR2 209 A3
Linkfield Rd TW7 130 D3
Link La SM6 220 A2
Linklea Cl NW9 27 C3
Link Prim Sch CR0 220 A4
Link Rd Dagenham RM9 103 D5
East Bedfont TW14 149 D4
Friern Barnet N11 31 A4
Hackbridge SM6 203 A1
Links Ave SM4 201 C5
Linkscroft Ave TW15 170 D4
Links Ct N20 14 B1
Links Dr N20 13 D3
Link Sec Sch CR0 220 B4
Links Gdns SW16 182 C3
Linkside Finchley N12 29 C4
Kingston u T KT3 177 C1
Linkside Cl EN2 4 C2
Linkside Gdns EN2 4 B2
Links Ind Est TW13 151 A1
Links Prim Sch SW17 181 A4
Links Rd Acton W3 88 C1
Ashford TW15 170 A5
Mitcham SW16, SW17 181 A4
West Wickham BR4 208 A1
Willesden NW2 67 D6
Woodford IG8 37 A5
Links Side EN2 4 C2
Link St E9 74 C3
Links The E17 53 A5
Linksview N2 48 D4
Links View Finchley N3 29 B3
Shooters Hill SE18 144 D4
Links View Cl HA7 25 A4
Links View Rd
Croydon CR0 223 C5
Hampton TW12 174 A6
Linksway NW4 28 D1
Links Way
Beckenham BR3 207 C3
Streatham SW17 181 A4
Links Yd
10 Spitalfields E1 96 A2
Spitalfields E1 243 D4
Link The Acton W3 88 D1
Chislehurst SE9 166 C1
Enfield EN3 7 A4
Hendon NW2 46 A1
Northolt UB5 63 B3
Pinner HA5 40 C2
Teddington TW11 174 D4
Wembley HA0 43 C1
Linkway Dagenham RM8 80 C4
Pinner HA5 22 D2
Stoke Newington N4 51 A2
West Barnes SW20 200 B5
Link Way Bromley BR2 210 A2
Richmond TW10 153 B2
Linkway The EN5 13 D5
Linkwood Wlk NW1 71 D1
Linley Cres RM7 59 D6
Linley Ct
1 Dulwich SE21 183 C6
Sutton SM1 218 A4
Linley Rd N17 33 C1
Linnell Cl NW11 47 D3
Linnell Dr NW11 47 D3
Linnell Ho
Spitalfields E1 243 C4
St John's Wood NW8 229 A6
Linnell Rd
Camberwell SE5 139 C3
Edmonton N18 34 A5
Linnet Cl Bushey WD23 8 A3
Lower Edmonton N9 18 D3
Woolwich SE28 124 C6
Linnet Ct CR4 180 C2
Linnet Mews SW12 159 A4
Linnett Cl E4 36 A6
Linom Rd SW4 138 A1
Linscott Rd E5 74 C4
Linsdell Rd IG11 101 A6
Linsey St
Bermondsey SE16 118 A2
Bermondsey SE16 118 A3
Linslade Cl
Hounslow TW4 151 A6
Pinner HA5 40 B6
Linslade Ho
10 Hackney E2 96 A6
Marylebone NW8 237 B6
Linstead St 1 NW6 69 C1
Linstead Way SW18,
SW19 157 A4
Linsted Ct SE9 167 C5
Linster Gr WD6 11 A6
Lintaine Cl W6 264 B5
Linthorpe Ave HA0 65 C2
Linthorpe Rd
Cockfosters EN4 2 C2
Stamford Hill N16 51 C2
Linton Cl
Carshalton CR4 202 D2
2 Greenwich SE7 121 C1
Welling DA16 146 B4
Linton Gdns E6 100 A1
Linton Gr SE27 183 A5
Linton Ho
Lower Holloway N7 72 B4
2 Tower Hamlets E3 97 C2
Linton Mead Prim Sch
SE28 124 B6
Linton Rd IG11 79 A1
Linton St N1 95 A6 235 B5
Lintons The
Barking IG11 79 A1
Finchley N3 29 B2
Linver Rd SW6 135 C3
Linwood Cl SE5 139 D3
Linwood Cres EN1 6 A4
Linzee Rd N8 50 A5
Lion Ave TW1 152 D3
Lion Cl Ladywell SE4 163 C5
Littleton TW17 192 A6
Lion Ct 12 NW9 46 A5
Lion Ctr The TW13 151 A1
Lionel Gdns SE9 165 D6
Lionel Ho Bowes Pk N22 32 B4
5 Kensal Town W10 91 A2
Lionel Mans 14 W14 112 D3
Lionel Mews 13 W10 91 A2
Lionel Rd SE9 165 D6
Lionel Road N TW8 110 A2
Lionel Road Prim Sch
TW8 110 A2
Lionel Road S TW8 110 B1
Lion Gate Gdns TW9 132 B2
Lion Gate Mews
SW18 157 C4
Lion House Sch SW15 134 D1
Lion Mills 36 E2 96 A5
Lion Park Ave KT9 214 C4
Lion Rd
Bexleyheath DA6 147 B1
Edmonton N9 18 A2
Newham E6 100 B2
Thornton Heath CR0 205 A4
Twickenham TW1, TW2 152 D3
Lions Cl SE12 165 D1
Lion Way TW8 131 D5
Lion Wharf Rd TW7 131 B2
Lion Yd SW4 137 D1
Liphook Cres SE23 162 C4
Liphook Rd WD19 22 D6
Lipton Cl SE28 124 C6
Lipton Ct N14 15 C4
Lipton Rd 9 E1 96 D1
Lisa Lo 5 EN5 13 D6
Lisbon Ave TW2 152 A2
Lisbon Cl E17 35 B1
Lisburne Rd NW3 70 D4
Lisford St SE15 139 D4
Lisgar Terr
W14 113 B2 254 C4
Liskeard Cl BR7 189 A4
Liskeard Gdns SE3 143 A4
Liskeard Ho SE11 261 B2
Lisle Cl SW17 181 B6
Lisle Ct NW2 69 A5
Lisle St WC2 115 D6 249 D6
Lismirrane Ind Pk WD6 9 B5
Lismore 9 SW19 179 B5
Lismore Cir NW5 71 A3
Lismore Cl TW7 131 A3
Lismore Rd
South Croydon CR2 221 C2
Tottenham N17 51 B6
Lismore Wlk 4 N1 73 A2
Lissant Cl KT6 197 D2
Lisselton Ho 3 NW4 46 D5
Lissenden Gdns NW5 71 A4
Lissenden Mans NW5 71 A4
Lisson Cotts NW1 237 B4
Lisson Gr NW1,
NW8 92 C3 237 A6
LISSON GROVE 92 B3
Lisson Ho NW1 237 A4
Lisson St NW1 92 C2 237 A4
Lister Cl Dagenham W3 89 B2
Mitcham SW19 180 C2
Lister Com Sch E13 99 B5
Lister Cotts WD6 9 A6
Lister Ct Hendon NW9 27 C1
Stoke Newington N16 73 C6
Lister Gdns N18 33 A5
Lister Ho
Greenwich SE3 142 C6
Hayes UB3 105 C2
Marylebone W1 238 C2
Spitalfields E1 96 A2
6 Wembley HA9 67 A5
West Heath SE2 124 D1
Lister Hospl
SW1 115 B1 258 C1
Lister Mews N7 72 B4
Lister Rd E11 54 D1
Lister Wlk SE28 124 D6
Liston Ho N21 16 B6
Liston Rd
Clapham SW4 137 C2
Tottenham N17 34 A2
Liston Way 1 IG8 37 C3
Listowel Cl 2 SW9 138 C5
Listowel Rd RM10 81 C5
Listria Lo N16 73 D6
Listria Pk N16 73 D6
Litcham Ho 23 E1 96 D4
Litchfield Ave
Morden SM4 201 B2
Stratford E15 76 C2
Litchfield Ct E17 53 C3
Litchfield Gdns NW10 68 A2
Litchfield Rd SM1 218 A4
Litchfield St WC2 249 D6
Litchfield Way NW11 48 A4
Lithgow's Rd TW14,
TW6 127 D1
Lithos Rd NW3 70 A2
Little Acre BR3 207 C6
Little Albany St NW1 238 D6
Little Argyll St W1 239 A1
Littleberry Ct NW7 28 C6
Little Birches DA15 167 C2
Little Boltons The
SW10 255 D1
Little Bornes SE21 183 C6
Littlebourne 2 SE13 164 C4
Little Britain EC1 242 A3
Littlebrook Cl CR0 206 D3
Little Brownings SE23 162 B2
Littlebury Rd SW4 137 D2
Little Bury St N9 17 C4
Little Bushey La WD23 8 B5
Little Cedars N12 30 A6
Little Chelsea Ho
SW10 266 B5
Little Chester St SW1 258 C6
Little Cloisters SW1 260 A6
Little College St SW1 260 A6
Littlecombe SE7 143 B6
Little Combe Cl 13
SW15 156 D5
Little Common HA7 9 A1
Littlecote Cl SW19 157 A4
Littlecote Pl HA5 23 B2
Little Cottage Pl SE10 141 D5
Littlecroft SE9 144 C2
Little Ct Harrow HA1 42 C2
West Wickham BR4 224 C6
Littledale SE2 146 A6
Little Deans Yd SW1 260 A6
Little Dell Lo 8 N3 29 B1
Little Dimocks SW12 159 B2
Little Dorrit Ct SE1 252 B2
Little Ealing La W5 109 C2
Little Ealing Prim Sch
W5 109 C3
Little Edward St NW1 231 D2
Little Elms UB3 127 B5
Little Essex St WC2 251 A6
Little Ferry Rd TW1 153 B3
Littlefield Cl
9 Kingston u T KT1 176 A1
Tufnell Pk N19 71 C4
Littlefield Ct UB7 126 A5
Littlefield Ho KT1 176 A1
Littlefield Rd HA8 27 A3
Little Friday Rd E4 20 C2
Little Gearies IG6 56 D5
Little George St SW1 250 A1
Little Gn TW9 131 D1
Little Grange UB6 87 A4
Little Green St NW5 71 B4
Littlegrove EN4 14 C5
Littlegrove Ct 3 EN4 14 C5
Little Halliards KT12 194 A3
LITTLE HEATH 58 B5
Little Heath Ilford RM6 58 B5
Woolwich SE7 122 A1
Littleheath Rd CR2 222 B1
Little Heath Rd DA7 147 B5
Little Heath Sch RM6 58 B5
Little Holt 10 E11 55 A4
LITTLE ILFORD 78 C3
Little Ilford La E12 78 B4
Little Ilford Sch E12 78 B3
Littlejohn Rd W7 86 D1
Little Larkins EN5 13 A5
Little London Cl UB8 82 D2
Little Marlborough St
W1 239 A1
Littlemead KT10 212 B4
Littlemede SE9 166 B1
Littlemoor Rd IG1 79 B5
Littlemore Rd SE2 124 A4
Little Moss La HA5 23 A1
Little Newport St WC2 249 D6
Little New St EC4 241 B2
Little Oak Cl TW17 192 B5
Little Orchard Cl HA5 23 A1
Little Oxhey La WD19 23 A6
Little Park Dr TW13 151 A2
Little Park Gdns EN2 5 B2
Little Pluckett's Way
IG9 21 D3
Little Portland St W1 239 A2
Little Potters WD23 8 C4
Little Queens Rd
TW11 174 D4
Little Rd UB3 105 D4
Little Redlands BR1 188 A1
Littlers Cl SW19 180 B2
Little Russell St WC1 240 A3
Little St James's St
SW1 249 A3
Little St Leonards
SW14 133 A2
Little Sanctuary SW1 250 A1
Little Smith St SW1 259 D6
Little Somerset St E1 243 C1
LITTLE STANMORE 26 B2
Littlestone Cl BR3 185 C4
Little Strand NW9 27 D1
Little Thrift BR5 211 A5
Little Titchfield St W1 239 A3
LITTLETON 192 C6
Littleton Ave E4 20 D3
Littleton CE Inf Sch
TW17 192 C6
LITTLETON COMMON
171 B3
Littleton Cres HA1 64 D6
Littleton Ho TW15 171 A3
Littleton La TW17,
TW18 192 A4
Littleton Rd
Harrow HA1 64 D6
Littleton TW15, TW17 171 A3
Littleton St SW18 158 A2
Little Trinity La EC4 252 B6
Little Turnstile WC1 240 C3
LITTLE VENICE 92 A2
Little Venice*
W9 92 A2 236 A4
Littlewood SE13 164 A5
Littlewood Cl W13 109 B3
Little Wood Cl BR5 190 A2
Littleworth Ave KT10 212 B3
Littleworth Common Rd
KT10 212 B5
Littleworth La KT10 212 B4
Littleworth Pl KT10 212 B4
Littleworth Rd KT10 212 C5
Livermere Ct 3 E8 95 D6
Livermere Rd E8 95 D6
Liverpool Gr
SE17 117 B1 262 C1
Liverpool Ho N7 72 C2
Liverpool Rd
Ealing W5 109 D4
Islington N1 234 B5
Islington N1, N7 72 C1
Kingston u T KT2 176 C3
Leytonstone E10 54 A3
Newham E16 98 C2
South Norwood CR7 205 A6
Liverpool St
EC2 95 C2 243 A3
Liverpool Street Sta
EC2 95 C2 243 A3
Livesey Cl
Kingston u T KT1 198 B6
Woolwich SE28 123 A3
Livesey Mus* SE15 140 B6
Livesey Pl SE15 140 A6
Livingstone Ct
Barnet EN5 1 A3
Leytonstone E10 54 A3
Stanwell TW19 148 A3
Livingstone Ho 16
SE5 139 A5
Livingstone Lo
13 Paddington W9 91 C2
Walthamstow E17 35 C1
Livingstone Pl E14 120 A1
Livingstone Prim Sch
EN4 2 B2
Livingstone Rd
14 Battersea SW11 136 B2
Bowes Pk N13 32 A5
Isleworth TW3 130 A1
Mill Meads E15 98 A6
Southall UB1 106 D6
South Norwood CR7 183 B1
Walthamstow E17 53 D3
Livity Sch The SW2 160 A6
Livonia St W1 239 B1
Lizard St EC1 95 A4 235 B1
Lizban St SE3 143 C5
Llandovery Ho 1 E14 120 A4
Llanelly Rd NW2 69 B6
Llanover Rd
Shooters Hill SE18 144 C5
Wembley HA9 65 D4
Llanthony Rd SM4 202 B4
Llanvanor Rd NW2 69 B6
Llewellyn Ct SE20 184 C2
Llewellyn Ho 10 N19 71 C5
Llewellyn St SE16 118 A4
Lloyd Ave SW16 182 A2
Lloyd Baker St
WC1 94 C4 234 A1
Lloyd Ct Ladywell SE13 163 D6
Pinner HA5 40 D4
6 West Norwood
SE27 160 D1
Lloyd Ho
3 Beckenham BR3 185 D4
Bromley BR1 187 B5
Stoke Newington N16 73 B5
Lloyd Mews EN3 7 C5
Lloyd Park Ave CR0 221 D4
Lloyd Park Ho E17 53 C6
Lloyd Park Sta CR0 221 D4
Lloyd Rd Dagenham RM9 81 B1
Newham E6 100 B6
North Cheam KT4, SM3 216 D5
Walthamstow E17 52 D5
Lloyd's Ave EC3 243 B1
Lloyd's Bldg*
EC3 95 C1 243 A1
Lloyd's Pl SE3 142 C3
Lloyd Sq WC1 94 C4 234 A2
Lloyd's Row EC1 94 D4 234 C1
Lloyd St WC1 94 C4 234 A2
Lloyds Way BR3 207 B4
Lloyd Villas SE4 141 C3
Loampit Hill SE13 141 D3
Loampit Vale SE13 142 A2
Loanda Cl 17 E8 95 D6
Loats Rd SW2 160 A5
Lobelia Cl 5 E6 100 A2
Locarno Cl 15 SW16 181 C5
Locarno Rd
6 Acton W3 111 A5
Greenford UB6 86 B3
Lochaber Rd SE13 142 C1
Lochaline St W6 134 C6
Lochan Cl UB4 85 A3
Lochbie 9 N4 50 A2
Lochinvar St SW12 159 B4
Lochleven Ho 9 N2 30 B1
Lochmere Cl DA8 147 D6
Lochmore Ho SW1 258 B3
Lochnagar St E14 98 A2
Lockbridge Ct 3 W9 91 C2
Lock Chase SE3 142 C2
Lock Cl UB2 108 A4
Locke Ho
Nine Elms SW8 269 A2
Stamford Hill N16 51 D1
Lockesfield Pl E14 119 D1
Lockesley Dr BR5 211 D3
Lockesley Sq KT6 197 D3
Locket Rd HA3 24 D1
Lockfield Ave EN3 7 B4
Lockgate Cl E9 75 B3
Lockhart Cl
Barnsbury N7 72 B2
Enfield EN3 18 B6
Lockhart Lo 4 E4 20 C4
Lockhart St E3 97 B3
Lockhurst St E5 74 D4
Lockier Wlk HA9 65 D5
Lockington Rd
SW8 137 B4 268 D2
Lockmead Rd
Lewisham SE13 142 A2
South Tottenham N15 52 A3
Lock Mews 9 NW1 71 D2
Lock Rd TW10 175 C6
LOCKSBOTTOM 226 D5
Lockside 17 E14 119 A6
Lock's La CR4 181 A1
Locksley St E14 97 B2
Locksmeade Rd TW10 175 C6
Lock View Ct 9 E14 119 A6
Lockwell Rd RM10 81 C5
Lockwood Cl SE26 184 D6
Lockwood Ct KT3 199 A5
Lockwood Ho 10 SE11 138 C6
Lockwood Ind Pk N17 52 B6
Lockwood Pl E4 35 C4
Lockwood Sq SE16 118 B3
Lockwood Way
Chessington KT9 214 C3
Higham Hill E17 34 D1
Lockyer Cl EN3 7 D5
Lockyer Est SE1 252 D1
Lockyer Ho
7 Greenwich SE10 120 D1
Putney SW15 134 D2
South Lambeth SW8 270 A4
Lockyer St SE1 252 D1
Locomotive Dr TW14 150 A3
Locton Gn 4 E3 97 B6
Lodden Lo 13 SM2 218 A1
Loddiges Ho 5 E9 74 C1
Loddiges Rd E9 74 C1
Loddon Ho NW8 236 D5
Loder St SE15 140 C5
Lodge Ave
Borehamwood WD6 10 B6
Croydon CR0 220 C5
Dagenham RM8, RM9,
IG11 80 B3
Harrow HA3 44 A5
Mortlake SW14 133 C2
Lodge Cl Edgware HA8 26 C4
Edmonton N18 33 A5
Hackbridge SM6 203 A1
Isleworth TW7 131 B4
Lodge Ct 3 HA0 66 A3
Lodge Dr N13 32 C6
Lodge Gdns BR3 207 B4
Lodge Hill
East Wickham DA16 146 B5
Redbridge IG4 56 A5
Lodgehill Park Cl HA2 63 D6
Lodge La Bexley DA5 168 D5
New Addington CR0 223 D1
North Finchley N12 30 A5
Lodge Mead Ct 5 N3 29 D3
Lodge Pl SM1 217 D3
Lodge Rd Bromley BR1 187 C3
Hendon NW4 46 C5
Lisson Gr NW8 92 C4 230 A1
Sutton SM1 217 D3
Thornton Heath CR0 204 D2
Wallington SM6 219 B3
Lodge The
9 Chiswick W4 111 C3
1 Sutton SM1 218 A4
Lodge Villas IG8 36 D4
Lodge Way
Charlton TW17 171 A1
Stanwell TW15 148 A2
Lodore Gdns NW9 45 C4
Lodore Gn UB10 60 A5
Lodore St E14 98 A1
Lodsworth Ho SW11 268 A1
Lofthouse Pl KT9 213 C2
Loftie St SE16 118 A4
Lofting Ho 8 N1 72 C1
Lofting Rd N1 72 C1
Lofts on the Park 24
E9 74 D2
Loftus Rd Barking IG11 79 A2
Shepherd's Bush W12 112 B5
Loftus Rd (Queens Park
Rangers FC) W12 112 B5
Logan Cl Enfield EN3 6 D4
Hounslow TW4 129 B2
Logan Mews W8 255 A4
Logan Pl W8 113 C2 255 A4
Logan Rd Edmonton N9 18 B2
Wembley HA9 66 A6
Loggetts SE21 161 C2
Logs Hill BR1, BR7 188 A2
Logs Hill Cl BR7 188 A2
Lohmann Ho 5 SE11 138 C6
Lois Dr TW17 192 D4
Lolesworth Cl E1 243 D3
Lolland Ho 8 SE7 122 A2
Lollard St
SE11 116 C2 261 A3
Lollards Twr SE1 260 C5
Loman St SE1 116 D4 251 D2
Lomas Cl CR0 224 A1
Lomas St E1 96 A2
Lombard Ave Enfield EN3 6 C4
Ilford IG3 57 C1
Lombard Bsns Pk
Merton SW19 179 D1
Thornton Heath CR0 204 B2
Lombard Ct
14 Acton W3 110 D5

Lombard Ct continued
City of London EC3 . . . . . . **252** D6
Lombard La EC4 . . . . **241** B1
Lombard Rd
Battersea SW11 . . . . .136 B3
Friern Barnet N11. . . . . . . .31 B5
Merton SW19 . . . . .179 D1
Lombard Rdbt CR0. . . . .**204** B2
Lombard St E3 . .95 B1 **242** D1
Lombard Trad Est
SE7. . . . . .121 B2
Lombard Wall SE7 . . . . .121 B2
Lombardy Pl W2. . . . . . .**245** D5
Lombardy Ret Pk UB3. .106 B6
Lomley Ho 10 SW2 . . . . .160 C5
Lomond Cl
Tottenham N15 . . . . .51 C4
Wembley HA0 . . . . .66 B1
Lomond Ct HA3. . . . . . . .42 D6
Lomond Gdns CR2 . . . . .223 A1
Lomond Gr SE5. . . . . . . .139 B5
Lomond Ho 10 SE5. . . . .139 B4
Loncroft Rd SE5 . . . . . . .139 C6
Londesborough Ho 1
N16 . . . . .73 C4
Londesborough Rd
N16 . . . . .73 C4
London Acadamy HA8. .26 B6
London Acad of
Computing & Electronics
SW17 . . . . .158 D1
London Aquarium★
SE1. . . . .**250** C1
London Bridge EC4.
SE1. . . . . .117 B6 **252** D6
London Bridge City Pier
SE1. . . . . .117 C5 **253** A4
London Bridge Hospl
SE1. . . . . .117 B5 **252** D6
London Bridge St
SE1. . . . . .117 B5 **252** D3
London Bridge Sta
SE1. . . . . .117 B5 **252** D3
London Bridge Wlk
SE1. . . . .**252** D4
London Britannia Coll
N1. . . . . .95 B4 **235** C2
London Business Sch
NW1. . . . . .92 D3 **237** C4
London Butterfly Ho★
TW8 . . . . .131 B4
London Canal Mus★
N1. . . . . .94 A5 **233** B4
London Central Mosque★
NW8 . . . . .92 C4 **230** B1
London Chest Hospl
E2 .96 C5
London City Airport
E16 . . . . .122 B5
London City Airport Sta
E16 . . . . .122 A5
London Clinic
NW1. . . . . .93 A3 **238** B5
London Coll of Advanced
Studies SE1 . . . .**252** C3
London Coll of Beauty
Therapy W1. . .93 C1 **239** B1
London Coll of Bsns &
Computer Studies
SW4 . . . . .137 D1
London Coll of
Communication (Sch of
Printing & Publishing)
SE1. . . . . .116 D3 **261** D5
London Coll of Economics
& Science NW10. . . . . . .89 A3
London Coll of Fashion
Broadgate EC2 . .95 C3 **243** B6
Marylebone W1. . . . .**238** D2
Marylebone W1. . . . .**238** B1
Marylebone W1. . . . .**238** C1
St Luke's EC1 . . .95 A3 **242** A5
London Coll of Fashion
(Mare St) E8 . . . . .74 A1
London Coll of
International Business
Studies WC1 . . . .**240** B3
London St 3 SW18 . .157 C6
London Docklands Visitor
Ctr★ E14. . . . . .120 A4
London Dungeon The★
SE1. . . . . .117 B5 **252** D4
London Electronics Coll
SW5 . . . . .113 C1 **255** C2
London Eye (Millennium
Wheel)★ SE1. .116 B4 **250** C2
London Fields East Side
E8 .74 B1
London Fields Prim Sch
E8 .96 B6
London Fields Sta E8 . .74 B1
London Fields West Side
E8 .74 A1
London Fire Brigade
Mus★ SE1. . . . .**252** A2
London Gas Mus The★ E3,
E16. . . . . .98 B3
London Group Bsns Pk
NW2. . . . . .46 A1
London Ho
Edgware HA8 . . . . .26 A6
13 Hammersmith W6 . . .112 A4
London Ho TW9 . . . . . . .132 B2
London Ho NW8 . . . .**230** B4
London Hospital Dental
Inst E1. . . . . .96 B2
London Independent
Hospl The E1. . . . . .96 D2
London Inst The
SW17 . . . . .181 B5

London Int Coll N7 . . . . .72 B5
London International Film
Sch WC2. . . . . .94 A1 **240** A1
London IT Coll IG2 . . . . . .56 C3
London La
Bromley BR1. . . . . .186 D3
Hackney E8 . . . . .74 B1
London Metropolitan
Univ
Islington N7 . . . . .72 C3
Whitechapel E1. . . . . .111 A1
Whitechapel E1. .95 D1 **243** C2
Whitechapel
EC3 . . . . .117 D6 **253** C6
London Metropolitan Univ
(Central Ho) E1 . . . . . .96 A1
London Metropolitan Univ
(Commercial Rd) E1. . .96 A1
London Metropolitan Univ
(Ladbrook Ho) N5 . . . . .72 D3
London Metropolitian Univ
(Moorgate)
EC2 . . . . .95 B2 **242** D3
London Metropolitian Univ
(Spring Ho) N1 . . . . . . .72 C2
London Mews W2 . . . .**236** D2
London Motorcycle Mus★
UB6. . . . . .86 A4
London Nautical Sch The
SE1. . . . . .116 C5 **251** B4
London Oratory Sch The
SW6 . . . . .135 C5 **265** A4
London Pavilion SW1 . .**249** C5
London Peace Pagoda★
SW3 . . . .**267** D4
London Rd
Ashford TW15, TW18, TW19,
TW14 . . . . .148 B2
Brentford TW7, TW8 . . . .131 B4
Bromley BR1. . . . . .186 D3
Carshalton CR4 . . . . .203 A2
Enfield EN2. . . . . .5 B1
Forest Hill SE22, SE23 . .162 C3
Hackbridge SM6, CR4 . . .219 B6
Harrow HA1. . . . . .64 C6
Hounslow TW3, TW7, TW1,
TW8. . . . . .130 B3
Kingston u T KT1, KT2. . .176 B1
Lambeth SE1. . .116 D3 **261** D6
Mitcham CR4. . . . . .180 D2
Morden SM4 . . . . .201 C6
Newham E13 . . . . .99 A5
Romford RM7, RM8. . . . . .59 C5
Stanmore HA7. . . . . .25 D6
Stoneleigh KT17, KT4,
SM3 . . . . .216 B3
Thornton Heath CR0, CR7,
SW16. . . . . .204 C3
Twickenham TW1. . . . . . .153 A4
Wembley HA9 . . . . .66 A2
London Road Rdbt
TW1. . . . . .153 A4
London Sch of Economics
& Political Science
WC2 . . . . .94 B1 **240** D1
London Sch of Jewish
Studies NW4 . . . . .46 D5
London St
City of London EC3 . . . . .**253** B6
Paddington W2 . .92 B1 **236** C1
London Stile 5 W4. . . . .110 C1
London Stock Exchange★
EC2. . . . .**242** A2
London Stone Bsns Est 15
SW11 . . . . .137 A3
London Terr 1 E2 . . . . .96 A5
London Tottenham Coll
N17. . . . . .33 D3
London Transport Mus★
WC2. . . . .**250** B6
London Wall
EC2. . . . . .95 B2 **242** D3
London Wall Bldgs
EC2. . . . .**242** D3
London Wetland Ctr★
SW13 . . . . .134 B5
London Wetland Visitor
Ctr★ SW13. . . . . .134 B4
London Wharf 4 E2 . . .96 B4
London Xtra Tuition Coll
N4. . . . . .72 B6
London Zoo★
NW1. . . . . .93 A5 **231** A4
Lonesome Prim Sch
CR4. . . . . .181 B1
Lonesome Way CR4. . .181 C2
Long Acre WC2 . .94 A1 **240** B1
Long Acre W13 . . . . .87 A2
Longacre Pl SM5 . . . . . .219 A2
Longacre Rd E17 . . . . . . .36 B2
Longbeach Rd SW11 . . .136 C2
Longberrys NW2. . . . . . . .69 B5
Longboat Row UB1 . . . . .85 B1
Longbridge Ho RM8. . . . .80 B4
Longbridge Rd
Barking IG11. . . . . .79 C3
Dagenham RM8. . . . . .80 B4
Longbridge Way SE13. .164 A6
Longbury Dr BR5. . . . . . .190 B2
Longchamp Ct 13 HA7. . .25 C5
Longcliffe Ho SW18. . . .157 D6
Longcroft SE9 . . . . .166 C1
Longcrofte Rd HA8. . . . . .26 D3
Long Deacon Rd E4. . . . .20 C3
LONG DITTON 197 C1
Long Ditton Inf Sch
KT6. . . . . .197 C1
London Wood BR2. . . . .226 A4
Longdown Rd SE6 . . . . .185 C6
Long Dr Dagenham W3 . .89 C1

Long Dr continued
Greenford UB6 . . . . .85 D6
Ruislip HA4. . . . . .62 D4
Long Elmes HA3. . . . . . . .24 A2
Longfellow Rd
North Cheam KT4. . . . . . .200 B1
Walthamstow E17. . . . . . . .53 B3
Longfellow Way SE1 . . .**263** D3
Longfield
3 Bromley BR1 . . . . . . .186 D2
Loughton IG10 . . . . .21 C6
Long Field NW9 . . . . .27 D3
Longfield Ave
Ealing W5 . . . . .109 C6
Enfield EN3 . . . . .6 C5
Hackbridge SM6 . . . . .203 A1
Hendon NW7. . . . . .28 A3
Walthamstow E17. . . . . . . .53 A5
Wembley HA9 . . . . .44 A1
Longfield Cres SE23,
SE26 . . . . .162 C1
Longfield Ct 4 N2. . . . . .48 A6
Longfield Dr
Mitcham SW19 . . . . .180 C2
Mortlake SW14 . . . . .154 D6
Longfield Est SE1. . . . . .**263** D3
Longfield Fst & Mid Schs
HA2 . . . . .41 C3
Longfield Ho
Ealing W5 . . . . .109 C6
Walthamstow E17. . . . . . . .53 B4
Longfield Rd W5. . . . . . . .87 C1
Longfield St SW18 . . . . .157 C4
Longford Ave
Feltham TW14. . . . . .149 B5
Southall UB1. . . . . .107 C6
Stanwell TW19 . . . . .148 A3
Longford Cl
Feltham TW13 . . . . .151 A1
Hampton TW12 . . . . .173 C6
Hayes UB4. . . . . .106 D6
Longford Com Sch
TW14 . . . . .149 D4
Longford Ct
1 Bedford Pk W12. . . . . .111 C4
2 Clapton Pk E5 . . . . .74 D4
Hampton TW12 . . . . .173 C6
3 Hendon NW4 . . . . .46 C5
Southall UB1. . . . . .107 C5
West Ewell KT19. . . . . . .215 A4
Longford Gdns
Hayes UB4. . . . . .106 D6
Sutton SM1 . . . . .218 A6
Longford Ho
1 Catford BR1. . . . . .186 B5
Hampton TW12 . . . . .173 C6
7 Stepney E1. . . . . .96 C1
Longford Ind Est
TW12 . . . . .173 D4
Longford Rd TW2. . . . . .151 B3
Longford St
NW1 . . . . .93 B3 **238** D6
Longford Way TW19 . . .148 A3
Longford Wlk 9 SW2 . .160 C4
Longhayes Ave RM6. . . . .58 D5
Longhayes Ct RM6. . . . . .58 D5
Longheath Gdns CR0. . .206 C4
Longhedge Ho SE26. . . .184 A6
Longhedge St SW11 . . .137 A3
Longhill Rd SE6. . . . . . . .164 B1
Long Ho SM5. . . . . .218 C6
Longhook Gdns UB5. . . . .84 B4
Longhope Cl SE15 . . . . .139 D6
Longhurst Ho 8 W9 . . . .91 B4
Longhurst Rd
Croydon CR0 . . . . .206 B3
Lewisham SE13. . . . . . . .164 C3
Long La
Bermondsey
SE1. . . . . . .117 B4 **252** D1
Croydon CR0 . . . . .206 C3
East Finchley N2 . . . . .48 B6
Erith DA7. . . . . .147 B4
Finchley N3 . . . . .29 C2
Hillingdon UB10 . . . . .82 D6
Holborn EC1 . . .94 D2 **241** D4
Stanwell TW15, TW19 . . .148 B3
Longland Ct
Bermondsey SE1. . . . . . .118 A1
Hackney E9 . . . . .75 A3
Longland Dr N20 . . . . . . .13 D2
LONGLANDS 167 B1
Longlands Ct
Higham Hill E17. . . . . .35 A2
Mitcham CR4. . . . . .181 A2
Notting Hill W11 . . . .**244** D6
Sidcup DA15 . . . . .167 D1
Longlands Park Cres
DA15. . . . . .167 C2
Longlands Prim Sch
DA15. . . . . .167 C1
Longlands Rd DA15 . . .167 D1
Longleat Ct 3 DA6 . . . .147 A1
Longleat Ho SW1. . . . . .**259** C2
Longleat Rd EN1. . . . . . . .17 C6
Longleat Way TW14. . . .149 B4
Longleigh Ho 8 SE5 . . .139 C4
Longleigh La SE2, DA7. .146 C5
Longlents Ho 3 NW10 . .89 B6
Longley Ave HA0. . . . . . . .88 B6
Longley Ho 5 N19 . . . . . .71 D4
Longley Rd Harrow HA1. . .42 B5
Thornton Heath CR0. . . . .204 D2
Upper Tooting SW17. . . . .180 C4
Long Leys E4. . . . . .36 A4
Longley St SE1 . . . . .118 A2
Longley Way NW2 . . . . . .68 C5
Longman Ho
9 Globe Town E2. . . . . . .96 D5
10 Shoreditch E8 . . . . . . .95 D6

Long Mark Rd 5 E16 . . .99 D2
Longmarsh La SE28 . . . .123 C5
Long Mead NW9 . . . . .27 D2
Longmead BR7 . . . . .188 C1
Longmead Dr DA14 . . . .168 D2
Longmead Ho SE27. . . .183 A5
Long Meadow 20 N7 . . .71 D3
Long Meadow Cl BR3,
BR4 . . . . .208 A2
Longmeadow Rd
DA15. . . . . .167 C3
Longmead Prim Sch
UB7. . . . . .104 A2
Longmead Rd
Hayes UB3. . . . . .105 D6
Thames Ditton KT7 . . . . .196 D2
Upper Tooting SW17. . . . .180 D5
Longmoor Point 14
SW15. . . . . .156 B3
Longmore Ave EN4, EN5 . .14 B5
Longmore St
SW1. . . . . .115 C2 **259** A3
Longnor Rd E1 . . . . .96 D4
Long Pond Rd SE3 . . . . .142 C4
Long Rd SW4 . . . . .137 A1
Longreach Ct IG11. . . . . .101 B5
Long Reach Rd IG11 . . .101 D3
Longridge Ho SE1 . . . . .**262** B5
Longridge La UB1. . . . . . .85 D1
Longridge Rd
SW5. . . . . .113 C2 **255** B3
Long Ridges N2 . . . . .49 A6
Longs Ct 2 TW9. . . . . . .132 B1
Long's Ct W1 . . . .**249** D5
Longshaw Prim Sch E4 . .20 B1
Longshaw Rd E4. . . . . . . .20 B1
Longshore SE8 . . . . .119 B2
Long St E2 . . . . .95 D4
Longstaff Cres SW18. . .157 C4
Longstaff Rd SW18. . . . .157 C5
Longstone Ave NW10 . . .89 D6
Longstone Rd SW17. . . .181 B5
Longthorne Ho 18 E3 . . .97 B4
Longthornton Rd
SW16. . . . . .181 D1
Longthorpe Ct 9 W6 . .112 A2
Longton Ave SE26 . . . . .184 A6
Longton Gr SE26. . . . . . .184 B6
Longville Rd SE11. . . . . .**261** D4
Longwalk Rd UB11. . . . . .104 D5
Long Wlk
Bermondsey SE1. . . . . . .**263** B6
Kingston u T KT3 . . . . . . .199 A6
Shooters Hill SE18 . . . . . .144 D4
Longwood Bsns Pk
TW16 . . . . .193 D4
Longwood Dr SW15. . . .156 A5
Longwood Gdns IG2, IG6,
IG5 . . . . .56 C6
Longwood Par IG6. . . . . .56 D6
Longworth Cl SE28. . . . .102 D1
Long Yd WC1. . . .94 B3 **240** C5
Loning The Enfield EN3. . . .6 C5
Hyde The NW9. . . . . .45 D5
Lonsdale Ave
Newham E6. . . . . .100 A3
Wembley HA9 . . . . .66 A3
Lonsdale Cl
Edgware HA8 . . . . .26 B5
Hillingdon UB8 . . . . .83 A2
Mottingham SE12 . . . . . .165 D1
Newham E6. . . . . .100 A3
Pinner HA5 . . . . .23 A2
Lonsdale Cres IG2. . . . . .56 D3
Lonsdale Dr EN2. . . . . . . .16 A6
Lonsdale Dr N EN2. . . . . . .4 A1
Lonsdale Gdns CR7,
SW16. . . . . .204 B5
Lonsdale Ho
Fulham SW6 . . . . .135 C2
6 Stoke Newington N4 . .51 A2
Lonsdale Mews
Notting Hill W11 . . . . .91 B1
4 Richmond TW9. . . . . .132 C4
Lonsdale Pl N1 . . . . .72 C1
Lonsdale Rd
Barnes SW13. . . . . .133 D5
Bexley DA7. . . . . .147 B3
Chiswick W4 . . . . .111 D2
Croydon SE25 . . . . .206 B5
Kilburn NW6 . . . . .91 B6
Leytonstone E11. . . . . . . .54 D2
Notting Hill W11 . . . . .91 B1
Southall UB2. . . . . .106 D3
Lonsdale Sq
Islington N1 . . . . .72 C1
Islington N1 . . . .**234** B6
Loobert Rd N15. . . . . .51 C6
Looe Gdns IG6. . . . . .56 D6
Loop Rd BR7 . . . . .189 A4
Lopen Rd N18. . . . . .33 C6
Lopen Works N18. . . . . . .33 C6
Lopez Ho 6 SW9 . . . . . .138 A2
Lorac Ct 10 SM2 . . . . . .217 C1
Loraine Cl EN3 . . . . .18 C6
Loraine Ct BR7. . . . . . . .188 D5
Loraine Ho 1 SM5. . . . . .219 B4
Loraine Rd
Chiswick W4 . . . . .132 D6
Islington N7 . . . . .72 B4
Lord Ave IG5 . . . . .56 B6
Lord Chancellor Wlk
KT2 . . . . .177 A2
Lord David Pitt Ho 8
SE24 . . . . .138 C1
Lordell Pl SW19 . . . . . . .178 C4
Lorden Wlk 13 E2. . . . . . .96 A4
Lord Gdns IG5. . . . . .56 B5
Lord Hills Rd W2 . . . . . . .91 D2

Lord Holland La 5
SW9. . . . . .138 C2
Lord Knyvetts Ct 3
TW19 . . . . .148 A5
Lord Napier Pl W6 . . . . .112 A1
Lord North St SW1. . . . .**260** A5
Lord Roberts Mews
SW6 . . . .**265** C3
Lord Roberts Terr
SE18 . . . . .122 C1
Lords Cl Feltham TW13 . .151 A2
West Norwood SE21. . . . .161 A2
Lord's Cricket Mus★
NW8 . . . . .92 B4 **229** D1
Lords Ct 3 HA8 . . . . .27 A3
Lordship Gr N16. . . . . . . .73 B6
Lordship Ho 3 N16. . . . .73 B6
Lordship La
Dulwich Village SE22. . . .161 D5
Tottenham N22 . . . . .33 B2
Lordship Lane Prim Sch
N22. . . . . .33 A2
Lordship Park Mews
N16. . . . . .73 A6
Lordship Pk N16. . . . . . . .73 B6
Lordship Pl SW3 . . . . . .**267** A5
Lordship Rd
Northolt UB5. . . . . .63 A1
Stoke Newington N16. . . . .73 B6
Lordship Terr N16 . . . . . .73 B6
Lord's Indoor Cricket Sch
NW8 . . . .**230** A2
Lord's (MCC & Middlesex
Cty Cricket Ground)★
NW8 . . . . .92 B4 **229** D1
Lordsmead Rd N17. . . . . .33 C1
Lord St E16. . . . . .122 A5
Lord's View NW8 . . . . . .**229** D1
Lord Warwick St SE18. .122 B3
Loreburn Ho 2 N7. . . . . .72 B4
Lorenzo St N1, WC1 . . .**233** C2
Loretto Gdns HA3. . . . . . .44 A5
Lorian Cl N12. . . . . .29 D6
Loring Rd
East Barnet N20 . . . . .14 C2
Isleworth TW7 . . . . .130 D3
Loris Rd W6 . . . . .112 C3
Lorn Ct SW9. . . . . .138 C3
Lorne Ave CR0. . . . . .206 D2
Lorne Cl NW8 . . .92 C4 **230** B1
Lorne Ct Harrow HA1 . . . .42 C2
Putney SW15. . . . . .156 D1
Lorne Gdns
Croydon CR0 . . . . .206 D2
5 Hammersmith W11 . .112 D4
Wanstead E11. . . . . .55 C5
Lorne Ho
Friern Barnet N11. . . . . . . .31 B5
Hornsey N4 . . . . .50 B2
7 Tower Hamlets E1. . . . .97 A5
Lorne Rd Finsbury Pk N4 . .50 B1
Forest Gate E7 . . . . .77 C4
Harrow HA3 . . . . .24 D1
3 Richmond TW10. . . . .154 B6
Walthamstow E17. . . . . . . .53 C4
Lorn Rd SW9 . . . . .138 C3
Lorraine Ct
Beckenham BR3 . . . . . . .186 A2
3 Belmont SM2. . . . . . . .217 C1
10 Camden Town NW1 . .71 B1
Lorraine Pk HA3 . . . . .24 C3
Lorrimore Rd SE17. . . . .138 D6
Lorrimore Sq SE17. . . . .138 D6
Lorton Ho 9 NW6 . . . . . .91 C6
Loseberry Rd KT10. . . . .212 B3
Lostock Ho 10 SW8 . . . .137 D3
Lothair Rd W5. . . . . .109 D4
Lothair Rd N N4 . . . . .50 D3
Lothair Rd S N4. . . . . .50 D2
Lothbury EC2. . .95 B1 **242** C2
Lothian Ave UB4. . . . . . . .84 B2
Lothian Cl HA0 . . . . .65 A5
Lothian Rd SW9 . . . . . . .138 D4
Lothrop St W10. . . . . .91 A4
Lots Rd SW10 . .136 A5 **266** B3
Loubet St SW17. . . . . . . .180 D4
Loudoun Ave IG6 . . . . . . .56 C4
Loudoun Rd
NW8 . . . . .92 A6 **229** B6
Loudwater Cl TW16 . . . .194 A5
Loudwater Rd TW16 . . .194 A5
Loughborough Ct 7
SW9. . . . . .138 D2
Loughborough Junction
Sta SW9 . . . . .138 D2
Loughborough Pk
SW9. . . . . .138 D2
Loughborough Prim Sch
SW9. . . . . .138 D3
Loughborough Rd SE5,
SW9. . . . . .138 D3
Loughborough St
SE11. . . . . .116 B1 **260** D1
Lough Rd N7 . . . . .72 B2
LOUGHTON 21 D5
Loughton Way IG9. . . . . .21 D3
Louie Black Ho 4
SW19. . . . . .179 A3
Louisa Cl E9 . . . . .96 D6
Louisa Ct
Twickenham TW2. . . . . . .152 C2
Wood Green N11. . . . . . . .31 D3
Louisa Gdns E1. . . . . .96 D3
Louisa Ho SW15 . . . . . . .133 D1
Louisa St E1. . . . . .96 D3
Louis Ct 3 RM10 . . . . . .81 D2
Louise Bennett Cl 9
SE24 . . . . .138 C1
Louise Ct
7 Bexley DA6 . . . . .147 A1

Lom–Low **341**

Louise Ct continued
4 Wanstead E11. . . . . . . .55 B4
Wood Green N22. . . . . . . .32 C2
Louise De Marillac Ho 26
E1 .96 C2
Louise Graham Ho 5
IG11. . . . . .101 B6
Louise Rd E15 . . . . .76 C2
Louise White Ho 1
N19 . . . . .49 D1
Louis Gdns BR7. . . . . . . .188 B6
Louis Mews N10 . . . . .31 B2
Louisville Rd SW17 . . . . .159 A1
Lousada Lo N14 . . . . .15 C5
Louvaine Rd SW11. . . . . .136 B1
Lovage App E6. . . . . .100 A2
Lovat Cl NW2 . . . . .67 D5
Lovat La EC3. . . . .**253** A5
Lovatt Cl HA8. . . . . .26 D4
Lovatt Ct SW12 . . . . .159 B3
Lovatt Dr HA4 . . . . .39 C4
Lovat Wlk TW5 . . . . .129 A5
Loveday Ho 2 SW2 . . . .160 C3
Loveday Rd W13. . . . . . . .109 B5
Lovegrove St SE1 . . . . . .140 A6
Lovegrove Wlk E14 . . . . .120 A5
Lovekyn Cl KT2 . . . . .176 B1
Love La Cheam SM3. . . . .217 A3
City of London
EC2 . . . . .95 A1 **242** B2
Croydon SE25 . . . . .206 B6
Long Ditton KT6 . . . . .213 C6
Mitcham CR4. . . . . .202 C6
Morden SM4 . . . . .201 D2
Old Bexley DA5. . . . . . . .169 C5
Pinner HA5 . . . . .41 A6
Tottenham N17 . . . . .33 D3
Woolwich SE18 . . . . .122 D2
Lovelace Ave BR2. . . . . .210 C3
Lovelace Gdns
Barking IG11. . . . . .80 A4
Surbiton KT6. . . . . .197 D2
Lovelace Gn SE9 . . . . . .144 B2
Lovelace Ho 12 E8 . . . . .95 C4
Lovelace Prim Sch
KT9. . . . . .213 C3
Lovelace Rd
East Barnet EN4 . . . . .14 C4
Surbiton KT6. . . . . .197 D2
West Norwood SE21. . . . .161 A3
Loveland Mans 7 IG11. .79 D1
Lovel Ave DA16 . . . . .146 A3
Lovelinch Cl SE15. . . . . .140 C6
Lovell Ho Hackney E8 . . . .96 A6
4 Merton SW19. . . . . . .180 A2
Lovell Pl SE16 . . . . .119 A3
Lovell Rd
Richmond TW10 . . . . . . .153 C1
Southall UB1. . . . . .85 D1
Loveridge Mews NW6. . .69 B2
Loveridge Rd NW6. . . . . .69 B2
Lover's Wlk
W1. . . . . .115 A5 **248** A3
Lovett Dr SW5 . . . . .202 B2
Lovette Ho 4 E3 . . . . .97 C4
Lovetts Pl SW18 . . . . . . .135 C1
Lovett Way NW10 . . . . . . .67 A3
Love Wlk SE5. . . . . .139 B3
Lovibonds Ave
Hillingdon UB7 . . . . .82 B1
Locksbottom BR6 . . . . . .226 D5
Lowbrook Rd IG1. . . . . . . .78 D4
Lowdell Cl UB7 . . . . .82 A1
Lowden Rd
Edmonton N9. . . . . .18 B3
Herne Hill SE24. . . . . . . .139 A1
Southall UB1. . . . . .107 A6
Lowder Ho 6 E1 . . . . . . .118 B5
Lowe Ave E16 . . . . .99 A2
Lowell Ho 10 SE5 . . . . . .139 A5
Lowell St E14. . . . . .97 A1
Lower Addiscombe Rd
CR0 . . . . .205 C2
Lower Addison Gdns
W14. . . . . .113 A4 **244** A1
Lower Belgrave St
SW1. . . . . .115 B3 **258** C5
Lower Boston Rd W7 . . .108 C4
Lower Broad St RM10 . .103 C6
Lower Camden BR7. . . . .188 B2
Lower Church St CR0 . . .220 B6
LOWER CLAPTON 74 C4
Lower Clapton Rd E5 . . .74 C4
Lower Clarendon Wlk 9
W11. . . . . .91 A1
Lower Comm S SW15 . .134 B2
Lower Coombe St
CR0 . . . . .221 A4
Lower Downs Rd
SW20. . . . . .178 D2
LOWER EDMONTON 18 B1
LOWER FELTHAM 149 C1
Lower Fosters NW4 . . . . .46 C4
Lower George St 13
TW10. . . . . .153 D6
Lower Gn W CR4 . . . . . . .202 C6
Lower Gravel Rd BR2. . .210 B3
LOWER GREEN 195 C1
Lower Green Gdns
KT4 . . . . .200 A1
Lower Grosvenor Pl
SW1. . . . . .115 B3 **258** C6
Lower Grove Rd TW10. .154 B6
LOWER HALLIFORD 193 C2
Lower Hall La E4 . . . . .35 A6

Lower Hampton Rd TW12, TW16 . . . . 172 D1
Lower Ham Rd KT2 . . . . 175 D4
LOWER HOLLOWAY . . 72 A3
Lower James St W1 . . . . 249 B6
Lower John St W1 . . . . 249 B6
Lower Kenwood Ave EN2 . . . . 16 A6
Lower Kings Rd KT2 . . . 176 A3
Lower Lea Crossing E14, E16 . . . . 120 C6
Lower Maidstone Rd N11 . . . . 31 C4
Lower Mall W6 . . . . 112 B1
Lower Marsh SE1 . . . . 116 C4 251 A1
Lower Marsh La KT1, KT5 . . . . 198 C5
Lower Merton Rise NW3 . . . . 70 C1
LOWER MORDEN 201 A2
Lower Morden La SM4 . . . . 201 A3
Lower Mortlake Rd TW9 . . . . 132 B2
Lower Park Rd
Belvedere DA17 . . . . . . 125 C2
Friern Barnet N11 . . . . . 31 C5
[4] Loughton IG10 . . . . . 21 D6
Lower Pk Acton W3 . . . . 89 A3
[5] Putney SW15 . . . . . 156 D6
LOWER PLACE 89 A5
Lower Place Bsns Ctr NW10 . . . . 89 A5
Lower Queen's Rd IG9 . . 21 D2
Lower Rd
Belvedere DA17 . . . . . . 125 D3
Finchley N2 . . . . 30 B2
Harrow HA2 . . . . 42 B1
Rotherhithe SE16 . . . . . 118 C4
Sutton SM1 . . . . 218 A4
Lower Richmond Rd
Mortlake SW14, TW9 . . 132 D2
Putney SW15 . . . . . . 134 C2
Lower Robert St WC2 . . 250 B5
Lower Sand Hills KT6 . . 197 C2
Lower Sloane St SW1 . . . . 115 A1 258 A2
Lower Sq TW7 . . . . 131 B2
Lower Strand NW9 . . . . 27 D1
Lower Sunbury Rd TW12 . . . . 173 C1
LOWER SYDENHAM . . 185 A6
Lower Sydenham Sta SE26 . . . . 185 B5
Lower Teddington Rd KT1 . . . . 175 D2
Lower Terr NW3 . . . . . . 70 A5
Lower Thames St EC3 . . . . 117 C6 253 A6
Lower Tub WD23 . . . . . . 8 B4
Lowerwood Ct W11 . . . . 91 A1
Lowestoft Cl [5] E5 . . . . 74 C6
Lowestoft Mews E16 . . 122 D4
Loweswater Ho E3 . . . . . 97 B3
Lowfield Rd
Dagenham W3 . . . . 89 A1
Hampstead NW6 . . . . . 69 C1
Low Hall Cl E4 . . . . 19 D4
Low Hall La E17 . . . . . . 53 A3
Lowick Rd HA1 . . . . . . 42 C4
Lowland Gdns RM7 . . . . 59 D3
Lowlands NW3 . . . . 70 C2
Lowlands Ct NW7 . . . . . 27 D5
Lowlands Rd
Harrow HA1 . . . . 40 C2
Pinner HA5 . . . . 40 C3
Lowman Rd N7 . . . . 72 B4
Lowndes Cl SW1 . . . . . 258 B5
Lowndes Ct
Knightsbridge SW1 . . . 257 D6
Marylebone W1 . . . . . 239 A1
Lowndes Lo Barnet EN5 . . 1 D2
SW1 . . . . 257 D6
Lowndes Pl SW1 . . . . 115 A3 258 A5
Lowndes Sq SW1 . . . . 114 D4 247 D1
Lowndes St SW1 . . . . 115 A3 258 A6
Lownds Ct BR1 . . . . . . 187 A1
Lowood Ct SE19 . . . . . 183 D5
Lowood Ho [12] E1 . . . . 118 C6
Lowood St E1 . . . . 118 B6
Lowry Cres CR4 . . . . . 180 C1
Lowry Ct [3] SE16 . . . . 118 B1
Lowry Ho N17 . . . . 33 D2
Lowry Lo [1] HA0 . . . . . 65 D3
Lowry Rd RM8 . . . . 80 B3
Lowther Cl WD6 . . . . . 10 B6
Lowther Dr EN2 . . . . . . 4 A1
Lowther Hill SE23 . . . . 163 A4
Lowther Ho
Pimlico SW1 . . . . . . 259 B1
[11] Shoreditch E8 . . . . 95 D6
Lowther Prim Sch SW13 . . . . 134 A6
Lowther Rd
Barnes SW13 . . . . . . 133 D4
Higham Hill E17 . . . . . 35 A1
Islington N7 . . . . 72 C3
Kingston u T KT2 . . . . 176 B2
Stanmore HA7 . . . . . . 44 B6
Lowth Rd SE5 . . . . . . 139 A3
Lowton Lo E17 . . . . . . 53 A6

LOXFORD 79 A3
Loxford Ave E6 . . . . 99 C5
Loxford Ho SW1 . . . . . 258 B3
Loxford La IG1 . . . . 79 B3
Loxford Rd IG11 . . . . . . 78 D2
Loxford Sch of Science & Tech IG1 . . . . 79 B3
Loxham Rd E4 . . . . 35 D3
Loxham St WC1 . . . . . . 233 B1
Loxley Cl SE26 . . . . . . 184 D5
Loxley Hall E11 . . . . 54 C2
Loxley Ho HA9 . . . . 66 A5
Loxley Rd
Feltham TW12 . . . . . . 173 B6
Wandsworth SW18 . . . 158 B3
Loxton Rd SE23 . . . . . 163 A3
Loxwood Cl TW14 . . . . 149 B3
Loxwood Rd N17 . . . . . . 51 C6
Loyola Prep Sch IG9 . . . 21 C3
LTC Coll London W1 . . 239 A2
Lubavitch House Sch (Jun Boys) E5 . . . . 51 D2
Lubbock Ct BR7 . . . . . 188 B3
Lubbock Ho [21] Canary Wharf E14 . . . . 119 D6
Orpington BR6 . . . . . 227 C6
Lubbock Rd BR7 . . . . . 188 B3
Lubbock St SE14 . . . . 140 C5
Lucan Ho N1 . . . . 235 D5
Lucan Pl SW3 . . 114 C2 257 B3
Lucan Rd EN5 . . . . 1 A2
Lucas Ave Harrow HA2 . . 63 C6
Newham E13 . . . . 99 B6
Lucas Ct
Battersea SW11 . . . . . 268 B1
Forest Hill SE26 . . . . . 185 A5
Lucas Gdns N2 . . . . 30 A1
Lucas Ho
[2] Clapham SW8 . . . . 137 C3
Walham Green SW10 . . 265 D4
Lucas Rd SE20 . . . . . . 184 C4
Lucas Sq NW11 . . . . . . 47 C3
Lucas St SE4, SE8 . . . 141 C4
Lucas Vale Prim Sch SE8 . . . . 141 C4
Lucerne Cl N14 . . . . . . 16 A1
Lucerne Ct
[5] Abbey Wood DA18 . . . . 125 A3
[8] Beckenham BR3 . . . 185 C3
Lucerne Gr E17 . . . . . . 54 B5
Lucerne Mews W8 . . . . 245 B4
Lucerne Rd Highbury N5 . 72 B4
Orpington BR6 . . . . . 211 D1
South Norwood CR7 . . 205 A5
Lucey Rd SE16 . . . . . . 118 A3
Lucey Way SE16 . . . . . 118 A3
Lucie Ave TW15 . . . . . 170 D4
Lucien Ho
Upper Tooting SW17 . . 181 A4
Wandsworth SW18 . . . 157 D2
Lucille Ho SE26 . . . . . 184 B4
Lucknow St SE18 . . . . 145 C5
Lucorn Cl SE12 . . . . . 164 D5
Lucraft Ho [12] SW2 . . . 160 A4
Luctons Ave IG9 . . . . . 21 C3
Lucy Ashe Ho SE17 . . . 261 D3
Lucy Brown Ho SE1 . . . 252 B3
Lucy Cres W3 . . . . 89 A3
Lucy Gdns RM8 . . . . . . 81 A5
Luddesdon Rd DA8 . . . 147 C5
Ludford Cl
Croydon CR0 . . . . . . 220 D4
Edgware NW9 . . . . . . 27 C1
Ludgate Broadway EC4 . . . . 241 D1
Ludgate Cir EC4 . 94 D1 241 D1
Ludgate Hill EC4 . . . . 94 D1 241 D1
Ludgate Ho EC4 . . . . . 241 D1
Ludgate Sq EC4 . . . . . 241 D1
Ludgrove Ct Enns 2 C1
Ludgrove Hall EN4 . . . . . 2 C1
Ludham NW5 . . . . 70 D3
Ludham Cl SE28 . . . . . 102 C1
Lud Lo TW15 . . . . 148 A2
Ludlow Cl Bromley BR2 . 209 A6
Harrow HA2 . . . . 63 B4
Ludlow Ct Acton W3 . . . 111 A4
East Barnet EN4 . . . . . 14 C6
Ludlow Rd Ealing W5 . . . 87 C3
Feltham TW13 . . . . . 172 A6
Ludlow St EC1 . . . . . . 242 A6
Ludlow Way N2 . . . . 48 A5
Ludovick Wlk SW15 . . . 133 C1
Ludwell Ho W14 . . . . . 254 B6
Ludwick Mews SE14 . . 141 A5
Luffield Rd SE2 . . . . . 124 B3
Luffman Rd SE12 . . . . 165 B1
Lugard Ho [2] W12 . . . . 112 B5
Lugard Rd SE15 . . . . . 140 B4
Lugg App E12 . . . . 78 C5
Luke Ho [32] E1 . . . . . . 96 B1
Lukes Ct N3 . . . . 47 C6
Luke St EC2 . . . . 95 C3 243 A6
Lukin Cres E4 . . . . 20 B1
Lukin St E1 . . . . 96 C1
Lullingstone Cl BR5 . . . 190 B3
Lullingstone Cres BR5 . 190 B3
Lullingstone Ho [21] SE15 . . . . 140 C6
Lullingstone La SE13 . . 164 B5
Lullingstone Rd [3] DA17 . . . . 147 B6
Lullington Garth
Borehamwood WD6 . . . 10 D6
Bromley BR1 . . . . . . 186 C3
Finchley N12 . . . . 29 B5
Lullington Rd
Dagenham RM9 . . . . . 81 A1
Penge SE20 . . . . 184 A3
Lulot Gdns N19 . . . . . . 71 B6
Lulworth
Camden Town NW1 . . . 71 D1
Walworth SE17 . . . . . 262 C2
Lulworth Ave
Hounslow TW5, TW7 . . 130 A5
Wembley HA9 . . . . 43 C2
Lulworth Cl HA2 . . . . . . 63 B5
Lulworth Cres CR4 . . . 180 C1
Lulworth Ct N14 . . . . . . 16 A1
Lulworth Dr HA5 . . . . . . 41 A2
Lulworth Gdns HA2 . . . . 63 B6
Lulworth Ho SW8 . . . . 270 C3
Lulworth Rd
Bexley DA16 . . . . . . 145 D3
Chislehurst SE9 . . . . 166 A4
Peckham SE15 . . . . . 140 B3
Lulworth Waye UB4 . . . . 84 B1
Lumen Rd HA0 . . . . 45 C5
Lumiere Bldg The E7 . . . 77 D3
Lumiere Ct [7] SW17 . . 159 A2
Lumina Bldg [1] E14 . . 120 A5
Lumley Cl DA17 . . . . . 125 C1
Lumley Ct WC2 . . . . . . 250 B5
Lumley Flats SW1 . . . . 258 A2
Lumley Gdns SM3 . . . . 217 A3
Lumley Ho KT3 . . . . . . 199 B1
Lumley Rd SM1, SM3 . . 217 A3
Lumley St W1 . . . . . . 238 B1
Lumsdon NW8 . . . . 91 D6
Luna Ho [6] SE16 . . . . 118 A4
Lunan Ho [14] E3 . . . . . 97 B5
Luna Rd CR7 . . . . 205 A6
Lundin Wlk WD19 . . . . . 22 D6
Lund Point E15 . . . . . . 98 A6
Lundy Dr UB3 . . . . . . 105 C2
Lunham Rd SE19 . . . . 183 C4
Luntley Pl E1 . . . . 96 A2
Lupin Cl Croydon CR0 . . 206 D1
Streatham SW2 . . . . . 160 D2
Lupin Cres IG11 . . . . . . 78 D2
Lupino Ct SE11 . . . . . 260 D4
Lupin Point SE1 . . . . . 253 D1
Lupton Cl SE12 . . . . . 187 B6
Lupton St NW5 . . . . 71 C4
Lupus Ct SE19 . . . . . . 183 B2
Lupus St SW1 . . 115 C1 259 B1
Luralda Gdns E14 . . . . 120 B1
Lurgan Ave W6 . . . . . . 134 C6
Lurline Gdns
SW11 . . . . 137 A4 268 B2
Luscombe Ct BR1 . . . . 186 C1
Luscombe Ho SW18 . . 157 B6
Luscombe Way SW8 . . . . 138 A5 270 A4
Lusher Ho SW15 . . . . . 156 D5
Lushington Ho KT12 . . 194 C3
Lushington Rd
Catford SE6 . . . . 185 D5
Willesden Green NW10 . . 90 B5
Lushington Terr [11] E8 . . 74 A3
Lutea Ho SM2 . . . . . . 218 A1
Luther Cl HA8 . . . . 11 A2
Luther King Cl E17 . . . . 53 A3
Luther Mews [2] TW11 . . 174 D5
Luther Rd TW11 . . . . . 174 D5
Luton Pl SE10 . . . . . . 142 A5
Luton Rd Newham E13 . . 99 A4
Sidcup DA14 . . . . . . 168 C1
Walthamstow E17 . . . . 53 B6
Luton St NW8 . . . 92 B3 236 D5
Luttrell Ave SW15 . . . . 156 B6
Lutwyche Rd SE6 . . . . 163 B2
Lutyens Ho [8] SW1 . . . 259 A1
Luxborough Ho W1 . . . 238 A4
Luxborough St W1 . . . . 93 A2 238 A4
Luxborough Twr W1 . . . 238 A4
Luxemburg Mews [2] E15 . . . . 76 C3
Luxemburg Gdns W6 . . 112 D2
Luxfield Rd SE9 . . . . . 166 A3
Luxford St SE16 . . . . . 118 D2
Luxmore St SE4 . . . . . 141 B4
Luxor St SE5 . . . . 139 A2
Lyall Ave SE21 . . . . . . 183 D6
Lyall Mews
SW1 . . . . 115 A3 258 A5
Lyall Mews W SW1 . . . 258 A5
Lyall St SW1 . . . 115 A3 258 A5
Lyal Rd E3 . . . . 97 A5
Lyce e Francais Charles de Gaulle (French Univ Coll) SW7 . . 114 B2 256 C4
Lycee The
SE11 . . . . 116 C1 261 B1
Lycett Ho [10] SW2 . . . 160 A4
Lycett Pl [3] W12 . . . . 112 A4
Lychgate Ct [4] N12 . . . 30 B5
Lychgate Manor HA1 . . . 42 C2
Lych Gate Wlk UB3 . . . 105 D6
Lyconby Gdns CR0 . . . 207 A2
Lydd Cl DA14 . . . . 167 C1
Lydden Ct SE9 . . . . . . 167 C5
Lydden Gr SW18 . . . . . 157 A4
Lydden Rd SW18 . . . . 157 A4
Lydeard Rd E6 . . . . 78 B1
Lydford NW1 . . . . 232 B5
Lydford Cl [22] N16 . . . . 73 C2
Lydford Rd
Brondesbury NW2 . . . . 68 D2
Paddington W9 . . . . . . 91 B3
Tottenham N15 . . . . . . 51 B4
Lydgate Ho [6] N16 . . . . 73 C3
Lydhurst Ave SW2 . . . 160 B2
Lydia Ct [2] N12 . . . . . 30 A4

Lydia Lodge HA1 . . . . . 64 C4
Lydney Cl
Camberwell SE15 . . . . 139 C5
Putney SW19 . . . . . . 157 A2
Lydon Rd SW4 . . . . . . 137 C2
Lydstep Rd DA7 . . . . . 147 D2
Lydwell Ho [29] SW8 . . . 137 D3
Lyford Rd SW18 . . . . . 158 C3
Lyford St SE7 . . . . 122 A4
Lygoe Ho [18] N6 . . . . . 49 D2
Lygoe Rd N2 . . . . 30 B2
Lygon Ho [2] E2 . . . . . . 96 A4
Lygon Pl SW1 . . . . . . 258 C5
Lyham Cl SW2 . . . . . . 160 A5
Lyham Rd SW2 . . . . . . 160 A5
Lyle Cl CR4 . . . . 203 A4
Lyle Ct SM4 . . . . 202 B3
Lyle Pk SW15 . . . . . . 156 D5
Lyly Ho SE1 . . . . 262 D5
Lyme Farm Rd SE12 . . 143 B1
Lyme Gr E9 . . . . 74 C1
Lyme Grove Ho [2] E9 . . 74 C1
Lymer Ave SE19 . . . . . 183 D5
Lyme Rd DA16 . . . . . . 146 B4
Lymescote Gdns SM1 . 217 C6
Lyme St NW1 . . . . 93 C6 232 A6
Lyminge Cl DA14 . . . . 189 D6
Lyminge Gdns SW17, SW18 . . . . 158 C3
Lymington Ave N22 . . . . 32 D1
Lymington Cl
Mitcham SW16 . . . . . 181 D1
[2] Newham E6 . . . . . 100 B2
Lymington Dr HA4 . . . . 61 B6
Lymington Gdns KT19 . 215 D3
Lymington Mans 69 D2
Lymington Rd
Dagenham RM8 . . . . . 58 D1
Hampstead NW6 . . . . . 69 D2
Lyminster Ct UB4 . . . . . 85 A2
Lympne N17 . . . . 33 B1
Lympstone Gdns SE15 . 140 A5
Lynbridge Gdns N13 . . . 32 D6
Lynbrook Gr SE15 . . . 139 C5
Lynchen Cl TW5 . . . . . 128 B4
Lynch Wlk [2] SE8 . . . 141 B6
Lyncott Cres SW4 . . . . 137 B1
Lyncourt SE3 . . . . 142 B3
Lyncroft Ave HA5 . . . . . 41 A4
Lyncroft Gdns
Ealing W13 . . . . 109 C5
Hampstead NW6 . . . . . 69 C3
Hounslow TW3 . . . . . 152 A6
Lyncroft Mans [4] NW6 . . 69 C3
Lyndale Ave NW2 . . . . . 69 B5
Lyndale Cl SE3 . . . . . 142 D6
Lyndean Ind Est SE2 . . 124 C3
Lynde Ho
[2] Clapham SW4 . . . 137 D2
Walton-on-T KT12 . . . 194 C3
Lynden Gate SW15 . . . 156 B4
Lyndenhurst SE3 . . . . 142 D2
Lynden Hyrst CR0 . . . . 221 D6
Lyndhurst BR7 . . . . . . 188 D4
Lyndhurst Ave
Colney Hatch N12 . . . . 30 D4
Edgware NW7 . . . . . . 27 C4
Mitcham SW16 . . . . . 181 D1
Pinner HA5 . . . . 22 B2
Southall UB1 . . . . . . 107 A5
Sunbury TW16 . . . . . 194 A6
Tolworth KT5 . . . . . . 198 D1
Twickenham TW2, TW4 . 151 C3
Lyndhurst Cl
Bexleyheath DA7 . . . . 147 D2
Neasden NW10 . . . . . . 67 B5
Orpington BR6 . . . . . 226 D4
South Croydon CR0 . . 221 D5
Lyndhurst Ct
[8] Belmont SM2 . . . . 217 C1
[11] Woodford E18 . . . . 37 A2
Lyndhurst Dr
Leytonstone E10 . . . . . 54 A2
New Malden KT3 . . . . 199 D3
Lyndhurst Gdns
Barking IG11 . . . . 79 C2
Enfield EN1 . . . . 5 C1
Hampstead NW3 . . . . . 70 B3
Hendon N3 . . . . 29 A2
Ilford IG2 . . . . 57 C2
Pinner HA5 . . . . 22 B2
Lyndhurst Gr SE5, SE15 . . . . 139 D3
Lyndhurst Ho [2] SW15 . . . . 156 A4
Lyndhurst House Prep Sch NW3 . . . . 70 B3
Lyndhurst Lo [3] E14 . . 120 D2
Lyndhurst Rd
Bexleyheath DA7 . . . . 147 D2
Chingford E4 . . . . 36 A3
Edmonton N18 . . . . . . 34 A6
Greenford UB6 . . . . . . 85 D3
Hampstead NW3 . . . . . 70 B3
Thornton Heath CR7 . . 204 C5
Tottenham N22 . . . . . . 32 C4
Lyndhurst Sch SE5 . . . 139 D3
Lyndhurst Sq SE15 . . . 139 D4
Lyndhurst Terr NW3 . . . 70 B3
Lyndhurst Way
Belmont SM2 . . . . . . 217 C1
Camberwell SE15 . . . . 139 D3
Lyndon Ave
Bexley DA15 . . . . . . 167 D6
Hackbridge SM6 . . . . 219 A5
Pinner HA5 . . . . 23 A4
Lyndon Rd DA17 . . . . . 125 C3
Lyndon Yd SW17 . . . . 179 D6

Lyndum Ct N22 . . . . . . 32 C2
Lyne Cres E17 . . . . 35 B2
Lyne Ct NW9 . . . . 45 B2
Lynegrove Ave TW15 . . 171 A5
Lyneham Wlk
Hackney E5 . . . . 75 A3
Pinner HA5 . . . . 39 D6
Lynette Ave SW4 . . . . 159 C5
Lynfield Ct SE23 . . . . 162 D4
Lynford Cl
Barnet Gate EN5 . . . . 11 D6
Burnt Oak HA8 . . . . . . 27 A2
Lynford French Ho SE17 . . . . 262 A2
Lynford Gdns
Edgware HA8 . . . . 10 D1
Ilford IG3 . . . . 79 D6
Lynford Terr N9 . . . . . . 17 D3
Lyngham Ct [10] N4 . . . . 50 A2
Lynhurst Cres UB10 . . . 61 B1
Lynhurst Rd UB10 . . . . . 61 A1
Lynmere Rd DA16 . . . . 146 B3
Lyn Mews [12] E3 . . . . . 97 B4
Lynmouth Ave
Enfield EN1 . . . . 17 D5
West Barnes SM4 . . . . 200 D2
Lynmouth Dr HA4 . . . . . 62 B5
Lynmouth Gdns
Heston TW5 . . . . 128 D4
Wembley UB6 . . . . . . 65 B1
Lynmouth Rd
Fortis Green N2 . . . . . 48 D5
Stamford Hill N16 . . . . 51 D1
Walthamstow E17 . . . . 53 A4
Wembley UB6 . . . . . . 87 B6
Lynn Cl Ashford TW15 . . 171 B5
Harrow HA3 . . . . 24 B1
Lynn Ct SW16 . . . . . . 181 D5
Lynne Cl [7] BR6 . . . . . 227 D2
Lynne Ct
Forest Hill SE23 . . . . 163 B4
Hampstead NW6 . . . . . 69 D1
South Croydon CR2 . . 221 C4
Wimbledon SW20 . . . 178 B2
Lynnett Ct E9 . . . . 75 A2
Lynnett Rd RM8 . . . . . . 58 D1
Lynne Way UB5 . . . . . . 84 C6
Lynne Wlk KT10 . . . . . 212 A3
Lynn Ho SE15 . . . . . . 140 A6
Lynn Mews E11 . . . . . . 76 C6
Lynn Rd Balham SW12 . . 159 B4
Ilford IG2 . . . . 57 B2
Leyton E11 . . . . 76 C5
Lynn St EN2 . . . . 5 B4
Lynsted Cl Bexley DA6 . . 169 D6
Bromley BR1 . . . . . . 187 C1
Lynsted Ct [4] BR3 . . . 185 A1
Lynsted Gdns SE9 . . . 143 D2
Lynton Ave Ealing W13 . . 87 A1
Isleworth TW7 . . . . . 130 D1
Willesden NW10 . . . . . 67 D3
Lynton Cl
Chessington KT9 . . . . 214 A4
Isleworth TW7 . . . . . 130 D1
Willesden NW10 . . . . . 67 D3
Lynton Cres IG2 . . . . . . 56 D3
Lynton Ct Bowes Pk N13 . 32 A5
[9] Dagenham W3 . . . . 89 A1
Penge SE20 . . . . 184 B2
Sutton SM2 . . . . 218 A4
Lynton Est SE1 . . . . . 118 A2
Lynton Gdns Enfield EN1 . 17 C4
Friern Barnet N11 . . . . 31 D4
Lynton Grange N2 . . . . . 48 D6
Lynton Ho [16] W2 . . . . 91 D1
Lynton Lo N5 . . . . 72 B2
Lynton Mans SE1 . . . . 261 A6
Lynton Mead N20 . . . . . 13 D2
Lynton Rd Acton W3 . . . 110 D6
Bermondsey SE1 . . . . 117 D2
Chingford E4 . . . . 35 D5
Harrow HA2 . . . . 63 A6
Hornsey N8 . . . . 50 A4
New Malden KT3 . . . . 199 B4
Paddington NW6 . . . . . 91 B5
Thornton Heath CR0 . . 204 C3
Lynton Terr [4] W3 . . . . 89 A1
Lynton Wlk UB4 . . . . . . 83 C4
Lynwood Cl Harrow HA2 . 63 A5
Woodford E18 . . . . . . 37 C2
Lynwood Ct TW15 . . . . 170 B5
Lynwood Dr KT4 . . . . . 216 A6
Lynwood Gdns
Southall UB1 . . . . 85 B1
Wallington CR0 . . . . . 220 B4
Lynwood Gr
Orpington BR6 . . . . . 211 C1
Southgate N21 . . . . . . 16 C3
Lynwood Rd Ealing W5 . . 88 A2
Thames Ditton KT7 . . . 196 D1
Upper Tooting SW17 . . 180 D6
Lynx Terr SW19 . . . . . 157 C1
Lynx Way E16 . . . . . . 121 D6
Lyon Bsns Pk IG11 . . . 101 C5
Lyon Cl HA4 . . . . 39 D1
Lyon Ho NW8 . . . . . . 237 A5
Lyon Meade HA7 . . . . . 25 C2
Lyon Park Ave HA0 . . . . 66 B2
Lyon Park Jun & Inf Schs HA0 . . . . 66 B1
Lyon Rd Harrow HA1 . . . 42 D3
Merton SW19 . . . . . . 180 A2
Lyonsdown Ave EN5 . . . 14 A5
Lyonsdown Ct EN5 . . . . 14 A6
Lyonsdown Sch EN5 . . . 14 A6
Lyons Pl NW8 . . 92 B3 236 C5
Lyon St N1 . . . . 72 B1

Lyons Wlk W14 . . . . . 254 A6
Lyon Way UB6 . . . . 86 C6
Lyoth Rd BR5 . . . . 227 A6
Lyric Dr UB6 . . . . 85 B7
Lyric Mews SE26 . . . . 184 C6
Lyric Rd SW13 . . . . . . 133 C4
Lysander [20] NW9 . . . . 27 C2
Lysander Ct [8] Eeltham E5 . . . 13 C6
Lysander Gdns KT5 . . . 198 B3
Lysander Gr N19 . . . . . 49 D1
Lysander Ho [10] E2 . . . 96 B5
Lysander Rd Ruislip HA4 . 61 B6
Wallington CR0 . . . . . 220 B2
Lysander Way BR6 . . . . 227 A5
Lysia Ct SW6 . . . . 134 C5
Lysias Rd SW12 . . . . . 159 B5
Lysia St SW6 . . . . 134 C5
Lysons Wlk SW15 . . . . 156 A6
Lytchet Rd BR1 . . . . . 187 B3
Lytchet Way EN3 . . . . . . 6 C4
Lytchgate Cl CR2 . . . . 221 C1
Lytcott Dr KT8 . . . . . . 195 B6
Lytcott Gr SE22 . . . . . 161 C6
Lytham Ave WD19 . . . . . 22 D5
Lytham Ct SE28 . . . . . 103 A3
Lytham Ct [5] UB1 . . . . . 85 D1
Lytham Gr W5 . . . . 88 B4
Lytham St
SE17 . . . . 117 B3 262 C1
Lyttelton Cl NW3 . . . . . 70 C1
Lyttelton Ct N2 . . . . . . 48 A4
Lyttelton Rd
Hampstead Garden Suburb N2 . . . . 48 A4
Leyton E10 . . . . 76 A5
Lytten Ct [6] W12 . . . . 112 A4
Lyttleton Ct UB4 . . . . . 84 C3
Lyttleton Ho [10] E9 . . . 74 C1
Lyttleton Rd N8 . . . . . . 50 C6
Lytton Ave Enfield EN3 . . . 7 A5
Southgate N13 . . . . . . 16 C2
Lytton Cl
Hampstead Garden Suburb N2 . . . . 48 A4
Northolt UB5 . . . . 63 B1
Lytton Ct WC1 . . . . . . 240 B3
Lytton Gdns SM6 . . . . 219 D4
Lytton Gr SW15 . . . . . 157 A5
Lytton Ho [3] TW12 . . . 173 D4
Lytton Rd
Leytonstone E11 . . . . . 54 C2
New Barnet EN5 . . . . . . 2 A1
Pinner HA5 . . . . 23 A3
Lytton Strachey Path [8] SE28 . . . . 124 B6
Lyveden Rd
Greenwich SE3 . . . . . 143 B5
Mitcham SW17, SW19 . 180 A1

M

Mabbett Ho [2] SE18 . . . 144 C6
Mabel Crout Ct SE9 . . . 145 B1
Mabel Evetts Ct UB3 . . 106 B6
Mabel Thornton Ho [12] N16 . . . . 73 B4
Maberley Cres SE19 . . 184 A3
Maberley Ct SE19 . . . . 184 A3
Maberley Rd SE19 . . . 182 C3
Mabledon Pl NW1, WC1 . . . . 232 D1
Mablethorpe Rd SW6 . . 264 A3
Mabley St E9 . . . . 75 A3
Mablin Lo [3] IG9 . . . . . 21 C3
McAdam Dr EN2 . . . . . . 4 D3
MacAllister Ho [8] SE18 . . . . 144 C6
Macaret Cl N20 . . . . . . 14 A4
MacArthur Cl E7 . . . . . . 77 A2
MacArthur Ho [4] SW2 . . . . 160 A4
Macartney Ho SE10 . . . 142 B5
Macaulay Ave KT10 . . . 212 C6
Macaulay CE Prim Sch SW4 . . . . 137 B1
Macaulay Ct SW4 . . . . 137 B1
Macaulay Ho
[2] Kensal Town W10 . . 91 A2
[10] Stoke Newington N16 . 73 C5
Macaulay Rd
Clapham SW4 . . . . . . 137 B2
Newham E6 . . . . 99 D5
Macaulay Sq SW4 . . . . 137 B1
Macaulay Way [2] SE28 . . . . 124 B5
McAuley Cl Eltham SE9 . 166 C6
Lambeth SE1 . . 116 C3 261 A6
MacAuley Mews SE13 . 142 A3
McAusland Ho [5] E3 . . . 97 B5
Macbean St SE18 . . . . 122 D3
Macbeth Ho [4] N1 . . . . . 95 C5
Macbeth St W6 . . . . . . 112 B1
McBride Ho [6] E3 . . . . . 97 B5
McCall Cl SW4 . . . . . . 138 A3
McCall Cres SE7 . . . . 122 A1
McCall Ho N7 . . . . 72 A4
Mccarthy Ct SW11 . . . 267 B1
McCarthy Rd TW13 . . . 172 D5
Macclesfield Rd
Croydon SE25 . . . . . . 206 C4
Shoreditch EC1 . . 95 A4 235 A2
Macclesfield St W1 . . . 249 D6
McClintock Pl EN3 . . . . . 7 C6
McCoid Way SE1 . . . . 252 A1
McConnell Ho SW8 . . . 269 C4
McCormick Ho [9] SW2 . . . . 160 C3
McCrone Mews [3] NW3 . . . . 70 B2

McCullum Rd E3........97 B6
McDermott Cl SW11 ...136 C2
McDermott Rd SE15 ...140 A2
MacDonald Ave RM10...81 D5
MacDonald Ct TW3 ....130 A1
McDonald Ho 1 KT2...176 B3
MacDonald Ho 2
SW11................137 A3
MacDonald Rd
Chingford E17..........36 A1
Dartmouth Pk N19 ......71 C6
Forest Gate E7 ....77 A4
Friern Barnet N11.......30 D5
McDonough Cl KT9....214 A4
McDougall Ct TW9.....132 C3
Mcdougall Ho E2.......96 A4
McDowall Cl E16 ....98 D2
McDowall Rd SE5......139 A4
Macduff Rd
SW11.........137 A4 268 B2
Mace Cl E1............118 B5
Mace Ho 2 E17 ....53 D6
McEntee Ave E17 ....35 A2
Mace St E2.............96 D5
McEwan Way E15.......98 B6
Macey Ho
Battersea SW11 ...... 267 A1
10 Greenwich SE10 ....142 A6
Macfarlane La TW7 ....131 A6
Macfarlane Rd W12....112 C5
Macfarren Ho 7 W10...91 A4
MacFarren Pl NW1.... 238 B5
McGlashon Ho 15 E1....96 A3
McGrath Rd E15........76 D2
McGregor Ct 8 N1 .....95 C4
MacGregor Ho 2
SW12................159 D3
McGregor Rd W11......91 B2
MacGregor Rd E16......99 C2
Mcguffie Ct E17 ....53 B6
Machell Rd SE15.......140 C2
McIndoe Ct N1 .... 235 C6
McIntosh Cl SM6.......220 A1
McIntosh Ho 14 SE16...118 C2
McIntyre Ct 19 SW4....138 A3
Mackay Ho 33 W12.....112 B6
McKay Rd SW20 ....178 C4
Mackay Rd SW4 ....137 B2
McKellar Cl WD23 ....8 A2
McKenna Ho 3 E3.......97 B5
Mackennal St
NW8 ....92 C5 230 B4
Mackenzie Cl 7 W12 ..112 B6
Mackenzie Ho
5 Dollis Hill NW2 ......68 A5
1 Hornsey N8 ....50 A5
Mackenzie Rd
Barnsbury N7 ....72 B2
Penge BR3.............184 D1
Mackenzie Wlk E14....119 C5
McKerrell Rd SE15.....140 A4
Mackeson Rd NW3......70 D4
Mackie Ho 18 SW2.....160 C4
Mackie Rd SW2........160 C4
McKiernan Ct 2
SW11................136 C3
Mc Killop Way DA14 ...190 C3
McKinlay Ct
Beckenham BR3 ....185 B1
Bexley DA16 ....146 C2
McKinnon Wood Ho 16
E2 ....96 A4
Mackintosh La E9.......74 D3
Macklin Ho SE23.......162 B2
Macklin St WC2..94 A1 240 B2
Mackonochie Ho EC1 . 241 A4
Mackrow Wlk 11 E14....120 A6
Macks Rd SE16 ....118 A2
Mackworth Ho NW1 .. 232 A2
Mackworth St NW1 ... 232 A2
Mac Laren Mews
SW15.................134 C1
Maclean Rd SE23 ......163 A5
McLeod Ct SE21 ....162 A3
McLeod Ho 3 SE23 ....162 C2
McLeod Rd SE2.........124 B2
MacLeod Rd N21 ....16 A6
McLeod's Mews
SW7..........113 D2 255 D4
MacLeod St
SE17 ....117 A1 262 B1
Maclise Rd
W14..........113 A3 254 A5
McManus Ho 3 SW11..136 B2
McMillan Ct 2 SE6 ....164 D3
Macmillan Ct HA2 ......41 C1
McMillan Ho SE4 ......141 A2
Macmillan Ho
Cricklewood NW4 ....68 B4
Lisson Gr NW8 .... 230 B1
McMillan St SE8.......141 C6
Macmillan Way SW17 ..181 B6
Mcmorran Ho 4 N7 ....72 A4
McNair Rd UB2........107 D3
Macnamara Ho SW10 . 266 C4
McNeil Rd SE5.........139 C3
McNicol Dr NW10.......89 A5
Macoma Rd SE18 ......145 B6
Macoma Terr SE18.....145 B6
Maconochies Rd 9
E14 ....119 D1
Macquarie Way E14....119 D2
McRae La CR4.........202 D2
Macready Ho W1 ...... 237 B3
Macready Pl 2 N7.......72 A4
Macroom Ho W9 ....91 B4
Macroom Rd W9 ....91 B4
Mac's Pl EC4 .... 241 B2
Madame Tussaud's*
NW1..........93 A3 238 A5
Mada Rd BR6..........226 D5
Maddams St E3.........97 D3
Madderfields Ct N11....31 D2
Maddison Cl
Finchley N2 ....30 A1
Teddington TW11 ......174 D4
Maddison Ct NW4 ......28 C1
Maddocks Cl DA14.....191 A5
Maddocks Ho 3 E1....118 B6
Maddock Way SE17 ....138 D6
Maddox Ct 1 E4........20 B3
Maddox St W1........ 248 D6
Madeira Ave BR1 ......186 C3
Madeira Gr IG8.........37 C4
Madeira Rd
Edmonton N13...........16 D1
Leytonstone E11 ....54 C1
Mitcham CR4...........202 D5
Streatham SW16........182 A5
Madeleine Cl RM6 ......58 C3
Madeley Ct W5..........88 A1
Madeley Rd W5..........88 A1
Madeline Gr IG1.........79 B3
Madeline Rd SE20 .....184 A3
Madge Gill Way 4 E6..100 A6
Madge Hill W7 ....108 C6
Madinah Rd E8..........74 A3
Madingley 11 KT1.....176 C1
Madingley Ct TW1 .....153 C6
Madison Apartments
N11 ....31 D3
Madison Cres DA7 .....146 C5
Madison Ct 15 RM10 ....81 D2
Madison Gdns
Beckenham BR2 ....208 D6
Bexley DA7 ....146 C5
Madison Ho E3 ....98 A4
Madras Ho IG1 ....78 D4
Madras Pl N7...........72 C2
Madras Rd IG1 ....78 D4
Madrid Rd SW13........134 A5
Madron St
SE17 ....117 C1 263 B2
Mafeking Ave
Brentford TW8 ....132 A6
Ilford IG2 ....57 B2
Newham E6............100 A5
Mafeking Rd Enfield EN1 ..5 D2
Newham E16...........98 D3
Tottenham N17 ....34 A1
Magdala Ave N19 ....71 C6
Magdala Rd
Isleworth TW7 ....131 A2
South Croydon CR2.....221 B1
Magdalen Ct SE25 .....206 A4
Magdalene Cl 7 SE15..140 B3
Magdalene Gdns E6 ...100 C3
Magdalene Ho 7
SW15.................156 D5
Magdalene Rd TW17 ...192 B6
Magdalen Pas E1...... 253 D6
Magdalen Rd SW18 ....158 B3
Magdalen St SE1 ..... 253 A3
Magee St SE11 ....138 C6
Magellan Ct 11 NW10 ...67 B1
Magellan Ho 16 E1.....96 D3
Magellan Pl 25 E14 ....119 C2
Magna Ct UB6 ....86 B4
Magnaville Rd WD23 .....8 D4
Magnet Rd HA9..........65 D6
Magnin Cl 5 E8 ....96 A6
Magnolia Cl
Kingston u T KT2.......176 D4
Leyton E10..............75 C6
Magnolia Ct
13 Belmont SM2........217 D1
Feltham TW14..........150 A3
2 Finchley N12 ....29 D6
Forest Hill SE26 ....184 C5
Harrow HA3 ....44 B2
Hillingdon UB10 ....60 D2
Northolt UB5............85 A3
Richmond TW9 ....132 D4
Wallington SM6.........219 B3
Wandsworth SW11 .....158 D5
Magnolia Gdns HA8.....27 A6
Magnolia Ho 13 SE8....141 B6
Magnolia Lo E4..........19 D1
Magnolia Pl
Clapham Pk SW4........160 A6
Ealing W5 ....87 D2
Magnolia Rd W4........132 D6
Magnolia Way KT19.....215 A3
Magnolia Wharf W4 ...132 D6
Magpie Cl Edgware NW9 .27 C1
Enfield EN1 ....6 A4
Forest Gate E7 ....76 D3
Magpie Hall Cl BR2 ....210 A3
Magpie Hall La BR2....210 B3
Magpie Hall Rd WD23....8 C2
Magpie Ho 7 E3 ....97 B6
Magpie Pl SE14.........141 A6
Magri Wlk 22 E1........96 C2
Maguire Dr TW10 ......175 C6
Maguire St
SE1 ....117 D4 253 D2
Mahatma Gandhi Ind Est
1 SE24 ....138 D1
Mahlon Ave HA4........62 B2
Mahogany Cl SE16.....119 A5
Mahon Cl EN1 ....5 D4
Mahoney Ho SE14 .....141 B4
Maida Ave Chingford E4 ..19 D4
Little Venice W2 .92 A3 236 B5
Maida Rd DA17 ....125 C3
MAIDA VALE 91 D4
Maida Vale W9..92 A4 229 A1
Maida Vale Sta W9......91 D4
Maida Way E4...........19 D4
Maiden Erlegh Ave
DA5 ....169 A3
Maiden La
Borough The
SE1.........117 A5 252 B4
Camden Town NW1.......71 D1
Strand WC2....116 A6 250 B6
Maiden Rd E15 ....76 C1
Maidenstone Hill
SE10 ....142 A4
Maids of Honour Row 4
TW9...................153 D6
Maidstone Bldgs SE1 . 252 C3
Maidstone Ct N11.......31 D4
Maidstone Ho 4 E14....97 D1
Maidstone Rd
Friern Barnet N11.......31 D4
Ruxley DA14 ....191 C3
Mail Coach Yd 23 E2....95 C4
Main Ave EN1 ....17 D6
Main Dr HA9 ....65 D5
Main Rd
Chislehurst BR5 ....190 C1
Sidcup DA14 ....167 C1
Mainridge Rd BR7,
SE9 ....188 C6
Main St TW13 ....172 D5
Mainwaring Ct 3
CR4 ....181 A1
Main Yd E9.............75 C2
Mais Ho SE26..........162 B2
Maismore St SE15 .....140 A6
Maison Alfort HA3 ......24 C2
Maisonettes The SM1 ..217 B3
Maitland Cl
3 Greenwich SE10 .....141 D5
Hounslow TW4 ....129 B2
Maitland Ct W2....... 246 C6
Maitland Ho
Chelsea SW1......... 269 A6
16 South Hackney E2 ....96 C5
MAITLAND PARK 70 D2
Maitland Park Rd NW3..70 D2
Maitland Park Villas
NW3 ....70 D2
Maitland Pl E5 ....74 C4
Maitland Rd
Penge SE26............184 D4
Stratford E15 ....76 D2
Majendie Rd SE18 .....123 B1
Majestic Ct N4 ....50 D1
Majestic Way CR4 .....180 D1
Major Cl SW9..........138 D2
Majorie Mews 6 E1 ....96 D1
Major Rd
22 Bermondsey SE16 ...118 A3
Stratford New Town E15..76 B3
Makepeace Ave N6 .....71 A6
Makepeace Mans N6....71 A6
Makepeace Rd
Northolt UB5...........85 A6
Wanstead E11...........55 A5
Makinen Ho 5 IG9 .....21 C3
Makins St SW3 .... 257 B3
Malabar Ct 20 W12.....112 B6
Malabar St E14 ....119 C4
Malam Ct SE11 .... 261 A3
Malam Gdns 3 E14....119 D6
Malatia CR2 ....221 A2
Malay Ho 2 E1.........118 C5
Malborough Ho 3 N20..14 D1
Malbrook Rd SW15 ....134 B1
Malbury Ct N22.........32 A3
Malcolm Cl SE20.......184 C3
Malcolm Cres NW4 .....46 A3
Malcolm Ct Ealing W5 ...88 B3
Hendon NW4............46 A3
Stanmore HA7...........25 C5
Stratford E7 ....76 D2
Malcolm Dr KT6 ....198 A1
Malcolm Ho 13 N1 .....95 C5
Malcolm Pl E2...........96 C3
Malcolm Prim Sch
SE20..................184 C3
Malcolm Rd
Bethnal Green E1 ....96 C3
Croydon SE25 ....206 A3
Ickenham UB10..........60 B4
Penge SE20............184 C3
Wimbledon SW19 ......179 A4
Malcolmson Ho SW1.. 259 D1
Malcolms Way N14 .....15 C6
Malcolm Way E11........55 A4
Malden Ave
Croydon SE25 ....206 B6
Northolt UB6...........64 C2
Malden CE Prim Sch
KT4...................199 C1
Malden Cres NW1 ......71 A2
Malden Ct
Stoke Newington N4.....51 A3
West Barnes KT3 ......200 B6
Malden Green Ave
KT4 ....200 A1
Malden Hill KT3 ....199 D6
Malden Hill Gdns KT3..199 D6
Malden Junc KT3 ......199 D4
Malden Manor Prim Sch
KT3...................199 C2
Malden Manor Sta
KT3...................199 C2
Malden Pk KT3 ....199 D3
Malden Pl NW5.........71 A3
Malden Rd
Camden Town NW5......71 A2
Cheam KT4, SM3.......216 D4
New Malden KT3, KT4...199 D2
Malden Way KT3.......200 A5
Malden Way (Kingston By
Pass) KT3, KT5 ....199 C4
Maldon Cl
Camberwell SE5 ....139 C2
Shoreditch N1........ 235 B6
Stratford New Town E15..76 B3
Maldon Ct Barking E6 ...100 C6
Wallington SM6.........219 C3
Maldon Rd Acton W3 ...111 A6
Edmonton N9............17 D1
Wallington SM6.........219 B3
Maldon Wlk IG8 ....37 C4
Malet Pl WC1......... 239 C5
Malet St WC1.....93 D2 239 D4
Maley Ave SE27........160 D2
Malford Ct E18 ....37 A1
Malford Gr E18 ....54 D6
Malfort Rd SE5 ....139 C2
Malham Cl N11 ....31 A4
Malham Rd SE23.......162 D3
Malham Road Ind Est
SE23..................162 D3
Malindi Ct N8 ....49 D4
Malins Cl EN5 ....12 C6
Malins Ct SW12........159 A5
Mallaig Ct HA8 ....10 D2
Mallams Mews 1
SW9..................138 D2
Mallard Cl
1 Hackney E9 ....75 B2
Hanwell W7...........108 C4
Kilburn NW6 ....91 C6
New Barnet EN5 ....14 B5
Twickenham TW4.......151 C4
Mallard Ct Chingford E4 ..20 B4
Ilford IG1 ....79 A6
Kingsbury NW9..........45 A2
Little Ilford E12..........78 B3
18 Richmond TW10.....153 D5
Walthamstow E17 ....54 B6
Mallard Ho
8 Camberwell SE15.....139 D4
St John's Wood NW8 .. 230 A3
Mallard Path 3 SE28 ...123 B3
Mallard Pl TW1.........153 A1
Mallard Point 6 E3.....97 C4
Mallards E11 ....55 A2
Mallards Rd
Barking IG11..........102 A3
Woodford IG8...........37 B3
Mallard Way NW9.......45 A2
Mallard Wlk
Beckenham BR3 ....206 D4
Sidcup DA14 ....190 C4
Mall Ct W5.............110 A6
Mallet Dr UB5 ....63 B3
Mallet Ho 11 SW15.....156 A6
Mallet Rd SE13 ....164 B5
Malling SE13 ....163 D6
Malling Cl CR0.........206 C3
Malling Gdns SM4 .....202 A3
Malling Ho 9 BR3 .....185 C3
Malling Way BR2 ......208 D2
Mallinson Ct 2 E11.....76 C6
Mallinson Rd
Wallington SM6.........219 D5
Wandsworth SW11......158 D6
Mallon Gdns E1 ...... 243 D3
Mallord St
SW3..........136 B6 266 D6
Mallory Bldgs EC1 .... 241 C5
Mallory Cl SE4.........141 A1
Mallory Gdns EN4.......15 A4
Mallory St NW8..92 C3 237 B6
Mallow Cl CR0.........206 D1
Mallow Ct
Colney Hatch N12 ....30 C4
Lewisham SE13 ....142 A3
Mallow Mead NW7......29 A3
Mallow St EC1 .... 242 C6
Mallows The UB10 ......60 D5
Mall Rd W6 ....112 B1
Mall Studios 9 NW3....70 D3
Mall The
6 Bexley DA6 ....147 C1
Brentford TW8 ....131 D6
4 Bromley BR1 ....209 A6
Ealing W5 ....110 A6
Harrow HA3 ....44 B3
Kingston u T KT6.......197 D4
Mortlake SW14.........155 A6
Palmers Green N14......16 A1
St James SW1. 115 D5 249 C3
Mall The (Prep Sch)
TW2 ....152 B1
Malmains Cl BR3 ......208 B5
Malmains Way BR3 ....208 B5
Malmesbury 30 E2 ......96 C5
Malmesbury Cl HA5.....40 A5
Malmesbury Prim Sch
Morden SM4 ....202 A3
Tower Hamlets E3.......97 B4
Malmesbury Rd Bow E3..97 B5
Morden SM4 ....202 A3
Newham E16.............98 C2
Woodford E18...........36 D2
Malmesbury Terr E16 ...98 D2
Malmsey Ho SE11..... 260 D2
Malmsmead Ho E9.......75 A3
Malorees Jun & Inf Schs
NW6...................68 D1
Malory Cl BR3 ....185 A1
Malpas Dr HA5 ....40 D4
Malpas Rd
Dagenham RM9..........80 D2
Hackney E8 ....74 B2
New Cross SE4 ....141 B3
Malta Rd E10............53 C2
Malta St EC1 .... 241 D6
Maltby Dr EN1............6 B5
Maltby Rd KT9.........214 C2
Maltby St SE1 ..117 D3 263 C6
Maltham Terr N18 ......34 B4
Malthouse Dr
Chiswick W4 ....133 D6
Feltham TW13.........172 D5
Malthouse Pas SW13...133 C3
Malthus Path 7 SE28 ..124 C5
Malting Ho E14.........119 B6
Maltings W4 ....110 C1
Maltings Cl SW13......133 C3
Maltings Lo W4........133 C5
Maltings Pl
Bermondsey SE1...... 253 B2
Parsons Green SW6 ... 265 D1
Maltings The BR6......211 D1
Malting Way TW7......130 D2
Malt Mill SE1......... 253 C3
Malton Ho SE25........205 C5
Malton Mews
1 Notting Hill W10 .....91 A1
Plumstead Comm SE18..145 C6
Malton Rd W10..........91 A1
Malton St SE18 ....145 C6
Maltravers St WC2.... 251 A6
Malt St SE1............140 A6
Malva Cl SW18.........157 D6
Malvern Ave
Chingford E4 ....36 B3
Erith DA7..............147 A5
Harrow HA2 ....63 B5
Malvern Cl Bushey WD23 ..8 A5
Ickenham UB10..........60 C6
Mitcham CR4..........203 C6
Notting Hill W10 ....91 B2
Penge SE20............184 A1
Surbiton KT6 ....198 A1
Malvern Ct
Belmont SM2..........217 C1
5 East Barnet N20 .....14 C2
15 Shepherd's Bush
W12 ....112 A4
South Kensington SW7 . 256 D4
3 Surbiton KT6 ....198 A1
Malvern Dr
Feltham TW13.........172 D5
Ilford IG3 ....79 D4
Woodford IG8...........37 C6
Malvern Gdns
Cricklewood NW2 ....69 A6
Harrow HA3 ....44 A5
Malvern Ho London N16 ..51 D1
SE17 .... 262 B1
Malvern Lo N12.........30 B6
Malvern Mews NW6.....91 C4
Malvern Pl NW6 ....91 B4
Malvern Rd Dalston E8 ...74 A1
Enfield EN3 ....7 A6
Hampton TW12 ....173 C3
Harlington UB3 ....127 C5
Hornsey N8.............50 C6
Leytonstone E11 ....76 D6
Maida Vale NW6.........91 C4
Newham E6............100 A6
Surbiton KT6 ....198 A1
Thornton Heath CR7 ....204 C5
Tottenham Hale N17 .....52 A6
Upper Holloway N19.....49 D1
Malvern Terr
Edmonton N9............17 D3
Islington N1 .... 234 A6
Malvern Way W13 ....87 B2
Malwood Rd SW12......159 B5
Malyons Rd SE13 ......163 D6
Malyons Terr SE13.....163 D6
Malyons The TW17.....193 B3
Managers St 8 E14....120 A5
Manatee Pl SM6 ....219 D5
Manaton Cl SE15.......140 B2
Manaton Cres UB1......85 C1
Manbey Gr E15 ....76 C2
Manbey Park Rd E15....76 C2
Manbey Rd E15..........76 C2
Manbey St E15 ....76 C2
Manbre Rd W6 ....134 C6
Manbrough Ave E6 ....100 C4
Manchester Ct E16 .....99 B1
Manchester Dr W10.....91 A3
Manchester Gr E14 ....120 A1
Manchester Ho SE17 .. 262 B2
Manchester Mans N19 ..49 D2
Manchester Mews W1 238 A3
Manchester Rd
Cubitt Town E14 ....120 A3
South Norwood CR7 ....205 A6
Tottenham N15 ....51 B3
Manchester Sq
W1...........93 A1 238 B2
Manchester St
W1...........93 A2 238 A3
Manchester Way RM10..81 D4
Manchuria Rd SW11 ...159 A5
Manciple St
SE1 ....117 B3 262 D6
Mandalay Ho 6 N16 ....73 B4
Mandalay Rd SW4 .....159 C6
Mandarin Ct
6 Deptford SE8 ....141 C6
Willesden NW10.........67 B2
Mandarin Way UB4 .....84 D1
Mandela Cl
36 Shepherd's Bush
W12 ....112 B6
Stonebridge NW10 ......67 A1
Mandela Ho
Plumstead Comm
SE18..................145 B6
18 Spitalfields E2 ....95 D4
Mandela Rd E16 ....99 A1
Mandela St
Camden Town
NW1.........93 C6 232 B6
Mandela St *continued*
Kennington SW9 ....138 C5
Mandela Way
SE1 ....117 C2 263 B4
Manderville Ho SE1... 263 D2
Mandeville Cl
5 Greenwich SE3 .....142 D5
Merton SW19 ....179 A2
Mandeville Ct
Hampstead NW3.........69 D3
Highams Pk E4 ....35 A6
Mandeville Ctyd SW11 268 A1
Mandeville Dr KT6.....197 D1
Mandeville Ho 8
SW4..................159 C6
Mandeville Pl W1..... 238 B2
Mandeville Prim Sch
E5....................74 D5
Mandeville Rd
Enfield EN3 ....7 A6
Isleworth TW7 ....131 A3
Littleton TW17.........192 C4
Northolt UB5...........63 C1
Osidge N14 ....15 C2
Mandeville Sch UB5 ....63 B2
Mandeville St E5 ....75 A5
Mandrake Rd SW17....158 D1
Mandrake Way 3 E15...76 C1
Mandrell Rd SW2 ......160 A6
Manesty Ct N14.........15 D4
Manette St W1 .... 239 D1
Manfred Ct 7 SW15 ...157 B6
Manfred Rd SW15......157 B6
Manger Rd N7..........72 A2
Mangold Way 4
DA18 ....125 A3
Manilla Ct RM6 ....58 B3
Manilla St E14 ....119 C4
Manister Rd SE2.......124 A3
Manitoba Ct 29 SE16 ...118 C4
Manitoba Gdns 6
BR6 ....227 D2
Manley Ct N16..........73 D5
Manley Ho SE11 ..... 261 A2
Manley St NW1 ...... 231 A6
Manly Dixon Dr EN3 .....7 A6
Mann Cl 3 CR0.........221 A5
Manneby Prior N1 .... 233 D3
Mannering Ho 16
SW2..................160 B6
Manning Ct 3 SE28....124 B5
Manningford Cl EC1 .. 234 C2
Manning Gdns HA3 .....43 D2
Manning Ho
3 Notting Hill W11 .....91 A1
6 Walthamstow E17 ....54 A6
Manning Pl TW10......154 B5
Manning Rd
Dagenham RM10.........81 C1
Walthamstow E17 ....53 A4
Manningtree Cl SW19..157 A3
Manningtree Rd HA4....62 B4
Manningtree St 2 E1...96 A1
Mannin Rd RM6..........58 B2
Mannock Mews IG8......37 B2
Mannock Rd N22 ....50 D6
Mann's Cl TW7 ....152 D6
Manns Rd HA8...........26 C4
Manny Shinwell Ho
SW6.................. 264 D5
Manoel Rd TW2 ....152 A2
Manor Ave
Hounslow TW4 ....128 D3
New Cross SE4 ....141 B3
Northolt UB5............63 B1
Manorbrook SE12, SE3..143 A1
Manor Circus TW9.....132 C2
Manor Cl Barnet EN5......1 A1
Edgware NW7...........27 B5
Higham Hill E17.........35 A1
Kingsbury NW9..........44 D4
New Malden KT4.......199 C1
Ruislip HA4 ....39 D1
Thamesmead SE28 .....102 C1
Manor Cottages App
N2 ....30 A1
Manor Cotts N2 ....30 A1
Manor Court Lo 12 E18..37 A2
Manor Court Rd W7 ...108 C6
Manor Cres KT5 ....198 C3
Manor Croft HA8 ....26 C4
Manor Ct
4 Barking IG11.........79 D1
7 Brixton SW2..........160 B6
Camberwell SE15 ......139 D4
Chingford E4 ....20 C3
Fortis Green N2 ....48 D4
Friern Barnet N20........14 D1
Gunnersbury W3 ....110 C2
5 Hackbridge SM6 .....219 A5
Harrow HA1 ....42 D3
Kingston u T KT2.......176 C2
Osidge N14 ....15 D2
Parsons Green SW6 ... 265 D1
Streatham SW16........160 A1
Surbiton KT5 ....198 C3
8 Sutton SM1 ....218 A4
Twickenham TW2.......152 A2
Walthamstow E10........53 D1
5 Wembley HA9 ....66 A3
Manordene Cl KT7.....197 A1
Manordene Rd SE28 ...102 D1
Manor Dr
East Barnet N14 ....15 B3
Edgware NW7...........27 B5
Feltham TW13..........172 D5
Friern Barnet N20........14 D1

Manor Dr *continued*
Hinchley Wood KT10 213 A5
Sunbury TW16 172 A1
Surbiton KT5 198 C3
Wembley HA9 66 B4
West Ewell KT19 215 C2
Manor Dr N KT3, KT4 199 B2
Manor Dr The KT4 199 D1
Manor Farm Ave
TW17 192 D3
Manor Farm Cl KT4 199 C1
Manor Farm Ct E6 100 B4
Manor Farm Dr E4 20 C1
Manor Farm Rd
Thornton Heath CR7,
SW16 182 C1
Wembley HA0 87 D5
Manorfield Cl 3 N19 71 C4
Manorfield Prim Sch
E14 97 D2
Manorfields Cl BR7 211 D6
Manor Gate UB5 63 A1
Manorgate Rd KT2 176 C2
Manor Gdns
8 Chiswick W4 111 C1
Clapham SW4 137 C3
Gunnersbury W3 110 C2
Hampton TW12 174 A3
Merton SW20 179 B1
Richmond TW10, TW9 132 B1
Ruislip HA4 62 C3
South Croydon CR2 221 D2
Sunbury TW16 172 A1
Upper Holloway N7 72 A5
Manor Gr
Beckenham BR3 185 D1
Deptford SE15 140 C6
Richmond TW9 132 C2
Manor Gt SW15 157 A6
Manor Hall Ave NW4 28 D1
Manor Hall Dr NW4 28 D1
Manor Hall Gdns E10 53 C1
Manor Ho
Brentford TW8 109 C1
Manor Pk E12 77 D4
Osidge N14 15 D3
Paddington NW1 237 B4
Twickenham TW2 152 C2
Wallington SM6 219 B3
Manor Ho The
Bexley DA5 169 D3
Chislehurst SE9 188 A5
Manor House Ct
Lower Halliford
TW17 192 D2
Paddington W9 236 A5
Manor House Dr NW6 68 D1
Manor House Est HA7 25 B5
Manor House Gdns E11 55 B3
Manor House Sta N4 50 D1
Manor House Way
TW7 131 B2
Manor Jun & Inf Schs
IG11 79 D2
Manor La
Feltham TW13 150 A2
Harlington UB3 127 B6
Hither Green SE12 164 C5
Sunbury TW16 172 B1
Sutton SM1 218 A3
Manor Lane Terr
SE13 164 C6
Manor Lo NW2 68 D2
Manor Mans
7 Hampstead NW3 70 C2
Tufnell Pk N7 72 A5
Manor Mead Sch
TW17 192 D4
Manor Mews
New Cross SE4 141 B3
Paddington NW6 91 C5
Manor Mount SE23 162 C3
Manor Oak Mans
SE22 162 B5
Manor Par Harrow HA1 42 D3
Stoke Newington N16 73 D6
MANOR PARK 78 A4
Manor Park Cl BR4 207 D1
Manor Park Cres HA8 26 C4
Manor Park Dr HA2 41 D6
Manor Park Gdns HA8 26 C4
Manor Park Par SE13 142 B1
Manor Park Prim Sch
SM1 218 A3
Manor Park Rd
Chislehurst BR7 189 B2
Dagenham NW10 89 D6
East Finchley N2 48 B6
Manor Pk E12 77 D4
Sutton SM1 218 A3
West Wickham BR4 207 D1
Manor Park Sta E12 77 D4
Manor Pk
Chislehurst BR7 189 B2
Lewisham SE13 164 C6
Richmond TW9 132 B1
Manor Pl
Chislehurst BR7 189 B1
East Bedfont TW14 150 A3
Mitcham CR4 203 C6
Newington
SE17 117 A1 262 A2
Sutton SM1 217 D4
Walton-on-T KT12 194 A2
Manor Prim Sch E15 98 C5
Manor Rd
Ashford TW15 170 C5
Manor Rd *continued*
Barking IG11 79 D2
Barnet EN5 1 A1
Beckenham BR3 185 D1
Belmont SM2 217 B1
Bowes Pk N22 32 A4
Dagenham RM6 58 D3
Ealing W13 109 A6
East Molesey KT8 196 B5
Enfield EN2 5 B3
Harrow HA1 43 A3
Hayes UB3 84 A1
Higham Hill E17 35 A1
Loughton IG10 21 B5
Merton SW20 179 B1
Mitcham CR4 203 C6
Newham E15, E16 98 C4
Old Bexley DA5 169 D3
Richmond TW10, TW9 132 B1
Ruislip HA4 39 B1
Sidcup DA15 168 A1
South Norwood SE25 206 A6
Stamford Hill N16 51 C1
Teddington TW11 175 B5
Tottenham N17 34 B2
Twickenham TW2 152 B2
Wallington SM5, SM6 219 B3
Walthamstow E10 53 C2
Walton-on-T KT12 193 D2
West Wickham BR4 223 D6
Manor Rd N
Hinchley Wood KT7 213 A6
Wallington SM5, SM6 219 B4
Manor Rd S KT10 212 C4
Manor Road Ho HA1 43 A3
Manor Sch NW10 90 C6
Manorside EN5 1 A1
Manorside Cl SE2 124 D2
Manorside Prim Sch
N3 30 A2
Manor Sq RM8 80 C6
Manor Street Est SW3 267 B6
Manor The
Dulwich SE23 162 C4
Mayfair W1 248 C5
Manor Vale TW8 109 C1
Manor View N3 29 D1
Manorway Enfield EN1 17 C4
Woodford IG8 37 C5
Manor Way
Beckenham BR3 207 C6
Bromley BR2 210 A3
Chingford E4 36 B6
Colindale NW9 45 C5
Greenwich SE3 143 A1
Gunnersbury W3 110 C2
Harrow HA2 41 D5
Mitcham CR4 203 C6
New Malden KT4 199 D1
Orpington BR5 211 A5
Ruislip HA4 39 D1
Sidcup DA5 169 C3
Southall UB2 106 D2
South Croydon CR2 221 D2
Manor Waye UB8 82 A6
Manor Way The SM6 219 B4
Manpreet Ct E12 78 B3
Manray Ct 2 N8 50 A4
Manresa Rd
SW3 114 C1 257 A1
Mansard Beeches
SW17 181 A5
Mansard Cl HA5 40 D6
Mansard Manor 4
SM2 218 A1
Manse Cl UB3 127 B6
Manse Ct DA14 190 C5
Mansel Ct SW11 267 B1
Mansel Gr E17 35 C2
Mansell Ho SW8 269 B2
Mansell Rd Acton W3 111 B4
Southall UB6 85 D2
Mansell St E1 95 D1 243 D1
Mansel Rd SW19 179 B4
Manse Rd N16 73 D5
Mansergh Cl SE18 144 A5
Mansfield Ave
East Barnet EN4 15 A5
Ruislip HA4 40 B1
Tottenham N15 51 B5
Mansfield Cl N9 18 A5
Mansfield Ct 27 E2 95 D6
Mansfield Dr UB4 83 C3
Mansfield Hill E4 19 D3
Mansfield Ho SW15 156 D5
Mansfield Hts N2 48 D4
Mansfield Mews W1 238 C3
Mansfield Pl 28 NW3 70 A4
Mansfield Rd Acton W3 88 D3
Chessington KT9 213 D3
Ilford IG1 78 C6
Maitland Pk NW3 70 D4
South Croydon CR2 221 B2
Walthamstow E17 53 B5
Wanstead E11 55 B3
Mansfield St
W1 93 B2 238 C3
Mansford St E2 96 A5
Manship Rd CR4 181 A2
Mansion Cl SW9 138 C4
Mansion Gdns NW3 69 D5
Mansion Ho* EC4 242 C1
Mansion House Pl EC3,
EC4 242 C1
Mansion House St EC2 242 C1
Mansion House Sta
EC4 117 A6 252 B6
Mansions The NW6 69 B3
Manson Mews
SW7 114 B2 256 C3
Manson Pl
SW7 114 B2 256 C3
Manstead Gdns RM6 58 C2
Manston
Camden Town NW1 71 C1
Tottenham N17 33 B1
Manston Ave UB2 107 C2
Manston Cl SE20 184 C2
Manstone Rd NW2 69 A3
Manston Gr KT2 175 D5
Manston Ho W14 254 B5
Mantell Ho SW4 159 C6
Manthorpe Rd SE18 123 A1
Mantilla Rd SW17 181 A6
Mantle Rd SE4 141 A2
Mantlet Cl SW16 181 C3
Mantle Way E15 76 C1
Manton Ave W7 109 A4
Manton Cl UB3 105 C6
Manton Ho N16 73 B5
Manton Rd Holdbrook EN3 7 C5
Plumstead SE2 124 A2
Mantua St 23 SW11 136 B2
Mantus Cl
Bethnal Green E1 96 C3
19 Stepney E1 96 C3
Mantus Rd E1 96 C3
Manus Way N20 14 A3
Manville Gdns SW17 159 B1
Manville Rd SW17 159 B1
Manwood Rd SE4 163 B5
Manwood St E16 122 B5
Manygate La TW17 193 A3
Many Gates SW12 159 B2
Mapesbury Ct NW2 69 A3
Mapesbury Mews 1
NW9 46 A3
Mapesbury Rd NW2 69 A2
Mapeshill Pl NW2 68 C2
Mapes Ho 7 NW6 69 A1
Mape St E2 96 B3
Maple Ave
East Acton W3 111 C5
Harrow HA2 63 D6
Walthamstow E4 35 B4
Yiewsley UB7 104 B6
Maple Cl
Buckhurst Hill IG9 21 D1
Clapham Pk SW4 159 D5
Finchley N3 29 C4
Hampton TW12 173 B4
Hayes UB4 84 D4
Mitcham CR4 181 B2
Petts Wood BR5 211 B4
Ruislip HA4 40 B3
South Tottenham N16 52 A3
Maple Cres DA15 168 A5
Maplecroft Cl E6 100 A1
Maple Ct Ashford TW15 171 B3
Catford SE6 163 D3
2 Croydon CR0 221 A4
7 Dagenham RM8 58 D2
Kingston u T KT3 199 B6
Newham E6 100 C2
6 Pinner HA5 22 C1
Sidcup DA14 190 B5
11 West Norwood
SW16 182 C5
3 Willesden NW2 68 D4
Mapledale Ave CR0 222 A5
Mapledene BR7 189 A5
Mapledene Est E8 74 A1
Mapledene Rd E8 74 A1
Mapledown Sch NW2 46 C2
Mapledurham Ct 3
N13 32 C6
Maple Gdns
Grahame Pk HA8 27 C3
Stanwell TW19 148 A2
Maple Gr
Brentford TW8 131 B5
Ealing W5 109 D3
Kingsbury NW9 45 A2
Southall UB1 85 B2
Maple Gr Bsns Ctr
TW4 128 C1
Maple Ho
2 Kingston u T KT6 198 A4
11 Maitland Pk NW3 70 D2
5 New Cross SE8 141 B5
4 Richmond TW9 132 D4
Teddington KT1 175 C3
13 Walthamstow E17 53 D6
Maplehurst 2 BR2 186 C1
Maplehurst Cl KT1 198 A5
Maple Ind Est TW13 150 A1
Maple Inf Sch KT6 197 D4
Maple Leaf Dr DA15 167 D3
Mapleleaf Gdns IG6 56 D6
Maple Leaf Sq 27
SE16 118 D4
Maple Lo
Buckhurst Hill IG9 21 D3
Putney SW15 157 A5
Welsh Harp NW9 67 B6
Maple Mews
Paddington NW6 91 D5
Streatham SW16 182 B5
Maple Pl
Marylebone W1 239 B5
Tottenham N17 34 A3
Yiewsley UB7 104 B6
Maple Rd Hayes UB4 84 D4
Kingston u T KT6 197 D4
Leytonstone E11 54 C3
Penge SE20 184 C2
Maples Pl E1 96 B2
Maple St
5 Bethnal Green E2 96 B5
Fitzrovia W1 93 C3 239 B5
Maplestead Rd
Dagenham RM9 102 B6
Streatham SW2 160 B4
Maples The 4 KT1 175 C3
Maplethorpe Rd CR7 204 D5
Mapleton Cl BR2 209 A3
Mapleton Cres
Enfield EN3 6 C5
Wandsworth SW18 157 D5
Mapleton Rd
Chingford E4 20 A1
Enfield EN1 6 B3
Wandsworth SW18 157 D5
Maple Tree Pl 7 SE3 144 A4
Maple Way TW13 150 B1
Maple Wlk W10 90 D3
Maplin Cl N21 16 B5
Maplin Ho 7 SE2 124 D4
Maplin Rd E16 99 B1
Maplin St E3 97 B4
Mapperley Cl 3 E11 55 A3
Mapperley Dr IG8 36 C3
Marabou Cl E12 78 A3
Marada Ho NW6 69 A1
Marais W4 133 A5
Maran Way DA18 124 D3
Marathon Way SE28 123 D4
Marban Rd W9 91 B4
Marble Arch*
W1 114 D6 247 D6
Marble Arch Sta
W1 92 D1 237 D1
Marble Cl W3 110 D5
Marble Dr NW2 46 D2
Marbleford Ct 4 N6 49 D2
Marble Hill* TW1 153 C4
Marble Hill Cl TW1 153 B4
Marble Hill Gdns TW1 153 B4
Marble Ho
Paddington W9 91 B3
Plumstead Comm SE18 123 D1
Marble Quay SE1 118 A5
Marbrook Ct SE12 165 C1
Marcella Rd SW9 138 C3
Marcellina Way BR6 227 D5
March 23 NW9 27 D2
Marchant Ho 13 SW2 160 B6
Marchant Rd E11 76 B6
Marchant St SE14 141 A6
Marchbank Rd
W14 135 B6 264 D6
March Ct SW15 134 B1
Marchmont Ho 10
SW16 181 C5
Marchmont Rd
Richmond TW10 154 B6
Wallington SM6 219 C1
Marchmont St
WC1 94 A3 240 A6
March Rd 7 TW1 153 A4
Marchside Cl TW5 128 D4
Marchwood Cl 9 SE5 139 C5
Marchwood Cres W5 87 D1
Marcia Rd SE1 117 C2 263 B3
Marcilly Rd SW18 158 B6
Marcol Ho W1 238 D2
Marcon Ct 29 E8 74 B3
Marconi Pl N11 31 B6
Marconi Rd E10 53 C1
Marconi Way UB1 85 D1
Marcon Pl E8 74 B3
Marco Rd W6 112 C3
Marcourt Lawns W5 88 A3
Marcus Ct
Brentford TW8 132 A5
Newham E15 98 C6
Marcus Garvey Mews
SE22 162 B6
Marcus Garvey Way 9
SE24 138 C1
Marcus Ho 14 SE15 139 D4
Marcus St
Wandsworth SW18 157 D5
West Ham E15 98 D6
Marcus Terr SW18 157 D5
Mardale Ct NW7 28 A3
Mardale Dr NW9 45 B4
Mardell Rd CR0 206 D4
Marden Ave BR2 209 A3
Marden Cres CR0 204 B3
Marden Ho 6 E8 74 B3
Marden Rd
Thornton Heath CR0 204 B3
Tottenham N17 33 C1
Marden Sq SE16 118 B3
Marder Rd W13 109 A4
Mardon HA5 23 B3
Mardyke Ho SE17 262 D4
Marechal Niel Ave
DA15 167 B1
Marechal Niel Par
DA15 167 B1
Maresby Ho E4 19 D2
Maresfield CR0 221 C5
Maresfield Gdns NW3 70 A2
Mare St E8 74 B1
Marey Ct 10 CR2 221 A3
Marfleet Cl SM5 218 C6
Margaret Ave E4 19 D5
Margaret Bondfield Ave
IG11 80 A1
Margaret Bondfield Ho
5 Bow E3 97 A5
22 Kentish Town N7 71 D3
Margaret Ct Barnet EN4 2 B1
Marylebone W1 239 A2
Margaret Gardner Dr
SE9 166 B2
Margaret Herbison Ho
SW6 264 D5
Margaret Hill Ho 1 N8 50 A4
Margaret Ho
16 Hammersmith W6 112 C1
2 Sutton SM1 217 D5
Margaret Ingram Cl
SW6 264 C5
Margaret Lockwood Cl
KT5 198 B5
Margaret Mcmillan Ho 10
N19 49 D2
Margaret Rd Barnet EN4 2 B1
Bexley DA5 168 D5
Stamford Hill N16 51 D1
Margarets Ct HA8 26 D5
Margaret's Ct E11 54 C2
Margaret St W1 93 C1 239 A2
Margaretta Terr
SW3 136 C6 267 B6
Margaretting Rd E12 55 C1
Margaret Way IG4 56 A3
Margaret White Ho
NW1 232 C2
Margate Rd SW2 160 A6
Margery Fry Ct N7 72 A5
Margery Park Rd E7 77 A2
Margery Rd RM8 80 D5
Margery St WC1 94 C4 234 A1
Margin Dr SW19 178 D6
Margravine Gdns
Hammersmith W6 112 D1
West Kensington W14 254 A2
Margravine Rd
W6 135 A6 264 A6
Marham Gdns
Morden SM4 202 A3
Wandsworth SW17,
SW18 158 C3
Mar Ho 4 SE7 143 C6
Maria Cl 13 SE1 118 A2
Maria Fidelis Convent Sch
(Lower) NW1 93 C4 232 B1
Maria Fidelis Convent Sch
(Upper) NW1 93 D4 232 C2
Marian Cl UB4 84 D3
Marian Ct Hackney E9 74 C3
1 Sutton SM1 217 D3
Marian Lo 5 SW20 178 D3
Marian Pl E2 96 B5
Marian Rd SW16 181 C2
Marian Sq E2 96 B5
Marian St 2 E2 96 B5
Marian Vian Prim Sch
BR3 207 A4
Marian Way NW10 67 D1
Maria Terr E1 96 D3
Maria Theresa Cl KT3 199 B4
Maribor 13 SE10 142 A5
Maricas Ave HA3 24 B2
Marie Curie SE5 139 C4
Marie Lloyd Ct 13
SW9 138 B1
Marie Lloyd Gdns 1
N19 50 A2
Marie Lloyd Ho N1 235 C3
Marien Ct E4 36 B5
Marie Stopes Ct 3
N19 50 A2
Marigold Cl UB1 107 A6
Marigold Rd N17 34 C3
Marigold St SE16 118 B4
Marigold Way CR0 206 D1
Marilea Ct W5 109 D4
Marillic Ho NW7 28 C6
Marina App UB4 85 A2
Marina Ave KT3 200 B4
Marina Cl 1 BR2 209 A6
Marina Ct 12 Bow E3 97 C4
Greenford UB6 85 D5
Marina Dr DA16 145 C3
Marina Gdns RM7 59 D4
Marina Pl KT1 175 D2
Marina Point 4 E14 119 D3
Marina Way TW11 175 D3
Marine Dr
Barking IG11 102 B4
5 Woolwich SE18 122 B2
Marinefield Rd SW6 135 D3
Marinel Ho 25 SE5 139 A5
Mariner Gdns TW10 153 C1
Mariner Rd E12 78 C4
Mariners Mews E14 120 B2
Marine St SE16 118 A3
Marine Twr 29 SE8 141 B6
Marion Ave TW17 192 D4
Marion Ct 4 SW17 180 C5
Marion Gr IG8 36 C6
Marion Rd Mill Hill NW7 28 A5
Thornton Heath CR0 205 B4
Marion Richardson Prim
Sch E1 96 D1
Marischal Rd SE13 142 B2
Maritime Ho
5 Clapham SW4 137 C2
14 Woolwich SE18 122 D2
Maritime Ind Est SE7 121 B2
Maritime Quay 5 E14 119 C1
Maritime St E3 97 B3
Marius Mans 3 SW17 159 A2
Marius Rd SW17 159 A2
Marjorie Gr SW11 136 D1
Marjorie McClure Sch
BR7 189 A2
Marjory Kinnon Sch
TW14 149 C6
Markab Rd HA6 22 A5
Mark Ave E4 19 D5
Mark Cl
Bexleyheath DA7 147 A4
Keston Mark BR2 226 A4
Southall UB1 107 D5
Markeston Gn WD19 22 D6
Market Ct W1 239 A2
Market Ctr The UB2 106 B2
Market La
Burnt Oak HA8 27 A2
Shepherd's Bush W12 112 C4
Market Mews
W1 115 B5 248 C3
Market Par
Croydon SE25 206 A5
1 Edmonton N9 18 A2
Feltham TW13 151 A2
Leyton E10 53 D3
Walthamstow E17 53 B6
Market Pavilion E10 75 C5
Market Pl 3 Acton W3 111 A5
1 Bermondsey SE16 118 B2
2 Bexleyheath DA6 147 C1
Brentford TW8 131 C5
East Finchley N2 48 C6
Enfield EN2 5 B2
Kingston u T KT1 175 D1
Marylebone W1 239 A2
Market Pl The NW11 47 D5
Market Rd Barnsbury N7 72 A2
Richmond TW9 132 C2
Market Sq
Bromley BR1 187 A1
Poplar E14 97 D1
Market Sq The N9 18 B2
Market St
Spitalfields E1 243 C4
Wallend E6 100 C5
Woolwich SE18 122 C2
Market Studios 14
W12 112 C4
Market The SM1, SM5 202 A1
Market Way Poplar E14 97 D1
2 Wembley HA0 66 A3
Market Yd Mews SE1 263 A6
Markfield Beam Engine &
Mus* N15 52 A4
Markfield Gdns E4 19 D4
Markfield Ho N15 52 A4
Markfield Rd N15 52 A4
Markham Ct NW4 46 C6
Markham Ho
1 Dagenham RM10 81 C5
9 Dulwich SE21 183 C6
Markham Pl SW3 257 C2
Markham Sq
SW3 114 D1 257 C2
Markham St
SW3 114 C1 257 B2
Mark Ho 3 E2 96 D5
Markhole Cl TW12 173 B3
Markhouse Ave E17 53 A3
Markhouse Pas E17 53 B3
Markhouse Rd E17 53 B3
Mark La EC3 117 C6 253 B6
Markland Ho W10 112 D6
Mark Lo 9 EN4 2 C1
Markmanor Ave E17 53 B2
Mark Mans W12 112 A4
Mark Rd N22 32 D1
Marksbury Ave TW9 132 C2
Marks Gate Jun & Inf Schs
RM6 59 A6
Mark Sq EC2 243 A6
Mark St Broadgate EC2 243 A6
Stratford E15 76 C1
Markstone Ho SE1 251 C1
Mark Wade Cl E12 55 D1
Markway The TW16 172 C1
Markwell Cl SE26 184 B6
Markyate Ho 6 W10 90 C3
Markyate Rd RM8 80 B3
Marland Ho SW1 257 D6
Marlands Rd IG5 56 B6
Marlang Ct BR3 186 B2
Marlborough
11 Putney SW19 156 D3
St John's Wood W9 229 A2
Marlborough Ave
Edgware HA8 10 D1
3 Hackney E8 96 A6
New Southgate N14 15 C1
Ruislip HA4 39 B3
Marlborough Cl
Broom Hill BR6 211 D3
Friern Barnet N20 14 D1
Mitcham SW19 180 C4
Newington SE17 261 D3
Marlborough Cres
Bedford Pk W4 111 C3
Harlington UB3 127 B5
Marlborough Ct
6 Beckenham BR3 185 C2
7 Bromley BR1 186 D3
7 Buckhurst Hill IG9 21 C2
Harrow HA1 42 B5
Kensington W8 255 A4
Marylebone W1 239 A1
Wallington SM6 219 C1
Marlborough Day Hospl
NW8 92 A5 229 A4
Marlborough Dr IG5 56 A6
Marlborough Flats
SW3 257 B4
Marlborough Fst & Mid
Sch HA1 42 C5
Marlborough Gdns
Friern Barnet N20 14 D1
Surbiton KT6 197 D2
Marlborough Gr SE1 118 A1
Marlborough Hill
Harrow HA1 42 C5
St John's Wood
NW8 92 A6 229 B5

Mar–May 345

Marlborough Ho
Marylebone NW1 238 D6
Richmond TW10 154 C6
Stoke Newington N4 51 A1
Marlborough Ho SW1 249 B3
Marlborough Ho SW19 156 D1
Marlborough La SE7 143 C5
Marlborough Lo
36 Stepney E1 96 C3
St John's Wood NW8 229 A3
Marlborough Mans 5 NW6 69 C3
Marlborough Mews 18 SW2 138 B1
Marlborough Par 1 UB10 82 D3
Marlborough Park Ave DA15 168 A3
Marlborough Pl NW8 92 A5 229 B4
Marlborough Prim Sch Chelsea SW3 114 C2 257 B3
Isleworth TW7 131 A4
Marlborough Rd
Acton Green W4 111 A1
Ashford TW15 170 A5
Bexley DA7 146 D2
Bowes Pk N22 32 B4
Brentford TW7 131 B5
Bromley BR2 209 C5
Chingford E4 35 D4
Dagenham RM8 80 C4
Ealing W5 109 D4
Edmonton N9 18 A3
Feltham TW13 150 D2
Hampton TW12 173 C4
Hillingdon UB10 82 D4
Leyton E15 76 C4
Mitcham SW19 180 C4
Richmond TW10 154 B5
Romford RM7 59 D5
Southall UB2 106 C3
South Croydon CR2 221 A1
St James SW1 115 C5 249 B3
Sutton SM1 217 C6
Upper Holloway N19 72 A6
Upton E7 77 C1
Wanstead E18 55 A6
Woolwich SE18 123 A3
Marlborough Sch DA15 168 A4
Marlborough St SW3 114 C2 257 B3
Marlborough Trad Est TW9 132 D4
Marlborough Yd N19 71 D6
Marlbury NW8 91 D6
Marler Rd SE23 163 B3
Marlesford Ct SM6 219 C4
Marlex Lo N3 29 D2
Marley Ave DA7 146 D6
Marley Cl Harringay N15 50 D5
Southall UB6 85 C4
Marley Ho 14 W11 112 D6
Marley Wlk NW2 68 C3
Marl Field Cl KT4 200 A1
Marlfield Ct KT3 199 D2
Marlin Cl TW16 171 C4
Marlin Ct 5 DA14 190 A6
Marling Ct TW12 173 B4
Marlingdene Cl TW12 173 C4
Marlings Cl BR7 211 C5
Marlings Park Ave BR7 211 C6
Marlin Ho SW15 157 A6
Marlins Cl 3 SM1 218 A3
Marloes Cl HA0 65 D4
Marloes Rd W8 113 D3 255 C5
Marlow Cl SE20 206 B6
Marlow Cres TW1 152 D5
Marlow Ct
Colindale NW9 45 D6
1 Ealing W7 108 C5
6 Finchley N3 29 C2
Harrow HA1 42 A3
Osidge N14 15 C4
Willesden NW6 68 D1
Marlow Dr SM3 216 D5
Marlowe Bsns Ctr 2 SE14 141 A5
Marlowe Cl BR7 189 B4
Marlowe Ct
Chelsea SW3 257 B3
2 Dulwich SE19 183 D5
6 Kingston u T KT2 175 D6
Marlowe Gdns SE9 166 C5
Marlowe Ho
Kingston u T KT1 197 D5
15 Stoke Newington N16 73 C4
Marlowe Lo CR0 223 A6
Marlowe Rd E17 54 A5
Marlowe Sq CR4 203 C5
Marlowes The NW8 92 B6 229 C6
Marlowe Way CR0 220 A6
Marlow Gdns UB3 105 B3
Marlow Ho
Bermondsey SE1 263 C6
15 Kensington W2 91 D1
44 Spitalfields E2 95 D4
Teddington TW11 175 A6
Wallington CR0 220 A5
Marlow Rd Newham E6 100 B4
Penge SE20 184 B1
Southall UB2 107 B3
Marlow Studio Workshops 43 E2 95 D4
Marlow Way SE16 118 D4
Marl Rd SW18 136 A1
Marlston NW1 231 D1
Marlton St SE10 120 D1
Marlwood Cl DA15 167 C2
Marmadon Rd SE18, SE2 123 D2
Marmara Apts 4 E16 121 A6
Marmion App E4 35 C6
Marmion Ave E4 35 B6
Marmion Cl E4 35 B6
Marmion Ho 13 SW12 159 B4
Marmion Mews 4 SW11 137 A2
Marmion Rd SW11 137 A1
Marmont Rd SE15 140 A5
Marmora Ho E1 97 A2
Marmora Rd SE22 162 C5
Marmot Rd TW4 128 D2
Marncrest Ct KT5 198 B4
Marne Ave
Friern Barnet N11 31 B6
Welling DA16 146 A2
Marnell Way TW4 128 D2
Marner Prim Sch E3 97 D3
Marne St W10 91 A4
Marney Rd SW11 137 A1
Marnfield Cres SW2 160 B3
Marnham Ave NW2 69 A4
Marnham Cres UB6 85 D5
Marnham Ct HA0 65 C3
Marnie Ct 11 E11 76 C6
Marnock Ho SE17 262 C2
Marnock Rd SE4 163 B6
Maroon St E14 97 A2
Maroons Way SE6 185 C5
Marqueen Twrs 1 SW16 182 B3
Marquess Rd N1 73 B2
Marquess Rd N N1 73 B2
Marquess Rd S 22 N1 73 A2
Marquis Cl HA0 66 B1
Marquis Ct Barking IG11 79 C3
Finsbury Pk N4 50 B1
1 Kingston u T KT1 198 A5
Stanwell TW19 148 A3
Marquis Rd
Bowes Pk N22 32 B4
Finsbury Pk N4 50 C1
Kentish Town NW1 71 D2
Marrabon Cl DA15 168 A3
Marrick Cl SW15 134 A1
Marrick Ho 19 NW6 91 D6
Marrilyne Ave EN3 7 B5
Marriner Ct UB3 105 C6
Marriott Cl TW14 149 B5
Marriott Ho 8 SE6 186 A6
Marriott Rd
Finsbury Pk N4 50 B1
Muswell Hill N10 30 D2
Newham E15 98 C6
Marriotts Cl NW9 45 D3
Marryat Cl TW3 129 B1
Marryat Ct 12 W6 112 B2
Marryat Ho SW1 259 A1
Marryat Pl SW19 179 A6
Marryat Rd SW19 179 A6
Marryat Sq SW6 264 A2
Marryatt Ct W5 88 B1
Marsala Rd SE13 141 D1
Marsalis Ho 3 E3 97 C4
Marsden Rd
Camberwell SE15 139 D2
Edmonton N9 18 B2
Marsden St NW5 71 A2
Marsden Way 2 BR6 227 D4
Marshall Cl
Brunswick Pk N11 15 B1
Harrow HA1 42 B2
Hounslow TW4 151 B6
Wandsworth SW18 158 A5
Marshall Ct SW4 270 B1
Marshall Dr UB4 83 D2
Marshall Ho
5 New Malden KT3 199 C5
Paddington NW6 91 B5
Shoreditch N1 235 D4
Walworth SE17 262 C2
Marshall Path 10 SE28 124 B6
Marshall Rd Leyton E10 75 D4
Tottenham N17 33 B2
Marshalls Gr SE18 122 A2
Marshall's Pl SE16 263 D5
Marshall's Rd SM1 217 D4
Marshall St W1 93 C1 239 B1
Marshalsea Rd SE1 117 A4 252 B2
Marsham Cl BR7 188 D5
Marsham Ct
19 Putney SW19 156 D3
Westminster SW1 259 D4
Marsham St SW1 115 D2 259 D4
Marsh Ave CR4 181 A1
Marshbrook Cl SE3 143 D2
Marsh Cl NW7 11 D1
Marsh Ct Dalston E8 74 A2
3 Merton SW19 180 A2
Marsh Dr NW9 45 D3
Marsh Farm Rd TW2 152 D3
Marshfield St E14 120 A3
Marsh Gate Bsns Ctr E15 98 A5
Marshgate Ctr The E15 97 D6
Marshgate La E15 75 D1
Marshgate Prim Sch TW10 154 B6
Marsh Green Prim Sch RM10 103 C5
Marsh Green Rd RM10 103 C6
Marsh Hall HA9 66 B5
Marsh Hill E9 75 A3
Marsh Ho
Nine Elms SW8 269 B2
Pimlico SW1 259 D1
Marsh La Edgware NW7 11 C1
Leyton E10 75 C6
Stanmore HA7 25 C4
Tottenham N17 34 B2
Marsh Point HA5 41 B5
Marsh Rd Pinner HA5 41 A5
Wembley HA0 87 D5
Marshside Cl N9 18 C3
Marsh St E14 119 D2
Marsh Wall E14 119 D4
Marshwood Ho 10 NW6 91 C6
Marsland Cl SE17 261 D1
Marsom Ho N1 235 C3
Marston SE17 262 B4
Marston Ave
Chessington KT9 214 A2
Dagenham RM10 81 C5
Marston Cl
Dagenham RM10 81 C5
South Hampstead NW6 70 A1
Marston Ct Barnet EN5 13 C6
Sidcup DA14 189 D6
Walton-on-T KT12 194 C1
Marston Ho 23 SW9 138 C3
Marston Rd TW11 175 B5
Marston Way SE19 183 A3
Marsworth Ave HA5 22 D2
Marsworth Cl UB4 85 A2
Marsworth Ho 8 E2 96 A6
Martaban Rd N16 73 D6
Martello St E8 74 B1
Martello Terr E8 74 B1
Martell Rd SE21 161 B1
Martel Pl E8 73 D2
Marten Rd E17 35 C1
Martens Ave DA7 147 D1
Martham Cl SE28 124 D6
Martha Rd E15 76 C2
Martha's Bldgs EC1 242 C6
Martha St E1 96 C1
Marthorne Cres HA3 24 B1
Martin Bowes Rd SE9 144 B2
Martinbridge Trad Est EN1 18 A6
Martin Cl
Lower Edmonton N9 18 D3
Uxbridge UB10 82 A5
Martin Cres CR0 204 C1
Martin Ct
15 Cubitt Town E14 120 A4
Lewisham SE12 164 D4
Merton SW19 179 C3
Southall UB2 107 B4
Martindale SW14 155 A6
Martindale Ave 2 E16 121 A6
Martindale Ho 23 E14 119 D6
Martindale Rd
Balham SW12 159 B4
Hounslow TW4 129 A2
Martin Dene DA6 169 B6
Martin Dr UB5 63 B3
Martineau Cl KT10 212 B4
Martineau Dr TW1 131 B1
Martineau Ho SW1 259 A1
Martineau Mews N5 72 D4
Martineau Rd N5 72 D4
Martingale Cl TW16 194 A5
Martingales Cl TW10 153 D1
Martin Gdns RM8 80 D4
Martin Gr SM4 201 C6
Martin Ho
Newington SE1 262 B5
7 New Malden KT3 199 C5
South Lambeth SW8 270 A4
Martini Dr EN3 7 C6
Martin Jun & Inf Schs N2 30 C1
Martin La EC4 252 D6
Martin Rd RM8 80 D4
Martin Rise DA6 169 B6
Martins Cl BR4 224 B6
Martins Mount EN5 1 D1
Martins Pl SE28 123 C5
Martin's Rd BR2 186 D1
Martin St SE28 123 C5
Martins The
Penge SE26 184 B5
Wembley HA9 66 B5
Martins Wlk
Muswell Hill N10 31 A2
Woolwich SE28 123 C5
Martin Way SW20, SM4 201 B6
Martlesham N17 33 C1
Martlesham Wlk NW9 27 C2
Martlet Gr 5 UB5 84 D4
Martlett Ct WC2 240 B1
Martlett Lo NW3 69 D4
Martley Dr IG2 56 D4
Martley Ho SW8 269 B2
Martock Cl HA3 43 A5
Martock Ct 10 SE15 140 B4
Martock Gdns N11 31 A5
Marton Cl SE6 163 C1
Marton Rd 2 N16 73 C5
Martyn Ct HA8 26 B6
Martyn Ho SE2 146 D6
Martynside 22 NW9 27 D2
Marvel Ho 5 SE5 139 B5
Marvell Ave UB4 84 A2
Marvels Cl SE12 165 B2
Marvels La SE12 165 C1
Marvels Lane Prim Sch SE12 187 C6
Marville Rd SW6 135 B5 264 C3
Marvin Ho 9 SE18 144 D6
Marvin St 8 E8 74 B2
Marwell Cl BR4 224 D6
Marwell Ct SE3 142 B3
Marwick Rd UB7 104 B4
Marwood Cl DA16 146 B2
Marwood Ct N3 29 D3
Marwood Dr NW7 28 D3
Mary Adelaide Cl
Kingston u T SW15 155 C1
Kingston u T SW15 177 C6
Mary Adelaide Ho W2 236 D4
Mary Ann Bldgs SE8 141 C6
Maryatt Ave HA2 63 D6
Marybank SE18 122 B2
Mary Cl HA7 44 B5
Mary Datchelor Cl SE5 139 B4
Mary Dine Ct SW8 270 D3
Mary Gn NW8 91 D6
Marygold Ho TW3 130 A4
Mary Ho
8 Hammersmith W6 112 C1
6 Stockwell SW9 138 B3
Mary James Ho 32 E2 96 A5
Mary Jones Ho 20 E14 119 C6
Maryland Ct KT1 176 D1
Maryland Pk E15 76 C3
Maryland Point E15 76 C2
Maryland Prim Sch E15 76 C3
Maryland Rd
Paddington W9 91 C3
South Norwood CR7 182 D2
Stratford New Town E15 76 B3
Tottenham N22 32 C4
Marylands Ind Est E15 76 C3
Maryland Sq E15 76 C3
Marylands Rd W9 91 D3
Maryland St E15 76 C3
Maryland Sta E15 76 C2
Maryland Way TW16 172 A1
Maryland Wlk N1 235 A6
Mary Lawrenson Pl 1 SE3 143 A5
MARYLEBONE 93 B1
Marylebone Ct 3 HA0 66 A2
Marylebone Flyover NW1 92 C2 237 A3
Marylebone High St W1 93 A2 238 B4
Marylebone La W1 93 A1 238 B2
Marylebone Mews W1 238 C3
Marylebone Pas W1 239 B2
Marylebone Rd NW1 92 D2 237 D4
Marylebone St W1 93 A2 238 B3
Marylebone Sta NW1 92 D3 237 C5
Marylee Way SE11 116 B2 260 D3
Mary McArthur Ho 12 N19 49 D2
Mary Macarthur Ho
8 Belvedere DA17 125 C3
11 Dagenham RM10 81 C5
15 Globe Town E2 96 D4
W14 264 A6
Marymount International Sch KT2 177 A3
Maryon Gr SE7 122 A2
Maryon Mews NW3 70 C4
Maryon Rd SE7 122 A2
Mary Peters Dr UB6 64 B3
Mary Pl W11 113 A6 244 A5
Mary Rose Cl TW12 173 C2
Mary Rose Mall E6 100 B2
Maryrose Way N20 14 B3
Mary's Ct NW8 237 B6
Mary Seacole Villas 19 NW10 67 B1
Mary Secole Cl 21 E8 95 D6
Mary Smith Ct SW5 255 B3
Mary St
5 Canning Town E16 98 D2
Shoreditch N1 95 A6 235 B5
Mary's Terr TW1 153 A4
Mary Tates Cotts CR4 202 D5
Mary Terr NW1 232 A5
Maryville DA16 145 D3
Mary Way WD19 22 C6
Mary Wharrie Ho 4 NW3 70 D1
Marzena Ct TW2 152 A6
Masbro' Rd W14 112 D3
Mascalls Ct 13 SE7 143 C6
Mascalls Rd SE7 143 C6
Mascotte Rd 2 SW15 134 D1
Mascotts Cl NW2 68 B5
Masefield Ave
Borehamwood WD6 10 D6
Southall UB1 107 C6
Stanmore HA7 24 D5
Masefield Cres N14 15 C5
Masefield Ct
New Barnet EN5 2 A1
Stoke Newington N5 73 B3
19 Surbiton KT6 197 D2
Masefield Gdns E6 100 C3
Masefield Ho 4 NW6 91 C4
Masefield La UB4 84 C3
Masefield Rd TW13 173 B6
Masefield View BR6 227 A5
Masefield Way TW19 148 B3
Masham Ho 13 DA18 124 D4
Mashie Rd W3 89 C1
Maskall Cl SW2 160 C3
Maskani Wlk SW16 181 C3
Maskell Rd SW17 158 A1
Maskelyne Cl SW11 136 C4 267 B2
Mason Cl
Bermondsey SE16 118 A1
Bexleyheath DA7 147 D2
Hampton TW12 173 B2
Newham E16 121 A6
Wimbledon SW20 178 D2
Mason Ct
4 Penge SE19 183 D3
Wembley HA9 66 C6
Mason Ho
15 Bermondsey SE1 118 A2
8 Friern Barnet N11 31 C5
16 Hackney E9 74 C1
Mason Rd Sutton SM1 217 D3
Woodford IG8 36 C6
Mason's Arms Mews W1 248 D6
Masons Ave HA3 42 D5
Mason's Ave
City of London EC2 242 C2
Croydon CR0 221 A5
Masons Hill
Bromley BR2 209 B5
13 Woolwich SE18 122 D2
Masons Ho NW9 44 D4
Mason's Pl
Finsbury EC1 235 A2
Mitcham CR4 180 D2
Mason St SE17 117 B2 262 D4
Mason's Yd
Finsbury EC1 234 D2
St James SW1 249 B4
Wimbledon SW19 178 D5
Massey Cl N11 31 B5
Massey Ct 6 E6 99 C6
Massie Rd E8 74 A2
Massingberd Way SW17 181 B6
Massinger St SE1, SE17 263 A3
Massingham St E1 96 D3
Masson Ave HA4 62 C2
Mast Ct 17 SE16 119 A2
Master Gunner's Pl 1 SE18 144 A4
Masterman Ho 1 SE5 139 B5
Masterman Rd E6 100 A4
Masters Cl SW16 181 C4
Masters Ct HA4 61 C6
Masters Dr SE16 118 B1
Masters Lo 24 E1 96 C1
Master's St 16 E1 96 D2
Mast House Terr E14 119 C2
Mastin Ho SW18 157 C3
Mastmaker Rd E14 119 C4
Maswell Park Cres TW3 152 A6
Maswell Park Rd TW3 130 A1
Matara Mews SE17 262 A1
Matcham Rd E11 76 D5
Matching Ct 14 E3 97 C4
Matchless Dr SE18 144 C5
Matfield Cl BR2 209 A4
Matfield Rd DA17 147 C6
Matham Gr SE22 139 D1
Matham Rd KT8 196 B4
Mathart Ct E4 36 B4
Matheson Lang Ho SE1 251 A1
Matheson Rd W14 113 B2 254 C3
Mathews Ave E6 100 C5
Mathews Park Ave E15 76 D2
Mathews Yd WC2 240 A1
Mathieson Ct SE1 251 D1
Mathieson Ho 10 E4 20 C4
Mathilda Marks-Kennedy Jewish Prim Sch NW7 27 B5
Mathison Ho SW10 266 A4
Matilda Cl SE19 183 B3
Matilda Ho E1 118 A5
Matilda St N1 94 B6 233 D6
Matlock Cl Barnet EN5 12 D6
Herne Hill SE24 139 A1
Matlock Cres SM3 217 A4
Matlock Ct
7 Herne Hill SE5 139 B1
St John's Wood NW8 229 A4
Woodford IG8 36 D2
Matlock Gdns SM1, SM3 217 A4
Matlock Pl SM1, SM3 217 A4
Matlock Rd E10 54 A3
Matlock St E14 97 A1
Matlock Way KT3 177 B2
Maton Ho SW6 264 C4
Matson Ct IG8 36 C3
Matson Ho
9 Bermondsey SE16 118 B3
16 Homerton E9 74 D2
Matthew Cl W10 90 D3
Matthew Ct
Mitcham CR4 203 D4
4 Walthamstow E17 54 A6
Matthew Parker St SW1 249 D1
Matthews Ct N5 73 A4
Matthews Ho 3 E14 97 C2
Matthews Rd UB6 64 B3
Matthews St SW11 136 D3
Matthias Ct 12 TW10 154 A5
Matthias Ho 2 N16 73 C3
Matthias Rd N16 73 C3
Mattingly Way 3 SE15 139 D5
Mattison Rd N4 50 D3
Mattock La W5, W13 109 C5
Maud Cashmore Way SE18 122 B3
Maude Ho 3 E2 96 A5
Maude Rd
Camberwell SE5 139 C4
Walthamstow E17 53 A4
Maudesville Cotts W7 108 C5
Maude Terr E17 53 A5
Maud Gdns
Barking IG11 101 D5
Newham E13 98 D5
Maudlins Gn E1 118 A5
Maud Rd Leyton E10 76 A5
Newham E13 98 D5
Maudslay Rd SE9 144 B2
Maudsley Ho TW8 110 A1
Maudsley Hospl The SE5 139 B3
Maud St E16 98 D2
Maud Wilkes Cl 10 NW5 71 C3
Maugham Ct 5 W3 111 A3
Mauleverer Rd SW2 160 A6
Maultway Ct KT19 215 B3
Maundeby Wlk NW10 67 C2
Maunder Rd 4 W7 108 D5
Maunsel St SW1 115 D2 259 C4
Maureen Campbell Ct TW17 192 D4
Maurer Ct 2 SE10 120 D3
Mauretania Bldg 11 E1 118 D6
Maurice Ave N22 32 D1
Maurice Browne Cl NW7 28 D4
Maurice Ct
3 Brentford TW8 131 D5
4 Mile End E1 97 A4
Wood Green N22 32 C2
Maurice Ho
Hither Green SE12 164 D5
1 Stockwell SW9 138 B3
Maurice St W12 90 B1
Maurice Wlk NW11 48 A5
Maurier Cl UB5 84 C6
Mauritius Rd SE10 120 C2
Maury Rd N16 74 A5
Mauveine Gdns TW3 129 C1
Mavelstone Cl BR1 188 A2
Mavelstone Rd BR1 188 A2
Maverton Rd E3 97 C6
Mavery Ct 5 BR1 186 D3
Mavis Ave KT19 215 C3
Mavis Cl KT19 215 C3
Mavis Ct 33 NW9 27 D1
Mavis Wlk 9 E6 100 A2
Mavor Ho N1 233 D5
Mawbey Ho SE1 263 D1
Mawbey Pl SE1 117 D1 263 D1
Mawbey Rd SE1 263 D1
Mawbey St SW8 270 A3
Mawdley Ho SE1 251 B1
Mawney Cl RM7 59 D6
Mawney Rd RM7 59 D6
Mawson Cl SW20 179 A1
Mawson Ct N1 235 D5
Mawson Ho EC1 241 A4
Mawson La W4 133 D6
Maxden Ct SE15 140 A2
Maxey Gdns RM9 81 A4
Maxey Rd
Dagenham RM9 81 A4
Plumstead SE18 123 A2
Maxfield Cl N20 14 A4
Maxim Apartments 3 BR2 209 B5
Maxim Rd N21 16 C5
Maxted Pk HA1 42 C2
Maxted Rd SE15 139 D2
Maxwell Cl
Croydon CR0 204 A1
Hayes UB3 106 A6
Maxwell Ct SE21 162 A3
Maxwell Gdns BR6 227 D5
Maxwell Ho
Bowes Pk N22 32 B4
Chislehurst BR7 188 D3
12 Shooters Hill SE18 144 D6
Maxwell Rd
Ashford TW15 171 A4
Fulham SW6 135 D5 265 D3
Welling DA16 146 A2
West Drayton UB7 104 B2
Maxwelton Ave NW7 27 B5
Maxwelton Cl NW7 27 B5
Maya Angelou Ct E4 36 A6
Maya Cl SE15 140 B3
Mayall Cl EN3 7 C5
Mayall Rd SE24 160 D6
Maya Pl N11 31 D3
Maya Rd N2 48 A5
Maybank Ave
Wembley HA0 65 A3
Woodford E18 37 B1
Maybank Gdns HA5 40 A4
Maybank Rd E18 37 C2
May Bate Ave KT2 175 D2
Maybells Commercial Est IG11 102 D5
Mayberry Pl KT5 198 B2

Maybourne Cl SE26 . . . .184 B5
Maybourne Grange
CR0 . . . . .221 C6
Maybrook Ct E11 . . . . . . .77 B6
Maybury Cl Enfield EN1. . . 6 B5
Petts Wood BR5 . . . . . .210 D4
Maybury Ct
Beckenham BR3 . . . . . . .185 B3
Croydon CR2 . . . . .220 D3
Harrow HA1 . . . . .42 B3
Marylebone W1 . . . . 238 B3
Maybury Gdns NW10 . . . 68 B2
Maybury Mews N6. . . . . 49 C2
Maybury Rd
Barking IG11. . . . . .102 A5
Newham E13 . . . . .99 C3
Maybury St SW17 . . . . .180 C5
Maychurch Cl HA7. . . . . .25 D3
May Cl KT9 . . . . .214 B2
Maycroft
2 Hayes BR2. . . . . . . .208 D1
Pinner HA5 . . . . 22 B1
Maycross Ave SM4. . . . .201 C5
May Ct 3 SW19. . . . . . .180 A2
Mayday Gdns SE3. . . . . .144 A3
Mayday Rd CR0, CR7. . . .204 D3
Mayday University Hospl
CR7. . . . . .204 D3
Maydeb Ct RM6. . . . . . . .59 B3
Maydew Ho SE16 . . . . . .118 C2
Maydwell Ho 6 E14 . . . .97 C2
Mayerne Rd SE9 . . . . . .165 D6
Mayesbrook Rd
Barking IG11. . . . . .101 D4
Dagenham RM8, IG3. . . . 80 B5
Mayesford Rd RM6. . . . . 58 C2
Mayespark Prim Sch
IG3. . . . . .80 A5
Mayes Rd N22 . . . . .32 B1
Mayeswood Rd SE12 . . .187 C6
MAYFAIR 115 B6
Mayfair Ave
Bexley DA7 . . . . .146 D4
Dagenham RM6 . . . . 58 D3
Ilford IG1 . . . . .56 C1
New Malden KT4. . . . . . .200 A1
Twickenham TW2. . . . . . .152 A4
Mayfair Cl
Beckenham BR3 . . . . . . .185 D2
Surbiton KT6. . . . . .198 A1
Mayfair Ct
2 Beckenham BR3. . . . .185 D2
7 Croydon CR0 . . . . . .221 D6
Edgware HA8 . . . . .26 B5
13 Wimbledon SW19 . . .179 A3
Mayfair Gdns
Tottenham N17 . . . . .33 B4
Woodford IG8. . . . . .37 A3
Mayfair Ho 11 SE1 . . . .118 A2
Mayfair Pl W1 . . . . 248 B1
Mayfair Terr N14 . . . . . .15 D4
Mayfield DA7. . . . . .147 B2
Mayfield Ave
Broom Hill BR6 . . . . . . .211 D2
Chiswick W4 . . . . .111 C2
Harrow HA3 . . . . .43 B4
North Finchley N12. . . . . .30 B6
Osidge N14 . . . . .15 D2
West Ealing W13. . . . . . .109 B4
Woodford IG8. . . . . .37 A4
Mayfield Cl
Ashford TW15. . . . . .170 D4
Clapham Pk SW4. . . . . . .159 D6
Dalston E8. . . . . .73 D2
Hillingdon UB10 . . . . . . .82 D4
Long Ditton KT7. . . . . . .197 B1
Penge SE20. . . . . .184 B2
Mayfield Cres
Enfield N9 . . . . 18 B5
Thornton Heath CR7 . . . .204 B4
Mayfield Ct SM2. . . . . . .218 A1
Mayfield Dr HA5 . . . . . . 41 B5
Mayfield Gdns
Ealing W7 . . . . .86 C2
Hendon NW4. . . . . .46 D3
Mayfield Ho
31 Bethnal Green E2 . . . .96 B5
Stamford Hill N16. . . . . . .51 C2
Mayfield Mans 4 IG11 . . .78 D1
Mayfield Prim Sch W7. . .86 B1
Mayfield Rd Acton W3 . . .110 D6
Bedford Pk W12 . . . . . . .111 C4
Bromley BR1. . . . . .210 A4
Chingford E4 . . . . .20 B2
Dagenham RM8. . . . . . . .58 C1
Dalston E8. . . . . .73 D1
Enfield EN3 . . . . .6 D3
Higham Hill E17. . . . . . . .35 A1
Hornsey Vale N8. . . . . . .50 B3
Merton SW19 . . . . .179 B2
Newham E13. . . . . .98 D3
South Croydon CR2. . . . .221 B1
Sutton SM2 . . . . .218 B2
Thornton Heath CR7 . . . .204 B4
Mayfields HA9 . . . . .66 C6
Mayfield Sch & Coll
RM8. . . . . .58 C1
Mayfields Cl HA9 . . . . . .66 C6
Mayfield Villas DA14 . . .190 C4
Mayflower Cl
Bermondsey SE16. . . . . .118 C2
Ruislip HA4 . . . . .39 A3
Mayflower Ho 2 IG11. .101 B6
Mayflower Lo
Hendon N3 . . . . .47 B6
Muswell Hill N10. . . . . . .31 A2

Mayflower Prim Sch
E14. . . . . .97 D1
Mayflower Rd SW9 . . . .138 A2
Mayflower St 1 SE16 . .118 C4
Mayfly Cl HA5 . . . . .40 C2
Mayfly Gdns 12 UB5. . . . .84 D4
Mayford
TW7. . . . . .130 D2
Mayford Cl
Balham SW12 . . . . .158 D4
Penge BR3. . . . . .206 D6
Mayford Rd SW12. . . . . .158 D4
May Gdns Elstree WD6 . . . 9 D5
Wembley HA0 . . . . .87 C4
Maygood Ho N1 . . . . . . 234 A4
Maygood St N1. . . 94 C5 234 A4
Maygrove Rd NW6. . . . . 69 B2
Mayhew Cl E4 . . . . .19 C1
Mayhew Ct 2 SE5 . . . . .139 B1
Mayhill Rd Barnet EN5 . . .13 A5
Greenwich SE7 . . . . . . .158 C5
Mayland Mans 4 IG11. . .78 D1
Maylands Dr DA14 . . . . .168 D1
Maylands Ho SW3 . . . . . 257 B3
Maylands Rd WD19 . . . . .22 C6
Maylie Ho 4 SE16 . . . . .118 B4
Maynard Cl
Fulham SW6 . . . 135 D5 265 D3
Tottenham N15 . . . . .51 C4
Maynard Ct EN3 . . . . . . .7 C5
Maynard Ho Mile End E1. . .97 A4
Plumstead SE18 . . . . . . .123 A2
Maynard Rd E17 . . . . . . .54 A4
Maynards Quay E1. . . . . .118 C6
Mayne Ct E8. . . . . .74 A4
Maynooth Gdns CR4 . . . .202 D2
Mayo Ct W13 . . . . .109 B3
Mayo Ho 10 E1 . . . . . . .96 C2
Mayola Rd E5 . . . . .74 C4
Mayo Rd
Thornton Heath CR0 . . . .205 B4
Walton-on-T KT12. . . . . .194 A2
Willesden NW10. . . . . . . .67 C2
Mayow Rd SE23, SE26. .184 D6
Mayplace Cl DA7. . . . . .147 D2
Mayplace La SE18. . . . .144 D6
Mayplace Rd W DA7 . . . .147 C1
Maypole Ct UB2 . . . . . . .107 B4
May Rd Chingford E4 . . . .35 C4
Newham E13. . . . . .99 A5
Twickenham TW2. . . . . . .152 C3
Mayroyd Ave KT6 . . . . . .214 C6
May's Buildings Mews
SE10 . . . . .142 B5
Mays Ct WC2 . . . . 250 A5
May's Ct SE10 . . . . .142 B5
Mays La EN5. . . . . .12 C5
Maysoule Rd SW11. . . . .136 B1
Mays Rd TW11, TW12 . . .174 B5
May St W14 . . . . 254 D1
Maystocks E18 . . . . .55 C6
Mayston Mews 3
SE18 . . . . .121 A1
May Terr IG1 . . . . .78 D4
Maythorne Cotts SE13. .164 B5
Maytime Prep Sch IG1. . .78 C5
Mayton St N7. . . . . .72 B5
Maytree Cl HA8 . . . . . . .11 A1
Maytree Ct
Mitcham CR4. . . . . .203 A6
Northolt UB5. . . . . .85 A4
May Tree Ho SE4 . . . . . .141 B2
Maytree La HA7 . . . . . . .24 D3
Maytree Wlk SW2. . . . . .160 C2
Mayville Prim Sch E11. . .76 C6
Mayville Rd Ilford IG1 . . .78 D3
Leyton E11. . . . . .76 C6
Mayward Ho 7 SE5 . . . .139 C4
May Wlk E13 . . . . .99 B5
Maywood Cl BR3. . . . . .185 D3
May Wynne Ho E16 . . . . .99 B1
Maze Hill SE10, SE3. . . .142 C6
Maze Hill Lodge 7
SE10 . . . . .142 B6
Maze Hill Sta SE10. . . . .142 C6
Mazenod Ave NW6. . . . . 69 C1
Maze Rd TW9. . . . . .132 C5
Mead Cl
3 Camden Town NW1 . .71 A1
Harrow HA3 . . . . .24 B2
Mead Cres
Carshalton SM1. . . . . . .218 C4
Chingford E4 . . . . .36 A4
Meadcroft Ho 4 KT3. . .199 C2
Meadcroft Rd SE17 . . . .138 D6
Mead Ct NW9. . . . . .45 B4
Meade Cl W4 . . . . .132 C6
Meader Ct SE14. . . . . . .140 D5
Meadfield HA8 . . . . .10 D2
Mead Field HA2 . . . . . . .63 B5
Meadfoot Rd SW16 . . . .181 C2
Mead Gr RM6. . . . . .58 D6
Mead Ho W11 . . . . 244 C4
Mead House La UB4 . . . .83 B3
Meadhurst Pk TW16 . . .171 C4
Mead Inf Sch The
KT19. . . . . .215 D4
Meadlands Dr TW10 . . .153 D2
Meadlands Prim Sch
TW10 . . . . .175 C6
Mead Lo W4. . . . . .111 B4
Meadow Ave CR0 . . . . . .206 D3
Meadowbank
Lewisham SE3. . . . . . . .142 D2
Primrose Hill NW3 . . . . . .70 D1
Southgate N21 . . . . .16 B5
Surbiton KT5. . . . . .198 B3
Meadow Bank 8
SW15. . . . . .157 B6

Meadowbank Cl SW6 . . .134 C5
Meadowbank Gdns
TW5. . . . . .128 B4
Meadowbank Rd NW9. . .45 B2
Meadowbanks EN5 . . . . .12 A6
Meadowbrook Ct
TW7. . . . . .130 D2
Meadow Cl Barnet EN5. . .13 B5
Bexley DA6 . . . . .169 B6
Catford SE6. . . . . .185 C5
Chingford E4 . . . . .19 D3
Chislehurst BR7 . . . . . . .188 D5
Enfield EN3 . . . . .7 A5
Hackney E9 . . . . .75 B3
Hinchley Wood KT10. . . .212 D6
Hounslow TW4 . . . . .151 C5
Northolt UB5. . . . . .85 C5
Richmond TW10 . . . . . . .154 A3
Ruislip HA4 . . . . .39 D3
Sutton SM1. . . . . .218 A6
West Barnes SW20. . . . .200 C5
Meadowcourt Rd SE3 . .142 D1
Meadowcroft 9 W4 . . . .110 C1
Meadow Croft BR1. . . . .210 B6
Meadowcroft Rd N13 . . .16 C2
Meadow Dr
Hendon NW4. . . . . .28 C1
Muswell Hill N10. . . . . . .49 B6
Meadowford Cl SE28. . .124 A6
Meadow Garth NW10 . . . 67 B2
Meadow Gate HA2. . . . . .63 D5
Meadowgate Cl NW7. . . .27 D5
Meadowgate Sch SE4. . .141 A2
Meadow Gdns HA8. . . . . .27 A4
Meadow High Sch UB8. . .82 A2
Meadow Hill KT3. . . . . . .199 C3
Meadow La SE12. . . . . . .165 B1
Meadow Mews SW8 . . . 270 C5
Meadow Pl
Chiswick W4 . . . . .133 C5
South Lambeth
SW8. . . . . . . .138 A5 270 B4
Meadow Rd
Ashford TW15. . . . . .171 B5
Barking IG11. . . . . .80 A1
Beckenham BR2 . . . . . . .186 C1
Carshalton SM1. . . . . . .218 C3
Claygate KT10. . . . . .212 C2
Dagenham RM9. . . . . . . .81 B2
Feltham TW13 . . . . .151 A2
Merton SW19 . . . . .180 A3
Pinner HA5 . . . . .41 A5
Southall UB1. . . . . .107 B6
South Lambeth
SW8. . . . . . . .138 B5 270 C4
Meadow Row SE1. . . . . 262 A5
Meadows Cl E10. . . . . . .75 C6
Meadows Ct SE4 . . . . . .172 A4
Meadows End TW16 . . . .172 A2
Meadowside
Eltham SE9 . . . . .143 C1
Twickenham TW1. . . . . . .153 D4
Meadow Stile CR0 . . . . .221 A5
Meadowsweet Cl
3 Newham E16 . . . . . . .99 D2
West Barnes KT3 . . . . . .200 C5
Meadowview The BR7 . . .189 A4
Meadowview TW17 . . . .193 A2
Meadow View
Blackfen DA15. . . . . . . .168 B4
Harrow HA1 . . . . .42 C1
Meadowview Rd
Catford SE6. . . . . .185 C5
Sidcup DA5 . . . . .169 B5
West Ewell KT19. . . . . . .215 C1
Meadow View Rd
Hayes UB4. . . . . .83 B3
Thornton Heath CR7. . . .204 D4
Meadow Way
Kingsbury NW9 . . . . .45 B4
Locksbottom BR6 . . . . . .226 C5
Ruislip HA4 . . . . .40 B3
Wembley HA9 . . . . .65 D4
Meadow Waye TW5. . . . .129 A5
Meadow Way The HA3 . . .24 C2
Meadow Wlk
Dagenham RM9. . . . . . . .81 B2
Hackbridge SM6. . . . . . .219 B5
Wanstead E18. . . . . .55 A5
West Ewell KT17, KT19. .215 D1
Meadow Wood Sch
WD23 . . . . .8 A6
Mead Pl Croydon CR0 . . .205 A2
Hackney E9 . . . . .74 C2
Mead Plat NW10. . . . . . . 67 A2
Mead Rd
Chislehurst BR7 . . . . . . .189 A4
Edgware HA8 . . . . .26 C4
Richmond TW10 . . . . . . .153 C1
Mead Road Inf Sch
BR7. . . . . .189 A4
Mead Row SE1 . . .116 C3 261 A6
Meads Ct E15. . . . . .76 D2
Meadside Cl BR3 . . . . . .185 A2
Meads La IG3 . . . . .57 D2
Meads Rd Enfield EN3. . . 7 A4
Tottenham N22 . . . . .32 D1
Meads The Cheam SM3. .217 A5
Edgware HA8 . . . . .27 B4
Hillingdon UB8. . . . . . . .82 A3
Mead The
Beckenham BR3 . . . . . . .186 A4
Ealing W13 . . . . .87 B2
Finchley N2 . . . . .30 A1
Ickenham UB10. . . . . . . .60 C6
Wallington SM6. . . . . . . .219 D2
West Wickham BR4. . . . .208 B1
Meadvale Rd
Croydon CR0 . . . . .206 A3
Ealing W5 . . . . .87 C3

Meadway
Ashford TW15. . . . . .170 C6
Barnet EN5 . . . . 1 C1
Beckenham BR3 . . . . . . .186 A2
Enfield EN3 . . . . .6 D6
Esher KT10 . . . . .212 A1
Hampstead Garden Suburb
NW11. . . . . .47 D3
Ilford IG3 . . . . .79 C4
Palmers Green N14. . . . . .16 A2
Tolworth KT5. . . . . .199 A1
Twickenham TW2. . . . . . .152 B3
West Barnes SW20. . . . .200 C5
Woodford IG8. . . . . .37 C5
Mead Way
Croydon CR0 . . . . .223 A6
Hayes BR2. . . . . .209 A3
Ruislip HA4 . . . . .39 B3
Meadway Cl Barnet EN5. . 1 C1
Hampstead Garden Suburb
NW11. . . . . .47 D3
Pinner HA5 . . . . .23 D4
Meadway Ct
Dagenham RM8. . . . . . . .81 B6
Ealing W5 . . . . .88 B2
Hampstead Garden Suburb
NW11. . . . . .47 D3
Meadway Gate NW11 . . .47 C3
Meadway Gdns HA4. . . . .39 B3
Meadway The
Buckhurst Hill IG9. . . . . .21 D3
Lewisham SE3. . . . . . . .142 B3
Meaford Way SE20. . . . .184 B3
Meakin Est SE1. . . . . . . 263 A6
Meakin Ho N7. . . . . .72 B3
Meanley Rd E12 . . . . . . .78 A3
Meard St W1 . . . . 239 C1
Meath Ho SE24 . . . . . . .160 D5
Meath Rd Ilford IG1 . . . .79 A5
Newham E15. . . . . .98 D5
Meath St SW11 . .137 B4 268 C2
Mecklenburgh Pl WC1 . . 240 C6
Mecklenburgh Sq
WC1. . . . . . . .94 B3 240 C6
Mecklenburgh St WC1. . 240 C6
Medburn St NW1 . . . . . . 232 C4
Medcalf Rd EN3 . . . . . . .7 B6
Medcroft Gdns SW14. . .133 A1
Medebourne Cl SE3. . . .143 A2
Mede Ho BR1. . . . . .187 B5
Medesenge Way N13. . . .32 D4
Medfield St SW15. . . . . .156 B4
Medhurst Cl 18 E3 . . . . . .97 A5
Median Rd E5 . . . . .74 C3
Medina Ave KT10 . . . . . .212 C5
Medina Cl N7 . . . . .72 C5
Medina Gr N7 . . . . .72 C5
Medina Ho SE15 . . . . . . .140 C1
Medina Rd N7 . . . . .72 C5
Medland Cl CR4 . . . . . . .203 A1
Medland Ho 11 E14 . . . .97 A6
Medlar Cl 11 UB5 . . . . . . .84 D5
Medlar Ho 3 DA15. . . . .168 A1
Medlar St SE5 . . . . .139 A4
Medley Rd NW6 . . . . . . .69 C2
Medora Rd SW2 . . . . . . .160 B4
Medresco Ho NW3. . . . . .70 B3
Medusa Rd SE6, SE13. . .163 D5
Medway Bldgs E3. . . . . .97 A5
Medway Cl
Croydon CR0 . . . . .206 C3
Ilford IG1 . . . . .79 A3
Medway Ct
South Norwood SE25 . . .205 C4
St Pancras WC1. . . . . . . 233 A1
Medway Dr UB6 . . . . .86 D5
Medway Gdns HA0. . . . . .65 A4
Medway Ho
Bermondsey SE1. . . . . . 252 D1
6 Kingston u T KT2 . . .175 D2
Paddington NW8. . . . . . . 237 A4
Stoke Newington N16. . . .73 B4
Medway Mews 35 E3. . . .97 A5
Medway Par 1 UB6. . . . .86 D5
Medway Rd E3 . . . . .97 A5
Medway St
SW1. . . . . . . .115 D3 259 D5
Medwin St SW4. . . . . . . .138 B1
Meecham Ct 1 SW11 . . .136 C3
Meerbrook Rd SE3. . . . .143 C2
Meers Ct SW20 . . . . . . .178 C2
Meeson Rd E15. . . . . . . .76 D1
Meeson St E5 . . . . .75 A4
Meeting House Alley 7
E1. . . . . .118 B5
Meeting House La
SE15 . . . . .140 B5
Mehetabel Rd E9 . . . . . .74 C3
Meister Cl IG1. . . . . .57 B1
Melanda Cl DA7 . . . . . . .188 B5
Melanie Cl DA7. . . . . . . .147 A4
Melba Way SE13 . . . . . .141 D4
Melbourne Ave
Bowes Pk N13. . . . . .32 B4
Ealing W13 . . . . .109 A5
Pinner HA2, HA5. . . . . . .41 D5
Melbourne Cl
Hackney N5. . . . . .72 C5
Muswell Hill N10. . . . . . .31 B3
Paddington W9 . . . . 236 B6
Penge SE20. . . . . .184 A3
Twickenham TW2. . . . . . .152 B3
Melbourne Gdns RM6. . . 59 A1
Melbourne Gr SE22 . . . .139 D1
Melbourne Ho
Hayes UB4. . . . . .84 C3
Kensington W8 . . . . 245 A3

Melbourne Ho continued
South Norwood SE25 . . .205 D5
Melbourne Mews
Brixton SW9 . . . . .138 C4
Catford SE6. . . . . .164 A4
Melbourne Pl WC2. . . . . 240 D1
Melbourne Rd
Ilford IG1 . . . . .56 D1
Leyton E10. . . . . .53 D2
Merton SW19 . . . . .179 C2
Newham E12. . . . . .100 B5
Teddington TW11 . . . . . .175 C4
Wallington SM6. . . . . . . .219 C3
Walthamstow E17. . . . . . .53 A5
Melbourne Sq 21
SW9. . . . . .138 C4
Melbourne Way EN1 . . . .17 D5
Melbray Mews 11
SW6. . . . . .135 B3
Melbreak Ho 11 SE22. . .139 C2
Melbury Ave UB2 . . . . . .107 D3
Melbury Cl
Claygate KT10. . . . . .213 B2
Elmstead BR7 . . . . .188 B4
Melbury Ct W8 .113 B3 254 D6
Melbury Dr SE5. . . . . . . .139 C5
Melbury Gdns SW20 . . .178 B2
Melbury Grange BR1. . . .188 A2
Melbury Ho
South Lambeth SW8 . . . 270 C4
Twickenham TW2. . . . . . .152 B2
Melbury Rd Harrow HA3. . 44 B4
Kensington
W14. . . . . . . .113 B3 254 D6
Melchester 5 W11. . . . . .91 B1
Melchester Ho 1 N19. . .71 D5
Melcombe Ct NW1. . . . . 237 C4
Melcombe Gdns HA3. . . .44 B3
Melcombe Ho SW8 . . . . 270 C3
Melcombe Pl NW1. . . . . 237 C4
Melcombe Prim Sch
W6 . . . . .134 D6
Melcombe St
NW1. . . . . . . .92 D3 237 D5
Meldex Cl NW7. . . . . . . .28 C4
Meldon Cl SW6 . . . . 265 D2
Meldone KT3. . . . . .199 B1
Meldone Cl KT5. . . . . . .198 D3
Meldrum Rd IG3. . . . . . . .80 A6
Melfield Gdns SE6. . . . .186 A5
Melford Ave IG11 . . . . . .79 D2
Melford Ct KT9 . . . . . . .214 B3
Melford Rd
Bermondsey SE1. . . . . . 263 B6
Dulwich SE22 . . . . .162 A4
Hackney E5 . . . . .74 B5
2 Sutton SM2 . . . . . . .218 A1
Melford St SE22. . . . . . .162 A4
Melford Rd
Dulwich SE21, SE22 . . .162 A4
Ilford IG1 . . . . .79 B6
Leyton E11. . . . . .76 C6
Newham E6. . . . . .100 B4
Walthamstow E17. . . . . . .53 B5
Melfort Ave CR7. . . . . . .204 D6
Melfort Rd CR7 . . . . . . .204 D6
Melgund Rd N5. . . . . . . .72 C3
Melina Cl UB3 . . . . .83 B2
Melina Ct Putney SW15. .134 A2
St John's Wood NW8 . . . 229 C1
Melina Pl NW8 . . .92 B4 229 C1
Melina Rd W12 . . . . . . .112 B4
Melior Ct N6 . . . . .49 C3
Melior Pl SE1. . . . . 253 A2
Melior St SE1. . .117 C4 253 A2
Meliot Rd SE6 . . . . .164 B2
Melisa Ct N6 . . . . .49 D2
Meller Cl SM6 . . . . .220 A5
Melling Dr EN1 . . . . .6 A4
Melling St SE18. . . . . . .145 C6
Mellington Ct 2 N16. . . .74 A5
Mellis Ave TW9 . . . . . . .132 D4
Mellish Cl IG11. . . . . . . .101 D6
Mellish Ct KT6. . . . . . . .198 A3
Mellish Flats E10 . . . . . .53 C2
Mellish Gdns IG8 . . . . . .37 A5
Mellish Ho 3 E1. . . . . . .96 B1
Mellish Ind Est SE18. . . .121 D3
Mellish St E14. . . . . . . .119 C3
Mellison Rd SW17 . . . . .180 C5
Mellitus St W12 . . . . . . .89 D1
Mellor Cl KT12. . . . . . . .195 B2
Mellor Ct 3 SW19 . . . . .180 A3
Mellor Ho 2 SE21 . . . . .183 C6
Mellow La E UB4. . . . . . .83 A4
Mellow Lane Sch UB4. . .83 A3
Mellow La W UB10. . . . . .83 A4
Mellows
Redbridge IG5. . . . . .56 B6
Wallington SM6. . . . . . . .219 D3
Mells Cres SE9 . . . . .188 B1
Mell St 6 SE10 . . . . . . .120 C1
Melody La N5 . . . . .73 A3
Melody Rd SW18. . . . . . .158 A6
Melon Pl W8 . . . . 245 B2
Melon Rd Leyton E11. . . .76 C5
Peckham SE15. . . . . . . .140 A4
Melrose Ave
Borehamwood WD6 . . . . .10 D6
Cricklewood NW2 . . . . . .68 C3
Greenford UB6 . . . . .85 D5
Mitcham CR4. . . . . .181 B3
Thornton Heath SW16. . .204 C6
Tottenham N22 . . . . .32 D2
Twickenham TW2. . . . . . .151 D4
Wimbledon SW19 . . . . . .157 C1
Melrose Cl
Greenford UB6 . . . . .85 D5
Grove Pk SE12. . . . . . . .165 B3
Hayes UB4. . . . . .84 A2
Melrose Cres BR6. . . . . .227 B3

Melrose Ct
5 Ealing W13. . . . . . . .109 A5
Wandsworth SW18. . . . . .157 B5
Melrose Dr UB1 . . . . . . .107 C5
Melrose Gdns
Edgware HA8 . . . . .26 D1
Hammersmith W6 . . . . . .112 C3
Kingston u T KT3. . . . . .199 B6
Melrose Ho
Maida Vale NW6 . . . . . . .91 C4
Pimlico SW1 . . . . 258 D2
Melrose Rd
1 Barnes SW13. . . . . . .133 D3
Merton SW19 . . . . .179 C2
Pinner HA5 . . . . .41 B5
Wandsworth SW18. . . . . .157 B5
Melrose Sch CR4 . . . . . .202 C6
Melrose Terr W6 . . . . . .112 C3
Melsa Rd SM4 . . . . .202 A3
Melthorne Dr HA4 . . . . . .62 C5
Melthorpe Gdns SE3 . . .144 A4
Melton Cl HA4 . . . . .40 C1
Melton Ct
11 Croydon CR0 . . . . . .221 D6
South Kensington SW7. . . 256 D3
Sutton SM2 . . . . .218 A1
1 Twickenham TW1. . . .153 B4
Melton Ho E5 . . . . .74 A6
Melton St NW1 . . 93 D4 232 C1
Melville Ave
Greenford UB6 . . . . .64 D3
South Croydon CR2 . . . .221 D3
Wimbledon SW20 . . . . . .178 A3
Melville Cl UB10 . . . . . . .61 B5
Melville Court Flats 8
W12. . . . . .112 B4
Melville Ct
4 Brentford W4. . . . . . .110 C1
Rotherhithe SE8 . . . . . . .119 A2
Melville Gdns N13 . . . . . .32 D5
Melville Ho
Lewisham SE10. . . . . . . .142 A4
New Barnet EN5 . . . . . . .14 B5
Melville Pl 4 N1 . . . . . . .73 A1
Melville Rd
Barnes SW13 . . . . .134 A4
Sidcup DA14 . . . . .168 C2
Stonebridge NW10. . . . . .67 B1
Walthamstow E17. . . . . . .53 B6
Melville Villas Rd W3 . . .111 B5
Melvin Rd SE20. . . . . . .184 C2
Melvin St 11 TW9 . . . . .132 C4
Melwood Ho 22 E1. . . . .96 B1
Melyn Cl N7 . . . . .71 C4
Memel Ct EC1 . . . . 242 A5
Memel St EC1. . . . . 242 A5
Memess Path 4 SE18 . .144 C6
Memorial Ave E15 . . . . . .98 C4
Memorial Cl TW5 . . . . . .129 B6
Memorial Hospl SE18 . .144 C3
Memorial Hts 12 . . . . . . .57 B3
Menai Pl 2 E3 . . . . .97 C5
Menard Ct EC1 . . . . 235 B1
Mendham Ho E1. . . . . . . 263 A6
Mendip Cl
Forest Hill SE26 . . . . . . .184 C6
Harlington UB3 . . . . . . .127 B5
North Cheam KT4 . . . . . .216 C6
Mendip Ct
12 Battersea SW11 . . . .136 A3
Deptford SE14. . . . . . . .140 C6
1 East Barnet N20 . . . .14 C2
Mendip Dr NW2, NW11. . .46 A4
Mendip Ho Harrow HA3 . .43 A3
2 Stoke Newington N4. . .51 B2
Mendip Hos 12 E2 . . . . .96 C4
Mendip Rd
Battersea SW11 . . . . . . .136 A2
Bushey WD23 . . . . .8 A5
Ilford IG2 . . . . .57 C4
Mendora Rd
SW6. . . . . . . .135 B5 264 C4
Menelik Rd NW2. . . . . . .69 B4
Menin Wks CR4. . . . . . .180 C1
Menlo Gdns SE19 . . . . . .183 B3
Mennie Ho SE18 . . . . . .144 B4
Mennis Ho SM5. . . . . . . .218 C6
Menon Dr N9. . . . . .18 B1
Menorah Foundation Sch
HA8 . . . . .27 A3
Menorah Prim Sch
NW11. . . . . .47 A2
Menotti St 6 E2. . . . . . . .96 A3
Menteath Ho 9 E14 . . . .97 C1
Mentmore Cl HA3. . . . . . .43 C3
Mentmore Terr E8 . . . . . .74 B1
Mentone Ct SW8. . . . . . 270 B2
Meon Ct TW7 . . . . .130 C3
Meon Rd W3 . . . . .111 A4
Meopham Rd CR4,
SW16. . . . . .181 C2
Mepham Cres HA3. . . . . .24 A3
Mepham Gdns HA3. . . . .24 A3
Mepham St
SE1 . . . . .116 C5 251 A8
Mera Dr DA7 . . . . .147 D1
Merantun Way SW19. . . .180 A3
Merbury Cl
Lewisham SE13. . . . . . . .164 B6
Woolwich SE28 . . . . . . .123 B5
Merbury Rd SE28 . . . . . .123 C4
Mercator Pl 4 E14 . . . . .119 C1
Mercator Rd SE13 . . . . .142 B1
Mercer Cl KT7. . . . . .196 C2
Merceron Ho 3 E2 . . . . .96 C4
Merceron St E1. . . . . . . .96 B3
Mercer Pl HA5. . . . . .22 C1
Mercers Cl SE10 . . . . . .120 D2
Mercer's Cotts 6 E3. . . .97 A1

Mercers Mews N7 . . . . . . 71 D4
Mercers Pl W6 . . . . 112 D2
Mercers Rd N19 . . . . 71 D5
Mercer St WC2 . . 94 A1 240 A1
Merchant Ct E1 . . . . 118 C5
Merchants Ct SE25 . . . . . 206 A5
Merchants Ho SE10 . . . . 120 B1
Merchants Lo 5 E17 . . . . 53 C5
Merchant St E3 . . . . 97 B4
Merchant Taylors' Almshouses SE13 . . . . 142 C1
Merchant Taylors Hall* EC3 . . . . 242 D1
Merchiston Rd SE6 . . . . 164 B2
Merchland Rd SE9 . . . . . . 167 A3
Merchon Ho N7 . . . . 71 C4
Mercia Gr SE13 . . . . 142 A1
Mercia Ho
9 Camberwell SE5 . . . . . 139 A3
Charlton TW15 . . . . 171 A2
Mercie Ct SE22 . . . . 162 A3
Mercier Rd SW15 . . . . . . 157 A6
Mercury 25 NW9 . . . . 27 D2
Mercury Ct
8 Brixton SW9 . . . . 138 C4
10 Millwall E14 . . . . 119 C2
Mercury Ctr TW14 . . . . . 150 A6
Mercury Ho
Brentford TW8 . . . . 109 D1
6 Old Ford E3 . . . . 97 C6
Mercury Rd TW8 . . . . 109 C1
Mercury Way SE14 . . . . . 140 D6
Mercy Terr SE13 . . . . 163 D6
Merebank La CR0, SM6 . . . . 220 B3
Mere Cl Orpington BR6 . . 226 D6
Putney SW15, SW19 . . . . 156 D4
Meredith Ave NW2 . . . . . . 68 C3
Meredith Cl HA5 . . . . 22 D3
Meredith Ho 17 N16 . . . . . 73 C3
Meredith Mews SE4 . . . . 141 B1
Meredith St
Finsbury EC1 . . . . 234 C1
Newham E13 . . . . 99 A4
Meredith Twr W3 . . . . . . 110 D3
Meredyth Rd SW13 . . . . 134 A3
Mere End CR0 . . . . 206 D2
Mere Rd TW17 . . . . 192 D3
Mereside BR6 . . . . 226 C6
Mereside Pk TW15 . . . . . 171 A6
Meretone Cl SE4 . . . . 141 A1
Mereton Mans 6 SE8 . . 141 C4
Meretune Ct SM4 . . . . . . 201 B6
Merevale Cres SM4 . . . . 202 A3
Mereway Industry TW2 . . . . 152 C4
Mereway Rd TW2 . . . . . . 152 C3
Merewood Cl BR1 . . . . . 188 C1
Merewood Gdns CR0 . . 206 D2
Mereworth Cl BR2 . . . . . 208 D4
Mereworth Dr SE18 . . . . 145 A5
Mereworth Ho 3 SE15 . . . . 140 C6
Merganser Ct 17 SE8 . . . 141 B6
Merganser Gdns SE28 . . 123 B3
Meridan Ct SE13 . . . . 142 B1
Meriden Cl BR1 . . . . 187 D3
Meriden Ct SW3 . . . . . . 257 A1
Meriden Ho
4 Barnet EN5 . . . . 1 A1
25 Hoxton N1 . . . . 95 C6
Meridian Building* SE10 . . . . 142 B5
Meridian Ct
4 Bermondsey SE16 . . . 118 A4
4 Catford SE6 . . . . 164 D3
Croydon CR0 . . . . 220 C4
Meridian Ho SE10 . . . . . . 120 C2
Meridian Pl E14 . . . . 120 A4
Meridian Prim Sch SE10 . . . . 142 B6
Meridian Rd SE7 . . . . 143 D5
Meridian Sq E15 . . . . 76 B1
Meridian Trad Est SE7 . . . . 121 B2
Meridian Way
Enfield EN3 . . . . 19 A5
Lower Edmonton N9, N18 . . . . 18 D1
Meridian Wlk N17 . . . . . . 33 C4
Merifield Rd SE9 . . . . 143 C1
Merino Cl E11 . . . . 55 C5
Merino Pl DA15 . . . . 168 A6
Merioneth Ct 7 W7 . . . . 86 D2
Merivale Rd
Harrow HA1 . . . . 42 A2
Putney SW15 . . . . 135 A1
Merlewood Dr BR7 . . . . 188 B2
Merley Ct NW9 . . . . 45 A1
Merlin 26 NW9 . . . . 27 D2
Merlin Cl Mitcham CR4 . . 202 C6
4 Northolt UB5 . . . . 84 C4
South Croydon CR0 . . . . 221 C4
Wallington SM6 . . . . 220 B2
Merlin Cres HA8 . . . . 26 B2
Merlin Ct
Beckenham BR2 . . . . 208 D5
6 Ealing W7 . . . . 86 D3
Mitcham CR4 . . . . 180 C2
Ruislip HA4 . . . . 61 B6
Stanmore HA7 . . . . 25 B5
Wood Green N22 . . . . 32 C2
Merling Cl KT9 . . . . 213 D3
Merlin Gdns BR1 . . . . 165 A1
Merlin Gr BR3 . . . . 207 C4
Merlin Ho
7 Chiswick W4 . . . . 111 B1
Enfield EN3 . . . . 18 D6
West Hampstead NW3 . . . 69 D4
Merlin Prim Sch BR1 . . 165 A1
Merlin Rd Bexley DA16 . . 146 A1
Wanstead E12 . . . . 77 D6
Merlin Rd N DA16 . . . . . . 146 A1
Merlins Ave HA2 . . . . 63 B5
Merlin Sch SW15 . . . . . . 157 A6
Merlins Ct WC1 . . . . 234 A1
Merlin St EC1 . . . . 94 C4 234 A1
Mermaid Ct
Bermondsey SE1 . . . . 117 B4 252 C2
Rotherhithe SE16 . . . . . . 119 B5
Stroud Green N4 . . . . 50 C3
Mermaid Ho 8 E14 . . . . 120 A6
Mermaid Twr 22 SE8 . . . 141 B6
Meroe Ct N16 . . . . 73 C6
Merredene St SW2 . . . . . 160 B5
Merriam Ave 2 E9 . . . . . . 75 B2
Merriam Cl E4 . . . . 36 A5
Merrick Rd UB2 . . . . 107 B3
Merricks Ct 5 SW14 . . . 132 D1
Merrick Sq SE1 . . . . 117 B3 262 C6
Merridale SE12 . . . . 164 D6
Merridene N21 . . . . 16 D5
Merrielands Cres RM9 . . . . 103 B5
Merrielands Ret Pk RM9 . . . . 103 B5
Merrilands Rd KT4 . . . . . 200 C1
Merrilees Rd DA15 . . . . . 167 C4
Merrilyn Cl KT10 . . . . . . 213 A2
Merriman Rd SE3 . . . . . . 143 C4
Merrington Rd SW6 . . . . 265 B6
Merrion Ave HA7 . . . . 25 D5
Merritt Gdns KT9 . . . . . . 213 C2
Merritt Rd SE4 . . . . 163 B6
Merrivale
Camden Town NW1 . . . . 232 B5
Southgate N14 . . . . 15 D6
Merrivale Ave IG4 . . . . . . 55 D5
Merrow Ct CR4 . . . . 180 B1
Merrow St SE17 . . . . 117 B1 262 C1
Merrow Way CR0 . . . . . . 224 A2
Merrow Wlk SE17 . . . . . 262 D2
Merrydown Way BR7 . . . 188 B2
Merry Fiddlers RM8 . . . . . 81 B6
Merryfield SE3 . . . . 142 D3
Merryfield Gdns HA7 . . . . 25 C5
Merryfield Ho SE12 . . . . 165 C1
Merryhill Cl E4 . . . . 19 D4
Merry Hill Rd WD23 . . . . . . 8 A3
Merryhills Ct N14 . . . . 15 C6
Merryhills Dr EN2 . . . . 4 A1
Merryhills Prim Sch EN2 . 4 B1
Merryweather Ct
13 Dartmouth Pk N19 . . . . 71 C5
1 New Malden KT3 . . . . 199 C4
Mersea Ho IG11 . . . . 78 D2
Mersey Ct 10 KT2 . . . . . . 175 D2
Mersey Ho 10 N7 . . . . 72 C3
Mersey Rd E17 . . . . 53 B6
Mersey Wlk UB5 . . . . 85 C5
Mersham Dr NW9 . . . . 44 D4
Mersham Pl
Penge SE20 . . . . 184 B2
South Norwood CR7 . . . 183 B1
Mersham Rd CR7 . . . . . . 183 B1
Merstone Ho SW18 . . . . 157 D5
Merten Rd RM6 . . . . 59 A2
Merthyr Terr SW13 . . . . 134 B6
MERTON 179 C2
Merton Abbey Mills SW19 . . . . 180 A2
Merton Abbey Prim Sch SW19 . . . . 179 D2
Merton Ave
Chiswick W4 . . . . 111 D2
Hillingdon UB10 . . . . 60 D1
Northolt UB5 . . . . 64 A3
Merton Coll SM4 . . . . . . 201 B4
Merton Court Sch DA14 . . . . 190 C6
Merton Ct Barnet EN5 . . . . . 1 D1
Welling DA16 . . . . 146 B3
Merton Gdns BR5 . . . . . . 210 D4
Merton Hall Gdns SW20 . . . . 179 A2
Merton Hall Rd SW19 . . 179 A2
Merton High St SW19 . . 180 A3
Merton Ho SW18 . . . . 157 C3
Merton Ind Pk SW19 . . . 180 A2
Merton La N6 . . . . 70 D6
Merton Lo
New Barnet EN5 . . . . 14 A6
3 Streatham SW16 . . . . 182 A5
Merton Mans SW20 . . . . 178 D1
MERTON PARK 179 C1
Merton Park Par SW19 . . . . 179 B2
Merton Park Prim Sch SW19 . . . . 179 C1
Merton Park Sta SW19 . . . . 179 C2
Merton Pl 9 SW19 . . . . . 180 A3
Merton Rd Barking IG11 . . 79 D1
Croydon SE25 . . . . 206 A4
Enfield EN2 . . . . 5 B5
Harrow HA2 . . . . 42 A1
Ilford IG3 . . . . 57 D2
Leytonstone E17 . . . . 54 A3
Merton SW19 . . . . 179 D3
Wandsworth SW18 . . . . . 157 C4
Merton Rise NW3 . . . . 70 C1
Merton Road Ind Est SW18 . . . . 157 C4
Merton Way
East Molesey KT8 . . . . . 196 A6
Hillingdon UB10 . . . . 60 D1
Merttins Rd SE15 . . . . . . 162 D6
Meru Cl NW5 . . . . 71 A3
Mervan Rd SW2 . . . . 138 C1
Mervyn Ave SE9 . . . . 167 A2
Mervyn Ct SE18 . . . . 145 C6
Mervyn Rd
Brentford W13 . . . . 109 A3
Shepperton TW17 . . . . . 193 A2
Mervyn Stockwood Ho 1 SE9 . . . . 167 A2
Messaline Ave W3 . . . . . . 89 A1
Messent Rd SE9 . . . . 165 D6
Messer Ct CR0 . . . . 220 D4
Messeter Pl SE9 . . . . 166 C5
Messina Ave NW6 . . . . 69 C1
Messiter Ho N1 . . . . 233 D5
Met Appts The SE12 . . . . 164 D6
Metcalfe Ho 23 SW8 . . . 137 D3
Metcalfe Wlk 2 TW13 . . . . 173 A6
Metcalf Rd TW15 . . . . . . 170 D5
Meteor St SW11 . . . . 137 A1
Meteor Way SM6 . . . . 220 A1
Metford Cres EN3 . . . . 7 C5
Metherell Ho N21 . . . . 17 B5
Metheringham Way NW9 . . . . 27 C2
Methley Ho 8 N7 . . . . 72 B6
Methley St SE11 . . . . 116 C1 261 B1
Methodist Central Hall* SW1 . . . . 115 D4 249 D1
Methuen Cl HA8 . . . . 26 C3
Methuen Pk N10 . . . . 49 B6
Methuen Rd
Belvedere DA17 . . . . 125 D2
Bexleyheath DA6 . . . . . . 147 B1
Edgware HA8 . . . . 26 C3
Methwold Rd W10 . . . . . . 90 D2
Metro Bsns Ctr The SE26 . . . . 185 B5
Metro Ctr UB4 . . . . 106 C6
Metro Ho E7 . . . . 77 B2
Metro Ind Ctr TW7 . . . . . 130 C3
Metropolis Apartments 5 SW12 . . . . 159 B3
Metropolitan Benefit Societies Almshouses 3 N1 . . . . 73 C2
Metropolitan Bsns Ctr 9 N1 . . . . 73 C1
Metropolitan Cl 23 E14 . . 97 C2
Metropolitan Ctr The UB6 . . . . 85 D6
Metro Trad Ctr HA9 . . . . . 66 D4
Meudon Ct KT6 . . . . 197 D4
Mews Pl IG8 . . . . 37 A6
Mews St E1 . . . . 118 A5
Mews The
Beckenham BR3 . . . . 185 C2
Hampton TW12 . . . . 174 A4
Hornsey N8 . . . . 50 C5
Redbridge IG4 . . . . 55 D4
Shoreditch N1 . . . . 235 B6
Thornton Heath SW16 . . . 182 B2
Tottenham N15 . . . . 51 C5
5 Upper Holloway N19 . . 50 A1
Woolwich SE18 . . . . 122 D1
Mexborough NW1 . . . . . 232 A5
Mexfield Rd SW15 . . . . . 157 B6
Meyer Gn EN1 . . . . 6 A5
Meyer Ho 1 SW12 . . . . . . 159 B4
Meymott St SE1 . . . . 116 D5 251 C3
Meynell Cres E9 . . . . 74 D1
Meynell Gdns E9 . . . . 74 D1
Meynell Rd E9 . . . . 74 D1
Meyrick Ct CR7 . . . . 204 C3
Meyrick Ho 8 E14 . . . . . . 97 C2
Meyrick Rd
Battersea SW11 . . . . 136 C2
Willesden NW10 . . . . 68 A2
Miah Terr 10 E1 . . . . 118 A5
Miall Wlk SE26 . . . . 185 A6
Micawber Ave UB8 . . . . . . 82 C3
Micawber Ct N1 . . . . 235 B2
Micawber Ho 27 SE16 . . 118 A4
Micawber St N1 . . 95 A4 235 B2
Michael Cliffe Ho EC1 . . 234 B1
Michael Faraday Ho SE17 . . . . 262 D1
Michael Faraday Sch SE17 . . . . 117 B1 262 D1
Michael Gaynor Cl W7 . . . . 108 D5
Michael Marshall Ho 2 SE9 . . . . 167 A2
Michaelmas Cl SW20 . . . 200 C6
Michael Rd
Leytonstone E11 . . . . 54 D1
Parsons Green SW6 . . . . 135 D4 265 D2
South Norwood SE25 . . . 205 C6
Michaels Cl SE13 . . . . . . 142 C1
Michael Sobell Sinai Sch HA3 . . . . 44 C3
Michaelson Ho 4 SE21 . . . . 183 C6
Michael Tippet Sch SE27 . . . . 161 A2
Michael Tippett Sch The SE11 . . . . 116 C2 261 B3
Michelangelo Ct 14 SE16 . . . . 118 B1
Micheldever Rd SE12 . . 164 D5
Michelham Gdns TW1 . . 152 D1
Michelle Ct Acton W3 . . . 111 B6
North Finchley N12 . . . . . . 30 A5
Michell Ho TW1 . . . . 152 D3
Michels Almshouses 11 TW10 . . . . 154 A6
Michelsdale Dr 3 TW9 . . . . 132 A1
Michelson Ho SE11 . . . . 260 D3
Michel's Row 2 TW9 . . 132 A1
Michel Wlk SE18 . . . . 122 D1
Michigan Ave E12 . . . . 78 B4
Michigan Ho E14 . . . . . . 119 C3
Michleham Down N12 . . 29 B6
Micklefield Ct CR0 . . . . . 204 D3
Mickledore NW1 . . . . 232 B3
Mickleham Cl BR5 . . . . . 190 A1
Mickleham Gdns SM3 . . 217 A2
Mickleham Rd BR5 . . . . . 190 A1
Mickleham Way CR0 . . . 224 B1
Micklethwaite Rd SW6 . . . . 135 C6 265 B5
Mickleton Ho 30 W2 . . . . 91 C2
Midas Bsns Ctr RM10 . . . 81 D4
Midas Metro Ctr SM4 . . 200 D2
Midcroft HA4 . . . . 39 C1
Middle Dene NW7 . . . . . . 11 B1
Middlefield NW8 . . . . 92 B6 229 C6
Middlefielde W13 . . . . 87 B2
Middlefield Gdns IG2 . . . 56 D3
Middle Green Cl 3 KT5 . . . . 198 B3
Middleham Gdns N18 . . . 34 A4
Middleham Rd N18 . . . . . 34 A4
Middle La Hornsey N8 . . . . 50 A4
Teddington TW11 . . . . . . 174 D4
Middle Lane Mews N8 . . 50 A4
Middle Mill KT5 . . . . 198 B6
Middle Park Ave SE9 . . . 165 D4
Middle Park Prim Sch SE9 . . . . 165 D4
Middle Rd
East Barnet EN4 . . . . 14 C5
Finchley N10 . . . . 30 C2
Harrow HA2 . . . . 42 B1
Mitcham SW16 . . . . 181 D1
12 Newham E13 . . . . 99 A5
Middle Row W10 . . . . 91 A3
Middle Row Prim Sch W10 . . . . 91 A3
Middlesborough Rd N18 . . . . 34 A4
Middlesex Bsns Ctr UB2 . . . . 107 B4
Middlesex Cl UB6 . . . . 85 D3
Middlesex Coll of Computing & Tech HA0 . . . . 66 A3
Middlesex Ct
5 Chiswick W4 . . . . 111 D2
6 Harrow HA1 . . . . 42 D4
Middlesex Cty Cricket Sch N3 . . . . 29 D1
Middlesex Ho
Marylebone W1 . . . . 239 B4
4 Penge SE20 . . . . 184 C3
Wembley HA0 . . . . 87 D6
Middlesex Pas EC1 . . . . 241 D3
Middlesex Pl 13 E9 . . . . . 74 C2
Middlesex Rd CR4 . . . . . 204 A4
Middlesex St E1 . . 95 D1 243 C2
Middlesex Univ N17 . . . . . 33 D4
Middlesex Univ (Cat Hill) EN4 . . . . 15 A6
Middlesex Univ (Enfield Campus) EN3 . . . . 18 C6
Middlesex Univ (Hendon Campus) NW4 . . . . 46 B5
Middlesex Univ Trent Park EN4 . . . . 3 C3
Middle St Croydon CR0 . . 221 A5
Holborn EC1 . . . . 242 A4
Middle Temple* EC4 . . . . 116 C6 251 A6
Middle Temple La EC4 . . . . 116 C6 251 A6
Middleton Ave
Chingford Green E4 . . . . . . 19 B1
Greenford UB5 . . . . 86 B5
Sidcup DA14 . . . . 190 C5
Middleton Cl E4 . . . . 19 B1
Middleton Ct
Bromley BR1 . . . . 187 B3
New Barnet EN5 . . . . 2 A1
Middleton Dr
Bermondsey SE16 . . . . . . 118 D4
Pinner HA5 . . . . 40 A6
Middleton Gdns IG2 . . . . 56 D3
Middleton Gr N7 . . . . 72 A3
Middleton Ho
Dalston E8 . . . . 73 D1
Newington SE1 . . . . 262 C5
Middleton Mews N7 . . . . . 72 A3
Middleton Pl W1 . . . . . . 239 A3
Middleton Rd
Carshalton CR4, SM5 . . . 202 B2
Dalston E8 . . . . 73 D1
Golders Green NW11 . . . . 47 C2
Hayes UB3 . . . . 83 B2
Middleton St E2 . . . . 96 B4
Middleton Way SE13 . . . 142 B1
Middleway NW11 . . . . 47 D4
Middle Way Hayes UB4 . . 84 C3
Mitcham SW16 . . . . 181 D1
Middle Way The HA3 . . . . 24 D1
Middlewich Ho 7 UB5 . . 85 B3
Midfield Prim Sch BR5 . . . . 190 A3
Midfield Way BR5 . . . . . . 190 B2
Midford Ho 1 NW4 . . . . . 46 D5
Midford Pl W1 . . . . 239 B5
Midholm
East Finchley NW11 . . . . . 47 D5
Wembley HA9 . . . . 44 C1
Midholm Cl NW11 . . . . . . 47 D5
Midholm Rd CR0 . . . . 223 A6
Midhope Ho WC1 . . . . . 233 B1
Midhope St WC1 . . . . . . 233 B1
Midhurst 1 SE26 . . . . 184 C4
Midhurst Ave
Muswell Hill N10 . . . . 49 A6
Thornton Heath CR0 . . . . 204 C2
Midhurst Ct N8 . . . . 50 A2
Midhurst Gdns UB10 . . . . 61 A1
Midhurst Hill DA6 . . . . . . 169 C6
Midhurst Ho 6 E14 . . . . . 97 B1
Midhurst Par N10 . . . . 49 A6
Midhurst Rd W13 . . . . . . 109 A3
Midhurst Way E5 . . . . 74 A4
Midland Mainline Terminal NW1 . . 93 D5 232 D3
Midland Pl E14 . . . . 120 A1
Midland Rd
Leytonstone E10 . . . . 54 A2
St Pancras NW1 . 94 A4 233 A2
Midland Terr
Cricklewood NW2 . . . . 68 D5
Dagenham NW10 . . . . 89 C3
Midlea Ho EN3 . . . . 6 C4
Midleton Rd KT3 . . . . 177 A1
Midlothian Ho NW2 . . . . . 68 B4
Midlothian Rd E3 . . . . 97 B3
Midmoor Rd
Merton SW19 . . . . 179 A2
Streatham SW12 . . . . 159 C3
Midship Cl SE16 . . . . 118 D5
Midship Point E14 . . . . . 119 C4
Midstrath Rd NW10 . . . . . 67 C4
Midsummer Apartments
7 SM2 . . . . 217 C1
Midsummer Ave TW4 . . 129 B1
Midsummer Ct
Blackheath Pk SE12 . . . . 143 A1
Edgware HA8 . . . . 10 D1
Harrow HA1 . . . . 42 B4
Midway SM3 . . . . 201 B2
Midway Ho EC1 . . . . 234 D2
Midwinter Cl 3 DA16 . . . 146 A2
Midwood Cl NW2 . . . . 68 B5
Mighell Ave IG4 . . . . 55 D4
Milan Ct N11 . . . . 31 D2
Milan Rd UB1 . . . . 107 B4
Milborne Gr SW10 . . . . . 256 B1
Milborne Ho 11 E9 . . . . . . 74 C2
Milborne St E9 . . . . 74 C2
Milborough Cres SE12 . . . . 164 C5
Milbourne La KT10 . . . . . 212 A3
Milbourne Lodge Jun Sch KT10 . . . . 212 A2
Milbourne Lodge Sen Sch KT10 . . . . 212 B2
Milbrook KT10 . . . . 212 A2
Milbrook Ct NW3 . . . . 48 A1
Milburn Dr 1 UB7 . . . . . 104 A6
Milburn Ho SW20 . . . . . . 178 B1
Milcote St SE1 . . . . 251 D1
Mildenhall Rd E5 . . . . 74 C5
Mildmay Ave N1 . . . . 73 B2
Mildmay Ct N1 . . . . 73 B3
Mildmay Gr N N1 . . . . 73 B3
Mildmay Gr S N1 . . . . 73 B3
Mildmay Ho 6 SW15 . . . 156 C6
Mildmay Mission Hospl E2 . . . . 95 D4
Mildmay Pk N1 . . . . 73 B3
Mildmay Rd Ilford IG1 . . . 78 D5
Stoke Newington N1 . . . . . 73 C3
Mildmay St N1 . . . . 73 B2
Mildon Ho EN3 . . . . 6 C3
Mildred Ave
Hayes UB3 . . . . 105 B3
Northolt UB5 . . . . 63 D3
Mildura Ct N8 . . . . 50 B5
MILE END 97 A3
Mile End Pl E1 . . . . 96 D3
Mile End Rd E1, E3 . . . . . 96 D3
Mile End Sta E3 . . . . 97 B4
Mile End The E17 . . . . 34 D2
Mile Rd
Hackbridge SM6 . . . . 203 A1
Wallington CR0, CR4, CR9 . . . . 203 D1
Miles Bldgs NW1 . . . . . . 237 A4
Miles Cl SE28 . . . . 123 B5
Miles Coverdale Prim Sch W12 . . . . 112 C4
Miles Ct Croydon CR0 . . . 220 D6
Stepney E1 . . . . 96 B1
Miles Dr SE28 . . . . 123 C5
Miles Ho 5 SE10 . . . . . . 120 C1
Miles Lo Harrow HA1 . . . . . 42 B4
Stratford New Town E15 . . 76 B3
Milespit Hill NW7 . . . . 28 C5
Miles Pl NW8 . . . . 236 D4
Miles Rd Hornsey N8 . . . . . 50 A6
Mitcham CR4 . . . . 202 C6
Miles St SW8 . . . 138 A6 270 B5
Milestone Cl
Edmonton N9 . . . . 18 A2
Sutton SM2 . . . . 218 B1
Milestone Ct TW7 . . . . . . 131 A4
Milestone Green SW14 . . . . 133 B1
Milestone Ho KT1 . . . . . . 197 D5
Milestone Rd SE19 . . . . . 183 D4
Miles Way N20 . . . . 14 C2
Milfoil St W12 . . . . 112 A6
Milford Cl SE2 . . . . 147 A6
Milford Ct
Southall UB1 . . . . 107 C5
3 Stamford Hill N16 . . . . . 51 C1
Milford Gdns
Croydon CR0 . . . . 206 D4
Edgware HA8 . . . . 26 C3
Milford Gdns *continued*
Wembley HA0 . . . . 65 D3
Milford Gr SM1 . . . . 218 A4
Milford La WC2 . . . . 116 C6 251 A6
Milford Mews SW16 . . . . 160 B1
Milford Rd Ealing W13 . . 109 B5
Southall UB1 . . . . 107 C6
Milk St Bromley BR1 . . . . 187 B4
City of London EC2 . . . . 95 A1 242 B2
Newham E16 . . . . 122 D5
Milkwell Gdns IG8 . . . . . . 37 B3
Milkwell Yd 7 SE5 . . . . . 139 A4
Milkwood Rd SE24 . . . . . 138 D1
Milk Yd E1 . . . . 118 C6
Millais Ave E12 . . . . 78 C3
Millais Cres KT19 . . . . . . 215 C3
Millais Ct 9 UB5 . . . . 84 D5
Millais Gdns HA8 . . . . 26 C1
Millais Rd Enfield EN1 . . . . 17 D6
Leyton E11 . . . . 76 B4
New Malden KT3 . . . . 199 C2
Millais Way KT19 . . . . . . 215 A4
Milland Ho 11 SW15 . . . . 156 A3
Millard Cl 21 N16 . . . . 73 C3
Millard Terr RM10 . . . . 81 C2
Millars Meadow Cl SE12 . . . . 165 A6
Millbank
Wallington SM6 . . . . 219 D3
Westminster SW1 . . . . 116 A2 260 A3
Millbank Ho KT6 . . . . 198 B2
Millbank Prim Sch SW1 . . . . 115 D2 259 D3
Millbank Way SE12 . . . . 165 A6
Millbourne Rd TW13 . . . 173 A6
Mill Bridge EN5 . . . . 13 B5
Millbrook 1 E18 . . . . 55 A6
Millbrook Ave DA16 . . . . 145 B1
Millbrooke Ct 7 SW15 . . . . 157 A6
Millbrook Gdns RM6 . . . . 59 A3
Millbrook Ho 4 SE15 . . . 140 A6
Millbrook Pl NW1 . . . . . 232 A4
Millbrook Rd
Brixton SW9 . . . . 138 D2
Edmonton N9 . . . . 18 B3
Mill Cl SM5 . . . . 219 A6
Mill Cnr EN5 . . . . 1 B4
Millcroft Ho SE6 . . . . 185 D6
Mill Ct Hendon NW7 . . . . . 29 A2
Leyton E10 . . . . 76 A5
14 Thamesmead SE28 . . . 124 B6
Millender Wlk SE16 . . . . 118 C2
Millennium Bridge* SE1, EC4 . . . . 252 A5
Millennium Bsns Ctr NW2 . . . . 68 B6
Millennium City Acad W1 . . . . 238 D3
Millennium Cl E16 . . . . . . 99 B1
Millennium Dr E14 . . . . . 120 B2
Millennium Harbour E14 . . . . 119 C4
Millennium Ho E17 . . . . . 52 D4
Millennium Pl 27 E2 . . . . 96 B5
Millennium Prim Sch SE10 . . . . 120 D3
Millennium Sq SE1 . . . . 253 D2
Millennium Way SE10 . . 120 C3
Miller Ave EN3 . . . . 7 C5
Miller Cl Bromley BR1 . . . 187 B5
Carshalton CR4 . . . . 202 D2
Pinner HA5 . . . . 22 C1
Miller Ct
Bexleyheath DA7 . . . . 147 D2
8 Hendon NW9 . . . . 46 A5
Miller Ho Harringay N15 . . 50 D5
9 Streatham SW2 . . . . . 160 A4
Miller Rd
Mitcham SW19 . . . . 180 B4
Thornton Heath CR0 . . . . 204 C1
Miller's Ave E8, N16 . . . . . 73 D3
Millers Cl NW7 . . . . 28 A6
Millers Ct 3 HA0 . . . . 88 A5
Miller's Ct 1 W4 . . . . 111 D1
Millers Green Cl EN2 . . . . . 4 D2
Miller's House Visitor Ctr*
1 E3 . . . . 98 A4
Millers Mead Ct SW19 . . 180 B3
Miller St NW1 . . . . 232 A4
Miller's Terr 1 E8 . . . . 73 D3
Miller's Way W6 . . . . 112 C4
Millers Wharf Ho E1 . . . 118 A5
Millers Yd N3 . . . . 29 D3
Miller Wlk SE1 . . . . 251 B3
Millet Rd UB6 . . . . 85 D5
Mill Farm Ave TW16 . . . . 171 C3
Millfarm Bsns Pk TW4 . . . . 151 A4
Mill Farm Cl HA5 . . . . 22 C1
Mill Farm Cres TW4 . . . . 151 A3
Millfield Charlton TW16 . . 171 B2
Finsbury Pk N4 . . . . 72 C6
Kingston u T KT1 . . . . . . 198 B6
Millfield Ave E17 . . . . 35 B2
Millfield La N6 . . . . 70 D6
Millfield Pl N6 . . . . 71 A6
Millfield Rd Hendon HA8 . 27 A1
Twickenham TW4 . . . . . . 151 B3
Millfields Com Sch E5 . . 74 C4
Millfields Rd E5 . . . . 74 C5
Mill Gdns SE26 . . . . 162 B1
Mill Gn CR4 . . . . 203 A2

Mill Green Bsns Pk CR4 203 A2
Mill Green Rd CR4 203 A2
Millgrove St 6 SW11 137 A3
Millharbour E14 119 D4
Millhaven Cl RM6 58 B3
MILL HILL 28 B5
Mill Hill SW13 134 A2
Mill Hill Broadway Sta NW7 27 C4
Mill Hill Circus NW7 27 D5
Mill Hill Cty High Sch NW7 11 C2
Mill Hill East Sta NW7 29 A3
Mill Hill Gr 11 W3 110 D5
Mill Hill Ind Est NW7 27 D4
Mill Hill Rd
Barnes SW13 134 A3
South Acton W3 110 D4
Mill Hill Sch NW7 28 B6
Mill Hill Terr 9 W3 110 D5
Mill Ho
4 Lewisham SE13 142 A2
Morden SM4 202 A5
Woodford IG8 36 D5
Millhouse Pl SE27 182 D6
Millicent Fawcett Ct N17 33 D2
Millicent Preston Ho 4 IG11 101 B6
Millicent Rd E10 53 B1
Milligan Ho SE23 163 B3
Milligan St E14 119 B6
Milliners Ho SW18 135 C1
Milling Rd HA8 27 B3
Millington Ho N16 73 B5
Millington Rd UB3 105 C3
Mill La Brondesbury NW6 69 B3
Carshalton SM5 219 A5
Croydon CR0 220 C5
Dagenham RM6 59 A3
Sewardstone E4 7 D2
Woodford IG8 36 D5
Woolwich SE18 122 C1
Mill Lane Trad Est CR0 220 B5
Millman Ct
Bloomsbury WC1 240 C5
Greenwich SE3 143 B5
Millman Mews WC1 240 C5
Millman Pl WC1 240 D5
Millman St WC1 94 B3 240 C5
Millmark Gr SE14 141 A3
Millmarsh La EN3 7 B3
Millmead Bsns Ctr N17 52 B6
Millmead Ind Ctr N17 52 B6
Mill Mead Rd N17 52 B6
MILL MEADS 98 B5
Millner Ct SE4 141 B3
Mill Pl Chislehurst BR7 188 D2
Kingston u T KT1 198 B6
Limehouse E14 97 A1
Mill Plat TW7 131 A3
Mill Plat Ave TW7 131 A3
Mill Pond Cl SW8 137 D5 269 D3
Millpond Est SE16 118 B4
Millpond Pl 2 SM6 219 A5
Mill Rd Ilford IG1 78 C5
Merton SW19 180 A3
Newham E16 121 B5
Twickenham TW2 152 A2
Mill Ridge HA8 26 C5
Mill River Trad Est EN3 7 A1
Mill Row N1 95 C6
Mills Cl UB10 82 C5
Mills Ct 9 Leyton E11 76 C5
Shoreditch EC2 95 C4
Mills Gr Hendon NW4 46 D6
1 South Bromley E14 98 A2
Mills Ho Nine Elms SW8 269 B2
Walthamstow E17 54 B6
Millshott Cl SW6 134 C4
Millside SM5 218 D6
Millside Pl TW7 131 B3
Millson Cl N20 14 B2
Mills Row W4 111 B2
Mill St
Bermondsey SE1 117 D4 253 D2
Kingston u T KT1 198 A6
Mayfair W1 249 A6
Millstream Cl N13 32 C5
Millstream Ho 14 SE16 118 B4
Millstream Rd SE1 117 D4 253 C1
Mill Trad Est The NW10 89 A4
Mill Vale BR2 186 D1
Mill View Cl KT17 215 D1
Mill View Gdns CR0 222 D5
MILLWALL 119 C3
Millwall Dock Rd E14 119 C3
Mill Way Edgware NW7 27 C5
Feltham TW14 150 B6
Millway Gdns UB5 63 B2
Millwood Rd TW3, TW7 152 A6
Millwood St 10 W10 91 A2
Mill Yd E1 118 A6
Milman Cl HA5 40 D6
Milman Rd NW6 91 A5
Milman's Ho SW10 266 C5
Milman's St SW10 136 B6 266 C5
Milne Ct Enfield EN2 4 C3
Milne Ct *continued*
4 Woodford E18 37 A2
Milne Field HA5 23 C3
Milne Gdns SE9 166 A6
Milne Ho 18 SE18 122 B2
Milner Bldg N16 73 B5
Milner Dr TW2 152 B4
Milner Ho
2 Battersea SW11 136 B2
Hayes UB4 84 B4
Milner Pl N1 94 C6 234 B6
Milner Rd
Dagenham RM8 80 C6
Kingston u T KT1 197 D6
Merton SW19 179 D2
Morden SM4 202 B4
Newham E15 98 C4
South Norwood CR7 205 B6
Milner Sq N1 72 D1
Milner St SW3 114 D2 257 C4
Milner Wlk SE9 167 B3
Milnthorpe Rd W4 133 B6
Milo Rd SE22 161 D5
Milrood Ho 5 E1 96 D2
Milroy Wlk SE1 251 C4
Milson Rd W14 113 A3 254 A6
Milsted Ho 23 E5 74 B3
Milton Ave Barnet EN5 13 B6
Becontree NW10 89 B6
Carshalton SM1 218 C4
Crouch End N6 49 C2
Kingsbury NW9 45 A6
Plashet E6 78 A1
Thornton Heath CR0 205 B2
Milton Cl
Bermondsey SE1 117 D2 263 C3
Carshalton SM1 218 B5
Hampstead Garden Suburb N2 48 A3
Hayes UB4 84 A1
Milton Court Rd SE14 141 A6
Milton Cres IG2 57 A3
Milton Ct Fulham SW6 135 A2
Ilford RM6 58 C2
Kingston u T KT2 176 A6
St Luke's EC2 242 C4
Twickenham TW2 152 C1
Uxbridge UB10 60 D5
9 Wandsworth SW18 157 C6
Milton Dr
Borehamwood WD6 10 D6
Littleton TW17 192 A5
Milton Gdns TW19 148 B3
Milton Gr
Friern Barnet N11 31 D5
Stoke Newington N16 73 C4
Milton Ho
12 Beckenham BR3 185 C3
19 Bethnal Green E2 96 C4
2 Camberwell SE5 139 B5
5 Kingston u T KT2 176 D4
Sutton SM1 217 C5
Milton House Mans E8 73 D4
Milton Lo
4 Sidcup DA14 190 A6
Southgate N21 16 D3
Twickenham TW1 152 D4
Milton Pk N6 49 C2
Milton Pl 3 N7 72 C3
Milton Rd Acton W3 111 B5
Belvedere DA17 125 C2
Bexley DA16 145 D4
Crouch End N6 49 C2
Ealing W7 108 D6
Hampton TW12 173 C3
Harrow HA1 42 C5
1 Hendon NW9 46 A2
Mill Hill NW7 28 A5
Mitcham CR4 181 A3
Mortlake SW14 133 B2
Sutton SM1 217 C4
Thornton Heath CR0 205 B2
Tottenham N15 50 D6
Tulse Hill SE24 160 D6
Uxbridge UB10 60 D4
Wallington SM6 219 D2
Walthamstow E17 53 C5
Wimbledon SW19 180 A4
Milton St EC1, EC2 95 B2 242 C4
Milton Way UB7 104 B2
Milverton NW5 71 A3
Milverton Dr UB10 61 A4
Milverton Gdns IG3 79 D6
Milverton Ho SE23 163 A1
Milverton Rd NW6 68 C1
Milverton St SE11 116 C1 261 B1
Milverton Way SE9 188 C6
Milward St E1 96 B2
Milward Wlk 14 SE18 144 C6
Mimosa N15 51 B4
Mimosa Ct
Colney Hatch N12 30 C4
South Lambeth SW4 270 B1
Mimosa Ho UB4 84 C2
Mimosa Rd UB4 84 C2
Mimosa St SW6 135 B4 264 D1
Mina Rd Merton SW19 179 C2
Walworth SE17 117 C1 263 B2
Minard Rd SE6 164 C3
Minchenden Cres N14 15 D1
Minchenden Ct N14 15 D2
Minchin Ho 10 E14 97 C1
Mincing La EC3 117 C6 253 A6
Minden Rd Cheam SM3 217 B6
Minden Rd *continued*
Penge SE20 184 B2
Minehead Ct HA2 63 C6
Minehead Rd
Harrow HA2 63 C5
Streatham SW16 182 B5
Mineral Cl EN5 12 C6
Mineral St SE18 123 C2
Minera Mews SW1 258 B4
Minerva Cl
Kennington SW9 138 C5
Sidcup DA14 189 C6
Minerva Rd
Becontree NW10 89 B4
Chingford E4 35 D3
Kingston u T KT1 176 B1
Minerva St E2 96 B5
Minerva Wlk EC1 241 D2
Minet Ave NW10 89 C5
Minet Ctry Pk UB2, UB3, UB4 106 C4
Minet Dr UB3 106 A5
Minet Gdns
Dagenham NW10 89 C5
Hayes UB3 106 B5
Minet Ho 20 E1 96 A1
Minet Jun & Inf Schs UB3 106 B5
Minet Rd SE5, SW9 138 D3
Minetta Ct 19 EN5 13 D6
Minford Gdns W14 112 D4
Mingard Wlk N7 72 B5
Ming St E14 119 C6
Minimax Cl TW14 150 A5
Ministry Way SE9 166 B2
Mink Ct TW4 128 C3
Minnie Bennett Ho SE3 143 C5
Minniedale KT5 198 B4
Minnow Wlk SE17 263 B3
Minories EC3 117 D6 253 C6
Minshaw Ct DA14 189 D6
Minshull Pl 23 BR3 185 C3
Minshull St SW8 269 C1
Minson Rd E9 96 D6
Minstead Gdns SW15 155 D4
Minstead Way KT3 199 C3
Minster Ave SM1 217 C6
Minster Ct EC3 253 B6
Minster Dr CR0 221 C4
Minster Gdns KT8 195 B5
Minsterley Ave TW16, TW17 193 C5
Minster Rd
Bromley BR1 187 B3
Brondesbury NW2 69 A3
Minster Wlk N8 50 A5
Minstrel Ct HA3 24 C1
Minstrel Gdns KT5 198 B5
Mint Bsns Pk 12 E16 99 A2
Mint Cl UB10 82 D4
Mintern Cl N13 16 D1
Minterne Ave UB2 107 C2
Minterne Rd HA3 44 B4
Minterne Waye UB4 84 C1
Mintern St N1 95 B5 235 D4
Minton Ho SE11 261 A4
Minton Mews 3 NW6 69 D2
Mint Rd SM5, SM6 219 B4
Mint St SE1 252 B2
Mint Wlk CR0 221 A5
Mirabel Rd SW6 135 B5 264 D4
Mirage Ctr The HA9 66 D4
Miranda Cl 19 E1 96 C2
Miranda Ct W3 88 B1
Miranda Ho
6 Belvedere DA17 125 C1
17 Hoxton N1 95 C5
Miranda Rd N19 49 C1
Mirfield Ct SE20 184 A1
Mirfield St SE7 121 D3
Miriam Ct DA14 190 B6
Miriam Rd SE18 123 C1
Mirravale Ct 11 IG9 21 C2
Mirravale Trad Est RM8 59 A2
Mirren Cl HA2 63 B5
Mirror Path SE12 165 C1
Misbourne Rd UB10 82 C6
Missenden SE17 262 D1
Missenden Cl TW14 149 D3
Missenden Gdns SM4 202 A3
Missenden Ho NW8 237 A6
Mission Gr E17 53 A4
Mission Grove Prim Sch E17 53 B5
Mission Pl SE15 140 A4
Mission Sq 13 TW8 132 A6
Mission The
13 Bermondsey SE16 118 B4
14 Poplar E14 97 B1
Missouri Ct HA5 40 C3
Misterton Ct SW11 266 D2
Mistletoe Cl CR0 206 D1
Mistley Thorn IG1 56 C2
Mistral SE5 139 C4
Mistral Ct E4 19 D1
Mistys Field KT12 194 C1
Mitali Pas 21 E1 96 A1
MITCHAM 202 D5
Mitcham Garden Village CR4 203 A4
Mitcham Ho 9 SE5 139 A4
Mitcham Ind Est CR4 181 A2
Mitcham Junction Sta CR4 203 A4
Mitcham La SW16 181 C5
Mitcham Pk CR4 202 C5
Mitcham Rd Ilford IG3 57 D2
Mitcham Rd *continued*
Newham E6 100 A4
Upper Tooting SW17 180 D5
Mitcham Sta CR4 202 C5
Mitchell 19 NW9 27 D2
Mitchell Brook Prim Sch NW10 67 C2
Mitchellbrook Way NW10 67 B2
Mitchell Cl
Abbey Wood SE2 124 C2
Belvedere DA17 125 D3
Mitchell Ct SW14 133 C1
Mitchell Ho
Gunnersbury W4 110 D1
6 Islington N1 72 C1
31 Shepherd's Bush W12 112 B6
Mitchell Rd
Edmonton N13 33 A5
Orpington BR6 227 D4
Mitchell's Pl SE21 161 C4
Mitchell St EC1 95 A3 242 B6
Mitchell Way
1 Bromley BR1 187 A2
Tokyngton NW10 67 A2
Mitchell Wlk E6 100 B2
Mitchison Rd N1 73 B2
Mitchley Rd N17 52 A6
Mitford Cl KT9 213 C2
Mitford Rd N19 72 A6
Mitre Bridge Ind Pk W10 90 B3
Mitre Cl
Shepperton TW17 193 B3
Sutton SM2 218 B1
Mitre Ct
Belvedere DA17 125 C1
1 Ilford RM6 58 B2
9 Woodford E18 37 A2
Mitre Ho RM7 59 D5
Mitre Rd
Lambeth SE1 116 C4 251 B2
Newham E15 98 C5
Mitre Sq EC3 243 B1
Mitre St EC3 95 C1 243 B1
Mitre The 9 E14 119 B6
Mitre Way W10 90 B2
Mizzen Ct E14 119 C4
Moatbridge Sch SE9 165 D5
Moat Cl BR6 227 D2
Moat Cres N3 47 D6
Moat Croft DA16 146 C2
Moat Ct Eltham SE9 166 B5
Sidcup DA15 167 D1
Moat Dr Harrow HA1 42 B5
5 Newham E13 99 C5
Ruislip HA4 39 C2
Moat Farm Rd UB5 63 B1
Moatfield NW6 69 A1
Moat Lodge The HA1 64 C6
Moat Pl Acton W3 88 D1
Stockwell SW9 138 B2
Moat Sch The SW6 135 A3
Moat Side Enfield EN3 6 D1
Feltham TW13 172 C6
Moat The KT3 177 C2
Moberly Rd SW4 159 D4
Mobey Ct SW4 270 A1
Moby Dick RM6 59 B5
Mocatta Ho 9 E1 96 B3
Modbury Gdns NW5 71 A2
Modder Pl SW15 134 D1
Model Cotts SW14 133 A2
Model Farm Cl SE9 166 A1
Modling Ho 8 E2 96 D5
Modoc Ho EN3 18 D6
Moelwyn Hughes Ct N7 71 D3
Moelyn Mews HA1 43 A4
Moffat Ct
Upper Tooting SW17 180 C6
Wimbledon SW19 179 C5
Moffat Ho 24 SE5 139 A5
Moffat Rd Bowes Pk N13 32 A4
South Norwood CR7 183 B1
Upper Tooting SW17 180 D6
Mogden La TW7 152 D6
Mohammedi Pk Complex UB5 85 C6
Mohawk Ho 33 E3 97 A5
Mohmmad Khan Rd E11 54 D1
Mohr Ct N22 32 B3
Moidart Ct HA8 10 D2
Moineau 18 NW9 27 D2
Moira Cl N17 33 C1
Moira Ct SW17 159 A2
Moira Ho 13 SW9 138 C4
Moira Rd SE9 144 B1
Molasses Ho 1 SW11 136 A2
Molasses Row 2 SW11 136 A2
Mole Abbey Gdns KT8 195 D6
Mole Ct
2 Bedford Pk W12 111 C4
West Ewell KT19 215 A4
Mole Ho NW8 236 D5
Molember Ct KT7 196 C5
Molember Rd KT8 196 C4
Molescroft SE9 167 A1
Molesey Ave KT12, KT8 195 B4
Molesey Bsns Ctr KT8 195 B4
Molesey Dr SM3 217 A5
Molesey Ho E2 243 C6
Molesey Hospl KT8 195 C4
Molesey Park Ave KT8 195 D4
Molesey Park Cl KT8 196 A4
Molesey Park Rd KT8 196 A4
Molesey Rd KT12 195 A2
Molesford Rd SW6 265 A1
Molesham Cl KT8 195 D6
Molesham Way KT8 195 D6
Molesworth Ho 9 SE17 138 D6
Molesworth St SE13 142 A2
Moliner Ct 4 BR3 185 C3
Mollie Davis Ct SE19 183 D4
Mollison Ave EN3 7 B5
Mollison Dr SM6 220 A1
Mollison Sq SM6 219 D1
Mollison Way HA8 26 C1
Molly Huggins Cl SW12 159 C4
Molton Ho N1 233 D5
Molvic Ct BR3 185 B1
Molyneux Dr SW17 181 B6
Molyneux Ho W1 237 B2
Molyneux St W1 92 C2 237 B3
Monarch Cl
Coney Hall BR4 224 D4
East Bedfont TW14 149 C4
Monarch Ct Ealing W5 87 C2
Hampstead Garden Suburb N2 48 A4
Monarch Dr E16 99 D2
Monarch Mews
Walthamstow E17 53 D3
West Norwood SW16 182 C5
Monarch Par CR4 180 D1
Monarch Pl
Buckhurst Hill IG9 21 C2
Sutton SM1 218 B3
Monarch Rd DA17 125 C3
Monarchs Ct
1 Edgware NW7 27 B5
Harrow HA2 41 C2
Monarch's Way HA4 39 C1
Monarch Way IG2 57 B3
Mona Rd SE15 140 C3
Mona St E16 98 D2
Monastery Gdns EN2 5 B3
Monaveen Gdns KT8 195 D6
Monck's Row SW18 157 B5
Monck St SW1 115 D3 259 D5
Monckton Ct W14 254 C6
Monclar Rd SE5 139 B1
Moncorvo Cl SW7 114 C4 247 A1
Moncrieff Cl 4 E6 100 A1
Moncrieff St SE15 140 A3
Mondial Way UB7 127 A5
Mondragon Ho SW8 270 B2
Monega Prim Sch E12 77 D2
Monega Rd E7, E12 77 D2
Monet Ct 15 SE16 118 B1
Moneyer Ho N1 235 C2
Monica Ct SW16 181 D4
Monica James Ho 12 DA14 168 A1
Monica Shaw Ct NW1 232 D3
Monier Rd E3 75 C1
Monivea Rd BR3 185 B3
Monkbretton Ho E2 96 A4
Monk Ct W12 112 A5
Monk Dr E16 121 A6
MONKEN HADLEY 1 A3
Monken Hadley CE Prim Sch EN4 1 C4
Monkfrith Ave N14 15 B5
Monkfrith Cl N14 15 B4
Monkfrith Prim Sch N14 15 A4
Monkfrith Way N14 15 B4
Monkham's Ave IG8 37 B5
Monkham's Dr IG8 37 B5
Monkham's La IG8 37 B6
Monkleigh Rd SM4, SW20 201 A5
Monkridge 3 N8 49 D2
Monks Ave
East Molesey KT8 195 B4
New Barnet EN5 14 A5
Monks Cl
Abbey Wood SE2 124 D2
Enfield EN2 5 A3
Harrow HA2 63 D6
Ruislip HA4 62 D4
Monks Cres KT12 194 B1
Monksdene Gdns SM1 217 D5
Monks Dr W3 88 C1
Monksfield N4 72 C6
MONKS ORCHARD 207 A3
Monks Orchard Rd BR3, CR0 207 C2
Monks Orchard Sch CR0 206 D4
Monks Park Gdns HA9 66 D1
Monks Pk HA9 67 A2
Monks Rd EN2 5 A3
Monk St SE18 122 C2
Monks Way
Beckenham BR3 207 C3
Crofton BR5 211 B1
Harmondsworth UB7 126 A6
Temple Fortune NW11 47 B5
Monkswell Ct N10 31 A2
Monkswell Ho E2 96 A4
Monkswood Gdns
Borehamwood WD6 11 B6
Ilford IG5 56 C6
Monk Terr SE23 163 B2
Monkton Ho
32 Bermondsey SE16 118 D4
22 Hackney E5 74 B3
Monkton Rd DA16 145 D3
Monkton St SE11 116 C2 261 B4
Monkville Ave NW11 47 B5
Monkville Par 1 NW11 47 B5
Monkwell Sq EC2 242 B3
Monmouth Ave
Teddington KT1 175 C3
Wanstead E18 55 B6
Monmouth Cl
Bedford Pk W4 111 B3
Bexley DA16 146 A1
Mitcham CR4, SW16 204 A5
Monmouth Ct 9 W7 86 D2
Monmouth Gr TW8 110 A2
Monmouth Ho
5 Camden Town NW5 71 B2
Wandsworth SW18 157 C5
Monmouth Pl W2 91 D1
Monmouth Rd
Dagenham RM9 81 B3
Hayes UB3 105 D2
Lower Edmonton N9 18 C2
Newham E6 100 B4
Notting Hill W2 91 C1
Monmouth St WC2 94 A1 240 A1
Monnery Rd N19 71 C5
Monnow Rd SE1 118 A2
Mono La TW13 150 B2
Monoux Almshouses E17 53 D5
Monoux Gr E17 35 C2
Monroe Cres EN1 6 B4
Monroe Dr SW14 154 D6
Monroe Ho
16 Crouch End N19 49 D2
Lisson Gr NW8 230 B1
Monro Gdns HA3 24 C3
Monro Ho
16 Hampstead NW3 70 A4
Putney SW15 156 B6
Monro Way E5 74 A4
Monsal Ct E5 75 A4
Monsell Ct 4 N4 72 D5
Monsell Rd N4, N5 72 D5
Monson Prim Sch SE14 140 D5
Monson Rd
Deptford SE14 140 D5
Willesden Green NW10 90 B5
Mons Way BR2 210 A3
Montacute Rd
Bushey WD23 8 C4
Carshalton SM4 202 B3
Forest Hill SE6 163 B4
Montagu Cres N18 34 B6
Montagu Ct W1 237 D3
Montague Ave
Brockley SE4 141 C1
Ealing W7 108 D5
Montague Cl
Borough The SE1 252 C4
Walton-on-T KT12 194 A2
Montague Ct 16 DA14 168 A1
Montague Fell HA0 64 D4
Montague Gdns W3 110 C6
Montague Pl WC1 93 D2 239 D4
Montague Rd
Ealing W13 87 B1
Hanwell W7 108 D4
Hornsey Vale N8 50 B4
Hounslow TW3 129 D2
Leytonstone E11 76 D6
Merton SW19 179 D3
Richmond TW10 154 A5
Shacklewell E8 74 A3
Southall UB2 107 A2
Thornton Heath CR0 204 D1
Tottenham Hale N15 52 A5
Uxbridge UB8 60 A1
Montague Sq SE15 140 C5
Montague St
Bloomsbury WC1 94 A2 240 A4
City of London EC1 242 A3
Montague Terr 1 BR2 209 A5
Montague Waye UB2 107 A3
Montague Works HA0 88 B5
Montagu Gdns
Edmonton N18 34 B6
Wallington SM6 219 C4
Montagu Ind Est N18 34 C6
Montagu Mans W1 92 D2 237 D3
Montagu Mews N W1 237 D3
Montagu Mews S W1 237 D2
Montagu Mews W W1 237 D2
Montagu Pl W1 92 D2 237 D3
Montagu Rd
Hendon NW4 46 A3
Lower Edmonton N9, N18 18 C1
Montagu Row W1 237 D3
Montagu Sq W1 92 D1 237 D2
Montagu St W1 92 D1 237 D2
Montaigne Cl SW1 259 D3
Montalt Ho IG8 36 D6
Montalt Rd IG8 36 D5
Montana Bldg 4 SE13 141 D4
Montana Gdns
Penge SE26 185 B5
5 Sutton SM1 218 A3
Montana Rd
Upper Tooting SW17 159 A1
Wimbledon SW20 178 C2
Montbelle Prim Sch SE9 188 C6
Montbelle Rd SE9 166 D1

Montcalm Cl
Hayes BR2 209 A3
Yeading UB4 84 B4
Montcalm Ho E14 119 C3
Montcalm Rd SE7 143 D5
Montclair Ct 21 N12 29 D6
Montclare St
E2 95 D3 243 C6
Monteagle Ave IG11 79 A2
Monteagle Ct
Barking IG11 79 A1
27 Hoxton N1 95 C5
Monteagle Prim Sch
RM9 102 B6
Monteagle Way
Nunhead SE15 140 B2
Shacklewell E5 74 A5
Montefiore Ct 2 N16 51 D1
Montefiore St 2 SW8 137 B3
Montego Cl 10 SW2 138 C1
Montem Prim Sch N7 72 B5
Montem Rd
Forest Hill SE23 163 B4
New Malden KT3 199 C5
Montem St N4 50 B1
Montenotte Rd N8 49 C4
Monteray Studios W10 91 A5
Monterey Cl NW7 27 C5
Montesole Ct 7 HA5 22 C1
Montesquieu Terr 3
E16 98 D1
Montford Pl
Kennington SE11 138 C6
Kennington SE11 261 A1
Montford Rd TW16 194 A5
Montfort Ho
4 Bethnal Green E2 96 C4
Cubitt Town E14 120 A3
Montfort Pl SW19 156 D3
Montgolfier Wlk UB5 85 A4
Montgomerie Ct 2
BR3 185 C2
Montgomery Ave
KT10 212 C6
Montgomery Cl
Blackfen DA15 167 D5
Mitcham CR4 204 A5
Montgomery Ct W4 133 A6
Montgomery Gdns
SM2 218 B1
Montgomery Ho 5
SW14 133 B2
Montgomery Lo 38 E1 96 C3
Montgomery Rd
Acton W4 111 A2
Edgware HA8 26 B4
Montholme Rd SW11 158 D5
Monthope Rd 17 E1 96 A2
Montolieu Gdns SW15 156 B6
Montpelier Ave
Ealing W5 87 C2
Sidcup DA5 168 D4
Montpelier Cl UB10 82 C6
Montpelier Ct
5 Beckenham BR2 208 D5
Ealing W5 87 D2
Montpelier Gdns
Ilford RM6 58 C2
Newham E6 99 D4
Montpelier Gr NW5 71 C3
Montpelier Mews SW7 257 B6
Montpelier Pl
Knightsbridge SW7 257 B6
21 Stepney E1 96 C1
Montpelier Prim Sch
W5 87 D2
Montpelier Rd
Ealing W5 87 D2
Finchley N3 30 A2
Peckham SE15 140 B4
Sutton SM1 218 A4
Montpelier Rise
Golders Green NW11 47 A2
Wembley HA9 43 D1
Montpelier Row
Blackheath Vale SE3 142 D3
Twickenham TW1 153 C4
Montpelier Sq
SW7 114 C4 247 B1
Montpelier St
SW7 114 C3 257 B6
Montpelier Terr SW7 247 B1
Montpelier Vale SE3 142 D3
Montpelier Way NW11 47 A2
Montpelier Wlk
SW7 114 C3 257 B6
Montpellier Ct KT12 194 B3
Montrave Rd SE20 184 C3
Montreal Ho
Catford SE6 163 D3
Hayes UB4 84 B4
Montreal Pl WC2 250 C6
Montreal Rd IG1 57 A2
Montrell Rd SW2 160 A3
Montrose Ave
Falconwood DA16 145 C2
Hendon HA8 27 B2
Kensal Rise NW6 91 A5
Sidcup DA15 168 A4
Twickenham TW2 151 D4
Montrose Cl
Ashford TW15 171 A5
Falconwood DA16 145 D2
Woodford IG8 37 A6
Montrose Cres
Finchley N12 30 A4
1 Wembley HA0 66 A2
Montrose Ct
2 Catford SE6 164 D2
Hendon NW9 27 A1
Montrose Ct *continued*
Knightsbridge
SW7 114 B4 246 D1
Temple Fortune NW11 47 B5
Montrose Gdns
Mitcham CR4 180 D1
Sutton SM1 217 D6
Montrose Ho
Belgravia SW1 248 B1
Millwall E14 119 C3
Twickenham TW2 151 D4
Montrose Pl
SW1 115 A4 248 B1
Montrose Rd
East Bedfont TW14 149 B5
Harrow HA3 24 D1
Montrose Villas 5
W6 112 A1
Montrose Way SE23 162 D3
Montserrat Ave IG8 36 B3
Montserrat Cl SE19 183 B5
Montserrat Rd SW15 135 A1
Montway Hts SW19 179 D3
Monument Gdns SE13 164 A6
Monument St
EC3 117 B6 252 D6
Monument Sta
EC3 117 B6 252 D6
Monument The* EC3 252 D6
Monument Way N17 51 D6
Monza Bldg The E1 118 C6
Monza St E1 118 C6
Moodkee St SE16 118 C3
Moody Rd SE15 139 D4
Moody St E1 96 D4
Moon Ct SE12 143 A1
Moon Ho HA1 42 D5
Moon La EN5 1 B2
Moon St N1 94 D6 234 C6
Moorcroft HA8 26 D2
Moorcroft Ct 4 N3 29 B1
Moorcroft Gdns BR1 210 A4
Moorcroft La UB8 82 C2
Moorcroft Rd SW16 160 A1
Moorcroft Sch UB8 82 B1
Moorcroft Way HA5 41 A4
Moordown SE18 144 D4
Moore Cl Mitcham CR4 181 B1
Mortlake SW14 133 A2
Wallington SM6 220 A1
Moore Cres RM9 102 B6
Moore Ct N1 234 C5
Moorefield Rd N17 33 D1
Moore Ho
16 Bethnal Green E2 96 C4
5 Greenwich SE10 120 D1
Hornsey N8 50 A5
7 Shadwell E1 118 C6
Wandsworth SW17 158 B1
1 West Norwood
SE27 183 A6
Mooreland Rd BR1 187 A2
Moore Park Ct SW6 265 D4
Moore Park Rd
SW6 135 D5 265 C3
Moore Rd SE19 183 A4
Moore St SW3 114 D2 257 C4
Moore Wlk E7 77 A4
Moorey Cl 2 E15 98 D6
Moorfield Ave W5 87 D3
Moorfield Rd
Chessington KT9 214 A3
Enfield EN3 6 C4
Moorfields EC2 95 B2 242 C3
Moorfields Ct 6
SW16 181 C6
Moorfields Eye Hospl
EC1 95 B4 235 C1
Moorfields Highwalk
EC2 242 C3
Moorgate EC2 95 B2 242 C3
Moorgate Pl EC2 242 C2
Moorgate Sta
EC2 95 B2 242 C3
Moorgreen Ho EC1 234 C2
Moorhead Way SE3 143 B2
Moorhouse 17 NW9 27 D2
Moorhouse Rd
Harrow HA3 43 D6
Notting Hill W2 91 C1
Moorings Ho 3 TW8 131 C5
Moorings The 5 E16 99 C2
Moor La
Broadgate EC2 95 B2 242 C3
Chessington KT9 214 A3
Moorland Cl TW4 151 C4
Moorland Ct N21 16 B5
Moorland Rd SW9 138 D1
Moorlands
Chislehurst BR7 188 D3
Northolt UB5 85 A6
17 Wallington SM6 219 B2
Moorlands Ave NW7 28 B4
Moor Lane Jun Sch
KT9 214 B3
Moormead Dr KT19 215 C3
Moor Mead Rd TW1 153 A5
Moor Park Gdns KT2 177 C3
Moor Park Ho N21 16 D4
Moor Pl EC2 242 C3
Moorside Ct W13 109 C5
Moorside Rd BR1 186 D6
Moor St W1 239 D1
Moortown Rd WD19 22 C6
Moot Ct NW9 44 C4
Morant Ho SW9 138 B3
Morant Pl N22 32 B2
Morant St E14 119 C6
Mora Prim Sch NW2 68 C4
Mora Rd NW2 68 C4
Mora St EC1 95 A4 235 B1
Morat St SW9 138 B4 270 D2
Moravian Cl SW3 266 D5
Moravian Pl
SW10 136 B6 266 D5
Moravian St 10 E2 96 C4
Moray Ave UB3 105 D5
Moray Cl HA8 10 D2
Moray Ho
11 Kingston u T KT6 198 A4
9 Mile End E1 97 A3
Moray Mews N4, N7 72 B6
Moray Rd N4, N7 72 B6
Mordaunt Gdns RM9 81 A1
Mordaunt Ho
4 Becontree NW10 89 B6
34 Clapham SW8 137 D3
Mordaunt Rd NW10 89 B6
Mordaunt St SW9 138 B2
MORDEN 201 D3
Morden Court Par
SM4 201 D5
Morden Ct SM4 201 D5
Morden Gdns
Greenford UB6 64 D3
Mitcham CR4 202 B5
Morden Hall SW19 201 D6
Morden Hall Rd SM4 202 A5
Morden Hill SE13 142 A3
Morden Ho
Morden SM4 201 C5
19 Tulse Hill SW2 160 C5
Morden La SE13 142 A4
Morden Lo BR2 186 B1
Morden Mount Prim Sch
SE13 141 D3
MORDEN PARK 201 A3
Morden Park Sch Sports
Ctr SM4 201 B4
Morden Prim Sch
SM4 201 C4
Morden Rd
Dagenham RM6 59 A2
Kidbrooke SE3 143 A3
Merton SW19 179 D1
Mitcham CR4, SM4 202 B5
Morden Road Mews
SE3 143 A3
Morden Road Sta
SW19 179 D1
Morden South Sta
SM4 201 C4
Morden St SE13 141 D4
Morden Sta SW19 201 D6
Morden Way SM3 201 C2
Morden Wharf Rd
SE10 120 C3
Mordern Ho NW1 237 B5
Mordon Rd IG3 57 D2
Mordred Rd SE6 164 C2
Morecambe Cl 3 E1 96 D2
Morecambe Gdns HA7 25 D6
Morecambe St
SE17 117 A1 262 B2
Morecambe Terr N18 33 B6
More Cl
Canning Town E16 98 D1
West Kensington
W14 113 A2 254 A3
Morecoombe Cl KT2 176 D3
Morecroft TW2 152 A2
Moredown Ho 3 E8 74 A3
Moree Way N18 34 A6
More House Sch
SW1 114 D3 257 D5
Moreland Ct 3 NW2 69 C5
Moreland Prim Sch
EC1 94 D4 234 D1
Moreland St
EC1 94 D4 234 D2
Moreland Way E4 20 A1
Morella Rd SW11,
SW12 158 D4
Morell Ho 5 SW9 138 B3
Morello Ave UB8 82 D2
Morello Ct HA9 66 B5
Moremead Rd SE6 185 C6
Morena St SE6 163 D4
Moresby Ave KT5 198 D2
Moresby Rd E5 52 B1
Moresby Wlk 6 SW8 137 B3
More's Gdn SW3 266 D5
Moreton Ave TW7 130 C4
Moreton Cl Mill Hill NW7 28 C4
Tottenham N15 51 B3
Upper Clapton E5 52 C1
Moreton Ho
Bermondsey SE16 118 B3
Upper Tooting SW17 180 B6
Moreton Pl
SW1 115 C1 259 B2
Moreton Rd
Croydon CR2 221 B3
North Cheam KT4 216 B6
Tottenham N15 51 B3
Moreton St
SW1 115 D1 259 C2
Moreton Terr
SW1 115 C1 259 B2
Moreton Terr Mews N
SW1 259 B2
Moreton Terr Mews S
SW1 259 B2
Moreton Twr 3 W3 110 D5
Morford Cl HA4 40 B2
Morford Way HA4 40 B2
Morgan Ave E17 54 B5
Morgan Cl RM10 81 C1
Morgan Ct
Ashford TW15 170 D5
Morgan Ct *continued*
5 Battersea SW11 136 B3
Carshalton SM5 218 D4
Morgan Ho
Nine Elms SW8 269 B2
Pimlico SW1 259 B3
Morgan Rd Islington N7 72 C3
Notting Hill W10 91 B2
Plaistow BR1 187 A3
Morgan's La UB3 83 B2
Morgan St
Canning Town E16 98 D2
Globe Town E3 96 D4
Morgan's Wlk SW11 267 A3
Morgan Terr RM6 58 C4
Moriah Jewish Day Sch
The HA5 41 A1
Moriatry Cl N7 72 A4
Morie St SW18 157 D6
Morieux Rd E10 53 B1
Moring Rd SW17 181 A6
Morkyns Wlk SE21 161 C1
Morland Ave CR0 205 C1
Morland Cl
Golders Green NW11 47 D1
Hampton TW12 173 B5
Mitcham CR4 202 C6
Morland Ct W12 112 B4
Morland Est E8 74 A1
Morland Gdns
Southall UB1 107 D5
Stonebridge NW10 67 B1
Morland Ho
Kilburn NW6 91 C6
Notting Hill W11 91 A1
Somers Town NW1 232 B3
Westminster SW1 260 A4
Morland Mews N1 72 C1
Morland Rd
Croydon CR0 205 D2
Dagenham RM10 81 C1
Harrow HA3 44 A5
Ilford IG1 78 D6
Penge SE20 184 D4
Sutton SM1 218 A3
Walthamstow E17 52 D4
Morley Ave Chingford E4 36 B3
Edmonton N18 34 A6
Tottenham N22 32 D1
Morley Cl BR6 226 D6
Morley Coll
SE1 116 C3 261 B6
Morley Cres
Edgware HA8 11 A2
Ruislip HA4 62 C6
Morley Cres E HA7 43 D6
Morley Cres W HA7 43 C6
Morley Ct Bromley BR3 186 B2
Chingford Hatch E4 35 B5
Lewisham SE13 142 A1
Shortlands BR2 208 D5
Morley Hill EN2 5 B5
Morley Ho
Stoke Newington N16 74 A6
Streatham SW2 160 A4
W1 238 D2
Morley Rd
Barking IG11 101 B6
Cheam SM3 201 B1
Chislehurst BR7 189 A2
Dagenham RM6 59 A4
Lewisham SE13 142 A1
Leytonstone E10 54 A1
Newham E15 98 D5
Twickenham TW1 153 D5
Morley St SE1 116 C4 251 B1
Morna Rd SE5 139 A3
Morning La E9 74 C2
Morningside Prim Sch
E9 74 C2
Morningside Rd KT4 216 C6
Mornington Ave
Bromley BR1 209 D6
Ilford IG1 56 C2
West Kensington
W14 113 B2 254 C3
Mornington Avenue Mans
W14 254 C3
Mornington Cl IG8 37 A6
Mornington Cres
Camden Town
NW1 93 C5 232 A4
Cranford TW5 128 B4
Mornington Crescent Sta
NW1 93 C5 232 A4
Mornington Ct NW1 232 A4
Mornington Gr E3 97 C4
Mornington Lo EN1 17 C6
Mornington Mews 2
SE5 139 A4
Mornington Pl
4 New Cross SE8 141 B5
Regent's Pk NW1 232 A4
Mornington Rd
Ashford TW15 171 A5
Chingford E4 20 B4
Greenford UB6 85 D3
Leytonstone E11 54 D1
New Cross SE14, SE8 141 B5
Woodford IG8 36 D6
Mornington St
NW1 93 B5 231 D4
Mornington Terr
NW1 93 B5 231 D4
Mornington Wlk
TW10 175 C6
Morocco St
SE1 117 C4 253 A1
Morpeth Gr E9 96 D6
Morpeth Rd E9 96 D6
Morpeth Sec Sch E2 96 C4
Morpeth St E2 96 D4
Morpeth Terr
SW1 115 C2 259 A4
Morpeth Wlk N17 34 B3
Morrab Gdns IG3 79 D5
Morrel Cl EN5 2 A2
Morrel Ct 11 E2 96 A5
Morris Ave E12 78 B3
Morris Blitz Ct 2 N16 73 D4
Morris Cl Croydon CR0 207 A4
Orpington BR6 227 C5
Morris Ct Chingford E4 19 D1
Croydon CR0 220 D4
3 Herne Hill SE5 139 B1
Morris Gdns SW18 157 C4
Morris Ho
17 Bethnal Green E2 96 C4
Lisson Gr NW8 237 A5
1 Stockwell SW4 138 A1
10 Tufnell Pk N19 71 C4
Morrish Rd SW2 160 A4
Morrison Ave
Chingford E4 35 C4
Tottenham N17 51 C6
Morrison Bldgs 5 E1 96 A1
Morrison Ct
7 Barnet EN5 1 A1
Finchley N12 30 C3
Morrison Ho SW2 160 C3
Morrison Rd
Barking IG11 103 A5
24 Brixton SW9 138 C3
Hayes UB4 84 B4
Morrison St SW11 137 A2
Morrison Yd N17 33 D1
Morris Pl N4 72 C6
Morris Rd
Bow Comm E14 97 D2
Dagenham RM8 81 B6
Isleworth TW7 130 D2
Leyton E15 76 C4
Morriss Ho
9 Bermondsey SE16 118 B4
5 Upper Clapton E5 74 B6
Morris St E1 96 B1
Morris Stephany Ho 4
SE27 182 D6
Morriston Cl WD19 22 C5
Morritt Ho 2 HA0 65 D3
Morse Cl E13 99 A4
Morshead Mans W9 91 C4
Morshead Rd W9 91 C4
Morson Rd EN3 19 A5
Morston Gdns SE9 188 B6
Mortain Ho 9 SE16 118 B2
Morten Cl SW4 159 D5
Morteyne Rd N17 33 B2
Mortgramit Sq SE18 122 C3
Mortham St E15 98 C6
Mortimer Cl
1 Child's Hill NW2 69 B5
Streatham SW16 159 D2
Mortimer Cres
Paddington NW6 91 D6
Worcester Pk KT4 215 B5
Mortimer Ct
St John's Wood NW8 229 B3
4 Whetstone N20 14 A2
Mortimer Dr EN1 17 C6
Mortimer Est NW6 91 D6
Mortimer Ho
6 Shepherd's Bush
W11 112 D5
West Kensington W14 254 B3
Mortimer Lo 11 SW19 157 A3
Mortimer Market WC1 239 B5
Mortimer Pl NW6 91 D6
Mortimer Rd
De Beauvoir Town N1 73 C1
Ealing W13 87 C1
Kensal Green NW10 90 C4
Mitcham CR4 180 D2
Newham E6 100 B4
Mortimer Sq W11 112 D6
Mortimer St W1 93 C2 239 B3
Mortimer Terr NW5 71 B4
MORTLAKE 133 A2
Mortlake Cl CR0 220 A5
Mortlake Dr CR4 180 C2
Mortlake High St
SW14 133 B2
Mortlake Ho 7 W4 111 A2
Mortlake Rd Ilford IG1 79 B4
Newham E16 99 B1
Richmond SW14, TW9 132 C4
Mortlake Sta SW14 133 A2
Mortlake Terr TW9 132 C5
Mortlock Cl SE15 140 B4
Mortlock Ct E12 77 D4
Morton Cl
Hillingdon UB8 82 B3
Stepney E1 96 C1
Wallington SM6 220 B1
Morton Cres N14 31 D6
Morton Ct UB5 64 A3
Morton Gdns SM6 219 C3
Morton Ho
Kennington SE17 138 D6
West Norwood SE27 183 B5
Morton Mews SW5 255 C3
Morton Pl SE1 261 A5
Morton Rd Islington N1 73 A1
Morden SM4 202 B4
Stratford E15 76 D1
Morton Way N14 31 D6
Morvale Cl DA17 125 B2
Morval Rd SW2 160 C6
Morven Rd SW17 158 D1
Morville Ho SW18 158 B5
Morville St E3 97 C5
Morwell St WC1 239 D3
Moscow Pl W2 245 C6
Moscow Rd
W2 113 D6 245 C6
Mosedale NW1 231 D1
Moseley Row SE10 120 D2
Moselle Ave N22 32 C1
Moselle Cl N8 50 B6
Moselle Ct N9 18 C1
Moselle Ho 2 N17 33 D3
Moselle Pl N17 33 D3
Moselle Sch (main site)
N17 33 C1
Moselle Sch (Upper)
N17 51 A6
Moselle St N17 33 D3
Mosque Tower 26 E1 96 A2
Mossborough Cl N12 29 D4
Mossbourne Com Acad
E8 74 A3
Mossbury Rd SW11 136 C2
Moss Cl Pinner HA5 23 A1
Spitalfields E1 96 A2
Mossdown Cl DA17 125 C2
Mossford Ct IG6 56 D6
Mossford Gn IG6 57 A6
Mossford St E3 97 B3
Moss Gdns
Feltham TW13 150 A2
South Croydon CR2 222 D1
Moss Hall Cres N12 30 A4
Moss Hall Ct N12 29 D4
Moss Hall Gr N12 29 D4
Moss Hall Inf Sch N12 29 D4
Moss Hall Jun Sch N3 29 D4
Mossington Gdns
SE16 118 C2
Moss La HA5 23 A1
Mosslea Rd
Bromley Comm BR2 209 D4
Orpington BR6 227 A5
Penge SE20 184 C4
Mossop St
SW3 114 C2 257 B4
Moss Rd RM10 81 C1
Mossville Gdns SM4 201 B5
Mosswell Ho 4 N10 31 A3
Moston Cl UB3 105 D1
Mostyn Ave HA9 66 B3
Mostyn Gdns NW10 90 D5
Mostyn Gr E3 97 C5
Mostyn Lo N5 73 A4
Mostyn Rd
Brixton SW9 138 C4
Bushey WD23 8 A6
Grahame Pk HA8 27 C3
Merton SW19 179 B1
Mosul Way BR2 210 A3
Motcomb St
SW1 115 A3 258 A6
Moth Cl SM6 220 A1
Mothers Sq The 13 E5 74 B4
Motley Ave EC2 243 A6
Motley St SW8 137 C3
MOTSPUR PARK 200 A3
Motspur Park Sta KT3 200 B4
Motspur Pk KT3 200 A3
MOTTINGHAM 165 D2
Mottingham Ct SE9 166 B3
Mottingham Gdns
SE9 165 D3
Mottingham La SE9 165 C3
Mottingham Prim Sch
SE9 166 B1
Mottingham Rd
Chislehurst SE9 166 B1
Ponders End N9 18 D4
Mottingham Sta SE9 166 B3
Mottisfont Rd SE2 124 B2
Moules Ct SE5 139 A5
Moulins Rd E9 74 C1
Moulsford Ho
5 Lower Holloway N7 72 A3
32 Paddington W2 91 C2
Moulton Ave TW3,
TW5 129 B3
Moundfield Rd N16 52 A3
Mound The SE9 166 C1
Mounsey Ho 13 W10 91 A4
Mountacre Cl SE26 183 D6
Mount Adon Pk SE21,
SE22 162 A4
Mountague Pl 2 E14 120 A6
Mountain Ho SE11 260 C2
Mountaire Ct NW9 45 B4
Mount Angelus Rd
SW15 155 D4
Mount Ararat Rd
TW10 154 A6
Mount Arlington 3
BR2 186 C1
Mount Ash Rd SE26 162 B1
Mount Ave Chingford E4 19 D1
Ealing W5 87 D2
Southall UB1 85 C1
Mountbatten Cl
Plumstead Comm
SE18 145 C6
6 West Norwood
SE19 183 C5
Mountbatten Ct 8 IG9 21 D2
Mountbatten Gdns
BR3 207 A5
Mountbatten Ho N6 49 A2
Mountbatten Mews
SW18 158 A3

Mountbel Rd HA7 25 A1
Mount Carmel 3 N7 72 B3
Mount Carmel RC Tech Coll for Girls N19 49 D1
Mount Cl Bromley BR1 188 A2
Cockfosters EN4 3 A1
Ealing W5 87 C2
Mountcombe Cl KT6 198 A2
Mountcombe Ho SW17 180 B5
Mount Ct
6 Kingston u T KT2 176 D3
West Wickham BR4 224 C6
Mount Culver Ave DA14 190 D4
Mount Dr Bexley DA6 169 A6
Harrow HA2, HA5 41 B4
Welsh Harp HA9 67 A6
Mountearl Gdns SW16, SW2 160 B1
Mount Eaton Ct W5 87 C2
Mount Echo Ave E4 19 D3
Mount Echo Dr E4 19 D3
Mount Ephraim La SW16 159 D1
Mount Ephraim Rd SW16 159 D1
Mount Felix KT12 193 D1
Mountfield NW2 69 B6
Mountfield Cl SE6 164 B4
Mountfield Ct SE13 164 B5
Mountfield Rd
Ealing W5 88 A1
East Finchley N3 47 C6
Wallend E6 100 C4
Mountford Ho EN2 4 D1
Mount Ford St E1 96 A1
Mountfort Cres N1 72 C1
Mountfort Terr 1 N1 72 C1
Mount Gdns SE26 162 B1
Mount Gr HA8 27 B6
Mountgrove Rd N5 73 A5
Mounthurst Rd BR2 208 D2
Mountier Ct 12 E11 55 A4
Mountington Park Cl HA3 43 D3
Mountjoy Cl SE2 124 B4
Mountjoy Ho EC2 242 A3
Mount Lo N6 49 C3
Mount Lodge SW4 137 D1
Mount Mews TW12 173 D2
Mount Mills EC1 234 D1
Mount Nod Rd SW16, SW2 160 B1
Mount Olive Ct W7 108 C4
Mount Par EN4 2 C1
Mount Park Ave HA1 64 C6
Mount Park Cres W5 87 D1
Mount Park Rd
Ealing W5 87 D1
Harrow HA1 64 B5
Pinner HA5 40 A4
Mount Pk SM5 219 A1
Mount Pl 7 W3 110 D5
Mount Pleasant
Cockfosters EN4 2 D1
Finsbury WC1 94 C3 241 A5
Ilford IG1 79 A3
Ruislip HA4 62 D6
Wembley HA0 88 B6
West Norwood SE27 183 A6
Mount Pleasant Cotts
Osidge N14 15 D4
Southall UB1 85 C1
Mount Pleasant Cres N4 50 B2
Mount Pleasant Hill E5 74 C6
Mount Pleasant La E5 52 B1
Mount Pleasant Pl SE18 123 B2
Mount Pleasant Rd
Ealing W5 87 C3
Higham Hill E17 35 A1
Kingston u T KT3 199 A6
Lewisham SE13 164 A5
Tottenham N17 33 C1
Willesden NW10 90 C6
Mount Pleasant Villas N4 50 B2
Mount Prim Sch The KT3 199 A6
Mount Rd Bexley DA6 169 A6
Chessington KT9 214 B3
Dagenham RM8 59 B1
Dollis Hill NW2 68 C5
East Barnet EN4 14 C6
Feltham TW13 151 A1
Hayes UB3 106 A4
Hendon NW4 46 A3
Kingston u T KT3 199 B6
Mitcham CR4 180 C1
South Norwood SE19 183 B4
Wimbledon SW18, SW19 157 D2
Mount Row W1 115 B6 248 C5
Mount Sch NW7 28 C5
Mountside HA7 25 A2
Mounts Pond Rd SE3, SE13 142 B3
Mount Sq The 6 NW3 70 A5
Mount St W1 115 A6 248 B5
Mount Stewart Ave HA3 43 D2
Mount Stewart Jun & Inf Schs HA3 43 D2
Mount Terr E1 96 B2
Mount The Bexley DA6 169 D6
Cheam SM1 217 C2
Chislehurst BR7 188 C2
Finchley N2 30 C1
Hampstead NW3 70 A5
Harrow HA1 64 C6
Kensington W8 245 A3
Kingston u T KT3 199 D6
North Cheam KT4 216 B4
Northolt UB5 63 D3
6 South Croydon CR2 221 A3
Upper Clapton E5 74 B6
Welsh Harp HA9 67 A6
Whetstone N20 14 A2
Mount Tyndal NW3 48 B1
Mount Vernon NW3 70 A4
Mountview
Edgware NW7 11 B1
Northwood HA6 22 A4
5 Streatham SW16 160 B1
Mount View Ealing W5 87 D3
Enfield EN2 4 B5
Southall UB2 106 D2
Mountview Cl NW11 48 A1
Mountview Cotts EN5 11 D5
Mountview Ct
Harringay N8 50 D5
3 Whetstone N20 14 A2
Mount View Rd
Chingford E4 20 B4
Claygate KT10 213 B1
Hornsey Vale N4 50 B3
Kingsbury NW9 45 B4
Mount Villas SE27 160 D1
Mountwood KT8 195 D6
Mountwood Ho W5 87 D3
Mourne Ho NW3 70 A2
Movers La IG11 101 C6
Movers Lane (Flyover) IG11 101 C5
Mowat Ct KT4 215 D6
Mowatt Cl N19 49 D1
Mowbray Ct
South Norwood SE19 183 D2
Wood Green N22 32 C2
Mowbray Gdns UB5 85 C6
Mowbray Ho 5 N2 30 B1
Mowbray Rd
Brondesbury NW6 69 A1
Edgware HA8 26 C6
New Barnet EN5 14 A6
Richmond TW10 153 C1
South Norwood SE19 183 D2
Mowlem Prim Sch E2 96 C5
Mowlem St E2 96 B5
Mowlem Trad Est N17 34 C3
Mowll St SW9 138 C5
Moxon Cl E13 98 D5
Moxon St Barnet EN5 1 B2
Marylebone W1 93 A2 238 A3
Moye Cl 10 E2 96 A5
Moyers Rd E10 54 A2
Moylan Rd W6 135 A6 264 B5
Moyle Ho SW1 269 B6
Moyne Ho 18 SW9 138 D1
Moyne Pl NW10 88 C5
Moynihan Dr N21 16 A6
Moys Cl CR0 204 A3
Moyser Rd SW16 181 B5
Mozart St W10 91 B4
Mt Carmel RC Prim Sch W5 109 C3
Muchelney Rd SM4 202 A3
Mudchute Sta E14 119 D2
Mudie Ho 8 SW2 160 A4
Mudlarks Blvd 3 SE10 120 D3
Muggeridge Cl CR2 221 B3
Muggeridge Rd RM10 81 D4
Muirdown Ave SW14 133 B1
Muir Dr SW18 158 C5
Muirfield W3 89 C1
Muirfield Cl
23 Bermondsey SE16 118 B1
South Oxhey WD19 22 C6
Muirfield Cres E14 119 D3
Muirfield Gn WD19 22 C6
Muirfield Rd WD19 22 C6
Muirhead Quay IG11 101 A5
Muirkirk Rd SE6 164 A3
Muir Rd E5 74 A5
Muir St E16 122 A5
Mulbarton Ct BR7 189 B4
Mulberry Ave TW19 148 A3
Mulberry Bsns Ctr SE16 118 D4
Mulberry Cl Barnet EN4 2 B1
Charlton SE7 143 D6
Chelsea SW3 266 D5
Chingford E4 19 C2
East Dulwich SE22 162 A5
Hampstead NW3 70 B4
Hendon NW4 46 C6
Hornsey N8 50 A4
Northolt UB5 85 A5
Streatham SW16 181 C6
Mulberry Cres
Brentford TW8 131 C5
West Drayton UB7 104 C4
Mulberry Ct
Barking IG11 79 D1
Bexley DA16 145 D3
Finchley N2 48 C6
Finsbury EC1 234 D1
Islington N5 72 D3
1 Leyton E11 76 B4
10 Paddington W9 91 B4
4 Surbiton KT6 197 D2
Twickenham TW1 152 D1
Willesden NW10 67 B2
Mulberry Ho
1 Bethnal Green E2 96 C4
8 Deptford SE8 141 B6
Mulberry House Sch The NW2 69 A3
Mulberry La CR0 205 D1
Mulberry Mews
New Cross SE14 141 B4
2 Wallington SM6 219 C2
Mulberry Par UB7 104 C4
Mulberry Pl
Chiswick W6 112 A1
Greenwich SE9 143 D1
Mulberry Prim Sch N17 34 A1
Mulberry Rd E8 73 D1
Mulberry Sch for Girls
Stepney E1 96 B1
St George in t East E1 118 B6
Mulberry St 7 E1 96 A1
Mulberry Trees TW17 193 B2
Mulberry Way
Ilford IG6 57 A5
Woodford E18 37 B1
Mulberry Wlk SW3 136 B6 266 D6
Mulgrave Chambers SM2 217 D2
Mulgrave Hall SM2 217 D2
Mulgrave Ho 10 SE18 122 B2
Mulgrave Manor SM2 217 D2
Mulgrave Prim Sch SE18 122 C2
Mulgrave Rd
Belmont SM2 217 C2
Ealing W5 87 D3
Harrow HA1 65 A6
South Croydon CR0 221 B5
West Kensington W14 264 C6
Willesden NW10 67 D4
Woolwich SE18 122 C2
Mulholland Cl CR4 181 B1
Mulkern Rd N19 49 D1
Mullard Ho WC1 239 C4
Mullards Cl CR4 202 D1
Mullens Ho 7 SW15 156 C6
Mullen Twr EC1 241 A5
Muller Ho SE18 122 C1
Muller Rd SW4 159 D5
Mullet Gdns 7 E2 96 A4
Mulletsfield WC1 233 B1
Mull Ho 17 E3 97 B5
Mullins Path SW14 133 B2
Mullion Cl HA3 23 D2
Mullion Wlk WD19 22 D6
Mulready St NW8 237 A5
Multi Way W3 111 C4
Multon Ho E9 74 C1
Multon Rd SW18 158 B4
Mulvaney Way SE1 252 D1
Mumford Rd SE24 160 D6
Muncaster Cl TW15 170 C6
Muncaster Rd
Ashford TW15 170 D5
Balham SW11 159 A6
Muncies Mews SE6 164 A2
Mundania Ct SE22 162 B5
Mundania Rd SE22 162 C5
Munday Ho SE1 262 C5
Munday Rd E16 121 A6
Munden Ho 5 E3 97 D4
Munden St W14 113 A2 254 A4
Mundesley Cl WD19 22 C6
Mundford Rd E5 74 C6
Mundon Gdns IG1 57 B1
Mund St W14 113 B1 254 D1
Mundy Ho 6 W10 91 A4
Mundy St N1 95 C4
Mungo-Park Cl WD23 8 A2
Munnery Way BR6 226 D6
Munning Ho 12 E16 121 B5
Munnings Gdns TW7 152 B6
Munro Ho
Bermondsey SE1 252 D1
Lambeth SE1 251 A1
Munro Mews W10 91 A2
Munro Rd WD23 8 A6
Munslow Gdns SM1 218 B4
Munstead Ct 12 SM2 218 A1
Munster Ave TW4 151 A6
Munster Ct
Fulham SW6 135 B3
Teddington TW11 175 C4
Munster Gdns N13 33 A6
Munster Ho N17 33 D2
Munster Rd
Fulham SW6 135 A5 264 B4
Teddington TW11 175 C4
Munster Residences SW6 264 B2
Munster Sq NW1 93 B3 238 D6
Munton Rd SE1, SE17 117 A2 262 B4
Murchison Ave DA5 169 A3
Murchison Ho 1 W10 91 A2
Murchison Rd E10 76 A6
Murdoch Ho 4 SE16 118 C3
Murdock Cl E16 98 D1
Murdock St SE15 140 B6
Murfett Cl SW19 157 A2
Muriel Ct 18 E10 53 D2
Muriel St N1 94 B6 233 D6
Murillo Rd SE13 142 C1
Murley Ct N21 17 A4
Murphy Ho SE1 261 D6
Murphy St SE1 116 C4 251 A1
Murray Ave
Bromley BR1 187 B1
Murray Ave *continued*
Hounslow TW3 151 D6
Murray Cl SE28 123 C5
Murray Cres HA5 22 D2
Murray Ct
5 Harrow HA1 42 D3
Southall TW7 108 C3
Twickenham TW2 152 A2
Murray Gr N1 95 B5 235 C3
Murray Grey Ho UB4 83 B2
Murray Ho
1 North Finchley N12 30 B5
20 Woolwich SE18 122 B2
Murray Mews NW1 71 D1
Murray Rd
Brentford W5 109 C2
Richmond TW10 153 C2
Wimbledon SW19 178 D4
Murray Sq E16 121 B6
Murray St NW1 71 D1
Murray Terr NW3 70 B4
Musard Rd W6 135 A6 264 B6
Musbury St E1 96 C1
Muscal W6 264 A6
Muscatel Pl SE5 139 C4
Muschamp Prim Sch SM5 218 C6
Muschamp Rd
Camberwell SE15 139 D2
Carshalton SM5 218 C6
Muscott Ho 15 E2 96 A6
Muscovy Ho DA18 125 A4
Muscovy St EC3 253 B6
Museum Ho 7 E2 96 C4
Museum in Docklands* E14 119 C6
Museum Mans WC1 240 A3
Museum of Brands* W11 91 B1
Museum of Domestic Design & Architecture* EN4 15 A6
Museum St WC1 94 A1 240 A2
Musgrave Cl EN4 2 A4
Musgrave Cres SW6 135 C4 265 B2
Musgrave Ct SW11 267 A2
Musgrave Rd TW7 130 D4
Musgrove Ho 1 E9 74 D2
Musgrove Rd SE14 141 A4
Musical Mus The* TW8 132 A6
Musjid Rd 7 SW11 136 B3
Muslim Coll The W5 110 C6
Mus of Childhood (V&A)* E2 96 C4
Mus of Culinary History & Alimentation* NW1 232 B4
Mus of Garden History* SE1 260 C5
Mus of London* EC2 95 A2 242 A3
Mus of Richmond* TW10 153 D6
Mus of the Great Eastern Rly* E16 122 C4
Mus of the Order of St John* EC1 94 D3 241 C5
Musquash Way TW4 128 C3
Muston Rd E5 74 B6
Mustow Pl 2 SW6 135 B3
Muswell Ave N10 31 B1
MUSWELL HILL 49 A6
Muswell Hill N10 49 C6
Muswell Hill Broadway N10 49 B6
Muswell Hill Pl N10 49 B5
Muswell Hill Prim Sch N10 49 B6
Muswell Hill Rd N10 49 A4
Muswell Mews N10 49 B6
Muswell Rd N10 31 B1
Mutrix Rd NW6 91 C6
Mutton Pl NW1 71 A2
Muybridge Rd KT3 177 A1
Myatt Garden Prim Sch SE4 141 B3
Myatt Ho SE5 138 D3
Myatt Rd SW9 138 D4
Myatts Field Ct SE5 139 A4
Mycenae Rd SE3 143 A6
Mychell Ho 8 SW19 180 A3
Myddelton Ave EN1 5 C5
Myddelton Cl EN1 5 D4
Myddelton Gdns N21 17 A4
Myddelton Ho N8 50 A6
Myddelton Pas EC1 94 C4 234 B2
Myddelton Pk N20 14 B2
Myddelton Rd N8 50 A5
Myddelton Sq EC1 94 C4 234 B2
Myddelton St EC1 94 C4 234 B1
Myddleton Ave N4 73 A6
Myddleton Ho 14 N2 30 B1
Myddleton Mews N22 32 A3
Myddleton Rd N22 32 B3
Myers Ho 5 SE5 139 A5
Myers La SE14 140 D6
Myherin Ct SE23 163 B2
Mylis Cl SE26 184 B6
Mylius Cl SE14 140 C4
Mylne Cl W6 112 A1
Mylne Ho N21 17 B5
Mylne St EC1 234 A3
Mynterne Ct 16 SW19 156 D3
Myra St SE2 124 A2
Myrdle Ct 14 E1 96 A1
Myrdle St E1 96 A1
Myrna Cl SW19 180 C3
Myron Pl SE13 142 A2
Myrtle Alley SE18 122 C3
Myrtle Ave
Hatton TW14 149 C6
Ruislip HA4 40 B2
Myrtle Cl Barnet EN4 14 D3
Hillingdon UB8 82 B2
West Drayton UB7 104 B3
Myrtledene Rd SE2 124 A1
Myrtle Gdns W7 108 C5
Myrtle Gr Enfield EN2 5 B5
Kingston u T KT3 177 A1
Myrtle Ho SE14 140 D4
Myrtle Rd Acton W3 111 A5
Croydon CR0 223 C5
Edmonton N13 17 B1
Hampton TW12 174 A4
Hounslow TW3 130 A3
Ilford IG1 78 D6
Newham E6 100 A6
Sutton SM1 218 A3
Walthamstow E17 53 A3
Myrtle Wlk 20 N1 95 C5
Mysore Rd SW11 136 D1
Myton Rd SE21 161 B1
Mytton Ho SW8 270 C3

N

N1 Shopping Ctr N1 94 C5 234 B4
Nacton Ct 2 RM6 58 C4
Nadine St SE7 121 C1
Nadir Ct E11 55 A2
Naffenton Rise IG10 21 D6
Nagle Cl E17 36 B1
Nags Head N7 72 B4
Nags Head Ct EC1 242 B5
Nag's Head La DA16 146 B2
Nags Head Rd EN3 6 D1
Nags Head Sh Ctr The N7 72 B4
Naima Jewish Prep Sch NW6 91 D5
Nainby Ho SE11 261 A3
Nairn Ct
3 Wallington SM6 219 C2
Wimbledon SW19 179 D4
Nairne Gr SE5, SE24 139 B1
Nairn Rd HA4 62 C2
Nairn St E14 98 A2
Naish Ct N1 233 B6
Naish Ho SW19 201 D6
Naldera Gdns SE3 143 A6
Nallhead Rd TW13 172 C5
Nalton Ho 4 NW6 70 A1
Namba Roy Cl SW16 182 B6
Namton Dr CR7, SW16 204 B5
Nan Clark's La NW7 11 D2
Nankin St E14 97 C1
Nansen Ct 1 E11 76 C6
Nansen Ho 8 NW10 67 B1
Nansen Rd SW11 137 A2
Nansen Village 5 N12 29 D6
Nant Ct NW2 69 B6
Nantes Cl SW18 136 A1
Nant Rd NW2 69 B6
Nant St E2 96 B4
Naomi Watts Ho 11 SW19 179 A3
Naoroji St WC1 234 A1
Napier 15 NW9 27 D2
Napier Ave
Deptford E14 119 C1
Fulham SW6 135 B2
Napier Cl
New Cross SE14, SE8 141 B5
West Drayton UB7 104 B3
West Kensington W14 254 C6
Napier Ct
13 Croydon CR0 221 D6
Fulham SW6 135 B2
Grove Pk SE12 165 B1
Hayes UB4 84 C3
Shoreditch N1 235 C4
1 Surbiton KT6 197 D2
12 Wallington SM6 219 B2
Wembley HA0 65 D2
Napier Gr N1 95 A5 235 B4
Napier Ho Eltham SE12 165 B1
Kennington SE17 138 D6
Napier Lo TW15 171 B4
Napier Pl W14 113 B3 254 C5
Napier Rd
Ashford TW15 171 B3
Belvedere DA17 125 B2
Bromley BR2 209 B5
College Pk NW10 90 B4
Croydon SE25 206 B5
Enfield EN3 18 D6
Isleworth TW7 131 A1
Kensington W14 113 B3 254 C5
Leyton E11 76 C5
Newham E15 98 C5
South Croydon CR2 221 B1
Tottenham N17 51 C6
Wallend E6 100 C5
Wembley HA0 65 D2
Napier Terr N1 72 D1
Napier Wlk TW15 171 B3
Napoleon Rd
Hackney E5 74 B5
Twickenham TW1 153 B4
Napton Cl UB4 85 A3
Narbonne Ave SW4 159 C6
Narborough Cl UB10 61 A6
Narborough St SW6 135 D3
Narcissus Rd NW6 69 C3
Nardini 12 NW9 27 D2
Naresby Fold HA7 25 C4
Narford Rd E5 74 A6
Narrow Boat Cl SE28 123 B4
Narrow St
6 Acton W3 110 D5
Limehouse E14 119 A6
Narrow Way BR2 210 A3
Nascot St W12 90 C1
Naseby Cl
Hounslow TW7 130 C4
South Hampstead NW6 70 A1
Naseby Ct DA14 189 D6
Naseby Rd
Dagenham RM10 81 C5
South Norwood SE19 183 B4
NASH 225 A2
Nash Cl SM1 218 B5
Nash Ct HA3 43 B3
Nashe Ho SE1 262 C5
Nash Gn BR1 187 A4
Nash Ho
5 Millwall E14 119 C3
Pimlico SW1 258 D1
1 Walthamstow E17 53 D5
Nash La BR2 225 A2
Nash Rd Brockley SE4 163 A6
Dagenham RM6 58 D5
Lower Edmonton N9 18 C2
Nash St NW1 231 D2
Nash Way HA3 43 B3
Nasmyth St W6 112 B3
Nassau Path 6 SE28 124 C5
Nassau Rd SW13 133 D4
Nassau St W1 239 A3
Nassington Rd NW3 70 D4
Natalie Cl TW14 149 B4
Natalie Mews TW2 152 B1
Natal Rd Bowes Pk N11 32 A4
Ilford IG1 78 D4
South Norwood CR7 205 B6
Streatham SW16 181 D4
Nathan Ct N9 18 C4
Nathan Ho SE11 261 B3
Nathaniel Cl E1 243 D3
Nathaniel Ct E17 53 A3
Nathans Rd HA0 65 C6
Nathan Way SE28, SE18 123 D3
National Army Mus* SW3 136 D6 267 D6
National Fan Mus* SE10 142 A5
National Film Theatre* SE1 250 D4
National Gallery* W1 115 D6 249 D5
National Hospl The WC1 94 A3 240 B5
National Maritime Mus* SE10 142 B6
National Physical Laboratory TW11 174 C4
National Portrait Gallery* W1 115 D6 249 D5
National Portrait Gallery (Annexe)* SW1 115 D5 249 D4
National Theatre* SE1 116 B5 250 D4
National Wks TW4 129 B2
Nation Way E4 20 A3
Natural History Mus* SW7 114 B3 256 C5
Nat West Twr* EC2 243 A2
Nautilus Bldg The EC1 234 B2
Naval Row E14 120 A6
Navarino Gr E8 74 A2
Navarino Mans E8 74 A2
Navarino Rd E8 74 A2
Navarre Rd E6 100 A5
Navarre St E2 243 C6
Navenby Wlk 13 E3 97 C3
Navestock Cl E4 20 A1
Navestock Cres IG8 37 C3
Navestock Ho IG11 102 B5
Navigation Ct E16 123 A6
Navigator Dr UB2 108 A4
Navy St SW4 137 D2
Naxos Bldg 9 E14 119 C4
Nayland Ho SE6 186 A6
Naylor Bldg W 4 E1 96 A1
Naylor Gr EN3 18 D6
Naylor Ho
33 Clapham SW8 137 D3
Walworth SE17 262 D2
5 West Kilburn W10 91 B4
Naylor Rd
Peckham SE15 140 B5
Whetstone N20 14 A2
Nayor Bldg E 6 E1 96 A1
Nazareth Cl SE15 140 B3
Nazrul St E2 95 D4
Neal Ave UB1 85 B3
Neal Cl HA6 22 A2
Nealden St SW9 138 B2
Neale Cl N2 48 A6
Neale Ct Dagenham RM9 80 B2
Muswell Hill N10 31 B3
Neal St WC2 94 A1 240 A1
Neal's Yd WC2 240 A1
Near Acre NW9 27 D2
NEASDEN 67 B4
Neasden Cl NW10 67 C3
Neasden Junc NW10 67 C4
Neasden La
Church End NW10 67 C3
Neasden NW10 67 B5

Neasden La N NW10 67 C5
Neasden Sta NW10 67 C3
Neasham Rd RM8 80 B3
Neate St SE5 139 D6
Neath Gdns SM4 202 A3
Neathouse Pl SW1 259 A4
Neats Acre HA4 39 B2
Neatscourt Rd E16 99 D2
Nebraska Bldg 11
SE13 141 D4
Nebraska St
SE1 117 B4 252 C1
Neckinger
SE16 117 D3 263 D6
Neckinger Est SE16 263 D6
Neckinger St SE1 263 D6
Nectarine Way SE13 141 D3
Nedahall Ct 4 NW11 47 B2
Needham Ct 20 EN3 7 C6
Needham Ho SE11 261 A3
Needham Rd W11 91 C1
Needham Terr NW2 68 D5
Needleman St SE16 118 D4
Needwood Ho N4 51 A1
Neela Cl UB10 60 D4
Neeld Cres Hendon NW4 46 B4
Wembley HA9 66 C3
Neeld Ct HA9 66 C3
Neeld Par HA9 66 B3
Neil Cl TW15 171 A5
Neilson-Terry Ct 9
SW9 138 B1
Neil Wates Cres 17
SW2 160 C3
Nelgarde Rd SE6 163 C4
Nella Rd W6 134 D6
Nelldale Rd SE16 118 C2
Nellgrove Rd UB10 82 D3
Nell Gwynn Ave TW17 193 B3
Nell Gwynn Ho SW3 257 B3
Nello James Gdns
SE27 183 B6
Nelson Cl
East Bedfont TW14 149 D3
Hillingdon UB10 82 D4
2 Paddington NW6 91 C4
Thornton Heath CR0 204 D1
Walton-on-T KT12 194 B1
Nelson Ct
5 Carshalton SM5 218 D5
Rotherhithe SE16 119 B5
Nelson Dock Pier
SE16 119 B5
Nelson Gdns
Bethnal Green E2 96 A4
Twickenham TW3, TW4 151 C5
Nelson Grove Rd
SW19 180 A2
Nelson Ho 1 W5 88 A4
Nelson Hospl SW20 179 B1
Nelson La UB10 82 D4
Nelson Mandela Cl
N10 31 A1
Nelson Mandela Rd
SE3 143 C2
Nelson Pas EC1 235 B2
Nelson Pl N1 234 D3
Nelson Prim Sch
Twickenham TW2 151 D5
Wallend E6 100 C5
Nelson Rd
Ashford TW15 170 A5
Bromley BR2 209 C5
Chingford E4 35 D4
Edmonton N9 18 B2
Enfield EN3 18 D5
Erith DA17 125 B1
Greenwich SE10 142 A6
Harmondsworth TW6 126 B4
Harrow HA1 42 C1
Hillingdon UB10 82 D4
Hornsey Vale N8 50 B3
Merton SW19 180 A3
New Malden KT3 199 B4
Sidcup DA14 190 A6
Stanmore HA7 25 C4
Tottenham N15 51 C5
Twickenham TW2, TW4 151 C5
Wanstead E11 55 B5
Nelson's Monument*
WC2 250 A4
Nelson Sq SE1 116 D4 251 C2
Nelsons Row SW4 137 D1
Nelson St Barking E6 100 C6
Canning Town E16 120 D6
Newham E6 100 B5
Stepney E1 96 B1
Nelsons Yd NW1 232 A4
Nelson Terr N1 234 D3
Nelson Trad Est
SW19 179 D2
Nemoure Rd W3 111 A6
Nene Gdns TW13 151 B2
Nene Rd TW6, UB7 126 D4
Nene Road Rdbt TW6 126 D4
Nepaul Rd 17 SW11 136 C2
Nepean St SW15 156 A4
Neptune Ct
Dagenham IG11 102 B4
13 Millwall E14 119 C2
Neptune Ho
2 Rotherhithe SE16 118 C3
14 Stoke Newington N16 73 C3
Neptune Rd
Harlington TW6 127 A4
Harrow HA1 42 B3
Neptune St SE16 118 C3
Nero Ct 6 TW8 131 D5
Nesbit Cl SE3 142 C2
Nesbit Rd SE9 143 D1
Nesbitt Ho DA6 169 D6
Nesbitt Sq SE19 183 C3
Nesham Ho 14 N1 95 C6
Nesham St E1 118 A5
Ness St 9 SE16 118 A3
Nesta Rd IG8 36 D4
Nestle's Ave UB3 105 D3
Nestor Ave N21 16 D5
Nestor Ho 13 E2 96 B5
Netheravon Rd
Chiswick W4 111 D1
Ealing W7 108 D5
Netheravon Rd S W4 111 D1
Netherbury Rd W5 109 D3
Netherby Gdns EN2 4 A1
Netherby Ho 23 SW8 137 D3
Netherby Rd SE23 162 C4
Nether Cl N3 29 C3
Nethercombe Ho 1
SE3 143 A6
Nethercott Ho 27 E3 97 D4
Nethercourt Ave N3 29 C4
Netherfield Gdns IG11 79 B1
Netherfield Rd
Finchley N12 29 D5
Upper Tooting SW17 159 A1
Netherford Rd SW4 137 C3
Netherhall Gdns NW3 70 A3
Netherhall Way NW3 70 A3
Netherlands Rd EN5 14 B5
Netherleigh Cl N6 49 B1
Nether St Finchley N3 29 D4
North Finchley N12 30 A5
Netherton Gr
SW10 136 A6 266 B5
Netherton Ho 1 UB5 85 B4
Netherton Rd
Isleworth TW1 153 B6
Tottenham N15 51 B3
Netherwood 24 N2 30 B1
Netherwood Rd W14 112 D4
Netherwood St NW6 69 C2
Nethewode Ct DA17 125 D3
Netley 18 SE5 139 C4
Netley Cl Cheam SM3 216 D3
New Addington CR0 224 A1
Netley Ct IG2 57 B4
Netley Dr KT12 195 B2
Netley Gdns SM4 202 A2
Netley Prim Sch
NW1 93 C4 232 A1
Netley Rd
Brentford TW8 132 A6
Cheam SM4 202 A2
Ilford IG2 57 B4
Walthamstow E17 53 B4
Netley St NW1 93 C4 232 A1
Nettlecombe NW1 71 D1
Nettleden Ave HA9 66 C2
Nettleden Ho SW3 257 B3
Nettlefold Pl SE27 160 D1
Nettlestead Cl 16 BR3 185 C3
Nettleton Rd
Harlington TW6 126 D4
Ickenham UB10 60 B4
New Cross Gate SE14 140 D4
Nettlewood Rd SW16 181 D3
Neuchatel Rd SE6 163 B2
Nevada Cl KT3 199 A5
Nevada St SE10 142 A6
Nevena Ct 3 SW2 160 C6
Nevern Mans SW5 255 A2
Nevern Pl SW5 113 C2 255 B3
Nevern Rd SW5 255 A3
Nevern Sq
SW5 113 C2 255 B3
Nevil Ho 7 SW9 138 D3
Nevill Ct SW10 266 A4
Neville Ave KT3 177 B2
Neville Cl Acton W3 111 A4
Hounslow TW3 129 D3
Leyton E11 76 D5
Paddington NW6 91 B5
Peckham SE15 140 A4
Sidcup DA15 189 D6
Somers Town NW1 232 D3
Neville Ct 10 SW12 159 C4
Neville Dr N2 48 A3
Neville Gdns RM8 80 D5
Neville Gill Cl SW18 157 D5
Neville Ho
Friern Barnet N11 31 A6
5 Twickenham TW1 153 A4
Neville Pl N22 32 B2
Neville Rd
Dagenham RM8 80 D5
Ealing W5 87 D3
Forest Gate E7 77 B1
Kingston u T KT1 176 C1
Paddington NW6 91 B5
Richmond TW10 153 C2
Thornton Heath CR0 205 B2
Neville's Ct NW2 68 A5
Neville St SW7 114 B1 256 C2
Neville Terr SW7 256 C2
Neville Wlk SM5 202 C2
Nevill Rd N16 73 C5
Nevin Dr E4 19 D3
Nevin Ho UB3 105 A3
Nevinson Cl SW18 158 B5
Nevis Rd SW17 159 A2
Nevitt Ho N1 235 D3
New Acres Rd SE28 123 C5
NEW ADDINGTON 224 B1
Newall Ho SE1 262 B6
Newall Rd TW6 127 A4
Newark Cres NW10 89 B4
Newark Ct KT12 194 C1
Newark Ho 3 SW9 138 D3
Newark Knok E6 100 C2
Newark Rd CR2 221 B2
Newark St E1 96 B2
Newark Way NW4 46 A6
New Ash Cl N2 48 B6
New Atlas Wharf E14 119 C3
New Barn Cl SM6 220 B2
NEW BARNET 14 A6
New Barnet Sta EN5 14 B6
New Barns Ave CR4 203 D5
New Barn St E13 99 B3
NEW BECKENHAM 185 A4
New Beckenham Sta
BR3 185 B3
New Belmont Ho 4
SE23 162 C3
New Bentham Ct 10 N1 73 A1
Newbery Ho N1 73 A1
Newbiggin Path WD19 22 C6
Newbold Cotts 4 E1 96 C1
Newbolt Ave SM3 216 D3
Newbolt Ho SE17 262 C2
Newbolt Rd HA7 24 D5
New Bond St
W1 115 B6 248 D6
Newborough Gn KT3 199 B5
Newborough Ho
SW19 180 B3
New Brent St NW4 46 C4
Newbridge Ct SW17 180 A6
Newbridge Point 3
SE23 162 D1
Newbridge Sch RM6 58 B4
New Bridge St
EC4 94 D1 241 C1
New Broad St
EC2 95 C2 243 A3
New Broadway
Ealing W5 109 D6
7 Hillingdon UB10 82 D3
Teddington TW12 174 B5
New Bsns Ctr The
NW10 89 D4
Newburgh Rd W3 111 A5
Newburgh St W1 239 B1
New Burlington Mews
W1 249 A6
New Burlington Pl W1 249 A6
New Burlington St W1 249 A6
Newburn Ct N12 30 A3
Newburn Ho SE11 260 D2
Newburn St
SE11 116 B1 260 D2
Newbury Ave EN3 7 B6
Newbury Cl UB5 63 B2
Newbury Cotts 4 IG2 57 A3
Newbury Ct Hackney E5 75 A3
Sidcup DA14 189 D6
7 Wanstead E11 55 A5
Newbury Gdns KT19 215 D4
Newbury Ho Barnet EN4 2 B1
Brixton SW9 138 D3
14 Kensington W2 91 D1
Wood Green N22 32 A2
Newbury Mews NW5 71 A2
NEWBURY PARK 57 B3
Newbury Park Prim Sch
IG2 57 B3
Newbury Park Sta IG2 57 B3
Newbury Rd
Bromley BR2 209 A6
Chingford E4 36 A4
Harmondsworth TW6 126 B4
Ilford IG2 57 C3
Newbury St EC1 242 A4
Newbury Way UB5 63 B2
New Butt La SE8 141 C5
Newby NW1 232 A2
Newby Cl EN1 5 C3
Newby Pl E14 120 A6
Newby St SW8 137 B2
New Caledonian Wharf
SE16 119 B3
New Campden Ct 9
NW3 70 A4
Newcastle Cl EC4 241 C2
Newcastle Ct EC4 252 B6
Newcastle Ho W1 238 A4
Newcastle Pl
W2 92 B2 236 D4
Newcastle Row EC1 241 B5
New Cavendish St
W1 93 B2 238 C3
New Change
EC4 95 A1 242 A1
New Chapel Sq TW13 150 B3
New Charles St EC1 234 D2
NEW CHARLTON 121 C2
New Church Ct 3
SE19 184 A3
New Church Rd
32 Camberwell SE5 139 A5
Camberwell SE5 139 B6
New City Prim Sch E13 99 C4
New City Rd E13 99 C4
New Cl Feltham TW13 173 A5
Morden SW19 202 A6
New Colebrooke Ct
SM5 219 A1
New College Ct 6
NW3 70 A2
New College Mews 7
N1 72 C1
New College Par 1
NW3 70 B1
Newcombe Gdns TW3 129 B1
Newcombe Ho N5 73 A3
Newcombe Pk
Edgware NW7 27 C5
Wembley HA0 88 B6
Newcombe Rise UB7 82 A1
Newcombe St W8 245 B4
Newcome Gdns SW16 182 A6
Newcome Ho E5 74 B5
Newcomen Ho 5 NW5 71 B4
Newcomen Rd
Battersea SW11 136 B2
Leyton E11 76 D5
Newcomen St
SE1 117 B4 252 C2
New Compton St
WC2 94 A1 240 A1
New Concordia Wharf
SE1 253 D2
Newcourt Ho 26 E2 96 B4
Newcourt St
NW8 92 C5 230 A3
New Covent Garden
Flower Market
SW8 138 A6 270 A5
New Covent Garden Fruit
& Vegetable Mkt
SW8 137 D5 269 C3
New Crane Pl E1 118 C5
New Crescent Yd 1
NW10 89 D5
Newcroft Cl UB8 82 B2
Newcroft Ho 10 NW10 67 B1
NEW CROSS 141 B4
New Cross SE14 141 B5
NEW CROSS GATE 140 D4
New Cross Gate SE14 140 D4
New Cross Gate Sta
SE14 141 A5
New Cross Hospl
SE14 140 C5
New Cross Rd SE14 141 A4
New Cross Sta SE14 141 B5
New Ct
City of London EC4 241 A1
26 Hampstead NW3 70 A4
Northolt UB5 63 D3
Stoke Newington N16 51 B1
Newdales Cl N9 18 A2
Newdene Ave UB5 84 D5
New Den (Millwall FC) The
SE16 118 C1
Newdigate Ho
6 Kingston u T KT2 176 D4
5 Poplar E14 97 B1
Newell St E14 97 B1
NEW ELTHAM 167 A2
New Eltham Sta SE9 166 D3
New End NW3 70 A5
New End Prim Sch
NW3 70 A4
New End Sq NW3 70 B4
New England Est
IG11 101 A5
Newent Cl
Camberwell SE15 139 C5
Carshalton SM5 202 D1
New Farm Ave BR2 209 A5
New Ferry App SE18 122 C3
New Fetter La
EC4 94 C1 241 B2
Newfield Cl TW12 173 C2
Newfield Prim Sch
NW10 67 D1
Newfield Rise NW2 68 B5
Newgale Gdns HA8 26 B2
New Garden Dr UB7 104 A4
Newgate CR0 205 A1
Newgate Cl TW13 151 A1
Newgate St
Chingford E4 20 C1
Holborn EC1 94 D1 241 D2
New Globe Wlk SE1 252 A4
New Goulston St E1 243 C2
New Green Pl SE19 183 C4
NEWHAM 98 D4
Newham Acad of Music
E6 100 A6
Newham Coll of FE
E6 100 B5
Newham Coll (Stratford
Campus) E15 76 C1
Newham Ctr for Mental
Health E16 99 D3
Newham General Hospl
E13 99 C3
Newham Gn N22 32 C2
Newham Sch of Nursing
E3 97 D3
Newham Sixth Form Coll
E13 99 B3
Newham Sixth Form Coll
(Stratford Ctr) E15 76 B1
Newham's Row SE1 253 B1
Newham Way
Beckton E6 100 B3
Canning Town E13 99 B2
Newhaven Cl UB3 105 D2
Newhaven Cres TW15 171 B5
Newhaven Gdns SE9 143 D1
Newhaven La 3 E16 99 A2
Newhaven Rd SE25 205 B4
New Heston Rd TW5 129 B5
New Horizons Ct TW8 131 A6
Newhouse 5 KT3 199 C2
Newhouse Ave RM6 58 D6
Newhouse Cl KT3 199 C2
Newhouse Wlk SM4 202 A2
Newick Cl DA5 169 D5
Newick Rd E5 74 C5
Newing Gn BR1 187 D3
NEWINGTON 116 D2
Newington Barrow Way
N7 72 B5
Newington Butts SE1,
SE11 116 D2 261 D3
Newington Cswy
SE1 117 A3 262 A6
Newington Gn N16 73 B3
Newington Green Mans
N16 73 B3
Newington Green Prim
Sch N16 73 B3
Newington Green Rd
N1 73 B3
Newington Ind Est
SE17 262 A3
New Inn Broadway
EC2 243 B6
New Inn Ct The KT8 196 B4
New Inn Sq EC2 243 B6
New Inn St EC2 243 B6
New Inn Yd EC2 95 C3 243 B6
New James Ct SE15 140 B2
New Jubilee Ct 1 IG8 37 A3
New Kelvin Ave TW11 174 C4
New Kent Rd
SE1 117 A2 262 B4
New King's Prim Sch
SW6 135 B3
New King's Rd
SW6 135 C4 265 B1
New King St SE8 141 C6
Newland Cl HA5 23 B4
Newland Ct
St Luke's EC1 242 C6
Wembley HA9 66 C6
Newland Dr EN1 6 B4
Newland Gdns W13 109 A4
Newland Ho
17 Deptford SE14 140 D6
Hornsey N8 50 A6
Newland House Sch
TW1 174 D6
Newland House Sch Annex
TW1 174 D6
Newland Rd N8 50 A6
Newlands NW1 232 A2
Newlands Ave KT7 196 C1
Newlands Cl
Edgware HA8 10 A1
Southall UB2 107 A1
Wembley HA0 65 C2
Newlands Croft SE20 184 D4
Newlands Ct
8 Eltham SE9 166 C5
6 Penge SE26 184 C4
Streatham SW16 182 A5
Newlands Pk SE26 184 D5
Newlands Pl EN5 12 D6
Newlands Quay E1 118 C6
Newlands Rd
Thornton Heath
SW16 182 A1
Woodford IG8 20 D2
Newland St E16 122 B5
Newlands The
Thames Ditton KT7 196 C1
Wallington SM6 219 D1
Newlands Way KT9 213 C3
Newling Cl E6 100 B1
New London St EC3 253 B6
New Lydenburg
Commercial Est SE7 121 C3
New Lydenburg St
SE7 121 C3
Newlyn NW1 232 B5
Newlyn Cl
Hillingdon UB8 82 C2
Orpington BR6 227 D4
Newlyn Gdns HA2 41 B2
Newlyn Ho
7 Pinner HA5 23 B3
7 Sutton SM1 218 A4
Newlyn Rd Barnet EN5 1 B1
Bexley DA16 145 D3
Tottenham N17 33 D2
NEW MALDEN 199 D5
New Malden Sta KT3 199 C6
Newman Ct
3 Bromley BR1 187 A2
8 Finchley N3 29 C2
Newman Ho 11 TW10 153 C1
Newman Pas W1 239 B3
Newman Rd
Bromley BR1 187 A2
Hayes UB3 106 B6
Newham E13 99 B4
Thornton Heath CR0 204 B1
Walthamstow E17 52 D4
Newman's Ct EC3 242 D1
Newman's Row WC2 240 D3
Newman St W1 93 C2 239 B3
Newman's Way EN4 2 A4
Newman Terr 9 CR4 202 D6
Newmarket Ave UB5 63 D3
Newmarket Gn SE9 165 D4
Newmarsh Rd SE28 123 D5
Newmill Ho E3 98 A3
New Mill Rd BR5 190 C2
Newminster Rd SM4 202 A3
Newmount NW3 70 B3
New Mount St E15 76 B1
Newnes Path SW15 134 B1
Newnham Ave HA4 40 C1
Newnham Cl
Loughton IG10 21 D5
Northolt UB5 64 A2
South Norwood CR7 183 A1
Newnham Gdns UB5 64 A2
Newnham Ho
Catford SE6 164 A1
Loughton IG10 21 D5
9 Putney SW15 156 D5
Newnham Jun & Inf Schs
HA4 40 C1
Newnham Lo 10 DA17 125 C1
Newnham Mews N22 32 C2
Newnham Rd N22 32 C2
Newnhams Cl BR1 210 B6
Newnham Terr SE1 261 A6
Newnham Way HA3 44 A4
New North Com Sch The
N1 73 B1
New North Pl EC2 243 A6
New North Rd
N1 95 B6 235 C5
New North Road Bridge
N1 235 C5
New North St
WC1 94 B2 240 C4
Newnton Cl N4 51 B2
New Oak Rd N2 30 A1
New Oxford St
WC1 94 A1 240 A2
New Palace Yd
SW1 116 A4 250 A1
New Par Ashford TW15 170 B6
Yiewsley UB7 104 A5
New Park Ave N13 17 B1
New Park Cl UB5 63 A2
New Park Ct 26 SW2 160 A4
New Park Est N18 34 C5
New Park Ho N13 32 B6
New Park Par 14 SW2 160 A4
New Park Rd
Ashford TW15 171 A5
Streatham SW2 160 A4
New Pl CR0 223 C2
New Place Sq SE16 118 B3
New Plaistow Rd E15 98 C6
New Pond Par HA4 62 A5
Newport Ave
Blackwall E14 120 B6
Newham E13 99 B3
Newport Cl EN3 7 A6
Newport Ct WC2 249 D6
Newport Ho 2 E3 97 A4
Newport Lo 2 EN1 17 C6
Newport Mead WD19 22 D6
Newport Pl WC2 249 D6
Newport Rd
Barnes SW13 134 A4
Harmondsworth TW6 126 C4
Hayes UB4 83 B2
Leyton E10 76 B6
Walthamstow E17 53 A5
Newport Sch E10, E11 76 A6
Newport St
SE11 116 B2 260 D4
New Priory Ct 9 NW6 69 C1
New Providence Wharf
E14 120 B5
Newquay Cres HA2 63 A6
Newquay Ho SE11 261 A2
Newquay Rd SE6 164 A2
New Quebec St W1 237 D1
New Rd Brentford TW8 109 D1
Carshalton CR4 203 A1
Chingford E4 36 A6
Dagenham RM10 103 D5
East Bedfont TW14 149 B5
East Molesey KT8 195 C6
Edmonton N9 18 B2
Elstree WD6 9 D5
Esher KT10 212 A4
feltham TW14 150 B3
Finchley N10 30 C2
Hanworth TW13 173 A5
Harlington TW6, UB7 127 A5
Harrow HA1 64 D4
Hendon NW7 29 A3
Hillingdon UB8 83 A2
Hornsey N8 50 A4
Hounslow TW3 129 D1
Ilford IG3 79 C6
Kingston u T KT2 176 C3
Littleton TW17 192 D6
Richmond TW10 175 C6
Stepney E1 96 B2
Tottenham N22 33 A2
Welling DA16 146 B3
West Heath SE2 124 D1
New River Cres N13 32 D6
New River Ct N5 73 B4
New River Sports &
Recreation Ctr N22 32 D3
New River Way N4 51 B2
New Row WC2 116 A6 250 A6
New Rush Hall Sch IG1 79 A6
Newry Rd TW1 153 A6
New St Sq EC4 94 C1 241 B2
Newsam Ave N15 51 B4
New Scotland Yard*
SW1 115 D3 259 C6
New Shepherd's Bush
Mkt* 6 W12 112 C4
Newsholme Dr N21 16 B6
NEW SOUTHGATE 31 C6
New Southgate Ind Est 10
N11 31 C5
New Southgate Sta
N11 31 B5
New Spitalfields Mkt
E10 75 C5
New Spring Gdns Wlk
SE11 260 B1
New Sq
East Bedfont TW14 149 A3
St Giles WC2 94 B1 240 D2
New Square Pas WC2 241 A2
New St EC2 95 C2 243 B3
Newstead Ave BR6 227 C6

Newstead Cl N12 30 C4
Newstead Ct UB5 85 A4
Newstead Ho
 Edmonton N9 17 D1
 Islington N1 234 B4
Newstead Rd SE12 164 D4
Newstead Way SW19 178 D6
Newstead Wlk SM5 202 A2
Newstead Wood Sch for Girls BR6 227 B5
New Street Hill BR1 187 C5
Newton Ave Acton W3 111 A4
 Muswell Hill N10 31 B2
Newton Cl Harrow HA2 63 C6
 Walthamstow E17 53 A3
Newton Farm Fst & Mid Sch HA2 63 B6
Newton Gr W4 111 C2
Newton Ho
 22 Clapham SW8 137 D3
 Paddington NW8 91 D6
 1 Stepney E1 118 B6
 10 Walthamstow E17 54 A6
Newton Ind Est RM6 58 D5
Newton Pl E14 119 C2
Newton Point 1 E16 98 D1
Newton Prep Sch SW8 137 B4 268 D2
Newton Rd Acton W3 111 A4
 Cricklewood NW2 68 C5
 Harrow HA3 24 C1
 Isleworth TW7 130 D3
 Kensington W2 91 D1
 South Tottenham N15 52 A4
 Stratford New Town E15 76 B3
 Welling DA16 146 A2
 Wembley HA0 66 B1
 Wimbledon SW19 179 A3
Newton St WC2 94 A1 240 B2
Newton's Yd 14 SW18 157 C6
Newton Terr BR2 209 D3
Newton Way N18 33 A5
Newton Wlk HA8 26 D2
New Tower Bldgs 21 E1 118 B5
Newtown Ct
 Battersea SW11 268 C1
 Clapham SW4 159 B6
New Trinity Rd 1 N2 30 B1
New Union Cl E14 120 A3
New Union St EC2 242 C3
New Victoria Hospl KT3 177 C2
New Wanstead E11 55 A3
New Way Rd NW9 45 C5
New Wharf Rd N1 94 A5 233 B4
New Woodlands Sch BR1 186 C6
NEWYEARS GREEN 38 B3
Newyears Green La UB9 38 B3
New Zealand Ave KT12 193 D1
Nexus Ct E11 54 C2
Niagara Ave W5 109 C2
Niagara Cl N1 235 B4
Niagara Ct 6 SE16 118 C3
Niagara Ho W5 109 C2
Nibthwaite Rd HA1 42 C4
Nicholas Cl UB6 85 D5
Nicholas Ct
 Chiswick W4 133 C5
 Golders Green NW11 47 C2
 Lewisham SE12 165 A3
 Newham E13 99 B4
Nicholas Gdns W5 109 D4
Nicholas Ho Ealing W13 87 C1
 Penge SE26 184 B4
 2 Putney SW15 156 A6
Nicholas La EC2, EC4 252 D6
Nicholas Pas EC3 252 D6
Nicholas Rd
 Bethnal Green E1 96 C3
 Borehamwood WD6 10 B6
 Dagenham RM8 81 B5
 Wallington CR0 220 A4
Nicholas Stacey Ho 3 SE7 121 B1
Nicholay Rd N19 49 D1
Nichol Cl N14 15 D3
Nicholes Rd TW3 129 C1
Nichol La BR1 187 A3
Nicholl Ho N4 51 A1
Nicholls Almshouses NW7 28 B5
Nicholls Ave UB8 82 C3
Nicholls Point E15 99 A6
Nicholl St E2 96 A6
Nichols Cl
 Chessington KT9 213 C2
 Finsbury Pk N4 50 C1
Nichols Ct E2 95 D5
Nichols Gn W5 88 A2
Nicholson Ct 9 N17 51 D6
Nicholson Ho SE17 262 C2
Nicholson Mews KT1 198 A5
Nicholson Rd CR0 205 D1
Nicholson St SE1 251 C3
Nickelby Cl SE28 102 C1
Nickleby Cl UB8 82 D1
Nickleby Ho
 18 Bermondsey SE1 118 A4
 7 Shepherd's Bush W11 112 D5
Nickols Wlk SW18 135 D1
Nicola Cl Harrow HA3 24 B1
Nicola Cl *continued*
 South Croydon CR2 221 A2
Nicola Terr DA7 147 A4
Nicol Cl 6 TW1 153 B5
Nicole Ho SE25 206 A6
Nicoll Ct
 Dagenham NW10 89 C6
 Muswell Hill N10 31 B3
Nicoll Pl NW4 46 B2
Nicoll Rd NW10 89 C6
Nicoll Way WD6 11 B6
Nicolson 14 NW9 27 D2
Nicolson Dr WD23 8 A2
Nicosia Rd SW18 158 C4
Niederwald Rd SE26 185 A6
Nield Rd UB3 105 D4
Nigel Bldg EC1 241 A4
Nigel Cl UB5 85 A6
Nigel Ct N3 29 D3
Nigel Fisher Way KT9 213 D1
Nigel Mews IG1 78 D4
Nigel Playfair Ave W6 112 B1
Nigel Rd Forest Gate E7 77 C3
 Peckham SE15 140 A2
Nigeria Rd SE7 143 D5
Nighthawk 16 NW9 27 D2
Nightingale Ave
 Chingford E4 36 C5
 Harrow HA1 43 B1
Nightingale Cl
 Carshalton SM5 219 A6
 Chingford E4 36 C6
 Chiswick W4 133 A6
 Pinner HA5 40 C4
Nightingale Ct
 14 Cubitt Town E14 120 A3
 Finsbury Pk N4 72 B6
 1 Harrow HA1 42 D3
 Penge SE19 183 D4
 Sutton SM1 218 A3
 1 Wanstead E11 55 B4
Nightingale Dr KT19 214 D2
Nightingale Gr SE13 164 B6
Nightingale Ho
 Hayes UB3 105 D2
 21 Hoxton E1 95 C6
 4 North Kensington W12 90 C1
 7 St George in t East E1 118 A5
 Woolwich SE18 122 C1
Nightingale La
 Balham SW11, SW12 159 A5
 Bromley BR1 187 D1
 Hornsey N8 50 A6
 Richmond TW10 154 A4
 Wanstead E11 55 B4
Nightingale Lo
 Edgware HA8 27 A4
 5 Paddington W9 91 C2
Nightingale Mans 4 SW12 159 A5
Nightingale Mews
 1 Bow E3 97 A5
 Newington SE11 261 C4
 8 Wanstead E11 55 B4
Nightingale Pl
 Shooters Hill SE18 144 D6
 West Brompton SW10 136 A6 266 B6
Nightingale Prim Sch
 Shacklewell E5 74 A4
 Wanstead E18 55 C5
 Wood Green N22 32 B2
 Woolwich SE18 122 D1
Nightingale Rd
 Carshalton SM5 219 A6
 Dagenham NW10 89 D5
 Ealing W7 108 D5
 East Molesey KT8 195 D4
 Hackney E5 74 B5
 Hampton TW12 173 C4
 Orpington BR5 211 A3
 Ponders End N9 18 C4
 Walton-on-T KT12 194 B2
 Wood Green N22 32 B3
Nightingale Sch SW17 158 C2
Nightingale Sq SW12 159 A4
Nightingales The TW19 148 B3
Nightingale Vale SE18 144 C6
Nightingale Way E6 100 A2
Nightingale Wlk SW18, SW4 159 B5
Nile Cl N16 73 D5
Nile Ct N12 30 C4
Nile Dr N9 18 C2
Nile Ho N1 235 C2
Nile Path 6 SE18 144 C6
Nile Rd E13 99 C5
Nile St N1 95 B4 235 C2
Nile Terr SE1, SE15 117 D1 263 D1
Nimegen Way 9 SE22 161 C6
Nimmo Dr WD23 8 B4
Nimrod 12 NW9 27 C2
Nimrod Cl UB5 84 D4
Nimrod Pas 4 N1 73 C2
Nimrod Rd SW16 181 B5
Nina Mackay Cl 10 E15 98 C6
Nine Acres Cl E12 78 A3
NINE ELMS 137 C5
Nine Elms Cl TW14 149 D3
Nine Elms La SW8 137 D6 269 C5
Nineteenth Rd CR4 204 A5
Ninhams Wood BR6 226 C4
Ninth Ave UB3 106 A6
Nisbet 13 NW9 27 C2
Nisbet Ho E9 74 D3
Nisbett Wlk DA14 190 A6
Nita Ct SE12 165 A3
Nithdale Rd SE18 145 A5
Nithsdale Gr UB10 61 A5
Niton Cl EN5 12 D5
Niton Rd TW9 132 C2
Niton St SW6 134 D5
No 1 St SE18 122 D3
No 2 Willow Rd* NW3 70 C4
Noam Prim Sch N12 29 D6
Nobel Dr TW6 127 C5
Nobel Ho 8 SE5 139 A3
Nobel Rd N18 34 C6
Noble Cnr TW5 129 C4
Noble Ct Mitcham CR4 180 B1
 Stepney E1 118 B6
Noblefield Hts N2 48 D4
Noble Ho 8 E1 118 A6
Noble St EC2 95 A1 242 A2
Noel 13 NW9 27 D2
Noel Baker Ct 5 E11 76 C6
Noel Coward Ho SW1 259 B3
Noel Ct TW4 129 B2
Noel Dene W5 109 C1
Noel Ho 3 NW3 70 B1
NOEL PARK 32 D1
Noel Park Prim Sch N22 32 C1
Noel Park Rd N22 32 C1
Noel Rd Acton W3 88 D1
 Islington N1 94 D5 234 D4
 Newham E6 100 A3
Noel Sq RM8 80 C4
Noel St W1 93 C1 239 B1
Noel Terr
 Forest Hill SE23 162 C2
 Sidcup DA14 190 B6
Noko NW10 90 D4
Nolan Way E5 74 A4
Noll Ho N7 72 B6
Nolton Pl HA8 26 B2
Nonsuch Ct SM3 217 A2
Nonsuch High Sch for Girls SM3 216 D1
Nonsuch Ho 5 SW19 180 B2
Nonsuch Prim Sch KT17 216 B3
Nook The SW19 180 A1
Noor Ul Islam Prim Sch E10 76 A6
Nora Gdns NW4 46 D5
NORBITON 176 C1
Norbiton Ave KT1, KT2 176 C1
Norbiton Common Rd KT1, KT3 198 D6
Norbiton Hall KT2 176 B1
Norbiton Rd E14 97 B1
Norbiton Sta KT1 176 C2
Norbreck Gdns NW10 88 B4
Norbreck Par NW10 88 B4
Norbroke St W12 111 D6
Norburn St W10 91 A2
NORBURY 182 C2
Norbury Ave
 Isleworth TW3 130 B1
 Thornton Heath CR7, SW16 182 C1
Norbury Cl SW16 182 D2
Norbury Court Rd SW16 182 A1
Norbury Cres SW16 182 C1
Norbury Cross SW16 204 A6
Norbury Ct N12 30 A6
Norbury Gdns RM6 58 D4
Norbury Gr NW7 11 C1
Norbury Hill SW16 182 D3
Norbury Manor Bsns & Enterprise Coll For Girls CR7 182 C2
Norbury Manor Prim Sch SW16 182 A2
Norbury Rd
 Chingford E4 35 C5
 Feltham TW13 149 D1
 South Norwood CR7 205 A6
Norbury Rise SW16 204 A6
Norbury Sch HA1 42 C4
Norbury Sta SW16 182 B2
Norbury Trad Est SW16 182 B1
Norcombe Gdns HA3 43 C4
Norcombe Ho 2 N19 71 D5
Norcott Cl UB4 84 C3
Norcott Rd N16 74 A5
Norcroft Gdns SE22 162 A4
Norcutt Rd TW2 152 C3
Norden Ho 25 E2 96 B4
Norden Point NW2 46 C1
Nore Ct NW10 68 A1
Norfolk Ave
 Edmonton N13 32 D4
 South Tottenham N15 51 D3
Norfolk Cl
 Cockfosters EN4 3 A1
 East Finchley N2 48 C6
 Edmonton N13 32 D4
 5 Twickenham TW1 153 B5
Norfolk Cres
 Paddington W2 92 C1 237 B2
 Sidcup DA15 167 C4
Norfolk Ct 5 Barnet EN5 1 A1
 4 Ilford RM6 58 B4
 Surbiton KT5 198 B3
 Wembley HA0 65 C2
Norfolk Gdns DA7 147 B4
Norfolk Ho 18 Acton W3 88 C1
 Beckenham BR2 208 D5
Norfolk Ho *continued*
 City of London EC4 252 A6
 Edgware HA8 26 B3
 Greenwich SE3 142 C6
 11 Merton SW19 180 A3
 Penge SE20 184 C2
 4 Putney SW15 156 C4
 Richmond TW10 154 C6
 Shacklewell E8 73 D4
 2 South Croydon CR0 221 B6
 3 Stanmore HA7 25 C5
 St Johns SE8 141 C4
 Westminster SW1 259 D4
Norfolk House Rd SW16 160 A1
Norfolk House Sch N10 31 B1
Norfolk Mans
 Battersea SW11 267 D1
 10 Wandsworth SW18 157 C6
Norfolk Mews 12 W10 91 A2
Norfolk Pl
 Paddington W2 92 B1 236 D2
 Welling DA16 146 A3
Norfolk Rd Barking IG11 79 C1
 Barnet EN5 1 C2
 Claygate KT10 212 C3
 Dagenham RM10 81 D3
 Enfield EN3 18 B6
 Feltham TW13 150 C3
 Harrow HA1 41 D4
 Higham Hill E17 34 D1
 Ilford IG3 57 C2
 Mitcham SW19 180 C4
 Newham E6 100 B6
 South Norwood CR7 205 A6
 St John's Wood NW8 92 B6 229 D5
 Willesden NW10 67 C1
Norfolk Row SE1, SE11 116 B2 260 C4
Norfolk Sq W2 92 B1 236 D2
Norfolk Sq Mews W2 236 D1
Norfolk St E7 77 A3
Norgrove St SW12 159 A4
Norhyrst Ave SE25 205 D6
Norland Ho 18 W11 112 D5
Norland Pl W11 113 A5 244 B3
Norland Place Sch W11 113 A5 244 A3
Norland Rd 16 W11 112 D5
Norlands Cres BR7 188 D2
Norland Sq W11 113 A5 244 B3
Norley Vale SW15 156 A3
Norlington Rd E10, E11 54 B1
Norlington Sch for Boys E10 54 B1
Norman Ave
 Feltham TW13 151 B2
 Southall UB1 107 A6
 Tottenham N22 33 A2
 Twickenham TW1 153 C4
Norman Butler Ho 10 W10 91 A3
Normanby Cl SW15 157 B6
Normanby Rd NW10 67 D4
Norman Cl
 Orpington BR6 227 A5
 Tottenham N22 33 A2
Norman Cres
 Heston TW5 128 D5
 Pinner HA5 22 C2
Norman Ct
 Dulwich SE22 162 A4
 5 Finchley N3 29 C2
 Finsbury Pk N4 50 C2
 8 Hampton TW12 173 C2
 Ilford IG2 57 B2
 West Norwood SW16 182 C5
 Willesden NW10 68 A1
 Woodford IG8 37 B5
Normand Croft Com Sch W14 135 B6 264 D6
Normand Mews W14 264 B6
Normand Rd W14 135 B6 264 C6
Normandy Ave EN5 1 B1
Normandy Cl SE26 163 A1
Normandy Dr UB3 83 A1
Normandy Ho
 8 Cubitt Town E14 120 A4
 4 Hendon NW4 28 D1
Normandy Rd SW9 138 C4
Normandy Terr E16 99 B1
Norman Gr E3 97 A5
Norman Ho
 1 Cheam SM1 217 C2
 Feltham TW13 151 B2
 7 Leyton E11 76 C6
 Lower Halliford TW17 192 C2
 South Lambeth SW8 270 A4
Normanhurst TW15 170 C5
Normanhurst Ave DA7 146 D4
Normanhurst Dr TW1 153 B6
Normanhurst Rd
 St Paul's Cray BR5 190 B1
 Streatham SW2 160 B2
 Walton-on-T KT12 194 D1
Normanhurst Sch E4 20 B4
Norman Par DA14 168 D2
Norman Rd
 Ashford TW15 171 B4
 Belvedere DA17 125 D3
 Greenwich SE10 141 D5
 Ilford IG1 78 D3
 Leyton E11 76 C6
 Merton SW19 180 A3
Norman Rd *continued*
 Newham E6 100 B3
 South Tottenham N15 51 D4
 Sutton SM1 217 C3
 Thornton Heath CR7 204 D4
Normans Cl
 Hillingdon UB8 82 A2
 Willesden NW10 67 B2
Normansfield Ave KT1, KT8 175 C3
Normanshire Dr E4 35 D6
Normans Mead NW10 67 B2
Norman St EC1 95 A4 235 B1
Normanton Ave SW18, SW19 157 C2
Normanton Ct CR2 221 C3
Normanton Ho 6 SW4 159 C5
Normanton Pk E4 20 C2
Normanton Rd CR2 221 C2
Normanton St SE23 162 D2
Norman Way Acton W3 88 D1
 Palmers Green N14 16 A2
Normington Cl SW16 182 C5
Norrice Lea N2 48 B4
Norris 11 NW9 27 D2
Norris Ho 12 Hoxton N1 95 C6
 15 South Hackney E9 96 C6
Norris St SW1 249 C5
Norroy Rd SW15 134 D1
Norrys Cl EN4 2 D1
Norrys Rd EN4 2 D1
Norse Ho 10 SE5 139 A3
Norseman Cl 3 IG3 58 B1
Norseman Way UB6 85 D6
Norstead Pl SW15 156 A2
North Access Rd E17 52 D3
North Acre NW9 27 C2
NORTH ACTON 89 B4
North Acton Rd NW10 89 B4
North Acton Sta W3 89 B2
Northampton Gr N1 73 B3
Northampton Pk N1 73 B2
Northampton Rd
 Croydon CR0 222 A6
 Enfield EN3 7 A1
 Finsbury EC1 94 C3 241 B6
Northampton Sq EC1 94 D4 234 C1
Northampton St N1 73 A1
Northanger Rd SW16 182 A4
North Audley St W1 115 A6 248 A6
North Ave Ealing W13 87 B2
 Edmonton N18 34 A6
 Harrow HA2 41 D3
 Hayes UB3 106 A6
 8 Richmond TW9 132 C4
 Southall UB1 107 B6
 Wallington SM5 219 A1
Northaw Ho 4 W10 90 C3
North Bank NW8 92 C4 230 A1
Northbank Rd E17 36 A1
North Beckton Prim Sch E6 100 B2
North Birkbeck Rd E11 76 B5
North Block 19 E1 118 C6
Northborough Rd SW16 182 A1
Northbourne BR2 209 A2
Northbourne Ho
 21 Hackney E5 74 B3
 Osidge N14 15 D4
Northbourne Rd SW4 159 D6
North Bridge House Sch NW3 70 A2
North Bridge House Senior Sch NW1 93 B6 231 C5
Northbrook CE Sch SE12 164 D6
Northbrook Rd
 Barnet EN5 13 A5
 Ilford IG1 78 C6
 Lewisham SE13 164 C6
 Thornton Heath CR0 205 B4
 Wood Green N22 32 A3
Northburgh St EC1 94 D3 241 D6
Northbury Jun & Inf Schs IG11 79 A2
North Carriage Dr W2 114 C6 247 B6
NORTH CHEAM 216 C6
Northchurch SE17 262 D2
Northchurch Ho 19 E2 96 A6
Northchurch Rd
 De Beauvoir Town N1 73 B1
 Wembley HA9 66 C2
Northchurch Terr N1 73 C1
North Circular Rd
 Edmonton N13 32 C5
 Finchley N2 30 B2
 Highams Pk E17 35 D2
 Ilford IG1, E12 78 C4
 Neasden NW2, NW10 67 C3
 Temple Fortune N3, NW2, NW4 47 A4
 Woodford E18 37 C1
North Cl Barnet EN5 12 C6
 Bexley DA6 146 D1
 Dagenham RM10 103 C6
 East Bedfont TW14 149 B5
 Merton SM4 201 A5
Northcliffe Cl KT4 215 C5
Northcliffe Dr N20 13 B3
North Colonnade The E14 119 D5
North Common Rd
 Ealing W5 110 A6
 Uxbridge UB8 60 A3
Northcote 3 HA5 22 C1
Northcote Ave
 Ealing W5 110 A6
 Isleworth TW7 153 A6
 Southall UB1 107 A6
 Tolworth KT5 198 D2
Northcote Ho UB4 84 D2
Northcote Lodge Sch SW11 158 D5
Northcote Rd
 Isleworth TW7 153 A6
 Kingston u T KT3 199 B6
 Sidcup DA14 189 C6
 Thornton Heath CR0 205 B3
 Walthamstow E17 53 A5
 Wandsworth SW11 158 D6
 Willesden NW10 67 C1
Northcott Ave N22 32 A2
North Countess Rd E17 35 B2
Northcourt W1 239 B4
NORTH CRAY 169 B1
North Cray Rd DA14 191 A5
North Cres Finchley N3 29 B1
 Marylebone WC1 239 C4
 Newham E16 98 B3
Northcroft Ct 8 W12 112 A4
Northcroft Rd
 Brentford W13 109 B3
 West Ewell KT19 215 C1
North Crofts SE21 162 B3
North Cross Rd
 East Dulwich SE22 162 A6
 Ilford IG6 57 A5
North Ct SW1 260 A5
North Dene
 Edgware NW7 11 B1
 Hounslow TW5 129 D4
Northdene Gdns N15 51 D3
Northdown Cl HA4 61 D5
Northdown Gdns IG2 57 C4
Northdown Rd DA16 146 C3
Northdown St N1 94 B5 233 C3
North Dr
 Beckenham BR3 207 D5
 Hounslow TW3, TW7 130 A3
 Orpington BR6 227 C4
 Ruislip HA4 39 C2
 Streatham SW16 181 C6
North Dulwich Sta SE21 161 B6
North Ealing Prim Sch W5 87 B3
North Ealing Sta W3 88 B1
NORTH END 70 A6
North End
 Buckhurst Hill IG9 21 C4
 Croydon CR0 221 A6
 North End NW3 70 B6
North End Ave NW3 70 A6
North End Cres W14 113 B2 254 C3
North End Ho W14 113 A2 254 B3
North End La BR6 226 D1
Northend Lodge 2 HA5 40 D6
North End Par W14 254 B3
North End Rd
 Golders Green NW11 47 D1
 Wembley HA9 66 D5
 West Kensington W14 113 B1 254 D1
North End Way NW3 70 A6
Northern Ave N9 17 D2
Northernhay Wlk SM4 201 A5
Northern Hts N8 49 D2
Northern Perimeter Rd TW6 127 C4
Northern Perimeter Rd (W) TW6 126 B4
Northern Rd E13 99 B5
Northern Relief Rd IG11 79 A2
Northern Star Ho N11 31 B5
Northesk Ho 6 E1 96 B3
North Eyot Gdns 5 W6 111 D1
Northey St E14 119 A6
NORTH FELTHAM 150 B6
North Feltham Trad Est TW14 128 B1
Northfield IG10 21 D6
Northfield Ave
 Pinner HA5 40 D5
 West Ealing W13, W5 109 B4
Northfield Cl
 Bromley BR1 188 A2
 Hayes UB3 105 D3
Northfield Cres SM3 217 A4
Northfield Gdns RM9 81 B4
Northfield Hall N6 49 A2
Northfield Ho
 2 Newham E13 99 C5
 3 Peckham SE15 140 A6
Northfield Ind Est HA0 88 C6
Northfield Par UB3 105 D3
Northfield Path RM9 81 B4
Northfield Pk UB3 105 D3
Northfield Rd
 Cockfosters EN4 2 C2
 Dagenham RM9 81 B4
 Enfield EN3 18 B6
 Heston TW5 128 D5
 Plashet E6 78 B1
 Stamford Hill N16 51 C2
 West Ealing W13 109 B4

Nor–Oak 353

- Northfields SW18 135 C1
- Northfields Prospect SW18 135 C1
- Northfields Rd W3 89 A2
- Northfields Sta W5 109 C3
- NORTH FINCHLEY 30 A6
- Northfleet Ho SE1 252 C2
- North Flower Wlk W2 114 B6 246 C5
- North Gate NW8 92 C5 230 A3
- Northgate Bsns Ctr EN1 6 B1
- Northgate Ct 14 SW9 138 C2
- Northgate Dr NW9 45 C3
- North Gates N12 30 A2
- North Gdns SW19 180 B3
- North Glade The DA5 169 B3
- North Gn NW9 27 C3
- North Gower St NW1 93 C4 232 B1
- North Gr Highgate N6 49 A2
  - Tottenham N15 51 B4
- North Greenwich Sta SE10 120 C4
- North Harringay Prim Sch N8 50 C5
- NORTH HARROW 41 D2
- North Harrow Sta HA2 41 D4
- North Hill N6 49 A3
- North Hill Ave N6 48 D3
- North Hill Ct N6 49 A2
- NORTH HILLINGDON 61 A2
- North Ho 3 SE8 119 B1
- NORTH HYDE 107 A1
- North Hyde Gdns UB2, UB3 106 A3
- North Hyde La UB2 107 A1
- North Hyde Rd UB3 105 D3
- Northiam Finchley N12 29 C6
  - St Pancras WC1 233 B1
- Northiam St E9 96 B6
- Northington St WC1 94 B3 240 D5
- NORTH KENSINGTON 90 D2
- North La TW11 174 D4
- Northlands 4 BR1 187 C1
- Northlands Ave BR6 227 C4
- Northlands St SE5 139 A3
- Northleigh Ho 36 E3 97 D4
- North Lo Clapham SW4 137 B1
  - Muswell Hill N22 31 D1
  - New Barnet EN5 14 A6
- North Lodge Cl SW15 156 D6
- North London Bsns Pk N11 15 A1
- North London Collegiate Sch The HA7, HA8 26 A5
- North London Nuffield Hospl EN2 4 C3
- North Mall The N9 18 B2
- North Mews WC1 94 B3 240 D5
- North Middlesex University Hospl N18 33 C5
- Northmoor 4 SE23 162 D1
- North Mount N20 14 A2
- Northolm HA8 27 B6
- Northolme Gdns HA8 26 C2
- Northolme Rd N5 73 A4
- Northolme Rise BR6 227 C6
- NORTHOLT 63 C1
- Northolt N17 33 C1
- Northolt Ave HA4 62 B3
- Northolt Gdns UB6 64 D3
- Northolt High Sch UB5 63 B2
- Northolt Park Inf Sch UB5 63 D3
- Northolt Park Sta HA2 63 D4
- Northolt Rd HA2 64 A5
- Northolt Sta UB5 63 C2
- Northolt Trad Est UB5 63 D1
- Northover BR1 164 D1
- North Par
  - Chessington KT9 214 B3
  - Edgware HA8 26 C1
  - Southall UB1 85 C1
- North Pas SW18 157 C6
- North Pk SE9 166 C5
- North Pl
  - Mitcham SW19 180 D3
  - Teddington TW11 174 D4
- Northpoint BR1 187 A2
- North Point UB7 104 A5
- Northpoint Cl SM1 218 A5
- Northpoint Sq 8 NW1 71 D2
- North Pole La BR2 225 A2
- North Pole Rd W10 90 C2
- Northport St N1 235 D5
- North Prim Sch UB1 107 B6
- North Rd Barnsbury N7 72 A2
  - Brentford TW8 132 A6
  - Bromley BR1 187 B2
  - Dagenham RM6 59 A4
  - Ealing W5 109 D3
  - East Bedfont TW14 149 B5
  - Edgware HA8 26 D2
  - Edmonton N9 18 B3
  - Erith DA17 125 D4
  - Finchley N2 30 C2
  - Hayes UB3 83 B2
  - Heston TW5 128 C6
  - Highgate N6 49 A2
  - Ilford IG3 79 C6
  - Plumstead SE18 123 C2
  - Richmond TW9 132 C3
  - Southall UB1 107 C6
  - Surbiton KT6 197 D3
  - West Drayton UB7 104 B3
  - 1 West Wickham BR4 207 D1
  - Wimbledon SW19 180 A4
- North Residence IG3 58 B4
- North Ride W2 114 C6 247 A5
- North Rise W2 237 B1
- Northrop Rd TW6 127 C4
- North Row W1 115 A6 248 A6
- NORTH SHEEN 132 C3
- North Sheen Sta TW10 132 C1
- Northside Prim Sch N12 30 A5
- Northside Rd BR1 187 A2
- North Side Wandsworth Comm SW18 158 B6
- Northspur Rd SM1 217 C5
- North Sq Edmonton N9 18 B2
  - Hampstead Garden Suburb NW11 47 C4
- North St Barking IG11 79 A1
  - Bexleyheath DA7 147 C1
  - Bromley BR1 187 A2
  - Carshalton SM5 218 D4
  - Clapham SW4 137 C2
  - Hendon NW4 46 C4
  - Isleworth TW7 131 A2
  - Newham E13 99 B5
- Northstead Rd SW2 160 C2
- North Tenter St E1 243 D1
- North Terr SW3 257 A5
- Northumberland Alley EC3 243 B1
- Northumberland Ave
  - Enfield EN1 6 B4
  - Falconwood DA16 145 C2
  - Hounslow TW7 130 D4
  - Wanstead E12 55 C1
  - Westminster WC2 116 A5 250 A4
- Northumberland Cl TW19 148 A5
- Northumberland Cres TW14 149 C5
- Northumberland Ct
  - 3 Hounslow TW3 129 D1
  - South Croydon CR2 221 C3
- Northumberland Gdns
  - Brentford TW7 131 A5
  - Bromley BR1 210 C5
  - Edmonton N9 17 D1
  - Mitcham CR4 203 D4
- Northumberland Gr N17 34 B3
- Northumberland Heath Prim Sch DA8 147 D5
- Northumberland Ho
  - Finchley N12 29 D4
  - Kentish Town NW5 71 C2
- Northumberland Mans E5 74 C4
- Northumberland Park Com Sch N17 34 A3
- Northumberland Park Ind Est N17 34 B3
- Northumberland Park Sports Ctr N17 34 A3
- Northumberland Park Sta N17 34 B3
- Northumberland Pk
  - Erith DA8 147 D5
  - Tottenham N17 34 A3
- Northumberland Pl
  - Notting Hill W2 91 C1
  - 26 Richmond TW10 153 D6
- Northumberland Rd
  - Harrow HA2 41 C4
  - New Barnet EN5 14 A4
  - Newham E6 100 A1
  - Walthamstow E17 53 C2
- Northumberland St WC2 250 A4
- Northumbria Ct 10 TW9 132 A1
- Northumbria St E14 97 C1
- North Verbena Gdns 2 W6 112 A1
- Northview 1 N7 72 A5
- North View Ealing W5 87 C3
  - Pinner HA5 40 C2
  - Wimbledon SW19 178 C5
- Northview Cres NW10 67 D4
- Northview Dr IG8 37 D1
- Northview Prim Sch NW10 67 D4
- North View Rd N8 49 D6
- North Villas NW1 71 D2
- Northway
  - Hampstead Garden Suburb NW11 47 D4
  - Merton SM4 201 A5
  - Wallington SM6 219 C4
- North Way
  - Friern Barnet N11 31 C4
  - Lower Edmonton N9 18 D2
  - Pinner HA5 40 D5
  - Queensbury NW9 44 D6
  - Uxbridge UB10 60 A1
- Northway Cir NW7 27 B6
- Northway Cres NW7 27 C6
- Northway Ct NW7 27 B6
- Northway Rd
  - Camberwell SE5 139 A2
  - Croydon CR0 205 D2
- Northway Sch NW7 11 B1
- Northways Par 2 NW3 70 B1
- Northweald La KT2 175 D5
- NORTH WEMBLEY 65 C6
- North Wembley Sta HA0, HA9 65 D5
- North Western Ave (Tylers Way) WD23 8 C6
- North Western Ave (Watford By-Pass) WD6 9 B4
- Northwest Pl N1 234 B4
- North Wharf Rd W2 92 B2 236 C3
- Northwick Ave HA3 43 B3
- Northwick Circ HA3 43 C3
- Northwick Cl
  - Harrow HA1 43 B1
  - Lisson Gr NW8 92 B3 236 C6
- Northwick Ho NW8 236 B6
- Northwick Park Hospl HA1 43 A2
- Northwick Park Rd HA1 42 D3
- Northwick Park Sta HA3 43 B2
- Northwick Rd
  - South Oxhey WD19 22 C6
  - Wembley HA0 87 D6
- Northwick Terr NW8 92 B3 236 C6
- North Wlk
  - Bayswater W2 114 A6 246 A5
  - New Addington CR0 224 A3
- Northwold Dr HA5 40 C6
- Northwold Prim Sch E5 74 A6
- Northwold Rd E5, N16 74 A6
- NORTHWOOD 22 A3
- Northwood Gdns
  - Greenford UB6 64 D3
  - Ilford IG5 56 C5
  - North Finchley N12 30 B5
- NORTHWOOD HILLS 22 A1
- Northwood Hills Cir HA6 22 A2
- Northwood Hills Sta HA6 22 A1
- North Wood Lo NW3 69 D4
- Northwood & Pinner Com Hospl HA6 22 A2
- Northwood Pl DA18 125 B3
- Northwood Prim Sch DA18 125 B3
- Northwood Rd
  - Forest Hill SE23 163 B3
  - Highgate N6 49 B2
  - South Norwood CR7 183 A1
  - Wallington SM5 219 A2
- Northwood Sch HA6 22 A2
- Northwood Twr 1 E17 54 A5
- Northwood Way
  - Northwood HA6 22 A3
  - 1 West Norwood SE19 183 C4
- NORTH WOOLWICH 122 D4
- North Woolwich Rd E16 121 B5
- North Woolwich Rdbt E16 121 D5
- North Worple Way SW14 133 B2
- Norton Ave KT5 198 D2
- Norton Cl Chingford E4 35 C5
  - Enfield EN1 6 B3
- Norton Ct
  - Beckenham BR3 185 B2
  - Ilford IG2 57 B3
- Norton Folgate E1 243 B4
- Norton Gdns SW16 182 A1
- Norton Ho
  - 14 Globe Town E2 96 D5
  - 6 New Malden KT3 199 C5
  - 30 Stepney E1 96 B1
  - 16 Stockwell SW9 138 B3
- Norton Rd
  - Walthamstow E10 53 B1
  - Wembley HA0 65 D2
- Norval Gn 1 SW9 138 C3
- Norval Rd HA0 43 B1
- Norvic Ho 5 SE5 139 A3
- Norway Gate SE16 119 A3
- Norway Pl E14 97 B1
- Norway St SE10 141 D6
- Norwegian Sch The SW20 178 C3
- Norwich Cres RM6 58 B4
- Norwich Ho 6 E14 97 D1
- Norwich Mews IG3 58 A1
- Norwich Pl 7 DA6 147 C1
- Norwich Rd
  - Forest Gate E7 77 A3
  - Greenford UB6 85 D6
  - Northwood HA6 39 D6
  - South Norwood CR7 205 A6
- Norwich St EC4 94 C1 241 A2
- Norwich Wlk HA8 27 A3
- Norwood Ave HA0 88 B5
- Norwood Cl
  - Cricklewood NW2 69 A5
  - Southall UB2 107 C2
  - Twickenham TW2 152 B2
- Norwood Dr HA2 41 C3
- Norwood Gdns
  - Hayes UB4 84 C3
  - Southall UB2 107 B2
- NORWOOD GREEN 107 C2
- Norwood Green Inf Sch UB2 107 B1
- Norwood Green Jun Sch UB2 107 A1
- Norwood Green Rd UB2 107 C2
- Norwood Heights Sh Ctr 13 SE19 183 C4
- Norwood High St SE27 183 A6
- Norwood Ho 25 E14 119 D6
- Norwood Hospl SE19 183 B4
- Norwood Junction Sta SE25 206 A5
- NORWOOD NEW TOWN 183 A4
- Norwood Park Rd SE27 183 A5
- Norwood Rd
  - Southall UB2 107 C2
  - West Norwood SE24, SE27 160 D3
- Norwood Sch SE19 183 A5
- Norwood Terr UB2 107 D2
- Notley St SE5 139 B5
- Notre Dame RC Girls Sch SE1 116 D3 261 D5
- Notre Dame RC Prim Sch SE18 144 D6
- Notson Rd SE25 206 B5
- Notting Barn Rd W10 90 D3
- Nottingdale Sq W11 244 A4
- Nottingham Ave E16 99 C1
- Nottingham Ct WC2 240 A1
- Nottingham Ho
  - 33 Camberwell SE5 139 A3
  - Stoke Newington N4 51 A1
- Nottingham Pl W1 93 A2 238 A4
- Nottingham Rd
  - Croydon CR2 221 A3
  - Isleworth TW7 130 D3
  - Leytonstone E10 54 A3
  - Upper Tooting SW17 158 D3
- Nottingham St W1 238 A4
- Nottingham Terr NW1 238 A5
- NOTTING HILL 113 B6
- Notting Hill & Ealing High Sch W13 87 B2
- Notting Hill Gate W11 113 C5 245 A4
- Notting Hill Gate Sta W11 113 C5 245 A4
- Nottingwood Ho W11 244 A6
- Nova Bldg 1 E14 119 C2
- Nova Ct E 3 E14 120 A5
- Nova Ct W 2 E14 120 A5
- Nova Mews SM4 201 A2
- Novar Cl BR6 211 D2
- Nova Rd CR0 205 A2
- Novar Rd SE9 167 A3
- Novello St SW6 135 C4 265 A2
- Nowell Rd SW13 134 A6
- Nower Ct HA5 41 B5
- NOWER HILL 41 B6
- Nower Hill HA5 41 B5
- Nower Hill High Sch HA5 41 C5
- Noyna Rd SW17 158 D1
- Nubia Way SE6 164 C1
- Nucleus NW10 89 A4
- Nuding Cl SE13 141 C2
- Nuffield Ct TW5 129 B5
- Nuffield Lo 14 W9 91 C2
- Nugent Ct
  - Streatham SW16 181 C6
  - 3 Upper Holloway N19 50 A1
- Nugent Rd
  - Finsbury Pk N19 50 A1
  - South Norwood SE25 205 D6
- Nugents Ct HA5 23 A2
- Nugent's Pk HA5 23 B2
- Nugent Terr NW8 92 A5 229 B3
- Numa Ct TW8 131 D5
- Nun Ct EC2 242 C2
- Nuneaton Rd RM9 81 A1
- Nuneham SW16 181 D6
- NUNHEAD 140 C1
- Nunhead Cres SE15 140 B2
- Nunhead Gn SE15 140 B2
- Nunhead Gr SE15 140 C2
- Nunhead La SE15 140 B2
- Nunhead Sta SE15 140 C3
- Nunnington Cl SE9 166 A1
- Nunn's Rd EN2 5 A3
- Nupton Dr EN5 12 C5
- Nurse Cl HA8 27 A2
- Nursery Ave
  - Bexleyheath DA7 147 B2
  - Croydon CR0 222 D6
  - Finchley N3 30 A1
- Nursery Cl
  - Broom Hill BR6 211 D2
  - Croydon CR0 222 D6
  - Dagenham RM6 58 D3
  - Enfield EN3 6 D4
  - Feltham TW14 150 B4
  - New Cross SE4 141 B3
  - Putney SW15 134 D1
  - Woodford IG8 37 B5
- Nursery Ct Ealing W13 87 A2
  - 8 Tottenham N17 33 D3
- Nursery Gdns
  - Chislehurst BR7 188 D4
  - Enfield EN3 6 D4
  - Hampton TW13 173 B6
  - Hounslow TW4 151 B6
  - Sunbury TW16 171 D1
- Nursery La
  - Forest Gate E7 77 A2
  - Hillingdon UB8 82 A3
  - North Kensington W10 90 C2
  - Shoreditch E2 95 D6
- Nurserymans Rd N11 15 A2
- Nursery Rd Finchley N2 30 B2
  - Hackney E9 74 C2
  - Loughton IG10 21 C6
  - Merton SW19 179 D1
- Nursery Rd *continued*
  - Mitcham CR4 202 C6
  - Osidge N14 15 C4
  - Pinner HA5 40 C6
  - South Norwood CR7 205 B5
  - Stockwell SW9 138 B1
  - Sunbury TW16 171 D1
  - Sutton SM1 218 A4
  - Wimbledon SW19 179 A3
- Nursery Row SE17 262 C3
- Nursery St N17 33 D3
- Nursery Walk Ct NW4 46 B6
- Nursery Wlk NW4 46 C6
- Nurstead Rd DA8 147 C5
- Nutborn Ho SW19 178 D4
- Nutbourne St W10 91 A4
- Nutbrook St SE15 140 A2
- Nutbrowne Rd RM9 103 B6
- Nutchford EN1 17 C5
- Nutcroft Rd SE15 140 B5
- Nutfield Cl
  - Carshalton SM5 218 C5
  - Edmonton N18 34 A4
- Nutfield Gdns Ilford IG3 80 A6
  - Northolt UB5 84 C5
- Nutfield Pl 1 CR7 204 D5
- Nutfield Rd
  - Dollis Hill NW2 68 A5
  - East Dulwich SE22 139 D1
  - Leyton E15 76 A4
  - Thornton Heath CR7 204 D5
- Nutfield Way BR6 226 D6
- Nutford Pl W1 92 D1 237 C2
- Nuthatch Cl TW19 148 B3
- Nuthatch Gdns SE28 123 B4
- Nuthurst Ave SW2 160 B2
- Nutkin Wlk UB8 60 A1
- Nutley Terr NW3 70 B2
- Nutmeg Cl E16 98 C3
- Nutmeg La E14 98 B1
- Nuttall St N1 95 C5
- Nutter La E11 55 C4
- Nutt Gr HA8 9 D2
- Nutt St SE15 139 D5
- Nutty La TW17 193 A6
- Nutwell St SW17 180 C5
- Nuxley Rd DA17 125 C1
- NW London Jewish Day Sch NW6 69 A1
- Nyanza St SE18 145 B6
- Nye Bevan Est E5 74 D5
- Nye Bevan Ho SW6 264 C4
- Nye's Wharf SE1, SE15 140 A6
- Nylands Ave TW9 132 C3
- Nymans Gdns SW20 200 B6
- Nynehead St SE14 141 A5
- Nyon Gr SE6 163 B2
- Nyton Cl N19 50 A1

O

- O2 Millennium Dome The* SE10 120 C5
- Oak Apple Ct SE12 165 A3
- Oak Ave Croydon CR0 223 D6
  - Enfield EN2 4 B5
  - Hampton TW12, TW13 173 A4
  - Heston TW5 129 A5
  - Hornsey N8 50 A5
  - Muswell Hill N10 31 B3
  - Tottenham N17 33 C3
  - Uxbridge UB10 60 D6
  - West Drayton UB7 104 C3
- Oak Bank CR0 224 A2
- Oakbank Ave KT12 195 B2
- Oakbank Gr SE24 139 A1
- Oakbark Ho 10 TW8 131 C5
- Oakbrook 3 BR3 185 D1
- Oakbrook Cl BR1 187 B6
- Oakbury Rd SW6 135 D3
- Oak Cl East Barnet N14 15 B4
  - Sutton SM1 218 A6
- Oakcombe Cl KT3 177 C2
- Oak Cottage Cl 11 SE6 164 D3
- Oak Cotts W7 108 C4
- Oakcourt 17 SE15 139 D5
- Oak Cres E16 98 C2
- Oakcroft SE12 165 B1
- Oakcroft Bsns Ctr KT9 214 B4
- Oakcroft Cl HA5 22 B1
- Oakcroft Ct SE3 143 A4
- Oakcroft Ho 3 KT3 199 C2
- Oakcroft Rd
  - Chessington KT9 214 B4
  - Lewisham SE13 142 B3
- Oakcroft Villas KT9 214 B4
- Oak Ct Bickley BR1 188 B1
  - Chingford E4 35 D4
- Oakdale
  - Beckenham BR3 186 A1
  - East Barnet N14 15 B3
- Oakdale Ave
  - Harrow HA3 44 A4
  - Pinner HA6 22 A1
- Oakdale Cl WD19 22 C6
- Oakdale Ct Chingford E4 36 A5
  - Upper Holloway N19 72 A6
- Oakdale Gdns E4 36 A5
- Oakdale Inf Sch E18 37 B1
- Oakdale Jun Sch E18 37 B1
- Oakdale Lo NW4 29 A2
- Oakdale Rd Leyton E11 76 B6
  - Nunhead SE15 140 C2
  - South Oxhey WD19 22 C6
  - Streatham SW16 182 A5
  - Tottenham N4 51 B3
  - Upton E7 77 B1
  - Woodford E18 37 B1
- Oakdale Way CR4 203 A2
- Oakdene
  - 3 Peckham SE15 140 B4
  - 1 West Norwood SE19 183 C5
- Oak Dene W13 87 B2
- Oakdene Ave
  - Chislehurst West BR7 188 C5
  - Thames Ditton KT7 197 A1
- Oakdene Cl HA5 23 B3
- Oakdene Ct
  - Feltham TW12 173 B6
  - 1 Streatham SW16 182 A5
- Oakdene Dr KT5 199 A1
- Oakdene Ho Enfield EN2 4 D2
  - 11 Stamford Hill N16 51 C1
- Oakdene Lo 3 SE20 184 B3
- Oakdene Mews SM3 201 B1
- Oakdene Pk N3 29 B3
- Oakdene Rd
  - Hillingdon UB10 82 D5
  - Orpington BR5 211 D4
- Oakden St SE11 116 C2 261 B4
- Oake Ct SW15 157 A6
- Oakeford Ho W14 254 B5
- Oakend Ho 10 N4 51 B2
- Oaken Dr KT10 212 D2
- Oakenholt Ho 1 SE2 124 D4
- Oaken La KT10 212 C3
- Oakenshaw Cl KT6 198 A2
- Oakes Cl E6 100 B1
- Oakeshott Ave N6 71 A6
- Oakey La SE1 261 A6
- Oak Farm WD6 11 A6
- Oak Farm Jun & Inf Schs UB10 82 D6
- Oakfield E4 35 D5
- Oakfield Ave HA3 43 B6
- Oakfield Cl
  - New Malden KT3 199 D4
  - Ruislip HA4 39 D3
- Oakfield Ct
  - Clapham Pk SW4 160 A5
  - 2 Ealing W5 110 C5
  - Finchley N3 29 D2
  - Finsbury Pk N8 50 A2
  - Hendon NW2 46 D2
  - South Croydon CR2 221 A2
- Oakfield Gdns
  - Beckenham BR3 207 C4
  - Carshalton SM5 202 D1
  - Edmonton N18 33 C6
  - Greenford UB6 86 B4
  - 3 West Norwood SE19 183 C5
- Oakfield Ho 2 IG1 78 D5
- Oakfield La BR2 225 C4
- Oakfield Lo 8 IG1 78 D5
- Oakfield Prep Sch SE21 161 B3
- Oakfield Rd
  - Ashford TW15 170 D5
  - Croydon CR0 205 A1
  - Finchley N3 29 D2
  - Finsbury Pk N4 50 C2
  - Higham Hill E17 35 A1
  - Ilford IG1 78 D5
  - Newham E6 100 A6
  - Palmers Green N14 16 A2
  - Penge SE20 184 B3
  - Wimbledon SW19 156 D1
- Oakfield Road Ind Est 11 SE20 184 B3
- Oakfields KT12 194 A1
- Oakfields Rd NW11 47 A3
- Oakfield St SW10 136 A6 266 A6
- Oakford Rd NW5 71 C4
- Oak Gdns Croydon CR0 223 C6
  - Hendon HA8 27 A1
- Oak Gr Ruislip HA4 40 B1
  - Sunbury TW16 172 B3
  - West Hampstead NW2 69 A4
  - West Wickham BR4 208 A1
- Oak Grove Rd SE20 184 C1
- Oakhall Ct
  - Ashford TW16 171 D5
  - Wanstead E11 55 B3
- Oakhall Dr TW16 171 D5
- Oak Hall Rd E11 55 B3
- Oakham Cl
  - Cockfosters EN4 2 D2
  - Forest Hill SE6 163 B2
- Oakham Dr BR2 208 D5
- Oakham Ho 5 W10 90 C3
- Oakhampton Rd NW7 28 D3
- Oakhill KT10 213 A2
- Oak Hill Chingford IG8 36 C3
  - Surbiton KT6 198 A2
- Oakhill Ave Pinner HA5 23 A1
  - West Hampstead NW3 69 D4
- Oak Hill Cl IG8 36 B3
- Oakhill Coll N14 15 A5
- Oak Hill Cres
  - Chingford IG8 36 C3
  - Surbiton KT6 198 A2
- Oakhill Ct
  - Honor Oak SE23 162 C5
  - Putney SW15 157 B6
  - 8 Surbiton KT6 198 A3
  - Wimbledon SW19 178 D3
- Oak Hill Ct IG8 36 C3
- Oak Hill Gdns E4 36 C2
- Oak Hill Gr KT6 198 A3
- Oakhill Ho BR5 190 A2

Oak Hill Lo NW3 ....69 D4
Oakhill Mans EN4 ....14 C5
Oak Hill Park Mews NW3 ....70 A4
Oak Hill Pk NW3 ....69 D4
Oakhill Pl SW15 ....157 C6
Oakhill Prim Sch IG8 ...36 C4
Oakhill Rd
Beckenham BR3 ....186 A1
Orpington BR6 ....227 D6
Putney SW15 ....157 B6
Sutton SM1 ....218 A5
Thornton Heath SW16 ...182 B2
Oak Hill Rd KT6 ....198 A3
Oak Hill Way NW3 ....70 A4
Oak Ho
13 Cubitt Town E14 ....120 A4
11 Finchley N2 ....30 B1
8 Maitland Pk NW3 ....70 D2
Penge SE20 ....184 B1
2 Richmond TW9 ....132 D4
13 Sidcup DA15 ....168 A1
9 Stoke Newington N16 .73 B6
Teddington TW11 ....175 C4
Wood Green N22 ....32 A3
Oakhouse Rd DA6 ....169 C6
Oakhurst Ave
East Barnet EN4 ....14 C4
Erith DA7 ....147 A5
Oakhurst Cl
Chislehurst BR7 ....188 B2
Snaresbrook E17 ....54 C5
4 Teddington TW11 ....174 C5
Oakhurst Ct E17 ....54 C5
Oakhurst Gdns
Chingford E4 ....20 D3
Erith DA7 ....147 A5
Snaresbrook E11, E17 ....54 C5
Oakhurst Gr SE22 ....140 A1
Oakhurst Rd KT19 ....215 B2
Oakington 14 KT1 ....176 C1
Oakington Ave
Harrow HA2 ....41 C2
Hayes UB3 ....105 B2
Wembley HA9 ....66 B5
Oakington Cl TW16 ....172 C1
Oakington Ct 1 EN2 ....4 D3
Oakington Dr TW16 ....172 C1
Oakington Manor Dr HA9 ....66 C3
Oakington Manor Prim Sch HA9 ....66 D3
Oakington Rd W9 ....91 C3
Oakington Way N8 ....50 A2
Oak La Finchley N2 ....30 B1
Friern Barnet N11 ....31 D4
Isleworth TW7 ....130 C1
Limehouse E14 ....119 B6
Twickenham TW1 ....153 A4
Woodford IG8 ....36 D6
Oakland Pl IG9 ....21 A2
Oakland Rd E15 ....76 C4
Oaklands
Chislehurst BR7 ....189 B4
Croydon CR0 ....220 D3
Ealing W13 ....87 A2
Southgate N21 ....16 B2
Twickenham TW2 ....152 A4
Oaklands Ave Enfield N9 .18 B5
Hounslow TW7 ....130 D6
Sidcup DA15 ....167 D4
Thames Ditton KT10 ....196 B1
Thornton Heath CR7 ....204 C5
West Wickham BR4 ....223 D5
Oaklands Cl
Bexley DA6 ....169 B6
Chessington KT9 ....213 C4
Orpington BR5 ....211 C3
Oaklands Ct
Beckenham BR3 ....186 A1
Dagenham NW10 ....89 C6
Orpington BR6 ....227 A6
5 Shepherd's Bush W12 ....112 B5
Wembley HA0 ....65 D3
Oaklands Dr TW2 ....152 A4
Oaklands Gr W12 ....112 A5
Oaklands Ho SE4 ....141 B2
Oaklands Mews 1 NW2 ....68 D4
Oaklands Park Ave IG1 ..79 A6
Oaklands Pas NW2 ....68 D4
Oaklands Pl 8 SW4 ....137 D1
Oaklands Prim Sch W7 ....108 D4
Oaklands Rd Barnet N20 .13 B4
Bexley DA6 ....169 B6
Bromley BR1 ....186 C3
Cricklewood NW2 ....68 D4
Ealing W7 ....108 D4
Mortlake SW14 ....133 B2
West Ealing W7, W13 ....109 A4
Oaklands Sch
Hounslow TW3 ....130 B2
Loughton IG10 ....21 D6
Oaklands Sec Sch E2 ....96 B4
Oaklands Way SM6 ....219 D1
Oakland Way KT19 ....215 C2
Oaklawn Ct HA7 ....25 B4
Oakleafe Gdns IG6 ....56 D6
Oaklea Pas KT1 ....197 D6
Oakleigh Ave
East Barnet N20 ....14 C3
Edgware HA8 ....26 D2
Tolworth KT6 ....214 D6
Oakleigh Cl N20 ....14 D1
Oakleigh Cres N20 ....14 C1
Oakleigh Ct
East Barnet EN4 ....14 C5
Hendon HA8 ....27 A1
7 Penge SE20 ....184 B3
Southall UB1 ....107 B5
Surbiton KT6 ....214 B6
Oakleigh Gdns
Edgware HA8 ....26 B5
Oakleigh Pk N20 ....14 B3
Orpington BR6 ....227 C4
Oakleigh Lodge IG3 ....80 A5
Oakleigh Mews 2 N20 ..14 A2
OAKLEIGH PARK 14 B3
Oakleigh Park Ave BR7 ....188 C2
Oakleigh Park Sta EN4 ..14 C4
Oakleigh Pk N N20 ....14 B3
Oakleigh Pk S N20 ....14 C3
Oakleigh Rd
Hillingdon UB10 ....61 A1
Pinner HA5 ....23 B4
Oakleigh Rd N N20 ....14 C2
Oakleigh Rd S N11 ....31 A6
Oakleigh Sch N20 ....14 D1
Oakleigh Way
Mitcham CR4 ....181 B2
1 Tolworth KT6 ....198 D1
Oakley Ave Barking IG11 .79 D1
Ealing W5 ....110 C6
Wallington CR0 ....220 A4
Oakley Cl Chingford E4 ...20 A1
Ealing W7 ....108 C6
Hounslow TW7 ....130 B4
7 Newham E6 ....100 A1
Oakley Cres EC1 ....234 D3
Oakley Ct
Carshalton CR4 ....203 A2
Harlington UB7 ....127 A5
Wembley HA0 ....65 A4
Oakley Dr
Keston Mark BR2 ....226 A5
Lewisham SE13 ....164 B5
New Eltham SE9 ....167 B3
Oakley Gdns
Chelsea SW3 ..136 C6 267 B6
Hornsey Vale N8 ....50 B4
Oakley Ho Chelsea SW1 257 D4
Ealing W5 ....110 C6
Oakley Pk DA5 ....168 C4
Oakley Pl SE1 ..117 D1 263 C1
Oakley Rd
Croydon SE25 ....206 B4
De Beauvoir Town N1 ....73 B1
Harrow HA1 ....42 C3
Keston Mark BR2 ....226 A6
Oakley Sq NW1 ..93 C5 232 B4
Oakley St SW3 ..136 C6 267 A6
Oakley Wlk W6 ....134 D6
Oak Lo
4 Ashford TW16 ....171 D3
Southgate N21 ....16 B5
10 Sutton SM1 ....218 A4
Wanstead E11 ....55 A2
6 Wembley HA0 ....65 D3
Oak Lodge 14 SE21 ....161 B2
Oak Lodge Cl HA7 ....25 C5
Oak Lodge Dr BR4 ....207 D2
Oak Lodge Sch
Balham SW12 ....159 A4
East Finchley N2 ....48 A5
Oaklodge Way NW7 ....27 D4
Oakman Ho 23 SW19 ....156 D3
Oakmead HA1 ....64 B5
Oakmead Ave BR2 ....209 A3
Oakmead Ct HA7 ....25 C6
Oakmeade HA5 ....23 C4
Oakmead Gdns HA8 ....27 B6
Oakmead Pl CR4 ....180 C2
Oakmead Rd
Balham SW12 ....159 B3
Wallington CR0 ....203 D3
Oakmere Rd SE2 ....146 A6
Oakmont Pl 6 BR6 ....211 B1
Oak Park Gdns SW19 ....156 D3
Oak Park Mews N16 ....73 D5
Oak Rd Ealing W5 ....109 D6
Kingston u T KT3 ....177 B1
Oakridge Dr N2 ....48 B6
Oakridge La BR1 ....186 B5
Oakridge Rd BR1 ....186 C6
Oak Rise IG9 ....21 D1
Oak Row CR4 ....181 C1
Oaks Ave
Feltham TW13 ....151 A2
North Cheam KT4 ....216 B4
West Norwood SE19 ....183 C5
Oaksford Ave SE26 ....162 B1
Oaks Gr E4 ....20 C2
Oakshade Rd BR1 ....186 B6
Oakshaw Rd SW18 ....157 D4
Oakshott Ct NW1 ....232 C3
Oaks La Ilford IG2 ....57 C5
South Croydon CR0 ....222 C5
Oaks Park High Sch IG2 ....57 C4
Oaks Rd CR0 ....222 C4
Oaks Sh Ctr The W3 ...111 A5
Oaks The
Brondesbury Pk NW6 ....68 D1
Chingford IG8 ....36 C3
Enfield EN2 ....4 D2
Finchley N12 ....29 D6
Hayes UB4 ....83 A5
Long Ditton KT6 ....213 C5
Ruislip HA4 ....39 C2
Southborough BR2 ....210 C3
Wallington SM6 ....219 C4
Willesden NW10 ....68 B1
Wimbledon SW19 ....179 A4
Woolwich SE18 ....123 A1
Oaks Way Surbiton KT6 ..197 D1
Wallington SM5 ....218 D1
Oakthorpe Ct N13 ....33 A5
Oakthorpe Prim Sch N13 ....33 A5
Oakthorpe Rd N13 ....32 C5
Oaktree Ave N13 ....16 D1
Oak Tree Ave N2 ....47 D6
Oak Tree Cl Ealing W5 ...87 C1
Stanmore HA7 ....25 C3
Oak Tree Ct Acton W3 ..110 D6
8 Clapham Pk SW4 ....160 A6
Elstree WD6 ....9 D5
Oak Tree Dell NW9 ....45 B4
Oak Tree Dr N20 ....13 D3
Oak Tree Gdns BR1 ....187 B5
Oaktree Gr IG1 ....79 B3
Oak Tree Ho W9 ....91 D3
Oak Tree Rd NW8 ....92 C4 230 A1
Oaktree Sch EN4 ....15 A5
Oaktrees Hostel HA8 ....11 A2
Oakview Gdns N2 ....48 B5
Oakview Gr CR0 ....207 A1
Oakview Lo NW11 ....47 B2
Oakview Rd SE6 ....185 D5
Oak Village NW5 ....71 A4
Oakway
Beckenham BR2 ....186 B1
West Barnes SW20 ....200 C5
Oak Way Croydon CR0 ...206 D3
East Acton W3 ....111 C5
East Barnet N14 ....15 B4
East Bedfont TW14 ....149 C3
Oakway Cl DA5 ....169 A5
Oakways SE9 ....166 D5
Oakwell Ho 24 SW8 ....137 D3
Oak Wlk CR4 ....203 A1
OAKWOOD 15 D6
Oakwood Ave
Beckenham BR2, BR3 ...186 A1
Bromley BR2 ....209 B6
Mitcham CR4 ....180 B1
Osidge N14 ....15 D4
Southall UB1 ....107 C6
Oakwood Cl
Chislehurst West BR7 ....188 C4
Lewisham SE13 ....164 B5
Southgate N14 ....15 C5
Oakwood Cres
Southgate N21 ....16 B5
Wembley UB6 ....65 B2
Oakwood Ct
Beckenham BR3 ....186 A1
6 Chingford E4 ....20 C4
Kensington W14 ....113 B3 254 C6
1 Newham E6 ....100 A6
17 Sutton SM1 ....218 A4
Oakwood Dr
Burnt Oak HA8 ....27 A4
West Norwood SE19 ....183 C4
Oakwood Gdns
Ilford IG3 ....79 D6
Orpington BR6 ....227 A6
Sutton SM1 ....217 C6
Oakwood La W14 ....113 B3 254 C6
Oakwood Park Rd N14 ..16 A5
Oakwood Pl CR0 ....204 C3
Oakwood Rd
Hampstead Garden Suburb NW11 ....47 D4
Orpington BR6 ....227 A6
Pinner HA5 ....22 B1
Thornton Heath CR0 ....204 C3
Wimbledon SW20 ....178 A2
Oakwood Sta N14 ....15 C6
Oakwood View N14 ....15 D4
Oakworth Rd W10 ....90 D2
Oarsman Pl KT8 ....196 C5
Oasis The 6 BR1 ....187 C1
Oast Ct 8 E14 ....119 B6
Oast Lo W4 ....133 C5
Oates Cl BR2 ....208 B6
Oatfield Ho 1 N15 ....51 C3
Oatfield Rd BR6 ....211 D1
Oat La EC2 ....95 A1 242 B2
Oatland Rise E17 ....35 A1
Oatlands Ct 3 SW19 ....156 D3
Oatlands Dr KT13 ....193 C1
Oatlands Rd EN3 ....6 C4
Oatwell Ho SW3 ....257 B3
Oban Cl E13 ....99 C3
Oban Ct HA8 ....10 D2
Oban Ho
5 Barking IG11 ....101 B5
South Bromley E14 ....98 B1
Oban Rd Newham E13 ....99 C4
South Norwood SE25 ....205 B5
Oban St E14 ....98 B1
Oberon Ho 5 N1 ....95 C5
Oberon Way TW17 ....192 A6
Oberstein Rd 15 SW11 ..136 B1
Oborne Cl SE24 ....160 D6
O'Brian Ho 10 E1 ....96 D4
Observatory Gdns W8. 245 B2
Observatory Mews E14 ....120 B2
Observatory Rd SW14 ..133 A1
Occupation La
Brentford W5 ....109 D2
Shooters Hill SE18 ....144 D4
Occupation Rd
Newington SE17 ....117 A1 262 A2
West Ealing W13 ....109 B4
Ocean St E1 ....96 D2
Ocean Wharf E14 ....119 C4
Ochre Ct TW13 ....149 D1
Ockbrook 3 E1 ....96 C2
Ockendon Rd N1 ....73 B2
Ockham Dr BR5 ....190 A3
Ockley Ct Sidcup DA14 ..167 C1
Sutton SM1 ....218 A4
Ockley Ho 8 KT2 ....176 D4
Ockley Rd
Streatham SW16 ....160 A1
Thornton Heath CR0 ....204 B2
Octagon Arc EC2 ....243 A3
Octagon The NW3 ....69 C4
Octavia Cl CR4 ....202 C4
Octavia Ho Catford SE6 .163 D4
Kensal Town W10 ....91 A3
Octavia Mews 1 W9 ....91 B3
Octavia Rd TW7 ....130 D2
Octavia St SW11 ....136 C4 267 B1
Octavia Way 12 SE28 ...124 B6
Octavius St SE8 ....141 C5
October Ct BR2 ....208 D6
October Pl NW4 ....46 D6
Odard Rd KT8 ....195 C5
Odell Cl IG11 ....79 D1
Odell Wlk SE13 ....142 A2
Odeon Ct
Dagenham NW10 ....89 C6
1 Newham E16 ....99 A2
Odeon Par Eltham SE9 ..144 A1
Wembley UB6 ....65 B2
Odeon The IG11 ....79 B1
Odessa Inf Sch E7 ....77 A3
Odessa Rd Leyton E7 ....76 D4
Willesden Green NW10 ...90 A5
Odessa St SE16 ....119 B3
Odette Ct N20 ....14 A1
Odette Duval Ho 29 E1 ..96 C2
Odette Ho 6 SE27 ....183 B6
Odger St SW11 ....136 D3
Odhams Wlk WC2 ....240 B1
Odin Ho 6 SE5 ....139 A3
O'Donnell Ct WC1 ....240 B6
O'Driscoll Ho 4 W12 ....90 B1
Odyssey Bsns Pk HA4 ...62 B3
Offa's Mead E9 ....75 A4
Offenbach Ho 12 E2 ....96 D5
Offenham Rd BR7, SE9 ..188 B6
Offers Ct KT1 ....198 B6
Offerton Rd SW4 ....137 C2
Offham Ho SE17 ....263 A3
Offham Slope N12 ....29 B5
Offley Ho 10 E9 ....74 D2
Offley Pl TW7 ....130 B3
Offley Rd SW9 ....138 C5
Offord Cl N17 ....34 A4
Offord Rd N1 ....72 B1
Offord St N1 ....72 B1
Ogden Ho TW13 ....173 A6
Ogilby St SE18 ....122 B2
Ogilvie Ho 12 E1 ....96 D1
Oglander Rd SE15 ....139 D2
Ogle St W1 ....93 C2 239 A4
Oglethorpe Rd RM10 ....81 C5
O'Gorman Ho SW10 ....266 B4
O'Grady Ct 17 W13 ....109 A5
O'Grady Ho 17 E17 ....53 D6
Ohio Bldg 13 SE13 ....141 D4
Ohio Rd E13 ....98 D3
Oil Mill La W6 ....112 A1
Okeburn Rd SW17 ....181 A5
Okehampton Cl N12 ....30 B5
Okehampton Cres DA16 ....146 C4
Okehampton Rd NW10 ..90 D6
Okeover Manor SW4 ...137 B1
Olaf Palme Ho TW13 ....150 B1
Olaf St W11 ....112 D6
Old Bailey EC4 ...94 D1 241 D1
Old Barn Cl SM2 ....217 A1
Old Barrack Yd SW1 ....248 A1
Old Barrowfield 7 E15 ..98 C6
Old Bellgate Wharf E14 ....119 C3
Oldberry Rd HA8 ....27 B4
Old Bethnal Green Rd E2 ....96 B4
OLD BEXLEY 169 D4
Old Bexley Bsns Pk DA5 ....169 D4
Old Bexley CE Prim Sch DA5 ....169 B3
Old Billingsgate Wlk EC3 ....253 A5
Old Bldgs WC2 ....241 A2
Old Bond St W1 ....115 C6 249 A5
Oldborough Rd HA0 ....65 C5
Old Brewery Mews NW3 ....70 B4
Old Bridge Cl UB5 ....85 C5
Old Bridge St KT1 ....175 D1
Old Broad St EC2 ....95 B1 242 D2
Old Bromley Rd BR1 ...186 B5
Old Brompton Rd SW5, SW7 ....114 A2 256 B3
Old Burlington St W1 ....115 C6 249 A5
Oldbury Ct E9 ....75 A3
Oldbury Pl W1 ...93 A2 238 B4
Oldbury Rd EN1 ....6 A3
Old Castle St E1 ....95 D1 243 D2
Old Cavendish St W1 ....238 C1
Old Change Ct EC4 ....242 A1
Old Chapel Pl 2 N10 ....49 B6
Old Charlton Rd TW17 ....193 A4
Old Chiswick Yd W4 ...133 C6
Old Church Ct N11 ....31 B5
Old Church La
Ealing UB6 ....87 A4
Stanmore HA7 ....25 C4
Welsh Harp NW9 ....67 B6
Old Church Path KT10 ..212 A4
Old Church Rd
Chingford E4 ....19 C1
Stepney E1 ....96 D1
Old Church St SW3 ....256 D1
Old Claygate La KT10 ..213 A3
Old Clem Sq 12 SE18 ...144 C6
Old College Ct DA17 ...125 D1
Old Compton St W1 ....93 D1 239 C1
Old Cote Dr TW5 ....129 C6
Old Court Ho W8 ....245 C1
Old Court (Mus & Liby)* HA0 ....65 C3
Old Court Pl W8 ....113 D4 245 C1
Old Covent Gdn* WC2 ....250 B6
Old Ctyd The BR1 ....187 B2
Old Cty H* SE1 ....250 C2
Old Dairy Mews
5 Balham SW12 ....159 A3
4 Camden Town NW5 ...71 B2
Old Dairy Sq The N21 ...16 C4
Old Deer Park Gdns TW9 ....132 A2
Old Devonshire Rd SW12 ....159 B4
Old Dock Cl TW9 ....132 C6
Old Dover Rd SE3 ....143 B5
Oldegate Ho 1 E6 ....99 D6
Old Farm Ave
Osidge N14 ....15 C4
Sidcup DA15 ....167 C2
Old Farm Cl TW4 ....129 B1
Old Farm Ct UB2 ....107 D2
Old Farm Rd
Hampton TW12 ....173 C4
London N2 ....30 B2
Old Farm Rd E DA15 ...168 A2
Old Farm Rd W DA15 ...167 D2
Oldfield Cl
Bromley BR1 ....210 B5
Greenford UB6 ....64 C2
Stanmore HA7 ....25 A5
Oldfield Farm Gdns UB6 ....86 B6
Oldfield Gr SE16 ....118 D2
Oldfield Ho
14 Chiswick W4 ....111 C1
Streatham SW16 ....181 B6
Oldfield House Unit TW12 ....173 B2
Oldfield La N UB6 ....64 B1
Oldfield La S UB6 ....86 A4
Oldfield Mews N6 ....49 C2
Oldfield Prim Sch UB6 ..86 B5
Oldfield Rd
Bedford Pk W3, W12 ....111 D4
Bexleyheath DA7 ....147 A3
Bromley BR1 ....210 B5
Hampton TW12 ....173 B2
Stoke Newington N16 ....73 C5
Willesden NW10 ....67 D1
Wimbledon SW19 ....179 A4
Oldfields Cir UB5 ....64 A2
Oldfields Rd SM1, SM3 ..217 C6
Oldfields Trad Est SM1 ....217 C5
Old Fire Station The SE18 ....144 D5
Old Fish St Hill EC4 ....252 A6
Old Fleet La EC4 ....241 C2
Old Fold Cl EN5 ....1 B4
Old Fold La EN5 ....1 B4
OLD FORD 97 B6
Old Ford Ho CR0 ....220 A5
Old Ford Prim Sch E3 ...97 B5
Old Ford Rd E2, E3 ....96 D5
Old Ford Trad Ctr 13 E3 ....97 C6
Old Forge Cl HA7 ....25 A6
Old Forge Cres TW17 ..192 D3
Old Forge Mews W12 ..112 B4
Old Forge Rd Enfield EN1 ..5 D5
Upper Holloway N19 ....71 D6
Old Forge Way DA14 ....190 B6
Old Gloucester St WC1 ....94 A2 240 B4
Old Hall Cl HA5 ....23 A2
Old Hall Dr HA5 ....23 A2
Oldham Ho 10 SE21 ....183 C6
Oldham Terr W3 ....111 A5
Old Hatch Manor HA4 ...40 A2
Old Hill Chislehurst BR7 ..188 C2
Orpington BR6 ....227 C2
Oldhill St N16 ....52 A1
Old Homesdale Rd BR2 ....209 C5
Old Hospital Cl SW12, SW17 ....158 D3
Old Ho The BR7 ....189 B2
Old House Cl SW19 ....179 A5
Old House Gdns 9 TW1 ....153 C5
Old Howlett's La HA4 ...39 B3
Olding Ho 6 SW12 ....159 C4
Old Jamaica Bsns Est 23 SE16 ....118 A3
Old Jamaica Rd SE16 ...118 A3
Old James St SE15 ....140 B2
Old Jewry EC2 ...95 B1 242 C1
Old Kenton La NW9 ....44 D4
Old Kent Rd
Deptford SE1, SE15 ....140 B6
Old Kent Rd *continued*
Walworth SE1 ..117 C1 263 B2
Old Kingston Rd KT4 ...215 A5
Old Laundry The 14 SW18 ....136 B1
Old Lodge Pl 7 TW1 ...153 B5
Old Lodge Way HA7 ....25 A5
Old London Rd KT2 ....176 A1
Old Maidstone Rd BR8, DA14 ....191 B3
OLD MALDEN 199 C1
Old Malden La KT4 ....215 C6
Oldman Ct SE12 ....165 B2
Old Manor Ct NW8 ....229 B4
Old Manor Dr TW7 ....152 A5
Old Manor House Mews TW17 ....192 C6
Old Manor Rd UB2 ....106 D2
Old Manor Way BR7, SE9 ....188 B5
Old Manor Yd SW5 ....255 C3
Old Market Ct SM1 ....217 D4
Old Market Sq 11 E2 ....95 D4
Old Marylebone Rd NW1 ....92 C2 237 B3
Oldmead Ho 8 RM10 ...81 D2
Old Mill Ct E18 ....55 C6
Old Mill Rd SE18 ....145 B6
Old Mitre Ct EC4 ....241 B1
Old Montague St E1 ...96 A2
Old Nichol St E2 ....95 D3 243 C6
Old North St WC1 ....240 C4
Old Nursery Pl TW15 ...170 D5
OLD OAK COMMON 89 D3
Old Oak Common La NW10 ....89 C3
Old Oak La NW10 ....89 D4
Old Oak Prim Sch W12 ..89 D1
Old Oak Rd W3 ....111 D6
Old Orch TW16 ....172 C1
Old Orchard Cl
Hadley Wood EN4 ....2 B5
Hillingdon UB8 ....82 C1
Old Orch The NW3 ....70 D4
Old Palace La TW9 ....153 C6
Old Palace Prim Sch E3 ....97 D4
Old Palace Rd CR0 ....221 A5
Old Palace Sch of John Whitgift CR9 ....220 D5
Old Palace Terr 8 TW9 ....153 D6
Old Palace Yd 2 TW9 ....153 D6
Old Paradise St SE11 ....116 B2 260 C4
Old Park Ave
Balham SW12 ....159 A5
Enfield EN2 ....5 A1
Old Park Gr EN2 ....5 A1
Old Park Ho N13 ....32 B6
Old Park La W1 ....115 B5 248 C3
Old Park Mews TW5 ...129 B5
Old Park Rd Enfield EN2 ...4 D2
Palmers Green N13 ....32 B6
Plumstead Comm SE2 ...124 A1
Old Park Rd S EN2 ....4 D1
Old Park Ridings N21 ...17 A6
Old Park View EN2 ....4 D2
Old Perry St BR7 ....189 C3
Old Post Office La SE3 ....143 B2
Old Pound Cl TW7 ....131 A4
Old Priory UB9 ....38 D2
Old Pye St SW1 ....259 C6
Old Pye Street Est SW1 ....259 C5
Old Quebec St W1 ....237 D1
Old Queen St SW1 ....115 D4 249 D1
Old Rd Enfield EN3 ....6 C4
Lewisham SE13 ....142 C1
Old Rectory Gdns HA8 ..26 C4
Old Redding HA3 ....24 A6
Oldridge Rd SW12 ....159 B4
Old Royal Free Pl N1 ..234 B5
Old Royal Free Sq N1 ....94 C6 234 B5
Old Ruislip Rd UB5 ....84 C5
Old St Andrews Mans NW9 ....67 B6
Old School Cl
3 Beckenham BR3 ....185 A1
Merton SW19 ....179 C1
Old School Cres E7 ....77 A2
Old School Ct 8 N17 ...51 D6
Old School Ho CR4 ....202 C6
Old School Ho The EN2 ..4 D2
Old School Pl CR0 ....220 C4
Old School Rd UB8 ....82 B3
Old School Sq
12 Poplar E14 ....97 C1
Thames Ditton KT7 ....196 D3
Old School The
Bloomsbury WC1 ....240 D4
Merton SW19 ....179 C1
Old Seacoal La EC4 ....241 C1
Old South Cl HA5 ....22 D2
Old South Lambeth Rd SW8 ....138 A5 270 B4
Old Spitalfields Mkt E1 ....95 D2 243 D4
Old Sq WC2 ....241 A2
Old St
Broadgate EC1 ....95 B3 242 D6
Newham E13 ....99 B5
Old Stable Mews N5 ....73 A5

Old Station Rd UB3 105 D3
Old Station Yard The 11 E17 54 A5
Oldstead Rd BR1 186 B6
Old Street Sta EC1 95 B3 242 D6
Old Studio Cl CR0 205 B2
Old Sun Wharf E14 119 A6
Old Swan Wharf SW11 266 D2
Old Swan Yd SM5 218 D4
Old Theatre Ct SE1 252 B4
Old Town
Clapham SW4 137 C2
Croydon CR0 220 D5
Old Tramyard SE18 123 C2
Old Twelve Cl W7 86 C3
Old Vicarage Sch TW10 154 A5
Old Vicarage The CR4 202 C6
Old Woolwich Rd SE10 120 B1
Old York Rd SW18 157 D6
Oleander Cl BR6 227 B3
O'Leary Sq E1 96 C2
Oleastor Ct IG5 56 A6
Olga Prim Sch E3 97 A5
Olga St 20 E3 97 A5
Olinda Rd N16 51 D3
Oliphant St W10 91 A4
Olive Blythe Ho 14 W10 91 A3
Oliver Ave SE25 205 D6
Oliver Bsns Pk NW10 89 A5
Oliver Cl W4 132 D6
Oliver Ct
Isleworth TW7 130 D2
2 Penge SE26 184 C4
Plumstead SE18 123 A2
Olive Rd
Cricklewood NW2 68 C4
Ealing W5 109 D3
3 Merton SW19 180 A3
Newham E13 99 C4
Oliver Gdns E6 100 A2
Oliver Goldsmith Prim Sch
Camberwell SE5 139 D4
Kingsbury NW9 45 B4
Oliver Gr SE25 205 D5
Oliver Ho
22 Bermondsey SE16 118 A4
Notting Hill W11 244 A5
South Lambeth SW8 270 A4
Oliver House Prep Sch SW4 159 B5
Oliver Mews SE15 140 A3
Oliver Rd
Kingston u T KT3 177 A1
Leyton E10 75 D5
Sutton SM1 218 B4
Walthamstow E17 54 A4
Oliver's Yd EC1 242 D6
Olive Tree Ho
7 Deptford SE15 140 C6
Stroud Green N4 50 C3
Olive Tree Sch The SE13 163 D5
Olivette St 1 SW15 134 D1
Olive Waite Ho NW6 69 D1
Olivia Ct 1 EN5 1 B1
Ollard's Gr IG10 21 D6
Ollerton Gn E3 97 B6
Ollerton Rd N11 31 D5
Olley Cl SM6 220 A2
Ollgar Cl W12 111 D5
Olliffe St E14 120 A3
Olmar St SE1 140 A6
Olney Ho NW8 237 B6
Olney Rd SE17 139 A6
Olron Cres DA6 169 A6
Olven Rd SE18 145 A6
Olveston Wlk SM5 202 B3
Olwen Mews HA5 22 D1
Olyffe Ave DA16 146 A3
Olyffe Dr BR3 186 A2
Olympia Ex Ctr* W14 113 A3 254 B5
Olympia Ind Est N22 50 B6
Olympian Ct 8 E14 119 C2
Olympia Way W14 113 A3 254 B5
Olympia Yd W2 245 D5
Olympic Ho 10 W10 90 C1
Olympic Ret Pk HA9 66 D4
Olympic Way
Greenford UB6 85 D6
Wembley HA9 66 C4
Olympus Gr N22 32 C2
Olympus Sq E5 74 A5
Oman Ave NW2 68 C4
Oman Ct NW4 68 B4
Ombersley Ho N4 51 A2
Omeara St SE1 252 B3
Omega Cl E14 119 D3
Omega Ho SW10 266 B4
Omega Pl N1 233 B3
Omega St SE14 141 C4
Omega Works E3 75 C1
Ommaney Rd SE14 141 A4
Omnibus Bsns Ctr N7 72 A3
Omnibus Way E17 35 C1
Ondine Rd SE15 139 D1
Onedin Point 10 E1 118 A6
Onega Gate SE16 119 A3
O'Neill Ho NW8 229 D3
O'Neill Path 11 SE18 144 C6
One Tree Cl SE23 162 C5
Ongar Cl RM6 58 C4
Ongar Ho 15 N1 73 B2
Ongar Rd SW6 135 C6 265 B6
Onra Rd E17 53 C2
Onslow Ave TW10 154 A6
Onslow Avenue Mans 10 TW10 154 A6
Onslow Cl Chingford E4 20 B2
Notting Hill W9 91 B4
Thames Ditton KT7 196 C1
Onslow Cres BR7 188 D2
Onslow Ct SW10 256 B1
Onslow Dr DA14 168 D2
Onslow Gdns
Chelsea SW7 114 B1 256 C2
Cranley Gdns N10 49 B4
Southgate N21 16 C6
Thames Ditton KT7 196 C1
Wallington SM6 219 C1
Wanstead E18 55 C6
Onslow Ho 1 KT2 176 B2
Onslow Lo 28 SW2 160 C4
Onslow Mews E SW7 256 C3
Onslow Mews W SW7 256 C3
Onslow Par N14 15 B3
Onslow Rd
Richmond TW10 154 A5
Thornton Heath CR0 204 C1
West Barnes KT3 200 A5
Onslow Sq SW7 114 B2 256 D3
Onslow St EC1 241 B5
Onslow Way KT7 196 C1
Ontario St SE1 116 D3 261 D6
Ontario Way E14 119 C6
Onyx Ct N11 31 D3
Onyx Ho KT4 199 B1
Onyx Mews 4 E15 76 D2
Opal Cl E16 99 D1
Opal Ct N11 31 D3
Opal Ho KT4 199 B1
Opal Mews 2 IG1 78 D6
Opal St SE11 116 D1 261 C2
Open Air Theatre, Regent's Pk* NW1 231 A1
Openshaw Rd SE2 124 B2
Openview SW17, SW18 158 B2
Opera Ct 7 N19 71 D5
Operating Theatre Mus & Herb Garret* SE1 117 B5 252 D3
Ophelia Gdns NW2 69 A5
Ophir Terr SE15 140 A4
Opie Ho NW8 230 B4
Opossum Way TW4 128 C2
Oppenheim Rd SE13 142 A3
Oppidan Apartments NW6 69 C2
Oppidans Rd NW3 70 D1
Opus Studios E13 99 A5
Orange Gr E11 76 C5
Orange Hill Rd HA8 27 A3
Orange Pl SE16 118 C3
Orangery Gallery The* W8 113 B4 244 C1
Orangery La SE9 166 B6
Orangery The TW10 153 C2
Orange St WC2 115 D6 249 D5
Orange Yd WC2 239 D1
Oransay Rd 25 N1 73 A2
Oratory La SW3 256 D2
Oratory RC Prim Sch SW3 114 C1 257 A2
Oratory The* SW7 114 C3 257 A5
Orbain Rd SW6 135 A5 264 B3
Orbel St SW11 136 C4 267 A1
Orb St SE17 117 B2 262 C3
Orchard Ave
Ashford TW15 171 A4
Carshalton CR4 203 A1
Croydon CR0 207 A1
East Finchley N3 47 C6
Erith DA17 147 B6
Hatton TW14 149 B6
Heston TW5 129 A5
Hinchley Wood KT7 213 A6
Kingston u T KT3 199 C6
Osidge N14 15 C4
Southall UB1 107 B5
Whetstone N20 14 B2
Orchard Bsns Ctr SE26 185 B5
Orchard Cl
Ashford TW15 171 A4
Bexleyheath DA7 147 A4
Bushey WD23 8 B3
Chingford E4 35 C6
Dollis Hill NW2 68 A5
Edgware HA8 26 A4
Honor Oak SE23 162 C5
Islington N1 73 A1
Kensal Town W10 91 A2
Northolt UB5 64 A2
Ruislip HA4 39 A2
Thames Ditton KT7 197 B2
Walton-on-T KT12 194 B2
Wanstead E11 55 B5
Wembley HA0 88 A6
West Barnes SW20 200 C5
West Ewell KT19 214 D2
Orchard Cotts
Chislehurst BR7 189 C4
Hayes UB3 105 C4
Orchard Cres
Edgware HA8 27 A5
Enfield EN1 5 D4
Orchard Ct
Barnes SW13 133 D2
Barnet EN5 1 D2
Croydon BR3 207 C1
Edgware HA8 26 B5
Orchard Ct *continued*
Hounslow TW7 130 B5
Marylebone W1 238 A2
New Malden KT4 200 A1
Penge SE26 184 D5
Southgate N14 15 C5
Wallington SM6 219 B3
Walthamstow E10 53 D1
1 Walton-on-T KT12 193 D1
Wood Green N22 32 A3
Orchard Dr
Blackheath Vale SE3 142 C3
Edgware HA8 26 B5
Upper Halliford TW17 193 C6
Orchard Gate
Colindale NW9 45 C5
Thames Ditton KT10 196 B1
Wembley UB6 65 B2
Orchard Gdns
Chessington KT9 214 A4
Sutton SM1 217 C3
Orchard Gn
Bromley BR1 187 C2
Orpington BR6 227 C6
Orchard Gr BR6 227 D6
Croydon CR0 207 A2
Edgware HA8 26 D2
Harrow HA3 44 B4
Orpington BR6 211 D1
Penge SE20 184 A3
Orchard Hill SE13 141 D4
Orchard Hill Coll SM6 219 B2
Orchard Ho
Camberwell SE5 139 A4
11 Rotherhithe SE16 118 C3
Shepherd's Bush W12 112 A5
Orchard Inf Sch The KT8 196 B5
Orchard Jun & Inf Sch The TW3 151 C6
Orchard La
Thames Ditton KT8 196 B3
Wimbledon SW20 178 B2
Woodford IG8 37 C6
Orchardleigh Ave EN3 6 C3
Orchard Lo N12 14 A1
Orchard Mead Ho NW11 69 C6
Orchardmede N21 17 B5
Orchard Mews N1 73 B1
Orchard Pl
Canning Town E14 120 C6
Tottenham N17 33 D3
Orchard Prim Sch E9 74 C1
Orchard Rd Barnet EN5 1 B1
Belvedere DA17 125 C2
Brentford TW8 131 C6
Bromley BR1 187 C2
Carshalton CR4 203 A1
Chessington KT9 214 A4
Dagenham RM10 103 C6
Enfield EN3 18 C6
Farnborough BR6 226 D3
Feltham TW14 150 A3
Hampton TW12 173 B3
Hayes UB3 106 A6
Highgate N6 49 B2
Hounslow TW4 151 C6
Isleworth TW1 153 B6
Kingston u T KT1 176 A1
Richmond TW9 132 C2
Sidcup DA14 189 C6
Sunbury TW16 172 B3
Sutton SM1 217 C4
Welling DA16 146 B2
Orchard Rise
Croydon CR0 207 B1
Kingston u T KT2 177 A2
Mortlake TW10 132 D1
Pinner HA5 39 D6
Orchard Rise E DA15 167 D6
Orchard Rise W DA15 167 C6
Orchard Sch DA14 190 B5
Orchard School Sports Ctr SE20 184 A2
Orchardson Ho NW8 236 D5
Orchardson St NW8 92 B3 236 D5
Orchard Sq W14 254 C1
Orchard St
Marylebone W1 238 B2
Walthamstow E17 53 A5
Orchard Terr EN1 18 A5
Orchard The
Acton Green W4 111 B2
Ealing W5 87 D2
East Barnet N14 15 B6
Edgware HA8 26 C5
Enfield N21 17 B5
Ewell KT17 215 D1
Hampstead Garden Suburb NW11 47 C4
Hounslow TW3 130 A3
Lewisham SE3 142 B3
Totteridge N20 13 D3
Orchard Villas BR7 189 C4
Orchard Way
Ashford TW15 148 B2
Croydon BR3, CR0 207 A3
Enfield EN1 5 C2
Esher KT10 212 A2
Sutton SM1 218 B4
Orchard Way Prim Sch CR0 207 A2
Orchestra Ct HA8 26 D3
Orchid Cl
Chessington KT9 213 C1
1 Newham E6 100 A2
Southall UB1 85 A1
Orchid Ct Catford BR1 164 B1
Orchid Ct *continued*
Harrow HA3 24 C2
Wembley HA9 66 A6
Orchid Gdns TW3 129 B1
Orchid Grange N14 15 C4
Orchid Lo N14 15 C4
Orchid Rd N14 15 C4
Orchid St W12 112 A6
Orde 6 NW9 27 D2
Orde Hall St WC1 94 B2 240 C4
Orde Ho 10 N16 73 B4
Ordell Ct 36 E3 97 B5
Ordell Rd E3 97 B5
Ordnance Cl TW13 150 A2
Ordnance Cres SE10 120 C4
Ordnance Hill NW8 92 B6 229 D5
Ordnance Mews NW8 229 D4
Ordnance Rd
Canning Town E16 98 D2
Enfield EN3 7 B6
Shooters Hill SE18 144 C6
Oregano Cl UB7 104 B6
Oregano Dr E14 98 B1
Oregon Ave E12 78 B4
Oregon Bldg 5 SE13 141 D4
Oregon Cl KT3 199 A5
Oregon Sq BR6 211 B1
Orestes Ct 9 E18 55 A6
Orestes Mews 1 NW6 69 C3
Orford Ct Stanmore HA7 25 C4
Wallington SM6 219 C3
West Norwood SE27 160 D2
Orford Gdns TW1 152 D2
Orford Rd Catford SE6 163 D1
Walthamstow E17 53 D4
Wanstead E18 55 B6
Organ Crossroads KT17 216 A1
Oriana Ct CR0 221 B6
Oriana Ho 3 E14 119 B6
Oriel Cl CR4 203 D6
Oriel Ct
6 Croydon CR0 205 B1
Hampstead NW3 70 A4
Oriel Dr SW13 134 C6
Oriel Gdns IG5 56 B6
Oriel Jun & Inf Sch TW13 151 A1
Oriel Rd Hackney E9 75 A2
Homerton E9 74 D2
Oriel Way UB5 63 D1
Oriental City NW9 45 B6
Oriental Rd E16 121 D5
Orient Ind Pk E10 75 C6
Orient St SE11 116 D2 261 C4
Orient Way
Lea Bridge E5 74 D5
Leyton E10 75 B6
Oriole Way SE28 124 B6
Orion Bsns Ctr SE14 118 D1
Orion Ct 10 HA8 26 D5
Orion Ctr The CR0 220 A6
Orion Ho 20 E1 96 B3
Orion Mews SM4 201 C5
Orion Point 5 E14 119 C2
Orion Prim Sch The NW9 27 D2
Orion Rd N11 31 A4
Orion Way HA6 22 A6
Orissa Rd SE18 123 C1
Orkney Ho N1 233 C6
Orkney St SW11 137 A3
Orlando Rd SW4 137 C2
Orleans Cl KT10 212 B6
Orleans Ct 9 TW1 153 B4
Orleans House Gallery* TW1 153 B3
Orleans Inf Sch TW1 153 B4
Orleans Park Sch TW1 153 B4
Orleans Rd
South Norwood SE19 183 B4
Twickenham TW1 153 C4
Orleston Mews N7 72 C2
Orleston Rd N7 72 C2
Orley Farm Rd HA1 64 C5
Orley Farm Sch HA1 64 B5
Orlop St SE10 120 C1
Ormanton Rd SE26 184 A6
Orme Ct W2 113 D6 245 C5
Orme Ct Mews W2 245 D5
Orme Ho 8 E8 95 D6
Orme La W2 113 D6 245 C5
Ormeley Rd SW12 159 B3
Orme Rd
Kingston u T KT1, KT3 176 D1
Sutton SM1 217 D2
Ormerod Gdns CR4 181 A2
Ormerod Ho 3 SW9 138 A2
Ormesby Cl SE28 124 D6
Ormesby Way HA3 44 B4
Orme Sq W2 245 C5
Ormiston Gr W12 112 B5
Ormiston Rd SE10 121 A1
Ormond Ave
Hampton TW12 173 D2
23 Richmond TW10 153 D6
Ormond Cl WC1 240 B4
Ormond Cres TW12 173 D2
Ormond Dr TW12 173 D3
Ormonde Ave BR6 227 A6
Ormonde Ct
Hendon NW4 46 D6
Putney SW15 134 C1
Ormonde Gate SW3 114 D1 257 D1
Ormonde Mans WC1 240 B4
Ormonde Pl SW1 258 B3
Ormonde Rd SW14 133 A2
Ormonde Rise IG9 21 C3
Ormonde Terr NW8 92 D6 230 C5
Ormond Ho 7 N16 73 B6
Ormond Mans WC1 240 C5
Ormond Mews WC1 240 B5
Ormond Rd
Finsbury Pk N4, N19 50 A1
Richmond TW10 153 D6
Ormond Yd SW1 249 B4
Ormrod Ct W11 91 B1
Ormsby SM2 217 D1
Ormsby Gdns UB6 86 A5
Ormsby Lo 7 W4 111 C3
Ormsby Pl N16 73 D5
Ormsby Point 6 SE18 122 D2
Ormsby St E2 95 D5
Ormside St SE15 140 C6
Ormskirk Rd WD19 22 D5
Ornan Rd NW3 70 C3
Orpen Ho SW5 255 B3
Orpen Wlk N16 73 C5
Orpheus Ho 25 N19 49 D2
Orpheus St SE5 139 B4
ORPINGTON 227 D6
Orpington Gdns N18 17 C1
Orpington Hospl BR6 227 D4
Orpington Mans N21 16 C3
Orpington Rd
Southgate N21 16 D3
St Paul's Cray BR7 211 C6
Orpington Sta BR6 227 C6
Orpwood Cl TW12 173 B4
Orsett Mews W2 92 A1 236 A2
Orsett St SE11 116 B1 260 D2
Orsett Terr
Bayswater W2 92 A1 236 A2
Woodford IG8 37 C3
Orsman Rd N1 95 C6
Orton Gr EN1 6 A4
Orton St E1 118 A5
Orville Rd SW11 136 B3
Orwell Cl UB3 105 C6
Orwell Ct Hackney E8 96 A6
Highbury N5 73 A4
Northolt UB5 85 A6
Orwell Ho W12 112 A6
Orwell Lo 2 E18 55 A5
Orwell Rd E13 99 C6
Osbaldeston Rd N16 52 A1
Osberton Rd SE12 165 A6
Osbert St SW1 259 C3
Osborn Cl E8 96 A6
Osborne Ave TW19 148 B3
Osborne Cl
Beckenham BR3 207 A5
Cockfosters EN4 2 D2
Feltham TW13 172 D5
Osborne Ct Ealing W5 88 A2
10 Surbiton KT6 198 A3
17 Walthamstow E10 53 D2
Osborne Gdns CR7 183 A1
Osborne Gr E17 53 B5
Osborne Mews E17 53 B5
Osborne Pl SM1 218 B3
Osborne Rd
Buckhurst Hill IG9 21 B3
Dagenham RM9 81 B3
Enfield EN3 7 A3
Erith DA17 147 B6
Finsbury Pk N4 50 C1
Forest Gate E7 77 B3
Hackney E9 75 B2
Hounslow TW3, TW4 129 B2
Kingston u T KT2 176 A3
Leyton E10 75 D6
Palmers Green N13 16 C1
South Acton W3 110 D4
Southall UB1 86 A1
South Norwood CR7 183 A1
Walton-on-T KT12 194 A1
Willesden NW2 68 B2
Osborne Sq RM9 81 B4
Osborne Terr 1 SW17 181 A5
Osborne Way KT9 214 B3
Osborn Gdns NW7 28 D3
Osborn La SE23 163 A4
Osborn St E1 95 D2 243 D4
Osborn Terr SE3 142 D1
Osbourne Ct HA2 41 D5
Osbourne Ho
Richmond TW10 154 C6
Twickenham TW2 152 A2
Oscar Faber Pl 8 N1 73 C1
Oscar St SE8 141 C3
Oseney Cres NW5 71 D2
Osgood Ave BR6 227 D3
Osgood Gdns 1 BR6 227 D3
OSIDGE 15 B2
Osidge Ct N14 15 B3
Osidge La N14 15 B3
Osidge Prim Sch N14 15 C3
Osier Cres N10 30 D2
Osier Ct E1 96 D3
Osier La SE10 120 D3
Osier Mews W4 133 D6
Osiers Ct 3 KT1 175 D2
Osiers Rd SW18 135 C1
Osier St E1 96 C3
Osier Way Leyton E10 75 D5
Mitcham CR4 202 D4
Oslac Rd SE6 185 D5
Oslo Ct Mitcham SW19 180 B3
St John's Wood NW8 230 A3
Oslo Ho 2 SE5 139 A3
Oslo Sq SE16 119 A3
Osman Cl N15 51 B3
Osmani Prim Sch E1 96 A2
Osman Rd Edmonton N9 18 A1
Hammersmith W6 112 C3
Osmington Ho SW8 270 D3
Osmond Cl HA2 64 A6
Osmond Gdns SM6 219 C3
Osmund St W12 89 D2
Osnaburgh St NW1 93 B3 238 D6
Osnaburgh Terr NW1 238 D6
Osney Ho 4 SE2 124 D4
Osney Wlk SM5 202 B3
Osprey 7 NW9 27 D2
Osprey Cl Cheam SM1 217 B3
Higham Hill E17 35 A3
Keston Mark BR2 210 A1
Newham E6 100 A2
Wanstead E11 55 A5
West Drayton UB7 104 A4
Osprey Ct 7 Ealing W7 86 D3
Hampstead NW3 69 D3
Thornton Heath SW16 182 B1
Osprey Ho
Camberwell SE15 139 D4
Isleworth TW7 131 B2
3 Limehouse E14 119 A6
Walthamstow E4 35 B4
Osprey Mews EN3 18 B6
Ospringe Cl 6 SE20 184 C3
Ospringe Ct SE9 167 B5
Ospringe Ho SE1 251 B3
Ospringe Rd NW5 71 C4
Osram Ct W6 112 C3
Osram Rd HA9 65 D5
Osric Path 8 N1 95 C5
Ossian Mews N4 50 B2
Ossian Rd N4 50 B2
Ossie Garvin Rdbt UB4 106 C6
Ossington Bldgs W1 238 A3
Ossington Cl W2 245 B5
Ossington St W2 113 D6 245 C5
Ossory Rd SE1 140 A6
Ossulston St NW1 93 D5 232 D4
Ossultan Pl N2 48 A6
Ossulton Way N2 48 A5
Ostade Rd SW2 160 B4
Ostell Cres EN3 7 C5
Osten Mews SW7 113 D3 255 D5
OSTERLEY 130 B5
Osterley Ave TW7 130 B5
Osterley Cl BR5 190 A2
Osterley Cres TW7 130 D4
Osterley Ct
Hounslow TW7 130 B4
7 Northolt UB5 84 C4
Osterley Gdns
Southall UB2 108 A4
South Norwood CR7 183 A1
Osterley Ho 5 E14 97 D1
Osterley La
Isleworth TW7 108 C1
Southall UB2, TW7 107 D1
Osterley Lo 1 TW7 130 C4
Osterley Park* TW7 108 B1
Osterley Park Rd UB2 107 B3
Osterley Park View Rd W7 108 C4
Osterley Rd
Hounslow TW7 130 C4
Stoke Newington N16 73 C4
Osterley Sta TW7 130 B5
Osterley Views UB2 108 B4
Osterly Lodge UB2 107 B3
Oster Terr E17 52 D4
Ostlers Dr TW15 171 A5
Ostliffe Rd N13 33 A5
Oswald Bldg SW8 268 C5
Oswald Rd UB1 107 A5
Oswald's Mead E9 75 A4
Oswald St E5 74 D5
Oswald Terr NW2 68 C5
Osward Pl N9 18 B2
Osward Rd SW12, SW17 158 D2
Oswell Ho 9 E1 118 B5
Oswin St SE11 116 D2 261 D4
Oswyth Rd SE5 139 C3
Otford Cl Bexley DA5 169 D5
Bromley BR1 210 C6
Penge SE20 184 C2
Otford Cres SE4 163 B5
Otford Ho
Bermondsey SE1 252 D1
6 Deptford SE15 140 C6
Otha Ho 13 SW9 138 A3
Othello Cl SE11 261 C2
Otho Ct 5 TW8 131 D5
Otis St E3 98 A4
Otley App IG2 56 D3
Otley Ct N11 31 A4
Otley Dr IG2 56 D3
Otley Ho N5 72 D5
Otley Rd E16 99 C1
Otley Terr E5 74 D5
Ottawa Ho 4 HA4 40 C1
Ottaway Ct E5 74 A5
Ottaway St E5 74 A5
Otterbourne Rd
Chingford E4 20 B1
1 Croydon CR0 221 A6
Otterburn Gdns TW7 131 A5
Otterburn Ho 12 SE5 139 A5

Otterburn St SW17 180 D4
Otter Cl E15 98 A6
Otterden Cl BR6 227 C4
Otterden St SE6 185 C6
Otterfield Rd UB7 104 A6
Otter Rd UB6 86 A3
Ottershaw Ho BR5 190 B2
Otto Cl SE26 162 B1
Ottoman Ct W5 109 D2
Otto St SE17 138 D6
Otway Ct N4 50 B3
Otway Gdns WD23 8 C4
Oulton Cl Erith SE28 102 C1
Upper Clapton E5 74 C6
Oulton Cres IG11 79 D3
Oulton Rd N15 51 B4
Oulton Way WD19 23 B6
Oundle Ave WD23 8 A5
Our Lady Immaculate RC Prim Sch KT6 198 D1
Our Lady of Dolours RC Prim Sch W2 91 D2
Our Lady of Grace RC Inf Sch NW2 68 C6
Our Lady of Grace RC Jun Sch NW2 68 B5
Our Lady of Grace RC Prim Sch SE7 143 B6
Our Lady of Lourdes RC Prim Sch
Finchley N12 30 A2
Friern Barnet N11 31 C5
Lewisham SE13 142 B2
Our Lady of Lourdes RC Sch NW10 89 A6
Our Lady of Lourds RC Prim Sch E11 55 A3
Our Lady of Muswell Prim Sch N10 49 A6
Our Lady of Muswell RC Prim Sch N10 31 A1
Our Lady of the Rosary RC Prim Sch DA15 167 C5
Our Lady of the Visitation RC Prim Sch UB6 86 A3
Our Lady of Victories RC Prim Sch
Putney SW15 134 D1
South Kensington SW7 114 A2 256 B3
Our Lady Queen of Heaven RC Sch SW19 156 D4
Our Lady RC Prim Sch
Camden Town NW1 93 C6 232 B6
Poplar E14 97 B1
Our Lady & St John's RC Jun & Inf Sch TW8 109 C1
Our Lady & St Joseph RC Prim Sch N1 73 C2
Our Lady & St Philip Neri RC Prim Sch SE26 185 A6
Our Lady's Convent RC High Sch N15 51 C2
Ouseley Rd SW12 158 D3
Outer Circ NW8 92 D5 230 D3
Outgate Rd NW10 67 D1
Outram Pl N1 94 A6 233 B6
Outram Rd
Croydon CR0 221 D6
Muswell Hill N22 31 D2
Newham E6 100 A6
Outwich St EC3 243 B2
Outwood Ct CR2 221 A1
Outwood Ho 3 SW2 160 B4
Oval Ct Burnt Oak HA8 27 A3
8 Teddington TW11 174 D5
Oval Mans SE11 270 D6
Oval Pl SW8 138 B5 270 D4
Oval Prim Sch CR0 205 C1
Oval Rd
Camden Town NW1 93 B6 231 C6
Croydon CR0 205 C1
Oval Rd N RM10 103 D6
Oval Rd S RM10 103 D5
Oval Sta SE11 138 C6
Oval The Hackney E2 96 B5
Sidcup DA15 168 A4
Oval The (Surrey Cnty Crkt Gd) SE11 138 C6
Oval Way SE11 116 B1 260 D1
Overbrae BR3 185 C5
Overbrook Wlk HA8 26 C3
Overbury 1 BR3 208 A6
Overbury Ave BR3 208 A6
Overbury Ho 3 E5 74 D4
Overbury Rd N4, N15 51 B3
Overbury St E5 74 D4
Overcliff Rd SE13 141 C2
Overcourt Cl DA15 168 B5
Overdale Ave KT3 177 B1
Overdale Rd W5 109 C3
Overdown Rd SE6 185 D6
Overhill Rd SE21, SE22 162 B4
Overhill Way BR3 208 B4
Overlea Rd E5 52 A2
Overmead DA15 167 B4
Oversley Ho 17 W2 91 C2
Overstand Cl BR3 207 C4
Overstone Gdns CR0 207 B2
Overstone Ho 19 E14 97 C1
Overstone Rd W6 112 C2
Overstrand Mans SW11 268 A1
Overton Cl
Hounslow TW7 130 D4
Tokyngton NW10 67 A2
Overton Ct E11 55 A2
Overton Dr Ilford RM6 58 C2
Wanstead E11 55 B2
Overton Grange Sch SM2 217 D1
Overton Ho SW15 155 D4
Overton Rd
Abbey Wood SE2 124 D3
Belmont SM2 217 C1
Brixton SW9 138 C3
Southgate N14 16 A6
Walthamstow E10 53 A1
Overton's Yd CR0 221 A5
Overy Ho SE1 251 C1
Ovesdon Ave HA2 41 B1
Ovett Cl SE19 183 C4
Ovex Cl E14 120 A4
Ovington Ct SW3 257 B5
Ovington Gdns SW3 257 B5
Ovington Mews SW3 257 B5
Ovington Sq SW3 114 C3 257 B5
Ovington St SW3 114 C2 257 B4
Owen Cl Hayes UB4 84 B4
Northolt UB5 63 A2
Thamesmead SE28 124 C5
Thornton Heath CR0 205 B3
Owen Ct UB4 84 B4
Owen Ho
Feltham TW14 150 A4
11 Tufnell Pk N19 71 C4
5 Twickenham TW1 153 B4
Owenite St SE2 124 B2
Owen Rd Edmonton N13 33 A5
Hayes UB4 84 B4
Owen's Ct EC1 234 C2
Owens Mews 10 E11 76 C6
Owen's Row EC1 234 C2
Owen St EC1 234 C3
Owens Way SE23 163 A4
Owen Way NW10 67 A3
Owen Wlk 7 SE20 184 A3
Owgan Cl SE5 139 B5
Oxberry Ave SW6 135 A3
Oxbridge Ct 4 W4 110 D1
Oxendon St SW1, W1 115 D6 249 C5
Oxenford St SE15 139 D2
Oxenham Ho 13 SE8 141 C6
Oxenholme NW1 232 B3
Oxenpark Ave HA9 44 A2
Oxestalls Rd SE8 119 A1
Oxford Ave
Harlington TW6 127 D5
Hounslow TW5 107 C1
Merton SW20 179 A1
Southgate N14 15 C3
Oxford & Cambridge Mans NW1 237 B3
Oxford Cir W1 93 C1 239 A1
Oxford Circus Ave W1 239 A1
Oxford Circus Sta W1 93 C1 239 A1
Oxford Cl Edmonton N9 18 B2
Littleton TW15, TW17 171 A3
Mitcham CR4 203 C6
Oxford Cres KT3 199 B3
Oxford Ct 16 Acton W3 88 C1
City of London EC4 252 C6
8 Ealing W7 86 D2
Gunnersbury W4 110 D1
17 Kingston u T KT6 198 A4
48 Paddington W2 91 C2
Sidcup DA14 189 D6
Oxford Dr
Bermondsey SE1 253 A3
Ruislip HA4 62 C6
Oxford Gardens Prim Sch W10 90 D1
Oxford Gate W6 112 D2
Oxford Gdns
Brentford W4 132 C6
Edmonton N21 17 A4
North Kensington W10 90 D1
Oakleigh Pk N20 14 B3
Oxford Ho N4 50 C1
Oxford Mews DA5 169 C4
Oxford Rd
Carshalton SM5 218 C3
Ealing W5 109 D6
Edmonton N9 18 B2
Enfield EN3 18 B6
Finsbury Pk N4 50 C1
Harrow HA1 42 A3
Ilford IG1 79 A3
Paddington NW6 91 C5
Putney SW15 135 A1
Sidcup DA14 190 B5
South Norwood SE19 183 B4
Stratford E15 76 B2
Teddington TW11, TW12 174 B5
Wallington SM6 219 C3
Wealdstone HA3 42 D6
Woodford IG8 37 D5
Oxford Rd N W4 110 D1
Oxford Rd S W4 110 D1
Oxford Sq W2 92 C1 237 B1
Oxford St W1 93 B1 238 D1
Oxford Way TW13 172 D6
Oxford Wlk UB1 107 B5
Oxgate Ct NW2 68 A6
Oxgate Ct Par NW2 68 A6
Oxgate Ctr NW2 68 B6
Oxgate Gdns NW2 68 B6
Oxgate La NW2 68 B6
Oxhawth Cres BR2 210 D3
Oxhey Dr WD19 22 B6
Oxhey Dr S HA6 22 B5
Oxhey La HA5 23 C5
Oxhey Ridge Cl HA6 22 B5
Oxhey Wood Prim Sch WD19 22 C6
Oxleas E6 100 D1
Oxleas Cl DA16 145 B3
Oxleay Rd HA2 41 C1
Oxleigh Cl KT3 199 C4
Oxley Cl SE1 118 A1
Oxleys Rd NW2 68 B5
Oxlip Cl 2 CR0 206 D1
Oxlow La RM10 81 C4
Oxonian St SE22 139 D1
Oxo Tower Wharf SE1 251 B5
Oxo Twr* SE1 251 B5
Oxted Cl CR4 202 B6
Oxted Ct N16 51 C1
Oxtoby Way SW16 181 D2
OYH Prim Sch NW4 46 D5
Oyster Catchers Cl E16 99 B1
Oyster Catcher Terr IG5 56 C6
Oyster Row E1 96 C1
Ozolins Way E16 99 A1

P

Pablo Neruda Cl 4 SE24 138 D1
Pace Pl E1 96 B1
Pacific Cl TW14 149 D3
Pacific Ho 15 E1 96 D3
Pacific Hts BR3 185 C3
Pacific Rd E16 99 A1
Pacific Wharf IG11 78 D1
Pacific Wharf SE16 118 D5
Packenham Ho
24 Crouch End N19 49 D2
21 Spitalfields E2 95 D4
Packham Ct KT4 216 C5
Packington Sq N1 95 A6 235 A6
Packington St N1 94 D6 234 D5
Packmores Rd SE9 167 B6
Padbury SE17 263 B1
Padbury Cl TW14 149 B3
Padbury Ct E2 95 D4
Padbury Ho NW8 237 B6
Padden Ct NW7 28 D3
Paddenswick Ct 2 W6 112 B3
Paddenswick Rd W6 112 A3
PADDINGTON 92 A2
Paddington Acad
Paddington W2 92 B2 236 C3
Paddington W9 91 C3
Paddington Cl UB4 84 D3
Paddington Com Hospl W9 91 C2
Paddington Ct
10 Ealing W7 86 D2
7 Wembley HA0 66 A2
Paddington Gn W2 92 B2 236 C4
Paddington Green Prim Sch NW8 92 B3 236 C5
Paddington St W1 238 A4
Paddington Sta W2 92 B1 236 C2
Paddock Cl
Forest Hill SE26 184 D6
Kidbrooke SE3 143 A3
New Malden KT4 199 C1
Northolt UB5 85 C5
Orpington BR6 226 D4
Paddock Ct SW20 200 C5
Paddock Gdns SE19 183 C4
Paddock Lo 13 EN1 17 C6
Paddock Rd
Bexley DA6 147 A1
Dollis Hill NW2 68 A6
Ruislip HA4 62 D5
Paddock Sch SW15 133 D1
Paddocks Cl HA2 63 D4
Paddocks Gn NW9 44 D1
Paddocks The
Addington CR0 223 C2
Cockfosters EN4 2 D2
Preston HA9 66 D6
Paddock The
Muswell Hill N10 49 B6
Uxbridge UB10 60 D4
Paddock Way
Chislehurst BR7 189 B3
11 Putney SW15 156 C4
Padfield Ct HA9 66 B5
Padfield Rd SE5 139 A2
Padley Cl KT9 214 B3
Padnall Ct RM6 58 D6
Padnall Rd RM6 58 D5
Padstone Ho 50 E3 97 D4
Padstow Cl BR6 227 D4
Padstow Ho 12 E14 119 B6
Padstow Rd EN2 4 D4
Padstow Wlk TW14 149 D3
Padua Rd SE20 184 C2
Pagden St SW8 268 D2
Pageant Ave NW9 27 C2
Pageant Cres SE16 119 B5
Pageantmaster Ct EC4 241 C1
Pageant Wlk CR0 221 C5
Page Cl Dagenham RM9 81 A3
Hampton TW12 173 A4
Harrow HA3 44 B3
Page Cres CR0 220 D3
Page Ct NW7 28 A3
Page Green Rd N15 52 A4
Page Green Terr N15 51 D4
Page Heath La BR1 209 D6
Page Heath Villas BR1 209 D6
Page High N22 50 C6
Page Ho SE10 142 A6
Pagehurst Rd CR0 206 B2
Page Mdw NW7 28 A3
Page Rd TW14 149 B5
Page's Ct N10 31 A1
Page's Hill N10 31 A1
Page's La N10 31 A1
Page St Hendon NW7 28 A3
Westminster SW1 115 D2 259 D4
Page's Wlk SE1 117 C3 263 B5
Page's Yd W4 133 C6
Paget Ave SM1 218 B5
Paget Cl TW12 174 B6
Paget Ct UB7 104 A4
Paget Gdns BR7 188 D2
Paget Ho 15 E2 96 C5
Paget La TW7 130 C2
Paget Pl
Kingston u T KT2 177 A4
Thames Ditton KT7 196 D1
Paget Rd
Hillingdon UB10 83 A3
Ilford IG1 78 D4
Stoke Newington N16 51 B1
Paget Rise SE18 144 C5
Paget St EC1 234 C2
Paget Terr SE18 144 D6
Pagham Ho 8 W10 90 C3
Pagin Ho N15 51 C4
Pagitts Gr EN4 1 D4
Pagnell St SE14 141 B5
Pagoda Ave TW9 132 B2
Pagoda Gdns SE3 142 B3
Pagoda Gr SE27 161 A2
Paignton Rd Ruislip HA4 62 A5
Tottenham N15 51 C3
Paine Ct SE3 142 D6
Paines Cl HA5 41 A6
Paine's La HA5 23 A1
Pain's Cl CR4 181 B1
Painsthorpe Rd 3 N16 73 C5
Painswick Ct 1 SE15 139 D5
Painters Mews SE16 118 A2
Painters Rd IG2, RM6 58 A6
Paisley Rd
Carshalton SM5 202 B1
Tottenham N22 32 D2
Paisley Terr SM5 202 B2
Pakeman Ho SE1 251 D2
Pakeman Prim Sch N7 72 B5
Pakeman St N7 72 B5
Pakenham Cl SW12 159 A3
Pakenham St WC1 94 B3 240 D6
Pakington Ho 22 SW9 138 A3
Palace Ave W8 113 D4 245 D2
Palace Court Gdns N10 49 C6
Palace Ct Bromley BR1 187 B2
Eltham SE9 166 B5
Hampstead NW3 69 D3
Harrow HA3 44 A3
Kensington W2 113 D6 245 C5
South Norwood CR7 205 B5
Streatham SW2 160 C2
Palace Garden Mews W8 245 B4
Palace Gate
Hampton KT8 196 C6
Knightsbridge W8 114 A4 246 A1
Palace Gate Mews 4 N8 50 A5
Palace Gates Rd N22 32 A1
Palace Gdns IG9 21 D3
Palace Gdns Mews W8 113 D5 245 D3
Palace Gdns Sh Ctr EN2 5 B1
Palace Gn
Kensington W8 113 D5 245 C3
New Addington CR0 223 B1
Palace Gr Bromley BR1 187 B2
Penge SE19 183 D3
Palace Mans W14 254 B4
Palace Mews
Belgravia SW1 258 B3
Fulham SW6 264 D4
Walthamstow E17 53 B5
Palace of Ind HA9 66 C4
Palace Par E17 53 C5
Palace Pl SW1 259 A6
Palace Rd Bromley BR1 187 B2
East Molesey KT8 196 B6
Hornsey N8 49 D4
Kingston u T KT1 197 D5
Penge SE19 183 D3
Ruislip HA4 63 A4
Streatham SE27, SW16, SW2 160 C2
Wood Green N11 32 A3
Palace Sq SE19 183 D3
Palace St SW1 115 C3 259 A6
Palace View
Bromley BR1 209 B6
Croydon CR0 223 B4
Grove Pk SE12 165 A2
Palace View Rd E4 35 D5
Palamos Rd E10 53 C1
Palatine Ave N16 73 C4
Palatine Rd N16 73 C4
Palazzo Apartments 11 N1 73 C1
Palemead Cl SW6 134 D4
Palermo Rd NW10 90 A5
Palestine Gr SW19 180 B2
Palewell Cl BR5 190 B1
Palewell Common Dr SW14 155 B6
Palewell Pk SW14 133 B1
Palfrey Pl SW8 138 B5 270 D4
Palgrave Ave UB1 107 C6
Palgrave Gdns NW1 92 C3 237 B6
Palgrave Ho
7 Camberwell SE5 139 A5
4 Maitland Pk NW3 70 D3
Twickenham TW2 152 A4
Palgrave Rd W12 111 D3
Palissy St 35 E2 95 D4
Palladino Ho 6 SW17 180 C5
Pallant Ho SE1 262 D5
Pallant Way BR6 226 C5
Pallester Ct NW11 47 A1
Pallet Way SE18 144 A4
Palliser Ct W14 254 A1
Palliser Ho
3 Greenwich SE10 142 B6
21 Stepney E1 96 D3
Palliser Rd W14 113 A1 254 A1
Pallister Terr SW15 155 D2
Pall Mall SW1 115 D5 249 C3
Pall Mall E SW1 115 D5 249 D4
Pall Mall Pl SW1 249 B3
Palmar Cres DA7 147 C3
Palmar Rd DA7 147 C3
Palm Ave DA14 190 D4
Palm Cl E10 75 D5
Palm Ct
Beckenham BR3 207 B6
18 Camberwell SE15 139 D5
Stoke Newington N16 73 B6
Wood Green N22 32 B3
Palmeira Rd DA7 146 D2
Palmer Ave KT4, SM3 216 C4
Palmer Cl Heston TW5 129 C4
Northolt UB5 63 A2
West Wickham BR4 224 B6
Palmer Cres KT1 198 A6
Palmer Gdns EN5 12 D6
Palmer Ho
6 Deptford SE14 140 D5
8 Kentish Town NW5 71 C4
5 Tufnell Pk N19 71 C5
Palmer Pl N7 72 C3
Palmer Rd
Dagenham RM8 58 D1
Newham E13 99 B3
Palmer's Ct 11 N11 31 C5
Palmers Gr KT8 195 C5
PALMERS GREEN 16 A1
Palmers Green High Sch N21 16 C2
Palmers Green Sta N13 32 B6
Palmers La EN3 6 C4
Palmers Rd
Globe Town E2 96 D5
Mortlake SW14 133 A2
Thornton Heath SW16 182 B1
Palmer's Rd N11 31 C5
Palmer St SW1 259 C6
Palmerston Cres
Bowes Pk N13 32 B5
Woolwich SE18 145 A6
Palmerston Ct
2 Buckhurst Hill IG9 21 C2
22 Globe Town E3 96 D5
9 Surbiton KT6 197 D2
7 Sutton SM1 218 A3
Walthamstow E17 53 B5
Palmerston Ctr HA3 42 D6
Palmerston Gr 11 SW19 179 C3
Palmerston Ho
Battersea SW11 268 B1
Kensington W8 245 A3
Palmerston Rd
Acton Green W3 111 A3
Bowes Pk N22 32 B4
Brondesbury NW6 69 B1
Buckhurst Hill IG9 21 C3
Farnborough BR6 227 A3
Hampstead NW6 69 C1
Harrow HA3 42 D6
Hounslow TW3 130 A4
Merton SW19 179 C3
Mortlake SW14 133 A1
Sutton SM1 218 A3
Thornton Heath CR0 205 B4
Twickenham TW2 152 C5
Upton E7 77 B2
Wallington SM5 219 A4
Walthamstow E17 53 B5
Palmerston Way SW8 268 D3
Palm Gr W5 110 A3
Palm Tree Ct 5 N17 33 D1
Palm Tree Ho 2 SE14 140 D5
Pamela Ct Finchley N12 29 D4
Willesden NW10 68 A1
Pamela Gdns HA5 40 B4
Pamela Ho 14 E8 95 D6
Pamir Ct 10 SM2 217 D2
Pamlion Ct N4 50 A2
Pams Way KT19 215 B3
Panama Ho 14 E1 96 D2
Panbro Ho SE18 144 B4
Pancras La EC2 242 C1
Pancras Rd NW1 93 D5 232 D4
Pandian Way 4 NW5 71 D2
Pandora Ct 4 KT6 198 A3
Pandora Rd NW6 69 C2
Panfield Mews IG2 56 C3
Panfield Rd SE2 124 A3
Pangbourne NW1 232 A1
Pangbourne Ave W10 90 C2
Pangbourne Ct
Oakleigh Pk N20 14 A4
Upper Tooting SW17 180 A6
Pangbourne Dr HA7 26 A5
Pangbourne Ho 4 N7 72 A3
Panhard Pl UB1 107 D6
Pank Ave EN5 14 A6
Pankhurst Ave 8 E16 121 B5
Pankhurst Cl
7 Deptford SE14 140 D5
Isleworth TW7 130 D2
Pankhurst Ho
2 Kensington NW10 90 C1
Streatham SW16 181 D5
Pankhurst Rd KT12 194 C2
Panmuir Rd SW20 178 B2
Panmure Cl N5 72 D4
Panmure Ct 11 UB1 86 A1
Panmure Rd SE26 162 B1
Panorama Ct N6 49 C3
Pansy Gdns W12 112 A6
Panther Dr NW10 67 B3
Pantiles Cl N13 32 D5
Pantiles The
Bickley BR1 210 A6
Bushey WD23 8 B3
Erith DA7 147 B5
Temple Fortune NW11 47 B4
Panton Cl CR0 204 D1
Panton St SW1 249 C5
Panyer Alley EC2 242 A2
Papermill Cl SM5 219 A4
Paper Mill Wharf E14 119 A6
Papillons Wlk SE3 143 A2
Papworth Gdns N7 72 B3
Papworth Way SW2 160 C4
Parade Mans
19 Camberwell SE5 139 A3
2 Hendon NW4 46 B4
Parade Mews SE27, SW2 160 D2
Parade The
Ashford TW16 171 D3
Battersea SW11 136 D5 267 D4
Claygate KT10 212 C2
Ilford IG2 57 B3
Thornton Heath CR0 204 A3
Thornton Heath CR7 204 C6
Waddon CR0 220 B3
Wembley UB6 65 B3
Paradise Pas N7 72 C3
Paradise Pl 15 SE7 122 A2
Paradise Rd
Richmond TW10 154 A6
South Lambeth SW4 138 A3
Paradise Row E2 96 B4
Paradise St SE16 118 B4
Paradise Wlk SW3 136 D6 267 D6
Paragon N8 50 C5
Paragon Cl E16 99 A1
Paragon Ct NW4 29 A2
Paragon Gr KT5 198 B3
Paragon Ho SE3 142 D3
Paragon Mews SE1 262 D4
Paragon Pl
Blackheath Vale SE3 142 D3
Surbiton KT5 198 B3
Paragon Rd E9 74 C2
Paragon The
Kidbrooke SE3 143 A3
Walworth SE17 262 D4
Paramount Bldg EC1 241 C6
Paramount Ct WC1 239 B5
Paramount Ho 10 E11 76 C5
Parbury Rd SE23 163 A5
Parbury Rise KT9 214 A2
Parchmore Rd CR7 205 A6
Parchmore Way CR7 182 D1
Pardes House Gram N3 29 B1
Pardes House Prim N3 29 B1
Pardoner St SE1 117 B3 262 D6
Pardon St EC1 241 D6
Parfett St E1 96 A1
Parfew Ct 2 SE22 162 B2
Parfitt Cl NW11 48 A1
Parfrey St W6 134 C6
Pargraves Ct HA9 66 C6
Parham Dr IG2 56 D4
Paris Gdn SE1 116 D5 251 C4
Parish CE Prim Sch BR1 187 A3
Parish Church CE Inf Sch CR0 220 D5
Parish Church CE Jun Sch CR0 220 D5
Parish Ct KT6 198 A3
Parish Gate Dr DA15 167 C5
Parish La SE20 184 D3
Paris Ho 12 E2 96 B5
Parish Wharf 6 SE7 122 A2
Park App DA16 146 B1
Park Ave Barking IG11 79 A2
Bromley BR6 226 C6
Edmonton N18 34 A6
Enfield EN1 17 C5
Finchley N3 29 D2
Golders Green NW11 47 D1

Park Ave *continued*
Ilford IG1 .... 56 C1
Mitcham CR4 .... 181 B3
Mortlake SW14 .... 133 B1
Palmers Green N13 .... 16 C1
Plaistow BR1 .... 187 A4
Ruislip HA4 .... 39 C3
Southall UB1 .... 107 C5
Stratford E15 .... 76 C2
Twickenham TW3 .... 151 D5
Upper Halliford TW17 .... 193 C6
Wallend E6 .... 100 C5
Wallington SM5 .... 219 A2
West Wickham BR4 .... 224 A6
Willesden NW2 .... 68 C2
Woodford IG8 .... 37 B5
Wood Green N22 .... 32 B2
Park Ave E KT17 .... 216 A2
Park Ave N
Dudden Hill NW10 .... 68 B3
Hornsey N8 .... 49 D5
Park Avenue Mews
CR4 .... 181 B3
Park Avenue Rd N17 .... 34 B3
Park Ave S N8 .... 49 D5
Park Ave W KT17 .... 216 A2
Park Chase HA9 .... 66 B4
Park Cl Dollis Hill NW2 .... 68 B5
Ealing NW10 .... 88 B4
Hampton TW12 .... 174 A2
Harrow HA3 .... 24 C2
Isleworth TW3, TW7 .... 152 A6
Kensington
W14 .... 113 B3 254 D6
Kingston u T KT2 .... 176 C2
Knightsbridge SW1 .... 247 C1
North Finchley N12 .... 30 B6
[13] South Hackney E9 .... 96 C6
Wallington SM5 .... 218 D2
Park Cotts [10] TW1 .... 153 B5
Park Cres Enfield EN2 .... 5 B1
Finchley N3 .... 30 A3
Harrow HA3 .... 24 C2
Regent's Pk W1 .. 93 B3 238 C5
Twickenham TW2 .... 152 B3
Park Crescent Mews E
W1 .... 238 D5
Park Crescent Mews W
W1 .... 238 C5
Park Croft HA8 .... 27 A2
Parkcroft Rd SE12 .... 164 D4
Park Ct Battersea SW11 268 C2
[2] Beckenham BR3 .... 207 D6
[2] Chingford E4 .... 20 A2
Clapham Pk SW4 .... 159 D6
Dulwich SE21 .... 161 B1
[12] Hammersmith W6 .... 112 A2
New Barnet EN5 .... 14 B4
New Malden KT3 .... 199 B5
North Finchley N12 .... 30 B5
Teddington KT1 .... 175 C2
Twickenham TW4 .... 151 D6
Upper Tooting SW12 .... 159 A3
Wallington SM6 .... 220 A3
Walthamstow E17 .... 53 D4
Wembley HA9 .... 66 A3
Wood Green N11 .... 31 D3
Parkdale N11 .... 31 D4
Parkdale Cres KT4 .... 215 B5
Parkdale Rd SE18 .... 123 C1
Park Dr Acton W3 .... 110 C3
Enfield N21 .... 17 A5
Golders Green NW11 .... 47 D1
Harrow HA2 .... 41 C2
Mortlake SW14 .... 133 B1
Stanmore HA3 .... 24 C4
Woolwich SE7 .... 144 A6
Park Dwellings [7]
NW3 .... 70 D3
Park End Bromley BR1 .... 186 D2
Hampstead NW3 .... 70 C4
Parker Cl Newham E16 .. 122 A5
Wallington SM5 .... 218 D2
Parker Ct Shoreditch N1 235 B6
South Lambeth SW4 .... 270 A1
Wimbledon SW19 .... 179 A3
Parke Rd Barnes SW13 .. 134 A4
Sunbury TW16 .... 194 A5
Parker Ho [4] SE18 .... 122 D1
Parker Mews WC2 .... 240 B2
Parker Rd CR0 .... 221 A4
Parkers Rd N10 .... 30 C2
Parkers Row [15] SE16 .... 118 A4
Parker's Row SE1 .... 253 D1
Parker St Newham E16 .. 122 A5
St Giles WC2 .... 94 A1 240 B2
Park Farm Cl
East Finchley N2 .... 48 A6
Pinner HA5 .... 40 B4
Park Farm Ct UB3 .... 105 C6
Park Farm Rd
Bromley BR1 .... 187 D2
Kingston u T KT2 .... 176 A3
Parkfield [3] TW7 .... 130 C4
Parkfield Ave
Feltham TW13 .... 150 A1
Harrow HA2 .... 24 A1
Hillingdon UB10 .... 82 D4
Mortlake SW14 .... 133 C1
Northolt UB5 .... 84 D5
Parkfield Cl
Edgware HA8 .... 26 D4
Northolt UB5 .... 85 A5
Parkfield Cres
Feltham TW13 .... 150 A1
Harrow HA2 .... 24 A1
Ruislip HA4 .... 63 A5
Parkfield Ct SE14 .... 141 B4
Parkfield Dr UB5 .... 84 D5
Parkfield Gdns HA2 .... 41 D6
Parkfield Ho HA2 .... 23 D2
Parkfield Ind Est
SW11 .... 137 A3
Parkfield Par TW13 .... 150 A1
Parkfield Prim Sch
NW4 .... 46 B2
Parkfield Rd
Feltham TW13 .... 150 A1
Harrow HA2 .... 64 A5
New Cross SE14 .... 141 B4
Northolt UB5 .... 85 A5
Uxbridge UB10 .... 60 D6
Willesden NW10 .... 68 B1
Parkfields Croydon CR0 .... 207 B1
Putney SW15 .... 134 C1
Parkfields Ave
Welsh Harp NW9 .... 45 B1
Wimbledon SW20 .... 178 B1
Parkfields Cl SM5 .... 219 A4
Parkfields Rd KT2 .... 176 B5
Parkfield St N1 .. 94 C5 234 B4
Parkfield Way BR2 .... 210 B4
Park Flats N6 .... 48 C2
Parkgate SE3 .... 142 D2
Park Gate Ealing W5 .... 87 D2
East Finchley N2 .... 48 B6
Southgate N21 .... 16 B4
Parkgate Ave EN4 .... 2 A4
Parkgate Cl KT2 .... 176 D4
Parkgate Cres EN4 .... 2 A4
Park Gate Ct TW12 .... 174 A5
Parkgate Gdns SW14 .... 155 B6
Parkgate House Sch
SW11 .... 137 A1
Parkgate Mews N6 .... 49 C2
Parkgate Rd
Battersea
SW11 .... 136 C5 267 B3
Wallington SM5, SM6 .... 219 B3
Park Gates HA2 .... 63 C4
Park Gdns
Kingston u T KT2 .... 176 B5
Queensbury NW9 .... 44 D6
Park Gr Bromley BR1 .... 187 B2
Edgware HA8 .... 26 B5
Newham E15 .... 99 A6
Wood Green N11 .... 31 D3
Park Grove Rd E11 .... 76 C6
Park Hall SE10 .... 142 B5
Park Hall Rd
Dulwich SE21 .... 161 B1
East Finchley N2 .... 48 C5
Park Hall Road Trad Est
SE21 .... 161 B1
Parkham Ct BR2 .... 186 C1
Parkham St
SW11 .... 136 C4 267 A1
Parkham Way N10 .... 31 C1
Park Heights Ct [21] E14 .. 97 B1
Park High Sch HA7 .... 25 D1
Park Hill Bromley BR1 .... 210 B5
Clapham Pk SW4 .... 159 D6
Ealing W5 .... 87 D2
Forest Hill SE23 .... 162 C3
Loughton IG10 .... 21 D6
Richmond TW10 .... 154 B5
Wallington SM5 .... 218 D2
Park Hill Cl SM5 .... 218 C3
Park Hill Ct
Croydon CR0 .... 221 C6
Ealing W5 .... 87 D2
Upper Tooting SW17 .... 158 D1
Parkhill Ho [1] SW16 .... 182 C5
Parkhill Inf Sch IG5 .... 56 C6
Park Hill Inf Sch CR0 .. 221 C5
Parkhill Jun Sch IG5 .... 56 C6
Park Hill Jun Sch CR0 .221 C5
Parkhill Rd Chingford E4 .. 20 A4
Maitland Pk NW3 .... 70 D3
Old Bexley DA5 .... 169 B4
Sidcup DA15 .... 167 C1
Park Hill Rd
Beckenham BR2 .... 186 C1
South Croydon CR0 .... 221 C5
Wallington SM6 .... 219 B1
Park Hill Rise CR0 .... 221 D5
Park Hill Sch KT2 .... 176 C3
Park Hill Wlk [10] NW3 .... 70 D3
Park Ho
[8] Camberwell SE5 .... 139 B4
Finsbury Pk N4 .... 72 D6
Forest Hill SE26 .... 184 A5
[35] Hackney E9 .... 74 C1
Richmond TW10 .... 154 A5
Sidcup DA14 .... 190 A5
Southgate N21 .... 16 B4
Parkholme Rd E8 .... 74 A2
Park House Gdns
TW1 .... 153 C6
Parkhouse St SE5 .... 139 B5
Park Hts NW4 .... 46 B6
Parkhurst Ct N7 .... 72 A4
Parkhurst Gdns [2]
DA5 .... 169 C4
Parkhurst Rd
Bowes Pk N22 .... 32 B4
Friern Barnet N11 .... 31 A5
Little Ilford E12 .... 78 C4
Lower Holloway N7 .... 72 A4
Sidcup DA5 .... 169 C4
Sutton SM1 .... 218 B4
Tottenham N17 .... 34 A1
Walthamstow E17 .... 53 A5
Parkin Ho SE20 .... 184 D3
Parkinson Ct
Finsbury N1 .... 235 C1
Shoreditch EC1 .... 235 D2
Parkinson Ho [6] E9 .... 74 C1
Park La Cheam SM3 .... 217 A2
Cranford TW5 .... 128 A5
Park La *continued*
Dagenham RM6 .... 58 D3
Edmonton N9 .... 17 D1
Harrow HA2 .... 63 D5
Hayes UB4 .... 83 C3
Mayfair W1 .... 115 A6 248 A5
Mill Meads E15 .... 98 B6
Richmond TW9 .... 131 D1
South Croydon CR0 .... 221 B5
Stanmore HA7 .... 9 A1
Teddington TW11 .... 174 D4
Tottenham N17 .... 34 A3
Wallington SM5, SM6 .... 219 A3
Wembley HA9 .... 66 A4
Parkland Ct
Kensington W14 .... 244 A2
Stratford E15 .... 76 C3
Parkland Gdns [12]
SW19 .... 156 D3
Parkland Gr
Ashford TW15 .... 170 C6
Hounslow TW7 .... 130 D4
Parkland Mead BR1 .... 210 D6
Parkland Rd
Ashford TW15 .... 170 C6
Woodford IG8 .... 37 B3
Wood Green N22 .... 32 B1
Parklands Bushey WD23 .... 8 A5
East Dulwich SE22 .... 162 B6
Highgate N6 .... 49 B2
Kingston u T KT5 .... 198 B4
[5] Whetstone N20 .... 14 A2
Parklands Cl
Hadley Wood EN4 .... 2 B5
Ilford IG2 .... 57 A2
Mortlake SW14 .... 155 A6
Parklands Ct TW5 .... 128 D3
Parklands Dr N3 .... 47 A6
Parklands Par TW5 .... 128 D3
Parklands Pl HA8 .... 26 B6
Parklands Rd SW16 .... 181 B5
Parklands Way KT4 .... 215 C6
Park Lane Cl N17 .... 34 A3
Park Lane Mans CR0 .... 221 B5
Park Lane Prim Sch
HA9 .... 66 A4
PARK LANGLEY 208 B4
Park Lawn CR7 .... 183 A1
Parklea Cl NW9 .... 27 C2
Park Lea Ct N16 .... 51 C2
Parkleigh Ct SW19 .... 179 D1
Parkleigh Rd SW19 .... 179 D1
Parkleys KT2, TW10 .... 175 D6
Park Lo [3] Ealing W5 .... 87 B3
North Finchley N12 .... 30 A5
[11] South Hampstead
NW8 .... 70 B1
[10] Wapping E1 .... 118 B5
Willesden NW2 .... 68 C4
Park Lofts [9] SW4 .... 160 A6
Park Lorne NW8 .... 230 B1
Park Mans
Battersea SW11 .... 267 C1
Bedford Pk W6 .... 111 D3
Forest Hill SE26 .... 162 C1
Fulham SW6 .... 264 B1
[5] Hendon NW4 .... 46 B4
Knightsbridge SW1 .... 247 C1
St John's Wood NW8 .. 230 A3
Vauxhall SW8 .... 270 B6
Parkmead SW15 .... 156 B5
Park Mead
Blackfen DA15 .... 168 B5
Harrow HA2 .... 63 D5
Parkmead Gdns NW7 .... 27 D4
Park Mews
Chislehurst BR7 .... 188 D4
Greenwich SE10 .... 120 D1
Kensal Rise W10 .... 91 A5
Stanwell TW19 .... 148 B4
Parkmore BR7 .... 188 D3
Parkmore Cl IG8 .... 37 A6
Park Nook Gdns EN2 .... 5 B6
Park Par Acton W3 .... 110 C3
Dagenham NW10 .... 89 D5
Hayes UB3 .... 83 C1
Kingsbury NW9 .... 45 B6
Park Pl
Canary Wharf E14 .... 119 C5
Ealing W5 .... 109 D5
Gunnersbury W3 .... 110 C2
Hampton TW12 .... 174 A4
Shoreditch N1 .... 235 D6
St James SW1 .. 115 C5 249 A4
Wembley HA9 .... 66 B4
Park Place Dr W3 .... 110 C3
Park Place Ho [8]
SE10 .... 142 B6
Park Place Villas W2 .. 236 B4
Park Prim Sch E15 .... 76 D1
Park Rd Ashford TW15 .... 170 D5
Beckenham BR3 .... 185 C3
Bromley BR1 .... 187 B2
Cheam SM3 .... 217 A2
Chipping Barnet EN5 .... 1 B1
Chislehurst BR7 .... 188 D4
Chiswick W4 .... 133 B6
Cockfosters EN4 .... 2 C1
Dagenham NW10 .... 89 C6
Ealing W7 .... 108 D6
East Finchley N2 .... 48 B6
East Molesey KT8 .... 196 A5
Edmonton N18 .... 34 A6
Feltham TW13 .... 172 D6
Hackbridge SM6 .... 219 B6
Hampton TW12 .... 174 A5
Hampton Wick KT1 .... 175 C2
Harringay N8, N15 .... 50 D5
Hayes UB4 .... 83 C2
Hendon NW4 .... 46 B3
Park Rd *continued*
Hornsey N8 .... 49 D4
Hounslow TW3, TW7 .... 152 A6
Ilford IG1 .... 79 B5
Isleworth TW7 .... 131 B3
Kingsbury NW9 .... 45 B2
Kingston u T KT2,
TW10 .... 176 C3
Leyton E10 .... 53 C1
Lisson Gr NW1,
NW8 .... 92 C3 237 B6
Lower Halliford TW17 .... 192 C1
Mitcham SW19 .... 180 C4
Newham E15 .... 99 A6
New Malden KT3 .... 199 B5
Osidge N14 .... 15 D4
Richmond TW10 .... 154 B5
South Norwood SE25 .... 205 C5
Sunbury TW16 .... 172 B3
Teddington TW11 .... 174 D4
Twickenham TW1 .... 153 C5
Upton Pk E6 .... 99 C6
Uxbridge UB8 .... 60 A2
Wallington SM6 .... 219 B3
Walthamstow E17 .... 53 B4
Wanstead E12 .... 77 B6
Wembley HA0 .... 66 A2
Wood Green N11 .... 31 D3
Park Rd E Acton W3 .... 111 A4
Uxbridge UB10 .... 82 A5
Park Rd N Chiswick W4 .. 111 B1
South Acton W3 .... 110 D4
Park Ridings N8 .... 50 C6
Park Rise
Forest Hill SE23 .... 163 A3
Harrow HA3 .... 24 C2
Park Rise Rd SE23 .... 163 A3
Park Road E [11] W3 .... 110 D4
Park Road Ho [3] KT2 .... 176 C3
Park Row SE10 .... 142 B6
PARK ROYAL 88 D4
Park Royal NW10 .... 88 D6
Park Royal Bsns Ctr
NW10 .... 89 A3
Park Royal Metro Ctr
NW10 .... 88 D3
Park Royal Rd NW10,
W3 .... 89 A3
Park Royal Sta W5 .... 88 C3
Park S SW11 .... 268 A1
Park St James NW8 .... 230 C5
Park Sch IG1 .... 56 D1
Park Sheen [3] SW14 .... 132 D1
Parkshot TW9 .... 132 A1
Parkside
[1] Beckenham BR3 .... 185 D1
Cheam SM3 .... 217 A2
Ealing W5 .... 110 A6
East Acton W3 .... 111 C5
Finchley N3 .... 29 D3
Greenwich SE3 .... 142 D5
Hampton TW12 .... 174 A5
Hayes UB3 .... 105 C6
Hendon NW7 .... 28 A4
Sidcup DA14 .... 168 B2
Wimbledon SW19 .... 178 D6
Park Side Chigwell IG9 .... 21 B2
Dollis Hill NW2 .... 68 B4
Parkside Ave
Bromley BR1 .... 210 A5
Wimbledon SW19 .... 178 D5
Parkside Bsns Est
SE8 .... 141 A6
Parkside Cl SE20 .... 184 C3
Parkside Cres
Highbury N7 .... 72 C5
Tolworth KT5 .... 199 A3
Parkside Ct
Bowes Pk N22 .... 32 B4
[2] Wanstead E11 .... 55 A3
Parkside Dr HA8 .... 10 C1
Parkside Est E9 .... 96 D6
Parkside Gdns
East Barnet EN4 .... 15 A4
Wimbledon SW19 .... 178 D6
Parkside Lo DA17 .... 125 D1
Parkside Prep Sch N17 .. 33 C2
Parkside (private) Hospl
SW19 .... 156 D1
Parkside Rd
Belvedere DA17 .... 125 D2
Hounslow TW3 .... 151 D6
Parkside St SW11 .... 268 A1
Parkside Terr N18 .... 33 B6
Parkside Way HA2 .... 42 A5
Park Sq E NW1 .. 93 B3 238 D6
Park Square Mews
NW1 .... 238 C5
Park Sq W NW1 .. 93 B3 238 C5
Park St
Borough The
SE1 .... 117 A5 252 B4
Croydon CR0 .... 221 A6
Mayfair W1 .... 115 A6 248 A5
Teddington TW11 .... 174 C4
Parkstead Rd SW15 .... 156 B6
Parkstone Ave N18 .... 33 D5
Parkstone Rd
[5] Peckham SE15 .... 140 A3
Walthamstow E17 .... 54 A6
Park Stps W2 .... 247 B6
Park Terr
Carshalton SM5 .... 218 C5
Enfield EN3 .... 7 A5
New Malden KT4 .... 200 A1
Park The Ealing W5 .... 109 D5
Forest Hill SE23 .... 162 C3
Golders Green NW11 .... 47 D1
Highgate N6 .... 49 A3
Sidcup DA14 .... 190 A5
Park The *continued*
Wallington SM5 .... 218 D3
Parkthorne Cl HA2 .... 41 D3
Parkthorne Dr HA2 .... 41 D3
Parkthorne Rd SW12 .... 159 D4
Park Twrs W1 .... 248 C3
Parkview UB6 .... 87 A4
Park View
Dagenham W3 .... 89 A2
Highbury N5 .... 73 A4
Kingston u T KT3 .... 199 D6
Morden SM4 .... 202 B4
Pinner HA5 .... 23 B2
Southgate N21 .... 16 B4
Wembley HA9 .... 66 D3
Willesden NW2 .... 68 C4
Yiewsley UB7 .... 104 A6
Park View Acad N15 .... 51 A5
Park View Cres N11 .... 31 B6
Parkview Ct
Fulham SW6 .... 135 A3
Harrow HA3 .... 24 C3
Ilford IG2 .... 57 C3
Penge SE20 .... 184 B2
Twickenham TW1 .... 153 C4
Park View Ct
Colney Hatch N12 .... 30 C6
Kingsbury NW9 .... 45 A5
Wandsworth SW18 .... 157 C5
Park View Dr CR4 .... 180 B1
Park View Gdns
Hendon NW4 .... 46 D4
Redbridge IG4 .... 56 B5
Wood Green N22 .... 32 C2
Park View Ho
Chingford E4 .... 35 C5
Hampton TW12 .... 174 A5
Streatham SE24 .... 160 D5
Parkview Lo BR3 .... 207 D6
Park View Mans N4 .... 50 D2
Park View Mews [24]
SW9 .... 138 B3
Parkview Rd
Chislehurst SE9 .... 166 D2
Croydon CR0 .... 206 A1
Park View Rd
Bexley DA16 .... 146 C2
Ealing W5 .... 88 A2
Finchley N3 .... 29 D2
Hillingdon UB8 .... 82 C1
Pinner HA5 .... 22 B3
Southall UB1 .... 107 C5
Tottenham N17 .... 34 A1
Willesden NW10 .... 67 D4
Park Village E
NW1 .... 93 B5 231 D3
Park Village W
NW1 .... 93 B5 231 C4
Park Villas RM6 .... 58 D3
Parkville Rd
SW6 .... 135 B5 264 C3
Park Vista SE10 .... 142 B6
Park Vista Apartments
E13 .... 98 D4
Park Walk Prim Sch
SW10 .... 136 B6 266 C5
Parkway
Abbey Wood DA18 .... 125 A3
Camden Town
NW1 .... 93 B6 231 C5
Hillingdon UB10 .... 60 D1
Ilford IG3 .... 79 D5
Palmers Green N14 .... 16 A2
West Barnes SW20 .... 200 D5
Woodford IG8 .... 37 C5
Park Way
East Molesey KT8 .... 195 D6
Edgware HA8 .... 26 D2
Enfield EN2 .... 4 C3
Feltham TW14 .... 150 B4
Friern Barnet N20 .... 30 D6
Gunnersbury W3 .... 110 C2
Ruislip HA4 .... 40 A1
Temple Fortune NW11 .... 47 A4
Park Way Ct HA4 .... 39 D1
Parkway Ho SW14 .... 133 B1
Parkway Prim Sch
DA18 .... 125 A3
Parkway The
Cranford TW5 .... 128 B5
Hayes UB2, UB3, UB4,
TW5 .... 106 B3
Yeading UB4 .... 84 D2
Parkway Trad Est
TW5 .... 128 C6
Park West W2 .... 92 C1 237 B1
Park West Pl W1,
W2 .... 92 C1 237 B2
Park Wlk
Chelsea
SW10 .... 136 B6 266 C6
Highgate N6 .... 49 A2
Parkwood
Beckenham BR3 .... 185 C3
Primrose Hill NW8 .... 230 C5
Parkwood Ave KT10 .... 196 A1
Parkwood Gr TW16 .... 194 A6
Parkwood Mews N6 .... 49 B3
Parkwood Prim Sch
N4 .... 72 D6
Parkwood Rd
Hounslow TW7 .... 130 D4
Old Bexley DA5 .... 169 B4
Wimbledon SW19 .... 179 B5
Parliament Ct NW3 .... 70 C4
Parliament Hill NW3 .... 70 C4
Parliament Hill Mans
NW5 .... 71 A4
Parliament Hill Sch
NW5 .... 71 A4
Parliament Mews
SW14 .... 133 A3
Parliament Sq*
SW1 .... 116 A4 250 A1
Parliament St
SW1 .... 116 A4 250 A2
Parliament View
Apartments SE11 .... 260 C4
Parma Cres SW11 .... 136 D1
Parminter Ind Est [24]
E2 .... 96 B5
Parmiter St E2 .... 96 B5
Parmoor Ct EC1 .... 242 A6
Parnall Ho [11] SE19 .... 183 C6
Parnell Cl Edgware HA8 .. 27 A6
Hammersmith W12 .... 112 B3
Parnell Ho WC1 .... 239 D2
Parnell Rd E3 .... 97 B6
Parnham Cl BR1 .... 210 D6
Parnham St E14 .... 97 A1
Parolles Rd N19 .... 49 C1
Paroma Rd DA17 .... 125 C3
Parr Cl N9 .... 34 B6
Parr Ct Feltham TW13 .... 172 C6
Shoreditch N1 .... 235 C4
Parrington Ho [1]
SW4 .... 159 D5
Parr Pl W4 .... 111 D2
Parr Rd Newham E6 .... 99 D6
Stanmore HA7 .... 26 A2
Parr's Pl TW12 .... 173 C3
Parr St N1 .... 95 B5 235 C4
Parry Ave E6 .... 100 B1
Parry Cl KT17 .... 216 A1
Parry Ho [32] E1 .... 118 B5
Parry Pl SE18 .... 122 D2
Parry Rd
South Norwood SE25 .... 205 C6
West Kilburn W10 .... 91 A4
Parry St SW8 .... 138 A6 270 B6
Parsifal Coll NW3 .... 69 C4
Parsifal Ho NW3 .... 69 C4
Parsifal Rd NW6 .... 69 C3
Parsley Gdns CR0 .... 206 D1
Parsloes Ave RM9 .... 81 A3
Parsloes Prim Sch RM9 .. 81 B2
Parsonage Cl UB3 .... 83 D1
Parsonage Ct WD6 .... 11 A6
Parsonage Gdns EN2 .... 5 A3
Parsonage La Enfield EN2 .. 5 B3
Sidcup DA14 .... 191 B6
Parsonage Manorway
DA17 .... 147 C6
Parsonage St E14 .... 120 A2
Parsons Cl SM1 .... 217 D5
Parsons Cres HA8 .... 10 C1
Parsons Gn
SW6 .... 135 C4 265 A1
PARSONS GREEN 135 C4
Parsons Green La
SW6 .... 135 C4 265 A2
Parsons Green Sta
SW6 .... 135 C4 265 A1
Parsons Hill SE18 .... 122 C3
Parsons Ho
Paddington W2 .... 236 C5
[21] Streatham SW12 .... 160 A4
Parsons Lo NW6 .... 69 D1
Parsons Mead KT8 .... 196 A6
Parson's Mead CR0 .... 204 D1
Parsons Rd
Edgware HA8 .... 10 C1
Newham E13 .... 99 C5
Parson St NW4 .... 46 C6
Parthenia Rd
SW6 .... 135 C4 265 B1
Partingdale La NW7 .... 28 D5
Partington Cl N19 .... 49 D1
Parton Lo [14] E8 .... 73 D2
Partridge Cl Barnet EN5 .. 12 C5
Bushey WD23 .... 8 A3
[1] Newham E16 .... 99 D2
Stanmore HA7 .... 26 A6
Partridge Ct EC1 .... 241 C6
Partridge Dr BR6 .... 227 A5
Partridge Gn SE9 .... 166 C1
Partridge Ho [22] E3 .... 97 B5
Partridge Rd
[8] Hampton TW12 .... 173 C4
Sidcup DA14 .... 189 C6
Partridge Sq [3] E6 .... 100 A2
Partridge Way N22 .... 32 A2
Pasadena Cl UB3 .... 106 B4
Pascall Ho SE17 .... 139 A6
Pascal St SW8 .. 137 D5 269 D4
Pascoe Rd SE13 .... 164 B6
Pasley Cl SE17 .... 262 A1
Pasquier Rd E17 .... 53 A6
Passey Pl SE9 .... 166 B5
Passfield Dr E14 .... 97 D2
Passfield Ho SE18 .... 123 B2
Passfield Path [13]
SE28 .... 124 B6
Passfields Catford SE6 .. 164 A1
West Kensington W14 .. 254 C1
Passing Alley EC1 .... 241 D5
Passingham Ho TW5 .... 129 C6
Passmore Edwards Ho
N11 .... 31 D3
Passmore Gdns N11 .... 31 D4
Passmore Ho [12] N9 .... 18 A1
Passmore St
SW1 .... 115 A1 258 A2
Pasters Ct EN1 .... 17 D5
Pasteur Cl NW9 .... 27 C1
Pasteur Gdns N18 .... 33 A5
Paston Cl SM6 .... 219 C5

Paston Cres SE12 165 B4
Pastor Ct N6 49 C3
Pastor St SE1, SE11 116 D2 261 D4
Pasture Cl Bushey WD23 8 A4
Wembley HA0 65 B5
Pasture Rd
Catford SE6 164 D3
Dagenham RM9 81 B3
Wembley HA0 65 B5
Pastures Mead UB10 60 C2
Pastures The N20 13 B3
Patcham Terr SW8 268 D2
Patch Cl UB10 82 B6
Patching Way UB4 85 A2
Pat Drew Ho BR1 187 C2
Patent Ho E14 97 D2
Paternoster La EC4 94 D1 241 D2
Paternoster Row EC2, EC4 95 A1 242 A1
Paternoster Sq EC4 94 D1 241 D2
Pater St W8 113 C3 255 A5
Pates Manor Dr TW14 149 B4
Pathfield Rd SW16 181 D4
Path The SW19 179 D2
Pathway Ho SW17 180 D4
Pathway Lo CR4 180 D2
Patience Rd SW11 136 C3
Patience Villas SE13 142 B2
Patio Cl SW4 159 D5
Patmore Ho 9 N16 73 C3
Patmore St SW8 137 C4 269 B2
Patmos Rd SW9 138 D4
Paton Cl E3 97 C4
Paton Ho 3 SW9 138 B3
Paton St EC1 235 A1
Patricia Ct
Chislehurst BR7 189 B2
Woolwich DA16 146 B5
Patrick Coman Ho EC1 234 C1
Patrick Connolly Gdns 41 E3 97 D4
Patrick Rd E13 99 C4
Patriot Sq E2 96 B5
Patrol Pl SE6 163 D5
Pat Shaw Ho 2 E1 96 D3
Patshull Pl NW5 71 C2
Patshull Rd NW5 71 C2
Patson Cl E5 74 D5
Pattenden Rd SE6 163 B3
Patten Ho N4 51 A1
Patten Rd SW18 158 C4
Patterdale NW1 231 D1
Patterdale Cl BR1 186 C4
Patterdale Rd SE15 140 C5
Patterson Ct SE19 183 D4
Patterson Rd SE19 183 D4
Pattina Wlk SE16 119 A5
Pattinson Point 10 E16 99 A2
Pattison Ho
Borough The SE1 252 B2
1 Stepney E1 96 D1
Pattison Rd NW2 69 C5
Pattison Wlk SE18 123 A1
Pat Williams Ho SE27 161 A1
Paul Byrne Ho 3 N2 48 A6
Paul Cl E15 76 C1
Paul Ct
7 Edmonton N18 34 A6
Hendon N3 29 A1
Paul Daisley Ct 2 NW6 69 A1
Paulet Rd SE5 138 D4
Paul Gdns CR0 221 D6
Paulhan Rd HA3 43 D5
Paul Ho 13 W10 91 A3
Paulin Dr N21 16 C4
Pauline Cres TW2 152 A3
Pauline Ho 21 E1 96 A2
Paulinus Cl BR5 190 C1
Paul Julius Cl E14 120 B6
Paul Robeson Cl E6 100 C4
Paulson Ho 7 IG11 78 D1
Paul St
Broadgate EC2 95 C3 243 A6
Newham E15 98 C6
Paultons Ho SW3 266 D6
Paultons Sq SW3 136 B6 266 D6
Paultons St SW3 136 B6 266 D5
Pauntley Ho 6 N19 49 C1
Pauntley St 4 N19 49 C1
Pavan Ct 20 E2 96 C4
Paved Ct 9 TW9 153 D6
Paveley Ct NW7 28 D3
Paveley Dr SW11 136 C5 267 A3
Paveley Ho N1 233 C3
Paveley St NW8 92 C3 237 B6
Pavement Mews 1 RM6 58 D2
Pavement Sq CR0 206 A1
Pavement The
Brentford W5 110 A3
Clapham SW4 137 C1
Leytonstone E11 54 A1
11 West Norwood SE27 183 A6
Pavet Cl RM10 81 D2
Pavilion Ct
Dagenham RM9 103 A6
7 Hampstead NW3 70 A4
Pavilion Ct *continued*
Hampstead NW3 70 B3
3 Paddington NW6 91 C4
5 South Norwood SW16 182 B3
3 Wimbledon SW19 179 A3
Pavilion L Ctr The BR1 187 A1
Pavilion Lo HA2 42 B1
Pavilion Mans 10 SW9 138 B1
Pavilion Mews N3 29 C1
Pavilion Rd
Knightsbridge SW1 114 D3 257 D5
Redbridge IG1 56 B2
Pavilion Sq SW17 158 D1
Pavilion St SW1 257 D5
Pavilions The BR3 185 C4
Pavilion Terr Ilford IG2 57 C4
8 North Kensington W12 90 C1
Pavilion Way
Burnt Oak HA8 27 A3
Ruislip HA4 62 C6
Pavillion Ct SW1 268 C6
Pavitt Ct NW10 68 A1
Pawleyne Cl SE20 184 C3
Pawsey Cl E13 99 A6
Pawson's Rd CR0 205 A4
Paxford Rd HA0 65 B6
Paxton Cl
Richmond TW9 132 B3
Walton-on-T KT12 194 C2
Paxton Ct
1 Forest Hill SE26 185 A6
Grove Pk SE9 165 C1
Mitcham CR4 180 D1
Paxton Ho SE17 262 B2
Paxton Pl SE27 183 C6
Paxton Prim Sch SE19 183 C4
Paxton Rd Chiswick W4 133 C6
Forest Hill SE23 163 A1
Plaistow BR1 187 A3
Tottenham N17 34 A3
Paxton Terr SW1 268 D6
Paymal Ho 33 E1 96 C2
Payne Cl IG11 79 D1
Payne Ho N1 233 D5
Paynell Ct SE3 142 C2
Payne Rd E3 97 D5
Paynesfield Ave SW14 133 B2
Paynesfield Rd WD23 8 D4
Payne St SE8 141 B6
Paynes Wlk W6 135 A6 264 A5
Payzes Gdns IG8 36 D5
Peabody Ave SW1 115 B1 258 D1
Peabody Bldgs
6 Camberwell SE5 139 B4
Walworth SE17 262 C3
Peabody Cl
Croydon CR0 206 C1
SW1 268 D6
Peabody Cotts N17 33 C2
Peabody Ct
9 Camberwell SE5 139 B4
25 Enfield EN3 7 C6
St Luke's EC1 242 B5
Peabody Est
18 Bethnal Green E2 96 B5
Borough The SE1 252 A3
Fulham SW6 135 B6 264 D6
17 Hammersmith W6 112 C1
Holborn EC1 241 B5
Lambeth SE1 251 B3
North Kensington W10 90 C2
4 Ratcliff E1 118 D6
7 St George in t East E1 118 A6
St Luke's EC1 242 B5
Strand WC2 240 C1
Streatham SE24 161 A4
Westminster SW1 259 B4
Peabody Hill SE21 161 A3
Peabody Sq SE1 251 C1
Peabody Twr EC1 242 B5
Peabody Yd N1 235 A6
Peace Cl
East Barnet N14 15 B6
Greenford UB6 86 B6
South Norwood SE25 205 C5
Peace Ct 10 NW9 46 A5
Peace Gr HA9 66 D5
Peacehaven Ct 8 N10 31 A3
Peace St SE18 144 C6
Peach Ct E4 35 C6
Peaches Cl SM2 217 A1
Peaches Ct SM2 217 A1
Peach Gr E11 76 B5
Peach Rd
Feltham TW14 150 A3
London W10 91 A4
Peach Tree Ave UB7 82 B1
Peachum Rd SE3 142 D6
Peach Walk Mews 24 E3 96 D5
Peacock Ave TW14 149 B3
Peacock Cl
Dagenham RM8 80 C6
Walthamstow E4 35 B3
Peacock Ct EN1 17 C5
Peacock Ind Est N17 33 D3
Peacock St SE17 116 D2 261 D3
Peacock Wlk E16 99 B1
Peacock Yd SE17 261 D3
Peaketon Ave IG4 55 D4
Peak Hill SE26 184 C6
Peak Hill Ave SE26 184 C6
Peak Hill Gdns SE26 184 C6
Peak Ho N4 51 A1
Peak The SE26 162 C1
Peal Gdns W13 87 A3
Peall Rd CR0 204 B3
Peall Rd Ind Est CR0 204 B3
Pear Ave TW17 193 C6
Pearce Cl 2 CR4 181 A1
Pearcefield Ave 5 SE23 162 C3
Pearce Ho
Camden Town N19 71 C5
7 Streatham SW2 160 A4
Westminster SW1 259 D3
Pear Cl Kingsbury NW9 45 B5
New Cross Gate SE14 141 A5
Pearcroft Rd E11 76 B6
Pear Ct 21 SE15 139 D5
Peardon St SW8 137 B3
Peareswood Gdns HA7 25 D2
Pearfield Ho 1 N5 73 A3
Pearfield Rd SE23 163 A1
Pearl Cl Hendon NW2 46 D2
Newham E6 100 C1
Pearl Ct 18 NW9 46 A5
Pearl Rd E17 53 C6
Pearl St E1 118 B5
Pearlstones Ct RM10 103 C6
Pearmain Cl TW17 192 D4
Pearmain Ho 9 SE13 142 A3
Pearman St SE1 116 C4 251 B1
Pear Pl SE1 251 A2
Pear Rd E11 76 C5
Pearscroft Ct SW6 135 D4 265 D1
Pearscroft Rd SW6 135 D4 265 D1
Pearse St 3 SE15 139 C6
Pearson Cl Barnet EN5 1 D2
4 Camberwell SE5 139 A4
Pearson Ct SM4 201 D4
Pearson Ho SW15 134 C3
Pearson's Ave SE8, SE14 141 C4
Pearson St E2 95 D5
Pearson Way CR4 181 A2
Pears Rd TW3 130 A2
Peartree Ave SW17 158 A1
Pear Tree Ave UB7 82 B1
Pear Tree Cl
Bromley BR2 209 D4
Chessington KT9 214 C3
Mitcham CR4 180 C1
23 Shoreditch E2 95 D6
Pear Tree Ct
Holborn EC1 241 B5
Putney SW15 134 B1
Woodford IG8 37 B2
Peartree Gdns RM8 80 B4
Pear Tree Ho
Brockley SE4 141 B1
Hayes UB8 83 A1
Peartree La E1 118 C6
Peartree Rd EN1 5 C2
Pear Tree Rd TW15 171 A5
Peartree St EC1 95 A3 242 A6
Peartree Way SE10 121 A2
Peary Ho 4 NW10 67 B1
Peary Pl E2 96 C4
Peaslake Ct SM2 218 A1
Peas Mead Terr E4 36 A6
Peatfield Cl DA15 167 C1
Pebworth Lo
2 Belmont SM2 217 D1
South Norwood SE25 205 D5
Pebworth Rd HA1 65 A6
Peckarmans Wood SE21, SE26 162 A1
Peckett Sq 3 N5 72 D4
Peckford Pl SW9 138 C3
PECKHAM 140 A4
Peckham Gr SE15 139 C5
Peckham High St SE15 140 A4
Peckham Hill St SE15 140 A5
Peckham Park Prim Sch SE15 140 A5
Peckham Park Rd SE15 140 A5
Peckham Rd SE5 139 C4
Peckham Rye
East Dulwich SE22 140 A1
Peckham SE15, SE22 140 B1
Peckham Rye Sta SE15 140 A3
Peckwater Ho 2 NW5 71 D2
Peckwater St NW5 71 C3
Pedlars Wlk N7 72 A3
Pedley Rd RM8 58 C1
Pedley St E1 95 D3 243 D5
Pedro St E5 74 D4
Pedworth Gdns 4 SE16 118 C2
Peebles Ct UB1 86 A1
Peek Cres SW19 178 D5
Peel Centre (Metropolitan Police Training Establishment) NW9 45 D6
Peel Cl Chingford E4 19 D2
Edmonton N9 18 A1
Peel Ct UB6 86 A4
Peel Dr Colindale NW9 45 D6
Redbridge IG5 56 A6
Peel Gr E2 96 C5
Peel Pass W8 245 A3
Peel Pl IG5 37 D1
Peel Prec NW6 91 C5
Peel Rd
Farnborough BR6 227 A3
Harrow HA3 42 D6
Wembley HA0, HA9 65 D5
Woodford E18 36 D2
Peel St W8 113 C5 245 A3
Peel Way UB8 82 A2
Peel Yates Ho 13 SE7 122 A2
Peerglow Est EN3 18 C6
Peerless St EC1 95 B4 235 C1
Pegamoid Rd N18 18 C1
Pegasus Cl N16 73 B4
Pegasus Ct 11 Acton W3 89 A1
Brentford TW8 110 B1
6 Buckhurst Hill IG9 21 D2
College Pk NW10 90 B4
Edmonton N21 17 A4
Harrow HA3 43 D4
Kingston u T KT1 197 D6
Sutton SM1 217 D6
Pegasus Ho 9 E1 96 D3
Pegasus Lo N21 17 A4
Pegasus Pl 2 SE11 138 C6
Pegasus Rd CR0, CR9 220 C2
Pegasus Way N11 31 B4
Peggotty Way UB8 82 D1
Pegg Rd TW5 128 D5
Peggy Quirke Ct 2 HA0 66 A2
Pegley Gdns SE12 165 A2
Pegwell Ho 19 E5 74 B3
Pegwell St SE18 145 C5
Pekin St E14 97 C1
Pekoe SE1 253 D3
Peldon Ct TW10 154 B6
Pele Ct N17 33 B3
Pelham Ave IG11 101 D6
Pelham Cl SE5 139 C2
Pelham Cotts DA5 169 D3
Pelham Cres SW7 257 A3
Pelham Ct SW3 257 A3
Pelham Ho W14 254 C3
Pelham Pl Chelsea SW7 257 A3
8 Ealing W7 86 D3
Pelham Prim Sch
Bexleyheath DA7 147 C2
Merton SW19 179 C3
Pelham Rd
Bexleyheath DA7 147 C2
Ilford IG1 79 B6
Merton SW19 179 C3
Penge BR3, SE20 184 C1
Tottenham N15 51 D5
Wanstead E18 55 B6
Wood Green N22 32 C1
Pelham St SW7 114 B2 256 D4
Pelican Ho 8 SE8 119 B2
Pelican Pas 3 E1 96 C3
Pelier St SE17 139 A6
Pelinore Rd SE6 164 C2
Pella Ho SE11 260 D2
Pellant Rd SW6 135 A5 264 B4
Pellatt Gr N22 32 C2
Pellatt Rd
East Dulwich SE22 161 D6
Wembley HA9 66 A6
Pellerin Rd N16 73 C3
Pellew Ho 15 E1 96 B3
Pellings Cl BR2 208 C6
Pelling St E14 97 C1
Pellipar Cl N13 16 C1
Pellipar Gdns SE18 122 B1
Pellipar Rd SE18 122 B1
Pelly Ct 4 E17 54 A5
Pelly Rd E13 99 A5
Pelter St E2 95 D4
Pelton Ct CR2 221 A2
Pelton Rd SE10 120 C1
Pembar Ave E17 53 A6
Pemberley Chase KT19 214 D3
Pemberley Cl KT19 214 D3
Pemberley Ho KT19 214 D3
Pember Rd NW10 90 D4
Pemberton Ct 18 E1 96 D4
Pemberton Gdns
Camden Town N19 71 C5
Dagenham RM6 59 A4
Pemberton Ho SE26 184 A6
Pemberton Pl
Esher KT10 212 A5
2 Hackney E8 74 B1
Pemberton Rd
East Molesey KT8 196 A5
Harringay N4 50 D4
Pemberton Row EC4 241 B2
Pemberton Terr N19 71 C5
Pembridge Ave TW4 151 B3
Pembridge Cres W11 113 C6 245 A6
Pembridge Gdns W2 113 C6 245 A5
Pembridge Hall Sch W2 113 C6 245 B5
Pembridge Mews W11 113 C6 245 A6
Pembridge Pl
Notting Hill W2 113 C6 245 B6
1 Wandsworth SW15 157 C6
Pembridge Rd W11 113 C6 245 A5
Pembridge Sq W2 113 C6 245 B5
Pembridge Villas W11 113 C6 245 A6
Pembroke W14 254 D3
Pembroke Ave
Enfield EN1 6 B4
Harrow HA3 43 B6
Islington N1 94 A6 233 B6
Surbiton KT5 198 D4
Pembroke Bldgs NW10 90 A4
Pembroke Cl SW1 248 B1
Pembroke Ct 11 W7 86 D2
Pembroke Gdns
Dagenham RM10 81 D5
West Kensington W8 113 B2 254 D4
Pembroke Gdns Cl W8 255 A5
Pembroke Hall NW4 46 C6
Pembroke Ho
Acton W3 111 A4
Chelsea SW1 258 A5
5 Clapham Pk SW2 160 A6
17 Kensington W2 91 D1
Putney SW15 156 A6
Upper Tooting SW17 180 B5
Pembroke Lo 2 SW16 160 B1
Pembroke Mews
8 Bow E3 97 A4
Bromley BR1 187 D1
Kensington W8 255 A5
Muswell Hill N10 31 A2
Pembroke Pl
Edgware HA8 26 C3
Isleworth TW7 130 C3
Kensington W8 255 A5
Pembroke Rd
Bromley BR1 187 D1
Edmonton N13 17 A1
Greenford UB6 85 D3
Hornsey N8 50 A5
Ilford IG3 80 A6
Kensington W8 113 C2 255 A4
Mitcham CR4 181 A1
Muswell Hill N10 31 A3
Newham E6 100 B2
Ruislip HA4 39 D1
South Norwood SE25 205 C5
South Tottenham N15 51 D4
Walthamstow E17 53 D4
Wembley HA9 65 D5
Pembroke Sq W8 113 C3 255 A5
Pembroke St N1 94 A6 233 B6
Pembroke Studios W8 254 D5
Pembroke Terr NW8 229 C5
Pembroke Villas
Kensington W8 255 A4
Richmond TW9 131 D1
Pembroke Way UB3 105 A3
Pembroke Wlk W8 255 A4
Pembry Cl SW9 138 C4
Pembury Ave KT4 200 A2
Pembury Cl Hackney E5 74 B3
Hayes BR2 208 D2
Pembury Cres DA14 169 A2
Pembury Ct UB3 127 B6
Pembury Ho
Camberwell SE5 139 C3
Keston Mark BR2 210 A1
Pembury Pl 15 E5, E8 74 B3
Pembury Rd
Croydon SE25 206 A5
Erith DA7 147 A6
Hackney E5 74 B3
Tottenham N17 33 D1
Pemdevon Rd CR0 204 C2
Pemell Cl 30 E1 96 C3
Pemell Ho 31 E1 96 C3
Pemerich Cl UB3 105 D1
Pempath Pl HA9 65 D6
Penair Lodge HA1 64 C5
Penally Pl N1 235 D6
Penang St E1 118 B5
Penard Rd UB2 107 D3
Penarth Ct SM2 218 A1
Penarth Ctr The SE15 140 C6
Penarth St SE15 140 C6
Penates KT10 212 B4
Penberth Rd SE6 164 A3
Penbury Rd UB2 107 B1
Penceat Ct SE20 184 C1
Pencombe Mews W11 244 D6
Pencraig Way SE15 140 B6
Pendall Cl EN4 2 C1
Penda Rd DA8 147 D5
Pendarves Rd SW20 178 C2
Penda's Mead E9 75 A4
Pendell Ave UB3 127 D5
Pendennis Ho 15 SE8 119 A2
Pendennis Rd
Streatham SW16 182 A6
Tottenham N17 51 B6
Penderel Rd TW3 151 C6
Penderry Rise SE6 164 B2
Penderyn Way N7 71 D4
Pendlebury Ho 5 SE18 144 A4
Pendle Ho 13 SE26 162 A1
Pendle Rd SW16 181 B5
Pendlestone Rd E17 53 D4
Pendley Ho 18 E2 96 A6
Pendolino Way NW10 66 D1
Pendragon Rd BR1 165 A1
Pendragon Sch BR1 165 A1
Pendragon Wlk NW9 45 C3
Pendrell Ho WC2 239 D1
Pendrell Rd SE4 141 A3
Pendrell St SE18 145 B6
Pendula Dr UB4 84 D3
Penelope Ho 20 SW9 138 C4
Penerley Rd SE6 163 D3
Penfield Lo 7 W9 91 C2
Penfields Ho N7 72 A2
Penfold Cl CR0 220 C5
Penfold Ct 7 CR4 181 A1
Penfold Ho 10 SE18 144 D6
Penfold La DA5 168 D3
Penfold Pl NW1 92 C2 237 A4
Penfold Rd N9 18 D3
Penfold St NW8 92 B3 236 D5
Penford Gdns SE9 143 D2
Penford St SE5 138 D3
Pengarth Rd DA5 168 D5
PENGE 184 D4
Penge East Sta SE20 184 C4
Penge La SE20 184 D3
Penge Rd Newham E13 99 C6
South Norwood SE25 206 A6
Penge West Sta SE20 184 B4
Penhall Rd SE7 121 D2
Penhill Rd DA5 168 C4
Penhurst Mans SW6 264 C2
Penifather La UB6 86 B4
Peninsula Ct E14 119 D3
Peninsular Cl TW14 149 C5
Peninsular Park Rd SE7 121 A2
Penistone Rd SW16 182 A3
Penketh Dr HA1 64 B5
Penmayne Ho SE11 261 B2
Penmon Rd SE2 124 A3
Pennack Rd SE15 139 D6
Penn Almshouses 1 SE10 142 A4
Pennant Mews W8 113 D2 255 C4
Pennant Terr E17 35 B1
Pennard Mans 5 W12 112 C4
Pennard Rd W12 112 C4
Pennards The TW16 194 C6
Penn Cl Greenford UB6 85 D5
Harrow HA3 43 C5
Penn Ct NW9 45 B6
Pennefather Ho N1 73 B2
Pennells Ct TW5 129 C6
Penner Cl SW19 157 A2
Penners Gdns KT6 198 A2
Pennethorne Cl E9 96 C6
Pennethorne Ho SW11 136 B2
Pennethorne Rd SE15 140 B5
Penn Gdns BR7 188 D1
Penn Ho
7 Edmonton N9 18 A1
Lisson Gr NW8 237 A5
Pennine Dr NW2 68 D6
Pennine La NW2 69 A6
Pennine Mans NW2 69 A6
Pennine Par NW2 69 A6
Pennine Way UB7 127 B5
Pennington Cl 10 SE27 183 B6
Pennington Ct
4 Rotherhithe SE16 119 A5
23 St George in t East E1 118 A6
Pennington Dr N21 16 A6
Pennington Lo 18 KT5 198 A4
Pennington St E1 118 B6
Pennington Way SE12 165 B2
Penniston Cl N17 33 A1
Penn La Bexley DA5 168 D5
Sidcup DA5 169 A5
Penn Rd N7 72 A4
Penn St N1 95 B6 235 D5
Penny Ct SW10 266 B6
Pennyfields E14 119 C6
Pennyford Ct NW8 236 C6
Penny La TW17 193 C2
Penny Mews SW12 159 B4
Pennymore Wlk W9 91 B3
Penny Rd NW10 88 D4
Penny Royal SM6 219 D2
Pennyroyal Ave E6 100 C1
Penpoll Rd E8 74 B2
Penpool La DA16 146 B2
Penray EN5 1 A2
Penrhyn Ave E17 35 C2
Penrhyn Cres
Mortlake SW14 133 A1
Walthamstow E17 35 C2
Penrhyn Gdns KT1 197 D5
Penrhyn Gr E17 35 C2
Penrhyn Rd KT1 198 A6
Penrith Cl
Beckenham BR3 185 D2
Putney SW15 157 A6
Penrith Pl SE27 160 D2
Penrith Rd
New Malden KT3 199 B5
South Norwood CR7 183 A1
Tottenham N15 51 B4
Penrith St SW16 181 C4
Penrose Gr SE17 117 A1 262 A1
Penrose Ho
Camberwell SE17 262 A1
Southgate N21 16 B6
Penrose St SE17 117 A1 262 A1
Penryn Ho SE11 261 C2
Penryn St NW1 93 D5 232 C4
Penry St SE1 263 B3
Pensbury Pl SW8 137 C3
Pensbury St SW8 137 C3
Pensford Ave TW9 132 C3
Penshurst 2 NW5 71 A2
Penshurst Ave DA15 168 A5
Penshurst Ct
Croydon CR2 220 D1

Penshurst Ct *continued*
1 Edgware HA8 ... 26 D5
Penshurst Gdns HA8 ... 26 D5
Penshurst Gn BR2 ... 208 D4
Penshurst Ho 1 SE15 .. 140 C6
Penshurst Rd
Erith DA7 ... 147 B4
Homerton E9 ... 74 D1
Thornton Heath CR7 ... 204 D4
Tottenham N17 ... 33 D3
Penshurst Way SM2 ... 217 C1
Penshurst Wlk 4
BR2 ... 208 D4
Pensilver Cl EN4 ... 2 C1
Penstemon Cl N3 ... 29 C4
Pentavia Retail Pk
NW7 ... 27 D3
Pentelow Gdns TW14 .. 150 A5
Pentire Rd E17 ... 36 B2
Pentland Ave
Edgware HA8 ... 10 D2
Littleton TW17 ... 192 C4
Pentland Cl
Cricklewood NW11 ... 69 A6
Lower Edmonton N9 ... 18 C2
Pentland Gdns SW18 ... 158 A5
Pentland Ho
17 Camden Town NW5 ... 71 A2
7 Stamford Hill N16 ... 51 D1
Pentland Pl UB5 ... 85 A6
Pentland Rd
Bushey WD23 ... 8 A5
1 Maida Vale NW6 ... 91 C4
Pentlands BR3 ... 186 A2
Pentlands Cl CR4 ... 203 B6
Pentland St SW18 ... 158 A5
Pentland Way UB10 ... 61 A5
Pentlow St SW15 ... 134 C2
Pentney Rd
5 Chingford E4 ... 20 B3
Merton SW19, SW20 ... 179 A2
Streatham SW12 ... 159 C3
Penton Gr N1 ... 234 A3
Penton Ho
3 Abbey Wood SE2 ... 124 D4
Islington N1 ... 234 A3
Sutton SM2 ... 218 A1
Penton Pl
SE17 ... 116 D1 261 D2
Penton Rise
WC1 ... 94 B4 233 D2
Penton St N1 ... 94 C5 234 A3
PENTONVILLE ... 94 B5
Pentonville Rd
N1 ... 94 B5 233 C3
Pentrich Ave EN1 ... 6 A5
Pentridge St SE15 ... 139 D5
Pentyre Ave N18 ... 33 B5
Penwerris Ave TW5,
TW7 ... 130 A5
Penwerris Ct TW7 ... 130 A5
Penwith Rd SW18 ... 157 D2
Penwood Ct HA5 ... 41 B5
Penwood Ho SW15 ... 155 D5
Penwortham Ct 1 N22 .. 32 C1
Penwortham Prim Sch
SW17 ... 181 B4
Penwortham Rd
SW16 ... 181 C4
Penylan Pl HA8 ... 26 C3
Penywern Rd
SW5 ... 113 C1 255 B2
Penzance Ho SE11 ... 261 B2
Penzance Pl
W11 ... 113 A5 244 B4
Penzance St
W11 ... 113 A5 244 A4
Peony Ct IG8 ... 36 C3
Peony Gdns W12 ... 112 A6
Peperfield WC1 ... 233 C1
Pepler Ho 17 W10 ... 91 A3
Pepler Mews SE1 ... 263 C1
Peploe Rd NW6 ... 90 D5
Pepper Cl E6 ... 100 B2
Peppercorn Cl CR7 ... 183 B1
Peppermead Sq SE13 .. 163 C6
Peppermint Cl CR0 ... 204 A2
Peppermint Pl 7 E11 ... 76 C5
Pepper St
Borough The SE1 ... 252 A2
Millwall E14 ... 119 D3
Peppie Cl N16 ... 73 C6
Pepsi Trocadero* W1. 249 C5
Pepys Cl UB10 ... 60 D4
Pepys Cres Barnet EN5 ... 12 C6
2 Newham E16 ... 121 A5
Pepys Ct SW20 ... 178 C1
Pepys Ent Ctr 18 SE8 ... 119 B2
Pepys Ho
14 Bethnal Green E2 ... 96 C4
Clapham Pk SW4 ... 159 D6
Pepys Rd
New Cross Gate
SE14 ... 140 D3
Wimbledon SW20 ... 178 C2
Pepys Rise BR6 ... 211 D1
Pepys St EC3 ... 117 C6 253 B6
Perak Ct KT5 ... 199 A2
Peralte Terr CR4 ... 204 A5
Perceval Ave NW3 ... 70 C3
Perceval Ct UB5 ... 63 C3
Percheron Cl TW7 ... 130 D2
Percheron Ct 3 SW9 .. 138 B2
Percheron Rd WD6 ... 11 B5
Perch St E8 ... 73 D4
Percival Ct N17 ... 33 D3
Percival Gdns RM6 ... 58 C3
Percival Ho 3 IG8 ... 37 A6
Percival Rd Enfield EN1 ... 5 D1
Feltham TW13 ... 149 D2
Percival Rd *continued*
Mortlake SW14 ... 133 A1
Orpington BR6 ... 226 D6
Percival St EC1 .. 94 D4 234 D1
Percival Way KT19 ... 215 B4
Percy Ave TW15 ... 170 C5
Percy Bilton Ct TW5 ... 129 D4
Percy Bryant Rd
TW16 ... 171 C3
Percy Bush Rd UB7 ... 104 B3
Percy Cir WC1 ... 94 B4 233 D2
Percy Ct 1 KT5 ... 198 B3
Percy Gdns Enfield EN3 .. 18 D6
Hayes UB4 ... 83 C4
5 Isleworth TW7 ... 131 A2
New Malden KT4 ... 199 C1
Percy Ho 4 SW16 ... 181 C6
Percy Laurie Ho 6
SW15 ... 134 D1
Percy Mews W1 ... 239 C3
Percy Pas W1 ... 239 C3
Percy Rd
Bexleyheath DA7 ... 147 A3
Carshalton CR4 ... 203 A2
Croydon SE25 ... 206 A4
Edmonton N21 ... 17 A4
Hampton TW12 ... 173 C3
Ilford IG3 ... 58 A2
Isleworth TW7 ... 131 A1
Leytonstone E11 ... 54 C2
Newham E16 ... 98 C2
North Finchley N12 ... 30 A5
Penge SE20 ... 184 D2
Romford RM7 ... 59 D6
Shepherd's Bush W12 ... 112 A4
Twickenham TW2 ... 152 A3
Percy St W1 ... 93 D2 239 C3
Percy Terr BR1 ... 210 D6
Percy Way TW2 ... 152 A3
Peregrine Cl NW10 ... 67 B3
Peregrine Ct
Bexley DA16 ... 145 D4
Streatham SW16 ... 182 B6
Peregrine Gdns CR0 ... 223 A6
Peregrine Ho
6 Battersea SW11 ... 136 C2
Finsbury EC1 ... 234 D2
Peregrine Rd
Sunbury TW16 ... 171 D1
Tottenham N17 ... 33 B3
Peregrine Way SW19,
SW20 ... 178 C3
Performing Arts & Tech
Sch SE25 ... 205 B3
Perham Rd
W14 ... 113 A1 254 B1
Peridot St E6 ... 100 A2
Perifield SE21 ... 161 A3
Perimeade Rd UB6 ... 87 C5
Period Wks E10 ... 53 A1
Periton Rd SE9 ... 143 D1
PERIVALE ... 87 B5
Perivale UB6 ... 86 D5
Perivale Gdns W13 ... 87 B3
Perivale Grange UB6 ... 87 A4
Perivale Ind Pk UB6 ... 87 B5
Perivale La UB6 ... 87 A4
Perivale Lo UB6 ... 87 A4
Perivale New Bsns Ctr
UB6 ... 87 C5
Perivale Prim Sch UB6 .. 87 C5
Perivale Sta UB6 ... 87 A5
Perkin Cl
Hounslow TW3 ... 129 D1
Wembley HA0 ... 65 B3
Perkins Ct TW15 ... 170 B5
Perkins Ho 15 E14 ... 97 B2
Perkins Rd IG2 ... 57 B4
Perkins Rents SW1 ... 259 C5
Perkins Sq SE1 ... 252 B4
Perks Cl SE3 ... 142 C2
Perley Ho 9 E3 ... 97 B2
Perotti Ho SW6 ... 135 D2
Perpins Rd SE9 ... 167 C5
Perran Rd SE24, SW2 ... 160 D2
Perren St NW5 ... 71 B2
Perrers Rd W6 ... 112 B2
Perrin Cl TW15 ... 170 B5
Perrin Ct TW15 ... 170 C6
Perring Est E3 ... 97 C2
Perrin Grange HA9 ... 66 B6
Perrin Rd HA0 ... 65 B4
Perrins Ct HA3 ... 44 B2
Perrin's Ct 20 NW3 ... 70 A4
Perrin's La NW3 ... 70 A4
Perrin's Wlk NW3 ... 70 A4
Perronet Ho SE1 ... 261 D5
Perry Ave W3 ... 89 B1
Perry Cl UB8 ... 82 D1
Perry Ct
6 Isle of Dogs E14 ... 119 C1
2 Kingston u T KT2 ... 176 A1
Sutton SM1 ... 217 C3
2 Tottenham N15 ... 51 C3
Perryfield Way
Richmond TW10 ... 153 B2
West Hendon NW9 ... 45 D3
Perry Garth UB5 ... 84 C6
Perry Gdns N9 ... 17 C1
Perry Hall Prim Sch
BR6 ... 211 D3
Perry Hill SE6 ... 163 B1
Perry Ho 24 SW2 ... 160 A4
Perry How KT4 ... 199 D1
Perryman Ho
Barking IG11 ... 101 A6
Tottenham N17 ... 34 B3
Perrymans Farm Rd
IG2 ... 57 B4
Perry Mead Bushey WD23 . 8 A5
Perry Mead *continued*
Enfield EN2 ... 4 D3
Perrymead St
SW6 ... 135 D4 265 C1
Perrymount Prim Sch
SE23 ... 162 D2
Perryn Ct 1 TW1 ... 153 A4
Perryn Ho W3 ... 111 C6
Perryn Rd Acton W3 ... 111 B6
1 Bermondsey SE16 ... 118 B3
Perry Rise SE23 ... 163 A1
Perry's Pl W1 ... 239 C2
Perry St BR7 ... 189 C4
Perry Street Gdns
BR7 ... 189 C4
Perry Vale SE23 ... 162 D2
Perrywood Ho 17 E5 ... 74 B3
Persant Rd SE6 ... 164 C2
Perseverance Pl SW9 .. 138 C5
Perseverance Works 17
E2 ... 95 C4
Pershore Cl IG2 ... 56 D4
Pershore Gr SM5 ... 202 B3
Pershore Ho 11 W13 ... 109 A5
Pert Cl N10 ... 31 B4
Perth Ave Hayes UB4 ... 84 C3
Kingsbury NW9 ... 45 B2
Perth Cl Northolt UB5 ... 63 C3
Wimbledon SW20 ... 178 A1
Perth Ct 5 SE5 ... 139 B1
Perth Ho 12 Acton W3 ... 88 C1
Barnsbury N1 ... 72 B1
Perth Rd Barking IG11 ... 101 B6
Beckenham BR3 ... 186 A1
Finsbury Pk N4 ... 50 C1
Ilford IG2 ... 56 D3
Newham E13 ... 99 B5
Tottenham N22 ... 32 D2
Walthamstow E10 ... 53 B1
Perth Terr IG2 ... 57 A2
Perwell Ave HA2 ... 41 B1
Perystreete SE23 ... 162 C2
Petavel Rd TW11 ... 174 C4
Petchey Acad The E8 ... 73 D3
Peter Ave NW10 ... 68 B1
Peter Best Ho 1 E1 ... 96 B1
Peterboat Cl SE10 ... 120 C2
Peterborough Ct EC4 . 241 B1
Peterborough Gdns
IG1 ... 56 A2
Peterborough Mews
SW6 ... 135 C3
Peterborough Prim Sch
SW6 ... 135 C3
Peterborough Rd
Carshalton SM5 ... 202 C3
Fulham SW6 ... 135 C2
Harrow HA1 ... 42 D2
Leytonstone E10 ... 54 B3
Peterborough Villas
SW6 ... 265 C2
Peter Bradley Ct RM9 ... 81 B1
Peter Butler Ho 9
SE1 ... 118 A4
Peterchurch Ho SE15 .. 140 B6
Peter Fagan Ho UB3 ... 105 C3
Petergate SW11 ... 136 A1
Peterhead Ct 12 UB1 ... 86 A1
Peter Heathfield Ho 4
E15 ... 98 B6
Peter Hills Ho 6
SE16 ... 118 A2
Peter Hills with St Mary's
& St Paul's CE Prim Sch
SE16 ... 118 D5
Peter Ho SW8 ... 270 A4
Peter James Bsns Ctr
UB3 ... 106 A4
Peter James Ent Ctr
NW10 ... 89 A4
Peter Kennedy Ct CR0 .. 207 B3
Peterley Bsns Ctr 21
E2 ... 96 B5
Peter Lyell Ct HA4 ... 62 B6
Peters Cl Bexley DA16 ... 145 C3
Dagenham RM8 ... 58 D1
Stanmore HA7 ... 25 D4
Peters Ct 9 W2 ... 91 D1
Peter's Ct SW4 ... 160 A5
Petersfield Cl N18 ... 33 A5
Petersfield Rd W3 ... 111 A4
Petersfield Rise SW15 .. 156 B3
PETERSHAM ... 154 A3
Petersham Cl
Richmond TW10 ... 153 D2
Sutton SM1 ... 217 C3
Petersham Dr BR5 ... 190 A1
Petersham Gdns BR5 .. 189 D1
Petersham Ho SW7 ... 256 C4
Petersham La SW7 ... 256 A6
Petersham Mews
SW7 ... 114 A3 256 B5
Petersham Pl
SW7 ... 114 A3 256 B6
Petersham Rd TW10 ... 154 A3
Petersham Terr CR0 ... 220 A5
Peter's La EC1 ... 241 D4
Peter's Lo HA8 ... 26 B4
Peter's Path SE26 ... 184 B6
Peter St W1 ... 115 D6 249 C6
Peterstone Rd SE2 ... 124 B4
Peterstow Cl SW19 ... 157 A2
Peterwood Pk CR9 ... 220 B6
Peterwood Way CR0 ... 220 B6
Petherton Ct
Brondesbury Pk NW10 .. 90 D6
10 Harrow HA1 ... 42 D3
Petherton Ho N4 ... 51 A1
Petherton Rd N5 ... 73 A3
Petiver Cl 26 E9 ... 74 C1
Petley Rd W6 ... 134 D5
Peto Pl NW1 ... 238 D6
Peto St N E16 ... 98 D1
Petrel Ct 8 SE21 ... 161 B2
Petrie Cl NW2 ... 69 A2
Petrie Ho 3 SE18 ... 144 C6
Petrie Mus of Egyptian
Archaeology*
WC1 ... 93 D3 239 C5
Petros Gdns 1 NW3 ... 70 A2
Pettacre Cl SE28 ... 123 A3
Petticoat Lane Mkt*
EC2 ... 95 D2 243 C3
Petticoat Sq E1 ... 243 C2
Petticoat Twr E1 ... 243 C2
Pettit's Pl RM10 ... 81 C3
Pettit's Rd RM10 ... 81 C3
Pettiward Cl SW15 ... 134 C1
Pettman Cres SE18,
SE28 ... 123 B3
Pettsgrove Ave HA0 ... 65 C3
Pett's Hill UB5 ... 63 D3
Petts La TW17 ... 192 C5
Pett St SE7 ... 122 A2
PETTS WOOD ... 211 B5
Petts Wood Rd BR5 ... 211 B4
Petts Wood Sta BR5 ... 211 A4
Petty France
SW1 ... 115 D3 259 C6
Petty Wales EC3 ... 253 B5
Petworth Cl UB5 ... 63 B1
Petworth Gdns
Hillingdon UB10 ... 83 A6
West Barnes SW20 ... 200 B6
Petworth Ho 16 SE22 ... 139 C2
Petworth Rd
Bexley DA6 ... 169 C6
Colney Hatch N12 ... 30 C5
Petworth St
SW11 ... 136 C4 267 B2
Petyt Pl SW3 ... 136 C6 267 A5
Petyward SW3 .. 114 C2 257 B3
Pevensey Ave Enfield EN1 .. 5 C3
Friern Barnet N11 ... 31 D5
Pevensey Cl TW7 ... 130 A5
Pevensey Ct
4 South Acton W3 ... 110 D4
West Norwood SW16 ... 160 C1
10 Woodford E18 ... 37 A2
Pevensey Ho 5 E1 ... 97 A2
Pevensey Rd
Feltham TW13 ... 151 A3
Forest Gate E7 ... 77 A4
Upper Tooting SW17 ... 180 B6
Peverel E6 ... 100 C1
Peverel Ho RM10 ... 81 C6
Peverett Cl N11 ... 31 B5
Peveril Dr TW11 ... 174 B5
Peveril Ho SE1 ... 262 D5
Pewsey Cl E4 ... 35 C5
Pewsham Ho N4 ... 51 A1
Pewterers Ct N3 ... 29 B2
Peyton Ho N11 ... 31 A6
Peyton Pl SE10 ... 142 A5
Pharamond NW2 ... 68 D2
Pharaoh Cl CR4 ... 202 D2
Pheasant Cl E16 ... 99 B1
Phelps Ho SW15 ... 134 D2
Phelp St SE17 ... 139 B6
Phelps Way UB3 ... 105 D2
Phene St SW3 ... 136 C6 267 B6
Philadelphia Ct SW10 .. 266 B3
Philbeach Gdns
SW5 ... 113 C1 255 A2
Phil Brown Pl 3 SW8 .. 137 B2
Philchurch Pl 36 E1 ... 96 A1
Philia Ho 4 NW1 ... 71 C1
Philimore Cl SE18 ... 123 C1
Philip Blairman Ho E1 243 C5
Philip Ct Enfield EN2 ... 5 B4
Paddington W2 ... 236 C4
Philip Gdns CR0 ... 223 B6
Philip Ho
East Barnet N20 ... 14 D2
12 Paddington NW6 ... 91 D6
Philip La N15 ... 51 C6
Philipot Almshouse
SE9 ... 166 B5
Philipot Path SE9 ... 166 B5
Philippa Gdns SE9 ... 165 D6
Philips Cl CR4 ... 203 A1
Philip St E13 ... 99 A3
Philip Turner Est 28 E9 .. 74 C1
Philip Wlk SE15 ... 140 A2
Phillimore Ct W8 ... 245 B1
Phillimore Gardens Cl
W8 ... 113 C3 255 A6
Phillimore Gdns
Kensington
W8 ... 113 C4 245 A1
Willesden NW10 ... 90 C6
Phillimore Pl
W8 ... 113 C4 245 A1
Phillimore Terr W8 ... 255 B6
Phillimore Wlk
W8 ... 113 C3 255 B6
Phillip Ho E1 ... 243 D3
Phillipp St N1 ... 95 C6
Phillips Ct Edgware HA8 .. 26 C4
Hayes UB4 ... 84 B4
Phillipson Ho 6 N12 ... 29 D5
Philpot La EC3 ... 253 A6
Philpot Sq SW6 ... 135 D2
Philpot St E1 ... 96 B1
Philson Mans 13 E1 ... 96 B1
Phineas Pett Rd SE9 ... 144 A2
Phipp's Bridge Rd CR4,
SW19 ... 202 B6
Phipps Bridge Sta
CR4 ... 202 B6
Phipps Hatch La EN2 ... 5 A5
Phipps Ho
1 Greenwich SE7 ... 121 B1
16 Shepherd's Bush
W12 ... 112 B6
Phipp St EC2 ... 95 C3 243 A6
Phoebeth Rd SE4 ... 163 C6
Phoenix Bsns Ctr 22 E3 . 97 C2
Phoenix Cl
18 Shoreditch E8 ... 95 D6
Walthamstow E17 ... 35 B1
West Wickham BR4 ... 224 C6
Phoenix Ct
4 Brentford TW8 ... 110 A1
Chingford E4 ... 19 D1
Croydon SE25 ... 206 A4
2 Deptford SE14 ... 141 A6
Enfield EN3 ... 6 C5
Feltham TW13 ... 171 C6
Millwall E14 ... 119 C2
8 New Barnet EN5 ... 2 A1
Phoenix Ctr The 1
SM6 ... 220 A1
Phoenix Dr BR2 ... 225 D5
Phoenix High Sch
W12 ... 112 A6
Phoenix Ho
Chelsea SW1 ... 258 A4
Kingston u T KT3 ... 199 D6
Phoenix Ind Est HA1 ... 42 D5
Phoenix Lodge Mans 1
W6 ... 112 C2
Phoenix Pk NW2 ... 68 A6
Phoenix Pl WC1 . 94 B3 240 D6
Phoenix Rd
Penge SE20 ... 184 C4
Somers Town
NW1 ... 93 D4 232 C2
Phoenix Sch E3 ... 97 B4
Phoenix Sch The NW3 ... 70 A2
Phoenix St WC2 ... 239 D1
Phoenix Trad Est UB6 ... 87 D6
Phoenix Trad Pk TW8 .. 109 D1
Phoenix Way TW5 ... 128 D6
Phoenix Wharf Rd SE1 253 D1
Phyllis Ave KT3 ... 200 B4
Phyllis Ho CR0 ... 220 D4
Phyllis Hodges Ho
NW1 ... 93 D5 232 C3
Physic Pl SW3 .. 136 D6 267 C6
Picador Ho 1 RM10 ... 81 D2
Picardy Manorway
DA17 ... 125 D4
Picardy Rd DA17 ... 125 C2
Picardy St DA17 ... 125 C3
Piccadilly W1 .. 115 C5 249 A4
Piccadilly Arc SW1 ... 249 A4
Piccadilly Cir*
W1 ... 115 D6 249 C5
Piccadilly Circus Sta
SW1 ... 115 D6 249 C5
Piccadilly Ct 5 N7 ... 72 B2
Piccadilly Pl W1 ... 249 B5
Pickard Cl N14 ... 15 D3
Pickard St EC1 ... 234 D2
Pickering Ave E6 ... 100 C4
Pickering Cl E9 ... 74 D1
Pickering Ct N22 ... 32 D2
Pickering Gdns
Croydon SE25 ... 205 D3
Friern Barnet N11 ... 31 A4
Pickering Ho
Brentford W5 ... 109 C2
18 Kensington W2 ... 91 D1
Stoke Newington N4 ... 51 B2
4 Woolwich SE18 ... 122 C2
Pickering Mews 9 W2 .. 91 D1
Pickering Pl SW1 ... 249 B3
Pickering St N1 ... 234 D6
Pickets Cl WD23 ... 8 C3
Pickets St SW12 ... 159 B4
Pickett Croft HA7 ... 25 D2
Pickett's Lock La N9 ... 18 D2
Pickford Cl DA7 ... 147 A3
Pickford La DA7 ... 147 A3
Pickford Rd DA7 ... 147 A2
Pickfords Wharf N1 ... 235 A3
Pickhurst Gn BR2 ... 208 D2
Pickhurst Inf Sch BR2 .. 208 D3
Pickhurst Jun Sch
BR2 ... 208 D3
Pickhurst La BR2, BR3,
BR4 ... 208 C2
Pickhurst Mead BR2 ... 208 D2
Pickhurst Pk BR2 ... 208 D4
Pickhurst Rise BR4 ... 208 B1
Pickwick Cl TW4 ... 151 A6
Pickwick Ct SE9 ... 166 B3
Pickwick Ho
21 Bermondsey SE16 ... 118 A4
3 Shepherd's Bush
W11 ... 112 D5
Pickwick Mews N18 ... 33 C5
Pickwick Pl HA1 ... 42 C2
Pickwick Rd SE21 ... 161 C4
Pickwick St SE1 ... 252 A1
Pickwick Way BR7 ... 189 A4
Pickworth Cl SW8 ... 270 B3
Picton Ho 1 SW4 ... 160 A4
Picton Pl
Marylebone W1 ... 238 B1
Tolworth KT6 ... 198 C1
Picton St SE5 ... 139 B5
Picture Ho 6 SW16 ... 160 A2
Pied Bull Ct WC1 ... 240 B3
Pied Bull Yd WC1 ... 240 B3
Piedmont Rd SE18 ... 123 B1
Pield Heath Ave UB8 ... 82 C3
Pield Heath House Sch
UB8 ... 82 A3
Pield Heath Rd UB8 ... 82 B3
Pier Head E1 ... 118 B5
Pierhead Wharf 37 E1 .. 118 B5
Pier Ho SW3 ... 267 B5
Piermont Pl BR1 ... 188 A1
Piermont Rd SE22 ... 162 B6
Pier Par 3 E16 ... 122 C5
Pierpoint Bldg 4 E14 .. 119 C4
Pier Rd Feltham TW14 ... 150 B6
Newham E16 ... 122 C4
Pierrepoint SE25 ... 205 C6
Pierrepoint Rd W3 ... 110 D6
Pierrepoint Row N1 ... 234 C4
Pierson Ho 12 SE19 ... 183 C6
Pier St E14 ... 120 A2
Pier Terr SW18 ... 136 A1
Pier Way SE18 ... 123 B3
Pigeon Ct E4 ... 36 A4
Pigeon La TW12 ... 173 C6
Piggott Ho 2 E2 ... 96 D5
Pigott St E14 ... 97 C1
Pike Cl Bromley BR1 ... 187 B5
Hillingdon UB10 ... 82 B6
Pike Rd NW7 ... 27 B6
Pike's End HA5 ... 40 B5
Pikestone Cl UB4 ... 85 A3
Pikethorne 1 SE23 ... 162 D2
Pilgrimage St
SE1 ... 117 B4 252 C1
Pilgrim Cl SM4 ... 201 D2
Pilgrim Hill SE27 ... 183 A6
Pilgrim Ho SE1 ... 262 D5
Pilgrims Cl Northolt UB5 .. 64 A3
Palmers Green N13 ... 32 B6
Pilgrims Cloisters 10
SE5 ... 139 C5
Pilgrims Ct Enfield EN1 ... 5 B3
Greenwich SE3 ... 143 A4
Pilgrim's La NW3 ... 70 B4
Pilgrims Mews 12 E14 .. 120 B6
Pilgrim's Pl 6 NW3 ... 70 B4
Pilgrim's Rise EN4 ... 14 C6
Pilgrim St EC4 ... 241 C1
Pilgrims Way
5 Newham E6 ... 100 A6
Upper Holloway N19 ... 49 D1
Wembley HA9 ... 44 D1
Pilgrim's Way CR2 ... 221 D3
Pilgrims Way Prim Sch
SE15 ... 140 C6
Pilkington Ct 1 NW9 ... 46 A5
Pilkington Rd
Orpington BR6 ... 227 A6
4 Peckham SE15 ... 140 B3
Pillions La UB4 ... 83 B3
Pilot Ind Ctr NW10 ... 89 C3
Pilsden Cl SW19 ... 156 D3
Piltdown Rd WD19 ... 22 D6
Pilton Est The CR0 ... 220 D6
Pilton Pl SE17 ... 262 B2
Pimento Ct W5 ... 109 D3
Pimilico Sta
SW1 ... 115 D1 259 C2
PIMLICO ... 115 C1
Pimlico Rd
SW1 ... 115 A1 258 B2
Pimlico Sch
SW1 ... 115 C1 259 B1
Pimlico Wlk 1 N1 ... 95 C4
Pinchbeck Rd BR6 ... 227 D2
Pinchin St E1 ... 118 A6
Pincombe Ho SE17 ... 262 C2
Pincott Pl SE4 ... 140 D2
Pincott Rd
8 Bexley DA6 ... 147 C1
Merton SW19 ... 180 A2
Pindar St EC2 ... 95 C2 243 A4
Pindock Mews W9 ... 91 D3
Pine Apple Ct SW1 ... 259 A6
Pine Ave
Stratford New Town
E15 ... 76 B3
West Wickham BR4 ... 207 D1
Pine Cl
11 Dartmouth Pk N19 ... 71 C6
London E10 ... 75 D6
Osidge N14 ... 15 C4
3 Penge SE20 ... 184 C2
Stanmore HA7 ... 25 B6
Pine Coombe CR0 ... 222 D4
Pinecrest Gdns BR6 ... 226 D4
Pinecroft
East Wickham DA16 ... 146 A5
Harrow HA3 ... 44 B4
Pinecroft Cres EN5 ... 1 A1
Pine Ct UB5 ... 85 A4
Pinedene 2 SE15 ... 140 B4
Pinefield Cl E14 ... 119 C6
Pine Gdns Ruislip HA4 ... 62 B6
Surbiton KT5 ... 198 C3
Pine Glade BR6 ... 226 B4
Pine Gr
Finsbury Pk N4, N19 ... 72 B6
Totteridge N20 ... 13 C3
Wimbledon SW19 ... 179 B5
Pine Ho Bow E3 ... 97 A6
21 Rotherhithe SE16 ... 118 C4
Pinehurst
Chislehurst BR7 ... 188 D4
Stanmore HA7 ... 25 A5
Pinehurst Ct 6 W11 ... 91 B1
Pinehurst Wlk 4 BR6 .. 211 B1
Pinelands Cl 7 SE3 ... 142 D5
Pine Lo SW15 ... 157 A5
Pinemartin Cl NW2 ... 68 C5
Pine Pl UB4 ... 83 D3

Pine Rd
Brunswick Pk N11 . . . . 15 A2
Cricklewood NW2 . . . . 68 D4
Pine Ridge SM5 . . . . 219 A1
Pines Ct 14 SW19 . . . . . . 156 D3
Pines Rd BR1 . . . . 188 A1
Pine St EC1 . . . . . 94 C3 241 A6
Pines The
Southgate N14 . . . . 15 C6
South Norwood SE19 . . . 182 D4
Sunbury TW16 . . . . 194 A6
Surbiton KT6 . . . . 214 A5
Woodford IG8 . . . . 21 A1
Pine Tree Cl TW5 . . . . . . 128 B4
Pine Tree Ho SE14 . . . . . 140 D5
Pine Tree Ho BR2 . . . . . . 208 D5
Pine Trees Dr UB10 . . . . . 60 A4
Pineview Ct 5 E4 . . . . . . 20 A3
Pine Wlk KT5 . . . . 198 C3
Pinewood BR7 . . . . 188 C4
Pine Wood TW16 . . . . . . 172 A2
Pinewood Ave
Hillingdon UB8 . . . . 82 B1
Pinner HA5 . . . . 23 D4
Sidcup DA15 . . . . 167 C3
Pinewood Cl
Crofton BR6 . . . . 211 B1
Croydon CR0 . . . . 223 A5
Pinner HA5 . . . . 23 D4
South Oxhey HA6 . . . . 22 B5
Pinewood Ct
Clapham Pk SW4 . . . . 159 D5
Enfield EN2 . . . . 4 D2
Merton SW19 . . . . 179 D3
Pinewood Dr BR6 . . . . . . 227 C3
Pinewood Gr W5 . . . . 87 C1
Pinewood Lo WD23 . . . . . . 8 B3
Pinewood Pl KT19 . . . . . 215 B4
Pinewood Rd
Bromley BR2 . . . . 209 A5
Feltham TW13 . . . . 150 B1
West Heath SE2 . . . . 146 D6
Pinfold Rd SW16 . . . . . . 182 A6
Pinglestone Cl UB7 . . . . 126 A5
Pinkcoat Cl TW13 . . . . . 150 B1
Pinkerton Ct KT2 . . . . . 176 D1
Pinkerton Pl SW16 . . . . 181 D6
Pinkham Mans W4 . . . . 110 C1
Pinkham Way (North Circular Rd) N12 . . . . . 31 A4
Pinkwell Ave UB3 . . . . . 105 B2
Pinkwell La UB3 . . . . . . 105 B2
Pinkwell Prim Sch
UB3 . . . . 105 A2
Pinley Gdns RM9 . . . . . 102 B6
Pinnace Ho E14 . . . . 120 A3
Pinnacle Hill DA7 . . . . . 147 D1
Pinnacle Hill N DA7 . . . 147 D1
Pinnacle Ho EC3 . . . . . . 253 A5
Pinnacle The
Dagenham RM6 . . . . 59 A3
7 Kingsland N1 . . . . 73 B2
Pinnell Rd SE9 . . . . 143 D1
PINNER 41 A6
Pinner Ct
Paddington NW8 . . . . . . 236 C6
Pinner HA5 . . . . 41 C5
Pinner Gn HA5 . . . . 22 C1
Pinner Gr HA5 . . . . 41 A4
PINNER GREEN 22 C1
Pinner Hill HA5 . . . . 22 B3
Pinner Hill Rd HA5 . . . . . 22 C1
Pinner Ho
30 Camberwell SE5 . . . . 139 A3
Pinner HA5 . . . . 41 A6
Pinner Park Ave HA2 . . . . 24 A1
Pinner Park Fst & Mid Schs HA5 . . . . 41 D6
Pinner Park Gdns HA2 . . 24 A1
Pinner Rd
Harrow HA1, HA2 . . . . 42 A3
Northwood HA6 . . . . 22 A1
Pinner HA2, HA5 . . . . 41 C5
Pinner Sta HA5 . . . . 41 A5
Pinner View HA1, HA2 . . . 42 A4
PINNERWOOD PARK . . . 22 C3
Pinner Wood Sch HA5 . . 22 C2
Pinn Way HA4 . . . . 39 C2
Pintail Cl E6 . . . . 100 A2
Pintail Ct 39 SE8 . . . . . . 141 B6
Pintail Rd IG8 . . . . 37 B3
Pintail Way UB4 . . . . 84 D2
Pinter Ho 30 SW9 . . . . . 138 A3
Pinto Cl WD6 . . . . 11 B5
Pinto Way SE3 . . . . 143 B1
Pioneer Cl W12 . . . . 90 B1
Pioneers Ind Pk CR0 . . . 204 A1
Pioneer St SE15 . . . . 140 A4
Pioneer Way W12 . . . . 90 C1
Piper Cl N7 . . . . 72 B3
Piper Rd KT1 . . . . 198 C6
Pipers Gdns CR0 . . . . . . 207 A2
Pipers Gn NW9 . . . . 45 A4
Pipers Green La HA8 . . . . 10 A1
Pipers Ho SE10 . . . . 120 B1
Piper Way IG1 . . . . 57 B1
Pipewell Rd SM5 . . . . . . 202 C3
Pippenhall SE9 . . . . 166 D5
Pippin Cl Croydon CR0 . . 207 B1
Dollis Hill NW2 . . . . 68 B5
Pippin Ct 5 EN4 . . . . 2 C1
Pippin Ho 17 W10 . . . . . 112 D6
Pippins Ct TW15 . . . . . . 170 D4
Piquet Rd SE20 . . . . 184 C1
Pirbright Cres CR0 . . . . 224 A2
Pirbright Ho 11 KT2 . . . . 176 D4
Pirbright Rd SW18 . . . . . 157 C3
Pirie St 6 E16 . . . . 121 B5
Pitcairn Cl RM7 . . . . 59 C5
Pitcairn Ct CR4 . . . . 180 D3
Pitcairne Ct N21 . . . . 16 B6
Pitcairn Ho 1 E9 . . . . 74 C1
Pitcairn Rd CR4 . . . . 180 D3
Pitchford St E15 . . . . 76 C1
Pitfield Cres SE28 . . . . . 124 A5
Pitfield Ho N5 . . . . 73 A3
Pitfield St N1 . . . . 95 C5
Pitfield Way Enfield EN3 . . 6 C4
Tokyngton NW10 . . . . 67 A2
Pitfold Cl SE12 . . . . 165 B5
Pitfold Rd SE12 . . . . 165 A4
Pit Ho NW10 . . . . 67 B5
Pitlake CR0 . . . . 220 D6
Pitman Ho
Southgate N21 . . . . 16 B6
4 St Johns SE8 . . . . 141 C4
Pitman St SE5 . . . . 139 A5
Pitmaston Ho 2 SE13 . . 142 A3
Pitsea Pl E1 . . . . 96 D1
Pitsea St E1 . . . . 96 D1
Pitshanger Ct 2 W5 . . . . . 87 C3
Pitshanger La W5 . . . . . . 87 C3
Pitshanger Manor Mus & Art Gallery* W5 . . . . . 109 D5
Pitt Cres SW19 . . . . 179 D6
Pitt Ho 4 SW11 . . . . 136 B1
Pittman Gdns IG1 . . . . . . 79 A3
Pitt Rd Harrow HA2 . . . . . 64 A6
Orpington BR6 . . . . 227 A4
Thornton Heath CR0,
CR7 . . . . 205 A4
Pitt's Head Mews W1 . . 248 B3
Pittsmead Ave BR2 . . . . 209 A2
Pitt St W8 . . . . . 113 C4 245 B2
Pittville Gdns SE25 . . . . 206 A6
Pixfield Ct BR2 . . . . 186 D1
Pixham Ct 5 SW19 . . . . 179 B5
Pixley St E14 . . . . 97 B1
Pixton 14 NW9 . . . . 27 C2
Pixton Way CR2 . . . . 223 B1
Place Farm Ave BR5,
BR6 . . . . 211 B1
Plains The 7 E4 . . . . 20 C4
PLAISTOW BR1 . . . . 187 A4
E13 . . . . 99 B4
Plaistow Gr
Bromley BR1 . . . . 187 B3
West Ham E15 . . . . 98 D6
Plaistow Hospl E13 . . . . . 99 C5
Plaistow La BR1 . . . . 187 C2
Plaistow Park Rd E13 . . . 99 B5
Plaistow Prim Sch E13 . . 99 B5
Plaistow Rd E13, E15 . . . . 98 D5
Plaistow Sta E13 . . . . 98 D5
Plane St SE26 . . . . 162 B1
Plane Tree Cres TW13 . 150 B1
Planetree Ct W6 . . . . 112 D2
Plane Tree Ho
Deptford SE8 . . . . 141 A6
Greenwich SE7 . . . . 121 D1
Plane Tree Wlk 4
SE19 . . . . 183 C4
Plantagenet Cl KT19 . . . 215 B4
Plantagenet Gdns RM6 . . 58 D2
Plantagenet Ho SE18 . . . 122 B3
Plantagenet Pl RM6 . . . . . 58 D2
Plantagenet Rd EN5 . . . . . 2 A1
Plantain Gdns E11 . . . . . . 76 B5
Plantain Pl SE1 . . . . 252 C2
Plantation La EC3 . . . . . 253 A6
Plantation The SE3 . . . . 143 A3
Plasel Ct E13 . . . . 99 B6
PLASHET 78 A2
Plashet Gr E6 . . . . 77 D1
Plashet Rd E13 . . . . 77 B1
Plashet Sch E6 . . . . 78 A1
Plassy Rd SE6 . . . . 163 D4
Platehouse The 3
E14 . . . . 119 D1
Platina St EC2 . . . . 242 D6
Platinum Ct RM7 . . . . 59 D6
Plato Pl 1 SW6 . . . . 135 B3
Plato Rd SW2 . . . . 138 A1
Platt Halls (a) 35 NW9 . . . 27 D1
Platt Halls (b) 37 NW9 . . . 27 D1
Platt Halls (c) 38 NW9 . . . 27 D1
Platt's Eyot TW12 . . . . . 173 C1
Platt's La NW3 . . . . 69 C5
Platts Rd EN3 . . . . 6 C4
Platt St NW1 . . . . 232 C4
Plaxdale Ho SE17 . . . . . 263 A3
Plaxtol Cl BR1 . . . . 187 C2
Plaxtol Rd DA8 . . . . 147 C5
Plaxton Ct E11 . . . . 76 D5
Playfair St W6 . . . . 112 C1
Playfield Cres SE22 . . . . 161 D6
Playfield Rd HA8 . . . . 27 A1
Playford Rd
Finsbury Pk N4 . . . . 72 B6
Finsbury Pk N4 . . . . 72 C6
Playgreen Way SE6 . . . . 185 C6
Playground Cl BR3 . . . . 184 D1
Playhouse Yd EC4 . . . . . 241 C1
Plaza Bsns Ctr EN3 . . . . . . 7 B3
Plaza Hts E10 . . . . 76 A5
Plaza Sh Ctr W1 93 C1 239 B2
Plaza Wlk NW9 . . . . 45 A6
Pleasance Rd
Putney SW15 . . . . 156 B6
St Paul's Cray BR5 . . . . . 190 B1
Pleasance The SW15 . . . 134 B1
Pleasant Gr CR0 . . . . 223 B5
Pleasant Pl N1 . . . . 72 D1
Pleasant Row NW1 . . . . . 231 D5
Pleasant View BR6 . . . . . 227 A3
Pleasant View Pl BR6 . . 227 A3
Pleasant Way HA0 . . . . . . 87 C5
Pleasaunce Ct SE9 . . . . . 144 B1
Plender Ct NW1 . . . . 232 B5
Plender St NW1 . 93 C6 232 B5
Pleshey Rd N7 . . . . 71 D4
Plevna Cres N15 . . . . 51 C3
Plevna Ho 1 N9 . . . . 18 A1
Plevna Rd Edmonton N9 . . 18 B1
Hampton TW12 . . . . 173 D2
Plevna St E14 . . . . 120 A3
Pleydell Ave
Chiswick W6 . . . . 111 D2
Penge SE19 . . . . 183 D3
Pleydell Ct EC4 . . . . 241 B1
Pleydell Gdns SE19 . . . . 183 D4
Pleydell St EC4 . . . . 241 B1
Plimsoll Cl E14 . . . . 97 D1
Plimsoll Rd N4 . . . . 72 D5
Plough Ct EC3 . . . . 252 D6
Plough Farm Cl HA4 . . . . 39 B3
Plough La
Dulwich Village SE22 . . . 161 D5
7 Teddington TW11 . . . . 175 A5
Wallington CR0, SM6 . . . 220 A3
Wimbledon SW17,
SW19 . . . . 180 A6
Plough Lane Cl CR0,
SM6 . . . . 220 A3
Ploughmans Cl NW1 . . . 232 C6
Ploughmans End TW7 . . 152 B6
Plough Mews 19
SW11 . . . . 136 B1
Plough Pl EC4 . . . . 241 B2
Plough Rd
Battersea SW11 . . . . 136 B1
West Ewell KT19 . . . . 215 B1
Plough St 16 E1 . . . . 96 A1
Plough Terr SW11 . . . . . 136 B1
Plough Way SE16 . . . . . . 119 A2
Plough Yd EC2 . . . . 243 B5
Plover Ho 4 SW9 . . . . . . 138 C5
Plover Way Hayes UB4 . . . 84 D2
Rotherhithe SE16 . . . . . . 119 A3
Plowman Cl N18 . . . . 33 B5
Plowman Ho SW19 . . . . . 156 D2
Plowman Way RM8 . . . . . 58 C1
Plumbers Row E1 . . . . 96 A1
Plumbridge St 7
SE10 . . . . 142 A4
Plum Cl TW14 . . . . 150 A3
Plumcroft Prim Sch
SE18 . . . . 145 A6
Plume Ho SE10 . . . . 141 D6
Plum Garth TW8 . . . . 109 D2
Plum La SE18 . . . . 145 A5
Plummer Ct SE13 . . . . . . 163 D5
Plummer La CR4 . . . . 180 D1
Plummer Rd SW4 . . . . . . 159 D4
Plumpton Cl UB5 . . . . 63 C2
Plumpton Ct SE23 . . . . . 163 A4
Plumpton Lo E5 . . . . 74 D5
Plumpton Way SM5 . . . . 218 C5
PLUMSTEAD 123 C2
PLUMSTEAD COMMON
. . . . 145 D6
Plumstead Common Rd
SE18 . . . . 145 A6
Plumstead High St SE18,
SE2 . . . . 123 C2
Plumstead Manor/Negus Sch SE18 . . . . 145 B6
Plumstead Rd SE18,
SE28 . . . . 123 A2
Plumstead Road Covered Mkt SE18 . . . . 122 D2
Plumstead Sta SE18 . . . 123 B2
Plumtree Cl
Dagenham RM10 . . . . 81 D2
Wallington SM6 . . . . 219 D1
Plumtree Ct EC4 . . . . . . 241 C2
Plymen Ho KT8 . . . . 195 C4
Plymouth Ho
10 Barking IG11 . . . . 80 A1
20 Lewisham SE10 . . . . . 141 D4
Plymouth Rd
Bromley BR1 . . . . 187 B2
Newham E16 . . . . 99 A2
Plymouth Wharf E14 . . . 120 B2
Plympton Ave NW6 . . . . . 69 B1
Plympton Cl 8 DA17 . . . . 125 A3
Plympton Pl NW1 . . . . . . 237 A5
Plympton Rd NW6 . . . . . . 69 B1
Plympton St NW8 . . . . . . 237 A5
Plymstock Rd DA16 . . . . 146 C5
Pocklington Cl NW9 . . . . . 27 C1
Pocklington Ct SW15 . . . 156 A3
Pocklington Lo 6
W12 . . . . 112 A3
Pocock Ave UB7 . . . . 104 B3
Pocock St SE1 . 116 D4 251 D2
Podmore Rd SW18 . . . . . 136 A1
Poets Cnr* SW1 . . . . . . 260 A6
Poet's Rd N5 . . . . 73 B3
Poets Way HA1 . . . . 42 C5
Pointalls Cl N3 . . . . 30 A1
Point Cl SE10 . . . . 142 A4
Pointer Cl SE28 . . . . 102 D1
Pointer Sch The SE3 . . . 143 A5
Pointers Cl E14 . . . . 119 D1
Point Hill SE10 . . . . 142 A4
Point Ho SE10 . . . . 142 A4
Point Pl HA9 . . . . 66 D1
Point Pleasant SW18 . . . 135 C1
Point Terr E7 . . . . 77 B3
Point The HA4 . . . . 62 A4
Point Wharf La TW8 . . . 132 A5
Poland Ho 3 E15 . . . . 98 B6
Poland St W1 . . . 93 C1 239 B1
Polaris Ct EN4 . . . . 14 B6
Polebrook Rd SE3 . . . . . 143 C2
Polecroft La SE6 . . . . . . 163 B2
Polehamptons The
TW12 . . . . 174 A2
Pole Hill Rd
Chingford E4 . . . . 20 A4
Hillingdon UB4 . . . . 83 A4
Polesden Gdns SW20 . . . 178 B1
Polesworth Ho 16 W2 . . . 91 C2
Polesworth Rd RM9 . . . . . 80 D1
Polish Inst & Sikorski Mus* SW7 . . . . 246 D1
Polish Univ Abroad
W6 . . . . 112 A2
Polish War Meml HA4 . . . 62 C2
Pollard Cl Islington N7 . . . 72 B4
Newham E16 . . . . 121 A6
Pollard Ct SM4 . . . . 202 C4
Pollard Ho Cheam KT4 . . 216 C4
Islington N1 . . . . 233 C3
Pollard Rd
East Barnet N20 . . . . 14 C2
Morden SM4 . . . . 202 B4
Pollard Row E2 . . . . 96 A4
Pollards Cl IG10 . . . . 21 C6
Pollards Cres SW16 . . . . 204 A6
Pollards Hill E SW16 . . . 204 B6
Pollards Hill N SW16 . . . 204 B6
Pollards Hill S SW16 . . . 204 B6
Pollards Hill W SW16 . . 204 B6
Pollard St E2 . . . . 96 A4
Pollards Wood Rd
SW16 . . . . 204 A6
Pollard Wlk DA14 . . . . . . 190 C4
Pollen St W1 . . . . 238 D1
Pollitt Dr NW8 . . . 92 B3 236 D6
Pollock Ho W10 . . . . 91 A3
Polperro Cl BR6 . . . . 211 D3
Polperro Mans 3 NW6 . . 69 C3
Polperro Mews SE11 . . . 261 C4
Polsted Rd SE6 . . . . 163 B4
Polsten Mews 2 EN3 . . . . 7 C6
Polthorne Gr SE18 . . . . . 123 B2
Polworth Rd SW16 . . . . . 182 A5
Polygon Rd
NW1 . . . . 93 D5 232 C3
Polygon The
1 Clapham SW4 . . . . 137 C1
St John's Wood NW8 . . . 229 D6
Polytechnic St SE18 . . . 122 C2
Pomell Way E1 . . . . 243 D2
Pomeroy Cl TW1 . . . . 131 B1
Pomeroy Ct W11 . . . . 91 A1
Pomeroy Ho 5 E2 . . . . 96 D5
Pomeroy St SE14 . . . . . . 140 C4
Pomfret Rd SE5 . . . . 138 D2
Pomoja La N19 . . . . 72 A6
Pomona Ho 10 SE8 . . . . 119 A2
Pond Cl
Colney Hatch N12 . . . . . . 30 C4
Kidbrooke SE3 . . . . 143 A3
Pond Cottage La BR3,
BR4 . . . . 207 C1
Pond Cotts SE21 . . . . . . 161 C3
PONDERS END 18 D6
Ponders End Ind Est
EN3 . . . . 19 A6
Ponders End Sta EN3 . . . 19 A6
Ponder St 5 N7 . . . . 72 B1
Pond Farm Est E5 . . . . . . 74 C5
Pondfield End IG10 . . . . . 21 C4
Pondfield Ho
4 Islington N5 . . . . 73 A3
West Norwood SE27 . . . 183 A5
Pondfield Rd
Dagenham RM10 . . . . 81 D3
Locksbottom BR6 . . . . . . 226 D5
West Wickham BR2 . . . . 208 C1
Pond Gn HA4 . . . . 61 C6
Pond Hill Gdns SM3 . . . . 217 A2
Pond Ho Chelsea SW3 . . 257 A3
Stanmore HA7 . . . . 25 B4
Pond Mead SE21 . . . . 161 B5
Pond Path BR7 . . . . 188 D4
Pond Pl SW3 . . . 114 C2 257 A3
Pond Rd
Blackheath Vale SE3 . . . 142 D3
Newham E15 . . . . 98 C5
Pondside Cl UB3 . . . . . . 127 B6
Pond Sq N6 . . . . 49 A1
Pond St NW3 . . . . 70 C3
Pond Way TW11 . . . . 175 C4
Pondwood Rise BR6 . . . 211 C2
Ponler St E1 . . . . 96 B1
Ponsard Rd NW10 . . . . . . 90 B4
Ponsford St E9 . . . . 74 C2
Ponsonby Ho 13 E2 . . . . . 96 C5
Ponsonby Pl
SW1 . . . . 115 D1 259 D2
Ponsonby Rd SW15 . . . . 156 B4
Ponsonby Terr SW1 . . . . 259 D2
Pontefract Ct UB5 . . . . . . 63 D3
Pontefract Rd BR1 . . . . . 186 D5
Ponton Ho SW2 . . . . 160 C3
Ponton Rd
SW8 . . . . 137 D6 269 D5
Pontoon Dock Sta
E16 . . . . 121 C5
Pont St Mews SW1 . . . . 257 C5
Pont St SW1 . . . 114 D3 257 D5
Pontypool Pl SE1 . . . . . 251 C2
Pool Cl Beckenham BR3 . . 185 C5
East Molesey KT8 . . . . . . 195 B4
Pool Ct SE6 . . . . 163 C2
Poole Cl HA4 . . . . 61 C6
Poole Court Rd TW5 . . . 129 A3
Poole Ct
De Beauvoir Town N1 . . . . 73 C1
Hounslow TW5 . . . . 129 A3
Poole Ho SE11 . . . . 260 D5
Pool End Cl TW17 . . . . . 192 C4
Poole Rd Homerton E9 . . . 74 D2
Poole Rd *continued*
West Ewell KT19 . . . . 215 B2
Pooles Bldgs EC1 . . . . . 241 A5
Pooles Ct IG3 . . . . 80 A5
Pooles La SW10 . . . . 266 A3
Pooles Park Prim Sch
N4 . . . . 72 B6
Pooles Pk N4 . . . . 72 C6
Poole St N1 . . . . . 95 B6 235 C5
Poole Way UB4 . . . . 83 C4
Pooley Ho E1 . . . . 96 D4
Pool Ho NW8 . . . . 236 D4
Poolmans St SE16 . . . . . 118 D4
Pool Rd
East Molesey KT12,
KT8 . . . . 195 B4
Harrow HA1 . . . . 42 B2
Poolsford Rd NW9 . . . . . . 45 C5
Poonah St E1 . . . . 96 C1
Pope Cl
East Bedfont TW14 . . . . . 149 D3
Mitcham SW17, SW19 . . . 180 B4
Pope Ct 10 KT2 . . . . 175 D6
Pope Ho
7 Bermondsey SE16 . . . 118 B2
3 Camberwell SE5 . . . . . 139 B5
Pope John RC Prim Sch
W12 . . . . 112 B6
Pope Rd BR2 . . . . 209 D4
Pope's Ave TW2 . . . . 152 C2
Popes Ct TW2 . . . . 152 C2
Popes Dr N3 . . . . 29 C2
Popes Gr CR0 . . . . 223 B5
Pope's Gr TW1, TW2 . . . . 152 D2
Pope's Head Alley EC3 . 242 D1
Pope's La W5 . . . . 110 A3
Pope's Rd SW9 . . . . 138 C2
Pope St SE1 . . . . 253 B1
Pope Street Ct SE9 . . . . 166 B3
Popham Cl TW13 . . . . . . 151 B1
Popham Ct N16 . . . . 73 C5
Popham Gdns TW9 . . . . 132 D2
Popham Rd N1 . . 95 A6 235 A6
Popham St Islington N1 . 234 D6
Shoreditch N1 . . . 95 A6 235 A6
Pop In Bsns Ctr HA9 . . . . 66 D3
POPLAR 97 C1
Poplar Ave
Mitcham CR4 . . . . 180 D2
Orpington BR6 . . . . 226 D6
Southall UB2 . . . . 107 D3
Yiewsley UB7 . . . . 104 B6
Poplar Bath St 11 E14 . . 119 D6
Poplar Bsns Pk E14 . . . . 120 A6
Poplar Cl Hackney E9 . . . . 75 B3
Pinner HA5 . . . . 22 D2
Poplar Cres KT19 . . . . . . 215 A2
Poplar Ct Chingford E4 . . . 35 D4
Northolt UB5 . . . . 84 C5
4 Streatham SW16 . . . . . 160 B1
13 Twickenham TW1 . . . . 153 C5
Wimbledon SW19 . . . . . . 179 C5
Poplar Farm Cl KT19 . . . 215 A2
Poplar Gdns KT3 . . . . . . 177 B1
Poplar Gr
Friern Barnet N11 . . . . 31 A4
Hammersmith W6 . . . . . . 112 C4
Kingston u T KT3 . . . . 199 B6
Wembley HA9 . . . . 67 A5
Poplar High St E14 . . . . 119 D6
Poplar Ho Brockley SE4 . . 141 B1
19 Rotherhithe SE16 . . . 118 D4
Poplar Mews 4 W12 . . . 112 C5
Poplar Mount DA17 . . . . 125 D2
Poplar Pl Hayes UB3 . . . . 106 A6
Kensington
W2 . . . . 113 D6 245 D6
Woolwich SE28 . . . . 124 C6
Poplar Prim Sch
SW19 . . . . 201 C6
Poplar Rd
Ashford TW15 . . . . 171 A5
Cheam SM3 . . . . 201 B1
Herne Hill SE24 . . . . 139 A1
Merton SW19 . . . . 179 C1
Poplar Rd S SW19 . . . . . 201 C6
Poplars Cl HA4 . . . . 39 C1
Poplars Ho 14 E17 . . . . . . 53 D6
Poplars Rd E17 . . . . 53 D3
Poplar Sta E14 . . . . 119 D6
Poplars The
East Barnet N14 . . . . 15 B6
Kentish Town NW5 . . . . . . 71 C3
Poplar View HA9 . . . . 65 D6
Poplar Way
Feltham TW13 . . . . 150 B1
Ilford IG6 . . . . 57 A5
Poplar Wlk
Croydon CR0 . . . . 205 A1
Herne Hill SE24 . . . . 139 A1
Poppins Ct EC4 . . . . 241 C1
Poppleton Rd E11 . . . . . . 54 C3
Poppy Cl
Belvedere DA17 . . . . 125 D4
Hackbridge SM6 . . . . 203 A1
Northolt UB5 . . . . 63 B2
Poppy Ct HA3 . . . . 42 C6
Poppy La CR0 . . . . 206 C1
Porchester Ct W2 . . . . 91 D1
Porchester Gate W2 . . . 246 A5
Porchester Gdn Mews
W2 . . . . 91 D1
Porchester Gdns
W2 . . . . 113 D6 245 D6
Porchester Ho 3 E1 . . . . 96 B1
Porchester Mead BR3 . . 185 D4
Porchester Mews W2 . . . 91 D1
Porchester Pl W2 . . . . . 237 B1
Porchester Rd
Kensington W2 . . . . 91 D1
Porchester Rd *continued*
Kingston u T KT1 . . . . 176 D1
Porchester Sq W2 . . . . . . 91 D1
Porchester Terr
W2 . . . . 114 A6 246 A6
Porchester Terr N W2 . . . 91 D1
Porch Way N20 . . . . 14 D1
Porcupine Cl SE9 . . . . . . 166 A2
Porden Rd SW2 . . . . 138 B1
Porland Ct SE1 . . . . 262 C6
Porlock Ave HA1, HA2 . . . 42 A1
Porlock Ho 5 SE26 . . . . 162 A1
Porlock Rd EN1 . . . . 17 D4
Porlock St SE1 . 117 B4 252 D2
Porrington Cl BR7 . . . . . 188 C2
Porson Ct SE13 . . . . 141 D2
Portal Cl Hillingdon UB10 . 60 B1
Ruislip HA4 . . . . 62 B4
West Norwood SE27 . . . . 160 C1
Portal Way W3 . . . . 89 B2
Portbury Cl 17 SE15 . . . . 140 A4
Portchester Cl SE24 . . . . 139 B1
Port Cres E13 . . . . 99 B3
Portcullis Lodge Rd EN1 . 5 B2
Porte 10 NW9 . . . . 27 D2
Portelet Ct 1 N1 . . . . 95 C6
Portelet Rd E1 . . . . 96 D4
Porten Hos W14 . . . . 254 A5
Porten Rd W14 . . . . 254 A5
Porter Rd E6 . . . . 100 B1
Porters Ave RM8, RM9 . . . 80 C3
Porter Sq N19 . . . . 50 A1
Porter St
Borough The
SE1 . . . . 117 A5 252 B4
Marylebone W1 . . . . 237 D4
Porters & Walters Almshouses N22 . . . . . . 32 B3
Porters Way UB7 . . . . . . 104 B4
Porteus Rd W2 . . . . 236 B4
Portfleet Pl 34 N1 . . . . 95 C6
Portgate Cl W9 . . . . 91 B3
Porthallow Cl BR6 . . . . . 227 D4
Porthcawe Rd SE26 . . . . 185 B6
Porthkerry Ave DA16 . . . 146 A1
Port Ho 6 SW11 . . . . 136 A2
Port House The 6
E14 . . . . 119 D1
Portia Ct 12 IG11 . . . . 80 A1
Portia Way E3 . . . . 97 B3
Porticos The SW3 . . . . . 266 C5
Portinscale Rd SW15 . . . 157 B6
Portishead Ho 29 W2 . . . . 91 C2
Portland Ave
Blackfen DA15 . . . . 168 A5
New Malden KT3 . . . . 199 D2
Stamford Hill N16 . . . . 51 D2
Portland Cl
Dagenham RM6 . . . . 59 A4
New Malden KT4 . . . . 200 B2
Portland Commercial Est
IG11 . . . . 102 C5
Portland Cotts
Feltham TW13 . . . . 173 A5
Wallington CR0 . . . . 203 D2
Portland Cres
1 Chislehurst SE9 . . . . . 166 A2
Feltham TW13 . . . . 171 B6
Southall UB6 . . . . 86 A2
Stanmore HA7 . . . . 25 D1
Portland Cres W HA7 . . . 43 D6
Portland Ct
7 De Beauvoir Town
N1 . . . . 73 C1
1 Deptford SE14 . . . . 141 A6
1 Sutton SM2 . . . . 217 D2
Portland Dr EN2 . . . . 5 C5
Portland Gdns
Harringay N4 . . . . 50 D3
Ilford RM6 . . . . 58 D4
Portland Gr
SW8 . . . . 138 B4 270 C2
Portland Ho 19 SW2 . . . . 160 C3
Portland Hospl for Women & Children The W1 . . 238 D5
Portland Mans SE25 . . . 206 B4
Portland Mews W1 . . . . 239 B1
Portland Pl
Croydon SE25 . . . . 206 A5
Marylebone W1 . . 93 B2 238 D3
Portland Place Sch
W1 . . . . 93 B2 238 D3
Portland Place Schs
W1 . . . . 93 B2 238 D4
Portland Rd
Ashford TW15 . . . . 148 A1
Bromley BR1 . . . . 187 C5
Chislehurst SE9 . . . . 166 A2
Croydon SE25 . . . . 206 B4
Hayes UB4 . . . . 83 C4
Kingston u T KT1 . . . . 198 B6
Mitcham CR4 . . . . 180 C1
Notting Hill
W11 . . . . 113 A5 244 B4
Notting Hill
W11 . . . . 113 A6 244 A5
Southall UB2 . . . . 107 B3
Tottenham N15 . . . . 51 D5
Portland Rise N4 . . . . 51 A1
Portland Sq 4 E1 . . . . . 118 B5
Portland St
SE17 . . . . 117 B1 262 C1
Portland Terr
Edgware HA8 . . . . 26 C3
Richmond TW9 . . . . 131 D1
Portland Village W6 . . . 112 C3
Portman Ave SW14 . . . . 133 B2
Portman Cl Bexley DA7 . . 147 A2
Marylebone W1 . . 93 A1 238 A2
Portman Dr IG8 . . . . 37 D1

Portman Gate NW1 237 B5
Portman Gdns
Hendon NW9 27 B1
Hillingdon UB10 60 C1
Portman Hall HA3 24 B5
Portman Hts 1 NW3 69 C5
Portman Lo N21 16 D6
Portman Mews S W1 238 A1
Portman Pl E2 96 C4
Portman Rd KT1 176 B1
Portman Sq W1 93 A1 238 A2
Portman St W1 93 A1 238 A1
Portman The NW11 47 C2
Portman Twrs W1 237 D2
Portmeadow Wlk SE2 124 D4
Portmeers Cl E17 53 C3
Portnall Rd W9 91 B4
Portobello Ct Est W11 91 B1
Portobello Ho 6 SW27 182 D5
Portobello Mews W11 245 A5
Portobello Rd W11 113 B6 244 D6
Portobello Road Mkt* W10 91 A2
Porton Ct KT6 197 C3
Portpool La EC1 94 C2 241 A4
Portree Cl N22 32 B3
Portree St E14 98 B1
Port Royal Pl 3 N16 73 C3
Portrush Ct 9 UB1 86 A1
Portsdown HA8 26 C5
Portsdown Ave NW11 47 B3
Portsdown Mews NW11 47 B3
Portsea Hall W2 237 B1
Portsea Ho 3 SW15 156 B3
Portsea Mews W2 237 B1
Portsea Pl W2 237 B1
Portslade Rd SW8 137 C3
Portsmouth Ave KT7 197 A2
Portsmouth Rd
Esher KT10 212 A5
Putney SW15 156 C4
Thames Ditton KT6, KT7 197 C3
Portsmouth St WC2 240 D1
Portsoken St E1, EC3 253 C6
Portswood Pl SW15 155 D5
Portugal Gdns TW2 152 A2
Portugal St WC2 94 B1 240 D1
Portway E15 98 D6
Portway Gdns SE18 143 D5
Portway Prim Sch E13 98 D6
Poseidon Ct
Dagenham IG11 102 B4
9 Millwall E14 119 C2
Postern Gn EN2 4 C2
Postern The EC2 242 B3
Post La TW2 152 B3
Postmasters Lodge HA5 41 A2
Postmill Cl CR0 222 D5
Post Office App E7 77 B3
Post Office Way SW8 137 D5 269 C4
Post Rd UB2 107 D3
Postway Mews 1 IG1 78 D5
Potier St SE1 262 D5
Potter Cl CR4 181 B1
Potteries The EN5 13 C6
Potterill Ct TW11 175 B3
Potterne Cl 5 SW19 156 D4
Potters Cl
5 Camberwell SE15 139 C5
Croydon CR0 207 A1
Pottersfield EN1 5 C1
Potters Fields SE1 117 C5 253 B3
Potters Gr KT3 199 A5
Potters Heights Cl HA5 22 B3
Potter's La Barnet EN5 1 C1
Streatham SW16 181 D4
Potters Lo E14 120 A1
Potters Mews 4 WD6 9 D5
Potters Rd SW6 136 A3
Potter's Rd EN5 1 D1
Potter St HA5 22 B2
Potter Street Hill HA5 22 B3
Pottery La W11 113 A5 244 B4
Pottery Rd TW8 132 A6
Pottery St SE16 118 B4
Pott St E2 96 B4
Poulett Gdns TW1 153 A3
Poulett Rd E6 100 B5
Poullett Ho SW2 160 D3
Poulters Wood BR2 225 D3
Poulton Ave SM1 218 B5
Poulton Cl E8 74 B2
Poultry EC2 95 B1 242 C1
Pound Cl
Long Ditton KT6 197 C1
Orpington BR6 227 B6
Pound Court Dr BR6 227 B6
Pound Farm Cl KT10 196 B1
Pound Green Ct 4 DA5 169 C4
Pound La NW10 68 A2
Pound Park Rd SE7 121 D2
Pound Pl SE9 166 C5
Pound St SM5 218 D3
Pountney Rd SW11 137 A2
Poverest Rd BR5 211 D4
Povey Ho
Tulse Hill SW2 160 C5
Walworth SE17 263 A3
Powder Mill La TW2, TW4 151 C3
Powell Cl
Chessington KT9 213 D3
Edgware HA8 26 B4
Wallington SM6 220 A1
Powell Ct Croydon CR2 221 A4
19 Walthamstow E17 53 D6
Powell Gdns RM10 81 C4
Powell Ho 10 SW19 179 A4
Powell Rd
Buckhurst Hill IG9 21 C4
Hackney E5 74 B5
Powell's Wlk W4 133 D6
Powell Terr CR4 204 A5
Powergate Bsns Pk NW10 89 B4
Power Ho 13 TW9 132 C4
Power Ho The W4 111 D2
Power Rd W4 110 C2
Powerscroft Rd
Lower Clapton E5 74 C4
Sidcup DA14 190 C4
Powers Ct TW1 153 D4
Powis Ct Bushey WD23 8 B3
Edgware HA8 26 B6
Powis Gdns
Golders Green NW11 47 B2
Notting Hill W11 91 B1
Powis Ho WC2 240 B2
Powis Mews W11 91 B1
Powis Pl WC1 94 A3 240 B5
Powis Rd E3 97 D4
Powis Sq W11 91 B1
Powis St SE18 122 D2
Powis Terr W11 91 B1
Powlesland Ct 21 E14 97 A1
Powle Terr IG1 79 B3
Powlett Ho NW1 71 B2
Powlett Pl NW1 71 B1
Pownall Gdns TW3 129 D1
Pownall Rd Hackney E8 96 A6
Hounslow TW3 129 D1
Pownsett Terr IG1 79 A3
Powrie Ho 4 SW11 136 B3
Powster Rd BR1 187 B5
Powys Cl DA7 146 D6
Powys Ct N11 32 A5
Powys La Bowes Pk N13 32 A5
Palmers Green N14 32 A6
Poynder Ct 3 N7 72 A3
Poynder Lo TW7 131 A4
Poynders Ct 9 SW4 159 C5
Poynders Gdns SW12 159 C4
Poynders Rd SW12, SW4 159 D4
Poynings Rd N19 71 C5
Poynings Way N12 29 C5
Poyntell Cres BR7 189 B2
Poynter Ct 11 UB5 84 D5
Poynter Ho
Paddington NW8 236 C6
10 Shepherd's Bush W11 112 D5
Poynter Rd EN1 18 A6
Poynton Rd N17 34 A1
Poyntz Rd SW11 136 D3
Poyser St E2 96 B5
Praed Mews W2 236 D2
Praed St W2 92 B1 236 D2
Pragel St E13 99 C5
Pragnell Rd SE12 165 B2
Prague Pl SW2 160 A6
Prah Rd N4 72 C6
Prairie St SW8 137 B3
Pratt Mews NW1 232 A5
Pratt St NW1 93 C6 232 A6
Pratt Wlk SE1, SE11 116 B2 260 D4
Prayle Gr NW2 46 D1
Preachers Ct EC1 241 D5
Prebend Gdns W4, W6 111 D2
Prebend Mans 4 W4 111 D2
Prebend St N1 95 A6 235 A6
Precinct Rd UB3 106 A6
Precincts The SM4 201 C3
Precinct The
Islington N1 235 A5
Islington N5 72 D3
Premier Corner NW6 91 B5
Premier Ct EN3 6 D5
Premier Ho 25 N1 72 D1
Premier League Hall of Fame* SE1 250 C2
Premier Lo N3 29 C2
Premier Park Rd NW10 88 D5
Premier Pk NW10 88 D5
Premier Pl 17 E14 119 C6
Prendergast Ho 7 SW4 159 D4
Prendergast Rd SE3 142 C2
Prendergast Sch SE4 141 C1
Prentice Ct 2 SW19 179 B5
Prentis Rd SW16 181 D6
Prentiss Ct SE7 121 D2
Presburg Rd KT3 199 C4
Prescelly Pl HA8 26 B2
Prescot St E1 117 D6 253 D6
Prescott Ave BR5 210 D3
Prescott Ho
Croydon CR0 220 C5
13 Kennington SE17 138 D6
Prescott Pl
Clapham SW4 137 D1
Streatham SW16 182 A3
Presentation Mews SW2 160 B3
Preshaw Cres CR4 202 C6
President Dr E1 118 B5
President Ho EC1 234 D1
President St EC1 235 A2
Prespa Cl N9 18 C2
Press Ho NW10 67 B5
Press Rd NW10 67 B5
Prestage Way 18 E14 120 A6
Prestbury Rd E7 77 C1
Prestbury Sq SE9 188 B6
Prested Rd SW11 136 C1
PRESTON 44 A1
Preston Ave E4 36 B4
Preston Cl
Twickenham TW2 152 C1
Walworth SE1 263 A4
Preston Ct
5 New Barnet EN5 2 A1
Northwood Hills HA6 22 A1
Sidcup DA14 189 D6
Walton-on-T KT12 194 C1
Preston Dr Bexley DA7 146 D4
Wanstead E11 55 C4
West Ewell KT19 215 D2
Preston Gdns Enfield EN3 7 A6
Redbridge IG1 56 A3
Willesden NW10 67 C2
Preston Hill HA3 44 B3
Preston Ho
Bermondsey SE1 263 C6
3 Dagenham RM10 81 C5
Walworth SE1 263 A4
1 Woolwich SE18 122 C2
Preston Manor High Sch HA9 66 B6
Preston Park Prim Sch HA9 43 D1
Preston Pl
Richmond TW10 154 A6
Willesden NW2 68 A2
Preston Rd
Leytonstone E11 54 C3
Littleton TW17 192 C4
South Norwood SE19 182 D4
Wembley HA3, HA9 66 A6
Wimbledon SW20 177 D3
Preston Road Sta HA3 44 A1
Prestons Rd BR2 225 A6
Preston's Rd E14 120 A5
Preston Waye HA3 44 A1
Prestwich Terr SW4 159 D6
Prestwick Cl UB2 107 A1
Prestwick Ct
Southall UB1 108 A6
Tottenham N17 34 A3
Prestwick Rd WD19 22 D6
Prestwood Ave HA3 43 B5
Prestwood Cl
East Wickham SE18 146 A6
Harrow HA3 43 B5
Prestwood Gdns CR0 205 A2
Prestwood Ho 3 SE16 118 B3
Prestwood St N1 235 B3
Pretoria Ave E17 53 A5
Pretoria Cres E4 20 A3
Pretoria Ho 3 HA4 40 C1
Pretoria Rd Chingford E4 20 B3
Ilford IG1 78 D3
Leytonstone E11 54 B1
Newham E16 98 D3
Streatham SW16 181 C5
Tottenham N17 33 D4
Pretoria Rd N N18 33 D4
Pretty Cnr HA6 22 A5
Prevost Rd N11 15 A2
Priam Ho 17 E2 96 B5
Price Cl Finchley NW7 29 A4
Upper Tooting SW17 158 D1
Price Ct HA1 43 A4
Price Ho N1 235 A5
Price Rd CR0 220 D3
Prices Ct SW11 136 B2
Price's St SE1 251 D4
Price's Yd N1 233 D5
Price Way TW12 173 A4
Prichard Ct
Battersea SW11 266 D1
Islington N7 72 B3
Pricklers Hill EN5 13 D5
Prickley Wood BR2 208 D1
Priddy's Yd 4 CR0 221 A6
Prideaux Ho WC1 233 D2
Prideaux Pl Acton W3 111 B6
St Pancras WC1 94 B4 233 D2
Prideaux Rd SW9 138 A2
Pride Ct N1 234 B4
Pridham Rd CR7 205 B5
Priestfield Rd SE23 163 A1
Priestlands Park Rd DA15 167 D1
Priestley Cl N16 51 D2
Priestley Gdns RM6 58 B3
Priestley Ho
2 Camden Town NW5 71 B2
St Luke's EC1 242 B6
3 Wembley HA9 67 A5
Priestley Rd CR4 181 A1
Priestley Way
Hendon NW2 46 A1
Walthamstow E17 52 D6
Priestman Point 25 E3 97 D4
Priestmead Fst & Mid Schs HA3 43 B6
Priest Park Ave HA2 63 C6
Priests Bridge SW14 133 C2
Priest's Ct EC2 242 A2
Prima Rd SW9 138 C5
Primrose Ave Enfield EN2 5 C4
Ilford RM6 58 B2
Primrose Cl 6 Bow E3 97 C5
Catford SE6 186 A5
Finchley N3 29 D1
Hackbridge SM6 203 B1
Primrose Cl *continued*
Harrow HA2 63 B5
Primrose Ct
2 Child's Hill NW2 69 B5
New Malden KT4 200 A2
Primrose Hill NW8 230 C5
11 Streatham SW12 159 D4
Primrose Gdns
Hampstead NW3 70 C2
Ruislip HA4 62 C3
PRIMROSE HILL 70 D1
Primrose Hill EC4 241 B1
Primrose Hill Ct NW3 70 D1
Primrose Hill Rd
Primrose Hill NW1, NW3 70 D1
Primrose Hill NW1, NW3 230 C6
Primrose Hill Sch NW1 93 A6 231 B6
Primrose Hill Studios NW1 231 A6
Primrose Ho
7 Peckham SE15 140 A4
1 Richmond TW9 132 B4
Primrose La CR0 206 D1
Primrose Mans SW11 268 A2
Primrose Mews 9 NW1 70 D1
Primrose Pl TW7 130 D3
Primrose Rd
Walthamstow E10 53 D1
Woodford E18 37 B1
Primrose Sq E9 96 C6
Primrose St EC2 95 C2 243 B4
Primrose Way HA0 87 D5
Primrose Wlk
Ewell KT17 215 D1
6 New Cross Gate SE14 141 A5
Primula St W12 90 A1
Prince Albert Ct
Primrose Hill NW8 230 C5
Sunbury TW16 171 C3
Prince Albert Rd NW8 92 D6 230 C5
Prince Arthur Ct 18 NW3 70 A4
Prince Arthur Mews 17 NW3 70 A4
Prince Arthur Rd NW3 70 A3
Prince Charles Dr NW2 46 C2
Prince Charles Rd SE3 142 D4
Prince Charles Way SM6 219 B5
Prince Consort Dr BR7 189 B2
Prince Consort Ho SE1 260 B2
Prince Consort Rd SW7 114 B3 256 C6
Princedale Rd W11 113 A5 244 B4
Prince Edward Mans W2 245 B6
Prince Edward Rd E9 75 B2
Prince George Ave N14 15 D6
Prince George Rd N16 73 C4
Prince George's Ave SW20 178 C1
Prince Georges Rd SW19 180 B2
Prince Henry Rd SE7 143 D5
Prince Imperial Rd
Chislehurst BR7 188 D3
Kidbrooke SE18 144 B4
Prince John Rd SE9 166 A6
Princelet St E1 95 D2 243 D4
Prince of Orange La 3 SE10 142 A5
Prince Of Wales Cl NW4 46 B5
Prince of Wales Dr SW11 137 A4 268 A2
Prince of Wales Mans
Battersea SW11 268 B2
Clapham SW4 159 B6
Prince of Wales Pas NW1 232 A1
Prince of Wales Prim Sch EN3 7 B6
Prince of Wales Rd
Blackheath Vale SE3 142 D4
Camden Town NW5 71 A2
Newham E16 99 C1
Prince Of Wales' Rd SM1 218 B6
Prince Of Wales Terr
Chiswick W4 111 C1
Kensington W8 245 D1
Prince Rd SE25 205 C4
Prince Regent E16 99 C2
Prince Regent Ct 2 SE16 119 A5
Prince Regent La E13 99 C3
Prince Regent Mews NW1 232 A1
Prince Regent Rd TW3 130 A2
Prince Regent Sta E16 121 C6
Prince Rupert Rd SE9 144 B1
Princes Arc SW1 249 B4
Princes Ave Acton W3 110 C3
Edmonton N13 32 C5
Finchley N3 29 D2
Muswell Hill N10 49 B6
Orpington BR5 211 C4
Princes Ave *continued*
Queensbury NW9 44 D5
Tolworth KT6 214 C6
Wallington SM5 218 D1
Woodford IG8 37 C6
Wood Green N22 31 D2
Prince's Ave UB1 85 D1
Princes Cir WC2 94 A1 240 A2
Princes Cl Edgware HA8 26 C5
Finsbury Pk N4 50 D1
Queensbury NW9 44 C5
Sidcup DA14 168 D1
Prince's Cl TW11, TW12 174 B6
Princes Coll WC1 240 A2
Princes Court Bsns Ctr 14 E1 118 B6
Princes Ct
Brondesbury NW2 69 A3
Hampstead NW3 70 B4
Kingston u T KT3 199 D6
Stepney E1 118 B6
Wembley HA9 66 A3
Prince's Ct SE16 119 B3
Princes Dr HA1 42 C6
Princes Gate SW7 114 B4 246 D1
Prince's Gate SW7 114 C4 247 A1
Princes Gate Ct SW7 246 D1
Princes Gate Mews SW7 114 B3 256 D6
Princes Gdns Acton W3 88 C2
Brompton SW7 114 B3 256 D6
Ealing W5 87 C3
Princes Ho W11 245 A5
Princes La N10 49 B6
Princes Mews TW3 129 C1
Prince's Mews
1 Hammersmith W6 112 B1
Kensington W2 113 D6 245 C6
Princes Par NW11 47 A3
Princes Park Ave
Hayes UB3 105 B6
Temple Fortune NW11 47 A4
Princes Park Circ UB3 105 B6
Princes Park Cl UB3 105 B6
Princes Park La UB3 105 B6
Princes Park Par UB3 105 B6
Princes Pl
Notting Hill W11 113 A5 244 A4
St James SW1 249 B4
Prince's Plain BR2 210 A1
Princes Plain Prim Sch BR2 210 A2
Princes Rd
Ashford TW15 170 B5
Buckhurst Hill IG9 21 C2
Ealing W13 109 B5
Edmonton N18 34 C6
Feltham TW13 149 D1
Ilford IG6 57 B5
Kew TW9 132 B4
Kingston u T KT2 176 C3
Penge SE20 184 D4
Richmond TW10 154 B6
Prince's Rd
Mortlake SW14 133 B2
Teddington TW11, TW12 174 B6
Wimbledon SW19 179 C4
Princes Rise SE13 142 A3
Princes Riverside Rd 7 SE16 118 D5
Princessa Ct EN2 17 B6
Princess Alexandra School of Nursing The E1 96 B2
Princess Alice Ho 1 W10 90 C3
Princess Alice Way SE28 123 B4
Princess Ave HA9 66 A6
Princess Beatrice Ho SW10 255 C1
Princess Cl SE28 102 D1
Princess Cres N4 72 D6
Princess Ct
Catford BR1 186 C4
3 Croydon CR0 221 D6
Hampstead NW6 69 D1
Hounslow TW4 128 C2
Kensington W2 245 D6
Marylebone W1 237 C3
11 Wimbledon SW19 178 D3
Princess Frederica CE Prim Sch NW10 90 C5
Princess Grace Hospl The W1 93 A3 238 A5
Princess La HA4 39 C1
Princess Louise Cl W2 236 D4
Princess Louise Hospl W10 90 C2
Princess Mary Ho SW1 259 D3
Princess May Prim Sch N16 73 D4
Princess May Rd N16 73 C4
Princess Mews
Hampstead NW3 70 B2
Kingston u T KT1 198 B6
Princess Par
Dagenham RM10 103 C5
Locksbottom BR6 226 C5
Princess Park Manor N11 31 A5
Prince's Sq W2 113 D6 245 C6
Princess Rd
Camden Town NW1 93 A6 231 B6
Paddington NW6 91 C5
Thornton Heath CR0 205 A3
Princess Royal University Hospl BR6 226 C5
Princess St Bexley DA7 147 B2
Newington SE1 261 D5
Princes St
Bexleyheath DA7 147 B1
Marylebone W1 238 D1
Sutton SM1 218 B4
Tottenham N17 33 C4
Prince's St
City of London EC2 95 B1 242 C1
Richmond TW10, TW9 154 A6
Prince St SE8 141 B6
Prince's Terr E13 99 B6
Princes Way Acton W3 110 C3
Buckhurst Hill IG9 21 C2
Coney Hall BR4 224 D5
Croydon CR0 220 B3
Putney SW15, SW19 157 A3
Ruislip HA4 63 A4
Princes Yd W11 244 B3
Princethorpe Ho W2 91 D2
Princethorpe Rd SE26 184 D6
Princeton Ct SW15 134 D2
Princeton Mans WC1 240 C3
Princeton Mews 3 KT2 176 C2
Princeton St WC1 94 B2 240 C4
Prince William Ct TW15 170 B5
Principal Cl N14 15 C3
Principal Sq E9 74 D3
Pringle Gdns SW16 181 C6
Pringle Ho N21 16 B6
Printers Mews E3 97 A6
Printer St EC4 241 B2
Printinghouse La UB3 105 C4
Printing House Yd 16 E2 95 C4
Printon Ho 16 E3 97 B2
Print Village Ind Est SE15 139 D3
Priolo Rd SE7 121 C1
Prior Ave SM2, SM5 218 C1
Prior Bolton St N1 72 D2
Prioress Ho 2 E3 97 D4
Prioress Rd SE27 160 D1
Prioress St SE1 262 D5
Prior Rd IG1 78 C5
Priors Croft E17 35 B1
Priors Field UB5 63 A2
Priors Gdns HA4 62 C3
Priors Lo 4 TW10 154 A5
Priors Mead EN1 5 C4
Prior St SE10 142 A5
Priors Wood KT10 212 D6
Prior Weston Prim Sch
Broadgate EC1 95 B3 242 C6
St Luke's EC1 95 A3 242 B5
Priory Ave
Bedford Pk W4 111 C3
Cheam SM3 216 D4
Chingford E4 19 C1
Hornsey N8 49 D5
Petts Wood BR5 211 B3
Walthamstow E17 53 C4
Wembley HA0 64 D4
Priory CE Prim Sch SW19 179 D5
Priory Cl Ashford TW16 172 A3
Barnet N20 13 B4
Beckenham BR3 207 A6
Chingford Green E4 19 B1
Chislehurst BR7 188 B2
East Barnet N14 15 B6
Finchley N3 29 B2
Hampton TW12 173 B2
Hayes UB3 106 B6
3 Merton SW19 179 D2
Ruislip HA4 39 D1
Stanmore HA7 8 D1
Wembley HA0 64 D4
Woodford E18 37 A2
Priory Cres
Cheam SM3 216 D4
South Norwood SE19 183 A3
Wembley HA0 65 A5
Priory Ct Bushey WD23 8 A3
Cheam SM3 217 A4
City of London EC4 241 D1
Hampton TW12 173 C3
Highgate N6 49 B3
Homerton E9 74 D3
Hounslow TW3 129 D2
Ilford RM6 58 B3
Newham E6 99 D6
Nunhead SE15 140 C1
Roehampton SW15 133 D1
South Lambeth SW8 137 D4 269 D2
Walthamstow E17 35 B1
4 Wembley HA0 88 A5
Priory Dr Stanmore HA7 8 D1
West Heath SE2 124 D1
Priory Field Dr HA8 26 D6
Priory Gdns
Ashford TW15 171 B5
Barnes SW13 133 D2
6 Chiswick W4 111 C2
Ealing W5 88 A4

Priory Gdns continued
Hampton TW12 . . . . .173 B2
Highgate N6 . . . . .49 B3
South Norwood SE25 . . . .205 D5
Wembley HA0 . . . . .65 A4
Priory Gn N1 . . . . 233 C4
Priory Gr Barnet EN5 . . . . 13 C6
South Lambeth
SW8 . . . . 138 A4 270 A1
Priory Grange N2 . . . . .48 D6
Priory Hill HA0 . . . . .65 A4
Priory Ho
3 Charlton SE7 . . . . .143 C6
Clerkenwell EC1 . . . . . . 241 C6
Pimlico SW1 . . . . 259 C2
Spitalfields E1 . . . . 243 C4
Priory Hospl Hayes Grove
The BR2 . . . . .225 A6
Priory Hospl The
SW15 . . . . .133 D1
Priory House Ct SE6 . . . .163 D3
Priory Htss N1 . . . . 233 D4
Priory La
East Molesey KT8 . . . . . .195 D5
Roehampton SW15 . . . . .155 D6
Priory Leas SE9 . . . . .166 A3
Priory Lo
7 Brentford W4 . . . . . . .110 C1
Coney Hall BR4 . . . . . . .224 C5
Ealing W5 . . . . .87 C1
Priory Mans
17 Maitland Pk NW3 . . . .70 D2
South Kensington SW10 . 256 B1
Priory Park Rd
Kilburn NW6 . . . . .91 B6
Wembley HA0 . . . . .65 A4
Priory Pk SE3 . . . . .142 D2
Priory Rd Barking IG11 . . .79 B1
Bedford Pk W4 . . . . .111 B3
Cheam SM3 . . . . .216 D4
Chessington KT9 . . . . . . .214 A5
Hampstead NW6 . . . . . . .69 D1
Hampton TW12 . . . . . . .173 C3
Hornsey N8 . . . . .49 D5
Hounslow TW3 . . . . .152 A6
Mitcham SW19 . . . . .180 B3
Newham E6 . . . . .99 D5
Richmond TW9 . . . . .132 C5
Thornton Heath CR0 . . . .204 C2
Priory Ret Pk SW19 . . . .180 B3
Priory Sch SE25 . . . . . . .205 D5
Priory St 13 E3 . . . . .97 D4
Priory Terr NW6 . . . . .91 D6
Priory The
Croydon CR0 . . . . .220 C5
Hornsey N8 . . . . .49 D5
21 Kingston u T KT6 . . . .198 A4
Lambeth SE1 . . . . 251 C1
Lewisham SE3 . . . . .142 D1
Priory View WD23 . . . . .8 C4
Priory Villas N11 . . . . .30 D5
Priory Way
Harmondsworth UB7 . . .126 A6
Harrow HA2 . . . . .41 D5
Southall UB2 . . . . .106 D3
Priory Wlk
South Kensington
SW10 . . . . . . .114 A1 256 B1
Sunbury TW16 . . . . .172 A3
Priscilla Cl N15 . . . . .51 A4
Priscilla Ho 8 TW16 . . . .172 A3
Pritchard Ho 38 E2. . . . . . .96 A5
Pritchard's Rd E2 . . . . . . .96 A5
Pritchett Cl 13 EN3 . . . . . . .7 C6
Priter Rd SE16 . . . . .118 A3
Priter Road Hostel 14
SE16 . . . . .118 A3
Private Rd EN1 . . . . .17 C6
Probert Rd SW2 . . . . .160 C6
Probyn Ho 9 SW1 . . . . . 259 D4
Probyn Rd SW2 . . . . .160 D2
Procter Ho 12 SE5 . . . . . .139 B5
Procter St WC1 . . 94 B2 240 C3
Proctor Cl CR4 . . . . .181 A2
Proctor Ho 5 SE1 . . . . . .118 A1
Proctors Ct TW14 . . . . . . .150 A3
Prodger 8 NW9 . . . . .27 D2
Progress Bsns Pk CR9 . .220 B6
Progress Way
Croydon CR0 . . . . .220 B6
Enfield EN1 . . . . .18 A6
Wood Green N22 . . . . . . .32 C2
Prologis Pk
Hounslow TW4 . . . . .128 C1
Wallington CR0 . . . . .203 D2
Prome Ho 3 N16 . . . . . . .73 B4
Promenade Approach Rd
W4 . . . . .133 C5
Promenade Mans HA8 . .26 C5
Promenade The W4 . . . . .133 C5
Pronto Trad Est UB4 . . . .83 C2
Prospect Cl
Belvedere DA17 . . . . . . .125 C2
Forest Hill SE26 . . . . . . .184 B6
Hounslow TW5 . . . . .129 B4
Ruislip HA4 . . . . .40 D2
Prospect Cotts SW18 . . .135 C1
Prospect Cres TW2 . . . . .152 A5
Prospect Hill E17 . . . . . . .53 D5
Prospect Ho
1 Dalston E8 . . . . .73 D2
Islington N1 . . . . 234 A3
3 Mitcham SW19 . . . . .180 B2
Newington SE1 . . . . 261 D5
14 North Kensington
W10 . . . . .90 D1
9 Walthamstow E17 . . . .54 A6

Prospect House Sch
SW15 . . . . .156 D4
Prospect Pl
Bromley BR2 . . . . .209 B6
5 Child's Hill NW2 . . . . .69 B5
2 Chiswick W4 . . . . . . .111 B1
6 Deptford SE8 . . . . . . .141 B6
East Finchley N2 . . . . . . .48 B5
17 Hampstead NW3 . . . .70 A4
4 Lower Holloway N7 . . .72 A4
Tottenham N17 . . . . .33 C3
Wapping E1 . . . . .118 C5
Wimbledon SW20 . . . . . .178 B3
Prospect Quay SW18 . . .135 C1
Prospect Rd Barnet EN5. . .1 D1
Child's Hill NW2 . . . . .69 C5
Kingston u T KT6 . . . . . .197 C3
Woodford IG8 . . . . .37 C5
Prospect Ring N2 . . . . . . .48 B6
Prospect St SE16 . . . . . . .118 B4
Prospect Vale SE7,
SE18 . . . . .122 A2
Prospect Wharf E1 . . . . . .118 C6
Prospero Ho 7 DA17 . . . .125 C1
Prospero Rd N19 . . . . .49 D1
Protea Cl E16 . . . . .98 D3
Protheroe Ho 11 N17 . . . .51 D6
Prothero Gdns NW4 . . . . . .46 B4
Prothero Ho 15 NW10 . . . .67 B1
Prothero Rd
SW6 . . . . .135 B5 264 C4
Proud Ho 16 E1 . . . . .96 B1
Prout Gr NW10 . . . . .67 D4
Prout Rd E5 . . . . .74 B5
Provence St N1 . . . . 235 A4
Providence 1 SE16 . . . . .118 A4
Providence Ave HA2 . . . . .41 C1
Providence Cl E9 . . . . .96 D6
Providence Ct
Harlington UB3 . . . . .127 B5
Islington N1 . . . . 234 C5
Mayfair W1 . . . . 248 B6
Providence La UB3 . . . . . .127 B5
Providence Pl N1 . . . . . . 234 C5
Providence Rd UB7 . . . . . .104 B5
Providence Row N1 . . . . 233 C3
Providence Row Cl 30
E1 . . . . .96 B4
Providence Sq 38 SE1 . .118 A4
Providence Yd 1 E2 . . . . . .96 A4
Provident Ind Est UB3 . .106 A4
Provincial Terr 2
SE20 . . . . .184 D3
Provost Ct NW3 . . . . .70 D2
Provost Rd NW3 . . . . .70 D1
Provost St N1 . . 95 B4 235 C2
Prowse Ave WD23 . . . . .8 A2
Prowse Pl NW1 . . . . .71 C1
Prudence La UB3 . . . . . . .127 B5
Pruden Cl N14 . . . . .15 C2
Prudent Pas EC2 . . . . . . 242 B1
Prusom's Island 8 E1 . . .118 C5
Prusom St E1 . . . . .118 B5
Pryors The NW3 . . . . .70 B5
Public Record Office
TW9 . . . . .132 D5
Puccinia Ct TW19 . . . . . . .148 A3
Pudding La EC3 . . . . 252 D6
Pudding Mill La E15 . . . . .97 D6
Pudding Mill Lane Sta
E15 . . . . .97 D6
Puddle Dock
EC4 . . . . .116 D6 251 D6
Puffin Cl Barking IG11 . . . .102 B4
Beckenham BR3 . . . . . . .206 D4
Puffin Ct 9 W13 . . . . .86 D3
Puffin Terr IG5 . . . . .56 C6
Puget Ct N12 . . . . .30 A5
Pugin Ct N1 . . . . .72 C1
Pulborough Rd SW18 . . .157 B4
Pulborough Way TW4 . . .128 C1
Pulford Rd N15 . . . . .51 B3
Pulham Ave N2 . . . . .48 B5
Pulham Ho SW8 . . . . 270 C3
Puller Rd EN5 . . . . .1 A3
Pulleyns Ave E6 . . . . .100 A4
Pullman Ct SW2 . . . . .160 B3
Pullman Gdns SW15 . . . .156 C5
Pullman Mews SE12 . . . .165 B1
Pullman Pl SE9 . . . . .166 A6
Pulross Rd SW9 . . . . .138 B2
Pulteney Cl
3 Isleworth TW7 . . . . . .131 A2
20 Old Ford E3 . . . . .97 B6
Pulteney Gdns 9 E18 . . . .55 B6
Pulteney Rd E18 . . . . .55 B6
Pulteney Terr
N1 . . . . .94 B6 233 D6
Pulton Ho 4 SE4 . . . . . . .141 A1
Pulton Pl SW6 . .135 C5 265 A3
Puma Ct E1 . . . . 243 C4
Puma Trade Pk CR4 . . . . .202 B5
Pump Alley 8 TW8 . . . . . .131 D5
Pump Cl UB5 . . . . .85 C5
Pump Ct EC4 . . . . 241 A1
Pump House Cl
Bromley BR2 . . . . .186 D1
Rotherhithe SE16 . . . . . .118 C4
Pumphouse Educational
Mus The* SE16 . . . . . . .119 A5
Pumping Ho 3 E14 . . . . . .120 B6
Pumping Station Rd
W4 . . . . .133 C6
Pump La Deptford SE14 . .140 C5
Hayes UB3 . . . . .106 A4
Pump Pail N CR0 . . . . . . .221 A5
Pump Pail S CR0 . . . . . . .221 A5
Punchard Cres EN3 . . . . . .7 B5
Punderson's Gdns E2 . . . .96 B4
Puran Ho E13 . . . . .99 C5

Purbeck Ave KT3 . . . . . . .199 D3
Purbeck Ct 2 N20 . . . . . .14 C2
Purbeck Dr NW2 . . . . .68 D6
Purbeck Ho SW8 . . . . . . 270 C3
Purbrook Est SE1 . . . . . . 253 B1
Purbrook Ho 2 SW15 . . .156 B3
Purbrook St SE1 . . . . 263 B6
Purcell Cres
SW6 . . . . .135 A5 264 A4
Purcell Ho
Chelsea SW10 . . . . 266 C5
Isleworth TW2 . . . . .152 B5
Southall UB1 . . . . .85 C1
Purcell Mews 2 NW10 . . .67 C1
Purcell Rd UB6 . . . . .85 D2
Purcells Ave HA8 . . . . .26 C5
Purcell St N1 . . . . .95 C5
Purchese St
NW1 . . . . .93 D5 232 D3
Purday Ho 4 W10 . . . . . . .91 B4
Purdey Ct 3 KT4 . . . . . . .200 A1
Purdon Ho 11 SE15 . . . . .140 A4
Purdy St E3 . . . . .97 D3
Purkis Cl UB3 . . . . .105 A6
Purland Cl RM8 . . . . .59 B1
Purland Rd SE28, SE18 . .123 D4
Purley Ave NW2 . . . . .69 A6
Purley Oaks Prim Sch
CR2 . . . . .221 B1
Purley Pl N1 . . . . .72 D1
Purley Rd Edmonton N9 . . .17 C1
South Croydon CR2 . . . . .221 B1
Purley View Terr CR2 . . .221 B1
Purley Way
Croydon CR0, CR9 . . . . .220 C3
Thornton Heath CR0 . . . .204 B1
Purley Way Cres CR0 . . .204 B2
Purneys Rd SE9 . . . . .143 D1
Purrett Rd SE18 . . . . .123 D1
Purser Ho 3 SW2 . . . . . .160 C5
Pursers Cross Rd
SW6 . . . . .135 B4 264 D2
Pursewardens Cl W13 . . .109 C5
Pursley Rd NW7 . . . . .28 B3
Purves Rd NW10 . . . . .90 C5
Purvis Ho CR0 . . . . .205 B2
Pusey Ho 20 E14 . . . . .97 C1
Puteaux Ho 6 E2 . . . . .96 D5
PUTNEY 156 C6
Putney Bridge App
SW6 . . . . .135 A2
Putney Bridge Rd
SW15 . . . . .135 B1
Putney Bridge Sta
SW6 . . . . .135 B2
Putney Comm SW15 . . . .134 C2
Putney Exchange
Shopping Ctr SW15 . . .134 D1
Putney Gdns RM6 . . . . . . .58 B4
PUTNEY HEATH 156 C4
Putney Heath SW15 . . . .156 C5
Putney Heath La
SW15 . . . . .156 D5
Putney High Sch
SW15 . . . . .156 D6
Putney High St SW15 . . .135 A1
Putney Hill SW15 . . . . . . .156 D6
Putney Park Ave
SW15 . . . . .134 A1
Putney Park La SW15 . . .156 B6
Putney Park Sch
SW15 . . . . .134 B1
Putney Pier SW15 . . . . . .135 A2
Putney School of Art &
Design SW15 . . . . .135 A1
Putney Sta SW15 . . . . . . .135 A1
PUTNEY VALE 156 A1
Putney Wharf Twr
SW15 . . . . .135 A2
Pycombe Cnr N12 . . . . . . .29 B6
Pycroft Way N9 . . . . .34 A6
Pykewell Lo 13 E8 . . . . . .74 A3
Pylbrook Rd SM1 . . . . . . .217 D5
Pylon Trad Est E16 . . . . . .98 B2
Pylon Way CR0 . . . . .204 A1
Pym Ct EN4 . . . . .14 B6
Pymers Mead SE21 . . . . .161 A3
Pymmes Brook Dr EN4 . . .2 C1
Pymmes Brook Ho 3
N10 . . . . .31 A3
Pymmes Cl
Bowes Pk N13 . . . . .32 B5
Tottenham N17 . . . . .34 B2
Pymmes Gdns N N9 . . . . .17 D1
Pymmes Gdns S N9 . . . . .17 D1
Pymmes Green Rd N11 . .15 C1
Pymmes Mews N13 . . . . . .32 A5
Pymmes Rd N13 . . . . .32 A5
Pynchester Cl UB10 . . . . .60 C6
Pyne Rd KT6 . . . . .198 C1
Pynfolds SE16 . . . . .118 B4
Pynham Cl SE2 . . . . .124 B3
Pynnacles Cl HA7 . . . . . . .25 B5
Pynnersmead SE24 . . . . .161 A6
Pyramid Ho N12 . . . . .30 A6
Pyrford Ho 12 SW9 . . . . .138 D1
Pyrland Rd
Richmond TW10 . . . . . . .154 B5
Stoke Newington N5 . . . .73 B3
Pyrmont Gr SE27 . . . . . . .160 D1
Pyrmont Rd W4 . . . . .132 C6
Pytchley Cres SE19 . . . . .183 A4
Pytchley Rd SE22 . . . . . .139 C2

Q

Quadrangle Cl SE1 . . . . . 263 A4
Quadrangle Ho The
E15 . . . . .76 C2
Quadrangle Lo SW19 . . .179 C4
Quadrangle The
Chelsea SW10 . . . . 266 B2
Fulham SW6 . . . . 264 A3
Herne Hill SE24 . . . . . . .161 A6
3 North Kensington
W12 . . . . .90 C1
Paddington W2 . . . . 237 A2
Stanmore HA7 . . . . .25 C3
Walthamstow E17 . . . . . .35 A1
Quadrant Arc W1 . . . . . . 249 B5
Quadrant Bsns Ctr
NW6 . . . . .91 A6
Quadrant Cl NW4 . . . . . . .46 B4
Quadrant Gr NW5 . . . . . . .70 D3
Quadrant Ho E15 . . . . .98 C4
Quadrant Rd
Richmond TW9 . . . . .131 D1
Thornton Heath CR7 . . . .204 D5
Quadrant The
4 Kensal Green W10 . . .90 D4
Richmond TW9 . . . . .132 A1
Sutton SM2 . . . . .218 A2
West Heath DA7 . . . . . . .146 D5
Wimbledon SW20 . . . . . .179 A2
Quad Rd HA9 . . . . .65 D5
Quaggy Wlk SE3 . . . . . . .143 A1
Quainton Hall Sch HA1. . .42 C4
Quainton St NW10 . . . . . . .67 B5
Quaker Ct EC1 . . . . 242 B6
Quaker La UB2 . . . . .107 C3
Quakers Course NW9 . . .27 D2
Quaker's Pl E7 . . . . .77 D3
Quaker St E1 . . .95 D3 243 C5
Quakers Wlk N21 . . . . . . .17 B5
Quality Ct WC2 . . . . 241 A2
Quantock Cl UB3 . . . . . . .127 B5
Quantock Ct
4 East Barnet N20 . . . . .14 C2
Greenford UB6 . . . . .64 C3
Quantock Dr KT4 . . . . . . .216 C6
Quantock Gdns NW2 . . . .68 D6
Quantock Ho N16 . . . . . . .51 D1
Quantock Mews 3
SE15 . . . . .140 A3
Quarles Park Rd RM6 . . . .58 C3
Quarrendon St SW6 . . . .135 C3
Quarr Rd SM5 . . . . .202 C3
Quarry Park Rd SM1 . . . .217 B2
Quarry Rd SW18 . . . . . . .158 A5
Quarry Rise SM1 . . . . . . .217 B2
Quarterdeck The E14 . . .119 C4
Quartermain Ho SM4 . . .202 A4
Quartermile La E10,
E15 . . . . .75 D4
Quayside Ct 6 SE16 . . . .118 D5
Quay West Ct TW11 . . . .175 B5
Quebec & Crown Wharves
E14 . . . . .97 B1
Quebec Ind Est SE16 . . .119 A3
Quebec Mews W1 . . . . . 237 D1
Quebec Rd Hayes UB4 . . .84 C1
Ilford IG1 . . . . .57 A2
Quebec Way SE16 . . . . . .119 A4
Quebec Wharf 32 E8 . . . .95 D6
Quedgeley Ct 3 SE15 . . .139 C6
Queen Adelaide Ct
SE20 . . . . .184 C4
Queen Adelaide Rd
SE20 . . . . .184 C4
Queen Alexandra Mans
WC1 . . . . 233 A1
Queen Alexandra's Ct
SW19 . . . . .179 B5
Queen Anne Ave BR2 . . .208 D6
Queen Anne Dr KT10 . . .212 C1
Queen Anne Gate
DA7 . . . . .146 D2
Queen Anne Mews
W1 . . . . 238 D3
Queen Anne Rd E9 . . . . . .74 D2
Queen Annes Cl TW2 . . .152 B1
Queen Anne's Gate
SW1 . . . . .115 D4 249 C1
Queen Anne's Gdns
Bedford Pk W4 . . . . .111 C3
Ealing W5 . . . . .110 A4
Enfield EN1 . . . . .17 C5
Mitcham CR4 . . . . .202 D6
Queen Anne's Gr
Bedford Pk W4 . . . . .111 C3
Ealing W5 . . . . .110 A4
Enfield EN1 . . . . .17 C5
Queen Anne's Pl EN1 . . .17 C5
Queen Anne St
W1 . . . . .93 B2 238 C3
Queen Anne Terr 9
E1 . . . . .118 B6
Queenborough Gdns
Chislehurst BR7 . . . . . . .189 B4
Ilford IG2 . . . . .56 C5
Queen Caroline St
W6 . . . . .112 C1
Queen Charlottes &
Chelsea Hospl W12 . . . .90 A1
Queen Ct WC1 . . . . 240 B5
Queen Elizabeth Ct
Barnet EN5 . . . . .1 B1
5 Kingsland N1 . . . . . . .73 B2
Queen Elizabeth Gdns
SM4 . . . . .201 C5
Queen Elizabeth Hall &
Purcell Room* SE1 . . 250 D4

Queen Elizabeth Ho
SW12 . . . . .159 A4
Queen Elizabeth Hospl
SE18 . . . . .144 A5
Queen Elizabeth II Con Ctr
SW1 . . . . 249 D1
Queen Elizabeth II Jubilee
Sch W9 . . . . .91 B3
Queen Elizabeth II Pier
SE10 . . . . .120 D5
Queen Elizabeth Rd
Kingston u T KT2 . . . . . .176 B1
Walthamstow E17 . . . . . .53 A6
Queen Elizabeth's Cl
N16 . . . . .73 B6
Queen Elizabeth's Coll 16
SE10 . . . . .142 A5
Queen Elizabeth's Dr
N14 . . . . .16 A3
Queen Elizabeth's Girls
Sch EN5 . . . . .1 B1
Queen Elizabeth's Hunting
Lodge Mus* E4 . . . . . . .20 D4
Queen Elizabeth St
SE1 . . . . .117 D4 253 C2
Queen Elizabeth's Wlk
Stoke Newington N16 . . .73 B6
Wallington SM6 . . . . .219 D4
Queen Elizabeth Wlk
SW13 . . . . .134 B4
Queenhithe EC4 . . . . 252 B6
Queen Margaret Flats 22
E2 . . . . .96 B4
Queen Margarets Ct
N1 . . . . .73 C3
Queen Margaret's Gr
N1 . . . . .73 C3
Queen Mary Ave SM4 . . .200 D4
Queen Mary Cl KT9 . . . . .214 C5
Queen Mary Ct TW19 . . .148 A3
Queen Mary Ho
Charlton TW17 . . . . .171 A1
South Norwood SE19 . . .182 D4
Queen Mary's Ave
SM5 . . . . .218 D1
Queen Mary's Gdns*
NW1 . . . . 231 A1
Queen Mary's Hospl
Hampstead NW3 . . . . . . .70 A5
Sidcup DA14 . . . . .190 A4
Queen Mary's Univ Hospl
SW15 . . . . .156 A5
Queen Mary, Univ of
London E1 . . . . .97 A3
Queen of Denmark Ct
SE16 . . . . .119 B3
Queen St PI EC4 . . . . . . 252 B6
Queens Acre SM3 . . . . . .217 A1
Queens Ave
Feltham TW13 . . . . .172 C6
Muswell Hill N10 . . . . . . .49 B6
Stanmore HA7 . . . . .25 C1
Whetstone N20 . . . . .14 B2
Queen's Ave Finchley N3 . 30 A2
Southall UB1 . . . . .86 A1
Southgate N21 . . . . .16 D3
Woodford IG8 . . . . .37 B5
Queensberry Ho 6
TW9 . . . . .153 D6
Queensberry Mews W
SW7 . . . . 256 C4
Queensberry Pl
Chelsea SW7 . .114 B2 256 C4
Plashet E12 . . . . .78 A3
Queensberry Way
SW7 . . . . 256 C4
Queensborough Ct N3 . . .47 B5
Queensborough Mews
W2 . . . . 246 A6
Queensborough Pas
W2 . . . . 246 A6
Queensborough Terr
W2 . . . . .113 D6 245 D6
Queensbridge Ct 2 E2. . .95 D5
Queensbridge Inf Sch
E8 . . . . .73 D1
Queensbridge Pk
TW7 . . . . .152 C6
Queensbridge Rd
Dalston E8 . . . . .73 D1
Shoreditch E2, E8 . . . . . .95 D6
QUEENSBURY 44 B6
Queensbury IG9 . . . . .21 B3
Queensbury Circ Par
HA3 . . . . .44 A6
Queensbury Ct CR7 . . . .183 A1
Queensbury Rd
Kingsbury NW9 . . . . .45 B2
Wembley HA0 . . . . .88 B5
Queensbury St N1 . . . . . . .73 A1
Queensbury Sta HA7,
HA8 . . . . .44 B6
Queensbury Station Par
HA8 . . . . .44 B6
Queen's CE Prim Sch The
TW9 . . . . .132 C5
Queen's Cir
SW11 . . . . .137 B5 268 C3
Queen's Cl Edgware HA8 . 26 C5
Wallington SM6 . . . . .219 B3
Queen's Club Gdns
W14 . . . . .135 A6 264 B6
Queen's Club The
W14 . . . . .113 A1 254 B6
Queen's Coll
W1 . . . . .93 B2 238 C3
Queenscourt HA9 . . . . . . .66 A4
Queens Cres TW10 . . . . .154 B6
Queen's Cres NW5 . . . . . .71 A2
Queenscroft Rd SE9 . . . .165 D5

Queens Ct
Battersea SW11 . . . . . . 268 C2
Beckenham BR3 . . . . . . .185 D3
Camberwell SE5 . . . . . . .139 C3
Leyton E10 . . . . .53 C2
4 Limehouse E14 . . . . . .119 B6
Sidcup DA14 . . . . .190 A6
Stanmore HA7 . . . . .25 B1
8 Temple Fortune
NW11 . . . . .47 B4
Walthamstow E17 . . . . . .53 C4
Queen's Ct
Barnes SW13 . . . . .134 A2
Beckenham BR3 . . . . . . .185 C2
Croydon CR2 . . . . .221 A3
8 Ealing W5 . . . . .87 C2
Hampstead Garden Suburb
NW11 . . . . .47 C4
Kensington W2 . . . . 245 D5
1 Kingston u T KT2 . . . .176 C3
Leytonstone E11 . . . . . . .54 C2
3 Richmond TW10 . . . .154 B5
St John's Wood NW8 . . . 229 C3
Thornton Heath CR7 . . . .204 C4
Queensdale W11 . . . . . . .112 C5
Queensdale Cres
W11 . . . . .112 D5
Queensdale Pl W11 . . . . 244 A3
Queensdale Rd
Notting Hill W11 . . . . . . .112 D5
Notting Hill
W11 . . . . .113 A5 244 A3
Queensdale Wlk W11 . . 244 A3
Queensdown Rd E5 . . . . . .74 B4
Queens Dr
Surbiton KT5 . . . . .198 C3
Walthamstow E10 . . . . . .53 C2
Queen's Dr Acton W3 . . . .88 C1
Finsbury Pk N4 . . . . .72 D2
Thames Ditton KT7 . . . . .197 A3
Queen's Elm Par SW3 . 256 D2
Queen's Elm Sq SW3 . . 256 D1
Queensferry Wlk N17 . . . .52 B5
Queensfield Ct SM3 . . . .216 C4
Queen's Gallery*
SW1 . . . . .115 B4 248 D1
Queen's Gate
SW7 . . . . .114 A3 256 B5
Queensgate Ct N12 . . . . .29 D5
Queensgate Gdns
SW15 . . . . .134 B1
Queens Gate Gdns
BR7 . . . . .189 B2
Queen's Gate Gdns
SW7 . . . . .114 A3 256 B5
Queensgate Ho 34 E3 . . .97 B5
Queen's Gate Mews
SW7 . . . . .114 A3 256 B5
Queensgate Pl 10 NW6 . .69 C1
Queen's Gate Pl
SW7 . . . . .114 A3 256 B5
Queen's Gate Pl Mews
SW7 . . . . .114 A3 256 B5
Queen's Gate Sch SW7 256 C5
Queen's Gate Terr
SW7 . . . . .114 A3 256 B5
Queens Gate Villas E9 . .75 A1
Queens Gdns NW4 . . . . . .46 C4
Queen's Gdns
Bayswater
W2 . . . . .114 A6 246 A6
Ealing W5 . . . . .87 C3
Heston TW5 . . . . .129 A4
Queen's Gr NW8 . 92 B6 229 D5
Queen's Grove Rd E4 . . .20 B3
Queen's Head Pas EC2 . 242 A2
Queen's Head St
N1 . . . . .94 D6 234 D5
Queen's Head Yd SE1 . . 252 C3
Queens Ho 1 SE17 . . . . .139 B6
Queen's Ho TW11 . . . . . .174 D4
Queen's House The*
SE10 . . . . .142 B6
Queens Keep 10 TW1 . .153 C2
Queens La
2 Ashford TW15 . . . . . .170 B6
Muswell Hill N10 . . . . . . .49 B6
Queensland Ave
Edmonton N18 . . . . .33 A4
Merton SW19 . . . . .179 D2
Queensland Cl E17 . . . . . .35 B1
Queensland Ct N10 . . . . .31 B3
Queensland Ho 2
E16 . . . . .122 C5
Queensland Rd N7 . . . . . .72 C4
Queens Lo HA7 . . . . .25 A5
Queens Manor Sch
SW6 . . . . .134 D5
Queens Mans
Hampstead NW6 . . . . . . .69 D3
Hendon NW4 . . . . .46 B4
Queen's Mans
Brook Green W6 . . . . . . .112 D2
Muswell Hill N10 . . . . . . .49 A6
Queensmead
Ashford TW15 . . . . .170 B5
St John's Wood
NW8 . . . . .92 B6 229 D6
Queens Mead HA8 . . . . . .26 B4
Queen's Mead Rd BR2 . .186 D1
Queensmead Sch HA4 . . .62 D4
Queensmere 4 SM1 . . . .217 D3
Queensmere Cl SW19 . .156 D2
Queensmere Rd SW13 . .134 A4
Queensmere Rd
SW19 . . . . .156 D2
Queens Mews 5 IG9 . . . .21 C2
Queen's Mews
W2 . . . . .113 D6 245 C6

Queensmill Rd SW6....134 D5
Queensmill Sch SW6...135 C3
Queen's Mkt E13.......99 C6
Queens Par Ealing W5 ... 88 B1
7 Hendon NW4........46 B4
3 Willesden NW2......68 C2
Queen's Par
3 Friern Barnet N11....30 D5
Wood Green N11........32 A3
Queens Parade Cl N11..30 D5
Queens Park Com Sch
NW6..................90 D6
Queens Park Ct 5
W10..................90 D4
Queens Park Gdns
TW13................149 D1
Queen's Park Prim Sch
W10..................91 A3
Queen's Park Sta NW6..91 B5
Queen's Pas BR7......188 D4
Queen's Pl SM4........201 C5
Queen Sq WC1 ..94 A2 240 B4
Queen's Quay EC4.... 252 B6
Queens Rd Hayes UB3 ...83 C1
Morden SM4..........201 C5
Twickenham TW1.......153 A3
West Drayton UB7 .....104 B4
Queen's Rd
Barking IG11..........79 A2
Beckenham BR3 ....185 A1
Bowes Pk N11..........32 A4
Bromley BR1..........187 A1
Buckhurst Hill IG9.......21 C2
Chislehurst BR7 ....188 D4
Ealing W5 ....88 A1
Edmonton N9...........18 B2
Enfield EN1..............5 C1
Feltham TW13.........150 B3
Finchley N3 ....30 A2
Hampton TW12 ....173 D6
Hendon NW4...........46 C4
Hounslow TW3 ....129 D2
Kingston u T KT2.......176 C3
Leytonstone E11 ....54 C2
Mitcham CR4..........202 B6
Mortlake SW14.........133 B2
New Cross Gate SE14,
SE15...............140 C4
Newham E13...........99 C6
New Malden KT3.......199 D4
Richmond KT2, TW10 ...176 C5
Richmond TW10 ....154 B5
Southall UB2..........107 A4
Teddington TW11 ......174 D4
Thames Ditton KT7 .....196 D4
Thornton Heath CR0....205 A3
Wallington SM6........219 B3
Walthamstow E17.......53 C3
Welling DA16..........146 B3
Wimbledon SW19 ......179 C4
Queen's Rd W E13......99 B5
Queens Reach KT8.....196 C5
Queen's Ride SW13....134 B2
Queen's Rise TW10....154 B5
Queen's Road Sta
SE15.................140 C4
Queen's Row SE17.....139 B6
Queen St
Bexleyheath DA7.......147 B2
City of London
EC4 ....117 A6 252 B6
Croydon CR0..........221 A4
Mayfair W1....115 B5 248 C4
Tottenham N17.........33 C4
Queens Terr
Harrow HA3...........24 C1
Newham E13...........99 B6
St John's Wood
NW8.........92 B5 229 C4
Queen's Terr TW7......131 A1
Queens Terr Cotts
W7...................108 C4
Queensthorpe Rd
SE26 ....184 D6
Queenstown Mews
SW8................268 C1
Queenstown Rd
SW8..........137 B5 268 C4
Queenstown Road Sta
SW8 ....137 B4 268 D2
Queensville Rd SW12,
SW4..................159 D4
Queens Walk Ho W5....87 C2
Queensway
Coney Hall BR4........224 D4
Croydon CR0..........220 B3
Enfield EN3..............6 C1
Kensington
W2........113 D6 245 D6
Orpington BR5.........211 A3
Sunbury TW16.........172 B1
Queens Way
Feltham TW13.........172 C6
Hendon NW4...........46 C4
Queensway Bsns Ctr
EN3......................6 C1
Queensway Sta
W2..........113 D6 245 D5
Queens Well Ave N20...30 C6
Queenswell Jun & Inf Schs
N20...................14 B2
Queens Wlk
Ashford TW15.........170 A6
Chingford E4...........20 B3
Harrow HA1 ....42 C5
Ruislip HA4 ....62 C5
Welsh Harp NW9 ....67 A6
Queen's Wlk Ealing W5 ..87 C2
St James SW1. 115 C5 249 A3
Queenswood Ave
Chingford E17..........36 A2
Hampton TW12.........173 D4
Hounslow TW3, TW5....129 B3
Thornton Heath CR7....204 C4
Wallington CR0, SM6...219 D4
Queenswood Ct
7 Clapham Pk SW4....160 A6
11 West Norwood
SE27................183 B6
Queenswood Gdns E11..55 B1
Queenswood Pk N3.....29 A2
Queenswood Rd
Blackfen DA15.........167 D5
Forest Hill SE23 ....163 A1
Queen's Wood Rd N6...49 B3
Queens Yd E9..........75 C2
Queen's Yd W1....... 239 B5
Queen Victoria Ave
HA0...................65 D1
Queen Victoria Meml*
SW1.................249 A2
Queen Victoria St
EC4 ....117 A6 252 A6
Queen Victoria Terr 12
E1 ....118 B6
Quelch Ho 2 N19.......71 D3
Quemerford Rd N7 .....72 B3
Quendon Ho 9 W10 ....90 C3
Quenington Ct 5
SE15 ....139 D6
Quenington Mans
SW6................. 264 C2
Quennel Ho 7 SW12...159 C4
Quentin Pl SE13 ....142 C2
Quentin Rd SE13.......142 C2
Quernmore Cl BR1.....187 A4
Quernmore Rd
Plaistow BR1..........187 A4
Stroud Green N4........50 C3
Querrin St SW6........136 A3
Quested Ct 27 E8 ....74 B3
Quex Mews NW6........91 C6
Quex Rd NW6...........91 C6
Quick Rd W4..........111 C1
Quicks Rd SW19.......179 D3
Quick St N1 .....94 D5 234 D3
Quick Street Mews N1 234 C3
Quickswood NW3.......70 C1
Quiet Nook BR2 ....225 D5
Quill La SW15 ....134 D1
Quill St Ealing W5 ......88 A5
Highbury N4 ....72 C5
Quilp St SE1.......... 252 A2
Quilter St
Bethnal Green E2 ....96 A4
Plumstead Comm SE18..123 D1
Quilting Ct 23 SE16 ....118 D4
Quince Ho TW13.......150 A3
Quince Rd SE13........141 D3
Quinta Dr EN5..........12 C6
Quintin Ave SW20......179 B2
Quintin Cl HA5..........40 B4
Quintin Ct W4..........133 A5
Quintin Kynaston Sch
NW8...........92 B6 229 C5
Quintock Ho 2 TW9....132 C4
Quinton Cl
Beckenham BR3 ....208 A6
Cranford TW5 ....128 B5
Wallington SM6........219 B4
Quinton Ho SW8...... 270 A4
Quinton Rd KT7........197 A1
Quinton St SW18.......158 A2
Quixley St 1 E14 ......120 B6
Quorn Rd SE22 ....139 C2
Quwwat-Ul-Islam Girls
Sch E7................77 B2

R

Rabbit Row W8....... 245 B4
Rabbits Rd E12 ....78 A4
Rabbs Farm Prim Sch
UB7..................104 A6
Rabinal Ho EN3.........18 D6
Rabournmead Dr UB5...63 A3
Raby Rd KT3...........199 B5
Raby St E14 ....97 A1
Raccoon Way TW4.....128 C3
Rachel Cl IG6 ....57 B6
Rachel Ct SM2.........218 B1
Racine 15 SE5 ....139 C4
Rackham Cl DA16......146 B3
Rackham Mews SW16..181 C4
Racs Flats 9 SE1......118 A2
Racton Rd
SW6..........135 C6 265 A5
Radbourne Ave W5.....109 C2
Radbourne Cl E5 ....74 D4
Radbourne Cres E17....36 B1
Radbourne Ct HA3......43 B3
Radbourne Rd SW12....159 D3
Radcliff Bldg EC1..... 241 A4
Radcliffe Ave Enfield EN2..5 A4
Willesden Green NW10...90 A5
Radcliffe Coll
Marylebone
W1..........93 C1 239 A1
Soho W1 ....93 D1 239 C2
Radcliffe Gdns SM5....218 C1
Radcliffe Ho 10 SE16...118 B2
Radcliffe Path 5
SW8...................137 B3
Radcliffe Rd
Bermondsey SE1...... 263 B6
Harrow HA3 ....25 A1
South Croydon CR0.....221 D5
Southgate N21 ....16 D3
Radcliffe Sq SW15.....156 D5
Radcliffe Way UB5......84 D4
Radcliff Mews TW12...174 A5
Radcot Point 2 SE23 ..162 D1
Radcot St SE11 .... 261 B1
Raddington Rd W10.....91 A2
Radfield Way DA15.....167 B4
Radford Ho
7 Bow Comm E14......97 D2
Islington N7 ....72 B3
Radford Rd SE13.......164 A5
Radford Way IG11 .....101 D4
Radipole Rd
SW6.........135 B4 264 C2
Radius Pk TW6 ....127 D1
Radland Rd E16.........99 A1
Radlet Ave SE23 ....162 B2
Radlett Cl E7...........76 D2
Radlett Pl NW8..92 C6 230 A6
Radley Ave IG3.........80 A4
Radley Cl TW14........149 D3
Radley Ct
4 Catford BR1........186 A6
25 Rotherhithe SE16....118 D4
Radley Gdns HA3 ....44 A5
Radley Ho
11 Abbey Wood SE2 ...124 D4
Marylebone NW1 ..... 237 C6
Radley Lo 30 SW19.....156 D3
Radley Mews W8 ..... 255 B5
Radley Rd N17..........33 C1
Radley's La E18.........37 A1
Radleys Mead RM10.....81 D2
Radley Sq E5 ....74 C6
Radley Terr 1 E16......98 D2
Radlix Rd E10 ....53 C1
Radnor Ave
Bexley DA16 ....168 B6
Harrow HA1 ....42 C4
Radnor Cl
Chislehurst BR7 ....189 C4
Mitcham CR4..........204 A5
Radnor Cres
Redbridge IG4..........56 B4
Woolwich SE18........146 A5
Radnor Ct Ealing W7....86 D1
6 Forest Hill SE23.....162 D1
Harrow HA3 ....24 D2
Radnor Gdns Enfield EN1..5 C4
Twickenham TW1.......152 D2
Radnor Gr UB10 ....82 C5
Radnor Ho
East Molesey KT8......196 B5
Thornton Heath SW16...182 B1
Radnor Lo W2......... 236 D1
Radnor Mews
W2............92 B1 236 D1
Radnor Pl W2 ...92 C1 237 A1
Radnor Rd Harrow HA1...42 C4
Kensal Rise NW6 ....91 A6
Peckham SE15.........140 A5
Twickenham TW1.......152 D2
Radnor St EC1...95 A4 235 B1
Radnor Terr
W14..........113 B2 254 C4
Radnor Way NW10......88 D3
Radnor Wlk
Chelsea
SW3....... 114 D1 257 C1
Croydon CR0..........207 A3
21 Millwall E14........119 C2
Radstock Ave HA3......43 B6
Radstock Cl N11.........31 A4
Radstock St SW11 ..... 267 A3
Radway Ho 38 W2 ......91 C2
Radwell Ho SW2........160 C6
Raebarn Ct 6 SW16 ...160 A1
Raebarn Gdns EN5......12 B6
Raeburn Ave KT5 ......198 D3
Raeburn Cl
Hampstead Garden Suburb
NW11..................48 A3
Teddington KT1........175 D3
Raeburn Ho
5 Belmont SM2........217 D1
6 Northolt UB5........84 D5
Raeburn Rd
Edgware HA8 ....26 C2
Hayes UB4.............83 B5
Sidcup DA15 ....167 C5
Raeburn St SW2........138 A1
Raffles Ct HA8..........26 B6
Raffles Ho NW4.........46 B5
Rafford Way BR1 ......209 B6
RAF Mus* NW9 ....28 A1
Ragged School Mus The*
E3.....................97 A2
Raggleswood BR7 .....188 C2
Raglan Cl TW4.........151 B6
Raglan Ct Brixton SW9 ..138 C2
Croydon CR0, CR2......220 D3
Lee SE12..............165 A6
Wembley HA9 ....66 C5
Raglan Jun & Inf Schs
EN1....................17 C4
Raglan Prim Sch BR2 ..209 D5
Raglan Rd
Belvedere DA17 ....125 B2
Bromley BR2..........209 C5
Enfield EN1 ....17 D4
Walthamstow E17 ....54 B4
Woolwich SE18 ....123 A1
Raglan St NW5 ....71 B2
Raglan Terr HA2........63 D4
Raglan Way UB5........64 A2
Ragley Cl W3..........111 A4
Ragwort Ct 1 SE26 ....184 B5
Rahere Ho EC1 .... 235 A2
Railey Mews NW5.......71 C3
Railshead Rd TW1,
TW7..................131 B1
Railton Rd SE24 ....160 D6
Railway App
Bermondsey SE1...... 252 D4
Harrow HA1, HA3 ....42 D5
Stroud Green N4........50 C3
11 Twickenham TW1....153 A4
Wallington SM6........219 B3
Railway Ave SE16......118 C4
Railway Cotts
Hammersmith W6......112 C4
Ilford IG6 ....57 B6
Railway Gr SE14 ....141 B5
Railway Pl DA17 ....125 C3
Railway Rd TW11 ......174 D6
Railway Rise SE22 .....139 C1
Railway Side SW13.....133 C2
Railway St Ilford RM6 ...58 C2
King's Cross N1....... 233 B3
Railway Terr
Chingford E17 ....36 A2
Feltham TW13, TW14 ...150 A3
Ladywell SE13.........163 D6
Rainborough Cl NW10...67 A2
Rainbow Ave E14 ......119 D1
Rainbow Ct 3 SE14....141 A6
Rainbow Ind Est
SW20.................178 B1
Rainbow Quay SE16.....119 A3
Rainbow Sch The
SW17 ....158 A2
Rainbow St SE5........139 C5
Rainbow Works N15 ....52 A4
Raine Gdns 4 IG8 ......37 A6
Raines Ct N16 ....73 D6
Raine's Foundation Lower
Sch E2.................96 B5
Raine's Foundation Sch
E2.....................96 C5
Raine St E1 ....118 B5
Rainford Ho 9 N7 ......72 B6
Rainham Cl Sidcup SE9..167 C5
Wandsworth SW11......158 C5
Rainham Ho NW1..... 232 B5
Rainham Rd NW10.......90 C4
Rainham Rd N RM10 ....81 D6
Rainham Rd S RM10 ....81 D4
Rainhill Way E3 ....97 C4
Rainsborough Ave
SE8 ....119 A2
Rainsford Cl HA7 ....25 C5
Rainsford Ct NW10......88 D5
Rainsford Ho 14 SW2...160 B6
Rainsford Rd NW10 .....88 D5
Rainsford St W2...... 237 A2
Rainstar Est N18........34 C6
Rainton Rd SE7.........121 A1
Rainville Rd W6 ....134 C6
Raisins Hill HA5 ....40 C6
Raith Ave N14 ....15 D1
Raleigh Ave Hayes UB4 ..84 B2
Wallington SM6........219 D4
Raleigh Cl Hendon NW4 ..46 C4
Pinner HA5 ....40 D2
Ruislip HA4 ....61 D6
Raleigh Ct
Beckenham BR3 ....185 D2
4 Dulwich SE19.......183 D5
Ealing W13 ....87 B2
7 Hammersmith W12 ..112 B4
2 Rotherhithe SE16....118 D5
Wallington SM6........219 B2
Raleigh Dr
East Barnet N20 ....14 C1
Esher KT10 ....212 B3
Tolworth KT5..........199 A1
Raleigh Gdns
Mitcham CR4..........202 D6
Tulse Hill SW2.........160 B5
Raleigh Ho
30 Clapham SW8 ......137 D3
Isle of Dogs E14 ....119 D4
1 Thames Ditton KT7 ..197 A2
Raleigh Mews
Islington N1 .... 234 D5
6 Orpington BR6......227 D3
Raleigh Rd Enfield EN2.... 5 B1
Feltham TW13.........149 D2
Finchley N10 ....30 C2
Hornsey N8 ....50 C5
Penge SE20...........184 D3
Richmond TW9 ....132 B2
Southall UB2..........107 A1
Raleigh St N1 ...94 D6 234 D5
Raleigh Way
Feltham TW13.........172 C5
Southgate N14 ....16 A3
Ralph Ct 8 W2..........91 D1
Ralph Perring Ct BR3 ..207 C5
Ralston St SW3 ...... 257 C1
Ramac Ind Est SE7......121 B1
Rama Cl SW16.........182 A3
Rama Ct HA1 ....64 C6
Ramac Way SE7 ....121 B1
Rama La SE19 ....183 D3
Ramar Ho 12 E1 ....96 A2
Rambler Cl SW16 ......181 C6
Rambler Ct 11 NW9 .....46 A5
Rame Cl SW17 ....181 A5
Ramilles Cl SW2 ....160 A5
Ramilles Ho W1 ...... 239 B1
Ramilles Pl W1 .93 C1 239 A1
Ramillies Rd
Bedford Pk W4 ....111 B3
Blackfen DA15.........168 B5
Edgware NW7...........11 C2
Ramillies St W1 ...... 239 A1
Ramney Dr EN3..........7 A6
Rampart St E1..........96 B1
Ram Pas KT1 ....175 D1
Rampayne St SW1 .... 259 C2
Rampton Cl E4 ....19 C1
Ramsay Ho NW8...... 230 A4
Ramsay Rd Acton W3 ...111 A4
Leyton E7 ....76 D4
Ramscroft Cl N9........17 C4
Ramsdale Rd SW17 ....181 A5
Ramsdean Ho 1
SW15.................156 B3
Ramsden Rd
Balham SW12 ....159 A4
Friern Barnet N11.......30 D5
Ramsey Cl
Greenford UB6 ....64 B3
West Hendon NW9 ......45 D3
Ramsey Ct
Croydon CR0..........220 D6
Hornsey N8............49 D4
Putney SW15..........156 C5
6 Upper Holloway N19 ..71 D6
Ramsey Ho
5 Battersea SW11 ....136 B1
14 Kennington SW9 ....138 C5
7 Merton SW19........179 D2
Ramsey Rd CR7........204 B3
Ramsey St E2...........96 A3
Ramsey Way N14 ....15 C4
Ramsfort Ho 4 SE16...118 B2
Ramsgate Cl 10 E16....121 B5
Ramsgate St E8 ....73 D2
Ramsgill App IG2.......57 D5
Ramsgill Dr IG2 ....57 D5
Rams Gr RM6...........59 A5
Ram St SW18..........157 D6
Ramulis Dr UB4.........84 D3
Ramus Wood Ave
BR6 ....227 C3
Rance Ho 12 SE7.......122 A2
Rancliffe Gdns SE9 ....144 A1
Rancliffe Rd E6........100 A5
Randal Cremer JMI Sch
E2.....................95 D5
Randall 9 NW9..........27 D2
Randall Ave NW2 ....67 D5
Randall Cl
SW11.........136 C4 267 A2
Randall Ct NW7.........28 A3
Randall Pl SE10........142 A5
Randall Rd
SE11 ....116 B2 260 C3
Randall Row SE11 .... 260 C3
Randell's Rd N1 . 94 A6 233 B6
Randisbourne Gdns
SE6 ....163 D1
Randle Rd TW10........175 C6
Randlesdown Rd SE6 ..163 D1
Randmore Ct 6 BR3...185 C3
Randolf Ct
Paddington NW6........91 D5
St John's Wood NW8 .. 229 A5
Randolph App E16......99 C1
Randolph Ave
W9...........92 A4 229 A1
Randolph Cl KT2.......177 A5
Randolph Cres
W9...........92 A3 236 A6
Randolph Ct HA5 ....23 C3
Randolph Gdns NW6....91 D5
Randolph Gr RM6.......58 C4
Randolph Mews
W9............92 A3 236 B5
Randolph Rd
Bromley BR2..........210 B1
Paddington W9 ..92 A3 236 B5
Southall UB1..........107 B4
Walthamstow E17.......53 D4
Randolph St NW1.......71 C1
Randon Cl HA2 ....23 D1
Ranelagh Ave
Barnes SW13 ....134 A3
Fulham SW6 ....135 B2
Ranelagh Cl HA8........26 C6
Ranelagh Ct HA8 ....26 C6
Ranelagh Dr
Edgware HA8 ....26 C6
Twickenham TW1.......153 C6
Ranelagh Gardens Mans
SW6..................135 A2
Ranelagh Gardens (site of
Chelsea Flower Show)*
SW1.........115 A1 258 B1
Ranelagh Gdns
3 Bedford Pk W6.......111 D3
Chiswick W4 ....133 A5
Fulham SW6 ....135 B2
Ilford IG1 ....56 C1
Wanstead E11..........55 C4
Ranelagh Gr
SW1..........115 A1 258 B2
Ranelagh Ho SW3 .... 257 C2
Ranelagh Mans 4
SW6..................135 B3
Ranelagh Pl KT3.......199 C4
Ranelagh Prim Sch
E15....................98 C5
Ranelagh Rd
Dagenham NW10 ....89 D5
Ealing W5 ....109 D4
Leyton E11.............76 C4
Newham E15...........98 C5
Pimlico SW1 ...115 C1 259 B1
Southall UB1..........106 D5
Tottenham N17 ....51 C6
Wallend E6 ....100 C5
Wembley HA0 ....65 D2
Wood Green N22........32 B2
Ranfurly Rd SM1.......217 C6
Rangdon St EC3 ..... 243 C1
Rangefield Prim Sch
BR1..................186 C5
Rangefield Rd BR1.....186 D5
Rangemoor Rd N15.....51 D4
Ranger's House (The
Wernher Collection)*
SE10 ....142 B4
Ranger's Rd
Buckhurst Hill IG9,
IG10...................21 A4
Chingford E4...........20 D4
Rangers Sq SE10.......142 B4
Range Villas TW17.....192 A2
Range Way TW17 ......192 C2
Rangeworth Pl DA15...167 D1
Rangoon Ho 5 N16.....73 B4
Rankin Cl NW9 ....45 C6
Rankine Ho SE1 ..... 262 A5
Ranleigh Gdns DA7 ....147 B5
Ranmere St SW12......159 B3
Ranmoor Cl HA1........42 B5
Ranmoor Gdns HA1.....42 C5
Ranmore Ave CR0 .....221 D5
Ranmore Ct
Kingston u T KT6.......197 D4
3 Wimbledon SW20 ...178 D2
Rann Ho 1 SW14 ......133 B2
Rannoch Cl HA8 ....10 D2
Rannoch Ct 9 KT6.....198 A4
Rannoch Rd W6 ....134 D6
Rannock Ave NW9 ......45 C2
Ransford Ho 16 SE21...183 C6
Ransomes Dock Bsns Ctr
SW11 .... 267 B3
Ransomes Mews
SW11................ 267 B4
Ransom Rd 1 SE7......121 C1
Ranston St NW1 ..... 237 A4
Ranulf Rd NW2 ....69 B4
Ranwell Cl 18 E3........97 B6
Ranwell Ho 17 E3.......97 B6
Ranworth Rd N9........18 C2
Ranyard Cl KT9 ....214 B5
Raphael Ct 9 SE16 ....118 B1
Raphael Dr KT7........196 D2
Raphael St SW7 ...... 247 C1
Rapide 15 NW9 ....27 C2
Rapley Ho 14 E2........96 A4
Rashleigh Ct 8 SW8...137 B2
Rashleigh Ho WC1 .... 233 A1
Rasper Rd N20 ....14 A2
Rastell Ave SW12 ......159 D3
RATCLIFF 118 D6
Ratcliffe Cl SE12.......165 A4
Ratcliffe Cross St E1....96 D1
Ratcliffe Ho 10 E14 .....97 A1
Ratcliffe La 16 E14......97 A1
Ratcliffe Orch 9 E1 ...118 D6
Ratcliff Rd E7 ....77 C3
Rathbone Ho
5 Canning Town E16....98 D1
Kilburn NW6 ....91 C6
10 Wimbledon SW19 ...178 D3
Rathbone Mkt 3 E16...98 D2
Rathbone Pl
W1...........93 D1 239 C2
Rathbone St
Canning Town E16.......98 D1
Fitzrovia W1 ....93 C2 239 B3
Rathcoole Ave N8 ......50 B4
Rathcoole Gdns N8 .....50 B4
Rathfern Prim Sch
SE6...................163 B3
Rathfern Rd SE6.......163 B3
Rathgar Ave W13 ......109 C5
Rathgar Cl N3 ....29 B1
Rathgar Rd SW9 ....138 D2
Rathmell Dr SW4 ......159 D5
Rathmore Rd SE7 ......121 B1
Ratier 16 NW9 ....27 C2
Rattray Ct 3 SE6 ......164 D2
Rattray Rd SW2........160 C6
Raul Rd SE15 ....140 A4
Raveley St NW5.........71 C4
Raven Cl NW9 ....27 C1
Ravendale Rd TW16.....171 D1
Ravenet Ct
Battersea SW11 ...... 268 C1
Clapham SW4 ....159 B6
Ravenet St
SW11.........137 B4 268 C1
Ravenfield Rd SW17 ...158 D1
Ravenhill Rd E13 ....99 C5
Raven Ho 10 SE16......118 D2
Ravenings Par IG3......58 A1
Ravenna Rd SW15 .....156 D6
Ravenor Ct UB6.........85 D3
Ravenor Park Rd UB6 ..86 A4
Ravenor Prim Sch UB6..85 C4
Raven Rd E18...........37 C1
Raven Row E1 ....96 B2
Ravensbourne Ave
Bromley BR2, BR3......186 C2
Catford BR2...........186 B3
Stanwell TW19 ....148 A3
Ravensbourne Bsns Ctr
BR2...................225 D4
Ravensbourne Coll of
Design &
Communication
BR7..................188 B5
Ravensbourne Ct SE6 ..163 C4
Ravensbourne Gdns
W13....................87 B2
Ravensbourne Ho
10 Catford BR1........186 B5
Paddington NW8...... 237 A4

Ravensbourne Ho *continued*
3 Twickenham TW1 153 C5
Ravensbourne Mans 9
SE8 141 C6
Ravensbourne Park Cres
SE6 163 B4
Ravensbourne Pk SE6 163 C4
Ravensbourne Pl
SE13 141 D3
Ravensbourne Rd
Bromley BR1, BR2 209 A6
Forest Hill SE23 163 B3
Twickenham TW1 153 C5
Ravensbourne Sch The
BR2 209 B5
Ravensbourne Sta
BR3 186 B3
Ravensbury Ave SM4 202 A4
Ravensbury Ct CR4 202 B5
Ravensbury Gr CR4 202 B5
Ravensbury La CR4 202 B5
Ravensbury Rd
Orpington BR5 211 D5
Wandsworth SW18 157 D2
Ravensbury Terr
SW18 157 D2
Ravenscar NW1 232 A5
Ravenscar Lo 14
SW19 178 D3
Ravenscar Rd
Catford BR1 186 C6
Surbiton KT6 214 B6
Ravens Cl Bromley BR2 186 D1
Enfield EN1 5 C3
Kingston u T KT6 197 D3
Ravenscourt
1 Shacklewell N16 74 A5
Sunbury TW16 171 D2
Ravenscourt Ave W6 112 A2
Ravenscourt Cl HA4 39 A2
Ravenscourt Gdns
W6 112 A2
Ravenscourt Ho 13
W6 112 B2
Ravenscourt Park Mans 1
W6 112 B3
Ravenscourt Park Prep
Sch W6 112 A2
Ravenscourt Park Sta
W6 112 B2
Ravenscourt Pk W6 112 A2
Ravenscourt Pl W6 112 B2
Ravenscourt Rd
Hammersmith W6 112 B2
St Paul's Cray BR5 190 B1
Ravenscourt Sq W6 112 A3
Ravenscourt Theatre Sch
W6 112 B2
Ravenscraig Rd N11 31 C6
Ravenscroft Ave
Golders Green NW11 47 B2
Wembley HA9 44 B2
Ravenscroft Cl 4 E16 99 A2
Ravenscroft Cres SE9 166 B1
Ravenscroft Ct NW11 47 B2
Ravenscroft Pk EN5 1 A1
Ravenscroft Point 26
E9 74 D2
Ravenscroft Prim Sch
E16 99 A3
Ravenscroft Rd
Acton W4 111 A2
Newham E16 99 A2
Penge BR3 184 D1
Ravenscroft Sch a Tech
Coll The N20 13 B4
Ravenscroft St E2 95 D4
Ravensdale Ave N12 30 B6
Ravensdale Commercial
Est N16 52 A3
Ravensdale Gdns
Hounslow TW4 129 A2
South Norwood SE19 183 B3
Ravensdale Mans N8 50 A3
Ravensdale Rd
Hounslow TW4 129 A2
South Tottenham N16 51 D3
Ravensdon St
SE11 116 C1 261 B1
Ravensfield Cl RM9 80 D4
Ravensfield Gdns
KT19 215 C4
Ravenshaw St NW6 69 B3
Ravenshill BR7 188 D2
Ravens Ho KT1 175 D1
Ravenshurst Ave NW4 46 C5
Ravenside KT6 197 D4
Ravenside Cl N18 34 D5
Ravenside Ret Pk N18 34 D5
Ravenslea Rd SW11,
SW12 158 D4
Ravensleigh Gdns
BR1 187 B5
Ravensmead Rd BR2 186 B3
Ravensmede Way W4 111 D2
Ravensroost SE19 183 B2
Ravenstone
SE17 117 C1 263 B1
Ravenstone Prim Sch
SW12 159 A2
Ravenstone Rd
Hornsey N8 50 C6
West Hendon NW9 45 D3
Ravenstone St SW12 159 A3
Ravensview Ct KT6 197 D4
Ravens Way SE3, SE12 165 A6
Ravenswood
Bowes Pk N22 32 B4
Sidcup DA5 169 A3
Ravenswood Ave
Tolworth KT6 214 C6
West Wickham BR4 208 A1
Ravenswood Cres
Harrow HA2 63 B6
West Wickham BR4 208 A1
Ravenswood Gdns
TW7 130 C4
Ravenswood Ind Est 5
E17 54 A5
Ravenswood Pk HA6 22 A4
Ravenswood Rd
Balham SW12 159 B4
Croydon CR0 220 D5
Walthamstow E17 54 A5
Ravens Wood Sch
BR2 225 D5
Ravensworth Ct SW6 265 A3
Ravensworth Rd
Chislehurst SE9 188 B6
College Pk NW10 90 B4
Raven Wharf SE1 253 C2
Ravey St EC2 95 C3 243 A6
Ravine Gr SE18 145 C6
Rav Pinter Cl N16 51 C2
Rawlings Cl
Beckenham BR3 208 A4
3 Orpington BR6 227 D3
Rawlings Cres HA9 66 D5
Rawlings St
SW3 114 D2 257 C4
Rawlins Cl Hendon N3 47 A6
South Croydon CR2 223 B1
Rawlinson Ct NW2 46 C2
Rawlinson Ho SE13 142 B1
Rawlinson Point 8
E16 98 D2
Rawnsley Ave CR4 202 C4
Rawreth Wlk N1 235 B6
Rawson Ct SW11 268 B1
Rawson St
SW11 137 B4 268 C1
Rawsthorne Cl E16 122 B5
Rawstone Wlk 5 E13 99 A5
Rawstorne Pl EC1 234 C2
Rawstorne St
EC1 94 D4 234 C2
Raybell Ct TW7 130 D3
Rayburne Ct
1 Buckhurst Hill IG9 21 C3
West Kensington W14 254 A6
Ray Cl KT9 213 C2
Ray Ct Ealing W13 109 B5
Stanmore HA7 25 B5
Woodford IG8 37 D4
Raydean Rd EN5 13 D6
Raydons Gdns RM9 81 A3
Raydons Rd RM9 81 A3
Raydon St N19 71 B6
Rayfield Cl BR2 210 A3
Rayford Ave SE12 164 D4
Ray Gdns Barking IG11 102 A5
Stanmore HA7 25 B5
Ray Ho
7 North Kensington
W10 90 D1
Shoreditch N1 235 D5
Rayleas Cl SE18 144 D4
Rayleigh Ave TW11 174 C4
Rayleigh Cl N13 17 B1
Rayleigh Ct
2 Kingston u T KT1 176 B1
Tottenham N22 33 A2
Rayleigh Rd
Edmonton N13 17 B1
Merton SW19 179 B2
5 Newham E16 121 B5
Woodford IG8 37 C3
Rayleigh Rise CR2 221 C2
Ray Lodge Prim Sch
IG8 37 D4
Ray Lodge Rd IG8 37 D4
Ray Massey Way 3
E6 100 A6
Raymead Ave CR7 204 C4
Raymede Twr W10 90 D2
Raymere Gdns SE18 145 C5
Raymond Ave
Brentford W13 109 A3
Woodford E18 36 D1
Raymond Bldgs WC1 240 D4
Raymond Cl SE26 184 C5
Raymond Ct N10 31 A3
Raymond Postgate Ct 5
SE28 124 B6
Raymond Rd
Beckenham BR3 207 A5
Ilford IG2 57 B2
Newham E13 99 C6
Wimbledon SW19 179 A4
Raymond Way KT10 213 A2
Raymouth Rd SE16 118 B2
Raynald Ho 15 SW16 160 A1
Rayne Ct
Bermondsey SE1 253 C2
Snaresbrook E18 54 D5
Rayne Ho
1 Balham SW12 159 A5
Paddington W9 91 D3
Rayner Ct 10 W12 112 C4
Rayners Cl HA0 65 D3
Rayners Cres UB5 84 B4
Rayners Gdns UB5 84 B4
Rayners La Harrow HA2 63 D6
Pinner HA5 41 B3
RAYNERS LANE 41 B1
Rayners Lane Sta HA5 41 B2
Rayner's Rd SW15 157 A6
Rayner Twrs E10 53 C2
Raynes Ave E11 55 C2
Raynes Ct NW2 69 A4
Raynesfield SW20 200 C6
RAYNES PARK 200 C6
Raynes Park High Sch
SW20 200 B6
Raynes Park Sta
SW20 178 C1
Raynham W2 237 A2
Raynham Ave N18 34 A5
Raynham Ho 1 E1 96 D3
Raynham Prim Sch
N18 34 A5
Raynham Rd
Edmonton N18 34 A5
Hammersmith W6 112 B2
Raynham Terr N18 34 A5
Raynor Cl UB1 107 B5
Raynor Pl N1 235 B6
Raynton Cl Harrow HA2 41 A2
Hayes UB4 83 D3
Raynton Dr Hayes UB4 83 C5
Hayes UB4 83 D3
Raynton Rd EN3 6 D6
Ray Rd KT8 195 D4
Rays Ave N18 34 C6
Rays Rd Edmonton N18 34 C6
West Wickham BR4 208 A2
Ray St EC1 241 B5
Ray Wlk N7 72 B6
Raywood Cl UB7 127 A5
Reachview Cl 17 NW1 71 C1
Read Cl KT7 197 A2
Read Ct E17 53 D3
Reade Ct 6 W3 111 A3
Reade Wlk 5 NW10 67 C1
Read Ho
Friern Barnet N11 30 D6
4 Kennington SE11 138 C6
Reading Ho
Paddington W2 236 A1
Peckham SE15 140 A6
Reading La E8 74 B2
Reading Rd
Northolt UB5 64 A3
Sutton SM1 218 A3
Reading Way NW7 29 A5
Readman Ct 8 SE20 184 B2
Reads Cl IG1 78 D6
Reapers Cl NW1 232 C6
Reapers Way TW7 152 B6
Reardon Ho 5 E1 118 B5
Reardon Path 31 E1 118 B5
Reardon St E1 118 B5
Reaston St SE14 140 D5
Reay Prim Sch
SW9 138 B5 270 D3
Rebecca Ct
3 Beckenham BR3 185 C2
Sidcup DA14 190 B6
Rebecca Ho 12 N12 29 D6
Reckitt Rd W4 111 C1
Record St SE16 140 C6
Recovery St SW17 180 C5
Recreation Rd
Bromley BR2 186 D1
Forest Hill SE26 184 D6
Southall UB2 107 A2
Recreation Way CR4,
SW16 204 A6
Rector St N1 95 A6 235 A5
Rectory Bsns Ctr 5
DA14 190 B6
Rectory Cl Chingford E4 19 C1
Finchley N3 29 B2
Littleton TW17 192 C6
Long Ditton KT6 197 C1
Sidcup DA14 190 B6
Stanmore HA7 25 B5
West Barnes SW20 200 C6
Rectory Cres E11 55 C3
Rectory Ct
Cranford TW5 128 C3
Feltham TW13 172 C6
Leyton E11 76 D5
Wallington SM6 219 C4
West Drayton UB7 104 A4
Woodford E18 36 D2
Rectory Field Cres
SE7 143 C5
Rectory Gdns
Beckenham BR3 185 C2
6 Clapham SW4 137 C2
Hornsey N8 50 A5
Northolt UB5 85 B6
Rectory Gn BR3 185 B2
Rectory Gr
Clapham SW4 137 C2
Croydon CR0 220 D6
Hampton TW12, TW13 173 B6
Rectory La Edgware HA8 26 C4
Long Ditton KT6 197 C1
Sidcup DA14 190 C6
Stanmore HA7 25 B5
Upper Tooting SW17 181 A5
Wallington SM6 219 C4
Rectory Orch SW19 179 A6
Rectory Paddock Sch
BR5 190 C1
Rectory Park Ave UB5 85 B4
Rectory Pl SE18 122 C2
Rectory Rd
Barnes SW13 134 A3
Beckenham BR3 185 C2
Cranford TW5 128 C3
Dagenham RM10 81 D1
Hayes UB3 84 A1
Keston BR2 225 D1
Rectory Rd *continued*
Little Ilford E12 78 B3
1 London W3 111 A5
Shacklewell N16 73 D5
Southall UB2 107 B3
Sutton SM1 217 D5
Walthamstow E17 53 D5
Rectory Road Sta N16 73 D5
Rectory Sq E1 96 D2
Rectory Way UB10 60 D5
Reculver Ho 2 SE15 140 C6
Reculver Mews N18 34 A6
Reculver Rd SE16 118 D1
Red Anchor Cl SW3 267 A5
Redan Pl W2 91 D1
Redan St W14 112 D3
Redan Terr SE5 138 D3
Red Barracks Rd 4
SE18 122 B2
Redberry Gr SE23,
SE26 162 C1
Redbourne Ave N3 29 C2
Redbourne Dr SE28 102 D1
Redbourne Ho
Finchley N3 29 C2
7 Poplar E14 97 B1
Redbourn Ho 10 W10 90 C3
REDBRIDGE 55 C3
Redbridge Coll RM6 58 B4
Redbridge Ct IG1 55 D3
Redbridge Ent Ctr IG1 79 A6
Redbridge Foyer IG1 79 A6
Redbridge Gdns SE5 139 C5
Redbridge La E IG4 56 A4
Redbridge La W E11 55 C3
Redbridge Prim Sch
IG4 56 A4
Redbridge Rdbt IG4 55 D3
Redbridge Sta IG4 55 D3
Redburn St
SW3 136 D6 267 C6
Redburn Trad Est EN3 18 D5
Redcar Cl UB5 63 D2
Redcar Ho SE26 184 B4
Redcar St SE5 139 A5
Redcastle Cl E1 118 C6
Red Cedars Rd BR6 211 C2
Redchurch St
E2 95 D3 243 C6
Redcliffe Cl SW5 255 C1
Redcliffe Ct 2 E5 74 B5
Redcliffe Gdns
Chiswick W4 132 D5
Fulham SW10 135 D6 265 D6
Ilford IG1 56 C1
Redcliffe Mews SW10 255 D1
Redcliffe Pl SW10 266 A5
Redcliffe Rd
SW10 136 A6 266 B6
Redcliffe Sch
SW10 136 A6 266 A6
Redcliffe Sq
SW10 113 D1 255 D1
Redcliffe St SW10 265 D6
Redclose Ave SM4 201 C4
Redclyffe Rd E6 99 C6
Redclyffe Terr 2
SM2 217 C1
Redclyf Ho 18 E1 96 C3
Redcroft 5 NW6 69 C2
Redcroft Rd UB1 86 A1
Red Cross Cotts SE1 252 B2
Redcross Way
SE1 117 A5 252 B3
Redding Ho SE18 122 A3
Reddings Ave WD23 8 A6
Reddings Cl NW7 27 D6
Reddings The NW7 11 D1
Reddins Rd SE15 140 A6
Reddons Rd BR3 185 A3
Rede Pl W2 113 C6 245 B6
Redesdale Gdns TW7 131 A5
Redesdale St SW3 267 C6
Redfern Ave TW2,
TW4 151 C4
Redfern Ho 6 E13 98 D6
Redfern Rd
Catford SE6 164 A4
Willesden NW10 67 C1
Redfield La
SW5 113 D2 255 C4
Redfield Mews SW5 255 B4
Redriff Est SE16 119 B3
Redford Ave
Thornton Heath CR7 204 B5
Wallington SM6 220 A2
Redford Cl TW13 149 D2
Redford Wlk N1 235 A6
Redgate Dr BR2 225 B6
Red Gates Sch CR9 220 C3
Redgate Terr SW15 156 D5
Redgrave Cl SE25 205 D3
Redgrave Rd SW15 134 D2
Red Hill BR7 188 D5
Redhill Ct SW2 160 C2
Redhill Dr HA8 27 A1
Red Hill Prim Sch
BR7 188 D5
Redhill St NW1 93 B4 231 D2
Red House* DA6 147 A1
Red House La DA6 147 A1
Red House Rd CR0 203 D3
Red House Sq 20 N1 73 A1
Redif Ho RM10 81 D4
Redington Gdns NW3 69 D4
Redington Ho N1 233 D4
Redington Rd NW3 69 D4
Redknap Ho TW10 153 C1
Red La KT10 213 A2
Redland Gdns KT8 195 B5
Redlands
Teddington TW11 175 A4
Tottenham N15 51 B5
Redlands Ct BR1 186 D3
Redlands Prim Sch E1 96 C2
Redlands Rd EN3 7 A4
Redlands The 5 BR3 185 D1
Redlands Way SW2 160 B4
Redleaf Cl DA17 147 C6
Redleaves Ave TW15 170 D4
Redless Cl TW7 131 A1
Red Leys UB8 60 A1
Red Lion Bsns Ctr
KT6 214 B5
Red Lion Cl 9 SE17 139 B6
Red Lion Ct
Holborn EC4 241 B1
Hounslow TW3 129 D2
Red Lion Hill N2 30 B1
Red Lion La SE18 144 C4
Red Lion Pl SE18 144 C4
Red Lion Rd KT6 214 C6
Red Lion Row SE17 139 A6
Red Lion Sq
WC1 94 B2 240 C3
Red Lion St
Gray's Inn
WC1 94 B2 240 C3
Richmond TW10 153 D6
Red Lion Yd W1 248 B4
Red Lo Ealing W5 88 A2
West Wickham BR4 208 A2
Red Lodge Rd BR3,
BR4 208 B2
Redlynch Ct
W14 113 A4 244 B1
Redlynch Ho 27 SW9 138 C4
Redman Bldg EC1 241 A4
Redman Cl UB5 84 C5
Redman Ho SE1 252 B1
Redman's Rd E1 96 C2
Redmayne Ho 15 SW9 138 B3
Redmead La E1 118 A5
Redmead Rd UB3 105 C2
Redmill Ho 24 E1 96 B3
Redmond Ho N1 233 D5
Redmore Rd W6 112 B2
Red Oak Cl BR6 226 D6
Redo Ho 3 E12 78 C3
Red Pl W1 248 A6
Redpoll Way DA18 124 D3
Red Post Hill SE21,
SE24 161 B6
Red Post Ho E6 77 C2
Redriffe Rd E13 98 D6
Redriff Prim Sch
SE16 119 A4
Redriff Rd SE16 119 A3
Redroofs Cl BR3 185 D2
Redrose Trad Ctr 1
EN4 14 B6
Red Rover SW13 134 A2
Redrup Ho 21 SE14 140 D6
Redruth Cl N22 32 B3
Redruth Gdns KT10 212 D1
Redruth Ho SM2 217 D1
Redruth Rd E9 96 C6
Red Sq The N16 73 B5
Redstart Cl
New Cross Gate
SE14 141 A5
Newham E6 100 A2
Redston Rd N8 49 D5
Redvers Rd N22 32 C1
Redvers St E2 95 C4
Redwald Rd E5 74 D4
Redway Dr TW2 152 A4
Redwing Path SE28 123 B4
Redwing Rd SM6 220 B1
Redwood Cl 4 Bow E3 97 C5
Chigwell IG9 21 B2
Hillingdon UB10 82 D5
Osidge N14 15 D4
Rotherhithe SE16 119 A5
Sidcup DA15 168 A3
South Oxhey WD19 22 D6
Redwood Ct
Brondesbury NW6 69 A1
Crouch End N19 49 D2
Northolt UB5 85 A4
10 Surbiton KT6 197 D2
Redwood Est TW5 128 B6
Redwood Gdns E4 19 D5
Redwood Gr W5 109 B2
Redwood Mews
Ashford TW15 171 B3
2 Clapham SW4 137 B2
Redwoods SW15 156 A3
Redwood Way EN5 12 D6
Redwood Wlk KT6 197 D1
Reece Mews SW7 256 C4
Reed Ave BR6 227 C5
Reed Cl Lee SE12 165 A6
Newham E16 99 A2
Reede Gdns RM10 81 D3
Reede Rd RM10 81 D2
Reede Way RM10 81 D2
Reedham Cl N17 52 B5
Reedham St SE15 140 A2
Reed Ho SW15 156 A5
Reedholm Villas N16 73 B4
Reed Mans 6 E11 55 A3
Reed Pl Clapham SW4 137 D1
Lower Halliford TW17 192 B1
Reed Rd N17 33 D1
Reedsfield Cl TW15 148 D1
Reedsfield Rd TW15 170 D6
Reed's Pl NW1 71 C1
Reedworth St
SE11 116 C2 261 B3
Reef Ho E14 120 A3
Reenglass Rd HA7 25 D6
Rees Dr HA7 26 A6
Rees Gdns CR0 205 D3
Rees Ho 6 N17 33 D3
Reesland Cl E12 78 C2
Rees St N1 95 A6 235 B5
Reets Farm Cl NW9 45 C3
Reeves Ave NW9 45 B2
Reeves Cnr CR0 220 D6
Reeves Cnr Sta CR0 220 D6
Reeves Ho Lambeth SE1 251 A1
Mayfair W1 248 A5
Reeves Mews
W1 115 A6 248 B5
Reeves Rd Bromley E3 97 D3
Shooters Hill SE18 144 D6
Reflection Ho 9 E2 96 A3
Reflection The E16 122 D4
Reflex Apartments 1
BR2 209 B5
Reform Row N17 33 D1
Reform St SW11 136 D3
Regal Cl Ealing W5 87 D2
Spitalfields E1 96 A2
Regal Cres SM6 219 B5
Regal Ct Edmonton N18 33 D5
2 Mitcham CR4 202 D6
Wembley HA0 65 D4
Regal Dr N11 31 B5
Regal Ho IG2 57 B3
Regal La NW1 231 B5
Regal Pl
8 Tower Hamlets E3 97 B4
Walham Green SW6 265 D3
Regal Way HA3 44 A3
Regan Ho 1 N18 33 D4
Regan Way N1 95 C5
Regatta Ho TW11 175 A6
Regatta Point TW8 132 B6
Regel Ct NW7 29 A2
Regency Cl Ealing W5 88 A1
Hampton TW12 173 B5
Regency Cres 3 NW4 28 D1
Regency Ct 9 Bow E3 97 B5
Enfield EN1 17 B6
4 Kingston u T KT5 198 B4
4 Penge SE19 184 A3
14 South Hackney E9 96 C6
Sutton SM1 217 D5
Wimbledon SW19 179 B3
7 Woodford E18 37 A1
Regency Dr HA4 39 C1
Regency Gdns KT12 194 C1
Regency Ho Finchley N3 29 B1
Marylebone NW1 238 D6
Regency Lo
1 Buckhurst Hill IG9 21 D2
Harrow HA3 42 C6
South Hampstead NW3 70 B1
Regency Mews
Beckenham BR3 186 A2
Camberwell SW9 138 D5
Isleworth TW7 152 C6
1 Willesden NW10 68 A2
Regency Pl SW1 259 D4
Regency St
SW1 115 D2 259 D3
Regency Terr SW7 256 C2
Regency Way DA6 147 A2
Regency Wlk
Croydon CR0 207 B3
8 Richmond TW10 154 A6
Regeneration Rd
SE16 118 D1
Regent Ave UB10 60 D1
Regent Bsns Ctr UB3 106 A4
Regent Cl
Cranford TW4 128 B4
Harrow HA3 44 A3
North Finchley N12 30 A5
Regent Ct
4 Finchley N3 29 D3
Lisson Gr NW8 230 A1
South Norwood SE19 182 D4
1 Stamford Hill N16 51 D2
Regent Gdns IG3 58 A2
Regent Ho W14 254 A4
Regent Pl Croydon CR0 205 D1
St James W1 249 B6
Wimbledon SW19 180 A5
Regent Rd
Surbiton KT5 198 C4
Tulse Hill SE24 160 D6
Regents Ave N13 32 C5
Regents Bridge Gdns
SW8 270 B4
Regents Canal Ho 19
E14 97 A1
Regents Cl Hayes UB4 83 C2
South Croydon CR2 221 C2
Regent's Coll
NW1 93 A3 238 A6
Regents Ct
22 Beckenham BR3 185 C3
Bromley BR1 186 D3
Edgware HA8 26 A6
Hackney E8 96 A6
1 Kingston u T KT2 176 A2
Regent's Ct HA5 22 D1
Regents Dr BR2 225 D3
Regents Gate Ho 20
E14 119 A6
Regents Lo 9 SW2 160 B3
Regents Mews
NW8 92 A5 229 B4
REGENT'S PARK 93 B4
Regent's Park*
NW1 93 A5 231 A3

Regent's Park Barracks NW1 ... 231 D3
Regent's Park Rd
Camden Town NW1 ... 93 A6 231 A6
Hendon N3 ... 47 B6
Primrose Hill NW3 ... 71 A1
Regent's Park Sta NW1 ... 93 B3 238 C5
Regent's Park Terr NW1 ... 231 C6
Regents Pl IG10 ... 21 D4
Regent's Pl SE3 ... 143 A3
Regents Plaza 2 NW6 .. 91 D5
Regent Sq
Belvedere DA17 ... 125 D2
23 Bromley E3 ... 97 D4
St Pancras WC1 . 94 A4 233 B1
Regent's Row E8 ... 96 A6
Regent St
Brentford W4 ... 110 C1
7 Kensal Green NW10 .. 90 D4
Mayfair W1 ... 115 C6 249 A6
Regents Wharf
3 Hackney E2 ... 96 B6
Islington N1 ... 233 C4
Regina Coeli RC Prim Sch CR2 ... 220 D1
Regina Ct TW11 ... 174 C5
Reginald Ct BR3 ... 186 A2
Reginald Pl 6 SE8 ... 141 C5
Reginald Rd
Deptford SE8 ... 141 C5
Forest Gate E7 ... 77 A2
Reginald Sorenson Ho E11 ... 54 B2
Reginald Sq SE8 ... 141 C5
Regina Point SE16 ... 118 C3
Regina Rd Ealing W13 ... 109 A5
Finsbury Pk N4 ... 50 B1
Southall UB2 ... 107 A2
South Norwood SE25 ... 206 A6
Regina Terr W13 ... 109 B5
Regis Ct
East Bedfont TW14 ... 149 B5
Hornsey N8 ... 50 B5
Marylebone NW1 ... 237 C4
Mitcham SW19 ... 180 C2
Regis Pl 17 SW2 ... 138 B1
Regis Rd NW5 ... 71 B3
Regnart Bldgs NW1 ... 232 B1
Regnolruf Ct KT12 ... 194 A2
Reid Cl Hayes UB3 ... 83 C1
Pinner HA5 ... 40 A5
Reid Ct SW14 ... 133 A3
Reidhaven Rd SE18 ... 123 C2
Reigate Ave SM1 ... 201 D1
Reigate Rd
Catford BR1 ... 164 D1
Grove Pk BR1, SE12 ... 165 A2
Ilford IG3 ... 79 D6
Reigate Way SM6 ... 220 A3
Reighton Rd E5 ... 74 A6
Reizel Cl N16 ... 51 D1
Relay Rd W12 ... 112 C5
Relf Rd SE15 ... 140 A2
Reliance Sq E2 ... 243 B6
Relko Gdns SM1 ... 218 B3
Relton Ct W3 ... 110 C4
Relton Mews SW7 ... 257 B6
Rembrandt Cl E14 ... 120 B3
Rembrandt Ct
10 Bermondsey SE16 ... 118 B1
Harrow HA3 ... 43 A3
West Ewell KT19 ... 215 D2
Rembrandt Rd
Edgware HA8 ... 26 C1
Lewisham SE13 ... 142 C1
Rembrant Cl SW1 ... 258 A3
Remembrance Ave N2 .. 47 D6
Remington Rd
Newham E6 ... 100 A1
Tottenham N15 ... 51 B3
Remington St N1 ... 94 D5 234 D3
Remnant St WC2 ... 240 C2
Remsted Ho 7 NW6 ... 91 D6
Remus Rd E3 ... 75 C1
Renaissance Ct SM1 ... 202 A1
Renaissance Wlk 4 SE10 ... 120 D3
Renbold Ho 5 SE10 ... 142 A4
Rendlebury Ho 17 SE18 ... 122 B2
Rendle Cl CR0 ... 206 A4
Rendlesham Ho 3 E5, N16 ... 74 A5
Rendlesham Rd
Enfield EN2 ... 4 D4
Shacklewell E5 ... 74 A5
Renforth St SE16 ... 118 C4
Renfree Way TW17 ... 192 C2
Renfrew Cl E6 ... 122 C6
Renfrew Ct TW5 ... 129 A3
Renfrew Ho
Paddington NW6 ... 91 D5
Walthamstow E17 ... 35 B1
Renfrew Rd
Hounslow TW5 ... 129 A3
Kingston u T KT2 ... 177 A3
Newington SE11 ... 116 D2 261 C3
Renmuir St SW17 ... 180 D4
Rennell Ho 18 E9 ... 74 D2
Rennell St SE13 ... 142 A2
Renness Rd E17 ... 53 A6
Rennets Cl SE9 ... 167 C6
Rennets Wood Ho SE9 ... 167 B6
Rennets Wood Rd SE9 ... 167 B6
Rennie Cotts 23 E1 ... 96 C3
Rennie Ct Holdbrook EN3 .. 7 C5
Lambeth SE1 ... 251 C4
Rennie Ho SE1 ... 262 A5
Rennie St SE1 .. 116 D5 251 C4
Renoir Ct 7 SE16 ... 118 B1
Renovation The E16 ... 122 D4
Renown Cl CR0 ... 204 D1
Rensburg Rd E17 ... 52 D3
Rensburg Villas E17 ... 52 D4
Renshaw Cl 7 DA17 ... 147 B6
Renshaw Cnr CR4 ... 181 A2
Renshaw Ct SW19 ... 179 A6
Renshaw Ho 11 SW27 .. 182 D5
Renters Ave NW4 ... 46 C3
Renton Cl SW2 ... 160 B5
Renwick Rd IG11 ... 102 B4
Repens Way UB4 ... 84 D3
Rephidim St SE1 ... 263 A5
Replingham Rd SW18 .. 157 C3
Reporton Rd SW6 ... 135 A5 264 B3
Repository Rd SE7, SE18 ... 122 B1
Repton Ave Hayes UB3 .. 105 B2
Wembley HA0 ... 65 C4
Repton Cl SM5 ... 218 C3
Repton Ct
Beckenham BR3 ... 185 D2
Southgate N21 ... 16 C3
Repton Ho SW1 ... 259 B3
Repton Rd Harrow HA3 ... 44 B5
Orpington BR6 ... 227 D5
Repton St E14 ... 97 A1
Reservoir Cl CR7 ... 205 B5
Reservoir Rd
New Cross Gate SE4 ... 141 A3
Ruislip HA4 ... 39 B5
Southgate N14 ... 15 C6
Reservoir Studios 14 E1 ... 96 D1
Resham Cl UB2 ... 106 C3
Resolution Way 14 SE8 ... 141 C5
Resolution Wlk SE18 ... 122 B3
Restell Cl SE3 ... 142 C6
Restmor Way SM5, SM6 ... 219 A6
Reston Pl SW7 ... 246 A1
Restons Cres DA15, SE9 ... 167 C5
Restoration Sq SW11 .. 266 D1
Restormel Cl TW3 ... 151 C6
Retcar Pl N19 ... 71 B6
Retford St E2 ... 95 C5
Retingham Way E4 ... 19 D2
Retlas Ct HA1 ... 42 B2
Retreat Cl HA3 ... 43 C4
Retreat Cvn Site The IG9 ... 21 A3
Retreat Ho 5 E9 ... 74 C2
Retreat Pl E9 ... 74 C2
Retreat Rd TW9 ... 153 D6
Retreat The Harrow HA2 . 41 C2
Kingsbury NW9 ... 45 B4
Mortlake SW14 ... 133 C2
North Cheam KT4 ... 216 B6
South Norwood CR7 ... 205 B5
Surbiton KT5 ... 198 B3
Reunion Row E1 ... 118 B6
Reveley Sq SE16 ... 119 A4
Revell Rd Cheam SM1 ... 217 B2
Kingston u T KT1 ... 176 D2
Revell Rise SE18 ... 145 D6
Revelon Rd SE4 ... 141 A2
Revelstoke Rd SW18, SW19 ... 157 C2
Reventlow Rd SE9 ... 167 A3
Reverdy Rd SE1 ... 118 A2
Reverend Cl HA2 ... 63 D5
Revesby Rd SM5 ... 202 C3
Review Lo RM10 ... 103 D5
Review Rd
Dagenham RM10 ... 103 D6
Willesden NW2 ... 67 D6
Rewell St SW6 .. 136 A5 266 A3
Rewley Rd SM4 ... 202 B3
Rew Lo 25 N2 ... 30 B1
Rex Ave TW15 ... 170 C5
Rex Ho TW13 ... 151 A1
Rex Par 2 IG8 ... 37 C4
Rex Pl W1 ... 115 A5 248 B4
Reydon Ave E11 ... 55 C3
Reygate Ct N4 ... 51 A3
Reynard Cl
Brockley SE4 ... 141 A2
Bromley BR1 ... 210 C6
Reynard Dr SE19 ... 183 D3
Reynard Mills Trad Est TW8 ... 109 C1
Reynard Pl SE14 ... 141 A6
Reynardson Rd N17 ... 33 A3
Reynardson's Ct 10 N17 ... 51 D6
Reynolah Gdns SE7 ... 121 B1
Reynolds Ave
Chessington KT9 ... 214 A1
Ilford RM6 ... 58 C2
Little Ilford E12 ... 78 C3
Reynolds Cl
Carshalton SM5 ... 202 D1
Golders Green NW11 ... 47 D2
Mitcham SW19 ... 180 B2
Reynolds Ct Ilford RM6 ... 58 D6
Leyton E11 ... 76 D5
Reynolds Dr HA8 ... 44 B6
Reynolds Ho Enfield EN1 . 18 A6
Finsbury Pk N4 ... 50 A1
Reynolds Ho *continued*
18 South Hackney E2 ... 96 C5
St John's Wood NW8 .. 229 D3
Westminster SW1 ... 259 D3
Reynolds Pl
Greenwich SE3 ... 143 B5
12 Richmond TW10 ... 154 B5
Reynolds Rd
Acton Green W4 ... 111 A3
Hayes UB4 ... 84 C3
New Malden KT3 ... 199 B2
Nunhead SE15 ... 140 C1
Reynolds Way CR0 ... 221 C4
Rheidol Mews N1 ... 235 A4
Rheidol Terr N1 . 95 A6 235 A5
Rhein Ho N8 ... 50 A6
Rheola Cl N17 ... 33 D2
Rhoda St E2 ... 95 D3 243 D6
Rhodes Ave N22 ... 31 C2
Rhodes Avenue Prim Sch N22 ... 31 C2
Rhodes Ho
Shepherd's Bush W12 ... 112 B5
Shoreditch N1 ... 235 C2
Rhodesia Rd Leyton E11 .. 76 B6
Stockwell SW9 ... 138 A3
Rhodes-Moorhouse Ct SM4 ... 201 C3
Rhodes St N7 ... 72 B3
Rhodeswell Rd E14 ... 97 B1
Rhodrons Ave KT9 ... 214 A3
Rhondda Gr E3 ... 97 B4
Rhyl Prim Sch NW5 ... 71 A2
Rhyl Rd UB6 ... 86 D5
Rhyl St NW5 ... 71 A2
Rhys Ave N11 ... 31 D3
Rialto Rd CR4 ... 181 A1
Ribble Cl IG8 ... 37 C4
Ribblesdale Ave
Friern Barnet N11 ... 31 A4
Northolt UB5 ... 63 D2
Ribblesdale Ho 11 NW6 ... 91 C6
Ribblesdale Rd
Hornsey N8 ... 50 B5
Streatham SW16 ... 181 B5
Ribbon Dance Mews SE5 ... 139 B4
Ribchester Ave UB6 ... 86 D4
Ribston Cl BR2 ... 210 B1
Ribstone Ho 12 E9 ... 74 D2
Ricardo Path 5 SE28 .. 124 C5
Ricardo St E14 ... 97 D1
Ricards Lodge High Sch SW19 ... 179 B5
Ricards Rd SW19 ... 179 B5
Riccall Ct 2 NW9 ... 27 C2
Riceyman Ho WC1 ... 234 A1
Richard Alibon Prim Sch RM10 ... 81 C3
Richard Anderson Ct 1 SE14 ... 140 D5
Richard Atkins Prim Sch SW2 ... 160 A4
Richard Burbidge Mans SW13 ... 134 C6
Richard Burton Ct 4 IG9 ... 21 C2
Richard Challoner Sch KT3 ... 199 B2
Richard Cl SE18 ... 122 A2
Richard Cloudesley Sch EC1 ... 95 A3 242 A5
Richard Cobden Prim Sch NW1 ... 93 C6 232 B5
Richard Ct
Ashford TW15 ... 170 B5
1 Barnet EN5 ... 1 A2
Richard Fell Ho 3 E12 .. 78 C4
Richard Fox Ho N4 ... 73 A5
Richard Ho 10 SE16 ... 118 C2
Richard House Dr E16 ... 100 A1
Richard Knight Ho SW6 ... 265 B2
Richard Neale Ho 2 E1 ... 118 B6
Richard Neve Ho 2 SE18 ... 123 C2
Richards Cl Bushey WD23 . 8 B4
Harlington UB3 ... 127 B6
Harrow HA1 ... 43 A4
Hillingdon UB10 ... 82 C6
Richards Ct BR3 ... 184 D2
Richard Sharples Ct 16 SM2 ... 218 A1
Richardson Cl 19 E8 ... 95 D6
Richardson Ct 20 SW4 ... 138 A3
Richardson Gdns 12 RM10 ... 81 D2
Richardson Ho
Isleworth TW7 ... 130 D2
10 Poplar E14 ... 97 C2
Richardson Rd E15 ... 98 C5
Richardson's Mews W1 ... 239 A5
Richards Pl E17 ... 53 C6
Richard's Pl SW3 ... 257 B4
Richard St 20 E1 ... 96 B1
Richbell WC1 ... 240 B4
Richbell Pl WC1 ... 240 C4
Richborne Terr SW8 ... 138 B5 270 D4
Richborough Ho
10 Deptford SE15 ... 140 C6
14 Hackney E5 ... 74 B4
Richborough Rd NW2 ... 69 A4
Richbourne Ct W1 ... 237 B2
Richens Cl TW3 ... 130 B3
Riches Rd IG1 ... 79 A6
Richfield Ct
4 Beckenham BR3 ... 185 B2
Wembley HA0 ... 66 A2
Richfield Rd WD23 ... 8 A4
Richford Gate W6 ... 112 C3
Richford Rd E15 ... 98 D6
Richford St W6 ... 112 C3
Richings Ho BR5 ... 190 A2
Rich La SW5 ... 255 C2
Richland Ho 4 SE15 ... 140 A4
Richlands Ave KT17 ... 216 A4
Richman Ho 10 SE8 ... 119 B1
RICHMOND ... 131 C1
Richmond Adult Com Coll TW9 ... 131 D1
Richmond Ave
Chingford E4 ... 36 B5
Feltham TW14 ... 149 C5
Hillingdon UB10 ... 60 D2
Islington N1 ... 94 B6 233 D6
Willesden NW10 ... 68 C2
Wimbledon SW20 ... 179 A2
Richmond Bldgs W1 .. 239 C1
Richmond Bridge TW1 ... 153 D5
Richmond Bridge Mans 1 TW1 ... 153 D5
Richmond Circus TW9 ... 132 A1
Richmond Cl
Borehamwood WD6 ... 11 B6
Walthamstow E17 ... 53 B3
Richmond Coll
Kensington W8 ... 113 D3 255 D6
Richmond TW10 ... 154 A4
Richmond Cres
Chingford E4 ... 36 B5
Edmonton N9 ... 18 A3
Islington N1 ... 94 C6 234 A6
Richmond Ct
Bromley BR1 ... 187 B3
12 Kingston u T KT2 ... 176 C3
Knightsbridge SW1 ... 247 D1
1 Loughton IG10 ... 21 D6
Mitcham CR4 ... 202 B6
4 New Southgate N11 ... 31 A4
Wembley HA9 ... 66 B6
Wimbledon SW20 ... 178 B1
Richmond Dr TW17 ... 193 B3
Richmond Gate TW10 ... 154 B4
Richmond Gdns
Harrow HA3 ... 24 D3
Hendon NW4 ... 46 A4
Richmond Gn CR0 ... 220 A5
Richmond Gr
Islington N1 ... 72 D1
Surbiton KT5 ... 198 B3
Richmond Healthcare Hamlet Hospl TW9 ... 132 A2
RICHMOND HILL ... 154 A5
Richmond Hill TW10 ... 154 A5
Richmond Hill Ct 5 TW10 ... 154 A5
Richmond Ho
12 Forest Hill SE26 ... 162 A1
Regent's Pk NW1 ... 231 D3
Walworth SE17 ... 262 C2
Richmond Ho (Hampton Com Coll) TW12 ... 173 B5
Richmond International Bsns Ctr 9 TW9 ... 132 B1
Richmond Mans
Earl's Ct SW5 ... 255 C2
Putney SW15 ... 135 A2
13 Twickenham TW1 ... 153 D5
Richmond Mews W1 .. 239 C1
Richmond Park* TW10 ... 155 A3
Richmond Park Rd
Kingston u T KT2 ... 176 A3
Mortlake SW14 ... 133 B1
Richmond Pk IG10 ... 21 D4
Richmond Pl SE18 ... 123 A2
Richmond Rd
Bowes Pk N11 ... 32 A4
Chingford E4 ... 20 B3
Dalston E8 ... 74 A1
Ealing W5 ... 110 A4
Finchley N2 ... 30 A1
Forest Gate E7 ... 77 B3
Ilford IG1 ... 79 A5
Isleworth TW7 ... 131 A2
Kingston u T KT2 ... 176 A4
Leyton E11 ... 76 B6
New Barnet EN5 ... 14 A6
Thornton Heath CR7 ... 204 D5
Tottenham N15 ... 51 C3
Twickenham TW1 ... 153 C4
Wallington CR0 ... 220 A5
Wimbledon SW20 ... 178 B2
Richmond St E13 ... 99 A5
Richmond Sta TW9 ... 132 A1
Richmond Terr SW1 ... 116 A4 250 A2
Richmond upon Thames Coll TW2 ... 152 C4
Richmond Way
Hammersmith W12, W14 ... 112 D4
Wanstead E11 ... 77 A6
Richmount Gdns SE3 ... 143 A2
Rich St E14 ... 119 B6
Rickard Cl Hendon NW4 .. 46 A5
Streatham SW2 ... 160 C3
Rickards Cl KT6 ... 214 A6
Rickett St SW6 ... 265 B6
Rickman Ho 23 E2 ... 96 C3
Rickman St 24 E1 ... 96 C3
Rickmansworth Rd HA5 ... 22 C1
Rick Roberts Way E15 .. 98 B5
Rickthorne Rd 7 N19 ... 72 A6
Rickyard Path SE9 ... 144 A1
Riddell Ct SE1 ... 263 C2
Riddell Lo EN2 ... 4 D3
Ridding La UB6 ... 64 D3
Riddons Rd SE12 ... 187 C6
Rideout St SE18 ... 122 B2
Rider Cl DA15 ... 167 C5
Ride The
Brentford TW8 ... 109 C1
Enfield EN3 ... 6 D2
Ridgdale St E3 ... 97 D5
Ridge Ave N21 ... 17 B4
Ridgebrook Rd SE3, SE9 ... 143 D2
Ridge Cl Hendon NW4 ... 28 D1
Kingsbury NW9 ... 45 B5
Plumstead SE28 ... 123 B4
Ridge Crest EN2 ... 4 B4
Ridge Hill NW11 ... 47 A1
Ridge Ho 4 KT2 ... 176 D3
Ridgeleigh Ct 3 EN5 ... 1 A2
Ridgemead Cl N13, N14 .. 16 A2
Ridgemont Gdns HA8 ... 27 A6
Ridgemount Ave CR0 .. 222 D6
Ridgemount Cl 4 SE20 ... 184 B3
Ridgemount Gdns EN2 ... 4 D3
Ridgeon Ct N22 ... 32 B4
Ridge Rd Cheam SM3 ... 201 B1
Child's Hill NW2 ... 69 B5
Edmonton N21 ... 17 B3
Hornsey Vale N8 ... 50 B3
Mitcham CR4 ... 181 B3
Ridges The E4 ... 35 C6
Ridge Terr N21 ... 17 A4
Ridge The Barnet EN5 ... 13 B6
Old Bexley DA5 ... 169 B4
Orpington BR6 ... 227 B6
Surbiton KT5 ... 198 C4
Twickenham TW2 ... 152 B4
Ridgeview Cl EN5 ... 12 D5
Ridgeview Ct EN4 ... 15 C6
Ridgeview Rd N20 ... 14 A1
Ridgeway Hayes BR2 ... 225 A6
11 Richmond TW10 ... 154 A5
Walton-on-T KT12 ... 193 D1
Woodford IG8 ... 37 C6
Ridge Way
Feltham TW13 ... 151 A1
7 West Norwood SE19 ... 183 C4
Ridgeway Ave EN4 ... 14 D5
Ridgeway Cres BR6 ... 227 C5
Ridgeway Crescent Gdns BR6 ... 227 C5
Ridgeway Ct HA5 ... 23 C3
Ridgeway Dr Acton W3 .. 110 C3
Grove Pk BR1 ... 187 B6
Ridgeway E DA15 ... 167 D6
Ridgeway Gdns
Crouch End N6 ... 49 C2
Redbridge IG4 ... 56 A4
Ridgeway Rd TW7 ... 130 C4
Ridgeway Rd N TW7 ... 130 C5
Ridgeway The
Acton W3 ... 110 C3
Chingford E4 ... 20 A3
Enfield EN2 ... 4 B5
Finchley N3 ... 29 D3
Friern Barnet N11 ... 30 D6
Golders Green NW11 ... 47 B1
Kenton HA3 ... 43 C3
Kingsbury NW9 ... 45 B5
Mill Hill NW7 ... 28 B6
North Harrow HA2 ... 41 D3
Palmers Green N14 ... 16 A2
Pinner HA2 ... 41 B4
Ruislip HA4 ... 40 A2
Stanmore HA7 ... 25 C4
Wallington CR0 ... 220 B5
Ridgeway W DA15 ... 167 C6
Ridgeway Wlk UB5 ... 63 A2
Ridgewell Cl
Dagenham RM10 ... 103 D6
Forest Hill SE26 ... 185 B6
Shoreditch N1 ... 235 B6
Ridgmount Gdns WC1 ... 93 D2 239 C4
Ridgmount Pl WC1 ... 239 C4
Ridgmount Rd SW18 ... 157 D6
Ridgmount St WC1 ... 93 D2 239 C4
Ridgway SW19, SW20 ... 178 D4
Ridgway Ct SW19 ... 178 D4
Ridgway Gdns SW19 ... 178 D3
Ridgway Pl SW19 ... 179 A4
Ridgway Rd SW9 ... 138 D2
Ridgway The SM2 ... 218 B1
Ridgwell Rd E16 ... 99 C2
Riding House St W1 ... 93 C2 239 A3
Ridings Ave N21 ... 17 A6
Ridings Cl N6 ... 49 C2
Ridings The Ealing W5 ... 88 B3
Oakleigh Pk EN4 ... 14 B4
Sunbury TW16 ... 172 A2
Surbiton KT5 ... 198 C4
Riding The NW11 ... 47 B2
Ridler Rd EN1 ... 5 C5
Ridley Ave W13 ... 109 B3
Ridley Cl IG11 ... 79 D1
Ridley Ct
Orpington BR6 ... 227 A4
Streatham SW16 ... 182 A4
Ridley Ho 14 SW11 ... 136 C2
Ridley Rd
Beckenham BR2 ... 208 D6
Dalston E8 ... 73 D3
Forest Gate E7 ... 77 C4
Merton SW19 ... 179 D3
Welling DA16 ... 146 B4
Willesden Green NW10 ... 90 A5
Ridley Road Mkt E8 ... 73 D3
Ridsdale Rd SE20 ... 184 B2
Riefield Rd SE9 ... 167 A6
Riesco Dr CR0 ... 222 C2
Riffel Rd NW2 ... 68 C3
Rifle Ct SE11 ... 138 C6
Rifle Pl W11 ... 112 D5
Rifle St E14 ... 97 D2
Riga Ho 12 E1 ... 96 D2
Rigault Rd SW6 ... 135 A3
Rigby Cl CR0 ... 220 C5
Rigby Ho 2 N17 ... 51 D6
Rigby La UB3 ... 105 A4
Rigby Mews IG1 ... 78 C6
Rigby Pl 8 EN3 ... 7 C6
Rigden St E14 ... 97 D1
Rigeley Rd NW10 ... 90 A4
Rigg App E10 ... 53 A1
Rigge Pl SW4 ... 137 D1
Rigg Ho 2 SW4 ... 160 A4
Riggindale Rd SW16 ... 181 D6
Rignold Ho 6 SE5 ... 139 C3
Riley Ho 9 Bow E3 ... 97 C3
Chelsea SW10 ... 266 C5
1 Streatham SW4 ... 159 D4
Riley Rd
Bermondsey SE1 ... 117 D3 263 C6
Enfield EN3 ... 6 C5
Riley St SW10 .. 136 B5 266 C4
Rill Ho 16 SE5 ... 139 C5
Rimini Ct SW12 ... 158 D3
Rinaldo Rd SW12 ... 159 B4
Ring Cl BR1 ... 187 B3
Ringcroft St N7 ... 72 C3
Ringer's Rd BR1 ... 209 A6
Ringford Ho SW18 ... 157 B6
Ringford Rd SW18 ... 157 C5
Ring Ho 15 E1 ... 118 C6
Ringlet Cl E16 ... 99 B2
Ringlewell Cl EN1 ... 6 B3
Ringmer Ave SW6 ... 135 A4 264 B1
Ringmer Gdns 3 N19 ... 72 A6
Ringmer Ho 15 SE22 ... 139 C2
Ringmer Pl N21 ... 17 B6
Ringmer Way BR1 ... 210 B4
Ringmore Rise SE23 ... 162 B4
Ring Rd W12 ... 112 C5
Ringsfield Ho SE17 ... 262 B1
Ringslade Rd N22 ... 32 B1
Ringstead Bldgs SE6 ... 163 D4
Ringstead Ct SM1 ... 218 B3
Ringstead Rd
Catford SE6 ... 163 D4
Sutton SM1 ... 218 B3
Ringway UB2 ... 107 A1
Ring Way N11 ... 31 C4
Ringwold Cl BR3 ... 185 A3
Ringwood Ave
Muswell Hill N2 ... 48 D6
Thornton Heath CR0 ... 204 A2
Ringwood Cl HA5 ... 40 C6
Ringwood Gdns
17 Millwall E14 ... 119 C2
Roehampton SW15 ... 156 A3
Ringwood Rd E17 ... 53 B3
Ringwood Way
Hampton TW12 ... 173 C6
Southgate N21 ... 16 D4
Ripley Cl Bromley BR1 ... 210 B4
New Addington CR0 ... 224 A2
Ripley Ct 1 CR4 ... 180 B1
Ripley Gdns
Mortlake SW14 ... 133 B2
Sutton SM1 ... 218 A4
Ripley Ho
13 Kingston u T KT2 ... 176 D4
Mortlake SW14 ... 133 C2
Nine Elms SW1 ... 269 A6
5 Penge SE26 ... 184 B5
Ripley Mews E11 ... 54 C3
Ripley Rd
Belvedere DA17 ... 125 C2
Enfield EN2 ... 5 A4
Hampton TW12 ... 173 C3
Ilford IG3 ... 79 D6
Newham E16 ... 99 C1
Riplington Ct SW15 ... 156 B4
Ripon Cl UB5 ... 63 C2
Ripon Ct 10 N11 ... 31 A4
Ripon Gdns
Chessington KT9 ... 213 D3
Redbridge IG1 ... 56 A2
Ripon Rd Edmonton N9 ... 18 B4
Shooters Hill SE18 ... 144 D6
Tottenham N17 ... 51 B6
Ripon Way WD6 ... 11 B6
Rippersley Rd DA16 ... 146 A4
Ripple Ct 10 IG11 ... 101 B6
Ripple Jun & Inf Schs IG11 ... 79 C1
Ripple Rd Barking IG11 ... 79 A1
Barking IG11 ... 101 C6
Castle Green RM9 ... 102 A6
Rippleside Commercial Est IG11 ... 102 C5
Ripplevale Gr N1 ... 72 B1
Rippolson Rd SE18 ... 123 D1

Ripston Rd TW15 171 B5
Risborough SE17 262 A4
Risborough Cl 4 N10 49 B6
Risborough Ct 5 N10 49 B6
Risborough Dr KT4 200 A2
Risborough Ho NW8 237 B6
Risborough St SE1 251 D2
Risdon Ho 26 SE16 118 C4
Risdon St 27 SE16 118 C4
Risedale Rd DA7 147 D2
Riseholme Ct E9 75 B2
Riseholme Ho 14
SE22 139 C2
Riseldine Rd SE23 163 A5
Rise The
Borehamwood WD6 10 B6
Buckhurst Hill IG9 21 D4
Chingford E4 20 C3
Edgware HA8 26 D5
Edmonton N13 32 C6
Harrow HA2 24 A1
Hendon NW7 27 D4
Hillingdon UB10 82 B5
Neasden NW10 67 B5
Sidcup DA5 168 C4
Wanstead E11 55 A4
Wembley HA0, UB6 65 A3
Risinghill St N1 234 A4
Risingholme Cl HA3 24 C2
Risingholme Rd HA3 24 C1
Risings The E17 54 B5
Rising Sun Ct EC1 241 D3
Risley Ave N17 33 B2
Risley Avenue Prim Sch
N17 33 C2
Risley Ho 7 E9 74 D2
Rita Rd SW8 138 B5 270 C4
Ritches Rd N15 51 A4
Ritchie Ho
Crouch End N19 49 D2
8 Rotherhithe SE16 118 C3
12 South Bromley E14 98 B1
Ritchie Rd CR0 206 B3
Ritchie St N1 94 C5 234 B4
Ritchings Ave E17 53 A5
Ritherdon Rd SW17 159 B2
Ritson Ho N1 233 C5
Ritson Rd E8 74 A2
Ritter St SE18 144 C6
Ritz Par W5 88 B3
Rivaz Pl E9 74 C2
Riven Ct 10 W2 91 D1
Rivenhall Gdns E11,
E18 54 D5
Riverains The SW11 266 C1
River Ave Southgate N13 16 D1
Thames Ditton KT7 197 A2
Riverbank KT8 196 C5
River Bank
Edmonton N21 17 A4
Thames Ditton KT7 196 D4
Riverbank Rd BR1 165 A1
Riverbank Way TW8 131 C6
River Barge Cl E14 120 A4
River Brent Bsns Pk
W7 108 C3
River Cl Ruislip HA4 39 D3
Southall UB2 108 A4
Wanstead E11 55 C3
River Cl BR5 190 C1
Rivercourt Rd W6 112 B1
River Crane Way
TW13 151 B2
River Ct
Kingston u T KT6 197 D4
Lambeth SE1 251 C5
Shepperton TW17 193 A2
Wanstead E11 55 C3
Riverdale Cl IG11 102 B3
Riverdale Ct N21 17 B6
Riverdale Dr SW18 157 D3
Riverdale Gdns TW1 153 C6
Riverdale Rd Erith DA8 125 D1
Feltham TW13 173 B6
Plumstead Comm SE18 123 D1
Sidcup DA5 169 B5
Twickenham TW1 153 C5
Riverdene HA8 11 A1
Riverdene Rd IG1 78 D5
Riverfleet WC1 233 B2
Riverford Ho 28 W2 91 C2
River Front EN1 5 C2
River Gdns
Carshalton SM5 219 A5
Feltham TW14 150 B6
River Gdns Bsns Ctr
TW14 128 B1
River Grove Pk BR3 185 B2
Riverhead Cl E17 34 D1
River Ho Barnes SW13 133 C3
1 Forest Hill SE26 162 B1
Riverholme KT8 196 C6
Riverhope Mans SE18 122 A3
Riverine Lo HA7 25 A5
River La TW10 153 D3
Riverleigh Ct E4 35 A5
Rivermead
East Molesey KT8 196 A6
Kingston u T KT6 197 D4
Rivermead Cl TW11 175 B5
Rivermead Ct
Ealing UB6 87 A4
Fulham SW6 135 B2
Rivermead Ho
Hackney E9 75 A3
Sunbury TW16 194 C6
River Meads Ave TW13,
TW2 151 D1
River Mount KT12 193 D2
Rivernook Cl KT12 194 C4
River Park Gdns BR2 186 B3
River Park Rd N22 32 B1
River Pl N1 73 A1
River Plate Ho EC2 242 D3
River Rd Barking IG11 101 D3
Buckhurst Hill IG9 21 D3
River Reach TW11 175 C5
River Road Bsns Pk
IG11 101 D4
Riversdale Gdns N22 32 C2
Riversdale Prim Sch
SW18 157 C3
Riversdale Rd
Highbury N5 73 A5
Thames Ditton KT7 197 A3
Riversdene N5 73 A5
Riversfield Rd EN1 5 C2
Rivers Ho 11 TW8 110 C1
Riverside
Battersea SW11 267 B4
Forest Hill SE6 185 B6
Greenwich SE7 121 B3
Hendon NW4 46 B2
Oatlands Pk TW17 193 C2
11 Rotherhithe SE16 118 C4
St Pancras WC1 233 B2
Sunbury TW16 172 D1
Twickenham TW1 153 B3
Riverside Apartments
N13 32 B5
Riverside Ave KT8 196 B4
Riverside Bsns Ctr
SW18 157 D3
Riverside Bsns Pk
SW19 180 A2
Riverside Cl
Chislehurst BR5 190 C1
Ealing W7 86 C3
Hackbridge SM6 219 B5
Kingston u T KT1 197 D5
Upper Clapton E5 74 C6
Riverside Ct
Chingford E4 19 D5
Lewisham SE12 142 D1
Nine Elms SW8 269 D6
Richmond TW11 175 C5
Riverside Dr
Chiswick W4 133 C4
Mitcham CR4 202 C4
Richmond TW10 153 B1
Temple Fortune NW11 47 A3
Riverside Est EN3 19 A5
Riverside Gdns
Enfield EN2 5 A3
Hammersmith W6 112 B1
Hendon N3 47 A6
Wembley HA0 88 A5
Riverside Ho
Finchley N12 29 D6
14 Islington N1 73 A1
Morden SW19 202 A5
20 Richmond TW10 153 D6
Riverside Ind Est
IG11 102 A4
Riverside Mans 4 E1 118 C5
Riverside Pl
New Southgate N11 15 C1
Stanwell TW19 148 A5
Riverside Prim Sch
SE16 118 A4
Riverside Rd
Mill Meads E15 98 A5
Sidcup DA14 169 A2
South Tottenham N15 52 A3
Stanwell TW19 148 A5
Wandsworth SW17,
SW19 158 A1
Riverside The KT8 196 B6
Riverside Wlk
Isleworth TW7 130 C2
3 West Wickham BR4 207 D1
Riverside Works IG11 78 D1
Riverside Workshops
SE1 252 B4
River St EC1 94 C4 234 A2
Riverstone Cl HA2 64 B6
Riverstone Ct KT2 176 B2
Riverston Sch SE12 165 A6
River Terr W6 112 C1
Riverton Cl W9 91 B4
Riverview TW17 193 B2
River View EN2 5 A2
Riverview CE Prim Sch
KT19 215 B4
Riverview Ct 14 DA17 125 C1
Riverview Gdns SW13 134 B6
River View Gdns TW1 152 D2
Riverview Gr W4 132 D6
Riverview Hts SE18 144 D5
Riverview Lo NW9 67 B6
Riverview Pk SE6 163 C2
Riverview Rd
Chiswick W4 132 D6
West Ewell KT19 215 B4
Riverway N13 32 C6
River Way
Canning Town SE10 120 D3
Twickenham TW13,
TW2 151 D2
West Ewell KT19 215 C3
River Wlk KT12 194 A3
Riverwood La BR7 189 B2
Rivet Ho SE1 263 D2
Rivington Ave IG8 37 D1
Rivington Cres NW7 27 D3
Rivington Ct
17 Dagenham RM10 81 D2
Willesden Green NW10 90 A6
Rivington Pl EC2 95 C4
Rivington St EC2 95 C4
Rivington Wlk 4 E8 96 A6
Rivulet Rd N17 33 A3
Rixon Ho SE18 144 D6
Rixon St N7 72 C5
Rixsen Rd E12 78 A3
Roach Rd E3 75 C1
Roads Pl N19 72 A6
Roan Ind Est CR4 180 D2
Roan St SE10 142 A6
Robart Ho 2 N12 30 A5
Robarts Cl HA5 40 B4
Robbins Hall EN3 18 D5
Robb Rd HA7 25 A4
Robert Adam St W1 238 A2
Roberta St E2 96 A4
Robert Bell Ho 2
SE16 118 A2
Robert Blair Prim Sch
N7 72 A2
Robert Browning Prim Sch
SE17 117 B1 262 C2
Robert Burns Ho N17 34 B3
Robert Cl Barking IG11 79 A2
Paddington W9 236 B5
Robert Clack Lower Sch
RM8 81 B6
Robert Clack Upper Sch
RM8 59 C1
Robert Dashwood Way
SE17 262 A3
Robert Gentry Ho W14 254 B1
Robert Gerard Ho 7
SE27 183 B6
Robert Ho 12 HA1 42 D4
Robert Jones Ho 3
SE16 118 A2
Robert Keen Cl 18
SE15 140 A4
Robert Lowe Cl SE14 140 D5
Roberton Dr BR1 187 C2
Robert Owen Ho
Fulham SW6 134 D4
8 Spitalfields E2 95 D4
Robert Owen Lo 4 E5 74 B4
Robertsbridge Rd
SM5 202 B2
Roberts Cl Cheam SM3 216 D1
New Eltham SE9 167 B3
South Norwood CR7 205 B6
Yiewsley UB7 104 A5
Roberts Ct
Chessington KT9 213 D3
Ealing W5 88 A1
Islington N1 234 D5
Penge SE20 184 C2
Willesden NW10 67 C2
Roberts Ho
Dagenham RM10 81 D1
Friern Barnet N11 31 B5
6 Kidbrooke SE18 144 A4
5 West Norwood
SE27 160 D1
Roberts Mews SW1 258 A5
Robertson Ho
Kidbrooke SE18 144 B4
11 Lewisham SE10 142 A4
1 Upper Tooting
SW17 180 C5
Robertson Rd E15 98 A6
Robertson St SW8 137 B3
Roberts Pl RM10 81 C2
Robert's Pl EC1 241 B6
Roberts Rd
Belvedere DA17 125 C1
Finchley NW7 29 A4
Highams Pk E17 35 D2
Robert St Croydon CR0 221 A5
Newham E16 122 D5
Plumstead SE18 123 B2
Regent's Pk
NW1 93 B4 231 D1
Strand WC2 250 B5
Robert Sutton Ho 20
E1 96 C1
Robeson St 7 E3 97 B2
Robina Cl DA6 146 D1
Northwood HA6 22 A2
Robin Cl Edgware NW7 11 C1
Hampton TW12 173 A5
Robin Cres E16 99 D2
Robin Ct
15 Cubitt Town E14 120 A3
Wallington SM6 219 C2
Wood Green N22 32 B3
Robin Gr
Brentford TW8 131 C6
Dartmouth Pk N6 71 A6
Harrow HA3 44 B3
Robin Hill Dr BR7 188 A4
Robin Ho NW8 230 A3
Robin Hood SW15 155 C1
Robinhood Cl CR4 203 C6
Robin Hood Ct 2
SM1 217 D3
Robin Hood Dr HA3 24 D3
Robin Hood Gdns 12
E14 120 A6
Robin Hood Inf Sch
SM1 217 C3
Robin Hood Jun Sch
SM1 217 D3
Robinhood La CR4 203 C6
Robin Hood La
Bexley DA6 169 A6
Blackwall E14 120 A6
Robin Hood La *continued*
Kingston u T SW15 177 C6
Sutton SM1 217 D3
Robin Hood Prim Sch
SW15 177 C5
Robin Hood Way UB6 64 D2
Robin Hood Way
(Kingston By Pass) KT2,
SW15, SW20 177 C5
Robinia Cl SE20 184 A2
Robinia Cres E10 75 D6
Robin La NW4 46 D6
Robinscroft Mews 18
SE10 141 D4
Robins Ct
Grove Pk SE12 165 C1
Richmond TW10 154 A5
South Croydon CR2 221 C4
Robin's Ct
Beckenham BR3 186 B1
Clapham Pk SW4 160 A5
Robinsfield Inf Sch
NW8 92 C5 230 A4
Robins Gr BR4 225 A5
Robinson Cl Enfield EN2 5 A2
11 Leyton E11 76 C5
Robinson Cres WD23 8 A3
Robinson Ct
5 Barnet EN4 14 D3
Islington N1 234 D6
4 Richmond TW9 132 B1
Thornton Heath CR0 204 D3
Robinson Ho
4 North Kensington
W10 90 D1
12 Tower Hamlets E14 97 C2
Robinson Rd
Dagenham RM10 81 C4
Mitcham SW19 180 C4
South Hackney E2 96 C5
Robinson's Cl W13 87 A2
Robinson St SW3 267 C6
Robinwood Gr UB8 82 B3
Robinwood Pl SW15 177 B6
Robsart St SW9 138 C3
Robson Ave NW10 68 A1
Robson Cl Enfield EN2 4 D3
Newham E6 100 A1
Robson Ct N12 30 A5
Robson Rd SE21, SE27 161 A1
Roby Ho EC1 242 A6
Roch Ave HA8 26 B1
Rochdale 8 SE19 183 C4
Rochdale Rd
Abbey Wood SE2 124 B2
Walthamstow E17 53 C2
Rochdale Way 4 SE8 141 C5
Roche Ho 15 E14 119 B6
Rochelle Cl SW11 136 B1
Rochelle Ct
Beckenham BR3 185 D3
14 Stepney E1 96 C1
Rochelle St 31 E2 95 D4
Rochemont Wlk 2 E8 96 A6
Roche Rd SW16 182 B2
Roche Sch The SW18 157 C6
Rochester Ave
Bromley BR1 187 B1
Feltham TW13 149 D2
Newham E13 99 C6
Rochester Cl
1 Blackfen DA15 168 B5
Enfield EN1 5 C4
Streatham SW16 182 A3
Rochester Ct
1 Bethnal Green E2 96 B3
9 Camden Town NW1 71 C1
Finchley N3 29 A1
Kingsbury NW9 45 B4
South Norwood SE25 184 A1
Rochester Dr
Old Bexley DA5 169 C5
Pinner HA5 40 D4
Rochester Gdns
Redbridge IG1 56 B2
South Croydon CR0 221 C5
Rochester Ho
Bermondsey SE1 252 D1
18 Deptford SE15 140 C6
Rochester Mews NW1 71 C1
Rochester Par TW13 150 A1
Rochester Pl NW1 71 C1
Rochester Rd
Carshalton SM5 218 D4
Kentish Town NW1 71 C2
Northwood HA6 39 D6
Rochester Row
SW1 115 C2 259 B4
Rochester Sq NW1 71 C1
Rochester St SW1 259 C5
Rochester Terr NW1 71 C2
Rochester Way
Eltham SE9 144 C2
Kidbrooke SE3, SE9 143 D2
Rochester Wlk SE1 252 C4
Roche Wlk SM5 202 B3
Rochford N17 33 C1
Rochford Ave RM6 58 C4
Rochford Cl 2 E6 99 D5
Rochford Way CR0 204 A3
Rochford Wlk 3 E8 74 A1
Rochfort Ho 4 SE8 119 B1
Rock Ave 13 SW14 133 B2
Rockbourne Rd SE23 162 D3
Rock Cl CR4 180 B1
Rockell's Pl SE22 162 B5
Rockfield Ho
Greenwich SE10 142 A6
2 Hendon NW4 46 D5
Rockford Ave UB6 87 B5
Rock Gdns RM10 81 D3
Rock Grove Way SE16 118 A2
Rockhall Rd NW2 68 D4
Rockhampton Cl 4
SE27 182 C6
Rockhampton Rd
South Croydon CR2 221 C2
West Norwood SE27,
SW16 182 C6
Rock Hill SE19 183 D6
Rockingham Cl SW15 133 D1
Rockingham Ct 19
BR3 185 C3
Rockingham Gate WD23 8 A5
Rockingham St
SE1 117 A3 262 A5
Rockland Rd SW15 135 A1
Rocklands N3 29 B3
Rocklands Dr HA7 25 C1
Rockley Ct 9 W14 112 D4
Rockley Rd W14 112 D4
Rockliffe Manor Prim Sch
SE18 145 D6
Rockmount Prim Sch
SE19 183 B4
Rockmount Rd
Plumstead Comm SE18,
SE2 123 D1
South Norwood SE19 183 B4
Rocks La SW13 134 A2
Rock St N4 72 C6
Rockstraw Ho 5 NW3 70 D1
Rockware Ave UB6 86 C6
Rockware Bsns Ctr
UB6 86 B6
Rockways EN5 11 D5
Rockwell Gdns SE19 183 C6
Rockwell Rd RM10 81 D3
Rockwood Ct N16 52 A2
Rocliffe St N1 94 D5 234 D3
Rocombe Cres SE23 162 C4
Rocque Ho SW6 264 C4
Rocque La SE3 142 D2
Rodborough Rd NW11 47 C1
Rodd Est TW17 193 B4
Roden Gdns CR0 205 C3
Rodenhurst Ct SW4 159 D6
Rodenhurst Rd SW4 159 D5
Roden St Ilford IG1 78 C5
Upper Holloway N7 72 B5
Roderick Ho 3 SE16 118 C2
Roderick Rd NW3 70 D4
Rodgers Cl WD6 9 D5
Rodgers Ho 4 SW4 159 D4
Rodin Ct N1 234 C5
Roding Ct 6 W12 111 C4
Roding Ho N1 234 A5
Roding Hospl IG4 55 D6
Roding La IG9 21 D3
Roding La N IG8 37 D1
Roding La S IG4 55 D5
Roding Lo IG1 55 D3
Roding Mews E1 118 A5
Roding Prim Sch RM8 80 C3
Roding Rd Hackney E5 75 A3
Newham E6 100 D2
Rodings Ct E4 36 B5
Rodings Row EN5 1 A1
Rodings The 4 IG8 37 C4
Roding Valley Sta IG9 37 D6
Roding View IG9 21 D3
Rodmarton St
W1 92 D2 237 D3
Rodmell WC1 233 B1
Rodmell Cl UB4 85 A3
Rodmell Slope N12 29 B5
Rodmere St SE10 120 C1
Rodmill La SW2 160 A4
Rodney Cl
New Malden KT3 199 C4
Pinner HA5 41 A2
Thornton Heath CR0 204 D1
Walton-on-T KT12 194 C1
Rodney Ct NW8 236 B6
Rodney Gdns
Hayes BR4 225 A4
Pinner HA5 40 C4
Rodney Ho
4 Cubitt Town E14 119 D2
Islington N1 233 D3
Notting Hill W11 245 A6
Rodney Pl
Merton SW19 180 A2
Newington
SE17 117 A2 262 B4
Walthamstow E17 35 B1
Rodney Rd
Mitcham CR4 202 C6
New Malden KT3 199 C4
Twickenham TW4 151 C4
Walton-on-T KT12 194 C1
Walworth SE17 117 B2 262 C3
Wanstead E11 55 B5
Rodney St N1 94 B5 233 D3
Rodwall Pl HA8 26 C3
Rodway Rd
Bromley BR1 187 B2
Putney SW15 156 A4
Rodwell Cl 2 HA4 40 C1
Rodwell Rd SE22 161 D5
Roe 5 NW9 27 D2
Roebourne Way E16 122 C4
Roebuck Cl
Feltham TW13 172 B6
Tottenham N17 33 D4
Roebuck Ct
Chingford E4 36 A3
2 New Malden KT3 199 C4
Roebuck Hts IG10 21 C4
Roebuck La IG9 21 C3
Roebuck Rd KT9 214 C3
Roedean Ave EN3 6 C5
Roedean Cl EN3 6 C4
Roedean Cres SW15 155 C6
Roe End NW9 45 A5
Roe Gn NW9 45 A4
Roe Green Jun & Inf Schs
NW9 44 D5
ROEHAMPTON 155 C4
Roehampton CE Prim Sch
SW15 156 B4
Roehampton Cl SW15 134 A1
Roehampton Ct SW13 134 A2
Roehampton Dr BR7 189 A4
Roehampton Gate
SW15 155 C5
Roehampton High St
SW15 156 A4
Roehampton La
Putney SW15 156 A5
Roehampton SW15 156 B3
Roehampton Univ (Digby
Stuart Coll) SW15 156 A6
Roehampton Univ
(Froebel Coll) SW15 155 D5
Roehampton Univ
(Southlands Coll)
SW15 156 A6
Roehampton Univ
(Whitelands Coll)
SW15 156 A4
Roehampton Vale
SW15 155 D2
Roe La NW9 45 A5
Roe Way SM6 220 A2
Roffey Ct 9 NW9 46 A5
Roffey St E14 120 A4
Rogate Ho E5 74 A5
Roger Ascham Prim Sch
E17 35 B2
Roger Dowley Ct 8 E2 96 C5
Roger's Almshouses 2
SW9 138 B1
Rogers Ct 16 E14 119 C6
Rogers Est 28 E2 96 C4
Rogers Gdns RM10 81 C3
Rogers Ho
9 Dagenham RM10 81 C5
Westminster SW1 259 D4
Rogers Rd
Canning Town E16 98 D1
Dagenham RM10 81 C3
Upper Tooting SW17 180 C6
Roger St WC1 94 B3 240 D5
Roger Stone Ct NW10 67 B6
Rogers Wlk N12 13 D1
Rohan Pl 4 IG4 56 B4
Rojack Rd SE23 162 D3
Rokeby Gdns IG8 37 A2
Rokeby Ho
9 Balham SW12 159 B4
Bloomsbury WC1 240 C5
Rokeby Pl SW20 178 B3
Rokeby Rd SE4 141 B3
Rokeby Sch
Kingston u T KT2 177 A3
Stratford E15 76 B1
Rokeby St E15 98 C6
Rokeland Ho SE4 141 A1
Rokell Ho BR3 185 D5
Roker Park Ave UB10 60 A4
Rokesby Cl DA16 145 B3
Rokesby Pl HA0 65 D3
Rokesly Ave N8 50 A4
Rokesly Jun & Inf Schs
N8 50 A4
Roland Ct SE19 183 D2
Roland Gdns
SW7 114 A1 256 B2
Roland Ho SW7 256 B2
Roland Mews 1 E1 96 D2
Roland Rd E17 54 B5
Roland Way
South Kensington
SW7 114 A1 256 B2
Walworth SE17 262 D1
Worcester Pk KT4 215 D6
Roles Gr RM6 59 A5
Rolfe Cl EN4 2 C1
Rolfe Ho N11 30 D6
Rolinsden Way BR2 225 D4
Rolland Ho W7 86 C2
Rollesby Rd KT19, KT9 214 C2
Rollesby Way SE28 102 C1
Rolleston Ave BR5 210 D3
Rolleston Cl BR5 210 D2
Rolleston Rd CR2 221 B1
Roll Gdns IG2 56 C4
Rollins St SE15 140 C6
Rollit Cres TW3 151 C6
Rollit Ho N7 72 C3
Rollit St N7 72 C3
Rollo Ct SW11 268 C1
Rolls Bldgs EC4 241 B2
Rollscourt Ave SE24 161 A6
Rolls Ct The E4 36 A5
Rolls Park Ave E4 35 D5
Rolls Park Rd E4 35 D5
Rolls Pas EC4 241 A2
Rolls Rd SE1 117 D1 263 D2
Rolt St SE8 141 A6
Rolvenden Gdns BR1 187 D3
Rolvenden Pl N17 34 A2
Roman Cl
Feltham TW14 150 C6
South Acton W3 110 D4
Roman Ct 4 N7 72 B2
Romanfield Rd SW2 160 B4
Romanhurst Ave BR2 208 C5

Romanhurst Gdns BR2,
BR3 208 C5
Roman Ind Est CR0 205 C2
Roman Lo 6 IG9 21 C3
Roman Rd
Chiswick W4 111 D2
Finchley N12 30 C2
Globe Town E2, E3 96 D5
Ilford IG1 78 D2
Muswell Hill N10 31 B3
Newham E6 100 A3
25 Old Ford E3 97 B6
Willesden NW2 68 C5
Roman Rise SE19 183 B4
Roman Road Prim Sch
E6 99 D3
Roman Sq SE28 124 A5
Roman Square Mkt 1
E3 97 B5
Roman Way
Barnsbury N7 72 B2
Croydon CR0 220 D6
4 Deptford SE15 140 C5
Enfield EN1 17 D6
Romany Gdns
Cheam SM3 201 C2
1 Higham Hill E17 35 A2
Romany Ho 8 N9 18 A1
Romany Prospect
SE19 183 B4
Romany Rise BR5 211 A1
Roma Rd E17 53 A6
Roma Read Cl SW15 156 B4
Romayne Ho SW4 137 D2
Romberg Rd SW17 159 A1
Romborough Gdns
SE13 164 A6
Romborough Way
SE13 164 A6
Romeland WD6 9 D5
Romeland Ct WD6 9 D5
Romer Ho 9 SW2 160 B6
Romero Cl SW9 138 B2
Romero Sq SE9 143 C1
Romeyn Rd SW16 160 B1
ROMFORD 59 D4
Romford Ho 17 N1 73 B2
Romford Rd
Forest Gate E7, E12 77 C3
Stratford E15 76 D2
Romford St E1 96 B2
Romilly Dr WD19 23 A6
Romilly Rd N4 72 D6
Romilly St W1 249 D6
Romily Ct SW6 135 A3
Rommany Ct SE27 183 B6
Rommany Rd SE27 183 B6
Romney Cl
Ashford TW15 171 A5
Chessington KT9 214 A4
7 Deptford SE14 140 C5
Harrow HA2 41 C2
North End NW11 48 A1
Tottenham N17 34 B2
Romney Ct
9 Hammersmith
W12 112 C4
9 Hampstead NW3 70 C2
15 Northolt UB5 84 D5
Romney Dr
Bromley BR1 187 D3
Harrow HA2 41 C2
Romney Gdns DA7 147 B4
Romney Ho
2 Blackwall E14 120 B6
Enfield EN1 18 A6
Sutton SM2 217 D2
Romney Mews W1 238 A4
Romney Par UB4 83 B5
Romney Rd
Greenwich SE10 142 B6
Hayes UB4 83 B5
New Malden KT3 199 B3
Romney Row NW2 68 D6
Romney St
SW1 116 A3 260 A5
Romola Rd SE24, SW2 160 D3
Romsey Cl BR6 226 D4
Romsey Gdns RM9 102 D6
Romsey Rd
Dagenham RM9 102 D6
Ealing W13 109 A6
Romulus Ct 7 TW8 131 D5
Ronald Ave E15 98 C4
Ronald Cl BR3 207 B4
Ronald Ct EN5 1 D2
Ronald Ho Eltham SE9 143 C1
4 Sutton SM1 218 B3
Ronald Ross Prim Sch
SW19 157 A4
Ronaldshay N4 50 C1
Ronalds Rd
Bromley BR1 187 A2
Islington N5 72 C3
Ronald St E1 96 C1
Ronaldstone Rd DA15 167 C5
Rona Rd NW3 71 A4
Ronart St HA3 42 D6
Rona Wlk 20 N1 73 B2
Rondu Rd NW2 69 A3
Ronelean Rd KT6 214 B5
Ron Leighton Way E6 100 A6
Ronnie La E12 78 C4
Ron Todd Cl RM10 103 C6
Ronver Lo E4 20 C1
Ronver Rd SE12 164 D3
Rood La EC3 117 C6 253 A6
Rookby Ct N21 16 D2
Rook Cl HA9 66 D5
Rookeries Cl TW13 150 C1
Rookery Cl NW9 45 D4
Rookery Cotts EN4 3 B2
Rookery Cres RM10 81 D1
Rookery Dr BR7 188 C2
Rookery La BR2 209 D3
Rookery Rd SW4 137 C1
Rookery Way NW9 45 D4
Rooke Way SE10 120 D1
Rookfield Ave N10 49 C5
Rookfield Cl N10 49 C5
Rook Lo IG1 55 D3
Rooks Heath High Sch
HA2 63 C5
Rooksmead Rd TW16 172 A1
Rooks Terr UB7 104 A4
Rookstone Rd SW17 180 D5
Rook Wlk E6 100 A1
Rookwood Ave
Wallington SM6 219 D4
West Barnes KT3 200 A5
Rookwood Gdns E4 20 D2
Rookwood Ho 2 IG11 101 B5
Rookwood Rd N16 52 A2
Roosevelt Ct 15 SW19 157 A3
Rootes Dr W10 90 D2
Ropemaker Rd SE16 119 A3
Ropemaker's Fields 7
E14 119 B6
Ropemaker St
EC2 95 B2 242 C4
Roper Ho 13 SE21 183 C6
Roper La SE1 117 C4 253 B1
Ropers Ave E4 36 A5
Roper's Orch SW3 267 A5
Roper St 1 SE9 166 C5
Ropers Wlk 13 SE24 160 C4
Roper Way CR4 181 A1
Ropery Bsns Pk SE7 121 C2
Ropery St E3 97 B3
Rope St SE16 119 A3
Ropewalk Gdns 18 E1 96 A1
Rope Yard Rails SE18 122 D3
Ropley St 6 E2 96 A5
Rosa Alba Mews N5 73 A4
Rosa Ave TW15 170 C6
Rosa Freedman Ctr
NW2 46 C1
Rosalind Ct 6 IG11 80 A1
Rosalind Ho 25 N1 95 C5
Rosaline Rd
SW6 135 A5 264 B3
Rosaline Terr SW6 264 B3
Rosamond St SE26 162 B1
Rosamund Cl CR2 221 B4
Rosamun St UB2 107 A2
Rosa Parks Ho 8
SW9 138 B3
Rosary Cl TW3, TW5 129 A3
Rosary Ct 17 E1 96 D2
Rosary Gdns
Ashford TW15 170 D6
Bushey WD23 8 C4
South Kensington
SW7 114 A2 256 B3
Rosary RC Inf Sch
TW5 129 C6
Rosary RC Jun Sch
TW5 129 C6
Rosary RC Prim Sch
NW3 70 C3
Rosaville Rd
SW6 135 B5 264 C3
Rosbury SW15 157 A5
Roscastle Rd SE4 163 A6
Roscoe St EC1 95 A3 242 B5
Roscoff Cl HA8 27 A2
Roscommon Ho 2
NW3 70 B3
Roseacre Cl Ealing W13 87 B2
Littleton TW17 192 C4
Roseacre Lo EN3 6 C1
Roseacre Rd DA16 146 B2
Rose Alley
Borough The SE1 252 B4
Broadgate EC2 243 B3
Rose Ave Mitcham CR4 180 D2
Morden SM4 202 A4
Woodford E18 37 B1
Rosebank
2 Dagenham W3 89 B1
Fulham SW6 134 C5
Penge SE20 184 B3
Rosebank Ave HA0 64 D4
Rosebank Cl
Colney Hatch N12 30 C5
Teddington TW11 175 A4
Rosebank Gdns Bow E3 97 B5
1 Dagenham W3 89 B1
Rosebank Gr E17 53 B6
Rosebank Rd
Hanwell W7 108 C4
Walthamstow E17 53 D3
Rosebank Villas E17 53 C5
Rosebank Way W3 89 B1
Rosebank Wlk
Camden Town NW1 71 D1
11 Woolwich SE7 122 A2
Rose Bates Dr NW9 44 C5
Rosebay Ho 20 E3 97 C2
Roseberry Gdns
Harringay N4 50 D3
Orpington BR6 227 C5
Roseberry Pl E8 73 D2
Roseberry St SE16 118 B2
Rosebery Ave
Finsbury EC1 94 C4 234 B1
Harrow HA2 63 B4
Kingston u T KT3 199 D6
Plashet E12 78 B2
Sidcup DA15 167 C4
Rosebery Ave *continued*
South Norwood CR7 183 A1
Tottenham N17 34 A1
Rosebery Cl SM4 200 D3
Rosebery Ct
Chessington KT9 214 B3
Holborn EC1 241 A6
Mayfair W1 248 C4
Rosebery Gdns
Ealing W13 87 A1
Hornsey N8 50 A4
Sutton SM1 217 D4
Rosebery Ho 21 E2 96 C5
Rosebery Ind Pk N17 34 B1
Rosebery Mews N10 31 C1
Rosebery Rd
Cheam SM1, SM2 217 B2
Clapham Pk SW2 160 A5
Isleworth TW3, TW7 152 A6
Kingston u T KT1 176 D1
Muswell Hill N10 31 C1
Rosebery Sq
Holborn EC1 241 A5
Kingston u T KT1 176 D1
Rosebine Ave TW2 152 B4
Rosebriars KT10 212 A3
Rose Bruford Coll
DA15 168 B3
Rosebury Ct SW16 182 B2
Rosebury Rd SW6 135 D3
Rosebury Vale HA4 62 A6
Rose Bush Ct NW3 70 D3
Rose Cotts KT10 212 B3
Rosecourt Rd CR0 204 B3
Rosecroft N22 32 B2
Rosecroft Ave NW3 69 C5
Rosecroft Gdns
Dollis Hill NW2 68 A5
Twickenham TW2 152 B3
Rosecroft Rd UB1 85 C3
Rosecroft Wlk
Pinner HA5 40 D4
Wembley HA0 65 D3
Rose & Crown Ct EC2 242 A2
Rose & Crown Yd SW1 249 B3
Rose Ct 7 Dalston E8 73 D1
Harrow HA2 64 A6
Ilford IG1 78 D2
Islington N1 234 C5
Muswell Hill N10 31 B3
3 Pinner HA5 40 C6
Spitalfields E1 243 D3
7 Wembley HA0 88 A5
10 Wimbledon SW19 179 B5
Rose Dale BR6 226 D6
Rosedale Ave UB3 83 B2
Rosedale Cl
Abbey Wood SE2 124 B3
Hanwell W7 108 D4
Stanmore HA7 25 B4
Rosedale Cnr BR7 188 B2
Rosedale Coll UB3 83 C1
Rosedale Ct N5 72 D4
Rosedale Dr RM9 80 B1
Rosedale Gdns RM9 80 B1
Rosedale Ho N16 51 B1
Rosedale Lo N14 15 B4
Rosedale Pl CR0 206 D2
Rosedale Rd
Dagenham RM9 80 B1
Forest Gate E7 77 C3
Richmond TW9 132 A1
Stoneleigh KT17 216 A3
Rosedale Terr W6 112 B3
Rosedene NW6 90 D6
Rosedene Ave
Morden SM4 201 C4
Southall UB6 85 C4
Streatham SW16 160 B1
Thornton Heath CR0 204 A2
Rosedene Ct HA4 39 C1
Rosedene Gdns IG2 56 C5
Rosedene Terr E10 75 D6
Rosedew Rd W6 134 D6
Rose End KT4 200 D1
Rosefield Cl SM5 218 C3
Rosefield Ct EN4 2 D1
Rosefield Gdns E14 119 C6
Roseford Ct 16 W12 112 D4
Rose Garden Cl HA8 26 A4
Rosegate Ho 32 E3 97 B5
Rose Gdns Ealing W5 109 D3
Feltham TW13 150 A2
Southall UB1 85 C3
Rose Glen NW9 45 B5
Rosehart Mews 8
W11 91 C1
Rosehatch Ave RM6 58 D6
Roseheath Rd TW4 151 B6
ROSEHILL 202 A1
Rosehill Claygate KT10 213 A2
Hampton TW12 173 C2
Rose Hill
Carshalton SM4, SM5 202 A2
Cheam SM1 201 D1
Rosehill Ave SM1, SM5 202 A1
Rosehill Ct SM4 202 A2
Rosehill Gdns
Greenford UB6 64 D3
Sutton SM1 218 A6
Rose Hill Park W SM1 218 A6
Rosehill Rd SW18 158 A6
Rose La RM6 59 A5
Roseland Cl N17 33 B3
Roseland Ho SW6 135 A2
Rose Lawn WD23 8 A3
Roseleigh Ave N5 72 D4
Roseleigh Cl 15 TW1 153 D5
Roselle Ct W5 88 A1
Rosemary Ave
East Finchley NW2 47 D5
East Molesey KT8 195 C5
Edmonton N9 18 B3
Enfield EN2 5 C4
Finchley N3 29 D1
Hounslow TW4 128 D3
Rosemary Branch Bridge
N1 235 D6
Rosemary Cl
Hillingdon UB8 82 C2
Thornton Heath CR0 204 A3
Rosemary Cotts 4
SW19 178 C3
Rosemary Ct 35 SE8 141 B6
Rosemary Dr
Redbridge IG4 55 D4
16 South Bromley E14 98 B1
Rosemary Gdns
Chessington KT9 214 A4
Dagenham RM8 59 B1
Mortlake SW14 133 A2
Rosemary Ho
Shoreditch N1 235 D5
Willesden NW10 90 B6
Rosemary La SW14 133 A2
Rosemary Rd
Bexley DA16 145 D4
Camberwell SE15 139 D5
Wandsworth SW17 158 A1
Rosemary St N1 235 D6
Rosemary Works Sch
N1 95 B6 235 D5
Rosemead NW9 46 A2
Rosemead Ave
Feltham TW13 149 D2
Mitcham CR4 181 C1
Wembley HA9 66 A3
Rosemead Prep Sch
SE27 161 A2
Rose Mews N18 34 B6
Rosemont Ave N12 30 A4
Rosemont Mans 11
NW3 69 D2
Rosemont Rd
Acton W3 110 D6
Kingston u T KT3 199 A6
Richmond TW10 154 A5
South Hampstead NW3 70 A2
Wembley HA0 88 A6
Rosemoor Ho 14 W13 109 A5
Rosemoor St
SW3 114 D2 257 C3
Rosemount Ct
2 Acton W3 110 D5
South Norwood SE25 205 C6
Rosemount Dr BR1 210 B5
Rosemount Lo W3 110 D6
Rosemount Point 10
SE23 162 D1
Rosemount Rd W13 87 A1
Rosemount Twrs 5
SM6 219 C2
Rosenau Cres SW11 267 C1
Rosenau Rd
SW11 136 D4 267 C2
Rosendale Prim Sch
SE21 161 A4
Rosendale Rd SE21,
SE24 161 A3
Roseneath Ave N21 16 D3
Roseneath Pl 2
SW16 182 B6
Roseneath Rd SW11 159 A5
Roseneath Wlk EN1 5 C1
Rosens Wlk HA8 10 D1
Rosenthal Ho SE6 163 D5
Rosenthal Rd SE6 164 A5
Rosenthorpe Rd SE15 162 D6
Roserton St E14 120 A4
Rosery The CR0 206 D3
Rose Sq SW7 256 D2
Rose St Holborn EC4 241 D2
Strand WC2 116 A6 250 A6
Roses The IG8 36 D3
Rosethorn Cl SW12 159 D4
Rosetta Cl SW8 270 B3
Rosetta Ct SE19 183 C3
Rosetta Prim Sch E16 99 B2
Rosetti Terr RM8 80 B4
Roseveare Rd SE12 187 C6
Roseville N21 16 C3
Roseville Ave TW3,
TW4 151 C6
Roseville Rd UB3 106 A2
Rosevine Rd SW20 178 C2
Rosewall Ct SW19 179 D5
Roseway SE21 161 B5
Rose Way Edgware HA8 27 A6
Lee SE12 165 A6
Rosewell Cl SE20 184 B3
Rose Wlk Surbiton KT5 198 D4
West Wickham BR4 224 B6
Rosewood Ave UB6 65 A2
Rosewood Cl DA14 168 C1
Rosewood Ct
Bromley BR1 187 D2
Dagenham RM6 58 C4
Kingston u T KT2 176 C3
2 Leyton E11 76 B4
Rosewood Dr TW17 192 B4
Rosewood Gdns SE13 142 A3
Rosewood Gr SM1 218 A6
Rosewood Ho 9 NW3 69 D2
Rosewood Sq W12 90 A1
Rosher Cl E15 76 B1
Roshni Ho SW17 180 C4
Rosh Pinah Prim Sch
Edgware HA8 10 D1
Edgware HA8 26 C6
Rosina Ct SW17 180 C5
Rosina St E9 74 D2
Roskeen Ct 1 SW19 178 C3
Roskell Rd SW15 134 D2
Roskild Ct HA9 66 B4
Roslin Ho 2 E1 118 D6
Roslin Rd W3 110 D3
Roslin Way BR1 187 A5
Roslyn Cl CR4 180 B1
Roslyn Rd N15 51 C4
Rosmead Rd
W11 113 A6 244 B6
Rosoman Pl EC1 241 B6
Rosoman St EC1 234 B1
Rossal Ct 2 SE20 184 B3
Rossall Cres NW10 88 B4
Rossanne Ho N3 29 D3
Ross Ave Dagenham RM8 59 B1
Finchley NW7 29 A5
Ross Cl Harrow HA3 24 A3
Hayes UB3 105 B2
Northolt UB5 64 B4
Ross Ct Chislehurst BR7 188 B3
Colindale NW9 45 C6
Ealing W13 87 B2
Edgware HA8 10 D2
1 Hackney E5 74 B4
4 Putney SW15 156 D4
South Croydon CR2 221 A2
Rossdale SM1 218 C3
Rossdale Dr
Ponders End N9 18 C5
Welsh Harp NW9 45 A1
Rossdale Rd SW15 134 C1
Rosse Gdns SE13 164 B5
Rosse Mews SE3 143 B4
Rossendale Cl EN2 4 D6
Rossendale Ho 7 E5 74 B6
Rossendale St E5 74 B6
Rossendale Way
NW1 93 C6 232 B6
Rossendon Ct 1 SM6 219 C2
Rossetti Ct WC1 239 C4
Rossetti Gdns Mans
SW3 267 C6
Rossetti Ho SW1 259 D3
Rossetti Mews NW8 229 D5
Rossetti Rd SE16 118 B1
Rossetti Studios SW3 267 B6
Ross Ho
2 Kidbrooke SE18 144 A4
Twickenham TW2 151 D2
18 Wapping E1 118 B5
Rossignol Gdns SM5 219 A6
Rossindel Rd TW3 151 C6
Rossington Cl EN1 6 B5
Rossington St E5 74 A6
Rossiter Fields EN5 13 B5
Rossiter Rd SW12 159 B3
Rossland Cl DA6 169 D6
Rosslyn Ave
Barnes SW13 133 D2
Chingford E4 20 D2
Dagenham RM8 59 C2
East Barnet EN4 14 C5
Feltham TW14 150 A5
Rosslyn Cl
Ashford TW16 171 C4
Coney Hall BR4 224 D5
Hayes UB3 83 B2
Rosslyn Cres
Harrow HA1 42 D5
Wembley HA9 66 A4
Rosslyn Ct NW3 70 C3
Rosslyn Hill NW3 70 B3
Rosslyn Ho 8 TW9 132 B4
Rosslyn Mans
8 Hampstead NW3 70 A2
South Hampstead NW6 70 A2
Rosslyn Mews 7 NW3 70 B4
Rosslyn Park Mews
NW3 70 B3
Rosslyn Rd Barking IG11 79 B1
Twickenham TW1 153 C5
Walthamstow E17 54 A5
Rossmore Cl EN3 6 D1
Rossmore Ct NW1 237 C6
Rossmore Rd
NW1 92 C3 237 B6
Ross Par SM6 219 B2
Ross Rd
South Norwood SE25 205 C6
Twickenham TW2 152 A3
Wallington SM6 219 C3
Ross Way SE9 144 A2
Rossway Dr WD23 8 B6
Rosswood Gdns SM6 219 C2
Rosswood Ho 13 SM6 219 B2
Rosswood Lo CR0 222 D6
Rostella Rd SW17 180 B6
Rostrever Gdns UB3 105 C5
Rostrevor Ave N15 51 D3
Rostrevor Gdns UB2 107 A1
Rostrevor Mans SW6 264 C2
Rostrevor Mews SW6 264 C1
Rostrevor Rd
Fulham SW6 135 B4 264 C2
Wimbledon SW19 179 C5
Rotary Ct KT8 196 C6
Rotary Lo 12 SE27 160 D1
Rotary St SE1 261 D6
Rothay NW1 231 D2
Rothbury Gdns TW7 131 A5
Rothbury Rd E9 75 C1
Rothbury Wlk N17 34 A3
Rotheley Ho 39 E9 74 C1
Rotherfield Ct
De Beauvoir Town N1 73 B1
Shoreditch N1 95 B6 235 C6
Rotherfield Prim Sch
N1 95 A6 235 B6
Rotherfield Rd
Enfield EN3 6 D6
Wallington SM5 219 A3
Rotherfield St
Islington N1 73 A1
Shoreditch N1 95 A6 235 B6
Rotherham Wlk SE1 251 C3
Rotherhill Ave SW16 181 D4
ROTHERHITHE 118 D3
Rotherhithe Bsns Est 6
SE16 118 C2
Rotherhithe New Rd
SE16 118 B1
Rotherhithe Old Rd
SE16 118 D2
Rotherhithe Prim Sch
SE16 118 D2
Rotherhithe St SE16 118 C4
Rotherhithe Sta SE16 118 C4
Rotherhithe Tunnel
SE16 118 D5
Rother Ho SE15 140 B1
Rotherwick Hill W5 88 B3
Rotherwick Rd NW11 47 C2
Rotherwood Cl SW20 179 A2
Rotherwood Rd SW15 134 D2
Rothery St N1 234 D6
Rothesay Ave
Merton SW20 179 A1
Mortlake SW14, TW10 132 D1
Northolt UB6 64 B2
Rothesay Ct
4 Catford SE6 164 D2
Grove Pk SE12 165 B1
13 Kennington SE11 138 C6
Rothesay Rd SE25 205 C5
Rothley Ct NW8 236 C6
Rothsay Rd E7 77 C2
Rothsay St SE1 117 C3 263 A5
Rothsay Wlk 10 E14 119 C2
Rothschild Rd W4 111 A3
Rothschild St SE27 182 D6
Rothwell Ct
2 Bromley BR1 187 B2
4 Harrow HA1 42 D4
Rothwell Gdns RM9 102 C6
Rothwell Ho TW5 129 C6
Rothwell Rd RM9 102 C6
Rothwell St
10 Hampstead NW1 70 D1
Primrose Hill NW1 230 D6
Roth Wlk N7 72 B6
Rotten Row
SW1 114 D4 247 C2
Rotterdam Dr E14 120 A3
Rouel Rd
Bermondsey SE16 118 A2
Bermondsey SE16 118 A3
Rougemont Ave SM4 201 C3
Roundabout Ho HA6 22 A2
Roundacre SW19 156 D2
Roundel Cl SE4 141 B1
Roundell Ho 14 SE21 183 C6
Rounders Ct 7 RM10 81 D2
Round Gr CR0 206 D2
Roundhay Cl SE23 162 D2
Roundhedge Way EN2 4 B5
Round Hill SE23 162 C1
Roundhill Dr EN2 4 B1
ROUNDSHAW 220 B1
Roundshaw Ctr SM6 220 A1
Roundtable Rd BR1 164 D1
Roundtree Rd HA0 65 B3
Roundways HA4 61 D5
Roundway The
Claygate KT10 212 D2
Tottenham N17 33 B2
Roundwood BR7 188 D1
Roundwood Ave UB11 105 A5
Roundwood Cl HA4 39 B2
Roundwood Rd NW10 67 D1
Rounton Rd E3 97 C3
Rountree Ct 9 UB1 85 D1
Roupell Ho 7 KT2 176 B3
Roupell Rd SW2 160 B3
Roupell St SE1 116 C5 251 B3
Rousden St NW1 71 C1
Rouse Gdns SE21 183 C6
Routemaster Cl E13 99 B4
Routh Ct TW14 149 B3
Routh Rd SW18 158 C4
Routh St E6 100 B2
Rover Ho 26 N1 95 C6
Rowallan Ct 3 SE6 164 D3
Rowallan Rd
SW6 135 A5 264 A3
Rowallen Par RM8 58 C1
Rowan N10 31 B1
Rowan Ave E4 35 B4
Rowan Cl Ealing W5 110 A4
Harrow HA7 24 D4
Ilford IG1 79 B3
Kingston u T KT3 177 C1
Streatham SW16 181 C2
Wembley HA0 65 A5
Rowan Cres SW16 181 C2
Rowan Ct
19 Camberwell SE15 139 D5
Forest Hill SE26 184 C6
11 Kingston u T KT2 176 C3
Newham E13 99 B5
Twickenham TW4 151 D6
Wandsworth SW11 158 D5
Wimbledon SW20 178 B1
Rowan Dr NW9 46 A6

Rowan Gdns CR0 221 D5
Rowan Ho 9 Bow E3 97 B6
  Dagenham NW10 89 C3
  East Bedfont TW14 149 B5
  Ilford IG1 79 B3
  5 Maitland Pk NW3 70 D2
  Sidcup DA14 167 D1
Rowan Pl UB3 105 D6
Rowan Rd
  Brentford TW8 131 B5
  Brook Green W6 112 D2
  DA7 147 A2
  Mitcham SW16 181 C1
  West Drayton UB7 104 A2
Rowans The
  Ashford TW16 171 D5
  Edmonton N13 17 A1
  7 Sutton SM2 217 D2
Rowan Terr W6 112 D2
Rowantree Cl N21 17 B3
Rowantree Rd
  Edmonton N21 17 B3
  Enfield EN2 4 D3
Rowan Way RM6 58 C6
Rowan Wlk BR2 226 B5
  7 Dartmouth Pk N19 71 C6
  Hampstead Garden Suburb N2 48 A4
  Kensal Town W10 91 A3
  1 New Barnet EN5 13 D6
Rowanwood Ave DA15 168 A3
Rowanwood Mews EN2 4 D3
Rowben Cl N20 13 D3
Rowberry Cl SW6 134 C5
Rowcross St SE1 117 D1 263 D2
Rowdell Rd UB5 85 C6
Rowden Par E4 35 C4
Rowden Park Gdns E4 35 C4
Rowden Rd
  Beckenham BR3 185 B2
  Chingford E4 35 D4
  West Ewell KT19 215 A4
Rowditch La SW11 137 A3
Rowdon Ave NW10 68 B1
Rowdowns Rd RM9 81 B1
Rowe Gdns IG11 102 A5
Rowe Ho E9 74 C2
Rowe La E9 74 C3
Rowena Cres SW11 136 C3
Rowe Wlk HA2 63 C5
Rowfant Rd SW12, SW17 159 A2
Rowhill Mans 11 E5 74 B4
Rowhill Rd E5 74 B4
Rowington Cl W2 91 D2
Rowland Ave HA3 43 C6
Rowland Ct E16 98 D3
  South Croydon CR0 221 C6
Rowland Gr SE26 162 B1
Rowland Hill Almshouses 7 TW15 170 C5
Rowland Hill Ave N17 33 B4
Rowland Hill Ho SE1 251 C2
Rowland Hill St NW3 70 C3
Rowlands Ave HA5 23 D4
Rowlands Cl
  Hendon NW7 28 A3
  Highgate N6 49 A3
Rowlands Rd RM8 81 B6
Rowland Way
  Ashford TW15 171 B3
  Merton SW19 179 D2
Rowley Ave DA15 168 B4
Rowley Cl HA0 66 B1
Rowley Ct EN1 17 C6
Rowley Gdns N4 51 A2
Rowley Green Rd EN5 12 A6
Rowley Ho SE8 141 C6
Rowley Ind Pk W3 110 D3
Rowley La EN5 11 D6
Rowley Rd N15 51 A4
Rowley Way NW8 229 A6
Rowlheys Pl UB7 104 A3
Rowlls Rd KT1 198 B6
Rowney Gdns RM9 80 C2
Rowney Rd RM9 80 B2
Rowntree Cl NW6 69 C2
Rowntree Clifford Cl 7 E13 99 B4
Rowntree Path 1 SE28 124 B5
Rowntree Rd TW2 152 C3
Rowse Cl E15 98 A6
Rowsham Ct HA1 64 C5
Rowsley Ave NW4 46 C6
Rowstock 1 NW5 71 D2
Rowstock Gdns N7 71 D3
Rowton Rd SE18 145 A5
Roxborough Ave
  Harrow HA1 42 C2
  Hounslow TW7 130 D5
Roxborough Pk HA1 42 C2
Roxborough Rd HA1 42 B3
Roxbourne Cl UB5 62 D2
Roxbourne Fst & Mid Schs HA2 63 A6
Roxburgh Rd SE27 182 D5
Roxburn Way HA4 61 D5
Roxby Pl SW6 135 C6 265 B6
ROXETH 64 A6
Roxeth Ct 6 TW15 170 C5
Roxeth Fst & Mid Sch HA2 64 B6
Roxeth Gr HA2 63 D4
Roxeth Green Ave HA2 63 D6
Roxeth Hill HA2 64 C6
Roxeth Manor Fst & Mid Schs HA2 63 C5
Roxeth Mead Sch HA2 64 B6
Roxford Cl TW17 193 C4
Roxford Ho 2 E3 97 D3
Roxley Rd SE13 163 D5
Roxton Gdns CR0 223 C3
Roxwell 10 NW1 71 B2
Roxwell Rd
  Barking IG11 102 A5
  Shepherd's Bush W12 112 A4
Roxwell Trad Pk E10 53 A2
Roxwell Way IG8 37 C3
Roxy Ave RM6 58 C2
Royal Academy of Dramatic Art* WC1 93 D2 239 C4
Royal Acad of Arts* W1 115 C6 249 A5
Royal Acad of Dance SW11 266 D1
Royal Acad of Music NW1 238 B5
Royal Albert Hall* SW7 114 B4 246 C1
Royal Albert Sta E16 122 A6
Royal Albert Way E6 122 B6
Royal Arc W1 249 A5
Royal Armouries The* E1 253 C5
Royal Ave SW3 114 D1 257 C2
  Worcester Pk KT4 215 C6
Royal Avenue Ho SW3 257 C2
Royal Ballet Sch The
  Hammersmith W14 112 D1
  St Giles WC2 94 A1 240 B1
Royal Ballet Sch (White Lodge) The TW10 155 B3
Royal Brompton Hospl
  Chelsea SW3 114 B1 256 C2
  Chelsea SW3 114 C1 257 A2
Royal Cir SE27 160 D1
Royal Cl Deptford SE8 141 B6
  Hillingdon UB7 82 B1
  Ilford IG3 58 A2
  Locksbottom BR6 226 D4
  Putney SW19 156 D2
  Stamford Hill N16 51 C1
  Worcester Pk KT4 215 C6
Royal College of Physicians Liby NW1 93 B3 238 D6
Royal College St NW1 93 C6 232 B6
Royal Coll of Anaesthetists WC1 240 C3
Royal Coll of Art SW7 114 B4 246 C1
Royal Coll of Art Sculpture Sch SW11 136 C5 267 A3
Royal Coll of Midwives W1 93 B2 238 C3
Royal Coll of Music SW7 114 B3 256 C6
Royal Coll of Obstetricians & Gynaecologists NW1 92 D3 237 C6
Royal Coll of Ophthalmologists NW1 238 A5
Royal Coll of Paediatrics & Child Health W1 238 D4
Royal Coll of Pathologists SW1 115 D5 249 C3
Royal Coll of Physicians NW1 93 B3 238 D6
Royal Coll of Radiologists W1 238 D4
Royal Coll of Science SW7 114 B3 256 C6
Royal Coll of Speech Language Therapists SE1 252 C3
Royal Coll of Surgeons WC2 94 B1 240 D2
Royal Connaught Apts E16 121 D5
Royal Courts of Justice WC2 94 C1 241 A1
Royal Cres Ilford IG2 57 B3
  Ruislip HA4 63 A5
  W11 113 A5 244 A3
Royal Crescent Mews W11 112 D5
Royal Crest Ho SM2 217 A1
Royal Ct
  City of London EC3 242 D1
  Enfield EN1 17 C5
  9 Kingston u T KT2 176 D3
  Mottingham SE9 166 B3
  Rotherhithe SE16 119 B3
  Ruislip HA4 40 A2
Royal Docks Com Sch The E16 99 C1
Royal Docks Rd E6 100 D2
Royal Dr N11 31 A5
Royal Duchess Mews SW12 159 B4
Royal Exchange* EC3 242 D1
Royal Exchange Bldgs EC3 242 D1
Royal Festival Hall* SE1 116 B5 250 D3
Royal Free Hospl NW3 70 C3
Royal Fusiliers Mus* E1 253 C5
Royal Gdns W7 109 A3
Royal Geographical Society SW7 246 D1
Royal Hill SE10 142 A5
Royal Hill Ct 2 SE10 142 A5
Royal Horticultural Society (Lawrence Hall & Conf Ctr) SW1 259 C5
Royal Horticultural Society (Lindley Hall) SW1 259 C4
Royal Hospital (Army Pensioners)* SW1 115 A1 258 A1
Royal Hospital Rd SW3 114 D1 257 D1
Royal Hospl and Home SW15 157 A5
Royal La Hillingdon UB7 82 B1
  Hillingdon UB8 82 B3
Royal Langford Apartments 3 NW6 91 D5
Royal London Est N17 34 B4
Royal London Est The NW10 89 B5
Royal London Homeopathic Hospl The WC1 94 A2 240 B4
Royal London Hospl Archives & Mus* E1 96 B2
Royal London Hospl (Mile End) The E2 96 D4
Royal London Hospl (St Clements) The E3 97 B4
Royal London Hospl (Whitechapel) The E1 96 B2
Royal Marsden Hospl SW3 114 B1 256 D2
Royal Mews KT8 196 C6
Royal Mews The* SW1 115 B3 258 D6
Royal Military Sch of Music (Kneller Hall) TW2 152 B5
Royal Mint Pl 6 E1 118 A6
Royal Mint St E1 117 D6 253 D6
Royal National Orthopaedic Hospl
  Regent's Pk W1 93 B3 238 D5
  Stanmore HA7 9 C2
Royal National TNE Hospl The WC1 94 B4 233 C2
Royal Nat TN&E Hospl The W5 87 C2
Royal Naval Pl SE14 141 B5
Royal Oak Ct
  Dagenham RM8 80 C6
  9 Shoreditch N1 95 C4
Royal Oak Mews 9 TW11 175 A5
Royal Oak Pl SE22 162 B5
Royal Oak Rd
  Bexley DA6 147 C1
  DA6 169 B6
  5 Hackney E8 74 B2
Royal Oak Sta W2 91 D2
Royal Oak Yd SE1 253 A1
Royal Obsy The* SE10 142 B5
Royal Opera Arc SW1 249 C4
Royal Orchard Cl SW18 157 A4
Royal Par
  Blackheath Vale SE3 142 D3
  Chislehurst BR7 189 A3
  11 Dagenham RM10 81 D2
  Ealing W5 88 A4
  Fulham SW6 264 A4
  12 Richmond TW9 132 C4
Royal Park Prim Sch DA14 169 A1
Royal Pl 11 SE10 142 A5
Royal Rd
  Kennington SE17 138 D6
  Newham E16 99 D1
  Sidcup DA14 168 D1
  Teddington TW11 174 B5
Royal Route HA9 66 B4
Royal Russell Sch CR0 222 B3
Royal Sch Hampstead The NW3 70 B4
Royal St SE1 116 B3 260 D6
Royal Tower Lo 3 SE1 118 A6
Royalty Ho W1 239 C1
Royalty Mews W1 239 C1
Royalty Studios W11 91 A1
Royal United Services Mus* SW1 250 A3
Royal Veterinary Coll NW1 93 D6 232 C5
Royal Victoria Pl 7 E16 121 B5
Royal Victoria Sq E16 121 B6
Royal Victoria Sta E16 121 A6
Royal Victor Pl E3 96 D5
Royal Wlk SM6 219 B5
Roycraft Ave IG11 101 D5
Roycroft Cl
  Streatham SW2 160 C3
  Woodford E18 37 B2
Roydene Rd SE18 123 C1
Roydon Cl 7 SW11 136 D3
Roy Gdns IG2 57 D4
Roy Gr TW12 173 D4
Royle Cres W13 87 A3
Roymount Ct TW2 152 C1
Roy Ridley Ho 6 SW4 137 D2
Roy Sq E14 119 A6
Royston Ave
  Carshalton SM1 218 B5
  Chingford E4 35 D3
  Wallington SM6 219 D4
Royston Cl
  Cranford TW5 128 B4
  Walton-on-T KT12 194 A1
Royston Ct
  Hinchley Wood KT10 212 D6
  New Cross SE4 141 B3
  1 Newham E13 99 A6
  Redbridge IG1 55 D3
  3 Richmond TW9 132 B4
  Ruislip HA5 40 C2
  Tolworth KT6 214 C6
Royston Gdns IG1 55 D3
Royston Gr HA5 23 C4
Royston Ho
  Friern Barnet N11 31 A6
  14 SE15 140 A6
Royston Lo SW19 180 A4
Royston Par IG1 55 D3
Royston Park Rd HA5 23 C5
Royston Prim Sch SE20 184 D2
Royston Rd
  Penge SE20 184 D2
  Richmond TW10 154 A6
Royston St 24 E2 96 C5
Roystons The KT5 198 D4
Rozel Ct 3 N1 95 C6
Rozelle Ct 1 CR7 204 C3
Rozel Rd SW4 137 C2
Rubastic Rd UB2 106 C3
Rubens Rd UB5 84 D5
Rubens St SE6 163 B2
Rubin Pl 14 EN3 7 C6
Ruby Ct TW13 149 D1
Ruby Rd E17 53 C6
Ruby St SE15 140 B6
  Stonebridge NW10 67 A1
Ruby Triangle SE15 140 B6
Ruckholt Cl E10 75 D5
Ruckholt Rd E10 75 D5
Rucklidge Ave NW10 90 A5
Rudall Cres NW3 70 B4
Rudbeck Ho 11 SE15 140 A5
Ruddington Cl E5 75 A4
Ruddock Cl HA8 27 A3
Ruddstreet Cl SE18 123 A2
Rudge Ho 1 SE16 118 A3
Rudgwick Terr NW8 92 C6 230 B5
Rudhall Ho 4 SW2 160 C5
Rudland Rd DA7 147 D2
Rudloe Rd SW12 159 C4
Rudolf Pl SW8 270 B5
Rudolph Ct SE22 162 B4
Rudolph Rd E13 98 D5
  Paddington NW6 91 C5
Rudstone Ho 10 E3 97 D4
Rudyard Ct SE1 252 D1
Rudyard Gr NW7 27 A4
Ruegg Ho 5 SE18 144 C6
Ruffetts Cl CR2 222 B1
Ruffetts The CR2 222 B1
Ruffle Cl UB7 104 B4
Rufford Cl HA3 43 A3
Rufford St N1 94 A6 233 B6
Rufford Street Mews N1 72 A1
Rufford Twr 5 W3 110 D5
Rufforth Ct 1 NW9 27 C2
Rufus Bsns Ctr SW18 157 D2
Rufus Cl HA4 63 A5
Rufus Ho SE1 263 D6
Rufus St N1 95 C4
Rugby Ave Edmonton N9 17 D3
  Northolt UB6 64 B2
  Wembley HA0 65 C4
Rugby Cl HA1 42 C5
Rugby Gdns RM9 80 C2
Rugby Mans W14 254 B4
Rugby Rd
  Bedford Pk W4 111 C4
  Dagenham RM9 80 C2
  Queensbury NW9 44 D5
  Twickenham TW1, TW2, TW7 152 C5
Rugby St WC1 94 B3 240 C5
Rugg St E14 119 C6
Rugless Ho 2 E14 120 A4
Rugmere 4 NW1 71 A1
RUISLIP 39 B2
Ruislip Cl UB6 85 D3
RUISLIP COMMON 39 B4
Ruislip Ct HA4 61 D6
RUISLIP GARDENS 61 D5
Ruislip Gardens Prim Sch HA4 61 D4
Ruislip Gardens Sta HA4 62 A4
Ruislip Lido* HA4, HA5 39 B5
Ruislip Lido Rly* HA4 39 B5
RUISLIP MANOR 40 A1
Ruislip Manor Sta HA4 40 A1
Ruislip Rd UB6, UB5 85 C4
Ruislip Rd E
  Ealing UB6, W7 86 D3
  Greenford UB6 86 B3
Ruislip St SW17 180 D6
Ruislip Sta HA4 39 D1
Rumball Ho 14 SE5 139 C5
Rumbold Rd SW6 135 D5 265 D3
Rum Cl E1 118 C6
Rumford Ho SE1 262 A5
Rumsey Cl TW12 173 B4
Rumsey Rd SW9 138 B2
Runacres Ct SE17 262 A1
Runbury Circ NW9 67 B6
Runcorn Cl N17 52 B5
Runcorn Pl W11 244 A6
Rundell Cres NW4 46 B4
Rundell Twr SW8 270 C2
Runes Cl CR4 202 C5
Runnelfield HA1 64 C5
Running Horse Yd 12 TW8 132 A6
Runnymede SW19 180 B2
Runnymede Cl TW2 151 D4
Runnymede Cres SW16 182 A2
Runnymede Ct
  Roehampton SW15 156 A3
  1 Wallington SM6 219 B2
Runnymede Gdns
  Greenford UB6 86 C5
  Twickenham TW2 151 D4
Runnymede Ho
  Hackney E9 75 A4
  Richmond TW10 154 C6
Runnymede Rd TW2 151 D5
Runway The HA4 62 C3
Rupack St 3 SE16 118 C4
Rupert Ave 6 HA9 66 A3
Rupert Ct W1 249 C6
Rupert Gdns SW9 138 D3
Rupert Ho SE11 261 B3
  8 Upper Holloway N19 71 D5
Rupert Rd
  Bedford Pk W4 111 C3
  Paddington NW6 91 B5
  Upper Holloway N19 71 D6
Rupert St W1 115 D6 249 C6
Rural Way SW16 181 B3
Rusbridge Cl E8 74 A3
Ruscoe Ho 12 SW27 182 D5
Ruscoe Rd E16 98 D1
Ruscombe Way TW14 149 D4
Rusham Rd SW12 158 D4
Rushbrook Cres E17 35 B2
Rushbrook Ho 20 SW8 137 D3
Rushbrook Rd SE9 167 A2
Rushbury Ct 4 TW12 173 C2
Rushby Ct SW4 270 A1
Rush Common Mews 18 SW2 160 B4
Rushcroft Rd
  Brixton SW2, SW9 138 C1
  Chingford E4 35 D3
Rush Croft Sch E4 35 D3
Rushcutters Ct 18 SE16 119 A2
Rushden Cl SE19 183 B3
Rushdene SE2 124 D3
Rushdene Ave EN4 14 C4
Rushdene Cl UB5 84 C5
Rushdene Cres UB5 84 C4
Rushdene Rd HA5 40 D3
Rushden Gdns
  Ilford IG5 56 C6
  Mill Hill NW7 28 C4
Rushen Wlk SM5 202 B1
Rushet Rd BR5 190 A1
Rushett Cl KT7 197 B1
Rushett Rd KT7 197 B2
Rushey Cl KT3 199 B5
Rushey Gn SE6 163 D4
Rushey Green Prim Sch SE6 163 D3
Rushey Hill EN2 4 B1
Rushey Mead SE4 163 C6
Rushford Rd SE4 163 B5
Rush Green Rd RM7, RM8, RM10 59 D1
Rushgrove Ave NW9 45 D5
Rushgrove Ct NW9 45 C4
Rushgrove St SE18 122 B2
Rush Hill Mews 3 SW11 137 A2
Rush Hill Rd SW11 137 A2
Rushlake Ho 3 SW11 137 A3
Rushley Cl BR2 226 A4
Rushman Villas KT3 199 D5
Rushmead
  5 Bethnal Green E2 96 B4
  Richmond TW10 153 B1
Rushmead Cl CR0 221 D4
Rushmere Ct KT4 216 A6
Rushmere Ho 2 SW15 156 A3
Rushmere Pl SW19 178 D5
Rushmon Pl SM3 217 A2
Rushmoor Cl HA5 40 B5
Rushmore Cl BR1 210 A6
Rushmore Cres 9 E5 74 D4
Rushmore Ho
  9 Kentish Town N7 71 D3
  W14 254 B5
Rushmore Prim Sch E5 74 D4
Rushmore Rd
  Clapton Pk E5 74 D4
  Hackney E5 75 A4
Rusholme Ave RM10 81 C5
Rusholme Gr SE19 183 C5
Rusholme Rd SW15 157 A5
Rushout Ave HA3 43 B3
Rush The SW20 179 B2
Rushton Ho 26 SW8 137 D3
Rushton St N1 95 B5 235 D4
Rushworth St SE1 116 D4 251 D1
Rushy Meadow La SM5 218 C5
Rushy Meadow Prim Sch SM5 218 C5
Ruskin Ave DA16 146 A3
  Feltham TW14 149 D5
  Plashet E12 78 A2
  Richmond TW9 132 C5
Ruskin Cl NW11 47 D3
Ruskin Ct
  Herne Hill SE5 139 B2
  SE9 166 B5
  Southgate N21 16 B4
Ruskin Dr
  North Cheam KT4 216 C6
  Orpington BR6 227 C5
  Welling DA16 146 A2
Ruskin Gdns Ealing W5 87 D3
  Harrow HA3 44 B5
Ruskin Gr DA16 146 A3
Ruskin Ho SW1 259 D3
Ruskin Par CR0 221 B3
Ruskin Park Ho SE5 139 B2
Ruskin Rd
  Belvedere DA17 125 C2
  Croydon CR0 220 D6
  Isleworth TW7 130 D2
  Southall UB1 107 A6
  Tottenham N17 33 D2
  Wallington SM5 219 A3
Ruskin Way SW19 180 B2
Ruskin Wlk BR2 210 B3
  Edmonton N9 18 A2
  Herne Hill SE24 161 A6
Rusland Ave BR6 227 B5
Rusland Hts HA1 42 C5
Rusland Park Rd HA1 42 C5
Rusper Cl
  Cricklewood NW2 68 C5
  Stanmore HA7 25 C6
Rusper Ct SW9 138 A3
Rusper Rd
  Dagenham RM9 80 C2
  Tottenham N17, N22 51 A6
Russel Cl BR3 208 A6
Russel Ct N14 15 D6
Russell Ave N22 32 D1
Russell Cl
  Bexleyheath DA7 147 C1
  Chiswick W4 133 D6
  Greenwich SE7 143 C5
  Ruislip HA4 62 C6
  Stonebridge NW10 67 A1
Russell Ct
  Battersea SW11 268 B1
  Bloomsbury WC1 240 A5
  Bromley BR1 186 D3
  12 New Barnet EN5 2 A1
  5 Peckham SE15 140 B3
  St James SW1 249 B3
  Streatham SW16 182 B5
  Surbiton KT6 198 A2
  Wallington SM6 219 C3
  4 Walthamstow E10 53 D2
  Wembley HA0 66 A1
Russell Gdns
  East Barnet N20 14 C2
  Ilford IG2 57 B2
  Richmond TW10 153 C2
  Temple Fortune NW11 47 A3
  W14 113 A3 254 A6
  West Drayton UB7 104 C1
Russell Gdns Mews W14 113 A3 254 A6
Russell Gr
  33 Brixton SW9 138 C4
  Edgware NW7 27 C6
Russell Ho
  21 Poplar E14 97 C1
  SW1 259 A2
Russell Kerr Cl W4 133 A5
Russell La N20 14 D2
Russell Lo
  5 Chingford E4 20 A2
  SE1 262 C6
Russell Mans WC1 240 B4
Russell Mead HA3 24 D2
Russell Par NW11 47 A3
Russell Pickering Ho 2 SW4 138 A2
Russell Pl
  Hampstead NW3 70 C3
  Rotherhithe SE16 119 A3
Russell Rd
  Bowes Pk N13 32 B4
  Buckhurst Hill IG9 21 C3
  Chingford Hatch E4 35 B6
  Crouch End N8 49 D3
  East Barnet N20 14 C2
  Enfield EN1 5 D5
  Leyton E10 53 D3
  Merton SW19 179 C3
  Mitcham CR4 202 C6
  Newham E16 99 B1
  Northolt UB5 64 A3
  Shepperton TW17 193 A2
  Tottenham N15 51 C4
  Twickenham TW1, TW2 152 D5
  W14 113 A3 254 B5
  Walthamstow E17 53 B6
  Walton-on-T KT12 194 A3
  West Hendon NW9 45 D3
Russell Sch The TW10 153 D3
Russell Sq WC1 94 A3 240 A5
Russell Square Ho WC1 240 A5
Russell Square Mans WC1 240 B4
Russell Square Sta WC1 94 A3 240 A5
Russell St WC2 116 A6 250 B6

Russell's Wharf 2 W9 . . 91 B3
Russell Way SM1 . . . . . . 217 D3
Russell Wlk 4 TW10 . . . 154 B5
Russet Ave TW16,
TW17 . . . . 193 C6
Russet Cl UB10 . . . . 83 A3
Russet Cres N7 . . . . 72 B3
Russet Ct 6 Barnet EN4 . . . 2 C1
Dollis Hill NW2 . . . . 68 B5
Feltham TW13 . . . . 149 C1
Russet Dr CR0 . . . . 207 A1
Russet Ho TW3 . . . . 129 B1
Russet House Sch EN1 . . . 6 B4
Russets Cl E4 . . . . 36 B6
Russettings 1 HA5 . . . . . 23 B3
Russett Way SE13 . . . . . . 141 D3
Russia Dock Rd SE16 . . . 119 A5
Russia La E2 . . . . 96 C5
Russia Row EC2 . . . . . . 242 B1
Russington Rd TW17 . . . 193 B3
Rusthall Ave W4 . . . . 111 B3
Rusthall Cl CR0 . . . . 206 C3
Rusthall Mans 3 W4 . . . 111 B2
Rustic Ave SW16 . . . . 181 B3
Rustic Pl HA0 . . . . 65 D4
Rustic Wlk E16 . . . . 99 B1
Rustington Wlk SM4 . . . 201 B2
Ruston Ave KT5 . . . . 198 D2
Ruston Gdns N14 . . . . 15 A5
Ruston Mews W11 . . . . . . 91 A1
Ruston Rd SE18 . . . . 122 A3
Ruston St E3 . . . . 97 B6
Rust Sq SE5 . . . . 139 B5
Rutford Rd SW16 . . . . 182 A5
Ruth Cl HA7 . . . . 44 B5
Ruth Ct 16 E3 . . . . 97 A5
Rutherford Cl
Hillingdon UB8 . . . . 82 B3
Sutton SM2 . . . . 218 B2
Rutherford Ct
Mitcham SW19 . . . . 180 B3
Southgate N21 . . . . 16 B6
Rutherford Ho
12 Bethnal Green E1 . . . . . 96 B3
Teddington TW11 . . . . . . 174 D5
4 Wembley HA9 . . . . 67 A5
Rutherford St
SW1 . . . . 115 D2 259 C4
Rutherford Twr 8 UB1 . . 85 D1
Rutherford Way
Bushey WD23 . . . . 8 C3
Wembley HA9 . . . . 66 C4
Rutherglen Rd SE2 . . . . . 146 A6
Rutherwyke Cl KT17 . . . 216 A2
Ruth Ho W10 . . . . 91 A3
Ruthin Cl NW9 . . . . 45 C3
Ruthin Rd SE3 . . . . 143 A6
Ruthven St E9 . . . . 96 D6
Rutland Ave DA15 . . . . . . 168 A4
Rutland Cl
Chessington KT9 . . . . 214 B2
DA5 . . . . 168 D3
Mitcham SW19 . . . . 180 C3
Mortlake SW14 . . . . 133 A2
Rutland Ct 15 Acton W3 . . 88 C1
Chislehurst BR7 . . . . 188 C2
Enfield EN3 . . . . 18 B6
Herne Hill SE5 . . . . 139 B1
Sidcup SE9 . . . . 167 A2
SW7 . . . . 247 B1
Twickenham TW2 . . . . 152 C1
Rutland Dr
Morden SM4 . . . . 201 C2
Richmond TW10 . . . . 154 A3
Rutland Gate
Beckenham BR2 . . . . 208 D5
Belvedere DA17 . . . . 125 D1
SW7 . . . . 114 C4 247 B1
Rutland Gate Mews
SW7 . . . . 247 A1
Rutland Gdns
Dagenham RM8 . . . . 80 C3
Ealing W13 . . . . 87 A2
South Croydon CR0 . . . . . 221 C4
Stoke Newington N4 . . . . . 51 A3
SW7 . . . . 114 C4 247 B1
Rutland Gdns Mews
SW7 . . . . 247 B1
Rutland Gr W6 . . . . 112 B1
Rutland Ho
Edgware HA8 . . . . 26 B4
6 Northolt UB5 . . . . 63 C2
2 Penge SE20 . . . . 184 C2
10 Putney SW15 . . . . 156 C4
Tolworth KT6 . . . . 198 C1
W8 . . . . 255 C5
15 Woolwich SE18 . . . . . 122 B2
Rutland Lo
Forest Hill SE6 . . . . 163 B2
Teddington TW11 . . . . . . 174 C5
Rutland Mews E SW7 . 257 B6
Rutland Mews S SW7 . 257 A6
Rutland Mews W SW7. 257 A6
Rutland Park Gdns 1
NW2 . . . . 68 C2
Rutland Park Mans 2
NW2 . . . . 68 C2
Rutland Pk
Forest Hill SE6 . . . . 163 B2
Willesden NW2 . . . . 68 C2
Rutland Pl Bushey WD23 . . 8 B3
EC1 . . . . 241 D4
Rutland Rd
Forest Gate E7 . . . . 77 D1
Harrow HA1 . . . . 42 A3
Hayes UB3 . . . . 105 B2
Ilford IG1 . . . . 78 D5
Mitcham SW19 . . . . 180 C3
Southall UB1 . . . . 85 C2
South Hackney E9 . . . . 96 D6
Rutland Rd continued
Twickenham TW2 . . . . 152 B2
Walthamstow E17 . . . . 53 C3
Wanstead E11 . . . . 55 B4
Rutland St SW7 . . . . . . 257 B6
Rutland Studios NW10 . . 90 A4
Rutland Wlk SE6 . . . . 163 B2
Rutley Cl SE11 . . . . 138 D6
Rutlish Rd SW19 . . . . 179 C2
Rutlish Sch SW20 . . . . . . 179 B1
Rutter Gdns CR4 . . . . 202 B5
Rutters Cl UB7 . . . . 104 C4
Rutt's Terr SE14 . . . . 140 D4
Rutts The WD23 . . . . 8 B3
Ruvigny Gdns SW15 . . . . 134 D2
Ruvigny Mans SW15 . . . 134 D2
Ruxbury Ct TW15 . . . . . . 148 A1
RUXLEY 191 A3
Ruxley Cl
Chessington KT19 . . . . . . 214 D3
Sidcup DA14 . . . . 191 A4
Ruxley Cnr DA14 . . . . 191 A4
Ruxley Corner Ind Est
DA14 . . . . 190 D4
Ruxley Cres KT10 . . . . . . 213 B1
Ruxley Ct KT19 . . . . 215 A3
Ruxley Gdns TW17 . . . . . 193 A4
Ruxley La KT19 . . . . 215 B3
Ruxley Mews KT19 . . . . . 214 D3
Ruxley Ridge KT10 . . . . . 213 A1
Ryall's Ct N20 . . . . 14 D1
Ryan Cl Ruislip HA4 . . . . . . 40 B1
SE9 . . . . 143 C1
Ryan Ct SW16 . . . . 182 A3
Ryan Dr TW8 . . . . 131 A6
Ryan Ho 3 HA1 . . . . 42 D4
Ryarsh Cres BR6 . . . . 227 C4
Rycott Path SE22 . . . . . . 162 A4
Rycroft Way N17 . . . . 51 D6
Ryculff Sq SE3 . . . . 142 D3
Rydal Cl NW4 . . . . 29 A2
Rydal Cres UB6 . . . . 87 C5
Rydal Ct Edgware HA8 . . . . . 26 B5
Wembley HA9 . . . . 44 A2
Rydal Dr DA7 . . . . 147 C4
West Wickham BR4 . . . . . 224 C6
Rydal Gdns
Kingsbury NW9 . . . . 45 C4
Kingston u T SW15 . . . . . 177 C5
Twickenham TW2, TW3 . . 151 D5
Wembley HA9 . . . . 43 C1
Rydal Ho 25 SW8 . . . . 137 D3
Rydal Lo N17 . . . . 34 A3
Rydal Rd SW16 . . . . 181 D6
Rydal Water NW1 . . . . . . 232 A1
Rydal Way Enfield EN3 . . . 18 C5
Ruislip HA4 . . . . 62 C4
Ryde Ho 1 NW6 . . . . 91 C6
Rydens Ho SE9 . . . . 165 C1
Rydens Rd KT12 . . . . 194 D1
Ryde Pl TW1 . . . . 153 D5
Ryder Cl BR1 . . . . 187 B5
Ryder Ct Leyton E10 . . . . . . 75 D6
SW1 . . . . 249 B4
Ryder Dr SE16 . . . . 118 B1
Ryder Ho
18 Bethnal Green E1 . . . . 96 C3
5 Merton SW19 . . . . 179 D2
Ryder St SW1 . . . . 249 B4
Ryder's Terr
NW8 . . . . 92 A5 229 A4
Ryder Yd SW1 . . . . 249 B4
Ryde Vale Rd SW12 . . . . 159 C2
Rydon Mews SW19 . . . . . 178 C3
Rydons Cl SE9 . . . . 144 A2
Rydon St N1 . . . . 235 B6
Rydston Cl 2 N7 . . . . 72 B1
Rye Cl DA5 . . . . 169 D5
Ryecotes Mead SE21 . . . 161 C3
Ryecroft Ave TW2 . . . . . . 151 D3
Ryecroft Cres EN5 . . . . . . 12 B6
Ryecroft Rd BR5 . . . . 211 B3
Lewisham SE13 . . . . 164 A6
South Norwood SW16 . . . 182 C4
Ryecroft St
SW6 . . . . 135 D4 265 C1
Rye Ct BR3 . . . . 185 B2
Ryedale SE22 . . . . 162 B5
Ryedale Ct 7 TW12 . . . . 173 C2
Ryefield Ave UB10 . . . . 60 D1
Ryefield Cres HA5, HA6 . . 22 A1
Ryefield Ct HA6 . . . . 22 A1
Ryefield Path 7
SW15 . . . . 156 A3
Ryefield Prim Sch
UB10 . . . . 83 B6
Ryefield Rd SE19 . . . . . . 183 A4
Ryegates 2 SE15 . . . . . . 140 B3
Ryehill Ct KT3 . . . . 199 D2
Rye Hill Pk SE15 . . . . 140 C1
Rye Ho 17 SE16 . . . . 118 C4
Rye La SE15 . . . . 140 A3
Ryeland Cl UB7 . . . . 82 A1
Ryelands Cres SE12 . . . . 165 C5
Ryelands Prim Sch
SE25 . . . . 206 B4
Rye Lane Mkt SE15 . . . . 140 A3
Rye Oak Sch SE15 . . . . . 140 B2
Rye Rd SE15 . . . . 140 D1
Rye The N14 . . . . 15 C4
Rye Way HA8 . . . . 26 B4
Rye Wlk SW15 . . . . 156 D6
Ryfold Rd SW19 . . . . 157 C1
Ryhope Rd N11 . . . . 31 B6
Ryland Cl TW13 . . . . 171 D6
Rylandes Rd NW2 . . . . 68 A5
Ryland Ho 11 SW16 . . . . 181 C5
Ryland Rd NW5 . . . . 71 B2
Rylett Cres W12 . . . . 111 D3
Rylett Rd W12 . . . . 111 D3
Rylston Rd
Edmonton N13 . . . . 17 B1
SW6 . . . . 135 B6 264 C5
Rylton Ho KT12 . . . . 194 A1
Rymer Rd CR0 . . . . 205 C2
Rymer St SE24 . . . . 160 D5
Rymill St E16 . . . . 122 C5
Rysbrack St SW1 . . . . . . 257 C6
Rythe Cl KT9 . . . . 213 C1
Rythe Ct KT7 . . . . 197 A2
Rythe Ho 7 BR1 . . . . 186 B5
Rythe Rd KT10 . . . . 212 C3

S

Saatchi Gallery Duke of
York's HQ*
SW3 . . . . 114 D1 257 D2
Sabah Ct TW15 . . . . 170 C6
Sabbarton St 9 E16 . . . . . 98 D1
Sabella Ct E3 . . . . 97 B5
Sabine Rd SW11 . . . . 137 A2
Sable Cl TW4 . . . . 128 C2
Sable Ct 3 KT3 . . . . 199 C4
Sable St N1 . . . . 72 D1
Sach Rd E5 . . . . 74 B6
Sacketts Ho 24 SW9 . . . . 138 C4
Sackville Ave BR2 . . . . . . 209 A1
Sackville Cl HA2 . . . . 64 B5
Sackville Gdns IG1 . . . . . . 56 B1
Sackville Ho
Hornsey N8 . . . . 50 A5
16 Streatham SW16 . . . . 160 A1
Sackville Rd SM2 . . . . . . 217 C1
Sackville St
W1 . . . . 115 C6 249 B5
Sacred Heart High Sch
W6 . . . . 112 C2
Sacred Heart Jun Sch
W6 . . . . 112 D2
Sacred Heart Language
Coll The HA3 . . . . 24 C1
Sacred Heart Prim Sch,
Battersea SW11 . . . . 136 C3
Sacred Heart RC Prim
Sch
East Barnet N20 . . . . 14 C2
Islington N7 . . . . 72 B3
Putney SW15 . . . . 156 A6
Ruislip HA4 . . . . 61 C6
Teddington TW11 . . . . . . 175 B3
West Barnes KT3 . . . . . . 200 A5
Sacred Heart RC Sec Sch
SE5 . . . . 139 A4
Saddlebrook Pk TW16 . . 171 C3
Saddlers Cl Barnet EN5 . . 12 B6
Borehamwood WD6 . . . . . 11 B5
Pinner HA5 . . . . 23 C5
Saddlers Mews SW8 . . . 270 B2
Teddington KT1 . . . . 175 C2
Wembley HA0 . . . . 64 D4
Saddlers Path WD6 . . . . . 11 B6
Saddlescombe Way
N12 . . . . 29 C5
Sadler Cl CR4 . . . . 180 D1
Sadler Ho
17 Bromley E3 . . . . 97 D4
EC1 . . . . 234 C2
Sadlers Ho EN1 . . . . 17 C6
Sadlers Ride KT8 . . . . . . 174 A1
Saffron Ave E14 . . . . 120 B6
Saffron Cl
Temple Fortune NW11 . . . 47 B3
Thornton Heath CR0 . . . . 204 A3
Saffron Ct
East Bedfont TW14 . . . . . 149 A4
10 Kingsland N1 . . . . 73 B2
Stratford E15 . . . . 76 C3
Saffron Hill EC1 . 94 C2 241 B4
Saffron Ho 6 TW9 . . . . . . 132 D4
Saffron St EC1 . . . . 241 B4
Saffron Way KT6 . . . . 197 D1
Saffron Wharf SE1 . . . . . 253 D2
Sage Cl 7 E6 . . . . 100 B2
Sage Mews SE22 . . . . 161 D6
Sage St E1 . . . . 118 C6
Sage Way WC1 . . . . 233 C1
Sage Yd KT6 . . . . 198 B1
Sahara Ct UB1 . . . . 107 A6
Saigasso Cl E16 . . . . 99 D1
Sailacre Ho 10 SE10 . . . . 120 D1
Sail Ct 10 E14 . . . . 120 B6
Sailmakers Ct SW6 . . . . 136 A2
Sail St SE11 . . . . 116 B2 260 D4
Saimet 3 NW9 . . . . 27 D2
Sainfoin Rd SW17 . . . . . . 159 A2
Sainsbury Rd SE19 . . . . . 183 C5
St Agatha's Dr KT2 . . . . . 176 B4
St Agatha's Gr SM5 . . . . 202 D1
St Agatha's RC Prim Sch
KT2 . . . . 176 B4
St Agnes Cl E9 . . . . 96 C6
St Agnes Pl SE11 . . . . 138 D6
St Agnes RC Prim Sch
E3 . . . . 97 D4
St Agnes RC Sch NW2 . . 69 A5
St Aidans Ct IG11 . . . . . . 102 B5
St Aidan's Prim Sch N4 . 50 C2
St Aidan's RC Prim Sch
IG1 . . . . 57 B1
St Aidan's Rd
East Dulwich SE22 . . . . . 162 B6
West Ealing W13 . . . . 109 B4
St Aiden's Ct W13 . . . . . . 109 C4
St Albans Ave
Bedford Pk W4 . . . . 111 B3
Feltham TW13 . . . . 172 D5
St Alban's Ave E6 . . . . . . 100 C4
St Alban's CE Prim Sch
EC1 . . . . 94 C2 241 A4
St Alban's Cl NW11 . . . . . 47 C1
St Albans Cres N22 . . . . . 32 C2
St Alban's Cres IG8 . . . . . 37 A2
St Alban's Gdns TW11 . . 175 A5
St Alban's Gr
Carshalton SM5 . . . . 202 C2
W8 . . . . 113 D3 255 D6
St Albans Ho 2 SW16 . . 182 C6
St Albans La NW11 . . . . . . 47 C1
St Albans Mans W8 . . . 255 D6
St Alban's Pl N1 . 94 D6 234 C5
St Alban's RC Prim Sch
KT8 . . . . 196 A4
St Albans Rd Barnet EN5 . . 1 A3
Cheam SM1 . . . . 217 B4
Ilford IG3 . . . . 57 D2
Kingston u T KT2 . . . . 176 A4
St Alban's Rd
Dagenham NW10 . . . . 89 C6
Dartmouth Pk NW5 . . . . . . 71 B5
Woodford IG8 . . . . 37 A3
St Alban's St SW1 . . . . . 249 C5
St Albans Studios W8 . 255 D6
St Albans Terr W6 . . . . 264 A6
St Alban's Villas NW5 . . . 71 A5
St Alfege Pas SE10 . . . . . 142 A6
St Alfege Rd SE7 . . . . 143 D6
St Alfege with St Peter's
CE Prim Sch SE10 . . . . 142 A6
St Aloysius RC Coll
N19 . . . . 49 C1
St Aloysius RC Inf Sch
NW1 . . . . 93 D4 232 C2
St Aloysius RC Jun Sch
NW1 . . . . 93 D5 232 C3
St Alphage Ct NW9 . . . . . 45 B6
St Alphage Gdn EC2 . . . 242 B3
St Alphage Highwalk
EC2 . . . . 242 B3
St Alphage Wlk HA8 . . . . 27 A1
St Alphege Rd N9 . . . . 18 C4
St Alphonsus Rd SW4 . . 137 D1
St Amunds Cl SE6 . . . . . . 185 C6
St Andrew & St Francis CE
Prim Sch NW2 . . . . 68 A2
St Andrews Ave HA0 . . . . 65 A4
St Andrew's (Barnsbury)
CE Prim Sch
N1 . . . . 94 B6 233 D6
St Andrew's CE Prim Sch
Enfield EN1 . . . . 5 C3
Osidge N14 . . . . 15 D3
Stockwell SW9 . . . . 138 A3
St Andrew's CE Sch
N20 . . . . 13 B2
St Andrews Chambers
W1 . . . . 239 B2
St Andrews Cl
25 Bermondsey SE16 . . . 118 B1
Erith SE28 . . . . 102 D1
Long Ditton KT7 . . . . 197 B1
Ruislip HA4 . . . . 62 D6
Stanmore HA7 . . . . 25 C1
Wimbledon SW19 . . . . . . 179 D4
St Andrew's Cl
Dollis Hill NW2 . . . . 68 B5
2 Hounslow TW7 . . . . . . 130 C4
North Finchley N12 . . . . . . 30 A6
Upper Halliford TW17 . . . 193 B5
St Andrews Ct W4 . . . . . . 133 A4
St Andrew's Ct
Carshalton SM5 . . . . 218 C5
2 Higham Hill E17 . . . . . . 35 A1
Kingston u T KT3 . . . . 199 D6
2 Wandsworth SW18 . . . 158 A2
St Andrews Dr HA7 . . . . . 25 C2
St Andrew's Gr N16 . . . . . 51 B1
St Andrew's Greek Sch
NW1 . . . . 71 C2
St Andrew's High Sch
CR0 . . . . 220 D4
St Andrew's Hill
EC4 . . . . 94 D1 241 D1
St Andrews Ho
11 Bermondsey SE16 . . . 118 B3
Bromley BR1 . . . . 187 B4
St Andrew's Hospl E3 . . . 97 D3
St Andrews Mans 9
E5 . . . . 74 B4
St Andrew's Mans W1 . 238 A3
St Andrews Mews
Greenwich SE3 . . . . 143 A5
4 Streatham SW12 . . . . 159 D3
St Andrew's Mews N16 . . 51 C1
St Andrew's Pl NW1 . . 238 D6
St Andrews RC Prim Sch
SW16 . . . . 182 A5
St Andrews Rd
Carshalton SM5 . . . . 218 C5
DA14 . . . . 168 D1
Higham Hill E17 . . . . 35 A1
Ponders End N9 . . . . 18 C4
Uxbridge UB10 . . . . 60 B1
Welsh Harp NW9 . . . . 45 B1
St Andrew's Rd
8 Croydon CR0 . . . . 221 A4
Dagenham W3 . . . . 89 C1
Enfield EN1 . . . . 5 B2
Hanwell W7 . . . . 108 C4
Hillingdon UB10 . . . . 82 B6
Leytonstone E11 . . . . 54 C3
Newham E13 . . . . 99 B4
Redbridge IG1 . . . . 56 B2
Surbiton KT6 . . . . 197 D3
Temple Fortune NW11 . . . 47 B3
W14 . . . . 264 B6
Willesden NW2 . . . . 68 B2
St Andrew's & St Mark's
CE Jun Sch KT6 . . . . . . 197 D4
St Andrew's Sq
Notting Hill W11 . . . . 91 A1
Surbiton KT6 . . . . 197 D3
St Andrew St EC4 . . . . . 241 B3
St Andrews Terr WD19 . . 22 C5
St Andrew's Twr UB1 . . 108 A6
St Andrews Way E3 . . . . . 97 D3
St Andrew's Wharf
SE1 . . . . 253 D2
St Angela's Ursuline
Convent Sch E7 . . . . 77 B2
St Anna Rd EN5 . . . . 12 D6
St Anne RC Prim Sch
E1 . . . . 96 A3
St Annes Catholic High
Sch for Girls (Upper)
N13 . . . . 32 C6
St Anne's CE Prim Sch
SW18 . . . . 157 D6
St Annes Cl WD19 . . . . . . 22 C6
St Anne's Cl N6 . . . . 71 A5
St Annes Ct 8 SM2 . . . . 217 D2
St Anne's Ct
Kensal Rise NW6 . . . . 91 A6
W1 . . . . 239 C1
St Anne's Flats NW1 . . 232 C2
St Annes Gdns NW10 . . . . 88 B4
St Anne's Pas E14 . . . . . . 97 B1
St Anne's RC High Sch for
Girls EN2 . . . . 5 B1
St Anne's RC Prim Sch
SE11 . . . . 138 B6 270 C6
St Anne's Rd Leyton E11 . 76 B6
Wembley HA0 . . . . 65 D3
St Anne's Row E14 . . . . . . 97 B1
St Anne St E14 . . . . 97 B1
St Anne's Trad Est 25
E14 . . . . 97 B1
St Ann's IG11 . . . . 101 A6
St Ann's CE Prim Sch
N15 . . . . 51 B4
St Ann's Cres SW18 . . . . 158 A5
St Ann's Ct NW4 . . . . 46 B6
St Ann's Ctr HA1 . . . . 42 C3
St Ann's Gdns NW5 . . . . . 71 A2
St Ann's General Hospl N4,
N15 . . . . 51 A4
St Ann's Hill SW18 . . . . . 158 A5
St Ann's Ho WC1 . . . . . . 234 A1
St Ann's La SW1 . . . . . . 259 D5
St Ann's Park Rd
SW18 . . . . 158 A5
St Anns Rd SW13 . . . . . . 133 D4
St Ann's Rd
2 Barking IG11 . . . . 101 A6
Edmonton N9 . . . . 17 D3
Harrow HA1 . . . . 42 C3
Shepherd's Bush W11 . . . 112 D6
Tottenham N15 . . . . 51 B4
St Ann's Sch Ealing W7 . 108 C5
Morden SM4 . . . . 201 D4
St Ann's St
SW1 . . . . 115 D3 259 D6
St Ann's Terr
NW8 . . . . 92 B5 229 D4
St Ann's Villas
W11 . . . . 113 A5 244 A3
St Ann's Way CR2 . . . . . . 220 D2
St Anselm RC Prim Sch
UB2 . . . . 107 B3
St Anselm's Ct SW16 . . . 182 A5
St Anselm's Pl W1 . . . . 248 C6
St Anselm's RC Prim Sch
Harrow HA1 . . . . 42 C2
Upper Tooting SW17 . . . . 159 A1
St Anselms Rd UB3 . . . . 105 D4
St Anthony's Ave IG8 . . . 37 C3
St Anthonys Cl SW17 . . . 158 C2
St Anthony's Cl 8 E1 . . . 118 A5
St Anthony's Ct
2 Balham SW12 . . . . 159 A5
Orpington BR6 . . . . 226 D6
Upper Tooting SW17 . . . . 159 A2
St Anthony's Flats
NW1 . . . . 232 C3
St Anthony's Hospl
KT4 . . . . 200 D1
St Anthony's RC Prim
Sch
East Dulwich SE22 . . . . . 162 A5
Penge SE20 . . . . 184 B2
Upton E7 . . . . 77 B1
St Anthony's Way
TW14 . . . . 127 D1
St Antony's RC Prim Sch
IG8 . . . . 37 A6
St Antony's Rd E7 . . . . 77 B1
St Arvans Cl CR0 . . . . 221 C5
St Asaph Ct SE4 . . . . 140 D2
St Asaph Rd SE4 . . . . 140 D2
St Aubins Ct N1 . . . . 235 D6
St Aubyns E18 . . . . 54 D5
St Aubyn's Ave
Hounslow TW3, TW4 . . . . 151 C6
Wimbledon SW19 . . . . . . 179 B5
St Aubyns Cl BR6 . . . . . . 227 D5
St Aubyn's Ct SW19 . . . . 179 A4
St Aubyns Gdns BR6 . . . 227 D6
St Aubyn's Rd SE19 . . . . 183 D4
St Aubyn's Sch IG8 . . . . . 36 D3
St Audrey Ave DA7 . . . . . 147 C3
St Augustine of
Canterbury CE Prim Sch
DA17 . . . . 125 B2
St Augustine's Ave
BR1, BR2 . . . . 210 A4
Ealing W5 . . . . 88 A4
St Augustine's Ave
continued
South Croydon CR2 . . . . . 221 A1
Wembley HA9 . . . . 66 A5
St Augustine's CE High
Sch NW6 . . . . 91 C5
St Augustine's CE Prim
Sch NW6 . . . . 91 D5
St Augustines Ct
Beckenham BR3 . . . . 185 A1
4 New Barnet EN5 . . . . . 14 A6
St Augustine's Ct E11 . . . 54 D1
St Augustine's Ho
NW1 . . . . 232 C2
Upper Tooting SW17 . . . . 180 D6
St Augustine's RC Prim
Sch
Ilford IG2 . . . . 56 D4
W6 . . . . 135 A6 264 B5
St Augustine's Rd
Camden Town NW1 . . . . . . 71 D1
DA17 . . . . 125 B2
St Augustines's RC Prim
Sch SE6 . . . . 186 A5
St Austell Cl HA8 . . . . 26 B1
St Austell Rd SE13 . . . . . 142 B3
St Awdry's Rd IG11 . . . . . 79 B1
St Barnabas CE Prim Sch
SW1 . . . . 115 A1 258 B2
St Barnabas Cl
Beckenham BR3 . . . . 186 A1
11 Dulwich Village
SE22 . . . . 161 C6
St Barnabas Ct HA3 . . . . . 24 A2
St Barnabas' Gdns
KT8 . . . . 195 C4
St Barnabas Ho CR4 . . . 181 A3
St Barnabas Rd
Mitcham CR4 . . . . 181 A3
Sutton SM1 . . . . 218 B3
Walthamstow E17 . . . . 53 C3
Woodford IG8 . . . . 37 C3
St Barnabas & St Philip's
CE Prim Sch
W8 . . . . 113 C3 255 A5
St Barnabas St SW1 . . . 258 B2
St Barnabas Terr E9 . . . . 74 D3
St Barnabas Villas
SW8 . . . . 138 A4 270 B2
St Bartholomews CE Prim
Sch SE26 . . . . 162 C1
St Bartholomew's CE Prim
Sch SE26 . . . . 184 C6
St Bartholomew's Cl
SE26 . . . . 184 C6
St Bartholomews Ct 6
E6 . . . . 100 A6
St Bartholomew's Hospl
EC1 . . . . 94 D2 241 D3
St Bartholomew's Rd
E6 . . . . 100 B5
St Bede's RC Inf Sch
SW12 . . . . 159 D3
St Bede's RC Prim Sch
RM6 . . . . 58 C4
St Benedict's Cl SW17 . . 181 A5
St Benedict's Jun Sch
W5 . . . . 87 C2
St Benedict's Sch W5 . . . 87 D2
St Benets Cl SW17 . . . . . 158 C2
St Benet's Gr SM5 . . . . . 202 A2
St Benet's Pl EC3 . . . . . 252 D6
St Bernadette RC Jun Sch
SW12 . . . . 159 C4
St Bernadette's Prim Sch
HA3 . . . . 44 B5
St Bernadette's RC Prim
Sch UB10 . . . . 82 D6
St Bernard Ho 6 E14 . . . 120 A3
St Bernards CR0 . . . . 221 C5
St Bernards Cl 8
SE27 . . . . 183 B6
St Bernards Ho 1
KT6 . . . . 214 A6
St Bernard's Rd E6 . . . . . 99 D6
St Blaise Ave BR1 . . . . . . 187 B1
St Bonaventure's RC Sch
E7 . . . . 77 A1
St Boniface RC Prim Sch
SW17 . . . . 180 D5
St Botolph St E1,
EC3 . . . . 95 D1 243 C2
St Brelades Ct N1 . . . . . 235 D6
St Bride's Ave EC4 . . . . 241 C1
Edgware HA8 . . . . 26 B2
St Brides Cl DA18 . . . . . . 124 D4
St Bride's Pas EC4 . . . . 241 C1
St Bride St EC4 . . 94 D1 241 C2
St Catherines Cl
Chessington KT9 . . . . 213 D2
Upper Tooting SW17 . . . . 158 C2
St Catherines Ct
TW13 . . . . 150 A3
St Catherine's Ct 8
W4 . . . . 111 C3
St Catherine's Dr
SE14 . . . . 140 D3
St Catherines Farm Ct
HA4 . . . . 39 A3
St Catherines Mews
SW3 . . . . 257 C4
St Catherine's RC Sch
EN5 . . . . 1 C1
St Catherine's RC Sch for
Girls DA6 . . . . 169 D6
St Catherines Rd
Chingford E4 . . . . 19 C2

St Catherines Rd *continued*
Ruislip HA4 39 B3
St Catherine's Sch
TW1 153 A2
St Catherines Twr 5
E10 53 D2
St Cecilia's CE Sch
SW18 157 B3
St Cecilia's Cl SM3 201 A1
St Cecilia's RC Prim Sch
SM3 216 D6
St Chads Cl KT6 197 C2
St Chad's Gdns RM6 59 A2
St Chad's Pl WC1 233 C2
St Chad's RC Prim Sch
SE25 205 C4
St Chad's Rd RM6 59 A2
St Chad's St WC1 233 B2
St Charles' Hospl W10 90 D2
St Charles Pl W10 91 A2
St Charles RC Prim Sch
W10 90 D2
St Charles RC Sixth Form
Coll W10 90 D2
St Charles Sq W10 90 D2
St Christina's Sch
NW8 92 C5 230 B4
St Christopher's Cl
TW7 130 C4
St Christophers Ct 15
N19 71 C5
St Christophers Dr
UB3 106 B6
St Christophers Gdns
CR7 204 C6
St Christopher's Ho
NW1 232 C3
St Christopher's Mews
SM6 219 C3
St Christopher's Pl
W1 238 B2
St Christopher's Sch
Beckenham BR3 186 A1
Hampstead NW3 70 B3
Wembley HA9 66 B5
St Clair Dr KT4 216 B4
St Clair Ho 17 E3 97 B4
St Clair Rd E13 99 B5
St Clair's Rd CR0 221 C6
St Clare Bsns Pk
TW12 174 A4
St Clare St EC3 243 C1
St Clement Danes CE Prim
Sch WC2 94 B1 240 C1
St Clement & St James CE
Prim Sch
W11 113 A5 244 A4
St Clements Ct
Barnsbury N7 72 B2
7 SE14 140 D6
8 Shepherd's Bush
W11 112 D6
St Clement's Ct EC3 252 D6
St Clements Ho E1 243 C3
Walton-on-T KT12 194 A2
St Clement's Hts SE26 184 A6
St Clement's La WC2 240 D1
St Clements Mans 3
SW6 134 D6
St Clements St N7 72 C1
St Cloud Rd SE27 183 B6
St Columba's Ct E15 76 C4
St Columbas Ho 2
E17 53 D5
St Columba's RC Boys Sch
DA6 169 D6
St Columb's Ho 11 W10 91 A2
St Crispins Cl NW3 70 C4
St Crispin's Cl UB1 85 B1
St Crispins Ct 1 UB1 85 B1
St Cross St EC1 94 C2 241 B4
St Cuthberts Gdns 2
HA5 23 B3
St Cuthberts Rd N13 32 C4
St Cuthbert's Rd NW2 69 B2
St Cuthbert with St
Matthias Prim Sch
SW5 113 D1 255 C2
St Cyprian's Greek
Orthodox Prim Sch
CR7 183 A2
St Cyprian's St SW17 180 D6
St Davids Cl
27 Bermondsey SE16 118 B1
Wembley HA9 67 A5
St David's Cl BR4 207 D2
St David's Coll BR4 207 D2
St Davids Ct 5 E11 55 B4
St David's Ct
Bromley BR1 210 D6
8 Southall UB1 86 A1
1 Walthamstow E17 54 A6
St David's Dr HA8 26 B2
St David's Pl NW4 46 B2
St David's Sch TW15 148 B1
St David's Sq E14 119 D1
St Denis Rd SE27 183 B6
St Dionis Rd SW6 135 B3
St Domingo Ho SE18 122 B3
St Dominic RC Prim Sch
NW5 70 D3
St Dominics RC Prim Sch
E9 75 A2
St Dominic's Sixth Form
Coll (RC) HA1 64 C6
St Donatt's Rd SE14 141 B4
St Dunstans SM1 217 B2
St Dunstan's Alley EC3 253 A5
St Dunstan's Ave W3 111 B6
St Dunstan's CE Prim Sch
SM3 217 A1
St Dunstans Cl UB3 105 D2
St Dunstan's Coll SE6 163 C3
St Dunstan's Ct EC4 241 B1
St Dunstan's Gdns W3 111 B6
St Dunstan's Hill
Cheam SM1, SM3 217 A3
EC3 253 A5
St Dunstan's La
Beckenham BR3 208 A4
EC3 253 A5
St Dunstans Rd E7 77 C2
St Dunstan's Rd
Cranford TW5 128 B3
Feltham TW13 149 D1
Hammersmith W6 112 D1
Hanwell W7 108 C4
South Norwood SE25 205 D5
St Edmund RC Sch
E14 119 C2
St Edmunds Ave HA4 39 B3
St Edmunds Cl DA18 124 D4
Upper Tooting SW17 158 C2
St Edmund's Cl NW8 230 C5
St Edmund's Ct NW8 230 C5
St Edmunds Dr HA7 25 A2
St Edmund's La TW2 151 D4
St Edmund's RC Prim
Sch
Edmonton N9 18 B3
Twickenham TW2 151 D4
St Edmunds Rd N9 18 A4
St Edmund's Rd IG1 56 B3
St Edmund's Sq SW13 134 C6
St Edmund's Terr
NW8 92 D6 230 C5
St Edward's CE Comp Sch
RM7 59 C3
St Edward's Cl NW11 47 C3
St Edwards Ct 3 E10 54 A2
St Edward's Ct NW11 47 C3
St Edwards RC Prim Sch
E6 99 C6
St Edward's RC Prim Sch
NW1 92 C3 237 B5
St Egberts Way E4 20 A3
St Elizabeth Ct
North Finchley N12 30 A6
9 Walthamstow E10 53 D2
St Elizabeth RC Prim Sch
E2 96 C5
St Elizabeth's RC Prim Sch
TW10 154 B5
St Elmo Rd W12 111 D4
St Elmos Rd SE16 119 A4
St Elphege's RC Inf Sch
SM6 220 A2
St Elphege's RC Jun Sch
SM6 220 A2
SS Peter & Paul's RC
Prim Sch
Ilford IG1 79 B5
Mitcham CR4 202 D5
St Erkenwald Mews
IG11 101 B6
St Erkenwald Rd IG11 101 B6
St Ermin's Hill SW1 259 C6
St Ervan's Rd W10 91 B2
St Eugene de Mazenod Rc
Prim Sch NW6 69 C1
St Faith's CE Prim Sch
SW18 158 A6
St Faith's Cl EN2 5 A4
St Faith's Rd SE24 160 D3
St Fillans Rd SE6 164 A4
St Francesca Cabrini Prim
Sch SE23 162 C5
St Francis Cl BR5 211 C3
St Francis de Sales RC Jun
& Inf Sch N17 33 D3
St Francis' Ho NW1 232 C3
St Francis Lodge HA0 64 D5
St Francis of Assisi RC
Prim Sch W11 112 D6
St Francis Pl SW12 159 B5
St Francis RC Prim Sch
SE15 140 A5
Stratford E15 76 C3
St Francis Rd SE22 139 C1
St Francis Way IG1 79 B4
St Francis Xavier Sixth
Form Coll SW12 159 B5
St Frideswides Mews 5
E14 98 A1
St Gabriel's CE Prim Sch
SW1 115 C1 259 A1
St Gabriels Cl 3 E14 97 D2
St Gabriel's Cl E11 55 B1
St Gabriels Ct N11 31 D3
St Gabriel's Rd NW2 68 D3
St George Ho SW11 268 B1
ST GEORGE IN THE EAST
118 A6
St George's Ave
Ealing W5 109 D4
Kingsbury NW9 45 B5
Southall UB1 107 B6
Tufnell Pk N7 71 D4
Upton E7 77 B1
St George's Battersea CE
Prim Sch
SW8 137 C5 269 B3
St George's Bickley CE
Prim Sch BR1 187 D1
St George's Bldgs
SE11 261 D5
St George's Cath NW1 231 D2
St George's Cath RC Jun &
Inf Sch SE1 116 D3 261 C6
St George's CE Prim Sch
SE5 139 C5
St George's Circ
SE1 116 D3 261 C6
St Georges Cl
Erith SE28 102 D1
Nine Elms SW8 269 B2
Wembley HA0 65 A5
St George's Cl NW11 47 B3
St Georges Coll N7 72 C5
St Georges Ct
Harrow HA3 43 A3
Newham E6 100 B3
Penge SE20 184 B2
Putney SW15 135 B1
Walthamstow E17 54 B4
St George's Ct
Brompton SW3 257 A4
Kensington SW7 256 A5
Newington SE1 261 C5
St George's Dr
Ickenham UB10 60 B6
South Oxhey WD19 23 A6
SW1 115 C1 259 A2
St George's Field
W2 92 C1 237 B1
St Georges Gdns KT6 214 D6
St George's Gr SW17 158 B1
St Georges Hanover Sq
Sch W1 115 A6 248 B5
St George's Ho NW1 232 B3
St George's Hospl
SW17 180 B5
St Georges Ind Est N22 32 D3
St George's Ind Est
KT2 175 D5
St George's La EC3 253 A6
St Georges Lo N10 49 C5
St Georges Mews 11
NW1 70 D1
St George's Mews
2 Rotherhithe SE8 119 B2
SE1 261 B6
St Georges Pl N7 71 D4
St George's RC Cath
SE1 116 C3 261 B6
St George's RC Prim Sch
Enfield EN2 5 B3
Harrow HA1 64 D5
St George's RC Sec Sch
W9 91 D5
St Georges Rd
Acton W4 111 B4
Bickley BR1 210 B6
Dagenham RM9 81 A4
Petts Wood BR5 211 B3
St George's Rd
Beckenham BR3 185 D2
Ealing W7 108 D5
Enfield EN1 5 D5
Feltham TW13 172 D6
Isleworth TW1 153 B6
2 Kingston u T KT2 176 C3
Leyton E10 76 A5
Mitcham CR4 203 B6
Newington SE1 116 D3 261 C5
Palmers Green N13 16 B2
Redbridge IG1 56 B2
Richmond TW9 132 B2
Sidcup DA14 190 D4
Temple Fortune NW11 47 B3
Upton E7 77 B2
Wallington SM6 219 B3
Wimbledon SW19 179 B4
St Georges Rd Ctr RM9 81 B4
St Georges Rd W BR1 188 A1
St George's Residences 4
SW2 160 C6
St Georges's Ct EC4 241 C2
St Georges Sh & L Ctr
HA1 42 C3
St Georges Sq 1 E14 119 A6
St George's Sq
Kingston u T KT3 199 C6
Rotherhithe SE8 119 B2
SW1 115 D1 259 C1
Upton E7 77 B1
St George's Square Mews
SW1 259 C1
St George St
W1 115 B6 248 D6
St Georges Terr
Hampstead NW1 70 D1
NW1 230 D6
St George's Way SE15 139 C6
St George's Wlk CR0 221 A5
St George the Martyr CE
Prim Sch WC1 94 B3 240 D5
St George Wharf SW8 270 A6
St Gerards Cl SW4 159 C6
St German's Pl SE3 143 A4
St German's Rd SE23 163 A3
St Gildas' RC Jun Sch
N8 50 A2
ST GILES 94 A1
St Giles Ave
Dagenham RM10 81 D1
Uxbridge UB10 61 A4
St Giles Cir
WC1 93 D1 239 D2
St Giles Cl BR6 227 B3
Dagenham RM10 81 D1
Heston TW3 129 A5
St Giles Coll
WC1 94 A2 240 B4
St Giles Ct Ealing W13 109 C5
WC2 240 A2
St Giles High St
WC2 93 D1 239 D2
St Giles Ho
2 New Barnet EN5 2 A1
Streatham SW16 160 A1
St Giles Hospl SE5 139 C4
St Giles Pas WC2 239 D1
St Giles Rd SE5 139 C4
St Giles' Sch CR2 220 D2
St Giles Twr 3 SE5 139 C4
St Gilles Ho 16 E2 96 D5
St Gothard Rd SE21,
SE27 183 B6
St Gregory Cl HA4 62 C4
St Gregory RC High Sch
HA3 43 D4
St Gregory's RC Prim Sch
W5 87 D2
St Helena Ho WC1 234 A1
St Helena Pier TW9 153 D6
St Helena Rd SE16 118 D2
St Helena St WC1 234 A1
St Helena Terr 31
TW9 153 D6
St Helens KT7 196 D2
St Helens Coll UB10 60 C1
St Helen's Cres SW16 182 B2
St Helen's Gdns W10 90 D1
St Helen's Pl EC3 243 A2
St Helen's RC Inf Sch
E17 54 A4
St Helen's RC Prim Sch
E13 99 A3
St Helen's RC Sch
SW9 138 C2
St Helens Rd 5 DA18 124 D4
St Helen's Rd
Ealing W13 109 C5
Redbridge IG1 56 B3
Thornton Heath SW16 182 B2
ST HELIER 202 B2
St Helier Ave SM4 202 A3
St Helier Ct 4 N1 95 C6
St Helier Hospl SM5 202 A1
St Heliers Ave TW3,
TW4 151 C6
St Helier's Rd E10 54 A3
St Helier Sta SM4 201 C3
St Hilary's Ct BR1 210 D6
St Hilda's Ave TW15 170 A5
St Hildas Cl SW17 158 C2
St Hilda's Cl NW6 68 D1
St Hilda's Rd SW13 134 B6
St Hildas Wharf E1 118 C5
St Hubert's Ho 2 E14 119 C3
St Hughes Cl SW17 158 C2
St Hugh's Rd SE20 184 B3
St Ignatius Coll EN1 6 B6
St Ignatius RC Prim Sch
TW16 172 A2
St Ignatius' RC Prim Sch
N15 51 D3
St Ives Ct NW2 69 A2
St Ivian Ct 3 N10 31 B1
ST JAMES 115 C5
St James Apartments 2
E17 53 A4
St James Ave
East Barnet N20 14 C1
Sutton SM1 217 C3
St James' Ave W13 109 A5
St James CE Jun Sch
E7 77 A3
St James CE Prim Sch
EN3 6 C3
St James' CE Prim Sch
SE16 118 A3
St James Cl Barnet EN4 2 B1
East Barnet N20 14 C1
St James' Cl
New Malden KT3 199 D4
Ruislip HA4 62 C6
St James Ct
26 Bethnal Green E2 96 A4
10 Brentford W4 110 C1
1 Bromley BR2 187 A1
Forest Hill SE23 163 A3
SE3 143 B4
Thornton Heath CR0 204 D2
Wanstead E12 77 C6
St James' Ct
Bedford Pk W4 111 B3
7 Kingston u T KT1 198 A6
SW1 259 B6
St James Gate IG9 21 B3
St James Gdns IG6 58 B5
St James' Gdns HA0 66 A1
St James Ho N5 72 C3
St James Hts 3 SE18 123 A1
St James Independent
Schs W14 113 A2 254 B4
St James Ind Mews 16
SE1 118 A1
St James Ind Sch for Boys
TW1 153 A2
St James' Mans NW6 69 C1
St James Mews E14 120 A3
St James' RC High Sch
NW9 27 D2
St James RC Prim Sch
BR5 210 D4
St James Rd
Carshalton SM5 218 C5
Kingston u T KT1 175 D1
Sutton SM1, SM2 217 C3
St James' Rd
Edmonton N9 18 B2
Forest Gate E15 76 D3
Mitcham CR4 181 A3
Surbiton KT6 197 D3
St James's SE14 141 A4
St James's App EC2 243 A5
St James's Ave
Beckenham BR3 207 A6
Hampton TW12 174 A5
South Hackney E2 96 C5
St James's CE Prim Sch
N10 49 A5
St James School Flats 5
N7 72 C3
St James's Cl NW8 230 C5
Upper Tooting SW17 158 D2
Woolwich SE18 123 A1
St James's Cloisters 2
SE22 139 D1
St James's Cotts 14
TW10 153 D6
St James's Cres SW9 138 C2
St James's Ct
8 Edmonton N18 34 A5
Harrow HA1 43 A3
St James's Dr
Balham SW12, SW17 158 D4
Upper Tooting SW17 158 D3
St James's Gdns
W11 113 A5 244 A4
St James's Gr SW11 136 D3
St James's Hatcham CE
Prim Sch SE14 141 A4
St James's La N10 49 B5
St James's Market
SW1 249 C5
St James's Mews E17 53 A4
St James's Pal*
SW1 115 C5 249 B3
St James's Park Sta
SW1 115 D3 259 C6
St James's Pas EC3 243 B1
St James's Pk* SW1 249 C2
St James's Pk CR0 205 A2
St James's Pl
SW1 115 C5 249 A3
St James's RC Prim Sch
TW2 152 C1
St James's Rd
Bermondsey SE1,
SE16 118 A2
Hampton TW12 173 D5
Peckham SE1 140 A6
Thornton Heath CR0 205 B2
St James's & St Michael's
CE Prim Sch
W2 114 A6 246 B6
St James's Sq
SW1 115 C5 249 B4
St James's St
SW1 115 C5 249 A4
Walthamstow E17 53 A4
St James St W6 112 C1
St James's Terr NW8 230 C6
2 Upper Tooting
SW12 159 A3
St James's Terrace Mews
NW8 230 C5
St James Street Sta
E17 53 A4
St James The Great RC
Prim Sch
Camberwell SE15 139 D4
South Norwood CR7 182 D1
St James Way DA14 191 A5
St James Wlk EC1 241 C6
St Jerome's Gr UB3 83 A1
St Joachim's RC Prim Sch
E16 99 C1
St Joan of Arc RC Prim
Sch N5 73 A4
St Joan's Rd N9 17 D2
St John Baptist CE Prim
Sch BR1 186 A6
St John Evangelist RC
Prim Sch N1 94 D5 234 C4
St John Fisher RC Fst &
Mid Sch HA5 41 C5
St John Fisher RC Prim
Sch
DA18 125 A3
Wembley UB6 87 C4
West Barnes SW20 200 D4
St John of Jerusalem CE
Prim Sch E9 74 C1
ST JOHNS 141 C3
St John & St James CE
Prim Sch
Edmonton N18 33 D5
Hackney E9 74 C3
St John's Angell Town CE
Prim Sch SW9 138 C3
St John's Ave
Dagenham NW10 89 D6
Friern Barnet N11 30 D5
Putney SW15 156 D6
St John's CE First Sch
HA7 25 A6
St John's CE JMI Sch
N11 30 D6
St John's CE Prim Sch
Buckhurst Hill IG9 21 B3
Croydon CR0 222 D5
Enfield EN2 4 D6
Fulham SW6 135 A4 264 B2
Kingston u T KT1 198 A6
Penge SE20 184 C3
SE17 117 A2 262 B3
South Hackney E2 96 C5
Whetstone N20 14 A2
St John's CE Sch
Stanmore HA7 25 A6
St John's Church Rd
E9 74 C3
St Johns Cl N14 15 C5
St John's Cl SW6 265 A4
Wembley HA9 66 A3
St Johns Concert Hall*
SW1 260 A5
St John's Cotts 2
SE20 184 C3
St John's Cres SW9 138 C2
St Johns Ct 39 E1 118 B5
St John's Ct
Buckhurst Hill IG9 21 B3
Finsbury Pk N4 72 D6
Hammersmith W6 112 B2
2 Harrow HA1 42 D3
Isleworth TW7 130 D3
Kingston u T KT1 198 A5
Lewisham SE13 142 A3
Leytonstone E11 54 D1
5 South Hampstead
NW3 70 A2
Saint John's Ct N5 72 D4
St Johns Dr KT12 194 C1
St John's Dr SW18 157 D3
St John's Est SE1 253 C1
St John's Gdns
W11 113 B6 244 C5
St John's Gr
3 Barnes SW13 133 D3
1 Richmond TW9 132 A1
Upper Holloway N19 71 C6
St John's Highbury Vale
CE Prim Sch N5 72 D5
St John's Hill SW11 136 B1
St John's Hill Gr
SW11 136 B1
St Johns Ho 5 SE17 139 B6
Streatham SW16 182 A4
St John's Ho 1 E14 120 A2
St John's La
EC1 94 D2 241 D4
St John's Lodge 8
SE8 141 C4
St John's Mans E5 74 C3
St John's Par
Ealing W13 109 B5
3 Sidcup DA14 190 B6
St John's Park Mans
N19 71 C5
St John's Path EC1 241 C5
St John's Pk SE3 143 A5
St John's Pl EC1 241 C5
St John's Prim Sch
W13 109 A6
St John's RC Prim Sch
SE16 119 A4
St Johns Rd Ilford IG2 57 C2
Kingston u T KT3 199 A6
St John's Rd
Barking IG11 101 C6
Battersea SW11 136 C1
Canning Town E16 99 A1
Carshalton SM5 218 C5
Chingford E4 35 D6
Croydon CR0 220 D5
DA16 146 B2
East Ham E6 100 A6
East Molesey KT8 196 B5
Feltham TW13 173 B6
Harrow HA1 42 D3
Isleworth TW7 130 D3
Orpington BR5 211 C3
Penge SE20 184 C4
Richmond TW9 132 A1
Sidcup DA14 190 B6
Southall UB2 107 A3
Sutton SM1 217 D6
Teddington KT1 175 C1
Temple Fortune NW11 47 B3
Tottenham N15 51 C3
Walthamstow E17 36 A1
Wembley HA9 66 A3
Wimbledon SW19 179 A4
St John's & St Clements
CE Prim Sch SE15 140 A2
St John's Sch HA6 22 B4
St John's Sq
EC1 94 D3 241 C5
St Johns Sta SE8 141 C3
St John St EC1 94 D3 241 C6
St John's Terr Enfield EN2 5 B6
North Kensington W10 90 D3
SE18 145 B6
Upton E7 77 B2
St Johnstone Ho 17
N12 29 D6
St John's Upper Holloway
CE Prim Sch N19 71 D6
St John's Vale SE8 141 C3
St John's Villas
4 Friern Barnet N11 30 D5
Upper Holloway N19 71 D6
W8 255 D5
St John's Way N19 49 D1
ST JOHN'S WOOD 92 B5
St John's Wood Ct
NW8 229 D1
St John's Wood High St
NW8 92 C5 230 A3
St John's Wood Park
NW8 92 B6 229 C6
St John's Wood Pre-Prep
Sch NW8 92 C4 230 A2
St John's Wood Rd
NW8 92 B4 229 D1
St John's Wood Sta
NW8 92 B5 229 C4
St John's Wood Terr
NW8 92 C5 230 A4

St John the Baptist CE Jun
Sch KT1. . . . . .175 D3
St John the Baptist CE
Prim Sch N1 . . .95 B5 235 D3
St John the Divine CE Jun
& Inf Sch SE5 . . . . .138 D5
St John Vianney RC Prim
Sch N8 . . . . .50 D5
St Joseph RC Prim Sch
W7 . . . . .108 C5
St Joseph's Acad SE3 . . .142 C2
St Josephs Cl BR6. . . . . .227 D4
St Joseph's Cl W10 . . . . .91 A2
St Joseph's Coll Mill Hill
Missionaries NW7 . . . . .27 D6
St Joseph's Convent Sch
E11. . . . . .55 A3
St Josephs Ct
  ③ Dagenham NW10. . . . .89 D5
  ⑳ Walthamstow E10 . . . .53 D2
St Joseph's Ct E4. . . . . . .20 B4
St Joseph's Dr UB1 . . . .107 B5
St Josephs Flats NW1 . .232 C2
St Josephs Gr NW4 . . . .46 B5
St Joseph's Ho W6 . . . . .112 D2
St Joseph's Hospice E9,
E8. . . . . .96 B6
St Joseph's RC Coll
SW16 . . . . .182 D4
St Joseph's RC Fst & Mid
Sch HA3 . . . . .25 A1
St Joseph's RC Inf & Jun
Schs
Hendon NW4 . . . . .46 B5
SE5 . . . . .139 A5
St Joseph's RC Inf Sch
Leyton E10. . . . . .75 C6
South Norwood SE19 . . .183 A4
St Joseph's RC Jun & Inf
Schs HA9 . . . . .66 B3
St Joseph's RC Jun Sch
South Norwood SE19 . . .183 A4
Walthamstow E10. . . . . .53 D1
St Joseph's RC Prim Sch
Barking IG11. . . . . .101 A6
Bermondsey SE16. . . . . .118 A4
Bromley BR1. . . . . .187 B3
Chelsea SW3. . .114 D2 257 C3
Dagenham RM9. . . . . . . .81 B4
Deptford SE8. . . . . .141 C5
Greenwich SE10 . . . . . . .120 C1
Kingston u T KT1. . . . . . .176 B1
Paddington W9 . . .92 A4 229 A1
Rotherhithe SE16 . . . . . .118 C3
St Giles WC2. . . . .94 A1 240 B2
Upper Holloway N19 . . . .49 B1
Wandsworth SW18 . . . . .157 C6
Willesden NW10 . . . . . . .67 C1
St Joseph's Rd N9 . . . . .18 C3
St Joseph's St SW8 . . . .268 C2
St Joseph's Vale SE3. . . .142 B2
St Jude & St Paul's CE
Prim Sch N1 . . . . .73 C2
St Jude's CE Prim Sch
SE24. . . . . .160 D4
St Judes Ho ⑥ W10. . . . .91 B4
St Jude's Prim Sch
SE1. . . . . . . .116 D3 261 C5
St Jude's Rd E2 . . . . . . .96 B5
St Jude St N16 . . . . .73 C3
St Julian's Cl SW16 . . . .182 C6
St Julian's Farm Rd SE27,
SW16. . . . . .182 D6
St Julian's Rd NW6 . . . . .91 C6
St Katharine's Ho N1 . .234 A4
St Katharine's Prec
NW1 . . . . .231 C4
St Katharine's Way
E1 . . . . .117 D5 253 D4
St Katherines Rd
DA18. . . . . .124 D4
St Katherine's Row
EC3 . . . . .243 B1
St Katherine's Wlk ①
W11. . . . . .112 D5
St Keverne Rd SE9. . . . .188 A6
St Kilda Rd BR6. . . . . . .211 D1
Ealing W13 . . . . .109 A4
St Kilda's Rd
Harrow HA1 . . . . .42 C3
Stamford Hill N16. . . . . .51 C1
St Kitts Terr SW13 . . . . .183 C5
St Laurence CE Jun Sch
KT8. . . . . .196 B5
St Lawrence Cl HA8. . . . .26 B3
St Lawrence Ct N1. . . . .235 D6
St Lawrence Dr HA5 . . . .40 B4
St Lawrence Ho SE1 . . .263 B6
St Lawrence RC Prim Sch
TW13 . . . . .150 B2
St Lawrence St E14 . . . .120 A5
St Lawrence Terr W10 . .91 A2
St Lawrence Way
SW9. . . . . .138 C3
St Leonards Ave E4 . . . .36 B4
St Leonard's Ave E4 . . . .36 B4
St Leonard's CE Prim Sch
SW16 . . . . .181 D1
St Leonards Cl ④
DA16. . . . . .146 A2
St Leonards Ct SW14. . .133 A2
St Leonard's Ct N1. . . . .235 D6
St Leonards Gdns IG1. . .79 A3
St Leonard's Gdns
TW5. . . . . .129 A4
St Leonard's Hospl N1. .95 C5
St Leonards Rd SW14 . .133 A2
St Leonard's Rd
Becontree NW10. . . . . . .89 B3

St Leonard's Rd continued
Claygate KT10. . . . . . . .212 D2
Croydon CR0. . . . . .220 D5
Ealing W13 . . . . .109 C6
Kingston u T KT6 . . . . . .197 D4
South Bromley E14 . . . . .98 A2
Thames Ditton KT7 . . . .197 A4
St Leonards Rise BR6 . .227 C4
St Leonard's Sq
Camden Town NW5. . . . .71 A2
Kingston u T KT6 . . . . . .197 D4
St Leonard's St E3 . . . . .97 C4
St Leonard's Terr
SW3. . . . . . . .114 D1 257 D1
St Leonard's Wlk
SW16. . . . . .182 B3
St Loo Ave
SW3. . . . . . . .136 C6 267 B6
St Loo Ct SW3 . . . . . . .267 C6
St Louis Rd SE27. . . . . .183 B6
St Loy's Rd N17. . . . . . . .51 D6
St Lucia Dr E15 . . . . .98 D7
St Luke Prim Sch E16. . .98 D1
St Luke's Ave
Clapham SW4 . . . . .137 D1
Enfield EN2 . . . . .5 B5
Ilford IG1 . . . . .78 D3
St Luke's CE Prim Sch
Cubitt Town E14 . . . . . .120 B2
Kingston u T KT2. . . . . .176 B2
Paddington W9 . . . . .91 B4
Shoreditch EC1 . .95 A4 235 B1
West Norwood SE27. . . .183 A5
St Luke's Cl
Croydon SE25 . . . . .206 B3
St Luke's EC1. . . .95 A3 242 B6
St Lukes Ct ⑥ E10 . . . . .53 D2
St Luke's Ct W11 . . . . . .91 B1
St Luke's Hospl
W1 . . . . .93 C3 239 A5
St Luke's Mews W11. . . .91 B1
St Luke's Path ① IG1 . . .78 D3
St Luke's RC Sixth Form
Coll DA14 . . . . .189 D5
St Luke's Rd
Notting Hill W11 . . . . . . .91 B2
Uxbridge UB10 . . . . .60 A1
St Luke's Sq E16. . . . . . .98 D1
St Luke's St SW3 . . . . .257 B2
St Luke's Woodside Hospl
N10. . . . . .49 A5
St Malo Ave N9 . . . . . . .18 C1
St Margaret Clitherow
RC Prim Sch
Neasden NW10 . . . . .67 B4
Woolwich SE28 . . . . . . .124 B5
ST MARGARETS 153 A5
St Margarets IG11. . . . .101 A6
St Margarets Ave
Ashford TW15. . . . . . . .170 D5
DA15. . . . . .167 B1
Hillingdon UB8 . . . . .82 C3
Whetstone N20 . . . . .14 A3
St Margaret's Ave
Cheam SM3. . . . . .217 A5
Harringay N8, N15 . . . . .50 D5
Harrow HA2 . . . . .64 A5
St Margarets Bsns Ctr ⑪
TW1. . . . . .153 B5
St Margaret's CE Prim
Sch
Barking IG11. . . . . .79 A1
Woolwich SE18 . . . . . . .123 A1
St Margaret's Cres
SW15. . . . . .156 B6
St Margaret's Ct
Leyton E15. . . . . .76 C4
Putney SW15. . . . . .134 B1
SE1. . . . . .252 C3
  ⑨ Twickenham TW1. . . .153 B5
St Margaret's Dr TW1. .153 B5
St Margaret's Gr
Leyton E11. . . . . .76 C4
SE18 . . . . .145 A6
Twickenham TW1. . . . . .153 A5
St Margaret's La
W8. . . . . .113 D3 255 C5
St Margaret's Lee CE Prim
Sch SE13. . . . . .142 C1
St Margarets Lo W3 . . .110 D4
St Margaret's Pass
SE13 . . . . .142 C2
St Margaret's Path ④
SE18 . . . . .123 A1
St Margarets Rd
Edgware HA8 . . . . .26 D5
Ruislip HA4 . . . . .39 B3
St Margaret's Rd
Brockley SE4. . . . . .141 B1
Hanwell W7. . . . . .108 C4
Isleworth TW1 . . . . .153 B6
Kensal Green NW10 . . . .90 C4
Tottenham N17 . . . . .51 C6
Wanstead E12. . . . . .77 C6
St Margarets Rdbt
TW1. . . . . .153 B6
St Margaret's Sch NW3 .69 D4
St Margaret's Sta
TW1. . . . . .153 B5
St Margaret St SW1. . . .250 A1
St Margaret's Terr
SE18 . . . . .123 A1
St Margret's Ct N11. . . .31 A6
St Mark's CE Acad
CR4. . . . . .181 B1
St Mark's CE Prim Sch
Bromley BR2. . . . . .209 A4
Croydon SE25 . . . . .206 A5

St Mark's CE Prim Sch
continued
Kennington
SE11. . . . . . .138 B6 270 D6
St Marks Cl ⑤ SE10 . . .142 A5
St Mark's Cl Barnet EN5. . .1 D2
Harrow HA1 . . . . .43 B1
St Mark's Cres
NW1 . . . . .93 A6 231 B6
St Mark's Ct
Hanwell W7. . . . . .108 C4
  ⑧ Walthamstow E10 . . .53 D2
St Marks Gate E9 . . . . . .75 B1
St Mark's Gr
SW10. . . . . . .135 D5 265 D4
St Mark's Hill KT6 . . . . .198 A3
St Marks Ho ⑥ SE17 . . .139 B6
St Mark's Ho ⑧ E17. . . .54 A5
St Mark's Hospl
EC1. . . . . .94 D4 234 D2
St Mark's Hts ㉕ KT6 . . .198 A4
St Marks Ind Est E16. . .121 D5
St Mark's Mans ⑭ N4. . .72 B6
St Mark's Pl
Notting Hill W11 . . . . . . .91 A1
Wimbledon SW19 . . . . .179 B4
St Mark's Prim Sch
Hanwell W7. . . . . .108 C4
Mitcham CR4. . . . . .180 D1
Upper Holloway N19 . . . .72 A6
St Mark's RC Sch
TW3. . . . . .129 C2
St Marks Rd ⑱ NW10 . .90 D1
St Mark's Rd
Bromley BR2. . . . . .209 B6
Croydon SE25 . . . . .206 A5
Ealing W5 . . . . .110 A5
Enfield EN1 . . . . .17 D6
Hanwell W7. . . . . .108 C4
Mitcham CR4. . . . . .181 A1
North Kensington W10 . .90 D2
Notting Hill W11 . . . . . . .91 A1
Teddington TW11 . . . . . .175 B3
St Mark's Rise E8. . . . . .73 D3
St Mark's Sq NW1 . . . .231 A5
St Mark St E1 . . .95 D1 243 D1
St Martha's Convent Jun
Sch EN5 . . . . .1 A1
St Martha's Senior Sch
EN4. . . . . .1 C4
St Martin-in-the-Fields
High Sch for Girls
SW2. . . . . .160 C3
St Martin of Porres RC
Prim Sch N11 . . . . .31 C4
St Martin's Almshouses
NW1 . . . . .232 A6
St Martin's App HA4 . . . .39 C2
St Martin's Ave E6. . . . . .99 D5
St Martins Cl DA18. . . . .124 D4
South Oxhey WD19 . . . . .22 C6
St Martin's Cl Enfield EN1 . .6 B4
NW1 . . . . .232 A6
St Martins Ct N1. . . . . . .95 C6
St Martin's Ct WC2. . . .250 A6
West Norwood SE27. . . .182 D7
St Martins La BR3. . . . .207 D4
St Martin's La
WC2. . . . . . . .116 A6 250 A5
St Martin's Le Grand
EC1. . . . . .242 A2
St Martin's Pl WC2. . . .250 A5
St Martin's Rd
Edmonton N9. . . . . .18 B2
Finchley N2. . . . . .30 B2
Stockwell SW9 . . . . . . .138 B3
St Martin's Sch NW7. . . .27 B5
St Martin's St WC2. . . .249 D5
St Martin's Way SW17. .158 A4
St Mary Abbots CE Prim
Sch W8. . . . . .113 D4 245 C1
St Mary Abbot's Ct
W14. . . . . .254 C5
St Mary Abbot's Pl W8 .254 D5
St Mary Abbots Terr
W14. . . . . .254 C5
St Mary at Hill
EC3 . . . . .117 C6 253 A5
St Mary Ave SM6. . . . . .219 B5
St Mary Axe EC3 . .95 C1 243 B2
St Marychurch St
SE16 . . . . .118 C4
St Mary Graces Ct E1 . .253 D5
St Mary Magdalene CE
Prim Sch
Islington N7 . . . . .72 C2
Paddington W2 . . . . .91 D2
Peckham SE15. . . . . . . .140 B3
Woolwich SE18 . . . . . . .122 C4
St Mary Magdalen's RC
Prim Sch
Brockley SE4. . . . . .141 A1
Mortlake SW14 . . . . . . .133 B2
St Mary Magdelen's RC
Jun Sch NW2 . . . . .68 B2
St Mary Newington Cl
SE17 . . . . .263 B2
St Mary of the Angels RC
Prim Sch W2 . . . . .91 C1
St Mary RC Prim Sch
W10 . . . . .91 A3
St Mary Rd E17 . . . . . . .51 D5
St Marys IG11 . . . . .101 B6

St Mary & St Joseph's RC
Sch DA14 . . . . .189 D5
St Mary & St Michael Prim
Sch E1. . . . . .96 C1
St Mary & St Pancras CE
Prim Sch
NW1. . . . . .93 D5 232 C3
St Mary's App E12 . . . . .78 B3
St Marys Ave UB2. . . . .107 D2
St Mary's Ave
Beckenham BR2 . . . . . .208 C6
Finchley N3 . . . . .29 B1
Teddington TW11 . . . . . .174 D4
Wanstead E11. . . . . .55 B2
St Mary's Bryanston
Square CE Sch
W1 . . . . .92 D2 237 C4
St Mary's CE High Sch
(Lower & Upper)
NW4. . . . . .46 C6
St Mary's CE High Sch
(Middle) NW4 . . . . .46 C6
St Mary's CE Inf Sch
N8. . . . . .50 B5
St Mary's CE Jun Sch
N8. . . . . .50 A5
St Mary's CE Prim Sch
Chessington KT9. . . . . .214 B2
East Barnet EN4 . . . . . . .14 C5
Finchley N3 . . . . .29 B3
Islington N1 . . .94 D6 234 D6
Long Ditton KT7 . . . . . .197 B1
Putney SW15. . . . . .134 D2
Walthamstow E17. . . . . .53 D5
Willesden NW10 . . . . . . .67 C2
St Mary's CE Prim Sch
(Inf) TW1 . . . . .153 A4
St Mary's CE Prim Sch
(Jun) TW1 . . . . .153 B4
St Mary's Church Ho ⑪
E17 . . . . .53 D5
St Mary's Cl BR5. . . . . .190 B1
Chessington KT9. . . . . .214 B1
Ewell KT17 . . . . .215 D1
Sunbury TW16. . . . . . . .194 A5
Tottenham N17 . . . . .34 A2
St Mary's Coll TW1 . . . .152 D1
St Mary's Cottage Hospl
TW12 . . . . .173 B2
St Mary's Cres
Hayes UB3. . . . . .105 D6
Hendon NW4 . . . . .46 B6
Hounslow TW7 . . . . .130 C5
St Marys Ct
Abbey Wood SE2 . . . . . .124 D2
Newham E6. . . . . .100 B3
SE7 . . . . .143 D5
St Mary's Ct
Bedford Pk W6 . . . . .111 D3
Ealing W5 . . . . .109 D4
Finchley N12. . . . . .30 A3
Kingston u T KT3 . . . . . .199 C6
Leytonstone E11. . . . . . .54 D1
Wallington SM6. . . . . . .219 C4
St Mary's Dr TW14 . . . .149 A4
St Mary's Est ② SE16 . .118 C4
St Mary's Flats NW1 . .232 C2
St Mary's Gate W8. . . .255 C5
St Mary's Gdns SE11 . .261 B4
St Mary's Gn ① N2 . . . . .48 A6
St Mary's Gr
Barnes SW13 . . . . .134 B2
Chiswick W4 . . . . .132 C6
Islington N1 . . . . .72 D2
Richmond TW10, TW9 . .132 B1
St Mary's Ho
Ealing W5 . . . . .109 D3
N1 . . . . .234 D6
St Mary's Hospl
W2 . . . . .92 B1 236 D2
St Mary's Hospl Medical
Sch W2. . . . . . .92 B1 236 D2
St Mary's Kilburn CE Prim
Sch NW6. . . . . .91 C6
St Mary's Lewisham CE
Prim Sch SE13 . . . . . . .163 D6
St Mary's Lo E11. . . . . . .55 B3
St Mary's Mans
Dagenham NW10 . . . . . .89 C6
Paddington W2 . .92 B2 236 C4
St Mary's Mews NW6 . .69 D1
St Mary's Path N1 . . . .234 D6
St Mary's Pl Ealing W5 .109 D4
Eltham SE9 . . . . .166 C5
Kensington W8 . .113 D3 255 C5
St Mary's RC High Sch
CR0. . . . . .205 A1
St Mary's RC Inf Sch
Carshalton SM5. . . . . . .218 D4
Croydon CR0. . . . . .205 B1
St Mary's RC Jun & Inf
Schs N15 . . . . .51 B4
St Mary's RC Jun Sch
Croydon CR0. . . . . .205 B1
Wallington SM5. . . . . . .218 D4
Walthamstow E17. . . . . .54 A6
St Mary's RC Prim Sch
Beckenham BR3 . . . . . .186 A3
Chingford E4. . . . . .20 B3
Chiswick W4 . . . . .133 C6
Clapham Pk SW4. . . . . .159 C6
Clapham SW8 . .137 B4 268 D2
Enfield EN3 . . . . .6 D1
Hammersmith W14. . . . .112 D3
Isleworth TW7 . . . . .131 A2
Merton SW19 . . . . .179 C3
Paddington NW6. . . . . . .91 C5
SE9 . . . . .166 C6
St Marys Rd IG1 . . . . . . .79 B6

St Mary's Rd
Dagenham NW10 . . . . . .89 C6
Ealing W5 . . . . .109 D5
East Barnet EN4 . . . . . . .14 C4
East Molesey KT8 . . . . .196 B4
Finchley N2 . . . . .30 B2
Golders Green NW11 . . .47 A2
Hayes UB3. . . . . .105 D6
Hornsey N8 . . . . .50 A5
Leyton E10. . . . . .76 A6
Long Ditton KT6 . . . . . .197 C1
Lower Edmonton N9 . . . .18 C3
Newham E13. . . . . .99 B5
Nunhead SE15. . . . . . . .140 C3
South Norwood SE25 . . .205 C6
Surbiton KT6. . . . . .197 D3
Wimbledon SW19 . . . . .179 B5
Worcester Pk KT4. . . . .215 C6
St Mary's & St John's CE
Prim Sch NW4 . . . . . . .46 B4
St Mary's & St Peter's CE
Prim Sch TW11. . . . . . .174 D5
St Mary's Sch Hampstead
NW3 . . . . .70 B3
St Mary's Sq Ealing W5 .109 D4
W2. . . . . .236 C4
St Mary's Stoke Newington
CE Prim Sch N16 . . . . .73 C6
St Mary St SE18. . . . . . .122 C2
St Mary's Terr W2 . . . .236 C4
St Mary's Twr EC1 . . . .242 B5
St Marys View HA3 . . . .43 C4
St Mary's Wlk
Hayes UB3. . . . . .105 D6
SE11 . . . . .261 B4
St Matthew's Ave SE19 .198 B1
St Matthew's CE Prim
Sch
Enfield EN3 . . . . .18 C6
Surbiton KT6. . . . . .198 A2
Wimbledon SW20 . . . . .178 A2
Yiewsley UB7 . . . . .104 A5
St Matthews Ct
Muswell Hill N10. . . . . . .31 A1
SE1 . . . . .262 A5
  ② Stratford E15. . . . . . .76 D1
  ⑦ Walthamstow E10 . . .53 D2
St Matthew's Ct ①
TW15. . . . . .170 C5
St Matthews Dr BR1 . . .210 B6
St Matthew's Ho ⑧
SE17 . . . . .139 B6
St Matthew's Lo NW1 . .232 B4
St Matthew's Rd
Clapham Pk SW2. . . . . .160 B6
Ealing W5 . . . . .110 A5
St Matthew's Row E2 . .96 A3
St Matthews Sch
Westminster
SW1. . . . . . . .115 D3 259 D6
St Matthew St W1 . . . .259 C5
St Matthias CE Prim Sch
E2. . . . . .95 D3 243 B6
St Matthias CI NW9 . . . .45 D4
St Matthias's CE Prim Sch
N16. . . . . .73 C4
St Mauritius Ho SE13. . .164 A6
St Maur Rd
SW6. . . . . . . .135 B4 264 D1
St Mellion Cl SE28 . . . .102 D1
St Merryn Cl SE18. . . . .145 B5
St Merryn Ct BR3. . . . . .185 C3
St Michael-at-Bowes CE
Jun Sch N13 . . . . .32 C4
St Michael RC Prim Sch
TW15. . . . . .170 C5
St Michael & St Martin RC
Prim Sch TW4 . . . . . . .129 B2
St Michael's Alley EC3 .242 D1
St Michaels Ave N9 . . . .18 C4
St Michael's Ave HA9 . .66 C2
St Michael's CE Prim Sch
Camden Town
NW1. . . . . .93 C6 232 A6
Enfield EN2 . . . . .5 A4
Forest Hill SE26 . . . . . .185 A6
Highgate N6 . . . . .49 A2
Wandsworth SW18 . . . . .157 B4
Wood Green N22. . . . . . .32 B2
St Michaels Cl BR1. . . . .210 A6
  ④ Newham E16 . . . . . . .99 D2
Worcester Pk KT4. . . . .215 D4
St Michael's Cl
Colney Hatch N12 . . . . . .30 C5
DA18. . . . . .124 D4
Finchley N3 . . . . .29 B1
St Michael's Cres HA5 . .41 A3
St Michaels Ct ② E14. . .98 C1
St Michael's Ct
Brunswick Pk N11. . . . . .15 A1
Golders Green NW11 . . .47 B2
St Michael's East Wickham
CE Prim Sch DA16. . . .146 C4
St Michael's Flats
NW1 . . . . .232 C3
St Michael's Gdns W10. .91 A2
St Michaels Ho SE26 . . .185 B6
St Michael's Hospl EN2. .5 A4
St Michael's RC Gram Sch
N12. . . . . .30 A5
St Michael's RC Prim Sch
E6. . . . . .100 B5
St Michael's RC Sch
SE16 . . . . .118 A4
St Michaels Rd TW15 . .170 C5
St Michael's Rd
Cricklewood NW2 . . . . . .68 C4
Croydon CR0. . . . . .205 A1

St J–St P 371

St Michael's Rd continued
DA16. . . . . .146 B2
Stockwell SW9 . . . . . . .138 B3
Wallington SM6. . . . . . .219 C2
St Michael's Rise
DA16. . . . . .146 B4
St Michael's St
W2. . . . . .92 C1 237 A2
St Michael Steiner Sch
The SW18. . . . . .157 C6
St Michael's Terr N22. . .32 A2
St Mildred's Ct EC2 . . .242 C1
St Mildreds Rd SE12,
SE6 . . . . .164 D4
St Mirren Ct ⑧ EN5 . . . .14 A6
St Monica's RC Prim Sch
Palmers Green N14. . . . .16 A1
Shoreditch N1. . . . . .95 C4
St Nicholas CE Prim Sch
TW17 . . . . .192 D3
St Nicholas Cl WD6 . . . . .9 D5
St Nicholas Ct E4 . . . . . .36 A4
St Nicholas Ctr ⑦
SM1. . . . . .217 D3
St Nicholas Dr TW17 . .192 C2
St Nicholas Elstree CE
Prim Sch WD6 . . . . .9 D5
St Nicholas' Flats NW1 .232 C3
St Nicholas Glebe
SW17. . . . . .181 A4
St Nicholas Ho SE8 . . . .141 B4
St Nicholas Mans
SW17. . . . . .158 D2
St Nicholas Rd
Plumstead SE18 . . . . . .123 D2
Sutton SM1 . . . . .217 D3
Thames Ditton KT7 . . . .196 D3
St Nicholas Sch NW9 . . .67 A6
St Nicholas St SE8 . . . .141 C4
St Nicolas La BR7. . . . .188 A2
St Ninian's Ct N20 . . . . .14 D1
St Norbert Gn SE4 . . . . .141 A1
St Norbert Rd SE4 . . . . .141 A1
St Olaf's Rd
SW6. . . . . . . .135 A5 264 B3
St Olaves Ct W2 . . . . . .245 C5
St Olave's Ct EC2 . . . . .242 C1
St Olave's Est SE1 . . . .253 B2
St Olave's Gdns SE11. . .261 A4
St Olave's Mans SE11 . .261 A4
St Olaves Prep Sch
SE9. . . . . .166 D2
St Olave's Rd E6. . . . . .100 C6
St Olave's Wlk SW16 . .181 D1
St Olav's Sq ㊷ SE16 . .118 C4
St Osmund's RC Prim Sch
SW13. . . . . .133 D4
St Oswald's Pl
SE11 . . . . .116 B1 260 C1
St Oswald's Rd SW16 . .182 D2
St Oswulf St SW1 . . . .259 D3
St Owen Ho SE1 . . . . . .263 B6
ST PANCRAS 232 C6
St Pancras Almshouses ⑱
NW5 . . . . .70 D2
St Pancras Commercial
Ctr NW1 . . . . .232 B6
St Pancras Ct
Finchley N2 . . . . .30 B1
  ⑥ Wembley HA0 . . . . . .66 A2
St Pancras Hospl
NW1. . . . . .93 D6 232 B5
St Pancras International
Sta WC1 . . . . .94 A4 233 A2
St Pancras Way
NW1. . . . . .93 D6 232 C6
St Patrick's Coll
W1. . . . . .93 D1 239 C2
St Patricks Ct IG8 . . . . .36 C3
St Patrick's RC Prim Sch
Camden Town NW5. . . . .71 B3
Plumstead SE18 . . . . . .123 B2
Walthamstow E17. . . . . .53 A5
St Paul's Acad SE2 . . . .146 A6
St Paul's & All Hallows CE
Jun & Inf Schs N17. . . .34 A3
St Paul's Ave
Harrow HA3 . . . . .44 B5
Rotherhithe SE16 . . . . . .118 D5
Willesden NW2 . . . . .68 C2
St Paul's Cath *
EC4. . . . . .95 A1 242 A1
St Paul's Cath Sch
EC4. . . . . .95 A1 242 A1
St Paul's CE Jun Sch
KT2. . . . . .176 C3
St Pauls CE Prim Sch
TW8 . . . . .131 D6
St Paul's CE Prim Sch
Chessington KT9. . . . . .214 A4
Friern Barnet N11. . . . . .31 B5
Hammersmith W6. . . . . .112 C1
Hampstead NW3. . . . . . .70 D1
Mill Hill NW7. . . . . .28 B6
SE17 . . . . .117 A1 262 D2
Southgate N21 . . . . .16 D4
St Paul's Church Yd
EC4. . . . . .95 A1 242 A1
St Pauls Cl Ealing W5 . .110 B4
Hayes UB3. . . . . .105 B1
St Paul's Cl
Ashford TW15. . . . . . . .171 A5
Borehamwood WD6 . . . .11 A6
Carshalton SM5. . . . . . .202 C1
Chessington KT9. . . . . .213 D4

St Paul's Cl *continued*
Greenwich SE7 121 D1
Hounslow TW3, TW4 129 A3
ST PAUL'S CRAY 190 A1
St Paul's Cray Rd BR7 189 B2
St Pauls Cres NW1 71 D1
St Paul's Ct
Clapham SW4 137 D1
Hounslow TW4 129 A2
6 Upper Holloway N19 72 A6
St Paul's Dr E15 76 B3
St Paul's Girls' Sch
W6 112 D2
St Pauls Ho N17 34 A3
St Pauls Mews NW1 71 D1
St Paul's Pl N1 73 B2
St Paul's RC Coll
TW16 172 A2
St Paul's RC Prim Sch
Thames Ditton KT7 196 C2
Wood Green N22 32 B1
St Pauls Rd
Barking IG11 101 A6
Richmond TW9 132 B2
St Paul's Rd
Brentford TW8 131 D6
Canonbury N1 73 A2
South Norwood CR7 205 A6
Tottenham N17 34 A2
St Pauls Rise N13 32 D4
St Paul's Sch SW13 112 A1
St Paul's Sq BR2 187 A1
St Paul's Sta
EC2 95 A1 242 A2
St Paul St N1 235 B5
St Paul's Terr SE17 138 D6
St Paul's Twr 14 E10 53 D2
St Pauls View WC1 234 A1
St Paul's Way
Finchley N3 29 D3
Tower Hamlets E3 97 C2
St Paul's Way Com Sch
E3 97 C2
St Paul's Whitechapel CE
Prim Sch E1 118 A6
St Paul's with St Michael's
Prim Sch E8 96 A6
St Paul's Wood Hill
BR5 189 D1
St Paul with St Luke CE
Prim Sch E3 97 B2
St Peter Chanel RC Prim
Sch DA14 190 C5
St Peter in Chains RC Inf
Sch N8 50 A3
St Peter & Paul RC Prim
Sch BR5 189 C1
St Peter & St Paul RC
Prim Sch EC1 94 D3 241 D6
St Peter's Alley EC3 242 D1
St Peters Ave N12 30 C3
St Peter's Ave
Edmonton N18 34 A6
37 Hackney E2 96 A5
Walthamstow E17 54 C5
St Petersburgh Mews
W2 245 C6
St Petersburgh Pl
W2 113 D6 245 C5
St Peter's CE Prim Sch
Chiswick W6 112 A1
Paddington W9 91 C3
SE17 117 B1 262 C1
St Peter's Church Ct
N1 234 D5
St Peters Cl BR7 189 B3
Ilford IG2 57 D5
Upper Tooting SW17 158 D2
St Peter's Cl Barnet EN5 12 B6
Bushey WD23 8 B3
Hackney E2 96 A5
Ruislip HA4 62 D6
St Peters Ct
East Molesey KT8 195 C5
New Cross SE4 141 B3
28 Stepney E1 96 C3
St Peter's Ct
Hendon NW4 46 C4
Lewisham SE12 164 D6
St Peter's Eaton Square
Prim Sch
SW1 115 B3 258 D5
St Peter's Gdns SE27 160 C1
St Peter's Gr W6 112 A2
St Peters Ho
Tottenham Hale N15 52 A5
WC1 233 B1
St Peter's Ho 4 SE17 139 B6
Stamford Hill N16 51 C2
St Peters La BR5 190 A1
St Peter's London Docks
CE Prim Sch E1 118 C5
St Peters Mews N4 50 D4
St Peter's Pl W9 91 D3
St Peter's Prim Sch
CR2 221 C2
St Peter's RC Prim Sch
Dagenham RM9 103 B6
Woolwich SE18 122 D2
St Peters Rd KT1 176 C1
St Peter's Rd
Chiswick W6 112 A1
Croydon CR0 221 B4
East Molesey KT8 195 C5
Edmonton N9 18 B3
Isleworth TW1 153 B6
Southall UB1 85 C2
St Peter's Sq
Chiswick W6 111 D1
Hackney E2 96 A5
St Peter's St
Croydon CR2 221 B3
Islington N1 94 D6 234 D5
St Peter's Street Mews
N1 234 D4
St Peter's Terr SW6 264 B3
St Peter's Villas 5
W6 112 A2
St Peters Way UB3 105 B1
St Peter's Way
De Beauvoir Town N1 73 C1
Ealing W5 87 D2
St Peter's Wharf 8
W6 112 A1
St Philip Ho WC1 234 A1
St Philip's Ave KT4 216 B6
St Philips Gate KT4 216 B6
St Philip Sq 1 SW8 137 B3
St Philip's Rd
Dalston E8 74 A2
Surbiton KT6 197 D3
St Philip's Sch
Chessington KT9 213 D2
SW7 114 A2 256 B3
St Philip St SW8 137 B3
St Philip's Way N1 235 B5
St Philomena's Sch
SM5 218 C3
St Quentin Ho SW18 158 B5
St Quentin Rd DA16 145 D2
St Quintin Ave W10 90 D2
St Quintin Gdns 21
W10 90 C2
St Quintin Rd E13 99 B5
St Raphaels Ho W13 109 C5
St Raphael's RC Prim Sch
UB5 84 B5
St Raphael's Way
NW10 67 A3
St Regis Cl N10 31 B1
St Regis Hts NW3 69 D5
St Richards Ct TW10 153 B1
St Richard's Ho NW1 232 C2
St Richard's with St
Andrew's CE Prim Sch
TW10 153 B1
St Robert Southwell RC
Prim Sch NW9 45 A3
St Ronan's 2 N3 29 C2
St Ronans Cl EN4 2 B5
St Ronans Cres IG8 37 A3
St Rule St SW8 137 C3
St Savior's CE Inf Sch
W5 109 D6
St Saviours SW4 137 B1
St Saviour's CE Prim Sch
Bow Comm E14 97 D2
Camberwell SE24 139 A2
Paddington W9 91 D3
Walthamstow E17 53 B2
St Saviour's Coll SE27 183 B6
St Saviours Ct
Harrow HA1 42 C4
Muswell Hill N22 31 D1
St Saviours Ho 35 SE1 118 A4
St Saviour's RC Prim Sch
SE13 142 A1
St Saviour's Rd
Clapham Pk SW2 160 B6
Thornton Heath CR0 205 A3
St Saviours & St Olaves CE
Sch SE1 117 B3 262 D5
St Saviour's Wharf
SE1 253 D2
St Scholastica's RC Prim
Sch E5 74 A5
Saints Cl SE27 182 D6
Saints Dr E7 77 D3
St Silas Pl NW5 71 A2
St Simon's Ave SW15 156 C6
St Stephen's Ave
Ealing W13 87 B1
Shepherd's Bush W12 112 B4
Walthamstow E17 54 A4
St Stephen's CE Jun Sch
TW1 153 B5
St Stephen's CE Prim
Sch
Paddington W2 91 C2
Shepherd's Bush W12 112 C4
St Johns SE8 141 C3
SW8 138 B5 270 C4
St Stephen's Cl
Maitland Pk NW5 70 D3
NW8 230 B5
Southall UB1 85 C2
Walthamstow E17 53 D4
St Stephen's Cres
Notting Hill W2 91 C1
Thornton Heath CR7 204 C6
St Stephens Ct
Ealing W13 87 B1
Enfield EN1 17 C5
Hornsey Vale N8 50 B3
St Stephens Gdns
Notting Hill W2 91 C1
4 Putney SW15 157 B6
Twickenham TW1 153 C5
St Stephen's Gr SE13 142 A2
St Stephens Ho 7
SE17 139 B6
St Stephen's Mews 34
W2 91 C2
St Stephens Par E6 77 C1
St Stephens Prim Sch
E6 77 C1
St Stephen's RC Prim Sch
DA16 146 A3
St Stephens Rd
Barnet EN5 12 D6
Upton E6 77 C1
St Stephen's Rd Bow E3 97 B5
Ealing W13 87 C1
Enfield EN3 6 D6
Hounslow TW3, TW4 151 C6
Walthamstow E17 53 D4
Yiewsley UB7 104 A5
St Stephen's Row EC4 242 C1
St Stephen's Terr SW8 270 C3
St Stephen's Wlk SW7 256 A4
St Swithin's La
EC4 117 B6 252 C6
St Swithun's Rd SE13 164 B6
St Swithun Wells RC Prim
Sch HA4 62 D5
St Teresa's RC Fst & Mid
Sch HA3 24 A2
St Teresa's RC Prim Sch
SM4 202 B3
St Teresa's RC Prim Sch
The RM8 80 C4
St Theresa Ct E4 20 B4
St Theresa's RC Sch
N3 47 D6
St Theresa's Rd TW14 127 D1
St Thomas a Beckett RC
Prim Sch SE2 124 A3
St Thomas Becket RC Prim
Sch SE25 206 A3
St Thomas' CE Prim Sch
W10 91 A3
St Thomas' Cl KT6 198 B1
St Thomas Ct
14 Camden Town NW1 71 C1
Sidcup DA5 169 C4
11 Walthamstow E10 53 D2
St Thomas' Ct HA5 23 A2
St Thomas' Dr BR5 211 A1
Pinner HA5 23 A2
St Thomas Gdns IG1 79 A2
St Thomas Ho 2 E1 96 D1
St Thomas More Language
Coll SW3 114 D2 257 C3
St Thomas More RC Comp
Sch SE9 166 C5
St Thomas More RC
Prim Sch
Bexley DA7 147 B3
SE9 144 A2
St Thomas More Sch
N22 32 C3
St Thomas of Canterbury
RC Prim Sch
Mitcham CR4 203 A6
SW6 135 B5 264 C4
St Thomas Rd
Newham E16 99 A1
Osidge N14 15 D4
St Thomas' Rd W4 133 A6
St Thomas's Gdns NW5 71 A2
St Thomas's Hospl
SE1 116 B3 260 C6
St Thomas's Hospl Medical
Sch SE1 116 B3 260 C5
St Thomas's Pl 20 E9 74 C1
St Thomas's Rd
Dagenham NW10 89 C6
Highbury N4, N5 72 C5
St Thomas's Sq E9 74 C1
St Thomas St
SE1 117 B5 252 D3
St Thomas's Way
SW6 135 B5 264 D4
St Thomas the Apostle
Coll The SE15 140 C4
St Timothy's Mews 3
BR1 187 B2
St Ursula Gr HA5 41 A4
St Ursula Rd UB1 85 C1
St Ursula's Convent Sch
SE10 142 B5
St Vincent Cl SE27 182 D5
St Vincent De Paul Ho 24
E1 96 C2
St Vincent De Paul RC
Prim Sch
SW1 115 C3 259 B6
St Vincent Ho SE1 263 C6
St Vincent Rd TW2 152 A5
St Vincent's Hospl HA5 39 D6
St Vincents La NW7 28 C6
St Vincents RC Prim Sch
SE9 188 A6
St Vincent's RC Prim Sch
Acton W3 110 D6
Dagenham RM8 80 C6
Marylebone W1 93 A2 238 B3
St Vincent's RC Sch
NW7 28 C5
St Vincent St W1 238 B3
St Wilfrid's Cl EN4 14 C6
St Wilfrid's Rd EN4 14 C6
St William of York RC
Prim Sch SE23 163 A3
St Winefride's Ave E12 78 B3
St Winefride's RC Prim
Sch E12 78 B3
St Winifred's RC Inf Sch
SE12 164 C6
St Winifred's RC Jun Sch
SE12 164 D4
St Winifred's Rd
TW11 175 B4
Sakura Dr N22 31 D2
Sala Ho SE3 143 B1
Salamanca Pl SE1 260 C3
Salamanca St SE1,
SE11 116 B2 260 C3
Salamander Cl KT2 175 C5
Salamander Quay
KT1 175 D2
Salcombe Dr
Dagenham RM6 59 B3
North Cheam SM4 200 D1
Salcombe Gdns
Clapham SW4 137 B1
Mill Hill NW7 28 C4
Salcombe Ho 6 SE23 162 C2
Salcombe Lo NW5 71 A4
Salcombe Pk IG10 21 D6
Salcombe Rd
Ashford TW15 148 A1
23 Stoke Newington N16 73 C3
Walthamstow E17 53 B2
Salcombe Sch N14 15 B4
Salcombe Villas 13
TW10 154 A6
Salcombe Way
Hayes UB4 83 C4
Ruislip HA4 62 A6
Salcot N4 72 B6
Salcott Rd
Wallington CR0 220 B4
Wandsworth SW11 158 D6
Salehurst Cl HA3 44 A4
Salehurst Rd SE4 163 B5
Salem Ho 13 E9 74 D2
Salem Pl CR0 221 A5
Salem Rd W2 113 D6 245 D6
Sale Pl W2 92 C1 237 A2
Salesian Coll
SW11 136 C4 267 A1
Sale St E2 96 A3
Salford Ho 5 E14 120 A2
Salford Rd SW12, SW2 159 D3
Salhouse Cl SE28 102 C1
Salisbury Ave
Barking IG11 79 C1
Cheam SM1, SM2 217 B2
Hendon N3 47 B6
Salisbury Cl SE17 262 C4
Worcester Pk KT4 215 D5
Salisbury Ct
15 Bermondsey SE16 118 A3
Chiswick W4 111 C2
EC4 241 C1
Edgware HA8 26 B6
Enfield EN2 5 B1
Finchley N3 29 B1
Hackney E9 75 A3
Northolt UB5 63 D3
Salisbury Gdns
5 Buckhurst Hill IG9 21 D2
Wimbledon SW19 179 A3
Salisbury Hall Gdns E4 35 C4
Salisbury Ho
2 Islington N1 72 D2
Islington N1 234 C6
3 Poplar E14 97 D1
1 Ruislip HA4 40 C1
Stanmore HA7 25 A4
5 Wallington SM6 219 B3
Westminster SW1 259 D2
Wimbledon SW19 156 D1
Salisbury Lower Sch
N9 18 C4
Salisbury Mans
Edmonton N9 18 A1
Harringay N4, N15 50 D4
Salisbury Mews
Bromley Comm BR2 210 A4
Fulham SW6 264 C3
Salisbury Pl
Camberwell SW9 138 D5
Marylebone W1 237 C4
Salisbury Prim Sch
E12 78 A3
Salisbury Rd Barnet EN5 1 A2
Bromley Comm BR2 210 A4
Chingford E4 19 C1
Croydon SE25 206 A3
Dagenham RM10 81 D2
East Bedfont TW6 149 A5
Enfield EN3 7 B6
Feltham TW13 150 C3
Forest Gate E7 77 A2
Harringay N4 50 D4
Harrow HA1 42 B4
Hounslow TW4 128 C2
Ilford IG3 79 C6
Kingston u T KT3 199 B6
Leyton E10 76 A6
Old Bexley DA5 169 C3
Pinner HA5 40 A5
Plashet E12 77 D3
Richmond TW9 132 A1
Southall UB2 107 A2
Tottenham N22 32 D1
Wallington SM5 218 D2
Walthamstow E17 54 A4
West Ealing W13 109 B4
Wimbledon SW19 179 A3
Worcester Pk KT4 215 C5
Salisbury Sq EC4 241 B1
Salisbury St
10 Acton W3 111 A4
NW8 237 A5
Salisbury Terr SE15 140 C2
Salisbury Upper Sch
N9 18 C4
Salisbury Wlk N19 71 C6
Salix Cl TW16 172 B3
Salix Ct N3 29 C4
Salliesfield TW2 152 B5
Sally Murray Cl E12 78 C4
Salmen Rd E13 98 D5
Salmond Cl HA7 25 A4
Salmon La E14 97 A1
Salmon Rd DA17 125 C1
Salmons Brook Ho EN2 4 D2
Salmons Rd
Chessington KT9 214 A2
Edmonton N9 18 A3
Salmon St
Kingsbury NW9 45 A2
13 Poplar E14 97 B1
Salomons Rd 2 E13 99 C2
Salop Rd E17 52 D3
Saltash Cl SM1 217 B4
Saltash Rd DA16 146 C4
Saltcoats Rd W4 111 C4
Saltcroft Cl HA9 44 D1
Saltdene N4 50 B1
Salter Cl HA2 63 B4
Salterford Rd SW17 181 A4
Salter Ho 8 SW16 181 C6
Saltern Ct IG11 102 B4
Salter Rd SE16 119 A5
Salters' Hall Ct EC4 252 C6
Salter's Hill SE19 183 B5
Salters Rd
North Kensington W10 90 D3
Walthamstow E17 54 B5
Salter St
College Pk NW10 90 A4
11 Poplar E14 119 C6
Salterton Rd N7 72 B5
Salt Hill Cl UB8 60 A3
Saltley Cl E6 100 A1
Saltoun Rd SW2, SW9 138 C1
Saltram Cl N15 51 D5
Saltram Cres W9 91 C4
Saltwell St E14 119 C6
Saltwood Gr SE17 262 C1
Saltwood Ho 19 SE15 140 C6
Salusbury Prim Sch
NW6 91 B6
Salusbury Rd NW6 91 A6
Salutation Rd SE10 120 C2
Salvador SW17 180 D5
Salvatorian RC Coll
HA3 24 C1
Salvia Gdns UB6 87 A5
Salvin Rd SW15 134 D2
Salway Cl IG8 37 A3
Salway Ho E10 75 D6
Salway Pl E15 76 C2
Salway Rd E15 76 B2
Salween Ho 2 N16 73 B4
Samantha Cl E17 53 B2
Samantha Ct E11 54 C2
Samaritan Hospl for
Women NW1 237 C4
Sam Bartram Cl SE7 121 C1
Sambrooke Ct EN1 17 D6
Sambrook Ho 25 E1 96 C2
Sambruck Mews SE6 163 D3
Samels Ct W6 112 A1
Samford Ho N1 234 A5
Samford St NW8 237 A5
Samira Cl E17 53 C3
Sam Manners Ho 7
SE10 120 C1
Sam March Ho 5 E14 98 B1
Samos Rd SE20 184 B1
Sampson Ave EN5 12 D6
Sampson Cl DA17 125 A3
Sampson Ct TW17 193 A4
Sampson St E1 118 A5
Samson Ct 5 DA17 125 C2
Samson Ho SE18 123 A2
Samson St E13 99 C5
Samuel Cl SE14 140 D6
Shoreditch E8 95 D6
Woolwich SE18 122 A2
Samuel Ct
Beckenham BR3 207 D6
Shoreditch N1 95 C4
Samuel Gray Gdns
KT2 175 D2
Samuel Ho
15 Shoreditch E8 95 D6
3 West Norwood
SE27 182 D6
Samuel Johnson Cl
SW16 182 B6
Samuel Jones Ind Est 7
SE15 139 C5
Samuel Lewis Bldgs
N1 72 C2
Samuel Lewis Trust
Dwellings
6 Camberwell SE5 139 A4
Chelsea SW3 257 A3
Walham Green
SW6 135 C5 265 B4
West Kensington W14 254 B4
Samuel Lewis Trust Est
N15 51 C3
Samuel Lo N3 29 B1
Samuel Rhodes Sch
N1 94 C6 234 A6
Samuel Richardson Ho
W14 254 C3
Samuel's Cl 2 W6 112 C2
Samuel St SE15 139 D5
Woolwich SE18 122 B2
Sancroft Cl NW2 68 B5
Sancroft Ct SW11 267 B2
Sancroft Ho SE11 260 D2
Sancroft Rd HA3 25 A1
Sancroft St
SE11 116 B1 260 D2
Sanctuary Mews 15 E8 73 D2
Sanctuary Rd TW19,
TW6 148 C5
Sanctuary St SE1 252 B2
Sanctuary The
Morden SM4 201 C3
Sidcup DA5 168 D5
35 Wapping E1 118 B5
Westminster
SW1 115 D3 259 D6
Sandale Cl N16 73 B5
Sandall Cl W5 88 A3
Sandall Ho 7 E3 97 A5
Sandall Rd Ealing W5 88 A3
Kentish Town NW5 71 C2
Sandal Rd
Edmonton N18 34 A5
New Malden KT3 199 C5
Sandal St E15 98 C6
Sandalwood Cl 11 E1 97 A3
Sandalwood Dr HA4 39 A2
Sandalwood Ho DA15 167 D1
6 Hampstead NW3 69 D2
Sandalwood Rd TW13 150 B1
Sandbach Pl SE18 123 A1
Sandbourne
4 Kensington W11 91 C1
14 Paddington NW8 91 D6
Sandbourne Ave
SW19 179 D1
Sandbourne Rd SE4 141 A3
Sandbrook Cl NW7 27 B4
Sandbrook Rd N16 73 C5
Sandby Ct BR3 185 B2
Sandby Gn SE9 144 A2
Sandby Ho
11 Camberwell SE5 139 C4
6 Kilburn NW6 91 C6
Sandcroft Cl N13 32 D4
Sandells Ave
Ashford TW15 171 A6
Ashford TW15 171 A6
Sandell St SE1 251 A2
Sanderling Ct 20 SE8 141 B6
Woolwich SE28 124 C6
Sanders Cl TW12 174 A5
Sanders Ho
Streatham SW16 182 A4
WC1 234 A2
Sanders La NW7 28 C3
Sanderson Cl NW5 71 B4
Sanderson Ho 7 SE8 119 B1
Sanderson Sq BR1 210 C6
Sanderstead Ave NW2 69 A6
Sanderstead Cl SW12 159 C4
Sanderstead Rd
South Croydon CR2 221 B1
Walthamstow E10 53 A1
Sanders Way 3 N19 49 D1
Sandfield WC1 233 B1
Sandfield Gdns CR7 204 D6
Sandfield Pl CR7 205 A6
Sandfield Rd CR7 204 D6
Sandford Ave N22 33 A2
Sandford Cl E6 100 B3
Sandford Ct Barnet EN5 1 D2
Stamford Hill N16 51 C1
Sandford Rd
Bexley DA7 147 A2
BR2 209 A5
Newham E6 100 B4
Sandford Row SE17 262 D2
Sandford St SW6 265 D3
Sandgate Ho
14 Beckenham BR3 185 C3
Ealing W5 87 C2
15 Hackney E5 74 B4
Sandgate La SW17,
SW18 158 C3
Sandgate Rd DA16 146 C5
Sandgate St SE15 140 B6
Sandgate Trad Est
SE15 140 B6
Sandham Ct SW4 270 B1
Sandham Point 10
SE18 122 D2
Sandhills CR0, SM6 219 D4
Sandhills Mdw TW17 193 A2
Sandhills The SW10 266 B6
Sandhurst Ave
Harrow HA2 41 D3
Tolworth KT5 198 D2
Sandhurst Cl
Queensbury NW9 44 C6
South Croydon CR2 221 C1
Sandhurst Ct SW2 138 A1
Sandhurst Dr IG3 79 D4
Sandhurst Ho 12 E1 96 C2
Sandhurst Jun & Inf Schs
SE6 164 C3
Sandhurst Mkt SE6 164 A3
Sandhurst Rd
Bexley DA5 168 D6
Catford SE6 164 B3
DA15 168 A1
Ponders End N9 18 D5
Queensbury HA8, NW9 44 C6
Sandhurst Way CR2 221 C1
Sandifer Dr NW2 68 D5
Sandiford Rd SM3 217 B6
Sandiland Cres BR2 224 D6
Sandilands CR0 222 A5
Sandilands Rd
SW6 135 D4 265 C1
Sandilands Sta CR0 221 D6
Sandison St SE15 140 A2
Sandland St WC1 240 D3
Sandling Rise SE9 166 C1
Sandlings Cl SE15 140 B3

Sandlings The
Tottenham N22 50 D6
5 Wood Green N22 32 C1
Sandmartin Way CR4 203 A1
Sandmere Rd SW4 138 A1
Sandon Cl KT10 196 B1
Sandon Ct IG3 80 A5
Sandon Ho 5 SW2 160 A4
Sandow Commercial Est
UB3 105 D3
Sandow Cres UB3 105 D3
Sandown Ave KT10 212 A3
Sandown Cl TW5 128 A4
Sandown Ct 12 SM2 217 D1
Sandown Gate KT10 212 B5
Sandown Ho
2 Acton Green W4 111 A1
Esher KT10 212 A4
Penge SE26 184 B4
Sandown Park KT10 212 A6
Sandown Rd
Croydon SE25 206 B4
Esher KT10 212 A4
Sandown Way UB5 63 B3
Sandpiper Cl
Higham Hill E17 34 D3
Rotherhithe SE16 119 B4
Sandpiper Ct
13 Cubitt Town E14 120 A3
1 SE8 141 C5
Sandpiper Rd SM1 217 B3
Sandpiper Terr IG5 56 D6
Sandpit Pl SE7 122 A1
Sandpit Rd BR1 186 C5
Sandpits Rd
Richmond TW10 153 D2
South Croydon CR0 222 D4
Sandra Cl
Hounslow TW3 151 D6
Tottenham N17 33 A2
Sandra Ho KT8 196 B4
Sandridge Cl
Hadley Wood EN4 2 C6
Harrow HA1 42 C5
Sandridge St 3 N19 71 C6
Sandringham Ave
SW20 179 A1
Sandringham Cl
Enfield EN1 5 C3
Ilford IG6 57 A6
1 Putney SW19 156 D3
Sandringham Cres
HA2 63 D6
Sandringham Ct
3 Beckenham BR3 186 A2
Edgware HA8 26 D6
Hillingdon UB10 83 A3
Kingston u T KT2 176 A2
Marylebone W1 239 B1
Putney SW15 156 D5
18 Rotherhithe SE16 118 D5
St John's Wood W9 229 B1
2 Twickenham TW1 153 A3
Sandringham Dr
Ashford TW15 170 A6
DA16 145 C3
Sandringham Flats
WC2 249 D6
Sandringham Gdns
Cranford TW5 128 A4
East Molesey KT8 195 C5
Finchley N12 30 B4
Hornsey Vale N8 50 A3
Ilford IG6 57 A6
Sandringham Ho
Richmond TW10 154 C6
W14 254 A4
Sandringham Lo BR6 226 C4
Sandringham Mews
TW12 173 B2
Sandringham Prim Sch
E7 77 C3
Sandringham Rd
Barking IG11 79 D2
BR1 187 A5
Dalston E8 73 D3
Forest Gate E7 77 C3
Golders Green NW11 47 A2
Leytonstone E10 54 B3
Northolt UB5 63 C1
Stanwell TW19, TW6 148 A6
Thornton Heath CR0 205 A4
Tottenham N22 33 A1
Willesden NW2 68 B2
Worcester Pk KT4 216 A5
Sandrock Pl CR0 222 D4
Sandrock Rd SE13 141 C2
SANDS END 136 A2
Sands End La
SW6 135 D4 265 D2
Sandstone TW9 132 C5
Sandstone La E16 121 B6
Sandstone Pl N19 71 B6
Sandstone Rd SE12 165 B2
Sandtoft Rd SE7 143 B6
Sandways 6 TW9 132 C4
Sandwell Cres 2 NW6 69 C2
Sandwell Mans 3
NW6 69 C2
Sandwich Ho
15 Rotherhithe SE16 118 C4
WC1 233 A1
Sandwich St
WC1 94 A4 233 A1
Sandwick Cl NW7 28 A3
Sandy Bury BR6 227 B5
Sandycombe Ctr TW9 132 C2
Sandycombe Rd
East Bedfont TW14 150 A3
Richmond TW9 132 C3
Sandycoombe Rd
TW1 153 C5
Sandycroft SE2 146 A6
Sandy Dr TW14 149 C3
Sandy Hill Ave SE18 122 D1
Sandy Hill La SE18 122 D2
Sandyhill Rd IG1 78 D4
Sandy Hill Rd SE18 122 D1
Sandy La Belmont SM2 217 A1
BR5 190 D2
Eastbury HA6 22 A6
Harrow HA3 44 A3
Mitcham CR4 181 A2
Richmond TW10 153 D2
Teddington KT8, TW11 175 B3
Walton-on-T KT12 194 C3
Sandy Lane N SM6 219 D3
Sandy Lane S SM6 219 C1
Sandy Lo N6 49 C2
Sandymount Ave HA7 25 D5
Sandy Rd NW3 69 D6
Sandy Ridge BR7 188 C4
Sandy's Row E1 243 B3
Sandy Way
Croydon CR0 223 B5
Walton-on-T KT12 193 D1
Sanford La 3 N16 73 D6
Sanford St SE14, SE8 141 A6
Sanford Terr N16 73 D5
Sanford Wlk SE14 141 A6
4 Stoke Newington N16 73 D6
Sangam Cl UB2 107 A3
Sanger Ave KT9 214 B4
Sangley Rd
Catford SE6 164 A3
South Norwood SE25 205 C5
Sangora Rd 17 SW11 136 B1
San Ho 20 E9 74 D2
Sankey Ho 22 E2 96 C5
Sansom Rd E11 76 D6
Sansom St
Camberwell SE5 139 B4
SE5 139 B5
Sans Wlk EC1 94 D3 241 C6
Santana SE18 144 D5
Santley Ho SE1 251 B1
Santley St SW4 138 B1
Santos Rd SW18 157 C6
Sapcote Trad Ctr
NW10 67 D2
Saperton Wlk SE11 260 D4
Saphora Cl BR6 227 B3
Sapperton Ct EC1 242 A6
Sapphire Cl
Dagenham RM8 58 C1
Newham E6 100 C1
Sapphire Ct 13 E1 118 A6
Sapphire Rd
Rotherhithe SE8 119 A2
Willesden NW10 67 A1
Saracen Cl CR0 205 B3
Saracen St E14 97 C1
Sarah Bonnell Sch E15 76 C2
Sarah Ct UB5 85 B6
Sarah Ho
Roehampton SW15 133 D1
8 Stepney E1 96 B1
Sarah Swift Ho SE1 252 D2
Sarah Turnbull Ho 2
SE18 122 B2
Sara Lane Ct 31 N1 95 C5
Saratoga Rd E5 74 C4
Sardeson Ho 13 SW27 182 D5
Sardinia Ho WC2 240 C1
Sardinia St WC2 240 C2
Sargents Hill N2 30 C2
Sarita Cl HA3 24 B1
Sarjant Path SW19 156 D2
Sark Cl TW5 129 C5
Sark Ho
9 Canonbury N1 73 A2
Enfield EN3 6 D5
Sark Twr SE28 123 A4
Sark Wlk E16 99 B1
Sarnersfield Ho SE15 140 B6
Sarnes Ct 4 N11 31 B6
Sarnesfield Rd EN2 5 B2
Sarratt Ho 6 W10 90 C2
Sarre Rd NW2 69 B3
Sarsden Bldgs W1 238 B1
Sarsen Ave TW3 129 C3
Sarsfeld Rd SW12,
SW17 158 D3
Sarsfield Rd UB6 87 C5
Sartor Rd SE15 140 D1
Sarum Hall Sch NW3 70 C1
Sarum Ho W11 244 D5
Sarwan Ho 1 E7 77 C1
Sassoon 4 NW9 27 D2
Sassoon Ho SE15 140 C3
Satanita Cl E16 99 D1
Satchell Mead NW9 27 D2
Satchwell Rd 17 E2 96 A4
Satin Ct NW9 45 D5
Saturn Ho 4 E3 97 C6
Saul Ct 4 SE15 139 D6
Sauls Gn E11 76 C5
Saunders Cl Ilford IG1 57 B1
14 Limehouse E14 119 B6
Saunders Ho 11 SW2 160 C3
Saunders Ness Rd
E14 120 B2
Saunders Rd
Hillingdon UB10 82 B6
Plumstead Comm SE18 123 D1
Saunders St SE11 261 A4
Saunders Way SE28 124 B6
Saunderton Rd HA0 65 B3
Saunton Ave UB3 127 D5
Saunton Ct UB1 108 A6
Savage Gdns EC3 253 B6
Newham E6 100 B1
Savana N16 73 C6
Savannah Cl 9 SE15 139 D5
Savernake Ct HA7 25 B4
Savernake Ho N4 51 B2
Savernake Rd
Enfield N9 18 A5
Maitland Pk NW3 70 D4
Savery Dr KT6 197 C2
Savile Cl
New Malden KT3 199 C4
Thames Ditton KT7 197 A1
Savile Gdns CR0 221 D6
Savill Ct IG8 36 D4
Saville Cres TW15 171 B4
Saville Ho E16 122 D5
Saville Rd
Bedford Pk W4 111 B3
Dagenham RM6 59 B2
Newham E16 122 A5
Twickenham TW1 152 D3
Saville Row Enfield EN3 6 D3
Hayes BR2 208 D1
W1 115 C6 249 A6
Savill Gdns SW20 200 A6
Savill Ho 2 SW4 159 D5
Savill Row IG8 36 D4
Savin Lo 7 SM2 218 A1
Savona Cl 16 SW19 178 D3
Savona Ct SW20 178 D2
Savona St SW8 137 C5 269 A3
Savoy Ave UB3 105 C1
Savoy Circus W3 111 D6
Savoy Cl Edgware HA8 26 C5
Newham E15 98 C6
Savoy Ct Earl's Ct SW5 255 B4
Strand WC2 250 B5
Savoy Hill WC2 250 C5
Savoy Mews SW9 138 A2
Savoy Par EN1 5 C2
Savoy Pier WC2 250 C5
Savoy Pl WC2 116 B6 250 C5
Savoy Row WC2 250 C6
Savoy St WC2 116 B6 250 C5
Savoy Stps WC2 250 C5
Savoy Way WC2 250 C5
Sawbill Cl UB4 84 D2
Sawkins Cl SW19 157 A2
Sawley Rd W12 112 A5
Sawmill Yd E3 97 A6
Sawtry Cl SM5 202 C2
Sawyer Cl N9 18 A2
Sawyer Ho 15 SE21 183 C6
Sawyer's Hill TW10 154 B4
Sawyers Lawn W13 87 A1
Sawyer St SE1 117 A4 252 A2
Saxby Rd SW2 160 A4
Saxham Rd IG11 101 D5
Saxlingham Rd E4 20 B1
Saxon Ave TW13 151 B2
Saxon Bsns Ctr SW19 180 A2
Saxonbury Ave TW16 172 B1
Saxonbury Cl CR4 202 B6
Saxonbury Ct
16 Kentish Town N7 71 D3
2 Lower Holloway N7 72 A3
Saxonbury Gdns KT6 197 C1
Saxon Cl Hillingdon UB8 82 A2
Surbiton KT6 197 D3
Walthamstow E17 53 C2
Saxoncroft Ho SW16 159 D1
Saxon Ct
Colney Hatch N12 30 C5
4 Edgware HA8 26 D5
Saxon Dr W3 88 D2
Saxonfield Cl SW2 160 B4
Saxon Gdns UB1 107 A6
Saxon Hall W2 245 C5
Saxon Ho
4 Clapham SW4 137 D1
Feltham TW13 151 B2
Saxon Prim Sch TW17 192 C4
Saxon Rd
Ashford TW15 171 B4
Bow E3 97 B5
Bromley BR1 186 D3
Ilford IG1 78 D3
Kingston u T KT2 176 A2
Newham E6 100 B3
Southall UB1 107 A6
South Norwood SE25 205 B4
Tottenham N22 32 D2
Wembley HA9 67 A5
Saxon Terr SE6 163 B2
Saxon Way N14 15 D5
Saxon Wlk DA14 190 C4
Saxony Par UB3 83 A2
Saxton Cl SE13 142 B2
Saxville Rd BR5 190 B1
Sayer Ho SE4 141 A1
Sayers Ho 4 N2 30 B1
Sayer's Wlk TW10 154 B4
Sayesbury La N18 34 A5
Sayes Court St SE8 141 B6
Sayes Ct SE8 141 B6
Sayline Ct CR0 221 B5
Scadbury Gdns BR5 190 A1
Scadbury Park Nature
Reserve* BR7 189 D4
Scads Hill Cl BR6 211 D3
Scafell NW1 232 A2
Scala St W1 239 B4
Scales Rd N17 52 A6
Scampston Mews 5
W10 90 D1
Scandrett St 38 E1 118 B5
Scarba Wlk N1 73 B2
Scarborough Rd
East Bedfont TW6 149 A5
Scarborough Rd *continued*
Finsbury Pk N4 50 C1
Leytonstone E11 54 B1
Ponders End N9 18 C4
Scarborough St E1 243 D1
Scarbrook Rd CR0 221 A5
Scardale Ho 12 E5 74 B6
Scarle Rd HA0 65 D2
Scarlet Rd SE6 164 C1
Scarlette Manor Wlk 10
SE24 160 C4
Scarsbrook Ho 2
SW2 160 C5
Scarsbrook Rd SE3 143 D2
Scarsdale Pl W8 255 C6
Scarsdale Rd HA2 64 A5
Scarsdale Villas
W8 113 C3 255 B5
Scarth Rd SW13 133 D2
Scawen Cl SM5 219 A4
Scawen Rd SE8 119 A1
Scawfell St E2 95 D5
Scaynes Link N12 29 C6
Sceptre Ho 10 E1 96 C3
Sceptre Rd E2 96 C4
Schiller International Univ
SE1 116 C5 251 A3
Schofield Wlk SE3 143 A5
Sch of Pharmacy
WC1 94 A3 240 B6
Scholars Cl EN5 1 A1
Scholars Ct 5 N19 49 D1
Scholars Ho 6 E4 20 B3
Scholars Rd
Chingford E4 20 B3
Streatham SW12 159 C3
Scholefield Rd N19 71 D6
Scholey Ho SW11 136 C2
Schomberg Ho SW1 259 D4
Schonfeld Sq N16 51 B1
School App 21 E2 95 C4
Schoolbank Rd SE10 120 D2
School Bell Cloisters 17
E3 97 A5
Schoolbell Mews 18 E3 97 A5
School Cotts
Bromley BR1 187 A3
Sidcup DA14 190 C5
School Flats SW8 270 A1
School Ho SE1 263 A4
Schoolhouse La E1 118 D6
School House La
TW11 175 C3
Schoolhouse Yd 9
SE18 122 D1
School La DA16 146 B2
Lower Halliford TW17 192 D2
Pinner HA5 41 A5
Surbiton KT6 198 B1
Teddington KT1 175 C2
School Pas
3 Kingston u T KT1 176 B1
Southall UB1 107 B6
School Rd
Ashford TW15 170 D4
Becontree NW10 89 B3
BR7 189 A3
Dagenham RM10 103 D6
East Molesey KT8 196 B5
Hampton TW12 174 A4
Hounslow TW3 130 A2
Ilford E12 78 B4
Littleton TW15 170 D3
Teddington KT1 175 C2
School Road Ave
TW12 174 A4
School Sq SE10 120 D3
Schoolway N12 30 B4
School Way RM8 80 C5
School Wlk TW16 193 D6
Schooner Cl
Barking IG11 102 B4
Cubitt Town E14 120 B3
1 Rotherhithe SE16 118 D4
Schubert Rd Elstree WD6 9 D5
Putney SW15 157 B6
Science Mus*
SW7 114 B3 256 C5
Scilly Isles KT10 212 C6
Sclater St E1 243 D6
Scoles Cres SW2 160 C3
Scope Way KT1 198 A5
Scoresby St SE1 251 C3
Scoresdale SE19 183 C2
Scorton Ave UB6 87 A5
Scorton Ho 2 N1 95 C5
Scotch Comm W13 87 B2
Scotch Ho
SW1 114 D4 247 C1
Scoter Cl IG8 37 B3
Scoter Ct 23 SE8 141 B6
Scot Gr HA5 22 D3
Scotia Bldg 10 E1 118 D6
Scotia Ct 3 SE16 118 C3
Scotia Rd 24 SW2 160 C4
Scotland Gn N17 33 D1
Scotland Green Rd
EN3 18 D6
Scotland Green Rd N
EN3 7 A1
Scotland Pl SW1 250 A3
Scotland Rd IG9 21 C3
Scotney Cl BR6 226 C4
Scotney Ho E9 74 C2
Scots Cl TW19 148 A3
Scotsdale Cl
Belmont SM3 217 A1
BR5 211 C5
Scotsdale Rd SE12 165 B6
Scotson Ho SE11 261 A3
Scotswood St
EC1 94 C3 241 B6
Scotswood Wlk N17 34 A3
Scott Cl
Thornton Heath
SW16 182 B2
West Drayton UB7 104 B2
West Ewell KT19 215 A3
Scott Ct Acton W4 111 B4
4 Clapham SW11 137 B3
17 Stoke Newington N16 73 C5
Scott Ellis Gdns
NW8 92 B4 229 C1
Scottes La RM8 58 D1
Scott Farm Cl KT7 197 B1
Scott Gdns TW5 128 D5
Scott Ho
2 Barnsbury N7 72 B2
3 Edmonton N18 34 A5
4 Erith DA17 125 B1
Islington N1 235 C6
Lisson Gr NW8 237 A5
17 Millwall E14 119 C4
6 Newham E13 99 A5
Richmond TW10 153 C2
3 Stonebridge NW10 67 B1
Scott Lidgett Cres
SE16 118 A4
Scott Rd HA8 26 D1
Scott's Ave
Ashford TW16 171 C3
Beckenham BR2 186 B1
Scotts Ct 6 W12 112 B4
Scotts Dr TW12 173 D3
Scotts Farm Rd KT19 215 A2
Scotts Ho DA16 146 C4
Scott's La BR2, BR3 186 B1
Scotts Park Prim Sch
BR1 187 C2
Scotts Rd BR1 187 A3
Southall UB2 106 D3
Scott's Rd
Leytonstone E10 54 A1
Shepherd's Bush W12 112 B4
Scott's Sufferance Wharf
SE1 253 D1
Scott St E1 96 B3
Scott's Way TW16 171 C3
Scott's Yd EC4 252 C6
Scott Trimmer Way
TW3 129 A3
Scottwell Dr NW9 45 D4
Scott Wilkie Prim Sch
E16 99 C1
Scoulding Ho 12 E14 119 C3
Scoulding Rd E16 99 A1
Scouler St E14 120 B6
Scout App NW10 67 C4
Scout La SW4 137 C2
Scout Way NW7 27 B6
Scovell Cres SE1 252 A1
Scovell Rd SE1 252 A1
Scratchwood Nature
Trail* NW7 11 B4
Scrattons Terr IG11 103 A5
Scriven Ct 2 E8 95 D6
Scriven St E8 95 D6
Scrooby St SE6 163 D5
Scrope Bldg EC1 241 A4
Scrubs La NW10, W10,
W12 90 B3
Scrutton Cl SW12 159 D4
Scrutton St EC2 95 C3 243 A5
Scudamore La NW9 45 A5
Scutari Rd SE22 162 C6
Scylla Cres
TW6&TW14 148 D4
Scylla Rd
East Bedfont TW14,
TW6 148 D5
Nunhead SE15 140 B2
Seabright St 27 E2 96 B4
Seabrook Dr BR4 224 C6
Seabrook Gdns RM7 59 C2
Seabrook Rd RM8 80 D5
Seacole Cl W3 89 B2
Seacole Ct N15 51 D4
Seacole Lo N21 16 B6
Seacon Twr 8 E14 119 C4
Seacourt Rd SE2 124 D4
Seacroft Gdns WD19 22 D6
Seafield Rd N11 31 D6
Seaford Cl HA4 61 B6
Seaford Ho 13 SE16 118 C4
Seaford Rd Ealing W13 109 B5
Enfield EN1 5 C1
Tottenham N15 51 C4
Walthamstow E17 53 D6
Seaford St WC1 233 B1
Seaforth Ave KT3 200 B5
Seaforth Cres N5 73 A3
Seaforth Gdns
Southgate N21 16 C3
Woodford IG8 37 C5
Worcester Pk KT19 215 D3
Seaforth Lo 2 SW13 133 D3
Seaforth Pl SW1 259 B6
Seagrave Lo SW6 265 B6
Seagrave Rd
SW6 135 C6 265 B6
Seagrove Cl E1 96 D2
Seagry Rd E11 55 B2
Seagull Cl IG11 102 A4
Seagull La E16 121 A6
Sealand Rd TW6 148 C5
Sealand Wlk UB5 85 A4
Seal Ho SE1 262 D6
Seal St E8 73 D4
Searle Ct 2 CR4 180 C2
Searle Pl N4 50 B1
Searles Cl
SW11 136 C5 267 B3
Searles Dr E6 100 D2
Searles Rd SE1 262 D4
Searson Ho SE17 261 D3
Sears Ret Pk UB6 86 C6
Sears St SE5 139 B5
Seasalter Ho 10 SW9 138 C4
Seasprite Cl 10 UB5 84 D4
Seath Ho 4 SE26 184 B5
Seaton Ave IG3 79 D3
Seaton Cl
Isleworth TW2 152 B5
6 Newham E13 99 A3
Roehampton SW15 156 B4
Seaton Dr TW15 148 A2
Seaton Gdns HA4 62 A6
Seaton Point E5 74 A4
Seaton Rd Bexley DA16 146 C5
Hayes UB3 105 B3
Mitcham CR4 180 C1
Twickenham TW2 152 A5
Wembley HA0 88 A5
Seaton Sq NW7 28 D3
Seaton St N18 34 A5
Seavington Ho 3 SE5 139 C2
Sebastian Ct 11 IG11 79 D1
Sebastian Ho 22 N1 95 C5
Sebastian St
EC1 94 D4 234 D1
Sebastopol Rd N9 34 A6
Sebbon St N1 72 D1
Sebergham Gr NW7 28 A3
Sebert Rd E7 77 B4
Sebright Ho 22 E2 96 A5
Sebright Pas 29 E2 96 A5
Sebright Rd EN5 1 A2
Sebright Sch E2 96 A5
Secker Cres HA3 24 A2
Secker Ho SW9 138 D3
Secker St SE1 251 A3
Second Ave
Chadwell Heath RM6 58 C4
Dagenham RM10 103 D5
East Acton W3 111 D5
Edmonton N18 34 C6
Enfield EN1 17 D6
Hayes UB3 105 D5
Hendon NW4 46 D5
Kensal Town W10 91 A3
Manor Pk E12 78 A3
Mortlake SW14 133 C2
Newham E13 99 A4
Walthamstow E17 53 C4
Walton-on-T KT12 194 B3
Wembley HA9 65 D6
Second Cl KT8 196 A5
Second Cross Rd
TW2 152 C2
Second Way HA9 66 D4
Secrett Ho 6 TW10 153 C1
Sedan Way
SE17 117 C1 263 A2
Sedcombe Cl DA14 190 C6
Sedcote Rd EN3 18 D6
Sedding St SW1 258 A4
Seddon Ho EC2 242 A4
Seddon Rd SM4 202 B4
Seddon St WC1 94 B4 233 D1
Sedgebrook Rd SE3 143 D2
Sedgecombe Ave HA3 43 C4
Sedgefield Ct UB5 63 D3
Sedgeford Rd W12 111 D5
Sedgehill Rd SE6 185 D5
Sedgehill Sch SE6 185 D5
Sedgemere Ave N2 48 A6
Sedgemere Rd SE2 124 C3
Sedgemoor Dr RM10 81 C4
Sedge Rd N17 34 C3
Sedgeway SE6 164 D3
Sedgewick Ho SW19 156 D2
Sedgewood Cl BR2 208 D2
Sedgley Ho N4 72 B6
Sedgmoor Pl SE5 139 C5
Sedgwick Ave UB10 60 D1
Sedgwick Rd E10 76 A6
Sedgwick St E9 74 D3
Sedleigh Rd SW18 157 B5
Sedlescombe Rd
SW6 135 C6 265 A6
Sedley Cl EN1 6 B5
Sedley Ct SE26 162 B2
Sedley Ho SE11 260 D2
Sedley Pl W1 238 C1
Sedum Cl NW9 44 D4
Seeley Dr SE21 183 C6
Seelig Ave NW9 46 A2
Seely Rd SW17 181 A4
Seething La
EC3 117 C6 253 B6
SEETHING WELLS 197 D3
Seething Wells Halls of
Residence KT6 197 C3
Seething Wells La
KT6 197 C3
Sefton Ave
Edgware NW7 27 B5
Harrow HA3 24 B2
Sefton Cl BR5 211 D5
Sefton Ct TW5 129 D4
Sefton Lo 2 TW1 153 C5
Sefton Rd Croydon CR0 206 A1
Orpington BR5 211 D5
Sefton St SW15 134 C2
Segal Cl SE23 163 A4
Sekforde St EC1 94 D3 241 C6
Sekhon Terr TW13 151 C1

Selan Gdns UB4 . . . . 84 B2
Selbie Ave NW10 . . . . 67 D3
Selborne 2 SW11 . . . . . 137 A2
Selborne Ave DA5 . . . . . 169 A3
Little Ilford E12 . . . . 78 C4
Walthamstow E17 . . . . 53 B5
Selborne Gdns
Hendon NW4 . . . . 46 A5
Wembley UB6 . . . . 87 A5
Selborne Ho SE1 . . . . . . 252 C1
Selborne Prim Sch
UB6 . . . . 86 D5
Selborne Rd
1 Camberwell SE5 . . . . . 139 B3
Ilford IG1 . . . . 78 C6
Kingston u T KT3 . . . . 177 C1
Palmers Green N14 . . . . . . 16 A1
Sidcup DA14 . . . . 190 B6
South Croydon CR0 . . . . . 221 D5
Walthamstow E17 . . . . 53 C4
Wood Green N22 . . . . 32 B2
Selborne Wlk E17 . . . . 53 B5
Selborne Wlk Sh Ctr
E17 . . . . 53 B5
Selbourne Ave KT6 . . . . 214 C5
Selbridge Ct SW19 . . . . . 179 C4
Selby Chase HA4 . . . . 62 B6
Selby Cl BR7 . . . . 188 C4
Chessington KT9 . . . . 214 A1
14 Newham E6 . . . . 100 A2
Selby Ct TW2 . . . . 152 B2
Selby Gdns UB1 . . . . 85 C3
Selby Gn SM5 . . . . 202 C2
Selby Ho 10 SW4 . . . . 159 C5
Selby Rd Ashford TW15 . . 171 A4
Carshalton SM5 . . . . 202 C2
Ealing W5 . . . . 87 C3
Leyton E11 . . . . 76 C5
Newham E13 . . . . 99 B2
Penge SE20 . . . . 184 A1
Tottenham N17 . . . . 33 C4
Selby Sq 1 W10 . . . . 91 A4
Selby St E1 . . . . 96 A3
Selden Ho 2 SE15 . . . . . 140 C3
Selden Rd SE15 . . . . 140 C3
Selden Wlk N7 . . . . 72 B6
Seldon Ho
Nine Elms SW8 . . . . 269 A3
Pimlico SW1 . . . . 259 A1
Selena Ct N20 . . . . 14 D1
SELHURST 205 B4
Selhurst Cl SW19 . . . . . . 156 D3
Selhurst New Ct SE25 . . 205 C3
Selhurst New Rd
SE25 . . . . 205 C3
Selhurst Park (Crystal Palace FC) SE25 . . . . . . 205 C5
Selhurst Pl SE25 . . . . 205 C3
Selhurst Rd
Edmonton N9 . . . . 17 C1
South Norwood SE25 . . . 205 C4
Selhurst Sta SE25 . . . . . . 205 C4
Selina Ho NW8 . . . . 236 D6
Selinas La RM8 . . . . 59 B2
Selkirk Ct N17 . . . . 33 C1
Selkirk Ho N1 . . . . 233 C6
4 Stoke Newington N16 . 73 C5
Selkirk Rd
Twickenham TW2 . . . . 152 A3
Upper Tooting SW17 . . . . 180 C6
Sellers Hall Cl N3 . . . . 29 C3
Sellincourt Prim Sch
SW17 . . . . 180 C4
Sellincourt Rd SW17 . . . 180 C4
Sellindge Cl BR3 . . . . 185 B3
Sellons Ave NW10 . . . . . . 89 D6
Sellsby Ct N11 . . . . 31 B5
Sellwood Dr EN5 . . . . 12 D6
Selma Ho 7 W12 . . . . 90 B1
Selman Ho 3 E9 . . . . 75 A2
SELSDON 223 A1
Selsdon Ave CR2 . . . . 221 B2
Selsdon Cl KT6 . . . . 198 A4
Selsdon High Sch
CR2 . . . . 222 D1
Selsdon Park Rd CR0,
CR2 . . . . 223 B1
Selsdon Rd
Newham E13 . . . . 99 C5
South Croydon CR2 . . . . . 221 B2
Wanstead E11 . . . . 55 A2
West Norwood SE27 . . . . 182 D6
Willesden NW2 . . . . 67 D6
Selsdon Road Ind Est
CR2 . . . . 221 B2
Selsdon Way E14 . . . . . . 119 D3
Selsea Pl N16 . . . . 73 C3
Selsey Cres DA16 . . . . . 146 D4
Selsey St E14 . . . . 97 C2
Selvage La NW7 . . . . 27 B6
Selway Cl HA5 . . . . 40 B6
Selway Ho SW8 . . . . 270 B2
Selwood Ho
Chislehurst BR7 . . . . 189 A4
1 Stoke Newington N4 . . 51 B2
Selwood Pl
SW7 . . . . 114 B1 256 C2
Selwood Rd
Cheam SM3 . . . . 201 B1
Chessington KT9 . . . . 213 D4
Croydon CR0 . . . . 206 B1
Selwood Terr SW7 . . . . 256 C2
Selworthy Cl E11 . . . . 55 A4
Selworthy Ho SW11 . . . . 266 D2
Selworthy Rd SE6 . . . . . . 163 B1
Selwyn Ave Chingford E4 . 36 A4
Ilford IG3 . . . . 57 D3
Selwyn Ave *continued*
Richmond TW9 . . . . 132 B2
Selwyn Cl TW4 . . . . 129 A1
Selwyn Cres DA16 . . . . . 146 B1
Selwyn Ct Edgware HA8 . . 26 D3
Lewisham SE3 . . . . 142 D2
8 Richmond TW10 . . . . . 154 B6
Walthamstow E17 . . . . 53 C4
Wembley HA9 . . . . 67 A5
Selwyn Ho 3 SW15 . . . . 156 D5
Selwyn Inf Sch E4 . . . . . . 36 A4
Selwyn Jun Sch E4 . . . . . . 36 A4
Selwyn Prim Sch E13 . . . 99 A6
Selwyn Rd Bow E3 . . . . 97 B5
Newham E13 . . . . 99 B6
New Malden KT3 . . . . 199 B4
Willesden NW10 . . . . 67 C1
Semley Gate E9 . . . . 75 B2
Semley Ho SW1 . . . . 258 C3
Semley Pl SW1 . 115 B2 258 C3
Thornton Heath SW16 . . . 182 B1
Semley Rd SW16 . . . . 182 A1
Senate St SE15 . . . . 140 C3
Senators Lo 31 E3 . . . . . . 97 A5
Senator Wlk 2 SE28 . . . 123 B3
Sencler Ho SE2 . . . . 146 D6
Sendall Ct 13 SW11 . . . . 136 B2
Seneca Rd CR7 . . . . 205 A5
Senga Rd SM6 . . . . 203 A1
Senhouse Rd SM3 . . . . . 216 D5
Senior St W2 . . . . 91 D2
Senlac Rd SE12 . . . . 165 B3
Sennen Rd EN1 . . . . 17 D4
Sennen Wlk SE9 . . . . 166 A1
Senrab St E1 . . . . 96 D1
Sentinel Cl UB5 . . . . 85 A3
Sentinel Ho NW4 . . . . 46 C5
Sentinel Sq NW4 . . . . 46 C5
September Ct UB1 . . . . . 107 D5
September Way HA7 . . . . 25 B4
Sequoia Cl WD23 . . . . 8 B3
Sequoia Gdns BR6 . . . . . 211 D2
Sequoia Pk HA5 . . . . 23 D4
Seraph Ct EC1 . . . 95 A4 235 A2
Serbin Cl E10 . . . . 54 A2
Serenaders Rd 20
SW9 . . . . 138 C3
Sergeant Ind Est The
SW18 . . . . 157 D5
Serica Ct 14 SE10 . . . . . 142 A5
Serjeants' Inn EC4 . . . . 241 B1
Serlby Ct W14 . . . . 254 C6
Serle St WC2 . . . . 94 B1 240 D2
Sermon La EC4 . . . . 242 A1
Serpentine Ct 10
SE16 . . . . 118 D4
Serpentine Gallery*
W2 . . . . 114 B4 246 D2
Serpentine Rd
W2 . . . . 114 D5 247 C3
Serpentine The*
W2 . . . . 114 C5 247 B3
Service Route No 1
E15 . . . . 76 B1
Service Route No 2 1
E15 . . . . 76 B1
Service Route No 3 2
E15 . . . . 76 B1
Serviden Dr BR1 . . . . 187 D2
Servite Ho
Beckenham BR3 . . . . 185 B2
Bromley BR1 . . . . 188 B1
East Barnet N14 . . . . 15 B6
Lewisham SE13 . . . . 141 D4
Penge SE26 . . . . 184 C4
Worcester Pk KT4 . . . . . . 215 D6
Servite RC Prim Sch
SW10 . . . . 136 A6 266 A6
Servius Ct 2 TW8 . . . . . . 131 D5
Sessions Terr CR4 . . . . . 180 D2
Setchell Rd
SE1 . . . . 117 D2 263 C4
Setchell Way SE1 . . . . . 263 C4
Seth St 25 SE16 . . . . 118 C4
Seton Ct 3 NW9 . . . . 46 A5
Seton Gdns RM9 . . . . 80 C1
Settle Point 11 E13 . . . . . 99 A5
Settlers Ct 11 E14 . . . . . 120 B6
Settles St E1 . . . . 96 A1
Settrington Rd SW6 . . . . 135 D3
Seven Acres
Carshalton SM5 . . . . 218 C6
Northwood HA6 . . . . 22 A4
Seven Dials
WC2 . . . . 94 A1 240 A1
SEVEN KINGS 57 D2
Seven Kings High Sch
IG2 . . . . 57 B2
Seven Kings Rd IG3 . . . . 79 D6
Seven Kings Sta IG3 . . . . 57 C1
Seven Kings Way KT2 . . 176 A2
Seven Mills Prim Sch
E14 . . . . 119 C4
Sevenoaks Rd BR6 . . . . . 227 D4
Catford SE4 . . . . 163 B5
Sevenoaks Way BR5 . . . 190 C1
Seven Sisters N15 . . . . . . 51 D4
Seven Sisters Prim Sch
N15 . . . . 51 B4
Seven Sisters Rd
Finsbury Pk N4 . . . . 72 D6
Stoke Newington N4, N7,
N15 . . . . 51 A2
Seven Sisters Sta N15 . . 51 C4
Seven Stars Cnr W12 . . 112 A3
Seven Stars Yd E1 . . . . . 243 D4
Seventh Ave
Hayes UB3 . . . . 106 A5
Ilford E12 . . . . 78 B4
Seven Ways Par IG2 . . . . 56 C4
Severnake Cl E14 . . . . . . 119 C2
Severn Ave 2 W10 . . . . . . 91 A4
Severn Ct 11 KT2 . . . . . . 175 D2
Severn Dr Enfield EN1 . . . . . 6 A5
Hinchley Wood KT10 . . . . 213 A6
Severn Way NW10 . . . . . . 67 D3
Severus Rd SW11 . . . . . . 136 C1
Seville Ho 11 E1 . . . . 118 A5
Seville Mews N1 . . . . 73 C1
Seville St SW1 . . . . 247 D1
Sevington Rd NW4 . . . . . . 46 B3
Sevington St W9 . . . . 91 D3
Seward Rd Penge BR3 . . 184 D1
West Ealing W7 . . . . 109 A4
Seward St EC1 . . . . 95 A4 235 A1
SEWARDSTONEBURY . . 20 C6
Sewardstone Gdns E4 . . . 19 D6
Sewardstone Rd
Chingford E4 . . . . 19 D6
South Hackney E2 . . . . 96 C5
Sewdley St E5 . . . . 74 D5
Sewell Ho 7 N16 . . . . 73 C3
Sewell Rd SE2 . . . . 124 B4
Sewell St E13 . . . . 99 A4
Sextant Ave E14 . . . . 120 B2
Sexton Ct 7 E14 . . . . 120 B6
Sexton's Ho 5 SE13 . . . . 142 A6
Seychelle Ct BR3 . . . . . . 185 D3
Seymour Ave
Tottenham N17 . . . . 34 A1
West Barnes SM4 . . . . . . 200 D2
Seymour Cl
East Molesey KT8 . . . . . . 196 A4
Pinner HA5 . . . . 23 B2
Seymour Ct
Chingford E4 . . . . 20 D2
Dollis Hill NW2 . . . . 68 B6
Muswell Hill N10 . . . . 31 A1
Putney SW15 . . . . 134 B1
Southgate N21 . . . . 16 B5
Upper Clapton N16 . . . . . . 52 A1
Seymour Dr BR2 . . . . 210 B1
Seymour Gdns
Brockley SE4 . . . . 141 A2
Feltham TW13 . . . . 172 C6
Kingston u T KT5 . . . . 198 B4
Redbridge IG1 . . . . 56 B1
Ruislip HA4 . . . . 40 D1
Twickenham TW1 . . . . 153 B4
Seymour Ho
Bloomsbury WC1 . . . . . . 240 A6
1 Clapham SW8 . . . . 137 C3
Ruislip HA4 . . . . 40 A5
Somers Town NW1 . . . . . 232 D1
Seymour Lo 14 KT1 . . . . 175 D2
Seymour Mews W1 . . . . 238 A2
Seymour Pl
Croydon SE25 . . . . 206 B5
Paddington W1 . . 92 D1 237 C2
Seymour Rd Acton W4 . . 111 A2
Carshalton CR4 . . . . 203 A2
Chingford E4 . . . . 19 D3
East Molesey KT8 . . . . . . 196 A4
Edmonton N9 . . . . 18 B2
Finchley N3 . . . . 29 D3
Hampton TW12 . . . . 174 A5
Harringay N8 . . . . 50 D4
Newham E6 . . . . 99 D6
Teddington KT1 . . . . 175 D2
Wallington SM5 . . . . 219 A3
Walthamstow E10 . . . . 53 B1
Wandsworth SW18 . . . . . 157 B5
Wimbledon SW19 . . . . . . 156 D1
Seymour St
Paddington
W1 . . . . 92 D1 237 D1
Woolwich SE18 . . . . 123 A3
Seymour Terr SE20 . . . . 184 B2
Seymour Villas SE20 . . . 184 A2
Seymour Way TW16 . . . . 171 C3
Seymour Wlk
SW10 . . . . 136 A6 266 A6
Seyssel St E14 . . . . 120 A2
Shaa Rd W3 . . . . 111 B6
Shabana Ct 3 W12 . . . . 112 B5
Shacklegate La TW11 . . 174 C6
Shackleton Cl SE23 . . . . 162 B2
Shackleton Ct
3 Dulwich SE21 . . . . 161 B2
2 Isle of Dogs E14 . . . . 119 C1
4 Shepherd's Bush
W12 . . . . 112 B4
7 Stanwell TW19 . . . . . . 148 A5
Shackleton Ho
5 Stonebridge NW10 . . . 67 B1
5 Wapping E1 . . . . 118 C5
Shackleton Lo SW16 . . . 181 D5
Shackleton Rd UB1 . . . . 107 B6
SHACKLEWELL 73 D4
Shacklewell Ho 3 E8 . . . . 73 D4
Shacklewell La E8 . . . . . . 73 D3
Shacklewell Prim Sch
E8 . . . . 73 D4
Shacklewell Rd N16 . . . . 73 D4
Shacklewell Row E8 . . . . 73 D4
Shacklewell St 30 E2 . . . . 95 D4
Shadbolt Ave E4 . . . . 35 A5
Shadbolt Cl KT4 . . . . 215 D6
Shad Thames
SE1 . . . . 117 D4 253 D2
SHADWELL 118 C6
Shadwell Ct UB5 . . . . 85 B5
Shadwell Dr UB5 . . . . 85 B4
Shadwell Gdns E1 . . . . . 118 C6
Shadwell Pierhead
E1 . . . . 118 C6
Shadwell Pl 1 E1 . . . . . . 118 C6
Shadwell Sta E1 . . . . 118 B6
Shady Bush Cl WD23 . . . . . 8 A4
Shaef Way TW11 . . . . 175 A3
Shaftesbury Ave
Enfield EN3 . . . . 6 D3
Feltham TW14 . . . . 150 A5
Kenton HA3 . . . . 44 A3
New Barnet EN5 . . . . 2 A1
Southall UB2 . . . . 107 C3
W1 . . . . 115 D6 249 D6
West Harrow HA1, HA2 . . 42 A1
Shaftesbury Circ HA2 . . . 42 A1
Shaftesbury Ct
Borough The SE1 . . . . . . 262 C6
1 Herne Hill SE5 . . . . . . 139 B1
Ilford RM6 . . . . 58 C2
Newham E6 . . . . 100 C1
Shoreditch N1 . . . . 235 C3
Streatham SW16 . . . . 159 D1
3 Thamesmead SE28 . . 124 C5
Shaftesbury Ctr NW10 . . . 90 D3
Shaftesbury Gdns
NW10 . . . . 89 C3
Shaftesbury High Sch
HA3 . . . . 23 D2
Shaftesbury Ho
11 Canning Town E16 . . . . 98 D1
Croydon SE25 . . . . 206 A3
13 Stoke Newington N16 . 73 C5
Upper Tooting SW17 . . . . 180 B6
W2 . . . . 245 D6
Shaftesbury Lo 9 E14 . . 97 D1
Shaftesbury Mews
2 Clapham Pk SW4 . . . . 159 C6
W8 . . . . 255 B5
Shaftesbury Park Chambers 1 SW11 . . . 137 A2
Shaftesbury Point E13 . . 99 B5
Shaftesbury Prim Sch
E7 . . . . 77 C1
Shaftesbury Rd
Beckenham BR3 . . . . 185 B1
Carshalton SM5 . . . . 202 C2
Chingford E4 . . . . 20 B3
Edmonton N18 . . . . 33 D4
Finsbury Pk N4, N19 . . . . . 50 A1
Leyton E10 . . . . 53 C1
Richmond TW9 . . . . 132 A2
Upton E7 . . . . 77 C1
Walthamstow E17 . . . . 53 D3
Shaftesbury St N1 . . . . . 235 C3
Shaftesburys The
IG11 . . . . 101 A5
Shaftesbury Way TW2 . . 152 B1
Shaftesbury Waye UB4 . . 84 C1
Shafteswood Ct SW17 . . 158 D1
Shafto Mews SW1 . . . . . 257 D5
Shafton Rd E9 . . . . 96 D6
Shaftsbury Park Prim Sch
SW11 . . . . 137 A3
Shafts Ct EC3 . . . . 243 A1
Shahjalal Ho 18 E2 . . . . . 96 A5
Shakespeare Ave
7 Becontree NW10 . . . . . 89 B6
Feltham TW14 . . . . 150 A5
Friern Barnet N11 . . . . 31 C5
Hayes UB4 . . . . 84 B2
Shakespeare Cl HA3 . . . . 44 C2
Shakespeare Cres E12 . . 78 B2
Shakespeare Ct EN5 . . . . . 1 D2
Shakespeare Dr HA3 . . . . 44 B3
Shakespeare Gdns N2 . . 48 D5
Shakespeare Ho
1 Erith DA17 . . . . 125 B1
3 Hackney E9 . . . . 74 C1
Osidge N14 . . . . 15 D2
Shakespeare Rd
Acton W3 . . . . 111 A5
Brixton SE24 . . . . 138 D1
DA7 . . . . 147 A4
Ealing W7 . . . . 108 D6
Finchley N3 . . . . 29 C2
Higham Hill E17 . . . . 34 D1
Mill Hill NW7 . . . . 28 A6
Shakespeare's Globe Theatre (site of)*
SE1 . . . . 252 B4
Shakespeare Twr EC2 . . 242 B4
Shakespeare Way
TW13 . . . . 172 C6
Shakspeare Mews 7
N16 . . . . 73 C4
Shakspeare Wlk N16 . . . . 73 C4
Shalbourne Sq E9 . . . . . . 75 B2
Shalcomb St
SW10 . . . . 136 A6 266 B5
Shalden Ho SW15 . . . . . . 155 D5
Shaldon Dr Ruislip HA4 . . . 62 C5
West Barnes SM4 . . . . . . 201 A4
Shaldon Rd HA8 . . . . 26 B1
Shalfleet Dr W10 . . . . . . 112 D6
Shalford
Willesden Green
NW10 . . . . 90 A6
3 Woodford IG8 . . . . 37 C4
Shalford Cl BR6 . . . . 227 A4
Shalford Ct N1 . . . . 234 C4
Shalford Ho SE1 . . . . . . 262 D6
Shalimar Gdns W3 . . . . . 111 A6
Shalimar Lo W3 . . . . 111 A6
Shalimar Rd W3 . . . . 111 A6
Shallons Rd SE9 . . . . 188 D6
Shalstone Rd SW14,
TW9 . . . . 132 D2
Shalston Villas KT5,
KT6 . . . . 198 B3
Shamrock Ct E7 . . . . 77 D3
Shamrock Ho
East Barnet N14 . . . . 15 B4
Forest Hill SE26 . . . . 184 A6
Shamrock Rd CR0 . . . . . 204 B3
Shamrock St SW4 . . . . . 137 D2
Shamrock Way N14 . . . . . 15 B3
Shandon Ct SE4 . . . . 141 A3
Shandon Rd SW4 . . . . . . 159 C5
Shand St SE1 . . . 117 C4 253 B2
Shandy St E1 . . . . 96 D3
Shane Ct EN2 . . . . 5 A3
Shan Ho WC1 . . . . 240 C5
Shanklin Gdns WD19 . . . . 22 C6
Shanklin Ho E17 . . . . 35 B1
Shanklin Rd Hornsey N8 . . 49 D4
Tottenham Hale N15 . . . . . 52 A5
Shannon Cl
Cricklewood NW2 . . . . 68 D5
Southall UB2 . . . . 106 D1
Shannon Cnr KT3 . . . . . . 200 A5
Shannon Cnr Ret Pk
KT3 . . . . 200 A5
Shannon Commercial Ctr
KT3 . . . . 200 A5
Shannon Ct
Croydon CR0 . . . . 205 A1
11 Peckham SE15 . . . . . 139 D5
Stoke Newington N16 . . . . 73 C5
Willesden NW10 . . . . 68 A2
Shannon Gr SW9 . . . . . . 138 B1
Shannon Pl
NW8 . . . . 92 C5 230 B4
Shannon Way BR3 . . . . . 185 D4
Shanti Ct SW18 . . . . 157 C3
Shap Cres SM5 . . . . 202 D1
Shapland Way N13 . . . . . . 32 B5
Shapla Prim Sch E1 . . . 118 A6
Shapwick Cl N11 . . . . 30 D5
Shardcroft Ave SE24 . . . 160 D6
Shardeloes Rd SE14 . . . . 141 B3
Shard's Sq SE15 . . . . 140 A6
Sharebourne Ho SW2 . . 160 C6
Sharland Cl CR7 . . . . 204 C3
Sharman Ct DA14 . . . . . . 190 A6
Sharman Ho 18 E14 . . . . . 98 A1
Sharnbrooke Cl DA16 . . 146 C2
Sharnbrook Ho W6 . . . 265 A6
Sharon Cl KT6 . . . . 197 C1
Sharon Ct 1 N12 . . . . 30 A4
Sharon Gdns E9 . . . . 96 C6
Sharon Rd
Chiswick W4 . . . . 111 B1
Enfield EN3 . . . . 7 A3
Sharpe Cl W7 . . . . 86 D2
Sharp Ho SW8 . . . . 137 B2
Sharples Hall St 8
NW1 . . . . 70 D1
Sharpness Cl UB4 . . . . 85 A2
Sharpness Ct 2 SE15 . . 139 D5
Sharps La HA4 . . . . 39 B2
Sharratt St SE15 . . . . . . 140 C6
Sharsted St
SE17 . . . . 116 D1 261 C1
Sharvel La UB5 . . . . 84 B6
Sharwood WC1 . . . . 233 D3
Shaver's Pl SW1 . . . . 249 C5
Shaw Ave IG11 . . . . 103 A5
Shawbrooke Rd SE9 . . . 143 D1
Shawbury Cl 9 NW9 . . . . 27 C2
Shawbury Ct SE22 . . . . . 161 D6
Shawbury Rd SE22 . . . . . 161 D6
Shaw Cl Bushey WD23 . . . . . 8 C2
Woolwich SE28 . . . . 124 B5
Shaw Cotts SE23 . . . . 163 A1
Shaw Cres 6 E14 . . . . 97 A1
Shaw Ct
8 Acton Green W3 . . . . 111 A3
12 Battersea SW11 . . . . 136 B2
Cheam SM4 . . . . 202 A2
Upper Holloway N19 . . . . . 72 A6
Shaw Dr KT12 . . . . 194 C2
Shawfield Ct UB7 . . . . . . 104 A3
Shawfield Pk BR1 . . . . . . 187 D1
Shawfield St
SW3 . . . . 114 C1 257 B1
Shawford Ct 8 SW15 . . . 156 A4
Shawford Rd KT19 . . . . . 215 B2
Shaw Gdns IG11 . . . . 103 A5
Shaw Ho 6 Erith DA17 . . 125 B1
5 Newham E16 . . . . 122 C5
Shaw Path BR1 . . . . 164 D1
Shaw Rd
Camberwell SE22 . . . . . . 139 C1
Catford BR1 . . . . 164 D1
Enfield EN3 . . . . 6 D4
Shaw Sq E17 . . . . 35 A2
Shaws Wood Cotts EN4 . . 3 C3
Shaw Way SM6 . . . . 220 A1
Shearing Dr SM4 . . . . . . 202 A2
Shearling Way N7 . . . . . . 72 A2
Shearman Rd SE3 . . . . . . 142 D2
Shears Ct TW16 . . . . 171 C3
Shearsmith Ho 19 E1 . . . 118 A6
Shears The TW16 . . . . . . 171 C3
Shears Way TW16 . . . . . . 171 C2
Shearwater Cl IG11 . . . . 102 A4
Shearwater Ct 24 SE8 . . 141 B6
Shearwater Rd SM1 . . . . 217 B3
Shearwater Way UB4 . . . . 84 D1
Sheaveshill Ave NW9 . . . 45 C5
Sheaveshill Ct NW9 . . . . 45 C5
Sheaveshill Par NW9 . . . . 45 C5
Sheba Ct N17 . . . . 34 A4
Sheba Pl E1 . . . . 243 D5
Sheen Common Dr SW14,
TW10 . . . . 154 C6
Sheen Court Rd TW10 . . 132 C1
Sheen Ct TW10 . . . . 132 C1
Sheendale Rd TW9 . . . . . 132 B1
Sheenewood SE26 . . . . . 184 B6
Sheen Gate Gdns
SW14 . . . . 133 A1
Sheengate Mans
SW14 . . . . 133 B1
Sheen Gr N1 . . . . . 94 C6 234 A6
Sheen La SW14 . . . . 133 A1
Sheen Mount Prim Sch
SW14 . . . . 154 D6
Sheen Pk TW10, TW9 . . . 132 A1
Sheen Rd
Orpington BR5 . . . . 211 D5
Richmond TW10, TW9 . . . 132 B1
Sheen Way SM6 . . . . 220 B3
Sheen Wood SW14 . . . . . 155 A6
Sheepcote Cl TW5 . . . . . 128 A5
Sheepcote La SW11 . . . . 136 D3
Sheepcote Rd HA1 . . . . . . 42 D3
Sheepcotes Rd RM6 . . . . . 59 A5
Sheephouse Way KT3 . . 199 C2
Sheep La E8 . . . . 96 B6
Sheepwalk TW17 . . . . . . 192 B3
Sheep Walk Mews 7
SW19 . . . . 179 A4
Sheerness Mews E16 . . 122 D4
Sheerwater Rd E16 . . . . . 99 D2
Sheffield Ho 15 SE15 . . . 139 D4
Sheffield Rd TW14,
TW6 . . . . 149 A6
Sheffield Sq 2 E3 . . . . 97 B4
Sheffield St WC2 . . . . . 240 C1
Sheffield Terr
W8 . . . . 113 C5 245 B3
Sheffield Way TW14,
TW6 . . . . 149 B6
Shefton Rise HA6 . . . . 22 A3
Shelbey Ct BR1 . . . . 186 D2
Shelbourne Cl HA5 . . . . . . 41 B6
Shelbourne Ho 20 N19 . . 49 D2
Shelbourne Rd N17 . . . . . 34 B2
Shelburne Ct SW15 . . . . 156 D6
Shelburne Dr TW4 . . . . . 151 C5
Shelburne Ho 9
SW16 . . . . 181 C5
Shelburne Rd N7 . . . . 72 B4
Shelbury Cl DA14 . . . . . . 168 A1
Shelbury Rd SE22 . . . . . 162 B6
Sheldon Ave N6 . . . . 48 D3
Sheldon Cl Penge SE20 . . 184 B2
SE12 . . . . 165 B6
Sheldon Ct Barnet EN5 . . . . 1 D1
SW8 . . . . 270 A3
Sheldon Ho
Chingford E4 . . . . 36 C4
9 Homerton E9 . . . . 74 D2
Teddington TW11 . . . . . . 175 A4
Sheldon Pl E2 . . . . 96 B5
Sheldon Rd
Cricklewood NW2 . . . . 68 D4
DA7 . . . . 147 B4
Dagenham RM9 . . . . 81 A1
Edmonton N18 . . . . 33 C6
Sheldon Sq W2 . . . . 236 B3
Sheldon St CR0 . . . . 221 A5
Sheldrake Cl E16 . . . . . . 122 B5
Sheldrake Ho 15 SE16 . . 118 D2
Sheldrake Pl
W8 . . . . 113 C4 245 A2
Sheldrick Cl CR4 . . . . 180 B1
Shelduck Cl E15 . . . . 76 D3
Shelduck Ct 37 SE8 . . . . 141 B6
Sheldwich Terr BR2 . . . . 210 A3
Shelford 20 KT1 . . . . 176 C1
Shelford Ct 7 E5 . . . . 52 B1
Shelford Pl N16 . . . . 73 B5
Shelford Rd EN5 . . . . 12 C5
Shelford Rise SE19 . . . . . 183 D3
Shelgate Rd SW11 . . . . . 158 D6
Shell Cl BR2 . . . . 210 A3
Shell Ctr SE1 . . . . 250 D3
Shellduck Cl NW9 . . . . 27 C1
Shelley N8 . . . . 50 A6
Shelley Ave
Greenford UB6 . . . . 86 B4
Plashet E12 . . . . 78 A2
Shelley Cl BR6 . . . . 227 C5
Edgware HA8 . . . . 26 C6
Greenford UB6 . . . . 86 B4
Hayes UB4 . . . . 84 A2
Peckham SE15 . . . . 140 B3
Shelley Cres
Heston TW5 . . . . 128 D4
Southall UB1 . . . . 85 B1
Shelley Ct
Finsbury Pk N4 . . . . 50 B1
9 Kingston u T KT2 . . . . 175 D6
SW3 . . . . 267 D6
13 Walthamstow E10 . . . . 53 D2
8 Wanstead E11 . . . . 55 A5
Wembley HA0 . . . . 65 C4
West Barnes KT3 . . . . . . 200 A4
Shelley Dr DA16 . . . . 145 C4
Shelley Gdns HA0 . . . . 65 C6
Shelley Ho
21 Bethnal Green E2 . . . . 96 C4
Chelsea SW1 . . . . 269 A6
9 Stoke Newington N16 . 73 C4
Walworth SE17 . . . . 262 B2
Shelley Rd NW10 . . . . 89 B6
Shelley Way SW17 . . . . . 180 B4
Shellgrove Rd N16 . . . . . . 73 C3
Shellness Rd E5 . . . . 74 B3
Shell Rd SE13 . . . . 141 D2
Shellwood Rd SW11 . . . . 136 D3
Shelly Lo EN2 . . . . 5 B4
Shelmerdine Cl E3 . . . . . . 97 C2
Shelson Ave TW13 . . . . . 171 D6
Shelton Ct N21 . . . . 16 C4
Shelton Rd SW19 . . . . . . 179 C2
Shelton St WC2 . . 94 A1 240 A1
Shene Bldg EC1 . . . . 241 A4
Shene Sch SW14 . . . . . . 133 C1
Shenfield Ho 3 SE18 . . . 143 D5
Shenfield Rd IG8 . . . . 37 B3
Shenfield St N1 . . . . 95 C5
Shenley Ave HA4 . . . . 39 D1
Shenley Ho 8 SW16 . . . . 182 B6

Shenley Rd
Camberwell SE5 ... 139 C4
Heston TW5 ... 129 A4
Shenstone W13 ... 109 C5
Shenstone Gdns IG2 ... 57 D4
Shenstone Ho SW16 ... 181 C5
Shepard Ho 18 SW11 ... 136 B2
Sheperdess Pl N1 ... 235 B2
Shepherd Cl
Feltham TW13 ... 173 A6
W1 ... 248 A6
Shepherdess Wlk
N1 ... 95 A5 235 B3
Shepherd Ho
Barnsbury N7 ... 72 A2
10 Poplar E14 ... 97 D1
Shepherd Mkt W1 ... 248 C3
SHEPHERD'S BUSH ... 112 B5
Shepherd's Bush (Central Line) Sta W12 ... 112 D4
Shepherd's Bush Gn W12 ... 112 C4
Shepherd's Bush (Hamm & City) Sta W12 ... 112 C5
Shepherd's Bush Market W12 ... 112 C4
Shepherd's Bush Pl W12 ... 112 D4
Shepherd's Bush Rd W6 ... 112 C3
Shepherds Cl
Dagenham RM6 ... 58 D5
Orpington BR6 ... 227 D5
Shepperton TW17 ... 192 D3
Stanmore HA7 ... 25 A5
Shepherd's Cl N6 ... 49 B3
Shepherds Ct
8 Hammersmith W12 ... 112 D4
13 Harrow HA1 ... 42 D3
Shepherds Gn BR7 ... 189 B3
Shepherd's Hill N6 ... 49 C3
Shepherds La SE28 ... 123 C5
Shepherd's La E9 ... 74 D2
Shepherds Leas SE9 ... 145 B1
Shepherds Path UB5 ... 63 A2
Shepherds Pl W1 ... 248 A6
Shepherd St
W1 ... 115 B5 248 C3
Shepherds Way CR2 ... 222 D1
Shepherds Wlk
Bushey WD23 ... 8 B2
Dollis Hill NW2 ... 68 A6
Shepherd's Wlk NW3 ... 70 B4
Shepiston La UB3 ... 105 A1
Shepley Cl SM5 ... 219 A5
Shepley Ct SW16 ... 181 C6
Shepley Mews EN3 ... 7 C6
Sheppard Cl Enfield EN1 ... 6 B5
Kingston u T KT6 ... 198 A5
Sheppard Dr SE16 ... 118 B1
Sheppard Ho
31 Hackney E2 ... 96 A5
8 Streatham SW2 ... 160 C3
Sheppard's Ct
Harrow HA1 ... 42 C2
Wembley UB6 ... 64 D2
Sheppard St E16 ... 98 D3
SHEPPERTON ... 193 A3
Shepperton Bsns Park
TW17 ... 193 A4
Shepperton Court Dr
TW17 ... 192 D4
Shepperton Ct TW17 ... 192 D3
SHEPPERTON GREEN
... 192 D5
Shepperton Rd
Littleton TW17, TW18 ... 192 A5
Orpington BR5 ... 211 A3
Shoreditch N1 ... 95 B6 235 C6
Shepperton Sta TW17 ... 193 A4
Shepperton Studios
TW17 ... 192 B6
Sheppey Gdns RM9 ... 80 C1
Sheppey Ho 16 E5 ... 74 B4
Sheppey Rd RM9 ... 80 C1
Shepton Ct SW11 ... 266 D2
Shepton Hos 11 E2 ... 96 C4
Sherard Ct N19 ... 72 A5
Sherard Ho 24 E9 ... 74 C1
Sherard Rd SE9 ... 166 A6
Sheraton Bsns Ctr UB6 ... 87 C5
Sheraton Cl WD6 ... 10 B6
Sheraton Ho SW1 ... 268 D6
Sheraton Lo HA3 ... 42 C6
Sheraton St W1 ... 239 C1
Sheraton The 22 KT6 ... 198 A4
Sherborne Ave
Enfield EN3 ... 6 C3
Southall UB2 ... 107 C2
Sherborne Cl UB4 ... 84 C1
Sherborne Cres SM5 ... 202 C2
Sherborne Ct SE20 ... 184 C1
Sherborne Gdns
Ealing W13 ... 87 B2
Queensbury NW9 ... 44 C6
Sherborne Ho
Pimlico SW1 ... 258 D2
South Lambeth SW8 ... 270 C3
Sherborne La EC4 ... 252 D6
Sherborne Rd BR5 ... 211 D4
Cheam SM3 ... 201 C1
Chessington KT9 ... 214 A3
East Bedfont TW14 ... 149 B3
Sherborne St
N1 ... 95 B6 235 C6
Sherboro Rd 1 N15 ... 51 D3
Sherbourne Ct
1 Hampton TW12 ... 173 C2
Sherbourne Ct *continued*
9 Sutton SM2 ... 218 A2
SW5 ... 255 C4
Sherbourne Gdns
TW17 ... 193 C2
Sherbourne Pl HA7 ... 25 A4
Sherbrooke Cl DA7 ... 147 C1
Sherbrooke Ho 9 E2 ... 96 C5
Sherbrooke Rd
SW6 ... 135 A5 264 B3
Sherbrooke Terr SW6 ... 264 B3
Sherbrooke Way KT4 ... 200 B2
Sherbrook Gdns N21 ... 16 D4
Sherbrook Ho 2 N3 ... 29 D3
Shere Cl KT9 ... 213 D3
Sheredan Rd E4 ... 36 C5
Shere Ho SE1 ... 262 C6
Shere Lo 1 SW19 ... 180 C3
Shere Rd IG2 ... 56 C4
Sherfield Cl KT3 ... 198 D5
Sherfield Gdns SW15 ... 155 D5
Sheridan N8 ... 50 C5
Sheridan Bldgs WC2 ... 240 B1
Sheridan Cl UB10 ... 83 A3
Sheridan Cres BR7 ... 188 D1
Sheridan Ct Ealing W7 ... 108 D6
Earl's Ct SW5 ... 255 C3
Harrow HA1 ... 42 B3
Hounslow TW4 ... 151 A6
South Hampstead NW6 ... 70 A1
South Lambeth SW9 ... 270 D1
Sheridan Gdns HA3 ... 43 D3
Sheridan Ho SE11 ... 261 B3
7 Stoke Newington N16 ... 73 C5
Sheridan Lo Barnet EN5 ... 1 D1
Bromley BR2 ... 209 C5
East Barnet N14 ... 15 B4
Sheridan Mews E11 ... 55 B3
Sheridan Pl
Barnes SW13 ... 133 D2
Hampton TW12 ... 174 A2
Harrow HA1 ... 42 C2
Sheridan Rd
Belvedere DA17 ... 125 C2
DA7 ... 147 A2
Leyton E7 ... 76 D5
Little Ilford E12 ... 78 B3
Merton SW19 ... 179 B2
Richmond TW10 ... 153 C1
Sheridan St 34 E1 ... 96 B1
Sheridan Terr UB5 ... 63 D3
Sheridan Way 5 BR3 ... 185 B2
Sheridan Wlk
Golders Green NW11 ... 47 C3
Wallington SM5 ... 218 D3
Sheringdale Prim Sch
SW18 ... 157 B3
Sheringham NW8 ... 229 D6
Sheringham Ave
Feltham TW13 ... 150 A1
Little Ilford E12 ... 78 B3
Southgate N14 ... 15 D5
Twickenham TW2 ... 151 C3
Sheringham Ct 1 N3 ... 29 C2
Sheringham Dr IG11 ... 80 A3
Sheringham Ho NW1 ... 237 B4
Sheringham Jun Sch
E12 ... 78 B4
Sheringham Mews 4
SW18 ... 158 A2
Sheringham Rd
Islington N7 ... 72 C2
Penge SE20 ... 206 C6
Sheringham Twr UB1 ... 107 D6
Sherington Ave HA5 ... 23 C3
Sherington Prim Sch
SE7 ... 143 B6
Sherington Rd SE7 ... 143 B6
Sheriton Ct SM1 ... 217 C5
Sherland Rd TW1 ... 152 D3
Sherleys Ct HA4 ... 61 C6
Sherlies Ave BR6 ... 227 C6
Sherlock Ct NW8 ... 229 C6
Sherlock Holmes Mus*
NW1 ... 92 D3 237 D5
Sherlock Mews W1 ... 238 A4
Sherman Gdns RM6 ... 58 C3
Sherman Rd BR1 ... 187 A2
Shernhall St E17 ... 54 A5
Shernwood Ho 1 E18 ... 55 A5
Sherrard Rd E7, E12 ... 77 D2
Sherrards Way EN5 ... 13 D5
Sherren Ho 35 E1 ... 96 C3
Sherrick Green Rd
NW10 ... 68 B3
Sherriff Ct NW6 ... 69 C2
Sherriff Rd NW6 ... 69 C2
Sherringham Ave N17 ... 34 A1
Sherrin Rd E10 ... 75 D4
Sherrock Gdns NW4 ... 46 A5
Sherry Mews IG11 ... 79 B1
Sherston Ct
Finsbury WC1 ... 234 A1
Newington SE1 ... 261 D4
Sherwin Ho 1 SE11 ... 138 C6
Sherwin Rd SE14 ... 140 D4
Sherwood 3 Barnet EN5 ... 1 D1
Brondesbury NW6 ... 69 A1
Long Ditton KT6 ... 213 D6
Sherwood Ave
Greenford UB6 ... 64 C3
Hayes UB4 ... 84 B3
Mitcham SW16 ... 181 D2
Ruislip HA4 ... 39 C3
Wanstead E18 ... 55 B6
Sherwood Cl
Barnes SW13 ... 134 B2
DA5 ... 168 C5
Ealing W13 ... 109 B5
Walthamstow E17 ... 35 B1
Sherwood Ct
11 Battersea SW11 ... 136 A2
Colney Hatch N12 ... 30 C5
2 South Croydon CR2 ... 221 A3
St Johns SE13 ... 141 D3
Sutton SM1 ... 217 C3
W1 ... 237 C3
6 West Wickham BR4 ... 207 D1
Sherwood Gdns
Barking IG11 ... 79 B1
Bermondsey SE16 ... 118 B1
Millwall E14 ... 119 C2
Sherwood Hall 7 N2 ... 48 A6
Sherwood Ho N4 ... 51 A2
Sherwood Park Ave
DA15 ... 168 B5
Sherwood Park Prim Sch
DA15 ... 168 B5
Sherwood Park Rd
Mitcham CR4 ... 203 D5
Sutton SM1 ... 217 C3
Sherwood Park Sch
SM6 ... 219 D5
Sherwood Rd
Croydon CR0 ... 206 B1
DA16 ... 145 C2
Hampton TW12 ... 174 A5
Harrow HA2 ... 64 A6
Hendon NW4 ... 46 C6
Ilford IG6 ... 57 B5
Merton SW19 ... 179 B3
Sherwood Sch The
CR4 ... 203 C5
Sherwood St W1 ... 249 B6
Whetstone N20 ... 14 B1
Sherwood Terr N20 ... 14 B1
Sherwood Way BR4 ... 224 A6
Shetland Cl WD6 ... 11 B5
Shetland Rd Bow E3 ... 97 B5
East Bedfont TW6 ... 149 A5
Shield Dr TW8 ... 131 A6
Shieldhall St SE2 ... 124 C2
Shield Rd TW15 ... 171 B6
Shifford Path SE23 ... 162 D1
Shillaker Ct W3 ... 111 D5
Shillibeer Ct N18 ... 34 B5
Shillibeer Pl W1 ... 237 B3
Shillingford Cl NW7 ... 28 D3
Shillingford Ho 40 E3 ... 97 D4
Shillingford St 23 N1 ... 72 D1
Shilling Pl TW8 ... 109 A5
Shillingstone Ho W14 ... 254 B5
Shine Ho 3 N3 ... 29 D3
Shinfield St W12 ... 90 C1
Shinglewell Rd DA8 ... 147 C5
Shinners Cl SE25 ... 206 A4
Shipka Rd SW12 ... 159 B3
Ship La SW14 ... 133 A3
Shiplake Ct SW17 ... 180 B6
Shiplake Ho 45 E2 ... 95 D4
Shipley Ct SE20 ... 184 A1
Shipley Ho 32 SW8 ... 137 D3
Shipman Rd
Forest Hill SE23 ... 162 D2
Newham E16 ... 99 C1
Ship & Mermaid Row
SE1 ... 253 A2
Ship St SE8 ... 141 C4
Ship Tavern Pas EC3 ... 253 A6
Shipton Cl RM8 ... 80 D5
Shipton Ho
7 Camden Town NW5 ... 71 A2
14 Haggerston E2 ... 95 D5
Shipton Rd UB8 ... 60 B4
Shipton St E2 ... 95 D4
Shipwright Rd SE16 ... 119 A4
Shipwright Yd SE1 ... 253 A3
Shirburn Cl SE23 ... 162 C4
Shirbutt St E14 ... 119 D6
Shirebrook Rd SE3 ... 143 D2
Shire Ct DA18 ... 124 D3
Ewell KT17 ... 215 D1
Shirehall Cl NW4 ... 46 D3
Shirehall Gdns NW4 ... 46 D3
Shirehall La NW4 ... 46 D3
Shirehall Pk NW4 ... 46 D3
Shire Ho E11 ... 76 D5
Shire Horse Way TW7 ... 130 D2
Shire La BR6 ... 227 B2
Shiremeade WD6 ... 10 B6
Shire Mews TW2 ... 152 A5
Shire Pl
12 Brentford TW8 ... 131 C5
Wandsworth SW18 ... 158 A4
Shires The TW10 ... 176 A6
Shirland Mews W9 ... 91 B4
Shirland Rd W9 ... 91 C3
SHIRLEY ... 206 C1
Shirley Ave
Carshalton SM1 ... 218 C4
Croydon CR0 ... 206 D1
DA5 ... 168 D3
Shirley Church Rd
CR0 ... 223 A5
Shirley Cl
Hounslow TW3 ... 152 A6
Walthamstow E17 ... 53 D4
Shirley Cres BR3 ... 207 A5
Shirley Ct
8 Ealing W13 ... 109 A5
Ilford IG2 ... 57 B4
Kingsbury NW9 ... 45 B4
2 South Norwood
SW16 ... 182 B3
Thornton Heath SW16 ... 204 B6
Shirley Dr TW3 ... 152 A6
Shirley Gdns
Barking IG11 ... 79 C2
Ealing W7 ... 108 D5
Shirley Gr
Clapham SW11 ... 137 A2
Ponders End N9 ... 18 D4
Shirley High Sch
Performing Arts Coll
CR0 ... 222 D5
Shirley Hills Rd CR0 ... 222 D3
Shirley Ho 18 SE5 ... 139 B5
Shirley House Dr SE7 ... 143 C5
Shirley Hts 6 DA6 ... 147 A1
Shirley Lo 4 SE26 ... 185 A6
SHIRLEY OAKS ... 207 A1
Shirley Oaks Hospl
CR0 ... 206 C2
Shirley Oaks Rd CR0 ... 222 D6
Shirley Park Rd CR0 ... 206 C1
Shirley Rd Acton W4 ... 111 B4
Croydon CR0 ... 206 B1
Enfield EN2 ... 5 A2
Sidcup DA15 ... 167 C1
Stratford E15 ... 76 C1
Shirley St E16 ... 98 D1
Shirley Way CR0 ... 223 B5
Shirlock Rd NW3 ... 70 D4
Shirwell Cl NW7 ... 28 D3
Shobden Rd N17 ... 33 B2
Shobroke Cl NW2 ... 68 C5
Shoebury Rd E6 ... 78 B1
Shoe La EC4 ... 94 C1 241 B2
Shoelands Ct NW9 ... 45 B6
Shona Ho E16 ... 99 C2
Shooters Ave HA3 ... 43 C5
SHOOTERS HILL ... 145 A4
Shooters Hill SE18 ... 144 C4
Shooters Hill Rd
Blackheath Vale SE3,
SE10 ... 142 C4
SE18, SE3, SE7 ... 143 D5
Shooters Rd EN2 ... 4 D4
Shoot-Up Hill NW2 ... 69 A2
Shopstop SW11 ... 136 C1
Shore Bsns Ctr 31 E9 ... 74 C1
Shore Cl Feltham TW14 ... 150 A4
Hampton TW12 ... 173 A5
Shorediche Cl UB10 ... 60 B5
SHOREDITCH ... 95 B5
Shoreditch Ct 2 E8 ... 73 D1
Shoreditch High St
E2 ... 95 C3 243 B6
Shoreditch Ho N1 ... 235 D1
Shore Gr TW13 ... 151 C2
Shoreham Cl
Croydon CR0 ... 206 C3
DA5 ... 168 D3
Wandsworth SW18 ... 157 D6
Shoreham Rd BR5 ... 190 B1
Shoreham Rd (E)
TW6 ... 148 A6
Shoreham Rd (W)
TW6 ... 148 A6
Shoreham Way BR2 ... 209 A3
Shore Ho SW8 ... 137 B2
Shore Mews 30 E9 ... 74 C1
Shore Pl E9 ... 74 C1
Shore Point 2 IG9 ... 21 B2
Shore Rd E9 ... 74 C1
Shore Way 26 SW9 ... 138 C3
Shorncliffe Rd
SE1 ... 117 D1 263 C2
Shorndean St SE6 ... 164 A3
Shorne Cl 3 DA15 ... 168 B5
Shornefield Cl BR1 ... 210 C6
Shornells Way SE2 ... 124 C1
Shorrolds Rd
SW6 ... 135 B5 264 D4
Shortcroft Mead Ct
NW10 ... 68 A3
Shortcroft Rd KT17 ... 215 D1
Shortcrofts Rd RM9 ... 81 B2
Shorter St EC3 ... 117 D6 253 D6
Shortgate N12 ... 29 B6
Short La TW15, TW19 ... 148 B3
SHORTLANDS ... 208 C6
Shortlands
Brook Green W6 ... 112 D2
Harlington UB3 ... 127 B6
Shortlands Cl DA17 ... 125 B3
Edmonton N18 ... 17 B1
Shortlands Gdns BR2 ... 186 C1
Shortlands Gr BR2 ... 208 B6
Shortlands Rd
Beckenham BR2, BR3 ... 208 C6
Kingston u T KT2 ... 176 B3
Walthamstow E10 ... 53 D2
Shortlands Sta BR2 ... 186 C1
Short Path SE18 ... 144 D6
Short Rd Chiswick W4 ... 133 C6
Leyton E11 ... 76 C6
Stanwell TW19 ... 148 A5
Shorts Croft NW9 ... 44 D5
Shorts Gdns
WC2 ... 94 A1 240 A1
Shorts Rd SM5 ... 218 C3
Short St 7 Hendon NW4 ... 46 C5
SE1 ... 251 B2
Shortway SE9 ... 144 A2
Short Way
Colney Hatch N12 ... 30 C4
Twickenham TW2 ... 152 A4
Shotfield SM6 ... 219 B2
Shott Cl SM1 ... 218 A3
Shottendane Rd
SW6 ... 135 C4 265 A2
Shottery Cl SE9 ... 166 A1
Shottfield Ave SW14 ... 133 C1
Shottsford 1 W11 ... 91 C1
Shoulder of Mutton Alley
10 E14 ... 119 A6
Shouldham St
W1 ... 92 C2 237 B3
Showers Way UB3 ... 106 A5
Shrapnel Cl SE18 ... 144 A5
Shrapnel Rd SE9 ... 144 B2
Shreveport Ho 23 N19 ... 49 D2
Shrewsbury Ave
Harrow HA3 ... 44 A5
Mortlake SW14 ... 133 B1
Shrewsbury Cl KT6 ... 214 A6
Shrewsbury Ho
Chelsea SW3 ... 267 A5
Kennington SE11 ... 270 D5
Shrewsbury House Sch
KT6 ... 214 A6
Shrewsbury La SE18 ... 144 D4
Shrewsbury Mews 33
W2 ... 91 C2
Shrewsbury Rd
Beckenham BR3 ... 207 A6
Carshalton SM5 ... 202 C2
Friern Barnet N11 ... 31 D4
Harlington TW14, TW6 ... 149 B5
Notting Hill W2 ... 91 C1
Plashet E7 ... 77 D2
Shrewsbury St W10 ... 90 C3
Shrewsbury Wlk 9
TW7 ... 131 A2
Shrewton Rd SW17 ... 180 D3
Shri Swaminarayan
Mandir* NW10 ... 67 B2
Shroffold Rd BR1 ... 164 D1
Shropshire Cl CR4 ... 204 A5
Shropshire Ct W7 ... 86 D1
Shropshire Ho WC1 ... 239 B5
Shropshire Rd N22 ... 32 B3
Shroton St NW1 ... 92 C2 237 B4
Shrubberies The
Ilford IG2 ... 57 D4
Woodford E18 ... 37 A1
Shrubbery Cl N1 ... 235 B5
Shrubbery Gdns N21 ... 16 D4
Shrubbery Rd
Edmonton N9 ... 18 A1
Southall UB1 ... 107 C5
Streatham SW16 ... 182 A6
Shrubbery The
2 Surbiton KT6 ... 198 A1
7 Wanstead E11 ... 55 B4
Shrub Ct 5 SM2 ... 218 A2
Shrubland Gr KT4 ... 216 C5
Shrubland Rd
Hackney E8 ... 96 A6
Leyton E10 ... 53 C2
Walthamstow E17 ... 53 C4
Shrublands Ave CR0 ... 223 C4
Shrublands Cl
Forest Hill SE26 ... 162 C1
Whetstone N20 ... 14 B2
Shrubsall Cl SE9 ... 166 A3
Shrubs Ho SW1 ... 259 D3
Shurland Ave EN4 ... 14 B5
Shurland Gdns SE15 ... 139 D5
Shurlock Dr BR6 ... 227 A4
Shuters Sq W14 ... 254 C1
Shuttle Cl DA15 ... 167 D4
Shuttlemead DA5 ... 169 B4
Shuttle St E1 ... 96 A3
Shuttleworth Rd
SW11 ... 136 C3
Sibella Rd SW4 ... 137 D3
Sibford Ct 5 CR4 ... 202 D6
Sibley Cl Bexley DA6 ... 169 A6
Bromley BR1 ... 210 A4
Sibley Ct
Beckenham BR3 ... 186 C1
Hillingdon UB8 ... 83 A2
Sibley Gr E12 ... 78 A1
Sibthorpe Rd SE12 ... 165 C4
Sibthorp Rd 2 CR4 ... 180 D1
Sibton Rd SM5 ... 202 C6
Sicilian Ave WC1 ... 240 B3
Sidbury St
SW6 ... 135 A4 264 A2
SIDCUP ... 190 A5
Sidcup By Pass Rd
Sidcup DA14 ... 189 C6
St Paul's Cray BR5, BR7 ... 190 B3
Sidcup Hill DA14 ... 190 B5
Sidcup Hill Gdns
DA14 ... 190 C5
Sidcup Pl DA14 ... 190 A5
Sidcup Rd SE9 ... 166 A3
Sidcup Sta DA15 ... 168 A2
Sidcup Tech Ctr DA14 ... 190 D4
Siddeley Dr TW4 ... 129 A3
Siddons Ct WC2 ... 240 C1
Siddons Ho 8 NW3 ... 70 D3
Siddons La
NW1 ... 92 D3 237 D5
Siddons Rd
Croydon CR0 ... 220 D5
Forest Hill SE23 ... 163 A2
Tottenham N17 ... 34 A2
Side Rd E17 ... 53 B4
Sidewood Rd SE9 ... 167 B3
Sidford Ho SE1 ... 260 D5
Sidford Pl SE1 ... 116 B3 260 D5
Sidgwick Ho 26 SW9 ... 138 A3
Sidi Ct 2 N15 ... 50 D6
Sidings Mews N7 ... 72 C4
Sidings The E11 ... 54 A1
Sidlaw Ho N16 ... 51 D1
Sidmouth Ave TW7 ... 130 C3
Sidmouth Dr HA4 ... 62 A5
Sidmouth Ho
18 Camberwell SE15 ... 140 A5
Marylebone W1 ... 237 B2
26 Streatham SW2 ... 160 C4
Sidmouth Mews WC1 ... 233 C1
Sidmouth Par NW2 ... 68 C1
Sidmouth Rd
Bexley DA16 ... 146 C5
Leyton E10 ... 76 A5
Willesden NW2 ... 68 C1
Sidmouth St
WC1 ... 94 B4 233 C1
Sidney Ave N13 ... 32 B5
Sidney Boyd Ct NW6 ... 69 C1
Sidney Elson Way E6 ... 100 C5
Sidney Gdns TW8 ... 131 D6
Sidney Godley (VC) Ho 31
E2 ... 96 C4
Sidney Gr EC1 ... 234 C3
Sidney Ho
4 Globe Town E2 ... 96 D5
SE18 ... 144 B4
Sidney Miller Ct 8
W3 ... 110 D5
Sidney Rd
Beckenham BR3 ... 185 A1
Croydon SE25 ... 206 A4
Harrow HA2 ... 42 A6
Stockwell SW9 ... 138 B3
Twickenham TW1 ... 153 B5
Walton-on-T KT12 ... 194 B1
Wanstead E7 ... 77 A5
Wood Green N22 ... 32 B3
Sidney Sq E1 ... 96 C2
Sidney St E1 ... 96 C2
Sidworth St 6 E8 ... 74 B1
Siebert Rd SE3 ... 143 A6
Siedle Ho 9 SE18 ... 144 C6
Siege Ho 14 E1 ... 96 B1
Siemens Rd SE18 ... 121 D3
Sienna SE28 ... 123 D3
Sienna Ct TW13 ... 149 D1
Sierra Dr RM9 ... 103 D5
Sigdon Rd E8 ... 74 A3
Sigers The HA5 ... 40 B3
Signal Ho 9 London E8 ... 74 B1
SE1 ... 252 A1
Signmakers Yd NW1 ... 231 D5
Sigrist Sq 4 KT2 ... 176 A2
Silbury Ave CR4 ... 180 C2
Silbury Ho 9 SE26 ... 162 A1
Silbury St N1 ... 235 C2
Silchester Ct
Stanwell TW15 ... 148 A2
Thornton Heath CR7 ... 204 C5
Silchester Rd W10 ... 90 D1
Silecroft Rd DA7 ... 147 C4
Silesia Bldgs E8 ... 74 B1
Silex St SE1 ... 116 D4 251 D1
Silicone Bsns Ctr UB6 ... 87 C5
Silk Cl SE12 ... 165 A5
Silkfield Rd NW9 ... 45 C4
Silk Ho NW9 ... 45 B6
Silk Mills Path SE13 ... 142 A2
Silk Mills Sq E9 ... 75 B2
Silks Ct E11 ... 54 C1
Silk St EC2 ... 95 A2 242 B4
Silkstream Par HA8 ... 27 A2
Silkstream Rd HA8 ... 27 A2
Sillitoe Ho N1 ... 235 D5
Silsoe Ho NW1 ... 231 D3
Silsoe Rd N22 ... 50 B6
Silverbell Ct 1 N12 ... 29 D5
Silver Birch Ave E4 ... 35 B4
Silver Birch Cl
Forest Hill SE6 ... 163 B1
Friern Barnet N11 ... 31 A4
Ickenham UB10 ... 60 A4
SE28 ... 124 A5
Silver Birch Ct EN3 ... 18 D6
Silver Birch Gdns E6 ... 100 B3
Silverbirch Wlk 1
NW3 ... 71 A2
Silverburn Ho 4 SW9 ... 138 D4
Silver Cl Harrow HA3 ... 24 B3
SE14 ... 141 A5
Silvercliffe Gdns EN4 ... 2 C1
Silver Cres W4 ... 110 D2
Silver Ct N19 ... 71 C5
Silverdale Enfield EN2 ... 4 A1
Forest Hill SE26 ... 184 C6
NW1 ... 232 A2
Silverdale Ave IG3 ... 57 D4
Silverdale Cl
Cheam SM1 ... 217 B4
1 Ealing W7 ... 108 D5
Northolt UB5 ... 63 B3
Silverdale Ct EC1 ... 241 D6
Silverdale Dr
Chislehurst SE9 ... 166 A2
Sunbury TW16 ... 172 B1
Silverdale Factory Ctr
UB3 ... 106 A3
Silverdale Gdns UB3 ... 106 A4
Silverdale Ind Est
UB3 ... 106 A4
Silverdale Par IG3 ... 57 D4
Silverdale Rd
Bexleyheath DA7 ... 147 D3
Chingford E4 ... 36 B4
Hayes UB3 ... 106 A4
Petts Wood BR5 ... 211 A5
Silverhall St TW7 ... 131 A2
Silverholme Cl HA3 ... 44 A2
Silver Ind Est N17 ... 33 D1
Silver Jubilee Way
TW4 ... 128 B3
Silver La BR4 ... 224 B6
Silverland St E16 ... 122 B5
Silverleigh Rd CR7 ... 204 B4
Silvermead 7 E18 ... 37 A2
Silvermere Rd SE6 ... 163 B5
Silver Pl W1 ... 249 B6

Silver Rd
Shepherd's Bush
W12...........................112 D6
St Johns SE13.........141 B1
Silvers 4 IG9.............21 C3
Silver Spring Cl DA8...147 D6
Silver St Edmonton N18...33 C6
Enfield EN1.....................5 B2
Silverstone Ct 8 BR1...187 C1
Silverston Way HA7.....25 C4
Silver Street Sta N18...33 D5
Silverthorn 17 NW6...91 D6
Silverthorne Rd SW8...137 B3
Silverthorn Gdns E4...19 C2
Silverton Lo SE19.......183 C3
Silverton Rd W6........134 D6
SILVERTOWN..............121 B4
Silvertown Way E16...121 A5
Silvertree La UB6........86 B4
Silver Way
Hillingdon UB10..........82 D5
Romford RM7...............59 D6
Silver Wing Ind Est
CR0.............................220 B2
Silver Wlk SE16.........119 B5
Silverwood Cl BR3....185 C3
Silvester Ho
27 Bethnal Green E2....96 C4
1 Notting Hill W11......91 B1
Pinner HA5..................40 A5
6 Stepney E1..............96 B1
Silvester Rd SE22.....161 D6
Silvester St SE1.........252 C1
Silwex Ho E1.............243 C5
Silwood St SE16........118 C1
Simba Ct TW1...........152 D3
Simla Ho SE1.............252 D1
Simmil Rd KT10.........212 C3
Simmonds Ct SW5.....255 C3
Simmons Cl
Chessington KT9.........213 C2
East Barnet N20...........14 C3
Simmons Dr RM8........81 A5
Simmons Gate KT10...212 A3
Simmons Ho
20 Bethnal Green E2....96 A4
Finsbury Pk N7............72 B6
Simmons La E4............20 B2
Simmons Rd SE18......122 C1
Simmons' Way N20.....14 C2
Simms Cl SM5.............218 C6
Simms Ct SW6............135 A2
Simms Gdns N2...........30 A1
Simms Rd SE1............118 A2
Simnel Rd SE12..........124 B4
Simon Cl W11...113 B6 244 D6
Simon Ct Paddington W9...91 C4
5 Woolwich SE28........124 B5
Simonds Rd E10...........75 C6
Simone Cl BR1............187 D2
Simon Lo 31 SW19.....156 D3
Simon Marks Jewish Prim
Sch N16........................73 D6
Simons Wlk E15...........76 B3
Simpson Cl N21............16 B6
Simpson Dr W3............89 B1
Simpson Ho
Lisson Gr NW8............230 A1
Vauxhall SE11.............260 C1
Wembley HA9..............65 D6
Simpson Rd
Hounslow TW4.............151 B5
Richmond TW10..........175 C6
Simpson's Rd BR2......209 A6
Poplar E14..................119 D6
Simpson St SW11......136 C3
Simpson Way KT6......197 C3
Sim's Cotts KT10.......212 D2
Sims Wlk SE3............142 D1
Sinclair Ct
21 Beckenham BR3.....185 C3
Canonbury N5...............73 A2
6 Croydon CR0...........221 D6
Sinclair Gdns W14.....112 D4
Sinclair Gr NW11........46 D3
Sinclair Ho Harrow HA7...24 D4
3 South Norwood
SW16........................182 B3
1 Streatham SW12.....159 D3
Sinclair Mans 13 W12...112 D4
Sinclair Pl SE4...........163 C5
Sinclair Rd
Chingford Hatch E4......35 B5
W14..............113 A3 254 A6
Sinclairs Ho 18 E3.......97 B5
Sinclare Cl EN1.............5 D4
Singapore Rd W13.....109 A5
Singer St EC2.............235 D1
Singlegate Prim Sch
SW19........................180 B3
Singleton Cl
Mitcham SW17............180 D3
Thornton Heath CR0...205 A2
Singleton Rd RM9........81 A5
Singleton Scarp N12...29 C5
Sinnott Rd E17............34 D2
Sion Ct TW1...............153 B3
Sion Ho SE13..............142 A1
Sion-Manning RC Sch
for Girls
Kensal Town W10.........91 A2
North Kensington W10...90 D2
Sion Rd TW1..............153 B3
Sippetts Ct IG1.............55 B3
SIPSON.......................126 C6
Sipson Cl UB7............126 C6

Sipson La UB3, UB7....126 D6
Sipson Rd
Harmondsworth UB7....126 C6
West Drayton UB7.......104 B2
West Drayton UB7.......104 C1
Sipson Way UB7........126 C5
Sir Abraham Dawes Cotts
SW15........................135 A1
Sir Alexander Cl W3....111 D5
Sir Alexander Rd W3...111 D5
Sir Arthur Bliss Ct 4
SW19........................180 D1
Sir Cyril Black Way 2
SW19........................179 C3
Sirdar Rd Mitcham CR4...181 A4
Tottenham N22.............33 A1
W11..............113 A4 244 A5
Sir Francis Drake Prim
Sch SE8......................119 A1
Sir George Monoux Sixth
Form Coll E17...............35 D1
Sir Henry Floyd Ct HA7...9 B2
Sirinham Point SW8....270 D5
Sirius Bldg 13 E1.........118 D6
Sir James Barrie Prim Sch
SW8................137 C4 269 B1
Sir John Cass Foundation
& Redcoat CE Sec Sch
E1................................96 D2
Sir John Cass's
Foundation Prim Sch
EC3...................95 C1 243 B1
Sir John Heron Prim Sch
E12..............................78 B4
Sir John Kirk Cl 33
SE5............................139 A5
Sir John Lillie Prim Sch
SW6................135 A6 264 B5
Sir Martin Bowes Ho 9
SE18..........................122 C2
Sir Oswald Stoll
Foundation The SW6...265 C4
Sir Thomas Abney Sch
N16.............................51 B1
Sir Thomas More Est
SW3................136 B6 266 D5
Sirus Rd HA6................22 A5
Sir William Burrough Prim
Sch E14........................97 A1
Sir William Powell's
Almshos SW6.............135 A2
Sise La EC4.................242 C1
Siskin Ho Edmonton N9...18 D3
14 Rotherhithe SE16...118 D2
Sisley Rd IG11............101 D6
Sispara Gdns SW18....157 B5
Sissinghurst Cl BR1....186 C5
Sissinghurst Ho 17
SE15..........................140 A5
Sissinghurst Rd CR0...206 A2
Sissulo Ct 8 E6...........99 C6
Sister Mabel's Way 15
SE15..........................140 A5
Sisters Ave SW11.......136 D1
Sistova Rd SW12........159 B3
Sisulu Pl SW9.............138 C2
Sitarey Ct 4 W12.......112 B5
Site of Changing of the
Guard* SW1...............249 A1
Sittingbourne Ave EN1...17 B5
Sitwell Gr HA7..............24 D5
Siverst Cl UB5..............63 D2
Sivill Ho 9 E2...............95 D4
Siviter Way RM10........81 D1
Siward Rd
Bromley BR2................209 C6
Tottenham N17..............33 B2
Wandsworth SW17.......158 A1
Six Bridges Ind Est
SE1............................118 A1
Sixpenny Ct IG11.........79 A2
Sixth Ave Hayes UB3...105 D5
Ilford E12.....................78 B4
West Kilburn W10..........91 A4
Sixth Cross Rd TW2....152 A1
Skardu Rd NW2............69 A3
Skeena Hill SW18,
SW19........................157 A4
Skeffington Rd E6.......100 B6
Skeffington St SE18....123 A3
Skeggs Ho 5 E14........120 A3
Skegness Ho 3 N7.......72 B1
Skelbrook St SW18......158 A2
Skelgill Rd SW15........135 D3
Skelley Rd E15.............76 D1
Skelton Cl 7 E8...........73 C2
Skelton Ho N16.............73 C3
Skelton Rd E7...............77 A2
Skelton's La E10...........53 D2
Skelwith Rd W6..........134 C6
Skenfrith Ho SE15......140 B6
Skerne Rd KT2...........175 D2
Skerne Wlk KT2.........175 D2
Sketchley Gdns SE16...118 D1
Sketty Rd EN1...............5 D2
Skiers St E15................98 C6
Skiffington Cl SW2.....160 C3
Skillen Lodge HA5.......22 D2
Skinner Ct E17.............53 C4
Skinner Pl SW1...........258 A3
Skinners Almshouses
N13.............................16 C1
Skinners Company Sch
(Upper) N16.................51 D2
Skinner's Company's
Lower Sch E5...............52 B1
Skinners La EC4...........242 B6
Hounslow TW5.............129 D4
Skinner St EC1....94 C3 241 B6
Skipper Ct 6 IG11......101 A6

Skipsea Ho SW18.......158 B5
Skipsey Ave E6..........100 B4
Skipton Cl N11.............31 A4
Skipton Dr UB3............105 A3
Skipton Ho SE4...........141 A1
Skipwith Bldg EC1......241 A4
Skipworth Rd E9..........96 C6
Skua Ct 33 SE8............141 B6
Skyline Ct SE1............263 C5
Skyline Plaza Bldg 19
E1................................96 A1
Skylines E14................120 A4
Sky Peals Rd IG8..........36 B3
Sky Studios E16..........122 C4
Sladebrook Rd SE3.....143 D2
Slade Ct Barnet EN5......1 D2
Brondesbury NW2.........69 A3
Muswell Hill N10............31 B3
Sladedale Rd SE18......123 C1
Slade Ho TW4............151 B5
Sladen Pl 12 E5............74 B4
Slades Cl EN2................4 A2
Slades Dr BR7.............189 A6
Slades Gdns EN2...........4 C2
Slades Hill EN2..............4 C2
Slades Rise EN2.............4 C2
Slade The SE18...........145 C6
Slade Twr E10...............75 C6
Slade Way CR4............181 A2
Slagrove Pl SE13.........163 D6
Slaidburn St
SW10................136 A6 266 B5
Slaithwaite Rd SE13....142 A1
Slaney Ct NW10............68 C1
Slaney Pl 1 N7..............72 C3
Slater Cl 15 SE18.........122 C2
Slatter 1 NW9................27 D2
Slattery Rd TW13........150 C3
Sleaford Ho 16 E3.........97 C3
Sleaford Ind Est
SW8................137 C5 269 B3
Sleaford St
SW8................137 C5 269 B3
Sleat Ho 11 E3...............97 B5
Sledmere Ct TW14......149 C3
Slievemore Cl 8 SW4...137 D2
Sligo Ho 8 E1................96 D3
Slingsby Pl WC2..........250 A6
Slippers Pl SE16..........118 B3
Slipway Ho 1 E14.......119 D1
Sloane Ave
SW3................114 C2 257 B3
Sloane Avenue Mans
SW3............................257 C3
Sloane Ct E SW3.........258 A2
Sloane Ct W SW3........258 A2
Sloane Gate Mans
SW1............................258 A4
Sloane Gdns
Belgravia
SW1................115 A2 258 A3
Orpington BR6.............227 A5
Sloane Ho 7 E9............74 C1
Sloane Hospl BR3........186 B2
Sloane Sq SW1............257 D3
Sloane Square Sta
SW1................115 A2 258 A3
Sloane St SW1...114 D3 257 D5
Sloane Terr SW1..........258 A4
Sloane Terr Mans
SW1............................258 A4
Sloane Wlk CR0..........207 B3
Sloan Ho RM10............81 D1
Slocum Cl SE28...........124 C6
Slough La NW9.............45 A3
Sly St 17 E1.................96 B1
Smaldon Cl UB7..........104 C3
Smallberry Ave TW7...130 D3
Smallberry Green Prim
Sch The TW7...............131 A4
Smallbrook Mews W2...236 C1
Smallbugh Mans HA0...65 B4
Smalley Cl N16..............73 D5
Smallwood Prim Sch
SW17........................180 B6
Smallwood Rd SW17...180 B6
Smarden Cl DA17.........125 C1
Smarden Gr SE9..........188 B6
Smart's Pl
Edmonton N18..............34 A5
WC1, WC2..................240 B2
Smart St E2..................96 D4
Smeaton Ct KT9..........213 D2
Smeaton Ct SE1..........262 A5
Smeaton Rd
Holdbrook EN3...............7 C6
Wandsworth SW18.......157 C4
Smeaton St E1............118 B5
Smedley St SW4.........137 D3
Smeed Rd E3.................75 C1
Smiles Pl SE13............142 A3
Smith Cl SE16.............118 D5
Smithers Ho 3 SE20....184 D3
Smithfield Mkt EC1......241 D3
Smithfield St
EC1...................94 D2 241 C3
Smithies Ct E15............76 A3
Smithies Rd SE2..........124 B2
Smith's Ct W1.............249 C6
Smithson Rd N17..........33 B2
Smiths Point E13...........99 A6
Smith Sq SW1...116 A3 260 A5
Smith St Surbiton KT5...198 B3
SW3...............114 D1 257 C1
Smith's Yd SW18.........158 A2
Smith Terr
SW3...............114 D1 257 C1
Smithwood Cl SW19....157 A2
Smithy St E1.................96 C2
Smithy Street Sch E1...96 C2

Smock Wlk CR0..........205 A3
Smoothfield TW3........129 C1
Smugglers Way SW18...135 D1
Smyrk's Rd
SE17................117 C1 263 B1
Smyrna Mans 8 NW6...69 C1
Smyrna Rd NW6...........69 C1
Smythe St E14.............119 D6
Snakes La EN4, N14......3 C1
Snakes La E IG8...........37 C4
Snakes La W IG8..........37 B4
Snakey La TW13..........172 B6
SNARESBROOK.............54 D6
Snaresbrook Coll E18...37 A1
Snaresbrook Dr HA7....26 A6
Snaresbrook Hall 12
E18..............................55 A6
Snaresbrook Ho E18....54 D5
Snaresbrook Prim Sch
E18..............................55 A5
Snaresbrook Rd E11....54 D5
Snaresbrook Sta E11....55 A4
Snarsgate St W10.........90 C2
Sneath Ave NW11........47 B2
Sneyd Rd NW2.............68 C4
Snowberry Cl E11.........76 B4
Snowbury Rd 6 SW6...135 D3
Snow Ct 4 HA0.............65 D3
Snowden Ave UB10.....82 D5
Snowden St
EC2...................95 C3 243 A5
Snowdon Cres UB3.....105 A3
Snowdon Dr NW9.........45 C3
Snowdon Rd TW6.......149 A5
Snowdown Cl SE20.....184 D2
Snowdrop Cl 2 TW12...173 C4
Snowe Ho SE27..........160 D1
Snow Hill EC1....94 D2 241 C3
Snowman Ho NW6........91 D6
Snowsfields
SE1................117 B4 252 D2
Snowsfields Prim Sch
SE1................117 C4 253 A2
Snowshill Rd E12.........78 A3
Snowy Fielder Waye
TW7..........................131 B3
Soames St SE15..........139 D2
Soames Wlk KT3.........177 C2
Soane Cl W5................109 D4
Soane Ct 10 NW1.........71 C1
Soane Ho SE17............262 D1
Soane Mus The*
WC2..................94 B1 240 C2
Soaphouse La TW8.....132 A5
Soham Rd EN3...............7 B6
SOHO...........................93 D1
Soho* W1.........93 D1 239 C2
Soho Mills SM6............203 B1
Soho Parish CE Prim Sch
W1...................93 D6 249 C6
Soho Sq W1.......93 D1 239 C2
Soho St W1.................239 C2
Sojourner-Truth Cl 11
E8................................74 B2
Sola Ct 8 CR0.............205 B1
Solander Gdns
13 Shadwell E1............118 C6
Stepney E1..................118 B6
Solar Ct N3...................29 D3
Soldene Ct N7...............72 B2
Solebay St E1...............97 A3
Solent Ct SW16...........182 B1
Solent Ho 6 E1..............97 A2
Solent Rd NW6.............69 C3
Solent Rise E13............99 A4
Soley Mews WC1........234 A2
Solidarity Ho 5 NW10...68 C2
Solna Ave SW15...........156 C6
Solna Rd N21................17 B4
Solomon Ave N9...........34 A6
Solomons Ct N12..........30 A3
Solomon's Pas SE15....140 B1
Solon New Rd SW4......138 A1
Solon Rd SW2..............138 A1
Solway Cl TW4............129 A2
Solway Ho 12 E1...........96 D3
Solway Rd
East Dulwich SE22........140 A1
Tottenham N22..............32 D2
Somaford Gr EN4..........14 B5
Somali Rd NW2.............69 B3
Somborne Ho 11
SW15........................156 A4
Sombrook Ho SE11......261 A4
Somerby Rd IG11..........79 B1
Somercoates Cl EN4.......2 C2
Somer Ct SW6..............265 A5
Somerfield Rd N4..........72 D6
Somerfield St SE16.......118 D1
Somerford Cl HA5..........40 A5
Somerford Gr
Shacklewell N16............73 D4
Tottenham N17..............34 A3
Somerford Grove Est
N16..............................73 D4
Somerford St E1............96 B3
Somerford Way SE16...119 A4
Somerhill Ave DA15....168 B4
Somerhill Rd DA16......146 B3
Somerleyton Rd SW9...138 C1
Somersby Est SE20.....184 C3
Somersby Gdns IG4......56 B4
Somers Cl NW1...........232 C3
Somers Cres W2..........237 A1

Somerset Cl
New Malden KT3..........199 C3
Tottenham N17..............33 B1
Woodford IG8................37 A2
Somerset Ct
10 Buckhurst Hill IG9...21 C2
Ealing W7.....................86 D1
2 Hampton TW12........173 C2
Somerset Gdns
Highgate N6..................49 A2
St Johns SE13.............141 D3
Teddington TW11..........174 C5
Thornton Heath SW16...204 B6
Tottenham N17..............33 C3
Somerset Hall N17........33 C3
Somerset Ho
WC2............116 B6 250 D6
Somerset Ho SW19......157 A1
Somerset Lo
9 Brentford TW8..........131 D6
5 New Barnet EN5........14 A6
Putney SW15...............134 B1
Somerset Rd
Bedford Pk W4.............111 B3
Brentford TW8.............131 C6
Ealing W13..................109 C5
Edmonton N18...............33 D5
Harrow HA1..................42 A4
Hendon NW4.................46 C5
Holdbrook EN3................7 C5
Kingston u T KT1..........176 B1
New Barnet EN5...........14 A6
Southall UB1.................85 C2
Teddington TW11..........174 C5
Tottenham N17..............51 D6
Walthamstow E17..........53 C3
Wimbledon SW19.........157 A1
Somerset Sq
W14............113 B4 244 C1
Somerset Waye TW5...129 A5
Somersham Rd DA7....147 A3
Somers Pl SW2...........160 B4
Somers Rd
Tulse Hill SW2..............160 B5
Walthamstow E17..........53 B5
SOMERS TOWN.............93 D4
Somers Town Est
NW1.................93 C5 232 B3
Somers Way WD23........8 A4
Somerton Ave TW9.....132 C2
Somerton Rd
Cricklewood NW2..........69 A5
Nunhead SE15..............140 B1
Somertrees Ave SE12...165 B2
Somervell Rd HA2.........63 C3
Somerville Ave SW13...134 C6
Somerville Ho 10
SW15........................156 D5
Somerville Point SE16...119 B4
Somerville Rd
Dagenham RM6.............58 C4
Penge SE20.................184 D3
Sonderburg Rd 13 N7...72 B6
Sondes St SE17...........139 B6
Songhurst Cl CR0........204 B3
Sonia Ct Edgware HA8...26 B3
North Finchley N12........30 A6
Sonia Gdns
Heston TW5.................129 C5
North Finchley N12........30 A6
Willesden NW10............67 D4
Sonning Ct CR0...........222 A6
Sonning Gdns TW12...173 A4
Sonning Rd 32 E2........95 D4
Sonning Rd CR0..........206 A3
Soper Cl
Chingford Hatch E4.......35 B5
4 Forest Hill SE23......162 D4
Soper Mews EN3...........7 C5
Sophia Ho 10
Hammersmith W6........112 C1
Tottenham N15.............51 D5
Sophia Rd Newham E13...99 B2
Walthamstow E10..........53 D1
Sophia Sq 18 SE16......118 A6
Sopwith 2 NW9.............27 D2
Sopwith Ave KT9........213 A3
Sopwith Cl KT2...........176 B5
Sopwith Rd TW5.........128 C5
Sopwith Way
Battersea
SW11...............137 B5 268 C4
Kingston u T KT2..........176 A2
Sorbus Ct EN2...............4 D3
Sorensen Ct 2 E10........75 D5
Sorrel Cl SE28.............124 A5
Sorrel Gdns E6.............100 A2
Sorrel Ho TW3............130 A4
Sorrel La 17 E14...........98 B1
Sorrell Cl
6 Brixton SW9.............138 C3
SE14..........................141 A5
Sorrento Rd SM1.........217 D5
Soseki Mus* SW4.......137 B2
Sotheby Rd N5..............73 A4
Sotheran Cl E8.............96 A6
Sotheron Pl SW6.........265 D3
Soudan Rd
SW11...............136 D4 267 C1
Souldern Rd 10 W14....112 D3
South Access Rd E17...53 A3
South Acre NW9............27 D1
Southacre Way HA5......22 C2
SOUTH ACTON.............110 C3
South Acton Sta W3,
W4..............................111 A3
South Africa Rd W12...112 B6
SOUTHALL...................107 A5

Southall Ct UB1..........107 B6
Southall Ent Ctr UB2...107 C4
Southall La TW5..........106 B1
Southall Norwood Hospl
UB2............................107 B3
Southall Pl SE1...........252 C1
Southall Sta UB1.........107 B4
Southall & West London
Coll UB1.....................107 A5
Southam Ho 9 W10.......91 A3
Southampton Bldgs
WC2............................241 A3
Southampton Gdns
CR4............................204 A4
Southampton Mews
E16.............................121 B5
Southampton Pl WC1...240 B3
Southampton Rd
Maitland Pk NW5...........70 D3
Stanwell TW19, TW6...148 B5
Southampton Row
WC1..................94 A2 240 B4
Southampton St WC2...250 B6
Southampton Way
SE5............................139 C5
South Audley St
W1................115 A5 248 B4
South Ave Chingford E4...20 A4
East Finchley NW11......47 D5
Richmond TW9............132 C3
Southall UB1...............107 B6
Wallington SM5............219 A1
South Avenue Gdns
UB1............................107 B6
Southbank KT7............197 B2
SOUTH BANK..............116 B4
South Bank KT6..........198 A4
South Bank Bsns Ctr
SW8................137 D6 269 D5
Southbank International
Sch NW3.......................70 A2
Southbank International
Sch (Westminster
Campus) W1.....93 B2 238 C4
Southbank Int Sch
W11................113 C6 245 A5
South Bank Lo 2 KT6...198 A4
South Bank Terr KT6...198 A3
South Bank Univ
London SW8.....137 D4 269 D2
SE1................116 C3 261 C6
SOUTH BEDDINGTON...219 C2
South Bermondsey Sta
SE16...........................118 C1
South Birkbeck Rd E11...76 B5
South Black Lion La 7
W6..............................112 A1
South Bldg SW1...........259 B6
South Block 20 E1........118 C6
South Bolton Gdns
SW10..........................255 D2
SOUTHBOROUGH.........197 C1
210 B3
Southborough Cl KT6...197 D1
Southborough High Sch
KT6............................214 C6
Southborough Ho
SE17..........................263 B2
Southborough La BR1,
BR2............................210 B4
Southborough Prim Sch
BR2............................210 C4
Southborough Rd
Bromley BR1, BR2.......210 A5
South Hackney E9.........96 D6
Surbiton KT6...............198 A1
Southborough Rd (The
Lane) KT6..................198 A1
Southbourne BR2.........209 A4
Southbourne Ave NW9...27 B1
Southbourne Cl HA5......41 A2
Southbourne Cres
NW4............................47 A5
Southbourne Ct NW9....27 A1
Southbourne Gdns
Ilford IG1......................79 A3
Ruislip HA4...................40 B1
SE12..........................165 B6
Southbridge Pl CR0.....221 C4
Southbridge Rd CR0....221 C4
Southbridge Way UB2...107 A4
SOUTH BROMLEY..........98 B2
Southbrook Mews
SE12..........................164 D5
Southbrook Rd
Hither Green SE12........164 D5
Thornton Heath SW16...182 A2
South Building* SE10...142 B5
Southbury NW8............229 B6
Southbury Ave EN1........6 A1
Southbury Prim Sch
EN3...............................6 C1
Southbury Rd Enfield EN1...5 D2
Enfield EN1, EN3............6 B1
Southbury Sta EN3.........6 B1
South Camden Com Sch
NW1.................93 D5 232 C4
South Carriage Dr SW1,
SW7...............114 D4 247 C2
South Chelsea Coll
SW9............................138 B1
Southchurch Ct
Bowes Pk N13...............32 B5
Newham E6..................100 B5
Southchurch Rd E6......100 B5
South Cl Barnet EN5.......1 B2
DA6............................146 D1
Dagenham RM10..........103 D4

South Cl *continued*
Highgate N6 49 B3
Morden SM4 201 C3
Pinner HA5 41 B2
Twickenham TW2 151 C1
West Drayton UB7 104 C3
South Colonnade The E14 119 D5
Southcombe St W14 254 A4
South Common Rd UB8 60 A2
Southcote Ave
Feltham TW13 150 A2
Tolworth KT5 198 D2
Southcote Rd
Croydon SE25 206 B3
Tufnell Pk N19 71 C4
Walthamstow E17 53 A4
Southcote Rise HA4 39 B2
Southcott Ho
31 Bromley E3 97 D4
W9 236 B5
South Countess Rd E17 53 B6
South Cres Newham E16 98 B3
WC1 239 C3
Southcroft SM1 218 C3
Southcroft Ave DA16 145 C2
West Wickham BR4 224 A6
Southcroft Rd BR6 227 C5
Streatham SW17 181 A4
South Cross Rd IG6 57 A4
South Croxted Rd SE21 183 B6
SOUTH CROYDON 221 B1
South Croydon Sta CR2 221 B3
South Ct 17 SW15 156 D5
Southdean Gdns SW19 157 B2
South Dene NW7 11 B1
Southdene Ct N11 15 C1
Southdown N7 72 A2
Southdown Ave W7 109 A3
Southdown Cres
Harrow HA2 42 A1
Ilford IG2 57 C4
Southdown Dr SW20 178 D3
Southdown Rd SW20 178 D2
South Dr
Orpington BR6 227 C3
Ruislip HA4 39 C1
South Ealing Cemy W5 109 D2
South Ealing Rd W5 109 D3
South Ealing Sta W5 109 D3
South Eastern Ave N9 17 D1
South Eastern Univ N7 72 B5
South Eaton Pl SW1 115 A2 258 B4
South Eden Park Rd BR3 207 D4
South Edwardes Sq W8 255 A5
SOUTHEND 186 B6
South End
Croydon CR0 221 A4
W8 113 D3 255 D6
Southend Cl SE9 166 D5
South End Cl NW3 70 C4
Southend Cres SE9 166 D5
South End Gn NW3 70 C4
Southend Ho SE9 166 C4
Southend La SE6 185 C6
Southend Rd
Beckenham BR3 185 C2
Plashet E6 78 B1
Woodford IG8 37 D1
South End Rd NW3 70 C4
Southend Road (North Circular Rd) E17, E18 36 C2
South End Row W8 113 D3 255 D6
Southern Ave
East Bedfont TW14 150 A3
South Norwood SE25 205 D6
Southerngate Way SE14 141 A5
Southern Gr E3 97 B3
Southernhay IG10 21 D6
Southern Perimeter Rd
Hatton TW14, TW6 149 B6
West Bedfont TW19, TW6 148 C5
Southern Rd
Fortis Green N2 48 D5
Newham E13 99 B5
Southern Road Prim Sch E13 99 B5
Southern Row W10 91 A3
Southern St N1 233 C4
Southern Way
Greenwich SE10 120 D3
Romford RM7 59 C3
Southerton Rd W6 112 C2
South Esk Rd E7 77 C2
Southey Ho SE17 262 B2
Southey Mews E16 121 A5
Southey Rd
Brixton SW9 138 C4
Merton SW19 179 C3
Tottenham N15 51 C4
Southey St SE20 184 D3
Southfield EN5 12 D5
Southfield Cl UB8 82 C4
Southfield Cotts W7 108 D4
Southfield Ct E11 76 D5
Southfield Gdns TW1, TW2 174 D6
Southfield Lo W4 111 B4
Southfield Pk HA2 41 D5
Southfield Prim Sch W4 111 C4
Southfield Rd
Acton W4 111 B4
Enfield EN3 18 C5
St Paul's Cray BR7 211 D6
SOUTHFIELDS 157 D3
Southfields
Hendon NW4 46 B6
Thames Ditton KT8 196 C3
Southfields Ave TW15 170 D4
Southfields Com Coll SW18 157 C3
Southfields Ct SM3 217 C6
Southfields Rd SW18 157 C5
Southfields Sta SW18 157 B3
Southfleet Rd BR6 227 C4
SOUTHGATE 16 B4
South Gate Ave TW13 171 B6
Southgate Cir 3 N14 15 D3
Southgate Coll N14 15 D2
Southgate Ct N1 73 B1
Southgate Gr N1 73 B1
Southgate Ho 7 E17 54 A6
Southgate Rd N1 95 B6 235 D6
Southgate Sch EN4 15 B6
Southgate Sta N14 15 D3
Southgate Way N2 30 C2
South Gdns
Mitcham SW19 180 B3
Wembley HA9 66 C6
South Gipsy Rd DA16 146 D2
South Glade The DA5 169 B3
South Gn NW9 27 C2
South Gr Highgate N6 49 A1
Tottenham N15 51 B4
Walthamstow E17 53 B4
South Greenford Sta UB6 86 C4
South Grove Ho N6 49 A1
South Grove Prim Sch E17 53 B3
SOUTH HACKNEY 96 C6
SOUTH HAMPSTEAD 70 A1
South Hampstead High Sch NW3 70 B2
South Hampstead High Sch Jun Dept NW3 70 A2
South Hampstead Sta NW8 70 A1
South Harringay Jun & Inf Schs N4 50 D4
SOUTH HARROW 63 D5
South Harrow Sta HA2 64 A5
South Hill BR7 188 B4
South Hill Ave HA1, HA2 64 B5
South Hill Gr HA1 64 C4
South Hill Pk NW3 70 C4
South Hill Pk Gdns NW3 70 C4
South Hill Rd BR2 208 C5
Southholme Cl SE19 183 C2
Southill La HA5 40 B5
Southill Rd BR7 188 B3
Southill St E14 97 D1
South Island Pl SW9 138 C5
SOUTH KENSINGTON 114 A1
South Kensington Sta SW7 114 B2 256 D4
South Kensington Station Arc SW7 256 D4
South Kenton Sta HA9 43 C1
South La
Kingston u T KT1 197 D6
New Malden KT3 199 B3
SOUTH LAMBETH 138 A4
South Lambeth Pl SW8 270 B6
South Lambeth Rd SW8 138 A5 270 B4
Southland Rd SE18 145 D5
Southlands Ave BR6 227 C3
Southlands Ct BR2 209 D5
Southlands Dr SW19 156 D2
Southlands Gr BR1 210 A6
Southlands Rd BR1, BR2 209 D5
Southland Way TW7 152 B6
South La W KT3 199 B5
South Lo
6 New Barnet EN5 13 D6
NW8 229 C2
Twickenham TW2 152 A5
South Lodge Ave CR4, CR7, SW16 204 A5
South Lodge Cres EN2 3 D1
South Lodge Dr N14 15 D6
South London Montessori Sch SW11 267 A1
South Mall The N9 18 A1
South Mead
Grahame Pk NW9 27 D2
West Ewell KT19 215 D1
Southmead Prim Sch SW19 157 A3
Southmead Rd SW19 157 A3
South Merton Sta SW20 201 B6
South Molton La W1 93 B1 238 C1
South Molton Rd E16 99 A1
South Molton St W1 93 B1 238 C1
Southmont Rd KT10 212 C5
Southmoor Way E9 75 B3
South Mount N20 14 A2
SOUTH NORWOOD 205 C6
South Norwood Ctry Pk* SE25 206 C5
South Norwood Hill SE19, SE25 183 D1
South Norwood Prim Sch SE25 206 A5
South Oak Rd SW16 182 B6
Southold Rise SE9 166 B1
Southolm St SW11 137 B4 268 D1
South Ordnance Rd EN3 7 C5
Southover BR1 187 A5
Finchley N12 29 C6
SOUTH OXHEY 22 B6
South Par
Acton Green W4 111 B2
Edgware HA8 26 C1
Wallington SM6 219 C2
South Parade SW3 114 B1 256 D2
South Park Bsns Ctr IG3 79 C6
South Park Cres
Catford SE6 164 D3
Ilford IG1 79 C5
Southpark Ct SW19 179 C4
South Park Ct 24 BR3 185 C3
South Park Dr IG3 79 C4
South Park Gr KT3 199 A5
South Park Hill Rd CR2 221 B4
South Park Mews SW6 135 D2
South Park Prim Sch IG3 79 C5
South Park Rd
Ilford IG1 79 B5
Wimbledon SW19 179 D4
South Park Terr IG1 79 C5
South Park Villas IG3 79 C4
South Park Way HA4 62 C3
South Pl
Broadgate EC2 95 B2 242 D3
Enfield EN3 18 C6
Surbiton KT5 198 B2
South Pl Mews EC2 242 D3
Southport Rd SE18 123 B2
South Quay Plaza E14 119 D4
South Quay Sta E14 119 D4
South Rd Brentford W5 109 D2
Edgware HA8 26 D2
Edmonton N9 18 A3
Feltham TW13 172 D5
Forest Hill SE23 162 D2
Hampton TW12 173 B4
Heston TW5 128 D6
Mitcham SW19 180 B4
Southall UB1 107 B5
Twickenham TW2 152 B1
West Drayton UB7 104 C3
South Residence IG3 58 B4
South Ridge BR2 209 C5
Southridge Pl SW20 178 D3
South Rise W2 247 B6
South Rise Prim Sch SE18 123 B1
South Rise Way SE18 123 B2
South Row SE3 142 D3
SOUTH RUISLIP 62 D4
South Ruislip Sta HA4 62 C3
Southsea Rd KT1 198 A5
South Sea St SE16 119 B3
Southside N7 71 D4
South Side W6 111 D3
Southside Comm SW19 178 D4
Southside Ind Est SW8 269 A2
Southside Quarter 4 SW11 136 D3
Southside Sh Ctr SW18 157 D5
Southspring DA15 167 B4
South Sq
Hampstead Garden Suburb NW11 47 D3
WC1 241 A3
South St Bromley BR1 187 A1
Enfield EN3 18 D6
Isleworth TW7 131 A2
Mayfair W1 115 A5 248 B4
South Tenter St E1 95 D1 243 D1
South Terr
Muswell Hill N22 31 D1
Surbiton KT6 198 A3
SW7 114 C2 257 A4
South Thames Coll (Battersea Ctr) SW11 136 D4 267 D1
South Thames Coll (Putney Ctr) SW15 156 D6
South Thames Coll (Roehampton Ctr) SW15 156 A5
South Thames Coll (Tooting Ctr) SW17 180 C5
South Thames Coll (Wandsworth Ctr) SW18 157 D6
SOUTH TOTTENHAM 51 D3
South Tottenham Sta N15 51 D4
South Vale Harrow HA1 64 C4
West Norwood SE19 183 C4
Southvale Rd SE3 142 C3
South View BR1 187 C1
Wimbledon SW19 178 D4
Southview Ave NW10 67 D3
Southview Cl SW17 181 A5
South View Cl DA5 169 B5
South View Cres IG2 56 D3
South View Ct
8 Forest Hill SE23 162 C3
South Norwood SE19 183 A3
Southview Dr E18 55 B6
Southview Gdns SM6 219 C1
Southview Rd BR1 186 B6
South View Rd
Hornsey N8 50 A6
Pinner HA5 22 B4
South Villas NW1 71 D2
Southville SW8 137 D4 269 D1
Southville Cl
East Bedfont TW14 149 C3
West Ewell KT19 215 B1
Southville Cres TW14 149 C3
Southville Jun & Inf Schs TW14 149 D3
Southville Rd
East Bedfont TW14 149 C4
Thames Ditton KT7 197 B2
SOUTHWARK 117 B5
Southwark Bridge SE1, EC4 117 A6 252 B5
Southwark Bridge Rd SE1 117 A5 252 B3
Southwark Cath* SE1 117 B5 252 C4
Southwark Coll SE1 116 D4 251 C2
Southwark Coll (Blackfriars Ctr) SE1 251 C3
Southwark Coll (Camberwell Ctr) SE5 139 C5
Southwark Coll (Grange Ctr) SE1 263 B5
Southwark Coll (Surrey Docks Ctr) SE16 118 B3
Southwark Park Est 11 SE16 118 B2
Southwark Park Prim Sch SE16 118 B3
Southwark Park Rd SE16 118 A2
Southwark Pl BR1 210 B6
Southwark St SE1 117 A5 252 A3
Southwater Cl
Beckenham BR3 185 D3
8 Poplar E14 97 B1
Southway
Hampstead Garden Suburb NW11 47 D4
Hayes BR2 209 A2
Totteridge N20 13 C2
Wallington SM6 219 C4
West Barnes SW20 200 D5
South Way
Croydon CR0 223 A5
Friern Barnet N11 31 C4
Harrow HA2 41 C5
Lower Edmonton N9 18 C2
Wembley HA9 66 C3
Southway Cl 9 W12 112 B4
Southwell Ave UB5 63 C2
Southwell Gdns SW7 256 A3
Southwell Grove Rd E11 76 C6
Southwell Ho
8 Bermondsey SE16 118 B2
13 Stoke Newington N16 73 C3
Southwell Rd
Camberwell SE5 139 A2
Harrow HA3 43 D3
Thornton Heath CR0 204 C3
South Western Rd TW1 153 B5
Southwest Rd E11 54 B1
South Wharf Rd W2 92 B1 236 D2
Southwick Mews W2 236 D2
Southwick Pl W2 237 A1
Southwick St W2 92 C1 237 A2
Southwick Yd W2 237 A1
SOUTH WIMBLEDON 179 D4
South Wimbledon Sta SW19 179 D3
South Wlk
Coney Hall BR4 224 C5
Hayes UB3 83 B2
Southwold Dr IG11 80 A3
Southwold Mans W9 91 C4
Southwold Prim Sch E5 74 B6
Southwold Rd DA5 169 D5
Upper Clapton E5 74 C6
Southwood Ave
Highgate N6 49 B2
Kingston u T KT2, KT3 177 A2
Southwood Cl BR1 210 B5
North Cheam KT4 200 D1
Southwood Ct EC1 234 C1
Hampstead Garden Suburb NW11 47 D4
Southwood Dr KT5 199 A1
South Woodford Sta E18 37 B1
Southwood Gdns
Hinchley Wood KT10 213 A5
Ilford IG2 56 D5
Southwood Hall N6 49 B3
Southwood Ho
New Eltham SE9 166 D2
Notting Hill W11 244 A6
Southwood Hospl (Geriatric) N6 49 A2
Southwood Hts N6 49 B2
Southwood La N6 49 A2
Southwood Lawn Rd N6 49 B2
Southwood Mans N6 49 B3
Southwood Park N6 49 A2
Southwood Prim Sch RM9 81 A4
Southwood Rd SE9 166 D2
Woolwich SE28 124 B5
Southwood Smith Ho 4 E2 96 B4
Southwood Smith St N1 234 C5
South Worple Ave SW14 133 C2
Southwyck Ho SW9 138 C1
South Yd EC1 242 C4
Sovereign Bsns Ctr EN3 7 B2
Sovereign Cl Ealing W5 87 C2
Ruislip HA4 39 C1
Stepney E1 118 B6
Sovereign Cres SE16 119 A6
Sovereign Ct BR2 210 B3
East Molesey KT8 195 B5
Harlington UB7 126 D5
3 Richmond TW9 132 B1
13 Stepney E1 118 B6
Sovereign Gr HA0 65 D5
Sovereign Ho
Ashford TW15 170 A6
23 Bethnal Green E1 96 B3
Chislehurst BR7 189 B3
Edgware NW7 27 B6
3 Wimbledon SW19 179 A4
Woolwich SE18 122 B3
Sovereign Mews
Barnet EN4 2 D2
6 Haggerston E2 95 D5
Sovereign Pk NW10 88 D3
Sovereign Pl HA1 42 D4
Sovereign Rd IG11 102 C4
Sovreign Ct HA6 22 A2
Sowerby Cl SE9 166 B6
Space Apartments N22 32 B3
Space Bsns Pk NW10 88 D4
Spa Central 1 SW16 182 A3
Spa Cl SE19 183 C2
Spa Ct
12 Bermondsey SE16 118 A3
Streatham SW16 182 B6
Spafield St EC1 241 A6
Spa Hill CR7, SE19 183 B2
Spalding Cl HA8 27 C3
Spalding Ct HA8 26 B6
Spalding Ho SE4 163 A6
Spalding Rd
Hendon NW4 46 C3
Streatham SW17 181 B5
Spanby Rd E3 97 C3
Spangate SE3 142 D2
Spaniards Cl NW11 48 B1
Spaniards End NW3 48 B1
Spaniards Rd NW3 70 A6
Spanish Pl W1 238 B2
Spanish Rd SW18 158 A6
Spanswick Lo 2 N15 50 D5
Spa Rd SE16 117 D3 263 D5
Sparkbridge Rd HA1 42 C5
Sparkes Cl BR2 209 B5
Sparke Terr 2 E16 98 D1
Sparkford Gdns N11 31 A5
Sparkford Ho SW11 266 D2
Sparks Cl Acton W3 89 B1
Dagenham RM8 80 D6
Hampton TW12 173 A4
Sparrow Cl TW12 173 A4
Sparrow Ct E4 36 A4
Sparrow Dr BR5 211 B1
Sparrow Farm Com Jun Sch KT17 216 B4
Sparrow Farm Dr TW14 150 D4
Sparrow Farm Inf Sch TW14 150 C4
Sparrow Farm Jun Sch TW14 150 C4
Sparrow Farm Rd KT17, KT4 216 B4
Sparrow Gn RM10 81 D5
Sparrow's Farm L Ctr SE9 167 A4
Sparrows Herne WD23 8 A4
Sparrows La SE9 167 A3
Sparrows Way WD23 8 A4
Sparsholt Rd
Barking IG11 101 C6
Finsbury Pk N19 50 B1
Sparta St SE10 142 A4
Spa Sch SE1 118 A2
Spa View 6 SW16 160 B1
Speakers' Corner* W1 114 D6 247 D6
Speaker's Ct 3 CR0 205 B1
Speakman Ho SE4 141 A2
Spearman St 8 SE18 144 C6
Spear Mews SW5 113 C2 255 B3
Spearpoint Gdns IG2 57 D5
Spears Rd N19 50 A1
Speart La TW5 129 A5
Spectacle Works E13 99 C4
Spectrum Ho NW5 71 A4
Spectrum Twr 1 IG1 79 A6
Spedan Cl NW3 70 A5
Speechly Mews E8 73 D3
Speed Ho EC2 242 C4
Speedwell Ct 9 N12 29 D6
Speedwell Ho 11 N12 29 D6
Speedwell St 5 SE8 141 C5
Speedy Pl WC1 233 A1
Speer Rd KT7 196 D3
Speirs Cl KT3 199 D3
Spekehill SE9 166 B1
Speke Rd CR7 183 B1
Speldhurst Cl 2 BR2 208 D4
Speldhurst Rd
Bedford Pk W4 111 B3
Homerton E9 74 D1
Spellbrook Wlk N1 235 B6
Spelman Ho 15 E1 96 A2
Spelman St E1 96 A2
Spelthorne Coll TW15 170 B6
Spelthorne Gr TW16 171 D3
Spelthorne Inf Sch TW15 171 B4
Spelthorne Jun Sch TW15 171 B4
Spelthorne La TW15, TW17 171 A2
Spence Cl SE16 119 B4
Spencer Ave
Bowes Pk N13 32 B4
Hayes UB4 84 A2
Spencer Cl BR6 227 D6
Church End N3 29 C1
Ealing NW10 88 B4
Woodford IG8 37 C5
Spencer Ct 5 BR6 227 A3
6 Finchley N3 29 D3
Wimbledon SW20 178 B2
Spencer Dr N2 48 A3
Spencer Gdns SW14 155 A6
Spencer Hill SW19 179 A3
Spencer Hill Rd SW19 179 A3
Spencer Ho
31 Clapham SW8 137 D3
Hendon NW4 46 B4
24 Putney SW19 156 D3
Vale of Health NW3 70 B5
Wimbledon SW19 156 D1
Spencer House Mus* SW1 115 C5 249 A3
Spencer Mews
Fulham W6 264 A6
South Lambeth SW9 270 C1
Spencer Park Ct SW18 158 B6
Spencer Pk
East Molesey KT8 196 A4
Wandsworth SW18 158 B6
Spencer Pl
16 Islington N1 72 D1
SW1 259 B5
Thornton Heath CR0 205 B2
Spencer Rd Acton W3 111 A5
Bromley BR1 186 D3
Carshalton CR4 203 A2
Chingford E17 36 A1
Chiswick W4 133 A5
East Molesey KT8 196 A4
Friern Barnet N11 31 B6
Harrow HA3 24 C1
Hornsey Vale N8 50 B4
Hounslow TW3, TW5, TW7 130 A4
Ilford IG3 57 D1
Mitcham CR4 203 A6
Newham E6 99 D6
South Croydon CR2 221 C3
Tottenham N17 34 A2
Twickenham TW2 152 C2
Wandsworth SW18 158 B6
Wembley HA0 65 C6
Wimbledon SW20 178 B2
Spencer Rise NW5 71 B5
Spencer St
Finsbury EC1 94 D4 234 C1
Southall UB2 106 D4
Spencer Wlk
23 Hampstead NW3 70 A4
Putney SW15 134 D1
Spencer Yd SE3 142 D3
Spenlow Ho 2 SE16 118 A3
Spenser Ct 5 TW10 175 D6
Spenser Gr N16 73 C4
Spenser Mews SE21 161 B3
Spenser Rd SE24 160 D6
Spenser St SW1 259 B6
Spens Ho WC1 240 C5
Spensley Wlk N16 73 B5
Speranza St SE18 123 D1
Sperling Rd N17 33 C1
Spert St E14 119 A6
Speyside N14 15 C5
Spey St E14 98 A2
Spezia Rd NW10 90 A5
Spice Ct
10 Battersea SW11 136 A2
2 St George in t East E1 118 A5
Spice Quay Htss SE1 253 D3
Spicer Cl
Brixton SE5, SW9 138 D3
Walton-on-T KT12 194 C3
Spicer Ct EN1 5 C2
Spicer Ho E2 96 A4
Spices Yd CR0 221 A4
Spigurnell Rd N17 33 B2
Spikes Bridge Rd UB1 107 A6
Spilsby Cl NW9 27 C1
Spindle Cl SE18 122 A3
Spindle Ho 8 DA15 168 A1
Spindlewood Gdns CR0 221 C4
Spindrift Ave E14 119 D2

Spinel Cl SE18 . . . . 123 D1
Spinnaker Cl IG11 . . . . 102 B4
Spinnaker Ct **2** KT1 . . . 175 D2
Spinnaker Ho **21** E14 . . . 119 C4
Spinnells Rd HA2 . . . . 41 B1
Spinney Cl
　Beckenham BR3 . . . . . . 207 D5
　New Malden KT3 . . . . . . 199 C4
　Worcester Pk KT4 . . . . . 215 D6
　Yiewsley UB7 . . . . 104 A6
Spinney Dr TW14 . . . . . . 149 A4
Spinney Gdns
　Dagenham RM9 . . . . 81 A3
　Dulwich SE19 . . . . 183 D5
Spinney Oak BR1 . . . . . . 188 B1
Spinneys The BR1 . . . . . 188 B1
Spinney The
　Barnes SW13 . . . . 134 B6
　Barnet EN5 . . . . 1 D3
　Cheam SM3 . . . . 216 C4
　DA14 . . . . 191 A5
　Edgware HA7 . . . . 26 A6
　Southgate N21 . . . . 16 C4
　Streatham SW16 . . . . . 159 D1
　Sunbury TW16 . . . . . . 172 A2
　Wembley HA0 . . . . 65 A5
Spire Ct **10** TW10 . . . . . 154 A5
Spire Ho W2 . . . . 246 B6
Spires The EN5 . . . . 1 A2
Spirit Quay E1 . . . . 118 B5
SPITALFIELDS 95 D2
Spital Sq E1 . . . . 95 C2 243 B4
Spital St E1 . . . . 96 A2
Spital Yd E1 . . . . 243 B4
Spitfire Bsns Pk CR0 . . . 220 C2
Spitfire Est The TW5 . . . 106 C1
Spitfire Rd SM6 . . . . 220 A1
Spitfire Way TW5 . . . . . . 106 C1
Splendour Wlk SE16 . . . . 118 C1
Spode Ho SE11 . . . . 261 A5
Spode Wlk NW3 . . . . 69 D3
Spondon Rd N15 . . . . 52 A5
Spoonbill Way UB4 . . . . . 84 D2
Spooner **8** NW9 . . . . 27 D3
Spooner Ho TW5 . . . . . . 129 C6
Spooner Wlk SM6 . . . . . 219 D3
Sporle Ct **6** SW11 . . . . 136 B2
Sportsbank St SE6 . . . . . 164 A4
Spottons Gr N17 . . . . 33 A2
Spout Hill CR0 . . . . 223 C3
Spratt Hall Rd E11 . . . . . . 55 A3
Spray St SE18 . . . . 122 D2
Spreighton Rd KT8 . . . . . 195 D5
Sprewell SW15 . . . . 157 A5
Spriggs Ho **14** N1 . . . . . 72 D1
Sprimont Pl
　SW3 . . . . 114 D1 257 C2
Springall St **9** SE15 . . . . 140 B5
Springalls Wharf **2**
　SE16 . . . . 118 A4
Springbank N21 . . . . 16 B5
Springbank Rd SE13 . . . 164 C5
Springbank Wlk NW1 . . . . 71 D1
Springbourne Ct BR3 . . . 186 A2
Spring Cl Barnet EN5 . . . . 12 D6
　Dagenham RM8 . . . . 58 D1
Springclose La SM3 . . . . 217 A2
Spring Cnr TW13 . . . . . . 149 D1
Spring Cott **10** W12 . . . . 112 A4
Spring Cotts KT6 . . . . . . 197 D4
Spring Court Rd EN2 . . . . . 4 C5
Springcroft Ave N2 . . . . . 48 D5
Spring Ct
　Brondesbury NW2 . . . . . . 69 B2
　Ealing W7 . . . . 108 B6
　Edgware HA8 . . . . 26 B5
　10 Wanstead E18 . . . . . . 55 B6
Springdale Rd N16 . . . . . . 73 B4
Spring Dr HA5 . . . . 40 A3
Springett Ho **15** SW2 . . . 160 B6
Springfield Bushey WD23 . . 8 B3
　South Norwood SE25 . . . 206 A6
　Upper Clapton E5 . . . . . . 52 B1
Springfield Ave
　Hampton TW12 . . . . . . 173 D4
　Hornsey N10 . . . . 49 C6
　Merton SW20 . . . . 201 B6
Springfield Cl
　Finchley N12 . . . . 29 D5
　Stanmore HA7 . . . . 9 A1
Springfield Com Prim Sch
　N16 . . . . 52 A3
Springfield Ct
　7 Dagenham W3 . . . . . 89 A1
　1 Friern Barnet N20 . . . 14 D1
　Hampstead NW3 . . . . . . 70 C1
　2 Ilford IG1 . . . . 78 D3
　9 Kingston u T KT1 . . . 198 A6
　Upper Clapton E5 . . . . . . 52 B1
　Wallington SM6 . . . . . . 219 B3
Springfield Dr IG2 . . . . . . 57 A3
Springfield Gdns BR1 . . . 210 B5
　Kingsbury NW9 . . . . 45 B4
　Ruislip HA4 . . . . 40 B1
　Upper Clapton E5 . . . . . . 52 B1
　West Wickham BR4 . . . . 223 D6
　Woodford IG8 . . . . 37 C3
Springfield Gr SE7 . . . . . 143 C6
　Sunbury TW16 . . . . . . 172 A2
Springfield Ho
　Acton W3 . . . . 111 A5
　1 Camberwell SE5 . . . . 139 C3
　13 Dalston E8 . . . . 73 D2
Springfield Hospl
　SW17 . . . . 158 C1
Springfield La NW6 . . . . . 91 D6

Springfield Mount
　NW9 . . . . 45 C4
Springfield Pl KT3 . . . . . 199 A5
Springfield Prim Sch
　TW16 . . . . 171 D2
Springfield Rd
　Ashford TW15 . . . . 170 B5
　Bexleyheath DA7 . . . . . 147 D1
　Bromley BR1 . . . . 210 B5
　Chingford E4 . . . . 20 C4
　Ealing W7 . . . . 108 C5
　Friern Barnet N11 . . . . . 31 C5
　Harrow HA1 . . . . 42 C3
　Hayes UB4 . . . . 106 C5
　Kingston u T KT1 . . . . . 198 A6
　Newham E15 . . . . 98 C4
　Penge SE26 . . . . 184 B5
　Plashet E6 . . . . 78 B1
　South Norwood CR7 . . . 183 A2
　St John's Wood
　　NW8 . . . . 92 A6 229 B5
　8 Teddington TW11 . . . 175 A5
　Tottenham Hale N15 . . . . 52 A5
　Twickenham TW2 . . . . . 151 C3
　Wallington SM6 . . . . . . 219 B3
　Walthamstow E17 . . . . . 53 B3
　Welling DA16 . . . . 146 B2
　Wimbledon SW19 . . . . . 179 B5
Springfield Rise SE26 . . . 162 B1
Springfields **18** EN5 . . . . 13 D6
Springfield Wlk
　3 BR6 . . . . 211 B1
　Paddington NW6 . . . . . . 91 D6
Spring Gdns
　East Molesey KT8 . . . . . 196 A5
　Islington N5 . . . . 73 A3
　SW1 . . . . 116 A5 250 A4
　Wallington SM6 . . . . . . 219 C3
　Woodford IG8 . . . . 37 C3
Spring Gr
　Brentford W4 . . . . 132 C6
　Hampton TW12 . . . . . . 173 D2
　Loughton IG10 . . . . 21 D5
　Mitcham CR4 . . . . 181 A4
SPRING GROVE 130 C3
Spring Grove Cres TW3,
　TW5 . . . . 130 A4
Spring Grove Prim Sch
　TW7 . . . . 130 B3
Spring Grove Rd
　Hounslow TW3, TW5,
　　TW7 . . . . 130 A4
　Richmond TW10 . . . . . . 154 B6
Springhallow Sch W13 . . 87 A1
Spring Hill
　Forest Hill SE26 . . . . . . 184 C6
　Upper Clapton E5 . . . . . . 52 A2
Springhill Cl SE5 . . . . . . 139 B2
Spring Ho
　Merton SW19 . . . . 179 B2
　WC1 . . . . 234 A1
Springhurst Cl CR0 . . . . . 223 B4
Spring La
　Croydon SE25 . . . . 206 B3
　Muswell Hill N10 . . . . . . 49 A6
　Upper Clapton E5 . . . . . . 52 B1
Spring Lake HA7 . . . . 25 B6
Spring Mews W1 . . . . . . 237 D4
SPRING PARK 223 B5
Spring Park Ave CR0 . . . 222 D6
Springpark Dr
　Beckenham BR3 . . . . . . 208 A6
　Stoke Newington N4 . . . . 51 A1
Spring Park Prim Sch
　CR0 . . . . 223 C5
Spring Park Rd CR0 . . . . 222 D6
Spring Pl
　Camden Town NW5 . . . . . 71 B3
　Church End N3 . . . . 29 C1
Springpond Rd RM9 . . . . . 81 A3
Spring Rd TW13 . . . . . . 149 D1
Springrice Rd SE13 . . . . 164 B5
Spring Shaw Rd BR5 . . . 190 A2
Spring St W2 . . . . 92 B1 236 C1
Spring Terr TW10 . . . . . . 154 A6
Springtide Cl **10** SE15 . . 140 A4
Spring Vale DA7 . . . . 147 D1
Springvale Ave TW8 . . . . 110 A1
Springvale Ct SE12 . . . . 143 A1
Springvale Terr **5**
　W14 . . . . 112 D3
Spring Villa Rd HA8 . . . . . 26 C3
Springwater WC1 . . . . . 240 C4
Springwater Cl SE18 . . . 144 C4
Springway HA1 . . . . 42 B2
Springwell Ave NW10 . . . 89 D6
Springwell Cl SW16 . . . . 182 B6
Springwell Ct TW5 . . . . . 128 D3
Springwell Jun & Inf Schs
　TW5 . . . . 129 A5
Springwell Rd
　Heston TW5 . . . . 128 D4
　West Norwood SW16 . . . 182 C5
Spring Wlk E1 . . . . 96 A2
Springwood Cl **8** E3 . . . . 97 C5
Springwood Cres HA8 . . . 11 A2
Springwood Ct CR2 . . . . 221 C4
Sprowston Mews E7 . . . . 77 A3
Sprowston Rd E7 . . . . . . 77 A3
Spruce Ct W5 . . . . 110 A3
Sprucedale Gdns CR0 . . . 222 D4
Spruce Hills Rd E17 . . . . 36 A1
Spruce Ho
　2 Brentford TW8 . . . . 131 C5
　16 Rotherhithe SE16 . . 118 D4
Spruce Pk BR2 . . . . 208 D5
Sprules Rd SE4 . . . . 141 A3
Spurfield KT8 . . . . 195 D6
Spurgeon Ave SE19 . . . . 183 B2
Spurgeon Rd SE19 . . . . . 183 B3

Spurgeon's Coll SE25 . . . 183 C1
Spurgeon St
　SE1 . . . . 117 B3 262 C6
Spur Ho **10** SW19 . . . . . 179 D2
Spurling Rd
　Dagenham RM8 . . . . 81 B2
　East Dulwich SE22 . . . . 139 D1
Spur Rd Brentford TW7 . . 131 B5
　Edgware HA8 . . . . 26 A6
　Feltham TW14 . . . . 128 B1
　SE1 . . . . 116 C4 251 A2
　Tottenham N15 . . . . 51 B5
　Wallend IG11 . . . . 101 A4
Spurstowe Rd E8 . . . . 74 B2
Spurstowe Terr E8 . . . . . . 74 B3
Spurway Par **2** IG2 . . . . 56 B4
Square Rigger Row **7**
　SW11 . . . . 136 A2
Square The
　Hammersmith W6 . . . . . 112 C1
　Hayes UB11 . . . . 105 B5
　Ilford IG1 . . . . 56 C2
　Leyton E10 . . . . 76 A5
　12 Richmond TW10 . . . 153 D6
　SW6 . . . . 265 A1
　Wallington SM5 . . . . . . 219 A3
　Woodford IG8 . . . . 37 A5
Squarey St SW17 . . . . . . 158 A1
Square St **2** EC2 . . . . . 205 C1
Squire Gdns NW8 . . . . . 229 C1
Squire's Almshouses **7**
　E17 . . . . 53 D5
Squires Bridge Rd
　KT17 . . . . 192 B5
Squires Ct Finchley N3 . . . 30 A2
　SW4 . . . . 270 B1
　Wimbledon SW19 . . . . . 179 C6
Squires Ho **3** SE18 . . . . 144 D6
Squires La N3 . . . . 30 A2
Squire's Mount NW3 . . . . 70 B5
Squires Rd TW17 . . . . . . 192 C5
Squires The RM7 . . . . 59 D3
Squires Wlk TW15 . . . . . 171 B3
Squires Wood Dr BR7 . . . 188 B3
Squirrel Cl TW4 . . . . 128 C2
Squirrel Mews W13 . . . . 109 A6
Squirrels Cl
　Hillingdon UB10 . . . . . . 60 C1
　North Finchley N12 . . . . . 30 A6
　Orpington BR6 . . . . 211 C1
Squirrels Ct KT4 . . . . 215 D6
Squirrels Gn KT4 . . . . . . 216 A6
Squirrel's La IG9 . . . . 21 D1
Squirrels The
　Bushey WD23 . . . . 8 B5
　Lewisham SE13 . . . . . . 142 B2
　Pinner HA5 . . . . 41 B6
Squirrels Trad Est
　UB3 . . . . 105 D3
Squirries St **2** E2 . . . . . 96 A4
Stable Cl
　Kingston u T KT2 . . . . . 176 B4
　Northolt UB5 . . . . 85 C5
Stable Ct **4** SE6 . . . . . 164 A4
Stable Ho **8** SE16 . . . . 118 C4
Stable Mews
　Twickenham TW1 . . . . . 152 D3
　West Norwood SE27 . . . 183 A5
Stables End BR6 . . . . . . 227 A5
Stables The IG9 . . . . 21 C4
Stables Way
　SE11 . . . . 116 C1 261 A2
Stable Way W10 . . . . 90 C1
Stable Wlk N2 . . . . 30 B2
Stable Yd Rd
　SW1 . . . . 115 C4 249 B2
Staburn Ct HA8 . . . . 27 A1
Stacey Ave N18 . . . . 34 C6
Stacey Cl E10 . . . . 54 B4
Stacey St Highbury N7 . . . 72 C5
　Soho WC2 . . . . . 93 D1 239 D1
Stack Ho SW1 . . . . 258 B3
Stackhouse St SW3 . . . . 257 C6
Stacy Path **13** SE5 . . . . 139 C5
Staddon Cl BR3 . . . . 207 A5
Stadium Bsns Ctr HA9 . . . 66 D5
Stadium Rd
　Hendon NW2 . . . . 46 C2
　SE7, SE18 . . . . 144 B6
Stadium Rd E NW2 . . . . . 46 C2
Stadium Ret Pk HA9 . . . . 66 C5
Stadium St
　SW10 . . . . 136 A5 266 B3
Stadium Way HA9 . . . . . . 66 C4
Staffa Rd E10 . . . . 53 A1
Stafford Cl Cheam SM3 . . 217 A2
　Maida Vale NW6 . . . . . . 91 C4
　Southgate N14 . . . . 15 C6
　Walthamstow E17 . . . . . *. . 53 B3
Stafford Cripps Ho
　30 Bethnal Green E2 . . . 96 C4
　SW6 . . . . 264 D5
Stafford Cross CR0 . . . . 220 B3
Stafford Cross Bsns Pk
　CR0 . . . . 220 B3
Stafford Ct
　Croydon CR0 . . . . 220 C4
　Ealing W7 . . . . 86 D1
　Kensington W8 . . . . . . 255 B6
　South Lambeth SW8 . . . 270 A2
Stafford Gdns CR0 . . . . . 220 B3
Stafford Ho SE1 . . . . 263 D2
Stafford Mans
　13 Hammersmith
　　W14 . . . . 112 D3
　14 Stockwell SW4 . . . . 138 A1
　SW11 . . . . 267 C3
Stafford Morris Ho **9**
　E15 . . . . 98 C6

Stafford Pl
　Richmond TW10 . . . . . . 154 B4
　SW1 . . . . 115 C3 259 A6
Stafford Rd Bow E3 . . . . . 97 B5
　Harrow HA3 . . . . 24 A3
　Kingston u T KT3 . . . . . 199 A6
　Maida Vale NW6 . . . . . . 91 C4
　Plashet E7 . . . . 77 D2
　Ruislip HA4 . . . . 61 D4
　Sidcup DA14 . . . . 189 C6
　Wallington CR0, SM6 . . . 220 A3
Staffordshire Ho N3 . . . . 47 A6
Staffordshire St
　Peckham SE15 . . . . 140 A4
　Peckham SE15 . . . . 140 B4
Stafford St W1 . . . . 249 A4
Stafford Terr
　W8 . . . . 113 C3 255 A6
Stag Cl HA8 . . . . 27 A1
Stag Ct **16** SM6 . . . . . . 219 B2
Stagg Hill EN4 . . . . 2 C6
Stag Hts **1** IG9 . . . . 21 B2
Stag La Chigwell IG9 . . . . 21 B2
　Edgware HA8, NW9 . . . . 45 A6
　Roehampton SW15 . . . . 155 D2
Stag Lane Fst & Mid Schs
　HA8 . . . . 26 C1
Stags Ct KT7 . . . . 197 A2
Stagshaw Ho **17** SE22 . . 139 C2
Stags Way TW7 . . . . 130 C6
Stainbank Rd CR4 . . . . . 203 B6
Stainby Cl UB7 . . . . 104 A3
Stainby Rd N15 . . . . 51 D5
Staincliffe Ho **5** SM1 . . 218 A4
Stainer Ho SE9 . . . . 143 C1
Stainer St SE1 . . . . 252 D3
Staines Ave SM3 . . . . . . 216 D6
Staines By-Pass
　TW15 . . . . 170 A4
Staines Rd
　East Bedfont TW14 . . . . 149 B4
　Feltham TW14, TW3 . . . . 150 C6
　Hounslow TW3 . . . . . . 129 C1
　Ilford IG1 . . . . 79 B4
　Twickenham TW2 . . . . . 152 A1
　Twickenham TW13,
　　TW2 . . . . 151 D1
Staines Rd E TW12,
　TW16 . . . . 172 C2
Staines Rd W TW15 . . . . 171 B3
Staines Wlk DA14 . . . . . 190 C4
Stainforth Cl TW15 . . . . 171 B5
Stainforth Rd Ilford IG2 . . 57 B2
　Walthamstow E17 . . . . . 53 C5
Staining La EC2 . . . . 242 B2
Stainmore Cl BR7 . . . . . 189 B2
Stainsbury St **2** E2 . . . . 96 C5
Stainsby Rd E14 . . . . 97 C1
Stainton Rd Enfield EN3 . . . 6 C4
　Lewisham SE13 . . . . . . 164 B4
Stalbridge Flats W1 . . . . 238 B1
Stalbridge Ho **1** NW1 . . 232 A3
Stalbridge St NW1 . . . . . 237 B4
Stalham St **1** SE16 . . . . 118 C3
Stambourne Ho SW8 . . . 270 B2
Stambourne Way
　Penge SE19 . . . . 183 D3
　West Wickham BR4 . . . . 224 A5
Stamford Bridge Stadium
　(Chelsea FC)
　SW6 . . . . 135 D5 265 C4
Stamford Brook Ave
　W6 . . . . 111 D3
Stamford Brook Gdns **1**
　W6 . . . . 111 D3
Stamford Brook Mans **2**
　W6 . . . . 111 D3
Stamford Brook Rd
　W6 . . . . 111 D3
Stamford Brook Sta
　W6 . . . . 111 D2
Stamford Cl
　Harrow HA3 . . . . 24 C3
　2 London NW3 . . . . . . 70 A5
　Southall UB1 . . . . 107 C6
　Tottenham Hale N15 . . . . 52 A5
Stamford Cotts SW10 . . . 265 D4
Stamford Ct
　Chiswick W6 . . . . 112 A2
　Edgware HA8 . . . . 26 B6
Stamford Dr BR2 . . . . . . 208 D5
Stamford Gdns RM9 . . . . 80 C1
Stamford Gr E **1** N16 . . . 52 A1
Stamford Gr W **4** N16 . . . 52 A1
STAMFORD HILL 51 D1
Stamford Hill N16 . . . . . . 51 D1
Stamford Hill Mans **1**
　N16 . . . . 51 D1
Stamford Hill Prim Sch
　N15 . . . . 51 B3
Stamford Hill Sta N16 . . . 51 C2
Stamford Ho N15 . . . . . . 52 A4
Stamford Hospl W6 . . . . 112 A2
Stamford Lo **2** N16 . . . . 51 D2
Stamford Mans **2** N16 . . 52 A1
Stamford Rd
　Dagenham RM9 . . . . 80 C1
　Kingsland N1 . . . . 73 C2
　Newham E6 . . . . 100 A3
　South Tottenham N15 . . . 52 A4
Stamford St
　SE1 . . . . 116 C5 251 B4
Stamp Pl E2 . . . . 95 D4
Stanard Cl N16 . . . . 51 C2
Stanborough Cl TW12 . . . 173 B4
Stanborough Ho **4** E3 . . . 97 B2
Stanborough Pas E8 . . . . 73 D2
Stanborough Rd TW3,
　TW7 . . . . 130 B2

Stanbridge Mans
　SW15 . . . . 134 C2
Stanbridge Pl N21 . . . . . . 16 D2
Stanbridge Rd SW15 . . . 134 C2
Stanbrook Ct W1 . . . . . . 249 A4
Stanbrook Rd SE2 . . . . . 124 B4
Stanburn Fst & Mid Schs
　HA7 . . . . 25 C3
Stanbury Ct **16** NW3 . . . . 70 D2
Stanbury Rd
　Nunhead SE15 . . . . 140 D3
　Peckham SE15 . . . . 140 B3
Stancroft NW9 . . . . 45 C4
Standale Gr HA4 . . . . 39 A4
Standard Ind Est E16 . . . 122 B4
Standard Pl **13** EC2 . . . . 95 C4
Standard Rd
　Becontree NW10 . . . . . . 89 B3
　Belvedere DA17 . . . . . . 125 C1
　DA6 . . . . 147 A1
　Enfield EN3 . . . . 7 A6
　Hounslow TW4 . . . . . . 129 A2
Standen Rd SW18 . . . . . 157 C4
Standfield Gdns RM10 . . . 81 C2
Standfield Rd RM10 . . . . 81 C3
Standish Ho
　6 Chiswick W6 . . . . . 112 A2
　SE9 . . . . 143 B1
Standish Rd W6 . . . . 112 A2
Standlake Point **1**
　SE23 . . . . 162 D1
Standor Ho **7** CR4 . . . . 202 D6
Stane Cl SW19 . . . . 179 D3
Stanedge Ct SW16 . . . . 182 A5
Stane Gr SW4 . . . . 138 A3
Stanesgate Ho **20**
　SE15 . . . . 140 A5
Stanetta Ct **3** RM6 . . . . . 58 B2
Stane Way SE18 . . . . . . 144 A5
Stanfield Ho
　8 Northolt UB5 . . . . . . 84 D5
　NW8 . . . . 236 B6
Stanfield Rd **14** E3 . . . . . 97 A5
Stanford Cl
　Hampton TW12 . . . . . . 173 B4
　Romford RM7 . . . . 59 D3
　Ruislip HA4 . . . . 39 A3
Stanford Ct
　Friern Barnet N11 . . . . . . 31 A5
　Kensington W8 . . . . . . 255 D5
　Walham Green SW6 . . . . 265 D1
Stanford Ho IG11 . . . . . . 102 B5
Stanford Pl
　SE1 . . . . 117 C2 263 A3
Stanford Prim Sch
　SW16 . . . . 181 D2
Stanford Rd
　Friern Barnet N11 . . . . . . 30 D5
　Thornton Heath SW16 . . 182 A1
　W8 . . . . 113 D3 255 D6
Stanford St SW1 . . . . . . 259 C3
Stanford Way SW16 . . . . 181 D1
Stangate SE1 . . . . 260 D6
Stangate Cres WD6 . . . . 11 C6
Stangate Gdns HA7 . . . . . 25 B6
Stangate Lo N21 . . . . 16 B4
Stangate Mansi TW1 . . . 152 D1
Stanger Rd SE25 . . . . . . 206 A5
Stanhope Ave
　Harrow HA3 . . . . 24 B2
　Hayes BR2 . . . . 209 A1
　Hendon N3 . . . . 47 B6
Stanhope Cl **23** SE16 . . . 118 D4
Stanhope Ct N3 . . . . 29 B1
Stanhope Gate W1 . . . . . 248 B6
Stanhope Gdns
　Crouch End N6 . . . . 49 C3
　Dagenham RM8 . . . . 81 B5
　Edgware NW7 . . . . 27 D5
　Redbridge IG1 . . . . 56 B1
　Stoke Newington N4 . . . . 51 A3
　SW7 . . . . 114 A2 256 B4
Stanhope Gr BR3 . . . . . . 207 B5
Stanhope Ho
　Crouch End N6 . . . . 49 C3
　5 Friern Barnet N11 . . . 31 B6
　4 Putney SW15 . . . . . 156 C6
　SE8 . . . . 141 B5
Stanhope Mews E
　SW7 . . . . 114 A2 256 B4
Stanhope Mews S
　SW7 . . . . 256 B3
Stanhope Mews W
　SW7 . . . . 114 A2 256 B4
Stanhope Par NW1 . . . . . 232 A2
Stanhope Park Rd UB6 . . 86 A3
Stanhope Pl W2 . . . . 237 C1
Stanhope Prim Sch
　UB6 . . . . 86 A3
Stanhope Rd
　Barnet EN5 . . . . 12 D5
　Crouch End N6 . . . . 49 C2
　DA7 . . . . 147 A3
　Dagenham RM8 . . . . 81 B5
　North Finchley N12 . . . . . 30 A5
　Sidcup DA15 . . . . 190 A6
　Southall UB6 . . . . 86 A2
　South Croydon CR0 . . . . 221 C5
　Wallington SM5 . . . . . . 219 A1
　Walthamstow E17 . . . . . 53 D4
Stanhope Row W1 . . . . . 248 C5
Stanhope St
　NW1 . . . . 93 C4 232 A1
Stanhope Terr
　W2 . . . . 114 B6 246 D6
Stanier Cl SW5 . . . . 254 D1
Stanlake Mews **7**
　W12 . . . . 112 C5
Stanlake Rd W12 . . . . . . 112 C5

Stanlake Villas **8**
　W12 . . . . 112 C5
Stanley Ave
　Barking IG11 . . . . 101 D5
　Beckenham BR2, BR3 . . . 208 A6
　Dagenham RM8 . . . . 59 B2
　Greenford UB6 . . . . 86 A6
　Wembley HA0 . . . . 66 A1
　West Barnes KT3 . . . . . 200 A4
Stanley Bldgs NW1 . . . 233 A6
Stanley Cl Eltham SE9 . . . 167 A3
　SW8 . . . . 270 C5
　Wembley HA0 . . . . 66 A1
Stanley Cohen Ho EC1 . . 242 A5
Stanley Cres
　W11 . . . . 113 B6 244 C6
Stanleycroft Cl TW7 . . . . 130 C4
Stanley Ct
　Belmont SM2 . . . . 217 D1
　11 Ealing W5 . . . . 87 C2
　Wallington SM5 . . . . . . 219 A1
　Wimbledon SW19 . . . . . 179 C4
Stanley Gardens Rd
　TW11 . . . . 174 C5
Stanley Gdns
　Bedford Pk W3 . . . . 111 A4
　Cricklewood NW2 . . . . . 68 C3
　Mitcham CR4 . . . . 181 A4
　W11 . . . . 244 C6
　Wallington SM6 . . . . . . 219 C2
Stanley Glynn Ct BR7 . . . 188 C5
Stanley Gr
　Clapham SW11 . . . . . . 137 A3
　Thornton Heath CR0 . . . 204 C3
Stanley Ho
　35 Clapham SW8 . . . . 137 D3
　Leytonstone E11 . . . . . . 54 C3
　22 Poplar E14 . . . . 97 C1
　Wembley HA0 . . . . 66 A1
Stanley Holloway Ct
　E16 . . . . 99 A1
Stanley Inf Sch KT11 . . . 174 C6
Stanley Jun Sch KT11 . . . 174 C6
Stanley Mans SW10 . . . 266 B6
　Upper Tooting SW17 . . . 158 D2
Stanley Park Dr HA0 . . . . 88 B4
Stanley Park High Sch
　SM5 . . . . 219 A2
Stanley Park Inf Sch
　SM5 . . . . 218 D1
Stanley Park Jun Sch
　SM5 . . . . 218 D1
Stanley Park Rd SM5,
　SM6 . . . . 219 A2
Stanley Rd
　Acton Green W3 . . . . . . 111 A3
　Ashford TW15 . . . . 170 A5
　Belmont SM2 . . . . 217 D1
　BR6 . . . . 211 D1
　Bromley BR2 . . . . 209 C5
　Chingford E4 . . . . 20 B3
　East Finchley N2 . . . . . . 48 B6
　Edmonton N9 . . . . 17 D2
　Enfield EN1 . . . . 5 C2
　Friern Barnet N11 . . . . . . 31 D5
　Harringay N15 . . . . 50 D5
　Harrow HA2 . . . . 64 A6
　2 Hendon NW9 . . . . . . 46 A2
　Ilford IG1 . . . . 79 B6
　Isleworth TW3 . . . . 130 A4
　Mill Meads E15 . . . . 98 B6
　Mitcham CR4 . . . . 181 A4
　Morden SM4 . . . . 201 C5
　Mortlake SW14 . . . . . . 132 D1
　Muswell Hill N10 . . . . . . 31 B4
　Northwood HA6 . . . . 22 A2
　Plashet E12 . . . . 78 A4
　Sidcup DA14 . . . . 168 A1
　Southall UB1 . . . . 107 A6
　Teddington TW11, TW2 . . 174 C5
　Thornton Heath CR0 . . . 204 C3
　Twickenham TW2 . . . . . 152 B1
　Wallington SM5 . . . . . . 219 A1
　Walthamstow E10 . . . . . 53 D3
　Wembley HA9 . . . . 66 B2
　Wimbledon SW19 . . . . . 179 C4
　Woodford E18 . . . . 36 D2
Stanley St SE14, SE8 . . . 141 B5
Stanley Studios SW10 . . 266 B6
Stanley Tech High Sch for
　Boys SE25 . . . . 205 D6
Stanley Terr **8** N19 . . . . 72 A6
Stanliff Ho **8** E14 . . . . . 119 C3
Stanmer St SW11 . . . . . 136 C3
STANMORE 25 A5
Stanmore Coll HA7 . . . . . 25 C4
Stanmore Gdns
　Richmond TW9 . . . . . . 132 B2
　Sutton SM1 . . . . 218 A5
Stanmore Hill HA7 . . . . . . 25 A6
Stanmore Ho **21** SW8 . . 137 D3
Stanmore Lo HA7 . . . . . . 25 B6
Stanmore Pl NW1 . . . . . 231 D1
Stanmore Rd
　Harringay N15 . . . . 50 D5
　Leytonstone E11 . . . . . . 54 D1
　Richmond TW9 . . . . . . 132 B2
Stanmore St N1 . . 94 B6 233 C6
Stanmore Sta HA7 . . . . . 25 C6
Stanmore Terr **3**
　BR3 . . . . 185 C1
Stanmuir Lo NW9 . . . . . . 45 A4
Stannard Cotts **27** E1 . . . 96 C5
Stannard Ct SE6 . . . . . . 163 D3
Stannard Mews E8 . . . . . 74 A2
Stannard Rd E8 . . . . 74 A2
Stannary Pl SE11 . . . . . 261 B1
Stannary St
　SE11 . . . . 116 C1 261 B1
Stannet Way SM6 . . . . . 219 C4

Stansbury Sq 3 W10 . . . 91 A4
Stansfeld Ho SE1 . . . . . 263 D3
Stansfeld Rd E6 . . . . 99 D1
Stansfield Rd
Cranford TW4, TW5 . . . . 128 B3
Stockwell SW9 . . . . 138 B2
Stansgate Rd RM10 . . . . . 81 C5
Stanstead Cl BR2 . . . . . . 208 D3
Stanstead Gr SE23 . . . . . 163 B3
Stanstead Ho E3 . . . . 98 A3
Stanstead Manor SM1 . . 217 C2
Stanstead Rd
Forest Hill SE23, SE6 . . . 163 A3
Wanstead E11 . . . . 55 B4
Stansted Cres DA5 . . . . . 168 D3
Stansted Express Terminal
EC2 . . . . 243 A4
Stansted Rd TW6 . . . . . . 148 B5
Stanswood Gdns SE5 . . 139 C5
Stanthorpe Cl SW16 . . . . 182 A5
Stanthorpe Rd SW16 . . . 182 A5
Stanton Ave TW11 . . . . . 174 C4
Stanton Cl
Chessington KT19 . . . . . 214 D3
North Cheam KT4 . . . . . 200 D1
Stanton Ct 5 DA15 . . . . 168 A1
Finchley N3 . . . . 29 C2
Stoke Newington N16 . . . 51 B2
Stanton Ho 9 SE10 . . . . 142 A6
Stanton Rd
Barnes SW13 . . . . 133 D3
Thornton Heath CR0 . . . 205 A2
Wimbledon SW20 . . . . . 178 D2
Stanton Sq SE26 . . . . . . 185 B6
Stanton Way SE26 . . . . . 185 B6
Stanway Ct 23 N1 . . . . . . 95 C5
Stanway Gdns
Acton W3 . . . . 110 C5
Edgware HA8 . . . . 27 A5
Stanway St N1 . . . . 95 C5
STANWELL 148 A3
Stanwell Fields CE Prim
Sch TW19 . . . . 148 A4
Stanwell Rd
Ashford TW15 . . . . 170 A6
East Bedfont TW14, TW19,
TW6 . . . . 148 D4
Stanwell TW15 . . . . 148 A1
Stanwick Rd
W14 . . . . 113 B2 254 C3
Stanworth Ct TW5 . . . . . 129 C5
Stanworth St SE1 . . . . . 253 D1
Stanyhurst SE23 . . . . . . 163 A3
Stapenhill Rd HA0 . . . . . . 65 B5
Staplefield Cl
Pinner HA5 . . . . 23 A3
3 Streatham SW2 . . . . . 160 A3
Stapleford N17 . . . . 33 C1
Stapleford Ave IG2 . . . . . 57 C4
Stapleford Cl
Chingford E4 . . . . 20 A1
Kingston u T KT1 . . . . . . 198 C6
Putney SW19 . . . . 157 A4
Stapleford Rd HA0 . . . . . . 65 D1
Stapleford Way IG11 . . . 102 B4
Staplehurst Ct SW11 . . . 158 D5
Staplehurst Ho 18 E5 . . . 74 B3
Staplehurst Rd
Lewisham SE13 . . . . 164 C6
Sutton SM5 . . . . 218 C1
Staple Inn WC2 . . . . 241 A3
Staple Inn Bldgs WC2 . 241 A3
Staples Cl SE16 . . . . 119 A5
Staples Corner Bsns Pk
NW2 . . . . 46 B1
Staples Corner (East)
NW2 . . . . 46 B1
Staples Corner Ret Pk
NW2 . . . . 46 B1
Staples Corner (West)
NW2 . . . . 46 B1
Staple St SE1 . . . 117 B4 252 D1
Stapleton Gdns CR0 . . . . 220 C3
Stapleton Hall N4 . . . . 50 B2
Stapleton Hall Rd N4 . . . 50 B2
Stapleton Ho 19 E2 . . . . 96 B4
Stapleton Rd DA7 . . . . . . 147 B6
Orpington BR6 . . . . 227 D5
Upper Tooting SW17 . . . . 159 A1
Stapley Rd DA17 . . . . 125 C1
Stapylton Rd EN5 . . . . 1 A2
Star Alley EC3 . . . . 253 B6
Star and Garter Hill
TW10 . . . . 154 A4
Starboard Way E14 . . . . 119 C3
Starbuck Cl SE9 . . . . 166 C4
Star Cl EN3 . . . . 18 C5
Starcross St
NW1 . . . . 93 C4 232 B1
Star Ct UB10 . . . . 83 A3
Stardome* NW1 . . . . 238 A5
Starfield Rd W12 . . . . . . 112 A4
Star & Garter Mans
SW15 . . . . 134 D2
Star La E16 . . . . 98 C3
Starliner Ct N7 . . . . 72 C2
Starling Cl
Beckenham BR3 . . . . 207 A3
Buckhurst Hill IG9 . . . . . . 21 A3
Pinner HA5 . . . . 40 C6
Starling Ct E13 . . . . 99 B6
Starling Ho NW8 . . . . . . 230 A4
Starling Wlk TW12 . . . . . 173 A5
Starmans Cl RM9 . . . . . . 103 A6
Star Path UB5 . . . . 85 C5
Star Pl E1 . . . . 118 A6
Star Prim Sch E16 . . . . . . 98 C3
Star Rd Hillingdon UB10 . . . 83 A3
Hounslow TW7 . . . . 130 B3
W14 . . . . 113 B1 254 C1
Star St W2 . . . . . . 92 C1 237 A2
Starts Cl BR6 . . . . 226 C5
Starts Hill Ave BR6 . . . . . 226 D4
Starts Hill Rd BR6 . . . . . 226 D4
Starveall Cl UB7 . . . . 104 B3
Star Works NW10 . . . . 90 A4
Star Yd WC2 . . . . . 94 C1 241 A2
State Farm Ave BR6 . . . . 227 A4
Stateland Ct 10 N11 . . . . . 31 B6
Staten Gdns TW1 . . . . . . 152 D3
Statham Ct N7 . . . . 72 A5
Statham Gr
Edmonton N18 . . . . 33 C5
Stoke Newington N16 . . . . 73 B5
Statham Ho SW8 . . . . . 269 A2
Station App
Ashford TW15 . . . . 170 B6
Belmont SM2 . . . . 217 A1
Bexleyheath DA7 . . . . . . 147 A3
Chislehurst BR7 . . . . 188 C1
Dagenham NW10 . . . . 89 D4
Elmstead BR7 . . . . 188 A4
20 Finchley N12 . . . . 29 D6
Forest Gate E7 . . . . 77 B4
Friern Barnet N11 . . . . 31 B5
Fulham SW6 . . . . 135 A2
Greenford UB6 . . . . 64 B1
Hampton TW12 . . . . 173 C2
Hayes BR2 . . . . 209 A1
Hayes Town UB3 . . . . 105 D3
Hinchley Wood KT10 . . . . 212 D5
4 Kingston u T KT1,
KT2 . . . . 176 C2
Lewisham SE3 . . . . 143 B2
Mottingham SE9 . . . . 166 B3
New Barnet EN5 . . . . 2 A1
6 New Malden KT4 . . . . 200 A1
Orpington BR6 . . . . 227 D6
Penge SE26 . . . . 185 B5
Pinner HA5 . . . . 41 A6
Richmond TW9 . . . . 132 C4
Ruislip HA4 . . . . 39 D1
Shepperton TW17 . . . . . . 193 A4
3 South Croydon CR0 . . 221 B6
South Ruislip HA4 . . . . . . 62 B3
Streatham SW16 . . . . 181 D5
Sunbury TW16 . . . . 172 A2
1 Surbiton KT6 . . . . 198 A3
Walthamstow E17 . . . . 53 C4
Wanstead E11 . . . . 55 A4
Welling DA16 . . . . 146 A3
Wembley HA0 . . . . 65 B2
2 Woodford E18 . . . . 37 B1
Woodford IG8 . . . . 37 B4
Woodford IG9 . . . . 37 D6
Worcester Pk KT19 . . . . . 216 A3
Yiewsley UB7 . . . . 104 A5
Station Approach Rd
W4 . . . . 133 A5
Station Ave
5 Brixton SW9 . . . . 138 D2
Kingston u T KT3 . . . . . . 199 C6
14 Richmond TW9 . . . . . 132 C4
West Ewell KT19 . . . . . . 215 D1
Station Bldgs
Catford SE6 . . . . 163 C4
Merton SW20 . . . . 178 C1
Station Blgs W5 . . . . 110 B5
Station Cl Finchley N3 . . . . 29 C2
Hampton TW12 . . . . 173 D2
Station Cres
Ashford TW15 . . . . 170 A6
Greenwich SE3 . . . . 121 A1
Tottenham N15 . . . . 51 B5
Wembley HA0 . . . . 65 B2
Station Ct
Mitcham CR4 . . . . 202 C5
5 Nunhead SE15 . . . . . . 140 C3
South Tottenham N15 . . . . 51 D4
Wembley HA9 . . . . 43 C1
Stationers Hall Ct EC4 241 D1
Station Est BR3 . . . . 206 D5
Station Est 1 E18 . . . . . . 37 B1
Station Estate Rd
TW14 . . . . 150 B3
Station Gdns W4 . . . . . . 133 A5
Station Gr HA0 . . . . 66 A2
Station Hill BR2 . . . . 225 A6
Station House Mews
N9 . . . . 34 A6
Station Mans 9 N3 . . . . . 29 C2
Station Mews Terr 4
SE3 . . . . 121 A1
Station Par Acton W3 . . . . 88 C1
1 Ashford TW15 . . . . . . 170 B6
Barking IG11 . . . . 79 A1
Belmont HA3 . . . . 25 A1
Cockfosters EN4 . . . . 3 A1
Cricklewood NW2 . . . . 68 C2
Dagenham RM10 . . . . 81 C2
Ealing W5 . . . . 110 B5
Edgware HA8 . . . . 26 A3
Feltham TW14 . . . . 150 B4
Northolt UB5 . . . . 63 D4
4 Osidge N14 . . . . 15 D3
Richmond TW9 . . . . 132 C4
Ruislip HA4 . . . . 61 B6
South Harrow HA2 . . . . . . 63 D4
4 Upper Tooting
SW12 . . . . 159 A3
2 Wanstead E11 . . . . 55 A4
Woodford IG9 . . . . 37 D6
Station Pas
New Cross Gate
SE15 . . . . 140 C4
Woodford E18 . . . . 37 B1
Station Pl N4 . . . . 72 C6
Station Rd
Ashford TW15 . . . . 170 B6
Barkingside IG6 . . . . 57 B6
Station Rd *continued*
Barnes SW13 . . . . 133 D3
Beckenham BR2 . . . . 186 C1
Belvedere DA17 . . . . 125 C3
Bexleyheath DA7 . . . . . . 147 A2
Bromley BR1 . . . . 187 A2
Camden Town N19 . . . . . . 71 C5
Carshalton SM5 . . . . 218 D4
Chadwell Heath RM6 . . . . . 58 D2
Chessington KT9 . . . . . . 214 A3
Chingford E4 . . . . 20 B3
Church End N3 . . . . 29 C1
Claygate KT10 . . . . 212 C3
Croydon CR0 . . . . 205 A1
Edgware HA8 . . . . 26 C4
Edgware NW7 . . . . 27 C4
Esher KT10 . . . . 212 B6
Forest Gate E7 . . . . 77 A4
Friern Barnet N11 . . . . 31 B5
Greenhill HA1 . . . . 42 D4
Hampton TW12 . . . . 173 D2
Hampton Wick KT1 . . . . . 175 D2
Hanwell W7 . . . . 108 C5
Harlesden NW10 . . . . 89 D5
Hayes UB3 . . . . 105 C2
Hendon NW4 . . . . 46 A4
Hounslow TW3 . . . . 129 D1
Ilford IG1 . . . . 78 D5
Kingston u T KT2 . . . . . . 176 C2
Lewisham SE13 . . . . 142 A2
Leyton E10 . . . . 76 A5
Manor Pk E12 . . . . 78 A4
Merton SW19 . . . . 180 A2
New Barnet EN5 . . . . 13 D6
North Harrow HA1, HA2 . . 41 D4
Orpington BR6 . . . . 227 D6
Penge SE20 . . . . 184 C4
Shepperton TW17 . . . . . . 193 A4
Sidcup DA14, DA15 . . . . . 168 A1
Southgate N21 . . . . 16 D3
South Norwood SE25 . . . 205 D5
Sunbury TW16 . . . . 172 A3
Teddington TW11 . . . . . . 175 A4
Thames Ditton KT7 . . . . . 196 D2
Tottenham Hale N17 . . . . . 52 A6
Twickenham TW1 . . . . . . 152 D4
Walthamstow E17 . . . . 53 A4
West Acton W5 . . . . 88 B1
West Barnes KT3 . . . . . . 200 B4
West Drayton UB7 . . . . . . 104 A4
West Wickham BR4 . . . . . 208 A1
Wood Green N22 . . . . 32 B1
Station Rd N DA17 . . . . . 125 D3
Station Rise SE27 . . . . . 160 D2
Station Sq BR5 . . . . 211 A4
Station St
Newham E16 . . . . 122 D5
Stratford E15 . . . . 76 B1
Station Terr
Camberwell SE5 . . . . 139 A4
Kensal Rise NW10 . . . . . . 90 D5
Station View UB6 . . . . 86 B6
Station Way
Cheam SM2, SM3 . . . . . . 217 A1
Claygate KT10 . . . . 212 C2
Woodford IG9 . . . . 37 D6
Station Yd TW1 . . . . 153 A4
Staton Ct 1 E10 . . . . 53 D2
Staunton Ho SE17 . . . . . 263 A3
Staunton Rd KT2 . . . . . . 176 B3
Staunton St SE8 . . . . 141 B6
Staveley NW1 . . . . 232 A2
Staveley Cl Hackney E9 . . . 74 C3
Lower Holloway N7 . . . . . . 72 A4
New Cross Gate SE15 . . . 140 C4
8 Peckham SE15 . . . . . . 140 B4
Staveley Ct 4 E11 . . . . . . 55 A4
Staveley Gdns W4 . . . . . 133 B4
Staveley Ho SE4 . . . . 163 A6
Staveley Rd
Ashford TW15 . . . . 171 B4
Chiswick W4 . . . . 133 B5
Stavers Ho 31 E3 . . . . 97 B5
Staverton Rd NW2 . . . . . . 68 C1
Stave Yard Rd SE16 . . . . 119 A5
Stavordale Lo W14 . . . . 254 D6
Stavordale Rd
Carshalton SM5 . . . . 202 A2
Highbury N5 . . . . 72 D4
Stayner's Rd E1 . . . . 96 D3
Stayton Rd SM1 . . . . 217 C5
Steadfast Rd KT1 . . . . . . 175 D2
Steadman Ct EC1 . . . . . . 242 B6
Steadman Ho 4 RM10 . . . 81 C5
Stead St SE17 . . 117 B2 262 C3
Steam Farm La TW14 . . 127 D1
Stean St E8 . . . . 95 D6
Stebbing Ho 8 W11 . . . 112 D5
Stebbing Way IG11 . . . . 102 A5
Stebondale St E14 . . . . . 120 A2
Stebon Prim Sch E14 . . . 97 C2
Stedham Pl WC1 . . . . . . 240 A2
Stedman Cl UB10 . . . . 60 C5
Steedman St
SE17 . . . . 117 A2 262 A3
Steeds Rd N10 . . . . 30 D2
Steel App IG11 . . . . 102 B5
Steele Rd
Acton Green W4 . . . . 111 A3
Becontree NW10 . . . . 89 A5
Isleworth TW7 . . . . 131 A1
Leyton E11 . . . . 76 C4
Tottenham N17 . . . . 51 C6
Steele's Mews N NW3 . . . 70 D2
Steele's Mews S NW3 . . . 70 D2
Steele's Rd NW3 . . . . 70 D2
Steele Wlk DA8 . . . . 147 D5
Steel's La 23 E1 . . . . 96 C1
Steen Way 7 SE22 . . . . . 161 C6
Steep Cl BR6 . . . . 227 D2
Steep Hill
South Croydon CR0 . . . . 221 C4
Streatham SW16 . . . . 159 D1
Steeple Cl Fulham SW6 . . 135 A3
Wimbledon SW19 . . . . . . 179 A5
Steeple Ct
19 Bethnal Green E1 . . . . 96 B3
Wimbledon SW19 . . . . . . 179 A5
Steeplestone Cl N18 . . . . 33 A5
Steepleton Ct E11 . . . . . . 54 A1
Steeple Wlk N1 . . . . 235 B6
Steerforth St SW18 . . . . 158 A2
Steering Cl N9 . . . . 18 C3
Steers Mead CR4 . . . . . . 180 D2
Steers Way SE16 . . . . . . 119 A4
Steetley Ct 14 SM2 . . . . 218 A1
Steinman Ct TW7 . . . . . . 130 D2
Stelfax Ho WC1 . . . . 233 D2
Stella Cl UB8 . . . . 82 D2
Stella Rd SW17 . . . . 180 D4
Stellar Ho 4 N17 . . . . 33 D4
Stellman Cl E5 . . . . 74 A5
Stembridge Rd SE20 . . . . 184 B1
Sten Cl 12 EN3 . . . . 7 C6
Stephan Cl E8 . . . . 96 A6
Stephen Cl BR6 . . . . 227 D5
Stephen Ct 18 SW19 . . . . 156 D3
Stephendale Rd SW6 . . . 136 A3
Stephen Fox Ho 7
W4 . . . . 111 C1
Stephen Hawking Sch
E14 . . . . 97 A1
Stephen Mews W1 . . . . . 239 C3
Stephen Pl SW4 . . . . 137 C2
Stephen Saunders Ct
SW11 . . . . 158 C6
Stephens Ct
Brockley SE4 . . . . 141 A2
E16 . . . . 98 D3
Stephens Lo N12 . . . . 14 A1
Stephenson Ct SM2 . . . . 217 B1
Stephenson Ho
2 Gospel Oak NW5 . . . . . 71 B4
6 Maitland Pk NW3 . . . . . 70 D3
Newington SE1 . . . . 262 A6
West Heath SE2 . . . . 124 D1
Stephenson Rd
Ealing W7 . . . . 86 D1
Twickenham TW4 . . . . . . 151 C4
Walthamstow E17 . . . . 53 A4
Stephenson St
Dagenham NW10 . . . . 89 D4
Newham E16 . . . . 98 C2
Stephenson Way
NW1 . . . . 93 C3 239 B6
Stephen's Rd E15 . . . . 98 C6
Stephen St W1 . . . . 239 C3
STEPNEY 96 D2
Stepney City E1 . . . . 96 C2
Stepney Cswy E1 . . . . 96 D1
Stepney Gn E1 . . . . 96 D2
Stepney Greencoat CE
Prim Sch The E14 . . . . . 97 B1
Stepney Green Ct 4
E1 . . . . 96 D2
Stepney Green Sch E1 . . 96 D2
Stepney Green Sta E1 . . 96 D3
Stepney High St E1 . . . . . 96 D2
Stepney Way
Mitcham CR4 . . . . 181 A2
Stepney E1 . . . . 96 C2
Sterling Ave HA8 . . . . 26 B6
Sterling Cl NW10 . . . . 68 A1
Sterling Gdns SE14 . . . . 141 A6
Sterling Ho SE9 . . . . 143 B1
Sterling Ind Est RM10 . . . 81 D4
Sterling Pl W5 . . . . 110 A2
Sterling Rd EN2 . . . . 5 B5
Sterling St SW7 . . . . 257 B6
Sterling Way (North
Circular Rd) N18 . . . . . . 33 C5
Stern Cl IG11 . . . . 102 C5
Sterndale Rd W14 . . . . . 112 D3
Sterne St W12 . . . . 112 D4
Sternhall La SE15 . . . . . . 140 A2
Sternhold Ave SW12,
SW2 . . . . 159 D2
Sterry Cres RM10 . . . . 81 C3
Sterry Dr
Thames Ditton KT7 . . . . . 196 C3
Worcester Pk KT19 . . . . . 215 C4
Sterry Gdns RM10 . . . . . . 81 C2
Sterry Rd Barking IG11 . . 101 D6
Dagenham RM10 . . . . 81 C3
Sterry St SE1 . . . . 252 C1
Steucers La SE23 . . . . . . 163 A3
Stevanne Ct 1 DA17 . . . 125 C1
Steve Biko Ct W10 . . . . . . 90 D3
Steve Biko La SE6 . . . . . 185 C6
Steve Biko Lodge 13
E13 . . . . 99 A5
Steve Biko Rd N7 . . . . 72 C5
Steve Biko Way TW3 . . . 129 C2
Stevedale Rd DA16 . . . . . 146 C3
Stevedore St 3 E1 . . . . . 118 B5
Stevenage Rd
Fulham SW6 . . . . 134 D4
Wallend E6 . . . . 78 C2
Stevens Ave E9 . . . . 74 C2
Stevens Cl
Beckenham BR3 . . . . 185 C4
Hampton TW12 . . . . 173 B4
Pinner HA5 . . . . 40 C4
Stevens Ct BR3 . . . . 185 C4
Stevens Gn WD23 . . . . 8 A3
Stevens Ho KT1 . . . . 175 D1
Stevens' La KT10 . . . . . . 213 A2
Stevenson Cl EN5 . . . . 14 B4
Stevenson Cres SE16 . . . 118 B1
Stevenson Ho
1 Battersea SW11 . . . . 136 D3
6 Clapham Pk SW2 . . . . 160 A6
NW8 . . . . 229 A6
Wembley HA9 . . . . 65 D6
Stevens Rd RM8 . . . . 80 C5
Stevens St SE1 . . . . 263 B6
Steventon Rd W12 . . . . . 111 D6
Stewards Holte Wlk 3
N11 . . . . 31 B6
Stewart Ave TW17 . . . . . 192 C5
Stewart Cl BR7 . . . . 188 D6
Hampton TW12 . . . . 173 A4
Kingsbury NW9 . . . . 45 A3
Stewart Fleming Prim Sch
SE20 . . . . 206 C6
Stewart Headlam Prim
Sch E1 . . . . 96 B3
Stewart Ho SE1 . . . . 263 A5
Stanmore HA7 . . . . 25 B5
Stewart Quay UB3 . . . . . 105 C4
Stewart Rainbird Ho 1
E12 . . . . 78 C3
Stewart Rd E15 . . . . 76 B4
Stewartsby Cl N18 . . . . . . 33 A5
Stewart's Gr
SW3 . . . . 114 C1 257 A2
Stewart's Rd
SW8 . . . . 137 C4 269 A2
Stewart St E14 . . . . 120 A4
Stew La EC4 . . . . 252 A6
Steyne Ho
15 Acton W3 . . . . 110 D5
11 Acton W3 . . . . 111 A5
Steyne Rd W3 . . . . 110 D5
Steyning Gr SE9 . . . . 188 B6
Steynings Way N12 . . . . . 29 C5
Steyning Way TW4 . . . . . 128 C1
Steynton Ave DA5 . . . . . 168 D2
Stickland Rd DA17 . . . . . 125 C2
Stickleton Cl UB6 . . . . 85 D4
Stifford Ho E1 . . . . 96 C2
Stilecroft Gdns HA0 . . . . . 65 B5
Stile Hall Gdns W4 . . . . 110 C1
Stile Hall Par 6 W4 . . . . 110 C1
Stileman Ho 4 E3 . . . . . . 97 B2
Stile Path TW16 . . . . 194 A5
Stiles Cl BR2 . . . . 210 B3
Erith DA8 . . . . 125 D1
Stillingfleet Rd SW13 . . 134 A6
Stillington St
SW1 . . . . 115 C2 259 B4
Stillness Jun & Inf Schs
SE23 . . . . 163 A5
Stillness Rd SE23 . . . . . . 163 B5
Stilwell Dr UB8 . . . . 82 B3
Stilwell Rdbt UB8 . . . . . . 104 D6
Stipularis Dr UB4 . . . . 84 D3
Stirling Ave Pinner HA5 . . 41 A2
Upper Halliford TW17 . . . 193 C6
Wallington SM6 . . . . 220 A1
Stirling Cl Sidcup DA14 . . 189 D6
Streatham SW16 . . . . 181 C2
Stirling Cnr EN5, WD6 . . . 11 B5
Stirling Ct
Clerkenwell EC1 . . . . . . 241 C6
Ealing W13 . . . . 109 B6
Strand WC2 . . . . 240 C1
Stirling Gr TW3 . . . . 130 A3
Stirling Ho 5 SE18 . . . . 122 D1
Stirling Ind Ctr WD6 . . . . 11 B6
Stirling Lo 7 EN5 . . . . . . 14 A6
Stirling Mans NW6 . . . . . . 70 A2
Stirling Rd Harrow HA3 . . 42 D6
Hayes UB3 . . . . 106 B6
Newham E13 . . . . 99 B5
South Acton W3 . . . . 110 D3
Stanwell TW19, TW6 . . . . 148 B5
Stockwell SW9 . . . . 138 A3
Tottenham N17 . . . . 34 A2
Twickenham TW2 . . . . . . 151 D4
Walthamstow E17 . . . . 53 A6
Wood Green N22 . . . . 32 D2
Stirling Ret Pk WD6 . . . . 11 B5
Stirling Way
Borehamwood WD6 . . . . . 11 B6
Thornton Heath CR0 . . . . 204 A2
Stiven Cres HA2 . . . . 63 B5
Stoatley Ho 10 SW15 . . . 156 A3
Stockbeck NW1 . . . . 232 B3
Stockbridge Ho EN2 . . . . . 4 D3
Stockbury Rd CR0 . . . . . 206 C3
Stockdale Rd RM8 . . . . . . 81 B6
Stockdove Way UB6 . . . . . 86 D4
Stocker Gdns RM9 . . . . . . 80 C1
Stockfield Rd
Claygate KT10 . . . . 212 C3
Streatham SW16 . . . . 160 B1
Stockford Ave NW7 . . . . . 28 D3
Stockholm Ho E1 . . . . . . 118 A6
Stockholm Rd SE16 . . . . 118 C1
Stockholm Way 9 E1 . . 118 A5
Stockhurst Cl SW15 . . . . 134 D3
Stockingswater La EN3 . . . 7 B2
Stockleigh Hall NW8 . . 230 B4
Stockley Acad UB8 . . . . . 82 B1
Stockley Cl UB7 . . . . 104 D4
Stockley Ctry Pk UB7 . . 104 C6
Stockley Farm Rd
UB7 . . . . 104 D3
Stockley Park Bsns Pk
UB11 . . . . 105 A5
Stockley Rd UB7, UB8,
UB11 . . . . 104 D4
Stock Orchard Cres N7 . 72 B3
Stock Orchard St N7 . . . . 72 B3
Stockport Rd SW16 . . . . 181 D2
Stocks Ct 5 E1 . . . . 96 D3
Stocksfield Rd E17 . . . . . 54 A6
Stocks Pl
Hillingdon UB10 . . . . 82 C6
16 Limehouse E14 . . . . . 119 B6
Stock St E13 . . . . 99 A5
Stockton Cl EN5 . . . . 2 A1
Stockton Gdns
Edgware NW7 . . . . 11 C1
Tottenham N17 . . . . 33 A3
Stockton Ho 16 E2 . . . . . . 96 B4
Harrow HA2 . . . . 41 C1
Stockton Rd
Edmonton N18 . . . . 34 B4
Tottenham N17 . . . . 33 A3
STOCKWELL 138 A2
Stockwell Ave SW9 . . . . 138 B2
Stockwell Cl BR1 . . . . . . 187 B1
Stockwell Gdns
SW9 . . . . 138 B4 270 C1
Stockwell Gn SW9 . . . . . 138 B3
Stockwell La SW9 . . . . . . 138 B3
Stockwell Park Cres
SW9 . . . . 138 B3
Stockwell Park Rd
SW9 . . . . 138 B4 270 D1
Stockwell Park Sch
SW9 . . . . 138 B4 270 C1
Stockwell Park Wlk
SW9 . . . . 138 C2
Stockwell Prim Sch
SW9 . . . . 138 B2
Stockwell Rd SW9 . . . . . 138 B3
Stockwell St SE10 . . . . . 142 A6
Stockwell Sta SW4 . . . . . 138 A3
Stockwell Terr SW9 . . . 270 C1
Stodart Rd SE20 . . . . 184 C2
Stoddart Ho SW8 . . . . . 270 D5
Stodmarsh Ho 28
SW9 . . . . 138 C4
Stofield Gdns SE9 . . . . . 165 D1
Stoford Cl SW19 . . . . 157 A4
Stokenchurch St
SW6 . . . . 135 D4 265 C1
STOKE NEWINGTON . . . 73 C6
Stoke Newington Church
St N16 . . . . 73 C6
Stoke Newington Comm
N16 . . . . 73 D6
Stoke Newington High St
N16 . . . . 73 D5
Stoke Newington Rd
N16 . . . . 73 D4
Stoke Newington Sch
N16 . . . . 73 B5
Stoke Newington Sta
N16 . . . . 73 D6
Stoke Pl NW10 . . . . 89 D4
Stoke Rd KT2 . . . . 177 A3
Stokesby Rd KT9 . . . . . . 214 B2
Stokes Ct N2 . . . . 48 C5
Stokesley St W12 . . . . 89 D1
Stokes Rd Croydon CR0 . . 206 D3
Newham E6 . . . . 100 A3
Stokley Ct N8 . . . . 50 A5
Stoll Cl NW2 . . . . 68 C5
Stoms Path SE6 . . . . 185 C5
Stonard Rd
Dagenham RM8 . . . . 80 B4
Palmers Green N13 . . . . . 16 C1
Stondon Pk SE23 . . . . . . 163 A5
Stondon Wlk 4 E6 . . . . . . 99 D5
Stonebanks KT12 . . . . . . 194 A2
Stone Bldgs
WC2 . . . . 94 B2 240 D3
STONEBRIDGE 89 A6
Stonebridge Ct 9
NW10 . . . . 67 B1
Stonebridge Ctr 6
NW10 . . . . 89 B6
Stonebridge Ctr The
N15 . . . . 52 A4
Stonebridge Park HA9 . . 66 D1
Stonebridge Park Sta
NW10 . . . . 66 D1
Stonebridge Pk NW10 . . . 67 B1
Stonebridge Rd N15 . . . . 51 D4
Stonebridge Sch The
NW10 . . . . 89 B6
Stonebridge Way HA9 . . . 66 D2
Stonechat Sq 6 E6 . . . . 100 A2
Stone Cl Clapham SW4 . . 137 C3
Dagenham RM8 . . . . 81 B6
Yiewsley UB7 . . . . 104 B5
Stonecot Cl SM3 . . . . 201 A1
Stonecot Hill SM3 . . . . . 201 A1
Stone Cres TW14 . . . . . . 149 D4
Stonecroft Way CR0 . . . 204 A2
Stonecrop Cl NW9 . . . . . . 45 B6
Stone Ct Southgate N21 . . 16 B6
4 Stratford E15 . . . . 76 D1
Stonecutter St EC4 . . . 241 C2
Stonefield N4 . . . . 72 B6
Stonefield Cl DA7 . . . . . . 147 C2
Ruislip HA4 . . . . 63 A3
Stonefield Mans N1 . . . 234 A5
Stonefield St
N1 . . . . 94 C6 234 B6
Stonefield Way
Ruislip HA4 . . . . 63 A3
SE7 . . . . 143 D5
Stonegate 8 NW5 . . . . . . 71 A2
Stone Gr HA8 . . . . 26 B5
Stone Grove Ct HA8 . . . . . 26 B5
Stonegrove Gdns HA8 . . . 26 A5
Stonegrove Ho HA8 . . . . . 26 B5
Stonehall Ave IG1 . . . . . . 56 A3
Stone Hall Rd N21 . . . . . . 16 C4
Stoneham Rd N11 . . . . . . 31 C5

Stonehaven BR3 185 D1
Stonehill Bsns Pk N18 34 D5
Stonehill Cl SW14 155 B6
Stonehill Ct E4 19 D4
Stonehill Rd
Brentford W4 110 C1
Mortlake SW14 155 B6
Stonehills Ct SE21 161 C1
Stonehill's Mans 3
SW16 160 A2
Stonehill Woods Pk
DA14 191 D4
Stonehorse Rd EN3 18 C6
Stonehouse NW1 232 B5
Stonehouse Ct EC2 243 B2
Stonehouse Ho 27 W2 91 C2
Stone Lake Ind Pk
SE7 121 C2
Stone Lake Ret Pk
SE7 121 C2
STONELEIGH 216 A3
Stoneleigh Ave
Enfield EN1 6 B4
North Cheam KT17,
KT4 216 A5
Stoneleigh Broadway
KT17 216 A3
Stoneleigh Cres KT19 215 D3
Stoneleigh Ct
Redbridge IG5 56 A6
6 Tottenham N17 33 D1
Stoneleigh Fst Sch
KT17 216 B4
Stoneleigh Lo 13 TW9 132 B4
Stoneleigh Mews 15
E3 97 A5
Stoneleigh Park Ave
CR0 206 D3
Stoneleigh Park Rd KT19,
KT4 216 A3
Stoneleigh Pl W11 112 D6
Stoneleigh Rd
Bromley BR1 210 D6
Carshalton SM5 202 C2
Redbridge IG5 56 B6
Tottenham N17 33 D1
Stoneleigh St W11 112 D6
Stoneleigh Sta KT19 216 A3
Stoneleigh Terr N19 71 B6
Stonell's Rd SW11 158 D6
Stonemasons Cl N15 51 B5
Stonenest St N4 50 B1
Stone Park Ave BR3 207 D5
Stone Pl KT4 216 A6
Stone Rd BR2 208 D4
Stones End St SE1 252 A1
Stonewall E6 100 C2
Stoneworth Ct SE25 206 A3
Stoney Alley SE18 144 C3
Stoneyard La E14 119 D6
Stoneycroft Cl SE12 164 D4
Stoney Deep TW11 175 A6
Stoneydown E17 53 A5
Stoneydown Ave E17 53 A5
Stoneydown Ho 2 E17 53 A5
Stoneydown Park Sch
E17 53 A5
Stoneyfields Gdns HA8 27 A6
Stoneyfields La HA8 27 A6
Stoney La E1 243 B2
Penge SE19 183 D4
Stoney St SE1 117 B5 252 C4
Stonhouse St SW4 137 D1
Stonor Rd W14 113 B2 254 C3
Stonycroft Cl EN3 7 A3
Stopes St SE15 139 D5
Stopford Rd
Newham E13 99 A6
SE17 261 D1
Stopher Ho SE1 251 D1
Storace Ho 6 SW4 138 A1
Store Rd E16 122 C4
Storers Quay E14 120 B2
Store St
Bloomsbury
WC1 93 D2 239 C4
Stratford New Town E15 76 B3
Storey Ct NW8 229 C1
Storey Ho 13 E14 119 D6
Storey Prim Sch E16 122 D5
Storey Rd Highgate N6 48 D3
Walthamstow E17 53 B5
Storey's Gate
SW1 115 D4 249 D1
Storey St E16 122 C4
Stories Rd SE5 139 C2
Stork Rd E7 77 A2
Storksmead Rd HA8 27 C3
Storks Rd SE16 118 A3
Stormont House Sch
E5 74 B4
Stormont Rd
Clapham SW11 137 A1
Highgate N6 48 D2
Stormont Way KT9 213 C3
Stormount Dr UB3 105 A4
Storrington WC1 233 B1
Storrington Rd CR0 205 D1
Story St N1 72 B1
Stotfold Rd BR1 188 A2
Stothard Ho 25 E1 96 C3
Stothard Pl E1 243 B4
Stothard St 12 E1 96 C3
Stott Cl SW18 158 B5
Stoughton Ave SM3 217 A3
Stoughton Cl
Roehampton SW15 156 A3
Stoughton Cl *continued*
SE11 260 D3
Stour Ave UB2 107 C3
Stourbridge Ho 8 UB5 85 B3
Stour Cl BR2 225 C4
Stourcliffe Cl W1 237 C2
Stourcliffe St W1 237 C1
Stour Ct UB1 86 B1
Stourhead Cl 6
SW19 156 D4
Stourhead Gdns
SW20 200 A6
Stour Rd
Dagenham RM10 81 C6
Hackney Wick E3 75 C1
Stourton Ave TW13 173 B6
Stowage SE8 141 D6
Stow Cres E17 35 A3
Stowe Cres HA4 39 A3
Stowe Gdns N9 17 D3
Stowe Ho
Hampstead Garden Suburb
NW11 48 A3
11 Stoke Newington N16 73 C5
Stowe Pl N15 51 C6
Stowe Rd W12 112 B4
Stowford Coll SM2 218 A1
Stowting Rd BR6 227 C4
Stox Mead HA3 24 B2
Stracey Rd
Becontree NW10 89 B6
Forest Gate E7 77 A4
Strachan Pl SW19,
SW20 178 C4
Stradbroke Gr
Buckhurst Hill IG9 21 D3
Redbridge IG5 56 C6
Stradbroke Rd N5 73 A4
Stradbrook Cl HA2 63 B5
Stradella Rd SE24 161 A5
Straffan Lo 8 NW3 70 C2
Strafford Ho 9 SE8 119 B1
Strafford Rd Acton W3 111 A4
Barnet EN5 1 A2
Hounslow TW3 129 B2
Twickenham TW1 153 A4
Strafford St E14 119 C4
Strahan Rd E3 97 A4
Straightsmouth SE10 142 A5
Straight The UB2 107 A4
Strait Rd E6 122 B6
Straker's Rd SE15 140 B1
Strale Ho 17 N1 95 C6
STRAND 116 B6
Strand
Strand WC2 116 B6 250 C6
Strand WC2 240 D1
Strand Ct SE18 123 D1
Strand Dr TW9 132 D5
Strandfield Cl SE18 123 C1
Strand Ho SE28 123 B5
Strand La WC2 250 D6
STRAND ON THE GREEN
132 C6
Strand-on-the-Green
W4 132 C6
Strand-on-the-Green
Schs W4 132 C6
Strand Pl N18 33 C6
Strang Ho N1 235 A5
Strangways Terr W14 254 C5
Stranraer Way
Barnsbury N1 72 A1
1 Stanwell TW6 148 A5
Strasburg Rd
SW11 137 B4 268 C1
Stratfield Ho SE12 165 A2
Stratfield Park Cl N21 16 D4
STRATFORD 76 A2
Stratford Ave UB10 82 B5
Stratford Bus Sta E15 76 B1
Stratford Cir (Newham 6th
Form Coll) E15 76 B2
Stratford Cl IG11 80 A1
Stratford Ct KT3 199 B5
Stratford Gr SW15 134 D1
Stratford House Ave
BR1 210 A6
Stratford International Sta
(under constr) E15 76 A2
STRATFORD MARSH 97 D6
STRATFORD NEW TOWN
76 A3
Stratford Office Village
The 1 E15 76 C1
Stratford Pl W1 238 C1
Stratford Rd
Harlington TW6 149 A6
Hayes UB4 84 B3
Hendon NW4 46 D5
Newham E13 99 A6
Southall UB2 107 A2
Thornton Heath CR7 204 D6
W8 113 C3 255 B5
Stratford Sch E7 77 A1
Stratford Sch (Annexe)
E7 77 B2
Stratford Sh Ctr E15 76 B1
Stratford Sta E15 76 B1
Stratford Studios W8 255 C5
Stratford Villas NW1 71 D1
Stratford Workshops
E15 98 B6
Strathan Cl SW18 157 A5
Strathaven Rd SE12 165 B5
Strathblaine Rd SW11 136 B1
Strathbrook Rd SW16 182 B3
Strathcona Rd HA9 65 D6
Strathdale SW16 182 B5
Strathdon Dr SW17 158 B1
Strathearn Ave
Harlington UB3 127 D5
Twickenham TW2 152 A3
Strathearn Ho W2 247 A6
Strathearn Pl
W2 114 C6 247 A6
Strathearn Rd
Sutton SM1 217 C3
Wimbledon SW19 179 C6
Stratheden Par SE3 143 A5
Stratheden Rd SE3 143 A5
Strathfield Gdns IG11 79 B2
Strathleven Rd SW2 160 A6
Strathmore Ct NW8 230 A2
Strathmore Gdns
Edgware HA8 26 D1
Finchley N3 29 D2
W8 245 B4
Strathmore Rd
Teddington TW11,
TW2 174 C6
Thornton Heath CR0 205 B2
Wimbledon SW19 157 C1
Strathmore Sch TW10 153 D2
Strathnairn St SE1 118 A2
Strathray Gdns NW3 70 C2
Strath Terr SW11 136 C1
Strathville Rd SW18 157 D2
Strathyre Ave SW16 204 C6
Stratton Ave EN2 5 B6
Stratton Cl DA7 147 A2
Edgware HA8 26 B4
Heston TW5 129 C4
Merton SW19 179 C1
Walton-on-T KT12 194 C1
Stratton Ct
4 De Beauvoir Town
N1 73 C1
10 Kingston u T KT6 198 A4
10 Pinner HA5 23 B3
Strattondale St E14 120 A3
Stratton Dr IG11 79 D2
Stratton Gdns UB1 85 C1
Stratton Ho HA8 26 B6
Stratton Lo 10 EN5 1 D1
Stratton Rd DA7 147 A2
Merton SW19 179 C1
Sunbury TW16 171 D1
Stratton St W1 115 B5 248 D4
Strauss Rd W4 111 B4
Strawberry Fields
BR6 226 D3
STRAWBERRY HILL 152 D1
Strawberry Hill Cl
TW1 152 D1
Strawberry Hill Rd
TW1 152 D1
Strawberry Hill Sta
TW2 152 D1
Strawberry La SM5 219 A5
Strawberry Terr N10 30 D2
Strawberry Vale
Finchley N2 30 B2
Twickenham TW1 153 A1
Strayfield Rd EN2 4 D6
Streakes Field Rd NW2 68 A6
Streamdale SE2 146 B6
Stream La HA8 26 D5
Streamline Mews
SE22 162 A3
Streamside Cl BR2 209 A5
Edmonton N9 17 D3
Stream Way DA17 147 C6
Streatfeild Ave E6 100 B6
Streatfield Rd HA3, HA7 43 D6
STREATHAM 182 A4
Streatham Cl SW16 160 A2
Streatham & Clapham
High Sch SW16 159 D1
Streatham Common N
SW16 182 B5
Streatham Common S
SW16 182 B4
Streatham Common Sta
SW16 181 D3
Streatham Ct SW16 160 A1
Streatham High Rd SW16,
SW2 182 A5
STREATHAM HILL 160 A3
Streatham Hill SW2 160 A3
Streatham Hill & Clapham
High Sch SW2 160 B3
Streatham Hill Sta
SW2 160 A2
STREATHAM PARK 181 C6
Streatham Pl SW2 160 A4
Streatham Rd CR4 181 A2
Streatham St WC1 240 A2
Streatham Sta SW16 181 D5
STREATHAM VALE 181 D3
Streatham Vale SW16 181 D3
Streathbourne Rd
SW17 159 A1
Streathem Wells Prim Sch
SW2 160 C2
Streatleigh Par 4
SW16 160 A2
Streatley Pl
27 Hampstead NW3 70 A4
Hampstead NW3 70 B4
Streatley Rd NW6 69 B1
Streeters La SM6 219 D5
Streetfield Mews SE3 143 A2
Streimer Rd E15 98 A5
Strelley Way W3 111 C6
Stretford Ct 1 SW19 179 A3
Stretton Lo W13 109 B6
Stretton Mans 16 SE8 141 C6
Stretton Rd
Croydon CR0 205 C2
Richmond TW10 153 C2
Strickland Ct SE15 140 A2
Strickland Ho 26 E2 95 D4
Strickland Row SW18 158 B4
Strickland St SE8 141 C4
Strickland Way 4
BR6 227 D4
Stride Rd E13 98 D5
Strimon Cl N9 18 C2
Stringer Hos 19 N1 95 C6
Strode Cl N10 31 A3
Strode Ho 3 SW2 160 C3
Strode Rd
Forest Gate E7 77 A4
SW6 135 A5 264 A4
Tottenham N17 33 C1
Willesden NW10 68 A2
Strome Ho NW6 91 D5
Strone Rd E7, E12 77 D2
Strone Way UB4 85 A3
Strongbow Cres SE9 166 B6
Strongbow Rd SE9 166 B6
Strongbridge Cl HA2 41 C1
Stronsa Rd W12 111 D4
Strood Ho
9 Penge SE20 184 C3
SE1 252 D1
Stroud Cres SW15 156 A1
Stroudes Cl KT4 199 D2
Stroud Field UB5 63 A2
Stroud Gate HA2 63 D4
STROUD GREEN 50 C3
Stroud Green Gdns
CR0 206 C2
Stroud Green Prim Sch
N4 50 C1
Stroud Green Rd N4 50 C1
Stroud Green Way
CR0 206 C3
Stroudley Ho SW8 269 B2
Stroudley Wlk E3 97 D4
Stroud Rd
Croydon SE25 206 A3
Wimbledon SW19 157 C1
Strouds Cl RM6 58 B4
Stroud Way TW15 171 A4
Strout's Pl 2 E2 95 D4
Struan Ho 15 E11 55 A4
Strudwick Ct SW4 270 B1
Strutton Ground
SW1 115 D3 259 C5
Strype St E1 243 C3
Stuart Ave Ealing W5 110 B4
Harrow HA2 63 B5
Hayes BR2 209 A1
Hendon NW9 46 A2
Walton-on-T KT12 194 B1
Stuart Cl UB10 60 C2
Stuart Cres
Croydon CR0 223 B5
Hayes UB3 83 A1
Wood Green N22 32 B2
Stuart Ct Chingford E4 20 D2
6 Croydon CR0 220 D5
2 Elstree WD6 9 D5
Stuart Evans Cl DA16 146 C2
Stuart Gr TW11 174 C5
Stuart Ho
Hammersmith W6 112 C3
1 Homerton E9 74 D1
Queensbury NW9 44 C5
5 Stockwell SW4 138 A1
W14 254 A4
Stuart Lo SE25 183 C1
Stuart Mill Ho N1 233 C3
Stuart Pl CR4 180 D2
Stuart Rd Acton W3 111 A5
Barking IG11 79 D1
DA16 146 B4
East Barnet EN4 14 D4
Harrow HA3 42 D6
Maida Vale NW6 91 C4
Nunhead SE15 140 C1
Richmond TW10 153 B1
South Norwood CR7 205 A5
Wimbledon SW19 157 C1
Stubbs Cl NW9 45 A4
Stubbs Dr SE16 118 B1
Stubbs Ho
Finsbury Pk N4 50 B1
1 Globe Town E2 96 D4
Stubbs Mews RM8 80 B4
Stubbs Point E13 99 B3
Stubbs Way SW19 180 B2
Stucley Pl 19 NW1 71 B1
Stucley Rd TW5, TW7 130 A5
Studdridge St SW6 135 C3
Studd St N1 94 D6 234 C6
Studholme Ct NW3 69 C4
Studholme St SE15 140 B5
Studio Mews 5 NW4 46 C5
Studio Pl SW1 247 D1
Studios NW8 229 A4
Studios Rd TW17 192 B6
Studios The
4 Clapham SW4 137 C1
SW8 269 D1
Studland SE17 262 C2
Studland Cl DA15 167 D1
Studland Ho E14 97 A1
Studland Rd Ealing W7 86 C1
Forest Hill SE26 184 D5
Kingston u T KT2 176 A4
Studland St W6 112 B2
Studley Ave E4 36 B3
Studley Cl E5 75 A3
Studley Ct
13 Blackwall E14 120 B6
Studley Ct *continued*
DA14 190 B5
Redbridge IG4 55 D3
Studley Dr IG4 55 D3
Studley Grange Rd
W7 108 D4
Studley Rd
Dagenham RM9 80 D1
South Lambeth SW4 138 A3
Upton E7 77 B2
Study Prep Sch The
SW19 178 C5
Study Sch The KT3 199 C4
Stukeley Rd E7 77 B1
Stukeley St
WC2 94 A1 240 B2
Stumps Hill La BR3 185 C4
Stunell Ho 23 SE14 140 D6
Sturdee Ho 2 E2 96 A5
Sturdy Ho 28 E3 97 A5
Sturdy Rd SE15 140 B3
Sturge Ave E17 35 D1
Sturgeon Rd
SE17 117 A1 262 A1
Sturges Field BR7 189 B4
Sturgess Ave NW4 46 B2
Sturge St SE1 117 A4 252 A2
Sturmer Way N7 72 B3
Sturminster Cl UB4 84 C1
Sturminster Ho SW8 270 D3
Sturrock Cl N15 51 B5
Sturry St E14 97 D1
Sturt St N1 235 B3
Stutfield St E1 96 A1
Stuttle Ho 14 E1 96 A3
Styles Gdns SW9 138 D2
Styles Ho SE1 251 C3
Styles Way BR3 208 A5
Stylus Apartments 25
E1 96 C1
Sudbourne Prim Sch
SW2 160 B6
Sudbourne Rd SW2 160 B6
Sudbrooke Rd SW12 159 A5
Sudbrook Gdns TW10 154 A1
Sudbrook La TW10 154 A2
SUDBURY 65 A4
Sudbury E6 100 C1
Sudbury Ave HA0 65 D4
Sudbury Court Dr HA1 65 A5
Sudbury Court Rd HA1 65 A5
Sudbury Cres BR1 187 A5
Wembley HA0 65 B3
Sudbury Croft HA0 64 D4
Sudbury Ct
1 Ilford RM6 58 B4
SW8 269 D2
Sudbury Gdns CR0 221 C4
Sudbury & Harrow Road
Sta HA0 65 B3
Sudbury Heights Ave
UB6 65 A3
Sudbury Hill HA1 64 C5
Sudbury Hill Cl HA0 64 D5
Sudbury Hill Harrow Sta
HA1 64 C4
Sudbury Hill Sta HA1 64 C4
Sudbury Ho SW18 157 D6
Sudbury Prim Sch HA0 65 B4
Sudbury Rd IG11 79 D3
Sudbury Town Sta UB6 65 B2
Sudeley St N1 94 D5 234 D3
Sudlow Rd SW18 157 C6
Sudrey St SE1 252 A1
Suez Ave UB6 86 D5
Suez Rd EN3 7 A2
Suffield Ho SE17 261 D2
Suffield Rd Chingford E4 35 D6
Penge SE20 184 C1
2 South Tottenham N15 51 D4
Suffolk Cl WD6 11 B6
Suffolk Ct
3 Dagenham RM6 58 C4
Ilford IG3 57 C3
Walthamstow E17 53 C2
3 West Norwood
SW16 182 C6
Suffolk Ho 11 Acton W3 88 C1
Beckenham BR2 208 D5
8 Dartmouth Pk NW5 71 C5
Edgware HA8 26 B4
Penge SE20 184 C2
4 South Croydon CR0 221 B6
Suffolk La EC4 252 C6
Suffolk Park Rd E17 53 A5
Suffolk Pl SW1 249 D4
Suffolk Rd Barking IG11 79 B1
Barnes SW13 134 A5
Dagenham RM10 81 D3
Enfield EN3 18 B6
Harrow HA2 41 C4
Ilford IG3 57 C3
4 Newham E13 99 A4
Sidcup DA14 190 C4
South Norwood SE25 205 D5
Tottenham N15 51 B3
Willesden NW10 67 C1
Worcester Pk KT4 215 D6
Suffolks Prim Sch EN1 6 B3
Suffolk St
Forest Gate E7 77 A4
SW1 115 D5 249 D4
Sugar House La E15 98 A5
Sugar Loaf Wlk 6 E2 96 C4
Sugden Rd
Clapham SW11 137 A1
Long Ditton KT7 197 B1
Sugden Way IG11 101 D5
Sulby Ho SE4 141 A1
Sulgrave Gdns 11 W6 112 C4
Sulgrave Rd W6 112 C3
Sulina Rd SW2 160 A4
Sulivan Ct SW6 135 C3
Sulivan Ent Ctr SW6 135 C2
Sulivan Prim Sch
SW6 135 C3
Sulivan Rd SW6 135 C2
Sulkin Ho 11 E2 96 D4
Sullivan Ave E16 99 D2
Sullivan Cl
Battersea SW11 136 C2
Hayes UB4 84 C2
Sullivan Ct
4 Croydon CR0 206 A1
Stamford Hill N16 51 D1
SW5 255 B4
Sullivan Ho
Chelsea SW1 268 D6
Isleworth TW2 152 B5
Vauxhall SE11 260 D3
Sullivan Rd
SE11 116 C2 261 B4
Sullivans Reach KT12 193 D2
Sullivan Way WD6 9 C5
Sultan Ho SE1 118 A1
Sultan Rd E11 55 B5
Sultan St Penge BR3 184 D1
SE5 139 A5
Sumal Ct E9 76 B6
Sumatra Rd NW6 69 C2
Sumburgh Rd SW12 159 A5
Summer Ave KT8 196 C4
Summercourt Rd E1 96 C1
Summer Crossing
KT7 196 C4
Summerene Cl SW16 181 C3
Summerfield 6 BR1 187 B2
Summerfield Ave
Colney Hatch N12 30 C4
Kensal Rise NW6 91 A5
Summerfield Ho RM9 80 D4
Summerfield La KT6 213 D6
Summerfield Rd
Ealing W5 87 B3
Loughton IG10 21 D5
Summerfield St SE12 164 D4
Summer Gdns KT8 196 C4
Summer Gr WD6 9 D5
Summer Hill
Borehamwood WD6 10 C6
BR7 188 C1
Summerhill Cl BR6 227 C5
Summerhill Gr EN1 17 C5
Summerhill Rd N15 51 B5
Summerhill Villas
BR7 188 D2
Summerhill Way CR4 181 A2
Summer Ho SE13 142 B1
Summerhouse Ave
TW5 129 A4
Summerhouse Rd N16 73 C6
Summerland Gdns N10 49 B6
Summerland Grange
N10 49 B6
Summerlands Ave
W3 111 A6
Summerlands Lo BR6 226 C4
Summerlee Ave N2 48 D5
Summerlee Gdns N2 48 D5
Summerley St SW18 157 D2
Summer Rd
East Molesey KT8 196 B4
Thames Ditton KT7,
KT8 196 D4
Summersby Rd N6 49 B3
Summers Cl
Belmont SM2 217 C1
Wembley HA9 44 D1
Summersell Ho SE27 183 B5
Summerside Prim Sch
N12 30 B4
Summerskille Cl N9 18 B2
Summers La N12 30 B3
Summers Row N12 30 C4
Summers St EC1 241 A5
SUMMERSTOWN 158 A1
Summerstown SW17 180 A6
Summerton Way
SE28 102 D1
Summer Trees TW16 172 B2
Summerville Gdns
SM1 217 B2
Summerwood Rd TW1,
TW7 152 D5
Summit Ave NW9 45 B4
Summit Bsns Pk The
TW16 172 A3
Summit Cl Edgware HA8 26 C3
Kingsbury NW9 45 B5
Osidge N14 15 C2
Summit Ct 5 Barnet EN5 1 B2
Brondesbury NW2 69 A3
Summit Dr IG8 37 D1
Summit Est N16 52 A2
Summit Rd Northolt UB5 63 C1
Walthamstow E17 53 D5
Summit Way
Brunswick Pk N14 15 B2
South Norwood SE19 183 C3
Sumner Ave SE15 139 D4
Sumner Bldgs SE1 252 A4
Sumner Cl BR6 227 A4
Sumner Ct SW8 270 A2
Sumner Gdns CR0 204 C1
Sumner Ho 1 E3 97 D2
Sumner Pl
SW7 114 B2 256 D3
Sumner Place Mews
SW7 256 D3
Sumner Rd Harrow HA1 42 A2

Sumner Rd continued
SE15 .... 139 D5
  Thornton Heath CR0 .... 204 D1
Sumner Rd S CR0 .... 204 C1
Sumner St SE1 .117 A5 252 A4
Sumpter Cl NW3 .... 70 A2
Sun Alley 6 TW9 .... 132 A1
Sunbeam Cres W10 .... 90 C3
Sunbeam Rd NW10 .... 89 B3
SUNBURY 194 B6
Sunbury Ave
  Edgware NW7 ...... 27 B6
  Mortlake SW14 .... 133 B1
Sunbury Cl KT12 .... 194 A3
SUNBURY COMMON .171 D3
Sunbury Court Island
  TW16 .... 194 D6
Sunbury Court Mews
  TW16 .... 172 D1
Sunbury Court Rd
  TW16 .... 172 C1
Sunbury Cres TW13 .. 171 D6
Sunbury Cross TW16 . 172 A3
Sunbury Cross Ctr 9
  TW16 .... 171 D3
Sunbury Ct
  3 Barnet EN5 .... 1 A1
  5 SE14 .... 140 D6
  Sunbury TW16 ...... 172 D1
Sunbury Ct (Con Ctr)
  TW16 .... 172 D1
Sunbury Gdns NW7 .. 27 B5
Sunbury Ho 38 E2 .... 95 D4
Sunbury Int Bsns Ctr
  TW16 .... 171 C2
Sunbury La
  Battersea
  SW11 ..... 136 B4 266 D2
  Walton-on-T KT12 .. 194 A3
Sunbury Manor Sch
  TW16 .... 171 D2
Sunbury Rd
  Cheam SM3 .... 217 A5
  Feltham TW13 ...... 171 D6
Sunbury St SE18 .... 122 B3
Sunbury Sta TW16 ... 172 A2
Sunbury Way TW13 .. 172 C1
Sunbury Workshops 39
  E2 .... 95 D4
Suncroft Pl SE26 .... 162 C1
Sun Ct EC3 .... 242 D1
Sunderland Ct
  Dulwich SE22 .... 162 A4
  12 Stanwell TW19 ... 148 A5
Sunderland Ho 28 W2 . 91 C2
Sunderland Mount
  SE23 .... 162 D2
Sunderland Point E16. 123 A5
Sunderland Rd
  Ealing W5 .... 109 D3
  Forest Hill SE23 .... 162 D2
Sunderland Terr W2 .. 91 D1
Sunderland Way E12.. 77 D6
Sundew Ave W12 .... 112 A6
Sundew Ct 9 HA0 .... 88 A5
Sundial Ave SE25 .... 205 D6
Sundorne Rd SE7 .... 121 C1
Sundown Rd TW15.... 171 A5
Sundra 23 E1 .... 96 D3
SUNDRIDGE 187 C4
Sundridge Ave
  Bromley BR1, BR7.... 188 A3
  DA16 .... 145 B2
Sundridge Ho
  Bromley BR1 .... 187 B5
  4 Homerton E9 ..... 74 D1
Sundridge Par BR1 .. 187 B3
Sundridge Park Sta
  BR1 .... 187 B3
Sundridge Rd CR0 ... 206 A1
Sunfields Pl SE3 .... 143 B5
Sun in the Sands SE3 . 143 B5
Sunken Rd CR0 .... 222 C3
Sun La SE3 .... 143 B5
Sunland Ave DA6 .... 147 A1
Sunleigh Ct HA0 .... 88 A6
Sunleigh Rd HA0 .... 88 A6
Sunley Gdns UB6 .... 87 A6
Sunley Ho E1 .... 243 D1
Sun Life Trad Est
  TW14 .... 128 A2
Sunlight Cl SW19 .... 180 A4
Sunlight Sq 29 E2 .... 96 B4
Sunmead Rd TW16 ... 194 A6
Sunna Gdns TW16 ... 172 B1
Sunna Lo TW16 .... 171 D3
Sunniholme Ct SE2 .. 221 A3
Sunningdale Ealing W13 . 87 B2
  Friern Barnet N14 .... 31 D5
Sunningdale Ave
  Barking IG11 .... 79 B1
  East Acton W3 .... 111 C6
  Feltham TW13 .... 151 A3
  Ruislip HA4 .... 40 C1
Sunningdale Cl
  22 Bermondsey SE16 .. 118 B1
  Erith SE28 .... 103 A1
  Newham E6 .... 100 B4
  Stanmore HA7 .... 25 A3
  3 Surbiton KT6 .... 214 A6
Sunningdale Ct
  13 Kingston u T KT2 .. 176 C3
  18 Southall UB1 .... 86 A1

Sunningdale Gdns
  Kingsbury NW9 .... 45 A4
  W8 .... 255 B5
Sunningdale Lo HA8 .. 26 B5

Sunningdale Rd
  BR1, BR2 .... 210 A4
  Cheam SM1 .... 217 B4
Sunningfields Cres
  NW4 .... 28 B1
Sunningfields Rd NW4 . 46 B6
Sunninghill Ct 9 W3 .. 111 A4
Sunninghill Gdns IG2 . 57 D4
Sunninghill Rd SE13 . 141 D3
Sunny Bank SE25 .... 206 A6
Sunny Cres NW10 .... 67 A1
Sunnycroft Rd
  Hounslow TW3 .... 129 D3
  Southall UB1 .... 85 C2
  South Norwood SE25 .. 206 A6
Sunnydale BR6 .... 226 C6
Sunnydale Gdns NW7 . 27 C4
Sunnydale Rd SE12 .. 165 B6
Sunnydene Ave
  Chingford E4 .... 36 B5
  Ruislip HA4 .... 62 A6
Sunnydene Gdns HA0 . 65 C2
Sunnydene St SE26 .. 185 A6
Sunnyfield NW7 .... 27 D6
Sunnyfields Prim Sch
  NW4 .... 46 B6
Sunny Gardens Par
  NW4 .... 28 B1
Sunny Gardens Rd
  NW4 .... 46 C6
Sunny Hill NW4 .... 46 B6
Sunnyhill Cl E5 .... 75 A4
Sunny Hill Ct NW4 .. 28 B1
Sunnyhill Prim Sch
  SW16 .... 182 B6
Sunnyhill Rd SW16 .. 182 A6
Sunnyhurst Cl SM1 .. 217 C5
Sunnymead Ave CR4 . 203 D6
Sunnymead Ct 9 W9 . 109 D6
Sunnymead Rd
  Kingsbury NW9 .... 45 B2
  Putney SW15 .... 156 B6
Sunnymede Ave 4 KT19 215 C1
Sunnymede Dr IG6 .. 56 D5
Sunny Nook Gdns
  CR2 .... 221 B2
Sunny Pl NW4 .... 46 C5
Sunny Rd The EN3 .... 6 D4
Sunnyside
  4 Child's Hill NW2 .. 69 B5
  Walton-on-T KT12 .. 194 D4
  Wimbledon SW19 .... 179 A4
Sunnyside Dr E4 .... 20 A4
Sunnyside Ho 3 NW2 . 69 B5
Sunnyside Pl SW19 .. 179 A4
Sunnyside Rd
  Crouch End N19 .... 49 D2
  Ealing W5 .... 109 D5
  Ilford IG1 .... 79 B5
  Teddington TW11 .... 174 B6
  Walthamstow E10 .... 53 C1
Sunnyside Rd E N9 .. 18 A1
Sunnyside Rd N N9 .. 18 A1
Sunnyside Rd S N9 .. 18 A1
Sunny View NW9 .... 45 B4
Sunny Way N12 .... 30 C3
Sun Pas 8 SE16 .... 118 A3
Sunray Ave BR2 .... 210 B3
  Herne Hill SE5, SE24... 139 B1
  Tolworth KT5 .... 214 A6
Sun Rd W14 .... 113 B1 254 C1
Sunrise Cl TW13 .... 151 B1
Sunrise View NW7 .. 27 D4
Sun St Pas EC2 . 95 C2 243 A2
Sunset Ave Chingford E4.. 19 D3
  Woodford IG8 .... 36 D6
Sunset Ct 4 IG8 .... 37 C3
Sunset Gdns SE25.... 183 D1
Sunset Ho HA3 .... 42 C6
Sunset Rd
  Herne Hill SE5 .... 139 B1
  SE28 .... 124 A5
  Wimbledon SW19 .... 178 B5
Sunset View EN5 .... 1 A3
Sunshine Way CR4.... 180 D1
Sun St EC2 .... 95 B2 242 D4
Sunwell Cl SE15 .... 140 B4
Superior Dr 4 BR6 .. 227 D2
Suraj Ho 6 N22 .... 32 C1
SURBITON 198 A2
Surbiton Boys Prep Sch
  KT6 .... 198 A4
Surbiton Cres KT1,
  KT6 .... 198 A5
Surbiton Ct KT6 .... 197 D3
Surbiton Hall Cl KT1 . 198 A5
Surbiton High Sch
  Girls Sch KT1 .... 198 A5
Surbiton Hill Pk KT5 . 198 C4
Surbiton Hill Rd KT6 . 198 A4
Surbiton Hospl KT6 .. 198 A3
Surbiton Par 11 KT6.. 198 A3
Surbiton Rd KT1 .... 198 A3
Surbiton Sta KT6 .... 198 A3
Surcot Ho 2 SW4 .... 137 D3
Surlingham Cl SE28 .. 124 D6
Surma Cl E1 .... 96 A3
Surmans Cl RM9 .... 102 C6
Surrendale Pl W9 .... 91 C3
Surrey Canal Rd SE14, SE16,
  SE8 .... 140 D6
Surrey Cl N3 .... 47 A6
Surrey Cres 1 W4 .... 110 C1
Surrey Ct 15 SM6 .... 219 B2
Surrey Gdns N4 .... 51 A3
Surrey Gr
  Carshalton SM1 .... 218 A5
  SE17 .... 263 A1

Surrey Ho Edgware HA8 .. 26 B4
  8 Rotherhithe SE16... 118 D5
Surrey La
  SW11 .... 136 C4 267 B1
Surrey Lo SW20 .... 178 C1
Surrey Mews SE27 .. 183 C6
Surrey Mount SE23 .. 162 B3
Surrey Quays Rd SE16. 118 C4
Surrey Quays Sh Ctr
  SE16 .... 118 D3
Surrey Quays Sta
  SE16 .... 118 D2
Surrey Rd Barking IG11 . 79 C1
  Dagenham RM10 ..... 81 D3
  Harrow HA1 .... 42 A4
  Honor Oak SE15 .... 162 D6
  West Wickham BR4... 207 D1
Surrey Row
  SE1 .... 116 D4 251 D2
Surrey Sq SE17 . 117 C1 263 B2
Surrey Square Inf Sch
  SE17 .... 117 C1 263 A2
Surrey Square Jun Sch
  SE17 .... 117 C1 263 A2
Surrey St Croydon CR0 . 221 A5
  4 Newham E13 ..... 99 B4
  WC2 .... 116 B6 250 D6
Surrey Terr SE17 .... 263 B2
Surrey Water Rd
  SE16 .... 118 D5
Surrey Wharf SE1 .... 140 A6
Surridge Ct 15 SW9 . 138 A3
Surridge Gdns SE19.. 183 B4
Surr St N7 .... 72 A3
Sury Basin KT2 .... 176 A2
Susan Constant Ct 18
  E14 .... 120 B4
Susan Lawrence Ho 4
  E12 .... 78 C4
Susannah St E14 .... 98 A1
Susan Rd SE3 .... 143 B3
Susan Wood BR7 .... 188 C3
Sussex Ave TW7 .... 130 C2
Sussex Cl
  New Malden KT3 .... 199 C5
  Redbridge IG4 .... 56 B4
  4 Twickenham TW1... 153 B5
  Upper Holloway N19 .. 72 A6
Sussex Cres UB5 .... 63 C2
Sussex Ct
  4 Barnes SW13 ..... 133 D3
  Greenwich SE10 ..... 142 A6
  Mitcham CR4 .... 204 A4
  Paddington W2 .... 236 C1
Sussex Gate N6 .... 48 D4
Sussex Gdns
  Chessington KT9 ..... 213 D2
  Fortis Green N6 .... 48 D4
  Harringay N4 .... 51 A4
  Paddington W2 .. 92 B1 236 D1
Sussex Ho Edgware HA8.. 26 B4
  Hampstead NW3 .... 70 C2
  Richmond TW9 .... 132 B3
Sussex House Sch
  SW3 .... 114 D3 257 C4
Sussex Lo W2 .... 236 D1
Sussex Mans
  South Kensington
  SW7 .... 256 C3
  Strand WC2 .... 250 B6
Sussex Mews SE6 .. 163 C3
Sussex Mews E W2 .. 236 D1
Sussex Mews W W2 .. 246 D6
Sussex Pl
  22 Hammersmith W6 .. 112 C1
  Lisson Gr NW1 .. 92 D3 237 C6
  New Malden KT3..... 199 C5
  Paddington W2 .. 92 B1 236 D1
Sussex Ring N12 .... 29 C5
Sussex Sq W2 .. 114 B6 246 D6
Sussex St Newham E13 ... 99 B4
  SW1 .... 258 B2
Sussex Way
  Cockfosters EN4 ..... 15 B6
  Upper Holloway N7.... 72 B5
  Upper Holloway N7, N19.. 72 A6
  Upper Holloway N19 .. 49 D1
Sutcliffe Cl NW11.... 47 D4
Sutcliffe Ho UB3 .... 84 A1
Sutcliffe Rd
  Bexley DA16 .... 146 C3
  SE18 .... 145 C6
Sutherland Ave
  Ealing W13 .... 87 B1
  Falconwood DA16 ..... 145 C1
  Hayes UB3 .... 106 A2
  Orpington BR5 .... 211 D4
  Paddington W9 .. 92 A3 236 A6
  Sunbury TW16 .... 171 D1
Sutherland Cl EN5 .. 1 A1
Sutherland Ct
  Kingsbury NW9 .... 44 D4
  3 Paddington W9 .... 91 C3
  Stoke Newington N16. 73 B5
Sutherland Dr SW19.. 180 B2
Sutherland Gdns
  Mortlake SW14 .... 133 C2
  North Cheam KT4 .... 200 B1
  Sunbury TW16 .... 171 D1

Sutherland Gr
  Putney SW18, SW19... 157 B2
  Teddington TW11 .... 174 C5
Sutherland Ho
  Ealing W13 .... 109 A6
  Kensington W8 .... 255 C5
  Kidbrooke SE18 .... 144 B4
  7 Putney SW15 .... 156 C4
  Richmond TW10 .... 153 C2
  9 South Hampstead
  NW6 .... 70 A2
Sutherland Pl W2 .... 91 C1
Sutherland Rd
  Belvedere DA17 ..... 125 C3
  Chiswick W4 .... 133 C6
  Ealing W13 .... 87 A1
  Edmonton N9 .... 18 B3
  Enfield EN3 .... 18 D6
  Southall UB1 .... 85 B1
  Thornton Heath CR0... 204 C2
  Tottenham N17 .... 34 A2
  Walthamstow E17 .... 53 A6
Sutherland Row SW1. 258 D2
Sutherland Sq
  SE17 .... 117 A1 262 A1
Sutherland St
  SW1 .... 115 B1 258 D2
Sutherland Wlk SE17. 262 B1
Sutlej Rd SE7 .... 143 C5
Sutterton St N7 .... 72 B2
SUTTON 218 A2
Sutton Cl
  Beckenham BR3 ..... 185 D2
  Pinner HA5 .... 40 A4
Sutton Coll of Liberal Arts
  SM1 .... 217 D3
Sutton Common Rd
  Cheam SM3 .... 201 C1
  Sutton SM1, SM3..... 217 D6
Sutton Common Sta
  SM1 .... 217 D6
Sutton Courtenay Ho
  SW17 .... 180 B6
Sutton Court Mans
  W4 .... 133 A6
Sutton Court Rd
  Chiswick W4 .... 133 A6
  Hillingdon UB10 .... 82 D6
  Newham E13 .... 99 C4
  Sutton SM1 .... 218 A2
Sutton Cres EN5 .... 12 D6
Sutton Ct Chiswick W4 . 133 A6
  Ealing W5 .... 110 A5
  East Molesey KT8.... 195 B4
  8 Hackney E5 .... 74 B4
  Penge SE19 .... 183 D3
  Sutton SM1 .... 218 A2
Sutton Dene TW3 .... 129 D4
Sutton Est
  SW3 .... 114 C1 257 B2
Sutton Est The 8 W10 . 90 C2
Sutton Gdns
  Barking IG11 .... 101 C5
  Croydon CR0 .... 205 D4
Sutton Gn IG11 .... 101 C6
Sutton Gr SM1 .... 218 B3
Sutton Gram Sch For Boys
  SM1 .... 218 A3
Sutton Hall Rd TW5.. 129 C5
Sutton High Sch SM1 . 217 D2
Sutton Ho N21 .... 16 B6
Sutton Hts SM2 .... 218 B1
Sutton La EC1 .... 241 D5
  Hounslow TW3, TW4,
  TW5 .... 129 B3
Sutton La N W4 .... 111 A1
Sutton La S W4 .... 133 A6
Sutton Par NW4 .... 46 C5
Sutton Park Rd SM1,
  SM2 .... 217 D2
Sutton Pl E9 .... 74 C3
Sutton Rd
  Barking IG11 .... 101 C6
  E13 .... 98 D3
  Heston TW5 .... 129 C4
  Higham Hill E17 ..... 34 D2
  Muswell Hill N10 .... 31 A2
Sutton Row W1 .... 239 D2
Sutton Sq Hackney E9 .. 74 C3
  Hounslow TW5 .... 129 B4
Sutton St E1 .... 96 C1
Sutton Sta SM2 .... 218 A4
Suttons Way EC1 .... 242 B5
Sutton Way
  Hounslow TW5 .... 129 B4
  North Kensington W10.. 90 C2
Sutton Wlk
  SE1 .... 116 B5 250 D3
Swaby Rd SW17, SW18. 158 A2
Swaffham Ct 1 RM6 .. 58 C4
Swaffield Prim Sch
  SW18 .... 158 A4
Swaffield Rd SW18 .. 158 A4
Swain Cl SW16 .... 181 B4
Swain Ho 4 SW18 .... 180 D3
Swain Rd CR7 .... 205 A4
Swains Cl UB7 .... 104 A4
Swain's La N6 .... 71 B6
Swainson Ho N7 .... 72 C4
Swainson Rd W3 .... 111 D4
Swains Rd CR4, SW17.. 180 D3
Swain St NW8 .. 92 C3 237 A6
Swakeleys Dr UB10 .. 60 C3
Swakeleys Rd UB10 .. 60 C4
Swakeleys Rdbt UB8,
  UB10 .... 60 A4
Swakeleys Sch UB10. 82 B5
Swaledale Cl N11 .... 31 A4
Swallands Rd SE6 .... 163 C1

Swallowbrook Bsns Ctr
  UB4 .... 106 D5
Swallow Cl Bushey WD23.. 8 A3
  New Cross Gate SE14.. 140 D4
Swallow Ct
  Chingford IG8 .... 36 B3
  Ilford IG2 .... 56 D4
  4 Paddington W9 .... 91 C2
  6 Ruislip HA4 .... 40 C1
  1 SE12 .... 165 A4
Swallow Dr
  Northolt UB5 .... 85 C5
  Willesden NW10 .... 67 B2
Swallowfield NW1 .. 231 D1
Swallowfield Rd SE7 . 121 B1
Swallowfield Way
  UB3 .... 105 B4
Swallow Gdns SW16 . 181 D5
Swallow Ho Hornsey N8. 50 B6
  NW8 .... 230 A4
Swallow Pk KT6 .... 214 B5
Swallow Pl
  24 Poplar E14 .... 97 B1
  W1 .... 238 D1
Swallows Ct 5 SE20 . 184 D3
Swallow St
  Newham E6 .... 100 A2
  W1 .... 115 C6 249 B5
Swaminarayan Sch The
  NW10 .... 67 B2
Swanage Ct 5 N1 .... 73 C1
Swanage Ho SW8 .... 270 C3
Swanage Rd
  Chingford E4 .... 36 A3
  Wandsworth SW18 ... 158 A5
Swanage Waye UB4... 84 C1
Swan And Pike Rd EN3.. 7 C5
Swan App E6 .... 100 A2
Swanbourne SE17 .. 262 A3
Swanbourne Ho NW8 . 237 A6
Swanbridge Rd DA7... 147 C4
Swan Bsns Ctr 8 W4 . 111 B2
Swan Ct Chelsea SW3 . 257 B1
  Parsons Green SW6 .. 265 A3
  Poplar E14 .... 97 B1
  Whetstone N20 .... 14 A2
Swan Ctr SW17 .... 158 A1
Swandon Way SW18 . 135 D1
Swan Dr NW9 .... 27 C1
Swanfield St E2 .... 95 D4
Swan Ho
  De Beauvoir Town N1. 73 B1
  Enfield EN3 .... 18 C6
Swan La EC4 .. 117 B6 252 C5
  Loughton IG10 .... 21 C4
  Whetstone N20 .... 14 A1
Swan Lane Pier
  EC4 .... 117 B6 252 C5
Swanlea Sec Sch E1 .. 96 B3
Swanley Ho SE17 .... 263 B2
Swanley Rd DA16 .... 146 C4
Swan Mead
  SE1 .... 117 C3 263 D6
Swan Mews
  Stockwell SW9 .... 138 B3
  SW6 .... 265 A2
Swanmore Ct SW18.. 158 A5
Swann Ct 8 TW7 .... 131 A2
Swanne Ho 12 SE10 .. 142 A5
Swan Pas 5 E1 .... 118 A6
Swan Pl SW13 .... 133 D3
Swan Rd Feltham TW13. 173 A6
  Greenwich SE18 ..... 121 D3
  Rotherhithe SE16 .... 118 C4
  Southall UB1 .... 85 D1
  West Drayton UB7 .. 104 A4
Swanscombe Ho
  1 BR5 .... 190 B1
  11 Shepherd's Bush
  W11 .... 112 D5
Swanscombe Point 7
  E16 .... 98 D2
Swanscombe Rd
  5 Chiswick W4 .... 111 C1
  Shepherd's Bush W11.. 112 D5
Swansea Ct E16 .... 122 D5
Swansea Rd Enfield EN3.. 6 C1
  Harlington TW4, TW6 . 149 B5
Swansland Gdns 2
  E17 .... 35 A2
Swan St Isleworth TW7. 131 B2
  SE1 .... 117 A4 252 B1
Swanston Ct TW1..... 152 D4
Swan The BR4 .... 224 B6
Swanton Gdns SW19. 156 D3
Swanton Rd DA8..... 147 D6
Swan Way EN3 .... 6 D3
Swanwick Cl SW15... 155 D4
Swan Wlk
  Oatlands Pk TW17..... 193 C2
  SW3 .... 136 D6 267 C6
Swan Yd N1 .... 72 D2
Swaton Rd E3 .... 97 C3
Swaylands Rd DA17... 147 C6
Swaythling Cl N18 .... 34 B6
Swaythling Ho SW15.. 155 D5
Swedenborg Gdns E1. 118 B6
Sweden Gate SE16.... 119 A2
Swedish Quays SE16. 119 A3
Swedish Sch The
  SW13 .... 134 A6
Sweeney Cres SE1 .. 253 D1
Sweet Briar Gn N9 .... 17 D1
Sweet Briar Gr N9 .... 17 D1
Sweet Briar Wlk N18. 33 D6
Sweetcroft La UB10... 60 C1
Sweetmans Ave HA5.. 40 D6

Sweets Way N20 .... 14 B2
Swell Ct E17 .... 53 D3
Swetenham Wlk SE18. 123 A1
Swete St E13 .... 99 A5
Sweyn Pl SE3 .... 143 A3
Swift Cl Harrow HA2 .. 63 D6
  Hayes UB3 .... 83 D1
  Higham Hill E17 ..... 35 A3
  Thamesmead SE28 ... 124 B6
Swift Ct SM2 .... 217 D1
Swift Ctr CR0 .... 220 B1
Swift Ho 16 Stepney E1. 96 C1
  15 Stoke Newington N16. 73 C5
  1 SW9 .... 138 C5
  4 Wanstead E18 .... 55 B6
Swift Rd Feltham TW13. 173 A6
  Southall UB1 .... 107 B3
Swiftsden Way BR1... 186 C4
Swift St SW6 .. 135 B4 264 C2
Swinbrook Rd W10 .. 91 A2
Swinburne Cres CR0 . 206 C3
Swinburne Ct 4 SE5. 139 B1
Swinburne Ho 15 E2 . 96 C4
Swinburne Rd SW15 . 134 A1
Swinderby Rd HA0 .. 66 A2
Swindon Cl IG3 .... 57 C1
Swindon Rd TW6 .... 149 A6
Swindon St W12 .... 112 C5
Swinfield Cl TW13 .. 173 A4
Swinford Gdns SW9.. 138 D2
Swingate La SE18 .. 145 C5
Swinfield St E2 .... 209 D4
Swinford Ho 4 E9 .... 96 C5
Swinley Ho NW1 .... 231 D2
Swinnerton St E9 .... 75 A3
Swinson Ho 12 N11 .. 31 C5
Swinton Cl HA9 .... 44 D1
Swinton Ho 21 E2.... 96 A4
Swinton Pl WC1 .... 233 C2
Swinton St WC1 . 94 B4 233 C2
Swires Shaw BR2 .... 225 D4
Swiss Cottage * NW3.. 70 B1
Swiss Cottage Sch
  South Hampstead NW3. 70 B1
  St John's Wood
  NW8 .... 92 B6 229 D6
Swiss Cottage Sta NW3. 70 B1
Swiss Re Building
  EC2 .... 95 C1 243 B2
Swiss Terr 7 NW3 .... 70 B1
Switch Ho 4 E14 .... 120 B6
Swithland Gdns SE9.. 188 C6
Swyncombe Ave W5... 109 B2
Swynford Gdns 7
  NW4 .... 46 A5
Sybil Elgar Sch UB2... 107 B3
Sybil Mews N4 .... 50 D3
Sybil Phoenix Cl SE8. 118 D1
Sybil Thorndike Casson Ho
  SW5 .... 255 B1
Sybil Thorndike Ho 12
  N1 .... 73 A2
Sybourn Inf Sch Annexe
  E10 .... 53 A1
Sybourn Jun & Inf Schs
  E17 .... 53 B2
Sybourn St E17 .... 53 B2
Sycamore Ave DA15... 167 D5
  Ealing W5 .... 109 D3
  East Finchley N3 ..... 47 D6
  Hayes UB3 .... 105 C6
  Old Ford E3 .... 97 B6
Sycamore Cl
  Carshalton SM5....... 218 D4
  Chislehurst SE9...... 166 A2
  East Acton W3....... 111 C5
  2 Edgware HA8 .... 27 A6
  Edmonton N9....... 34 A6
  Feltham TW13....... 150 A1
  New Barnet EN4 ..... 14 B5
  Newham E16........ 98 C3
  Northolt UB5........ 85 A6
  South Croydon CR2... 221 C3
  Yiewsley UB7 .... 104 B6
Sycamore Ct
  4 Beckenham BR3... 185 C2
  Forest Gate E7 .... 77 A2
  3 Forest Hill SE26.. 184 C6
  Golders Green NW11... 47 A3
  Hendon NW4 .... 28 C1
  Hillingdon UB8....... 82 C3
  Hither Green SE12.... 164 D5
  Hounslow TW4 .... 129 A1
  Kilburn NW6 .... 91 C6
  Surbiton KT6 .... 198 A2
  Tufnell Pk N19....... 71 D5
  10 West Norwood
  SE16 .... 182 C6
Sycamore Gdns
  Hammersmith W6,
  W12 .... 112 B3
  Mitcham CR4 .... 180 B1
  Tottenham N15 .... 51 D5
Sycamore Gr
  Kingsbury NW9 .... 45 A2
  Kingston u T KT3 .... 199 C6
  Lewisham SE6 .... 164 A5
  Penge SE20 .... 184 A2
Sycamore Hill N11 .. 31 A4
Sycamore Ho
  4 Buckhurst Hill IG9... 21 D2
  21 Finchley N2 .... 30 B1
  10 Maitland Pk NW3. 70 D2
  8 Penge SE20 .... 184 D4
  17 Rotherhithe SE16.. 118 D4

Sycamore Ho *continued*
3 Shepherd's Bush W6 112 B4
2 Stoke Newington N16 73 B6
Teddington TW11 175 C3
Twickenham TW1 152 D2
Sycamore Lo
7 Ashford TW16 171 D3
Putney SW15 134 B2
Sycamore Lodge HA2 64 B6
Sycamore Mews 4 SW4 137 C2
Sycamore Rd SW19, SW20 178 C4
Sycamore St EC1 242 A5
Sycamore Way TW11 175 C4
Sycamore Wlk
Ilford IG6 57 A5
1 Kensal Town W10 91 A3
Sydcote SE21 161 A3
Sydenham Ave
Penge SE26 184 B5
Southgate N21 16 B6
Sydenham High Sch SE26 162 B1
Sydenham High Sch GDST SE26 184 B5
Sydenham Hill SE21, SE22, SE23, SE26, SE19 162 A1
Sydenham Hill Sta SE21 161 D1
Sydenham Ho 18 KT6 197 D2
Sydenham Ind Est SE26 185 B5
Sydenham Park Mans 2 SE26 162 C1
Sydenham Park Rd SE23, SE26 162 C1
Sydenham Pk SE26 162 C1
Sydenham Rd
Forest Hill SE26 185 A6
Thornton Heath CR0 205 B2
Sydenham Rise SE23 162 B2
Sydenham Sta SE26 184 C6
Sydenham Station App 4 SE26 184 C6
Sydmons Ct SE23 162 C4
Sydner Mews N16 73 D4
Sydner Rd N16 73 D4
Sydney Chapman Way EN5 1 B3
Sydney Cl SW3 256 D3
Sydney Cotts KT10 212 D2
Sydney Cres TW15 170 D4
Sydney Ct Hayes UB4 84 C3
Surbiton KT6 214 A6
Sydney Gr NW4 46 C4
Sydney Ho
4 Chiswick W4 111 C2
Muswell Hill N10 31 B3
Sydney Mews SW3 256 D3
Sydney Pl SW7 257 A3
Sydney Rd
Abbey Wood SE2 124 D3
Bexley DA6 146 D1
Ealing W13 109 A4
East Bedfont TW14 150 A3
Enfield EN2 5 B1
Hornsey N8 50 C5
Muswell Hill N10 31 B3
Richmond TW10, TW9 132 A1
Sidcup DA14 189 C6
Sutton SM1 217 C4
Teddington TW11 174 D5
Wanstead E11 55 B3
West Barnes SW20 178 D1
Woodford IG8 37 A6
Sydney Russell Sch The RM9 80 D3
Sydney St SW3 114 C1 257 A2
Sydney Terr KT10 212 D2
Sylva Cotts 3 SE8 141 C4
Sylva Ct 3 SW15 156 D4
Sylvana Cl UB10 82 B6
Sylvan Ave
Church End N3 29 C1
Dagenham RM6 59 B3
Edgware NW7 27 D4
Wood Green N22 32 C3
Sylvan Ct Finchley N12 29 D6
1 Kilburn NW6 91 D6
South Croydon CR2 221 A2
Sylvan Gdns KT6 197 D2
Sylvan Gr
Hampstead NW2 68 D4
SE15 140 B6
Sylvan Hill SE19 183 C2
Sylvan Ho N21 16 B6
Sylvan Rd Ilford IG1 79 A6
South Norwood SE19 183 D2
Upton E7 77 B2
Walthamstow E17 53 C4
Wanstead E11 55 A4
Sylvan Way
Coney Hall BR4 224 C4
Dagenham RM8 80 B5
Sylvan Wlk BR1 210 B6
Sylverdale Rd CR0 220 D5
Sylvester Ave BR7 188 B4
Sylvester Ct HA0 65 D3
Sylvester Ho 7 E8 74 B2
Sylvester Path 8 E8 74 B2
Sylvester Rd Finchley N2 30 B1
Hackney E8 74 B2
Walthamstow E17 53 B2
Wembley HA0 65 C3
Sylvestrus Cl KT1 176 C1
Sylvia Ave HA5 23 B4
Sylvia Ct N1 235 C3
Wembley HA9 66 D1
Sylvia Gdns HA9 66 D1
Sylvia Lawla Ct N22 32 B1
Sylvia Pankhurst Ho
10 Dagenham RM10 81 C5
14 Globe Town E2 96 D4
Sylvia Young Theatre Sch NW1 237 B5
Symes Mews NW1 232 A4
Symington Ho SE1 262 C5
Symington Mews E9 74 D3
Symister Mews N1 95 C4
Symons St SW3 114 D2 257 D3
Symphony Cl HA8 26 D3
Symphony Mews 15 W10 91 A4
Syon Gate Way TW7, TW8 131 B5
Syon Ho & Pk* TW8 131 C4
Syon La
Brentford TW7, TW8 131 B5
Hounslow TW7 130 D6
Syon Lane Sta TW7 131 A5
Syon Lo 6 SE12 165 A4
Syon Park Cotts TW8 131 C4
Syon Park Gdns TW7 130 D5
Syon Park Sch TW7 131 B4
Syringa Ho SE4 141 B2

T

Tabard Ct 6 E14 98 A1
Tabard Ho SE1 262 D6
Teddington KT1 175 C2
Tabard St SE1 117 B3 262 C6
Tabernacle Ave 7 E13 99 A3
Tabernacle St EC2 95 B3 242 D6
Tableer Ave SW4 159 D6
Tabley Rd N7 72 A4
Tabor Ct 3 SM3 217 A2
Tabor Gdns SM2, SM3 217 B1
Tabor Gr SW19 179 B3
Tabor Rd W6 112 B3
Tachbrook Est SW1 115 D1 259 D1
Tachbrook Mews SW1 259 A4
Tachbrook Rd
East Bedfont TW14 149 D4
Southall UB2 106 D2
Tachbrook St SW1 115 C2 259 B3
Tack Mews SE4 141 C2
Tadbourne Ct 1 HA8 27 A3
Tadema Ho NW8 236 D5
Tadema Rd SW10 136 A5 266 B3
Tadlow KT1 198 C6
Tadmor Cl TW16 193 D5
Tadmor St W12 112 D5
Tadworth Ave KT3 199 D4
Tadworth Ct 5 N11 31 A4
Tadworth Ho SE1 251 C1
Tadworth Rd NW2 68 A6
Taeping St E14 119 D2
Taffrail Ho 2 E14 119 D1
Taffy's How CR4 202 C6
Taft Way 44 E3 97 D4
Taggs Ho KT1 175 D1
Tailors Ct 9 SW16 181 C6
Tailworth St 16 E1 96 A2
Tait 7 NW9 27 D3
Tait Ct 16 Old Ford E3 97 B6
SW8 269 D2
Tait Ho SE1 251 B3
2 Tufnell Pk N19 71 C4
Tait Rd CR0 205 C2
Tait Rd Ind Est CR0 205 C2
Takhar Mews SW11 136 C3
Talacre Rd NW5 71 A2
Talbot Ave N2 48 B6
Talbot Cl N15 51 D5
Talbot Cres NW4 46 A4
Talbot Ct EC3 252 D6
Neasden NW9 67 B5
Talbot Gdns IG3 80 A6
Talbot Grove Ho 10 W11 91 A1
Talbot Ho Highbury N7 72 C5
Poplar E14 97 D1
Talbot Pl SE3 142 C3
Talbot Rd
Ashford TW15 170 A5
Camberwell SE22 139 C1
Dagenham RM9 81 B1
Ealing W13 109 A5
Forest Gate E7 77 A4
Harrow HA3 24 D1
Highgate N6 49 A3
Isleworth TW1, TW7 131 A1
Notting Hill W2 91 C1
Notting Hill W11 91 B1
Southall UB2 107 A2
South Norwood CR7 205 B5
Tottenham N15 51 D5
Twickenham TW2 152 D3
Wallend E6 100 C5
Wallington SM5 219 A3
Wembley HA0 65 D2
Wood Green N22 31 C2
Talbot Sq W2 92 B1 236 C1
Talbot Wlk
Notting Hill W11 91 A1
Willesden NW10 67 C2
Talbot Yd SE1 252 C3
Talcott Path 12 SW2 160 C3
Talfourd Pl SE15 139 D4
Talfourd Rd SE15 139 D4
Talgarth Rd
Hammersmith W6 112 C1
W14 113 A1 254 B2
Talgarth Wlk NW9 45 C4
Talia Ho E14 120 A3
Talina Ctr SW6 266 A1
Talisman Cl 2 IG3 58 B1
Talisman Sq SE26 184 A6
Talisman Way HA9 66 B5
Tallack Cl HA3 24 C3
Tallack Rd E10 53 B1
Tall Elms Cl BR2 208 D4
Talleyrand Ho SE5 139 A3
Tallis Cl E16 99 B1
Tallis Gr SE7 143 B6
Tallis St EC4 251 B6
Tallis View NW10 67 B2
Tallow Rd TW8 131 C5
Tall Trees SW16 204 B6
Talma Gdns TW2 152 C4
Talmage Cl SE23 162 C4
Talman Gr HA7 25 D4
Talma Rd SW2 138 C1
Talmud Torah Chaim Meirim Sch N16 51 D1
Talmud Torah Machzikei Hadass Sch E5 52 A2
Talmud-Torah Yetev-Lev N16 52 A1
Talwin St E3 97 D4
Tamar Cl 24 E3 97 B6
Tamar Ho
10 Cubitt Town E14 120 A4
SE11 261 B2
Tamarind Ct 8 W3 89 A1
Tamarind Ho 4 SE15 140 A5
Tamarind Yd 5 E1 118 A5
Tamarisk Sq W12 111 D6
Tamar Sq IG8 37 B4
Tamar St SE7 122 A2
Tamar Way N17 52 A6
Tame Ho 3 UB5 85 B4
Tamesa Ho TW17 192 C2
Tamesis Gdns KT4 215 C6
Tamian Ind Est TW4 128 C1
Tamian Way TW4 128 C1
Tamil Ho SE6 163 C2
Tamworth N7 72 A2
Tamworth Ave IG8 36 C4
Tamworth La CR4 203 B6
Tamworth Pk CR4 203 B6
Tamworth Pl 3 CR0 221 A6
Tamworth Rd CR0 221 A6
Tamworth St SW6 135 C6 265 A5
Tancred Rd N4 50 D3
Tandem Ctr SW19 180 B2
Tandridge Ct SM2 217 D2
Tandridge Dr BR6 211 B1
Tandridge Pl 2 BR6 211 B1
Tanfield Ave NW2 67 D5
Tanfield Rd CR0 221 A4
Tangier Rd TW10 132 D2
Tangleberry Cl BR1 210 B5
Tangle Tree Cl N3 29 D1
Tanglewood Cl
Hillingdon UB10 82 C3
South Croydon CR0 222 C5
Stanmore HA7 8 C2
Tanglewood Lo HA8 27 A4
Tanglewood Way TW13 150 B1
Tangley Gr SW15 155 D4
Tangley Park Rd TW12 173 B4
Tanglyn Ave TW17 192 D4
Tangmere
Tottenham N17 33 B1
WC1 233 C1
Tangmere Gdns UB5 84 C5
Tangmere Gr KT2 175 D5
Tangmere Way NW9 27 C1
Tanhurst Ho 27 SW2 160 A4
Tanhurst Wlk SE2 124 D3
Tankerton Rd KT6 214 B6
Tankerton St WC1 233 B1
Tankerton Terr CR0 204 B3
Tankerville Rd SW16 182 A3
Tankridge Rd NW2 68 B6
Tanner Ho
1 Merton SW19 180 A2
SE1 253 B1
Tanner Point E13 99 A6
Tanners Cl KT12 194 B3
Tanners End La N18 33 C5
Tanner's Hill SE8 141 C4
Tanners La IG6 57 A6
Tanners Mews SE8 141 B4
Tanner St Barking IG11 79 A2
SE1 117 C4 253 B1
Tanners Yd 33 E2 96 B5
Tannery Cl
Beckenham BR3, CR0 206 D4
Dagenham RM10 81 D5
Tannery Ho 22 E1 96 A2
Tannington Terr N5 72 C5
Tannsfeld Rd SE26 184 D5
Tansley Cl N7 71 D3
Tanswell St SE1 251 A1
Tansy Cl E6 100 C1
Tantallon Rd SW12 159 A3
Tant Ave E16 98 D1
Tantony Gr RM6 58 D6
Tanworth Gdns HA5 22 C1
Tanyard Ho 8 TW8 131 C5
Tan Yard La DA5 169 C4
Tanza Rd NW3 70 D4
Tapestry Cl SM2 217 D1
Tapley Ho 11 SE1 118 A4
Taplow NW3 70 B1
Taplow Ct CR4 202 C5
Taplow Ho 36 E2 95 D4
Taplow Rd N13 33 A6
Taplow St N1 95 A5 235 B3
Tappesfield Rd SE15 140 C2
Tapping Cl 5 KT2 176 C3
Tapp St E1 96 B3
Tapster St EN5 1 B2
Tara Ct 4 BR3 185 D1
Taranto Ho 14 E1 96 D2
Tarati Ct HA0 65 D1
Tarbert Rd SE22 161 C6
Tarbert Wlk E1 118 C6
Target Cl TW14 149 C5
Target Ho W13 109 B5
Target Rdbt UB5 85 B6
Tariff Rd N17 34 A4
Tarleton Ct 2 N22 32 C1
Tarleton Gdns SE23 162 B3
Tarling Cl DA14 168 B1
Tarling Rd
Canning Town E16 98 D1
Finchley N2 30 A1
Tarling St E1 96 C1
Tarnbank EN2 16 A6
Tarnbrook Ct SW1 258 A3
Tarn St SE1 117 A3 262 A5
Tarns The NW1 232 A2
Tarnwood Pk SE9 166 B3
Tarplett Ho 22 SE14 140 D6
Tarquin Ho SE26 184 A6
Tarragon Cl SE14 141 A5
Tarragon Gr SE26 184 D4
Tarranbrae NW6 69 A1
Tarrant Ho E2 96 C4
Tarrant Pl W1 237 C3
Tarrantt Ho W14 254 A6
Tarriff Cres SE8 119 B2
Tarrington Cl SW16 159 D1
Tartan Ho 12 E14 98 A1
Tarver Rd SE17 116 D1 261 D2
Tarves Way SE10 141 D5
Tash Pl N11 31 B5
Tasker Cl UB7 127 A5
Tasker Ho
3 Barking IG11 101 B5
17 Poplar E14 97 B2
Tasker Lo W8 245 A2
Tasker Rd NW3 70 D3
Tasman Ct
Ashford TW16 171 C3
9 Cubitt Town E14 119 D2
Tasman Ho 17 E1 118 B5
Tasmania Terr N18 33 A4
Tasman Rd SW9 138 A2
Tasman Wlk E16 99 D1
Tasso Rd W6 135 A6 264 A6
Tasso Yd W6 264 A5
Tatam Rd NW10 67 B1
Tatchbury Ho SW15 155 D5
Tate Britain* SW1 116 A2 260 A3
Tate Gdns WD23 8 C4
Tate Ho 13 E2 96 D5
Tate Modern* EC4 116 D5 251 D4
Tate Rd Newham E16 122 B5
Sutton SM1 217 C3
Tatham Pl NW8 92 B5 229 D4
Tatnell Rd SE23 163 A5
Tattersall Cl SE9 166 A6
Tatton Cres E5, N16 51 D2
Tatum St SE17 117 B2 262 D3
Tauheed Cl N4 73 A6
Taunton Ave
Hounslow TW3 130 A3
Wimbledon SW20 178 B1
Taunton Cl SM3 201 C1
Taunton Dr Enfield EN2 4 C2
Finchley N2 30 A1
Taunton Ho W2 236 A1
Taunton Mews NW1 237 C5
Taunton Pl NW1 92 D3 237 C6
Taunton Rd
Greenford UB6 85 D6
Lewisham SE12 164 D6
Taunton Way HA7 26 A1
Tavern Cl SM5 202 C2
Tavern Ct SE1 262 B5
Taverner Ho N16 73 B5
Taverners Cl W11 244 A3
Taverners Ct HA9 66 B6
Taverners Lo EN4 15 A6
Taverner Sq 4 N5 73 A4
Taverners Way E4 20 C3
Tavern La SW9 138 C3
Tavistock Ave
Mill Hill NW7 28 D3
Walthamstow E17 53 A6
Wembley UB6 87 A5
Tavistock Cl N16 73 C3
Tavistock Cres
Mitcham CR4 204 A5
Notting Hill W11 91 B2
Tavistock Ct
1 Croydon CR0 205 B1
WC1 239 D6
Tavistock Gdns IG3 79 C4
Tavistock Gr CR0 205 B2
Tavistock Ho 3 W11 91 B2
Tavistock Mews 3 W11 91 B1
Tavistock Pl
Bloomsbury WC1 94 A3 240 A6
East Barnet N14 15 B5
Tavistock Rd
4 Beckenham BR2 208 D5
Carshalton SM5 202 B1
Croydon CR0 205 B1
DA16 146 C4
Dagenham NW10 89 D5
Edgware HA8 26 C2
Leyton E7 76 D4
Notting Hill W11 91 B2
Stratford E15 76 D2
Tottenham N4, N15 51 B3
Uxbridge UB10 61 A3
Wanstead E18 55 A6
Tavistock Sq WC1 93 D3 239 D6
Tavistock St WC2 116 A6 250 B6
Tavistock Terr N19 71 D5
Tavistock Twr SE16 119 A3
Tavistock Wlk SM5 202 B1
Taviton St WC1 93 D3 239 C6
Tavy Bridge SE2 124 C4
Tavy Cl SE11 261 B2
Tawney Rd SE28 124 B6
Tawny Cl Ealing W13 109 B5
Feltham TW13 150 A1
Tawny Way SE16 118 D2
Tayben Ave TW2 152 C5
Taybridge Rd SW11 137 A1
Tayburn Cl E14 98 A1
Tayfield Cl UB10 61 A5
Tay Ho 10 E3 97 B5
Tayler Ct NW8 229 C6
Taylor Ave TW9 132 D3
Taylor Cl Deptford SE8 141 B6
Hampton TW12 174 A5
Hounslow TW3 130 A4
3 Orpington BR6 227 D4
Tottenham N17 34 A3
Taylor Ct Ealing W13 109 C5
Penge SE20 184 C1
Stratford New Town E15 76 A3
Taylor Ho
Carshalton SM5 218 C6
10 Streatham SW2 160 C3
Taylor Rd Mitcham CR4 180 C3
Wallington SM6 219 B3
Taylor's Bldgs SE18 122 D2
Taylors Cl DA14 167 D1
Taylors Ct TW13 150 A2
Taylor's Gn W3 89 C1
Taylor's La Barnet EN5 1 B4
Forest Hill SE26 184 B6
Willesden NW10 67 C1
Taylorsmead NW7 28 A5
Taymount Grange 2 SE23 162 C2
Taymount Rise SE23 162 C2
Tayport Cl N1 72 A1
Tayside Ct 6 SE5 139 B1
Tayside Dr HA8 10 D2
Taywood Rd UB5 85 B3
Teak Cl SE16 119 A5
Tealby Ct N7 72 B2
Teal Cl Enfield EN3 6 C6
Newham E16 99 D2
Teal Ct 30 SE8 141 B6
Wallington SM6 219 C3
Willesden NW10 67 B2
Teale St E2 96 A5
Tealing Dr KT19 215 B4
Teal Pl SM1 217 B3
Teal St 1 SE10 120 D3
Teasel Cl CR0 206 D1
Teasel Cres SE28 123 C5
Teasel Way E15 98 C4
Teather St 12 SE5 139 C5
Tebbs Ho 14 SW2 160 C4
Tebworth Rd N17 33 D3
Technology Pk NW9 45 C6
Teck Cl TW7 131 A3
Tedder 5 NW9 27 D3
Tedder Cl
Chessington KT9 213 C3
Hillingdon UB10 60 B1
Tedder Rd CR2 222 D1
TEDDINGTON 175 C5
Teddington Meml Hospl TW11 174 C4
Teddington Park Rd TW11 174 D6
Teddington Pk TW11 174 D5
Teddington Sch TW11 175 C4
Teddington Sta TW11 175 A4
Ted Hennem Ho RM10 81 D5
Tedman Ct SE13 142 A1
Ted Roberts Ho 25 E2 96 B5
Tedworth Gdns SW3 257 C1
Tedworth Sq SW3 114 D1 257 C1
Tees Ave UB6 86 D5
Tees Ct W7 86 B1
Teesdale Ave TW7 131 A4
Teesdale Cl E2 96 B5
Teesdale Gdns
Isleworth TW7 131 A4
South Norwood SE25 183 C1
Teesdale Rd E11 54 D2
Teesdale St E2 96 B5
Teesdale Yd 34 E2 96 B5
Teeswater Ct DA18 124 D3
Tee The W3 89 C1
Teevan Cl CR0 206 A2
Teevan Rd CR0 206 A2
Teign Mews SE9 166 A2
Teignmouth Cl
6 Clapham SW4 137 D1
Edgware HA8 26 B1
Teignmouth Gdns UB6 87 A4
Teignmouth Par UB6 87 B5
Teignmouth Rd
Bexley DA16 146 C3
Brondesbury NW2 68 D2
Tejas Ct N3 47 A5
Tej Ct E7 77 D3
Telcote Way HA4 40 C2
Telegraph Hill NW3 69 D5
Telegraph La KT10 212 D3
Telegraph Mews
Ilford IG3 58 A1
Seven Kings IG3 57 D1
Telegraph Pl E14 119 D2
Telegraph Rd SW15 156 C4
Telegraph St EC2 242 C2
Telemann Sq SE3 143 B2
Telephone Pl SW6 264 D6
Telfer Cl 4 W3 111 A4
Telfer Ho
8 Dulwich SE21 183 C6
EC1 234 D1
Telferscot Prim Sch SW12 159 D3
Telferscot Rd SW12 159 D3
Telford Ave SW12, SW2 160 A3
Telford Avenue Mans 7 SW2 160 A3
Telford Cl Penge SE19 183 D4
Walthamstow E17 53 A2
Telford Ct EN5 13 C6
Telford Dr KT12 194 C2
Telford Ho
2 Belvedere DA17 125 C3
8 Kensal Town W10 91 A2
SE1 262 A6
Telford Parade Mans 8 SW2 160 A3
Telford Rd
3 Hendon NW9 46 A3
Kensal Town W10 91 A2
Sidcup SE9 167 B2
Southall UB1 85 D1
Twickenham TW4 151 C4
Telford Rd (North Circular Rd) N11 31 C5
Telford's Yd 21 SE1 118 A6
Telford Terr SW1 269 A6
Telford Way
Dagenham W3 89 C2
Hayes UB4 85 A2
Telham Rd E6 100 C5
Tell Gr SE22 139 D1
Tellson Ave SE18 144 A4
Telscombe Cl BR6 227 C6
Telscombe Ho SW11 268 A1
Temair Ho 1 SE10 142 A5
Temeraire Pl TW8 110 B1
Temeraire St SE16 118 C4
Tempelhof Ave NW2 46 C2
Temperley Rd SW12 159 A4
Templar Ct RM7 59 D5
Templar Dr SE28 102 D1
Templar Ho
Hampstead NW2 69 B2
7 Upper Clapton E5 74 C6
Templar Pl TW12 173 C3
Templars Ave NW11 47 B3
Templars Cres N3 29 C1
Templars Dr HA3 24 B4
Templars Ho E15 75 D3
Templar St SE5 138 D3
Temple Ave
Croydon CR0 223 B5
Dagenham RM8 59 C1
EC4 116 C6 251 B6
Oakleigh Pk N20 14 B4
Temple Cl Finchley N3 29 B1
Leytonstone E11 54 C2
Woolwich SE18 123 A3
Templecombe Rd E9 96 C6
Templecombe Way SM4 201 A4
Templecroft TW15 171 B4
Temple Ct Stepney E1 96 D2
SW8 270 A3
Templedene BR2 186 B1
Temple Dwellings 7 E2 96 B5
TEMPLE FORTUNE 47 A4
Temple Fortune Ct 9 NW11 47 B4
Temple Fortune Hill NW11 47 C4
Temple Fortune Ho 3 NW11 47 B4
Temple Fortune La NW11 47 C3
Temple Fortune Par 5 NW11 47 B4
Temple Gdns
Dagenham RM8 80 D5
Edmonton N21 16 D2
Temple Fortune NW11 47 B3
Temple Gr Enfield EN2 4 D2
Golders Green NW11 47 C3
Temple Hall Ct E4 20 B2
Temple Ho
13 Battersea SW11 136 C2
4 Tufnell Pk N7 71 C5
11 Walthamstow E17 53 D6
Temple La EC4 94 C1 241 B1
Temple Lo EN5 14 B4
Templeman Rd W7 86 D2
Templemead Cl W3 89 C1
Temple Mead Cl HA7 25 B4
Templemead Ho E9 75 A4
Temple Mill La E10, E15 76 A4
TEMPLE MILLS 75 D3
Temple Mills Rd E9 75 C4
Templemore DA14 190 B5

Temple Par EN5 14 B4
Temple Pk UB8 82 C4
Temple Pl WC2 116 B6 250 D6
Temple Rd
Acton Green W4 111 A3
Cricklewood NW2 68 C5
Croydon CR0 221 B4
Ealing W5 109 D3
Hornsey N8 50 B5
Isleworth TW3 130 A1
Newham E6 100 A6
Richmond TW9 132 B2
Temple Sheen SW14 155 A6
Temple Sheen Rd SW14 133 A1
Temple St E2 96 B5
Temple Sta WC2 116 C6 251 A6
Temple Terr N22 32 C1
Templeton Ave E4 35 D6
Templeton Cl
South Norwood SE19 183 B2
25 Stoke Newington N16 73 C3
Templeton Ct Enfield EN3 6 C5
Walthamstow E10 53 D1
Templeton Pl SW5 113 C2 255 B3
Templeton Rd N4, N15 51 B3
Temple Way SM1 218 B5
Temple West Mews SE11 261 C5
Templewood W13 87 B2
Templewood Ave NW3 69 D5
Templewood Gdns NW3 69 D5
Templewood Point NW2 69 B6
Tempsford Cl EN2 5 A2
Tempsford Ct HA1 42 D3
Temsford Cl HA2 24 A1
Tenbury Cl E7 77 D3
Tenbury Ct SW12 159 D3
Tenby Ave HA3 25 B1
Tenby Cl Dagenham RM6 59 A3
Tottenham N15 51 D5
Tenby Ct E17 53 A4
Tenby Gdns UB5 63 C2
Tenby Ho Hayes UB3 105 A3
Islington N7 72 C4
W2 236 A1
Tenby Rd DA16 146 D4
Dagenham RM6 59 A3
Edgware HA8 26 B1
Enfield EN3 6 C1
Walthamstow E17 53 A4
Tench St E1 118 B5
Tenda Rd SE16 118 B2
Tendring Ho SW2 160 C5
Tendring Way RM6 58 C4
Tenham Ave SW2 159 D2
Tenison Ct W1 249 A6
Tenison Way SE1 251 A3
Tenniel Cl W2 245 D6
Tennison Ave WD6 10 D6
Tennison Rd SE25 205 D4
Tennis St SE1 117 B4 252 C2
Tenniswood Rd EN1 5 C4
Tennyson Ave
Kingsbury NW9 45 A6
Plashet E12 78 A1
Twickenham TW1 152 D3
Wanstead E11 55 A2
West Barnes KT3 200 B4
Tennyson Cl DA16 145 D4
Enfield EN3 18 D6
Feltham TW14 150 A5
Tennyson Ct 3 TW10 175 D6
Tennyson Ho
2 Erith DA17 125 B1
SE17 262 B2
Southall UB1 85 C1
Tennyson Rd
Ashford TW15 170 A5
Ealing W7 108 D6
Hounslow TW3 130 A3
Kilburn NW6 91 B6
Leyton E10 75 D6
Mill Hill NW7 28 A5
Penge SE20 184 D3
Stratford E15 76 C1
Walthamstow E17 53 B3
Wimbledon SW19 180 A4
Tennyson St SW8 137 B3
Tensing Ct TW19 148 A3
Tensing Ho N1 72 D2
Tensing Rd UB2 107 C3
Tentelow La UB2 107 D3
Tenterden Cl
Hendon NW4 46 D6
SE9 188 B6
Tenterden Dr NW4 46 D6
Tenterden Gdns
Croydon CR0 206 A2
Hendon NW4 46 D6
Tenterden Gr NW4 46 D6
Tenterden Ho SE17 263 B2
Tenterden Rd
Croydon CR0 206 A2
Dagenham RM8 81 B6
Tottenham N17 33 D3
Tenterden St W1 238 D1
Tenter Ground E1 243 C3
Tent Peg La BR5 211 A4
Tent St E1 96 B3
Tenzing Ct 4 SE9 166 A2
Tequila Wharf E14 97 A1
Terborch Way 6 SE22 161 C6
Tercelet Terr NW3 70 A4
Teredo St SE16 118 D3
Terence Ct 6 DA17 147 B6
Teresa Mews E17 53 C5
Teresa Wlk N10 49 B4
Terling Cl E11 76 D5
Terling Ho 9 W10 90 C2
Terling Rd RM8 81 C6
Terling Wlk N1 235 A6
Terminal Four Rdbt TW6 149 A5
Terminus Pl SW1 258 D5
Tern Ho 9 SE15 139 D4
Terrace Gdns SW13 133 D3
Terrace Ho 2 N20 14 A1
Terrace La TW10 154 A5
Terrace Rd Hackney E9 74 C1
Newham E13 99 B6
Walton-on-T KT12 194 B3
Terraces The 6 SW20 178 D3
Terrace The
Barnes SW13, SW14 133 C3
Chingford E4 20 C1
Cranley Gdns N2 49 A5
EC4 241 B1
Kilburn NW6 91 C6
10 Rotherhithe SE8 119 B2
1 Woodford IG8 37 A4
Terrace Wlk RM9 81 A3
Terrall Apartments 7 N17 51 D6
Terrano Ho 1 TW9 132 D4
Terrapin Ct SW17 159 B1
Terrapin Rd SW17 159 B1
Terrapins KT6 197 D2
Terrick Rd N22 32 A2
Terrick St W12 90 B1
Terrilands HA5 41 B6
Territorial Ho SE11 261 B3
Terront Rd N15 51 A5
Terry Ct 8 SM6 219 C2
Terry Ho SW2 160 C3
Terry Lodge 2 CR7 204 C4
Tersha St TW9 132 B1
Tessa Sanderson Pl 6 SW8 137 B2
Tessa Sanderson Way UB6 64 B3
Testerton Wlk 3 W11 112 D6
Testwood Ct W7 108 C6
Tetcott Rd SW10 136 A5 266 A3
Tetherdown N10 49 A6
Tetherdown Prim Sch N10 49 A5
Tetty Way BR1, BR2 187 A1
Teversham La SW8 138 A4 270 B2
Teviot Cl DA16 146 B4
Teviot St E14 98 A2
Tewkesbury Ave
Forest Hill SE23 162 B4
Pinner HA5 41 A4
Tewkesbury Cl
Barnet EN4 2 B1
Tottenham N15 51 B3
Tewkesbury Ct N11 31 D4
Tewkesbury Gdns NW9 44 D6
Tewkesbury Rd
Carshalton SM5 202 B1
Ealing W13 109 A6
Tottenham N15 51 B3
Tewkesbury Terr N11 31 D4
Tewson Rd SE18 123 C1
Teyham Ct SW11 158 D5
Teynham Ave EN1 17 B5
Teynham Ct N12 30 A6
Teynham Gn BR2 209 A4
Teynham Ho SE9 167 B5
Teynton Terr N17 33 A2
Thackeray Ave N17 34 A1
Thackeray Cl
Hayes UB8 82 D1
Isleworth TW7 131 A3
Wimbledon SW19 178 D3
Thackeray Ct
Chelsea SW3 257 C2
Ealing W5 88 B1
West Kensington W14 254 A5
Thackeray Dr RM6 58 B2
Thackeray Ho
College Pk NW10 90 A4
WC1 240 A6
Thackeray Manor SM1 218 A3
Thackeray Mews E8 74 A2
Thackeray Rd
Clapham SW8 137 B3
Newham E6 99 D5
Thackeray's Almshouses SE6 163 D5
Thackeray St W8 255 D6
Thackery Lo TW14 149 B5
Thackrah Cl N2 30 A1
Thakeham Cl SE26 184 B5
Thalia Cl SE10 142 B6
Thame Rd SE16 118 D4
Thames Ave
Dagenham RM9 103 D3
Sands End SW10 136 A4 266 B2
Wembley UB6 86 D5
Thames Bank SW14 133 A3
Thamesbank Pl SE28 102 C1
Thames Barrier Visitor Ctr* SE18 121 D3
Thames Christian Coll SW11 136 B2
Thames Circ E14 119 C2
Thames Cl TW12 173 D1
Thames Cnr TW16 194 C6
Thames Cres W4 133 C5
Thames Ct Ealing W7 86 C1
Edmonton N9 18 C1
10 SE15 139 D5
West Molesey KT8 173 D1
THAMES DITTON 197 B2
Thames Ditton Fst Sch KT7 196 D3
Thames Ditton Island KT7 197 A3
Thames Ditton Jun Sch KT7 196 D2
Thames Ditton Sta KT7 196 D2
Thames Dr HA4 39 A3
Thames Eyot 8 TW1 153 A3
Thamesfield Ct TW17 193 A2
Thamesfield Ho TW17 193 A2
Thamesfield Mews TW17 193 A2
Thamesgate Cl TW10 175 B6
Thames Gateway Pk RM9 103 B4
Thames Haven KT6 197 D4
Thames Hts SE1 253 C2
Thameside TW11 175 D3
Thameside Ctr TW8 132 B6
Thameside Ind Est E16 121 D4
Thameside Pl KT1 175 D2
Thames Link Ho 7 TW9 132 A1
Thames Mdw KT12, TW17 193 C1
THAMESMEAD 124 A5
Thames Mead KT12 194 A3
Thames Meadow KT8 195 C6
Thamesmead Sec Sch TW17 193 B3
Thamesmead Sh Ctr SE28 124 A6
Thamesmere Dr SE28 124 A6
Thames Pl SW15 134 D2
Thamespoint TW11 175 D3
Thames Quay
Millwall E14 119 D4
SW10 266 B1
Thames Rd
Barking IG11 102 A4
Chiswick W4 132 D6
Newham E16 121 D5
Thames Reach
Fulham W6 134 C6
Woolwich SE28 123 C4
Thames Road Ind Est E16 121 D4
Thames Row TW9 132 B6
Thames Side
Teddington KT1 175 D2
Thames Ditton KT7 197 B3
Thames St
Hampton TW12 173 D1
Kingston u T KT1, KT2 175 D1
SE10 141 D6
Sunbury TW16 194 B6
Walton-on-T KT12 193 D2
Thamesvale Cl TW3 129 C3
Thames Valley Univ W5 109 D5
Thames View 2 IG1 79 A6
Thames View Ho TW12 194 A3
Thames View Inf Sch IG11 102 A5
Thames View Jun Sch IG11 101 D5
Thames View Lo IG11 101 C4
Thames Village W4 133 A4
Thames Wlk SW11 136 C5 267 A4
Thane Mans N7 72 B5
Thanescroft Gdns CR0 221 C5
Thanet Ct 14 W3 88 C1
Thanet Dr BR2 225 D5
Thanet Ho WC1 233 A1
1 West Norwood SE27 160 D1
Thanet Lo NW2 69 A2
Thanet Pl CR0 221 A4
Thanet Rd DA5 169 C4
Thanet St WC1 94 A4 233 A1
Thane Villas N7 72 B5
Thane Works N7 72 B5
Thanington Ct DA15 167 C5
Thant Cl E10 75 D5
Tharp Rd SM6 219 D3
Thatcham Ct N20 14 A4
Thatcham Gdns N20 14 A4
Thatcher Cl UB7 104 A4
Thatchers Way TW7 152 B6
Thatches Gr RM6 59 A5
Thavies Inn EC4 241 B2
Thaxted Ct N1 235 D3
Thaxted Ho
Bermondsey SE16 118 C2
Dagenham RM10 81 D1
Thaxted Lo 3 E18 55 B6
Thaxted Pl 9 SW20 178 D3
Thaxted Rd
Buckhurst Hill IG9 21 D4
SE9 167 A2
Thaxton Rd W14 135 B6 264 D6
Thayers Farm Rd BR3 185 A2
Thayer St W1 93 A1 238 B2
Theatre Mus* WC2 250 B6
Theatre Sq E15 76 B2
Theatre St SW11 136 D2
Theberton St N1 94 D6 234 C6
Theed St SE1 116 C5 251 B3
Thelbridge Ho 28 E3 97 D4
Thelma Gdns SE3 144 A4
Thelma Gr TW11 175 A4
Theobald Cres HA3 24 A2
Theobald Rd
Croydon CR0 220 D6
Walthamstow E17 53 C2
Theobalds Ave N12 30 A6
Theobalds Ct N4 73 A6
Theobalds Park Rd EN2 4 D6
Theobald's Rd WC1 94 B2 240 C4
Theobald St SE1 262 C5
Theodora Way HA5 39 D6
Theodore Ct SE13 164 B5
Theodore Ho 1 SW15 156 A6
Theodore Rd SE13 164 B5
Therapia La
Thornton Heath CR0 204 A2
Thornton Heath CR0 204 A3
Wallington CR0 203 D2
Therapia Lane Sta CR0 204 A2
Therapia Rd SE22 162 C5
Theresa Rd W6 112 A2
Therfield Ct N4 73 A6
Thermopylae Gate E14 119 D2
Theseus Ho
2 South Bromley E14 98 B1
2 E14 98 B1
Theseus Wlk N1 234 D3
Thesiger Rd SE20 184 D3
Thessaly Ho SW8 269 A3
Thessaly Rd SW8 137 C4 269 B2
Thetford Cl N13 32 D4
Thetford Ct
3 Dulwich SE21 162 B2
New Malden KT3 199 C4
Thetford Gdns RM9 103 A6
Thetford Ho SE1 263 C6
Thetford Rd
Ashford TW15 148 A1
Dagenham RM9 80 D1
New Malden KT3 199 C4
Thetis Terr TW9 132 C6
Theydon Gr IG8 37 C4
Theydon Rd E5 74 C6
Theydon St E17 53 B2
Thicket Cres SM1 218 A4
Thicket Ct 14 SM1 218 A4
Thicket Gr
Dagenham RM9 80 C2
Penge SE20 184 A3
Thicket Rd Penge SE20 184 B3
Sutton SM1 218 A4
Thicket The UB7 82 A1
Third Ave
Chadwell Heath RM6 58 C3
Dagenham RM10 103 D5
East Acton W3 111 D5
Enfield EN1 17 D6
Hayes UB3 105 D5
Little Ilford E12 78 B3
3 Newham E13 99 A4
Walthamstow E17 53 C4
Wembley HA9 65 D6
West Kilburn W10 91 A4
Third Cl KT8 196 A5
Third Cross Rd TW2 152 B2
Third Way HA9 66 D4
Thirleby Rd Hendon HA8 27 B2
SW1 115 C3 259 B5
Thirlestane Ct N10 31 A1
Thirlestane Ho TW12 173 D6
Thirlmere NW1 231 D2
Thirlmere Ave UB6 87 C4
Thirlmere Gdns HA9 43 D1
Thirlmere Ho
Isleworth TW1 152 D6
19 Stoke Newington N16 73 B4
Thirlmere Rd
Muswell Hill N10 31 B2
Streatham SW16 181 D6
Thirlmere Rise BR1 186 D4
Thirsk Cl UB5 63 C2
Thirsk Rd
Clapham SW11 137 A1
Mitcham CR4 181 A3
South Norwood SE25 205 B5
Thistlebrook SE2 124 C3
Thistlebrook Ind Est SE2 124 C4
Thistlecroft Gdns HA7 25 D1
Thistle Ct N17 52 B5
Thistledene KT7 196 C3
Thistledene Ave HA2 63 A5
Thistledown Ct SE25 205 C6
Thistlefield Cl DA5 168 D3
Thistle Gr SW7 256 B1
Thistle Ho 10 E14 98 A1
Thistlemead BR7 188 D1
Thistlewaite Rd E5 74 B5
Thistlewood Cl 3 N7 72 B6
Thistleworth Cl TW7 130 B5
Thistley Cl N12 30 C4
Thistly Ct SE8 141 D6
Thomas a' Beckett Cl HA0 64 D4
Thomas Arnold Prim Sch RM9 81 B1
Thomas Baines Rd SW11 136 B2
Thomas Burt Ho 9 E2 96 B4
Thomas Buxton Jun & Inf Sch E1 96 A3
Thomas Cribb Mews E6 100 B1
Thomas Crowell Ct 29 N1 73 C3
Thomas Ct RM8 80 C6
Thomas Dean Rd SE26 185 B6
Thomas Dinwiddy Rd SE12 165 B2
Thomas Doyle St SE1 261 D6
Thomas Fairchild Com Sch N1 95 A5 235 B4
Thomas Gamuel Prim Sch E17 53 C3
Thomas Hardy Ho N22 32 B2
Thomas Hewlett Ho HA1 64 C4
Thomas Ho
9 Belmont SM2 217 D1
3 Hackney E9 74 C2
4 Stockwell SW4 138 A1
Thomas Hollywood Ho 3 E2 96 C5
Thomas Jones Prim Sch W11 91 A1
Thomas' La SE6 163 C4
Thomas Lo E17 53 D4
Thomas Milner Ho 8 SE15 140 A5
Thomas More Bldg The HA4 39 C1
Thomas More Ho EC2 242 A3
Thomas More Sq E1 118 A6
Thomas More St E1 118 A5
Thomas More Way N2 48 A6
Thomas North Terr 4 E16 98 D2
Thomas Pl W8 255 C5
Thomas Pooley Ct KT6 198 A2
Thomas Rd E14 97 C2
Thomas Road Ind Est 2 E14 97 C1
Thomas Shearley Ct DA5 169 D4
Thomas's London Day Schs SW11 136 B4 266 D1
Thomas's Prep Sch Clapham SW11 158 D6
Thomas St SE18 122 D2
Thomas Tallis Sch SE3 143 B2
Thomas Wall Cl SM1 217 D3
Thomas Watson Cottage Homes The EN5 13 A6
Thompson Ave
Richmond TW9 132 C2
6 SE5 139 A5
Thompson Cl Ilford IG1 79 A6
Morden SM3 201 C1
Thompson Ho
11 Kensal Town W10 91 A3
SE14 140 D6
Southall UB1 107 A6
Thompson Rd
Dagenham RM9 81 B5
Dulwich Village SE22 161 D5
Hounslow TW3 129 D1
Uxbridge UB10 60 A1
Thomson Cres CR0 204 C1
Thomson Ct 4 E8 74 A2
Thomson Ho
Pimlico SW1 259 D1
Walworth SE17 263 A3
Thomson Rd HA3 42 C6
Thorburn Ho SW1 248 A1
Thorburn Sq SE1 118 A2
Thorburn Way SW19 180 B2
Thoresby Ho N16 73 B5
Thoresby St N1 95 A4 235 B2
Thorkhill Gdns KT7 197 B1
Thorkhill Rd KT7 197 B2
Thornaby Gdns N18 34 B5
Thornaby Ho 15 E2 96 B4
Thorn Ave WD23 8 A3
Thornbill Ho 1 SE15 140 A5
Thornbridge Ct 10 EN5 13 D6
Thornbury 3 NW4 46 C5
Thornbury Ave TW7 130 B5
Thornbury Cl
Edgware NW7 28 D3
Stoke Newington N16 73 C3
Thornbury Ct
Croydon CR2 221 B3
Hounslow TW7 130 C5
W11 245 A6
Thornbury Ho N6 49 C1
Thornbury Lo EN2 4 D2
Thornbury Rd
Clapham Pk SW2 160 A5
Hounslow TW7 130 B4
Thornbury Sq N6 49 C1
Thornby Rd E5 74 C5
Thorn Cl BR2 210 C3
Northolt UB5 85 B4
Thorncliffe Ct SW2 160 A5
Thorncliffe Rd
Clapham Pk SW2 160 A5
Southall UB2 107 B1
Thorncombe Rd SE22 161 C6
Thorncroft HA2 64 A5
Thorncroft Rd SM1 217 D4
Thorncroft St SW8 138 A5 270 A3
Thorndale BR7 188 B3
Thorndale Ho 10 N16 51 C1
Thorndean St SW18 158 A2
Thorndene Ave N11 15 A3
Thorndike Ave UB5 84 D6
Thorndike Cl SW10 136 A5 266 A4
Thorndike Ho SW1 259 C2
Thorndike Rd 21 N1 73 B2
Thorndike St SW1 115 D2 259 C3
Thorndon Cl BR5 189 D1
Thorndon Gdns KT19 215 C4
Thorndon Rd BR5 189 D1
Thorndyke Ct HA5 23 B3
Thorne Cl
Claygate KT10 213 A1
DA8 147 D6
Leyton E11 76 C4
Littleton TW15 171 A3
Newham E16 99 A1
Thorne Ho
34 Bethnal Green E2 96 C4
4 Cubitt Town E14 120 A3
Thorneloe Gdns CR0, CR9 220 D3
Thorne Pas 7 SW13 133 D3
Thorne Rd SW8 138 A5 270 B3
Thorne's Cl BR3 208 A6
Thorness Ct SW18 158 A5
Thorne St SW13, SW14 133 C2
Thornet Wood Rd BR1 210 C6
Thornewill Ho 8 E1 118 C6
Thorney Cres SW11 136 B5 266 D3
Thorneycroft Cl KT12 194 C3
Thorneycroft Dr EN3 7 C6
Thorneycroft Ho 11 W4 111 C1
Thorney Ct W8 246 A1
Thorney Hedge Rd W4 110 D2
Thorney St SW1 116 A2 260 A4
Thornfield Ave NW7 29 A2
Thornfield Ct NW7 29 A2
Thornfield Ho 5 E14 119 C6
Thornfield Par NW7 29 A3
Thornfield Rd W12 112 B4
Thornford Rd SE13 164 A6
Thorngate Rd W9 91 C3
Thorngrove Rd E13 99 B6
Thornham Gr E15 76 B3
Thorn Ham Ho SE1 262 D6
Thornham St SE10 141 D6
Thornhaugh St WC1 239 D5
Thornhill Ave SE18 145 C5
Surbiton KT6 214 A6
Thornhill Bridge Wharf N1 233 C5
Thornhill Cres N1 72 B1
Thornhill Ct N8 49 D3
Thornhill Gdns
Barking IG11 79 C1
Leyton E10 75 D6
Thornhill Gr N1 72 C1
Thornhill Ho
12 Chiswick W4 111 C1
Islington N1 72 C1
Thornhill Mews SW15 135 B1
Thornhill Prim Sch N1 72 C1
Thornhill Rd
Ickenham UB10 60 C4
Islington N1 94 C6 234 A6
Leyton E10 75 D6
Surbiton KT6 214 B6
Thornton Heath CR0 205 A2
Thornhill Sq N1 72 B1
Thornhill Way TW17 192 C4
Thornicroft Ho 12 SW9 138 B3
Thornlaw Rd SE27 182 D6
Thornley Cl N17 34 A3
Thornley Dr HA2 63 D6
Thornley Pl 2 SE10 120 C1
Thornsbeach Rd SE6 164 A2
Thornsett Pl SE20 184 B1
Thornsett Rd
Penge SE20 184 B1
Wandsworth SW18 157 D3
Thornsett Terr SE20 184 B1
Thornton Ave
Chiswick W4 111 C2
Streatham SW2 159 D3
Thornton Heath CR0 204 B3
West Drayton UB7 104 B3
Thornton Cl UB7 104 B3
Thornton Ct
Lower Holloway N7 72 A3
West Barnes SW20 200 D4
Thornton Dene BR3 185 C1
Thornton Gdns SW12 159 D3
Thornton Gr HA5 23 C4
THORNTON HEATH 204 D3
Thornton Heath Pond CR7 204 C4
Thornton Heath Sta CR7 205 A5
Thornton Hill SW19 179 A3
Thornton Ho SE17 263 A3
7 Wanstead E11 55 A3
Thornton Lo
South Norwood CR7 205 A6
8 Wimbledon SW19 179 A3
Thornton Pl W1 237 D4
Thornton Rd Barnet EN5 1 A2
Belvedere DA17 125 D2
BR1 187 A5
Carshalton SM5 202 B1

Thornton Rd *continued*
Ilford IG1 78 D4
Leyton E11 76 B6
Lower Edmonton N18 18 C1
Mortlake SW14 133 B2
Streatham SW12, SW2 159 D3
Thornton Heath CR0, CR7 204 B3
Wimbledon SW19 178 D3
Thornton Rd E SW19 178 D4
Thornton Rd Ind Est CR0 204 B3
Thornton Row CR7 204 C4
Thornton St SW9 138 C3
Thornton Way NW11 47 D4
Thorntree Ct W5 88 A2
Thorntree Prim Sch SE7 121 D1
Thorntree Rd SE7 121 D1
Thornville Gr CR4 180 B1
Thornville St SE8 141 C4
Thornwell Ct W7 108 C4
Thornwood Cl E18 37 B1
Thornwood Gdns W8 245 A2
Thornwood Lo W8 245 A2
Thornwood Rd SE13 164 C6
Thornycroft Ct TW9 132 B3
Thorogood Gdns E15 76 C3
Thorold Ho SE1 252 A2
6 Streatham SW2 160 A4
Thorold Rd Ilford IG1 57 A1
Wood Green N22 32 A3
Thorparch Rd SW8 137 D5 269 D3
Thorpebank Rd W12 112 A5
Thorpe Cl BR6 227 C6
Forest Hill SE26 184 D6
Notting Hill W10 91 A1
Thorpe Coombe Hospl E17 54 A6
Thorpe Cres E17 35 B1
Thorpe Ct Enfield EN2 4 D2
Upper Tooting SW17 180 C6
Thorpedale Gdns IG6 56 D5
Thorpedale Rd N4 50 B1
Thorpe Hall W5 87 D2
Thorpe Hall Prim Sch E17 36 B2
Thorpe Hall Rd E17 36 A2
Thorpe Ho N1 233 D5
Thorpe Rd Barking IG11 79 B1
Chingford E17 36 A1
Kingston u T KT2 176 A3
Leyton E7 76 D4
Newham E6 100 B6
Tottenham N15 51 C3
Thorpewood Ave SE23, SE26 162 B2
Thorpland Ave UB10 61 A5
Thorsden Way 2 SE19 183 C5
Thorverton Rd NW2 69 A5
Thoydon Rd E3 97 A5
Thrale Almshouses SW16 182 A5
Thrale Rd SW16 181 C5
Thrale St SE1 252 B3
Thrasher Cl 20 E8 95 D6
Thrawl St E1 95 D2 243 D3
Thrayle Ho 2 SW9 138 B2
Threadgold Ho 8 N1 73 B2
Threadneedle St EC2, EC3 95 B1 242 D1
Three Bridges Bsns Ctr UB2 108 A4
Three Bridges Prim Sch UB2 107 D3
Three Colts La E2 96 B3
Three Colt St E14 119 B6
Three Corners DA7 147 D3
Three Cups Yd WC1 240 D3
Three Kings Yd W1 248 C6
Three Meadows Mews HA7 24 D2
Three Mill La E3 98 A4
Three Mills Studios E14 98 A4
Three Nun Ct EC2 242 B2
Three Oak La SE1 253 C2
Three Oaks Cl UB10 60 B5
Threshers Pl W11 244 A6
Thriffwood SE23, SE26 162 D1
Thrigby Rd KT9 214 B2
Thring Ho 2 SW9 138 B3
Throckmorten Rd E16 99 B1
Throgmorton Ave EC2 95 B1 242 D2
Throgmorton St EC2 95 B1 242 D2
Throwley Cl SE2 124 C3
Throwley Rd SM1 217 D3
Throwley Way SM1 217 D3
Thrupp Cl CR4 181 B1
Thrush Gn HA2 41 C5
Thrush St SE17 262 A2
Thunderer Rd RM9 103 B3
Thurbarn Rd SE6 185 D5
Thurbin Ho UB4 83 B2
Thurland Ho 3 SE16 118 B2
Thurland Rd SE16 118 A3
Thurlby Cl HA1 43 A3
Thurlby Croft NW4 46 C6
Thurlby Rd Wembley HA0 65 D2
West Norwood SE27 182 C6
Thurleigh Ave SW12 159 A5
Thurleigh Ct SW12 159 A5
Thurleigh Rd SW12 159 A5
Thurleston Ave SM4 201 A4
Thurlestone Ave Colney Hatch N12 30 D4
Ilford IG3 79 D4
Thurlestone Cl TW17 193 A3
Thurlestone Ct 1 UB1 85 D1
Thurlestone Par TW17 193 A3
Thurlestone Rd SE27 182 C6
Thurloe Cl SW7 257 A4
Thurloe Ct SW3 257 A3
Thurloe Pl SW7 114 B2 256 D4
Thurloe Place Mews SW7 256 D4
Thurloe Sq SW7 114 C2 257 A4
Thurloe St SW7 114 B2 256 D4
Thurlow Cl E4 35 D4
Thurlow Ct 5 E11 55 A4
Thurlow Gdns HA0 65 D3
Thurlow Hill SE21 161 A2
Thurlow Ho 17 SW16 160 A1
Thurlow Park Rd SE21, SE24 161 A2
Thurlow Rd Hampstead NW3 70 B3
West Ealing W7 109 A4
Thurlow St SE17 117 C1 263 A1
Thurlow Terr NW5 71 A3
Thurlow Twrs SE27 160 C1
Thurlow Wlk SE17 263 A1
Thurlston Rd HA4 62 A5
Thurnby Ct TW2 152 C1
Thurnscoe NW1 232 A5
Thursland Rd DA14 191 A5
Thursley Cres CR0 224 B1
Thursley Gdns SW19 156 D2
Thursley Ho 3 Kingston u T KT2 176 D3
10 Streatham SW2 160 B4
Thursley Rd SE9 166 B1
Thurso Ho NW6 91 D5
Thurso St SW17 180 B6
Thurstan Rd SW20 178 B3
Thurston Ho 4 BR3 185 D4
Thurston Ind Est SE13 141 D2
Thurston Rd Southall UB1 85 B1
St Johns SE8, SE13 141 D3
Thurtle Rd E2 95 D5
Thurza Ct TW7 130 D3
Thyer Cl BR6 227 A4
Thyme Cl SE3 143 C2
Thyme Ct NW7 29 A3
Thyra Gr N12 29 D4
Tibbatt's Rd E3 97 D3
Tibbenham Pl SE6 163 C2
Tibbenham Wlk E13 98 D5
Tibberton Sq N1 235 A6
Tibbets Cl SW19 156 D3
Tibbet's Corner SW19 156 D4
Tibbet's Ride SW19 156 D4
Tiber Cl 10 E3 97 C6
Tiber Gdns N1 233 B5
Ticehurst Cl BR5 190 A3
Ticehurst Rd SE23 163 A2
Tickford Cl SE2 124 C4
Tickford Ho NW8 230 A1
Tidal Basin Rd E16 120 D6
Tidbury Ct SW8 269 A3
Tideham Ho SE28 123 B5
Tidelock Ho SE28 123 B4
Tidemill Prim Sch SE8 141 C5
Tidenham Gdns CR0 221 C5
Tideside Ct SE18 122 A3
Tideslea Path SE28 123 B5
Tideslea Twr SE28 123 A4
Tideswell 10 NW5 71 B4
Tideswell Rd Croydon CR0 223 C5
Putney SW15 134 C1
Tideway Cl TW10 175 C6
Tideway Ct 9 SE16 118 D5
Tideway Ho E14 119 C4
Tideway Ind Est SW8 137 C6 269 B5
Tideway Wharf SW13 133 C3
Tideway Yd SW13 133 C3
Tidey St E3 97 C2
Tidford Rd DA16 145 D3
Tidworth Ho 18 SE22 139 C2
Tidworth Rd E3 97 C3
Tiepigs La BR2, BR4 208 D1
Tierney Ct 4 CR0 221 D6
Tierney Rd SW2 160 A3
Tierney Terr SW2 160 A3
Tiffin Girls' Sch The KT2 176 A4
Tiffin Sch KT2 176 B1
Tiger Ho WC1 232 D1
Tiger La BR2 209 B5
Tiger Way E5 74 B4
Tignel Ct W3 110 C4
Tigris Cl N9 18 C2
Tilbrook Rd SE3 143 C2
Tilbury Cl 14 Camberwell SE15 139 D5
St Paul's Cray BR5 190 B1
Tilbury Ho 4 SE14 140 D6
Tilbury Rd Leytonstone E10 54 A2
Newham E6 100 B5
Tildesley Rd SW15 156 C5
Tile Farm Rd BR6 227 B5
Tilehurst NW1 231 D1
Tilehurst Point 2 SE2 124 C4
Tilehurst Rd Cheam SM3 217 A3
Wandsworth SW17, SW18 158 B3
Tile Kiln La Edmonton N13 33 A5
Harefield UB9 38 D2
Upper Holloway N6 49 C1
Tileyard Rd N7 72 A1
Tilford Ave CR0 224 A1
Tilford Gdns SW19 156 D3
Tilford Ho 8 SW2 160 B4
Tilia Cl SM1 217 B3
Tilia Rd E5 74 B4
Tilia Wlk 21 SW9 138 D1
Tiller Ho 28 N1 95 C6
Tiller Rd E14 119 C3
Tillet Sq SE16 119 A4
Tillett Cl NW10 67 A2
Tillet Way 6 E2 96 A4
Tilley Rd TW14 150 A3
Tillingbourne Gdns N3 47 B6
Tillingbourne Way N3 47 B5
Tillingham Way N12 29 D6
Tilling Ho 1 SE15 140 B2
Tilling Rd NW2 46 C2
Tilling Way HA9 65 D6
Tillman Ho 8 SW2 160 B3
Tillman St E1 96 B1
Tilloch St 9 N1 72 B1
Tillotson Ct SW8 269 D3
Tillotson Rd Edmonton N9 17 D2
Harrow HA3 23 D3
Ilford IG1 56 C2
Tilney Ct EC1 242 B6
Kingston u T KT6 197 D4
Woodford IG9 21 A2
Tilney Dr IG9 21 A2
Tilney Gdns 12 N1 73 B2
Tilney Rd Dagenham RM9 81 B2
Southall UB2 106 C2
Woodford IG9 21 A2
Tilney St W1 248 B4
Tilson Cl 2 SE15 139 C5
Tilson Gdns SW2, SW4 160 A4
Tilson Ho SW2 160 A4
Tilson Rd N17 34 A2
Tilston Cl E11 76 D5
Tilton St SW6 264 B5
Tiltwood The W3 111 A6
Tilt Yard App SE9 166 B5
Timber Cl BR7 188 C1
Timbercroft KT19 215 C4
Timbercroft La SE18 145 C5
Timbercroft Prim Sch SE18 145 C5
Timberdene NW4 28 D1
Timberland Cl 16 SE15 140 A5
Timberland Rd E1 96 B1
Timber Mill Way SW4 137 D2
Timber Pond Rd SE16 118 D4
Timber St EC1 242 A6
Timberwharf Rd N16 52 A3
Time Sq E8 73 D3
Times Sq SM1 217 D3
Timor Ct UB1 107 D5
Timothy Cl Bexley DA6 169 A6
1 Clapham Pk SW4 159 C6
Timothy Ho DA18 125 A4
Timsbury Wlk 5 SW15 156 A3
Tina Ct Forest Hill SE6 163 B4
West Norwood SW16 160 C1
Tindal St SW9 138 D4
Tinniswood Cl N5 72 C3
Tinsley Cl SE25 206 B6
Tinsley Rd E1 96 C2
Tintagel Cres SE22 139 D1
Tintagel Ct EC1 241 C6
Tintagel Dr HA7 25 D6
Tintagel Ho SE20 184 A3
Tintern Ave NW9 44 D6
Tintern Cl Putney SW15 157 A6
Wimbledon SW19 180 A4
Tintern Ct W13 109 A6
Tintern Gdns N14 16 A4
Tintern Ho Belgravia SW1 258 C3
Regent's Pk NW1 231 D3
Tintern Path NW9 45 C3
Tintern Rd Carshalton SM5 202 B1
Tottenham N22 33 A2
Tintern St SW4 138 A1
Tintern Way HA2 41 D1
Tinto Rd E16 99 A3
Tinwell Mews WD6 11 B6
Tinworth St SE11 116 A1 260 B2
Tippett Ct E6 100 B5
Tippetts Cl EN2 5 A4
Tipthorpe Rd SW11 137 A2
Tipton Dr CR0 221 C4
Tiptree 7 NW1 71 B1
Tiptree Cl E4 20 A1
Tiptree Cres IG5 56 C6
Tiptree Ct EN2 5 B1
Tiptree Dr EN2 5 B1
Tiptree Rd HA4 62 B4
Tirlemont Rd CR2 221 A1
Tirrell Rd CR0 205 A3
Tisbury Ct W1 249 C6
Tisbury Rd SW16 182 A1
Tisdall Pl SE17 117 B2 262 D3
Tissington Ct 4 SE16 118 D2
Titan Bsns Est 8 SE8 141 C5
Titan Ct TW8 110 B1
Titchborne Row W2 237 B1
Titchfield Rd Carshalton SM5 202 B1
Enfield EN3 7 A6
Paddington NW8 92 D6 230 C6
Titchfield Wlk SM5 202 B2
Titchwell Rd SW18 158 B3
Tite St SW3 136 D6 267 C6
Tithe Barn Cl KT2 176 B2
Tithe Barn Way UB5 84 B5
Tithe Cl Hayes UB4 83 D2
Hendon NW7 28 A2
Walton-on-T KT12 194 B3
Tithe Ct NW4 28 A2
Tithe Farm Ave HA2 63 C5
Tithe Farm Cl HA2 63 C5
Tithe Wlk NW7 28 A2
Titian Ave WD23 8 C4
Titley Cl E4 35 C5
Titmus Cl UB8 83 A1
Titmuss Ave SE28 124 B6
Titmuss St W12 112 C4
Tivendale N8 50 A6
Tiverton Ave IG5 56 C6
Tiverton Cl CR0 205 D2
Tiverton Dr SE9 167 A3
Tiverton Prim Sch N15 51 B3
Tiverton Rd Brondesbury Pk NW6, NW10 90 D6
Edgware HA8 26 B1
Edmonton N18 33 C5
Hounslow TW3 130 A3
Ruislip HA4 62 A5
Tottenham N4, N15 51 B3
Wembley HA0 88 A5
Tiverton St SE1 117 A3 262 A6
Tiverton Way Chessington KT9 213 D3
Edgware NW7 28 D3
Tivoli Ct SE16 119 B5
Tivoli Gdns 11 SE7 122 A2
Tivoli Rd Hornsey N8 49 D4
Hounslow TW4 129 A1
West Norwood SE27 183 A5
Toad La TW4 129 B1
Tobago St 12 E14 119 C4
Tobin Cl NW3 70 C1
Toby Ct N9 18 C4
Toby La E1 97 A3
Toby Way KT5, KT6 214 D6
Todber Ho W14 254 A6
Todd Ho 3 N2 30 B1
Todds Wlk N7 72 B6
Tokenhouse Yd EC2 242 C2
TOKYNGTON 66 D2
Tokyngton Ave HA9 66 C2
Toland Sq SW15 156 A6
Tolcairn Ct 2 DA17 125 C1
Tolcarne Dr HA5 40 B6
Tolchurch 2 W11 91 C1
Toldos Yakov Yosef sch N16 51 C1
Toley Ave HA3, HA9 44 A2
Tolhurst Dr 4 W10 91 A4
Tollbridge Cl W10 91 A3
Tollesbury Gdns IG6 57 B6
Tollet St E1 96 D3
Tollgate Dr Dulwich SE21 161 C2
Hayes UB4 106 D6
Tollgate Ho 1 NW6 91 D5
Tollgate Prim Sch Croydon CR0 206 C3
Newham E13 99 C3
Tollgate Rd E6 100 A2
Tollhouse Way N19 71 C6
Tollington Ct N4 72 B6
Tollington Ho 4 N19 72 A5
Tollington Pk N4 72 B6
Tollington Pl N4 72 B6
Tollington Rd N7 72 B4
Tollington Way N7 72 A5
Tolmers Sq NW1 93 C3 239 B6
Tolpaide Ho SE11 261 A3
Tolpuddle Ave 1 E13 99 C6
Tolpuddle St N1 94 C5 234 A4
Tolsford Rd E5 74 B3
Tolson Ho 4 TW7 131 A2
Tolson Rd TW7 131 A2
Tolverne Rd SW20 178 C2
TOLWORTH 214 C6
Tolworth Broadway KT6 198 D1
Tolworth Cl KT6 198 D1
Tolworth Gdns RM6 58 D4
Tolworth Girls' Sch KT6 214 B5
Tolworth Hospl KT6 214 C6
Tolworth Inf Sch KT6 198 B1
Tolworth Junc KT6 214 D6
Tolworth Jun Sch KT6 198 B1
Tolworth Par RM6 59 A4
Tolworth Park Rd KT6 214 B6
Tolworth Rd KT6 214 A6
Tolworth Rise N KT5 198 D1
Tolworth Rise S KT5 198 D1
Tolworth Sta KT5 214 D6
Tolworth Underpass KT5, KT6 214 D6
Tomahawk Gdns 4 UB5 84 D4
Tom Coombs Cl SE9 144 A1
Tom Cribb Rd SE18, SE28 123 B3
Tom Groves Cl E15 76 B3
Tom Hood Cl E15 76 B3
Tom Hood Sch E11 76 D5
Tom Jenkinson Rd 5 E16 121 A5
Tomkyns Ho SE11 261 A3
Tomline Ho SE1 252 A3
Tomlin's Gr E3 97 C4
Tomlinson Cl 5 Gunnersbury W4 110 D1
Spitalfields E2 95 D4
Tomlins Orch IG11 101 A6
Tomlin's Terr E14 97 A1
Tomlins Wlk 4 N7 72 B6
Tom Mann Cl IG11 101 C6
Tom Nolan Cl E15 98 C5
Tompion Ho EC1 241 D6
Tompion St EC1 234 D1
Tom Smith Cl SE10 142 C6
Tom Smith Ho 3 E17 54 A4
Tomson Ho SE1 263 C6
Tom Williams Ho SW6 264 C5
Tonbridge Cres HA3 44 A5
Tonbridge Hos WC1 233 A1
Tonbridge Rd KT12, KT8 195 B5
Tonbridge St WC1 94 A4 233 A1
Toneborough 16 NW8 91 D6
Tonfield Rd SM3 201 B1
Tonge Cl BR3 207 C4
Tonsley Hill SW18 157 D6
Tonsley Pl SW18 157 D6
Tonsley Rd SW18 157 D6
Tonsley St SW18 157 D6
Tonstall Rd CR4 181 A1
Tony Law Ho SE12 165 A6
Tooke Cl HA5 23 A2
Tookey Cl HA3 44 B2
Took's Ct EC4 241 A2
Tooley St SE1 117 C5 253 A3
Toorack Rd HA3 24 B1
Tooting Bec Gdns SW16 181 D6
Tooting Bec Lido SW16 181 C6
Tooting Bec Rd Furzedown SW17 181 B6
Streatham SW16 181 C5
Tooting Bec Sta SW17 159 A1
Tooting Broadway SW17 180 D5
Tooting Broadway Sta SW17 180 C5
Tooting Gr SW17 180 C5
TOOTING GRAVENEY 180 B5
Tooting High St SW17, SW19 180 C5
Tooting Mkts SW17 180 D6
Tooting Sta SW17 180 D4
Tootswood Rd BR2, BR3 208 C5
Topaz Ct TW13 149 D1
Topaz Ho KT4 199 B1
Topaz Wlk NW2 46 D2
Topcliffe Dr BR6 227 B4
Topham Ho 8 SE10 142 A5
Topham Sq N17 33 A2
Topham St EC1 241 A6
Top House Rise E4 20 A4
Topiary Sq TW9 132 B2
Topley St SE9 143 D1
Topmast Point 23 E14 119 C4
Top Pk BR3 208 C4
Topsfield Cl N8 49 D4
Topsfield Par N8 50 A3
Topsfield Rd N8 50 A4
Topsham Rd SW17 181 A6
Tora Ct 9 IG9 21 C2
Torbay Ct 13 NW1 71 B1
Torbay Mans NW6 91 B6
Torbay Rd Brondesbury NW6 69 B1
Harrow HA2 63 A6
Torbay St 15 NW1 71 B1
Torbitt Way IG2 57 D4
Torbridge Cl HA8 26 A3
Torbrook Cl DA5 169 A5
Torcross Dr SE23 162 C2
Torcross Rd HA4 62 C5
Tor Ct W8 245 B2
Torfell 5 E18 36 D1
Tor Gdns W8 113 C4 245 A2
Tor Gr SE28 123 C5
Tor Ho N6 49 B3
Tormead Cl SM1 217 C2
Tormount Rd SE18 145 C6
Tornay Ho Hackney E9 74 C1
N1 233 C4
Toronto Ave E12 78 B4
Toronto Rd IG1 57 A1
Torquay Gdns IG4 55 D5
Torquay Ho 1 SM6 219 D3
Torquay St W2 91 D2
Tor Rd DA16 146 C4
Torrence Ho 6 N19 71 C6
Torrens Ct SE5 139 B2
Torrens Rd Clapham Pk SW2 160 B6
Stratford E15 76 D2
Torrens Sq E15 76 D2
Torrens St EC1 94 D5 234 C3
Torres Sq E14 119 C1
Torre Wlk SM5 202 C1
Torrey Dr SW9 138 C3
Torriano Ave NW5 71 D3
Torriano Cotts NW5 71 C3
Torriano Jun & Inf Schs NW5 71 D3
Torriano Mews NW5 71 C3
Torridge Gdns SE15 140 C1
Torridge Rd CR7 204 D4
Torridon Ct HA8 10 D2
Torridon Ho NW6 91 D5
Torridon Jun & Inf Schs SE6 164 B2
Torridon Rd SE13, SE6 164 B3
Torrington Ave N12 30 B5
Torrington Cl Claygate KT10 212 C2
North Finchley N12 30 B6
Torrington Ct Forest Hill SE26 184 A5
Harrow HA2 63 D5
North Finchley N12 30 B6
Torrington Dr HA2 63 D5
Torrington Gdns Friern Barnet N11 31 C4
Wembley UB6 65 C1
Torrington Gr N12 30 C5
Torrington Pk N12 30 B6
Torrington Pl Bloomsbury WC1 93 D2 239 C4
St George in t East E1 118 A5
Torrington Rd Claygate KT10 212 C2
Dagenham RM8 59 B1
Ruislip HA4 62 A5
Wanstead E18 55 A6
Wembley UB6 87 C6
Torrington Sq Bloomsbury WC1 93 D3 239 D5
Thornton Heath CR0 205 B2
Torrington Way SM4 201 C3
Torr Rd SE20 184 D3
Tortington Ho 1 SE15 140 B5
Torver Rd HA1 42 C5
Torver Way BR6 227 B5
Torwood Rd SW15 156 A6
Totham Lo SW20 178 B2
Tothill Ho SW1 259 D4
Tothill St SW1 115 D4 249 D1
Totland Ho SW18 157 D5
Totnes Rd DA16 146 C5
Totnes Villas N11 31 C5
Totnes Wlk N2 48 B5
Tottan Terr E1 96 D1
Tottenhall 5 NW1 71 A1
Tottenhall Inf Sch N13 32 C4
Tottenhall Rd N13 32 D4
TOTTENHAM 33 D1
Tottenham Court Rd W1 93 C2 239 B4
Tottenham Court Road Sta W1 93 D1 239 D2
Tottenham Gn E 3 N15 51 D5
Tottenham Gn E South Side 4 N15 51 D5
TOTTENHAM HALE 52 A6
Tottenham Hale N15 52 A5
Tottenham Hale Ret Pk N15 52 A5
Tottenham Hale Sta N17 52 B6
Tottenham La N8 50 B4
Tottenham Mews W1 239 B4
Tottenham Rd N1 73 C2
Tottenham St W1 93 C2 239 B4
Totterdown St SW17 180 D5
TOTTERIDGE 13 C3
Totteridge Comm N20 12 C3
Totteridge Gn N20 13 C2
Totteridge Ho Barnet N20 13 B3
Battersea SW11 136 B3
Totteridge La N20 13 D3
Totteridge Pk N20 12 D3
Totteridge Rd EN3 6 D6
Totteridge Village N20 13 B3
Totteridge & Whetstone Sta N20 14 A2
Totternhoe Cl HA3 43 C4
Totton Rd CR7 204 C6
Toucan Cl NW10 88 C4
Touchard Ho N1 235 D1
Toulmin St SE1 117 A4 252 A1
Toulon St SE5 139 A5
Toulouse Ct 2 SE16 118 B1
Tounson Ct SW1 259 D3
Tournay Rd SW6 135 B5 264 D4
Toussaint Wlk 18 SE16 118 A3
Tovil Cl SE20 184 B1
Tovy Ho 6 SE1 118 A1
Towcester Rd E3 98 A3
Tower 42* EC2 95 C1 243 A2
Tower Bldgs 22 E1 118 B5
Tower Br App E1, EC3 253 C5
Tower Bridge* E1, EC3, SE1 117 D5 253 C4
Tower Bridge Bsns Complex SE16 118 B3
Tower Bridge Bsns Sq SE16 118 B2
Tower Bridge Mews HA0 64 D4
Tower Bridge Piazza SE1 253 C3

Tower Bridge Prim Sch SE1 117 D4 253 C2
Tower Bridge Rd SE1 117 C4 253 A1
Tower Bridge Sq SE1 253 C2
Tower Bridge Wharf SE1 118 A5
Tower Cl
Hampstead NW3 70 B3
Orpington BR6 227 D5
Penge SE20 184 B3
Tower Ct Brockley SE4 141 A1
Stamford Hill E5 51 D2
St Giles WC2 240 A1
St John's Wood NW8 230 B4
Tower Gardens Rd N17 33 B2
Towergate SE1 263 A4
Towergate Cl UB8 60 A3
Towergate Ho 35 E3 97 B5
Tower Gateway Sta EC3 117 D6 253 C6
Tower Gdns KT10 213 A1
Tower Gr KT13 193 C1
TOWER HAMLETS 97 B2
Tower Hamlets Coll
Poplar E14 97 D1
Poplar E14 119 D6
Stepney E1 96 D1
Tower Hamlets Rd
Forest Gate E7 76 D3
Walthamstow E17 53 C6
Tower Hill EC3 117 D6 253 D5
Tower Hill Sta EC3 117 D6 253 C6
Tower La HA9 65 D5
Tower Mans SE1 263 C5
Tower Mews
Hackney E5 75 A3
Walthamstow E17 53 C5
Tower Millennium Pier EC3 117 C5 253 B4
Tower Mill Rd 1 SE15 139 C5
Tower Pl E EC3 253 B5
Tower Pl W EC3 253 B5
Tower Rd DA7 147 D1
Orpington BR6 227 D5
Twickenham TW1, TW2 152 D1
Willesden NW10 68 A1
Tower Rise TW9 132 A2
Tower Royal EC4 252 C6
Towers Ave UB10 83 A4
Towers Bsns Pk HA9 66 D4
Towers Ct UB10 83 A4
Towers Pl TW10 154 A6
Towers Rd Pinner HA5 23 A2
Southall UB1 85 C3
Tower St WC2 240 A1
Towers The
Dartmouth Pk NW5 71 B5
1 Richmond TW9 132 B1
Tower Terr
Brockley SE4 141 A1
Wood Green N22 32 B1
Tower The* EC3 117 D6 253 C5
Towerview SE13 163 C6
Tower View
Bushey WD23 8 C4
Croydon CR0 207 A2
Tower Wharf SE1 253 C2
Tower Wlk SE1 263 A4
Towfield Ct TW13 151 B2
Towfield Rd TW13 151 B2
Towncourt Cres BR5 211 B5
Towncourt La BR5 211 B2
Towncourt Path N4 51 A1
Townend Ct 6 BR1 186 D2
Towney Mead UB5 85 B5
Towney Mead Ct UB5 85 B5
Townfield Rd UB3 105 D5
Townfield Sq UB3 105 D6
Town Field Way TW7 131 A3
Town Hall Approach Rd N15 51 D5
Townhall Ave 3 W4 111 B1
Town Hall Rd SW11 136 D2
Townholm Cres W7 108 D3
Town Hos EC1 241 D5
Town La TW19 148 A2
Townley Ct E15 76 D2
Townley Gram Sch for Girls DA6 169 B6
Townley Rd DA6 169 B6
Dulwich Village SE22 161 C6
Townley St SE17 117 B1 262 C2
Townmead Bsns Ctr SW6 136 A2
Town Meadow TW8 131 D5
Townmead Rd
Richmond TW9 132 D3
Sands End SW6 136 A3
Town Quay IG11 100 D6
Town Quay Wharf IG11 100 D6
Town Rd N9 18 B2
Townsend Ave N14 31 D6
Townsend Ct NW9 45 B2
Townsend Ho 14 SE1 118 A2
Townsend Ind Est NW10 89 A5
Townsend La NW9 45 B3
Townsend Mews 3 SW18 158 A2
Townsend Prim Sch SE17 117 C2 263 A4
Townsend Rd
Ashford TW15 170 A5
Southall UB1 107 A5
Townsend Rd *continued*
South Tottenham N15 51 D4
Townsend St SE1, SE17 117 C2 263 A4
Townsend Way HA6 22 A3
Townsend Yd N6 49 B1
Townshend Cl DA14 190 C4
Townshend Ct NW8 230 B4
Townshend Est NW8 92 C5 230 A4
Townshend Ho 16 SE18 122 B2
Townshend Rd
Chislehurst BR7 188 D5
Primrose Hill NW8 92 C6 230 A5
Richmond TW9 132 B1
Townshend Terr TW9 132 B1
Towns Ho 4 SW4 137 D2
Townson Ave UB5 84 B5
Townson Way UB5 84 A5
Town The EN2 5 B2
Town Tree Rd TW15 170 C5
Towpath TW17 192 B1
Towpath Way CR0 205 D4
Towpath Wlk E9 75 B3
Towton Rd SE27 161 A2
Toxteth Ho N4 51 A2
Toynbec Cl BR7 188 D6
Toynbee Rd SW19, SW20 179 A2
Toynbee St E1 95 D2 243 C3
Toyne Way N6 48 D3
Tracey Ave NW2 68 C3
Tracy Ct HA7 25 C3
Tracy Ho 15 E3 97 B4
Trade Cl N13 32 C6
Trader Rd E6 100 D1
Tradescant Ho 15 E9 74 C1
Tradescant Rd SW8 138 A5 270 B3
Trade Twr 8 SW11 136 A2
Trade Winds Ct 1 E1 118 A5
Trading Estate Rd NW10 89 A3
Traemore Ct SW16 160 C1
Trafalgar Ave
North Cheam KT4, SM3, SM4 200 D1
SE15 139 D6
Tottenham N17 33 C4
Trafalgar Bsns Ctr IG11 101 D3
Trafalgar Cl 1 SE16 119 A2
Trafalgar Ct
Barking E6 100 C6
Hounslow TW3 129 B2
West Barnes KT3 200 B6
Trafalgar Gdns
Stepney E1 96 D2
W8 255 D6
Trafalgar Gr SE10 142 B6
Trafalgar Ho
Barking IG11 102 B4
SE17 262 B2
Trafalgar Inf Sch TW2 152 B2
Trafalgar Jun Sch TW2 152 B2
Trafalgar Mews E9 75 B2
Trafalgar Pl
Edmonton N18 34 A5
Wanstead E11 55 A5
Trafalgar Point 2 N1 73 B1
Trafalgar Rd
Greenwich SE10 120 C1
Merton SW19 180 A3
Twickenham TW2 152 B2
Trafalgar Sq* SW1 115 D5 249 D4
Trafalgar St SE17 117 B1 262 D2
Trafalgar Terr HA1 42 C1
Trafalgar Trad Est EN3 7 A1
Trafalgar Way
Canary Wharf E14 120 A5
Croydon CR0 220 C6
Trafford Cl E15 75 D3
Trafford Ho N1 235 D4
Trafford Rd CR7 204 B3
Trafford Villas CR0 204 B4
Tragail SW15 157 A6
Traherne Lo 5 TW11 174 D5
Trahorn Cl E1 96 B3
Traitors Gate* EC3 117 D5 253 C4
Tralee Ct 31 SE16 118 B1
Tramsheds Ind Est The CR0, CR4 203 D2
Tramway Ave
Ponders End N9 18 C4
Stratford E15 76 B1
Tramway Cl SE20 184 C2
Tramway Path CR4 202 C5
Trance Way W3 110 C3
Tranmere Ct 5 SM2 218 A1
Tranmere Ho 7 N7 72 C3
Tranmere Rd
Edmonton N9 17 D4
Twickenham TW2 151 D4
Wandsworth SW17, SW18 158 A2
Tranquil Pas SE3 142 D3
Tranquil Vale SE3 142 C3
Transept St NW1 237 B3
Transmere Cl BR5 211 A3
Transmere Rd BR5 211 A3
Transom Cl SE16 119 A2
Transom Sq E14 119 D1
Transport Ave TW8 131 B6
Tranton Rd SE16 118 B3
Trappes Ho 2 SE16 118 B2
Traps La KT2, KT3 177 C2
Travellers Way TW5 128 C3
Travers Cl E17 34 D2
Travers Ho 6 SE10 142 B6
Travers Rd N7 72 C5
Travis Ho SE10 142 A4
Treacy Cl WD23 8 A2
Treadgold Ho 7 W11 112 D6
Treadgold St W11 112 D6
Treadway St E2 96 B5
Treasury Bldgs SW1 250 A2
Treasury Cl SM6 219 D3
Treaty Ctr TW3 129 D2
Treaty St N1 94 B6 233 C5
Trebeck St W1 248 C3
Treborough Ho W1 238 A4
Trebovir Rd SW5 113 C2 255 B3
Treby St E3 97 B3
Trecastle Way 2 N7 71 D4
Tredegar Mews 10 E3 97 B4
Tredegar Rd Bow E3 97 B5
Wood Green N11 31 D3
Tredegar Sq E3 97 B4
Tredegar Terr E3 97 B4
Trederwen Rd E8 96 A6
Tredown Rd SE26 184 C5
Tredwell Cl BR2 210 A5
Tredwell Rd SE27 182 D6
Tree Cl TW10 153 D3
Treehouse Sch N10 49 A5
Treen Ave SW13 133 D2
Tree Rd E16 99 C1
Trees The N16 51 B2
Tree Tops 1 IG8 37 A6
Treetops Cl SE2 125 A1
Treetops Ct CR7 205 A4
Treetops View IG10 21 D4
Treeview Cl SE19 183 C2
Treewall Gdns BR1 187 B6
Trefgarne Rd RM10 81 C6
Trefil Wlk N7 72 A4
Trefoil Ho DA18 125 A4
Trefoil Rd SW18 158 A6
Trefusis Ct TW5 128 B4
Tregaron Ave N8 50 A3
Tregaron Gdns KT3 199 C5
Tregarvon Rd SW11 137 A1
Tregenna Ave HA2 63 C4
Tregenna Cl 1 N14 15 C6
Tregenna Ct HA2 63 C4
Tregony Rd BR6 227 D4
Trego Rd E9 75 C1
Tregothnan Rd SW9 138 A2
Tregunter Rd SW10 114 A1 256 A1
Treherne Ct
Brixton SW9 138 D4
Upper Tooting SW17 181 A6
Trehern Rd 12 SW14 133 B2
Trehurst St E5 75 A3
Trelawney Cl E17 53 D5
Trelawney Est E9 74 C2
Trelawney Ho SE1 252 A2
Trelawn Rd Leyton E10 76 A5
Tulse Hill SW2 160 C6
Trellis Ho SW19 180 A3
Trellis Sq 1 E3 97 B4
Treloar Gdns SE19 183 B4
Tremadoc Rd SW4 137 D1
Tremaine Cl SE4 141 C3
Tremaine Rd SE20 184 B1
Trematon Ho SE11 261 B2
Trematon Pl TW11 175 C3
Tremlett Gr N19 71 C5
Tremlett Mews N19 71 C5
Trenance Gdns IG3 80 A5
Trenchard Ave HA4 62 B4
Trenchard Cl
Grahame Pk NW9 27 C2
Stanmore HA7 25 B4
Trenchard Ct SM4 201 C3
Trenchard St SE10 120 B1
Trenchold St SW8 138 A6 270 A5
Trend Ct W13 109 B5
Trendell Ho 8 E14 97 C1
Trenholme Cl 6 SE20 184 B3
Trenholme Rd SE20 184 B3
Trenholme Terr SE20 184 B3
Trenmar Gdns NW10 90 B4
Trent Ave W5 109 C3
Trent CE Prim Sch EN4 2 D1
Trent Ct
1 South Croydon CR2 221 A3
Wanstead E11 55 A4
Trent Ctry Pk* EN4 3 A3
Trent Gdns N14 15 B5
Trentham Ct W3 89 B2
Trentham Lo 8 EN1 17 C6
Trentham St SW18 157 C3
Trent Ho
4 Kingston u T KT2 175 D2
Nunhead SE15 140 C1
Trent Rd
Buckhurst Hill IG9 21 B3
Clapham Pk SW2 160 B6
Trent Way Hayes UB4 83 C4
North Cheam KT4 216 C5
Trentwood Side EN2 4 B2
Treport St SW18 157 D4
Tresco Cl BR1 186 C4
Trescoe Gdns HA2 41 A2
Tresco Gdns IG3 80 A6
Tresco Ho SE11 261 A2
Tresco Rd SE15 140 B1
Tresham Cres NW8 92 C3 237 A6
Tresham Rd IG11 79 D1
Tresham Wlk E9 74 C3
Tresidder Ho 10 SW4 159 D4
Tresilian Ave N21 16 B6
Tressel Cl 20 N1 72 D1
Tressillian Cres SE4 141 C2
Tressillian Rd SE4 141 C2
Trestis Cl UB4 84 D2
Treswell Rd RM9 103 A6
Tretawn Gdns NW7 11 C1
Tretawn Pk NW7 27 C6
Trevallyn Lo 1 KT2 176 D2
Trevanion Rd W14 254 B2
Treve Ave HA1 42 B2
Trevelyan Ave E12 78 B4
Trevelyan Cres HA3 43 D2
Trevelyan Ct KT3 199 D2
Trevelyan Gdns NW10 90 C6
Trevelyan Ho
16 Globe Town E2 96 D4
SE5 138 D5
6 Twickenham TW1 153 C5
Trevelyan Rd
Leyton E15 76 D4
Upper Tooting SW17 180 D4
Trevenna Ho 13 SE23 162 D1
Trevera Ct EN3 19 A6
Treveris St SE1 251 D3
Treversh Ct 7 BR1 186 D2
Treverton St W10 90 D3
Treverton Twr W10 90 D2
Treves Cl N21 16 B6
Treves Ho E1 96 A3
Treville St SW15 156 B4
Treviso Rd SE23 163 A2
Trevithick Cl TW14 149 D3
Trevithick Ho
13 Bermondsey SE16 118 B2
3 Gospel Oak NW5 71 B4
SW8 269 C2
Trevithick St SE8 141 C6
Trevone Gdns HA5 41 A3
Trevor Cl Harrow HA3 24 D3
Hayes BR2 209 A2
Isleworth TW7 152 D6
New Barnet EN4 14 B5
Northolt UB5 84 C5
Trevor Cres HA4 61 D4
Trevor Gdns
Hendon HA8 27 B2
Northolt UB5 84 C5
Ruislip HA4 62 A4
Trevor Pl SW7 114 C4 247 B1
Trevor Rd Hayes UB3 105 C4
Hendon HA8 27 B2
Wimbledon SW19 179 A3
Woodford IG8 37 A3
Trevor Roberts Tutorial Coll NW8 70 B1
Trevor Sq SW7 114 C4 247 B1
Trevor St SW7 114 C4 247 B1
Trevose Ho SE11 260 D2
Trevose Rd E17 36 B2
Trewenna Dr KT9 213 D3
Trewince Rd SW20 178 C2
Trewint St SW18 158 A2
Trewsbury Ho 2 SE2 124 D4
Trewsbury Rd SE26 184 D5
Triandra Way UB4 84 D2
Triangle Ct
4 Newham E16 99 C2
SE1 252 B3
Triangle Ctr UB1 108 B5
Triangle Est The SE11 261 A1
Triangle Ho SE1 253 C2
Triangle Pl SW4 137 D1
Triangle Rd 7 E8 96 B6
Triangle The
Barking IG11 79 A2
Crouch End N19 49 D2
EC1 241 D6
Hackney E8 96 B6
Kingston u T KT3 177 A1
Tribune Ct 16 NW9 46 A5
Tricorn Ho SE28 123 B5
Trident Bsns Ctr SW17 180 D5
Trident Gdns 6 UB5 84 D4
Trident Ho
14 South Bromley E14 98 A1
Woolwich SE28 123 B5
Trident St SE16 118 D2
Trident Way UB2 106 B3
Trieste Ct SW12 158 D3
Trig La EC4 252 A6
Trigon Rd SW8 138 B5 270 D4
Trilby Rd SE23 162 D2
Trillington Ho W12 112 A5
Trillo Ct IG1 57 C2
Trimdon NW1 232 B5
Trimmer Ct TW7 130 D2
Trimmer Wlk 11 TW8 132 A6
Trim St SE8 141 B6
Trinder Gdns N19 50 A1
Trinder Mews 10 TW11 175 A5
Trinder Rd Barnet EN5 12 C6
Finsbury Pk N4, N19 50 A1
Tring Ave Ealing W5 110 B5
Southall UB1 85 B1
Wembley HA9 66 C2
Tring Cl IG2 57 B4
Tring Ct TW1 175 A6
Trinidad Ho 17 E14 119 B6
Trinidad St E14 119 B6
Trinity Ave
East Finchley N2 48 B6
Enfield EN1 17 D5
Trinity Church Rd SW13 134 B6
Trinity Church Sq SE1 117 A3 262 B6
Trinity Cl
3 Clapham SW4 137 C1
Hounslow TW4 129 A1
Keston Mark BR2 210 A1
Lewisham SE13 142 B1
Leyton E11 76 C6
Trinity Cotts TW9 132 B2
Trinity Cres SW17 159 A2
Trinity Ct
8 Chingford E4 20 A2
Edmonton N18 33 D4
Eltham SE9 166 D5
Finsbury WC1 240 C6
Forest Hill SE23 162 C1
Greenwich SE7 121 D2
2 Hoxton N1 95 C6
Rotherhithe SE16 119 A4
Southgate N21 16 D3
Thornton Heath SE25 205 C3
Twickenham TW2 152 C2
Wallington SM6 219 C1
Willesden NW2 68 C3
Wimbledon SW19 179 C4
Trinity Dr UB8 83 A1
Trinity Gdns E16 98 D2
Stockwell SW2, SW9 138 B1
11 Wanstead E18 55 B6
Trinity Gn E1 96 C2
Trinity Gr 8 SE10 142 A4
Trinity Ho SE1 262 B6
5 Walthamstow E17 53 D6
Trinity Homes 14 SW2 138 B1
Trinity Mews
Penge SE20 184 B2
SE9 167 B5
Wandsworth SW18 157 C3
Trinity Par TW3 129 D2
Trinity Pl
Bexleyheath DA6 147 B1
City of London EC3 253 C5
Trinity RC High Sch (Lower) IG8 37 A6
Trinity RC High Sch (Upper) IG8 37 A6
Trinity RC High Sch (Upper Sch) IG8 36 D6
Trinity Rd
East Finchley N2 48 B6
Ilford IG6 57 A6
Richmond TW9 132 B2
Southall UB1 107 A5
Wandsworth SW17, SW18 158 C4
Wimbledon SW19 179 C4
Wood Green N22 32 A3
Wood Green N22 32 B2
Trinity Rise SE24, SW2 160 D4
Trinity St Mary's CE Prim Sch SW12 159 A3
Trinity Sch
Croydon CR0 222 C6
Dagenham RM10 81 C4
Trinity Sq EC3 117 C6 253 B6
Trinity St Enfield EN2 5 A3
9 Newham E16 99 A2
SE1 117 B3 262 C6
Trinity Terr IG9 21 B4
Trinity Way
East Acton W3 111 D6
Walthamstow E4 35 B4
Trio Pl SE1 117 A4 252 B1
Triscott Ho UB3 106 A5
Tristan Ct 33 SE8 141 B6
Tristan Sq SE3 142 C2
Tristram Cl E17 54 B6
Tristram Dr N9 18 A1
Tristram Rd BR1 186 D6
Triton Ct EC2 242 D5
Woodford IG9 21 A2
Triton Ho 2 E14 119 D2
Triton Sq NW1 239 A6
Tritton Ave CR0 220 A4
Tritton Ho N21 17 B5
Tritton Rd SE21, SE27 161 B1
Triumph Cl UB7 127 A4
Triumph Ho IG11 102 A4
Triumph Rd E6 100 B1
Triumph Trad Est N17 34 A4
Trocette Mans SE1 263 B6
Trojan Ct
Brondesbury NW6 69 A1
9 Ealing W7 109 A5
Trojan Ind Est NW10 67 D2
Trojan Way CR0 220 B5
Troon Cl
34 Bermondsey SE16 118 B1
Erith SE28 102 D1
Troon Ct UB1 108 A6
Troon Ho 9 E14 97 A1
Troon St E1 97 A1
Tropical Ct 2 W10 90 D4
Trosley Rd DA17 147 C6
Trossachs Rd SE22 161 C6
Trothy Rd SE1 118 A2
Trotman Ho 1 SE14 140 C4
Trott Rd N10 31 A3
Trott St SW11 136 C4 267 A1
Trotwood Ho 3 SE16 118 B4
Troubridge Ct 12 W4 111 A1
Troughton Rd SE7 121 B1
Troutbeck NW1 231 D1
Troutbeck Rd SE14 141 A4
Trouville Rd SW4 159 C5
Trowbridge Rd E9 75 B2
Trower Ho 5 E9 75 A2
Trowlock Ave TW11 175 C4
Trowlock Island TW11 175 D4
Trowlock Way TW11 175 D4
Troy Ct W8 255 A6
5 Woolwich SE18 122 D2
Troyes Ho NW3 70 D3
Troy Rd SE19 183 B4
Troy Town SE15 140 A2
Troy Town Flats SE15 140 A2
Trubshaw Rd UB2 107 D3
Trulock Ct N17 34 A3
Trulock Rd N17 34 A3
Truman Cl 2 HA8 27 A3
Truman's Rd 24 N16 73 C3
Trumpers Way W7 108 D3
Trumpeters Inn TW9 153 C6
Trumpington Rd E7 76 D4
Trump St EC2 242 B1
Trundlers Way WD23 8 C3
Trundle St SE1 252 A2
Trundleys Rd SE8 141 A6
Trundley's Rd SE8 118 D1
Trundley's Terr SE8 118 D2
Truro Ct 2 N8 49 D4
Truro Gdns IG1 56 A2
Truro Ho
25 Paddington W2 91 C2
Pinner HA5 23 B2
Truro Rd
Walthamstow E17 53 B5
Wood Green N22 32 B3
Truro St NW5 71 A2
Truro Way UB4 83 C4
Truscott Ho 3 CR7 204 C3
Trusedale Rd E6 100 B1
Truslove Rd SE27 182 D5
Trussley Rd W6 112 C3
Trust Wlk SE21 160 D3
Tryfan Cl IG4 55 D4
Tryon Cres E9 96 C6
Tryon St SW3 114 D1 257 C2
Trystings Cl KT10 213 A2
Tuam Rd SE18 145 B6
Tubbenden Cl BR6 227 C5
Tubbenden Dr BR6 227 B4
Tubbenden Jun & Inf Schs BR6 227 B4
Tubbenden La BR6 227 C5
Tubbenden La S BR6 227 B3
Tubbs Rd NW10 89 D5
Tudor Ave
Hampton TW12 173 C3
North Cheam KT4 216 B4
Tudor Cl Ashford TW15 170 A6
BR7 188 B2
Cheam SM3 217 A2
Chessington KT9 214 A3
Crouch End N6 49 C2
Hampstead NW3 70 C2
Hampton TW12 174 A5
Hendon NW7 28 A4
Pinner HA5 40 A4
Tulse Hill SW2 160 B5
Wallington SM6 219 C1
Welsh Harp NW9 67 A6
Woodford IG8 37 B5
Tudor Coll WC1 233 A1
Tudor Court N HA9 66 C3
Tudor Court S HA9 66 C3
Tudor Cres EN2 5 A4
Tudor Ct 2 Barnet EN5 1 B1
3 Ealing W13 87 C1
Feltham TW13 172 C6
Kingsland N1 73 C2
5 Rotherhithe SE16 118 D5
Sidcup DA14 168 A1
South Acton W5 110 C4
4 Stanwell TW19 148 A5
Teddington TW11 174 D4
Walthamstow E17 53 B2
Tudor Dr
Kingston u T KT2 176 A5
Walton-on-T KT12 194 D1
West Barnes SM4 201 A3
Tudor Ent Pk HA3 42 B6
Tudor Est NW10 88 D5
Tudor Gables NW7 27 D6
Tudor Gdns Acton W3 88 C1
Harrow HA3 24 B1
Mortlake SW14 133 C2
Twickenham TW1 152 D3
Welsh Harp NW9 67 A6
West Wickham BR4 224 A5
Tudor Gr E9 74 C1
Tudor Ho
Brook Green W14 112 D2
Feltham TW13 172 C6
34 Hackney E9 74 C1
Mitcham CR4 181 A2
6 Muswell Hill N10 31 A3
Queensbury NW9 44 C5
Tolworth KT6 198 C1
Tudor Lo 4 N12 29 D5
Tudor Mews
Walthamstow E17 53 B5
2 Willesden NW10 68 A2
Tudor Par
Dagenham RM6 58 D2
SE9 144 A1
Tudor Pl SW19 180 C3
Tudor Prim Sch
Finchley N3 30 A2
Southall UB1 107 A6
Tudor Rd
Ashford TW15 171 B4
Barking IG11 101 D6
Barnet EN5 1 D2
Beckenham BR3 208 A6
Chingford E4 35 D4

Tudor Rd *continued*
Croydon SE25 206 B4
Hackney E9 96 B6
Hampton TW12 173 C3
Harrow HA3 24 B1
Hayes UB3 83 B1
Isleworth TW3 130 B1
Kingston u T KT2 176 C3
Newham E6 99 C6
Penge SE19 183 D3
Pinner HA5 22 C1
Ponders End N9 18 C4
Southall UB1 107 A6
Tudor Sq UB3 83 B2
Tudor St EC4 116 C6 251 B6
Tudors The 2 BR3 185 D1
Tudor Way BR5 211 B3
Hillingdon UB10 60 C2
Osidge N14 15 D3
South Acton W3 110 C4
Tudor Well Cl HA7 25 B5
Tudor Wlk DA5 169 A5
Tudway Rd SE3, SE9 143 C1
Tufnell Ct 19 E3 97 B6
Tufnell Mans 7 N7 71 D4
TUFNELL PARK 71 D4
Tufnell Park Mans 2 N7 72 A5
Tufnell Park Prim Sch N7 71 D4
Tufnell Park Rd N19, N7 71 D4
Tufnell Park Sta N19 71 C4
Tufton Ct SW1 260 A5
Tufton Gdns KT8 173 D1
Tufton Rd E4 35 C6
Tufton St SW1 116 A3 260 A5
Tugboat St SE28 123 C4
Tugela Rd CR0 205 B3
Tugela St SE6 163 B2
Tugmutton Cl BR6 226 D4
Tuke Sch SE15 140 B4
Tulip Cl Croydon CR0 206 D1
Hampton TW12 173 B4
5 Newham E6 100 B2
Southall UB2 108 A4
Tulip Ct 1 HA5 40 C6
Tulip Gdns Chingford E4 20 B1
Ilford IG1 78 D2
Tullis Ho 12 E9 74 C1
Tull St CR4 202 D2
Tulse Cl BR3 208 A6
TULSE HILL 160 D4
Tulse Hill
Tulse Hill SW2 160 C4
Tulse Hill SW27 160 D2
Tulse Hill Sta SE27 160 D2
Tulse Ho SW2 160 C5
Tulsemere Rd SE21, SE27 161 A2
Tumbling Bay KT12 194 A3
Tummons Gdns SE25 183 C1
Tump Ho SE28 123 C5
Tunbridge Ct 1 SE26 162 A1
Tunbridge Ho EC1 234 C2
Tuncombe Rd N18 33 C6
Tunis Rd W12 112 B5
Tunley Gn 12 E14 97 B2
Tunley Rd
Dagenham NW10 89 C6
Upper Tooting SW12, SW17 159 A2
Tunmarsh La E13 99 C4
Tunnan Leys E6 100 C1
Tunnel Avenue Trad Est SE10 120 B4
Tunnel Gdns N11 31 C3
Tunnel Link Rd TW6 148 C5
Tunnel Rd SE16 118 C4
Tunnel Rd E TW6 126 D3
Tunnel Rd W TW6 126 D4
Tunstall Cl BR6 227 C4
Tunstall Ct 14 TW9 132 B4
Tunstall Rd
Croydon CR0 205 C1
Stockwell SW9 138 B1
Tunstall Wlk 10 TW8 132 A6
Tunstock Way DA17 125 A3
Tunworth Cl NW9 45 A3
Tunworth Cres SW15 155 D5
Tun Yd SW8 137 B2
Tupelo Rd E10 75 D6
Tupman Ho 26 SE16 118 A4
Tuppy St SE28 123 A3
Turberville Ho 1 SW9 138 B2
Turenne Cl SW18 136 A1
Turin Rd N9 18 C4
Turin St E2 96 A4
Turkey Oak Cl SE19 183 C2
Turkey St EN1, EN3 6 C6
Turkey Street Sta EN3 6 C6
Turks Cl UB8 82 C4
Turk's Head Yd EC1 241 C4
Turks Row SW3 114 D1 257 D2
Turle Rd Finsbury Pk N4 72 B6
Thornton Heath SW16 182 A1
Turleway Cl N4 50 B1
Turley Cl E15 98 C6
Turnagain La EC4 241 C2
Turnage Rd RM8 59 A1
Turnant Rd N17 33 A2
Turnberry Cl
24 Bermondsey SE16 118 B1
Hendon NW4 28 D1
Turnberry Quay 1 E14 119 D3
Turnberry Way BR6 211 B1
Turnbull Ho N1 234 D6
Turnbury Cl SE28 102 D1
Turnchapel Mews 1 SW4 137 B2
Turner Ave
Mitcham CR4 180 D2
Tottenham N15 51 C5
Twickenham TW2 152 A1
Turner Cl
7 Brixton SW9 138 D4
Hampstead Garden Suburb NW11 47 D3
Hillingdon UB4 83 A4
Wembley HA0 65 D2
Turner Ct
9 Herne Hill SE5 139 B1
24 Rotherhithe SE16 118 C4
Turner Dr NW11 47 D3
Turner Ho
Finsbury Pk N4 50 B1
24 Millwall E14 119 C4
St John's Wood NW8 230 A4
Strand WC2 250 B5
6 Twickenham TW1 153 D5
Westminster SW1 259 D3
Turner Lo 10 SW19 156 D3
Turner Mews SM2 217 D1
Turner Pl SW11 158 C6
Turner Rd Edgware HA8 26 B1
New Malden KT3 199 B2
Walthamstow E17 54 A6
Turners Cl N20 14 D1
Turners Ct Leyton E15 76 A4
New Barnet EN5 13 D5
Tottenham N15 51 B4
Turners Meadow Way BR3 185 B2
Turner's Rd E3 97 B2
Turner St
Canning Town E16 98 D1
Stepney E1 96 B2
Turners Way CR0 220 C6
Turneville Rd W14 135 B6 264 C6
Turney Prim & Sec Specl Sch SE21 161 A4
Turney Rd SE21 161 B4
Turnham Green Sta W4 111 C2
Turnham Green Terr W4 111 C2
Turnham Ho SE4 141 A1
Turnham Prim Sch SE4 141 A1
Turnham Rd SE4 141 A1
Turnmill Ho 8 SW2 160 C6
Turnmill St EC1 94 D2 241 C4
Turnour Ho 31 E1 96 B1
Turnpike Cl SE8 141 B5
Turnpike Ct DA6 146 D1
Turnpike Ho EC1 234 D1
Turnpike La Hornsey N8 50 C6
Sutton SM1 218 A3
Uxbridge UB10 82 A5
Turnpike Lane Sta N15 50 D6
Turnpike Link CR0 221 C6
Turnpike Mews N8 50 C6
Turnpike Way TW7 131 A4
Turnpin La 3 SE10 142 A6
Turnstone Cl
Edgware NW9 27 C1
Newham E13 99 A4
Uxbridge UB10 60 D3
Turnstone Terr 11 W13 86 D3
Turpentine La SW1 115 B1 258 D1
Turpin Cl 15 EN3 7 C6
Turpington Cl BR2 210 A2
Turpington La BR2 210 A3
Turpin Ho SW11 268 C2
Turpin Rd TW14 149 D5
Turpin Way
Upper Holloway N19 49 D1
Wallington SM6 219 B1
Turquand St SE17 262 B3
Turret Gr SW4 137 C2
Turret Ho KT2 176 A4
Turton Ho 5 SE18 144 D6
Turton Rd HA0 66 A3
Turville Ho NW8 237 A6
Turville St E2 243 C6
Tuscan Ho 36 E2 96 C4
Tuscan Rd SE18 123 B1
Tuscany Ho E17 35 B1
Tuskar St SE10 120 C1
Tutorial Coll of West London UB1 107 B5
Tuttlebee La IG9 21 A2
Tuttle Ho SW1 259 D1
Tweedale Ct E15 76 A3
Tweed Ct W7 86 C1
Tweeddale Gr UB10 61 A5
Tweeddale Prim Sch SM5 202 B2
Tweeddale Rd SM5 202 B1
Tweed Ho E14 98 A3
Tweedmouth Rd E13 99 B5
Tweedy Cl EN1 17 D6
Tweedy Rd BR1 187 A2
Tweezer's Alley WC2 251 A6
Twelve Acre Ho 5 E12 78 C5
Twelvetrees Bsns Pk E16 98 B3
Twelvetrees Cres E3 98 A3
Twentyman Cl IG8 37 A5
Twice Times Montessori Sch SW6 135 C3
TWICKENHAM 152 D4
Twickenham Bridge TW9 153 C6
Twickenham Cl CR0 220 B5
Twickenham Gdns
Harrow HA3 24 C3
Wembley UB6 65 A3
Twickenham Pl KT7 212 D6
Twickenham Prep Sch TW12 174 A2
Twickenham Rd
Isleworth TW1, TW7 131 A2
Leyton E11 76 B6
Richmond TW1, TW9 131 C1
Teddington TW11 175 A6
Twickenham TW13 151 B1
Twickenham Rugby Football Union Ground TW2 152 C5
Twickenham Sta TW1 153 A4
Twickenham Trad Ctr TW1 152 D5
Twig Folly Cl 21 E2 96 D5
Twilley St SW18 157 D4
Twine Cl IG11 102 B4
Twine Ct E1 118 C6
Twineham Gn N12 29 C6
Twining Ave TW2 152 B1
Twinn Rd NW7 29 A4
Twin Tumps Way SE28 124 A6
Twisden Rd NW5 71 B4
Twiss Ho 6 SE18 122 D1
Twist Ho E10 75 D6
Two Bridges Ind Est CR0 221 B2
Twybridge Way NW10 67 A1
Twyford Abbey Rd NW10 88 B4
Twyford Ave Acton W3 110 C6
Muswell Hill N2 48 D6
Twyford CE High Sch W3 110 D5
Twyford Cres W3 110 C5
Twyford Ct Acton W3 110 C6
Muswell Hill N10 49 A6
6 Wembley HA0 88 A5
Twyford Ho Highbury N5 72 D5
6 Tottenham N15 51 C3
Twyford Par KT6 198 C1
Twyford Rd
Carshalton SM5 202 B1
Harrow HA2 41 D2
Ilford IG1 79 A3
Twyford St N1 94 B6 233 C6
Twynholm Mans SW6 264 A4
Tyas Rd E16 98 D3
Tybenham Rd SW19 201 C6
Tyberry Rd EN3 6 C2
Tyburn La HA1 42 D2
Tyburn Tree (site of)* W2 247 C6
Tyburn Way W1 247 D6
Tye La BR6 227 A3
Tyer's Est SE1 253 A2
Tyers Gate SE1 117 C4 253 A1
Tyers Ho 1 SW16 181 C5
Tyers St SE11 116 B1 260 C2
Tyers Terr SE11 116 B1 260 D1
Tyeshurst Cl SE2 125 A1
Tylecroft Rd SW16 182 A1
Tylehurst Gdns IG1 79 A3
Tyler Cl Erith DA8 147 D5
Haggerston E2 95 D5
Tyler Ho SE3 142 B3
Tyler Rd UB2 107 D3
Tylers Ct
4 Walthamstow E17 53 C5
5 Wembley HA0 88 A5
Tylers Gate HA3 44 A3
Tylers Path SM5 218 D4
Tyler St
Greenwich SE10 120 C1
SE10 142 C6
Tylney Ave SE19 183 D5
Tylney Ho 10 E1 96 B1
Tylney Rd BR1 187 D1
Forest Gate E7 77 C4
Tymperley Ct SW19 157 A3
Tynamara KT1 197 D5
Tynan Cl TW14 150 A3
Tyndale La N1 72 D1
Tyndale Mans N1 72 D1
Tyndale Terr 13 N1 72 D1
Tyndall Gdns E10 76 A6
Tyndall Rd DA16 145 D2
Leyton E10 76 A6
Tyne Ct W7 86 C1
Tyneham Cl 10 SW11 137 A2
Tyneham Rd SW11 137 A2
Tyne Ho 8 KT2 175 D2
Tynemouth Cl E6 100 D1
Tynemouth Dr EN1 6 A5
Tynemouth Rd
Mitcham CR4 181 A3
Plumstead Comm SE18 123 C1
Tottenham N15 51 D5
Tynemouth St SW6 136 A3
Tynemouth Terr 9 N15 51 D5
Tyne St E1 243 D2
Tynsdale Rd NW10 67 C2
Tynte Ct E9 75 A3
Tynwald Ho 14 SE26 162 A1
Type St E2 96 D5
Tyrawley Rd SW6 265 C2
Tyrell Cl HA1 64 C4
Tyrell Ct SM5 218 D4
Tyrells Ct 3 SE15 140 B2
Tyrols Rd SE23 162 D3
Tyrone Ct SW16 181 D5
Tyrone Rd E6 100 B4
Tyron Way DA14 189 D5
Tyrrell Ave DA16 168 B6
Tyrrell Ho Catford BR3 185 D5
SW1 269 B6
Tyrrell Rd SE22 140 A1
Tyrrell Sq CR4 180 C2
Tyrrel Way NW9 46 A2
Tyrwhitt Rd SE4 141 C2
Tysoe Ave EN3 7 B6
Tysoe St EC1 234 B1
Tyson Rd SE23 162 C4
Tyssen Com Prim Sch N16 52 A1
Tyssen Rd N16 73 D5
Tyssen St Dalston E8 73 D2
Hoxton N1 95 C5
Tysson Ho E9 75 A1
Tytherton 20 E2 96 C5
Tytherton Rd N19 71 D5

U

Uamvar St E14 97 D2
Uckfield Gr CR4 181 A2
Uckfield Rd EN3 6 D6
Udall St SW1 259 B3
Udimore Ho 11 W10 90 C2
Udney Park Rd TW11 175 A4
Uffington Rd
West Norwood SE27 182 C6
Willesden Green NW10 90 B6
Ufford Cl HA3 23 D3
Ufford Rd HA3 23 D3
Ufford St SE1 116 C4 251 B2
Ufton Ct UB5 84 D4
Ufton Gr N1 73 B1
Ufton Rd N1 73 C1
Uhura Sq 19 N16 73 C5
Ujima Ct
Finsbury Pk N19 50 A1
Streatham SW16 182 A6
Ujima Ho SW16 182 A6
UK Coll of Bsns & Computing IG2 56 C3
Uk Cotts UB3 105 B4
Ullathorne Rd SW16 181 C6
Ulleswater Rd N14 16 B1
Ullin St E14 98 A2
Ullswater SW15 156 D5
Ullswater Cl
Bromley BR1 186 C3
Hayes UB4 83 C5
Kingston u T KT2, SW15 177 B6
Ullswater Cres SW15 177 B6
Ullswater Ct
Harrow HA2 41 C2
2 Woodford E18 37 A1
Ullswater Ho SE15 140 C6
Ullswater Rd
Barnes SW13 134 A5
West Norwood SE27, SW16 160 D2
Ulster Ct KT2 175 D4
Ulster Gdns N13 33 A6
Ulster Pl NW1 238 C5
Ulster Terr NW1 238 C6
Ulundi Rd SE3 142 C6
Ulva Rd SW15 134 D1
Ulverscroft Rd SE22 162 A6
Ulverstone Rd SE27 160 D2
Ulverston Rd E17 36 B1
Ulysses Rd NW6 69 B3
Umberston St E1 96 B1
Umbria St SW15 156 A5
Umfreville Rd N4 50 D3
Umoja Ho N22 32 B1
Una Ho 7 NW5 71 B2
Undercliff SE10 142 A4
Undercliff Rd SE13 141 D2
UNDERHILL 13 C6
Underhill EN5 13 C6
Underhill Ct EN5 13 C6
Underhill Ho 7 E14 97 C2
Underhill Jun & Inf Schs EN5 13 A6
Underhill Pas NW1 231 D6
Underhill Rd SE21, SE22 162 B4
Underhill St NW1 231 D5
Underne Ave N14 15 B2
Undershaft EC3 95 C1 243 A1
Undershaw Rd BR1 164 D1
Underwood CR0 224 A3
Underwood Ct 3 E10 53 D1
Underwood Ho
East Molesey KT8 195 C4
Hammersmith W6 112 B3
Underwood Rd
Bethnal Green E1 96 A3
Chingford E4 35 D5
Woodford IG8 37 D3
Underwood Row N1 235 B2
Underwood St N1 95 A4 235 B2
Underwood The SE9 166 B2
Undine Rd E14 119 D2
Undine St SW17 180 D5
Uneeda Dr UB6 86 B6
Unicorn Bldg 14 E1 118 D6
Unicorn Prim Sch BR3 207 D4
Unicorn Sch TW9 132 B4
Unicorn Works N17 34 C3
Union Cl E11 76 B4
Union Ct
45 Paddington W2 91 C2
2 Richmond TW10 154 A6
South Lambeth SW4 138 A3
Union Dr E1 97 A3
Union Gr SW8 137 D3
Union Mews 32 SW9 138 A3
Union Pk 11 SE10 120 D1
Union Rd BR2 209 D4
Clapham SW8 137 D3
Friern Barnet N11 31 D4
Northolt UB5 85 C5
Thornton Heath CR0 205 A2
Wembley HA0 66 A2
Union Sq N1 95 A6 235 B5
Union St Barnet EN5 1 A2
Kingston u T KT1 175 D1
Mill Meads E15 98 B6
SE1 117 A5 252 A3
Union Terr HA2 41 C1
Union Wharf N1 235 B4
Union Wlk E2 95 C4
Union Yd W1 238 D1
Unity Cl
West Norwood SE19 183 A5
Willesden NW10 68 A2
Unity Mews NW1 232 C4
Unity Rd EN3 6 C6
Unity Terr HA2 63 D6
Unity Way SE18 121 D3
Univ Coll Jun Sch NW3 70 A4
Univ Coll London
Bloomsbury WC1 93 D3 239 C6
Bloomsbury WC1 94 A3 240 B6
Univ Coll London (Windeyer Inst) W1 93 C2 239 B4
Univ Coll London (Wolfson Ho) NW1 93 C4 232 B1
University Cl NW7 27 D3
University Coll Hospl WC1 93 C3 239 B6
University Coll Sch NW3 70 A3
University Gdns DA5 169 B4
University Mans SW15 134 D2
University Pl DA8 147 D5
University Rd SW19 180 B4
University St WC1 93 C3 239 B5
University Way E16 122 D6
Univ of California WC1 93 D2 239 D3
Univ of East London
Barking RM8 80 A4
Newham E16 122 C6
Stratford E15 76 C2
Univ of East London (Duncan Ho) E15 98 B6
Univ of East London (Holbrook Ctr) E15 98 D5
Univ of Greenwich SE10 142 B6
Univ of Greenwich Avery Hill Campus Mansion Site SE9 167 A5
Univ of Greenwich Avery Hill Campus Southwood Site SE9 167 B4
Univ of Greenwich Rachel Mcmillan Campus SE8 141 C6
Univ of Greenwich Riverside Ho Annexe SE18 122 C3
Univ of London WC1 93 D3 239 D5
Univ of London (King's Coll Hall) SE5 139 B2
Univ of London Obsy NW7 27 D4
Univ of London (Queen Mary & Westfield Coll) E1 97 A3
Univ of Westminster NW1 93 C3 239 A6
Univ of Westminster (Cavendish Campus) W1 93 C2 239 A4
Univ of Westminster (Harrow Campus) HA1 43 A2
Univ of Westminster (Marylebone Campus) W1 93 A2 238 A4
Univ of Westminster (Regent Campus) W1 93 C2 239 A3
Univ of Westminster (Regent Campus, Univ HQ) W1 93 B1 238 D2
Uno Apartments 4 BR1 187 A2
Unwin Ave TW14 149 B6
Unwin Cl SE15 140 A6
Unwin Rd
Isleworth TW7 130 C2
SW7 114 B3 256 D6
Upbrook Mews W2 92 A1 236 B1
Upcerne Rd SW10 136 A5 266 B3
Upchurch Cl 8 SE20 184 B3
Upcott Ho
33 Bromley E3 97 D4
4 Hackney E9 74 C1
Upcroft Ave HA8 27 A6
Updale Rd DA14 189 D6
Upfield CR0 222 B5
Upfield Rd W7 86 D2
Upgrove Manor Way 12 SE24 160 C4
Uphall Prim Sch IG1 78 D3
Uphall Rd IG1 78 D3
Upham Park Rd W4 111 C2
Uphill Dr Edgware NW7 27 C5
Kingsbury NW9 45 A4
Uphill Gr NW7 27 C6
Uphill Rd NW7 27 C6
Upland Ct SE23 162 C2
Upland Prim Sch DA7 147 B2
Upland Rd
Croydon CR2 221 B3
DA7 147 B2
East Dulwich SE22 162 A5
8 Newham E13 99 A3
Sutton SM2 218 B1
Uplands
Beckenham BR3 185 C1
Woolwich SE18 122 D1
Uplands Ave E17 34 D1
Uplands Bsns Pk E17 52 D6
Uplands Cl SW14 154 D6
Uplands Ct N21 16 C4
Uplands Park Rd EN2 4 C3
Uplands Rd
East Barnet EN4 15 A3
Hornsey Vale N8 50 B4
Ilford RM6 58 D6
Woodford IG8 37 D3
Uplands The HA4 40 A1
Uplands Way N21 16 C6
Upnall Ho 16 SE15 140 C6
Upney Ct 2 IG11 79 D1
Upney La IG11 79 D1
Upney Sta IG11 79 D1
Upnor Way SE17 263 B2
Uppark Dr IG2 57 A3
Upper Abbey Rd DA17 125 C2
Upper Addison Gdns W14 113 A4 244 A2
Upper Bank St E14 119 D5
Upper Bardsey Wlk 7 N1 73 A2
Upper Belgrave St SW1 115 A3 258 B6
Upper Berkeley St W1 92 D1 237 D1
Upper Beulah Hill SE19 183 C2
Upper Brighton Rd KT6 198 A2
Upper Brockley Rd SE4 141 B3
Upper Brook St W1 115 A6 248 A6
Upper Butts TW8 131 C6
Upper Caldy Wlk 18 N1 73 A2
Upper Camelford Wlk 14 W10 91 A1
Upper Cavendish Ave N3 47 C6
Upper Cheyne Row SW3 136 C6 267 A6
UPPER CLAPTON 52 B1
Upper Clapton Rd E5 74 B6
Upper Clarendon Wlk 12 W11 91 A1
Upper Dengie Wlk N1 235 A6
UPPER EDMONTON 34 B5
UPPER ELMERS END 207 B3
Upper Elmers End Rd BR3 207 A4
Upper Farm Rd KT8 195 B5
Upper Fosters NW4 46 C5
Upper Gn W CR4 180 D1
Upper Gr SE25 205 D5
Upper Grosvenor St W1 115 A6 248 A5
Upper Grotto Rd TW1 152 D2
Upper Ground SE1 116 C5 251 A4
Upper Grove Rd DA17 147 B6
Upper Gulland Wlk 23 N1 73 A2
UPPER HALLIFORD 193 B5
Upper Halliford Rd TW17 193 C6
Upper Halliford Sta TW16 171 C1
Upper Hampstead Wlk 29 NW3 70 A4
Upper Ham Rd KT2, TW10 175 D6
Upper Handa Wlk 2 N1 73 A2
Upper Harley St NW1 238 B5
Upper Hawkwell Wlk N1 235 B6
UPPER HOLLOWAY 71 D6
Upper Holloway Sta N19 71 D6
Upper Holly Hill Rd DA17 125 D1
Upper James St W1 249 B6
Upper John St W1 249 B6
Upper Lismore Wlk 8 N1 73 A2
Upper Lodge Mews TW12 174 A4
Upper Mall W6 112 B1
Upper Marsh SE1 116 B3 260 D6
Upper Montague St W1 92 D2 237 C3

Upper Mulgrave Rd
SM2 ... 217 A1
Upper North St E3, E14 ... 97 C2
UPPER NORWOOD ... 183 C3
Upper Park Rd
Belvedere DA17 ... 125 D2
BR1 ... 187 C2
Friern Barnet N11 ... 31 C5
Kingston u T KT2 ... 176 C4
Maitland Pk NW3 ... 70 D3
Upper Phillimore Gdns
W8 ... 113 C4 245 A1
Upper Pk IG10 ... 21 D6
Upper Ramsey Wlk 19
N1 ... 73 B2
Upper Rawreth Wlk
N1 ... 235 B6
Upper Rd Finchley N2 ... 30 C2
Newham E13 ... 99 A4
Wallington SM6 ... 219 D3
Upper Richmond Rd
SW15 ... 134 C1
Upper Richmond Rd W
TW10, SW14, SW15 ... 133 A1
UPPER RUXLEY ... 191 C3
Upper St Martin's La
WC2 ... 250 A6
Upper Selsdon Rd
CR2 ... 221 D1
Upper Sheridan Rd 3
DA17 ... 125 C2
UPPER SHIRLEY ... 222 D4
Upper Shirley Rd CR0 ... 222 D5
Upper Sq TW7 ... 131 A2
Upper St N1 ... 94 D6 234 C5
Upper Sunbury Rd
TW12 ... 173 C2
Upper Sutton La TW5 ... 129 C4
UPPER SYDENHAM ... 184 A6
Upper Tachbrook St
SW1 ... 259 B4
Upper Talbot Wlk 7
W10 ... 91 A1
Upper Teddington Rd KT1,
KT8 ... 175 C2
Upper Terr NW3 ... 70 A5
Upper Thames St
EC4 ... 117 A6 252 B6
Upper Tollington Pk
N4 ... 50 C1
Upperton Rd DA14 ... 189 D5
Upperton Rd E E13 ... 99 C4
Upperton Rd W E13 ... 99 C4
UPPER TOOTING ... 158 D1
Upper Tooting Park Mans
1 SW17 ... 159 A2
Upper Tooting Pk
SW17 ... 158 D2
Upper Tooting Rd
SW17 ... 158 D1
Upper Town Rd UB6 ... 85 D3
Upper Tulse Hill SW2 ... 160 B3
Upper Vernon Rd
SM1 ... 218 B3
UPPER WALTHAMSTOW
... 54 C6
Upper Walthamstow Rd
E17 ... 54 B6
Upper Wickham La
DA16 ... 146 B4
Upper Wimpole St
W1 ... 93 A2 238 B4
Upper Woburn Pl NW1,
WC1 ... 93 D4 232 D1
Uppingham Ave HA7 ... 25 C1
Upsdell Ave N13 ... 32 C4
Upshire Ho E17 ... 35 B1
Upstall St SE5 ... 138 D4
UPTON ... 77 B1
Upton Ave E7 ... 77 A1
Upton Cl
Cricklewood NW2 ... 69 A5
Sidcup DA5 ... 169 B5
Upton Cross E13 ... 99 A6
Upton Cross Prim Sch
E13 ... 99 B6
Upton Ct Penge SE20 ... 184 C3
Southall UB1 ... 107 D5
4 Wimbledon SW19 ... 178 D3
Upton Day Hospl DA6 ... 147 A1
Upton Dene SM2 ... 217 D1
Upton Gdns HA3 ... 43 C3
Upton Hts E7 ... 77 A1
Upton La E7 ... 77 A1
Upton Lo E7 ... 77 A2
Upton Lodge Cl WD23 ... 8 A4
UPTON PARK ... 99 D6
Upton Park Rd E7 ... 77 B1
Upton Park Sta E13 ... 99 C6
Upton Prim Sch DA5 ... 169 B5
Upton Rd Bexley DA6 ... 169 A6
Edmonton N18 ... 34 A5
Hounslow TW3 ... 129 C2
SE18 ... 145 A6
South Norwood CR7 ... 183 B1
Upton Rd S DA5 ... 169 B5
Upton Villas 4 DA6 ... 147 A1
Upway N12 ... 30 C4
Upwood Rd SE12 ... 165 A5
Thornton Heath SW16 ... 182 A2
Urban Mews N4 ... 50 D2
Urlwin St SE5 ... 139 A6
Urlwin Wlk SW9 ... 138 D4
Urmston Dr SW19 ... 157 A3
Urmston Ho 4 E14 ... 120 A2
Urquhart Ct BR3 ... 185 B3
Ursula Lo DA14 ... 190 B5
Ursula Mews N4 ... 51 A1
Ursula St
SW11 ... 136 C4 267 A1
Ursuline High Sch
SW20 ... 178 D2
Ursuline Prep Sch
SW19 ... 178 D3
Urswick Gdns RM9 ... 81 A1
Urswick Rd
Dagenham RM9 ... 81 A1
Hackney E5, E9 ... 74 C3
Usborne Mews SW8 ... 270 D4
Usher Hall NW4 ... 46 B5
Usher Rd E3 ... 97 B5
Usk Rd SW11 ... 136 A1
Usk St E2 ... 96 D4
Utah Bldg 3 SE13 ... 141 D4
Utopia Ho 3 NW2 ... 68 A2
Utopia Village
NW1 ... 93 A6 231 A6
Uvedale Rd
Dagenham RM10 ... 81 C5
Enfield EN2 ... 17 B6
Uverdale Rd
SW10 ... 136 A5 266 B3
UXBRIDGE ... 82 A6
Uxbridge Coll
Hayes UB3 ... 106 A6
Uxbridge UB8 ... 60 A2
Uxbridge High Sch
UB8 ... 82 A5
Uxbridge Rd
Acton W3, W5 ... 110 C5
Ealing W13 ... 109 C6
Feltham TW13 ... 150 D2
Hampton TW12, TW13 ... 173 D5
Hayes UB4 ... 106 C6
Hillingdon UB10, UB4 ... 83 C2
Kingston u T KT1, KT6 ... 197 D4
Shepherd's Bush W12 ... 112 B5
Southall UB1, UB2, W5,
W7 ... 108 B5
Stanmore HA7 ... 25 A5
Uxbridge Road (Harrow
Weald) HA3 ... 24 B3
Uxbridge Road (Hatch
End) HA5 ... 23 B3
Uxbridge Road (Pinner)
HA5 ... 22 D1
Uxbridge St
W8 ... 113 C5 245 A4
Uxendon Cres HA3, HA9 ... 44 A1
Uxendon Hill HA9 ... 44 B2
Uxendon Manor Prim Sch
HA3 ... 44 A4

V

Vadnie Bish Ho NW5 ... 71 C2
Vaine Ho 4 E9 ... 75 A2
Valance Ave E4 ... 20 D3
Valan Leas BR2 ... 208 C6
Vale Ave WD6 ... 10 D6
Vale Cl Muswell Hill N2 ... 48 D6
Orpington BR6 ... 226 C4
St John's Wood
W9 ... 92 A4 229 A1
Twickenham TW1 ... 153 A1
Vale Cres SW15 ... 177 C6
Vale Croft
Claygate KT10 ... 212 D1
Pinner HA5 ... 41 A4
Vale Ct Barnet EN5 ... 1 D1
East Acton W3 ... 111 D5
St John's Wood
W9 ... 92 A4 229 A1
Wembley HA0 ... 65 C5
Vale Dr EN5 ... 13 C6
Vale End SE22 ... 139 D1
Vale Est The W3 ... 111 C5
Vale Farm Sports Ctr
HA0 ... 65 B4
Vale Gr Acton W3 ... 111 B5
Stoke Newington N4 ... 51 A2
Vale La W3 ... 88 C2
Vale Lo SE23 ... 162 C2
Valence Ave RM8 ... 80 D6
Valence Cir RM8 ... 81 A5
Valence House Mus*
RM8 ... 81 A6
Valence Jun & Inf Schs
RM8 ... 80 D6
Valence Wood Rd RM8 ... 81 A5
Valencia Rd HA7 ... 25 C6
Valens Ho 1 SW2 ... 160 C3
Valentia Pl SW9 ... 138 C1
Valentine Ave DA5 ... 169 A3
Valentine Ct Elstree WD6 ... 9 D5
3 Forest Hill SE23 ... 162 D2
Valentine Ho
11 Clapham Pk SW4 ... 159 C5
26 Old Ford E3 ... 97 B6
Valentine Pl
SE1 ... 116 D4 251 C2
Valentine Rd
Harrow HA2 ... 64 A5
Homerton E9 ... 74 D2
Valentine Row SE1 ... 251 C1
Valentines High Sch
IG2 ... 56 C3
Valentines Rd IG1 ... 56 D1
VALE OF HEALTH ... 70 B5
Vale of Health NW3 ... 70 B5
Vale Rd BR1 ... 188 C1
Claygate KT10 ... 212 D1
Mitcham CR4 ... 203 D5
Stoke Newington N4 ... 51 A2
Sutton SM1 ... 217 D4
Upton E7 ... 77 B2
Worcester Pk KT19,
KT4 ... 215 D5
Vale Rd N KT6 ... 214 A6
Vale Rd S KT6 ... 214 A6
Valerian Way E15 ... 98 C4
Valerie Ct
Belmont SM2 ... 217 D1
Bushey WD23 ... 8 A4
Vale Rise NW11 ... 47 B1
Vale Row N5 ... 72 D5
Vale Royal N7 ... 72 A1
Valery Pl TW12 ... 173 C3
Vale Sch The SW7 ... 256 A5
Valeside Ct 2 EN5 ... 1 D1
Valeswood Rd BR1 ... 186 D5
Vale Terr N4 ... 51 A3
Vale The Ashford TW16 ... 172 A4
Cricklewood NW11 ... 69 A6
Croydon CR0 ... 222 D6
East Acton W3 ... 111 C5
Feltham TW14 ... 150 B5
Heston TW5 ... 129 A6
Muswell Hill N10 ... 31 A2
Ruislip HA4 ... 62 C4
Southgate N14 ... 16 A4
SW3 ... 136 B6 266 D6
Woodford IG8 ... 37 A3
Valetta Gr E13 ... 99 A5
Valetta Rd W3 ... 111 D4
Valette Ct N10 ... 49 B5
Valette Ho E9 ... 74 C2
Valette St E8 ... 74 B2
Valiant Cl 13 UB5 ... 84 D4
Valiant Ho
9 Cubitt Town E14 ... 120 A4
5 Greenwich SE7 ... 121 C1
SW11 ... 266 D1
Valiant Way E6 ... 100 B2
Vallance Rd
Bethnal Green E1 ... 96 A3
Muswell Hill N22 ... 31 C1
Vallentin Rd E17 ... 54 A5
Valley Ave N12 ... 30 B6
Valley (Charlton Athletic
FC) The SE7 ... 121 C1
Valley Cl HA5 ... 22 B1
Valley Ct IG8 ... 37 B3
Valley Dr NW9 ... 44 D3
Valleyfield Rd SW16 ... 182 B5
Valley Fields Cres EN2 ... 4 C3
Valley Gdns
Mitcham SW19 ... 180 B3
Wembley HA0 ... 66 B1
Valley Gr SE7 ... 121 C1
Valley Ho
4 Edmonton N9 ... 18 A1
Upper Clapton E5 ... 52 C1
Valleylink Est EN3 ... 19 A5
Valley Mews TW1 ... 153 A2
Valley Pl KT6 ... 198 A3
Valley Point Ind Est
CR0 ... 204 A2
Valley Prim Sch BR2 ... 186 D1
Valley Prospect 3
SE19 ... 183 C4
Valley Rd
Beckenham BR2 ... 186 C1
BR5 ... 190 B2
Streatham SW16 ... 182 B6
Uxbridge UB10 ... 82 A5
Valleyside SE7 ... 121 D1
Valley Side E4 ... 19 C3
Valley Side Par E4 ... 19 C2
Valley View EN5 ... 13 A5
Valley Wlk CR0 ... 222 C6
Valliere Rd NW10 ... 90 A4
Valliers Wood Rd
DA15 ... 167 C3
Vallis Way
Chessington KT9 ... 213 D4
Ealing W13 ... 87 A2
Val McKenzie Ave N7 ... 72 C5
Valmar Rd SE5 ... 139 A4
Valmar Trad Est SE5 ... 139 A4
Valnay St SW17 ... 180 D5
Valognes Ave E17 ... 35 A2
Valois Ho SE1 ... 263 C6
Valonia Gdns SW18 ... 157 B5
Vambery Rd SE18 ... 145 A6
Vanbern Ho NW5 ... 71 A2
Vanborough Ct 4
SM2 ... 218 A2
Vanbrough Cres UB5 ... 84 C6
Vanbrugh Cl 2 E16 ... 99 D2
Vanbrugh Ct SE11 ... 261 B3
Vanbrugh Dr KT12 ... 194 C3
Vanbrugh Fields SE3 ... 142 D5
Vanbrugh Hill SE10,
SE3 ... 142 D6
Vanbrugh Ho 8 E9 ... 74 C1
Vanbrugh Mews KT12 ... 194 C2
Vanbrugh Park Rd
SE3 ... 142 D5
Vanbrugh Park Rd W
SE3 ... 142 D5
Vanbrugh Pk SE3 ... 142 D5
Vanbrugh Rd W4 ... 111 B3
Vanbrugh Terr SE3 ... 142 D4
Vanburgh Cl BR6 ... 211 C1
Vanburgh Ct 6 EN5 ... 1 A1
Vanburgh Ho E1 ... 243 C4
Vancouver Rd
Edgware HA8 ... 26 D2
Forest Hill SE23 ... 163 B2
Hayes UB4 ... 84 B3
Richmond TW10 ... 175 C6
Vancover Ho 33 E1 ... 118 B5
Vanderbilt Rd SW18 ... 158 A3
Vanderbilt Villas 1
W12 ... 112 D4
Vanderville Gdns N2 ... 30 B1
Vandome Cl E16 ... 99 B1
Vandon Ct SW1 ... 259 B6
Vandon Pas SW1 ... 259 B6
Vandon St SW1 ... 259 B6
Van Dyck Ave KT3 ... 199 B2
Vandyke Cl SW15 ... 156 D5
Vandyke Cross SE9 ... 166 A6
Vandy St EC2 ... 243 A5
Vane Cl Hampstead NW3 ... 70 B4
Harrow HA3 ... 44 B3
Vane Ho 18 N2 ... 30 B1
Vanessa Cl DA17 ... 125 C1
Vane St SW1 ... 259 B4
Vanfame Ct KT3 ... 199 D6
Vange Ho 12 W10 ... 90 C2
Van Gogh Cl 11 TW7 ... 131 A2
Van Gogh Ct E14 ... 120 B3
Vanguard Bldg 6
E14 ... 119 C4
Vanguard Cl
Newham E16 ... 99 B2
Thornton Heath CR0 ... 204 D1
Vanguard Ho
11 Hackney E8 ... 74 B1
7 Merton SW19 ... 180 A3
6 Stanwell TW19 ... 148 A5
Vanguard St SE8 ... 141 C4
Vanguard Trad Ctr E15 ... 98 A6
Vanguard Way
Hatton TW6 ... 127 C3
Wallington SM6 ... 220 A1
Van Lang Ho EN3 ... 18 D6
Vanneck Sq SW15 ... 156 A6
Vanner Point 27 E9 ... 74 D2
Vanoc Gdns BR1 ... 187 A6
Vansittart Rd E7 ... 77 A4
Vansittart St 7 SE14 ... 141 A5
Vanston Pl
SW6 ... 135 C5 265 B4
Vantage Ct
Harlington UB3 ... 127 C5
4 South Norwood
SW16 ... 182 B3
Vantage Mews 7 E14 ... 120 A5
Vantage Pl W8 ... 255 B5
Vant Rd SW17 ... 180 D5
Vantrey Ho SE11 ... 261 A3
Varcoe Rd SE16 ... 118 C1
Vardens Rd SW11 ... 136 B1
Varden St E1 ... 96 B1
Vardon Cl W3 ... 89 B1
Vardon Ho SE10 ... 142 A4
Vardy Ho HA7 ... 25 B5
Varey Ho E1 ... 97 A4
Varley Ho 5 NW6 ... 91 C6
Varley Par NW9 ... 45 C5
Varley Rd E16 ... 99 B1
Varley Way CR4 ... 180 B1
Varma Ct SE3 ... 143 A4
Varna Rd
Hampton TW12 ... 173 D2
SW6 ... 135 B5 264 C3
Varndell St
NW1 ... 93 C4 232 A2
Varsity Dr TW1, TW7 ... 152 D5
Varsity Row SW14 ... 133 A3
Vartry Rd N15 ... 51 C3
Vascroft Est NW10 ... 88 D3
Vassall Ho 3 E3 ... 97 A4
Vassall Rd SW9 ... 138 C5
Vat Ho SW8 ... 270 B4
Vauban Est SE16 ... 263 D5
Vauban St
SE16 ... 117 D3 263 D5
Vaudeville Ct N4 ... 72 C6
Vaughan Almshouses
TW15 ... 170 D5
Vaughan Ave
Chiswick W6 ... 111 D2
Hendon NW4 ... 46 A4
Vaughan Cl TW12 ... 173 A4
Vaughan Est 3 E2 ... 95 D4
Vaughan Fst & Mid Sch
HA1 ... 42 A3
Vaughan Gdns IG1 ... 56 B2
Vaughan Ho SE1 ... 251 C2
Vaughan Rd
Camberwell SE5 ... 139 A2
DA16 ... 145 D3
Harrow HA1 ... 42 B3
Stratford E15 ... 76 D2
Thames Ditton KT7 ... 197 B2
Vaughan St SE16 ... 119 B4
Vaughan Way E1 ... 118 A5
Vaughan Williams Cl
SE8 ... 141 C5
VAUXHALL ... 116 A1
Vauxhall Bridge Rd
SW1 ... 115 C2 259 B3
Vauxhall Cross SE1,
SW8 ... 116 A1 260 B1
Vauxhall Gdns CR2 ... 221 A2
Vauxhall Gr
SW8 ... 138 B6 270 C6
Vauxhall Prim Sch
SE11 ... 116 B1 260 D2
Vauxhall St
SE11 ... 116 B1 260 D2
Vauxhall Sta
SE11 ... 116 A1 260 B1
Vauxhall Wlk SE11 ... 260 C2
Vawdrey Cl E1 ... 96 C3
Vaynor Ho N7 ... 72 A4
Veals Mead CR4 ... 180 C2
Vectis Ct SW18 ... 157 D5
Vectis Gdns SW17 ... 181 B4
Vectis Rd SW17 ... 181 B4
Veda Rd SE13 ... 141 C1
Vega Cres HA6 ... 22 A5
Vega Rd WD23 ... 8 A4
Veitch Cl TW14 ... 149 D4
Veldene Way HA2 ... 63 B5
Velde Way 1 SE22 ... 161 C6
Vellacott Ho 3 W12 ... 90 B1
Velletri Ho 17 E2 ... 96 D5
Vellum Dr SM5 ... 219 A5
Venables Cl RM10 ... 81 D4
Venables St
NW8 ... 92 B2 236 D4
Vencourt Pl W6 ... 112 A2
Venetian Rd SE5 ... 139 A3
Venetia Rd Ealing W5 ... 109 D4
Harringay N4 ... 50 D3
Venice Ct 14 SE5 ... 139 A5
Venita Manor SE27 ... 182 C5
Venmead Ct 7 DA17 ... 125 C2
Venner Rd SE26 ... 184 C5
Venn Ho N1 ... 233 D5
Venn St SW4 ... 137 C1
Ventnor Ave HA7 ... 25 B1
Ventnor Dr N20 ... 13 D2
Ventnor Gdns IG11 ... 79 C2
Ventnor Mans IG11 ... 79 C2
Ventnor Rd
Belmont SM2 ... 217 D1
SE14 ... 140 D5
Ventnor Terr N15 ... 52 A5
Ventura Ho 12 SW2 ... 138 A1
Venture Cl DA5 ... 169 A4
Venture Ct 3 SE12 ... 165 A4
Venue St E14 ... 98 A2
Venus Ho
7 Millwall E14 ... 119 C2
8 Old Ford E3 ... 97 C6
Venus Mews CR4 ... 202 C6
Venus Rd SE18 ... 122 B3
Vera Ave N21 ... 16 C6
Vera Ct
1 Kensington W2 ... 91 D1
Tottenham N22 ... 32 D2
Vera Lynn Cl 5 E7 ... 77 A4
Vera Rd SW6 ... 135 A4 264 B2
Verbena Cl E16 ... 98 D3
Verbena Gdns 4 W6 ... 112 A1
Verdant Ct 3 SE6 ... 164 C4
Verdant La SE6 ... 164 C3
Verdayne Ave CR0 ... 222 D6
Verdi Cres W10 ... 91 A5
Verdun Rd
Barnes SW13 ... 134 A5
SE18 ... 146 A6
Vere Bank SW19 ... 157 B3
Vereker Dr TW16 ... 194 A6
Vereker Rd W14 ... 254 B1
Vere St W1 ... 93 B1 238 C1
Verity Cl W11 ... 91 A1
Verity Ct N9 ... 18 D3
Verity Ho 20 E3 ... 97 B4
Vermeer Ct E14 ... 120 B3
Vermillion Ct TW13 ... 149 D1
Vermont Cl EN2 ... 4 D1
Vermont Ho E17 ... 35 B1
Vermont Rd
Sutton SM1 ... 217 D5
Wandsworth SW18 ... 157 D5
West Norwood SE19 ... 183 C4
Verne Ct 9 W3 ... 111 A3
Verneer Gdns SE15 ... 140 C1
Verney Gdns RM9 ... 81 A4
Verney Ho
Isleworth TW3 ... 130 A1
Lisson Gr NW8 ... 237 A6
South Kensington SW10 266 A6
Verney Rd
Bermondsey SE16 ... 118 B1
Dagenham RM9 ... 81 A4
Verney St NW10 ... 67 B5
Verney Way SE16 ... 118 B1
Vernham Rd SE18 ... 145 A6
Vernon Ave Ilford E12 ... 78 B4
West Barnes SW20 ... 178 D1
Woodford IG8 ... 37 B3
Vernon Cl
Stanwell TW19 ... 148 A3
West Ewell KT19 ... 215 A2
Vernon Cres EN4 ... 15 A5
Vernon Ct
Child's Hill NW2 ... 69 B5
Ealing W5 ... 109 C6
Stanmore HA7 ... 25 B2
Vernon Dr HA7 ... 25 A2
Vernon Ho
Hyde The NW9 ... 45 D4
SE11 ... 260 D1
Vernon House Sch
NW10 ... 67 B3
Vernon Mews W14 ... 254 B3
Vernon Pl WC1 ... 240 B3
Vernon Rd Bow E3 ... 97 B5
Feltham TW13 ... 149 D2
Hornsey N8 ... 50 C6
Ilford IG3 ... 57 D1
Leytonstone E11 ... 54 C1
Mortlake SW14 ... 133 B2
Stratford E15 ... 76 C1
Sutton SM1 ... 218 B3
Walthamstow E17 ... 53 B4
Vernon Rise
Greenford UB6 ... 64 B3
WC1 ... 233 D2
Vernon Sq WC1 ... 233 D2
Vernon St W14 ... 113 A2 254 B3
Vernon Yd
W11 ... 113 B6 244 C6
Veroan Rd DA7 ... 147 A3
Verona Ct Chiswick W4 ... 111 C1
10 SE14 ... 140 D6
Verona Dr KT6 ... 214 A6
Verona Rd E7 ... 77 A1
Veronica Gdns CR4,
SW16 ... 181 C2
Veronica Ho
Brockley SE4 ... 141 B2
46 Bromley E3 ... 97 D4
Veronica Rd SW17 ... 159 B2
Veronique Gdns IG6 ... 57 A4
Verran Rd SW12 ... 159 B4
Versailles Rd SE20 ... 184 A3
Verulam Ave E17 ... 53 B2
Verulam Bldgs WC1 ... 240 D4
Verulam Ct
Hendon NW9 ... 46 A2
4 Southall UB1 ... 86 A1
Verulam Ho 1 W6 ... 112 C4
Verulam Rd UB6 ... 85 C3
Verulam St EC1 ... 94 C2 241 A4
Vervain Ho 2 SE15 ... 140 A5
Verwood Dr EN4 ... 2 D2
Verwood Ho SW8 ... 270 D3
Verwood Lo 1 E14 ... 120 B2
Verwood Rd HA2 ... 24 A1
Veryan Ct 3 N8 ... 49 D4
Vesage Ct EC1 ... 241 B3
Vesey Path 15 E14 ... 97 D1
Vespan Rd W12 ... 112 A4
Vesta Ct SE1 ... 253 A1
Vesta Ho 9 E3 ... 97 C6
Vesta Rd SE4, SE14 ... 141 A3
Vestris Rd SE23 ... 162 D2
Vestry House (Mus)*
E17 ... 53 D5
Vestry Mews 12 SE5 ... 139 C4
Vestry Rd
Camberwell SE5 ... 139 C4
Walthamstow E17 ... 53 D5
Vestry St N1 ... 95 B4 235 C2
Vevey St SE23, SE6 ... 163 B2
Veysey Gdns RM10 ... 81 C5
Viaduct Pl 28 E2 ... 96 B4
Viaduct Rd N2 ... 30 C1
Viaduct St E2 ... 96 B4
Viaduct The
Harrow HA2 ... 64 A5
Woodford E18 ... 37 B1
Vian St SE13 ... 141 D2
Vibart Gdns SW2 ... 160 B4
Vibart Wlk N1 ... 233 B6
Vicarage Ave SE3 ... 143 A5
Vicarage Cl
New Malden KT4 ... 199 C1
Northolt UB5 ... 63 B1
Ruislip HA4 ... 39 B2
Vicarage Cres
SW11 ... 136 B4 266 C1
Vicarage Ct
Beckenham BR3 ... 207 A6
East Bedfont TW14 ... 149 A4
Finchley N12 ... 29 D5
7 Putney SW15 ... 156 A4
W8 ... 245 C2
Vicarage Dr
Barking IG11 ... 79 A1
Beckenham BR3 ... 185 C2
Mortlake SW14 ... 155 B6
Vicarage Farm Ct
TW5 ... 129 B5
Vicarage Farm Rd TW3,
TW4, TW5 ... 129 A4
Vicarage Fields KT12 ... 194 C3
Vicarage Field Sh Ctr The
IG11 ... 79 A1
Vicarage Gate
W8 ... 113 D5 245 C3
Vicarage Gdns
Mitcham CR4 ... 202 C6
Mortlake SW14 ... 155 B6
W8 ... 245 B3
Vicarage Gr SE5 ... 139 B4
Vicarage Ho 1 KT1 ... 176 B1
Vicarage La Ilford IG1 ... 57 B1
Stratford E15 ... 76 D1
Wallend E6 ... 100 C4
Vicarage Mans N15 ... 51 A5
Vicarage Pk SE18 ... 123 A1
Vicarage Prim Sch E6 ... 100 B4
Vicarage Rd
Ashford TW16 ... 171 D4
Croydon CR0 ... 220 C5
DA5 ... 169 D3
Dagenham RM10 ... 81 D1
Hampton Wick KT1 ... 175 C2
Hendon NW4 ... 46 A3
Kingston u T KT1 ... 175 D1
Mortlake SW14 ... 155 B6
Stratford E15 ... 76 D1
Sutton SM1 ... 217 D5
Teddington TW11 ... 175 A5
Tottenham N17 ... 34 A2
Walthamstow E10 ... 53 D1
Woolwich SE18 ... 123 A1
Vicarage The N8 ... 50 B3
Vicarage Way
Harrow HA2 ... 41 C2
Neasden NW10 ... 67 B5
Vicarage Wlk
SW11 ... 136 B4 266 D2
Vicars Bridge Cl HA0 ... 88 A5
Vicar's Cl Enfield EN1 ... 5 C3
Newham E15 ... 99 A6
South Hackney E9 ... 96 C6
Vicar's Green Prim Sch
HA0 ... 87 C5
Vicars Hill SE13 ... 141 D1
Vicar's Moor La N21 ... 16 D4
Vicars Oak Rd SE19 ... 183 C4
Vicar's Rd NW5 ... 71 A3
Vicar's Wlk RM8 ... 80 B5
Viceroy Cl N2 ... 48 C6

Viceroy Ct
5 Croydon CR0 ....205 B1
NW8 ....230 B4
Viceroy Lo 6 KT6....198 A4
Viceroy Par N2....48 C6
Viceroy Rd
SW8....138 A4 270 A2
Vic Johnson Ho 21 E3...97 B6
Vickers Cl SM6....220 B1
Vickers Ct 10 TW19....148 A5
Vickery Ct EC1....242 B6
Vickery Ho 13 SW4....138 A1
Vickery's Wharf 3 E14..97 C1
Victor Cazalet Ho N1 . 234 C6
Victor Gr HA0....66 A1
Victor Ho 2 N20....14 D1
Victoria & Albert Mus*
SW7....114 B3 256 D5
Victoria Arc SW1....258 D5
Victoria Ave Barnet EN4...2 B1
East Molesey KT8....195 D6
EC2....243 B3
Finchley N3....29 B2
Hackbridge SM5, SM6...219 A5
Hillingdon UB10....60 D1
Hounslow TW3, TW4....151 C6
Newham E6....99 D6
Surbiton KT6....197 D3
Wembley HA9....66 D2
Victoria Bglws DA14...191 B3
Victoria Bldgs 13 E8....96 B6
Victoria Bsns Ctr
DA16....146 B3
Victoria Chambers
EC2....243 A6
Victoria Cl Barnet EN4....2 B1
East Molesey KT8....195 C6
Harrow HA1....42 D3
Hayes UB3....83 B1
Victoria Coach Sta
SW1....115 B2 258 C3
Victoria Coll WC2....241 A2
Victoria Cotts Ilford IG6 . 57 A4
Muswell Hill N10....31 A1
7 Richmond TW9....132 C4
3 Spitalfields E1....96 A2
Victoria Cres
Tottenham N15....51 C4
West Norwood SE19....183 C4
Victoria Ct
5 Clapham Pk SW4....159 D5
3 Penge SE26....184 C4
South Acton W3....110 C4
4 St George in t East
E1....118 A6
1 Wanstead E18....55 B6
Wembley HA9....66 C2
Victoria Dock Rd E16..121 B6
Victoria Dr SW19....156 D3
Victoria Emb
WC2....116 C6 251 A5
Victoria Gdns
Heston TW5....129 A4
W11....113 C5 245 A4
Victoria Gr
North Finchley N12....30 B5
W8....114 A3 256 A6
Victoria Gr Mews W2 . 245 C5
Victoria Hall 15 E16....121 A5
Victoria Ho
6 Clapham Pk SW4....159 D5
Edgware HA8....26 D4
2 Shepherd's Bush
W12....112 A4
SW1....258 C2
Victoria Ind Est W3....89 C2
Victoria Jun Sch
TW13....150 B3
Victoria La Barnet EN5....1 B1
Hayes UB3....105 B1
Victoria Lo 5 SW19....178 C3
Victoria Mans
8 Islington N7....72 C3
Willesden NW10....68 B1
Victoria Mews
Kilburn NW6....91 C6
Wandsworth SW18....158 A3
Victoria Mills 1 E15....98 B6
Victorian Gr N16....73 C5
Victorian Hts 7 SW8...137 B3
Victorian Rd N16....73 D5
Victoria Park Ct 11 E9...74 C1
Victoria Park Ind Ctr
E9....75 B1
Victoria Park Lofts E9...96 D6
Victoria Park Rd E9....74 D1
Victoria Park Sq E2....96 C4
Victoria Pas NW8....236 C6
Victoria Pl 10 TW10....153 D6
Victoria Place Sh Ctr
SW1....115 B2 258 D4
Victoria Point 10 E13....99 A5
Victoria Rd
Barking IG11....78 D2
Barnet EN4....2 B1
Bexley DA6....147 C1
Bromley Comm BR2....209 D4
Buckhurst Hill IG9....21 D2
Chingford E4....20 C3
Chislehurst West BR7...188 C5
Dagenham RM10....81 D3
Ealing W5....87 B2
Edgware NW7....27 D5
Edmonton N9....17 D1
Feltham TW13....150 B3
Finsbury Pk N4....50 B1
Hendon NW4....46 D5
Victoria Rd *continued*
Kensington W8 114 A3 256 A6
Kilburn NW6....91 B6
Kingston u T KT1....176 B1
Leyton E11....76 C4
Mitcham CR4....180 D3
Mortlake SW14....133 B2
Muswell Hill N22....31 D2
Newham E13....99 A5
North Acton NW10....89 C3
Ruislip HA4....62 B4
Sidcup DA15....168 A1
Southall UB2....107 B3
Surbiton KT6....197 D3
Sutton SM1....218 B3
Teddington TW11....175 A4
Tottenham Hale N15....52 A5
Twickenham TW1....153 B4
Walthamstow E17....36 A1
Wanstead E18....55 B6
Victoria Ret Pk HA4....62 D3
Victoria Rise SW4....137 B2
Victoria Sq SW1....258 D6
Victoria St Erith DA17...125 B1
Stratford E15....76 C1
SW1....115 C3 259 B5
Victoria Sta
SW1....115 B2 258 D4
Victoria Terr
Dagenham NW10....89 C3
Finsbury Pk N4....50 C1
Harrow HA1....42 C1
Victoria (Underground)
SW1....115 B3 258 D5
Victoria Villas TW9....132 B1
Victoria Way SE7....143 C6
Victoria Wharf E14....119 A6
Victoria Yd 28 E1....96 A1
Victor Mills Cotts BR8..191 C3
Victor Rd
College Pk NW10....90 B4
Harrow HA2....42 A6
Penge SE20....184 D3
Teddington TW11....174 C6
Victors Dr TW12....173 A4
Victor Seymour Inf Sch
SM5....218 D4
Victors Way EN5....1 B2
Victor Villas N9....17 B1
Victory Ave SM4....202 A4
Victory Bsns Ctr The
TW7....130 D1
Victory Cl TW19....148 A3
Victory Ct IG11....102 B4
Victory Pl
6 Limehouse E14....119 A6
SE17....117 B2 262 C4
West Norwood SE19....183 C4
Victory Rd
Merton SW19....180 A3
Wanstead E11....55 B5
Victory Road Mews 5
SW19....180 A3
Victory Sch
SE17....117 A2 262 B4
Victory Way
Hounslow TW5....106 C1
Rotherhithe SE16....119 A4
Victory Wlk SE8....141 C4
Video Ct N4....50 A2
Vidler Cl KT9....213 C2
Vienna Cl IG5....37 D1
View Cl Harrow HA1....42 B5
Highgate N6....48 D2
View Cres N8....49 D4
Viewfield Cl HA3....44 A2
Viewfield Rd DA5....168 C3
Wandsworth SW18....157 B5
Viewland Rd SE18....123 D1
Viewpoint Ealing W5....110 B6
3 Islington N5....72 D3
Lewisham SE3....142 D2
View Point N20....14 A4
Viewpoint Ct 8 HA5....22 C1
View Rd N6....48 D3
Viewside Lo N6....49 C3
View The SE2....125 A1
Viga Rd N21....16 C5
Vigilant Cl SE26....184 A6
Vignoles Rd RM7....59 C2
Vigo St W1....115 C6 249 A5
Vi & John Rubens Ho
IG2....56 C3
Viking Cl 18 E3....97 A5
Viking Ct
Hampton TW12....173 D2
New Barnet EN4....14 B6
Viking Gdns E6....100 A3
Viking Ho
3 Camberwell SE5....139 A3
3 Woolwich SE7....122 A2
Viking Pl E10....53 B1
Viking Prim Sch UB5....84 D4
Viking Rd UB1....107 A6
Villacourt Rd SE18....146 A6
Village Arc The 2 E4....20 B3
Village Cl Chingford E4...36 A5
Hampstead NW3....70 B3
Village Ct
Blackheath SE3....142 C2
Walthamstow E17....53 D4
Village Gate TW17....192 D4
Village Home The IG6 . 57 A6
Village Hts IG8....36 D5
Village Inf Sch RM10....81 C1
Village Mount 10 NW3 . 70 A4
Village Park Cl EN1....17 C5
Village Rd Enfield EN1....17 C6
Hendon N3....29 A1
Village Row SM2....217 C1
Village Sch The NW3....70 D2
Village The
Battersea SW11....136 D2
SE7....143 D6
Village Way
Ashford TW15....170 C6
Beckenham BR3....207 C6
Dulwich Village SE21....161 B5
Ilford IG6....57 A6
Pinner HA5....41 A2
Willesden NW10....67 B4
Village Way E HA2....41 C2
Villa Rd SW9....138 C2
Villas On The Heath
NW3....70 A5
Villas Rd SE18....123 A2
Villa St SE17....117 B1 262 D1
Villiers Ave
Kingston u T KT5....198 B5
Twickenham TW2....151 B3
Villiers Cl
Kingston u T KT5....198 B5
Leyton E10....75 C6
Villiers Ct
Oakleigh Pk N20....14 A4
SW11....267 B2
Villiers High Sch UB1..107 B5
Villiers Ho W5....109 D6
Villiers Rd
Isleworth TW7....130 C3
Kingston u T KT1....198 B6
Penge BR3....184 D1
Southall UB1....107 B5
Willesden NW2....68 A2
Villiers St WC2....250 B4
Vincam Cl TW2....151 C4
Vince Ct N1....235 D1
Vincent Ave KT5....215 A6
Vincent Cl
Avery Hill DA15....167 C3
Barnet EN5....1 D2
Bromley BR2....209 B5
Harmondsworth UB7....126 C6
Vincent Ct
Finsbury Pk N4....50 A1
Hendon NW4....46 D5
Marylebone W1....237 C2
Ruislip HA4....62 B3
South Lambeth SW9...270 D1
Vincent Dr
Hillingdon UB10....82 B6
Upper Halliford TW17...193 C6
Vincent Gdns NW2....67 D5
Vincent Ho KT3....199 D5
Vincent Mews 1 E3....97 C5
Vincent Rd
Acton Green W3....111 A3
Chingford E4....36 B4
Croydon CR0....205 C2
Dagenham RM9....81 A1
Hounslow West TW4....128 D2
Kingston u T KT1....198 C6
Osterley TW7....130 B4
Tottenham N15....51 A5
Wembley HA0....66 B1
Wood Green N22....32 C1
Woolwich SE18....122 D2
Vincent Row TW12....174 A5
Vincents Cl SE16....119 A4
Vincents Path UB5....63 A2
Vincent Sq
SW1....115 D2 259 C4
Wood Green N22....32 C1
Vincent St
Canning Town E16....98 D2
Westminster
SW1....115 D2 259 D4
Vincent Terr N1 . 94 D5 234 D4
Vince St EC1 ... 95 B4 235 D1
Vine Cl Surbiton KT5....198 B3
Sutton SM1....218 A5
West Drayton UB7....104 C2
Vine Cotts
3 Ealing W7....108 C5
Southall UB2....107 D2
Vine Ct Harrow HA3....44 A3
Spitalfields E1....96 A2
Vinegar St E1....118 B5
Vinegar Yd SE1....253 A2
Vine Gdns IG1....79 A3
Vine Gr UB10....60 C1
Vine Hill EC1....241 A5
Vine La Hillingdon UB10....82 B6
SE1....117 C5 253 B3
Uxbridge UB10....60 B1
Vine Lo N12....30 A4
Vine Pl Ealing W5....110 A5
Hounslow TW3....129 D1
Vine Rd Barnes SW13....133 D2
BR6....227 D2
East Molesey KT8....196 A5
Stratford E15....76 D1
Vineries Bank NW7....28 B5
Vineries Cl
Dagenham RM9....81 B2
Harmondsworth UB7....126 C6
Vineries The Enfield EN1 . 5 C2
Southgate N14....15 C5
Viners Cl KT12....194 C3
Vine St Bridge EC1....241 B5
Vines Ave N3....29 D2
Vine Sq W14....254 D1
Vines Sch The SW11...137 A1
Vine St W1....249 B5
Whitechapel
EC3....95 D1 243 C1
Vinewood Ct E17....54 B4
Vineyard Ave NW7....29 A3
Vineyard Cl
Forest Hill SE6....163 C3
Vineyard Cl *continued*
Kingston u T KT1....198 B6
Vineyard Gr N3....29 D2
Vineyard Hill Rd
SW19....179 C6
Vineyard Path SW14...133 B2
Vineyard Rd TW13....150 A1
Vineyard Row KT1,
KT8....175 C2
Vineyard Sch The
TW10....154 A5
Vineyards The TW13...150 A1
Vineyard Studios 3 E7..77 C1
Vineyard The TW10....154 A6
Vineyard Wlk EC1....241 A6
Viney Ct 9 SW4....159 D5
Vine Yd SE1....252 B2
Viney Rd SE13....141 D2
Vining St SW2, SW9....138 C1
Vinlake Ave UB10....60 C5
Vinson Ho N1....235 D3
Vinter Ct TW17....192 C4
Vintners Ct EC4....252 B6
Vintry Mews 3 E17....53 C5
Viola Ave
Feltham TW14....150 C5
SE2....124 B1
Stanwell TW19....148 A3
Viola Ct HA8....26 D3
Viola Sq W12....111 D6
Violet Ave Enfield EN2....5 B5
Hillingdon UB8....82 B2
Violet Cl Cheam SM3....201 A1
Hackbridge SM6....203 A1
Newham E16....98 C3
32 SE8....141 B6
Violet Ct 2 E15....76 C1
Violet Gdns CR0....220 D3
Violet Hill NW8 . . 92 A5 229 A3
Violet Hill Ho NW8....229 A3
Violet La CR0....220 D3
Violet Rd Bromley E3....97 D3
Walthamstow E17....53 C3
Woodford E18....37 B1
Violet St E2....96 B3
Violet Terr UB8....82 C2
Violette Szabo Ho 4
SE27....183 B6
VIP Trad Est SE7....121 C2
Virgil Pl W1....237 C3
Virgil St SE1....116 B3 260 D6
Virginia Cl KT3....199 A5
Virginia Ct
Ashford TW15....170 A6
7 Rotherhithe SE16....118 D4
Virginia Ho
3 Blackwall E14....120 A6
Teddington TW11....175 A5
Virginia Prim Sch E2....95 D4
Virginia Rd
South Norwood CR7....182 D2
19 Spitalfields E2....95 D4
Virginia St E1....118 A6
Virginia Wlk SW2....160 B5
Viridian Ct TW13....149 D1
Viscount Cl N11....31 B5
Viscount Ct
9 Kensington W11....91 C1
1 Littleton TW15....171 A3
Viscount Dr E6....100 B2
Viscount Gr 3 UB5....84 D4
Viscount Point 6
SW19....179 C3
Viscount Rd TW19....148 A3
Viscount St EC1....242 A4
Viscount Way TW6....127 C1
Vista Ave EN3....6 D3
Vista Bldgs 19 E3....97 B4
Vista Bldg The 14
SE18....122 C2
Vista Dr IG4....55 D4
Vista Ho 2 SW19....180 B2
Vista Hts SE23....163 A4
Vista The Chingford E4....20 B4
SE9....165 D4
Sidcup DA14....189 D5
Vista Way HA3....44 A3
Vitae Apartments 7
W6....112 A3
Vita Et Pax Sch N14....15 B6
Vittoria Ho N1....233 D5
Vittoria Prim Sch
N1....94 C5 234 A4
Viveash Cl UB3....105 D3
Vivian Ave Hendon NW4..46 B4
Wembley HA9....66 C2
Vivian Comma Cl 3
N4....72 D5
Vivian Ct Finchley N12....29 D5
Paddington NW6....91 D5
Vivian Gdns HA9....66 C3
Vivian Ho N4....51 B2
Vivian Mans 1 NW4....46 B4
Vivian Rd E3....97 A5
Vivian Sq SE15....140 B2
Vivian Way N2....48 B4
Vivien Cl KT9....214 A1
Vivienne Cl TW1....153 D5
Voce Rd SE18....145 B5
Voewood Cl KT3....199 D3
Vogans Mill SE1....253 D2
Vogler Ho 3 E1....118 C6
Vogue Ct 8 BR1....187 B2
Vollasky Ho 5 E1....96 A2
Volta Cl N9....18 C1
Voltaire
2 Camberwell SE5....139 D4
15 Richmond TW9....132 B4
Voltaire Ct 13 SW11....137 A3
Voltaire Rd SW4....137 D2
Voltaire Way UB3....105 C6
Volt Ave NW10....89 C4
Volta Way CR0....204 B1
Voluntary Pl E11....55 A3
Vora Ho HA0....65 D2
Vorley Rd N19....71 C6
Voss Ct SW16....182 A4
Voss St E2....96 A4
Voyager Bsns Est 10
SE16....118 A3
Voyagers Cl IG11....102 C1
Voysey Cl N3....47 A6
Vulcan Cl E6....100 C1
Vulcan Gate EN2....4 C3
Vulcan Rd SE4....141 B3
Vulcan Sq E14....119 C2
Vulcan Terr SE4....141 B3
Vulcan Way N7....72 B2
Vyne Ho SM5....218 D2
Vyner Ct E5....74 A6
Vyner Rd W3....111 B6
Vyners Sch UB10....60 B4
Vyner St E2....96 B6
Vyners Way UB10....60 C3
Vyne The DA7....147 D2
Vyvyan Ho SE18....144 C4

W

Wadbrook St KT1....175 D1
Wadcroft Ct SE4....141 B2
Waddesdon Lo HA3....43 A3
Wadding St
SE17....117 B2 262 C3
Waddington Cl EN1....5 C1
Waddington Rd E15....76 B2
Waddington St E15....76 B2
Waddington Way
SE19....183 B2
WADDON....220 C4
Waddon Cl CR0....220 C5
Waddon Court Rd
CR0....220 C5
Waddon Inf Sch CR9...220 C3
Waddon Marsh Sta
CR0....220 C6
Waddon Marsh Way
CR0....204 B1
Waddon New Rd CR0 . 220 D6
Waddon Park Ave
CR0....220 C5
Waddon Rd CR0....220 D5
Waddon Sta CR0....220 C4
Waddon Way CR0, CR2,
CR9....220 D2
Wade Ct
Muswell Hill N10....31 B3
Wembley HA0....65 D5
Wade Ho
16 Bermondsey SE1....118 A4
1 Enfield EN1....17 C6
Wade's Gr N21....16 C4
Wade's Hill N21....16 C4
Wade's La TW11....175 A5
Wadeson St E2....96 B5
Wade's Pl E14....119 D6
Wadeville Ave RM6....59 B2
Wadeville Cl DA17....125 C1
Wadham Ave E17....35 D3
Wadham Cl TW17....193 A2
Wadham Gdns
Greenford UB6....64 B2
Primrose Hill
NW3....92 C6 230 A6
Wadham Ho N18....33 D5
Wadham Rd
Highams Pk E17....35 D2
Putney SW15....135 A1
Wadhurst Cl SE20....184 B1
Wadhurst Ct E6....100 C5
Wadhurst Rd W4....111 B3
Wadley Rd E11....54 C2
Wadsworth Bsns Ctr
UB6....87 C5
Wadsworth Cl
Enfield EN3....18 D6
Wembley UB6....87 C5
Wadsworth Ct E10....54 A3
Wadsworth Rd UB6....87 C5
Wager St E3....97 B3
Waggoners Rdbt TW5..128 B4
Waggon Mews N14....15 C3
Waggon Rd EN4....2 B6
Waghorn Rd
Harrow HA3....43 D6
Newham E13....99 C6
Waghorn St SE15....140 A2
Wagner St SE15....140 C5
Wagon Rd EN4, EN5....1 D6
Wagstaff Gdns RM9....80 C1
Wagtail Cl NW9....27 C1
Wagtail Wlk BR3....208 A4
Waights Ct KT2....176 A2
Waikato Lo IG9....21 C3
Wainford Cl SW19....156 D3
Wainwright Gr TW7....130 B1
Wainwright Ho 3 E1....118 C5
Waite Davies Rd SE12 . 164 D4
Waitelands Ho KT3....199 B5
Waite St SE15....139 D6
Waithman St EC4....241 C1
Wakefield Ct 4 SE26....184 C4
Wakefield Gdns
Redbridge IG1....56 A3
South Norwood SE19...183 C3
Wakefield Ho
Dulwich SE22....162 B3
6 Peckham SE15....140 A4
Wakefield Mews WC1 . 233 B1
Wakefield Rd
Friern Barnet N11....31 D5
20 Richmond TW10....153 D6
South Tottenham N15....51 D4
Wakefield St
Edmonton N18....34 A5
Newham E6....100 A6
St Pancras WC1 . 94 A4 233 B1
Wakeford Cl SW4....159 C6
Wakehams Hill HA5....41 B6
Wakeham St 9 N1....73 B2
Wakehurst Rd SW11...158 D6
Wakeling Ct E7....77 C2
Wakeling Ho 8 SE27...160 D1
Wakeling La HA0....65 B5
Wakeling Rd W7....86 D2
Wakeling St 11 E14....97 A1
Wakelin Ho
Forest Hill SE23....163 A4
19 Islington N1....72 D1
Wakelin Rd E15....98 C5
Wakeman Ho HA8....26 A6
Wakeman Rd NW10....90 D4
Wakemans Hill Ave
NW9....45 B4
Wakering Rd IG11....79 A1
Wakerley Cl 6 E6....100 B1
Wakley St EC1....94 D4 234 C2
Walberswick St SW8 . 270 B3
Walbrook EC4....252 C6
10 Wanstead E18....55 A6
Walbrook Ct 32 N1....95 C5
Walbrook Ho N9....18 C2
Walbrook Wharf EC4 . . 252 C6
Walburgh St E1....96 B1
Walcorde Ave SE17....262 B3
Walcot Ct CR0....222 A6
Walcot Gdns SE11....261 A4
Walcot Ho 9 SE22....139 C2
Walcot Rd EN3....7 B3
Walcot Sq
SE11....116 C2 261 B4
Walcott St SW1....259 B4
Waldair Ct E16....122 D4
Waldeck Gr SE27....160 D1
Waldeck Rd
Brentford W4....132 C6
Ealing W13....87 B1
Mortlake SW14....133 A2
Tottenham N15....50 D6
Waldeck Terr SW14....133 A2
Waldegrave Ct
11 Barking IG11....101 B6
1 Teddington TW11....174 D5
Waldegrave Gdns
TW1....152 D1
Waldegrave Ho 5
SW15....156 C6
Waldegrave Pk TW1...174 D6
Waldegrave Rd BR1....210 B5
Dagenham RM8....80 C6
Ealing W5....110 B6
Hornsey N8....50 C6
Penge SE19....183 D3
Teddington TW11....174 D6
Waldegrave Sch TW2 . 152 B1
Waldegrove CR0....221 D5
Waldemar Ave
Ealing W13....109 C5
Fulham SW6....135 A3
Waldemar Avenue Mans
SW6....264 A1
Waldemar Rd SW19....179 C5
Walden Ave BR7....188 B6
Edmonton N13....33 A6
Walden Cl DA17....125 B1
Walden Ct SW8....269 D2
Walden Gdns CR7,
SW16....204 B5
Walden Ho Barnet EN4....2 C1
8 Clapham SW11....137 A3
SW1....258 B3
Walden Rd BR7....188 B4
Tottenham N17....33 B2
Waldenshaw Rd SE23 . 162 C3
Walden St E1....96 B1
Walden Way NW7....28 D4
Waldo Cl SW4....159 C6
Waldo Ind Est BR1....209 D6
Waldo Pl SW19....180 C3
Waldo Rd BR1....209 D6
College Pk NW10....90 B4
Waldorf Cl CR2....220 D1
Waldram Cres SE23....162 C3
Waldram Park Rd
SE23....162 D3
Waldram Pl 6 SE23....162 C3
Waldrist Way DA18....125 B4
Waldron Gdns BR2....208 B6
Waldron Ho 17 SW2....160 B6
Waldronhyrst CR0,
CR2....220 D4
Waldron Mews SW3 . . 266 D6
Waldron Rd
Harrow HA1, HA2....42 C1
Wandsworth SW18....158 A1
Waldrons The CR0....221 A4
Waldron's Yd HA2....64 B6
Waldstock Rd SE28....124 A6
Waleran Cl HA7....24 D4
Walerand Rd SE13....142 A3
Waleran Flats SE1....263 A4
Wales Ave SM5....218 C3
Wales Cl SE15....140 B6
Wales Farm Rd W3....89 B2
Waleton Acres SM6....219 C2
Waley St 1 E1....97 A2
Walfield Ave N20....13 D4
Walfield Ho N20....14 A4
Walford Ho 28 E1....96 B1

Walford Rd N16 . . . . .73 C4
Walfrey Gdns RM9 . . . . . . .81 A1
Walham Ct 15 NW3 . . . . . .70 D2
Walham Gr
SW6. . . . . .135 C5 **265** A4
WALHAM GREEN 135 D5
Walham Green Arc
SW6. . . . .**265** B4
Walham Rise 1 SW19.179 A4
Walham Yd SW6. . . . . . .**265** A4
Walkden Rd BR7. . . . . . .188 C5
Walker Cl Ealing W7 . . . .108 C5
East Bedfont TW14 . . . . . .149 D4
Frijern Barnet N11. . . . . . . .31 C6
Hampton TW12 . . . . .173 B4
Plumstead SE18 . . . . . . .123 A2
Walker Ho NW1 . . . .**232** C3
Walker Mews 9 SW2.160 C6
Walker Prim Sch N14 . .15 D2
Walkerscroft Mead
SE21 . . . . .161 A3
Walker's Ct W1. . . . . . .**249** C6
Walkers Lo 18 E14. . . . .120 A4
Walker's Pl SW15. . . . . .135 A1
Walkinshaw Ct 9 N1 . .73 A3
Walks The N2 . . . . .48 B6
Walk The
Ashford TW16 . . . . .171 D3
Palmers Green N13. . . . . .16 C1
Walkynscroft 1 SE15 .140 B3
Wallace Cl SE28 . . . . . . .124 D6
Upper Halliford TW17 . . . .193 B3
Uxbridge UB10 . . . . .82 A5
Wallace Collection ★
W1 . . . .**238** A2
Wallace Cres SM5 . . . . .218 D3
Wallace Ct 19 Enfield EN3 . .7 C6
NW1. . . . .**237** B3
Wallace Ho N7 . . . . .72 B2
Wallace Lo N4. . . . . .50 C1
Wallace Rd N1, N5 . . . . .73 A2
Wallasey Cres UB10 . . . .60 C5
Wallbrook Bsns Ctr
TW4 . . . . .128 B2
Wallbutton Rd SE4. . . . .141 A3
Wallcote Ave NW2 . . . . .46 D1
Wall Ct N4 . . . . .50 B1
Walled Garden Cl
BR3 . . . . .207 D5
Walled Gdn The ★
TW16 . . . . .194 B6
WALLEND 100 C6
Wall End Ct E6 . . . . .100 C6
Wall End Rd E6. . . . . .78 C1
Waller Dr HA6 . . . . .22 A2
Waller Rd SE14 . . . . .140 D3
Wallers Cl RM9 . . . . .103 B6
Wallett Ct 11 NW1 . . . . .71 C1
Wallflower St W12. . . . . .111 D6
Wallgrave Rd SW5. . . . .**255** C3
Wallingford Ave W10 . . .90 D1
WALLINGTON 219 A2
Wallington Cl HA4 . . . . .39 A3
Wallington Ct 10 SM6 . .219 B2
Wallington Cty Gram Sch
SM6 . . . . .219 B5
Wallington Green
SM6. . . . . .219 B4
Wallington Rd IG3. . . . . .57 D2
Wallington Sq 4 SM6.219 C2
Wallington Sta. 219 B2
Wallis Alley SE1. . . . . . .**252** B2
Wallis Ct SW11 . . . . .136 B2
Wallis Ho
5 New Cross Gate
SE14. . . . . .141 A4
Ruislip HA4 . . . . .39 A1
Ruislip HA4 . . . . .39 B1
Wallis Rd
Hackney Wick E9. . . . . . .75 C2
Southall UB1 . . . . .85 D1
Wallorton Gdns SW14.133 B1
Wallside EC2 . . . .**242** B3
Wall St N1 . . . . .73 B2
Wallwood Rd E11. . . . . . .54 B2
Wallwood St E14 . . . . . . .97 B2
Walmar Cl EN4 . . . . .2 B4
Walmer Cl BR6. . . . . .227 B4
Chingford E4 . . . . .19 D2
Walmer Gdns W13. . . . . .109 A4
Walmer Ho
8 North Kensington
W10. . . . . .90 D1
6 Penge SE20 . . . . .184 C3
Walmer Pl W1. . . . .**237** C4
Walmer Rd
North Kensington W10 . . .90 C1
W11. . . . . .113 A6 **244** A5
Walmer Terr SE18 . . . . . .123 B2
Walmgate Rd UB6 . . . . . .87 B6
Walmington Fold N12. . .29 C4
Walm La NW2 . . . . .68 C2
Walmsley Ho 1 SW16.181 C6
Walney Wlk 6 N1 . . . . . .73 A2
Walnut Ave UB7 . . . . . . .104 C3
Walnut Cl Hayes UB3 . . .105 C6
Ilford IG6 . . . . .57 A5
SE8 . . . . .141 B6
Wallington SM5. . . . . . . .218 D3
Walnut Ct 2 E17 . . . . . . .54 A5
Walnut Gdns E15 . . . . . . .76 C3
Walnut Gr EN1. . . . . .17 B6
Walnut Ho 11 E3. . . . . . .97 B6
Walnut Mews SM2. . . . . .218 A1
Walnut Rd E10. . . . . .75 D6
Walnut Tree Ave CR4.202 C6
Walnut Tree Cl
Barnes SW13 . . . . .133 D4
Chislehurst BR7 . . . . .189 A2

Walnut Tree Cotts
SW19. . . . . .179 A5
Walnut Tree Ho SW10.**265** D6
Walnut Tree Rd
Brentford TW8 . . . . .132 A6
Charlton SE7 . . . . .171 A1
Dagenham RM8. . . . . .81 A6
Greenwich SE10 . . . . . . .120 C1
Heston TW5. . . . . .129 B6
Walnut Tree Walk Prim
Sch SE11. . . .116 C2 **261** A4
Walnut Tree Wlk
SE11 . . . . . . .116 C2 **261** A4
Walnut Way
Buckhurst Hill IG9. . . . . . .21 D1
Ruislip HA4 . . . . .62 C2
Walpole Ave TW9. . . . . . .132 B3
Walpole Cl Pinner HA5 . . .23 C4
West Ealing W13. . . . . . .109 C4
Walpole Cres 10
TW11. . . . . .174 D5
Walpole Ct Ealing W5 . . .109 D5
7 Hammersmith W14 . . .112 D3
South Hampstead NW6. . . .70 A1
Twickenham TW2. . . . . . .152 C2
2 Wallington SM6 . . . . .219 B3
Walpole Gdns
Acton Green W4 . . . . . . .111 A1
Twickenham TW2. . . . . . .152 C1
Walpole Ho
Chislehurst BR7 . . . . .189 B2
East Molesey KT8 . . . . . .195 C4
Walpole Lo W13. . . . . . . .109 C5
Walpole Mews NW8. . . .**229** C5
Walpole Pl
9 Teddington TW11. . . .174 D5
3 Woolwich SE18 . . . . .122 D2
Walpole Rd Bromley BR2.209 D4
Mitcham SW19. . . . . .180 B4
South Croydon CR0. . . . .221 B6
Surbiton KT6. . . . . .198 A3
Teddington TW11. . . . . . .174 D5
Tottenham N17 . . . . .33 A1
Tottenham N17 . . . . .51 A6
Twickenham TW2. . . . . . .152 C2
Upton E6 . . . . .77 C1
Walthamstow E17. . . . . . .53 A5
Woodford E18. . . . . .36 D2
Walpole St
SW3. . . . . . . .114 D1 **257** D2
Walrond Ave HA9. . . . . . .66 A3
Walsham Cl SE28 . . . . . .124 D6
Upper Clapton N16. . . . . .52 A1
Walsham Ho
New Cross Gate
SE14. . . . . .140 D3
SE17 . . . .**262** C2
Walsham Rd
Feltham TW13 . . . . .150 B4
New Cross Gate SE14. . . .140 D3
Walsh Lodge HA4 . . . . . .40 B3
Walsingham Ho 1 . . . . .**229** D6
KT19. . . . . .215 D3
Walsingham Ho
Chingford E4. . . . . .20 B4
Twickenham TW2. . . . . . .152 B2
Walsingham Lo SW13 .134 A4
Walsingham Mans
SW6. . . . .**265** D4
Walsingham Pk BR7 . . . .189 B1
Walsingham Pl SW4,
SW11. . . . . .159 A5
Walsingham Rd BR5 . . . .190 B2
Ealing W13 . . . . .109 A5
Enfield EN1 . . . . .17 B6
Mitcham CR4. . . . . .202 D4
Shacklewell E5 . . . . .74 A5
Walsingham Wlk
DA17 . . . . .147 C6
Walter Besant Ho 20
E1 . . . . .96 D4
Walter Ct 3 W3 . . . . . . .89 A1
Walter Green Ho
SE15 . . . . .140 C4
Walter Ho SW10 . . . .**266** C4
Walter Hurford Par 5
E12 . . . . .78 C4
Walter Northcott Ho 2
NW6 . . . . .69 C3
Walter Rodney Cl E12. . .78 B2
Walter Savill Twr E17 . . .53 C3
Walters Cl Hayes UB3. . .105 C4
SE17 . . . .**262** B3
Walters Ho
3 Camberwell SE5. . . . .139 C3
Islington N1 . . . .**234** D2
10 Kennington SE17 . . . .138 D6
Walter Sickert Hall N1 .**235** A3
Walter's Rd SE25 . . . . . .205 C5
Walter St Globe Town E2. .96 D4
2 Kingston u T KT2 . . . .176 A2
Walters Way SE23 . . . . . .162 D5
Walter Taylor Ct SE4. . . .141 B5
Walter Terr E1 . . . . .96 D1
Walterton Rd W9 . . . . . . .91 C3
Walter Wlk HA8 . . . . .27 A4
Waltham Ave
Hayes UB3. . . . . .105 B3
Preston NW9 . . . . .44 C3
Waltham Ct
Chingford E17. . . . . .36 A2
Whetstone N20 . . . . .14 B1
Waltham Dr HA8. . . . . . . .44 C4
Waltham Forest Coll
E17 . . . . .35 D1
Waltham Gdns EN3 . . . . .6 C6

Waltham Green Ct
SW6. . . . .**265** C3
Waltham Ho NW8. . . . . .**229** A6
10 Stockwell SW9 . . . . .138 B3
Waltham Park Way
E17 . . . . .35 C3
Waltham Pk E17 . . . . .35 C2
Waltham Rd
Carshalton SM5. . . . . . . .202 C1
Southall UB2 . . . . .107 A3
WALTHAMSTOW 53 D6
Walthamstow Acad
E17. . . . . .35 B2
Walthamstow Ave E4 . . .35 C3
Walthamstow Ave (North
Circular Rd) E4. . . . . . . .35 A2
Walthamstow Bsns Ctr
E17. . . . . .36 A1
Walthamstow Central Sta
E17. . . . . .53 C4
Walthamstow Mkt E17 . . .53 C5
Walthamstow Queens
Road Sta E17. . . . . .53 C4
Walthamstow Sch for Girls
E17. . . . . .53 D5
Waltham Way E4 . . . . . . .19 C2
Waltheof Ave N17 . . . . . .33 B2
Waltheof Gdns N17 . . . . .33 B2
Walton Ave
Cheam SM3. . . . . .217 C5
Harrow HA2 . . . . .63 B4
New Malden KT3. . . . . . .199 D5
Wembley HA9 . . . . .66 D5
Walton Bridge Rd KT12,
TW17. . . . . .193 C2
Walton Cl
Dollis Hill NW2 . . . . .68 B6
Harrow HA1 . . . . .42 B5
Lea Bridge E5 . . . . .74 D5
SW8. . . . . .138 A5 **270** B4
Walton Croft HA1. . . . . .64 C4
Walton Ct EN5. . . . . .14 A6
Walton Dr Harrow HA1 . . .42 B5
Willesden NW10. . . . . . . .67 B2
Walton Gdns Acton W3 . .88 D2
Feltham TW13 . . . . .171 D6
Wembley HA9 . . . . .66 A6
Walton Gn CR0 . . . . .224 A1
Walton Ho E2 . . . .**243** D6
Ealing W5 . . . . .109 D2
1 Edmonton N9. . . . . . . .34 A6
4 Kingston u T KT2 . . . .176 A3
Upper Holloway N7. . . . . .72 B5
10 Walthamstow E17 . . . .53 D6
Wandsworth SW18. . . . . .157 C5
Walton La
Oatlands Pk KT13,
TW17. . . . . .193 B1
Shepperton TW17 . . . . . .193 B2
Walton Oak Prim Sch
KT12. . . . . .194 C1
WALTON-ON-THAMES
. . . . .194 C2
Walton Pl SW3 . . . .**257** C6
Walton Rd
East Molesey KT8,
KT12. . . . . .195 C5
Harrow HA1 . . . . .42 B5
Little Ilford E12. . . . . . . .78 C4
Newham E13. . . . . .99 C5
Sidcup DA14 . . . . .168 C1
Tottenham N15 . . . . .51 B5
Walton-on-T KT12&KT8. .194 D4
Walton St Enfield EN2 . . . .5 B4
SW3. . . . . .114 C3 **257** B5
Walton Way Acton W3 . . .88 D2
Mitcham CR4. . . . . .203 C5
Walt Whitman Cl 6
SE24 . . . . .138 C1
WALWORTH 117 B1
Walworth Pl
SE17 . . . . .117 A1 **262** B1
Walworth Rd
SE17 . . . . .117 A1 **262** B1
Walworth Sch
SE17. . . . . . . .117 C1 **263** B1
Walwyn Ave BR1. . . . . . .209 D6
Wanborough Dr SW15 .156 B3
Wanderer Dr IG11. . . . . .102 C4
Wandle Bank
Mitcham SW19. . . . . .180 B3
Wallington SM6. . . . . . . .220 A5
Wandle Court Gdns
CR0. . . . . .220 A5
Wandle Ct
4 Bedford Pk W12. . . . .111 C4
Wallington CR0 . . . . . . .220 A5
West Ewell KT19. . . . . . .215 A4
Wandle Ho
6 Catford BR1. . . . . . . .186 B5
NW8 . . . .**237** A4
Wandsworth SW18. . . . . .157 D4
Wandle Lo CR0 . . . . .220 A5
Wandle Lodge SM6 . . . . .219 B6
Wandle Pk Sta CR0 . . . .220 C6
Wandle Rd
Croydon CR0 . . . . .221 A5
Hackbridge SM6 . . . . . . .219 B6
Morden SM4. . . . . .202 B4
Upper Tooting SW17. . . . .158 C2
Wallington CR0 . . . . .220 A5
Wandle Side
Hackbridge SM6 . . . . . . .219 B5
Wallington CR0 . . . . .220 B5
Wandle Tech Pk CR4 . . .202 D2
Wandle Trad Est CR4 . . .202 D2
Wandle Valley Sch
SM5 . . . . .202 C2
Wandle Way
Mitcham CR4. . . . . .202 D4

Wandle Way continued
Wandsworth SW18. . . . . .157 D3
Wandon Rd
SW6. . . . . .135 D5 **265** D3
WANDSWORTH 157 C5
Wandsworth Bridge Rd
SW6. . . . . .135 D4 **265** C1
Wandsworth Common Sta
SW12 . . . . .158 D3
Wandsworth Common
West Side SW18 . . . . . . .158 A3
Wandsworth Gyratory
SW18. . . . . .157 D6
Wandsworth High St
SW18. . . . . .157 D6
Wandsworth Mus ★
SW18 . . . . .157 C6
Wandsworth Plain
SW18. . . . . .157 D6
Wandsworth Rd
SW8. . . . . .138 A5 **270** A3
Wandsworth Road Sta
SW4 . . . . .137 C3
Wandsworth Town Sta
SW18. . . . . .135 D1
Wangey Rd RM6 . . . . . . .58 D2
Wangford Ho 13 SW9 . .138 D1
Wanless Rd SE24 . . . . . .139 A2
Wanley Rd SE5 . . . . .139 B1
Wanlip Rd E13. . . . . .99 B3
Wansbeck Ct EN2. . . . . . . .4 D2
Wansbeck Rd E3, E9. . . . .75 B1
Wansdown Pl
SW6. . . . . .135 D5 **265** C4
Wansey St
SE17 . . . . .117 A2 **262** B3
Wansford Rd IG8 . . . . . . .37 C2
WANSTEAD 55 C3
Wanstead Church Sch
E11. . . . . .55 A4
Wanstead Cl BR1 . . . . . .187 C1
Wanstead High Sch
E11. . . . . .55 B5
Wanstead Hospl E11. . . .55 B5
Wanstead Hts E11. . . . . .55 A4
Wanstead La IG1. . . . . . .56 A3
Wanstead Park Ave
E12 . . . . .77 D6
Wanstead Park Rd IG1. .56 A1
Wanstead Park Sta E7 . .77 B4
Wanstead Pl E11 . . . . . . .55 A4
Wanstead Rd BR1. . . . . .187 C1
Wanstead Sta E11 . . . . . .55 B3
Wantage Rd SE12. . . . . .164 D6
Wantz Rd RM10. . . . . . . .81 D3
WAPPING 118 B5
Wapping Dock St 19
E1 . . . . .118 B5
Wapping High St E1 . . . .118 B5
Wapping La E1 . . . . .118 B5
Wapping Sta E1 . . . . . . .118 C5
Wapping Wall E1 . . . . . .118 C5
Warbank La KT2. . . . . . . .177 D3
Warbeck Rd W12 . . . . . . .112 B4
Warberry Rd N22 . . . . . . .32 B1
Warboys App KT2. . . . . .176 D4
Warboys Cres E4 . . . . . . .36 A5
Warboys Rd KT2. . . . . . .176 D4
Warburg Ho E2. . . . . .96 A4
Warburton Cl
6 Kingsland N1 . . . . . . .73 C2
Stanmore HA3. . . . . .24 B4
Warburton Ct
Peckham SE15. . . . . .140 A2
Ruislip HA4 . . . . .62 A6
Warburton Ho 5 E8 . . . .96 B6
Warburton Rd
8 Hackney E8 . . . . .96 B6
Twickenham TW2. . . . . . .151 D3
Warburton St 6 E8. . . . . .96 B6
Warburton Terr E17 . . . . .35 D1
Wardalls Ho 12 SE8 . . . .141 B6
Ward Cl CR2. . . . . .221 C3
Wardell Cl NW7 . . . . . . .27 C3
Wardell Ct N1. . . . . .48 B6
Wardell Ho 7 SE10 . . . . .142 A6
Warden Ave HA2. . . . . . .41 B1
Warden Rd NW5. . . . . . . .71 A2
Wardens Field Cl 2
BR6 . . . . .227 D2
Wardens Gr SE1 . . . .**252** A3
Wardle St E9 . . . . .74 D3
Wardley Lo E11. . . . . . . .54 D3
Wardley St SW18 . . . . . .157 D4
Wardlow 8 NW5 . . . . . . .71 B4
Wardo Ave
SW6. . . . . .135 A4 **264** A2
Wardour Mews W1 . . . . .**239** B1
Wardour St W1. .93 D1 **239** D1
Ward Point SE11. . . . . . .**261** A3
Ward Rd
Camden Town N19. . . . . .71 C5
Mill Meads E15. . . . . . . .98 B6
Wardrew Ct 9 EN5 . . . . .14 A6
Wardrobe Pl EC4 . . . . . .**241** D1
Wardrobe Terr EC4 . . . . .**251** D6
Wardrobe The 3
TW9. . . . . .153 D6
Wards Cotts TW19 . . . . .148 A4
Wards Rd IG2 . . . . .57 B2
Wards Wharf App
E16 . . . . .121 D2
Ware Ct Cheam SM1 . . . .217 B4
Edgware HA8 . . . . .26 A6
Wareham Ct 3 N1 . . . . . .73 D1
Wareham Ct 2 N1. . . . . .73 C1
Wareham Ho SW8. . . . . .**270** C4
Warehouse W E16 . . . . . .121 B6
Waremead Rd IG2. . . . . .56 D4
Ware Point Dr SE28. . . . .123 B4

Warfield Rd
East Bedfont TW14 . . . . .149 C1
Hampton TW12 . . . . .173 D2
Kensal Green NW10 . . . . .90 D4
Warfield Yd 6 NW10. . . . .90 D4
Wargrave Ave N15 . . . . . .51 D3
Wargrave Ho 46 E2 . . . . .95 D4
Wargrave Rd HA2. . . . . . .64 C3
Warham Rd
Croydon CR2 . . . . .221 A3
Harringay N4. . . . . .50 D4
Harrow HA3 . . . . .24 D1
Warham St SE5. . . . . . . .138 C5
Waring Cl BR6. . . . . .227 D2
Waring Dr BR6 . . . . .227 D2
Waring Ho 22 E2. . . . . . .96 A4
Waring Rd DA14 . . . . . . .190 C4
Waring St SE27 . . . . .183 A6
Warkworth Gdns TW7.131 A5
Warkworth Rd N17 . . . . .33 B3
Warland Rd SE18 . . . . . .145 C5
Warley Ave
Dagenham RM8. . . . . .59 B2
Hayes UB4. . . . . .84 A1
Warley Cl E10 . . . . .53 B1
Warley Ho N1 . . . . .73 B2
Warley Rd Hayes UB4 . . .84 A2
Lower Edmonton N9 . . . . .18 C2
Woodford IG8 . . . . .37 B3
Warley St E2. . . . . .96 D4
Warlingham Rd CR7 . . .204 D5
Warlock Rd W9. . . . . .91 C3
Warlow Cl 6 EN3. . . . . . . .7 C6
Warlters Cl N7 . . . . .72 A4
Warlters Rd N7. . . . . .72 A4
Warltersville Mans
N19 . . . . .50 A2
Warltersville Rd N4, N8,
N19 . . . . .50 A2
War Meml Homes W4.133 B5
Warming Cl E5 . . . . .74 D5
Warmington Rd SE24 . . .161 A5
Warmington St 8 E13 . . .99 A3
Warminster Gdns
SE25 . . . . .184 A1
Warminster Rd SE25 . . . .184 A1
Warminster Sq SE25 . . .184 A1
Warminster Way CR4 . . .181 B1
Warmsworth NW1 . . . . . .**232** A6
Warmwell Ave NW9. . . . .27 C2
Warndon St SE16 . . . . . .118 C2
Warneford Rd HA3 . . . . . .44 A6
Warneford St E9. . . . . . . .96 B6
Warne Pl 4 DA15. . . . . . .168 B5
Warner Ave SM3. . . . . . .217 A6
Warner Cl
Hampton TW12 . . . . . . .173 B5
Harlington UB3. . . . . . . .127 B5
Hendon NW9. . . . . .46 A2
Stratford E15 . . . . .76 C3
Warner Ct SM3 . . . . .217 A6
Warner Ho
1 Beckenham BR3. . . . .185 D4
Harrow HA1 . . . . .42 B2
4 Homerton E9 . . . . . . .74 D2
Lewisham SE13. . . . . . . .141 D3
NW8 . . . .**229** A2
Warner Pl E2. . . . . .96 A4
Warner Rd
Bromley BR1. . . . . .186 D3
Camberwell SE5 . . . . . . .139 A4
Hornsey N8 . . . . .49 D5
Walthamstow E17. . . . . . .53 A5
Warners Cl IG8. . . . . .37 A5
Warner St EC1. . . . .94 C3 **241** A5
Warner Yd EC1. . . . .**241** A5
Warnford Ho SW15 . . . . .155 C5
Warnford Ind Est UB3. .105 C4
Warnford Rd BR6. . . . . . .227 D3
Warnham WC1 . . . .**233** C1
Warnham Court Rd
SM5. . . . . .218 D1
Warnham Ho 6 SW2. . . . .160 B4
Warnham Rd N12. . . . . . .30 C5
Warple Mews W3. . . . . . .111 C4
Warple Way W3, W12. . . .111 C4
Warren Ave
Bromley BR1. . . . . .186 C3
Leyton E11. . . . . .76 B5
Mortlake SW14, TW10. . . .132 D1
Orpington BR6. . . . . .227 D3
South Croydon CR2. . . . .222 D1
Warren Cl DA6 . . . . .169 C6
Esher KT10 . . . . .212 A4
Hayes UB4. . . . . .84 C2
Ponders End N9. . . . . . . .18 D4
Wembley HA9 . . . . .65 D6
West Norwood SE21. . . . .161 A4
Warren Comp Sch The
RM6 . . . . .59 B4
Warren Cres N9 . . . . .17 D4
Warren Ct
17 Beckenham BR3. . . . .185 C3
5 Croydon CR0 . . . . . . .205 C1
6 Ealing W5. . . . . .87 C2
Greenwich SE7 . . . . .143 C6
N1 . . . .**234** A4
Tottenham Hale N17 . . . .52 A6
Warren Cutting KT2. . . .177 B3
Warrender Prim Sch
HA4 . . . . .39 D2
Warrender Rd N19. . . . . .71 C4
Warrender Way HA4 . . . .40 A2
Warren Dr
Greenford UB6 . . . . .86 A3
Ruislip HA4 . . . . .40 D2
Warren Dr N KT5, KT6 . .198 D1
Warren Dr S KT5. . . . . . .199 A1
Warren Dr The E11 . . . . .55 C2

Warren Farm Cotts
RM6. . . . . .59 B5
Warren Fields HA7. . . . . .25 C6
Warren Gdns E15 . . . . . . .76 B3
Warren Hill IG10. . . . . . . .21 C6
Warren Ho 21 E3 . . . . . . .97 C4
Warren Jun Sch RM6 . . .59 B4
Warren La Stanmore HA7. .9 A4
Woolwich SE18 . . . . .122 D3
Warren Mews W1 . . . . . .**239** A5
Warren Park Rd SM1. . .218 C2
Warren Pk KT2 . . . . .177 A4
Warren Pond Rd E4. . . . .20 D4
Warren Rd
Ashford TW15 . . . . .171 C4
Bexleyheath DA6. . . . . . .169 C6
Bushey WD23 . . . . .8 B3
Chingford E4 . . . . .20 A2
Croydon CR0 . . . . .205 D1
Hayes BR2. . . . . .225 A6
Ickenham UB10. . . . . . . .60 B4
Ilford IG6 . . . . .57 B4
Isleworth TW2. . . . . .152 B5
Kingston u T KT2 . . . . . .177 A4
Leyton E10. . . . . .76 A5
Mitcham SW19 . . . . .180 C4
Sidcup DA14 . . . . .168 C1
Wanstead E11. . . . . .55 C2
Willesden NW2 . . . . .67 D6
Warren Rise KT3. . . . . . .177 B2
Warren Road Prim Sch
BR6. . . . . .227 D4
Warrens Shawe La
HA8 . . . . .10 D2
Warren St W1 . . .93 C3 **239** A5
Warren Street Sta
NW1 . . . . .93 C3 **239** B6
Warren Terr RM6 . . . . . . .58 D5
Warren The Hayes UB4. . .84 A1
Heston TW5. . . . . .129 B5
Manor Pk E12 . . . . .78 A4
Worcester Pk KT19. . . . . .215 B5
Warren Way
Edgware HA8 . . . . .26 D1
Finchley NW7 . . . . .29 A4
Warren Wlk 1 SE7 . . . . .143 C6
Warren Wood Cl BR2 . . .225 A6
Warriner Dr N9 . . . . .18 A1
Warriner Gdns
SW11. . . . . . . .137 A4 **268** A1
Warrington Cres
W9. . . . . .92 A3 **236** A6
Warrington Ct
4 Croydon CR0 . . . . . . .220 D5
2 Merton SW19. . . . . . .179 C3
Warrington Gdns W9 . . .**236** A5
Warrington Rd
Croydon CR0 . . . . .220 D5
Dagenham RM8. . . . . .81 A6
Harrow HA1 . . . . .42 C4
22 Richmond TW10. . . . .153 D6
Warrington Sq RM8. . . . .80 D6
Warrior Cl SE28 . . . . . . .123 C5
Warrior Sq E12. . . . . .78 C4
Warsaw Cl HA4 . . . . .62 B2
Warspite Ho 3 E14 . . . . .119 D2
Warspite Rd SE18. . . . . .122 A3
Warton Rd E15 . . . . .98 A6
Warwall E6. . . . . .100 D1
Warwick W14 . . .113 B2 **254** D3
Warwick Ave
Edgware HA8 . . . . .11 A1
Harrow HA2 . . . . .63 B4
Paddington W9 . .92 A3 **236** A6
Warwick Avenue Sta
W9 . . . . .92 A3 **236** A5
Warwick Bldg SW8 . . . .**268** C5
Warwick Chambers
W8. . . . .**255** A6
Warwick Cl Bushey WD23 . .8 C4
DA5. . . . . .169 A4
Hampton TW12 . . . . . . .174 A3
New Barnet EN4 . . . . . . .14 B6
Warwick Cres
Hayes UB4. . . . . .83 D3
Little Venice W2 . .92 A3 **236** A4
Warwick Ct
1 Beckenham BR2. . . . .186 C1
Ealing W7 . . . . .108 D6
5 East Finchley N2 . . . .48 A6
Friern Barnet N11. . . . . .31 D4
Harrow HA1 . . . . .42 C4
Merton SW19 . . . . .179 B2
13 New Barnet EN5 . . . .13 C6
Northolt UB5. . . . . .63 C3
Surbiton KT6. . . . . .214 A6
3 Upper Clapton E5. . . .74 B6
WC1. . . . .**240** D3
Warwick Dene W5. . . . . .110 A5
Warwick Dr SW15. . . . . .134 B2
Warwick Gdns
Harringay N4. . . . . .51 A4
Ilford IG1. . . . . .56 D1
Thames Ditton KT7 . . . . .196 D4
Thornton Heath CR7 . . . .204 C5
W14. . . . . .113 B2 **254** D4
Warwick Gr
Surbiton KT5. . . . . .198 B2
Upper Clapton E5 . . . . . .52 B1
Warwick Ho
9 Acton W3 . . . . .88 C1
6 Brixton SW9 . . . . . . .138 C3
6 Kingston u T KT2 . . . .176 A2
6 Putney SW15 . . . . . . .156 C4
Stoke Newington N4 . . . . .51 A1
5 Wimbledon SW19 . . . .179 A3

Warwick House St
SW1 249 D4
Warwick La EC4 . 94 D1 241 D1
Warwick Lo
Brondesbury NW2 69 A3
Cheam SM1 217 B4
Twickenham TW2 151 D1
Warwick Mans SW5 255 A4
Warwick Par HA7 25 B1
Warwick Pas EC4 241 D2
Warwick Pl Ealing W5 109 D4
Little Venice W9 .92 A2 236 A4
Warwick Pl N SW1 259 A3
Warwick Rd
Ashford TW15 170 A5
Barnet EN5 1 D1
Bexley DA16 146 C2
Chingford E4 35 C5
Ealing W5 110 A5
Edmonton N18 33 D6
Enfield EN3 7 B6
Friern Barnet N11 31 D4
Hounslow TW4 128 B2
Kingston u T KT3 199 A6
Penge SE20 206 B6
Plashet E12 78 A3
Sidcup DA14 190 B5
Southall UB2 107 B3
Stratford E15 76 D2
Sutton SM1 218 A3
Teddington KT1 175 C2
Thames Ditton KT7 196 D4
Thornton Heath CR7 204 C6
Twickenham TW2 152 C3
Walthamstow E17 35 B1
Wanstead E11 55 B4
West Kensington W14,
SW5 113 B2 254 D4
Yiewsley UB7 104 A5
Warwick Row
SW1 115 B3 258 D6
Warwick Sch for Boys
E17 54 A5
Warwickshire Path
SE8 141 B5
Warwick Sq
Holborn EC4 241 D2
Pimlico SW1 115 C1 259 A2
Warwick Sq Mews
SW1 259 A3
Warwick St
W1 115 C6 249 B6
Warwick Terr
Leytonstone E17 54 B4
SE18 145 B6
Warwick Way
SW1 115 B2 258 D4
Warwick Yd EC1 242 B5
Wasdale NW1 231 D1
Washbourne Ct N9 18 A2
Washbrook Ho SW2 160 C5
Washington Ave E12 78 B4
Washington Bldg 1
SE13 141 D4
Washington Cl 45 E3 97 D4
Washington Ct SW17 180 D4
Washington Ho SW1 247 C1
Walthamstow E17 35 B1
Washington Rd
Barnes SW13 134 A5
Kingston u T KT1 176 C1
North Cheam KT4 200 B1
Upton E6 77 C1
2 Woodford E18 36 D1
Wastdale Rd SE23 162 D3
Watchfield Ct 7 W4 111 A1
Watcombe Cotts TW9 132 C6
Watcombe Rd SE25 206 B4
Waterbank Rd SE6 186 A6
Waterbeach Rd RM9 80 C2
Water Brook La NW4 46 C4
Watercress Pl N1 73 C1
Waterdale Rd SE2 146 A6
Waterden Cres E9 75 C3
Waterden Rd E15 75 C2
Waterer Ho 7 SE6 186 A6
Waterer Rise SM6 219 D2
Waterfall Cl N14 15 C1
Waterfall Cotts SW19 180 B4
Waterfall Rd
Mitcham SW19 180 B4
New Southgate N11, N14 15 C1
Waterfall Terr SW17 180 C4
Waterfield Cl
Belvedere DA17 125 C3
Woolwich SE28 124 B5
Waterfield Gdns SE25 205 C4
Waterford Ct 16 W13 109 A5
Waterford Rd
SW6 135 D5 265 C3
Waterford Way NW10 68 A3
Watergardens The
Kingston u T KT2 177 A4
Woodford IG8 37 A5
Water Gardens The
W2 92 C1 237 B2
Watergate EC4 251 C6
Watergate Ho 5
SE18 122 C2
Watergate Sch SE6 185 D5
Watergate St SE8 141 C6
Watergate Wlk WC2 250 B4
Water Gdns HA7 25 B4
Waterglade Ctr The
W5 109 D6
Waterhall Ave E4 36 C6
Waterhall Cl E17 34 D2
Waterhead NW1 232 A2
Waterhedge Mews
EN1 17 D6
Waterhouse Cl
Hammersmith W6 112 D1
Hampstead NW3 70 B3
Newham E16 99 D2
Waterhouse Ct 7
TW11 174 D5
Wateridge Cl E14 119 C3
Wateringbury Cl BR5 190 B1
Water La
16 Camden Town NW1 71 B1
Edmonton N9 18 B4
Ilford IG3 79 D5
Richmond TW10, TW9 153 D6
SE14 140 C5
Sidcup DA14 169 B2
Stratford E15 76 C2
Teddington KT1 175 D2
Twickenham TW1 153 A3
Water Lane Ho 29
TW10 153 D6
Water Lily Cl UB2 108 A4
Waterloo Bridge SE1,
WC2 116 B6 250 D5
Waterloo Cl
East Bedfont TW14 149 D3
Hackney E9 74 C3
Waterloo Ct 4 HA0 66 A2
Waterloo East Sta
SE1 116 C5 251 B3
Waterloo Gdns
26 Islington N1 72 D1
South Hackney E2 96 C5
Waterloo Int Sta
SE1 116 B4 250 D2
Waterloo Pier SE1 250 C2
Waterloo Pl Kew TW9 132 C6
9 Richmond TW9 132 A1
SW1 115 D5 249 C4
Waterloo Rd
Dollis Hill NW2 68 A6
Forest Gate E7 76 D3
SE1 116 C4 251 B2
Sutton SM1 218 B3
Upton E6 77 C1
Walthamstow E10 53 C2
Waterloo Sta
SE1 116 C4 251 A2
Waterloo Terr N1 72 D1
Waterlow Ct NW11 47 D2
Waterlow Rd N19 49 C1
Waterman Bldg 2
E14 119 C4
Watermans Ct
12 Brentford TW8 131 D6
2 Brentford TW8 132 A6
Watermans Mews 1
W5 110 A6
Waterman St SW15 134 D2
Waterman Way E1 118 B5
Watermark Ct RM6 58 B3
Watermead TW14 149 C3
Watermead Ho E9 75 B3
Watermead La CR4 202 D2
Watermeadow La
SW6 136 A3
Watermead Rd SE6 186 A6
Watermead Way N17 34 B1
Watermen's Sq 1
SE20 184 C3
Water Mews SE15 140 C1
Watermill Bsns Ctr EN3 7 B3
Watermill Cl TW10 153 C1
Watermill Ct SE13 141 D2
Watermill La N18 33 C5
Watermill Way SW19 180 A2
Water Mill Way TW13 151 C2
Watermint Quay N16 52 A2
Water Rd HA0 88 B6
Watersedge KT19 215 A4
Water's Edge SW6 134 C4
Watersfield Way HA8 26 A3
Waters Gdns RM10 81 C3
Watershipdown Ho 4
E11 54 D2
Waterside
11 Beckenham BR3 185 C2
N1 235 A3
Walthamstow E17 52 C3
Waterside Ave BR3 207 D4
Waterside Cl
Barking IG11 80 A4
30 Bermondsey SE16 118 A4
Northolt UB5 85 B4
Old Ford E3 97 B6
Surbiton KT6 214 A6
Woolwich SE28 123 D5
Waterside Ct
3 Hackbridge SM6 219 A5
Lewisham SE13 142 B1
Waterside Dr KT12 194 B4
Waterside Pl NW1 231 B6
Waterside Point SW11 267 B4
Waterside Rd UB2 107 C3
Waterside Sch SE18 123 B1
Waterside Trad Ctr
W7 108 C3
Waterside Way SW17 180 A5
Watersmeet Way
SE28 102 D1
Waterson St E2 95 D4
Waters Pl SW15 134 C3
Watersplash Cl KT1 198 A6
Watersplash La
Hayes UB3 106 A2
Southall TW5 106 B1
Watersplash Rd TW17 192 C5
Waters Rd Catford SE6 164 C1
Waters Rd *continued*
Kingston u T KT1 176 D1
Waters Sq KT1 198 D6
Water St WC2 251 A6
Water View Cl DA6 168 D6
Waterview Ho 13 E14 97 A2
Waterville Lo 6 N12 30 A5
Waterways Bsns Ctr EN3 7 C5
Waterworks Cnr E17 36 C1
Waterworks La E5 74 D6
Waterworks Rd SW2 160 B5
Waterworks Yd 4
CR0 221 A5
Watery La DA14 190 B4
Hayes UB3 105 B1
Merton SW19, SW20 179 B1
Northolt UB5 84 C5
Wates Way CR4 202 D3
Wateville Rd N17 33 A2
Watford Cl SW11 267 B2
Watford Rd Elstree WD6 9 C5
Harrow HA1 43 A1
Newham E16 99 A2
Northwood HA6 22 A4
Sudbury HA0, HA1 65 B4
Watford Way NW4 46 A5
Watford Way (Barnet By-
Pass) NW9 27 D3
Watkin Mews 18 EN3 7 C6
Watkin Rd HA9 66 D5
Watkins Ho
11 Cubitt Town E14 120 A4
Harrow HA1 42 D4
Watkinson Rd N7 72 B2
Watling Ave HA8 27 B2
Watling Ct EC4 242 B1
1 Elstree WD6 9 D5
Watling Gate NW9 45 C5
Watling Gdns NW2 69 A2
Watling Ho 10 SE18 144 C6
Watlings Cl CR0 207 A3
Watling St
Bexleyheath DA7 147 D1
4 Camberwell SE15 139 C6
City of London
EC4 95 A1 242 B1
Watlington Gr SE26 185 A5
Watney Cotts SW14 133 A2
Watney Mkt* E1 96 B1
Watney Rd SW14 133 A2
Watneys Rd CR4 203 D4
Watney St E1 96 B1
Watson Ave
Cheam SM3 217 A6
Wallend E6 78 C1
Watson Cl
Mitcham SW19 180 C3
Stoke Newington N16 73 B3
Watson Ho 3 SW2 160 A4
Watsons Lo 4 RM10 81 D2
Watsons Mews W1 237 B3
Watsons Rd N22 32 B2
Watson's St SE8 141 C5
Watson St E13 99 B5
Wattisfield Rd E5 74 C5
Watts Cl N15 51 C4
Wattsdown Cl E13 99 A6
Watts Gr E3 97 D2
Watts Ho 6 W10 91 A2
Watt's La
Chislehurst BR7 189 A2
Teddington TW11 175 A5
Watts Rd KT7 197 A2
Watts St SE15 139 D4
Wapping E1 118 B5
Wat Tyler Ho N8 50 A6
Wat Tyler Rd SE10 142 B4
Wauthier Cl N13 32 D5
Wavel Ct
7 Streatham SW16 160 A1
7 Wapping E1 118 C5
Wavell Dr DA15 167 C5
Wavell Ho N6 49 A3
Wavel Mews
Hampstead NW6 69 D1
Hornsey N8 49 D5
Wavel Pl SE26 183 D6
Wavendon Ave W4 111 B1
Waveney Ave SE15 140 B1
Waveney Cl E1 118 A5
Waveney Ho SE15 140 B1
Waverley Ave
Chingford Hatch E4 35 B6
Sutton SM1 217 D6
Tolworth KT5 199 A3
Twickenham TW2, TW4 151 C3
Walthamstow E17 54 B6
Wembley HA9 66 B3
Waverley Cl BR2 209 D4
East Molesey KT8 195 C4
Hayes UB3 105 B2
Woodford E18 37 C1
Waverley Cres SE18 123 B1
Waverley Ct
5 Brondesbury NW6 69 A1
Enfield EN2 5 A2
North Finchley N12 30 B6
W1 238 B4
Waverley Gdns
Barking IG11 101 C5
Ealing NW10 88 B5
Ilford IG6 57 B6
Newham E6 100 A2
Northwood HA6 22 A2
Waverley Gr N3 47 A6
Waverley Ind Pk HA1 42 B6
Waverley Pl
Finsbury Pk N4 50 D1
St John's Wood
NW8 92 B5 229 C4
Waverley Rd
Croydon SE25 206 B6
Enfield EN2 4 D2
Finsbury Pk N8 50 A2
Harrow HA2 41 A1
Plumstead SE18 123 B1
Southall UB1 107 C6
Stoneleigh KT17, KT4 216 B3
Tottenham N17 34 B3
Walthamstow E17 54 A6
Woodford E18 37 C2
Waverley Sch EN3 6 C1
Waverley Way SM5 218 C2
Waverly Ct NW3 70 D2
Waverton Ho 2 E3 97 B6
Waverton Rd SW18 158 A4
Waverton St
W1 115 B5 248 C4
Wavertree Ct 9 SW2 160 A3
Wavertree Rd
Streatham SW2 160 B3
Woodford E18 37 A1
Waxham NW5 70 D3
Waxlow Cres UB1 85 C1
Waxlow Ho UB4 84 C2
Waxlow Rd NW10 89 B5
Waxlow Way UB5 85 B3
Waxwell Cl HA5 22 D1
Waxwell La HA5 22 D1
Wayatt Point 1 SE28 123 A3
Wayborne Gr HA4 39 A3
Waye Ave TW5 128 A4
Wayfarer Rd UB5 85 A4
Wayfield Link SE9 167 B5
Wayford St SW11 136 C3
Wayland Ave E8 74 A3
Wayland Ho 12 SW9 138 C3
Waylands UB3 83 B2
Waylands Ct IG1 79 B4
Waylands Mead BR3 185 D2
Waylett Ho SE11 261 A1
Waylett Pl Wembley HA0 65 D4
West Norwood SE27 160 D1
Wayman Ct E8 74 B2
Wayne Cl BR6 227 D5
Waynflete Ave CR0 220 D5
Waynflete Sq
18 North Kensington
W10 90 D1
16 Shepherd's Bush
W10 112 D6
Waynflete St SW18 158 A2
Wayside
Chislehurst BR7 189 B2
Golders Green NW11 47 A1
Mortlake SW14 155 A6
New Addington CR0 223 D2
Wayside Ave WD23 8 B5
Wayside Cl N14 15 C5
Wayside Commercial Est
IG11 102 A5
Wayside Ct
Isleworth TW7 130 C3
Twickenham TW1 153 C5
Wembley HA9 66 C5
Wayside Gdns RM10 81 C3
Wayside Gr BR7, SE9 188 B6
Wayside Mews IG2 56 C4
Weald Cl
16 Bermondsey SE16 118 B1
BR2 226 A6
Weald Fst & Mid Schs
HA3 24 D3
Weald La HA3 24 B2
Weald Rd UB10 82 C5
Weald Rise HA3 24 D2
Weald Sq E5 74 B6
WEALDSTONE 42 D6
Wealdstone Rd SM3 217 B6
Weald The BR7 188 B4
Weald Way Hayes UB4 83 C4
Romford RM7 59 D3
Wealdwood Gdns HA5 23 D4
Weale Rd E4 20 B1
Weall Ct HA5 41 A5
Weardale Ct EN5 12 C6
Weardale Gdns EN2 5 B4
Weardale Ho N4 51 A2
Weardale Rd SE13 142 B1
Wearmouth Ho 1 E3 97 B2
Wear Pl 13 E2 96 B4
Wearside Rd SE13 141 D1
Weatherbury 6 W2 91 C1
Weatherbury Ho 3
N19 71 D5
Weatherill Ct SE25 206 B3
Weatherley Cl E3 97 B2
Weathersfield Ct SE9 166 B5
Weaver Cl
Newham E16 122 D6
South Croydon CR0 221 D4
Weaver Ct 2 E2 96 B3
Weaver Ho
12 Bethnal Green E1 96 A3
1 Northolt UB5 85 B3
Weavers Cl TW7 130 C1
Weavers Ho 4 E11 55 A3
Weaver's La
SE1 117 C5 253 B3
Weaver St E1 96 A3
Weavers Way
6 Camden Town NW1 71 D1
NW1 232 C6
Weaver Wlk SE27 182 D6
Webb Cl NW10 90 C3
Webb Ct 6 SE28 124 B6
South Acton W3 110 D4
Webber Cl WD6 9 D5
Webber Ho 6 IG11 78 D1
Webber Row
SE1 116 D4 251 C1
Webber St SE1 116 D4 251 C1
Webb Est E5 52 A2
Webb Gdns 1 E13 99 A3
Webb Ho
2 Dagenham RM10 81 C5
Feltham TW13 151 A1
SW8 269 D3
Webb Pl NW10 89 D4
Webb Rd SE3 142 D6
Webbscroft Rd RM10 81 D4
Webbs Rd UB4 84 B4
Webb's Rd SW11 158 D6
Webb St SE1 117 C3 263 A5
Webheath 6 NW6 69 B1
Webley Ct 22 EN3 7 C6
Webster Gdns W5 109 D5
Webster Ho 16 N16 73 C3
Webster Rd
Bermondsey SE16 118 A3
Leyton E11 76 A5
Weddell Ho 23 E1 96 D3
Wedderburn Rd
Barking IG11 101 C6
Hampstead NW3 70 B3
Wedgewood Ct
1 Beckenham BR2 208 D5
DA5 169 B4
Wedgewood Ho SW1 259 A1
Thames Ditton KT7 196 D1
Wedgewood Mews
W1 239 D1
Wedgewood Wlk NW3 69 D3
Wedgwood Ho
17 Globe Town E2 96 D4
SE11 261 A5
Wedgwood Way SE19 183 A3
Wedlake St W10 91 A3
Wedmore Gdns N19 71 D6
Wedmore Rd UB6 86 B4
Wedmore St N19 71 D5
Weech Rd NW6 69 C4
Weedington Rd NW5 71 A3
Weedon Ho W12 90 A1
Weekley Sq SW11 136 B2
Weeks Ho TW10 175 C6
Weigall Rd SE12, SE3 143 A1
Weighhouse St W1 238 B1
Weighton Rd
Harrow HA3 24 B2
Penge SE20 184 B1
Weihurst Ct SM1 218 C3
Weihurst Gdns SM1 218 B3
Weimar St SW15 135 A2
Weirdale Ave N20 14 D2
Weir Hall Ave N18 33 B4
Weir Hall Gdns N18 33 B5
Weir Hall Rd N18 33 B4
Weir Ho 5 SW12 159 C4
Weir Rd Sidcup DA5 169 D4
Streatham SW12 159 C4
Walton-on-T KT12 194 A3
Wimbledon SW18,
SW19 157 D1
Weir's Pas NW1 232 D2
Weiss Rd SW15 134 D2
Welbeck Ave
Grove Pk BR1 187 B6
Hayes UB4 84 B3
Sidcup DA15 168 A3
Welbeck Cl
New Malden KT3 199 D4
North Finchley N12 30 B5
Stoneleigh KT17 216 A1
Welbeck Ct Hayes UB4 84 B3
W14 254 C4
Welbeck Mans 10 NW6 69 C3
Welbeck Rd
Carshalton SM1 218 B6
Carshalton SM5 202 C1
East Barnet EN4 14 C5
Harrow HA2 41 D1
Newham E6 99 D4
Welbeck St W1 93 B1 238 C2
Welbeck Villas N21 17 A3
Welbeck Way W1 238 C2
Welbeck Wlk SM5 202 B1
Welbourne Prim Sch
N17 52 A6
Welbury Ct E8 73 C1
Welby Ho N19 49 D2
Welby St SE5 138 D4
Welch Pl HA5 22 C2
Welcome Ct E17 53 C2
Weldon Cl HA4 62 B2
Weldon Ct
Southgate N21 16 B6
St Johns SE8 141 C3
7 Sutton SM1 218 B3
Thornton Heath CR7 204 D4
Weldon Dr KT8 195 B5
Weld Pl N11 31 B5
Welfare Rd E15 76 C1
Welford Cl E5 74 D5
Welford Ct
12 Camden Town NW1 71 B1
7 Clapham SW8 137 C3
Welford Ho 4 UB5 85 B3
Welford Pl SW19 179 A6
Welham Rd SW16,
SW17 181 B4
Welhouse Rd SM5 202 C1
Wellacre Rd HA3 43 B3
Wellan Cl DA15, DA16 168 B6
Welland Ct SE6 163 B2
Welland Gdns UB6 86 D5
Welland Ho SE15 140 C1
Welland Mews E1 118 A5
Wellands Cl BR1 188 B1
Welland St SE10 142 A6
Well App EN5 12 C6
Wellbrook Rd BR6 226 C4
Wellby Cl N9 18 A3
Wellby Ct 1 E13 99 C5
Well Cl Ruislip HA4 63 A5
Streatham SW16 182 B6
Wellclose Sq E1 118 A6
Wellclose St 20 E1 118 A6
Well Cottage Cl E11 55 C2
Well Ct EC4 242 B1
Wellday Ho 2 E9 75 A2
Welldon Cres HA1 42 C3
Welldon Ct Harrow HA1 42 C4
1 West Dulwich SE21 161 B2
Welldon Park Fst Sch
HA2 64 A4
Welldon Park Mid Sch
HA2 64 A4
Weller Ho 23 SE16 118 A4
Weller Mews 6 BR2 209 B5
Weller St SE1 252 A2
Welles Ct 15 E14 119 C6
Wellesley Ave W6 112 B3
Wellesley Cl 8 SE7 121 C1
Wellesley Court Rd 1
CR0 221 B6
Wellesley Cres TW2 152 C1
Wellesley Ct
Cheam SM3 201 A1
St John's Wood
W9 92 A4 229 A2
Twickenham TW2 152 C1
Wellesley Gr CR0 221 B6
Wellesley Ho NW1 232 C1
12 Wimbledon SW19 179 A3
Wellesley Park Mews
EN2 4 D3
Wellesley Pl
Camden Town NW5 71 A3
NW1 232 C1
Wellesley Rd
Croydon CR0 205 A1
Gospel Oak NW5 71 A3
Gunnersbury W4 110 D1
Harrow HA1 42 C4
Ilford IG1 57 A1
Sutton SM2 218 A2
Twickenham TW2 152 C1
Walthamstow E17 53 C3
Wanstead E11 55 A4
Wood Green N22 32 C1
Wellesley Road Sta
CR0 221 B6
Wellesley St E1 96 D2
Wellesley Terr
N1 95 A4 235 B2
Wellfield Ave N10 49 B6
Wellfield Rd SW16 182 B6
Wellfit St 6 SE24 138 D2
Wellgarth UB6 65 B2
Wellgarth Rd NW11 47 D1
Well Gr N20 14 B3
Wellgrove Sch N20 14 B3
Well Hall Par SE9 144 B1
Well Hall Pleasaunce*
SE9 144 A1
Well Hall Rd SE9 144 B1
Well Ho 11 N9 18 A1
Wellhouse Rd BR3 207 C5
Wellhurst Cl BR6 227 D1
WELLING 146 B2
Wellingfield Ct 1
DA16 146 A2
Welling High St DA16 146 B2
Welling Sch DA16 146 B4
Wellings Ho UB3 106 B5
Welling Sta DA16 146 A3
Wellington
1 Grahame Pk NW9 27 D3
Hornsey N8 50 A5
Wellington Arch*
SW1 248 B2
Wellington Ave
Chingford E4 19 D2
DA15 168 A5
Edmonton N9 18 B1
Hounslow TW3, TW4 151 C6
North Cheam KT4 216 C5
Pinner HA5 23 B2
South Tottenham N15 52 A3
Wellington Bldgs
15 Bow E3 97 C4
SW1 258 B1
Wellington Cl
Kensington W11 91 C1
New Cross Gate SE14 140 D4
Walton-on-T KT12 193 D1
Wellington Cres KT3 199 A6
Wellington Ct
Ashford TW15 170 A6
Knightsbridge SW1 247 C1
Stanwell TW19 148 A4
St John's Wood NW8 229 D3
Strand WC2 250 A6
5 Surbiton KT6 198 A3
Teddington TW12 174 B5
4 Upper Tooting
SW17 180 C4
Wandsworth SW18 158 C6
Wellington Gdns
Greenwich SE7 121 C1
Teddington TW12, TW2 174 B6
Wellington Gr SE10 142 B5
Wellington Ho
4 Ealing W5 88 A4
18 Maitland Pk NW3 70 D2
Northolt UB5 63 C1
6 Ruislip HA4 40 C1
Stanmore HA7 9 A1

Wellington Hospl The
NW8 . . . . . 92 B5 229 D3
Wellington Mans
Shacklewell N16 . . . . 73 D4
1 Walthamstow E10 . . . 53 C1
Wellington Mews
East Dulwich SE22 . . . 140 A1
3 Islington N7 . . . . 72 B2
SE7 . . . . . 143 C6
Streatham SW16 . . . . 159 D1
Wellington Mus (Apsley Ho)* SW1 . . . 115 A4 248 B2
Wellington Par DA15 . . . 168 A6
Wellington Park Est
NW2 . . . . . 68 A6
Wellington Pas 7 E11 . . 55 A4
Wellington Pl
East Finchley N2 . . . . 48 C4
St John's Wood
NW8 . . . . . 92 B4 229 D2
Wellington Prim Sch
Bow E3 . . . . . 97 C4
Chingford E4 . . . . . 19 D2
Hounslow TW3 . . . . 129 B3
Wellington Rd
Ashford TW15 . . . . 170 A5
Bexley DA5 . . . . . 168 D6
Brentford W5 . . . . 109 C3
Bromley BR2 . . . . . 209 C5
Enfield EN1 . . . . . 17 C6
Erith DA17 . . . . . 125 B1
Harrow HA3 . . . . . 42 C6
Hatton TW14 . . . . . 149 C6
Kensal Green NW10 . . . 90 D4
Leyton E7 . . . . . 76 D4
Newham E6 . . . . . 100 B5
Pinner HA5 . . . . . 23 B2
St John's Wood
NW8 . . . . . 92 B5 229 D3
Teddington TW12, TW2 . . 174 B6
Thornton Heath CR0 . . . 204 D2
Walthamstow E10 . . . . 53 A1
Walthamstow E17 . . . . 53 A5
Wanstead E11 . . . . . 55 A4
Wimbledon SW19 . . . . 157 C2
Wellington Rd N TW4 . . 129 B2
Wellington Rd S TW4 . . 151 B6
Wellington Row E2 . . . . 96 A4
Wellington Sq
SW3 . . . . . 114 D1 257 C2
Wellington St
1 Barking IG11 . . . . 101 A6
WC2 . . . . . 116 B6 250 C6
Woolwich SE18 . . . . 122 C2
Wellington Terr
Harrow HA1 . . . . . 42 B1
2 Wapping E1 . . . . 118 B5
Wellington Way E3 . . . . 97 C4
Welling Way DA16 . . . . 145 B2
Well La SW14 . . . . . 155 A6
Wellmead IG3 . . . . . 58 A2
Wellmeadow Rd
Brentford W7 . . . . 109 A2
Catford SE13, SE6 . . . 164 C3
Wellow Wlk SM5 . . . . 202 B1
Well Rd Barnet EN5 . . . . 12 C6
Vale of Health NW3 . . . 70 B5
Wells Cl 2 Northolt UB5 . . 84 C4
South Croydon CR2 . . . 221 C3
Wells Ct
21 Hampstead NW3 . . . 70 A4
4 Mitcham CR4 . . . . 180 C2
1 Paddington NW6 . . . 91 C5
Stoke Newington N1 . . . 73 C3
Wells Dr NW9 . . . . . 45 B1
Wells Gdns
Dagenham RM10 . . . . 81 D3
Redbridge IG1 . . . . . 56 A2
Wells Ho
4 Barking IG11 . . . . 80 A1
Ealing W5 . . . . . 109 D6
Finsbury EC1 . . . . . 234 C2
12 Kensal Town W10 . . . 91 A3
New Cross Gate SE4 . . . 141 A3
Plaistow BR1 . . . . . 187 B5
9 Rotherhithe SE16 . . . 118 C3
Wells Ho The 2 NW3 . . . 70 B4
Wells House Rd NW10 . . 89 C2
Wellside Gdns SW14 . . . 155 A6
Wells Mews W1 . . . . . 239 B2
Wellsmoor Gdns BR1 . . 210 C6
Wells Park Ct SE26 . . . . 184 B6
Wells Park Rd SE26 . . . . 184 B6
Wells Pl SW18 . . . . . 158 A4
Wells Prim Sch IG8 . . . . 37 A6
Wellspring Cres HA9 . . . . 66 D5
Wells Rd BR1 . . . . . 188 B1
Hammersmith W12 . . . . 112 C4
Wells Rise NW8 . . 92 D6 230 C5
Wells Sq WC1 . . . . . 233 D1
Wells St W1 . . . . 93 C1 239 B2
Well St Hackney E9 . . . . 74 C1
Stratford E15 . . . . . 76 C2
Wellstead Ave N9 . . . . 18 D4
Wellstead Rd E6 . . . . 100 C5
Wells Terr N4 . . . . . 72 C6
Wells The N14 . . . . . 15 D4
Wells Way
Brompton
SW7 . . . . . 114 B3 256 C6
Camberwell SE5 . . . . 139 C6
Well Wlk NW3 . . . . . 70 B5
Wellwood Ct SW15 . . . . 134 C1
Wellwood Rd IG3 . . . . 58 A2
Welmar Works SW4 . . . 137 D1
Welsby Ct W5 . . . . . 87 C2
Welsford St SE1 . . . . 118 A2
Welsh Cl E13 . . . . . 99 A4
WELSH HARP 45 C1
Welsh Harp Field Centre
NW9 . . . . . 45 B1
Welsh Ho 14 E1 . . . . 118 B5
Welshpool Ho 22 E8 . . . 96 A6
Welshpool St 1 E8 . . . . 96 B6
Welshside NW9 . . . . . 45 C3
Welshside Wlk NW9 . . . 45 C3
Welstead Ho 29 E1 . . . . 96 B1
Welstead Way W4 . . . . 111 D2
Weltje Rd W6 . . . . . 112 A1
Welton Ct SE5 . . . . . 139 C4
Welton Ho E1 . . . . . 96 D2
Welton Rd SE18 . . . . 145 C5
Welwyn Ave TW14 . . . . 149 D5
Welwyn St E2 . . . . . 96 C4
Welwyn Way UB4 . . . . 83 C3
WEMBLEY 65 D2
Wembley HA0 . . . . . 65 D2
Wembley Arena HA9 . . . 66 C4
Wembley Central Sta
HA9 . . . . . 66 A3
Wembley Commercial Ctr
HA9 . . . . . 65 D6
Wembley Conference Ctr
HA9 . . . . . 66 C4
Wembley Exhibition Halls
HA9 . . . . . 66 C4
Wembley High Tech Coll
HA0 . . . . . 65 C5
Wembley Hill Rd HA9 . . . 66 B4
Wembley Hospl HA0 . . . 65 D2
Wembley Mkt
1 Wembley HA0 . . . . 66 A3
1 Wembley Pk HA9 . . . 66 C4
WEMBLEY PARK 66 C5
Wembley Park Bsns Ctr
HA9 . . . . . 66 D5
Wembley Park Dr HA9 . . 66 B5
Wembley Park Sta HA9 . . 66 C5
Wembley Prim Sch
HA9 . . . . . 66 A5
Wembley Rd TW12 . . . . 173 C2
Wembley Stadium HA9 . . 66 C3
Wembley Stadium Ind Est
Wembley HA9 . . . . . 66 C5
Wembley HA9 . . . . . 66 D4
Wembley Stadium Sta
HA9 . . . . . 66 B3
Wembley Way HA9 . . . . 66 D2
Wemborough Rd HA7 . . . 25 C3
Wembury Mews N6 . . . . 49 C2
Wembury Rd N6 . . . . . 49 B2
Wemyss Rd SE3 . . . . . 142 D3
Wendela Ct HA1 . . . . . 64 C6
Wendell Park Prim Sch
W12 . . . . . 111 D4
Wendell Rd W12 . . . . . 111 D4
Wenderholme CR2 . . . . 221 B3
Wendle Ct SW8 . . . . . 270 A5
Wendling NW5 . . . . . 70 D3
Wendling Rd SM1 . . . . 218 B6
Wendon Ct 13 SM6 . . . . 219 C2
Wendon St E3 . . . . . 97 B6
Wendover
SE17 . . . . . 117 C1 263 A1
Wendover Cl UB4 . . . . 85 A3
Wendover Ct Acton W3 . . 88 D3
Becontree W3 . . . . . 89 A3
Bromley BR2 . . . . . 209 B6
4 Child's Hill NW2 . . . 69 C5
W1 . . . . . 238 A3
Wendover Dr KT3 . . . . 199 D3
Wendover Ho
Bowes Pk N22 . . . . . 32 B5
W1 . . . . . 238 A3
Wendover Lo NW9 . . . . 45 D3
Wendover Rd
Blackheath SE9 . . . . 143 D2
Bromley BR1, BR2 . . . . 209 B6
Dagenham NW10 . . . . 89 D5
Wendover Way
Bexley DA16 . . . . . 146 A1
Bushey WD23 . . . . . 8 A5
Wendy Cl EN1 . . . . . 17 D5
Wendy Ho 3 N12 . . . . 30 B5
Wendy Way HA0 . . . . . 88 A6
Wengham Ho W12 . . . . 112 A6
Wenham Ho SW8 . . . . . 269 A3
Wenlake Ho EC1 . . . . . 242 A6
Wenlock Ct N1 . . . . . 235 D3
Wenlock Gdns 13 NW4 . . 46 A5
Wenlock Rd
Burnt Oak HA8 . . . . . 27 A4
Shoreditch N1 . . . 95 A5 235 B3
Wenlock St N1 . . 95 B5 235 C3
Wennington Rd E3 . . . . 96 D5
Wensdale Ho E5 . . . . . 74 A6
Wensley Ave IG8 . . . . . 37 A3
Wensley Cl
6 Barnet N11 . . . . . 31 A4
SE9 . . . . . 166 B5
Wensleydale Gdns
TW12 . . . . . 173 D3
Wensleydale Ho 8 N4 . . 51 A2
Wensleydale Rd
TW12 . . . . . 173 D3
Wensley Rd N18 . . . . . 34 B4
Wentland Cl SE6 . . . . 164 B2
Wentland Rd SE6 . . . . 164 B2
Wentway Ct W13 . . . . . 87 A3
Wentwood Ho 1 E5 . . . 74 B6
Wentworth Ave
Borehamwood WD6 . . . 10 B6
Finchley N3 . . . . . 29 C3
Wentworth Cl
Ashford TW15 . . . . . 170 D6
Finchley N3 . . . . . 29 D3
Hayes BR2 . . . . . 225 A6
Long Ditton KT6 . . . . 213 D6
Wentworth Cl *continued*
Morden SM4 . . . . . 201 C2
Orpington BR6 . . . . 227 C3
Thamesmead SE28 . . . 102 D1
Wentworth Cres
Hayes UB3 . . . . . 105 B3
SE15 . . . . . 140 A5
Wentworth Ct
Barnet EN5 . . . . . 1 A2
7 Chingford E4 . . . . 36 B5
20 Kingston u T KT6 . . . 198 A4
Southall UB2 . . . . . 106 C2
2 Surbiton KT6 . . . . 214 A6
Twickenham TW2 . . . . 152 C1
W6 . . . . . 264 A5
Wandsworth SW18 . . . 157 D5
Wentworth Dr HA5 . . . . 40 A4
Wentworth Dwellings
E1 . . . . . 243 C2
Wentworth Gdns N13 . . . 16 D1
Wentworth Hall NW7 . . . 28 C5
Wentworth Hill HA9 . . . 44 B1
Wentworth Ho
Enfield EN1 . . . . . 17 C5
4 Greenwich SE3 . . . 143 A5
Wentworth Lo N3 . . . . 29 D3
Wentworth Mews E3 . . . 97 B4
Wentworth Pk N3 . . . . 29 D3
Wentworth Pl HA7 . . . . 25 B4
Wentworth Rd
Manor Pk E12 . . . . . 77 D4
Southall UB2 . . . . . 106 D2
Temple Fortune NW11 . . 47 B3
Thornton Heath CR0 . . . 204 C2
Wentworth St
E1 . . . . . 95 D2 243 D3
Wentworth Tutorial Coll
NW11 . . . . . 46 D3
Wentworth Way HA5 . . . 41 A5
Wenvoe Ave DA7 . . . . 147 D3
Wepham Cl UB4 . . . . . 84 D2
Wernbrook St SE18 . . . 145 A6
Werndee Rd SE25 . . . . 206 A5
Werneth Hall Rd IG5 . . . 56 C6
Werrington St
NW1 . . . . . 93 C5 232 B3
Werter Rd SW15 . . . . . 135 A1
Wesleyan Pl NW5 . . . . 71 B4
Wesley Ave
Becontree NW10 . . . . 89 B4
Hounslow TW3 . . . . . 129 B3
Newham E16 . . . . . 121 B5
Wesley Cl
Finsbury Pk N7 . . . . 72 B6
Harrow HA2 . . . . . 64 A6
SE17 . . . . . 261 D3
Wesley Ct W1 . . . . . 238 B3
Wesley Ho SE24 . . . . . 161 B5
Wesley Rd
Becontree NW10 . . . . 89 A6
Finchley N10 . . . . . 30 C2
Hayes UB3 . . . . . 84 A1
Leytonstone E10 . . . . 54 A2
Wesley Sq W11 . . . . . 91 A1
Wesley St W1 . . . . . 238 B3
Wessex Ave SW19 . . . . 201 C6
Wessex Cl
Hinchley Wood KT10,
KT7 . . . . . 212 D6
Ilford IG3 . . . . . 57 C3
Kingston u T KT1, KT2 . . 176 D2
Wessex Ct
Putney SW15 . . . . . 156 D6
5 Stanwell TW19 . . . . 148 A5
Wembley HA9 . . . . . 66 B6
Wessex Dr HA5 . . . . . 23 A3
Wessex Gardens Prim Sch
NW11 . . . . . 47 A1
Wessex Gdns NW11 . . . 47 A1
Wessex Ho SE1 . . . . . 263 D1
4 Tufnell Pk N19 . . . . 71 D5
Wessex La UB6 . . . . . 86 B5
Wessex St E2 . . . . . 96 C4
Wessex Way NW11 . . . . 47 A1
Wesson Ho 3 CR0 . . . . 206 A1
West 12 Sh Ctr W12 . . . 112 D4
Westacott UB4 . . . . . 83 C2
Westacott Cl N19 . . . . 49 D1
WEST ACTON 88 C1
West Acton Prim Sch
W3 . . . . . 88 D1
West Acton Sta W3 . . . . 88 C1
West App BR5 . . . . . 211 A4
West Arbour St E1 . . . . 96 D1
West Ave
East Finchley N2 . . . . 47 D6
Finchley N3 . . . . . 29 C4
Hayes UB3 . . . . . 105 D6
Hendon NW4 . . . . . 46 D4
Pinner HA5 . . . . . 41 B2
Southall UB1 . . . . . 107 B6
Wallington SM6 . . . . 220 A3
Walthamstow E17 . . . . 53 D4
West Avenue Rd E17 . . . 53 D5
West Bank
Barking IG11 . . . . . 100 D6
Enfield EN2 . . . . . 5 A3
Stamford Hill N16 . . . . 51 C2
Westbank Rd TW12 . . . . 174 A4
WEST BARNES 200 C4
West Barnes La KT3,
SW20 . . . . . 200 B5
WEST BEDFONT 148 B4
Westbeech Rd N22 . . . . 50 C6
Westbere Ct HA7 . . . . 25 D5
Westbere Dr HA7 . . . . 25 D5
Westbere Rd NW2 . . . . 69 A3
West Block 18 E1 . . . . 118 C6
Westbourne Ave
Cheam SM3 . . . . . 217 A6
Westbourne Ave *continued*
Dagenham W3 . . . . . 89 B1
Westbourne Cl UB4 . . . 84 C3
Westbourne Cres W2 . . 246 C6
Westbourne Ct
Cheam SM3 . . . . . 217 A6
W2 . . . . . 236 A2
Westbourne Dr SE23 . . . 162 D2
Westbourne Gdns W2 . . . 91 D1
Westbourne Gr
Notting Hill W2, W11 . . . 91 C1
W11 . . . . . 113 B6 244 D6
WESTBOURNE GREEN
. . . . . 91 D3
Westbourne Gr Mews 7
W11 . . . . . 91 C1
Westbourne Gr Terr
W2 . . . . . 91 D1
Westbourne Ho
Heston TW5 . . . . . 129 C6
SW1 . . . . . 258 C2
8 Twickenham TW1 . . . 153 B4
Westbourne Par 4
UB10 . . . . . 82 D3
Westbourne Park Rd
Notting Hill W2 . . . . 91 C1
Notting Hill W11 . . . . 91 B1
Westbourne Park Sta
W11 . . . . . 91 B2
Westbourne Park Villas
W2 . . . . . 91 D2
Westbourne Pl N9 . . . . 18 B1
Westbourne Prim Sch
SM1 . . . . . 217 C5
Westbourne Rd
Barnsbury N7 . . . . . 72 B2
Croydon CR0 . . . . . 205 D3
DA7 . . . . . 147 A5
Feltham TW13 . . . . . 149 D1
Hillingdon UB8 . . . . 82 D3
Penge SE26 . . . . . 184 D4
Westbourne St
W2 . . . . . 114 B6 246 C6
Westbourne Terr
W2 . . . . . 92 A1 236 B2
Westbourne Terrace Mews
W2 . . . . . 236 A2
Westbourne Terrace Rd
W2 . . . . . 92 A2 236 A3
Westbridge Cl W12 . . . . 112 A5
Westbridge Prim Sch
SW11 . . . . . 267 A2
Westbridge Rd
SW11 . . . . . 136 C4 267 A2
WEST BROMPTON 135 D6
West Brompton Sta
SW5 . . . . . 113 C1 255 B1
Westbrook Ave TW12 . . . 173 B3
Westbrook Cl EN4 . . . . 2 B2
Westbrook Cres EN4 . . . 2 B2
Westbrook Ct SE3 . . . . 143 B4
Westbrooke Cres
DA16 . . . . . 146 C2
Westbrooke Rd
Bexley DA16 . . . . . 146 C2
DA15 . . . . . 167 B2
Westbrooke Sch
DA16 . . . . . 146 D2
Westbrook Ho
5 Bethnal Green E2 . . . 96 C4
5 Clapham Pk SW4 . . . 159 C6
Westbrook Rd
Heston TW5 . . . . . 129 B5
SE3 . . . . . 143 B4
South Norwood CR7 . . . 183 B1
Westbrook Sq EN4 . . . . 2 B2
West Brow BR7 . . . . . 188 D5
Westbury Ave
Claygate KT10 . . . . . 212 D2
Southall UB1 . . . . . 85 C3
Tottenham N22 . . . . . 32 D1
Wembley HA0 . . . . . 66 A1
Westbury Cl Ruislip HA4 . . 40 A2
Shepperton TW17 . . . . 192 D3
Westbury Ct
3 Barking IG11 . . . . 101 B6
Beckenham BR3 . . . . 185 D2
1 Buckhurst Hill IG9 . . . 21 C2
Clapham SW4 . . . . . 159 B5
11 New Barnet EN5 . . . 14 A6
Tottenham N22 . . . . . 33 A1
Westbury Gr N12 . . . . 29 C4
Westbury Ho
1 Walthamstow E17 . . . 53 C5
6 Willesden NW10 . . . 67 C1
Westbury House Sch
KT3 . . . . . 199 B4
Westbury La IG9 . . . . . 21 C2
Westbury Lodge Cl
HA5 . . . . . 40 D6
Westbury Pl 2 TW8 . . . 131 D6
Westbury Rd
Barking IG11 . . . . . 101 B6
Beckenham BR3 . . . . 207 A6
Bowes Pk N11 . . . . . 32 A4
Bromley BR1 . . . . . 187 D2
Buckhurst Hill IG9 . . . 21 C3
Ealing W5 . . . . . 88 A1
Feltham TW13 . . . . . 150 D3
Finchley N12 . . . . . 29 D5
Ilford IG1 . . . . . 78 C6
New Malden KT3 . . . . 199 B4
Penge SE20 . . . . . 184 D2
Thornton Heath CR0 . . . 205 B3
Upton E7 . . . . . 77 B2
Walthamstow E17 . . . . 53 C5
Wembley HA0 . . . . . 66 A1
Westbury Terr E7 . . . . 77 B2
Westbush Ct 1 W12 . . . 112 B4
West Carriage Dr
W2 . . . . . 114 C5 247 A4
West Central St WC1 . . . 240 A2
West Chantry HA3 . . . . 23 D2
Westchester Ct NW4 . . . 46 D6
Westchester Dr NW4 . . . 46 D6
Westchester Ho W2 . . . 237 C1
West Cl Ashford TW15 . . . 170 A6
Barnet EN5 . . . . . 12 B6
Cockfosters EN4 . . . . 3 A1
Edmonton N9 . . . . . 17 D1
Greenford UB6 . . . . . 86 A5
Hampton TW12 . . . . . 173 A4
Wembley HA9 . . . . . 44 B1
Westcliff Ho 13 N1 . . . . 73 B2
Westcombe Ave CR0 . . . 204 B2
Westcombe Ct 1 SE3 . . . 142 D5
Westcombe Dr EN5 . . . . 13 C6
Westcombe Hill SE3,
SE10 . . . . . 143 A6
Westcombe Lodge Dr
UB4 . . . . . 83 B2
Westcombe Park Rd
SE3 . . . . . 142 D5
Westcombe Park Sta
SE3 . . . . . 121 A1
West Common Rd
BR2 . . . . . 225 B5
Westcoombe Ave
SW20 . . . . . 177 D2
Westcote Rd SW16 . . . . 181 C5
Westcote Rise HA4 . . . . 39 A2
Westcott Cl BR1 . . . . . 210 A4
2 South Tottenham N15 . 51 D3
Westcott Cres W7 . . . . 86 C2
Westcott Ho 1 E14 . . . . 119 D6
Westcott Rd SE17 . . . . 138 D6
West Cotts NW6 . . . . . 69 C3
Westcroft 1 SM5 . . . . . 219 A4
Westcroft Cl Enfield EN3 . . 6 C5
West Hampstead NW2 . . . 69 A4
Westcroft Ct
3 Chiswick W6 . . . . . 112 A2
Kingsbury NW9 . . . . . 44 D4
Westcroft Gdns SM4 . . . 201 B5
Westcroft Ho 2 SM5 . . . 219 A4
Westcroft Rd SM5,
SM6 . . . . . 219 A4
Westcroft Sq W6 . . . . . 112 A2
Westcroft Way NW2 . . . . 69 A4
West Cromwell Rd
W14 . . . . . 113 B1 254 D2
West Cross Ctr TW8 . . . . 131 B6
West Cross Route W10,
W11 . . . . . 112 D6
West Cross Way TW8 . . . 131 B6
West Croydon Sta
CR9 . . . . . 205 A1
West Ct Hounslow TW7 . . 130 A5
Sunbury TW16 . . . . . 172 B1
Walthamstow E17 . . . . 53 D5
Wembley HA0 . . . . . 65 C6
Westdale Rd SE18 . . . . 144 D6
Westdean Ave SE12 . . . 165 C3
Westdean Cl SW18 . . . . 157 D5
Westdown Rd
Catford SE6 . . . . . 163 C4
Leyton E15 . . . . . 76 A4
West Dr Stanmore HA3 . . . 24 B4
Streatham SW16 . . . . 181 C6
WEST DRAYTON 104 B4
West Drayton Park Ave
UB7 . . . . . 104 A3
West Drayton Prim Sch
UB7 . . . . . 104 A4
West Drayton Rd UB8 . . . 82 D1
West Drayton Sta
UB7 . . . . . 104 A5
West Drive Gdns HA3 . . . 24 B4
WEST DULWICH 161 A2
West Dulwich Sta
SE21 . . . . . 161 B3
WEST EALING 109 B5
West Ealing Bsns Ctr
W13 . . . . . 109 A6
West Ealing Sta W13 . . . 109 B6
West Eaton Pl SW1 . . . 258 A4
West Eaton Pl Mews
SW1 . . . . . 258 A4
West Ella Rd NW10 . . . . 67 C1
West End Ave
Leytonstone E10 . . . . 54 B4
Pinner HA5 . . . . . 40 D5
West End Cl
Stonebridge NW10 . . . . 67 A1
Willesden NW10 . . . . 67 A1
West End Ct
Hampstead NW6 . . . . 69 D1
Pinner HA5 . . . . . 40 D5
West End Gdns UB5 . . . . 84 C5
West End La
Hampstead NW6 . . . . 69 D2
Harlington UB7 . . . . . 127 A5
Pinner HA5 . . . . . 40 D5
West End Rd
Ruislip HA4, UB5 . . . . 62 A4
Ruislip UB5 . . . . . 62 C1
Southall UB1 . . . . . 107 A5
Westerdale Ct N5 . . . . 72 D4
Westerdale Rd 2
SE10 . . . . . 121 A1
Westerfield Rd 1 N15 . . . 51 D4
Westergate W5 . . . . . 88 A2
Westergate Rd SE2 . . . . 147 A6
Westerham
13 Kingston u T KT6 . . . 198 A4
NW1 . . . . . 232 A5
Westerham Ave N9 . . . . 17 C1
Westerham Dr DA15 . . . 168 C5
Westerham Ho SE1 . . . 262 D6
Westerham Lo 10 BR3 . . 185 C3
Westerham Rd
Keston BR2 . . . . . 225 D2
Walthamstow E10 . . . . 53 D2
Westerley Cres SE26 . . . 185 B5
Westerley Ct HA4 . . . . 62 B3
Western Ave
Dagenham W3 . . . . . 89 B1
Hendon NW11 . . . . . 46 D3
Hillingdon HA4, UB4, UB5,
UB10 . . . . . 61 C1
Northolt UB5, UB6 . . . . 85 B6
Ruislip UB8, UB9, UB10 . . 60 B3
Wembley UB6 . . . . . 87 C4
Western Avenue Bsns Pk
W3 . . . . . 88 D3
Western Beach Apts
E16 . . . . . 121 A5
Western Ct
4 Dagenham W3 . . . . 89 B1
Finchley N3 . . . . . 29 C4
3 Kilburn W9 . . . . . 91 B5
Southall UB2 . . . . . 107 A3
Western Dr TW17 . . . . . 193 B3
Western Eye Hospl The
NW1 . . . . . 92 D2 237 C4
Western Gateway E16 . . 121 A6
Western Gdns W5 . . . . . 110 C6
Western Ho 3 W9 . . . . . 91 B3
Western Hts SM1 . . . . . 217 C3
Western International
Market UB2 . . . . . 106 B2
Western La SW12 . . . . . 159 A4
Western Mews W9 . . . . . 91 B3
Western Par EN5 . . . . . 13 D6
Western Pl 19 SE16 . . . . 118 C4
Western Rd
Becontree NW10 . . . . 89 A3
Brixton SW9 . . . . . 138 C2
Ealing W5 . . . . . 109 D6
Fortis Green N2 . . . . 48 D5
Mitcham CR4, SW19 . . . 180 C1
Newham E13 . . . . . 99 C5
Southall UB2 . . . . . 106 D2
Sutton SM1 . . . . . 217 C3
Walthamstow E17 . . . . 54 A4
Wood Green N22 . . . . 32 B1
Western Terr 3 W6 . . . . 112 A1
Western View UB3 . . . . 105 D4
Westernville Gdns IG2 . . 57 A2
Western Way
New Barnet EN5 . . . . 13 D5
Plumstead SE28 . . . . 123 C4
Western Wharf 2
SE15 . . . . . 140 A6
WEST EWELL 215 C1
West Ewell Inf Sch
KT19 . . . . . 215 B3
West Farm Ct EN4 . . . . 2 D2
Westferry Cir E14 . . . . 119 C5
Westferry Rd E14 . . . . 119 C3
Westferry Sta E14 . . . . 119 C6
Westfield 1 BR6 . . . . . 227 A3
Loughton IG10 . . . . . 21 C6
West Hampstead NW3 . . . 69 C4
Westfield Cl
Cheam SM1 . . . . . 217 B4
Enfield EN3 . . . . . 7 A2
Kingsbury NW9 . . . . . 45 A6
SW10 . . . . . 266 A3
Westfield Ct
1 Kensal Green W10 . . . 90 D4
Kingston u T KT6 . . . . 197 D4
Westfield Dr HA3 . . . . 43 D5
Westfield Gdns
Harrow HA3 . . . . . 43 D5
Ilford RM6 . . . . . 58 C3
Westfield Ho 6 SE16 . . . 118 D2
Westfield La HA3 . . . . 43 D5
Westfield Pk HA5 . . . . 23 B3
Westfield Rd
Beckenham BR3 . . . . 185 B1
Cheam SM1 . . . . . 217 B4
Croydon CR0 . . . . . 220 D6
Dagenham RM9 . . . . . 81 B4
Ealing W13 . . . . . 109 A5
Edgware NW7 . . . . . 11 C1
Kingston u T KT6 . . . . 197 D4
Mitcham CR4 . . . . . 180 D1
Walton-on-T KT12 . . . . 195 A2
Westfields SW13 . . . . . 133 D2
Westfields Ave SW13 . . . 133 C2
Westfields Rd W3 . . . . 88 D2
Westfield St SE18 . . . . 121 D3
Westfield Way
Mile End E1 . . . . . 97 A3
Ruislip HA4 . . . . . 61 D5
West Finchley Sta N3 . . . 29 D4
West Garden Pl W2 . . . 237 B1
West Gate W5 . . . . . 88 A4
Westgate Bsns Ctr
2 Kensal Town W10 . . . 91 A3
North Kensington W10 . . . 90 D3
Westgate Ct
6 Beckenham BR3 . . . . 186 A2
15 Brixton SW9 . . . . . 138 C2
Lewisham SE12 . . . . . 165 A3
Westgate Est TW14 . . . . 148 D3
Westgate Rd
Beckenham BR3 . . . . 186 A2
Croydon SE25 . . . . . 206 B5
Westgate St E8 . . . . . 96 B6
Westgate Terr
SW10 . . . . . 135 D6 265 D6
West Gdns
Mitcham SW19 . . . . . 180 C4
Stepney E1 . . . . . 118 B6

Westglade Ct HA3 .... 43 D4
West Gr
Lewisham SE10 .... 142 B4
Woodford IG8 .... 37 C5
WEST GREEN 51 A5
West Green Pl UB6 .... 86 B6
West Green Prim Sch N15 .... 51 A5
West Green Rd N15 .... 51 B5
Westgrove La SE10 .... 142 A4
West Grove Prim Sch N14 .... 15 D4
West Halkin St SW1 .... 115 A3 258 A6
West Hallowes SE9 .... 166 A3
West Hall Rd TW9 .... 132 D4
WEST HAM 99 B6
West Ham Church Prim Sch E15 .... 98 D6
West Ham La E15 .... 76 C1
WEST HAMPSTEAD 69 C4
West Hampstead Mews NW6 .... 69 D2
West Hampstead Sta NW6 .... 69 C2
West Hampstead Thameslink Sta NW6 .. 69 C2
West Ham Sta E15 .... 98 C4
West Harding St EC4 .. 241 B2
WEST HARROW 42 A2
West Harrow Sta HA1 .... 42 A3
West Hatch Manor HA4 .... 39 D2
Westhaven SM1 .... 217 C3
Westhay Gdns SW14 .... 154 D6
WEST HEATH 146 D6
West Heath Ave NW11 .. 47 C1
West Heath Cl NW3 .... 69 C5
West Heath Ct NW11 .... 47 C1
West Heath Dr NW11 .... 47 C1
West Heath Gdns NW3 .. 69 C5
West Heath Rd
SE2, DA7 .... 146 D6
West Hampstead NW3 .... 69 D5
WEST HENDON 45 D3
WEST HILL 157 B5
West Hill Harrow HA2 .... 64 C6
Highgate N6 .... 49 A1
Putney SW15 .... 157 A5
South Croydon CR2 .... 221 C1
Wembley HA9 .... 44 B1
Westhill Ct W11 .... 244 D6
West Hill Ct N6 .... 71 A5
West Hill Hall HA2 .... 64 C6
Westhill Pk
Dartmouth Pk N6 .... 71 A6
Highgate N6 .... 70 D6
West Hill Prim Sch SW18 .... 157 C6
West Hill Rd SW18 .... 157 B5
West Hill Way N20 .... 13 D3
West Ho Barking IG11 .... 78 D2
4 Penge SE20 .... 184 D3
9 Streatham SW12 .... 159 C4
Westholm NW11 .... 47 D5
Westholme BR6 .... 211 D2
Westholme Gdns HA4 .... 40 A1
Westhope Ho 29 E2 .... 96 A4
Westhorne Ave SE9, SE12 .... 165 C5
Westhorpe Gdns NW4 .... 46 C6
Westhorpe Rd SW15 .... 134 C2
West House Cl SW19 .... 157 A3
Westhurst Dr BR7 .... 188 D5
West India Ave E14 .... 119 C5
West India Dock Rd E14 .... 119 C6
West India Ho 1 E14 .. 119 C6
West India Quay Sta E14 .... 119 C6
WEST KENSINGTON .. 113 A2
West Kensington Ct W14 .... 254 C2
West Kensington Mans W14 .... 254 C1
West Kensington Sta W14 .... 113 B1 254 C2
WEST KILBURN 91 A4
West La SE16 .... 118 B4
Westlake 12 SE16 .... 118 C2
Westlake Cl Hayes UB4 .. 85 A3
Palmers Green N13 .... 16 C1
Westlake Rd HA9 .... 65 D6
Westland Cl TW19 .... 148 A5
Westland Ct 9 UB5 .... 84 D4
Westland Dr BR2, BR4 .. 224 D6
Westland Ho 1 E16 .... 122 C5
Westland Lo 1 BR1 .... 187 C1
Westland Pl N1 .... 235 C2
Westlands Cl UB3 .... 106 A2
Westlands Ct KT8 .... 196 C5
Westlands Terr 3 SW12 .... 159 C5
Westlea Rd W7 .... 109 A3
West Lea Sch N9 .... 17 C1
Westleigh Ave SW15 .. 156 C6
Westleigh Ct
Finchley N12 .... 29 D4
16 Wanstead E11 .... 55 A4
Westleigh Dr BR1 .... 188 A2
Westleigh Gdns HA8 .... 26 C1
West Links HA0 .... 87 D4
Westlinton Cl NW7 .... 29 A4
West Lodge Ave W3 .... 110 C5
West Lodge Ct W3 .... 110 C5
West Lodge Fst & Mid Schs HA5 .... 40 D5
West Lodge Sch DA15 .. 168 A1
West London Acad
Northolt UB5 .... 63 A1
Northolt UB5 .... 85 A6
West London Shooting Grounds UB5 .... 84 B5
West London Stad The W12 .... 90 B2
Westly Ct NW2 .... 68 D2
Westly Ho N9 .... 18 B3
Westmacott Dr TW14 .. 149 D3
Westmacott Ho NW8 .... 236 D5
West Mall W11 .... 245 B4
Westmark Point 13 SW15 .... 156 B3
Westmead SW15 .... 156 B5
West Mead Ruislip HA4 .... 62 C4
West Ewell KT19 .... 215 C2
Westmead Cnr SM5 .... 218 C4
Westmead Rd SM1 .... 218 B4
Westmeath Ho NW2 .... 68 A5
Westmere Dr NW7 .... 11 B1
West Mersea Cl 9 E16 .... 121 B5
West Mews SW1 .... 259 A3
West Middlesex Univ Hosp TW7 .... 131 A3
Westmill Ct N4 .... 73 A6
WESTMINSTER 115 C4
Westminster Abbey* SW1 .... 116 A3 260 A6
Westminster Abbey Choir Sch SW1 .... 115 D3 259 D6
Westminster Acad NW1 .... 92 C2 237 A4
Westminster Acad (Sch of English) W1 .... 93 C1 239 B2
Westminster Ave CR7 .. 182 D1
Westminster Boating Base SW1 .... 269 C6
Westminster Bridge SE1, SW1 .... 116 A4 250 B1
Westminster Bridge Rd SE1 .... 116 B4 250 C1
Westminster Cath* SW1 .... 115 C3 259 A5
Westminster Cath Choir Sch SW1 .... 115 C2 259 B4
Westminster Cath RC Prim Sch SW1 .... 115 D1 259 D2
Westminster City Hall SW1 .... 259 B6
Westminster City Sch SW1 .... 259 B6
Westminster Cl
East Bedfont TW14 .... 150 A3
Teddington TW11 .... 175 A5
Westminster Coll of Computing HA9 .... 66 A3
Westminster Ct
22 Rotherhithe SE16 .... 118 D5
South Norwood CR7 .... 183 A1
5 Wandsworth SW18 .. 157 C6
Wanstead E11 .... 55 B3
Westminster Dr N13 .... 32 A5
Westminster Gdns
Barking IG11 .... 101 C5
Chingford E4 .... 20 C3
SW1 .... 260 A4
Westminster Ind Est SE18 .... 121 D3
Westminster Kingsway Coll
Battersea SW11 .... 137 A4 268 B2
St Pancras WC1 .94 B4 233 C1
Westminster Kingsway Coll (Regent's Park Ctr) NW1 .... 93 C3 239 A6
Westminster Pier SW1 250 B1
Westminster Rd
Carshalton SM1 .... 218 B6
Ealing W7 .... 108 C5
Edmonton N9 .... 18 B3
Westminster Sch SW1 .... 116 A3 260 A6
Westminster Sta SW1 .... 116 A4 250 B1
Westminster Under Sch SW1 .... 115 D2 259 C3
Westmoat Cl BR3 .... 186 A3
WEST MOLESEY 195 C5
Westmont Rd KT10 .... 212 C6
Westmoor Gdns EN3 .... 6 D3
Westmoor Rd EN3 .... 6 D3
Westmoor St SE7 .... 121 D3
Westmore Ct SW15 .... 157 A6
Westmoreland Ave DA16 .... 145 C1
Westmoreland Dr SM2 .... 217 D1
Westmoreland Ho NW10 .... 90 A4
Westmoreland Pl
5 Bromley BR1 .... 209 A6
Ealing W5 .... 87 D2
Pimlico SW1 .... 258 D1
Westmoreland Rd
Barnes SW13 .... 134 A4
Beckenham BR2, BR3 .... 208 D5
Bromley BR2 .... 209 A5
Camberwell SE17 .... 139 B6
Queensbury NW9 .... 44 B5
Westmoreland St W1 . 238 B3
Westmoreland Terr
10 Penge SE20 .... 184 B3
SW1 .... 115 B1 258 D1
Westmorland Cl
3 Twickenham TW1 .... 153 B5
Westmorland Cl *continued*
Wanstead E12 .... 77 D6
Westmorland Ct
12 Surbiton KT6 .... 197 D2
Sutton SM1 .... 218 A5
Westmorland Rd BR2 .. 209 A5
Harrow HA1 .... 41 D4
Walthamstow E17 .... 53 C3
Westmorland Way CR4 .... 203 D4
Westmount Ct W5 .... 88 B2
Westmount Rd SE9 .... 144 C1
WEST NORWOOD 161 A1
West Norwood Sta SE27 .... 160 D1
West Oak BR3 .... 186 B2
Westoe Rd N9 .... 18 B2
Weston Ave
East Molesey KT8 .... 195 B5
Thames Ditton KT10, KT7 .... 196 C2
Westonbirt Ct 6 SE15 .... 139 D6
Weston Ct Highbury N4 .... 73 A5
3 Kingston u T KT1 .... 198 A6
Oakleigh Pk N20 .... 14 A4
Weston Dr HA7 .... 25 B2
Weston Ed Ctr The SE5 .... 139 A3
West One Ho W1 .... 239 A3
Westone Mans 6 IG11 .. 79 D1
West One Sh Ctr W1 .... 93 B1 238 C1
Weston Gdns TW7 .... 130 C4
Weston Gn
Dagenham RM9 .... 81 B4
Thames Ditton KT7 .... 196 C1
Weston Gr 1 BR1 .... 186 D2
WESTON GREEN 196 D1
Weston Green Prep Sch KT7 .... 196 C1
Weston Green Rd KT7 .. 196 C2
Weston Ho
6 Brondesbury NW6 .... 69 A1
8 South Hackney E9 .... 96 C6
Weston Lo KT7 .... 196 D1
Weston Park Cl KT7 .... 196 C1
Weston Park Prim Sch N8 .... 50 B4
Weston Pk
Hornsey Vale N8 .... 50 B3
Kingston u T KT1 .... 176 A1
Thames Ditton KT10, KT7 .... 196 C1
Weston Rd
Acton Green W4 .... 111 A3
Bromley BR1 .... 186 D3
Dagenham RM9 .... 81 A4
Enfield EN2 .... 5 B3
Thames Ditton KT7 .... 196 C1
Weston Rise N1, WC1 .... 94 B4 233 D2
Weston St SE1 .. 117 B4 252 D2
Weston Wlk 3 E8, E9 .... 74 B1
Westover Hill NW3 .... 69 C6
Westover Rd SW18 .... 158 A5
Westow Hill SE19 .... 183 D4
Westow St SE19 .... 183 C4
Westpark 5 W5 .... 87 D1
West Park Ave TW9 .... 132 D4
West Park Cl
Heston TW5 .... 129 B6
Ilford RM6 .... 58 D4
West Park Rd
Richmond TW9 .... 132 C4
Southall UB2 .... 108 B5
West Parkside
Greenwich SE10 .... 120 D3
Greenwich SE10 .... 121 A2
West Pk SE9 .... 166 A3
West Pl SW19 .... 178 C5
West Plaza E14 .... 119 D5
Westpoint
Beckenham BR2 .... 208 B6
Putney SW15 .... 156 D5
West Point 2 SE1 .... 118 A1
Westpoint Apartments N8 .... 50 B5
Westpoint Trad Est W3 .. 88 D2
Westpole Ave EN4 .... 3 B1
Westport Ct UB4 .... 84 C3
Westport Rd E13 .... 99 B3
Westport St E1 .... 96 D1
West Poultry Ave EC1 . 241 C3
West Quarters W12 .... 90 A1
West Quay Dr UB4 .... 85 A2
West Ramp TW6 .... 126 C4
West Rd
Chelsea SW3 .... 136 D6 267 D6
Clapham Pk SW4 .... 159 D6
Dagenham RM6 .... 59 A3
Ealing W5 .... 88 A2
East Barnet EN4 .... 15 A3
East Bedfont TW14 .... 149 B4
Finchley N2 .... 30 B2
Kingston u T KT2, KT3 .... 177 A2
Tottenham N17 .... 34 B4
West Drayton UB7 .... 104 B3
West Ham E15 .... 98 D6
West Ridge Gdns UB6 .... 86 A5
Westrow SW15 .... 156 C5
West Row W10 .... 91 A3
Westrow Dr IG11 .... 80 A2
Westrow Gdns IG3 .... 79 D5
WEST RUISLIP 61 B6
West Ruislip Ct HA4 .... 61 B6
West Ruislip Elementary Sch UB10 .... 61 A5
West Ruislip Sta HA4 .... 61 A6
West Sheen Vale TW9 .. 132 B1
Westside
11 Hammersmith W6 .... 112 A2
Hendon NW4 .... 28 B1
Muswell Hill N2 .... 48 D6
West Side Comm SW19 .... 178 C5
Westside Ct 1 W9 .... 91 C3
West Silvertown Sta E16 .... 121 A5
West Smithfield EC1 .... 94 D2 241 D3
West Sq SE11 .... 116 D3 261 C5
West St
30 Bethnal Green E2 .... 96 B5
Bexleyheath DA7 .... 147 B2
Bromley BR1 .... 187 A1
Carshalton SM5 .... 218 D4
Croydon CR0 .... 221 A4
Harrow HA1 .... 42 C1
Leyton E11 .... 76 C5
Soho WC2 .... 93 D1 239 D1
Sutton SM1 .... 217 D3
Walthamstow E17 .... 53 D4
West Street La SM5 .... 218 D4
West Street Pl 1 CR0 .. 221 A4
West Surrey Est TW15 .. 171 A2
West Sutton Sta SM1 .. 217 C4
West Temple Sheen SW14 .... 154 D6
West Tenter St E1 .... 95 D1 243 D1
West Terr DA15 .... 167 C3
West Thames Coll TW7 .... 130 C4
West Thamesmead Bsns Pk SE28 .... 123 D3
West Thornton Prim Sch CR0 .... 204 B3
West Towers HA5 .... 40 D3
West Twyford Prim Sch NW10 .... 88 C5
Westvale Mews W3 .... 111 C4
Westview W7 .... 86 C1
West View
Dagenham RM6 .... 58 C4
East Bedfont TW14 .... 149 A4
Westview Cl
North Kensington W10 .... 90 C1
Willesden NW10 .... 67 D3
Westview Cres N9 .... 17 C4
Westview Ct
3 Elstree WD6 .... 9 D5
1 Whetstone N20 .... 14 A2
Westview Dr IG8 .... 37 D1
West View Gdns WD6 .... 9 D5
Westville Rd
Shepherd's Bush W12 .... 112 A4
Thames Ditton KT7 .... 197 A2
Westward Rd E4 .... 35 B5
Westward Way HA3 .... 44 A3
West Warwick Pl SW1 259 A3
Westway
Shepherd's Bush W10, W12 .... 112 A6
West Barnes SW20 .... 200 C5
West Way BR5 .... 211 B4
Burnt Oak HA8 .... 27 A4
Croydon CR0 .... 223 A5
Edmonton N18 .... 33 B6
Hounslow TW5 .... 129 B4
Neasden NW10 .... 67 B5
Pinner HA5 .... 40 D5
Ruislip HA4 .... 39 D1
Shepperton TW17 .... 193 B3
West Wickham BR4 .... 208 C3
Westway Cl SW20 .... 200 B6
Westway Ct UB5 .... 85 C6
Westway (Elevated Rd) W10 .... 91 B2
West Way Gdns CR0 .... 222 D6
Westway Lo 35 W2 .... 91 C2
Westways KT19 .... 215 D4
West Ways HA6 .... 22 A1
Westwell 4 NW5 .... 71 A2
Westwell Rd SW16 .... 182 A4
Westwell Road App SW16 .... 182 A4
Westwick 7 KT1 .... 176 C1
Westwick Gdns
Cranford TW4, TW5 .... 128 B3
Hammersmith W14 .... 112 D4
WEST WICKHAM 224 C6
West Wickham Sta BR3 .... 208 A2
West Wimbledon Prim Sch SW20 .... 200 B6
West Wlk
East Barnet EN4 .... 15 A3
Hayes UB3 .... 106 A5
Westwood Ave
Harrow HA2 .... 63 D4
South Norwood SE19 .... 183 A2
Westwood Bsns Ctr NW10 .... 89 C3
Westwood Cl BR1 .... 209 D6
Esher KT10 .... 212 A5
Ruislip HA4 .... 38 D3
Westwood Coll DA16 .... 145 C1
Westwood Ct
Enfield EN1 .... 17 C5
3 Forest Hill SE23 .... 162 C3
7 Wimbledon SW19 .... 179 B5
Westwood Gdns SW13 .... 133 D2
Westwood Hill SE26 .... 184 B6
Westwood Ho
6 Shepherd's Bush W12 .... 112 C5
Westwood Ho *continued*
5 Stoke Newington N4 .. 51 B2
Westwood La DA16 .... 145 D1
Westwood Language College for Girls SE19 .... 183 B3
Westwood Lo N12 .... 30 C5
Westwood Park Trad Est W3 .... 88 D3
Westwood Pk SE23 .... 162 B4
Westwood Pl SE26 .... 184 A6
Westwood Rd
Barnes SW13 .... 133 D2
Ilford IG3 .... 58 A2
Westwood Sch WD23 .... 8 B2
West Woodside DA5 .... 169 A3
Wetheral Ct SW17 .... 180 B6
Wetheral Dr HA7 .... 25 C1
Wetherby Cl UB5 .... 63 D2
Wetherby Ct SE25 .... 183 C1
Wetherby Gdns SW5 .... 114 A2 256 A3
Wetherby Mans SW5 .. 255 C2
Wetherby Mews SW5 . 255 D2
Wetherby Pl SW7 .... 114 A2 256 B3
Wetherby Rd EN2 .... 5 A4
Wetherby Way KT9 .... 214 A1
Wetherden St E17 .... 53 B2
Wetherell Rd E9 .... 96 D6
Wetherill Rd N10 .... 31 A2
Wevco Wharf SE15 .... 140 B6
Wexford Ho 11 E1 .... 96 C2
Wexford Rd SW12 .... 158 D4
Weybourne St SW18 .... 158 A2
Weybridge Ct 19 SE16 .. 118 B1
Weybridge Ho N4 .... 51 A2
Weybridge Point 11 SW11 .... 136 D3
Weybridge Rd CR7 .... 204 C5
Wey Ct KT19 .... 215 A4
Weydown Cl SW19 .... 157 A3
Weyhill Ho 28 SE5 .... 139 A3
Weyhill Rd 11 E1 .... 96 A1
Wey Ho 6 Northolt UB5 .. 85 B3
NW8 .... 236 D5
Weylands Cl KT12 .... 195 B1
Weylond Rd RM8 .... 81 B5
Weyman Rd SE3 .... 143 C4
Weymarks The N17 .... 33 B4
Weymouth Ave
Brentford W5 .... 109 C3
Edgware NW7 .... 27 C5
Weymouth Cl 1 E6 .... 100 D1
Weymouth Ct
Belmont SM2 .... 217 C1
5 Haggerston E2 .... 95 D5
15 Streatham SW2 .... 160 B4
Weymouth Ho
Bromley BR2 .... 186 D1
Edgware HA8 .... 26 B4
Fitzrovia W1 .... 238 D4
South Lambeth SW8 .... 270 C3
Weymouth Mews W1 .... 93 B2 238 C4
Weymouth Rd UB4 .... 83 C4
Weymouth St W1 .... 93 B2 238 C4
Weymouth Terr E2 .... 95 D5
Weymouth Wlk HA7 .... 25 A4
Whadcoat St N4 .... 72 C6
Whaddon Ho
10 Camberwell SE5 .... 139 C2
SW1 .... 247 D1
Whalebone Ave RM6 .... 59 B3
Whalebone Gr RM6 .... 59 B3
Whalebone La E15 .... 76 C1
Whalebone Lane N RM6 .... 59 A6
Whalebone Lane S RM6, RM8 .... 59 B2
Whales Yd E15 .... 76 C1
Wharfdale Cl N11 .... 31 A4
Wharfdale Rd N1 .... 94 A5 233 B4
Wharfedale Ct 5 E5 .... 74 D4
Wharfedale Gdns CR7, SW16 .... 204 B6
Wharfedale St SW10 .. 255 C1
Wharf La 19 Poplar E14 .... 97 B1
Twickenham TW1 .... 153 A3
Wharf Pl E2 .... 96 B6
Wharf Rd Enfield EN3 .... 19 A5
King's Cross NW1 .... 93 D6 232 D5
Shoreditch N1 .... 95 A5 235 A3
Wharf Road NW1 .... 94 A5 233 A4
Wharfside HA0 .... 88 A6
Wharfside Rd E16 .... 98 C2
Wharf St E16 .... 98 C2
Wharf View Ct 15 E14 .... 98 A1
Wharncliffe Dr UB1 .... 108 B5
Wharncliffe Gdns SE25 .... 183 C1
Wharncliffe Ho 3 SW15 .... 156 C6
Wharncliffe Rd SE25 .... 183 C1
Wharton Cl NW10 .... 67 C2
Wharton Ho SE1 .... 263 C6
Wharton Rd BR1 .... 187 B2
Wharton St WC1 .... 94 B4 233 D1
Whateley Rd
East Dulwich SE22 .... 161 D6
Penge SE20 .... 184 D3
Whatley Ave SW20 .... 201 A6
Whatman Ho 10 E14 .... 97 B1
Whatman Rd SE23 .... 162 D4
Wheatcroft Ct SM1 .... 201 D1
Wheatfields Enfield EN3 .... 7 A3
Newham E6 .... 100 D1
Wheatfield Way KT1 .... 176 A1
Wheathill Ho SE20 .... 184 B1
Wheathill Rd SE20 .... 206 B6
Wheat Ho TW19 .... 148 A3
Wheatland Ho 7 SE22 .... 139 C2
Wheatlands TW5 .... 129 C6
Wheatlands Rd SW17 .. 159 A1
Wheatley Cl NW4 .... 28 A1
Wheatley Cres UB3 .... 106 A6
Wheatley Gdns N9 .... 17 C2
Wheatley Ho
Gospel Oak NW5 .... 71 B4
3 Putney SW15 .... 156 A4
Wheatley Mans 8 IG11 .... 80 A1
Wheatley Rd TW7 .... 130 D2
Wheatley St W1 .... 238 B3
Wheatsheaf Cl UB5 .... 63 A3
Wheat Sheaf Cl E14 .... 119 D2
Wheatsheaf La
Fulham SW6 .... 134 C5
SW8 .... 270 B4
Wheatsheaf Par 7 BR4 .... 207 D1
Wheatsheaf Terr SW6 . 264 D3
Wheatstone Cl SW19 .. 180 C2
Wheatstone Ho 7 W10 . 91 A2
Wheatstone Rd W10 .... 91 A2
Wheeler 2 NW9 .... 27 D3
Wheeler Ct 5 SW11 .... 136 B2
Wheeler Gdns N1 .... 233 B6
Wheeler La E1 .... 243 C4
Wheeler Pl 2 BR2 .... 209 B5
Wheelers Cross IG11 .. 101 B5
Wheelers Dr HA4 .... 39 A3
Wheeler's St SM1 .... 217 C5
Wheelhouse The 4 E14 .... 119 D1
Wheelock Cl DA8 .... 147 D5
Wheelwright St N7 .... 72 B1
Whelan Way SM6 .... 219 D5
Wheldon Ct SE1 .... 253 C2
Wheler Ho E1 .... 243 C5
Wheler St E1 .... 95 D3 243 C5
Whellock Rd W4 .... 111 C3
Whernside Cl SE28 .... 124 C6
WHETSTONE 14 A2
Whetstone Cl N20 .... 14 B2
Whetstone Park WC2 .... 94 B1 240 C2
Whetstone Rd SE3 .... 143 D4
Whewell Rd N19 .... 72 A6
Whichcote St SE1 .... 251 A3
Whidborne Bldgs WC1 233 A1
Whidborne Cl SE8 .... 141 C3
Whidborne St WC1 .... 233 B1
Whimbrel Cl SE28 .... 124 C6
Whimbrel Way UB4 .... 84 D2
Whinchat Rd SE18, SE28 .... 123 B3
Whinfell Cl SW16 .... 181 D5
Whinyates Rd SE9 .... 144 A2
Whippendell Cl BR5 .... 190 B2
Whippendell Way BR5 . 190 B1
Whippingham Ho 22 E3 .... 97 B4
Whipps Cross E17 .... 54 B4
Whipps Cross Ho E17 .... 54 B4
Whipps Cross Hospl E10, E11 .... 54 B3
Whipps Cross Rd E11 .... 54 C3
Whiskin St EC1 .. 94 D4 234 C1
Whisperwood Cl HA3 .... 24 C3
Whistler Gdns HA8 .... 26 B1
Whistler Mews
Dagenham RM8 .... 80 B3
23 SE15 .... 139 D5
Whistlers Ave SW11 .... 136 B5 266 D3
Whistler St N5 .... 72 D3
Whistler Twr SW10 .... 266 A3
Whistler Wlk SW10 .... 266 B4
Whiston Ho 18 N1 .... 72 D1
Whiston Rd E2 .... 96 A6
Whitakers Lo EN2 .... 5 B4
Whitbread Cl N17 .... 34 A2
Whitbread Ctr EC1 .... 242 C5
Whitbread Rd SE4 .... 141 B1
Whitburn Rd SE13 .... 142 A1
Whitby Ave NW10 .... 88 D4
Whitby Ct
6 Lower Holloway N7 .... 72 A4
3 New Southgate N11 .... 31 A4
Whitby Gdns
Carshalton SM1 .... 218 B6
Queensbury NW9 .... 44 C6
Whitby Ho NW8 .... 229 A5
Whitby Par HA4 .... 62 C6
Whitby Rd
Carshalton SM1 .... 218 B6
Harrow HA2 .... 64 A5
Ruislip HA4 .... 62 C6
Woolwich SE18 .... 122 B2
Whitby St E1 .... 243 C6
Whitcher Cl SE14 .... 141 A6
Whitcher Pl NW1 .... 71 C2
Whitchurch Ave HA8 .... 26 B3
Whitchurch Cl HA8 .... 26 B4
Whitchurch Ct SW17 .... 180 B6
Whitchurch Fst & Mid Schs HA7 .... 25 D3
Whitchurch Gdns HA8 .. 26 B4
Whitchurch Ho
Catford SE6 .... 164 A1
16 North Kensington W10 .... 90 D1
Whitchurch La HA8 .... 26 B3

Whitchurch Par HA8 … 26 C3
Whitchurch Rd W11 … 112 D6
Whitcomb Ct W1 … 249 D5
Whitcomb St WC2 … 115 D6 249 D5
Whitcome Mews TW9 … 132 D4
Whiteacre Mews SE11 261 B1
Whiteadder Way E14 … 119 D2
Whitear Wlk E15 … 76 B2
Whitebarn La RM10 … 103 C6
Whitebeam Ave BR2 … 210 C3
Whitebeam Cl SW9 … 270 D3
Whitebeam Ho 3 NW3 … 70 D2
White Bear Pl 1 NW3 … 70 B4
White Bear Yd EC1 … 241 A5
White Bridge Ave CR4 … 202 B6
White Bridge Cl TW14 … 149 D5
White Butts Rd HA4 … 62 D5
WHITECHAPEL … 95 D1
Whitechapel High St E1 … 95 D1 243 D2
Whitechapel Mkt E1 … 96 A2
Whitechapel Rd E1 … 96 B2
Whitechapel Sta E1 … 96 B2
Whitechurch La 3 E1 … 96 A1
Whitechurch Pas 1 E1 … 96 A1
White City W10 … 90 C1
White City Cl W12 … 112 C6
White City Est W12 … 112 B6
White City Rd W12 … 112 C6
White City Sta W12 … 112 C6
Whitecliff Ho SW18 … 157 D5
White Conduit St N1 … 234 B4
Whitecote Rd UB1 … 86 A1
White Craig Cl HA5 … 23 C5
Whitecroft Cl BR3 … 208 B5
Whitecroft Way BR3 … 208 B5
Whitecross Pl EC2 … 242 D4
Whitecross St EC1 … 95 A3 242 B5
White Cube The, Art Gallery* N1 … 95 C4
Whitefield Ave NW2 … 46 C1
Whitefield Cl SW15 … 157 A5
Whitefield Sch
Chingford E17 … 36 A1
Hendon NW2 … 46 D2
Whitefoot La BR1 … 164 B1
Whitefoot Terr BR1 … 164 D1
Whitefriars Ave HA3 … 24 C1
Whitefriars Ct 9 N12 … 30 B5
Whitefriars Dr HA3 … 24 C1
Whitefriars Fst & Mid Sch HA3 … 24 C1
Whitefriars St EC4 … 94 C1 241 B1
Whitefriars Trad Est HA3 … 24 B1
White Gate Gdns HA3 … 24 D3
Whitegates 4 EN5 … 13 D6
White Gdns RM10 … 81 C2
Whitehall SW1 … 250 A2
Whitehall Cres KT9 … 213 D3
Whitehall Ct SW1 … 116 A5 250 B3
Whitehall Gdns
Acton W3 … 110 C5
Chingford E4 … 20 C3
Chiswick W4 … 132 D6
SW1 … 250 A3
Whitehall La IG9 … 21 A2
Whitehall Lo
Muswell Hill N10 … 49 A6
Woodford IG8 … 21 A1
Whitehall Mans 3 N19 … 49 C1
Whitehall Park Rd W4 … 132 D6
Whitehall Pk N19 … 49 C1
Whitehall Pl
Wallington SM5 … 219 B4
WC2, SW1 … 116 A5 250 A3
Whitehall Prim Sch E4 … 20 C2
Whitehall Rd
Bromley BR2 … 209 D5
Chingford E4 … 20 C2
Harrow HA1 … 42 C2
Thornton Heath CR7 … 204 C4
West Ealing W7 … 109 A4
Woodford IG8 … 21 A1
Whitehall St N17 … 33 D3
White Hart Ave SE28, SE18 … 123 D3
White Hart La
Mortlake SW13 … 133 C2
Willesden NW10 … 67 D2
White Hart Lane Sec Sch N22 … 32 D3
White Hart Lane Sta N17 … 33 D3
White Hart Lane (Tottenham Hotspur FC) N17 … 34 A3
Whitehart Lo SW19 … 180 A4
White Hart Rd SE18 … 123 C2
White Hart Rdbt UB5 … 84 D5
White Hart St
Holborn EC4 … 241 D2
Kennington SE11 … 116 C1 261 B2
White Hart Terr N17 … 33 D3
White Hart Yd SE1 … 252 C3
Whitehaven Cl BR2 … 209 A5
Whitehaven Ct 5 DA6 … 147 A1
Whitehaven St NW8 … 237 A5
Whitehead Cl
Edmonton N18 … 33 B5
Wandsworth SW18 … 158 A4
Whitehead Ct
Muswell Hill N10 … 31 A2
Twickenham TW1 … 152 D4
Whitehead Ho 8 SW15 … 156 D6
Whitehead's Gr SW3 … 114 C2 257 B3
White Heart Ave UB8 … 83 A2
Whiteheath Ave HA4 … 39 A2
Whiteheath Inf Sch HA4 … 39 A3
Whiteheath Jun Sch HA4 … 39 A2
White Heron Mews TW11 … 174 D4
White Ho
2 Battersea SW11 … 136 B3
Lower Edmonton N9 … 18 C2
3 Streatham SW4 … 159 D4
Whitehorn Ho 6 E1 … 118 C5
White Horse Hill BR7, SE9 … 188 C6
Whitehorse La SE25 … 205 C5
White Horse La E1 … 96 D2
Whitehorse Manor Inf Sch CR7 … 205 B5
Whitehorse Manor Jun Sch CR7 … 205 B5
Whitehorse Mews SE1 261 C6
Whitehorse Rd
South Norwood CR0, CR7 … 205 B3
Tower Hamlets E1 … 97 A2
White Horse Rd
Limehouse E1 … 97 A1
Newham E6 … 100 B4
White Horse St W1 … 115 B5 248 D3
White Horse Yd EC2 … 242 C2
White Ho The NW1 … 238 D6
Tottenham N17 … 51 C6
Upper Tooting SW17 … 180 D5
White House Ct
1 Beckenham BR3 … 186 A2
Osidge N14 … 15 D2
White House Dr HA7 … 25 C6
Whitehouse Est E10 … 54 A3
White House La EN2 … 5 A4
Whitehouse Way N14 … 15 B1
White Kennett St E1 … 243 B2
Whitelands Cres SW18 … 157 A4
Whitelands Ho SW3 … 257 D2
Whiteledges W13 … 87 C1
Whitelegg Rd E13 … 98 D5
Whiteley Ho 9 SW4 … 159 D4
Whiteley Rd SE19 … 183 B5
Whiteleys Ctr 19 W2 … 91 D1
Whiteleys Ho TW13 … 151 C1
Whiteleys Par 5 UB10 … 82 D3
Whiteleys Way TW13 … 151 C1
White Lion Ct EC3 … 243 A1
White Lion Hill EC4 … 116 D6 251 D6
White Lion St N1 … 94 C5 234 B3
White Lo 7 Ealing W5 … 87 C2
Golders Green NW11 … 47 B1
South Norwood SE19 … 182 D3
Whitelock Ho 21 E9 … 74 D2
White Lodge Cl
Hampstead Garden Suburb N2 … 48 B3
Isleworth TW7 … 131 A3
Sutton SM2 … 218 A1
White Lodge Ct TW16 … 172 C2
Whitely Ct TW13 … 151 B1
White Lyon Ct EC2 … 242 A4
Whiteness Ho 18 SW9 … 138 C4
White Oak Dr BR3 … 186 A1
White Oak Gdns DA15 … 167 D4
Whiteoak Ho SE19 … 183 A3
Whiteoaks La UB6 … 86 B5
White Orchards
Barnet N20 … 13 B3
Stanmore HA7 … 25 A5
White Post La E9 … 75 C2
White Post St SE14, SE15 … 140 C5
White Rd E15 … 76 C1
Whites Ave IG2 … 57 C3
Whites Dr BR2 … 208 D2
White's Grounds SE1 … 117 C4 253 B2
White's Grounds Est SE1 … 253 B2
White's Mdw BR1 … 210 C5
Whitespar DA14 … 189 D6
White's Row E1 … 95 D2 243 C3
White's Sq SW4 … 137 D1
White St UB1 … 106 D4
Whitestile Rd TW8 … 109 D1
Whitestone La NW3 … 70 A5
Whitestone Wlk NW3 … 70 A5
Whitethorn Ave UB7 … 104 B6
Whitethorn Gdns
Croydon CR0 … 222 B6
Enfield EN2 … 17 B6
Whitethorn Pl UB7 … 104 B5
Whitethorn St E3 … 97 C2
Whiteways NW4 … 46 D5
Whitewebbs Way BR5 … 189 D2
Whitfield Ct
3 Dulwich SE21 … 183 C6
Redbridge IG1 … 56 B2
SW4 … 270 A1
West Barnes SW20 … 178 D1
Whitfield Gdns W1 … 239 B4
Whitfield Ho NW8 … 237 A5
Whitfield Pl W1 … 239 B5
Whitfield Rd DA7 … 147 B5
Upton E6 … 77 C1
Whitfield St W1 … 93 C2 239 B4
Whitford Gdns CR4 … 202 D6
Whitgift Ave CR2 … 221 A3
Whitgift Ct CR2 … 221 A3
Whitgift Ctr CR0 … 221 A6
Whitgift Ho
Battersea SW11 … 267 A2
Croydon CR2 … 221 A3
Lambeth SE11 … 260 C4
Whitgift Sch CR2 … 221 A3
Whitgift St
Croydon CR0 … 221 A5
SE11 … 116 B2 260 C4
Whiting Ave IG11 … 78 D1
Whitings Hill Prim Sch EN5 … 12 C6
Whitings Rd EN5 … 12 C6
Whitings The IG2 … 57 C4
Whitings Way E6 … 100 C2
Whitington Ave EC3 … 243 A1
Whitland Rd SM5 … 202 B1
Whitley Cl TW19 … 148 A5
Whitley Ho SW1 … 269 B6
Whitley Rd N17 … 33 C1
Whitlock Dr SW19 … 157 A3
Whitman Ho 20 E2 … 96 C4
Whitman Rd E3 … 97 A3
Whitmead Cl CR2 … 221 C2
Whitmore Cl N11 … 31 B5
Whitmore Gdns NW10 … 90 C5
Whitmore High Sch HA1, HA2 … 42 A1
Whitmore Ho
Friern Barnet N11 … 30 D6
20 Hoxton E1 … 95 C6
Whitmore Prim Sch N1 … 95 B6 235 D5
Whitmore Rd
Beckenham BR3 … 207 B6
Harrow HA1 … 42 A2
Hoxton N1 … 95 C6
Whitnell Ct 7 SW15 … 156 D6
Whitnell Way SW15 … 156 D6
Whitney Ave IG4 … 55 D5
Whitney Ho 6 SE22 … 139 C2
Whitney Rd E10 … 53 D2
Whitney Wlk DA14 … 191 A4
Whitstable Cl
Beckenham BR3 … 185 B2
Ruislip HA4 … 61 C6
Whitstable Ho 11 W10 … 90 D1
Whitstable Pl 9 CR0 … 221 A4
Whitsters Ho SE1 … 253 C2
Whitstone La BR3 … 207 D4
Whittaker 3 NW9 … 27 D3
Whittaker Ave TW10, TW9 … 153 D6
Whittaker Ct SW4 … 270 B1
Whittaker Pl 28 TW10 … 153 D6
Whittaker Rd
Cheam SM3 … 217 B5
Forest Gate E6 … 77 D1
Whittaker St SW1 … 258 A3
Whittaker Way 19 SE1 … 118 A2
Whittam Ho SE27 … 183 A5
Whitta Rd E12 … 77 D4
Whittell Gdns SE26 … 162 C1
Whitten Lo N12 … 30 C6
Whittingham 6 N17 … 34 B3
Whittingham Com Prim Sch E17 … 35 A2
Whittingham Ct W4 … 133 C5
Whittingstall Mans SW6 … 264 D1
Whittingstall Rd SW6 … 135 B4 264 D1
Whittington Ave UB4 … 83 D2
Whittington Ct
Fortis Green N2 … 48 D4
Penge SE20 … 184 B1
Whittington Hospl The N19 … 71 C6
Whittington Mews N12 … 30 A6
Whittington Rd N22 … 32 A3
Whittington Way HA5 … 41 A4
Whittle 4 NW9 … 27 D3
Whittlebury Cl SM5 … 218 D1
Whittlebury Ho N4 … 51 A2
Whittle Cl Southall UB1 … 85 D1
Walthamstow E17 … 53 A2
Whittle Rd
Heston TW5 … 128 C5
Southall UB2 … 107 D4
Whittlesea Cl HA3 … 24 A3
Whittlesea Path HA3 … 24 A2
Whittlesea Rd HA3 … 24 A2
Whittlesey St SE1 … 116 C5 251 B3
WHITTON … 152 A4
Whitton NW3 … 70 D1
Whitton Ave W UB5, UB6 … 64 B3
Whitton Cl UB6 … 65 B2
Whitton Dene TW3, TW7 … 152 B6
Whitton Dr UB6 … 65 A2
Whitton Manor Rd TW7 … 152 A5
Whitton Rd
Hounslow TW3 … 151 D6
Twickenham TW1 … 153 A4
Whitton Road Rdbt TW1 … 152 D5
Whitton Sch TW2 … 151 D2
Whitton Sta TW2 … 152 A4
Whitton Waye TW2, TW3 … 151 C5
Whitton Wlk E3 … 97 C4
Whitwell Ho 11 E5 … 74 B6
Whitwell Rd E13 … 99 A4
Whitworth Cres 1 EN3 … 7 C6
Whitworth Ho SE1 … 262 B5
Whitworth Rd SE18 … 144 C5
South Norwood SE25 … 205 D5
Whitworth St SE10 … 120 C1
Whorlton Rd SE15 … 140 B2
Whychcote Point NW2 … 46 C2
Whymark Ave N22 … 50 D6
Whytecroft TW5 … 128 D5
Whyteville Ho E7 … 77 B2
Whyteville Rd E7 … 77 B2
Whytlaw Ho 10 E3 … 97 B2
Wickersley Rd SW11 … 137 A3
Wickers Oake SE19 … 183 D6
Wicker St 24 E1 … 96 B1
Wicket Rd UB6 … 87 A4
Wickets The TW15 … 170 A6
Wicket The CR0 … 223 C3
Wickfield Ho 32 SE16 … 118 A4
Wickford Ho 5 E1 … 96 C3
Wickford St E1 … 96 C3
Wickford Way E17 … 52 D5
Wickham Ave
Cheam KT4, SM3 … 216 C3
Croydon CR0 … 207 A1
Wickham Chase BR4 … 208 C2
Wickham Cl Enfield EN3 … 6 C2
New Malden KT3 … 199 D4
Stepney E1 … 96 C2
Wickham Common Prim Sch BR4 … 225 A4
Wickham Court Rd BR4 … 224 A6
Wickham Court Sch BR4 … 224 B4
Wickham Cres BR4 … 224 A6
Wickham Ct DA16 … 145 C3
Wickham Gdns SE4 … 141 B2
Wickham Ho SW15 … 156 D5
Wickham La SE2 … 146 A6
Wickham Mews SE4 … 141 B3
Wickham Rd
Beckenham BR3 … 207 D6
Brockley SE4 … 141 B2
Chingford E4 … 36 A3
Croydon CR0 … 207 B1
Harrow HA3 … 24 B1
Wickham St
Bexley DA16 … 145 C3
Vauxhall SE11 … 116 B1 260 C2
Welling DA16 … 146 A4
Wickham Way BR3 … 208 A4
Wick Ho 1 KT1 … 175 D2
Wick La Hackney E3 … 75 B1
Stratford Marsh E3 … 97 C6
Wickliffe Ave N3 … 29 A1
Wickliffe Gdns HA9 … 66 D6
Wicklow Ct SE26 … 184 C5
Wicklow Ho N16 … 51 D1
Wicklow St WC1 … 94 B4 233 C2
Wick Rd Hackney E9 … 74 D2
Hackney E9 … 75 A2
Teddington TW11 … 175 C3
Wicks Cl SE12 … 187 D6
Wickstead Ho TW8 … 110 B1
Wicksteed Ho SE1 … 262 B5
Wickway Ct 7 SE15 … 139 D6
Wickwood St SE5 … 138 D3
Widdenham Rd N7 … 72 B4
Widdicombe Ave HA2 … 63 A6
Widdin St E15 … 76 C1
Widecombe Ct N2 … 48 B4
Widecombe Gdns IG4 … 56 A5
Widecombe Ho 32 SE5 … 139 A3
Widecombe Rd SE9 … 166 A1
Widecombe Way N2 … 48 B5
Widegate St E1 … 243 B3
Widenham Cl HA5 … 40 C4
Wide Way CR4 … 203 D6
Widewing Cl TW11 … 175 B3
Widford 8 NW1 … 71 B2
Widford Ho N1 … 234 C3
Widgeon Cl E16 … 99 B1
Widgeon Path SE28 … 123 B3
Widley Rd W9 … 91 C3
Widmer Ct TW5 … 129 A3
WIDMORE … 188 A1
Widmore Lodge Rd BR1 … 187 D1
Widmore Rd BR1 … 187 C1
Hillingdon UB8 … 82 D3
Widnes Ho 6 N7 … 72 C3
Wieland Rd HA6 … 22 A3
Wigan Ho E5 … 52 B1
Wigeon Way UB4 … 84 D1
Wiggins La TW10 … 153 C2
Wiggins Mead NW9 … 27 D3
Wigginton Ave HA9 … 66 D2
Wigham Ho IG11 … 79 A1
Wightman Rd N4, N8 … 50 C4
Wighton Mews TW7 … 130 C3
Wigley Rd TW13 … 150 D3
Wigmore Ct 4 W13 … 109 A5
Wigmore Hall* W1 … 238 C2
Wigmore Pl W1 … 93 B1 238 C2
Wigmore Rd SM5 … 202 C1
Wigmore St W1 … 93 A1 238 B2
Wigmore Wlk SM5 … 218 B6
Wigram Ct SW11 … 267 A2
Wigram Ho 7 E14 … 119 D6
Wigram Rd E11 … 55 C3
Wigram Sq E17 … 54 A6
Wigston Cl N18 … 33 C5
Wigston Rd E13 … 99 B3
Wigton Gdns HA7 … 26 A2
Wigton Pl SE11 … 261 B1
Wigton Rd E17 … 35 B2
Wilberforce Ct
Edgware HA8 … 26 B6
2 SE28 … 124 C5
Wilberforce Ho 4 SW11 … 136 B2
Wilberforce Mews 9 SW4 … 137 D1
Wilberforce Prim Sch W10 … 91 A4
Wilberforce Rd
Finsbury Pk N4 … 72 D6
Hendon NW9 … 46 A3
Highbury N4, N5 … 73 A5
Wilberforce Way SW19 … 178 D4
Wilbraham Ho SW8 … 270 A3
Wilbraham Pl SW1 … 258 A4
Wilbury Prim Sch N18 … 33 B5
Wilbury Way N18 … 33 B5
Wilby Mews W11 … 113 B5 244 D4
Wilcox Cl SW8 … 270 B4
Wilcox Gdns TW17 … 192 B6
Wilcox Ho 5 E3 … 97 B2
Wilcox Pl SW1 … 259 B5
Wilcox Rd Sutton SM1 … 217 D4
SW8 … 138 A5 270 A4
Teddington TW11 … 174 B6
Wildcroft Gdns HA8 … 25 D4
Wildcroft Manor SW15 … 156 C4
Wildcroft Rd SW15 … 156 C4
Wild Ct WC2 … 94 B1 240 C2
Wilde Cl E8 … 96 A6
Wilde Pl Edmonton N13 … 32 D4
Wandsworth SW18 … 158 B4
Wilder Cl HA4 … 40 B1
Wilde Rd DA8 … 147 D5
Wilderness Mews SW4 … 137 B1
Wilderness Rd BR7 … 188 D3
Wilderness The
East Molesey KT8 … 196 A4
Hampton TW12 … 173 D6
Wilderton Rd N16 … 51 C2
Wildes Cotts SM3 … 217 A2
Wildfell Rd SE6 … 163 D4
Wild Goose Dr SE14 … 140 C4
Wild Hatch NW11 … 47 C3
Wilding Ho 17 E9 … 74 D2
Wild Marsh Ct EN3 … 7 A6
Wild's Rents SE1 … 117 C3 263 A6
Wild St WC2 … 94 B1 240 C1
Wildwood Cl SE12 … 164 D4
Wildwood Gr NW3 … 48 A1
Wildwood Rd NW11 … 48 A2
Wildwood Rise NW11 … 48 A1
Wildwood Terr NW3 … 48 A1
Wilford Cl EN2 … 5 B2
Wilford Ho 3 SE18 … 122 D1
Wilford Rd CR0 … 205 A2
Wilfred Fienburgh Ho N7 … 71 D4
Wilfred Owen Cl SW19 … 180 A4
Wilfred St SW1 … 115 C3 259 A6
Wilfrid Gdns W3 … 89 A2
Wilkes Rd 3 TW8 … 132 A6
Wilkes St E1 … 95 D2 243 D4
Wilkie Ho SW1 … 259 D2
Wilkins Cl Hayes UB3 … 105 D1
Mitcham CR4 … 180 C2
Wilkins Ho SW1 … 269 A6
Wilkinson Cl UB10 … 83 A6
Wilkinson Ct SW17 … 180 B6
Wilkinson Gdns CR7 … 183 C2
Wilkinson Ho
Isleworth TW7 … 130 D2
N1 … 235 D3
Twickenham TW2 … 152 B2
Wilkinson Rd E16 … 99 C1
Wilkinson St SW8 … 138 B5 270 C3
Wilkinson Way W4 … 111 B4
Wilkin St NW5 … 71 B2
Wilks Gdns CR0 … 207 A1
Wilks Pl N1 … 95 C5
Willan Rd N17 … 33 C1
Willan Wall E16 … 120 D6
Willard St SW8 … 137 B2
Willbury Ho 4 N7 … 71 D3
Willcocks Cl KT9 … 214 A5
Willcott Rd W3 … 110 D5
Will Crooks Gdns SE9 … 143 D1
Willenfield Rd NW10 … 89 A5
Willenhall Ave EN5 … 14 A5
Willenhall Ct EN5 … 14 A5
Willenhall Dr UB3 … 105 C6
Willenhall Rd SE18 … 122 D1
Willersley Ave
Blackfen DA15 … 167 D4
Orpington BR6 … 227 B5
Willersley Cl DA15 … 167 D3
WILLESDEN … 67 D1
Willesden Community Hospl The NW10 … 68 A1
WILLESDEN GREEN … 90 B6
Willesden Green Sta NW2 … 68 C2
Willesden Junction Sta NW10 … 89 D4
Willesden La NW2, NW6 … 68 D2
Willes Rd NW5 … 71 B2
Willett Cl BR5 … 211 C3
3 Northolt UB5 … 84 C4
Willett Ho
7 Newham E13 … 99 A5
Willett Ho *continued*
Stockwell SW9 … 138 A2
Willett Pl CR7 … 204 C4
Willett Rd CR7 … 204 C4
Willett Way BR5 … 211 C3
William Allen Ho HA8 … 26 B3
William Ash Cl RM9 … 80 B2
William Atkinson Ho N17 … 33 C3
William Banfield Ho 10 SW6 … 135 B3
William Barefoot Dr SE9 … 166 C1
William Bellamy Jun & Inf Schs RM10 … 81 C6
William Blake Ho 2 SE15 … 140 A3
William Bonney Est 10 SW4 … 137 D1
William Booth Meml Training Coll SE5 … 139 B3
William Booth Rd SE20 … 184 A2
William Brown Ct SE27 … 160 D2
William Byrd Sch UB3 … 127 A6
William Carey Way HA1 … 42 C3
William Caslon Ho 28 E2 … 96 B5
William Channing Ho 6 E2 … 96 B4
William C Harvey Sch N17 … 33 B1
William Cl
26 Finchley N2 … 30 B1
Lewisham SE13 … 142 A2
Southall UB2 … 108 A4
William Covell Cl EN2 … 4 B5
William Ct
4 Belvedere DA17 … 125 C2
4 Ealing W5 … 87 C2
Ilford IG6 … 57 B5
William Davies Prim Sch E7 … 77 D2
William Davis Prim Sch E2 … 96 A3
William Dr HA7 … 25 B5
William Dromey Ct NW6 … 69 B1
William Dunbar Ho NW6 … 91 B5
William Dyce Mews 1 SW16 … 181 D6
William Ellis Sch NW5 … 71 A5
William Ellis Way 16 SE16 … 118 A3
William Evans Ho 9 SE8 … 118 D2
William Ford CE Jun Sch RM10 … 81 C1
William Gdns SW15 … 156 B6
William Guy Gdns 47 E3 … 97 D4
William Harvey Ho 1 SW19 … 157 A3
William Ho N13 … 32 D4
William Hogarth Prim Sch The W4 … 111 C1
William Hunt Mans SW13 … 134 C6
William IV St WC2 … 116 A6 250 A5
William Margrie Cl 1 SE15 … 140 A3
William Marsden Ho 2 SE27 … 182 D6
William Mews SW1 … 114 D4 247 D1
William Morley Cl E6 … 99 D6
William Morris Acad W6 … 112 D1
William Morris Cl E17 … 53 B6
William Morris Gallery* E17 … 53 C6
William Morris Ho W6 … 134 D6
William Morris Prim Sch CR4 … 203 D6
William Morris Sch E17 … 35 A2
William Morris Way SW6 … 136 A3
William Patten Prim Sch N16 … 73 D6
William Perkin Ct UB6 … 64 C2
William Pl 37 E3 … 97 B5
William Rainbird Ho 9 N17 … 33 D3
William Rathbone Ho 3 E2 … 96 B4
William Rd
Regent's Pk NW1 … 93 C4 232 A1
Sutton SM1 … 218 A3
Wimbledon SW19 … 179 A3
William Rushbrooke Ho 4 SE16 … 118 A2
Williams Ave E17 … 35 B2
William Saville Ho 2 NW6 … 91 B5
William's Bldgs 1 E2 … 96 C3
Williams Cl SW6 … 135 A5 264 B4
Williams Coll EC1 … 241 B3
Williams Dr TW3 … 129 C1

Williams Gr
Kingston u T KT6 . . . . . .**197** C3
Wood Green N22 . . . .**32** C2
Williams Ho 10 Bow E3 . . .**97** C4
9 Hackney E9 . . . .**96** B6
14 Streatham SW2 . . . . .**160** C4
7 Tottenham N17 . . . . . .**33** D3
Willesden NW2 . . . .**68** C5
Williams La
Morden SM4 . . . .**202** A4
Mortlake SW14 . . . .**133** A3
William Smith Ho 10
DA17 . . . .**125** C3
Williamson Cl SE10 . . . .**120** D1
Williamson Ct SE17 . . . .**262** A1
Williamson Rd N4 . . . . . .**50** D3
Williamson St N7 . . . .**72** A4
Williamson Way NW7 . . . .**29** A4
William Sq 15 SE16 . . . . .**119** A6
Williams Rd UB2 . . . .**107** A2
William's Rd W13 . . . . . .**109** A5
William St Barking IG11 . .**79** A1
Carshalton SM5 . . . .**218** D5
SW1 . . . .**114** D4 **247** D1
Tottenham N17 . . . .**33** D3
Walthamstow E10 . . . .**53** D3
Williams Terr CR0 . . . . . .**220** C2
William Torbitt Prim Sch
IG2 . . . .**57** D4
William Tyndale Prim Sch
N1 . . . .**15** A1
William Wilberforce Ho 1
SE27 . . . .**182** D6
William Winter Ct 29
SW2 . . . .**160** C4
William Wood Ho 3
SE26 . . . .**162** C4
Willifield Way NW11 . . . . .**47** C4
Willingale Cl IG8 . . . .**37** C4
Willingdon Rd N22 . . . . . .**32** D1
Willingham Cl 4 NW5 . . .**71** C3
Willingham Terr NW5 . . . .**71** C3
Willingham Way KT16 . . .**176** C1
Willington Ct E5 . . . .**75** A5
Willington Prep Sch
SW19 . . . .**179** B5
Willington Rd SW9 . . . . .**138** A2
Willis Ave SM2, SM5 . . . .**218** C2
Willis Ct CR7 . . . .**204** C3
Willis Ho 2 Ilford E12 . . .**78** C5
8 Poplar E14 . . . .**119** D6
Willis Rd E15 . . . .**98** D5
Thornton Heath CR0 . . . .**205** A2
Willis St E14 . . . .**97** D1
Willis Yd N14 . . . .**15** D4
Willows The CR0 . . . .**223** A6
Will Miles Ct 8 SW19 . . .**180** A3
Willmore End SW19 . . . .**179** D1
Willoughby Ave CR0 . . . .**220** B4
Willoughby Gr N17 . . . . . .**34** B3
Willoughby Ho 2 . . . . .**242** C3
34 Wapping E1 . . . .**118** B5
Willoughby La N17 . . . . . .**34** B3
Willoughby Mews N17 . . .**34** B3
Willoughby Park Rd
N17 . . . .**34** B3
Willoughby Rd
Hampstead NW3 . . . .**70** B4
Hornsey N8 . . . .**50** C5
Kingston u T KT2 . . . . . .**176** B2
Twickenham TW1 . . . . . .**153** D6
Willoughby St WC1 . . . . .**240** A1
Willoughbys The
SW14 . . . .**133** C1
Willoughby Way SE7 . . . .**121** B2
Willow Ave
Barnes SW13 . . . .**133** D3
DA15 . . . .**168** A5
Yiewsley UB7 . . . .**104** B6
Willowbank SW6 . . . . . .**135** A2
Willow Bank TW10 . . . . .**153** B1
Willowbank Rd SE15 . . . .**139** D6
Willowbay Cl EN5 . . . .**12** D5
Willow Bridge Rd N1 . . . .**73** A2
Willow Brook Prim Sch
E10 . . . .**53** C1
Willowbrook Rd
Southall UB2 . . . .**107** C3
Stanwell TW19 . . . .**148** A2
Willow Bsns Pk SE26 . . .**162** C1
Willow Cl BR2 . . . .**210** B4
Brentford TW8 . . . .**131** C6
Buckhurst Hill IG9 . . . . . .**21** D1
12 Catford SE6 . . . .**164** D3
Sidcup DA5 . . . .**169** B5
Willow Cotts
Carshalton CR4 . . . .**202** D2
Feltham TW13 . . . .**151** A1
Richmond TW9 . . . .**132** C6
Willowcourt Ave HA3 . . . .**43** B4
Willowcroft SE3 . . . .**142** D1
Willow Ct
Ashford TW16 . . . .**171** C3
5 Beckenham BR3 . . . .**185** C2
Brixton SW9 . . . .**138** C4
Chiswick W4 . . . .**133** C5
8 Dagenham RM8 . . . . .**58** D2
EC2 . . . .**243** A6
Edgware HA8 . . . .**26** A6
6 Finchley N12 . . . .**29** D6
Harrow HA3 . . . .**24** D2
Headstone HA2 . . . .**24** A1
Ilford IG1 . . . .**79** A3
Islington N7 . . . .**72** B3
Kingston u T KT3 . . . . . .**198** D6
8 London E11 . . . .**76** C6
Mitcham CR4 . . . .**202** C5

Willow Ct continued
40 Paddington W2 . . . . . .**91** C2
3 Streatham SW16 . . . .**160** B1
Thornton Heath CR7 . . . .**205** B4
Willow Ctr The CR4 . . . .**202** D3
Willow Dean HA5 . . . .**22** D1
Willowdene
Highgate N6 . . . .**48** D2
1 Peckham SE15 . . . . .**140** B4
5 SE15 . . . .**140** B5
Willow Dene WD23 . . . . . .**8** C4
Willowdene Cl TW2 . . . . .**152** A4
Willowdene Ct N20 . . . . . .**14** A4
Willow Dene Sch
SE18 . . . .**145** C4
Willow Dr EN5 . . . .**1** A1
Willow End
Northwood HA6 . . . .**22** A4
Surbiton KT6 . . . .**198** A1
Totteridge N20 . . . .**14** A4
Willow Farm La SW15 . . .**134** B2
Willowfields Ct SE18 . . . .**123** C1
Willowfield Sec Sch
E17 . . . .**52** D6
Willow Gdns
Heston TW5 . . . .**129** C4
Ruislip HA4 . . . .**61** D6
Willow Gn
Borehamwood WD6 . . . . .**11** B6
Grahame Pk NW9 . . . . . .**27** C2
Willow Gr BR7 . . . .**188** D4
Newham E13 . . . .**99** A5
Ruislip HA4 . . . .**39** D1
Willow Hall NW3 . . . .**70** B4
Willowhayne Dr KT12 . . .**194** B2
Willowhayne Gdns
KT4 . . . .**216** C4
Willow Ho TW14 . . . .**150** B6
17 Finchley N2 . . . .**30** B1
9 Maitland Pk NW3 . . . . .**70** D2
North Kensington W10 . . .**90** D3
Teddington TW11 . . . . . .**175** C3
Willow La
Mitcham CR4 . . . .**202** D3
Woolwich SE18 . . . .**122** C2
Willow Lo
6 Ashford TW16 . . . . . .**171** D3
Fulham SW6 . . . .**134** D4
New Barnet EN5 . . . .**14** A6
Putney SW15 . . . .**134** B2
Willow Lodge 10 SW8 . .**137** B2
Willow Manor SM1 . . . . .**217** B4
Willowmead Cl W5 . . . . . .**87** D2
Willowmere
Esher KT10 . . . .**212** A4
Ladywell SE13 . . . .**163** D6
Willow Mount CR0 . . . . . .**221** C5
Willow Pl SW1 . . .**115** C2 **259** B4
Willow Rd
Dagenham RM6 . . . .**59** A3
Ealing W5 . . . .**110** A4
Enfield EN1 . . . .**5** C3
Hampstead NW3 . . . .**70** B4
New Malden KT3 . . . . . .**199** A5
Wallington SM6 . . . .**219** B1
Willows Ave SM4 . . . . . .**201** D4
Willows Cl HA5 . . . .**22** C1
Willows Ct 3 SW19 . . . .**179** C3
Willows Sch The UB4 . . . .**84** D3
Willow St
Broadgate
EC2 . . . .**95** C3 **243** A6
Chingford E4 . . . .**20** B4
Willows Terr NW10 . . . . . .**89** D5
Willows The
Beckenham BR3 . . . . . .**185** C2
Claygate KT10 . . . .**212** C2
Loughton IG10 . . . .**21** D6
Wallend E12 . . . .**78** C1
Whetstone N20 . . . .**14** A1
Willowtree Cl UB10 . . . . . .**61** A5
Willow Tree Cl
Hayes UB4 . . . .**84** C3
Northolt UB5 . . . .**63** A2
10 Old Ford E3 . . . .**97** B6
Wandsworth SW18 . . . .**157** D3
Willow Tree Ct DA14 . . .**189** D5
5 Wembley HA0 . . . .**65** D3
Willow Tree La UB4 . . . . . .**84** C3
Willow Tree Prim Sch
UB5 . . . .**63** A2
Willowtree Way SW16 . . .**182** C2
Willow Tree Wlk BR1 . . .**187** B2
Willow Vale BR7 . . . .**188** D4
Shepherd's Bush W12 . . .**112** A5
Willow View SW19 . . . . .**180** B2
Willow Way Finchley N3 . .**29** D3
Forest Hill SE26 . . . . . .**162** C1
9 Shepherd's Bush
W11 . . . .**112** D6
Sunbury TW16 . . . .**194** A5
Twickenham TW2 . . . . . .**151** D2
Wembley HA0 . . . .**65** A5
West Ewell KT19 . . . . . .**215** B2
Willow Wlk
Bermondsey
SE1 . . . .**117** D2 **263** C4
Cheam SM1, SM3 . . . . .**217** B5
15 Finchley N2 . . . .**30** B1
Harringay N15 . . . .**50** D5
Locksbottom BR6 . . . . .**226** D5
Southgate N21 . . . .**16** B5
Walthamstow E17 . . . . . .**53** B4
Willow Wood Cres
SE25 . . . .**205** C3
Willridge Ct E11 . . . .**54** B2
Willrose Cres SE2 . . . . . .**124** B1
Willsbridge Ct 1
SE15 . . . .**139** D6

Wills Cres TW3 . . . .**151** D5
Wills Gr NW7 . . . .**28** B5
Will Thorne Pav The
E16 . . . .**100** A1
Wilman Gr E8 . . . .**74** A1
Wilmar Cl UB4 . . . .**83** B3
Wilmar Gdns BR4 . . . . . .**207** D1
Wilmcote Ho W2 . . . .**91** D2
Wilment Ct NW2 . . . .**68** C5
Wilmer Cl KT2 . . . .**176** B5
Wilmer Cres KT2 . . . .**176** B5
Wilmer Gdns 22 N1 . . . . . .**95** C6
Wilmer Ho 6 E3 . . . .**97** A5
Wilmer Lea Cl E15 . . . . . .**76** B1
Wilmer Pl N16 . . . .**73** D6
Wilmers Ct 5 NW10 . . . . .**89** B6
Wilmer Way N14 . . . .**31** D5
Wilmington Ave W4 . . . . .**133** B5
Wilmington Ct SW16 . . . .**182** A3
Wilmington Gdns IG11 . . .**79** D1
Wilmington Sq
WC1 . . . .**94** C4 **234** A1
Wilmington St WC1 . . . . .**234** A1
Wilmot Cl Finchley N2 . . . .**30** A1
SE15 . . . .**140** A5
Wilmot Ho 14 SM2 . . . . . .**218** A2
Wilmot Pl
Camden Town NW1 . . . . .**71** C1
Ealing W7 . . . .**108** C5
Wilmot Rd Leyton E10 . . . .**75** D6
Tottenham N17 . . . .**51** B6
Wallington SM5 . . . .**218** D3
Wilmot St E2 . . . .**96** B3
Wilmount St SE18 . . . . . .**122** D2
Wilna Rd SW18 . . . .**158** A4
Wilnett Ct 4 RM6 . . . .**58** B2
Wilnett Villas 3 RM6 . . . .**58** B2
Wilsham St
W11 . . . .**113** A5 **244** A4
Wilshaw Cl NW4 . . . .**46** A6
Wilshaw Ho 10 SE8 . . . .**141** C5
Wilshaw St SE14 . . . . . .**141** C4
Wilsmere Dr
Harrow HA3 . . . .**24** C3
Northolt UB5 . . . .**63** A3
Wilson Ave CR4 . . . .**180** C2
Wembley HA9 . . . .**44** B2
Wilson Cl Croydon CR2 . .**221** B3
Wembley HA9 . . . .**44** B2
9 SE28 . . . .**123** A3
Wilson Dr Iver **44** B2
Wilson Gdns HA1 . . . .**42** A2
Wilson Gr SE16 . . . .**118** B4
Wilson Ho
39 Clapham SW8 . . . . .**137** D3
2 SE7 . . . .**143** C6
South Hampstead NW6 . . .**70** A1
Wilson Rd
Camberwell SE5 . . . . . .**139** C4
Chessington KT9 . . . . . .**214** B2
Newham E6 . . . .**99** C4
Redbridge IG1 . . . .**56** B2
Wilson's Ave 4 N17 . . . . . .**33** D1
Wilson's Pl E14 . . . .**97** B1
Wilson's Rd W6 . . . .**112** D1
Wilson's Sch SM6 . . . . . .**220** A4
Wilson St
Broadgate
EC2 . . . .**95** B2 **242** D4
Southgate N21 . . . .**16** C4
Walthamstow E17 . . . . . .**54** A4
Wilstone Ct UB4 . . . .**85** A3
Wiltern Ct NW2 . . . .**69** A2
Wilthorne Gdns RM10 . . . .**81** D1
Wilton Ave W4 . . . .**111** C1
Wilton Cres
Merton SW19 . . . .**179** B2
SW1 . . . .**115** A4 **248** A1
Wilton Ct
3 Edgware HA8 . . . .**26** D5
Muswell Hill N10 . . . .**31** A1
4 Richmond TW10 . . . .**154** A6
7 Stepney E1 . . . .**96** B1
7 Woodford IG8 . . . .**37** A4
Wilton Est E8 . . . .**74** A2
Wilton Gdns
East Molesey KT8 . . . . .**195** C6
Walton-on-T KT12 . . . . .**194** D1
Wilton Gr
Merton SW19 . . . .**179** B2
New Malden KT3 . . . . . .**199** D3
Wilton Ho
8 Camberwell SE22 . . .**139** C2
Chislehurst BR7 . . . . . .**189** B2
Ealing W13 . . . .**109** B6
Wilton Mews
SW1 . . . .**115** A3 **258** B6
Wilton Par TW13 . . . .**150** B2
Wilton Pl
2 Beckenham BR3 . . . .**208** A6
1 Harrow HA1 . . . .**42** D3
SW1 . . . .**115** A4 **248** A1
Wilton Rd
Abbey Wood SE2 . . . . . .**124** C2
Cockfosters EN4 . . . .**2** D1
Hounslow TW4 . . . .**128** D2
Mitcham SW19 . . . .**180** C3
Muswell Hill N10 . . . .**31** A1
Westminster
SW1 . . . .**115** C2 **259** A4
Wilton Row SW1 . . . .**248** A1
Wilton Sq N1 . . . .**95** B6 **235** C6
Wilton St SW1 . .**115** B3 **258** C6
Wilton Terr SW1 . . . .**258** A6
Wilton Villas N1 . . . .**235** C5
Wilton Way E8 . . . .**74** A2
Wiltshire Cl
Edgware NW7 . . . .**27** D5
SW3 . . . .**257** C3
Wiltshire Ct
Barking IG11 . . . .**79** A2

Wiltshire Ct continued
2 Finsbury Pk N4 . . . . . .**50** B1
Wiltshire Gdns
Stoke Newington N4 . . . .**51** A3
Twickenham TW2 . . . . . .**152** A3
Wiltshire La Pinner HA5 . .**40** A5
Ruislip HA4 . . . .**39** D6
Wiltshire Rd
Brixton SW9 . . . .**138** C2
Thornton Heath CR7 . . . .**204** C6
Wiltshire Row
N1 . . . .**95** B6 **235** D5
Wilverley Cres KT3 . . . . .**199** C3
Wimbart Rd SW2 . . . .**160** B4
WIMBLEDON **179** B4
Wimbledon Bridge
SW19 . . . .**179** B4
Wimbledon Central
SW19 . . . .**179** B4
Wimbledon Chase Prim
Sch SW20 . . . .**179** A2
Wimbledon Chase Sta
SW20 . . . .**179** A1
Wimbledon Cl 2
SW20 . . . .**178** D3
Wimbledon Coll
SW19 . . . .**178** D3
Wimbledon Common* . . .**178** B6
Wimbledon Common Prep
Sch SW19 . . . .**178** D3
Wimbledon High Sch
SW19 . . . .**179** A4
Wimbledon Hill Rd
SW19 . . . .**179** B4
Wimbledon Lawn Tennis
Mus* SW19 . . . .**157** A1
Wimbledon Park Ct
SW19 . . . .**157** B3
Wimbledon Park
Montessori Sch
SW18 . . . .**157** C2
Wimbledon Park Prim Sch
SW19 . . . .**157** D2
Wimbledon Park Rd SW18,
SW19 . . . .**157** B3
Wimbledon Park Side
SW19 . . . .**156** D3
Wimbledon Park Sta
SW19 . . . .**157** C1
Wimbledon Rd SW17 . . . .**180** A6
Wimbledon Sch of Art
SW19 . . . .**179** A2
Wimbledon Sch of Art
Annexe SW19 . . . . . .**179** C3
Wimbledon Sta SW19 . . .**179** B4
Wimbledon Stad
SW17 . . . .**180** A6
Wimbledon Stadium Bsns
Ctr SW17 . . . .**157** D1
Wimbledon Windmill
Mus* SW19 . . . .**156** C1
Wimbolt St E2 . . . .**96** A4
Wimborne 2 DA14 . . . . . .**190** B6
Wimborne Ave
Hayes UB4 . . . .**84** B1
Southall UB2 . . . .**107** C2
St Paul's Cray BR5, BR7 . .**211** D5
Wimborne Cl
Buckhurst Hill IG9 . . . . . .**21** C2
Lewisham SE12 . . . .**164** D6
North Cheam KT4 . . . . . .**200** C1
Wimborne Ct 1 UB5 . . . . .**63** C2
Wimborne Dr
Pinner HA5 . . . .**41** A2
Queensbury NW9 . . . . . .**44** C6
Wimborne Gdns W13 . . . . .**87** B2
Wimborne Ho
Canning Town E16 . . . . .**120** D6
Croydon CR0 . . . .**206** C4
Marylebone NW1 . . . . . .**237** B6
South Lambeth SW8 . . . .**270** D3
Upper Tooting SW12 . . . .**159** C1
Wimborne Rd
Edmonton N9 . . . .**18** A2
Tottenham N17 . . . .**33** C1
Wimborne Way BR3 . . . . .**207** A3
Wimbourne Ct
Mitcham SW19 . . . .**180** B3
N1 . . . .**235** C4
South Croydon CR2 . . . .**221** C2
Wimbourne St
N1 . . . .**95** B5 **235** C4
Wimbush Ho 3 N12 . . . . . .**29** D5
Wimpole Cl
Bromley BR2 . . . .**209** C5
1 Kingston u T KT1 . . . .**176** C1
Wimpole Mews
W1 . . . .**93** B2 **238** C3
Wimpole St W1 . .**93** B1 **238** C2
Wimshurst Cl CR0 . . . . . .**204** A1
Winans Wlk SW9 . . . .**138** C3
Winant Ho 19 E14 . . . . . .**119** D6
Wincanton Cres UB5 . . . . .**63** C3
Wincanton Ct 2 N11 . . . . . .**31** A4
Wincanton Gdns IG6 . . . . .**56** D6
Wincanton Rd SW18 . . . .**157** B4
Winchcombe Rd SM5 . . . .**202** C1
Winchcomb Gdns SE9 . . .**143** D2
Winchelsea Ave DA7 . . . .**147** B5
Winchelsea Cl SW15 . . . .**156** C6
Winchelsea Ho 16
SE16 . . . .**118** C4
Winchelsea Rd
Becontree NW10 . . . .**89** B6
Forest Gate E7 . . . .**77** A4
Tottenham N17 . . . .**51** C6
Winchelsey Rise CR2 . . . .**221** D2
Winchendon Rd
Fulham SW6 . .**135** B4 **264** D2

Winchendon Rd continued
Teddington TW11,
TW12 . . . .**174** B6
Winchester Ave
Brondesbury NW6 . . . . . .**69** A1
Heston TW5 . . . .**129** B6
Queensbury NW9 . . . . . .**44** C6
Winchester Cl
Beckenham BR2 . . . . . .**208** D6
Enfield EN1 . . . .**17** C6
Kingston u T KT2 . . . . . .**176** D3
11 Newham E6 . . . . . .**100** B1
SE17 . . . .**261** D3
Winchester Ct
15 Belvedere DA17 . . . .**125** C1
1 Higham Hill E17 . . . . .**35** A2
Richmond TW9 . . . .**132** B2
W8 . . . .**245** C2
Winchester Dr HA5 . . . . . .**40** D4
Winchester Ho
5 Barking IG11 . . . .**80** A1
Bayswater W2 . . . .**236** A1
Chelsea SW3 . . . .**266** D5
1 Greenwich SE18 . . . .**143** D5
24 Tower Hamlets E3 . . .**97** B4
Twickenham TW1 . . . . . .**153** C4
Winchester Mews
KT4 . . . .**216** D6
Winchester Pal* SW1 . . .**252** C4
Winchester Pk BR2 . . . . .**208** D6
Winchester Pl
6 Dalston E8 . . . .**73** D3
Highgate N6 . . . .**49** B1
Winchester Rd
Beckenham BR2 . . . . . .**208** D6
Bexley DA7 . . . .**146** D3
Chingford E4 . . . .**36** A3
Edmonton N9 . . . .**18** A3
Harlington UB3 . . . .**127** C5
Harrow HA3 . . . .**44** A5
Highgate N6 . . . .**49** B1
Ilford IG1 . . . .**79** B5
Northwood HA6 . . . .**40** A6
South Hampstead NW3 . . .**70** B1
St Margarets TW1 . . . . .**153** B5
Twickenham TW13 . . . . .**151** B1
Walton-on-T KT12 . . . . .**194** A1
Winchester Sq SE1 . . . . .**252** C4
Winchester St
Acton W3 . . . .**111** A4
SW1 . . . .**115** B1 **258** D2
Winchester Wlk SE1 . . . .**252** C4
Winchet Wlk CR0 . . . . . .**206** C3
Winchfield Cl HA3 . . . .**43** C3
Winchfield Ho SW15 . . . .**155** D5
Winchfield Rd SE26 . . . . .**185** A5
Winch Ho
Isle of Dogs E14 . . . . . .**119** D3
SW10 . . . .**266** B4
Winchilsea Cres KT8 . . . .**174** A1
Winchilsea Ho NW8 . . . . .**229** D1
WINCHMORE HILL **16** A4
Winchmore Hill Rd N14,
N21 . . . .**16** A4
Winchmore Hill Sta
N21 . . . .**16** B2
Winchmore Sch N21 . . . . .**17** A2
Winchmore Villas N21 . . . .**16** A4
Winchstone Cl TW17 . . . .**192** B5
Winckley Cl HA3 . . . .**44** B4
Wincott St
SE11 . . . .**116** C2 **261** B3
Wincrofts Dr SE9 . . . . . .**145** B1
Windall Cl SE20 . . . .**184** C4
Windborough Rd SM5 . . .**219** A1
Windcott Ct HA3 . . . .**43** C2
Windermere NW1 . . . . . .**231** D2
12 Putney SW15 . . . . .**156** D5
Windermere Ave
Golders Green N3 . . . . . .**47** C6
Kensal Rise NW6 . . . . . .**91** A6
Merton SW19 . . . .**201** D6
Ruislip HA4 . . . .**40** D2
Wembley HA9 . . . .**43** C1
Windermere Ct BR6 . . . . .**226** D5
East Bedfont TW14 . . . . .**149** D3
Stanwell TW19 . . . .**148** A2
Windermere Ct
Barnes SW13 . . . .**133** D6
Barnet EN5 . . . .**1** D1
Carshalton SM5 . . . .**219** A5
Wembley HA9 . . . .**43** C1
Windermere Gdns IG4 . . . .**56** A4
Windermere Gr HA9 . . . . . .**43** C1
Windermere Hall HA8 . . . . .**26** B5
Windermere Ho
Isleworth TW1 . . . .**152** D6
Tower Hamlets E3 . . . . . .**97** B3
Windermere Point 3
SE15 . . . .**140** C5
Windermere Rd
Brentford W5 . . . .**109** C3
Croydon CR0 . . . .**205** D1
Kingston u T SW15 . . . .**177** C5
Mitcham SW16 . . . .**181** D1
Muswell Hill N10 . . . .**31** B2
Southall UB1 . . . .**85** B2
Upper Holloway N19 . . . . .**71** C6
West Wickham BR4 . . . .**224** C6
Windermere Way UB7 . . .**104** B5
Winders Rd SW11 . . . . . .**136** C3
Windfield Cl SE26 . . . . . .**184** D6
Windham Rd TW9 . . . . . .**132** B2
Winding Way RM8 . . . .**80** C5
Windlass Pl SE8 . . . .**119** A2
Windlesham Gr SW19 . . .**156** D3
Windley Cl SE23 . . . .**162** C2
Windmill WC1 . . . .**240** C4
Windmill Alley 7 W4 . . . .**111** C2
Windmill Ave UB2 . . . . . .**108** A4

Windmill Bridge Ho 1
CR0 . . . .**205** C1
Windmill Bsns Ctr
UB2 . . . .**108** A5
Windmill Bsns Village
TW16 . . . .**171** C2
Windmill Cl
Ashford TW16 . . . .**171** C3
12 Bermondsey SE1 . . .**118** C2
Kingston u T KT6 . . . . . .**197** C2
4 Lewisham SE13 . . . . .**142** A3
Windmill Ct
Brentford W5 . . . .**109** C2
Brondesbury NW2 . . . . . .**69** A2
Bushey WD23 . . . .**8** B3
Windmill Dr BR2 . . . .**225** C4
Clapham SW4 . . . .**159** B6
Cricklewood NW2 . . . . . .**69** A5
Windmill Gdns
Brixton SW2 . . . .**160** B5
Enfield EN2 . . . .**4** C2
Windmill Gr CR0 . . . .**205** A3
Windmill Hill Enfield EN2 . . .**5** A2
1 Hampstead NW3 . . . . .**70** A4
Hampstead NW3 . . . .**70** A5
Ruislip HA4 . . . .**39** D1
Windmill Ho
4 Millwall E14 . . . .**119** C2
SE1 . . . .**251** B3
Windmill La
Barnet Gate EN5 . . . .**11** D5
Bushey WD23 . . . .**8** C3
Greenford UB6 . . . .**86** A2
Isleworth TW7, UB2,
W7 . . . .**108** C2
Southall UB2 . . . .**108** A4
Stratford E15 . . . .**76** B2
Thames Ditton KT7 . . . .**197** B2
Windmill Lo TW16 . . . . . .**171** C2
Windmill Pas 10 W4 . . . .**111** C2
Windmill Pl UB1 . . . .**108** A5
Windmill Rd
Brentford TW8, W5 . . . .**109** C1
Charlton TW16 . . . .**171** C2
Chiswick W4 . . . .**111** C2
Edmonton N18 . . . .**33** B6
Hampton TW12 . . . .**174** A5
Mitcham CR4 . . . .**203** C5
Roehampton SW19 . . . .**156** B1
Thornton Heath CR0 . . . .**205** A2
Wandsworth SW18 . . . .**158** B5
Windmill Rd W TW16 . . . .**171** C1
Windmill Rise KT2 . . . . . .**176** D3
Windmill Row SE11 . . . . .**261** A1
Windmill St
Bloomsbury
W1 . . . .**93** D2 **239** C3
Bushey WD23 . . . .**8** C3
Windmill Terr TW17 . . . .**193** C2
Windmill Trad Est
CR4 . . . .**203** C5
Windmill Way HA4 . . . .**39** D1
Windmill Wlk SE1 . . . . . .**251** B2
Windmore Cl HA0 . . . .**65** A3
Windrose Cl SE16 . . . . . .**118** D4
Windrush NW4 . . . .**199** A5
Windrush Cl
Battersea SW11 . . . . . .**136** B1
Chiswick W4 . . . .**133** A5
Ickenham UB10 . . . .**60** B4
Windrush Ho NW8 . . . . . .**236** D4
Windrush La SE23 . . . . . .**162** D1
Windrush Prim Sch
SE28 . . . .**124** B5
Windrush Rd NW10 . . . . . .**89** B6
Windsock Cl 1 SE16 . . . .**119** B2
Windsor Ave
Cheam SM3 . . . .**217** A5
East Molesey KT8 . . . . .**195** C6
Edgware HA8 . . . .**10** C1
Higham Hill E17 . . . .**35** A1
Hillingdon UB10 . . . .**60** D1
Merton SW19 . . . .**180** A2
New Malden KT3 . . . . . .**199** A4
Windsor Cl
Brentford TW8 . . . .**131** B6
Chislehurst BR7 . . . . . .**188** D5
Harrow HA2 . . . .**63** C5
Hendon N3 . . . .**29** A1
Pinner HA6 . . . .**22** A1
West Norwood SE27 . . . .**183** A6
Windsor Cres
Harrow HA2 . . . .**63** C5
Wembley HA9 . . . .**66** D5
Windsor Ct
Battersea SW11 . . . . . .**136** B3
Bayswater W2 . . . .**245** C6
Bickley BR1 . . . .**210** A6
Bushey WD23 . . . .**8** A4
Chelsea SW3 . . . .**257** B2
2 Clapham SW4 . . . . .**137** C1
Edgware HA8 . . . .**26** B3
Friern Barnet N11 . . . . . .**30** D5
Fulham SW6 . . . .**135** A2
Osidge N14 . . . .**15** C4
20 Rotherhithe SE16 . . .**118** D5
17 Sidcup DA14 . . . . . .**168** A1
South Norwood SE19 . . .**183** C2
Sunbury TW16 . . . .**172** A3
Temple Fortune NW11 . . .**47** A3
Walthamstow E17 . . . . . .**53** B6
4 Wandsworth SW18 . .**157** C6
West Hampstead NW3 . . .**69** C4
5 West Wickham BR4 . .**207** D1
Windsor Ctr The SE27 . .**183** A6
Windsor Dr EN4 . . . .**14** D1
Windsor Gdns
Hayes UB3 . . . .**105** B3
Paddington W9 . . . .**91** C3
Wallington CR0 . . . .**220** A6

Windsor Gr SE27 183 A6
Windsor Hall 11 E16 121 B5
Windsor Ho
4 Acton Green W4 111 A1
Brondesbury NW2 69 A2
4 Globe Town E2 96 D4
2 Hendon NW4 28 D1
7 Northolt UB5 63 C2
Queensbury NW9 44 C5
Regent's Pk NW1 231 D2
Shoreditch N1 235 B4
Stanmore HA7 25 B5
Stoke Newington N4 51 A1
Windsor Lo KT3 199 A4
Windsor Mews
Catford SE6 164 A3
Forest Hill SE23 163 A3
Windsor Park Rd UB3 127 D5
Windsor Pk SW19 180 A2
Windsor Pl SW1 259 B4
Windsor Rd
Ashford TW16 172 A4
Barnet EN5 12 D5
Chingford E4 35 D6
Cranford TW4, TW5 128 C3
DA6 147 A1
Dagenham RM8 81 A5
Ealing W5 110 A6
Forest Gate E7 77 C3
Harrow HA3 24 B2
Hendon N3 29 A1
Ilford IG1 79 A4
Kingston u T KT2 176 A3
Leyton E10 75 D6
Palmers Green N13 16 C1
Richmond TW9 132 B3
Southall UB2 107 B3
South Norwood CR7 182 D1
Teddington TW11 174 B5
Tottenham N17 34 A1
Upper Holloway N7 72 A5
Wanstead E11 77 A6
Willesden NW2 68 B2
Worcester Pk KT4 216 A6
Windsor St N1 94 D6 234 D6
Windsor Terr
N1 95 A4 235 B2
Windsor Way
W14 113 A2 254 A4
Windsor Wharf E9 75 B3
Windsor Wlk
Camberwell SE5 139 B3
Walton-on-T KT12 194 D1
Windspoint Dr SE15 140 B6
Windus Rd N16 51 D1
Windus Wlk N16 51 D1
Windy Ridge BR1 188 A2
Windy Ridge Cl SW19 178 D5
Wine Cl E1 118 C6
Wine Office Ct EC4 241 B2
Winery La KT1 198 B6
Winey Cl KT9 213 C1
Winfield Ho 3 SW11 136 B3
Winford Ct 16 SE15 140 A4
Winford Ho E3 75 B1
Winford Par 6 UB1 85 D1
Winforton St SE10 142 A4
Winfrith Rd SW18 158 A3
Wingate Cres CR0 204 A3
Wingate Ho
26 Bromley E3 97 D4
8 Stoke Newington N16 73 B4
Wingate Rd
Hammersmith W6 112 B3
Ilford IG1 78 D3
Sidcup DA14 190 C4
Wingate Trad Est 11
N17 33 D3
Wingfield Ct
5 Blackwall E14 120 B6
Sidcup DA15 167 D3
Wingfield Ho
Paddington NW6 91 D5
16 Spitalfields E2 95 D4
Wingfield Mews SE15 140 A2
Wingfield Prim Sch
SE3 143 B2
Wingfield Rd
Kingston u T KT2 176 C4
Leyton E15 76 C4
Walthamstow E17 53 D4
Wingfield St SE15 140 A2
Wingfield Way HA4 62 B2
Wingford Rd SW2 160 A5
Wingham 3 NW5 71 A2
Wingham Ho 3 SE26 184 B5
Wingmore Rd SE24 139 A2
Wingrad Ho 18 E1 96 C2
Wingrave SE17 262 C3
Wingrave Rd W6 134 C6
Wingreen 15 NW8 91 D6
Wingrove Ho E4 19 D4
Wingrove Rd SE6 164 C2
Wings Cl SM1 217 C4
Winicotte Ho W2 236 D4
Winifred Cl EN5 11 D5
Winifrede Paul Ho 7
NW5 71 B4
Winifred Pl N12 30 A5
Winifred Rd
Dagenham RM8 59 A1
Hampton TW12 173 C6
Merton SW19 179 C2
Winifred St E16 122 B5
Winifred Terr EN1 17 D4
Winkfield Rd
Newham E13 99 B5
Wood Green N22 32 C2
Winkley Ct
Cranley Gdns N10 49 B5
Winkley Ct *continued*
Harrow HA2 63 C5
Winkley St 6 E2 96 B5
Winkworth Cotts 14 E1 96 C3
Winlaton Rd BR1 186 B6
Winmill Rd RM8 81 B5
Winn Bridge Cl IG8 37 D2
Winn Common Rd
SE18 145 C6
Winnett St W1 249 C6
Winningales Ct IG5 56 A6
Winnings Wlk UB5 63 A6
Winnington Cl N2 48 B3
Winnington Ho
19 Kensal Town W10 91 A3
8 SE5 139 A5
Winnington Rd
Enfield EN3 6 C6
Hampstead Garden Suburb
N2 48 B3
Winnipeg Dr 3 BR6 227 D2
Winnipeg Ho UB4 84 B3
Winn Rd SE12 165 B3
Winns Ave E17 53 B6
Winns Mews N15 51 C5
Winns Prim Sch The
E17 35 B1
Winns Terr E17 53 C6
Winsbeach E17 36 B1
Winscombe Cres W5 87 D3
Winscombe Ct W5 87 D3
Winscombe St N19 71 B6
Winscombe Way HA7 25 A5
Winsford Rd SE6 163 B1
Winsford Terr N18 33 B5
Winsham Gr SW11 159 A6
Winsham Ho NW1 232 D2
Winslade Ho 4 E5 74 B6
Winslade Rd SW2 160 A6
Winslade Way SE6 163 D4
Winsland Mews W2 236 C2
Winsland St W2 92 B1 236 C2
Winsley St W1 239 B2
Winslow SE17 263 A1
Winslow Cl
2 Neasden NW10 67 C5
Pinner HA5 40 B3
Winslow Gr E4 20 C2
Winslow Rd W6 134 C6
Winslow Way TW13 151 A1
Winsmoor Ct EN2 4 D2
Winsor Prim Sch E6 100 C1
Winsor Terr E6 100 C2
Winstanley Rd SW11 136 B2
Winston Ave NW9 45 C2
Winston Cl Harrow HA3 24 D4
Romford RM7 59 D5
Winston Ct 7 BR1 187 B2
Harrow HA3 23 D3
Winston Ho WC1 239 D6
Winston Rd N16 73 B4
Winston Way IG1 79 A5
Winston Wlk 2 W4 111 B2
Winter Ave E6 100 A6
Winterberry Ct 22 N12 29 D6
Winterborne Ave BR6 227 B5
Winterbourne Ho W11 244 A5
Winterbourne Inf Sch
CR7 204 C5
Winterbourne Jun Boys'
Sch CR7 204 C5
Winterbourne Jun Girls'
Sch CR7 204 C5
Winterbourne Rd
Dagenham RM8 80 C6
Forest Hill SE6 163 B3
Thornton Heath CR7 204 C5
Winter Box Wlk TW10 154 B6
Winterbrook Rd SE24 161 A5
Winterburn Cl N11 31 A4
Winterfold Cl SW19 157 A2
Wintergreen Cl 7 E6 100 A2
Winterleys 7 NW6 91 B5
Winter Lo 17 SE16 118 A1
Winter's Ct E4 19 D1
Winterslow Ho 20 SE5 139 A3
Winters Rd KT7 197 B2
Winterstoke Gdns NW7 28 A5
Winterstoke Rd SE6 163 B3
Winterton Ct KT1 175 D2
Winterton Ho 15 E1 96 C1
Winterton Pl SW10 266 B6
Winterwell Rd SW2 160 A6
Winthorpe Rd SW15 135 A1
Winthrop Ho 10 W12 112 B6
Winthrop St E1 96 B2
Winthrop Wlk HA9 66 A5
Winton Ave N11 31 C3
Winton Cl N9 18 D4
Winton Ct 15 KT6 197 D2
Winton Gdns HA8 26 B3
Winton Prim Sch
N1 94 B5 233 C3
Winton Rd BR6 226 D4
Winton Way SW16 182 C5
Wintour Ho HA9 65 D6
Wirrall Ho 15 SE26 162 A1
Wirral Wood Cl BR7 188 C4
Wisbeach Rd CR0 205 B4
Wisbech 5 N4 50 B1
Wisden Ho SW8 270 D5
Wisdom Ct 7 TW7 131 A2
Wisdons Cl RM7, RM9 59 D1
Wise La NW7 28 A4
Wiseman Ct 12 SE19 183 C5
Wiseman Rd E10 75 C6
Wise Rd E15 98 B6
Wiseton Rd SW17 158 D3
Wishart Rd SE3 143 D3
Wishaw Wlk N13 32 A4
Wisley Ho SW1 259 C2
Wisley Rd
Balham SW11 159 A6
St Paul's Cray BR5 190 B3
Wistaria Cl BR6 226 D6
Wisteria Cl
Edgware NW7 27 D4
Ilford IG1 78 D3
Wisteria Ho SE4 141 A2
Wisteria Rd SE13 142 B1
Wistow Ho 14 E2 96 A6
Witanhurst La N6 49 A1
Witan St E2 96 B4
Witchwood Ho 10
SW9 138 C2
Witcombe Point 14
SE15 140 A4
Witham Ct Leyton E10 75 D5
Upper Tooting SW17 158 D1
Witham Ho 33 SE5 139 A3
Witham Rd
Dagenham RM10 81 C3
Ealing W13 109 B5
Hounslow TW7 130 B4
Penge SE20 206 C6
Witherby Cl CR0 221 C4
Witherington Rd N5 72 C3
Withers Cl KT9 213 C2
Withers Mead NW9 27 D2
Withers Pl EC1 242 B6
Witherston Way SE9 166 C1
Withington Rd N2 30 C2
Withycombe Rd SW19 156 D4
Withy Ho 4 E1 96 D3
Withy La HA4 39 A4
Withy Mead E4 20 B1
Witley Cres CR0 224 A2
Witley Ct Southall UB2 107 B2
WC1 240 A5
Witley Gdns UB2 107 B2
Witley Ho 2 SW2 160 B4
Witley Ind Est UB2 107 B2
Witley Point 8 SW15 156 B3
Witley Rd N19 71 C6
Witney Cl
Ickenham UB10 60 B4
Pinner HA5 23 B4
Witney Path SE23 162 D1
Wittenham Way E4 20 B1
Witten Ho KT3 199 B1
Wittering Cl KT2 175 D5
Wittering Ho 9 SW11 136 D3
Wittersham Rd BR1 186 D5
Witts Ho KT2 198 B6
Wivenhoe Cl SE15 140 B2
Wivenhoe Ct TW4 129 B1
Wivenhoe Rd IG11 102 B5
Wiverton Rd SE26 184 C5
Wixom Ho SE9 143 C1
Wix Prim Sch SW4 137 B1
Wix Rd RM9 102 D6
Wix's La SW4 137 B1
Woburn W13 87 B2
Woburn Cl Bushey WD23 8 A5
SE28 102 D1
Wimbledon SW19 180 A4
Woburn Ct
32 Bermondsey SE16 118 B1
Croydon CR0 205 A1
1 DA6 147 A1
Richmond TW9 132 B2
4 Woodford E18 37 A1
Woburn Pl WC1 94 A3 240 A5
Woburn Rd
Carshalton SM5 202 C1
Croydon CR0 205 A1
Woburn Sq
WC1 93 D3 239 D5
Woburn Twr 14 UB5 84 D4
Woburn Wlk WC1 232 D1
Wodeham Gdns 1 E1 96 B2
Wodehouse Ave SE15 139 D4
Wodehouse Ct 10 W3 111 A3
Woffington Cl KT1,
KT8 175 C2
Woking Cl SW15 133 D1
Wolcot Ho NW1 232 B3
Woldham Pl BR2 209 C5
Woldham Rd BR2 209 C5
Wolds Dr BR6 226 C4
Wolfe Cl Hayes BR2 209 A3
Yeading UB4 84 B4
Wolfe Cres
Greenwich SE7 121 D1
34 Rotherhithe SE16 118 D4
Wolfe Ho 19 W12 112 B6
Wolferton Rd E12 78 B4
Wolffe Gdns 2 E15 76 D2
Wolf Fields Prim Sch
UB2 107 B2
Wolfington Rd SE27 182 D6
Wolfram Cl SE13 164 C6
Wolfson Ct
4 Barnet EN4 14 D3
Golders Green NW11 47 A2
SE1 253 D2
Wolfson Hillel Prim Sch
N14 15 D5
Wolftencroft Cl SW11 136 B2
Wollaston Cl SE1 262 A4
Wollotan Ho N1 234 B4
Wolmer Cl HA8 26 D6
Wolmer Gdns HA8 10 C1
Wolmer Rd HA8 26 D6
Wolseley Ave SW18,
SW19 157 C2
Wolseley Gdns W4 132 D6
Wolseley Rd Acton W4 111 A2
Carshalton CR4 203 A2
Harrow HA3 42 C6
Wolseley Rd *continued*
Hornsey N8 49 D4
Upton E7 77 B1
Wood Green N22 32 B2
Wolseley St
SE1 117 D4 253 D1
Wolsey Ave
Thames Ditton KT7 196 D4
Wallend E6 100 C4
Walthamstow E17 53 B6
Wolsey Cl
Isleworth TW3 130 A1
Kingston u T KT2 176 D2
Southall UB2 108 A3
Wimbledon SW20 178 B3
Worcester Pk KT19,
KT4 216 A4
Wolsey Cres SM4 201 B2
Wolsey Ct Bromley BR1 186 D3
SE9 166 B5
South Hampstead NW6 70 A1
Wolsey Dr
Kingston u T KT2 176 A4
Walton-on-T KT12 194 D1
Wolsey Gr HA8 27 B3
Wolsey Ho
2 Hampton TW12 173 D4
3 Kentish Town NW5 71 D2
Wolsey Inf Sch CR0 224 A1
Wolsey Jun Sch CR0 224 A1
Wolsey Mews
Kentish Town NW5 71 C2
Orpington BR6 227 D3
Wolsey Rd
Ashford TW15 170 B6
East Molesey KT8 196 B5
Enfield EN1 6 B3
Hampton TW12 174 A4
Stoke Newington N1 73 B3
Sunbury Comm TW16 171 D4
Wolsey St E1 96 C2
Wolsey Way KT9 214 C3
Wolstenholme HA7 25 B5
Wolstonbury N12 29 C5
Wolvercote Rd SE2 124 D4
Wolverley St E2 96 B4
Wolverton SE17 263 A2
Wolverton Ave KT2 176 C2
Wolverton Gdns
Brook Green W6 112 D2
Ealing W5 110 B6
Wolverton Mans W5 110 B5
Wolverton Rd HA7 25 B3
Wolverton Way N14 15 C6
Wolves La N22 32 C4
Womersley Rd N4, N8 50 B3
Wonford Cl KT2, KT3 177 C2
Wontner Cl 5 N1 73 A1
Wontner Rd SW12,
SW17 158 D2
Wooburn Cl UB8 82 D3
Wooburn Ct N14 15 D3
Woodall Cl
Chessington KT9 213 D2
15 Poplar E14 119 D6
Woodall Ho TW7 130 D2
Woodall Rd EN3 18 D5
Woodbank Rd BR1 164 D1
Woodbastwick Rd
SE26 185 A5
Woodberry Ave
Edmonton N21 16 D2
Harrow HA2 42 A5
Woodberry Cl
Ashford TW16 172 A4
Mill Hill NW7 28 D3
Woodberry Cres N10 49 B6
Woodberry Down N4 51 A2
Woodberry Down Com
Prim Sch N4 51 A2
Woodberry Gdns N12 30 A4
Woodberry Gr
Finchley N12 30 A4
Stoke Newington N4 51 A2
Woodberry View N6 49 A3
Woodberry Way
Chingford E4 20 A4
Finchley N12 30 A4
Woodbine Cl TW2 152 B2
Woodbine Gr Enfield EN2 5 B5
Penge SE20 184 B3
Woodbine La KT4 216 C5
Woodbine Pl E11 55 A3
Woodbine Rd DA15 167 C3
Woodbines Ave KT1 197 D6
Woodbine Terr E9 74 C2
Woodborough Rd
SW15 134 B1
Woodbourne Ave
SW16 159 D1
Woodbourne Cl SW16 160 A1
Woodbourne Dr KT10 212 D2
Woodbourne Gdns
SM6 219 B1
Woodbridge Cl
4 Dollis Hill NW2 68 A5
10 Finsbury Pk N7 72 B6
Woodbridge Ct
Forest Gate E7 77 D3
Stoke Newington N16 73 B5
Woodbridge High Sch
IG8 37 B3
Woodbridge Ho E11 54 D1
Woodbridge Rd IG11 79 D3
Woodbridge St
EC1 94 D3 241 C6
Woodbrook Rd SE2 146 B6
Woodbrook Sch BR3 185 B2
Woodburn Cl NW4 46 D4
Woodbury Cl
Croydon CR0 221 D6
Wanstead E11 55 B5
Woodbury Ct 1 W13 87 B3
Woodbury Gdns
Bromley SE12 187 B6
Eltham SE12 165 B1
Woodbury Ho 4 SE26 162 B1
Woodbury Park Rd
W13 87 B3
Woodbury Rd E17 53 D5
Woodbury St SW17 180 C5
Woodchester Sq W2 91 D2
Woodchurch Cl DA14 167 B1
Woodchurch Dr BR1 187 D3
Woodchurch Ho 15
SW9 138 C4
Woodchurch Rd NW6 69 D1
Wood Cl
Bethnal Green E2 96 A3
Harrow HA1 42 B2
Kingsbury NW9 45 B2
Woodclyffe Dr BR7 188 C1
Woodcock Ct HA3 44 A2
Woodcock Dell Ave
HA3 43 D2
Woodcock Hill HA3 43 C3
Woodcock Ho 4 E14 97 C2
Woodcocks E16 99 D2
Woodcombe Cres
SE23 162 C3
Woodcote Ave
Mill Hill NW7 28 C4
Thornton Heath CR7 204 D5
Wallington SM6 219 B1
Woodcote Cl Enfield N9 18 C5
Kingston u T KT2 176 B5
Woodcote Ct 14 SM6 219 B2
Woodcote Dr BR6 211 B2
Woodcote Ho 4 SE8 141 B6
Woodcote Mews
Loughton IG10 21 D4
Wallington SM6 219 B2
Woodcote Pl 1 SE27 182 D5
Woodcote Rd
Wallington SM6 219 C1
Wanstead E11 55 A2
Woodcott Ho 1
SW15 156 A4
Woodcroft SE9 166 B1
South Croydon CR0 221 C5
Southgate N21 16 C3
17 Stanmore HA7 25 C5
Wembley UB6 65 A2
Woodcroft Ave
Edgware NW7 27 C4
Stanmore HA7 25 A2
Woodcroft Cres UB10 82 D6
Woodcroft Mews SE8 119 A2
Woodcroft Prim Sch
HA8 27 C3
Woodcroft Rd CR7 204 D3
Wood Dene 6 SE15 140 B4
Wood Dr BR7 188 A4
Woodedge Cl E4 20 D3
Woodend
South Norwood SE19 183 A4
Sutton SM1 218 A6
Thames Ditton KT10 212 A6
WOOD END 83 D1
Wood End UB3 83 C1
Wood End Ave HA2 64 A4
Wood End Cl UB5 64 B3
Woodend Gdns EN2 4 A1
Wood End Gdns UB5 64 A3
WOOD END GREEN 83 C2
Wood End Green Rd
UB3 83 C1
Wood End Inf Sch UB5 64 B3
Wood End Jun Sch
UB6 64 B3
Wood End La UB5 63 D3
Wood End Park Com Sch
UB3 105 A6
Woodend Rd E17 36 A1
Wood End Rd HA1, UB5 64 B4
Wood End Way UB5 64 A3
Wooder Gdns E7 77 A4
Wooderson Cl SE25 205 C5
Wooderson Ct 9 BR3 185 C2
Woodfall Ave EN5 13 B6
Woodfall Rd N4 72 C6
Woodfall St SW3 257 C1
Woodfarrs SE5 139 B1
Woodfield SW16 182 B2
Wood Field NW3 70 D3
Woodfield Ave
Colindale NW9 45 C5
Ealing W5 87 C3
Streatham SW16 159 D1
Wallington SM5 219 A1
Wembley HA0 65 C5
Woodfield Cl
1 Enfield EN1 5 C1
South Norwood SE19 183 A3
Woodfield Cres W5 87 B3
Woodfield Ct SW16 159 D1
Woodfield Dr EN4 15 A3
Woodfield Gdns KT3 199 D4
Woodfield Gr SW16 159 D1
Woodfield Ho
11 Forest Hill SE23 162 D1
Hinchley Wood KT7 212 D6
New Malden KT3 199 D4
6 Upper Clapton E5 74 B6
Wood Green N11 31 D4
Woodfield Pl W9 91 B3
Woodfield Rd
Cranford TW4, TW5 128 B3
Ealing W5 87 C3
Woodfield Rd *continued*
Hinchley Wood KT10,
KT7 212 D6
Kensal Town W9 91 B2
Woodfield Rise WD23 8 B4
Woodfield Sch NW9 45 C1
Woodfields Ct SM1 218 A5
Woodfield Way N11 31 D3
WOODFORD 37 D5
Woodford Ave IG2, IG4, IG5,
IG8 56 B5
Woodford Bridge Rd
IG4 56 A5
Woodford Cres HA5 22 B1
Woodford Ct 15 W12 112 D4
Woodford Cty High Sch
IG8 36 D4
Woodforde Ct UB3 105 B1
WOODFORD GREEN 37 B3
Woodford Green Prep Sch
IG8 37 A4
Woodford Green Sch
IG8 36 D5
Woodford Ho 13 SE18 144 D6
5 Wanstead E18 55 A5
Woodford New Rd
Upper Walthamstow
E17 54 C6
Woodford E18 36 D3
Woodford Pl HA9 44 A1
Woodford Rd
Forest Gate E7 77 B4
Wanstead E18 55 A6
Woodford Sta IG8 37 B4
Woodford Trad Est
IG8 37 D1
WOODFORD WELLS 21 B1
Woodgate Ave KT9 213 D3
Woodgate Cres HA6 22 A4
Woodgate Dr SW16 181 D3
Woodgate Ho 12 KT6 198 A3
Woodger Rd W12 112 C4
Woodget Cl E6 100 A1
Woodglen SM4 202 C4
Woodgrange Ave
Ealing W5 110 C5
Enfield EN1 18 A5
Finchley N12 30 B4
Harrow HA3 43 D4
Woodgrange Cl HA3 43 D4
Woodgrange Ct 1
BR2 208 D1
Woodgrange Gdns EN1 18 A5
Woodgrange Ho W5 110 B5
Woodgrange Inf Sch
E7 77 B4
Woodgrange Mans
HA3 43 C4
Woodgrange Park Sta
E12 77 D3
Woodgrange Rd E7 77 A3
Woodgrange Terr EN1 18 A5
WOOD GREEN 32 B2
Wood Green Sh City
N22 32 C1
Wood Green Sta N22 32 C1
Woodhall NW1 232 A1
Woodhall Ave
Dulwich SE21 161 D1
Pinner HA5 23 A2
Woodhall Dr
Dulwich SE21 161 D1
Pinner HA5 23 A2
Woodhall Gate HA5 22 D3
Woodhall Ho SW18 158 B5
Woodhall La WD19 23 A6
Woodhall Prim Sch
WD19 23 A6
Woodhall Rd HA5 22 D4
Woodham Ct E11 54 D5
Woodham Rd SE6 164 A1
Woodhatch Cl 16 E6 100 A2
Woodhaven Gdns IG6 57 A5
Woodhayes BR7 188 D4
Woodhayes Rd SW19,
SW20 178 C4
Woodhead Dr BR6 227 C6
Woodheyes Rd NW10 67 C3
Woodhill SE7, SE18 122 A2
Woodhill Cres HA3 43 D3
Woodhill Prim Sch
SE18 122 A2
Wood Ho
4 Clapham SW4 137 D3
6 Paddington NW6 91 B5
Woodhouse Ave UB6 86 D5
Woodhouse Cl
Hayes UB3 105 C3
Wembley UB6 86 D5
Woodhouse Eaves HA6 22 A5
Woodhouse Gr E12 78 A2
Woodhouse Rd
Colney Hatch N12 30 C4
Leyton E11 76 D5
Woodhouse Sixth Form
Coll N12 30 B4
Woodhurst Ave BR5 211 A3
Woodhurst Rd
Acton W3 111 A6
SE2 124 A2
Woodington Cl SE9 166 C5
Woodison St E3 97 A3
Woodknoll Dr BR7 188 B2
Wood La
Dagenham RM10 81 A5
Highgate N6 49 B3
Hounslow TW7 130 D5

Wood La continued
Kingsbury NW9 . . . . 45 B2
Ruislip HA4 . . . . 61 C6
Shepherd's Bush W12. . . .112 C6
Stanmore HA7 . . . . 9 B2
Woodford IG8 . . . . 36 D5
Woodland App UB6 . . . . 65 A2
Woodland Cl
Kingsbury NW9 . . . . 45 A3
Uxbridge UB10 . . . . 60 D6
West Ewell KT19 . . . . . . .215 C4
West Norwood SE19 . . . .183 C4
Woodford IG8 . . . . 21 B1
Woodland Cres
18 Rotherhithe SE16. . . .118 D4
SE10 . . . . .142 C6
Woodland Ct
Cheam SM1 . . . . .217 C2
Temple Fortune NW4 . . . 47 A4
13 Wanstead E11 . . . . . . 55 A4
Woodland Gdns
Cranley Gdns N10 . . . . . . 49 B4
Isleworth TW7 . . . . .130 C2
Woodland Gr SE10 . . . .120 C1
Woodland Hill SE19 . . .183 C4
Woodland Hts SE3 . . . .142 C6
Woodland Mews
SW16. . . . . .160 A1
Woodland Rd
Chingford E4 . . . . 20 A3
Friern Barnet N11. . . . . . . 31 B5
Penge SE19 . . . . .183 C4
Thornton Heath CR7 . . . .204 C5
Woodland Rise
Cranley Gdns N10 . . . . . . 49 B5
Wembley HA0 . . . . 65 A2
WOODLANDS 130 C2
Woodlands
Beckenham BR3 . . . . . . .185 D3
Clapham SW4 . . . . .137 B1
Finchley N12 . . . . 30 A4
Harrow HA2 . . . . 41 C5
Temple Fortune NW11 . . 47 A4
Walthamstow E11. . . . . . . 54 B2
West Barnes SW20. . . . . .200 D5
Woodlands Ave
Acton W3. . . . . .110 D5
DA15. . . . . .167 C3
Dagenham RM6. . . . . 59 A2
Finchley N3 . . . . 30 A2
Kingston u T KT3 . . . . . . .177 B2
Ruislip HA4 . . . . 40 D2
Wanstead E11 . . . . 55 B1
Worcester Pk KT4. . . . . . .216 A6
Woodlands Cl BR1 . . . . .188 B1
Claygate KT10. . . . . .212 D1
Temple Fortune NW11 . . 47 A4
Woodlands Ct
9 Bromley BR1 . . . . . . .186 D2
Brondesbury Pk NW10 . . 90 B4
Dulwich SE22 . . . . .162 B4
Southall UB1 . . . . .107 C4
Woodlands Dr
Harrow HA7 . . . . 24 D4
Sunbury TW16. . . . . .172 C1
Woodlands Fst & Mid Sch
HA8 . . . . 26 B2
Woodlands Gdns E17 . . 54 C5
Woodlands Gr TW7 . . . .130 C3
Woodlands Gt SW15 . . .157 B6
Woodlands Jun & Inf Schs
IG1 . . . . 79 B3
Woodlands Par TW15 . .171 A4
Woodlands Park Rd
SE10 . . . . .142 C6
Tottenham N15 . . . . 51 A4
Woodlands Rd
Barnes SW13 . . . . .133 D2
Bexleyheath DA7. . . . . . .147 A2
Bickley BR1 . . . . .188 B1
Enfield EN2 . . . . 5 B4
Harrow HA1 . . . . 42 D4
Ilford IG1 . . . . 79 A5
Isleworth TW7 . . . . .130 C3
Leyton E11. . . . . 76 C6
Lower Edmonton N9 . . . . 18 C3
Southall UB1 . . . . .106 D5
Surbiton KT6. . . . . .197 D2
Walthamstow E17. . . . . . . 54 A6
Woodlands St SE13 . . . .164 B4
Woodland St 2 E8. . . . . 73 C2
Woodlands The
East Barnet N14 . . . . 15 B3
Harrow HA1 . . . . 64 C6
Highbury N5 . . . . 73 A4
12 Hornsey N8 . . . . 50 A2
Isleworth TW7 . . . . .130 C3
Lewisham SE13 . . . . .164 B4
Mitcham CR4. . . . . .203 A6
South Norwood SE19 . . .183 A3
Stanmore HA7 . . . . 25 B5
Thames Ditton KT10 . . . .212 A6
Woodlands Way
SW15. . . . . .157 B6
Woodland Terr SE7 . . . .122 A2
Woodland Way
Abbey Wood SE2 . . . . . .124 D2
Croydon CR0 . . . . .207 A1
Edgware NW7. . . . . 27 D4
Merton SM4 . . . . .201 B5
Mitcham CR4. . . . . .181 A3
Petts Wood BR5 . . . . . . .211 A4
Southgate N21. . . . . 5 B4
Tolworth KT5. . . . . .214 D6
West Wickham BR4. . . . . .224 A5
Woodford IG8 . . . . 21 B1

Woodland Wlk
Chessington KT19 . . . . . .214 C2
9 Greenwich SE10 . . . .120 C1
Hampstead NW3 . . . . 70 C3
Wood Lane High Sch
W12. . . . . 90 B1
Woodlawn Cl SW15 . . . .157 B6
Woodlawn Cres TW2. . .151 D2
Woodlawn Dr TW13. . . .150 D2
Woodlawn Rd SW6 . . . .134 D4
Woodlea Dr BR2 . . . . . .208 C4
Woodlea Lo EN1 . . . . . . 17 C5
Woodlea Rd N16. . . . . . . 73 C5
Woodleigh
1 Kingston u T KT5 . . . .198 B4
3 Woodford E18. . . . . . 37 A2
Woodleigh Ave N12. . . . . 30 C4
Woodleigh Ct N22 . . . . . . 32 B2
Woodleigh Gdns
SW16. . . . . .160 A1
Woodley Cl SW17 . . . . . .180 D3
Woodley La SM1, SM5 . .218 C5
Woodlodge 4 SW19 . . .179 B5
Wood Lodge Gdns
BR1. . . . . .188 A3
Wood Lodge La BR4 . . . .224 A5
Woodman La E4 . . . . 20 C6
Woodman Mews TW9 . . .132 D4
Woodman Par 4 E16 . .122 C5
Woodmans Ct HA7. . . . . . 44 A6
Woodmans Gr NW10 . . . . 67 D3
Woodmans Mews W12. . . 90 B2
Woodman St E16 . . . . . .122 C5
Woodmansterne Prim Sch
SW16. . . . . .181 D2
Woodmansterne Rd
Mitcham SW16. . . . . .181 D2
Sutton SM5 . . . . .218 C1
Wood Mead N17. . . . . . . 34 A4
Woodmere SE9 . . . . . . .166 B3
Woodmere Ave CR0. . . .206 D2
Woodmere Cl
11 Clapham SW11 . . . .137 A2
Croydon CR0 . . . . .206 D2
Woodmere Ct N14 . . . . . 15 B4
Woodmere Gdns CR0 . . .206 D2
Woodmere Way BR3 . . .208 B4
Woodnook Rd SW16 . . . .181 B5
Woodpecker Cl
Bushey WD23 . . . . 8 A3
Enfield N9 . . . . 18 B5
Harrow HA3 . . . . 24 D7
Woodpecker Ct TW2. . . .151 D4
Woodpecker Ho E17. . . . 53 C6
Woodpecker Mews
SE13 . . . . .142 B1
Woodpecker Rd
6 SE14. . . . . .141 A6
Woolwich SE28 . . . . .124 C6
Wood Point 8 E16. . . . . . 99 A2
Woodquest Ave SE24. . . .161 A6
Wood Rd
Littleton TW17. . . . . .192 C5
Willesden NW10 . . . . 67 A1
Wood Retreat SE18 . . . .145 B5
Wood Ride Barnet EN4 . . . 2 B4
Orpington BR5. . . . . .211 C5
Woodridge Cl EN2 . . . . . . 4 C4
Woodridge Prim Sch
N12. . . . . 13 C1
Woodridings Ave HA5. . . 23 B2
Woodridings Cl HA5. . . . 23 B3
Woodridings Ct N22 . . . 31 D2
Woodriffe Rd E11. . . . . . 54 B2
Wood Rise HA5. . . . . 40 A4
Woodrow SE18 . . . . . . .122 B2
Woodrow Ave UB4. . . . . 83 D3
Woodrow Cl UB6 . . . . . . 65 B1
Woodrow Ct 3 N17. . . . 34 B3
Woodruff Ho 12 SW2. . .160 C5
Woodrush Cl 4 SE14 . . .141 A5
Woodrush Way RM6 . . . . 58 D5
Woodseer St E1 . . . . . . 96 A2
Woodsford SE17. . . . . . .262 C1
Woodsford Sq
W14. . . . . .113 A4 244 B2
Woodshire Rd RM10 . . . 81 D5
Woods Ho SW8. . . . . . . .269 A2
WOODSIDE 206 A4
Woodside
Buckhurst Hill IG9. . . . . . . 21 C2
Hampstead Garden Suburb
NW11. . . . . 47 C4
Muswell Hill N10. . . . . 49 A6
Walton-on-T KT12. . . . . . .194 A1
Wimbledon SW19 . . . . . .179 B5
Woodside Ave
Chislehurst BR7 . . . . . . .189 A5
Croydon SE25 . . . . .206 B4
Fortis Green N6 . . . . 48 D5
North Finchley N12 . . . . . 30 A6
Thames Ditton KT10 . . . .196 C2
Wembley HA0 . . . . 88 A4
Woodside Cl Ruislip HA4 . 39 B3
Stanmore HA7. . . . . 25 B5
Tolworth KT5. . . . . .199 A4
Wembley HA0 . . . . 88 A4
Woodside Court Rd
CR0. . . . . .206 A2
Woodside Cres DA15. . . .167 C1
Woodside Ct
Ealing W5 . . . . .110 A5
Enfield EN2 . . . . 4 D4
10 Finchley N12 . . . . . . 29 D6
Palmers Green N13. . . . . . 16 C1
Wanstead E12. . . . . 55 C1
Woodside End HA0 . . . . . 88 A4
Woodside Gdns
Chingford E4 . . . . 35 D4
Tottenham N17 . . . . 33 D1

Woodside Gn SE25. . . . .206 A3
Woodside Gr N12. . . . . . . 14 A1
Woodside Grange Rd
N12. . . . . 29 D6
Woodside Ho SW19 . . . .179 B4
Woodside Jun & Inf Sch
CR0. . . . . .206 A2
Woodside La DA15. . . . . .168 D5
Whetstone N12. . . . . 14 A1
WOODSIDE PARK 29 C6
Woodside Park Ave
E17 . . . . 54 B5
Woodside Park Int Sch
N11. . . . . 30 D5
Woodside Park Rd N12. . 30 A6
Woodside Pk SE25. . . . . .206 A3
Woodside Pl HA0 . . . . . . 88 A6
Woodside Rd BR1. . . . . . .210 A4
Coombe KT3 . . . . .177 C1
Croydon SE25 . . . . .206 B3
Kingston u T KT2. . . . . . .176 A3
Newham E13. . . . . 99 C3
Northwood HA6. . . . . 22 A3
Sidcup DA15 . . . . .167 C1
Sutton SM1. . . . . .218 A5
Woodford IG8 . . . . 37 A6
West Green N22. . . . . 32 C3
Woodside Sch
Belvedere DA17 . . . . . . .125 D2
Walthamstow E17 . . . . . . 54 A6
Woodside Sta SE25 . . . .206 B3
Woodside Way
Croydon CR0. . . . . .206 C3
Streatham CR4 . . . . .181 C2
Wood's Mews
W1. . . . . .115 A6 248 A6
Woodsome Rd NW5. . . . . 71 B5
Wood's Pl SE1. . . . . .263 B5
Woodspring Rd SW19. . .157 A2
Wood's Rd SE15 . . . . . . .140 B4
Wood St Barnet EN5 . . . . 1 A1
Carshalton CR4. . . . . .203 A2
Chiswick W4 . . . . .111 C1
City of London
EC2 . . . . .95 A1 242 B2
Custom Ho E16. . . . . .121 B6
Kingston u T KT1. . . . . . .175 D1
Kingston u T KT2. . . . . . .176 A2
Walthamstow E17. . . . . . . 54 B5
Woodstar Ho 3 SE15 . .140 A5
Woodstead Gr HA8. . . . . 26 A4
Woods The
Eastbury HA6 . . . . 22 A5
Uxbridge UB10 . . . . 60 D4
Woodstock Ave
Brentford W13 . . . . .109 A3
Cheam SM3. . . . . .201 B2
Golders Green NW11 . . . 47 A2
Isleworth TW7 . . . . .153 A6
Southall UB1 . . . . 85 B4
Woodstock Cl DA5. . . . . .169 B3
Stanmore HA7. . . . . 26 A1
Woodstock Cres N9. . . . . 18 B5
Woodstock Ct
Kingston u T KT2 . . . . . . .176 D1
Lee SE12 . . . . .165 A5
Vauxhall SE11 . . . . .260 D2
Woodstock Dr UB10. . . . 60 B4
Woodstock Gdns
Beckenham BR3 . . . . . . .185 D3
Hayes UB4. . . . . 83 D2
Ilford IG3 . . . . 80 A6
Woodstock Gr W12 . . . .112 D4
Woodstock Grange
W5. . . . . .110 A5
Woodstock Ho
Hayes UB3. . . . . 83 B2
2 Highbury N5. . . . . . . 73 A4
Woodstock Lane N
KT6 . . . . .197 D2
Woodstock Lane S KT6, KT9,
KT10 . . . . .213 C4
Woodstock Mews W1. . .238 B3
Woodstock Rd
Bedford Pk W4 . . . . .111 C3
Bushey WD23 . . . . 8 D4
Chingford E17 . . . . 36 B1
Finsbury Pk N4 . . . . 50 C1
Golders Green NW11 . . . 47 B1
South Croydon CR0 . . . . .221 B5
Upton E7 . . . . 77 C1
Wallington SM5, SM6 . . .219 A3
Wembley HA0 . . . . 66 B1
Woodstock Rise SM3. . . .201 B2
Woodstock St W1 . . . . . .238 C1
Woodstock Studios 17
W12. . . . . .112 D4
Woodstock Terr E14 . . . .119 D6
Woodstock The SM3 . . . .201 B2
Woodstock Way CR4 . . . .181 C2
Woodstone Ave KT17,
KT4 . . . . .216 A3
Wood Street Sta E17. . . . 54 B5
Woodsyre SE26 . . . . . . .183 D6
Woodthorpe Rd
Ashford TW15 . . . . .170 A6
Putney SW15. . . . . .134 B1
Woodtree Cl NW4. . . . . . 28 C1
Wood Vale
Cranley Gdns N10. . . . . . . 49 C4
Dulwich SE22 . . . . .162 B4
Woodvale Ave SE25. . . . .183 D1
Woodvale Ct BR1 . . . . . .187 B1
South Norwood SE25. . . .205 D4
Woodvale Way NW11 . . . 68 D5
Woodvale Wlk SE27. . . . .183 A5
Woodview Ave E4 . . . . . . 36 A6
Woodview Cl
Finsbury Pk N4 . . . . 50 D2
Kingston u T SW15 . . . . .177 B6

Woodview Cl continued
Orpington BR6. . . . . .227 A6
Woodville SE3 . . . . .143 B4
Woodville Cl SE12 . . . . . .165 A6
Teddington TW11 . . . . . .175 A6
Woodville Ct
3 Lewisham SE10 . . . . .142 A4
Southgate N14 . . . . 15 C6
Woodville Gdns
Ealing W5 . . . . 88 A1
Hendon NW11 . . . . 46 D2
Ilford IG6 . . . . 56 D5
Ruislip HA4 . . . . 39 A2
Surbiton KT6 . . . . .197 D2
Woodville Gr 2 DA16 . . .146 A2
Woodville Ho SE1. . . . . . .263 C6
Sutton SM1 . . . . .217 D4
Woodville Rd Barnet EN5. . 1 D2
Ealing W5 . . . . 87 D1
Golders Green NW11 . . . 47 A2
Leytonstone E11 . . . . 54 C1
Morden SM4 . . . . .201 C5
Paddington NW6 . . . . 91 B5
Richmond TW10 . . . . . . .153 C1
South Norwood CR7 . . . .205 B6
Stoke Newington N16 . . . 73 C3
Walthamstow E17. . . . . . . 53 B5
Woodford E18. . . . . 37 B1
Woodville 16 SE16. . . . .122 A2
Woodville The W5. . . . . . 87 D1
Woodward Ave NW4 . . . . 46 A4
Woodward Cl KT10. . . . . .212 D2
Woodwarde Rd SE22. . . .161 C5
Woodward Gdns
Dagenham RM9. . . . . 80 C1
Harrow HA7 . . . . 24 D3
Woodward Rd RM9 . . . . . 80 C1
Wood Way BR6 . . . . .226 C6
Woodway Cres HA1. . . . . 43 A3
Woodwell St SW18. . . . . .158 A6
Wood Wharf SE10 . . . . . .142 A6
Woodyard Cl NW5 . . . . . . 71 A3
Woodyard La SE21. . . . . .161 C4
Woodyates Rd SE12. . . . .165 B4
Woolacombe Rd SE3. . . .143 C3
Woolacombe Way
UB3 . . . . .105 C2
Woolcombes Ct 4
SE16 . . . . .118 D5
Woolden Ho 2 E4. . . . . . 20 C4
Wooler St
SE17 . . . . .117 B1 262 D2
Woolf Cl SE28 . . . . .124 B5
Woolf Ct 7 W3. . . . . . . .111 A3
Woolf Mews WC1. . . . . . .240 A6
Woollaston Rd N4 . . . . . . 50 D3
Woolley Ho SW9 . . . . . . .138 D2
Woollon Ho 1 E1. . . . . . 96 C1
Woolmead Ave NW9 . . . . 46 A2
Woolmer Gdns N18. . . . . 34 A5
Woolmer Ho 2 E5. . . . . . 74 B6
Woolmer Rd N18. . . . . . . 34 A5
Woolmore Prim Sch
E14. . . . . .120 A6
Woolmore St E14. . . . . . .120 A6
Woolneigh St SW6. . . . . .135 D3
Woolpack Ho 1 E9. . . . . 74 C2
Wool Rd SW20. . . . . .178 B4
Woolridge Way E9. . . . . . 74 C1
Woolstaplers Way
SE16 . . . . .118 A2
Woolston Cl E17. . . . . . . 34 D1
Woolstone Ho 7 E2. . . . . 96 A6
Woolstone Rd SE23 . . . .163 A2
Woolven Ho SE3. . . . . . .142 D6
WOOLWICH 122 D3
Woolwich Arsenal Sta
SE18 . . . . .122 D2
Woolwich Church St SE7,
SE18 . . . . .122 A3
Woolwich Comm
SE18 . . . . .144 C6
Woolwich Ct EN3 . . . . 7 C5
Woolwich Dockyard Ind
Est SE18 . . . . .122 A3
Woolwich Dockyard Sta
SE18 . . . . .122 B2
Woolwich High St
SE18 . . . . .122 C3
Woolwich Manorway
E16. . . . . .122 D4
Woolwich Manor Way
Beckton E6 . . . . .100 C1
North Woolwich E16 . . . .122 D5
Woolwich New Rd
SE18 . . . . .122 D2
Woolwich Poly Sch for
Boys SE28. . . . . .124 A5
Woolwich Rd
Belvedere DA17 . . . . . . .125 C1
DA7. . . . . .147 C2
Erith SE2 . . . . .125 B1
Greenwich SE7, SE10 . . .121 C2
Woolwich Sta SE18 . . . . .122 D1
Woosters Gdns E14. . . . . 98 B1
Wooster Mews HA2. . . . . 42 A6
Wooster Pl SE1. . . . . . . .262 D4
Wootton Cl KT10 . . . . . . .212 A4
Wootton Gr N3 . . . . 29 C2
Wootton Ho SE9 . . . . . . .167 B5
Wootton St
SE1 . . . . .116 C5 251 B3
Worbeck Rd SE20. . . . . . .184 C1
Worcester Ave N17 . . . . . 34 A3
Worcester Cl
Croydon CR0 . . . . .223 C6
Dollis Hill NW2 . . . . 68 B5
Mitcham CR4. . . . . .181 A1

Worcester Ct
Ashford TW15 . . . . .170 D5
Ealing W7 . . . . 86 D1
Finchley N12 . . . . 29 D5
Harrow HA1 . . . . 42 C6
44 Paddington W2 . . . . . 91 C2
12 Sutton SM2 . . . . . . .217 D2
Walton-on-T KT12 . . . . . .194 C1
Worcester Pk KT4. . . . . . .215 C5
Worcester Dr
Ashford TW15 . . . . .170 D5
Bedford Pk W4 . . . . .111 C4
Worcester Gdns
Northolt UB6 . . . . 64 B2
Redbridge IG1 . . . . 56 A2
Wandsworth SW11. . . . . .158 D6
Worcester Pk KT4. . . . . . .215 C5
Worcester Ho
Bayswater W2 . . . . .236 A1
3 Islington N1. . . . . 73 A1
Lambeth SE11. . . . . .261 A5
9 Putney SW15. . . . . . .156 C4
Worcester Mews 2
NW6 . . . . 69 D2
WORCESTER PARK 215 C4
Worcester Park Rd
KT4 . . . . .215 B6
Worcester Park Sta
KT4 . . . . .200 A1
Worcester Rd
Belmont SM2. . . . . .217 D1
Higham Hill E17. . . . . 34 C1
Ilford E12 . . . . 78 D4
11 Wimbledon SW19 . . .179 B5
Worcesters Ave EN1 . . . . 6 A5
Worcesters Prim Sch
EN1. . . . . 5 B5
Wordsworth Ave N8. . . . . 50 C5
Wordsworth Ave
Greenford UB6 . . . . 86 B5
Plashet E12. . . . . 78 A1
Snaresbrook E18. . . . . . . 54 D6
Wordsworth Ct
Harrow HA1 . . . . 42 B2
New Barnet EN5 . . . . 14 A6
Wordsworth Dr KT4,
SM3. . . . . .216 C4
Wordsworth Gdns WD6 . .10 C5
Wordsworth Ho
Maida Vale NW6 . . . . 91 C4
15 SE18. . . . . .144 C6
Wordsworth Par 1
N15. . . . . 50 D5
Wordsworth Pl 11 NW5. . 70 D3
Wordsworth Rd
Bermondsey SE1. . . . . . .263 D3
Bexley DA16 . . . . .145 C4
Hampton TW12, TW13. . .173 B6
Penge SE20. . . . . .184 D3
Stoke Newington N16. . . . 73 C4
Wallington SM6. . . . . . . .219 D2
Wordsworth Way SW7 . .104 B2
Wordsworth Wlk NW11 . 47 C5
Worfield St
SW11. . . . . .136 C5 267 B3
Worgan St
Rotherhithe SE16. . . . . . .118 D2
SE11. . . . . .116 B1 260 C2
Working Men's Coll The
NW1. . . . . .93 C5 232 B4
Worland Rd E15. . . . . 76 C1
World Bsns Ctr TW6 . . . .127 A4
WORLD'S END 4 C1
Worlds End Ho BR6 . . . . .227 D1
World's End La EN2. . . . . 4 B1
World's End Pas SW10 . .266 C4
World's End Pl SW10. . . .266 B3
World Trade Ctr London
E14. . . . . .119 D4
Worley Ct NW2 . . . . 68 D5
Worleys Dr BR6. . . . . . . .227 B4
Worlidge St W6 . . . . .112 C1
Worlingham Rd SE22. . . .139 D1
Wormholt Park Prim Sch
W12. . . . . .112 A6
Wormholt Rd W12 . . . . . .112 A5
Wormwood St EC2. . . . . .243 A2
Wornington Rd W10 . . . . 91 A2
Woronzow Rd
NW8 . . . . .92 C6 230 A5
Worple Ave
Isleworth TW7 . . . . .153 A6
Wimbledon SW19 . . . . . .178 D3
Worple Cl HA2. . . . . 41 B1
Worple Ct SW19 . . . . . . .179 A4
Worple Prim Sch
TW7 . . . . .131 A1
Worple Rd
Isleworth TW7 . . . . .131 A1
Wimbledon SW19,
SW20. . . . . .178 D2
Worple Road Mews
SW19. . . . . .179 B4
Worple St SW14 . . . . . . .133 B2
Worple Way
Harrow HA2 . . . . 41 B1
Richmond TW10 . . . . . . .132 A1
Worship St EC2. . .95 C3 243 A5
Worslade Rd SW17. . . . . .180 B6
Worsley Bridge Jun Sch
BR3. . . . . .185 A3
Worsley Bridge Rd BR3,
SE6 . . . . .185 C5
Worsley Ct N3. . . . . 29 C4
Worsley Gr E5 . . . . 74 A4
Worsley Grange BR7. . . .189 A4
Worsley Ho 9 SE23. . . . .162 B2
Worsley Rd E11. . . . . 76 C4
Worsopp Dr SW4 . . . . . . .159 C6
Worth Cl BR6. . . . . .227 C6

Worthfield Cl KT19. . . . . .215 B1
Worth Gr SE17. . . . . .262 C1
Worthing Cl 5 E15. . . . . 98 C6
Worthing Rd TW5. . . . . . .129 B6
Worthington Cl CR4. . . . .203 B6
Worthington Ho EC1. . . . .234 B2
16 Streatham SW2. . . . .160 C4
Worthington Rd KT6 . . . .198 B1
Wortley Rd
Forest Gate E6 . . . . 77 C1
Thornton Heath CR0 . . . .204 C2
Worton Ct TW7 . . . . .130 C1
Worton Gdns TW7 . . . . . .130 B3
Worton Hall Ind Est
TW7 . . . . .130 C1
Worton Rd TW7 . . . . .130 C1
Worton Way TW3,
TW7. . . . . .130 B3
Wotton Ct 14 E14 . . . . . .120 B6
Wotton Rd
Cricklewood NW2 . . . . . . 68 C5
16 SE8. . . . . .141 B6
Wouldham Rd E16. . . . . . 98 D1
Wragby Rd E11. . . . . 76 C5
Wrampling Pl N9 . . . . 18 A3
Wrangthorne Wlk
CR0. . . . . .220 C4
Wray Ave IG5. . . . . 56 C6
Wrayburn Ho 28 SE16 . . .118 A4
Wray Cres N4 . . . . 72 B6
Wray Ct N4. . . . . 72 B6
Wrayfield Rd SM3. . . . . . .216 D5
Wray Ho 11 SW2. . . . . . .160 A3
Wraysbury Cl TW4 . . . . . .151 A6
Wrays Way UB4. . . . . 83 C3
Wrekin Rd SE18 . . . . . . .145 A5
Wren Ave
Cricklewood NW2 . . . . . . 68 C4
Southall UB2 . . . . .107 B2
Wren Cl E16 . . . . 98 D1
Lower Edmonton N9 . . . . 18 D3
Wren Cres WD23. . . . . 8 A3
Wren Ct 1 Barnet EN4 . . .14 D3
Croydon CR0 . . . . .221 B4
Wren Gdns RM9 . . . . 80 D3
Wren Ho 29 Bow E3 . . . . 97 A5
4 Hampton TW12. . . . . .173 D4
SW1. . . . . .259 C1
Wren Landing E14. . . . . .119 C5
Wrenn Ho SW13 . . . . . . .134 C6
Wren Path SE28 . . . . . . .123 B4
Wren Rd
Camberwell SE5 . . . . . . .139 A4
Dagenham RM9. . . . . 80 D3
Sidcup DA14 . . . . .168 C1
Wrens Ave TW15. . . . . . .171 A6
Wren's Park Ho E5 . . . . . 74 B6
Wren St WC1 . . . .94 B3 240 D6
Wrentham Ave NW10 . . . 90 D5
Wrenthorpe Rd BR1. . . . .186 C6
Wren View N6. . . . . 49 C1
Wrenwood Way HA5 . . . . 40 B5
Wrestlers Ct EC3 . . . . . . .243 A2
Wrexham Rd E3 . . . . 97 C5
Wricklemarsh Rd SE3 . . .143 D4
Wrigglesworth St
SE14. . . . . .140 D5
Wright Cl SE13 . . . . .142 B1
Wright Gdns SW17. . . . . .192 C4
Wright Ho SW15 . . . . . . .156 B6
Wrighton Ct SM1 . . . . . . .217 B2
Wright Rd TW5 . . . . .128 C5
Wrights Cl RM10. . . . . . . 81 D4
Wright's Gn SW4 . . . . . .137 D1
Wright's La
W8. . . . . .113 D3 255 C6
Wrights Pl NW10 . . . . 67 A2
Wright's Rd SE25. . . . . . .205 C6
Wright's Rd E3 . . . . 97 B5
Wright's Row SM5 . . . . . .219 B4
Wrights Wlk SW14 . . . . . .133 B2
Writtle Ho 38 NW9 . . . . . 27 D1
Wrotham Rd
Beckenham BR3 . . . . . . .185 B3
SE1. . . . . .262 D6
13 Camden Town NW1. . . 71 C1
DA16. . . . . .146 C4
Ealing W13 . . . . .109 C5
Wrottesley Rd SE18 . . . .145 A6
Willesden Green NW10. . . 90 A5
Wroughton Rd SW11. . . .159 A6
Wroughton Terr NW4 . . . 46 B5
Wroxall Rd RM9 . . . . 80 D2
Wroxham Gdns N11. . . . . 31 D3
Wroxham Rd SE28 . . . . . .124 D6
Wroxton Rd SE15 . . . . . .140 C3
Wr Twr Cl UB8. . . . . 60 A3
Wr Twr Hill CR0 . . . . .221 B4
Wr Twr Pl N1. . . . . .234 C5
Wrythe Gn 2 SM5 . . . . . .218 C5
Wrythe Green Rd
SM5. . . . . .218 C5
Wrythe La SM1, SM5,
SM4. . . . . .218 C5
WRYTHE THE 218 D6
Wulfstan St W12. . . . . 89 D1
Wyatt Cl Bushey WD23 . . . 8 C4
Feltham TW13 . . . . .150 D3
Hayes UB4. . . . . 84 A2
Rotherhithe SE16. . . . . . .119 B4
Wyatt Ct HA0. . . . . 66 A1
Wyatt Ho
Blackheath Vale SE3 . . . .142 D3
NW8 . . . . .236 D5
Wyatt Park Mans 1
SW2. . . . . .160 A2
Wyatt Park Rd SW2 . . . . .160 B2
Wyatt Rd Forest Gate E7 . .77 A2

Wyatt Rd *continued*
Highbury N5 73 A5
Wyatt's La E17 54 A6
Wybert St NW1 239 A6
Wyborne Ho NW10 67 A1
Wyborne Prim Sch
SE9 166 D3
Wyborne Way NW10 67 A1
Wyburn Ave EN5 1 B2
Wyche Gr CR2 221 A1
Wycherley Cl SE3 142 D5
Wycherley Cres EN5 13 D5
Wychwood Ave
Edgware HA8 25 D4
South Norwood CR7 205 A6
Wychwood Cl
Ashford TW16 172 A4
Edgware HA8 25 D4
Wychwood End N6 49 C2
Wychwood Gdns IG5 56 C5
Wychwood Ho N4 51 A2
Wychwood Way SE19 183 B4
Wyclif Ct EC1 234 C1
Wycliffe Cl DA16 145 D4
Wycliffe Ho 13 N16 73 C4
Wycliffe Rd
Battersea SW11 137 A3
Wimbledon SW19 179 D4
Wyclif St EC1 234 C1
Wycombe Ct SE3 143 A5
Wycombe Gdns NW11 69 C6
Wycombe Ho NW8 237 A6
Wycombe Pl SW18 158 A5
Wycombe Rd
Redbridge IG2 56 B4
Tottenham N17 34 A2
Wembley HA0 88 C6
Wycombe Sq W8 245 A3
Wydehurst Rd CR0 206 B2
Wydell Cl SM4 200 D3
Wydeville Manor Rd
SE12 187 B6
Wye Cl Ashford TW15 170 D6
BR6 211 D2
Ruislip HA4 39 A3
Wye Ct W13 87 B2
Wyemead Cres E4 20 C2
Wyersdale Ho N4 51 A2
Wye St SW11 136 B3
Wyevale Cl HA5 40 A6
Wyfold Ho 8 SE2 124 D4
Wyfold Rd
SW6 135 A5 264 A3
Wyke Cl TW7 130 D6
Wyke Gdns W7 109 A3
Wykeham Ave RM9 80 C2
Wykeham Cl UB7 126 C6
Wykeham Ct
Chislehurst BR7 189 C4
Hendon NW4 46 C4
Wykeham Gn RM9 80 C2
Wykeham Hill HA9 44 B1
Wykeham Ho SW19 179 C2
Wykeham Prim Sch
NW10 67 C5
Wykeham Rd
Harrow HA3 43 B5
Hendon NW4 46 C4
Wykeham Rise N20 13 A3
Wykehurst Ho SW17 180 B5
Wyke Rd
Hackney Wick E3 75 C1
Merton SW20 178 C1
Wylchin Cl HA5 39 D6
Wyldes Cl NW11 48 A1
Wyldfield Gdns N9 17 D2
Wyld Way HA9 66 D2
Wyleu St SE23 163 A4
Wylie Rd UB2 107 C3
Wyllen Cl E1 96 C3
Wylo Dr EN5 12 A5
Wymering Mans 9 W9 91 C4
Wymering Rd W9 91 C4
Wymondham Ct NW8 229 D6
Wymond St SW15 134 C2
Wynan Rd E14 119 D1
Wynash Gdns SM5 218 C3
Wynaud Ct N22 32 B4
Wynbourne Ct SE20 184 B1
Wyncham Ave DA15 167 C3
Wynchgate Harrow HA3 24 C3
Southgate N14 16 A4
Wyncroft Cl BR1 210 B6
Wyndale Ave NW9 44 C3
Wyndcliff Rd SE7 143 B6
Wyndcroft Cl EN2 4 D2
Wyndham Cl
Belmont SM2 217 C1
Orpington BR6 211 A1
Wyndham Cres
Camden Town N19 71 C5
Hounslow TW4 151 C5
Wyndham Ct
Brentford W7 109 A2
1 Thornton Heath
CR0 204 D3
Wyndham Deedes Ho 30
E2 96 A5
Wyndham Ho SW1 258 A3
Wyndham Lo TW7 130 C4
Wyndham Mews W1 237 C3
Wyndham Pl W1 237 C3
Wyndham Rd
Barnet EN4 14 D3
Brentford W13 109 B3
Forest Gate E6 77 D1
Kingston u T KT2 176 B3
SE5 139 A5
Wyndhams Ct 4 E8 73 D1
Wyndham St
W1 92 D2 237 C4
Wyndham Yd W1 237 C3
Wyndhurst Cl CR2 220 D1
Wyneham Rd SE24 161 B6
Wynell Rd SE23 162 D1
Wynford Pl DA17 147 C6
Wynford Rd N1 94 B5 233 D4
Wynford Way SE9 166 B1
Wynlie Gdns HA5 22 B1
Wynndale Rd E18 37 B2
Wynne Ct 6 TW7 131 A2
Wynne Ho SE14 140 D4
Wynne Rd SW9 138 C3
Wynn's Ave DA15 168 A6
Wynnstay Gdns
W8 113 C3 255 B6
Wynter Ho 20 SW9 138 B3
Wynter St SW11 136 A1
Wynton Gdns SE25 205 D4
Wynton Pl W3 88 D1
Wynyard Ho SE11 260 D2
Wynyard Terr SE11 260 D2
Wynyatt Ho EC1 234 C2
Wynyatt St EC1 94 D4 234 C2
Wyre Gr Edgware HA8 10 D1
Hayes UB3 106 A2
Wyresdale Cres UB6 86 D4
Wyteleaf Cl HA4 39 A3
Wytham Ho NW8 236 D5
Wythburn Ct W1 237 C2
Wythburn Pl W1 237 C2
Wythenshawe Rd RM10 81 C5
Wythens Wlk SE9 166 D5
Wythes Cl BR1 188 B1
Wythes Rd E16 122 A5
Wythfield Rd SE9 166 B5
Wyvenhoe Rd HA2 64 A5
Wyvern Est The KT3 200 A5
Wyvil Prim Sch
SW8 138 A5 270 B4
Wyvil Rd SW8 138 A5 270 A4
Wyvis St E14 97 D2

X

Xavier Ho E17 35 B1

Y

Yabsley St E14 120 A5
Yaldam Ho SE1 263 A3
Yalding Ho 30 E5 74 B3
Yalding Rd SE16 118 A2
Yale Cl TW4 151 B6
Yale Ct NW6 69 D3
Yarborough Rd 1
SW19 180 B2
Yardley Cl E4 19 D6
Yardley Ct SM3 216 D4
Yardley La E4 19 D6
Yardley Prim Sch E4 20 A5
Yardley St WC1 234 A1
Yard The N1 233 B3
Yarlington Ct N11 31 A5
Yarmouth Cres N17 52 B4
Yarmouth Pl W1 248 C3
Yarnfield Sq 15 SE15 140 A4
Yarnton Way DA17,
DA18 125 B3
Yarrow Cres E6 100 A2
Yarrow Ho
12 Cubitt Town E14 120 A3
16 North Kensington
W10 90 C2
Yateley St SE18 121 D3
Yatesbury Ct E5 75 A3
Yates Ct NW2 68 D2
Yates Ho 22 E2 96 A4
Yatton Ho 15 W10 90 C2
YEADING 84 D3
Yeading Ave HA2 41 A1
Yeading Ct UB4 84 C3
Yeading Fork UB4 84 C3
Yeading Gdns UB4 84 B2
Yeading Ho UB4 84 D2
Yeading Jun & Inf Schs
UB4 84 C2
Yeading La Hayes UB4 84 B2
Northolt UB4, UB5 84 C4
Yeadon Ho 14 W10 90 C2
Yeames Cl W13 87 A1
Yearby Ho W10 90 C3
Yeate St N1 73 B1
Yeatman Rd N6 48 D3
Yeats Cl NW10 67 C2
Yeend Cl KT8 195 C5
Yeldham Ho W6 112 D1
Yeldham Rd W6 112 D1
Yellowhammer Ct NW9 27 C1
Yelverton Lo TW1 153 C4
Yelverton Rd SW11 136 B3
Ye Market CR0 221 B3
Yenston Cl SM4 201 C3
Yeoman Cl
Newham E16 122 D6
West Norwood SE27 160 D1
Yeoman Ct
Heston TW5 129 B5
8 Sutton SM1 218 B3
Yeoman Dr TW19 148 A3
Yeoman Rd UB5 63 A1
Yeomans Acre HA4 40 A3
Yeomans Mews TW7 152 B6
Yeoman's Row
SW3 114 C3 257 B5
Yeoman St SE8 119 A2
Yeomans Way EN3 6 C3
Yeoman's Yd E1 253 D6
Yeo St E3 97 D2
Yeovil Cl BR6 227 C6
Yeovil Ho Finsbury Pk N7 72 B6
North Kensington W10 90 C3
Yeovilton Pl KT2 175 C5
Yerbury Prim Sch N19 71 D5
Yerbury Rd N19 71 D5
Yeshivo Horomo
Tadmudical Coll N16 51 B1
Yesodey Hatorah Sch
N16 51 D2
Yester Dr BR7 188 A3
Yester Pk BR7 188 B4
Yester Rd BR7 188 B3
Yet Lev Ct E5 52 A1
Yew Ave UB7 104 A6
Yew Cl IG9 21 D2
Yewdale Cl BR1 186 C4
Yewfield Rd NW10 67 D2
Yew Gr NW2 68 D4
Yew Ho SE14 141 B3
Yews The TW15 170 D6
Yew Tree Ave N2 47 D6
Yewtree Cl Harrow HA2 41 D5
Wood Green N22 31 C2
Yew Tree Cl DA16 146 A4
3 Lewisham SE13 142 A2
New Malden KT4 199 C1
Southgate N21 16 C4
Yew Tree Cotts KT10 212 B6
Yew Tree Ct Elstree WD6 9 D5
8 Stoke Newington N16 73 B6
8 Sutton SM2 218 A1
4 Temple Fortune
NW11 47 B4
Yew Tree Gdns RM6 59 A4
Yew Tree Grange 2
W5 109 C6
Yew Tree Ho
New Malden KT4 199 C1
5 Surbiton KT6 198 A1
Yew Tree Lo 10 SW16 181 C5
Yewtree Rd BR3 207 B6
Yew Tree Rd
East Acton W12 111 D6
Hillingdon UB10 82 B6
Yew Trees TW17 192 B5
Yew Tree Wlk TW4 151 B6
Yew Wlk HA1 42 C1
YIEWSLEY 104 A6
Yiewsley Ct UB7 104 A5
Yoakley Rd N16 73 C6
Yoke Cl N7 72 A2
Yolande Gdns SE9 166 A6
Yonge Pk N4, N7 72 C5
York Ave Ealing W7 108 C5
Hayes UB3 83 A1
Mortlake SW14 155 A6
Sidcup DA15 167 D2
Stanmore HA7 25 B1
Walworth SE17 262 B2
York Bldgs
WC2 116 A6 250 B5
York Bridge
NW1 93 A3 238 A6
York Cl
17 Camberwell SE5 139 A3
Ealing W7 108 C5
Morden SM4 201 D5
Newham E6 100 B1
York Ct Beckenham BR3 186 B2
Kingston u T KT2 175 D4
York Ct *continued*
Palmers Green N13 16 A1
Wallington SM6 219 C3
York Gate NW1 238 B5
Southgate N14 16 A4
York Gr SE15 140 C4
York Hill SE27, SW16 160 D1
York Ho Acton W3 111 A6
Chelsea SW3 257 D2
Chingford E4 35 C6
Edgware HA8 26 B4
Enfield EN2 5 B4
Forest Hill SE26 184 C5
1 Hendon NW4 28 D1
1 Ilford IG1 78 D6
Islington N5 72 C3
Kensington W8 245 C2
11 Kentish Town N7 71 D2
Kew TW9 132 C4
4 Kingston u T KT2 176 B3
Lambeth SE1 116 B3 260 D5
Marylebone W1 237 C4
Pentonville N1 233 C3
Richmond TW10 154 C6
South Norwood SE25 205 C5
10 West Acton W3 88 C1
York House Pl
W8 113 D4 245 C2
Yorkland Ave DA16 145 D1
Yorkley Ho 3 W10 90 C3
York Mans
Battersea SW11 268 B2
2 Hendon NW9 46 A3
Marylebone W1 238 A4
Walworth SE17 262 B2
York Mews
Camden Town NW5 71 B3
Ilford IG1 78 C5
York Par
Brentford TW8 109 D1
Hendon NW9 46 A3
York Pl
Battersea SW11 136 B2
Ilford IG1 78 C6
WC2 250 B5
York Place Mans NW1 237 D4
York Rd
Battersea SW11,
SW18 136 B2
Belmont SM1, SM2 217 C1
Brentford TW8 109 D1
Chingford E4 35 C5
Dagenham W3 89 B1
Ealing W5 109 C3
Edmonton N18 34 B5
Forest Gate E7 77 A2
Friern Barnet N11 31 D4
Hounslow TW3 129 D2
Ilford IG1 78 C6
Kingston u T KT2 176 B3
Leyton E10 76 A5
New Barnet EN5 14 B6
Pinner HA6 22 A1
4 Richmond TW10 154 B6
SE1 116 B4 250 D2
Southgate N21 17 B4
Teddington TW11 174 C6
Thornton Heath CR0 204 C2
Walthamstow E17 52 D4
Wimbledon SW19 180 A4
York Rise BR6 227 C6
Dartmouth Pk NW5 71 B5
York Road Bsns Ctr
SW11 136 B3
York St Chambers W1 237 C4
Yorkshire Cl N16 73 C5
Yorkshire Gdns N18 34 B5
Yorkshire Grey SE9 165 D6
Yorkshire Grey Pl 13
NW3 70 A4
Yorkshire Grey Yd
WC1 240 C3
Yorkshire Rd
Limehouse E14 97 A1
Mitcham CR4 204 A5
York Sq 12 E14 97 A1
York St Carshalton CR4 203 A2
Paddington W1 92 D2 237 D4
Twickenham TW1 153 A3
York Terr EN2 5 A5
York Terr E
NW1 93 A3 238 B5
York Terr W
NW1 93 A3 238 A5
Yorkton St E2 96 A5
York Way
Barnsbury N1, N7,
NW1 72 A1
Chessington KT9 214 A1
Friern Barnet N20 14 D1
N1 233 B5
Twickenham TW13 151 B1
York Way Ct
Islington N1 233 C5
Islington N1 233 B5
Youngmans Cl EN2 5 A4
Young Rd E16 99 C1
Young's Bldgs EC1 242 B6
Youngs Brewery Visitor
Ctr* SW18 157 D6
Youngs Ct SW11 268 B1
Youngs Rd IG2 57 B4
Young St W8 113 D4 245 C1
Yoxall Ho 2 W10 90 C3
Yoxford Ct 6 RM6 58 B4
Yoxley App IG2 57 A3
Yoxley Dr IG2 57 A3
Yukon Rd SW12 159 B4
Yunus Khan Cl E17 53 C4

Z

Zambezie Dr N9 18 C1
Zampa Rd SE16 118 C1
Zander Ct E2 96 A4
Zangwill Ho NW6 91 B5
Zangwill Rd SE18, SE3 143 D4
Zealand Ave UB7 126 A5
Zealand Ho
11 Camberwell SE5 139 A3
4 Woolwich SE7 122 A2
Zealand Rd E3 97 A5
Zenith Lo 7 N3 29 D3
Zennor Rd SW12 159 C3
Zenoria St SE22 139 D1
Zermatt Rd CR7 205 A5
Zetland Ho W8 255 C6
Zetland St E14 98 A2
Zeus Ho N1 235 C1
Zion Ho 6 E1 96 C1
Zion Pl CR7 205 B5
Zion Rd CR7 205 B5
Zircon Ct N11 31 D3
ZK Pk CR0 220 B5
Zoar St SE1 117 A5 252 A4
Zodiac Ct CR0 204 D1
Zodiac Ho 3 E3 97 C3
Zoffany St N19 71 D6

List of numbered locations

This atlas shows thousands more place names than any other London street atlas. In some busy areas it is impossible to fit the name of every place.

Where not all names will fit, some smaller places are shown by a number. If you wish to find out the name associated with a number, use this listing.

The places in this list are also listed normally in the Index.

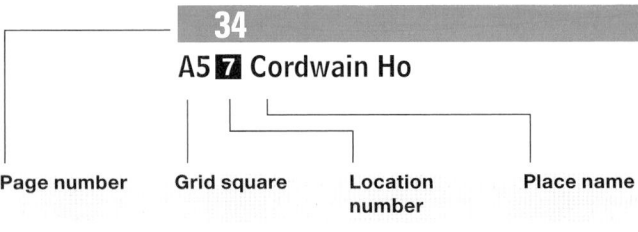

34

A5 7 Cordwain Ho

Page number	Grid square	Location number	Place name

1

A1 1 Hertswood Ct
2 Abingdon Lo
3 Sunbury Ct
4 Meriden Ho
5 Norfolk Ct
6 Vanburgh Ct
7 Morrison Ct
8 Kingshill Ct
9 Baronsmere Ct
10 Chartwell Ct
A2 1 Richard Ct
2 Alston Ct
3 Ridgeleigh Ct
4 Bartletts Cotts
5 Leathersellers Cl
6 Holkham Ho
7 Leinster Mews
B1 1 Olivia Ct
2 Tudor Ct
3 Gordon Mans
B2 1 Brake Shear Ho
2 Durham Ct
3 Huntingdon Ct
4 Cambridge Ct
5 Summit Ct
D1 1 Cranleigh Ct
2 Valeside Ct
3 Sherwood
4 Bradbury Ct
5 Chester Ho
6 Graham Ho
7 Highfield Ct
8 Amberley Ho
9 Hadley View
10 Stratton Lo
11 Gainsborough Ct
12 Christopher Ct
13 Bowmar Lo

2

A1 1 Hanover Ho
2 St Giles Ho
3 Henrietta Ho
4 Byron Ct
5 Preston Ct
6 Clivedon Ct
7 Battle House Mews
8 Phoenix Ct
9 Landsdown Cl
10 Comer Ho
11 Basil Ct
12 Russell Ct
13 Alice Cl
C1 1 Braeburn Ct
2 Bramley Ct
3 Cox Ct
4 Golden Ct
5 Pippin Ct
6 Russet Ct
7 High Birch Ct
8 Joystone Ct
9 Mark Lo
10 Edgeworth Ct

4

D3 1 Oakington Ct
2 Elderberry Ct
3 Blueberry Ct
4 Butterfield Ho

5

C1 1 Woodfield Ct
2 Fielders Cl

7

A2 1 Amethyest Ct
2 Bradmore Ct
3 Acer Ct
4 Cornell Ct
5 Durnsford Ct
6 Feldspar Ct
C6 1 Whitworth Cres
2 Polsten Mews
3 Aldis Mews
4 Dundas Mews
5 Colt Mews
6 Warlow Cl
7 Barrass Cl
8 Rigby Pl
9 Gunner Dr
10 Colgate Pl

11 Baddeley Cl
12 Sten Cl
13 Pritchett Cl
14 Rubin Pl
15 Turpin Cl
16 Island Centre Way
17 Hispano Mews
18 Watkin Mews
19 Wallace Ct
20 Needham Ct
21 Dryer Ct
22 Webley Ct
23 Frosbery Ct
24 Jacob Ct
25 Peabody Ct
26 Greener Ct
27 Bren Ct

9

D5 1 Watling Ct
2 Stuart Ct
3 Westview Ct
4 Potters Mews

13

D6 1 Rowan Wlk
2 Ford Ho
3 Glenwood Ho
4 Whitegates
5 Lisa Lo
6 South Lo
7 Hockington Ct
8 Lysander Ct
9 Ashwood Lo
10 Thornbridge Ct
11 Invergarry Ct
12 Eysham Ct
13 Warwick Ct
14 Chaucer Ct
15 Coleridge Ct
16 Springfields
17 Bure Ct
18 Florence Ct
19 Minetta Ct

14

A1 1 Belmont Ct
2 Terrace Ho
3 Croft Mews
4 Bluebell Ct
A2 1 Westview Ct
2 Oakleigh Mews
3 Mountview Ct
4 Mortimer Ct
5 Parklands
A6 1 Chiltern Ct
2 Gills Ct
3 Beaufort Ct
4 St Augustines Ct
5 Somerset Lo
6 Carlyle Lo
7 Stirling Lo
8 St Mirren Ct
9 Wardrew Ct
10 Apex Lo
11 Westbury Ct
B2 1 Davis Ct
2 Deerings Ct
3 Ashcroft Ct
B6 1 Redrose Trad Ctr
2 Lancaster Road Ind Est
C2 1 Mendip Ct
2 Purbeck Ct
3 Brendon Ct
4 Quantock Ct
5 Malvern Ct
6 Chiltern Ct
C5 1 Feline Ct
2 Brookhill Ct
3 Littlegrove Ct
4 Desmond Ho
D1 1 Springfield Ct
2 Victor Ho
3 Malborough Ho
4 Coopers Ct
5 Joiners Ct
D2 1 Bantock Ct
2 Burgess Ct
3 Heaton Ct
4 Bordley Ct
5 Garside Ct
6 Cranston Ct

7 Gleave Ct
D3 1 Wren Ct
2 Homerton Ct
3 Emmanuel Ct
4 Wolfson Ct
5 Robinson Ct
6 Gonville Ct

15

C6 1 Tregenna Cl
2 Catherine Ct
3 Conisbee Ct
4 Ashmead
D3 1 Dennis Par
2 Broadway The
3 Southgate Cir
4 Station Par
5 Bourneside
6 Bourneside Cres

17

C6 1 Wade Ho
2 Newport Lo
3 Halcyon Ho
4 Lerwick Ct
5 Anchor Ct
6 Grassmere Ct
7 Datchworth Ct
8 Trentham Lo
9 Austin Ct
10 Cedar Grange
11 Brookview Ct
12 Chestbrook Ct
13 Paddock Lo
14 Hamlet Ct
15 Haven Lo

18

A1 1 Plevna Ho
2 Lea Ho
3 Brook Ho
4 Valley Ho
5 Chiltern Ho
6 Blenheim Ho
7 Penn Ho
8 Romany Ho
9 Gilpin Ho
10 Anvil Ho
11 Well Ho
12 Passmore Ho
13 Durbin Ho
A2 1 Market Par
2 Beechwood Mews
3 Keats Par
4 Cedars Rd
5 Cross Keys Cl
6 Dorman Pl
7 Concourse The

20

1 Lea Ct
2 Park Ct
3 Conference Cl
4 Berrybank Cl
5 Russell Lo
6 Brunswick Lo
7 Kenilworth Ct
8 Trinity Ct
9 Kingsmead Lo
10 Fairlawns
A3 1 Knight Ct
2 Grant Ct
3 Chantry The
4 Bowyer Ct
5 Pineview Ct
6 Ellen Ct
7 Leeview Ct
8 Chelsea Ct
9 Bramley Ct
10 Garenne Ct
11 Kendal Ct
12 Fairways
13 Avon Ct
B3 1 Maddox Ct
2 Village Arc The
3 Cambridge Rd
4 Crown Bldgs
5 Pentney Rd
6 Scholars Ho
7 Cranworth Cres
C4 1 Connaught Ct
2 Woolden Ho
3 Fairmead Ct

4 Lockhart Lo
5 Cavendish Ct
6 Oakwood Ct
7 Plains The
8 Hadleigh Ct
9 Forest Ho
10 Mathieson Ct

21

B2 1 Stag Hts
2 Shore Point
3 Buckhurst Hill Ho
4 Beech Ave
5 High Road Buck-hurst Hill
6 Highclears
C2 1 Westbury Ct
2 Palmerston Ct
3 Ibrox Ct
4 Richard Burton Ct
5 Queens Mews
6 Gunnels Ct & Hastingwood Ct
7 Marlborough Ct
8 Avenue The
9 Tora Ct
10 Somerset Ct
11 Mirravale Ct
C3 1 Rayburne Ct
2 Laurels The
3 Mablin Lo
4 Silvers
5 Makinen Ct
6 Roman Ct
D1 1 Highview Ho
2 Hornbeam Ho
3 Highview Ho
4 Bourne Ho
D2 1 Regency Lo
2 Kings Ct
3 Beech Ct
4 Sycamore Ho
5 Salisbury Gdns
6 Pegasus Ct
7 Buckhurst Ct
8 Mountbatten Ct
9 Atrium
D6 1 Richmond Ct
2 Highview Ct
3 Collins Ct
4 Lower Park Rd
5 Homecherry Ho

22

C1 1 Daniel Ho
2 Hawthorn Ct
3 Northcote
4 Edwin Ware Ct
5 Chalfont Wlk
6 Maple Ct
7 Montesole Ct
8 Viewpoint Ct

23

B3 1 Russettings
2 St Cuthberts Gdns
3 Cherry Croft Gdns
4 Claire Ct
5 Cornwall Ct
6 Falmouth Ho
7 Newlyn Ho
8 Chestnuts The
9 Dunford Ct
10 Stratton Ct
11 Hanover Ct

25

C5 1 Belgrave Gdns
2 Heywood Ct
3 Norfolk Ho
4 Garden Ct
5 Chatsworth Ct
6 Chartridge Ct
7 Hardwick Ct
8 Cheltenham Ct
9 Cargrey Ho
10 Holbein Ho
11 Goodwood Ct
12 Ascot Pl
13 Longchamp Ct
14 Halfacre
15 Burnham Ct
16 Dingle Ct

17 Woodcroft
18 Daneglen Ct
19 Buckingham Par
C6 1 Bickley Ct
2 Kelmscott Ct
3 Elstree Ho
4 Brompton Ct
5 Kenmare Ct
6 Burlington Park Ho
7 Gressenham Ct
8 Amora

26

D5 1 Penshurst Ct
2 Cranbourne Ct
3 Wilton Ct
4 Saxon Ct
5 Abbey Ct
6 Kenlor Ct
7 Daniel Ct
8 Hillcrest Ct
9 Hunters Lo
10 Orion Ct

27

A1 1 Colesworth Ho
2 Crokesley Ho
3 Curtlington Ho
4 Clare Ho
5 Kedyngton Ho
A3 1 Tadbourne Ct
2 Truman Cl
3 Lords Ct
4 Hutton Row
5 Compton Cl
6 Botham Cl
7 Bradman Row
A6 1 Iris Wlk
2 Sycamore Cl
3 Aster Ct
4 Firethorn Cl
5 Berberry Cl
6 Hibiscus Cl
B5 1 Monarchs Ct
2 Kensington Ct
3 Grosvenor Ct
4 Chasewood Ct
C2 1 Rufforth Ct
2 Riccall Ct
3 Lindholme Ct
4 Driffield Ct
5 Jack Ashley Ct
6 Folkingham La
7 Debden Cl
8 Holbeach Cl
9 Shawbury Cl
10 Daniel Ct
11 Leander Ct
12 Nimrod
13 Nisbet
14 Pixton
15 Rapide
16 Ratier
D1 1 Gauntlet
2 Guilfoyle
3 Grebe
4 Gates
5 Galy
6 Folland
7 Firefly
8 Halifax
9 Debussy
10 Crosbie
11 Grant Ct
12 Ham Ct
13 Deal Ct
14 Ember Ct
15 Canterbury Ct
16 Beaumont Ct
17 Cirrus
18 Defiant
19 Dessouter
20 Douglas
21 Cobham
22 Clayton
23 Camm
24 Bradon
25 Boarhound
26 Bodmin
27 Bleriot
28 Blackburn
29 Audax

30 Anson
31 Albatross
32 Arran Ct
33 Mavis Ct
34 Goosander Ct
35 Platt Halls (a)
36 Writtle Ho
37 Platt Halls (b)
38 Platt Halls (c)
D2 1 Slatter
2 Sopwith
3 Saimet
4 Sassoon
5 Roe
6 Orde
7 Osprey
8 Prodger
9 Randall
10 Porte
11 Norris
12 Nardini
13 Noel
14 Nicolson
15 Napier
16 Nighthawk
17 Moorhouse
18 Moineau
19 Mitchell
20 Lysander
21 Lillywhite
22 Martynside
23 March
24 Kemp
25 Mercury
26 Merlin
27 Hudson
28 Hawker
29 Hawfinch
30 Heracles
31 Hector
32 Concourse The
D3 1 Wellington
2 Wheeler
3 Whittaker
4 Whittle
5 Tedder
6 Cranwell Ct
7 Tait
8 Spooner

28

D1 1 York Ho
2 Windsor Ho
3 Regency Cres
4 Normandy Ho
5 Allerton Ct
6 Beaulieu Ho
7 Dewlands Ct
8 Knightshayes Ho

29

A3 2 Frances & Dick James Ct
3 Farthing Ct
4 Coniston Ct
B1 1 Carlisle Lo
2 Laburnum Lo
3 Eden Ct
4 Moorcroft Ct
5 Clifford Lo
6 Acacia Lo
7 Cumberland Ct
8 Little Dell Lo
9 Cyprus Ct
10 Cyprus Ho
C2 1 Sheringham Ct
2 St Ronan's
3 Crescent Rise
4 Elm Ct
5 Norman Ct
6 Marlow Ct
7 Dancastle Ct
8 Newman Ct
9 Station Mans
10 Alice Ct
D3 1 Hadley Ct
2 Sherbrook Ho
3 Shine Ho
4 Regent Ct
5 Lodge Mead Ct
6 Spencer Ct
7 Zenith Lo
8 Burberry Ct

D5 1 Silverbell Ct
2 Inverey Ho
3 Wimbush Ho
4 Tudor Lo
5 Duncan Ct
6 Phillipson Ho
D6 1 Brookfield Ct
2 Magnolia Ct
3 Dunbar Ct
4 Haughmond
5 Nansen Village
6 Willow Ct
7 Birch Ct
8 Beechcroft Ct
9 Speedwell Ct
10 Woodside Ct
11 Speedwell Ho
12 Rebecca Ct
13 Ashbourne Ct
14 Forest Ct
15 Beecholme
16 Greville Lo
17 St Johnstone Ho
18 Ashbourne Cl
19 Clements Ct
20 Station App
21 Montclair Ct
22 Winterberry Ct
23 Caroline Ct

30

A4 1 Sharon Ct
2 Lydia Ct
3 Beatrice Lo
4 Grange Ct
5 Blissland Ct
A5 1 Archgate Bsns Ctr
2 Robart Ho
3 Danescroft
4 Cornelius Ct
5 Gable Lo
6 Waterville Lo
7 Chand Ho
B1 1 New Trinity Rd
2 Garden Ho
3 Todd Ho
4 Sayers Ho
5 Mowbray Ho
6 Bouchier Ho
7 Cleveland Ho
8 Goodyear Ho
9 Lochleven Ho
10 Berwick Ho
11 Oak Ho
12 Hilton Ho
13 East View Ho
14 Myddleton Ho
15 Willow Wlk
16 Craven Ho
17 Willow Ho
18 Vane Ho
19 Adelphi Ct
20 Annette White Lo
21 Foskett Ho
22 Elmfield Ho
23 Sycamore Ho
24 Netherwood
25 Rew Lo
26 William Cl
B5 1 Murray Ho
2 Damon Ho
3 Wendy Ho
4 Lychgate Ct
5 Clarence Ct
6 Carley Ct
7 Hermiston Ct
8 Cardrew Ct
9 Whitefriars Ct
D5 1 Halliwick Ct
2 Halliwick Court Par
3 Queen's Par
4 St John's Villas
5 Hartland Ct
6 Kennard Mans
7 Bensley Ct
8 Leadbeaters Cl
9 Gibson Ct
10 Burton Ct
11 Knights Ct
12 Constable Cl
13 Alderman Ct

31
A3 1 Campe Ho
2 Betstyle Ho
3 Pymmes Brook Ho
4 Mosswell Ho
5 Cavendish Ho
6 Tudor Ho
7 Kingsfield Ho
8 Peacehaven Ct
9 Hatch Ho
10 Hampden Ct
11 Crown Ct
A4 1 Cheddar Cl
2 Wincanton Ct
3 Whitby Ct
4 Richmond Ct
5 Tadworth Ct
6 Wensley Cl
7 Howeth Ct
8 Kilnsey Ct
9 Harrogate Ct
10 Ripon Ct
B1 1 Cedar Ct
2 Carisbrook
3 St Ivian Ct
4 Barrington Ct
5 Essex Lo
B6 1 Grovefield
2 Lapworth
3 Stewards Holte Wlk
4 Sarnes Ct
5 Stanhope Ho
6 Holmsdale Ho
7 Crosby Ct
8 Leyland Ct
9 Boundary Ct
10 Stateland Ct
C5 1 Barbara Martin Ho
2 Jerome Ct
3 Limes Cl
4 Arnos Grove Ct
5 Cedar Ct
6 Betspath Ho
7 Curtis Ho
8 Mason Ho
9 Danford Ho
10 New Southgate Ind Est
11 Palmer's Ct
12 Swinson Ho
13 Jackson Ho

32
A4 1 Brownlow Lo
2 Brownlow Ct
3 Latham Ct
4 Fairlawns
5 Beaumaris
C1 1 Penwortham Ct
2 Tarleton Ct
3 Holmeswood Ct
4 Kwesi Johnson Ct
5 Sandlings The
6 Suraj Ho
C6 1 Hazelwood Ct
2 Ashbourne Lo
3 Mapledurham Ct

33
D1 1 Kenmare Dr
2 Ashling Ho
3 Honeysett Rd
4 Wilson's Ave
5 Palm Tree Ct
6 Stoneleigh Ct
7 Brook St
D3 1 Charles Ho
2 Moselle Ho
3 Ermine Ho
4 Kathleen Ferrier Ct
5 Concord Ho
6 Rees Ho
7 Williams Ho
8 Nursery Ct
9 William Rainbird Ho
10 Gibson Bsns Ctr
11 Wingate Trad Est
D4 1 Regan Ho
2 Isis Ho
3 Boundary Ct
4 Stellar Ho
5 Cooperage Cl

34
A5 1 Angel Pl
2 Cross St
3 Scott Ho
4 Beck Ho
5 Booker Rd
6 Bridport Ho
7 Cordwain Ho
8 St James's Ct
9 Highmead
A6 1 Walton Ho
2 Alma Ho
3 Brompton Ho
4 Field Ho
5 Bradwell Mews
6 Angel Corner Par
7 Paul Ct
8 Cuthbert Rd
9 Brockenhurst Mews
B3 1 Kenneth Robbins Ho
2 Charles Bradlaugh Ho
3 Woodrow Ct
4 Cheviot
5 Corbridge
6 Whittingham
7 Eastwood Cl
8 Alnwick
9 Bamburgh
10 Bellingham
11 Briaris Cl

35
A1 1 Clayton Ct
2 St Andrew's Ct
3 Aranya Ct
4 Fitzwilliam Ho
A2 1 Romany Gdns
2 Swansland Gdns
3 Garnett Way
4 Claymore Ct
5 Winchester Ct
C5 1 Ainslie Ho
2 Lewis Ho

36
B5 1 Hedgemoor Ct
2 Hewitt Ho
3 Castle Ho
4 Bailey Ct
5 Harcourt Ho
6 Gerboa Ct
7 Wentworth Ct
D1 1 Chatham Rd
2 Washington Rd
3 Cherry Tree Ct
4 Grosvenor Lo
5 Torfell
D2 1 Hillboro Ct
2 Dorchester Ct

37
A1 1 Chiltons The
2 Ullswater Ct
3 Leigh Ct
4 Woburn Ct
5 Alveston Sq
6 Eaton Ct
7 Regency Ct
8 Cowley Ct
9 High Oaks Lo
A2 1 Lindal Ct
2 Hockley Ct
3 Woodleigh
4 Milne Ct
5 Cedar Ct
6 Elizabeth Ct
7 Silvermead
8 Laurel Mead Ct
9 Mitre Ct
10 Pevensey Ct
11 Lyndhurst Ct
12 Manor Court Lo
A3 1 New Jubilee Ct
2 Chartwell Ct
3 Greenwood
4 Clementine Wlk
A4 1 Terrace The
2 Broomhill Ct
3 Clifton Ct
4 Fairstead Lo
5 Hadleigh Lo
6 Broadmead Ct
7 Wilton Ct
8 Fairfield Ct
9 Higham Ct
10 Aston Ct
A6 1 Tree Tops
2 Cranfield Ct
3 Percival Ho
4 Raine Gdns
B1 1 Station Est
2 Station App
3 James Ct
C3 1 Liston Way
2 Elizabeth Ct
3 Coopersale Cl
4 Sunset Ct
5 Lambourne Ct
C4 1 Hope Cl
2 Rex Par
3 Shalford
4 Rodings The
5 Lawrence Ct
6 Cowan Lo

40
C1 1 Salisbury Ho
2 Rodwell Cl
3 Pretoria Ho
4 Ottawa Ho
5 Swallow Ct
6 Wellington Ho
7 Canberra Ho
C6 1 Tulip Ct
2 Hyacinth Ct
3 Rose Ct
4 Iris Ct
D6 1 Ashburton Ct
2 Northend Lodge

42
D3 1 Nightingale Ct
2 St John's Ct
3 Gayton Ct
4 Wilton Pl
5 Murray Ct
6 Cymbeline Ct
7 Knowles Ct
8 Charville Ct
9 Lime Ct
10 Petherton Ct
11 Garth Ct
12 Chalfont Ct
13 Shepherds Ct
D4 1 Crystal Cntr The
2 Blue Point Ct
3 Ryan Ho
4 Rothwell Ct
5 Bruce Ho
6 Middlesex Ct
7 Ingram Ho
8 Arless Ho
9 Leaf Ho
10 Becket Fold
11 Brandan Ho
12 Robert Ho

46
A2 1 Milton Rd
2 Stanley Rd
A3 1 Mapesbury Mews
2 York Mans
3 Telford Rd
A5 1 Pilkington Ct
2 Cousins Ct
3 Seton Ct
4 Frensham Ct
5 Chatton Ct
6 Geraldine Ct
7 Swynford Gdns
8 Miller Ct
9 Roffey Ct
10 Peace Ct
11 Rambler Ct
12 Lion Ct
13 Wenlock Gdns
14 Dogrose Ct
15 Harry Ct
16 Tribune Ct
17 Bonville Gdns
18 Pearl Ct
B4 1 Vivian Mans
2 Parade Mans
3 Georgian Ct
4 Florence Mans
5 Park Mans
6 Cheyne Ct
7 Queens Par
8 Central Mans
C5 1 Courtney Ho
2 Golderton
3 Thornbury
4 Ferrydale Lo
5 Studio Mews
6 Brampton La
7 Short St
8 Belle Vue Rd
9 Longford Ct
10 Ashwood Ho
D5 1 Midford Ho
2 Rockfield Ho
3 Lisselton Ho
4 Acrefield Ho

47
B2 1 Berkeley Ct
2 Exchange Mans
3 Beechcroft Ct
4 Nedahall Ct
B3 1 Charlton Lo
2 Clifton Gdns
B4 1 Hallswelle Par
2 Belmont Par
3 Temple Fortune Ho
4 Yew Tree Ct
5 Temple Fortune Par
6 Courtleigh
7 Arcade Ho
8 Queens Ct
9 Temple Fortune Ct
B5 1 Monkville Par
2 Ashbourne Par

48
A6 1 St Mary's Gn
2 Dunstan Cl
3 Paul Byrne Ho
4 Longfield Ct
5 Warwick Ct
6 Branksome Ct
7 Sherwood Hall

49
B6 1 Dorchester Ct
2 Old Chapel Pl
3 Athenaeum Pl
4 Risborough Cl
5 Risborough Ct
C1 1 Calvert Ct
2 Academy The
3 Whitehall Mans
4 Pauntley St
5 Archway Hts
6 Pauntley Ho
D1 1 Louise White Ho
2 Levison Way
3 Sanders Way
4 Birbeck Ho
5 Scholars Ct
D2 1 Eleanor Rathbone Ho
2 Christopher Lo
3 Monkridge
4 Marbleford Ct
5 High London
6 Garton Ho
7 Hilltop Ho
8 Caroline Martyn Ho
9 Arthur Henderson Ho
10 Margaret Mcmillan Ho
11 Enid Stacy Ho
12 Mary McArthur Ho
13 Bruce Glasier Ho
14 John Wheatley Ho
15 Keir Hardie Ho
16 Monroe Ho
17 Iberia Ho
18 Lygoe Ho
19 Lambert Ho
20 Shelbourne Ho
21 Arkansas Ho
22 Lafitte Ho
23 Shreveport Ho
24 Packenham Ho
25 Orpheus Ho
26 Fayetville Ho
27 Bayon Ho
D4 1 Kelland Cl
2 Truro Ct
3 Veryan Ct
4 Coulsdon Ct

50
A1 1 Beeches The
2 Lambton Ct
3 Nugent Ct
4 Lambton Mews
5 Mews The
A2 1 Marie Lloyd Gdns
2 Edith Cavell Cl
3 Marie Stopes Ct
4 Jessie Blythe La
5 Barbara Rudolph Ct
6 Hetty Rees Ct
7 Leyden Mans
8 Brambledown
9 Lochbie
10 Lyngham Ct
11 High Mount
12 Woodlands The
A4 1 Margaret Hill Ho
2 Manray Ct
3 Hermiston Ct
4 Carleton Ho
A5 1 Mackenzie Ho
2 Stowell Ho
3 Campsbourne Ho
4 Palace Gate Mews
B1 1 Lawson Ct
2 Wiltshire Ct
3 Fenstanton
4 Hutton Ct
5 Wisbech
D5 1 Wordsworth Par
2 Spanswick Lo
3 Barker Ho
D6 1 Langham Cl
2 Sidi Ct
3 Ince Terr

51
A2 1 Finmere Ho
2 Keynsham Ho
3 Kilpeck Ho
4 Knaresborough Ho
5 Leighfield Ho
6 Lonsdale Ho
7 Groveley Ho
8 Wensleydale Ho
9 Badminton Ct
B2 1 Selwood Ho
2 Mendip Ho
3 Ennerdale Ho
4 Delamere Ho
5 Westwood Ho
6 Bernwood Ho
7 Allerdale Ho
8 Chattenden Ho
9 Farningham Ho
10 Oakend Ho
C1 1 Godstone Ct
2 Farnham Ct
3 Milford Ct
4 Cranleigh Ct
5 Haslemere Ct
6 Belmont Ct
7 Hockworth Ho
8 Garratt Ho
9 Fairburn Ho
10 Thorndale Ho
11 Oakdene Ho
12 Briardale Ho
C3 1 Perry Ct
2 Henrietta Ho
3 Bournes Ho
4 Chisley Rd
5 Twyford Ho
6 Langford Cl
7 Hatchfield Ho
D1 1 Stamford Hill Mans
2 Montefiore Ct
3 Berwyn Ho
4 Clent Ho
5 Chiltern Ho
6 Laindon Ho
7 Pentland Ho
8 Powell Ct

52
D4 1 Westerfield Rd
2 Suffield Rd
D5 1 Laseron Ho
2 Greenway Cl
3 Tottenham Gn E
4 Tottenham Gn E South Side
5 Deaconess Ct
6 Elliot Ct
7 Bushmead Cl
8 Beaufort Ho
9 Tynemouth Terr
D6 1 Holcombe Rd
2 Rigby Ho
3 Chaplin Rd
4 Keswick Apartments
5 Ambleside Cl
6 Lauriston Apartments
7 Terrall Apartments
8 Old School Ct
9 Nicholson Ct
10 Reynardson's Ct
11 Protheroe Ho

52
A1 1 Stamford Gr E
2 Stamford Mans
3 Grove Mans
4 Stamford Gr W
B1 1 Hawkwood Mount
2 Holmbury View
3 High Hill Ferry
4 Leaside Ho
5 Courtlands
6 Ivy Ho
7 Shelford Ct

53
A4 1 Hammond Ct
2 St James Apartments
3 Grange The
A5 1 Bristol Park Rd
2 Stoneydown Ho
3 Callonfield
4 Hardyng Ho
C1 1 Wellington Mans
2 Clewer Ct
3 Cochrane Ct
C5 1 Westbury Ho
2 Hatherley Ho
3 Vintry Mews
4 Tylers Ct
5 Merchants Lo
6 Gillards Mews
7 Blacksmiths Ho
8 Central Par
D1 1 Fitzgerald Ct
2 Bechervaise Ct
3 Underwood Ct
D2 1 Staton Ct
2 Howell Ct
3 Atkinson Ct
4 Russell Ct
5 St Catherines Twr
6 St Lukes Ct
7 St Matthews Ct
8 St Mark's Ct
9 St Elizabeth Ct
10 Emanuel Ct
11 St Thomas Ct
12 Beaumont Ho
13 Shelley Ct
14 St Paul's Twr
15 Flack Ct
16 King Ct
17 Osborne Ct
18 Muriel Ct
19 All Saints Twr
20 St Josephs Ct
D5 1 Nash Ho
2 St Columbas Ho
3 Attlee Terr
4 Astins Ho
5 Lindens The
6 Kevan Ct
7 Squire's Almshouses
8 Berry Field Cl
9 Connaught Ct
10 Holmcroft Ho
11 St Mary's Church Ho
D6 1 Hallingbury Ct
2 Mace Ho
3 Gaitskell Ho
4 Hancocke Ho
5 Trinity Ho
6 Fanshaw Ho
7 Hilltop
8 Batten Ho
9 Bradwell Ho
10 Walton Ho
11 Temple Ho
12 Gower Ho
13 Maple Ho
14 Poplars Ho
15 Cedars Ho
16 Kimm Ho
17 O'Grady Ho
18 Latham Ho
19 Powell Ho
20 Crosbie Ho

54
A2 1 Ayerst Ct
2 Dare Ct
D3 1 Sherboro Rd
2 Westcott Cl
3 Cadoxton Ave

9 St Edwards Ct
A4 1 Collard's Almshouses
2 Ellen Miller Ho
3 Tom Smith Ho
A5 1 Northwood Twr
2 Walnut Ct
3 Albert Whicher Ho
4 Pelly Ct
5 Ravenswood Ind Est
6 Holland Ct
7 Emberson Ho
8 St Mark's Ho
9 Alfred Villas
10 Leonard Ho
11 Old Station Yard The
A6 1 St David's Ct
2 Golden Par
3 Chestnuts Ct
4 Matthew Ct
5 Gilbert Ho
6 Manning Ho
7 Southgate Ho
8 Boyden Ct
9 Prospect Ho
10 Newton Ho
D2 1 Buxton Ct
2 Hanbury Dr
3 Forest Lea
4 Watershipdown Ho

55
A3 1 Aldham Hall
2 Parkside Ct
3 Mapperley Cl
4 Weavers Ho
5 Cyna Ct
6 Reed Mans
7 Thornton Ho
8 Hardwick Ct
A4 1 Kingsley Grange
2 Station Par
3 Gwynne Ho
4 Staveley Ct
5 Thurlow Ct
6 Devon Ho
7 Wellington Pas
8 Wanstead Hts
9 Hollies The
10 Little Holt
11 Hunter Ct
12 Mountier Ct
13 Woodland Ct
14 Dudley Ct
15 Struan Ho
16 Westleigh Ct
A5 1 Shernwood Ho
2 Orwell Lo
3 Hermitage Ct
4 Gowan Lea
5 Woodford Ho
6 Eagle Ct
7 Newbury Ct
8 Shelley Ct
9 Hardy Ct
10 Dickens Ct
11 Byron Ct
A6 1 Millbrook
2 Half Acre
3 Elmbrook
4 Grange The
5 Glenavon Lo
6 Glenwood Ct
7 Ferndown
8 Embassy Ct
9 Orestes Ct
10 Walbrook
11 Helmsley
12 Snaresbrook Hall
B4 1 Nightingale Ct
2 Chelston Ct
3 Grosvenor Ct
4 Louise Ct
5 St Davids Ct
6 Cedar Ct
7 Shrubbery The
8 Nightingale Mews
B5 1 Great Hall The
2 Clock Ct
3 Langham Ho
B6 1 Victoria Ct
2 Kenwood Gdns
3 Thaxted Lo
4 Albert Rd
5 Albert Ho
6 Falcon Ct
7 Deborah Ct
8 Swift Ho
9 Pulteney Gdns
10 Spring Ct
11 Trinity Gdns

56
B4 1 High View Par
2 Spurway Par
3 Florence Root Ho
4 Rohan Pl
5 Homeheather Ho

57
A3 1 Catherine Ct
2 Lincoln Ct
3 Ivy Terr
4 Newbury Cotts

58
B1 1 Caledonian Cl
1 Talisman Cl
2 Norseman Cl
3 Frank Slater Ho
4 Brook's Mans
5 Brook's Par
B2 1 Mitre Ct
2 Coppins The
3 Stanetta Ct
4 Wilnett Ct
5 Wilnett Villas
B4 1 Sudbury Ct
2 Dunwich Ct
3 Cromer Terr
4 Norfolk Ct
5 Framlingham Ct
6 Yoxford Ct
C4 1 Swaffham Ct
2 Nacton Ct
3 Suffolk Ct
D2 1 Pavement Mews
2 Chadview Ct
3 Granary Ct
4 Bedwell Ct
5 Chapel La
6 Faulkner Cl
7 Maple Ct
8 Willow Ct
9 Cedar Terr

63
C2 1 Wimborne Ct
2 Haydock Green Flats
3 Brighton Dr
4 Blaydon Ct
5 Fakenham Cl
6 Rutland Ho
7 Windsor Ho

65
D3 1 Lowry Lo
2 Morritt Ho
3 Charles Goddard Ho
4 Snow Ct
5 Willow Tree Ct
6 Oak Lo

66
A2 1 Montrose Cres
2 Peggy Quirke Ct
3 Marylebone Ct
4 Waterloo Ct
5 Euston Ct
6 St Pancras Ct
7 Paddington Ct
8 Copland Mews
9 Coronet Par
10 Aylestone Ct
11 Charlotte Ct
A3 1 Wembley Mkt
2 Market Way
3 Lodge Ct
4 Central Sq
5 Manor Ct
6 Rupert Ave
7 Lily Ho
C4 1 Wembley Mkt

67
A5 1 Curie Ho
2 Darwin Ho
3 Priestley Ho
4 Rutherford Ho
5 Fleming Ho
6 Lister Ho
7 Edison Ho
B1 1 Biko Ho
2 Kingthorpe Terr
3 Scott Ho
4 Peary Ho
5 Shackleton Ho
6 Amundsen Ct
7 Brentfield Ho
8 Nansen Ho
9 Stonebridge Ct
10 Newcroft Ho
11 Magellan Ct
12 Leadbetter Ct
13 Jefferies Ho
14 Cowan Ct
15 Prothero Ho
16 Crawford St
17 Clark Ct
18 Diamond St
19 Mary Seacole Villas
C1 1 Beveridge Rd
2 Purcell Mews
3 George Lansbury Ho
4 Charles Hobson Ho
5 Reade Wlk
6 Westbury Ho
7 Bridge Ct
C4 1 Grange Ct
2 Green Ct
C5 1 Hazelwood Ct
2 Winslow Cl

68
A2 1 Regency Mews
2 Tudor Mews
3 Utopia Ho
4 Bell Flats
5 Angel Ct

A5 1 Bourne Ho
2 Carton Ho
3 Bidwell Ho
4 Woodbridge Cl
5 Mackenzie Ho
6 Banting Ho
C2 1 Rutland Park Gdns
2 Rutland Park Mans
3 Queens Par
4 Harcourt Ho
5 Solidarity Ho
6 Electra Ct
7 Cassandra Ct
8 Carlton Ct
D4 1 Oaklands Mews
2 Acer Ct
3 Maple Ct
4 Argyle Mans

69

A1 1 Christ Church Ct
2 Paul Daisley Ct
3 Fountain Ho
4 Kingston Ho
5 Waverley Ct
6 Weston Ho
7 Mapes Ho
8 Athelstan Gdns
9 Leff Ho
B1 1 Alma Birk Ho
2 Brooklands Ct
3 Brooklands Court Apartments
4 Cleveland Mans
5 Buckley Ct
6 Webheath
B5 1 Mortimer Cl
2 Primrose Ct
3 Sunnyside Ho
4 Sunnyside
5 Prospect Pl
C1 1 Linstead St
2 Embassy Ho
3 Acol Ct
4 Kings Wood Ct
5 Douglas Ct
6 King's Gdns
7 Carlton Mans
8 Smyrna Mans
9 New Priory Ct
10 Queensgate Pl
11 Brondesbury Mews
C2 1 Dene Mans
2 Sandwell Cres
3 Sandwell Mans
4 Hampstead West
5 Redcroft
C3 1 Orestes Mews
2 Walter Northcott Ho
3 Polperro Mans
4 Lyncroft Mans
5 Marlborough Mans
6 Alexandra Mans
7 Cumberland Mans
8 Cavendish Mans
9 Ambassador Ct
10 Welbeck Mans
11 Inglewood Mans
12 Dennington Park Mansions
C5 1 Portman Hts
2 Hermitage Ct
3 Moreland Ct
4 Wendover Ct
D2 1 Beswick Mews
2 Worcester Mews
3 Minton Mews
4 Doulton Mews
5 Laurel Ho
6 Sandalwood Ho
7 Iroko Ho
8 Banyan Ho
9 Rosewood Ho
10 Ebony Ho
11 Rosemont Mans
12 Exeter Mews

70

A1 1 Harrold Ho
2 Glover Ho
3 Byron Ct
4 Nalton Ho
A2 1 Petros Gdns
2 Heath Ct
3 Imperial Twrs
4 Fairhurst
5 St John's Ct
6 New College Ct
7 Chalford
8 Rosslyn Mans
9 Sutherland Ho
A4 1 Windmill Hill
2 Highgrove Point
3 Gainsborough Ho
4 Holly Bush Hill
5 Heath Mans
6 Holly Bush Steps
7 Pavilion Ct
8 Holly Berry La
9 New Campden Ct
10 Holly Bush Vale
11 Benham's Pl
12 Prospect Pl
13 Yorkshire Grey Pl
14 Gardnor Mans
15 Ellerdale Cl
16 Monro Ho
17 Prince Arthur Mews
18 Prince Arthur Ct
19 Village Mount
20 Perrin's Ct
21 Wells Ct
22 Bakers Pas
23 Spencer Wlk
24 Bird In Hand Yd
25 Kings Well
26 New Ct
27 Streatley Pl
28 Mansfield Pl
29 Upper Hampstead Wlk
A5 1 Hampstead Sq
2 Stamford Cl
3 Mount Sq The
B1 1 New College Par
2 Northways Par
3 Noel Ho
4 Campden Ho
5 Centre Hts
6 Hickes Ho
7 Swiss Terr
8 Leitch Ho
9 Jevons Ho
10 Langhorne Ct
11 Park Lo
12 Avenue Lo
B2 1 Belsize Park Mews
2 Baynes Mews
3 McCrone Mews
B3 1 Belsize Court Garages
2 Roscommon Ho
3 Akenside Ct
B4 1 White Bear Pl
2 Wells Ho The
3 Boades Mews
4 Flask Cotts
5 Coach House Yd
6 Pilgrim's Pl
7 Rosslyn Mews
C2 1 Banff Ho
2 Glenloch Ct
3 Havercourt
4 Holmefield Ct
5 Gilling Ct
6 Howitt Cl
7 Manor Mans
8 Straffan Lo
9 Romney Ct
10 Lancaster Stables
11 Eton Garages
D1 1 Hancock Nunn Ho
2 Higginson Ho
3 Duncan Ho
4 Mary Wharrie Ho
5 Rockstraw Ho
6 Cleaver Ho
7 Chamberlain St
8 Sharples Hall St
9 Primrose Mews
10 Rothwell St
11 St Georges Mews
D2 1 Alder Ho
2 Hornbeam Ho
3 Whitebeam Ho
4 Aspen Ho
5 Rowan Ho
6 Beech Ho
7 Chestnut Ho
8 Oak Ho
9 Willow Ho
10 Sycamore Ho
11 Maple Ho
12 Hazel Ho
13 Elaine Ct
14 Faircourt
15 Walham Ct
16 Stanbury Ct
17 Priory Mans
18 Wellington Ho
19 Grange The
D3 1 Cayford Ho
2 Du Maurier Ho
3 Isokon Flats
4 Palgrave Ho
5 Garnett Ho
6 Stephenson Ho
7 Park Dwellings
8 Siddons Ho
9 Mall Studios
10 Park Hill Wlk
11 Wordsworth Pl
12 Fraser Regnart Ct
13 St Pancras Almshouses

71

A1 1 Bridge Ho
2 Hardington
3 Mead Cl
4 Rugmere
5 Tottenhall
6 Beauvale
7 Broomfield
A2 1 Silverbirch Wlk
2 Penshurst
3 Wingham
4 Westwell
5 Chislet
6 Burmarsh
7 Shipton Ho
8 Stonegate
9 Leysdown
10 Headcorn
11 Lenham
12 Halstow
13 Fordcombe
14 Cannington
15 Langridge
16 Athlone Ho
17 Pentland Ho
18 Beckington
19 Hawkridge
20 Edington
B1 1 Ferdinand Ho
2 Harmood Ho
3 Hawley Rd
4 Hawley Mews
5 Leybourne St
6 Barling
7 Tiptree
8 Havering
9 Candida Ct
10 Lorraine Ct
11 Donnington Ct
12 Welford Ct
13 Torbay Ct
14 Bradfield Ct
15 Torbay St
16 Water La
17 Leybourne Rd
18 Haven St
19 Stucley Pl
20 Lawrence Ho
B2 1 Ashington
2 Priestley Ho
3 Leonard Day Ho
4 Old Dairy Mews
5 Monmouth Ho
6 Alpha Ct
7 Una Ho
8 Widford
9 Heybridge
10 Roxwell
11 Hamstead Gates
B4 1 Denyer Ho
2 Stephenson Ho
3 Trevithick Ho
4 Brunel Ho
5 Newcomen Ho
6 Faraday Ho
7 Winifrede Paul Ho
8 Wardlow
9 Fletcher Ct
10 Tideswell
11 Grangemill
12 Hambrook Ct
13 Calver
C1 1 Cherry Tree Ct
2 Chichester Ct
3 Durdans Ho
4 Philia Ho
5 Bernard Shaw Ct
6 Foster Ct
7 Bessemer Ct
8 Hogarth Ct
9 Rochester Ct
10 Soane Ct
11 Wallett Ct
12 Inwood Ct
13 Wrotham Rd
14 St Thomas Ct
15 Caulfield Ct
16 Bruges Pl
17 Reachview Cl
18 Lawfords Wharf
C3 1 Eleanor Ho
2 Falkland Pl
3 Kensington Ho
4 Willingham Cl
5 Kenbrook Ho
6 Aborfield
7 Great Field
8 Appleford
9 Forties The
10 Maud Wilkes Cl
11 Dunne Mews
12 Dowdeny Cl
C4 1 Benson Ct
2 Tait Ho
3 Manorfield Cl
4 Greatfield Cl
5 Longley Ho
6 Lampson Ho
7 Davidson Ho
8 Palmer Ho
9 Lambourn Cl
10 Morris Ho
11 Owen Ho
C5 1 Hunter Ho
2 Fisher Ho
3 Lang Ho
4 Temple Ho
5 Palmer Ho
6 Carlisle Ho
7 Durham Ho
8 Suffolk Ho
9 Lincoln Ho
10 Llewellyn Ho
11 Fell Ho
12 Aveling Ho
13 Merryweather Ct
14 Brennands Ct
15 St Christophers Ct
16 Francis Terrace Mews
C6 1 Flowers Mews
2 Archway Cl
3 Sandridge St
4 Bovingdon Cl
5 Cavell Ct
6 Torrence Ho
7 Rowan Wlk
8 Laurel Cl
9 Forest Way
10 Larch Cl
11 Pine Cl
12 Alder Mews
13 Aspen Cl
D1 1 Hillier Ho
2 Gairloch Ho
3 Cobham Mews
4 Bergholt Mews
5 Blakeney Cl
6 Weavers Way
7 Allensbury Pl
D2 1 Rowstock
2 Peckwater Ho
3 Wolsey Ho
4 Pandian Way
5 Busby Mews
6 Caledonian Sq
7 Canal Bvd
8 Northpoint Sq
9 Lock Mews
10 Carters Cl
11 York Ho
12 Hungerford Rd
13 Cliff Road Studios
14 Cliff Ct
15 Camelot Ho
16 Church Studios
17 Camden Terr
D3 1 Blake Ho
2 Quelch Ho
3 Lee Ho
4 Willbury Ho
5 Howell Ho
6 Holmsbury Ho
7 Leith Ho
8 Betchworth Ho
9 Rushmore Ho
10 Dugdale Ho
11 Horsendon Ho
12 Colley Ho
13 Coombe Ho
14 Ivinghoe Ho
15 Buckhurst Ho
16 Saxonbury Ct
17 Charlton Ct
18 Apollo Studios
19 Barn Cl
20 Long Meadow
21 Landleys Field
22 Margaret Bondfield Ho
23 Haywood Lo
D4 1 Fairlie Ct
2 Trecastle Way
3 Dalmeny Avenue Est
4 Hyndman Ho
5 Carpenter Ho
6 Graham Ho
7 Tufnell Mans
D5 1 Melchester Ho
2 Norcombe Ho
3 Weatherbury Ho
4 Wessex Ho
5 Archway Bsns Ctr
6 Harford Mews
7 Opera Ct
8 Rupert Ho
9 All Saints Church
D6 1 Bowerman Ct
2 Gresham Pl
3 Hargrave Mans
4 Church Garth
5 John King Ct
6 Ramsey Ct

72

A3 1 Kimble Ho
2 Saxonbury Ct
3 Poynder Ct
4 Pangbourne Ho
5 Moulsford Ho
A4 1 Arcade The
2 Macready Pl
3 Cardwell Rd
4 Mcmorran Ho
5 Crayford Ho
6 Whitby Ct
7 Prospect Pl
A5 1 Northview
2 Tufnell Park Mans
3 Fulford Mans
4 Tollington Ho
A6 1 Bracey Mews
2 Christie Ct
3 Ringmer Gdns
4 Kingsdown Rd
5 Cottenham Ho
6 St Paul's Ct
7 Rickthorne Rd
8 Stanley Terr
9 Arundel Lo
10 Landseer Ct
B1 1 Kerwick Cl
2 Rydston Cl
3 Skegness Ho
4 Frederica St
5 Ponder St
6 Kings Ct
7 Freeling St
8 Coatbridge Ho
9 Tilloch St
B2 1 Burns Ho
2 Scott Ho
3 Wellington Mews
4 Roman Ct
5 Piccadilly Ct
B3 1 Culverin Ct
2 Garand Ct
3 Mount Carmel
B4 1 Buckmaster Ho
2 Loreburn Ho
3 Cairns Ho
4 Halsbury Ho
5 Chelmsford Ho
6 Cranworth Ho
B6 1 Berkeley Wlk
2 Lazar Wlk
3 Thistlewood Cl
4 Tomlins Wlk
5 Andover Ho
6 Barmouth Ho
7 Chard Ho
8 Methley Ho
9 Rainford Ho
10 Woodbridge Cl
11 Allerton Wlk
12 Falconer Wlk
13 Sonderburg Rd
14 St Mark's Mans
15 Athol Ct
C1 1 Mountfort Terr
2 Avon Ho
3 Buckland Ho
4 Dovey Lo
5 Carfree Cl
6 Mitchell Ho
7 New College Mews
8 Lofting Ho
9 Brooksby Ho
10 Cara Ho
C3 1 Slaney Pl
2 Eastwood Cl
3 Milton Pl
4 Hartnoll Ho
5 St James School Flats
6 Widnes Ho
7 Tranmere Ho
8 Victoria Mans
9 Formby Ct
10 Mersey Ho
11 Birkenhead Ho
12 Drayton Park Mews
C6 1 Brookfield
2 Churnfield
D1 1 Islington Park Mews
2 Evelyn Denington Ct
3 Bassingbourn Ho
4 Cadmore Ho
5 Adstock Ho
6 Garston Ho
7 Flitton Ho
8 Datchworth Ho
9 Battishill St
10 Almeida St
11 Edward's Cotts
12 Hyde's Pl
13 Tyndale Terr
14 Spriggs Ho
15 Barratt Ho
16 Spencer Pl
17 Chadston Ho
18 Whiston Ho
19 Wakelin Ho
20 Tressel Cl
21 Canonbury Ct
22 Halton Ho
23 Shillingford St
24 Highbury Mans
25 Premier Ho
26 Waterloo Gdns
D2 1 Hampton Ct
2 Salisbury Ho
D3 1 De Barowe Mews
2 Fieldview Ct
3 Viewpoint
4 Ashurst Lo
D4 1 Chestnuts The
2 Bowen Ct
3 Peckett Sq
D5 1 Hurlock Ho
2 Blackstock Ho
3 Vivian Comma Cl
4 Monsell Ct

73

A1 1 Astey's Row
2 Lincoln Ho
3 Worcester Ho
4 Melville Pl
5 Wontner Cl
6 Hedingham Cl
7 Laundry La
8 Base Apartments
9 Walkinshaw Ct
10 New Bentham Ct
11 Bentham Ct
12 Haslam Ho
13 Horsfield Ho
14 Riverside Ho
15 Eric Fletcher Ct
16 Annette Cres
17 Ashby Ho
18 Lindsey Mews
19 Cardigan Wlk
20 Red House Sq
A2 1 Crowline Wlk
2 Upper Handa Wlk
3 Handa Wlk
4 Lismore Wlk
5 Bardsey Wlk
6 Walney Wlk
7 Upper Bardsey Wlk
8 Upper Lismore Wlk
9 Sark Ho
10 Guernsey Ho
11 Guernsey Rd
12 Sybil Thorndike Ho
13 Clephane Rd
14 Florence Nightingale Ho
15 Jersey Ho
16 Jethou Ho
17 Islay Wlk
18 Upper Caldy Wlk
19 Caldy Wlk
20 Alderney Ho
21 Gulland Wlk
22 Marquess Rd S
23 Upper Gulland Wlk
24 Church Rd
25 Oransay Rd
A3 1 Pearfield Ho
2 Larchfield Ho
3 Beresford Terr
4 Pondfield Ho
5 Ashfield Ho
6 Elmfield Ho
A4 1 Fountain Mews
2 Woodstock Ho
3 Henson Ct
4 Taverner Sq
B1 1 Downham Ct
2 Trafalgar Point
B2 1 John Kennedy Ct
2 John Kennedy Lo
3 Ball's Pond Pl
4 Haliday Wlk
5 Queen Elizabeth Ct
6 Canonbury Hts
7 Pinnacle The
8 Threadgold Ho
9 Wakeham St
10 Saffron Ct
11 Callaby Terr
12 Tilney Gdns
13 Westcliff Ho
14 Ilford Ho
15 Ongar Ho
16 Greenhills Terr
17 Romford Ho
18 Bute Wlk
19 Upper Ramsey Wlk
20 Rona Wlk
21 Thorndike Rd
B4 1 Ledo Ho
2 Salween Ho
3 Prome Ho
4 Arakan Ho
5 Rangoon Ho
6 Mandalay Ho
7 Karen Ho
8 Wingate Ho
9 Jubet Ho
10 Orde Ho
11 Chindit Ho
12 Mabel Thornton Ho
13 Crawshay Ho
14 Avon Ho
15 Connaught Mans
16 Jonson Ho
17 Herrick Ho
18 Donne Ho
19 Thirlmere Ho
20 Grasmere Ho
B6 1 Chestnut Cl
2 Sycamore Ho
3 Lordship Ho
4 Clissold Ho
5 Beech Ho
6 Laburnum Ho
7 Ormond Ho
8 Yew Tree Ct
9 Oak Ho
C1 1 Dorchester Ct
2 Wareham Ct
3 Dorset Ct
4 Stratton Ct
5 Swanage Ct
6 Blandford Ct
7 Portland Ct
8 Oscar Faber Pl
9 Metropolitan Bsns Ctr
10 Lancaster Cl
11 Palazzo Apartments
C2 1 Kingsland Gn
2 Kingsland Pas
3 Metropolitan Benefit Societies Almshouses
4 Nimrod Pas
5 De Beauvoir Pl
6 Warburton Cl
7 Buckingham Mews
8 Aztec Ct
C3 1 Hewling Ho
2 Matthias Ho
3 Port Royal Pl
4 Cressington Cl
5 King Henry's Yd
6 Bronte Ho
7 Sewell Ho
8 Lydgate Ho
9 Patmore Ho
10 Congreve Ho
11 Elton St
12 Conrad Ho
13 Southwell Ho
14 Neptune Ho
15 Campion Ho
16 Webster Ho
17 Meredith Ho
18 Beckford Ho
19 Ashley Ct
20 Hayling Cl
21 Millard Cl
22 Lydford Cl
23 Salcombe Rd
24 Truman's Rd
25 Templeton Cl
26 John Campbell Rd
27 Gillett Pl
28 Bradbury St
29 Thomas Crowell Ct
C4 1 Londesborough Ho
2 Knebworth Ho
3 Knebworth Rd
4 Bransby Ct
5 Imperial Ave
6 Leonard Pl
7 Shakspeare Mews
8 Binyon Ho
9 Shelley Ho
10 Browning Ho
11 Burns Ho
12 Andrew Marvell Ho
13 Wycliffe Ho
14 Blake Ho
15 Marlowe Ho
16 Fletcher Ho
17 Chaucer Ct
C5 1 Gujarat Ho
2 Marton Rd
3 Painsthorpe Rd
4 Selkirk Ho
5 Defoe Ho
6 Edward Friend Ho
7 Sheridan Ho
8 Barrie Ho
9 Arnold Ho
10 MacAulay Ho
11 Stowe Ho
12 Carlyle Ho
13 Shaftesbury Ho
14 Lillian Cl
15 Swift Ho
16 Dryden Ho
17 Scott Ct
18 Kingsfield Ho
19 Uhura Sq
20 Hartopp Ct
D1 1 Hilborough Rd
2 Shoreditch Ct
3 Evergreen Sq
4 Wyndhams Ct
5 Festival Ct
6 Fortune Ct
7 Rose Ct
8 Ability Plaza
D2 1 Prospect Ho
2 Woodland St
3 Crosby Wlk
4 Kirkland Wlk
5 Bowness Cl
6 Carlisle Wlk
7 Skelton Cl
8 Camerton Cl
9 Buttermere Wlk
10 Houghton Cl
11 Hayton Cl
12 Kingsland Sh Ctr
13 Springfield Ho
14 Parton Lo
15 Sanctuary Mews
D3 1 Miller's Terr
2 Chow Sq
3 Drysdale Flats
4 Gateway Mews
5 Birkbeck Mews
6 Winchester Pl
D4 1 Coronation Ave
2 Morris Blitz Ct
3 Shacklewell Ho
4 Alexandra Ct
D5 1 Lawrence Bldgs
2 Cottage Wlk
3 Batley Pl
D6 1 Garnham St
2 Garnham Cl
3 Sanford La
4 Sanford Wlk
5 Abney Gdns
6 Fleet Wood

74

A1 1 Aldington Ct
2 Bayton Ct
3 Rochford Wlk
A2 1 Burdon Ct
2 Thomson Ct
3 Bruno Ct
A3 1 Kingsdown Ho
2 Glendown Ho
3 Moredown Ho
4 Blakeney Cl
5 Beeston Cl
6 Benabo Ct
7 David Devine Ho

8 Kreedman Wlk
9 Hermitage Row
10 Grafton Ct
11 Lushington Terr
12 Aspen Ct
13 Pykewell Lo
14 Albion Works Studios
A5 1 Ravenscourt
2 Mellington Ct
3 Rendlesham Ho
4 Carroll Ct
A6 1 Cazenove Mans
2 Chedworth Ho
3 Aldergrove Ho
4 Abbotstone Ho
5 Briggeford Cl
6 Inglethorpe Ho
7 Ashdown Ho
8 Epping Ho
9 Cypress Cl
B1 1 Fortescue Ave
2 Pemberton Pl
3 Weston Wlk
4 Bayford St Ind Ctr
5 Bayford St
6 Sidworth St
7 Helmsley St
8 Cyntra Pl
9 Signal Ho
10 All Nations Ho
11 Vanguard Ho
12 Hacon Sq
B2 1 Bohemia Pl
2 Graham Mans
3 Marvin St
4 Boscobel Ho
5 Royal Oak Rd
6 Colonnades The
7 Sylvester Ho
8 Sylvester Path
9 Doctor Spurstowe Almshouses
10 Great Eastern Bldgs
11 Sojourner-Truth Cl
B3 1 Birchington Ho
2 Bicknor Ho
3 Boxley Ho
4 Adisham Ho
5 Cranbrook Ho
6 Marden Ho
7 Broome Ho
8 Crandale Ho
9 Cheriton Ho
10 Ditton Ho
11 Langley Ho
12 Dymchurch Ho
13 Elham Ho
14 Davina Ho
15 Pembury Ho
16 Downs Ct
17 Perrywood Ho
18 Staplehurst Ho
19 Pegwell Ho
20 Yalding Ho
21 Northbourne Ho
22 Monkton Ho
23 Milsted Ho
24 Athlone Ct
25 Clarence Pl
26 Gould Terr
27 Quested Ct
28 Brett Pas
29 Marcon Ct
30 Appleton Ct
B4 1 Ross Ct
2 Downs La
3 Gaviller Pl
4 Robert Owen Lo
5 Apprentice Way
6 Arrowe Ct
7 Gilwell Ct
8 Sutton Ct
9 St Andrews Mans
10 Kinnoull Mans
11 Rowhill Mans
12 Sladen Pl
13 Mothers Sq The
14 Richborough Ho
15 Sandgate Ho
16 Sheppey Ho
B5 1 De Vere Ct
2 Redcliffe Ct
3 Greville Ct
4 Anthony Kendal Ho
B6 1 Wentwood Ho
2 Woolmer Ho
3 Warwick Ct
4 Winslade Ho
5 Morriss Ho
6 Woodfield Ho
7 Rossendale Ho
8 Ettrick Ho
9 Charnwood Ho
10 Boyne Ho
11 Whitwell Ho
12 Scardale Ho
13 Hendale Ho
14 Brampton Cl
15 Aveley Ct
16 Aldeburgh Cl
17 Dennington Cl
C1 1 Pitcairn Ho
2 Lyme Grove Ho
3 Shakespeare Ho
4 Upcott Ho
5 Loddiges Ho

6 Parkinson Ho
7 Sloane Ho
8 Vanbrugh Ho
9 Cambridge Pas
10 Lyttleton Ho
11 Victoria Park Ct
12 Tullis Ho
13 Fairchild Ho
14 Forsyth Ho
15 Tradescant Ho
16 Mason Ho
17 Capel Ho
18 Cordwainers Ct
19 Bridgeman Ho
20 St Thomas's Pl
21 Barclay Ho
22 Clayton Ho
23 Danby Ho
24 Sherard Ho
25 Catesby Ho
26 Petiver Cl
27 Leander Ct
28 Philip Turner Est
29 Grendon Ho
30 Shore Mews
31 Shore Bsns Ctr
32 Kendal Ho
33 Classic Mans
34 Tudor Ho
35 Park Ho
36 Enterprise Ho
37 Alpine Gr
38 Clarendon Cl
39 Rotheley Ho
40 Bernie Grant Ho
C2 1 Woolpack Ho
2 Elvin Ho
3 Thomas Ho
4 Hockley Ho
5 Retreat Ho
6 Butfield Ho
7 Brooksbank Ho
8 Cresset Ho
9 Brooksbank St
10 Lennox Ho
11 Milborne Ho
12 Collent Ho
13 Middlesex Pl
14 Elsdale Ho
15 Devonshire Hall
16 Brent Ho
C6 1 Haybridge Ho
2 Framlingham Cl
3 Halesworth Cl
4 Harleston Cl
5 Lowestoft Cl
6 Howard Ho
7 Templar Ho
D1 1 Stuart Ho
2 Gascoyne Ho
3 Chelsfield Point
4 Sundridge Ho
5 Banbury Ho
6 Lauriston Ho
D2 1 Musgrove Ho
2 Cheyney Ho
3 Haynes Ho
4 Warner Ho
5 Gilby Ho
6 Gadsden Ho
7 Risley Ho
8 Baycliffe Ho
9 Sheldon Ho
10 Offley Ho
11 Latimer Ho
12 Ribstone Ho
13 Salem Ho
14 Fieldwick Ho
15 Lever Ct
16 Matson Ho
17 Wilding Ho
18 Rennell Ho
19 Dycer Ho
20 Granard Ho
21 Whitelock Ho
22 Harrogate Ho
23 Cass Ho
24 Lofts on the Park
25 Heathcote Point
26 Ravenscroft Point
27 Vanner Point
28 Hensley Point
29 San Ho
D4 1 Cromford Path
2 Longford Ct
3 Overbury Ho
4 Heanor Ct
5 Wharfedale Ct
6 Ladybower Ct
7 Ilkeston Ct
8 Derby Ct
9 Rushmore Cres
10 Blackwell Cl
11 Belper Ct

75
A2 1 Chigwell Ct
2 Wellday Ho
3 Selman Ho
4 Vaine Ho
5 Trower Ho
B2 1 Mallard Cl
2 Merriam Ave
3 Gainsborough St
D6 1 Hammond Ct
2 Sorensen Ct
3 Hinton Ct

76
B1 1 Service Route No 2
2 Service Route No 3
B4 1 Mulberry Ct
2 Rosewood Ct
3 Gean Ct
4 Blackthorn Ct
5 Cypress Ct
C1 1 Stratford Office Village The
2 Violet Ct
3 Mandrake Way
4 Brimstone Ho
5 Hibiscus Lo
6 Glasier Ct
C3 1 Bordeaux Ho
2 Luxembourg Mews
3 Basle Ho
C5 1 Acacia Bsns Ctr
2 Brook Ct
3 Gainsfield Ct
4 Artesian Wlk
5 Doreen Capstan Ho
6 Apollo Pl
7 Peppermint Pl
8 Denmark St
9 Mills Ct
10 Paramount Ho
11 Robinson Cl
C6 1 Nansen Ct
2 Mallinson Ct
3 Barbara Ward Ct
4 Caradon Ct
5 Noel Baker Ct
6 Corigan Ct
7 Norman Ho
8 Willow Ct
9 Lime Ct
10 Owens Mews
11 Marnie Ct
12 Cotton Cl
D1 1 Flint Cl
2 St Matthews Ct
3 Ammonite Ho
4 Stone Ct
D2 1 Common The
2 Wolffe Gdns
3 College Pt
4 Onyx Mews
5 Candlelight Ct
6 Boltons The

77
A4 1 Bronte Cl
2 Anna Neagle Cl
3 Brownlow Rd
4 Carrington Gdns
5 Vera Lynn Cl
C1 1 Sarwan Ho
2 Bridgepoint Lofts
3 Vineyard Studios

78
C3 1 Stewart Rainbird Ho
2 Abraham Fisher Ho
3 Redo Ho
4 George Comberton Wlk
C4 1 Cardamom Ct
2 Annie Taylor Ho
3 Richard Fell Ho
4 Susan Lawrence Ho
5 Walter Hurford Par
6 John Cornwell VC Ho
7 Alfred Prior Ho
C5 1 Charlbury Ho
2 Willis Ho
3 Arthur Walls Ho
4 Blakesley Ho
5 Twelve Acre Ho
6 Beech Ct
7 Golding Ct
D1 1 Aveley Mans
2 Harlow Mans
3 Danbury Mans
4 Mayland Mans
5 Bowers Ho
6 Webber Ho
7 Paulson Ho
8 Collins Ho
9 Jack Cook Ho
D3 1 St Luke's Path
2 Springfield Ct
D5 1 Postway Mews
2 Oakfield Ho
3 Janice Mews
4 Kenneth More Rd
5 Clements Ct
6 Handforth Rd
7 Churchill Ct
8 Oakfield Lo
9 Langdale Ct
10 Ilford Chambers
D6 1 York Ho
2 Opal Mews
3 Florentine Ho
4 Kingsley Mews
5 Hainault Bridge Par

79
A6 1 Spectrum Twr
2 Thames View
3 City View
4 Centreway
D1 1 Gibbards Cott
2 Upney Ct
3 Edgefield Ct
4 Manor Ct
5 Lambourne Gdns
6 Westone Mans
7 Loveland Mans
8 Edward Mans
9 Clarke Mans
10 Dawson Gdns
11 Sebastian Ct

80
A1 1 Bristol Ho
2 Canterbury Ho
3 Durham Ho
4 Wells Ho
5 Winchester Ho
6 Rosalind Ct
7 Exeter Ho
8 Wheatley Mans
9 Greenwood Mans
10 Plymouth Ho
11 Graham Mans
12 Portia Ct

81
C5 1 Markham Ho
2 Webb Ho
3 Preston Ho
4 Steadman Ho
5 Hyndman Ho
6 Clynes Ho
7 Henderson Ho
8 Blatchford Ho
9 Rogers Ho
10 Sylvia Pankhurst Ho
11 Mary Macarthur Ho
12 Ellen Wilkinson Ho
D2 1 Picador Ho
2 Centurion Lodge
3 Louis Ct
4 Watsons Lo
5 Carpenters Ct
6 Bell Ho
7 Rounders Ct
8 Oldmead Ho
9 Jervis Ct
10 Bartletts Ho
11 Royal Par
12 Richardson Gdns
13 Forsyth Ct
14 Eldridge Ct
15 Madison Ct
16 Bowery Ct
17 Rivington Ct

82
D3 1 Marlborough Par
2 Blenheim Par
3 Lea Ct
4 Westbourne Par
5 Whiteleys Par
6 Hillingdon Par
7 New Broadway

84
C4 1 Dilston Cl
2 Wells Cl
3 Willett Cl
4 Merlin Cl
5 Glyndebourne Ct
6 Albury Ct
7 Osterley Ct
8 Hatfield Ct
9 Gayhurst Ct
D4 1 Caravelle Gdns
2 Farman Gr
3 Viscount Gr
4 Tomahawk Gdns
5 Martlet Gr
6 Trident Gdns
7 Latham Ct
8 Jupiter Ct
9 Westland Ct
10 Seasprite Cl
11 Convair Wlk
12 Mayfly Gdns
13 Valiant Ct
14 Woburn Twr
15 Brett Ct
16 Friars Ct
D5 1 Medlar Cl
2 Cranberry Cl
3 Lely Ho
4 Girtin Ho
5 Cotman Ho
6 Raeburn Ho
7 Gainsborough Twr
8 Stanfield Ho
9 Millais Ho
10 Hunt Ct
11 Poynter Ct
12 Hogarth Ho
13 Constable Ho
14 Bonnington Ct
15 Romney Ct
16 Landseer Ho

85
B1 1 St Crispins Ct

B3 1 Weaver Ho
2 Caldon Ct
3 Ashby Ho
4 Welford Ho
5 Hertford Ho
6 Wey Ho
7 Middlewich Ho
8 Stourbridge Ho
B4 1 Netherton Ho
2 Keadby Ho
3 Tame Ho
4 Dorset Ct
D1 1 Thurlestone Ct
2 Disley Ct
3 Burgess Ct
4 Bayliss Cl
5 Lytham Ct
6 Winford Par
7 Brunel Pl
8 Rutherford Twr
9 Rountree Ct

86
A1 1 Farnham Ct
2 Gleneagles Twr
3 Birkdale Ct
4 Verulam Ct
5 Hartsbourne Ct
6 Ferndown Ct
7 Deal Ct
8 St David's Ct
9 Portrush Ct
10 Alnmouth Ct
11 Panmure Ct
12 Peterhead Ct
13 Sunningdale Ct
D2 1 Denbigh Ct
2 Devon Ct
3 Dorset Ct
4 Glamorgan Ct
5 Gloucester Ct
6 Hereford Ct
7 Merioneth Ct
8 Oxford Ct
9 Monmouth Ct
10 Paddington Ct
11 Pembroke Ct
12 Chadwick Ct
13 Cotts Ct
D3 1 Berkshire Ct
2 Buckingham Ct
3 Cardigan Ct
4 Carmarthen Ct
5 Cornwall Ct
6 Merlin Ct
7 Osprey Ct
8 Pelham Pl
9 Puffin Ct
10 Fulmar Ct
11 Turnstone Terr
D5 1 Medway Par
2 Brabstone Ho
3 Cotswold Ct

87
B3 1 Woodbury Ct
2 Edward Ct
3 Park Lo
C1 1 Hurley Ct
2 Amherst Gdns
3 Tudor Ct
4 Hilton Ho
C2 1 Hutton Ct
2 Cain Ct
3 Langdale Ct
4 William Ct
5 Castlebar Ct
6 Warren Ct
7 White Lo
8 Queen's Ct
9 King's Ct
10 Cheriton Cl
11 Stanley Ct
12 Juniper Ho
C3 1 Holtoake Ct
2 Pitshanger Ct
3 Holtoake Ho

88
A4 1 Nelson Ho
2 Gordon Ho
3 Frobisher Ho
4 Wellington Ho
5 Fairfax Ho
A5 1 Carlyon Mans
2 Ainslie Ct
3 Millers Ct
4 Priory Ct
5 Tylers Ct
6 Twyford Ct
7 Rose Ct
8 Laurel Ct
9 Sundew Ct
10 Campion Ct
11 Foxglove Ct
C1 1 Buckingham Ho
2 Chester Ct
3 Devon Ct
4 Essex Ho
5 Fife Ct
6 Gloucester Ct
7 Hereford Ho
8 Inverness Ct
9 Warwick Ho
10 York Ho
11 Suffolk Ho
12 Perth Ct
13 Norfolk Ho
14 Thanet Ct
15 Rutland Ho

16 Oxford Ct

89
A1 1 Avon Ct
2 Bromley Lo
3 Walter Ct
4 Lynton Terr
5 Acton Ho
6 Fells Haugh
7 Springfield Ct
8 Tamarind Ct
9 Lynton Ct
10 Aspen Ct
11 Pegasus Ct
12 Friary Park Ct
B1 1 Rosebank Gdns
2 Rosebank
3 Edinburgh Ho
4 Western Ct
5 Kilronan
B6 1 Carlyle Rd
2 Bernard Shaw Ho
3 Longlents Ho
4 Mordaunt Ho
5 Wilmers Ct
6 Stonebridge Ctr
7 Shakespeare Ave
C5 1 Futters Ct
2 Barrett Ct
3 Elms The
4 Fairlight Ct
D5 1 New Crescent Yd
2 Harlesden Plaza
3 St Josephs Ct
4 Jubilee Ct
5 Ellery Cl

90
B1 1 Holborn Ho
2 Clement Danes Ho
3 Vellacott Ho
4 O'Driscoll Ho
5 King Ho
6 Daley Ho
7 Selma Ho
8 Garrett Ho
C1 1 Latimer Ind Est
2 Pankhurst Ho
3 Quadrangle The
4 Nightingale Ho
5 Gordon Ct
6 Ducane Cl
7 Browning Ho
8 Pavilion Terr
9 Ivebury Ct
10 Olympic Ho
C2 1 Galleywood Ho
2 Edgcott Ho
3 Cuffley Ho
4 Addlestone Ho
5 Hockliffe Ho
6 Sarratt Ho
7 Firle Ho
8 Sutton Est The
9 Terling Ho
10 Danes Ho
11 Udimore Ho
12 Vange Ho
13 Binbrook Ho
14 Yeadon Ho
15 Yatton Ho
16 Yarrow Ho
17 Clement Ho
18 Danebury
19 Coronation Ct
20 Calderon Pl
21 St Quintin Gdns
C3 1 Princess Alice Ho
2 Yoxall Ho
3 Yorkley Ho
4 Northaw Ho
5 Oakham Ho
6 Markyate Ho
7 Letchmore Ho
8 Pagham Ho
9 Quendon Ho
10 Redbourn Ho
11 Ketton Ho
12 Hillman Dr
D1 1 Kelfield Ct
2 Downing Ho
3 Crosfield Ct
4 Robinson Ho
5 Scampston Mews
6 Girton Villas
7 Ray Ho
8 Walmer Ho
9 Goodrich Ct
10 Arthur Ct
11 Whitstable Ho
12 Kingsnorth Ho
13 Bridge Cl
14 Prospect Ho
15 St Marks Rd
16 Whitchurch Ho
17 Blechynden Ho
18 Waynflete Sq
19 Bramley Ho
20 Dixon Ho
D4 1 Westfield Ct
2 Tropical Ct
3 Chamberlayne Mans
4 Quadrant The
5 Queens Park Ct
6 Warfield Yd
7 Regent St
8 Cherrytree Ho
9 Artisan Mews
10 Artisan Quarter

91

91
A1 1 Malton Mews
2 Lancaster Lo
3 Manning Ho
4 Galsworthy Ho
5 Hudson Ho
6 Cambourne Mews
7 Upper Talbot Wlk
8 Kingsdown Cl
9 Lower Clarendon Wlk
10 Talbot Grove Ho
11 Clarendon Wlk
12 Upper Clarendon Wlk
13 Camelford Wlk
14 Upper Camelford Wlk
15 Camelford Ct
A2 1 Murchison Ho
2 MacAulay Ho
3 Chesterton Ho
4 Chiltern Ho
5 Lionel Ho
6 Watts Ho
7 Wheatstone Ho
8 Telford Ho
9 Golborne Mews
10 Millwood St
11 St Columb's Ho
12 Norfolk Mews
13 Lionel Mews
A3 1 Sycamore Wlk
2 Westgate Bsns Ctr
3 Buspace Studios
4 Bosworth Ho
5 Golborne Gdns
6 Appleford Ho
7 Adair Twr
8 Gadsden Ho
9 Southam Ho
10 Norman Butler Ho
11 Thompson Ho
12 Wells Ho
13 Paul Ho
14 Olive Blythe Ho
15 Katherine Ho
16 Breakwell Ct
17 Pepler Ho
18 Edward Kennedy Ho
19 Winnington Ho
A4 1 Selby Sq
2 Severn Ave
3 Stansbury Sq
4 Tolhurst Dr
5 John Fearon Wlk
6 Mundy Ho
7 Macfarren Ho
8 Bantock Ho
9 Banister Ho
10 Batten Ho
11 Croft Ho
12 Courtville Ho
13 Mounsey Ho
14 Bliss Mews
15 Symphony Mews
B1 1 Silvester Ho
2 Golden Cross Mews
3 Tavistock Mews
4 Clydesdale Ho
5 Melchester
6 Pinehurst Ct
7 Denbigh Ho
B2 1 Blagrove Rd
2 All Saints Ho
3 Tavistock Ho
4 Leamington Ho
B3 1 Octavia Mews
2 Russell's Wharf
3 Western Ho
4 Kelly Mews
B4 1 Boyce Ho
2 Farnaby Ho
3 Danby Ho
4 Purday Ho
5 Naylor Ho
6 St Judes Ho
7 Leeve Ho
8 Longhurst Ho
9 Harrington Ct
10 Mulberry Ct
11 Kilburn Ho
B5 1 Claremont Ct
2 William Saville Ho
3 Western Ct
4 Bond Ho
5 Crone Ct
6 Wood Ho
7 Winterleys
8 Carlton Ho
9 Fiona Ct
C1 1 Shottsford
2 Tolchurch
3 Casterbridge
4 Sandbourne
5 Anglebury
6 Weatherbury
7 Westbourne Gr Mews
8 Rosehart Mews
9 Viscount Ct
10 Hereford Mans
11 Hereford Mews
C2 1 Ascot Ho
2 Ashgrove Ct

91 C2

3 Lockbridge Ct
4 Swallow Ct
5 Nightingale Lo
6 Hammond Lo
7 Penfield Lo
8 Harvey Lo
9 Hunter Lo
10 Barnard Lo
11 Falcon Lo
12 Johnson Lo
13 Livingstone Lo
14 Nuffield Lo
15 Finch Lo
16 Polesworth Ho
17 Oversley Ho
18 Derrycombe Ho
19 Buckshead Ho
20 Combe Ho
21 Culham Ho
22 Dainton Ho
23 Devonport Ho
24 Honwell Ho
25 Truro Ho
26 Sunderland Ho
27 Stonehouse Ho
28 Riverford Ho
29 Portishead Ho
30 Mickleton Ho
31 Keyham Ho
32 Moulsford Ho
33 Shrewsbury Mews
34 St Stephen's Mews
35 Westway Lo
36 Langley Ho
37 Brindley Ho
38 Radway Ho
39 Astley Ho
40 Willow Ct
41 Larch Ct
42 Elm Ct
43 Beech Ct
44 Worcester Ct
45 Union Ct
46 Leicester Ct
47 Kennet Ct
48 Oxford Ct
49 Fazerley Ct
C3 1 Westside Ct
2 Byron Mews
3 Sutherland Ct
4 Fleming Cl
5 Hermes Cl
C4 1 Pentland Rd
2 Nelson Cl
3 Pavilion Ct
4 Masefield Ho
5 Austen Ho
6 Fielding Ho
7 Argo Bsns Ctr
8 John Ratcliffe Ho
9 Wymering Mans
C5 1 Wells Ct
2 Cambridge Ct
3 Ely Ct
4 Durham Ct
C6 1 Ryde Ho
2 Glengall Pass
3 Leith Yd
4 Daynor Ho
5 Varley Ho
6 Sandby Ho
7 Colas Mews
8 Bishopsdale Ho
9 Lorton Ho
10 Marshwood Ho
11 Ribblesdale Ho
12 Holmesdale Ho
13 Kilburn Vale Est
14 Kilburn Bridge
D1 1 Vera Ct
2 Alexander Mews
3 Gurney Ho
4 Burdett Mews
5 Greville Lo
6 Hatherley Ct
7 Bridge Field Ho
8 Ralph Ct
9 Peters Ct
10 Pickering Mews
11 Riven Ct
12 Cervantes Ct
13 Bishops Ct
14 Newbury Ho
15 Marlow Ho
16 Lynton Ho
17 Pembroke Ho
18 Pickering Ho
19 Whiteleys Ctr
D3 1 Ellwood Ct
D5 1 Tollgate Ho
2 Regents Plaza
3 Royal Langford Apartments
D6 1 Sylvan Ct
2 Birchington Ct
3 Farndale Ho
4 Abbey Rd Motorist Ctr
5 Greville Mews
6 Goldsmith's Pl
7 Remsted Ho
8 Bradwell Ho
9 Cheshunt Ho
10 Haliwell Ho
11 Broadoak Ho

12 Philip Ho
13 Hillsborough Ct
14 Sandbourne
15 Wingreen
16 Toneborough
17 Silverthorn
18 Kington Ho
19 Marrick Ho

95

C4 1 Pimlico Wlk
2 Aske Ho
3 Hathaway Ho
4 Haberdasher Pl
5 Fairchild Ho
6 Burtt Ho
7 Enfield Cloisters
8 McGregor Ct
9 Royal Oak Ct
10 Hoxton Mkt
11 Bath Pl
12 Chapel Pl
13 Standard Pl
14 Cleeve Workshops
15 Cleeve Ho
16 Printing House Yd
17 Perseverance Works
18 Crooked Billet Yd
19 Drysdale Ho
20 Castlefrank Ho
21 School App
22 Basing House Yd
23 Mail Coach Yd
C5 1 Bracer Ho
2 Scorton Ho
3 Fern Cl
4 Macbeth Ho
5 Oberon Ho
6 Buckland Ct
7 Crondall Ct
8 Osric Path
9 Caliban Twr
10 Celia Ho
11 Juliet Ho
12 Bacchus Wlk
13 Malcolm Ho
14 Homefield St
15 Crondall Pl
16 Blanca Ho
17 Miranda Ho
18 Falstaff Ho
19 Charmian Ho
20 Myrtle Wlk
21 Arden Ho
22 Sebastian Ho
23 Stanway Ct
24 Jerrold St
25 Rosalind Ho
26 Cordelia Ho
27 Monteagle Ct
28 John Parry Ct
29 James Anderson Ct
30 Ben Jonson Ct
31 Sara Lane Ct
32 Walbrook Ct
C6 1 Portelet Ct
2 Trinity Ct
3 Rozel Ct
4 St Helier Ct
5 Corbiere Ho
6 Kenning Ho
7 Higgins Ho
8 Cavell Ho
9 Girling Ho
10 Fulcher Ho
11 Francis Ho
12 Norris Ho
13 Kempton Ho
14 Nesham Ho
15 Crossbow Ho
16 Catherine Ho
17 Strale Ho
18 Horner Hos
19 Stringer Hos
20 Whitmore Ho
21 Nightingale Ho
22 Wilmer Gdns
23 Arrow Ho
24 Archer Ho
25 Meriden Ho
26 Rover Ho
27 Bowyer Ho
28 Tiller Ho
29 Canalside Studios
30 Kleine Wharf
31 Benyon Wharf
32 Quebec Wharf
33 Belvedere Ct
34 Portfleet Pl
D4 1 Gorsuch Pl
2 Strout's Pl
3 Vaughan Est
4 George Loveless Ho
5 Baroness Rd
6 James Brine Ho
7 Arthur Wade Ho
8 Robert Owen Ho
9 Sivill Ho
10 Georgina Gdns
11 Old Market Sq
12 Cuff Point
13 Bakers Rents
14 Leopold Bldgs
15 Dunmore Point
16 Wingfield Ho
17 Gascoigne Pl
18 Mandela Ho

19 Virginia Rd
20 Briggs Ho
21 Packenham Ho
22 Gowan Ho
23 Kirton Gdns
24 Chambord Ho
25 Ducal St
26 Strickland Ho
27 Alliston Ho
28 Gibraltar Wlk
29 Equity Sq
30 Shacklewell St
31 Rochelle St
32 Sonning Ho
33 Culham Ho
34 Hurley Ho
35 Palissy St
36 Taplow Ho
37 Chertsey Ho
38 Sunbury Ho
39 Sunbury Workshops
40 Datchett Ho
41 Hocker St
42 Coll Sharp Ct
43 Marlow Studio Workshops
44 Marlow Ho
45 Shiplake Ho
46 Wargrave Ho
47 Iffley Ho
D5 1 Queensbridge Ct
2 Godwin Ho
3 Kent Ct
4 Brunswick Ho
5 Weymouth Ct
6 Sovereign Mews
7 Dunloe Ct
8 Cremer Bsns Ctr
9 James Hammett Ho
10 Allgood St
11 Horatio St
12 Cadell Ho
13 Horatio Ho
14 Shipton Ho
D6 1 Hilborough Ct
2 Scriven Ct
3 Livermere Ct
4 Angrave Ct
5 Angrave Pas
6 Benfleet Ct
7 Belford Ho
8 Orme Ho
9 Clemson Ho
10 Longman Ho
11 Lowther Ho
12 Lovelace Ho
13 Harlowe Ho
14 Pamela Ho
15 Samuel Ho
16 Acton Ho
17 Loanda Cl
18 Phoenix Cl
19 Richardson Cl
20 Thrasher Cl
21 Mary Secole Cl
22 Canal Path
23 Pear Tree Cl
24 Hebden Ct
25 Charlton Ct
26 Laburnum Ct
27 Mansfield Ct
28 Garden Pl
29 Amber Wharf
30 Haggerston Studios

96

A1 1 Whitechurch Pas
2 Manningtree St
3 Whitechurch La
4 Naylor Bldg W
5 Morrison Bldgs
6 Nayor Bldg E
7 Mulberry St
8 Albany Ct
9 Cornell Bldg
10 Dryden Bldg
11 Weyhill Rd
12 Colefax Bldg
13 Fordham St
14 Myrdle St
15 Buckle St
16 Plough St
17 Goodman's Stile
18 Ropewalk Gdns
19 Skyline Plaza Bldg
20 Minet Ho
21 Mitali Pas
22 Basil Ho
23 Bernhard Baron Ho
24 Hogarth Ct
25 Delafield Ho
26 Chandlery Ho
27 Berner Terr
28 Victoria Yd
29 Batson Ho
30 Harkness Ho
31 Drewett Ho
32 Dowler Ho
33 Bicknell Ho
34 Danvers Ho
35 Philchurch Pl
36 Hadfield Ho
37 Kindersley Ho
38 Langmore Ho
39 Halliday Ho

A2 1 Arthur Deakin Ho
2 Albert Cotts
3 Victoria Cotts
4 Boden Ho
5 Vollasky Ho
6 Daplyn St
7 Hobsons Pl
8 Hanbury Ho
9 Huguenot Ct
10 Links Yd
11 Casson Ho
12 Ramar Ho
13 Greatorex Ho
14 Chicksand Ho
15 Spelman Ho
16 Tailworth St
17 Monthope Rd
18 Evelyn Ho
19 Bloomfield Ho
20 Davenant Ho
21 Pauline Ho
22 Tannery Ho
23 Don Gratton Ho
24 Green Dragon Yd
25 Fieldgate Mans
26 Mosque Tower
A3 1 Bentworth Ct
2 Hawksmoor Pl
3 Kerbela St
4 Fuller Cl
5 Kinsham Ho
6 Menotti St
7 Barwell Ho
8 Grimsby St
9 Reflection Ho
10 Fleet Street Hill
11 Bratley St
12 Weaver Ho
13 Cornerstone Ct
14 Stuttle Ho
15 McGlashon Ho
16 John Pritchard Ho
A4 1 Providence Yd
2 Lygon Ho
3 Brabner Ho
4 Delta St
5 Delta Point
6 Tillet Way
7 Mullet Gdns
8 Lampern Sq
9 Kite Pl
10 Elver Gdns
11 Cobden Ho
12 Eversley Ho
13 Lorden Wlk
14 Rapley Ho
15 Dence Ho
16 McKinnon Wood Ho
17 Satchwell Rd
18 Dickinson Ho
19 Hutton Ho
20 Simmons Ho
21 Swinton Ho
22 Yates Ho
23 Johnson Ho
24 Jeremy Bentham Ho
25 Waring Ho
26 St James Ct
27 Ebony Ho
28 Azure Ho
29 Westhope Ho
30 Hague St
A5 1 London Terr
2 Sturdee Ho
3 Maude Ho
4 Haig Ho
5 Jellicoe Ho
6 Ropley St
7 Guinness Trust Bldgs
8 Ion Ct
9 Columbia Rd
10 Moye Cl
11 Morrel Ct
12 Courtauld Ho
13 Drummond Ho
14 Gurney Ho
15 Atkinson Ho
16 Halley Ho
17 Goldsmith's Sq
18 Shahjalal Ho
19 Ken Wilson Ho
20 April Ct
21 Crofts Ho
22 Sebright Ho
23 Beechwood Ho
24 Gillman Ho
25 Cheverell Ho
26 Besford Ho
27 Dinmont Ho
28 Elizabeth Mews
29 Sebright Pas
30 Wyndham Deedes Ho
31 Sheppard Ho
32 Mary James Ho
33 Hadrian Est
34 Blythendale Ho
35 George Vale Ho
36 Lion Mills
37 St Peter's Ave
38 Pritchard Ho
A6 1 Broke Wlk
2 Rochemont Wlk
3 Marlborough Ave
4 Rivington Wlk
5 Magnin Cl
6 Gloucester Sq

7 Woolstone Ho
8 Marsworth Ho
9 Cheddington Ho
10 Linslade Ho
11 Cosgrove Ho
12 Blisworth Ho
13 Eleanor Ct
14 Wistow Ho
15 Muscott Ho
16 Boxmoor Ho
17 Linford Ho
18 Pendley Ho
19 Northchurch Ho
20 Debdale Ho
21 Broadway Market Mews
22 Welshpool Ho
23 Ada Ho
B1 1 Peter Best Ho
2 Mellish Ho
3 Porchester Ho
4 Dickson Ho
5 Joscoyne Ho
6 Silvester Ho
7 Wilton Ct
8 Sarah Ho
9 Bridgen Ho
10 Tylney Ho
11 Greenwich Ct
12 Damien St
13 Philson Mans
14 Siege Ho
15 Jacob Mans
16 Proud Ho
17 Sly St
18 Barnett St
19 Kinder St
20 Richard St
21 Hungerford St
22 Colstead Ho
23 Melwood Ho
24 Wicker St
25 Langdale St
26 Chapman Ho
27 Burwell Cl
28 Walford Ho
29 Welstead Ho
30 Norton Ho
31 Turnour Ho
32 Luke Ho
33 Dunch St
34 Sheridan St
35 Brinsley St
B2 1 Wodeham Gdns
2 Castlemaine St
3 Court St
B3 1 Rochester Ct
2 Weaver Ct
3 Greenheath Bsns Ctr
4 Glass St
5 Herald St
6 Northesk Ho
7 Codrington Ho
8 Heathpool Ct
9 Mocatta Ho
10 Harvey Ho
11 Blackwood Ho
12 Rutherford Ho
13 Bullen Ho
14 Fremantle Ho
15 Pellew Ho
16 Ashington Ho
17 Dinnington Ho
18 Bartholomew Sq
19 Steeple Ct
20 Orion Ho
21 Fellbrigg St
22 Eagle Ho
23 Sovereign Ho
24 Redmill Ho
25 Berry Ho
26 Grindall Ho
27 Collingwood Ho
B4 1 Charles Dickens Ho
2 Adrian Bolt Ho
3 William Rathbone Ho
4 Southwood Smith Ho
5 Rushmead
6 William Channing Ho
7 John Cartwright Ho
8 Charles Darwin Ho
9 Thomas Burt Ho
10 John Fielden Ho
11 Gwilym Maries Ho
12 Joseph Priestley Ho
13 Wear Pl
14 John Nettleford Ho
15 Thornaby Ho
16 Stockton Ho
17 Barnard Ho
18 Gainford Ho
19 Stapleton Ho
20 James Middleton Ho
21 Kedleston Wlk
22 Queen Margaret Flats
23 Hollybush Ho
24 Horwood Ho
25 Norden Ho
26 Newcourt Ho

27 Seabright St
28 Viaduct Pl
29 Sunlight Sq
30 Providence Row Cl
B5 1 Dinmont St
2 Marian St
3 Claredale Ho
4 Keeling Ho
5 Maple St
6 Winkley St
7 Temple Dwellings
8 Argos Ho
9 Helen Ho
10 Lysander Ho
11 Antenor Ho
12 Paris Ho
13 Nestor Ho
14 Hector Ho
15 Achilles Ho
16 Priam Ho
17 Peabody Est
18 Felix St
19 Cambridge Cres
20 Peterley Bsns Ctr
21 Beckwith Ho
22 Brookfield Ho
23 Parminter Ind Est
24 Ted Roberts Ho
25 Cambridge Ct
26 Millennium Pl
27 William Caslon Ho
28 Hugh Platt Ho
29 West St
30 Mayfield Ho
31 Apollo Ho
32 Tanners Yd
33 Teesdale Yd
B6 1 Welshpool St
2 Broadway Ho
3 Regents Wharf
4 London Wharf
5 Warburton Ho
6 Warburton St
7 Triangle Rd
8 Warburton Rd
9 Williams Ho
10 Booth Cl
11 Albert Cl
12 King Edward Mans
13 Victoria Bldgs
14 Andrews Wharf
C1 1 Woollon Ho
2 Dundalk Ho
3 Anne Goodman Ho
4 Newbold Cotts
5 Kerry Ho
6 Zion Ho
7 Longford Ho
8 Bromehead St
9 Athlone Ho
10 Jubilee Mans
11 Harriott Ho
12 Brayford Sq
13 Clearbrook Way
14 Rochelle Ct
15 Winterton Ho
16 Swift Ho
17 Brinsley Ho
18 Dean Ho
19 Foley Ho
20 Robert Sutton Ho
21 Montpelier Pl
22 Glastonbury Pl
23 Steel's La
24 Masters Lo
25 Stylus Apartments
26 Arta Ho
C2 1 Fulneck
2 Gracehill
3 Ockbrook
4 Fairfield
5 Dunstan Hos
6 Cressy Ct
7 Cressy Hos
8 Callahan Cotts
9 Lindley Ho
10 Mayo Ho
11 Wexford Ho
12 Sandhurst Ho
13 Addis Ho
14 Colverson Ho
15 Beckett Ho
16 Jarman Ho
17 Armsby Ho
18 Wingrad Ho
19 Miranda Cl
20 Drake Ho
21 Ashfield Yd
22 Magri Wlk
23 Jean Pardies Ho
24 St Vincent De Paul Ho
25 Sambrook Ho
26 Louise De Marillac Ho
27 Dagobert Ho
28 Le Moal Ho
29 Odette Duval Ho
30 Charles Auffray Ho
31 Boisseau Ho
32 Clichy Ho
33 Paymal Ho
C3 1 William's Bldgs
2 Donegal Ho
3 Pelican Pas

4 Frederick Charrington Ho
5 Wickford Ho
6 Braintree Ho
7 Doveton Ho
8 Doveton Ho
9 Cephas Ho
10 Sceptre Ho
11 Bancroft Ho
12 Stothard St
13 Redclyf Ho
14 Winkworth Cotts
15 Amiel St
16 Hadleigh Ho
17 Hadleigh Cl
18 Ryder Ho
19 Mantus Cl
20 Kenton Ho
21 Colebert Ho
22 Ibbott St
23 Rickman St
24 Rickman St
25 Stothard Ho
26 Barbanel Ho
27 Stannard Cotts
28 St Peters Ct
29 Rennie Cotts
30 Pemell Cl
31 Pemell Ho
32 Leatherdale St
33 Gouldman Ho
34 Lamplighter Cl
35 Sherren Ho
36 Marlborough Lo
37 Hamilton Lo
38 Montgomery Lo
39 Cleveland Gr
40 Cromwell Lo
41 Bardsey Pl
42 Charrington Ho
43 Hayfield Yd
44 Allport Mews
45 Colin Winter Ho
C4 1 Mulberry Ho
2 Gretton Ho
3 Merceron Ho
4 Montfort Ho
5 Westbrook Ho
6 Sugar Loaf Wlk
7 Museum Ho
8 Burnham Est
9 Globe Terr
10 Moravian St
11 Shepton Hos
12 Mendip Hos
13 Academy Ct
14 Pepys Ho
15 Swinburne Ho
16 Moore Ho
17 Morris Ho
18 Burns Ho
19 Milton Ho
20 Whitman Ho
21 Shelley Ho
22 Keats Ho
23 Dawson Ho
24 Bradbeer Ho
25 Forber Ho
26 Hughes Ho
27 Silvester Ho
28 Rogers Est
29 Pavan Ct
30 Stafford Cripps Ho
31 Sidney Godley (VC) Ho
32 Butler Ho
33 Butler St
34 Thorne Ho
35 Bevin Ho
36 Tuscan Ho
C5 1 Evesham Ho
2 James Campbell Ho
3 Thomas Hollywood Ho
4 James Docherty Ho
5 Ebenezer Mussel Ho
6 Jameson Ct
7 Edinburgh Cl
8 Roger Dowley Ct
9 Sherbrooke Ho
10 Calcraft Ho
11 Burrard Ho
12 Dundas Ho
13 Ponsonby Ho
14 Barnes Ho
15 Paget Ho
16 Maitland Ho
17 Chesil Ct
18 Reynolds Ho
19 Cleland Ho
20 Goodrich Ho
21 Rosebery Ho
22 Sankey Ho
23 Cyprus Pl
24 Royston St
25 Stainsbury St
26 Hunslett St
27 Baildon
28 Brockweir
29 Tytherton
30 Malmesbury
31 Kingswood
32 Colville Ho
C6 1 Halkett Ho
2 Christchurch Sq
3 Helena Pl

4 Swingfield Ho
5 Greenham Ho
6 Dinmore Ho
7 Anstey Ho
8 Weston Ho
9 Carbroke Ho
10 Bluebell Cl
11 Cherry Tree Cl
12 Georgian Ct
13 Park Cl
14 Regency Ct
15 Norris Ho
D1 1 Pattison Ho
2 St Thomas Ho
3 Arbour Ho
4 Bladen Ho
5 Antill Terr
6 Majorie Mews
7 Billing Ho
8 Dowson Ho
9 Lipton Rd
10 Chalkwell Ho
11 Corringham Ho
12 Ogilvie Ho
13 Edward Mann Cl
14 Reservoir Studios
15 Lighterman Mews
D2 1 Roland Mews
2 Beatrice Ho
3 Morecambe Cl
4 Stepney Green Ct
5 Milrood Ho
6 Panama Ho
7 Galway Ho
8 Jacqueline Ho
9 Crown Mews
10 Caspian Ho
11 Darien Ho
12 Riga Ho
13 Flores Ho
14 Taranto Ho
15 Aden Ho
16 Master's St
17 Rosary Ct
D3 1 Raynham Ho
2 Pat Shaw Ho
3 Colmar Cl
4 Withy Ho
5 Stocks Ct
6 Downey Ho
7 Bay Ct
8 Sligo Ho
9 Pegasus Ho
10 Barents Ho
11 Biscay Ho
12 Solway Ho
13 Bantry Ho
14 Aral Ho
15 Pacific Ho
16 Magellan Ho
17 Levant Ho
18 Adriatic Ho
19 Genoa Ho
20 Hawke Ho
21 Palliser Ho
22 Ionian Ho
23 Weddell Ho
24 Carlyle Mews
25 Greencourt Ho
26 Sundra Wlk
D4 1 Stubbs Ho
2 Holman Ho
3 Clynes Ho
4 Windsor Ho
5 Gilbert Ho
6 Chater Ho
7 Ellen Wilkinson Ho
8 George Belt Ho
9 Ayrton Gould Ho
10 O'Brian Ho
11 Sulkin Ho
12 Jenkinson Ho
13 Bullards Pl
14 Sylvia Pankhurst Ho
15 Mary Macarthur Ho
16 Trevelyan Ho
17 Wedgwood Ho
18 Pemberton Ct
19 Leatherdale St
20 Walter Besant Ho
21 Barber Beaumont Ho
22 Brancaster Ho
23 Litcham Ho
D5 1 Kemp Ho
2 Piggott Ho
3 Mark Ho
4 Sidney Ho
5 Pomeroy Ho
6 Puteaux Ho
7 Doric Ho
8 Modling Ho
9 Longman Ho
10 Ames Ho
11 Alzette Ho
12 Offenbach Ho
13 Tate Ho
14 Norton Ho
15 St Gilles Ho
16 Harold Ho
17 Velletri Ho
18 Bridge Wharf
19 Gathorne St
20 Bow Brook The
21 Twig Folly Cl
22 Palmerston Ct
23 Lakeview
24 Peach Walk Mews
25 Caesar Ct

97
A1 1 Hearnshaw St
2 Berry Cotts
3 Causton Cotts
4 Elizabeth Blount Ct
5 Carr St
6 Shaw Cres
7 Darnley Ho
8 Mercer's Cotts
9 Troon Ho
10 Ratcliffe Ho
11 Wakeling St
12 York Sq
13 Anglia Ho
14 Cambria Ho
15 Caledonia Ho
16 Ratcliffe La
17 Bekesbourne St
18 John Scurr Ho
19 Regents Canal Ho
20 Basin App
21 Powlesland Ct
A2 1 Waley St
2 Edith Ramsay Ho
3 Andaman Ho
4 Atlantic Ho
5 Pevensey Ho
6 Solent Ho
7 Lorne Ho
8 Cromarty Ho
9 Dakin Pl
10 Greaves Cotts
11 Donaghue Cotts
12 Ames Cotts
13 Waterview Ho
14 Limehouse Fields Est
A3 1 Formosa Ho
2 Galveston Ho
3 Arabian Ho
4 Greenland Ho
5 Coral Ho
6 Anson Ho
7 Cambay Ho
8 Lindop Ho
9 Moray Ho
10 Azov Ho
11 Sandalwood Cl
12 Broadford Ho
A4 1 Imperial Ho
2 Newport Ho
3 Vassall Ho
4 Maurice Ct
5 Creed Ct
6 Christopher France Ho
7 Beaumont Ct
8 Pembroke Mews
A5 1 Nightingale Mews
2 Bunsen Ho
3 Bunsen St
4 Beatrice Webb Ho
5 Margaret Bondfield Ho
6 Wilmer Ho
7 Sandall Ho
8 Butley Ct
9 Josseline Ct
10 Dalton Ho
11 Brine Ho
12 Ford Cl
13 Viking Cl
14 Stanfield Rd
15 Stoneleigh Mews
16 Ruth Ct
17 School Bell Cloisters
18 Schoolbell Mews
19 Medhurst Cl
20 Olga St
21 Conyer St
22 Diamond Ho
23 Daring Ho
24 Crane Ho
25 Exmoor Ho
26 Grenville Ho
27 Hyperion Ho
28 Sturdy Ho
29 Wren Ho
30 Ardent Ho
31 Senators Lo
32 Hooke Ho
33 Mohawk Ho
34 Ivanhoe Ho
35 Medway Mews
B1 1 Dora Ho
2 Flansham Ho
3 Gatwick Ho
4 Ashpark Ho
5 Newdigate Ho
6 Midhurst Ho
7 Redbourne Ho
8 Southwater Cl
9 Andersens Wharf
10 Whatman Ho
11 Butler Ho
12 Fitzroy Ho
13 Salmon St
14 Mission The
15 Aithan Ho
16 Britley Ho
17 Cheadle Ho
18 Elland Ho
19 Wharf La
20 Docklands Ct
21 Park Heights Ct
22 Grosvenor Ct
23 Lime House Ct
24 Swallow Pl
25 St Anne's Trad Est
B2 1 Wearmouth Ho
2 Elmslie Point
3 Grindley Ho
4 Stileman Ho
5 Wilcox Ho
6 Huddart St
7 Robeson St
8 Couzens Ho
9 Perley Ho
10 Whytlaw Ho
11 Booker Cl
12 Tunley Gn
13 Callingham Cl
14 Bowry Ho
15 Perkins Ho
16 Printon Ho
17 Tasker Ho
B4 1 Trellis Sq
2 Sheffield Sq
3 Howcroft Ho
4 Astra Ho
5 Frye Ct
6 Byas Ho
7 George Lansbury Ho
8 Regal Pl
9 Coborn Mews
10 Tredegar Mews
11 Cavendish Terr
12 Lyn Mews
13 Buttermere Ho
14 Coniston Ho
15 Tracy Ho
16 Hanover Pl
17 St Clair Ho
18 Longthorne Ho
19 Vista Bldgs
20 Verity Ho
21 Icarus Ho
22 Whippingham Ho
23 Hamilton Ho
24 Winchester Ho
B5 1 Roman Square Mkt
2 John Bond Ho
3 McKenna Ho
4 Dennis Ho
5 McAusland Ho
6 McBride Ho
7 Libra Rd
8 Dave Adams Ho
9 Regency Ct
10 Tay Ho
11 Sleat Ho
12 Brodick Ho
13 Ewart Pl
14 Lunan Ho
15 Cruden Ho
16 Anglo Rd
17 Mull Ho
18 Sinclairs Ho
19 Driftway Ho
20 Clayhall Ct
21 Berebinder Ho
22 Partridge Ho
23 Barford Ho
24 Gullane Ho
25 Gosford Ho
26 Dornoch Ho
27 Dunnet Ho
28 Enard Ho
29 Fraserburgh Ho
30 Forth Ho
31 Stavers Ho
32 Rosegate Ho
33 Crowngate Ho
34 Queensgate Ho
35 Towergate Ho
36 Ordell Ct
37 William Pl
B6 1 Hampstead Wlk
2 Waverton Ho
3 Elton Ho
4 Locton Gn
5 Birtwhistle Ho
6 Clare Ho
7 Magpie Ho
8 Hornbeam Sq
9 Rowan Ho
10 Barge La
11 Walnut Ho
12 Birdsfield La
13 Atkins Ct
14 Willow Tree Cl
15 Jasmine Sq
16 Tait Ct
17 Ranwell Ho
18 Ranwell Cl
19 Tufnell Ct
20 Pulteney Cl
21 Vic Johnson Ho
22 Lea Sq
23 Iceni Ct
24 Tamar Cl
25 Roman Rd
26 Valentine Ho
C1 1 Landin Ho
2 Thomas Road Ind Est
3 Vickery's Wharf
4 Abbotts Wharf
5 Limehouse Ct
6 Charlesworth Ho
7 Gurdon Ho
8 Trendell Ho
9 Menteath Ho
10 Minchin Ho
11 Donne Ho
12 Old School Sq
13 Anglesey Ho
14 Gough Wlk
15 Baring Ho
16 Gladstone Ho
17 Hopkins Ho
18 Granville Ho
19 Overstone Ho
20 Pusey Ho
21 Russell Ho
22 Stanley Ho
C2 1 Bredel Ho
2 Linton Ho
3 Matthews Ho
4 Woodcock Ho
5 Limborough Ho
6 Maydwell Ho
7 Underhill Ho
8 Meyrick Ho
9 Ambrose Ho
10 Richardson Ho
11 Carpenter Ho
12 Robinson Ho
13 Bellmaker Ct
14 Lime Tree Ct
15 Bracken Ho
16 Bramble Ho
17 Berberis Ho
18 Bilberry Ho
19 Ladyfern Ho
20 Rosebay Ho
21 Invicta Cl
22 Phoenix Bsns Ctr
23 Metropolitan Cl
24 Busbridge Ho
C3 1 Fairmont Ho
2 Healy Ho
3 Zodiac Ho
4 Buick Ho
5 Consul Ho
6 Bentley Ho
7 Cresta Ho
8 Daimler Ho
9 Riley Ho
10 Jensen Ho
11 Lagonda Ho
12 Ireton St
13 Navenby Wlk
14 Burwell Wlk
15 Leadenham Ct
16 Sleaford Ho
17 Bow Triangle Bsns Ctr
C4 1 Bow Ho
2 Denmark Pl
3 Marsalis Ho
4 Lovette Ho
5 Drapers Almhouses
6 Mallard Point
7 Creswick Wlk
8 Bevin Ho
9 Huggins Ho
10 Williams Ho
11 Harris Ho
12 Marina Ct
13 Electric Ho
14 Matching Ct
15 Wellington Bldgs
16 Grafton Ho
17 Berkeley Ho
18 Columbia Ho
C5 1 Vincent Mews
2 Menai Pl
3 Heathfield Ct
4 Redwood Cl
5 Acorn Ct
6 Primrose Cl
7 Briar Ct
8 Springwood Cl
C6 1 Ironworks
2 Juno Ho
3 Chariot Cl
4 Saturn Ho
5 Hadrian Cl
6 Mercury Ho
7 Forum Cl
8 Venus Ho
9 Vesta Ho
10 Tiber Cl
11 Gemini Ho
12 Crown Close Bsns Ctr
13 Old Ford Trad Ctr
D1 1 Colebrook Ho
2 Essex Ho
3 Salisbury Ho
4 Maidstone Ho
5 Osterley Ho
6 Norwich Ho
7 Clarissa Ho
8 Elgin Ho
9 Shaftesbury Lo
10 Shepherd Ho
11 Jeremiah St
12 Elizabeth Cl
13 Chilcot Cl
14 Fitzgerald Ho
15 Vesey Path
16 Ennis Ho
17 Kilmore Ho
18 Cygnet House N
19 Cygnet House S
D2 1 Sumner Ho
2 David Hewitt Ho
3 St Gabriels Cl
4 Limehouse Cut
5 Colmans Wharf
6 Foundary Ho
7 Radford Ho
D3 1 Broxbourne Ho
2 Roxford Ho
3 Biscott Ho
4 Stanborough Ho
5 Hillstone Ct
D4 1 Bradley Ho
2 Prioress Ho
3 Alton Ho
4 Foxley Ho
5 Munden Ho
6 Canterbury Ho
7 Corbin Ho
8 Barton Ho
9 Jolles Ho
10 Rudstone Ho
11 Baxter Ho
12 Baker Ho
13 Insley Ho
14 Hardwicke Ho
15 Glebe Ct
16 Priory St
17 Sadler Ho
18 Ballinger Point
19 Henshall Point
20 Dorrington Point
21 Warren Ho
22 Fairlie Ct
23 Regent Sq
24 Hackworth Point
25 Priestman Point
26 Wingate Ho
27 Nethercott Ho
28 Thelbridge Ho
29 Bowden Ho
30 Kerscott Ho
31 Southcott Ho
32 Birchdown Ho
33 Upcott Ho
34 Langmead Ho
35 Limscott Ho
36 Northleigh Ho
37 Huntshaw Ho
38 Chagford Ho
39 Ashcombe Ho
40 Shillingford Ho
41 Patrick Connolly Gdns
42 Lester Ct
43 Franklin St
44 Taft Way
45 Washington Cl
46 Veronica Ho
47 William Guy Gdns
48 Denbury Ho
49 Holsworthy Ho
50 Padstone Ho

98
A1 1 Glenkerry Ho
2 Carradale Ho
3 Langdon Ho
4 Balfron Twr
5 St Frideswides Mews
6 Tabard Ct
7 Delta Bldg
8 Findhorn St
9 Kilbrennan Ho
10 Thistle Ho
11 Heather Ho
12 Tartan Ho
13 Sharman Ho
14 Trident Ho
15 Wharf View Ct
A2 1 Mills Gr
2 St Michaels Ct
3 Duncan Ct
A4 1 Miller's House Visitor Ctr
B1 1 Lansbury Gdns
2 Theseus Ho
3 Adams Ho
4 Jones Ho
5 Sam March Ho
6 Arapiles Ho
7 Athenia Ho
8 Julius Ho
9 Jervis Bay Ho
10 Helen Mackay Ho
11 Gaze Ho
12 Ritchie Ho
13 Blairgowrie Ct
14 Circle Ho
15 Dunkeld Ho
16 Rosemary Dr
17 Sorrel La
18 East India Dock Road Tunnel
B3 1 Crescent Court Bsns Ctr
2 Ashmead Bsns Ctr
3 Forward Bsns Ctr The
B6 1 Victoria Mills
2 Hallings Wharf Studios
3 Poland Ho
4 Peter Heathfield Ho
5 Burford Rd
C5 1 Abbey Lane Commercial Est
2 Greenway Ct
C6 1 Barnby Sq
2 Barnby St
3 Brassett Point
4 David Lee Point
5 Worthing Cl
6 Bexhill Wlk
7 Old Barrowfield
8 Elmgreen Cl
9 Stafford Morris Ho
10 Nina Mackay Cl
11 Lime Wlk
D1 1 Newton Point
2 Sparke Terr
3 Montesquieu Terr
4 Crawford Point
5 Rathbone Ho
6 George St
7 Emily St
8 Fendt Cl
9 Sabbarton St
10 Briary Ct
11 Shaftesbury Ho
D2 1 Radley Terr
2 Bernard Cassidy St
3 Rathbone Mkt
4 Thomas North Terr
5 Mary St
6 Hughes Terr
7 Swanscombe Point
8 Rawlinson Point
9 Kennedy Cox Ho
10 Cooper St
D6 1 Harris Cotts
2 Moorey Cl
3 Euro Bsns Ctr
4 Ladywell St
5 Caistor Ho
6 Redfern Ho

99
A2 1 Odeon Ct
2 Edward Ct
3 Newhaven La
4 Ravenscroft Cl
5 Douglas Rd
6 Ferrier Point
7 Harvey Point
8 Wood Point
9 Trinity St
10 Pattinson Point
11 Clinch Ct
12 Mint Bsns Pk
A3 1 Webb Gdns
2 Eric Shipman Terr
3 Warmington St
4 Jellicoe Rd
5 Frank St
6 Seaton Cl
7 Tabernacle Ave
8 Upland Rd
9 Clove St
10 Edward St
A4 1 Bob Anker Cl
2 Lea Ct
3 Third Ave
4 Suffolk Rd
A5 1 Lettsom Wlk
2 Ashburton Terr
3 Grasmere Rd
4 Dimsdale Wlk
5 Rawstone Wlk
6 Scott Ho
7 Willett Ho
8 James Cl
9 Cordwainers Wlk
10 Victoria Point
11 Settle Point
12 Middle Rd
13 Steve Biko Lodge
14 Lady Helen Seymour Ho
A6 1 Royston Ct
B4 1 Barbers Alley
2 Grengate Lodge
3 Augurs La
4 Surrey St
5 Dongola Rd W
6 Bemersyde Point
7 Rowntree Clifford Cl
C2 1 Alliance Rd
2 Salomons Rd
3 Barnes Ct
4 Triangle Ct
5 Moorings The
C5 1 Wellby Ct
2 Northfield Ho
3 Bishop Wilfred Wood Ct
4 Castle Point
5 Moat Dr
C6 1 Tolpuddle Ave
2 Crown Mews
3 Lilac Ct
4 Hamara Ghar
5 Greenleaf Rd
6 Massey Ct
7 Florence Rd
8 Sissulu Ct
9 Austin Ct
D2 1 Partridge Cl
2 Vanbrugh Cl
3 Meadowsweet Cl
4 St Michaels Cl
5 Long Mark Rd
6 Congreve Wlk
D5 1 Foxcombe Cl
2 Rochford Cl
3 Kylemore Cl
4 Stondon Wlk
5 Imperial Mews
6 Dominica Cl
D6 1 Oldegate Ho
2 Gaitskell Ho
3 Cabot Way

100
A1 1 Hadleigh Wlk
2 Hawksmoor Cl
3 Fraser Cl
4 Moncrieff Cl
5 Burlington Cl
6 Dundonald Cl
7 Oakley Cl
8 Ashwell Cl
A2 1 Orchid Cl
2 Bellflower Cl
3 Partridge Sq
4 Larkspur Cl
5 Lobelia Cl
6 Stonechat Sq
7 Wintergreen Cl
8 Garnet Wlk
9 Mavis Wlk
10 Beacons Cl
11 Abbess Cl
12 Elmley Cl
13 Chetwood Wlk
14 Selby Cl
15 Denny Cl
16 Woodhatch Cl
A6 1 Oakwood Ct
2 Harrow Rd
3 Ray Massey Way
4 Madge Gill Way
5 Pilgrims Way
6 St Bartholomews Ct
B1 1 Bowers Wlk
2 Barton Cl
3 Clayton Cl
4 Dixon Cl
5 Gautrey Sq
6 Wakerley Cl
7 Canterbury Cl
8 Goose Sq
9 Coventry Cl
10 Butterfield Sq
11 Winchester Cl
B2 1 Fleetwood Ct
2 Lymington Cl
3 Holyhead Cl
4 Bondfield Rd
5 Tulip Cl
6 Ambrose Cl
7 Sage Cl
8 Lindwood Cl
D1 1 Weymouth Ct
2 Founder Cl
3 Admirals Ct

101
A6 1 Wellington St
2 St Ann's Rd
3 Cooke St
4 Gateway Ho
5 Ardleigh Ho
6 Skipper Ct
7 Hewetts Quay
B5 1 Anderson Ho
2 Rookwood Ho
3 Tasker Ho
4 Crispe Ho
5 Oban Ho
6 Earlsdown Ho
B6 1 Jarvis Cl
2 Mayflower Ho
3 Westbury Ct
4 Millicent Preston Ho
5 Louise Graham Ho
6 Grange Ho
7 Basing Ho
8 Barnes Ho
9 Lexham Ho
10 Ripple Ct
11 Waldegrave Ct
12 Howard Ct

104
A6 1 Milburn Dr
2 Cousins Cl
3 Leacroft Cl

108
C5 1 Marlow Ct
2 Andrewes Ct
3 Vine Cotts
4 Benjamin Ct
5 Broadway Bldgs
6 Clocktower Mews
7 Amberley Ho
8 Diamond Ct
D5 1 Silverdale Cl
2 Burdett Cl
3 Hopefield
4 Maunder Rd
5 Clare Ho

109
A5 1 Glastonbury Ct
2 Evesham Ct
3 Lacock Ct
4 Wigmore Ct
5 Melrose Ct
6 Brownlow Rd
7 Chignell Pl
8 Shirley Ct
9 Trojan Ct

10 Hatfield Rd
11 Pershore Ho
12 Hyde Ho
13 Hugh Clark Ho
14 Rosemoor Ho
15 Leeland Mans
16 Waterford Ct
17 O'Grady Ct
C6 1 Abbey Lo
2 Yew Tree Grange
3 Abinger Ct

110

A1 1 Burford Ho
2 Hope Cl
3 Centaur Ct
4 Phoenix Ct
A6 1 Watermans Mews
2 Hills Mews
3 Grosvenor Ct
4 Elton Lo
5 Hambledon Ct
C1 1 Surrey Cres
2 Forbes Ho
3 Haining Cl
4 Melville Ct
5 London Stile
6 Stile Hall Par
7 Priory Lo
8 Kew Bridge Ct
9 Meadowcroft
10 St James Ct
11 Rivers Ho
C5 1 Grosvenor Par
2 Oakfield Ct
3 Hart Grove Ct
4 Grosvenor Ct
D1 1 Churchdale Ct
2 Cromwell Cl
3 Cambridge Rd S
4 Oxbridge Ct
5 Tomlinson Cl
6 Gunnersbury
Mews
7 Grange The
8 Gunnersbury Cl
9 Bellgrave Lo
D4 1 Cheltenham Pl
2 Beaumaris Twr
3 Arundel Ho
4 Pevensey Ct
5 Jerome Twr
6 Anstey Ct
7 Bennett Ct
8 Gunnersbury Ct
9 Barrington Ct
10 Hope Gdns
11 Park Road E
D5 1 Lantry Ct
2 Rosemount Ct
3 Moreton Twr
4 Acton Central Ind
Est
5 Rufford Twr
6 Narrow St
7 Mount Pl
8 Sidney Miller Ct
9 Mill Hill Terr
10 Cheltenham Ct
11 Mill Hill Gr
12 Benjamin Ho
13 Arlington Ct
14 Lombard Ct
15 Steyne Ho

111

A1 1 Arlington Park
Mans
2 Sandown Ho
3 Goodwood Ho
4 Windsor Ho
5 Lingfield Ho
6 Ascot Ho
7 Watchfield Ct
8 Belgrave Ct
9 Beverley Ct
10 Beaumont Ct
11 Harvard Rd
12 Troubridge Ct
13 Branden Lo
14 Fromow's Cnr
A2 1 Chiswick Green
Studios
2 Bell Ind Est
3 Fairlawn Ct
4 Dukes Gate
5 Dewsbury Ct
6 Chiswick Terr
7 Mortlake Ho
A3 1 Blackmore Twr
2 Bollo Ct
3 Kipling Twr
4 Lawrence Ct
5 Maugham Ct
6 Reade Ct
7 Woolf Ct
8 Shaw Ct
9 Verne Ct
10 Wodehouse Ct
11 Greenock Rd
12 Garden Ct
13 Barons Gate
14 Cleveland Rd
15 Carver Cl
16 Chapter Cl
17 Beauchamp Cl
18 Holmes Ct

19 Copper Mews
A4 1 Belgrave Cl
2 Buckland Wlk
3 Frampton Ct
4 Telfer Cl
5 Harlech Twr
6 Corfe Twr
7 Barwick Ho
8 Charles Hocking
Ho
9 Sunninghill Ct
10 Salisbury St
11 Jameson Pl
12 Castle Cl
A5 1 Rectory Rd
2 Derwentwater
Mans
3 Market Pl
4 Hooper's Mews
5 Cromwell Pl
6 Locarno Rd
7 Edgecote Ct
8 Harleyford Manor
9 Coopers Ct
10 Avingdor Ct
11 Steyne Ho
B1 1 Chatsworth Lo
2 Prospect Pl
3 Townhall Ave
4 Devonhurst Pl
5 Heathfield Ct
6 Horticultural Pl
7 Merlin Ho
8 Garth Rd
9 Autumn Rise
B2 1 Disraeli Cl
2 Winston Wlk
3 Rusthall Mans
4 Bedford Park
Mans
5 Essex Place Sq
6 Holly Rd
7 Homecross Ho
8 Swan Bsns Ctr
9 Jessop Ho
C1 1 Glebe Cl
2 Devonshire Mews
3 Binns Terr
4 Ingress St
5 Swanscombe Rd
6 Brackley Terr
7 Stephen Fox Ho
8 Manor Gdns
9 Coram Ho
10 Flaxman Ho
11 Thorneycroft Ho
12 Thornhill Ho
13 Kent Ho
14 Oldfield Ho
C2 1 Chestnut Ho
2 Bedford Ho
3 Bedford Cnr
4 Sydney Ho
5 Bedford Park Cnr
6 Priory Gdns
7 Windmill Alley
8 Castle Pl
9 Jonathan Ct
10 Windmill Pas
11 Chardin Rd
12 Gable Ho
C3 1 Fleet Ct
2 Ember Ct
3 Emlyn Gdns
4 Clone Ct
5 Brent Ct
6 Abbey Ct
7 Ormsby Lo
8 St Catherine's Ct
9 Lodge The
C4 1 Longford Ct
2 Mole Ct
3 Lea Ct
4 Wandle Ct
5 Beverley Ct
6 Roding Ct
7 Crane Ct
D1 1 Miller's Ct
2 British Grove Pas
3 British Grove S
4 Berestede Rd
5 North Eyot Gdns
D2 1 Flanders Mans
2 Stamford Brook
Mans
3 Linkenholt Mans
4 Prebend Mans
5 Middlesex Ct
D3 1 Stamford Brook
Gdns
2 Hauteville Court
Gdns
3 Ranelagh Gdns

112

A1 1 Chisholm Ct
2 North Verbena
Gdns
3 Western Terr
4 Verbena Gdns
5 Montrose Villas
6 Hammersmith Terr
7 South Black Lion
La
8 St Peter's Wharf
A2 1 Hamlet Ct
2 Derwent Ct
3 Westcroft Ct
4 Black Lion Mews
5 St Peter's Villas

6 Standish Ho
7 Chambon Pl
8 Court Mans
9 Longthorpe Ct
10 Charlotte Ct
11 Westside
12 Park Ct
A3 1 Elizabeth Finn Ho
2 Ashchurch Ct
3 King's Par
4 Inver Ct
5 Ariel Ct
6 Pocklington Lo
7 Vitae Apartments
A4 1 Becklow Gdns
2 Victoria Ho
3 Lycett Pl
4 Kylemore Ct
5 Alexandra Ct
6 Lytten Ct
7 Becklow Mews
8 Northcroft Ct
9 Bailey Ct
10 Spring Cott
11 Landor Wlk
12 Laurence Mews
13 Hadyn Park Ct
14 Askew Mans
15 Malvern Ct
B1 1 Prince's Mews
2 Aspen Gdns
3 Hampshire Hog La
4 Blades Ct
B2 1 Albion Gdns
2 Flora Gdns
3 Lamington St
4 Felgate Mews
5 Galena Ho
6 Albion Mews
7 Albion Ct
8 King Street Clois-
ters
9 Dimes Pl
10 Clarence Ct
11 Hampshire Hog La
12 Marryat Ct
13 Ravenscourt Ho
B3 1 Ravenscourt Park
Mans
2 Paddenswick Ct
3 Ashbridge Ct
B4 1 Westbush Ct
2 Goldhawk Mews
3 Sycamore Ho
4 Shackleton Ct
5 Drake Ct
6 Scotts Ct
7 Raleigh Ct
8 Melville Court
Flats
9 Southway Cl
B5 1 Arlington Ho
2 Lugard Ho
3 Shabana Ct
4 Sitarey Ct
5 Oaklands Ct
6 Davenport Mews
B6 1 Abercrombie Ho
2 Bathurst Ho
3 Brisbane Ho
4 Bentinck Ho
5 Ellenborough Ho
6 Lawrence Ct
7 Mackenzie Cl
8 Carteret Ho
9 Calvert Ho
10 Winthrop Ho
11 Auckland Ho
12 Blaxland Ho
13 Havelock Cl
14 Hargraves Ho
15 Hudson Ct
16 Phipps Ho
17 Lawson Ho
18 Hastings Ho
19 Wolfe Ho
20 Malabar Ct
21 Commonwealth
Ave
22 Charnock Ho
23 Canning Ho
24 Cornwallis Ho
25 Commonwealth
Ave
26 Champlain Ho
27 Grey Ho
28 Durban Ho
29 Baird Ho
30 Campbell Ho
31 Mitchell Ho
32 Denham Ho
33 Mackay Ho
34 Evans Ho
35 Davis Ho
36 Mandela Cl
C1 1 Bridge Avenue
Mans
2 Bridgeview
3 College Ct
4 Beatrice Ho
5 Amelia Ho
6 Edith Ho
7 Joanna Ho
8 Mary Ho
9 Adela Ho
10 Sophia Ho
11 Henrietta Ho
12 Charlotte Ho
13 Alexandra Ho

14 Bath Pl
15 Elizabeth Ho
16 Margaret Ho
17 Peabody Est
18 Eleanor Ho
19 Isabella Ho
20 Caroline Ho
21 Chancellors Wharf
22 Sussex Pl
C2 1 Phoenix Lodge
Mans
2 Samuel's Cl
3 Broadway Arc
4 Brook Ho
5 Hammersmith
Broadway
6 Broadway Ctr The
7 Cambridge Ct
8 Ashcroft Sq
C4 1 Verulam Ho
2 Grove Mans
3 Frobisher Ct
4 Library Mans
5 Pennard Mans
6 New Shepherd's
Bush Mkt
7 Kerrington Ct
8 Granville Mans
9 Romney Ct
10 Rayner Ct
11 Sulgrave Gdns
12 Bamborough Gdns
13 Hillary Ct
14 Market Studios
15 Lanark Mans
C5 1 Linden Ct
2 Frithville Ct
3 Blomfield Mans
4 Poplar Mews
5 Hopgood St
6 Westwood Ho
7 Stanlake Mews
8 Stanlake Villas
9 Alexandra Mans
D3 1 Grosvenor Resi-
dences
2 Blythe Mews
3 Burnand Ho
4 Bradford Ho
5 Springvale Terr
6 Ceylon Rd
7 Walpole Ct
8 Bronte Ct
9 Souldern Rd
10 Brook Green Flats
11 Haarlem Rd
12 Stafford Mans
13 Lionel Mans
14 Barradell Ho
D4 1 Vanderbilt Villas
2 Bodington Ct
3 Kingham Cl
4 Clearwater Terr
5 Lorne Gdns
6 Cameret Ct
7 Bush Ct
8 Shepherds Ct
9 Rockley Ct
10 Grampians The
11 Charcroft Ct
12 Addison Park
Mans
13 Sinclair Mans
14 Fountain Ct
15 Woodford Ct
16 Roseford Ct
17 Woodstock Stu-
dios
D5 1 St Katherine's Wlk
2 Dorrit Ho
3 Pickwick Ho
4 Dombey Ho
5 Caranday Villas
6 Mortimer Ho
7 Nickleby Ho
8 Stebbing Ho
9 Boxmoor Ho
10 Poynter Ho
11 Swanscombe Ho
12 Darnley Terr
13 Norland Ho
14 Hume Ho
15 Boundary Ho
16 Norland Rd
17 Helix Ct
D6 1 Frinstead Ho
2 Hurstway Wlk
3 Testerton Wlk
4 Grenfell Wlk
5 Grenfell Twr
6 Barandon Wlk
7 Treadgold Ho
8 St Clements Ct
9 Willow Way
10 Florence Ho
11 Dora Ho
12 Carton Ho
13 Agnes Ho
14 Marley Ho
15 Estella Ho
16 Waynflete Sq
17 Pippin Ho
18 Baseline Business
Studios

118

A1 1 Hope Ct
2 West Point
3 Centre Point

4 East Point
5 Proctor Ho
6 Tovy Ho
7 Avondale Pave-
ment
8 Brettinghurst
9 Colechurch Ho
10 Harman Cl
11 Avondale Ho
12 Lanark Ho
13 George Elliston
Ho
14 Eric Wilkins Ho
15 Six Bridges Ind
Est
16 St James Ind
Mews
17 Winter Lo
18 Fern Wlk
19 Ivy Ct
20 Fallow Ct
21 Culloden Cl
22 Archers Lo
A2 1 Cadbury Way
2 Robert Bell Ho
3 Robert Jones Ho
4 William Rush-
brooke Ho
5 Helen Taylor Ho
6 Peter Hills Ho
7 Charles Macken-
zie Ho
8 Drappers Way
9 Racs Flats
10 Abbey Gdns
11 Mayfair Ho
12 Windmill Cl
13 Maria Ct
14 Townsend Ho
15 Mason Ho   *
16 Kotree Way
17 Hannah Mary Way
18 Langdon Way
19 Whittaker Way
A3 1 Rudge Ho
2 Spenlow Ho
3 Darnay Ho
4 Carton Ho
5 Giles Ho
6 Bowley Ho
7 Casby Ho
8 Sun Pas
9 Ness St
10 Voyager Bsns Est
11 Dockley Road Ind
Est
12 Spa Ct
13 Discovery Bsns Pk
14 Priter Road Hostel
15 Salisbury Ct
16 William Ellis Way
17 John McKenna
Wlk
18 Toussaint Wlk
19 Gillison Wlk
20 Bromfield Ct
21 Ben Smith Way
22 Major Rd
23 Old Jamaica Bsns
Est
A4 1 Providence
2 Springalls Wharf
3 Flockton St
4 Meridian Ct
5 East La
6 Luna Ho
7 Axis Ct
8 Farthing Alley
9 Peter Butler Ho
10 Brownlow Ho
11 Tapley Ho
12 Copperfield Ho
13 Dombey Ho
14 Fleming Ho
15 Parkers Row
16 Wade Ho
17 Bardell Ho
18 Nickleby Ho
19 John Felton Ho
20 Flockton St
21 Pickwick Ho
22 Oliver Ho
23 Weller Ho
24 Haredale Ho
25 Havisham Ho
26 Tupman Ho
27 Micawber Ho
28 Wrayburn Ho
29 Dartle Ct
30 Waterside Cl
31 Burnaby Ct
32 Wickfield Ho
33 Fountain Ho
34 Fountain Green
Sq
35 St Saviours Ho
36 Providence Sq
A5 1 Trade Winds Ct
2 Spice Ct
3 Leeward Ct
4 Bridgeport Pl
5 Tamarind Yd
6 Cape Yd
7 Nightingale Ho
8 St Anthony's Cl
9 Stockholm Way
10 Miah Terr
11 Seville Ho
12 Douthwaite Sq
13 Codling Cl

14 Hermitage Ct
15 Capital Wharf
16 Cinnabar Wharf
East
17 Cinnabar Wharf
Central
18 Cinnabar Wharf
West
19 Halcyon Wharf
A6 1 Conant Mews
2 Hanson Ho
3 Royal Tower Lo
4 Victoria Ct
5 Swan Pas
6 Royal Mint Pl
7 Peabody Est
8 Florin Ct
9 Flank St
10 Onedin Point
11 Liberty Ho
12 Ensign Ct
13 Sapphire Ct
14 Graces Alley
15 George Leybourne
Ho
16 Fletcher St
17 Hatton Ho
18 Noble Ho
19 Shearsmith Ho
20 Wellclose St
21 Telford's Yd
22 Breezer's Ct
23 Pennington St
B1 1 Hockney Ct
2 Toulouse Ct
3 Lowry Ct
4 Barry Ho
5 Lewis Ct
6 Gainsborough Ct
7 Renoir Ct
8 Blake Ct
9 Raphael Ct
10 Rembrandt Ct
11 Constable Ct
12 Da Vinci Ct
13 Gaugin Ct
14 Michelangelo Ct
15 Monet Ct
16 Weald Cl
17 Jasmin Lo
18 Birchmere Lo
19 Weybridge Ct
20 Florence Ho
21 Gleneagles Cl
22 Sunningdale Cl
23 Muirfield Cl
24 Turnberry Cl
25 St Andrews Cl
26 Kingsdown Cl
27 St Davids Cl
28 Galway Cl
29 Edenbridge Cl
30 Birkdale Cl
31 Tralee Ct
32 Woburn Ct
33 Belfry Cl
34 Troon Cl
35 Holywell Cl
B2 1 Market Pl
2 Trappes Ho
3 Thurland Ho
4 Ramsfort Ho
5 Hambley Ho
6 Holford Ho
7 Pope Ho
8 Southwell Ho
9 Mortain Ho
10 Radcliffe Ho
11 Southwark Park
Est
12 Galleywall Road
Trad Est
13 Trevithick Ho
14 Barlow Ho
15 Donkin Ho
16 Landmann Ho
17 Fitzmaurice Ho
18 Dodd Ho
B3 1 Perryn Rd
2 Chalfont Ho
3 Prestwood Ho
4 Farmer Ho
5 Gataker Ho
6 Gataker St
7 Cornick Ho
8 Glebe Ho
9 Matson Ho
10 Hickling Ho
11 St Andrews Ho
B4 1 Butterfield Cl
2 Janeway Pl
3 Trotwood Ho
4 Maylie Ho
5 Cranbourn Pas
6 Cranbourn Ho
7 Cherry Garden Ho
8 Burton Ho
9 Morriss Ho
10 Dixon's Alley
11 King Edward The
Third Mews
12 Cathay St
13 Mission The
14 Millstream Ho
B5 1 Wellington Terr
2 Stevedore St
3 Portland Sq
4 Reardon Ho
5 Lowder Ho

7 Meeting House
Alley
8 Farthing Fields
9 Oswell Ho
10 Park Lo
11 Doughty Ct
12 Inglefield Sq
13 Chopin's Ct
14 Welsh Ho
15 Hilliard Ho
16 Clegg St
17 Tasman Ho
18 Ross Ho
19 Wapping Dock St
20 Bridewell Pl
21 New Tower Bldgs
22 Tower Bldgs
23 Chimney Ct
24 Jackman Ho
25 Fenner Ho
26 Franklin Ho
27 Frobisher Ho
28 Flinders Ho
29 Chancellor Ho
30 Beechey Ho
31 Reardon Path
32 Parry Ho
33 Vancover Ho
34 Willoughby Ho
35 Sanctuary The
36 Dundee Ct
37 Pierhead Wharf
38 Scandrett St
39 St Johns Ct
B6 1 Newton Ho
2 Richard Neale Ho
3 Maddocks Ho
4 Cornwall St
5 Brockmer Ho
6 Dellow Ho
7 Bewley Ho
8 Artichoke Hill
9 Queen Anne Terr
10 King Henry Terr
11 King Charles Terr
12 Queen Victoria
Terr
13 Sovereign Ct
14 Princes Court
Bsns Ctr
15 Kingsley Mews
C2 1 Damory Ho
2 Antony Ho
3 Roderick Ho
4 Pedworth Gdns
5 Banner Ct
6 Rotherhithe Bsns
Est
7 Beamish Ho
8 Corbetts Pas
9 Gillam Ho
10 Richard Ho
11 George Walter Ho
12 Westlake
13 Adron Ho
14 McIntosh Ho
C3 1 Blick Ho
2 Neptune Ho
3 Scotia Ct
4 Murdoch Ho
5 Edmonton Ct
6 Niagara Ct
7 Columbia Point
8 Ritchie Ho
9 Wells Ho
10 Helen Peele Cotts
11 Orchard Ho
12 Dock Offices
13 Landale Ho
14 Courthope Ho
15 Hithe Gr
16 China Hall Mews
C4 1 Mayflower St
2 St Mary's Est
3 Rupack St
4 Frank Whymark
Ho
5 Adams Gardens
Est
6 Hatteraick St
7 East India Ct
8 Bombay Ct
9 Stable Ho
10 Grannary The
11 Riverside
12 Cumberland
Wharf
13 Seaford Ho
14 Hythe Ho
15 Sandwich Ho
16 Winchelsea Ho
17 Rye Ho
18 Kenning St
19 Western Pl
20 Ainsty St
21 Pine Ho
22 Beech Ho
23 Larch Ho
24 Turner Ct
25 Seth St
26 Risdon Ho
27 Risdon St
28 Aylton Est
29 Manitoba Ct
30 Calgary Ct
31 Irwell Est
32 St Olav's Sq
33 City Bsns Ctr
C5 1 John Rennie Wlk
2 Malay Ho

3 Wainwright Ho
4 Riverside Mans
5 Shackleton Ho
6 Whitehorn Ho
7 Wavel Ct
8 Prusom's Island
C6 1 Shadwell Pl
2 Gosling Ho
3 Vogler Ho
4 Donovan Ho
5 Knowlden Ho
6 Chamberlain Ho
7 Moore Ho
8 Thornewill Ho
9 Fisher Ho
10 All Saints Ct
11 Coburg Dwellings
12 Lowood Ho
13 Solander Gdns
14 Chancery Bldgs
15 Ring Ho
16 Juniper St
17 Gordon Ho
18 West Block
19 North Block
20 South Block
21 Ikon Ho
D2 1 John Kennedy Ho
2 Brydale Ho
3 Balman Ho
4 Tissington Ct
5 Harbord Ho
6 Westfield Ho
7 Albert Starr Ho
8 John Brent Ho
9 William Evans Ho
10 Raven Ho
11 Egret Ho
12 Fulmar Ho
13 Dunlin Ho
14 Siskin Ho
15 Sheldrake Ho
16 Buchanan Ct
17 Burrage Ct
18 Biddenham Ho
19 Ayston Ho
20 Empingham Ho
21 Deanshanger Ho
22 Codicote Ho
23 Buryfield Ct
D4 1 Schooner Cl
2 Dolphin Cl
3 Clipper Cl
4 Deauville Ct
5 Colette Ct
6 Coniston Ct
7 Virginia Ct
8 Derwent Ct
9 Grantham Ct
10 Serpentine Ct
11 Career Ct
12 Lacine Ct
13 Fairway Ct
14 Harold Ct
15 Spruce Ho
16 Cedar Ho
17 Sycamore Ho
18 Woodland Cres
19 Poplar Ho
20 Adelphi Ct
21 Basque Ct
22 Aberdale Ct
23 Quilting Ct
24 Chargrove Ct
25 Radley Ct
26 Greenacre Sq
27 Maple Leaf Sq
28 Stanhope Cl
29 Hawke Pl
30 Drake Cl
31 Brass Talley Alley
32 Monkton Ho
33 James Ho
34 Wolfe Cres
D5 1 Clarence Mews
2 Raleigh Ct
3 Katherine Cl
4 Woolcombes Ct
5 Tudor Ct
6 Quayside Ct
7 Princes Riverside Rd
8 Surrey Ho
9 Tideway Ct
10 Edinburgh Ct
11 Falkirk Ct
12 Byelands Cl
13 Gwent Ct
14 Lavender Ho
15 Abbotshade Rd
16 Bellamy's Ct
17 Blenheim Ct
18 Sandringham Ct
19 Hampton Ct
20 Windsor Ct
21 Balmoral Ct
22 Westminster Ct
23 Beatson Wlk
D6 1 Barnardo Gdns
2 Roslin Ho
3 Glamis Est
4 Peabody Est
5 East Block
6 Highway Trad Ctr The
7 Highway Bsns Pk The
8 Cranford Cotts
9 Ratcliffe Orch
10 Scotia Bldg
11 Mauretania Bldg
12 Compania Bldg
13 Sirius Bldg
14 Unicorn Bldg
15 Keepier Wharf

119

A2 1 Trafalgar Cl
2 Hornblower Cl
3 Cunard Wlk
4 Caronia Ct
5 Carinthia Ct
6 Freswick Ho
7 Graveley Ho
8 Husbourne Ho
9 Crofters Ct
10 Pomona Ho
11 Hazelwood Ho
12 Cannon Wharf Bsns Ctr
13 Bence Ho
14 Clement Ho
15 Pendennis Ho
16 Lighter Cl
17 Mast Ct
18 Rushcutters Ct
19 Boat Lifter Way
A5 1 Edward Sq
2 Prince Regent Ct
3 Codrington Ct
4 Pennington Ct
5 Cherry Ct
6 Ash Ct
7 Beech Ct
8 Hazel Ct
9 Laurel Ct
A6 1 St Georges Sq
2 Drake Ho
3 Osprey Ho
4 Fleet Ho
5 Gainsborough Ho
6 Victory Pl
7 Challenger Ho
8 Conrad Ho
9 Lock View Ct
10 Shoulder of Mutton Alley
11 Frederick Sq
12 Helena Sq
13 Elizabeth Sq
14 Sophia Sq
15 William Sq
16 Lamb Ct
17 Lockside
18 Adriatic Bldg
19 Ionian Bldg
20 Regents Gate Ho
B1 1 Gransden Ho
2 Daubeney Twr
3 North Ho
4 Rochfort Ho
5 Keppel Ho
6 Camden Ho
7 Sanderson Ho
8 Berkeley Ho
9 Strafford Ho
10 Richman Ho
11 Hurleston Ho
12 Grafton Ho
13 Fulcher Ho
14 Citrus Ho
B2 1 Windsock Cl
2 St George's Mews
3 Linberry Wlk
4 Lanyard Ho
5 Golden Hind Pl
6 James Lind Ho
7 Harmon Ho
8 Pelican Ho
9 Bembridge Ho
10 Terrace The
11 George Beard Rd
12 Colonnade The
13 Pepys Ent Ctr
B6 1 Hamilton Ho
2 Imperial Ho
3 Oriana Ho
4 Queens Ct
5 Brightlingsea Pl
6 Faraday Ho
7 Ropemaker's Fields
8 Oast Ct
9 Mitre The
10 Bate St
11 Joseph Irwin Ho
12 Padstow Ho
13 Bethlehem Ho
14 Saunders Ct
15 Roche Ho
16 Stocks Pl
17 Trinidad Ho
18 Grenada Ho
19 Kings Ho
20 Dunbar Wharf
21 Limekiln Wharf
22 Belgrave Ct
23 Eaton Ho
C1 1 Hudson Ct
2 Shackleton Ct
3 De Gama Pl
4 Mercator Pl
5 Maritime Quay
6 Perry Ct
7 Amundsen Ho
C2 1 Nova Bldg
2 Apollo Bldg
3 Gaverick Mews
4 Windmill Ho
5 Orion Point
6 Galaxy Bldg
7 Venus Ho
8 Olympian Ct
9 Poseidon Ct
10 Mercury Ct
11 Aphrodite Ct
12 Cyclops Mews
13 Neptune Ct
14 Artemis Ct
15 Hera Ct
16 Ares Ct
17 Ringwood Gdns
18 Dartmoor Wlk
19 Rothsay Wlk
20 Ashdown Wlk
21 Radnor Wlk
22 Ironmonger's Pl
23 Britannia Rd
24 Deptford Ferry Rd
25 Magellan Pl
26 Dockers Tanner Rd
C3 1 Bowsprit Point
2 St Hubert's Ho
3 John Tucker Ho
4 Broadway Wlk
5 Nash Ho
6 Fairlead Ho
7 Crosstrees Ho
8 Stanliff Ho
9 Keelson Ho
10 Clara Grant Ho
11 Gilbertson Ho
12 Scoulding Ho
13 Hibbert Ho
14 Cressall Ho
15 Alexander Ho
16 Kedge Ho
C4 1 Anchorage Point
2 Waterman Bldg
3 Jefferson Bldg
4 Pierpoint Bldg
5 Franklin Bldg
6 Vanguard Bldg
7 Edison Bldg
8 Seacon Twr
9 Naxos Bldg
10 Express Wharf
11 Hutching's Wharf
12 Tobago St
13 Bellamy Cl
14 Dowlen Ct
15 Cochrane Ho
16 Beatty Ho
17 Scott Ho
18 Laybourne Ho
19 Ensign Ho
20 Beaufort Ho
21 Spinnaker Ho
22 Bosun Cl
23 Topmast Point
24 Turner Ho
25 Constable Ho
26 Knighthead Point
C6 1 West India Ho
2 Berber Pl
3 Birchfield Ho
4 Elderfield Ho
5 Thornfield Ho
6 Gorsefield Ho
7 Arborfield Ho
8 Colborne Ho
9 East India Bldgs
10 Compass Point
11 Salter St
12 Garland Ct
13 Bogart Ct
14 Fonda Ct
15 Welles Ct
16 Rogers Ct
17 Premier Pl
18 Kelly Ct
19 Flynn Ct
20 Mary Jones Ho
21 Cannon Dr
22 Horizon Bldg
D1 1 Slipway Ho
2 Taffrail Ho
3 Platehouse The
4 Wheelhouse The
5 Chart House The
6 Port House The
7 Beacon Ho
8 Blasker Wlk
9 Maconochies Rd
D2 1 Brassey Ho
2 Triton Ho
3 Warspite Ho
4 Rodney Ho
5 Conway Ho
6 Exmouth Ho
7 Akbar Ho
8 Arethusa Ho
9 Tasman Ct
10 Cutty Sark Ho
D3 1 Turnberry Quay
2 Balmoral Ho
3 Aegon Ho
4 Marina Point
D6 1 Westcott Ho
2 Corry Ho
3 Malam Gdns
4 Blomfield Ho
5 Devitt Ho
6 Leyland Ho
7 Wigram Ho
8 Willis Ho
9 Balsam Ho
10 Finch's Ct
11 Poplar Bath St
12 Lawless St
13 Storey Ho
14 Abbot Ho
15 Woodall Cl
16 Landon Wlk
17 Goodhope Ho
18 Goodfaith Ho
19 Winant Ho
20 Goodspeed Ho
21 Lubbock Ho
22 Goodwill Ho
23 Martindale Ho
24 Holmsdale Ho
25 Norwood Ho
26 Constant Ho

120

A2 1 St John's Ho
2 Betty May Gray Ho
3 Castleton Ho
4 Urmston Ho
5 Salford Ho
6 Capstan Ho
7 Frigate Ho
8 Galleon Ho
A3 1 Cardale St
2 Hickin St
3 John McDonald Ho
4 Thorne Ho
5 Skeggs Ho
6 St Bernard Ho
7 Kimberley Ho
8 Kingdon Ho
9 Killoran Ho
10 Alastor Ho
11 Lingard Ho
12 Yarrow Ho
13 Sandpiper Ct
14 Nightingale Ct
15 Robin Ct
16 Heron Ct
17 Ferndown Lo
18 Crosby Ho
A4 1 Llandovery Ho
2 Rugless Ho
3 Ash Ho
4 Elm Ho
5 Cedar Ho
6 Castalia Sq
7 Aspect Ho
8 Normandy Ho
9 Valiant Ho
10 Tamar Ho
11 Watkins Ho
12 Alice Shepherd Ho
13 Oak Ho
14 Ballin Ct
15 Martin Ct
16 Grebe Ct
17 Kingfisher Ct
18 Walkers Lo
19 Antilles Bay
A5 1 Lumina Bldg
2 Nova Ct W
3 Nova Ct E
4 Aurora Bldg
5 Arran Ho
6 Kintyre Ho
7 Vantage Mews
8 Managers St
9 Horatio Pl
10 Concordia Wharf
A6 1 Discovery Ho
2 Mountague Pl
3 Virginia Ho
4 Collins Ho
5 Lawless Ho
6 Carmichael Ho
7 Commodore Ho
8 Mermaid Ho
9 Bullivant St
10 Anderson Ho
11 Mackrow Wlk
12 Robin Hood Gdns
13 Prestage Way
B2 1 Verwood Lo
2 Fawley Lo
3 Lyndhurst Lo
4 Blyth Cl
5 Farnworth Ho
6 Francis Cl
B6 1 Quixley St
2 Romney Ho
3 Pumping Ho
4 Switch Ho
5 Wingfield Ct
6 Explorers Ct
7 Sexton Ct
8 Keel Ct
9 Bridge Ct
10 Sail Ct
11 Settlers Ct
12 Pilgrims Mews
13 Studley Ct
14 Wotton Ct
15 Cape Henry Ct
16 Bartholomew Ct
17 Adventurers Ct
18 Susan Constant Ct
19 Atlantic Ct
C1 1 Bellot Gdns
2 Thornley Pl
3 King William La
4 Bolton Ho
5 Miles Ho
6 Mell St
7 Sam Manners Ho
8 Hatcliffe Almshouses
9 Woodland Wlk
10 Earlswood Cl
D1 1 Baldrey Ho
2 Christie Ho
3 Dyson Ho
4 Cliffe Ho
5 Moore Ho
6 Collins Ho
7 Lockyer Ho
8 Halley Ho
9 Kepler Ho
10 Sailacre Ho
11 Union Pk
D3 1 Teal St
2 Maurer Ct
3 Mudlarks Blvd
4 Renaissance Wlk
5 Alamaro Lo

121

A1 1 Layfield Ho
2 Westerdale Rd
3 Mayston Mews
4 Station Mews Terr
A5 1 Capulet Mews
2 Pepys Cres
3 De Quincey Mews
4 Hardy Ave
5 Tom Jenkinson Rd
6 Kennacraig Cl
7 Charles Flemwell Mews
8 Gatcombe Rd
9 Badminton Mews
10 Holyrood Mews
11 Britannia Gate
12 Dalemain Mews
13 Bowes-Lyon Hall
14 Lancaster hall
15 Victoria Hall
A6 1 Clements Ave
2 Martindale Ave
3 Balearic Apts
4 Marmara Apts
5 Baltic Apts
6 Coral Apts
7 Aegean Apts
8 Capital East Apts
B1 1 Phipps Ho
2 Hartwell Ho
3 Nicholas Stacey Ho
4 Frank Burton Ho
B5 1 Beaulieu Ave
2 Charles Whincup Rd
3 Audley Dr
4 Julia Garfield Mews
5 Rayleigh Rd
6 Pirie St
7 Royal Victoria Pl
8 Pankhurst Ave
9 West Mersea Cl
10 Ramsgate Cl
11 Windsor Hall
12 Munning Ho
13 Drake Hall
14 Jane Austen Hall
15 Eastern Quay
C1 1 Ransom Rd
2 Linton Cl
3 Cedar Pl
4 Gooding Ho
5 Valiant Ho
6 Chaffey Ho
7 Benn Ho
8 Wellesley Cl
9 Gollogly Terr

122

A2 1 Harden Ct
2 Albion Ct
3 Viking Ho
4 Zealand Ho
5 Glenalvon Way
6 Parish Wharf
7 Elsinore Ho
8 Lolland Ho
9 Denmark Ho
10 Jutland Ho
11 Tivoli Gdns
12 Rance Ho
13 Peel Yates Ho
14 Rosebank Wlk
15 Paradise Pl
16 Woodville St
B2 1 Bowling Green Row
2 Sarah Turnbull Ho
3 Brewhouse Rd
4 Red Barracks Rd
5 Marine Dr
6 Hastings Ho
7 Centurion Ct
8 Cambridge Ho
9 Churchill Ct
10 Elizabeth Ct
11 Cambridge Barracks Rd
12 Len Clifton Ho
13 Granby Ho
14 Harding Ho
15 Rutland Ho
16 Townshend Ho
17 Rendlebury Ho
18 Milne Ho
19 Mulgrave Ho
20 Murray Ho
21 Chatham Ho
22 Biddulph Ho
23 Carew Ho
24 Eleanor Wlk
C2 1 Preston Ho
2 Lindsay Ho
3 Fraser Ho
4 Pickering Ho
5 Watergate Ho
6 Grinling Ho
7 Glebe Ho
8 Elliston Ho
9 Sir Martin Bowes Ho
10 Jim Bradley Cl
11 Bathway
12 Limavady Ho
13 Slater Cl
14 Vista Bldg The
C5 1 Westland Ho
2 Queensland Ho
3 Pier Par
4 Woodman Par
5 Shaw Ho
6 Glen Ho
7 Brocklebank Ho
D1 1 Branham Ho
2 Ford Ho
3 Wilford Ho
4 Parker Ho
5 Stirling Ho
6 Twiss Ho
7 Hewett Ho
8 De Haviland Dr
9 Schoolhouse Yd
D2 1 Beresford Ho
2 Central Ct
3 Walpole Pl
4 Anglesea Ave
5 Troy Ct
6 Ormsby Point
7 Haven Lo
8 Green Lawns
9 Eardley Point
10 Sandham Point
11 Bingham Point
12 Anglesea Mews
13 Masons Hill
14 Maritime Ho

123

A1 1 Glenmount Path
2 Claymill Ho
3 St James Hts
4 St Margaret's Path
5 George Akass Ho
A3 1 Wayatt Point
2 Albert Ho
3 Building 50
4 Building 49
5 Building 48
6 Building 47
7 Building 36
8 Blenheim Ho
9 Wilson Ct
B1 1 Bert Reilly Ho
B3 1 Apollo Way
2 Senator Wlk
3 Mallard Path
4 Fortune Wlk
C1 1 Fox Hollow Cl
2 Goldsmid St
C2 1 Gavin Ho
2 Richard Neve Ho
3 Bateson St
4 Lewin Ct

124

B5 1 Rowntree Path
2 MacAulay Way
3 Manning Ct
4 Chadwick Ct
5 Simon Ct
B6 1 Beveridge Ct
2 Hammond Way
3 Leonard Robbins Path
4 Lansbury Ct
5 Raymond Postgate Ct
6 Webb Ct
7 Curtis Way
8 Lytton Strachey Path
9 Keynes Ct
10 Marshall Path
11 Cross Ct
12 Octavia Way
13 Passfield Path
14 Mill Ct
15 Besant Ct
C3 1 Hermitage Cl
2 Chantry Cl
C4 1 Binsey Wlk
2 Tilehurst Point
3 Blewbury Ho
4 Coralline Wlk
5 Evenlode Ho
C5 1 Kingsley Ct
2 Wilberforce Ct
3 Shaftesbury Ct
4 Hazlitt Ct
5 Ricardo Path
6 Nassau Path
7 Malthus Path
8 Bright Ct
9 Cobden Ct
D4 1 Oakenholt Ho
2 Trewsbury Ho
3 Penton Ho
4 Osney Ho
5 St Helens Rd
6 Clewer Ho
7 Maplin Ho
8 Wyfold Ho
9 Hibernia Point
10 Duxford Ho
11 Radley Ho
12 Limestone Wlk
13 Masham Ho
14 Jacob Ho

125

A3 1 Harlequin Ho
2 Dexter Ho
3 Argali Ho
4 Mangold Way
5 Lucerne Ct
6 Holstein Way
7 Abbotswood Cl
8 Plympton Cl
9 Benedict Ct
B1 1 Shakespeare Ho
2 Tennyson Ho
3 Dickens Ho
4 Scott Ho
5 Lansbury Ho
6 Shaw Ho
7 Chestnuts The
C1 1 Stevanne Ho
2 Tolcairn Ct
3 Chalfont Ct
4 Alonso Ho
5 Ariel Ct
6 Miranda Ho
7 Prospero Ho
8 Laurels The
9 Camden Ct
10 Newnham Lo
11 Court Lo
12 Flaxman Ct
13 Hertford Wlk
14 Riverview Ct
15 Winchester Ct
C2 1 Brushwood Lo
2 Bletchington Ct
3 Upper Sheridan Rd
4 William Ct
5 Samson Ct
6 Cowper Rd
7 Venmead Ct
C3 1 Cressingham Ct
2 Telford Ho
3 Kelvin Ho
4 Faraday Ho
5 Jenner Ho
6 Keir Hardie Ho
7 Lennox Ho
8 Mary Macarthur Ho
9 Elizabeth Garrett Anderson Ho
10 William Smith Ho
11 Baden Powell Ho
12 Baird Ho
13 Boyle Ho

129

D1 1 Heathwood Ct
2 Aldermead
3 Northumberland Ct

130

C4 1 Osterley Lo
2 St Andrew's Cl
3 Parkfield
4 Fairways
5 Granwood Ct
6 Grovewood Ct

131

A2 1 Brewery Mews Bsns Ctr
2 Forge Lo
3 Pulteney Cl
4 Tolson Ho
5 Percy Gdns
6 Wynne Ct
7 Wisdom Ct
8 Swann Ct
9 Shrewsbury Wlk
10 King's Terr
11 Van Gogh Cl
12 Holme Ct
C5 1 Canute Ho
2 Spruce Ho
3 Moorings Ho
4 Jessops Wharf
5 Corsell Ho
6 Barnes Qtr
7 Dorey Ho
8 Tanyard Ho
9 Booth Ho
10 Oakbark Ho
11 Bordeston Ct
12 Shire Pl
D5 1 Galba Ct
2 Servius Ct
3 Maurice Ct
4 Leo Ct
5 Otho Ct
6 Nero Ct
7 Romulus Ct

8 Pump Alley
D6 1 Brockshot Cl
2 Westbury Pl
3 Brook La N
4 Braemar Ct
5 Brook Ct
6 Clifden Ho
7 Cedar Ct
8 Cranbrook Ct
9 Somerset Lo
10 Alexandra Rd
11 Berkeley Ho
12 Watermans Ct
13 Ferry Quays Ctyd

132

A1 1 St John's Gr
2 Michel's Row
3 Michelsdale Dr
4 Blue Anchor Alley
5 Clarence St
6 Sun Alley
7 Thames Link Ho
8 Benns Wlk
9 Waterloo Pl
10 Northumbria Ct
A6 1 Ferry Sq
2 Watermans Ct
3 Wilkes Rd
4 Albany Par
5 Charlton Ho
6 Albany Ho
7 Alma Ho
8 Griffin Ct
9 Cressage Ho
10 Tunstall Wlk
11 Trimmer Wlk
12 Running Horse Yd
13 Mission Sq
14 Distillery Wlk
B1 1 Towers The
2 Longs Ct
3 Sovereign Ct
4 Robinson Ct
5 Calvert Ct
6 Bedford Ct
7 Hickey's Almshouses
8 Church Estate Almshouses
9 Richmond International Bsns Ctr
10 Abercorn Mews
B4 1 Primrose Ho
2 Lawman Ct
3 Royston Ct
4 Garden Ct
5 Capel Lo
6 Devonshire Ct
7 Celia Ct
8 Rosslyn Ho
9 Branstone Ct
10 Lamerton Lo
11 Kew Lo
12 Dunraven Ho
13 Stoneleigh Lo
14 Tunstall Ct
15 Voltaire
C4 1 Clarendon Ct
2 Quintock Ho
3 Broome Ct
4 Lonsdale Mews
5 Elizabeth Cotts
6 Sandways
7 Victoria Cotts
8 North Ave
9 Grovewood
10 Hamilton Ho
11 Melvin Ct
12 Royal Par
13 Power Ho
14 Station Ave
15 Blake Mews
D1 1 Hershell Ct
2 Deanhill Ct
3 Park Sheen
4 Furness Lo
5 Merricks Ct
D4 1 Terrano Ho
2 Oak Ho
3 Aura Ho
4 Maple Ho
5 Cedar Ho
6 Saffron Ho
7 Lime Ho
8 Lavender Ho
9 Juniper Ho

133

B2 1 Rann Ho
2 Craven Ho
3 John Dee Ho
4 Kindell Ho
5 Montgomery Ho
6 Avondale Ho
7 Addington Ct
8 Dovecote Gdns
9 Firmston Ho
10 Glendower Gdns
11 Chestnut Ave
12 Trehern Rd
13 Rock Ave
D3 1 Melrose Rd
2 Seaforth Lo
3 St John's Gr
4 Sussex Ct
5 Carmichael Ct

6 Hampshire Ct
7 Thorne Pas
8 Brunel St
9 Beverley Path

134

D1 1 Olivette St
2 Mascotte Rd
3 Glegg Pl
4 Crown Ct
5 Charlwood Terr
6 Percy Laurie Ho
D6 1 Cobb's Hall
2 Dorset Mans
3 St Clements Mans
4 Bothwell St
5 Hawksmoor St

135

B3 1 Plato Pl
2 Mustow Pl
3 Laurel Bank Gdns
4 Ranelagh Mans
5 Churchfield Mans
6 Bear Croft Ho
7 Elysium Gate
8 Ethel Rankin Ct
9 Arthur Henderson Ho
10 William Banfield Ho
11 Melbray Mews
D3 1 Brightwells
2 Broughton Road App
3 Bulow Ct
4 Langford Rd
5 Elizabeth Barnes Ct
6 Snowbury Rd

136

A2 1 Molasses Ho
2 Molasses Row
3 Cinnamon Row
4 Calico Ho
5 Calico Row
6 Port Ho
7 Square Rigger Row
8 Trade Twr
9 Ivory Ho
10 Spice Ct
11 Sherwood Ct
12 Mendip Ct
13 Chalmers Ho
14 Coral Row
15 Ivory Sq
16 Kingfisher Ho
B1 1 Burke Ho
2 Fox Ho
3 Buxton Ho
4 Pitt Ho
5 Ramsey Ho
6 Beverley Cl
7 Florence Ho
8 Linden Ct
9 Dorcas Ct
10 Johnson Ct
11 Agnes Ct
12 Hilltop Ct
13 Courtyard The
14 Old Laundry The
15 Oberstein Rd
16 Fineran Ct
17 Sangora Rd
18 Harvard Mans
19 Plough Mews
B2 1 Benham Cl
2 Milner Ho
3 McManus Ho
4 Wilberforce Ho
5 Wheeler Ct
6 Sporle Ct
7 Holliday Sq
8 John Parker Sq
9 Carmichael Cl
10 Fenner Sq
11 Clark Lawrence Ct
12 Shaw Ct
13 Sendall Ct
14 Livingstone Rd
15 Farrant Ho
16 Jackson Ho
17 Darien Ho
18 Shepard Ho
19 Ganley Ct
20 Arthur Newton Ho
21 Chesterton Ho
22 John Kirk Ho
23 Mantua St
24 Heaver Rd
25 Candlemakers
B3 1 Archer Ho
2 White Ho
3 Winfield Ho
4 Powrie Ho
5 Morgan Ct
6 Fairchild Cl
7 Musjid Rd
C2 1 Kildoran Ct
2 Lanner Ho
3 Griffon Ho
4 Kestrel Ho
5 Kite Ho
6 Peregrine Ho
7 Hawk Ho
8 Inkster Ho
9 Harrier Ho
10 Eagle Hts

11 Kingfisher Ct
12 Lavender Terr
13 Temple Ho
14 Ridley Ho
15 Eden Ho
16 Hertford Ct
17 Nepaul Rd
C3 1 Meecham Ct
2 McKiernan Ct
3 Banbury St
4 Colestown St
5 Crombie Mews
6 Frere St
D3 1 Stevenson Ho
2 Ambrose Mews
3 Harling Ct
4 Southside Quarter
5 Latchmere St
6 Dovedale Cotts
7 Roydon Ct
8 Castlemaine
9 Wittering Ho
10 Berry Ho
11 Weybridge Point

137

A2 1 Shaftesbury Park Chambers
2 Selborne
3 Rush Hill Mews
4 Marmion Mews
5 Crosland Pl
6 Craven Mews
7 Garfield Mews
8 Audley Cl
9 Basnett Rd
10 Tyneham Cl
11 Woodmere Cl
A3 1 Hopkinson Ho
2 MacDonald Ho
3 Rushlake Ho
4 Bishopstone Ho
5 Dresden Ho
6 Millgrove St
7 Farnhurst Ho
8 Walden Ho
9 Kennard St
10 Langhurst Ho
11 Atkinson Ho
12 Kennard Ho
13 Voltaire Ct
14 Barloch Ho
15 London Stone Bsns Est
B2 1 Turnchapel Mews
2 Redwood Mews
3 Phil Brown Pl
4 Bev Callender Cl
5 Keith Connor Cl
6 Tessa Sanderson Pl
7 Daley Thompson Way
8 Rashleigh Ct
9 Abberley Mews
10 Willow Lodge
11 Beaufoy Rd
B3 1 St Philip Sq
2 Montefiore St
3 Gambetta St
4 Scott Ct
5 Radcliffe Path
6 Moresby Wlk
7 Victorian Hts
C1 1 Polygon The
2 Windsor Ct
3 Trinity Cl
4 Studios The
5 Bourne Ho
C2 1 Clapham Manor Ct
2 Clarke Ho
3 Gables The
4 Sycamore Mews
5 Maritime Ho
6 Rectory Gdns
7 Floris Pl
C3 1 Seymour Ho
2 Lucas Ho
3 Durrington Twr
4 Amesbury Twr
5 Fovant Ct
6 Allington Ct
7 Welford Ct
8 Ilsley Ct
9 Blake Ct
D1 1 Kendoa Rd
2 Felmersham Cl
3 Abbeville Mews
4 Saxon Ho
5 Gifford Ho
6 Teignmouth Cl
7 Holwood Pl
8 Oaklands Pl
9 Wilberforce Mews
10 William Bonney Est
D2 1 Chelsham Ho
2 Lynde Ho
3 Greener Ho
4 Towns Ho
5 Hugh Morgan Ho
6 Roy Ridley Ho
7 Lendal Terr
8 Slievemore Cl
9 Cadmus Cl
10 Clapham North Bsns Ctr
D3 1 Haltone Ho

2 Surcot Ho
3 Kingsley Ho
4 Wood Ho
5 Dalemain Ho
6 Fallodon Ho
7 Dartington Ho
8 Esher Ho
9 Kneller Ho
10 Lostock Ho
11 Croxteth Ho
12 Donnington Ho
13 Farnley Ho
14 Hardwick Ho
15 Bradfield Ho
16 Brocket Ho
17 Colchester Ho
18 Clive Ho
19 Chessington Ho
20 Rushbrook Ho
21 Stanmore Ho
22 Newton Ho
23 Netherby Ho
24 Oakwell Ho
25 Rydal Ho
26 Rushton Ho
27 Harcourt Ho
28 Metcalfe Ho
29 Lydwell Ho
30 Raleigh Ho
31 Spencer Ho
32 Shipley Ho
33 Naylor Ho
34 Mordaunt Ho
35 Stanley Ho
36 Alderley Ho
37 Effingham Ho
38 Grant Ho
39 Wilson Ho
40 Fraser Ho

138

A1 1 Morris Ho
2 Gye Ho
3 Clowes Ho
4 Thomas Ho
5 Stuart Ho
6 Storace Ho
7 Bedford Ho
8 Ascot Ct
9 Ascot Par
10 Ashmere Ho
11 Ashmere Gr
12 Ventura Ho
13 Vickery Ho
14 Stafford Mans
15 Beresford Ho
A2 1 Callingham Ho
2 Russell Pickering Ho
3 Ormerod Ho
4 Lopez Ho
5 Coachmaker Mews
A3 1 Barling Ct
2 Jeffrey's Ct
3 Brooks Ct
4 Dalmeny Ct
5 Fender Ct
6 Fishlock Ct
7 Bedser Ct
8 Gover Ct
9 Clarence Wlk
10 Barton Ct
11 Allom Ct
12 Garden Ho
13 Otha Ho
14 Hayward Ho
15 Surridge Ct
16 Knox Ct
17 Jephson Ct
18 Holmes Ct
19 McIntyre Ct
20 Richardson Ct
21 Cassell Ho
22 Pakington Ho
23 Bain Ho
24 Enfield Ho
25 Fawcett Ho
26 Sidgwick Ho
27 Jowett Ho
28 Beckett Ho
29 Arden Ho
30 Pinter Ho
31 Barrington Ct
32 Union Mews
B1 1 Freemens Hos
2 Roger's Almsshouses
3 Gresham Almsshouses
4 Exbury Ho
5 Glasbury Ho
6 Dalbury Ho
7 Fosbury Ho
8 Chalbury Ho
9 Neilson-Terry Ct
10 Pavilion Mans
11 Daisy Dormer Ct
12 George Lashwood Ct
13 Marie Lloyd Ct
14 Trinity Homes
15 Lethaby Ho
16 Edmundsbury Ct Est
17 Regis Pl
18 Marlborough Mews
19 Alpha Ho
20 Beta Pl

21 Cedars Ho
B2 1 Turberville Ho
2 Thrayle Ho
3 Percheron Ct
4 Draymans Ct
B3 1 Maurice Ho
2 Thring Ho
3 Paton Ho
4 Huxley Ho
5 Morell Ho
6 Mary Ho
7 Beale Ho
8 Rosa Parks Ho
9 Birrell Ho
10 Waltham Ho
11 Burford Ho
12 Thornicroft Ho
13 Addington Ho
14 Goffton Ho
15 Redmayne Ho
16 Norton Ho
17 Aytoun Ct
18 Colwall Ho
19 Burrow Ho
20 Wynter Ho
21 Crowhurst Ho
22 Lidcote Gdns
23 Cumnor Cl
24 Park View Mews
C1 1 Electric Mans
2 Electric La
3 Connaught Mans
4 Clifton Mans
5 Hereford Ho
6 Chaplin Ho
7 Brixton Oval
8 Lord David Pitt Ho
9 Marcus Garvey Way
10 Montego Cl
11 Bob Marley Way
12 Leeson Rd
C2 1 Buckmaster Cl
2 Albemarle Ho
3 Goodwood Mans
4 Angell Park Gdns
5 Fyfield Rd
6 Howard Ho
7 Harris Ho
8 Broadoak Ct
9 Burgate Ct
10 Witchwood Ho
11 Blacktree Mews
12 Chartham Ct
13 Chilham Ct
14 Northgate Ct
15 Westgate Ct
16 Dover Mans
C3 1 Norval Gn
2 Hilda Terr
3 Burton La
4 Church Gn
5 Lord Holland La
6 Sorrell Cl
7 Burton Rd
8 Holles Ho
9 Leys Ct
10 Warwick Ho
11 Fairfax Ho
12 Wayland Ho
13 Dudley Ho
14 Denchworth Ho
15 Fitzgerald Ho
16 Lambert Ho
17 Chute Ho
18 Bedwell Ho
19 Ferrey Mews
20 Serenaders Rd
21 Boatemah Wlk
22 Ireton Ho
23 Marston Ho
24 Morrison Rd
25 Fir Grove Rd
26 Shore Way
C4 1 Hector Ct
2 Jason Ct
3 Creon Ct
4 Hermes Ct
5 Argos Ct
6 Cadmus Ct
7 Appollo Ct
8 Mercury Ct
9 County Ho
10 Seasalter Ho
11 Downbarton Ho
12 Garlinge Ho
13 Moira Ho
14 Alvanley Ho
15 Woodchurch Ho
16 Durlock Ho
17 Hallam Ho
18 Whiteness Ho
19 Bromstone Ho
20 Penelope Ho
21 Melbourne Sq
22 Cloisters The
23 Cliffsend Ho
24 Sacketts Ho
25 Hanway Ho
26 Brickworth Ho
27 Redlynch Ho
28 Stodmarsh Ho
29 Kingsgate Ho
30 Chardin Ho
31 Annesley Ho
32 Knowlton Ho
33 Russell Gr
34 Eamann Casey Ho
C5 1 Swift Ho
2 Listowel Cl

3 Deal Wlk
4 Plover Ho
5 Aigburth Mans
6 Glencoe Mans
7 Glenshaw Mans
8 Cleveland Mans
9 Leda Ct
10 Jupiter Ct
11 Juno Ct
12 Healy Ho
13 Ashton Ho
14 Ramsey Ho
15 Annesley Ho
16 Cowley Rd
C6 1 Sherwin Ho
2 Pegasus Pl
3 Kilner Ho
4 Read Ho
5 Lohmann Ho
6 Hornby Ho
7 Abel Ho
8 Blythe Ho
9 Key Ho
10 Lockwood Ho
11 Alverstone Ho
12 Blades Ho
13 Rothesay Ct
D1 1 Mahatma Gandhi Ind Est
2 Dylan Rd
3 Bessemer Park Ind Est
4 Pablo Neruda Cl
5 Langston Hughes Cl
6 Walt Whitman Cl
7 James Joyce Wlk
8 Alice Walker Cl
9 Louise Bennett Cl
10 Chadacre Ho
11 Burwood Ho
12 Pyrford Ho
13 Wangford Ho
14 Ashford Ho
15 Kenwood Ho
16 Moyne Ho
17 Elveden Ho
18 Carrara Cl
19 Broughton Dr
20 Angela Davis Ind Est
21 Tilia Wlk
22 County Ho
D2 1 Mallams Mews
2 Amberley Ct
3 Harper Ho
4 Leicester Ho
5 Station Ave
6 Wellfit St
7 Loughborough Ct
8 Belinda Rd
9 Higgs Ind Est
D3 1 Langport Ho
2 Iveagh Ho
3 Newark Ho
4 Edgehill Ho
5 Hopton Ho
6 Ashby Ho
7 Nevil Ho
D4 1 Fairbairn Gn
2 Hammelton Gn
3 Foxley Sq
4 Silverburn Ho
5 Butler Ho
6 Dalkeith Ho
7 Turner Cl
8 Bathgate Ho
9 Black Roof Ho
D6 1 Faunce Ho
2 Garbett Ho
3 Harvard Ho
4 Doddington Pl
5 Kean Ho
6 Jephson Ho
7 Cornish Ho
8 Bateman Ho
9 Molesworth Ho
10 Walters Ho
11 Cruden Ho
12 Brawne Ho
13 Prescott Ho
14 Chalmer's Wlk
15 Copley Cl
16 King Charles Ct

139

A3 1 Bergen Ho
2 Oslo Ho
3 Viking Ho
4 Jutland Ho
5 Norvic Ho
6 Odin Ho
7 Baltic Ho
8 Nobel Ho
9 Mercia Ho
10 Kenbury Gdns
11 Zealand Ho
12 Elsinore Ho
13 Norse Ho
14 Denmark Mans
15 Dane Ho
16 Canterbury Cl
17 York Cl
18 Kenbury Mans
19 Parade Mans
20 Winterslow Ho
21 Lilford Ho
22 Bartholomew Ho
23 Guildford Ho
24 Boston Ho

25 Hereford Ho
26 Weyhill Ho
27 Lichfield Ho
28 Lansdown Ho
29 Honiton Ho
30 Pinner Ho
31 Baldock Ho
32 Widecombe Ho
33 Nottingham Ho
34 Witham Ho
35 Barnet Ho
36 Empress Mews
A4 1 Bertha Neubergh Ho
2 Mornington Ho
3 Badsworth Rd
4 Pearson Cl
5 Elm Tree Ct
6 Samuel Lewis Trust Dwellings
7 Milkwell Yd
8 Keswick Ho
9 Mitcham Ho
A5 1 Boundary Ho
2 Day Ho
3 Burgess Ho
4 Carlyle Ho
5 Myers Ho
6 Thompson Ave
7 Palgrave Ho
8 Winnington Ho
9 Brantwood Ho
10 Lowell Ho
11 Jessie Duffett Ho
12 Otterburn Ho
13 Crossmount Ho
14 Venice Ct
15 Bowyer St
16 Livingstone Ho
17 Gothic Ct
18 Coniston Ho
19 Harlynwood
20 Carey Ct
21 Finley Ct
22 Grainger Ct
23 Hayes Ct
24 Moffat Ho
25 Marinel Ho
26 Hodister Cl
27 Arnot Ho
28 Lamb Ho
29 Kipling Ho
30 Keats Ho
31 Kenyon Ho
32 New Church Rd
33 Sir John Kirk Cl
B1 1 Shaftesbury Ct
2 Mayhew Ct
3 Morris Ct
4 Swinburne Ct
5 Perth Ct
6 Tayside Ct
7 Matlock Ct
8 Hunter Ct
9 Turner Ct
B3 1 Selborne Rd
2 Hascombe Terr
B4 1 Joiners Arms Yd
2 Butterfly Wlk
3 Cuthill Wlk
4 Colonades The
5 Artichoke Mews
6 Peabody Bldgs
7 Brighton Ho
8 Park Ho
9 Peabody Ct
10 Lomond Ho
11 Lamb Ho
12 Kimpton Ct
13 Belham Wlk
14 Datchelor Pl
15 Harvey Rd
B5 1 Masterman Ho
2 Milton Ho
3 Pope Ho
4 Chester Ct
5 Marvel Ho
6 Flecker Ho
7 Landor Ho
8 Leslie Prince Ct
9 Evelina Mans
10 Langland Ho
11 Drinkwater Ho
12 Procter Ho
13 Shirley Ho
14 Drayton Ho
15 Bridges Ho
16 Cunningham Ho
17 Hood Ho
18 Herrick Ho
19 Dekker Ho
20 Houseman Way
21 Coleby Path
B6 1 Queens Ho
2 Arnside Ho
3 Horsley St
4 St Peter's Ho
5 St Johns Ho
6 St Marks Ho
7 St Stephens Ho
8 St Matthew's Ho
9 Red Lion Cl
10 Boyson Rd
11 Bradenham
C2 1 Harfield Gdns
2 Karen Ct
3 Seavington Ho
4 Appleshaw Ho
5 Birdsall Ho
6 Whitney Ho

7 Wheatland Ho
8 Wilton Ho
9 Walcot Ho
10 Whaddon Ho
11 Melbreak Ho
12 Ledbury Ho
13 Tidworth Ho
14 Riseholme Ho
15 Ringmer Ho
16 Petworth Ho
17 Stagshaw Ho
18 Ivybridge Ho
19 Inwood Ho
20 Gatcombe Ho
21 Felbridge Ho
22 Cowdray Ho
C3 1 Springfield Ho
2 Craston Ho
3 Walters Ho
4 Edgecombe Ho
5 Fowler Ho
6 Rignold Ho
7 Chatham Ho
C4 1 Barnwell Ho
2 Brunswick Villas
3 St Giles Twr
4 Bentley Ho
5 Dawson Ho
6 Dryden Ho
7 Mayward Ho
8 Longleigh Ho
9 Fairwall Ho
10 Bodeney Ho
11 Sandby Ho
12 Vestry Mews
13 Netley
14 Lakanal
15 Racine
C5 1 Tower Mill Rd
2 Tilson Cl
3 Granville Sq
4 Edgar Wallace Cl
5 Potters Cl
6 Dorton Cl
7 Samuel Jones Ind Est
8 Dibden Ho
9 Marchwood Cl
10 Pilgrims Cloisters
11 Beacon Ho
12 Teather St
13 Stacy Path
14 Rumball Ho
15 Ballow Cl
16 Rill Ho
C6 1 Downend Ct
2 Andoversford Ct
3 Pearse St
4 Watling St
5 Gandolfi St
D1 1 Dulwich Mews
2 St James's Cloisters
D4 1 Colbert
2 Voltaire
3 Finch Mews
4 Charles Coveney Rd
5 Bamber Rd
6 Crane St
7 Curlew Ho
8 Mallard Ho
9 Tern Ho
10 Crane Ho
11 Falcon Ho
12 Bryanston Ho
13 Basing Ct
14 Marcus Ho
15 Sheffield Ho
D5 1 Painswick Ct
2 Sharpness Ct
3 Mattingly Way
4 Hordle Prom N
5 Burcher Gale Gr
6 Calypso Cres
7 Hordle Prom S
8 Cinnamon Cl
9 Savannah Cl
10 Thames Ct
11 Shannon Ct
12 Amstel Ct
13 Danube St
14 Tilbury Cl
15 Hordle Prom E
16 Indus Ct
17 Oakcourt
18 Palm Ct
19 Rowan Ct
20 Blackthorn Ct
21 Pear Ct
22 Lidgate Rd
23 Whistler Mews
24 Boathouse Wlk
D6 1 Willsbridge Ct
2 Cam Ct
3 Quedgeley Ct
4 Saul Ct
5 Quenington Ct
6 Westonbirt Ct
7 Wickway Ct

140
A3 1 William Margrie Cl
2 William Blake Ho
3 Quantock Mews
4 Choumert Sq
5 Parkstone Rd
6 Atwell Rd

A4 1 Canal Head Public Sq
2 Angelina Ho
3 Jarvis Ho
4 Richland Ho
5 Honeywood Ho
6 Wakefield Ho
7 Primrose Ho
8 Hardcastle Ho
9 Dunstall Ho
10 Springtide Cl
11 Purdon Ho
12 Flamborough Ho
13 Lambrook Ho
14 Witcombe Point
15 Yarnfield Sq
16 Winford Ct
17 Portbury Cl
18 Robert Keen Cl
A5 1 Thornbill Ho
2 Vervain Ho
3 Woodstar Ho
4 Tamarind Ho
5 Hereford Retreat
6 Haymerle Ho
7 Furley Ho
8 Thomas Milner Ho
9 Applegarth Ho
10 Freda Corbett Cl
11 Rudbeck Ho
12 Henslow Ho
13 Lindley Ho
14 Collinson Ho
15 Sister Mabel's Way
16 Timberland Cl
17 Hastings Cl
18 Sidmouth Ho
19 Budleigh Ho
20 Stanesgate Ho
21 Breamore Ho
22 Ely Ho
23 Gisburn Ho
A6 1 Bowles Rd
2 Western Wharf
3 Northfield Ho
4 Millbrook Ho
5 Denstone Ho
6 Deerhurst Ho
7 Caversham Ho
8 Battle Ho
9 Cardiff Ho
10 Bridgnorth Ho
11 Exeter Ho
12 Grantham Ho
13 Aylesbury Ho
14 Royston Ho
B2 1 Tilling Ho
2 Goodwin Ho
3 Tyrells Ct
4 Citron Terr
5 Basswood Cl
6 Cheam St
B3 1 Walkynscroft
2 Ryegates
3 Hathorne Cl
4 Pilkington Rd
5 Russell Ct
6 Heaton Ho
7 Magdalene Cl
B4 1 Willowdene
2 Pinedene
3 Oakdene
4 Beechdene
5 Hollydene
6 Wood Dene
7 Staveley Cl
8 Carnicot Ho
9 Martock Ct
10 Cherry Tree Ct
11 Kendrick Ct
B5 1 Tortington Ho
2 Credenhill Ho
3 Bromyard Ho
4 Hoyland Cl
5 Willowdene
6 Ashdene
7 Acorn Par
8 Havelock Ct
9 Springall St
10 Harry Lambourn Ho
11 Grenier Apartments
C3 1 Honiton Gdns
2 Selden Ho
3 Hathway Ho
4 Hathway St
5 Station Ct
C4 1 Trotman Ho
2 Boddington Ho
3 Heydon Ho
4 Boulter Ho
5 Astbury Bsns Pk
C5 1 Ambleside Point
2 Grasmere Point
3 Windermere Point
4 Roman Way
5 Laburnum Cl
6 Juniper Ho
7 Romney Cl
8 Hammersley Ho
9 Hutchinson Ho
10 Hammond Ho
11 Fir Tree Ho
12 Glastonbury Ct
13 Highbridge Ct
14 Filton Ct
15 Chiltern Ct

16 Cheviot Ct
C6 1 Penshurst Ho
2 Reculver Ho
3 Mereworth Ho
4 Camber Ho
5 Chiham Ho
6 Otford Ho
7 Olive Tree Ho
8 Aspen Ho
9 Lewis Silkin Ho
10 Richborough Ho
11 Dover Ho
12 Eynsford Ho
13 Horton Ho
14 Lamberhurst Ho
15 Canterbury Ind Pk
16 Upnall Ho
17 Sissinghurst Ho
18 Rochester Ho
19 Saltwood Ho
20 Leybourne Ho
21 Lullingstone Ho
D1 1 Laxton Path
2 Barlings Ho
3 Bayfield Ho
4 Coston Wlk
5 Coverham Ho
6 Gateley Ho
7 Dereham Ho
8 Greenwood Ho
9 Hilton Ho
10 Goodall Ho
11 Horsley Ho
12 Jordan Ho
D5 1 Richard Anderson Ct
2 Palm Tree Ho
3 Edward Robinson Ho
4 Antony Ho
5 Gerrard Ho
6 Palmer Ho
7 Pankhurst Cl
D6 1 Harrisons Ct
2 Grantley Ho
3 Sunbury Ct
4 Tilbury Ho
5 Graham Ct
6 Connell Ho
7 St Clements Ct
8 Henderson Ct
9 Jemotts Ct
10 Verona Ct
11 Heywood Ho
12 Francis Ct
13 Hind Ho
14 Donne Ho
15 Carew Ct
16 Burbage Ho
17 Newland Ho
18 Dobson Ho
19 Dalton Ho
20 Greene Ct
21 Redrup Ho
22 Tarplett Ho
23 Stunell Ho
24 Gasson Ho
25 Bryce Ho
26 Barnes Ho
27 Barkwith Ho
28 Bannister Ho
29 Apollo Ind Bsns Ctr

141
A4 1 Archer Ho
2 Browning Ho
3 Hardcastle Ho
4 Brooke Ho
5 Wallis Ho
A5 1 Batavia Ho
2 Marlowe Bsns Ctr
3 Batavia Mews
4 Woodrush Cl
5 Alexandra St
6 Primrose Wlk
7 Vansittart St
8 Granville Ct
9 Cottesbrook St
10 Ewen Henderson Ct
11 Fordham Ho
A6 1 Portland Ct
2 Phoenix Ct
3 Rainbow Ct
4 Hawke Twr
5 Chubworthy St
6 Woodpecker Rd
7 Hercules Ct
B5 1 Austin Ho
2 Exeter Way
3 Crossleigh Ct
4 Mornington Pl
5 Maple Ho
B6 1 Chester Ho
2 Lynch Wlk
3 Arlington Ho
4 Woodcote Ho
5 Cornbury Ho
6 Prospect Pl
7 Akintaro Ho
8 Mulberry Ho
9 Laurel Ho
10 Linden Ho
11 Ashford Ho
12 Wardalls Ho
13 Magnolia Ho
14 Howard Ho
15 Larch Cl
16 Ibis Ct

17 Merganser Ct
18 Wotton Rd
19 Kingfisher Sq
20 Sanderling Ct
21 Dolphin Twr
22 Mermaid Twr
23 Scoter Ct
24 Shearwater Ct
25 Brambling Ct
26 Kittiwake Ct
27 Diana Cl
28 Guillemot Ct
29 Marine Twr
30 Teal Ct
31 Lapwing Twr
32 Violet Cl
33 Skua Ct
34 Tristan Ct
35 Rosemary Ct
36 Cormorant Ct
37 Shelduck Ct
38 Eider Ct
39 Pintail Ct
C4 1 Admiralty Cl
2 Harton Lodge
3 Sylva Cotts
4 Pitman Ho
5 Heston Ho
6 Mereton Mans
7 Indiana Bldg
8 St John's Lodge
C5 1 Sandpiper Ct
2 Flamingo Ct
3 Titan Bsns Est
4 Rochdale Way
5 Speedwell St
6 Reginald Pl
7 Fletcher Path
8 Frankham Ho
9 Cremer Ho
10 Wilshaw Ho
11 Castell Ho
12 Holden Ho
13 Browne Ho
14 Resolution Way
15 Lady Florence Ctyd
16 Covell Ct
17 Albion Ho
C6 1 Dryfield Wlk
2 Blake Ho
3 Hawkins Ho
4 Grenville Ho
5 Langford Ho
6 Mandarin Ct
7 Bittern Ct
8 Lamerton St
9 Ravensbourne Mans
10 Armada St
11 Armada Ct
12 Benbow Ho
13 Oxenham Ho
14 Caravel Mews
15 Hughes Ho
16 Stretton Mans
D4 1 Washington Bldg
2 California Bldg
3 Utah Bldg
4 Montana Bldg
5 Oregon Bldg
6 Dakota bldg
7 Idaho Bldg
8 Atlanta Bldg
9 Colorado Bldg
10 Arizona Bldg
11 Nebraska Bldg
12 Alaska Bldg
13 Ohio Bldg
14 Charter Bldgs
15 Flamsteed Ct
16 Friendly Pl
17 Dover Ct
18 Robinscroft Mews
19 Doleman Ho
20 Plymouth Ho
D5 1 Finch Ho
2 Jubilee The
3 Maitland Cl
4 Ashburnham Retreat

142
A2 1 Bankside Ave
2 Elder Wlk
3 Yew Tree Cl
4 Mill Ho
A3 1 Ellison Ho
2 Pitmaston Ho
3 Aster Ho
4 Windmill Cl
5 Hertmitage The
6 Burnett Ho
7 Lacey Ho
8 Darwin Ho
9 Pearmain Ho
A4 1 Penn Almshouses
2 Jervis Ho
3 Woodville Ho
4 Darnall Ho
5 Renbold Ho
6 Lindsell St
7 Plumbridge St
8 Trinity Gr
9 Hollymount Cl
10 Cade Tyler Ho
11 Robertson Ho
A5 1 Temair Ho
2 Royal Hill Ct

3 Prince of Orange La
4 Lambard Ho
5 St Marks Cl
6 Ada Kennedy Ct
7 Arlington Pl
8 Topham Ho
9 Darnell Ho
10 Hawks Mews
11 Royal Pl
12 Swanne Ho
13 Maribor
14 Serica Ct
15 Queen Elizabeth's Coll
A6 1 Crescent Arc
2 Greenwich Mkt
3 Turnpin La
4 Durnford St
5 Sexton's Ho
6 Bardsley Ho
7 Wardell Ho
8 Clavell St
9 Stanton Ho
10 Macey Ho
11 Boreman Ho
12 Clipper Appts
B6 1 Frobisher Ct
2 Hardy Cotts
3 Palliser Ho
4 Bernard Angell Ho
5 Corvette Sq
6 Travers Ho
7 Maze Hill Lodge
8 Park Place Ho
D5 1 Westcombe Ct
2 Kleffens Ct
3 Ferndale Ct
4 Combe Mews
5 Mandeville Cl
6 Pinelands Cl

143
A5 1 Mary Lawrenson Pl
2 Bradbury Ct
3 Dunstable Ct
4 Wentworth Ho
A6 1 Nethercombe Ho
2 Holywell Cl
B6 1 Capella Ho
2 Collington Ho
C6 1 Warren Wlk
2 Wilson Ho
3 Priory Ho
4 Mar Ho
5 Langhorne Ho
6 Games Ho
7 Erskine Ho
8 Ducie Ho
9 Downe Ho
10 Bayeux Ho
11 Elliscombe Mount
12 Harold Gibbons Ct
13 Mascalls Ct
14 Leila Parnell Pl
15 East Mascalls
16 Birch Tree Ho
17 Cherry Tree Ct
18 Elm Tree Ct
19 Cedar Ct
D5 1 Winchester Ho
2 Brentwood Ho
3 Shenfield Ho
4 Chesterford Ho

144
A4 1 Master Gunner's Pl
2 Ross Ho
3 Dickson Ho
4 Horne Ho
5 Pendlebury Ho
6 Roberts Ho
7 Maple Tree Pl
C6 1 Lawson Ho
2 Mabbett Ho
3 Petrie Ho
4 Memess Path
5 Ruegg Ho
6 Nile Path
7 Leslie Smith Sq
8 Spearman Ho
9 Siedle Ho
10 Watling Ho
11 O'Neill Path
12 Old Clem Sq
13 Jefferson Wlk
14 Milward Wlk
15 Wordsworth Ho
16 Fenwick Cl
D6 1 Acworth Ho
2 Griffiths Ho
3 Squires Ho
4 Cowen Ho
5 Turton Ho
6 Alford Ho
7 Boxshall Ho
8 MacAllister Ho
9 Marvin Ho
10 Kelham Ho
11 Kimber Ho
12 Maxwell Ho
13 Woodford Ho
14 Penfold Ho

146
A2 1 Wellingfield Ct
2 Woodville Gr
3 Midwinter Cl

4 St Leonards Cl

147
A1 1 Woburn Ct
2 Arundel Ct
3 Longleat Ct
4 Upton Villas
5 Whitehaven Ct
6 Shirley Hts
7 Louise Ct
8 Bethany Ct
B6 1 Bevercote Wlk
2 Lullingstone Rd
3 Benjamin Ct
4 Charton Cl
5 Terence Ct
6 Renshaw Ct
7 Grove Rd
C1 1 Friswell Pl
2 Market Pl
3 Geddes Pl
4 Janet Ct
5 Broadway Sh Ctr
6 Mall The
7 Norwich Pl
8 Pincott Rd

148
A5 1 Stranraer Way
2 Deri Dene Cl
3 Lord Knyvetts Ct
4 Tudor Ct
5 Wessex Ct
6 Vanguard Ho
7 Shackleton Ct
8 Fleetwood Ct
9 Clifton Ct
10 Vickers Ct
11 Bristol Ct
12 Sunderland Ct

153
A3 1 Katharine Rd
2 Sandringham Ct
3 Garfield Rd
4 Arragon Rd
5 Flood La
6 John Wesley Ct
7 King Street Par
8 Thames Eyot
A4 1 Perryn Ct
2 Ivybridge Cl
3 Heritage Ho
4 Brook Ho
5 Neville Ho
6 Latham Cl
7 March Rd
8 Berkley Ct
9 Cole Court Lo
10 Cheltenham Ave
11 Railway App
A5 1 Greenways The
2 Cole Park View
B4 1 Melton Ct
2 Amyand Park Gdns
3 Crown Ct
4 Burrell Ho
5 Owen Ho
6 Brentford Ho
7 Leeson Ho
8 Westbourne Ho
9 Orleans Ct
10 Lebanon Ct
B5 1 Grove The
2 Cumberland Cl
3 Westmorland Cl
4 Sussex Ct
5 Norfolk Cl
6 Nicol Cl
7 Old Lodge Pl
8 Kelvin Ct
9 St Margaret's Ct
10 Park Cotts
11 St Margarets Bsns Ctr
12 Amyand Cotts
C1 1 Benson Ho
2 Bowes Lyon Ho
3 Cavendish Ho
4 Bentinck Ho
5 Clarke Ho
6 Secrett Ho
7 Edwards Ho
8 Field Ho
9 Greig Ho
10 Hawkins Ho
11 Newman Ho
12 Leyland Ho
13 Hornby Ho
14 Hatch Ho
C5 1 Howmic Ct
2 Sefton Lo
3 Ravensbourne Ho
4 Arlington Ct
5 Georgina Ct
6 Trevelyan Ho
7 Caradon Ct
8 Green Hedges
9 Old House Gdns
10 Queens Keep
11 Beresford Ct
12 Langham Ct
13 Poplar Ct
D5 1 Richmond Bridge Mans
2 Heatherdene Mans
3 Kenton Ct
4 Lennox Ho

5 Leicester Ct
6 Turner Ho
7 Blanchard Ho
8 Arosa Rd
9 Ashe Ho
10 Bevan Ct
11 Lawley Ho
12 Darling Ho
13 Richmond Mans
14 Beaulieu Cl
15 Roseleigh Cl
16 Mallard Ct
D6 1 Garrick Cl
2 Old Palace Yd
3 Wardrobe The
4 Maids of Honour Row
5 Hunters Ct
6 Queensberry Ho
7 Green The
8 Old Palace Terr
9 Paved Ct
10 Golden Ct
11 Brewers La
12 Square The
13 Lower George St
14 St James's Cotts
15 Church Wlk
16 Church Ct
17 Victoria Pl
18 Castle Yd
19 Lewis Rd
20 Wakefield Rd
21 Church Terr
22 Warrington Rd
23 Ormond Ave
24 Glovers Lo
25 Holbrooke Pl
26 Northumberland Pl
27 Heron Sq
28 Whittaker Pl
29 Water Lane Ho
30 Riverside Ho
31 St Helena Terr

154
A5 1 Lancaster Cotts
2 Lancaster Mews
3 Bromwich Ho
4 Priors Lo
5 Richmond Hill Ct
6 Glenmore Ho
7 Hillbrow
8 Heathshott
9 Friars Stile Pl
10 Spire Ct
11 Ridgeway
12 Matthias Ct
A6 1 Lichfield Terr
2 Union Ct
3 Carrington Lo
4 Wilton Ct
5 Egerton Ct
6 Beverley Lo
7 Bishop Duppa's Almshouses
8 Regency Wlk
9 Clear Water Ho
10 Onslow Avenue Mans
11 Michels Almshouses
12 Albany Pas
13 Salcombe Villas
B5 1 Chester Ct
2 Evesham Ct
3 Queen's Ct
4 Russell Wlk
5 Charlotte Sq
6 Jones Wlk
7 Hildtch Ho
8 Isabella Ct
9 Damer Ho
10 Eliot Ho
11 Fitzherbert Ho
12 Reynolds Pl
13 Chisholm Rd
B6 1 Alberta Ct
2 Beatrice Rd
3 Lorne Rd
4 York Rd
5 Connaught Rd
6 Albany Terr
7 Kingswood Ct
8 Selwyn Ct
9 Broadhurst Cl

156
A3 1 Farnborough Ho
2 Rushmere Ho
3 Horndean Cl
4 Highcross Way
5 Timsbury Wlk
6 Foxcombe Rd
7 Ryefield Path
8 Greatham Wlk
9 Gosport Ho
10 Stoatley Ho
11 Milland Ho
12 Clanfield Ho
13 Fareham Ho
14 Grayswood Point
A4 1 Woodcott Ho
2 Lyndhurst Ho
3 Wheatley Ho
4 Allbrook Ho

156 A4

156
5 Bordon Wlk
6 Chilcombe Ho
7 Vicarage Ct
8 Shawford Ct
9 Eastleigh Wlk
10 Kings Ct
11 Somborne Ho
A6 1 Theodore Ho
2 Nicholas Ho
3 Bonner Ho
4 Downing Ho
5 Jansen Ho
6 Fairfax Ho
7 Devereux Ho
8 David Ho
9 Leigh Ho
10 Clipstone Ho
11 Mallet Ho
12 Arton Wilson Ho
B3 1 Ramsdean Ho
2 Purbrook Ho
3 Portsea Ho
4 Blendworth Point
5 Eashing Point
6 Hindhead Point
7 Hilsea Point
8 Witley Point
9 Buriton Ho
10 Grateley Ho
11 Hascombe Ho
12 Dunhill Point
13 Westmark Point
14 Longmoor Point
15 Cadnam Point
C4 1 Cumberland Ho
2 Devonshire Ho
3 Cornwall Ho
4 Norfolk Ho
5 Leicester Ho
6 Warwick Ho
7 Sutherland Ho
8 Carmarthen Ho
9 Worcester Ho
10 Rutland Ho
11 Paddock Way
C6 1 Inglis Ho
2 Ducie Ho
3 Wharncliffe Ho
4 Stanhope Ho
5 Waldegrave Ho
6 Mildmay Ho
7 Mullens Ho
D3 1 Sandringham Cl
2 Eastwick Ct
3 Oatlands Ct
4 Banning Ho
5 Grantley Ho
6 Caryl Ho
7 Duncombe Ho
8 Chilworth Ct
9 Kent Lo
10 Turner Lo
11 Marlborough
12 Parkland Gdns
13 Lewesdon Cl
14 Pines Ct
15 Ashtead Ct
16 Mynterne Ct
17 Arden
18 Stephen Ct
19 Marsham Ct
20 Doradus Ct
21 Acorns The
22 Heritage Ho
23 Conifer Ct
24 Spencer Ho
25 Chartwell
26 Blenheim
27 Chivelston
28 Greenfield Ho
29 Oakman Ho
30 Radley Lo
31 Simon Lo
32 Admirals Ct
D4 1 Brett Ho
2 Brett House Cl
3 Sylva Ct
4 Ross Ct
5 Potterne Ct
6 Stourhead Cl
7 Fleur Gates
8 Greenwood
D5 1 Balmoral Cl
2 Glenalmond Ho
3 Selwyn Ho
4 Keble Ho
5 Bede Ho
6 Gonville Ho
7 Magdalene Ho
8 Armstrong Ho
9 Newnham Ho
10 Somerville Ho
11 Balliol Ho
12 Windermere
13 Little Combe Cl
14 Classinghall Ho
15 Chalford Ct
16 Garden Royal
17 South Ct
18 Anne Kerr Ct
19 Ewhurst
D6 1 Geneva Ct
2 Laurel Ct
3 Cambalt Ho
4 Langham Ct
5 Lower Pk
6 King's Keep
7 Whitnell Ct
8 Whitehead Ho
9 Halford Ho
10 Humphry Ho
11 Jellicoe Ho

157
A3 1 William Harvey Ho
2 Highview Ct
3 Cameron Ct
4 Galgate Cl
5 Green Ho The
6 King Charles Wlk
7 Florys Ct
8 Augustus Ct
9 Albert Ct
10 Hertford Lo
11 Mortimer Lo
12 Allenswood
13 Ambleside
14 Hansler Ct
15 Roosevelt Ct
A6 1 Claremont
2 Downside
3 Cavendish Cl
4 Ashcombe Ct
5 Carltons The
6 Espirit Ho
7 Millbrooke Ct
8 Coysh Ct
9 Keswick Hts
10 Lincoln Ho
11 Avon Ct
B6 1 Keswick Broadway
2 Burlington Mews
3 Cambria Lo
4 St Stephen's Gdns
5 Atlantic Ho
6 Burton Lo
7 Manfred Ct
8 Meadow Bank
9 Hooper Ho
10 Aspire Bld
C6 1 Pembridge Pl
2 Adelaide Rd
3 London Ct
4 Windsor Ct
5 Westminster Ct
6 Fullers Ho
7 Bridge Pk
8 Lambeth Ct
9 Milton Ct
10 Norfolk Mans
11 Francis Snary Lo
12 Bush Cotts
13 Downbury Mews
14 Newton's Yd
D6 1 Fairfield Ct
2 Blackmore Ho
3 Lancaster Mews
4 Cricketers Mews
5 College Mews
6 Arndale Wlk

158
A2 1 Beemans Row
2 St Andrew's Ct
3 Townsend Mews
4 Sheringham Mews

159
1 Upper Tooting Park Mans
2 Cecil Mans
3 Marius Mans
4 Boulevard The
5 Elmfield Mans
6 Holdernesse Rd
7 Lumiere Ct
A3 1 Heslop Ct
2 St James's Terr
3 Boundaries Mans
4 Station Par
5 Old Dairy Mews
A4 1 Hollies Way
2 Endlesham Ct
A5 1 Rayne Ho
2 St Anthony's Ct
3 Earlsthorpe Mews
4 Nightingale Mans
B3 1 Holbeach Mews
2 Hildreth Street Mews
3 Coalbrook Mans
4 Hub Buildings The
5 Metropolis Apartments
B4 1 Meyer Ho
2 Faraday Ho
3 Hales Ho
4 Frankland Ho
5 Graham Ho
6 Gibbs Ho
7 Dalton Ho
8 Ainslie Wlk
9 Rokeby Ho
10 Caistor Ho
11 Ivanhoe Ho
12 Catherine Baird Ct
13 Marmion Ho
14 Devonshire Ct
15 Blueprint Apartments
C4 1 Limerick Ct
2 Homewoods
3 Jewell Ho
4 Glanville Ho
5 Dan Bryant Ho
6 Olding Ho
7 Quennel Ho
8 Weir Ho
9 West Ho
10 Neville Ct
11 Friday Grove Mews
C5 1 Joseph Powell Cl
2 Cavendish Mans
3 Westlands Terr
4 Cubitt Ho
5 Hawkesworth Ho
6 Normanton Ho
7 Eastman Ho
8 Couchman Ho
9 Poynders Ct
10 Selby Ho
11 Valentine Ho
12 Gorham Ho
13 Deauville Mans
14 Deauville Ct
C6 1 Timothy Ct
2 Shaftesbury Mews
3 Brook Ho
4 Grover Ho
5 Westbrook Ho
6 Hewer Ho
7 Batten Ho
8 Mandeville Ho
9 George Beare Lo
D3 1 Sinclair Ho
2 MacGregor Ho
3 Ingle Ho
4 St Andrews Mews
D4 1 Riley Ho
2 Bennett Ho
3 White Ho
4 Rodgers Ho
5 Dumphreys Ho
6 Homan Ho
7 Prendergast Ho
8 Hutchins Ho
9 Whiteley Ho
10 Tresidder Ho
11 Primrose Ct
12 Angus Ho
13 Currie Ho
D5 1 Parrington Ho
2 Savill Ho
3 Blackwell Ho
4 Bruce Ho
5 Victoria Ct
6 Victoria Ho
7 Belvedere Ct
8 Ingram Lo
9 Viney Ct
10 Bloomsbury Ho
11 Belgravia Ho
12 Barnsbury Ho

160
A1 1 De Montfort Ct
2 Leigham Hall Par
3 Leigham Hall
4 Endsleigh Mans
5 John Kirk Ho
6 Raeburn Ct
7 Wavel Ct
8 Homeleigh Ct
9 Howland Ho
10 Beauclerk Ho
11 Bertrand Ho
12 Drew Ho
13 Dowes Ho
14 Dunton Ho
15 Raynald Ho
16 Sackville Ho
17 Thurlow Ho
18 Astoria Mans
A2 1 Wyatt Park Mans
2 Broadlands Mans
3 Stonehill's Mans
4 Streatleigh Par
5 Dorchester Ct
6 Picture Ho
A3 1 Beaumont Ho
2 Christchurch Ho
3 Staplefield Cl
4 Chipstead Ho
5 Coulsdon Ho
6 Conway Ho
7 Telford Avenue Mans
8 Telford Parade Mans
9 Wavertree Ct
10 Hartswood Ho
11 Wray Ho
A4 1 Picton Ho
2 Rigg Ho
3 Watson Ho
4 MacArthur Ho
5 Sandon Ho
6 Thorold Ho
7 Pearce Ho
8 Mudie Ho
9 Miller Ho
10 Lycett Ho
11 Lafone Ho
12 Lucraft Ho
13 Freeman Ho
14 New Park Par
15 Argyll Ct
16 Dumbarton Ct
17 Kintyre Ct
18 Cotton Ho
19 Crossman Hos
20 Cameford Ct
21 Parsons Ho
22 Brindley Ho
23 Arkwright Ho
24 Perry Ho
25 Brunel Ho
26 New Park Ct
27 Tanhurst Ho
28 Hawkshaw Cl
A6 1 King's Mews
2 Clapham Court Terr
3 Clapham Ct
4 Clapham Park Terr
5 Pembroke Ho
6 Stevenson Ho
7 Queenswood Ct
8 Oak Tree Ct
9 Park Lofts
10 Ashby Mews
B1 1 Carisbrooke Ct
2 Pembroke Lo
3 Willow Ct
4 Poplar Ct
5 Mountview
6 Spa View
B3 1 Charlwood Ho
2 Earlswood Ho
3 Balcombe Ho
4 Claremont Cl
5 Holbrook Ho
6 Gwynne Ho
7 Kynaston Ho
8 Tillman Ho
9 Regents Lo
10 Hazelmere Ct
11 Dykes Ct
B4 1 Archbishop's Pl
2 Witley Ho
3 Outwood Ho
4 Dunsfold Ho
5 Deepdene Lo
6 Warnham Ho
7 Albury Lo
8 Tilford Ho
9 Elstead Ho
10 Thursley Ho
11 Brockham Ho
12 Capel Lo
13 Leith Ho
14 Fairview Ho
15 Weymouth Ct
16 Ascalon Ct
17 China Mews
18 Rush Common Mews
B6 1 Beatrice Ho
2 Florence Ho
3 Evelyn Ho
4 Diana Ho
5 Brixton Hill Ct
6 Austin Ho
7 Manor Ct
8 Camsey Ho
9 Romer Ho
10 Gale Ho
11 Byrne Ho
12 Farnfield Ho
13 Marchant Ho
14 Rainsford Ho
15 Springett Ho
16 Mannering Ho
17 Waldron Ho
C3 1 Valens Ho
2 Loveday Ho
3 Strode Ho
4 Ethelworth Ct
5 Harbin Ho
6 Brooks Ho
7 Godolphin Ho
8 Sheppard Ho
9 McCormick Ho
10 Taylor Ho
11 Saunders Ho
12 Talcott Path
13 Derrick Ho
14 Williams Ho
15 Baldwin Ho
16 Churston Cl
17 Neil Wates Cres
18 Burnell Ho
19 Portland Ho
C4 1 Ellacombe Ho
2 Booth Ho
3 Hathersley Ho
4 Brereton Ho
5 Holdsworth Ho
6 Dearmer Ho
7 Cherry Cl
8 Greenleaf Cl
9 Longford Wlk
10 Scarlette Manor Wlk
11 Chandlers Way
12 Upgrove Manor Way
13 Ropers Wlk
14 Tebbs Ho
15 Bell Ho
16 Worthington Ho
17 Courier Ho
18 Mackie Ho
19 Hamers Ho
20 Kelyway Ho
21 Harriet Tubman Cl
22 Estoria Cl
23 Leckhampton Pl
24 Scotia Rd
25 Charles Haller St
26 Sidmouth Ho
27 Hunter Ct
28 Onslow Lo
29 William Winter Ct
30 Langthorne Lo
C5 1 Eccleston Ho
2 Scarsbrook Ho
3 Purser Ho
4 Rudhall Ho
5 Hardham Ho
6 Heywood Ho
7 Haworth Ho
8 Birch Ho
9 Lansdell Ho
10 Lomley Ho
11 Laughton Ho
12 Woodruff Ho
13 Bascome St
14 Dudley Mews
15 Herbert Mews
16 Blades Lo
17 Dick Shepherd Ct
18 Charman Ho
19 Morden Ho
20 Bishop Ct
21 Blackburn Ct
22 Leigh Ct
23 John Conwey Ho
24 Bristowe Ct
C6 1 Crownstone Ct
2 Brockwell Ct
3 Nevena Ct
4 St George's Residences
5 Hanover Mans
6 Fleet Ho
7 Langbourne Ho
8 Turnmill Ho
9 Walker Mews
10 Cossar Mews
11 Carter Ho
D1 1 Thanet Ho
2 Chapman Ho
3 Beaufoy Ho
4 Easton Ho
5 Roberts Ho
6 Lloyd Ct
7 Kershaw Ho
8 Wakeling Ho
9 Edridge Ho
10 Jeston Ho
11 Lansdowne Wood Cl
12 Rotary Lo

161
B2 1 Welldon Ct
2 Coppedhall
3 Shackleton Ct
4 Bullfinch Ct
5 Gannet Ct
6 Fulmar Ct
7 Heron Ct
8 Petrel Ct
9 Falcon Ct
10 Eagle Ct
11 Dunnock Ct
12 Dunlin Ct
13 Cormorant Ct
14 Oak Lodge
15 Corfe Lodge
C6 1 Velde Way
2 Delft Way
3 Arnhem Way
4 Isel Way
5 Kempis Way
6 Terborch Way
7 Steen Way
8 Deventer Cres
9 Nimegen Way
10 Hilversum Cres
11 St Barnabas Cl

162
A1 1 Tunbridge Ct
2 Harrogate Ct
3 Bath Ct
4 Leamington Ct
5 Porlock Ho
6 Cissbury Ho
7 Eddisbury Ho
8 Dundry Ho
9 Silbury Ho
10 Homildon Ho
11 Highgate Ho
12 Richmond Ho
13 Pendle Ho
14 Tynwald Ho
15 Wirrall Ho
16 Greyfriars
A6 1 Dorothy Charrington Ho
2 Keswick Ct
3 Kendall Ct
4 Halliwell Ct
B1 1 River Ho
2 Fordington Ho
3 Arbury Terr
4 Woodbury Ho
5 Gainsborough Mews
6 Forest Hill Ct
B2 1 Bromleigh Ct
2 Parfew Ct
3 Thetford Ct
4 Attleborough Ct
5 Dunton Ct
6 Frobisher Ct
7 Julian Taylor Path
8 Grizedale Ct
9 Worsley Ho
C1 1 Forest Lo
2 Sydenham Park Mans
3 William Wood Ho
C2 1 Fitzwilliam Hts
2 Taymount Grange
3 McLeod Ho
4 Featherstone Ave
5 Kingswear Ho
6 Salcombe Ho
7 Glynwood Ct
C3 1 Harlech Ct
2 Angela Ct
3 Westwood Ct
4 New Belmont Ho
5 Pearcefield Ave
6 Waldram Pl
7 Horniman Grange
8 South View Ct
9 Heron Ct
10 Katherine Ct
D1 1 Standlake Point
2 Radcot Point
3 Newbridge Point
4 Northmoor
5 Kelmscott
6 Radnor Ct
7 Heathwood Point
8 Ashleigh Point
9 Deepdene Point
10 Rosemount Point
11 Woodfield Ho
12 Clairville Point
13 Trevenna Ho
14 Hyndewood
D2 1 Pikethorne
2 Andrew Ct
3 Valentine Ct
4 Soper Cl

164
C4 1 Beaumont Terr
2 Littlebourne
3 Verdant Ct
D2 1 Kinross Ct
2 Montrose Ct
3 Rattray Ct
4 Rothesay Ct
D3 1 Edinburgh Ct
2 McMillan Ct
3 Rowallan Ct
4 Meridian Ct
5 Braemar Ct
6 Barrow Ct
7 Blair Ct
8 Darlington Ct
9 Hamilton Ct
10 Inverness Ct
11 Oak Cottage Cl
12 Willow Cl
13 Keswick Ct

165
A4 1 Swallow Ct
2 Honeysuckle Ct
3 Venture Ct
4 Cheriton Ct
5 Askham Lo
6 Syon Lo

166
A2 1 Portland Cres
2 Bourdillon Ct
3 Hillary Ct
4 Tenzing Ct
5 John Hunt Ct
A6 1 Horsfeld Gdns
2 Foxhole Rd
C5 1 Roper St
2 Arcade The
3 Elm Terr
4 Imber Ct
5 Ashcroft Ct
6 Fairlands Ct
7 Brecon Ct
8 Newlands Ct
9 Harvard Ct
10 Garden Ct
11 Chiltern Ct
12 Fairway Ct

167
A2 1 Mervyn Stockwood Ho
2 Michael Marshall Ho
3 Keith Sutton Ho

168
A1 1 Ham Shades Cl
2 Aspen Ho
3 Medlar Ho
4 Cornel Ho
5 Stanton Ct
6 Hornbeam Ho
7 Beech Ho
8 Spindle Ho
9 Hunters Lo
10 Edam Ct
11 Monica James Ho
12 Oak Ho
13 Crescent Ct
14 Freeland Ct
15 Montague Ct
16 Windsor Ct
B5 1 Rochester Cl
2 Cobham Cl
3 Shorne Cl
4 Warne Pl

169
C4 1 Close The
2 Parkhurst Gdns
3 Chichester Ct
4 Pound Green Ct

170
B6 1 Station Par
2 Queens La
3 Copthorne Chase
4 Canterbury Ct
5 Church Par
C5 1 St Matthew's Ct
2 Dencliffe
3 Crest Ho
4 Bourne Ho
5 Elms The
6 Roxeth Ct
7 Rowland Hill Almshouses

171
A3 1 Viscount Ct
2 Blackthorne Ct
D3 1 Bishops Ct
2 Ash Lo
3 Lime Lo
4 Oak Lo
5 Elm Ct
6 Willow Lo
7 Sycamore Lo
8 Priscilla Ho
9 Sunbury Cross Ctr
10 Isobel Ho

173
A6 1 Gabriel Cl
2 Metcalfe Wlk
3 Dunmow Cl
4 Burgess Cl
5 Chamberlain Wlk
C2 1 Sherbourne Ct
2 Somerset Ct
3 Jubilee Ho
4 Rushbury Ct
5 Blenheim Ct
6 Hemming Cl
7 Ryedale Ct
8 Norman Ct
C4 1 Begonia Ho
2 Snowdrop Cl
3 Hyacinth Ct
4 Cyclamen Cl
5 Jonquil Gdns
6 Gladioli Cl
7 Daffodil Pl
8 Partridge Rd
D4 1 Acorn Cl
2 Wolsey Ho
3 Lytton Ho
4 Wren Ho
5 Faraday Ho

174
C5 1 Knaggs Ho
2 Keeling
3 Elizabeth Ct
4 Oakhurst Cl
5 Charles Ct
6 Harold Ct
D5 1 Waldegrave Ct
2 Luther Mews
3 Alice Mews
4 Gresham Ho
5 Traherne Lo
6 Fishers Ct
7 Waterhouse Ct
8 Oval Ct
9 Walpole Pl
10 Walpole Cres
11 Bychurch End

175
A5 1 Cherrywood Ct
2 Cambridge Ho
3 Cairngorm Cl
4 Gleneagles Ct
5 Christchurch Ave
6 Hales Ct
7 Plough La
8 Springfield Rd
9 Royal Oak Mews
10 Trinder Mews
C3 1 Belgravia Ho
2 Ash Ho
3 Crieff Ct
4 Maples The
D2 1 Wick Ho
2 Spinnaker Ct
3 Osiers Ct
4 Trent Ho
5 Arun Ho
6 Medway Ho
7 Avon Ho
8 Tyne Ho
9 Clyde Ho
10 Mersey Ct
11 Severn Ct
12 John William Cl
13 Henry Macaulay Ave
14 Seymour Lo
15 Falmouth Ho
16 Earlsfield Ho
D6 1 Byron Ct
2 Coleridge Ct
3 Tennyson Ct
4 Herrick Ct
5 Spenser Ct
6 Marlowe Ct
7 Brooke Ct
8 Gray Ct
9 Shelley Ct
10 Pope Ct

11 Dryden Ct

176

A1 1 Cleave's Almshos
2 Perry Ct
3 Drovers Ct
4 Gough Ho
5 Eden Wlk
6 Alderman Judge Mall
7 Lady Booth Rd
8 Caversham Ho
9 Littlefield Cl
10 Bentall Sh Ctr The
11 Adams Wlk
12 Ceres Ct
A2 1 Regents Ct
2 Walter St
3 Canbury Bsns Pk
4 Sigrist Sq
5 Ashway Ctr
6 Warwick Ho
7 Hedingham Ho
8 Alexander Ho
9 Bramber Ho
10 Carisbrooke Ho
11 Dartmouth Ho
12 Garland Ho
A3 1 Walton Ho
2 Berkeley Cl
3 Canbury Ct
4 King's Penny Ho
B1 1 Vicarage Ho
2 Rayleigh Ct
3 School Pas
4 Chippenham
5 Camm Gdns
B2 1 Onslow Ho
2 Dowler Ct
B3 1 McDonald Ho
2 Elm Ho
3 Dale Ct
4 York Ho
5 Florence Ho
6 Florence Rd
7 Roupell Ho
8 Delft Ho
C1 1 Wimpole Cl
2 Burwell
3 Caldecote
4 Fordham
5 Connington
6 Chesterton Terr
7 Westwick
8 Eureka Rd
9 Fulbourn
10 Comberton
11 Madingley
12 Grantchester
13 Cambridge Grove Rd
14 Oakington
15 Harston
16 Graveley
17 Croxton
18 Brinkley
19 Impington
20 Shelford
21 Duxford
22 Cascadia Ho
C2 1 Farthings The
2 Brae Ct
3 Princeton Mews
4 Station App
C3 1 Queen's Ct
2 St George's Rd
3 Park Road Ho
4 Dagmar Rd
5 Tapping Cl
6 Arthur Rd
7 Borough Rd
8 Belvedere Ct
9 Braywick Ct
10 Dean Ct
11 Rowan Ct
12 Richmond Ct
13 Sunningdale Ct
14 Hawker Ct
15 Cromwell Ct
16 Kings Ct
D2 1 Trevallyn Lo
2 Chichester Ho
3 Beechcroft
4 Cedars The
5 Liddlesdale Ho W
6 Liddlesdale Ho E
7 Deerhurst
8 Brockworth
9 Alderton
D3 1 Bramley Ho
2 Abinger Ho
3 Thursley Ho
4 Ridge Ho
5 Clone The
6 Mount Ct
7 Hillside Ct
8 Hill Ct
9 Royal Ct
10 Lakeside
11 High Ashton
D4 1 Godstone Ho
2 Hambledon Ho
3 Kingswood Ho
4 Leigh Ho
5 Milton Ho
6 Newdigate Ho
7 Farleigh Ho
8 Ockley Ho
9 Effingham Ho
10 Dunsfold Ho
11 Pirbright Ho
12 Clandon Ho
13 Ripley Ho

178

C3 1 Roskeen Ct
2 Chimneys Ct
3 Aston Ct
4 Rosemary Cotts
5 Victoria Lo
D2 1 Beaufort Ho
2 Kinnear Ct
3 Ranmore Ct
4 Lantern Ct
5 Crescent Ho
D3 1 Kings View Ct
2 Wimbledon Cl
3 Beryl Harding Ho
4 Upton Ct
5 Marian Lo
6 Terraces The
7 Lanherne Ho
8 Cumberland Cl
9 Thaxted Pl
10 Rathbone Ho
11 Princess Ct
12 Claremont Lo
13 Downs Ct
14 Ravenscar Lo
15 Haverley
16 Savona Cl
17 Beaumont Ct
18 Gordon Ct
D5 1 Lancaster Pl
2 Haygarth Pl
3 Allington Cl
4 Homefield Pl

179

A3 1 Stretford Ct
2 Brunswick Ct
3 Pavilion Ct
4 Louie Black Ho
5 Warwick Ho
6 Erica Ho
7 Adyar Ct
8 Thornton Lo
9 Ash Ct
10 Broughton Ho
11 Naomi Watts Ho
12 Wellesley Ho
13 Mayfair Ct
A4 1 Walham Rise
2 Grosvenor Ct
3 Sovereign Ho
4 Holly Lo
5 Florence Ct
6 Linden Cotts
7 Sheep Walk Mews
8 Emerson Ct
9 Hill Ct
10 Powell Ho
B4 1 Aspen Lo
2 Gladebury Ct
3 Centre Court Sh Ctr
B5 1 Lawns The
2 Prentice Ct
3 Catherine Ct
4 Woodlodge
5 Pixham Ct
6 Lake Cl
7 Westwood Ct
8 Brambles The
9 Lismore
10 Rose Ct
11 Worcester Rd
12 Leopold Ct
C3 1 Ashbourne Terr
2 Sir Cyril Black Way
3 Willows Ct
4 Harefield Ct
5 Broadway Ho
6 Viscount Point
7 Carrington Ho
8 Cloisters Ho
9 Downing Ho
10 Bickley Ct
11 Palmerston Gr
12 Gladstone Ct
13 Warrington Ct
D2 1 Gilbert Cl
2 Becket Cl
3 Priory Cl
4 Hudson Ct
5 Ryder Ho
6 Eleanor Ho
7 Ramsey Ho
8 Colborne Ct
9 Falcon Ho
10 Spur Ho
D3 1 Hamilton Road Mews
2 Dowman Cl
3 Burleigh Lo
4 Horatio Ho

180

A2 1 Tanner Ho
2 May Ct
3 Marsh Ct
4 Lovell Ho
A3 1 Fiske Ct
2 Mellor Ct
3 Olive Rd
4 Allerton Ho
5 Victory Road Mews
6 Will Miles Ct
7 Vanguard Ho
8 Mychell Ho
9 Merton Pl
10 De Burgh Ho
11 Norfolk Ho
12 Hotham Road Mews
B1 1 Ripley Ct
2 Brooklands Ct
3 Horner La
B2 1 Yarborough Rd
2 Vista Ho
3 Prospect Ho
4 Independence Ho
5 Nonsuch Ho
6 Baron Ho
C2 1 Linford Ct
2 Searle Ct
3 Gunnell Ct
4 Wells Ct
5 Hartley Ct
C3 1 Shere Lo
2 Goodwin Ct
3 Cairn Ho
C4 1 Douglas Ct
2 Lannock Ct
3 Gateway Ho
4 Wellington Ct
C5 1 Robertson Ho
2 Dewar Ho
3 Jean Ho
4 Marion Ct
5 Gravenel Gdns
6 Palladino Ho
D1 1 Elms Cotts
2 Sibthorp Rd
3 Armfield Cotts
4 Sir Arthur Bliss Ct
5 Fountain Ho
6 Gladstone Ho
7 Chart Ho

181

A1 1 Kennedy Cl
2 Pearce Cl
3 Mainwaring Ct
4 Coningsby Ct
5 Laburnum Ct
6 Beaumont Ct
7 Penfold Ct
8 Fitch Ct
10 Lea Cotts
A5 1 Osborne Terr
2 Limetree Wlk
C5 1 Tyers Ho
2 Boothby Ho
3 Adams Ho
4 Burney Ho
5 Boswell Ho
6 Chesterfield Ho
7 Garrick Ho
8 Levett Ho
9 Shelburne Ho
10 Marchmont Ho
11 Ryland Ho
12 Flather Cl
13 Bank Bldgs
14 Carriage Pl
15 Locarno Cl
C6 1 Walmsley Ho
2 Chambers Ho
3 Fordyce Ho
4 Percy Ho
5 Langton Ho
6 Moorfields Ct
7 Hidaburn Ct
8 Salter Ho
9 Tailors Ct
10 Yew Tree Lo
D6 1 William Dyce Mews
2 Doctor Johnson Ho

182

A3 1 Spa Central
A5 1 Oakdene Ct
2 Hopton Par
3 Merton Lo
4 Bouverie Ct
5 Deerhurst
6 Farnan Hall
A6 1 Central Mans
2 Central Par
B3 1 Marqueen Twrs
2 Shirley Ct
3 Sinclair Ho
4 Vantage Ct
5 Pavilion Ct
B6 1 Ashleigh Ho
2 Roseneath Pl
3 Shenley Ho
4 Blytheswood Pl
C5 1 Parkhill Ho
2 Ash Ct
3 Alder Ct
4 Beech Ct
5 Acacia Ct
6 Blackthorn Ct
7 Cypress Ct
8 Hawthorn Ct
9 Hazel Ct
10 Sycamore Ct
11 Maple Ct
12 Laburnam Ct
13 Fern Lo
14 Colyton La
C6 1 James Boswell Cl
2 St Albans Ho
3 Suffolk Ct
4 Rockhampton Cl
5 Delphian Ct
6 Heather Ct
D5 1 Woodcote Pl
2 Joe Hunte Ct
3 Cork Tree Ho
4 Lake Ho
5 Cedars Ho
6 Portobello Ho
7 Cooper Ho
8 Farnsworth Ho
9 Hook Ho
10 Crest The
11 Renshaw Ho
12 Ruscoe Ho
13 Sardeson Ho
D6 1 William Wilberforce Ho
2 William Marsden Ho
3 Samuel Ho
4 Morris Stephany Ho
5 Church Ct

183

A6 1 Moore Ho
2 Chaucer Ho
3 Bushell Ho
4 Bligh Ho
5 Hobbs Rd
6 Hogarth Ho
7 Goodbehere Ho
8 Astley Ho
9 Elder Gdns
10 Elderberry Gr
11 Pavement The
12 Dunkirk St
B6 1 Josef Perrin Ho
2 Jean Humbert Ho
3 Charles Staunton Ho
4 Violette Szabo Ho
5 Lilian Rolfe Ho
6 Odette Ho
7 Robert Gerard Ho
8 St Bernards Cl
9 Champness Cl
10 Pennington Cl
11 Queenswood Ct
C4 1 Northwood Way
2 High Limes
3 Valley Prospect
4 Plane Tree Wlk
5 City Prospect
6 Bankside Way
7 Ridge Way
8 Rochdale
9 Barrington Wlk
10 Gatestone Ct
11 Childs La
12 Carberry Rd
13 Norwood Heights Sh Ctr
C5 1 Oakdene
2 Thorsden Way
3 Oakfield Gdns
4 Georgetown Cl
5 Bridgetown Cl
6 Mountbatten Cl
7 Brabourne Cl
8 Alexandra Wlk
9 Compton Ct
10 Battenburg Wlk
11 Burma Terr
12 Wiseman Ct
C6 1 Linley Ct
2 Mellor Ho
3 Whitfield Ct
4 Michaelson Ho
5 Holberry Ho
6 Hovenden Ho
7 Huntley Ho
8 Telfer Ho
9 Markham Ho
10 Oldham Ho
11 Parnall Ho
12 Pierson Ho
13 Roper Ho
14 Roundell Ho
15 Sawyer Ho
16 Ransford Ho
17 Carmichael Ho
18 Bonne Marche Terr Mews
D3 1 Hetley Gdns
2 Claybourne Mews
3 Highland Lo
4 Mason Ct
5 Kendall Ct
6 High View
D5 1 Glenhurst Ct
2 Marlowe Ct
3 Grenville Ct
4 Raleigh Ct
5 Beechwoods Ct
6 Burntwood View

184

A3 1 Hanover Ct
2 Brunswick Ct
3 New Church Ct
4 Regency Ct
7 Owen Wlk
8 Bargrove Cl
9 Beaver Cl
B2 1 Dorset Ho
2 Collingwood Cl
3 Chartwell Way
4 Essex Twr
5 Appletree Cl
6 Ditton Pl
7 Kelvin Ct
8 Readman Ct
9 Glen Ct
10 Kingsbridge Ho
11 Carlton Ct
12 Benhurst Ct
13 Carole Ho
14 Dover Ho
15 Bettswood Ct
B3 1 Avery Ct
2 Rossal Ct
3 Oakdene Lo
4 Ridgemount Cl
5 Blakewood Ct
6 Trenholme Cl
7 Oakleigh Ct
8 Upchurch Cl
9 Devon Ho
10 Westmoreland Terr
11 Oakfield Road Ind Est
B5 1 Ragwort Ct
2 Firs The
3 Wingham Ho
4 Seath Ho
5 Ripley Ho
6 Lathwood Ho
7 Hurst Ho
8 George Ho
9 Browne Ho
10 Beacon Ho
11 Bailey Ho
12 Agate Ho
C2 1 Challin St
2 Rutland Ho
3 Pine Cl
C3 1 Watermen's Sq
2 St John's Cotts
3 Gladstone Mews
4 Middlesex Ho
5 Bethesda Ct
6 Ospringe Cl
7 Goudhurst Ho
8 Walmer Ho
9 Strood Ho
10 Greatstone Ho
11 John Baird Ho
C4 1 Midhurst
2 Oliver Ct
3 Victoria Ct
4 Wakefield Ct
5 Fountain Ct
6 Newlands Ct
C6 1 Homewalk Ho
2 Grace Path
3 Sycamore Ct
4 Sydenham Station App
5 Greenways
6 Faircroft
D3 1 Groombridge Ho
2 Provincial Terr
3 Smithers Ho
4 West Ho
5 Swallows Ct
6 Hornbeam Ho
7 Blenheim Centre

185

A1 1 Clock House Ct
2 Blandford Ave
3 Old School Cl
4 Lynsted Ct
5 Florence Rd
A6 1 Paxton Ct
2 Kenton Ct
3 Grove Ct
4 Shirley Lo
B2 1 Ashton Ct
2 Coombe Ct
3 Fontaine Ct
4 Richfield Ct
5 Sheridan Way
C1 1 Christ Church Rd
2 Lea Rd
3 Stanmore Terr
C2 1 Erindale Ct
2 Montgomerie Ct
3 Rebecca Ct
4 Sycamore Ct
5 Willow Ct
6 Marlborough Ct
7 Bearsted Terr
8 Berwick Ct
9 Wooderson Ct
10 Beck River Pk
11 Waterside
C3 1 Gardenia Ct
2 Brackendale Ct
3 Daniel Ct
4 Moliner Ct
5 Chartwell Lo
6 Randmore Ct
7 Dover Ho
8 Lucerne Ct
9 Malling Ho
10 Westerham Lo
11 Brasted Lo
12 Milton Ho
13 Bradsole Ho
14 Sandgate Ho
15 Adelaide Ct
16 Nettlestead Cl
17 Warren Ct
18 Alton Ct
19 Rockingham Ct
20 Camellia Ct
21 Sinclair Ct
22 Regents Ct
23 Minshull Pl
24 South Park Ct
D1 1 Parkside
2 Tudors The
3 Oakbrook
4 Tara Ct
5 Redlands The
6 Cambria
7 Hillworth
8 Kelsey Gate
9 Burrells
10 Lincoln Lo
11 Courtlands
12 Fairleas
13 Ashdown Cl
14 Barons
D2 1 Clifton Ct
2 Mayfair Ct
3 Lait Ho
4 Fire Station Mews
D4 1 Warner Ho
2 Clifford Ho
3 Lloyd Ho
4 Thurston Ho
5 Byron Ho
6 Blake Ho
7 Keats Ho

186

A2 1 White House Ct
2 Hunters The
3 Sandringham Ct
4 Glenhurst
5 Copperfields
6 Westgate Ct
A6 1 Dedham Ho
2 Flatford Ho
3 Langthorne Ct
4 Radley Ct
5 Hoover Ho
6 Brunner Ho
7 Waterer Ho
8 Marriott Ho
9 Bourbon Ho
B5 1 Longford Ho
2 Ingrebourne Ho
3 Brent Ho
4 Darent Ho
5 Beverley Ho
6 Wandle Ho
7 Rythe Ho
8 Ember Ho
9 Crane Ho
10 Ravensbourne Ho
C1 1 Warwick Ct
2 Maplehurst
3 Mount Arlington
4 Arundel Ct
D2 1 Weston Gr
2 Gibbs Ho
3 Longfield
4 Hammelton Ct
5 Bracken Hill Cl
6 Townend Ct
7 Treversh Ct
8 Cameron Ho
9 Woodlands Ct
10 Blythwood Pk
11 Bromley Pk
D3 1 Homecoppice Ho
2 Linden Ct
3 Kimberley Gate
4 Inglewood Ct
5 Mavery Ct
6 Glen Ct
7 Marlborough Ct
8 Cawston Ct
9 Blendon Path

187

A1 1 St James Ct
A2 1 Mitchell Way
2 Harrington Ho
3 Newman Ct
4 Uno Apartments
5 Bromley Ho
B2 1 Dainton Cl
2 Rothwell Ct
3 St Timothy's Mews
4 Andringham Lo
5 Kendall Lo
6 Summerfield
7 Winston Ct
8 Vogue Ct
9 Laurels The
C1 1 Westland Lo
2 Eastland Ct
3 Dairsie Ct
4 Northlands
5 Beechfield Cotts
6 Oasis The
7 Cromarty Ct
8 Silverstone Ct

188

A6 1 Beaconsfield Par
2 Cranley Par
3 Kimmeridge Gdns
4 King & Queen Cl
C2 1 Ivybridge Ct
2 Greenbank Lo

190

A6 2 Cyril Lo
3 Hazlemere
4 Milton Ho
5 Marlin Ct
6 Conroy Ct
7 Glenwood Ct
8 Culverton Ct
9 Holmbury Manor
B1 1 Swanscombe Ho
2 Haverstock Ct
3 Arrandene Ho
4 Broomfield Ho
5 Headley Ho
6 Kenley Ho
7 Ladywell Ho
B6 1 Chudleigh
2 Wimborne
3 St John's Par
4 Holly Ct
5 Rectory Bsns Ctr

193

D1 1 Orchard Ct
2 Bridge Ct

197

A2 1 Raleigh Ho
2 Leicester Ho
3 Gresham Ho
D2 1 Napier Ct
2 Darlington Ho
3 Charminster Ct
4 Mulberry Ct
5 Leander Ct
6 Clinton Ho
7 Hollingsworth Ct
8 Gloucester Ct
9 Palmerston Ct
10 Redwood Ct
11 Hursley Ct
12 Westmorland Ct
13 Lawson Ct
14 Alexander Ct
15 Winton Ct
16 Sydenham Ho
17 Caroline Ct
18 Ellswood Ct
19 Masefield Ct

198

A1 1 Ash Tree Cl
2 Shrubbery The
3 Malvern Ct
4 Gate Ho
5 Yew Tree Ho
A3 1 Station App
2 South Bank Lo
3 Bramshott Ct
4 Pandora Ct
5 Wellington Ct
6 Glenbuck Ct
7 Leighton Ho
8 Oakhill Ct
9 Downs View Lo
10 Osborne Ct
11 Surbiton Par
12 Woodgate Ho
13 Godwyn Ho
14 Ashby Ho
A4 1 Effingham Lo
2 Maple Ho
3 Channon Ct
4 Falconhurst
5 Ferndown
6 Viceroy Lo
7 Frensham Ho
8 Kingsley Ho
9 Rannoch Ct
10 Stratton Ct
11 Moray Ho
12 Dulverton Ct
13 Westerham
14 Hill Ct
15 Assheton-Bennett Ho
16 Hatfield Ho
17 Oxford Ct
18 Pennington Lo
19 Austin Ho
20 Wentworth Ct
21 Priory The
22 Sheraton The
23 Christopher Ct
24 Hobart Ho
25 St Mark's Hts
A5 1 Marquis Ct
2 Garrick Ho
A6 1 College Rdbt
2 Edinburgh Ct
3 Weston Ct
4 Grebe Terr
5 Heron Ct
6 Agar Ho
7 St James' Ct
8 Grove Ct
9 Springfield Ct
10 College Wlk
B3 1 Percy Ct
2 Holmwood
3 Middle Green Cl
4 Herbert Ct
B4 1 Woodleigh
2 Highcroft
3 Caernarvon Ct
4 Regency Ct
D1 1 Oakleigh Way
2 Chandler Ct

199

C2 1 Goodland Ho
2 Furzeland Ho
3 Oakcroft Ho

4 Meadcroft Ho
5 Newhouse
C4 1 Merryweather Ct
2 Roebuck Ct
3 Sable Ct
C5 1 Acacia Ho
2 Kingston Lo
3 Carrington Ct
4 Fairholme Ho
5 Marshall Ho
6 Norton Ho
7 Martin Ho

200

A1 1 Brookside Cres
2 Beverley Gdns
3 Purdey Ct
4 Avenue The
5 Briarwood Ct
6 Station App

202

D6 1 Fair Green Ct
2 Regal Ct
3 Lewes Ct
4 Esher Mews
5 Sibford Ct
6 Deseret Ho
7 Standor Ho
8 Langdale Par
9 Newman Terr

204

A2 1 Barcom Trad Est
2 Croydon Valley
Trade Pk
C3 1 Rozelle Ct
2 Dunheved Ct
3 Truscott Ho
C4 1 Brigstock Par
2 Terry Lodge
3 Justin Ct
D3 1 Wyndham Ct
D5 1 Nutfield Pl
2 Braidwood Ho
3 Elliott Ho

205

B1 1 Tavistock Ct
2 Chartwell Ct
3 Speaker's Ct
4 Cumberland Ct
5 Viceroy Ct
6 Oriel Ct
7 Cherry Orchard
Gdns
8 Sola Ct
9 Gamma Ct
C1 1 Windmill Bridge
Ho
2 Squire Ct
3 Houston Ct
5 Warren Ct
D1 1 Hastings Pl
2 Grant Pl

3 Clive Ho
4 Havelock Ho
5 Bellmore Ct
6 Hereford Ct
7 Chequers Ct
8 Havelock Hall

206

A1 1 Farleycroft
2 Edgecumbe Ct
3 Wesson Ho
4 Sullivan Ct
5 Kenley Ho
6 Christopher Ct
7 Jayson Ct
A6 1 Leybourne Ct
2 Lestock Cl
3 Croftside The
D1 1 Cottongrass Cl
2 Oxlip Cl
3 Eyebright Cl

207

1 North Rd
2 Sussex Rd
3 Riverside Wlk
4 Christie Ho
5 Windsor Ct
6 Sherwood Ct
7 Wheatsheaf Par
D6 1 Linden Ct
2 Park Ct
3 Chilchester Ct
4 Iveagh Ct

208

A6 1 Overbury
2 Wilton Pl
D1 1 Woodgrange Ct
2 Maycroft
3 Farnborough Cres
D4 1 Knowlton Gn
2 Speldhurst Cl
3 Bidborough Cl
4 Penshurst Wlk
D5 1 Wedgewood Ct
2 Birches The
3 Eccleshill
4 Tavistock Rd
5 Montpelier Ct

209

A5 1 Montague Terr
2 Chatsworth Ho
A6 1 Marina Cl
2 Cheveney Wlk
3 Bromley Manor
Mans
4 Mall The
5 Westmoreland Pl
B5 1 Reflex Apartments
2 Wheeler Pl
3 Maxim Apart-
ments
4 Exchange Apart-
ments
5 Axiom Apartments
6 Weller Mews

211

B1 1 Gleneagles Gn
2 Tandridge Pl
3 Springfield Wlk
4 Pinehurst Wlk
5 Cromer Pl
6 Oakmont Pl

214

A6 1 St Bernards Ho
2 Wentworth Ct
3 Sunningdale Cl
4 Arklow Mews
5 Edward Pinner Ct

216

1 Lansdowne Copse
2 Lansdowne Ct

217

A2 1 Cheam Court Flats
2 Farnham Ct
3 Tabor Ct
C1 1 Lancaster Ct
2 Redclyffe Terr
3 Kenilworth Terr
4 Lincoln Terr
5 Garden Ct
6 Ashwood Pk
7 Midsummer
Apartments
8 Lyndhurst Ct
9 Lorraine Ct
10 Gloucester Ct
11 Banbury Ct
12 Camilla Ct
13 Lorac Ct
14 Kingswood Mans
15 Claremont Ho
16 Holly Ct
17 Castle Ho
18 Balmoral Ct
19 Davington Ct
20 Hereford Ct
C2 1 Norman Ho
2 Hawthorns The
3 Limes The
4 Alexa Ct
5 Kristina Ct
6 Beverley Ct
7 Chestnut Ct
D1 1 Holmeswood
2 Pebworth Lo
3 Addison Ct
4 Kingslee Ct
5 Raeburn Ho
6 Girtin Ho
7 Leith Towers
8 Courtlands
9 Thomas Ho
10 Grayshott Ct
11 Hadrian Ct
12 Sandown Ct
13 Magnolia Ct
14 Dunsfold Ct
15 Camberley Ct
16 Berrylands Ct
17 Brockham Ct

18 Alford Ct
19 Lansdowne Ho
20 Larchvale Ct
D2 1 Portland Ct
2 Durnston Ct
3 Barton Ct
4 Aplin Ct
5 Hannah Ct
6 Honeysuckle Ct
7 Rowans The
8 St Annes Ct
9 Bonnington Ho
10 Pamir Ct
11 Bradbourne Ct
12 Worcester Ct
D3 1 Marian Ct
2 Robin Hood Ct
3 Distin Ct
4 Queensmere
5 Grosvenor Ho
6 Cromer Mans
7 St Nicholas Ctr
D5 1 Dorothy Pettingel
Ho
2 Margaret Ho

218

A1 1 Beauclere Ho
2 Melford Ct
3 Elmhurst Lo
4 Mansard Manor
5 Tranmere Ct
6 Beechcroft Lo
7 Savin Lo
8 Yew Tree Ct
9 Avondale Ct
10 Devonshire Ho
11 Hidcote Ho
12 Munstead Ct
13 Lodden Lo
14 Steetley Ct
15 Grampian Cl
16 Richard Sharples
Ct
A2 1 Grosvenor Ct
2 Forest Dene Ct
3 Cedar Ct
4 Vanborough Ct
5 Shrub Ct
6 Evergreen Ct
7 Grasmere Ct
8 Heathfield Ct
9 Sherbourne Ct
10 Kinsale Grange
11 Linden Ct
12 Jubilee Ct
13 Langley Ct
14 Wilmot Ho
15 Farendon Ho
16 Alexander Ho
A3 1 Goossens Cl
2 Cliffe Wlk
3 Marlins Cl
4 Clowser Cl
5 Montana Gdns
6 Bournemouth Ct
7 Palmerston Ct
A4 1 Lodge The

2 Hazelwood Ho
3 Chesterton Ho
4 Clevedon Ho
5 Staincliffe Ho
6 Denewood Ho
7 Newlyn Ho
8 Manor Ct
9 Glenrose Ho
10 Oak Lo
11 Briar The
12 Fernhead
13 Branch Ct
14 Thicket Ct
15 Adam Ct
16 Arndell Ho
17 Oakwood Ct
B3 1 Hogarth Ho
2 Gillray Ho
3 Cramhurst Ho
4 Ronald Ho
5 Blythewood
6 Hillsde
7 Weldon Ct
8 Yeoman Ct
D5 1 Kynersley Cl
2 Wrythe Gn
3 Bedford Villas
4 Chateau The
5 Nelson Ct
6 Errington Manor
7 Leeds Ct
8 Blair Ct

219

A4 1 Westcroft
2 Westcroft Ho
A5 1 Burnside Ct
2 Millpond Pl
3 Waterside Ct
4 Stable Ct
5 Manor Ct
B2 1 Runnymede Ct
2 Dolphin Ct
3 Kings Ct
4 Cheyne Ct
5 Hendfield Ct
6 Ellerslie Ct
7 Embassy Ct
8 Chandler Ct
9 Hambledon Ct
10 Wallington Ct
11 Jasmine Ct
12 Napier Ct
13 Rosswood Ho
14 Woodcote Ct
15 Surrey Ct
16 Stag Ct
17 Moorlands
B3 1 Cornelion Cotts
2 Walpole Ct
3 Farmstead Ct
4 Derby Ho
5 Salisbury Ho
6 Chatham Ho
B4 1 Loraine Ho
2 Harcourt Lo
3 Coniston Ct
4 Alcester Ct

2 Friars Ct
6 Campbell Ct
7 Brodie Ho
8 Lesley Ct
9 Birch Ct
10 Airborne Ho
C2 1 Rossendon Ct
2 Mulberry Mews
3 Nairn Ct
4 Wallington Sq
5 Rosemount Twrs
6 Connell Ho
7 Ashby Grange
8 Terry Ct
9 Leigham Cl
10 Clyde Works
11 Chandos Bsns Ctr
12 Beech Ho
13 Wendon Ct
D3 1 Torquay Ho
2 Ashburton Ho
D5 1 Goodwood Lo
2 Haydock Lo
3 Kempton Lo

220

A1 1 Phoenix Ctr The
2 Ensign Way
3 Hunter Cl
4 Cirrus Ct
D5 1 Latimer Rd
2 Cromwell Ho
3 Arundel Ct
4 Warrington Ct
5 Grace Ct
6 Stuart Ct
7 Bridge Par

221

A3 1 Trent Ct
2 Sherwood Ct
3 Archers Ct
4 Keepers Ct
5 Lincoln Ct
6 Mount The
7 Fairhaven Ct
8 Brockham Ct
9 Chelwood Ct
10 Marey Ct
11 Landau Ct
A4 1 West Street Pl
2 Maple Ct
3 St Andrew's Rd
4 Albury Ct
5 Chestnut Ct
6 Elgin Ct
7 Beechfield Ct
8 Barham Ct
9 Whitstable Pl
10 Ledbury Pl
A5 1 Fellmongers Yd
2 Halstead Cl
3 Mann Cl
4 Waterworks Yd
5 Chanderia Ct
6 Katherine Ho
A6 1 Otterbourne Rd
2 Charrington Rd

3 Tamworth Pl
4 Priddy's Yd
5 Hospital of the
Holy Trinity (Alm-
shouses)
B6 1 Wellesley Court
Rd
2 Norfolk Ho
3 Station App
4 Suffolk Ho
5 Cherry Orchard
Gdns
6 Harrington Ct
D6 1 Cheyne Ct
2 Fourways
3 Princess Ct
4 Tierney Ct
5 Sinclair Ct
6 Guinness Ct
7 Mayfair Ct
8 Bishopscourt
9 Gloucester Lo
10 Beverley Hyrst
11 Melton Ct
12 Cecil Ct
13 Napier Ct

227

A3 1 Westfield
2 Farnborough Ct
3 Fern Hill Pl
4 Churchill Ct
5 Spencer Ct
6 Ladycroft Gdns
7 Crabbs Croft Cl
8 Clifton Cl
D2 1 Brittenden Cl
2 Wardens Field Cl
3 Winnipeg Dr
4 Superior Dr
5 Huron Cl
6 Manitoba Gdns
7 Lynne Cl
8 Flint Cl
9 Bakers Mews
D3 1 Osgood Gdns
2 Amberley Cl
3 Rawlings Cl
4 Beblets Cl
5 Fir Tree Cl
6 Raleigh Mews
7 King Henry Mews
D4 1 Healy Dr
2 Marsden Way
3 Taylor Cl
4 Strickland Way
5 Dryland Ave
6 Adcot Wlk
7 Lichlade Cl

Hospitals

Hospitals with Accident and Emergency departments

Central Middlesex Hospital   89 A4
Acton Lane, Park Royal, London NW10 7NS
☎ 020 8965 5733

Charing Cross Hospital   112 D1
Fulham Palace Road, London W6 8RF
(A&E entrance off St Dunstan's Road)
☎ 020 8846 1234

Chase Farm Hospital   4 C5
The Ridgeway, Enfield, Middlesex EN2 8JL
☎ 020 8375 1010

Chelsea and Westminster Hospital   136 A6   266 B5
369 Fulham Road, London SW10 9NH
☎ 020 8746 8080

Ealing Hospital   108 B4
Uxbridge Road, Southall, Middlesex UB1 3HW
☎ 020 8967 5613

Hammersmith Hospital   90 B1
Du Cane Road, London W12 0HS
☎ 020 8383 1111

Hillingdon Hospital   82 B2
Pield Heath Road, Uxbridge, Middlesex UB8 3NN
☎ 01895 238282

Homerton University Hospital   74 D3
Homerton Row, E9 6SR
☎ 020 8510 5555

King George Hospital   58 A4
Barley Lane, Goodmayes, Ilford, Essex IG3 8YB
☎ 020 8983 8000

King's College Hospital   139 B3
Denmark Hill, (A&E in Ruskin Wing) SE5 9RS
☎ 020 3299 9000

Kingston Hospital   176 D2
Galsworthy Road, Kingston-upon-Thames, Surrey KT2 7QB
☎ 020 8546 7711

Lewisham Hospital   163 D6
High Street, Lewisham, London SE13 6JH
☎ 020 8333 3000

Mayday University Hospital   204 D3
Mayday Road, Thornton Heath CR7 7YE
☎ 020 8401 3000

Moorfields Eye Hospital (eyes only)   95 B4   235 C1
162 City Rd, London EC1V 2PO
☎ 020 7253 3411

Newham General Hospital   99 C3
Glen Road, Plaistow, London E13 8SL
☎ 020 7476 4000

North Middlesex University Hospital   33 C5
Sterling Way, Edmonton, London, N18 1QX
☎ 020 8887 2000

Northwick Park Hospital   43 A2
Watford Road, Harrow, Middlesex HA1 3UJ
☎ 020 8864 3232

Princess Royal University Hospital   226 C5
Farnborough Common, Orpington BR6 8ND
☎ 01689 863000

Queen Elizabeth Hospital   144 A5
Stadium Rd, Woolwich SE18 4QH
☎ 020 8836 6000

Queen Mary's Hospital   190 A4
Frognal Avenue, Sidcup,Kent DA14 6LT
☎ 020 8302 2678

Royal Free Hospital   70 C3
Pond Street, London NW3 2QG
☎ 020 7794 0500

Royal London Hospital (Whitechapel)   96 B2
Whitechapel Road, London E1 1BB
☎ 020 7377 7000

St George's Hospital   180 B5
Blackshaw Road, London SW17 0QT
☎ 020 8672 1255

St Helier Hospital   202 A1
Wrythe Lane, Carshalton, Surrey SM5 1AA
☎ 020 8296 2000

St Mary's Hospital   92 B1   236 D2
Praed Street, Paddington W2 1NY
(A&E entrance on South Wharf Rd)
☎ 020 7886 6666

St Thomas' Hospital   116 B3   260 C6
Lambeth Palace Road, London SE1 7EH
☎ 020 7188 7188

University College Hospital   93 C3   239 B6
235 Euston Rd, London NW1 2BU
☎ 0845 155 5000

West Middlesex University Hospital   131 A3
Twickenham Road, Isleworth, Middlesex TW7 6AF
☎ 020 8560 2121

Whipps Cross Hospital   54 B3
Whipps Cross Road, Leytonstone London E11 1NR
☎ 020 8539 5522

Whittington Hospital   71 C6
Highgate Hill, London, N19 5NF
☎ 020 7272 3070

Acton Hospital W3   110 C4
Ashford Hospital TW15 3AA   148 A2
Athlone House (The Middlesex Hospital) N6   48 D1
Atkinson Morley Hospital SW20   178 B3
Barking Hospital IG11   79 D1
Barnes Hospital SW14   133 C2
Beckenham Hospital BR3   185 B1
Bethlem Royal Hospital The BR3   207 C2
Blackheath Hospital SE3   142 C2
Bolingbroke Hospital The SW11   158 C6
Bowden House Hospital (Private) HA1   64 C6
British Home and Hospital for Incurables SW16   182 D5
Bromley Hospital BR2 9AJ   209 B5
Brompton Hospital SW3   114 B1   256 D2
BUPA Bushey Hospital WD2   8 D3
Carshalton, War Memorial Hospital SM5   218 D2
Cassel Hospital TW10   175 D6
Castlewood Day Hospital SE18   144 C4
Central Middlesex Hospital NW10 7NS   89 A4
Central Public Health Laboratory NW9   45 C6
Chadwell Heath Hospital RM6   58 B4
Charing Cross Hospital W6 8RF   112 D1
Charter Nightingale Hospital The NW1   92 C2   237 B4
Chase Farm Hospital EN2 8JL   4 C5
Chelsea Hospital for Women SW3   114 C1   257 A2
Chelsea and Westminster Hospital SW10 9NH   136 A6   266 B5
Chingford Hospital E4   20 A1
Chiswick Maternity Hospital W4   111 D1
Clayponds Hospital and Day Treatment Ctr TW8   110 A2
Clementine Churchill Hospital The HA1   64 D5
Colindale Hospital NW9   45 C6
Connaught Day Hospital E11   54 C3
Coppetts Wood Hospital N10   30 D2
Cromwell Hospital SW5   113 D2   255 C4
Devonshire Hospital W1   93 A2   238 B4
Dulwich Hospital SE22   139 C1
Ealing Hospital UB1 3HW   108 B4
East Ham Memorial Hospital E7   77 D1
Eastman Dental Hospital WC1   94 B4   240 C6
Edgware General Hospital HA8   26 D3
Elizabeth Garrett Anderson and Obstetric Hospital WC1   93 C3   235 B5
Farnborough Hospital BR6   226 C4
Finchley Memorial Hospital N12   30 A3
Fitzroy Nuffield Hospital W1   92 D1   237 C2
Garden Hospital The NW4   46 C6
Goldie Leigh Hospital SE2   146 C6
Goodmayes Hospital IG3   58 A4
Gordon Hospital The SW1   115 D2   259 C3
Great Ormond St Hospital for Children WC1   94 B3   240 C5
Grovelands Priory N14   16 A3
Guy's Hospital SE1   117 B5   252 D2
Hackney Hospital E9   75 A3
Hamlet (Day) Hospital The TW9   132 A2
Hammersmith Hospital W12   90 B1
Harrow Hospital HA2   64 C6
The Heart Hospital W1   93 B2   238 C3
Hillingdon Hospital UB8   82 B2
Homerton University Hospital E9   74 D3

Hornsey Central Hospital N8   49 D4
Hospital for Tropical Diseases WC1   232 C5
Hospital of St John and St Elizabeth NW8   92 B5   229 C3
Inverforth House Hospital NW3   70 A6
Jewish Home and Hospital at Tottenham The N15   51 D5
King George Hospital IG3   58 A4
King's College Hospital SE5   139 B3
Kings Oak Hospital (Private) The EN2   4 C5
Kingsbury Hospital NW9   44 C5
Kingston Hospital KT2   176 D2
Langthorne Hospital E11   76 B5
Lewisham Hospital SE13   163 D6
Lister Hospital SW1   115 B1   258 C1
London Bridge Hospital SE1   117 B5   252 D4
London Chest Hospital E2   96 C5
London Clinic NW1   93 A3   238 B5
London Foot Hospital W1   93 C3   239 A5
London Hospital (Mile End) The E2   96 D4
London Hospital (St Clements) The E3   97 B4
London Independent Hospital The E1   96 D2
Maida Vale Psychiatric Hospital W9   92 A3   236 B6
Manor House Hospital NW11   47 D1
Marlborough Day Hospital NW8   92 A5   229 A4
Maudsley Hospital The SE5   139 B3
Mayday University Hospital CR7   204 D3
Memorial Hospital SE18   144 C3
Mildmay Mission Hospital E2   95 D4
Molesey Hospital KT8   195 C4
Moorfields Eye Hospital EC1   95 B4   235 C1
Morland Road Day Hospital RM10   103 C6
National Hospital for Neurology and Neurosurgery N2   48 C5
National Hospital The WC1   94 A3   240 B5
National Physical Laboratory TW11   174 C4
Nelson Hospital SW20   179 B1
New Cross Hospital SE14   140 C5
New Victoria Hospital KT3   177 C2
Newham General Hospital E13   99 C3
Normansfield Hospital KT8   175 C3
North London Nuffield Hospital N2   4 C3
North Middlesex University Hospital N18   33 C5
Northwick Park Hospital HA1   43 A2
Northwood Pinner and District Cottage Hospital HA6   22 A2
Norwood Hospital SE19   183 B4
Orpington Hospital BR6   227 D4
Paddington Com Hospital W9   91 C2
Penny Sangam Day Hospital UB2   107 B3
Plaistow Hospital E13   99 C5
Portland Hospital for Women and Children The W1   93 B3   238 D5
Princess Grace Hospital The W1   93 A3   238 A5
Princess Louise Hospital W10   90 C2
Princess Royal University Hospital BR6   226 C5
Priory Hospital The SW15   133 D1
Putney Hospital SW15   134 C2
Queen Charlotte's Hospital W12   90 B1
Queen Elizabeth Hospital for Children The E2   96 A5
Queen Elizabeth Hospital SE18   144 A5
Queen Mary's Hospital DA14 6LT   190 A4
Queen Mary's Hospital NW3   70 A5
Queen Mary's University Hospital SW15   156 A5
Queen's Hospital CR0   205 A3

Roding Hospital IG4   55 D6
Royal Brompton and Nat Heart Hospital The SW3   114 C1   257 A2
Royal Ear Hospital WC1   93 C3   239 B5
Royal Free Hospital NW3   70 C3
Royal Hospital SW15   157 A5
Royal London Homeopathic Hospital The WC1   94 A2   240 B4
Royal London Hospital(Whitechapel) E1   96 B2
Royal Marsden Hospital SW3   114 B1   256 D2
Royal Masonic Hospital W6   112 A2
Royal National Orthopaedic Hospital HA7   9 C2
Royal National Orthopaedic Hospital W1   93 B3   238 D5
Royal Nat TN&E Hospital The W5   87 C2
Royal Nat TN&E Hospital The WC1   94 B4   233 C2
St Andrew's Hospital E3   97 D3
St Ann's General Hospital N4, N15   51 A4
St Anthony's Hospital KT4   200 D1
St Bartholomew's Hospital EC1   94 D2   241 D3
St Charles' Hospital W10   90 D2
St Christopher's Hospice SE26   184 C5
St George's Hospital SW17   180 B5
St Giles Hospital SE5   139 C4
St Helier Hospital SM5   202 A1
St Joseph's Hospice E9, E8   96 B6
St Leonard's Hospital N1   95 C5
St Luke's Hospital W1   93 C3   239 A5
St Luke's Woodside Hospital N10   49 A5
St Mark's Hospital EC1   94 D4   234 D2
St Mark's Hospital HA1   43 A2
St Mary's Cottage Hospital TW12   173 B2
St Mary's Hospital W2   92 B1   236 D2
St Michael's Hospital EN2   5 B4
St Pancras Hospital NW1   93 D6   232 C5
St Thomas's Hospital SE1   116 B3   260 C6
St Vincent's Hospital HA5   39 D6
Samaritan Hospital for Women NW1   237 C4
Shirley Oaks Hospital CR0   206 C2
Sloane Hospital BR3   186 B2
South Western Hospital SW9   138 B2
Southwood Hospital (Geriatric) N6   49 A2
Springfield Hospital SW17   158 C1
Stepney Day Hospital E1   96 C1
Surbiton Hospital KT6   198 A3
Teddington Memorial Hospital TW11   174 C4
Thorpe Coombe Hospital E17   54 A6
Tolworth Hospital KT6   214 C6
Travel Clinic, Hospital for Tropical Diseases WC1   93 C3   239 B5
University College Hospital WC1   93 C3   239 B6
Upton Day Hospital DA6   147 A1
Wanstead Hospital E11   55 B5
Wellington Hospital (North) NW8   92 B5   229 D3
Wellington Hospital (South) NW8   92 B5   229 D3
Wembley Hospital HA0   65 D2
West Middlesex University Hospital TW7 6AF   131 A3
Western Hospital The NW1   92 D2   237 C4
Whipps Cross Hospital E11 1NR   54 B3
Whittington Hospital N19 5NF   71 C6
Willesden Community Hospital The NW10   68 A1
Winifred House Hospital EN5   11 D5

Places of interest

Central

West End

Admiralty Arch SW1 . . . . 249 D4
Apple Market WC2 . . . . 250 B6
Banqueting House SW1 . . . . 250 A3
Big Ben SW1 . . . . 250 B1
British Library NW1 . . . . 93 D4 232 D2
British Mus WC1 . . . . 94 A2 240 A3
BT Tower W1 . . . . 93 C2 239 A4
Buckingham Palace SW1 .115 C4 249 A1
Cabinet War Rooms SW1 .115 D4 249 D2
Carnaby Street W1 . . . . 93 C1 239 A4
Cenotaph SW1 . . . . 250 A2
Changing of the Guard
  (site of) SW1 . . . . 249 A1
Chinatown W1 . . . . 115 D6 249 D6
Clarence House SW1 . . . . .115 C5 249 B3
Cleopatra's Needle WC2 . .116 B5 250 C5
Courtauld Galleries WC2 . . . . 250 C6
Covent Garden WC2 . . . . . 116 A6 250 B6
Dickens House
  Mus WC1 . . . . 94 B3 240 D5
Downing Street SW1 . . . . . 116 A4 250 A2
Eros W1 . . . . 115 D6 249 C5
Green Park SW1,W1 . . . . . .115 B4 248 D2
Guards Mus SW1 . . . . .115 C4 249 B1
Holocaust Memorial
  Garden W2 . . . . .114 D4 247 D2
Horse Guards
  Parade SW1 . . . . .115 D5 249 D3
Houses of
  Parliament SW1 . . . . 116 A3 260 B6
Hyde Park W2 . . . . .114 D5 247 C3
Leicester Square WC2 . . . .115 D6 249 D5
London's Transport Mus WC2 . . . . 250 B6
Marble Arch W1 . . . . .114 D4 247 D6
Methodist Central
  Hall SW1 . . . . .115 D4 249 D1
National Gallery W1 . . . . . .115 D6 249 D5
National Portrait
  Gallery W1 . . . . .115 D6 249 D5
Nelson's Monument WC2 . . . . 250 A4
New Scotland Yard SW1 . .115 D3 259 C6
Parliament Square SW1 . .116 A4 250 A1
Pepsi Trocadero W1 . . . . 249 C5
Piccadilly Circus W1 . . . . . .115 D6 249 C5
Queen Victoria Memorial SW1 . . . . 249 A2
Queen's Gallery SW1 . . . . .115 B4 248 D1
Rotten Row SW1 . . . . .114 D4 247 C6
Royal Academy
  of Arts W1 115 C6 249 A5
Royal Mews SW1 . . . . .115 B3 258 D6
Royal United Services
  Mus SW1 . . . . 250 A3
St James's Palace SW1 . . 115 C5 249 B3
St James's Park SW1 . . . . 249 C2
Serpentine Gallery W2 . . .114 B4 246 D2
Soho W1 . . . . 93 D1 239 C2
Somerset House WC2 . . .116 B6 250 D6
Speakers' Corner W1 . . . . .114 D6 247 D6
Tate Britain SW1 . . . . .116 A2 260 A3
Theatre Mus WC2 . . . . 250 B6
Trafalgar Square W1 . . . . .115 D6 249 D4
Tyburn Tree (site of) W2 . . . . 247 C6
Wallace Collection W1 . . . . 238 A2
Wellington Arch SW1 . . . . 248 B2
Wellington Mus
  (Apsley House) SW1 . . . .115 A4 248 B2
Westminster Abbey SW1 . .116 A3 260 A6
Westminster
  Cathedral SW1 . . . . .115 C3 259 A5

City

Bank of England EC2. . . . . 242 C1
Barbican Arts and
  Conference Centre EC2 . . 95 A2 242 B4
Central Criminal Court
  (Old Bailey) EC4 . . . . 94 D1 241 D6
Custom House EC3 . . . . . .117 C6 253 A5

Dr Johnson's House EC4 . . . . 241 B1
Gray's Inn WC1 . . . . 94 B2 240 D4
Guildhall EC2 . . . . 95 A1 242 D1
Inner Temple EC4 . . . . 251 A6
John Wesley's House &
  Mus EC1 . . . . 242 D6
Lincoln's Inn WC2 . . . . 94 B1 240 D2
Lloyd's Building EC3 . . . . . 95 C1 243 A1
Mansion House EC4 . . . . 242 C1
Merchant Taylors Hall EC2R 242 D1
Middle Temple EC4 . . . . . .116 C6 251 A6
Monument, The EC3 . . . . 252 D6
Mus of London EC2 . . . . . . 95 A2 242 A3
Nat West Tower EC2 . . . . 243 A4
National Postal
  Mus EC1 . . . . 95 A1 242 A2
Petticoat Lane Market EC2 95 D2 243 C3
Public Record Office
  Mus EC4,WC2 . . . . 241 A2
Royal Exchange EC3 . . . . 242 D1
St Katharine Dock E1 . . . .117 D5 253 D4
St Mary le Bow Church EC2 . . . . . . 242 B1
St Paul's Cathedral EC4 . . . 95 A1 242 A1
Sir John Soane's
  Mus WC2 . . . . 94 B1 240 C2
Spitalfields Market E1 . . . . 95 D2 243 C4
Stock Exchange EC2 . . . . 241 D1
Tower Bridge E1,EC3,SE1 . .117 D5 253 C5
Tower of London EC3 . . . . .117 D6 253 C5
Traitors Gate EC3 . . . . .117 D5 253 C4
Ye Olde Cheshire Cheese EC4 . . . . 241 B2

Northern

Business Design Centre N1 94 C6 234 B5
Camden Market NW1 . . . . . 93 B6 231 D6
London Canal Mus N1 . . . . 94 A5 233 B4
London Central
  Mosque NW8 . . . . 92 C4 230 B1
London Zoo NW1 . . . . 93 A5 231 A4
Lord's Cricket Ground NW8 92 B4 229 D2
Madame Tussaud's NW1 . . 93 A3 238 A5
Open Air Theatre, Regent's
  Park NW1 . . . . 231 A1
Planetarium NW1 . . . . 93 A3 238 A5
Primrose Hill NW1. . . . . 92 D6 230 C6
Queen Mary's Gardens NW1 . . . . . 231 A1
Regent's Park NW1 . . . . 93 A4 231 A3
St George's Cathedral NW1 . . . . . . 231 D2
Sherlock Holmes
  Mus NW1 . . . . 92 D3 237 D5

Southern

Battersea Park SW11 . . . . .137 A5 268 A3
Battersea Power
  Station SW8 . . . . .137 B6 268 D6
Brompton Oratory SW7 . . .114 C3 257 A5
Bear Gardens
  Mus SE1 . . . . .117 A5 252 A4
Bermondsey Market SE1 . .117 C3 263 B8
Borough Market SE1 . . . . 252 C3
Design Mus SE1 . . . . .117 D4 253 D2
Florence Nightingale
  Mus SE1 . . . . 250 D1
Gabriel's Wharf SE1 . . . . 251 A4
George Inn SE1 . . . . 252 C3
Globe Theatre SE1 . . . . 252 A5
Hayward Gallery SE1 . . . . .116 B5 250 D4
HMS Belfast SE1 . . . . 253 B4
Imperial War
  Mus SE1 . . . . .116 C3 261 B5
Lambeth Palace SE1 . . . . . .116 B3 260 C5
London Aquarium SE1 . . . . 250 C1
London Dungeon SE1 . . . . .117 B5 252 D4
London Eye SE1 . . . . .116 B4 250 C2
London Peace Pagoda SW11 . . . . 267 D4
Millennium Bridge SE1,EC4 . . . . . . 252 A5
Mus of Garden History SE1 . . . . . . 260 C5
National Film Theatre SE1 . . . . 250 D4
National Theatre SE1 . . . . .116 B5 250 D4
Old County Hall SE1 . . . . 250 C2

Operating Theatre Mus and Herb
  Garret SE1 . . . . .117 B5 252 D3
Oxo Tower SE1 . . . . 251 B5
Royal Festival Hall SE1 . . .116 B5 250 D3
Saatchi Gallery SE1 . . . . 250 C2
St George's RC
  Cathedral SE1 . . . . .116 C3 261 B6
Shakespeare's Globe Theatre
  (site of) SE1 . . . . 252 B4
Southwark Cathedral SE1 .117 B5 252 C4
Tate Modern SE1 . . . . .116 D6 251 D4
Vinopolis SE1 . . . . .117 B5 252 C4

Western

Albert Memorial SW7 . . . .114 B4 246 C1
Carlyle's House SW3 . . . . 267 A5
Chelsea Barracks SW1 . . .115 A1 258 B1
Chelsea Physic
  Garden SW3 . . . . .115 A1 267 C6
Commonwealth
  Institute W8 . . . . .113 C3 255 A6
Geological Mus SW7 . . . . .114 B3 256 D5
Kensington Gardens W2 . .114 A5 246 B3
Kensington Palace W8 . . .113 D5 245 D3
Leighton House W14 . . . . 254 D6
Lindsey House SW10 . . . . 266 D4
Little Venice W9 . . . . 92 A2 236 A4
National Army
  Mus SW3 . . . . .136 D6 267 D6
Natural History
  Mus SW7 . . . . .114 B3 256 D5
Ranelagh Gardens SW1 . .115 A1 258 B1
Royal Albert Hall SW7 . . . .114 B4 246 C1
Royal Hospital (Army
  Pensioners) SW1 . . . . . . .115 A1 258 A1
Science Mus SW7 . . . . .114 B3 256 D5
Victoria and Albert
  Mus SW7 . . . . .114 B3 256 D5

East

Canary Wharf E14 . . . . .119 D5
Docklands Mus E14 . . . . 119 D6
Epping Forest IG10 . . . . 21 B6
Geffrye Mus E2 . . . . 95 D5
London Docklands Visitor
  Centre E14 . . . . .120 A4
London Gas Mus E16 . . . . 98 B3
Mus of Childhood (V&A) E2 . . . . 96 C4
Museum of the Great Eastern
  Railway E16 . . . . .122 C4
Queen Elizabeth's Hunting
  Lodge Mus E4 . . . . 20 D4
Ragged School Mus E3 . . . . 97 A2
Vestry House (Mus) E17 . . . . 53 D5
Whitechapel Art Gallery E1 . . . . 95 D1

North

Alexandra Palace N22 . . . . 31 D1
Barnet Mus EN5 . . . . 1 A1
Battle of Britain Mus NW9 . . 27 D1
Bruce Castle Mus N17 . . . . 33 C2
Church Farm House Mus NW4 . . 46 B6
Coppetts Centre N12 . . . . 30 D3
Forty Hall EN2 . . . . 5 D4
Freud Mus NW3 . . . . 70 A2
Grange Mus of Community History
  NW10 . . . . 67 D4
Hampstead Heath NW3 . . . . 70 B6
Harrow Mus and Heritage Centre
  HA2 . . . . 42 A6
Highgate Cemetery N19 . . . . 71 B6
Kensal Green Cemetery
  (All Souls) NW10 . . . . 90 C4
Kenwood House NW3 . . . . 48 C1
Old Court (Mus and Library) HA0 .65 C3
RAF Mus NW9 . . . . 28 A1

Ruislip Lido HA4,HA5 . . . . 39 B5
Ruislip Lido Railway HA4 . . . . 39 B5
White Cube N1 . . . . 95 C4

South east

Blackheath SE3 . . . . .142 C4
Brockwell Park SE24 . . . . .160 D5
Cutty Sark SE10 . . . . .142 A6
Docklands Heritage Mus SE16 . . .119 B5
Dulwich Picture Gallery SE21 . . . .161 C4
Eltham Palace SE9 . . . . .166 A4
Flamsteed House SE10 . . . . .142 B5
Gipsy Moth IV SE10 . . . . .142 A6
Greenwich Park SE10 . . . . .142 C5
Horniman Mus and Gardens SE23 162 B3
Livesey Mus SE15 . . . . .140 B6
Meridian Building SE10 . . . . .142 B5
Millennium Dome SE10 . . . . .120 C5
National Maritime Mus SE10 . . . . .142 B6
Old Royal Observatory
  Greenwich SE10 . . . . .142 B5
Queen's House SE10 . . . . .142 B6
Rotunda Mus SE18 . . . . .122 B1
Scadbury Park Nature
  Reserve BR7 . . . . .189 D4
South Norwood Country
  Park SE25 .206 C5
Thames Barrier Visitor
  Centre SE18 . . . . .121 D3
Well Hall Pleasaunce SE9 . . . . .144 A1

South west

Barnes Common SW13 . . . . .134 A2
Clapham Common SW4 . . . . .137 C1
Fulham Palace SW6 . . . . .135 A3
Hampton Court Palace KT8 . . . . . .196 D6
Kingston Mus KT1 . . . . .176 A1
Wandsworth Mus SW15 . . . . .135 A1
Wetland Centre SW13 . . . . .134 B5
Wimbledon Common SW19 . . . . . .178 B6
Wimbledon Lawn Tennis
  Mus SW19 . . . . .157 A1
Wimbledon Windmill Mus SW19 . .156 C1

West

Chiswick House W4 . . . . .133 B6
Eel Pie Island TW1 . . . . .153 A3
Gunnersbury Park Mus W3 . . . . . .110 C3
Ham House TW10 . . . . .153 C2
Kew Bridge Steam Mus TW8 . . . . .110 B1
Kew Gardens
  (Royal Botanic Gardens) TW9 . . .132 A4
Kew Observatory TW9 . . . . .131 C2
Kew Palace TW9 . . . . .132 A5
London Butterfly House TW8 . . . . .131 B4
Marble Hill TW1 . . . . .153 C4
Mus of Richmond TW10 . . . . .153 D6
Musical Mus TW8 . . . . .132 A6
Osterley Park TW7 . . . . .108 B1
Pitshanger Manor Mus and
  Art Gallery W5 . . . . .109 D5
Portobello Road Market W10 . . . . . 91 A2
Richmond Park TW10 . . . . .155 A3
Syon House TW8 . . . . .131 C4
Walled Garden TW16 . . . . .194 B6

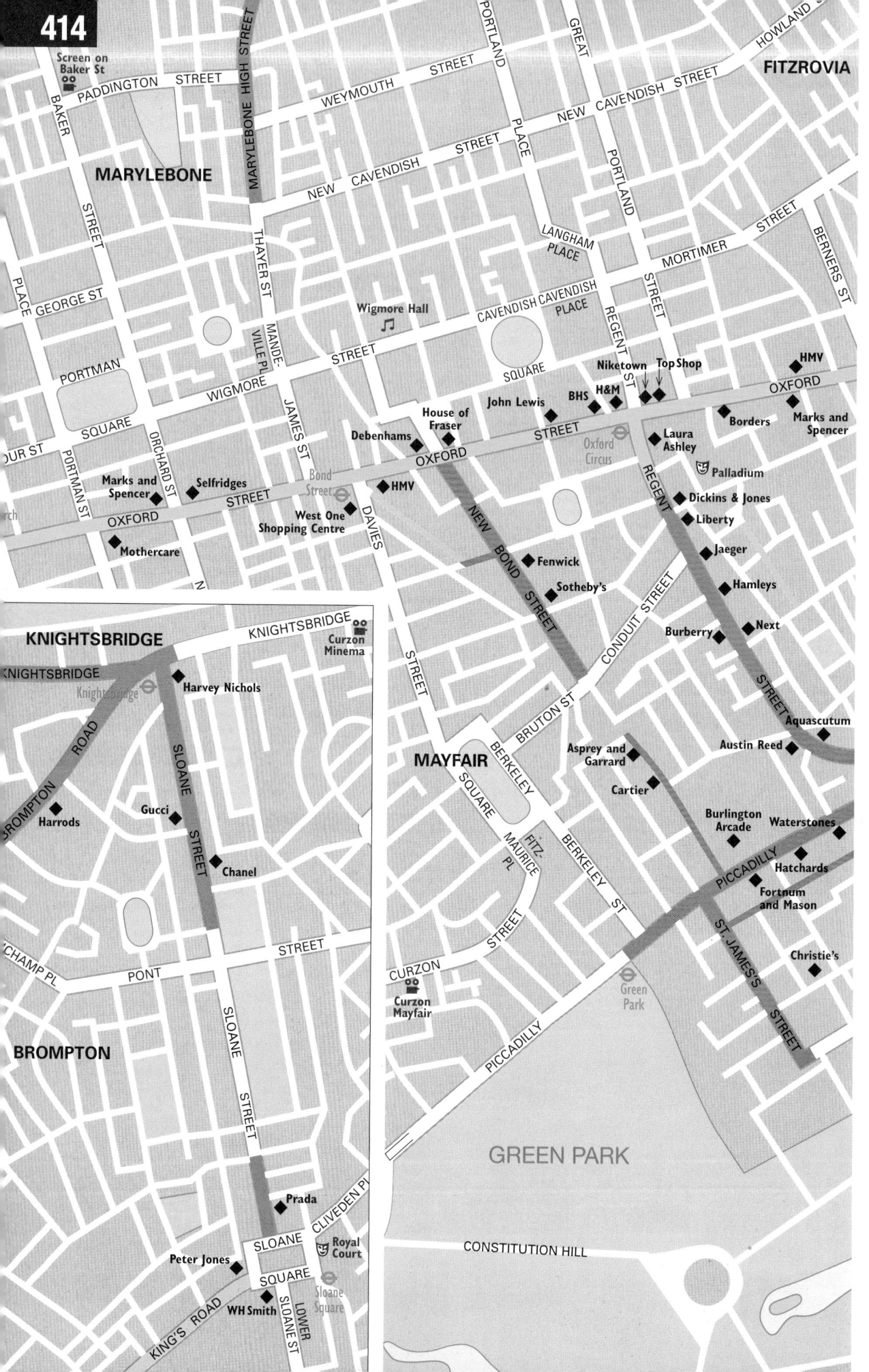

MARYLEBONE

FITZROVIA

Screen on Baker St

PADDINGTON STREET

BAKER STREET

MARYLEBONE HIGH STREET

WEYMOUTH STREET

PORTLAND STREET

NEW CAVENDISH STREET

GREAT

THAYER ST

NEW CAVENDISH STREET

PORTLAND PLACE

MORTIMER STREET

BERNERS ST

GEORGE ST

MANDE- VILLE PL

Wigmore Hall

CAVENDISH CAVENDISH PLACE

LANGHAM PLACE

REGENT ST

PORTMAN SQUARE

WIGMORE STREET

SQUARE

HMV

Niketown Top Shop

H&M BHS

OXFORD

PORTMAN ST

OUR ST

JAMES ST

John Lewis

House of Fraser

Borders

Marks and Spencer

Debenhams

OXFORD STREET

Oxford Circus

Laura Ashley

Palladium

Marks and Spencer

Selfridges

HMV

Bond Street

OXFORD STREET

Dickins & Jones

Liberty

REGENT STREET

Mothercare

West One Shopping Centre

DAVIES

NEW BOND STREET

Jaeger

Hamleys

Fenwick

Conduit Street

Burberry

Next

Sotheby's

KNIGHTSBRIDGE

KNIGHTSBRIDGE

Curzon Minema

STREET

Aquascutum

KNIGHTSBRIDGE

Knightsbridge

Harvey Nichols

BRUTON ST

Asprey and Garrard

Austin Reed

MAYFAIR

BERKELEY

Cartier

BROMPTON ROAD

SLOANE STREET

Gucci

Harrods

Chanel

SQUARE

Burlington Arcade

Waterstones

FITZ MAURICE PL

BERKELEY ST

PICCADILLY

Hatchards

Fortnum and Mason

'CHAMP PL

PONT STREET

SLOANE STREET

CURZON STREET

ST. JAMES'S STREET

Christie's

BROMPTON

Curzon Mayfair

Green Park

Prada

CLIVEDEN PL

SLOANE

Royal Court

PICCADILLY

GREEN PARK

Peter Jones

SQUARE

KING'S ROAD

WH Smith

Sloane Square

LOWER SLOANE ST

CONSTITUTION HILL

Cinemas, theatres shopping streets

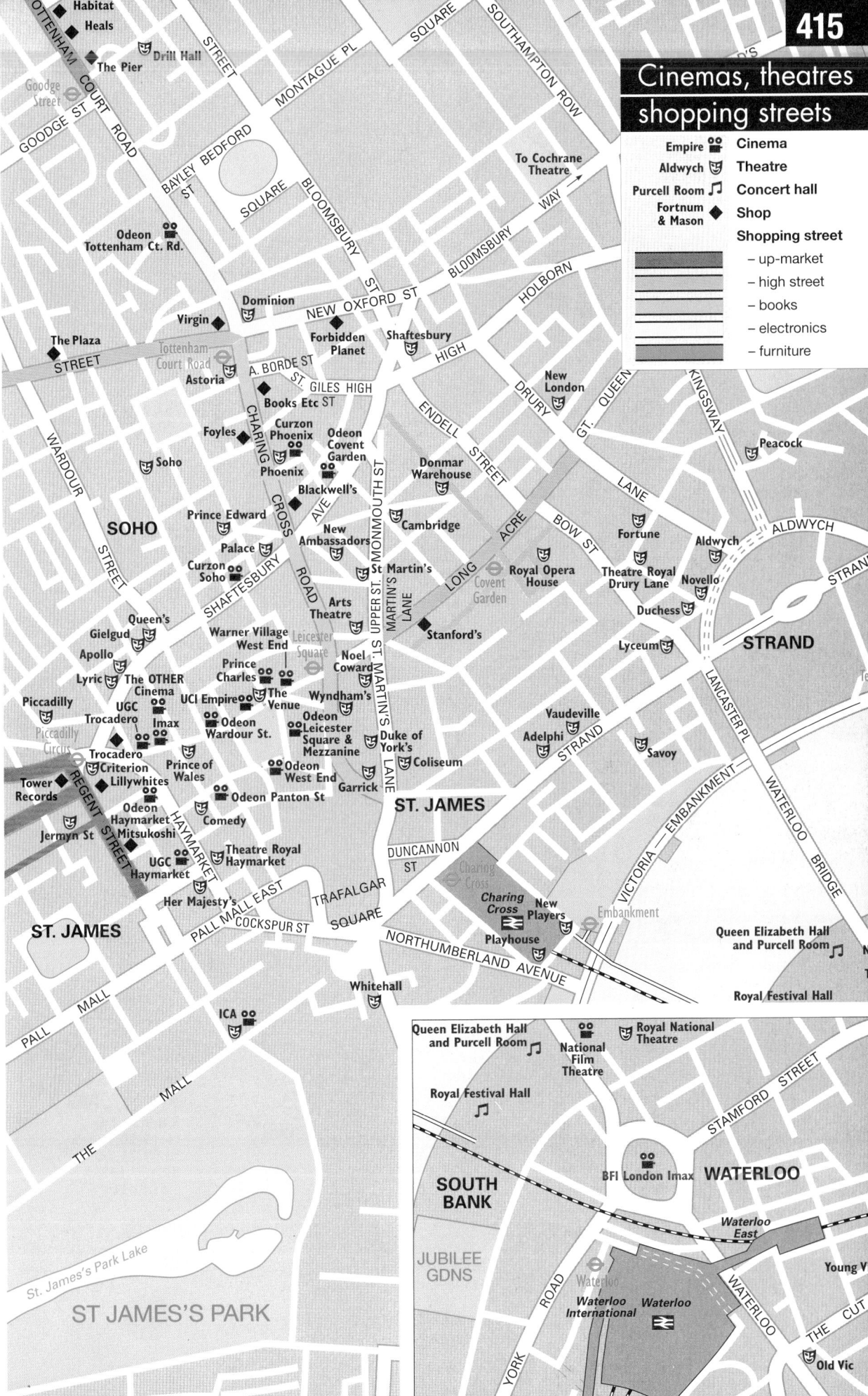
Empire Cinema
Aldwych Theatre
Purcell Room Concert hall
Fortnum & Mason Shop
Shopping street
– up-market
– high street
– books
– electronics
– furniture
Habitat
Heals
The Pier
Drill Hall
Goodge Street
TOTTENHAM COURT ROAD
GOODGE ST
STREET
BAYLEY ST
BEDFORD SQUARE
MONTAGUE PL
SQUARE
SOUTHAMPTON ROW
BLOOMSBURY ST
BLOOMSBURY WAY
To Cochrane Theatre
Odeon Tottenham Ct. Rd.
Dominion
NEW OXFORD ST
HOLBORN
Virgin
Forbidden Planet
Shaftesbury
The Plaza
STREET
Tottenham Court Road
Astoria
A. BORDE ST
ST. GILES HIGH ST
HIGH
Books Etc
New London
DRURY LANE
GT. QUEEN
KINGSWAY
Peacock
Foyles
Curzon Phoenix
Phoenix
Odeon Covent Garden
CHARING CROSS ROAD
WARDOUR STREET
Soho
ENDELL STREET
Donmar Warehouse
Blackwell's
AVE
MONMOUTH ST
SOHO
Prince Edward
Cambridge
New Ambassadors
Palace
Curzon Soho
SHAFTESBURY
St Martin's
LONG ACRE
BOW ST
Fortune
Aldwych
ALDWYCH
Royal Opera House
Covent Garden
Theatre Royal Drury Lane
Novello
STRAND
Queen's
Arts Theatre
UPPER ST. MARTIN'S LANE
Duchess
Gielgud
Warner Village West End
Leicester Square
Stanford's
Lyceum
STRAND
Apollo
Prince Charles
Noel Coward
Lyric
The OTHER Cinema
Piccadilly
UGC Trocadero
UCI Empire
The Venue
Wyndham's
Imax
Odeon Wardour St.
Odeon Leicester Square & Mezzanine
ST. MARTIN'S LANE
Duke of York's
Vaudeville
Adelphi
STRAND
Savoy
LANCASTER PL
Piccadilly Circus
Trocadero
Criterion
Prince of Wales
Odeon West End
Coliseum
Tower Records
Lillywhites
Garrick
REGENT STREET
Odeon Haymarket
HAYMARKET
Odeon Panton St
Comedy
ST. JAMES
VICTORIA — EMBANKMENT
WATERLOO BRIDGE
Jermyn St
Mitsukoshi
UGC Haymarket
Theatre Royal Haymarket
DUNCANNON ST
Charing Cross
Her Majesty's
PALL MALL EAST
TRAFALGAR SQUARE
COCKSPUR ST
Charing Cross
New Players
Playhouse
Embankment
ST. JAMES
NORTHUMBERLAND AVENUE
Queen Elizabeth Hall and Purcell Room
Royal Festival Hall
Whitehall
PALL MALL
ICA
THE MALL
St. James's Park Lake
ST JAMES'S PARK
Queen Elizabeth Hall and Purcell Room
National Film Theatre
Royal National Theatre
Royal Festival Hall
STAMFORD STREET
SOUTH BANK
BFI London Imax
WATERLOO
Waterloo East
JUBILEE GDNS
Waterloo
Waterloo International
Waterloo
YORK ROAD
WATERLOO
THE CUT
Old Vic

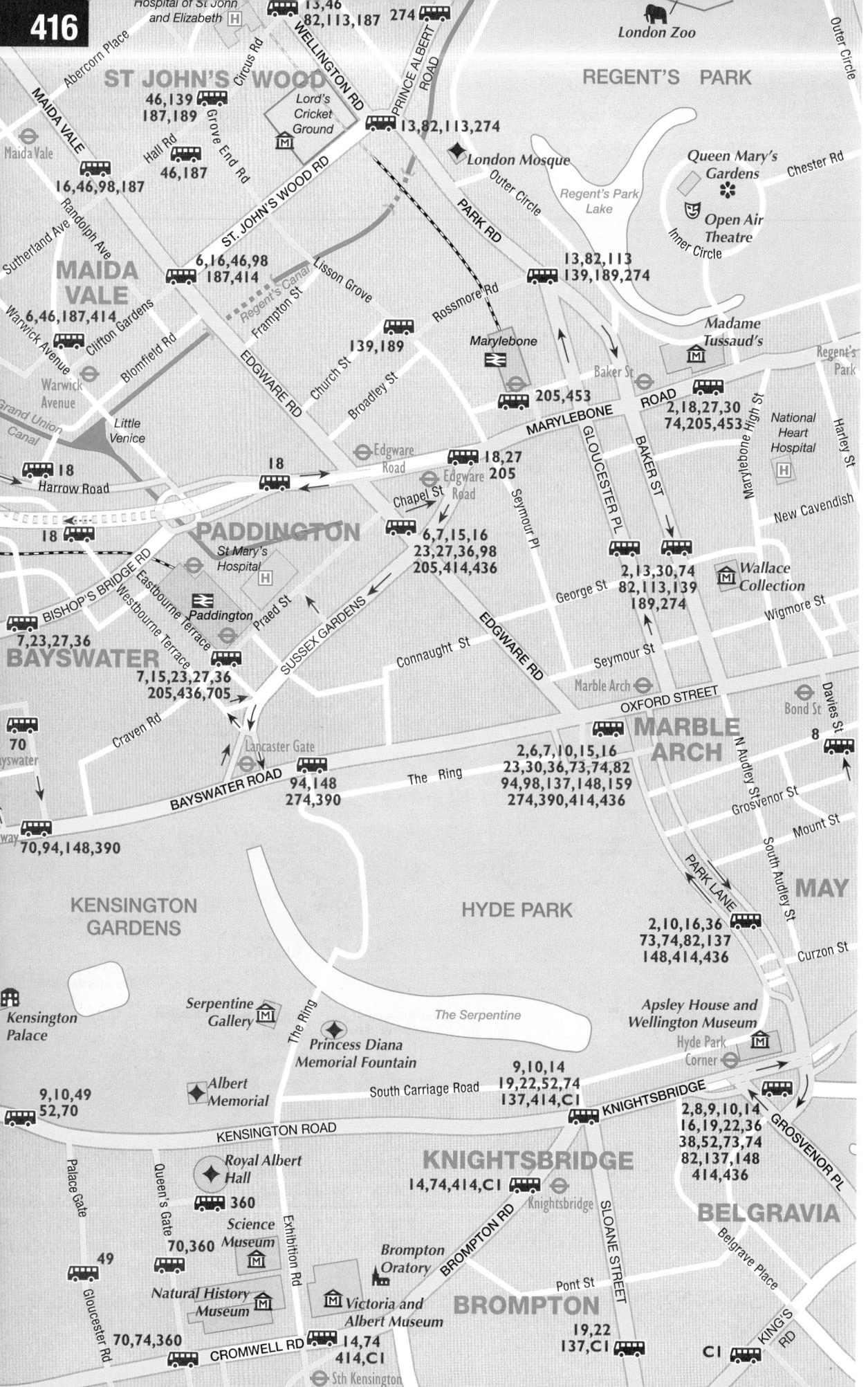

ST JOHN'S WOOD

Hospital of St John and Elizabeth

13,46
82,113,187
274

13,82,113,274

REGENT'S PARK

London Zoo

Queen Mary's Gardens

Chester Rd

Outer Circle

London Mosque

Regent's Park Lake

Open Air Theatre

Inner Circle

46,139
187,189

Lord's Cricket Ground

Abercorn Place

MAIDA VALE

Maida Vale

Hall Rd
46,187

16,46,98,187

Grove End Rd

Circus Rd

WELLINGTON RD

PRINCE ALBERT ROAD

PARK RD

Outer Circle

MAIDA VALE

6,16,46,98
187,414

6,46,187,414

Sutherland Ave

Randolph Ave

Warwick Ave

Clifton Gardens

Blomfield Rd

Lisson Grove

Frampton St

Regent's Canal

ST. JOHN'S WOOD RD

EDGWARE RD

Church St

Broadley St

139,189

Rossmore Rd

Marylebone

205,453

13,82,113
139,189,274

Baker St

Madame Tussaud's

Regent's Park

2,18,27,30
74,205,453

National Heart Hospital

Harley St

Marylebone High St

New Cavendish

Warwick Avenue

Little Venice

Grand Union Canal

18

Harrow Road

18

18

PADDINGTON

St Mary's Hospital

Paddington

Edgware Road

18,27
205

Chapel St

Edgware Road

6,7,15,16
23,27,36,98
205,414,436

Seymour Pl

GLOUCESTER PL

BAKER ST

2,13,30,74
82,113,139
189,274

George St

Wigmore St

Wallace Collection

BAYSWATER

7,23,27,36

Bishop's Bridge Rd

Eastbourne Terrace

Westbourne Terrace

7,15,23,27,36
205,436,705

Praed St

Sussex Gardens

Connaught St

EDGWARE RD

Seymour St

Marble Arch

Seymour St

OXFORD STREET

N Audley St

MARBLE ARCH

Bond St

Davies St

8

8

70
Bayswater

Craven Rd

Lancaster Gate

BAYSWATER ROAD

94,148
274,390

The Ring

2,6,7,10,15,16
23,30,36,73,74,82
94,98,137,148,159
274,390,414,436

Grosvenor St

Mount St

70,94,148,390

KENSINGTON GARDENS

HYDE PARK

2,10,16,36
73,74,82,137
148,414,436

Park Lane

South Audley St

MAY

Curzon St

Kensington Palace

Serpentine Gallery

The Ring

The Serpentine

Apsley House and Wellington Museum

Hyde Park Corner

Princess Diana Memorial Fountain

Albert Memorial

South Carriage Road

9,10,14
19,22,52,74
137,414,C1

KNIGHTSBRIDGE

2,8,9,10,14
16,19,22,36
38,52,73,74
82,137,148
414,436

GROSVENOR PL

9,10,49
52,70

KENSINGTON ROAD

Royal Albert Hall

360

14,74,414,C1

Knightsbridge

KNIGHTSBRIDGE

BROMPTON RD

SLOANE STREET

Belgrave Place

BELGRAVIA

Palace Gate

Queen's Gate

Science Museum

70,360

Exhibition Rd

Brompton Oratory

Pont St

49

Natural History Museum

70,74,360

CROMWELL RD

Victoria and Albert Museum

14,74
414,C1

BROMPTON

19,22
137,C1

C1

KING'S RD

Sth Kensington

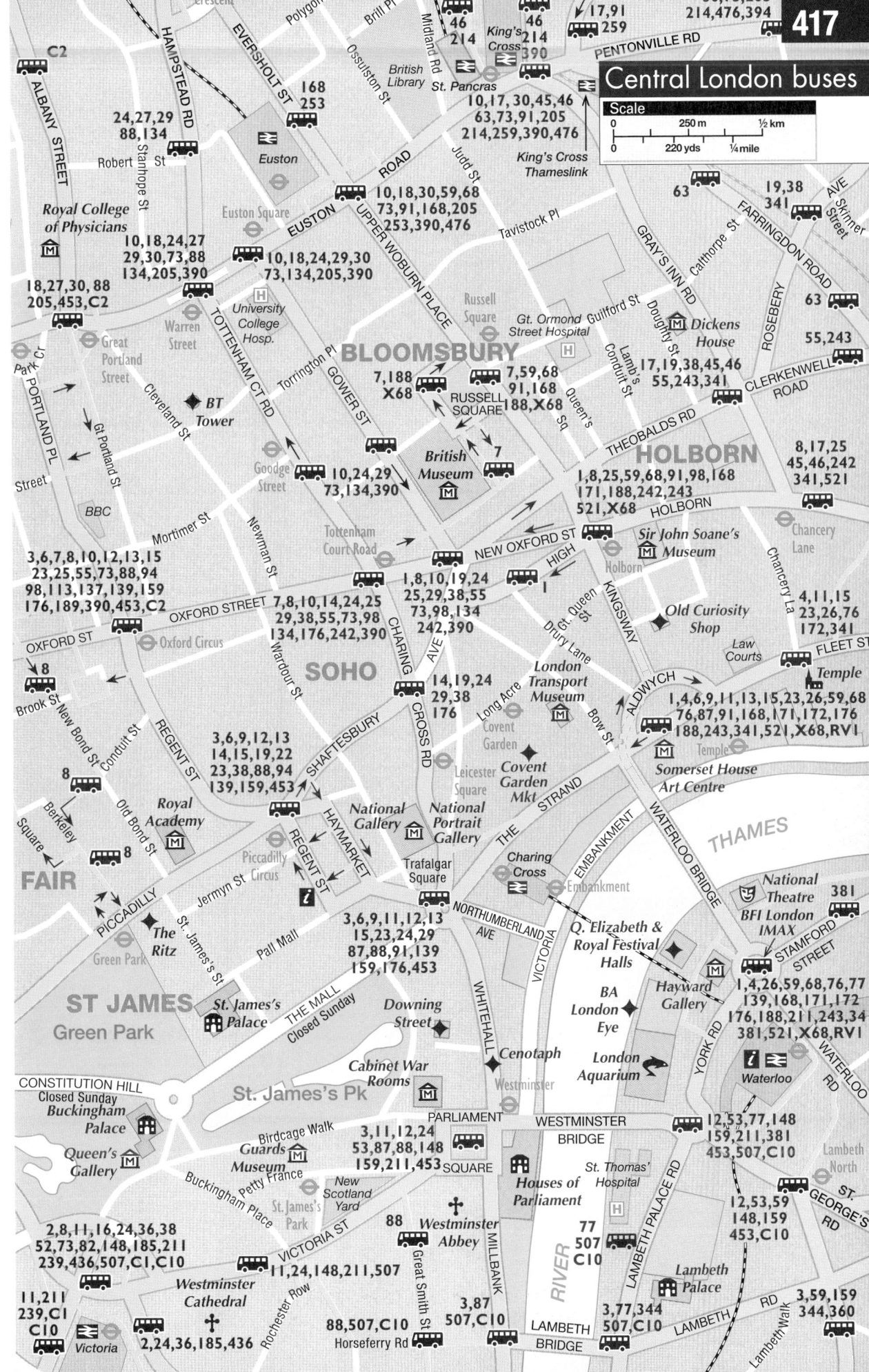

Central London buses

Scale
0   250 m   ½ km
0   220 yds   ¼ mile

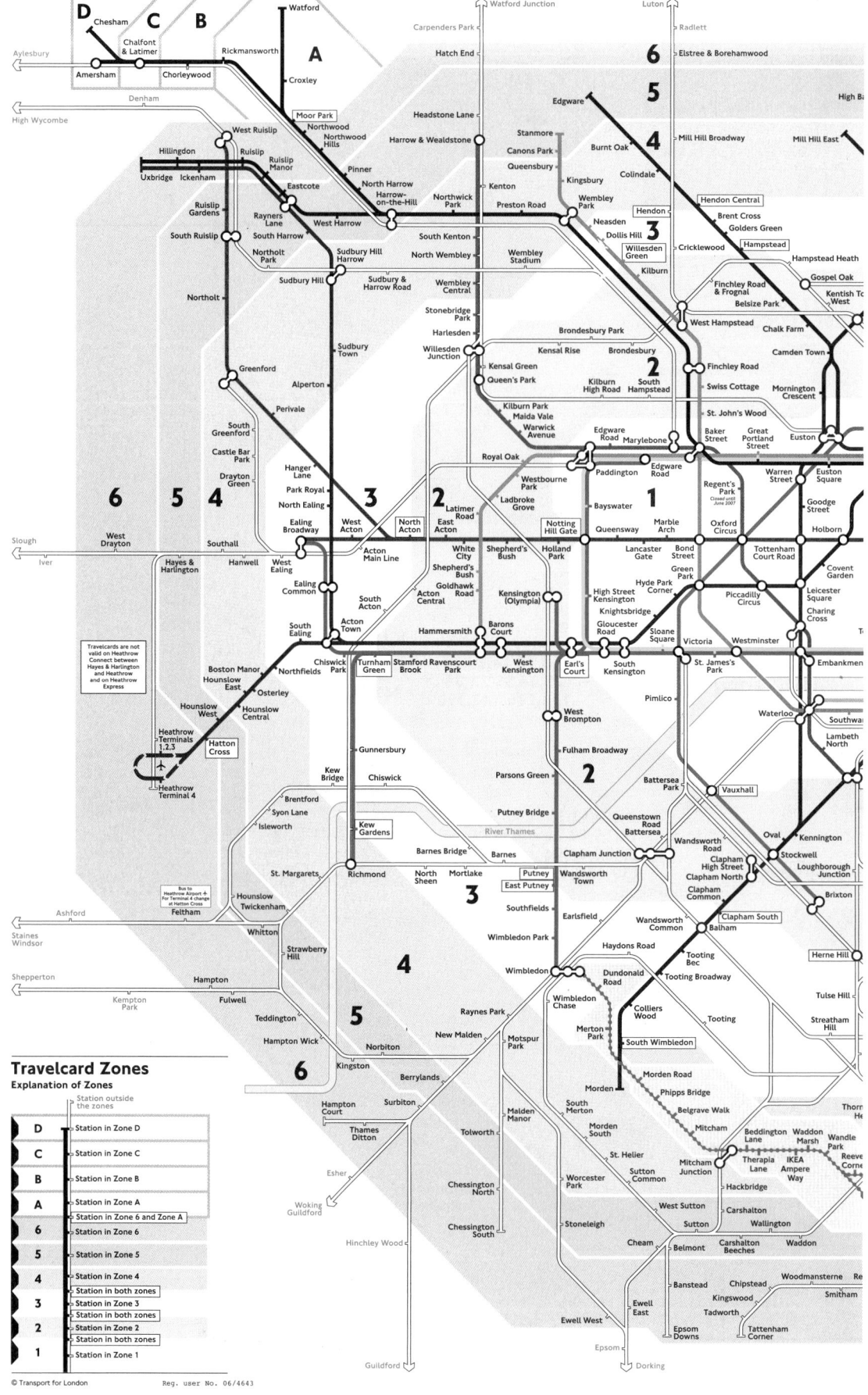

Travelcard Zones

Explanation of Zones

	Station outside the zones
D	Station in Zone D
C	Station in Zone C
B	Station in Zone B
A	Station in Zone A
	Station in Zone 6 and Zone A
6	Station in Zone 6
5	Station in Zone 5
4	Station in Zone 4
3	Station in both zones
	Station in Zone 3
2	Station in both zones
	Station in Zone 2
1	Station in both zones
	Station in Zone 1

© Transport for London   Reg. user No. 06/4643

MAYOR OF LONDON

i 24 hour travel information
020 7222 1234

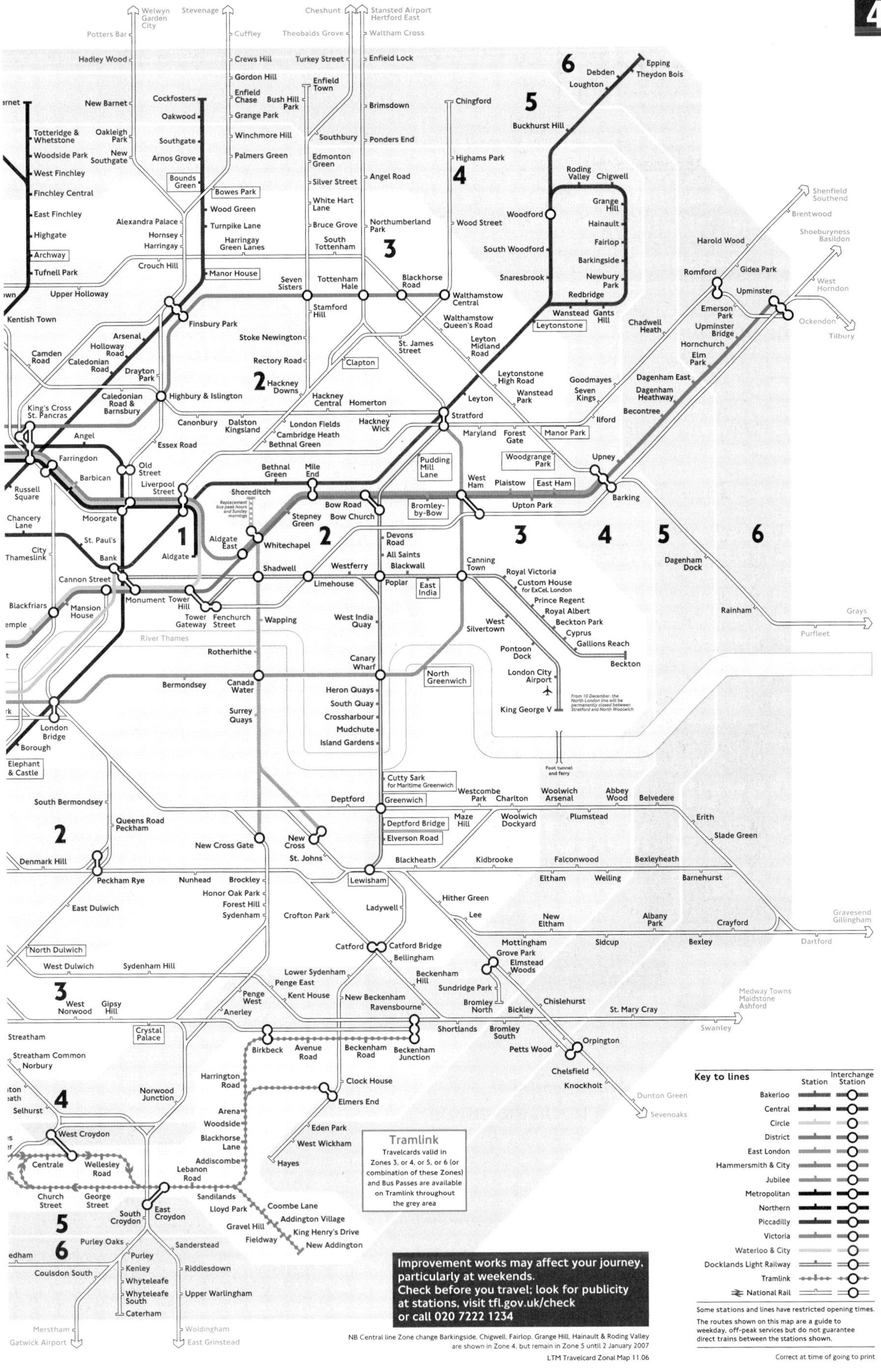

Website
tfl.gov.uk

Textphone
020 7918 3015

Transport for London

PHILIP'S MAPS

the Gold Standard for drivers

◆ **Philip's street atlases cover every county in England, Wales, Northern Ireland and much of Scotland**

◆ Every named street is shown, including alleys, lanes and walkways

◆ Thousands of additional features marked: stations, public buildings, car parks, places of interest

◆ Route-planning maps to get you close to your destination

◆ Postcodes on the maps and in the index

◆ Widely used by the emergency services, transport companies and local authorities

For national mapping, choose
Philip's Navigator Britain
the most detailed road atlas available of England, Wales and Scotland. Hailed by Auto Express as 'the ultimate road atlas', the atlas shows every road and lane in Britain.

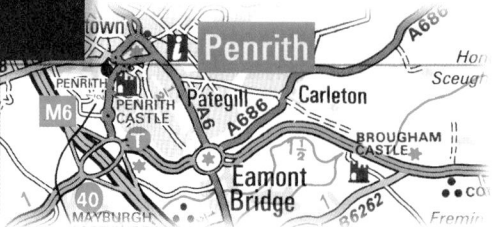

Street atlases currently available

England
Bedfordshire
Berkshire
Birmingham and West Midlands
Bristol and Bath
Buckinghamshire
Cambridgeshire
Cheshire
Cornwall
Cumbria
Derbyshire
Devon
Dorset
County Durham and Teesside
Essex
North Essex
South Essex
Gloucestershire
Hampshire
North Hampshire
South Hampshire
Herefordshire Monmouthshire
Hertfordshire
Isle of Wight
Kent
East Kent
West Kent
Lancashire
Leicestershire and Rutland
Lincolnshire
London
Greater Manchester
Merseyside
Norfolk
Northamptonshire
Northumberland
Nottinghamshire
Oxfordshire
Shropshire
Somerset
Staffordshire
Suffolk
Surrey

East Sussex
West Sussex
Tyne and Wear
Warwickshire
Birmingham and West Midlands
Wiltshire and Swindon
Worcestershire
East Yorkshire Northern Lincolnshire
North Yorkshire
South Yorkshire
West Yorkshire

Wales
Anglesey, Conwy and Gwynedd
Cardiff, Swansea and The Valleys
Carmarthenshire, Pembrokeshire and Swansea
Ceredigion and South Gwynedd
Denbighshire, Flintshire, Wrexham
Herefordshire Monmouthshire
Powys

Scotland
Aberdeenshire
Ayrshire
Dumfries and Galloway
Edinburgh and East Central Scotland
Fife and Tayside
Glasgow and West Central Scotland
Inverness and Moray
Lanarkshire
Scottish Borders

Northern Ireland
County Antrim and County Londonderry
County Armagh and County Down
Belfast
County Tyrone and County Fermanagh

PHILIP'S MAPS

the Gold Standard for drivers

◆ **Philip's street atlases cover every county in England, Wales, Northern Ireland and much of Scotland**

- ◆ Every named street is shown, including alleys, lanes and walkways
- ◆ Thousands of additional features marked: stations, public buildings, car parks, places of interest
- ◆ Route-planning maps to get you close to your destination
- ◆ Postcodes on the maps and in the index
- ◆ Widely used by the emergency services, transport companies and local authorities

For national mapping, choose
Philip's Navigator Britain
the most detailed road atlas available of England, Wales and Scotland. Hailed by Auto Express as 'the ultimate road atlas', the atlas shows every road and lane in Britain.

Street atlases currently available

England

Bedfordshire
Berkshire
Birmingham and West Midlands
Bristol and Bath
Buckinghamshire
Cambridgeshire
Cheshire
Cornwall
Cumbria
Derbyshire
Devon
Dorset
County Durham and Teesside
Essex
North Essex
South Essex
Gloucestershire
Hampshire
North Hampshire
South Hampshire
Herefordshire Monmouthshire
Hertfordshire
Isle of Wight
Kent
East Kent
West Kent
Lancashire
Leicestershire and Rutland
Lincolnshire
London
Greater Manchester
Merseyside
Norfolk
Northamptonshire
Northumberland
Nottinghamshire
Oxfordshire
Shropshire
Somerset
Staffordshire
Suffolk
Surrey

East Sussex
West Sussex
Tyne and Wear
Warwickshire
Birmingham and West Midlands
Wiltshire and Swindon
Worcestershire
East Yorkshire Northern Lincolnshire
North Yorkshire
South Yorkshire
West Yorkshire

Wales

Anglesey, Conwy and Gwynedd
Cardiff, Swansea and The Valleys
Carmarthenshire, Pembrokeshire and Swansea
Ceredigion and South Gwynedd
Denbighshire, Flintshire, Wrexham
Herefordshire Monmouthshire
Powys

Scotland

Aberdeenshire
Ayrshire
Dumfries and Galloway
Edinburgh and East Central Scotland
Fife and Tayside
Glasgow and West Central Scotland
Inverness and Moray
Lanarkshire
Scottish Borders

Northern Ireland

County Antrim and County Londonderry
County Armagh and County Down
Belfast
County Tyrone and County Fermanagh

How to order Philip's maps and atlases are available from bookshops, motorway services and petrol stations. You can order direct from the publisher by phoning **01903 828503** or online at **www.philips-maps.co.uk** For bulk orders only, e-mail philips@philips-maps.co.uk